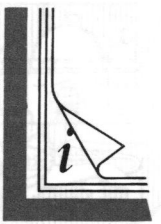

THE

HISTORY AND ANTIQUITIES

OF THE

COUNTY OF LEICESTER

THE
HISTORY AND ANTIQUITIES
OF THE
COUNTY OF LEICESTER

BY

JOHN NICHOLS

VOLUME I, PART II

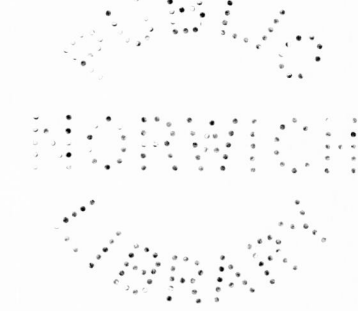

Republished 1971 by S.R. Publishers, Limited,
in association with Leicestershire County Council
Originally published by John Nichols, London, 1815

PUBLISHERS' NOTE

This book comprises four volumes, each divided into two parts, intended to be bound separately. They were issued as follows:

Vol. I, part 1		The Town of Leicester	1795
I	2	The Town of Leicester + indexes	1815
II	1	The Hundred of Framland	1795
II	2	The Hundred of Gartree	1798
III	1	The Hundred of East Goscote	1800
III	2	The Hundred of West Goscote	1804
IV	1	The Hundred of Guthlaxton (second edition, with some corrections, 1810, reprinted in the new edition)	1807
IV	2	The Hundred of Sparkenhoe	1811

REDUCTION FACTOR

The standard reduction factor used throughout the work for text and illustrations is 15 per cent; in a few instances however the length of the text has imposed a higher reduction factor of up to 28 per cent to maintain the standard format of the new edition.

NOR:RA

R
942
·54

Rf 577713

Reprinted in England by Scolar Press Ltd.
Menston, Yorkshire, U.K.

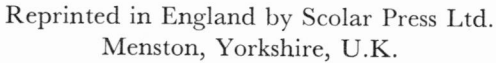

J. Jackson pinxit 1811.

H. Meyer sculp.^t

JOHN NICHOLS, F.S.A. ÆTAT. LXVI.

THE

HISTORY AND ANTIQUITIES

OF THE

COUNTY OF LEICESTER.

By JOHN NICHOLS, F.S.A.

VOLUME I. PART II.

CONTAINING A CONTINUATION OF

THE HISTORY OF THE TOWN OF LEICESTER:

INCLUDING AN ACCOUNT OF ITS

RELIGIOUS FOUNDATIONS, PUBLIC INSTITUTIONS, AND PAROCHIAL HISTORY.

WITH

ANNALS OF THAT ANTIENT BOROUGH;

CONSISTING OF ORIGINAL CHARTERS, AUTHENTIC CORPORATION RECORDS, AND
MISCELLANEOUS EVENTS, DIGESTED ACCORDING TO THE SERIES OF TIME.

TO WHICH ARE ADDED,

GENERAL INDEXES TO THE WHOLE WORK;

WITH

AN APPENDIX OF ADDITIONS AND CORRECTIONS.

LONDON:

PRINTED BY AND FOR NICHOLS, SON, AND BENTLEY,
RED LION PASSAGE, FLEET STREET.
1815.

PREFATORY ADVERTISEMENT.

I HAVE now the pleasure of presenting to the Publick my last labours on the " History and Antiquities of Leicestershire."

Having nearly worn out my eyes in the service of the County, I was under the absolute necessity of seeking for aid in compiling the General Indexes; and I consider myself fortunate in having met with such able Assistants.

Well knowing the Abilities and Industry of my Friend and late Apprentice Mr. JOSEPH STRUTT, I had great satisfaction in confiding the Index to his care; but more important engagements compelled him to relinquish it after COMPLETING THE FIRST VOLUME. I cannot communicate his ideas on the plan he adopted more appropriately, than in a Letter which he wrote to me on the subject:

" WORTHY SIR,   *December* 22, 1813.

" I have at length the satisfaction to announce to you, that my labour in compiling the Index to your First Volume has been crowned with the former part of that issue which I had hardly the hope to look forward to, namely, that of being spared to put the finishing stroke to the task, and that, too, as you have kindly declared to me, unto your satisfaction: And herewith I transmit once more to you the last portion of manuscript, having revised it, and made such amendments therein as you were pleased to indicate as requiring correction. The latter period of my labour is still in reversion: I mean, the confirmatory approbation of your candid Readers; this I anxiously look forward to, humbly trusting that my endeavours will not pass altogether unacknowledged.

" Perhaps, Sir, it may be expedient to offer some apology or explanation to yourself and to your readers as to the voluminous extent which my Index has attained. It is observable, that (except in the two hundred pages comprising the histories of the Earls of Leicester) far the larger portion of this First Volume, in the Town-annals especially, is occupied with minor notices relative to numerous personages and matters, classed chronologically where the series is continuous, as in the said Annals; and here alone might have been found materials sufficient for a *chronological* index; but oftentimes these notices are widely dispersed, and introduced incidentally: so that the personal and alphabetical arrangement cannot be much less copious as to quantity and wording, than the original passages referred to: indeed, in this transfer of order from chronological to alphabetical, the latter will require considerably more language to express particulars than the former, where the matters following each other in one paragraph, or at one view, one general head or wording serves for the whole; which will require to be repeated to each, when disorganized and renewed alphabetically. And in order, in some measure, to atone for this necessary length of repetition, it seemed that the introduction of some *new* memoranda, besides the additions and corrections which might occur, would be no unpleasing relief to the reader: I have therefore, where opportunity served, given explanations of ambiguous terms and antiquated usages, when the passage of text referred to had no note of illustration subjoined (for many of which explanations I am indebted to that useful work, Cowel's Interpreter); and these appeared to me the more desirable, as I look upon this Introductory Volume as the *clavis*, by which the portal into the subsequent portions of this Work is to be opened, and also as the grand *depôt* where *prolegomena* of every denomination, as well as explications of antient usages, should be largely collected, and the rather, for the reader's convenience, that, these explanations being given once for all, he may not be troubled to turn over page after page of successive Volumes in quest of desired information, and, after all, perhaps, meet with little to gratify his wishes:—I mean that, in the parochial collections for this County, each particular place (with a few restrictions) has its tenures, usages, customs, &c. *mutatis mutandis*, in conformity with its neighbour-place: under which, then, of these places should these explanatory notices be placed so conveniently, to avoid repetition (not easy to be avoided in a Work of such magnitude as the present), as in an introductory volume, in a common-place order?

" If any real apology on my part be requisite, it is, Sir, that, in two or three instances, I have given a turn of *badinage* to a pleasant occurrence,—but never at the expence of truth; again, in requital, on a few subjects I have launched into digressions with the *gravity* of a philosopher or a preacher (saving the lack of eloquence;) and, once in particular, I have *forced* a reference, or rather an article of references, in order to exhibit fairly the (much controverted) character of the great EARL OF LEICESTER*. As to my observations under the word *Ruled* Bible, I trust, Sir, to you, as a Father and Patron of Literature, they will not be found altogether unacceptable; and that your readers will be pleased not to consider them as too intrusive.

" As to the plan of the Index, and an explication of the abridged terms and characters employed therein, I inclose a schedule of remarks thereon; and will be obliged to you, if you will subjoin it to your prefatory observations.

" I cannot but repeat what I mentioned at the commencement of this Letter, that it is one source of great satisfaction to myself, that what I have been enabled and spared to execute and finish, has attained your approbation. Believe me, Sir, since first I entered upon the task, I have enjoyed but few moments free from bodily pain. Often, in the midst of my labours, have I looked forward with an almost desponding glance, at the portion of the Volume which still remained unexamined; then would I revert to the piles of rough-draught manuscript already travelled through, and scarcely a transitory hope whispered

---

* See the article *Hero,* in the General Index.

whispered in my ear, that it would be my task to fit them for the public inspection: but a good and beneficent Providence has been pleased to guide me to the end of this toilsome journey, and still I can look up to Heaven with gratitude for sparing mercies to myself and my numerous family. A recollection, too, of my obligations to you, Sir, which so many years have been increasing, inspirited me with much energy towards accomplishing my task:—and in presenting it in the whole to you, I feel it a duty incumbent on me, as well as a mark of becoming gratitude, to acknowledge myself,

Worthy Sir,

Your ever dutiful, greatly obliged, and grateful Servant,

Joseph Strutt."

Explanatory Hints relative to some peculiarities of method adopted in compiling the double Index to the First Volume.

By way of previous remark, it will not be amiss to examine cursorily with the reader the principal heads or grand divisions under which the subject-matter of this Volume is comprehended; because each of these divisions has its distinct mode of paging, and will be found so distinguished in the Indexes.

The parts, then, of the Work, are chiefly four: viz. 1. The *prolegomena*: 2. The Tables of Benefactions: 3. The Subject-matter of the Volume; *i. e.* The History of the Town of Leicester, including Memoirs of its Earls: and, 4. An Appendix, preserving the Charters and other documents which could not with propriety have broken a continuous narrative in the body of the work.

The pages of the *prolegomena* are marked by the numerical letters, i, ii, iii, iv, &c.; so are they in the Index: now, these run on uninterruptedly till p. liv, where the Dissertation on the Domesday-book closes; and then follows a series of 24 (unpaged) pages, *Conspectus Tabellaris Leicestriæ*. The paging then takes a retrograde course to xli; so that there is a double series from xli. to liv: and, in order to distinguish the latter from the former, the interposed pages are included in [ ] brackets: this too is complied with, in the Index. Again: the Tables of Benefactions are indicated by arithmetical figures; as is the whole of the subject-matter of the Volume; only, as the series of paging is renewed in each of these parts of the Work, the pages of the former are, for distinction-sake, included in brackets, both in the body of the Work, and in the Index. The pages of the *Appendix* have the abridged word *App.* prefixed to them.

One other peculiarity of paging, common both to the Work and the Index, is that of marking the pages with an asterisk; as xlvii*, 5*, &c.; signifying their interposition, and the places where they are to be inserted.

The pages of reference inclosed within ( ) the parenthetical character, relate solely to the method of the Index, independently of any correspondent distinction in the body of the Work: and it may be necessary to explain this peculiarity somewhat at large to the reader, and to adduce an example by way of illustration.—It is obvious, that, in a work of the miscellaneous kind as is the present, many *incidental* matters present themselves in such a way, that, were they to be analysed in the progressive order of the pages, and so laid before the reader, it would indeed seem an assemblage of anachronisms, an incongruous jumble; as, oftentimes, the first notice we have of a person is by means of an occurrence which, in an Index, should claim the last place. The second Simon de Montfort, for instance, whose memoir occupies upwards of a hundred pages in this Volume, is first introduced to the reader's notice by his having banished the Jews from Leicester: this is told *incidentally*: that is, the subject under consideration is the *Jewry-wall*; and this, again, occurs nearly a hundred pages before the memoir of the said Simon commences, and in the course of the memoir is again noticed, as also in the Appendix.—Farther, this Earl's funeral is spoken of, p. 107, at the very outset of his memoir: whereas p. 208, his death, the incidents previous thereto, and the consequences thereof, are stated at large; and thither I have deferred the anticipated notice, inclosing it in a *parenthesis*, and subjoining it to its proper place of connexion.

In a word, the parenthetically-included pages of reference may with propriety be denominated *retrospective references;* which term, and the above and subsequent example, may perhaps suffice to give the reader a clear insight into the method of analysis proposed and adopted by the compiler throughout: it has been his aim to trace *events* regularly, though the *order of pages* be not progressive :|yet that, probably, is of small moment, if the notice sought be shewn by a correct reference.

So, *Peter* (Aigleblanche) is mentioned as *dead*, p. 127: he appears on the stage of action, pp. 130, 132, &c. &c. The notice of his death, inhumation, &c. is reserved for the end of the article in a parenthesis.——On a like account, the three references are subjoined to the article William Earl of *Ferrers*.

Sometimes, but rarely, the parenthesis *looks forward;* as may be seen in the article of Leicester *Town.* The grand idea suggested for the employment of this distinctive character, whether *prospective* or *retrograde*, is to concentrate in the most suitable and concinnous place all discrepant as well as (for an analytical assemblage) disorganized particulars.

The figures, then, included in a parenthesis, will be found to be smaller numbers following larger ones: and suitable harmony of matters in progressive dependence on each other is the result.

Now, as the *parenthesis* serves as a *retrospective* guide, the reader may be conducted *progressively* to *repeated* matters by a series of figures separated from each other by a *semicolon:* the substance of each article is compressed into one head, and any essential differences of statement are brought under one view; the figures following the whole, as just noticed.

Sometimes expletive words, various readings of the same name, corrective exceptions, illustrative comparisons, parallel passages diversely stated, and supplementary memoranda, all, however, amended or deducible from the Work itself, will be found comprehended under the parenthesis.—The articles included in brackets, and, where of any length, marked by the antient useful character ¶, are such, for the most part, as the Compiler has been enabled to supply without reference to the Volume itself.

In the Index of Names, the word *sir* printed in italicks, as after Pexale, Pycsale, Raynes, &c. shews those gentlemen to have been of the *Clergy;* as is mentioned under the article *Sir*, in the General Index.

Where the reader is referred from one passage to another for information, the precise word for his consultation is shewn in the *italic type*, or, if it be an article of larger importance, in the small-capital character: for it does happen that, in referring to a person for instance, there may be others of a similar surname, so that the distinguishing Christian-name is requisite to be set down also. Thus, under "Burton, John de;" this direction is given: "see John de *Knighton;*" and, in the next line, after William *Burton*, it is said, "see Richard *Elvet*." The particular words *Elvet* and *Knighton*, are those to which the reader must look. Again: under *Otho*, the reference stands thus: "see Henry *Grismond*, duke of Lancaster;" where *Grismond* determines the reference.

Concerning the unavoidable bulk of this Compilation, an apology has been offered, or at least an explanation of the reason and necessity thereof has been adduced, in the letter inclosing this schedule of remarks. To surmount this inconvenience as far as possible, it has been contrived to bring each article within the compass of a single paragraph;—not, as is usual in indexes, to make each reference a distinct paragraph, or break-line, subordinate to its leading word. That each reference may stand clear without discontinuance of the line, a small dash closes the sentence, and fresh matter of reference is immediately annexed; and, when greater distinction is requisite, a somewhat larger or double dash is used. By this contrivance, and that of the *prospective semicolon* and *retrospective parenthetical reference* spoken of above, (if the Reader will be pleased to consult one of the longer articles of this Index, he will readily perceive that,) great acquisition of space has been retrieved.

It

It is trusted that the interchanged classification of *names* and *titles*, and of *titles* and *names*, which *vice versâ* will be found in this double Index, is an arrangement not entirely without its advantage. For instance; in the Index of Names, we have Bellomont, the first Norman earl of Leicester, noticed by his family-name; whence the Reader is directed to the word Leicester, where, under the earls of that title, all the references where the said earl Bellomont occurs, are shewn. So of Le Bossu his son, and of Blanchmaines his grandson; each of whom is, in like manner, under his several name, referred to the same titular appellation in this Index. That is, in one word; in the Index of Names, under the several titles of nobility, every personage will be found ranged by his patronymic appellation according to the order of his succession to the title and dignity set above his name. But, in the General Index, this method is reversed: for, under the patronymicks, the titles also being annexed, the several matters of reference are collected. It is obvious that, if all the Earls of Leicester had been set down; in the General Index, under the word *Leicester*, it would have incumbered the word too much; there being perhaps no fewer than thirty of the said Earls, besides the accumulation of local matters which fall under that word. By consulting the Index of Names, all the Earls of Leicester will be found at one view, and the order of seniority determines the arrangement of their names. So of the other noble persons mentioned in this History.

Another remark.—It has been already suggested, that the notices selected for the compilation of the analysis do not lie in the Volume accommodated for that purpose. A person's epitaph may first occur perhaps; then we find him elected mayor probably; then we find him a benefactor to some charitable institution, &c. &c. To preserve greater harmony, it has been my endeavour to get a good starting-place for each article, so as to lead the Reader forward in due method. With the *mayors* of Leicester, for instance, and other town-officers, I begin with their election; and the *vicars* are commenced with their induction: for it must be observed, that these gentlemen are afterwards frequently styled from their respective offices, as their actions spring from the execution of the same. An epitaph may declare a man to have been *twice mayor* of Leicester; but it is my wish to exhibit the time of his election, &c. By thus conducting the Reader as it were to the fountain-head, one grand desideratum is acquired; namely, a *date*, (of which, in many places of this History, there is a great dearth;) by knowing when-about such a one flourished, the subsequent notices respecting him are more usefully applicable; and many persons of exactly similar names are kept distinct: (and to preserve this distinction has been the greatest source of labour in the compilation of this Index.)

To say a word or two respecting the title *Rev.* following a name, in the General Index. Where, after the name the first mention is, that he was the incumbent of such a place, the *Rev.* is needless; therefore omitted: thus of Mr. Angell, I say: " Angell, John, vicar of St. Nicholas's," &c.—Now the case is different with Mr. Bickerstaffe: he was no vicar, nor perhaps have I found occasion in my references to point out his being a *clergyman*, at least without too much circumlocution: all which information the Reader has at the outset in one word, viz. " Bickerstaffe, *Rev.* William, usher," &c.

But, in the Index of Names, the *reverend* gentlemen are always mentioned as such: thus; Angel, rev. John; Bickerstaffe, rev. William; &c. (Thus accommodating one Index to another; as throughout it has been attempted to render each subservient in illustration to the other by exhibiting the *names* as well as *titles* of the more dignified characters, as already largely noticed.)

I have not, as a gentleman once said to me, *squired the squires;* nor, except in some instances, could I have done it, being an entire stranger to all the gentlemen mentioned:—neither are the *M. D. s* and *D. D. s* discriminated; which also to do I had not competent information.—Under these disadvantages, I have been obliged to leave more for the Reader's developement than I could have wished.

The Reader will be pleased farther to remark, that when any king's name is mentioned; if he be *of England,* it is not expressed so in the Index. Thus Isabel, " daughter of king John, marries," &c.; not the " daughter of John king of England," &c.

It will be expected that *general* terms, such, for instance, as *instrument, award, deed, charter,* &c. should not find leading places in this Index; except in some few particulars, the insertion of these has been carefully guarded against: but the following is one of the instances where a *general* term is employed, and the reason assigned. An article concerning Thos. de Cantelupe is thus worded: " Cantelupe, Thos. de, sent by and on the part of the Earl of Lei-" cester to Amiens, to await the award of the king of France, 148."—What king of France?—What *award?* and on what occasion? and betwixt what parties? (may the Reader say.) Turn to the word *award,* (is the reply;) and there it is said, that " it was of St. Lewis of France; and betwixt Henry III. of England and the barons."—To have said all this under Cantelupe (many others besides him being concerned) would have had too much dilated the article.

Again; epistolary writing is oft-times peculiarly instructive, and highly pleasing to many readers: and as this Volume comprises transcripts of many curious original *letters,* they are indicated at one view, under that word.

Monumental inscriptions, too, are perused with pleasure; they afford not only general instruction, but also particular information. These (or at least the detached ones) are severally referred to under the above head. When I say that the *detached* epitaphs are collected and indicated, I mean all that do not occur in the parochial histories, but lie here and there dispersed through the book: for, under each parish described, the epitaphs are given together after the account of each church.

Thus much respecting the occasional use of *general* terms. Other reasons might have been assigned for employing them; but a more enlarged specification would be a labour of needless assumption.

To conclude; I most fervently hope the candid Reader will forgive one thing which I have proposed to myself as an invariable rule from which I never mean to recede; I mean that of retaining our true English orthography; the Work itself too, in this respect, formed my exemplar. The modern system of pruning (too lenient a term, by-the-by, because then some good might be expected), of maiming our native language, is really unpardonable.—Well for our discontented mal-orthographical innovators, that Dr. Johnson is far removed from witnessing their temerity. —Can an Englishman bear to see such words as *labor, armor, endeavor, rumor,* &c. obtruded upon him as *English* terms? No surely.——In what has our *k* final * offended, that it must be discarded without a particle of regard to its use in strengthening the pronunciation† ?——Why, too, must our lordly *z* be converted into the simpering *s*? And this is even extended to words of pure Greek original. But I do not believe our innovators have quite the effrontery to destroy the distinction in every particular: *seise* for *seize* I am unconscious of having seen, nor does it seem to have found its way into those receptacles of modern miscalled improvements,—spelling-books. But I must not here enlarge on this subject. J. S.

The Reader having an opportunity of judging for himself, I scarcely need add, that this Index was compiled to my entire satisfaction. A more complete Analysis of any Work, than that which is included in the General Index to the First Volume, has seldom been presented to the Publick. For the truth of this assertion, it is only necessary to refer to any of the more prominent articles—*Simon de* Montfort (II. or the *younger)* Earl of Leicester, for instance; where all the leading particulars of this gallant

* To such a pitch of upstart temerity has this system of lopping prevailed, that even in family-names, where long prescriptive usage might have pleaded an irrefragable claim, exclusive of the general arbitrary orthography of patronymicks allowed by hereditary hypercritical decision, for retaining the complement of letters constituting such names ,—even in these appellations, I say, transmitted from father to son in uniform semblance, our modern refining correctors cannot withhold the exercise of their sharp talents, but impertinently slash away what they are pleased to style *unnecessary* letters. But there is one consolation: these dogmatic correctors constitute an abject minority, in advocating the disfigurement of our language.—J. S.

† It may be conveniently spared in an Adjective to distinguish it from a Substantive. Thus, in the present Work, I write " a *pnblic* man;" but should say " the good of the *publick*."

Warrior and eminent Nobleman, mentioned in the Volume, are shown at one view, with the advantage of being digested into a better arrangement than was practicable in compiling the History, as additional information was continually arising, after the previous matter had been printed off; a circumstance wholly unavoidable in so extended a Work.

Not content, however, with giving the Reader all the particulars comprised in the Volume, Mr. STRUTT has frequently introduced Additional Information, chiefly illustrative of the Manners and Customs of former times; as well as noticed such Corrections as his accurate eye discovered in the perusal of the Volume.

I have great pleasure in paying this well-deserved attestation to modest merit; and have no doubt the Reader will find this Index (what few Indexes can boast) at the same time instructive and amusing.

Desireable, however, as such an extended Analytical Index may be, I was aware that the plan could not be carried into execution with all the Volumes; nor, perhaps, from the different nature of their contents, did the same necessity exist. I therefore engaged the assistance of another literary friend, Mr. JAMES PELLER MALCOLM, F. S. A. the Modern Historian of London; who, with great expedition, performed the laborious task, on a plan which I suggested to him.

The " Personal Index to the Second, Third, and Fourth Volumes," embraces every individual of consequence mentioned in those portions of the Work. The names of *all the Landholders* are given, under this restriction, that when Lands or Manors remained for a century or more in a Family bearing the same name, *that name* is seldom mentioned more than *once* in the same page, in the Index, though there may be ten or more members of the family noticed as succeeding to the property. The names of the Patrons and Incumbents, and the principal Epitaphs, are also given.

Previously to the Reformation, the word *Priest* points out the Clergy; and, subsequently to that event, *Rev.* is used. To distinguish individuals of the same Christian and Sur Names, the *years* in which they lived are commonly given. This plan, it is hoped, by facilitating research, will be found useful.

The " Local and Miscellaneous Index to the Second, Third, and Fourth Volumes," speaks for itself.

When I consider the great bodily sufferings of Mr. MALCOLM while compiling this Index, I am astonished at his fortitude and perseverance. "The Almighty," says my afflicted Friend, " has been so merciful to me, as to enable me to complete your Index; and thus have been fulfilled your benevolent intentions towards myself and family. Surely, never before was an Index compiled under an equal continuance of pain: but it was a kind of refuge and solace against affliction; and often has it turned aside the severest pangs."

To the late Mr. BARAK LONGMATE I paid a willing tribute of regard early in the Work. (See Vol. II. p. 182.)—To his SON (the worthy Successor of a worthy Father), I am indebted for Indexes to the Arms and Pedigrees in the whole Work, as well as for much useful heraldic information, and professional assistance, in the course of my labours.

By the kindness of the Rev. MATTHEW DRAKE BABINGTON, I am enabled to enrich my Appendix with an ample Pedigree of his antient and respectable Family*.

The Rev. HENRY WOODCOCK, Vicar of Barkby, has also very obligingly favoured me with a Plate of very curious Sepulchral Relicks.

In conclusion, after again sincerely thanking all the Friends who have in any manner assisted in bringing these Volumes before the Publick; I trust I shall not be accused either of querulousness or ingratitude, when I observe, that, in a pecuniary point of view, not only the labour of more than thirty years has been in a great measure frustrated ; but I have actually suffered an immense loss— arising, at first, from the tardy patronage received at the commencement of the publication, and the very confined sale of a Work which now cannot be obtained under at least three times its original very cheap price—and, secondly, from the melancholy destruction of by far the greater part of the impression.

I trust, however, that I may be allowed to indulge a hope, that the few existing copies of the Work will secure to its Author an honourable and a lasting reputation: And am truly thankful to a gracious Providence, for being permitted to say, that, on the day of an Anniversary which with me completes the allotted age of man, I am enabled to put a finishing hand to " The History and Antiquities of the County of Leicester."

Highbury Place, [Feb. 2, O. S.] Feb. 14, *N. S.* 1815.   J. NICHOLS, *Septuagenarius.*

---

* To be placed between p. 954 and p. 955, of Vol. III.

₊ *To gratify the wishes of a dutiful Son, the following article is here introduced, extracted from the Eighteenth Number of a very elegant Work, intituled, " British Gallery of Contemporary Portraits."*

BRIEF MEMOIRS of the AUTHOR.

" JOHN NICHOLS, the son of Edward and Anne Nichols, was born at Islington, February 2, 1744-5; and received his education in that village, at the academy of Mr. John Shield. In 1757, he was placed under the care of the learned Printer, Mr. William Bowyer, who, in a short time, received him into his confidence, and entrusted to him the management of his Printing-office.

" In 1766, having previously become a Freeman of London, and a Liveryman of the Company of Stationers, he entered into partnership with his Master; with whom, in 1767, he removed from White Friars into Red Lion Passage, Fleet-street. This union continued till the death of Mr. Bowyer, in 1777.

" In August 1778, he became associated with Mr. David Henry in the management of the Gentleman's Magazine; to which he has ever since been an extensive contributor, and for many years sole Editor.

" In 1781, he was elected an honorary member of the Society of Antiquaries of Edinburgh; in 1785, received the same distinction from the Society of Antiquaries of Perth; and, in 1810, was elected a Fellow of the Society of Antiquaries of London.

" In December 1784, he obtained a seat in the Common Council of London, for the Ward of Far-ringdon Without, of which he was also Deputy from 1787 to 1797; and finally resigned his seat in December 1811.

" On January 8, 1807, by an accidental fall, he fractured one of his thighs; and on February 8, 1808, experienced a far greater calamity, by a fire, which occasioned the total destruction of his Printing-office and warehouses, with the whole of their valuable contents.

" Under these accumulated misfortunes he experienced the sympathy and aid of extensive friendship; his mind gradually recovered its vigour; and his first efforts were exerted to complete his great literary undertaking, " The History of Leicestershire," which alone seems to demand the labour of a whole life.

" In 1800, he associated with himself in partnership John-Bowyer Nichols, his son; and, in 1812, Mr. Samuel Bentley, his nephew.

" The publications, of which Mr. Nichols has been either Author or Editor, are very numerous. The following more particularly may be attributed to him:

" The Origin of Printing," 1774, 8vo.; a joint production of Mr. Bowyer and himself; reprinted in 1776; and a Supplement added in 1781.

" Three Supplemental Volumes to the ' Works of Dean Swift,' with Notes, 1775, 1776, 1779; and, in 1801, a complete edition of ' Swift's Works,' 19 vols. 8vo.; reprinted in 1803, 24 vols. 18mo.; and again in 1808, in 19 vols. 8vo.

" The Original Works, in Prose and Verse, of William King, LL.D. with Historical Notes," 1776, 3 vols. small 8vo.

" Brief Memoirs of Mr. Bowyer," 1778, 8vo. distributed, as a tribute of respect, amongst a few select friends. Subsequent communications, and an extension of the plan, produced, in 1782, ' Biographical and Literary Anecdotes of William Bowyer, Printer, F.S.A. and of many of his learned Friends,' 4to. This was again reprinted in 1812, with a vast accession of biography and correspondence, under the title of ' Literary Anecdotes of the Eighteenth Century.' Of this, eight large Volumes, 8vo. have appeared, and a ninth is very far advanced in the press.

" A Collection of Royal and Noble Wills." 1780, 4to.

" A Select Collection of Miscellaneous Poems, with Historical and Biographical Notes," 8 vols. small 8vo. 1780—1782.

" Bibliotheca Topographica Britannica," a series of articles of British topography, begun in 1780, and completed in 1790, in fifty-two numbers, or parts, forming eight vols. 4to.

" Biographical Anecdotes of William Hogarth." 1781, 8vo. Republished in 1782 and 1785; and again in 1810, in two quarto volumes, with 160 plates, accurately copied in that size from the originals.

" Biographical Memoirs of William Ged." 1781, 8vo.

" History and Antiquities of Hinckley, in Leicestershire," 1782, 4to; and a new edition, in folio, in 1813; to which is added, a " History of Witherley," &c.

" Bishop Atterbury's Epistolary Correspondence, with Notes." 4 vols. 8vo. 1783—1787; reprinted in 1799 with Memoirs of the Bishop, and a fifth volume of additional Correspondence, &c.

" A Collection of Miscellaneous Tracts, by Mr. Bowyer and some of his learned Friends." 1785, 4to.

" History and Antiquities of Lambeth Parish." 1786, 4to.

" The Works, in Verse and Prose, of Leonard Welsted, Esq. with Notes, and Memoirs of the Author." 1787, 8vo.

" The History and Antiquities of Aston Flamvile and Burbach, in Leicestershire," 1787, 4to.

" Sir Richard Steele's Epistolary Correspondence, with Biographical and Historical Notes," 1788, 2 vols. small 8vo. Reprinted, with large additions, in 1809.

" The Progresses and Royal Processions of Queen Elizabeth." 3 vols. 4to. 1788—1804.

" The History and Antiquities of Canonbury, with some Account of the Parish of Islington." 1788, 4to.

" The Lover and Reader," by Sir Richard Steele. 1789, 8vo. And in 1790 and 1791, Sir Richard's " Town Talk," and other Miscellanies. 2 vols. 8vo.

" Collections towards the History and Antiquities of the Town and County of Leicester," 1790, 2 vols. 4to.

" Miscellaneous Antiquities, in continuation of the Bibliotheca Topographica Britannica." Six numbers, 4to. 1792—1798.

" The History and Antiquities of the Town and County of Leicester," begun in 1795, and concluded in 1815; in eight parts, forming four very large volumes, folio.

" Illustrations of the Manners and Expences of Ancient Times in England." 1797, 4to.

" Letters on various Subjects, to and from Archbishop Nicolson." 1809, 2 vols. 8vo.

" A new Edition of " Fuller's Worthies," with brief Notes. 2 vols. 4to, 1811.—&c. &c. &c.

" Mr. Nichols, in 1766, married Anne, daughter of Mr. William Cradock, of Leicester, by whom, who died in 1776, he has two daughters*; and again, in 1778, Martha, daughter of Mr. William Green, of Hinckley, who died in 1788, and by whom he has one son and four daughters†."

* See Vol. III. p. 1149.　　　　　† See Vol. IV. p. 709.　　　CON-

CONTENTS.

LIST OF PLATES.

FRONTISPIECES TO THE EIGHT PARTS.

The HISTORY and ANTIQUITIES

OF THE

RELIGIOUS FOUNDATIONS in LEICESTER.

RES ANTIQVAE LAVDIS ET ARTIS
INGREDIOR, SANCTOS AVSVS RECLVDERE FONTES.

VIRGIL.

VETERA MAIESTAS QVAEDAM, ET, VT SIC DIXERIM, RELIGIO COMMENDAT.

QVINTIL.

In refuming the Local Hiftory of LEICESTER, it is our intention firft to defcribe the feveral religious foundations; then to give briefly, in the way of annals, fuch general particulars of the town of Leicefter as occurred previous to the diffolution; and, finally, the feparate defcription of each parifh.

MONASTERIES, COLLEGES, RELIGIOUS HOUSES, AND HOSPITALS.

UNDER this head, I find fo valuable an Introduction prepared by Mr. STAVELEY, that it would be injuftice to his memory if I were not to give it as nearly as poffible in his own words.

"Being now," fays this learned Lawyer, "come to fpeak of the Monafteries, Colleges, Frieries, and Religious Houfes, fituate in and about Leicefter, it will not, I hope, be impertinent to premife fomething touching the original of a monaftic life and profeffion. For, the name, or word, *monachus*, a monk, it is well known to be derived from the Greek word μόνος, *folus*, fignifying fuch a one as lives folely and alone; for when, in the infancy of Chriftianity, great perfecutions were raifed againft the profeffors thereof, many of the Chriftians retreated into the woods and deferts for protection and fhelter againft thefe ftorms[1]; therein following, as fome fay, Samuel the prophet, Helyfeus, and Helyas, who lived in poor cottages and defert places near the river Jordan; as St. John the Baptift long time after did in the wildernefs; imitated, as fome alfo fay, by St. Mark; and after thefe, we hear much of Paul the Hermit, St. Anthony, St. Hilarion, St. Bafil, St. Hierom, and others. But of thefe Paul the Hermit was of greateft note for his retired living, who, to avoid the perfecution raifed under Decius, betook himfelf to the wildernefs, where he is faid to have lived ninety-three years unknown to any one[2]; and frequent it alfo was, towards the primitive times, and when there was no imminent perfecution, for feveral perfons, out of devotion, melancholy, or other regards, to leave the world, and betake themfelves to fuch a fequeftrated courfe of life. But, at the firft, thefe men had no certain rule or order; for, every one, being free, regulated himfelf as he faw beft for his fpiritual advantage, exercifing devout prayers, frequent faftings, hard ftudies, with mean and flender diet, which they acquired by labour of their hands, thereby giving great examples of pious living to all pofterity.

"St. Anthony is the firft unto whom fome do chiefly refer the original of this monaftic profeffion, in regard he fo greatly raifed up the defires of men to lead this kind of life, and firft inftituted fome rules for monks, as St. Bafil did afterwards in Greece, and St. Hilarion in Syria. This Anthony lived in the defert of Thebes, in Egypt, and there built a monaftery; where, with his difciples, Sarmatus, Amatues, and Macharius, wholly exercifing himfelf in devotion, he fed upon nothing but bread and water; and fo famous was he for holinefs, that Helena, the mother of Conftantine, commended herfelf and fon to him by letters. He died in the wildernefs in the year 360, aged 105 years.

"After him, as is faid, Bafil, the bifhop of Cæfarea in Cappadocia, about the year 370, being very famous for his learning and piety, prefcribed fome orders alfo to monks; and obliged fuch as fhould enter into thofe holy orders to obferve poverty, chaftity, and obedience to their fuperiors.

"Then, about 166 years after the death of Anthony, one Benedictus Nurfinus[3], born in Umbria, a territory in Italy, having lived long in folitude, came at length to Sublacum[4], a place diftant from Rome about 40 miles, now called Sollago, according to Leander; but, to avoid great company, in regard many for his great fanctity reforted to him, he not long after betook himfelf to Caffinum, an antient place in that country; and, there fettling, he fet himfelf to gather together many difperfed and wandering monks into one monaftery, inftituting certain rules and forms for their obfervance, and affigning them a fpecial kind of habit, forms of prayers, and rules of diet[5].

"But, touching the beginning of a monaftic life here in England, if we look after particular perfons that, in times of perfecution, fled unto woods, caves, and deferts, for prefervation, it will be hard to point out the firft that did fo retire themfelves.

[1] Polydore Vergil, de Invent. lib. vii. cap. 1.
[3] *Nurfi* in the dukedom of Spoletti in Italy. R. F.
[5] Vid. Reiner. Apoftolat. Benedict.

[2] Catal. Sanct. Pet. Natal. lib ii. cap. 60.
[4] A defert called *Subla.um* [Subiaco]; Deering, p. 53. R. F.

" If we confider their firft being gathered into any convent or monaftery, then certainly thofe of Glaſtonbury in Somerſetſhire, and Bangor in Cheſhire, in the times of the Britains, will appear to be the firft[1]; in the latter whereof, as Bede relates, there was fo great a number, that, being divided into feven parts, each having a feveral ruler, every part was no lefs in number than 300, all living by the labour of their hands[2]. And yet thefe cannot be faid to have lived under any other rule than the Effeans in Paleſtine, as Polydore obferves.

" The firft monks tranſplanted hither were the Benedictines, who were brought over by Auſtin the Monk about the year 595, the converſion of the Saxons being alſo about this time wrought. By this Auſtin, and his followers, epifcopacy was eſtabliſhed in feveral places, and monaſteries by degrees built for monks obferving the rules of Benedict; fo that for a long time after there was none in England but of that order, even to the time of the Norman Conqueſt. Nay, all the Mitred or Parliamentary Abbeys in England, except the priors of the Hoſpitallers, were of this order, as fome have obferved.

" Thefe Benedictines, and feveral other orders, increaſing much in the world, and at feveral times and by degrees coming into England, the devotion of the middle and darker times running chiefly in that channel, there became fuch a breed and fuperfetation of monks and friers (of the diſtinction of which denomination we ſhall fay fomething prefently) that it is as difficult as unneceffary for our purpofe to have their defcent and pedigrees, through all the commixtures, coalitions, and refinements, that have been made amongft them; and that will fufficiently appear by giving only their names; as Auguſtinians, Benedictines, Cluniacks, Ciſtercians, Celeſtines, Cumalduenſes, Umbrenſes, Montolivitenſes, Grandimontenſes, Bernardines, Premonſtratenſes, Silveſtrenſes, Heremites of St. Hierom, Carthuſians, Gilbertines, Dominicans, Crouched Friers, Carmelites, White, Black, and Grey, Friers, Cordeliers, Capuchins, Minorites (Obſervantes), Minimes, Recollects, Theatines, Robertines, Trinitarians, Bons-homes de Pœnitentiâ Jefu (Fratres de Saccâ), Bethlemites, Francifcans, Jefuits, Jefuats, Oratorians, with many more, differing both fpecifically and gradually from one another, and amongft themfelves; befides thofe of the female fex, as the She-Benedictines, Nuns of St. Clere, She-Auguſtinians, Gilbertines, Brigetteans, and feveral others, almoſt as numerous in England as monks and friers; as having, although not fo many orders, yet many more of the fame order, that fex being experienced more zealous and eager than the males in any thing, as might fufficiently appear in Gilbertines, that hermophroditical order, admitting both men and women under the fame roof; for, during the life of Gilbert, their firft founder, for 700 brethren, there were 1100 fifters entered into that order[3].

" Of the people which enliſted themfelves in a religious profeffion, under the denominations above, fome of them were efteemed and called monks, and fome friers; which fometimes and with fome are undiſtinguiſhedly confounded together, and in fome reſpects they might all be called by either name[4]; but the differences between them confiſted chiefly of thefe particulars, according to the different fentiments of fome; as fome make monks the genus, and friers but the fpecies, fo that all friers were monks, but, è converſo, all monks were not friers. Others fay, that monks were confined to their cloiſters, whilſt more liberty was allowed to the friers to go about, preach, and beg in the country; others, that monks were properly in thofe convents where they had a biſhop over them, as Canterbury, Norwich, Durham, &c. but never any friers, or at leaſtwife fo called, were. The biſhop was the fupreme; and they had fome hand in this election. But the moſt effential difference was,

that monks had nothing in propriety, but all in common; friers had nothing either in propriety or in common; but, being mendicants, had all their ſubfiſtence from the continued current charity of others. They had indeed fome houfes, cells, or fites, to dwell in, but no endowments, properties, or poffeffions; and when it hath fometimes been debated, whether a frier may be faid to be the owner of his cloaths that he weareth, it hath been for the moſt part concluded in the negative. But yet, notwithſtanding this, certain it is, that fome convents of friers had large and ample revenues, as may appear by the catalogues and accounts given of our religious houfes[5]; but then we muſt know, that from the beginning it was not fo; the firft inſtitution of the friers was otherwiſe; and the addition of lands and poffeffions to fome of them was of a late date, by the bounty of fome extraordinary benefactors: for, as is faid before, they generally had no endowments, but went their walks and circuits, up and down the country, with boys or valets at their heels, to collect the charity of others, who knew the precife time of their coming, againſt which their charity was made ready. But then this rural excurſion of the friers proved very prejudicial to the pariſh-prieſt, who dully repeating mafs, were very ignorant and lazy; but the friers were far more nimble fellows, ſlipping upon every occaſion into all pulpits, which, by virtue of fome papal privileges, they might do at their pleafure without reſtraint; and fo, by their frequent preaching, they infinuated much into the good will and affections of the people, whilſt the dull, idle prieſts became contemned as unprofitable and ufelefs: and then, when any perſon of quality ſtood in need of confeffion on his deathbed, a frier muſt always be fent for to do that office, who feldom or never failed to obtain the party's fepulture in his convent; and then the corpfe was always accompanied with fome good legacy and gifts; the great fcuffling between the friers and prieſts about thefe perquifites being fet forth to life by the moſt witty Erafmus, in his Dialogue Funus[6]. And little lefs were the animofities between the monks and friers, in regard the activity and pragmaticalnefs of thefe expofed the other as idle and infignificant fellows; and hence it is that we find Thomas Walfingham, Matthew Paris, and other monks, always fnarling and girding at the poor friers; particularly Matthew Paris, upon the coming of the Fratres de Saccâ into England, and the Bethlemites, faith that they brought confufion along with them[7]; and Walfingham, when the friers minors had got the heart of queen Eleanor to be buried in their convent, fays they were like a company of greedy dogs, always flocking about a dead corpfe, every one fnatching for a bit[8].

" To give fome diſtinction to thefe monks and friers, the feveral orders had their peculiar habits[9] for colour and fafhion, of which it is not worth the while to make farther enquiry or defcription here; yet in this they agreed, to have their crowns ſhaven; and in that ufage they conceive fome weighty myſteries are contained. For the original of this cuſtom there have been feveral conjectures. An old author[10] relates it thus: that, whilſt St. Peter preached at Antioch, the Gentiles there, by way of contumely towards the name of Chriſtians, ſhaved the top of his head, which was afterwards practifed by the monks and prieſts, as a teſtification of their glorying and honour in conforming to that which the faints fuffered for Chriſt's fake[11]; and hence probably it was, that that part of the head which was ſhaved became to be called corona, the crown. Thefe votaries alfo generally have the hair of their beards ſhaven; and this is done, they fay, by thofe whofe office it is to celebrate the mafs, that no part of the facramental wine, the blood of Chriſt, might hang upon or ſtick to their hairs; and then to the myſteries of ſhaving;

---

[1] Camden's Britannia, fol. 227.　　　[2] Eccl. Hiſt. lib. ii. cap. 2.　　　[3] Weever's Funeral Monuments, fol. 148.
[4] Hofpinian, de origine & progreffu monachatûs; Zechias de Republ. Ecclefiæ.
[5] See Speed's Catalogue, and Dugdale's Mon. Angl.　　　[6] Erafmus, Coll. Funus.　　　[7] Matth. Paris, fol. 949.
[8] Walſingham, in Edw. III.　　　[9] Vid. Monaſt. Angl.　　　[10] Johan. Tinemuthenfis.
[11] Vide Stellart. de coronis et tonfuris, lib. iii. cap. 1.

6

whereas

whereas the Abantes, an antient people of Thrace [1], and the Curetes, fo called *à tonfurâ*, both warlike people, ufed to fhave themfelves, that their enemies in fight might not catch or entangle them by the hair [2]; fo, thefe votaries being enlifted to fight againft a multitude of fpiritual enemies, they fhould not afford them the leaft advantage; no, not fo much as a hair. Plutarch, in the Life of Thefeus, relates this occafion and cuftom of the fhaving of the Abantes; and alfo that Alexander the Great commanded his captains to caufe all the Macedonian foldiers to be fhaven, that their enemies might not have the advantage of their hairs. He alfo tells, that it was a cuftom in Greece, for the young men, when they came to man's eftate, to offer their hair to Apollo in his temple at Delphi, and that Thefeus did fo; as our profeffed Romanifts initiate themfelves in their refpective orders by the tonfure of their heads. Farther, as hairs are accounted but fuperfluous excrements; by the fhaving them off is fignified, that a religious devotee fhould lay afide all fuperfluous things, and retain only what is neceffary. Befides, as at their admiffion thefe Romifh profeffors lofe their hairs, fo thereby they teftify that they fhall be ready to lofe their heads alfo in that caufe wherein they have thus enrolled themfelves. But, upon the trial of fome of the confpirators in the late plot difcovered by Dr. Oates, moft of whom were priefts, Jefuits, and Benedictines, it was averred, that this ceremony of fhaving is omitted or difpenfed withal to fuch Englifh priefts as take orders beyond the feas, and come into England to promote the Catholic caufe, to prevent difcovery, they having made themfelves liable to the penal laws by taking fuch orders.

" And here, I know not whether it be worthy of remembrance, a conceit of the Jews, going traditionally amongft them, who, though they acknowledge our Saviour Chrift to have been an extraordinary perfon, yet, amongft their fables of him, this is one: that, after he was dead, the Jews buried him in a fecret place, left his body fhould be found and worfhiped by his followers; when a noble woman that adhered to his doctrine fo prevailed with the Roman governor, that he threatened to kill the Jews unlefs they produced the body; which they, digging up, found uncorrupted, retaining the amiable favour that he had when alive; only the hair was fallen from his crown, imitated, as they fay, by the Romifh friers [3].

" Certain it is, that this ufage of fhaving the crowns of priefts was very antient; for, after the converfion of the Saxons here by Auftin the monk and his followers, who endeavoured to bring the Britifh Chriftians to an entire conformity to the Roman rites, there were differences a long time agitated between them, touching the time of the celebration of Eafter and the tonfure of priefts; the Britains therein following the Eaftern ufage, differing from that of the Romans; concerning which there is a notable epiftle (exemplified by Bede [4]) of Cleolfrid, a Northern abbot, to Naitanus king of the Picts, by which he endeavours to fet him right in thofe matters; and intimating, that tonfure arofe firft from the imitation of St. Peter, but upon an account different from that of John Tinemuthenfis remembered before. In regard, as he fays, St. Peter was fhaven in memorial of Chrift's fuffering, fo it did become his followers to bear the figns of his paffion even on the crowns of their heads, as their chiefeft glory and crown, where Chrift had worn a crown of thorns, as all churches on their fummits bore the fign of this crofs: all which, he fays, do teach, that for his fake we fhould crucify the flefh, and offer ourfelves to derifion for his fake, as he was content to be mocked for us; and by that means hope at laft to obtain the crown of glory. He hinteth alfo, that Simon Magus was alfo fhaven, but in a different manner from St. Peter; and that he expoftulated with one Adamnanus, a foreign abbot, for following therein the fafhion of Simeon, perfuading him to conform to the other. But for their fhaving thus much.

" I fhall not here, as I faid before, undertake to give a perfect account of all religious profeffed votaries, fome of which I have already only named or mentioned, but fhall confine myfelf to thofe of them that were feated in or near this town of Leicefter; of which the canons regular of the order of St. Auguftin, of whofe great monaftery here we fhall fpeak more prefently, being the moft eminent, I will defcribe them with as much brevity and certainty as I can.

" Moft people or nations have endeavoured to deduce their defcents from high and facred originals; and fome from the gods themfelves, as thofe of Italy and others: in competition with which, all religious orders and votaries, whofe originals were any whit uncertain, to win the greater reverence, would boaft the moft holy and glorious men to have been founders of their order. But for the canons regular there is very great uncertainty about their beginning [5]; fome refer their original to one pope, and fome to another; and others to feveral reputed faints and holy men; but they themfelves generally owned the famous St. Auguftin bifhop of Hippo to have been the firft inftitutor of their order [6]: but fome go much higher, amongft whom Thomas Aquinas, and fay they were firft inftituted by the Apoftles themfelves. In which variety, the common opinion fettled them upon St. Auguftin at laft; and thofe of this order pretend and profefs to live according to the rules that he prefcribed; which rules have alfo been embraced by feveral religious votaries of other names, and are exemplified at large in the beginning of the fecond volume of the " Monafticon Anglicanum:" but, as thofe rules are fpurioufly afcribed to that holy man, fo certain it is, that the lives of thefe canons regular were altogether different and unconformable to the moft pious and chriftian life of that great doctor of the church.

" But, whoever was the founder, certainly they were much efteemed here; and there was no county but what was plentifully ftored with them in great monafteries, and thofe very richly endowed, as may be collected from the catalogues of the religious houfes exhibited by Speed in his Hiftory and others [7]; and for their habit, as Polydore Vergil faith, it was a white coat and a linen furplice under a black cloak, with a hood, when pulled up, covering their head and neck; under all having doublet, breeches, and white ftockings, with fhoes and flippers; and, when they go abroad, a black cornered cap, or a broad hat, their crowns being fhaven, but not fo much as other monks [8].

" There was another fort of religious votaries who pretended the great St. Auguftin to have been their founder, and thefe were a fort of mendicant friers, not endowed like the canons regular; for they fay, that St. Auguftin inftituted their order when he lived in the wildernefs, and therefore they are called *Auguftiniani Eremitani*, or Eremite Auguftin Friers; and great contention hath been between the canons regular and them, who fhould engrofs fo eminent a founder; infomuch that moft of the Romifh learned men do fufpect, whilft others generally are affured, that St. Auguftin was no inftitutor either of the one or the other of them, according to the import of thefe old verfes:

" *Mendici fratres induti veftibus atris;*
Auguftinus ego nomen habere nego.

" Thefe begging friers, that in black are clad,
Nor name, nor habit, from St. Auftin had.

" Thefe Auguftinians, the firft order of the begging friers [9], came into England out of Italy about the year 1250, and obtained many feats here, as the Auguftin friers in London [10] (which was built for them by Humphrey Bohun earl of Hereford and Effex), and many other cloifters in England, did heretofore belong to this order of friers. They wear a

[1] Euftath. in Homer. [2] Strabo, lib. x. [3] Sandys's Travels, fol. 147. [4] Eccl. Hift. lib. v. cap. 22.
[5] Onuphr. Panvinius, in annotationibus ad Platinam. Sabellicus, Ennead. 9. lib. 9.
[6] Bale, Cent. 7. Polyd. Vergil, lib. iii. cap. 3. [7] Polydore Vergil, de Invent. lib. vii. cap. 3.
[8] Deering fays, p. 58, " Their crowns to be fhaved like other friers." R. F.
[9] Bale, Cent. 7. cap. 89. [10] Matth. Weftm. in anno 1250.

long white coat of cloth down to their heels all loose, with a cowl or hood of the same when they are in their cloifters; but, when they go abroad, they wear another black coat over the other, with another cowl, and then all bound close to their bodies with a broad leather girdle or belt; and this girdle is esteemed to have very great virtue in it, which they call St. Auftin's girdle; and many persons of great quality, and some queens, often wear it; but yet none but such as are special benefactors and pay well for it. But now those of this order beyond the feas (though they are competently rich, especially in Italy and Spain) have of late years not been of so great esteem, because Dr. Martin Luther, who revolted from the church of Rome, and was so great an agent in the Reformation of the Church, was a frier of this order: but that the reflection is by this time somewhat worn off; and at this day they are in pretty good repute in those places where they are [1].

" I confess I can hardly forbear the giving of some account of some other orders of monks and friers that once flourished in England, but that I fear the digreffion would be enlarged too far, though I hope it may be pardoned hitherto. But for those of them that had their situation in this our town of Leicefter I shall speak something particularly, as I meet with them in the pursuit of this discourse upon the place, which may give some light to the underftanding, in some measure, the nature of all the rest; premising, as is hinted before, that their numbers, differences, distinctions, and degrees, make it as difficult as unneceffary to make exact specification of them all.

" Now, for the monafteries, frieries, and religious houses, in and about Leicefter, we will begin with that great and eminent abbey of St. Mary de Pratis [2], or de la Pre, so called because situate with a pleasing profpect upon the meadows. This was first founded in the year 1143, with the advice of Alexander bishop of Lincoln and other discreet persons, by Robert Fitz-Robert, or Robert Boffu, of whom we have already spoken amply [3], for such monks as were canons regular of the order of St. Auftin, and in honour of the Affumption of the bleffed Virgin St. Mary: for he, having been very ftubborn, and undutiful to his prince, and a great ftickler in some dangerous commotions, when growing in years meditated the expiation of such crimes, particularly the injuries he had brought upon Leicefter, by founding and endowing of this and some other religious houfes; and into this, after the same was finished, he entered himself a canon regular, with the confent of his lady Amicia, where he lived in that profeffion fifteen years, and there died, and was buried [4].

" In the fame train of devotion this great earl founded a monaftery for Ciftercian or White Monks at Gerendon in this county; and, that his lady might fympathize with him in such a derelidion of the world, he and she, or one of them, founded a nunnery at Nun-Eaton, in Warwickshire; where she, by his confent, enrolled herself a nun, and in that profeffion there died [5].

" The fon of this Robert Boffu was Robert Blanchmains, of whom also we have already fully spoken [6]. He married Petronel, daughter of Hugh Grentefmainel, baron of Hinckley and lord high fteward of England; which lady Petronel built a fair church to the said abbey, which was dedicated in the year 1279, and was buried in the choir thereof before the high altar [7]. It is memorable also of this lady, that in a devotional fit, she made a long rope or plait of her own hair, to be used with a pulley to draw up the great lamp or light in the choir; which was afterwards kept there for a long time as a precious relick.

" Though this great abbey was not always and to all purposes reckoned amongft the Mitred Abbeys, which were held by barony, and whofe abbots were fummoned to fit with the peers in parliament, yet in revenue and ftate it far exceeded many of the others, the firft founder being very liberal in its endowments, befides the liberality of many fubfequent benefactors. The more eminent and hofpitable it alfo was, in regard of its excellent and convenient fituation, being a competent diftance from the town, fo that it was not crowded with other houfes, or town-bound. It was feated in an extraordinary rich and fertile foil, both giving and receiving a delicate profpect, and having all imaginable accommodations for receipt and provifions in its demefnes, granges, paftures, feeding, tithes, mills, woods, fifhings, boons, rents, tenants, &c. and ftanding juft upon the great road from London into the North, it was frequented by, and gave entertainment to, perfons of all qualities, and gave great relief to the neighbourhood and poor of the country.

" And here it would not be improper to give fome account or an inventory of the lands and poffeffions of this houfe, which indeed were many and large; and I prefume we fhall not be able to attain the knowledge or difcovery of them all; but fo much touching the fame as can be collected out of the Regiftry of this Abbey, ftill preferved in that noble treafury of antiquity fir Robert Cotton's library, or other good evidence, we will caft all together at the latter end of the difcourfe upon the fame.

" Thus much at prefent, and in general, touching the endowments and poffeffions of this great monaftery. How it ftood in honour and parliamentary privilege we come now to enquire; and for this purpofe we muft know, that all monafteries had a chief, commonly called Abbot or Prior, Cænobiarcha. An Abbat, or Abbot, was fo called from the Syriac word abba, father [8]; and Prior, from the Latin, denoting his priority, being both fpiritual governors, having rule and pre-eminence over a religious houfe [9]. Some of thefe were mitred abbots and barons of parliament; and thofe that were mitred or lords of parliament were exempt from the jurifdiction of the diocefan, having within themfelves epifcopal authority within their precincts, and were called abbots fovereign; and, as there were abbots, fo there were lords priors alfo, who had both exempt jurifdiction, and were lords of parliament. In the reign of king Henry III, when fummons of peers to parliament became more certain than before, all the abbots and priors of quality were fummoned to parliament; and in the 49th year of his reign no lefs than fixty-four abbots and thirty-fix priors were fummoned to parliament [10]: but in fubfequent parliaments their numbers were uncertain, fometimes more and fometimes lefs: for, when parliaments became more frequent, fome abbots and priors that lived at great diftance, by reafon of age or infirmities, or idlenefs, or comparative inability of their houfes, obtained leave to be freed of their honourable, but troublefome, attendance in parliament: for, in thofe days, there was not fuch labouring to be parliament-men as we now fee there is, it being antiently efteemed a great burden, and a trouble to ferve in that office in either of the houfes; and therefore the knights and burgeffes of the houfe of commons had wages from the feveral counties and places for which they ferved. But now we fee many thoufand pounds fpent in an election, when perfons, out of faction, ambition, or fome private defign, labour to be chofen members of parliament; a matter much wifhed, and fometimes endeavoured, to be regulated by a law [11].

But to return to our Spiritual Barons.

[1] Lewis Owen, fol. 35.
[2] Leland obferves that " the waulles of St. Marie abbey be 3 quarters of a mile aboute." Itinerary, vol. I. p. 16.
[3] See before, p 24—68.   [4] H. Knighton, fol. 2346; Leland, Collectanea, vol. I. fol. 70.
[5] Dugdale, Warwickfhire, in Nun-Eaton; and fee our Appendix, p. 15.   [6] See before, p. 67—90.
[7] Leland notices no more than one tomb in Leicefter abbey; and feems to have been uncertain whether it was this lady's, or the founder's. He fays, " Other Robert Boffue, erle of Leircefter, or Petronilla, a countefs of Leicester, was buried in a tumbe ex marmore chalch. donico yn the waul of the South of the high altare of S. Marie abbay of Leyrcefter." Itinerary, ubi fupra.
[8] Vide Powel, in voc. Abbat.   [9] Stat. 9 Ric. II. cap. 4.   [10] Dorf. Clauf. 49 Hen III. m. 11.
[11] The reader will recollect that thefe are the words of Mr. Staveley, at leaft a hundred years back.

" King

" King Edward III. was the firft who fixed upon a fet number of abbots and priors to be fummoned unto parliament ; and after him they fettled into the number of twenty-fix [1], generally reckoned thefe :

1. St. Alban's.	15. Shrewfbury.
2. Glaftonbury.	16. Gloucefter.
3. St. Auftin's, Cant.	17. Bardney.
4. Weftminfter.	18. Be'net in Holm.
5. St. Edmondfbury.	19. Thorney.
6. Peterborough.	20. Ramfey.
7. Colchefter.	21. Hide.
8. Evefham.	22. Malmefbury.
9. Winchelcomb.	23. Cirencefter.
10. Crowland.	24. St. Mary, York.
11. Battell.	25. Selby.
12. Reading.	26. Prior of St. John of
13. Abingdon.	Jerufalem, firft ba-
14. Waltham.	ron of England.

" All thefe held of the king *in capite, per baroniam* ; and if the king had called an abbot or prior by writ to parliament, who held not of the king *per baroniam*, he might take his liberty, and refufe to fit and ferve in parliament [2] ; and though fuch a one had been often called by writ, he might have obtained difcharge from that fervice, as feveral did, amongft which the abbot of Leicefter was one ; for, in the reign of king Edward III. it was that this abbot obtained a difcharge from the king by his patent, becaufe he held not of the king by barony, and that his predeceffors had not been conftantly fummoned, but *interpolatis vicibus* only, after the 49th of Henry III.[3] The words of the patent itfelf fhall be given in the Appendix [4].

" The parliament wherein this was obtained was fummoned by writs, dated 15 Nov. 25 Edward III. to fit upon St. Hilary's day following [5], which is the 13th of January ; and the 15th of February following (in the 26th year of his reign, he beginning the 25th of January) this patent or grant is dated ; and in the Claufe Rolls of that fummons of 25 Edward III, the abbot's name is cancelled, and thefe words are written againft it, ' *Abbas Leiceftriæ* cancellatur, quia habet cartam regis quod non compellatur venire ad parliamentum [6] ;' yet in 27 Edward III. the abbot of Leicefter appears fummoned again to the great council held in that year at Weftminfter [7], as alfo in the 29th year of that king : but his name is alfo there again cancelled, and the fame words written over againft it as before ; fo hard a thing was it to get fo great a privilege, as that was then efteemed to be, completed. And in thofe days, when multitudes of abbots and priors were called to parliament by writ, it may be obferved by the Records that feveral mafters of orders, officials, deans and priors of cathedral churches, whofe convents were chapters to them and the bifhops, were called alfo by writs to parliament [8]. But then, in time, they, and all fuch as held not by barony, but were called only by writ, upon petition that they and their houfes were burdened by their attendance in parliament, obtained difcharges for them and their fucceffors ; amongft which, as is faid before, the abbot of Leicefter was one, whofe name we find not in the foregoing lift ; for, the abbey of Leicefter, as hath been faid before, being founded by Robert Boffu earl of Leicefter (although the pa-

tronage thereof came to the crown by the forfeiture of Simon de Montfort earl of Leicefter), yet, being of a fubjeft's foundation, it could not be held *per baroniam*, and fo the abbot was incapable to be legally called to parliament [9] ; whereupon the king, upon the petition and agency of *William le Clowne*, an eminent abbot of that place, did grant, that the faid abbot and his fucceffors fhould for ever after be eafed and difcharged of their attendance in parliament ; for which the faid William le Clowne is celebrated as a great benefactor to his houfe. The like liberty the prior of Coventry alfo obtained ; and fo was it adjudged, in the parliament at York, in the cafe of the abbot of St. James near Northampton.

" Having mentioned that William le Clowne was a benefactor to this monaftery for the purpofe aforefaid, it will not, I hope, be amifs to give you a farther inventory of his good qualities and virtues, as I find them recorded, with fome admiration, by a canon of that houfe [10]. He was, faith he, a prudent and moderate governor ; a lover of peace ; ftudious of reformation ; of a pleafing afpect, both to his fuperiors and inferiors ; by his good example, the members of his houfe grew fo noted and eminent, that in his time two of them were called forth and chofen abbots ; viz. one of the monaftery of Miffenden [11], and the other of Wellow [12] : two others to be priors ; one of Tortington [13], and the other of Motesfont [14] : two, out of extreme devotion, turned anchorites ; one at Chefter ; the other at Leicefter, in St. Michael's church there : and two others promoted to good ecclefiaftical benefices. In his time two churches were appropriated to his abbey, Hungarton and Humberfton ; and two manors obtained, Ingwardby and Kirkby Malory ; with divers lands, rents, and poffeffions, in Hertyfhorn, Mofeley, Bytefwell, Leicefter, Humberfton, Belgrave, Dalby, and Burftall. Befide the charter of privilege for not coming to parliament before mentioned, he obtained alfo that, upon vacancy by death of the abbot, the king's efcheator fhould not enter into or upon any of the poffeffions of the monaftery, but upon the fite of the abbey only ; and that there he fhould ftay but one day and night for feifin (for in fuch cafes thofe officers would be very troublefome and chargeable) ; and this by charter from king Edward III. ratified and confirmed in 1377 by his fucceffor king Richard II. And with all perfons he was fo taking, that none could fcarcely deny him any thing ; infomuch that, to humour the king, who extremely delighted in dogs and hunting, he obtained a market for hounds and all kinds of dogs for hunting, in which fports he frequently accompanied the king, prince, and great lords : but he would privately tell his friends, that he took no other delight in thofe fports but to gain opportunity to infinuate with thofe great men for fome *advantages* to his houfe. And, after he had moft commendably governed his houfe 33 years, he died xi kal. Feb. 1377 [15].

" Other abbots alfo of note have been of this houfe, amongft which Gilbert Foliot is very memorable ; and in this Bale [16] hath difcovered the error of Matthew of Weftminfter, who faith he was abbot of Gloucefter [17].

" Philip de Repingdon was firft canon, then abbot of Leicefter. He was eminent for wit, learning, and

---

[1] *Tewkfbury* and *Taviftock* are taken into the Mitred Abbeys by Godwin, Willis, &c. though omitted by Tanner. R. F.

[2] Coke, 4 Inft. cap. i. p. 45.

[3] The abbots of Leicefter, as appears by the Claufe Rolls and Lifts of Summons in the Tower of London, were fummoned to the parliaments, or great councils, in the following years : 49 Hen. III ; 23. 27 (D. 17. 18.) Edw. I ; 12 (D. 11.) 13. 14 (D. 5. 23) 16 to 20 Edw. II ; 1 (D. 3. 16) 2 (D. 15. 31) 4 (D. 19. 41) 5 (D. 7. 25) 6 (D. 4. 9. 19. 36) 7, 8, 9 (D. 2. 18) 10 (D. 1. 5) 11 (D. 8. 11. 40) 12, 13 (D. 1. 28) 14 (D. 23. 33) 15 to 18, 20, 21 (D. 9. 28) 22 (D. 7. 32) 23, 24 (25 cancellatur) 27 fummoned again, & 29 (D. 7) Edw. III. cancellatur. Appendix to Stevens's Monafticon, vol. II. p. 13.

[4] See Appendix, p. 60.   [5] Prynne's Parliamentary Writs, vol. I. p. 142.   [6] Rot. Clauf. 25 Edw. III. m. 5.

[7] In the fecond edition of Selden's Titles of Honour, p. 724, fect. 29. is thus fet down : " Writs of fummons to parliament, bearing date at Woodftock, anno 19 Edward III. were directed to thefe regulars ; amongft others, " Abbati de Leiceftre," &c. Likewife in the 4th and 5th years of Edward III. (when the number of abbots fo fummoned was much diminifhed, as being reduced to 27, befides three priors) the abbot of Leicefter was ftill fummoned ; and 25 Edward III, in the Roll the abbot of Leicefter's name is cancelled. So likewife anno 29 ; yet, in the fummons of the 27th of the fame king to a great council, the abbot of Leicefter is amongft the reft." In p. 727, the king's patent of difcharge to the abbot of Leicefter is fet down at large ; the reafon therein given, becaufe the abbot held his lands, not *per baroniam*, but in frank-almoine.

[8] Selden's Titles of Honour, p. 602.   [9] Rot. Parl. 26 Edw. III. p. 1. m. 22 ; Hale's Pleas of the Crown, fol. 183.

[10] H. Knighton, fol. 2630 ; and fee our Appendix, p. 68.   [11] In Bucks. Tanner, Not. Mon. *Bucks*.

[12] Or *Welhove*, near Grimfby, co. Linc. Ibid. p. 257.   [13] In Suffex, near Arundel. Ibid. p. 560.

[14] In Hampfhire. Ibid. p. 165.   [15] See more of him hereafter.   [16] Cent. iii. fol. 215.   [17] See hereafter, p. 260.

other qualities. His wit, which is supposed to have been very modish, appears in a smart repartee to Alexander Nequam, alias Necham, from whom having received salute,

Phi nota fœtoris, lippus malus omnibus horis ;
Phi fœtor lippus: semper malus ergo Philippus ;

he returned thus :

Es niger et nequam cum sis cognomine Necham,
Nigrior esse potes, nequior esse nequis.

Which *Nequam* being so liable in his name, it is also said, that once suing to be admitted into St. Alban's monastery; he received this answer :

Si bonus sis, venias ; si nequam, nequaquam.

And, to prevent the like again, he is said to have changed his name to *Neckham* [1].

" Henry de Knighton, so called because born at Knighton, a neighbouring town, was a canon of this house in the reigns of Edward III. Richard II. and Henry IV; Mr. Burton [2] mistaking when he says he was abbot there. But, whatever was his office in the abbey, he wrote in it a useful history, *De Eventibus Angliæ* ; in the first book whereof he briefly treats on public events from the earliest Saxon kings to the year 1066 ; in the three next books he is transcriber only of Ranulphus Cestrensis; after which he goes on with his own collections to the deposition of king Richard II; in which work of his, several material circumstances may be found, which may in vain be sought elsewhere [3].

" To omit many other memorable persons that had residence in this sumptuous abbey, certain it is, that it flourished a great while, being very opulent in revenues, and thence enabled to be, on all occasions, subsidiary to the king, charitable to the neighbourhood and the poor, and hospitable to strangers and travellers.

" In the year 1337, king Edward III. laid a tax of wool throughout England ; and from this abbey had eighteen sacks, every sack valued at 19 marks.

" Several kings have here been entertained and lodged in their journeys to and from the North ; particularly a great entertainment and lodging was once given to king Richard II. and his queen, with their retinue [4]; amongst which were the duke of Ireland, earl of Suffolk, archbishop of Canterbury, bishop of Chichester, &c. ; and it is well known, that in this abbey died that famous cardinal and legate *à latere* Thomas Wolsey, archbishop of York, 1530, in the 22d year of king Henry the Eighth, and that he was here buried [5].

" And as those of this religious foundation were not wanting in their charity and relief to others, so were they, upon occasion, no less careful of their own rights, of which I shall deliver one memorable passage or two.

" In 1351, a very great difference happened between *John Laurence* and *Stephen Laurence* his brother, and other inhabitants of Belgrave, about the bounds and limits of their fields and ground in a place called *Le Stocking* ; whereupon one night the men of Belgrave, in a tumultuous and riotous manner, pulled up the stakes and fences which the abbot had made in that place; and, not therewith content, but the more to despite the abbot and monks, stopped up the Foss-way over the river Soar, and made barricadoes at the end of the bridge, so that the tenants of the abbey could not bring with carriages the usual provisions to the abbey, to the great grievance of the convent. Hereupon the abbot obtained the king's writ to certain justices, viz. sir Robert Herle, sir John de Folvile, Simon Pakeman, and Laurence Hauberk ; before whom twenty-five men of Belgrave were indicted for the offence; and, being found guilty, the ring-leader, John Laurence, was bound in £40. for better behaviour, and paid 100s. for damages. All the rest, who had been drawn into the fact by him, had only a fine of £10. set on them, to be paid among them all ; and

were pardoned, upon condition that they should repair the Foss-way at Coweswalk (or Culverwater), and clear the way thence to the bridge, along the Willows and the Penny-green, and should lay the way open over the bridge ; and the said John Laurence to release all the right that he claimed to have in the place where the abbot's fences had been pulled down ; and so the difference was ended [6].

" In the 33d year of king Edward III, John de Arden, a powerful man in Warwickshire, impleaded the abbot of Leicester for the manor of Berwode, and the advowson of Crudworth, in the county of Warwick, given to the canons of this house by some of his ancestors ; whereupon the abbot, fearing partiality in the hearing of the cause, for it was to be tried at Warwick, procured the king's letters to the judges of that circuit, viz. sir John de Mowbray and Thomas Hyngylby, requiring them to do equal right ; whereupon verdict and judgement passed for the abbot [7].

" And now it is time to speak of the dissolution of this great monastery; concerning which, we shall premise something touching the means and manner of the dissolution of all such religious foundations in this kingdom; in order to which matter, we may first remember and reflect, that, about the eighth, ninth, and tenth ages of the church, upon the fall of the Roman Empire, Christendom became generally overspread with barbarism ; all Learning, with the Arts and Sciences, being decayed almost to extinguishment, of which the notices and complaints are too evident : particularly we find Genebrard thus speaking of the ninth age ; ' *Infelix hoc seculum,*' &c. ' This unhappy age, void of men eminent for wit or learning, neither shewing any famous or worthy princes or priests ; in which nothing happened worthy to be remembered by posterity [8] :' at which time a certain monster was found with a dog's head, by all the other members those of a man, which wonderfully represented the state of those times.' And in this island we read of one of our Saxon kings, Whitredus by name, who was altogether ignorant of letters, insomuch that he could not write his own name ; for, in the conclusion of a charter of privileges by him granted to the church, are these words : ' Ego Whitredus rex Cantie, &c. omnia superscripta confirmavi, atque a me dictata propriâ manu signum sanctæ crucis, pro *ignorantiâ literarum*, expressi [9].'' But then, upon this foundation of ignorance, the priests and churchmen of the times raised a strong dominion in and over the consciences of men : for then, pretended miracles, visions, and revelations, obtained wonderfully, and were imposed upon the world ; whereby such a fervour of blind devotion and zeal, by the agency of the priests, became kindled in the world, as gave birth to many religious orders and foundations, and endowments to many, nay multitudes of religious houses, for the entertainment of religious votaries of all sorts, as monks, friers, canons, nuns, &c. ; in all of which, the zeal of these and some other times grew so intense, that it was thought fit and necessary here, by some acts of state, to restrain those excessive donations to such houses.

" But then, as nothing that is violent is long permanent, there came afterwards a reviviscence of Knowledge, Learning, and the Arts ; by which the abuses and corruptions in these institutions, as well as in matters of doctrine, being discovered, and the necessity of some reformation appearing, these monastic foundations, with divers other excesses which had sprung up in the middle and dark times, were rooted up ; the procedure of which amongst us in this island appears to have been thus.

" The beginnings and progress of the doctrines of Luther and other eminent reformers are so well known, that it need not here be repeated ; how, upon the

---

[1] Camden's Remains, art. *Allusions.* Of Repingdon, see more hereafter.   [2] Pp. 155. 163.
[3] Scripsit Chronicon de eventibus Angliæ ab anno DCCCCL. ad MCCCXCV. lib. v. Horum primo res a Saxonicis regibus usque ad A. D. MLXVI gestas breviter percurrit ; tres sequentes, qui ad annum usque MCCCLXXVII pertingunt, ex Ranulphi Higdeni Cestrensis Polychronico ferè verbatim exscripsit. Historiam depositionis Ricardi II. lib. i. Extat utrumque opus inter Scriptores Decem Historiæ Anglicanæ, Lond. 1652, p. 2311. 2743. Cave.
[4] H. Knighton, fol. 2696.   [5] Burton, p. 163 ; and see hereafter. p. 263.   [6] Knighton, fol. 2616.
[7] Dugdale, Warwickshire, vol. II. p. 927 ; from H. Knighton's MS. fol. 163. b.
[8] Genebrardi Chron. lib. iv. initio 10 seculi.   [9] Spelman's Concilia, tom. I. p. 198 ; Janus Angl. lib. i.

pope's fetting his indulgences to fale in Germany in fo grofs and fcandalous a manner, that, for a little money, any man might preferve himfelf, and deliver his friends out of purgatory[1]; which, with many other corruptions in the church, being detected by Luther and others, whofe writings were difperfed in England, it was ftrange to fee how greatly they were liftened to and embraced by the people, by the juft prejudices they had conceived againft the ignorances and lives of the priefts and clergy. They had en-groffed the greateft part of the power and riches of Chriftendom; and the corruptions of their doctrines, worfhip, and practice, were fuch, that a fmall pro-portion of common fenfe, with a little looking into the New Teftament (which about that time was tranf-lated into Englifh), did eafily difcover and detect them; nor had the Romanifts any varnifh to colour their corruptions with, but the authority and traditions of the Church; and then many learned men, looking into the Fathers and Councils, found a vaft difference between the primitive and modern Chriftianity; for, as in the firft ages Piety and Learning prevailed; in the middle and latter, Ignorance had almoft buried all the Learning; and for Piety, only a little mifguided devo-tion was retained; the reftlefs ambition and ufurpation of the popes being fomewhat fupported by the feem-ing holinefs of the mendicant friers, and pitiful learn-ing that ran among the canonifts, fchoolmen, and cafuifts.

" The art of Printing arriving alfo at this time to fome degree of perfection, the tranflated Scriptures and other good books became difperfed abroad, whereby men were convinced, and taught to pray and praife God in fuch language as they underftood; whereby the authority of the mafs, and the reverence to ecclefiaftical orders, mightily fell. And, as the keeping of the myfteries of Religion in the hands of priefts only had been a principal means, in all times, of making the priefthood facred and venerable; complaints were now made, that the priefts withhold-ing the Scriptures from the people was a tacit ac-knowledgement that there was an oppofition between the Scriptures and their doctrines; that the monks and religious orders engroffing the riches, as the popes did the dominion of the world, it was not confiftent with their defigns, nor with the arts ufed to promote them, to let the Scriptures be much known; and therefore legends, ftrange ftories of vifions and miracles, with other devices, were thought far more proper for keeping up their credit, and carrying on their defigns, which had no warranty from the Scrip-tures. Then, it appearing that the foundation of thefe monaftical houfes had been laid on the fuperftitious conceit of redeeming fouls out of pergatory, by fay-ing maffes for them there; and that they whofe of-fice it was to be employed in the miniftry of fuch fuperftitious purpofes had, by counterfeiting of re-licks, by forging of miracles, and many other impof-tures, heaped up vaft wealth, to the enriching of their convents, and the magnifying of their faints, of which perhaps many never went to heaven, and others never were in being; thefe arts and practices being detected, together with the great vicioufnefs of the profeffed votaries in fome places, and in all their great abufe of Religion, made it feem unfit that they fhould be continued any longer.

" Now, as a prelude to the general diffolution of monafteries, as it proved, there came a political pro-ject into the head of cardinal Wolfey, feconded or approved by others in this juncture who were for the fupport of the papal and facerdotal dominion; that is, to wipe off the imputation of ignorance, and to fet up Learning againft Learning. The king alfo natu-rally loving Learning; the cardinal, as well for the purpofes aforefaid, as to do a thing acceptable to the king, refolved to fet up fome colleges, in which there fhould be both great encouragement for fome emi-nent fcholars to profecute their ftudies, and good fchools for teaching and training up of youth; and fo, by thefe learned men, the teachers of and difputers for the new doctrines (as they were called) would be confronted, and poffibly fome ftop put to the current

of reformation then coming on. The cardinal, there-fore, applied himfelf to have two colleges (one at Oxford, the other at Ipfwich, the place of his birth) well conftituted and nobly endowed. But towards this it was neceffary, by the aids and leave of the pope and king, to fupprefs fome few fmall monafteries; which was thought as juftifiable and lawful as it had been, in fome former ages, to change fecular prebends into canons regular, the devoted goods being ftill applied to a religious ufe; and it was full as reafon-able as to fay that the pope had an abfolute power of difpenfing the fpiritual treafure of the church, and to tranflate the merits of one man and apply them to another; it being infinuated too that this would be a means to keep up all the reft, feeing fome then thought that in this kingdom the number was become exceffive.

" And now, to fee what great effects fuch a con-currence of fmall motives will produce. The car-dinal being fo much confidered at Rome as a pope of another world, that it was not hard for him to obtain almoft any thing there, the pope (Clement VII.) con-fented to the project; and the king was not averfe, forefeeing that fuch a beginning made it lawful to make bold with the reft, in cafe of urgent national neceffity; and at prefent the pulfes of the people might hereby be felt, how they would refent a farther change; and fo the cardinal proceeded to the finifhing of that defign.

" It was not long after when the occafions or ne-ceffities of the king inclined him to be dealing with fome of the other monafteries and religious houfes: for, having exafperated the pope in point of his fu-premacy, and his revenue funk by reafon of wars and troubles, in the 27th year of his reign, the parliament gave to the king, his heirs and fucceffors, all monaf-teries, priories, and other religious houfes of monks, canons, nuns, &c. which had not above the clear yearly value of £200. and all ornaments, jewels, goods, and debts, which they had on the 1ft of March, 1535: and thus became the leffer monafteries diffolved, being in number 376, the yearly revenues thereof being rated at about £32,000.; and the goods and chattels, at low rates, at £100,000.; and it is not improbable that the commiffioners were as care-ful to enrich themfelves as to increafe the king's re-venue. The churches and cloifters were, for the moft part, pulled down; and the lead, bells, and other materials, fold.

" Afterwards, by the parliament, in the 31ft year of the king's reign, all monafteries, abbeys, priories, nunneries, colleges, hofpitals, houfes of friers, and other religious houfes, above the yearly value of £200. were given to the king, his heirs and fucceffors, in as large and ample a manner as the governors thereof held them in right of their houfes[2]. And at this time it was that our great abbey of Leicefter went down. But yet we muft know, that moft, if not all thefe, were diffolved or furrendered to the king fome time before, but confirmed thus to him by act of parliament; the inftruments of which furrenders are preferved, and ftill to be feen, in the Augmentation-office.

" And then, after all this, by parliament, in the 37th of that king's reign[3], all colleges, free chapels, chantries, hofpitals, fraternities, guilds, brotherhoods, and other promotions made to have continuance for ever, and chargeable with firft fruits and tenths, with their houfes, lands, &c. were adjudged in actual pof-feffion of the king, his heirs and fucceffors. And then, by computation, the number of the monafteries and religious houfes, firft and laft, fuppreffed in Eng-land and Wales, appeared to be thus: monafteries, 648; colleges, 90; chantries and free chapels, 2374; and hofpitals, 110[4]; the yearly value of all which being accounted to amount unto £161,100; being above a third part of all fpiritual revenues; befides ornaments, money, goods, plate, jewels, lead, bells, &c. invaluable[5].

" But then, to make thefe great revolutions and tranfactions more plaufible and current with the peo-ple, who became greatly ftartled, as not knowing where fuch mutilations would end, there was much

---

[1] Sleidan's Commentaries. [2] Stat. 31 Hen. VIII. cap. 13. [3] Stat. 37 Hen. VIII. cap. 4. [4] Camden. [5] Speed.

art

art ufed; it being infinuated and declared, firft, that this was done for the neceffary fupply of the king's neceffities, and to enable him to fortify and defend his kingdom againft foreign enemies, then become formidable; then, whereas no fmall fupply was requifite for thofe purpofes, by this means the charge and burden would be fhifted from the king's loyal and good fubjects upon thofe who were fautors and maintainers of the pope's ufurped fupremacy againft the rights of the king and kingdom [1]. In the next place, there was a great declaiming againft the vicious and lewd lives of monaftical perfons, difcovered by the commiffioners and inquifitors, and declared by the whole parliament in the preamble to the Statutes of Diffolution, and confeffed by the abbots and monks themfelves in divers preambles to their inftruments of furrender. Again, it was faid to be apparent, that the lands and revenues of their houfes were not employed according to the direct intent of the owners and founders. Then, to be fure, was not forgotten the multitudes of fuperftitions, and forging of miracles and relicks that were found in thofe houfes. And, laftly, the declaration of the king's patent, to employ moft, or fome, of the revenues to other and better religious ufes. But, to make a full fcrutiny and enquiry into the vicious lives of the abbots, priors, monks, nuns, friers, canons, &c. a vicar-general (Thomas lord Cromwell) was inftituted, and vifitors were fent abroad, with articles and inftructions, to make enquiry into the manners and behaviour of the religious of both fexes. Thefe vifitors or commiffioners acquitted themfelves vigoroufly in their difcoveries; for, by their letters, ftill extant, to the vicar-general, it appears that in moft houfes they found monftrous diforders; that many of the votaries fell down upon their knees, and prayed to be difcharged, fince they had been forced to make vows againft their wills, who thereupon were fet at liberty by the vifitors [2]; that they found great factions in the houfes, and barbarous cruelties exercifed by one faction againft another, as either of them prevailed; that they were all extremely addicted to idolatry and fuperftition; and that in fome of them they found the inftruments and tools for multiplying and coining; that the lewdnefs of the confeffors of nunneries was moft abominable, many of the nuns being found to be with child; and that the diffolutenefs of abbots, monks, and friers, was notorious, not only with whores, but married women; befides unnatural and brutal practices amongft themfelves, equal to thofe of Sodom. All which mifdemeanors were recorded in a black book; and, being fo notorious in fome, and vehemently fufpected in others, caufed many of them, out of confcioufnefs, to make furrenders of themfelves to the king; and then fome of them were employed as agents or commiffioners to incline others to furrender, as the prior of Gifeburn in Yorkfhire for one; in which matter the canons of Leicefter being fomewhat fturdy and backward, the commiffioners told them they could charge them with adultery, &c. if they would not fubmit [3]; fo that, by one way or other, moft of them were brought in to furrender before the ftatute of 31 Henry VIII, which confirmed all to the king, as is before noted; and fome abbots, particularly thofe of Glaftonbury, Reading, and Colchefter, and feveral priors and monks, were attainted of treafon, and executed, for joining with, or fending aid to, the rebels in Yorkfhire; who, upon thefe charges, rofe in great numbers, ftyling their rebellion the Pilgrimage of Grace.

" This great monaftery being diffolved, the large poffeffions thereof were fold, and conveyed by parcels to feveral of the king's fubjects, whofe heirs or affigns enjoy them at this day. I will not prefume to fpecify the particular and refpective prefent owners of all the lands and poffeffions of this houfe; but for the fite thereof, with a fair proportion of lands, grounds, &c. thereunto adjoining and belonging, ...
............[Here Mr. Staveley has a chafm, which we fhall endeavour hereafter to fupply. He proceeds:]

" And now I come to make my promife good, in giving fome account of the lands and poffeffions of this great monaftery; and in the firft place we muft know, that the founder thereof, Robert Boffu earl of Leicefter, found in St. Mary's church in the caftle of Leicefter certain canons fecular, there placed and endowed by his father, Robert earl of Mellent; which canons, with all their poffeffions, he tranfplanted to this abbey of St. Mary of the Meadows [4]; viz. five yard-lands without the North-gate, and eight dwelling-houfes; and in another part of the city, three yard-lands and three bovates of land; and fix pounds a year rent in Leicefter, with all the churches of Leicefter both within and without the walls that were at his difpofal (fue ditionis), and all the profits thereunto belonging; alfo the church of Lilburn, with the lands and tithes thereunto belonging, and £60. a year rent in that town; three carucates and one yard-land in Thurmodefton; one yard-land, of the gift of Ifabel his mother, in Burton; in Segrave fix carucates and three bovates of land, and the entire manor of Asfordby, with the mill, &c.; all which were the poffeffions of the canons of the church of St. Mary within the caftle.

" The founder alfo gave to his new Abbey one carucate of land at the North bridge, near to the fite of the Mint; the houfes alfo which Gilbert the dean held of him at the South-gate; the mill that had been the bifhop's; all that Ofbert the chaplain held of him in the foke of Shepefhed and in the foke of Halfo, with all the churches of both fokes; the church of Sygrefham in the parifh of Brackley, with all lands, tithes, &c.; the church of Ildfley in Berks, with the lands, tithes, &c. He gave them alfo every day three loads of wood for fuel out of his forefts; with free feeding for their cattle there, without pannage. And thefe were all the poffeffions that the founder gave in his firft charter; by which he confirmed alfo all the gifts that had been given by others; namely, the church of Thurnby, of the gift of Ralph Pincerna; and the church of Thedingworth, of the gift of Robert Pincerna his fon; the churches of Clifton and Thorpe juxta Melton, and one mark rent a year in Leicefter, of the gift of Ernald de Bofco; the church of Bulkington, half a hide of land in Brankote, and a meadow in Wefton, of the gift of Roger de Watervile, with all lands, tithes, &c.; and the lands in Bruntingfthorp, which Seward Pitefridus held of him, of the gift of the faid Seward. The founder alfo gave unto the abbot and convent the church of Cofby, that had belonged to the church of St. Auguftin of Leicefter; alfo the church of Aldeby (now Enderby) and chapel of Whetftone. On the day on which he affumed the religious habit, he gave them the whole townfhip of Stoughton, except fuch part of it as was of the fee of Ralph Friday. He gave them alfo, together with the mill of Belgrave, two yard-lands at the Weft-gate; the manor of Pynflade, with four yard-lands there; the manor of Knighton; one yard-land in Whatton; and 3000 eels, to be taken at Nun-Eaton. By this charter he releafed to the abbot and convent, their fervants, tenants, and villans, all fervices whatfoever.

" They had alfo five fhillings and fixpence yearly rent in Bruntingfthorp, out of one croft and one bovate of land, of the lands of Thomas Walche.

" The countefs Amicia, wife of the founder, gave to this monaftery four pounds yearly rent, out of certain lands in Everley in Wiltfhire.

" Earl Robert Blanchmains, fon of the founder, by his charter, confirmed all that his father or others had before given to this houfe; as, of the gift of the founder, the manor of Knighton, with the mill, &c.; of the gift of the countefs Amicia, the four pounds rent in Everley; of the gift of Ernald de Bofco, the churches of Thorpe, Evington, and Humberfton; the place called Stockingforth, and 40 fhillings in Welton, of the gift and confirmation of the founder; alfo the profits of the houfes that Godwinus Bena held, being four yard-lands in Leicefter, the land

---

[1] Coke's Inft. 4. fol. 44.   [2] Lord Herbert, Hift. p. 399.   [3] On this head, fee more fully hereafter.
[4] His charter bears date in 1137.

which

which Jocelinus Marefcallus had given, five affarts on the North of the wood, and the ground before the chapel; the land called Nedlebede, of the gift of Geffrey de Turvill; one carucate of land, of the gift of William de Alnei; part of his wood, with all the affart thereof; the church of Aldeby, the vill of Stoðon, and the mill of Belgrave, of the gift of the founder.

" The faid Robert the fon alfo gave to the abbot and convent one ftag on the day of the Affumption, and another on the day of the Nativity of the Bleffed Virgin Mary yearly; and liberty of fifhing in his great pool at Groby four times in the year, on the Vigils of the Purification, the Annunciation, the Affumption, and the Nativity of the Bleffed Virgin Mary; pafturage at Desforth for ten cows; and two acres of alder-ground, between the highway and the land which mafter Ralph de Wolfcroft held.

" After him, Robert Fitz Parnell, by his charter, confirmed all that his grandfather, father, or others, had given; and farther gave to the abbot and convent pafturage in the foreft of Leicefter, between the way to Groby and the way to Anfty; and an additional load of wood every day in that foreft. He alfo gave them 24 yard-lands, the vill of Anfty, and four cottages, with their tofts.

" The faid Robert Fitz-Parnell alfo gave them lands at Farningo and Sirefham; and Weftcote, with the appurtenances, which earl Robert his grandfather had given to the church of Lincoln in exchange for the manor of Knighton, &c. And this was for their lands in Asfordby and Segrave, which, by affent and compromife, were given to the church of Lincoln for peace fake.

" The countefs Petronell confirmed all that her fon Robert had given; and farther gave them all her meadow in Thurmodefton, called Belloholm, and her houfes in Leicefter, with land and garden beyond the Weft-bridge.

" Simon Montfort earl of Leicefter, who had married Amicia, the elder daughter and coheirefs of Robert Fitz-Parnell, gave to this abbey a wood called Doveland; and land and wood towards Anfty, which was called Ofulves-hawe; and one piece of land that William de Belgrave held.

" Simon Montfort the younger confirmed all that his father and anceftors had given; and farther gave them, by feoffment, 300 acres of land and wood in the foreft of Leicefter adjoining, which land lay from the way of Anfty-crofs to Dalfyke, and from Dalfyke beyond Storkyfhall unto Oldfeld over againft Cropfton, and from Oldfeld along by the fields of Belgrave, and all the cleyhedges, with the vefture thereof.

" Margaret de Quincy, the youngeft daughter of Robert Fitz-Parnell, and wife to Saer de Quincy, confirmed all that her anceftors had given; and farther gave to the abbot and convent one yard-land lying in Shepefhed, with a toft, croft, and the mill of Shepefhed[1], with a grove of alders adjoining: with all the multure or grinding of Shepefhed and Hathern, and of her own houfe at Shepefhed; and that neither fhe nor her heirs would ever erect any other mill in Shepefhed or Hathern. She alfo gave them houfebote and haybote, and wood out of Charnwood Foreft, to repair their houfes and mill, toties quoties; alfo one ftag out of Charnwood yearly on the day of the Nativity of the Bleffed Virgin Mary. She granted to them, and to their men-fervants and tenants of Brackley, Sirefham, Weftcote, Halfo, Farningo, Wefton, Clifton, Bulkington, Brancote, Bernangul, Sow, Merfton, Stocton, Lokinton[2], Shepifhed, Hemington, Anfty, Thurmafton, Clenfeld, and Burton, that they fhould be quit and free from all fecular fervice, exactions, demands, fuit of court, view of frankpledge, and all foreign fervice whatfoever.

" Saer de Quincy confirmed the grants of his wife; which were again confirmed by Roger de Quincy their fon; who commanded R. Chamberleyn, his fteward, to give the abbot and convent feifin of all; giving

them alfo feveral loads of wood for firing, and the tithe and tenth of all fales of wood in his woods of Acle and Wyffely, and the right fhoulder of every deer killed in his park of Acle, with liberty to make ftalls for cattle, and free paffage into the foreft. He gave them one yard-land in Wefton, which Richard Kyrke held; and common in all his purparty of the foreft of Leicefter; alfo ten fhillings a year rent in Schevifby, from the prior of Chaucomb; and three fhillings and four-pence at Hemington, from the heirs of Hugh de Derby and his partners, in exchange for their right of fifhing in Groby pool; the homage and fervice of Helias de Lynfey and Alice his wife; four yard-lands in Thurmafton, and certain other lands there, with the fervices of the tenants, as alfo of the tenants of the prior of Caldwell there.

" Alan la Zouch confirmed all that his anceftors, the earls of Leicefter and Winchefter, had given to this monaftery.

" We made mention before of Ernald de Bofco, or de Bois, a good benefactor to this houfe; in reference to whom, we may here obferve, that Robert earl of Mellent in Normandy came in with William the Conqueror; and, according to the politic proceeding of the Conqueror, who rewarded his friends and followers with the lands and poffeffions of the fubdued Englifh; this Robert obtained the earldom, confulate, or government of Leicefter, with vaft poffeffions both in this and other counties; which defcended to his fon Robert Boffu our founder. And then thefe great Normans, to carry on the policy, parcelled out great fhares of their lands to their followers and fervants; amongft whom Ernald de Bois, fteward to Robert Boffu, had a large partage, and, fymbolizing with his lord's devotion, gave to this monaftery (as is in part fpecified before) the church of Clifton, with the chapels of Wovere (Brownfover) and Rokeby, the church of Thorpe near Melton, and thofe of Humberfton[3] and Evington.

" To this Ernald fucceeded three Ernalds de Bois fucceffively; and we find the fecond Ernald confirming all that his father had given; and alfo all that Roger Watervile had given, mentioned before (for he was heir to this Watervile) adding fome land, with a meadow, park, &c. at Creffewell.

" Then Ernald de Bois the third confirmed all that his grandfather or father had given; and farther gave himfelf one bovate of land in Thorpe Ernald, with a toft and croft, and common of pafture for fix fcore fheep, and ten acres of meadow in a certain place called Redinwalde.

" After him, Ernald the fourth confirmed all again; and farther granted to the abbot and convent common for ten cattle, eight oxen and two cows, with his cattle in his own pafture.

" King Stephen, by charter, made a confirmation of all hitherto; alfo 20 meafures of falt out of the Wiches, of the gift of Waleran earl of Mellent; and two carucates of land in Rolei, called Hanecheftofr, with the wood adjoining, of the gift of Ranulph earl of Chefter; giving and granting to them alfo freedom from all fecular fervices, with liberty to hold courts, fac and foc, tol and theam, infangenetheof, and all other cuftoms and privileges, as he had granted to any church within his land.

" In the next place, king Henry II, by charter, confirmed all that the founder or others had given or fhould give to this abbey; and alfo the churches of Knaptoft, Ernefby, and Staunton; the church of Langton, with the chapels of Thorpe and Tur Langton, of the gift of William de Novo Mercato and Roger de Bouden; the church of Barrow, of the gift of Ranulph earl of Chefter, the chapel of Querndon, with the lands, tithes, &c. and one carucate of land of his demefnes in Barrow and Querndon; the church of Narborough, with the chapel of Huncote, of the gift of Roger earl of Warwick; a meadow in Sigefwold, of the gift of Geffery de Dalry; the vill of Conkyfbury, with the mill, the cliff, and 20 acres of land in Haddon, and the church of Adftock, of the gift of W. Avenel;

[1] Plac. Affif. in com. Leic. 12 Edw. I. Rot. 5. de molendino in Shepefhed.
[2] Efch. Leic. 7 Edw. II. m. 36. de dimid. feodi mil. in Lokington; & Rot. 8 Edw. III. p. 1. m 6. de manerio in Lokington
[3] Rec. in Scacc. 7 Hen. VI. Mich. Rot. 4. de terris in Humberfton.

[X x x]   one

one yard of land in Effewell, of the gift of H. Tuchet; two parts of the garbs of the demefnes of Gayam, of the gift of Robert earl of Leicefter; the moiety of the church of Chefham, and of the church of Billefdon, with the chapels of Rollefton and Godeby, of the gift of Robert de Sifrewaft; the church of Billing, of the gift of W. Barre; the churches of Thornton and Sirefham, of the gift of T. Sorrell; the church of Blaby, with the chapel of Countefs Thorpe, of the gift of William de Lodbroke; the church of Hufbands Borefworth, and one carucate of land there, of the gift of Robert de Borefworth, and one yard-land in the fame, of the gift of Roger Samfon; the church of North Kilworth, of the gift of Robert Rabaz; two yard-lands in Mufele, of the gift of Reginald de Mufele; one yard-land in Humberfton, of the gift of Ralph de Martinwaft; one yard-land in Norton, of the gift of Robert de Burton; the churches of Barkby and Hungarton, with the chapels, of the gift of Walter de Power; the church of Eaton [1], of the gift of William de Evermeu; the churches of Eaftwell and Bittefwell, of the gift of Robert de Arraby; the church of Crudworth, with the hermitage, the wood of Brewood, and the mill, of the gift of Hugh de Ardena; one carucate in Sutton, of the gift of Geffery de Craft; one carucate in Stoke, of the gift of R. de Craft; the church of Craft, of the gift of Ralph de Turvile; one bovate of land in Shuckburg, of the gift of Ofbert de Lemington; the church of Wanlip, and fix yard-lands in the fame town, of the gift of Richard l'Abbé; one carucate of land in Empingham, of the gift of the faid Richard; three yard-lands in Kilby; five yard-lands in Bittefwell, of the gift of Godefrid Patroc; one carucate of land in Thedingworth, of the gift of William de Kerby; the whole manor of Cokeram, of the gift of William de Lancafter, with the church of the fame town, and the chapel of Elhale; the church of Queniborough, with lands, tithes, &c. of the gift of Ralph de Queniburg, one yard-land in Lilburn, of the gift of Richard l'Abbé; three yard-lands in the fame, of the gift of Geffrey de Dalby; one yard-land in Foxton, of the gift of Robert de Cotes; the church of Thedingworth, of the gift of Ralph Pincerna; the churches of Knipton and Harefton, of the gift of Robert the fon of Ralph, fo as neverthelefs that his fon Gervafe fhould enjoy the fame during his life.

" And then king John, by his charter, confirmed all, together with the exchanges that had been made with the bifhop of Lincoln mentioned before [2].

" Within the gift of the founder was alfo comprized the Abbey-gate, a ftreet of houfes beyond St. Sunday's bridge, heretofore belonging to the abbey.

" Befides all which, it appears that feveral other churches, tithes, lands, and poffeffions, were impropriated and given refpectively to this abbey, as the manor of Ingwardby, or the greateft part thereof, fome time belonging to the lords Percy [3], and by them given to this abbey; feveral lands in Kilby, held by this abbey in frankalmoigne, of the gift of William la Zouch; the church of Lokington, with the chapel of Hemington; the church of Shepefhed; befides the lands and privileges therein before-mentioned.

" The church of Thurnby in this county being given to this abbey, as is mentioned before, and appropriated thereunto, Stoughton fell in with the fame, as being within the parifh of Thurnby; near unto which they had a great grange, with excellent fifhpools belonging to it, where ftores and provifions of corn, grain, cattle, fifh, fruits, &c. were made and laid in for the ufe and maintenance of the abbot and convent." Thus far Mr. Staveley.

We fhall now introduce fuch additional particulars as have occurred in various refearches; with fome farther account of their poffeffions; a lift of the abbots; and the prefent ftate of the fite of the abbey.

Mr. Burton fays, " Of this houfe was fome time abbot that moft learned Gilbert Foliot [4]," who was after made bifhop of Hereford, 1149; and thence tranflated to the fee of London 1161. Memorable for two things; the one, his allegiance and fidelity to his king, being always true and faithful to king Henry the Second in all thofe ftirs between the king and Thomas Becket archbifhop of Canterbury; for which caufe he was twice excommunicated. The other, for a refolute anfwer made to an unknown voice heard by him; for (as Matthew Paris [5] reporteth it) coming one night from the king, after long conference had with him, of thefe troubles with the faid archbifhop Becket, as he lay meditating and mufing thereon in his bed, a terrible and unknown voice founded thefe words in his ears,

O Gilberte Foliot,
Dum revolvis tot eft tot,
Deus tuus eft Aftaroth;

which he, taking to come from the Devil, anfwered as boldly,

Mentiris, Demon; Deus meus eft Sabaoth.
[———— O Gilbert Foliot,
While you compute what's to be got,
Your God's the God of Aftarot.
Devil or man, you lie, you fot;
My God's the God of Sabaot. F. P.]

He wrote an Apology for King Henry the Second, againft the archbifhop; and an invective againft him; and another book of his fudden and proud rifing; one book of Epiftles, and fix books upon the Canticles. He died in 1187, 34 Henry II."

The circumftance of Foliot's having been abbot of Leicefter, already noticed by Mr. Staveley, p. 455, is evidently a miftake; his name not being in the lift of abbots in their regifter; nor does he mention this among his preferments in the following account of himfelf, extracted by Mr. Peck from a curious MS. formerly belonging to the priory of Belvoir, and ftill preferved among the literary treafures of the duke of Rutland in the muniment-room at Belvoir, intituled,

" GILBERTI FOLIOTH Epiftolæ."

Literis rubris, ad imum paginæ primæ, fic funt infcriptæ:

" Hunc librum dedit frater Willielmus de Belvero, prior ejufdem ecclefie, Deo & Beate Marie de Belvero; quem qui alienaverit vel deleverit anathema fit. Anima dicti Willielmi & anime omnium fidelium defunctorum requiefcant in pace. Amen."

In hujus codicis folio quinto decimo a fine retro (pagina 1. col. a.) de feipfo & fuis in ecclefiâ dignitatibus fic fcribit Foliothus:

" In promotione meâ primâ Cluniaci prior quidam fum conftitutus in ordine. Dehinc prior Abbatis ville [6]. Hinc abbas Gloeceftrie [7]. Poftea epifcopus Herefordie [8]. Hinc tranflatus Londonie [9]. Confidenter affero, quod ad nullum horum ambivi; quorum tamen unumquodque, permittente Domino, confequutus obtinui."

Mr. Peck (from whofe MSS. this account of Foliot's book is copied) adds, " It appears by the life of Gilbert Foliot in Wharton de Epifcop. London, p. 60, & feqq. that Wharton never met with any more than feven letters of G. Foliot's; fo that this MS. is really a very great rarity. The fcarcity of copies, as I take it, is owing to Foliot's adhering to the king againft Thomas Becket; for, Becket being fainted, and Foliot twice excommunicated by him, it was meritorious to deftroy the letters of the Martyr's adverfary.

" The epiftles in this volume are thus numbered:

I. Gilleberti Hereford. epi, domino Radulpho decano Hereford'—Sic incipit—A te longe pofiti, p. 1.

II. [Anonymo.] Poteram me cohibere filentio, p. 3.

III. Patri fuo & domino H. Winton, Dei gratiâ, epifcopo, & S. fedis apoftolice legato, frater Gilbertus ecclefie B. Petri Gloceft. dictus abbas, totius obedientie & caritatis obfequium. Quum difcretioni noftre, in Chrifto amabilis pater, &c. P. 4.

---

[1] Plac. Affif. in com. Leic. Rot. 15. de advoc. ecclefie de Eytou.
[2] Cart. 2 Johannis, n. 44.
[3] " This lordfhip longgid once to one Algernoune, and after it was gyven to Leyrcefter abbay. Now it is Brian Caves, that boute it of the king It ftondith very well, and the grounde aboute it is very riche of pafture. From Belleg eve to Ingrefby a 4 miles, partely by corne, pafture, and woody ground." Leland, Itin. vol. I. p. 22.
[4] He was a native of Devonfhire. Price's Worthies, p. 289.
[5] Fol. 108.
[6] Abbeville in Picardy, where there was a Cluniac priory.
[7] Sept. 5, 1148. To this the archdeaconry of Oxford was added in the latter end of 1151. Le Neve.
[7] 11 id. Junii, 1139. Willis.
[9] April 28, 1163. Ibid.

IV. Patri

IV. Patri fuo & domino Sim. Wigorn' epifcopo, frater Gilbertus ecclefie B. Petri Gloc. dictus abbas, cum pietate fructus operari jufticie. Compellit me caritas. p. 5.

V. Patri fuo & domino fummo Dei gratiâ pontifici Celeftino, Fr. Gilbertus B. Petri Gloc. dictus abbas, totum quod obedientie & obfequii valet humilis & primitiva devotio. Fidelis dominus de omnibus verbis fuis. p. 6.

VI. Patri fuo & domino T. Cant. Dei gratiâ archiepifcopo, Fr G. ecclefie B. Petri Gloc. dictus abbas, totum quod pacis, quod gratie, quod falutis. Gratias ago benevolentie veftre, in Chrifto dilecte pater, ib.

There is not one copy of this book mentioned in the Oxford or Cambridge or Cotton Catalogues, or in the other Englifh or Irifh libraries. F. PECK."

In 1148, the abbot and convent of Leicefter obtained feveral material privileges from pope Eugenius III; which were confirmed by fucceeding pontiffs.

A compofition between Paul abbot of Leicefter and the prior of Trentham in Staffordfhire, relative to the church of Brackley, was confirmed by pope Celeftine III. in 1191 [1].

In the time of the fame abbot, about 1200, a feoffment occurs, to Wigan de la Mare, of two tofts in Thedingworth, near the church, on the North fide, in the tenure of Almer and William Chubbe, for his homage and fervice; to hold to the feoffee, in cafe he fhould have any heir of lawful marriage; otherwife to revert to the feoffors. " Teftibus; magiftro A. de Wilnâ, Petro de Sais, magiftro Waltero Medico, Willelmo de Ceftriâ, Heliâ nepote abbatis, Roberto de Ofulvefton & Bertrammo fervientibus abbatis; & multis aliis [2].

In 1210, the right of the abbot and convent of Leicefter to the chapelry of Clay Coton, in Northamptonfhire, was determined at law [3]; and by another fuit, in 1229, their right to divers liberties within the manor of Sirefham, Farningho, and Brackley [4], and to the advowfon of Eydon, all in the fame county [5], was fully eftablifhed.

In 1234, Stephen de Segrave, who had been juftice of England, falling into the king's difpleafure, and being called to an account for his adminiftration, fled to this abbey, pretending that he was a prieft, and refolved to fhave his crown again, to be a canon of this houfe. Upon fecond thoughts, he made his peace with the king, and came into action again; but died a canon regular here, Nov. 9, 1241 [6].

Robert abbot of Leicefter, about 1245, granted permiffion to Solomon, chaplain to the hofpital at Brackley, to found a church within that hofpital [7].

In 1250, Henry Rotheley, abbot of Leicefter, with others, were prefent at the agreement made by the Eremites of St. Auftin in Atherfton with the parfon of Manceter, about the tithes of the fite of their houfe [8], &c.

In 1252, the abbot and convent had a charter of confirmation from king Henry III, for 300 acres of wood in the foreft near Leicefter [9].

In 1254, the oldeft " Rentale" of this abbey was compiled by a monk named " Le Pin."

In 1257, the abbot of Leicefter was directed to return into the king's court all fuch rolls of pleas, that had been held before Stephen de Segrave, as had been left in that abbey at his death [10].

In 1269, the king's letters patent were obtained, relative to the cuftody of this monaftery during the vacancy of an abbot [11].

In 1270, a general chapter of the clergy was held at Leicefter, at which the prior of Barnwell prefided in the place of the abbot of Leicefter; and among the

MSS. in the library cf Corpus Chrifti college, Oxford, is one (D. 1. p. 414.) intituled, " Statuta in capitulo generali Leyceftr', tento in octab. Sancti Trinitatis, A. D. MCCLXXVI; præfidentibus in eodem capitulo domini priore de Bernewell loco abbatis de Leyceftriâ, & priore de Ycon' [12]."

William Shepefhed, abbot of Leicefter, was one of thofe who had a protection granted to him by king Edward I, in 1275, when he obliged all monafteries to take fuch protection [13].

In 1279, the abbey church was folemnly dedicated.

In 1291, on the Tuefday after the feaft of All Saints, abbot William de Malverna obtained an inftrument, under the common feal of the abbey, teftifying that the convent was then indebted to divers creditors in the fum of 2060 marks, 10s. 6d. [14].

In 1296, Robert Winchelfey, archbifhop of Canterbury, by the pope's concurrence, publifhed the conftitution of pope Boniface VIII. forbidding the giving any thing to laymen; and king Edward I. at his parliament held at St. Edmund's, demanded a twelfth of the laity and a large fubfidy of the clergy. The archbifhop and clergy, not knowing how to comply, on account of the new conftitution, without confulting the pope, broke up, and returned home. Hereupon the temporalties of the clergy were feized; but many of them, and particularly the abbot of Leicefter, compounded, and received the king's protection [15].

In 1300, Robert, fon of Robert of Burfiall, had liberty to grant lands to this abbey [16]; and in the fame year it was found that prince Edmund, earl of Leicefter, the king's brother, was their patron [17].

At the feaft of the Annunciation following, the abbey poffeffed 21 filver falt-cellars, and 43 filverdifhes; out of which the abbot had for his own ufe 12 difhes and 8 falt-fellars; the others were affigned to the ufe of the convent, and delivered ad coquinam [18].

In 1305, Richard de Brickeley had licence to give Anfty mill to this abbey [19].

In 1310-11, Anthony Bek, bifhop of Durham, had licence to give 74 acres of land at Ratby [20].

In 1311, William Aunfelys and Richard Whileby gave certain lands and tenements in the Abbey Gate [21].

In the fame year, a commiffion iffued from archbifhop Reynolds, to Thomas de Bray, a canon of Leicefter, on a difpute between the abbot and convent and the parifhioners of St. Nicholas, concerning the prefentation of a vicar [22].

In 1312, in a full court of Huftings, in the Guildhall of the city of London, Hugh de Chaundeler, John de Stratford, and John de Eure, executors of the laft will of William de Langley, clerk, affigned to the abbot and convent a confiderable eftate, confifting of feveral houfes, &c. in the parifh of St. Sepulchre, in the Suburbs of London; part of which extended from St. Sepulchre's church yard to Holborn-bridge; with 14 fhops in Cock-lane; the rent of a meffuage called the Reindeer, and of a meffuage in Weft Smithfield near the Pool [23].

At the death of archbifhop Winchelfey in 1318, Thomas Plantagenet, earl of Lancafter and Leicefter, fent a requeft to the pope, that this archbifhop, for the fake of his holy and ftrict life, of his excellent merits, and glorious miracles done by him, might have the honour he deferved, of being folemnly canonized for a Saint; but in vain [24].

In 1320, the king having iffued writs [25] to call the clergy together to confider of a fubfidy for the war, fent a mandate to archbifhop Reynolds for them to meet on the morrow of the tranflation of fir Thomas the Martyr [26]: the archbifhop's letter [27] fummoned

them

---

[1] Appendix, p. 68.　　[2] Madox, Formulare Anglicanum, p. 598.—Wiganus de Mara occurs in a record, 8 Hen. III.
[3] See hereafter, under the poffeffions of the abbey, a few pages farther on.
[4] Mich. Rec. 14 Hen. III. Rot. 30. This point was again litigated in 1319. See hereafter under the poffeffions of the abbey.
[5] This alfo was again contefted at law in 1290; but was determined in favour of the abbey. See this alfo hereafter.
[6] Matth. Paris, p. 772.　　[7] Appendix, p. 61.　　[8] Dugdale, Warwickfhire, vol. II. p. 1085.
[9] Cart. 37 Hen. III. m. 3.　　[10] Appendix, p. 61.　　[11] Pat. 54 Hen. III. m. 4. vel 5.
[12] Gen. Cat. 1621. 154.　　[13] Stevens, vol. I. p. 175. b.　　[14] Appendix, p. 72.
[15] Stevens, Monafticon, vol. I. pp. 175. 327.　　[16] Appendix, p. 61.　　[17] See before, p. 222; and Appendix, pp. 23. 61.
[18] Appendix, p. 72.　　[19] Ibid. p. 61.　　[20] Ibid p. 62. See his feal, plate XVII. fig. 1.　　[21] Appendix, p. 62.
[22] Ibid. p. 62.　　[23] See p. 275; and Appendix, p. 73.　　[24] Somner, Antiq. Cant. p. 130.
[25] Printed in Wilkins's Concil. vol. II. p. 456. Reg. Reynolds, fol. 73. a.
[26] Wilkins, ibid. p. 444. Reg. Reynolds, fol. 105. b.　　[27] Wilkins, ibid. p. 538. Reg. Reynolds, fol. 207. a.

2

them to Leicester, and gave a proxy *(procuratorium[1])* to the bishops of London and Winchester to assist at it. In his register[2] is a commission and proxy to appear there for him; the king's letter to convoke the clergy; and his writ to prorogue the council.

On the attainder of the earl of Lancaster, in 1322, the abbot and convent experienced some temporary inconveniences; a considerable part of their property being distrained, on the idea of its belonging to that nobleman. In this situation was one of the grants of Simon earl of Montfort, of £6. rent at Leicester, a load of fuel daily from his wood, and pannage for their hogs; and a similar grant of wood which they had enjoyed from the time of their foundation[3].

In 1323, *John de Tours* had licence to found a chantry in this abbey; and to endow it with 88 acres of arable land, and four acres and a half of meadow at Burstall, Leicester, and Stanton under Burton[4].

In 1325, they were disturbed in the possession of the tithes of Bagworth Park; which they had long enjoyed as a member of their church of Thornton[5].

In 1326, the amount of lambs received by the abbey for tithes in the High Peak of Derby was 237; of fleeces 426 reckoning by the great hundred, which weighed 87 stone[6].

Among the records in the Tower during the reign of Edward III. occurs, " Litera missa domino papæ, de licentiâ dandâ abbati & conventui de Leicestrè, quod ipsi adquirere valeant ecclesiam de Humberston, diocef. Lincolnienfis. Data apud Eltham, 30 Martii[7].

In 1329, the abbot and convent were, by the king's writ, put into possession of a parcel of wood at Halliwellhagh near Loughborough, which they had purchased from Henry de Beaumont[8].

In 1334, *John de Spondon* vicar of Lockington, and *William de Wivelleston* vicar of Shepefhed, had licence to grant lands at Shepefhed to this abbey[9]; and in 1337, *John de Spondon* and *William de Afton* had licence to grant lands, &c. at Skeffington[10].

Of William Geryn, a canon of this houfe, to whom in 1341 the abbey was indebted for the compilation of a " Rentale," the following benefactions are recorded. He gave the pulpit in the refectory, a picture in the chapel of our Lady, the cieling and painting of the whole choir and body of the abbey-church, a table at the altar of St. Mary, a silver cross with the images of St. John and Mary, a picture of the crucifix, and of Mary and John, with several others[11].

In 1344, Richard abbot of Leicester was directed to find a proper and strong house in his abbey, to receive the moneys collected for the tenth and fifteenth; and allow free ingress and egress to the collectors, who were to answer for them to the king[12].

In 1349, *William la Zouch*, formerly dean (and then archbishop) of *York*, and fir *Roger la Zouch*, knt. had liberty to grant fix messuages and several parcels of lands at Lubbesthorpe[13].

In 1352, *Henry* duke of *Lancaster* granted licence to the abbot and convent to impark their wood, and gave them deer to store it out of his forest of Leicester; and, by his personal mediation with the Pope, procured for them liberty to appropriate the churches of Humberston and Hungarton to the abbey, which was this year effected; in consideration whereof, they remitted and quitted-claim to him their right in their

lands and tenements of Everley in Wiltshire, and a cart-load of wood, which they had used to receive daily out of the forest of Leicester[14].

In 1352, *Simon de Ifip*, archbishop of *Canterbury*, had licence to found a chantry here; and to endow the same with 7 messuages, 4 tofts, 2 carucates, and 5 virgates of arable land, two acres of meadow, and 14s. annual rent, in Babbegrave, Stoughton, Cofby, and Little Thorpe; the manor of Ingwardby, and the advowson of Willoughby[15].

In 1361, *Simon Pakeman, Thomas de Roppele,* clerk, and *Richard of Leicester,* had licence to grant to this abbey the manor and advowson of Kirkby Malore, with their appurtenances; 7 messuages, a mill, 5 virgates of arable, 10 acres of meadow, 62s. 1d. annual rent, and an acknowledgement of two pounds of cumin, at Bittefwell, with the advowson of that church[16].

In 1364, some persons, designing to rob the abbey church, got into it through the window over the altar of St. John the Evangelist; but, being soon discovered by the sacrist, they were forced to depart before they had done any damage[17].

In 1370, pope Gregory XI. granted to this abbey the liberty of eating white meats made of milk during the season of Advent *(comedendi lactcinia in tempore Adventûs Domini[18])*. In this year also, at the request of abbot Clowne, king Edward III. granted a pardon to brother Henry de Knighton, for the offence he had committed in harbouring Robert de Killingworth, a minorite, and his servant boy, *felones regis[19]*. This seems to have been the period when Henry de Knighton, the able Chronicler already commended in p. 257, became first a canon of this abbey; which, by the indulgences of divers popes, had the privilege of affording sanctuary, to a considerable extent, to such as chose to associate themselves into their fraternity; and the crime of Henry de Knighton, in concealing two felons, was not of too grievous a dye to exclude him from this privilege. As a native of the neighbouring village of Knighton, he was probably indebted to this abbey, or some of its monks, for his education; and it is certain that, after his admission, he applied himself so sedulously to study[20] as to compile one of the most satisfactory Chronicles in our language.

In 1371, the abbot and convent fold three virgates of land in Bufby[21].

To the account of abbot Clowne, who died in 1377, the " Rentale" of Charyte enables us to add, that in his time the gates of the abbey were new-built with brick; the abbot's hall was built, which cost upwards of £39.; and more than £33. expended on Brackley chancel. He obtained an exemption from the payment of a hariot *(cupam vel palfredum)* on the death of an abbot; ordained the several chantries of the convent; and changed the use of black shoes to black boots *(ufum nigrarum botarum a nigris caligis cum nigris fotularibus[22])*. The singular grant of a dog-market, or fair, which he obtained from king Edward I, as noticed in p. 255, was not established[23].

In 1382, Philip de Repingdon (who had been a student of Broadgate-hall, in St. Aldate's parish, Oxford, and was then D. D. of Pembroke college) was accused of being an advocate for the doctrines of Wicklift, both in preaching, and in open disputation in the university, and also in his writings; amongst

[1] Wilkins, Concil. vol. II. p. 539. Reg. Reynolds, fol. 207. b.   [2] Reg. Reynolds, fol. 207. b. 208. a.

[3] Appendix, p. 59.   [4] Ibid. p. 62.   [5] Ibid. p. 59.   [6] Ibid. p. 69.   [7] Rotulus Romæ, 3 Edw. III.

[8] Appendix, p. 62.   [9] Ibid.   [10] Ibid.   [11] Ibid. p. 68.   [12] Ibid. p. 60.   [13] Ibid. p. 62.

[14] Knighton, fol. 2605.   [15] Appendix, p. 63. See this archbishop's seal, plate XVII. fig. 2.

[16] Appendix, p. 63.   [17] Knighton, fol. 2628.

[18] Wheatley, in his " Illustration of the Common Prayer," says, *Whitfunday* was fo called, " quia prædecessores nostri omne lac ovium et vaccarum suarum folebant dare pauperibus illo die, pro Dei amore, ut puriores efficerentur ad recipiendum donum Spiritus Sancti."—" Et certè quod de lacte vaccarum refert, illud percognitum habeo, in agro Hamptonienfi (an et alibi nefcio) decimas lacticiniorum venire vulgò fub hoc nomine, *The whites of kine*; apud *Leiceftrenfes* etiam lacticinia vulgariter dicuntur *Whitemeat*."

[19] Rot. 44 Edw. III. p. 3.

[20] " Totum fe dedicavit lectioni autorum, qui de rebus Anglicis fcripferunt; hoc confilio, quod præstantius effe duxerit hiftoriam fuæ gentis, qualicunque editam ftylo, pernofcere, quam alterius cujufvis remotæ nationis originem, ac fortia facta vel ab ipfis Liviis fcripta. Sed poftea quam in incepto pulchrè procefsiffet opere, venit illi in mentem, ut recentiorum temporum res geftas in ordinem redigeret. Itaque multa felegit ex libris, quos in confilium vocavit, multa etiam privatim ex illis, quorum longo domi militiæque claruerat experientia, didicit, ac pofteritati tanquam per manus tradidit." Tanner, Bibl. Brit. p. 458.

[21] Appendix, p. 69.   [22] Ibid. p. 68.

[23] Knighton, inter Decem Scriptores, 2631. 45, &c. " Abbas verò noluit in ftare circa negotium."

which,

which, one book was a profeffed " Defence of Wick-liffe," and another of his " Moral Doctrine." He wrote alfo a book of Homilies for the year; and others, on the Gofpels upon the Sabbath-days, of Secular Government; and of Queftions difcuffed [1].

" This man," fays Fox, " was a canon of Leicefter, and had before taken his firft degree unto doctorfhip; who preaching the fame time at Brodgates, for the fame fermon he became fufpected and hated of the Pharifaical brood of the friers; but, through the great and notable dexterity of his wit (which all men did behold and fee in him), accompanied with like mo-defty and honefty, he did fo overcome, or at the leaft affuage, this cruelty and perfecution which was to-wards him, that fhortly after, by the confent of the whole fellowfhip, he was admitted doctor; who, as foon as he had taken it upon him, ftepped forth in the fchools, and began to fhew forth that which he had long diffembled. Now the day of Corpus Chrifti aforefaid approaching near, when the friers under-ftood that this man fhould preach, fearing left that he would rub the galls of their religion, they con-vented with the archbifhop of Canterbury, that the fame day, a little before that Philip fhould preach, Wickliff's conclufions, which were privately con-demned, fhould be openly defamed in the prefence of the whole univerfity. The doing of which matter was committed to Peter Stokes, frier, ftandard-bearer and chief champion of that fide againft Wickliff. There were alfo letters fent unto the commiffary, that he fhould help and aid him in publifhing of the fame conclufions, as is before declared. Thefe things thus done and finifhed, Repingdon at the hour ap-pointed proceeded to his fermon. In the which fer-mon, among many other things, he was reported to have uttered thefe fayings, or to this effect: ' That the popes or bifhops ought not to be recommended above temporal lords. Alfo, that in moral matters he would defend Mafter Wickliff as a true Catholic doctor. Moreover, that the duke of Lancafter was very earneftly affected and minded in this matter, and would that all fuch fhould be received under his pro-tection;' befides many things more which touched the praife and defence of Wickliff. And finally, in concluding his fermon, he difmiffed the people with this fentence; ' I will (faid he) in the fpeculative doc-trine, as appertaining to the matter of the facrament of the altar, keep filence and hold my peace, until fuch time as God otherwife fhall inftruct and illu-minate the hearts of the clergy.' When the fermon was done, Repingdon entered into St. Fridefwide's church, accompanied with many of his friends; who, as the enemies furmifed, were privily weaponed under their garments, if need had been. Frier Stokes, the Carmelite aforefaid, fufpecting all this to be againft him, and being afraid of hurt, kept him within the fanctuary of the church, not daring as then to put out his head. The vicechancellor and Repingdon, friendly faluting one another in the church-porch, fent away the people; and fo departed every man home to his own houfe. There was not a little joy through the whole univerfity for that fer-mon; but, in the mean time, the unquiet and bufy Carmelite declared the whole order of the matter unto the archbifhop, exaggerating the perils and dangers, and requiring his help and aid."

Various proceedings were had on feveral different days in the priory of the Friers Preachers in London; and on the 20th of June fome conceffions were made by Repingdon and " Mafter Nicholas Herford," who was involved with him in the accufation [2]. Yet we find them again appearing before the archbifhop, on the 28th of June, in the chapel of his manor of Ot-ford; whence (as the archbifhop had not at that time the prefence of the doctors in divinity, and of the canon and civil law) the hearing was adjourned till the firft of July, in the chief houfe of the arch-bifhop's church at Canterbury; on which day, nei-ther Repingdon nor Herford appearing, fentence of excommunication was pronounced againft them both; which, in confequence of a mandate from the arch-bifhop, dated at his manor-houfe of Lambeth, July 13, was folemnly denounced by the preacher at Paul's Crofs, " by holding up a crofs, and lighting up a candle, and then throwing down the fame on the ground." Repingdon and Herford fled to the duke of Lancafter for fuccour; and, in the mean time, great fearch was made for them, to cite and to apprehend them wherefoever they might be found. On the 25th of July, the fentence of excommunication againft them both was repeated at Oxford; after which, not find-ing the protection which was expected from the duke, Repingdon contrived to make his peace; for we find, by a letter in the Lambeth Regifters, dated Oct. 23, that he was then reconciled to the archbifhop, and admitted to his fcholaftical acts in the univerfity [3]; and on the 24th of November, in the prefence of the prelates and the clergy, in the chapter-houfe of St. Fridefwide, made the following abjuration:

" *In Dei nomine, amen.* I Philip Repingdon, canon of the houfe of Leicefter, acknowledging one Catholic and Apoftolic faith, do curfe and abjure all herefy, namely, thefe herefies and errors under-written, con-demned and reproved by the decrees canonical, and by you, moft reverend father, touching which I have hitherto been defamed; condemning moreover and re-proving both them and the authors of them; and do confefs the fame to be catholically condemned. And I fwear alfo by thefe holy Evangelifts, which here I hold in my hand, and do promife, never by any per-fuafions of men, nor by any way hereafter, to defend, or hold as true, any of the faid conclufions under-written; but do and will ftand and adhere in all things to the determination of the holy Catholic church, and to yours, in this behalf. Over and be-fides, all fuch as ftand contrary to this faith, I do pro-nounce them, with their doctrine and followers, worthy of everlafting curfe; and, if I myfelf fhall prefume at any time to hold or preach any thing con-trary to the premifes, I fhall be content to abide the feverity of the canons. Subfcribed with mine own hand, and of mine own accord, *William Repingdon* [4]."

In 1389, William Courtney, archbifhop of Canter-bury, vifited the diocefe of Lincoln. On the feaft of St. Faith the Virgin (Oct. 6.) he vifited the cathedral of Lincoln; and on the Sunday before All Saints came for the fame purpofe to the abbey of Leicefter, and ftayed there feveral days; during which, inform-ation was given him, that Roger Dexter, Nicholas Taylor, Richard Wagftaffe, Michael Scrivener, Wil-liam Smith, John Henry, William Parchmentar, and Roger Goldfmith, inhabitants of Leicefter, held opi-

[1] " Repingtonus a literis fuo fæculo commendatiffimus, in numero fcriptorum merito quidem ponendus. Sic fama, fic me-moria, fic virtus jubet, quibus pro dignitate obtemperandum certè. Scholis in Ifiacis fub ipfum adolefcentiæ florem multa tulit fecitque, diligentiâ plane admirabili ufus; quam nec ante intenfam remittebat, quam fcopum attigiffet deftinatum. Tum verò inftructiffimus philofophus idemque theologus, doctorum fedulo imitatus exemplum, ad fcribendum fe totum contulit, multaque non infeliciter commentatus eft; e quibus extant in Evangelia lucubrationes, " Dominicalia," lib. i. Pr. pr. " Evangelicæ tubæ comminatio." Pr. I. " Dominici adventus tempus quater." MS. Cantab. in colleg. Caii, K. 59. et in aula Pembr. MS. 49.—Sermones Repington extabant olim MS. in bibl. eccl. S. Pauli. Dugdale, 283. " De fæculari dominio," lib. i. " Quæfti-ones difputatas," lib. i. " Scripfit etiam Defenforium Wiclevi," lib. i. " Pro doctrina [ejus de moribus, Add. Bal. Lel.] morali ejufdem," lib. i. " Homelias per annum," lib. i. Tanner, Bibl. Brit. p. 622.

[2] Extat MS. bibl. Bodl. Muf. 163. f. 67. a. ejus et Nic. Hereford. refponfio ad xxiv concl. damnatus in fynodo MCCCLXXXII. Pr. " Proteftamur ut alias publice:" et Angl. MS. bibl. Bodl. Arch. B. 83. Et in vol. III. Concil. M. Brit. et Hib. p. 161. feqq. ejus et Nicol. Heref. recantatio in domo fratrum minorum, 19 Jun. MCCCLXXXII. coram archiepifcopo Cantuar. Ibid. Vid. Concil. M. Brit. et Hib. vol. III. p. 172." Tanner, Bibl. Brit. p. 622.

[3] " Reftitutio domini Phil. Repyngdon, canonici Leyceftr. ad actus fcholafticos et priftinam famam per Willielm. archiep. Cant. mandatum, dat. 23 Oct. MCCCLXXXII. extat apud Twinum, A 262. et in Concil. M. Brit. et Hib. vol. III. p. 169. et 172. feq." Tanner, ibid.

[4] See thefe proceedings more fully detailed, from the Lambeth Regifters, in Fox's Acts and Monuments, vol. I. p. 498—508.

nions

nions concerning the Sacrament of the Altar, &c. contrary to the church of Rome; whereupon he caused them to be cited to appear before him at the abbey next day; which they not doing, he, on All Saints day, celebrating mass at the high altar in the monastery, denounced them and all their adherents excommunicate. He also caused the said excommunication to be published in all the parish-churches; and laid the whole town under an interdict so long as any of them should remain in the same, until they should obtain absolution from him [1]. Of these eight persons, Mr. Carte supposes that the last, Roger Goldsmith, died under the sentence of excommunication, and therefore was buried in the back-lanes, at the place which from him is to this day known by the name of *Goldsmith's Grave*. William Smith, Roger Dexter, and Alice his wife, at length recanted: and thereupon had the following penance enjoined them:

"That, the Sunday next after their returning to their proper goods, they the said William, Roger, and Alice, holding every of them an image of the Crucifix in their hands, and in their left hands every one of them a taper of wax, weighing half a pound weight, in their shirts (having none other apparel upon them) do go before the cross three times, during the procession of the cathedral church of our Lady of Leicester; that is to say, in the beginning of the procession, in the middle of the procession, and in the latter end of the procession; to the honour of him that was crucified, in the memorial of his Passion, and to the honour of the Virgin his mother; who also, devoutly bowing their knees and kneeling, shall kiss the same crucifix, so held in their hands. And so with the same procession they, entering again into the church, shall stand during all the time of the holy Mass, before the image of the cross, with their tapers and crosses in their hands. And, when the Mass is ended, the said William, Roger, and Alice, shall offer to him that celebrated that day the Mass. Then, upon the Saturday next ensuing, the said William, Roger, and Alice, shall in the full and public market, within the town of Leicester, stand in like manner in their shirts, without any more cloaths upon their bodies, holding the aforesaid crosses in their right hands; which crosses three times they shall (during the market) devoutly kiss, reverently kneeling upon their knees; that is, in the beginning of the market, in the middle of the market, and in the end of the market. And the said William (for that he somewhat understandeth the Latin tongue) shall say this Anthem with the Collect, *Sancta Katharina*; and the aforesaid Roger and Alice, being unlearned, shall say devoutly a *Pater Noster*, and an *Ave Maria*. And thirdly, the Sunday next immediately after the same, the said William, Roger, and Alice, in their parish-church of the said town of Leicester, shall stand and do as upon the Sunday before they stood and did in the cathedral church of our Lady aforesaid in all things. Which done, the aforesaid William, Roger, and Alice, after Mass, shall offer to the priest or chaplain that celebrated the same, with all humility and reverence, the wax-tapers which they shall carry in their hands. And because of the cold weather that now is, left the aforesaid penitents might peradventure take some bodily hurt standing so long naked (being mindful to moderate partly the said our rigour) we give leave, that after their entrance into the churches abovesaid, whilst they shall be in hearing the aforesaid Masses, they may put on necessary garments to keep them from cold, so that their heads and feet notwithstanding be bare and uncovered [2]." This ceremony being fully

performed, they were all absolved. The instrument for this purpose is dated at Dorchester, Nov. 17, 1389.

Whilst the archbishop was at Leicester, complaint was made to him of Matilda, a recluse in the church-yard of St. Peter's church in Leicester, as one that was tainted with the like principles as the others. Upon his excommunication of her, he, apprehending her answers to be subtle and unsatisfactory, appointed her on a day prefixed to appear personally before him in the monastery of St. James at Northampton; and in the mean time ordered the abbot of Leicester to put her into safe custody. Upon her appearance at Northampton, she gave the archbishop some better satisfaction, recanted the opinions charged upon her, and, being enjoined 40 days penance, was remitted to her recluse abode at Leicester again [3].

In 1392, *John Oxcliff*, *John Coiton*, *John Twywell*, *John Ansty*, *Richard Gameston*, *Robert of the Halle*, and *Richard Barwe*, had licence to give to the abbey at Leicester 6 messuages, 15 cottages, 3 virgates, 1 bovate, 1 acre, and 1 rood of arable, 3 acres of meadow, 4*d*. yearly rent, and an acknowledgement of a pound of cumin, in Leicester and its Suburbs, Humberston, Burstall, Barkby, and Lockington [4].

In 1393, on the resignation of William de Kerby, Philip de Repingdon, who in the registry at Lincoln is styled "Sacr' pag' professor [5]," was elected abbot of this house [6]. In 1395, he obtained a writ to compel Giles Jordan of Loughborough to restore the tithes of Woodhouse, a chapelry of Barrow, which had been unjustly detained [7]; and in 1399 obtained for his abbey, from king Henry IV, an annual grant of £245. being the whole profits of the alien priory of Ware, which had been seized by king Edward III, during his wars with France, as a cell to the abbey of St. Ebrulph in Normandy. He obtained also from the king a charter of exemption from all corrodies [8], and a confirmation of all the possessions of the abbey; procured for them a beautiful transcript of all the privileges they had received from the different popes [9], archbishops, and bishops [10]; and, in 1402, completed an agreement with John bishop of Lichfield for settling their respective boundaries on each side the Trent, in the townships of Sallowe and Lockington [11]. He had the honour of being chancellor of the university of Oxford in the years 1397, 1400, 1401, and 1402; and, in a writing, dated May 5, 1400, at which time several statutes were made concerning the election of the chancellor and other officers, he is styled " clericus specialissimus illustris principis D. regis " Henrici;" and " Vir potens & Deum timens, amans " veritatem, & detestans avaritiam [12]," &c. He was confessor also to the king; and, in the brief Register of Prior Charyte, we find this entry: " Memorandum, quod Henricus IV, finito magno bello in campo Salopie, et victoriâ habitâ, confestim fecit proclamationem per totum exercitum suum, si aliquis servus abbatis Leycestrie fuerit ibi. Statim venit unus servus dicti abbatis; cui rex tradidit annulum de digito suo, donans ei c solidos, precipiendo quod cum omni festinatione pergeret ad dominum Philippum abbatem Leycestrie, et nullo modo quiescat, donec traderet ei dictum annulum, et diceret ei, quod rex vivit, habens victoriam de inimicis suis, benedictus Deus. Item iste venerabilis pater Philippus simul & semel fuit abbas Leyc', doctor theologie, cancellarius universitatis Oxonie, & confessor domini regis Anglie, & postea episcopus Lincoln' [13]." On bishop Beaufort's translation to Winchester in 1405, Dr. Repingdon obtained the see of Lincoln; and after this became such a persecutor of the Wicklevians, that he

[1] Knighton, col. 2733.   [2] Fox's Acts and Monuments, vol. I. p. 577.   [3] Ibid. p. 576.   [4] Appendix, p. 64.
[5] This seems equivalent to the modern S. T. P. *sacræ theologiæ professor*.   [6] Reg. Bokingham, pars secunda.   [7] Appendix, p. 64.
[8] A corrody was a sum of money, or allowance of meat, drink, and cloathing, due to the king, or any other founder of an abbey or religious house, towards the reasonable subsistence of any servant he thinks fit to bestow it on. Fitzherbert, Nat. Br. 250. sets down all the corrodies and pensions certain that abbeys, when they stood, were bound to perform to the king. For an elucidation of the subject, see hereafter, p. 267.
[9] See these in our Appendix, p. 70.   [10] The confirmations of divers archbishops of Canterbury are enumerated in Charyte's Rentale, p. clxxv. a. b; of bishops of Coventry and bishops of Lincoln, p. clxxv. b; and of archbishops of York, p. clxxvi.
[11] Appendix, p. 64; and see his good deeds more particularly specified, Appendix, p. 71.
[12] Gutch's History and Antiquity of the Colleges, &c. at Oxford, p. 622; Appendix, pp. 34—36.
[13] Cotton MSS. Vitellius F. XVII.

was commonly called *Philip Rampington*. Whilft he was bifhop, we find a commiffion, addreffed to his fucceffor Richard Rotheley, for the examination of Ifolda N. who was defirous to exchange the pomps of the world, and the fnares of worldly converfation, for the riches of eternal treafure, by becoming an anchoret in the cemetery of St. Peter at Leicefter[1]. He was made a cardinal by pope Gregory XII in 1409[2]; refigned his bifhoprick in 1419[3]; and lived private from that time till his death, which happened in 1424; in which year, on the firft of Auguft, his will was proved in the new collegiate church at Leicefter. Of this will Mr. Gough has the following abftract in Mr. Anftis's copy of Godwin : " Ego Phil. de Ripyndon, nuper ecclefie Linc. epus, compos mentis, appropinquante confimiliter viâ mortis meæ.—Miffa funeralis in ecclefiâ paroch. S. Margaretæ infra claufum Linc. pro animâ meâ—in die miffæ meæ funeralis veftiantur c pauperes—Corpus meum extra limen porticûs ecclefiæ parochialis Scæ Margaretæ prædict', ex parte borealis ejufdem ecclefiæ, *fub plano & aperto firmamento cœli*; non in ecclefiâ vel monafterio, quia ad hoc me indignum reputo, fepeliri nudum & in facco miferum faciant tumulari." He was however buried in his cathedral, near the South wall, by bifhop Groffetefte's tomb ; with this infcription on a brafs plate in the middle of a plain flab :

Marmoris in tumba fimplex fine felle columba
Repington natus jacet hic Philippus humatus.
Flos Adamas cleri, paftor gregis, et preco veri,
Vivat ut in cælis quem pofcat quique fidelis[4]."

In 1408, another " Rentale" of this houfe was compiled by a canon of the name of Bathe.

In 1409, whilft John Rotheley was abbot, the chancel of St. Martin's at Leicefter was rebuilt[5].

In the regifter of archbifhop Arundel, an inftrument is preferved, under the Title of " Relaxatio interdicti Monafterii B. M. de Pratis Leyceft', & abfolutio procuratoris ejufdem. Dat. apud Forde, A. D. 1410[6]."

In 1414, a parliament was held at Leicefter, in which 110 religious houfes, called Alien Priories[7], were fuppreffed entirely, and their poffeffions given to the king and his heirs for ever[8]; moft of which were afterwards given by Henry the Sixth to other monafteries and houfes of learning, efpecially King's College in Cambridge, and Eaton College, of that king's foundation. Several compofitions which the abbey of Leicefter had entered into with that of St. Ebrulph, refpecting tithes of various places in Leicefterfhire, were transferred to the prior and convent of Jefus of Bethlehem of Shene ; with whom the abbot and convent of Leicefter entered into a new engagement; which, for the annual rent of twelve pounds a year, fecured to them all they had before on leafe from the abbot and convent of St. Ebrulph ; confifting of tithes at Braunfton, Kerby, Kirkby Malory, Thorpe-Ernald, Stoughton, Bufhby, Evington, Humberfton, Great Wigfton, Thornton, Bagworth, Enderby, Doveland, the earl of Leicefter's demefne in the South and Weft gates of Leicefter, in a place called the *affartum* of Simon Danet in the Suburbs of Leicefter, and in feveral places called Culleferland, Edwynerys, and Stocking[9].

At the firft fuppreffion of the alien priories, that of Ware[10] was given by king Henry V. to the monks at Shene ; but was afterwards in 1422[11] transferred to the abbey of Leicefter, which had for a confiderable time received from it a large annual income. It was, however, again reftored to the priory of Shene; and, as parcel of their poffeffions, was granted by king Henry VIII. to Trinity College, Cambridge.

About the year 1420, Thomas Langley, bifhop of Durham, one of the executors of the will of John of Gaunt duke of Lancafter, gave to this abbey the patronage of a chantry for two chaplains founded by the duke's directions in the New College at Leicefter[12].

In 1421, the canons of the order of St. Auftin reminded king Henry V, that they had lately applied to him, when at Leicefter, for the grant of a proper feminary at Oxford, for the education of the young canons of their order ; and requefted that a convenient place for that purpofe might be purchafed at Candyche, near the monks of Durham, without the walls of the city, and beftowed on them by the king. This appears by the Rolls of Parliament[13]. And we learn from Stevens's Monafticon, that the canons obtained, from the fingular devotion of that monarch, a warrant under his fignet, with a commiffion from the lord treafurer, to purchafe lands at Oxford for a manfion-place ; but, the king's will being not fully performed, the canons for that time were fruftrated of their defigns, totally difperfed, and their bufinefs came to nought ; wherefore, to renew it again, and that they might be privileged in having a nurfery for the young canons of their order[14] in the univerfity, as others had, the prior of the Holy Trinity in London, the abbot of Waltham, the prior of Twynham, the abbot of Leicefter, the prior of Gifeburn[15], the prior of Bridlington, the prior of St. Ofwald in Noftel, the prior of Hexham, and the prior of Catliol, in the name of the reft, with a joint confent, petitioned king Henry VI, that the work, which had flept for many years, might be carried on ; wherefore the faid king, by his letters patent, dated Dec. 24, 1435, gave leave to Thomas Holden, efq. and Elizabeth his wife (whom thefe canons had before procured), to give and affign to the prior of St. Trinity, London, and to his fucceffors for ever, in the name of the whole order, one meffuage, with gardens thereunto belonging, lying in the parifhes of St. Peter and St. Michael at Northgate, within the walls of the city (fituated between the inn commonly called the Star-Inn, and the lane[16] that goes from Bocardo to New-Inn, on the Weft fide of the ftreet[17]) to the yearly value of 40s. beyond reprifes; which the faid Thomas and Elizabeth held of the king in free burgage. Having obtained this houfe, they afterwards in procefs of time much enlarged it with buildings, both at the entry into the little lane or alley leading from the High-ftreet thereunto, as alfo on the other fide almoft oppofite to New-Inn-Hall[18]. The pious founder, willing to extend his charity farther, laid the foundation of a chapel, intending a library over it ; but he dying Auguft 17, 1440, before it was quite built, ordered, in his will, for the finifhing thereof, as much money as would ferve for the neceffary expences ; befides £103. 6s. 8d. in which the abbot of Leicefter, the abbot of St. Ofyth in Effex, and the prior of Gifeburn in Yorkfhire, were, by their three obligations, bound to him for, towards other expences in building ; befides a veftment for

---

[1] Appendix, p. 65.

[2] " Epifcopus Lincolnienfis (provifus ab Innocentio VII. papa 13 kal. Decemb. Reg. Arundel.) confecratus eft 29 Martii MCCCCV, et poft triennium (Sept. 18, MCCCCVIII.) purpureo infignitus galero a Gregorio XII, tit. SS. Nerei et Achillei."

[3] " MCCCCXIX. Ecclefia Lincoln. per refign. Philippi epifcopi Lincoln. per ipfius procur. in manus domini Martini papæ V, vicefimo die Nov. anno prædicto in curia factam, et in craftino ejufd. diei autoritate domini papæ admiffam vacavit, et a primo die menfis Februarii idem Philippus, olim epifcopus, ab omni exercitio jurifdictionis penitus abftinebat." Reg. Fleming.

[4] Willis's Cathedrals, vol. II. p. 54 ; Sepulchral Monuments of Great Britain, vol. II. p. 68.

[5] Appendix, p. 72.   [6] Reg. Arundel, fol. 123. a.

[7] Thefe foundations were fo called becaufe they belonged to foreign monafteries ; and their fuperiors abroad ufed to fend over French and Normans, who tranfplanted the wealth of thefe houfes to thofe of the fuperiors, as well as communicated the fecrets of the kingdom to other powers ; two fufficient caufes in policy for their fuppreffion. By the united labours of Dr. Ducarel, Mr. Gough, and the Publifher of the prefent Hiftory, a tolerably complete account of the Alien Priories was publifhed in 1779, in two fmall octavo volumes.

[8] Rot. Parl. 2 Hen. V. m. 9 ; Coke, 2 Inft. p. 432.   [9] See farther particulars in the Appendix, p. 73.

[10] The priory of Ware had lands in Leicefterfhire, at Belgrave, Carleton, Great Peatling, Shevefby, and Earl's Shilton.

[11] De abbatiâ beatæ Mariæ de Pratis, pro prioratu de Ware alienig. fibi annectand. Pat. 1 Hen. VI. p. 1. m. 41.

[12] Appendix, p. 65.   [13] Rot Parl. vol. IV. p. 159; 9 Hen. V. See Appendix, p. 60.

[14] A general chapter of canons regular was held at Leicefter in 1425. Kennet, Parochial Antiquities, p. 572.

[15] Alias Gifeburg, in Yorkfhire. Tanner, Not. Mon. p. 650.   [16] Wood-ftreet. A. Wood.   [17] Northgate-ftreet. A. W.

[18] The building was ftanding in 1723, and had been fome time before employed as a meeting-houfe for Quakers. Stevens.

the

the prieft, with a cope or hood lined with red fattin, on which he would have both his and his wife's arms worked; and, after the death of his faid wife, they fhould have for ever his better veftment and ornaments for the chapel, as alfo £20. to be beftowed upon books for the library there. The lands that belonged to this college were few or none; for the canons thereof were maintained by the greater abbeys of this order, who fent them here to gain academical learning, fome more, and fome of a lefs number; and after two or three years or more, when they were graduated, were taken home to teach their fellows,

and others put in their places [1]. The chapel here, with the college, was dedicated to the Virgin Mary; and in it were the bodies of the founder, who died in 1440, and Elizabeth his wife, depofited under a fair marble ftone, with their images curioufly cut on brafs.

Wood fays, " Though this college had but a fmall continuance, yet it hath left fufficient memory behind : it gained more repute than thofe of a longer ftanding; and which was the breeding and entertaining feveral learned men; Erafmus [2], and others. Thus far may be faid of this place fo long as it was a priory [3]."

[1] " Befides thefe regulars, there were fecular monks, as they are called in their ftatutes, which were commoners and battlers, both which, efpecially the canons regular, were governed by a prior, and both he and they by ftatutes, which were confulted of by a convocation of that order at St. James's near Northampton, 1446, and committed to the difcretion of Thomas the abbot of Oufney, for the framing and completing of them; who two years after, upon examination and approbation, publifhed them in this college, under the faid abbot's feal, to whofe overfight this place did pertain, which, though made for monks, yet feem to be extracted from fome of the ftatutes of our ancienteft colleges, viz. in our chapel duties, the ufual way of performing divine fervice, their folemn days wherein High-mafs was faid, efpecially on St. Auguftin's-day, the father of this order, the dedication of the chapel, with other commemorations for the founder and the like; and the mulcts impofed on the abfent, as well as the regulars, as commoners and battlers, they had their facrift and præcentor or *rector chori* [*], as we now call him, chofe annually amongft them, whofe office was to have the cuftody of veftments, books, utenfils, and other ornaments of the chapel; the præcentor to give notice what prayers to be faid, when fuch or fuch fervice to be performed, what hymn, verficle, or collect to be fung; and, on all high feftival days, both feculars and battlers to be at his command, in the office of offering wax, frankincence, and blowing the organs; but in the leffer feftival days, the feculars were not bound to be prefent, but to go to the parifh-church wherein they lived. Their hall-duties alfo, for the moft part, like thofe of the college; as reading a Latin chapter every day in the term-time; fpeaking always of Latin (except gaudy-days) both in the hall and the limits of the college; not dining in their chambers without fpecial leave from the prior, and the like; with many other ftatutes relating to feveral matters." Stevens, Monafticon, vol. II. p. 128. Wood's MS Hiftory and Antiquities of the City of Oxford, in the Afhmolean Mufeum, F. 29.

[2] Erafmus, when he was at Oxford in 1497 and 1498, as appears by his Epiftles to John Sixtine and Will. Mountjoy, ftudied and had his abode in this college of the Virgin Mary; and hence alfo his Epiftle before his " Difputatio de tædio & pavore Chrifti" was dedicated to John Colet, then profeffor of divinity in Oxford. Knight's Life of Erafmus, p. 20, 21, and of Colet, p. 32. Jortin's Life of Erafmus, p. 11. Hence he went to Cambridge, where he began to write in 1510, as appears from an Epiftle to Andreas Ammonius. It is remarkable, that the apartments where Erafmus was lodged in both our univerfities are now pulled down. That at Queen's College, Cambridge, was demolifhed about 30 years ago.

[3] From Wood's MS Hiftory of the City of Oxford, which is on loofe papers, and does not feem to have been prepared for publication, Mr. Gutch has favoured me with the following continuation of the hiftory of St. Mary's college : " This priory did not much fuffer deftruction of its walls when it was diffolved; neither was it rendered up in the king's hands till 1541; and then, Oct. 7, Mr. Jarvis Markham being then prior or rector, there was an inventory taken of the goods and implements therein; and employed a fmall while, till 1547 or thereabouts, for the ufe of fcholars as a hall; but into whofe poffeffion it came afterwards, I am as yet uncertain, unlefs it was the lord Williams; for I find that he, in the 3d and 4th of Philip and Mary, fold timber and flate from hence to the city by Mr. Wayt. In the fame year alfo, viz. 1556, I meet with one John Feteplace, efq. who, for the fingular favour he bore to the univerfity, did, by his charter, dated 8 Oct. the fame year, give and confirm to the chancellor and fcholars thereof, and their fucceffors for ever, all this his tenement, called by the name of St. Mary's College, and which before was known by the name of Berill's Place. This he did conditionally, that they fhould pray both for his and his parents' fouls, and number him in their prayers as a benefactor of this univerfity. Upon this donation, the vice-chancellor, willing to keep that place from ruin and defolation, which was then much inclining thereto, gave commiffion to Alexander Elcock, mafter of arts, and feveral other fcholars that were of the faid Elcock's acquaintance, to poffefs the fame as a hall, and he to be their principal, paying fuch a fum of money annually for the rent; but with this provifo, that if cardinal Pole would have it employed to its former ufe (times being then turned), for the entertainment of the regular canons again, then they were willingly and freely to refign up their whole right in the faid hall; but this coming not to pafs, they did for three or four years or more poffefs the fame, though at firft they were denied poffeffion thereto by John Wayt citizen of Oxon aforefaid, who pretended that he had intereft therein, and that he was lord of the fame. Thus we find it given to the univerfity by a liberal benefactor; and by them for fome years freely enjoyed, having 13s. 4d. rent paid to them annually by the principal thereof : but whether Feteplace's title to it was bad, or what the reafon of it fhould be, I am yet in doubt; the univerfity afterwards loft it; and, coming into the hands of the earls of Huntingdon, Catharine the widow of Frances earl thereof, with earl Henry his fon and lord Haftings, did, in the year 1562, grant and feoffee John Wayt, then mayor of Oxon, and others, of all the fite, with the houfe thereof; which, as it appeareth by another inftrument of the feoffees, was given and taken to the intent to maintain ten poor children, to be taught and brought up there; and likewife to maintain ten poor perfons, to be fet on work, upon the cofts and charitable relief of the citizens of Oxon; fo that this place then, and for fome years after, was known by the name of Bridewell; to which alfo, according to the intention of the donor, for the better encouragement of the poor folk there, it was enacted, by a mayor of Oxon and his council, 11 July, anno Eliz. 7[?], that the mayor of the time being fhould pay weekly for their maintenance 6d. the aldermen 4d. the bailiffs 3d. the chamberlains 2d. the common council 1d. and fo to laft till farther order was taken. But this fum did not continue long; for on the 19th of Auguft following they leffened it, and ordained, that the mayor for the time being fhould pay towards their relief 3s. 4d. quarterly; the aldermen each of them and the other eight likewife, 3s. quarterly; the bailiffs 2s. apiece; the chamberlains 16d. apiece; the common council 12d. apiece, all quarterly; and this to endure for a whole year, commencing from the Midfummer preceding; which when that alfo was finifhed, they enacted, 28 June, anno Eliz. 8, that Mr. Mayor, and the thirteen, with the bailiffs, fhould tax all men according to their difcretions for their maintenance another year. What became of their maintenance afterward I know not; neither do I find any more mention of it † ; only fome well-difpofed people would at the time of their death leave a fmall portion of money towards their fuftenance; among whom, and the greateft fum that I have yet met with, was the gift of Richard Williams, twice mayor fome time of this city; who, dying 1579 ‡, 21 Eliz. did leave to them £4. towards their apparelling, who always were habited with blue coats. Will. Tipping, of Draycot, co. Oxon. £300. towards the building of the New Bridewell without Northgate, which was built anno 1635.—The chapel, with a garden adjoining, was demifed in 1575 by the mayor and commonalty to John Wait (who alfo before held it) for 21 years, as alfo part of the cloifter for as many years to Mr. Tarlton; the one paying 26s. 8d. the other 2s. yearly rent; by whofe ufage efpecially the cloifter, which led from the chapel towards the great gate [ftill ftanding 1796] almoft oppofite to New-Inn Hall, was much ruinated and demolifhed; and the faid chapel, which was a very fair fabrick, built with free-ftone, and very good workmanfhip to be feen about it, was given to Brazen-Nofe college by the owner thereof, to lay the foundation of their own chapel; which for that ufe was demolifhed and taken away in 1656."

[*] Wood is not quite accurate in his fuggeftion that heretofore *præcentor* and *rector chori* were terms always fynonymous. In the ftatutes of Lichfield and Lincoln, in Wilkins, Concil. vol. I. p. 498 & p. 536, under title " De Officio Cantorum," it appears there was at Lichfield *cantor* (i. e. precentor) et *fuccentor* (fub-chanter); and that in both cathedrals there was *cantor* cum aliis *rectoribus chori*. Somner, in Antiquities of Canterbury, p. 93, mentions his having noticed in a regifter of Chrift Church priory *inferior* and *fuperior chorus*; interpreted, by Battely, to fignify the upper ftalls from the lower. But query, does it not allude to the feating of the finging monks on each fide of the choir for the performance of the alternate chant; and that the precedency or fuperiority was given to the South or right fide, as it ftill is to the decanal fide in choirs, where the firft verfe of the firft pfalm is fung; though Mr. Denne is inclined to think, from an expreffion in a ftatute of archbifhop Winchelfey, that the fuperior chorus might originally fing only half the verfe, as pointed by : a colon; and that the other half was fung by the monks on the oppofite fide (Wilkins, Concil. vol. II. p. 244.) According to Somner, Supprior, *precentor*, and one of the penitentiaries, were to take to them four other brothers; two from the right fide of the choir, and two from the left fide, &c. Thefe brethren Mr. Denne fuppofes to have been what are in the Statutes of Lichfield and Lincoln ftyled *rectores chori*; but at Canterbury, it feems, they had the title of Cardinals (Somner, Appendix, p. 57), as they had in St. Paul's cathedral; in which, as in many other cathedrals of the old foundations, there is ftill a prebendary denominated *precentor*, and a minor canon called *cardinal*.

† " Prior and fellowes of Brazen Colledge did let it for 30 yeares (20 Jan. 24 Eliz.) to Dr. Lloyd, law profeffor, by the name of Bridewell, vel S. Marie's Hofpitall." Reg. Antiq. Br. Coll. fol. 75. b. ‡ Super tumulum in Ecclefiâ S. Aldati.

John

John Mackworth being dean of Lincoln in the time of William Sadyngton, who was abbot from 1420 till 1442, and a vacancy happening in the fee of Lincoln; he would have visited the abbey of Leicester, because, in the composition made between Boniface archbishop of Canterbury and the dean and chapter of Lincoln, the dean was allowed to visit, *jure episcopali*, two monasteries, during every vacancy of the bishoprick, in each archdeaconry; but there being an exception of such monasteries as were under the patronage of the king; and the earldom of Leicester, to which the patronage of the abbey belonged, being by this time united with the crown; therefore, when the dean came to the abbey, the abbot sent his gentleman, Richard Taylerd, to the gates, forbidding him entrance; upon which the dean, with his attendants, went to the town, and did not make any farther attempt to visit the abbey[1].

In 1434, the lady Joane Beauchamp, lady of Bergavenny, and relict of sir William Beauchamp, devised by her last will[2], " that in every cathedral church or conventual, where her body should rest a night, toward the place where her body was to be buried (the choir of the Friers Preachers at Hereford), the dean, abbot, or prior, to have 6s. 8d.; and every canon, monk, vicar, priest or clerk, present at the dirige at the mass in the morning, to have 12d." She farther ordained, " that, anon after her burying, there should be done for her soul 5000 masses in all the best haste that they might goodly." In obedience to these directions, we find an agreement between the abbot and convent of Leicester, and Bartholomew Brokesby, one of her executors, for the celebration of a mass for her soul at the altar of St. John the Baptist and Saint Austin, on the South side of their monastery[3].

In 1445, a lease occurs, from abbot John Pomerey, and Walter Pomerey of Leicester, to John German and others, of a messuage and garden in St. Margaret's[4].

In 1458, a circular letter was sent, from this abbey, to all the neighbouring churches, requesting their prayers for the souls of all the benefactors to the abbey, and of all the abbots and canons departed[5].

In 1466, a commission was issued, to William Sutton master of Burton Lazars, Richard Neel of Prestwold, then a serjeant-at-law, John Pulteney, esq. and Robert Staunton, on the representation of John Pomerey abbot of Leicester, to enquire whether the abbey of Leicester was exempt from the imposition of corrodies; when it appeared that this monastery, being of private foundation and of frank almoigne, though the patronage had devolved to the crown in 1265 by the attainder of Simon Montfort, was undoubtedly entitled to that exemption, both by the nature of their foundation, and by a charter of king Edward III[6]; yet that, at the request of several of their patrons[7], the abbots had afforded relief to some old dependants[8].

In the interval between Midlent Sunday and Palm Sunday, 1470, king Edward IV. came to Leicester abbey, and departed to Combe abbey and Coventry[9].

In 1473, the abbot and convent demised their capital mansion in St. Sepulchre's, London, to sir Thomas Littleton, one of the judges of the king's bench, for 40 years, at an annual rent of 16s. with a covenant of for-

feiting 40d. if the rent should not be paid half-yearly, and the lease to be void if a year should so elapse[10].

In 1482, the abbot and convent ordained an especial daily service in honour of William Charyte, 43 years a resident in this abbey; whose good deeds were such as to entitle him to very peculiar notice[11], and who lived to be eminently serviceable to the abbey for twenty years longer. He occurs as prior in 1471; and, at the time he was thus noticed, had given to the abbey a chalice of gold, an image of our Lady gilt, and several sums of money for the public use of the convent; had bought for them the windmill at Stoughton, with several lands and tenements in Hungarton, Bagrave, &c. But his principal assistance to them was in compiling the " Rentale Novum generale," which bears his name, and which furnishes so many useful articles to the present History of the Abbey[12]. This Register, compiled with incredible labour, and transcribed with his own hand in a folio volume of 219 leaves closely written on both sides, was begun in 1477, and finished in 1502, when he was in his 81st year, 63 years after his first having embraced the religious profession. He frequently observes, that there had been a great and general decrease in the value of all their estates between the years 1335 and 1493, occasioned principally by the plague of 1346[13]; and in many parts it is noticed that their lands, &c. afforded a much greater rent *ante annum pestilentiæ* than afterwards. A rent-roll is given of the value of the several chapels, farms, and manors, *ante pestilentiam*[14]; a comparative view of the different state of their property at the periods of 1254, 1341, 1408, and 1477[15]; another such comparison of the rents received in grain in 1393, 1399, 1401, and 1470[16]; and again in 1477[17], distinguished into wheat, rye, barley, peas, and oats, and, in some few cases, mixed grain *(mixtorum bladiorum)*; a rental of receipts in capons, hens, cocks, and eggs[18]; and of those *in pipere, cumino, rosis, cirotecis, flectis, & calcaribus*[19]; the customs of their tenants[20]; the places where they had a right to free-warren[21], hariots[22], view of frankpledge, &c. and of those where they till lately *(infra breve)* had neifes *(nativos)*[23]. An inventory is entered, of all the existing leases from the abbey, whether of offices, farms, mills, tenements, or lands[24]; among which, we find one from the prior, ascertaining the weight and value of all their jewels; two from the precentor, an inventory of the books delivered to him by his predecessor, and a list of such books as were lent out to any of the canons; and an inventory from the sub-chanter of all the books in his custody. Engagements were likewise taken (between the officer going out of place and his successor) from the sacrist and sub-sacrist, the treasurer, the almoner, the steward *(firmarius)*, the celarer, the master of the grange, the sub-celarer, the *hospitiarius*[25], the chaplain, the chamberlain *(camerarius)*, the abbot's butler, and the keepers of his buttery, wine and ale cellar, and pantry *(butterie, taberni*[26]*, celarii, & pantrie)*. There were engagements also from the abbot's granges of West-gate, Stoughton, Medoplek, and Ingwarby, of all their goods and chattels, of the books and religious vestments, and of the household goods, at each respec-

---

[1] Appendix, p. 65. [2] See some farther particulars of this will, under Kirkby Beler, vol. II. p. 227.
[3] Appendix, p. 72. [4] Carte, MS. [5] Appendix, p. 65. [6] See before, p. 264.
[7] In the Parliament Rolls, vol. I. p 156, we find, in 1302, a petition to king Edward I, from Gilbert de Bed, who had been his *sumeter* more than 20 years, ten of them in the wars at home and abroad *en garnesterre*; stating, that, having in the king's last residence in Scotland been taken prisoner and wounded by the Scotch, he was unable to help himself; and praying the king to grant him his letter to some religious house not already burdened with any person for subsistence, as he had indulged others of his old servants. In answer to this petition, he was informed, that, if he pointed out any monastery that was not already so burdened, the king would write for him. On which he named the monasteries of Bardney and Leicester.— The office of *sumeter* here mentioned may have been that of master of the *sumpter* or baggage horses, there being in the Wardrobe account of king Edward I. 1299-1300, this allowance, p. 77; Rob'to atte Grove, pro uno equo liardo pomele empto de eodem apud Ebor' et lib' ibidem Will'o Mone fometar' ad unum fomerum pro armis reg', mense Novemb', £10.—But, whatever was Gilbert de Bed's business, he was *en garnesterre*, ready equipped or accoutred, which added to his expence and loss.
[8] What the nature of this relief was, see in our Appendix, p. 61. [9] Dugdale, Warwickshire, vol. I. p. 143.
[10] Appendix, p. 74. [11] See them specified, Appendix, p. 71.
[12] See the full title of this work, with a character of it by Mr. Thomas Hearne, Appendix, p. 53; and its contents, p. 67.
[13] Appendix, p. 68. [14] Charyte, fol. clxx. b. [15] Ibid. fol. cli. b. [16] Ibid. fol. clxxviii. a—clxx. a. [17] Ibid. fol. clxxi. a. b.
[18] Appendix, p. 77. [19] Ibid. p. . [20] Ibid. p. . [21] Ibid. p. 77. [22] Ibid. p. 76.
[23] This species of vassalage (of which see the Dissertation on Domesday, p. xlv.) was gradually wearing away at the very period when Charyte was compiling his " Rentale."—In an act of resumption passed in 1485, provision is made, that the act should not prejudice any manumission of villanage, or *neifte*, granted to any person, either by king Henry VI, king Edward IV, or the sovereign then reigning. Rot. Parl. 1 Hen. VII; vol. VI. p. 339.
[24] Appendix, p. 69. [25] *Hospitiarius*, or *hostiarius*. His business was to accommodate strangers. Tanner.
[26] *Taberna*, a wine cellar. Du Cange, in voce.

tive

tive manor-houfe. The parties to all thefe were the celarer *egrediens* and the celarer *ingrediens*[1]. The engagement of each chaplain was made with the abbot's chamberlain for all that was contained in the wardrobe; with his butler for what was in the ftorehoufe (*provituarium*[2]), buttry, ale and wine cellar; and with the pantler for the contents of the pantry[3].

The *ordinationes vicariarum* are given for Barkby, Bittefwell, Billefdon, Carleton, Curdworth, Difeworth, Eaton, Glenfield, Godeby, Hamilton, Hungarton, Ilfton, Shepefhed, Lockington, Nofeley, Thedingworth, Thornton, Thorpe Ernald, &c.; with feveral contefts and compofitions about the patronage and rights of the vicarage of Blaby[4], and of the churches of Eaton[5], Harefton, Hathern, and Houghton; and concerning the rights and patronage of the churches of Hufbands Bofworth, Croft, Difhley, Kilworth, and Narborough[6]. Under Wykingefton, there is no mention of the vicarage; but of the rights of the rectory, and the interefts of the abbey and convent of Leicefter, of St. Ebrulf, and of the priory of Lenton, there is much. Under Barrow there are feveral fettlements and compofitions about the vicarage worth obferving, with an accurate terrier of the parifh. Of Stoughton Grange and Thurnby, there are full accounts[7]. The advowfon of Wanlip, and a virgate of glebe land, which had been given to the abbot and convent by William Walfh, lord of Wanlip, they afterwards exchanged with him for a meadow on the North fide of Leicefter, called Walfh's meadow, or the Oftler's aker. They had an unlimited right of fifhing at Wanlip, *cum retibus & fagenis*, which they alfo gave up for a rent of 6*s*. a year at Barkby, and the homage and fervice of William fon of Roger de Rotheley of Syfton[8].

Charyte wrote alfo with his own hand twenty-five different books or rolls on fubjects of importance; the laft of which he began in 1502, in his 81ft year. One of thefe, a fmall quarto, on 40 leaves of vellum, is called, "Breve opufculum compilatum per fratrem W. Charyte, ad cognofcendum nomina fundatorum noftrorum & benefactorum, & donationes eorum quas illi nobis dederunt in villis fubfcriptis, ut illorum memoria noftris in mentibus & omnibus ferventiùs hereatur;" and, on another leaf is explained to be, "Repertorium Chartarum Abbatie de Leicefter; continens privilegia apoftolica; nomina fundatorum & benefactorum, & donationes illorum; & confirmationes & libertates regum abbati & monachis conceffas; & nomina abbatum, a Ricardo primo abbate ad Joannem Penney, qui erat vicefimus fecundus, anno xi° R. Henrici VII, anno MCCCXCVI; compilatum per fratrem Willielmum Charite, anno MCCCCLXXXVII; & poftea continuatum.—Nota quod in ifto brevi opufculo fubfcripto manifeftum eft quomodo aliqui redditus noftri antiqui tam de fpiritualibus quam de temporalibus decreverunt ab anno Domini M.CCC.XXXV°. ad annum Dominiм. cccc. nonagefimum tertium, &c." This MS. at the fire in the Cotton Library was confiderably damaged. About two thirds, however, of each leaf remain legible, the upper part only being confumed. It is marked Vitellius F. XVII; and, though in fome refpects it may be called an abridgement of the "Rentale" at Oxford, contains feveral particulars that are not in the larger volume. Of the above-mentioned Regifters an abftract, by fir William Dugdale, is preferved in the Afhmolean Mufeum, F. 2. p. 327; under the title of "Analecta & tranfcripta ex duobus

Regiftris abbathiæ de Leiceftriâ, de terris, &c. eodem conceffis in com. Warwic', 1638, per me W. D."[9]

Another of Charyte's works which has been preferved is called "Regiftrum Librorum Monafterii B. M. de Pratis, Leiceftrie, renovatum tempore fratris W. Charyte, hic precentoris;" from which it appears that the abbey had no mean collection of books; and the induftry of the compiler is fully difplayed[10].

In 1484, the abbot of Leicefter was appointed a collector of the taxes of all the benefices charged or difcharged within the archdeaconry of Leicefter. In September that year, the abbot and convent obtained a charter for a fair at Leicefter, on the feaft of Saint Leonard, within the faid abbey; and in the parifh of Saint Leonard two days before the faid feaft, and two days after[11]. In February 1484-5, they had licence to appropriate the church of Stoke[12].

On the 27th of November, 1493, Richard Befton, chaplain of Woodhoufe, performed his accuftomed fealty in the chapter-houfe of Leicefter abbey to Gilbert the abbot, in the prefence of John Penny, prior, William Charyte, *quondam* prior, fir John Noris, fir Richard Palet, chaplain, and others[13].

John Penny, whofe birth-place Wood could not difcover, was educated at Lincoln college, Oxford, LL. D. there; and an eminent canonift. He was prior of the abbey of St. Mary de Pratis at Leicefter in 1493; admitted abbot there 7 kal. Julii, 1496; and on the 14th of September, 1503, obtained the fmall priory of Bradley *in commendam*; both which he continued to hold with the bifhoprick of Bangor, to which he was nominated in 1504, and confecrated 1505[14]; after which period, we find an agreement of his with Thomas Stoke, efq. of Elsford, co. Stafford, by which the patronage and advowfon of Hufbands Bofworth is conveyed to the faid Thomas Stoke, in confideration of divers fums of money by him paid, and in return for divers lands and tenements given to the abbey by Thomas Stoke and his anceftors[15]. Bifhop Penny refigned this abbey and the priory of Bradley[16], on being tranflated to the fee of Carlifle[17]; the pope's bull for which tranflation was dated 10 kal. Octob. 1508. He died at the end of the year 1519, or the beginning of 1520, on a vifit at Leicefter-abbey; where it is fuppofed that he was buried; and that, on the fuppreffion of the monaftery, his monument was removed to St. Margaret's church in Leicefter, to the re-building of which church Mr. Willis defcribes him to have been a good benefactor[18], and where, near the Eaft end of the North aile, on an uninfcribed monument (the work of no inferior artift) raifed about three quarters of a yard from the floor, his effigies ftill remains in his epifcopal habit, with a ring on the fourth finger of his right hand, and on the firft and fourth fingers of the left; befides which, there feem to be traces of another ring, which appears to have been flipped off[19]. He embraces, with his left arm, a paftoral ftaff, formed with a head like a mace, and reaching to his feet[20]. The figure is five feet feven inches and a half long, including the mitre, which exceeds the head two inches. Leland fays, "John Penny, firft abbate of Leircefter, then bifhop of Bangor and Cairluel, is here buried in an alabafter tumbe[21];" and adds, "This Penny made the new bricke workes of Leicefter abbey, and much of the bricke walles."

The manor and demefne of Cokeram were demifed in 1515, by Richard Pexal, abbot of Leicefter, to William Calvert junior, for £14. 13*s*. 4*d*.[22]

---

[1] Thefe diftinctions do not occur in Du Cange.   [2] This word is not in Du Cange.   [3] Appendix, p. 69.
[4] Plac. coram rege 2 Hen. V. Rot. 62. de advoc. ecclefie de Blaby.
[5] See in the Appendix, pp. 92, 93, two agreements between the abbots of Leicefter and Croxton, concerning the tithes of Eaton, in 1220 and 1228; and, in p. 94, the recovery of the patronage of that church by the abbot of Leicefter in 1292.
[6] Carte, MS.   [7] Thefe will be given in our Appendix, as abftracted by Mr. Hearne.   [8] Charyte's Rentale, fol. x.
[9] Sir William Dugdale's extracts will be given in the Appendix, p. 75.—Another abridgement of this brief Regifter is preferved at Oxford, under the title of "Collectanea doctiff. Ric. Jamefii, ex Regiftro Leiceftrenfi." MSS. Bodl. James, 24, 113. This alfo we have collated (fee Appendix, p. 68); and in fome inftances it has fupplied the deficiencies of the Cotton MS.
[10] An analyfis of this Catalogue may be feen in the Appendix, p. 79.   [11] Cart. 2 Ric. III.   [12] Harl. MSS. 433. p. 79. b.
[13] Charyte's Rentale, fol. cxlix.   [14] The licence for confecration was dated penult. Aug. 1505. Reg. Warham.
[15] Append. p. 66.   [16] Reg. Smith.   [17] "Spiritualia non feifita ante 20 Jan. 1508, & liberata 20 Jan. 1509." Reg. Warham, f. 12.
[18] Mr. Bickerftaffe remembered there being a mitre in the window next the veftry; but it was gone in 1790.
[19] Might not thefe fuppofed four rings, worn by prior, abbot, and bifhop Penny, have a reference to the four *quafi* fpiritual wives which he wedded? Might they not allude to his having been abbot of St. Mary de Pratis, prior of Bradley, and bifhop, firft of Bangor and afterwards of Carlifle?   [20] This monument fhall be engraved with the view of St. Margaret's church.
[21] Burton mentions a marble monument of a bifhop John Middleton, with arms, Quarterly, fretty . . . . and a canton Gules; which has been fuppofed to be this of bifhop Penny. But, as Wyrley's notes preferve an epitaph on "John Middleton, gent." mayor of Leicefter in 1578, who died in 1588; we may conclude, that Burton confounded the two tombs, and that Middleton's has been demolifhed; the one now remaining being undoubtedly bifhop Penny's.   [22] Appendix, p. 66.

In 1530, this abbey was rendered famous by being the laft refidence of cardinal Wolfey; "the whole ftory of whofe life and death and acts by him done," Mr. Burton obferves, " is exceedingly well-penned by John Stow in his Annals;" and from this account, as Wolfey's conduct after the king's favour was withdrawn has frequently been mifreprefented, it may not be here impertinent to cite fome particulars.

" Cardinal Wolfey, having licence of the king to repair unto Richmond, was there lodged within the lodge of the great park, which was a very pretty houfe. There my lord lay until Lent, with a pretty number of his fervants; for the reft went to board-wages. Cromwell went to London; and my lord removed out of the lodge into the Charter-houfe at Richmond, where he lay in a lodging which doctor Collet made for himfelf, until he removed Northward, which was in the Paffion-week; and every day reforted to the Charter-houfe there; and in the afternoons would fit in contemplation with one of the moft antient fathers of that houfe in their cells, who converted him, and caufed him to defpife the vain glory of the world, and gave him fhirts of hair to wear, the which he wore divers times after. When Mr. Cromwell came to the court, he fhewed my lord of Norfolk that my lord would gladly go Northward, but for lack of money, wherein he defires his help to the king. Then was the king moved therein, as well by mafter Cromwell as by the council: which matter the king referred to determine, and affigns to the council, who were in divers opinions, fo that, after long debating, it was concluded that he fhould have, by way of preft, a thoufand marks of his penfion out of Winchefter. When this determination was concluded, they declared the fame to the king, who ftraightway commanded the fame thoufand marks to be delivered out of hand to mafter Cromwell; and fo it was. The king commanded mafter Cromwell to refort to him again, when he had received the fame fum of money; at whofe return to the king, the king faid, " Shew my lord, although our council have affigned no fum of money for to bear his charges; yet ye fhall fhew him in my behalf, that I have fent a thoufand pounds of my benevolence; and tell him that he fhall not lack; and bid him be of good cheer." Mafter Cromwell, humbly in my lord's behalf, thanked the king, and therefore departed, and came to Richmond to my lord, to whom he delivered the money, and whereof it was levied, that the council fent him, and of the money which the king fent him, adding thereto the king's comfortable fayings, wherein my lord did not a little rejoice. Then my lord prepared all things for his journey, and fent to London for livery-cloaths for his fervants that fhould ride with him; fo that, all things being furnifhed towards his journey, in the beginning of Paffion-week before Eafter he fet forward, and rode from Richmond to a place of the abbot of Weftminfter, called Hendon: the next day he removed to a place where the lady Parry lay, called the Rie: the next day to Royfton, where he lodged in the priory: the next day to Huntington, and there lodged in the abbey: and the next day he removed to Peterborough, and there lodged in the abbey, making there his abode all the next week, where he kept his folemn feaft of Eafter, with all his train, in number 160 perfons, having with him 12 carts to carry his ftuff of his own, which he fent for from his college of Oxford, that were there provided, befide threefcore other carts of his daily carriage of neceffaries for his buildings: upon Palm-Sunday he went in proceffion with the monks: and upon Maundy-Thurfday he made his maundy there in our Lady chapel, having 59 poor men, whofe feet he wafhed and kiffed after he had wiped them; he gave every of the faid poor men twelve-pence in money, three ells of good canvas to make them fhirts, a pair of new fhoes, a caft of red-herrings and three white herrings, and one of them had two fhillings. Upon Eafter-day he rofe to the refurrection, &c. On Thurfday next he removed to mafter Fitz Williams, knight (fome time a merchant-tailor of London, and then of the king's council, who dwelt within three or four miles of Peterborough), where he was joyfully received, and had honourable entertainment: on Monday next he removed unto Stamford, and the next day to Grantham, and was lodged in the houfe of mafter Hall. The next night he lodged in the caftle of Newark, where he remained the next day; and from thence rode to Southwell, and there continued the moft part of that fummer, not without great refort of the moft worfhipful of the country; and divers noblemen, having occafion to repair into the fame county there, thought it good to vifit my lord as they travelled, of whom they were moft gladly entertained, and had right good cheer; whofe noble and gentle behaviour caufed him to have much love in the country of all kind of people. He kept there a noble houfe, where was both plenty of meat and drink for all comers, and alfo much alms given at his gate unto the poor of the town and country. He ufed much charity and clemency among his tenants and other; he made many agreements between gentlemen and gentlemen, and between fome gentlemen and their wives, and other mean perfons, the which had been long before afunder and in great trouble; making for every of them (as occafion ferved) great affemblies and feafts, not fparing his purfe where he might make amity.

It chanced upon Corpus Chrifti even, in the night, when my lord and all his houfehold were at reft in their beds, there knocked at the gate two gentlemen, the one named mafter Brierton, one of the gentlemen of the king's privy chamber, and mafter Writherley, who were come from the king in poft to fpeak with my lord. Thefe were let in. My lord was raifed, and came to them into the dining-chamber; they, feeing him in his night-apparel, did to him due reverence, whom he took by the hands, demanding how the king his fovereign lord did. " Sir," faid they, " right well and merry: we muft defire to talk with you apart." " With a good will," quoth he. After long talk, they took forth of a little mail a little coffer covered with green velvet, and bound with bars of filver and gilt, with a lock and a gilt key, with the which they opened the cheft, out of the which they took an inftrument or writing, containing more than a fkin of great parchment, having many feals hanging to the fame, whereunto they put more wax for my lord's feal; the which my lord fealed, and fubfcribed his name with his own hand, and delivered the fame again unto them, defiring them to take a bed, for it was fomewhat paft midnight; but they faid they would ftraightway ride to the earl of Shrewfbury, to be with him ere he were ftirring; fo my lord caufed them to eat fuch cold meat as was ready, and to drink a bowl or two of wine: that done, he gave each of them four old fovereigns of fine gold, and fo they departed. In this fort and manner my lord lay at Southwell until about the latter end of grafs-time; then he removed to Newik, an abbey to Rufford and Blith abbey, and fo to Scroby, where he continued till after Michaelmas, exercifing many deeds of charity; and commonly every Sunday he would travel unto fome poor parifh-church, and there would fay his divine fervice, and caufe one of his chaplains to preach unto the people: that done, he would dine in fome honeft houfe of the town, where fhould be diftributed to the poor a great alms in meat and drink, as well as of money. About the feaft of St. Michael, he removed to Cawood Caftle, within feven miles of York, where he lay long after with much honour and love of the country, doing deeds of charity, and held there an honourable houfehold for all comers; and alfo built and repaired the caftle, having artificers and labourers above the number of 300 perfons daily in wages, &c. At length, being thereunto perfuaded by the doctors of the church of York, he determined to be ftalled there at York minfter the next Monday after Alhallows-day; againft which time due preparation was made for the fame, but not in fo fumptuous wife as were his predeceffors. My lord fent his gentleman-ufher to York, to forefee things there that fhould be ordered and provided for the folemnity, which fhould have been as mean as could be. Upon Alhallows-day, one of the head-officers of the church of York, which fhould have the moft doings in all this ftallation, was with my lord

4

at dinner at his houfe at Cawood; and, fitting at dinner, they fell in communication of this matter, and of the order thereof, faying that my lord fhould go on foot from a chapel of St. James, without the gates of the city, unto the minfter, upon cloth, the which fhould be diftributed among the poor after his paffage. My lord, hearing this, made anfwer in this wife: " Although our predeceffors did go upon cloth fo, we intend to go on foot from thence without any fuch glory; for, I take God to witnefs, I do not intend to go thither for any triumph or glory, but only to perform the rules of the church, to which I am bound. And therefore I defire you all, and will command other my fervants, to go as humble thither without any fumptuous or gorgeous apparel, otherwife than in decent manner; for I do purpofe to come to York upon Sunday at night next, and to lodge in the dean's houfe: and upon Monday to be ftalled, and there to make but a dinner for you of the Clofe, and for other worfhipful gentlemen that fhall chance to come thither to the fame, and to fup with the refidencies; and the next day to dine with the mayor, and then to prepare home hither again."

The day being once known unto all the country, which could not be hid, the worfhipful gentlemen and others, as abbots and priors, fent in fuch provifion of victuals that it is almoft incredible, as of fat beafts and muttons, wild fowl, and venifon both red and fallow, and other dainty things, fuch as would have plentifully furnifhed the feaft; all which things were unknown to my lord; for as much as he being prevented and difappointed of his purpofe, by reafon that he was arrefted of high treafon, as ye fhall hear hereafter, fo that moft part of this fummer provifion was fent unto York that fame day of his arreft, and the next day following; for his arreft was kept as clofe and fecret from the country, becaufe they doubted the common people, which had him in great eftimation and love for his great charity and liberality which he ufed daily amongft them. It is appointed by the king and council, that fir Walter Walfh, knight, one of the king's privy chamber, fhould be fent down with a commiffion into the North unto the earl of Northumberland, who was fome time brought up in houfe with the cardinal; and they twain being jointly in commiffion to arreft the cardinal of high treafon, mafter Walfh took his horfe at the court-gate about noon upon Alhallows-day, toward the earl of Northumberland.

Now the appointed time drew near of his ftallation; and fitting at dinner upon the Friday next before the Monday, on the which day he intended to be ftalled at York, the earl of Northumberland and mafter Walfh, with a great company of gentlemen of the earl's houfe and of the country, whom he had gathered together in the king's name, came into the hall at Cawood, the officers being at dinner, and the cardinal not fully dined, being then in his fruits. The firft thing that the earl did after he had fet order in the hall, he commanded the porter at the gates to deliver him the keys thereof. Of all thefe doings knew the cardinal nothing; for they ftopped the ftairs, fo that none went up to the cardinal's chamber; and they that came down, could no more go up again. At the laft one efcaped, who fhewed the cardinal that the earl was in the hall; whereat the cardinal marvelled, and would not believe him, but commanded a gentleman to bring him the truth; who, going down the ftairs, faw the earl of Northumberland, and returned and faid it was very he: " Then," quoth the cardinal, " I am forry that we have dined; for I fear our officers be not provided of any ftore of good fifh, to make him fome honourable cheer: let the table ftand," quoth he. With that he rofe up, and going down the ftairs, he encountered the earl coming up with all his train; and as foon as the cardinal efpied the earl, he put off his cap, and faid, " My lord, ye be moft heartily welcome;" and fo embraced each other; then the cardinal took the earl by the hand, and had him up into his chamber, whom followed all the number of the earl's fervants; from thence he led him into his bed-chamber, and they being there all alone, the earl faid unto the cardinal with a foft voice, laying his hand upon his arm,

6

" My lord, I arreft you of high treafon." With which words the cardinal being marvelloufly aftonifhed, ftanding both ftill a good fpace, at the laft quoth the cardinal, " What authority have you to arreft me?" " Forfooth, my lord," quoth the earl, " I have a commiffion fo to do." " Where is your commiffion," quoth he, " that I may fee it?" " Nay, fir, that you may not," faid the earl. " Well then," quoth the cardinal, " I will not obey your arreft." But, as they were debating this matter between them in the chamber, fo bufy was mafter Walfh in arrefting doctor Auguftine at the door in the palace, faying unto him, " Go in, traitor, or I fhall make thee." At the laft mafter Walfh, being entered the cardinal's chamber, began to pluck off his hood, and after kneeling down to the cardinal, unto whom the cardinal faid, " Come hither, gentleman, and let me fpeak with you, fir; here my lord of Northumberland hath arrefted me; but by whofe authority he fheweth not; if ye be joined with him, I pray you fhew me." " Indeed, my lord," quoth mafter Walfh, " he fheweth you the truth." " Well then," quoth the cardinal, " I pray you let me fee it, fir." " I befeech you," quoth mafter Walfh, " hold us excufed; there is annexed to our commiffion certain inftructions which you may not fee." " Well," quoth the cardinal, " I trow ye are one of the king's privy chamber; your name is Walfh; I am content to yield to you, but not to my lord of Northumberland, without I fee his commiffion: the worft in the king's privy chamber is fufficient to arreft the greateft peer of the realm by the king's commandment, without any commiffion; therefore put your commiffion and authority in execution; fpare not; I will obey the king's will. I take God to judge, I never offended the king in word nor deed." Then the earl called into the chamber divers gentlemen of his own fervants, and after they had taken the cardinal's keys from him, they put him in cuftody of the earl's gentlemen; and then they went about the houfe to fet all things in an order; then fent they doctor Auguftine away to London with as much fpeed as they could, who was bound unto the horfe like a traitor; but it was Sunday toward night ere the cardinal was conveyed from Cawood, and lodged that night in the abbey of Pomfret. The next day he removed toward Doncafter, and was there lodged at the Black Friers; the next day he was removed to Sheffield-park, where the earl of Shrewfbury, with his lady, and a train of gentlemen and gentlewomen, received him with much honour; and the cardinal, being thus with the earl of Shrewfbury, continued there eighteen days after; upon whom the earl appointed divers gentlemen to attend continually, to fee that he fhould lack nothing, being ferved in his own chamber as honourably as he had been in his own houfe; and once every day the earl would repair unto him and commune with him. After the cardinal had thus remained with the earl of Shrewfbury about a fortnight, it came to pafs at a certain time as he fat at his dinner in his own chamber, having at his board's end a mefs of gentlemen and chaplains to keep him company; toward the end of his dinner, when he was come to eating his fruits, his colour was perceived often to change, whereby he was judged not to be in good health; whereupon one of his gentlemen faid, " Sir, mefeems you are not well at eafe." To whom he anfwered with a loud voice, " Forfooth, no more I am; for I am," quoth he, " taken fuddenly with a thing about my ftomach, that lieth there along, as cold as a whetftone, which is no more but wind: I pray you go to the apothecary, and enquire of him, if he have any thing that will break wind upward." Then went he to the earl, and fhewed him what eftate the cardinal was in, and what he defired. With that the earl caufed the apothecary to be called before him, and demanded of him if he had any thing that would break wind upwards in a man's body? and he anfwered, he had fuch gear. " Then," quoth the earl, " fetch me fome." Then the apothecary fetched a white confection in a fair paper, and fhewed it to the earl, who commanded one to give the affay thereof before him, and then the fame to be brought to the cardinal, who

received

received it up all at once into his mouth; but immediately after surely he voided much wind upwards. "Lo," quoth he, " ye may fee that it was but wind, and now I am well eafed, I thank God;" and fo he rofe from the table, and went to his prayers; and that done, there came on him fuch a loofenefs, that it caufed him to go to his ftool. And not long after the earl of Shrewfbury came into the gallery to him, with whom the cardinal met; and then fitting down upon a bench, the earl afked how he did; and he moft lamentably anfwered him, and thanked him for his gentle entertainment: " Sir," quoth the earl, " if ye remember, ye have often wifhed to come before the king to make your anfwer, and I have written to the king in that behalf, making him privy of your lamentation that ye inwardly have received for his difpleafure; who accepteth all your doings therein, as friends be accuftomed to do in fuch cafes; wherefore I would advife you to pluck up your heart, and be not aghaft at your enemies. I doubt not but this your journey to his highnefs fhall be much to your advancement. The king hath fent for you that worfhipful knight mafter Kingfton, and with him 24 of your old fervants, now of the guard, to the intent ye may fafely come to his majefty." " Sir," quoth the cardinal, " I trow mafter Kingfton is conftable of the Tower." " Yea, what of that?" quoth the earl. " I affure you, he is elected by the king for one of your friends." " Well," quoth the cardinal, " as God will, fo be it; I am fubject to fortune, being a true man, ready to accept fuch chances as fhall follow, and there an end. I pray you, where is mafter Kingfton?" Quoth the earl, " I will fend for him." " I pray you fo do," quoth the cardinal: at whofe meffage he came; and as foon as the cardinal efpied him, he made hafte to encounter him, and at his coming he kneeled to him, and faluted him in the king's behalf; whom the cardinal bareheaded offered to take up, and faid, " I pray you ftand by; kneel not to me; I am but a wretch replete with mifery, not efteeming myfelf but as a vile abject, utterly caft away, without defert, as God knoweth[1]." Then mafter Kingfton ftood up, and faid, with humble reverence, " Sir, the king hath him commended unto you." " I thank his highnefs," quoth the cardinal: " I truft he be in health." " Yea," quoth mafter Kingfton, " and he commanded me to fay to you, that you fhould affure yourfelf that he beareth you as much good will as ever he did, and willeth you to be of good cheer; and where report hath been made that ye fhould commit againft him certain heinous crimes, which he thinketh to be untrue, yet he can do no lefs than to fend for you to your trial, and take your journey to him at your own pleafure, commanding me to be attendant upon you. There-

fore, fir, I pray you, when it fhall be your own pleafure to take your journey, I fhall be ready to give attendance." " Mafter Kingfton," quoth my lord, " I thank you for your good news; and, fir, if I were as able as I have been but of late, I would not fail to ride with you in poft; but I am difeafed with a flux (at which time it was apparent that he had poifoned himfelf[2]), that maketh me very weak. But, mafter Kingfton, all the comfortable words that you have fpoken unto me be fpoken but for a purpofe, to bring me into a fool's paradife. I know what is provided for me. Notwithftanding, I thank you for your good will and pains taken about me. And I fhall with all fpeed make me ready to ride with you to-morrow."

When night came, the cardinal waxed very fick. Therefore, in confideration of his infirmity (by the advice of Dr. Nicholas, a doctor of phyfic) they caufed him to tarry all that day; and the next day he took his journey with mafter Kingfton and them of the guard, till he came to a houfe of the earl of Shrewfbury's, called Hardwick-hall, where he lay all night very evil at eafe. The next day he rode to Nottingham, and there lodged that night more fick; and the next day he rode to Leicefter abbey, and by the way waxed fo fick, that he had almoft fallen from his mule, fo that it was night before he came to the abbey of Leicefter; where, at his coming in at the gates, the abbot with all his convent met him with divers torches light, whom they right honourably received and welcomed[3]; to whom the cardinal faid, " Father abbot, I am come hither to lay my bones among you;" riding ftill on his mule, till he came to the ftairs of his chamber, where he alighted. Mafter Kingfton, holding him by the arm, led him up ftairs; who told me afterwards that he never felt fo heavy a burthen in all his life; and, as foon as he was in his chamber, he went ftraight to bed. This was upon Saturday, and fo he continued. On Monday in the morning, as I ftood by his bedfide, about eight of the clock in the morning, the windows being clofe fhut, and having wax lights burning upon the cupboard, I thought I perceived him drawing towards death. He, perceiving my fhadow upon the bedfide, afked, " Who was there?" " Sir," quoth I, " it is I." " How do you," quoth he, " well?" " Aye, fir," quoth I, " if I might fee your grace well." " What is it a clock?" quoth he. I anfwered, " It was about eight of the clock." Quoth he, " That cannot be;" rehearfing " eight of the clock" divers times. " Nay, nay," quoth he, " that cannot be; for at eight of the clock fhall you lofe your mafter, for my time draweth near that I muft depart this world." With that, one Dr. Palmes[4], a worfhipful gentleman, being his chaplain and ghoftly father, ftanding by, bade me afk him if he would be fhriven, to make

[1] After this paffage our extracts are enlarged from the MS. of Mr. Cavendifh, who was prefent, and is more circumftantial.

[2] This parenthefis is an interpolation, not to be found in the MS. copies of Mr. Cavendifh. " Philipot, in his Catalogue of the chancellors, fays, the cardinal died, ' not without fufpicion of poifon, which he had prepared for himfelf, and given to his apothecary to deliver when he called for it.' And Baker, in his Chronicle, fays, ' But whether it were he took it in too great a quantity, or that there was fome foul play ufed, he fell foon after into fuch a loofenefs, &c.' The former of thefe authors infinuates, that the cardinal poifoned himfelf; and the latter, that he, perhaps, might be poifoned by others; and yet, I dare fay, they both of them made ufe of Mr. Cavendifh; infomuch that the whole weight of the evidence refts folely upon his teftimony. But then, on the other hand, it muft be confeffed that Mr. Cavendifh's authority is very great, and abundantly fufficient in this caufe. His narrative of the life and death of his mafter muft be read, it is true, with diftinction, as requiring fome care and difcernment; for, whilft he relates fuch incidents as he was not actually privy to, he is liable to the fame errors that other biographers are, and confequently has been contradicted upon fome points; but, in fuch matters where he was perfonally prefent, there is no room to fufpect his fidelity, for in them he is a moft competent witnefs, very fair, and very impartial." Thefe are the remarks of the late learned and Rev. Dr. Pegge, who has fome curious papers on this fubject in Gent. Mag. vol. XXV. pp. 25. 299; vol. LIII. p. 751.—In vol. LIII. p. 1021, is alfo a fatisfactory collation, by Mr. Ayfcough, of two of the copies of Cavendifh in the Britifh Mufeum (Harl. MSS. 428. and Birch MSS. 4233.) by which it appears that the fentence on the poifon (which was originally printed in brackets) is not in either of thofe MSS; but that there was fufficient caufe for fufpicion; as the cardinal twice mentions his apprehenfion of the defign of his enemies to difpatch him, which might be done to take off the fufpicion of doing it himfelf; the declaring to Mr. Cavendifh the knowledge of his latter days; and again, when he was taken ill before the arrival of Mr. Kingfton, the fymptoms were ftrongly thofe of poifon.

[3] In Shakespeare's hiftorical play of King Henry VIII, the laft moments of Wolfey are thus beautifully defcribed:

" At laft, with eafy roads, he came to Leicefter,
Lodg'd in the abbey; where the reverend abbot,
With all his convent, honourably receiv'd him;
To whom he gave thefe words,—O father abbot,
An old man, broken with the ftorms of ftate,
Is come to lay his weary bones among ye;
Give him a little earth for charity!—
So went to bed: where eagerly his ficknefs

Purfued him ftill; and, three nights after this,
About the hour of eight (which he himfelf
Foretold fhould be his laft), full of repentance,
Continual meditations, tears, and forrows,
He gave his honours to the world again,
His bleffed part to heaven, and flept in peace.——
——So may he reft; his faults lie gently on him!"
[A portrait of the Cardinal is given in plate XVII.]

[4] George Palmes, LL. D. rector of Collingham, co. Nottingham; prebendary of Gevendale 1539—1543; archdeacon of York, Weft Riding, 1543; prebendary of Langtoft, 1546—1558; and of Wetwang, 1558; all in the church of York. He was deprived in 1559. See Wood, Fafti Oxon. vol. I. p. 65.

him

him ready for God, whatever chanced to fall out; which I did: but he was very angry with me, and afked, "What I had to do to afk him fuch a queftion?" till at laft mafter Doctor took my part, and talked with him in Latin, and pacified him.

At afternoon mafter Kingfton fent for me, and faid, "So it is, the king hath fent unto me letters by mafter Vincent, one of your old companions, who hath been in trouble in the Tower for money that my lord fhould have at his laft departure; a great part of which money cannot be found; wherefore the king, at this Vincent's requeft, for the declaration of the truth, hath fent him hither with his grace's letters, that I fhould examine my lord, and have your counfel therein, that he may take it well and in good part. And this is the caufe of my fending for you; therefore I defire your counfel therein for the true acquittal of this poor gentleman, mafter Vincent." "Sir," quoth I, "according to my duty, you fhall; and, by my advice, you fhall refort unto him in your own perfon to vifit him; and, in communication, break the matter unto him; and, if he will not tell the truth therein, then may you certify the king thereof; but, in any cafe, name not, nor fpeak of, my fellow Vincent: alfo I would not have you to track the time with him, for he is very fick, and I fear that he will not live paft a day or two. And accordingly mafter Kingfton went to my lord, and demanded the money; faying, "that my lord of Northumberland found in a book at Cauwood-houfe that you had but lately borrowed £1500[1]; and it will not be found, no not fo much as one penny thereof; who hath made the king privy to the fame: wherefore the king hath written to me to know what is become thereof; for it were pity that it fhould be holden from you both. Therefore I require you, in the king's name, to tell me the truth, that I may make a juft report thereof unto his majefty of your anfwer?" With that quoth my lord, "Oh good Lord! how much doth it grieve me that the king fhould think any fuch thing in me, that I fhould deceive him of one penny, feeing I have nothing, nor never had (God be my judge), that I ever efteemed fo much mine own as his majefty's, having but the bare ufe of it during my life, and after my death to leave it wholly to him; wherein his majefty hath prevented me. But for this money that you demand of me, I affure you it is none of my own; for I borrowed it of divers of my friends to bury me, and to beftow amongft my fervants, who have taken great pains about me; notwithftanding, if it be your pleafure to know, I muft be content; yet I befeech his majefty to fee it fatisfied, for the difcharge of my confcience to them that I owed it to." "Who be they?" quoth mafter Kingfton. "That fhall I tell you," quoth my lord; "I borrowed £200. thereof of fir John Allen of London; and other £200. of fir Richard Grefham of London; and £200. of the Mafter of the Savoy; and alfo £200. of Dr. Heyden, dean of my college at Oxford; £200. of the treafurer of the church; and £200. of parfon Ellis my chaplain; and another £200. of a prieft that was then his fteward, whofe name I have forgotten. I hope the king will reftore it again, forafmuch as it is none of mine." "Sir," quoth mafter Kingfton, "there is no doubt in the king, whom you need not diftruft: but, fir, I pray you, where is the money?" Quoth he, "I will not conceal it, I warrant you; but I will declare it unto you before I die, by the grace of God. Have a little patience with me, I pray you; for, the money is fafe enough in an honeft man's hands, who will not keep one penny thereof from the king." So mafter Kingfton departed for that time, my lord being very weak; and about four

of the clock in the next morning, as I conceived, I afked him how he did? "Well," quoth he, "if I had any meat—I pray you give me fome." "Sir," quoth I, "there is none ready." Then he faid, "you are much to blame; for you fhould have always meat for me in readinefs, whenfoever that my ftomach ferves me; I pray you get fome ready for me; for I mean to make myfelf ftrong to-day, to the intent I may go to confeffion, and make me ready for God." Quoth I, "I will call up the cooks to prepare fome meat; and alfo I will call mafter Palmes, that he may difcourfe with you till your meat be ready." "With a good will," quoth my lord. And fo I called mafter Palmes, who rofe and came to my lord. Then I went and acquainted mafter Kingfton that my lord was very fick, and not like to live. "In good faith," quoth mafter Kingfton, "you are much to blame to make him believe he is ficker than he is." "Well, fir," quoth I, "you cannot fay but I gave you warning, as I am bound to do." Upon which words he arofe and came unto him; but, before he came my lord cardinal had eaten a fpoonful or two of callis made of chicken; and after that he was in his confeffion the fpace of an hour: and then mafter Kingfton came to him, and bade him good morrow, and afked him how he did? "Sir," quoth he, "I watch but God's pleafure to render up my poor foul to him. I pray you have me heartily commended unto his royal majefty, and befeech him on my behalf to call to his princely remembrance all matters that have been between us from the beginning and the progrefs; and efpecially between good queen Katharine and him; and then fhall his grace's confcience know whether I have offended him or not. He is a prince of a moft royal carriage, and hath a princely heart; and, rather than he will mifs or want any part of his will, he will endanger the one half of his kingdom. I do affure you, I have often kneeled before him, fometimes three hours together, to perfuade him from his will and appetite; but could not prevail. And, mafter Kingfton, had I but ferved God as diligently as I have ferved the king, he would not have given me over in my grey hairs: but this is the juft reward that I muft receive for my diligent pains and ftudy, not regarding my fervice to God, but only to my prince. Therefore, let me advife you, if you be one of the privy council, as by your wifdom you are fit, take heed what you put in the king's head; for you can never put it out again. Mafter Kingfton, farewell. I wifh all things may have good fuccefs; my time draws on; I may not tarry with you; I pray you remember my words." Now began the time to draw near; for he drew his fpeech at length, and his tongue began to fail him, his eyes perfectly fet in his head, his fight failed him. Then we began to put him in mind of Chrift's paffion, and caufed the yeomen of the guard to ftand by privately to fee him die, and bear witnefs of his words and his departure, who heard all his communications. And incontinently the clock ftruck eight. And then gave he up the ghoft, and thus he departed this prefent life[2]. And calling to remembrance how he faid the day before, that at eight of the clock we fhould lofe our mafter, as it is before rehearfed, one of us looking upon another, fuppofing that either he knew or prophefied of his departure. Yet, before his departure, we fent for the abbot of the houfe to annoyle him; who made all the fpeed he could, and came to his departure, and fo faid certain prayers before the breath was fully out of his body. After that he was thus departed, mafter Kingfton fent a poft to the king, advertizing him of the departure of the cardinal by one of the guard

---

[1] In the printed copies of Mr. Cavendifh's "Memoirs" it is £10,000.

[2] "The great ftory of this abbey has a virtuous tendency. Within its walls was once exhibited a fcene more humiliating to human ambition, and more inftructive to human grandeur, than almoft any which Hiftory hath produced. Here the fallen pride of Wolfey retreated from the infults of the world. All his vifions of ambition were now gone; his pomp and pageantry; and crouded levees! On this fpot he told the liftening monks, the fole attendants of his dying-hour, as he ftood around his pallet, That he was come to lay his bones among them; and gave a pathetic teftimony to the truth and joys of religion, which preaches beyond a thoufand lectures.—The death of Wolfey would make a fine moral picture, if the hand of any mafter could give the pallid features of the dying ftatefman, that chagrin, that remorfe, thofe pangs of anguifh, which in thofe laft bitter moments of his life poffeffed him. The point might be taken when the monks are adminiftering the comforts of religion, which the defpairing prelate cannot feel. The fubject requires a gloomy apartment, which a ray through a Gothic window might juft enlighten, throwing its force chiefly on the principal figure, and dying away on the reft. The appendages of the piece need only be few and fimple; little more than the crozier and red hat, to mark the cardinal, and tell the ftory." Gilpin, Northern Tour.

3

THOMAS WOLSEY, CARDINAL, ARCHBISHOP OF YORK,
AND LORD CHANCELLOR OF ENGLAND,
DIED NOV. 29. 1529.

Plate XVII. p.272.

AN AUGUSTINE MONK OF St MARY DE PRATIS.

J. Swaine. sc.

Fig.1.   p.261.

Fig.3. p.274.

Fig.2. p.262.

Fig.5. p.308.

Fig.8. p.296.

Regiſtrum libroꝝ[.]

Fig.12.
p.300.

Fig.7. p.294.

Fig.10. p.299.

Fig.4. p.274.

Fig.11. p.299.

Fig.9.   p.297.   Fig.13.   p.301.

Longmate. sc.

that faw and heard him die. Then was mafter Kingfton and the abbot in confultation about the funeral, which was folemnized the day after; for mafter Kingfton would not ftay the return of the poft. They thought good that the mayor of Leicefter and his brethren fhould be fent for, to fee him perfonally dead, to avoid falfe rumours that might fpread to fay that he was ftill alive. Then was the mayor and his brethren fent for; and in the mean time the body was taken out of the bed where he lay dead, who had upon him next his body a fhirt of hair, befides his other fhirt, which was of very fine holland, which was not known to any of his fervants being continually about him in his chamber, faving to his ghoftly father; which fhirts were laid in a coffin made for him of boards, having upon his dead corpfe all fuch ornaments as he was invefted in when he was made bifhop and archbifhop, as mitre, crofs, ring, and pall, with all other things due to his order and dignity. And, lying thus all day in his coffin open and bare-faced, every man that would might fee him there dead, without fayning, even as the mayor, his brethren, and others did. Lying thus watched from four or five at night, he was carried down into the church with great folemnity by the abbot, and conducted with much torch-light and fervice-fong due for fuch funerals. And, being in the church, the corpfe was fet in our Lady's chapel, with divers tapers of wax, and divers poor men following about the fame, holding torches in their hands, who watched about the corpfe all night, while the chanons fung *Dirige* and other divine oryfons. And, about four of the clock in the morning, mafter Kingfton and we the cardinal's fervants came into the church, and there tarried the execution of divers ceremonies in fuch cafes, as is ufual about the corpfe of a bifhop. Then went they to mafs; at which mafs the abbot and divers others did offer. And, that done, they went to bury the corpfe in the middle of the faid chapel, where was made for him a ftate [1]. And by that time he was buried, and all ceremonies ended, it was fix of the clock in the morning. Then went we and prepared us to horfe-back, being St. Andrew's day the Apoftle, and fo took our journey to the court, riding that fame day, being Wednefday, to Northampton; and the next day to Dunftable; and the next day to London, where we tarried until St. Nicholas' even; and then we rode to Hampton Court, where the king and council lay; giving all our attendance upon them, for our difcharge. And the next day, being St. Nicholas' day, I was fent for, being in mafter Kingfton's chamber then in the court, to come to the king; whom I found fhooting in the rounds in the park, on the back-fide of the garden; and perceiving him occupied in fhooting, thought it not good to trouble him, but, leaning to a tree, attended there until he had made an end of his difport; which ended, the king gave his bow to the yeoman of the bows, and went his way inward. Then mafter Norris commanded me to go to the king, who ftood behind the door, in his night-gown of ruffet velvet furred with fables, before whom I kneeled the fpace of an hour; during which time his majefty examined me of divers particulars concerning my lord cardinal, wifhing rather than twenty thoufand pounds that he had lived. He afked me concerning the fifteen hundred pounds

which mafter Kingfton moved to my lord. Quoth I, " I think I can perfectly tell your grace where it is, and who hath it." " Can you?" quoth the king. " I pray you tell me, and you fhall not be unrewarded." " Sir," quoth I, " after the departure of mafter Vincent from my lord at Scroby, who had the cuftody thereof, leaving it with my lord in divers bags, he delivered it to a certain prieft, fafely to be kept to his ufe." " Is this true?" quoth the king. " Yea," quoth I, without doubt; the prieft will not deny it before me, for I was at the delivery thereof, who hath gotten divers other rich ornaments, which are not regiftered in the book of my lord's inventory [2] or other writings, whereby any man is able to charge him therewith but myfelf." " Then," faid the king, " let me alone for keeping this fecret between me and you. Howbeit, three may keep council if two be away; and if I knew my cap were privy to my council, I would caft it into the fire and burn it : and for your honefty and truth, you fhall be our fervant in our chamber, as you were with your mafter. Therefore go you your ways to fir John Gage our vice-chamberlain, to whom we have fpoken already, to admit you our fervant in our chamber; and then go to the lord of Norfolk, and he fhall pay you your whole year's wages, which is ten pounds. Is not it fo?" quoth the king. " Yes forfooth," quoth I; " and I am behind for three quarters of a year of the fame wages." " That is true," quoth the king; " therefore you fhall have your whole year's wages, with our reward, delivered you by the duke of Norfolk." So I received ten pounds of the duke for my wages, and twenty pounds for my reward; and his majefty gave me a cart and fix horfes, the beft that I could choofe out of my lord's horfes, to carry my goods, and five marks for my charge homewards [3]."

Mr. Carte fays, " Upon my enquiries about the place of Wolfey's burial [4], the moft probable account that I have met with is from Mr. John Hafloe, whofe grandfather Arthur Barefoot was gardener to the countefs of Devonfhire, who lived at the Abbey before the war. He tells me, that the church ftood, part of it in what is now a little garden, and the Eaft end of it in the orchard (which was formerly called the New Garden), where his grandfather, with others, digging, found feveral ftone coffins [5], the cavities of which did not lye uppermoft, but were inverted over the bodies; that one of thefe was taken up, of about fix feet and a half long, four wide, and two deep; that it feemed very found at firft, but when it was expofed to the air it foon mouldered away; that he obferved that all of them had a round hole about the middle of them near five inches diameter, but for what ufe he could not tell; that among thefe he difcovered cardinal Wolfey's (Mr. Hafloe forgets by what means he knew it); which the countefs would not fuffer to be ftirred, but ordered it to be covered again, and his grandfather laid a great heap of gravel over it, that he might know the place; which ftill remains there."— Mr. Browne Willis, in a letter to Dr. Chartlett, dated Whaddon-hall, April 19, 1716, adds, " I was greatly pleafed with the above-mentioned anfwer to fome queries I fent to Leicefter fome time ago; from which place I received this anfwer on Tuefday, from the Rev. Mr. Samuel Carte, a noted antiquary there,

---

[1] The funeral was attended by the mayor and corporation with their formalities and in their uniforms.

[2] This refers to a curious MS. preferved in the Harleian Collection, intituled, N° 428, " An Inventorie of Cardinal Wolfey's rich Houfhold Stuff," written by his own officers, and including all the furniture at Hampton Court and York Houfe. This Inventory is brought down to the year of the Cardinal's death; and is well worthy the attention of the Society of Antiquaries.

[3] Here the printed copy ends; but there are feveral more pages of the MS. in which is the following : That, in going from the king, Mr. Cavendifh met Mr. Kingfton coming from the council, who commanded him to go before the council, but to take heed of what he faid; for he fhould be examined of certain words fpoken by my lord his mafter at his departure (the which I knew well enough); and if I tell them the truth (quoth he) what he faid, I fhould undo myfelf; for in any wife they may not hear of it, therefore be circumfpect what anfwer you make to their demands. Why, quoth I, how have you done therein yourfelf? Quoth he, I have utterly denied that I heard any fuch words; and he that opened the matter firft is fled for fear, which was the yeoman of the guard that rode to the king from Leicefter, &c.

[4] The obfcurity of Wolfey's burial-place is thus alluded to by bifhop Corbet, in his " Iter Boreale :"

" And though from his own ftore Wolfey might have
A Palace *, or a College †, for his grave;
Yet here he lies interr'd, as if that all
Of him to be remember'd were his fall.

Nothing but ea.th to earth, nor pompous weight
Upon him, but a pebble or a quoit.
If thou art thus neglected, what fhall we ‡
Hope after death, that are but fhreds of thee?"

[5] Thefe coffins were probably thofe of the founder, and other benefactors to the abbey.

* Whitehall.　　　† Chrift Church.　　　‡ Students of Chrift Church.

among

among other things relating to that borough [1]. I have written ſince to him concerning more particulars in relation to the diſcovery. In ſhort, as I have been ever zealous concerning our founder Cardinal Wolſey, ſo I cannot but be pleaſed in whatever I diſcover about him; and it would be a great ſatisfaction to me, and I ſhould be willing to contribute much, if his body could be tranſlated to Chriſt Church. This our College ought in gratitude to do; and, dear Doctor, if you have an opportunity of ſpeaking with any of them, as doubtleſs you have many, found the thing, and ſee how it will agree with their notions. Methinks, though I am but a mean perſon, I could gladly undergo the charge of removing the Cardinal's body, if it were into the next pariſh-church, rather than it ſhould reſt ſo obſcurely there [2]."—The farther proceedings are thus related by Mr. Carte: "That great lover of antiquity, Browne Willis, eſq. having an extraordinary veneration for cardinal Wolſey, as the original founder of Chriſt church in Oxford, of which he and his father were members, deſired me to try if I could find out the ſepulchre of the Cardinal; which I did, hoping that, when I had provided tools and labourers, ſome others would have contributed with me towards the expence; but, finding that only one perſon would contribute twelve-pence, I deſiſted [3]."

John Bourchier, abbot of Leiceſter, ſubſcribed to the king's ſupremacy, Auguſt 11, 1534; and in that year a commiſſion iſſued from the king, to take an eccleſiaſtical ſurvey of the county of Leiceſter, directed to ſir John Villers, knight, ſir John Nevill, knight, ſir Thomas Pulteney, knight, ſir William Turvile, knight, John Harrington, Roger Radcliff, Roger Wygſton, William Aſhby, Chriſtopher Villers, Thomas Trye, John Beaumont, Thomas Waldram, Peter Ithiell, and Robert Wyngfield. In their return, the revenues of this abbey are thus ſtated [4]:

	£.	s.	d.	£.	s.	d.
In Spirituals,	247	7	8¾	785	7	8¾
In Temporals,	538	0	0			
The outgoings were,						
To the biſhop of Lincoln,	2	0	0			
——- chapter of Lincoln,	5	0	0			
——- Lichfield cathedral,	6	13	4			
——- York cathedral,	2	13	4			
—— archdeacon of Bedford,	0	7	7¾			
————- Bucks,	0	2	9¾			
————- Derby,	0	12	7¾			
————- Northampton,	0	7	5¾			
————- Richmond,	0	7	7¾			
—— prior of Clerkenwell,	0	13	4			
————- St. John of Jeruſalem,	0	4	0			
————- Lenton,	0	3	4			
————- Shene,	12	14	0			
————- Trentham,	5	13	4	83	4	10¾
To augment vicarages [5]:						
———— Billeſdon,	3	0	0			
———— Bitteſwell,	1	0	0			
———— Brackley,	5	4	4			
———— Coſby,	0	8	0			
———— Galby,	1	6	8			
———— Hungarton,	3	0	0			
———— St. Leonard,	5	6	8			
———— St. Mary de Caſtro,	4	0	0			
———— Melton,	5	0	0			
———— Queniborough,	5	6	8			
———— Sharnbrook,	1	0	0			
———— Thornton,	3	0	0			
———— Thurnby,	3	0	0			
———— Youlgrave,	5	0	0			

In 1539, when all the great religious houſes that were above the yearly value of £200. were given to the king, it is obſerved by Mr. Browne Willis [6] (who refers to Collier's Eccleſiaſtical Hiſtory for his authority) that this abbot withſtanding the diſſolution of his monaſtery, the viſitors charged *him* and his canons with adultery, &c. But in Collier [7] the *canons* only are mentioned as being threatened with a proſecution. As Henry intended to promote Bourchier to an epiſcopal ſee at Shrewſbury; and as he was actually nominated by queen Mary, in 1558, to the ſee of Glouceſter [8]; it can hardly be ſuppoſed that his character was open to ſo opprobrious an accuſation. On the contrary, in a letter from Richard Layton, one of the commiſſioners, to the lord Cromwell, the abbot is repreſented as "an honeſt man," but the canons as "obſtinate and factious." And, in a letter ſent by this abbot to Thomas lord Cromwell, he expreſly ſays, "I have ſent by mye ſervant, the barer herof, the hundred pounds whiche I promyſed to you for your greate and manyfold payns takyn in my favour; and that I ſend it with as good will as ever I ſent anye thing in mye lyef; humblye beſeching your infynyt goodnes to contynue continuallye your former favour; the which, God beyng mye record, I prefer above all my lyvyng. Wheras your Mayſterſhip did requyre me for the ferme of Yngwordſby in maiſter Richard's favour, I have as vehementlye moved mye brotherne therfor, as I woold have doon for a ryght hygh matyer; but byecauſe it ever was the demeane lands of the houſe, and that withought the ſame ferme we can bryng upe nether bevs ne muttons for the mayntynans of our hoſpytalytes, I cannot bend them to yt; for, my predeceſſour dyd bring our pour monaſterye to the hindrans that it is yn by lettyng that ferme. Therfor, ſyns your pleaſur is that I ſhall proſpour, bycauſe I am of your Maiſterſhip's advauncement eſpecially, I with knelyng hart beſech your goodnes not to requyre it; partlye bycauſe my brotherne in noo wyeſs will graunt or agree to yt, eſpecially bycauſe the lacke of that ferme is the extream undoyng of our houſſe. Thus, your good maiſterſhip extendyng your old goodnes to me your bedyman, I and all mye brotherne ſhall be bonden to pray for your proſperouſe helthe [9]." This was dated April 19; and in a ſhort time after, the abbot and convent, having no hopes of a fair trial or impartial judges, conſented to ſurrender up the valuables and large revenues of the abbey, to ſecure the penſions for life which were promiſed them on their ſo doing. The original inſtrument, for this purpoſe, dated . . . . die . . . . . . anno regni illuſtriſſimi domini regis triceſimo" (the day of the month having never been filled up) is ſigned by *John Bourchier*, abbot of *Leiceiſtere*; *Richard Duckytt*, [prior ;] *Richard Webbe*, ſubprior; *Richard Clarke*; *Robert Sapcott*; *John Dingſworth*; *Thomas Jurdane*; *John Boſworth*; *Thomas Kendall*; *John Lacie*; *John Revell*; *John Bux*^m^; *Gregory Kyng*, *Hugh Sheppe*; *William Clarke*; *William Bylſbe*; *Jamys Lowe*; *Thomas Weſtys*; *William Parmyter*; *Thomas Gamſwett*. Two double ſeals [10] appended to this ſurrender, with a *fac ſimile* of the names of the abbot and ſome of the monks, are given in plate XVII. fig. 3, 4.

In 1553, there remained in charge here £3. 6s. 8d. fees; £32. 19s. 4d. in annuities; and the following penſions: *John Bourchier*, laſt abbot, £.200; *Richard Duckytt* £.10; *John Buckeſham* £.6; *Richard Webbe* £.6; *John Lacie* £.6; *Hugh Shepey* £5. 6s. 8d.; *John Revell* £5. 6s. 8d.; *Gregory King* £5. 6s. 8d.; *William Parmyter* £5; *James Lowe* £5; and *Thomas Weſtys* £5. [11]

[1] Mr. Carte's letter may be ſeen at length in the Bibliotheca Topographica Britannica, vol. VIII. p. 556.

[2] From Ballard's MSS. in the Bodleian Library, XVIII. 86.

[3] As a labourer was digging in 1787 for potatoes upon the ſpot where the high-altar of the chapel was ſuppoſed to ſtand, he found a human ſkull, with ſeveral other human bones, all perfect. From the ſituation of the place and other circumſtances, it was conjectured at the time that this might be the identical ſkull of cardinal Wolſey. Cambridge Chronicle, June 2, 1787.

[4] See an account of their revenues in ſpirituals and temporals in 1292 in our Appendix, p. 79.

[5] The vicar of Bulkington had 16s. 8d. given him; and nine acres of glebe land. Cotton MSS. Vitellius F. XVII. fol. 29.

[6] Hiſtory of Mitred Abbeys, vol. II. p. 112.

[7] Vol. II. p. 158.

[8] "Ep'us electus Gloceſtr." Geo. Lilius, in vitâ Fiſheri Roff. p. 31; Baker's MS Hiſtory of St. John's College, p. 283. in margine.—On the death of Dr. Brokes, biſhop of Glouceſter, which happened Sept. 7, 1558; John Bourſher, S. T. B. had, on the 25th of October, the cuſtody of the temporalities of that ſee. Godwin de Præſulibus, p. 552; from Rymer, Fœd. vol. XV. p. 489. Queen Mary died in the month following; and the ſee remained vacant till 1562.

[9] See the Introductory Volume, p. cxlii.

[10] Another ſeal of this abbey is engraved in fig. 5.

[11] Willis's Mitred Abbeys, vol. II. p. 112.

A lift of the abbots of Leicefter, extracted by the Rev. Henry Hall from a MS. in the Lambeth library[1]; compared with another MS. formerly in the Cotton library, and now in the Britifh Mufeum[2].

1. Ricardus, electus anno 1144, 8 Steph. præfuit an' 24[3].

2. Willielmus de Kalewyken, electus 1167, 14 Hen. I. præfuit an' 10.

3. Willielmus de Broke, electus 1177, 23 Hen. II. præfuit an' 9. [He refigned in 1186, on becoming abbot of the Ciftercians.]

4. Paulus[4], electus 1186, 8 Ric. I. præfuit an' 19.

5. Willielmus Pepyn, electus 1205, 15 Joh. præfuit an' 19.[5]

6. Ofbertus[6], electus 1224, 8 Hen. III. præfuit an' 5.

7. Matthias de Bray[7], electus 1229, 13 Hen. III. præfuit an' 6. On his refignation,

8. Alanus de Ceftreham[8], electus 1235, 19 Hen. III. 5 kal. Nov. præfuit an' 9. This abbot appears to have been fufpended in 1236[9], and re-appointed.

9. Robertus Furmenteyn[10], electus 1244, 28 Hen. III. non. Nov. præfuit an' 3.

10. Henricus de Roiley, or Rotheleye[11], electus 1247, 10 cal. Aug. 31 Hen. III. præfuit an' 23.

11. Willielmus Schepifhed[12], electus 1270, 54 Hen. III. 2 non. Octob. præfuit an' 21.

12. Willielmus de Malverniâ[13], electus 1291, 19 Edw. I. 5 id. Sept. præfuit ann' 26.

13. Ricardus Towrs[14], electus 1317, 11 Edw. II. 13 cal. Jan. præfuit an' 28.

14. Willielmus Clowne[15], electus 1345, 19 Edw. III. cal. 12 Nov. præfuit an' 32. Ob. 1377, 11 cal. Feb.

15. Willielmus de Kerby[16], electus 1377, 1 Ric. II. 3 non. Feb. præfuit an' 16.

16. Philippus de Repingdon[17], electus 1393, 17 Ric. II. præfuit an' 11.

17. Ricardus Rothele[18], electus 1404, 6 Hen. IV. 5 cal. Maii, præfuit an' 16.

18. Willielmus Sadyngton[19], electus 1420, 8 Hen. VI. 13 cal. Nov. præfuit an' 22.

19. Johannes Pomerey[20], electus 1442, 21 Hen. VI. 16 cal. Jun. præfuit an' 32.

20. Johannes Schepifhed, electus 1474, 14 Edw. IV. 11 cal. Sept. præfuit an' 11.

21. Gilbertus Manchefter[21], electus 1485, 1 Hen. VII. 2 cal. Oct. præfuit an' 11.

22. Johannes Penney[22], electus 1496, 11 Hen. VII. 7 cal. Julii; præfuit an' 13.

23. Ricardus Pexal[23], 3° Martii, 1509; occurs 1533.

24. John Bourchier[24] occurs in 1534[25] and 1537; and furrendered up his office in 1539[26]. On the death of queen Mary, her intended favour of making him a bifhop becoming of no avail, he left England; and, on the 29th of January, 1576, he, with two other Leicefterfhire perfons, Henry Jolliffe, clerk, and John Pott, fchool-mafter, were returned into the Exchequer as fugitives[27]; but, in Auguft 1584, a general pardon to " John abbot late of Leicefter" is noticed in a grant in the Britifh Mufeum[28]; fo that he feems to have been one of the laft furviving abbots.

By a letter to lord Cromwell, from Francis Cave, one of the commiffioners, dated Aug. 20, 1539, it appears that the furrender was then completed, and the writings in the cuftody of Mr. Cave[29]; who fays; " By your lordfhippes goodnefs towardes me, I now ame in the poffeffion of the houfe, and all the demeynes wiche was unlett at the tyme of our repare thether. We founde the houfe indettyd to dyvers creditors in £410. 10s. over and befides certain fums of money the houfe was indebted to the kinges heyghnes, wherof we make no reconinge; and for the difcharge therof we have made fale of the ftoke and ftore, withe the houfhold ftuffe and ornaments of the church, which amounte unto £223. The plate is onfolde, wiche maifter Freman takith the charge of, and is valuyd at, by weyght, 190 pounds. The lead,

---

[1] Vitellius F. XVII. in Bibl. Cotton.   [2] MSS. Lambethan DLXXV. 215.

[3] " On the authority of Bale, it has been believed that Gilbert Foliot was abbot of Leicefter; and Bale is fo confident of his miftake, that he is not content to affirm that he was thence tranflated to the fee of Hereford; but that he never was abbot of Gloucefter, as fome fuppofe. In this he is followed by Pits, Burton, and Cave. On the other hand, Leicefter abbey was founded 1143; the firft abbot was Richard, elected 1144, who held the abbacy 24 years. He was fucceeded by William, fecond abbot, 1167, who died 1177. This is clear from Henry Knighton and an old regifter of the abbey." Wharton, de Epifcopis London. p. 64. —This point has been already difcuffed, on Foliot's own authority, in p. 260.

[4] Paulinus occurs abbot 8 Ric. I. Dodfworth's Collections. Kennet.

[5] William occurs abbot 1204. He was abbot in the time of pope Alexander III. and Robert prior of Kenelworth. MS. Kennet.

[6] He died 1229. Chron. Dunftap. p. 185. He is called de Dunton in the king's affent to his election, 22 Aug. 8 Hen. III. Kennet.

[7] Licence to elect an abbot on the death of Ofbert, 22 Jan.—Rex confentit electioni M. de Bray prioris Leic. in abbatem ejufdem, 29 Jan. Pat. 13 Hen. III. m. 10.

[8] " Fr. Alanus de Cefterfham, petitâ & obtentâ a rege licentiâ, per refignationem Matthie, admiff' in abbatem Sancte Marie de Pratis, Leyc'. mandat. J. archidiac' Leyc'." Reg. Groffetefte, ann. 1.—Licentia eligendi abb. de Leic. 4 Sept. Rex confentit electioni Alani canonici Leic. in abbatem ejufdem 16 Sept. Pat. 19 Hen. III. m. 4 & 29 Sept. m. 3.

[9] Robert (Groffetefte) bifhop of Lincoln vifited the monafteries in his diocefe, and removed [or rather fufpended] the abbot of Leicefter 1236, and caufed another to be placed therein. Chron. Dunftap. p. 239. Pegge's Life of Grotietefte, p. 48.

[10] Licentia eligendi abb. Leic. 13 Nov. 29 Hen. III. Rex prebet affenfum electioni Rob. Fermentin in abb. Leic. & mandatum eft magiftro Rob. de Marifco, officiali Linc. ep'i, 26 Nov. Pat. 29 Hen. III. m. 10.

[11] Rex prebuit affenfum electioni Ric. de Rottel. 23 Sept. 31 Hen. III.—" Henricus Rothelegh, canonicus Sancte Marie de P.atis, Leyc', ad abbatiam ejufdem, benedictus per fratrem W. quondam epifcopum Karl', ad rogatum epifcopi." Ibid. ann. 13. Walter Mal-clerk had refigned the bifhoprick of Carlifle 1246.

[12] Pat. 54 Hen. III. Prior & conventus S. Marie de Pratis pro fine 40 marc. habent cuftodiam dicte abb'ie per ceffionem vel deceffum Henrici abbatis fui.—13 Sept. ceffit; & habuerunt licentiam eligendi 25 Sept. " Fr. Willielmus de Sepefheved, electus abbas 7 Oct. per ceffionem Henrici; confirmatus 18 kal. Nov." Reg. Gravefend, ann. 12.—William Schepifhed, recorded as a writer in bifhop Tanner's Bibliotheca Britannica, p. 666, was a monk of Crokefden in Staffordfhire; and wrote " Annals of England," in the Cotton library, Fauftina B. VI. 6; but feems to be a different perfon from our abbot.

[13] Pat. 19 Edw. I. licentia eligendi per mortem W. Sept. 11. Rex confentit electioni W. de Malverne, 21 Sept. Temporalia fua traduntur 6 Oct.—" Fr. William de Malvernia fit abbas S. Marie de Pratis, Leicetr. per mortem Will' de Shepefheved, 4 kal. Oct. 1294." Reg. Sutton, ann. 11.—He occurs 31 Edw. I. MS. Kennet.

[14] " Fr. Ric. Towrs, electus per mortem fratris Will' de Malverniâ, confirmatus 3 non. Feb. 1317." Reg. Dalderby, ann. 17. The abbot of Leicefter was the firft of the four " venditores, five affeffores," appointed to enquire into the value of nones of fheaves, wool, and lands, granted by parliament in the 14th year of Edw. III. A. D. 1341: therefore Richard Towrs muft have been the abbot in this commiffion, for he was elected in 1317; and continued abbot till 1345.

[15] " Per mortem Richardi de Tours; confirmatus 6 kal. Dec. 1345." Reg. Beke. See p. 262; & X Scriptores, col. 2620.

[16] " Per mortem Will' de Cloune; confirmatus 7 kal. April." Reg. Bokingham.

[17] " Fr. Phil. de Repyndon, fac. pag. profeffor, electus abbas per refig. fratris Will'i de Kereby, admiff. 23 Jun. 1393." Ib.

[18] " Fr. Ric. Rotheley electus abbas B. M. de Pratis Leyceft. 1404; confirmatus 12 Jun. 1405." Reg. Repingden, ann. 1.

[19] " Fr. Will. Sadyngton electus abbas B. M. de Pratis Leyc. confirmatus 8 Nov. 1420." Reg. Flemmyng, 17 Jun. 1442.

[20] " Frater Joh. Pomerey, electus per mortem fratris Will'i Sadyngton, confirmatus 17 Junii." Reg. Alnewyk. See p. 264.

[21] Charyte's " Rentale" having been made in the time of this abbot, is fometimes called " Rentale abbatis Gilberti."

[22] He was a monk here in 1477; and had the priory of Bradley in commendam 14 Sept. 1508. Reg. Smith. See before, p. 266; and fee under Bradley (in vol. II. p. 508.) a general pardon to him as bifhop of Bangor and abbot of Leicefter.

[23] " Ric. Pexal electus in abb. Leic. confirmatus ultimo die Martii 1509." Reg. Smith. He occurs abbot in a deed dated July 10, 1520; and as fuch fubfcribed by proxy at the convocation holden April 5, 1533. Willis, Mitred Abbeys, vol. II. p. 112.

[24] Cleopatra, E. IV.   [25] P. 170.

[26] " Omnibus, &c. Johannes Bourchier abbas monafterii B. V. de Pratis Leyc. & ejufdem loci conventus falutem in Domino fempiternam. Noveritis nos, &c.—Fidem & teftimonium nos prefati abbas & conventus huic prefenti fcripto noftro figillum noftrum appofuimus, anno dicti illuftriffimi domini noftri regis 30°." Rymer, tom. XIV. p. 639.

[27] Strype, Ecclef. Mem. vol. II. Append. p. 103. Peck, Defid. Cur. vol. I. Book II. p. 26.   [28] Harl. MSS. 433. p. 76.

[29] We find Mr. Cave again employed as a commiffioner in this county, under queen Mary, in 1554: " De Francifco Cave & aliis, affignatis ad inquirendum fuper certis articulis in comitatu Leiceftriæ." Pafchæ Commiffiones, 1 Mariæ, Rot. 4.

by eſtimacõn, is valuyd at £1000; the bells at £88. For the diſchargeynge of thabbot, convent, and ſervants of the ſeide monaſtery, there haithe beyne payde, as dothe apere more particularly by the bouke we ſend yowr lordſhippe, £149. And for as moche as thabbot hathe not receyvyd of us but £20, he hath requyride me to defyer your lordſhippe to be ſo good lorde unto hym, he may have 20 pounds, or 20 marks more. The church and houſe remeynethe as yet undefacede, and in the cherche be many thynges to be made ſale of; for the wiche yt may pleſe yowr lordſhippe to let me knawe yowre pleyſure, as well for the further ſale to be made, as for the defaſinge of the chirche and other ſuperfluous byldinges wiche be abowt the monaſtery. A hundrithe marks yerly will not ſuſteyne the charges in reparyng this houſe, yf all byldinges be lett ſtande, as your lordſhippe ſhall knowe more hereafter[1]." This was a prelude to the total demolition; which ſpeedily followed.

The dreſs of the monks of this houſe hath been already deſcribed, from Polydore Vergil[2]. Among the indulgences granted to them by the popes, that of the abbot's being permitted to wear a cap[3] (uti pileo), notwithſtanding any conſtitution or cuſtom to the contrary, is noticed as a conceſſion of pope Nicholas IV. From pope Gregory IV. they had a regulation reſpecting their boots and ſhoes; and it is noticed among the good deeds of abbot Clowne, that he changed their black boots to black ſhoes[4].

The abbey of Leiceſter had the uſual ſuite of officers that are found in the larger religious houſes[5].

The power and dignity of their abbot was conſiderable. He gave the ſolemn benediction, conferred the leſſer orders, wore a mitre a little different from that of a biſhop, who carried the croſier in his left hand, but an abbot in his right hand; wore ſandals[6], &c.—He had apartments with every ſuitable office, and regular ſervants[7], for his own immediate uſe. He preſided of courſe on all material occaſions; and occaſionally, on great ſolemnities, dined with the monks in their refectory; and was ſometimes, as we have ſeen, ſummoned to parliament, till, at the requeſt of abbot Clowne, the privilege of being excuſed from that attendance[8] was granted by king Edward III.

The prior, like the preſident under the maſter in the colleges at Cambridge, was next to the abbot in dignity. He had the care of the jewels and plate; which, in 1300, conſiſted of 21 ſilver ſalt-cellars, and 43 ſilver diſhes[9]. William Geryn, about 1340, gave a ſilver crucifix, with the images of St. John and Mary, and ſeveral paintings[10]; and prior Charyte, about 1470, gave a gold chalice.

The ſub-prior was of courſe aſſiſtant to the prior.

Three ſcriptores, or regiſters, are noticed here in an early deed[11]. They were to write and return letters, and manage the learned employments in the monaſtery.

The camerarius, or chamberlain, kept the keys of the treaſurer, and received and iſſued all conſiderable ſums of money; "in which notion," ſays Fuller[12], "the chamberlain of London holdeth his name."

The precentor and ſubchanter had the ſuperintendance of the library; and made regular entries of ſuch books as were occaſionally lent to any of the brethren.

The cellerarius, or cellerar, was the burſar, who bought in all proviſions, and appointed the pittances for the monks; and two ſuch are noticed in this houſe in 1371. "The cellerars," Fuller ſays, "were brave blades, much affecting ſecular gallantry; for I find it

complained of, that they uſed to ſwagger with their ſwords by their ſides like lay-gentlemen[13]."

Of the original abbey, or of its church, we know but little. The only ſhadow I have ever found of a view of either is in the ſlight ſketch given at the corner of plate XVII. from Speed's map (not publiſhed till 1610); but even this will give ſome little idea of the original, which appears to have conſiſted of three bays of building, beſides the church.

Leland ſcarcely mentions the church; only obſerving, that there was a marble tomb in the wall of the South of the high altar. Whether this was the founder's, or the counteſs Petronell's, he knew not; but it was probably the latter, as the founder's tomb was generally on the North ſide of the high altar.

The principal chapel, dedicated to the Virgin Mary, was ornamented with paintings, the gift of William Geryn, ſome time treaſurer; who built a new cieling to the choir and body of the church, and had the whole new painted[14]. In this chapel Wolſey was buried.

The chapel of St. Auguſtine was on the South ſide of the church; as were the altars of St. Auguſtine and St. John the Baptiſt[15]. Other altars enumerated in Charyte's Catalogue of their miſſals (of which they had a conſiderable number), are the high altar of the Virgin; with thoſe of the Trinity, and of Saints Gabriel, Stephen, Michael, Leonard, Andrew, Katharine, and Anne; and a portable altar, which they poſſeſſed by an eſpecial indulgence of pope Gregory IV. There were alſo four diſtinct chantries here.

A liſt may be ſeen in the Appendix[16] of the eminent perſonages, who, in conſequence of liberal gifts, were admitted canons of the houſe; and of thoſe who gave certain lands with their bodies[17]. Malcolm de Morvill, brother to Richard, conſtable of the king of Scotland[18], was buried in their cemetery.

As we know ſo little of the abbey itſelf, it will not be expected that we ſhould attempt a deſcription of the various parts; of which the bounding wall, and the circular gate-way ſhewn in the North view, plate XVIII, are perhaps the only remnants. It certainly was extenſive, and contained all the uſual apartments of a religious houſe; which are ſo minutely deſcribed by Dr. Fuller, that I ſhall only obſerve, that the abbot's hall here, rebuilt by abbot Clowne, the refectory, library, and infirmary, were particularly eminent.

The refectory was furniſhed with a pulpit[19] whilſt William Geryn was treaſurer; whence the monks, whoſe dinner-hour was fixed at twelve o'clock, were daily edified by a portion of divinity from the lecturer; all the others being ſtrictly enjoined to ſilence, whenever they were either in the church, the cloiſter, the dormitory, or the refectory[20].

They had alſo a Locatorium, or parlour, where they were freely permitted to diſcourſe; and an Oriol, which ſeems to have been a dining-parlour for viſitors, or for the uſe of ſuch as were ſlightly indiſpoſed[21].

The number and value of their books appears by Charyte's "Regiſtrum Librorum[22];" where they are arranged under a variety of diſtinct heads; amongſt which is one of Aſtronomy, with a liſt of their aſtronomical inſtruments, conſiſting of a large aſtrolabe and one of a ſmaller ſize; a ſphere and a radius, both of latten [de auricalco]; two triangles and a trigonometer; a catalogue, or map, of the ſtars[23] [ſtellarium]; and a green table for pointing out[24] the dominical letter [viridis tabula ad cognoſcend' literam dominicalem.]

---

[1] See the Introductory Volume, p. cxliii.   [2] See before, p. 253; and a figure of one of the monks in plate XVII.

[3] "Ds. official' monuit D. Joh'em Haſtyngs de Wylmington capellan' quod de cætero non utatur an hatte ſub pœnâ excommunicationis." Act. Cur. Conſiſt Roffenſe, April 3, 1447, fol. 68. b.   [4] See before, p. 262; and Gent. Mag. vol. LXVI. p. 384.

[5] Titles of ſeveral other of the officers of this houſe have been already given, p. 267.   [6] Burton's Monaſticon, p. 62.

[7] A deed, in the Appendix, p. 55, is witneſſed, among others, by William Diſpenſator, and by Roger, John, and Peter, who are ſtyled famuli abbatis.

[8] "After the fixation of parliamentary abbots in a ſet number, the ſame was eftſoons ſubject to variety. The prior of Coventry played at in and out, and declined his appearance there; ſo did the abbot of Leiceſter, who may ſeem to have worn but half a mitre on his head; ſo alſo the abbot of St. James by Northampton may be ſaid to ſit but on one hip in parliament, he appears ſo in the twilight betwixt a baron and no baron in the ſummons thereunto. But afterwards the firſt of theſe three was confirmed in his place; the two laſt on their earneſt requeſt obtained a diſcharge." Fuller, Church Hiſtory, Book VI. p. 293.

[9] P. 71.   [10] See before, p. 262.   [11] Appendix, p. 55.   [12] Church Hiſtory, book VI. p. 284.   [13] Ibid. p. 285.

[14] Appendix, p. 71.   [15] Ibid. p. 72.   [16] Ibid. p. 70.   [17] Ibid p. 71.

[18] This office had been held by Roger de Quincy; whoſe ſeal, under that character, may be ſeen in the Introductory Volume, plate XII. Appendix, p. 40; and again, ſomewhat different, under the pariſh of Long Whatton.

[19] See a picture and deſcription of ſuch a pulpit at Beaulieu in Hampſhire, in Gent. Mag. vol. LXVI. p. 290.

[20] "Ne ſolæ fauces ſumant cibum, ſed & aures percipiant Dei verbum." Fuller, p. 219.   [21] See hereafter, p. 278.

[22] See a ſpecimen of his writing in plate XVII. fig. 6; and another, from his "Rentale," in plate I. N° VI.

[23] This article, and ſeveral other parts of the Catalogue, will be illuſtrated in the Appendix, pp. 92 & ſeqq.   [24] Ibid.

There

There occurs alſo a diſtinct head of books of Phyſic, with an entry that they were purchaſed by W. Cadyngton, and had formerly been the property of John Bokedene, a phyſician.

Though we cannot aſcertain the particulars of the Infirmary ; we know that, at the foundation [1] of the abbey, there was an eſpecial proviſion for it by the bounty of the counteſs Amicia [2] ; and find *Johannes de Infirmatorio* a witneſs to an early deed [3], and *Johannes Medicus* (perhaps the ſame perſon) to another. They were in fact the only phyſicians of the neigbourhood. In this Infirmary, which was furniſhed with a miſſal, and with ſeveral portiforia, " perſons downright ſick (trouble to others, and troubled by others, if lodging in the dormitory), had the benefit of phyſick, and attendance private to themſelves. No Lent or faſting-days came over the threſhold of this room ; ſickneſs being a diſpenſation for the eating of fleſh. It was puniſhable for any to eat therein, except ſolemnly deſigned for the place [4]."

Biſhop Tanner, in his " Notitia Monaſtica," while appreciating the merits of the monkiſh orders, did not mention their knowledge of medicine and their motives for practiſing it ; but Dr. Freind, in his Hiſtory of Phyſic, was very ſevere in his ſtrictures on the clergy, both regular and ſecular, for interfering in a profeſſion that was foreign to their vows, and incompatible with their calls of duty ; and he attributed to the monks, in great meaſure, the ſlow progreſs that was made in the ſcience of phyſic before the Reformation.

Vol. II. p. 257. " One may obſerve in reading this author (Arnoldus de Villâ novâ), that though the phyſical ſchools were then in a flouriſhing condition, particularly at Salernum, Naples, and Bologna, and bred up men of learning and experience, yet the practice of phyſick was in a great degree incroached upon both by the regular and ſecular clergy. This cuſtom had been long growing in the church ; and the author of the Antiquities of the Univerſity at Paris reckons it one of the devil's ſtratagems to ſupplant religion, by drawing them out of their convents under a ſpecious pretence of doing good to their ſick languiſhing brethren : but the abuſe of it in a little time became ſo infamous, that the Roman council, aſſembled by pope Innocent II. in 1139, abſolutely forbad all the clergy to meddle with phyſick. In the council of Tours, 1163, where Alexander III. preſided, this more ſevere order was made, " That no one, after having taken the vow, and profeſſed himſelf, ſhould go out to hear any lecture in phyſic ; and if any one did go out, and not return to his cloiſter in two months, he ſhould be avoided as an excommunicated perſon : and farther, upon his return, ſhould be turned down below all the reſt, and be incapable of any promotion, unleſs the pope thought fit." The canon adds, " that all biſhops, abbots, and priors, who conſent to ſuch enormities, and correct them not, ſhall be deprived of their dignities, and expelled from the church." And this order was re-inforced by the ſame pope in 1179 ; and revived by Honorius the Third in 1216. Notwithſtanding theſe edicts, either they grew into neglect, or the monks found the way to evade them ; and it was chiefly owing to the multitudes employed in our faculty, that at length the colleges of Salernum and Montpelier began to decay. There might be ſome reaſons in theſe ages, why this ſet of men ſhould be made choice of, where their power over the conſciences of others was very great, eſpecially in caſes which required ſecreſy. But the Reformation, I think, has put an end to the enormity ; and perhaps it is no great prejudice to the publick, that, in our times, there are no more preaching divines, who either cannot be well qualified in their own profeſſion, or muſt be very unſkilful in ours."

P. 266. " I muſt not paſs over this period of time without looking a little at home, and taking a ſhort view how the affairs of phyſic ſtood in our own country. The progreſs it made here was indeed very little ; and it is no wonder it made no more, when there was ſcarce any encouragement for the ſtudy of it, either at court or in the univerſities ; and when the monks, who had very little learning in any of the liberal arts or ſciences, made a ſort of monopoly of this profeſſion, and kept it chiefly in their own hands. However there were ſome even in that age, unknowing as it was, who endeavoured to diſtinguiſh themſelves in this way, both in their practice and their writings. The firſt practical writer extant, which this nation has produced, flouriſhed about this time ; I mean Gilbert, called Anglicus : Bale places him in 1220, in the reign of king John ; but Leland ſays, though he does not acquaint us upon what grounds he ſays ſo, that he was more modern."

P. 410. " Linacre had ſtill farther views for the advantage of our profeſſion. He ſaw in how low a condition the practice of phyſic then was, that it was moſt engroſſed by illiterate monks and empiricks, who, in an infamous manner, impoſed upon the publick."

As it was the deſign of Dr. Freind to expoſe the incongruity of an alliance between divinity and phyſic, he was rather unlucky in citing the authority of Linacre, who late in life entered into holy orders, and who, whilſt preſident of the College of Phyſicians that was eſtabliſhed under his auſpices, was a pluraliſt in parochial benefices and in prebends. " And if," as obſerved Democritus junior, one of the luminaries of the county of Leiceſter, " any phyſician in the mean time ſhall infer, *ne ſutor ultra crepidam*, and find himſelf grieved that I have inruded into his profeſſion, I will tell him in brief, I do not otherwiſe by them than they do by us if it be for their advantage. I know many of their ſect which have taken orders, in hope of a benefice ; it is a common tranſition ; and why may not a melancholy divine, that can get nothing but by ſimony, profeſs phyſic ? Druſianus, an Italian (Cruſianus, but corruptly, Trithemius calls him), *becauſe he was not fortunate in his practice, forſook his profeſſion, and wrote afterwards in divinity. Marcilius Ficinus was ſemel & ſimul a prieſt* and a phyſician at once ; and *T. Linacer* in his old age took orders. The *Jeſuits* profeſſed both at the ſame time ; divers of them, *permiſſu ſuperiorum*, chirurgeons, bawds, panders, midwives, &c. Many poor country vicars, for want of other means, are driven to their ſhifts, to turn mountebanks, quackſalvers, empiricks ; and, if our greedy patrons hold us to ſuch hard conditions as they commonly do, they will make moſt of us work at ſome trade, as Paul did ; at laſt turn taſkers, maltſters, coſter-mongers, graziers, ſell ale, as ſome have done, or worſe. However, in undertaking this taſk, I hope I ſhall commit no great error or *indecorum* ; if all be conſidered aright, I can vindicate myſelf with *Georgius Braunus* and *Hieronymus Hemingius* ; thoſe two learned divines, who (to borrow a line or two of mine elder brother, Mr. William Burton, Preface to Hiſtory of Leiceſterſhire), drawn by a *natural love, the one of pictures and maps, proſpectives and corographical delights, writ that ample theatre of cities ; the other to the ſtudy of genealogies, penned* Theatrum Genealogicum [5]."

The caſe was, that Dr Freind, whilſt zealous for the craft, did not well conſider that before the Reformation literature and ſcience were almoſt totally confined to eccleſiaſtics of the various claſſes ; and ſome there were, who, regard being had to the times in which they lived, made diſtinguiſhed figures in ſtudies that appertained to the preſervation of life. And the firſt upon this liſt was a monk, the incomparable frier Bacon, whoſe treatiſe on the means of avoiding the infirmities of age, founded on the knowledge of chemiſtry, has been much and juſtly admired by many eminent phyſicians.

Dr. Freind has quoted three canons, which were probably as little obſerved by the monks as divers other injunctions impoſed by popes and councils ; and it is believed that there was not any like poſitive reſtriction to which the regulars in this country were ſubject by a ſpecial conſtitution. But if the monks were, by reading, obſervation, and trial, acquainted with the ſalutary properties of herbs and drugs, they were of more uſe in their generation than they are commonly allowed to have been, by the application of them in reſtoring health to the ſick, and ſtrength to the convaleſcents.

---

[1] At a ſtill earlier period, the mill at the North bridge was given by Robert earl of Mellent to the canons of St. Mary de Caſtro, *ad veſtitum infirmorum.* Appendix, p. 54.

[2] Appendix, p. 55.   [3] Ibid. p. 56.   [4] Fuller.

[5] Anatomy of Melancholy, Preface to the Reader, p. 15, 16.

In monasteries, the *infirmatorius*, the warden or president of the infirmary, ought not to have been deemed qualified for his office, if he were ignorant of the medical science[1]; there is, however, room to suspect that his chief employment might be to attend to the mode of living of the monks who were put under his care, from a persuasion that many of them would feign illness to obtain a greater latitude in their diet. Whereas the want of the infirm was only to be regarded, and not a voluptuous indulgence of the appetite; and, when a monk who had been ill first appeared in the chapter, he was to supplicate absolution of the prior for having eat and drunk such viands as were not permitted by the Benedictine rules[2]. By a statute of archbishop Winchelsey, the monks of Christ Church, Canterbury, when any seculars were present, were to abstain from eating flesh, except at the table of the master in the infirmary, in the chambers of the sick, *in deporto*[3], in the chamber of the prior, and in the strangers' hall; where, if duly licensed, they might partake of it for their own regale, and the solace of others. But, in order to prevent all junketings in the infirmary, it was a general rule, that no monk, if in health, should eat in the infirmary; nor was any layman to enter it, except the servants and medical practitioners; for, the monks were permitted to consult skilful physicians[4]; and, in the priory of St. Andrew in Rochester, a lay-apothecary was retained by agreement on these terms: that he was to receive flesh, fish, and bread with ale, as much as he pleased. It appears that John Bishop was the person engaged in 1498; and that, at an episcopal visitation of the convent, there was a complaint against him for neglecting the sick[5].

The monks of some orders were in the habit of being blooded five times in the year; and the operation might be performed by a layman. Heretofore, among the laity, the same persons were barbers-chirurgeons[6]; and perhaps the Benedictines might occasionally apply both razor and lancet. Thus far it is on record, that, till the reign of Henry III, the members of St. Augustine's monastery, near Canterbury, were obliged to shave one another; but that, about the year 1265, on account of the wounds suffered, and the dangers likely to be incurred from their not using the lancet

dexterously, the then abbot granted that a room should be prepared for the purpose near the baths, and that the monks might be shaved by seculars. As a memorial of this kind indulgence, abbot Robert was enrolled among the benefactors; and it was ordained, that on shaving days three collects should be recited for the health of his soul[7].

At Croyland, " the serjeantry of the infirmary was given to Wifin Barbour, who took an oath of obedience and fidelity in full chapter. His duty, then read to him, was to shave the whole convent in their turn, unless it should happen that a senior wanted to be shaved before a junior; to wait on the monks at table in the infirmary, particularly on the sick, whose provision he was to fetch from the cellarer, and be always ready in the infirmary at their call. If two were confined to their beds by sickness, he was to attend the elder of them and lie with him; and the younger was to be attended and slept with by the clerk of the infirmary; and if a third, by the infirmary cook; and these three servants to be respectively assisting to each other. If the sick party had received extreme unction, the first night the serjeant of the infirmary and the serjeant cutter of the shoemaker[8] were to sit up with him; the second night the clerk of the infirmary and the serjeant shoemaker; and the third night the cook of the infirmary and the shoemaker's washerman[9]; and so for nine nights successively by turn: and the serjeant of the infirmary was to have for his trouble of every monk that died a tunic or four shillings, or something of equal value, which he must sell only to a monk of the same house. The rest, who sat up with the deceased, were to have two-pence out of his effects, which were all to be sold by the prior and chamberlain, and the money given to the poor, for the good of his soul, or to the inferior clerks, to sing for him. Every sick monk might choose one of his brethren to attend him, provided the infirmarer[10] took his place in the convent; and the serjeant of the infirmary might assist the prior in celebrating, or the clerk of the infirmary the infirmarer, or any other senior disposed to celebrate there, if not otherwise engaged about the sick, for which he was to have an allowance as one of the abbot's servants, and four shillings a year for his pay. If the whole convent

[1] Si ægritudo adeo invaluerit ut frater in conventu remanere non possit, præcipiat abbas fratri cui cujusmodi cura impositum est ut ducet ægrum in cellam infirmorum; in qua domo serviatur ei secundum possibilitatem loci, tam de communibus cibi, quam de esu carnis, ut nullius rei, si fieri possit, indigentiam patiatur. Lanfranci Constitut. Wilkins, Concil. vol. I. p. 357.

[2] Jussus surgere, hæc, vel similia verba dicat, " Domine, infirmitate meâ gravatus, in domo infirmorum diu fui, et cibo & potu, & aliis multis offendi, & contra ordinem feci, & inde peto absolutionem vestram." Ibid.

[3] It is not unlikely that the apartment which in the abbey of St. Alban's (see Gent. Mag. vol. LXVI. p. 300.) was styled *Oriolanum* (porticus atrium), might in the priory of Christ Church be termed *Deportum*; and that what in the statutes of archbishop Winchelsey might be so denominated, afterwards acquired the appellation of *La Gloriette* vel *Honneurs*; about which rooms Somner and Batteley differed in opinion, as may be seen in Antiquities of Canterbury, p. 106; and in Cantuaria Sacra, pp. 92, 93. In *La Gloriette* and *Maister Honneurs*, which were situated not far from the priors lodging and the infirmary, such guests seem to have been entertained as were of too much consequence to be intermixed with strangers of all degrees *in Aulâ Hospitum*. The etymology of *Deportum* is still, however, a desideratum. And, qu. Is it not to be deduced from some old French word? S. D.

[4] Statuta R. Winchelsey, archiepisc. Cantuar. Art. VII. De infirmatorio, & extra refectorium comedentibus.

Item monachi de cætero omnes in conspectu communi secularium tam in claustro inferiori quam exteriori domus vestræ a carnium esu, exceptis locis inferius annotatis, abstineant; scilicet, quod solum in mensâ magistri in infirmatorio, & cameris infirmorum, in *deporto*, & camerâ prioris, aut in aulâ hospitum, cum ab hoc ritu licentiati extiterint, vescantur carnibus ad suam recreationem idoneam, vel ad solatium aliorum.

Item fratres non infirmi, nisi quandoque ad honestum infirmorum solatium, & hoc de præsidentis licentiâ, in infirmatorio non sedeant, nec morentur ultra quam ter dici voleat dominicalis oratio " Pater Noster;" nec in eo bibant aut comedant, nisi sit eis a præsidente concessum.—Item commune ferculum infirmorum ex consuetudine prius habita distributum in aliud sibi competentius, si sit necesse, mittatur, & in magnâ indulgentiâ superaddatur aliquid opportunum; in quo casu respectus ad solam infirmorum indigentiam, non autem ad appetitum voluptuarium habeatur. Hæc caute consideret præsidens in licentiâ taliter concedenda. Wilkins, Concil. vol. II. p. 247.

Litera abbatum in capitulo provinciali Angliæ apud Northampton celebrato præsidentium anno Dom. MCCCXLIII. cap. XII. de curâ infirmorum.

Medicinalia etiam juxta peritorum consilia medicorum eis (infirmis) præcipimus exhiberi. Secularem autem nullum cum infirmis comedere volumus, aut aliqualiter misceri; medicis & servientibus ad eorum curam et custodiam deputatis duntaxat exceptis.

[5] Visitat. Ricardi Episcopi Roffen. in Ecclef. Cathedral. per venerabiles viros Thomas Cutfolde, decretor. doctor. et Johannem Edmund, Sac. Theolog. Baccal. Commiss.

Ds. primus Charnock camerarius; ad ii. iii. iiii. &c. Artic. Concordat in omnibus, cum prior' test', &c. excepto quod dicit quod egri laborand' infirmitat' jacend' in firmario non sunt custodit' ficut deberent in defectu cujusdam Johannis Bishop, laici habent' feod' ad custodiend' infirm', &c.—Dicit ulterius quod præfat' Johannes Bishop, laicus, habet ex mandato proprio, carnes, aquatica, & panes cum servisia ex monast. prædict' invito celerario loci. Act. Cur. Consist. fol. 319.

[6] Minutor—venæ incisor—Rasor et minutor; chirurgicusque expertissimus. Du Cange.

[7] Chronica W. Thorn; X Script. col. 1915.—Quando incepit rasura fratrum per seculares.

Usque ad tempus hujus Rogeri abbatis radebant se mutuo fratres in claustro, set iste propter tonsuras & diversa pericula quæ frequenter contigerunt inter eos quia rudes & nescii erant in officio radendi, ordinavit, cum consensu conventus, quod rasura fieret in camera juxta balneatorium per seculares quotiens opus esset. Et quod diebus rasuræ post *verba mea* in capitulo dicantur tres collectæ, scilicet, *absolve, inclina,* & *fideles,* in memoriam illius beneficii, pro anima Rogeri abbatis, &c.

[8] *Cissor de sartrina.*   [9] *Lotarius de sartrina.*   [10] *Infirmarius.*

eat in the refectory, and none were fick, the faid ferjeant was not to go to his dinner before the bell rang; but if the monks for their own pleafure and eafe, or becaufe they had been bled [1], chofe to eat in the refectory, the fervant of the infirmary was to attend them till all their provifion was fet on, and then retire to his own dinner; unlefs wanted by the prior or any of the feniors who might be fick; and then to take his bread, and the fick monks were to give him a fhare [2] of their provifion; and fo every fucceeding day the cook's fervant to have their leavings; and if none, then the almoner was to find him provifion. All thefe fervants were ftrictly charged not to let any feculars, men, women, or children, from the town or elfewhere, into the infirmary; nor was any fecular perfon to be fhaved or bled there, without fpecial leave from the abbot or prior. Thefe three fervants were to lie every night in the infirmary, and not abfent themfelves without exprefs leave from the prior [3]."

Farther extracts relating to the practice and habit of the monks about bleeding, de minutione Sanguinis.

Cuftumale Roffenfe—De lavatoribus.

P. 32. " Ejus eft focum facere contra quod *fratres minuere* debent, et *minutorem* fummonere, ut paratus fit fratres minuere."

P. 30. " De famulo infirmatorii—in focietate—*minutorum* ordinate ferviet ita facete, ut nullus indigeat petere aliquid, et maxime tunc cuftodiet hoftium ab ingreffu laicorum, ne aliquis abfque licentiâ magiftri fui introeat."

Du Cange—*Minuere*. " Stata erant minutionis tempora in monafteriis, extra quæ *fanguinem minuere* fas non erat, nifi gravis urget infirmitas."

" Quinquies in anno fient generalis *minutiones*—Prima eft in Septembri; fecunda eft ante Adventum; tertia eft ante Quadragefimam; quarta poft Pafcha; quinta poft Pentecoften: tribus diebus minutio durabit," &c. &c.—Many other inftances might be added. Gunton's Peterborough, p. 296.

" Before his [abbot Robert de Lyndefey's] time there had been great difcord and murmuring, contention and envy frequently happened among the brethren, *propter minuiionem*, about blood-letting (which was very neceffary fome time to thofe fedentary people, who were fubject to repletion); and no wonder, becaufe nobody could *accipere minutionem*, be let blood, without an order from the prior; who let fome have it oftener, others more rarely; fome after five weeks, others after fix, and others not till after eight, or ten, or fifteen, or perhaps half a year. To take away, therefore, all trouble out of their minds about this matter, this abbot ordered that the convent fhould be divided into fix parts, and, upon the day of letting blood, he that was the fenior of that part, whofe turn it was to have the benefit of it, fhould afk *licentiam minuendi* (and that under his hand) for his brethren from the prior. In the margin of the book there is this note. That in abbot Walter's time this mode of minution was thus far altered, that they may be divided into five parts, and then *minuerentur modo fupradicta*. For Robert Groffetefte, bifhop of Lincoln, in his vifitation, had forbidden the eating of flefh altogether unto the monks every where; except only in the infirmary, or in the abbot's chamber; which was accounted by them an unfupportable burden. It is

farther noted, that the convent, in former times, had liberty, at three feafons in the year, to eat as much flefh as they pleafed in a houfe deputed for that purpofe; and in the *domus hofpitum*, houfe where they entertained ftrangers; and in all places where they eat out of the refectory they might eat flefh. Which liberty was quite taken away by the above-named inhibition of the bifhop. They who were *minuti*, let blood, were formerly refrefhed in the refectory three times a day with a regular diet, as appears by the antient cuftomary of this church."

Extracts from Warton's Hiftory of Poetry in England, concerning the knowledge and practice of phyfick by ecclefiaftics.

Vol. I. p. 442. note *(S)*. " It has been before obferved, that at the introduction of philofophy into Europe, by the Saracens, the clergy only ftudied and practifed the medical art. This fafhion prevailed a long while afterwards. The prior and convent of St. Swithin's in Winchefter granted to Thomas of Shaftefbuty, clerk, a corrody, confifting of two difhes daily from the prior's kitchen, bread, drink, robes, and a competent chamber in the monaftery, for the term of his life. In confideration of all which conceffions, the faid Thomas paid them fifty marks; and moreover is obliged to " defervire nobis *in arte medicinæ*." Dat. in dom. capitul. Feb. 15, A. D. 1319 [4]." The learned and accurate Fabricius [5] has a feparate article on Theologici Medici. In the romance of fir Guy, a monk heals the knight's wounds. Signature G. iiii.

There was a *monke* beheld him well
That could of *leach craft* fome dell.

In Geoffrey of Monmouth, who wrote in 1128, Eopa, intending to poifon Ambrofius, introduces himfelf as a phyfician. But, in order to fuftain this character with due propriety, he firft fhaves his head, and affumes the habit of a monk, lib. VIII. cap. 14. John Arundale, afterwards bifhop of Chichefter, was chaplain and firft phyfician to Henry VI. in 1468 [6]. Farilius, abbot of Abingdon, about 1110, was eminent for his fkill in medicine; and a great cure performed by him is recorded in the regifter of the abbey [7]. King John, whilft fick at Newark, made ufe of William de Wodeftoke, abbot of the neighbouring monaftery of Croxton, as his phyfician [8].

Thus much (principally in the words of a moft refpectable Antiquary [9]) by way of digreffion on a fubject not generally noticed, though not uninterefting to the hiftory of monaftic orders in general.

We return to the particular hiftory of the poffeffions of this abbey; which, at the time of the fuppreffion, Speed fays, was eftimated to expend £1062. 0s. 4¼d. a year; according to Dugdale, £951. 14s. 5¾d. [10]

The feveral churches from which this abbey received penfions in 1477 may be feen in the Appendix. At that period they had, in Leicefterfhire and other counties, 35 churches and 32 chapels appropriated [11], for which they paid procurations [12]; and 25 more churches licenfed for appropriation [13]. And it is remarked in the " Regiftrum Breve," that their poffeffions were fo numerous, that they had for every monk a church, a chapel, a mill referved in demefne, and a mill from which they received tithes. I do not find that the number of the regular monks in this houfe at any time exceeded twenty [14].

---

[1] *Pro minutione.*   [2] *Campanagium.*   [3] Hiftory of Croyland, p. 38.   [4] Regiftrum Priorat. S. Swithin, Winton. MS

[5] Bibl. Gr. XII. 739. feq.   See alfo Gianon. Iftor. Neapol. I. X. chap. xi. fect. 419.

[6] Wharton, Angl. Sacr. vol. I. p. 777.   [7] Hearne, Bened. Abbas, Præf. p. xlvii.

[8] Belvoir Chron. MS. Harl. apud Hearne, Præfat. ut fupra, p. xlix.   And fee before, under Croxton Abbey, p. 152.

[9] The Rev. Samuel Denne, M. A. F. S. A. vicar of Wilmington and Darenth, on whom the mantle of the late learned Antiquary Dr. Pegge appears to have fallen.

[10] A MS. in the Cotton Library (Cleopatra E. IV. fol. 283.) reconciles thefe fums, by giving the firft of them as the grofs value, and the other as the nett amount.   [11] See thefe churches enumerated, Appendix, p. 66.

[12] The original ground of procurations was by reafon of the damage that the bifhop and his fucceffors were like to fuftain after an appropriation made, becaufe the parfon was to give entertainment to the bifhop when he vifited ecclefiatim.

[13] Appropriation, from the French *appropier*, properly fignifies, in our law (as Cowell obferves), a fevering a benefice ecclefiaftical, which originally and in nature is *juris divini & in patrimonio nullius*, to the proper and perpetual ufe of fome religious houfe or the like; for, without the confent of the bifhop, no religious order could receive any appropriation or tithes, as by a decree of the council of Lateran it was decreed 1180. An appropriation of a church muft be made by the patron by licence of the king and bifhop, provided always that according to the 15th of Richard II. and 4 Henry IV. it be performed; for by thofe acts as provided, that in every licence which fhould be made it fhould be exprefsly contained, that the diocefan, according to the value, fhould appoint a convenient fum to be paid yearly out of the fruits and profits of the church to the poor of the parifh; and alfo fhould ordain a vicar, which fhould be well and fufficiently endowed, fo that he might do divine fervice, and keep hofpitality there. See before, under Abkettleby, p. 12.

[14] This was the number that figned the furrender; and the fame number occurs, in 1477, in the Catalogue of their books.

They

They had four several granges, where the corn-rents were regularly depofited; at each of which one of their members refided under the title of prior, or mafter of the grange. One was fituated at the Weft-gate of Leicefter (now called Weftcotes[1]); two others at Ingwardby[2] and Stoughton[3] in this county; the fourth at Medoplek[4] in the High Peak of Derbyfhire.

Enough for the prefent has been faid of their pof-feffions within the county of Leicefter; where, befides lands, rents, and tithes, they had liberty of procuring fuel and keeping cattle in divers manors; the particulars of which will appear under each refpective townfhip. They had property alfo *(redditum voluntarium vel liberum[5], feu penfionem, portionem, vel decimas)* in many other counties, which fhall now be briefly noticed.

In *Bedfordfhire*, they had at Camefton [Kempfton] the church and manor, the gift of Ifabel countefs of Northampton[6].

At Scharnbroke, the church was appropriated to them about the year 1220 by William Triket, being then valued at 20 marks, exclufive of a penfion of 20s. to the archdeacon of Bedford. They had alfo a rent of 2d. and 24 acres of arable land in that lordfhip, five acres of which were fituated between the abbot's manor-houfe and the church.

"Habemus, ex conceffione Hugonis Linc' epi, cum affenfu Wilti decani & totius capituli, ecclefiam de Scharnbroke poft deceffum Ricardi rectoris ejufdem[7].

"Vicaria confiftit in toto altaragio dicte ecclefie, exceptis principalibus legatis, que ufibus abbatis & conventûs Leic', per ordinationem Johannis epi Linc', refervantur; qui quidem religiofi, fecundum eandem ordinationem, omnia onera ordinaria & extraordinaria fuftinebunt in perpetuum, &c. Et folvent loci ordinario annuatim xxs."—The abbot and convent contributed 20s. a year towards augmenting the vicarage.

At Sowrdrop, in the fame county, they had a rent of 13s. 4d. for a place called *Bolfworth Land*[8].

In *Berkfhire*, they had originally the church of Ildfley, the gift of the founder[9]; but, as this place is not noticed in Charyte's Rentale, it was probably foon exchanged for other property.

In *Buckinghamfhire*, William Avenel gave them the advowfon of the church of Adftock, which was confirmed to them by king Henry II. about 1166. The abbot and convent in 1422 affigned over this advowfon to fir Richard Vernon and his heirs; and it continued, with the manor, in the poffeffion of that family till it came, with their other demefnes at Adftock, by marriage, to the families of Manners and Fortefcue; and in 1707 was given to the bifhoprick of Lincoln[10].

They had a portion of fuch lands as the monks of Bitulfden held in culture, at Bitulfden, Whitefeld, and Sirefham, as were within the limits of Brackley and Sirefham[11].

At Chefham-Leyceter, they had a moiety of the profits of the church, and of the chapel of St. Leonard at Chefham Boys[12], the gift of Robert de Sifrewaft; which in 1220 was valued at 30 marks, and the temporalities of the abbey at 30s. 5½d. The following extract is from an original terrier[13].

"Chefham Leycet' in the com. of Buk, perteyninge to the towne of Chefham, and wythin the conftabulwyke there. Yt is to be remembered and to be underftonde that theis prefent fcripcons folowing, makyng mencyon wher that all the glebis and tythes of bladis and of heyze, and alfo of all the rentes, fute, fervyce, and demayne londis, with ther apperten', ben and ow it to be hadde, receyved, gadered, and layde wythin the lymytes, markes, and boundes of the parifche and the park of Chefham Leyceter forfeyde, in

the faid com. of Buk, the which ben perteyning and belonging, by dew and right of old cuftome, unto the rectorye and parfonage ther of the lord abbot and covent of the monaftery of the bleffed Mary Virgin in the mede of Leyceftr', be the right of her chyrche, called the chyrche of Chefham Leycet', in the feide com. of Buk, as be the hameletis and conftabulwykes in thofe fubfcripcons thereof hereafrur wreten and made plenarly apperyng; the whiche ben renewed, atte Chefham Leycet' forfayde, at the tide of the yere called Hokketyde, in the yere of our Lord MCCCCLXVIII, and the VIII yere of the reigne of kynge Edwarde the IIII, be Wylliam Wedin bayly of Chefham forfaide, and fermar alfo unto the fayde abbot and covent of theyre feyde chirche and parfonage; and alfo be the concentyng and avice, knowlyfhyng, tellyng, utteryng, and declaryng of the moft aged men and beft theryn, and therof avifed of all the feyd pariffche and parifshoners, and alfo of all themits there of the feide abbot and covent.

Wythyn the conftabulwyke of Chefham towne forfeyde. In the foreft all the glebys and tythes of the landys, with appertenances, called Coppid-thorne, of Thomas Lynde, efquir, lord of the manor of Chefham Bury, lying in a field there, called Churche-felde, &c. The terrier is continued through more than 13 folio pages of an exact defcription of all the lands and tithes belonging to the abbey, "within the conftabulwyke of the duchey of Langcaftell there, and alfo of the lordfhippe of Latimer there" (out of which the abbot and convent affigned "the tithes of tithes, otherwife the tenth part of ten parts of tithes, to the chapel and chaplain of Chefham Boys"); "the hamelett of Layhull, the hamelett of Whelpley Wyth, in the conftabulwyke there of the honour of Walyngforde;" the hamelettis of Alcheley Grene, Belenden, Afsherugge, Charderrugge, Hunrugge (in which were fome lands held under the abbot and convent of Muffenden), Chefham Dene, otherwife Chefham Water Wyth, in which were lands of John Stoketon, alderman and mercer of London; and Botteley.

The abbefs of Burnham, in Buckinghamfhire, as lady of the manors of Holmer and Little Miffenden[14], had fuit of court from certain lands at Holmer, given by Henry de Rokeby to the abbot and convent of Leicefter in free and perpetual alms; confifting of all the lands he had in the townfhip, with the appurtenances, both within and without the town, the woods, meadows, &c. which had been given to him by Richard de Camvile[15] in exchange for the advowfon of the chapel of Rokeby, which was a member of Clifton, and belonged to that abbey; touching which chapel there was a fuit betwixt the faid Henry and the abbot in the year 1200; which ended not, it feems, till 1220, when a fine was levied between the abbot and Henry Rokeby, by which it was concluded that the faid Henry and his heirs fhould exhibit a fit clerk to the abbot and his fucceffors, whom they might prefent to the bifhop; which clerk fhould pay to them yearly the antient and due penfions they had wont to receive thence; and, to perfect this agreement, the faid Henry gave to that abbey for ever a yard-land in Holme. This land, which brought in a rent of 18s. was given by the abbey to Roger de Miffenden, clerk, for his homage and fervice[16]. The right to this portion of land was again confirmed by a procefs at law in 1299; after which we find feveral fucceffive entries in the "Rentale" of the receipt of the rent from 1310 to 1323, when a regular acquittance of certain arrears occurs, figned by abbot Richard Tourfe, on condition of the rent being regularly paid in future.

---

[1] Of which an account will be found under Bruntingthorpe, in the parifh of St. Mary de Caftro.

[2] The gift of archbifhop Iflip. See p. 262; and a farther account under the parifh of Hungarton.

[3] See an account of this grange under the parifh of Thurnby.   [4] See hereafter, p. 277.

[5] *Redditus liber* is evidently the fame as *redditus affifus*; and is defcribed fo by Du Chefne. S. Carte.

[6] Charyte's Rentale, fol. xxxiv.   [7] Ibid. fol. cxxiv.   [8] Charyte, fol. cxxx.   [9] Appendix, p. 54.

[10] Charyte's Rentale, fol. xi; Willis's Buckingham, p. 123.   [11] Charyte's Rentale, fol. xxii.

[12] Charyte's Rentale, fol. xxxv. Fin. Buckingham. 14 Joan. de advoc. capellæ S. Leonardi de Ceftrefham.

[13] Cotton MSS. Galba E. III. p. 131. & feqq.

[14] Clauf. 13 Edw. III. p. 1. m. 29. pro man. de Holmere & Miffenden Parvâ, ex conceff' Rogeri le Strange.—Mifled by fir William Dugdale's extracts from the "Regiftrum Breve," I have (in the Index to Charyte's Rentale, p. 67) placed *Holmer* in Warwickfhire. The name of *Homer Green* is ftill to be found near Miffenden in the maps of the county of Buckingham.

[15] The Camviles were benefactors to the priory of Burchefter.

[16] Cotton MSS. Vitellius F. XVII; ex Plac. 2 John, Rot. 26. & Rot. Mich. 5 Hen. III; and Charyte, fol. lxii.

Sir John Brows[1], or Brewofe, held in 1154 a meffuage, with a virgate of land, and the wood near
Holmers-hill, formerly in the tenure of William Miffenden, a rent of 18s. payable at three terms in the
year. Of this land William Capon rented a field
near the water called le Brech, containing eight acres;
John Dunefmore, a field called Argentefield, and a
toft called Argentefcroft, containing also eight acres;
John Baldewyn, a croft called Oldfield; and two
others called Hechyager, containing nine acres. From
all which, fir John Brewofe received no more than 20s.

The prior of Burcefter[2] in Oxfordfhire held one
toft, and the wood, where William de Miffenden
dwelt, with a field called Dichefeld, and another
called Hunefred, containing more than twenty acres.

William Inngefby had the wardfhip of Henry de
Rokeby whilft under age, as far as related to the
lands which the faid Henry gave to Leicefter abbey,
the fame being within his fee.

In *Derbyfhire*, they had a confiderable property in
the High Peak; particularly the church of Youlgrave,
with the chapels of Cratton, Elton, Mydulton, and
Wynfter, &c. the gift of *Robert* the fon of *Robert
Coll*, confirmed about 1250 by pope Innocent IV;
the whole townfhip of Conkyfbery, with the mill,
cliff, &c. and the townfhips of Newbyggen and Medoplek, the gift of *William Avenel*, confirmed by the
bifhop of *Coventry*; and eftablifhed by regular procefs at law in 1339[3] and 1423[4]; after which the
abbey gave £5. a year to augment the vicarage of
Youlgrave.—The church of Youlgrave was rated in
1220 at 30 marks, and Medoplek, &c. at 68s.

In Byrchover, Herthull in the parifh of Bakewell,
Lyes, and Smerill Grange, various lands and tithes.

At Haddon, 20 acres, the gift of William Avenel.

At Medoplek they had in 1292 two bovates of land,
of the annual value of 14s; the mill worth 10s;
mines worth 2s; affife rents 10s; pleas and perquifites 2s; a meadow worth 6s. 6d; and other receipts
to the value of 68s. a year.

At Stanton, lands given by Adam de Stanton.

At Hertyfhorn, in the fame county, they had the
manor-houfe of Schorthafull, the gift of William
Afton; and three other meffuages, two virgates, 101
acres and a half of arable land, with woods, meadows,
paftures, &c. to the amount of 26s. 8d. a year. This
manor, with all its appurtenances, in Hertyfhorn or
elfewhere, was granted to *Chriftopher Dean*, by whom
they were conveyed in 1544 to *Thomas Boyde*, yeoman,
for a fee-farm rent of 3s. 4d.; which rent, being afterwards purchafed from the crown, became vefted in
fir Samuel Barnadifton, of Kedelton, Suffolk, bart.
who held it in 1727; at which time Robert Charnell,
of Snarefton, efq. was owner of the manor-houfe and
other property; Edward Dawfon, of Long Whatton,
efq. poffeffed a meffuage, lands, &c. part of the faid
manor; and Jofeph Clark, of Blaugherby, and Jofeph
Mould, Thomas Broad, Mary Madin, and William
Madin, had divers lands, &c. within the lordfhip[5].

At Okethorpe (a hamlet of Seile in Leicefterfhire)
Thomas Lathbury gave them all the lands and tenements, meadows, and paftures, with their appurtenances, which he held under the gift and feoffment
of his mother Elizabeth Norton, confirmed by William Norton and Thomas Bytfwell, confifting of a
meffuage and toft, four virgates of land, and the
moiety of a rent of 38s. 8d. He gave them alfo, by
his laft will, all the tenements he had lately acquired
in the townfhips of Cateby and Okethorpe, and in

Naneby field; and directed that a lamp, or large wax
candle, fhould be provided for ever, to be burnt before the image of the Virgin in St. Mary's chapel in
the abbey. Richard Glover was their tenant here at
a rent of 28s. 8d. for a meffuage, three tofts, and
three virgates of land; for which they paid 2s. to the
king for fuit of court[6]. They had other lands, the
gift of Thomas Elsforde and his anceftors[7].

In *Lancafhire*, they had the manor and church of
Cokeram, with the chapels of Elhale and Thurnham,
which in 1220 were valued at 26 marks; with lands
at Afsheton, Kirkelow, Geyrftang, and Halouth[8]; the
gift of William, the fon of Gilbert, who was fummoned
to parliament by the title of William of Lancafter, baron of Kendale, and married Gundreda the dowager
countefs of Warwick, who joined her hufband in a
gift to the canons of Leicefter of two bovates of land
at Cokeram, " unde heredes fui minus tenent in capite." This grant was confirmed to our abbey by a
charter of John lord of Ireland, earl of Morteigne,
Cornwall, and Nottingham (afterwards king of England), and by a bull of pope Innocent IV.

John Oxcliff and John Corton gave to the abbey
of Leicefter a meffuage, 12 acres of arable land, and
4 of meadow, at Cokeram[9]; foon after which, whilft
Philip de Repingdon was abbot, they obtained, with
great labour and expence, a grant of quit-claim[10]
from the lady Philippa de Conor, dutchefs of Ireland[11],
and a charter of confirmation from king Henry IV.

The chancel of Cokeram church was rebuilt in 1442
whilft John Pomerey was abbot[12].

On a part of the land belonging to the abbey of
Leicefter, at Cokerfand, where formerly ftood an
hofpital, the abbey of Cokerfand was afterwards
founded; as appears by the following agreement:
" Ad univerforum notitiam perveniat, inter Paulum
abbatem & conventum de Leiceftria in pratis, & canonicis de Cokerfand, ita conveniffe, quod jam dictus
Paulus & conventus de Leiceftriā, intuitu pietatis &
religionis, dederunt prefatis canonicis de Cokerfand
locum in quo domus hofpitalis de Cokerfand fita eft,
in puram & perpetuam eleemofinam; ita ut liceat eis
abbathiam conftruere, & abbatem habere, fcilicet de
tribus rubris ufque ad divifum de Thurnham, per me-
diam moffam[13]." For this land the abbey of Leicefter
had an annual rent of 5s. 8d.[14]

Cokerfand was at firft the habitation of Hugh an
hermit, then converted to an hofpital, under Lancafter
abbey, endowed by William de Lancafter, temp. Henry II; but about 1190 changed, by authority of pope
Clement, to an abbey of Premonftratenfian canons,
valued at £157. " Coker river maketh no great
courfe or he come to the fands by Cokerham village
not a mile off. Thens to Cokerfande an abbey of
Ciftertienfes, about half a mile of, ftanding very
blekely an object to all winds[15]."

The fite of Cokerham abbey is now (1796) the
property of *John Dalton*, efq. (who is of an antient
catholic family) of Thurnham hall; whofe anceftors,
fince the diffolution of the abbey, have been buried in
the chapter-houfe, which is a Gothic ftructure of an
octagonal form, fupported by a ftone pillar, now
greatly out of repair, though it is the moft perfect
part of the abbey; much of the ruins of the building
having been wafhed away by the fea. It is three miles
diftant from Thurnham hall; to which tradition, as is
ufual, fays there was a fubterraneous paffage. The
farm here has been many years in the occupation of
Mr. *Holt*; and is confidered as extra-parochial[16].

---

[1] This family appears to have been feated in Buckinghamfhire earlier than is generally fuppofed. The town of Buckingham
came to William de Browfe by frank marriage, as appears by Pat. 7 John, m. 23. Dugdale, Bar. vol. I. p. 419; and Willis's
Buckingham, p. 26.   [2] Fin. Buckingham, 46 Hen. III. n. 52. de carucatā terræ in Miffenden.

[3] Plac. de quo warranto in com. Derb. 4 Edw. III. Rot. 3. dorfo.

[4] Fin. Derb. 2 Hen. VI. Hill. Rot. 452. pro manerio de Medoplec & terris in Conkyfbery.

[5] From an original deed.   [6] Charyte, fol. cxiv. b. See farther on this hamlet under Seile.

[7] Appendix, p. 66. A terrier of their lands may be feen in a Cotton MSS. Galba E. III. fol. 155. & feqq.

[8] Charyte, fol. xxxix—xlvi. [9] Appendix, p. 64; Pat. 12 Edw. II. p. 1. m. 18. de libertatibus in Lancaftr. [10] Appendix, p. 68.

[11] The duke of Ireland's vifiting Leicefter abbey has been mentioned in p. 256. John de Vere, feventh earl of Oxford,
was created marquis of Dublin in 1385, the title of *marquis* being then new and unheard-of in England, and in the year following duke of Ireland. Thefe rapid promotions made him fo haughty and infolent, that he put away his wife Philippa; who was
daughter to Ingelram earl of Bedford, by Ifabel his wife, daughter of Edward III. Dugdale, Bar. vol. I. p. 194.

[12] Appendix, p. 69.   [13] Dugdale, Mon. Angl. vol. II. p. 636.   [14] Charyte's Rentale, fol. xlvi.

[15] Leland, vol. V. p. 84.   [16] From the information of Mr. John Eccles, who vifited the ruins in May 1796.

In

In *Lincolnshire*, they had at Benington an annual rent of six quarters of salt, worth 20*s*; and at Botulston [Boston] Walter Gerun gave them, *cum corpore suo*, all his land in the High-street next the sea, and the homage and service of several persons. They had also divers rents, &c. the gift of Warner de Engaine, John Gerun, and others, amounting in the whole to 76*s*. 7½*d*. a year; which originally had produced £7. 12*s*. The representative of the Gerun family paid annually a pound of pepper and a pound of cumin.

Reginald, son of William de Benington, gave to master Gerard, son of Baldric archdeacon of Leicester, for his service and homage, certain lands, to hold for the rent of 12*d*. a year; which 12*d*. was given to the church of All Saints at Benington, to found a lamp in the said church. All these lands Gerard gave to the abbey and convent of St. Mary at Leicester, by whom they were conveyed to Warner de Engayne, on condition of his paying annually six quarters of salt at Bostom, and 12*d*. to the church of Benington[1]. The property of the abbey here was taxed in 1292 at £4.

In *Middlesex*, they had, in the parish of St. Sepulchre, in the suburbs of London, a considerable estate, as already noticed, p. 261; given them in 1312[2] by William de Langley, clerk; consisting of a capital mansion, with several houses, shops, and cellars, the Saracen's-head inn[3], and a moiety of the fountain[4]. This parcel of land, extending in length from the highway leading from Newgate to Holborn-bridge, was bounded on the East by St. Sepulchre's church[5], and a tenement which William de Langley at the same time devised for a chantry[6]; on the West by the tenements of Gerard the Barber and the prioress of Haliwell; on the South by the king's highway; and on the North it took in the site of Cock Lane and part of Smithfield. The abbot and convent had also a release of all claims to the above-mentioned property from Thomas master of the hospital of St. Giles without the bars of the Old Temple and the brethren and sisters of that hospital, reserving their right to an antient ground-rent; and another release, from Humfrey prior of the church of St. Mary in Southwark, and his convent, of 3*s*. annual rent, payable out of land in Smithfield. They bought ten feet of ground, from Richard archdeacon of Ely, to enlarge the kitchen of their house in Smithfield; where they possessed a plot of ground near Chick-lane, 55 feet in length *de pedibus Sancti Pauli*; 27 feet wide towards the East, and 27 in front towards the West; which they demised for 10*s*. a year to John Bukonite; and which was by him under-let to William the Carpenter of Smithfield; a rent of 8*s*. in Cock-lane, the gift of Peter of Southampton, alias de la Hull, and Agnes his wife, payable out of tenements which extended from his own gate to the residence of John Morrice; and a tenement on the North side of St. Sepulchre's church-yard, near Newgate, called the Reindeer, the gift of Hugo the Frenchman, a baker, and Dionisia his wife, with a release from sir

John de Woburn of 13*s*. annual rent for the same. This was first demised by the abbey to Christiana, daughter of Ralph the Smith, of Newgate, for a rent of 21*s*.; and after to the master and brethren of St. Bartholomew's for 20*s*. From Warinus of Naples, prior of the hospital of St. John of Jerusalem, they had a grant of so much of the land of that priory as was bought of Thomas Tornatus, for a rent of 2*s*. and a pound of incense; and other land, 24 feet wide, extending in length to the Horse-market, for a rent of 6*d*.

Of this estate, which was confirmed to them by a charter of king Edward I, the principal messuage, or manor-house, was leased to sir Thomas Littleton, one of the judges of the court of king's bench, as stated in p. 266, for an annual rent of 16*s*.

William Strette had a lease of the Saracen's-head, for £7. 13*s*. 4*d*.

Eleanor Bredon, a cottage and a chamber joining to the Saracen's-head, at a rent of 20*s*.

John Rutt, an adjoining tenement, for 26*s*. 8*d*.

Richard Burstal, another tenement, for 50*s*.

William Mynt, a messuage near the Pool[7] in Smithfield, for 53*s*. 4*d*. This messuage, with two cottages, the convent sold to William Mynt for 100 marks; and laid out the money in an advantageous purchase in Leicestershire. Total receipts, £16. 19*s*. 4*d*.

The outgoings were,

	s.	*d.*
To the master of St. Giles's Hospital a ground-rent for a tenement in Smithfield,	20	0
Another tenement near the Saracen's-head,	6	8
To the monks of Clerkenwell, from the Saracen's-head,	13	4
To the hospital of St. John of Jerusalem; from a tenement in Smithfield called Blackgate,	2	0
To the same, in lieu of a pound of incense,	0	8
To the same, from a tenement near Chicklane,	0	6
To St. Sepulchre's church, *pro quadam pendula*[8] *ultra cemeterium in hospitio de Sarsonheyd*,	2	0
Summa,	45	2

In a "Taxatio cleri infra dioc' London'[9]," the abbey of Leicester is thus rated for this property:

"In parochiâ Sancti Sepulchri,   XL.*s̃*.
Inde decima,   IIII*s̃*.
Medietas,   II*s̃*.

At Old Ford, in the parish of Stepney, they had the mill called Algodismilne, demised to Henry de Calabre for a rent of two marks to the abbey, and of 10*s*. to the lord of the manor; and afterwards let to John of Honilane, citizen of London, for 28*s*. a year.

In *Northamptonshire*, they had a yearly pension of 6*s*. 8*d*. from the rectory of Aynho[10].

They once possessed the advowson of Billing Magna, with a pension of 20 marks, the gift of William Barre; but this was legally recovered from them by Robert Wauton[11].

---

[1] Charyte's Rentale, fol. xxv. a. xxvi. a. b.   [2] Pat. 14 Edw. II. p. 2. m. 4. de tenementis in London.

[3] " Near to this church is a fair and large inn for receipt of travellers, and hath to sign the Saracen's-head." Strype's Stow, edit. 1720, book III. p. 245; and fee edit. 1598, p. 311.

[4] Situated at Holbourn-cross, where a conduit was first erected in 1498, and rebuilt in 1577 by William Lambe.

[5] " The fair parish church, called St. Sepulchre's, in the Baily, or by Chamberlain-gate, was newly re-edified about the reign of Henry VI. or Edward IV. in a fair churchyard, though not so large as of old time; for the same is letten out for buildings and a garden plot." Strype's Stow, ubi supra.

[6] No notice is taken, by the Historian of London, either of this chantry, or the property of the abbot and convent of Leicester, or the tenement of the prioress of Haliwell.

[7] " Smithfield Pond of old time in records was called Horse Pool, for that men watered horses there, and was a great water. In 1418 a new building was made in the West part of Smithfield, betwixt the said Pool, and the river of the Wells, or Turnmill Brook, in a place then called The Elms; for that there grew many elm trees; and this had been the place of execution for offenders. Since the which time, the building there hath been so increased, that now remaineth not one tree growing. This place was in use for executions in 1219, and, as it seems, long before; for a Clause Roll, 4 Hen. III. mentions *Furcæ factæ apud ulmellos com. Middlesex, ubi prius factæ fuerunt.*" Stow, 1598, p. 311; or edit. Strype, p. 238.

[8] *Pendulum* in a French deed in Du Cange is a part of a mill: " Concessi domui infirmorum Sancti Quintini molendinum de Rovereco, cum raëriâ & pendulo, perpetuò tenendum." Charta A. 1165. apud Hemeræum in Augustâ Viromand. Charpentier supposes it the same with *pencellum*, a *penstock*, or dam of a water-mill; and *raëria* is a *sluice*. Du Cange *in voc*. But, as the situation here assigned seems too distant from any *water*-course or stream, quere, if it be another term for *penticius*, a *penthouse*; which is properly supposed by Johnson to be a corruption of *pentice*, and is thus defined in his Dictionary; " a shed hanging out, a slope from the main wall;" a *lean-to*, as it is now called in Leicestershire, and many other parts of the kingdom.

[9] Harl. MSS. 60. fol. 161. b.   [10] Bridges, vol. I. p. 138.

[11] Charyte, fol. lxix. Bridges, in his account of Great Billing, vol. I. p. 405, does not notice their having had this advowson.

The

The rectory and advowfon of Brackley, with the chapels of Halfo and Sigrefham, were given by the founder, whofe defcendants were liberal benefactors[1]. The abbot had a penfion of half a mark.

In 1191, a compofition with the prior of Trentham, relative to this rectory, was confirmed by pope Celeftine; in 1220 the rectory was valued at 56 marks; and, about 1223, permiffion was given by Richard abbot of Leicefter to erect the chapel of St. John the Baptift within the precincts of the hofpital at this place, with the privileges of fepulture, &c.[2]

"The parfonage of St. Peter's was impropriate to the abbey of Leircefter; and there was a vicar endowed[3]." This endowment, which was made in 1225, confifted "in tertiâ parte decime garbarum de Brackele & de Halfo, & in medietate altaragiorum, cum manfo vicario affignato. Confiftit etiam in duabus partibus decime garbarum de octo virgatis terre in campo de Evenley; & in decimis duarum virgatarum in Parvâ Whitefeld, cum curiâ Thome de Ermenters, &c. in decimis feni & molendini[4]."

In 1272, the abbot of Leicefter had a grant of common of pafture here[5]; and in 1295 recovered the right of prefentation to the vicarage, againft John de Ferrars, Eleanor la Zouch, and Elizabeth countefs of Boughan. In 1302, he prefented Robert Caftelyen de Humberfton[6]; in 1313, was certified to hold a fourth part of a knight's fee in Brackley of Alan la Zouch[7]; and in 1329 claimed to have view of frankpledge, with other liberties in his lands here, and had his claim allowed[8].

The chapel of Brackley hofpital was rebuilt about 1360, at the expence of more than £34; and the abbey of Leicefter paid yearly £5. 4s. 4d. towards the augmentation of this vicarage[9].

At Brixworth[10], the abbey had lands in the feveral fields; the particulars of which, not noticed in Bridges, may be feen in a MS. in the Cotton library[11].

At Cley Cotys, or Coton, they had once the advowfon of the chapel, as a member of the church of Lilburn. This was alienated, in 1210, by a fine paffed between Thomas de Eftley, demandant, and William abbot of Leicefter, deforcient[12]; and in 1254, the chapel (deducting a penfion of 20s. to the abbot of Leicefter) was valued at 8 marks[13].

They had the tithes at Evenley, as a member of the church of Brackley, the gift of their founder; and demifed them in 1323 to William Marton[14], vicar of Brackley, for 13s. 4d. a year; and again, in 1348, to William Swan[15], another vicar. They were afterwards let to the farmer of the abbot's lands at Brackley, one of whom was Stephen Chamberleyn, for the fame fum[16].

The church of Eydon was appropriated to this abbey, in 1202, by Richard fon of Henry Wale; confirmed, in 1219, by a fine levied at Northampton[17]; again, in 1229, by another fine at Weftminfter between Richard Wale, demandant, and William abbot of Leicefter, deforcient[18]; and, in 1291, the abbot and convent prefented Richard Ryder, of Leicefter, clerk, to this rectory, having proved their right to the patronage againft Thomas lord Wale, who had prefented John de Martin[19].

They had the church of Farningho, of the gift of their founder; and the abbot's penfion from it was four marks[20]. The abbot and convent occur as patrons in 1219[21] (when the churches of Farningho and Sirefham were valued at £18. 1s. 8d.); and in 1290 prefented Aymo de Vienna; who had a fecond prefentation in 1291, by reafon that he had not obtained prieft's orders within the year[22]. The abbot and convent had free-warren granted them at Farningho, Sirefham, and other places, in 1300[23]; and in 1329[24] were cited (as they had been in 1229[25]), to fhew by what right they claimed from their tenants in Farningho and Sirefham, Brackley and Halfo, view of frankpledge, weifs, affife of bread and beer, &c. exemption from gelds, danegelds, and all other aids, either in wapentakes, hundreds, or fhires, from meadows, fcutages, and affizes, and all worldly fervices, with fac and foc, tol and theam, and infangenthef, together with an exemption from pannage, pontage, tolls, or ftallage, throughout all the cities and boroughs in the kingdom[26]. Their right was on this occafion fully eftablifhed; and the inhabitants of Farningho were enjoined to make a perambulation once at leaft in every fix years, to fee that the boundaries of the abbot's lands were maintained, for which they were to be allowed 12d. to buy drink (ad emend' poculenta), drinkings being always found abfolutely neceffary in all perambulations[27]. The total receipt of the abbey from Farningho was £12. 18s. 10d.[28]

At Halfo (now called Hawes, and generally reckoned a hamlet of Brackley, though originally the lordfhip of which Brackley itfelf was a member[29]), they had the chapel, with the tithes of garbs and hay, the gift of their founder. The church of Brackley was bound to provide a refident chaplain, and the hamlet of Halfo to repair the chapel; the abbot and convent having been ever exonerated from that expence. The abbot and convent, however, in 1398, at the efpecial requeft of fir John Lovell, after entering a folemn proteft of their right of exemption, agreed to repair the roof and windows of the chancel for that time only, fir John Lovell contributing thereto fix good oak-trees out of his woods at Bagworth, and 40s. in money[30].

At Hothorpe (a chapelry of Thedingworth in Leicefterfhire) they had the tithes of garbs and hay, as belonging to the mother-church. For the tithe of 20 acres of hay, they received 6s. 8d.[31]

The impropriate rectory and advowfon of the vicarage of Lilburn, with an annual rent from that lordfhip, originally given by Robert earl of Mellent to the church of St. Mary de Caftro, were transferred by him to the abbey[32]. One yard-land here was given by Richard l'Abbé, and three more by Geffrey de Dalby. In 1220, this church was valued at 10 marks; and the temporalities of the abbey here at 60[33].

Richard de Morvill, conftable to the king of Scotland, gave an annual rent of 10s. payable by the abbot and convent of Dryburgh in Scotland, in lieu of half a carucate of land, given by Alexander de Sancto Martino for the murder of the conftable's brother Malcolm de Morvill, who was buried in the cemetery of Leicefter abbey. Several difputes having arifen concerning the payment of this fum, the abbot and convent at length accepted an affignment of 5s. a year, to be paid by the abbot and convent of St. James at Northampton out of a penfion of two marks and a half a year, for the church of Bozeate; which the abbot and convent of Dryburgh affigned after-

---

[1] Leland, vol. VII. p. 12.

[2] Appendix, p. 61. See a view of Brackley church, and of the ruins of this chapel, in Bridges, vol. I. p. 150.

[3] Appendix, p. 11; and Charyte, fol. xxvi.   [4] Rot. Hugonis Wells, annis 15 & 20.

[5] Plac. 1 Edw. I. m. 17. de communi pafturâ Brackele.

[6] Reg. Sutton, ann. 3. Their being patrons on this occafion is not noticed by Bridges.

[7] Bridges, vol. I. p. 143.   [8] See under Farningho.   [9] Appendix, p. 68.   [10] Charyte, fol. xxix.

[11] Galba E. III. fol. 125.   [12] Fin. Northampton. 12 Johan de ecclefiâ de Cotes.

[13] Charyte, fol. xxxviii; Bridges, vol. I. p. 549.   [14] This vicar is omitted by Bridges.   [15] Bridges calls him Sweyn.

[16] Charyte, fol. lvii. Bridges, vol. I. p. 165.   [17] Fin. Northampton. de advoc. ecclefie de Eyndon.

[18] Appendix, p. 61; Charyte, fol. lv.   [19] Reg. Sutton. See Appendix, p. 61; and Bridges, vol. I. p. 123.

[20] Charyte, fol. lviii; Bridges, vol. I. p. 170.   [21] Reg. Sutton.   [22] Ibid.   [23] Clauf. 29 Edw. I. N° 27.

[24] Plac. de quo warranto in com. Northampt. 3 Edw. III. Rot. 13. de privilegiis in Farningho, Sirefham, &c.

[25] See before, p. 261.   [26] Rot. Quo warranto apud Northampton, coram Juftic. Itinerant. 3 Edw. III.

[27] See Addenda to Lambeth Hiftory, p. 364.—Drinke for the children, 6d.—1586, For making honeft men drinke when we went to Vicar's Oke in perambulation, 2s. 6d.

[28] Charyte, fol. lviii. b. A terrier of their lands here fills ten pages in a Cotton MS. Galba E. III. fol. 101. & feqq.

[29] Bridges, vol. I. p. 153.   [30] Appendix, p. 74; Charyte, fol. lix. b.

[31] Charyte, fol. cxiv. This is not noticed by Bridges. See more of this chapelry under Thedingworth.

[32] Charyte, fol. cv; Bridges, vol. I. p. 573.   [33] A terrier of their lands here may be feen in Galba E. III. p. 150.

wards to the prior and convent of St. Andrew[1] at Northampton, on condition of their paying 5s. a year to the abbey of Leicester[2].

At Siresham, they had the church, the gift of Thomas Sorell, lord of the manor in the reign of king Henry II; and, in 1254, the rectory was valued at 15 marks; and the abbot's pension was half a mark[3]. At Siresham, they had also lands called Westerles, or Westcotes; which originally were given by Robert Boffu, their founder, to the church of Lincoln, in exchange for Knighton and the Suburbs of Leicester; but the bishop and chapter, in after-times, complaining of this disposition, Robert Fitz Parnell, his grandfon, took them back, and bestowed them on the abbey; giving to the chapter of Lincoln, with consent of the monks, certain lands in Asfordby and Segrave, which belonged to the convent. In 1315, the abbots of Leicester and Bitulsden, with John de Chetwode, were certified to be lords of Siresham and Westcote[4].

At Standeford, Robert de Standeford gave a virgate of land to the almoner of Leicester abbey[5].

At Welton, they had a rent of 43s. arising from a water-mill in the possession of John Hynckley[6]; which in 1559 was sold by the crown to Mr. Thompson for twenty years purchase[7].

In 1340, the spiritualities of the abbey of Leicester in the archdeaconry of Northampton were thus taxed:
The church of Brackley 36 marks.
The church of Lilburn 10 marks.
A pension at Siresham, 6s. 8d.
———————— Farningho, 4 marks.
———————— Cley Coton, 20s.
In all, 52 marks; which paid 34s. 6d. for tenths. Their temporalities in that archdeaconry were taxed,
At Farningo and Siresham, £18. 20d.
At Lilburne, 60s.
At Astwell and Empingham in Rutland, 8s.
In all, £21. 9s. 8d.; taxed at 21s. 6d.[8]

In *Nottinghamshire*, Hugo de Dyva and Helwysia his wife gave to this abbey two parts of the tithes of the garbs of her demesne lands at Gotham, which was confirmed by Robert earl of Leicester[9].

In *Rutland*, they had at Ashwell (*Essewell juxta Ocham*) an annual rent of 3s. the gift of Henry Touchet, lord of that manor[10].

At Empingham, four bovates, the gift of Richard l'Abbé; four others, the gift of Robert Fitz Philip; and several small rents[11].

From the prior and convent of Shene in *Surrey*, they had a lease of tithes in various parts of Leicestershire, at an annual rent of £12.[12] From this priory they had also an annual acknowledgement of a rose.

In *Warwickshire*, they had the chapel of Ansty, with that of Shelton, both hamlets of Bulkington, the gift of Roger de Watervile; for which the prior of Coventry paid them by composition £10. a year[13].

At Bernangull, or Bernacle, another hamlet of Bulkington, they had the tithes and certain lands, given by Roger de Watervile, and a virgate by Alice Temple, *cum corpore suo*. Four yard-lands here, of the fee of Ernald de Bois, were given antiently to the abbey

by Henry the son of Fulco de Merston, who afterwards became a canon of their house; and the gift was confirmed by Ernald de Bois, and by king Henry II. Thomas earl of Lancaster confirmed to them a carucate in 1284. The abbot had a court-leet there for his own tenants, with other privileges, which he claimed to have had time out of mind. They granted to Guy, a knight, lord thereof, an oratory in his own house, provided the priest should swear, in the presence of the vicar of Bulkington, that it might be no damage to the mother-church[14].

At Berwode, a hamlet of Curdworth, Hugh de Ardena gave the manor and a hermitage; with one messuage, two carucates, one mill, 60 acres of meadow, 60 acres of pasture, 300 acres of wood, and 10s. rent in Curdworth; which were confirmed by William and Waleran earls of Warwick, of whose fee they were held. The abbot and convent had the patronage of the rectory, and the tithes and various parcels of land, &c. from John de Ardena and others of that family, on condition of finding two canons to celebrate divine service in the chapel of Berwode-hall; but John Ardena[15], being a powerful man and a knight, impleaded the abbot of Leicester in 1339 for the manor of Berwode, with the advowson of the church of Curdworth, being given to that house by his ancestors many years before. By the prudence of abbot Clowne, this cause was terminated in favour of the monastery of Leicester. An early terrier of the manor of Berwode will be found in our Appendix[16].

The lands which Richard de Camvile had in the manor of Bigging, within the lordship of Newton, being granted to Henry de Rokeby from Richard de Camvile, were by the canons of Leicester obtained, temp. Henry II. in consideration of the chapel of Rugby, given by them to him and his heirs, which chapel was a member of Clifton; but the mill they had from Robert the son of Fulco de Holme[17].

At Bramcote[18], another hamlet of Bulkington, the tithes and the mill, with eight yard-lands, the gift of Geffrey l'Abbé, Robert de Watervill, &c. The abbot and convent, as in other their lands in Warwickshire, claimed a court-leet in 1284, as granted by the king's progenitors, for which they then produced their charters. What they then had amounted to the third part of a knight's fee; for, in 1346, it was certified, that so much they held of the earl of Lancaster, who then had the honour of Leicester. They had here also the homage and relief of their free tenants, two instances of which are recorded in 1342 and 1470; with weyfs and strays, hariots, *auxilia, & merchetas*[19].

At Bromwych, they had certain lands, held under them by Thomas de Bromwych; " sicut patet in placito quod est in veteri registro cum nigro cooperterio." This Thomas de Bromwych gave them certain common of pasture in Berwode[20].

Roger de Watervile gave the rectory and advowson of Bulkington, with two yard-lands belonging to it, together with its chapels of Bernangul, Weston, Ryton, Merston, Shelton, Ansty, and Bramcote; all which were confirmed by Ernald de Bois I, and three suc-

[1] Of this priory, see our Introductory Volume, p. cxlii.
[2] Charyte, fol. cxiii; Cotton MSS. Vitellius, F. XVII. fol. 16. b; and Bridges, MS. vol. I. p. 161.
[3] Charyte, fol. cxxix; Bridges, vol. I. p. 194. [4] Appendix, p. 61; Bridges, vol. I. p. 169, 170.
[5] Charyte, fol. cxxxi; not noticed by Bridges. [6] Charyte, fol. cxlvi. [7] Harl. MSS. 608. p. 8. See Bridges, vol. I. p. 96.
[8] Bridges, MS. ex Offic. Primit. [9] Charyte, fol. lix; Thoroton, p. 18. [10] Charyte, fol. lvii; not noticed by Wright.
[11] Charyte, fol. lvi; not noticed by Wright. [12] See before, p.
[13] Charyte's Rentale, fol. cxxviii; Dugdale's Warwickshire, vol. I. pp. 65. 123. [14] Appendix, p. 79; Dugdale, vol. I. p. 63.
[15] Edward Arden, a gentleman, though not inferior to the rest of his ancestors in those virtues wherewith they were adorned, had the hard hap to come to an untimely death, 27 Elizabeth; the charge laid against him being no less than high treason against the queen, as privy to some foul intentions that Mr. Somerton, his son in law, a Roman Catholic, had towards her person. For which he was prosecuted with so great rigour and violence by the earl of Leicester's means, whom he had irritated in some particulars (as I have credibly heard), partly in disdaining to wear his livery, which many in the county of Warwick of his rank thought no small honour to them in those days; but chiefly for galling of him by certain hard expressions about his private accesses to the countess of Essex before she was his wife; that, through the testimony of one Hall, a priest, he was found guilty of the fact, and lost his life in Smithfield. " Tristis his exitus nobilis viri," says Camden, " qui sacerdotiis insidiis illectis & ejusmodi testimonio perculsus, Leicestrii invidiæ vulgò vertebatur. Certum enim est illum Leicestrii invidiam nec immeritò incunisse, cui in omnibus quibus poterat se temerè objecerat, quasi adultero obtrectaverat, & ut homini novo detraxerat." Upon whose attainder, his lands were given to Edward Darcy, esq. and his heirs; but recovered all by Robert his son, except Curdworth and Minworth. Dugdale, vol. II. p. 931.
[16] Appendix, p. 79; Dugdale, vol. II. pp. 925, 926, 927. 932. And see before, p. 256.
[17] Cotton MS. Vitellius F. XVII; Dugdale, vol. I. p. 13.
[18] From a copy of a terrier of lands in the tenure of William Lucas and Richard Orchard, in Cotton MSS. Galba E. III. p. 91.
[19] Appendix, p. 80; Dugdale, vol. I. p. 62. [20] Charyte, fol. xxx; Dugdale, vol. II. p. 886.

ceeding

ceeding Ernalds[1]. The church was valued in 1220 at 26 marks; and, at the endowment of the vicarage, a penfion of 26s. 8d. was referved. William Orchard, one of their tenants here, paid a yearly rent of a pair of gloves[2].

The rectory and advowfon of Clifton, and its chapels of Brownfover, Rokeby, and Newton, the gift of the firft Ernald de Bofco, confirmed by fucceeding Ernalds; of whom the fourth gave permiffion to the tenants of the abbey to have common of pafture with their own tenants. They had alfo the meadow called Flexdames, given by Thomas Truan, Robert de la Beauvifme, and T. de Landa[3]; and a bovate of land, *cum corpore fuo,* by Robert fon of Robert le Sweyn. The church of Clifton, dedicated to the Affumption of our Lady, was antiently a prebend of St. Mary de Caftro at Leicefter; but, being afterwards granted to the abbey, was appropriated by Geffrey Mufchamp, bifhop of Coventry and Lichfield[4]. In 1220 this church was valued at 25 marks.

The church of St. Nicholas at Curdworth, with the hermitage and divers chapels, the gift of Hugo de Arden, valued in 1220 at 7 marks and a half; and divers lands there, the gift of Thomas de Ardena[5]. Within this lordfhip the abbot of Leicefter, in 1284, claimed a court-leet, &c.; and, to juftify this challenge, exhibited the charters of Henry II. and Richard I. whereby the canons of that houfe had fundry general privileges granted to them throughout all their poffeffions; whereupon the jury finding they had enjoyed a court-leet, with affife of bread and beer, time out of mind, thofe liberties were allowed; and, forafmuch as it appeared that in the time of abbot Henry a gallows had been fet up, and a thief there taken adjudged to death, and hanged by his bailiffs, the fame privilege was likewife allowed. The endowment of this vicarage may be feen in our Appendix[6].

At Dunton, a hamlet of Curdworth, they had certain tithes, received by the vicar; and fome land leafed to William Bracebridge[7].

At Holme, in the parifh of Newton (which in the Conqueror's time had been a village, but was afterwards depopulated) this abbey had the tithes, the gift of the firft Ernald de Bofco; and half a virgate of land, with a toft and croft, &c. the gift of Robert the fon of Fulco de Holm, and Humfrey de Newton. The rent was 13s. 4d.; and had originally been 20s. The name of this place was taken from its fituation, lying in a nook between the river Avon and a fmall brook which comes from Shawell in Leicefterfhire. It was afterwards called New Bigging[8].

At Ilmefdon [Elmedon], they had the church, with lands, tithes, &c. the gift of their founder[9].

At Merfton Jabet, a chapelry of Bernangul, they had tithes, and four virgates of land, the gift of Henry, furnamed Jabet, fon to Fulco de Merfton, which had been fettled as a dower on Alice his wife. For this gift, he was admitted a canon of the houfe, and his wife a fifter[10].

At Minworth, a hamlet of Curdworth, they had the homage and fervice of Simon fon of Nicholas, an annual acknowledgement of a rofe from the heir of John Philip, and certain lands the gift of William de Ardena[11].

At Newhay, a member of Stockingford, Henry de Lilburn and his heirs paid 10s. a year, for 30 acres of arable land, to Stephen de Segrave; who granted to this abbey the homage and fervice of Henry de Lilburn and his heirs, and the income arifing from the

wood at Newhay, with its appurtenances. This wood the prior of the neighbouring convent of Erdbury rented from the abbey of Leicefter for 13s. 4d. a year[12].

At Newton, a chapelry of Clifton, they had the tithes of garbs and hay, the gift of their founder; a toft, 120 feet long, given by Bertram de Newton, for an annual acknowledgement of 4d.; which rent was afterwards releafed by his daughter and heir. They had the barn and croft alfo of the demefne; with the tithes of the hades & leys; and, inftead of the tithe of hay there, a meadow called Wafford, given to them by the parifhioners, producing eight cart-loads, worth on an average 8d. a year; and the tithes of the demefne mill, called Cuttulmylne, worth 3s. 4d. a year. This was recovered to the abbey by a fentence in the Court of Arches, July 31, 1452[13].

The lordfhip of Nuneaton, with all its dependencies, except what was poffeffed by the abbot and convent of Leicefter in the hamlet of Stockingford, and by the monaftery *de Cafâ Dei* in Eaton and Atleberg, was given by earl Robert Boffu, and confirmed by his fon Robert Blanchmaines[14] to the nuns of that place; who were to pay to the abbey of Leicefter a rent of 30 *fterlingæ* and 3000 eels yearly[15]. Thefe nuns poffeffed in Leicefterfhire two carucates of land at Waltham in the Wolds, with pafture there for 300 fheep, the gift of Ifabel the founder's daughter, and of Simon earl of Northampton her fon; two virgates of land in Swinford, given by Richard Malore; with 2s. rent from a houfe in Leicefter, held by Guy Broadleas.

Among the gifts of *Ernald de Bofco,* they had the advowfon of the chapel of Rugby, which was a member of the church of Clifton; and concerning which there was a fuit, in the king's court, in the year 1200, between Paul abbot of Leicefter and Henry de Rokeby[16], which terminated in a renunciation of right on the part of the faid Henry; and an admiffion from the abbot that Henry and his heirs fhould have liberty for their homage and fervice, after the death of Simon the dean, to nominate a clerk; whom the abbot and convent, if he were fit, would prefent to the church, on his paying them an annual penfion of 20 fhillings, the faid Henry and his heirs being fureties for the payment; and the clerk fo prefented undertaking *percipere fingulis annis crifma de matrice ecelefia*[17]. A final agreement was after this made, between William abbot of Leicefter and Henry de Rokeby; who was to nominate in future to the abbot and his fucceffors a fit and proper clerk, to be by them prefented to the bifhop for induction; which clerk fhould be bound to pay to the abbey their accuftomed penfion of 20 fhillings. The matter of this penfion was afterwards agitated in the confiftorial court of the bifhop of Lichfield about 1350, between abbot Clowne and Peter de Bilney the then rector; and decided in favour of the abbey. Yet it was again contefted in 1465 by another rector, John Stone; and again recovered by abbot Pomerey[18].

At Ryton, a chapelry of Bernangul, this abbey had the tithes, and a rent of 46s. 8d. given by Roger de Watervill[19].

At Shelton, they had the chapel, with that of Anfty, as parcel of the church of Bulkington; for which the prior of Coventry, by compofition, paid 10s. yearly to the canons of Leicefter; a difpute concerning which was amicably fettled, as will be fhewn under Scraptoft. They had here alfo a rent of two pounds of pepper[20].

Ofbert de Lemington granted an oxgang of land

---

[1] Appendix, p. 80; Dugdale, vol. I. p. 57, 58.
[2] Appendix, p. 69.
[3] Appendix, p. 80; Dugdale, vol. I p. 8, 9. A terrier of their lands here fills five pages. Galba E. III p. 94, &c.
[4] Cotton MSS. Vitellius F. XVII; and Dugdale, ubi fupra, ex vetufto exemplari penes decan. & capit. Lichfield.
[5] Plac. quo warranto in com. Warwic. 13 Edw. I. Rot. 3. & 4. de privilegiis tenentium de Curdworth.
[6] Appendix, p. 80; Dugdale, vol. II. p. 924.
[7] Appendix, p. 80; Dugdale, vol. II. p. 932.
[8] Appendix, p. 80; Dugdale, vol. I. p. 13. See a terrier of their lands here, Cotton MSS. Galba E. III. fol. 143.
[9] Charyte, fol. lxvii; not noticed by Dugdale.
[10] Appendix, p. 81; Dugdale, vol. I. p. 63.
[11] Appendix, p. 81; Dugdale, vol. II. p. 932.
[12] Appendix, p. 81; Dugdale, vol. II. p. 1070.
[13] Appendix, p. 81; Dugdale, vol. I. p. 12.
[14] See this charter, Appendix, p. 15; and fee vol. II. p. 580.
[15] Appendix, p. 81; Dugdale, vol. II. p. 106. b.
[16] Plac. 2 Johan. Mich. Rot. 29. dorf. de advoc. capellæ de Rokeby.
[17] The confecrated oil or unguent ufed at baptifm. Regularly the parochial clergy were to have it from the cathedral church. But it fhould feem the ftipulation here was, that the clerk prefented to the chapel of Rugby fhould have the crifm from the mother-church of Clifton, of which it is exprefsly faid to be a member.
[18] Appendix, p. 82; Dugdale, vol. I. pp. 23, 24.
[19] Appendix, p. 82; Dugdale, vol. I. p. 62.
[20] See under the hiftory of that parifh; and Appendix, p. 82.

lying within the precincts of Shuckborough Superior. This was confirmed by king Henry II; and in a short time was given by them to Thomas the son of Oliver de Shuckborough, for 9s. rent a year; afterwards reduced to 2s. [1]

At Sow, they had one croft, for which John Naseby paid 8d. rent. They had frankpledge also and suit of court, as was determined by an inquisition taken by the king's command. The altarage of the chapels of Sow and Wyken, both dependent on the rectory of St. Michael in Coventry, was valued at £4; and the tithes of Sow and Woodend at £10. 13s. 4d. " The royalty of Sow was bequeathed, by will of Lucy countess of Bedford, to Mr. George Purefoy, of Belgrave, co. Leicester, who enjoyed it in 1640 [2]."

The whole of Stockyngford, a member of Nuneaton, the gift of William de Novo Mercato, with the assent of Robert earl of Leicester, who had exchanged this place for Whitwick. They had the chapel also, the gift of Geffrey de Turvile; and other lands there, the gift of Geffrey the Eremite; but they gave most of it to the nuns of Eaton. This manor the abbot and convent permitted William Boteler, William Babyngton, Thomas Warner, and John Catby, to assign over to the prior of Erdbury, reserving to the abbey of Leicester their accustomed fealty, and a security for the payment of 63s. 4d. as a relief on every vacancy of the priory [3].

At Stretton, a virgate of land was held under this abbey by Robert Torr [4].

At Weston in Arden, they had the tithes " garbarum, feni, & bosci, & decimas molendini [5]," as a chapelry belonging to Bulkington.

Threescore years and more before the Conquest, Ulfric Spot, a potent man in those days, and founder of Burton abbey, co. Stafford, gave Wibtoft (a chapelry of Cleybrook in Leicestershire) to one Athelne by will for life, and afterwards to the said monastery; but in the Conqueror's time it was possessed by the earl of Mellent [6]. Ralph de Arraby, cum corpore suo, gave to this abbey one third part of the hamlet, which produced a rent of 4l. 17s. (originally £6. 17s.) [7]. This grant was confirmed by Ernald de Bois; and consisted of 7 messuages, 10 crofts, 5 yard-lands and a half, and a mill; wherein the abbot claimed a court-leet and the privileges he had in Bulkington, and was allowed them.

A question arose between the abbot of Leicester and the rector of Sutton, concerning the tithes of nine virgates of land at Wigginhull juxta Crudworth; six of which, being in the fee of the earl of Warwick, belonged to the church of Sutton; and the other three, being of the fee of Thomas de Ardena, to the church of Crudworth. This dispute was settled before judges delegated by apostolical authority; who decreed that two parts of the tithe should be paid to Sutton, and one third to Crudworth; and that such persons as dwelt within the six virgates of the earl of Warwick's fee should visit the mother-church of Sutton on the day of the Assumption of the Virgin, and at Easter, when they were to communicate there, and also make the proper confessions during Lent, receive extreme unction from the chaplain of Sutton, bury their dead there, and pay all small tithes to that church; but, as they were at a great distance from the mother-church, all other offerings were to be given to the chaplain officiating at Crudworth, who was to minister to them in spiritual cases as need should require. The chaplain of Sutton was to pay 3d. to the church of Crudworth, at Easter, to buy frankincense; and the inhabitants of the three virgates in the fee of Thomas de Ardena were to be answerable for all oblations whatever to the mother-church of Crudworth [8].

At Wover (Brounsover) they had the chapel, as a member of Clifton, worth £8. a year, (originally £15.) the gift of the first Ernald de Bosco [9].

In *Wiltshire*, they had at Everley four *libratæ terræ*, being one ninth of the whole township, the gift of Amicia, wife to their founder, confirmed by her husband and her son, for the sustentation of the poor brethren in the Infirmary; or, as it is in another place expressed, *ad pitanciam conventûs*. These lands in 1220 were valued at four marks; and paid 5s. towards a subsidy of a tenth; but, in the taxation of 1292 it is stated, " Modo abbas exoneratur de predict' vs. per placitum;" and the lands were afterwards surrendered by the abbot to Henry duke of Lancaster, in exchange for Hungarton and Humberston churches [10].

If this statement of the property of the abbey should not be considered sufficient, the reader may consult a magnificent volume in the British Museum, containing, among other articles, a Chronicle of the kings of England from 1178 to the death of Richard II; a Register of the benefactors to Christ Church, Canterbury, and a Chronicle from the death of Canute to 1286; with several other articles relative to the church of Canterbury and to Becket. That part of the volume which relates to Leicester abbey is intituled, " Transcriptio, tempore regis Henrici Septimi, diversarum rerum tangentium monasterium de Pratis juxta Leicester. Ex scriptis ejusdem ecclesiæ, domini Latimer, Roberti Brudnell, Johannis Turvile, Willielmi Cottorr, Thome Esulryk, & aliorum [11]." It begins at p. 81; fills 90 leaves; and consists chiefly of antient terriers of several (but not all) of their possessions, some in Latin, others in English, too long to be copied here; but for the sake of those who may wish to consult this MS. we give the names of the places to be found in it:

Barkby,	fol. 82	Kilby,	fol. 153
Barrow,	87	Kyrkebye juxta Melton,	147
Bagworth,	119	Lilburn,	150
Barkby,	119. b.	Lockington,	107
Belgrave,	120	Moseley,	151
Billesdon,	88. 121	Noseley,	154
Boresworth,	124	Oadby,	157
Blaby,	122	Octhorpe,	155
Bramcote,	91	Porta Occidentalis [12],	107
Brickelsworth,	125	Pynslade [13],	111
Brontingsthorpe,	125	Queniborough,	95
Burstall,	127	Querndon,	159
Burton Overy,	129	Reresby,	161
Cosby,	97	Scharnbroke,	112
Cossington,	138	Shepished,	112
Chesham,	131	Shakerston,	162
Clifton,	94	Shucburgh,	162
Croxton,	140	Skeffington,	163
Eaton,	99	Stanton,	165
Farningho,	101	Stoke,	167
Godeby,	142	Stretton,	168
Gaddesby,	142	Thornton,	113
Glenfelde,	135	Thorpe Ernald,	114
Holme,	143	Thorp Norboro,	168
Horspole,	188	Thurmaston,	118
Houghton,	144	Walton,	169
Humberston,	144	Whatton,	169 b.
Kerbye,	146	Wover,	170

King Henry VIII, Feb. 14, 1544, granted to *Richard, Roger,* and *Robert Taverner,* several of the lands and tenements in Leicester, if not all, belonging to the abbey; as appears by an instrument, dated March 27, 1545, by which Richard, Roger, and Robert Taverner, granted to *John Dicks,* gentleman, one tenement in the Ward-gate, one tenement in the Abbey-gate in the parish of St. Leonard, which had been part of the possessions of the abbey, and which

---

[1] Charyte, fol. ccxviii; Dugdale, vol. I. p. 308.   [2] Charyte, fol. cxxx; Dugdale, vol. I. p. 212.
[3] Charyte, fol. cxxxi; Dugdale, vol. II. p. 1070.   [4] Charyte, p. v. a; not noticed by Dugdale.
[5] Charyte, fol. cxlvi; Dugdale, vol. I p. 61.   [6] Burton Register, in the possession of the earl of Uxbridge.
[7] Charyte, fol. cxlvii; and Cotton MSS. Vitellius F. XVII. See more of this hamlet under the parish of Cleybrook.
[8] Appendix, p. 82; Dugdale, vol. II. p. 920.   [9] Charyte, fol. cxlix; Dugdale, vol. II. p. 11.
[10] Appendix, p. 55; Charyte, fol. lvii.   [11] Cotton MSS. Galba E. III. p. 81.
[12] A terrier of lands in the West Gate, including Bruntingthorpe (which was taken in the year 1381) fills 9 pages in the above-mentioned MS. p. 107. Another terrier of Bruntingthorpe in 1447 occurs in p. 125.
[13] *Bulkyngton* occurs p. 93. b; and *Pynslade* in p. 111; but the terrier of neither of those places was entered.

they

they held of the king in free burgage and common focage, by fealty only, and not *in capite* [1].

By another deed, 25 Aug. 1545, John Dycks, of Leicefter, yeoman, granted to *Thomas Creffy*, gent. one of the burgeffes of Leicefter, an orchard in St. Peter's parifh, and a tenement in Abbey-gate, parcel of the poffeffions of the late abbey of St. Mary de Pratis, which he had by grant of Richard Taverner, efq. Roger and Robert Taverner, gentlemen, in as full manner as was granted them by king Henry VIII, &c. [2]

In the Bodleian library is a fmall printed poem [3], with the following title : " Heere beginneth a mery Jeft of Dane Hew, Munk of Leiceftre, and how he was foure times flain and once hanged;" beginning,

" In olde time there was in Lecefter town
An abbay of munks of great renown,
As ye fhall now after heer ;
But amongft them all was one there
That pafs'd all his brethren I wis,
His name was Dane Hew, fo have I blis."

In 1547, Thomas Day [4], clerk, a native of Leicefter, who had been fome time a canon of this abbey, and alfo a prebendary of St. Stephen's in Weftminfter (and who, it is believed, in 1554 obtained the vicarage of Stepney), contributed £20. towards the fum of £80 ; which the corporation of Leicefter gave that year to Thomas Danet, of Brumkinthorpe, efq. for his office of bailiff to the king in the liberties of Leicefter, of which office Mr. Danet had a patent for life [5].

It has generally been ftated that king Henry VIII. beftowed fome part of the poffeffions of this abbey on Mr. *Cavendifh* ; " who, in the reign of queen Mary, wrote the Life and Death of Cardinal Wolfey, to whom he had been gentleman ufher ; and, having been admitted to more intimacy with his lord, and let more into fecrets, than any other fervant, would not defert him in his fall, but honourably waited on his old mafter, when he had no office and no falary to beftow upon him. The king himfelf had heard of the abilities and fidelity of this gentleman ; and therefore fent him word in the cardinal's laft ficknefs, by one of his privy chamber, ' how the king's majefty bore unto him his principal favour, for the love and diligent fervice that he had performed to his lord ; and for which it was the king's pleafure that he fhould be about him as chief, in whom his highnefs would put a great confidence and truft.' To give a more lafting teftimony of his gratitude to the cardinal, he drew up a fair account of his life and death, of which the oldeft copy is in the hands of the noble family of Pierpoint [6], into which the author's daughter was married ; for, without exprefs authority, we may gather from circumftances, that this very writer was the fame perfon with the immediate founder of the prefent noble family, *William Cavendifh*, of Chatfworth, co. Derby, efq. who, being a man of learning and bufinefs, was found out and employed by king Henry VIII ; and, in the 31ft of his reign, was made one of the auditors of the court of augmentation, and difcharged the truft with fuch fidelity and expedition, that the king promoted him, anno regni 27, not only to be treafurer of his chamber, but to be one of his privy council. He bore the fame relation to king

Edward VI. and queen Mary ; receiving the honour of knighthood, and a large acceffion of eftate, by grant of lands belonging to feveral diffolved priories and abbeys, in exchange for his manors of Northal in Hertfordfhire, and Northawbery in Lincolnfhire, &c." [7]

In 1551, the fite of Leicefter abbey was purchafed by *William* lord *Parr*, marquis of *Northampton*; and alienated about 1562 to *Henry Haftings* third earl of *Huntingdon*, who built a fair houfe on it out of the old materials, and fold it to fir *Edward Haftings*, knt.

In 1571, we find a grant to fir *Chriftopher Hatton*, knight, of the fite of the monaftery of St. Mary de Pratis at Leicefter, and of the water-mill adjoining, with the curtilages, buildings, and certain lands, called the Barn-yard, Afhe Clofe, Sterpe Orchard, Overbiggin, Nether-biggin, Read's Clofe, Pynder's Clofe, Whitley Typpet, Merewell Clofe, Calverhaye, Childe Clofe, 103 acres of meadow adjoining in the Northe Meadowe, Afhe Clofe Meadow, Leicefter Meadow, and Halmore Meadow ; 56 acres in the Hermitage Field and Peafe Field ; the meadow called Leicefter Meadow; the wood called Stocking Wood, and Doveland Coppice ; the park called Leicefter Park, otherwife the Little Park of Leicefter, lately belonging to the abbey, then to William marquis of Northampton, and afterwards to fir Edward Haftings ; which park William marquis of Winchefter, fir Walter Myldmay, knight, and fir Edward Haftings, had affigned over to the queen *(nobis barganizaverunt)* by deed, dated Dec. 19, 1571. Tefte 11° Februar. anno regni 14°." [8] This feems to have been an affignment preparatory to a new grant to *Henry* earl of *Huntingdon* ; from whom it was re-purchafed, in 1580, by fir *Edward Haftings*, as appears by the following record :

" Whereas the abbey of Leicefter, in the county of Leicefter, is feized into her majefty's hands for the debt of Henry late earl of Huntingdon, at twenty pounds *per annum*, and the fame charged in the accompt of William Skypwith, efq. now fheriff of the faid county ; and whereas this Court was informed, in Trinity Term laft paft, by fir Edward Haftings, knt. tenant of the faid Abbey, that he purchafed the faid Abbey of the faid late earl in the 22d year of her majefty's reign ; and that all the debts of the faid earl due to her majefty before the time of his purchafe were anfwered ; and prayed that procefs might be ftayed, and offered to enter into bond in this Court to pay the faid feizure, or elfe procure his difcharge before the end of this term; which this Court thought reafonable ; and the faid Edward Haftings entered into bond accordingly. Now, forafmuch as this Court is farther informed by Mr. Morgan, being of counfel with the faid fir Edward Haftings, that the faid fir Edward, by reafon of extreme ficknefs, wherewith he hath been vifited almoft ever fince (and at this time is in great peril of death), could not proceed in pleading his difcharge, and humbly craved longer time for the fame, and that no advantage fhould be taken by reafon of his faid bond : It is ordered by this Court, the 20th day of November, this term, that the faid fir Edward Haftings fhall have day given until the next term, to procure his difcharge of the faid feizure ; and his faid bond to remain as it now doth, and no procefs to be made thereupon [9]."

---

[1] Carte, MS. ex chartis quibufdam penes J. Haflock.   [2] Ibid.

[3] " Imprinted at London, at the long fhop adjoining unto Saint Mildred's Church in the Pultrie, by John Alde, 1596;" Art. 4° C. 39. Selden. See Herbert's Ames, p. 892.

[4] According to Le Neve, Fafti, p. 62, Thomas Day, LL. B. was collated to the precentorfhip of Chichefter in 1547 ; and, at p. 234, it is mentioned that Thomas Day was the firft canon appointed to the third ftall in Chrift Church, Oxford, in 1547. The faid Thomas Day had been inftalled in the fecond prebend of Ofney college. He was buried in Chrift Church, Feb. 22, 1567. Browne Willis's Survey, vol. II. p. 451.

[5] Carte, MS. from the records of the borough of Leicefter.

[6] Two other copies of this MS. in the Britifh Mufeum have been already noticed, p. 271 ; materially differing from the printed work, which firft appeared under the title of " The Negotiations of Thomas Wolfey, the great Cardinall of England ; containing his Life and Death ; viz. 1. The Original of his Promotion ; 2. The Continuance in his Magnificence ; 3. His Fall, Death, and Buriall. Compofeed by one of his owne Servants, being his Gentleman Ufher, 1641," 4to ; and afterwards under the following variations of title : 1. " The Life and Death of Thomas Wolfey, Cardinall ; once Archbifhop of York, and Lord Chancel'our of England, 1667," 8vo.—2. " The Memoirs of that great Favourite Cardinal Wolfey, with Remarks on his Rife and Fall, &c. 1706," 8vo.—3. " Sir William Cavendifh's Memoirs of the Life of Cardinal Wolfey, Legate of the Pope, Archbifhop of York, Bifhop of Winchefter, Lord High Chancellor of England, and principal Minifter of State in the Reign of King Henry the Eighth, 1708," 8vo.—In Gutch's " Collectanea Curiofa," vol. I. p. 283, is " An Account of Plate, Gold and Silver, made for Cardinal Wolfey, from the Ninth Year of Henry VIII. unto the Nineteenth Year; wherein is fet forth what he gave to the Abbey of St. Alban's, and to St. Fridefwide's College at Oxford ;" and in p. 334, " A farther Account of Plate, Gold and Silver, made for Cardinal Wolfey, from the Twentieth Year of Henry VIII. unto the Twenty-firft Year ; wherein is fet forth what he gave to the College of Ipfwich."

[7] Kennet's Memoirs of the Family of Cavendifh.

[8] Originalia temp. Eliz. pars 2. Rot. 106. & 108.   [9] From the Original in the Exchequer, 20 November, 21 Eliz.

In

In 1606, *Charles Blount* lord *Mountjoy*, who in 1603 had been created earl of *Devonshire*, died without lawful issue, possessed of some property here[1].

The site of Leicester abbey was in 1622 the inheritance of *William Cavendish*, the second earl of *Devonshire* of that name. This noble earl was beloved and admired in parliament, and a great speaker in both houses. Mr. Hobbes, in his Epistle Dedicatory of his History of Thucydides to his son, gives this shining character of him; " By the experience of many years I had the honour to serve him, I know this, there was not any who more really, and less for glory's sake, favoured those that studied the liberal arts liberally, than my Lord your father did; nor in whose house a man should less need the University than in his. For his own study, it was bestowed, for the most part, in that kind of learning which best deserved the pains and hours of great persons, History, and Civil Knowledge; and directed, not to the ostentation of his reading, but to the government of his life and the public good; for he so read, that the learning, he took in by study, by judgement he digested and converted into wisdom and ability, to benefit his country: to which he also applied himself with zeal, but such as took no fire, either from faction or ambition; and, as he was a most able man for soundness of advice, and clear expression of himself in matters of difficulty and consequence, both in public and private, so also was he one whom no man was able either to draw or justle out of the straight path of justice. Of which virtue, I know not whether he deserved more by his severity in imposing it (as he did to his last breath) on himself; or by his magnanimity in not exacting it himself from others. No other man better discerned of men, and therefore was he constant in friendship, because he regarded not the *fortune* or *adherence,* but the men; with whom also he conversed with an openness of heart, that had no other guard than his own security, and that *Nil conscire*. To his equals he carried himself equally; and to his inferiors familiarly; but maintaining his respect fully, and only with the native splendour of his worth. In sum, he was one in whom might plainly be perceived, that *honour* and *honesty* are but the same thing, in the different degrees of persons."—He contracted a vast debt by his excessive gallantry, and splendid way of living; died at his house near Bishopsgate, in London (where Devonshire-square is now built), on June 20, 1628; and was buried in the vault of All Saints church in Derby, with Elizabeth countess of Shrewsbury, his grandmother, on July 11 following[2]; where a most stately monument is erected to his memory, his own statue of white marble standing upright in the midst of it. *William,* the third earl, his son and heir, by the lady *Christiana Bruce*[3], was ten years, eight months, and ten days old, at the death of his father, being then a knight[4]. He was made knight of the Bath at the coronation of Charles I.[5]; and his mother, the countess dowager, getting the wardship of him, he was under her care. She was a woman of considerable celebrity, and of a singular character. She had brought to her husband £10,000, the gift of king James I. Her clear jointure was no less than £5000. a year, to which she added £4000. by her own prudent management. She seems indeed to have imbibed a due portion of the profitable wisdom of her lord's grandmother, the famous countess of Shrewsbury, who laid such ample foundations

of wealth for her family. Her son's estate was charged and complicated with near thirty law-suits, which, by the cunning and power of her adversaries, were made as perplexed and as tedious as possible; yet, by right, managed by diligence and resolution, she went through them all with satisfaction; so as king Charles jestingly said to her, " Madam, you have all my judges at your disposal." The discharging of the estate from those numerous law-suits was not the only thing that required her care; there was a great debt to be satisfied, which was another specimen of her trouble, as well as patience. Her lord had, before his death, obtained an act of parliament for cutting off an entail, in order to the sale of lands; a thing not usual in those times, and " had not then been effected, but for the sakes of those for whom it was done," as king Charles was pleased to express it. Yet this bore no proportion towards the payment of that vast debt for which it was designed; but with what money the sale of those lands brought in, together with her own care and management, the debt was discharged by her. Whilst these controversies were depending, she committed her son to his father's tutor, Mr. Hobbes, who instructed him in the family for three years; and then, about 1634, travelled with him as his governor into France and Italy. This countess was a lady of that sweet affability and sweet address, with so great a wit and keen a judgement, as captivated all who conversed with her; and of such strict virtue and morals, that she was an example to her sex. Prayers and pious readings were her first business; the remainders of the day were determined to her friends; in the entertainment of whom, her conversation was so tempered with courtship and heartiness, her discourses so sweetened with the delicacies of expression, that such as did not well know the expence of her time would have thought she had employed it all in address and dialogue. In both which she exceeded most ladies; and yet never affected the title of a wit; carried no snares in her tongue, nor counterfeited friendships; and, as she was never known to speak evil of any, so neither would she endure to hear of it, from any, of others; reckoning it not only a vice against good-manners, but the greatest indecency also, in the entertainment of friends, and therefore always kept herself within the measures of civility and religion. Her gestures corresponded to her speech, being of a free, native, genuine, and graceful behaviour; as far from affected and extraordinary motions as they from discretion. These admirable qualities drew the poor to her gates, and strangers to her table, and the city and court to her conversations. She had so easy and such an obliging address, without the least allay of levity and disdain, that every one departed with the highest satisfaction; she ever distributing her respects according to the quality and merit of each; steering the same steady course in the country also; between which and the town she commonly divided the year. Her country feats were many and noble; and, when her son came of age, she delivered up to him his great houses in Derbyshire, all ready furnished; she herself living in that of *Leicester Abbey* (near to which she had purchased a considerable estate) until the rebellion broke out."[6]

Having met with severe domestic losses, by the death of her only daughter Anne[7], the wife of Robert lord Rich[8], son and heir to the earl of Warwick, and her

<hr/>

[1] Esch. 5 Jac. I.   [2] MS. J. 8. in Offic. Arm fol. 18.

[3] " She was daughter of Edward lord Bruce of Kinlofs, and called Christiana because she was born on Christmas-day. Her father, being nobly descended from a brother of him who carried the crown of Scotland with great lustre, was ambassador here in the decline of queen Elizabeth; and he, in conjunction with secretary Cecil (afterwards earl of Salisbury), had procured of all the great men of this kingdom an engagement in writing, that they should adhere to the succession in the Scots Protestant line. This service was justly rewarded by many royal favours, and by this especially, that the king promoted the matching this lady into so great an English family, and in the marriage was pleased to act the father's part, and gave her with his own hand to William the second earl of Devonshire." Kennet's Memoirs of the Family of Cavendish.

[4] Inq. 17 Sept. 4, Car. I; Cole's Escheats, vol. III. p. 240. in Bibl. Harl.   [5] Catalogue of Knights, MS.

[6] Life of Christiana Countess of Devonshire, passim; and Kennet's Memoirs of the Family of Cavendish.

[7] " A lady of those rare endowments of mind and body, that her memory is celebrated by the Wits and Orators of her own time, the lord Falkland, Mr. Waller, Mr. Godolphin, and others." Kennet, p. 99. This lady died young, about 1644, of a feverish disorder, caught, as Waller expresses it, in —— " the curs'd Essexian plains,
    Where hasty death and pining sickness reigns."
Her husband married a second wife, Oct. 3, 1645 (Lyfons, vol. II. p. 415); and yet, by some mistake, she is confounded, in all the editions of Collins's Peerage, with her niece Anne, sister of the first duke (who was married to John Cecil, lord Burleigh afterwards earl of Exeter, with whom she travelled twice to Rome, and died June 18, 1703).

[8] He succeeded his father as earl of Warwick in 1658; and, having outlived his only son, died May 29, 1659. See p. 291.

second

fecond fon the brave Charles Cavendifh [1], her thoughts became more devoted to national affairs, and fhe then began to take an active part in the interefting politicks of thofe times. She retired to Greenwich towards the latter end of the rebellion ; and, reflecting on the deplorable condition of the king and church, endeavoured, with her utmoft fkill and diligence, to recover the dignity of the crown and the liberties of the people ; foliciting the earls of Effex and Holland to expiate their former engagements by efpoufing the royal caufe. They are faid both to have been very much encouraged by her earneft folicitations and prudence ; that Effex would have given the fureft demonftration of his loyal purpofes, had not death prevented him [2] (not without fufpicion of poifon) Sept. 13, 1646 ; and that Holland was urged by her to the rafh enterprize which, on the 9th of March, 1648, occafioned his being beheaded. When the army had made themfelves mafters of the king's perfon, and were carrying him in their triumph from place to place, they let him reft a night or two at Latimers, a feat of this family in Buckinghamfhire, where this noble lady happened then to be, with her fon the earl of Devonfhire, and his majefty had much private confultation with them concerning the ftate of his affairs ; and, at the fame time, expreffed both to her and the earl the great

fenfe he had of the faithful fervices they had done him. After the fatal fight at Worcefter, Sept. 3, 1651, fhe was infinitely concerned for the fafety of the king's perfon, and could not conceal her joy when fhe heard of his fafe arrival in France : fhe took care of the only remains he left in England, his domeftic fervants, many of whom fhe received into her own family, and retained them with good refpect and fupport till their royal mafter's happy return. By three years privacy at her brother the earl of Elgin's houfe, at Ampthill, fhe had lightened her griefs and expences, and became able to renew her hofpitality and charity, in a feat which fhe purchafed for the pleafant fituation, Roehampton, in Surrey. She was diftinguifhed as the patronefs of the wits of that age, who frequently affembled at her houfe. Waller frequently read his verfes there ; and William earl of Pembroke wrote a volume of Poems in her praife, publifhed afterwards, and dedicated to her, by Donne. Other contemporary wits exercifed their talents in celebrating the virtues and accomplifhments of herfelf and her beautiful daughter lady Rich. At this houfe fhe alfo entertained many of the king's friends, and concerted meafures with them for the Reftoration, correfponding at the fame time with fome of the principal Royalifts on the Continent. Her letters were written in cypher, in which fhe was affifted by her nephew lord

[1] This young nobleman, bred to books and arms, was in both a glory of the latter age. He was born in London May 20, 1620 ; the king was his godfather, and named him Charles. After a ftrict tuition in his father's houfe, at eigh cen years of age he was fent to travel with a governor. He went firft to Paris, and hearing much of the French army, then in the field near Luxemburg, was fo impatient for fuch a view, that he ftole away to the camp, without the knowledge of his governor, who, hearing of the frolick, followed him in great pain, and brought him back to his ftudies at Paris. He fpent the year following in Italy, making his chief ftages at Naples, Rome, and Venice ; whence, in the next fpring, he embarked for Conftantinople, dropping his governor and Englifh fervants, as knowing that a traveller may learn moft from ftrangers After a long circuit by land through Natolia, he went by fea to Alexandria, thence to Cairo, and was brought, by way of Malta, to Spain, and back to Paris ; and, after fome converfation with the court, returned to England about the end of May, 1641. When he had paid his duty to his mother, he was prefented to the king and queen, and was gracioufly received by them, and much careffed by the moft eminent perfons about the court. His inclinations determined him to arms ; and therefore his mother, the countefs, defigned to have bought for him colonel Goring's regiment of foot in Holland : fo he went over to be trained up there in the prince of Orange's army, the moft eminent fchool of war. When he had paffed one campaign, he came over again to England, about the end of November, 1641 ; and when, foon after, the king, by tumults in the ftreets, and greater diftractions in the two houfes, was forced to retire to York, the earl of Devon and his brother Mr. Cavendifh repaired thither to offer their duty and fervice to their diftreffed prince. He was a perfon of fo much addrefs and valour, that thofe brave gentlemen of the Temple, who offered themfelves as a guard to the king's perfon, chofe him for their captain, knowing he would thither lead them, where law, honour, and confcience, would oblige them to follow. At York, Mr. Cavendifh put himfelf among the noblemen and gentlemen volunteers, who defired to be under command for the king's fervice ; and made it his choice to ride in the king's own troop, commanded by my lord Bernard Stuart, his kinfman, brother to the duke of Richmond ; among fo many confiderable perfons for qualities and fortunes, that the king was heard to fay, " The revenues of thofe in that fingle troop would buy the eftates of my lord of Effex, and of all the officers in his army." He marched in this troop till the battle of Edge-Hill, Oct. 23, 1642 ; when the king, in refpect and tendernefs to thofe gallant men, would not expofe them to equal hazard with the reft of the cavalry, but referved them for a guard to his own perfon. Mr. Cavendifh, fuppofing this to be no poft of danger, and therefore not of honour, prevailed with the lord Bernard Stuart, that they fhould wait upon the king, and entreat his leave to be drawn up on the right hand of the right wing of the horfe, as the moft open and moft honourable place in the battle ; to which his majefty, upon their importunity, confented. And this indeed proved to be the poft of hotteft fervice, and greateft fuccefs ; wherein Mr. Cavendifh fo diftinguifhed himfelf by a perfonal valour, that, the lord Aubigny (who commanded the duke of York's troop) being flain, he was preferred to that charge before any other pretenders of eminent birth and merit. This troop was foon after put into the prince of Wales's regiment, wherein the fuperior officer put fomething on captain Cavendifh, which he thought an indignity ; and therefore he defired his majefty to affign him £1000. (which his own brother, the earl of Devonfhire, had prefented to the king,) promifing, that, if his majefty would be pleafed to let him have the duke of York's troop out of the prince of Wales's regiment, he would go into the North, and raife the duke a complete regiment of horfe before the army could take the field ; to which the king confented, affuring him the honour of being colonel of his new regiment. In order to complete it, he accepted of Thomas Markham, efq. to be his lieutenant-colonel, and Mr. Tuke for the captain of his firft troop ; and took his head-quarters at Newark, keeping under many of the rebel garrifons at Nottingham, and other neighbouring parts ; and, by degrees, became mafter of the whole country ; fo that the king's commiffioners for Lincolnfhire and Nottinghamfhire defired his leave to petition the king, that he might have the command of all the forces of the two counties in quality of colonel-general ; which he complied with, and the king granted. In this command he beat the enemy from Grantham, gained a complete victory near Stamford, and reduced feveral of their garrifontowns, by the affiftance of colonel Welby and other brave officers. After many glorious actions, being lieutenant-general of the horfe to his kinfman the marquis of Newcaftle, he had the honour to receive the queen in her march to Newark, who immediately took notice, that fhe faw him laft in Holland, and was very glad now to meet him again in England. The countefs of Derby fitting at the end of the queen's coach, entertained her majefty with great commendations of the general ; and, when the queen was to give the word to major Tuke, fhe gave that of CAVENDISH.—The copy of his life breaks off with his convoying the queen to Newark ; but thence, with a noble guard, he waited on her majefty towards Oxford ; and in his way, with her confent, took Burton upon Trent by ftorm on July 2, 1643 ; encouraging his foldiers, by his own example, to fwim over the river, and fcale the works, and enter under fhowers of bullets, defying all the moft dreadful images of death, as if his life had been as immortal as he hath made his honour. The royal caufe declining, made him only the more daring and defperate. In his laft action, near Gainfborough, in the latter end of July, he was driven with fome of his foldiers into a quagmire, where he received his death-wound, by a thruft under the fhort ribs, by lieutenant-colonel Bury, as was triumphantly ftated in a letter from Cromwell to the parliamentary committee. He deferved the character given by the writer of his mother's life, " that he was a gentleman fo furnifhed with all the interior and politer parts of learning (obtained at home and abroad, both by reading books and men) as well as courage, that he was prepared to defend his prince with his head and hand, by the ftrongeft reafon and moft generous valour ;" and was the more capable of arms by his great knowledge in the mathematical arts (See Harl. MS. 6797 16, 17.). Some of his papers, that fhew a profound fkill in numbers and meafures, were in the hands of that eminent collector of valuable papers, Dr. John Moore, lord bifhop of Ely. When his body was brought to Newark to be interred, the whole town was fo fond of it (even dead) that that they would not fuffer it, for fome days, to be laid into the ground, but wept over and admired it ; and, not without the greateft reluctance, at laft committed him to his dormitory, covering his hearfe with tears and laurels. And when, about thirty years after, his body was removed to be interred at Derby with his mother (fee p. 290), frefh lamentations were made, by thofe who knew, and others that had heard, his fame ; and the whole people of Newark expreffed the moft forrowful unwillingnefs to part with the relicks of fo dear a perfon, who had been, when alive, the ornament and defence of that place. Waller wrote an Epitaph upon Colonel Charles Cavendifh.

[2] Dugdale's Baronage, vol. II. p. 182.

Bruce,

Bruce, and Mr. Gale her chaplain. She became at laft a fufpected perfon, and was in danger of being fent to the Tower—a feafonable bribe to the council of ftate proved her protection. She afterwards entered into a correfpondence with general Monk ; who, at the time that his conduct was moft myfterious, is faid to have made known to her, by a private fignal, his intentions of reftoring the king. When Charles II. returned to England, he fhewed the fenfe he entertained of her zeal for his fervice by frequently vifiting her at Roehampton, in company with the queen-mother and the royal family, with whom fhe enjoyed an unufual intimacy till her death [1], which happened Jan. 16, 1674-5. She was buried with her hufband; and it was her exprefs will, that the remains of her fon Charles fhould be removed from Newark, and accompany her own. Her corpfe paffing through Leicefter, due refpects were paid to her memory ; the magiftrates of that place attending in their formalities, and the gentry of the country meeting there at the fame time, waited on it out of town. The fame honourable reception was paid to both of them at Derby, where they were interred in the burial-place of the family [2].

A Life of the Countefs was publifhed, in 1685, by Thomas Pomfret ; and there is an original portrait of her in the duke of Bedford's Collection at Wooburn, by Theodore Ruffell (a fcholar of Vandyke) ; from which a beautiful plate has been lately copied by his grace's permiffion [3].

In the ftreet called The Abbey gate, this excellent lady founded a fmall afylum, called " The Countefs's Hofpital," for fix poor women, maids or widows; and endowed it with £30. a year, to be paid quarterly, being £1. 5s. to each perfon.

Her houfehold-books [4], now at Chatfworth, began in her widowhood, April 1, 1635, or rather Lady-day 1635. The firft is a thick volume folio, including 1636, 1637.

The other, Privy-purfe book, is thin, and begins Lady-day 1651, and reaches to 1655 inclufive, paged, and every page figned. Book coft 8s. ; and the writing is by Mr. Vivian.

They are not properly her own books, but her fteward's ; running thus : " Delivered . . . . . for the ufe of my honourable Lady." However, fhe figns moft items, in a large hand, " C. DEVONSHIRE ;" and fhe figned moft bills before they were paid.

Mr. William Booth is fteward ; examiner H. P. who, Nov. 28, had a trunk with writings.

She had a book for her privy-purfe.

Perhaps Humphrey Pool lived in London in Devonfhire houfe, Devonfhire-fquare, in Bifhopgate-ftreet, and parifh of St. Botolph.

Young earl abroad in France, April 16, 1635.
Pages' garters, points, and rofes, April 26.
Coachman, poftilion, and four footmen, April 31.
Dutch bottles, 20 dozen at 3s.
May, footboy at £3. per annum.
Kitchin book.
Soap, weight 15 pounds, coft 14s. Another, 16s.
Loaf fugar.
Leicefter (this muft be the abbey of St. Mary) ; a chapel there, with a pulpit. There was a chimney, but it was walled up.
Venice glafs 15s. and 16s. per dozen.
Elder vinegar.

Bread for *Bedlam* [5] 2s. per week ; and again 30 Jan. in another part.
She goes to Bath 25th, and ftays five weeks ; and then to Leicefter.
At Chatfworth Sept. 3.
Clerk of the kitchen, £18. per annum.
July 25. Hobbes [6] has £60. per annum.
Vamping pages' boots 2s.
Auguft. Feather for lady's wear.
Sept. 24. A mutton, a veal.
26. et paffim. Account of provifion.
Half a year, from Lady-day 1635 to Michaelmas, £1947. 17s. 8d.; to Lady-day, £1573. 5s. 11d.; to Michaelmas, £2524. 13s. 11d.
To Lady-day, 1637, £3873. 1s. 2d. ; Michaelmas, £1637. 12s. 8d.
Mr. Gale, who lived in the houfe, had £.40 a year, and was probably chaplain at Leicefter abbey. Mrs. Gale has £.10 a year. She, I think, was houfe-keeper. His ftudy is mentioned 20 March, 1636.
Stags at Chatfworth killed that fummer ; 12 bucks, 2 ftags. N. B. Mr. Fullwood half a buck given, and Mr. Long.
Oct. 14. Kitchener at £2. per annum.
27. *Endfor* and *Enfor* [7] occur.
Nov. 1. Claret £6. 10s. per hogfhead ; fack 5s. 4d. per gallon.
Stag pies.
24. Rufhes for Hardwick 2s. Before for Chatfworth.
She goes from Hardwick to Leicefter in her way to London by Wellingborough (45 perfons) and Lewton a fumpter-mare.
She ftaid at Ampthill and Harding.
Dec. 4. Young lord is in Italy.
Six fhillings fee for a doe ; 10s. before for a buck ; afterwards 10s. a doe, Feb. 24 ; and afterwards £2. a ftag ; July 4, £1. half ftag ; fo two hinds £2.
9. Lady Bruce.
15. Gilt paper and cut paper [8].
St. Martin's [9] filver lace at 1s. 4d. per yard ; again Aug. 20, 1637.
26. Bettony, beer, and ale.
29. Dr. Worral has £4. per annum for his tithes. He was rector of St. Botolph's without Bifhopfgate ; his name Thomas ; he occurs afterwards.
Fifty fervants at 2d. per head is 8s. 4d.
30. Five pounds of damafk powder to fweeten [10] linen, Jan. 3 ; fo p. 9, vol. 2. fweet bags ; and often.
Jan. 1. Blacke fheet. Work done about it. 3 pounds of worfted coft £1. 16s. for lady's bed.
3. Water-bottles dreffed with flowers, before with ribbons.
Feb. 20. Planifhing, burnifhing, &c. of filver.
23. Charles, fecond fon [11], lived with the countefs.
24. Mafk at the Temple.
25. Sweet wood for the hall 1s. ; cedar occurs before.
March 12. Given faltpetre-men [12] not to break up the ftables.
March 15. Lady Maie, fir Humphrey May vice-chamberlain's lady.
24. Coachman and poftilion in purple ; fo pages' cloak and hofe, &c.
Gingerlyne [13] cloth for a fcreen, May 27, and thrice after ; and June 16, 1637.
1636. Poor cefs 5s. per week ; 10s. May 7.

[1] Roehampton houfe defcended, after the countefs's death, to her fon William, the third earl of Devonfhire, who died there in 1684 ; and, after the death of his countefs, in 1689, appears to have been alienated to fir Jeffery Jefferys, alderman of London, who died there in 1707. Lyfons's Environs of London, vol. I. p. 433.

[2] The monument for her and her hufband is an octagon dome, fupported by four Ionic pillars, two at front and two behind, with two arches, North and South. In the centre ftand their ftatues. On the outfide are four bufts, one of them female ; all moft vilely executed. No infcription. Arms : *Cavendifh* ; impaling, a chief in a canton Ermine a lion rampant ; in bafe a faltire.

[3] See this plate in Lyfons's Environs, vol. I. p. 432.

[4] For this epitome of the countefs's houfehold-books, I am indebted to my late worthy friend Dr. Pegge ; to whom the originals were lent, in October 1776, by the prefent duke of Devonfhire.

[5] Probably a benefaction to the hofpital of Bedlam, not far from her town refidence in Devonfhire-fquare.

[6] At Chatfworth is a portrait of Hobbes, a chearful look, with a glafs of liquor in his hand.

[7] Or Edinfor, the parifh in which Chatfworth ftands.

[8] The amufement among the ladies of cutting and raifing paper brought from France into this country before 1600, and was much in fafhion within thefe few years.

[9] This probably was the ornamenting of St. Martin's church at Leicefter, which was done very fumptuoufly in 1635, on account of the king's coming. This appears by the churchwardens' accompts. See afterwards, p. 292, " St. Martin's ribbons."

[10] Rofe powder. [11] See before, p. 289.

[12] In 1625, faltpetre-makers were permitted to dig the floors of all dove-houfes, ftables, &c. for the fake of the falts contained in them, very fmall quantities of faltpetre being then brought from the Eaft Indies. [13] Q. Hingerlyne ? See p. 292.

April 13. Spanish tables; also before and after.
16. Mrs. Murray, Mr. Osberston.
The countess had an embroidered saddle.
Running footman.
May 4. Three leather jacks cost 10s.
May 7. King's drawing-chamber in Devonshire-square.
King and queen entertained, May 12, 1636; cost £380. 9s. 7d.
15. Picture by sir Anthony Vandike of the countess, copied by Corcellis [1], cost £10.
To Corcellis, for pictures of the Lord Steward, earl of Pembroke, and my Lord Chamberlain, in little, £3.
27. Bills of sickness delivered by parish-clark.
Countess goes to Raynham [2] and Pergoe [3], and Rochford [4], Essex.
The state, and before the ninth 3½ yards of tawney taffety.
Watchet taffety sarsenet at 40s. per ell.
College pots to silversmith.
Wall candlestick.
June 20. Vault is a great room; and before, as May 27, the making clean the heads in the vault. This was for the king's entertainment.
Running money to footmen.
July 4. Countess at Byfleet [5]; king and queen entertained there; stayed till Feb. 18.
Oct. 5. Countess plays at shovel-board.
Dec. 6. Young lord seems to be come home.
12. Masking night, and after, cost £17.
Jan. 4. Two pages; they play on lute and harp, and are richly dressed in sattin.
5. Latymers.
18. A play; ribbons, pasteboard, &c. and joiner, £1. 4s. 6d.
Quere, if countess and earl did not remove from Byfleet to Hampton Court for a few days?
A lamb cost 10s.
23. Earl again in France.
Portage and porterage; alibi.
Artichoaks scarce.
Clerk of kitchen has £7. per annum, and is different from caterer, who purchased accators, and was a kind of purveyor.
Feb. 18. Went to Leicester, with 16 horses, 21 persons, from Byfleet, Shepperton, Berkhamsted, Stratford, Wellingborough, &c.; was also at Ampthill, or Ampthill Lees.
March 6. Creeper, andiron.
16. Isabella [6]-coloured stockings for pages, often after, and in second volume.
21. Laid out at Leicester abbey £424. 8s. 6d.
22. Two salt-stoanes [7] for the dove-house, 3s. 9d.
1637, April 2. Earl of Warwick (her brother in law); elsewhere frequently.
May 7, lord Elgin [8] at Leicester abbey.
10. Holland for boot hose.
May 6. Lord of Newcastle's chamber at Leicester; so June 3.
12. Young lord at Leicester, for Hobbes is there.
June 6. Son Charles went to France, and is there Aug. 20.
July 20. Countess went to Hardwick.
29. She and young lord dine at Langwith Park.
31. Went to Chatsworth.
Dr. Belcankewell [Balcanqual] [9] at Tutbury.
Aug. 6. Mr. Bisben has £60. per annum.
30. Countess seems to go to Hardwick.
Queen of Scots' chamber at Chatsworth.
Keepers of Peak Forest bring a stag Sept. 25.

Sept. 1. Countess and young earl went to the chamber in the Peak Forest.
20. Starching cloth for landerye 3s.
1635. At Ln° Barm and before.
Countess at Bath.
A cord to maile [10] up a box.
Citrons 3s. apiece; also 3s. 6d.
King and queen supped at Devonshire-house May 15, 1636.

	£	s.	d.
Expence of diet was —	203	11	8
Banquet, — —	57	10	11
Other expences to king's servants, cooks, &c. — }	56	6	0
More to carpenters, joiners, and Mr. Corcellis, — }	37	10	9
Charcoal, — —	22	8	0
Billets, &c. — —	32	4	0
	409	11	4

The king gave 60 ounces of gilt plate at 5s. 4d; £16. when afterwards changed away.
July 4, 1636. Prince Elector supped at Byfleet.
Feb. 18. Pheasants sent to Leicester cost 8s. apiece.
June 3, 1637. A marchpane £1. 10.
Dec. 15, 1635. To air by fire.
A small maudling cup £1. 5s. 6d. plate.
Nov. 21. Newton, draper of Chesterfield.
Mar. 1637. Seventy-five yards of vermilion for a bed.
May 27. Slese silk [11], and elsewhere.
Wages £436. 2s.

	£.	s.	d.
£416. 16s. 8d.; but liveries, &c. came to }	472	5	3
And next year,	508	15	0

Dec. 9, 1635. Dr. Cragg sends a present.

SMALL BOOK.

Holland for smocks 3s. 6d. per ell, after 4s. 2d.; lace for them at 4s. 10d. per yard.
Perfumed cordevant gloves, 2s. 2d.
Lady Anne; she was daughter, and married Rich.
Mask at Putney £1; door-keeper 2s. 6d.
Sir Paul Pinder [12], glass-man.
Dr. Nurfs, given to him £10.; and p. 34, £2.; and p. 45, £5.; and p. 79, she pays apothecary's bill, apothecary's or doctor, £5.
Searching books at Worcester house about Peak Forest 1s.
25. Half a year is £324. 17s. 6d.; next half year, £392. 14s. 11d.; so from Lady-day, 1652, to Michaelmas, £384. 15s. 3d.; from Michaelmas 1652, to Lady-day, £317. 11s. 9d.; to Michaelmas £481. 10s. 1cd.; Lady-day, £300. 3s. 6d.; Michaelmas 1654, £275. 17s. 8d.; to Lady-day, 1655, £493. 13s. 4d.; to Michaelmas, 1655, £296. 5s. 9d.
30. Fuller, minister of Bishopsgate, given him £2.
33. Lady Anne Cavendish [13]; a purse for lady Betty.
33. Wax-book 6d. in wax-chandler's bill.
34. Mr. Harding seems to be a preacher; so p. 48.
35. Mr. Rich [14] is at Cambridge in March 1651; and the countess sends him £5.
36. Gorgett, neck-handkerchiefs.
She lived at Roehampton; so p. 56, and afterwards.
Mr. Glenn is a person at good exhibition, and Mrs. Glenn has £5. given her; and Glenn and wife have £7. p. 177.
Gallery of heroic women [15], 18s. a book.
Hair-coloured ribbon alibi.
Spirit of sack; and so before.
Lawn peake and square lace for them.

---

[1] This artist has escaped the noble author of the Anecdotes of Painting.
[2] The seat of the Townsend family in Norfolk.   [3] The seat of the Chekes.   [4] The seat of the St. Johns.
[5] The seat of Henry lord Jermyn, treasurer of the household to king Charles I; master of the horse to his queen; and afterwards earl of St. Alban's.   [6] Orange-coloured.
[7] A salt cat, as it is now called, is a mass of clay mixed up with salt, and placed in pidgeon-houses to induce the birds to drink, and to draw off their attention from tiling, to which they do great mischief by picking out the mortar.
[8] Thomas, the first earl of Elgin, and lord Bruce of Whatton. He was brother to our countess.
[9] Dean of Rochester. See Archæologia, vol. XII. 122. 128. 129. & seq.   [10] To make it tight, to go upon a pillion.
[11] Ravelled silk.   [12] He was her neighbour in Bishopsgate-street. See Gent. Mag. vol. LXV. p. 750.
[13] This was her niece; afterwards countess of Exeter. See p. 288.
[14] The hon. Robert Rich, the countess's grandson, and the only son of Robert lord Rich by the lady Anne. He married, Nov. 11, 1657, the lady Anne Cromwell, youngest daughter to the Protector. He died Feb. 16, 1657-8, aged 23; his grandfather April 18, 1658; and his father May 29, 1659. Peck, Desiderata Curiosa, vol. II. Book XIII. n. 13.
[15] A book by Le Moyne, so intituled.

Froft-coloured.

She goes to various churches.

Lord Cavendifh [1] in 1653 is her grandfon.

Poor have 2s. given at the gate every Sunday, p. 102; and on leaving town, &c.

Three lawn-pantletts £1. 4s. 6d.

Brief at Putney church 5s. anno 1653.

Luteftring hingerline laced £1. 17s. p. 158; mohair hingerline with pleats, and buttons and loops, £1. 17s. 10d.

P. 110. She goes to fee a dog-match at Hamptoncourt 1653.

111. Arris-powder one pound 1s. 6d.

119. Lord Warwick lives at Lees [2].

122. One pound of orange-powder 6s. for hair; p. 136.

143. To Mr. Maikerne, for a picture of General Cavendifh, £8. 1654.

153. Nonefuch water.

164. Given to Dr. Myarne £3; fir Theodore Mayerne, fir Theodore Myron, p. 166, 1654. [3]

Given to Lake £3.

169. Dr. Harvey, for his opinion and writing of and to lord Cavendifh, £2. 1s. 6d.

172. Dr. Nurfe £2.; more £3.; more £3. p. 181; more £10. p. 185.

178. Paid my lady Bruce for a fann handle fet with fmall diamonds and rubies, with two pendants fuitable to it, £30; another afterwards cofts £33.

181. Given to Dr. Witherbourne £3; after £2. and £5. and £2.

188. *Cedann*, i. e. fedan, 1654.

196. To Mrs. Gale, in new two-pences, one pound, 1655; this is elfewhere called *fmall-money*.

197. For St. Martin's [4] ribbons, £1 15s. 8d.

198. Upper gloves two pair, 4s. 6d.—N. B. often mentioned.

209. Lord Protector fent a brief £. 1655; and the countefs vifited lady Claypole.

217. Lady Oxford's picture and frame £12. 10.

225. Little ladies at Latimer's are Bruces, I think.

226. For bone-lace for fix coyfs and crofs-clothes, and two handkerchiefs, and fix under crofs-clothes, £4. 11s. 10d.

Holland at 12s. 6d. the ell, for handkerchiefs.

1655. Cloaths bought for lord Cavendifh, £17. 12s.

Silver bone-lace at 5s. 8d. *per* oz. bought by oz.

Silver-plate bone-lace at 5s. 4d. alfo by yards 10s. 6d.

Donations are made to L. Ar. £20. at a time, and £10. 9s. Ufher archbifhop of Armagh.

Mr. Rich is in France 1655.

Ribboning and ribbons.

Farrendon, a kind of ftuff for petticoats.

Morella ftuff for gown.

Ampthill belonged to Bruce; having been given by Charles II, 1660, to Robert Bruce, whom he created vifcount Bruce of Ampthill, and earl of Ailefbury.

Roehampton was purchafed by Chriftian countefs of Devonfhire.

Account Book of CHRISTIAN countefs of Devonfhire.

May 15, 1636. Charge of diet, and other necef-fary expences, for the king and queen's entertainment on the 12th of May, 1636:

	£.	s.	d.
Paid for all forts of fowl and poultry, as appears by particulars, —	76	12	0
Paid for butcher's meat, —	18	4	11
Paid for frefh fifh of feveral forts,	12	0	0
Paid for grocery, &c. ufed in the kitchen,	16	17	7
Paid for wine fpent of all forts,	16	19	0
Paid for fruits and herbs, —	22	7	0
Paid for 240 pounds of butter fpent,	6	0	0
Paid for 13 hundred and a half of eggs,	2	14	0
Paid for bread and flour fpent,	5	10	8
Paid for milk and creams,	3	9	11
Paid for dry'd tongues, bacon, anchovy, &c. — —	3	18	4
Paid for oranges and lemons,	5	6	6
Paid for olives, capers, and fallads, &c.	4	14	9
Paid for wax-lights fpent, —	8	17	0

Hitherto diet, which comes to £203. 11s. 8d.

Charges of the banquet.

	£	s	d
Paid for making the 4 voiders, and 100 of bafkets, with filvering them, &c.	19	16	0
Paid for artificial flowers to adorn them,	7	10	0
Paid for the fweet-meats of all forts, according to the particulars, —	30	4	11

Total of the banquet £57. 15s. 11d.

Several other charges about this entertainment, viz.

	£	s	d
Given amongft cooks and labourers,	30	14	0
Gifts and rewards to the king's fervants and others, —	21	0	0
Paid for two loads of charcoal 56s. and for four loads of faggots,	4	12	0
	317	8	7

Yet charges about the king's entertainment.

	£	s	d
Paid for carpenters, joiners, and bricklayers work, according to bills,	8	15	2
Paid for feveral neceffary things bought to ufe in feveral offices, parts of them yet remaining, —	5	18	7
Paid for portage of feveral things, both diet and things borrowed;	4	12	8
Paid for flowers and ftrewings,	3	1	0
Paid for hire of hangings, carpets, &c.	4	0	0
Paid for the loan of water-pots, glaffes, &c.	0	13	0
Paid (by Mr. Corcellis) for joiner's work, portage, &c. about this occafion, as by his bill, — —	1	10	4
Given to Mr. Corcellis, for his pains herein, by my honourable lady's appointment, — —	10	0	0

Charges about beautifying the vault in Devonfhire houfe, London, againft this time, viz.

	£	s	d
Paid (by Mr. Corcellis) to Monf. Le Soire, for the finifhing about the great glafs, with 14d. portage, —	4	1	2
Paid for painting and gilding it, &c.	1	12	0
Paid for painting the landfcape there,	5	10	0
Paid for joiners' work about the cornice of the glafs, making frames for the two oval doors to ftrain the painted canvas upon, for pedeftals for the flower-pots, mending the doors there, for four fire-pans, &c. as by Mr. Corcellis's bills,	1	17	1
Paid for canvas and painting the two door-frames,	3	0	0
Paid for light Italian chairs for the vault to Mr. Buckatt, at 24s. *per* piece,	9	12	0
Paid for two large flower-pots for the vault, painted and gilded, bought of Mr. Chriftmas, — —	3	10	0

The whole charge of this entertainment, 54 11 0

Yet charges about the entertainment, viz. according to particulars contained in the two former pages; and above on this page is £380. 9s. 7d.

The countefs, when fhe refided at Byfleet in Surrey, July 4, 1636, entertained lord Holland, the Maids of Honour, and the Elector Palatine.

	£	s	d
Given to my lord chamberlain's pantler for fruit that night my lord Holland fupped at Byfleet, and for fruit at other times, — —	1	0	0
Given to my lord chamberlain's cooks,	3	10	0
Given a cook of Byfleet,	0	5	0
Given for the hire of brakes, and pans and racks, — —	0	10	0
Given to the helpers in the kitchen,	0	5	0
Given to my lord chamberlain's man that brought the plate, —	0	10	0
Given to the wardrobe-keeper for the hire of two chairs, —	0	10	0

---

[1] William, afterwards the firft duke. [2] Lees priory in Effex. [3] Phyfician to the court.
[4] For the ornamenting of St. Martin's church at Leicefter. See before, p. 290.

2

Paid

South View.

Buck del. 1730.

North View from the Meadow.

W. N.W. Prospect.

South View.

J. Pridden del. July 8. 1786.

Paid for the hire of a tent, —	0	11	0
Given the keeper that brought the ftag, by Mrs. Gale, —	2	0	0
Given to the fidlers, —	2	10	0
Paid the mafon for moving a range,	0	3	0
Given to fir Henry Maning's keeper that brought a buck, —	0	12	0
To the fidlers when the maids of honour fupped at Byfleet, —	1	10	0
Paid for the hire of two carts to carry the tent and other things from Oatlands and back again, — —	0	10	0
Paid to the fidlers when the Prince Elector fupped at Byfleet, —	1	10	0
Paid for the portage of divers things this time, — —	0	3	0
Paid for 24 fmall cheefes, —	0	3	0
To Mr. Cawood's maid that brought a prefent, — —	0	1	0

We find by the manuscript Diary of Richard Symonds, that Leicefter abbey was in 1645 the regular refidence of the countefs of Devonfhire; that it was occupied by the king as his head quarters from the 30th of May to the 2d of June; and that feveral of his officers received there the honour of knighthood [1]. It was neverthelefs burnt by his troops [2], perhaps to prevent its being ufeful to the enemy; though the demolition has by fome been attributed to envy on the part of Henry Haftings the then lord Loughborough, who marched from Afhby de la Zouch, where he was governor for the king, for the exprefs purpofe of burning this noble manfion.

The fite of Leicefter abbey, after the death of the countefs of Devonfhire, devolved to her eldeft fon *William* earl of *Devonfhire* [3]; who died at Roehampton Nov. 23, 1684; and was fucceeded by his fon *William*, who in 1694 was created duke of Devonfhire [4]; and died Aug. 18, 1707; leaving his property at Leicefter to *William* the fecond duke [5]; on whofe death, June 4, 1729, it paffed to *William*, the third duke; by whom, in the year 1733, it was alienated to lord *William Manners* (brother to the duke of Rutland); who gave it to his fon *John* Manners, efq.; and on his death, 1792, it defcended to his fon *William* Manners, efq. who in 1793 was created a baronet,

and is the prefent owner of the fite of the abbey, with about 1500 acres of land. He is lord alfo of the manor of three parifhes in Leicefter, St. Mary's, St. Leonard's, and St. Margaret's (with its chapelry of Knighton).

A fmall part only of the old houfe is preferved for any ufeful purpofe; a low building with a leaded roof; the remainder being merely a mafs of ruins [6]; to the Eaft-fouth-eaft of which are three large clofes walled in, with gates, and a handfome communication to each other. Thefe clofes, where the traces of fifh-ponds, terraces, walks, &c. may yet be feen, are chiefly ufed as orchards, being well ftocked with cherries, &c.

Of the South front, copied in Plate XVIII. from Buck's view in 1730, the fmall part now remaining will appear on comparing it with three other views taken by Mr. Pridden in 1786 [7]; namely,

1. A North view, from the meadow.
2. A Weft-north-weft view, fhewing part of the North front, and an infide view of the only remaining part of the South front.
3. Another South view, which fhews the infide of the North front.

The following admeafurements of the buildings were communicated to me by the late Rev. Mr. Bickerftaffe:

"The back of the Abbey-houfe is 42 yards long from the Soar end to the ovens; and thence, through a fpace to continued foundations, 27 yards more of fpace, a good part of which might be ftables.

"A recefs within that part of the abbey-wall which is brick, and which embraces the grafs ground beyond the gardens, and is neareft Leicefter, has over the entrance a fingle blank efcutcheon, freeftone, having three fides equilateral, 8 inches and a half to its bottom, a pointed fquare on an exergue fcalloping, like the *calix* of a flower, half as wide as the efcutcheon, the radii or rays three inches long. The freeftone inclofure is 1 foot 5 inches, and has a laft inclofure, exergue, or edging, of brick, two inches and a half thick. The entrance to this recefs, refembling a door-way, is a yard wide, pointed at top of its arch, and paffing through the wall, which feems two bricks' length in thicknefs, or a foot and a half. From the ground upwards it is 3 feet 4 inches, and then 9 inches to the point at top over the entrance. It goes farther backward, beyond the level of the wall, 1 foot

[1] See under Harborough, vol. II. p. 506.

[2] "The countefs of Devonfhire's we demolifhed with fire." Gutch's "Collectanea Curiofa," vol. I. p. 441.

[3] "This earl was fo much a Cavendifh in the very outward appearance, that Mr. Hobbes called him the image of his father, being of a comely fhape and afpect; and therefore he ended an epiftle to him with a prayer, 'that it would pleafe God to give him virtues fuitable to the fair dwelling he had prepared for them.' He is faid to have been feafoned with the juft tincture of all private and public virtues, and to have made an early expreffion of the fevereft loyalty, mixed with the nobleft refolution, in that famous occafion of the earl of Strafford's bill, and many others; being then firm to the true intereft of his prince and country. He followed the king in the North; and at York, on June 1642, was one of thofe noble peers who fubfcribed a declaration of their bearing teftimony of his majefty's frequent and earneft declarations and profeffions of his abhorring all defigns of making war upon his parliament. When he faw a party in the two houfes too ftrong to be fatisfied, he fupplied the king with money, attended him in his parliament at Oxford, and was one of the peers who figned there, on January 27, 1643-4, his majefty's declaration of fuch means as might probably fettle the peace of the king; after which he lent him his own brother to take the field; and then retired beyond the feas, to wait for peace at home. This recefs could give him no repofe; he was thruft into the number of delinquents; his great eftate was fequeftered; and when, by the mediation of his friends, an ordinance was depending for his compofition, on October 23, 1645, order was given for his return from beyond the feas by a certain day. Though he had been fo great a fufferer for his loyalty, he fought for no employment at court on the Reftoration; but his majefty fhewed his confidence in him, by conftituting him lord lieutenant of the county of Derby, Aug 20, 1660. In fir William Temple's Letters, vol. II. p. 70, is a letter to lord Cavendifh, dated July 18, 1669, relative to an attack made upon him at Paris, from which he extricated himfelf with fpirit and honour. He lived in great plenty and refpect, a true Englifh peer, honoured by his prince, and beloved by the people; becaufe fteady in the meafures of maintaining the juft prerogatives of the one, and the legal liberties of the other. Many perfons of honour, his cotemporaries, agree in the remembrance of him, that he was a man of as much confcience and honour, religion and virtue, prudence and goodnefs, as they ever knew in the world. His tendernefs and good nature to friends and relations was very exemplary. He was fo extraordinarily fond of his grandfon, the fecond duke, then a youth, that he could not be eafy without him; and affiduoufly affected to have him as much in his company as poffible. He was virtuous in his whole life, and prudent in all his affairs; improved his large inheritance, and took care to let it defcend entire to his fucceffor.

[4] This noble duke had all the advantages of education, both by ftudies and travels, and was a gentleman of gracefulnefs and gallantry, becoming a prince's court. The companion and guide of his travels was Dr. Killigrew, afterwards mafter of the Savoy, &c. who gave him a juft and true relifh in poetry, and all the refinements of fenfe and wit. He was a poet, not by genius only, but by learning and judgement. The lord Rofcommon made him a conftant revifer of his verfes. He was a mafter of Horace, and would talk of the other antients with great relifh and knowledge. He had nothing profane or indecent in any line. Between the wit and the gentleman he knew the difference, and nicely obferved it.

[5] He was trained to the public fervice from his youth; and in 1692 ferved as a volunteer under king William in Flanders. As foon as he came of age, he was returned a member of the houfe of commons; and, on the peace concluded at Ryfwick, made a tour to France. He was elected one of the knights for the county of Derby in 1695, 1698, and 1700; and one of the knights for Yorkfhire in 1702, 1705, and 1707, when he fucceeded to the peerage. While he was marquis of Hartington her majefty conftituted him captain of the yeomen of her guard; and, fucceeding his father in his honours, the queen likewife conferred on him his places of dignity and truft, with this moft gracious expreffion, "that fhe had loft a loyal fubject and good friend in his father, but did not doubt to find them both again in him."

[6] "From fo rich an endowment as the abbey of Leicefter formerly poffeffed, we expected many beautiful remains, as it is ftill in a kind of fequeftered ftate; but in that expectation we were difappointed. Not the leaft fragment of a Gothic window is left; not the mereft mutilation of an arch. Its prefent remains afford as little beauty as the ruins of a common dwelling." Gilpin, Northern Tour. [7] Two different views, by Mr. Throfby, may be feen in Grofe's Antiquities.

4 inches,

4 inches, and more. The hollow overhead between the wall and the back part, meafuring from the arch's point, is 1 foot 5 inches; the thicknefs of the ftone or timber-feat was 8 inches; for, fuch is the width of the chafm in the lower part of the wall facing the entrance, where it feems to have been inferted nine inches deep from the floor, or rather ground, within. On the back, about two inches up, appears an horizontal niche. It is by the way-fide at prefent, facing the North, on which fide the brick wall extends a great way to join the freeftone part, but its other end is near the firft houfe in the Abbey-gate. There the wall runs Weft, having an ornamented vacant niche at the curve, and an arm of the old Soar before it, and foon lofes itfelf in the freeftone continuation; which, after a fhort progrefs the breadth of the Abbey-clofe, bears Southerly, parallel with the Soar, fo tutelary, fo near, as fometimes to wafh the mural foundation. Why the wall for a great extent on the North fide the Abbey-pafture or grafs ground, is only brick, unfriended by a facing of water, and the oppofite fide coafting with the Soar is freeftone, I wifh to account for: the interfecting freeftone walls, which run North and fouth, fupply in fome meafure the impotence of the fubftantial wall of brick.

" Beginning to meafure from the Abbey-gate end of the brick wall. To the firft door 6 chains; to the feat under the radiated efcutcheons one chain more lacking 2 yards; to the little gate beyond the two-leaved gate 23 chains; to the end of the wall from the beginning 26 chains, 44 links; the whole length, i. e. from Weft to North. Then, beginning at the North end of the wall, are 5 chains to the firft dome; but 10 chains 80 links to the centre of the fecond dome; 14 chains 60 links to the middle of the dome at the Eaft end, which contains the breadth in a line with the wall, which fquares off from Eaft to Weft on the fide of the Soar; 62 yards 2 feet 1 inch from the recefs to the door into the clofe; 113 paced yards from the recefs to the end of the brick wall, where the ftone one begins; 2 chains 85 links, 90 yards, from the ftone wall to the door-feat; 34 feet from the gate to the dome on the other fide, three fquare outwards, three half feet three inches from the wall; 11 half feet two inches. To the end of this wall it may be 100 yards; no dome, or work, or pinnacle, the reft of the way on this fide. This fide looks to the Northern road, through Mountforrel, Loughborough, &c. It then fquares from North to Weft. About 60 yards, probably, from the end is a fingle door by another high pair of gates, a yard and four inches wide, within the wooden door-frame, which is half a foot broad, two feet two or three inches thick: the ftone wall at this door-place 11 half feet high; the door-place within the frame 62 half feet three inches; 16 half feet the interval; half a foot two inches one fide-poft of the fecond great entrance; 20 half feet and four inches wide the two gates or folding doors. This wall goes on till it joins at a good diftance the brick wall which has the recefs. No pinnacle or dome on this fide; much ivy fpreads feveral yards high and broad.

" On the Eaft, in and on the wall, was a porter's lodge, a rotunda at top, lead-capt in my time, high folding-doors on its fide leading to the Abbey, a few yards within; on the Weft no lodge, but alfo lofty gates, leading to another fide of the edifice; but no piece of water in front of either. The North-eaft gate is convenient for the Northern and Eaft by South London road, at an eafy diftance; the other gate feems rather defigned to admit from Leicefter, and is nearly as well fituated for the Northern road traveller as the North-eaft gate. No fortification, edifice, or pleafure-houfe, on the Weft; but the plain wall of ftone proceeding a good way, till it meets the mural brick I have fpoken of. I cannot fee how the garrifon from Mountforrel entered the Abbey; for, no walls on the Eaft fide or Weft, which fo readily occur, have been impaired; but they muft either have forced the gates, or mounted the wall near a gate, and admitted their affociates, if they had not confpirators

within, and worked perhaps by night, or knew the place to be ungarrifoned, or but weakly. The wet ditch that goes to Belgrave bridge, commencing at St. Sunday's bridge, and rejoining Old Soar before its arrival at Belgrave, making the Abbey-meadow an ifland, but for a fmall ifthmus or path in the Abbey-meadow, feems hardly the effect of accidental coincidence. Old Soar guards Leicefter on the Weft and North.

" At the garden's end, on the water's edge wefterly, three yards one foot broad, as meafured by the eye, directing my walking-ftaff on the bank on the oppofite fide, over an interval of a few yards of old Soar water, is a circular ftone dome or fummer-houfe, in the Abbey-meadow, as it is called, the old race-ground, on the other fide the river (fee plate XIX.); and which once afforded a pleafing profpect, at an eafy diftance, of the elegant tower-church of St. Margaret, being little more than the breadth of the meadow diftant [1].

" Twenty yards from the circular dome, is a fquare one ftanding, like the other, not two yards in the river forward from the wall, with two loop-holes South-eaft, and one on each fide. From the fame wall with the above two, and alfo on the garden's edge, another fquare dome, ftanding three yards or more continued in the water, perhaps 60 yards below the other, more than three yards broad from the wall to the front, in the water; and which front feems twice the length of the other, and is arched on each fide, to humour the courfe of the river; a loop-hole is on each fide, but a blind wall towards the meadow; a door in the wall about three yards from this neceffary-houfe (I will call it) on the ftream, and a flight of feven or eight fteps. Some connoiffeurs have ferioufly confidered thefe domes as fortifications. One of them juts from the wall, refting on an arch, a few yards upon Soar, calculated, I will venture to fay, ' to give their daily cates a watery grave.'

" From this place a door on the Weft by its North fide pierces the ftone wall running from South-Eaft to North-weft, feparating the garden from the grafs-ground, whofe breadth meafures from the end of St. Sunday's Bridge extra; as the wall from the garden continues ftill on the Soar fide, now with no domes, but a door at 40 or 50 yards diftance, opening to a terrace of two or three yards breadth, with many loop-holes in the wall, which, as it advances to the town-fide, with an interval of the Abbey-meadow, a quarter of a mile over, has many breaches, even to the furface of the earth, efpecially feveral yards before it arrives at the junction of the wall which runs from the Soar Northerly, coafting on its ditch, till it meets at not half the clofe breadth on the Weft fide with the brick wall near the Abbey-gate.

" About 40 yards from it is a garden-wall, which runs from the Soar wall South eaft to North-weft, feemingly half a yard thick. Perhaps 20 yards from that, down the ftream, prefenting five fquares, is another dome, alfo from the wall, on the river, about as widely extended from the wall as the firft at the other end, without loop-holes; but has an edging of three broken pinnacles like the wall, and of the fame height; they feem too near each other to have been windows. At the end of this wall is the Abbey water-mill [2], and there the wall fquares from South-eaft to North-weft; and at its angle a fix-fquare dome, with an equilateral window-frame near half a yard diameter, about the height of the wall, looking North-eaft.

" Not 100 yards from this is another dome, three fquare, to the North-eaft, and edged, as the wall at top, about three yards jutting from the wall.

" One hundred yards farther is the porter's lodge, which commands the front view of the Abbey ruins; 17 feet three inches from this to the court-gate; i. e. from the two-leaved gate, which is 10 feet wide, and its top very high, fo that a continuation of the wall covers it. This lodge has a loop-hole on the gate-fide eight inches wide, two feet two inches long, three feet fquare, about four feet from the wall outwards, but going much deeper backwards behind the wall, as a correfponding circle. Three yards two feet four inches is the breadth of its front."

---

[1] In this meadow was found, in May 1796, the gold ring engraved in plate XVII. fig. 7; on which are deeply engraved the words **tn bon an**. The ring, which appears to have been a new-year's gift, is in the poffeffion of Mr. J. Tailby, of Slaufton.
[2] This mill has lately been pulled down. It is fhewn in plate XIX.

DOMI-

Malcolm 1794

View of LEICESTER, taken within the ABBEY WALL.

Malcolm 1796

Rev. Rob. Throsby. del. 1796   B. Cary sculp

A View from the ABBEY MEADOW.

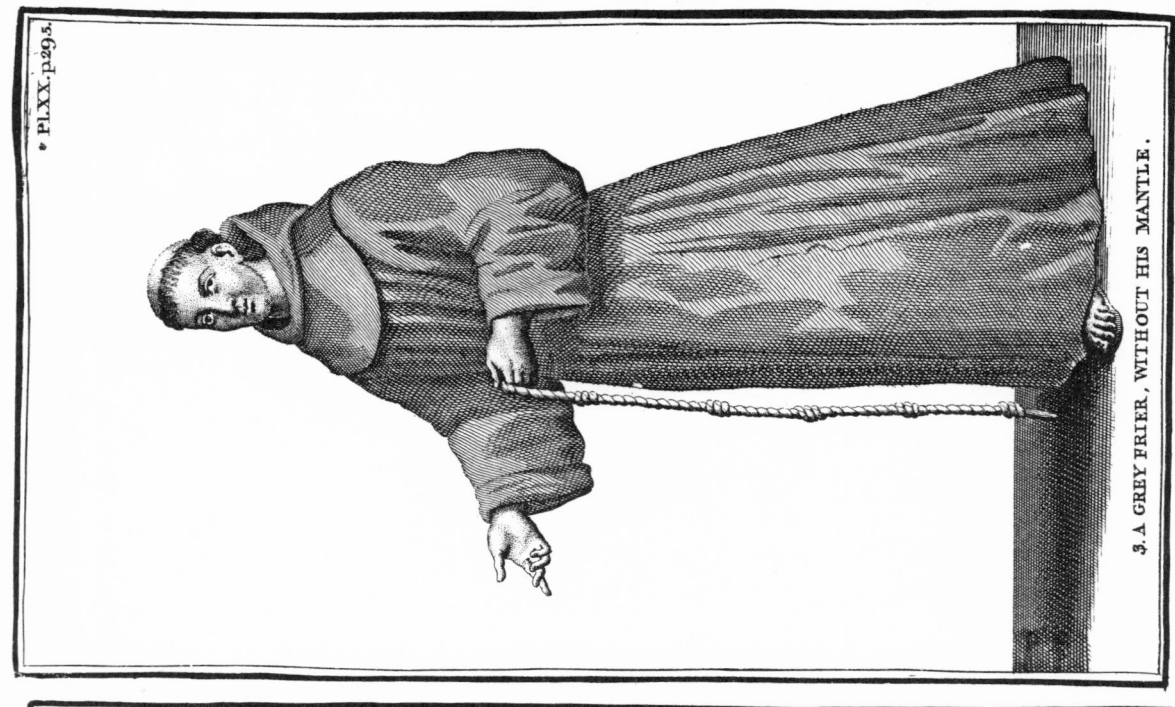

3. A GREY FRIER, WITHOUT HIS MANTLE.

Fig. 4.
p.299.

2. A FRANCISCAN OR GREY FRIER OF LEICESTER.

1. A DOMINICAN OR BLACK FRIER OF LEICESTER.

DOMINICANS, OR BLACK FRIERS.

The Mendicant Friers, it may be proper to obferve, were divided into four diftinct orders; which, according to Mofheim [1], were thus claffed; the Dominicans, Francifcans, Carmelites, and the Hermits of St. Auguftine [2]. And the fame learned writer obferves, that " The enthufiaftic attachment to thefe fanctimonious beggars went fo far, that, as we learn from the moft authentic records, feveral cities were divided or cantoned out into four parts, with a view to thefe four orders; the *firft* part being affigned to the *Dominicans*; the fecond to the Francifcans; the third to the Carmelites; and the *fourth* to the Auguftinians [3].

The order of Friers Preachers, or Black Friers, was begun in the pontificate of Innocent III, by St. Dominick, a Spaniard; who, being at firft a canon, with a few who chofe to be his companions, inftituted a new rule of ftrict and holy living; and, left they fhould grow fluggifh in the fervice of God by ftaying at home, he appointed them, in imitation of our Saviour, to travel far and wide to preach the Gofpel; which order Honorius III. confirmed; and Gregory IX. canonized the founder. They were called Dominicans, from the founder; Preaching Friers from their office to preach; and Black Friers from their garments. Their firft habit was the fame as that of the Auftin canons; and they followed the fame rule; but they foon changed their drefs, and had a white caffock, with a white hood over it; and, when they went abroad, a black cloak, with a black hood over their veftments [4]. They came into England in 1217 [5].

Frieries were feldom endowed, the friers being by their profeffion mendicants, and to have no property. Yet many of them were large and ftately buildings, in which many great perfons chofe to be buried. The fite of thofe in Leicefter is well known; but there had been no tradition for a long time to diftinguifh precifely their different orders. Hence, in the plan of Leicefter drawn by Mr. Thomas Roberts (which for the part of a furveyor is very exact), we find near the North-gate the *White* [6] friers, and out of the Weft-gate the *Black* [7] friers; which are fo ftyled by him on conjecture, becaufe he thought that he muft give them fome name or other, to diftinguifh them: but he is clearly miftaken; for, it is believed, there never was any houfe of White friers in Leicefter [8]; and the others are mifplaced [9].

The church of the Dominicans, or Friers Preachers, in Leicefter, commonly called Black Friers of St. Cle-

ment's, or Le Blak Frears in le Afhes [10], was founded by *Simon de Montford* the fecond earl of *Leicefter* of that name [11]; and was dedicated to St. Clement.

The Matriculus of 1220 informs us that the vicarage of St. Clement's was then fo poor, that it was fcarcely fufficient to maintain a chaplain; and therefore it is likely that the church was providently given to thefe Friers Preachers to officiate in; and Mr. Carte fuppofed " in le Afhes" related to the many afh-trees which of old grew in their precincts, and that they had the title of St. Clement's becaufe fituated in that parifh. It appears from fome old writings that a lane from the North-gate, turning Weftward to the Friers adjoining, and then running Southward between the faid Friers and the back fides of the houfes oppofite to All Saints church, is called St. Clement's lane; and therefore it is probable that the church was fituated in or near it; and that, upon its being demolifhed, the parifh was united to St. Nicholas, or All Saints, or partly to one, and partly to the other. The Matriculus of 1220 informs us, it was then fo poor that it was fcarcely fufficient to maintain a chaplain [12].

In Mr. Le Neve's Regifter relating to the church of Lichfield, there is a delegation to the guardians of the Friers Preachers [13] and Minors at Leicefter, to hear and determine a difference about tithes (at Bakewell, it is believed, in Derbyfhire) between the dean and chapter of Lichfield and the prior and convent of Lenton in Nottinghamfhire, from pope Innocent IV. anno pont. 10°; and the guardian of the Friers Minors finifhed the fame " die Sabbati poft Purificationem Sce Marie, 1252 [14]."

In 1285, *Robert Willoughby* and *Alice* his wife were benefactors to the Dominican priory at Leicefter [15].

" Juratores dicunt, quòd non eft ad dampnum dni regis nec aliorum, licèt dnus rex concedat Roberto de Willouby & Alicie uxori ejus, quòd dant fratribus predicatoribus ville Leiceftrie duas placeas in eâdem villâ; & quòd predicte placee terre tenentur de domino Edwardo comite Leic', per fervitium ixd. per annum, & continet in longitudine ciii pedes, & in latitudine LXXX [16]."

In 1321, *Thomas* earl of *Lancafter* and *Leicefter* was alfo a benefactor [17].

In 1337 and 1345, the poffeffions of this priory were confirmed by the letters patent of king Edward III [18].

In 1357, *Henry* duke of *Lancafter*, earl of *Derby*, *Lincoln*, and *Leicefter*, granted to the Friers Prea-

---

[1] Ecclefiaftical Hiftory, Cent. XIII. chap. II. fect. xxii.

[2] Somner fays that the Eremites of St. Auguftine was one, and the firft, of the four orders of Begging Friers; but, in the funeral proceffion, p. 299, the precedency is allowed to the Dominicans, and the Friers Eremites of St. Auguftine follow the three other orders.

[3] Mofheim, ubi fupra, fect. xxiii. p. 53. [4] See plate XX. fig. 1.

[5] " Hubert de Burgo earl of Kent was their prime patron, beftowing his palace in the fuburbs of London upon them, which afterwards they fold to the archbifhops of York, refiding therein, till, by fome tranfactions betwixt king Henry the Eighth and cardinal Wolfey, it became the royal court, now known by the name of Whitehall. Afterwards, by the bounty of Gregory Rokefley, lord-mayor of London, and Robert Kilwarby, archbifhop of Canterbury, they were more conveniently lodged in two lanes on the bank of Thames, in a place enjoying great privileges, and ftill retaining the name of Black Friers. No fewer than fourfcore famous Englifh writers are accounted of this order." Fuller, Church Hiftory, Book VI. p. 270.

[6] Thefe fhould have been called the Dominicans, or Black Friers. [7] And thefe the Friers Eremites of St. Auguftine.

[8] See, however, the funeral proceffion defcribed in p. 299.

[9] They are rightly diftinguifhed in our map, which is that of Dr. Stukeley. See plate III. p. 6.

[10] Rymer, vol. XIV. p. 621. [11] Stow's MS. Rec. 18 Edw. III. [12] See the Introductory Volume, p. lv.

[13] The word *Prædicatores* was not exclufively appropriated to this order of mendicants; the Francifcan or *Grey* Friers being ftyled *Prædicatores* as well as *Minorites*. This is evident from different paffages cited by Mofheim (Ecclefiaftical Hiftory, Cent. XIII. Part II. cap. 11. l. xxvi. note x.) from the Hiftoria Major of Matthew Paris —" *Fratres Minores* & *Prædicatores* (fays he) invitos ut credimus, jam fuos fecit dominus papa"—" non ceffavit papa pecuniam aggregare, faciens de *Prædicatoribus* & *Minoribus*, etiam invitis, non jam pifcatores hominum, fed nummorum." " Erant Minores & *Prædicatores* magnatum confiliarii & nuncii"—" Facti funt eo tempore *Prædicatores* & *Minores* regum confiliarii & nuncii fpecialis." And in Du Cange, ad voc. *Minores*—" Sub his diebus *Prædicatores*, qui appellati funt Minores, favente papâ Innocentio, emergentes terram reppleverunt, &c. &c. Conrad. Abbas Ufperg. ann. 1219."

[14] Tanner's Notitia Monaftica.

[15] Inq. 13 Edw. I. de duabus placeis in villâ Leiceftriæ. Peck, MSS. vol. V. (Harl. MSS. 4938.)

[16] Peck, MSS. vol. V. (Harl. MSS. 4938. p. 12.); ex Inq. ad quod dampn. 13 Edw. I. 1285. N° 55. Leic.

[17] Pat. 15 Edw. II. p. 2. m. 14. confirm. cujufdam placæ terræ in villâ de Leycefter, conceff. per Thomam comitem Lancaftr' fratribus prædicatoribus."

[18] Pat. 10 Edw. III. p. 1. m. 2. vel 3. Pat. 18 Edw. III. p. 1. m. 2. vel 3.

chers

chers of Leicefter liberty to fifh three days weekly (Wednefdays, Fridays, and Saturdays) in the river Soar, with a net of convenient mefh, fo as not to deftroy the young fifh :

" As touz ceux qe ceftes tres verront ou orront, Henri duc de Lancaftre, conte de Derby, de Nicole, & de Leiceftre, & fenefchal d'Engleterre, falute en Dieu. Sachez nous de ñre grace efpeciall avoir done conge a nos cħs en Dieu le prior & le convent de Frers Precheurs de Leiceftre, qu'ils puiffent chefcone fymaigne trois jours, c'eft affavoir, Mykerdy, Vendredy, & Samedy, pecher ove une fluv de convenable mefh fanz deftruction de ťfcoyn pefceon, & meanment pvable de refone, en la ryvere de Sore defouz lour clos, & iffuñ qu'ils pefchent de jour, & nemye de noct. En tefmoignage de quele chofe, nos avons fait faire ceftes noz tres patentes, enfeallez de ñre feal, & doñ a ñre chaftel de Leiceftre, le darrein jour de Fevrier, & l'an du regne ñre feigneur le roi Edward Tiers puis le Conqueft trentifme [1]."

William Layton[2] was prior of this convent in 1505; and to him, and his fucceffors, the corporation of Leicefter, by act of common hall, Sept. 21, in that year, granted the pafture of two cows in their common pafture, called the Cow hey; for which the prior paid 20 marks, and engaged that his houfe fhould pray for them for ever. In 1531, the wardens and company of fhoe-makers agreed to pay them yearly ten marks, over and above the ufual offering duties, to have their prayers.

Ralph Burrell, the laft prior, furrendered this convent[3] 10 November, 1539.

" Omnibus Chrifti fidelibus, &c. Frater Radus Burrell, prior domûs five prioratûs Sancti Clementis de Leyceſter, ordinis Sci Dominici, vulgariter nuncupat' Le Blak Frears in le Afhes, in com. Leycefter, alias dictus frater Radus Burrell, prior domûs five prioratûs fratrum predicantium, vulgariter nuncupat' le Blakfreears de Leycefter, in com' Leic', & ejufdem loci conventus, &c. Nov. 10, anno regni 30°.

Per me Radm Burrell, priorem, ac doctorem fac' theologie.

Per me Will'm Hopkyn, fub-priorem.
Per me Johannem Harford.
Per me Ricardum Yngylby.
Per me Elizeum Jem.
Per me Johannem Hern.
Per me Johannem Kok.
Per me Ricum Blafvyn.
Per me Edwardum Whonarck.
Per me Robertum Sutton."

The minifters accompts in the Augmentation-office thus defcribe the lands and poffeffions of the late houfe of Dominican Friers (fratrum Dominicalium) in the town of Leicefter[4].

" The account of Thomas Catelyn, gent. collector of the rents thereof.

He anfwers for £2. for a houfe within the precinct of the late houfe of friers aforefaid, called Robert Orton's Houfe, with the appurtenances, together with the gardens and clofes, and alfo with a grove of willows near the Soar, and alfo with the churchyard there, in the tenure of Chriftopher Lambrige; as alfo the herbage of all lands within the limits and precincts of the faid houfe; demifed to Thomas Catlyn, gent. by indenture under the common feal of the faid late houfe, dated 10th September, 30 Henry VIII.

exemplified by decree of the Court of Augmentations, under the decree of the chancellor and council of that court; to have and to hold, to the faid Thomas Catlyn and his affigns, from the day of the date of the indenture, for fixty years, at the rent of 40s. at Lady-day and Michaelmas; with a covenant that the leffee fhall have ' Hedgboote, Lope, Tope, Croppe,' of all manner, woods and underwoods. The leffee to be charged with all repairs, ' exceptis lapidibus, maeremio, fundulis, & clavis.'

The fite of the late houfe aforefaid.

He anfwers alfo for 20d. for rent of the Cloifter-yard, with the refidue of the ground and land moft apt for tenements, within the precinct of the faid houfe, referved in the hands of the prior and convent.

Sum total, — £2. 1s. 8d."

Leland, fpeaking of the religious houfes here fays, " I faw in the quire of the Blake Freres the tumbe of . . . . and a flat alabafter ftone, with the name of lady Ifabel, wife to fir John Beauchamp of Holt. And in the North-crofs ifle a tombe having the name of Roger Poynter, of Leicefter, armid, and another tombe there of a knight without fcripture. Thefe things brevely I markid at Leyrcefter [5]."

Aug. 7, 1547, the king granted to Henry marquis of Dorfet and Thomas Duport, and the heirs of the marquis, the whole houfe, and the fite of it, together with fuch fifhings as can be proved to have been belonging to the friers in Leicefter.

" Septimo die Augufti, 38 Hen. VIII. rex conceffit Henrico marchioni Dorfet & Thome Duport, & heredibus marchionis, totam domum & fcitum domûs dudum fratrum Dominicalium, vulgariter nuncupat' les Black-freyers [6]."

At the entrance of this friery [7] from the North-gate of the town, upon Mr. Noble's erecting a houfe there, in 1718, was found a pot full of Roman coins.

In 1754, two elegant mofaic pavements, with the fragment of a third, were found in a piece of ground in this friery [8], then belonging to the late Rogers Ruding, efq. of Weftcotes, who died March 27, 1795 [9]; and now to the younger branches of his family. Some other pavements alfo feem to run under the prefent building [10].

" The North Bridge, now commonly called St. Sunday's Bridge, has eight wet arches, the midmoft high and wide; two more on the town fide, fmall and ufelefs, obftructed on both fides by dyers' buildings, and made-ground. It is 98 yards one foot long, five yards two feet wide; parapet walls about a yard high, their thicknefs one foot two inches. One of its arches, the neareft the town, is pointed; the other nine are round. From the top of the parapet to the water is four yards three quarters; the common depth of the water one yard eight inches, near the middle of the bridge, by the middle of the arch. I believe that, when the two dry arches of Sunday's Bridge poffeffed each a ftream, the waters fupplied a channel, or wet ditch, on the South-eaft edge of the Abbey-meadow; as the other arches, the river, or North-weft current, by the Abbey; and it became an ifland, in the manner of the Old Soar and Back Soar, whofe water circulates here, running off by the North-weft fide of Belgrave through its bridge [11]."

---

[1] Copied by Mr. Carte, 1716, from the original deed, then in the poffeffion of Mr. Thomas Noble of Leicefter.

[2] " Not Cleyton, as in the Addenda to Willis's Hiftory of Abbeys, p. 328." Mr. Cole of Milton, MS.

[3] See the feal affixed to this furrender, plate XVII. fig 10; and the hand-writing of the prior and fub-prior, plate XX.

[4] Communicated by John Caley, Efq. F. S. A. and keeper of the records in that office.   [5] Itinerary, vol. I. p. 16.

[6] From a deed communicated to Mr. Carte, by Mr. T. Noble, in 1710.

[7] See before, p. *4; where the coins are faid to have been found in the White friers; a miftake accounted for in p. 295.

[8] From this fpot they were traced under the ftables of the Bath, now called Vauxhall.

[9] Gent. Mag. vol. LXV. p. 352.   [10] See before, p. 11; and plates VII. VIII. IX.

[11] Mr. Bickerftaffe, MS. See before, p. 294.

FRAN-

FRANCISCANS, or GREY FRIERS.

St. Francis was born of noble extraction at Affife in Umbria, a province of Italy [1]. His order, called *Minores*, was confirmed by Innocent III. in 1207; by Honorius III. about 1220; and by Gregory IX. in 1229. They firft came into England in 1224, two years before the death of St. Francis [2]; and, when their order flourifhed here, this province was divided into feven diftricts, called *cuftodies*; of which the fifth was the cuftody or wardenfhip of Oxford, which had eight monafteries; Oxford, Reading, Bedford, Stamford, Nottingham, Northampton, Leicefter, and Grantham [3]. They were called Francifcans from their founder; Grey Friers from their cloathing; and Friers minors out of their pretended humility. Their habit was a fingle coat of grey colour, girt with a cord, and reaching down to their ancles, with a cowl of the fame, and a cloak over it when they went abroad [4]. They went barefoot, and poffeffed nothing, but lived on charity.

Their priory at Leicefter was founded by *Simon Montfort* the fecond earl of Leicefter of that name. In fome collections, however, made by Mr. Stow (a MS. formerly in the poffeffion of John Anftis, efq. Garter king of arms) out of the records of 23 Edward III, the houfe is faid to have been founded by one *Gilbert Luenor* and *Ellen* his wife [5]; and Mr. Peck, in one of his MSS. mentions *John Pickering*, of Stampwick, either as the founder or as an early benefactor.

This priory ftood on the South fide of St. Martin's church-yard, towards which there is a portal remaining, but all the other building is quite demolifhed.

Their church was probably that mentioned in Charyte's Rentale as " Ecclefia Sanctæ Trinitatis," which is plainly defcribed to be within the parifh of St. Martin; and is probably the fame that is fketched in the funeral proceffion exhibited in plate XVII. fig. 11.

In 1252, the guardian of this houfe made an award in a difpute concerning tithes between the church of Lichfield and priory of Lenton [6].

In 1402, the mafter of the Friers Minors of Leicefter, being convicted of treafon, was hanged at Tyburn, at the fame time with fir Roger Clarendon, a natural fon of the famous Black Prince. Stevens [7] fays, that, in 1402, fome affirmed that king Richard II. was alive, and a confpiracy was difcovered, for which fome were put to death; among thefe, fome were Grey friers; of which one Richard Frifeley, doctor of divinity, being afked what he would do if king Richard were prefent, anfwered, " that he would fight in his quarrel againft any man, even to death;" whereupon he was drawn and hanged in his religious habit [8]. Shortly after, fir Roger Clarendon, baftard fon of the Black Prince, and with him a fquire and yeoman, were beheaded; and eight Grey friers hung and beheaded at London, and two at Leicefter; all which had publifhed king Richard to be alive [9].

William of Leicefter, a Francifcan frier, educated at Oxford, is noticed by Wood as an early prælector at Hereford [10].

Brother *Gregory de Rofellis*, of this order, and bred in the fchool at Oxford, was prælector in their priory at Leicefter [11].

Robert of Leicefter [12], a frier of this order, was educated at Oxford, where he obtained the degree of D. D. and became afterwords prælector in divinity in the Francifcan priory in his native town. Leland fays of him, " Splendidam ex literis gloriam fibi comparavit, quo titulo inter Francifcanos totus eluxit. Scripfit " Commentarios" Longobardum illuftrantes; " Quodlibeta" etiam, ac libellum " de paupertate Chrifti." He wrote alfo " De computo Latinorum ad Ricardum Swinfeld epifcopum Hereford. tom. i." Two works of his are preferved in the Bodleian Library (Digb. 212.) 1. " De ratione temporum, five de computo Hebræorum, aptato ad kalendarium Latinorum," divided into four parts; and " De computo Hebræorum, lib. i." A MS. in Pembroke Hall, Cambridge, mentions alfo, by this author, " Lecturas fcripturarum lib. i;" and " Diftinctiones, lib. i." He died at Lichfield in 1348, and was buried there in the Francifcan priory [13].

Mafter *John of Leicefter*, parfon of Whethamfted, obtained the privilege of that manor temp. Edward I. [14]

Richard of Leicefter (it is not quite clear that he was a Francifcan) wrote " De articulorum fimboli diftributione fecundum Numerum Apoftolorum ;" a MS. formerly preferved in the library of Sion College [15].—This feems to be the " mafter Richard Rider, of Leicefter," whofe father's tomb Leland noticed in St. Mary's church; the fame that in thofe dayes, as apperith by his works, was a great clerke [16]."

Peter Swynerfted, the 8th provincial of the Grey Friers in England, and William Nottingham [17], S. T. P. the 19th provincial, were both buried in the church of this priory [18].

Adam Bill was warden 1521 [19]; but the laft warden was William Gyles, who, with feven other friers, furrendered his convent 10 Nov. 1539.

" Frater Willus Giles, gardianus domûs feu prioratûs Sancti Francifci de Leicefter, ordinis Sci Francifci, vulgariter nuncupat' le Gray Freers in com' Leic', alias dictus Willis Giles, prior domûs five prioratûs vulgariter nuncupat' le Gray Freers de Leyceftr', in com' Leyc', & ejufdem loci conventus. Nov. 10, anno regni 30°.

Per me Wyllum Gylys, gardianū.

Per me fratrem Simonem Harve, lectorem.

Per me fratrem Henricum Schepzed.

Per me fratrem Johannem Standyfche.

Per me Robertum Afftun.

Per me Radulphum Hyryk.

Per me Wyllum Abbot.

Recognitum fuit hoc prefens fcriptum per fupranominat' capitulum & conventum 13° die Novembris, anno tricefimo, coram nobis, Johe Catlyn, Georgio Afheby, & Johe Smith, commiffionariis dni ñri regis, &c. [20]"

In Speed's Catalogue, no revenues are accounted for as belonging to this houfe; whence they are fuppofed to have fubfifted upon alms [21]; but the Minifters Accompts in the Augmentation office thus defcribe their lands and poffeffions [22]:

[1] Matthew Paris, p. 286.   [2] Batteley, Antiquities of Canterbury, p. 54.   [3] Stevens, Monafticon, vol. I. p. 95, 96.
[4] See their drefs, with and without the mantle, in plate XX. fig. 2, 3.   [5] Tanner, Notitia Monaftica.
[6] See before, p. 295.   [7] Monafticon, vol. I. p. 112.   [8] Stow's Chronicle, p. 347.   [9] Ibid.
[10] Hift. & Antiq. Univerfitatis Oxon. p. 69.   [11] Stevens, vol. I. p. 127.
[12] Another *Robert of Leicefter* was archdeacon of Ely 1238—1241. See Le Neve, p. 73.   [13] Tanner's Bibl. Brit. p. 636.
[14] Salmon's Herts, p. 146.   [15] Tanner, Bibl. Brit. p. 636.   [16] Itinerary, vol. I. p. 16.
[17] William of Nottingham, a canon and chanter of York cathedral. None of his works are printed; but there are feveral of them in the libraries of England; and, among others, fome Queftions upon the Four Gofpels, Reflections upon all the Gofpels of the Year, Queftions upon the Lord's Prayer, and a Treatife againft the Errors of Pelagius. He died Oct. 5, 1336. Dupin, 14th Cent. p. 63.   Leland's account of him, with notes, is in Tanner, Bibl. Brit. p. 362. Le Neve, Fafti, p. 316, puts him among the præcentors of York.   Having gone through the office of profeffor, he fucceeded Richard in that of provincial minifter; in the catalogue of which minifters, we have thefe words concerning him : " B. William Notyngham, doctor of Oxford, who made the famous Expofition on the Four Gofpels, lies at Leicefter." Stevens, Monafticon, vol. I. p. 132.—Quære de Will'o Nottingham circa 1330. Bale, p. 414.
[18] Hiftory of the Grey Friers, part 2. p. 12; and Stevens, vol. I. p. 97. a.
[19] Mr. Cole of Milton, MS. in a letter to Dr. Farmer.
[20] From the original furrender in the Augmentation-office. See the feal, plate XVII. fig. 11; and a fac-fimile of the handwriting of the guardian and prælector in plate XX.
[21] Hiftory of the Grey Friers, London, 1726, 4to, part 2. p. 29.   [22] Communicated by Mr. Caley.

Rents

Rents of affize.

" Four fhillings for free-rent of the heirs of William Wigfton, for land and foil, where a certain houfe of poor is fituated.

Site of the late houfe, with the lands within the precinct.

Twenty fhillings for the rent of the foil and land where the buildings of the faid houfe were conftructed, with all other lands and gardens within the precinct of the fame, being in the hands and occupation of the late prior and co-brethren.

Sum total — £1. 4s."

" The Gray Freres of Leircefter ftode at the ende of the hofpital of Mr. Wigefton. Simon Mountefort, as I lernid, was founder thereof; and there was byried king Richard III. flayne at Bofworth-field, and a knight caullid Mutton, fumtyme mayre of Leyrcefter [1]."

" The dead corps of Richard was as fhamefullie carried to the towne of Leicefter as he gorgeouflie the day before with pompe and pride departed out of the fame towne; for his bodie was naked and defpoiled to the very fkin, and nothing left about him, not fo much as a clout to cover his privy parts; and was truffed behind a purfevant of arms, one Blanch Senglier, or White-boar, like a hog or calf; his head and arms hanging on the one fide of the horfe, and his legs on the other fide; and all befprinkled with mire and bloud, he was brought to the Graie Friers church within the town, and there laie like a miferable fpectacle [2]; and afterward, with fmall funeral pomp, was there interred [3]."—" But to leave the tyrant as he died, you fhall underftand king Henry the Seventh caufed a tomb to be made, and fet up over the place where he was buried, with a picture of alabafter reprefenting his perfon [4]; which at the fuppreffion of that monaftery was utterly defaced: fince when, his grave, over-grown with nettles and weeds, is not to be found; only the ftone cheft wherein his corpfe lay is now made a drinking-trough for horfes, at a common inn in Leicefter, and retaineth the only memory of this monarch's greatnefs. But his body (as is reported) was carried out of the city, and contemptuoufly beftowed under the end of Bow-bridge [5], which giveth paffage over a branch of Stowre, upon the Weft fide of the town. Upon this bridge (the like report runneth) ftood a ftone of fome height; againft which king Richard, as he paffed toward Bofworth, by chance ftruck his fpur; and againft the fame ftone, as he was brought back, hanging by the horfe's fide, his head was dafhed and broken, as a wife woman forfooth had foretold; who, before his going to battle, being afked of his fuccefs, faid, that where his fpur ftruck his head fhould be broken. But thefe are but reports [6]."

" After revenge and rage had fatiated their barbarous cruelties upon his dead body, they gave his royal earth a bed of earth, honourably, appointed by the order of king Henry the Seventh, in the chief church of Leicefter, called St. Mary's, belonging to the order and fociety of the Grey Friers; the king in fhort time after caufing a fair tomb of mingled-coloured marble, adorned with his ftatue, to be erected thereupon; to which fome grateful pen had alfo deftined an epitaph, the copy whereof (never fixed to his ftone) I have feen

in a recorded manufcript book chained to a table in a chamber in the Guildhall of London, which (the faults and corruptions amended) is thus reprefented, together with the title thereunto prefixed, as I found it [7]:

" Epitaphium Regis Richardi Tertii, fepulti ad Leiceftriam, juffu et fumptibus Sti Regis Henrici Septimi.

" Hic ego, quem vario tellus fub marmore claudit,
  Tertius a jufta [a] voce Richardus eram.
Tutor eram patriae [b], patrius pro jure nepotis;
  Dirupta, tenui regna Britanna, fide.
Sexaginta dies binis duntaxat ademptis
  Æftatefque tuli tunc [c] mea fceptra duas.
Fortiter in bello certans [d] defertus ab Anglis,
  Rex Henrice, tibi, feptime, fuccubui.
At fumptu, pius ipfe, tuo, fic offa dicaras [e],
  Regem olimque facis regis honore coli.
Quatuor exceptis jam tantum, quinque bis annis,
  Acta trecenta quidem, luftra falutis erant.
Anteque Septembris undena luce kalendas,
  Reddideram rubræ jura petita [f] Rofæ.
At mea, quifquis eris, propter commiffa precare,
  Sit minor ut precibus pœna levata [g] tuis."

*** Various readings in this epitaph, in a copy given by Sandford, p. 435, from the Heralds College MSS. vol. I. p. 3: [a] Multa. [b] Nam patriæ tutor. [c] Non. [d] Merito. [e] Decoras. [f] Dedita jura. [g] Fienda.

Englifhed:

" I who am laid beneath this marble ftone,
Richard the Third, poffefs'd the Britifh throne.
My Country's guardian in my nephew's claim,
By truft betray'd I to the kingdom came.
Two years and fixty days, fave two, I reign'd;
And bravely ftrove in fight; but, unfuftain'd,
My Englifh left me in the lucklefs field,
Where I to Henry's arms was forc'd to yield.
Yet at his coft my corfe this tomb obtains, }
Who pioufly interr'd me, and ordains }
That regal honours wait a king's remains. }
Th' year thirteen hundred 'twas and eighty-four, }
The twenty-firft of Auguft, when its power }
And all its rights I did to the Red Rofe reftore. }
Reader, whoe'er thou art, thy prayers beftow,
T'atone my crimes, and eafe my pains below."

" The wicked and tyrannical prince king Richard III, being flain at Bofworth, his body was begged by the nuns [friers] at Leicefter (aliter Grey friers), and buried in their chapel there; at the diffolution whereof, the place of his burial happened to fall into the bounds of a citizen's garden; which being (after) purchafed by Mr. Robert Heyrick (fome time mayor of Leicefter), was by him covered with a handfome ftone pillar, three feet high, with this infcription: " Here lies the body of Richard III. fome time king of England." This he fhewed me (Chriftopher [8] Wren, B. D.) walking in the garden, 1612 [9]."

The Rev. Samuel Carte, vicar of St. Martin's in Leicefter, fays, in 1720, " I know no other evidence that the ftone coffin formerly ufed for a horfe-trough was king Richard's, but the conftancy of the tradition. There is a little part of it ftill preferved at the White Horfe Inn, in which one may obferve fome appearance of the hollow, fitted for retaining the head and the fhoulders."

---

[1] Probably Moton; but no fuch name occurs in the lift beginning in 1268. If he was mayor, it muft be before that time.

[2] Holinfhed, p. 760. " Then was the corps of Richarde, late king, fpoyled and naked as he was borne, cafte behynd a man, and fo caryed unreverently overthwarte the horfebacke unto the Fryers at Leycefter: where after a feafon that he had been that all men myght beholde him, he was there with lytell reverence buryed." Fabian, p. 418.

" Occidit in bello miferanda cæde Richardus
Crinibus attractus dum ferro fævit hoftis."

Dr. John Hird, in Hift. Angl. cited by Buck, in The Complete Hiftory of England, vol. I. p. 542.—" And after all," fays Buck, " to complete their barbarifm, they threw his body behind one upon a jade, and fo conveyed it to Leicefter."—" The body, after many indignities and reproaches, was obfcurely buried; for though the king [Henry VII.] of his noblenefs gave charge unto the friers of Leicefter to fee an honourable interment to be given unto it; yet the religious people themfelves, being not free from the humours of the vulgar, neglected it." Lord Bacon's Life of Henry VII. Ibid. 578.—T. Carte, vol. II. p. 818, fays, " Richard's corpfe, with a rope about his neck, thrown like a calf acrofs a horfe, was carried, and, after being treated with horrible indignities, was at laft buried in the church of the Grey Friers without any folemnity."

[3] Baker's Chronicle, p. 251.—Grafton, p. 852, fays, " he was with no leffe funerall pompe and folemnitie enterred then he would to be done at the burrying of his innocent nephewes, whom he caufed cruelly to be murthered, and unnaturally to be quelled."

[4] Holinfhed, v. II. p. 761. I cannot find Mr. Hutton's authority for calling this a fcrubby monument. See his Bofworth Field, p. 142.

[5] See hereafter, p. 301.   [6] Baker, ubi fupra.   [7] Buck's Richard III, in the Complete Hiftory of England, vol. I. p. 577.

[8] At that time tutor, at St. John's College, Oxford, to the eldeft fon of fir William Heyrick of Beaumanor; in whofe family feveral curious letters of Mr. Wren's are preferved.   [9] Wren's Parentalia, p. 114.

Mr.

Mr. Throfby adds, " When I was a boy, the end that then remained ftood as a part of a heap of rub-bifh, in the inn-yard, of brick-ends, ftones, &c. and was in appearance like the fketch here annexed [1]."

And Mr. Hutton fays, " I took a journey to Lei-cefter in 1758, to fee a trough which had been the repofitory of one of the moft fingular bodies that ever exifted; but found it had not withftood the ra-vages of time. The beft intelligence that I could ob-tain was, that it was deftroyed about the latter end of the reign of George the Firft, and fome of the pieces placed as fteps in a cellar at the fame inn where it had ferved as a trough [2]."

In 1513, the king's letters patent were obtained, by *William, Thomas,* and *Roger Wigfton,* for founding the hofpital of St. Urfula, now called Wigfton's Hofpital, on ground which was within the precincts of the Grey Friers; to which, in 1520, *William Fifher,* the firft mafter of that hofpital, obtained the addition of St. Francis's garden. For all this, the heirs of William Wigfton engaged to pay for ever to the Crown an annual quit-rent of 4s.

A proceffion to a funeral [3] in this church is thus defcribed in the MSS. of Mr. Peck:

" Proceffio quedam funebris antiqua, quâ cadaver vefpillonibus tedas ferentibus preceffum eft, & Fra-tribus Mendicantibus afportatum, fequente magnâ collachrymantium turbâ.—1. Vefpillones atratis vefti-bus cereos magnos cadaveri preferentes.—2. Frater niger, five predicator, ordinis Sancti Dominici.—3. Frater leucopheatus, five minor, ordinis Sancti Fran-cifci.—4. Frater albus, five Carmeliticus [4], ordinis beate Marie de Monte Carmeli.—5. Frater Eremiticus, ordinis Sancti Auguftini.—6. Confanguinei, affines, proximi, pauperes, populique plurimi alii fubfequentes, condolentefque.

Notandum eft, quòd cùm unicuique domui mendi-cantium aliquam eleemofinam dono dederit vir mortuus, tum cadaver ejus vefte fratris mendicantis indutum eft; idemque uniufcujufque ordinis frater unus linteolis ad ecclefiam fepulchrum versùs afportat, & in hunc mo-dum eorum omnium confratri agnofcitur mortuus, & bonorum operum cujufcunque ordinis mendicantium (uti afferitur) fit particeps. Nec mirum igitur, quòd fuper tumulos fuos, & monumenta fepulchralia, laico-rum etiam mortuorum effigies, veftibus religiofis à fculptoribus indute, non rarò videntur expreffe [5].

The fite of the Grey Friers was granted, in 1536, to *John Bellowe,* efq. and *John Broxholme,* gentleman; who had before obtained the manor of Willoughby, with many very confiderable poffeffions in this and feveral other counties [6]; and, on the 31ft of Auguft that year, paid £200. to fir *John Williams,* knt. trea-furer of the Augmentation of the provifions of the Crown, as the laft payment on the fum of £2370. 19s. 0¼d. due for their immenfe purchafe; amongft which were the fite of the late *Grey Friers* of *Leicefter;* the 4s. quit-rent paid yearly to the faid houfe of friers by the heirs of *William Wigfton;* the fite of the *Friers*

Auguftines within the fame town [7], and all the tene-ments belonging to that priory.

The Particular for this grant of the Grey Friers, &c. is in the Augmentation-Office, and agrees with the Minifters' Accompt before-mentioned, with this addi-tion, that the houfe and lands were valued at the faid fum of £1. 4s. by the officers of the king at the time of the furrender; and there is alfo to the Particular this note: " Memorandum, the king's highnes hathe no more lands and tenements belonging to the faid late Fryer-houfe then be above-mentioned, to the au-ditor's knowledge. Thefe premifes were fold to *Bel-low* and *Broxholme* at twenty years purchafe."

The church was foon after demolifhed; as we find among the payments of the churchwardens of St. Mar-tin's, in 1545, fix load of freeftone from the *Freers* at 18s. the load; 7d. a day to the chief workmen; and 4d. to the ordinary ones; and again, in 1561, a charge of 15s. for a beam to be laid on the high roof, fetched from the *Freers* [8].

The fite of the Grey Friers [9] became afterwards the property of Sir *Robert Catlyn;* from whom it paffed to Alderman *Robert Heyrick* [10], who died June 14, 1618; and, by his laft will, charged this eftate with the following annual payments; one fhilling to each of the poor people in Trinity Hofpital (then 110); 40s. to poor widows of the Borough; and 13s. 4d. to the fchool-mafter that teacheth the petties, or under-ufher of the free-fchool in Leicefter [11].

This part of the Alderman's property was fold, in 1711, by his great grandfon, *Samuel Heyrick,* clerk, to *Thomas Noble,* efq. whom Mr. Carte, in 1720, defcribes as then having " a very fair houfe within the precincts of the priory of the Grey-friers."

About the year 1731, a brafs feal [12] was dug up in a garden in the Frier-lane, belonging to a houfe of Mr. Simpfon, within the precincts alfo of this priory. In the centre, under a rude Gothic arch, IȠS, and round it, ЄST AṀOR ṀЄ', making, when complete, Iefus eft Amor meus [13]; an infcription not unfrequent on old monuments and on rings [14].

" The fine fpacious grounds belonging to this friery extended from the upper-end of the Market-place nearly to the Frier-lane meeting-houfe; much of which has been built on in my time. When the work-men were digging for the cellars to the range of houfes which face St. Martin's church, they caft up, I re-member, many human bones; one fkeleton entire [15]."

The late *Rogers Ruding,* efq. devifee of Mr. *Noble,* after allotting a piece of ground throughout for a common ftreet, now called New-ftreet, in which many good houfes are fince built, fold the fite of the Grey-friers, to different purchafers.

The manfion-houfe and gardens were fold by Mr. Ruding to Mr. *Garle* in 1752, and by Mr. Garle's heirs in 1776 to *Thomas Pares,* junior, efq. F. A. S. who has lately beautified the houfe, and added two extenfive wings to it. From this houfe the original quit-rent ftill continues to be paid.

---

[1] Throfby's Leicefter, p. 291. See this copied in plate XX. fig. 4.

[2] Hutton's Bofworth Field, p. 142.   [3] See plate XVII. fig. 11.

[4] If this fketch of a funeral was originally made for one that took place in the church of the Grey Friers at Leicefter, as Mr. Peck fuppofed, it fhould feem as if there had once been a fmall cell of Carmelites, or White Friers, in this town.

[5] Peck, MSS. vol. V. (Harl. MSS. 4938.) p. 11.

[6] See feveral grants to them in 36 & 37 Hen. VIII. in Jones's Index, vol. I. under the Originalia temp. Hen. VIII.

[7] Stevens's Monafticon, Appendix, p. 4, 5.   [8] Churchwardens' Accompts of St. Martin's parifh.

[9] It was called, in title-deeds to property which it bounded, " lands formerly belonging to fir Robert Catlyn, knt. deceafed, and now the land of the heirs of Robert Heyrick, gent. deceafed;"—this in 1620. Robert died in 1618.—In another; dated 9 Car. " formerly, &c. and now the lands of the heirs of Tobye Heyricke, clerk." Tobias died in 1627.—In another, dated 1653, " formerly, &c. and now the land of John Heyrick, gent."

[10] In a letter to his brother Sir William, Jan. 8, 1615-16, Mr. Robert Heyricke fays, " For the Blake Fryars, I never ment, nor doe not, to part with them, but you fhall be pryvy to it or yt go; although Mr. Archdeacon and 2 or 3 more have fent to me to know if I would fell yt. And I thinke I doe yt fomewhat too deare to them; yet one was fo round with me that I tolld him I muft except that yf a frend of myne wolld challenge my former promes, I muft perform yt." And in another letter, Dec. 17, 1616, " This morning, about 9 of the clok, as I was coomyng forthe of my chambre, the bells at Sent Marten's very fodenly rung aloud; and prefently word was brought me, that the fire was at Fryars; and prefently word cam that yt was a kylln of Robart Cocke adjoyning to the Fryars, in a very dangerous place, where the ftac of corn and hay lay nere; but, the Lord be praifed! it was quickly quenched." From the originals at Beaumanor.

[11] This appears from " Certain Braunches of the will of Mr. Robert Heyrick, one of the Aldermen of this Burrow of Lei-cefter," hung up in the Town-hall parlour by the fide of the picture, and printed under Houghton on the Hill, vol. II. p. 617.

[12] See plate XVII. fig. 10.

[13] In the will of William of Wickham is this bequeft: " Item, lego domino meo archiepifcopo Cantuarienfi unum anulum aureum, cum lapide de ruby. Item, unum par precum de auro appenfum ad unum monile de auro, habens hæc verba in-fculpta, I. H. C. eft Amor meus." Dr. Lowth's Life of that Prelate, Appendix, p. xxxviii.

[14] Gent. Mag. vol. LXVI. p. 458.   [15] Throfby's Leicefter, p. 291.

FRIERS EREMITES OF ST. AUGUSTINE.

According to Mofheim[1], the *hermits* of St. *Auguftine* had for their founder Alexander IV.[2] who, obferving that the *hermits* were divided into feveral focieties, fome of which followed the maxims of their famous *William*, and others the rule of St. *Auguftine*, while others were again diftinguifhed by different denominations, formed the wife project, in 1256, of uniting them all into one religious order[3], and fubjecting them to the fame rule of difcipline as that of St. Auguftine.

" *Auguftinian Eremites* lag laft, of far later date than *Auguftinian Monks*, as who firft entered England, anno 1252[4]; and had (if not their *firft*) their *faireft* habitation in St. *Peter's the Poor*, London; thence probably taking the denomination of *Poverty* (otherwife at this day one of the richeft parifhes in the city) becaufe the faid *Auguftinian Eremites* went under the notion of *begging friers*. Mean time, what a mockery was this, that thefe fhould pretend to be *Eremites*, who, inftead of a *wide wildernefs*, lived in *Broad-ftreet, London*, where their church at this day belongeth to the Dutch congregation! To give thefe Auguftine friers their due, they were good *difputants*; on which account they are remembered ftill in *Oxford*, by an act performed by *candidates* for mafterfhip, called *Keeping of Auguftine*[5]."

They had for their habit a white garment and fcapulary, when they were in the houfe; but in the choir, and when abroad, they had over the former a cowl, and a large hood, both black, which were girt with a black leathern thong[6].

The houfe of the friers Eremites at Leicefter was called " The Priory of St. Katharine;" or, more commonly, " The Auguftine Friers of Leicefter;" but when it was built, or by whom founded, is uncertain.

" Thefe Friers," fays Mr. Carte, I have found ftyled " St. Katharine's Auftin Friers;" I fuppofe becaufe their church or chapel was dedicated to St. Katharine; and I take them to be thofe who were fettled without the Weft gate Northwards, between the two channels of the river.

In 1304, *Thomas* earl of *Lancafter* obtained the king's permiffion to give to the friers Eremites of the order of St. Auftin, in the county of Leicefter, three meffuages, fituated contiguous to their priory *(manfo dilectorum in Chrifti fratrum Hermitarum ordinis Sancti Auguftini Leiceftr', in fuburbio ejufdem ville, contigua)* for the purpofe of enlarging their place of habitation[7] *(ad elargationem manfi fui ibidem)*.

In 1377, the Auguftine friers obtained leave to eat flefh, upon condition that they fhould keep the faft of the Friers Minors before Chriftmas[8].

Bifhop Tanner, in his Bibliotheca Britannica-Hibernica, p. 613, has recorded Thomas Ratcliff[9], a learned native of [Radcliffe] on the Wreke in this county, an excellent preacher *(concionator)*, who was an Auguftine Eremite at Leicefter, D. D. and at length a bifhop, though of what fee neither Bale nor

Pitts with certainty knew. Pitts fuppofed 'him to be bifhop of Lincoln, perhaps becaufe Leicefter was within that diocefe. He flourifhed, according to Bale[10], in 1360; or, as Pitts[11], in 1370. His principal works were, " Lecturæ Scholafticæ;" lib. i. " Pro introitu fententiarum," lib. i; and " Conciones ad vulgum," lib. i. Wharton[12] mentions a Thomas Ratcliffe, bifhop of Dromore in Ireland, and *chorepifcopus* of Durham, who died a little before 1489; who is alfo noticed by Ware[13].

On the 23d of February 1532, it was agreed before Mr. Nicholas Rennold, then mayor, by confent of the wardens and all the company of journeymen-fhoemakers, that they fhould give yearly to the Auftin friers in Leicefter, for all the brethren and fifters to be prayed for, in ready money, 10s. to be paid at two times in the year, befides the offering days before ufed.

Richard Prefton, the laft prior, furrendered this convent[14] 10 November, 1539.

" Omnibus, &c. Richardus Prefton, prior domûs five prioratûs Sancte Katherine de Leycefter, ordinis Sancti Auguftini, in com' Leyceftr', alias dictus frater Richardus Prefton, frater domûs five prioratûs vulgariter nuncupat' Auguftin friers de Leyceftr', in com' Leyceftr', & ejufdem loci conventus, &c. Dat' 10° die Novembris, anno regni 30°.
Richard Prefton, prior.
Richard Holman, fub-prior.
John Whyte. John Greer."

Extracts from the Minifters Accounts, co. Leicefter, 34 Henry VIII. in the Augmentation-Office[15].

Lands and poffeffions of the Houfe of Auftin Friers, in the town of Leicefter.

Eight fhillings for the farm of a clofe within the precinct of the late houfe there, called *The Water Clofe*, with the appurtenances, demifed to John Smythe, by indenture under the conventual feal, dated 7 Oct. 29 Henry VIII. for 21 years.

Eight fhillings for a clofe lying within the precinct of the faid houfe, called *Le Bake-broke Clofe*, demifed to the faid John Smythe, by conventual leafe, dated 19 September, 30 Henry VIII.

One fhilling and eight-pence for the farm of one curtilage, lying out of the Weft-gate of the town of Leicefter, demifed to Thomas Creffey. Sum, 17s. 8d.

Site of the faid late houfe, with the lands and buildings of the fame.

Four fhillings and four-pence for the rent of the foil and land within the precinct of the late houfe aforefaid, including 12d. for a certain parcel of land there, called *The Pree*, containing, by eftimation, half a rood; and a certain vacant place on the South fide of the church there, containing half a rood and 20 perches, being in the hands of the late prior and convent aforefaid.—Sum total, £1. 2s.

---

[1] Ecclef. Hift. cent. XIII. ch. II. fect. xxii.   [2] This edict of pope Alexander IV. is to be found in the new edition of the *Bullarium Romanum*, tom. I. p. 110. See alfo *Acta Sanctorum*. menf. Februar. tom. II. p. 472.

[3] Innocent had a defign of uniting all thefe orders of friers into one, and it was executed by his fucceffor Alexander IV. who made one conventual of them under a general, and called them *Hermits of St. Auguftine*, though he had drawn them from their hermitages to live in towns, and to employ them in the affairs of the church. Dupin, Ecclef. Hift. cent. XIII. p. 157.

[4] Somner, Antiquities of Canterbury, p. 16, affigns from Bale the fame period for their introduction into England.

[5] Fuller's Church Hiftory, Book VI. Hiftory of Abbeys, p. 273; cited by Newcourt, in Repertory, vol. I. p. 289.

[6] See the drefs of a frier of this order in plate XXI.   [7] Pat. 32 Edw. I. m. 1.   [8] Leland, Coll. vol. I. pars 2. p. 308.

[9] In Godwin de Præfulibus, Radcliffe does not occur among the furnames; and, according to Godwin and Le Neve, John Gynewell, alias Gyndwell, was bifhop from 1351 to 1362. Suppofing, therefore, as Tanner has fuggefted, Thomas Ratcliff, the Eremite frier, to have been an Englifh bifhop, he could be only a fuffragan. It fhould feem that this famous *concionator* never publifhed any of his performances, as he is not noticed in Dupin's Hiftory of Ecclefiaftical Writers; or rather, it may be fairly prefumed that his performances had not in them a fufficient degree of excellence to countenance their being printed; and it is not clear, from the account of Tanner, where the MSS. are depofited. Nor of the fourteenth century does Dupin mention any other frier Eremite or Hermit of St. Auguftine, whofe chriftian name was Thomas, than Thomas of Strafburg, vol. XII. p. 71.   [10] Cent. xvi. fol. 463.   [11] P. 504.   [12] Anglia Sacra, tom. I. p. 778.

[13] De Præfulibus, p. 93. Thomas Ratcliffe, mentioned by Wharton and Ware as bifhop of Dromore in Ireland, and as having died a little before 1489, is a century too late for a man reported by Bale to have flourifhed in 1360, and by Pitts in 1370.

[14] See the feat affixed to this furrender, and the hand-writing of the prior and fub-prior, plate XVII. fig. 8.

[15] Communicated by Mr. Caley.

Leland

3. A NUN OF THE ORDER OF PENANCE AT LEICESTER.

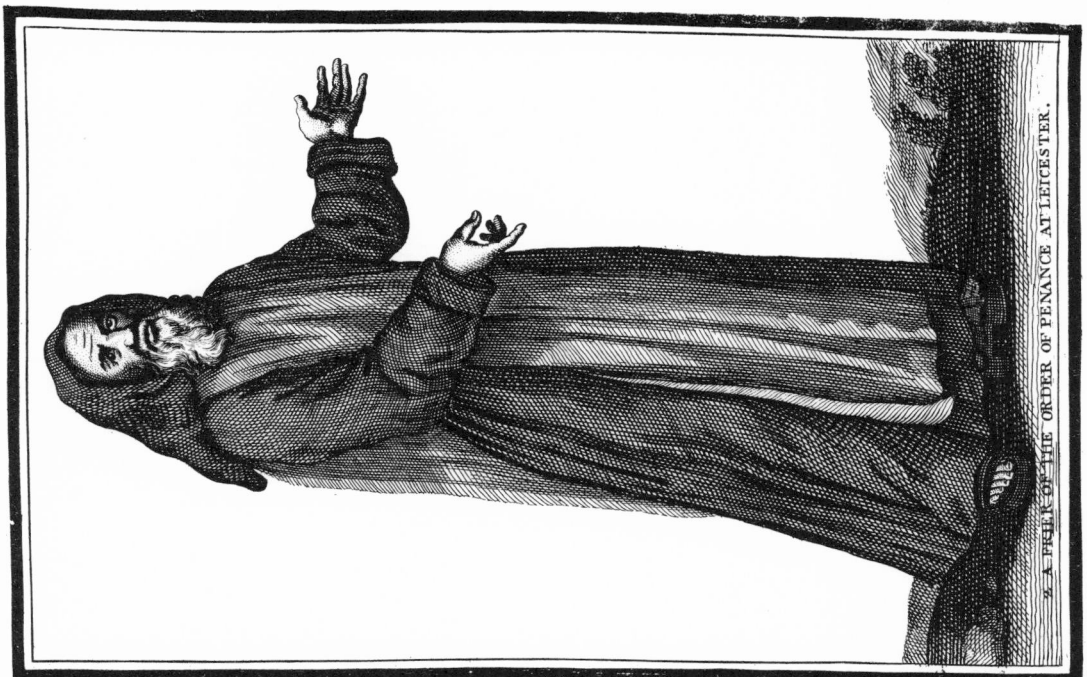

2. A FRIER OF THE ORDER OF PENANCE AT LEICESTER.

1. AN EREMITE AUGUSTINE OF LEICESTER.

BOW BRIDGE, the Property of

Joseph Cradock Esqr M. A. F. A.

Published as the Act directs, by T. Woodcock, May 1, 1795.

Leland thus defcribes this priory and its church :

" A little above the Weft-bridge the Sore cafteth out an arme ; and fone after it cummith in again, and maketh one ftreame. Wythin this ile ftandeth the Blake[1] Frieres very pleafauntly ; and harde by the freres is alfo a bridge of ftone over th* arme of Sore. And after the hole water creping aboute half the toune cummith thorough the North bridge of a vii. or viii. arches of [ftone.] And there Sore·brek[eth into two] armes againe, wher[of the biggeft] goith by S. Maries a[bbey ftanding] on the farther ripe; and the other, caullid the Bifshoppes water, bycaufe the bifhop of Lincoln's tenentes have privilege on it, and after fone methith with the bigger arme, and fo infulatith a right large and plefaunt medow ; wherapon the abbay, as I fuppofe, in fum writinges is caullid S. Maria de Pratis. (Sore cumming again fhortely to one botom goith a 4 miles of by the ruines of the caftel of Mountforelle.) Over the midle part of this arme of Bifshops water is a meane ftone bridge: and a litle beyond it is a nother ftone bridge, thorough the which paffit a litle land broke, cumming from villages not far of, and fo rennith into Bifshops water. And by Bifshops water is a chapel longging to the hofpital of S. John[3]."

" If I am not very much miftaken, the traces of the foundation of this priory church are now difcoverable : by which it appears that its direction was from Eaft to Weft, agreeable with the cuftom of church-building ; and was in length about 150 feet, and in width 90. It ftood near by the centre of what Leland calls the " ile" between the arms of the Sore. I have examined people who have lately dug in this place to make a garden ; by whom it appears that the foundations of buildings were found almoft all the way, Southwardly, from the fite of the church, in various directions; many of which indeed I faw taken up myfelf: whence an opinion may be hazarded, that the houfe of the Auguftine Friers ftood on, or rather occupied all, or a great part of the ground on the South fide of the church. On the North fide no foundations are to be traced[4]."

" On the South-eaft fide of the Weft-bridge[5] is a dwelling-houfe, refting on its edge, the water paffing under it through the arch neareft the town; and the back part continuing above the water on ftone-work : once a chapel, with a bell on the Southweft without, near the top ; the frame of which ftill remains, though the window, through which it might play, is ftopped up. Here two mendicant friers afked alms, for the benefit of the neighbouring priory[6]."

" There was alfo till very lately a foot-bridge covered wholly over with ivy, and called *Bow-bridge*, becaufe it confifted of one large arch like a bow, ftriding from the Friers near the Weft-bridge, over a back water of the Soar, to the clofe or garden called Bow church-yard[7] ; and, by the narrownefs of it, was evidently only a foot-bridge for the ufe of the friers to a conftant fpring of limpid water, on the paved road fide, a few paces diftant, called *St. Auftin's Well*[8], ftill overflowing with contributions to the back water ; and it is probable that the ground by the fide of it, now inclofed with a brick-wall, was a garden belonging to the priory. The well is three quarters of a yard broad, and the fame in length within its inclofure ; the depth of its water from the lip or backedging on the earth, where it commonly overflows, is half a yard. It is covered with a mill-ftone, and inclofed with ftone and brick on three fides; that towards Bow-bridge and the town is open[9]. This elegant and eafy curved arch is about 145 yards Wefterly from the Weft-bridge ; its length, from abutment to

abutment, ten yards and a half ; the breadth two yards thirteen inches and a half ; the height from a middle ftream (i. e. a middle height of water, neither high nor low) to the top of the abutment, is two yards, thirteen inches and a half ; the elevation or height, from the ftream in the centre to the top of the arch, three yards, one foot, ten inches and a half.

" A few yards to the South-eaft is another bridge, called Bow-bridge likewife[10], which leads from Bow church-yard to the town, confifting of five arches, rather low, which receives the ftream at a fmall diftance from the Braunfton-gate bridge to deliver it to Bow, thence to pafs at a fmall diftance into the conflux of the Soar. From this bridge to St. Auftin's well is 74 yards. The former Bow-bridge, confifting of one arch, only ferved to convey paffengers from the Friery to Bow church, and was without parapet walls ; which the other has, 2½ feet high, where, Baker's Chronicle fays, king Richard's fpur ftruck ; and the event was conftrued into an omen, that his head fhould be bruifed there. The length of this bridge is 23½ yards ; the breadth of it about five feet four inches: the arches are round.—The Bofworth, Hinckley, and Coventry road, from Leicefter, is over the Braunfton-gate bridge ; and its exiftence at that time might be doubted, except that the king might take this (i. e. Bow-bridge) as a bye-way, to efcape the crowd of the army, which yet he muft rejoin at the other end of the lane, beyond Danet's-hall garden. The common breadth of the road by the terrace by Danet's-hall clofe, called a Roman-way, feems about four feet in a hollow road between a regular defcent of clofe ground. From this bottom to the furface of the terrace, which is only a part of the defcent, is fourteen feet in height or more. The breadth of this terrace is about the fame breadth with the hollow way; that is, fourteen feet. The terrace has no ftone furface, but feems an eafy continuation of the clofes on its Eaft fide towards the town. Braunfton-gate Bridge[11], over a difcharge from the Back Soar, is 51 yards ; in the middle; and as far as the arches extend, three yards 28 inches wide ; the parapet walls are a yard high ; five yards and three quarters wide, at the North-weft end, which leads to the town, to near the firft arch. Here are four high arches pointed at top, 25 yards from the town's end to the narrower part[11]."

The fite of the peninfula on which this priory ftood was granted, in 1536, to *John Bellowe*, efq. and *John Broxholme*, gentleman[13] ; and in 1597 was the property of *Robert Temple* of Leicefter, as appears by the counterpart of an indenture between the faid *Robert Temple* and *Thomas Temple* his fon and heir apparent of the one part, and *Robert Heyricke* one of the comburgeffes of the town of Leicefter in the county of Leicefter aforefaid, ironmonger, of the other part. In confequence of £120. to the faid Robert and Thomas Temple by the faid Robert Heyricke then paid ; they, the faid Temples, did bargain, fell, and alien, unto the faid Robert Heyricke, his heirs, and affigns; " all that the fcyte, cyrcuite, and precynóte of the late dyffolved religyoufe howfe, or frerye, commely called or knowne by the name of, *The Auguftyne Freers*, fcytuate, lyeing, and being, in or neare adjoynyng to the Weft parte of the towne of Leiĉ aforefaid, and all the feyte and grouude therein conteyned, in quantytie by eftemacyon three akers, be yt more or leffe, nowe in the tenure and occupyeing of the faid Robᵗ Temple, or of his affigne or affignes; and one peece of meadowe-grounde, devyeded by a lytle gutture of water one the North parte of the faid

---

[1] The Eremite friers are here meant, whofe hàbit was *black*. Leland had before briefly noticed the Dominicans ; fee p. 296.

[2] Of this chapel, fee more hereafter. [3] Itinerary, vol. I. p. 18. [4] Throfby, MS.

[5] The Weft-bridge fpans the Soar, confifts of four arches, and is fituated near the Caftle. [6] Bickerftaffe, MS.

[7] Why Mr. Bickerftaffe chofe to call this Bow churchyard, or whether either of the demolifhed churches was Bow-church, I cannot difcover. It might have been conjectured that St. Sepulchre's *extra muros* ftood here, if Mr. Carte had not ftated that this was at the end of Southgate-ftreet. Or the friers of Penance might have had a fmall church or chapel here.

[8] Bow-bridge was repaired by the corporation in 1688, at an expence of £15. 12s. ; and St. Auftin's well for £2. 14s. 8d.

[9] Since this was written, it has been entirely deftroyed, occafioned by widening the road.

[10] The fite of thefe two bridges will readily be comprehended by referring either to plate XXII. or XXIII.—Fig. 1. fhews the prefent Bow Bridge ; fig. 2. the fite of the Auftin Friers ; fig. 3. St. Nicholas's church ; fig. 4. the foot-bridge to St. Auftin's Well.

[11] This bridge is in St. Mary's parifh ; as are all the houfes beyond the bridge towards Braunfton, and all the land in the liberty.

[12] Bickerftaffe, MS. who adds, " This bridge, which croffes the old Soar South-wefterly, was widened with brick, and the lane leading to it, called Dun's Lane, made commodious for paffengers, in 1792." [13] See before, p. 298.

fcyte next adjoynyng; and alfo one clofe of pafture, with the appurteñies, called *The Bowebryge-clofe*, conteyning by eftimacyon three akers of grounde, be yt more or lefs, late pcell of the faid late dyffolved relygyoufe howfe, or fryerye, lyeing weftwarde betweene the water of Wye, devyedyng yt from the faid fryers of the Eaft partie, and the grounde of Leonard Dannett, efquyer, of the Weft parte; and alfo one parcell of grounde, conteynynge one gardaine, one yarde, and certaine buyldings for dvife purpofes in and upon parte of the fame yarde, coñionly called *St. Frauncys Gardaine*, in Leicefter aforefaid, with the faid buyldings, romethes, and eafements, ftanding, fet, lyeing, and being, in the town of Leiĉ aforefaid, and nowe in the occupyeing of Thomas Sampfon, pfeffor of God's moft holy worde, and mafter of the Hofpytall of Willm Wigfton, in the towne of Leiĉ aforefaid, of the foundacyon of the fame Willm, adjoyñge to the North parte of the late dyffolved relygyoufe howfe, or fryerye, coñionly called *The Grey Freres*; faving and alwayes excepting out of this bargaine and fale one lyttell pcell or platt of grounde, whereupon a lyttyl howfe is buylded and lyeth weftwarde betwixt the Soare and the walle of the faid Auguftyne fryers, and is taken as pcell of the fame fryers, and was lately rented at xxᵈ by the yeare; and alfo all and fingler howfes, &c. franchyfes, libertyes, waters, fyfhings, &c. w'foever they or any of them been or bee, to the faid late dyffolved relygyoufe howfe of the Auguftyne freres, Bowebryge-clofe, Seynt Frauncys Gardayne, or to any of theym belonginge, &c.; and all and every the rents referved upon any leafe or demyfe thereof, or any part thereof demifed, and now being in force, and not expyred; faving to the chaplaynes and poore of the faid hofpytal of Willm Wigfton, and their fucceffors, their leafe and terme of yeares therin conteyned dureing the contyneance of the fame terme of yeares, payeinge the yarly rent of iiiiˢ to the faid Robᵗ Heiricke, his heires or affignes, thereupon referved; to hold unto and to the ufe of the faid Robᵗ in fee."

The fite of the Auguftine Friers is now the property of *Jofeph Cradock*, efq. of Gumley, in this county; to whofe good tafte my readers are obliged for a faithful engraving of Bow-bridge[1], from a drawing which was fortunately taken by Mr. Schnebbelie in 1791, a few weeks only before its final demolition[2].

FRIERS DE PŒNITENTIA JESU CHRISTI.

This fhort-lived order of mendicant friers is of great antiquity; having been eftablifhed, long before the general union of the Friers Eremites, in the time of pope Innocent III, who died in 1216. Their firft introduction into England was in 1257; in which year, fays Matthew Paris, " there were feen in London a new order of friers, called *De Pœnitentiâ Jefu*, or *Fratres de Saccâ*, becaufe they were apparelled in fack-cloth, who had their houfe in London, near unto Alderfgate without the Gate, and had licence of Henry III, in the 54th year of his reign [1270] to remove to any other place; and in 1272 he gave them the Jews fynagogue in Lothbury[3]."

" This fraternity admitted both men and women, who yet were not in ftriĉtnefs efteemed *religious*, though they profeffed a certain religious kind of life; and therefore, as it was not a perfeĉt or complete religion, it was not a true order. They were permitted to have *property*; and, if they were married perfons, to continue in that ftate; and though, after their admiffion into the order, they could not lawfully or regularly marry, yet, fhould they happen to do fo, the marriage was reputed valid. In fhort, they were deemed ecclefiaftical perfons; but, whether they enjoyed the perfonal and real privileges of clerks and religious perfons, authors are not agreed. The men of this profeffion were called *Fratres de Pœnitentiâ Jefu Chrifti*, *Fratres Saccii*, *Sacci*, *Saccini*, *Saccitæ*, *Saccati*, *Freres aux Sacs*, *Fraires enfaques*, *de viridi vallæ*, *Sacs*, *Sac-Friars*, *de Saccis*, or *de Sacco*; for I cannot approve of the term *de Saccâ*, which I find in Stowe and Weever, and from them in bifhop Tanner. They were alfo ftyled *Continentes*, not becaufe they profeffed abfolute chaftity, for they lived in wedlock, but only as being obliged to abftain from their wives on certain days of the week. The women, on their part, were termed *Sorores de Pænitentiâ*, and *Sackettes*. As to the fack, whence the greater part of thefe appellations is taken, fome fay it was borrowed from the fack-cloth wherewith they were cloathed; others, becaufe it was fhaped like a fack; others, becaufe the brethren carried facks; and others again, that the fifters were called *de Sacco*, on account of the fcapulary made of fack-cloth, *de fachino panno*, which they wore out of humility. However, the profeffors of both fexes together are reprefented as numerous; and Stowe even pretends they had many good fcholars amongft them; a faĉt which I think may be juftly called in queftion, fince they appear to have been only *Fraterculi*, or *Fratricelli*, in any refpeĉt[4]."

Plate XXI. fhews the drefs of a frier and a nun.

This order is faid to have been included in the profcription of the council of Lyons 1275; when all mendicant orders were fuppreffed, excepting only the Dominicans, Franĉifcans, Auguftinians, and Carmelites[5]. But it is evident that at firft little regard was paid here to that decree; and that the houfes of this order in England, which were ten in number, each of which had its prior, were not immediately evacuated upon it. Certain it is, that in 1283 a priory of thefe friers fubfifted in a houfe long before eftablifhed in the Suburbs of Leicefter; though it appears that they were at that time involved in a fuit at law[6]; which probably terminated in their fuppreffion.

The order in general was naturally on the decline; and was peremptorily fuppreffed in England[7] in 1307 (in which year the prior of Lynne was their provincial), and univerfally by the council of Vienne in 1311[8].

---

[1] See plate XXII.—The view in plate XXIII. (originally engraved to accompany Mr. Peck's accotint of Richard's natural fon, in his " Defiderata Curiofa," vol. VII. N° 8,) was introduced into the Leicefterfhire Colleĉtions, under the Hiftory of Burbach; but, though correĉt as to fituation, was rendered abfurd by mifñaming the Auguftine friery, and ftill more fo by introducing a military proceffion over the foot-bridge. Both thefe defeĉts being removed, the view is now repeated.

[2] The bridge was wafhed away, on the 19th of November 1791, by a heavy flood, which had fwelled the river to nearly a level with its banks. The whole difappeared in an inftant; yet not even a blade of grafs on the banks feemed to have been damaged by the fide walls. During the preceding fummer, Mr. Cradock, with his accuftomed liberality, had been at fome expence in repairing this fine remnant of antiquity; and, after the accident, wifhed much to have had it completely reftored; but, on infpeĉtion by fome mafter-builders, when the flood had fubfided, it was found to be demolifhed paft all recovery. See Gent. Mag. vol. LXI. p. 980.

[3] Stow's London, ed. 1528, p. 220.   [4] Dr. Pegge, in Archæologia, vol. III. p. 126.   [5] Stevens, Monafticon, vol. II. p. 272.

[6] Plac. Affif. in com. Leic. 12 Edw. I. Rot. 3. de injufte diffeif. lib. ten. in Suburb. Leiceftr', Rot. 4. dorfo, contra Ricardum priorem fratrum de Pœnitentiâ Jefu Chrifti de Leyceftr', pro meff' in Bruntingfthorp.

[7] Peter-Houfe College, Cambridge, was founded in 1280 by Hugh de Balfham, bifhop of Ely, on the ruins of two hoftels of this order, which had been " monuments of the higheft antiquity." Carter's Hiftory of that Univerfity, p. 18.—Their chapel in Lothbury was granted in 1305 to Robert Fitz Walter, whofe adjoining houfe was in the place where now ftands Grocer's Hall; and the chapel, after being the refidence of feveral lord-mayors of London, was converted into the Windmill Tavern. Stow and Stevens, ubi fupra.   [8] Dr. Pegge, ubi fupra, p. 127.

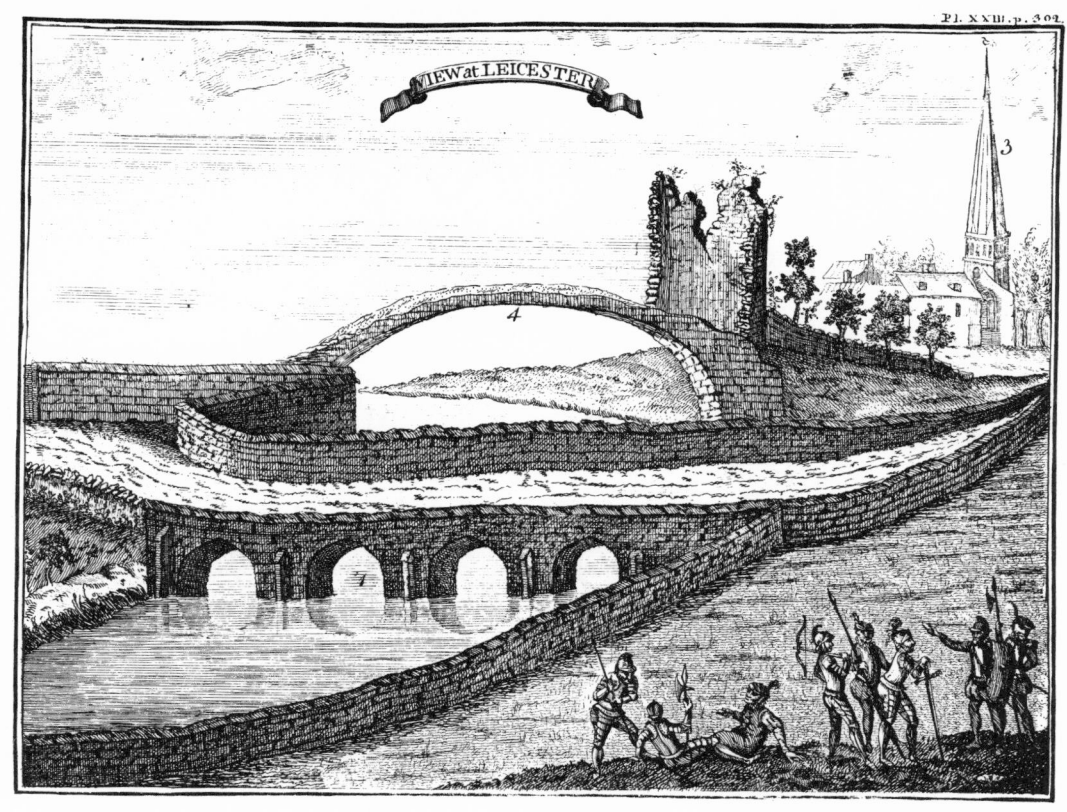

Pl. XXIII. p. 304.

VIEW at LEICESTER

CHAPEL OF St JOHN'S HOSPITAL.

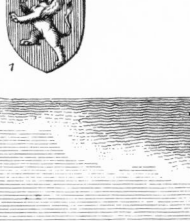  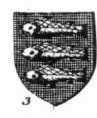  

The SPITAL HOUSE, in Belgrave Gate.

Plan for rebuilding St LEONARDS CHURCH.

Malcolm 1794

St. MARY'S, S.W.

M. 1794

A diftant View, with the CANAL.

Rev. Rob Throsby. del. 1796.

THE COLLEGIATE CHURCH OF ST. MARY DE CASTRO.

In the time of the Saxons there was a collegiate church situated a little below the castle [1] *(infra & juxta castellum)*, whose founder is unknown; which, having been destroyed, or at least very considerably damaged, as was the castle itself, at the Norman invasion, was completely repaired in 1107 [2], and dedicated to the Virgin *Mary*, by *Robert de Bellomont*, earl of *Mellent* and *Leicester*, who placed in it a dean and twelve secular canons; to whom he restored all the antient possessions which had belonged to the former church, with considerable additions; confirmed to them the churches of All Saints, St. Peter, and St. Martin, with all the lands and tithes thereto belonging; 60s. rent out of his rents at Lilburn, and 30s. rent in Blingessit and Thurmedeston, which had been given by *Ralph Boteler* to augment the prebends; and appropriated to them all the other churches in Leicester and its suburbs, except St. Margaret's [3]. He gave them the mill at the North bridge, for the cloathing of their sick; and, among other benefactions, all the churches that were within the soke of Shepeshed (which then included Shepeshed, Dixley, Hathern, Whatton, and Lockington); all those within the soke of Halso in Northamptonshire, and a confirmation grant of the church of Lilburn [4]. They had moreover, of the gift of the countess *Isabel*, one virgate of land in Burton; and, from the charitable donations of other benefactors, possessed the manor of Asfordby, with divers lands in that lordship and at Segrave [5].

The church of Clifton in Warwickshire, dedicated to the Assumption of our Lady, was antiently one of the prebends of this collegiate church, who possessed lands at Bigging in that county; which were given by *Henry de Rokeby*, in consideration of their resigning to him the chapel of Rugby. They had the mill also at Bigging, the gift of *Fulco de Holme* [6].

After the death of earl Robert de Bellomont, the canons of this church, with all their property, were in 1137 transferred, by his son *Robert Bossu* earl of Leicester [7], to the abbey of St. *Mary de Pratis*, which he in that year founded: but, that he might not totally seem to destroy his father's foundation, he, with the consent of Richard the first abbot, placed eight canons in the church of St. Mary de Castro [8]; one of whom was at length made dean. These were all instituted by the abbot; except one that was afterwards called vicar of the parish, who was instituted by the bishop: but this regulation was changed in 1400 [9]; when, by the consent and advice of Bp. Beaufort, the abbot and convent ordained that, for the future, either the dean or the sacrist should also be the vicar.

In the "Rentale" of William Charyte, the state of the second foundation is thus described:

"Patronus hujus ecclesie abbas Leycestr', sicut patet in matriculo in his verbis: ' Ecclesie Sce Marie de Castro patronus abbas Sce Marie de Pratis, habens eam in proprios usus [cum decimis garbarum [10], &c.] à fundatione canonicorum totam, exceptis oblationibus & obventionibus altaris, que deputate sunt septem clericis deservientibus in eâdem in propriis personis; qui etiam debent de suis portionibus duos capellanos ministrantes exhibere in eâdem; & exceptâ tertiâ parte garbarum de tribus carucatis terre, quas percipit abbas Sci Ebrulfi ab antiquo.

"Portio abbatis valet circiter LX solidos.

"Et notandum, quòd in compositione inter nos & abbatem de Sco Ebrulfo dictus abbas locavit abbati Leyc' ad perpetuam firmam omnes decimas garbarum de communâ comitis Leycestr' de South & West, que respondebat pro IIII carucatis terre, cum prato, sicut patet in extentis manerii Leycestr' & ejusdem comitis.

"In cartâ ordinationis canonicorum ecclesie Sce Marie de Castro sic scribitur: ' Universis Sce matris ecclesie filiis Robertus comes Leycestr' salutem. Notum sit universitati vestre, quòd Ricardus abbas & conventus ecclesie Sce Marie de Prato providerunt, ex consensu & consilio meo, &c. octo clericos honestos, &c. ad serviendum in ecclesiâ Sce Marie de Castello, ab eis eligendos; ad quorum sustentationem concesserunt omnes oblationes & omnes decimas, exceptis manipulis frugum; & omnia beneficia parochie illius ecclesie, que antea commune vocabatur. Ita quòd due portiones cedent sacriste qui ecclesie servitio providebit, cum XX s. de scaccario, &c. Relique sex portiones dabuntur sex clericis cum eo, &c. Octavus erit capellanus, qui ad sustentationem suam habebit quod priores capellani ante eum habere solebant. Sacramento singuli fidelitatem & canonicam subjectionem ecclesie Sce Marie de Prato promittent, &c. Capitulo illius ecclesie abbas presideat, vel alius canonicorum quem ad hoc mittere voluerit, semel in septimanâ, vel quoties voluerit, & leviores clericorum excessus ibidem emendet. Et si quis clericorum de prenominatis viciis vel de quolibet majori excessu accusatus in capitulum canonicorum veniet, super hoc abbatis & capituli judicium pariturus.

"Decanus & ceteri canonici instituendi sunt per abbatem. Vicarius instituendus est per episcopum, qui solebat habere de nobis ad sustentationem suam XXVI s. VIII d. Sed illud mutatum est ex assensu & consilio episcopi Lincoln'; & ordinatum est per abbatem & conventum, anno Domini MCCCC, quòd quicunque de cetero erit decanus, vel sacrista ipse, idem erit & vicarius; & habebit ad sustentationem suam duas portiones. Sic solebat habere, cum XX s. de scaccario, &c. ut in ordinatione eorundem octo clericorum.

"Compositionem vicarie require in libro parliamenti.

"Habemus ex scaccario dni regis, ex eleemosinâ antiquâ per fundatorem nostrum concessâ, & per cartam suam confirmatâ, VI li. [11]

"Abbas solvit, archidiacono Leycestrie, pro procurationibus, synodalibus, & denariis Sci Petri, ecclesie Sce Marie, IX s. ob. q. [12]

"Capella *Sancti Sepulchri* extra muros spectat ad ecclesiam Sce Marie de Castello, & est propria canonicorum ibidem, & debet deserviri per capellanum eorundem. Clericus illius ecclesie instituendus & imponendus est per abbatem."

---

[1] This is exactly the site of the present church; as may be seen in the two views in plate XXIV; in both of which the old *Mount* belonging to the Castle and the back front of the Castle itself (the only part that is antient) are represented. All Saints church, with the arms, given in the same plate, will be described hereafter.

[2] Cart. Antiq. CC. n. 23. anno 1107.   [3] Register of Leicester Abbey.   [4] See before, vol. I. p. 22; and Appendix, p. 54.

[5] Afterwards exchanged, by the abbot and convent of St. Mary de Pratis, for the manor of Knighton and the Suburbs of Leicester. See Appendix, p. 83.   [6] See before, under Leicester Abbey, p. 284, 285.

[7] Robertus comes Legrecestr' dedit eis præbendas & possessiones quæ fuerunt canonicorum secularium ecclesiæ S. Mariæ infra castellum de Legrecestrie. Hæ donationes factæ fuere tempore Hen. I. Alexandro episcopo Linc." Leland, Coll. I. i. 28.

[8] There remained till very lately in the vestry a kind of press called an *Ark*, containing seven cranes for the purpose of hanging up the vestments of the canons, with a socket for the eighth crane, which had long been lost. This press was destroyed in 1795, when the old vestry gave place to a new one.—"Churches collegiate may be evinced from their form across (as almost all of them are built); from stalls in the chancel; and a place where the priests used to hang their vestments." Gibson's Additions to Camden.—"Very many chancels, however, have stalls in them at the West end, without there being the least ground to imagine that the churches were of the collegiate kind: in these stalls were probably seated the curates of chapels dependent on the officiating priests at the private altars, who were expected to be attending on the parochial incumbent at the high altar on the great festivals, and on the day of the dedication of the churches. And it is not unlikely that the choir-singers of the parish might occasionally make use of these seats." S. D.

[9] In the Registers of the diocese of Lincoln, may be seen an instrument intituled, " Portionis permutatio;" on which Mr. Tyringham Stephens remarks, " Et ibi adverte inquisitionem quæ videtur facere per jurisdictionem abbatis monasterii de Pratis Leic' in dictam ecclesiam & prebendarios ejusdem." See the Introductory Volume, p. xcix.

[10] These three words are in the Abbey Register, but not in the Matriculus. See the Introductory Volume, p. lv.

[11] Charyte's Rentale, fol. xcix.   [12] Ibid. fol. ciii. a.

The

The church of St. Mary de Caſtro was parochial long before it ceaſed to be collegiate; and it appears by the preceding extracts that the chapel of St. Sepulchre once belonged to it. This church alſo was one of the earlieſt in Leiceſter that was provided with a regular cemetery [1]; and, in a taxation made about the year 1220, was rated at four marks [2].

In 1300, on a fine being paid into the Exchequer, *Peter of Leiceſter*, clerk, obtained liberty to give a meſſuage in Leiceſter, with the appurtenances, to the dean and canons of St. Mary de Caſtro, not ſubject to mortmain. Teſte rege, apud Karliol, 4° die Julii [3].

In 1323, it was proved that the prebendaries of this church were entitled to receive 10s. a year from the revenues of the earldom of *Leiceſter*, as a part of their founder's benefactions [4].

In 1358-9, king Edward III. by his letters patent, permitted the dean and canons of St. Mary in the Newark to ſettle an annual payment of 51s. 7d. on the ſacriſt, canons, and vicar, of St. Mary de Caſtro. Teſte rege, apud Weſtm. 24° die Januarii [5].

The advowſon of the church of Hathern, which belonged to the abbot and convent of Leiceſter as part of the ſoke of Shepeſhed, was granted by the abbot and convent, and confirmed in 1379 by the letters patent of king Richard II, to the ſacriſt and canons of St. Mary de Caſtello, reſerving to the abbot the accuſtomed penſion of 40s. and under a penalty of 500 marks not to alienate the ſame [6].

In 1408, the dean, ſacriſt, and canons of St. Mary de Caſtro (having, for a fine of 20 marks, procured licence from king Henry IV. to hold lands to the annual value of ten pounds) obtained letters patent to receive a grant from *Thomas Thorpe*, of Leiceſter, chaplain, *William Freman*, and *John Hornyngwould*, of twelve meſſuages, eleven tofts, a rood of arable land, the moiety of an acre of meadow, and 6s. 10d. rent, and the farther rent of one halfpenny, held under the king as duke of *Lancaſter*, and parcel of the honour of *Leiceſter* [7].

Theſe are all the grants which we have been able to trace to this collegiate church; yet, it may not be unneceſſary to obſerve, that the grant of Kempsford in Glouceſterſhire, and the appropriation of Higham Ferrars in Northamptonſhire, both which are ſaid in Tanner to have been given to this church, were the property of the collegiate church of St. Mary in the Newark, and will be there particularly noticed [8].

Leland ſays, "There was afore the Conqueſte a collegiate church of prebendes *intra caſtrum*; the landes wherof gyven by Robert Boſſu, erle of Leirceſtre, to the abbay of chanons made by him withoute the walles. A new chirch of the reſidew of the old prebendes was erected *withoute* the caſtelle, and dedicate to S. Marie, as the olde was [9]."

The preſent building has been erected at different times, and conſiſts of what may be termed an old and a new or additional church.

The old church, mutilated as it is to accommodate its modern neighbour, ſtill retains many curious ſpecimens of architecture in the Saxon or early Norman ſtyle [10]; and at preſent conſiſts of a nave, a chancel, a ſmall North croſs, a narrow North aile, and a large modern veſtry-room.

The chancel is very antient. Near and about the end without are ſome fine pieces of Saxon ornamented work. Of theſe parts two ſeparate ſketches are given in plate XXV; fig. 2. repreſenting the North ſide, and fig. 3. the South ſide and the Eaſt end.

Within, in the South wall, are three ſtalls [11], with zigzag arches on eight round columns, ſeparated in pairs, ſtanding in diſtinct rows before each other, and having flowered capitals; and at the Weſt end of this chancel, on either ſide, the tops of two large arches ſtill remain, on which ſtood, probably, the tower of the original church. A Gothic Eaſt window completely fills up that end: and has in it the earl of *Lancaſter's* arms, Gules, three lions paſſant guardant in pale Or; a label of *France* [12].

The North ſide has five windows, divided into days by ſlender pillars with flowered capitals; but three of them are in part blocked up. On the South ſide were alſo five round zigzag windows, one only of which remains; a ſecond has been changed to later Gothic; and the upper parts of the other three are ſeen over the two lofty arches (within which are ſcreens) ſeparating this chancel from that of the new or South church. Beyond theſe, the nave has on this ſide one lofty pointed arch, and four lower ones obtuſely pointed; over which are twelve clereſtory windows. On the North ſide are five arches nearly ſimilar to thoſe on the South, but ſomewhat more lofty, and pointed; and twelve clereſtory windows, four only in the original circular form, eight others being changed to Gothic windows.

The preſent Weſtern door-way is Gothic; but on the left ſide of this door are plain veſtiges of the original door-way, with a ſemi-circular arch, and hatched zigzag mouldings. Above this door-way a large Gothic window occupies the whole Weſt end.

On the North ſide of the nave is a narrow aile, part of the original church, which, from the appearance on the outſide, ſeems to have extended farther into the caſtle-yard. In this part of the church is a lodging chamber [13] belonging to the porter of the caſtle [*janitor caſtri*]; whoſe houſe joins to the North ſide of the church at the Weſt end, and forms part of a range of antient buildings, which have evidently been prebendal houſes.

"From the level of the South wall of this church," ſays Mr. Bickerſtaffe, "near its centre, and coeval with it, projects a cloſet, with loop-holes, or oblong apertures in front, looking into the church-yard; backed, a few years ago, by a door, which I well remember opening into the church; called by tradition "Little Eaſe," ſuppoſed to have been a place of diſcipline; where ſcarcely above one at a time could be admitted, and that only in an erect poſture [14]."

On the left of the pulpit-ſtairs, as you aſcend, and cloſe to them, are three compaſs ſeats adjoining, or in one frame; that which takes the right of the other two, when occupied, has a turn-up fitting-board, decorated with a ſemi-circle *ex adverſo*, in alto relievo, over a tree, well ſtemmed, and well cluſtered with berries, like grapes [15].

At the Eaſt end of this aile is a ſmall North croſs, or chapel, formerly called St. Anne's chapel, which contained ſeveral images, three tables of alabaſter, and an altar, part of which was remaining in 1722. This

---

[1] Originally in Leiceſter were only two church-yards, viz. St. Mary's within the walls, and St. Margaret's without the walls. All Saints, St. Martin's, and St. Nicholas, were provided about the latter end of the twelfth century. Carte, MS.
[2] Cotton MSS. Nero D. X. p. 133.   [3] Pat. 28 Edw. I. m. 1.   [4] Inq. ad quod dampnum, 17 Edw. II. m. 130. Leic.
[5] Pat. 32 Edw. III. pars 2. m. 2.
[6] Charyte's Rentale, fol. lxi.; Inq. ad quod dampnum, 2 Ric. II. 102. Leic. ; & Pat. 3 Ric. II. p. 1. m. 41.
[7] Pat. 10 Hen. IV. pars 2. m. 8.
[8] It may be proper alſo to ſtate, that Mr. Naſmith is unluckily wrong in both his conjectures, reſpecting this church, in a note on St. John's Hoſpital; the author of the Additions to Camden being perfectly correct in ſtating that the hoſpital and chapel of the Newark ſtill exiſt on ſtipends paid out of the dutchy of Lancaſter; and the hoſpital referred to by Chauncey being that of Wigſton, where Richard Clarke was ſome time maſter, and has an epitaph.—In Tanner's account of the Frieries alſo the words " in an iſland above the bridge" ſhould be transferred from the *Black* to the *Auſtin* Friers. See before, p. 301, note.
[9] Itinerary, vol. I. p. 16.
[10] The Saxon arch was higher than the Norman, which ſucceeded it, till the pointed arch was introduced after the time of Henry II.
[11] Plate XXV. fig. 4.—Might not theſe three ſeats be for the accommodation of the three principal officers of the guild, the ſteward and the two wardens? They paid regular wages to only *one* prieſt.   [12] See Plate XXV. fig. 17.
[13] This chamber, though actually within the walls of the church, is extraparochial. It is inhabited by a ſervant of the county juſtices, called the *Caſtle-keeper*.
[14] What Mr. Bickerſtaffe here deſcribes is probably only the aſcent to the rood-loft. Many ſuch are noticed by Mr. Bridges.
[15] Three ſeats in a ſimilar frame are near the landing of the South gallery ſtairs at St. Martin's; and ſomething of the ſame kind in St. Margaret's chancel.

chapel

Fig. 4. In North Chancel.　　Fig. 7. In South Chancel.　　Fig. 8. In S. Chancel.

Fig. 2. N: Side of Old Chancel.　　Fig. 3. S: Side of Old Chancel, & East End.

Fig. 9.　　Fig. 26.　　Fig. 24.

Longmate del. et sc.

chapel is flated ¹. An old veſtry ², which joined it to the Eaſt, was rebuilt in 1795; when the old doorway ³ on the North ſide of the chancel, which was round-arched, and profuſely adorned with zigzag mouldings, was removed.

The new church, which by tradition is ſaid to have been built by John of Gaunt (not long before the year 1400, at which period St. Mary's became parochial) is conſiderably wider than the old one, being 33 feet within the walls. When it was built, great apertures were made in what had been the outward South-wall of the collegiate church, that an eaſy communication might be had between the two churches.

It is aſtoniſhing how this South wall could have been ſo perforated, three lofty arches and four ſmaller ones having been cut through it, without diſturbing the upper works; among which, over the ſmall arches, are the twelve clereſtory windows, nine of which are now open; and, among theſe, on the ſide next to the new church, many of the fine ornaments and ſmall circular pillars, once external, are well preſerved.

The chancel of this church, which does not extend ſo far Eaſt as that of the old church by ſix yards, has at the Eaſt end two large ſemicircular windows with a ſmall oval window over them, and on the South ſide one large pointed window. In the South wall are three pointed ſtalls of different heights ⁴, with zigzag and dentals in the inner, and nail-head quatrefoils in the outer mouldings. The pillars are double, ſtanding in pairs as the former, and have flowered capitals. At a diſtance Eaſt of them is a ſmall plain piſcina ⁵.

The font is circular ⁶; very curious, and rudely carved with heads and angels, much defaced by plaſtering.

The nave has two large pointed windows, with two ſmall circular ones; and over the whole eight clereſtory windows.

At the Weſt end, ſtanding as it were within the church, it not being ſkreened off, is a ſubſtantial tower (in which are five good bells) ſurmounted by four handſome pinnacles, and a lofty crocketed ſpire. See plates XXIV. and XXV.

The leaded roof of this additional church has been conſiderably lowered, as may be ſeen in plate XXV. The South door is pointed; and the wooden door has a rich top. The porch is large and modern.

On the South ſide of the church a large old wall is continued to the ſmaller Newark-gate.

In the year 1489, at Chriſtmas, the pariſhioners agreed that the ſeats ſhould be made in the nave of the old church; for which purpoſe a collection was made of what every one pleaſed to give every Sunday, from Chriſtmas till Midſummer. So likewiſe in 1490.

Mr. Mayor's pew was made in 1491.

The dean of St. Mary's college was bound to be at the charge of ſome things belonging to the church, and the pariſhioners of others; but the dean often gave ſeveral things of his good-will; and there is entered, in the churchwardens' accompts of 1498, a memorandum, " quod non pertinet ad decanum ad ſolvendum, neque pro reparatione veſtimentorum neque pro lotione eorum, neque pro organis, neque pro reparatione librorum neque coparum; ſed tamen ad inveniendum thus ad uſum ſummi altaris, ſtramentum eccleſiæ, & unum creſſet de ſebo ardente a feſto Omnium Sanctorum uſque ad Purificationem Beatæ Mariæ in nocte; & propter hoc recipit annuatim de auditore domini regis 10s."

The images in this church were the Rood and another Crucifix, Mary and John, the Virgin Mary, St. James, St. Hugo, St. George, &c.; a repreſentation of the Holy Trinity, and another of the five wounds, before which there was a light burning. The high altar had a lamp before it, and candleſticks belonging to it, and a canopy over it. The veſtments, altar-cloths, and other utenſils uſed in the church, were hallowed in the Abbey, for which a ſmall fee was paid.

The church being dedicated to St. Mary, her image was more eſpecially adorned with cloaths, and a crown, and placed in a tabernacle, with a candleſtick and light before it, and a table or picture (tabula) repreſenting her coronation.

From this church there uſed to be a ſolemn proceſſion every Whit-Monday to St. Margaret's church, in which the image of the Virgin Mary was carried under a canopy borne by four perſons, with a minſtrel, harp, or other muſic, and 12 perſons repreſenting the 12 Apoſtles ⁷, each of which had the name of the apoſtle whom he repreſented written on parchment fixed on his bonnet, and 14 perſons bearing banners, with the virgins in the pariſh attending. When they came to St. Margaret's, among other oblations, there were two pair of gloves, whereof one is ſaid to be for God, the other for St. Thomas of India.

In this church there were five ſolemnities on which oblations were made; and on the ſame days there were gatherings for the uſe of the building (ad opus fabricæ eccleſiæ); on the day of dedication of the church, otherwiſe called the Church holy-day, on the day of the Aſſumption of the Bleſſed Virgin, on All Saints Day, at Chriſtmas, and at Eaſter.

They uſed to have church ales, and the profit made by them was accounted for by the churchwardens at Chriſtmas and at Eaſter. Theſe were frequent in the reign of Henry VII; but ſeem in a great meaſure to have been left off in the time of Henry VIII.

At the Eaſt end of the South aile, near that called the Greater or Trinity Choir, a guild, or fraternity, called the Guild of the Holy Trinity, was founded by ſir Richard Sacheverel, knight, and the good lady Hungerford ⁸; in which new deſks were made in 1495, with little images before them, for the expence whereof collections were made of the pariſhioners every Sunday ſucceſſively that year. The ſame year the ſtone of William the firſt lord Haſtings's arms, as a knight of the noble order of the Garter, was placed in the South wall of the old church, where it ſtill remains ⁹.

This guild uſed to make four gatherings in a year of the brethren and ſiſters belonging to it in the church, for defraying the expences of it, which conſiſted chiefly in the wages for their prieſt, which was paid quarterly, and their feaſts, the chief of which was a dinner on Trinity Sunday; beſide which, they had a ſupper that evening, and a breakfaſt next day, when the officers gave up their accompts, and new one were choſen for the year enſuing. The officers were a ſteward and two wardens; but after 1511 four wardens. The firſt I have met with were Mr. John Whatton, ſteward, and John Chamberleyn and Richard Morgan, wardens; who gave up their accompt in 1508, when Trinity Sunday happened on the 18th of June. By their accompt it appears that a dozen of ale coſt 20d.; a fat wether 2s. 4d.; ſeven lambs 7s.; fourteen goflings 4s. 8d.; fifteen capons 5s.; thirty chicken 23d.; two gallons of cream 8d.; a gallon of honey and a quart 10d.; three quarters of charcoal 15d.; half a quarter of malt 2s.; a buſhel of wheat meal and a peck 22d.; fourteen geeſe 4s. 3d.; twelve capons 4s.; two loads of wood 22d.; four gallons of milk 4d.; for a pig 5d. &c. &c.

The guild had a ſtock of £9. 13s. 4d. which was paid into the hands of the ſteward and wardens; who thereupon engaged to make the dinner on Trinity Sunday, 1511, at their own coſt and charges, which they did, and next day paid in that ſtock, and gave account of what had been gathered at the ſeveral collections from the brethren and ſiſters, which example was followed by their ſucceſſors, by which means the ſtock increaſed in 1517 to £20.

¹ See, in p. 311, a charge for new flating it in 1513.
² A part of the old veſtry is ſhewn in the North view of the old chancel, plate XXV. fig. 2.
³ Plate XXV. fig. 5, 6.   ⁴ Ibid. fig. 7.   ⁵ Ibid. fig. 8.   ⁶ Ibid. fig. 9.   ⁷ See more at the bottom of p. 314.
⁸ Daughter and heir of ſir Thomas Hungerford, ſon of Robert, ſon of Walter lord Hungerford. She was married to Edward the ſecond lord Haſtings, who died November 8, 1507, leaving iſſue, by her, George the firſt earl of Huntingdon. After her firſt huſband's death, ſhe was married to ſir Richard Sacheverel, of Ratcliffe upon Soar, co. Nottingham (ſon of Ralph Sacheverel, of Hopwell in Derbyſhire), who died in 1553; and was buried in the church of St. Mary in the Newark.
⁹ Argent, a maunch Sable. The arms are within a Garter, with the uſual motto of the order; and at each corner is repeated the family creſt, a buffalo's head, eraſed, Sable, crowned and gorged with a ducal coronet, and armed, Or. See Plate XXV. fig. 10.

In 1512, it is faid, " Omnia erant cara; modium frumenti 18d."

In 1514, a table was ordered to be made, with the names of all the brethren and fifters, quick and dead, which was to ftand on the Trinity altar.

The lady Mary Hungerford and fir Richard Sacheverel were prefent at the dinner, and gave them £20.

Mr. William Wigfton was a witnefs to the accompts paffed in 1518 and 1519; in which laft year Richard Brokefby, dean of Haftings, and chaplain to king Henry VIII. was chofen fteward.

For thefe particulars the reader is indebted to the refearches of Mr. Carte; who has farther furnifhed, on this fubjeft, the following extracts from a book concerning Trinity Guild.

	£.	s.	d.
Imprimis, pro pane, Johanni Barton, 3 dozen and a half, — —	o	3	6
Item, to William Fuk, for 2 dozen and 8 penny-worth, — —	o	2	8
Item, for a dozen of ale bought,	o	1	8
Malt was gadyrd for the renneland. Item, for bringing of the fame to Lawrence Hedeley's wife, —	o	o	6
Item, for bayffe and leggs of moten for pyes, — — —	o	4	3
Item, to Robert Bolton, for a gude fat wedyr, — — —	o	2	4
Item, for 7 lames bought, —	o	7	o
Item, for 14 gefullings [goflings] that John Chamberlayn bought, —	o	4	8
Item, for 15 capons, — —	o	5	o
Item, for 30 chekins, —	o	2	3
Item, for butter, — —	o	o	7
Item, for 2 gallons of creme, to Mrs. Smith, — — —	o	o	8
Item, for 2 gallons to Mrs. Rede,	o	o	1
Item, for a gallon to John Brown,	o	o	4
Item, for all manner of fpyce, —	o	8	1
Item, for a gallon of honey and a quart,	o	o	10
Item, for falt and oatmeal, —	o	o	2
Item, for 3 quarters of charcoal,	o	1	3
Item, for half a quarter of malt,	o	2	o
For a bufhell of wheat meal and a peck,	o	1	10
Item, for 14 geefe, —	o	4	8
Item, 12 capons, with feeding,	o	4	o
Item, for 2 lode of woode, —	o	1	10
Item, for eggs, —	o	o	5
Item, for 4 gallons of mylke, —	o	o	4
Item, for vergeys, —	o	o	2
For a quarter of a lamb and odyr moton, for the brekefaft for the count in craftino,	o	o	6
Item, for a pig, —	o	o	5
Item, paid for drynking potts,	o	o	4
Item, for veffell to St. John's,	o	o	4

Item, to Nicholas Hayn, coke, for dreffing the dynar and fepar and brekefaft in craftino: he found fpytts and odyr, and fetchyed and bare home ye fpytts and odyr, and veffel, and found all maner of folks to turn and to help him, of hys own coft, and gafe to the broderhode, to be brodyr and his wyff fyfter, 6 —   o 5 o

| Item, payed to the priefts, for faying maffe, in reward for the hole year, | o | 13 | 4 |

Summa totalis, £4. os. 3d.

Memorandum, that John Chamberlayn, warden of the fraternity of the Holy Trinitye, Thomas Roban and Robert Edwards, ftewards of the fame, made their account on the morn aftyr Trinitye Sunday, the which was the 4th of June, the year of our Lord 1509, afore Mr. W. Mafon, comeffary, Mr. William Gibfon, Mr. J. Whatton, fir T. Derby, dean, and divers moo of the parifhioners then being prefent.

Fyrft, the recetts gadurryd in the chyrch of the bredren and fyfters divers times, — — —   1 0 0
Sum total gadurryd at the dynar, 4 marc, o 4 11
Sum total, — —   4 18 3
Summa expenf' of Thomas Roban, for the dynar, —   1 2 2
Summa expenf' of Robert Edward, for the dynar, —   2 0 0
Sum total of both,   3 2 2

3

| Item, paid to the priefts, | — | o | 13 | 4 |
| Remain overplus illius anni, | — | o | 2 | 10 |

Memorandum, that John Chamberlayn, warden of the fraternity of the Holy Trinitye, and Thomas Knolesford and Robert Edwards, have delivered to John Whyte and William Prowit, of the money in hoole £8. wanting 5d.

And the parifhyoners chofe Robert Edwards to be warden for the year to cum; and John Whyte and William Prowet to be ftewards.

Memorandum, that John Whatton, ironmonger, Richard Morgan, kepar of the caftle, Thomas Grene, farmer, and John Marfton, fherman, receyved the forfaid £9. 13s. 4d. and promyfed to make the dynar on Trinitye Sunday next coming apon their own cofts; and the money that thei gadur in the yer of the bredren and fyftren, and at the dynar on Trinitye Sunday, truly to gyf account thereof, and delyver hit to the paryfhioners, with the old ftokke, on the morn affter Trinitye Sunday; and yf hit happen the 4 forfayd perfons any of them to deceffe within the yer, thei that are on lyffe, or he that is on lyffe, fhall anfwer for the hoole duty afoorwrytyn; and the paryfhioners fayd that thefe fhould be made an obligation; and thei that occupie the ftokke fhall be bounden therein to bryng in the fayd ftokke, in payn of forfeiting £40. yerely, on the morn affter Trinitye Sunday.

A memorandum, that thes forfayd perfons laudably and wyrfhypfully made the dinnar on ther own cofts and charges od Trinitye Sunday, in the year of our Lord 1511, and the yer of the reygn of king Henry the Eighth the 3d yer, the firft perfons that made the dinar of their own cofts, the Holy Trinite be lowyde and quite them; and there was gaduryd at the fayd dinar 5 marc and 3s.

Item, gaduryd twife in the church of the bredren and fyftern, —   o 10 3
Of the bredren and fyftern at dynar, o 7 8

They chofe 4 guardians for the enfuing year, and delivered to them the old ftock £9. 13s. 4d. upon conditions as above, and agreed to chufe 4 yearly the day after Trinity Sunday.

Et concordatum eft—alfo that every brother and fifter that is of this fraternity and gyld fhall be in charity and loving either to other; quia Deus charitas eft, et qui manet in charitate in Deo manet, et Deus in eo quod nobis concedat qui fine fine vincit et regnat; amen.

In 1512, they chofe 2 of the old and 2 new guardians; and, by the accounts which were given up that year in aulâ caftri, among others coram dño Henrico Crofby, vicario ecclefiæ, it appears that fir Robert was prieft of the fraternity.

Et memorandum, quod epifcopi fecerunt jentaculum in fefto Sanctæ Trinitatis, 22° die Maii; et tamen omnia erant cara; modium frumenti, 1s. 6d.

Gathred at dinner, —   2 1 4
And the prieft for his wages gathered, o 19 0

Memorandum, quod folvi pro obitu tent' in die Martis prox' poft feftum Sanctæ Trinitatis, inprimis mihi (fcil' decano, qui tunc erat guardianus) et fociis quatuor 2s. Et duobus cantoribus 16d. clerico paroch' 2d. pulfatoribus 6d.

Et memorandum, we paid the prieft for his quarter at Lammas more than was gathered of the brethren and fifters every one of us 4 guardians 2s. 5d.; fum,   o 9 8
We paid, die Sancti Edmundi, for his 2d quarter at Martlemas, each 2s. 6d. fum o 10 0
And, in die Sancti Matthiæ, for his 3d quarter at Candlemas, every man of 4 of the ftokke 2s. 7d.; fum, —   o 10 5
Et memorandum, we paid the prieft, fir Robert, for his 4th quarter, at Invention of the Holy Crofs, or May-day, at the dinner on Trinitye Sunday, 4 nobles gathered of the brethren and fiftern, and made hoole the ftokke every man,   3 10 0
Item, Mr. Dean paid for mending the Trinitie banner that was torn, —   o o 3
Item, Mr. Booth paid for writing under our chapter-feal, that my lady Hungerford gave — —   o 1 4

Anno

Anno Domini 1514, festum Sanctæ Trinitatis, erat in festo Sancti Barnabæ Apostoli.

The same day, sir Thomas Derby, dean, Mr. Edward Booth, Mr. John Whatton, Edward Lydyrland, stewards of the Trinity Gilde, made the dinner of their own costs; and passed accounts on the morn after in this manner following.

Imprimis, the priest paid his wages for the whole year after the rate of 8 marks.

Item, they delivered the whole stock received the year past.

And received the said Trinitye Sunday, of good lady the lady Mary Hungerford, and sir Richard Sacheverel, knt. — 1 0 0

Of other brethren and sisters at the dinner, with the reward of Mr. Thomas Ashby of Quenby, — 0 10 0

Mr. Doctor . . . . . . Darby, parson of Northborough, one crown of gold, value 0 4 0

And for all charges deduct as hereafter doth follow:

First, the priest Robert's wages.

For the cook, John Brown, and his help, 0 5 0

For dirige and messe, priests and clarks, 0 2 6

Item, for ringers, — — 0 0 10

Item, for a certain writing in parchment, given to the good lady Hungerford and sir Richard Sacheverel, knt. founders of the said fraternity or gilde, 0 1 4

Item, for the obligation of the year past, 0 0 6

Item, for parchment to make a table of names, — — 0 0 8

For mending the Trinity banner of sylke, 0 0 3

Item, remains in keeping, for the entent to make a table with the names of the bretheren and sisters, quick and dead, stand on the Trinity altar, — 0 3 6

And so remaineth clearly in the hands of John Marston and Robert Edward, churchwardens of this gylde, money for the more surety, £4. of good and lawfull money above, and beside £14. afore rehearsed the old stock of the other year.

And the parishioners chose new stewards for the year following; Mr. John Whatton, sir Henry Crosby, vicar of Hungarton, Thomas Greene, farmer, and John Brown; and every of the 4 received of the old stock £3. 10s. and promissed to bring it in crastino Sanctæ Trinitatis next coming; and of their charity, the dynar, and bounden by an obligation, as others have been before them.

Costs for the dinner:

Imprimis, in pane, — 0 9 8

In meal, 5 strikes, price — 0 4 4

In sp'ebus 7s. in potu 19 dozen 16d. 1 5 0

In beef, — — 0 6 0

In motton, — — 0 0 7

For 5 lambs and a half, — 0 6 5

Two calves, — — 0 4 0

Item, venison, given by my lord Hastings, 2 bucks, and my lady his madam.

Item, in reward to them that brought the venison, — — 0 2 0

Item, milke and cream, — 0 2 2

In eggs and butter, — 0 2 6

In capons 40, echone 4d. — 0 13 4

In geese 40, echone 4d. — 0 13 4

In chickens 40, echone 1d. — 0 3 4

In rabbits, 6 couple. — 0 1 8

Item, wood and charcoal, — 0 2 10

Item, for vessels borrowed of our Lady Gilde, St. John's, and St. Margaret's, — — 0 0 8

Item, for potts to drink in, — 0 0 9

Item, for keeping the yates and killing calves, to Lawrence, — 0 0 8

Item, to Barth. Chamberlain, 0 0 4

Item, for honey, — 0 0 4

Item, for baking venison at Prewet's, ut putatur, — — 0 1 0

Sum, — — 5 7 0

The people at dinner 56 messe; and 40 at supper; and on the morn 8 messe. Laus eternaliter Deo.

In the year 1517, the stock came to £20. each steward having in his hand £5.

George Villers, of Scraptoft, was one of the stewards in 1517, 1518, 1519.

In 1534, the payments from St. Mary's church were,

To the dean, — —	13	0	0
To the prior of Shene,	0	1	6
To the king, — —	1	12	0
To John Park, vicar, —	4	0	0
To John Brewer, a prebendary,	2	0	0

On the dissolution of religious houses the value of this collegiate church was thus stated:

" Colleg' B. Marie juxta Castrum Leic', valet in Reddit' & firm' omn' terr' & ten' pdict' colleg' ptinen', dimiss' diversis psonis tam ad volunt' quam p indenturam, solvend' ad festa Annunc' B. Marie & Sci Michis Archangeli equaliter prout ptclr p rentale inde fact' & renovat' apparet, p ann' XXIIIIl. XIXs. VId.

Reddit' mobil' annuatim de diversis liberis tentis pd' recipiend', viz. de precio XVII gallinarum IIs. IId. quelibet gallina appretiatur ad IId.; & IX capon' IIs. IIId. quilibet capo appreciatur ad IIId.; in toto solvend' ad festa pd', prout ptclr p rentale inde fact' & renovat' apparet' p ann' Vs. Id.

Firma mansionis ibm p ann' valuat' — — Vs. VIIId.

——————

XXVl. IXs. IIId.

——————

Inde repris', viz.

In reddit' resolut' diversis personis sequent', viz.

Dño regi ut ducat' sui Lancastr', VIs. Id. nuper prioratui de Shene XVIIId. & castro Leic' VIIId. in toto p ann' — VIIIs. IIId.

Feod' ballivi ibm p ann' XLs.

Feod' supervisor' omn' terr' & tenem' pd' p ann' — XXs.

Stipend' Radi Cockley, decani ibm, p ann', Xs.

Stipend' VI al' capellan' & clericor' ibm, cuilibet eor' ad XLVIIs. IId. ob. p ann', in toto XIIIIl. IIIs. IIId.

Annuitate sive annuali pensione solut' Rico Fowler per decan' & colleg' pd' p ann' XXs.

Decimis dño regi anntr inde solut' p ann' — XLVIIs. IIId. ob.

——————

XXVl. XVIIIs. IXd. ob.

Et sic habent surplus, VIIIs. VId. ob.

——————

" The said college was founded by Robert earle of Leicester for the fyndyng of eight priests for ever, to sing mass, and to pray for the soul of the said founder within the parish church of our Lady. Howbeit there be at these presents but seven of the said priests now resydent there, so that there is one rowme voyde; and there be within the said parish D houselyng people; and there ys a mansion house for all the said prests, which is before valued. Also the said college church is within the parish church of our Lady, where there ys a vicar endowed, and hath a pention of the king's majesty of VIIIl. by the yeare, by reason of the dissolution of the monasterie of Leicester; and hath no other profytts but only hys mansion house and a little garden, set upon the West part of the said college, next to Gunne dyke. Also there hath been no lands, or any other possessions to the same belonging sold or mynyshed sythen the tyme before limited; nor no plate, jewels, ornaments, or other moveable goods, to the same also belonging."

Of the deans and prebendaries of this church, we are not able to furnish any thing that approaches to a list; but shall here give the names that have occurred.

[6 K] DEANS.

DEANS.

Gubertus decanus occurs in 1344 [1].

Thomas Derby became dean in 1488; and was fucceded in 1514 or 1515 by

Sir John Pexfal or Pycfale, who died in 1520.

Richard Pexal, figned the compofition, as dean, with Wigfton's Hofpital in 1520; and at the convocation, holden April 5, 1533, fubfcribed by proxy.

Richard Fowler was dean in 1534.

Ralph Cockley was dean at the diffolution, 1539.

PREBENDARIES.

Two vacancies in the prebends of this church were filled by king Edward III. in 1328 and 1339.

Thomas de Melborne [2], April 25, 1372, was prebendary of the ftall marked *E* in the collegiate church of St. Mary juxta Caftrum; which he exchanged with

Peter de Dalton, prebendary of Ketton in the church of Lincoln, 1372.

Roger de Bury, chaplain, prebendary of the ftall marked *H*, exchanged it, 3 kal. Dec. 1372, with

John de Swafham, rector of Netelham, 1372.

John Welley, prebendary of the ftall called *B*, had licence to exchange it with John Martyn for the vicarage of Hyllebourne, in the diocefe of Lincoln, both being in the patronage of the Abbey of Leicefter, July 14, 1411 [3].

John Boroughe, a prebendary of this church, and warden of Sapcote, was buried in the chancel [4].

John Brewer was a prebendary here in 1534.

Nov. 1, 1505, *Charles Villars* conveyed to *Richard Reynolds, Richard Gyllot*, and others, a meffuage and two cottages, with their appurtenances, in Leicefter, in the ftreet called the *Swyne-market*, between the tenant of *Robert Crofte* on the one fide, and the lands of St. *Mary de Caftro* on the other, and extending from the Swyne-market to the *Church-lane*.

The lands and poffeffions belonging to the late college of the bleffed Virgin Mary over againft the caftle in Leicefter, were demifed to *Edward Holt*, efq. by queen Elizabeth; and at length by her granted, with other property, to the corporation of *Leicefter* in feefarm; under which title they occur in the chamberlain's accompts annually, at a rental of £32. 13s. 10d.; with £5. 3s. 6d. more, for Lammas tithes and herbage due for grounds in St. Mary's parifh.

Dec. 22, 1577, there was a parifh meeting, at which the churchwardens gave up their accompts, and new ones were chofen. At this accompt it was agreed by the whole confent of the affembly there, that thirteen of the chief of the parifh fhould be chofen, to fet order for fuch things as fhall be done for the church behoof; and without the confent of them, or moft part of them, as concerned the church-work, charges at vifitation, and fuch like, nothing fhould be done. The names of the thirteen then chofen were, Mr. Danet, Mr. Ruding, Mr. Worfhip, Mr. Temple [5], Mr. Ludlam, Robert Burftal, Henry Newbold, Thomas Chamberleyn, Thomas Worthe, John Worfhip, John Walker, John Wright, William Taylor. It was agreed alfo that every one of the parifh that had heretofore paid for church-works 4d. fhould pay 4d.; and each one that had paid 2d. fhould pay 4d.; and he that paid 1d. fhould pay 2d.; and every one that paid a halfpenny fhould pay 1d. from this time following. And that every fervant taking wages fhould pay by the year 1d.

Dec. 13, 1584, the thirteen were Mr. Pannit, Mr. Worfhip, Mr. Ludlam, Robert Burftal, Henry Newbold, Thomas Chamberlayn, Thomas Moor, John Worfhip, John Walker, John Wright, William Taylor, Robert Nyx, and Richard Burftall, who made feveral ftanding orders for the better government of the parifh. The three firft concerned the clerk and fexton, regulating the time and manner of their ringing for prayers on Sundays, holy-days, and their evens, and enjoining their attendance on and dutiful behaviour towards the minifter; by the fourth, every of the thirteen abfent from church-accompt, or quarterly-meeting, when warned, forfeited 1s.; by the fifth, fuch poor as being able and come not to church on Wednefdays and Fridays, were to have no relief; by the fixth, they determined a certain fum to be gathered by the churchwardens, or levied by the thirteen, to mend the minifter's wages; by the feventh, they obliged every parifhioner and inmate to pay, yearly, quarterly, monthly, or weekly, what fhould be levied on them by the thirteen, or feven of them, towards relieving the poor, mending the minifter's wages, to the clerk, and other duties, on pain of 1s. for every default; by the eighth, every houfeholder was obliged to pay, or fee to be paid, for his inmates, what they fhould be levied at for the purpofes aforefaid, on pain of 1s. for every default. All the forfeitures were applied to the poor man's box.

By the churchwardens' accompts it appears, that, on Dec. 1, 1560, there was delivered to the churchwardens an indenture, bearing date the 4th of September, in the 30th year of Henry the Eighth's reign, fealed with the feal of the college of St. Mary [6], for a houfe and garden, which was bought out of the church-ftock, for the maintenance of the prieft. How this houfe and garden came to be alienated does not appear, but fo in fact it was.

The corporation, being entitled to all the profits which the dean and canons enjoyed, had confequently the church-yard, the fmall tithes, and offerings, which in other places belong to the vicar; fo that the vicar here had nothing to depend on for his fubfiftence, but a fmall penfion of £8. a year from the crown, and the voluntary contributions of the parifhioners. But, Aug. 13, 1 Jac. I. the corporation agreed that Mr. Jeffon Clarke, ftipendiary minifter of the parifh church of St. Mary, fhould be tenant to the town of the Eafter-book, or duties of St. Mary's parifh, and of the tithe-pigs, and chrifoms, as Richard Normond had them, and fhould alfo have the mortuaries from Michaelmas following, from year to year, upon his honeft behaviour, during the town's pleafure, not exacting any tithes in other fort than heretofore they have been paid at Eafter, paying yearly to the town upon Tuefday in Eafter-week 40s. and paying alfo thenceforth the 2s. a year which was due to the vicarage of St. Nicholas. At length the town granted to the vicar of St. Mary's £10. a year, to be paid him by the chamberlains. And the vicar having no houfe belonging to him, one Mrs. Lacy offered the parifh of St. Mary, upon their paying her £20. to fettle on the vicars for ever the houfe late in the occupation of Mr. Jofiah Bond, vicar of the faid parifh; whereupon, March 12, 1679, at the petition of the parifh, the town granted them £5. out of the chamber of the town, towards the payment of it. And, Aug. 13, 1706, at a common-hall, it was ordered that Mr. Fox (the vicar) fhould have the rent of St. Mary's church-yard till the end of Mr. Wilkins's leafe; and after that the ufe and benefit of the church-yard fo long as the hall fhould think fit; and on June 10, 1709, it was again ordered, that Mr. Fox, vicar of St. Mary's, fhould be tenant of St. Mary's church-yard, paying yearly for the fame 10s. and enjoy it during the pleafure of the hall; and that the 3s. 4d. charged on him for the Eafter-book and other dues of the parifh fhould not for the future be fuperfeded, but that he fhould pay the fame; but at the fame time it was ordered, that he fhould be paid by the chamberlains 13s. 4d. over and above the 10s. already granted him during the pleafure of the hall.

In 1564, the officiating minifter of St. Mary's was ftyled "curate;" and there were then 120 families in the parifh [7].

In 1650, the value of the vicarage was returned to be £13. 6s. 8d.; and the vicar altogether infufficient, fcandalous, and a pluralitan [8].

In the king's books it is valued at £8.; and the clear yearly value is ftated at £60.

---

[1] He bought feveral houfes that year in the South gate of Leicefter.
[2] He died in 1388.
[3] Reg. Arundel, Archiep. Cant. pars 2. fol. 85.
[4] See his epitaph, p. 314.
[5] Robert Nyx was chofen, in the room of Temple, Dec. 19, 1582.
[6] See this feal in plate XVII. fig. 4.
[7] See the Introductory Volume, p. lxxxvii.
[8] Ibid. p. xcviii.

Obfervations

Obſervations on, and Extracts from, the Accompts of the Churchwardens of St. Mary de Caſtro.

1491. Mr. Mayor's pew was made.

1493. Paid for the roodlight,	£.0	2	8
Paid for holly for the church ob in 1494,	0	0	8
Paid to the wardens of the ſepulchre light,	2	2	0

There were then organs in the church.

Paid at Whitſuntide, for bread, ale, fleſh, &c. for the apoſtles and others,	0	3	4
Paid to the clerk, for bringing of Our Lady auter by —— ——	0	0	6

Paid quarterly to Thomas Walker, 10 d. (So alſo in 1494 and 1504; and to Thomas Cowdelow 1505.)

Recept. in 1493, die Dedicationis, de parochianis, ad opus ecclefiæ, ——	0	4	6
Rec. in die Aſſumptionis Virginis, ad opus ecclefiæ, —— —— ——	0	2	9
In die Omnium Sanctor', ad opus ecclefiæ,	0	5	9
Rec. pro oblatione in die Natalis Domini,	0	5	5½
Rec. de decano et canonicis, pro obitu Margaretæ Kegworth, —— ——	0	1	0

1494. The churchwardens are called churchmaſters, and ſo in other years.

Paid for coles for holy fire, ——	0	0	1½

A candleſtick mended that ſtood near the high altar.

Memorand', quòd parochiani ecclefiæ B. Mariæ de Caſtro, Leic', elegerunt Johannem Lokkey et Will. Fukes yconomos dictæ ecclefiæ in vigiliâ Sci Adelmi epi, in menſe Maii; et dñs Thomas Derby, decanus, accipiebat hos per manus ſuas ad veſperas in eâdem die Dominicâ, et in pulpito demonſtravit ad parochianos; et nemo contradicebat, ſed omnes conſenſerunt.

1495. Rec. of Mr. William Gibſon, for the third bell 2 s.; for his wife's obit for the bells 4 s.

Item, of Mr. William Gibſon, to the frame of the bells, for Margaret his wife's ſoul, in vigiliâ exalt', —— ——	0	4	4
Three bells, or third bell, ——	0	1	0
All the five bells, —— ——	0	4	0
For Katharine Clarke's, ——	0	1	2
For three peals of all the bells, ——	0	2	8

For 4 bells ringing, 2 s. 4 d.; other years, 2 s. 6 d.

Rec. of Mr. Gerard Danet [1], for waſting of torches for his lady, ——	0	3	0
Rec. on Pace-day for the church-work of the pariſhioners, —— ——	0	12	9
For waſte of torches, —— ——	0	4	0
Rec. upon the kirk holy-day, ——	0	4	1
Rec. of the church ale clearly, ——	0	19	0

Received at St. Margaret's 6 d. and ſo yearly.

N. B. Here was a Lady light, and a Sepulchre light.

Received clearly of the church ale at St. Laurenttide 4 nobles.

Received for the offering on our Lady day's Aſſumption, to the church work,	0	2	8
Item, on Wedneſday after Relique Sunday, our church holiday, ——	0	4	0
Received clearly of the church ale on Holy-rood day, —— —— ——	0	5	4
Item, on Allhallows day, to the church-work, of the pariſhioners, ——	0	5	8
Rec. de oblat' in die Natal' Dñi,	0	5	8
—— in die Paſchæ de oblat', ——	0	10	6
—— on the church holyday for the offerings, —— —— ——	0	4	2
Item, on our Lady's Aſſumption for the offering, —— —— ——	0	3	2
Item, on Allhallow day, for the offering to the church-work, ——	0	5	4
On Chriſtmas-day, for the church-work,	0	5	5

Memorandum, on St. Vincent day, the churchmaſters began to gadyr for the deſks in the great quire, and received 21 d.; Sexageſima Sunday received 11 d.; and ſo they continued to gather every Sunday.

Mem. the frames for all the bells made this year; carpenters received 6 d. per diem for work; inferior ſervants under them 3 d. per diem; labourers 4 d. a day.

Paid for ſweeping the ſepulchre,	0	0	6
Paid for tallow-candles for the church on Chriſtmas-day, —— ——	0	0	8
Paid for wax for the rood-light at Chriſtmas-day, —— —— ——	0	2	11
Paid for free-ſtone for the deſks,	0	8	4
Paid for carrying the ſame, ——	0	0	2
Paid for ſawing timber for the deſks, and other matters about the deſks, which this year were made in the great quire, (N. B. there were old deſks before)	0	4	7
Paid for painting the little images for the deſks in the great quire, ——	0	1	4
For 13 candleſticks, —— ——	0	18	5
For making the images before the deſks,	0	6	8
For ſetting-in the ſtone of lord Haſtings's arms in the wall, ——	0	16	0
To Wygley, for painting the ſame,	0	3	0
For painting the candleſticks in the rood-loft, —— —— ——	0	3	4
For the rood-light wax and making,	0	5	2

Annual obits in St. Mary's church.

Katharine Clerk, in die Sti Valentini 20 d.; paid by Nicholas Clerk. The churchwardens paid for ringing her obit 6 d.; ſometimes received only 14 d. viz. clearly paid by the dean, 1495, &c.

1495. Received of Iſabel Large, for her huſband's obit, —— ——	0	1	0
Rec. of John Prowet, for three bells for his wife's obit, —— ——	0	1	0
Rec. pro obitu Agnetis Kebull, pro campanis, —— —— ——	0	4	0

Of this nature, not annual, are many in other years.

Mem. Mr. Dean gave voluntarily ſeveral ſums towards playing on the organs every year, —— ——	0	13	4
Our Lady's tabernacle, ——	0	3	4
Item, he gave a good blew ſilk cloth to hold the paten of the chalice on,	0	1	0

1498. The glaſs windows made this year or mended; gatherings were made for that purpoſe often.

Rec. for all the bells and burial, and 2 torches, —— —— ——	0	12	4
For all the bells and burial in the church,	0	10	8
Rec. for waſte of 4 torches, ——	0	1	4

Several ſums were given and bequeathed towards making our Lady's tabernacle.

Mem', quòd dicti yconomi Johes Whatton & Johes Chamberlayne fecerunt ſuum computum coram M'ro Gibſon et parochianis ecclefiæ colleg' B. Mariæ de Caſtro Leic', in feſto Reliquiarum, viz. in vigiliâ Sancti Swithuni.

1499. The dean, of his devotion, cauſed the lamp before the high altar and the candleſtick on the high altar to be

mended, and which coſt him ——	0	1	2
Item, he gave a cenſer, ——	0	4	0
Item, he cauſed an image of the Holy Trinity to be painted on the quire walls, and another of St. Hugo, ——	0	2	0
Paid for mending of the clerk's chamber in ſlating and lyme, ——	0	1	0
Paid for a play in the church, in Dominicâ infra octav' Epiph', ——	0	2	0
Item, paid for hallowing Mr. Pryke's cloth, 2 ſtolis, and 2 corporaſes, &c.	0	1	2
Memorandum, quòd decanus fecit feneſtram borealem pro ſuo memoriale, & ſolvit propterea, —— —— ——	1	3	4

Item, for painting St. James, and underſetting the body of the church there, and making the tabernacle, 4 marks.

Item, for mending 7 images' hands and feet, —— —— ——	0	2	0
1500. Making of Our Lady candleſtick,	0	5	0
For painting the ſame, ——	0	0	4
Paid for hallowing a veſtment, and three altar cloths at the abbey, ——	0	1	8
For making the ſilver candleſtick,	0	0	10
For thakking upon the ſtore-houſe,	0	0	4

The organiſt quarterly 3 s. 4 d.; and the dean, I think, paid him.

[1] See hereafter, p. 316.

1501, Richard Morgan, janitor castri, was chosen one of the churchwardens. The churchwardens usually continued in two years, and some four.

1502. Paid for coles for the holy fire, 0 0 1
Paid for clensing 3 tables of alabaster and divers images in St. Anne's chapel, 0 3 0
Nails to fasten the tables and images, 0 0 1
Jan. 19. Paid by the dean and canons for Margaret Kegworth's obit, — 0 1 0½

1504. The clerk, for hanging the altars yearly 6d. (He had 8d. in 1595.)
Paid to the bell-ringer (who seems to be sexton) quarterly 10d.
Linen for the clerk's rochet, 4 yards, 0 1 7
Agnes Mass, for making the said rochet, 0 0 6
Charcoal and a cord for the vail, 0 0 2
Paid for mending the garment of Jesus and the cross painting, — 0 1 3
Paid for a pound of hemp to mend the angels heads, 0 0 4
Paid for linen cloth for the angels heads and Jesus' hose, making in all, 0 0 9

Et memorandum, quod dūs Tho. Derby, decanus, eodem anno fecit fieri de novo, de suis propriis expensis, unum crucifixum, cum Mariâ et Johanne, stantem supra clauftrum magni chori Scæ Trinitatis; et unam tabulam coronationis Beatæ Mariæ stantem super summum altare in diebus festis; et solvebat pro illis 4 marcas.

Paid quarterly for playing on the organs 20d. by the parish, and as much by the dean.

1505. The organ player was Roger Okley.
Paid for making the candlesticks on the high altar, — — 0 0 4
Paid for mending the candlesticks afore the said high altar, — — 0 2 6
Paid for soldering the holy-water-stock at the North-door of the church, 0 0 7
Paid for slating the revestry; and lath, nails, lime and sand, and slates, — 0 8 4
Paid for the plank that lies afore the high altar, — — 0 1 4
Paid for mending 3 white copes, 0 3 6
For the black cope, — 0 2 6
For ribband for it, — — 0 0 8
Four tapers of wax for the rood-light, 0 0 4
Memorandum, the dean gave the stone, and paved the church-porch, — 0 0 8
Ad Natale Dñi for the high-rood light, 0 3 10
Paid for making the copper-cross, scouring the other cross and censer, ... ing the altar, and sweeping the windows, 0 1 4
For freshing the canopy over the altar that the sacrament is in, — 0 0 8
For making the foot of the holy-water stock at the vestry-door, — — 0 1 0
For 8 pound of wax and making, to the high-rood, — — 0 4 8
For setting of Our blessed Lady in the church, — — 0 1 0

Memorandum, quod omnia jocalia et ornamenta data ecclesiæ visa fuerunt à parochianis in festo Sancti Andreæ apostoli in magno choro post nonam ei, &c.

1506. Received on Allhallow-day for the offering [1] to the church-work, — 0 3 6
Paid for making the four St. George's crosses on the steeple-shaft, — 0 1 8
Paid at several times to one for playing on the organs 2d. a day; and the dean paid as much.
Paid to a frier-preacher, for playing on the organs in die Assumpt. B. Mariæ, 0 0 6
For horning the lantern, — 0 0 5
For playing on the organs in die Omn. Sanctorum to one of the abbey 4d.; the dean as much, and meat, drink, and beds.
Paid to Henry Pye, for Midsummer-quarter, for his wages of sexton there, 0 0 10
Paid to Henry Yerle, for his quarter at Michaelmas, — — 0 0 10

1507. Paid to Henry Yerle Pye, bell-ringer, for his quarter of Michaelmas 20d. and so in following years.
Paid for 20 pounds of lead, — 0 0 8
Paid for a pound of hemp for the heads of the angels, — 0 0 3
Paid for painting the wings and scaff, &c. 0 0 8
Item, the dean paid for the glasing a light of St. Anne in St. Anne chapel, 0 6 8
And of his own, 0 3 4
Item, the young men paid for the ... on the candlesticks, with a branch of 5 lights on the long perke of the king's money, and some of our Lady light, 1 2 0
The clerk's surplice washing and mending, 0 0 2
Paid to the ringers of all the bells for our king Harry the Seventh, the which deceased the 25th of April, — 0 1 2

1509. Paid for 3 ells of cloth linen for the clerk's surplice and half a yard 2s. 3d. for making the same 4d. — 0 2 7
Paid for making the silver candlestick, 0 0 6
Paid for mending the candlestick of iron afore the Trinity, — 0 0 4
Paid to the clerk for playing on the organs for Christmas quarter, — 0 1 8
Paid by the dean as much of his devotion; and so in following years.
Paid for our Lady's crown, — 0 1 6
For mending the banner of the Trinity, 0 0 2
Paid for the canopy for the sacrament, 0 1 8
Paid to the painters of the tabernacle for the first payment £9. for full payment £9.; the dean gave 20s. Some other payments were about it.

1511. Rec. for linen cloth that was bought for the vicar's surplice, — 0 0 3
Paid for a surplice for the vicar, 0 6 8
Paid for a lanthorn for the church, 0 0 6
Obit of John Geffrey, to be kept for ever annually, for all the bells, 0 4 0
Obit of Andrew Langton, annually, 0 4 0

1512. Anno Henrici VIII. 4°; et Tho. Derby, decani collegii, 24°.
Rec. of Mr. William Wigston the younger, for his father's soul, which God pardon, to be prayed for, — 0 10 0
Paid for binding the silver Gospel books and covering the back with leather, 0 0 4
Paid for mending a streamer, the which was king Edward's standard.
Paid for bread for St. Philippe, 0 0 1
For binding the Gospel-book covered with silver; the dean paid as much, 0 0 4
For mending a silk streamer, which was torn on Whitson Monday, — 0 0 4
The clerk's wages at Michaelmas, 0 1 8
The sexton's, — — — 0 1 0

1513. Rec. cognat' Tho...... le Fryth, pro tertiâ campanâ pro uxore suâ quæ obiit apud Leyc. at Poul End, & veniebat de Markefield ex infirmitate pestilentiæ, 12d.; et sepulta est in cemeterio Sanctæ Mariæ; et dabat unam vaccam pro mortuo; cujus animæ propitietur Deus, Amen. 7 die infra Octav. Nat. Beatæ Mariæ.—Et memorand. quod in Vigiliâ Sancti Martini episcopi, ... Sawyear died at Mr. Morgan's, whose name was Lawrence, dwelling in Tyndale, and had but two bells; his mortuary a white horse, performed by Lawrence Hedley, &c. 10s.
Rec. for all the bells for Mr. Doctor Mason, commissary, in festo Sancti Magni Martyris, 4s.
Paid for mending a stone over the Trinity quire on the South side, — 0 0 4
Paid for slating St. Anne's chapel, 0 6 8
On the feast of St. Augustin in August was a great flood.
1515. Robert Edwards and Tho. Crosse passed their accounts coram dño Johe Pexsel, decano ecclesiæ.
The preceding accounts seem to have been made in the time of Thomas Derby, dean, who now, it is supposed, was dead.

---

[1] Ergo, what was received for the church-works were offerings of the parishioners on certain days for that purpose. T. C.

Paid for 6 yards of linen cloth, to make the clerk a surplice, — — 0 2 10
Paid for making the fame, — 0 0 4
Paid for wafhing the vicar's furplice, 0 0 1
Paid for a board for the turnftile, 0 0 4
John Chamberlayn, for the bifhop, 0 1 8
1516. Paid to the 12 apoftles and the bearers of banners and other things down at Pentecoft, for wafhing, and 4 that beryd Henry, and other things done, 0 5 8
1517. Rec. for the obit of Henry Cartt, 0 0 4
1520. This year churchwardens are firft fo called, being before ftyled churchmafters.
Received for the obit of my lord bifhop of Carlifle, 2 0 0
Received for the obit of the dean, 0 8 0
Item, received of the king's game, 2 6 0
1521. Received for burial of George Typping, for all the bells, — 0 4 0
For the fame George's lying in the church, 0 6 8
For the obit of Mr. Peccal, dayen, 0 4 0
Paid for fprinkles of the church, 0 0 2
Paid for cord for the rood-loft and for the tabernacle of our Lady, — 0 0 4
Paid for 2 ftrike of charcoal to make the hallowed fire, — — 0 0 3
Paid for wafhing the lawn-bands for the faints in the church, — 0 0 2
1523. Paid for making the light afore the five wounds, — — 0 0 2
1525. Paid for hallowing the 3 albes, 0 0 8
John Coke, glafier, agreed to mend all the glafs windows in the church for life, receiving yearly — — 0 1 8
Paid for the tabul of St. Ann's altar, 0 0 8
Paid for the dreffing of our Lady, 0 2 0
For making 2 rochets to the children, 0 0 4
The church-porch built.
Edward Lydurland and George Baynesford, churchwardens, with confent of the parifh, bought 3 copes, with a veftment, and 2 . . . . . . of which. . . . . . damafke flowered with . . . . . flower de luces, 20 0 0
1526. Paid for wax for the rood-loft and the 5 wounds, — — 0 3 0

1543. The church is indebted to William Tebb, which the churchwardens borrowed of him, 20s.
Item, the faid church is in debt to the faid Mr. Tebb, for tymber, 5s. 8d.; which money and timber is borrowed towards making the North aile.
1544. At the time of accounts, the church being indebted to the churchwardens £3. 6s. 8d.; a chalice was given them to pledge; which chalice was next year fold, and the debt difcharged.
1555. The churchwardens are called church-reves.
Memorandum, that the mayor, the churchwardens, and the body of the whole parifh, have, on this prefent day, Dec. 10, 1555, hired fir William Burrows, clerk, to ferve the church for one whole year, from the feaft of St. Thomas the Apoftle next, and have given him one penny in earneft, promifing to pay him his accuftomed wages due for the fame, every half year.
1571, Aug. 24. Thomas Smith, plumber, undertook to keep in repair the glafs windows and leads of the church (except the chancel and veftry) for 8 years, for the rate of 8s. per annum. This year a great many of the poorer fort denied payment of their church-works.
1571, Sept. 19. Delivered to the churchwardens hands what was taken out of the poor men's box; and remained of fuch money as had been given at communions before this day, £1. 17s.
Particulars of feveral fee-farm rents arifing from the poffeffions of the diffolved college of St. Mary de Caftro, as ftated in 1712, will be given in a future page, with thofe of the collegiate church of St. Mary in the Newark.
In a book of the collectors of the poor, beginning in 1620, is a note, 1625, of them that hold land and clofes in the parifh, and are to pay 12d. a quarter for every £20. a year; in which lands bearing names in the parifh are, The Dutch Holm, Burgefs Meadow, Stone Meadow, The Cow Clofe, Chapel Clofe, Gofling Clofe, The Tippel, Hill Clofe, Cow Drift, Wye Clofe, Walchhall Clofe, &c.
In an indenture, Dec. 9, 3 Annæ, 1704, about Robert Loughton or George Billet's houfe, it is faid to be in the parifh of St. Nicholas, in or near a ftreet or lane called Silver-ftreet, leading to the Black Friers, and on the Weft part or fide of the ftreet, and was heretofore part of the poffeffions of this college.

VICARS, &c.

Roger de Wileweby occurs in 1237.
Nicholas de Beby, 1240.
John Paffelew, 1250.
Richard de . . . . . . 1248.
Thomas de Northampton, 1263.
Henry de Hinkel, 1263.
Hugo de Burftall, 1263.
Henry de Aylefton, 1285.
Henry Crofby, 1512.
John Park, 1534, when the vicarage was valued at £4. a year.
Sir William Burrows, clerk, was the officiating minifter, 1555.
Richard Normond, 1602.
Jeffon Clarke, 1603; occurs 1625.
John Bonnet, 1618.
John Willowes, 1632.
William Croft, 1640.
———— Holden, 1648.
Thomas Peftell, 1658.
Jofiah Bond[1], 1659; died Sept. 26, 1679.
Theophilus Tapper[2], M. A. curate, 1680.
William Fox, curate 1683; vicar 1688.
Thomas Pocklington, M. A. June 27, 1737; died May 23, 1768, in his 77th year[3].
John Simmonds[4], M. A. Oct. 17, 1768; died Aug. 29, 1778.
Thomas Robinfon[5], M. A. 1778; the prefent vicar, 1796.

PATRONS.

The abbot and convent of Leicefter.

The corporation of Leicefter.

The king.

[1] See his epitaph, p. 314.   [2] Of Queen's College, Cambridge; B. A. 1664; M. A. 1668.
[3] He was more than 52 years rector of Rotherby; where fee his epitaph.   [4] See his epitaph, p. 314.
[5] The firft volume of "Scripture Characters; or, a Practical Improvement of the principal Hiftories in the Old and New Teftament, from Adam to Jofhua inclufive; by Thomas Robinfon, M. A. Vicar of St. Mary's, Leicefter, and late fellow of Trinity College, Cambridge;" was publifhed in 12mo, 1789; the fecond in 1790; the third and fourth in 1792. An octavo edition has been publifhed fince. Mr. Robinfon is alfo the author of "A ferious Exhortation to the Inhabitants of Great Britain, with reference to the approaching Faft, 1795;" and of "An Addrefs to the loyal Leicefter Volunteer Infantry, at the Confecration of their Colours, in the Parifh Church of St. Martin, Leicefter, Oct. 19, 1795. To which is annexed the Prayer ufed on that occafion;" 8vo.

Though

Though it is not our immediate intention to bring forward the parochial history of St. Mary de Castro; some account of the present state of the church, with the benefactions, monuments, &c. shall here be given:

A remarkable high wind, March 14, 1757, blew out a steeple window of this church, and much damaged the rest of the steeple, which was that year repaired, entirely lined with brick, girt with five braces of iron, and strengthened with perpendiculars of the same metal, for £110.

The steeple was struck by lightning June 15, 1763; and repaired the same year, at the expence of £80.

In another dreadful storm, July 10, 1783, the lightning struck the highest steeple window, N. E. cracked the inclosed brick work, and threw off the free-stone shell, which was half a foot thick, down to the next window inclusive, upwards of six yards perpendicularly; and nearly a yard broad all the way, splitting the stone-work as low as the battlements; part of whose wall, N. E. passed with the other fragments through the leads into the church; whose roof was repaired at £46. expence; and the spire taken down and rebuilt by Mr. Cheshire for the sum of £245. 10s. exclusive of the old materials. The new steeple was to be 61 yards from the ground; 25 yards and a foot from the battlements: the same proportion to be observed in the new erection, with additional decorations to the battlements.

Burton and Wyrley describe the following ten coats in St. Mary's church; Plate XXV. fig. 11—20:

Quarterly, *France* and *England.*

Quarterly, 1. and 4. Argent, three lozenges, conjoined in fess, Gules, within a border Sable, *Montagu*; 2. and 3. Or, an eagle displayed Vert, beaked and membred Gules, *Mounthermer.*

Gules, three lions passant guardant, in pale Or; a label Argent. *De Brotherton.*

Gules, a cinquefoil Ermine. Old earls of *Leicester.*

Gules, three cinquefoils Ermine. *Hamilton.*

Quarterly, Or and Gules. *Saye.*

Quarterly, Ermine, and Paly of six Or and Gules.

Barry of six, Argent and Gules, within a bordure Sable bezanté. *Shareshull.*

Barry, wavy of six, Argent and Gules, within a border Sable bezanté. *Shareshull.*

Argent, a maunch Sable, *Hastings*; impaling, Gules, three lions passant guardant, in pale Or; a label of three points Azure, each charged with three fleurs de lis; Earl of *Lancaster* [1].

The seven following shields are communicated by Francis Townsend, Esq. from a MS. in the College of Arms [2].

In St. Mary's church.

I. A shield of nine quarterings, for *Leonard Danet.*

1. Sable, gutté d'Or, a canton Ermine. *Danet.*

2. Argent, two bars Gules, each charged with three lions rampant of the field. *De la hay.*

3. Azure, three eagles displayed Or, membered Gules.

4. Azure, three eagles displayed Or. *Billesworth.*

5. Gules, a fess checky Argent and Sable, six crosses formé fitché at the feet, Argent. *Boteler.*

6. Or, two bendlets Gules. *Sudeley.*

7. Bendy of ten, Or and Azure. *Montfort.*

8. Checky, Argent and Sable. *Ellenbridge.*

9. Argent, six annulets Sable, 3. 2. 1. *Manvers.*

II. A shield for *George Talbot,* earl of *Shrewsbury,* who married *Anne,* daughter of *William* lord *Hastings,* and aunt to *George* the first earl of *Huntingdon:*

1. Gules, a lion rampant within a bordure engrailed Or. *De Belesmo.*

2. Azure, a lion rampant within a bordure Or. *Talbot.*

3. Gules, a saltire Argent, charged with a martlet Sable. *Nevill.*

4. Argent, a bend between six martlets Gules. *Furnivall.*

5. Or, a fret Gules. *Verdon.*

6. Argent, two lions passant in pale Gules. *Strange.*

Impaling;

Argent, a maunch Sable. *Hastings.*

III. Quarterly, 1. and 4. *Hastings*; 2. and 3. Gules, a fess Or between three sheldrakes proper; *Herle*; impaling sixteen coats:

1. Sable, two bars Argent, in chief three plates. *Hungerford.*

2. Per pale indented Gules and Vert, a chevron Or. *Hungerford.*

3. Barry of six, Ermine and Gules. *Hussee.*

4. Azure, three garbs Argent, banded Gules, a chief Or. *Peverell.*

5. Argent, a lion rampant Gules, crowned Or, within a bordure engrailed Sable, bezantée. *Cornwall.*

6. Argent, three torteaux, a bend compony Or and Azure. *Courtney.*

7. Gules, a griffin rampant segreant Or. *Redvers.*

8. Checky, Or and Gules, on a bend Azure, three horseshoes Argent. *Botreaux.*

9. Argent, three toads erect Sable. *Botreaux.*

10. Argent, two bars Gules, in chief three torteaux. *Moeles.*

11. Argent, three lozenges in fess Gules. *Montacute.*

12. Argent, a bend Sable, a label of three points Gules. *St. Leo.*

13. Argent, three escallops Gules. *Clivedon.*

14. Sable, on a chief Argent three lozenges Gules. *Molyn.*

15. Gules, three pallets wavy Or. *Mauduit.*

16. Sable, on a chief Argent three mullets of the field.

IV. *Hastings*; impaling, Sable, two bars Argent in chief three plates. *Hungerford.*

In Mr. *Ruding's* house at *Westcotes.*

V. Quarterly:

1. Argent, on a bend between two lions rampant Sable, a wyvern, wings open of the field. *Ruding.*

2. Argent, on two bars Vert three plates. *Clerke.*

3. Sable, femé of cross crosslets fitché, and three fleurs de lis Argent, a canton Ermine. *Watercroft.*

4. As the first.

Impaling;

Per chevron, Argent and Sable, in chief two fleurs de lis Azure, in base a castle triple-towered Or. *Littel.*

Ruding's crest, a wivern's head Argent, collared and lined Or, in the mouth a lion's jambe erased Sable.

Littel's crest, a goat's head Sable, armed and gorged with a ducal coronet Or.

VI. Quarterly of nine, in a lozenge, for *Elizabeth Chambers,* daughter of *Richard Chambers,* of *Gaddesby*; who died Dec. 19, 1584:

1. Gules, a chevron between three cinquefoils Or. *Chambers.*

2. Ermine, a fess checky Or and Azure. *Arden.*

3. Sable, gutté d'Or a canton Ermine. *Danet.*

4. Argent, two bars Gules, each charged with three lions rampant of the field. *De la hay.*

5. Azure, three eagles displayed Or. *Billesworth.*

6. Barry wavy of six Argent and Gules.

7. Argent, a fess dancette, plain cotized between six mullets Gules.

8. Gules, a chevron between three castles Argent. *Allen.*

9. Gules, a fess between three ducks, within a bordure engrailed Or. *Whatley.*

VII.

1. Argent, on a cross Gules, five escallops Or. *Villiers* modern.

2. Per pale, Gules and Sable, a lion rampant Argent. *Beler.*

3. Gules, a fess between three .... Argent.

4. Sable, a fess between three cinquefoils Argent. *Villiers* antient.

[1] This coat still remains.

[2] Vincent, N° 94. p. 261. And see Plates XXVI. XXVII.

3

5. Azure,

5. Azure, a bend between fix mullets of fix points pierced Argent. *Houby.*
6. As the firft.

Impaling;

1. Azure, femé de lis, and a lion rampant Or. *Beaumont.*
2. Gules, three garbs Or. *Comyn.*
3. Gules, feven mafcles voided and conjoined Or, 3. 3. and 1. *Quincey.*
4. Gules, a cinquefoil Ermine. *Bellomont.*
5. Azure, a lion rampant Argent, crowned Or. *Galloway.*
6. Argent, within a double treffure flory Gules, an efcutcheon of the laft.
7. Azure, three garbs Or. *Chefter.*
8. Gules, a lion rampant Vaire. *Everingham.*
9. Azure, a fefs Argent, between three cinquefoils Or. *Maureward.*

On the tablet over the Mayor's feat, under which, on an oblong fhield, are the arms of the town.

" John Abney, mayor; William Bunney, Edmund Johnfon, chamberlains, 1700.

Robert Winfield [1], mayor; John Earpe, Gabriel Newton, chamberlains, 1721.

Humphrey Chapman, mayor; William Lewin, Jofeph Bunney, chamberlains, 1723.

Thomas Ludlam, mayor; Thomas Johnfon, William Lee, chamberlains, 1725.

Thomas Chapman, mayor; Hamlet Clarke, John Fifher, chamberlains, 1754.

Edm. Johnfon, John Winfield, churchwardens, 1699. John Tyler, Thomas Goodrich, 1709."

On the South-eaft wall is a table of the different benefactions and annuities given by divers benefactors to the poor of this parifh of St. Mary, Leicefter, collected out of the old records, from the year 1685.

Chriftmas.

⚑ Part of an annuity of John Poultney, efq. of Mifterton in this county; the gift to all the parifhes being £10.

⚑ Annuity of Mr. James Ellis, once Mayor of this Borough, 16s. 8d.; the whole gift being £8.

⚑ Annuity of Mr. Robert Heyrick, thrice Mayor of this Borough, 5s.; the whole gift being 40s. to five widows.

⚑ Annuity of Mr. Hugh Botham [2], 6s. 8d. to three parifhes only.

New Year's Day.

⚑ Part of fir William Courtney's [3] and Mr. Evington's lottery, 10s. 8d.; the whole being £4. 10s. for four-penny bread.

Candlemas Day.

⚑ Of Mr. Robert Heyrick aforefaid, the whole to the Corporation, being £5.; to be given in twopenny bread.

March or April.

Part of the gift of Mr. John Norrice, Mayor of this Borough, the whole gift being £10.; to be given by Aldermen who have wards, or part of wards, in this parifh.

Lady Day.

Part of a gift of widow Hobby, out of the rent of a houfe in the South Gate, given to widows in twopenny bread, 2s.; the whole gift being 4s.

Out of another houfe of the faid widow Hobby, in the South Gate, to be given to the poor, 1s.

Lent.

To fend twenty poor people of this parifh to St. Martin's church every Friday in Lent at morning prayer; there each to receive a two-penny loaf, the gift of Mr. William Ive [4], thrice Mayor of this Borough.

Friday before Eafter.

⚑ Part of a gift of the Countefs Dowager of Devonfhire; the whole gift to the Corporation; and St. Leonard's gift to the parifh, being £3. yearly for ever.

⚑ The latter payment of Mr. Hugh Botham's annual gift, 6s. 8d.

Thurfday before Whit-funday.

⚑ The Eafter payment of fir William Courtney's and Mr. Evington's lottery, 10s.

July 20th.

⚑ Part of the gift of king Charles the Firft, out of the rent of forty acres of land in Leicefter Foreft, to the poor houfe-keeper, being a freeman, 6s.; the gift being £6.

⚑ Part of Mrs. Elizabeth Offiter's annual gift to poor houfe-keepers for coals; the whole gift being £6.

⚑ The annual gift of Mr. John Nurce, of Leicefter, being 13s. 4d.; paid yearly on St. Thomas the Apoftle.

⚑ Of Hugh Botham, gent. to the poor of this parifh, 13s. 4d.; paid on St. Thomas and Whitfunday by equal portions.

⚑ Mr. Jofeph Wright's gift, paid at Candlemas yearly, 13s. 4d.

⚑ Mr. Watts's gift, paid by Mr. Simpfon yearly, 10s.

Mr. Peter Palmer's gift, out of a houfe in St. Martin's parifh, 1s.

Mrs. Elizabeth Clarke, late of this Borough, gave to the poor of this parifh the fum of £100.

N. B. Marked ⚑, paid by the Chamberlain, or Overfeers of charitable works [5].

An evening lecture in this church was founded by a parifhioner [Mr. Jofeph Wheatley] in the year 1778. The deed of truft, declaring the ufes, and appointing the truftees, is enrolled in the Court of Common Pleas, in Trinity Term 1778; and the roll is numbered 47. It is alfo copied in the regiftry at Lincoln.

Extracts from the Regifters of St. Mary de Cafiro.

" Anno 1603, William Cheyney, fonne of Chriftofer Cheyney, of Grayes Inne in the county of Middlefex, efquier, was borne at the houfe of fir Thomas Cave, knight, in the Newarke by Leicefter, being *in this parifh*, the 27 day of Nov. being the firft year of our moft gratious foveraigne lord king James, and was baptifed in this church the 4th of Dec. then next following [6]."

" Chriftian, the wife of Thomas Cademan, buried 9th of July, 1611. Thomas Cademan, buried 27th of July. Edward, fonne of Thomas Cademan, buried Auguft 9. Thomas, fonne of Thomas Cademan, buried 12th of Auguft [7]."

" 1625, Roger, fonne of Henry Hemminge, of the *Newarke, within* this parifh, baptized the 22 July [8]."

	£.	s.	d.
Money raifed for the poor within the year ending at Eafter 1776, —	571	17	2
Expended in county rates, &c.	39	18	10
——— on the poor,	531	18	4
Rent of workhoufe [9] and habitations,	1	13	9
Expended in litigations, —	33	11	9
Money raifed for 1783, —	668	16	10
——————— 1784, —	719	17	8
——————— 1785, —	704	0	1
Medium of thefe three years,	697	11	6
——— of county expences,	23	11	0
——— of expences not relating to the poor; repairs of churches, roads, &c.	33	1	10
——— of nett annual expences,	640	18	8
——— of attending on magiftrates,	0	0	0
——— of entertainments at meetings,	0	0	0
——— of law expences, —	13	7	3
——— of fetting the poor to work,	1	8	0

[1] See his epitaph, p. 319.
[2] Hugh Botham entered his Pedigree at Leicefter at the Vifitation of 1619. His firft wife was Grace Jackfon; and he was at that time married to Margaret daughter of William Barrett. [3] This fhould be fir William Courteen.
[4] He lies, with his wife, in St. Martin's chancel; with a legible Englifh infcription, their figures cut on the floor-ftone.
[5] See the return made to Parliament, p. 126. [6] Regifter of St. Mary, Leicefter, p. 8, Old Regifter.
[7] Ibid. p. 50. [8] Ibid. p. 120. [9] The workhoufe at that time was capable of accommodating 112 perfons.

MONUMENTAL INSCRIPTIONS.

On the floor of the *Old Chancel* (or Corporation Chancel, as it is usually called) are several painted tiles, on which are inscribed the letters ℂ and L[1]. Frequent interments have demolished, or disperfed, many others. The ℂ Mr. Bickerstaffe (somewhat too fancifully) took to be the initial of *Municipium*, the borough, and L for *Leiceftria*, as they are on separate squares; and observes that a few others were decorated with the cinquefoil, one of which was at the head of the inscription over *Boroughe's* grave, as a token that the interment was acknowledged to be within the privilege of the Corporation.

At the West end of this chancel, near the feat at the bottom of the pulpit-stairs, there formerly lay a white stone, not quite two feet broad, and three feet two inches long, with the figure of a prieft delineated on it; and round it,

" Orate pro a'i'a ðñi
Ioh'is Boroughe, q'nd'm huj' eccl'ie
p'bendar' ac gardiani
de Sapcote cuj' a'i'e mifereat' Deus. Amen."

This stone has been lately removed somewhat farther into the chancel; changing place with a larger and darker one, (fig. 24.) five feet seven inches and a half long, two feet four inches and a half wide, which bears a tall broad crofs; a Bible on its right, on its left a chalice; at its foot, under a curious bafe, a short and imperfect inscription:

" Orate pro a'i'a ðñi Wilhelmi . . . ."

Adjoining this laft is a large blue flab, with the figure of a prieft and a fcroll over his head; and another near it, with a prieft, and an inscription round the verge; but from both thefe the braffes are torn.

In this chancel, a few years ago, a paten was dug up, which had been buried with one of the priefts.

Leland, who vifited Leicefter about the year 1538, fays, " In this church of St. Marie extra caftrum I faw the tumbe in marble of *Thomas Rider*, father to mafter *Richard of Leicefter*. This Richard I take to be the fame that yn thofe dayes, as it apperith by his workes, was a greate clerke[2]. Befide this grave I faw few thinges there of any auncient memorie within the chirch[3]."

A mifcellaneous volume in the Cotton Library, however, preferves in MS the following epitaph on a lady; whofe effigies in a fhroud-drefs still remains perfectly diftinct on a large blue flab, though the brafs is torn off:

" St. Mary chirche at Leiceftr. in the South quere:

" Hic jacet Matilda de La hay[4],
uror Thome de La hay;
que obiit rr° Maii,
año ðñi mcccclrrriv.
cuj' a'i'e ppicietur deus. amen[5]."

Arms: Argent, two bars Gules, each charged with three lions rampant of the field; *De la Hay*; fig. 25.

On a small flip of white marble, inlaid on the laft-mentioned blue flab:

" Jofiah Bond, hujus ecclefiæ per 19 annos elapfos myfta fedulus.
Quodque fui mortale fuit, hic
depofuit, Sept. 26, A. D. 1678[6], ætat. fuæ 47."

On tablets againft the North wall:
1. " WILLIAM BILLERS, GENT.
AGED 76 YEARS, DIED AN.
DOM. 1658; AND LEFT ISSUE
EDWARD, WILLIAM, BENJAMIN, AND JOSEPH.
HIS WIFE ALICE, AGED 71 YEARS,
DIED ANNO DOM. 1662.
THEY WERE BOTH INTERRED IN ONE GRAUE
NEERE THIS PLACE."

2. " Near unto this place lies interred
the bodies of George Beckett, of
the Newark, near Leicefter, gent. and
Hannah his wife; he was one of the Aldermen,
and twice Mayor, of this Corporation;
they both died in his fecond Mayoralty;
fhe died on the 27th of December, 1691, and
he on the 11th of Auguft, 1692,
being aged 64 years; her age 59.
This monument was erected for them by his
executors anno Dom. 1700."

3. " Sacred to the memory of John Harris,
who departed this life May 11, 1782, aged 65 years.'

On the South wall:
" To the memory of Philip Bamford, gent.
who departed this life the 9th day of Dec. 1759,
aged 66 years;
and of Elizabeth his wife,
who died July 4, 1783, aged 77 years."

On the Eaft wall:
1. " Sacred
to the memory of
the Rev. John Simmonds, M. A.
from Lullington, in the county of
Derby; curate and vicar of this parifh
32 years; and vicar of Enderby,
in this county, 22 years. He died
Aug. 29, 1778, in the 58th
year of his age.
He was a man of exemplary piety
and univerfal beneficence,
not refting in the mere fpeculation
of religious truths,
but enforcing by
his own example
the precepts of that moft holy Gofpel,
of which he was a minifter.
In the difcharge of all Chriftian duties
none was more affiduous;
within the circle of his acquaintance
none more efteemed.
Thefe truths are infcribed, to excite
in the reader an endeavour
to imitate fo eminent an example."

The following addition to this epitaph was written by Mr. Bickerftaffe:
" Loft to the world, is now with God, we truft,
The humble owner of this fleeping duft;
Rich in each heavenly grace which Chrift infpir'd;
O much regretted, and O much defir'd!
Say, grateful Want, if thou canft utter aught,
How well he practis'd what fo well he taught.

---

[1] Plate XXV. fig. 22, 23.

[2] See before, p. 283.— This " Mafter Richard of Leicefter" was prefented by the abbot and convent of St. Mary de Pratis, in 1291, to the rectory of Eydon in Northamptonfhire; which he held till 1316. Fruitlefs has been the refearch in Dupin for an account of Richard de Leicefter's literary abilities; and probably his name, as a learned clerk, was confined to his own country. Tanner, in Bibl. Britan. p. 626, has noticed only a fingle MS. penned by this learned clerk; and might not this MS, even though the title of it be Articles of the Creed, be principally calculated for the meridian of Leicefter? Might it not have fome reference to the proceffion, on Whit Monday, from the church of St. Mary de Caftro to that of St. Margaret, in which, as ftated at p. 305, there were, attending on the image of the Virgin Mary, twelve perfons reprefenting the twelve apoftles, each of which had the name of the apoftle whom he reprefented written on parchment fixed on his bonnet?—" Scripfit de Articulorum Symboli diftributione fecundum *numerum Apoftolorum*." Could this MS. be examined, there might be found in it fome particulars illuftrative of this folemn proceffion. According to Tanner, this MS. was in Sion library (Bibliotheca Sion). Qu. did he mean the nunnery of Sion, co. Middlefex. In Notit. Monaft. (Edit. Nafmith) it is mentioned, that, in the library of Corpus Chrifti College, Cambridge, there is a Regifter or Catalogue of the MSS. that were in Bibl. Monaft. de Sion.

At p. 310, 1498, paid at Whitfuntide, for bread, ale, and flefh, for the apoftles and others, 3s. 4d.
At p. 312, 1516, fee another entry of a payment to the twelve apoftles.
[3] Itin. p. 17.
[4] This lady occurs as a tenant to the abbot of Leicefter, for a garden in St. Peter's parifh, at an annual rent of two capons. See Appendix, p. 78.   [5] Cotton MSS. Vefpafian D. XVII. fol. 53.
[6] In the parifh-regifter Mr. Bond's burial is entered, not in 1678, but in 1679.

I

Twice

Twice widow'd orphan'd forrows, how they weep !
They've loft the faithful fhepherd of his fheep.
Hunger and Nakednefs their lofs deplore:
Simmonds is dead, and Charity no more."

2. " To the memory of Phœbe Chatwyn,
who died Jan. 22, 1783, aged 48 years."

The kindeft mother, and of wives the beft,
From mortal ills hath found eternal reft.
Art thou a hufband, happy in thy wife;
Or child, whofe mother loves thee dear as life ?
With foul unmov'd thou fhalt not read this ftone,
But feel our grief, and make the lofs thy own."

On flat ftones in the old chancel:
1. " Rafe Watton died June 3, 1631, aged 19."

2. " Here lieth the body of Robert ... ol [1]
of the Newark within the borough of Leicefter,
who departed this life June 21, 16.6,
aged 74."

3. " Under this ftone lies the body
of John Norrice, gent.
late mafter of the family of the Norrices.
He left behind him only one daughter;
and died in the 59th year of his age,
July the 19th, A. D. 1700."

4. " Here lyeth the body of
Mary Mawfon, wife of
Richard Mawfon, of the New-
ork near Leicefter,
who departed this life
May 2, A. D. 1702,
aged 69.
Here lyes interred
the body of Richard
Mawfon, gent. who
was governor of the
Magazine in the New-
ork 55 years. He de-
parted this life May
the 23, 1715, aged 79."

5. " Here lieth interred the body of
Tyringham Stephens, of
the Newark near the Borough of Leicefter, gent.
regifter to the bifhop of Lincoln, and archdeacon
of Leicefter for the archdeaconry of Leicefter,
fecond fon of Nathaniel Stephens,
of Horton, in the county of Gloucefter, gent.
by Elizabeth daughter of Robert Tyringham [2], of
Wefton Favell, in the county of Northampton, efq.
who departed this life the 20th of June,
A. D. 1710, ætatis fuæ 75."

6. " Here alfo lies interred Tyringham Stephens,
of the Middle Temple, efq.
eldeft fon of the faid Tyringham, by
Milicent his wife, daughter of William Inge, of
Thorpe Conftantine, in the county of Stafford, efq.
who departed this life the 5th day of June,
anno Domini 1710, ætatis fuæ 38."

7. " Here lieth interred the body of Milicent Stephens,
widow and relict of Tyringham Stephens, gent.
late of the Newark ;
fhe departed this life the 21ft day of November,
A. D. 1721, aged 71 years."

8. " Here lie the remains of Frances Stephens,
daughter of Tyringham Stephens, gent. and
Milicent, his wife ;
fhe departed this life the 4th day of Auguft 1768,
aged 78."

9. " In memory of Richard Stephens, gent.
who died July 30, 1745, aged 60 ;
and of Sarah his wife,
who died June 17, 1745 ; aged 73."

10. " Here lieth the body of W. Homer,
the fon of Henry and Sarah Homer,
who departed this life the May 8, 1724, aged 4 years."

11. " Hìc jacet corpus Roberti,
filii Thomæ Pocklington, hujus ecclefiæ vicarii,
qui obiit Aug. 14, 1738, æt. 11."

12. " Here lieth the body of John Farmer, gent.
late of the parifh of Nuneaton,
in the county of Warwick.
He departed this life the 23rd day of Sept.
in the year of our Lord 1727, aged 63 years."

13. " Here lieth the body of Mary,
the eldeft daughter of Richard Farmer
by Hannah his wife,
who departed this life the 17th day of Ap. 1743,
aged 6 years and 10 weeks;
alfo John, their eldeft fon, aged 11 days.
Thefe both died young; more happy they
Than thofe that do here longer ftay."

14. " Nathan, the fon of William Wright, efq.
born the 25th of Auguft, 1735,
died the 15th of March following. *Flebilis occidit.*"

15. On a brafs plate, removed in 1761 on making a
new vault for the family of an alderman :
" Hic jacet
Quod mori potuit Henrici Gilberti Cooper,
Infantis defideratiffimi,
Filii natu maximi
Joannis Gilberti Cooper,
De Thurgarton in agro Notting. arm.
Et Sufannæ uxoris ejus.
Natus 25to die Jul. denatus 26to, anno 1749.
Atavis erat editus antiquis ;
Nullâ aliâ in re claruit,
Nec potuit.
Flofculus enim, in ipsâ quoque dulci ætatulæ
Primâ gemmâ pullulaturus,
Parcarum, heu! parcere nefciarum,
Fatali afflatu contactus,
Exaruit.
Mœftus itaque & mœrens pater ipfius
Chariffimi infantuli fui memoriæ
Hoc, etfi inane munus,
Amoris monumentum
Collocavit."

16. " Here lieth interred the body
of Thomas Chapman, late Alderman,
and once Mayor, of this Corporation.
He died the 20th day of November, 1768,
in the 71ft year of his age."

17. " Here lieth interred the body of Ann Rawfon,
wife of Mr. William Rawfon of Nottingham,
and daughter of Mr. Humphrey Chapman,
late one of the Aldermen, and once Mayor,
of this Borough.
She departed this life the 26th day of October, 1768,
in the 60th year of her age.
Here alfo lieth the body of Mary Wilfon,
the wife of Mr. John Wilfon of this borough,
and daughter of Mr. Humphrey Chapman.
She departed this life the 6th day of June, 1761,
aged 62 years."

On a flat ftone at the South-weft end of the church,
towards the caftle, lately covered by a new gallery :
" Propè repofiti funt cineres
viri reverendi Thomæ Gee [3],
ecclefiæ Chrifti reformatæ in villâ Leic.
per viginti ferè annos paftoris docti feduli & fidelis;
qui, cum pietate fincerâ in Deum,
juftitiâ & charitate erga homines,
& eximiâ morum modeftiâ & temperantiâ,
Chriftum imitatus,
religionem tam vitâ quàm doctrinâ adornâffet,
ex mortalium cœtu ad cœleftium fedes
gravi febre præmaturè extinctus emigravit,
die menfis Septembris duodevigefimo, A. D. 1729,
natus annos 43."

On another compartment of the fame ftone :
" Juxta item jacet

[1] Perhaps Robert Wincoll, fon of John Wincoll, efq. counfellor of the Middle Temple, whofe Pedigree is entered, as of Leicefter, in the Vifitation of 1619.
[2] Robert Tyringham, of Leicefter, M. A. was ejected from a fellowfhip of Peterhoufe, Cambridge in 1644; and reftored in 1660.
[3] This Mr. Thomas Gee was preacher at the great or Prefbyterian meeting near the But-clofe; and, as Mr. Bickerftaffe's mother informed him, firft introduced the Lord's prayer in his miniftry. Before this erection, their houfe of worfhip was, what is now a barn, in Bonner's lane, by the Horfepool ftreet.

Thomæ

Thomæ Benion quod reliquum eft,
fupralaudati Thomæ Gee privigni,
filii verò Samuelis Benion, Salop.
nuper magni nominis medici, nec minùs eximii theologi,
primordiis vitæ,
tam virtute quàm ingenio maturus effulfit,
ætate folâ non grandis.
Vixit annos 22, obiit 18 Nov. 1727.
Catharina Benion, avuncula infra-dicti Thomæ Benion,
hìc etiam requiefcit, beatâ fpe refurgendi.
Deceffit 18 Aug. 1728, nata annos 42."

On another compartment:
" Juxta funt fiti
hujufce Thomæ Gee & chariff. conjugis liberi,
Maria Gee, nat. 24 Maii, 1712, denat' 24 Oct. 1719.
Jana Gee, nat. 17 Sept. 1714, denat. 10 Nov. 1719.
Robertus Gee, nat. 26 Nov. 1716, denat. 7 Nov. 1719.
Anna Gee, nat. 5 Jun. 1718, denat. 26 Jun. 1719.
Catharina Gee, nat. 21 Feb. 1721, denat. 17 Oct. 1724.
Hunc cippum, in amoris & officio ergò,
pia & mœftiffima conjux poni curavit."

On another flat ftone under the new gallery:
" Here lies interred the body of
Capt. John Phillips of . . . . . . in Huntingdonfhire,
who, being wounded in Nafeby fight,
in the caufe of
the glorious King and Martyr Charles the Firft,
died here July 8, 1645."

On a flat ftone in the nave :
" In memory of John,
fon of John and Ruth Brown,
who died Feb. 28, 1794, aged 26 years."

In the chancel of the South aile.
Mr. Wyrley notices,
" Leonardus Danet, de Danet's Hall, ob. 1582."

Of this tomb we cannot now difcover the fituation ;
but at Tiltey-abbey, in Effex, on a flab with the effigies
of a man and his wife, fix fons and fix daughters, are
the arms of *Danet* (Sable, guttée Argent a canton
Ermine [1],) and this infcription:
" Hic jacet fepultus, cum conjuge Wazia, Gezazdus Danet
de Bzonkynfthorpe [2], in com. Leceftrie, azm. fezeniffimi regis
Henrici octavi confiliazius. Ob. 4 Maij, 1520, an. regni Hen.
UIIII. 20. Quozum animabus propitietur Deus. Amen."

Mr. Burton fays, " In this church lyeth buried the
virtuous lady, and moft worthy of all honour, Mabell,
late wife of fir Henry Haftings, knt. fonne of fir Edward Haftings, knight, third fonne of Francis earle
of Huntington. She was daughter to Anthony Faunt,
of Fofton, in the countie of Leicefter, efq. and departed this life 1619." (This is alfo gone.)

On a grave-ftone erected againft the North corner of
the Eaft-wall are the arms of *Watts*, three greyhounds'
erafed, ducally gorged Or; creft, a greyhound Sable,
ducally gorged Or; fig. 27; and this infcription:

" *Tempora mutantur, et nos mutamur.*
Here lieth the body of Hugh Watts the elder, gent.
fometimes Major and Alderman of this Corporation,
who deceafed in the 61 yeare of his age, an° Dñi 1643."

Over this, on a large and high monument, are the
arms of *Watts*; impaling, Sable, a chevron between
three owls Argent, crowned Or, *Burton* of Stockerfton [3]; fig. 28.
" To the precious memory of Hugh Watts, gent.
fon and heir of Hugh Watts, the elder, gent.
who married Jane,
fourth daughter of fir Thomas Burton, of Stockerfton,
in the county of Leicefter, knight and baronet.
He had iffue one fon and four daughters ;
and died in the faith of Chrift, Aug. 26, 1656.

Dignum laude virum Mufa vetat mori.
Her generous male, his noble female twines
Still with her arms, and thus her faint enfhrines
In liquid marble of immortal lines ;
Her guardian angel urged her fo to frame
Pure precious unction, fure conferve of fame ;
And hurle eternal perfumes on his name,
Whofe fpotlefs life, religion's crown and teft,
Rule, and example, was for all the beft,
And charm'd down deafeft vices in the reft ;
What earlie deaws of graces did prevent
His rare, and juft, and pondered temper'ment,
Would afke a volume half to reprefent ;
Yet by his gracious fadd relict alone,
His large foul's opulence will beft be fhowne,
By fympathetic virtues of her own.
Aged 45 years."

At the top of this monument there remained in
1682 a penon, with the arms of *Watts* without the
creft; and another penon, with the arms of *Watts* impaling *Burton* as above defcribed [4].

On a flat ftone, at fome diftance :
" HERE LIETH INTERRED ROSE WATTES,
DAUGHTER TO HUGH AND MARY WATTES,
WHO DEPARTED THIS LIFE THE THIRD OF JUNE,
ANNO DOM. 1636, ÆTATIS SUÆ 19."

On an adjoining flab of white marble :
" HERE LIETH THE BODIE OF JOHN SWANN,
OF THE NEWARKE NEERE THE BOROUGH
OF LEICESTER, WHO DEPARTED THIS LIFE
THE 15TH DAY OF AUG. A. D. 1639,
WHOSE SOULE WE HOPE IS IN THE HAND OF
THE LORD; TO WHOM BE PRAISE FOR
EVERMORE! AMEN."

Againft the South wall was alfo a penon of thefe
arms, for the wife of Captain *Sherman* of Leicefter:
Or, a lion rampant Sable between three leaves
Vert; impaling, Argent, a fefs embattled between
three unicorns' heads erafed; fig. 27.

On another penon, Azure, a lion rampant between
femé of fleurs de lis Or, *Beaumont*; impaling *Burton* as
before [5]; fig. 30.

On a large flab:
" Under this ftone is interred
the body of lady Jane Beaumont, aged 44 years,
wife to fir Thomas Beaumont,
of Stoughton Grange in this county, baronet,
being daughter to fir Thomas Burton,
of Stockerfton, in the fame county, baronet.
And here is likewife buried with her
Thomas Watts, aged 16 years, her only fone,
begotten by her former hufband Hugh Watts,
of the Newarke near Leicefter, efq.
Their bodies were both laid here together
upon the 4 day of October,
in the year of our Lord 1670."

The following memorials of the family of *Ruding* [6]
are on flat ftones, except where otherwife mentioned :

1. On an alabafter flab, within the altar rails,
(Plate XXVI.) are the figures of a man and his wife,
feven fons and four daughters. At the four corners
of this ftone are four fhields; on the firft and fourth
of which are, *Ruding*, as in p. 312. The bearings of the
fecond and third fhields are obliterated. Round the verge,

" Hic jacet Joh'es Rudyng genof' et . . . .
. . . . atq' libe eor'd'. Que quide Jocofa obiit
riiii die meffis novebris, anno
dñi m.ccccpliiii. Quor' a'i'ab' ppiciet' dez. Amen."

2. On a fimilar flab, alfo within the altar-rails
(Plate XXVII.), the figures of a man and woman;

[1] Salmon's Effex, p. 200; Weever, p. 63; but not noticed by Morant. Of Gerard Danet's wife fee before, p. 309.
[2] A liberty within St. Mary's parifh, and nearly adjoining to the town of Leicefter. The antient family of *Danett* had formerly confiderable poffeffions here, a part of which, with their capital manfion-houfe, is now the property of William Bentley, efq.
[3] Thefe arms and the infcription are much defaced. [4] Vifitation-Notes, 1682, in the College of Arms. [5] Ibid.
[6] This family have long been the owners of a capital manfion called Weftcoates (formerly one of the Granges belonging to the Abbey of St. Mary de Pratis), and a confiderable eftate within the liberty of Bronkinfthorpe, now poffeffed by *Walter Ruding*, efq. See fome arms from this houfe in p. 312.—At Bigglefwade is an infcription to the memory of *John Ruding*, archdeacon of Buckingham, who died in 1481; engraved in Mr. Gough's " Sepulchral Monuments in Great Britain," vol. II. plate CII. p. 273; but he was of a different family, as appears from his arms in Willis's Buckingham, where two different coats are affigned to him, p. 62.

Pl. **XXVI.** *p.* 316.

Monument of John Ruding and Joice
(Purefoy) his Wife in the Chancel of
St. Mary's Church in Leicester

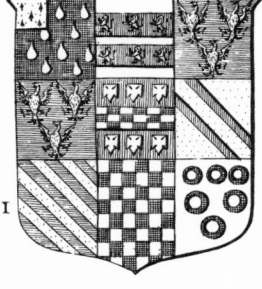

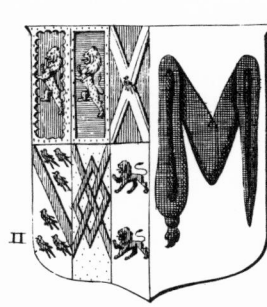

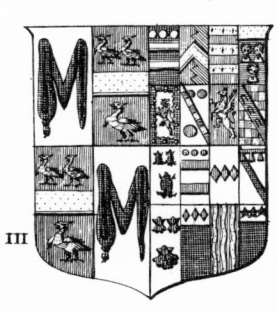

Pl. XXVII. *p.317.*

Monument of Richard Ruding &
Anne (Drivet) his Wife in y° Chancel
of S.t Mary's Church in Leicester.

MINE ❧ 1582

RICHARD RVDING OF WESCOTHS GENT LEMAN : DESEASED

THE EAGHT DAY OF OCTOBER ANNO DO

R:R.

IV

V

VI

VII

and in two compartments below three fons and three daughters. Arms: 1. and 4. *Ruding*; 2. *Clerke*; 3. *Watercrofte* [1]; as in p. 312; with this infcription on the verge:

"HERE LIETH RICHARD RUDING, OF WESCOTHS, GENTLEMAN, DESEASED
THE EAGHT DA OF OCTOBER, ANNO DOMINE 1582."

3. " HERE LIETH INTERRED THE BODIE OF
WALTER RUDINGE, ESQUIER,
WHO DEPARTED THIS LIFE ON
THE 12TH DAY OF NOVEMBER, ANNO
DOMINI 1655, HIS AGE 78.
HE WAS SON AND HEIR OF RICHARD
RUDINGE, OF THE WEST C....."

4. " HERE LIETH ALSO THE BODIE
OF ELIZABETH, THE WIFE OF WALTER RUDINGE,
ESQUIER, WHO DEPARTED THIS LIFE
THE .. OF JUNE, 1657,
HIR . . . ."

5. " HERE LIETH THE BODY OF
ELIZABETH HUNGATE, THE
DAUGHTER OF HENRY HUNGATE, ESQ.
AND LUCY HIS WIFE, WHO WAS
DAUGHTER OF WALTER RUDING
AND ELIZABETH HIS WIFE. SHE
DEPARTED THIS LIFE THE 26TH
OF SEPTEMBER, ANNO DOM. 1667;
HER AGE 18 YEARE AND 6 MUNTH."

6. " HERE LIES JOHN, THE
SONNE OF WALTER RUDINGE, OF WESTCOTE,
ESQ. AND JANE HIS WIFE,
WHO DEPARTED THIS LIFE FEBRUARY
THE THIRD, ANNO DOMINI MDCLXX,
AGED XIX."

7. Againft the wall of the North-eaft end, on a fmall tablet, *Ruding*, with the quarterings as in fig. 31; impaling, Argent, a chevron between three goats' heads erafed Sable, *Inge*; fig. 32.
" Near unto this place is interred the body of Jane, late wife of Walter Ruding, of the Weft Coates, nere the Borrough of Leicefter, efq. only daughter of Richard Inge, of Knighton, gent. and Jane Ive his wife, who departed this life Oct. the 9th, 1685, being aged 64."

8. " Here lyeth the body of John Ruding, third fon of Walter Ruding, of Weftcoats, Efq. and Sarah his wife, who departed this life May 25, 1709, aged 11 weeks."

9. Arms: Quarterly, as in fig. 31.
" Here lyeth the body of William Ruding, of Weftcoats, efq. who departed this life the 4th of July, 1712, aged 72 years."

10. " Here lyeth interred (in hopes of a glorious refurrection) the body of John Rogers, archdeacon of Leicefter, who departed this life May 7, 1715, aged 67."

11. A mural monument is alfo fixed for him againft the South wall, with this infcription :
" Hic
felicem præftolantes refurrectionem
deponuntur exuviæ
reverendi viri
JOHANNIS ROGERS, A. M.
archidiaconi Leiceftrienfis, rectoris de Segrave,
olim coll. divi Johannis apud Oxon. Socii,
comis, benefici, pii, pervigilis,
inter
bonorum gemitus, fuorum querimonias,
ecclefiæ defideria, pauperum efflagitationes,

è mediis laboribus et malis
mortalium vel optimos obfidentibus,
ad emeritorum otia,
plufquam victorum triumphos,
confummatorum beatitudines evocati
nonis Maii,
Anno $\left\{\begin{array}{l}\text{Salutis 1715.}\\ \text{ætatis 67."}\end{array}\right.$

12. " Here lyes the body of Sarah Rogers, wife of John Rogers, Archdeacon of Leicefter. She departed this life January 27, 1722, aged 65. Here alfo lyeth the body of Anne-Lucy, fifter to the faid Sarah Rogers, who departed this life January 29, 1722, aged 69."

13. " Here lies the body of Jane Ruding, fecond daughter of Walter Ruding, of Weft Coates, efq. and Sarah his wife; fhe departed this life Jan. 31, 1716, aged 2 years and 1 months."

14. " Here lies the body of Anne Ruding, third daughter of Walter Ruding, of Weftcoats, efq. and Sarah his wife. She departed this life September 26, 1717, aged 2 years and 3 months."

15. In a lozenge, *Ruding* [2]; impaling, Checquy, Or and Gules, on a bend Ermine, a fleur de lis Gules, *Clifton*; fig. 33.
" Here lieth the body of Abigail Ruding, wife of William Ruding, of Weftcoats, in the county of Leicefter, efq. and eldeft daughter of Henry Clifton, of Toftrees [3], in the county of Norfolk, efq. She departed this life the 13th day of February, 1726, aged 84."

16. Arms, *Ruding* alone (lions rampant guardant).
" Here lieth the body of Walter Ruding, of Weft Coats, efq. the only fon of William Ruding, efq. who departed this life May the 6th, 1748, aged 73."

17. In a lozenge, *Ruding*; impaling Argent a chevron between three bucks' current, Sable; *Rogers*; fig. 34.
" Here lieth the body of Sarah Ruding, the wife of Walter Ruding, of Weft Coats, efq. and daughter of the Rev. Mr. John Rogers, A. M. archdeacon of Leicefter. She departed this life the 12th day of March, 1761, aged 75 years."

18. Arms, *Ruding* alone.
" Here lieth the body of William Ruding, efq. the eldeft fon of Walter Ruding, of Weft Coats, efq. who departed this life the 27th of February, 1762, aged 54."

19. *Ruding*. On an efcutcheon of pretence, Gules, a lion rampant Or within a border Vaire; *Skrymfher*; fig. 35.
" Beneath are interred the remains of Anne, the wife of Rogers Ruding, efq. of Weftcotes, and daughter and fole heirefs of James Skrymfher, efq. of Hill Hall, in the parifh of High Offley, and county of Stafford; fhe was born June 5, 1721, and departed this life, at Derby, March 4, 1791."

---

[1] The quarterings, Numbers 2, and 3, are much defaced, as may be feen in the Plate; but ftill enough remains to afcertain them to have been originally as defcribed above. They are engraved complete in Plate XXV. fig. 31.
[2] The lions in *Ruding*'s arms are here (by miftake) rampant guardant.
[3] On a flat ftone in the chancel of Toftes church : " In memory of Jane Ruding, daughter of William Ruding, of Weftcoates, efq. and Abigail his wife, daughter of Henry Clyfton, of Tofte, efq. She died Jan. 3, 1709, aged 38 years. Alfo of Martha Ruding, daughter of William Ruding and Abigail his wife; and three fons, William, Clifton, and Richard."

20. " Here

20. " Here lieth the body of Rogers Ruding, efq.
of Weftcotes, the fourth
fon of Walter Ruding, efq. of Weftcotes, and
Sarah (the daughter of John Rogers, M. A.
archdeacon of Leicefter) his wife.
He was born the 27th of October, 1710,
and departed this life, at Warwick,
on the 27th of March, 1795."
At top, arms of *Ruding* and *Skrymfher* as before.

On a fmall tablet of black marble on the South wall :

Arms: Argent, on a chevron between three lozenges Sable, three ftags' heads cabofled of the firft ;
Staveley ; impaling, Or, a chevron Vert, between three
towers Gules ; *Oneby* ; fig. 36.

" Near this place is interred the body
of Thomas Staveley, efq.
who, having faithfully ferved GOD,
his king, and country, many years,
departed this life the 2d of January, 1683,
in the 57th year of his age [1].
He had iffue, by Mary his wife,
who was the fourth daughter of John
Oneby, efq.
three fons and four daughters."

On an adjoining white marble monument :
" Near this place lye interred
the body of Mr. James Palmer,
Mrs. Frances Palmer his wife,
Mr. James Palmer their fon,
and alfo that of Mrs. Jane Palmer their daughter ;
fhe was a gentlewoman very exemplary
for her piety, virtue, and great charity.
She deceafed April 30, 1718,
in the 39th year of her age ;
who while living did always exprefs a very
dutiful veneration for her parents ;
and to whofe memory fhe, the faid Mrs. Jane Palmer,
by her laft will and teftament, did enjoin
this fmall monument to be erected."

On flat ftones near the altar :
" P. M. S.
Sarah, pia & chariffima uxor Thomæ Ludlam,
obiit 4° Novemb', 1713."

" Here was interred the remains of
Richard Ludlam [2], M. B.

Obiit Aug. 13, 1728, ætat. 48.
And near this place lieth Anne his wife,
and daughter of William Drury, efq. of Nottingham.
Obiit May 3, 1739, ætat. 47."
On the South wall :
" In memory of William Ludlam [3], B. D.
many years fellow of St. John's college, Cambridge,
(fon of Richard Ludlam, M. B.)
who died March 16, 1788, aged 71 years.
And of William his fon, aged 3 years."

[The following elegant epitaph, intended for the above
tomb, has been communicated by a Friend :
" Here refts a Man, whom Genius gave to fway
Through the bright compafs of etherial Day ;
Whofe bound, nor Time, nor diftance could controul,
But bore him boldly on from Pole to Pole,
Pierc'd the dark regions of all-covering Night,
And gave to Newton's felf a clearer Light."]

Under the table of benefactions, on a fmall tablet :
" Mrs. Lucy Fownes
was buried in this church May the 6th, 1716,
who by her laft will and teftament
gave the fum of twenty pounds
to the poor of this parifh ; which
fum the officers of the faid parifh have received, and do promife
and intend to diftribute the fum of
twenty fhillings, being the intereft
of the faid twenty pounds, to the
poor of this parifh, yearly, for ever."

On flat ftones in the chancel :
1. " Hic jacet Elizabetha, quondam uxor Laurencii
Carter, generofi ; & filia natu maxima Thomæ
Wadland, generofi, quæ 29° Septembris, anno D'ni
1671, obiit ; cujus pietatem, probitatem,
charitatem, ac patientiam, Deus in cœlis coronavit,
et in die refurrectionis omnibus patefaciet.
Virtus poft funera vivit."

2. " To the memory of
Laurence Carter [4], of the Neworks near Leicefter,
Efq. thrice Member of Parliament
for the Borough of Leicefter [5], and here
interred in 1710, aged 69.
Here alfo is interred Mary his fecond wife, daughter of
Thomas Potter, of the city of London, gent."

---

[1] It appears by the Parifh Regifter that he was buried on the 8th of January ; and that his brother-in-law Dr. Richard Mafon, who died March 26, 1668, was alfo buried in this church ; where, tradition fays, is a flat ftone in memory of him and his children, now covered by the pews.

[2] Dr. Ludlam left two fons, William and Thomas, both clergymen. Of William, fee the following note. The Rev. Thomas Ludlam, of St. John's college, Cambridge, B. A. 1748 ; M. A. 1752 ; is the prefent Confrater of Wigfton's Hofpital, and rector of Fofton in this county. Dr. Ludlam's only daughter was the fecond wife of Jofeph Cradock, efq. father to the prefent owner of Gumley Hall.

[3] The Rev. William Ludlam, rector of Cockfield in Suffolk, and vicar of Norton by Galby ; fellow of St. John's College, Cambridge ; B. A. there 1738 ; M. A. 1742 ; B. D. 1749 ; was highly celebrated for his fkill in mechanics and mathematics. He was author of " Aftronomical Obfervations made in St. John's College, Cambridge, in the years 1767 and 1768 ; with an Ac-count of feveral Aftronomical Inftruments, 1769," 4to. " Two Mathematical Effays ; the firft on Ultimate Ratios, the fecond on the Power of the Wedge, 1770," 8vo. " Directions for the ufe of Hadley's Quadrant ; with Remarks on the Conftruction of that Inftrument, 1771 ;" 8vo. " The Theory of Hadley's Quadrant ; or Rules for the Conftruction and Ufe of that In-ftrument demonftrated, 1771 ;" 8vo. " An Effay on Newton's Second Law of Motion, 1780," 8vo. " The Rudiments of Mathematics ; defigned for the Ufe of Students at the Univerfities ; containing an Introduction to Algebra ; Remarks on the firft fix books of Euclid ; and the Elements of Plane and Spherical Trigonometry ; 1785 ;" 8vo. " An Introduction to, and Notes on, Mr. Bird's Method of dividing Aftronomical Inftruments, 1786," 4to. " Mathematical Effays ; 1. on the Properties of the Cycloïd ; 2. on Def. 1. Cor. 1. prop. 10 ; Cor. 1. prop. 13 ; Book I. of Newton's Principia ; 1787 ;" 8vo. " Effays ; on Scripture Metaphors ; Divine Juftice ; Divine Mercy ; and the Doctrine of Satisfaction, 1787," 8vo. " Two Effays ; on Juftification, and the Influence of the Holy Spirit," in addition to the foregoing, 1788. He alfo publifhed, in the " Philofophical Tranfactions," 1. " Account of a new-conftructed Balance for the Woollen Manufacture," vol. LV. p. 205 ; 2. " Obfervations on the Tranfit of Venus and Eclipfe of the Sun at Leicefter, June 3, 1769," LIX. 236 ;" 3. 4 and 5. " Aftronomical Obfervations there," LX. 355. LXV. 366. 370 ; 6. " Eclipfe of the Sun at Leicefter, 1778," LXVIII. 1019 ; 7. " An Engine for turning Ovals in Wood or Metal, and drawing Ovals on Paper," LXX. 378. In Gent. Mag. vol. XXXV. p. 412, is his Report to the Board of Longitude on the Merits of Mr. Harrifon's Watch ; and in vol. XLII. p. 562. a fhort ac-count of Church-Organs. He was alfo, in early life, an occafional writer in the Monthly Review.

[4] This gentleman, who was father to the Baron, obtained in 1685, from the Corporation of Leicefter, a leafe of the Caftle-mill, and feveral fifheries on the Soar ; with liberty, at his own expence, to make cifterns within the High Crofs, in the Borough of Leicefter, for building and furnifhing with water fuch pipes as he fhould lay down in the faid *Borough*, the *Bifhop's Fee, Newark*, and *Caftle* of Leicefter, or any of them.—" Thefe water-works were completed at an expence, it is faid, of £4000 ; Alderman John Wilkins undertaking the execution. They were ferved from the Caftle mill, where remain in the wall pot pipes. The water-houfe pump, as it is yet called, is in St. Martin's parifh, adjoining to St. Mary's.—Wilkins was a man of many fchemes, a moft mechanical genius. He entertained journeymen in various profeffions. All the houfes in Leicefter faced with imagery and other external decorations were the acts of his people. His genius was unbounded ; he projected an appa-ratus, or complicated machine, to fow and harrow, if not plough, at the fame time ; he feemed to poffefs no fmall portion of a like fpirit with the mechanical Bifhop his name-fake. It was reported that the Corporation were jealous of his abilities, and dared not truft him with a whole year's mayoralty ; but he was once fupplemental mayor of Leicefter (1691), and found means to detach fome property of the Corporation. He perfuaded his brethren to part with fome land in different places for a confideration he held forth ; part of which he re-fold to St. Mary's parifh, to build a work-houfe, with garden ground. The remaining fpot at the end of this was offered to my father by Wilkins's eldeft fon, after his father's deceafe ; but, as the writings to the title to this were wanting, it lay a long time unappropriated and wafte. The heads of the claiming family, two brothers, dying in untoward circumftances, after having facrificed in contention the whole of their patrimony ; the fpot we advert to, having many years after their deaths been unoccupied, is of late mounded and cultivated." W. B. [5] In 1688, 1690, and 1701.

On the same stone:

3 " Under this stone lie the remains of
Thomas Carter, of the Neworks,
Clerk of the Peace for this county,
son to Laurence Carter by Mary
his wife. He departed out of this life
1747, and in the year of his age 65.
Here also is deposited Judith his
wife, daughter of John Ward,
of Leicester, gent."

4. " Here lies Ursula Carter,
wife of the rev. Isaac Carter,
rector of Heather in Lincolnshire,
and one of the prebendaries of Lincoln.
She died Aug. 24, 1721, aged 68.
Here likewise lies Lucy Carter,
daughter of the said Isaac and Ursula Carter.
She died Nov. 24, 1738, aged 30."

5. " Here lieth the body of the Rev. Mr. John Carter,
late fellow of Trinity College, Cambridge,
and one of the sons of Thomas Carter,
late of the New-work near Leicester, esq.
Clerk of the Peace of this county.
He died Dec. 25, 1758, aged 32."

6. " To the memory of Anne Carter,
daughter of Laurence Carter,
late of the New-work near Leicester, esq.
She departed this life the 25th day of March, 1760,
aged 78 years."

7. " To the memory of Edward Carter, esq.
eldest son of Thomas Carter,
late of the New-work near Leicester, esq.
He died the 21st day of August, 1779, aged 49."

On a fair marble, on a wall which parts the pulpit
stairs from the South aile:

Arms: Quarterly, 1. and 4. Gules, two lions
counter-combatant, Or, *Carter*; 2. and 3. Argent,
on a pale Sable, three lions' gambs couped Argent.
Crest, a lion's head erased Or; fig. 37.

" Near this place
lie interred the remains
of the honourable sir Laurence Carter [1], knight,
late one of the Barons of his Majesty's
Court of Exchequer,
son of Laurence Carter, esq.
and Mary his wife,
who was daughter of Thomas Wadland,
esq. of the Neworke.
He was thrice Member of Parliament
for the Borough of Leicester,
and Recorder of the same.
He was eminent in his profession,
and in every station of his life
acquitted himself with integrity and honour.
He departed this life
the 14 day of March, 1744,
in the 73d year of his age."

On an atchievement within the North chapel:

Ermine, on a chief Gules a bezant between two
billets Or; impaling *Carter*. Crest, a lozenge Gules
between two wings Argent; fig. 38.

On other flat stones in the chancel:

1. Near the communion-steps:
" M. S.
Gulielmi, filii Johannis & Elizabethæ Cheshire,
plebeiâ non orti stirpe;
qui vitæ humanæ complevit catastrophen
die 10mo Maii, 1758,
anno ætatis 32, redemptionis 1758.
Hoc amoris ergo, mœrore
haud pote communi commotus,
perfici curàvit pater, M. D.

Devenit mater, die 17 Junii,
anno Christi 1760, ætat. 68.
Devenit Johannes-Cheshire, M. D.
qui obiit Apr. 30, 1762, ætat. 67."

2. Arms: Azure, a lion rampant within a sémi of
cross crosslets fitché Or, *Jordain*; impaling, Argent,
on a chief Gules a lion passant, guardant, crowned Or.
Noble. Crest, a cubit arm habited and gloved,
holding a broken spear; fig. 39.

" Here lieth the body of Thomas Jordain, gent.
He was Town-clerk to this Corporation 30 years.
He departed this life June 9, 1745, aged 63."

3. Same arms; but the crest an eagle displayed:
" To the memory of Mary Jordain,
widow of Thomas Jordain, gent.
and daughter of
Thomas Noble, armigr.
She departed this life May 5, 1788."

4. " Here
lieth the body of Robert Winfield,
Mayor of this Burrough, who departed this life the 14 day of Novem.
1720, being the day on which the anniversary feast happened, aged 44 years.
Also Elizabeth his wife, who
departed this life the 23 day of March,
1724, aged 49 years.
Also Robert their son, one of
the Aldermen of this Burrough,
who departed this life the 11 day of
June, 1738, aged 34 years.
Also of Elizabeth Lee, relict of
William Lee, and daughter of the above
Robert and Elizabeth Winfield, who
departed this life the 20th day of May, 1785,
aged 76 years."

Within the stalls on the South side:
" Near this place are interred the remains
of Mary Robinson,
wife of the Rev. Thomas Robinson, A. M.
vicar of this parish;
she died in the year of our Lord 1791, aged 43.
Her object was
rather to be, than to seem, a Christian.
While she fixed and maintained an entire dependance
upon the blood of Jesus
for the pardon of her sins,
she studied to approve herself to God,
and to evince her love of her Redeemer
by a rigid attention to every relative duty,
and by a calm, yet persevering, course of
unaffected devotion.
The hope of the Gospel supported her
through a lingering illness;
and her end was peace and joy.
O! Reader!
dost not thou learn thy own duty in her example!
She had eleven children;
five of whom died before her in their infancy;
six survived."

On flat stones in the South aile:

1. " Here lie the bodies of
Onesiphorus and John Raworth,
sones of Onesiphorus Raworth by Mary his 2nd wife.
They both departed this life 22 Feb. 1693;
Onesiphorus aged 1 yeare and a halfe;
and John 2 mounths."

2. " Here lieth the body of Thomas Hartshorn,
one of the Aldermen of this Borough,
who departed this life May 27, 1702,
in the 69 year of his age."

[1] This gentleman, being a barrister at law, and son to the worthy projector of the scheme for supplying Leicester with water, was fixed on almost unanimously, Sept. 1, 1698, to succeed sir Nathan Wrighte in the Recordership of that Borough, in which office he continued till 1729. He was chosen representative in parliament for this town in 1698, 1701, 1722; was made a serjeant at law, 1723; king's serjeant, April 30, 1724; knighted May 4, 1724; and made a baron of the Exchequer Oct. 16, 1726. He resided in the Newark, in the house now Mr. Coltman's, on the site of which stood the beautiful collegiate church. Dying a bachelor, he left his estates to his half-brother Thomas Carter, esq.

2

3. " Here

3. " Here lieth the body of Marmion Gee, gent.
of the Borough of Leicefter,
who departed this life June 7, 1702, aged 62."

4. " Here lieth the body of Marmion Gee,
of Leicefter, gent. who departed this life
December 3, 1769."

5. " Here lieth interred the body of Martha,
the wife of Samuel Tuffley.
She departed this life Aug. 4, 1761, aged 25 years."

6. " Here lieth the body of Samuel Tuffley,
who departed this life Feb. 18, 1779, aged 16 years."

7. " Here lieth interred
the body of Mr. William Sharpe.
He departed this life Feb. 4, 1761,
aged 59 years.
Here alfo lie the remains of Martha,
the wife of Mr. William Sharpe,
who departed this life the 17th day of Aug. 1784,
aged 75 years."

8. " Beneath are interred
the remains of Sampfon Chapman,
who departed this life the 1st of April, 1782,
aged 57 years.
Alfo three fons by Hannah his wife,
who died in their infancy."

9. " Here lieth the body of Mrs. Martha Borrough,
relict of Dr. William Borrough,
rector of Sapcote in this county,
who departed this life the 18th of March, 1726, æt. 87.
And near this place the body of Mr. John Borrough,
fon of the faid William and Martha,
who departed this life June 3, 1722, æt. 52."

On a fmall tablet of white marble on a North pillar :
" In memory of two children of
Thomas and Mary Leach ;
Mary died March 21, 1793, aged 1 year ;
William died Jan. 20, 1794, aged 5 months."

In the church-yard :

1. On an altar tomb :
Arms: Per pale, Gules and Azure, three bucks'
heads erafed Or, *Lewin*; impaling, a fefs between three
efcallops. Creft, a buck trippant, quarterly, Or and
Azure ; fig. 40.
On the North fide :
" Here lieth the body of John Lewin,
who departed this life October 26, 1766,
in the 64th year of his age."

On the South fide :
" Here lieth the body of Sufanna Lewin,
wife of John Lewin,
who departed this life June 11, 1768,
in the 64th year of her age."

At the Eaft end :
" Near this place lie
three children of John and Sufanna Lewin ;
Sufannah, aged 7 weeks ;
James, aged 14 years ;
and Thomas, aged 21 years."

2. " Gabriel, the fon of Gabriel Hill, brewer,
by Elizabeth his wife, deceafed [1] this life
Sept. 26, 1679, aged 3 years and 2 days."

3. " Here lieth the body of John Coleman.
In great affliction he did wait, and dyed at 38 ;
Is [2] mother aged 68 and fomat more, dyed in 1704."

4. " In memory of William Bickerftaff,
who died Feb. 7, 1728, aged 41 years,
and Hannah his wife,
who died Oct. 31, 1769, aged 72 years.
Alfo of Hannah and Hannah, two of their children,
who died in their infancy."

5 " In memory of the Rev. William Bickerftaff [3],
forty-eight years an ufher of the
Grammar-fchool in this town ;
he died January 26, 1789, aged 60.
No noify vain applaufe, no dazzling blaze !
Mark'd the progreffion of his quiet days :
Yet let this monumental tablet tell
That praife, which living he deferv'd fo well ;
His joys were, Nature's forrows to relieve :
He gave the needy all he had to give,
To claffic lore he led the mind of youth,
And taught to all the heavenly paths of truth.
His humble life with great examples fraught—
Himfelf the mirror of the truths he taught.
If, Reader, one more perfect you would know,
Trace him in Heaven—fuch are not here below!"

6. " To the memory of Richard Gamble.
He died the 30th of December, 1772, aged 47 years.
Stranger, if the folemn fcene before thee
fhould arreft thy footfteps,
contemplate on the uncertainty
of all fublunary enjoyments, and be admonifhed
by thefe awful wrecks of human nature
to fhun the path of diffipation,
as an enemy to temporal and eternal peace."

7. " *Time how fhort! Eternity how long!*
To the memory of John Burley, junior,
who departed this life Auguft 19, 1784, aged 17 years.
Look! O look on this monument, ye gay and carelefs ;
Attend on this date, and boaft no more of to-morrow."

8. " In memory of Elizh Robinfon,
an humble follower of the Saviour,
who entered into his reft
April 3, in the year of our Lord 1790,
of her age 35.
Reader, pray for thyfelf, that thy
life and latter end may be like hers."

9. The following infcription was placed on a head-
ftone here, by the liberality of Mr. W. Firmadge, as a
token of friendfhip, and as a tribute to departed genius :
" This grave
contains the perifhable part of
CHARLES ROZZELL [4]:
an offspring of parents, both of the Irifh nation,
whofe duft mingles with his.
Reader,
this is the memorial of a man,
not more diftinguifhed for the eccentric bent of his
conduct, than for the
fuperior endowments of his mind ;
who, by the ftrength of natural genius,
unaided by the advantages which wealth affords,
exhibited thofe rare and genuine qualities
which conftitute the Wit, the Orator, and the Poet.
He was born in Leicefter, September 21, 1754 ;
and died July 25, 1792.
Whether he's fummon'd in life's early morn,
Or in old age drops like an ear of corn,
Full ripe he falls on Nature's nobleft plan,
Who lives to Reafon, and who dies a Man.
CHURCHILL."

10. " Richard Kirton died April 13, 1794, aged 85."

---

[1] Sic. [2] Sic.

[3] The Rev. William Bickerftaffe, fon of William and Anne Bickerftaffe, born in St. Mary's parifh at Leicefter June 17, 1728, was appointed mafter of the Lower Free Grammar School in that town Jan. 30, 1749-50 ; ordained in December, 1770 ; and from that period was occafionally a curate at moft of the churches in Leicefter, particularly at St. Mary's, his native parifh, and alfo at Great Wigfton and Aylefton, two villages at no great diftance. On the morning of Feb. 26, 1789, after having retired to bed the preceding night as well in health as he had been for fome time, he was found dead, appearing to have expired, as he had always wifhed, without a ftruggle or a groan. He was in the 61ft year of his age ; and had not long before reprefented his cafe to the Lord Chancellor, from whom he had hopes of fome fmall preferment. With great claffical knowledge, he poffeffed a ftrong vein of pleafantry and fatire. The duties of his function he difcharged very affiduoufly ; and, bei poffeffed of much medical knowledge, employed it in comforting the afflicted, as he did the fmall furplus of his little revenue in alleviating diftrefs. To the improvement of the " Leicefterfhire Collections" he was particularly attentive ; and, in the defcription of various parts of Leicefter, his communications will appear fagacious and entertaining. To the Gentleman's Magazine he was alfo a confiderable contributor ; and in vol. LIX. p. 203, are fome of his letters, which will give a better idea of his merit, than can be conveyed by the moft laboured panegyrick.
[4] See Gent. Mag. vol. LXII. p. 767.

The Hofpital and Church of St. LEONARD.

St. *Leonard's* Hofpital is faid to have been built by *William Leprofus* [1], youngeft fon of *Robert Blanch-maines* [2] earl of *Leicefter*; who, being himfelf a leper, erected an hofpital for relief of perfons labouring under that dreadful malady. The brethren of this hofpital enjoyed, from their firft inftitution, a rent of 60 s. from the bailiwick *(prepofitura)* of Hinckley; which they refigned to *Simon de Montfort*, earl of Leicefter, on his giving them the larger rent of 7l. 19s. 1½d. from his bailiwick *(provoflrie)* of Leicefter [3].

In 1307, three meffuages and certain lands were given to this hofpital by *Thomas* earl of *Lancafter*:

" Juratores dicunt, quòd non eft ad dampnum dni regis, &c. fi rex concedat Thome comiti Lancaftrie, quòd ipfe tria meffuagia, quatuor acras & unam rodam prati, & xxiis. redditûs, cum pertinentiis, in Sharneford, Burftall, Leiceftriâ, & Suburbio Leiceftrie, dare poffit fratribus hofpitalis Sci Leonardi Leiceftrie; & quòd per ipfum comitem tenentur de dno rege in capite, ut de honore Leic', per fervicium militare [4]."

In 1321-2, the brethren and fifters preferred the following petition to king Edward II:

" A lour feignour le roi e a foun counfeil pent les povs freres e foers de le hofpital de Seint Leonard de Leyceftre, ke il voile de fa grace par Dieu graunter bref a foun gardeyn de Leyc', ke il les face paier une rente par an de feet liveres dis e nef foutz un dener e maile, des aunciens aumofnes iffauntz de la provoftrie de Leyceftr', autre ficome la chartre fir Simon de Mounfort, jadis counte de Leyceftre, feefte a les dites freres & foers, tefmoigne; de laquelle rente il ount efte tousjours pleinement paie de tems de la confeccioun la chartre le dit fire Symoun de Mountfort taunt q̃ a la fyn de la vie fire Thomas jadis counte de Lanc'."—To which was anfwered: " Oftendant cartas in cancellariâ, & fiat eis ibidem jufticia [5]."

They thus obtained redrefs in the following year:

" Rex dilecto fuo Willielmo Davy, receptori fuo de Tuttebury & Leiceftriâ, falutem. Quia accepimus per inquifitionem, quam per dilectos & fideles noftros Hugonem de Preftwold & Robertum de Gaddefby fieri fecimus, quòd Simon de Monteforti, quondam comes Leiceftrie, per cartam fuam, pro fe & heredibus fuis, intuitu caritatis, conceffit fratribus hofpitalis Sci Leonardi Leiceftr', & fuccefforibus fuis, feptem libras, decem & novem folidos, & unum denarium & unum obolum, percipiendos fingulis annis de prepofiturâ Leiceftrie; quòdque pro conceffione predictâ fratres dicti, pro fe & fuccefforibus fuis, prefato comiti & heredibus fuis LX folidos, quos in prepofiturâ ipfius comitis de Hynkell percipere folebant, quietos clamaverunt; & quòd iidem fratres & eorum predeceffores de predictis viili. xixs. 1d. ob. à tempore confectionis carte predicte, femper hactenùs per manus receptoris comitis Leiceftrie, qui pro tempore fuit, fingulis annis feifiti fuerant, quoufque terre & tenementa Thome nuper comitis Lancaftrie & Leiceftrie per forisfacturam ipfius comitis, ad manus noftras devenerunt; & quòd iidem fratres redditum illum receperunt apud Leiceftriam ad tres anni terminos (viz. ad fefta Purificationis beate Marie, Pentecofte, & Sci Michaelis), per equales portiones: Nos, eifdem fra-

tribus quod juftum fuit fieri volentes in hâc parte, vobis mandamus, quòd fratribus predictis id quod eis à retro eft de viili. xixs. 1d. ob. predictis, à tempore quo terre & tenementa predicti Thome, ut premittitur, ad manus noftras devenerunt; & etiam ex nunc hujufmodi viili. xixs. 1d. ob. fingulis annis, ad terminos predictos, quamdiu terre ille & tenementa illa in manu noftrâ extiterunt, dictis fratribus habere facias. Et nos vobis indè in compoto veftro ad fcaccarium noftrum debitam allocationem habere faciemus. T. rege apud Conik. x11º Jan'. Per petit' de confilio [6]."

In 1328, they had three meffuages and five virgates and a half at Frifby given them by *Philip Danet*:

" Juratores dicunt, quòd non eft ad dampnum, fi rex concedat Philippo Danet, quòd ipfe tria meffuagia, & quinque virgatas terre & dimidiam, cum pertinentiis, in Frifby juxta Galby, co. Leic', dare poffit magiftro hofpitalis Sci Leonardi de Leiceftriâ, ad inveniendum quendam capellanum; & quòd Henricus de Bello Monte tenuit eadem tenementa de dno rege in capite, ut de honore de Winton'; & quòd remanent eidem Philippo terre & tenementa apud Whefton & Craft [7]."

In 1348, a moft dreadful, univerfal, and contagious diftemper broke out in the Eaftern part of the globe, and fpread into the Weftern countries, raging nowhere with more violence than at Leicefter; and Henry of Knighton, a monk of Leicefter abbey, relates, that above 380 perfons died of it within this little parifh of St. Leonard; in that of the Holy Crofs above 400; in St. Margaret's above 700; and fo in other parifhes proportionably.

The mafter of St. Leonard's hofpital paid an annual acknowledgement of 10 s. to the abbot and convent of St. *Mary de Pratis*, to whom the church of St. Leonard belonged, for the liberty of free accefs to their chapel for the celebration of divine fervice; as appears from a difpute which arofe on this fubject between Philip de Repindon abbot of Leicefter and Richard the mafter of St. Leonard's; which was amicably adjufted, in the prefence of *John* of *Gaunt* duke of *Lancafter*, in 1396, when certain regulations were entered into for the regulation of future mafters; in virtue of which, we find two fucceffive abbots exercifing their vifitatorial powers, in 1396 and 1405; and in 1438, by order from another abbot, the facrift diftraining a Miffal for non-payment of the rent; which brought the mafter of the hofpital, *Robert Matfeyn*, to a public payment.

The facts are thus ftated in Charyte's Rentale:

" Parochia Sci *Leonardi*. Ecclefia reddit circa viii. xs. communibus annis. Habemus eam in propriis ufibus, cum decimis, &c. ex dono fundatoris noftri ibidem. Et notandum eft, quòd anno Domini mccccxxxvii. ordinatum fuit per abbatem & conventum, cum affenfu epifcopi Lincoln', & confilio diverforum proborum, quòd aliquis capellanus electus & conftitutus per abbatem deferviret ecclefie Sci Leonardi, & miniftraret omnia facramentalia vice vicarii, quia beneficium illud fuit & adhuc eft ita exile, quòd non potuit nec poteft dignè aliquem vicarium exhibere; & folvimus predicto capellano liiis. iiiid. per annum pro falario fuo.

---

[1] So Dugdale, Mon. II. 454, from Knighton's Chronicle; and fo alfo Tanner, Not. Mon.—But my late learned friend Mr. Ruffell doubted (fee before, p. 90.) whether *William* was the founder's name. Blanchmaines had four fons. *William* de Britelio, the eldeft, for whofe anniverfary his mother fettled an annual penfion of 11s. on the monks of Lira, died before his father; but the youngeft might alfo have been a *William.*—And perhaps, after all, it was *The Spital*, and not this Hofpital, which he founded. See p. 323.

[2] Ralph Brooke fays, that Robert de Bellomont, or Beaumont, third earl of Leicefter, was called *Blanchmaines* from his white hands; but qu. if this title may not rather be derived from the white fcurf of the leprofy (then moft common in France and England), than from the beauty of his hands? efpecially as his fon William was fo infected with that malady, that he founded an hofpital for it in Leicefter; and, more efpecially, if we confider that thefe fobriquets, or furnames, fo common in thefe times, were often impofed from imperfections or deformities; as William the Baftard; Robert Boffu, earl of Leicefter, fo named, no doubt, from his crooked make; and many others eafy to be named if requifite; as Edmund Crouchback; Henry Torto Collo (Wryneck), duke of Lancafter. Mr. Cole of Milton, MSS. vol. XXI. p. 218.

[3] See the records fubfequently quoted. [4] Peck, MSS. vol. V. p. 34 ;ex Inq. ad quod dampnum, N° 55. Leic.

[5] Petitiones in Parliamento, 15 & 16 Edw. II. Rot. Parl. vol. I. p. 390.

[6] Peck, MSS. vol. V. p. 38; ex Rot. Clauf. 15 Edw. II. m. 15. dorf. de terris forisfact. ; & 16 Edw. II. m. 16.

[7] Ibid. p. 366; ex Inq. ad quod dampnum, 1 Edw. III. N° 135. Leic.

" Habemus

" Habemus xᷓ. per annum [1] à magiſtro hoſpitalis Sᶜᵗi Leonardi, pro ingreſſu & egreſſu in capellam ſuam ad celebrand' divina, &c. ut patet per indenturas factas inter abbatem Philippum Leyceſtr' & Ricardum magiſtrum hoſpitalis Sᶜᵗi Leonardi ejuſdem ville, die concordie coram illuſtriſſimo principe d'no Johanne, duce Lancaſtr', &c. anno Dñi MCCCXCVI, VIII° die Martii; per quas indenturas predictus magiſter & ſucceſſores ſui tenentur ad diverſas conſtitutiones obſervandas, ut patet in eiſdem indenturis.

" Mem', quòd dominus Philippus abbas Leyc' viſitavit dominum Ric' Mannefeld, magiſtrum hoſpitalis Sᶜᵗi Leonardi, & fratres ejus, xxı° die menſis Martii, anno Domini MCCC° nonageſimo-ſexto. Et dominus Ric' Rodley, abbas Leyc', viſitavit eundem Ricardum, magiſtrum ejuſdem hoſpitalis, & fratres ejus, ſecundo die menſis Martii, anno Domini M°CCCC quinto, ſicut patet in inſtrumentis magiſtrorum Willi de Welton & Johis Erneſby, notariorum pupplicorum.

" Mem', quòd anno Dñi M°CCCC°XXXVIII°, feriâ v° in Capite Ramorum, frater Johes Schepiſhed, tunc ſacriſta, venit in capellam magiſtri hoſpitalis Leyc', annexam ecclefie Sᶜᵗi Leonardi Leyc'; & ibi accepit unum Miſſale, nomine diſtrictionis, pro redditu xᷓ. à retro exiſtentium, & ſecum aſportavit. Et feriâ v° in cenâ Domini proximo ſequente d'nus Robertus Matſeyn, magiſter dicti hoſpitalis, venit in abbathiam monaſterii Leyc', in domo capitulari, coram Willo Sadyngton, tunc abbate dicte abbathie, & ſolvebat dicto Johi Schepiſhed ſacriſte x ᷓ. predictos, ut in rotulo dicti Johis Schepiſhed de officio ſacriſte & fabrice [2]."

" Abbas ſolvit archidiacono Leiceſtrie, pro procurationibus, ſynodalibus, & denariis Sᶜᵗi Petri ecclefie Sᶜᵗi Leonardi, ıxᷓ. xd̄. ob. q̄." [3]

The maſter of St. Leonard's Hoſpital paid alſo to the abbot of St. Mary an annual acknowledgement of two hens, for a toft in All Saints' pariſh [4].

In 1439, a piece of diſcipline was put in practice, which may ſeem ſtrange in our days: On Eaſter-day, John Bayford, chaplain to Robert Matſeyn, then maſter of this hoſpital, permitted two of the maſter's ſervants to receive the ſacrament in the chapel, to the prejudice of the rights of the abbot; whoſe complaint having been regularly heard before John Wardale, commiſſary to the biſhop of Lincoln, the chaplain was directed, by way of penance, to attend in the church on the following Sunday, previous to the proceſſion, bare-footed and bare headed [5], & ſine camiſiâ, carrying in his hands a wax taper of three pounds' weight; and, ſtanding in the middle of the choir, inter crucem & chorum, on the entrance of the proceſſion, to repeat ſeven pſalms [6].

In little-more than 20 years after this, the hoſpital was diſſolved; and its revenues, with thoſe of the Hoſpital of St. John, were given by king Edward IV. on his acceſſion to the crown, to ſir William Haſtings, as a reward for his faithful ſervices, in 1456, when ſheriff of the county, to his father Richard duke of York. Sir William, amongſt other grants, had the appointment of ſteward of the honour of Leiceſter, and of the manors and caſtles of Leiceſter, Higham Ferrers, and Donington, and all other the king's manors in the counties of Warwick, Leiceſter, Nottingham, Northampton, and Huntingdon, parcel of the dutchy of Lancaſter; was conſtable of the caſtles of Leiceſter, Higham Ferrers, and Donington; and ranger of Leiceſter Foreſt; and in 1461 was created baron Haſtings, and admitted into the order of the Garter. The lands of St. Leonard's hoſpital he beſtowed on the church of St. Mary in the Newark; as appears by an agreement dated Feb. 12, 1477-8, in which Dean Chauntre and his chapter covenanted with William lord Haſtings, to pay him an annuity of £20.

for his life, and to keep a ſpecial obit for him in their church, in return for his benefactions [7].

There is now no part of the building remaining; but the ſituation is pointed out in Charyte's Rentale, where the chapel of the hoſpital is ſaid to be annexa ecclefie Sancti Leonardi.

After the diſſolution of the college of St. Mary in 1548, the lands of the hoſpitals of St. Leonard and St. John were granted, 2 Edw. VI. as parcel of their poſſeſſions, to Robert Catlyn [8]; and the leaſe of the lands belonging to both thoſe hoſpitals was afterwards conveyed to Stephen Harvey and George Tatam; by whom, about 1592, they were ſold to the Corporation of Leiceſter for £340.

In 1776, Mr. Freeman, an ingenious painter, of Cambridge, preſented to Mr. Cole of Milton an impreſſion of the ſeal of this hoſpital, from the original braſs ſeal which had been then lately found at Saffron Walden in Eſſex, where a family of the name of Catlyn had long been ſettled; and Mr. Cole thought it not improbable that the ſeal and writings of St. Leonard's hoſpital might have been in that family, and the ſeal by accident loſt there. " It is of an oval form [9], of three inches depth, having the full figure of St. Leonard dreſſed as an abbat, with a ſhort ſquab mitre on his head, a crofier in his left hand, a book in his right, and a pair of manacles or collar, and chains hanged from them to expreſs the nature of his charitable employment in redeeming captives. Under an arch below his feet is the half figure of one of the brethren of the hoſpital praying to him. The ſaint ſtands under a beautiful Gothic canopy, and the whole is ſurrounded with this legend:

𝕾𝖎𝖌𝖎𝖑𝖑𝖚' 𝖈𝖔𝖒'𝖚𝖓𝖊 𝕸𝖆𝖌𝖎𝖘𝖙𝖗𝖎 𝖊𝖙 𝕱𝖗𝖆𝖙𝖗𝖚𝖒 𝕳𝖔𝖘𝖕𝖎𝖙𝖆𝖑' 𝕾𝖈'𝖎 𝕷𝖊𝖔𝖓𝖆𝖗𝖉𝖎 𝕷𝖊𝖈𝖊𝖘𝖙𝖗𝖎𝖊." [10]

The CHURCH of St. Leonard, with the temporal revenues of the pariſh, was antiently given to the abbot and convent of St. Mary in Pratis (as almoſt all the other eccleſiaſtical beneſices in Leiceſter had been) in proprios uſus. Its annual value in 1220 was two marks; and in a taxation made about that period, it was rated at 50s.; when All Saints, St. Clement's, St. Michael's, St. Nicholas's, and St. Peter's, were all marked nichil [11].

The annnal revenues of this rectory produced, for the advantage of the abbey, 6l. 10s. communibus annis; but the vicarage was ſo ſmall that it could not ſufficiently maintain a vicar; wherefore, in 1437, it was ordained by the abbot and convent, with the approbation of the biſhop of Lincoln, that any chaplain appointed by the abbot ſhould ſerve the cure inſtead of a reſident vicar, and that he ſhould receive 53s. 4d. by the year, out of the revenues of the rectory.

Mr. Wyrley ſays, " St. Leonard's is an old church, beyond the North bridge, near unto the ſometime ſtately abbey of St. Mary de Pratis. In this church are:

Gules, a lion rampant Argent. Mowbray.
Gules, ſeven maſcles voided and conjoined Or. Quincy.
Sable, three fiſhes naiant in pale Argent.

And in the chapel of St. Andrew, founded by William Leproſus, are theſe arms:

Argent, three leopards' heads jeſſant Sable, Sodington.
Gules, three fiſhes naiant in pale, Arg. a bend Sable [12].

VICARS of St. Leonard's.
Adam de .... 1242.
William Capellanus, 1238.
Robert de Herdeby, 1242.
Robert de Naileſton, 1247.
Robert de Bulk .... 1258.
Moyſes Capellanus, 1267.
William Payn, 1270.
John Halifax, 1276.

In 1650, the vicar is ſtated to be " the ſame man that hath All Souls, weak, and a pluralitan."

---

[1] This ſum of ten ſhillings continued to be paid to the dean and chapter of St. Mary in the Newark after they became poſſeſſed of this hoſpital.   [2] Charyte's Rentale, fol. xciv. b.   [3] Ibid. fol. ciii. a. ccvii. b.   [4] Appendix, p. 77.
[5] So Martin, biſhop of Ely, pranced about his church, after walking three weeks on the highway to take poſſeſſion of his church. G. A.   [6] Appendix, p. 65.   [7] See under the hiſtory of the church of St. Mary in the Newark.
[8] To this Robert Catlyn the manor of Beby in Leiceſterſhire was alſo granted, 3 Edw. VI.; and to him and William Thomas ſeveral other lands in the ſame county. Orig. 3 Edw. VI. Pars 3. Rot. 98; & Pars 4. Rot. 80.
[9] See Plate XVII. fig. 13.   [10] Letter from Mr. Cole of Milton to J. Nichols, 1781.   [11] Cotton MSS. Nero D. X.
[12] See Plate XXIII. fig. 1—5. The ſame arms are deſcribed in the Viſitation of 1619; where 1. 2. 3. are ſaid to be in St. Leonard's church; and 4. and 5. " in eccleſiâ Hoſpitalis;" ſo that St. Andrew's chapel was poſſibly a part of the church of St. Mary in the Newark.

The

The parifh of St. *Leonard* is not within the limits of the Town of Leicefter, nor within the precincts of the Borough; but the magiftrates of the County and Borough have a concurrent jurifdiction. It confifts principally of the ftreet called *The Abbey-Gate* [1]; and comprifes feveral pieces of inclofed ground belonging to different proprietors. The adjoining places are the lordfhips of *Anftey*, *Beaumont-Leys*, and the lands formerly enjoyed by this once rich and flourifhing Abbey. The public mint alfo, which is noticed in Domefday-book, was fituated in this parifh [2].

The old church, which is faid to have been a fmall and very neat ftructure, ftood over againft the farther end of the North bridge [3]; but, being ruinous, was rebuilt a little time before the unhappy rebellion (in the reign of king Charles I.) difturbed the tranquillity of thefe three kingdoms. The fituation of it was fuch, that it commanded the bridge; and therefore, when the town of Leicefter was made a garrifon in the diftracted times of the civil war, and was befieged by the army of the parliament under lord Fairfax, military policy requiring its demolition, it fell a victim to the public rage; and not having had the good fortune to rife again from its afhes, the parifhioners of St. Leonard have attended divine fervice in the church of St. Margaret, in confideration of their paying to the church-levies, and making a due recompence to the vicar of that church; who formerly officiated under a fequeftration of the church of St. Leonard, granted him by the ecclefiaftical court [4]; but is now generally prefented to the vicarage of St. Leonard's, which of late has been augmented by the addition of queen Anne's bounty.—The inhabitants of St. Leonard's, however, continue feparately to maintain their own poor, and bury in their own church-yard; and there was lately an intention of rebuilding the church, on a plan fhewn in Plate XXIII.

On tomb-ftones in St. Leonard's church-yard:

Ifaiah Garle died Feb. 19, 1709, aged 60.
Elizabeth Garle, Oct. 14. 1721, aged 75.
Ann Denfher, April 21, 1721; aged 71.
William Jarvis, Sept. 8, 1730, aged 85.
Martha Wilfon, Jan. 28, 1735, aged 78.
Ifabella Dencher, June 23, 1750, aged 84.
Thomas Burley, Sept. 14, 1758, aged 84.
Ifabella Burley, Aug. 20, 1762, aged 78.
Elizabeth Payne, March 28, 1774, aged 68.
Richard Philips, Jan. 1781, aged 70.
Francis Davis, Feb. 2, 1781, aged 81.

	£	s.	d.	£	s.	d.
					Abbey Liberty.	
Money raifed for the poor of St. *Leonard's* in the year ending at Eafter 1776,	77	15	1	76	14	0
Expended in county rates, &c.	12	19	0	3	9	4
————— on the poor, &c.	63	5	4	2	0	0
Rent of workhoufe [5], &c.	5	8	6	2	0	0
Expended in litigations,	13	9	7	0	0	0
Money raifed for 1783,	153	17	6	3	19	11
——————— 1784,	122	12	1	12	19	9
——————— 1785,	135	16	8	17	6	4
Medium of thefe three years,	137	8	9	11	8	8
———— of county expences,	7	9	0	4	18	8
———— of expences not relating to the poor; repairs of roads, &c.	1	0	0	4	17	10
———— nett annual expences,	128	19	9	1	12	2
———— attending upon magiftrates,	0	0	0	0	0	0
———— entertainments at meetings,	1	16	0	0	8	4
———— law expences,	1	3	11	0	0	0
———— fetting the poor to work,	0	0	0	0	0	0

The SPITAL,

another diftinct hofpital, faid alfo to have been founded by *William Leprofus*, and ftyled the houfe of St. *Edmund* the Confeffor and Archbifhop (who died in 1244), was fituated on the Eaft fide of the town, near the chapel of St. John's Hofpital, which Leland defcribes as ftanding by "the Bifhops' water." Soon after the foundation (before 1250) the abbot and convent of *Croxton* were benefactors to this hofpital:

"Memorandum, quòd Galfridus abbas & conventus de Crcxton conceffcrunt Deo & beate Marie, & domui Sci Edmundi confefforis & archiepifcopi in Leyceftriâ, & pauperibus fratribus ibidem manentibus, in feodo Rogeri Blundi, totam terram quam habuimus in Galby & Fryfeby, de dono Amicie filie Mauricii de Hampton, cum toftis, meffuagiis, gardinis, pratis, &c. in puram eleemofinam warentizabimus [6]," &c.

Knighton, in his Chronicle, mentions that certain followers of Wickliffe kept their rendezvous "in the chapel of St. John the Baptift without Leicefter, near the houfe of the Lepers."

In 1618, Alderman *Robert Heyrick*, among other benefactions to the Corporation, gave 3*l*. 6*s*. 8*d*. for ever out of *The Spital-houfe Clofe*.

This houfe [7] is particularly pointed out in Speed's map; but has long fince been demolifhed, and its place fupplied by a fmall building on *The Cock-muck-hill*, at the end of Belgrave-gate, which affumed the fame name, and which in 1720 Mr. Carte defcribes as "belonging to the county, and ufually containing fix poor people, put in by the juftices; but not limited to any certain number. The treafurer of the county paid to each of them weekly 14*d*.; and they who were in it at Michaelmas yearly prefented to Mr. *Thomas Noble* twelve chicken, on account of an eftate which he enjoys at Rearfby in this county, which formerly belonged to the family of *Keble* there, and by two coheireffes defcended to *Noble* and *Orton*, during which divifion each received fix chicken; but Orton's part coming to *Faunt*, and being fince purchafed by Mr. Noble, he is entitled to the whole. It is probable that this right was grounded on Keble's giving the fite of the houfe for the ufe of the hofpital."

In 1782, this afylum again experienced a revolution; the houfes being then pulled down [8], to widen the ftreet, and fix others built in their ftead in St. Margaret's church lane, as will farther appear under that parifh.

[1] A ftreet, or row of houfes, without the North gate, leading from a place called The Hare and Hounds, on St. Sunday's Bridge, to the Abbey of St. Mary de Pratis, to which, before the diffolution, it belonged; and undoubtedly received its name from being the road or accefs to and from that religious houfe. Three meffuages and divers lands in the Abbey-Gate were given to that Abbey by William de Aunfelys in 1311; fee Appendix, p. 62. And in Charyte's Rentale, fol. lxxxvi. a. lxxxvii. b. is this entry: "Habemus in Leyceftr' plures redditus tam liberos quàm voluntarios, ex donis diverforum, ficut patuerunt per proprias cartas eorum hic fubfequentes." Then follows an enumeration of their poffeffions in the "Vicus Abbathie," in the following ftyle: "Habemus, ex conceffione, dimiffione, & quietâ clamatione Hugonis & Roberti filiorum Mathei de Elmele & Dionifie filie ejufdem, quandam cameram, cum curtilagio, &c." Nothing particular occurs throughout. Their poffeffions in the "Wodegate," and in the "Vicus Borealis, vel extra Portam borealem." follow in the fame manner at fol. lxxxviii; but nothing material occurs. At fol. lxxxviii. b. is "The Skeyth," a fimilar enumeration; in which the only thing worth norice is, "Habemus ibi, ex dono Petri filii Rogeri de Glenfield, unum meffuagium, cum placeâ terre eidem pertinent', ad fuftentationem unius cerei ad altare Sancti Thome." In fol. lxxxix. are the like for "Belgrave and Humberfton-gates." And in fol. xciv. a. under the title of "Tenores cartarum fundatorum noftrorum," is an account of tenants in the "Vicus Abbathie."

[2] In the Abbey Gate, Mr. Carte, in 1712, notices "The Countefs's Hofpital," founded by the countefs of Devonfhire, in the reign of king Charles I, for fix poor women, maids or widows, and endowed with £30. a year, from which 25*s*. was paid to each of them quarterly. The houfes, Mr. Throfby fays, were down, or nearly fo, feveral years; but were rebuilt about 1773. I am forry to add that in 1796 the very traces of this benefaction had vanifhed—*Etiam perîére ruinæ*.

[3] Since Mr. Bickerftaffe's particular defcription of this bridge, p. 296, was written, having been much damaged by the great flood in 1795, the greater part of it was rebuilt in the fummer of 1796.   [4] Sir T. Cave, MS.

[5] Seven perfons were accommodated in this workhoufe in 1776.   [6] Peck, MSS. 4935. p. 28; from Croxton Abbey Regifter.

[7] The dean and canons of St. Mary in the Newark paid an annual acknowledgement for it of two capons and four hens.

[8] A fingle houfe, at the end of Belgrave-gate, ftill preferves the name of *The Spital houfe*. See Plate XXIII.

The

The HOSPITAL, or COLLEGE, of St. JOHN the Baptiſt and St. JOHN the Evangeliſt,

in the pariſh of All Saints, is another charitable foundation of very great antiquity; but neither the date nor the founder can now be diſcovered.

In 1235, the firſt year after biſhop Groſſeteſte obtained the ſee of Lincoln, we find him recogniſing an agreement entered into by Gervaſe maſter of this hoſpital with John de Winton, the ſucceſſor to Groſſeteſte in the rectory of St. Margaret's, Leiceſter:

"Noverint univerſi veſtri nos cartam fratris Gervaſii, magiſtri Hoſpitalis Sancti Johannis Leyc', & omnium aliorum tam fratrum quàm ſororum ejuſdem domûs inſpexiſſe, in hec verba: "Univerſis Chriſti fidelibus magiſtri Hoſpitalis Sancti Johannis de Leyc' ſalutem. Noverit univerſitas veſtra nos dediſſe magiſtro J. de Winton, rectori eccleſie Sancte Margarete de Leiceſtriâ, & ſucceſſoribus ſuis, pro decimis curtilagii noſtri, & pro decimis gardinis quas magiſter R. Groſſeteſte, quondam rector ejuſdem eccleſie, petebat coram judicibus delegatis, tofium noſtrum quod jacet conjunctum cemeterio capelle Sancti Johannis, in parochiâ dictâ eccleſie Sancte Margarete ex parte occidentali. Teſte A. Coſtein[1]." Nos igitur, de conſenſu W. decani & capituli noſtri Lincolnie, omnia in predictâ cartâ contenta, quantum ad nos pertinet, epiſcopali & Lincolnie eccleſie confirmavimus auctoritate. Teſtibus; W. decano, R. archidiacono Linc', Joħe precentore, W. cancellario, W. theſaur', W. ſubdec'; J. Norťhť', W. Stowe, J. Leyc', G. Hunt', A. Bedf', archidiaconis; W. de Avalon; magiſtris R. de Gravel, J. de Ciſſeſtr', R. de Bolleſhover, R. de Wiſbech, capellanis; R. de Warvill, P. de Hungart'; magiſtro R. de Brinkel, W. de Winchcumb, & Tho. de Aſkes, diaconis; magiſtro Tho. Walens, R. de Oxon', J. de Crakhall, ſubdiaconis, canonicis Linc'. Dat' in capitulo Linc', kal' Aprilis, Pont' i (dorſ')."

This deed removes the doubt concerning biſhop Groſſeteſte's having once been rector of St. Margaret's, which Dr. Pegge ſuggeſts in his Life of that Prelate, p. 26.—Groſſeteſte held that rectory when archdeacon of Leiceſter; as did the ſucceeding archdeacons till 1276, when this vicarage was endowed.

In 1308, *Philip Danet* gave meſſuages and lands to this hoſpital, at Whetſtone, Croft, and Friſby:

"Juratores dicunt, quòd non eſt ad dampnum dñi regis nec aliorum, ſi dñus rex concedat Philippo Danet, quòd ipſe quinque meſſuagia, ſeptem virgatas terre & dimidiam, cum pertinentiis, in Weſton, Croft, & Friſeby juxta Galby in com' Leic', dare poſſit magiſtro & fratribus hoſpitalis Sci Johannis Leiceſtrie. Et dicunt, quòd tria meſſuagia & quinque virgate terre & dimidia in Friſeby juxta Galby tenentur de Roberto Burdet per ſervicium xxˢ̄. per annum; & unum meſſuagium & una virgata terre in Weſton tenentur de Henrico de Bello-monte per ſervicium vˢ̄. per annum; & unum meſſuagium & una virgata terre in Croft tenentur de Hugone Turville per ſervicium viˢ̄. per annum; & centum ſolidati terre & redditûs, cum pertinentiis, in Leiceſtriâ & Northburg, Craft, & Weſton, tenentur de comite Leiceſtrie per ſervicium militare[2]."

"Rex omnibus ad quos, &c. ſalutem. Licèt de communi conſilio, &c. per finem tamen quem Philippus Danet fecit nobiſcum, conceſſimus & licentiam dedimus, pro nobis & heredibus noſtris, quantum in nobis eſt, eidem Philippo, quòd ipſe v meſſuagia & vii virgatas terre & dimidiam, cum pertinentiis, in Weſton, Craft, & Friſeby juxta Galby, dare poſſit & aſſignare dilectis nobis in Chriſto magiſtro & fratribus Sci Johannis Leiceſtrie; habenda & tenenda eiſdem magiſtro & fratribus hoſpitalis Sci Johannis Leic' & ſucceſſoribus ſuis, ad inveniendum quendam capel-

lanum, divina ſingulis diebus in eccleſiâ Sci Johannis hoſpitalis predicti, pro animâ ipſius Philippi, & animabus anteceſſorum ſuorum & omnium fidelium defunctorum, celebraturum imperpetuum; & eiſdem magiſtro & fratribus, quòd ipſi predicta meſſuagia & terram, cum pertinentiis, à prefato Philippo recipere poſſint & tenere, ſibi & ſucceſſoribus ſuis, ad inveniendum dictum capellanum, divina ſingulis diebus pro animabus predictis celebraturum imperpetuum, ſicut predictum eſt, tenore preſentium, licentiam dedimus ſpecialem, nolentes quòd predictus Philippus vel heredes ſui, ſeu predicti magiſter & fratres, aut ſucceſſores ſui, ratione ſtatuti antedicti, per nos vel heredes noſtros indè occaſionentur ſeu graventur; ſalvis tamen capitalibus dominis feodi illius ſerviciis indè debitis & conſuetis. In cujus, &c. Teſte rege apud Ebor', xxvii die Feb'. Per finem xl ſolidorum[3]."

In 1346, on the aid granted to the king for making his eldeſt ſon a knight, the maſter of St. John's hoſpital was aſſeſſed at 16 d. for the thirtieth part of a knight's fee in Hungarton, of the fee of *Cheſter* and *Huntingdon*; and 16 d. for the like quantity of land in Queniburgh, of the fee of Tutbury[4].

The maſter of St. *John's* Hoſpital was bound to pay a penſion of 10 s. to the biſhop of Lincoln[5].

In the Archiepiſcopal Regiſtry at Lambeth we find, "Certificatorium ſuper collatione ſive proviſione factâ auctoritate dñi archiepi de Hoſpitali Sci Joħis Leiceſtr. jure devoluto dño Willo Hyll[6] preſbytero, in ſacrâ theologiâ baccalaureo. Dat' Leiceſtr', in domo capitulari S. Joħis Leiceſtrie, 11 die menſis Sept. 1424[7]."

Thomas de Bretford, maſter of St. John's, and the brethren and ſiſters of that Hoſpital, gave to Leiceſter abbey a plot of ground *(placeam terre)*, with the appurtenances, part of the land in their tenure, near the cemetery of the church "Sce Trinitatis" on the Eaſt, and the Hoſpital's land on the Weſt[8].

In the church belonging to this hoſpital was founded, 1478, the guild of St. John, by *Peers Celler* and his wife:

"This compoſition and agreement, made Sept. 20, 17 Edw. IV. betwixt ſir Robert Syleby, maſter of the hoſpital of St. John Evangeliſt and St. John Baptiſt of Leiceſter and the brethren of the ſame place, of the one part; and Richard Wiggeſton of Leiceſter, ſteward of the gyld of the ſame St. John, of the other part; witneſſeth, that the ſaid Richard and his ſucceſſors for the time being, ſtewards of the ſaid gild, with the advice of the ſaid maſter and his ſucceſſors, ſhall find evermore, during the ſaid gylde, a prieſt to ſay or ſing maſs in the gylde chappel of St. John aforeſaid, and two days in the week in the chappel of St. John ſet at the town's end of Leyceſter, except that the maſter or his ſucceſſors at any time will ſay maſs ther themſelf; and what time they ſay maſs ther, or be forth of town, that then the ſaid gyld prieſt ſhall ſyng or ſay maſs at the high alter of the ſaid St. John, helping the ſaid maſter and his ſucceſſors to ſyng and rede in the quere ther every holy day in the yere divine ſervice, praying eſpecially for the ſouls of Peers Celler and his wife, and for the welfare and the ſouls of all the brethren and ſiſters of the ſaid gyld and houſe, and in general for oder good benefactors of the ſaid houſe or gylde; and the ſaid maſter and his ſucceſſors ſhall gyffe to the ſaid gylde prieſt mete and drynk ſufficiently, or elſe every yere for his borde 40 s. of lawfull money; and the ſaid ſteward and his ſucceſſors to pay him the rembland of his ſalary as they can agree, and find him a chamber within the ſaid St. John; and, if it happen that the ſaid gyld prieſt fail, and have not his borde nor 40 s. as he ought, in default of the

---

[1] Afterward rector of Aſhby Folvile.
[2] Peck, MSS. vol. V. p. 32; ex Inq. ad quod dampnum, 2 Edw. III. N° 103. Leic.
[3] Pat. 2 Edw. III. pars i. m. 38.   [4] Rot. Aux. 20 Edw. III.   [5] See the Introductory Volume, p. lxxxviii.
[6] Mr. Hyll in 1424 reſigned the rectory of Staunton Wyvile. Reg. Chicheley, archiep. Cant. fol. 246. b.
[7] Reg. Chicheley, fol. 245. b. 246. a.   [8] Charyte's Rentale, fol. xcvii.

maſter

mafter or his fucceffors, then it fhall be lawfull to the faid fteward and his fucceffors to enter into a place, with the appurtenances of St. John aforefaid, fet with Eft yate of Leycefter between the meys of the gylde of Corpus Chrifti in St. Martin churche of the Weft fide, and St. Marget-lane of the Eft part, now in the tenour of Thomas Davye, grocer, and there to take a diftreffe for the faid 40s. and it to bere away as oft-times as ther ys defaulte of his borde or payment of the faid 40s. yerly. In witnefs whereof, as well the common feal of the faid houfe, as the feal of the faid fteward, alternately to thefe indentures be putt [1]."

That the dean and canons of St. Mary in the New-ark were the proprietors or guardians of this hofpital, in 1484, appears by the following curious indulgence, containing fome particulars very common in licences of this caft, communicated to Sir Thomas Cave in 1760 by the Rev. George Burton [2], rector of Elden in Suffolk, from the original, in the poffeffion of the feoffees for preferving fome charity-lands in the adjoining pſr ſh of Ickingham St. James. There is an oval feal in red wax appendant to it, with the impreffion of a phœnix upon its neft, the letter R on his head, and a ftar on each fide. (See Plate XXIII.)

" Univerfis fancte matris ecclefie filiis ad quos prefentes litere pervenerint, decanus & canonici ecclefie collegiate beate Marie Novi Operis Leiceftrie, proprietarii five cuftodes hofpitalis Sanctorum Johis Evangelifte & Johis Baptifte, ejufdem loci confratribus, falutem, ac utriufque hominis continuum incrementum ver'. Dilectioni veftre innotefcimus per prefentes, quòd omnes qui de facultatibus & bonis fuis eiſdem à Deo collatis nobis fubvenerint, aut in veftram confraternitatem funt affumpti, poffint fibi eligere idoneum confefforem, qui ipfos & eorum quemlibet ab omnibus & fingulis criminibus, exceffibus, & peccatis, plenam haberet poteftatem eadem abfolvendi, nifi talia fint fuper quibus fedes apoftolica fit meriiò confulendum, videlicet votis, beatorum Petri & Pauli & Sci Jacobi duntaxat exceptis. [Imprimis, cariffimus in Chrifto papa, pater & dominus Innocentius Septimus, conceffit omnibus fratribus & fororibus, necnon benefactoribus, & feptimam partem penitencie in Domino relaxavit; Nichus papa tertius conceffit octo annos & XL dies; Bonefacius papa tertius feptem annos & totidem XL; Clemens papa fextus, Johes papa vicefimus, quilibet eorum octo annos & XL dies; dnus Martinus papa quintus feptem annos & totidem XL; Nichus papa quintus, Calixtus papa tertius, quilibet eorum tres annos & XL dies; dnus Pius papa fecundus tres annos & XL dies; & dnus Sixtus papa quartus [3]] omnes & fingulas indulgentias per predictos predeceffores conceffas auctoritica confirmavit, & in plenam participationem omnium miffarum & aliarum devotionum fingulis ecclefiis per univerfum orbem Deo offerendar', & femel in vità & in tempore mortis plenam remiffionem omnium peccatorum, ac etiam in vifitand' locum predictum annuatim à fefto Sci Mathei apoftoli ufque feftum fanctorum Crifpini & Crifpiani, tam in caufis refervatis quàm non refervatis, plenam remiffionem. Perfonis autem ecclefiafticis qui in veftram confraternitatem funt affumpti,

qui propter vota irregularitatis à fententiis canonicis, vel hominibus contractis, qui pro beneficio abfolutionis ad curiam Romanam debuiffent accedere, ut id à dicto confeffore valeant recipere, mifericordìter concefferint, ac fic ab eodem propter omiffionem horarum canonicarum in divinis pro recompenfo plenam remiffionem, & ut qui in veftram confraternitatem funt affumpti, fi dum ecclefie ad quas pertinent à divinis officiis fuerint interdicte eis mori contigerit, eifdem ecclefiafticam fepulturam non negent, nifi vinculo excommunicationis nominatìm fuerint innodati : Unde nos decanus & canonici, proprietarii five cuftodes collegii & hofpitalis antedicti, auctoritate apoftolicâ, vigoreque noftrorum privilegiorum, in noftram confraternitatem recipientes Thomam Burton & Margeriam uxorem ejus, participes privilegiorum, indulgentiarum, & aliorum pietatis operum, in omnibus fecimus per prefentes, figillo noftro confraternitatis fignato. Dat' apud Leyceftriam, in domo noftrâ capitulari, anno Dñi miſſimo quadringentefimo octogefimo-quarto."

On the back is endorfed the following abfolution :
" Auctoritate Dñi noftri Jhefu Chrifti, & fpeciali gratiâ mini concefsâ à fanctiffimo domino noftro papâ, ego te abfolvo ab omnibus peccatis, que contra Deum & teipfum fecifti; necnon ab omnibus fententiis, interdictionibus, fufpenfionibus, & excommunicationibus, concedo tibi plenam remiffionem, fi in hâc infirmitate deceffieris, & in mortis articulo alioqũ ex mifericordiâ Dei falva fit tibi gratia, dum fueris in mortis articulo conftitut' [3]. Amen !"

Leland fays, " St. John's hofpital landes for the moft parte was given by Edward IV. to the college of Newark in Leyrcefter;" probably in 1477, by the fame means, and on the fame terms, as the hofpital of St. Leonard was conferred on them (fee p. 322.) At length thefe lands, with thofe belonging to the other colleges, which were then in the crown, were purchafed from queen Elizabeth by the Corporation; who receive, as appears in the chamberlain's rent-roll, 2l. 0s. 2d. for an orchard, or piece of ground, formerly *Thomas Chapman's*, efq. afterwards Dr. *Hartopp's*, on which ftood a houfe called *St. John's*; which, Mr. Carte obferves, is near " Bifhop's water, where is a chapel longging to the hofpital of St. John: at this chapel lyeth Mr. *Boucher* [4]."

Chief rents belonging to the Hofpitals of St. John and St. Leonard, payable at Michaelmas, 1712.

	£	s	d
The warden of Wigfton's hofpital,	0	1	4½
The heirs or executors of Mr. Boon, for a meſſuage or tenement in Gallowtree-gate, known by the fign of The Black Lion,	0	0	6
The earl of Stamford, for Thurmafton mill, — —	0	6	8
Sir William Rawlinfon, for lands in Oadby, late fir Henry Beaumont's, and late Mr. Waldron's land, — —	0	5	11½
For the vicarage-houfe in Oadby	0	1	0½
William Davenport of Oadby, for lands there, late Mary Hall's land, —	0	0	6
Samuel Winterton, for a houfe in Senvey-gate, late John Turlington's,	0	0	9

[1] Catalogue of the Lock-book for fines, in the cuftody of the mayor of Leicefter.

[2] Some account of this gentleman has been given in vol. II. p. 258; and his epitaph in p. 423. The communication from him, printed above, was accompanied with the following defcription of his fituation, in anfwer to an enquiry after Mr. Burton the Hiftorian: " As your author was of another family, and ours have never been refident in the county, I am a perfect ftranger to the antiquities of it. Did you fee the county I live in (where, give me leave to affure you, here you would meet with a hearty welcome) you would conclude from the face of it, that we ftudy Nature rather than Books; for, though my parifh is at leaft fixteen miles round, I cannot mufter up above three or four fcore, unlefs I admit fheep and rabbits, the fight of which is fo numerous, that Don Quixote would be provoked to put himfelf in a pofture of defence, fince they tell by thoufands. It is greatly to be wifhed, that gentlemen of fortune and leifure would apply themfelves to the rational amufement of books, which affords fuch a variety of employment for every kind of genius. I truly condole with you on fo confiderable and irreparable a lofs as that of a bofom friend, who had endeared herfelf by an experience of 23 years' tender affection. The relation of your prefent fuffering has awakened in me a remembrance of what I myfelf not many years fince have gone through, and makes me truly fympathize with you in your diftrefs; for, in the year 1752, I was burnt out of my houfe, and knew not that I had a bed left to lie upon. My wife and prefent daughter expofed for many hours (upwards of ten) to all the rage of a moft tempeftuous wind—with not one friendly fhed to cover them—furrounded by the bulk of my parifh, more deftitute and friendlefs than myfelf (fee Gent. Mag. XII. 285,)—all that I had, as I then apprehended, confuming before my eyes—the two moft engaging comforts in life both upon the very brink of deftruction at once. In this dark and gloomy period of time (which I think can fcarce be imagined greater)—that indulgent hand of Providence, which ever kindly difpenfes comforts while it fends trials, weakened the edge of my own forrows by feeling for others—till reafon could come to my affiftance—and taught me to acquiefce, and to divert the gloom of melancholy by applying myfelf more affiduoufly than common to the ftudy of books. I found relief by it; and am glad to hear you have fallen into the fame tract; which I hope will in time leffen the weight of an affliction that is remedilefs, and render it tolerable."

[3] All the words between hooks are in red ink in the original.

[4] As Leland was at Leicefter in 1538, or 1539, the Mr. Boucher here mentioned may poffibly be the abbot of Leicefter, who was about that time *ejected* from his abbey. The expreffion *lyeth* I take to mean *liveth*; as it is not likely that any one fhould have been *buried* in this little chapel.

On taking down the old town-gaol in 1792, the ruins of St. John's chapel were difcovered; and an accurate fketch of them by Mr. Throfby is given in plate XXIII. [1]

July 5, 1592, the fite of this hofpital, with the appurtenances, were granted, by the Corporation, to Mr. *Thomas Clark*, for term of life, paying the queen's rent, to make a wool-hall thereof, at his own charge, he promifing to leave the fame to the corporation. This wool-hall growing into difufe in the time of James I. or Charles I. fix poor widows were placed in it; who in 1682 were removed up into chambers then fitted up for them [2]; and, for their better fubfiftence, it was agreed by the clergy of the town, to preach, in their turn, a fermon [3] upon charity or almfgiving, annually, on St. John's day, Dec. 27, at the hofpital, or the church of All Saints near it; whereupon, Dec. 27, 1688, at a common hall, the two companies, of twenty-four and forty-eight, obliged themfelves, without fummons, to attend the mayor on that day yearly in their gowns, to hear the faid fermon, or, if abfent, to fend feverally to the chamberlains 12d. if the abfentee was one of the twenty-four, and 6d. if one of the forty-eight.

In 1718, Mr. Carte copied thefe benefactions:

	£.	s.	d.
Mr. William Morton, who was thrice mayor of this borough, gave them yearly	0	18	0
Mr. Robert Heyrick, alderman, gave	0	4	0
Mr. John Heyrick, alderman, gave	1	6	8
Widow Hobby gave	0	0	6
Mrs. Elizabeth Ward, widow, daughter of Mr. Morton aforefaid, gave	2	0	0
Mrs. Anne Pufie, widow, another daughter of Mr. Morton, gave	1	4	0
Mrs. Elizabeth Twickten, widow, daughter of William Ward, alderman, gave them	2	0	0
Robert Langton, fen. fellmonger, gave	0	6	8
Mr. John Norris, alderman, and once mayor, gave	0	6	8
William Franck, efq. alderman and mayor of the borough, and high fheriff of the county of Leicefter, gave	0	6	0
Mr. John Clay, alderman, and twice mayor, gave	0	10	0
Mrs. Cook, widow, gave	2	8	0
Jofeph Wright, one of the 48, gave two pair of fhoes	0	0	0
Mary, relict of Mr. William Stanley, alderman, and twice mayor, gave	1	0	0
Mr. Richard Palmer, alderman, and once mayor, gave	0	1	0
Mrs. Katharine Henfhaw gave	0	2	0

Mr. Edward Palmer, by will, gave a clofe of pafture or meadow ground, in the liberties of Botchefton, containing four acres, then rated at 3l. 10s. a year, to the mayor, bay-liffs, and burgeffes, in truft to pay them yearly (the refidue to the Mayor for the the time being) — — 3 0 0

		£.	s.	d.
W. Springthorpe, of the Wood-gate, gave	0	14	0
Mr. Birkhead, minifter of Houghton,	0	10	0
Mr. David Deakin gave yearly for ever	0	6	0
Mr. George Beckett, of the Newark, yearly	0	12	4
Matthew Simons [4], efq. gave, to make up the gift of Mrs. Cook,		2	6	0
And moreover gave them yearly		2	0	0
Mr. Thomas Ayre, once mayor, gave to the mayor, bailiffs, &c. in truft, to pay to the faid widows yearly —		1	0	0

£23 5 2

Mr. Thomas Blunt, alderman, and twice mayor, gave to each of the fix poor widows, every third year, a pair of fhoes.

John Joanes, of Aylefton, clerk, minifter of Belgrave, added two to the fix widows, allowing them 6d. a week and gowns during his life.

Mrs. Hannah Aires, of the Northgate, gave them 20s. by her laft will.

Mr. Thomas Topp, hofier, gave them the like fum.

Over the front of BENT's HOSPITAL:

" Mr. *John Bent*, once Mayor of this Corporation, gave lands [5] to the yearly value of £24. for the maintenance of four poor widows here for ever, *anno Domini* 1703. Edmund Cradock, Mayor;
Thomas Helmfley, } Chamberlains."
John Smalley, }

The four widows were to be placed, by the mafter and governors of the Trinity Hofpital, when any vacancy happened; and, by Mr. Bent's will, each to have 2s. a week, amounting to

	£.	s.	d.
each to have 2s. a week, amounting to	20	16	0
To be laid out on them in the fpring in wood and coals — —	2	10	0
For oatmeal and candle —	0	14	0

24 0 0

June 5, 1704, At a common hall, certain orders were made concerning thefe four widows, to be obferved by them [6]; and it was decreed that 6d. a week fhould be paid by the town to a keeper, to look to them in their illnefs; the keeper to make them a fire in the morning; and that the chamberlain fhould make the fpare room below ftairs fit for the keeper to lie in. The four widows and the nurfe inhabit ground-rooms.

The widows now receive 3s. every Friday morning, the nurfe 2s.; and each of them has 10s. 8d. every year, left by Mr. Harris, and a gown every other year.

[1] " In this plate, *aa* fhews the bounding wall of Northgate-ftreet; *bb* the paffage to the prifon-houfe; the arch againft *cc* found in the back of a large chimney in the gaol-cellar; *ee* Gaol-lane; *ff* (the fite of St. John's and Bent's Hofpitals) is a wall corref-ponding with *bb*; both which, by appearance, formed a kind of arched roof, and perhaps fupported a turret. The fine Saxon arch, which ftood at the Weft end of the nave, (fcreened from fight by the bending wall of the ftreet,) efcaped demolition. The walls in general were three feet eight inches in thicknefs; and that marked *h* was continued 14 feet to the Eaft. The fpan of the arches was 9 feet; the columns only 6 feet high, and 5 feet 8 inches in girth; and on their rude capitals lay crofs-ways four large oak beams; which, from their fituation in the line marked *i*, could not have been originally fo placed. They were wrought into grooves beneath on each fide except the two end-ones, which were only wrought on one fide that forms the end-wall; and, as they were much corroded, were perhaps originally part of the roof, and afterwards let down to figure as principals for the floor which covered them." Throfby's Leicefter, p. 386.

[2] Thefe chambers now contain eight widows; fix of whom receive 14s. quarterly, and a fmall ftipend weekly, making together fomewhat more than 2s. a week; the other two about 1s. 6d. They have firing allowed them; and two of them have by turns 2s. 6d. each annually in lieu of a pair of fhoes.

[3] The annual fermon is now preached at St. Martin's church on the Sunday next after St. John's day.

[4] This gentleman founded a feparate charity which bears his name. See p. 327.

[5] Some clofes at Enderby, which in 1720 were in the poffeffion of Daniel Alcock.

[6] The rules to be obferved are: At their admiffion, to bring with them to their houfe their bed, a bedftead, and hangings, or curtains, one bolfter, two pillows, two pairs of fheets and pillow-drawers, two blankets, one rug or quilt, one cheft or coffer, one chair, and two towels; and to be left to the houfe, or difpofed of by them at their death; and, if difpofed of at their death, the perfon, or perfons, to whom they are given, is to give the keeper, or woman that affifts them, 5s. To have new gowns, made of ferge of 2s. per yard, once in three years; on the left breaft of each gown a half-badge is to be fixed, and they to wear the faid gowns when they go to church, and at all other public appearance; and the gowns are refpectively to be left, at their feveral deaths, to the fucceffor and fucceffors. That at the death of each of the feveral widows that now do, or hereafter fhall, dwell in the faid houfe, and enjoy this charity, the houfe or place enjoyed by the deceafed fhall ftand empty, and no one be admitted into it, nor have any pay, for 8 weeks from the death of any of the faid widows fo dying, the two fhillings a week for the faid 8 weeks amounting to 16s. to be put into the common box, to be equally divided between the three furvivors, and the keeper, or woman that affifts, fhare and fhare alike. That the keeper, or woman that doth or fhall affift the faid four widows, fhall make the firft fire in the morning for the faid widows in the common room, and fweep and cleanfe the fame, and carry the afhes and dirt out of it every morning; and what fires are to be made after the morning in each and every day, and cleanfing the faid common room, fhall be done by the four widows, by their feveral turns, every one for a week, till all have done; and fo begin again, and continue it. That the garden fhall be enjoyed between the Upper Houfe and the Nether Houfe, as it is now fet out; viz. that part on the right hand from the entry and far-end to the Upper Houfe, and the other part on the left hand to the Nether Houfe.—Thefe houfes are pointed out, with the new Town-Gaol, in Plate XXVIII.

I   Another

Pl. XXVIII. p. 326.

CASTLE.

FREE SCHOOL.

COUNTY GAOL.

TOWN GAOL.

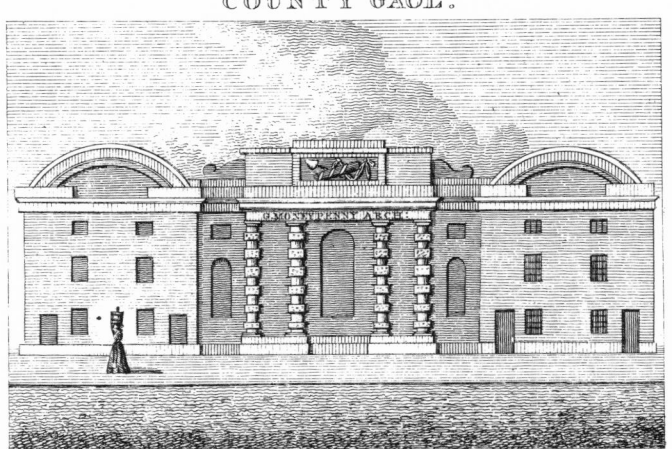

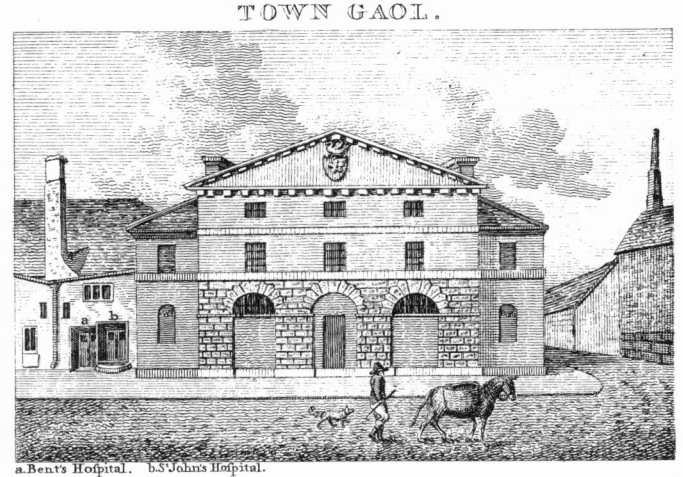

a. Bent's Hospital.   b. S.t John's Hospital.

EXCHANGE.

INFIRMARY, N.

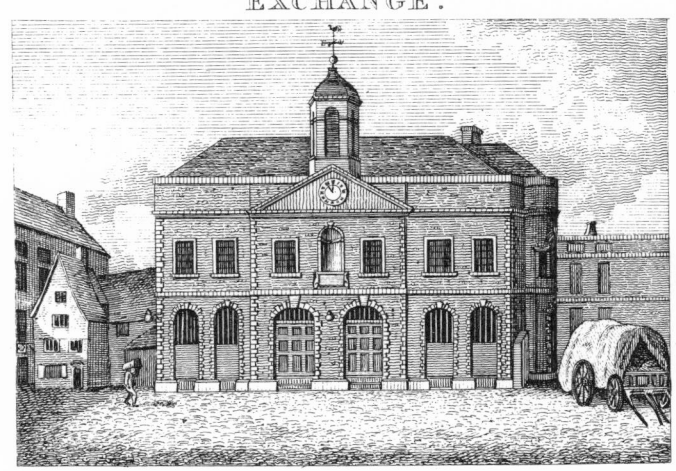

INFIRMARY, S.

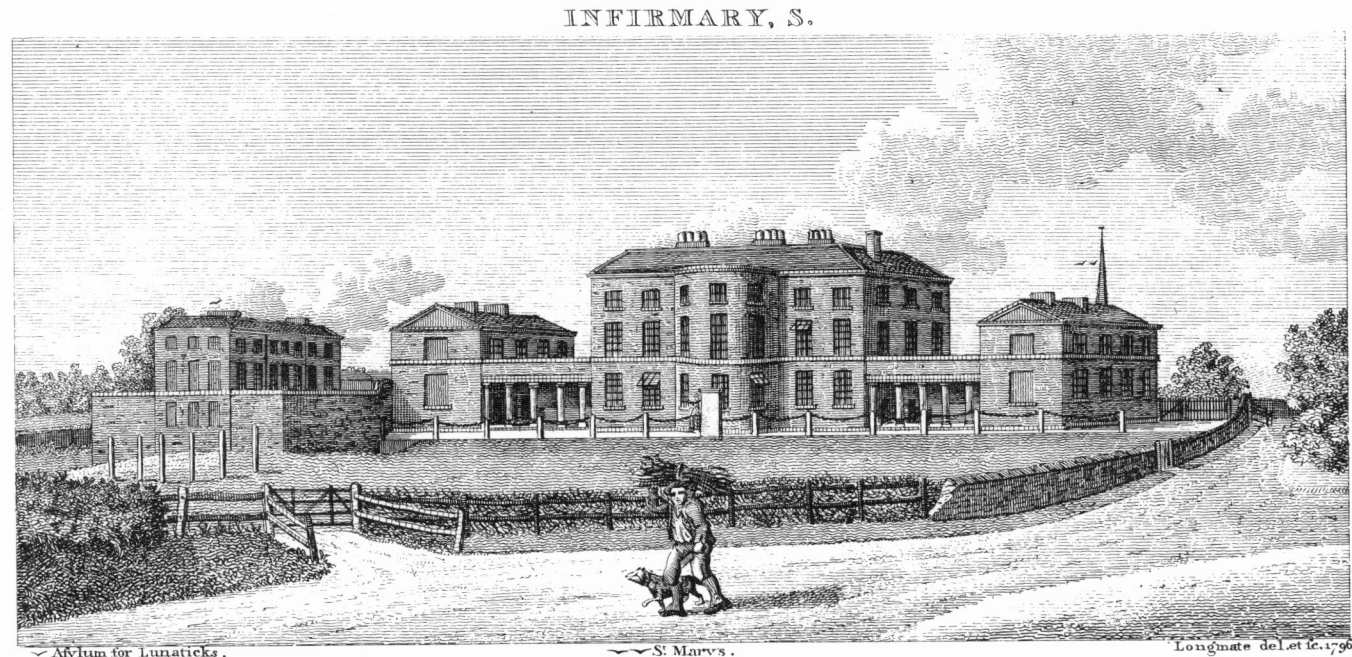

Asylum for Lunaticks.   S.t Marys.   Longmate del. et sc. 1796.

Another charitable inftitution [1] may here be noticed, founded by MATTHEW SIMONS, Efq. who, having purchafed a houfe in Blue-boar lane about 1700, after having repaired and fitted it up for the purpofe, placed therein fix fingle women about 1703; and at his death, about 1714, ordained a fucceffion of that number to be continued for ever; affigning to them a good garden and a good cellar in common, and to each woman £3. a year to be paid quarterly, and 15 hundred of coals, coft what they will; and enjoined his executor or truftees to keep the houfe in repair. The fame Mr. Simons gave about £103. for other lafting charities.

St. MICHAEL'S Church

was fituate in thofe which are called the Back-lanes, the houfes whereof were demolifhed or burnt down in 1173 [2].

William Eyton occurs vicar of St. Michael 1221; and Henry de Sco Martino in 1233 [3].

The church continued a confiderable time afterwards; for in it a monk, who was educated under William le Cloune, abbot of Leicefter 1345—1377, is faid to have turned anchoret; and, in 1487, it is thus noticed in Charyte's Rentale:

" Memorandum, quòd Andreas Burgeis dedit ecclefie Sci Michaelis quandam terram, in longitudine intra terram ipfius ecclefie & terram Gregorii Makepays, & in latitudine intra venellam & veterem murum Leyc', &c.

" Memorandum, quòd Matheus le Marchat, capellanus, dedit ecclefie Sancti Michaelis quandam terram, in longitudine intra terram pertinentem ad eandem ecclefiam & terram que fuit Gregorii Makepays, & in latitudine intra longam venellam & murum Leyc' [4]."

" Memorandum, quòd omnia emolumenta ad vicariam Sancti Michaelis fpectantia, durante vacatione vicarie predicte, pertinent, & debent pertinere, ad abbatem & conventum monafterii Leyceftr', & non ad epifcopum Lincoln', ficut patet in placito inter ipfos.

Ecclefia Sci Michaelis reddit vli. xiiii s." [5]

The church was foon after demolifhed.

Richard Orton, April 29, 1586, gave to the mayor and burgeffes of Leicefter a rent of 12d. yearly, out of a clofe lying in the late parifhes of St. Peter's and St. Mychill's of Leicefter, between the ground fometime William Purefei's and Thomas Pallet's of the Weft part, and the queen's highway of old called Torchemer, near to a place there where formerly ftood a crofs of the Eaft part, and extending from a lane called Feill-lane, otherwife called Storehall-lane, of the South, unto a lane called St. Mighill's lane of the North, and now in the tenure of Robert Johnfon, roughlayer [6].

" This indenture, made the 27th day of April, in the 33d year of our fovereign lady Elizabeth, and in the year of our Lord 1591, between the mayor and burgeffes of the town of Lifter on the one part, and William Dethick, town-clerk of the faid town, on the other part, witneffeth, that the faid mayor and burgeffes, for, and in confideration of, the full fatisfaction and payment of the faid William, for the making fundry writings, conveyances, and teftaments, at divers times, for and about the affairs and bufinefs of the corporation of faid town, and for divers other good caufes and confiderations them the faid mayor and burgeffes prefently moving, have, upon condition hereafter expreffed, granted, bargained, fold, enfeoffed, and confirmed, and, by thefe prefents, under and upon the conditions hereafter expreffed, do, for them and their fucceffors, covenant, bargain, fell, enfeoff, and confirm, unto the faid William Dethick, his heirs and affigns, one parcel of ground, or croft, with the appurtenances, called St. Michael's churchyard, together with one lane at the Weft end thereof, lying and being together in the parifh of St. Peter's in the town of Lifter aforefaid, and now in the tenure of one Robert Pilkington, or of his affigns, and is parcell of the lands and poffeffions of the antient dutchy of Lancafter, and belonging the honour of Lifter, in the faid county of Lifter [7]."

June 16, 1606, an agreement occurs between George Neville and Thomas Bidale, concerning two acres of pafture lately in St. Michael's parifh, but then united to All Saints.

St. PETER'S

parifh included part of the High-Crofs-ftreet, and lay between All Saints and St. Martin's.

The Church is thus noticed in Charyte's Rentale:

" Patronus hujus ecclefie abbas Leicefti'. Vicarius ibidem inftitutus per epifcopum. Penfio vicarii ab antiquo v marc'. Ordinatio ejus per Hugonem epifcopum patet in le Chartwary. Clericus eligendus eft per abbatem [8]."

All that is farther faid of St. Peter's in the Rentale is, that the Abbey of Leicefter poffeffed a few fingle meffuages in the parifh [9].

[10] VICARS of St. Peter's.

Robertus Capellanus, 1221.
R.... de L..... capellanus, 1226.
Henry de Shirle, 1270.
William de Eafton, 1273.

In 1283, " R. clericus S. Petri de Leiceftriâ & fubdiaconus" occurs as witnefs to a deed [11].

In this church, fir William Marmion performed homage to fir Robert Burdett, in 1309, for the lordfhip of Galby [12].

" Sciant prefentes & futuri, quòd nos Johes Hefylton capellanus, Johes Hornyngwold de Leiceftriâ, & Wiltus Outhorp de eâdem, dedimus, conceffimus, & hâc prefenti cartâ noftrâ confirmavimus, Wilto Derby de Leiceftriâ, tayllour, unam placeam terre, cum edificiis & omnibus pertinentiis, in Leyceftrâ, in parochiâ Sci Petri ejufdem ville, jacent' inter terram Sce Marie ecclefie Sci Petri, que quondam fuit Hugonis le Carter, ex parte unâ, & terram quondam Wilh le Cook, ironmonger, ex parte alterâ, & extendit fe à venellâ vocat' Wylughby-lane ufque ad terram Willi Danet; quam quidem placeam terre, cum edificiis & omnibus pertinentiis fuis, nuper habuimus ex dono & conceffione Thome Benytt capellari, & quam placeam terre, cum edificiis & omnibus pertinentiis fuis, idem Thomas nuper, fimul cum Johe Gybbefton de Syleby,

---

[1] One other inftitution of a fimilar nature, by a worthy individual ftill living, will be duly noticed in a future page.
[2] The Back-lanes, which are in All Saints parifh, and formerly a very populous part of Leicefter, have never been rebuilt fince this almoft general deftruction. [3] Charyte's Rentale, fol. xc. a. [4] Ibid. fol. xcvi b. xcvii. a.
[5] The endowment of the vicarage is in the Lincoln regifter. [6] Carte, MS. from the Town Records.
[7] Extracted from a deed in the poffeffion of Mr. Cobley, of Leicefter, who owns the ground alluded to; a part of which was lately fold to the parifhioners of All Saints, in addition to their church-yard.
[8] Charyte's Rentale, fol. xcvii. b. [9] Ibid. fol. xc. a. [10] The endowment of the vicarage is in the Lincoln regifter.
[11] Dugdale, Warwickfhire, ed. 1. p. 391. [12] See vol. II. p. 598.

jam

jam defuncto, habuit ex dono & conceffione Willi Pykwell de Syleby; habend' & tenend' predictam placeam terre, cum edificiis & omnibus pertinentiis fuis, prefato Willo Derby, heredibus & affignatis fuis, liberè, quietè, benè, & in pace, in perpetuum, de capitalibus dominis feodi illius, per fervicia indè debita & de jure confueto: Et nos verò prefati Johes Hefylton, Johes Hornyngwold, & Willus Outhorp, & heredes noftri, predictam placeam terre, cum edificiis & omnibus pertineniis fuis, prefato Willo Derby, heredibus & affignatis fuis, contra omnes gentes warantizabimus, & in perpetuum defendemus. In cujus teftimonium, huic prefenti carte noftre figilla noftra appofuimus. Hiis teftibus; Willo Pacy, tunc majore ville Leiceftrie; Henrico Forfter, tunc ballivo ejufdem ville; Henrico Derby, Johe Nyghtyngale, Willo York, ballivis & . . . . .; Willo Maloyn de Leyceftriâ; & aliis. Dat', apud Leyceftr', 12° die menfis Maii, anno regni regis Henrici Quinti poft conqueftum octavo, & anno Domini 1412 [1]."

One of the Back-Lanes in 1522 was called " Venella Sci Petri."

About October, 1563, an account being taken of the four bells in this church, it was found that the great bell weighed 11 cwt. 16 lb. the fecond bell 8 cwt. 26 lb. the third bell 6 cwt. 18 lb. the firft bell 5 cwt. 10 lb.; that the timber of the church fhould be taken down, and kept in fafety with the lead.

June 30, 1564, it was ordered, that one of the bells fhould be fold, for repair of the fchool-houfe; whence it appears that there was a fchool-houfe here before the prefent free fchool (fee Plate XXVIII.) was erected.

Nov. 16, 1570, at a Common hall, it was agreed, that the timber of St. Peter's church fhall be taken down, and kept in fafety, with the lead, till farther orders.

In 1571, the following deed occurs of *Richard Darker:*

" Omnibus, &c. Sciatis me dediffe Willo Dakyn meff' feu tent', & gardinum jacent', in parochiâ Sci Petri, in le High-ftreet, quod abuttat fe versùs auftrum fuper gardinum Leonardi Danet, armigeri, & versùs partem borealem fuper venellam vocat' Willoughby-lane, & versùs partem orientalem fuper communem ftratum vocat' le High-ftreet, & versùs partem occidentalem fuper peciam terre majoris & communitatis Leic'; ac etiam dediffe prefato Willo claufum meum quod abuttat fe versùs auftralem fuper venellam voc' St. Peter's lane, & versùs domum manfionalem vicarii Sci Petri fuper partem borealem, & versùs cemeterium Sci Petri fuper partem occidentalem, & terram Willi Gilbert fuper partem orientalem. Dat' 20 Aprilis, anno regni Elizabethe regine 21° [2]."

April 7, 1573, an indenture was made, between the mayor and co-burgeffes of Leicefter, whereby the queen, for £35. to be paid to the general receiver of the dutchy of Lancafter, and other caufes, granted to the mayor and co-burgeffes all the lead, ftone, and timber, of the decayed church of St. Peter, which lead by commiffioners was certified to be 4 fodders and 400 lb.; and the mayor and co-burgeffes covenanted to erect a fubftantial fchool-houfe, within a year after the date, covered with flate, and the fame from time to time to repair; and to employ the faid lead, ftone, and timber, in edifying the fame; and to employ the overplus, if any fhould be, in bringing a conduit of frefh water into the town.

The church being thus entirely demolifhed, it was thought convenient that the parifh fhould be united to fome other; and it lying between St. Martin's parifh and All Saints' parifh, when the matter came to be confidered in a common hall, March 26, 1591, there arofe a great debate between the members which were of thofe parifhes; but at length it was carried that it fhould be united to All Saints, which was completed in the time of queen Elizabeth; the procefs of which will be given under that parifh.

On the fite of this church was afterwards built the County Gaol; a view of which is given in Plate XXVIII.

Other DEMOLISHED CHURCHES and CHAPELS.

1. St. *Andrew's* chapel is noticed by Mr. Wyrley in 1590 as belonging to St. Leonard's hofpital; or poffibly was a chapel within the church of the Newark [3].

2. At the Eaft end of the church of St. Nicholas there ftood, in very early times, two churches or chapels under the fame roof; the one dedicated to St. *Auguftine*, the other to St. *Columbanus*; which are fuppofed to have been demolifhed either at the Conqueft, or in the troubles of 1087 [4]. Neither of them is mentioned in the Matriculus of 1220.

3. Hugh Capellanus was prefented to the vicarage of St. *Clement's* [5] in 1221, " per epifcopum authoritate concilii [6]." The church was foon after given to the Grey Friers; whofe fate it fhared [7].

4. The church of St. *Crofs*, which has fometimes been noticed in old writings, is only another name for St. *Martin's*. The oblations *ad fanctam crucem* at Eafter in this church were a part of the vicar's endowment. The *High Crofs* was alfo within this parifh, and a chantry called *Corpus Chrifti*.

5. The chapel of the *Holy Sepulchre* was fituated at the extremity of the Borough, without the walls, towards the South, at the end of South-gate ftreet, where thofe who were to be hanged at the gallows ufed to be interred. This chapel was appropriated to the church of St. Mary de Caftro, and was regularly ferved by a chaplain from that church, under the appointment of the abbot of St. *Mary de Pratis* [8].

6. St. *James's* chapel had fome of its walls ftanding within the memory of perfons living in Mr. Carte's time; and, confidering that in a hall-book, 1 Richard III. one of the wards of the town is defcribed to be " from the South-gate unto the Sepulchre church," and in another hall-book, 4 and 5 Philip and Mary, the fame is defcribed to extend " from the South-gate to St. James's chapel," this chapel was perhaps the fame with The Sepulchre church, or at leaft ftood very near it, and poffibly might be *The Hermitage*.

7. St. *Trinity's* was only another name for the choir in the South aile of St. *Mary's* church.

---

[1] From the original deed, communicated to Mr. Carte, by Mr. Noble, in 1725.   [2] Ibid.   [3] See before, p. 322; and hereafter, p. 339.

[4] It was demolifhed, according to the Saxon Chronicle, p. 194, " per Hugonem fub A. D. 1087," in the confpiracy againft William Rufus in favour of his brother Robert, when this Hugh ravaged the counties of Leicefter and Northampton; as is obferved by Maurice Johnfon, efq. who, in Dr. Stukeley's Plan of Roman Leicefter, Itin. I. Pl. 92. (which has been introduced in a former part of the prefent volume, p. 6) has written, " Ad Orientem Sancti Nicholai, ecclefiæ Sancti Auguftini & Sancti Columbani fub duobus tectis conjunctis fuper medias columnas;" and adds, " The Rev. Samuel Carte, M. A. an aged and very learned Antiquary, and my honoured friend, in converfation on the fpot at the place, and in his own ftudy there, give me a copy of a record from the Rentale B. M. V. in Pratis Leyc. ' quod ecclefia de Cofby pertinuit ad ecclefias Sancti Auguftini Leyc. & Sancti Columbani ibidem, vocat' Holybones;' not being parochial, and fo not entitled to perfonal tithes; not having any prædial, being pent up and inclofed *infra burgum*." M. JOHNSON, MS.—Mr. Johnfon fuppofed that the church of St. Mary de Caftro was built on the foundation of a Roman temple.

[5] The abbot and convent of Croxton poffeffed an annual rent of 12d. and two capons, given them by *Peter* rector of Eaftwell, to be received from a meffuage in the parifh of St. Clement, in the tenure of *Richard de Walton*; which rent the abbot and convent beftowed on the friers-preachers of Leicefter. Regifter of Croxton Abbey.

[6] The endowment of the vicarage may be feen in the Lincoln Regifters.

[7] See before, p. 298.   [8] See before, p. 303.

The

Longmate sc.

Fig.18. TRINITY HOSPITAL, 1796.

Longmate del.et sc.

6      FLEE IDILNES AND BE WEL OCCVPIED 1579   4   5

22

23   THIS BELONGITH TO THE OLDE OSPITALL   21   ANNO REGNI REGINÆ ELIZABETH ANGLIÆ

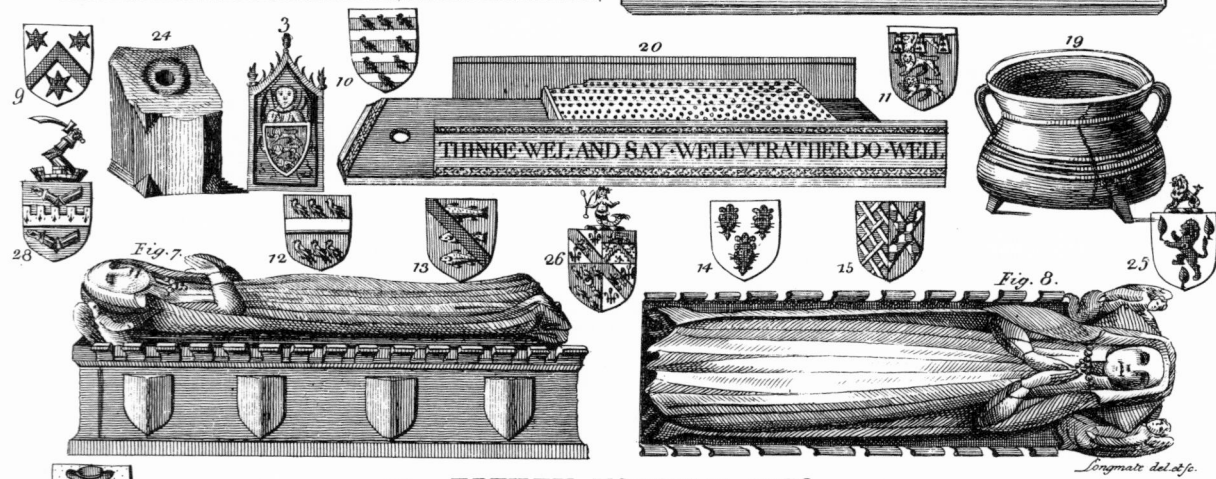

9   24   3   10   20   11   19

THINKE WEL AND SAY WELL VT RATHER DO WELL

28   12   13   26   14   15   25

Fig.7.   *Fig.8.*

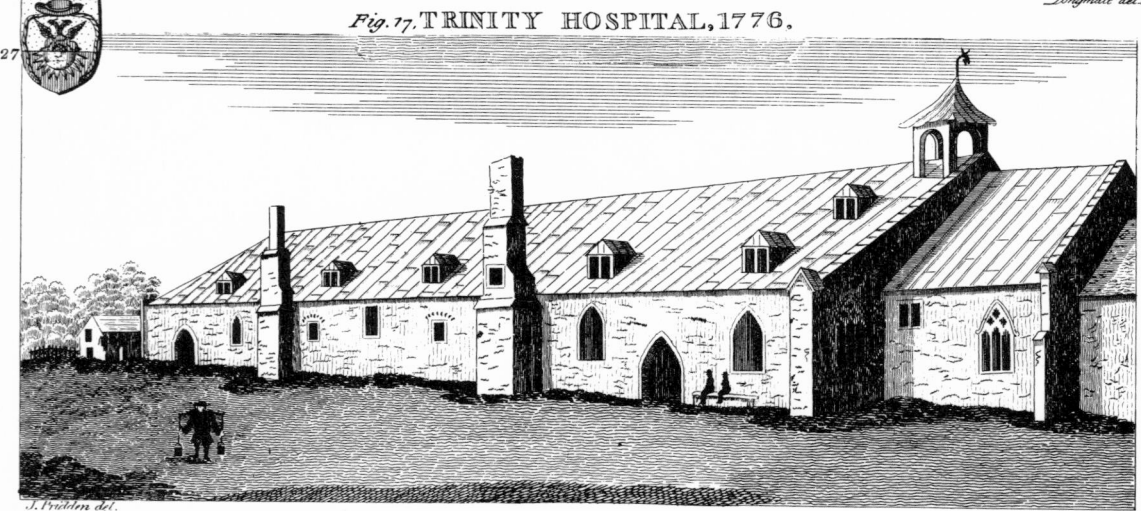

Longmate del.et sc.

Fig.17. TRINITY HOSPITAL, 1776.

27

J.Prudden del.   *Cook Sculp.*

The HOSPITAL and COLLEGE of the NEWARK.

The Newark, a diſtrict of four acres, was originally ſurrounded, except towards the river, with high ſtone walls embattled, of which ſeveral parts remain, though many breaches are made in them. It has two lofty gates; one towards the South-gate ſtreet [1], very large and handſome, made uſe of for the county-magazine [2]; the other, which ſeparates the Newark from the Caſtle-yard, was handſomely turreted till very lately, when the upper part was houſe-topped; and the arms of the duke of *Lancaſter* (Plate XXIX. fig. 3.) deſtroyed; but there ſtill remain ſome emblems of its illuſtrious founders, fig. 4, 5.—The fragment in fig. 6. is from a window in the Caſtle-yard.

The Old Hoſpital was founded by *Henry* earl of *Lancaſter*, who in 1322 ſucceeded his brother *Thomas* in the earldom of *Leiceſter*; in 1327, on the reverſal of his brother's attainder, obtained the earldom of *Lancaſter*; and in 1330 procured the king's letters patent, dated at Woodſtock, 2 April, 4 Edw. III. for founding, in a certain place belonging to him in Leiceſter, containing within itſelf four acres, an hoſpital [3], in honour of God and the Virgin Mary, for the maintenance of 50 infirm old men, and 5 women as nurſes, under the management of a maſter, four chaplains, and two clerks; and alſo a regular chapel *(oratorium)*, and proper houſes for the habitation of the maſter and chaplains; with liberty to confer on his foundation four acres of land in Leiceſter, and the advowſon of the church of Ircheſter [4] in Northamptonſhire; and authorizing the maſter and chaplains to hold the ſaid lands, and appropriate the ſaid church, for the maintenance of themſelves and the poor of the hoſpital, notwithſtanding the ſtatute of mortmain [5]. To this gift, in 1333, was added the advowſon of the church of Duffield in Derbyſhire [6].

Earl Henry died in 1345; and was buried with great pomp in the chapel of this hoſpital [7], where a fair tomb was afterwards erected for him. But his charitable intentions were purſued with unabated ardour by *Henry* his ſon and ſucceſſor, who, in 1348, acquired for this new foundation the lordſhip and advowſon of Haringdon [8] in Northamptonſhire, which had fallen into the king's hands on the diſſolution of the Knights Hoſpitallers; and in 1349 obtained from Pope Clement III. " a bull of relaxation from penance to all who ſhould viſit the hoſpital founded by Henry earl of Leiceſter; which the ſaid earl, and Henry earl of Lancaſter his ſon, relinquiſhing the place of ſepulture in which the remains of their anceſtors were depoſited, had choſen for their own interment; dated at Avignon, 3 id. Aprilis, pont. 7°." [9] He procured alſo, in 1350, from archbiſhop Iſlip, an indulgence of 40 days to all who ſhould viſit the church of this

hoſpital for eight days preceding the feaſt of St. Michael, and of 30 days to thoſe who ſhould viſit it once in a year; dated at Maghefeld, 1350 [10].

He was in 1351 advanced to the dignity of a duke. In 1354, he conſiderably enlarged the original foundation, by engrafting on it a collegiate church in honour of the Annunciation of the bleſſed Virgin; " Henry Plantagenet, firſt duke of Lancaſter, founded a place by the South gate, called the New work, the moſt beautiful abbey in England [11]." And in the ſame year it was found to be of no prejudice, if the king permitted his couſin *Henry* duke of *Lancaſter* to give the advowſons of Thorpe Edmere and Wymondham to the dean of St. Mary's church in Leiceſter [12].

The ſtatutes for the regulation of the new foundation were completed, 9 kal. Aprilis, 1355; " preſentibus, fratre Willo de Cloune abbate monaſterii beate Marie de Pratis Leyc', dominis Hen' de Walton archidiacono Richm', Willo de Donne archidiacono Leyc', Willo de Louteburgh archidiacono Lewen', Willo de Grenburgh archidiacono Stafford' [13];" and on the ſame day, *Richard de Hanſlape*, the firſt dean, with his brethren the prebendaries, were admitted; and, agreeably to the ſuperſtition of the age, received from their founder a celebrated relick, which he had then lately brought from France, a thorn ſaid to have been part of the crown of Jeſus [14].

May 18, 1356, the duke obtained full powers, from the pope and the king, to convert the church belonging to his hoſpital into a collegiate church [15]. To the 50 almſmen and 5 nurſes originally placed in the hoſpital, he added 50 more men and 5 more nurſes [16]; who were all placed under the care and guardianſhip of the dean and canons, and provided for by an aſſignment of a rent-charge from various lands belonging to his dutchy. He gave them alſo his manor of Kempsford, with part of the manor of Chedworth, in Glouceſterſhire; the manor of Ingleſham in Wiltſhire; and the advowſons of Thorpe Edmere, Wymondham, Higham Ferrars [17], Raundes [18], Preſton, Kempsford, and Chedworth [19]; the reverſion of his manor of Wolaſton in Northamptonſhire after the death of *Simon Symyon* [20], who held it for his life, ſubject to a yearly payment of 40 s. to St. David's hoſpital near Northampton. This noble grant was dated 4 March, 29 Edw. III; and on the 12th of June following the duke ſecured to the dean and canons, on divers others of his lordſhips, an annual rent-charge of £1000. if they ſhould be diſturbed in the poſſeſſion of his former grant [21]. He had for ſome time before reſided at Kempsford; but, his beloved child and only ſon having come to an untimely end, he quitted that part of the country, and employed him-

---

[1] See two views of this gate in Plate XXIX. fig. 1, 2.

[2] " Newark-gate (the arſenal of arms) is juſt 51 yards from the South-gate; the approach to which ſeems to have been under the command of the garriſon. The extent of the front, as it faces the North-eaſt, or South-gate ſtreet, 54 feet 6 inches in front, 29 feet 1 inch in breadth; 32 feet from the Magazine to the end of the ſhops on the Newark ſide; thence to Bunney's wall 44 feet 7 inches; which together make 76 feet 7 inches." W. B.

[3] " Eodem anno Henricus comes Lancaſtrie cœpit conſtruere novum hoſpitale juxta caſtrum Leiceſtrie, ſcil', anno Gratie mccxxx; & comes cœpit oculis caligare in cœcitatem, & feneſcere." Knyghton, Chron. inter x Script. col. 2559.

[4] Pat. 14 Edw. III. pro eccleſiâ de Irenceſtre.—This vicarage was endowed in 1348; and a vicar was in 1349 preſented " per cuſtodem & fratres hoſpitalis." Bridges, vol. II. p. 180. [5] Appendix, p. 109.

[6] Pat. 5 Edw. III. p. 1. m. 12. pro eccleſiâ de Duffield. A fee-farm rent of £24. iſſuing from this rectory, and which, after the diſſolution of the collegiate church, had been long applied towards the maintenance of the hoſpital, was alienated about the year 1678. [7] See before, p. 226.

[8] Pat. 22 Edw. III. pars 2. m. 20. " Pro decano Leyc. de manerio de Haringdon, cum advocatione ecclefie ejuſdem ville appropriatâ." [9] Appendix, p. 109; from Reg. Iſlip, archiep. Cant. f. 24. a. [10] Ibid. from the ſame Regiſter, f. 34. b.

[11] Carte, MS. from Knighton. In the Regiſter of the Biſhop of Lincoln is preſerved " Hoſpitalis beate Marie ordinatio, & cantarie mutatio in eccleſiâ conventuali pro animâ domini Roberti Byrd ordinate."

[12] Peck, MSS. 4937, p. 162; from Inq. ad quod dampnum, 28 Edw. III. N° 2. Leic.

[13] Theſe ſtatutes are preſerved in the Regiſters at Lincoln. Reg. Gynewell, fol. 278—293. 320.

[14] Knighton, col. 2605. See before, p. 219.

[15] Pat. 30 Edw. III. " Henricus dux Lanc. filius Henrici comitis Lanc. auctoritate papæ & regis, obtinuit ut ecclefia hoſpitalis Leyc. mutaretur in eccleſiam collegiatam, pro uno decano & certo numero canonicorum, 18 Maii."

[16] Knighton miſtakes, in ſuppoſing the foundation to be for 50 men and 50 women.

[17] Higham Ferrars was appropriated, with the chapels of Chelverſton and Caldecote, 28 Edw. III. Bridges, vol. II. p. 174.

[18] The vicarage of Raundes was endowed in 1356. The firſt preſentation made by the dean and chapter to the vicarage was in 1390. The preceding incumbent (who was rector) had been preſented by " John Gynewell, Henr. com. Lanc. attorn. gen." who was afterwards (1351) biſhop of Lincoln. Bridges, vol. II. p. 186. [19] Appendix, p. 109.

[20] Bridges, vol. II. p. 200. This is probably the ſame perſon with *Simon Synden*, whoſe endowment of a chantry is preſerved in the Regiſters of the Biſhop of Lincoln. See the Introductory Volume, p. xcix. [21] Appendix, p. 109.

ſelf

felf chiefly in fuperintending his magnificent building at Leicefter. On his departure from Kempsford, his horfe happening to caft a fhoe, the inhabitants nailed it to the church-door; where it remained in 1712 [1], and probably ftill preferves his memory.

In 1357, the dean and canons obtained a charter of free-warren for their lands in Wolafton; and for their manors of Kynemeresford, Chedfworth, Haryngdon, and Inglefham [2]; and in 1358 the duke had the king's permiffion to grant to them four acres and a half of land in Leicefter, being near their dwelling, *in elargationem manfi fui.* " Tefte rege, apud Weftm', 15° die Januarii [3];" in the fame year, the duke and his dutchefs *Ifabella* obtained for them a confirmation-grant of the manor and advowfon of Haringdon [4]; and in 1358-9, they agreed to make a yearly payment of 51s. 7½d. to the facrift and canons of the collegiate church of St. Mary de Caftro. " Tefte rege, apud Weftm', 24° die Januarii [5]."

May 10, 1361, the dean and canons, taking notice that their hofpital and college, with divers of the lands thereunto belonging, were defcribed in the charters of their founders and benefactors to be fituated within the borough *(villa)* of Leicefter; and apprehenfive that their exempt jurifdiction might be hereafter difputed by the Corporation; they obtained the letters patent of king Edward III; which, after a brief recital of the various benefactions to the hofpital and college, and declaring them both to be fituate in the Suburbs, and not within the town, permitted the duke of Lancafter to give to the dean and canons two whole lanes *(venellas)* and a plot of ground next the Caftle, for the enlargement of their houfe and church [6]. In this year, the duke died; and, by the exprefs direction of his will, was buried in this church [7].

In 1363, the dean and canons had licence to appropriate the advowfon of Llanvaylog *(aliàs* Llan Defailog, or Llandeveylogg,) in Carmarthenfhire [8]; where they poffeffed alfo the church of Pen Bre [9].

In 1369, *John de Knighton, John de Burton,* and *John de Banbury,* chaplains, gave three fhops, one toft, fix acres of arable land, and two acres of meadow, in the Suburbs of Leicefter, then of the yearly value of 6s. 8d.; which the dean and canons were enabled to receive, and hold in perpetuity, at the annual value of £5. as a part of £10. a year, which by former letters patent they had been empowered to acquire. " Tefte rege, apud Weftm', 5° die Maii [10]."

In 1374, as a farther part of the annual ten pounds abovementioned, they were empowered to receive from *John de Stockton* and *William de Swepfton,* chaplains, one meffuage, 5 tofts, 15 acres of arable land, and the third part of another meffuage, in the Suburbs of Leicefter; and from *William Chefelden, John de Knighton,* and *John de Banbury,* chaplains, one toft in the fame Suburbs; being together of the annual value of 9s. 5½d. " Tefte rege, apud Weftm', 4° Nov' [11]."

In 1380, they obtained the advowfon of Cranfley in Northamptonfhire, where this college poffeffed a manor appropriated to the dean and canons [12].

Thomas de Brytwell, profeffor of divinity at Oxford, prebendary of St. Margaret's, Leicefter, was examined, in 1382, before archbifhop Courtney, as a witnefs on the articles of Wickliff [13]. He was afterwards chancellor of the univerfity of Oxford, and dean of the church of our Lady in the Newark; and to him was directed, in 1389, the curious procefs concerning the Lollards performing penance in this church, already noticed under the Hiftory of Leicefter Abbey [14].

In 1391, Sir *Maurice Berkeley,* fon of *Thomas,* releafed to the dean and canons all claim to the tithes of Wolafton, co. Northampton [15].

In 1392, *William Burton* and *Richard Elvet,* clerks, had licence to give to the dean and canons 9 meffuages, 9 fhops, 16 tofts, 6 acres of arable land, 11 acres and 1 rood of meadow, a rent of 9s. and an annual acknowledgement of a capon, a hen, and half a pound of cumin, with the appurtenances, in Leicefter and its Suburbs; which completed their £10. a year. " Tefte rege, apud Nottingham, 9° Augufti [16]."

In 1398, *Gilbert Elvet, John de Stukley,* and *Peter Burnell,* had licence to give " unum molendinum aquaticum de Thamifiâ in Harrindon, unà cum gurgite, multurâ bladorum, & fitu eidem molendino pertinentibus, ac pifcariam eorundem molendini & gurgitis, necnon medietatem unius hide terre, cum pertin', in eâdem villâ. Tefte rege, apud Weftm', 1° die Septemb' [17]."

Soon after, this church loft an efpecial benefactor, by the death of *John* of *Gaunt* duke of *Lancafter,* who, during his refidence in the caftle of Leicefter [18], had taken great delight in this fplendid foundation of his father and grandfather [19]; and, by his laft will, dated from his chamber in the caftle, Feb. 3, 1397-8, gave to this church his red garment of velvet embroidered with gold funs, and all the apparel to the faid garment belonging, with the whole of his Miffals, and fuch books belonging to his chapel as were according to the ufe of the church of Salifbury, and not otherwife fpecifically devifed [20]. In his lifetime he had fecured to them an annuity of 100 marks, in lieu of 700 marks fettled on them at their foundation, which he had taken away [21].

In 1399, King *Henry* IV. reciting that *Henry* duke of *Lancafter,* his grandfather, had begun the foundation of a collegiate church at Leicefter, and buildings for the habitation of canons and clerks, and infirm people there dwelling; and that *John* duke of Lancafter, his father, had been defirous to complete the fame; and approving their pious intentions; affigned John de Byngham and others, to provide mafons, carpenters, and other workmen, to the number of four and twenty, and to provide timber and ftone for carrying on and finifhing the work; commanding all mayors, bayliffs, &c. to be aiding and affifting [22].

---

[1] Sir Richard Atkyns, Gloucefterfhire, p. 490; who miftakes, however, in fuppofing the grant to have been made to the church of St. Mary de Caftro. And fee Bigland's Collections, vol. II. p. 121.

[2] Lib. Feod. Mil. penes Rememb. Reg. Scaccarii; and Bridges, vol. II. p. 200; & Cart. 30 Edw. III. n. 14. In a book of Warrants, temp. Hen. V. in the Dutchy-office, f. 9. 11. & 61. thefe feveral manors are noticed as belonging to this college. Tanner's Notitia Monaftica, ed. Nafmith. [3] Pat. 32 Edw. III. pars 1. m. 2. [4] Appendix, p. 109. [5] Pat. 32 Edw. pars 2. m. 2.—" Ratificatio cujufdam compofitionis facte inter decanos & canonicos ecclefiarum collegiatarum, viz. beate Marie juxta caftrum & Novi Operis." Reg. Gynewell. [6] Pat. 34 Edw. III. pars 1. m. 15. [7] See before, p. 241; where feveral particulars of his will are given.—" Anno Domini MCCCLXI. nobilis dux Lancaftrie Henricus tumulatus eft in ecclefiâ collegiali & hofpitali extra portam auftralem Leyceftrie, quam ipfe conftruxerat, & quam prefecerat uno decano & xii canonicis prebendariis, & totidem vicariis, ac aliis miniftris fufficientèr requifitis; & centum pauperibus debilibus, & decem fortibus mulieribus, que debilibus defervirent, & procurarent in efculentis & poculentis, & aliis neceffariis, jugitèr die ac nocte; dictamque hofpitalitatem pauperum, cum collegio canonicorum fufficjentèr donavit, ubi jacet fepultus." H. Knyghton, ubi fuprà, lib. IV.—" Erat in terrâ Anglie vir quidam, vitâ venerabilis, & gratiâ benedictus, nomine Henricus, dux Lancaftrie primus. Hic, ex regali profapiâ progenitus, fuit filius Henrici, qui fuit filius Edmundi, filii Henrici regis tertii, fepultus eft Leiceftrie in monafterio novo curiofo, & plurimùm fumptuofo, quod ipfemet integralitèr conftruxit, immenfifque poffeffionibus donavit, ac canonicis fecularibus & pretiofis reliquiis adornavit, ubi hofpitale benè difpofitum & diftinctum pro infirmis & mulieribus, juxta monafterium, edificavit; & fic ad plenum omnia eis neceffaria providit, ut nullum hofpitale in Anglia eò commodiùs reperiatur." Ex Chron. Tho. Otterburne, MS. in Bibl. Bodl.

[8] Pat. 37 Edw. III. p. 2. m. 8. & 41. [9] Bacon's Liber Regis, p. 1022; from the original furvey in Offic. Primit. & Decim. [10] Pat. 42 Edw. III. pars 1. m. 15. [11] Pat. 47 Edw. III. p. 2. m. 16. [12] Bridges, vol. II. pp. 90, 91. [13] Fox's Acts and Monuments, vol. I. p. 497. [14] See before, p. 264. [15] Clauf. 15 Ric. II. m. 32. [16] Pat. 16 Ric. II. pars 1. m. 18. [17] Pat. 22 Ric. II. pars 2. m. 5. [18] The caftle-houfe, now inhabited by Mr. Brown, and fuppofed to have been the duke's refidence, is a good old building, with many fpacious rooms, a noble cellar, and a large apartment called *John of Gaunt's kitchen.* The two great chambers in this houfe were originally one, as is evident from the regular arrangement and continuation of the wooden buttreffes. The rooms were 7 yards broad, and, taken together, about 18 yards long. The rooms are on the North-weft fide of the manfion, by St. Mary's church, next the porter's lodge, beyond the gates which open to the caftle-yard. On the North-eaft fide of this houfe, on the edge of the garden, which defcends thence by a great flope to the mud, and looking up St. Mary's church lane, was an old ftone fummer-houfe, with the Lancafter arms in mortar, lately demolifhed, to mend the garden-view, and admit of palifades. [19] See before, p. 239. [20] See farther particulars of this will, p. 240. [21] Rot. Parl. vol. V. p. 186. See p. 332. [22] Appendix, p. 110.

In

In 1405, *William Allmanbury* and *John Northburg* clerks, and *Thomas de Quenby*, had licence to give 3 meffuages, 5 fhops, three acres of land, and 16 s. 10 d. with the farther rent of a capon and three hens, and the appurtenances, in Leicefter and its Suburbs, and in Wykingfton [1].

The manors of Fillebert's Court and Grey's Court, at Southrop, co. Gloucefter, were given to this church in 1406, by the lady *Mary Harvey* [2], for the endowment of a chantry for one prieft; and, about the fame time, another chantry for two priefts, the patronage of which was given to the abbot and convent of St. *Mary de Pratis* [3], was founded in this church by *Thomas de Langley* bifhop of *Durham*, as executor of the will of *John* duke of *Lancafter*, to whom he had been fecretary. This eminent prelate, who was afterwards lord chancellor of England and a cardinal, by his will, Dec. 21, 1436, gave feveral books to the library of this church.

July 13, 1407, many ample privileges were granted by king Henry IV. to the dean and canons; fome of them to continue fo long only as the rebellion in Wales (where they had large eftates) fhould laft, others in perpetuity [4].

Jan. 11, 1407 8, *Thomas Quenby, Thomas Maundevile,* and *William Almanbury*, clerks, were permitted to convey to the dean and canons two meffuages and two tofts, with the appurtenances, in Leicefter and its Suburbs, as part of the permiffion which had been granted by king Richard II. to appropriate lands to the annual amount of £40. in augmentation of the revenues of this church, and the performance of divine fervice therein [5].

In 1410, the dean and college had licence to appropriate the advowfon of Arnold, or Arnhale, in Nottinghamfhire [6]. The fame year, they appear to have poffeffed certain tenements in the Strand, London [7].

On the 23d of July, 1412, king Henry IV. gave the manor of Draicote, in the parifh of Burton fupra Dunfmore, co. Warwick, to the dean and canons, and their fucceffors for ever, referving the rent of ten marks to be yearly paid by them out of the fame to the chantry-priefts in that church, to celebrate divine fervice, for the good eftate of him the faid king, and for the health of the fouls of his father John duke of Lancafter, and Conftance his mother, whofe bodies lay interred there [8].

Some privileges were confirmed to them by king Henry V. in 1411 [9]; and in 1416, they obtained the church of Bradford in Yorkfhire [10].

July 10, 1417, *Thomas* duke of *Clarence*, by his teftament then dated, appointed that his executors fhould purchafe the patronage of fome church of forty marks a year value, and procure the fame to be appropriated to the dean, canons, and vicars of this college, to fupport two fitting priefts, to celebrate divine fervice, for the fouls of his father and mother, himfelf and Margaret his wife, his anceftors, and all the faithful deceafed [11].

In 1422, many confiderable privileges were granted to this church by king Henry VI. [12]

May 6, 1424, *Thomas Haliwell* and *John White*, clerks, and *John Hornyngwold*, had liberty to convey to the dean and canons a meffuage and 2 tofts in Leicefter and its Suburbs, parcel of the honour of *Leicefter*; 2 tofts, 39 acres and half a rood of arable land, one acre of meadow, and three roods of pafture, with the appurtenances, of the annual value of 13 s. 8 d. On the fame day, the fame perfons were allowed to give 2 meffuages, 8 tofts, 24 acres of arable land,

an annual rent of 3 s. 2 d. and another of a pound of pepper, the homages and fervices of *Robert Pecoke* and *Robert Smithe*, pafture for 28 *averia*, and view of frankpledge, with the appurtenances, in Little Thorpe near Northburg, held under the king as of the honour of *Chefter*; as well in and for the fuftentation of the dean and canons, as for the founding a chantry for two chaplains in their church, to pray perpetually for the king whilft he lived, for his foul after death, and for the fouls of *John* late duke of *Lancafter* and his confort *Conftance* [13].

In this year, Archbifhop *Chicheley* vifited the diocefe of Lincoln *jure metropolitico*. He was at Lincoln, July 27; at Leicefter, Aug. 1 (on which day the will of Philip de Repyngdon, bifhop of Lincoln, was proved before him in this collegiate church); and thence proceeded to Higham Ferrers [14].

At this vifitation, a compofition was entered into between the archbifhop and the members of this college; under which, the patronage of Higham Ferrers continued for fome time alternate; the archbifhop prefenting an incumbent in 1429 and 1444, and the dean and canons in 1437 and 1462 [15].

In 1439, *Henry* cardinal of England and bifhop of *Winchefter, Henry* archbifhop of *Canterbury*, and fir *Walter Hungerford*, feoffees of Henry V, late king of England, of certain lands in the dutchy of Lancafter, granted and fettled on " the collegiate church of our Lady of Leicefter', and their fucceffors, a rent-charge of c marks, to be had and perceyved yerely, to them and to their fucceffours, in free, pure, and perpetuall almeffe for evermore, of and in the manors, lordfhips, tounes, wapentaches, and focage of Wyrkefworth and Effeburn, with the hameletts of Irton, Mattelok, Underwode, Bradlowe, Bentley, Thorp, Mapulton, Ayton, Hunfyndon, Alforde, Penerwig, Hednafton, Cladlowe, Carfyngton, Cromford, Snyterton, Wednefley, Hopton, Middleton, and Over Bountfall, in the county of Derby, and parcel of the dutchy of Lancafter, with their membres and appurtenances hole, at the termes of Seint Michell and Pafch by even portions [16]."

The preferments of this church feem in general to have been beftowed on perfons of fafhion.

William Walefby [17], who refigned the deanry in 1450, was chaplain to king Henry VI; and was fucceeded by Richard Andrew, who was fecretary to that king. This uncommon pluralift, a native of Abberbury in Oxfordfhire, educated firft at Winchefter fchool, removed to New College, Oxford, where he was admitted fcholar in 1419, was afterwards fome years a fellow, and in 1433 a benefactor to their library [18], became familiar with the founder, archbifhop Chicheley; who made him chancellor of the diocefe of Canterbury in 1437, appointed him in the fame year the firft warden of All Souls college [19]; and in 1438 collated him to the rectory of St. Vedaft, London [20], which he refigned in 1440, in which year he was prolocutor of the fynod then held in London [21], and one of the perfons to whom the king granted the cuftody of the alien priories belonging to the Crown [22]. Oct. 28, 1441, he was collated to the archdeaconry of Salifbury [23]; in which cathedral he held the prebend of Farindon; in 1442, refigned his wardenfhip of All Souls, the College then being fufficiently finifhed for the reception of its members. In 1443 he was appointed the king's fecretary; and, refigning his archdeaconry of Salifbury in 1444, was employed in that capacity in an embaffy of great importance, being

---

[1] Inq. ad quod dampnum, 7 Hen. IV. N° 4.

[2] Pat. 7 Hen. IV. p. 1. m. 22. And fee p. 330.—The endowment of this chantry is in the Regifters of the Bifhop of Lincoln.

[3] Appendix, p. 65. In Charyte's Rentale, fol. ciii. a to civ. a. is an enumeration of the charters " Collegii Novi Operis."

[4] Pat. 8 Hen. IV. n. 2.   [5] Pat. 9 Hen. IV. pars 1. m. 17.

[6] Pat. 11 Hen. IV. m. 1; Bacon's Liber Regis, p. 175; Thoroton, p. 237.

[7] Pat. 11 Hen. IV. m. 23. & Clauf. 29 Hen. IV. m. 35. pro diverfis tenementis in le Strande, London.

[8] Dugdale, Warwickfhire, vol. I. p. 291. & Bar. vol. II. p. 197.

[9] De quibufdam brevibus regis de libertatibus decano & canonicis nove ecclefie collegiate beate Marie Leyc. conceffis," Irrot. Hill. Rec. 2 Hen. V. Rot. 14.   [10] Pat. 3 Hen. V. p. 2. m. 29. pro eccl. de Bradford; Bacon's Liber Regis, p. 1154.

[11] Royal and Noble Wills, p. 231.   [12] Cart. 1 Hen. VI. n. 11.   [13] Pat. 3 Hen. VI. pars 3. m. 23. 25.

[14] Reg. Chicheley, f. 374.   [15] Bridges, vol. II. p. 174; and fee our Appendix, p. 111.

[16] Pat. 19 Hen. VI. p. 1. m. 17. recit. cartam Henrici epifcopi Winton. & aliorum feffatorum.

[17] He had been collated to the prebend of Leighton Bozard, in the church of Lincoln, 1439; and to North Kelfey in 1456.

[18] Gutch's Hiftory of the Colleges at Oxford, p. 197.   [19] Ibid. p. 265.   [20] Newcourt, Repertorium, vol. I. p. 565.

[21] Wilkins, Concilia, tom. III. p. 535.   [22] Rymer, Fœd. vol. V. pars I. p. 91.   [23] Le Neve's Fafti, p. 275.

one of the ambaffadors fent to France to treat of a peace concerning the two kingdoms, and of a marriage between king Henry V. and Margaret of Anjou[1]; both which being effected, he was appointed to attend the new queen in France, and to conduct her to England. In confideration of thefe fervices, the king, by writ of privy feal, dated May 15, 1445, and confirmed by parliament, granted to him an annuity of £100[2]. He was afterwards employed in various treaties with Scotland both by Henry VI. and Edward IV.[3] Wood fays he was keeper of the privy feal: but this is not certain; for, at the time he was fecretary, Adam Moleyns enjoyed that office[4]. Dec. 1, 1450, he obtained, by the refignation of Thomas Redman[5], the fifth prebend in our church of St. Mary in the Newark at Leicefter, which on the 20th of the fame month he exchanged for the firft prebend and the deanry[6]; and Redman was reftored to the fifth prebend. Dean Andrew continued not long at Leicefter; for in 1451 he was inftalled canon of Windfor[7], and in the fame year elected dean of York[8]; which, Wood fays, was by a turbulent election, by two canons only and the prior of St. Ofwald, the reft of the canons having truly chofen one John Bermyngham to that office. Much trouble there was about that election; and the three electors abovementioned lodged an appeal againft the election of Bermyngham. The reafon of this difunion cannot be difcovered; nor the grounds upon which the appeal was founded. Mr. Gutch[9] conjectures that it was in confequence of a recommendation from the king; who, after this "vicious and unjuft election," as it is called, granted Andrew a licence to accept of this deanry by a bull of provifion iffued from pope Nicholas V. which vacated Bermyngham's election. This was attributed to the bribery of Andrew; "& fic factum fuit Romæ per pecunias prædicti Ricardi[10]; a charge probably founded on bare fufpicion. The canons refufing to admit Andrew into the deanry, many of them were excommunicated, and the cathedral of York was for feveral weeks interdicted; but at length he was confirmed dean Jan. 21, 1451-2; though not perfonally admitted till June, 1454[11]. Nov. 8, 1462, he poffeffed the archdeaconry of Bucks; but the date of that preferment is unknown[12]; and in 1465 was vicar-general to the archbifhop of York[13]. He had been a great benefactor to All Souls College, not only by his advice and affiftance at the time of its foundation, but by various gifts of copes and other ecclefiaftical veftments, of chalices, and of books; and at different times had expended 100 marks on the buildings of the college, particularly the kitchen: confideration of which benefits, the college admitted him, quoad fuffragia, a brother of their fociety, April 20, 1469; and engaged, Oct. 26, 1471, to celebrate his obit annually, and to give 4d. on the day preceding to the bellman of the city, to invite by proclamation all good Chriftians to offer a prayer for his foul[14]. Before his death, he refigned all his ecclefiaftical preferments; his archdeaconry of Bucks in in 1473; and his deanry of York June 2, 1477; and, by his laft will, left various legacies; among others, to the poor of Abberbury, and to the cathedral of St. Afaph[15]; to All Souls college two lavatories filver-gilt, and the fum of £40. on condition that

certain Pfalms and prayers for the fafety of his foul fhould be daily faid in the hall after dinner; which condition, on the receipt of the legacy, the College engaged to perform[16]. He died in 1477 (between Sept. 12, when his will was dated, and Nov. 5, when it was proved); and was buried in the South crofs aile of the cathedral at York, where he had founded a chantry. An infcription was placed on his graveftone, which is now perifhed[17].

In an act of refumption, 1450, provifion was made, that "it fhould not affect an annuity of c marks yearly, granted to the dean and canons of the collegiate church of our Lady of Leyceftr', and to their fucceffors, by Henry cardinal of England, Henry archbifhop of Canterbury, and Walter lord Hungerford, by their letters patent, wherynne they were enfeoffed by the moft noble prynce of perpetuell memorie our lord our fadre, and confermed by us under the feale of oure faid duchie, in pure and perpetuell almoife, in fuftentation of the grete importable charges of the feid church; the which c marcs was given by John fometyme duke of Lancaftre, in recompence of vii c marks given to theym in theire foundation, and by the feid John taken awey; whereof they alwey fithen have be poffeffed[18]."

Another provifo occurs, "that the feide act of refumption ftreeche not nor extende to the graunt made by us to the dean and chanons of the church collegiate of our Lady of Leyceftr', and their fucceffors, of a tunne of wynne graunted to theym by us, to be taken and perceyved yerely, by the handes of oure chief boteler of England for the tyme being, or his depute, in our port of Kyngefton uppon Hull, of ye wyne yat fhall be taken and furveyed in the feide port for us; confideryng that they hadde never no wyne graunted to theym by us, nor none of our progenitores, afore this tyme, to fing with nor otherwife[19]."

William Witham, LL.D. prebendary of Banbury in the church of Lincoln, 1446; of Stoke, 1457; obtained the deanry of St. Mary in the Newark in 1450; was archdeacon of Stow, 1454; of Leicefter, 1456; and dean of Wells in 1467. He died July 16, 1472; and was buried at Wells, with this epitaph, long fince defaced:

Infignis legum doctor, decus atque decanus,
Ecclefie gemina, cujus hic una fuit;
Altera Leiftzenfis, fimul archidiaconus illuc,
Willhelmus Witham nobilis hic recubat.
Dapfilis ac hilaris fuit hofpitio, wiferorum
Solamen culto juftitie requies.
Juftorum fp——, bonitatis tutor, et auctor
Pacis, concilii fons, pugil ecclefie.
Hunc mors eripuit vitam tribuens morienti,
Umbra mi——; at mors modo vita mori,
Anno milleno C quater LX duodeno,
In fetodeno claubitur hic tumulo.

In 1472-3, king Edward IV, "callyng to remembrance howe that Henr' late duke of Lancaftr', of his grete devotion, founded at Leyceftr', in the counte of Leyceftr', a churche called the Churche newe Collegiat of oure Lady Seynt Marye of Leycefter, of a deane, xii chanons, xiii vicars, iii clerkes, vi chorefters, and a verger perpetuell, and uppon that fundation yave unto theym the deane and chanons

[1] Rymer, Fœd. vol. V. pp. 130. 133. [2] Ibid. p. 142.
[3] Ibid. pars II. pp. 10. 12, 13. 15, 16. 25. 32. 34. 41. 47. 85, 86. 127. 131. [4] Ibid. pars I. p. 133.
[5] " Primo die menfis Dec. 1450, admiffus fuit magifter Ricardus Andrewe, fecretarius d'ni regis, ad canonicat. & quintam prebendam, quos nuper obtinuit d'n's Tho. Redman in novâ ecclefiâ collegiatâ B. M. Leyceftr', Lincoln. dioc. fede vacante, per refignationem ejufdem Thome, ultimi poffefforis eorundem, vacant. ad prefentationem d'ne Margarete regine Anglie, vere ipfius prebende patrone." Reg. Stafford & Kemp, archiep. Cant. fol. 107. a.
[6] " 20° die Dec. 1450, apud Croydon, admiffus fuit mag. Ric. Andrewe ad decanat. ecclefie nove collegiate B. M. Leyc. Linc. diœc. vacant. & primam prebendam in eâdem, per refignationem mag. Will. Walefby ult. decani ac canonici & præbendarii ibid. vac. ad prefentationem domine Margarete regine Anglie, vere, &c.—Eodem die admiffus fuit d'ns Thomas Redman ad canonicatum & quintam prebendam quos nuper obtinuit mag. Ric. Andrewe in eccl. novâ collegiatâ B. M. Leiceftrie, per refignationem mag. Ric. ult. poffefforis eorundem, vacant. ad prefentationem d'ne Margarete regine Angliæ, fede vacante, &c." Ibid. fol. 107. a. b. [7] Le Neve, p. 379. [8] Willis's Cathedrals, vol. II. p. 68. [9] Hiftory of Colleges, p. 266.
[10] Tho. Gafcoigne, in Dictionar. Theolog. MS. [11] Le Neve, p. 315; Drake's York, p. 464.
[12] Willis's Cathedrals, vol. I. p. 68. Le Neve, p. 68. [13] Gutch, p. 266. [14] Regifter of that College, I. 24. a.
[15] Willis, from this circumftance, fuppofes that he had fome preferment at St. Afaph.
[16] This obligation is dated Nov. 30, 1479; whence Wood fuppofed that to have been the year of his death.
[17] Gutch, p. 267.
[18] Rot. Parl. vol. V. pp. 186. A like provifo occurs in 1451, and again in 1455 and 1461. Ibid. pp. 222. 305. 521.
[19] Ibid. p. 189. a.

3

of that churche, and to their fucceffours, certeyn londes, tenementes, and poffeffions, and ordeyned and eftablifhed, amonge other, devyne fervice perpetuell there to be obferved and execute by the fame deane, chanons, vicars, clerks, chorefters, and verger, and their fucceffours; and that the fame dean and chanons, and their fucceffours, perpetuelly fhuld fynde cx pore men and women, in a houfe their by the feid duke therfore ordeyned and bilded, and diftribute every Friday wekely for evermore, to every pore man and woman of the faid nombre of a cx perfones there for the tyme beyng, viid, and certeyn maffes dailly to be feid there, afore the fame pore men and women, in a chapell within the fame hous dedicate. And for that the fame charges fo ordeyned were over grete to be founden and born of the lyvelode yoven unto the dean and chanons of the feid church at tyme of the feid fundation, one Marye that was the wyf of William Hervy, to th'entent that the deane and chanons of the feid chirche the chargies to the fame bilongyng fhuld nowe the better fuppor, bere, and for ever contynue, of her grete devotion, by the licence of Henry the VIte late in dede and not in right kyng of Englond, yave unto the dean and chanons of the feid chirche, one Ric' Elvethan beyng deane of the fame, the manoir of Southrop called Filibertifcourt, with th'appurtenauncez, in the counte of Glouceftr', and the manoir of Southrop called Greyefcourt, with th'appurtenauncez, in the fame counte, and one meafe, one toft, and 11 yerds and an half of lande, in Southrop in the fame counte, and one yerde and an half of lande in the towne of Southrop biforefeid, and in Leecheturvile in the fame counte; to have and to hold to the feide deane and chanons, and to their fucceffours, in helpyng of the fuftentation and fupporte of the feid charges for evermore: the which manoirs and other premiffes, with their appurtenances, the deane and chanons of the feid churche, alwey after the feid yeft, hiderto have occupied; and which manoirs and other premiffes, with th'appurtenauncez, the kynges noble progenitour kyng Edward the thyrdde, by his lettres patentes fealed with his grete feale, yave unto the feid William Hervy, and to the faid Marye then his wyf; to have and to hold to theym and to their heires males of their bodies comyng: unto the which Marye therof beyng feifed, after the deth of the feid William Hervy, for that he died withoute iffue male bitwixt theym hadde, and other dyvers confiderations, Henr' the Vth late in deed and not in right kyng of Englond, by his lettres patentes fealed with his grete fele, releffed all his right, title, and intereffe, that he had in the fame: and howe alfoe divine fervicez and other charges abovefeid, alwey contynuelly fith the feid fundation hiderto have be duely obferved and kept, to the verrey honour and worfhipp of God, and grete releyf and fuftenaunce of pore people: the Kyng oure foveraigne lord, of his mooft bleffed difpofition, mere motion, and certeyne fcience, by th'advis and affent of the lords fpirituelx and temporelx, and of the commens of this reame, in this his prefent parlement affembled, and by auctorite of the fame, ordeyneth, enacteth, and eftabliffeth, that all and every actes and acte made in any of the parlementes holden fith the firft day of his reigne, or in this prefent parlement made or to be made, be not in any wife prejudiciall or hurtyng to the feid nowe deane and chanons, to their predeceffors or fucceffours, or to the predeceffours or fucceffours of any of theym, in any maner wife, as for, in, or of, the feid manoirs and other premiffes; but that all and every actes and acte made fith the feid firft day, or in this prefent parlement made or to be made, the which be or may be prejudiciall or hurtyng to the feid deane and chanons, their predeceffours or fucceffours, of, in, or for the fame, or any parcell therof, be aneynft theym, as to the feid manoirs and other premiffes, and for every parcell therof, voide and of none effecte; and that the feid nowe deane and chanons, and their fucceffours, and every of theym, and

the fucceffours of every of theym, may entre into the feid manoirs, landes, and tenementes, and other premiffes, and have, hold, and enjoy all the fame manoirs and other premiffes, and every parcell therof, accordyng to the tenure of the faid yefte therof made to the deane and chanons of the feid churche by the feid Marye; the feid acte and actes, the kynges affumption of eftate roiall, the kynges lettres patentes, or any other thyng by hym done, or any myfreherfell of the premiffes in any wife notwithftondyng, by what name or names the feid manoirs, meafe, toft, and lande, with th'appurtenauncez, and the feid nowe deane and chanons, or any of their predeceffours, or the predeceffours of any of theym, be or were named or called in eny graunte or grauntes, lettres patentes, or other evydences therof as is biforefeid made, or by what name or names the feid churche or college, in any lettres patentes of any of the kynges of Englond be named or called : faved to every of the kynges liege people, and to their heires, all fuch right, title, and intereffe, the which they or any of theym have or had in or to any of the premiffes, the feid thrydde day of Marche or any tyme fith, other then by lettres patentes of the kynge oure foverayne lord that nowe is[1]."

Feb. 12, 1477-8, *William Chauntre*, dean of St. Mary's in the Newark, with the approbation of his chapter, covenanted with *William* lord *Haftings* to pay him an annuity of £20. out of their manors, lands, &c. in Leicefter, Higham Ferrers, and other places; and engaged, that, whenever he fhould die, they would keep a fpecial obit for him in their church on the day of his funeral, and every year celebrate an anniverfary for the foul of him and Catharine his wife; and that the provoft of their church fhould yearly on that day, at the end of mafs, pay to the dean 3s. 4d. and to every canon then prefent 2s. to every clerk 6d. to every chorifter 4d. and to the verger 4d. and to every poor man and woman of the hofpital there 1d. out of the profits of the hofpital of St. Leonard, by reafon that the lord Haftings had obtained that hofpital from the king, and given it to their college for ever [2]. The patronage and revenues of St. John's Hofpital [3] were alfo given to them at the fame time by the lord Haftings.

In 1480, the dean and canons were regularly incorporated, by the letters patent of king Edward IV.; and enabled to fue and be fued, to hold lands, &c. [4]

William Dudley, third fon of John the eighth baron Dudley, of Univerfity college, Oxford, M. A. and prebendary of Stillington in the church of York, was prefented by king Edward IV. to a prebend of this church, Aug. 5, 1472; and on the 17th of that month was elected dean. He held alfo a canonry at Wells, and one at Wolverhampton; was dean of Windfor, 1473; archdeacon of Middlefex, 1475; and in 1476 obtained the bifhoprick of Durham. He was a great benefactor to Dudley church, and to other of the collegiate churches in which he was preferred; and, dying Nov. 29, 1483, was buried in the chapel of St. Nicholas in Weftminfter abbey; where he has a handfome monument, with a rich canopy of three arches, and two others forming tabernacles with pedeftals, to which defcend animals, and over the whole ten pierced arches, and a cornice of angels holding fcrolls. On the altar, whofe fide is adorned with four blank fhields in ftarred quatrefoils, was the figure inlaid in brafs, and this infcription :

Hic jacet Gulielmus de Dudley, e familia baronum de Dudley, Dunelm. epifcopus. Obiit anno Dom. 1483 [5].

John Morgan (alias Yonge), a native of Wales, LL. D. of Oxford, and dean of Windfor 1484, obtained this deanry in December, 1485 [6]; which he refigned in 1496, on being promoted to the bifhoprick of St. David's. He died in 1504; and, by his laft will, defired to be buried in his cathedral at St. David's, and a chapel to be erected over his grave in the beft manner that might be, according to the difpofition of his executors [7].

---

[1] Rot. Parl. 12 & 13 Edw. IV. vol. VI. p. 49.
[3] See before, p. 325, under the Hiftory of that Hofpital, chapter of this collegiate church, ftyling themfelves the *proprietarii*, or *cuftodes*, of the hofpital.
[5] See Plate XXX; from Mr. Gough's "Sepulchral Monuments in Great Britain," vol. II. p. 285.
[6] See p. 336.
[7] Wood, Ath. Oxon. vol. I. p. 647.

[2] Clauf. 17 Edw. IV, pars unica, dorfo.
a grant of admiffion into their confraternity from the dean and
[4] See our Appendix, p. 111.

The form of a prefentation to one of the prebends during the fhort reign of king Edward V. is here given:

"Rex, &c. Sciatis nos, de grâ ñrâ spâli, ex ctâ fcienciâ & mero motu ñris, dediffe & conceffiffe dilectis nobis A. B. & C. D. & affign' fuis, advocacõem, collacõem, donacõem, & libam difpoficionem, ac auctoritatem & poteftatem conferendi feu donandi, cuicũq̃ idonee pſone, quãcunq̃ p̄bendam in ecclîâ novâ collegiat' beate Marie Leyceftr' px' vacatâ, cum p̄ mortem, refignacõem, ceffionem, p̃mutacõem, vel dimiffionem, feu quocũq̃ alio modo h̃mod' p̄benda vacare contigit, p̃ unicâ & px' vacacõe; & quòd benè liceat eifdem A. B. & C. D. ac eoẕ alt' & affignat' fuis, auctoritate p̄ſent' conceffionis m̄ē h̃mod' p̄bend', cum px' ut p̄dictum vacant', idonee pſone îrate conferre feu dare, ac omia & fingula que circa p̄miffa neceffaria fuerint, feu quomodoît opportuerit ageret p̄implere, adeò plenè & integrè put nos fecerimus fi conceffio ñra facta non fuiffet [1]."

In 1483-4, we find the following order:

"Richard III. &c. kynge of Englande and of Fraunce, and lorde of Yrelande, to all juftices, ftuerdes, ſhereffes, maiers, recevours, baillies, reves, conftables, and all other oure officers, miniftres, trueliegemen, and fubjects, w'in our lordfhipps of Carmarden, Kedwelly, and Carnewaltham, in Wales, and to every of them hering or feing thefe our lres, greting. Forfemoche as it hath be fhewed unto us, on ye behalve of oure trufty and welbeloved the deane and chanons of our new collegiat churche of our bleffed lady of Leiceftre, that the revenues & duetees which w'in our faid lordfhips have of their lyveloods there hertofor growen unto them (by might & power of evill-difpofed pſones having rule in thefe ptes) and alfo by others whome they have favored, maynetened, & fupported, have from ye faid deane and chanons ben kept and w'drawen, to thear gret hurt and damage, and alfo to our gret difpleafur: We therfore, not willinge them herafter fo to be entreated, wronged, and appreched, have commanded the faid deane and chanons, yt they fhall name and appointe one of themfelff, or fuche anoyr able and pollitique pſone as they fhall thinke for ye wele of their place good and profitable, to be their proctor in that behalve, and him to fende unto our faid lordfhips, there to take a view of their faid livelods, and the fame, by their auctorities to him committed, to graunt and fet to ferme to fuch wele-difpofed pſones as wele and truely woll anfwere and paye fuch dueties as fhall growe unto them by reafon of the fame: And, if any pſone or pſones then, whatfoever he or they be, which hertofore hath or have had or receved, or herafter fhall have or receive, anye parte of the revenues of their faid lyvelods and the duetes therof, which unto the faid deane and chanons be well owen and due, or herafter fhall be owing or due, will not content and pay as right willeth; then the fame proctour therof, in the name of the faid dean and chanons, do feafe and take fufficient diftreffes, wherby they may have fuche good and fure contentations as fhall accorde wt reafon, the fame diftreffes to be demeaned and detayned according to the lawes & cuftomes ther defirend; and praing you, that unto the faid proctr, or any other officers or ſvñts which by the faid dean and chanons fhall at any tyme herafter be fent thider for the execucion of the p̃miffes, ye will geve your aide and affiftence, when ye by them on our behalve be required. So doe, not failling, &c. Yaven, &c. yt xi day of Febr̄, aº primo [2]."

May 16, 1511, *William Wygefton*, junior, of Leicefter, merchant of the Staple of Calais, *Thomas Wygefton* clerk, *Roger Wygefton*, and *William Colte*, obtained the king's letters patent for building a houfe, and founding a chantry here [3]; in purfuance of which, an indenture quadripartite was made, Jan. 20, 1512, between, 1, the faid William Wigfton; 2, John Yonge the dean, and the canons of the collegiate church; 3, Richard abbot of St. Mary de Pratis, with his convent; and, 4, Richard Gyllot mayor, and the burgeffes of Leicefter; in which it is ftated, that the faid *William Wygefton*, at his proper cofts, had newly built a manfion-place, and inclofed it, with an adjoining garden, within the precincts and walls of the college, for the manfion-place of two chantry-priefts by him, with God's grace, to be founded within the fame college, to the honour of Almighty God, our bleffed Lady, St. Urfula, and St. Katharine; which manfion and garden were fet between the manfion-place and gardens of Mr. Thomas Wygefton, then prebendary of the thirteenth prebend, on the Eaft part, and the Caftle-way on the Weft part, and extending from the church-yard of the faid college on the South to the garden of the Bedehoufe on the North part; and, for the foundation of the forefaid chantry and chantry-prieft, by licence of the dean and canons, at his proper cofts, had newly erected, to the honour of Almighty God, our bleffed Lady, St. Urfula, and St. Katharine, a new chapel, inclofed with coftly works wrought and made of latten, fixed and laid betwixt two pillars in the body of the church of the aforefaid college on the North fide, to the intent that the aforefaid chantry-priefts and their fucceffors fhould there daily perpetually minifter divine fervice. The dean and canons agree to grant a leafe of the chapel, houfe, and garden, for 99 years, to the abbot and mayor in truft, for the two priefts, with a covenant of renewal when 90 years fhould be expired, and alfo to keep the fame in conftant repair; the faid William Wygefton undertaking to affign to the dean and canons in fee fimple the manor of Chefter by the Water, and other lands in the county of Northampton, and two meffuages and two yard-lands at Knighton, of the clear yearly value of £20. and upwards; in confideration of which, the dean and canons were to pay to each of the two priefts £7. a year; and perpetually, on the 26th of January, to obferve a folemn obit, with Dirige and mafs on the morrow, with fong and bells to be rung, for the good eftate of the faid William Wigfton the younger during his life, and for his foul perpetually after his death, after like manner as they ufe to keep and do in other folemn obits: And the faid dean, canons, and other minifters of the faid college, and their fucceffors for the time being, and every of them, being prefent at all the Dirige and mafs of the faid yearly obit, or the more part of them, fhall, for the fame obit fo keeping and being prefent, have, perceive, and take perpetually every year, by the hands of the dean or his deputy, or by the hands of the provoft of the fame college for the time being, to be diftributed in manner as hereafter followeth; to the dean, if he be prefent, 2 s.; every canon 12 d.; every vicar 6 d.; every chief clerk 6 d.; and each of the faid chantry-priefts 6 d.; and other chantry-priefts of the faid college, every of them faying Dirige for the fouls above rehearfed, 4 d.; every of the chorifters 3 d.; and the verge-bearer 3 d. And, if any of the faid canons or other minifters at the time of the faid obit be out of the town of Leicefter at their recreations or other bufinefs, that they fhall perceive and take every man after his degree and the rate above fpecified, as they fhould do if they were prefent; but, if in the town or precinct, and not prefent, to have nothing: And the dean and canons engage perpetually, at the time of Dirige and mafs of the faid obit, to find four wax tapers, fuch as they find at other obits, to burn at the hearfe of the faid William; and to pay, on the day of the faid obit, the following fums; to the mayor of the town of Leicefter and his brethren, and minifters of the faid town, reforting to the faid college on the day of the faid obit, and offering there at the mafs, and faying at the door of the faid new latten chapel, before they depart out of the faid college, the Pfalm "De Profundis" for the foul of the faid William Wygefton, 3 s. in this form to be applied and paid; to the mayor for the time being 8 d.; and to every fix of his moft antient brethren of the fame town 4 d.; and to the mayor's fergeant 2 d.; and to

---

[1] Harl. MSS. 433. p. 21. b.   [2] Ibid. p. 152. a.
[3] "Aº 2 Hen. VIII. Will's Wygefton de Leyceftr', junior, mercator Stapule Cales, Thomas Wygefton clericus, Rogerus Wygefton, & Will's Colte, habent licentiam de cantariâ fundandâ ad altare beate Marie Virginis, Sanctarumque Urfule & Katarine virginum & martyrum, infra ecclefiam collegiatam beate Marie Novi Operis Leiceftrie in com' Leiceftr'. Tefte, &c. 16º die Maii." See Appendix, p. 112.

Pl. XXX. p. 335.

SGVI · MV · D · · · YDAM · · · VM DE DVDLEY QVNL II · ORV II · DOMINI ·

Monument of

BISHOP DVDLEY,

in

Westminster Abbey

1483.

Schnebbelie del.   Basire sc.

the mayor's clerk 2 d.; and to the bellman, to make relation and notice throughout the town the day and time of the said obit, as he doth at other special obits, 2 d.; and the dean and canons to distribute among poor people, on the day of the said obit, 2 s. in money; and every year cause to be made 24 penny-tapers of wax, to be set upon the candlestick of the said new latten chapel, and to be renewed twice in a year, against the feastes of Easter and All Saints; and also to be lighted by the clerks of the said college, or their deputies, at the eight principal feasts solemnized in the said college, and at all the feasts of our Lady, and in the feast of St. Katharine and St. Ursula, in the times of high mass and Magnificat. The dean and canons every year to pay to the clerks of the said college, for their labour in lighting and doing out of the tapers, at the times of the said feasts, 16 d.; and, for the scowering of the said latten chapel, 4 d.; and find for the two chantry-priests bread, wine, and wax-candle, for their mass, when need requires. The said William Wigston endowed his chapel with these ornaments and anonements; two chalices of silver and gilt with their patents, &c.; one of them whole gift, containing 18 ounces with the patents; and the other parcel gilt, containing 11 ounces; two mass-books imprinted; four corporaxes and corporax-cases; five vestments, with mobes and orfrayes sorting to the vestments; the first vestment of blue velvet, set with silk and gold; and the second white damask, with flowers of silk and gold; the third, red sarsenet flowered with flowers of silk and gold; the fourth black worsted of St. Omer's, set with flowers of silk and gold; and the fifth of blue satin of Sipers, flowered and set with flowers of silk and gold; four hangings for the altar, for above the altar and beneath, with altar-cloths and frontels sorting to the same; the first hanging blue velvet, set with flowers of silk and gold; the second with white damask, set with flowers of silk and gold; and the third of black worsted of St. Omer's, with flowers of silk and gold; and the fourth of red and green satin Sipers flowered like damask, set with flowers of silk and gold; four pairs of curtains of sarfenet; and four single chest clothes; all which ornaments and anonements the dean and canons covenant to keep for the same new chapel, there to be occupied and worn, and no where else; and bind themselves and their successors to repair, maintain, renew, and to make and cause to be made, new like ornaments, or other of like value, at their proper costs and charges, as often as need shall require, to be worn and occupied in the said new latten chapel, so that the said chapel be always endowed and anoned with like ornaments and anonements as is above expressed; or at the least with three suits of vestments, and three hangings for the altar as well above as beneath, with all other things thereto belonging, in like manner and form as is above expressed, over and besides all other ornaments above rehearsed; to be occupied and used in the said chapel, and by the said chantry-priests for the same chantry, and their successors, and not otherwise nor elsewhere, without lett, interruption, or taking away, by the said dean and canons, or their successors. For which agreement and grants William Wigston paid to the said dean and canons the day of the date of these presents 100 marks sterling; and farther it was agreed, that the dean and canons pay to the provost of the said college 6 s. 8 d. per annum for his pains in the premisses, for which William Wigston paid the said dean and canons ten marks more [1].

In consequence of this agreement, *Thomas Wygeston* clerk, *William Wygeston* the younger, merchant of the Staple of Calais, *Roger Wygeston*, and *William Fisher* clerk (the first master of the Hospital then newly

founded by W. Wygeston), obtained licence from the crown, Oct. 5, 1512, to bestow on the new collegiate church of St. Mary at Leicester the manor of Chester by the Water, with several rents and tenements in Little Chester, Irynchester, Chester by the Water, and Artleborow, co. North'ton [2]; and at Knighton, co. Leic' [3].

John Yong, LL. D. and master of the Rolls, was elected dean of this church, Jan. 3, 1512-13 [4]; obtained the prebend of Absthorpe, in the cathedral of York, April 6, 1514; was elected dean there, May 7; and obtained the prebend of Bugthorp, Sept. 18, that year; in 1515 resigned his deanry at Leicester, for a pension of £20. a year payable out of it; died April 15, 1516; and was buried in the Rolls chapel; where, against the North wall, is his effigies in a scarlet robe and four-cornered cap, with this epitaph:

" *Dominus firmamentum meum.*
Jo. Yong, Legum Doctori, Sacrorum
Scriniorum, & hujus Domûs
Custodi; Decano olim Ebor.
vitâ defuncto xxv Aprilis,
sui fideles Executores
hoc posuerunt MCXVI."

His successor in the deanry at Leicester was William Knight [5]; who was a native of London, bred in Winchester-school, and admitted fellow of New College, Oxford, 1493; where having followed the study of the civil law, he was appointed one of the secretaries to king Henry VII; obtained the chapelry of Kibworth Harcourt in 1502; and was afterwards employed by king Henry VIII. on an embassy to the emperor Maximilian; who, for his eminent virtues, and as a reward for many services to the English king, in exposing his life to danger, wearing it out in continual labours for him, and ready for the future to do the like if occasion should require, granted him the following arms: " Party per fess, Or and Gules, a demi-rose and a demi-sun conjoined, counterchanged of the field; on the top of the demi-rose two eagles' heads issuing thence Sable, and from each side an eagle's wing displayed of the third: over the whole a cardinal's cap;" which grant was also confirmed to him by letters patent dated July 20, 1514 [6]. In the next year he obtained this deanry at Leicester, by stipulating to pay an annuity of £20. to his predecessor Dr. Yong. He relinquished this preferment in 1522; in which year he was admitted archdeacon of Chester Nov. 11; and archdeacon of Huntingdon, Sept. 17, 1523. In 1527, being then secretary to the king, he was sent to the pope on the business of the divorce; and in December, 1529, being then a prebendary of St. Stephen's at Westminster, and newly returned from Rome, was made archdeacon of Richmond. In 1531, he was incorporated LL. D. at Oxford, as he had stood in a foreign university. He surrendered his archdeaconry of Chester, May 20, 1541, on its being dissevered from the church of Lichfield, that the king might the better annex it to his new intended see at Chester; and in nine days after was rewarded the bishoprick of Bath and Wells. In the latter of these cities a magnificent colonade in the centre of the market-place, with a beautiful arched roof, bore the next year this testimony to his liberality: " Ad honorem Dei Omnipotentis, & commodum pauperum mercatum Welliæ frequentantium, impensis Gulielmi Knight episcopi, & Richardi Wooleman, hujus ecclesiæ cathedralis olim decani, hic locus erectus est. Laus Deo, pax vivis, requies defunctis. Amen. A. D. 1542 [7]." He died Sept. 29, 1547; and, by his last will, dated Aug. 12, that year, bequeathed £100. [8] for conveying his body from London to Wells for interment in that cathedral, and for a tomb to be laid or set over it; £40. to

[1] Palmer's MS Cases, p. 82.
[2] A fine of this manor had been levied by William Wyggeston the younger, demandant, and William Coope and Joan his wife deforcients, 2 Hen. VIII. Bridges, vol. II. p. 182.   [3] Inq. ad quod dampnum, 5 Oct. 4 Hen. VIII.
[4] " Magister Johannes Yong, LL. D. presentatus per regem ad decanatum ecclesie collegiate Beate Marie Novi Operis, Leyc', per mortem magistri Jacobi Whiston, Jan. 3, 1512." Reg. Smith.
[5] " Magister Will' Knyght, utriusque juris doctor, presentatus per regem ad decanatum ecclesie nove collegii Beate Marie, Leyc', per resignationem magistri Joh' Yong, LL. D. 4 Dec. 1515; solvend' penf' ann' 20 lib' resignanti." Reg. Atwater.
[6] See Wood's History of the University of Oxford, by Gutch, vol. III. pp. 192. 195. The arms still remain in the second South window of the refectory at New College. See Plate XXVIII. fig. 27.
[7] Wood, Athen. Oxon. vol. I. p. 675, says he was buried in the nave of that cathedral: but Godwin, p. 387, says (from MS. Trin. p. 91) " Obiit apud Wivelescomb, ibique sepultus jacet."   [8] Godwin de Præsulibus, p. 387.

New College, and £20. to Wykeham's College at Winchester.

Robert Boune, the next and laſt dean of this church, was elected in 1522, and about the ſame time was preſented to the rich rectory of Hanſlope in Bucks, which in that year had been appropriated to the dean and canons of St. Mary in the Newark[1] (and of which church he was the laſt rector, as the impropriation was given, at the diſſolution of this College, to the Corporation of Lincoln[2]).

With thirty others, Dean Boune, Aug. 11, 1534, ſubſcribed to the king's ſupremacy; and at that period the yearly payments of this church are thus ſtated[3]:

	£.	s.	d.
To the Dean, Mr. Robert Bone	40	0	0
To the 13 prebendaries, each 13l. 6s. 8d.	173	6	8
To 13 vicars, each £6. —	78	0	0
To 7 choriſters, each 6l. 13s. 4d.	44	13	4
To the provoſt —— ——	10	0	0
To the treaſurer —— ——	1	0	0
Cantori collegii —— ——	2	0	0
	349	0	0

Mr. Richard Layton, one of the viſitors of religious houſes in 1539, reported to the Lord Cromwell, " that the College of the Newark, with an Hoſpital, was well kept, and honeſt men therein ; £300. in their treaſury beforehand;" but " that the biſhop of Lincoln (Longland) had commanded the preachers of this college, that they ſhould no more preach but in their own benefices[4]." Nov. 12, 1543, dean Boune preſented Thomas Rigmayden, clerk, one of the prebends of his church, to the vicarage of Ircheſter, co. Northampton[5]; and Nov. 5, 1547, this dean was ſummoned to Convocation; almoſt immediately after which the college was diſſolved[6]. His name occurs in the archiepiſcopal regiſters at York[7], Sept. 8, 1553; and he died rector of Hanſlope in 1554.

The Founder of this Hoſpital, beſides the poor, deſigned a maſter and certain chaplains to have the care and management of them; but, when they were put under the government of the dean and chapter, one of the canons was entruſted therewith; who, in 1539, was Richard Fowler, treaſurer of the church, who paid them yearly 176l. 0s. 3d. for their daily food and proviſion in ſickneſs; whereof paid every Friday 7d. to each of the poor, and 10d. to each of the nurſes every week. He alſo paid £10. yearly for buying 50 taberdes, or gowns; ſo that every two years each poor man might have a new garment. Beſides which, there was given among them yearly, on every Good Friday, 20s.; they had alſo 12l. 10s. to make porridge, and £6. for fuel, a year. All this was of the gift of the founder; but their fivepenny money was of the gift of the lady Mary Harvey, which, with 6d. per annum to each of the poor by another charity, came to 4l. 11s. 6d.—This appears by the following certificate from John biſhop of Lincoln; Richard biſhop of Coventry and Lichfield; ſir Richard Manners, knight; ſir Richard Cattiſbie, knight; William Lee, eſq.; John Beamonte, eſq.; William Ryggs and Clement Throckmorton, gentlemen; commiſſioners of the king for ſurvey of chauntries, hoſpitals, colleges, free chapels, fraternities, brotherhoods, gilds, and ſtipendiary prieſts, within the county

of Leiceſter, by virtue of the king's majeſty's commiſſion, 31° regni.

" Collegium Novi Operis Leiceſtr', infra villam Leiceſtr', valet in redd' & firm' totius manerii de Draycote, in com' Warw', xiiii li. xii s. viii d. & in redd' & firm' diverſ' manerior', rectoriar', terr', & ten', in diverſis aliis comitatibus, in toto per annum ccccxvi li. iiii s. v d. ob. q̃.

Redd' reſolut' diverſis exeunt' de oĩbus terr' & poſſeſſion' predict', per annum vi li. xv s. v d. ob.

Stipend' decani ejuſdem collegii, per ann' xl li.

Stipend' xii canonicorum infra collegium prædict' annuatim reſiden', cuilibet eorum ad xiii li. vi s. viii d. per annum —— cLxi li.

Stipend' xiii vicar' ejuſdem collegii, cuilibet eor' ad iiii li. xiii s. iiii d. in toto per annum LXii li. xiii s. iiii d.

Stipend' Hugonis Aſton, magiſtri organor' & choriſt' ib', per annum —— x li.

Stipend' iiii clericor' cantar' chori & unius vergiferi ac vi choriſt' ibid', cuilibet eor' ad Liii s. iiii d. in toto, per annum xxix li. vi s. viii d.

Stipend' unius alii choriſt' ibidem, ex fundatione Willi Derby nuper canonici ibidem xL s.

Denarii ſolut' Ricardo Fowler, clerico, theſaur' eccleſ' collegiat' præd', pro vad' centum pauperum hoĩum in domo orator' dicti collegii infra precinctum ejuſdem, ac pro vad' decem mulier' attendend' ſuper eos pro cibis ſuis quotidiè parandis & tempore ægritud' illor' pauper', viz. cuilibet hoĩ predict' vii d. per ſeptiman', ſolut' quâlibet ſeptiman' diebus Veneris, per annum cLxxvi s. iiii d.

Denar' ſolut' quolibet anno pro panno laneo empt' pro 50 taberdes vel togis pro coöperiend' ex fundatione fundator', ut in ſpatio duor' annor' quilibet pauper habeat novum veſtimentum, per annum —— —— —— x li.

Eleemoſinis dat' pauperibus præd' in die Pharaſeph', ex ordinatione fundator', inter eos annuatim dividend' per annum —— xx s.

Denar' ſolut' dictis pauperibus orantibus pro animâ Mariæ Harvy, voc' Five-penny money, per ipſam fundat', viz. cuilibet homini pauperi v d. per ann', & in al' eleemoſinâ eiſdem & pauperibus, cuilibet eorum ex aliâ ordinatione ad vi d. per annum —— —— iiii li. xi s. viii d.

Conſimilibus denar' ſolut' eiſdem pauperibus pro oleribus, voc' La Porage[8], pro ſuſtentatione eorundem pauperum quotidiè ex fundat', per annum —— —— xii s. x d.

Denar' ſolut' pro focal' pro prædict' pauperibus inter hos annuatim expendend', per annum vi li.

Feod' diverſ' officiar' & ſervien' præd' colleg' pertinen', eis conceſſ' tam per literas paten' quàm ad voluntat', prout, &c. per annum xLii li. xvi s. viii d.

Synodal' & procurationibus annuatim ſolut' diverſ' archidiac' & al' officiar' ibidem, per annum —— —— xLii li. xvi d.

Denar' ſolut' annuatim pro cuſtubus & expenſ' obit' anniverſariorum regum Angliæ, diverſ' fundator', ac al' benefactor', in denariis diſtribut' decano, prebendar', & omnibus miniſtris chori dicti collegii, ac pauperibus, quolibet anno, per ſtatuta & ordinacõnes, ſcil' per annum LXvi li. xiii s. viii d.

Reprin' in

---

[1] " A. 14 Hen. VIII. rex xxvii die Junii conceſſit decano & canonicis collegii B. Marie Leyc', & ſucceſſoribus ſuis, advocationem eccleſie parochialis de Hanſlope, com. Durh.; habend' ſibi & ſucceſſoribus." From the Original in the Rolls Chapel.

[2] Bacon's Liber Regis, p. 499.   [3] See the Introductory Volume, p. lxxxii.

[4] See the Introductory Volume, p. cxlii.—They appear to have in ſome degree purchaſed this good report; for, we find that, in 1548, William Cannam, clerk, was preſented to the vicarage of Raundes, by George Wooderoffe, gent. and John Holland, " patronis pro hâc vice, per conceſſ. decani & capituli Novi Operis, modò diſſolut.;" and in 1550 the rectory of Cranſley in Northamptonſhire was in the preſentation of Francis Cave, Roger Gyllot, &c. " conceſſ. per Collegium Novi Operis Leyc." Bridges, vol. II. p. 91.   [5] Ibid. vol. II. p. 181.

[6] " The king," in the quaint words of Dr. Fuller, " made three meals (or one meal of three courſes) on Abbey lands, beſides what Cardinal Wolſey (the king's taſter herein) had eat beforehand, when aſſuming ſmaller houſes to endow his two colleges.——The religious houſes under £200. a year were granted to him by the parliament in 1535; the greater monaſteries in 1538; and the colleges, chantries, and free chapels, in 1545.—The firſt of theſe were moſt in number; the ſecond, richeſt in revenue; the third in this reſpect better than the former, becauſe, they being ſpent and conſumed, theſe alone were left to ſupply his occaſions. But the enſuing death of king Henry VIII, for a time, preſerved the life of theſe houſes, which were totally demoliſhed by act of parliament in the firſt year of king Edward VI." Church-Hiſtory, Book VI. p. 350.

[7] Rob. Boune, 1553, decanus eccleſie collegiate Beate Marie Novi Operis, Leic', 8 Sept. Reg. Holgate, regiſt. Ebor.

[8] Hence the uſe of the great porridge-pot; ſee p. 343.

Denar'

Denar' solut' domino episcopo Lincoln' & officiar' suis, pro perpetuâ decimâ domino regi de collegio prædict' debit', ultra solut' subf' cùm acciderit, per annum   LIX li. X s. IX d.

Stipend' diverf' cantaristarum annuatim solut' in pecuniis numerat' per decanum & capitulum collegii præd', pro diversis cantariis infra ecclesiam collegiat' prædict' fundat', ut sequitur; viz. Willielmo Wilson, cantaristæ cantariæ Mariæ Harvey, CVI s. VIII d.; Ricardo Waterworth, cantaristæ cantariæ Willielmi Bedell, IIII li. VI s. VIII d.; Thomæ Marshall & Willielmo Blakewell, cantaristis cantariæ Johannis nuper ducis Lanc', inter eos equaliter dividend', VI li. XIII s. IIII d.; Humfro Ellyot & Johanni Hardye, cantaristis cantariæ Will' Wigston, XIII li.; Thomæ Hornecourt, celebrant' infra nuper hospitale Sancti Johannis Baptist' infra villam Leic' præd', LX s.; in toto per annum   —   XXXIII li. VI s. VIII d.

Altone omnium terrar' & ten' præd' vocat' Obitt lands jacent' infra villam Leic' & precinct' ejusdem, eò quòd annualiter dividentur inter decanum & præbendar' ac vicar' dicti collegii ex ordinacõne composicõne per certum rotulum, voc' Porcõn' roll, cuilibet' partem, scil' ultra reprif' allocat', viz. decano duas partes, & cuilibet canonic' unam partem, & cuilibet vicar' tertiam partem pertinen' decan' & canonic', per annum   XXIIII li. XVII s. I d. ob.

Solut' for' an^{le} ut in reparacõnes tenementor' & vacat' ejusdem, tam infra præd' villam Leic' & precinct' ejusdem, quàm in diverf' al' villar' in diverf' com' attingen', cõibus annis, per estimat'. sicut apparet in annis præceden' per diverf' comp' dicti collegii, ad minus, ultra LXXVIII li. XVII s. VII d. ob. pro subf' domino regi cùm acciderit, per annum   —   LXVI li. XIII s. IIII d.

(margin: Reprif' in)

CCCCXLII li. XIII s. IIII d.

Et remanet clarè per annum XIIII li. XXIII d. ob. q^a.

Cantaria dominæ Mariæ Harvey, fundat' infra predict' ecclesiam Novi Operis, Leicstr', val' in quâdam pencõne annuatim recipiend' per Will' Wilson, cantaristam cantariæ præd', per manus decani & capituli præd' collegii, in pecuniis numeratis, ad IIII anni terminos, per annum   —   CVI s. VIII d.

Cantaria, vocat' Elvett's Chauntry, infra dictam ecclesiam Novi Operis, Leyc', valet in quâdam annuitate five annuali pensione pro cantaristâ cantariæ prædictæ recipiend' per manus decani & capituli Collegii Novi Operis, Leic', p̄d' in pecuniâ numeratâ, ad quatuor anni terminos, æqualiter per ann' CVI s. VIII d.

Cantaria Will' Wigston, fundat' infra præd' ecclesiam Novi Operis, val' in quâdam annuitate five annuali pencõne annuatim recipiend' per Johannem Hardy & Humfrum Gyllot, cantaristas ibidem, per manus decani & capituli Novi Operis, Leic', equaliter, per annum,   —   XIIII li.

Cantaria vocat' Beddel's chantrie, infra præd' ecclesiam Novi Operis fundat', val' in quâdam annuali pencõne annuatim recipiend' per Ricardum Waterworth, cantaristam ibidem, de prædicto decano & cap' collegii prædict', ad quatuor anni terminos equaliter, per annum   —   IIII li. VI s. VIII d.

Cantaria, vocat' John à Gaunt's chantry, fundat' pro duobus capellan' infra præd' ecclesiam Novi Operis, Leic', val' in quâdam annuali pencõne annuatim recipiend' per Will' Blakwell & Thomam Marshall, cantaristas cantariæ ejusdem, viz. per manus prædict' decani & capituli VI li. XIII s. IIII d. ac per dominum regem extra cur' augmentat' revenc' coronæ suæ ut in jure nuper monasterii de Vaudyâ in com' Lincoln', VI li. XIII s. IIII d. in toto per annum   XIII li. VI s. IIII d.

By a survey at the same time taken of all the houses belonging to the said college of Leicester, situate and being within the walls and precincts of the same, it appears that the then members of it were the dean Robert Boune, sir Richard Paget, sir Nicholas Bradshaw, sir Anthony Skevington, sir William Weston, sir Richard Bawdwyn, sir Richard Fowler, sir Christopher Marshall, sir John Vincent, sir John Leigh, sir Gabriel Raynes, sir Edward Burton, sir William Gyllot, canons; whereof the dean's salary or stipend was £40. and his house, garden, and orchard, valued at 40 s. a year. The stipend of the thirteen vicars was to each 4 l. 13 s. 4 d. &c.

There were five chantries founded in the church:

1. John of Gaunt's, of two chaplains, William Blackwell and Thomas Marshall; their joint salary was 13 l. 6 s. 8 d. and their house 10 s. a year.

2. The lady Mary Harvey's, of one priest, William Wilson, who had 5 l. 6 s. 8 d.

3. Elvett's, of one priest, who had 5 l. 6 s. 8 d., these two had one house, 10 s. a year.

4. William Wigston's, of two priests, John Hardy and Humfry Gyllot, alias Ellyott, who had between them £14. and a house, 10 s. a year.

5. Beddel's chantry, of one priest, Richard Waterworth, of 4 l. 6 s. 8 d. a year.

The lodging between the gates was valued at 20 s. and the lodging between the church and the great steeple at 5 s. a year.

This collegiate church had several sums to receive from the abbot and convent of St. Mary's, and several other sums to pay to them; the particulars of which are specified in the Appendix, from Charyte's Rentale [1].

In 1547, a considerable part of their possessions was granted by king Edward VI. to *John Beaumont* and *William Gyes* [2].

In 1553, an account being taken of the pensions payable to the members of the dissolved religious houses, the following return was made:

Leicester; Collegium Novi Operis, seu Newark.

John Leyghe, William Gillot, John Vincent, Richard Fowler, Christopher Marshall, William Weston, William Pachett, Nicholas Bradshaw, Thomas Rigmayden [3],	Prebendarii; to each £10.
Richard Berton, John Parke, George Charlett, John Borough, William Hethecote [4], Thomas Berwyke, Richard Pedder,	Prebendarii minores; to each 2 l. 17 s. 3 d.
Robert Wangle, Thomas Mylver, Thomas Westons, John Midleton, William Borough,	Vicarii; to each £6.
William Blackwall, Thomas Harrryson,	Vicarii cantaristæ; to each £6.
Thomas Harcourt, William Mansfelde,	cantores; to each £5.
William Kyttes, Thomas Arden [5], Robert Weston [6], John Palfreyman,	Ministri in eodem collegio; to each 4 l. 13 s. 4 d.

The reason why there were so many members of this collegiate church and so few of the abbey, whose pensions remained in charge, was because the abbey had been dissolved in 1539; whereas this college continued till 1547. The dean was provided for by the rectory of Hanslope; and it may be presumed that such of the prebendaries as are not mentioned in this report were dead, or disposed of in some preferment.

---

[1] Appendix, p. 69.   [2] 1 Pars Original. 2 Edw. VI. Rot. 106.   [3] Vicar of Irchester, 1543—1566.

[4] Afterwards rector of Aylestone; where see a portrait of him from the brass on his tomb.

[5] One so named was installed prebendary of Worcester in the third stall in 1558, afterwards deprived as a bigoted Papist. Strype, Annals, vol. I. pp. 243. 356. Browne Willis's Survey, vol. I. p. 671.

[6] Robert Weston, LL.D. dean of Wells in 1570, subscribes to articles, Feb. 5, 1562, as proctor in convent for Lichfield and Coventry. Strype, Ann. vol. I. p. 290; his character, 291. See Wood's History and Antiquities of Oxford, vol. II. p. 40.—Qu. whether the same person?

DEANS of St. MARY in the NEWARK.

1. Richard de Hampflap de Toneworth[1], prefbyter, was admitted the firft dean, 9 cal. Apr. 1355.
2. John Porter[2], admitted 7 id. Jan. 1361.
3. Thomas Brightwell[3], S. T. D. 1382.
4. Richard Elveden, 1408.
5. William Walefby, one of the king's chaplains, occurs dean in 1422[4]; and in 1437 was rector of Church Langton. He refigned in 1450.
6. Richard Andrewe[5], admitted December 20, 1450.
7. William Witham died dean in 1472[6].
8. William Dudley, 1472—1476[7].
9. William Chauntre[8], one of the king's chaplains, Oct. 20, 1476; died 1485.
10. John Morgan[9], LL.D. Dec. 1485; promoted to the fee of St. David's in 1496. He died in 1504.
11. Robert Middleton[10], LL. D. a canon of this church, Dec. 5, 1496. He died Jan. 14, 1499.
12. William Stokedale[11], S. T. P. 1499.
13. James Whifton[12], LL. D. rector of Charlebury, in Oxfordfhire, 1495; and fucceffively prebendary of Welton, Brinkhall, Gretton, and Banbury, all in the church of Lincoln, was elected Nov. 23, 1500. He died in 1512.
14. John Young, LL.D. elected Jan. 3, 1512-13; refigned in 1515 for a penfion of £20. a year payable out of this deanry; and died April 25, 1516[13].
15. William Knight, LL. D. of New college, Oxford, Dec. 4, 1515. He refigned in 1522; in 1541 became bifhop of Bath and Wells; and died in 1547[14].
16. Robert Boune, the laft dean, admitted in 1522, was dean at the diffolution; and died rector of Hanflope in 1554.

PREBENDARIES.

Oct. 2, 1366. Robert de Newton, rector of Wardley in Rutland, held the fifth prebend (*cujus verus valor in pecuniâ numeratâ confiftit in* xx *marc'*[15].)

1382, 22 Aug. Walter Hanloo exchanged the prebend of Taunton, in the church of Wells, for the ninth prebend in this church[16].

1424, 3 Aug. Henry Rofe was prefented to the feventh prebend, and admitted by the archbifhop in perfon at Laund priory[17].

27 Oct. William Aflakby exchanged the twelfth prebend with William Browne, dean of the collegiate church of Lanchefter, dioc. Durham[18].

1425, June 16. William Holwell was prefented to the fifth prebend, *vice* Walter Denton, deceafed[19].

1450. William Williams refigned the fifth prebend.

1450, Dec. 1. Richard Andrewe, *fecretarius regis*, was admitted to the fifth prebend, on the refignation of Thomas Redman[20].

Dec. 20, Richard Andrewe obtained the firft prebend, and was at the fame time elected dean[21].

1450, 20 Dec. Thomas Redman again fucceeded to the fifth prebend, on the refignation of Andrewe[21].

1472, 5 Aug. William Dudley was prefented to the third prebend[22].

1484, June. Laurence Squier was prefented to a prebend, *vice* James Letes deceafed[23].

1484, Auguft. William Duffeld was prefented to the fourth prebend, *vice* John Billefdon deceafed[24].

1484, William Raulyns refigned the fourth prebend. William Villers was prefented to the third prebend, *vice* William Raulyns, Dec. 1484[25].

1484-5, Feb. Robert Morne was prefented to the fourth prebend, on the death of John Billefdon[26].

1492-3. Hugh Lovered refigned the twelfth prebend, by exchange, to William Ibbefton[27].

1495. Thomas Ridley refigned the fifth prebend.

1495, July 4. Edward Shuldham, LL. D. was prefented to the fifth prebend, *vice* Ridley[28].

1513, Thomas Wigfton[29] held the 13th prebend.

1534. ——— Wullock (fee p. 344.)

[1] Ricardus de Hampflap de Toneworth, prefbyter, primus decanus, prefentatus per Henricum ducem Lancaftrie, 9 kal. Apr. 1355; & 13 prebendarii fimiliter admiffi eodem die, quorum nomina regiftrantur in Reg. Gynewell, ep. Linc'.

[2] Magifter Joh' Porter, prefb', admiffus fecundus decanus ecclefie nove collegiate Beate Marie, Leyc', ad prefentationem Mathei de Afsheton & Johannis de Stafford nobilis domini, domine Matilde de Lancaftr' filie & heredis domini Henrici, nuper ducis Lancaftrie, defuncti, attornat', 7 id. Jan. 1361. Reg. Gynewell.   [3] See before, p. 303.

[4] See Appendix, p. 111; and vol. II. under Langton.   [5] See before, p. 331.   [6] See p. 332.

[7] Will' Dudley, elect' in decan' collegiat' ecclefie beate Marie, Leyc', per mortem magiftri Will' Witham, admiffus 17 Aug. 1472. Reg. Rotheram. He was afterward bifhop of Durham, 1476. See p. 333.

[8] Magifter Will' Chauntre, per prefidentem & capitulum ecclefie nove collegiate Beate Marie, Leyceftrie, in decanum ejufdem ecclefie, per refignationem magiftri Will' Dudley, electus, & per regem prefentatus; admiffus 20 Oct. 1476. Reg. Rotheram. W. Chauntre was appointed archdeacon of Derby in 1473. Browne Willis's Survey, vol. I. p. 421.

[9] Magifter Joh' Morgan ad decanatum ecclefie collegiate Novi Operis, Leyc', per mortem magiftri Willielmi Chauntre, ad prefentationem regis, Dec. 1485. Reg. Ruffel. See p. 333; and Wood, Athen. Oxon. vol. I. p. 647.

[10] Magifter Robertus Middleton, LL. D. canonicus ecclefie collegiate Novi Operis, Leyc', ac unus de duobus canonicis ejufdem collegii, in decanum ipfius collegii, per munus confecrationis domini Johannis Morgan, Menevenfis epifcopi, per capitulum ibidem domino regi Hen' VIII°, ipfius collegii racione ducatûs Lancaftrie fundatore & patrono, electus & nominatus, per eundem dominum regem prefentatus ad dictum decanatum, 5 Dec. 1496, admiffus. Reg. Smith.—He was prebendary of Norton Epifcopi in the cathedral church of Lincoln, 1474; and of Donnington in the cathedral of York, which he refigned in 1496.

[11] Magifter Will' Stokedale, S. T. D. prefbyter, prefentatus per regem ad decanatum collegii five ecclefie collegiate Novi Operis, Leyc', per mortem magiftri Roberti Middleton, 14 Jan. 1499. Reg. Smith.—William Stockdale is mentioned as proctor in 1477. Fuller's Hiftory of Cambridge, p. 84.

[12] Magifter Jacobus Whifton, decr' doctor, prefbyter, prefentatus per abbatem & conventum de Eynefham ad vicariam de Cherleburg, per refignationem domini Willielmi Welwyn, 1495 (Reg. Smith.); prefentatus per regem ad decanatum infra ecclefiam collegiatam Novi Operis juxta caftrum Leyceftrie, per mortem Johannis [Willielmi] Stokedale, 23 Nov. 1500. Ibid.

[13] See p. 335.   [14] Ibid.   [15] Reg. Langham, arch. Cant. fol. 28. a.   [16] Reg. Buckingham.

[17] 1424, 3 die Augufti, in prioratu de Landâ admifit d'nus Henricum Rofe capellanum ad feptimam prebendam infra novam ecclefiam collegiatam beate Marie Leiceftrie, Linc. diœc. ad prefentationem domine Katarine regine Anglie, matris regis Anglie & Francie, filie Caroli regis Francie, & d'ni Hibernie, vere ipfius prebende patrone. Reg. Chicheley, arch. Cant. pars 1. f. 243. a. b.

[18] 1424, 27 die Octobris recept. fuit certif. d'ni Thomæ Dunelm. ep'i, de & fuper exped. permutat. facte inter mag. Will. Aflakby rect. eccl. paroch. de Walton Lync. diœc. ac præbendarum præbendæ duodecimæ in eccl. nov. collegiatâ B. M. Leiceftriæ ejufdem diœc. dict. eccl. de Walton ad præfentat. d'ni H. regis Angliæ, &c. & dictam duodecimam præbendam ad præfentationem d'næ reginæ Angliæ, matris regis Angliæ & Franciæ, filie Karoli regis Franciæ & d'ni Hiberniæ, veræ, &c. Et Will. Broun, decanum eccl. collegiate de Langchiftre, Dunelm. diœc. Reg. Chicheley, pars 1. fol. 249. b. And fee Hutchinfon's Durham, vol. II. p. 357.   [19] Reg. Chicheley, arch. Cant. pars 1. fol. 259. a.

[20] Reg. Stafford & Kemp, fol. 107. a.   [21] Ibid.   [22] Reg. Rotheram. See p. 333.   [23] Appendix, p. 112.

[24] Harl. MSS. 433. p. 77. a.—William Duffeld occurs archdeacon of Stafford in 1497. Browne Willis, I. 415.

[25] Harl. MSS. 433. p. 87. b.   [26] Ibid. p. 97. b.   [27] Reg. Ruffel.   [28] Reg. Smith.

[29] He obtained the rectory of Houghton in 1534. See vol. II. p. 613.

Leland,

Leland, who vifited Leicefter whilft the church continued in full fplendour, fays in his " Collectanea [1]," Newark college has a revenue of £800. and confifts of 12 prebendaries, befides a dean and finging men." And in his " Itinerary" he thus defcribes it: " The collegiate chirch of Newarke, and the area of it, yoinith to another peace of the caftelle ground. The college chirch is not very great, but it is exceeding fair. There lyith on the North fide of the high altare Henry erle of Lancafter, withowt a creunet, and two men childern under the arche next to his hedde. On the Southe fide lyith Henry the firft duke of Lancafter; and yn the next arch to his hedde lyith a lady, by likelihod his wife. Conftance, doughtter to Peter, king of Caftelle, and wife to John of Gaunt, liith afore the high altare in a tumbe of marble, with an image of braffe (like a quene) on it. There is a tumbe of marble in the body of the quire. They told me that a countes of Darby [2] lay biried in it; and they make her, I wot not how, wife to John of Gaunt, or Henry the IV. Indeade Henry the IV. wille John of Gaunt livid was caullid erle of Darby. In the chapelle of St. Mary, on the Southe fide of the quire, ly buried to of the Shirleys, knights, with their wives; and one Brokefby, an efquier. Under a piller yn a chapelle of the South croffe ifle lyith the lady Hungreford, and Sacheverel her feeund hufbande [3]. In the Southe fide of the body of the chirch lyith one of the Bluntes, a knight, with his wife. And on the North fide of the church, ly 3 Wigeftons [4], greate benefactors to the college. One of them was a prebendarie there, and made the free grammar fchole. The cloifters ftanding on the South-wefte fide of the chirch is large and faire; and the houfes in the cumpace of the area of the college for the prebendaries be al very praty. The waulles and gates of the college be ftately. The riche cardinal of Winchefter [5] gildid all the floures and knottes in the voulte of the chirch. The large almofe houfe ftondith alfo withyn the quadrante of the area of the college [6]."

This church appears to have been demolifhed before the vifitation of Mr. Wyrley in 1590 [7]; who fays, " Henry Plantagenet firft duke of Lancafter founded a place called *The Newark* by the South gate of this town. This piece of building hath been commended by knights and fquires to have been the moft faireft that ever they had feen. By this abbey [college] the faid Henry founded a ftately hofpital, which yet remaineth. In it is a very fair and ftately monument of a lady, curioufly wrought, but of no note or mark [8]."

In this chapel alfo Mr. Wyrley defcribes thefe arms [9]:

9. Argent, a chevron between three mullets of fix points pierced Sable.

10. Barry of eight, Argent and Gules, eight martlets, 3. 2. 2. and 1. Sable.

11. Gules, three lions of *England*; a label of three points, each charged with as many fleurs de lis, Sable, *Lancafter*.

12. Gules, a fefs between fix martlets Argent.

13. Gules, three fifhes naiant in pale, Argent a bend Sable.

14. Argent, three leopards' heads jeffant Sable. *Sodington* [10].

15. Azure fretty Argent, *Cave*; impaling Gules, a faltire Vaire.

The Hofpital at that time continued under the patronage of the queen, in right of the dutchy of Lancafter; by her authority the wardens were appointed; and, by her grants, moft of the houfes and lands were transferred to the Corporation of Leicefter; with feveral fee-farm rents, amounting to 4l. 2s. 5d. belonging to the Newark, feven of which were from houfes fituated within that liberty, and others at Knighton, Carleton Curlew, Burton, Sileby, and Glenfield.

In the early part of James the Firft's reign, *William Fowkes* was mafter, or warden, under a regular patent, which he had the power of transferring; and accordingly fold it for 26l. 13s. 4d. to *Henry* earl of *Huntingdon*; who in 1609 offered it to the Corporation of Leicefter, upon condition that they would pay for it as much as he gave to Mr. Fowkes; which was agreed to at a meeting of the twenty-four aldermen, and twenty-four of the feniors of the company of 48, Feb. 19, 1609-10; and that fum was accordingly paid; and alfo, for charges of fuing out the fame in the name of the mayor, bailiffs, and burgeffes, 37l. 14s." [11]

At a common hall, March 28, 1610, it was agreed that the fee of 13l. 6s. 8d. due to the mafter of the hofpital in the Newark fhould yearly be paid to the ufe of the chamber; and that, as the poor in the houfe fhould die, one other poor perfon of the town to be chofen to fupply that room, by the mayor and twenty-four; and the poor of every parifh to be placed one parifh after another, a fpecial regard being had to the parifhes which had moft poor.

Feb. 7, 1613-14, they purchafed " The Grange near the borough of Leicefter, with the appurtenances, together with all lands, meadows, feedings, and pafturages, to the fame belonging, or ufually occupied; and the clofe called Gofling-croft, with the appurtenances, in the borough of Leicefter, and in the fields of Leicefter; the tack of cattle to be depaftured in the Cow-lees and South-fields of Leicefter; the water-mill called the Newark-mill; the holme called Goofe-holme, with the water; a tenement at the corner of the lane leading to the mill; the Land-fwanne; a meadow called Beed-houfe-mead; being 16 yard-lands [12] in the whole; with all and fingular the meffuages, mills, houfes, edifices, ftructures, barns, ftables, dove-houfes, orchards, gardens, fhops, cellars, lands, tenements, chapels, church-yards, meadows, feedings, pafturage, commons, waftes, void way, grounds lately briers, moors, marfhes, waters, fifheries, fifhings, woods, underwoods, trees, and all the land, ground and foil of the fame woods, underwoods, &c.; and all reverfions, mines, quarries, fervices, &c. parcel of the late College of the Newark;" all which had been given by the Crown to

[1] Vol. I. p. 74.
[2] This was Mary Bohun, firft wife of Henry IV, mother to king Henry V; who died before her hufband's acceffion to the crown; and who (Knighton, c. 2741, expreffly fays) was buried at Leicefter.—" Had Henry IV. died earl of Derby, it is probable he would have been buried among his anceftors in the collegiate church of their founding at Leicefter; fo that it is no improbable conclufion that his wife, who died countefs of Derby, was actually carried thither, to his family, rather than to her own, efpecially as the conjectures about her do not depofit her among any of her very near relations, if they were at all related to her." Gough's Sepulchral Monuments in Great Britain, vol. II. p. 35.—This is a fufficient confutation of Sandford's idea that fhe was buried in Canterbury cathedral, and that Henry, out of regard to her, chofe that church for his own fepulture, as well as of the appropriation of a figure in Hereford cathedral to her. Under the North window of the chapel of the prefent Hofpital remains a monument, which, in 1590, Mr. Wyrley notices as " a fair and ftately monument of a lady, curioufly wrought, but of no note or mark;" and which might be fuppofed to have belonged to this countefs, were it not that, as the college-church, which Leland defcribes, is certainly long fince demolifhed, we muft conclude the monument perifhed with it, and look for fome other appropriation of that in the chapel, which, being only the original *oratorium* of the Old Hofpital, gives a very inadequate reprefentation of the " not very great, but exceeding fair," collegiate church.
[3] Thoroton, in his Antiquities of Nottingham, p. 11, informs us that fir Richard Sacheverel, knight, whofe wife was lady Mary Hungerford, was here buried, 25 Hen. VIII. This lady, by her firft hufband, was mother to George earl of Huntingdon.
[4] In the chapel erected by William Wigfton for his chantry. The prebendary was Thomas, brother of William Wigfton, who made the free grammar-fchool, whence it appears that thefe Wigftons where all dead when Leland vifited Leicefter.
[5] Beaufort. [6] Leland's Itinerary, vol. I. p. 17. [7] MS notes in the College of Arms.
[8] This ftill remains on the North fide of the altar; and is engraved, Plate XXIX. fig. 7, 8. See it defcribed hereafter, p. 347.
[9] See Plate XXIX. fig. 9—15.
[10] The two coats, marked 13, 14, are elfewhere faid to be in the chapel of St. Andrew. See p. 322.
[11] Extracted by the Rev. Sam. Carte, vicar of St. Martin's, from the Corporation Records.
[12] They before poffeffed two yard-lands bought of Wightman in 1589, and two others bought of Archers in 1592. To thefe half a yard-land more was added in 1622, bought of Mr. Wadland, which completed the 20 yard-lands and a half enjoyed by the Corporation in the South Fields. Carte, MS.

I

Francis

Francis Morris and *Francis Philips*, and by them fold to fir *William Smith*, knight, of Leicefterfhire, and *Humphrey Smith*, citizen of London; from whom they were bought, in truft for the Corporation, by *Thomas Sacheverell, Robert Gilliott, James Andrew, Thomas Parker, William Ive*, and *Rowland Pufey*, all of the borough of Leicefter, gentlemen, for the fum of £1000. This purchafe, as it was a favourite one, appears alfo to have been fo beneficial to the Corporation, that they difpofed of feveral of their fee-farm rents to raife the money for it. They had bought in 1586, for £600. a moiety of a leafe then held of the faid Grange by *Francis Haftings*, efq. and in 1592 obtained for themfelves a reverfionary leafe of 31 years, on a referved rent of 32l. os. 6d.

They were foon after favoured by king James, through the mediation of their powerful friend the earl of Huntingdon, with letters patent of incorporation, under the title of " The Mafter, Affiftants, Chaplain, and Poor, of the Hofpital of the Holy Trinity in the Newark near the Borough-town of Leicefter, in the county of Leicefter, of the foundation of James I. king of England [1]."

See their common feal in Plate XXVIII. fig. 16.

In completing the purchafe of the Grange, and in foliciting new letters patent, the Corporation had much affiftance from Sir William Heyrick, as appears by the following original letters [2]:

1. " Right worfhipful; after our hartie commendations, with thanks for yo[r] love and great care of us and our Corporation: Underftandinge by yo[r] let[re] to your brother Mr. Robert Heyricke, that one Gibb [3], an almfman in o[r] Hofpital in the Newarke of Leicefter, hath exhibited a petition to the Kinge's Ma[tie], and of his Highnes reference thereof to oure honorable good frende Mr. Chancellor of the Duchie, and of his good likeinge thereof, for the incorporating of the fayde Hofpital: We have therefore thought fitt to fend upp this bearer, our lovinge friende Thomas Nurfe, to repaire to the fayde Gibb, and to knowe of him how farr he hath proceeded therein, and fully to acquainte you therewith; that, as his proceedinge therein hitherto may be to yo[r] good likinge, and likelie to be broughte to pafs, wee are therefore the boulder to intreate y[r] Worfhipp's good direction, and to advife with o[r] Recorder [4] howe to incorporate the fayde Hofpital; and that the Maior of our fayde borough (for the tyme beinge) and certen of his brethren (in the name of o[r] Corporation) maie for ever be maifters thereof (yf fo it maie be obtayned). Thus farr prefuming of y[r] Worfhipp[s] fav[r] and paynes in this fuite, wee commend you to the protection of the Almightie; and allwaies reft your verie loveinge frends,

Leicefter, the 17 daie of November, 1613.   THOMAS MANBIE, Maior. ROBART HEYRICKE. W[m] MORTON. JAMES ELLYS. JAMES ANDREWE. T. PARKER. Jo. FREAKE."

To the right worfhipfull Sir William Heyricke, knight, at London, bee theefe d'd."

2. " I muft neds confes that I am now far behind, not only for lettars, but allfo for matters which fholld have bene involved in them; and cheflly and efpefyally for youre great paynes and care, for youre good-will in oure towne bufynes, for which you have not only won Mr. Wadland and his copartnors that were with him; but allfo, by their meaynes and myne, making it knowne to the hole company, they will nevar forget youre payns and kyndnes. And for youre ordynary good will in feafting of the Hawfes, and Cytes, the Sanfords, the reft, with the Withringtons, and Douglaffis, and Parrees, all redounds to youre immortall

fame. And thoughe we will no whit imytate you, nor coom nere, we have celebrated the feaft of Natyvety in the beft fort we can. I had a fat doe fent me of the even; and when we had, acording to auntient cuftom, gon ovar all oure neabors and tennaunts; that being done, coomes ovar Mr. Samuell Clarke, parfon of Kingfthorp [5], two myle of this fyde Northampton, and mafter of the New Ofpytall called Wigfton's Ofpytall, and one Mr. Henry Clarke [6], his eeldar brother, who is Recordar of Rocheftar, and dwellethe there, a counfelar of the Temple, and by report a very good lawyer and a proper man. Thefe two came to fee my daughter Dorkas, and to afk my goodwill of her; Mr. Henry being procured by his brothar to take fo longe a journey at this tyme of the yeare, and had not tyme to ftay, but muft prefently return into Kent, and backe agayne to the tearme. Good lyking of all fides; for, if I fhall beftow her of a clergyman, I doe thinke, of his yeares, I fhall hardly fynd his equall in England; an excelent preacher, very wyffe, and lykly of great preferments. He is great with Sir Thomas Parry, my lord of London's chaplen, and in great favour with the Metropolytan. Yf you talke afar of anny tyme with Mr. Fanfhawe, he will tell you as moche of them as anny I know; and I pray you doe, and let me but here two woords after from you. And if you have ocafyne to ufe a lawyer, as I know you have, if you doo but make tryall of the faid Mr. Henry, I thinke you fhall fynd him to be learned and carfull of youre bufynes. And fo, comedyng all thes matters to Him that rulethe all, I feace to troble you furder at this tyme. Leicefter, the 12 of January, 1613-14.

Your ever loving brother,   ROBART HEYRICKE.
To the right worthy his loving brother, &c."

3. " After our hearty commendations; underftanding by Mr. Wadland of your great paynes and care of us to Sir William Smyth, in the purchafing of our Grange; for the w[ch] wee and o[r] wholl Corporation acknowledge o[r] felves much bounde unto you, and reft your debtor for your approved love towards us: foe fhall o[r] fucceedinge age have juft caufe to acknowledge the fame (althoughe the purchafe bee verie deare); earneftle intreatinge your advice and paynes once againe for the incorporatinge the Hofpital; and for the followinge of which bufines wee have fent up Mr. Wadlande, whoe will bee readie to attende you therin; and by him have fent unto Sir William Smyth the firfte five hundreth markes, and fecurytie for the reft, and x1l. in gold for the lady Smyth; but, in refpect of o[r] povertie at this tyme, yf you can content her with x l. wee fhall tak it as a greate kindnes, defireing yo[r] prefence when the affurance is to paffe unto us. And thus beinge (as wee have allwayes beene) bould to trouble you, wee comend y[u] to the protection of the Almightie; and allwayes reft your affured lovinge frendes,

Leicefter, 23 Jan. 1613-4.   THOMAS MANBY, Maior.
To Sir William Heyricke.   ROBART HEYRICKE."

4. " My ague would not fuffer me to wryte by the carryar, as I would have doone, to geve yow manny and harty thanks for your late kynde lettar and coppy therein of parchment; which we bothe doe unfaynedly give you great thanks for, and do acknowledge ourefellfes much bound unto you, and indepted to doe the like, or any thing ells for you that doth lye in our powers. I pray you, at youre convenyent leafure, let one fearch yf this be inroled anny wher, or whether it be a fecret bargon; which, if yt be inrolled, will, I think, appeare where the recognefencis were acknowledged. My good cofin Harvay is gone from my Lord, which I thought to let you underftand, and, as Mr. Haftings tells me, dothe re-

---

[1] Newark Hofpital. fundat. Leic. 1 Pars Original. 12 Jac. I. Rot. 76. This charter is in the Hofpital cheft.

[2] Communicated by John Herrick, Efq. of Beaumanor, from the originals preferved by his anceftor Sir William.   [3] See p 344.

[4] Francis Harvey, efq. of Northampton, a bencher of the Middle Temple, was then recorder. He was made a ferjeant at law in 1614; and a judge of the common pleas in 1624.

[5] Mr. Clarke was rector of St. Peter's in Northampton (of which Kingfthorpe is a chapel) from 1608 to 1640. See a farther account of him under Wigfton's Hofpital.

[6] Henry Clarke was a ferjeant at law; and a reprefentative in parliament for Rochefter in the firft year of the reign of Charles I. as was his fon fir Francis in the reigns of Charles II. and James II. and Francis the grandfon in the reign of William and Mary. Henry Clarke and his family are noticed in Harris's Kent (from Philipott's Villare), pp. 127. 324; and in Hafted's Kent, vol. II. pp. 238. 423.—Dugdale is the authority contained in the note in the latter page.

porte himfellfe to be worth £7000. Yt may be, that he may doe you as much plefure in fuche matters as you tolld me of as he collde before. Thus, with our kyndeft comēdacyons to my Lady and yourfelf doone, with defire of youre prayers to God for Mr. Mayor, who is in great daungar, and fell ficke yᵉ 23ᵈ of January even, as he was putting his hand to the bonds for fir Willyam Smyth's laft payments; we comēd you to God's bleffed proteftion. Leicefter, this 3ᵈ of Feb. 1613-4. Your loving brother, Ro. HEYRICKE."

5. " For the Parlement, we do heare that the writs be forthe ; and my Lord is not forgettfull of us, that we fholld not be unprovyded of burgeffes when the tyme farves. To that end he hath fent for Robart Hawford, and tolld him, that, before we fholld want, he woold provide his brother Geordg Haftings and Sir Henry Ritche [1]. I have fpoken with Mr. Maior, Mr. Morton, and foom of the chefeft, that they will thinke of fuche as be freemen, and well willars to Corporacyons, wherof I know you to be one; and alfo I put them in remembraunce of Mr. Recordar [2], which they colld not but think well of. So the matter ftays; and my defyre is that I may have your letter touchyng thys matter fo foon as may be, the rather yf you have anny intention to be one. Leicefter, the 22 of Feb. 1613-14. ROBART HEYRICKE."

6. " For the place of a burges, I went prefently into the chamber, and found Mr. Maior and Mr. Morton together; and told them that I had inftantly receayved a lettar from you, wherin you commended you kindly unto the Town; and told them that now I had receayved from you touching a burges' place, which before I had broke with them of; and red the lettar unto them. Then they bothe tolld me agayne of the meayns my Lord had made ; " but," fay they, " in anny cafe, we muft offar one place to Mr. Recordar ;" and yf he fhould refufe yt, as yt is thought he will, then I make no dout but yt is redy for you: but for my Lord's brother, Mr. Geordg Haftings," faythe Mr. Morton, " we may in no wife fay my Lord nay ; for he will," faythe he, menyng my Lord, " fpeke concerning the Ofpytall to the Chauncelar, to the Kinge, nay, if ther be caus, my Lord will moove the Parlement Hous." I replyd, on your advice, that you did advife them to take freemen; as by ftatute, I told them, we ought : but, yf they woold take anny not refyaunt or inhabeting within the Borow, then I told them that Mr. Recordar and you are both fworne men to the Towne, yourefelfe born and bred and fworn; fo that, yf Mr. Recordar fay nay, as I thinke he will, then I do not dout but one place is youres. I will not be unmyndfull of it; and let you knowe as foone we can procure the Recordar's anfwer. Leicefter, the 26 of February, 1613-4. Your loving brother, ROBART HEYRICKE."

7. " I have told Mr. Maior, that he fholld be fuaf to have lettars from the Chauncelor, which in the end are coom, and we colld not hellp yt ; for yet to this day we cannot get the precept from the fherive, which I thinke is helld away by fome pollefy : yet I have tolld our cheffe men that youre cytefens be chofen fuche a day, and othar places have done, as you wrote unto me. In the end, we have fent this day to Cotham [3], hoping to have Mr. Recordar there; fo this nyght we fhall knowe his mynde. And now my Lord wrytes that he hopes his brother fhal be one of the knyghts of the fhyre: but for Sir Henry Ritche he is very importunate, but I thinke Sir Henry will not put you by; but the voyce goes in oure hall, thatt yf Mr. Chauncelor be faid nay for Mr. Henry Faylton, then oure olld Ofpytall is quite gon ; fo that, you fee, manny heads, manny braynes. But fo foon as I can wryte anny fartenty, ethar I or no, you fhall be partaker, God willing, by the firft. And fo, with manny thanks for all your frendfhips, I end, fartefying you that our Recordar hath

now fayde nay. And now I think they will fend to my Lord, to fe yf he will be content to releafe us of Sir Henry Riche, which by no meanes we woold have yf we coold get his Ho. confent; and then it will coom to youre lot. But, fince I wrote this, we have met all oure company of 24 and 48 this afternone, being the 14 of this moonthe ; and thus concluded, that Robart Hawford muft go to-morrow in the morning to my Lorde, to entreat my Lord to nominate one, and that he will be plefed to let Mr. Chauncelor nomynat the the other. To-morrow at night we fhall know his mynd; and then by the caryar I hope to wryte furder to you; but you fe alredy how yt fall out. And fo, till the next, God have you in his keping. Leicefter, the 14 of March, 1613-14. ROBART HEYRICKE."

8. " My cofin Heyricke being fent from hence of Thurfday laft, with a letter to yourfealfe, and one other to Mr. Chauncelar, to fygnifye unto his Honor that we were all willing to grant his requeft, and withall to defyr him that Mr. Henry Faylton might prefently repayre to us to take his othe ; but, before Robert Heyricke cold be at London, we refayved a fecond lettar from Mr. Chauncellar, wherin he fignifyethe that Mr. Faylton's bufynefs is fouche that he cannot entende that farvis, but requyres that he may have the nominacyon of another gentellman, whom he greatly comēnds, but doeth not name him; and after his lettar wrytes a poftfkript, that, as we expeft any favor at his hand anny way, not to fay him nay in this his requeft; fo that I doe imagen that cofin Heyricke ftays the longar to bring the gentleman with him. Yf evar I live for to fee another parlement fummoned, and that you have intencyon to be one of the Hows, we will take no other courfe, but have you fpeake to Mr. Chauncellar to wryte but two lynes to oure Towne, that you may be one ; yt will be as fure as any ackt of parlement. To-morrow, being Thurfday, and our county day, our knights of the fhire are to be chofen betwyxt 8 and 9 of the cloke in the forenoon [4], and the farmon is to begin for the judges and juftefis affembled about the fame tyme; and the chardge to be given will not be long after, if it be not before. Leicefter, this 22 of March, 1613-14. ROBART HEYRICKE."

9. " Leicefter, the 13 of Aprill, 1614. Youre longexpeckted lettar I receayved of Sayturday laft, and one othar breefe one befydes; for which bothe, as for your good counfell therin to Mr. Maior and us, and for youre news allfo, I rendar all poffyble thankes. Thus hoping that till we may fe you we may fometymes heare from you, I end, and comēd you to the bleffed proteftion of the Allmyghty, who kepe you, and defend you in your journey from evells. My comēdacyons, my wyfe's and doughter's, to yourfelfe and my Lady doon, I doe leave you to the fafe kepeng of the Lord Jefus. ROBART HEYRICKE."

10. " I muft not forget to geve you thanks, from Mr Maior and us all, for all your former care and paynes for our Towne cawfes; and to entreate your furder favour, if Mr. Wadland doe defyre it, to bring him once acquainted with Mr. Chauncelor, Sir Danniell Day, or anny other burgefis, or others that may doe him good in his fute for the incorporating of the Ofpytall. The Lord be with you! Leicefter, the 10 of May, 1614. ROBART HEYRICKE."

11. " Towchyng the New-woorke myles, there is no fuche forwardnes in fellyng of them as Tō Stamford tolld you; but fince we are fo far in dept, that I feare we fhall be conftrained in the end ethar to part with them, or foom othar good thinge: but affure yourfelfe, that nethar the myles nor no fuche thinge fhall goe, but you fhal be pryve to yt in tyme; and well woorthy, for we fhall have non that will offar no fuche kyndnes as you doe. Leicefter, the 24 of May, 1614. Your loving brother, ROBART HEYRICKE."

---

* Second fon to Robert earl of Warwick. He was one of the burgeffes for Leicefter in 1608 and 1613; made knight of the Bath in 1610; created lord Kenfington in 1622, and earl of Holland in 1624; and, for his loyalty to king Charles, was beheaded March 9, 1648-9.
² Mr. Harvey; fee p. 340. ³ In Nottinghamfhire, the family-feat of the Markhams.
⁴ Sir Henry Rich and Sir Francis Leigh were elefted burgeffes for Leicefter in March, 1613-14.

12. " I and all the reſt moſt hartely thanke you for youre greate paynes. I went to Mr. Mayor, and willed him to ſend for foom half doffin or more of the eeldors; which preſently he did, and met them at the hall; but yt was 9 of the cloke or we colld mete: and at oure meeting we received likewiſe two ſeverall lettars from Mr. Wadland, wherin he ſignefyethe the greate care and paynes you have taken for the Towne; and requireth that Robart Hauford may coom up with ſpeede; which preſently we thought neceffary to doe: and therefore we have ſent him with ſuch a coppy of an order forth of the Duchye, which ſhewes that the Duke did founde the Oſpitall for the relefe of 110 perſons to be taken out of the towne and county of Leiceſter, and with ſuch other inſtrucktions as we colld for the fooden furnyſhe him; deſyring of God, yf yt be his good pleaſure, that we may enjoy the Oſpytall here during the King's good pleſhure; and the incorporating to reſt till we have more monney and fewer ennemyes. Thus concluding at xi of the clocke this Fryday nyght, being the 27 of May, 1614; praying to God longe to contynnew you, to his glory and your heart's deſire. Ro. Heyricke."

13. " I thanke you, and ſo we doe, and have all good cares, for your greate care and paynes you have taken for oure Towne buſynes; which though we cannot, yet I hope God will reward you for it. Leiceſtar, 9 June, 1614. Robart Heyricke."

14. " Right worſhipful; after our great thanks for your great paines and all your kindenes, theiſe are to certifie you, that wee have over-intreated Mr. Sacheverill to come up in our behalfe about our ſuite concerninge the Olde Hoſpital, to doe what he cann therein for a while, until Mr. Wadland ſhall come up. We weare the more importunate with him to undertake this journey, for that (for his knowledge of the wholl buſines, and his experience in Hoſpital matters) wee thought him as likelie at this tyme to doe good therein as any other that wee could have gotten. And therefore wee pray that you will take the paines to goe wth him to Mr. Moſeley ſo ſoone as you maie, and to make him knowne unto him to be the man whom wee have deſired to repayre unto his Worſhipp about our ſuite; and as touching the meſſage which he ſent to us by our Towne-clarke, that Mr. James Andrew is the man whom wee deſire and thinke the fitteſt to be named in the booke for the firſt man, if one particular perſon muſt be named therein; and if the general name of ' The Mayor and Aldermen of the Borough of Leiceſter for the tyme beinge' maie not ſerve in this caſe. And ſo intreatinge earneſtly the contynuence of y^r love, notwithſtanding the tediouſneſs of the ſuite, wee commend you, by our prayers, unto the rich rewarding of him that pitied Ninivi.
Your worp$^{p's}$ much bounden to be commanded,
Thomas Manbie, Mai^r. James Andrew.
William Morton. Thomas Parker.
Leiceſter, 23 June, 1614."

15. " Right worſhipfull; underſtanding by our good friends Mr. Sacheverill and Mr. Wadland of your greate paines, travell, and good endeavours, to many perſons, and ſeveral places, in the behalfe of our poor Towne, concerninge our Hoſpital; for the which we acknowledge ourſelves muche beholdinge unto you, not onlie in this, but for dyvers other your lovinge fauours done unto us and our wholl Corporation, hartilye deſiringe the contynuance of your kinde favours towards us and our poore Town; for, upon yourſelfe wee and our wholl Corporation are bound whollie to relye, without which we know not what might befall us: Wee have ſent by this bearer, Mr. Chamblin Heyrike, to paie unto Sr Wm Smyth the five hundred marks due upon Saturdaie nexte, beinge the ſeconde paiement for our Graunge, which wee purchaſed by your good meanes of him. Thus beinge, as wee have allwaies been, trobleſome, wee commende you to the protection of the Allmightie; and ever reſt your Worſhipp's aſſured frends,
" Leiceſter, 2 Aug. 1614. Thomas Manbie, Maior.
To the right worſhipfull Robart Heyricke.
our eſpeciall good frende William Morton.
Sr Wm Heyricke, knight. John Freake."

16. " I colld wiſhe that for the Oſpital mattar, you might grow to an end with yt, that, yf the pencyon will not willingly be confirmed, yt myght be ended without yt, yt is ſo trobleſoom to you, and will be chardgable to the Toune; and lingring brede delays. 1 thank you for all your newes contayned in all your papers; as alſo for the copy of the Sarmon; and the rather for that yt is, I parſayve, my godſon's doing. I pray God bles him, and make him a good man. Leiceſtar, the 7 of Novembre, 1614.
Your faythfull and loving brother, Ro. Heyricke."

17. " For the Oſpytall byſynes, we are all bound unto you; and for the cup you have given to Mr. Attorney, I pray you wryte unto me in your next what it coſt. And looke, what yt was under £10. I will gev it them agayne; for, they are pore and nedy; and ſhortly, God ſo willing, I hope Mr. Wadland will coom, and take ſoom of the burden from you. Leiceſtar, the 2 of January, 1614-15. Ro. Heyricke."

18. " Sir, my duty firſt done, and my harty thanks premiſed for all your kindneſſes; theſe are only to informe you touching £100. which my father hath undertaken ſhall be readie in your hand towards the laſt payment (that our Toune is to make) unto Sir William Smith, which is to be about the 5 or 6 of February at the furtheſt. So it is, that that £100. myſelf and divers of my frends here have it made up amongſt us, to be lent to the Toune after the rate of £8. in the 100; and that 8 alſo is alreadie determined to be beſtowed and given to a certeine godly uſe here within this Towne. But we are deſirous, for good reaſons, to have the money lent in my brother Stringer's name, that dwellith by Aburgany houſe a little above Ludgate, who hath promiſed to repaye it of his oune money after a whyle, yf all things fall out with his mynde. And therefore theſe are to pray ycu to let him have yt, yf he come to you for it, to pay it himſelfe to them that are to make the payment to Sir W. Smith for the Towne, to the end to take away all ſuſpicion that the money is not his. But if he doe not come to you for it (as I thinke rather that he cannot conveniently by reaſon of his gowte), then I pray you ſo to order the matter (when you are to paye it to them that ſhall come for the Towne) as that it may not be knowne nor ſuſpected otherwiſe but that he hath left it in your hands readie for the Townes uſe aforeſayd, as I had intreated him, and as he had promiſed me that he would doe; and ſo you to receive the Town's bond over to him for the money when you deliver the mony, yf you have not either word before that tyme that the bond is otherwiſe delivered, either to himſelf, or to ſome other to his uſe. And of this my requeſt for ſecrecye I pray you to have care, to keepe me as free from ſuſpicion or knowledge as is poſſible, becauſe the knowledge of it in our Towne would bring upon me many ſuits and inconveniences for my love to the Towne, that moved me chiefely to this action, to ſave them forty ſhillings a year, their chardg of intereſt; beſides that the example of it hath brought doune alreadye ſundry others of their creditours to 8 and to 9 in the 100. And thus craving pardon for my bouldnes in being ſo trobleſome unto you, with my harty prayers both for yourſelf, my Lady, and your whole family, I take my leave. Leiceſter, the 24 of Januarie. Your much indetted kinſman, Thomas Sacheverill."

19. " According to your deſyre, here was a ſarmon preached in the New-worke, on Monday the 20th of May, by Mr. Sacheverill. His text was out of Matthew the xxvth; *When I was hungry, you gave me meate.* And he did not only learnedly, but alſo zelouſly, handele the ſame. There was warnynge given to bothe our companys to mete Mr. Maior at the Hall at ix of the cloke, and ſo to go downe with him to the Oſpytall; which we did, and had a tilt ſet up agaynſt the wall of the Oſpytall alonge the chauncell, and foorms next to the wall for the bettar ſort, and divers other before them toward the long alley, where at the ſyde of the alley the pulpit ſtoude. His voyce was very well harde, and yt helld fayre all the day without rayne. But the old ſaying is, where God

5 buyllds

buylds his Chirche, the Devil will build his Chappell; for, by what meayns I will not fay, but all them of the New-work abfented themfelves; and all the gentlemen in the Town, not one of them there only Mr. Wadland. And yet there was gathered, at the coming forthe of the New-worke gate, 5l. 12s. which made them 12d. apiece; which was prefently diftributed amongft them. In the mydft of the farmon comes one of Sir Henry's men to Sergeaunt Befwicke, and bad him tell Mr. Maior, that my Lady fent him word that Sir Henry was not well, and that he fhould not carry up his mace as he went forth of the New-work; notwithftanding, he did carry it. Sir Henry hath got a ftomake againft Mr. Maior, and fekes to be revenged by any meaynes he may. As God woolld, we had fent to the bifhop of Lincoln for his allowance, that by good hap we had under his hand; that, if we had not, they would furely have complayned prayfently to him. Thus much I thought good to fignifye unto you for the prefent, and more as occafion farves. Leicefter, this 22d of May, 1616.

Your loving brother, ROBART HEYRICKE."

20. "Right worfhipfull; the point I would now inform you of is, about all our gentryes and the men of Newark's abfence from the late Sermon; whereas (to have it done with good-will of all parts) we had not only gotten our Bifhop's allowance under his own hand, but alfo Sir Henry Haftings and the Doctor Chip [1] had granted us their good-will. But it feemed they did after repent, partly uppon fir H. falling out into bitter words with Mr. Maior, and partly being urged thereunto by Sherman, &c. whom it grieved to fee the Towne (as it weare) there, in that place, about the which he had received the overthrow; and therefore they drew that meeting into the quarrel about the jurifdiction of the Newark, &c.; informing that word was fent to Mr. Maior in the fermon-tyme (by an old Lady's man dwelling nere, and in her name), that he fhould not let his mace be borne up as he fhould goe home; and Sir Henry being fick that day, and pleading that he would have bene there yf he had been well, yet he did that afternoone fend word to Mr. Maior that he did take offence at his carrying up his mace; and it is out of doubt that there would not have been fo generall an abfence, but uppon their knowledge of his mynde to have it fo: but Sherman and his fonn Hemings were abroad openly at that tyme, that all might fee that they did refufe to come. Now the doeings about the Sermon hath increafed the difpleafure and hart-burnings againft Mr. Maior; and in lykelyhood may provoke him to doe the more agaynft him or his Towne by way of certificate into the Dutchy. And fo, craving pardon for my tedioufnes, I take my leave. June 11, 1616. Your worp's much bounden, THOMAS SACHEVERILL."

21. "Right worfhipfull; the greate love we have foe often found in you heretofore towards our Towne doeth make us the more boulde to requeft your helpe nowe againe allfoe at this tyme; and it is onelie that you would be pleafed to goe with Mr. Wadland to Mr. Attorney of the Duchie, for the deliveringe of a letter of ours unto him, and to intreate his lawfull favour towards us in the matters conteyned in that letter, the particulars whereof we leave unto Mr. Wadland's relation. And foe, with due thanks for all your kindneffes, wee doe moft hartilie commende yourfelfe and all yours into the Almighties gracious protection; reftinge, both now and evere,

Your worfhippes in all love to be commanded,
WILL. IVE, Maior. JAMES ELLICE.
ROBART HEYRICKE. JAMES ANDREWE.
WILLIAM MORTON. THO. PARKER.
Leicefter, the eleaventh of June, 1616."

22. "I marvel you did not wryte of the death of fir Thomas Parry [2]; but, though God have taken him away, yet I doubt not but he hathe provyded a bettar for us, and the rather by your good helpe, which as we have hertofore fully founde, fo, for the good of your pore natyfe toune, I pray you let us ftill retayne. I know Mr. Maior hathe wrytten to you, but yet it is not coom to my hand for my hand; but yt will. We have great neede of your helpe agayne, though we have made fmall recompence for all your former paynes and chardges. Our nebors in the Newarke, as I am enformed, make great brags, that they will wreft the Mafterfhip from us; and that bufy fellow Gibb [3] is turned from us, and making fute to Mr. Attorney; and fays, that yf he cannot fynde his favor, he will go to the Kinge. Yf you colld tell how to have him, I thinke he wolld tell you his greeffe. Leicefter, the 12 of June, 1616. ROBART HEYRICKE."

23. "Sir, the Sermone on Monday was not fo profperous, but in the afternoone we did meete with as great croffing, and efpecially two wayes. Firft, by the under-clerke Mr. Baylie, that had Gibb's booke to engroffe; who firft to Mr. Attorney did oppofe himfelf as a great frend on the other fide, by alledging that our warrant tended to the difinheriting of the King, to the excluding of the country-poore out of the Hofpitall: that it was contrary to his former warrants, in which cafe they were to wayte for the King's owne refolution; that Mr. Dackombe [4] was ignorant what had bene done before in the cafe; that they muft alter all the booke if it was drawne, and in effect make a new; and that the perpetuity to the Mayor and his fucceffors would never paffe, when the King fhould be tould what hurt he fhould do to himfelf; and yf yt did paffe (unleffe we had the better counfell to draw the booke anew for the purpofe) the patent would be overthrowne agayne as unfufficient within one yere. Secondly, Mr. Attorney himfelf was much dafhed with the aforefaid fpeaches; but more, when he founde his owne unability to alter and reforme the paper book according to our warrant in fundry refpects, and namely to bring in handfomely the affiftants that be added to the Maior, and to joyne the particular perfon and the Maior and his fucceffors in one booke; whereuppon he was readie to caft off all, and to have put us to get a new warrant, or els the booke to be new drawne, by fuch as had fkill and leafure to doe it, at our coft. At length we were glad to offer to be content to paffe with the particular perfon only; and to have Tho. Manby nominated and fet downe (in the blank left in the book) for the Mafter uppon whom the Hofpital fhold be incorperated; which Mr. Attorney did himfelf put into their paper booke, and fent it fo by his man to Mr. Bailey; who feemeth unwilling to do it, alledging that he is loath to give us the benefit of their booke; but, we offering him to pay him well for our coppye and what he fhall doe for us, he fayd he would confeder of it; and if he did it, he could not poffibly do it before the next weeke. Now the cafe being fo, that yf Baily will not be brought to doe it thus, then we muft pafs untill we have procured a new booke to be drawn, which we fhall hardly get downe in hafte. 2. If Bayly will

---

[1] John Chippindale, doctor of the Civil Law, and commiffary to the bifhop of Lincoln.

[2] Chancellor of the dutchy of Lancafter.

[3] "Brother and Sifter, my hartie commendations to you, and my wife's. Concernyng the letter I receyved of you laft, they faie it is all of my owne doinge, becaufe I beare fome mallis againft the towne; therefore I woulde wifh you to gett fir Henrie Haftings good will, and to drawe a petition, and gett the juftices hands to it of your owne eftate; for, I have certified Mr. Attorney that I will complaine to the Kinge if I maie not have remedie for it. As for the howfe you fhoulde builde me, if Mr. Maior will not give waie, let it alone till I come home. And, I praye you, haft up the retorne of your commiffion, and labour with the juftices to gett too there hands concernynge your booke of orders for placynge of the countrie people; for, there is greate bragge made of there S'mon, that they are foe much goode to you, which the countrie woulde never doe the like. And foe I leave you all this tyme, committinge you to God. Your loving brother JOHN GIBB, to his power.
This to be delivered to William Hyde, at the olde Hofpital."
It is not unlikely that this was the fame John Gib, a Scotchman, who was an old fervant of king James, and of whom Wilfon, in his Life of that Monarch, p. 219, records a remarkable anecdote, of his being kicked by the King, who afterwards, finding that he had been in an error, knelt down to entreat Gib's pardon.

[4] John Dackombe, efq. Chancellor of the Dutchy of Lancafter, was knighted Aug. 31, 1616.

doe it, yet it will not be in fuch haft but our adverfaryes will have their full tyme to croffe us both with the King and with Mr. Attorney Generall if they can, and the hazard of lofing all our chardge of all the fees before it cometh to paffe the King's hand. I am in great doubt wheather it be not beft to leave our earneft fute for the drawing or making ready of our booke untill the King hath been at Leicefter [1], and we perceeve how the bufines will prove; and now only to labour to make fure to them of their booke; for we weare better (yf fo it might be) that we fhould continue to hold it, as we doe by the patents we have, *durante beneplacito*; but that we cannot doe, if the incorporating goe forward; which yf the King refolve that it fhall, then it will lye in this queftion, wheather the warrant we have, and our meanes to mayntaine it, will kepe them from obtaining a new warrant for Cave from the King; or be able to ftay fome of the neceffary warrants of the three under-officers (that muft make readie this booke, and allow it with their hands before it be offered to his Majeftie) from fuffering them to have their booke ingroffed with a blanke; for either want of a new warrant from the King, or the fure ftanding of either the fheref (or of either of the Atturnes for us uppon pretenfe of our warrant), will keepe them from proceeding; and then either Cave may give over in difpayer, or Gibb may be glad to agree to this, or uppon fome particular perfon that we like of, if the incorporation go forward, or the King may conclude of them. Or at leaft we fhall fee (after the brunt is paft) what is beft for us to doe, better than now, and not hazard all out fo much chardges. Now, the cafe ftanding thus, Mr. Wadland is wonderfully defirous to be gone hence on Thurfday in the morning fo early as to be at Leicefter on Friday at night; and therefore I would intreat you (if you may poffibly) that you would be at London, and fpeak with him, on Wenfday at night, to confer and conclude with him on the premiffes. He will leave his man Edward here, after he is gone himfelf, three weekes, to doe any good that he can in the matter, which will be almoft as much as his mafter. And fo, craving pardon for my tedious fcribbling, with my dutie to my Ladie, I commend yourfelf, fhe, and all yours, unto the fafe keping of the great Lord Keeper of Ifrael. London, this Thurfday in the morning [June .... 1616]. Your moft affured, to his uttermoft power, THOMAS SACHEVERILL.

" Since I did underftand of Bailyes mafter, Mr. Corat, that Baily tould him abfolutely that he would not make their booke readie for us; whereuppon going to Mr. Chauncelor with our warrant, I requefted his commandment to Mr. Baily, written uppon our warrant, by his kinfman Mr. Edward Thomas (to whom you fpake), who did go with me to Baily; who fayd that he had delivered Gibb the paper booke agayne now this morning, peremptorily denying to put in our name in their boke, as ackting verry unreafonable. But, through Mr. Thomas his perfuafion, he hath promifed to draw one for us after to-morrow; having before alledged that he did affure himfelf Gibb would get a contrary warrant before we fhould be able to bring ours to be figned by the King, and fo we fhould lofe a great deal more chardges. Yet we thought good to let there be at leaft a paper booke drawne for us, that fo we may come by a coppy, which otherwife we know not how to get. I have met Gibb twife to-day; at firft ftarke mad; the latter tyme he came to more temper than the former; he was going to Mr. Dackombe's, to have wyled there, but founde him not at home; and fince, it feemeth, he was with Sir Roger, who, he faith, will meet with Dackombe, and Gibb faith he is his elder brother.
To the right worfhipfull Sir William Heirick, knight, at Richmond, with fpeede."

24. " After a million of hartye thanks from us all; thefe are only to fignifie unto you two things by occafion of your laft letter directed unto me. The former, that (the matter having bene in that danger which you write of) we feare leaft the fame occafion that made him fo willing to have given it over, may mak

him ftill (and now in your fo long abfence from him) leffe willing to effect the bufines, or even to neglect it and to doe nothing in it. And therefore we thinke that it would be a happye thing for us, yf your affayres might permitt you to be here (in the manner you have follicited him in that matter) where the King fhal be here; and that our wifh for your prefence here at that tyme may be alfo the more by reafon of Mr. Sherman's geafts lyeing (as you write) at his houfe. The other matter is, that I perceave that a wrong information is given unto Mr. Dackombe touching the fumme of the whole pencion payed to the Hofpitall in former tymes; which is not £255. as you write, but only 238*l*. 8*s*. 8*d*. I dare fay uppon myne owne certeine knowledge. There be indeed two other pencions (the one myne of £10. and the other Mr. Rudiard's of £6. a yere), both making up £16. which with the 238*l*. 8*s*. 8*d*. doeth make a fumme nere to £255. And hence (I think) it came, that Gibb did informe you of that fumme; becaufe both he and Mr. Sherman have fought by this meanes to get our fayd pencions away from us (as well as the mafterfhip of the Hofpitall from the Maior), even by getting the King's grant of them to the Hofpitall in ppetuity; which you know will make voyde our patents, that be only *durante beneplacito*. But, as I knew you would not be any meanes to further them in hurting of us; fo I affure you, that it hath caufed a wrong information to be given to Mr. Dackombe; for, 1. neither of the fayd pencions be any of the Hofpitall payments; but both of them are altogeather and mearely arifing out of the diffolved Church of New-ark, without refpect of the Hofpitall; at the diffolution of which Church and Colledge, when the pfons (that before had their livings in it) wear all put to their pencions for their lives, in lieu and confideration of their livings (there being therein two companyes), the Canons weare allowed £10. apiece, and the other company (which weare called Vickars) weare allowed £6. apiece. Now my pencion was originally one Wullock's pencion, who was one of the Canons of Newarke; and Mr. Rudiard's £6. was one of the Vicker's pencions, namely, old Parfon Heathcot's of Elfton, untill within 16 yeres agoo, when Mr. Rudiard fucceded him, and gott it to be newly put into his patent (as the confideration wherefore the King fhould pay it to him) that he fhould adminifter the communion in the Hofpital for it. But for my pencion of the £10. (after the firft Canon that had it for his life, uppo the confideration of his living which he loft by the diffolution of the church in the 2 of Edw. VI.) the next that had it had it given him to pray in the Towne of Leicefter (without any mention of the Hofpitall), and that becaufe the Towne was a parcell of the Dutchye, whence the fayd pencion is payed; and becaufe they loft (by the diffolution of the fayd Church of Newark) that preaching which the Towne did enjoy by it when it ftode. And with that exprefs cofideration alone (to pray in the Towne of Leicefter as parcell of the Dutchie) the Preachers of Leicefter from tyme to tyme have had it expreffed in their patents. So that (as it is moft certeine that neither it nor Mr. Rudiard's £6. be any part of the Hofpitall's whole pencion or payments; but of another nature, meerly and exprefsly arifing out of the Church, as it is a diftinct thyng from the Hofpitall, and the Hofpitall from it,) fo it maketh it to be an untruth (that canot be truly affirmed or faid) that fo much as £255. hath beene payed fince Edwarde the Seconde tyme, or fro the firft founding of the fayd Hofpitall, becaufe the two pencions of £10. and £6. have beene payed but fince Edward the VI. his tyme, and not as Hofpitall payments at all, but for other refpects and cofiderations. And therefore (yf I finde oportunity) I will make Mr. Dackombe to be better informed in the poynts of the true fuffes of all the Hofpitall payments, when he paffeth by us. But Gibb's meaning in that muft be good, becaufe he doeth well know the difference, and did in playne termes pmife me not to meddle at all with our two pencions; and did himfelf tell me that he knew the whole Hofpitall pay to be but 238*l*. 8*s*. 8*d*. I pray God, therefore, that he doe carry a truer meaning to the Towne than he doeth unto

[1] The King vifited Leicefter in 1612, 1614, and 1616. See vol. II. p. 627.

us;

us; for I doe heare by one in fecret, that Mr. Loveden hath written to Mr. Sherman this laſt weeke that there is ſome hope to get Mr. Dackombe (our frend) out of the buſines, by reaſon we pforme not with him; and therefore I thinke Mr. Loveden did heare by Gibb of that alteration in Mr. Dackombe which you founde, and did reporte in your laſt letter. What is to be conjectured thereby, I leave unto youreſelf. And ſo, wiſhing that (touching your coming) which I dare not requeſt, I take leave, with my dewtyfull remẽbrance of my Ladie, and moſt hartye prayers for yourſelf and all that is yours. Your W. much boundẽ and to be cõmanded, THOMAS SACHEVERILL. Leiceſter, the 9th of Auguſt, 1616."

25. " Right worſhipfull; after our hartieſt commendacõns, with thanks for yorkinde remembrance unto us in yor letter concernynge Mr. Dackombe, the new Chauncellar of the Duchie, ſince whych tyme we have not bene unmindful; and nowe have ſent upp this bearer, Roger Cotes, one of or Chamberlins, unto yu, that, by yr Worſhipp's directions, he may provide a ſilver and gilte cupp with a cover, as to yr diſcretion ſhal be thought fitt; deſiring yu to cõmende the ſayde cuppe to Mr. Chauncellar, as a ſmall taſt of our faithfull love and true affection towards him, with much deſire of contynuance of his honble love and favour towards our poore towne, being one of the moſt auncient townes in all the wholl Duchie. Thus beinge (as wee allwaies have been) bold to trouble you, wee cõmend you to the protection of the Allmightie; and allwaies reſt your Worpp's verie lovinge freinds,

" To the right worſhipfull our verie lovinge frend Sir William Heyricke, knight, bee theſe d'd.

" Leiceſter, this laſt of June, 1616."

WILL. IVE, Maior.
ROBART HEYRICKE.
W. MORTON.
JAMES ELLIS.
JAMES ANDREWE.
THOMAS PARKER.
THOMAS MANBIE."

26. " Towchyng the cup which you wrote of for Mr. Chauncellar, I red your letter to Mr. Maior; and though we be in poor eſtate, yet they geve you great thanks for your care of us, and are very willing to perfourm yt you doe think well of; and to that end have partly ſent up this bringer, Mr. Chamberlin Cotes, who, I pray you, in anny caſe let him be with you at the delyvery, as though he brought it of purpoſe from Leiceſtar. Thus, with my kyndeſt love to youreſelfe and my Lady, I end; cõmending you both, with all yours, to the bleſſed protection of the Allmighty. Leiceſter, this 1 of July, 1616.
Your loving brother, ROBART HEYRICKE."

27. After many harty thanks; firſt unto God, for directing and proſpering your endeavours ſo happily as he hath; and next unto yourſelf, for your ſo great pains and care taken in the behalf of this Hoſpital; theſe are only at this time to certifye you, in caſe you have not already reſolved about the form of the badge, that my father and I do both think that a little roume would do well for that purpoſe, as fit to ſignifye that this King is their ſecond friend [1]. But for the ſeale [2] and the badge both, wee ſhall be the better able to give advice, if there be neede, after we have ſeen the device, and you wryte that you will ſend it hither by the next fit meſſenger; for then it will be time enough, becauſe neither of them do neede ſo much haſte but that you may well allow yourſelf time enough before you reſolve of them. And ſo I ceaſe to trouble you any further at this time; with my humble duty to my Lady, and my harty prayers for yourſelf and all yours. Leiceſter, the 7th of January. Your worſhip's much beholden, and ready to be cõmanded, THOMAS SACHEVERILL."

28. " Right worſhippfull; may yt pleaſe you to underſtande, wee, whoſe names are underwritten, are bould both to crave your advice, and to acquaint you with a grievance which not onely ourſelves but many others doe undergoe. Soe yt is: yt hath pleaſed his Majeſtie, both by his publique proclamation beareinge date the 24th of March, 1618, and by his gratious

letters pattents beareinge date the 29th of March, 1617, to ſignifie his Highnes pleaſure, that the ſtaple for wool and woolfells ſhould be removed from beyond the ſeas, and that from thenceforth the ſtaple ſhould be houlden at certeine citties and townes in the ſaid proclamation and pattent mentioned: and for that there was not a ſufficient number of merchants in thoſe places to meinteine the ſaid ſtaple, and by reaſon of a pattent graunted to the right honourable Lord Fenton, with power to nominate 200 men to bee free merchants of the ſtaple, diverſe of his Majeſtie's ſubjects that have uſed tradeinge in wools (for the better meintenaunce of themſelves and families) have not onely been drawne to buie their freedomes with great ſummes of mony, namely 1111 l. the man, to the utter undoeinge of many of them, but alſo have taken corporall oath to be juſticiable to the Companie of Merchants, and to dee nothinge that may be derogative or hurtfull to the generalitie of the ſaid Staple. Yet, notwithſtandinge theſe paſſages, wee heare that the pattent either is, or like to be, called in queſtion; which gives cauſe to feare that wee ſhall both loſe our monies and priviledge, except yt pleaſe the honourable Courte of Parliament to releive us, by takinge order that wee ſhall either have our monies repayd us, or our freedome continued, which ſhall ſeeme beſt to their wiſedomes. Nowe our humble ſuite to your Worſhip is, yf you would be pleaſed to adviſe us, whether wee ſhould exhibitt a bill for this grieveance into the Parliament-houſe or not; or, if there be one alreadie preferred by any others, then that yt would pleaſe you to be meanes for us of Leiceſter, that we may fare as others do.

Soe ſhall wee ever pray for your Worſhip's proſperous ſucceſſe; and reſt, ever at your ſervice,
" To the right worſhipful Sir NICHOLAS GILLIOT.
William Heiricke, knight, JAMES ELLIS.
Burgeſſe for the Burrough RIC. INGE."
of Leiceſter, give theſe. Leiceſter, April 29, 1621."

In 1647, when the parliament ſeized the revenues of the crown, the poor of Trinity Hoſpital were included in the wreck. But the Corporation of Leiceſter (who, greatly to their honour, have ever been conſiderable benefactors ſince they firſt held the wardenſhip,) laudably appropriated a portion of their own inheritance towards their maintenance, till the year 1650, when the following fee-farm rents were granted by Parliament to truſtees, and by them aſſigned to the mayor of Leiceſter and his aſſiſtants, maſters of the old Hoſpital in the Newark, for paying the poor people in the ſaid Hoſpital for ever:

	£.	s.	d.
Out of the fee-farm rents of the manor of Earl Shilton —	1	1	10
Out of 38 meſſuages, half a yardland, and one fourth of cuſtomary lands and parcels of demeſne lands and meadows, and ſix half-yard lands called Deer lands, and 172 acres of demeſne lands	18	12	8¼
Out of the increaſe of the cuſtomary and demeſne lands —	0	11	6
Out of hens and eggs payable by tenants in Shilton and Elmeſthorpe,	0	16	0¼
Out of cottages in Shilton —	5	19	3¼
Out of Conygree-cloſe in Shilton, and 14 acres called Smith Waſt, and out of the warren, and Shilton Halby wood, and the fiſhing — — —	4	6	9
Shilton milne — —	2	7	4
The fee-farm rent of Tooley Park, containing 578 acres — —	40	0	0
The fee-farm rent of the manor of Hinckley — — —	24	3	7½
Hinckley wood — — —	3	5	0
The fee-farm rent of the manor of Foxton — — — —	4	9	2¼
The fee-farm rent of the manor of Stapleford — — -—	23	6	8
The fee-farm of the manor of Eaſt Langton — — —	9	7	3
The fee-farm for the horſe-milne and two tenements in the town of Leiceſter	4	3	4

[1] See the inſcription here alluded to in p. 348.

[2] The ſeal is noticed in p. 340.

[4 U]

The

	£.	s.	d.
The fee farm of the lands, tenements, meadows, and paſtures, of the late hoſpital of St. John Baptiſt and St. Leonard, granted to the mayor and burgeſſes of Leiceſter — —	31	12	3
The fee-farm reſerved out of the Town-obit lands, and the lands and tenements of St. Margaret's guild, granted to the mayor and burgeſſes of Leiceſter	42	18	1
The fee-farm iſſuing out of the lands, tenements, &c. belonging to the college of the Virgin Mary near the caſtle of Leiceſter, granted to the mayor and burgeſſes of Leiceſter — —	20	8	11
The fee-farm iſſuing out of divers houſes in the Newark, with the lands, tenements, &c. belonging to Corpus Chriſti guild, granted to the mayor and burgeſſes — — —	18	8	6¼
Parcel of the lands and poſſeſſions, &c. of the hoſpital and priory of St. John of Jeruſalem in England, &c. out of the free and cuſtomary tenements in Bareſby in the pariſh of Aſhby Folvile —	2	8	9
The free and cuſtomary tenants in Gaddeſby, in the pariſh of Rothley,	5	17	0

From the free and cuſtomary tenements in	£.	s.	d.
South Croxton	0	17	6
In Somerby —	0	19	7
In South Marefield —	0	1	4
In Tilton — —	0	6	6
In Keame — —	3	11	0
In Saxulby — —	0	17	4

	£.	s.	d.
In all, — —	7	16	0
From the free and cuſtomary tenants in Grimſton, in the pariſh of Rothley,	1	5	0
From the free and cuſtomary tenants in Caldwell and Wickham —	2	0	3
From the free and cuſtomary tenants in Wartnaby — —	3	18	8
The fee-farm rent for tithe of grain and hay in the pariſh of Gaddeſby, with a barn to the ſaid tithe belonging	11	13	4
	289	17	3¼

The order of payments and allowances to the poor in the old Hoſpital.

	£.	s.	d.
The chamberlains are to pay on every Friday 3*l.* 7*s.* 9*d.*; that is, 6*s.* 8*d.* apiece to the ten keepers; 8*d.* to the widows of St. John's; and 5*d.* to be ſpent in bread and drink, and diſtributed among the officers of the houſe; which in the year amounts to — — —	176	3	0
Item, to the four men, about Eaſter or Spring, to pay for proviſion of wood and coals — — —	14	15	4
Item, drovers' money, payable half on Aſh-wedneſday, and half on Good Friday	2	0	0
Item, to Mr. Mayor, as maſter of the ſaid Hoſpital — —	13	6	8
To the chaplain, for reading daily prayers, to be paid quarterly —	5	0	0
To the lecturer of St. Martin's, for preaching there once in the quarter	10	0	0
Item, to the vicar of All Saints —	6	0	0
Item, for repairs of the ſaid houſe	4	0	0
Item to the widows of St. John's, to buy them a load of coals, 6*s.* 8*d.* or	0	7	8
Item, more to the ſaid widows, on All Saints day, in ready money —	0	2	0

Particular ſums paid by the chamberlains to the ſaid Hoſpital on Friday before St. Andrew's day yearly.

	£.	s.	d.
For the maintenance of the lamp or watch-candle — —	1	0	0
For bread and wine for the communion 6*s.* 8*d.* — — —	0	7	8
For ſixpenny-money — —	2	10	0
For fivepenny-money —	2	1	8
For halfpenny-money, alias 1*l.* 6*s.* 8*d.* alias	10	16	8
For livery-money for 50 of the poor yearly, to buy them gowns, at 4*s.* apiece	10	0	0

Soon after the Reſtoration, the old payments of the Hoſpital returned nearly back through their former channel, and from its own poſſeſſions.

	£.	s.	d.
The whole ſums at that time allowed by the king for maintenance of the Hoſpital of the Holy Trinity amounted to	229	1	7
Towards which the Corporation paid in fee-farm rents, by two equal portions of 56*l.* 13*s.* 10¾*d.* at Lady-day and Michaelmas; which fee-farm rents were for certain lands and tenements belonging to certain religious houſes, diſſolved, and granted in fee-farm to the Corporation;	113	7	9½
For the lands belonging to the Hoſpitals of St. John and St. Leonard	15	16	1½
Town-obit lands / St. Margaret's guild —	21	9	0½
The college of the bleſſed Virgin Mary juxta Caſtrum — —	10	4	5½
Corpus Chriſti guild —	7	6	2¾
Rents of houſes in the Newark, collected by the Corporation —	1	18	0½
Total for the half year's rent of all theſe,	56	13	10¾
Theſe the auditors allowed towards payment of the poor, and at their audit at Lady-day paid over and above in money	37	1	1
Which amounted in the whole to	93	14	11¾
Alſo at their audit at Michaelmas for the fee-farm rents the auditors paid in ready money, over and above the allowance of thoſe rents, 11*l.* 19*s.* 6*d.* *in toto*	68	13	4
Alſo the Corporation was to receive at Michaelmas of the auditors at Tutbury	66	13	4
All which three ſeveral ſums amounted to	229	1	7

being the whole and only allowance of the King for the ſaid Hoſpital, towards their maintenance, attire, gowns, chaplains, repairs, and other neceſſary proviſions[1].

Fees uſually paid to the auditor at Michaelmas only upon payment of the fee-farm rents.

	£.	s.	d.
Exchequer fees for the rents of St. John and St. Leonard — —	0	17	8
For Corpus Chriſti guild —	0	8	4
For the Newark — —	0	5	4
Debentures — —	0	2	8
Acquittances to Mr. Receiver —	0	8	0
For Town obit-lands — —	0	16	4
For *Quietus eſt* — —	0	5	0
In toto — — —	2	15	4

In 1683 the receipts were theſe:	£.	s.	d.
Paid by Mr. Dyſon, —	113	13	11¼
Other rents paid by ditto, —	25	6	8
From the honour of Tutbury,	66	13	4
	205	13	11¼

The money which had been advanced for the poor during Cromwell's uſurpation, and expences in petitiors, &c. afterwards, left the Hoſpital indebted to the Corporation, in 1684, 546*l.* 11*s.* 8*d.* Till that year the warden's fee of 13*l.* 6*s.* 8*d.* was conſtantly paid; and the ſum is ſtill charged to the debt due from the Hoſpital to the Corporation[2].

Sir William Heyrick in 1614 had laid the foundation of a ſmall addition to the income of the poor of the Trinity Hoſpital, by a voluntary gift of 20*s.* for an annual ſermon on Whit-monday in the Hoſpital-yard;

[1] Carte, MS. out of the long paper-book in cuſtody of the Mayor, fol. 28.

[2] Throſby.

and

and 20*s.* more for the poor; when a collection was also made from such inhabitants of the town as those to attend divine service. And this for a long series of years was regularly continued by his descendants. At the sermon in 1687 the collection amounted to £9.

Among several other preachers on those occasions, we find the names of Dr. Bright, of Loughborow; Dr. Camfeild, of Ilston; Mr. Beverege, of Barrow; Mr. Alsop, of Langton; Dr. Alefounder, of Thurcaston; Mr. Faulkingham, of Glenfield; Mr. Herricke, of Harborough; Mr. Rogers, of Segrave; and Mr. Pagett, of Barwell.

In 1695, Sir Nathan Wrighte, being then recorder of Leicester, drew out an account of the income of the Hospital; in which it appeared that there was received from the king, before the dissolution, 216*l.* 11*s.* 8*d.*; since, for a chaplain, £5.; for repairs, £4.; and for fuel, by gift, £4.; in all, 229*l.* 11*s.* 8*d.*

Expended thus:

	£.	s.	d.
To 100 poor men and women, to each 7 *d.* weekly	2	18	4
Ten keepers, each 10 *d.*	0	8	9
	3	7	1
For the year	174	8	4
Wood-money,	10	0	0
Halfpenny-money, the gift of Simpkin Simpson,	11	16	8
Fivepenny-money, the gift of Lady Harvey,	2	1	8
Sixpenny-money, the founder's gift,	2	10	0
Lamp-money	1	0	0
Livery-money	12	0	0
To six widows of St. John's	2	15	0
	216	11	8
Chaplain, repairs, and fuel-money, stated above	13	0	0
In all	229	11	8

From what cause is now not known, but, we believe, from a personal offence which had been given by some leading men in the Corporation, the annual sermon was discontinued in 1698, as appears by the following letter, written that year,

"To William Herrick, Esq. Beaumanor.

"Sir, you were pleased, last Whitsontide, to provide no preacher; nor make the allowance to the poor of the Old Hospital, which had been continued so long, to the honour and esteeme of your family. If any offence hath been taken from any particular person, I hope you will not impute that to the whole body; especially when you consider that the charity, given by your ancestors, is the cause of a further increase and releife to the poor on that day, which, upon consideration, yourselfe will think it great pitty to take away. I beg the favour of an answer to your faithful servant, JOHN CRACROFT, Mayor."

The answer to this application does not appear. But the loss which the Hospital had sustained was soon after supplied by an equal benefaction from the Rev. William Staveley, rector of Cossington.

"The chief endowment of the Hospital," says Mr. Carte in 1712, "was by an annual rent-charge issuing out of the lands of the Dutchy, which restored to each of the poor 7 *d.* weekly. But, after the sale of the chief rents in the time of king Charles the Second, the revenue being lessened, the number of the poor (by direction of the officers in the Dutchy Court, as the Lord Keeper Wrighte informed me) was reduced to about 90. And they would have a poor subsistence, were it not for some modern benefactors, and the yearly contributions of the members of the Corporation and other inhabitants of the town. The King, as heir to the Lancaster estates, has the sole disposal of the places when vacant; and his deputy is the Chancellor of the Dutchy of Lancaster."

The sum of £1125. was given in 1766 by Mr. John Holmes, an inhabitant of Leicester, on condition that the Corporation should pay him interest for life.

Mr. Thomas Heselrige, Lady Moyer, the late rev. Gerard Andrewes, and the late Joseph Cradock Esq; may also be added to the list of benefactors[1].

Previous to 1768, the Mayor used to nominate to vacancies, at the end of three months after vacancies occurred, as of right. In that year, in consequence of searches from an attempted innovation by the Corporation of the Dutchy right within the Castle-view) some of their leading members having entertained an idea that the Corporation magistrates had a concurrent jurisdiction with the county-magistrates therein), it was discovered that the right of presentation was in the Chancellor of the Dutchy, and in the Mayor only in the case of his omission for three months; which accounts for stopping the payment till that time. Lord Strange, then Chancellor, asserted his right; and it has ever since continued with his successors, who have paid only such attention to recommendations as they have thought proper.

Our present most gracious Sovereign, having been informed that the building was much out of repair, directed an estimate to be prepared; which was accordingly made by an eminent surveyor at Derby, to the amount of £1600; from which sum £1000. being deducted for the lead and other old materials (the present building being flated, and reduced about one third in the width), the remainder of the expence (being £600.) was defrayed by the royal bounty.

Before the late alteration, the old building consisted of three ailes, of which only the Northern one is now standing, what is now the front wall having before been a range of fine arched pillars on the side of a spacious aile. Mr. Carte describes it as "comprehending, under one large roof covered with lead, a chapel at one end of it, and cells or apartments for the poor, divided into ten wards, to each of which belonged a nurse; and adjoining to the building a large kitchen, with other proper offices."

At the East end is still the chapel in its original state (the ante-chapel wider from North to South than the chancel), which has a handsome window on each side. The East window consists of three lancets.

Under the North window, on an altar-tomb, a figure of a lady[2] in a rich mantle, with a high-standing cape, long sleeves reaching to her wrists, garment folded over her feet; angels at her head support two cushions, the undermost tasseled. An embattled moulding to the slab, and four shields on the side of the tomb.

The chaplain to this Hospital holds his place by patent from the Dutchy.

The rev. Mr. Fox, vicar of the adjoining parish of St. Mary, in the memory of persons now living, held this office, and read the daily prayers himself. Since his time, the chaplains have usually hired one of the almsmen to do this part of their duty.

The rev. John Dawes Ross is the present chaplain, and signs the presentations for admission as such.

The Confrater of Wigston's Hospital has an augmentation to his stipend, by patent from the Dutchy, during pleasure, for which he preaches four times a year in this chapel; and divine service is also performed twice a year by the vicar of St. Mary's.

The following orders were exemplified under the seal of the Dutchy of Lancaster, in February, 1780:

An augmentation of forty pounds a year being ordered by the King's most excellent Majesty to the use of this Hospital; and the Dutchy Court having directed that, after Lady-day 1780, the regulations herein-after mentioned shall take place; the following orders were printed, for the information of the foremen, keepers, and poor of this hospital.

"It is ordered, that the several annual sums following (instead of being divided and paid as heretofore), shall, after Lady-day 1780, be made one common fund for the purposes herein-after mentioned:

The Michaelmas rents and gifts, £116 18 4

---

[1] See the Returns made to Parliament, p. 132.
[2] This is the monument described by Mr. Wyrley, the only one which remained in 1590. See p. 339.

The

The Lady-day rents and gifts, —	79	15	4
Lady Moyer's donation, — —	20	0	0
Mr. Holmes's donation, — —	45	0	0
The drovers money, livery money, lamp money, half-penny money, and fix-penny money, — — — —	23	6	6
The old pay of 8d. per week, to the eight keepers, — — — — —	13	17	4
Old pay of 7d. per week, to 80 poor,	121	6	8
The old allowance for repairs, —	4	0	0
The like for fuel, — — —	9	11	1
	433	15	3

To the above muft be added, a faving made to the poor in 1776, by the voluntary bounty of the Dutchy officers, in giving up all their fees and poundage, which till then had been paid to them out of the Dutchy allowance ever fince the reign of Edward the Sixth, amounting to the annual fum of — 14 15 0

And his Majefty's additional grant *per annum* is — — — — — 40 0 0

Making in the whole, 488 11 0

By the new orders, this fum of £488. 11s. is directed to be paid and applied as follows.

	Weekly allow.			Annual amount.		
	£.	s.	d.	£.	s.	d.
To the eight keepers, for foap for wafhing, — —	0	1	8	4	6	8
To the eight keepers, 2s. 4d. each, in lieu of all other allowances and perquifites,	0	18	8	48	10	8
To the two women entitled to Mr. Billers's donation, and exclufively thereof, 10d. each, — — —	0	1	8	4	6	8
To the remaining 80 poor, 1s. 10d. each, — —	7	6	8	381	6	8
So that the fum to be divided on Friday morning in every week is £8. 8s. 8d.; which amounts to £438. 10s. 8d. a year, — —	8	8	8	438	10	8
To an apothecary, to be appointed by the mafter annually, to vifit the poor in ficknefs, and for medicines, not to exceed — — — — —				10	0	0
For fuel, not to exceed — —				11	0	0
For lamps and candles, not to exceed				5	0	0
To the foremen, for collecting the rents, 7s. 6d. at Lady-day, and 7s. 6d. at Michaelmas, — — —				0	15	0
And the remaining fum of £23. 5s. 4d. together with all favings of pay for vacant houfes three months after every vacancy, are to be kept as a fund by the mafter and affiftants for the future repairs of the hofpital, — — —				23	5	4
Total as above —				488	11	0

All the reft of the poors money to be divided as heretofore accuftomed.

It is alfo ordered, that all the rents and gifts fhall be continued to be received by the foremen in the ufual manner; but they are to pay the fame over to the chamberlains of Leicefter for the time being, to be carried to the account of the above fund.

Item, The chamberlains are, out of the faid fund, to iffue and pay to the foremen the above fum of £8. 8s. 8d. every Friday morning weekly, to be by them immediately diftributed amongft the keepers and the poor in manner above-mentioned.

Item, After every vacancy, the weekly pay for the vacant houfes is to be ftopped for three calendar months; and applied towards the expence of keeping the hofpital in good repair.

And, laftly, all the keepers and poor are at their own expence to keep in good repair the windows, bedfteads, floors, fhutters, partitions, doors, hinges, locks and faftnings, of their refpective rooms or houfes (every one his and her own); and in default thereof, the foremen are to repair the fame, and ftop the expences out of the pay of the defaulters, to the intent the revenue of the hofpital may not be charged with the repairs of the rooms, nor any one perfon contribute to the expences of the repairs of another perfon, but that every one of the keepers and poor may keep his and her room in the aforefaid particulars in fit and decent repair."

A view of the old building, taken in 1776, is given in Plate XXVIII. fig. 17; and fig. 18. fhews the prefent building; over the door of which is infcribed:

" Founded
By Henry Earl of Lancafter, 1331;
Rebuilt
By George III. 1776."

And on a frame within the chapel:

" Henry Grifmond, duke
of Lancafter, and earl of
Leicefter. He was Founder
of this Hofpital in the year
of our Lord God 1332;
and fince granted,
by charter by our late
gracious Sovereign King James,
to be called the
Holy Trinity, the 12th year of
his reign."

In this hofpital is a remarkably large bell-metal pot, called *the Duke of Lancafter's porridge-pot*, which holds fixty-one gallons [1]; and a curious old nutmeg-grater, called *Queen Elizabeth's Pocket-piece*, ornamented with a border of rofes, and quartered; and on the top of it is engraved ANNO REGNI REGINÆ ELIZABETH: ANGLIÆ," On one fide " THINKE WEL, AND SAY WEL, BUT RATHER DO WEL;" on the other fide, " FLEE IDILNES, AND BE WEL OCCUPIED, 1579." On the bottom, " THIS BELONGITM . TO . THE . OLDE OSPITALL [2]."

In the open yard, near the door of the chapel, is placed a large ftone, which appears to have been the bafe of an old font [3].

John Whatton [4], efq. of the Newark, died in 1656.

Thomas Lanie, of the Newark, (fon of John Lanie of Cratfield, Suffolk, and brother to John Lanie, recorder of Suffolk,) entered his pedigree in the Vifitation of 1619. His wife was *Gertrude*, daughter of *John Hunte* of Lyndon in Rutland. His arms were, Quarterly, 1. and 4, Argent on a bend between two fleurs de lis Gules, a lion paffant; 2. .... a chevron engrailed between three cinquefoils, and on a chief Gules, a lion paffant ......; 3. Gules, a crefcent Ermine within an orle of martlets Or. Creft, a mermaid proper, wreathed about the temples, Or and Vert, holding a fprig [5].

John Sherman, of the Newark, entered his pedigree at the fame Vifitation [5]. By *Anne*, daughter of *William Cave*, he had two fons, *William*, aged 31; and *Thomas*, aged 18; and fix daughters, the eldeft of whom, *Faith*, was married to *Henry Heming*, then alfo of the Newark. His arms; Argent, a lion rampant Sable, charged on the fhoulder with an annulet Argent, between three holly leaves Vert. Creft, a fea-lion fejant Ermine [6]. His widow occurs among the benefactors to the Hofpital.

The name of Alderman Becket, of the Newark, is alfo among the lift of benefactors.

Edmund Brudenell [7], efq. of the Newark (who married *Mary* daughter of Thomas Staveley, efq. of Belgrave) died in February, 1686-7; and his brother, *Richard Brudenell*, efq. Feb. 28, 1687-8.

[1] See Plate XXVIII. fig. 19.   [2] Ibid. fig. 20—23.   [3] Ibid. fig. 24.
[4] See his epitaph, and fome account of him, under the hiftory of St. Martin's parifh.
[5] See Plate XXVII. fig. 25.   [6] Ibid. fig. 26.   [7] See an account of his defcendants in vol. II. under Church Langton.

Mr.

Mr. Carte, in 1712, speaking of the Newark says, "The church stood in Mr. Carter's garden, and the foundations of it were dug up about 1690, when the garden was reduced into the form which it is now of. There are three very fair houses, belonging to *William Franke* [1], esq. *Lawrence Carter* [2], esq. and Mrs. *Stephens*; but they are all of late erection. I believe that Mrs. Stephens's stands where the prebendal house of Thomas Wigston was situated, because the house which William Wigston built for his two chantry priests adjoins to it; over the portal of which there is his coat of arms. Of the old buildings scarcely any thing remains except this house of Wigston's, and another much like it now settled on the vicar of St. Mary's."

Of the three "fair houses," that which was Mr. Franke's was afterwards inhabited by the late *Joseph Bunney*, esq. and now by *John Pares*, esq. an eminent manufacturer of hosiery (who is owner of this Liberty); Mr. Carter's (formerly *Skeffington house*) was some time the residence of Mr. *Coultman*, and has since been sold in lots; and Mrs. Stephens's, in which Mr. *Wrighte* the Recorder resided, has been, with additions, converted into two houses. Besides these, there are several other good houses in the Newark, which is now the handsomest part of the town.

In the Return made to Parliament in 1776, the Newark is entered as extraparochial [3]; and so continues. The expence of the poor that year was only 20s.; of which 13s. was for rent.

In 1783, the sum raised for the poor of this Liberty was 18l. 12s.; in 1784, 33l. 18s.; in 1785, 10l. 2s.; medium, 20l. 17s. 4d.

On six large tables in the chapel are recorded:

Benefactors of the perpetuities bequeathed towards the maintenance of the poor in the old Hospital.

	£.	s.	d.
Henry Plantagenet, earl of Grismond, duke of Lancaster, and earl of Leicester, the first and chief founder of it, A. D. 1332, for 110 poor people.			
Sir William Heyrick, knt. gave 20s. for a sermon on Whit-monday, and 20s. to the poor of the hospital for ever; but these charities have been withdrawn since 1698 by William Heyrick, late of Beaumanor, esq. heir of the said sir William.			
William Staveley, late rector of Cossington, in the county of Leicester, supplied the said defect, giving 20s. for a sermon on the said day exhorting to charity, and 20s. to the poor of the said hospital; in all	2	0	0
The lady Mary Harvey gave out of her manor of Southorp called Fillibert's Court, and the manor of Southorp called Grey's Court, in the county of Gloucester,	26	16	0
Mr. William Taylor, merchant-tailor of London, by will, dated May 6, 1619, gave an annuity of 40s. payable out of his lands in Bowden, co. Kent, at Michaelmas and Lady-day, to buy them oatmeal,	2	0	0
Mr. Robert Heyrick, thrice mayor of Leicester, by his will, dated June 14,			

1618, gave out of his ground land, called the Grey or Franciscan Friers in Leicester, to each of the then poor [4] one shilling, payable at or before Nov. 11, ... 5 10 0

	£.	s.	d.
1618, gave out of his ground land, called the Grey or Franciscan Friers in Leicester, to each of the then poor [4] one shilling, payable at or before Nov. 11,	5	10	0
Mr. Tobias Heyrick, rector of Houghton, co. Leicester, by will, dated June 13, 1627, gave out of the Grey Friers 2s. yearly, to two of the said poor, payable the same day with the donation bequeathed by his father Robert Heyrick, —	0	2	0
Mr. John Heyrick, once mayor of Leicester, by will, dated July 17, 1633, gave two houses in the Southgate, then of the rent of 40s. a year, which were both pulled down in the time of war [5]; the ground and backsides of them are in the tenure of Anne Webster, widow, and of the rent of 20s. yearly; whereof 13s. 4d. to the town, and 6s. 4d. to the hospital, payable at Michaelmas and Lady-day,	0	6	8
Mrs. Mary Heyrick, spinster, sister of the said John Heyrick, gave a little close in the parish of St. Margaret, adjoining to the But-Close, in tenure of George Palmer, which close was afterwards confirmed to the said hospital by her brother John Heyrick, by deed 28 Aug. 1626, and is of the rent of —	0	18	8
William Morton, clerk, son of William Morton, archdeacon of Durham, and grandson of William Morton, thrice mayor of Leicester, gave one acre, called Mary Acre, in Burgess-meadow, in the tenure of John Hall, glazier, of the yearly rent of —	1	1	0
And also two messuages in St. Martin's parish, whereof one in the tenure of William Springthorp, cordwainer, —	1	0	0
The other in tenure of Jane Reed, spinster, of the rent of —	0	15	0
Mr. William Ive, thrice mayor of Leicester, by deed dated 14 Car. I. gave an annuity of £5. 10s. out of a house in the Southgate, pulled down in time of war, and also out of two meadows near the water-mills called Newark Mills, to be paid the first week in clean Lent yearly,	5	10	0
Mrs. Jane Ive, wife of the said William Ive, gave also an annuity of 20s. a year, payable out of the said house and meadows the first week in clean Lent,	1	0	0
Mr. James Ellis, senior, twice mayor of Leicester, by will, dated Nov. 7, 1617, gave a piece of ground or orchard over against the Vineyard in the parish of All Saints, now in the tenure of William Noon the younger, of the yearly rent of	10	0	0

Mr. James Ellis, junior, once mayor, by will, dated Jan. 16, 1628, gave two messuages and a piece of ground lying on the Town-wall; whereof the one messuage was in the parish of St. Mary's, and then of the rent of £4. but was pulled down in time of war; but now the

---

[1] Arms granted to William Franke, of the New Works: Azure, a fess embattled Ermine between two dexter arms in armour, fess-ways, Argent, garnished Or. Crest, out of a mural crown Or, an arm embowed in armour proper, holding a sword Argent, hilt and pomel Or; fig. 28. (Harl. MSS. 1171. p 64. b.)—This William Franke was high sheriff of the county in 1674. He married a daughter of Gilbert Armstrong, of Rampstone, co. Notts, esq. and sister of Katharine, the wife of John Heyrick, of the Grey Friers in Leicester, gent.; died in 1679, and was buried at St. Martin's, where see his epitaph; and occurs among the benefactors to the Hospital, p. 347. His son William Franke married Anne daughter of sir Richard Levett, lord mayor of London in 1700; by whom he had a son, the Rev. Levett Franke, vicar of Caythorpe, co. Lincoln, who died in 1734; a daughter, married to the Rev. Caleb Robinson, vicar of Glen; see p. 437; and several other children.

[2] Afterwards Sir Lawrence Carter, and a baron of the Exchequer. See his epitaph at St. Mary's, p. 319.

[3] "The Corporation, finding several inconveniences to arise from the exemption of the Castle, Newark, &c. from the franchises, made several attempts to have them brought under their jurisdiction, which at length they obtained a grant of, in the charter of 41 Eliz. in very ample terms; with a saving to all persons of whatsoever rights, liberties, and jurisdictions, they had and enjoyed before the making of that charter." Carte, MS. 1712.—The Corporation-Magistrates have, therefore, a concurrent jurisdiction with those of the County in all these places, except the Castle-view.

[4] The poor are now reduced to 90; and 4l. 10s. (being 1s. to each) is paid to them by Thomas Pares, jun. esq. the present owner of the principal part of the Grey Friers.

[5] April 20, 1713, John Cooper, mayor, John Rogers, a deacon, and William Fox, vicar of St. Mary's, as arbitrators about differences relating to these two houses (then rebuilt), determined that a lease should be made from the hospital to Humphry Chapman and Thomas Gamble, executors of Robert Gamble, and from Lady-day last, for 999 years, under the clear yearly rent of £2. 13s. 4d. to be paid half-yearly to the poor; and 13s. 4d. as a fee-farm rent to the town.

ground

ground and backfide, with a dovecote, is in the tenure of John Atkinfon, gent. and of the rent of £2. 6s. 8d. payable at Michaelmas and Lady-day, —   2 6 8

The other meffuage or tenement is in Parliament-lane, in the parifh of All Saints, in tenure of Edward Chulmley, gent. and of the rent of £5. payable at Michaelmas and Lady-day,   5 0 0

The piece of ground lying on the Town-wall adjoins to the orchard, garden, and backfide of the meffuage or tenement of the faid Edward Chulmeley, and is in tenure of Lawrence Dawfon, of the yearly rent of 20s. payable at Michaelmas and Lady-day, —   1 0 0

Robert Brookefby, efq. by deed, dated Dec. 31, 5 Jac. 1. gave an annuity of 26s. 8d. payable out of his lands and tenements in Great Afhby at Michaelmas and Lady-day   1 6 8

He gave alfo an annuity of 13s. 4d. out of a meffuage or tenement and two beafts paftures in Wartnaby, in tenure of Robert Brifcoe, payable at Michaelmas and Lady-day, — —   0 13 4

Chriftopher Tamworth, of Gray's Inn, efq. by will[1], dated May 9, 1624, gave to the Corporation of Leicefter £20. to purchafe lands of inheritance for augmentation of the annual revenues of this hofpital for relief of the poor there for ever; with which was purchafed a cottage or tenement in Whefton, fix roods of land, and two beaft-paftures, now in tenure of John Green, and of the yearly rent of   1 0 0

Mr. John Clarke, twice mayor of Leicefter, gave an annuity of £3. 6s. 8d. out of a piece of ground, barn, and malting-kiln, in the parifh of St. Nicholas, in tenure of John Berkhead, fenior, payable at Michaelmas and Lady-day, —   3 6 8

Mr. John Norrice, fenior, once mayor of Leicefter, gave an annuity of £1. 13s. 4d. out of lands in Willoughby Waterlefs, which the earl of Stamford purchafed of the faid Mr. Norrice, payable on Friday before Eafter yearly, —   1 13 4

Mr. Hugh Watts, fenior, once mayor of Leicefter, by will, dated Feb. 1, 1642, gave an annuity of 28s. iffuing out of a meffuage in Shambles-lane, in the parifh of St. Nicholas, in tenure of Anthony Biggs, baker, to buy for every of the poor a penny-loaf on the eve of Chriftmas, Eafter, and Whitfuntide, for ever,   1 8 0

Mr. Julius Billers, fenior, gent. by will, Jan. 10, 1634, gave to the corporation £100. in truft, to pay to the poor of this hofpital £5. 12s. yearly, to be diftributed equally among them on Tuefday before Eafter, — — —   5 12 0

Mr. William Speechly, once mayor of Leicefter, by will, dated Dec. 8, 1651, gave an annuity of 20s. out of his clofes called The Foards, in the parifh of Barwell and Stapleton, now in tenure of Thomas Smith, payable at Michaelmas and Lady-day, — —   1 0 0

Mr. John Nurfe, by will, gave an annuity of — —   0 13 4

John Hinman, of the Newark, yeoman, by deed 22 Oct. 1 Elizabeth, gave a third part of a yard-land arable, lying in St. Margaret's fields, in the tenure of John Harris, of the yearly value of 40s. and the bringing of a load of fand and a load of clay yearly to the faid hofpital,   2 0 0

Mr. John Hinde, fenior, twice mayor, by his will, gave £10.; enjoining his executors and overfeers of his will to purchafe a piece of land or fome annuity with it, which might remain to the faid hofpital for ever.

Mr. John Hind, junior, by will, dated Sept. 11, 1652, gave an annuity of 24s. out of a clofe and parcel of ground, and two tenements, in the Northgate-ftreet, joining upon the Mill-lane, to be paid upon St. Thomas's day yearly, —   1 4 0

Peter Palmer, of Leicefter, labourer, by will, dated July 10, 1610, gave an annuity of 2s. out of an orchard and garden, and houfe thereon, called the Water Caggs, in tenure of George Mountney, gent. payable at Michaelmas and Lady-day yearly, — —   0 2 0

Margaret Hobby, widow, gave an annuity of 2s. 9d. out of a meffuage in the Southgate, late in tenure of Robert Meffenger, which was pulled down in the time of war; the ground and backfide thereof now in tenure of Robert Hartfhorne, payable at Michaelmas and Lady-day,   0 2 6

John Smart, of Thurlefton, co. Leicefter, yeoman, gave an annuity of 2s. 6d. out of a clofe near his houfe, called the Lodge, payable July 16, or thereabouts,   0 2 6

Ralph Smalley, of Leicefter, gent.   2 0 0

Mrs. Elizabeth Ware, daughter of Mr. William Morton, alderman, and thrice mayor, gave — —   1 0 0
Befides 40s. to St. John's hofpital.

Mr. William Pippin, of Knighton,   1 0 0

Mr. John Clay, alderman, and twice mayor, gave — —   1 0 0
Befides 10s. to the widows of St. Jones's.

Mrs. Elizabeth Cook gave £66. and Mr. Matthew Symons, her fon-in-law, added to it £100. to buy £8. per annum, whereof £4. 18s. to buy 56 pair of ftockings for 56 of the hofpital, and 14s. to buy bread for 56 of the poor that have not ftockings that year [the reft for the widows of St. John's, viz. £2. 8s.]   5 12 0

Mr. Francis Noble, alderman, and twice mayor, gave a houfe worth   2 0 0

Mr. Jofeph Becket, of Houghton on the Hill, out of a half yard-land in Houghton-field, gave —   0 10 0

Mr. William Billers, thrice mayor, by will, dated April 10, 1657, gave to the corporation a rent-charge of £12. a year, payable out of that parcel of meadow ground, called Leazow, and the clofes adjoining, which he had purchafed of Thomas Chapman, efq. to be paid the 25th of March and the 29th of September at the Guildhall: if behind 40 days, then by legal authority to enter and diftrain, and to have and drive the diftreffes and keep them till the rent is paid; upon truft, to pay two almfwomen, placed by Mr. Billers in the faid hofpital, each of them weekly on Friday 12d.; and for a gown every year for one of them 20s.; alfo to pay to the poor of the hofpital, being 110, £5. 10s. on Friday next after May 1 and November 1; and the other 6s. to buy oatmeal; all the money to be paid into the hands of the governors of the hofpital. And

---

[1] "I will moreover, that my executors fhall caufe to be laid in every year into the coal-houfe of the faid Hofpital, for fo long time as Mr. Walter Ruding's leafe made to me of certain lands in Braunftonthorp, alias Bromkinfthorpe, in the county of Leicefter, fhall continue, fix loads of Coleorton pit-coal, to make the poor people of the faid hofpital fires before Allhallows-tide, and after St. George's day, if the weather require it; and thofe fix loads of coal to be laid by themfelves from their other coals which they have from their founder. Item, I give to the poor people inhabiting in all the parifhes of the town of Leicefter 20 nobles, to be diftributed among them by the difcretion of the mayor of Leicefter, and the curate or vicar of every parifh in Leicefter, and the chamberlains of Leicefter. Item, I give to Willoughby and Eme Achor, of the hofpital of St. Trinity nigh Leicefter, five marks apiece."—He gave alfo 200 marks for the performance of divine fervice twice every day at St. Martin's church; where, and at Tilton, fee more of him.

it is inferted in the faid will, that the poor women to be placed fhall not pay any money to the houfe during the vacancy.

Mr. William Stanley, alderman, by will, gave to the poor of the old hofpital 20s. a year; for fecurity of which fum, and of £4. given by his brother Mr. John Stanley, for feveral charitable ufes, he charged a clofe called Beadhoufe Meadow, in the occupation of Mr. Robert Hartfhorne, with an annuity of £5.

William Franke, efq. by his will, dated 25 March, 31 Charles II. gave as followeth; " I give to the mafter, affiftants, chaplain, and poor of the hofpital of the Holy Trinity, three meffuages, cottages, or tenements, in Leicefter, late in tenure of George Heggs, John Noon, and Laurence Cooper, by me purchafed of John Atton, to enjoy the fame, paying yearly to the fix poor widows in St. John's hofpital 6s. on the 21ft of December; and the refidue of the profits I give to the poor of the hofpital of the Holy Trinity; and in cafe the mafterfhip fhall be taken away from the mayor of the borough, fo as he cannot execute the fame, then I give the faid three meffuages to the corporation and their affigns, in truft, that they fhall demife the fame at the beft rent they can get; and the whole rents and profits thereof yearly difpofe as follows, viz. 6s. to the fix poor widows of St. John's hofpital; and the reft to the poor people of the faid borough, in fuch proportion as the mayor and aldermen fhall think convenient."

Jofeph Wright, one of the 48, by will, gave the acre of meadow ground, which he was feifed of in the Abbey-meadow of Leicefter, and is of the yearly value of 40s. or thereabouts, to the poor of the old hofpital for ever, to buy them oatmeal.

William Staveley, rector of Coffington, by will, dated Sept. 21, 1702, appointed his executors, John Allen, John Rogers, and Thomas Benfkin, their heirs and affigns for ever, to pay 20s. to fuch preacher as they fhould appoint, for a fermon, exhorting to charity, to be preached on Whit-Monday, at the hofpital of the Holy Trinity in the Newark, Leicefter; and farther pay 20s. more towards the collection for the poor of the faid hofpital on that day.

Mr. Thomas Blunt, alderman, and twice mayor, gave 40 pair of fhoes.

Mr. Becket, of the Newark in Leicefter, alderman, and twice mayor, gave to the poor of this hofpital and St. John's the ufe of £134. 10s.

Margaret, relict of Mr. John Sherman, of the Newark in Leicefter, gave a filver communion-bowl, with a chalice, to the value of £7.

Befides thefe benefactions, whofe charity they ftill annually partake of, there are others which were temporary.

Mrs. Amy Coles, widow, during her life gave annually 20s.

Ralph Difon, gent. gave £1. per annum for ten years.

Mr. Anthony Major gave to each of the poor that fhould be in this houfe at the time of his deceafe 2s. 6d.

Mr. George Crofts gave 12d. apiece to the poor.

Others, at the time of their death, gave them:

	£	s.	d.
John Major, of Leicefter, gent.	10	0	0
Mrs. Alice Chapman, of Foxton, widow,	2	0	0
Mr. Danet Abney, alderman, and twice mayor,	5	12	0
Mr. John Brewin, of Belgrave, gent.	5	0	0
Mr. William Brewin, of Belgrave,	5	12	0
George Reafon, of Leicefter, gent.	5	0	0
Elizabeth, wife of William Warbarton,	5	0	0
Mr. William Stubbing, alderman,	3	0	0
Anne, wife of Mr. David Dekins,	5	0	0
Mr. Thomas Ludlam, alderman, and once mayor,	5	0	0
Mr. Robert Spence, of Leicefter,	5	0	0
Mr. Thomas Ward, of this Borough,	5	0	0
Mrs. Sarah Glover,	5	0	0
Mrs. Joanna Ayres, widow, in the North-gate, Leicefter,	5	0	0
Mr. Thomas Topp, one of the 48, gave to the poor of this hofpital	5	0	0
Mr. Henry Pate, alderman, and once mayor, to this and St. John's hofpital,	5	0	0

Obfervations by the Rev. Samuel Carte, taken out of the Rental of the Chamberlains, 1711-12; which is of all the lands and tenements which the mayor, bailiffs, and burgeffes, were then feifed of, in fee fimple, and otherwife.

		£	s.	d.
1. Rents of affize and rents at will in the borough of Leicefter, &c. —		29	0	7
2. Receipts of the whole Grange, with the appurtenances, and the four yard-land, and two yard-land, called Archer's Land; and half a yard-land the town purchafed of the lord Spencer in fee fimple, with the Newark mill and windmill, &c. (The particulars amount to 20 yard-lands, 7 acres, befides clofes, barns, &c.)		177	12	7
3. The Bead-houfe meadow,		27	10	3
4. Other rents, for lands and tenements, which the faid mayor, bailiffs, and burgeffes, held in fee-farm of the hofpital of St. John and St. Leonard, heretofore belonging to the late college of the Newark of Leicefter, amount to —		53	0	2
5. Other rents of lands and tenements, parcel of the Town Obit-lands, St. Margaret's Guild, and parcel of the fee-farm rents heretofore demifed by queen Elizabeth to Mr. Hawkes and Bakes, by indenture expired, amount to —		20.	4	4
6. Rents for lands and tenements, parcel of the manor of Leicefter, heretofore granted to the mayor, &c. in fee-farm,		4	5	6
7. Rents of Corpus Chrifti Guild, parcel of the lands and tenements, with the manor, &c. purchafed of queen Elizabeth,		13	18	0
8. Rents, parts of the poffeffion of the late Guild in Leicefter, parcel of the Town Obit-lands, — —		22	18	4
9. Part of Mr. Wylde's rents,		5	9	8

10. A rental of the lands and poffeffions of the College of the bleffed Virgin Mary over againft the caftle of Leicefter, heretofore demifed by queen Elizabeth to *Edward Holt*, efq. and by her majefty granted, among other things, to the corporation in fee-farm; tranfcribed by Mr. Carte.

	£	s.	d.
Widow Bellamy, for a meffuage or tenement in Swines-market, in fee-farm,	0	6	8
Robert Langton, for part of a tenement in occupation of Martin Beeby,	0	2	0
Ralph Wells, for a clofe near Aylefton highway, late the land of Mr. Robert Heyrick, in fee-farm, —	0	5	0
Elias Wallin, for a garden, or piece of ground, or backfide of a meffuage or tenement, near the South-gate, heretofore the land of Mr. Hugh Watts,	0	1	0
Thomas Jackfon, clerk, for a tenement in Soar Lane near Red Crofs Street, in occupation late of John Colfton, and now of Thomas Kitchin, in fee-farm,	0	10	0
Samuel Dewick and Mrs. Windfor, for a tenement in Soar-lane near Red Crofs Street, heretofore fold to John Underwood, in fee-farm, —	0	5	0
Edward Smith, or William Dawfon, for a houfe or garden in the fame lane, heretofore Robert Stevenfon's, —	0	12	0
Heirs of Gabriel Hill, for a meffuage in Red Crofs Street, and a garden in Chaff-lane adjoining to the faid houfe, now in occupation of John Savage, being the fign of the Bird-in-hand, in fee-farm,	1	0	0
The heirs or executors of Robert Atton, butcher, for a meffuage or tenement in Soar-lane, in fee-farm, —	1	6	8
Robert Wringmore, for a tenement or garden in Soar-lane, heretofore fold to John Launder, in fee-farm, —	0	12	0
Mr. Hill, or Robert Fawcett, for a garden in Soar-lane in occupation of Thomas Trantum, in fee-farm, —	0	0	8

Mr.

Mr. John Abney, for a parcel of ground belonging to a tenement in the South-gates, ruined in time of war, and for a croft, in fee-farm, — 0 16 0

William Franke, efq. for a piece of ground adjoining to Friers-lane, in occupation formerly of William Cullis, and lately of John Burbage, in fee-farm, 0 0 4

Mr. John Wilkins, now Mr. Fox, for herbage of St. Martin's church-yard, 0 10 0

Mr. John Farmer, for a clofe near Cowdriff land and Mr. Herdman's land, 1 0 0

Mr. Barwell, for the tithe-hay in Burgefs-meadow, South-field, and tithable meadows beyond the mills, in fee-farm, 5 0 0

William Franke, efq. for St. James's chapel yard and clofe at the Nether end of the South-gates, heretofore fold to one Mr. Simpfon, late Mr. Sherman's land, 1 6 8

Richard Brown, now Thomas Griffin, for a houfe and garden, or back-fide, in the parifh of St. Nicholas, by leafe, 3 0 0

John Denfhire, for a houfe and garden in the fame parifh, late the land of Daniel Murfin, butcher, in fee-farm, — 1 0 0

Mr. Watts and Mrs. Lucy Fownes, for the tithes, vicarial tenths, herbage, and other dues, belonging to Danet's hall, St. Mary's mills, and the Holmes, by leafe, 5 0 0

Mr. Samuel Heyrick, for tithes, tenths of all thofe grounds fome time parcel of Danet's hall, by leafe, — — 2 0 0

William Ruding, efq. for all the tithes, vicarial tenths, herbage, and other duties belonging to the fame, payable out of all thofe grounds and parcels of land belonging to the Weftcotes, by leafe, 5 0 0

The executor of Nathanael Sims, for a garden in Senvey-gate, late Woodford's land, in occupation of Henry Sands, 0 1 0

Matthew Symonds, efq. for a garden, or piece of ground, fome time a well-yard, heretofore the land of Thomas Chettleton, late Robert Griffin's, in occupation of Hugh Jordan, in fee-farm, — 0 1 4

Executor of Mr. Edmund Townfend, for an orchard and garden in Silver-ftreet, 0 2 0

Mr. Ralph Wells, for the third part of a clofe near Cowdrift, in fee-farm, 0 4 0

The poor of the Old Hofpital, for part of Dovehoufe Clofe, beyond the Weftbridge, in occupation of John Winter, 0 1 6

Richard Haffel, for a piece of meadowground in Glen field, in occupation of John Carr, in fee-farm, — 0 0 6

Mr. Thomas Helmefley, for a clofe near St. Margaret's cow-pafture, heretofore Bennet's land, in fee-farm, 0 8 4

Mr. Watts, for lands and leys in the Weft fields of Leicefter, heretofore land of Thomas Bennet, efq. in fee-farm, 0 2 6

The poor of the Old Hofpital, for a piece of meadow-ground in Burgefs-meadow, called Lady-acre, in fee-farm, 0 8 4

William Ruding, for a clofe in Braunfton-gate, in fee-farm, — — 0 5 0

Robert Hobfon, for a houfe and clofe in occupation of John Holmes, 1 10 0

Mr. Fox, vicar of St. Mary's, for the Eafter-book and other duties of the faid parifh, — — 0 3 4

For a garden and tenement in Soarlane, near Red Crofs Street, heretofore in occupation of George King, and lately of Richard Bruce, at will. — 0 13 4

Anthony Abel and William Lyon, for a garden in Hotgate-ftreet, alias Thornton-lane, late the land of Thomas Pare, now Elizabeth Power, in fee-farm, 0 5 0

Mr. Thomas Palmer, attorney, for a garden in Swines-market lately built upon, in occupation formerly of Thomas Ludlam, lockfmith, and now of himfelf, 0 1 2

More for a fhop, heretofore fold to Chriftopher Needham, late in occupation of William Tompfon, in fee-farm, 0 2 6

11. Rents belonging to the Newark.

	£.	s.	d.
The heirs or executors of Mr. Hugh Watts, for a meffuage, or tenement, formerly Dr. Chippendale's and Mr. Walker's, fituate in the Newark, in occupation of Mr. Bayly, in fee-farm, —	1	6	8
Mrs. Frances Palmer, widow, for a houfe there, late Dr. Walker's, in occupation of Oliver Grace, in fee-farm,	0	13	4
Matthew Judd, for a houfe in Newark, late Mr. Hollingworth's, in occupation of Francis Hall, in fee-farm, —	0	13	4
Richard Inge, of Knighton, for two parts of Mr. Chamberlain's land,	0	12	4
Jeffrey Palmer, of Carleton Curlieu, efq. for certain lands there, in fee-farm,	0	1	6
The heirs or executors of James Carr, of Bowden Magna, for land there, in occupation of John Carrol, in fee-farm,	0	1	0
The heirs or executors of Mr. Godfrey Barrowdale, for lands in Sileby,	0	0	6
William Needham, of Glenfield, for lands there, in fee-farm, —	0	0	3

12. Other rents [1] of the town and manor of Leicefter, and parcel of the lands and poffeffions of the dutchy of Lancafter.

	£.	s.	d.
The executor of William Higgs, mercer, for a meffuage or tenement, heretofore the land of Mr. Ellis, in occupation of Mr. John Brockefby, in fee-farm,	0	16	8
Mr. Thomas Palmer, attorney, for a houfe in the Swines-market, fold to Bartholomew Parnel, in fee-farm, —	1	13	4
William Franke, efq. for a piece of ground, being part of the town-wall, near the Frier-lane, late Mr. Manby's,	0	2	6
Robert Langton, for two pieces of land taken off the common dunghill, in the lane near the Weft-bridge, in fee-farm,	0	0	10
Abraham Pougher, for two tenements in Parchment-lane, late the land of Mr. John Heyrick, in occupation of ——— Paul and others, in fee-farm, —	0	3	4
Mr. Alfop, for a fhop under the Gainfborough, by leafe, now The Spencer,	0	10	0
13. Other rents received of new, &c.	56	6	4
14. Rents given to the free-fchool and other charitable ufes,	150	5	0
15. Rents for fhops and ftalls in Saturday-market, — —	13	6	8
16. Chief rents belonging to the hofpitals of St. John and St. Leonard,	0	16	9½
17. To Corpus Chrifti Guild, —	4	14	4
18. To St. Margaret's Guild, —	4	5	6½
19. A rental of Lammas tithes and herbage due for grounds in St. Mary's parifh, parcel of the poffeffions of the college of St. Mary over againft the caftle,	5	3	6

[1] Amongft the places mentioned in the Rent-roll of 1694, the following defcriptions occur: In the gardens of Wigfton's Hofpital, a piece of ground called The Normandy; the Water-laggs; Chaffe-lane near Redcrofs-ftreet; a clofe in All Saints parifh near Plank Well; Dove-houfe Clofe near the New Market; Tippet Clofe; a clofe called the Paradife; Gofling Clofe; Soar-lane, or Walker-lane, near the North-gate; a piece of meadow, called The Shield, in St. Mary's Meadow; a houfe or piece of ground, called The Hermitage, near St. James's Chapel clofe; a piece of ground in All Saints parifh called The Vineyard; a piece of ground, called The Lyon-yard, in St. Martin's parifh; Frogmir Bridge; Dead Man's Lane; Cowdrift; Applegate-ftreet; The Mayor's Old Hall; an orchard, whereupon heretofore ftood a houfe called St. John's; St. Margaret's bed; Archdeacon-lane; Butt Clofe; Chaffle-lane; Dove-houfe Clofe beyond the Weft-bridge; Lady-acre in Burgefs Meadow; College Clofe; Hott-gate-ftreet; Clerk Barne; Shire-hall Clofe; Ironmonger-lane; Bakehoufe-lane; and the Mott Orchard.

Pl. XXXI. p.353.

1. LEICESTER CROSS.

built 1557; taken down 1769.

The TOWN HALL.

Over the entrance of the door, in one frame, the arms of king Charles the First, and thofe of the Company of Merchant Taylors, plate XXXI. fig. 2, 3, with this infcription : " Sur Thomas White[1], knight, merchant-tailor and citizen of London 1616.

" Lo ! here a fhip, a merchant-royal, fraught
With ftore of wealth, from whoes rich fides unfought,
Plentie of metall hath been largelie given,
White name, White gifts, White foule, White faint
   in heaven ;
Whoes arms wee (left wee fhew ourfelfs ingrate)
Properly blazon'd here doe celebrate ;
The which eternall monumente fhal be
Of White's renowne, to all pofteritie.
Dye then, and rot, and ftinke, you hulks of fhame,
Who, charg'd with wealth, have nothing but the name
Of dying rich, whofe tombs fhall never fpeak
Your praife ; one White fhall all your credits break."

At the upper end of the Hall, on the right fide of the town-arms, fir Thomas White, knight, in the drefs of lord-mayor of London, with gold chain and collar of SS ; he has a black cap and pointed beard ; his gloves in his right hand ; and on the little-finger of his left hand a ring.

Over his head :
" Quum viginti quatuor urbes hujus regni Angliæ
   fuis ditáffet opibus ;
   annis et honore plenus obiit Feb. 16,
   anno Domini 1566, ætatis fuæ 72."

On the right hand corner :
" Cernitur hic Thomas Whitus fub imagine piĉtâ ;
Cernitur hâc vitâ melius fub imagine verâ ;
Et pater & prætor Londini, miles in illo ;
Providus Oxoniæ fautor, fundator in illâ ;
Briftolii decus eximium ; laus prima Redingæ ;
Gloria Tunbrigiæ ; tibi caufa, Coventria, famæ ;
Urbis honos, orbis prudentia, gemma feneĉtæ."

Over his left fhoulder :
Gules, an annulet Argent, a border Sable charged with three eftoiles Or ; on a canton Ermine a lion rampant of the fecond. Creft, on a wreath a ftork

Argent, beaked and legged Or, fig. 4. Motto, Auxilium meum a Domino.
Round the frame :
" THOMAS WHITE, MILES,
ALDERMANUS CIVITATIS LONDON.
FUNDATOR COLLEGII SANTI JOHANNIS BAPTISTÆ
ET AULÆ GLOCESTRENSIS OXONIÆ.
GULIELMUS HEYRICKE, EQUES,
AMORIS ERGO DEDIT, 1616."

2 On the fame fide is a portrait of James Wigley, efq. of Scraptoft Hall, one of the reprefentatives in parliament for the borough of Leicefter from 1737 till his death in 1765. He is in a full-dreffed fuit of crimfon velvet, and full-bottomed wig.

3. To the left is a portrait of Henry Haftings, fifth earl of Huntingdon of that name, in his robes, and collar and ribbon of the Garter ; a pointed beard ; black cap, and large ruff ; in his right hand a white wand.

Round the frame :
" HENRIE EARLE OF HUNTINGDON, LORD HASTINGS, HUNGERFORD, BOTREUX, MULINS, AND MOULES, KNIGHT OF THE MOST NOBLE ORDER OF THE GARTER, AND LORD PRESIDENT OF THE QUEENE'S COUNSELL IN THE NORTH PARTS OF INGLANDE."

In a compartment at the top of the portrait :
" This noble Peere gave an hundred markes a yeare for ever to fundrie godly ufes ; as thirtie pounds to a publique preacher for the whole town of Leicefter ; ten pounds to the chiefe fchoolemafter their ; ten pounds to four poore fchollers ; and twentye nobles a yeare to the poore of Wigfton's Hofpital in Leicefter ; befides many bookes for a librari, and a ftock of twentie poundes to provide coles at the beft hand for the generall good of the poore ; and fundrie other greate favours which he did for this Corporation, 1623."

On the left fide of the Hall, over the door leading to the Mace-parlour, the arms of the earl of Huntingdon are painted very large on the wall : Within the order of the Garter, Argent a maunch Sable.

[1] Sir Thomas White, a citizen and merchant-taylor of London in 1546, from a noble intention, paid into the hands of the mayor and commonalty of the city of Coventry £1400. to purchafe lands, the rents of which were to be paid to fir Thomas during the remainder of his life, and then to be applied as under. The purchafe brought him in annual.y £70. ; and he dying Feb. 11, 1566, aged 72, his will direĉted that there fhould be given out of it, firft to twelve poor men of the city of Coventry, 40s. a year each, free gift ; next he willed £40. of the refidue to four young men of the fame place, tradefmen, £10. each, for nine years, without intereft, provided they were free of the fame city, and gave fecurity. When the nine years were expired, the faid truft were to pay yearly £20. each, to two young men, free of Coventry, to be continued for thirty years, each holding the money for nine years as before, without intereft ; and at the expiration of that time they were to pay one other freeman of Coventry £40. for nine years, without intereft, and fo on as before for ever. In the fecond year after the expiration of the thirty years, it was alfo ordered that they were to pay to the town of Northampton £40. the Corporation of which was direĉted to lend the fame to four young freemen, inhabitants of that place, £10. each, for nine years, as in the firft inftance, and fo on to four other young men for ever. In the third year after the expiration of the thirty years, they were alfo ordered to pay £40. to the town of Leicefter, to be difpofed of in the fame manner as that at Northampton. In the fourth year the fame fum, and in the like manner, to Nottingham ; in the fifth to Warwick ; and the fixth to Coventry, where the whole £40. were then to be paid to one freeman of the city for nine years, and fo on for ever. It was willed that no perfon was to have it twice ; and to be paid in one month after the deceafe of the principal ; and the perfon to be chofen without partiality. The eftate being much improved in the year 1700, the Corporations preferred a bill in Chancery, for an equitable diftribution of the improved rents, which, upon hearing, was given againft the Corporations ; but, not being fatisfied with this decifion, they brought their claim before the Houfe of Lords the enfuing year ; when it was fettled to their advantage. It happened, upon examining the eftate and fettling the accompts in 1709, that the eftate was improved to the value of £709. 2s. 2d. It was therefore fettled that the firft year, beginning March 25, the whole of the above annual fum fhould go to the city of Coventry, to be difpofed of to the purpofe following, viz. to 121 poor men 40s. each, and to one other poor man 23s. ; in all £243. 3s. ; to be given according to the deed of free-gift to the donor ; and £42. 4s. 2d. to be put out in free-loan, according alfo to the donor's intention. The reft was given to the Merchant-taylors Company, referving a certain portion to the mayor, recorder, and aldermen of Coventry ; and a divifion alfo of it to the fteward and town-clerk of that city ; the whole amounting to the fum of £700. 2s. 2d. This fum the fucceeding year, beginning March 25, was to be divided as follows : to the city of Coventry £243. 3s. to be given to the poor men as before. To the Merchant-taylors, mayor, &c. £60. 15s. ; and to Northampton £405. 4s 2d. Then to Leicefter ; fo on each fucceeding year to Nottingham and Warwick. Various fuits were after this had in Chancery, which were finally adjufted by decree, dated Dec. 20, 1722 ; and on Lady-day 1725, the whole rental amounted to £932 2s. and was then in a ftate of great probable improvement. The fum now in the gift of the mayor and aldermen of Leicefter, arifing from the gift of fir T. White, is faid to amount to £7500. and is lent without intereft to tradefmen freemen of Leicefter, in fums of £40. and £50. ; no perfon being allowed to have more than one 50 and one £40. during his life, and thefe fums never at one time ; no petition of that nature being complied with till after the payment of the firft loan. The Corporation have been very careful that pofterity fhould not fuffer from their negligence or indulgence in lending the money upon hazardous fecurity ; and few inftances have happened detrimental to the intereft of fucceeding generations. Some years ago, when the Corporation built their new Exchange, they intended to have perpetuated the memory of this benefaĉtor, by placing his ftatue in a niche they left for that purpofe in the front of the fame building. Why this was not accomplifhed we have not heard. That the predeceffors of this body of gentlemen poffeffed the warmeft fenfe of the bleffings which through his means have been given to the hand of induftry here, the lines written under his arms in the Town hall will teftify.

Creft,

Creft, on a wreath a buffalo's head erafed, armed, ducally crowned and gorged Or; and this motto, HONORANTES ME HONORABO; fig. 5.

On the oppofite wall, equally large, the arms of the Town are blazoned; fig. 6.

4. Next to the earl of Huntingdon's is a portrait of John Darker, efq. F. R. and A. SS. and one of the reprefentatives in parliament for the borough of Leicefter; who died Feb. 8, 1784, aged 62. He is in a plain modern coat, with a fmall round wig.

In the frame for the mace the town arms are repeated; with the dates 1586, 1702, 1786.

In the Mace-parlour, over the mayor's feat, are the king's arms between two pyramids; under which is written, "Ex dono R. Inge, majoris, anno Dom. 1637."

In the windows of this room in the firft light at the entrance is the figure of a threfher, and two fheaves of corn; and over it " September;" fig. 7.

2d light, a face and portcullis; the border battered, and repaired.

3d light, a large cinquefoil.

4th light, a faint figure of a man; under that a fmall ear of corn, with a few flowerets.

5th light inclofes H. R. and a crown, over which are two chalices, with ihc; fig. 8; and under it two others.

6th light, Prince of Wales's arms and motto, with a P on the right fide, included in a circlet or edging, like a glory or radii-like flames, furrounded with " Honi soit qui mal y pense" in the radius, which inclofes two hands with only two thumbs, fingers out of fight or in gloves, and the arms continued with the coat fleeves, a leg and foot, and part of the thigh, the foot inclining upwards; fig. 9.

7th light, three chalices; and under them June; a man in a cap, bare leg and thigh, ftockings down to the ancles; has a belt, from which hangs another; behind him a building with turrets; before him a wooden fork holds a ftump of a branch upwards, while a hook-like ftick-head pulls down a ragged leaf like holly; fig. 10.

8th light, a royal crown.

9th light, a cinquefoil Azure.

10th light, four chalices, and ihc; fig. 11.

11th light, a winged figure, fig. 12.

12th light, one chalice, and to the right a bear's head, with a fort of flag-ftaff, fig. 13.

13th light, the knot engraved, fig. 14; with five chalices above, and four below it.

In this parlour is a portrait of —— Bond, citizen and goldfmith of London, dated ÆTATIS SUÆ 30; ANNO 1594. He has a picked beard and whifkers, black hair, large ruff round his neck, a dark brown clofe drefs, his wrift covered with a very rich lace, his left hand refting on an ornamented cufhion, his gloves in his right hand.

Arms on the right fide, Argent, on a chevron Sable between three hurts, three eftoiles Argent; on a chief Gules, three cinquefoils Argent; Bond; fig. 15.

On the left fide, Quarterly, 1. and 4. Gules, a leopard's face affronté Or; 2. and 3. Azure, a covered cup between two buckles in fefs Or; the Goldfmiths Company of London; fig. 16.

An excellent portrait of Alderman Robert Heyrick is alfo placed here, painted at the expence of the Corporation; an old man, with a long beard, black cap, ruff round his neck, black drefs, his right hand holding both his gloves, and at the left this infcription:

" His picture whom you here fee,
When he is dead and rotten,
By this fhall he remember'd be
When he fhould be forgotten."

On the right: Quarterly, 1. and 4. Argent, a fefs Vaire, Or and Gules, Heyrick; 2. and 3. Bond as above. Creft, on a wreath a buffalo's head erafed Argent, gorged with a chaplet of rofes proper, leaves Vert; fig. 17.

Near this picture, in a frame, are " Certain Branches of Mr. Heyrick's Will;" fee vol. II. p. 617.

In another frame is fairly written, " A Part of the

laft Will and Teftament of Mr. Alderman Thomas Ludlam the Elder; Nov. 4, 1742;" in which, among other things, he gave £100. towards the repairs of the Trinity Hofpital.

Arms and feals of Leicefter, as framed and glazed in one tablet, over a door at the fide of the chimney of the mace-parlour.

1. Left hand feal at top, on a red ground this circumfcription, a little cinquefoil before the firft word, " SIGILLUM COMMUNITATIS :: BURGI LEICESTRIE." The above is the great common feal for deeds, conveyances, &c. kept by the mayor and two chamberlains, under two keys.

2. The feal for ftatutes, kept by the mayor for the time being; i. e. the Virgin Mary, with a child on her left arm, a long-ftemmed, or crofier crucifix in her right hand, reaching over her right fhoulder, under her feet a cinquefoil on a red ground, circumfcribed, " SIGILL. STAT. MAJO. BURGI LEICESTRI."

3. A fmall cinquefoil, red ground, circumfcribed, " BURGUS LEICESTRIE." This feal for capias's, letters, &c.

4. A larger cinquefoil than the laft, " ✠ SIGILLUM STATUT, BURGI LEICESTRIE." This is another feal for the ftatutes, kept by the clerk of the ftatutes.

5. Three arrow heads, the middlemoft continued as a perfect arrow, with fide feathers, &c.; on their left a cinquefoil, on their right a ferpentine label, infcribed, " IN ANTITRINITARIOS;" and circumfcribed, " SIGIL. HOSPITALIS S'CTE TRINITATIS, IN NOVO OPERE, LEIC." This is the feal of Trinity hofpital in the Newark[1], kept by the mayor and two chamberlains, alfo under two keys.

6. A large cinquefoil, over it a cafque, and over that a dragon, ftyled the arms of the borough of Leicefter.

7. Three lions paffant under a coronet (the duke of Lancafter's arms).

" Thefe are the arms and town feales, ufed by the mayor and burgeffes of the borough of Leicefter, incorporated by the name of mayor, bayliffe, and burgeffes, of the faid borough of Leicefter, and enabled with many great and large privileges and immunities by many of the ancient Kings of England, and fince confirmed and enlarged by King James, and laftly by our moft gracious Souveraign that now is, 20 Jan. anno 16 Car. II. with a refervation to his Majefty, his heirs and fucceffors, of approving the recorder, fteward, follicitor, and town clark; of which faid borough, at the time of the fecond Vifitation, viz. 23 Martii, 1681, George Bent, efq. was mayor; Edmund Sutton, Philip Abney, John Roberts, and John Goodall, juftices of the peace within the faid borough, being the fower laft perfons who ferved the office of mayor; Mr. William Major, and Mr. William Elliott, bayliffs; Thomas Staveley, barrifter at law, fteward of the faid borough; William Storingthorpe and Henry Pate, chamberlains; Nathan Wright, barrifter at law, recorder; and John Huckle, town clark; and William Browne, follicitor. The aldermen are in number twenty-four, and the common-councell forty-eight.—Attefted under the hand of George Bent, mayor."

The Town Cross (Plate XXXI.) was erected in 1577, to replace an older one, which had been taken down before 1569, as appears by an entry in the accompts of the churchwardens of St. Martin's for that year[2]. The late Crofs, which was a light handfome building, was taken down in 1773, when the prefent fubftitute for it was made from one of the pillars.

The Exchange at Leicefter was built in alderman Smalley's mayoralty in 1747[3]. The lower part, intended as fhambles[4] for the town-butchers, was but a fhort time ufed for that purpofe. The upper rooms, one of which is fpacious, and rather elegantly furnifhed, were intended, and are ufed to fupply the place of the old Gainfborough, which ftood likewife in the market-place prior to the prefent building. Here the magiftrates for the borough affemble on certain days to determine fuch judicial matters as are brought before them.

---

[1] See Plate XXVIII. fig. 16.   [2] " Payd to Bodely for carying the ftones and ramell away from where the Croffe ftood viii d."
[3] See the propofal in 1762 to convert it into an infirmary; Gent. Mag. vol. XXXII. p. 196.
[4] This was but a modern building when deftroyed, and it was equal to moft both for utility and ornament. The ruins of this building were ufed to make the foundation for the Exchange. The fhambles which now remain in Leicefter, near St. Nicholas' church, were built for the week-day market; but have been long fince difufed.

ANNALS OF LEICESTER;

Confifting of ORIGINAL CHARTERS, AUTHENTIC CORPORATION RECORDS; and MISCELLANEOUS EVENTS, digefted according to the Series of Time.

THE early Hiftory of this antient and famous Borough, from the firft dawning of rude tradition, through the fucceffive periods of its domination under the Romans, and the fucceffive ftruggles between the native Britains and the invading Saxons, Jutes, and Angles, has already been amply difcuffed. The Angles[1], we may briefly repeat, took poffeffion of *The Midland*—the moft noble of all the intruding party; not only as under king Egbert they gave name to the whole united kingdom, but as our anceftors were always proud of the appellation of *Angles*, when their enemies in contempt called them *Saffons*[2]. Egbert, by public edict, commanded that the feveral provinces united fhould be called *Angles-land*. The memories of the Jutes being worn out, and the name of the Saxons fuppreffed, the Angles only remained, who, in refpect of their number, might feem to challenge by right the denomination.

LEICESTER, during the Heptarchy, was a part of the kingdom of *Mercia*; of whofe dukes, or earls, an accurate lift has been given[3]; and alfo of the ravages of the Danes from the ninth to the eleventh century[4].

Of the Saxon earls of Leicefter before the period of the Conqueft enough has been already faid[5]; and the ftate of Leicefter at that memorable epoch defcribed from a public record of moft unqueftionable authority[6].

I fhall now endeavour to collect, in as fuccinct a manner as may be, the regular Annals of the Town of Leicefter, and of the remarkable events with which it has been connected; and fhall, under this head, introduce the various Charters at different times obtained by its inhabitants, with fuch interefting particulars as an attentive examination of original documents can produce. But firft it may be neceffary to recapitulate briefly what has been already detailed; which cannot be more concifely performed than from the words of Mr. Burton's MS. which, when the former part was printing, I had not had the opportunity of confulting.

"LEICESTER, called alfo by antient writers, and in old records, *Legracefter*, *Legecefter*, *Legeocefter*, *Leogora*, and *Caër-Lerion*; fo named, not of that fabulous king Leir, whom Geffrey of Monmouth will have to be the firft builder thereof[7]; but for that it ftandeth upon the river of *Legra*, or *Leir*, now called *Soar*, as Leland holdeth[8], and William of Malmefbury[9], fignifying as much as the City ftanding upon the river Leir. Many other cities and places in this land fo denominated, as *Colchefter* upon the river *Colne*, *Excefter* upon the river *Exe*, *Riblechefter* upon the river *Rible*. It ftandeth in the centre and heart of the fhire; the fhire (as I have elfewhere faid[10]) bearing the proportion of an heart, and being in the very midft and heart of the land, as by all writers, and by the topography thereof, doth appear; and upon the great road-way called *The Fofs* (as Ranulph Higden affirmeth), which goeth from the South into the North, which begins at Totnefs in Devonfhire, and endeth at Catnefs in the utmoft part of Scotland, paffing through Lincoln[11]. It is fituated in a moft rich, delicate, and pleafant foil, and a delicious air;

and, whether you refpect health or wealth, pleafure or profit, it is in this place afforded. To parallel it with other Cities, is not my purpofe; but, had it a Navigable River[12], whereby it might have trading and commerce, it might compare with many of no mean rank. For the antiquity thereof, I fhall fpeak what I have either read or found in the beft and moft approved writers. That this was a City in the Britains time, before the coming of the Romans, I fhould conjecture by the name thereof fet down by Nennius in his Catalogue of Cities[13], viz. *Caer Lerion*, that is, the City upon Leir. And Henry of Huntingdon, in his Hiftory[14], fetting down the names of all the Cities which were in this ifland in the Britains time, there nameth this City to be one, in thefe words, viz. *Caër Lerion*, i. e. *Leiceftria*. That this fhould be *Rata*, mentioned in Antonine's Itinerarium, as Mr. Camden in the late editions of his Britannia would have it, I cannot affent unto; but muft reduce *Rata* to *Ratby*, a village diftant fome three miles hence, where firft Mr. Camden placed it, and of which opinion he was in the firft editions of his book; and that very rightly, as hereafter, when I come to Ratby, I fhall fet down more plainly, by reafon of certain intelligences and antiquities which I have both heard and feen fince the firft edition of this book; yet, neverthelefs, I will not deny but that the Romans had fome refiding here. And that this was a great Roman ftation, thefe Roman antiquities (here found and affirmed) will give ftrength and confirmation[15].

"Firft, the antient temple here, dedicated to Janus, which had a *flamen*, or high prieft, here refident; in which place great ftore of bones of beafts (which here have been facrificed) have been digged up and found, and the place yet called thereof *The Holy Bones*; which all hiftories do agree to have been here, and furely was the foundation of the Romans, as appeareth by their god Janus Bifrons, to whofe honour the firft temple was built in Rome by Romulus and Tatius; or, as others fay, Numa Pompilius, in a place called *Argiletum*; and not founded by that feigned king Leir to the honour of Janus, as Geffrey of Monmouth, and, (of latter days) John Harding and John Rous of Warwick, will have it; which how fabulous and improbable it is, any ordinary capacity may conceive, in that it is known to all that Janus was not adored or thought of ever of any but the Romans. And this king Leir died (at leaft) 300 years before Rome was built, as by their own chronology and computation will appear[16]: but this, and many fuch improbabilities and contradictions, will eafily convince this forged hiftory of Brute and of his progeny: fome whereof are cited by Richard Verftegan, in his "Reftitution of decayed Intelligence in Antiquities," p. 90; and exceeding well difcovered by Mr. Speed, in his Hiftory, fol. 163. Part of the wall of this temple is yet to be feen ftanding at the Weft end of St. Nicholas's church; a wonderful antient piece of work as any, I think, to be found in this kingdom, made of Roman large bricks and fmall flints, bound with fo folid a mortar, that with an ordinary tool it

---

[1] "Angles—moft probably from that part of Denmark (yet retaining the name of Angle) which lieth between Juitland and Holfatia. From them came the Eaft Angles, the Mercians, and Northumbers." Hiftorie of Great Britaine, 1606, p. 187. [2] Kennett's Parochial Antiquities, p. 23. [3] See before, in this volume, p. 14. [4] Pp. 14—16. [5] Pp. 16. 17. [6] See the extracts from Domefd-y, p. 17. [7] Hift. l. i. c. 15. [8] Collect. tom. II. p. 323. [9] De Geftis Pontif. lib. 4. fol. 165. [10] See vol. II. p. 1. [11] Henry de Huntington, fol. 171. b. Aluredus Beverlacenfis, in cap. de Dunvallone. [12] An advantage it has of late years very fortunately obtain-d. See before, p. clxi. [13] P. 227. [14] Lib. I. fol. 170. b. [15] Of the *Rawdykes*, a Roman fortification in the neighbourhood, fee before, p. 4; and under Aylefton, in vol. IV. p. 25. [16] See Dr. George Hakewell, in his "Apology or Declaration of the Power and Providence of God in the Government of the World," fol. 8.

cannot

cannot be pierced [1]; which well may be perceived, in that since the foundation thereof it hath (though uncovered) withstood the fury of Time almost 1700 years. The wall is between four and five feet thick, about 23 or 24 feet high without, vaulted in the walls; which I have viewed, and well obferved, not without much admiration thereof. Next, the many Roman antiquities here found, their medaglies and coins in great abundance, both in filver and copper; of Vefpafian, Domitian, Trajan, Hadrian, Antonine, and others, which I myfelf have feen, and have of them. About ten years before the firft edition of this book (about 1612), near unto the town, without and between the North and Weft gates, fomewhat deep in the ground, was found a piece of work of ftone arched over, the ftones whereof it was made being very fmall, about an inch long, and half an inch broad and thick, neatly jointed together; and (as fince it hath been related unto me) the pavement thereof was of quarries of curious workmanfhip [2], fome fquare, fome round, whereon were drawn the lively proportions of flowers, knots, frets, and other inventions, in exceeding orient colours. In the walls were fet little ftatues and antickes, imboffed and cut out; the roof covered with a like kind of quarry of the fame workmanfhip, wherein were many fmall and earthen pipes; it was in length near fix yards, in breadth near four. This I guefs to be a *ftouphe*, or hothoufe [3], to bathe in; for, as Vitruvius writeth, the Romans growing to the height of riotoufnefs and excefs, ufed thefe baths to wafh and clarify themfelves withal, and that every day ufually before meals. And within the Roman empire they grew fo famous and coftly, that, as Seneca writeth [4], he feemeth to be but of mean and poor eftate, whofe bath walls did not fhine with precious ftones, and were adorned with pictures of feveral coloured ftones; the vaults arched with cryftal and Thafian ftones; the cocks of filver, to fpout out water; the building fupported with curious pillars, graced with lively ftatues, and the floor fet with rich jewels; and (as Pliny hath it [5]) in fome the whole fides, feats, and pavement, were of pure filver, fo bright that they could hardly go thereon for fliding; which were accuftomed, for their further delight (as Rofinus [6] faith), to be anointed with rich and fweet ointments. Thefe baths were of two forts; thofe which had only the ufe of warm water brought in pipes, and let in by cocks, whereof Seneca fpake in his epiftle above vouched; or thofe which were by fire made hot, as this here in this place fpoken of; and that whereof Sextus Aurelius Victor writeth [7], which Conftantine the Great Emperor caufed to be made fo wonderfully hot, that, having put thereinto Flavia Maximiana Faufta his wife (for that fhe had, upon falfe fuggeftions of inceftous attempts, caufed the faid Conftantine to put to death his eldeft fon Crifpus Cæfar by his firft wife) fhe was inftantly ftifled. In both thefe forts of baths men and women entered promifcuoufly together; a filthy cuftom amongft the antients, whereof Plutarch complaineth that the Grecians learned it of the Romans [8]. Dio writeth [9], that Agrippa firft inftituted thefe mixed baths at Rome; which the wife Emperor Hadrian endeavoured to fupprefs, erecting for each fex feveral baths, as Dio and Ælian Spartianus,

in his life, do fhew; but it fhould feem they lafted not long; for Antoninus Philofophus (as it is in Julius Capitolinus) made a law againft thefe promifcuous baths, which was kept till the time of Heliogabalus, who abrogated it. Alexander Severus (as Lampridius writeth) reftored Antoninus's laws again; but with no long fuccefs, forafmuch as the antient Chriftians did formerly ufe and frequent thefe mixed baths, which by the Clementine Conftitutions [10] were prohibited; and alfo by fynodal decrees in the Council of Laodicea, can. 30; yet, notwithftanding, this uncivil fafhion continued long after; and Juftinian the Emperor, amongft the lawful caufes of divorces, fetteth this down for one; ' if a wife do enter into a bath with men, not having firft obtained licence of her hufband for the fame [11].'

" This City was after called by the Saxons *Legrecefter*, and thofe other variations above named, in the fame fenfe, as is before fhewed. And in that divifion of the kingdom into an Heptarchy, it came to the king of Mercia; and king Ethelred, dividing his kingdom into bifhopricks in the year 680 (but, as the right reverend bifhop Dr. Godwin in his Catalogue of Bifhops faith, in the year 737) placed here an epifcopal fee [12], making Sexulfe the firft bifhop, to whom fucceeded (as William of Malmefbury writeth [13]) Wilfrid, Hedda, Aldwine, Totta, Edbert, Unwon [14], Werenbert, Rethun [15], Aldred, Ceolred, and Leofwine the laft bifhop; in whofe time, and in the reign of king Edgar, about the year 970, it was united to Lincoln. This City falling to decay (either upon the diffolution of the kingdom of Mercia, or through the Danifh cruelty), was after repaired by Egelfleda [16], wife of Etheldred a prince of Mercia, and daughter of king Alfred, in the 14th year of the reign of king Edward fenior, 914; and which was by her fo well walled and fortified, that it continued for many years after, and was termed by Matthew of Paris (who wrote in the time of king Henry III.) to be impregnable [17].

" At the Conqueft time it was well peopled and frequented, and had many burgeffes in it; out of which number they were bound, by an antient cuftom (as appeareth by the book of Domefday made by William the Conqueror), to fend twelve with the king, fo often as he went in perfon to the wars; but, if he made a voyage by fea againft his enemies, then they were to fend four horfes to carry armour and ammunition as far as London. This City paid yearly to the king 30l. by tale, and 20 by weight, and 25 fexterces or meafures of honey. At that time there were fix churches in this town; a mint; and 322 houfes within the king's demefne, or held under him *in capite*; which, however, does not fhew the complete number of houfes; for many of thefe burgage-tenants had under-tenants, not noticed in the general furvey.

" *Robert de Bellemont* (in his mother's right earl of *Mellent* in Normandy), fon to *Roger* de Bellemont, and coufin in the fourth degree to the Conqueror [18]; attending his kinfman into England, and fighting valiantly in the battle of Haftings [19], was by him rewarded with vaft poffeffions [20], being, at the time of this furvey, feifed of 64 lordfhips in Warwickfhire, 16 in Leicefterfhire, 7 in Wiltfhire, 3 in Northamptonfhire, and 1 in Gloucefterfhire [21].

---

[1] This wall is particularly defcribed and engraved in pp. 5, 6; with the famous Roman milliary, found long after Mr. Burton's time.

[2] This difcovery has been noticed in p. 9, from the Chetwynd MS; but I have thought proper to give it here in the original words of Mr. Burton; who obferves, that " thefe kinds of pavement are at large defcribed by Petrus Crinitus, in his Commentaries de Honeftâ Difciplinâ, lib. xxii. c. 1."—Many others have fince been difcovered in and near Leicefter. See pp. 9—14.

[3] The figure of them you may fee in Boifard's Antiquities of Rome, tom. II. iii. 5. and tom. III. ii. 1; who, in fix tomes, hath collected the chiefeft antiquities now in Rome, curioufly cut in copper by Theodore de Bryij; printed in folio, 1597.

[4] Epift. 86.   [5] Lib. xxiii. cap. 12.   [6] De Antiquit. Rom.

[7] Fol. 179 edit Steph. 1544   [8] In the life of M. Cato.   [9] Lib. xlix.   [10] Lib. i. cap. 6. 9.

[11] Juftin. Novell. 117.   [12] Florentius Wigornenfis, fol. 562.   [13] Lib. iv. Pontif. fol. 165.

[14] Unwon bifhop of Leicefter is a witnefs to the charter of Kenulph king of Mercia, made to the abbey of Crowland, dated anno 806. See Ingulphus, fol. 486. b.

[15] Rethun is a witnefs to the charter of Bertulph king of Mercia, made to the abbey of Crowland, dated 851. Ingulphus, fol. 490.   [16] Hen. Huntingdon, lib. v. fol. 204. Florentius Wigornenfis, fol. 346.

[17] In the year 942 (as it is in Florentius Wigornenfis, fol. 351.) king Edmund, brother to king Athelftan, did free from the power of the Danes five cities, viz. Lincoln, Nottingham, Derby, Leicefter, and Stamford; and brought all Mercia wholly under his own government.   [18] Gul. Gemeticenfis, pp. 312, 650, 688.

[19] Gul. Pictavienfis, p. 197.   [20] William of Malmefbury.   [21] See Domefday Book, under thefe feveral counties.

" Within

" Within the town was a houfe of *Francifcan* or *Grey Friers*, built by Simon Montfort earl of Leicef-ter[1]; whither (after Bofworth field) the dead body of king Richard III. naked, truffed behind a purfui-vant of arms, all dafhed with mire and blood, was brought, and there homely buried; where afterward king Henry VII. (out of a royal difpofition) erected for him a fair alabafter monument, with his picture cut out, and made thereon. Sir William Moton, of Peckleton, knight, was buried in this houfe in 1362.

" Here alfo was founded a Chapel of St. *Andrew*, or (as others fay) an Hofpital, by *William the Leper*[2], fon to Robert Blanchmaines earl of Leicefter.

" About the midft of the town, near St. Martin's church, ftood the houfe of *Black Friars* (there is a lane thereby yet called *Black Friars Lane*); by whom built I know not[3]. To them, in 1285, Robert de Willoughby and Alice his wife gave two parcels of ground in Leicefter[4]. In the cloifter, in a niche in the wall, not long fince was found a coffin of ftone, wherein was a corpfe laid in bond leather.

" There was alfo in Leicefter the hofpital of *St. Leonard*, to which Simon de Montfort earl of Lei-cefter gave much land; and in 1307, Thomas earl of Lancafter gave thereto three meffuages, four acres, and a quarter of a rood of meadow, in Leicefter, Burftall, and Sharnford[5].

" There was alfo an hofpital of *St. John* in Leicefter, to which Philip Danet, in 1329, gave five meffuages and feven yard lands and a half in Whetftone, Croft, and Frifby juxta Gaulby[6]. All the lands belonging to this houfe were afterward granted by king Henry IV. to the new College in Leicefter called *Newark*.

" In the Suburb without the South gate ftood the *Au-guftine Friers*, to which houfe Thomas earl of Lancafter was a great benefactor; who gave them three mef-fuages in the faid fuburbs of Leicefter in 1304[7]. In the year 1629, in a lane called Millftone-lane, near to the Horfe-fair leys, without the South gate, was found and digged up a great ftone coffin covered, wherein was a coffin of lead, and therein the bones of a body; fo that I fhould guefs that this was the fite of the faid friery, wherein this corpfe had been interred."

Thus far in the words of Mr. Burton, from his MS additions to the printed book. I fhall now pro-ceed to fuch particular events as can be collected from the beft hiftorical records; in the courfe of which the judicious refearches of our venerable pre-deceffor will occafionally be very ferviceable.

HENRY I.

About the year 1102, the prohibition of priefts' marriages, which had been ordained by archbifhop Anfelm in a Council at London, was publifhed at Leicefter; but was received with great heat, and re-jected by many of the married clergy[8].

" The firft that was honoured with the title of earl of *Leicefter* after the Conqueft was *Robert de Bellemont*, already noticed as the follower of the Conqueror under the title of earl of *Mellent*; who, in the differences between king Henry I. and Ro-bert de Curthofe his brother, faithfully adhering to the king, was by him advanced to the earl-dom of Leicefter[9], the City being then in the hands of four lords, viz. the King, the Bifhop of Lincoln, Earl Simon, and Ivo the fon of Hugo [Grentefmenill][10]; which Ivo, being then in rebel-lion, deprived of the king's favour, and fined in a great fum, endeavoured to obtain a reconciliation by the mediation of the faid earl of Mellent; but, dying foon after in a pilgrimage beyond fea, this earl fub-jected it all to his power, after which he exceeded all the nobles of the realm in riches and grandeur, being alfo efteemed the wifeft man betwixt England and Jerufalem (as Henry of Huntingdon faith[11]) in worldly affairs. He repaired the caftle of Leicefter; in the limits of which, in the time of the Saxons,

there was a collegiate church (of whofe foundation is not known); which, being ruined at the Norman in-vafion, was in 1107 re-built by *Robert* earl of *Mel-lent* and *Leicefter*, and dedicated to the Bleffed Virgin; wherein he placed a dean and 12 fecular canons, re-ftoring to them all the antient poffeffions belonging to that church[12]. He founded the Hofpital of Brack-ley, co. Northampton, and was a great benefactor to the abbey of Preaux in France (which was of the foundation of Humphry de Vitulis his grandfather); in which abbey, retiring from the world, he became a monk, and, dying in 1118, his body was there buried; but his heart was fent to Brackley[13]."

To this earl was owing the abolition of the trial by battle for lands and tenements in burgage; in return for which, the payment called *Gavel pence* (which was a penny a-year for every houfe which had a gable in the front) was firft levied. To him alfo was owing the eftablifhment in Leicefter of the com-pany of *Twenty-four* (of which more fully hereafter); and the privilege of fetching wood from Leicefter Foreft on the payment of a very moderate acknow-ledgement; which, from being collected at the bridges of the town, was called *Brigg-filver*.

William, the eldeft fon, fucceeded his father in the earldom of *Mellent*; and *Robert* furnamed *Boffu* (or *Crouchback*), the fecond fon, obtained the earldom of Leicefter. He was much favoured by king Henry I. to whom he continued conftantly faithful.

STEPHEN.

In works of piety earl *Robert Boffu* far furmounted his father. By the advice of Alexander bifhop of Lincoln, and permiffion of king Stephen, between the years 1137 and 1143, he founded an abbey (without the walls) at Leicefter, dedicated to the ho-nour of the Affumption of the Bleffed Virgin. Of this magnificent abbey and its large poffeffions an account has been already given, very far beyond what at the commencement of this undertaking I had even hoped to obtain; but of which the fol-lowing very brief recapitulation in the words of Mr. Burton's MS. may not be unacceptable.

" *Robert Boffu* earl of *Leicefter* founded the moft fumptuous and goodly monaftery of *St. Mary de Pra-tis*, without the walls, for canons regular of the order of St. Auftin[14]; fo called, for that it ftood upon the edge of the meadows, and had the delicious and plea-fant profpect of them and the water; into which houfe the faid Robert Boffu became a canon regular pro-feffed by the fpace of fifteen years, that fo, by re-pentance, he might expiate his former treafons com-mitted to his king and fovereign; endowing the fame with the prebends' lands and poffeffions belonging to the canons fecular of the collegiate church. But, in return for what he thus took away from the church of St. Mary, he founded a new college there, dedi-cated to the Virgin Mary, called after (for diftinction fake) *Collegium Beatæ Mariæ Minoris*, for a mafter and feven fellows[15]. This abbey had in this fhire twenty fix parifh churches appropriated unto it; which at the fuppreffion thereof was valued yearly to difpend 1062*l.* 4*d.* ob. q. It was endowed by divers kings with many and large privileges, as by king Edward I. Edward II. and Edward III. with grant of free warren in all the demefne lands, and by name, in 16 feveral lordfhips in feveral fhires. King Henry IV. granted to them, that no purveyor, or taker of the king's, fhould enter into their fee, or upon their lands take any corn, cattle, carriages, grain, or other manner of purveyance. The abbot of this houfe had a place in parliament till 26 Edw. III.; at which time, upon petition made by William Clowne, then abbot, he was difcharged of fummons or appearance there, by the king; for that, as he alledged, he had not a whole barony, or held not *per baroniam*[16].

In 1149, Theobald archbifhop of Canterbury, being

---

[1] See p. 297.   [2] See p. 323.   [3] It was founded, about 1250, by the fecond earl Simon de Mountfort. See p. 295.
[4] 13 Edw. I. N° 55.   [5] See p. 321.   [6] See p. 324.   [7] See before, p. 310.
[8] See p. 22.   [9] Ordericus Vitalis, p. 700.   [10] Ibid. p. 805.
[11] Henry of Huntingdon, MS. de contemptu mundi, in Bibl. Cotton. fol. 3.   [12] Cart. Antiq. CC. n. 23, 1107.
[13] Burton, MS. citing H. Knighton, MS.   [14] Leland, tom. 1. fol. 30.   [15] See before, p. 303.
[16] Pat. 26 Edw. III. pars prima, m. 22. and Hen. de Knighton, temp. Edw. III.

at Leicefter in the regular courfe of his metropoli-
tical vifitation, called thither the monks of Coventry,
to elect a bifhop for that fee.

In 1151, the famous agreement was entered into
between Robert de Boffu earl of Leicefter and Ranulph de Gernoniis earl of Chefter, for afcertaining
the boundaries of their refpective properties[1].

HENRY II.

To earl Robert Boffu the burgeffes of Leicefter
were indebted for a confirmation of the feveral privileges granted by his father; and for remitting the
payment of the Gavel-pence. He died in 1167; and
his lady Amicia became a nun in the monaftery of
Nuneaton. He was buried in Leicefter abbey, in the
South wall of the high altar, in a tomb *ex marmore
Chalcedonico*, as Leland termeth it in his Itinerary.

To him fucceeded *Robert*, his fon and heir, furnamed *Blanchmaines*; who, in the year 1173, involved
himfelf and nearly the whole town of Leicefter in one
common ruin. In the early part of that year, king
Henry II. being then in France on account of the re-
volt of his fon (whom he had not long before caufed
to be crowned in his life-time), the earl of Leicefter
obtained from Richard de Lucy, regent of the realm
during the king's abfence, permiffion to vifit his poffeffions in Normandy. Previous to his departure, the
walls and gates of Leicefter, by the earl's care, and
the zeal of his burgeffes, were rendered fo ftrong,
and fo well provided with other means of defence, as
to be confidered impregnable; and the town and
caftle were placed by him under the government of
David brother to William king of Scotland. When
arrived at his caftle of Breteuil in Normandy, the earl
of Leicefter, who had collected vaft fums of money
from all quarters, declared himfelf openly on the part
of the young king, in whofe fervice he very actively
engaged. That caftle was in confequence befieged,
and deftroyed by the elder Henry; the earl of Leicefter having precipitately fled from it to join the
king of France. The town of Leicefter alfo fell a
victim to the monarch's rage; who, early in the
fummer, to revenge the earl's defection, fent fpecial
orders to Richard de Lucy to go againft that town;
which was accordingly attacked on the 3d of July;
and, in confequence of an accidental fire, was fpeedily
fubdued, and the inhabitants compelled to purchafe
the privilege of retiring with their property[2].

"By the rebellion of Robert Blanchmaines," fays
Mr. Burton, "the inhabitants of Leicefter were reduced to great mifery; the town being facked and
burnt by the king's forces[3], the walls caft down, and
the inhabitants forced to pay 300 marks for their
ranfom; whereupon they had licence to depart to
any of the king's cities or caftles; but divers of
them, through fear, took fanctuary at St. Alban's,
St. Edmund's Bury, and elfewhere."

The earl of Leicefter, cut to the heart at this dif-
aftrous event, repaired to England, early in October,
with an army of 10,000 Flemings; and, fighting unfuccefsfully near St. Edmund's Bury, loft the battle
and his liberty, he and his lady being both taken prifoners. A heavy fine was in confequence inflicted on
him; his lands and tenements were feized into the
king's hands; his caftles of Leicefter, Groby, and
Mountforell, demolifhed; and his perfon for a confiderable time detained in cuftody: but, in the beginning of the year 1177, he was again received into
the king's favour; and *all Leicefter* (that is, the borough and earldom, with its feveral knights fees and

tenements) were reftored to him[4]; after which, intending a pilgrimage to the Holy Land, he confirmed
the grants made by his anceftors to the monks of
Lyra and St. Ebrulph.

In 1185, Ralph fon of Godwin and others were
fined, for fending to Leicefter for a coat of mail[5].

RICHARD I.

Earl Robert Blanchmaines died in 1190 on his
voyage to the Holy Land, leaving, by Parnell his
wife, daughter of Hugh de Grentemefnill, *Robert
Fitz Parnell*, his fon and heir; who, Feb. 1, 1190-1,
was invefted in the earldom of Leicefter at Meffina in
Sicily; whence, attending the king into the Holy
Land, he there unhorfed and flew the Soldan in a
tournament.

In 1194, we find the earl of Leicefter indebted to
Aaron the Jew in the fum of 452l. 6s. 8d. on a
mortgage of feveral of his effects. After his return,
in 1196, he was taken prifoner by the French, and
forced to give 2000 marks and the caftle of Pacy to
the French king for his redemption.

JOHN.

"We are now arrived at that grand epocha," to
ufe the words of an ingenious native of Leicefter,
"which diftinguifhes the reign of king John from all
others. The tyranny of the fix preceding monarchs
of the Norman race, and his own imbecillity and bafe-
nefs of heart, after a violent ftruggle, gave us the
bulwark of Englifh Liberty, *Magna Charta*; but,
prior to this, he had given particular grants and
privileges to many large towns in the kingdom; and
much earlier than the completion of that noble deed,
he had granted feveral charters to this town, perhaps,
in fome meafure, from motives of compaffion, to
fofter its inhabitants, children of adverfity; who
even then felt anguifh from that fcourge of vengeance and revenge brought on them for the crimes
of an imperious nobleman, their lord and governor[6]."

A charter of this monarch, whilft he was only lord
of Ireland and earl of Mortaigne, bears date at Leicefter, where he appears to have been at leaft an occafional refident; and on his acceffion to the throne,
in the firft year of his reign, June 29, 1199, the
earl of Leicefter obtained from him a charter "de Libertatibus[7];" and on the 26th of December the
king granted and confirmed to the burgeffes of Leicefter, that all thofe buyings and fellings of the
lands of the town of Leicefter, which had been, or
fhould be, reafonably made in court, called *The
Portman Mote* of the fame town, fhould remain firm
and valid; and another, for the free paffage and trading of the burgeffes of Leicefter through the whole
kingdom, without paying any manner of toll, ftallage, &c.[8]

The great kindnefs of this noble earl to the burgeffes of Leicefter is evinced by a charter exempting
them from all payments in lieu of perfonal fervice in
the gathering-in of his harveft, and alfo from the
penalties incurred for cattle impounded[9]. They were
alfo indebted to him for the gift expreffed in the following undated charter, tranflated from a Corpora-
tion-book of References:

"Know all men prefent and to come, that I Robert earl of Leicefter have given, granted, and by
this my prefent charter confirmed, to the free burgeffes of the town of Leicefter, certain limits, being
according as they have been appointed, divided, and
fet out, by my direction, upon the view of lawful

---

[1] See the prefent volume, p. 26.   [2] See p. 72.

[3] Roger de Hoveden Annalium pars pofterior, fol. 307. b. Matthew Paris, fol. 172. Matthew of Weftminfter, Flor. Hiftor. lib.
li. fol. 38. Mr. Carte was of opinion, that the quarter of the town which lies between the North and South gates, and is called
The Back Lanes, was never rebuilt from the time of this grand demolition. The wall is reprefented as having been almoft impregnable; and fo indiffoluble was the cement, that fome remarkable pieces of it remained for above 400 years after, as
appears by an order, made March 26, 33 Elizabeth, that no one decay or pull down the town wall, by getting ftones, except
by licence of a common hall, on pain of twenty fhillings. The late Rev. William Ludlam, in a letter with which he feveral
years ago favoured me, obferves, that "the plan of Leicefter, as it ftood before that event, is eafily to be traced. In the
heart of the town, on each fide the principal ftreet, are a number of large orchards; feparated not with one common fence as
ufual, but a double fence; a wall belonging to each, with public ways between the two walls, called *Back Lanes*. Thefe
back lanes were manifeftly the ftreets, and the orchards the fite of houfes and yards deftroyed, and never fince rebuilt. The
traces of the town-wall and ditch are in many places to be feen."

[4] See p. 78.   [5] Madox, Hiftory of the Exchequer, p. 391.   [6] Throfby, p. 56.   [7] Harl. MS. 84. fol. 104. b.
[8] See both thefe charters in p. 97.   [9] See this deed at length in p. 97.

men:

men: A certain pasture which is called *Cowhaye*, without *The South Gates*; with free ingress and egress appertaining unto the said pasture, through my lordship; to wit, a pasture which is between my pasture which is called *Oxbey* and near the mill of *Amaris Danet* on the one part, and *Tackholme* on the other part; to have and to hold the said pasture, with the said appurtenances, to my said burgesses and their heirs and assigns, of me and my heirs, freely and quietly for ever; they honourably paying thereout to me, and my heirs and successors, for every cow joisted or to be joisted, and for every beast in the said pasture joisted or to be joisted, 3*d*. by the year. And, for this grant and confirmation, the said burgesses have given me a certain sum of money in hand, by way of fine, that neither I the said Robert, nor my heirs, my successors, nor any other person by us nor for us, may have any challenge or claim unto the said pasture hereafter. In witness whereof, I have confirmed this charter with my seal. Testibus; Willo de Semfell, Thomâ Esterling, Radulpho Mortivall, Ernest de . . . ., Gilberto Miners, Galfrido Costeyn, . . . de Cranford, &c."

An early grant from king John to this earl Robert, of property in the Strand, has been already printed[1]; and an undated grant from the same earl to *Geoffrey the Smith*, of land without the South gate of Leicester, which had been held in serjeanty by Richard the son of Herbert, grandfather to the said Geoffrey, has also been noticed on account of the rarity of the seal[2].

In 1201, king John summoning the barons, and other immediate tenants of the crown, to attend him at Portsmouth, in order to embark for his transmarine dominions, and reduce the province of Poictou to his obedience, which had revolted; the barons, instead of obeying the king's summons, assembled at Leicester, and from thence sent a message to the king, that they would not attend him in this voyage, unless he would restore them their antient rights and privileges; whereupon the king immediately marched against them with what troops he had about him; and, having taken Belvoir castle, which they had fortified, the barons were so terrified by this sudden attack, which they were not prepared to oppose, that they all submitted, and came to the rendezvous at Portsmouth[3].

In 1202, the public records preserve a deed under the title of " Pardonatio Roberti comitis Mellent[4]."

William son of *Heneric* (or rather *William Fitz Lewerick*, for so his name occurs as a witness to a deed) appears to have been an alderman of the gild of Leicester in 1203; and is the earliest person that the attentive researches of Mr. Carte could discover under that denomination[5].—" The government of the town," Mr. Carte adds, " is now vested in 24 aldermen, whereof one is mayor, with a recorder, and the company of 48, who are the common council. But, by such records or passages in antient writings as I have seen, I judge that the corporation originally consisted of a gild of merchants, whereof the master was styled alderman: I have met with several with that title; and the entry of freemen in the town books was long continued under the title of *Gilda mercatorum*. At the same time as there began to be a mayor, the company of twenty-four was also established; out of whom one is chosen annually, Sept. 21, to be mayor, who enters on his office Sept. 29; and on the Monday after Martinmas swore fealty to the earl of Leicester, as he does now to the king as duke of Lancaster[6]."—"' The Borough of Leicester is an antient corporation of a mayor and aldermen, incorporated by king John. Within the said Borough there be four justices of peace. The mayor is justice for four years after; and as there be new mayors, there be new justices; and they go forth after the time of four years expired[7]."

Robert Fitz Parnell married *Lora*, or *Loretta*, daughter to *William* lord *Braose* of Brember; and, dying without issue in 1204, was buried in the abbey of Leicester; leaving all that great inheritance which he had from his ancestors to his two sisters, *Amicia* the wife of *Simon de Montfort* (who was great-grandchild to Almaric, an illegitimate son to Robert king of France), and *Margaret*, who was married to *Saher de Quency* (afterward earl of *Winchester*)[8]; upon partition whereof, the moiety of the earldom of Leicester, with the Honour of Hinckley and the office of High Steward of England, were allotted to *Simon de Montfort*, who was created earl of *Leicester*[9].

In 1204, *Petronella* countess of *Leicester* gave to the king 3000 marks, that she might enjoy Leicester, with its appurtenances, as also all the fees and demesnes belonging to the Honour of Grentesmainell, both within Leicestershire and without, as her proper inheritance[10].

Saher de Quency also gave 1000 marks for the custody of all the lands in England which had belonged to that earl, as well in demesne as fee, excepting the Honour of Grentesmainell, and the dowry of the two countesses (mother and wife of the late earl), and the castle of Mountsorell, which the king retained; and with a proviso for any claim that might be made by *Avicia* countess of *Montfort*. The king also gave him the manors of Bagworth, Croft, Weston, and Seneby, in Leicestershire, and Hungerford in Berkshire[11].

In the same year, earl Simon de Montfort gave a ton of wine of Auxerre, on sealing a reconciliation, *pro apponendo sigillo concordie*, made between himself and William bishop of Lincoln[12]; and granted to *Richard Suard*, for his liege homage, 20 marks of rent in his præfecture of Leicester[13]. And *William de Langton* paid a fine to the king, for seisin of one carucate of land in the Suburbs of Leicester, which had been given to him by the late earl of Leicester for his homage and scutage; as did *Richard le Burgeis*, respecting a suit which he had with *William Fitz Walter*, touching a messuage in the same Suburbs[14].

Jan. 18, 1204-5, king John confirmed to Master *Gilbert de Aquila* 100*s*. rent in the præfecture of Leicester, which earl Robert Fitz Parnell had given to the said Gilbert for his homage and service[15].

April 28, 1205, king John sent his precept to the sheriff of Leicester, to make livery to *Saher de Quency* of all that land, without the wall of Leicester, which had belonged to *Robert Fitz Parnell* late earl of Leicester (whereof he had so granted him the custody); provided it were no part of the Honour of Grentesmainell, nor of the dowry of the countess; and excepting likewise to the said countess all that land which the king had commanded to be given unto her in exchange for the lands of the Honour of Grentesmainell, which the earl had passed to the Bishop of Lincoln by an agreement between them; and excepting to the abbot and convent of St. *Mary de Pratis* in *Leicester* those lands which had been given to them by the before specified earl[16]. And soon after, in consideration of a fine of 5000 marks, the king gave him also livery of all the lands and fees of the Honour of Grentesmainell, which he had formerly assigned to the countess Petronella, but had afterward re-assumed[17].

About the same time we find the following grant:

" Johannes, Dei gratiâ, rex Anglie, &c. Sciatis nos, intuitu Dei, & ob amorem karissimi nepotis nostri domini O. Romanorum regis illustris, dedisse, concessisse, & præsenti cartâ nostrâ confirmâsse magistro Willielmo de Leicestr', clerico ejusdem regis, xxx marcas singulis annis percipiendas ad Scaccarium nostrum London'; scilicet, xv marcas ad Festum Sancti Michaelis & xv marcas ad Festum Pasche, quousque ei in certo beneficio ecclesiastico usque ad estimationem xL marcarum redditûs providerimus. Testibus; dominis J. Norwic' & H. Sarum. Dat' per

---

[1] See Appendix to vol. I. p. 38; from Harl. MSS. fol. 189. Q. 7. in Arce Lond.   [2] See p. 97.
[3] Modern History, vol. XVI. p. 440.   [4] Rot. Pat. 4 John, m. 2. n. 7.   [5] See before, p. 97.
[6] Carte, MS.   [7] Burton, MS.   [8] H. Knighton, ut supra.   [9] Rot. penès Thesaur. & Cam. Scaccarii.
[10] Rot. Fin. 6 John, m. 10. & Rot. Pip. 6 John.   [11] Rot. Fin. 6 John, m. 1.
[12] Pat. 6 John; Rot. 176. Warr' & Leic'.   [13] Original Charters in the British Museum, 83 G. 45.
[14] Rot. Fin. 6 John.   [15] Cart. 6 John.   [16] Rot. Clauf. 6 John, de terris Normannis datis, m. 3.
[17] Rot. Fin. 7 John, m. 4.

manum J. Bathon' electi, apud Winlefhoram, 2° die Maii, anno regni noſtri ſeptimo [1]."

In 1206, *Petronella* counteſs dowager of *Leiceſter* had a grant concerning the *anabagium* and landing of boats *(de anabagio & karkid battellorum)*, and alſo for a market and bridge, in the town of Ware [2].

March 5, 1206-7, the king ratified the agreement which had been made, before himſelf and his barons, by *Simon de Montfort* earl of *Leiceſter* and *Saher de Quency* earl of *Winton*, concerning the partition which had been made of the lands of *Robert* late earl of Leiceſter; excepting to earl Simon the third penny of the earldom of Leiceſter, and the office of ſteward to the king; provided that 40l. land of earl Simon's purparty ſhould remain to earl Saher, till earl Simon ſhould ſecure to him certain lands in Normandy; after the death of the two counteſſes, *Petronella* the mother and *Loretta* the widow of earl Robert, their dowries to be divided equally between earls Simon and Saher [3]. At the ſame time, the king granted to *Saher de Quency* a yearly rent of 10l. out of the revenues of the county of Leiceſter [4]; and (probably) the ſame ſum to *Simon de Montfort*; which two ſums Mr. Ruſſell very acutely ſuppoſed to be the 20l. originally paid out of the iſſues of the county to *Hugo de Grentefmaineil*, as recorded in Domeſday.

In 1207, *Loretta* the widow of *Robert* earl of Leiceſter obtained a grant " de libertatibus [5]."

In 1208, Saher de Quency gave to the king three excellent courſers for the chaſe, for livery of a moiety of the Suburbs of Leiceſter; which was thereupon divided by a jury, by virtue of the king's precept [6].

" Saherus de Quency reddit compotum de tribus optimis caſzuris, pro habendâ medietate Suburbii Leiceſtrie, quod partitum fuit per juratam legalium hominum ultimò factum per preceptum regis [7]."

After having fully taken poſſeſſion of his wife's purparty, Simon de Montfort retired into France, where his paternal eſtate lay; and in 1209 was choſen general of the cruſade which pope Innocent had ordered to be carried on againſt the Albigenſes; and the king of England and his dominions, which had been ſmarting two years under a papal interdict, were now further puniſhed with a regular excommunication.

In 1210, Saher de Quency gave to the king another good courſer (ſuch a one as the king already had) called *Liard*, and a good *pied brache* [8]; and in 1211, being then fully ſeiſed of his moiety of the Honour of Leiceſter, he obtained a ſpecial diſcharge from the ſcutage of Scotland, then required for the ſame [9].

In 1212, Lewis the Dauphin invading England, Simon de Montfort ſupported him with his intereſt in this kingdom; whereupon the earldom of Leiceſter appears to have been forfeited; for, in the ſubſequent year, it was accounted for at the Exchequer among the eſcheats of the crown.

In 1213, *William Heneric* (or *Fitz Lewerick*) again occurs as an alderman of the gild of Leiceſter [10].

June 15, 1215, the Great Charter was ſigned at Runnymede; and in this year the king placed the earldom of Leiceſter in the hands of Montfort's near relation *Ranulph Blundeville* earl of *Cheſter* [11], to the uſe of Simon de Montfort, then in France. He gave alſo to the earl of Cheſter " totam terram Simonis de Monteforti, cum Foreſtâ [11]."

In this ſtate things ſeem to have continued till the death of king John, which happened Oct. 19, 1216.

HENRY III.

In 1218, Ranulph earl of Cheſter, Saher de Quency earl of Wincheſter, William de Albini earl of Arundel, and Henry Bohun earl of Hereford, went with ſoldiers into the Holy Land [13]. In this year alſo *Simon de Montfort* died, unreſtored, being ſlain with a ſtone before the city of Touloufe, then beſieged by Louis of France. He left iſſue, by *Amicia* his wife, *Almaric* earl of *Montfort* and conſtable of France, and *Simon*; and at this period we find the earldom of Leiceſter in the charge of *Stephen de Segrave*, one of the young king's chief favourites.

In 1219, king Henry III. by charter, granted to the mayor and burgeſſes of Leiceſter, that no free burgeſs ſhould be impeached for the debt of another, if the principal were of ability to ſatiſfy the ſame [14]; and in this year the earldom of Leiceſter was again committed to *Ranulph* earl of *Cheſter*, not improbably on account of ſome debt or mortgage incurred either by the earl of Leiceſter or the Crown [15]; and a commiſſion was iſſued for ſurveying the Foreſts of Leiceſterſhire and Rutland [16].

In 1222, the earls of *Wincheſter* and *Hereford* both died in the Holy Land [17].

In 1224, the earl of *Cheſter*, with many of the nobility, kept their Chriſtmas at Leiceſter; whence they ſent word to king Henry III. who was then at Northampton, that, unleſs he would forbear to demand his caſtles, and to hearken to the counſels of Hubert de Burgh, they would take up arms againſt him; but the archbiſhop of Canterbury and his ſuffragans, being then with the king, ſending them word on the next day, that, unleſs they ſurrendered their caſtles, &c. they would excommunicate them, they thought it beſt to ſubmit.

Matthew of Paris tells us [18], that in 1225, a young maid, a religious recluſe, died at Leiceſter; who, for ſeven years together next before her death, eat no food, ſaving that on Sundays ſhe received the ſacrament of the body and blood of Chriſt; that Hugh the biſhop of Lincoln, hearing of her abſtinence, had cauſed her to be watched, that, if there had been any impoſture, it might have been diſcovered; and that her face was as white as a lily, with a delicate mixture of a roſy colour, which was eſteemed a great evidence of her purity and chaſtity.

In 1227, there was a general perambulation of the king's foreſts in Leiceſterſhire [19].

Feb. 5, 1228-9, king Henry III. granted to the good men [20] of Leiceſter, that the fair which uſed to be held there for 15 days, viz. on the eve, day, and morrow, of St. Peter, &c. ſhould thenceforth be held on the day of the Purification of our Lady, and for 14 days after. Teſtibus; J. Bathon', A. Dunelm', epiſcopis; Huberto de Burgo, & aliis. Dat' apud Weſtm', 5° die Feb. [21].

Soon after the earl of Cheſter's death, which happened in 1232, *Almaric* earl of *Montfort*, eldeſt ſon of the firſt earl Simon Montfort, preparing for his journey into the Holy Land, propoſed to the king, that his younger brother *Simon* ſhould quit France, and become entirely Engliſh; and that he would ſurrender all his right in the earldom of *Leiceſter*, provided the king would confer it on his brother: whereupon *Simon* was reſtored to the earldom of Leiceſter and ſtewardſhip of England, made high ſeneſchal of Gaſcoign [22]; and, with the conſent of Almaric, the king granted to the ſaid Simon all the lands in England which had belonged to their father [23].

" In 1233, were ſeen five ſuns at one time together; after which followed ſo great a dearth, that people were conſtrained to eat horſe-fleſh and barks of trees; and in London 20,000 died for want of food [24]."

In this year, we find the names of *William Teynlo* and *Simon Curlewache*, or *Carlewake*, preſiding over

[1] Rot. Pat. 7 John; Harl. MSS. 85. fol. 320. b. AA 41. in Arce Lond.   [2] Rot. Pat. 8 John, m. 2. n. 12.
[3] Harl. MSS. 84. fol. 112. Chartæ Antiquæ K. in Turre Lond. n. 29. And ſee the Appendix to vol. I. p. 39.
[4] Dugdale, Bar. Angl. vol. I. p. 687.   [5] Rot. Pat. 9 John, m. 2. n. 18.   [6] Rot. Pip. 10 John.
[7] Mag. Rot. 10 John, Rot. 3. a.   [8] Rot. Pip. 12 John.   [9] Rot. Pip. 13 John.   [10] Carte, MS.
[11] Matthew of Weſtminſter, p. 279.   [12] Rot. Pat. 17 John, m. 19. n. 75.   [11] Hakluyt, vol. II. p. 32.
[14] From a Collection of the Town Charters, made in 1623, Mr. John Hinde, mayor.   [15] See p. 104.
[16] Rot. Pat. 4 Hen. III. m. 4.   [17] Hakluyt, ubi ſupra.   [18] See p. 437.   [19] Rot. Clauf. 11 Hen. III. m. 19.
[20] *Probi hominibus*—good, and as formerly uſed for good in condition; in leading, reſpectable, ſuperior ſort of people.
[21] Cart. 13 Hen. III.   [22] Regiſtrum Magnum, in Offic. Ducat. Lanc.
[23] Rot. Pat. 16 Hen. III. m. 6. And ſee the Appendix to vol. I. p. 41.
[24] From an old liſt of Mayors, formerly belonging to the Rev. Mr. Topp.

the town of Leicefter, as aldermen, being the firft that occur in that capacity in the Corporation-books.

In 1238, the earl of Leicefter had fo far improved himfelf in the king's favour, that, on the day after 'the feaft of Epiphany, he gave him in marriage, with his own hand, his fifter *Eleanor*, the widow of *William Marefchall* the younger, earl of *Pembroke* [1]; and a grant at the fame period occurs, " Pro Simone de Monteforti & Alianorâ uxore ejus, forore regis [2]."

The names of *William Teynlo* and *Simon Curlewache* occur again in conjunction in 1239, and fo probably continued for feveral fucceeding years; and during this feeming dawn of corporation government, Simon de Montfort gave to the burgeffes of Leicefter the following confirmation of the grant of a preceding earl:

" To all faithful Chriftians who fhall infpect this prefent writing of Simon de Montfort earl of Leicefter, health in the Lord. Be it known unto all people, that whereas Robert fome time earl of Leicefter, my predeceffor, has feoffed, by his charter to my burgeffes of Leicefter, a certain pafture called *Cowhey*, and lying in the *South fields* of Leicefter, between my paftures on either fide; that I have newly remifed, releafed, and entirely from me and my heirs for ever quit-claimed all right and claim which I have had, or might have had, unto the faid pafture, to my free burgeffes of Leicefter, which are or fhall be (for the time being); to wit, to thofe unto whom the faid pafture ought to belong, and that they may have and hold the faid pafture, with the appurtenances, of me and my heirs, freely and quietly, without wafte; paying thereout yearly to me and my heirs, or my fucceffors, for every beaft joifted, or to be joifted, 3d. as in the time of my predeceffors was accuftomed to be paid. And for this remife, releafe, and quitclaim, my faid burgeffes have given me a colt, of the value of one hundred fhillings, in hand, that neither I the faid Simon, nor my heirs or fucceffors, nor any of us, nor on our part, may joift or depafture our cattle in the faid pafture, but from all depafturing and joifting we may be for ever excluded. In witnefs whereof to this prefent writing of quitclaim my feal is put; thefe being witneffes: Philip Calewan, Richard de Harecourt, Alexander de Harecourt, Henry Cofteyn, Peter fon of Roger, Hugo Tafch, William Tafch, Richard fon of Goffelyn, William Wakeleyn, Theobald Clerk, and others. Dated at Leicefter, on the feaft of the Invention of the Holy Crofs, in the 23d year of king Henry the fon of king John [3]."

June 21, 1239, the earl of Leicefter affifted at the ceremony of baptizing Prince Edward, the firft and new-born fon of king Henry III. On the 9th of Auguft, he attended with his countefs at the public churching of the queen; but this gave the king an occafion to reproach him with having difhonoured his fifter; which induced the earl to take the crofs, with an intent to make a pilgrimage to the Holy Land, to expiate the fin of having married a lady who had entered into vows of chaftity [4].

In 1240, the Patent Rolls record an " Inhibitio Torneamenti apud Leyceftr' [5]."

In 1243, another grant occurs, " Pro Simone de Monteforti comite Leiceftrie & Alianorâ uxore ejus, forore regis, ac quondam uxore W. Marefcalli comitis Pembrochie, poftea dos ejus in Hiberniâ, cccc lï." [6]

In 1245, an inquifition was taken, " de omnibus terris, redditibus, & feodis militum, que tenentur de honore Leiceftrie in comitatu Suffex [7]."

In 1246, *Peter Fitz Roger* governed the town of Leicefter alone as an alderman; and under that title he feems to have prefided till 1248, when, according to the antienteft catalogue of the mayors of Leicefter which can be difcovered, this *Peter Fitz Roger* appears to have been chofen the firft mayor, and to have continued in that office for nine years [8].

Jan. 10, 1248-9, Simon de Montfort, *forarius regis*, was fent to Theobald king of Navarre, &c. and Count Palatine, to fettle all mifunderftandings [9].

Robert Groffetefte, bifhop of Lincoln, having complained to Pope Innocent, that many of the Religious in his diocefe had prefumed to take the tithes and poffeffions of churches *in proprios ufus*, without the confent of his chapter; and having obtained a bull from the Pope for their refumption; he, in the year 1250, cited all the Religious in his diocefe to appear at Leicefter, on the feaft of St. Hilary, to hear the mandate of the Pope; but, when they were met, the Templars, Hofpitallers, and many other exempts, refufed to obey it, appealing to the Pope. The good Bifhop, attended by the archdeacon of Oxford, went to Rome, to anfwer their appeal; but they, with their money, had fo fecured the Pope's favour, that he returned with difappointment [10].

In 1250, a difpute between Simon de Montfort, at that time the king's reprefentative in Vafconia, " contra formam pacis inter regem & cives Burdegaliæ," is recorded in the Patent Rolls [11]; and repeated in 1251, when the king fent his young fon Prince Edward with authority to adjuft the differences [11].

In the fame year, a confirmation grant occurs, to *Roger de Quency* earl of *Winton*, one of the heirs of Robert formerly earl of Leicefter, " de libertatibus fuis in medietate comitatûs Leyceftr' [13]."

In 1253, *Roger de Quency*, earl of *Winton*, married *Eleanor* wife of *William de Vallibus* [14].

By an inquifition taken this year, it appears that the charters, whereby the former earls had remitted the payment of gavel-pence and brig-filver, with other writings, being in the cuftody of one Lambert, they were burnt, together with his houfe; which a perfon, who had taken the bailiwick of Leicefter to farm, taking advantage of, exacted thofe payments afrefh; which being reprefented to Simon Montfort the fecond, then earl of Leicefter, he, by indenture, quitted claim to thofe payments for the future; *Robert Fitz Roger*, the then mayor, and the burgeffes, on their part, quitting claim alfo to fome demands which they had of him; to which were witneffes, fir Ernald de Bois, fir Ralph Baffett, fir Richard de Havering, fir Thomas de Eftleye, &c.

About the fame time, the earl granted a charter of the fame import with that of Robert Fitz Parnell (mentioned p. 358.), exempting them from any demands for the reap of his domains, and pafturage of their cows and cattle; for which they gave him 15 marks. Witneffes; fir Stephen de Segrave, fir Thomas de Menill, fir Gilbert de Segrave, fir Nicholas de Leftres, &c. He alfo ftipulated, that for the future, *ufque in finem mundi*, no Jews fhould be permitted to refide within the town of Leicefter [15].

In 1254, it was found that *Matthew le Venour*, at

---

[1] Matthew Paris, anno 1238.   [2] Rot. Pat. 22 Hen. III. m. 2.
[3] Tranfcribed from the Corporation Book of References, noticed in p. 358.   [4] See the particulars at large in p. 108.
[5] Rot. Pat. 25 Hen. III. m. 3.—At this period, the practice of meeting in Tournaments was become fo prevalent, and fo much danger was apprehended from it to the ftate, that it was thought neceffary frequently to prohibit them by public proclamation; which was the cafe in 1218 at Northampton, and afterwards at Leicefter, and feveral other great towns. Rot. Pat. 1 Hen. III. à tergo, " De torneamento refpectuand' apud North';" 3 Hen. III. m. 3. apud Stanes; ibid. m. 4. n. 2. apud Northampton; and again, in numberlefs inftances, to 5 Edw. III. inclufive. Thefe Tournaments were regular military contentions, and confifted of many men in troops; in which refpect they differed materially from what, as the age grew more refined, was practifed under the title of Jufts, which were ufually between two men fingly, with fpears, on horfeback; and were regular exercifes between martial men and perfons of honour.
[4] Rot. Pat. 28 Hen. III. m. 11.   [7] Efch. 30 Hen. III. n. 40.
[8] " The Corporation confifts of a mayor, recorder, and 24 aldermen, a fteward, bailiff, and 48 common-council-men. The burgeffes in parliament are elected by the inhabitants paying fcot and lot, and freemen not receiving alms, and the mayor is returning officer." Willis, Notit. Parl. pp. 31, 302.
[9] Rot. Pat. 33 Hen. III. m. 7.   [10] Matthew Paris, pp. 1026, 1027.   [11] Rot. Pat. 35 Hen. III. m. 12.
[12] Rot. Pat. 36 Hen. III. m. 7.   [13] Ibid. m. 4.   [14] Rot. Pat. 37 Hen. III. m. 19.
[15] See all thefe deeds in the Appendix to vol. I. p. 38.

his

his death, had in Leicefter 4s. 9d. rent of *William Sadynton* and *Roger de Cramford* ; and that *Robert* his fon and next heir was aged 28[1].

In 1255, a circumftance took place, which was of very confiderable importance to the inhabitants of Leicefter ; that whereas the law called *Borough Englifh*, whereby the youngeft fon ufed to be heir to his father, prevailed in this town ; it was altered, and the right of inheritance conferred on the eldeft. At the petition and with the confent of all the burgeffes, the earl of Leicefter obtained, " Quod omnes filii primogeniti de legitimo matrimonio in villâ Leyceftrie & ejus fuburbiis, poft mortem patris eorum, hereditatem paternam & habitationem pacificè, &c. de utero habeant & obtineant, & fine eis heredes de uteris legitimi[2]."

Bartholomew of *Dunftable* was mayor of Leicefter in 1257 ; in which year earl Simon de Montfort was permitted to make a teftamentary difpofition of all his lands ; and a deed occurs, " De hereditate ejufdem comitis recipiend' à Rege Franciæ[3]."

A deed alfo occurs under the title of " Debitum Regis Simoni de Monteforti comiti[4]."

In 1258, the barons, at the inftigation of the earl of Leicefter, compelled the king, at a parliament held at Oxford, to delegate his regal power to 24 perfons, 12 to be chofen from among the king's minifters, and the reft by the barons ; referving only to the king the chief place in all public affemblies. The earl of Leicefter was at the head of this fupreme council, to which the legiflative power was thus in reality transferred ; and on the 4th of May, a deed occurs, " De difceptione inter Regem & Simonem de Montforti, comite Leiceftrie, concernen' terras pro debito ejufdem comitis ; in quâ de xxiv ex parte Regis, &c. elect' & conventur' apud Oxon' à die Pentecoftes prox' futur' in unam menfem[5]."

In the fame year, *Henry de Rodington* was mayor of Leicefter, and fo continued till 1268.

In March 1258-9, Simon de Montfort earl of Leicefter, Robert de Clare earl of Gloucefter and Hereford, Peter of Savoy, J. Maunfell treafurer of York, Jo. de Baillol, and Robert Wallerand, were appointed, " Nuncii Regis ad tractand' cum Rege Franciæ de negotiis regis ;" and at the fame time, by other letters patent, were empowered to treat either jointly or feparately[6]. And about the fame time, the earl of Gloucefter, John Maunfell, and Robert Wallerand, were authorized to fettle all difputes between the king and Simon de Montfort and Eleanor his wife, the king's fifter. Several noblemen alfo entered into a bond of 3000 marks to certain merchants, for the debt due from the king to the earl of Leicefter ; who, jointly with Eleanor his wife, had a grant of the manor and foke of Gunthorp in Nottinghamfhire ; and alfo of feveral other manors to the annual value of 50 l.[7]. Soon after which, the earl of Leicefter, enraged at the oppofition he met with from his own party, pretended to throw up all concern in Englifh affairs, and retired wholly into France[8].

At a royal feaft, on St. Edward's day, March 18, 1259-60, Henry fon of Richard king of Almaine officiated as the earl of Leicefter's deputy in his office of high fteward of England[9].

On the 18th of May, 1261, an order was iffued, " De depellendo omnes extraneos à regno, quos Simon de Monteforti comes Leiceftrie nititur introducere[10] ;" and on the 20th of July, the king fubmitted all differences between himfelf and the earl and countefs of Leicefter to the arbitration of Margaret queen of France, fifter to the queen of England[11].

Jan. 18, 1262-3, the king difpatched letters to the king of France, " de negotio comitis Leicefter[12] ;" and in 1263, the earl of Leicefter having reconciled

himfelf to the king, obtained a fafe conduct for himfelf, his wife, and children[13] ; the king granted to Simon de Montfort junior, fon of Simon earl of Leicefter, all the poffeffions in England which had belonged to John Maunfell[14] ; and in July this year, on the Thurfday before the feaft of St. Margaret, a new great feal was folemnly delivered to the cuftody of Nicholas archdeacon of Ely, in the prefence of the earl of Leicefter and other *magnates* of the realm[15].

When the fatal differences between king Henry III. and his barons broke out into acts of hoftility, the earl of Leicefter was the chief ringleader in the enfuing war ; and, coming over fecretly from France, collected all the forces of his party ; and, entering into open rebellion, Prince Edward, the life and foul of the royal party, was by him taken prifoner, in October 1263, in a parley at Windfor ; after which, the king and the barons once more agreed to fubmit their differences to the arbitration of the king of France[16].

In December this year, we find the agreement and oaths of king Henry III. his fon prince Edward, and his barons, made to Lewis king of France, to obferve all the ordinances that had been made at Oxford, concerning the difputes between the king and his barons, dated at Windfor, " Dominicâ proximè poft feftum Sanctæ Luciæ Virginis[17]."

On the 13th of March, 1263-4, meffengers were fent from the king to Simon de Montfort and the other barons, to require them to anfwer certain articles at Brackley, in the prefence of John de Valentinis, the king of France's envoy[18].

On the 14th of May, the earl of Leicefter, then general of the confederate barons, took the king, and his brother Richard king of the Romans, prifoners at the battle of Lewes ; whereupon he affumed and kept the fole government of the kingdom ; and appointed his nephew *Henry de Montfort* to be conftable of Dover Caftle, and warden of the Cinque Ports[19].

On the 11th of June, peace was proclaimed in London between the king and his barons ; " in quâ notandum, quod Rex tempore turbationis recepit omnes Judeos London', ut eos protegeret à violentiis[20] ;" and on the 23d, Stephen bifhop of Chichefter, Simon de Montfort earl of Leicefter, and Gilbert de Clare earl of Gloucefter and Hereford, were allowed to nominate nine of the king's council, to be fent by the king and his barons to Lewes[21].

An agreement occurs, Auguft 25, between Simon de Montfort and Roger de Mortimer and the other Lords Marchers of Wales[22]. Simon de Montfort earl of Leicefter was appointed by the king to treat with Robert de Ferrariis, " circa ardua negotia regis[23] ;" and, Sept. 4, the king requefted that Henry fon of Richard king of Almaine (at that time detained by the Englifh barons as a hoftage in the caftle of Dover, under the cuftody of Henry de Montfort, *contra voluntatem regis)* might be allowed to pafs over to the king of France, to negotiate peace between the king and his barons ; the faid Henry firft binding himfelf by oath before the king and his *magnates*, that he would in no wife act againft the faid barons, and that he would return and furrender himfelf again into the cuftody of Henry de Montfort ; for the due performance of which, feveral noblemen entered into a bond of 20,000 marks[24].

In December this year, the earl of Leicefter had the cuftody of all the lands of Richard brother to the king of the Romans[25] ; and about the fame time a writ was iffued, to enquire whether *Roger de Quency* had recently before his death granted to *Robert* de Quency, late earl of *Winton*, the manor of Stiventon in fpecial tail, namely, to the then heir male of Robert the donor ; and at the fame time feveral public

---

[1] Efch. 39 Hen. III.   [2] Carte, MS.   [3] Rot. Pat. 41 Hen. III. m. 12, 13. n. 16.   [4] Ibid. m. 15.
[5] Rot. Pat. 43 Hen. III. m. 9. n. 28.   [6] Ibid. m. 11. n. 24, 25.   [7] Ibid. m. 5. n. 24 ; m. 12. n. 29 ; dorf. n. 4.
[8] Annal. Burton. p. 427.   [9] Rot. Pat. 44 Hen. III. m. 2. n. 3.   [10] Rot. Pat. 45 Hen. III. dorf. n. 3.   [11] Ibid. m. 17. 21. 33.
[12] Rot. Pat. 47 Hen. III. m. 19. n. 53.   [13] Ibid. m. 8. n. 30.   [14] Ibid. m. 5. n. 16.   [15] Ibid. m. 6. n. 21.
[16] Matthew Paris, p. 669.
[17] Rot. Pat. 48 Hen. III. m. 18. n. 75.   [18] Ibid. m. 16. n. 57. 58. m. 17. n. 64.   [19] Ibid. m. 13. n. 47.
[20] Ibid. m. 12. n. 41.   [21] Ibid. m. 10. n. 57.   [22] Ibid. m. 5. n. 19.   [23] Ibid. m. 5. n. 22.
[24] Ibid. m. 4. n. 16.   [25] Rot. Pat. 49 Hen. III. m. 27. n. 111.

inftruments,

inftruments were figned, as well on the part of the king, as of the earl of Leicefter and the other then oppofing barons, to fubmit all matters in contention to the arbitration of the king of France[1].

Jan. 3, 1264-5, feveral prifoners taken at Northampton were ordered to be releafed, the earls of Leicefter and Gloucefter having undertaken that they fhould attend on the king when commanded ; and on the 17th, certain " milites fcutiferi de partibus borealibus" had the earl of Leicefter's fafe conduct, and that of Roger de St. John, for the like purpofe[2].

In February, this year, the earls of Leicefter and Gloucefter, and feveral other noblemen, were prohibited from holding a tournament at Dunftable ; and were ordered to attend the king, refpecting the liberation of prince Edward[3].

March 10, prince Edward and Henry fon of the king of the Romans, who, after the battle of Lewes, had been detained by Henry de Montfort as hoftages, were delivered out of cuftody ; and, for the fecurity of the realm, the caftles of Dover, Scarborough, Bamburgh, Nottingham, &c. were committed to the cuftody of the barons[4].

In April 1265, Simon de Montfort, earl of Leicefter and high fteward of England, had a grant in fee of the caftle and honour of Chefter, the caftle and honour of the Peak, and Newcaftle under Lyne[5].

May 20, a treaty of peace and amity between the earls of Leicefter and Gloucefter was publifhed throughout the realm[6] ; but on the 8th of June, the bifhop of London was directed to excommunicate prince Edward and Gilbert de Clare earl of Gloucefter, and their adherents, who were then in rebellion, in oppofition to the treaty which had recently been concluded[7].

On the 9th of June, the town and caftle of Briftol were ordered, by Roger de St. John and Giles de Argenton, the king's juftices, to be guarded, for the fole ufe of the king and Simon de Montfort, againft Edward the king's fon, and all other perfons[8] ; and on the 12th, the earl of Leicefter and Roger de St. John the king's fecretary were empowered to treat with Lewin Fitz Griffin prince of Wales, who obtained from them his pardon, and was placed over all the nobles of Wales, on payment of 30,000 marks[9].

Prince Edward, after a year and half's imprifonment, making his efcape, the king's letters were fent to Simon de Montfort the younger, and to feveral other *cuftodes comitatuum*, June 28, to put them on their guard againft the rebellious conduct of the young prince and others, who had engaged in a new warfare at Monmouth[10].

On the 4th of Auguft, the earl of Leicefter was, together with Henry his eldeft fon, flain at the battle of Evefham ; when the conquerors, at the head of whom was the young prince Edward, to their eternal difgrace, cut off the earl of Leicefter's head, and fent it, as a daftardly token of victory, to his wife.

Upon the breaking out of the war, the caftles at Leicefter and Mountforell had been repaired, and put into a pofture of defence ; but, foon after, the latter was deftroyed by order of Henry III. ; and the former was but little made ufe of during this turbulent reign, notwithftanding that the town of Leicefter, at the beginning of the troubles, was the refort of the barons, where they met for the purpofe of raifing their army, and fortifying the caftle. It is exceedingly probable that the town of Leicefter, about this period, had increafed in population : it had efcaped the diftrefs which others unfortunately endured in confequence of the war ; it had become a fanctuary to many unhappy people, who were driven from their dwellings where the fcourge of war had paffed. The charters of its great earls, and thofe granted by king John, with the profpect of a more regular mode of government, which was rifing into confequence and ufefulnefs, had rendered

it a place defirable. They were again, however, forced to purchafe the king's favour by the payment of a confiderable fum of money.

On the 1ft of October, the letters patent were revoked, which had been granted to feveral perfons, "de pardonatione debitorum Judæorum," whilft the king, after the battle of Lewes, was in the cuftody and in the power of Simon de Montfort, formerly earl of Leicefter, his enemy ; who had ufed the royal feal at his own pleafure, and fealed with it divers letters contrary to the king's will, and in general to thofe who had oppofed him and his eldeft fon. Another patent, which had in like manner been given to Almaric de Montfort, of the treafurerfhip of the church of York, was alfo revoked[11].

On the 6th of October, for the good fervices performed by Gilbert de Clare earl of Gloucefter and Hereford, Thomas de Clare, and John Giffard, at the battle of Evefham, the king remitted the offence of their having adhered to Simon de Montfort at the battle of Lewes[12] ; and on the 25th, the pofterity of Montfort being difinherited by parliament, the king granted to his fecond fon *Edmund Crouchback*, in fee, " comitatum & honorem Leiceftrie, ac fenefcalciam Anglie, nuper Simonis de Monteforti, quondam comitis Leiceftrie[13] ;" together with all other the lands of the earl of Leicefter, with thofe of *Robert* earl *de Ferrariis*, *Nicholas* lord *Segrave*[14], and other vaft poffeffions ; and advanced him to the earldoms of *Lancafter*, *Leicefter*, and *Derby*.

In 1268, *Jordain Wardefton* was mayor of Leicefter, and *Alexander Bourn* in 1269 ; in which year, it was found that the " honor, villa, & manerium de Leiceftriâ," had been forfeited to the king, by the attainder of Simon de Montfort ; and in the fame year, the office of high fteward was affigned for life to the king's fecond fon earl Edmund.

" Edwardus, &c. militibus, liberis hominibus, & omnibus aliis tenentibus de comitatu & honore Leyceftrie, fenefcalciâ Anglie, & de omnibus terris & tenementis que fuerunt Simonis de Monteforti quondam comitis Leyceftrie, falutem. Sciatis quod dedimus & conceffimus Edmundo filio noftro predicto comitatum, honorem, fenefcalciam, terras, & tenementa, que fuerunt prefati Simonis inimici noftri, exceptis dominicis noftris ; habendum & tenendum de nobis & heredibus noftris eidem Edmundo & heredibus fuis in perpetuum, faciendo fervitium inde debitum & confuetum. Et ideo vobis mandamus, quod eidem Edmundo tanquam domino veftro in omnibus que ad predictum comitatum, honorem, fenefcalciam, terras, & tenementa pertinent, de cetero intendentes ficut predictum eft. In cujus, &c. Tefte, &c.[15]"

On the 20th of April in this year, at the inftance of earl Edmund, a charter was obtained, under the title of " Libertates pro majore Leiceftrie[16] ;" by which it was granted to the mayor and burgeffes of Leicefter, "that neither their perfons nor goods, in any place of the king's dominions, fhould be arrefted for any debt whereof they were not fureties or principal debtors, unlefs the debtors were of their community, and under their power, having wherewith to fatisfy the debts in whole or in part, and the mayor and burgeffes were deficient in doing juftice to their creditors ; and this fhould be made reafonably to appear."

From this period the inhabitants of Leicefter may date the growth of their profperity. Their former loffes were fpeedily recovered under their Lancaftrian earls ; who frequently honoured the town with their refidence, adorned it with public and ftately ftructures, and procured for it feveral privileges and immunities ; in which flourifhing condition it continued, till its lords, having obtained the fovereignty of the kingdom, brought it under the immediate government of the Crown.

In 1270, *Alexander Bourn* was again mayor of Leicefter ; and in this year another inftance occurs of a tournament being prohibited in this town[17].

[1] Rot. Pat. 48 Hen. III. m. 12, 13.   [2] Rot. Pat. 49 Hen. III. m. 25. n. 106. 107.   [3] Ibid. m. 23. n. 100. 101.   [4] Ibid. m. 20. n. 87 ; m. 21. n. 91.   [5] Ibid. m. 18. n. 79.   [6] Ibid. m. 15. n. 61.   [7] Ibid. m. 13. n. 54.   [8] Ibid. n. 53.   [9] Ibid. n. 47. 49.   [10] Ibid. m. 12. n. 45.   [11] Ibid. m. 6. n. 27 ; m. 7. n. 33.   [12] Ibid. m. 5. n. 25.   [13] Ibid. m. 1. n. 7.   [14] Ibid. m. 2.   [15] Selden, Titles of Honour, p. 605.   [16] Rot. Pat. 53 Hen. III. m. 18. n. 40.   [17] Rot. Pat. 55 Hen. III. m. 18. n. 40.

EDWARD I.

In 1272, the Honour of Leicester was again demised, by the young king, to his brother *Edmund* earl of *Cornwall*[1].

In 1274, *John Alfay* was mayor of Leicester; and in this year it was found that *Thomas de Nevill* held the fourth part of a knight's fee in Leicester and Rotherby, late parcel of the possessions of sir *Robert de Montalt*, out of which sir Robert and his heirs ought to have wards, services, and reliefs[2].

William Leef was mayor of Leicester in 1274, and continued in office till 1277; in which year occurs, a "Participatio feudorum militum de Rogero Quenci, quondam comitis Wintonie, apud S. Neotam, inter coheredes ejufdem hereditatis."

William English was mayor of Leicester in 1279 and 1280; *Thomas Gamfrey*, 1281—1284.

In 1285, at Michaelmas, *John de Canp*, and another named *Salomon*, justices in eyre, held a session at Leicester, when *Godfrey Manclarke* was mayor, and again in 1286; *Thomas Gamfrey* in 1287 and 1288; *John Alfay*, 1289; *Thomas Gamfrey*, 1290; and *Lawrence Miller*, 1291; in which year a record occurs, under the title of "Muragium pro villâ Leiceftrie[3]."

Thomas Gamfrey was again mayor of Leicester in 1292; *William English*, 1293; *Thomas Gamfrey*, 1294; *Ralph Ionick*, 1295; in which year, Master *William Bois* enfeoffed dame *Milicent de Montalt* in his rent of Leicester[4].

In 1296, *Robert de Vere* earl of *Oxford*, at his death, held divers lands in the town of Leicester; and *Robert* his son and heir was then of full age[5]. *Peter Humphrey* was then mayor; and so continued till 1299, in which year *Edmund* earl of *Lancaster* was sent into Gascoigne with an army; and, dying the same year at Bayonne, his body was brought into England, and interred in the abbey at Westminster[6]. At the inquisition taken on this occasion, it was found that, at the time of his death, he held the town of Leicester[7]. He was succeeded by *Thomas* his eldest son.

Thomas Gamfrey was again mayor in 1300, and *William English* in 1301; in which year we find a grant for erecting a prison in the town of Leicester, to prevent the inconvenience of sending their prisoners to the gaol at Warwick; "de prisonâ in villâ Leiceftrie conftruend', pro prisonâ comitatûs, qui ante ufque gaolam Warwici duci solebant[8]."

William Palmer was mayor in 1302 and 1303; *Robert Willoby*, 1304; and *Roger Willoby*, 1305.

Nov. 8, 1305, king Edward I. granted to *Thomas* earl of *Lancaster* and his heirs a yearly fair, to be held on the morrow of the Holy Trinity, and 14 days after, at his manor of Leicester. "Teftibus; venerabilibus patribus Johanne Cicestr' epifcopo, cancellario noftro; Johanne epifcopo Norw'; Hen' de Lacy, comite Linc'; Petro de Gavefton, comite Cornubie; Roberto de Clifford; Milone de Stapleton, fenefcallo hofpitii noftri; & aliis. Dat' apud manerium noftrum apud Weftmon', 8° die Novembris. Per ipfum regem, nuncio Willielmo Inget[9]."

Lawrence Caedge was mayor of Leicester in 1306.

EDWARD II.

John Celar was mayor of Leicester in 1307; and *John Caedge* in 1308.

Aug. 2, 1309, the king, being then at Stanford, sent his letters to the sheriff of Leicester; signifying, that whereas the late king Edward his father, for the more convenience of the inhabitants of Leicestershire, had, with the consent of Thomas earl of Lancaster, ordained, that a public prison should be made in the town of Leicester, for the safe keeping of all prisoners taken within the said county; and that whereas he himself, after the death of his said father, had, by his writ, commanded that the said prison, then not wholly finished, should be forthwith completely perfected; so that no prisoner should thenceforth be carried out of the said county of Leicester (as until then was the cuftom) to the prison at Warwick; and that whereas he was now credibly given to understand, that the said prison was at length accordingly finished; he therefore required, that the said sheriff should cause all such prisoners as should be thenceforth apprehended in the county of Leicester to be safely brought and kept in the said new prison at Leicester, until they should be thence delivered by due course. Tefte Rege, apud Staunford, 9° Augufti[10].

John Alfay was mayor of Leicester from 1309 to 1312; in which year, *Thomas* earl of *Lancafter*, siding with the barons against Pierce Gavefton, was made their general; for which, in 1314, he obtained the king's pardon, though it seems he was not restored to his favour. This Thomas was earl of Lancaster, Leicester, and Derby, as heir to his father; and of Lincoln and Salisbury, as some say, in right of *Margaret* his wife, only daughter of *Henry de Lacy* earl of *Lincoln*.

Walter Basley was mayor of Leicester in 1313; *John Knight*, 1314; *John Alfay* in 1315, 1316; *John Marrow*, 1317; *William Weanhoufe*, 1318; in which year, the Pope sent two cardinals, *Cancellino* and *Lucas de Teifio*, into England, to mediate a peace between king Edward II. and his kinsman Thomas earl of Lancaster and Leicester, and between the king of England and Robert Bruce king of Scotland[11]. The cardinals, therefore, with the king and queen, and archbishop of Canterbury, with all the bishops of the province, the earls and barons, and the other great men of the kingdom, came to Leicester; and on a day appointed, the earl, marching with a retinue of 18,000 men, met the king at Syroches Brigge, which now (says H. Knighton) is called Sotes Brige, where the king and the earl very kindly saluted each other; and, so far as appeared to those present, were made good friends, and thereupon the cardinals soon set forwards towards the North. The same year, certain articles were agreed on at Leicester, between earl Thomas and the clergy, which were afterwards confirmed at London by the cardinals, the archbishop of Canterbury, the bishop of Durham, and other prelates of the province of Canterbury, and then sent to the earl at Tutbury[12].

Peter Kent was mayor of Leicester in 1319, 1320; *John Marrow* in 1321; in which year, the barons again taking arms, on pretence of removing the Spencers (and then potent favourites), the earl of Leicester appeared at the head of them, forcing the king to a dishonourable accord; but the next year, being forsaken by the Mortimers and several leading barons of the faction, he was by the king routed at Burton upon Trent, pursued Northward, and taken at Boroughbrig, co. Ebor; and on the third day after, in the king's presence, condemned, and beheaded on the 22d of March at his castle of Pontrefact[13]. He died without issue, so that *Henry* his brother succeeded him; who, notwithstanding his brother's attainder, found such favour at the king's hands, that, in 1324, he had a grant of the title and honour of the earldom of Leicester[14].

William Lyndrige was mayor of Leicester in 1322; *John Norton*, 1323; *John Alfay*, 1324; and *Robert Strayton*, 1325; when it was found that *Roger Beler*, deceased, and *Alice* his wife, had held one messuage and three shops in the town of Leicester, by the service of 2s. *per annum*; and that there was a certain burgage there, and 3s. rent due from the free tenants in Belgrave-gate, which the said Roger held of *William la Zouch*, by the service of 6d. *per annum*[15].

Robert Strayton was again mayor of Leicester in 1326; in which year, sir *John de Vaus*, knt. came to the Abbey of Leicester, on the nones of October, with choice armour, rich cloaths, great horses, and a vast quantity of treasure, belonging to the lord Hugh de Spenfer earl of Winchester, being on his march to

[1] Rot. Pat. 56 Hen. III.   [2] Burton, p. 295.   [3] Rot. Pat. 17 Edw. I. m. 17.
[4] Efch. 23 Edw. I. N° 19. Leic.   [5] Efch. 24 Edw. I. N° 62. Leic.
[6] See a full account of him, and two splendid engravings of his monument, in vol. I. p. 222.
[7] Efch. 25 Edw. I. N° 51. Leic.   [8] Rot. Clauf. 29 Edw. I.   [9] Cart. 33 Edw. I. N° 26.   [10] Clauf. 3 Edw. II.
[11] Peck, lib. X. p. 12; H. Knighton, col. 2534.   [12] Ibid. col. 2535.   [13] See before, p. 224.
[14] Rot. Fin. 14 Edw. II.   [15] Efch. 29 Edw. II. N° 98. Leic.

the earl of Leicefter, who defigned to affift the king againft queen Ifabel and her fon prince Edward [1]: but the men belonging to Henry earl of Lancafter and Leicefter, happening at that time to be affembled at the Caftle of Leicefter in great numbers, came by night to the Abbey, and befieged him there; whereupon fir John de Vaus, perceiving that he could not profecute the bufinefs of his lord, in the next morning went to the earl of Lancafter, then refiding at his Caftle of Leicefter. As foon as he was gone out, the people entered the Abbey, and, feizing all the things which he had brought thither, carried them to the Caftle. Within three days after this, the earl, with all the forces which he could raife, departed hence to join the queen at Dunftable; and the king, being taken on the 18th of November, was committed to his cuftody in Kenilworth Caftle, where during the whole winter he was treated with great kindnefs and humanity; but the next year, the earl refufed to have the guardianfhip of him any longer, becaufe a report was fpread abroad, that fome of the abettors of the old king had formed a project to fteal him out of the caftle of Kenelworth, when the earl was elfewhere employed on his neceffary affairs [2]. The unfortunate monarch furvived till the 21ft of the following September, when he was cruelly murdered in Berkeley Caftle.

EDWARD III.

In the firft Parliament held by the new king at Weftminfter, March 9, 1326-7, *Henry* earl of *Lancafter* obtained an act for reverting the attainder of his brother *Thomas*; on which occafion it was found that *Thomas* earl of *Lancafter*, at his death, had held of lord Edward, late king of England, father of the king who now is, the Caftle and Honour of *Leicefter*, by the fervice of two knights fees and a half; and the manors of Hinckley, Shulton, and Desford, co. Leic. as parcel of the Caftle aforefaid, by the aforefaid fervice; alfo 30s. 10d. rent, arifing out of divers free tenements in Swanington and Ravenfton; and that *Henry* de Lancafter, brother of the faid earl Thomas, was his next heir [3].

In 1327, *John Norton* was mayor of Leicefter; and in this year king Edward III. returning from Scotland, held his fecond parliament at Lincoln, where he was advifed by his mother queen Ifabel, Roger Mortimer, and others, to demand a fubfidy of the clergy; upon which the bifhops defired time of deliberating concerning an anfwer to be given to the king at the feaft of All Saints at Leicefter.

In 1327-8, the king obtained a grant of the twentieth penny of the temporalities, and of the tenth of the fpiritualities [4]; which was made at Leicefter, at the inftance of Henry earl of Lancafter.

Whilft the king continued at Leicefter, the monks and inhabitants of Coventry obtained a patent, Jan. 6, for the taking toll of all vendable commodities brought into that city for fix years to be fold, towards their charges of inclofing the fame. Sir William Dugdale [5] fuppofes this was for inclofing it with a rampire of earth; for the licence to inclofe it with a wall of lime and ftone was granted in 1364.

In 1328, the new earl of *Lancafter*, out of diflike of the proceedings of the king's mother and Mortimer, refufed to be prefent at the parliament held at Salifbury, where John of Eltham was made earl of Cornwall, Roger Mortimer earl of March, Edmund Boteler earl of Ormond; all of whom, with their adherents, gathered a great army, and ravaged the lands of the earl of Lancafter; and particularly coming to Leicefter, on the day before the nones of January, ftaid there and in the adjacent country eight days, making great havock and fpoils, deftroying the woods, parks, and fifh-pools, and carrying away all they could lay their hands on, whether valuable or not; gold, filver, grain, utenfils, arms, and garments, wild and tame beafts, oxen, fheep, geefe, hens, and the very ornaments of the churches, leaving nothing in them or elfewhere which they could meet with [6]. And all this out of fpite to the earl of Lancafter, who at that time was marching from the South part to encounter them with a great power, having with him fuch of the nobility as formerly had been adherents to Thomas earl of Lancafter.

John Alfay was mayor of Leicefter in 1328, and *Henry Merlin* in 1329; in which year he occurs as a witnefs to the following deed:

" Sciant prefentes & futuri, quod ego Ricardus Cagge de Leicefter dedi, conceffi, & hâc prefenti cartâ meâ confirmavi Roberto de Rerifby de Leicefter, quinque eycras terre, cum pertinentiis, & cum crofto ibidem crefcente, in parochiâ S. Margarete, in le Merfh lane, continentes feptuaginta pedes; que jacent inter terram quondam Willielmi le Cu & terram Johannis de Burgo, & extendit de dictâ venellâ ufque ad terram meam propriam; habendum & tenendum dicto Roberto, heredibus & fuis affignatis, liberè, quietè, benè, & in pace, in perpetuum, de capitalibus dominis feodi illius, per fervicia inde debita & confueta. Et ego dictus Richardus & heredes mei dictas quinque eycras terre, cum pertinentiis, dicto Roberto, heredibus & fuis affignatis, contra omnes gentes warantizabimus in perpetuum. In cujus rei teftimonium prefentem cartam figillo meo fignavi. Hiis teftibus; Henrico Merlin, majore Leiceftrie; Willielmo de Clounâ, ballivo; Willielmo de la Waynhoufe, Johanne de Sallowe, Johanne de Lidington, Willielmo le Porter, Willielmo Bonifeaun, Roberto de Beby, Stephano clerico, & aliis. Datum Leiceftrie, die Martis proximè poft feftum Apoftolorum Simonis & Jude, anno regni regis Edwardi tertii poft Conqueftum quarto [7]."

Aug. 11, 1329, king Edward III. granted to *Henry de Burgherfh* bifhop of *Lincoln*, and his fucceffors in that fee, liberty of free-warren in all their demefne lands at Leicefter and Esfordeby [8].

Henry Merlin was again mayor of Leicefter in 1330; in which year a grant of pontage *(conceffio pontagii)* was obtained for three years, for the repair of the bridge at Leicefter [9].

John Marrow was mayor of Leicefter in 1331 and 1332.

" Without the South gate, *Henry* earl of *Lancafter*, in 1332, founded an Hofpital, or Bede-houfe, for four chaplains, two clerks, fifty men, and five women, which continueth in good ftate at this day. This Hofpital hath in it about 110 perfons; their ordinary pay is 7d. ob. a week. The mayor of Leicefter is the mafter thereof. Sir William Herrick of Beaumanor, knight, hath given 10s. yearly for a fermon to be preached there on Monday in Whitfun week yearly, for the fame end that the Hofpital fermons in London are. This Hofpital was incorporated by king James, by the name of *The Hofpital of the Holy Trinity*; the feal, a triple dart iffuant out of a flame in chief; with this word, *In Antitrinitarios* [10]. And near unto the fame, Henry duke of Lancafter, fon to the faid Henry, built a moft magnificent and goodly College, called (for diftinction from the former) *The New Work* (which name ftill it beareth), for a dean, twelve prebends, and certain chorifters; which, whilft it ftood, was no fmall ornament and beauty to the city; but, at the general fuppreffion of abbeys in the time of king Henry VIII. it was pulled down [11]."

John Martin was mayor of Leicefter in 1333; *John Leverych*, 1334; *John Alfay*, 1335; *William Warren*, 1336; *William Clanney*, 1337; in which year, in fummer, the king had a general fubfidy of wool; at which time he received of the abbey of Leicefter

---

[1] Knighton, col. 2546. [2] Ibid. col. 2551. [3] Efch. 1 Edw. III. N° 88 Leic.

[4] Knighton, col. 2552. [5] Warwickfhire, ed. 1730, vol. I. p. 140. [6] Knighton, col. 2554.

[7] Peck, MS. ex autogr. penès virum Rev. Joh. Kilby, vic. S. Marg. Leic. 1729. [8] Cart. 4 Edw. III. N° 46.

[9] Clauf. 4 Edw. III. pars 2. m. 24.

[10] See this feal engraved in vol. I. Plate XXVIII. fig. 16. In the fame Plate are two views of the Hofpital, taken in 1776 and 1796.

[11] Burton, MS.—Of both thefe fplendid foundations an account has been given in vol. I. pp. 329—352.

18 facks, and fet the rate of nine marks upon each fack; but when it was tranfported to Brabant, each fack was fold for 20l.[1]

John Martin was mayor of Leicefter in 1338; *Jeffery Kent* in 1339 and 1340; in which year, in fummer time, there was a ftrange kind of ficknefs common in England, which in an efpecial manner reigned in Leicefterfhire[2]. The paroxyfms of the fits were attended with intolerable pains, and caufed the patients to make a noife like the barking of dogs[3].

Jeffery Kent was again mayor of Leicefter in 1341; *Richard Leverych*, 1342; *John Martin*, 1343; and *Richard Leverych*, 1344; in which year, at the feaft of St. Andrew, there was a folemn tournament held at Leicefter by *Henry* earl of *Derby*, fon of Henry earl of Lancafter, on occafion of the marriage of his daughter *Maud*; and in the Eafter week, *John de Alithwerl*, clerk, was murdered in his own houfe by his wife and man-fervant, and others their accomplices, and then carried and laid upon the bank of the Soar, under the Abbey; for which crime his wife *Emma* was burnt, and his fervant hanged, but the reft efcaped[4].

John Waynhoufe was mayor of Leicefter in 1345; when Henry earl of Lancafter was buried in his own collegiate church at Leicefter with great pomp, the king and queen, with many of the nobility, attending the funeral in perfon[5].

In the fame year, a general chapter of the order of St. Auguftine was held at Leicefter abbey.

John Hayward was mayor of Leicefter in 1346; when *Thomas Le Beke*, bifhop of *Lincoln*, on the aid then granted for knighting Edward of Woodftock, the king's eldeft fon, was affeffed 20s. for half a knight's fee in the Suburbs of Leicefter[6].

John Hayward was again mayor in 1347; when it was found that *William de Herle*, deceafed, had held one meffuage at Leicefter of the earl of *Leicefter*, by the fervice of 2s. *per annum*[7]. At the fame time, the warden and fcholars of *Merton College* held 8s. rent in the town of Leicefter[8]. In this year, the king, being engaged in war with France, in purfuance of the aid granted him, received from the county of Leicefter 333 facks of wool; from that of Derby 252, &c.; each fack containing 26 ftone, and each ftone 14 pound weight[9]. In thofe days, a fack of wool being tranfported to Brabant ufed to be fold for 20l.

In 1348, *John Hayward* was a third time mayor; and in this year died at Lichfield *Robert de Leicefter*, a native of Leicefter, and ftudent at Oxford. He was a Francifcan friar, and a great divine; and efteemed, in a particular manner, by his patron the bifhop of Hereford. He wrote many books, whofe merit gained him the reputation of a good writer and fchoolman.—In this year, the moft dreadful and univerfal plague raged in England that was ever known; which, arifing in the Eaftern parts of the world, fpread itfelf Weftward, and came into England; and particularly at Leicefter it raged fo, that (as Henry Knighton, a monk of the abbey there, tells us[10]) there died, in the little parifh of St. Leonard, above 380, in that of the Holy Crofs above 400, in that of St. Margaret above 700, and fo in other parifhes proportionably. In the fame year, there was fuch a rot of fheep, and that putrefied them in fuch a manner, that neither birds nor beafts would touch them. And the calamity was fo great, and every one fo apprehenfive of imminent death, that nobody minded riches or any thing elfe, fo that every thing was extremely cheap; for (as Knighton tells us, without doubt from what he obferved at Leicefter) a man might buy a horfe, which before was worth 40s. for half a mark; a fat ox for 4s. a cow for 12d. a heifer for 6d. a fat mutton for 4d. a fheep for 3d. a lamb for 2d. a great hog for 5d. a ftone of wool for 9d. &c. It was ob-

ferved, that the peftilence this year feized chiefly the meaner fort of people.

Jeffery Kent was mayor of Leicefter in 1349; in which year, in the parliament adjourned to Leicefter, the commons fell fo feverely upon the duke of Suffolk, that the king thought fit to banifh him, with a fecret defign to recal him; but he was beheaded at fea.

William Goldfmith was mayor of Leicefter in 1350, and again in 1351; in which year king Edward III. granted here a market and a fair to *Henry* the newly-created duke of *Lancafter*; which fair the faid duke prefently after granted to the mayor and burgeffes of Leicefter, and their fucceffors, to be governed by the mayor and two or three of the burgeffes of the fame borough, to be yearly chofen, and to have the appointment of the ftalls and ftandings, and are now called the ftewards of the fair: the fame fair to be free from tolls, &c.

Roger Knightcote was mayor of Leicefter in 1352; *Jeffery Kent*, 1353; *John Paitling*, 1354; and *William Dunftable*, 1355; in which year, 9 kal. Aprilis, the ftatutes of the foundation of Newark college are dated; wherein the founder then inftituted a dean, thirteen canons fecular, thirteen vicars, three clerks, fix choifters, and one minifter[11].

Roger Knightcote was mayor of Leicefter in 1356; *William Dunftable*, 1357 and 1358; and *John Cook*, 1359 and 1360; in which year, on the 20th of July, king Edward III. in lieu of a fair which Henry duke of Lancafter and earl of Leicefter, and his anceftors, before then held yearly at Leicefter, on the feaft of the Invention of the Holy Crofs, and 15 days after, granted to the faid duke and his heirs one other fair, to be held at Leicefter, three days before, upon the feaft, and three days after, the feaft of St. Michael; provided that all ftrangers reforting to the faid fair fhould be free from toll, ftallage, picage[12], and all cuftoms and payments due to the faid earl or his heirs.

" Edwardus, Dei gratiâ, rex Anglie et Francie, et dominus Hibernie, archiepifcopis, &c. falutem. Supplicavit nobis dilectus confanguineus et fidelis nofter Henricus dux Lancaftrie et comes Leiceftrie, quod cum ipfe habeat, et ipfe et anteceffores fui et alii qui comites Leiceftrie pro tempore fuerunt à tempore quo memoria non exiftit fingulis annis habuerunt, unam feriam apud villam Leiceftrie, que de nobis tenetur in capite ut dicitur, in fefto Invencionis Sancte Crucis et per quindecim dies proximè fequentes duraturam; velimus ei concedere quod ipfe et heredes fui, loco ferie predicte, habere poffint unam aliam feriam, apud villam predictam et fuburb' ejufdem, fingulis annis per feptem dies, videlicet, tribus diebus proximè ante feftum Sancti Michaelis Archangeli, et in eodem fefto, ac tribus diebus proximè fequentibus, in perpetuum duraturam; ita quod quilibet indigena five alienigena ad villam et fuburb' predicta, causâ ferie predicte veniens, ibidem moram faciens, et exinde recedens, tam ante dictam feriam quam poft, in perpetuum, fit quietus de theolonio, ftallagio, picagio, et aliis cuftumis et preftacionibus quibufcumque, eidem duci, feu dictis heredibus fuis, racione dicte ferie qualitercumque fpectantibus, folvend': Nos, optentum laudabilis et fructuofi obfequii ipfius ducis nobis à diu impenfi, volentes fupplicacioni fue anime in hâc parte, de gratiâ noftrâ fpeciali conceffimus, et hâc chartâ noftrâ confirmavimus, pro nobis et heredibus noftris, eidem duci, quod ipfe et heredes fui, loco dicte antique ferie, exnunc habeant unam aliam feriam, apud villam et fuburbium predictam, fingulis annis, per feptem dies, videlicet, tribus diebus ante feftum Sancti Michaelis Archangeli, et in eodem fefto, et tribus diebus proximè fequentibus, in perpetuum duraturis, nifi feria illa fit ad nocumentum vicinarum feriarum: Quare volumus et

firmiter

[1] Knighton, col. 2570. [2] Ibid. col. 2580.
[3] In the Philofophical Tranfactions, n. 270. p. 799, Dr. J. Freind gives an account of two families at Blackthorn in Oxfordfhire, who in the years 1700 and 1701 were afflicted with a diftemper much like this of 1340. Dr. Willis, in his account of it, calls it *morbus novus Cynicus*. See Camden, Annals of Ireland, p. 188.
[4] See before, p. 226. [5] Knighton, col. 2584. [6] Rot. Aux. 20 Edw. III.
[7] Efh. 21 Edw. III. Nº 44. Leic. [8] Ibid. Nº 91. Leic. [9] Knighton, col. 2595. [10] Ibid. col. 2599.
[11] Carte, MS. from a communication of Browne Willis. [12] A duty paid for breaking the ground to fet up ftalls.

firmiter precipimus, pro nobis et heredibus noftris, quod idem dux et heredes fui in perpetuum habeant dictam feriam apud villam et fuburbium predictum, cum omnibus libertatibus et liberis confuetudinibus ad hujufmodi feriam pertinentibus; falvo femper, quod quilibet indigena five alienigena, ad dictam villam et fuburbium causâ ferie predicte veniens, ibidem moram faciens, et exinde recedens, tam in dictâ feriâ, quam ante et poft, in perpetuum, fit quietus de theolonio, ftallagio, picagio, et aliis cuftumis et preftacionibus quibufcumque, eidem duci feu dictis heredibus fuis, racione ferie predicte, qualitercumque fpectantibus folvend', nifi feria illa fit ad nocumentum vicinarum feriarum, ficut predictum eft; et quod dicta antiqua feria exnunc ceffet omnino. Hiis teftibus; Simone archiepifcopo Cantuar', W. epifcopo Winton' cancellario, & J. Roffen' epifcopo, thefaurario noftro; Ricardo de Arundell, Roberto de Ufford, Suff', & Radulpho de Stafford, comitibus; Waltero de Mannye, Johanne de Bello-Campo, & Guidone de Brian, fenefcallo, hofpitii noftri, & aliis. Dat' per manum noftram apud Weftm', fecundo die Julii, anno regni noftri Anglie 34°, regni vero noftri Francie 21°¹."

William Goldfmith was mayor of Leicefter in 1361; in which year a plague happened; not fo univerfally fatal as that of 1348, but much more deftructive of the nobility and gentry; and among others the great, valiant, and liberal prince *Henry Plantagenet*, duke of *Lancafter*; who came to the earldom, by the death of his father, in 1345; was created duke March 6, 1350; and died at Leicefter, in Lent, 1361, much lamented by all; having, by his many good deeds, obtained the name of the *good* duke of Lancafter. He had made his will a few days before, it bearing date March 15, 1360, at his Caftle of Leicefter, in which he prefcribed the order of his funeral; and according to which he was buried in the Newark, in the collegiate church which he had founded². He held, at his death, the Caftle, Manor, and Honour of Leicefter, of the king *in capite*³.

William Tubbe was mayor of Leicefter in 1362; in which year, *Maud*, wife of *William* duke of *Barr* [*Bavaria*], at her death, held the Caftle, Manor, and Honour of Leicefter, of the king *in capite*; and *Blanch* her fifter was her next heir⁴.

Roger Belgrave was mayor in 1363; about which time, according to Knighton, the following circumftance occurred. A certain man, who was called *Walter Winkborn*, was hanged in Leicefter, upon the profecution of brother John Dingley, mafter of Dalby, of the order of the Knights Hofpitallers; who being taken down from the gallows, after hanging the ufual time, was put into a cart; but, as he was taking to St. Sepulchre's chapel to be buried, he revived; which the priefts perceiving, they took him into the chapel, and there protected him from the civil officers, who would have taken him again to the gallows to have fuffered. At this time king Edward III. was at the abbey, where he had refted on a journey; and the ftory of the man's recovery being related to him, the king was gracioufly pleafed to grant him his pardon, faying, " Deus tibi dedit vitam, & nos tibi dabimus curtum," as Knighton⁵ relates, who was then in the king's prefence, and heard him utter the words.

In 1364, *John Martin* was mayor of Leicefter; in which year it was found, that fir *Robert de Herle*, at his death, held 38*s.* yearly rent, to be received out of a certain meffuage in Leicefter, held of the duke of *Lancafter*, as of the Honour of Leicefter, by the fervice of 12*d. per annum*⁶.

William Sifton was mayor of Leicefter in 1365; *John Stafford*, 1366; *Thomas Bebee*, 1367; *John Coke*, 1368 and 1369; *John Stafford*, 1370; in which year a writ occurs, " De officio Cambiatoris Caleffæ commiffo Johanni de Leyceftrie. Tefte Rege, apud Weftmonafterium, 6° Septembris⁷."

In 1371, *William Greene* was mayor of Leicefter;

Henry Clipfon, 1372; *Henry Petling*, 1373; *William Ferror*, 1374 and 1375; *William Taylor*, 1376; in which year *John* of *Gaunt*, ftyling himfelf " king of *Caftile* and *Leon*, duke of *Lancafter*," by indenture, to ferm let to the mayor, burgeffes, and commonalty of Leicefter, the bailiwick of the town, fuburbs, and fields of Leicefter, with the appurtenances of the fame, with all executions within the fame, and all other profits; the profits of the portmote courts, of the fairs, markets, and all other courts, rents, ferms, goods and chattels; of fugitives, felons, forfeitures of wafte, the year and day of them; deodands, treafure-trove, &c. &c. with the keeping of all manner of prifoners—except the Caftle of Leicefter, the mill under the fame, and rents and fervices levied by the porter of the faid Caftle by old time accuftomed, and the court of the fame, &c.; to hold the premifes for the term of ... years from Michaelmas next, yielding therefore to the faid duke yearly 20*l.* And he alfo granted to them and their fucceffors fufficient timber, in the woods of the Honour of Leicefter, belonging to the faid duke, for all manner of reparations for all manner of fhops, houfes, fhambles, with all other claufures to the fame belonging, by the overfight of the mafter forefter of the Foreft of Leicefter. Given at Leicefter, the Monday next after the feaft of the Affumption of our Lady⁸.

William Ferror was mayor of Leicefter in 1377; in which year king Edward died on the 21ft of June.

RICHARD II.

In 1377, king Richard II. held a great council of war at Stamford, to confult about an expedition into France: but it came to nothing in that inactive reign. However, it was this year ordered in Parliament, that certain fmall barges, called *balingers*, fhould be made and got ready, by feveral cities and good towns of England, againft the firft day of March next. The king commanded the bailiffs and good men of the town of Staunford and of the town of Leicefter to make forthwith, and get ready, one competent *balinger*, having between forty and fifty oars, againft the faid day, at the cofts of the more fufficient and richer men of the faid town only, and not of others; and not by any means to charge any other men, of ordinary or inferior condition, to the expence of the faid *balinger*. Afterwards, becaufe it feemed to the king and his council, that the men of the faid town of Staunford, who had poffeffions, goods, or chattels, to the value of 5*l.* and more, might reafonably contribute to the making of the faid *balinger*; the king, by his letters patent, appointed fir William Bufhy, knight, fir Thomas de Burton, knight, John Harowedon, and John Broun, alderman, of Staunford, three or two of them, to caufe all fuch men of the town of Staunford, as had poffeffions, goods, or chattels, amounting to the value of 5*l.* and not under; to wit, each of them to be reafonably taxed and affeffed, according to the rate of the value of fuch their poffeffions, goods, or chattels, to the coft of making the faid *balinger* for the faid town, and to caufe the fums fo taxed and affeffed to be levied; and to compel all perfons who were rebellious or contrariant in this matter, either by diftreffes if need were, or by other lawful ways and means; and to certify the king, from time to time, of the names of fuch rebels. Thefe things the king commanded the faid commiffioners to do and execute with all fpeed in form aforefaid; and alfo commanded the bailiffs and good men of the faid town to be intendant and obedient to the commiffioners, or to any three or two of them, in the execution of this mandate. Tefte Rege, apud Weftmonafterium, 6° die Aprilis⁹.

William Ferror was again mayor of Leicefter in 1378; and king Richard II. having the laft year commanded the men of Staunford and Leicefter to fit out a *balinger* for the wars, which they accordingly did; he, on the 8th of February 1378-9, with the advice of his parliament, in confideration of the great charge

¹ Cart. 34 Edw. III. n. 18.   ² See the former part of this volume, p. 231.   ³ Efch. 35 Edw. III. Pars 1. N° 122.
⁴ Efch. 36 Edw. III. Pars 1. N° 37.   ⁵ Col. 2627.   ⁶ Efch. 38 Edw. III. N° 23. Leic.
⁷ Catalogue des Rolles François, vol. II. p. 103.   ⁸ Cart. 49 Edw. III.   ⁹ Pat. 1 Ric. II. pars 5. m. 36. dorfo.

which the men of Leicefter had been at in fitting out the faid *balinger*, confirmed a grant which had been obtained in 1199 from John earl of Mortaigne, about buying and felling o lands in the portman mote there:

" Rex omnibus ad quos, &c. falutem. Infpeximus cartam domini Johannis quondam Regis Anglie, progenitoris noftri, in hec verba: [*Here the grant already printed in p. 97 is literally recited.*] Nos autem conceffionem & confirmationem prediĉtas ratas habentes & gratas, eas, pro nobis & heredibus noftris, quantum in nobis eft, burgenfibus prediĉte ville Leiceftrie, heredibus & fucefforibus fuis, burgenfibus ville prediĉte, ratificamus, approbamus, concedimus, & confirmamus, ficut carta prediĉta rationabiliter teftatur, & prout hujufmodi emptiones & venditiones terre ville prediĉte haĉtenus rationabiliter faĉte extiterunt. Tefte Rege, apud Weftmonafterium, 8° die Februarii. Per ipfum Regem & Confilium in Parliamento, quia fecerunt quandam Balinger cum hominibus ville Stanford [1]."

Richard Clipfton was mayor of Leicefter in 1379; when a deed occurs, " De libertatibus olim pertinentibus & modò clamatis & allocatis Henrico de Lancafter, in villis de Lilborne, Efthaddon, Hameldon, Dodeford, & Wedon, parcell' Honoris de Leicefter [2]."

Richard Gamelfton was mayor in 1380; when it was found that *Roger Beler*, at his death, held 30s. rent of certain burgeffes of Leicefter, payable at Candlemas, which the faid burgeffes held of the duke of *Lancafter* [3].

John Stafford was mayor in 1381; *Richard Knightcote*, 1382; *Richard Gamelfton*, 1383; *Henry Ferror*, 1384, in which year, the great Reformer Wickliffe died [4]; *Henry Bebee* in 1385, when, on the feaft of the Tranflation of St. Thomas the Martyr, the king and queen paffed through Leicefter, in their way towards Scotland, and were followed by the chief of their army [5].

Henry Bebee was again mayor in 1386; *Richard Braunfton*, 1387 and 1388; in which year there was fuch plenty, that in Leicefter market 100 quarters of barley were fold for 100s.; and the king and queen, in their progrefs towards York, on the morrow of St. Valentine, called at the abbey of Leicefter, and lodged that night at the lord Beaumont's at Beaumanor; and on their return the king and queen lay at Groby, 14 kal. September; and 16 kal. Oĉtober, the king and queen lodged at the abbey of Leicefter, and with them the duke of Ireland, the earl of Suffolk, the archbifhop of York, and bifhop of Chichefter [6].

William Stretton, of Whetftone, gave 12d. yearly rent, and the reverfion of a meffuage and two yard lands, to Richard Braumfton, mayor of Leicefter, &c. die Mercurii, in fefto Sanĉti Botulfi abbatis (1388).

Henry Clipfton was mayor of Leicefter in 1389; *William Humberftone*, 1390; *Jeffery Okeham*, alias *Clark*, 1391; when it was found that *Mary* wife of *Roger Beler* (married firft to *John Seintclere*) held at her death 30s. rent in Leicefter of the lord duke of *Lancafter*, by the fervice of 2s. *per annum* [7]; and alfo that *Robert de Swillington*, knight, held at his death one meffuage in the town of Leicefter, called *Wingesplace*, of the duke of *Lancafter*, as of the Honour of *Leicefter* [8].

Richard Braunfton was again mayor of Leicefter in 1392, in which year archbifhop Courtney vifited the abbey of Leicefter [9]; and *William Mercer* and *William Spencer*, Sept. 14, gave to the mayor and corporation of Leicefter divers lands and tenements in Leicefter, Whetftone, and Great Glen, towards the amendment and reparation of the fix bridges within the town of Leicefter, and for other charges within the faid town arifing, to be maintained according to the appointment of the faid William Mercer and William Spencer; but this aĉt of theirs being contrary to the ftatute of mortmain, before it could take effeĉt, there was firft

an " Inquifitio de ad quod dampnum," and then a licence from the king, of neceffity to be had for that purpofe; but which were as follows:

" Juratores dicunt, quod non eft ad dampnum, fi Rex concedat Willielmo Mercer & Willielmo Spenfer, quod ipfi viii meffuagia, xv cotagia, ii fhopas, unum toftum, vi virgatas & ix acras terre, vi acras & unam rodam prati, & xxv folidatas, ix denaratas & obolum redditûs, & redditum unius galli & ii gallinarum, cum pertinentiis, in Leiceftriâ, Whefton, & Magnâ Glenne, dare poffint majori ville Leiceftrie. Dicunt etiam, quod ii meffuagia, v cotagia, ii fhope, unum toftum, xviiis. redditûs, & reverfio ii meffuagiorum, & una roda terre cum pertinentiis in Leicefter tenentur de domino duce Lancaftrie; per quod fervicium ignorantur; & ipfe de domino Rege. Et dicunt, quod funt in Whefton fex meffuagia, x cotagia, vi virgate terre, & ix aciâ terre, vi acre & una roda prati, xiii đ. oƀ. redditûs, & redditus unius galli & ii gallinarum, que tenentur de domino Johanne de Bellomonte per fervicium iiis. xđ. & feĉte curie de tribus in tres; & ipfe de domino Rege. Et quod remanent ultra in villâ Leiceftrie terre ad valenciam xxt. per annum [10].

" Rex omnibus ad quos, &c. falutem, Licet, &c. de gratiâ tamen noftrâ fpeciali, & pro xx libris quas dileĉti nobis major & communitas ville Leiceftrie, nobis folverunt, conceffimus & licentiam dedimus, pro nobis & fucefforibus noftris, quantum in nobis eft, Willielmo Mercer & Willielmo Spencer, quod ipfi viii meffuagia, xv cotagia, ii fhopas, unum toftum, fex virgatas & ix acras terre, fex acras & unam rodam prati, xxv folidatas, ix denariatas & unam obolum redditûs, & redditûm unius galli & ii gallinarum, cum pertinentiis, in Leicefter, Whefton, & Magna Glenne (que de nobis non tenentur) dare poffint & affignare prefatis majori & communitati; habend' & tenend' fibi & fucefforibus fuis, ad emendationem & reparationem fex pontium infra villam de Leiceftriâ prediĉtam, ac ad alia onera infra eandem villam emergentia, juxta ordinationem ipforum Willielmi & Willielmi in hâc parte faciendam, fupportandum, &c. Tefte Rege, apud Nottingham, 23° Septembris [11]."

Richard Humberfton was mayor of Leicefter in 1393; *Thomas Wakefield*, 1394; in which year *Conftantia*, eldeft daughter and coheir of *Peter* king of *Caftile* and *Leon*, fecond wife of *John* duke of *Lancafter* (whom he had married about 1371) died, and was very honourably interred at Leicefter on Sunday next after the feaft of St. Peter and St. Paul. And on Monday, being the next day, *Mary de Bohun*, younger daughter and coheir of *Humphrey* earl of *Hereford*, *Effex*, and *Northampton*, the firft wife of *Henry* earl of *Derby* (afterwards king Henry IV.), fon of the duke of Lancafter, was buried at the New College in Leicefter [12].

Henry Bebee was again mayor of Leicefter in 1395; *Thomas Bayley*, 1396; *John Houghton*, 1397; and *Ralph Fifher*, 1398; in which year, *John* duke of *Lancafter* dying about Candlemas, his fon *Henry* (who had been banifhed the foregoing year) landed in England in July, and to him king Richard furrendered himfelf the 20th of Auguft, 1399; whereupon the duke brought him to Leicefter, and thence to London, where, on Michaelmas day, he refigned his crown to the duke, who thereupon was declared king, by the name of

HENRY IV.;

whereby the dukedom of Lancafter and earldom of Leicefter were united to the crown. But feveral confpiracies were made againft him; which being difcovered, many fuffered on that account [13].

Roger Humberfton was mayor of Leicefter in 1399; in which year, Nov. 5, the king granted to *Thomas Horneby* of Leicefter the cuftody of the court called

---

[1] Pat. 2 Ric. II. pars 2. m. 3. 32.   [2] Rot. Clauf. 3 Ric. II. n. 2.   [3] Efch. 4 Ric. II. N° 14. Leic.
[4] Of whom a full account is given in the Fourth Volume, under Lutterworth.   [5] H. Knighton, col. 2675.
[6] Ibid. 2693. 2696.   [7] Efch. 15 Ric II. Pars 1. N° 5.   [8] Ibid. N° 62.
[9] See the proceedings on this occafion in the former part of this volume, p. 262.   [10] Efch. 16 Ric. II. Pars 1. n. 97.
[11] Pat. 16 Ric. II. pars 1. m. 6.   [12] Knighton, col. 2741.   [13] Anglia Sacra, vol. II. p. 364.

The

The Prince's Court, co. Leicester, late *William Outeby's*. "Rex omnibus ad quos, &c. falutem. 'Sciatis, quod, de gratiâ noftrâ fpeciali, conceffimus dilecto nobis Thome Horneby de Leiceftrie cuftodiam curie vocate le Prince Court in comitatu Leiceftrie, habendam pro tempore vite fue, cum omnibus exitibus & proficuis curie predicte pertinentibus, ufque ad valorem quatuor marcarum per annum : quod quidem officium Willielmus Outeby habuit, de dono Ricardi nuper regis Anglie Secundi poft Conqueftum. In cujus, &c. Tefte Rege, apud Weftmonafterium, 5° die Octobris[1]."

William Spencer was mayor in 1400 ; *John Loveday*, 1401 ; *Peter Clark*, 1402 ; in which year, fome affirmed that king Richard II. was alive ; and a confpiracy was difcovered, for which fome were put to death. Among thefe fome were Grey friars ; of which one *Richard Trifeley*, doctor of divinity, being afked what he would do if king Richard were prefent, anfwered, " that he would fight in his quarrel againft any man, even to death ;" whereupon he was hanged and drawn in his religious habit. Shortly after fir Roger Clarendon, baftard fon of the Black Prince, and with him a 'fquire and yeoman, were beheaded, and eight Grey friers hanged and beheaded at London, and two at Leicefter ; all which had publifhed king Richard to be alive[2].

In the fame year, *Roger* fon of *Roger Ironmonger* granted to *John Caumbrigge* and others one mefluage in St. Martin's parifh, in Holyrood-lane ; and fix cottages in Baldwingate, in St. Nicholas's parifh, in the town of Leicefter[3].

John London was mayor in 1403 ; *John Church*, 1404 ; *Richard Fawkner*, 1405 ; *Thomas Wakefield*, 1406 ; and *Ralph Humberfton*, 1407 ; when fir *John Lovel*, knt. died feifed of 6s. 8d yearly rent, arifing out of a certain mefluage in Leicefter[4].

John Grefley was mayor in 1408 ; *John Church*, 1409 ; *Thomas Bayley*, 1410 ; in which year, the king was at Leicefter, in November ; for on the 15th of that month are the letters patent dated, whereby he empowers *Ifabel*, relict of *Fulco de Penbruge*, chevalier, *Walter Swan*, and *William Mofse*, clerks, to found the collegiate church of Tonge in Shropfhire.

Roger Humberfton was mayor in 1411 ; and *Thomas Walgrave*, 1412 ; in which year, March 20, king Henry IV. died.

HENRY V.

Robert Randolph was mayor of Leicefter in 1413 ; and *Robert Evington* in 1414, in which year a parliament was held in this town ; but not at the period which has generally been afcribed to it by our Hiftorians, mifled by the authority of Prynne, who, in his " Abridgement of the Records," ftates, that the Parliament 2 Hen. V. which was fummoned to meet at Weftminfter on the Monday after the Octaves of St. Martin, was afterwards prorogued to Leicefter.

The fact is, there were two diftinct parliaments in this year ; and it was the earlieft of thefe, which, by the king's writ, was convened at Leicefter, on Monday the 30th of April, ' *en une graunae Sale pres l'Efglife & la Manfion des Frieres Menours a Leycefter*.' And of the acts of this parliament, as Prynne has not mentioned them, I fhall give a fhort epitome.

The king's uncle, bifhop of Winchefter and lord chancellor, having taken for his theme, *Pofuit cor fuum ad inveftigandum leges*, opened the meeting by a learned fpeech ; in which he demonftrated that no kingdom can exift in fafety without a due reverence for the Supreme Being, and a proper refpect for the laws ; and that both the Church and State had been much endangered by the herefy of the Lollards. He recommended that proper remedies might be devifed for the maintenance of peace and good order ; and ftated alfo, by the king's command, that though it had been cuftomary with his predeceffors to afk from the commons a fubfidy of tenths and fifteenths from the laity, he would for the prefent difpenfe with fuch requeft, and leave it to fome future time ; but, that

juftice might be done to all perfons, he recommended that triers of petitions fhould be appointed ; and the commons were directed to affemble in *Le Fermerie*, a houfe belonging to the Friars Minors, there to elect a fpeaker, to be prefented to the king on the following day. This they accordingly did ; and Mr. Walter Hungerford was prefented as fpeaker, and gracioufly accepted.

The Triers of Petitions for England, Ireland, Wales, and Scotland, were appointed to meet *en le Fraitour ou Refectoire des Frieres Menours* ; and thofe for Gafcoigne and other places beyond fea *en le Maifon appellée le Chapitrehous as Frieres Menours*.

A fubfidy was in this parliament granted to the king of 3s. a tun upon all wine exported and imported, except for the king's own ufe ; and of 12d. in the pound upon all merchandize imported and exported, except wool, hides, and fkins ; and except alfo all manner of grain, flour, preferved fifh, and cattle, imported ; and corn for the victualling of Calais.

At the particular requeft of the lords and commons, the king created his brother John of Lancafter earl of Kendal and duke of Bedford ; his other brother Humphrey of Lancafter earl of Pembroke and duke of Gloucefter ; and Richard of York earl of Cambridge.

Edward duke of York, for the good fervices he had performed to the king's father, and to the king himfelf, was reftored, by a declaration of the king in parliament, to all the honours of which he had been deprived by a judgment againft him in the parliament of 1 Henry IV.

In like manner Thomas duke of Clarence the king's brother, and his uncle Thomas Beauford earl of Dorfet, were refpectively reftored to their titles and honours.

A certificate from Robert Hakebeche, fheriff of Cambridgefhire, that John de Wyndefore, who had been ordered to attend the parliament at Leicefter on a writ of *Scire facias*, had in the mean time died.

Thomas Montague earl of Salifbury, fon and heir of John Montague late earl of Salifbury, petitioned that the judgment paffed againft his father in 1401 might be reverfed, on feveral grounds of error ; which he ftrongly enforced by comparifon with the cafes of Thomas fometime earl of Lancafter in 1320, and of Roger de Mortimer earl of March in 1331. A day of anfwer was appointed to him againft the next parliament.

The following petitions prefented in this parliament were of a public nature :

1. That the Church might enjoy its accuftomed privileges ; the lords fpiritual and temporal and other liege fubjects, the franchifes granted by the king's predeceffors ; and that the great charter, the charter of the Foreft, and fuch other ftatutes as were unrepealed, might continue in full force. Granted.

2. A complaint was prefented againft the officers of the Ecclefiaftical Court, that exorbitant charges were made for probates of wills, &c. ; the officials and commiffaries frequently exacting *fynes, fees, raunfeons, & extorfions*, to the amount of 100l. 40l. 20l. or more or lefs, in an arbitrary manner ; whereas, by the old accuftomed law, 2s. 6d. was the proper charge. In anfwer to which, the prelates engaged that due remedy fhould be provided within half a year after the fee of Canterbury, then vacant, fhould be filled up.

3. It being reprefented to the king in parliament, that the revenues of divers Hofpitals throughout the realm, founded by his royal predeceffors, or by liberal individuals, for the maintenance of aged men and women, lazars, lunaticks, pregnant women, and other diftreffed perfons, had been groffly mifapplied : Order was given for their proper vifitation and reform.

4. The commons petition, that in future all perfons againft whom a writ of *Certiorari corpus cum caufá* fhall be iffued, may not be improperly bailed, nor releafed without bail unlefs by the confent of the plaintiff. Granted.

---

[1] Pat. 1 Hen. IV. pars 1. m. 34.   [2] Stowe's Chronicle, p. 347.   [3] Clauf. 4 Hen. IV. m. 16.
[4] Efch. 9 Hen. IV. N° 29. Leic.

5. The commons complain againſt improper con⸗duct in the Spiritual Courts. Ordered to be redreſſed.

6. They complain alſo, that the ſtatutes for the regulation of labourers and artificers are evaded, by the flight of that deſcription of perſons from one county to another, by which they eſcaped from juſtice. Ordered to be amended by holding ſeſſions uniformly throughout the kingdom in one and the ſame week; and the ſheriff of each county to attend this part of his office under pain of forfeiting 20l.

7. The commons complain, that they are often impleaded in the Spiritual Courts for tithe of timber trees of 20 or 40 years growth, under the name of *Silve cedue*; and pray that no trees may be reckoned titheable that are of more than 21 years growth. Being an affair of great conſequence, the conſideration was adjourned to the next parliament, when the Clerk of the Parliament is to bring it forward at an early period.

8. The commonalty of Northumberland repreſent that murders, treaſons, homicides, robberies, &c. are frequently committed by the inhabitants of the privileged places of Tyndale, Riddeſdale, and Exhamſhire, bordering on the Marches of Scotland, by reaſon of their being ſo privileged; and that they unlawfully harbour and protect certain natives of Scotland, and countenance them in murder and rapine. Due remedy is directed to be provided.

9. The commons pray that, in caſe of a peace with France, the poſſeſſions of the Alien Priories may not be reſtored to the foreign houſes, but reſerved to the king's uſe; to the intent that divine ſervice may for the future be more regularly performed in them by Engliſhmen than had lately been done by Frenchmen; with the exception, however, of the poſſeſſions of ſuch alien priories as were conventual, of priors regularly inducted, and alſo ſuch as had been ſettled by king Henry IV. on the maſter and college of Fodrynghay; and ſaving alſo to all perſons, whether ſpiritual or temporal, any ſuch of the ſaid poſſeſſions as they may have legally purchaſed from their former owners, or received as a grant from the crown, they paying thereout all proper charges, penſions, annuities, and corrodies. Granted.

10. The commons aſſert, that the commonalty of the land is, and ever has been, " a member of the king's parliament, as well Aſſenters as Petitioners;" and pray that nothing which they may aſk through the mouth of their Speaker may paſs into a law in any way that may change the intention of what they aſk. The king grants that nothing ſhall be enacted that may bind them without their aſſent; reſerving his real prerogative, " to grant and deny what him luſt of their petitions and aſkings." And, having a great deſire to amend whatever may be found amiſs, he, by the advice and conſent of the lords ſpiritual and temporal, and at the requeſt of the commons, agrees to the ſeveral following Statutes which appeared to be neceſſary and profitable:

11. A Statute againſt murder, robbery, ſpoiling of goods, breaking through treaties and ſafe-conducts, within the realms of England, Ireland, Wales, and the high ſeas.

12. A Statute againſt Hereticks and Lollards.

13. A Statute for the more effectual ſuppreſſion of riotous and unlawful aſſemblies.

14. Another Statute againſt murders, homicides, robbers, &c. who, having committed the ſaid ſeveral offences, by ſecreting themſelves in woods or other lurking-places, avoided the then exiſting laws.

Thus ended the public buſineſs of the parliament at Leiceſter; in the courſe of which the following petitions were preſented to them, on what in modern language would be ſtyled private buſineſs.

1. William Cryche, prior of Mountagu in Somerſetſhire, repreſented that his priory, being a cell to Clugny in France, had been ſeized by king Edward III. and was afterwards given by king Henry IV. to Fraunceys de Baugiaco, predeceſſor to the petitioner; and therefore prayed, as the brethren of the houſe were all Engliſhmen, that they might remain in quiet poſſeſſion. Granted.

2. John Rypon, abbot of Founteynes (who, in obedience to a papal bull, had, by the king's order, been put into legal poſſeſſion), having a legal proceſs againſt Roger Frank, a monk (who had intruded himſelf into the ſaid abbey, and taken from it ſeveral ornaments and goods) was way-laid, on the edge of Welbeck Park, by Olyver Frank brother to the ſaid Roger, and Robert Frank his couſin, with at leaſt 40 other perſons, and dangerouſly wounded; for which he requeſted redreſs. He was referred to ſeek his remedy by common law.

3. Another petition of the ſame abbot John Rypon is alſo entered, ſtating that his abbey had been plundered of ſeveral chalices, jewels, and other church ornaments; alſo of the common ſeal; and that 500 oxen and 700 ſheep had been forcibly taken away; and that, whilſt he was on his journey to London, to anſwer in the courts of king's bench to a writ iſſued thence againſt him, he was forcibly attacked near Welbeck, as repreſented in his former petition; and praying relief. Again referred to common law.

4. Roger Frank, monk, and of right abbot of Founteynes, repreſents that he was lately made abbot there, agreeably to the ſtatutes and privileges of the Ciſtertian order, and duly put into poſſeſſion and confirmed by the ſuperior of that order in a general chapter; till one John Rypon, lately abbot of Meux, by untrue ſuggeſtions to the pope, had obtained a bull to ouſt him from the ſaid abbey, to the great prejudice of the king and his crown, and contrary to law; and praying to be reſtored to his abbey. There being a writ pending between the parties on the Statute of Proviſions, as Maſter William Hankeford chief juſtice of the king's bench aſſerted; the king directed both parties to await the iſſue of that trial.

5. A petition of Thomas duke of Clarence, Eſmond earl of March, Thomas earl of Saliſbury, Henry le Scrop lord of Maſham, John Nevill ſon and heir of Ralph earl of Weſtmoreland, and Lucy relict of Edward late earl of Kent; ſtating, that John duke of Milan and the commonalty of that city had neglected to pay 70,000 florins, which they had engaged to pay by bonds entered into on the marriage of Edward late earl of Kent with Lucy daughter of Barnabo late duke of Milan; and praying that letters of marque and repriſal may be granted for the effectual recovery of the ſame. Granted.

6. A petition of John Barndeſley, reſpecting the manor of Shorteley in Coventry, formerly the property of Roger Leedaile, eſq. whoſe widow the ſaid John had married, by whom he had a ſon William; and complaining that they were unjuſtly diſſeiſed of the ſaid manor by Baldwin ſon and heir of Baldwin Frevile. *Le Roy vorra faire gree ceſte partie, à l'inſtance & requeſte des Co'es eſteantz en ceſt Parlement.*

7. The tenants of Darleton and Ragenell in Nottinghamſhire ſtate, that they have always enjoyed common of paſture belonging to their freeholds; but of late ſir Richard Stanhope had forcibly incloſed all the common fields, meadows, and paſtures, to their great injury. As this petition relates to *frank tenement*, the king will be further adviſed on it.

8. Oliver Billyng, of Wympeton, in the county of Nottingham, and Agnes his wife, widow of John Sewale of the ſame place, ſtate, that the ſaid John Sewale, by his laſt will, had appointed the ſaid Agnes and John Sewale of Coventry, her brother, her executors; and that, after his death, the laſt mentioned John being old and impotent, had renounced the executorſhip, and Agnes had ſolely adminiſtered: Yet, nevertheleſs, ſir Richard Stanhope, under the ſanction of John Sewale's name, had taken all the goods and chattels of her late huſband to the amount of 60l. and all her own goods worth 20l. more, with all her cloaths except what ſhe was then wearing, and all the debts which were due to her amounting to 19l.; and praying relief. The petition was openly read in parliament in the preſence of ſir Richard Stanhope; who denied all the allegations it contained.

9. A petition of the chancellor and ſcholars of the Univerſity of Cambridge, complaining of the great inconveniences ſuſtained by being under the frequent
neceſſity

neceffity of anfwering to indictments of felony, in cafes wherein they had in no wife offended; and praying, that the chancellor of the Univerfity and certain burgeffes of the town may be authorized to take cognizance of fuch fuppofed offences. The king will provide proper remedies for both Univerfities.

10. John Bryn, Roger Leney, Robert Swynnerton, Thomas Marchall, and Henry Herdley, complain, that Robert Corbett and Richard Lacum, who in the laft parliament had been returned knights of the fhire for the county of Salop, had malicioufly named the faid petitioners to be collectors of the tenths and fifteenths granted in that parliament; and, in further profecution of their malice, had by force of arms obftructed them in the execution of their duty, and violently affaulted and wounded them, and killed their horfes, to the detriment of the king's revenue, and the difhonour of his crown and dignity. The anfwer to this petition appears in the large fchedule annexed.

11. The large fchedule, above referred to, enumerates many inftances of interruption received by the faid collectors, at Eton, Moreton Corbet, Oldbury, and Shrewfbury; and the particulars of an attack made at Dunftable (where the king then was) on two of the faid collectors, who were deputed by their brethren to carry their collection to the Exchequer, when they were cruelly beat and wounded by Roger Leney. Ordered to be tried, by due form of law, in the court of king's bench.

12. Edmund le Ferrers, efq. complains that Hugh Erdefwyck and divers other perfons of the counties of Chefter and Stafford had made a violent affault on his town of Charteley, in the county of Stafford, killed John Page one of his fervants, and demolifhed his park pales; and praying redrefs. The Statute of 13 Henry IV. provides a fufficient remedy.

13. A counter petition of Hugh Erdefwyck, efq. complains of riotous proceedings on the part of Edmund Ferrers; of which feveral inftances are produced. The fame Statute is fufficient for this alfo [1].

In 1414, *Francis Keble*, efq. died feifed of one meffuage, with the appurtenances, in Leicefter; which was held of the king, as of his dutchy of *Lancafter*, by fealty, and the fervice of 3*s.* 9*d. per annum* [2].

In 1415, *Ralph Humberfton* was mayor of Leicefter; in which year, Oct. 24, was the famous battle of Agincourt [3].

Thomas Saborne was mayor in 1416; *John Earnfby*, 1417; *Henry Bebe*, 1418 (in which year the lord Cobham and fir John Oldcaftle were hanged [4]); *William Pacy*, 1419; and *Thomas Walgrave*, 1420; in which year *Robert Shillington* died feifed of one meffuage and two fhops in Leicefter; which were held of the king, as of the Honour of *Leicefter* [5].

In 1421, *Ralph Humberfton* was mayor of Leicefter; and *John Church* in 1422; in which year, on the 31ft of Auguft, king Henry V. died, at the age of 34.

HENRY VI.

In 1423, *Henry Fofter* was mayor of Leicefter; in which year, *Maud* wife of fir *John Lovel*, knt. died feifed of 6*s.* 8*d.* yearly rent, arifing out of a certain meffuage in the town of Leicefter; which was held of *Katherine* Queen of England, as of the Honour of *Leicefter*; alfo of a certain parcel of meadow in the fame place, held of the fame Queen [6].

In this year, *Richard Hynam*, of Leicefter, had licence to go out of the kingdom [7].

Henry Darby was mayor of Leicefter in 1424; and *William Newby* in 1425.

In 1425-6, a parliament was held at Leicefter, the writs for which, dated at Weftminfter, Feb. 7, and returnable at Leicefter Feb. 18, were thus directed:

Rex, &c. chariffimo avunculo fuo Johanni duci Bedfordie, &c.

Humfrido duci Gloceftrie.
Thome duci Exonie.
Johanni duci Norfolcie.

Henrico comiti Northumberland.
Humfrido comiti Stafford.
Jacobo de Berkley chevalier.
Magiftro Thome de la War.
Willielmo de Ferrariis de Groby chevalier.
Johanni de Wells, chevalier.
Johanni baroni de Grayftock, chevalier.
Reginaldo Gray de Ruthin, chevalier.
Johanni Latimer, chevalier.
Roberto de Poynings, chevalier.
Willielmo Bottreaulx, chevalier.
Johanni Dacre de Gilfland, chevalier.
Willielmo Clinton, chevalier.
Willielmo Harrington, chevalier.
Jacobo de Audley, chevalier.
Johanni Gray de Codenor, chevalier.
Radulpho Cromwell, chevalier.
Lodovico Robefart, chevalier.
Ricardo Strang, chevalier.
Johanni le Scroop de Mafham, chevalier.
Willielmo Lovell, chevalier.
Willielmo la Zouch de Harringworth.
Waltero Hungerford.
Johanni Tibetot, chevalier.
Reginald le Warr, chevalier.
Thome de Morle, chevalier.
Willielmo Cheyn, Capitali Jufticiarie.

The Parliament was accordingly holden, on Monday the 18th day of February, in the great hall of the Caftle of Leicefter, the lords and commons being there, in due form affembled; when Henry bifhop of Winchefter, chancellor of England, declared,

1. that the king's will was, that the Englifh Church, and all the king's liege fubjects of every defcription, fhould enjoy their liberties.

2. He then took for his theme the words of St. Paul, *Sic facite ut falvi fitis*; the which he divided into three parts. The firft to God's protecting the faith of the Church againft the innovations of the Hereticks and the Lollards. The fecond, by imparting found counfel. The third, by granting liberal fubfidies; from which, he affirmed, a threefold benefit' would follow; viz. glory to God, by protecting his faith; honour to the king, by receiving found counfel; and peace to the fubjects by liberal granting. Wherefore he willed the prelates, peers, and commons, refpectively, to labour therein.

3. He then directed the commons to affemble themfelves *in quâdam baffâ camerâ eifdem communibus pro eorum domo communi ordinatâ & affignatâ*, there to elect a fpeaker, to be prefented next day to the king.

4, 5, 6, 7. Receivers and triers of petitions were then appointed. Thofe for England, Ireland, Wales, and Scotland, to meet in the chapter-houfe of the collegiate church of St. Mary de Caftro; and thofe for Gafcoigne and other foreign parts in the North chapel of the fame church.

8. The king appointed, by letters patent, John duke of Bedford his commiffioner, to prorogue and diffolve the parliament.

9. On the 28th of February, the commons prefented before the king Richard Vernon, knight, to be their fpeaker; with whom, after the accuftomed proteftation, *Rex benè fe contentavit*.

10. Upon the commons difliking the diffention between the nobles, the duke of Bedford and other lords made a folemn decree amongft themfelves, that every of them fhould, without affection, hear and end the diffention between the duke of Gloucefter and the bifhop of Winchefter, fo as neither of them fhould be encouraged to break the peace: to which order, after every of the lords were fworn, they fent the copy thereof to the commons; it being alfo ordered, that none of the lords, or their followers, fhould repair to the parliament with weapons.—["In this town (as Robert Fabian, alderman of London, writeth in his Chronicle [8]) was kept, in 1425-6, the famous *Parliamentum Fuftium*, or *Parliament of Bats*; fo called, for that parliamentary men being forbidden to wear

[1] Rot. Parl. 2 Hen. V. Pars I.; fee the printed Rolls, vol. IV. pp. 15—33.
[2] Efch. 2 Hen. V.   [3] From the Roll of Mayors of Leicefter.   [4] Ibid.   [5] Efch. 8 Hen. V. N° 71. Leic.
[6] Efch. 1 Hen. VI. N° 51. Leic.   [7] Catalogue des Rolles François, vol. II. p. 241.   [8] Fol. 186. b. 201. b.

fwords

fwords or weapons, they then ufed bats and ftaves; which alfo likewife being inhibited, they wore in their fleeves great ftones and plummers of lead [1]."]

11. On the 5th of March: "Concordatum fuit & ordinatum, quod proclamatio fieret in villa Leyceftrie, quod univerfi & finguli in villâ prediftâ exiftentes, qui aliqua annuitates, feoda, vel officia habent, ex concef-fione vel confirmatione domini regis, compareant co-ram domino rege & confilio fuo, in Caftro Leyceftrie, die Mercurii tunc proximè futuro, ad faciend' & reci-piend' quod per dictum dominum regem & confilium fuum tunc ibidem contingeret ordinari."

12. The difference between the duke of Gloucefter and the bifhop of Winchefter, by their formal inftruments, was compromitted to certain bifhops and lords, who, by like formality, make a full order between them; viz. that the bifhop fhould firft fubmit himfelf to the king; which he did: whereupon the duke of Bedford, in open parliament, by the king's commandment, pro-nounced the faid bifhop excufed, as well of that it is faid that the faid bifhop had procured one to have murthered the king, being prince, as the murtherer confeffed (who having been delivered to the earl of Arundel, the faid earl *lete fake him forthwith, and drownyd hym in the Thamyfe*); as alfo for that it was faid that the bifhop fhould counfel, and would have it procured, by king Henry V. being prince, to have deprived king Henry IV. his father.

13. Moreover they awarded, that the faid bifhop fhould acknowledge to the faid duke of Gloucefter an offence, and by his fubmiffion to pray his favour; and that the duke fhould promife the fame; and that, in token thereof, either of them fhould take the other by the hand. Which was done, in token of re-conciliation.

14. On the 13th day of March, the bifhop of Winchefter, for fundry caufes, prayed to be dif-charged of the great feal, whereof by common con-fent he was difcharged. The bifhop of Bath, trea-furer of England, was of his office alfo difcharged.

15. On the 18th day of March, John bifhop of Bath and Wells, late treafurer of England, by a writ of privy feal, delivered unto the duke of Bedford the king's great feal of gold in a leather bag; the which the duke took, and fhewed openly, and then fealed it up with his own feal; and after delivered the fame to John bifhop of London, chancellor of Eng-land.

16. On the 8th of February, the bifhop of Dur-ham, by virtue of a privy feal to him directed, deli-vered the laft will and teftament, with a codicil on paper thereto annexed, of king Henry V. which was fealed with the great and privy feal, and the privy fignet to the lords of the privy council; who deli-vered the fame over, fafely to be kept, to Mafter William Alnewyk, keeper of the privy feal.

17. It is enacted that the lords of the council fhall have full power to bind the king, his heirs and fuc-ceffors, to his creditors, for one affurance for the fum of 40,000l.

18. At the petition of the earl of Huntingdon, the king, by common confent, releafed to Lewis of Bur-bon, earl of Vendofme, who had been taken prifoner at the battle of Agincourt, all arrears of ranfom.

19. The duke of Bedford, who had the keeping of the caftle at Berwick, to him and his heirs male, with the fee of 500 marks, had licence, by common con-fent, to appoint a deputy there, at the king's pleafure.

20. It is enacted, that any of the feoffees of king Henry V. may take the homage of fealty of any te-nants holding under them.

21. It is enacted, that the king's council, by au-thority of parliament, fhall have power to end all fuch petitions relative to private bufinefs as fhall not have been ended by parliament.

22. It is decreed, by common affent of the lords, that the late fubfidy of tonnage and poundage to the king granted ought fimply to be paid, notwithftand-ing any condition.

23. On the 27th day of March, before the lords and commons, the bifhop of London, chancellor of Eng-land, by the king's commiffary's commandment, pro-rogued the parliament, from the fame day, till Mon-day next after the feaft of St. George, at Leicefter.

24. On the 1ft day of June, being the laft day of parliament, the commons, by affent of the bifhops and lords, granted to the king the fubfidy of wools, tonnage, and poundage.

25. The king, by common confent, granteth, by his letters patent, that the prior of St. Trinity in York, being a cell of the abbey of Meremoftier in France, fhall be denizens.

26. The king grants to Thomas Cornyfh, of Woxebrigge, co. Middlefex (on the humble petition of Margaret his wife), a pardon for ftealing of fheep from a clofe belonging to Alice Scolecroft.

27. At the requeft of the merchants of the Hans in Germany, the king, in conformity to their privi-leges, appointeth to them fir William Crowmere, one of the aldermen of London, to be a judge between party and party of the fame company of Hans in all fuits; and that, within one month after the death, or leaving over, of the faid alderman, there be ap-pointed to them one other alderman to fupply the fame.

28. Petitions of the commons, with the anfwers.

Upon motion of the commons, it was granted, that all fuch merchants as had paid fubfidy for their wools, and could prove before the council that the fame or any part thereof was perifhed, might fhip the fame quantity without cuftom.

29. That no man make a prefentation, collation, or induction, to any alien, of any benefice or ecclefi-aftical dignity, on pain of Premunire. The king will be advifed.

30. That no man of good name be impeached by the accufation of any being in fanctuary, unlefs fure-ties be bound that proof be made thereof. The Sta-tutes already made fhall be obferved.

31. That every patron may prefent a-new, in cafe of non-refidence of the incumbent. The bifhops have promifed to take order therein.

32. The print againft bribery of fheriffs, chap. 4. agrees with the record.

33. That all ftrangers being within the realm about queen Joan may depart out of the realm. The Statutes thereupon made fhall be obferved.

34. That the chancellor of England for the time being may, for reafonable fines, grant licences to the king's tenants that hold in chief, to alien their lands; and to the king's widows, to marry themfelves ac-cording to the antient cuftom. The king will be ad-vifed.

35. The print touching the mifprifion of clerks of the king's courts, chap. 3. agrees with the record.

36. The print touching knights of parliament, chap. 4, agrees with the record.

37. The print touching exportation of provifions, chap. 5, agrees with the record.

38. The print touching affizes and protections, chap. 2, agrees with the record [2].

At Whitfuntide this year, the duke of Bedford, re-gent of France, knighted the young king Henry VI. who thereupon immediately conferred the like honour on Richard earl of Cambridge, and about 40 more. At this parliament alfo the faid earl of Cambridge was not only reftored in blood, which was inherited by his father, but alfo was created duke of York; which enabled him afterwards, as he did, to put in and profecute claim to the crown.

In 1426, *John Picwell* was mayor of Leicefter; *William Hufly*, 1427; *William Pacy*, 1428; and *Wil-liam Humberftone*, 1429; in which year, the follow-ing *Gentlemen* of this county were fummoned to attend the king, for the defence of the realm:

"*Leiceftr'.* Will' Truffell, chevalier, Rob' Nevill, chevalier, Tho' Pulteney, arm', Johannes Perwick, arm', Alanus Moton, arm', Everardus Digby, arm',

---

[1] Burton, MS.
[2] Prynne's Abridgement of the Records, pp. 582—585. Rot. Parl. 4 Hen. VI.; printed Rolls, vol. IV. pp. 295—308.

Tho' Nevill, arm', Rob' Wiwell, arm', Johannes Charnel, arm' [1]."

In 1430, *Thomas Walgrave* was mayor of Leicester; *John Loughborough*, 1431 (in which year, Dec. 7, king Henry VI. was crowned at Paris) ; *Thomas Clarke*, 1432 ; *William Newby*, 1433 (in which year the arbitration concerning *The South Field near Leicester* was made, which will be elsewhere noticed [2]) ; *John Reynolds*, 1434 ; *Adam Pacy*, 1435 [3] ; and *Walter Pomerey*, 1436 ; in which year, fir *Richard Haftinges*, knt. died feifed of three crofts in Leicester, held of the abbot of St. *Mary de Pratis* in that town [4].

William Hafty was mayor of Leicester in 1437 ; *John Coventre*, 1438 ; *John Reynolds*, 1439 ; *Adam Racye*, 1440 ; *Thomas Charity*, 1441 ; *William Wimefwold*, 1442 ; *William Grantham*, 1443 (in which year, Feb. 1, *Paul's Steeple* was burnt [5]) ; *William Newby*, 1444 ; *Thomas Green*, 1445 ; *John Brynight* (or *Bennet*), 1446 ; *Ralph Furnys*, alias *Fifher*, 1447 ; *William Wigfton*, 1448 ; and *William Stringer*, 1449 ; in which year the parliament, which was fummoned to meet at Weftminfter on the 6th of November, was, *ob aëris infeétionem in villâ Weftm' & aliis locis circumvicinis*, adjourned to the City of London; where, on the 4th of December, they were affembled in the houfe of the Black Friers; and for fome time continued to fit, till on the 30th of December they were prorogued, to meet at Weftminfter on the 22d of January, 1449-50.

At the commencement of this parliament, there being great difcontents againft the dukes of Somerfet and Suffolk, upon the lofs of Normandy ; and the commons having impeached William de la Pole, duke of Suffolk ; he was imprifoned, but foon after releafed out of the Tower, and reftored to his former place about the king again ; which fo incenfed the people, that there was danger of an infurreétion [6].

The *infalubritas aëris* ftill continuing to prevail in Weftminfter, the parliament was, on the 30th of March, 1450, prorogued to the 29th of Auguft, and then to meet at Leicefter; at which place the ufual fubfidy was granted [7]. But the commons perfevering in their profecution of the duke of Suffolk, and very few of the nobility appearing at Leicefter, the parliament was re-adjourned to Weftminfter.

Whilft the archbifhop of Canterbury was at Leicefter, in his attendance upon this parliament, Reginald Peacock, on his tranflation from St. Afaph to the fee of Chichefter, made his profeffion of obedience to him on the 31ft of March [8].

John Reynolds was mayor of Leicefter in 1450; *William Clarke*, 1451; *William Wimefwold*, 1452; and *Thomas Charyte*, 1453.

May 23, 1454, was the battle near St. Alban's.

In 1455, fir *Leonard Haftings*, knt. died feifed of three crofts in Leicefter, held of the abbot of St. *Mary de Pratis* [9].

Thomas Dalton was mayor of Leicefter 1454—1456; *Thomas Green*, 1457; and *John Reynolds*, 1458.

In the Records of the Corporation of Leicefter is preferved the following very curious entry:

" It is to have in mind that *John Fryfley*, of Leicefter, burgefs, came into the court of Portman moot of Leicefter, the Monday next after the feaft of St. Valentine, 1458-9, afore *John Reynolds* the elder, at that time being mayor of the faid town, and his brethren; and there, wilfully, devoutly, and holily, bearing in mind the unftablenefs of this prefent life, and alfo the infecurity of people left after a man's prefent life in miniftration of his temporal goods, any thing to the health of his foul, and alfo the great worfhip and pleafure to the mayor for the

time being, and all his brethren, hath given to the mayoralty of Leicefter, perpetually to endure, certain lyflode and tenement, as in divers deeds and muniments thereof made more plainly doth under this condition appear that followeth ; *i. e.* the mayor for the time being fhall find a prieft perpetually to fing for the faid John Fryfley, his wife, his father and mother, the mayor and his brethren for the time being, and in all time to come, and all his benefactors. And if the mayor be negligent, and no prieft will have, then the feoffours which fhall be feoffed in the faid livelode and tenement, fhall have a prieft to fing, fay, and pray, for the health of the fouls of the faid John Fryfley, his wife, father and mother, the mayor, his brethren, and all his benefactors, in the church where the faid John lieth, as long as the mayor for the time being is without a prieft. Alfo the faid mayor which for the time fhall be, with the provenues coming and growing of the faid lyflode and tenement, fhall yearly pay and content the faid prieft his falary, and keep all manner of reparations neceffary to the faid lyflode and tenement, by the good advice of the faid feoffees. And if the mayor will no prieft find, then the feoffees to find a prieft, and pay him his falary, and with the overplus to make reparations. And the faid John Fryfley chargeth the feoffees that they make new feoffees after three or four of them have deceafed [10]."

In 1459, was the battle at Blore Heath [11]; and the following perfons were appointed commiffioners for this county, to feleét proper archers for the defence of the realm.

" Johannes vicecomes Beaumont, abbas Leyceftrie, Edwardus Grey de Groby, Willielmus Haftings, Johannes Bellers, Thomas Palmer, Willielmus Fildinge, Thomas Berkeley, Ricardus Nele, Ricardus Hotofte."

William Wigfton was mayor of Leicefter in 1459.

The battle of Northampton [11] was fought July 9, 1460 ; in which year, *Robert Shillingham* was elected mayor of Leicefter ; and during his mayoralty the battle of Wakefield, commonly called *York field* [11], was fought, Dec. 31 ; and on the 4th of March, 1460-1, king Henry VI. was depofed.

EDWARD IV.

March 29, 1461, king Edward obtained a decifive victory over the forces of the late king Henry at Towton [11]; and in this year it was found that *Everard Digby*, attainted of high treafon, was feifed of one meffuage in Leicefter [12].

The following entry is alfo of this period:

" It is to have in mind that *John Reynolds* the elder, of Leicefter, burgefs, the 3d of May 1461, for the goodly zeal that he had to the honourable and worfhipful office of mayoralty of the town of Leicefter, the which was by him four fundry years miniftered, gave to the mayoralty aforefaid perpetually a tenement in the High Street of Leicefter, by the High Crofs there fet, between the tenement of John Roberts on the South and the tenement of John Danet on the North, as in certain muniments thereof made appeareth, to have and to hold the faid tenement, with the appurtenances, to the mayoralty of the town of Leicefter perpetually, in manner, and all conditions, means, and rules, as the livelode, lands, and tenements, late of John Fryfley above fpecified, were given by the faid John Fryfley to the office of mayoralty of the town of Leicefter [13]."

Robert Rawlett was elected mayor of Leicefter in 1461; and on the 15th of May, 1462, king Edward IV. for fervice done by the mayor and burgeffes of Leicefter againft the king's enemies, granted them 20 marks

---

[1] Nomina illorum qui [per fingulos Angliæ comitatus] arma antiqua portantium, qui ad regem veniendum, pro defenfione regni fummoniti funt, 1429. [2] See under *The South Field* in the Hundred of Guthlaxton.
[3] In this year was a great froft, endured from . . . . . to Feb. 14; fo that neither fhips might fail, nor boats be rowed, in the river of Thames ; and therefore all the vintages were carried to London in carts by land. (From the Roll of Mayors.)
[4] Efch. 15 Hen. VI. N° 58. Leic.   [5] From the Roll of Mayors.
[6] This year rofe the commons in Kent ; and made there a captain, named John Cade. (From the Roll of Mayors.)
[7] Rot. Parl. 28 Hen. VI. vol. V. p. 172.   [8] He was deprived in 1457 ; and fent to the abbey of Thornley.
[9] Efch. 34 Hen. VI.   [10] Extracted by Mr. Carte from the Lock Book for Fines, in cuftody of the mayor of Leicefter.
[11] From the Roll of Mayors.   [12] Efch. 1 Edw. IV. N° 7. Leic.
[13] From the Lock Book, as before; in which follow fome feoffments made of John Fryfley's lands, before John Reynolds fenior, then mayor, and Peter Curteys, bailiff, 24 and 26 Dec. 17 Edw. IV.

yearly,

yearly, from Michaelmas paft, for 20 years. This grant was at the Caftle of Leicefter, by the labour of *Robert Rawlett* then mayor, and of Thomas Green and John Roberds, then being burgeffes of the parliament.

John Yoman was elected mayor of Leicefter in 1462; and in his mayoralty, in April 1463, was the battle of Hexham[1].

John Reynolds was elected mayor of Leicefter in 1463; and in his mayoralty, king Edward IV. by his letters patent under the feal of the duchy of Lancafter, dated at his caftle of Leicefter, June 2, 1464, " gave to his well-beloved fervant Mauryce Arnolde, fquire, his ferjeant porter, all the iffues and profits to him due and growing, of a place called *Blanckchapillon*, with all the lands belonging to the fame, in the city of London[2]. And in the fame year, in an act of refumption of grants, there was a claufe for faving the grant of 20 marks to the town of Leicefter, which had been granted them in 1462. A provifo alfo occurs, that an act of refumption " fhall not be prejudicial to Richard Chambre, of a grant committing the keeping to him of one mece, with the appurtenances, in Leicefter, late by us, by our letters patent, under our great feal made[3]."

On the 24th of Auguft, 1464, king Edward IV. for the greater fecurity and quiet of the corporation of Leicefter, granted to the then mayor and burgeffes, and to their fucceffors for ever; 1. that the mayor for the time being and four of the difcreeteft comburgeffes, with one perfon fkilled in the laws (to be called the recorder) fhould be juftices to keep and caufe to be kept the ftatutes of fervants, artificers, and labourers. 2. That the faid mayor and comburgeffes, or any three or two of them, with the recorder, fhould have the full correction, privilege, power, and authority, of knowing, inquiring, hearing, and determining of all matters of tranfgreffion, mifprifion, and extortion, and of all other caufes, complaints, and mifdemeanors, within the faid town and liberties, as fully and entirely as any other juftices of fervants, labourers, and artificers in the county of Leicefter, have elfewhere therein; matters of felony therein, matters of felony, and of melting, clipping, wafhing, and other falfifying of the coin only excepted. 3. That no juftice of the peace, or other juftice or commiffioner of the king or his heirs, in the county, fhould intermeddle there in any matter, except as before excepted. 4. That neither they the mayor and burgeffes, or their fucceffors, any conftable of the town of Leicefter, or any other perfon there fojourning, fhould be bound or compelled to appear before any other juftice of the peace, or any other juftice or commiffioner of the king or his heirs, either within or without the faid town, to enquire or do any thing in the matters aforefaid, happening in the faid town and liberties (except as before excepted), fave only before the mayor and four of the difcreeter comburgeffes, and their fucceffors, as is abovefaid. 5. That if any mayor, burgefs, conftable, or other perfon within the faid town or liberties thereof abiding, fhould be fummoned or impanelled, and refufe to appear before any other juftice about any fuch matter, or to fwear or enquire about any heads or articles thereunto belonging, that, for fuch his refufal, he fhould not be put in contempt, or incur any lofs or penalty to the king or his heirs. 6. That the mayor of the 24 comburgeffes fhould yearly, upon the feaft of St. Matthew the Evangelift, elect four of the faid 24 to be juftices of the peace for the year enfuing; and two of the faid 24 to be coroners; and no other coroner to intermeddle. 7. Laftly, that they, the mayor and burgeffes and their fucceffors, fhould not be impanelled on any affifes, juries, jurifdictions or recognizances (though they concern either the king or his heirs, or any other of his liege people) or be fworn or put upon the trial of any amerciament of any affize or panal before any juftices or commiffioners of the king or his heirs, about any thing, caufe, or

matter, happening without Leicefter, when the trial is to be taken out of the faid borough.

" Edwardus, Dei gratiâ, rex Anglie et Francie, et dominus Hibernie, omnibus ad quos prefentes litere pervenerint, falutem. Sciatis quod nos, volentes fecuritati et quieti dilectorum ligeorum noftrorum majoris et burgenfium ville five burgi noftre Leyceftrie, conceffimus, pro nobis et heredibus noftris, quantum in nobis eft, et per prefentes concedimus *Johanni Yoman*[4], nunc majori ejufdem ville five burgi, et burgenfibus ejufdem, ac fuccefforibus fuis pro tempore exiftentibus, quod hujufmodi major et quatuor de difcretioribus comburgenfibus ville five burgi illius, in formâ fubfequendâ eligendis et nominandis, quamdiu in hujufmodi officiis majoratûs aut burgenfium fuerint, cum uno legifperito in perpetuo nominando Recordatore Leyceftrie, fint jufticiarii noftri et heredum noftrorum ad pacem infra villam five burgum predictum, procinctus et limites ejufdem ville five burgi, necnon ad ftatuta et ordinaciones de fervientibus, artificibus, et laboratoribus edita, confervandum et cuftodiri faciendum in perpetuum. Et quod iidem major et quatuor comburgenfes ville five burgi illius pro tempore exiftentes, tres vel duo eorum, cum dicto recordatore, plenam habeant correctionem, punitionem, poteftatem, et auctoritatem cognofcendi, inquirendi, audiendi, et terminandi omnes res et materias, tam de omnibus feloniis, tranfgreffionibus, mifprifionibus, et extortionibus, quam de omnimodis aliis caufis, querelis, et moleftiis quibufcumque, infra eandem villam five burgum, procinctus et limites ejufdem, qualitercunque contingentibus five emergentibus, adeo plenè et integrè ficut cuftodes pacis noftre et jufticiarii ad felonias, tranfgreffiones, et alia malefacta audiendum et terminandum affignati et affignandi, ac jufticiarii fervientium, laboratorum, et artificium, in comitatu Leyc', extra villam five burgum ac procinctus predictos, habent, feu in futurum qualitercumque habebunt; terminationibus de omnimodis feloniis, ac de contrafacturâ, tonfurâ, loturâ, et aliâ falfitate monete regni noftri Anglie, duntaxat exceptis; et quod nullus cuftos pacis, jufticiarius, aut commiffionarius noftri, vel heredum noftrorum, ad premiffa, five aliquod premifforum, in comitatu predicto audiendum et terminandum affignatus, in aliquo intromittat infra villam five burgum predictum, aut procinctus et limites ejufdem, feu extra eandem villam five burgum, procinctus et limites ejufdem, pro premiffis, aut aliquo premifforum, infra villam five burgum predictum, ac procinctus ejufdem, qualitercumque facta five emergentia, exceptis preexceptis; nec infra villam five burgum predictum, aut procinctus ejufdem, aliquod officium fuum de premiffis, five aliquo premifforum, exceptis preexceptis, infra dictam villam five burgum ac procinctus ejufdem, qualitercumque factis five emergentibus aliqualiter faciendum, inquirendum, vel exequendum, ingrediantur, nec ingredi prefumant. Conceffimus etiam eifdem majori et burgenfibus, et fuccefforibus fuis, quod ipfi et fucceffores fui, feu eorum aliquis, aut aliquis conftabularius ville five burgi illius pro tempore exiftens, aut aliquis alius infra villam five burgum predictum commorans feu commoraturus, non arctentur neque compellantur, non arctetur nec compellatur, ad comparendum coram aliquibus jufticiariis pacis noftre, vel heredum noftrorum, in comitatu predicto, vel coram jufticiariis noftri vel heredum noftrorum, ad felonias, tranfgreffiones, et alia malefacta, in eodem comitatu, audiendum et terminandum affignati vel affignandi, aut aliquibus aliis jufticiariis vel commiffionariis noftri aut heredum noftrorum, extra villam five burgum predictum, ac procinctus et limites ejufdem, neque infra eandem villam five burgum, procinctus et limites ejufdem, ad inquirendum vel aliquid aliud faciendum pro premiffis vel aliquo premifforum, infra eandem villam five burgum, procinctus aut limites ejufdem, factis, emergentibus five contingentibus, exceptis preexceptis, preterquam coram prefatis majore et quatuor

---

[1] From the Roll of Mayors.   [2] Rot. Parl. vol. V. p. 548.   [3] Ibid. p. 541.
[4] *John Yoman*, though mentioned by name in this charter, was the mayor of the preceding year, as is evident by the uniform teftimony of various Rolls of Mayors; and *John Reynolds* is recognized as mayor Sept. 10, 1464, in a deed abridged in p. 375.

de difcretioribus comburgenfibus et fucceſſoribus fuis pro tempore exiſtentibus, ut predictum eſt. Et ſi aliquis major, burgenſis, conſtabularius, vel aliquis alius, infra dictam villam five burgum, procinctus et limites ejuſdem reſidens, vel extunc reſidere contingens, exnunc ſummoneatur aut impanelletur ad comparendum coram aliquibus hujuſmodi cuſtodibus aut juſticiariis pacis, laboratorum et artificium noſtri, vel heredum noſtrorum, in comitatu predicto, vel coram juſticiariis aut commiſſionariis noſtris, vel heredum noſtrorum, ad felonias, tranſgreſſiones, et alia malefacta ibidem perpetrata, audiendum et terminandum, aſſignati vel aſſignandi, exceptis preexceptis, et ipſe coram eis defaltam fecerit, vel ad jurand' ſui inquirend' de vel pro aliquibus articulis infra villam five burgum predictum factis five perpetratis, exceptis preexceptis, recuſaverit, non propter hoc ponatur in contemptu, nec ullum deperditum aut gravamen erga nos vel heredes noſtros ex hâc causâ incurrat. Et inſuper conceſſimus, et per preſentes concedimus, prefatis majori et burgenſibus, et eorum ſucceſſoribus, quod iidem major et viginti quatuor comburgenſes ville five burgi predicti, et eorum ſucceſſores pro tempore exiſtentes, de anno in annum, in feſto Sancti Matthei Evangeliſte, eligere poſſint, de ipſis viginti quatuor comburgenſibus predictis, quatuor diſcretiores comburgenſes, eſſendi juſticiarii noſtri et heredum noſtrorum, ad premiſſa five premiſſorum infra villam five burgum predictum, procinctus et limites ejuſdem, exceptis preexceptis, cognoſcendi, inquirendi, audiendi, et terminandi; ac, de eiſdem viginti quatuor comburgenſibus, duos coronatores, qui officium coronatoris infra villam five burgum predictum, procinctus et limites ejuſdem, facient et exequantur; et quod iidem coronatores ſic electi, et ſucceſſores ſui qui pro tempore erunt, in perpetuum habeant et exerceant officium coronatoris noſtri et heredum noſtrorum in villâ five burgo predicto, et procinctibus et limitibus ejuſdem, tam in preſentiâ noſtrâ et heredum noſtrorum, quam in abſentiâ noſtrâ et heredum noſtrorum, in omnibus rebus, prout aliquo tempore ante datum preſentium aliquis coronator noſter infra villam five burgum predictum, ac procinctus ejuſdem, officium coronatoris ibidem exercere conſuevit; ac etiam in omnibus aliis rebus infra eandem villam five burgum, aut procinctus ejuſdem, accidentibus, contingentibus, five emergentibus in futuro, que ad officium coronatoris quoviſmodo pertinent five ſpectant, et que ſi infra aliquem comitatum regni noſtri Anglie acciderent aut emergerent per coronatores feu coronatorem ejuſdem comitatûs exerceri, compareri, feu fieri deberent, adeò plenè et integrè, pacificè et quietè, prout iidem coronatores five coronator alterius comitatûs regni noſtri Anglie hujuſmodi officium coronatoris, et omnia alia officium illud tangentia, occupant feu exercent, occupat feu exercet, aut occuparunt five exercuerunt, occupare feu exercere quoviſmodo legitimè poterint vel poterit in futuro, fine occaſione, impetitione, vel impedimento noſtri, vel heredum noſtrorum, aut aliorum officiariorum feu miniſtrorum noſtrorum quorumcumque; ita quod nullus alius coronator noſtri vel heredum noſtrorum fe pro aliquo ad officium coronatoris pertinens infra villam five burgum predictum, ac procinctus ejuſdem, emergente five accidente, aliqualiter intromittat, nec villam feu burgum illum ad aliquod ad officium coronatoris pertinet faciendum ingrediatur. Conceſſimus etiam, pro nobis, heredibus et ſucceſſoribus noſtris, prefatis majori et burgenſibus, et eorum ſucceſſoribus, quod nec ipſi nec eorum aliquis ponantur neque ponatur, impanellentur neque impanelletur, in aliquibus aſſiſis, juratis, inquiſitionibus, feu recognitionibus, licet tanget nos vel heredes noſtros, vel aliquos alios ligeos noſtros; nec jurentur nec onerentur, nec ullus eorum juretur feu oneretur, ſuper triatione arraiamenti alicujus aſſiſe five panelli coram aliquibus juſticiariis feu commiſſionariis noſtris vel heredum noſtrorum, de vel pro aliquâ re, causâ,

vel materiâ quâcumque; extra villam five burgum predictum emergente five contingente, capiendam extra villam five burgum predictum. In cujus rei teſtimonium, has literas noſtras fieri fecimus patentes. Teſte meipſo, apud Wodeſtoke, 24° die Auguſti, anno regni noſtro quarto. Per breve de privato ſigillo, ac de datâ predictâ, auctoritate Parliamenti '."

Sept. 10, 1464, the mayor and commonalty of Leicefter let, for 12 years, to *Ranulph Beryngton*, taylor, for 12*d. per annum*, a piece of land lying in the pariſh of St. Margaret, in *Le Water Croftes*, between the land of St. Margaret's and the land of St. John Leicefter; *John Reynolds* then being mayor, *Peter Curteis* bailiff, &c.

William Holbech was elected mayor of Leicefter in September 1464; *Roger Wigſton*, 1465; and *John Fryſley*, 1466.

" It is agreed for ever, in time of the mayoralty of William Fryſley, by the wardens and all the occupation of the craft of taylors, that there ſhall no taylor fet up his craft as a maſter within the town of Leicefter, but the wardens of the ſaid craft ſhall bring in 10*s*. in money, and pay it to the chamberlains, for his duty to the chapman's gild, a fortnight before the chamberlains enter into their accompt, upon pain of forfeiting 20*s*. of the gild of taylors' money, to be levied by the chamberlains ²."

Richard Gyllott was elected mayor of Leicefter in 1467; and at a common hall holden the Friday before the feaſt of St. Luke, it was ordained, " that if any perſon enter and abyde within the gild hall at any comon hall holden at the day of election of the mayor, or other comon hall, except he be of the forty-eight; that he, by comand of the mayor, be forthwith comitted to warde, to continue forty days on the mayor's grace, paying 40*d*. to the chamberlains to the uſe of the town, without pardon or grace of any part. And alſo if any perſon of what degree foever name one of the mayor's brethren to the office of mayoralty till ſuch time as the mayor hath comanded the cryer to make an noy and read the ordinance before time made, and declared the liberty of election, and diſcharged himſelf according to the antient cuſtom; for the ſame ſhall pay like forfeiture and penalty as before is rehearſed. And if any mayor be verily known innocent [negligent] in execution of theſe ordinances, he ſhall forfeit to the chamber 20*s*. to be witholden by the chamberlains of the mayre's fee ²."

Then follow ſeveral orders, made by Richard Gillot, mayor, at a common hall, on Thurſday before St. Simon and Jude; whereof ſome are:

" That no one in town bear any weapon except in ſupport of the mayor; but a knight or eſquire may have a ſword borne after hym. Every countryman to leave his weapon at his inn, and bear it not in town, on forfeit of the weapon, and his body to priſon as long as the mayor likes.

That no one walk, after nine of the bell be ſtricken in the night, without light, or without cauſe reaſonable.

That bakers [take care] that the town lack no bread white or brown, on pain of impriſonment.

That ſuch as bring wine to town fell none without leave of the mayor, on like pain.

That brewers fell the beſt ale for 1¼*d*.; the ſecond, 1*d*.; the third, ½*d*. a gallon; and by meaſure ſealed.

That butchers bring the ſkins and tallow with the fleſh to the market; and no butcher to kill a bull till baited, nor buy fleſh of other butchers to fell again.

That geeſe be fold for 4*d*. apiece, and the beſt pig for 6*d*.

That none lay muck at his door, nor ſtones, timber, or clay, &c. within the four gates, and four ſtreets of the ſuburbs, but remove it within three days.

That no one play for filver at any unlawful game forbidden by the ſtatute.

That no writer fet the mayor to witnefs in any ſcripture without his knowledge.

That no franchiſed perſon fue another by ſpiritual

---

¹ Pat. 4 Edw. IV. Pars 1. m. 12.

² S. Carte, ex Libro Villæ Leyceſtriæ, temp. Edw. IV. Ric. III. Hen. VII. & part. Hen. VIII.

or temporal law, but only before the mayor, if due remedy can there be had, on pain of imprisonment, &c.

That no woman wash cloaths or other corruption at the comon wells, or High-street.

That scoldes be punished by the mayr on a cuck-stole before their door, and then carried to the four gates of the town.

That no buyer of corn cheapen it till ten of the bells be stricken on Saturday.

That such as have gates or doors on the Town-wall against the market leave them not open on a market-day, on pain of 20d. and imprisonment forty days.

That butchers sell their meat, not at their house, but the common shambles, on pain of 12d.

That no ducks be let abroad in any street within the four gates.

That every man be ready, at every affray in the town, to assist the mayor; and if he come not when sent for, the mayor may fetch him; and if he shut his door, the mayr may break it open, and imprison him while he liketh.

That no man lend others in the country any weapon but in support of the mayr.

That all inhabitants sumoned come to the common hall, or to attend the mayr to ride against the king, or for riding of the George, or any other thing to the pleasure of the mayr and worship of the town, on payn to the mayr's brethren 2s. and a comoner 12d.

That every person opening a shop pay yearly 3s. 4d. till he enter into the Chapman's gild.

That every one keeping corn in his house from market-day to market-day for any person of the country forfeit 12d.

Charcoal to be sold, from All Saints to Easter, for 7d. the quarter, and from Easter to All Saints for 6d; as that none sell it for above 1¼d. a strike [1]."

King Edward IV. in consideration of his good services, granted to Peter Curteys, his servant, one messuage, with the appurtenances, in Leicester, situate in the High-street, near the South gate there; which messuage was forfeited to the king, by the attainder of Edward Digby, esq. then convicted of rebellion. Teste Rege, apud Westmon', 25° die Aprilis [2]."

A proviso occurs in 1464, and is repeated in 1467-8, that an act of resumption " shall not in any wife be prejudicial or hurting into our right well beloved servant Richard Kestven, squier, of, to, or for, the graunte by us to him made of a horsmylne and two mesuages, with th' appurtenaunce, lying in a strete called Swyne-market, within our town of Leycestre, not exceeding the yearly value of 8l. 16s. 8d.; ne to Pyers Courteys and William Truffell, of or for the loppes and croppes of woode, falled withyne our Fryth of Leycestre, for the brusyng of our dere there, or for repreacyon of the pale there, to theym graunted by oure lettres patentez; ne to the maire and burgeis or comaltee of oure towne of Leycestre, of or for 13l. 6s. 8d. to theym graunted, terme of 20 yeres, by oure lettres patentez [3]."

In 1468, Philip Purefoy died seised of three messuages and seven tofts in Leicester; and John Purefoy was his next heir [4].

Richard Yates was elected mayor of Leicester in 1468; John Wigston, 1469 (in which year was the battle beside Banbury [5]); and Robert Shillingham, 1470.

March 1, 1470-1, king Edward IV. after his flight into Holland, returning landed at Ravenspur in Yorkshire, and went thence to York, and Wakefield, and Sowdal, Doncaster, Nottingham, and thence to Leicester, where 3000 able men and well armed came to him, thence he came before the walls of Coventry, where the earl of Warwick lay with 6 or 7000 men, but would not come out to battle.

On Easter Sunday, the 14th of April, 1471, there was a battle at Barnet field [5]; and another, May 9, at Tewkfbury [5].

John Parsons was elected mayor of Leicester in 1471; and in 1471-2, the king, for service done by the mayor and burgesses of Leicester against his enemies, and in consideration of their great costs, granted them 20l. yearly, from Michaelmas then last past, for the term of 20 years; to be received of the profits of the Honour of Leicester, unless within the time he should give them lands and tenements to that value. Dat. sub sigillo ducatûs Lancastrie, apud Westm', 2° Januarii, anno regni 11.

Roger Wigston was elected mayor of Leicester in 1472; when Joan (late wife of John Lovel, knight) died seised of two burgages, five cottages, one garden, and six acres of meadow, with the appurtenances, in Leicester, which were held of the king as of the Honour of Leicester; and Francis Lovel was their son and heir [6].

On the 2d of April, 1473, king Edward IV. by the charter which here follows, granted to the mayor and burgesses of Leicester licence to hold a fair in the town and suburbs of Leicester three days before, upon the feast of St. Philip and St. James, and three days after, yearly for ever; the profits and government of the said fair, with all its liberties and privileges, to belong to the mayor and corporation.

" Edwardus, Dei gratiâ, rex Anglie et Francie, et dominus Hibernie, archiepiscopis, &c. salutem. Sciatis quod nos, ob affectionem et dilectionem quas habemus ad villam nostram Leicestrie, necnon dilectis et fidelibus nostris majori et burgensibus ibidem commorantibus, de gratiâ nostrâ speciali, ac ex certâ scientiâ et mero motu nostris, concessimus, et per presentes confirmamus, eisdem majori et burgensibus ejusdem ville Leicestrie, et successoribus suis, quandam feriam apud eandem villam Leicestrie et suburb' ejusdem, singulis annis, per septem dies, videlicet, tribus diebus ante festum Apostolorum Philipi et Jacobi, et in eodem festo, et in tribus diebus proximè sequentibus in perpetuum duraturam; ita quod quilibet indigena sive alienigena ad dictam villam Leicestrie et suburb' causâ ferie predicte veniens, ibidem moram faciens, et exinde recedens, tam in dictâ feriâ, quam ante et post in perpetuum, sit quietus de theolonio, stallagio, picagio, et aliis custumis et prestacionibus quibuscumque, nobis seu heredibus nostris racione ferie predicte qualitercumque spectantibus. Volumus insuper et concedimus, pro nobis et heredibus nostris predictis, ac per presentes confirmamus, prefatis majori et burgensibus predicte ville Leicestrie, et successoribus suis in perpetuum, omnimodo ordinacionem, gubernacionem, et assignationem stallorum et placearum, ac totum regimen predicte ferie, et omnium et singularum libertatum et aliarum consuetudinum ad eandem feriam spectantium, per majorem ejusdem ville Leicestrie qui pro tempore fuerit, et duos vel tres de probioribus et melioribus hominibus ejusdem ville in auxilium ipsius majoris ad hoc annuatim electis, deputatos et juratos per dictos majorem et burgenses suos, sine impedimento seu perturbacione nostri vel heredum nostrorum, seu aliorum ministrorum nostrorum quorumcumque. Hiis testibus; venerabilibus patribus in Christo Thomâ Cardinali, archiepiscopo Cantuarie; R. Bathon' & Wellen', cancellario nostro Anglie, & Thomâ Lincoln', custode privati sigilli nostri, episcopis; ac prechariffimis fratribus nostris, Georgio Clarencie, & Ricardo Glouceftrie, ducibus; necnon consanguineis chariffimis nostris, Henrico Essex', thesaurario nostro Anglie, & Johanne Wiltes', capitali pincernâ nostro Anglie, comitibus; dilectisque fidelibus nostris Thomâ Stanley de Stanley, senescallo hospitii nostri, & Willielmo Hastings de Hastings, camerario hospitii nostri, militibus; & aliis. Dat' per manum nostram, apud palacium nostrum Westm', secundo die Aprilis, anno regni nostri tercio decimo [7]."

Sept. 7, 1473, the mayor and commonalty of Leicester let for 99 years to John Whittewell a piece of

[1] Ex Libro Villæ Leycestriæ temp. Edw. IV. &c.
[2] Rot. Pat. 7 Edw. IV.   [3] Rolls of Parliament, 4 Edw. IV. vol. V. p. 547; and 7 & 8 Edw. IV. p. 603.
[4] Esch. 8 Edw. IV. N° 29. Leic.   [5] Roll of Mayors.   [6] Esch. 12 Edw. IV. N° 7. Leic.   [7] Cart. 13 Edw. IV. n. 5.
land

land lying apud le Southgate end, & continet in longitudine a cemiterio Sancti Sepulchri verfus Auftrum, & in latitudine a terris gildæ corporis Chrifti, &c. he paying yearly 4d.

Robert Rawlett was elected mayor in 1473; and in November, 1474, *John Roberts* (being then mayor), *Peter Curteis*, bailiff, and *Thomas Tayllor* of Whetftone, gave to the mayor and commonalty of Leicefter a rent-charge of 6d. *per annum*, payable out of his lands at Scraptoft. Dated at Whetftone, in fefto S. Lucæ.

In the fame year, in a grant of a fifteenth and twentieth, for raifing 51,147l. 4s. 7¾d. Leicefterfhire was taxed at 1043l. 19s. 8¼d. [1]

William Holbech was elected mayor of Leicefter in 1475; and *Peter Wyndwode* in 1476.

Thus far the lift of mayors has been compiled from a comparifon of a variety of antient Rolls; which, though agreeing in the main, have occafionally fome flight variation. By the induftry, however, of the Rev. Samuel Carte, for many years vicar of St. Martin's, I am enabled not only to continue the feries with exactnefs, but to enrich thefe Annals with extracts, which it is hoped will be gratifying to Antiquarian curiofity, and honourable to the antient Borough from whofe very valuable and authentic Records they have been tranfcribed.

In the beginning of an antient MS. intituled, "Liber Villæ Leyceftriæ, temp. Edw. IV. Ric. III. Hen. VII. & part. Hen. VIII." are the following forms of the oath of the Mayors; of the Jurier for the year; of them that enter into the Chapman Gilde; of the Chamberlains; of Fifh Sayers; Flefh Sayers; of Conftables; of Ale Tafters; of Leather Sayers; of the Recorder; of the Occupations, &c.

The Oath of the MAYOR.

" I fhall maintain the peace of our Lord the King; and the affrayers thereagainft and the difturbers thereof I fhall do to be areft and punifh as the law woll. I fhall maintain the affize of bread, wine, and ale, and all other maner of victualls; and the trefpaffers with them I fhall punifh as the law woll. I fhall affay all maner of weights and meafures; and the fals I fhall dampe, and the trefpaffers with them I fhall punifh as the law woll. I fhall fuffer no foreftaller nor regrater dwell within this town, nor the fraunches of the fame. I fhall do even right as well to the poor as to the rich; and all other good cuftoms and fraunchifes of this town I fhall fupport and maintain during the time of mine office. So help me God and all Saints [2]."

The Oath of the JURIER.

" This hear you, Mayor and Juries, and ye Brethren of the Gilde, that I fhall yield lawfull judgment; fhall do lawfully as well to the poor as to the rich after the quantity of their trefpafs. I fhall come continually to the court of Portmote, and at the fummons of my mayor, when I fhall be warnynde by his officers, if I be in the town, without a reafonable excufe. And that I fhall maintain lawfully the affize of bread, wine, and ale, and all other victualls, with Mr. Mayor; and I fhall maintain the fraunches and good cuftoms of this town, and the fame keep. So help me God and all Saints."

The Oath of them that enter into the CHAPMAN GILDE.

" This hear you, Mayor and ye Brethren of the Gilde, that I truly the cuftoms of my Gilde fhall lawfully hold, and my Gild in all things fve. I fhall lote and fcot with my brethren of the Gild, whether I dwell in the town, frauncheſes, or in the Bifhop Fee, or in any other place. Alfo I fhall warne Mr. Mayor and the good folks of the town if I know any man that merchandizeth within the fraunches of this town, that been able to enter into the Chapman Gilde. And alfo I fhall be obedient and ready at Mr. Mayor's commandment and fommons; and the

good cuftoms and fraunchiffes of this town to my power I fhall maintain, as God me help and all Saynts."

The Oath of the CHAMBERLAINS.

" We fhall faithful and true officers be unto our mafter the Mayor, diligent of attendance at all times, obedient to his commandment, and ready to do his precepts. We fhall improve the livelode belonging unto the coialte of this town of Leicefter, to the moft behove of the fame town; and alfo the tenements thereof we fhall well and fufficiently repare during our office. We fhall endeavour alfo for to emprove the Chapman Gilde to the uttermoft of our powers. We fhall be attendant at the Cornwall on the Saturday during our year, and the fame to our powers we fhall order; and all traunters that there can be found we fhall prefent to our mafter the Mayor; and all horfes and mares that there can be found we fhall caufe them to be had from the Cornwall, and out of the market-place. And moreover we fhall well and truly charge and difcharge ourfelf of all lands and rents belonging to this town and of the Chapman Gilde, and of all other money as fhall come to our hands belonging unto the coialte of this town, and thereof a true accompt fhall yield up to the auditours affigned in the end of our year; and all other things lawfull that belongeth or partaineth to our office well and truly to our powers we fhall do. So help us God and all Saints."

The Oath of the CONSTABLES.

" I fhall true Conftable be, and true areft make of all affrayers and difturbers of the king's peace, and of all felons within my office; and fhall true oath give unto the watchmen, and in due hour during the time of the fame I fhall maintain all maner of officers of the King within my Conftablefhip during the time of my faid office; and all other things that appertaineth to my office I fhall duly and truly execute to my power and knowledge. So help me God and all Saints."

The FISH SAYER's Oath.

" You fhall take a lawfull affay and view of fifh; and weekly, on the market-days and other days, fearch that if it be falt, and fweet, and good for man's body; and if you find any defective, you fhall caufe fuch fifh and the perfon owner thereof to be brought before Mr. Mayor; and alfo fhall prefent all foreftallers, regueters, and ingroffers of fuch victual within this Borough. Thefe and all other things belonging or appertaining to the office of a Fifh Sayer you fhall truly execute and do, to the beft of your power, knowledge, fkill, and ability. So help you God."

The FLESH SAYER's Oath.

" You fhall take a lawfull affay and view of all manner of flefh offered to be fold within this Borough, that it be not tached with pock, morrein, mefle, nor with any other infectious difeafe or fault, but that it be good, wholefome, found, convenient meat for man's body. You fhall weekly, as well on the market days as one other week days, make due fearch for defective flefh; and if you find any defective, both the flefh and the owner thereof you fhall bring before Mr. Mayor. Thefe and all other things that belong or appertain to Flefh Sayers you fhall duly and truly do and execute, to the beft of your knowledge, fkill, and ability, fo long as you continue in the faid office. So help you God."

The ALE TASTER's Oath.

" You fhall diligently and truly fearch and take a lawful affay of all manner of Ale and Beer brewed to be fold within the precincts of this Borough; and that which is not good and well brewed you fhall not allow of, as if it be raw red, or long ropy, or have any other fault; and fhall not fpare any perfon for any favour, kin, or alliance, nor do any wrong out of envy or hatred; but you fhall deal juftly and do right to every one, to the beft of your power and fkill;

[1] Rot. Parl. 14 Edw. IV. vol. VI. p. 116. a.
[2] Mr. Carte has alfo copied the more modern oath of the Mayor; but the older one is here preferved.

and

and that Ale and Beer that you fhall find defective, you fhall true prefentment make thereof, and of the owners of the fame, to Mr. Mayor and the juftices of the peace. All thefe things you fhall duly and truly do and execute at all times fo long as you fhall continue in your office. So help you God."

SEARCHERS AND SEALERS OF LEATHER.

" You fhall duly and truly fearch and take a lawfull affay of all maner of Tanned Leather within this Borrough of Leicefter, that it be well and fufficiently barked, tanned, and good, and alfo of all manner of wares made of Leather within this borough; and if you find any Leather, or wares made of Leather, within the faid Borough, defective, fuch Leather and wares and the offenders you fhall caufe to be attached, and them brought before Mr. Mayor. Thefe and all other things that belong and appertain to your faid office you fhall well and truly execute for the year enfuing, according to the laws and ftatutes in fuch cafes made and provided, according to the beft of your knowledge, fkill, and ability. So help you God."

The Oath of SEARCHERS OF HYDES AND TALLOW.

" You fhall duly and truly fearch and take a ftrict view of all Hydes and Tallow brought to this market, that the faid Hydes and Tallow be good and merchantable, according to the ftatutes in that cafe made and provided; and if you find any defective, that then you inform Mr. Mayor therewith, and alfo of the perfons offending: And you fhall do and execute all other things belonging to the faid office for this enfuing year, according to the beft of your knowledge, fkill, and ability. So help you God."

The Oath of the RECORDER.

" You fhall fwear to be true to our lyche Lady the Queen [1], and her heirs Kings. You fhall juftly do juftice as well to the poor as to the rich; and all other things to your office of Recorderfhip belonging you fhall well and truly do to your power. So help you God, &c."

The Oath of the OCCUPATIONS to their Ordinals.

" You fhall do and execute all good rules and cuftoms contained and fpecified within your Ordinal. You fhall be obedient to your fteward and wardens' commandment, at all convenient times; you fhall duly and truly pay all fuch duties and forfeits mentioned in your Ordinal to be due for any offence, matter, or thing, therein contained; and all other good rules and lawful cuftoms therein expreffed you fhall maintain and keep, to the beft of your power, fkill, and ability. So help you God."

The Oath of the MAYOR'S OFFICERS, his CLERK, and SERJEANT.

" I fhall true and faithfull officer be unto my mafter the Mayor for this year being, and to his lieutenant in his abfence, and to all other their fucceffors, Mayors and lieutenants of the fame town, during the time of my office and fervice. The counfel and fecrets of this town I fhall not utter nor difclofe, but faithfully keep. I fhall be diligent and ready at the Mayor's commandment, and in like wife to his lieutenant, for the town bufynez. So help me God, &c."

Then follows a regular entry of elections:

" Die Dominicâ, in fefto S. Matthei Apoftoli, 17° Edw. IV. Petrus Wynwode amotus eft ab officio majoratûs; et in loco ejus electus eft pro anno fequenti Johannes Reynolds fenior, major; et Willielmus Chaunler pro communitate camerarius, et Willielmus Pekefale pro majore.

Cuftodes pacis; Johannes Reynolds fenior, major; Petrus Wynwode, Willielmus Holbeche, Johannes Parfons, Johannes Roberdes.

Senefchalli Nundinorum. Election of the Stewardys of the Faire; chofen, furft, one for the new maire; and the fecond be the old maire; and the thirde for the commons: Robertus Sheryngham, Willielmus Holbeche, Johannes Rokeden.

At a common hall holden at Leicefter, Jan. 12, in the year afore-written, for a parliament to be holden at Weftminfter the 16th of the fame month, was chofen, be my mafter the maire and all his brethren, Peers Curtes for to be one of their brethren of the benche. And alfo the fame day the faid Peers Curtes was chofen by the commons to be burges of the faid parliament. And, bi the election of the maire and his brethren, was chofen at the fame time John Wygfton.

M^{dm}. The parliament began to be holden at Weftminfter on ye 17th Jan. yn the 17 of Edw. IV.; which parliament was diffolved on the 25th day of February next following yn the fame yere.

At a common hall at Leyc', 26th March, in the year aforewritten, the pleyers which pleid the Paffion play the yere next afore brought yn a byll, the which was of [certain deuties] of mony; and wheder the Paffion fhal be put to crafts to be bounden, or nay. And at that time the feid pleyers gaff to the pachents ther mony which that thei had getten yn playing of the feid play ever fore to that day; and all the raymentts with all maner of ftuff that they had at that tyme. And at the fame comen hall, be the advyfe of all the comons, was chofen thies perfons after-named for to have the gydyng and rulle of the feid play; Roger Wigfton, Robert Sheringham, &c.

Gilda Mercatorum, 9.

[Hic datur Rentale terrarum et tenementorum majoris et communitatis in Whefton.]

" To the honour of Almighty God, and increafe of unity and worfhip of the mayor and of his brethren of the bynke of the town of Leyc', &c. on the feaft of St. Edward the king, 17 Edw. IV. by the affent of John Reynolds then mayor, and of all his brethren, it was ordeyned that none of the faid brethren, fecretly nor openly, in no caufe ne matter, reprove ne difhonour, by word ne deed, none of theire order; but that every of them, in abfence and prefence, report and fay well be oder, on pain of forfeit to the chamber of the town, the firft time 3s. 4d. the fecond time 6s. 8d. to be forthwith levied by the mayor and the two mafters of Corpus X^{ti} gild. And if any refufe to pay his penalty, then he to be comitted by the mayre to ward, there to continue without redemption till the paine be levied. And if the mayor be lacheous in execution on that behalf, the fame penalties to be levied upon the mayor by the mafters of Corpus X^{ti} gild. And if any of the faid brethren be obftinate, and will not be reconciled, and be war by the penalties afore noted, the third time, he to be depofed and difcharged of the bynke, and excluded the fellowfhip of the brethren for evermore. And if any of the faid brethren have any reafonable caufe or matter to other, every of them that findeth himfelf agrieved fhew his caufe or grief to the mayor and mafters of Corpus X^{ti} gild; and they to take a rule between the parties; and for love, favour, or alliance, as right and good confcience requireth, to determine, award, and end the caufe. And that none of the parties difobey the warde of the faid mayor and mafters, on the penalties afore-mentioned. And alfo that every of the faid brethren do their uttermoft to fave and increafe the honour of the majoralty, and continually report in every place and company, by their mayor, the moft honour, worfhip, and goodnefs, they can or may. And to their hearing or knowledge, if any other perfon, in word or deed, reprove or difhonour their mayor, that then every of the faid brethren ufe his moft effectual endeavour to rebuke, reconcile, and reform, every fuch fimple perfon to his power, on the pain and depofition afore written. Moreover it is ordained, that if any of them difclofe or utter to any perfons any manner of counfell moved or determined among them, or to his power alter or contrary any manner of agreement among themfelves concluded, as in naming of the new mayor upon St. Matthew's even, or for choofing of burgefs for the parliament, or any other matter concerning good rule or profit to the town, the mayor, or his brethren; he or they forthwith to be depofed and difcharged from the bynke, and excluded of the fellowfhip of the faid brethren for ever. Alfo it is ordered, that no mayor hereafter fet no man upon the bynke without

[1] This, probably, is not older than the reign of Queen Elizabeth. Mr. Carte has alfo copied one ftill more modern.

advife

advife and councell of all or moft part of his brethren, in pain of himfelf to be difcharged of the bynke,
and excluded of the fellowfhip of the faid brethren for
evermore after the time of his office of the mayoralty.

The mayor and his brethren, being by writing
and otherwife informed that the king and certain of
his lords have knowledge of divers ungodly rules and
demeanings afore-time ufed at the comon halls ; and
for thofe take fuch difpleafure, that without a remedy
found it is likely to turn to the undoing of the large
liberties and franchifes of this town, &c. For a remedy and amendment, &c."

[The orders aforegoing, with thofe made 7 Edw.
IV. (p. 375.) feem to be part of the " Books of the
Ordinances of the town," mentioned by William Wygefton fenior (fee hereafter, 3 Hen. VIII. 1511),
which " went from mayor to mayor."]

" At a comon halle, holden at Leyc' on the xxvi
day of Marche (17 Edw. IV.) in the yeare afore
written ; att the which comon halle the pleyers the
which pleed the Paffion play the yere next afore
brought yne a byll, the whiche was of ften dewtes of
mony ; and wheder the Paffion fhul be put to crafts
to be bounden, or nay ; and at that tyme the feid
pleyers gaff to the pachents their mony which that
thei had getten in playing of the feid play everfore
to that day, and all the raymentts with all other
manner of for' that they had at that tyme : And at the
fame comon halle, be the advyfe of all the Comons,
was chofen thies perfones after-named, for to have the
gydynge and rulle of the feid play[1]." (Here follow
the names of about twenty of the Corporation.)

Richardus Elkefley, nuper de Leyc' capellanus, gave
to the mayor, chamberlains, and commonalty of Leyc',
a meffuage in Belgrave gate, extending thence to
Barkby lane, to the intent that the chamberlains
fhould expend 20d. for celebrating his obit in St.
Margaret's church on the 11th of Auguft, paying
the vicar 3d. &c. Dated, Fefto Inventionis S. Crucis,
18 Edw. IV.; John Reynolds then being mayor, and
John Bayhuwe vicar of St. Margaret's church.

Die Lunæ, in fefto S. Matth. 18 Edw. IV. Johannes
Reynoldes amotus eft ab officio majoratûs ; et electus
eft *Thomas Thowithby.*—*Gilda Mercatorum,* 10.

N. B. The *Auditores Compotorum* are chofen for the
Eafter quarter ; Swyne's market, South quarter,
North quarter ; for each three.

Die Martis, in fefto S. Matth. 19 Edw. IV. Thomas Totheby amotus eft ab officio majoratûs ; et in
loco ejus electus eft *Johannes Perfons.*
Gilda Mercatorum, 16.

Die Jovis, in fefto S. Matth. 20 Edw. IV. Johannes
Perfons amotus eft ab officio ; et *Johannes Wyggefton*
electus eft major.—*Gilda Mercatorum,* 15.

Die Veneris, in fefto S. Matth. 21 Edw. IV. *Johannes Penny* electus eft major.
Gilda Mercatorum, 14 (inter quos Ricardus Wod
hofyer, Johannes Clough hofyer.)

Die Sabbati, in fefto S. Matth. 22 Edw. IV. Johannes Penny amotus eft ; et electus eft *Petrus Curtes*
major.—*Gilda Mercatorum,* 19 ; inter quos, Thomas
Lynalls, clericus majoris predicti.

At a comon hall, on Friday after the feaft of St.

Dennys, 22 Edw. IV. ordeined, that none of the
mayre's brethren of the benke fhail bake or brew to
fell, on pain to be depofed and difcharged of the benke.

At a common hall, Friday next before the feaft of
the Epiphany, 22 Edw. IV. there were chofen burgeffes for the parliament, i. e. for the commons, Mr.
Maire (viz. Mr. Peers Courteis), and John Robardes
for the maire's bredren.

In an act of refumption 1482, provifion is made,
that it " extend not, ne in any wife be prejudiciall,
unto the maire and communalte of the town of Leyceftr', of or for any graunte or grauntes to them
made by the kyng's grace undre any of his letters patentes fealed with his grete feale[2]."

On the 9th of April following, 1483, king Edward IV. died at Weftminfter, of a furfeit, in the 23d
year of his reign, and 42d of his age.

EDWARD V.

The crown, which only hovered over the head of
young Edward, fettled for a fhort time on that of
Richard, who was at once the uncle, protector, and
murderer of the young king, who was only 12 years
old at the death of his father. Richard, an ambitious
prince, but renowned as a foldier and politician, fent
the young king and his brother to the Tower, and
removed, partly by carnage, all their friends from
their prefence. In two months they were no more.

Sir Thomas More fays, " that one Tyrrel was appointed by Richard to murder them ; and he procured one Miles Forreft and John Dighton to be the
immediate inftruments thereof. The former (fays he)
was a fellow flufhed in murder beforetime ; and the
latter a horfe-keeper, a big, broad, fquare knave.
About midnight, all others being removed, thefe two
ruffians entered the princes' apartments, and fuddenly
wrapped up their bed-clothes, and forced them againft
their mouths with all their ftrength, till they ceafed
to ftruggle under the preffure of their weighty bodies;
which when thefe monfters perceived, they lay their
dead bodies naked upon the bed, and then fetched
Tyrrel, their employer, to be fatisfied of the completion of the horrid deed, who caufed their bodies to
be buried under the ftairs."

This fhort but eventful reign proved fatal, among
others, to the lord Haftings, Anthony Woodvile earl
Rivers' brother to the dowager queen, and to her father lord Richard Grey, who were beheaded by order
of the Protector ; and the young king's life and reign
concluded June 22, 1483, in 2 months and 18 days.

RICHARD III.

Die Lunæ, in fefto S. Matth. 1 Ric. III. Petrus
Courteis amotus eft ab officio ; et electus eft *Johannes
Roberdes* major.—*Gilda Mercatorum,* 14.

At a common hall, Wednefday 12 Jan. 1 Ric. III.
in the mairalty of John Roberds, by power of the
king's writte unto the mayre and his brethren and the
coialte of the fame direct, for the election of the burgeffes of the parliament, to begin 23 day of January,
there is chofen by the mayre's brethren[3] to be burges
John Roberds ; and by the coialtie[4] ther is chofen
Peres Curtis.

---

[1] Extracted from the Hall Books belonging to the Corporation of Leicefter.   [2] Rot. Parl. 22 Edw. IV. vol. VI. p. 202.

[2] The government of the town being antiently lodged in 24 perfons, ftyled " The mayor and his brethren," thefe feparately made choice of one of the members of parliament, and the comminalty of the town chofe the other. This diftinct
choice lafted a good while in king Henry the Eighth's reign ; but I cannot tell the precife time when they began to choofe
jointly. S. CARTE.

[3] The commons concerned in the election of their members were all the inhabitants of the town, whether freemen or others,
till 4 Henry VII. when the king, by the advice of his council of the dutchy, to prevent the diforders which frequently happened in the election of mayor, burgeffes of parliament, and making affeffments, ordered the mayor and 24 comburgeffes to
call unto them only 48, whom they fhould judge to be the wifeft and graveft of the commonalty, upon thefe occafions (fee p. 382.)
At the next election of annual officers, Sept. 21, 5 Hen. VII. the commons at large infifting upon their antient privilege in a
tumultuous manner, the king in parliament that year ordained, that the mayor and his brethren fhould from time to time
choofe 48 of the moft difcreet inhabitants of the town, who, with the mayor and his brethren, or more part of them, fhould make
yearly election of all the mayors and other officers of the faid borough, and their election fhould be good, &c. (fee p. 383.) The
election of parliament-men is not exprefsly mentioned in this act ; neverthelefs, all elections of them were in fact made agreeable to the tenor of it till the Reftoration of king Charles II. when fir John Pretyman made intereft with the commons at large,
and, upon a hearing in the houfe of commons, was admitted to be duly elected in virtue of their votes : and now the right of
election is vefted in the freemen at large, not receiving alms, and in the inhabitants paying fcot and lot, not being perfons
certificated from other places. As to the perfons elected, it is obfervable that of old they were always inhabitants and members of the borough : the firft inftance which I have met of any country gentleman's election being in the firft parliament of
queen Mary, when William Faunt and Thomas Farnham, efqrs. were chofen. S. CARTE.

At a comyn hall holden at Leyc', 7 April, 1 Ric. III. it was ordeyned as follows: "In nomine Dei, Amen. Wheras, for the grete rumor and fhlander that runns upon the town of Leyc', as well of divers evil difpofed perfons, as of broken pavements, ftones, timber, and muck, to the great noyfance of the king's people, and deftruction of this faid town, without due remedy therein be had: It is therefore ordeyned and ftablifhed, by the hole affent and agreement as well of the right honourable and worfhipfull John Roberds, efq. at that time being mayre, and all his brethren coburges of the fame town, as by the worfhipful coialtie of the fame; that the faid town fhall be divided in twelve wards; and in every of the faid wards one of the mayre's brethren for the time being, dwelling within the fame ward or next thereunto, to be called an *Aldreman*; and to have full power and authority to correct and punifh all fuch people as been afore rehearfed, or at any time doing a trefpafs, after the quantity of his trefpafs. And if any fuch perfon will not obey the correction and punifhment of the faid aldreman, that then the faid aldreman fhall fhew his name and dealing unto the mayre; and he, accorling to juftice, to correct and punifh the faid trefpaffer, until he fhall with benevolence fubmit himfelf unto his faid aldreman, and afk pardon of him, of his ungodly difobeying and demeaning againft him. And at every time as it fhall happen any fuch aldreman to deceafe, or to be mayre, that then, at the next comyn hall to be holden after his deceafe, one other of the mayre's brethren to be chofen an aldreman, and to have the faid power and correction, &c.

Firft; it is agreed and ordeyned, by the hole affent, confent, and agreement, of the mayre, his brethren, and comminaltie aforefaid;

That the firft ward fhall begin at the High Crofs in Leicefter, on both fides the ftrete Northward, to the Mayre's hall, with Apullgate, to St. Nicholas church, the lane behind the faid church, and the Black Freres lane.

The fecond warde to begin in the High ftrete at the Mayre's hall lane, and the Dede lane, on both fides the ftrete, unto the North gate, with St. Peter's church-yard lane, and St. John's lane.

The third warde to begyn from the North gate without unto the North bryge on both fides, Senvy gate on both fides, unto St. Margaret's church and Sore lane.

The fourth warde to begin at St. Margaret's chirch, unto the corner at the little brige without the Eaft gate, and Belgrave gate on both fides, unto the corner forgeinft the Berhill Crofs.

The fifth warde to begyn at Humberftone gate on both fides, Galewtre gate on both fides, and the Roundell.

The fixth warde to begin from the Eaft gate on both fides the ftrete unto Roger Trig's and Pekefhull.

The feventh warde to begyn at Roger Trig's and William Pekefhul, unto the High Crofs on both fides.

The eighth warde to begyn in the Shepe market on both fides, Lowefby lane on both fides, unto Thomas Phelip's, and the Church lane, unto the High ftreet.

The ninth warde to begyn in the Cank at Thomas Phelip's, on both fides the Saturday market, unto the Eaft gate.

The tenth warde to begin at the High Crofs Southward, on both fides the ftrete, unto the Grey Freres lane, and to the Sore lane, the Hofe gate, and fo forth, to the Weft brige, and without as far as the fraunches goes.

The eleventh warde to begin at the faid Grey Freres lane and Sore lane unto the South gate on both fides, the Sore lane to Fofsbrok, Bukkons lane, and Gun dyk.

The twelfth warde to begin at the South gate on both fides, unto the Sepulcre chirch.

In 1483, it was found that Edward late king of England, by his letters patent, bearing date at Weftminfter, Auguft 9, 7 Edw. IV. granted the office of the ftewardfhip of the Honour of Leicefter, parcel of his Duchy of Lancafter; the office of the Conftablefhip or Wardenfhip of the Caftle of Leicefter; the office of Chief Forefter of the Foreft and Chace of Leicefter; and the office of the Keeper of the Park of the Frith of Leicefter, called Leicefter Frith, to *William* lord *Haftings*, deceafed; and that the faid William lord Haftings was alfo feifed of one meffuage, three gardens, and 2s. rent, in Leicefter [1].

Die Martis, in fefto S. Matth. 2 Ric. III. electus major *Robertus Croft.—Gilda Mercatorum*, 15.

Richard afcended the throne with but little of the common exultations of the people; but with many fecret execrations. The mourning relatives of the unfortunate fufferers formed a defign to banifh him from the throne, to place thereon Richmond, a defcendant of John of Gaunt, who was then an exile in Britanny. Richmond accepted the offer to marry the late king Edward the Fourth's daughter Elizabeth, and thereby effect an union with the oppofite factions of York and Lancafter. He foon landed an army of 2000 men in Wales; and, being joined by numbers on his march, haftened to attack Richard, who had fixed his ftandard at Nottingham, and was forcing recruits into his fervice.

On the 21ft of Auguft 1485, " with a frowning fterne countenance, but yet in great pompe, Richard entered the town of Leicefter after the fun was fet, being full of indignation, and fwelling in anger, which fomewhat he affuaged with threats of revenge [2]."

" His army chiefly confifted of foot, which he feparated into two divifions; the firft marched five in a rank, then followed the baggage; then himfelf, gorgeoufly dreffed, upon a large white courfer, richly caparifoned, attended by his body guards. The fecond divifion marched five a-breaft alfo. The horfe formed the wings, and kept near the centre; and, in the manner they marched, this army muft have covered at leaft three miles of the road [3]."

Richard flept at the Blue Boar Inn [4], part of which houfe is fuppofed to be now ftanding, oppofite the Free-fchool. The bedftead [5] whereon he is fuppofed to have lain is ftill preferved; and its hiftory is thus handed down. In the year 1613, Mrs. Clark, keeper of that inn, was robbed by her fervant maid and feven men; and the relation is thus given by fir Roger Twifden, who had it from perfons of undoubted credit, who were not only inhabitants of Leicefter, but faw the murderers executed: " When king Richard III. marched into Leicefterfhire againft Henry earl of Richmond, afterwards Henry VII. he lay at the Blue Boar Inn, in the town of Leicefter, where was left a large wooden bedftead, gilded in fome places, which, after his defeat and death in the battle of Bofworth, was left, either through hafte, or as a thing of little value (the bedding being all taken from it) to the people of the houfe: thenceforward this old bedftead, which was boarded at the bottom (as the manner was in thofe days), became a piece of ftanding furniture, and paffed from tenant to tenant with the inn. In the reign of queen Elizabeth this houfe

[1] Efch. 1 Ric. III. N° 32. Leic.　　　[2] Speed.　　　[3] Hutton.

[4] The principal part of Leicefter was then that ftreet which leads from the North to the South gate. The chief inn ftood oppofite the Free-fchool; where the king lay, then the fign of the Boar, " his cognizance," fays Mr. Speed: but, upon his defeat, all the figns of the Boar being torn down as an infult to his memory, it feems probable that this inn afterwards became the fign of the Blue Bell. The Rev. Mr. Pigot, of Leicefter, had once a piece of glafs, now in the poffeffion of Mifs Simons, the prefent occupier of that houfe, which was taken from one of the windows, on which is painted a blue bell. The prefent name of the lane, in which part of this houfe ftands, feems compounded of the former and latter figns, "Blue Boar lane." The building (of which two views are here given in Plate XXXII.) evidently fhews the age of Richard, and the chimney which appears in Blue Boar lane of an earlier age; it is built of thin brick or tiles, ornamented with fome wrought ftone. The room in which it is faid he flept is very large, and now open to the roof; the timber which fupports it is painted with vermillion, in a rude vine-tree tendril form. There is on the left, as you approach the old fteps which lead into this room, a low door, the pannels of which are handfomely carved.　　[5] See a reprefentation of it in Plate XXXII.

Blue Boar Inn at Leicester.

Vol. I. Pl. XXXII. p. 380.

FENDR. M. MAGT.

The length, 2 f. 8 in.

Found near the Lords Place in Leicester: See p. 533.

IN: GOUDE

Richard the Thirds 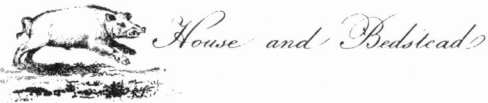 House and Bedstead.

was kept by one Mr. Clark, who put a bed on this bedftead; which his wife going to make haftily, and jumbling the bedftead, a piece of gold dropped out. This excited the woman's curiofity; fhe narrowly examined this antiquated piece of furniture, and, finding it had a double bottom, took off the uppermoft with a chiffel, upon which fhe difcovered the fpace between them filled with gold, part of it coined by Richard III. and the reft of it in earlier times. Mr. Clark (her hufband) concealed this piece of good fortune, though by degrees the effects of it made it known; for he became rich from a low condition, and, in the fpace of a few years, mayor of the town; and then the ftory of the bedftead came to be rumoured by the fervants. At his death, he left his eftate to his wife, who ftill continued to keep the inn, though fhe was known to be very rich; which put fome wicked perfons upon engaging the maid fervant to affift in robbing her. Thefe folks, to the number of feven, lodged in the houfe, plundered it, and carried off fome horfe-loads of valuable things, and yet left a confiderable quantity of valuables fcattered about the floor. As for Mrs. Clark herfelf, who was very fat, fhe endeavoured to cry out for help, upon which her maid thruft her fingers down her throat, and choaked her; for which fact fhe was burnt, and the feven men, who were her accomplices, were hanged at Leicefter fome time in the year 1613."

After this, the bedftead came into the hands of a fervant of that inn; and, before it came into the hands of Mr. Alderman Drake, it had been many years in the Redcrofs-ftreet, where it had been cut to make it fit for a low room. The feet which were cut off were 2 feet 6 long, and each fquare 6 inches. The prefent feet are modern.—It is not probable that the king would carry fuch a bedftead about with him; but it feems more likely that he was put on the beft bed in the houfe; and that the money was fecreted, in fome convenient and obfcure part of the bedftead, till his return after the battle; or, in the hurry of the preparation next morning, it might be forgotten. Half the money which has been found in old houfes was hidden during fome violent troubles in the country, and, through the fudden death of the owner, has remained there till fome change has taken place in the thing or houfe in which the money was hidden [1].

The two armies met in Sutton field, near Market Bofworth in this county, where the great leaders harangued their refpective armies before the battle. Richmond's army confifted of about 5000 men, and Richard's 12,000. Richmond advanced towards Richard with the found of trumpet for battle; they fought, but Richard's followers fought not like their leader. When all was loft but his life, ftern Richard rufhed into the arms of death, to feek for Richmond; but was furrounded by his enemies, after performing the moft brilliant and warlike atchievements that Hiftory has related. He died by the hands of a multitude, who cut his body in the moft fhocking and barbarous manner, while he was breathing his laft. It is faid that his body was fo fhamefully mangled, that it had the appearance of only a mafs of blood.

" Richard's body being ftripped naked, all tugged and torn, and not fo much as a clout left to cover his fhame, was truffed, behind a purfuivant at arms, like a hog or a calf; his head and arms hanging on one fide the horfe, and his legs on the other, all befprinkled with mire and blood, and was fo carried to Leicefter [2]."—" No king," fays Mr. Hutton, " was ever fo degraded a fpectacle; humanity and decency ought not to have fuffered it." Mr. Carte fays, " they tied a rope about his neck, more to infult the helplefs dead, than to faften him to the horfe."

It fhould feem that this Blanch Sanglier, an officer in Richard's army, was fuffered, perhaps from importunity, to take the body of his mafter to Leicefter for a decent burial; for it cannot be fuppofed that Richmond would fend the body to be buried at Lei-

cefter, unlefs it were to convince the world that Richard was dead. However, whether the body lay expofed in the town-hall, then at the bottom of Blue Boar lane, where the hofpital called *Symonds* now ftands, by the order of Richmond, the requeft of the mayor and his brethren, or while the officer who brought the body could procure a fit place for its interment, I know not. But this we are informed from the beft authority, that at the end of the fecond day it was taken to the church of the Grey Friars, near St. Martin's church, and there buried in a ftone coffin. From thefe circumftances may be hazarded an opinion, which is probable, that the body lay at the town-hall, not to meet the infults of the rabble, but only while a fhell of ftone was formed to contain it, at the expence of fome who might detect the actions of the man, while they pitied fallen Majefty. All were not like Richmond, who, while in the poffeffion of a complete victory, was totally deftitute of that mercy and compaffion which ennobles man!

Henry VII. neither from motives of love nor compaffion, we may apprehend, erected afterwards over king Richard's remains an ordinary alabafter monument to his memory, on which was the figure of the king; but at the diffolution of religious houfes, in the fucceeding reign, about 50 years after his death, it was ruinated with the church, the grave ranfacked, and his bones taken in triumph through the ftreets; and at laft thrown over the bridge over which he rode to the fatal battle. The ftone coffin which contained his body was fold or given to an innkeeper, in whofe poffeffion and his fucceffors it remained, as an horfe-trough, till the beginning of the eighteenth century [3].

Two days after the battle, Catefby, Richard's confidential minifter, with fome others who were taken prifoners, without any ceremony or decency, were executed at Leicefter; and " Tradition informs us that the town's-people, with the promptitude with which the lower orders of mankind engage in every purpofe that is either recommended by novelty or example, obliged the proprietor of the inn where Richard flept to change the White Boar, his fign, for that of the Blue. The fluctuations of the human mind are remarkable. The tide of applaufe runs parallel with the tide of profperity; when this falls, the voice of popular favour falls with it. While the Houfe of York fwayed the Britifh fceptre, the white rofe was held in repute, bloomed on the bofom of beauty, and on the fign-poft of the public; but, when that Houfe fell, it faded with it, and from that moment was elevated no more. Even now, if ever we fee the fign of the rofe, it is always a red: nay, it was but recently that this innocent and lovely flower recovered its priftine credit; for, in the contefts between the Houfes of Stuart and Brunfwick, it was fuppofed to be tainted with the fmell of treafon [4]."

An act of attainder, paffed in 1485, begins thus: " Forafmoche as every King, Prince, and Liege Lord, the more hie that he be in eftate and preheminence, the more fingularly he is bound to the advancement and preferring of that indefferent vertue Juftice; and promoteinge and rewardinge Vertue, and bi oppreffinge and punifhinge Vice: Wherefore oure Soveraigne Lord, calleinge unto hys bleffed remembrannce thys high and grete charge adjoyned to hys Royall Majeftie and Eftate, not oblivious nor puttinge out of hys godly mind the unnaturall, mifcheivous, and grete perjuries, treafons, homicides, and murdres, in fhedding of infants blood, with manie other wronges, odious offences, and abominacōns ayenft God and man, and in efpall oure faid Soveraigne Lord, committed and doone by Richard late Duke of Glouc', calleinge and nameinge hymfelf, by ufurpacōn, King Richard the IIId; the which, with John late duke of Norff', Thomas erle of Surrie, Francis Lovell knt vifc' Lovell, Walter Devereux knt, late lord Ferrers, John lord Zouche, Robert Harrington, Richard Charleton, Richard Rat-

---

[1] Throfby, p. 62.   [2] Holinfhed and Speed.
[3] See farther particulars of this tomb, and the epitaph infcribed on it, in a former part of this Hiftory, p. 298.   [4] Hutton.

cliffe,

cliffe, William Berkeley of Welley, Robert Braken-
bury, Thomas Pilkinton, Robert Midletoune, James
Harrington, knīts; Walter Hopton, William Catesby, Roger Wake, William Sapcott, Humfrey
Stafford, William Clerke of Wenlocke, Jeffrey Sᵗ
Jermin, Richard Watkins, herrauld of armes, Richard Revell of Derbishyre, Thomas Poulter of the
countee of Kent the younger, John Walsh otherwyse
called Haftinges, John Kendale, late fecretarie to the
said Richard late duke, John Buck, Andrew Ratt,
and William Bramton of Burford, the xxıˢᵗ daie of
Auguft, the firft yere of the reigne of oure Soveraigne Lord, assembled to theyme atte Leiceftre in
the countee of Leyceftre a grete hofte, traiteroufly
intendinge, imagininge, and confpireinge, the de-
ftruccōn of the Kinges royall pfoune, oure Soveraigne Leige Lord. And they, with the fame hofte,
with banners fpred, mightyly armed and defenced
with all manner armes, as gunnes, bowes, arrowes,
fperes, gleves, axes, and all other manner articles
apt or needfull to gef and caufe mightie battaille
agen oure faid Soveraigne Lord, kept togedre from
the faid xxııᵈ daie of the faid month thanne next followinge, and theyme conduced to a feld within the
faid fhyre of Leiceftre, there bi grete and continued
deliberacōne, traiteroufly levied warre ayenft oure
faid Soverayne Lord, and his true fubjeɛts there
being in his fervice and affiftance under a banner of
oure faid Soveraine Lord, to the fubverfion of this
realme, and cōmon weale of the fame [1]."

By this aɛt, the above perfons are all declared
traitors, and their eftates forfeited; with an exception in favour of John Catefbie, knight, Thomas
Kennell, and William Afhby, efquires, for the manor
of Kirbie upon Wretheck in the county of Leicefter,
and of other lands and tenements in Kirbie, Stretton,
Somerby, Thorp Segfeld, and Godebie, which they
had of the gift and feoffment of Thomas Davis and
John Bye [2].

HENRY VII.

In fefto S. Matth. 1485, 1 Hen. VII. eleɛtus major
Thomas Swyke.

Die Jovis, in fefto S. Matth. 2 Hen. VII. Thomas
Swyke amotus eft ab officio majoratûs, et pro anno
fequenti eleɛtus eft *Thomas Palet.*

At a comyn hall holden Wednefday before the feaft
of Corpus Xp̄i day, 1487, 3 Hen. VII. it was ordayned,
that no perfon, franchift or unfranchift, fue any of
his neighbours by fpiritual law nor temporal law,
neither for debt, trefpafs, nor furety of the peace,
&c. without licence of the maire, but only before the
faid maire of this town, in pain of imprifonment for
forty daies, and of making his cofts good that he
made his neighbour to lofe; and alfo, after this day,
he that fo dothe, fhall lofe his franches and his freedom of the town for ever, and forfeit 40s. to the town.

Alfo ordeined, that if any perfon make a fray at
the High Crofs of Leicefter, and blood be drawn, he
fhall forfeit 6s. 8d.; if no blood be drawn, he fhall
forfeit 3s. 4d.

Item, a fray made in any part of the town, on the
market day, 6s. 8d. The maker to pay, if blood be
drawn, not on market day, 3s. 4d.; if blood be not
drawn, 1s. 8d.

"Henry, by the grace of God, kynge of England
and of France, and lord of Ireland. To all to whom
thefe ires fhall be fhewed, gretynge. Knowe ye that,
in confideration of the true and faithful farvice that
the mayers and burgeffes of our towne of Leycefter
have don unto us, and hereafter intend to doo, and
alfo the gret coftes and charges that they have fuf-
teigned and borne, by oure commandement, in oure
journees, fields, and battailles; and the coftes that
they dyde and made upon oure fervants wounded and
maymed in our firft field, to ther cofte and charge of
clxxxlī.; and to thentent that they fhuld be ftrong
hereafter, better to kepe our lawes and peax within
our faid towne; and alfo that the faid maires and burgeffes fhall fupport and helpe to be kept our mercats

on Wednefday, Freyday, and Satturday, every weke
ther to be holden; and for the affeɛtion that we have
and beare to our fubjeɛtes of our faid town, for ther
prudence and hy merits reherfed: Wee, of our grace
efpeciall, have geven and graunted unto the mayer
and burgeffes, and ther fucceffurs, an annuite and annuele rent of xxlī. fterling, to be hade and received
yearly frome the feaft of Saint Michell the Archangele laft paffed, for the terme of every yere then next
enfuyng, by the hand of our receiver and baylyff of
our faid towne and honour of Leicefter for the tyme
beinge, at the feafte of St. John Baptift and of Saint
Mychell the Archangele, by even porcyons. In witnes whereoff, we have caufed to be made this oure
ires patentz. Geven at oure cite of London, under
oure feall of our Duchy, the xvı day of Februare,
the thyrd yere of our reigne.

In fefto St. Matth. 3 Hen. VII. eleɛtus major
Roger Wygfton.—*Gilda Mercatorum,* 21.

"Henry, king of England and France, and lord of
Ireland, to our trufty and welbeloved the mayr,
bayliff, comburgy, and burgy of our town of Leyc',
parcel of our Duchy of Lancafter, greeting: And forafmuch as we be enformed, that at every election of
the mayr ther, or burges of the parliaments, or at
affeffing of any lawfull impofition, the cōialtie of our
faid town, afwell poor as rich, have alway affembled
at the cōmon hall; whenas fuch perfons as be of
little fubftance or reafon, and not contributors, or
elfe full little, to the charge fufteined in fuch behalf,
and have had great intereft, through their exclamations and hidynefs, to the fubverfion not only of the
good policy of our faid town, but likely to the often
breach of the peax, and other inconveniences, en-
creafing and caufing the full myfery and decline of
our faid town, and to the great difcorage of you the
governors ther: For reformation whereof, and to the
entent that good rule and fubftantial order may be
had and entertained there from henceforth, we will
and ftriɛtly charge you, and alfo cōmand you, the
faid mayr, bayliff, and 24 comburgeffes of our faid
town now being, and that for the time fhall be, that
at all cōmon halls and affemblies hereafter to be
holden there, afwell for the eleɛtion of the mayr, of
the juftices of the peace, and burgeffes of our parliaments, as alfo at affeffing of any lawfull impofitions,
or otherwife, ye jointly chofe and call unto you our
bayliffe of our faid town for the time being, and only
48 of the moft wife and fad cōmoners inhabitants
ther, after the difcretions of the fame cōialtie, and
no more; and ye then to order and direɛt all matters
occurrent or fupervening among you, as by the reafon and confcience fhall be thought lawfull and moft
expedient. Given at our palace of Weftminfter,
under our feal of our faid Duchy, the 2d day of Auguft, the 4th year of our reign.

Per confilium ducatûs Lancaftrie."

Feft. S. Matth. 4 Hen. VII. eleɛtus major *Thomas
Davy.*—*Gilda Mercatorum,* 16.

22 Dec. 4 Hen. VII. At a common hall, were
chofen to be burges of the parliament, to begyn 13
of January next, Peter Curteys and Roger Wigfton.

Note, that in the time of Thomas Davy's being
mayor, 17 Sept. 5 Hen. VII. the mayor and his 24
brethren took an oath, that no one of the 24 fhould
take upon him the office of mayor, or other office,
at the eleɛtion of the commonalty; but only at the
eleɛtion of the mayor and his brethren, and the 48 of
the commonalty, on pain of being excluded from the
bench, and the number of the 24, without a contrary
command had from the king, &c.

Fefto S. Matth. 5 Hen. VII. Thomas Davy amotus
fuit ab officio fuo; & in loco ejus eleɛtus fuit pro anno
fequenti *Rogerus Tryg,* per prefatum Thomam Davy
& confratres fuos, & per 48 nomine totius commni-
tatis, fecundum ordinationem & preceptum domini
noftri regis & confilii fui, ut patet in fcriptis fub magno
figillo fuo ducatûs fui Lancaftrie prefatis majori &
confratribus fuis direɛtis. Et eodem die Thomas
Toutheby eleɛtus fuit pro anno fequenti per commu-

[1] Rot. Parl. 1 Hen. VII. vol. VI. p. 276.   [2] Ibid. p 277.

nitatem

nitatem ville predicte, contra ordinationem & preceptum domini noſtri regis predicti. Et ſuper controverſiam & diſconcordiam illam, & ad evidend' majorem moovementiam, ad inſtantiam dicti domini noſtri regis, per literas ſuas ſub privato ſigillo ſuo prefato Thome Davy directas, & ad inſtantiam parium ſuorum & 48, dictus Thomas Davy occupavit officium majoratûs ville predicte pro anno ſequenti.—*Gilda Mercatorum*, 22.

In 1489, " Billa, formam Actûs ſimiliter in ſe continens, porrecta fuit Domino Regi, in Parliamento predicto, ex parte inhabitancium ville Leyceſtrie, que in ſe ſeriem verborum ſequentium continebat. ' To the Kyng oure Sovereigne Lorde. Foraſmoch as of late greate dyvyſions and diſcordes have growen and been had, as well in the townes and bourghes of Leyceſtre and Northampton, as in other dyvers townes and burghes corporate within the realme of England, amongeſt the inhitauntes of the ſame, for eleccion and choiſe of maires and other officers within the ſame, by reaſon that ſuch multitude of the ſaid inhabitauntes, beyng of litill ſubſtaunce and havour, and of no ſadnes, diſcrecion, wiſdome, ne reaſon, which oft in nombre excede in their aſſembles others that been approved, diſcrete, ſadde, and well-diſpoſed pſones, have, by their multitude, and their bandys, confederacies, exclamations, and heedneſſe, uſed in the ſaid aſſembles, cauſed greate trobles, dyvyſions, and diſcordes amongeſt themſelfe, aſwell in the ſaid elections, as in aſſeſſyng of the lawfull charges and impoſitions amongeſt theym, to the ſubverſyon of the goode rule, governaunce, and polytike demeanyng of the bourghes, and oftetymes to the great brech of the kyng's peaſe within the ſame, to the fere, drede, and manyfold perills that therby may enſue. For reformacion wherof, and for the more quyet and reſtfullnes of the kyng's ſubgiets herafter, and for the conſervacion of the kynge's peas more fermely to be obſerved and kept, it is ordeyned, eſtabliſhed, and enacted, by the advyſe and aſſent of the Lordes Spuall and Temporall, and Comens, in this parliament aſſembled, and by auctorite of the ſame, that from henſforth the elleccions of maires and other officers, and alſo the aſſeſſyng of all lawfull charges and impoſitions, that herafter ſhall be made and had in the bourgh of Leyceſtre, ſhall be had, made, and uſed, after the fourme folowyng: That is to ſay, the maire of the towne of Leyceſtre and his brethren for the tyme beyng, or the more parte of theym, upon their othes and diſcreſſions, ſhall name and choſe XLVIII pſohes, of the moſt wiſe, diſcrete, and beſt-diſpoſed perſones of the inhitauntes within the ſaid towne; and the ſame pſones, or parte of theym, from tyme to tyme herafter to chaunge, when 'and as ofte as they or the more parte of theym ſhall ſeme moſt neceſſarie and behovfull; which perſones ſo by them choſen and named, and the ſaid maire and his brethren, or the more parte of theym, ſhall have and make yerly elleccions of all the maires that herafter ſhall be maires of the ſaid bourgh and towne; and elleccions by them or the more parte of theym ſo made, to ſtande and be goode and effectuall in the lawe, yerly herafter for ever to endure, in lyke maner, fourme, and condition, as yf the elleccions were made by ſuche waye, maner, and fourme, as aforetyme hath been uſed and accuſtumed, in, of, and for the ſame elections in the ſame bourgh; and that the voices of every other pſone or pſones, other then been afore reherced, in all eleccions within the ſaid towne, as to choſyng any officers of the ſame, be voide, and of none effecte in the lawe: And over this, that all other officers of the ſaid towne, that by dutie of their offices owe to be attendant upon the maire and maires that nowe be, or that herafter in the ſaid bourgh ſhall be electe, choſen and made, only by the ſaid maire and his brethren for the tyme beyng, or the more parte of theym, without aſſemble of any other pſones, inhitauntes of, in, or for the ſame. Provided alway, that yf in the ſaid eleccions, or any of theym, the voices be evenly divided and equall for ſondry parties, then the voice of the maire for the

tyme beyng to ſtand and be reputed for 11 voices in the ſame election; and if any eleccion or eleccions herafter happe to be made of maire or maires in the ſaid towne in other wiſe then in this acte afore is reherced, then that ellection or elleccions to be taken voide, and of no ſtrength ne effecte. And over this, be yt ordeyned by the ſaid auctorite, that yf any of the inhitauntes nowe beyng, or that herafter ſhall be inhabited in the ſaid borough and towne, attempte or do to the breche, ympedyment, or lett of this preſent acte; that then the ſaid pſone or pſones to forfeite the ſume of xli.; the moite therof to be to the kyng, and the other moite to be to the maire of the ſaid towne for the tyme beyng, to employe to the charges of the ſaid towne. And that yt ſhall be leſull to the maire of the ſaid bourgh and towne for the tyme beyng to comytte every ſuch pſone or pſones, troblyng or lettyng the ſaid elleccion, to priſon within the ſame towne, and there to remayne without baille or maynprize, till the ſaid ſome or ſomes of money be fully levyed and paide.'—Cui quidem bille perfecte & intellecte per dominum regem, auctoritate & aſſenſu predictis, ut ſequitur reſpondebatur. Le Roy le vuelt'."

At a common hall, 6 Nov. 5 Hen. VII. at the inſtance of the king's writing to the ſame mayre directed, it was agreed, that for and towards the charge of the ſaid mayre, he ſhall have, over and above his fee accuſtomed, the ſum of 7*l*. ſterling; ſo that this grant hereafter be no precedent, &c.

At a common hall, 25 May, 1490, the chamberlayns were ordered to pay of their proper goods a certain ſum (viz. 10*l*. &c. for half a fifteen) to the king, in name of the town, in like manner as other chamberlayns have done for ſuch like charges and other charges to the ſaid town appertaining, untill ſuch time as they may levy it again of the revenues and other receipts of the ſaid town.

It was alſo agreed, that John Aſhby ſhould ride to London, to have communication with the counſell of the Dutchy, and with my Lady York's counſell, for the matter concerning taking toll and paſſage money of the inhabitants of this town by the officers of Grantham; and that he ſhould have, daily, in going and coming, 12*d*. for his coſts of himſelf and horſe, and for his reward.

Agreed, Sept. 3, 6 Hen. VII. in the mayoralty of Thomas Davy, by conſent of the mayor and his brethren named the twenty-four, that whoſoever of the twenty-four hereafter be mayor ſhall, by reaſon of his oath, endeavour in all things to juſtify all ſuch matters, cauſes, and puniſhments, as the mayres before him have done or entered in, for the weal, worſhip, and honour of the ſaid town or office, as effectually as it were done or begun within his year of mayoralty.

St. Matthew's day, 6 Hen. VII. at a common hall, it was agreed, that any of the twenty-four choſen to be mayre (ſo that he be not put upon the ſame office within ſeven years next following), if he refuſe to ſerve, he ſhall forfeit 20*l*.; and for lack of payment, the mayr may commit him to ward, without bayl, till payment be made of the ſaid 20*l*. whereof 10*l*. to be paid to the mayr for the time being towards his charge, over and above his accuſtomed fee; and the other 10*l*. to the chamberlains for uſe of the town: And if the mayor neglect to puniſh and levy the ſume aforeſaid, then the mayr to be deduct of his fee of 10*l*. 6*s*. 8*d*. and no fee to have for that year, at jopardy of the chamberlains if they pay him.

And it is enacted, that if any inhabitant of the ſaid town be named or choſen by the mayr or his brethren, or the forty-eight, to be chamberlain, and he refuſes to ſerve, they are to proceed to a new election, and he is to pay to the chamberlains 5*l*. for uſe of the town, and then he is to be reputed as a chamberlain; but, in caſe of non-payment, the mayr is to comit him to ward without bayl; and if the mayr neglect to do ſo, he is to forfeit 5*l*. out of his fee, at the jopardy of the chamberlains if they pay him.

Feſto S. Matthei, 6 Hen. VII. Thomas Davy amotus

' Rot. Parl. 5 Hen. VII. vol. VI. p. 432.

eft & *Roger Tryg* electus eft major.—*Gilda Mercatorum*, 15.

Fefto S. Matthei, 7 Hen. VII. *William Gibfon* electus major.

The view taken 22 May, 7 Hen. VII. in the tyme of marfaltie of William Gybfon, of the charts, deeds, indentures, and other munyments, &c. as hereafter followeth, within the trefore houfe, then being and remaining:

Imprimis, of three charters of Michaelmas fayr, and one of the new fayr, knyt togadr in a box.

Item, two charters of the grant of king John; one of felling and buying of lands and tenements within portmote to be forme and ftable; and another of grant to pafs through all England without payment of any toll, paffage-money, &c.; and another charter of the fame of king Henry.

Item, the confirmation of all the grants confermed at a parliament holden 4 Hen. VI.

Item, the grant of the election of the mayr, and of the affeffing of impofitions by the mayr, his brethren, and 48.

Item, a ple of warantize.

Item, a box of the charter of the juftices of the peace and coroners.

Item, a rede paper, with three charters in it, of divers grants.

Item, a box of the tenements in Dede lane, conteyning the evidences of the fame.

Item, a box of the evidences of the lands and tenements in Whefton.

Item, a box of evidences of the lands and tenements in Ratclyff, Thruffington, and Cofington.

Item, a box of evidences of a tenement in Belgrave gate, that Richard Illefley, chapelain, gaf unto the town of Leyc'.

Item, a box of evidences of the lyvelode at the High Crofs that was John Frefley's.

Item, a box of evidences of a houfe at the Weft Bryg, and other at the North Bryg; and of the rent 6*d*. a year in Mekyll Afhby.

Item, a box of evidences of divers tenements in the North gate.

Ad communem aulam, tent' 23 Aug. anno fupradicto pro burgenfibus parliamenti inceptur' 17 die Octobris, anno fupradicto (electi funt) pro communitatu villæ prædictæ Petrus Curteys, & pro majore & comburgenfibus Robertus Croft.

Fefto S. Matth. 8 Hen. VII. *Thomas Swyke* electus major.—*Gilda Mercatorum*, 26.

Fefto S. Matth. 9 Hen. VII. *Robert Crofte* electus major.—*Gilda Mercatorum*, 12.

Fefto S. Matth. 10 Hen. VII. *Thomas Hurft* electus major.—*Gilda Mercatorum*, 14.

Fefto S. Matth. 11 Hen. VII. *Andrew Langton* electus major.—*Gilda Mercatorum*, 5.

Fefto S. Matth. 12 Hen. VII. *William Rowlet* electus major.—*Gilda Mercatorum*, 16.

John Wayffe paid for the chamberlainfhip (i. e. to be excufed from bearing it) 2*l*. 13*s*. 4*d*.

Fefto S. Matth. 13 Hen. VII. *Richardus Gillot* electus major.—*Gilda Mercatorum*, 16.—(Three perfons fined for the chamberlainfhip, each paying 2*l*. 13*s*. 4*d*.; as four did next year.)

Fefto S. Matth. 14 Hen. VII. *William Wygfton* fenior electus major.—*Gilda Mercatorum*, 11.

At a common hall, 21 Sept. 14 Hen. VII. agreed, that every of the forty-eight that hath been chamberlayn fhall pay, to the upholding of St. George's gyld, by the year, 6*d*.; and they that have not been chamberlains fhall pay at leaft 4*d*.

Item, that every of the forty-eight fhall pay to the wayts 2*d*. a quarter.

Item, that if any of the mayor's brethren, being within the fhire, fhall be abfent from the court of portmote three court-days togather, contrary to his oath, if he be not fick, he fhall forfeit 12*d*. to be levied by the chamberlains, to the ufe of the town.

Fefto S. Matth. 15 Hen. VII. *William Wygfton* junior electus major.—*Gilda Mercatorum*, 18.—[The

order made 7 April, 1 Ric. III. was this year renewed, 22 Nov. 15 Hen. VII.; and the 12 wards fet out as before.]

At the fame common hall, 22 Nov. 15 Hen. VII. it was ordained, that no brewer run forth their ale to their cuftomers till the ale-tafters had approved it, on pain of 3*s*. 4*d*.; nor till, after it be clenfed, it have ftood an hour at leaft, and fettled.

Alfo ordained, that the fine for chamberlainfhip be 5*l*.

Alfo typlers, felling ale by unlawful meafure, or not fealed, to forfeit 2*d*.

21 Sept. 16 Hen. VII. at a common hall, it was enacted, that no one fhould break any pavement within the precincts of the market-place, for pitching of booths, on pain of 2*c*d. apiece, to be levied by the chamberlains, &c.

Alfo agreed, that the chamberlains fhall pay yearly 13*s*. 4*d*. to a perfon appointed by the mayor and his brethren, to keep clear the market-place, and convey the filth to a place to be affigned to him.

Agreed, that the mayor fhall keep the court at Whefton every year by Michaelmas next after his election, on pain of 6*s*. 8*d*.

It was agreed, that no one lay any muck or filth in the precincts of the Saterday market, on pain of 12*d*. to be levied by the chamberlains.

Fefto S. Matth. 16 Hen. VII. *William Gibfon* major.—*Gilda Mercatorum*, 7.—*Thomas Jakys*, recordator. [This is the firft time that the recorder is mentioned by name; and this fame perfon, viz. Thomas Jakys, continues to be fo mentioned till 1 Henry VIII.]

At a common hall, on the feaft of St. Vincent, 16 Hen. VII. certain perfons were appointed to conferr with certain of the canons of the Abbey, about a chief rent concerning which there was a variance between the Town and Abbey.

At the fame hall ordered, that no vintner fell wyne in pots unfealed, but bring their pots to William Coke to be fealed; and he, for three pots fealing, to have 4*d*. Unfealed pots, after a fortnight, be feized by W. Coke, and kept to his proper ufe.

Fefto S. Matth. 17 Hen. VII. *Roger Tryg* electus major.—*Gilda Mercatorum*, 22.

The King's Roll of all the Lords, Knights, Efquires, and Gentlemen, refyent in the County of Leicefter, 17 Henry VII.

Gray marchio Dorfettiæ	Willielmus Charnells, arm.
Dominus Harrington	Johannes Beamonte, arm.
Dn's Ferrers de Chartley	Edmund Shepey, arm.
Dominus Haftings	Barthus Brokefby, arm.
Radulphus Shirley, miles	Johannes Villers, arm.
Mauritius Barkley, miles	vicecomes
Johannes Digby, miles	Thomas Stockes, arm.
Thomas Kebill, arm.	Johannes Woodford, arm.
Thomas Nevill, arm.	Thomas Hafelrigge, arm.
Thomas Morton, arm.	Willielmus Wigefton
William Afhebye, arm.	Henricus Sotell
Thomas Sherard, arm.	Thomas Antefwefilt
Everardus Feldinge, arm.	Chriftopherus Nele
Willielmus Turpine, arm.	Gerardus Danett
Johannes Turvile, arm.	Robertus Stonefbye
Thomas Purfrey, arm.	Thomas Geraide[1]."

Fefto S. Matth. 18 Hen. VII. *William Fryfley* electus major.—*Gilda Mercatorum*, 14.

Fefto S. Matth. 19 Hen. VII. *Johannes Norys* electus major.—*Gilda Mercatorum*, 16.

Ad communem aulam tent' die Jovis prox' ante feftum Natalis Domini 19 Hen. VII. electi fuerunt burgenfes parliamenti incepturi 26 Jan. prox' futur' Robertus Orton pro communitate, & Willielmus Wigfton junior pro majore & confratribus.

Ordered at the faid hall, that no one dwelling in the franchife of the town pin any cattle at the Caftle; but complain to the alderman of the ward where he or the trefpaffer dwells, and ftand to his award.

Fefto S. Matth. 20 Hen. VII. John Reed agreed to pay 5*l*. to be difcharged of the chamberlainfhip. *Robert Orton* elected mayor.—*Gilda Mercatorum*, 6.

King Henry the Seventh, in the 20th year of his

[1] Harl. MS. 6166. p. 116.

reign, doth, by his charter, confirm the former charter of the fourth of Edward the Fourth; and granteth further to the mayor and burgesses of Leicester, that the mayor, recorder, and four discreetest burgesses of the fame town, shall be justices of peace within the said borough, and limits thereof; and gives them power to enquire, hear, and determine of all offences against divers statutes, and of all felonies, murders, and other malefactors; and against another statute for the counterfeiting, clipping, washing, and falsifying of money *(non obstante* the execution in the former charter), and to punish the offenders in the premisses: And also they, or two of them, to bind men to the peace, or good behaviour, and to commit to prison any person refusing to find sureties for the peace or good behaviour : And granteth likewise, that the mayor, recorder, and four justices, or five, four, three, or two of them, quorum the recorder to be one, shall have power to hold sessions, and to enquire, by the oaths of lawful men of the said borough, of all treasons, murders, felonies, rapes, trespasses, &c.: And the justices to have wages as the justices of the county have, and to take indictments concerning the premisses; and the same to hear and determine, and thereupon to grant procefs, until the offenders be taken and outlawed, in as large and ample manner as any justices of the county may do; and to assess fines and inflict punishment upon the delinquents in the premisses as the justices in the county may do: And that when any subsidy, fifteenth, or tenth, or any other tax, shall be granted by the parliament to the king, his heirs or successors, that the inhabitants of the borough of Leicester shall be taxed and assessed by themselves, and not with the county; and that commission shall be awarded to the mayor and four discreet burgesses for the taxing and assessing of the burgesses within the said town and limits thereof, to be affociated by the king, his heirs or successors: And that the tax of the fifteenth or twentieth shall be 21l., *ultra* 5l. 13s. 4d. allowed to the collectors, being the antient charge or tax for the fifteenth or twentieth for the said borough of Leicester; and that commission shall be awarded to the mayor and four burgesses, to nominate collectors for the subsidies and fifteenths, so as the said inhabitants there shall not be taxed, ceffed, or charged, by any other commission: And that the mayor and commissioners shall chuse such a collector as they will answer for, and to certify his name to the Exchequer; and that such collector shall be only charged with the subsidies and fifteenths of the town, and not of the county: And that no free burgess being resident in the town shall hereafter be chosen collector for the subsidy or fifteenth, forth of the town, for any lands or goods which he hath in the county. But take the record:

Rex omnibus ad quos, &c. falutem. Inspeximus literas patentes domini Edwardi nuper regis Anglie Quarti, majori et burgensibus ville five burgi sui Leyceftrie, factas, in hec verba: " Edwardus, Dei gratià," [&c. ut supra, p. 374]. " Nos autem literas predictas, ac omnia et singula in eisdem contenta, rata habentes et grata, ea pro nobis et heredibus nostris, quantum in nobis eft, acceptamus et approbamus; et dilecto et fideli servienti nostro Roberto Orton nunc majori, et burgensibus dicte ville five burgi, tenore presentium, ratificamus et confirmamus, prout litere predicte in se rationabiliter testantur. Et ulterius, de uberiori gratià nostrà, ac ad inftantiam et specialem requisitionem dilecti et fidelis servientis nostri Roberti Orton, nunc majoris ville five burgi predicti, necnon ob singularem affectionem et dilectionem quas penes predictos majorem et burgenses five inhabitantes predicte ville five burgi gerimus et habemus, ac pro conservatione pacis noftre, ac fano regimine et pro bono reipublice, ville, et burgensium five inhabitantium predictorum augendo, dedimus et concessimus, ac per presentes literas nostras damus et concedimus, pro nobis et heredibus nostris, quantum in nobis eft, prefatis nunc majori et burgensibus ville predicte, suburb' et procinctuum ejusdem, et successoribus suis

majoribus five burgensibus predictis, quod de cetero dicti nunc major ejusdem ville, et successores sui qui pro tempore erunt, ac quatuor de discretioribus burgensibus ejusdem ville, simul cum majore et recordatore ejusdem ville, sint custodes et justiciarii pacis nostre, et heredum et successorum nostrorum, infra villam predictam, suburb' et procinctuum ejusdem, quorum dictus recordator ejusdem ville pro tempore existens erit unus, ad omnia ordinaciones et ftatuta apud Westm', Wynton', et Northampton', pro conservatione pacis noftre, heredum et successorum nostrorum, necnon ad ftatuta et ordinationes ibidem et alibi, de venatoribus, operariis, artificibus, servitoribus, hoftellariis, ponderibus, menfuris, vendicione victualium, mendicantibus, et vagabundis, ac aliis hominibus mendicantibus qui se nominant *Travelyngz-men*, ac ad ftatuta et ordinationes apud Westm', anno regni Henrici Quarti nuper regis Anglie primo et fecundo, de libertatibus, ac aliis libertatibus pannorum minime dandis, nec eifdem libertatibus aliqualiter utendis, et de omnibus feloniis, murdris, et aliis malefactoribus; ac ad quoddam aliud ftatutum de contrafacturâ, tonfurâ, loturâ, et aliis falfitatibus alicujus monete edite five facte, predictâ exceptione de hujufmodi terminationibus de omnimodis feloniis, ac de contrafacturâ, tonfurâ, loturâ, et aliis falfitatibus monete regni nostri Anglie, duntaxat exceptis, in dictis literis patentibus domini Edwardi nuper regis Anglie Quarti contentâ et specificatâ, in contrarium inde factâ, non obstantibus; ac ad omnia et singula alia ftatuta et ordinationes pro bono pacis, et quieto regimine et gubernatione populi nostri, edita, et in posterum edenda, de et in omnibus suis articulis, juxta vim, formam, et effectum eorundem, infra dictam villam Leyceftrie, suburbia et procinctus ejusdem, custodiendum et custodiri faciendum, inquirendum, audiendum, et terminandum, ac ad omnes illos quos contra formam ordinationum et ftatutorum predictorum, aut eorum alicujus, delinquentes invenerunt caftigandum et puniendum, caftigare et punire faciendum, prout fecundum formam et effectum ordinationum et ftatutorum eorundem, predictâ excepcione non obftante, fuerit faciendum; et ad omnes illos qui aliquibus de populo nostro infra villam predictam, suburbia et procinctus ejusdem, minas fecerint de corporibus suis, vel de incendio domorum suarum, ad sufficientem securitatem de pace et bono geftu suo, erga nos, heredes et successores nostros pro tempore existentes, et cunctum populum nostrum inveniendum, coram eis seu eorum duobus, per debitam legis formam venire faciendum; et si hujufmodi securitates invenire recufaverint, tunc eos in prifonâ noftrâ ville predicte, quoufque hujufmodi securitates invenerint, salvo cuftodiri faciendum. Volumus etiam et concedimus prefatis nunc majori et burgensibus, et successoribus suis, quod dicti major, recordator, et alii quatuor burgenses ejusdem ville pro tempore existentes, sex, quinque, quatuor, tres, et duo eorum, quorum recordator ejusdem ville pro tempore existens omnino erit unus, de tempore in tempus futuris temporibus fint et erint justiciarii nostri, heredum et successorum nostrorum, ad inquirendum per facramentum proborum et legalium hominum de villâ predictâ et suburb' ac procinctibus ejusdem, per quos rei veritas melius fciri poterit, de omnibus proditionibus, murdris, feloniis, raptibus mulierum, et aliis feloniis quibufcumque, ac de quibufcumque tranfgreffionibus, riotis, routis, et conventiculis illicitis, imbraciariis, manutenenciis, ambidextriis, extortionibus, confederationibus, confpirationibus, tranfgreffionibus, regratariis et foreftallariis, infra villam predictam, suburbia et procinctus ejusdem, per quofcumque et qualitercumque factis five perpetratis, et exnunc fieri five perpetrari contingentibus, necnon ad omnia indictamenta quecumque ad hujufmodi tranfgreffiones et alia malefacta quecumque infra villam predictam, et suburbia ac procinctus ejusdem, coram prefatis majore, recordatore, fex, quinque, quatuor, et tribus eorum, audiendum et terminandum, quorum recordator ejusdem ville pro tempore

pore exiftens erit unus, jufticiarii noftri et heredum et
iucceſſorum noſtrorum, de premiſſis feu aliquo premiſſorum, ac ad proceſſus inde faciendum verſus
omnes quos coram jufticiariis noftris, et heredum et
fucceſſorum noſtrorum, de premiſſis feu aliquo premiſſorum de cetero judicari contigerit, quouſque
capiantur, reddantur, vel utlagentur, faciendum et
continuandum ; necnon ad omnia et fingula que contra formam ordinationum et ſtatutorum predictorum,
feu in evaſionem eorundem, feu eorum alicujus,
infra villam predictam, fuburbia et procinctus
ejuſdem, facta, perpetrata, feu attemptata fuerint,
et que ibidem in poſterum fieri, perpetrari, feu at-
temptari contigerit, tam ad fectam noftram quam
aliorum quorumcunque, coram eiſdem jufticiariis, pro
nobis, heredibus et fucceſſoribus noftris, aut pro fe-
ipfis, conqueri aut profequi volentium, audiendum,
ac fecundùm legem et confuetudinem regni noftri
Anglie, ac juxta formam ordinationum et ſtatutorum
predictorum terminandum, in tam amplis modo et
formâ prout aliqui alii jufticiarii pacis noftre, heredum
et fucceſſorum noftrorum, alibi in aliquo comitatu
regni noftri Anglie inquirere, audire, feu terminare
poſſint et poterint, necnon tranſgreſſiones forſtalla-
rum predictarum, ac omnia alia fuperius ad deter-
minandum, non declarat' ad fectam noftram tamen,
et ad omnia alia que virtute aliquorum ordinationum
five ftatutorum per cuftodes pacis noftre, heredum
et fucceſſorum noftrorum, ac jufticiarios noftros, heredum et fucceſſorum noftrorum, hujuſmodi difcuti et
terminari debent, audiendum et terminandum ; et ad
quofcunque contra formam ordinationum et ſtatutorum predictorum, feu eorum alicujus delinquentium,
per fines, redemptiones, et amerciamenta, ac alio modo, pro dilectis fuis caftigandum et puniendum, prout
ante ordinationem et punitionem corporalem hujuſmodi delinquentibus pro delictis fuis exhibendum
factum fieri confuevit alibi infra regnum noftrum
Anglie pertinent feu pertinebunt, faciendum, exercendum, audiendum, et terminandum ; falvis nobis,
heredibus et fucceſſoribus noftris, finibus, recognitionibus, redemptionibus, exitibus, et amerciamentis, nobis, heredibus et fucceſſoribus noftris, ratione jufti-
ariorum predictorum, in fingulis ceſſionibus ipforum
majoris, recordatoris, et aliorum noftrorum predictorum in hâc parte nobis adjudicandis et afferandis
five pertinentibus. Volumus tamen quod predicti jufticiarii noftri, et eorum quilibet, de et fuper fingulis
finibus et exitibus in ceſſionibus predictis forisfacturis et affidendis habeant, et eorum quilibet habeat,
tanta vadia et feoda, prout finguli jufticiarii et cuftodes pacis in dicto comitatu Leyceſtrie juxta formam ſtatuti inde editi habentis percipiunt, licet officium jufticiarii in villâ five burgo predicto poft ſtatutum predictum ordinatum pro hujuſmodi vadiis percipiendis per
dictum pregenitorem noftrum ordinatum fuerit; et
quod aliqui alii jufticiarii pacis noftre, heredum aut fucceſſorum noftrorum, aut aliqui alii jufticiarii heredum
aut fucceſſorum noftrorum, aliqua ordinatiorum et ſtatuta de premiſſis, aut aliqua premiſſorum, edita five ordinata, infra villam predictam, fuburbia et procinctus ejuſdem, emergentium five contingentium, aut ad
aliqua premiſſorum, aut ad aliquod officium de aut
pro iiſdem feu eorum aliquibus ibidem exercendum,
faciendum, feu exequendum in aliquo ibidem, fe non
intromittant, nec eorum aliquis fe intromittat, aut
aliquam jurifdictionem inde habeant feu exerceant.
Et ulterius, de uberiori gratiâ, fcientiâ, et mero motu
noftris, dedimus et conceſſimus, ac per prefentes
damus et concedimus, prefatis nunc majori ville five
burgi predicti, et burgenfibus predictis, et fucceſ-
foribus fuis, quod quandocunque et quotieſcun-
que acciderit feu contigerit exnunc unquam in
futuro aliquam quintamdecimam et decimam, quotam, taxam, auxilium, fubfidium, aut annuam vel
certam pecunie fummam, vel alia onera quecumque,
quocunque nomine aut formâ concedantur aut concedi contigerint, nobis, heredibus aut fucceſſoribus
noftris regibus Anglie, per communitatem noftri
Anglie, ac per cives et burgenfes civitatum et burgorum ejuſdem regni, auctoritate parliamenti five
communis confilii, aut aliter quovis modo, et ex

quâcumque urgente causâ, nobis five heredibus vel
fucceſſoribus noftris, concedi, preſtari, aut con-
ferri ullo modo, quod fuper moderatione, taxa-
tione, ordinatione, affeſſione, collectione, leva-
tione, receptione, et percepcione omnium et fingularum, five alicujus aut aliquarum hujuſmodi quintarumdecimarum, decimarum, quotarum, taxarum,
auxiliorum, fubfidiorum, aut annue vel certe pecunie fumme cujuſcunque, vel alicujus inde parcelle, aut aliorum onerum quorumcunque, nullus
aut nulli commiſſionariorum, moderatorum, affeſſa-
torum, ordinatorum, vel taxatorum, in predicto
comitatu Leyceſtrie, pro corpore ejuſdem comitatûs
aſſignati five aſſignandi in eâ parte, de cetero aſſig-
netur five aſſignentur per commiſſionem regiam noftri,
heredum aut fucceſſorum noftrorum, five per aliud
mandatum regni quodcumque, ad moderandum,
taxandum, ordinandum, five aſſidendum, aliquem
five aliquos burgenfes, commorantes five inhabitantes aut refidentes infra villam five burgum predictum et fuburbia ejuſdem, pro bonis, catallis, terris,
tenementis, aut rebus fuis, infra villam five burgum
predictum aut fuburbia ejuſdem adtunc exiſtentibus, five extunc exiſtere contingentibus, cum hundredis, burgis, villis, villatis, terris, tenementis, et
hamelettis, perfonis, bonis, catallis, terris, aut tenementis, infra dictum comitatum Leyceſtrie exiſtentibus, ut parcella oneris ejuſdem comitatûs contributoria
five oneranda; fed volumus, ordinamus, et tenore
prefentium, quantum in nobis eſt, pro nobis, heredibus ac fucceſſoribus noftris, ſtabilimus, ac per
prefentes concedimus, prefatis nunc majori et burgenfibus ville five burgi predicti, et fucceſſoribus
fuis, quod prefatus major ejuſdem ville five burgi
nunc exiſtens, ac finguli fucceſſores fui, major
ibidem pro tempore exiſtens, et qui exnunc pro
tempore fuerit, ac quatuor probiores, difcretiores,
et fagaciores burgenfes ejuſdem, eidem majori pro
tempore exiſtente aſſociandi, per nos, heredes ac
fucceſſores noftros pro tempore exiſtentes, per commiſſionem regiam, de tempore in tempus, cum hujuſmodi cafus evenerit, aut conceſſiones hujuſmodi
fieri contigerint, in premiſſis aſſignentur, et poteſ-
tatem ac auctoritatem de cetero in perpetuum habeant infra villam five burgum predictum, ad or-
dinand', moderand', taxand', et aſſidend', per feipfos, majorem, et quatuor difcreciores viros ville
five burgi predicti fic aſſignand', ex commiſſione
regiâ, feparatos à commiſſionariis corporis dicti comitatus Leiceſtrie exnunc aſſignand', fuper et in
fingulis hujuſmodi conceſſionibus, oneracionibus,
et preſtacionibus quintarumdecimarum, decimarum,
quotarum, taxarum, auxiliorum, fubfidiorum, aut
alterius contribucionis vel oneris cujuſcumque, nobis,
heredibus aut fucceſſoribus noftris, fiend', et quibuf-
libet inde parcelle, omnes et fingulos burgenfes, refidentes, commorantes et inhabitantes ville five
burgi illius et fuburb' ejuſdem pro tempore exiſten',
pro ratâ et porcione fuâ bonorum, cattallarum, terrarum, et tenementorum fuorum, infra villam five
burgum ill' contingen' de jure contributorum et
onerabilium, taxand' five apporcionand' vel affidend' ; videlicet, ad quamlibet integram quintam-
decimam et decimam viginti et unam libras pro
taxâ ejuſdem ville nobis et heredibus noftris folvend',
ultra fummam centum et trefdecim folidorum et
quatuor denariorum, pro taxâ ville five burgi illius
in fingulis folucionibus hujuſmodi deducend', et
eiſdem burgenfibus, ac eorum collectoribus inde
deputand' allocand', prout villa five burgus predicta antiquitus fit contribuere et taxari, ac in de-
ductione fuâ predictâ exonerari aut allocari hactenus
pro parte et porcione ejuſdem ville five burgi confuevit cum dicto corpore tocius comitatûs Leyceſtrie fupradicti, dum eidem corpori ipfius comitatûs Leyceſtrie in collectione et folucione fuâ
contribuet fuit. Et volumus ac ordinamus quod nos,
heredes ac fucceſſores noftri, ac quilibet noſtrorum,
fingulas commiſſiones noftras majori et quatuor dif-
crecioribus burgenfibus dicte ville five burgi pro
tempore exiſtentibus, pro fingulis talibus taxacioni-
bus, deputacionibus, et nominacionibus collectorum
infra

infra villam five burgum ill' deputand' dirigi faciemus exequendas; ita quod de cetero in perpetuum
villa five burgus predict', ac omnes et finguli majores, burgenfes, refidentes, commorantes, et inhabitantes ejufdem et fuburb' inde, de folucione quinte-
decime et decime predict', et aliarum conceffionum,
preftacionum, et contribucionum predict', cum aliis
villis, burgis, villatis, hundredis, hamelettis, et
locis, de corpore dicti comitatûs Leyceftrie, pro porcione fuâ inde quocienfcunque evenerit contribu-
end' nullatenus oneretur aut onerentur, fet pro
eâdem porcione fuâ ville five burgi illius ad fummam fupradictam, et pro parte rate fue ejufdem,
ultra deduccionem predictam, per moderatores,
taxatores, et affeffores predicte ville five burgi
illius, per nos, heredes et fucceffores noftros, reges
Anglie pro tempore exiftentes, ut premittitur, tantummodo affignand', onerentur et taxentur; ita
quod per aliquos commiffionarios, affeffores, five taxatores de dicto comitatu Leyceftrie, feu aliquos
alios generales commiffionarios noftros infra regnum
noftrum Anglie exiftentes, ordinari aut nominari
contingentes, pro corpore dicti comitatûs Leyceftrie
feu alibi deputand' five affignand', extra villam five
burgum ill', aliquomodo non taxentur, affidentur,
aut folvere vel aliquo modo onerari conantur vel dif-
tringantur feu occafionentur; quodque dicti major
et ceteri contaxatores, moderatores, affeffores, et
ordinatores, infra villam five burgum ill' et fuburbia inde, pro tempore de cetero exiftentes, per
nos, heredes et fucceffores noftros, ut premittitur,
affignati et affignandi, per fe, divifi ab aliis commiffionariis de corpore dicti comitatûs Leyceftrie,
tantos et tales fufficientes collectores quintarumdecimarum, decimarum, quotarum, taxarum, auxiliorum, fubfidiorum, et cujufcumque ulterius oneris
et contribucionis, et parcell' eorumdem, infra villam five burgum predict' et fuburbia ejufdem, nobis, heredibus aut fuccefforibus noftris, pertinent' et
pertinere contingent', quando et quociens cafus hujufmodi conceffionum inde colligendi et levandi
evenerit feu contigerit, pro quibus refpondere voluerint, nominare, deputare, affignare, ordinare,
aut onerare, valeant et debeant, ac de eorum nominibus, quotiens fic fieri contigerit, de tempore in
tempus, nobis, heredibus et fuccefforibus noftris,
in Scaccarium noftrum aut alibi, prout pro conceffionibus hujufmodi fieri contingent, per feipfos folos,
et divifos ab aliis commiffionariis corporis dicti comitatûs Leyceftrie, fub eorum figillis debitè certi-
ficent; et quod finguli predicti collectores dicte
ville five burgi, fic de tempore in tempus quociens
et quando nominati, deputati, ordinati, aut onerati
fuerint in formâ predictâ, in hujufmodi cafu, de cetero non onerentur cum collectoribus corporis dicti
comitatûs Leyceftrie in aliquo modo, nec de pluribus aliis five majoribus fummis, in compotis fuis,
cum dictis collectoribus de corpore dicti comitatûs
Leyceftrie refpondeant; fed quod ipfi collectores
infra dictam villam five burgum de cetero, in formâ
predictâ, ut premittitur, deputandi et nominandi,
de tantis et talibus fummis, unde dicta villa five
burgus, ac finguli burgenfes commorantes, inhabitantes, ac refidentes ibidem, et fuburbiis inde,
pro fe, à dicto corpore predicti comitatûs Leyceftrie
divifis, pro ratâ et onere ejufdem burgi, prout cafus
eveniet, onerari aut affidi per dictos affeffores infra
villam five burgum predict', per fe, ut premittitur, affidend' onerabuntur, et à quibufcumque
collectionibus, contributionibus, et folutionibus
fuis, cum collectoribus de et pro corpore dicti comitatûs Leyceftrie, et aliis collectoribus quibufcumque extra villam five burgum predict' deputandis,
fint exnunc in perpetuum penitus feparati, divifi, et
onerati, licet ipfi burgenfes five inhabitantes infra
dictam villam five burgum et fuburbia inde, per
commiffionarios de corpore dicti comitatûs Leyceftrie exnunc quovis modo cum collectoribus ejufdem comitatûs deputentur aut deputari contigerint.
Concedimus eciam majori, burgenfibus, et fuccef-

foribus fuis predictis, quod nullus burgenfis refi-
dens ville five burgi qui nunc eft, et exnunc fore
contigerit, de cetero non fiat nec fit, aut oneretur
fore, collector aliquorum premifforum in aliquo loco
five aliquibus locis infra dictum comitatum Leyceftrie, feu alibi extra villam five burgum predictum
aut fuburbia inde exiftentibus, per aliquos commiffionarios de dictâ corporatione predicti comitatûs Leyceftrie, feu aliquos alios extra villam five burgum
ill' deputand', affignand', aut nominand', ratione
aliquorum bonorum, cattallorum, terrarum, aut tenementorum fuorum in dicto comitatu Leyceftrie, feu
alibi extra villam five burgum predictum et fuburbia inde exiftentia aut exiftere contingentia; fed
quod ipfi burgenfes et eorum finguli, ac eorum
heredes et fucceffores, et eorum quilibet burgenfis
ville five burgi predicti exnunc in perpetuum, tenore et auctoritate prefencium, de cetero et de tempore in tempus, de fingulis hujufmodi collectionibus
fuis, ac omnibus folucionibus ratione dictarum col-
lectionum contingentibus, in dicto comitatu Leyceftrie, feu alibi extra villam five burgum predict', in
hâc parte penitus erga nos et heredes noftros exonerati et quieti exiftant, et eorum quilibet exiftat;
eo quod expreffa mencio de vero valore annuo premifforum, aut de aliis donis five conceffionibus per
nos, progenitores five predeceffores noftros, eifdem
majori et burgenfibus ante hec tempora factis in prefentibus facta non exiftit, aut aliquo ftatuto, actu,
ordinacione, five reftrictione, in contrarium premifforum, facto, ordinato, edito, five provifo, aut
aliquâ aliâ re, caufâ, feu materiâ quacumque, in aliquo non obftante. In cujus, &c. Tefte Rege,
apud Weftm', quarto die Marcii.

Per ipfum Regem, et de dato, &c. pro trefdecim
folidis et quatuor denariis folutis in Hanaperio [1]."

21 May, 21 Hen. VII. enacted by Robert Orton
mayor, by confent of the twenty-four and forty-
eight, firmly hereafter to be obferved, that, from
the faid 21 May to Michaelmas next come twelvemonth, the Sheeps market fhall be kept in the Saturday market, and the profits thereof be received for
the ufe of the town by fuch perfons as are deputed
by the mayor and his brethren, &c.; the mayor to
forfeit 40s. and every of his brethren 20s. if he attempt to break the faid ordinance.

21 Sept. 21 Hen. VII. At a common hall, it is
agreed, and given to Frere William Seyton, prior of
the Black Friers of Leicefter, and to all his fucceffors
for ever, the pafture of two kye in our commonalty
called *The Cow-hey*, to be as free to them as any of
us, without let or impediment of any of us; for the
which he gave us twenty fhillings, and he and his
houfe to pray for us for ever. In witnefs of the fame,
we gave him and his houfe our feal of office.

Fefto S. Matth. 21 Hen. VII. *Richard Reynolds*
elected mayor.—*Gilda Mercatorum*, 7.

Fefto S. Matth. 22 Hen. VII. *John Waffe*, alias
Wayes, elected mayor.—*Gilda Mercatorum*, 7.

Fefto S. Matth. 23 Hen. VII. *Walter May* elected
mayor.—*Gilda Mercatorum*, 8.

Some made free are ftated to have confented to
pay at Michaelmas next 5s. and at Chriftmas next 5s.

Ad communem aulam tent' die Veneris prox' poft
Feftum Sancti Ricardi Epifcopi, 23 Hen. VII.

It is agreed, that the Sheeps market fhall be henceforth holden ftill in the Market-place; and the profits to be to behoof of the town.

And at the fame common hall William Clarke
taketh the profits of the Sheeps market, with the 122
craches for the fheeps penns, for feven years; to
pay yearly to the chamber of the town 3l.; and at the
end of the term to have as many craches, and fufficiently repaired. [Several agreements and arbitra-
tions concerning private perfons were made before
the Mayor, and entered in the Hall-book.]

Several perfons paid five nobles, or 33s. 4d. as a
fine for the chamberlainfhip; and one paid 53s. 4d.

Mem. That it is enacted that no one fhall lay any
manner of muck or fweepings within the four gates

---

[1] Pat. 20 Hen. VII. Pars 1. m. 18.

of the town, but without in fuch places as ben affigned, viz. in the nether ende of Belgrave gate, and in the field without Galtre gate end, and beyond the Horfe fair, under payn for every default 40d. For the Weft quarter at the Sore fide, at the comyn drawts.

Fefto S. Matth. 24 Hen. VII. *Miles Lamberd* elected mayor.—*Gilda Mercatorum*, 10.

About this period the poffeffions of the abbot and convent of *Croxton* in the town of Leicefter are thus defcribed in the Regifter of that Abbey :

" Habemus in Leyceftriâ, de dono Simonis filii Willielmi Kipping, cum corpore fuo, capitale meffuagium fuum, cum camerâ & omnibus pertinentiis fuis, in liberam eleemofinam, fine aliquo retenemento ; quod fcilicet jacet in parochiâ S. Martini, falvo fervicio debito dominis feodi. Warentizabit, &c.

Item Radulfus le Tanur, & Alicia Kipping uxor fua conceff erunt & confirmaverunt etiam nobis quandam domum cum pertinentiis in orientali parte folarii, & redditum inde provenientem ; tenendam nobis benè & in pace, faciendo fervicia que pertinent ad capitales dominos. Warantizabunt, &c.

Item Cecilia Kipping, filia Willielmi Kipping, in plenâ poteftate & viduitate fua, confirmavit nobis, in puram eleemofinam, pro fe & heredibus fuis, totum jus & clameum quod habuit, vel habere poterit, in predictis meffuagio & folario verfus orientem, cum omnibus pettinentiis fuis ; & quandam domum in parte orientali folarii, cum pertinentiis fuis, & redditum inde provenientem ; habendam & tenendam benè & in pace, fine aliquo retenemento, faciendo fervicium quod ad capitales dominos pertinet. Warentizabit, &c.

Item habemus, de dono ejufdem Cecilie Kipping, in liberam, puram, & perpetuam eleemofinam, homagium & totum fervicium Henrici filii Reginaldi Howel de Leyceftriâ & heredum fuorum ; fcilicet, annuum redditum xiid. & unius flette, de quadam terrâ cum pertinentiis & edificiis in Leyceftriâ, in alto vico orientali, in parochiâ Sancti Martini ; quam fcilicet terra dicta Cecilia habuit de dono patris fui, nichil juris vel clamei fibi & heredibus in predictâ terrâ retinens, vel in homagiis & ferviciis predicti Henrici vel heredum fuorum. Warantizabit, &c.

Item habemus remiffionem & quietam clamationem Willielmi de Odifton de annuo redditu xiid. quem de nobis percipere folebat, de tenemento quod habemus de dono predicti Simonis Kipping, retinendo fibi & heredibus fuis alios xiid. ; ita quod nec ipfe nec heredes fui, ratione homagii, relevii, fecte alicujus, auxilii, five cujufcunque confuetudinis, de predicto tenemento ad unquam exigere poterunt imperpetuum. Et fi contingat quod diftringamur vel implacitemur de homagiis & releviis & arreragiis ad predictum tenementum pertinentibus, pro fe & heredibus, five capitali domino & heredibus fuis vel affignatis faciendis, predictus Willielmus & heredes fui nobis warantizabunt in perpetuum.

Item habemus, de dono Petri quondam perfone de Eftwelle, annuum redditum xiid. & ii caponum in eâdem villâ, in puram eleemofinam ; recipiendum de quodam meffuagio in parochiâ Sancti Clementis, quod Ricardus de Walton tenuit. Quem quidem redditum fratres predicatores [1] manentes in Leyceftriâ habent de dono noftro, intuitu caritatis, in perpetuum.

Item habemus, de dono Warini Rufi, quandam terram in eâdem villâ, cum edificiis in eâdem conftructis, que jacet inter terram quam Ricardus de Wyteby tenuit & terram Roberti Albi.

Item habemus, de dono Rogeri Blundi, annuum redditum xviiid. & ii gallinarum & unius galli, in puram eleemofinam ; quem Warinus predictus fibi reddere folebat pro predictâ terrâ, quam idem Warinus nobis dedit.

Item recepimus, de tenemento quod habemus de dono predicti Warini, vs. per annum ad tres terminos, per manum Rogeri Curteys [2].

Item Henricus filius Rogeri Howel, & heredes fui,

tenent de nobis quoddam tenementum cum edificiis in eâdem villâ, in parochiâ Sancti Martini ; quod fcilicet emit de Ceciliâ Kipping ; reddendo nobis xiid. & unam flettam (viz. ad Purificationem iiiid. ad Pentacoften iiiid. ad S. Michaelem iiiid. & ad Natale unam flettam) ; & faciendo nobis omnia fervicia debita & confueta, fecundùm confuetudinem ville ; & etiam reddendo nobis is. ad Natale, pro conftructione gabli folarii fui fuper gablum folarii noftri.

Robertus de Feure de Leyceftre & Alicia uxor ejus tenent de nobis unum meffuagium in altâ ftratâ orientali Leyceftrie, ad terminum xl annorum ; reddendo nobis annuatim v s. ad tres terminos.

Summa totius redditûs noftri in eâdem viis. ō. unam flettam. Expaiamus xiid. [3]"

HENRY VIII.

Fefto S. Matth. 1 Hen. VIII. *Richard Eyr* elected mayor.—*Gilda Mercatorum*, 9.

Thomas Jackys, the recorder, is here, laft of all, mentioned among the juftices of peace.

In this year Robert Orton was Bailiff of Leicefter. This officer is called the King's Bailiff; and was, prior to the office of Mayor, called the Earl's Bailiff. He holds his place for life, and is chofen alternately by the earls of Huntingdon and the 24 aldermen. The Huntingdon family obtained this privilege from James I. The office, whatever it might have been, is now in a great meafure honorary ; excepting that the gentleman who holds it is returning officer, in conjunction with the Mayor, at elections for Members to ferve in Parliament. The Corporation are addreffed as a body by the names of " Mayor, Bailiffs, &c." though there is but one Bailiff.

Mem. quod Dec. 20, 1 Hen. VIII. Radulphus Swyllington admiffus eft in gildam mercatorum iftius villæ ; & infuper, die & anno fupradicto, prædictus Radulphus admiffus eft unus combergenfium ejufdem villæ ; provifo femper quod non oneretur ad aliquod officium ibidem occupandum, nec fit ad [fummonitionem] majoris aliqualiter pro aliquâ caufâ nifi ad placitum ipfius Radulphi.

Fefto S. Matth. 2 Hen. VIII. *William Wygfton* junior elected mayor.—*Gilda Mercatorum*, 29.

It is enacted, that henceforth no one fhall redeem his chamberlainfhip under 4l.

Alfo, that the mayor for the time being fhall every year take the accompts for the church of St. Martin's within his time, under pain of 40s.

Alfo, that all brewers that brew to fell fhall give twelve gallons of their beft ale for 12d.

Item, it is enacted that the mayor's ferjeant fhall have, of every prifoner committed to the hall for a fray, 4d. ; and of every prifoner fo committed for any other trefpafs, 2d. in name of a fee, to mend his wages, &c.

Alfo, that no man fhall put no more beafts in the Cowhey above two and a bullik.

Fefto S. Matth. 3 Hen. VIII. *William Wigfton* fenior elected mayor.—*Gilda Mercatorum*, 7.

William Wygfton the elder (was) fon and heir and executor of Roger Wygfton, efq.—Robert Gaddifby was at that time clerk to the mayor ; and the chandlers engaged to fell candles at 1¼d. the pound.

Mem. that I William Wygefton the elder, mayor of Leicefter, received of William Wygefton the younger, laft mayor, thefe parcells ; firft, the mayor's feal of offyce, fylver ; the common feal, copper and gilt, in a purfe, with four keyes ; alfo a box, with two grants, concerning the liberties of the town ; one of them under the broad feal, and the other under the feal of the Dutchy.

Item, a great book lokett ; two other books concerning the ordinances of the town, and fying good ale and other vetell.

Item, a broken metwand.

Item, a quartern weight of brafs.

---

[1] Of the Friers Preachers at Leicefter, commonly called the Dominican or Grey Friers, fee before, vol. I. p. 295.

[2] Peter Curteys occurs in 1467 as owner of a houfe in the Weft Gate.

[3] Peck's MS. in the Britifh Mufeum, 4935. ex cod. MS. in 4to, apud Belvoir, fol 28. a.

Item,

Item, two half ftones of brafs of 14lb. weight.

Item, three other brazen weights, each lefs than other.

Item, a gallon of brafs.

Fefto S. Matth. 4 Hen. VIII. *Richard Gyllot* elected mayor.—*Gilda Mercatorum*, 8.

Fefto S. Matth. 5 Hen. VIII. *Richard Reynold* elected mayor.—*Gilda Mercatorum*, 6.

Fefto S. Matth. 6 Hen. VIII. *Thomas Burton* elected mayor.—*Gilda Mercatorum*, 9.

Ad communem aulam tent' die Lunæ prox' ante feftum Affumptionis Beatæ Mariæ, 7 Hen. VIII.

Agreed that a fubfidy of 21l. fhall be levied and gedered within the town, to content the town's debt; and there were affefors appointed for each of the 12 wards, and one collector with the conftable in each ward.

1 May, *Robert Orton* was bailiff.

Fefto S. Matth. 7 Hen. VIII. *Thomas Cotton* elected mayor.

Fefto S. Michaelis Archangeli 8 Hen. VIII. *John Reede* elected mayor.—*Gilda Mercatorum*, 18.

Fefto S. Matth. 9 Hen. VIII. *Thomas Smyth* elected mayor.—*Gilda Mercatorum*, 30.

Mem. that in the feft of St. Leonard, in 9 Hen. VIII. William Prowdlof, in the houfe, rebuked the mayor and his brethren for the feffing of the fifteenth penny in the time of meraltie of Thomas Smyth. Sir William Lewcas, preft, Chriftopher Grevys, Thomas Leyx, Richard Rutter, fworn and examined, feyn upon their oaths, that the faid William Prowdlof faid that he had as redy 20 nobles in his perfe as any knaff of the bench that fat upon the feffment of the fifteenth penny, or of the beft churles of herlotts of them all. Wherupon, according to reafon, was the faid William Prowdlof comytted to ward, and there punyfhed eight days; and fo after came into the cort of portmote, and there upon his knees afkyt the meyr and his bredren openly forgyffnes in the face of the cort, and fo was pardoned.

[This is placed in the book before 20 Hen. VII.]

Fefto S. Matth. 10 Hen. VIII. *Richard Beefton* elected mayor.—*Gilda Mercatorum*, 6.

Fefto S. Matth. 11 Hen. VIII. *William Bartlatt* elected mayor; and the following undated order is believed to have been made in his time.

" By the King. [Henry VIII.] Trufty and welbe-loved, we grete you well. And forafmuch as we, for diverfe confiderations us moving, intend to have almaner perfons refeant, inhabiting, and abiding, or hereafter to be refeant, inhabiting, and abiding, within that our town of Leicefter and the liberties thereof, liable to do unto us fervice of war when the caas fhall require, to be at the leading and conducing of our right trufty and well-beloved counfellor the lord Haftyngs, fteward of our faid towne : We there-fore will and command you, and every of you, that ye in no wife fuffer any of the faid perfonnes to be taken by any maner perfonne or perfonnes whatfoever they be, nor reteigned to any of them; but that they be allways in a redynes and furthcomyng to geve at-tendaunce upon our faid counfaillor, to do unto us fervice of war when we fhall geve unto hym co-mmaundement in that behalf; any our lettres, placards, or other our lettres of commiffions or commaundement maide or to be maide to the contrary thereof notwith-ftandyng. And that ye faile not thus to do, as ye intend to pleafe us, and woll efchue the contrary. Geven under our fignet, at our manor of Efthamp-fted, the 17th day of July."

Fefto S. Matth. 12 Hen. VIII. *Wm. Wygfton* fenior elected mayor the third time.—*Gilda Mercatorum*, 5.

The 13 Jan. fir Nicholas Wagftaffe, prieft, and vicar of St. Martin's in Leicefter, owned a debt be-fore the mayor, and gave fureties to pay it.

Die Jovis, viz. die Depofitionis Sancti Antonii 12 Hen. VIII. At a common hall, agreed that Mr. Har-ward buy at London, for the common wealth of the town, a lawful ftrike of brafs, a gallon of brafs, a yard of brafs by the ftandard, and all other weights and meafures needful; and the chamberlains to con-tent and pay to the faid Robert Harward bill, cofts, and charges of the fame.

Die Veneris prox' ante Feftum S. Hugonis, 12 Hen. VIII. At a common hall, ordered that no baker of the country bring any bread into the town but on the market-day, i. e. Wednefday and Friday, and to fet their bread at the High Crofs, and there fell it by the pennyworth or twopennyworth; and carry bread to none of their cuftomers, in pain of forfeiting their bread to the king, and their bodies to be imprifoned at the mayor's commandment; and on Saturday to bring their bread to the Saturday market, and there to fell it.

Alfo agreed, that the firft Friday in clean Lent every mayor hold a common hall; and there the chamberlain's accounts to be fhewed, that it may be known in what degree the town ftands. [Three fining for the Chamberlainfhip, paid each 4l. 4s.]

Alfo agreed, that all bakers that bake for fale make good wholefome bread, according to the affize, on pain of forfeiting the firft time 3s. 4d. and the fecond time 6s. 8d.; and fo to double as often as they make default.

Alfo that brewers make good ale, and wholefome, and mighty of the corn, according to the ftatute, and to fell 13 gallons for 2s. 6d.; and, upon default, forfeit the firft time 3s. 4d. the fecond 6s. 8d. and fo to double as often as they make default; alfo to make good wholefome ale for the poor people of ob. the gallon; and they that find themfelves grieved to have remedy of Mr. Mayor.

Alfo, that no brewer fet forth no ale till the alder-man of the ward and two of the forty-eight have tafted it, on forfeiture the firft time 3s. 4d. and fo to double as often as they make default; and if the al-derman of the ward be a brewer, then thofe of the forty-eight to call the alderman of the next ward to tafte : for they that be brewers fhall be no tafters.

Alfo, that no tipler fell ale but with meafure fealed according to the king's ftatute, on pain of 4d. *toties quoties*.

Alfo, that all meafures, as ftrikes, gallons, pottles, quarts, pints, and all other meafures, both fealed and unfealed, be brought before the Mayor; and thofe that be able fhall be admitted, and thofe that be not able to be mended.

Die Lunæ prox' ante Feftum S. Matth. Apoftoli 13 Hen. VIII. At a common hall, enacted that no man fhall redeem the chamberlainfhip under the fum of 5l.; and if any Mayor do or would break this act, he is to forfeit 6l. to be levied by the Mayor fuc-ceeding; and if he will not execute it, he is to forfeit 10l. to be levied to the common wealth of the town.

Alfo, it is agreed that there fhall be found, at the charge of Mr. Mayor and his brethren and the forty-eight, ten able archers in harnefs, with bows and arrows, fwords and bucklers, with other able harnefs for their bodies; and five of them to be harneffed at the charge and coft of the twenty-four, and five at the charge of the forty-eight, to be ready within a day's warning, when the king pleafes to fend for them.

Fefto S. Matth. Apoftoli 13 Hen. VIII. *Robert Harward* elected mayor.—*Gilda Mercatorum*, 8.

The King, being about to declare war againft France, caufed a furvey to be made of all the lands in England, much in the nature of Domefday, in order to get an account of the wealth and eftates of his fubjects; which, when he had received, he fent commiffionors to demand money of them by way of loan.

" Capitales redditus ville Leyceftrie, in tempore ma-joratûs Roberti Harward.

Inprimis, 11s. 1vd. de uno tenemento apud Pontem Borealem, quondam Johannis London, modò in te-nurâ Roberti Walton, barber.

Item, 11s. de uno tenemento in le Northgate, modò in tenurâ Nicholai Cley, quondam Willielmi Whel-ton, per annum.

Item, xviiid. & 11 gallos de duabus cotagiis in le Northgate, de Thomâ Gaddifby, per annum.

Item, 11s. & 1 gallum de unâ peciâ terre infra clau-furam dicti Thome Gaddifby in le Afhlane, per annum.

Item, viiis. de uno meffuagio apud Portam Occi-dentalem, quondam Thome Hiklyn, per annum.

Item, 11id. de uno tenemento juxta Portam Auf-tralem, nuper in tenurâ Petri Davy, modò vocato le Pynfold, per annum.

Item,

Item, iiiid. de uno tenemento in parochiâ Sancti Nicholai Leyceſtrie, quondam Ricardi Cawthorn, nuper conceſſo communitati ville Leyceſtrie, per annum, in perpetuum.

Wheſtone, iiiid. de capitali redditu exeunte de tenemento W. Stretton in Wheſton predict', per annum.

Item, id. exeunt' unius tofti & dimidie virgate terre in tenurâ Willielmi Yannill in Wheſton, per annum.

Item, ixs. exeunt' unius tofti & dimidie virgate terre in tenurâ Johannis Skevyngton in Wheſton, per annum.

Item, ixs. exeunt' unius meſſuagii & dimidie virgate terre in tenurâ Thome Bodicote.

Item, vid. exeunt' unius meſſuagii in Coſby, juxta eccleſiam ibidem, in tenurâ Willielmi Dawbyn, alias vocati Broughton, per annum.

Item, vid. exeunt' de omnibus terris & tenementis in Scraptoft, modò Tho' Taylor de Wheſton, per ann'.

Item, ivd. de terris & tenementis Johannis Skevyngton in Wheſton, pro relaxatione ſecte curie ibidem.

Item, iid. exeunt' de terris & tenementis Willielmi de Webſter in Wheſton per annum [1]."

Die Veneris prox' ante Feſtum Sancti Clementis 13 Hen. VIII. At a common hall, enacted that brewers make good ale, and ſell for 1½d. a gallon.

Alſo, that tallow-chandlers ſell candles at 1d. the pound, on pain of 3s. 4d.

Alſo, that no perſon receive bread out of the country till it be ſeen and weighed before Mr. Mayor or his officers, and by the warden of the bakers, on pain to forfeit every time 12d. to be levied by the chamberlains, for the wealth of the town.

Alſo, that Mr. Mayor and his brethren ſhall prove all ordinals of all the occupations within the town; and thoſe that be good to allow them, and thoſe that be evil to damn them.

Alſo, that no one ſhall receive any corn that comes on the market-day to be ſold till it has been in the common market-places, and there ſet down till the market be full gathered, whether it be ſold or unſold, in pain of default, the firſt time, 12d. and every time to double.

Alſo, that all treſpaſſers that are committed for puniſhment to Mr. Mayor's hall ſhall take their victuals of the ſerjeant, except mens' ſons and prentices.

Alſo, that all bakers that ſell horſe-bread within the houſes to any gueſt ſell but two loaves for 1d. on pain of 3s. 4d.

Alſo, that all perſons on the market-day, having unladen their horſes, geldings, or mares, lead them out of the market-place, on pain of 2d. for every horſe, &c. taken in the market-place, to be levied by the chamberlains.

Die Veneris, 1ma Septimanâ Quadrageſimæ 13 Hen. VIII. At a common hall, the ſheep-penns were ſet to two perſons, whereof each to pay 33s. 4d.

In purſuance of a commiſſion from the King, March 30, 13 Hen. VIII. the conſtables were ſworn to preſent all perſons ſpiritual and temporal, widows, and all that were 16 years of age, ſhewing what harneſs they had meet for war, and the value of their goods, and the yearly value of their lands, tenements, and other profits, what they have or be worth, in their ſeveral wards; and if there be any retained, and to whom; and whether there be any aliens or ſtrangers born out of the king's allegiance; and who be lords, and whoſe tenants, and of whom they hold.

Die Veneris prox' poſt Feſtum Sancti Hugonis epiſcopi 13 Hen. VIII. At a common hall, ordered that brewers make good and wholeſome ale, and ſell for 1¼d. a gallon under the hair ſieve, and to give 13 gallons to the dozen, with God's good to the ſame; and that no brewer tun out till the ale-taſters have taſted their ale, on pain of 3s. 4d. the firſt time, and 6s. 8d. the ſecond time, &c.

Feſto S. Matth. 14 Hen. VIII. *William Bolte* elected mayor.—*Gilda Mercatorum,* 2.

At a common hall, on Friday next after the Annunciation of our Lady, 14 Hen. VIII. there were choſen burgeſſes for the preſent parliament, for the commons Mr. William Bolte mayor, and Mr. Roger Wygſton for the mayor's brethren.

Feſto S. Matth. 15 Hen. VIII. *Richard Reynolds* elected mayor.—*Gilda Mercatorum,* 18.

Die Veneris prox' poſt Feſtum Sancti Hugonis epiſcopi 15 Hen. VIII. Ordered, that all brewers make good and wholeſome ale, and ſell 14 gallons for 16d.

Alſo, that all brewers brew with no hops to be medyllyd within their maſhfat nor zelyngfat, on pain the firſt time of 3s. 4d. the ſecond 6s. 8d. the third 10s.

Alſo, that no brewers tun out ale till the ale-taſters have abyllyd it, on pain of 3s. 4d. Alſo, that no typlers ſell ale with unſealed meaſures, on pain of 12d.

Alſo, that tallow-chandlers make good candles, of good ſtuff and good wick, and to ſell 13lb. for 18d.; and 6½lb. for 9d.; and 3¼lb. for 4½d. on pain the firſt time 3s. 4d. the ſecond 6s. 8d. &c.

Allſo it is enactyd at the ſame comon hall, be the ſaid meyr and his brether' the xxiiii. and the xlviii electyd of the comyns, that this acte foloyng to be of effect, and evermore to theym that ſhall hereafter to be ferme and ſtable, that whoſoever be the marſter of Seynt Georgis gylde ſhall cauſe the George to be rydyn, accordyng to the olde auncient coſtome, that ys to ſey betewxt Sent George's day and Whytſondey, except a cauſſe reaſſonnable; and he or they that make defaute in rydyng of the ſeyd Georg of the ſeid maiſter or maiſters to forfet, frome the day of this acte forthwards, vli.; and that to be levied of the ſeid maiſter or maiſters, to the behew and uſe of the ſeyd gyld, by the meir for the tyme beyng and the chamburleyns: And yf the ſeyd meyr and chamberleyns be necligent in ataching or levyeng of the ſcid forfet, that then the meire to forfet xxvis. viiid. and eyther chamburleyn to forfet vis. viiid. and to be peyd to the profet of the ſame gyld.

Moreover, that all forfeits made by the maſters ſince the laſt time that the George was ridden, ſhall be paid to the profit of the ſame gild, of every wrangler behind 26s. 8d.

Alſo, that no waterman carry no burne upon the Sunday without cauſe reaſonable, on pain of impriſonment.

Alſo, that the Swines market ſhall be kept, from this day forth, in the Parchment lane, and no more in the High ſtreet [and] in the Eaſt gate.

Alſo, that all bakers that carry into the country ſhall bring their bread on horſeback to the mayor, or to the wardens of the craft, and there to be weighed, and ſeen that it be able paſte and wholeſome, on pain of forfeit the firſt time 12d. the ſecond time 20d. the third time 3s. 4d. &c.

Alſo, that every one abſent from the common hall pay the old forfeit, without a cauſe reaſonable; i. e. every one of the twenty-four 12d. and of the forty-eight 6d. to be levied by the chamberlains.

Feſto S. Matth. 16 Hen. VIII. *Robert Staples* elected mayor.

Ralph Swyllyngton, recorder, died this year; and in his room was choſen *Thomas Brokſby,* alias *Broxby.* —*Gilda Mercatorum,* 21.

Robertus Staples nuper defunctus eſt in die Epiphaniæ Domini; & ad communem aulam tent' die Lunæ prox' poſt Feſtum Sancti Hilarii electus erat *Henricus Gillot* in loco ipſius Roberti in officium majoratûs per totum conſilium confratrum & XLVIII.

Et in feſto S. Matth. 17 Hen. VIII. dictus Robertus & Henricus Gillot amoti ſunt ab officio majoratûs, & in loco eorum electus eſt *Edward Beyr.*

Feſto S. Matth. 18 Hen. VIII. *John Weſtwiſe* elected mayor.—*Gilda Mercatorum,* 12.

In this year the Corporation of Leiceſter thought it expedient to procure the following exemplification, under the great ſeal of England:

" Henricus Octavus, Dei gratiâ, &c. omnibus ad quos, &c. ſalutem. Inſpeximus quoddam breve noſtrum de certiorand', Theſaurario & Camerariis noſtris direct', necnon certificationem ejuſdem nobis in Cancellariam noſtram miſſam, & in filaciis ejuſdem Cancellarie reſidentem, in hec verba: ' Henricus Octavus,

[1] Carte, MS.

&c.

&c. Thefaurario & Camerariis fuis falutem, Volentes, certis de caufis, certiorari utrum villa noftra Leyceftrie, alias dicta *Ledecefter*, fit de antiquo dominico Corone Anglie necne, vobis mandamus, quod, fcrutatis rotulis, recordis, & aliis memorandis noftris, penes vos remanentes, de eo quod inde inveneritis, tenores earundem nobis in Cancellariam noftram, fub figillis veftris, diftincte & aperte, fine dilatione mittatis, una cum hoc breve, ut, infpectis tenoribus predictis, ulterius inde fieri faciamus quod juris fuerit & rationis, & per eandem curiam Cancellarie noftre confideratum fuerit in hac parte & decretum. Tefte meipfo, apud Weftm', 19° die Novembris, anno regni noftri decimo octavo. PEXSALL.'

" Refponfio Thefaurarii & Camerariorum: 'Scrutato Libro veftro de *Domefday*, in Thefauraria veftra fub cuftodia noftra exiftente, & de eo quod invenimus tangente villam infrafcriptam vobis mittimus in quadam fcedula huic brevi confuta.

' In Libro de Domefday, inter alia, continetur fic; videlicet, ' *LEDECESTRESCYRE*.

Civitas de Ledeceftre tepore Regis Edwardi reddeb' p annu Regi . xxx lib' ad numerum de xxᵗⁱ . in ora . 7 xv . fextar' mellis.

Quando Rex ibat in exercitu per terra :' de ipfo burgo xii . burgenfes ibant cu eo . Si u per mare in hofte ibat ; :' mittebant ei . iiii . equos de eod' burgo ufque Londonia . ad coportand' arma uel alia quæ opus . eet.

Modo ht Rex . W . p omib' redditib' ciuitatis ej'dem 7 comitat' . xl . ii . lib' 7 x . folid' ad pond'.

Pro i accipitre x lib' ad numer' p fumario xxᵗⁱ fol'. De monetarijs . xx . lib' per annu de . xx . in ora . De his xx lib' ht Hugo de Grentemaifnil teiu denariu.'

[*&c. &c. as in vol. I. p. 1. ending with*] Silva tot' Vicecomitat' *Herefwode* vocat' ht iiii leu' in lg, & i leu' in lat'.'

" Nos autem renorem certificationis predicte, ad inftanciam majoris & comitatus ville predicte, duximus exemplificandam per prefentes. In cujus rei teftimonium, has literas noftras fieri fecimus patentes. Tefte meipfo, apud Weftm', vicefimo tertio die Novembris, anno regni noftri decimo octavo. PEXSALL.

Exʳ per { Will'm Throkmerton, Radulphum Pexfall, } Clericos."

Fefto S. Matth. 19 Hen. VIII. *Thomas Burton* elected mayor.—*Gilda Mercatorum*, 7.

Fefto S. Matth. 20 Hen. VIII. *Roger Gyllat* elected mayor.—*Gilda Mercatorum*, 5.

At a common hall, holden at Corpus Chrifti hall 11th of Auguft, 21 Hen. VIII. it was agreed to give to John Beaumont, gent. 6s. 8d. fee, to anfwer in fuch caufes as the town fhall need and require.

Fefto S. Matth. 21 Hen. VIII. *Thomas Bett* elected mayor.

At the common hall this day agreed, that if any of the forty-eight be elected by the mayor and his brethren comburgeffes to be of the faid comburgeffes, and refufe it, that then he forfeit 10l. to be levied by the chamberlains.

Mem. the 27th day of March, there was brought to Thomas Bett, then mayor of Leicefter, hawthorn budytt furth, baene flowres, and a cullumbell flour.

Fefto S. Matth. 22 Hen. VIII. *William Tebb* elected mayor. In this year Cardinal Wolfey died in Leicefter Abbey.

Friday after St. Hugh's day, at a common hall, enacted that brewers fhall give twelve gallons for 15d. and fmall ale ob. the gallon; and they to make good ale. Alfo, that no chandler fell above 2½d. the pound till Candlemas, on pain of 6s. 8d.; and fhall not fell dozens or half dozens by wholefale into the country except by licence of the mayor, on forfeiture of 6s. 8d.

The eldeft fon of a freeman paid 2d. others 10s. to be made free. [What each perfon paid is firft mentioned 15 Hen. VIII.]

Fefto S. Matth. 23 Hen. VIII. *Nicholas Rennold* elected mayor. Thomas Cattelyn was then bailiff.—*Gilda Mercatorum*, 3.

Mem. there was brought to Mr. Nicholas Reynolds, on St. Leonard's day, a chefter of appletree blooms. Here follows the charter of 4 Edward IV. which

Vol. I.

has been printed in p. 374; and after that an account of feveral tranfactions and orders paffed in time of feveral mayors aforegoing, as followeth in part:

A letter of Henry VIII. to the juftices of Leicefterfhire, with a proclamation for enforcing the laws for purfuit and fuppreffion of robbers and rioters.

Another of Jan. 31, 1 Hen. VIII. about vagabonds and beggars.

[Here ends the old Hall Book, ufed temp. Edw. IV. Ric. III. and till 23 Hen. VIII. The following book contains the reft of the reign of Henry VIII. Edward VI. and Mary.]

23 Feb. at a common hall, enacted that no man enter into the chapman's gild but he fhall pay the 10s. within the year.

Agreed by the twenty-four, the 5th April, that Mr. Chriftopher Clught fhould not ride the George this year, for divers confiderations.

Mem. It was agreed before Nicholas Rennold, then mayor of Leicefter, by confent of the wardens and all the company of journeymen fhoemakers in the town, that they fhall give yearly to the Auftin Freers in Leicefter, for all the brethren and fifterne to be prayed for, in ready money 10s. to be paid at two times in the year, befides the offering-days afore-ufed.

Fefto S. Matth. 24 Hen. VIII. *John Barton* elected mayor.—*Gilda Mercatorum*, 12.

22 Nov. at a common hall, it was agreed, in cafe of coming late to a common hall (upon reafonable warnings), the mayor's brethren to pay 6d. if the mayor be fitting; and if they come after, each to pay 12d.; and if any of the forty-eight come too late, he is to pay 3d. if the mayor be fitting; and if after he is up, then to pay 6d.

Alfo, that no brewer fell above 2d. the gallon.

Roger Redcliff, efq. (high fheriff in 1529) was appointed by the king's writ, June 30, 1534, to take the ecclefiaftical furvey of the county of Leicefter.

Fefto S. Matth. 25 Hen. VIII. *Chriftopher Clught*, alias *Clough*, elected mayor.—*Gilda Mercatorum*, 10.

20 Nov. at a common hall, agreed that no brewer that is a common brewer fell above 1¼d. a gallon; and that no brewer fell in his houfe above 3d. a gallon; and that no chandler fell above 1½d. per pound, and carry none into the country except they afk leave of the mayor.

Fefto S. Matth. 26 Hen. VIII. *William Bolte* elected mayor.—*Gilda Mercatorum*, 12.

Fefto S. Matth. 27 Hen. VIII. *Thomas Burton* elected mayor.—*Gilda Mercatorum*, 9.

19 Nov. at a common hall, enacted that brewers fell ale for 2d. a gallon; and that chandlers fell caudles at 1½d. per pound, and 13 to the dozen.

Fefto S. Matth. 28 Hen. VIII. *Roger Gyllot* elected mayor.—*Gilda Mercatorum*, 27.

Mr. *Thomas Bruxby* continued to be recorder till the laft year inclufive; but this year *John Baymond* was recorder, and fo continued till 33 Hen. VIII.

Thomas Catlyn was then bailiff of Leicefter.

Fefto S. Matth. 17 Hen. VIII. *Randyll Awood* elected mayor.—*Gilda Mercatorum*, 14.

Nov. 16, 29 Hen. VIII. at a common hall, agreed that brewers fell for 1d. a gallon: and chandlers fell for 1½d. a pound, and 13 to the dozen.

Fefto S. Matth. 30 Hen. VIII. *William Pratt* elected mayor.—*Gilda Mercatorum*, 10.

Fefto S. Matth. 31 Hen. VIII. *Nicholas Reynold* elected mayor the fecond time. The fine for abfence of any of the twenty-four was made 8d.; of the forty-eight 4d.—*Gilda Mercatorum*, 17.

Leicefter Abbey fuppreffed in this year.

18 Jan. at a common hall, it was enacted that no craftfmen nor vitteller, being foreigners, fhall fell ware or victuals, except by wholefale, on the marketday within the town.

Jan. 29, the occupation of Smiths gave to the chamber of the town 13s. 4d. towards the charges of the town now at this term, &c. The Butchers gave 26s. 8d.; and the Bakers gave 6s. 8d.

King Henry VIII. granted to the mayor and burgeffes of Leicefter two fairs, to be held five days apiece; the one upon the feaft of the Nativity of St.

John the Baptift, and the other on the feaft-day of the Conception of our Lady, and two days before and two after, free from toll, ftallage, &c. with the government of the fair and ordering of the ftalls to the mayor and two or three burgeffes, to be yearly chofen, now called Stewards of the fair.

"Henricus Octavus, Dei gratiâ, Anglie et Francie rex, fidei defenfor, dominus Hibernie, et in terrâ fupremum caput Anglicane ecclefie, omnibus ad quos prefentes litere pervenerint falutem. Sciatis quod nos, ob affeccionem et dileccionem quas habemus et gerimus ad villam noftram Leyceftrie, ac ad communem utilitatem ejufdem, necnon dilectis et fidelibus noftris majori et burgenfibus ibidem commorantibus, de gratiâ noftrâ fpeciali, ac ex certâ fcientiâ et mero motu noftris, conceffimus, ac per prefentes, quantum in nobis eft, pro nobis, heredibus et fuccefforibus noftris, concedimus eifdem majori et burgenfibus ville noftre Leyceftrie predicte, et fuccefforibus fuis in perpetuum, quandam feriam apud eandem villam Leyceftrie et fuburbia ejufdem, fingulis annis, per quinque dies duraturam; videlicet, duobus diebus ante feftum Nativitatis Sancti Johannis Baptifte, et in die ejufdem fefti, et duobus diebus idem feftum proximè fequentibus. Et infuper fciatis quod nos, pro confideracionibus predictis, conceffimus, ac per prefentes concedimus et confirmamus, prefatis majori et burgenfibus predicte ville Leyceftrie, et fuccefforibus fuis, quandam aliam feriam apud eandem villam Leyceftrie, et fuburbia ejufdem, fingulis annis per quinque dies duraturum; videlicet, duobus diebus proximè ante feftum Conceptionis beate Marie Virginis, et in die ejufdem fefti, et in duobus diebus idem feftum proximè fequentibus, in perpetuum; ita quod quilibet indigena five alienigena ad dictam villam Leyceftrie et fuburbia ejufdem, caufâ feriarum predictarum feu earum alicujus veniens, et ibidem moram faciens, et exinde recedens, tam in dictis feriis et in earum quâlibet, quam ante et poft, in perpetuum, fit quietus de theoloneo, ftallagio, picagio, et aliis cuftumis et preftacionibus quibufcumque, nobis, heredibus vel fuccefforibus noftris, racione feriarum predictarum feu eorum alicujus qualitercumque fpectantibus, accedentibus, five pertinentibus. Volumus infuper et concedimus, pro nobis, heredibus et fuccefforibus noftris, ac per prefentes confirmamus, prefatis majori et burgenfibus predicte ville Leyceftrie, et fuccefforibus fuis in perpetuum, omnem et omnimodò ordinacionem, gubernacionem, et affignacionem ftallorum et placearum in predictis feriis et in earum quâlibet, ac totum regimen earundem feriarum, et earum cujuflibet, et omnium fingularum libertatum et aliarum confuetudinum ad eafdem ferias et quamlibet eorum fpectantium, per majorem ejufdem ville Leyceftrie qui pro tempore fuerit, et duos vel tres de probioribus et melioribus hominibus ejufdem ville, in auxilium ipfius majoris ad hoc annuatim electis, deputatis et juratis per dictos majorem et burgenfes, fine impedimento feu perturbacione noftri vel heredum noftrorum, feu aliorum miniftrorum noftrorum quorumcumque; ita quod predicte ferie, feu earum aliqua, non fint vel fit in prejudicium vel nocumentum aliquarum feriarum vicinarum; eo quod expreffa mencio de vero valore annuo, aut de certitudine premifforum, vel eorum alicujus, aut de aliis donis five conceffionibus per nos vel per aliquem progenitorum noftrorum prefatis majori et burgenfibus ante hec tempora factis in prefentibus minimè factis exiftat, aut aliquo ftatuto, actu, ordinacione, five provifione, inde in contrarium factis, editis, ordinatis, five provifis, aut aliâ re, caufâ, vel materiâ quâcumque, in aliquo non obftante. In cujus rei teftimonium, has literas noftras fieri fecimus patentes. Tefte meipfo, apud Walden, vicefimo die Marcii, anno regni noftri 31°."[1]

12 March, the King having granted to the town two fairs (Midfummer fair, and the Conception of our Lady before Chriftmas), over and befides two fairs antiently granted by the King's progenitors;

Towards the charges of the charter under the great feal, the mafters, wardens, and ftewards of the gilds of Corpus Chrifti and St. Margaret's, in the name of the brotherhood, gave 20l.; viz. each of the gilds 10l. And it was agreed that this fhould be regiftered in the Town-book, to remain for ever.

Received of the mafter and ftewards of Corpus Chrifti gild, towards the charges of labouring the King's charter for two new fairs for the town of Leicefter, 10l.; of the gild of St. Margaret's, for the fame, 10l.; of the occupation of Bakers, 6s. 8d.; of the Butchers, 26s. 8d.; of the Smiths, 13s. 4d. In all, 22l. 6s. 8d.

The chamberlains paid to Mr. Barton, for riding to London and Waldyng, and for fealing the charter, 10l. 2s. 11d.; to Robert Cotton, for like charges, 9l. 14s. 10d.; to Mr. Gyllot, for the town's bufinefs, 6s. 8d.; to Mr. Wood, for the like, 6s. 8d.; to Mr. Bolte, for riding to London, 40s. In all, 22l. 11s. 1d.

So that the town was at no more charge than 4s. 5d.

Fefto S. Matth. 32 Hen. VIII. *Robert Gaddifby* elected mayor.—*Gilda Mercatorum,* 14.

This year, in the account of the election, the King has given him the title of "Fidei Defenfor, & in terrâ Supremum Caput Anglicanæ Ecclefiæ," and fo often to the end of the book.

Fefto S. Matth. 33 Hen. VIII. *Hugh Afton* elected mayor.—*Gilda Mercatorum,* 13.

This year *John Baymond* is mentioned as recorder; but his name is blotted out, and inftead thereof is inferted *Edward Gryffyn* recorder, who continued fo till 3 Edw. VI. inclufive.

Ale under the fieve for 1½d. a gallon, 13 to the dozen; candles 1½d. a pound, 13 to the dozen.

Fefto S. Matth. 34 Hen. VIII. *Thomas Creffy* elected mayor.—*Gilda Mercatorum,* . . .

Fefto S. Matth. 35 Hen. VIII. *Chriftopher Clugh* elected mayor.—*Gilda Mercatorum,* 10.

Oct. 5, at a common hall, Mr. Mey, mafter of St. George's gild, becaufe the George was not ridden, paid 40s.

Fefto S. Matth. 36 Hen. VIII. *William Ollyffe* elected mayor.—*Gilda Mercatorum,* 9.

Fefto S. Matth. 37 Hen. VIII. *Robert Cotton* elected mayor.—*Gilda Mercatorum,* 10.

"One William Foxby having fallen afleep, could not be awaked, by pinching and burning, till after fourteen days; and when awaked was found, in all points, as if he had fleep butt one night[2]."

19 March. At a common hall, enacted, that if the mayor and his brethren choofe any of the forty-eight to be one of the 24 comburgeffes, and he refufe, he fhall pay 10l. half to the king, and half to the town; and for non-payment, to be put into wards.

At the fame hall, enacted, that if any inhabitant fummoned by the conftable or mayor's officers come not to the common hall at any hour appointed, or to attend the mayor, to ride to meet the king, or to do any other thing that fhall be to the pleafure or worfhip of the town, without reafonable caufe or fpecial licence of the mayor, he fhall forfeit, if of the twenty-four, 12d.; and the forty-eight, or other, 6d.: And if any of the twenty-four or forty-eight refufe to pay, the mayor may commit him to ward till he pay; and if the mayor be negligent or forgetful in executing this act, then he is to forfeit 2s. and the fucceeding mayor fhall have power to levy it; and if he refufe payment, to commit him till he pay all fuch forfeitures. [This act was firft made at a common hall, on Thurfday before St. Simon and Jude, 7 Edw. IV. Mr. Richard Gyllot being mayor; and, laft of all, confirmed 29 Jan. 1 Mary, in the mayoralty of Mr. Thomas Davinport, for ever to endure.]

20 Nov. Mr. Robert Cotton, then mayor, &c. purchafed, in name of the town, of Richard Roger and Robert Taverner, gents. a chief going out of a piece of ground of 12d. a year to the King, belonging to the Court of Augmentation (which piece of ground

---

[1] Pat. 31 Hen VIII.   [2] In the margin of a book containing a lift of the Mayors of Leicefter.

was

was given to the town by the earl of Huntingdon), paying, for the said chief of 12*d.*, 20*s.*

Festo S. Matth. 28 Henry VIII. *Robert May* elected mayor.—*Gilda Mercatorum*, 11.

Ale under the sieve, 1½*d.*; stale ale, 2*d.* a gallon, and 13 to the dozen; candles, 2*d. per* pound, 13 to the dozen.

EDWARD VI.

King Edward VI. in the first year of his reign, re-citing the charter of King John, for freedom of toll; and the patent of Edw. III. for Michaelmas fair; the patent of Ric. II. for confirmation of the patent of King John, for fines in the portmote court; and the patent of 13 Edw. IV. for May-day fair; and the charter of 4 Edw. IV. for making of justices of peace; and the charter of Hen. VII. for confirmation of that patent, and for the enlargement of the authority of justices of peace; doth approve, ratify, and confirm all the said charters [1].

About the 13th of May, Robert Maye being mayor, the town purchased of Thomas Danet, of Bronkynsthorp, esq. and bailiff to the king in the liberties of Leicester, the office of the said bailiwick, for which he had a patent for his life; for which they gave him 80*l.*; of which Thomas Dey, clerk, born in Leicester, and some time canon of the late monastery of St. Mary in Leicester, and also prebendary of St. Stephen's in Westminster, gave them 20*l.*

Festo S. Matth. 1 Edw. VI. *Ranulph Wood* elected mayor.—*Gilda Mercatorum*, 12.

Nov. 20, Thomas Dave, by consent of the parish of St. Margaret, paid 3*l.* 6*s.* 8*d.* towards the maintenance of the chamber of the town of Leicester.

Ale, 1¼*d.* 13 to the dozen; candles, 2*d. per* pound.

Many years before and after, the eldest son paid 2*d.* the second son 5*s.* others 10*s.* for their freedom; and 2*d.* for swearing.

18 April, " Rex concessit Thome Hawkins molendinum equinum, ac unum tenementum, ac quatuor shopas, cum omnibus pertinentiis, &c. situat' infra villam Leicestrie, in Foro ibidem vocato Swynesmarket, habend' pro termino vite."

Money gathered for setting forth 11 horsemen, to go with sir Richard Manners into Scotland, 6 Aug. 2 Edw. VI.; Randall Wood mayor the second time:

Paid, for the 11 horses and harness, with other furniture at the same time, 47*l.* 4*s.* 8*d.*

Gathered, of divers churches in the town, towards the said charge, 48*l.* 3*s.* 4*d.*; viz.

Received of the churchwardens of St. Peter's, towards the same, 2*l.* 13*s.* 4*d.*; of the churchwardens of Allhallows, 6*l.*; of St. Margaret's, 10*l.*; of the churchwardens of St. Nicholas, 3*l.*; of St. Martin's, 18*l.* 10*s.*; of St. Mary's, 8*l.*—in all 48*l.* 3*s.* 4*d.*; of which the surplus is 18*s.* 8*d.* Which was put into the hands of the chamberlains, Mr. Nicholas Reynolds being mayor.

Festo S. Matth. 2 Edw. VI. *John Gatlyff* elected mayor.—*Gilda Mercatorum*, 7.

Festo S. Matth. 3 Edw. VI. *Nicholas Reynold* elected mayor.—*Gilda Mercatorum*, 14.

" The coppy of my lord of Huntyngdon's lett*r* sent to Mr. Mayor and his brethren, with the eyght and forty, as herafter follyth:

' To my assuered friends the mayor of Leycester and his brethr'n and to evry of them, geve this wythe spede.

' After my ryght harty comendacõns: thes be to advtyse you that I am commaunded by the Kyng's Ma*tie*, and hys moste honorable councell, to sve in the parties beyond the sees, wythe suche a numbre as to me by them ys appoynted to be ther generell captane in the hole jurney (of whych numbre I am assygnyd to have of myne owne furnyture ccc able men), they to be levyed, by vertue of the Kyng's Ma*ties* highe comyssyon under hys brod seale, of my frends, favorers, tenaunts, and servaunts: And for that I have

at all tymes reckneyd you to be my very frends, as heretofore I have approvyd the same; therfore nowe I hartely requyre you to furnyche unto me to goe in thys jurney suche and as many able men, wherof as many of them to be good archers and gunners, well furnyshed with armour, weapon, money, and horses, to serve them to the see syde, as ye may convenyently make; and ther horses shal be sent home to you agayne: And that I maye be assueryd from you to have them here at London with me within x days; for my tyme ys but xiiii days to tarye here, before I take my leave of the Kyng's Ma*tie* and hys honorable councell, to accomplyshe hys Grace's plesure and comaundement in hys affayers. And your frendshyps, to me shewed at thys presente, shall bynd me in frend-shype towards you, every of you, duryng my lyff. And thus I byd you hartily farewell. Wrytten the xiiii*th* of November, 1549.

Your friend, FRAUNCIS HUNTINGDON [2].'

" Money gathered for my lord Huntyngdon the xix*th* day of November, in the thyrd yere of the reigne of our Soveraigne Lord Kyng Edward the Sext, &c. in the tyme of may'alty of Mr. Nich'is Reynolds then beying mayor, of the benevolent wyll of the xxiiii and the xlviii, as folloythe.

[Here follow the names of the mayor and 19 of the aldermen (probably the then whole number), amongst whom were Mr. Nicholas Heyrek and Mr. John Heyrek; and the sums set against each of their names, as paid, are 5*s.* each, except that against the name of one of the aldermen, Mr. Otlyff, nothing is put; so he subscribed nothing.]

[Here follow the names of the whole forty-eight, all of whom subscribed something (except two); one of them subscribed 3*s.* 4*d.* many of them 2*s.* 8*d.* some 2*s.* others less. The whole amount was 10*l.*]

' 21 Nov. 3 Edw. VI. A copy of a receipt from Robert Templeman, servant to Mr. Thomas Hastyngs, by the hands of the mayor of Leicester, of the benevolent wyll of the said mayor and his brethren the xxiiii and the whole xlviii, in the name of the hole body of the seid towne of Leyc', of 10*l.* towards the furnyture of ccc men into Bulloign wythe th'erle of Huntyngdon.'

" The answere of the letter sent for the receypt of the seyd money:

' After my ryght hartye comendacõns; sygnyfyeng you that I have receyvyd from you consernyng my late requests made unto you, for my Sovayn affayres beyond the sees, wherby I perceve the lovyng, frendly, and hartye good wyll of you and every of you to me wards; wherfore I hartely thank you, and wil be glad, when yt shall plese God to send me prosperous retorne, and at a merye metyng, to shew you and every of you semblable plesure. And for that I cannot be in the countrey thys Crystmas, to have the company of you, wherof I wold have bene glad; my trustye servant Mychill Purpherey shall delyver you for a token, whensoever you shall call upon hym from me, two does, to make merye with at your plesures. And thus I byd you all hartily farewell. From my house in London, the xxv*th* of this present November, 1549.

Your frend assuered, FRAUNCIS HUNTYNGDON."

Festo S. Matth. 4 Edw. VI. *Robert Newcom* elected mayor. The foregoing year *Edward Gryffyn* was recorder; but this year *John Beamont* was recorder, and so continued 5 Edward VI.—*Gilda Mercatorum*, 31.

The sheep-penns were set for 8*l. per annum.*

At a common hall, it was agreed by the mayor, aldermen, and common-council-men, " That every man having any cattel goyng or pasturyng within the Cowhey shal fynde yerly, when nede shal requyre, a man to worke a day's worke about the same for the fencyng and safe kepeyng of the same pasture." It appears also, by this agreement, that those who refused were to pay 6*d.* for every beast; and the chamberlains of the town for the time being were empowered

---

[1] Pat. 1 Edw. VI. p. 6. n. 1.
[2] Extracted from the Town Book of Acts belonging to the Corporation of Leicester; xiiii° die Novembris, anno Regis Edwardi VI. tercio, in tempore Maiorält' Nicholai Reynolds.

to hire men and fet them at work in repairing and ditching the faid Cowhey.

16 Jan. At a common hall, the twenty-four agreed to pay each 2s. and the forty-eight 12d. each, towards charges of the fuit for agiftment in Beamont Leafe; and promifed to pay more, if more fhould need.

Money gathered for the fuit of Beaumont Leas, at two times, in the mayoralty of Mr. Robert Newcom, 20 February; viz. each time of the twenty-four, 2s. and of the forty-eight, 12d. apiece; at both times, 9l. 8s.

Item, given to the marquis of Dorfet, when he went to the North, two geldings, price 16l. 13s. 4d.; that is to fay, the twenty-four paid 5s. and the forty-eight 2s. 6d. each, which came to 11l. 15s.; and the reft was paid by the churches and by the chamberlains.

On the 20th of April, John Corbet doth grant, before Henry marquis of Dorfet, that the poor of Leicefter fhall have their milch kye going weekly (viz. in Beaumont Lees), from May-day till Lammas, after the rate of three half-pence a week, and the rich after the rate of 2d. a week, for every of them. Alfo the faid Corbet doth grant, that the poor of Leicefter fhall have their labouring horfes going from May-day to Lammas after the rate of 3d. the week, and the rich 4d. the week apiece; and fo to have them going, from year to year, as long as the faid Corbet doth occupy it.

6 Sept. there was allowed 6l. 13s. 4d. for keeping four poft-horfes; the twenty-four paying 3s. 4d. and the forty-eight 1s. 8d. each.

20 Sept. Thefe parcels are to be delivered from mayor to mayor, for the town's ufe. One great mace; four little maces; one lock-book; a purfe with five keyes, and the mayor's feal therein; three books for the common hall; one great paper-book for areafts; two books of the acts of parliament; one bag with . . . . weights for bread, after Troy weight, of four pounds; a bag of brafen weights, from fix pounds to half a pound; one brafen ftandard; one brafen ftrike; a brafen gallon; a pair of fcales for bread.

Fefto S. Matth. 5 Edw. VI. *Thomas Wilcocks* elected mayor.—*Gilda Mercatorum*, 10.

Johannes Beamont, Magifter Rotulorum Curiæ Cancellariæ Domini Regis, & Recordator Villæ Leic'.

20 Dec. At a common hall, agreed that if any one cut down any boughs, to fet at their doors or windows, out of any clofe, garden, or orchard, within the liberties of the town, he fhall forfeit 12d. and his body to prifon.

11 March. At a common hall, agreed that labour fhall be made immediately to London, to fee if they can get the land given by the Bifhop of Carlifle [1] to found a free fchool in Leicefter, in the parifh of St. Margaret, which land Mr. John Beamont hath 12 years paft fold away; and alfo to get the bailiwick of Leicefter in fee-farm to the town; and alfo to get the Bifhop's Fee joined with the faid town; and hath fent up for the fame Mr. Boughton, clerk, &c.; of whofe charges the parifh of St. Margaret one-half, and the town the other half.

20 June. At a common hall, agreed that, yearly, each of the twenty-four fhall make two carfeys, and each of the forty-eight one, to fet the poor to work; each carfey to be 18 yards long, and brought to the mayor's hall to be fealed; and upon failing, to forfeit 3s. 4d. to the poor man's box.

Agreed, that the bailiwick of Leicefter remain to one of the brethren that hath not been Mayor, to occupy every man in his order upon the bench; and if any of the twenty-four in his courfe refufe it, he to pay 40s. or to be committed.

Fefto S. Matth. 6 Edw. VI. *Nicholas Heyrek* elected mayor. *John Huntt* recorder.—*Gilda Mercatorum*, 8.—Candles at 3d. per pound.

Nov. 30, Mr. Overend promifed to pay to the chamberlains 40s. 20 Jan. next, for not occupying the bailiwick of the town.

The wayts collars, three weighing 23 ounces and 3 quarters.

19 May. At a common hall, agreed that no one fhall put any cattle into the Cowhey but two cows, or one cow and two heifers, which are his own, and neither ox nor fteer; yet a freeman may hire a milch cow or two, and put into the pafture for his own ufe; but not, under colour of hiring one cow, to find pafture for another, on pain, between May day and Lammas day, of 2s. 6d. for the firft time, 5s. the fecond, and the third time to lofe his freedom.

MARY.

In fefto S. Matth. Apoftoli, 1 Mariæ, *Willielmus Overend* electus eft in officium majoratûs; quod recufavit excercere, & petitus ad finem fuam admitti; & admittitur ad 20l. inde folvend'.

Ale at 2½d. and 13 to the dozen; candles 2¼d. and 13 to the dozen.

Fefto S. Matth. 1 Mariæ, *Thomas Davynport* elected mayor.—*Gilda Mercatorum*, 12. [Here was written *Johannes Hunt* recordator; but it is blotted out, and there is inferted *Francifcus Fernham* recordator, who continued to 3 and 4 Philip and Mary.]

Burgenfes Parliamenti villæ Leyc', *Willielmus Faunt, Thomas Farnebam*, armigeri.

At a common hall, 17 Nov. (a man having been killed in the ftreet in a night) it is enacted, that no perfon, of what degree fo ever, inhabiting in the town or fuburbs, go abroad in the ftreet after nine o'clock at night, and after the curfew bell leaves ringing, except officers and the watch: And if any perfon dwelling in town or fuburbs after nine o'clock be found in the ftreet, or keeping company out of his own houfe in any inn, tavern, or ale-houfe, without reafonable caufe to be known before the mayor or alderman of the quarter, he fhall forfeit the firft time 12d.; the fecond, 2s.; the third, fuffer imprifonment at the will of the mayor, or alderman of the ward: Alfo fuch keeper of the inn, tavern, or ale-houfe, for every time, fhall forfeit 12d. and fuffer imprifonment for fourteen days without favour; but ftrangers may have lawful paftime in their inns, but not go abroad without the good man of the houfe, or fome of his fervants, on pain of going to the ward, there to remain till examined by the mayor or juftices: And if any innkeeper or other occupying the lodging of guefts receive into their houfe any ftranger after the faid time, he fhall report the names and dwelling-places of fuch guefts on the morrow to the alderman of the ward, or his deputy, on pain of fuffering imprifonment for fourteen days without favour. And that the faid bell be rung, nightly, from Michaelmas till Lady-day in Lent; for which the twenty-four to pay 2d. and the forty-eight 1d. each.

At the fame hall [ordered that proclamation be made], that no perfon dwelling in Leicefter, or the fuburbs, cut down or carry any wood out of the New Park, Abbey Park, Stocking and Afhe clofe, or any other wood of the Queen's or any other perfons about the town, not being bought, on pain to be punifhed by the juftices of the fhire where he fhall be taken, and fent to the town to be likewife punifhed at the mayor and juftices' pleafure, and to be ordered as vagabonds, and banifhed the town for ever.

29 Nov. Mr. Smyth, for refufing to occupy the bailiwick, promifed to pay 40s.

Queen Mary, in the 1ft year of her reign, by charter, reciting the charter of Henry VIII. for two fairs to be held; the one at Midfummer day, and two days before and two days after; and the other at the Conception of our Lady, and two days before and two after; and the charter of Edw. VI. laft mentioned, and the confirmation of the former charter therein recited; doth alfo confirm, ratify, and allow the fame for her heirs and fucceffors [2].

19 Jan. At a common hall, it was agreed that a levy be made, in the manner of a fifteenth, for the charge of the confirmation of the charter, with other things; i. e. each of the twenty-four to pay 5s.

---

[1] Dr. John Penny, bifhop 1509—1520. See hereafter, under St. Margaret's parifh.   [2] Pat. 1 Mariæ, p. 2. m. 10.

and

and of the forty-eight 2s. 6d. and the reft to be gathered of the commoners of the town.

[In the title of this laft act the Queen has the ftyle of " Supreme Head of the Church of England and Ireland;" which is afterwards left out.]

16 March, 1 Mary. At a common hall, there were chofen burgeffes of the parliament, to be held at Oxford 2d April, *Francis Fernam* recorder, and *Thomas Jenkinfon* mercer.

[Here ends this book. The next book begins with the year aforegoing, and ends 10 Elizabeth.]

22 July, 2 Mary. At an affembly of the twenty-four, agreed that, at the requeft of the earl of Huntingdon, Anthony Gay fhall have the office of the mayor's ferjeantfhip at the next avoydance.

Die S. Matth. 21 Sept. 1 & 2 Philip & Mary, *John Berredge* elected mayor.—*Gilda Mercatorum*, 12.

26 Oct. At a common hall were chofen burgeffes of parliament, *Francis Fernham* recorder, and Mr. *Hugh Afton*.

9 Dec. At an affembly of the twenty-four, Mr. Jones, Mr. Hervy, and Mr. Welche, brought in an injunction for grinding at their mills; which was thought hurtful to the town, and to the King and Queen's mills of the Caftle. Agreed to fupprefs it; and thereupon the mayor and his brethren remitted the faid forfeiture: but this is to be no precedent to any that offend in like matter.

A letter fent from my Lord Chancellor to Mr. Mayor and his brethren, for the wearing of their apparel, in the time of the mayoralty of Mr. John Berredge. " After commendations; I underftand, by advertifement from the town, that diverfe of you, being rather defirous of new-fanglednefs, than contented to follow fuch ancient and laudable cuftoms as have had time out of mind their continuance, you have of late fought means to breke and abolifh fuch thereof whereby the common wealth is moft countenanced and fet forth; whereupon I thought meet to require fo many of you as be thus fondly affected, that, leaving of fuch vain fancies, ye would henceforth remain quiet, and contented to follow and allow fuch laudable cuftoms and rules as have alwaies been time out of mind ufed among you. Thus fare you well. At my houfe in London, this 8th of January, your loving friend."

8 March. At a common hall, agreed that every one chofen to the mayoralty fhall, during his office, wear fcarlet, on pain of forfeiting 5s. according as of old times it hath been accuftomed.

Alfo, agreed that when any venifon comes to the twenty-four and forty-eight by gift of any nobleman or gentleman, it fhall be eaten at the only cofts of the faid twenty-four and forty-eight, and no part of the charge to be borne by the chamber of the town.

Die S. Matth. 21 Sept. 2 & 3 Philip & Mary, *Robert Jonys, Johens,* feu *Jones,* elected mayor.—*Gilda Mercatorum*, 20.

Ale, 3d. per gallon, 12 gallons to the dozen, with fmall drink and grains; and to make penny ale for the poor at ob. per gallon; and the typlers to fell after 3½d.; candles 2d. per pound, 12 to the dozen.

Die S. Matth. 21 Sept. 3 & 4 Philip & Mary, *William Maube* elected mayor.—*Gilda Mercatorum*, 6.

Ale, 4d. the gallon, and 12 gallons to the dozen; typlers to fell after 4½d. the gallon; candles 3d. per pound, 13 to the dozen.

This year, Sept. 21, Mr. *Francis Fernham* was recorder; but at a common hall, 7 May, it was agreed that Mr. *Francis Gytton* fhall be recorder.

7 May. At a common hall, agreed that if any one caft into the Soar or river any weeds, or other filth, near any place where burne is taken up, he fhall forfeit the firft time 6d. the fecond 12d. and fo double; and afterwards imprifonment, as the mayor and juftices will.

Die S. Matth. 21 Sept. 4 & 5 Philip & Mary, *John Heireke, Eyrycke,* or *Heyryke,* elected mayor. *Francis Gytton,* recorder.—*Gilda Mercatorum*, 10.

Ale, 3d. per gallon, 13 to the dozen, and the typlers 3½d.; candles 3d. per pound, and no tallow-chandler to fell by wholefale.

Vol. I.

20 Nov. At a common hall, candles of late years having been very fcant and dear, which is fuppofed to be becaufe much tallow hath been fold to ftrangers; it is enacted that no town butcher fell tallow to any ftranger, from Michaelmas to Candlemas, on forfeiture of 12d. for every ftone; except the ftranger, with two tradefmen, will be bound to the mayor to bring to the town, for every ftone of tallow, 12lb. of candles on the next market-day. [Here is firft inferted the names of all the twenty-four and forty-eight.]

The ten wards of the town of Leicefter:

The firft ward from South gate to St. James's chapel.

Second, from South gate to the High Crofs, with the Soar lane and Redcrofs ftreet.

Third, from the High Crofs to the North gate.

Fourth, from the North gate to North bridge and Senvy gate, with the Soar lane.

Fifth, St. Nicholas parifh, and fo without the Weft gate.

Sixth, the Swine's market; i.e. from High Crofs to the Eaft gate.

Seventh, from the High ftreet beyond the Hels houfe, and fo all the Church gate down to Mr. Nicholas Heyrick's and Parchment lane.

Eighth, all the Market-place, Cank-well, and to the Eaft gate.

Ninth, Belgrave gate and St. Margaret's Church gate.

Tenth, from the bridge by the Antelope, the Roundell, and Gallowtre gate.

Jan. 11. At a common hall, there were chofen for burgeffes of parliament Robert Breame recorder, and Mr. Maurice Tyrrell. [*Robert Breame,* alias *Breham,* alias *Braham,* being chofen recorder about this time, continued fo till 16 Eliz. inclufive.]

At the fame common hall, agreed that no one fhall work wax in tapers or candles to be fold, but thofe that be wax-chandlers, or will become of their company; provided that none of the faid occupation fhall take, for the making other tapers or other candle, above 1d. per pound.

4 March. At a common hall, agreed that the charge of Whefton court fhall not amount, nor be chargeable to the town, above 10s. at a day.

Ale, 2½d. per gallon, 12 to the dozen; candles, 2½d. per pound.

Fefto S. Matth. 5 & 6 Philip & Mary, Robert Harby paid 20l. as a fine for the mayoralty. *Robert Fletcher* elected mayor.—*Gilda Mercatorum*, 23.

Ale, 3d. per gallon, 13 to the dozen; typlers to fell for 3½d.: And ordered, that none that brew head ale in their houfes fell above 4d. per gallon; candles, 3d. per pound.

In fome part of the reign of Queen Mary the following letter was written:

" Broughton to Coñyfby.

Grace and peace from God, &c. As I cannot but wifh unto you all health and felicity in our Lord Jefus, moft gentle Mr. Coñyfby; even fo can I not but render unto you moft hearty and Chriftian thanks for your moft Chriftian and gentle benevolence; which the Lord (when I cannot) render unto you in the day of his coming! Amen.—And now, Sir, you fhall underftand, that Mafter Mayer hath entreated me urgently, as this bringer fhall more at large declare unto you, to whom I pray you give credit: for, immediately as we were come to Laycefter, he fent me forthwith to the moft vile prifon called Gaynsborrow, and then offered to put gyves and fetters upon my legs, and fo to lye upon the hard planchers without bed or ftraw, and without company or comfort; and all for becaufe that, when I could not entreat him to fhew me his lawful favour, I bad him then to do his worft; with the which word he was brought into fuch a fury, or rather frenfye, that he called me knave, villain, yea, vile and wrangling knave, and alfo roonagate. And all thefe words fo multiplied at once upon me upon none other caufe than is above mentioned, as I fhall anfwer before the Judgment-feat of God in the laft day. But you fhall underftand all by this bringer. And now I fhall defire you, that for as much as I cannot, and, if I could, dare not, by myfelf or my friends, in the dangerous bands of good abering; and do therefore, not only to my great coft and charges, but alfo to my utter undoing, remain in prifon; it would pleafe you, for Chrift his fake (the caufe of my imprifonment confidered to be utterly vain and falfe, as I before the Queen's Commiffioners have offered, and do ftill offer, to prove; yea, and that upon the peril of life and death), to be fo much my friend, as to fpeak to the right honourable and my fpecial good mafter and yours fir Edward Haftynges, that he will fpeak to the Commiffioners and Lords of the Counfel, that I may be releafed and reftored to liberty: and fo fhall I have caufe, as I am bound already, to pray unto God both for him and you. And thus, for this time, I bid you in Chrift moft heartily well to fare. Amen.

Yours at commaundement, Robert Broughton[1]."

ELIZABETH.

Queen Elizabeth, in the firft year of her reign, by her charter, reciting the laft charter of Queen Mary of confirmation, and the former charters therein mentioned, doth, for her, her heirs and fucceffors, ratify, approve, confirm, and allow the fame[2].

Fefto S. Matth. 1 Eliz. *Thomas Stanforde* elected mayor.—*Gilda Mercatorum*, 23.

28 April. At a common hall, agreed that Mr. Mayor and two or three of his brethren fhall go to London, at the term following, to try the liberties of the town, and to do other bufinefs; and have appointed John Eyrycke to be lieutenant in his abfence for that time being. [Here is, the fecond time, the names of all the twenty-four and forty-eight.]

29 October. Agreed, at a common hall, that a levy be made in the town, in manner of a fifteenth, for the charges of confirming the charter and other things; viz. every of the twenty-four to pay 3s. 4d. (of which three were lacking), and of the forty-eight 2od. each, and the refidue to be gathered of the commonalty.

The twenty-one came to 3l. 10s. the forty-eight to 4l. the commonalty to 3l. 14s.; the total 11l. 4s.

Fefto S. Matth. 2 Eliz. *Richard Derker* elected mayor.—*Gilda Mercatorum*, 22.

Ale, 3d. per gallon, 12 to the dozen; typlers to fell 3½d. and head ale 4½d. per gallon; candles, 3d. per pound.—Here, and fo annually for the mayor, are fet down the names of the twenty-four and forty-eight.

Fefto S. Matth. 3 Eliz. *Thomas Hallam* elected mayor.—*Gilda Mercatorum*, 15.

This year fome made free paid 20s. others 10s. &c.; and for fwearing, 2d.

20 Feb. 4 Eliz. At a common hall, ordered that no new matter be put into any ordinal, but it fhall be firft agreed upon at a common hall, or at leaft by the mayor and two juftices of the peace.

Item, that there be of every houfe one at every fermon on Wednefday and Friday, on pain of every houfholder making default to forfeit 4d.

Item, that no victualler keep open his door in fervice-time upon the Sabbath-day or holy days; to forfeit, for every default, 3s. 4d. common innkeepers only excepted; and that no one keep open their fhop-windows nor door in fervice-time on like pain.

Item, that in every parifh two be chofen to make collection for the poor.

Item, that every ftranger that hath not been prentice in the town, nor born in the fame, fhall pay for his freedom 20s.; and otherwife not to be made free.

6 July, 4 Eliz. At a common hall, agreed that each of the twenty-four pay 20s. and of the forty-eight 10s. to the chamberlain, on Friday next, towards repairing the town againft the Queen's coming; and that every alderman bring in the names of every one of the commonalty in his ward able to be taxed on Wednefday next, to be taxed by the mayor and juftices, according to his ability and their difcretion: Alfo, that every one pave before his door and compafs of his houfe immediately.

Here is inferted the oath of the Mayor, of the Mayor's Brethren, of them that enter into the Chapmans' Gild, of the Chamberlains, of the Fifh Sayers, of the Flefh Sayers, of the Conftables, of the Third Borowes, of the Ale Tafters, of the Leather Sayers, of the Occupations, and of the Recorder.

Fefto S. Matth. 4 Eliz. *William Reynolds* elected mayor.—*Gilda Mercatorum*, 37.

Jan. 16, 1562-3, a great tempeft of wind and thunder happened in the town of Leicefter; which uncovered 411 baies of houfes, and overturned many[3].

20 Nov. 5 Eliz. At a common hall, agreed that no one fhall receive or keep in his houfe any ftranger above three days, without giving notice to the mayor or to the alderman of the ward, unlefs he knows from whence he comes, and knows him to be honeft, and will undertake for him, on pain of forfeiting for every day 6s. 8d.

21 Nov. At a common hall, agreed that no butcher fell any flefh on a Sunday after feven o'clock in the morning, till all divine fervice be done in the parifh churches, on pain of 12d.

Item, that no milner nor loadfman carry any corn, malt, or meal, to or from their milns on Sundays till Evening prayer be done in all or moft parifh churches, on pain of 12d.

Item, that all good cuftoms made, and in this book written, fhall ftand in force.

Item, that no one that hath appeared depart any common hall till the mayor depart, without licence of the mayor, on pain of 6d.

Item, that no perfon lay muck in any other place in the ftreets or lanes than fuch as is or fhall be appointed, on pain of 4d.

2 Dec. *Robert Breham* recorder, and *Robert Broxby*, efq. were, at a common hall, chofen burgeffes for the parliament.

5 May. At a common hall, agreed that the order for orphans' goods fhall be entered, and take effect.

Fefto S. Matth. 5 Eliz. *Richard Davye* elected mayor.—*Gilda Mercatorum*, 14.

The weight of the bells of St. Peter's: The great bell, 11 cwt. 16 lb.; the third bell, 8 cwt. 26 lb.; the fecond bell, 6 cwt. 18 lb.; the forebell, 5 cwt. 10 lb. Summa totalis, 32 cwt. 13 lb.

19 Nov. 6 Eliz. At a common hall, agreed that no town-dwellers fhall fit and tipple in any alehoufe; but if any fuch will drink ale or beer, they fhall fend for the fame to their own houfes, on pain, for every default, to forfeit 3s. 4d. [3s. 4d. is ftruck out, and there is put in 12d.]

At a common hall, held Jan. 7, it was agreed, by the wholl confent of the fame theire affembled, that there fhold be gyven my lorde of Huntyngdon, for his welcome to the towne, one yoke of fat oxfon of x li. pce; and a fchore of fat wethers, pce . . . . . to be gyven to my lorde Haftyngs of Loughborowe, for theire frendfhip and good wyll towards this towne of Leic' fhewed.

The laft of June, 6 Eliz. At a common hall, enacted that if any one, dwelling within the liberties of Leicefter, be vifited with the plague, and prefume to go among them that are clear within two months after, that any one die in his houfe, he or fhe fhall forfeit 5l. to the chamber; and if not able to pay, then he fhall lofe his freedom, and be banifhed for ever out of the town without any redemption.

Alfo enacted, that if any man being at a common hall difclofe any fecrets there fpoken, he fhall forfeit 5l. to the chamber.

Alfo agreed, that one of the bells of St. Peter's church fhould be fold to repair the fchool-houfe.

Fefto S. Matth. 6 Eliz. *Simon Nix* elected mayor.—*Gilda Mercatorum*, 16.

Ballivi, *William Reynolds* and *Thomas Fowler*.

Ale under the fieve, 2d. the gallon, 13 to the dozen; typlers to fell 2¼d. per gallon; candles, 3d. per pound, and 13 to the dozen, on pain of 6s. 8d.

The total fums of money gathered for the fecond moiety of the fifteenth and tenth, to be paid into the

---

[1] Harl. MSS. 416. 49. fol. 87.   [2] Pat. 1 Eliz. p. 2. n. 6.

[3] Stow's Chronicle, Abridgment by Edm. Howes, p. 284.

Exchequer before 10 Nov. 1564:

	£.	s.	d.
Of the twenty-four – – – –	6	0	0
Of the forty-eight – – – –	5	18	6
In the ward of Thomas Stanford –	0	16	4
Robert Fletcher – –	0	16	0
John Tatam – – –	0	16	10
Thomas Fowler – –	0	16	0
Robert Wylcocks –	2	3	2
William Maubey –	0	16	0
Thomas Hallam – –	2	2	8
Nicholas Englyfhe –	2	6	8
James Clarke – –	0	10	11
William Norys – –	0	16	1

Fefto S. Matth. 7 Eliz. *Thomas Fowler* elected mayor.—*Gilda Mercatorum,* 28.

Ballivi, *William Reynolds, John Tatam.*

The total fums of money gathered for the firft moiety of the one fubfidy, to be paid into the Exchequer before 1 April, 1566:

	£.	s.	d.
Of the twenty-four – – –	3	0	0
Of the forty-eight – – –	3	0	0
Of the ward of William Beryge –	2	4	0
James Clark –	0	13	0
William Noris –	2	4	0
Nicholas Englifh –	0	15	0
Thomas Fowler –	2	11	0
William Manbye –	2	19	8
Simon Nixe –	1	14	0
Robert Fletcher –	1	14	0
Thomas Hallam –	3	10	8
Thomas Stanford –	2	1	0

Fefto S. Matth. 8 Eliz. *John Tatam* elected mayor. *Gilda Mercatorum,* 17.

Ballivi, *William Norys* and *Thomas Newcombe.*

Ale, 3d. per gallon, 12 to the dozen; typlers to fell after 3½d.; candles, 3d. per pound, 13 to the dozen.

The wayts collars weighed 21 ounces and a quarter, and half the half-quarter.

11 July. At a common hall, enacted that the ordinal of Tanners fhall continue for ever in force; fo there be nothing therein contained that fhall be prejudicial to the Queen's laws.

Fefto S. Matth. 9 Eliz. *William Norris* elected mayor.—*Gilda Mercatorum,* 29.

Ballivi, *Jacob Clarke* and *Thomas Newcombe.*

The total fums of money gathered for the firft moiety of a fifteenth and tenth, to be paid into the Exchequer at or before Nov. 1, 1567:

	£.	s.	d.
Of the twenty-four – – –	3	0	0
Of the forty-eight – – –	3	0	0
Of the ward of William Manbie –	0	8	0
Thomas Stanford –	0	8	8
Thomas Hallam –	0	11	4
Thomas Fowler –	0	8	0
James Clarke –	0	6	0
Robert Fletcher –	0	8	0
Richard Darker –	0	8	0
Simon Nixe – – –	0	11	7
John Tatam – –	0	8	5
Nicholas Englifh –	0	13	4

[The very fame fums were collected for the fecond moiety of the fifteenth and tenth.]

22 Nov. At a common hall, the town ftock having been decayed by great gifts, in country as well as town, to noblemen and women and others, as alfo at the banquets of venifon; of gifts and rewards given to players, muficians, jefters, noblemens' bearwards, and fuch like; it is enacted, that from the faid day no fuch great allowance fhall be paid out of the town ftock; but that the fpenders thereof, as at the banquets of venifon, plays, bear-baitings, &c. every of the twenty-four and forty-eight being required by the commandment of Mr. Mayor to be there, fhall bear every one his portion: Alfo, that no manner of gift be given to any noble perfon (out of the town ftock), except by confent of the mayor and four or five of the antienteft of his brethren, and as many of the antienteft of the forty-eight, except 5s. or under the value thereof, which may be beftowed by order of the mayor, as oft as occafion fhall move him. This act to be for ever.

Alfo, agreed that the lecture upon Wednefday and Friday in every week fhall begin after feven o'clock in the forenoon, and end at eight o'clock, according to a decree made by the advice and confent of Henry earl of Huntingdon, in the mayoralty of Mr. Thomas Fowler.

21 Feb. At a common hall, agreed that no butcher of town or country fhall ftand on the Eaft fide of the gutter that lieth from the end of the Gainfborow towards the Eaft gate; but to ftand in the fhambles appointed for Saturdays, and on the North fide of the faid gutter, and on the North fide of the faid Gainfborow toward the Eaft end of the faid fhambles; and alfo along without and by the North fide of the fame fhambles, toward the Weft end, and at the Weft end of the faid fhambles, on pain for every default of 3s. 4d.

Further agreed, that no perfon, having lands or tenements in the town or fuburbs of Leicefter, fhall take upon him to put into his houfes or tenements any perfon to be his tenant before he have prefented fuch foreign perfon before the mayor, and alderman of the ward where he fhall inhabit, to be examined from whence he cometh, and what honeft behaviour he is of, on pain of 6s. 8d. for every default, to be paid by the owner of the houfes.

March 10. At a common hall, agreed that in every parifh there be appointed a fubftantial perfon to collect the fums following, for relief of the poor and impotent, over and above the collection by virtue of the Queen's ftatute; viz. every of the twenty-four fhall pay, at every time of his wedding, to the collector of the parifh where he dwells, 2s. 8d.; and every of the forty-eight 16d. and the beft of commoners 8d. and every fecond commoner 4d. Alfo, there fhall be no feafts made at any churchings, fave only one competent mefs of meat provided for the goffips and midwives; and in confideration thereof every of the twenty-four fhall pay, at every churching of his wife, 2s. 8d. and the forty-eight 16d.; and commoners of the beft fort 8d. and fecond commoners 4d.; and at every wedding and churching the parfon, vicar, minifter, or clerk, fhall receive the faid fums, and deliver them to the collector by a bill indented. And further it is agreed, that one poor man, which fhall be apparelled with a black gown, and a badge upon his fleeve, fhall be appointed to go, with a box locked, to every inn and other places where ftrangers refort, to afk alms towards the univerfal relief of the poor; of which box the mayor, or one of the chief of the twenty-four, fhall keep the key: and the mayor or receiver, with confent of three or four of the moft antient of the twenty-four, fhall diftribute to the poor as oft as occafion ferves. Alfo it is agreed, that the feveral collectors fhall make accompt quarterly, and openly in the church, or other convenient place, to Mr. Mayor, and as many of the twenty-four and forty-eight as will be there; and then the mayor, with confent of three or four of the chief of the twenty-four, fhall diftribute the fame, and the furplus, if any, to be kept in the chamber to the ufe of the poor.

The fums gathered for the fecond moiety of a fubfidy, to be paid into the Exchequer before April 1, 1568:

	£.	s.	d.
Of the twenty-four – – –	3	0	0
Of the forty-eight – – –	3	0	0
Of the ward of Richard Darker –	2	3	2
William Manbey –	2	15	2
Simon Nixe –	1	9	4
Nicholas Englifh –	0	12	6
Thomas Stanford –	7	12	2
John Tatam –	1	15	0
James Clarke –	0	10	11
Robert Fletcher –	1	2	6
Thomas Hallam –	2	18	6
Thomas Fowler –	2	5	0

11 Aug. At a common hall, agreed that there fhall be put into the general lottery ten lots; viz. 5l. out of the ftock of the town; and if any of the faid lots be returned with any gain, it fhall be put into the ftock of the town; and if any part of the faid lottery be loft in the adventure, it fhall be made up

by

by the twenty-four and forty-eight, half by one, and half by the other company.

Festo S. Matth. 10 Eliz. *William Maubie* elected mayor second time.—*Gilda Mercatorum*, 10.

Ballivi, *Nicholas English* and *Thomas Newcombe*.

Here ends the foregoing Hall-book.

The next book is from anno 10 to 28 Elizabeth.

In the beginning is written the oath of the Mayor, of the Mayor's Brethren, of them that enter into the Chapman's Gild, of Chamberlains, of the Constables, of the Freeboroughs, of the Recorder, of the Mayor's Officers, his Clerk and Serjeant, of the Occupations, of the Fish Sayers, Flesh Sayers, Leather Sayers, of the Mayor for Orphans.

5 Nov. 10 Eliz. At a common hall, agreed that a perfect survey shall be taken of the lands belonging to the chamber of the town of Leicester by the mayor and auditors therefore appointed.

4 March, 11 Eliz. An act was made for keeping four post-horses, for which allowed 26s. 8d. each; to be paid by the twenty-four and forty-eight and commoners.

Item, it was agreed that the mayor may appoint the Court of Whetton to be kept at any time of the year which he thinks best; and he may, at keeping of it, go himself with other of his brethren, or send one of his chamberlains and his steward to keep the same.

26 August. At a common hall, agreed that a general levy or collection be made through the whole liberties of Leicester, for buying ten morrys pycks and ten new corseletts, furnished, to remain in the Treasure-house of the town, to serve the Queen in her affairs of war, if cause require.

Festo S. Matth. 11 Eliz. *Jacob Clarcke* elected mayor.—*Gilda Mercatorum*, 19.

Ballivus, *William Shingleton*.

Brewers to sell ale for 2½d. per gallon; typlers to sell out of their houses for 3d.; within them 4d. per gallon; candles 2¾d. per pound, 13 to the dozen.

Ale-tasters to enquire the defaults of tanners and typlers and common drunkards, &c.

Festo S. Matth. 12 Eliz. *Nicholas Englysshe* elected mayor.—*Gilda Mercatorum*, 18.

Ballivus, *William Shingleton*.

4 Jan. At a common hall, agreed that a general levy be made, to accomplish such extraordinary charges as the Corporation hath been at about the Queen's affairs in the late rebellion in the North; viz. the twenty-four to pay each 6s. 8d. and the forty-eight 3s. 4d.; and that every commoner, as well of good as mean ability, shall pay as they shall be assessed by discretion of the mayor and his brethren, to be collected by the chamberlains within a month: And that all tenants in Whetton that hold of the town of Leicester shall be contributors with the inhabitants of Leicester, according to the tenor of their leases, to be collected within forty days.

Item, agreed that every common victualler inhabiting within the liberties of the same town shall set forth an outward sign of his victualling, on pain of 6s. 8d. for every month's default.

18 Feb. At a common hall, enacted that every one holding lands, houses, or other hereditaments, shall sufficiently pave and repair the common streets and pavements, so far as the same extend before their lands, houses, and hereditaments, on pain of 3s. 4d. for every month's default. This act to continue for ever.

There being a collection made of such acts and orders as tended to the good government of the town, it was agreed, April 13, at a common hall, that every mayor once in his year, between Michaelmas and Lady-day, at a common hall, cause all and every act and acts, thing and things, therein specified, to be circumspectly perused and examined in presence of the said assembly, that the better reformation may be had, if any thing amiss shall happen therein to be contained.

At the same common hall, agreed that six post-horses be kept; and that 33s. 4d. be allowed for each.

27 April, 13 Eliz. At a common hall, agreed that 40l. be lent to a clothier, to set the poor on work; and towards that each of the twenty-four 16s. 8d. and of the forty-eight 8s. 4d.

Festo S. Matth. 13 Eliz. *William Gyllot* elected mayor.—*Gilda Mercatorum*, 13.

Ale under the sieve, 2d. the gallon; typlers out of doors, 2½d. per gallon; within doors, 1d. per quart.

16 Nov. At a common hall, agreed that the timber of St. Peter's church shall be taken down, and kept in safety, with the lead, till further order.

Item, that the serjeants shall have gowns one year, and the wayts another.

17 April, 14 Eliz. At a common hall, *Robert Braham* recorder, and *John Stanford*, were chosen burgesses for the parliament to be holden at Westminster 8 May next.

Item, agreed that six post-horses be kept for 12 months; the twenty-four to pay 2s. each, and the forty-eight 12d.; the residue to be gathered of the commons; 26s. 8d. to be allowed for each horse.

Item, that no tresses, hurdles, bordes, nor blocks, used on the market-days by artificers, be left in the Market-place when market is done, on pain of 12d.

Item, that no one in the liberty of Leicester take an apprentice but by indenture made by the mayor's clerk, for which he shall have 16d. and no more, for every pair; and to be sealed and recorded before the mayor by his clerk, and he to have of the master 4d. upon pain of 6s. 8d.

Item, the mayor's serjeant to have, for every one committed to the mayor's hall, 6d.

At a common hall, before Mr. William Gyllot, mayor, the twenty-four, and forty-eight, it was agreed that the mayor shall have, yearly, for ever hereafter, 20 marks fee for the better maintenance of his house-keeping, to be paid by the chamberlains at the times that were used when there was but 10l. paid.

Festo S. Matth. 14 Eliz. *John Eyricke* elected mayor. Freemen, 8.

At this election of the mayor, it was agreed that the mayor's clerk should have four nobles a year more wages than ever hath been paid; and that same to be paid by the chamberlains.

This page is subscribed by *William Dedyck*, clericus. His hand-writing seems to begin at a common hall held the year before, when William Gyllot was mayor, held the last of February, 14 Eliz. 1571-2. He presently after writes his name *Deadyck*, and after 17 Eliz. *Deathyck*, till 20 Eliz.; and then continued to write it *Dethyck* as long as he was town-clerk, which was till 1608.

Feb. 28. At a common hall, agreed for payment for a salt of silver gilt, bought of Mr. James Clarke, one of the twenty-four, the price 10l. 0s. 6d.; to be paid of the town stock. The salt to be lent to the mayor for his year, and so to his successors, &c.

Whereas Thomas Bradgate, of Gloucester, clothier, at the special request of Henry earl of Huntingdon, is minded to set up clothing within the town of Leicester; the twenty-four and forty-eight, at this present assembled, on desire of the said earl, have agreed to lend to the said Thomas Bradgate the sum of 100 marks for seven years, scil' to Michaelmas 1579; of which sum the twenty-four to advance 20s. apiece, and the forty-eight 10s. each, and the residue to be paid out of the town stock; and for re-payment, sufficient bonds to be taken by the mayor or his successors.

17 April. At a common hall, among other acts then made, it was appointed that the hall, or any part thereof, or implements belonging to the same, shall not at any time be lent to the parators, nor no other person nor persons, neither by the mayor nor no other officer, and on pain of 6s. 8d. for every default.

Here follows the oath of the mayor for observing, in all points, the act made for orphans' goods.

At the same hall, April 17, agreed that the following act for ever stand in force: If any person dwelling within the liberties of the town, franchised or unfranchised, making a will, or dying intestate, bequeath or leave to his own or other children any legacy or goods, then the executor or administrator, warned by the mayor's serjeant, shall come before the mayor and chamberlains, within eight days after the

said

faid perfon's death, and give, in writing, his name, and how many children he left, with their names, legacies, or portions in their keeping, and bring in fufficient townfmen, to be fureties, to be bound to the mayor and chamberlains in a fum to be by them limited, to be forfeited to fuch child or children on the condition hereafter mentioned, on pain of 20*s.* to be forfeited to the town. And it is agreed, that the executor or adminiftrator, or perfon that has the cuftody of fuch legacy, fhall, within a month after the perfon's death, come and give good fureties of townfmen for payment of the faid legacies to the children at fuch times as are appointed; and if the executor or adminiftrator refufe the cuftody of the faid legacy, then the mayor and chamberlains fhall take to the next of blood, being franchifed, and in the town dwelling, finding furety as aforefaid; and if they refufe it, then the mayor and chamberlains fhall put it to fuch other franchifed men as they think beft, upon good fureties as aforefaid: And if the executor or adminiftrator, or other perfon as aforefaid, having convenient warning by the mayor's ferjeant, come not at the day appointed, he fhall forfeit, for every day after, 6*s.* 8*d.* : And the party receiving the childrens' ftocks fhall, at fealing the bond, pay to the mayor 3*s.* 4*d.* if the ftock be above 20*l.* and if under then but 20*d.*; and to the mayor's clerk, for making the bond, 2*s.* 6*d.* and to the mayor's ferjeant 12*d.* be the ftock much or little: And at payment of the ftock to the orphans, they are to pay to the chamberlains, for the ufe of the chamber, 3*s.* 4*d.* if the ftock be above 20*l.* and if under but 20*d.*; and the refidue of the children, when they receive their portions, fhall pay to the mayor a gallon of wine. If any furety die, thofe furviving fhall bring to the mayor and chamberlains other fureties as aforefaid to be bound within twenty days after fuch perfon's death, or elfe furrender the legacies that they were fureties for to the mayor and chamberlains, on pain of 40*s.* for every day's default.

Item, that the party that will have the cuftody of the orphans' goods fhall, of his own goods and chattels, find the orphans meat, drink, clothes, and all other things meet for them, as long as they remain in his cuftody; or elfe the faid goods and legacies fhall be ordered as the mayor, his brethren, and chamberlains, fhall think beft for the profit of the children. If any furety depart the town, the party that hath the cuftody of the child fhall, within a month, put in new fureties of fufficient townfmen, on pain of 6*s.* 8*d.* for every day after the month paft.

[In the mayor's oath, it is required that he fhould, once in his year, enquire if any of the fureties were dead, or departed the town, or decayed in his fubftance, and take fuch order as fhould feem beft for affurance of the orphans; and that he fhould call before him and the chamberlains, on Thurfday the fifft week of Lent, every perfon bound of furety, to fee them to be fufficient to difcharge their bonds, &c.]

Here are the names of thofe who lent money towards the fum of 100 marks lent to Thomas Bradgate, clothier, according to the act the laft of Feb. 14 Eliz. The twenty-four lent 23*l.* the forty-eight 24*l.* the chamber of Leicefter 19*l.*; the total 66*l.*

Here are the names of the twenty-four and forty-eight that lent money to the clothier; and have, 15 Eliz. received one-half of the faid money from the chamberlains, and the other half been given to the ufe of the chamber of the faid town of Leicefter. They of the twenty-four received 10*l.* 10*s.* of the forty-eight 11*l.* 10*s.*; fum total, 22*l.*

An indenture, made 7 April, 15 Eliz. between the Queen and mayor and coburgeffes of the town of Leicefter; witneffeth, that the Queen, for 35*l.* to be paid to the general receiver of the duchy of Lancafter, and other caufes, doth fell and grant to the mayor and coburgeffes of Leicefter all the lead, ftone, and timber, that now is, or fince 20 Jan. laft was being, in and on the decayed church of St. Peter's in Leicefter, being parcel of the poffeffions of the duchy of Lancafter, which lead, by commiffion, was certified to be four fowders and 500 pounds; and the

Queen grants them to take and convert the fame to their moft commodity: And the faid mayor and coburgeffes covenant to erect a fubftantial fchool-houfe in the faid town, within a year after the date hereof, covered with flate, and the fame from time to time repair, and alfo to employ the faid lead, ftone, and timber, in edifying the fame; and to employ the overplus, if any be, in bringing a conduit of frefh water into the faid town.

Mem. this year, in the mayoralty of Mr. John Eyrick, was the fchool-houfe begun to be erected, &c.

8 May. At a common hall, agreed that William Moreton, a coburgefs of Leicefter, fhall have to him, his heirs and affigns, a tenement called the Stocks houfe in the High ftreet, between the land of the faid William on the North and South, and doth extend itfelf from the common ftreet there of the Weft to the land of the faid William on the Eaft; in confideration whereof the faid William Moreton grants abfolutely to the mayor and coburgeffes, and their fucceffors and affigns for ever, a piece of ground, in the High ftreet, extending from Dead lane on the South to a piece of ground of the faid town of Leicefter on the North part, 61 feet, and butteth from the King's highway on the Weft unto a garden-place or orchard of the faid William Moreton on the Eaft, 22 feet by the ftandard: And the faid William Moreton muft pay, at the fealing of the affurance for the exchange, to the ufe of the town, 40*s.*

The act about election of chamberlains, made on St. Matthew's day, 6 Hen. VII. was repealed 21 Sept. 15 Eliz.; when it was ordained, that henceforth it fhall be lawful for the mayor elected to nominate and choofe his chamberlain, and for the commonalty to choofe and elect for their chamberlain as well any fuch perfon as hath not before fined, as any fuch as have fined and difpenfed for the fame; neverthelefs with this confideration, that fuch election be made of fuch as have fined for the fame, in order as they be moft antient in election: And if any of the aforefaid perfons, inhabitants of the faid town, fo elected, do obftinately refufe, and will not ferve in the office of chamberlain as aforefaid, that . . . . . . [The reft is wanting, and a blank leaf follows.]

Controverfy having been between Thomas Hallam and others about a gutter or water-courfe from Dead lane into a piece of ground there, fold by the Corporation to the faid Thomas Hallam, the matter was referred to Thomas Sampfon, gent.; mafter and warden of Wigfton's Hofpital; and Samuel Culverwell, gent.; who, 14 May 1578, ordered, that the water in Dead lane fhall have its iffue into the faid piece of ground in and through the old current or gutter which, by appointment of Mr. John Tatam now mayor, fhall be opened, and made a perfect water-courfe, with a grate of iron to the fame; and for ever fo be kept by the chamberlains of the town.

Here is an account of writings of private houfes depofited in the chamber of the town, &c.

Fefto S. Matth. 15 Eliz. *Thomas Stanford* elected mayor. Freemen, 26.

20 Nov. 16 Eliz. At a common hall: Whereas evil perfons have ufed to fell apparel, houfhold ftuff, &c. and have been called brogers or pledge-women, it is appointed that two certain perfons are to exercife the trade of brokers, and no others; and they to have for their pains one penny in the fhilling, and no more; and they to fell in their fhops at their houfes, or at their ftandings in the market and fairs; and to be bound yearly for their honeft dealing.

7 May, 16 Eliz. Ad communem aulam. Agreed that four poft-horfes (there had ufed to be fix) be kept, to ferve on an hour's warning; for two of which there be allowed 26*s.* 8*d.* and for the other two 40*s.*; and the faid fum of 3*l.* 6*s.* 8*d.* to be levied, of the twenty-four 20*d.* and of the forty-eight 10*d.* apiece, and the refidue of the commons, &c.; out of which fum the faid five marks to be paid, and the 40*s.* remaining to be paid towards the charge of the coals, &c.

Alfo, that the twenty-four this year pay 12*d.* and the forty-eight 6*d.* towards carriage of the coals, &c.

Alfo,

Alfo, that the twenty-four pay 2s. and the forty-eight 12d. each, towards building a new houfe at the end of the fchool-houfe, and the repairing of the briggs.

In this year was the fchool-houfe built and finifhed, and a new houfe erected at the North end of the fame fchool-houfe, which is appointed for the head fchoolmafter to dwell in; and thereto is laid all the back fide late in the occupation of Johnfon, mafon, paying therefore yearly to the chamber of the town 20s.

Fefto S. Matth. 16 Eliz. *Thomas Hallam* elected mayor. Freemen, 10. Thofe admitted of the company of twenty-four paid 12d. and of the company of forty-eight 6d. apiece. Candles 3½d. per pound, 12 to the dozen; new ale, 3d. per gallon; tiplers, 3½d.; and a quart for one penny.

9 Nov. At a common hall, agreed that none ufing tipling fhall brew of their own, but fhall tun-in of the common brewers; and none to be common brewers but fuch as now ufe the fame, or that fhall be admitted by the mayor and the moft antient coburgeffes: And no common brewer to fell ale by retail, viz. pennyworth, or halfpennyworth; yet any may fell by the gallon; and common innkeepers and others may do as before they have done, but not fell, on pain of 40s.: Alfo, that the common brewers fhall become a fellowfhip, and have orders and decrees made among them, by confent of the mayor, before the 2d of March next; and among them appoint wardens and other officers, to be allowed by the mayor.

Alfo, that no perfons living out of the town or fuburbs (victuallers only excepted) fhall, within the town and liberties, on the market or other days (the fairs only excepted), fell, exchange, or utter, any wares whatfoever but only to fuch perfons as fell them again by retail, inhabiting within the town of Leicefter, till they have agreed with the mayor and coburgeffes for fuch liberty, and agree to pay fuch fine as by them fhall be affeffed.

In mufters taken in 1574 and 1575, the number of able men in Leicefterfhire was 1260; armed men, 400; felected men, 400; artificers and pioneers, 800; demilances, 4; light horfe, 66; the able men, at the fame period, for the whole kingdom, being 182,929; armed men, 62,462; felected men, 11,882; artificers and pioneers, 12,563; demilances, 269; light horfe, 2566 [1].

25 Feb. 17 Eliz. At a common hall, agreed that one townfman fhall not fue another, but complain to the mayor, or alderman of the ward, who is to agree them without fuit of law; or if he cannot, the party aggrieved is to demand licence to fue in the court of portmote; if any do contrary, he to pay 6s. 8d.

Alfo agreed, that no ftrangers be admitted freemen under 5l.

Alfo, for executing the act, made 21 Feb. 10 Eliz. againft landlords taking ftrangers to be their tenants till prefented to the mayor and alderman of the ward, and examined by them: And it is agreed that, yearly, in every ward the mayor fhall appoint two difcreet perfons, who have no lands of their own, to fearch their ward every month, to find any doing contrary to the faid act, and to fee that there be not above one tenant in a houfe; the fearchers to make monthly prefentments to the mayor; and landlords offending to pay 6s. 8d.

Allowed to Mr. John Stanford, for the charges in fuit between this town and Nottingham for paying toll, 18l. 2s. 6d. over and befides 5l. which he recovered of the faid town for charges by fuit of law; in confideration whereof, he faith, this town fhall there go toll-free.

Till this year the town-clerk ufed to have but 2d. for fwearing freemen, but now he received 6d.; and the eldeft fons of a freeman ufed only to pay the clerk 2d., but this year they began to pay a pottle of wine, befides 6d. to the clerk. The payments for freedom are, this year, to the town, 33s. 4d.—20s.—15s.—13s. 4d. and 10s.

29 April, 17 Eliz. At a common hall, agreed, for four poft-horfes, to allow 6l. 13s. 4d.; that is, 33s. 4d. each; the twenty-four to pay 2s. and the forty-eight 12d. each, and the reft to be levied on the inhabitants.

Alfo, it being fuppofed that the Queen will come to Leicefter, it is ordered, that, for a ftock of money, the twenty-four pay 40s. and the forty-eight 20s. each to the chamberlains, upon a fortnight's warning; and that the mayor, and fuch as have been mayors, meet her in fcarlet gowns; and that the reft of the twenty-four wear black gowns, made of a new comely fafhion; alfo the forty-eight at that prefent to wear coats of fine black cloth, and to be guarded with velvet, and to meet her Majefty on horfeback.

And that every houfeholder forthwith amend and beautify the fore front of their houfes, and amend the pavement; and this to be done, at furtheft, within a fortnight after Whitfuntide next.

Alfo, that henceforth the ferjeants of this town fhall, every third year, be allowed 20s. apiece towards buying them gowns.

Alfo, for better maintenance of the mayor's clerk, ordered, that every one chofen to be of the twenty-four fhall give him 12d. for adminiftering the oath, and recording their names; and every one chofen to be of the forty-eight to pay 6d. for recording his name; and every perfon made free 6d. over and befides for every one that is his father's eldeft fon to the mayor for the time being a pottle of wine: Alfo, every perfon made free of any occupation by force of their ordinal, to give likewife to the mayor's clerk 6d. for adminiftering the oath, and recording his name.

James Ellis, draper, appointed to be one of the twenty-four in the court of portmote, took his oath, and paid the fees to the officers; fcil', to the mayor's clerk 12d. and to mayor's ferjeant 6s. 8d.

Mem. on Saturday, July 2, 1575, in the afternoon, a fudden great rain, with marvellous thundering and tempeft, continued four or five hours in fuch fort that the ftreets ftood full of water—the like never feen.

July 9, 1575, received 6l. given by the earl of Huntingdon to buy coals for the poor.

[Hitherto *Robert Braham* continued recorder; but] Monday, July 18, 1575, the oath was adminiftered to Mr. *Richard Parkins*, then appointed to be recorder, who died July 3, 1603.

Fefto S. Matth. 17 Eliz. *Richard Davye* elected mayor the fecond time. Freemen, 22.

18 Nov. 18 Eliz. At a common hall, ordered that no one fuffer wood or timber to lie againft their houfes nor under their eves in any ftreet, on pain of lofing the wood towards paving the ftreet.

Item, that one at leaft of every houfe in town and fuburbs come to St. Martin's church to the fermon every Wednefday and Friday, on pain of 12d.

Freemen paid this year 3l.—20s.—10s. &c.

16 March. At a common hall, agreed to have 24 leather buckets; two of the twenty-four, and four of the forty-eight, to find a bucket; each of the twenty-four to pay 16d. and of the forty-eight 8d.

Alfo, that the inhabitants of the town and liberties, by command of the mayor, fhall find an able perfon, for one day's work, to gather and fetch ftones, and dig and carry fand, for repairing fuch ways and pavements as the town-chamber is charged with: Alfo the mafter of the houfe to pay 12d.

Alfo, Mr. John Stanford, burgefs of parliament, upon making his bill of charges, fhall be allowed, out of the ftock of the chamber, fuch confideration as by law he ought to have, and by his confcience is thought fufficient.

Here was an order made about reception of the Queen; but fhe came not.

Fefto S. Matth. 18 Eliz. *John Stanford* elected mayor. Freemen, 16.

23 Nov. 19 Eliz. At a common hall, agreed that the mayor and fuch as have been mayors fhall, for ever hereafter, wear fcarlet gowns; and they that lack are to provide them againft Whitfunday, and then to wear them, on pain of 10l.

---

[1] Peck, Defiderata Curiofa, Part II. Chap. 2.

Alfo, that the wayts have gowns provided them before Chriftmas next.

This year perfons of the country, for their freedom, paid fome 20s. and 2s. 6d. yearly at May-day; another 10s. and at May-day 4s. yearly, &c.

The wayts collars weighed 36 ounces, and coft the town 12l.

1 March, 19 Eliz. At a common hall, agreed that the twenty-four pay weekly 4d. and the forty-eight 2d. for relief of the poor and other inhabitants, to be affeffed according to ability.

10 May, 19 Eliz. At a common hall, agreed for four poft-horfes, 26s. 8d. each, &c.

Agreed alfo, that there fhall be in the High ftreet a crofs or market-houfe new erected this fummer.

12 June, 19 Eliz. Whereas the Queen and council charge the town to have ten able perfons in readinefs for her fervice, with culivers, flafks, tuchboxes, morions, fwords, and daggers, &c. to be trained three times in the year, four days together, and they to be allowed 8d. each every day; the twenty-four are to pay 5s. and the forty-eight 2s. 6d. each.

Fefto S. Matth. 19 Eliz. *John Tatam* elected mayor the fecond time. Freemen, 27.

22 Nov. 20 Eliz. Agreed, that the twenty-four pay 4d. and the forty-eight 2d. weekly each, towards relief of the poor; and none to be fuffered to go a begging.

It is agreed to have wayts as aforetime hath been ufed; and they to have this year coats of orange colour, and the cinquefoil on their fleeves, &c.

Alfo, that the ferjeants have their gowns this year.

Alfo, William Shilton, his fine being 5l. for refufing the chamberlainfhip, had one-half remitted, and he to pay 50s.

14 March, 20 Eliz. At a common hall, agreed that the 78l. 4s. 4d. at the foot of the account of the year paft, is allowed, over and befides the money gathered of the twenty-four and forty-eight, towards the charge of the crofs then erected: Alfo, that the reft of the charge of the faid crofs paid by the late chamberlains, viz. 17l. 13s. 7d. fhall be paid by the chamber of the town; in confideration whereof Mr. Stanford promifes to finifh the crofs at his proper charges in all things before Michaelmas next, and the fame to be covered with lead.

Alfo, agreed that the twenty-four pay 5s. and the forty-eight 2s. 6d. each to the prefent chamberlains, and the commons to be affeffed reafonably, towards certain charges of the town.

And that fuch as lack fcarlet gowns, who ought to wear them, provide them before May-day next, on pain of 5l.; and they to be worn, on pain of 10s. on Chriftmas-day, New-year's-day, Twelfth-day, Eafterday, Whitfunday, and at the fairs, fuch as fhall be then appointed; and alfo on the days next after Chriftmas, Eafter, and Whitfunday.

Four poft-horfes to be kept, for which allowed for each 26s. 8d.

[This order is repeated for many following years.]

For freedom there was paid this year, 33s. 4d.—20s.—13s. 4d.—10s. &c.

Fefto S. Matth. 20 Eliz. *John Middleton* elected mayor. Freemen, 35.

29 Sept. At a common hall, agreed that the [old] chamberlains who buy the coals fhall have the felling of them, and fell them for 5d. *per* hundred, and pay the money to the new chamberlains within a week when they are all fold, or fo much as they have received, when required by the mayor.

Alfo, that the wayts have coats, and the ferjeants gowns, for this year.

21 Nov. 21 Eliz. At a common hall, ordered that no perfon fit or refort to any inn on any Wednefday, Friday, Sunday, or other holiday, in time of fermon, divine fervice, or catechifm, on pain of 12d.; and upon non-payment thereof, imprifonment; and that none on other days tarry there tipling, otherwife than about their lawful bufinefs, above an hour in a day, upon the like pain.

Alfo, that no miller of this town or the country buy malt or other corn on the market-day, on pain

of 10s. otherwife than for their own provifion to fpend in their houfes, and that upon licence of the mayor firft obtained.

All wood lying in the common ftreets to be prefently avoided, on pain of forfeiture of the wood, to be given to the poor by the alderman of the ward.

Mem. Dec. 22, the deputy of the queen's clerk of the market, examining our ftandards, found or made them fit. Note, that all yard wands are to be fealed at both ends; and that in all places out of London the ale quart and wine quart (as he faith) ought to be all one; and he faith, that the City of London payeth 100 marks a year for the allowing and fuffering of their wine meafures.

13 March. At a common hall, appointed that, towards the charge of the four poft-horfes, the training the foldiers, and repairing the North bridge, a levy be made on all perfons, burgeffes, dwelling out of the Corporation, as well as within, and of the inhabitants, and of fuch houfes as any keep in their hands to lie at their pleafure, though not duly inhabited; the twenty-four to pay 10s. and the forty-eight 5s. apiece.

Item, it is enacted for ever, that if any freeman go to dwell out of the liberties of the town a whole year and a day, and afterwards fhall come and dwell again here, and hath not during fuch time borne fuch charges as other freemen have done, he fhall not be fuffered to ufe any trade, or be reputed as a freeman, till he be fworn anew to the Corporation, and pay a fine, which fhall be at leaft 10s.

Item, that none fhall keep an apprentice above 40 days unbound, on pain of 10s. and then enroll him before the mayor within ten days; for which he fhall pay the mayor's clerk, if he make the indenture, but 4d.; or elfe, for every pair enrolling by any other made, 8d. upon pain of 10s.

None fhall wafh cloaths or other things at the common wells, having once warning to the contrary, on pain of 12d.

Item, that every one that maketh honey in the fummer fhall bring one barrel at leaft, yearly, to fell in Lent time, on market-days, in the open market, on pain of 2s. 6d.

Item, that Mr. Mayor fhall do his good will to take the town in fee-farm.

Item, that all chandlers of the town and others pay 40d. apiece, for breaking the affize.

22 July. At a town-hall, agreed that the twenty-four pay 12d. and the forty-eight 6d. apiece, towards keeping the vifited of the plague, as oft as need requires, during its continuance; and all other inhabitants to be charged to the fame.

Item, it is agreed to buy the bailiwick to the ufe of the town; and Mr. John Stanford, who bought Mr. John Danet's patent, hath now fold it to the town for 4l. befides his charges; and the town muft enter upon it at Michaelmas next, fo foon as the audit is finifhed.

Fefto S. Matth. 21 Eliz. *William Noryce* elected mayor the fecond time. Freemen, 18.

At this faid feaft, agreed that Mr. Recorder fhall have a fcarlet gown at the charge of the town, towards which Mr. John Stanford promifes to give 40s. and the reft of the company promife 5s. apiece.

Mem. At this election Mr. Noryce, then elected mayor, was abfent at London; and on Michaelmasday being abfent, he was fined 5l.; [but it is faid] *Non fol'*.

20 Nov. 22 Eliz. At a common hall, ordered that fuch as fell ale by retail provide quart and pint pots of pewter before Chriftmas next, on pain of 12d. and then provide them within three weeks, on pain of 2s. and then to provide them within three weeks, on pain of being difmiffed of victualling for ever: And that none of them fell by other meafure (but they may have little glaffes or crufes to drink out of), nor fell lefs than a quart for 1d. how ftrong foever their ale or beer be; and any perfon that takes lefs than a quart for 1d. or in any other meafure than abovefaid, he fhall pay, if of the twenty-four, 4d.; of the forty-eight, 2d.; other commoner, 1d.

30 March.

30 March. *William Bullbrocke* being dead, Thomas Skeffington, efq. by letter to Mr. Mayor, recommended *Thomas Wurfhippe* to be mace-bearer ; who was appointed to that office, and fworn.

On Monday and Tuefday in Whitfun-week our ten trained foldiers were fent to Melton, and trained there two days. The charge was 40*s*. 5*d*.

Mem. This year a new commiffion was fent to the juftices of the county of Leicefter for general mufters; whereupon the town of Leicefter fued out one for the general mufters to be taken within the town ; or elfe the juftices of the county would have intermeddled within our Corporation. Our commiffion, and fending for it, coft 40*s*.

T. Goddard of Anfty, for freedom at fairs and market-days, paid 20*s*. ; and, yearly, 2*s*. 6*d*. on May-day.

Fefto S. Matth. 22 Eliz. *George Tatam* elected mayor. Freemen, 17.

At this common hall, it was agreed that every child, eight years old and upwards, fhall be taught the Lord's Prayer, the Articles of their Belief, and alfo to anfwer certain points of the Catechifm, upon penalty to the parents : And mufters of fuch as are not idiots, &c. as follows ; viz. the twenty-four, 12*d*. ; the forty-eight, 6*d*. ; and other commoners, 3*d*. apiece, or three days imprifonment.

17 Feb. 23 Eliz. At a common hall, agreed that the act for orphans be amended.

Item, that the twenty-four give 12*d*. and the forty-eight 6*d*. apiece yearly to the mayor's ferjeant.

Alfo, that fuch of the forty-eight as fhall fo offend as to deferve punifhment fhall be punifhed at the new hall, and not at the old hall ; but it fhall be at Mr. Mayor's pleafure, whether the door fhall be locked upon any fuch offender or not.

This year two fifteenths and a fubfidy were granted to the Queen.

Wednefday before Pentecoft, at a common hall, agreed that, towards the firft fifteenth, the twenty-four pay 5*s*. and the forty-eight 2*s*. 6*d*. apiece, and the inhabitants to be charged towards it ; the fifteenth is 21*l*. and 10*s*. allowed for charge.

Item, agreed that Mr. Breham and Mr. John Stanford, burgeffes of the faid parliament, fhall be paid their charges allowed by ftatute.

Arthur Tatam was difmiffed the company of forty-eight, for diforders and for libelling, &c.

Fefto S. Matth. 23 Eliz. *Philip Freake* elected mayor. Freemen, 14.

At this hall, agreed that the chamberlains fhall ever hereafter keep a dinner at the hall, according to the old cuftom, on pain of 5*l*.

17 Nov. 24 Eliz. At a common hall, Arthur Tatam was difmiffed the company of forty-eight again, for his diforder committed againft Mr. Hallam and Mr. Ellys, &c.

9 March. At a common hall, the chamberlains' accompts were read and allowed ; faving, that fome did miflike that Mr. Stanford hath been allowed his charge for the Parliament laft paft ; for that they fay he faid, when he was chofen burgefs, he would not crave his charge except he did good to the town ; whereupon it is, by fome part of the hall, agreed, that if the faid Mr. Stanford do, at any time hereafter (by reafon of his burgefsfhip), any good to the town, then his charge to be allowed ; otherwife he to repay again that which he hath received for his charge for the two Parliaments paft.

Alfo, Mr. Francis Haftings delivered to Mr. Mayor and certain of his brethren a letter from the Council, and another from the earl of Huntingdon, on behalf of Simon Crofts, touching the fheep-pens ; which were read ; and thereupon moft part agreed, that Simon Crofts (and his wife after him, if fhe furvives), during his and her life, and that leafe the town holdeth the fheep-penns by in being, fhall enjoy the fheep-penns in fuch manner as heretofore, upon the rent he now payeth, viz. 9*l*. 6*s*. 8*d*. not letting them forth of his hands ; provided that he fhall not exact more for the penns than he ufually did ; and fhall not fet any penns on the Cornwall on market days, with-

out licence of the mayor, otherwife than hath been ufed.

Alfo, granted that the brewers have an ordinal for orders among themfelves, and tiplers and victuallers ; fo that the orders be feen and allowed firft by the mayor, recorder, and juftices, &c.

7 May, the twenty-four paid 5*s*. for the fecond fifteenth, and 20*d*. apiece for the poft-horfes. The forty-eight paid 2*s*. 6*d*. each towards the fifteenth, and 10*d*. towards the poft-horfes.

19 Sept. 1582, the fecond payment of the fubfidy was affeffed ; the total fum whereof did amount to 20*l*. 5*s*.

Strangers, for their freedom, paid 20*s*. each.

Things bought this year towards furnifhing the recorder's chamber at the hall ; a trufs bedftead, a cubbarde, and a trundle bed—26*s*. 8*d*.

Fefto S. Matth. 24 Eliz. *William Morton* elected mayor. Freemen, 20.

16 Nov. At a common hall, agreed that the old gallons fhall be ufed again, and made as big as they were before they were cut by Mr. William Norrice, in the fecond time of his mayoralty.

Item, that all inhabitants and others that have houfes in their hands uninhabited fhall caufe the ftreets before their houfes, and thereto belonging, to be weekly made clean, and the filth to be carried away, on pain for every default to pay 3*s*. 4*d*.

Item, that henceforth no fee or reward fhall be given by the chamber of the town, nor any of the twenty-four or forty-eight be charged with any payment, towards any bear-wards, bear-baitings, players, plays, interludes, or games (except the queen, or lords of the privy council) ; nor any players be fuffered to play at the town-hall (except before excepted), and then but only before the mayor and his brethren, on pain of 40*s*. to be loft by the mayor that fuffer the contrary ; to be levied by his fucceffor, on pain of 5*l*. if he make default therein, &c.

Item, that the act, made in the fecond time of the mayoralty of Mr. Thomas Hallam, touching admitting ftrangers to the freedom of the town, fhall ftand in force, and no mitigation of the fine therein mentioned (which is 5*l*.) to be had or fuffered.

Item, that every houfekeeper (of reafonable ability) fhall be taxed, at the difcretion of the mayor, what they fhall, quarterly, give to the wayts ; in confideration whereof, the wayts fhall play every night and morning orderly, both winter and fummer, and not go forth of the town to play except to fairs or weddings, and then by licence of the mayor.

Item, that no ftrangers, viz. wayts, minftrels, or other muficians, be fuffered to play within this town at weddings or fairs, or any other time whatfoever.

Item, that fuch as have, or fhall have, any children taught of the free fchool, being ftrangers, fhall give, yearly, fome reafonable contribution towards the living of the under ufher, by confent of the mayor.

22 Feb. 25 Eliz. At a common hall, agreed that the chamberlains fhall, before the next affize, at charge of the town, furnifh the chamber at the town-hall with bedding and other furniture for the recorder to lie at when he comes to town.

Item, that henceforth there be no more allowance given to the collector of the fifteenth of the town, towards his charges for payment of the faid fifteenth and tenth.

Item, that the twenty-four fhall each give 12*d*. and the forty-eight 6*d*. a quarter to the wayts, and the other inhabitants fhall be taxed by the mayor : And that no ftrangers or others, being muficians or players, though they dwell in the town, if not of the company of town-wayts, fhall be fuffered to play at or in any man's houfe, doors, window, or at any wedding, the time of the general affizes only excepted, and then to play only to ftrangers, provided the town-wayts keep the town, and play about the town, both evening and morning, continually and orderly, at reafonable times.

Item, if a victualler be chofen to be mayor, then two of the company, that be not victuallers, according

to

to the ftatute (3 Hen. VIII.) in that cafe made and provided, fhall be chofen, and fworn with the mayor, to affize the price of victual; and that the mayor fhall not, without the confent of the faid two perfons, alter any affize of victual, or alter any meafure.

Item, that the keeper of any alehoufe that fuffers any townfmen to remain in his houfe after the curfew bell hath rung (without lawful caufe) fhall forfeit 12d., to be paid prefently, or elfe to remain in ward that night.

May 3, 1583. At a meeting of the mayor and certain of the twenty-four, it was agreed that the twenty-four pay 12d. each, for three weeks, towards keeping the vifited folk, and the forty-eight 6d. each; and the inhabitants to be taxed according to ability. This affeffment is to continue from three weeks to three weeks, till it pleafe God to ceafe the fame.

Fefto S. Mich. 25 Eliz. *Thomas Clarke* elected mayor. Freemen, 22.—John Heyrick and William Morton appointed according to the ftatute for affizing of victuals.—From 25 Eliz. and fo forward, the town-clerk takes notice of the fwearing of the mayor on Sept. 29; which is fcarcely mentioned before, and yet it is faid to be done according to the cuftom of the town of Leicefter.

22 Nov. 26 Eliz. At a common hall, agreed that the wayts and their boys fhall have coats bought them; and two fcutcheons or cinquefoils to be made for the boys, to wear with lace about their necks.

A letter to the mayor, charging the town with two demilances and four light-horfemen, to be rated of the moft wealthy men in town, to be ready at an hour's warning. Dated Michaelmas-day, 1583[1].

Letters relating to the clothiers[1].

Jan. 12, 1583. Blace Vyilers, merchant of the Staple of England, and free of London, was made free of this town, and paid for his freedom 10s.; and the fame day he was made of the forty-eight, and then one of the twenty-four; and paid, for redemption of the chamberlainfhip, 50s.

Jan. 14. William earl of Worcefter licenfed certain perfons, his fervants, to go abroad to play, requiring all officers to permit them to pafs, and give them fuch entertainment as other noblemen's players have.

Mr. Mayor gave the faid players an angel towards their dinner; and willed them not to play at prefent, being Friday March 6. About two hours after, they defired the mayor to let them play in their inn; he faid they fhould not—they faid they would, and ufed contemptuous words, &c.: but at length they fubmitted, and begged pardon[1].

On Tuefday March 3, 1583, came certain players, the Queen's fervants, who had licence from Mr. Edmund Tilney, mafter of the Rolls[1].

More ftuff bought for the recorder's chamber:

A feathered tick, 14s. 6d.; five ftone and one pound of feathers, 26s. 9d.; a wool mattrefs, 8s.; another covering, 8s.; two bolfters and one pillow, 8s. 8d.; 16 ells of filk wool for a coverlid, 24s.; another mattrefs, 5s. The tick, bolfters, and pillows, of themfelves, without feathers, weigh 10 lbs.

Bought four yards of daringe for a carpet for the hall parlour, 7s. 8d.

Thomas Clarke the mayor's letter to fir Francis Walfingham, fecretary of ftate, fent with fome printed books feized here, that were againft the Common Prayer, &c.; and prefcribing a form of reformation. Dated May 16, 1584[1].

Aug. 17. A letter of Thomas Clarke, mayor, to . . . . . . afferting the right of exemption from toll[1].

13 March, 26 Eliz. At a common hall, agreed that the twenty-four and forty-eight fhall give fome yearly portion or falary to Mr. Johnfon the preacher, towards his better maintenance, together with other inhabitants of the town.

Item, it is ordered (and the rather for the repreffing of ftrong ale) that the brewers proceed with an ordinal, according to the order in Mr. Freak's mayoralty.

Item, that the mayor, with fix of the antienteft brethren, and the chamberlains, fhall fet and order fuch town-lands within the town as are out of leafe.

Item, that none duft, drefs, or winnow any malt or other corn in the Crofs, or hang any clothes or other things in or on it, on pain of 12d.

2 Jan. 26 Eliz. Mr. Hynde having been fined 5l. for difobedience to the mayor, it was upon his fubmiffion forgiven, fave only 10s. which he paid; which 10s. was given towards repairing the well near St. Martin's church.

A great fire having been at Nantwich, it is agreed that the twenty-four give 12d. and the forty-eight 6d. each; and the inhabitants to be affeffed under the rate for poft-horfes, &c.

Item, agreed that Mr. George Tatam fhall have the dealing of the coals till May-day next, and then deliver to the mayor and chamberlains the whole ftock, which is 57l. 14s. 4½d. and for the increafe for the two years paft which he hath had the dealing in, 40s.; and alfo he promifes to give for the increafe for the laft year, ending at May-day, 4l. The whole 63l. 14s. 4½d.

Nota, that the earle of Leicefter came to the towne of Leicefter of Thurfday the xviii[th] daie of June, anno fupradicto, and then laye at therle of Huntingdon's houffe; at which tyme his fifter the countys of Huntingdon dyd receyve him there.

At this his comynge to Leicefter from the bathes oute of Derbyfhier, he came into Leicefter by the Abbye, upp the Abbye gate, the North gate, and Hie ftreete, to the Hie Croffe, where, ageynft the fchoole-howffe, the mayor, his bretherene, and the eighte and fortye, mett his honor, but not in fkarlett. The preyfent gyven to hym was, a hoggefheade of clarett wyne, which coft iiii l. xs.; and two verye fatt oxen, which coft xx marks.

Alfo his honor gave twentie nobles, to be diftributed amongeft the poore. The number of the poor then was 118 perfons; and it came to 1½d. apiece, and 18d. over, in every ward; and was diftributed by Mr. Mayor, Mr. Sparks and Mr. Johnfon preachers, and other of the aldermen. Alfo, out of the fame, to the new hofpital, 3s.; the old hofpital, 5s.; and to the prifoners of the county and bridewell, 3s.

Alfo his honor did geve unto the twoe companyes, viz. the xxiiii[ti] and eight and fortye, to be delyv'ed by his feid fifter the countis of Huntingdon, vi bucks.

Alfo his honor ftaied but one night in Leicefter; and was goun of the Fridaye morninge, by fyve of the clocke, &c.

22 Jan. At a common hall, towards the foregoing charges, it was agreed that the twenty-four give 6s. 8d. and the forty-eight 3s. 4d. each; and all the beft inhabitants to be affeffed, with the Bifhop's fee, according to our compofition.

Strangers this year paid for freedom 15s.; 13s. 4d.; 4l.

Fefto S. Matth. 26 Eliz. *Robert Heyrycke* elected mayor. Freemen, 26.—Agreed, that Mr. William Worfhip be fpared from being mayor four years; he giving bond, that, if he die or do not ferve then being elected, he will pay to the town 10l.

Item, ordered that John Hitche fhall be a brewer and victualler, but not an innkeeper; viz. not to fet out any fign or fign-poft.

Oct. 6, 1584. At a meeting of the mayor and certain of his brethren, agreed that 100l. be taken up for the clothier, and the intereft to be yearly levied on the companies and commonalty; and that the clothier fhall have the 100l. two years; and longer, as his dealing fhall be liked.

Oct. 20. At another like meeting, agreed that the reft of the twenty-four fhall ftand bounden to thofe two of the twenty-four that are bound for the 100l. if the party lending it will not take affurance of the land from the Corporation.

Oct. 28. At another like meeting, agreed that as much land fhall be affured to the two bound for the 100l. lent to the clothier as comes to 6l. yearly rent; with a provifo, if they be faved harmlefs, to be void.

---

[1] Thefe feveral articles were copied by Mr. Carte, from the Files in the Town-clerk's chamber.

Nov. 12, 26 Eliz. At a common hall, the sheriff's precept (which is in English) being read, and after that sir Ralph Sadler's letter for nomination of both our burgesses, and other letters; it is agreed, that sir Ralph Sadler, knt chancellor of the dutchy of Lancaster, shall have the nomination of one of the burgesses; who thereupon nominated Henry Skipwith, esq.; and the other chosen was Thomas Johnson, one of her Majesty's serjeants at arms: and either of them promised to bear their own charges.

Item, agreed that the twenty-four pay 14d. and the forty-eight 7d. apiece, quarterly, towards payment of the 100l. lent to the clothier, and for making the writings.

Commissioners for disarming Recusants, 1584:

Sir Edward Hastings, Francis Hastings, Thomas Cave, Henry Skipwith, Thomas Ashbye, Brian Cave, Thomas Skevington, and William Cave.

In this year, when the whole number of men appeared to be trained throughout the realm was 9670, the town of Leicester was to provide 20; and the rest of the county 130 [1].

Justices of Peace, 1584. (Henry Turvile sheriff.)

Thomas Bromley miles, dominus camerarius.
Willielmus dñs Burghley, dominus thesaurarius.
Edvardus comes Rutland.
Henricus comes Huntingdon, dominus præses.
Henricus dominus Cromwell.
Christoferus Hatton, miles, vicecamerarius.
Thomas Meade, unus justiciariorum.
Robertus Streat, secundus baro Scaccarii.

Georgius Hastinges miles.	Johannes Harrington.
Franciic' Hastinges miles.	Franciscus Beaumont.
Henricus Grey.	Thomas Cave.
Franciscus Cave.	Edwardus Leigh.
Adrianus Stockes.	Leonardus Dannet.
Brianus Cave.	Andreas Nowell.
Nicholaus Beamonde.	Willielmus Cave.
Franciscus Smyth.	Franciscus Brown.
Edwardus Afton.	Thomas Skevington.
Henricus Poole.	Edwardus Turvill.
Henricus Scipwith.	Henricus Turvill.
Thomas Ashbye.	Anthonius Fant [2].
Mauritius Barkley.	

Nov. 20, 1584, 27 Eliz. At a common hall, ordered that the common wells henceforth be kept in repair by the inhabitants of that ward or quarter wherein they stand; and the alderman to appoint, yearly, two in every ward, called Well-reeves, to oversee the same.

Item, that no more shops, stalls, lean-tos, be erected in the market-place, on pain of 5l. to be forfeited by the builder, and 10l. by the mayor that doth suffer the same.

Jan. 29. At a common hall, agreed that a survey be made of all the town-land, and what wood is upon it, and to value every tree, &c.

At this hall the new mace was shewn. Agreed, that neither the salt nor the old mace shall be sold for payment of the new mace, but it shall be paid as follows; viz. the twenty-four 3s. 4d., the forty-eight 20d. apiece, and the residue out of the town-stock.

Item, agreed that John Marshall, tanner, shall be acquitted against the tanners for the 5l. which they claim of him for his freedom; and they to have the 20s. which they have received of him, and the town to have the 4l. which is already paid.

March 5. At a common hall, agreed that no kilns be new erected within the town or suburbs, without consent of the twenty-four, or major part of them, on pain of 5l.

April 23, 1585. At a common hall, five of the twenty-four and five of the forty-eight were impowered, till May 1, 1586, to sell or exchange any lands, tenements, woods, &c. of the Corporation's; and to buy or take on lease any other.

Christopher Bringys, a freeman, being gone to live forth of the town, continued his freedom, by paying 12d. yearly at Michaelmas.

Mem. that Anthony Dugdale, bellman of Leices-

ter, being dead, his wife claimed the bell as hers; saying her husband bought it; but, that being proved untrue, she delivered the bell to the mayor, who delivered it to Henry Bland the beadle, to be bellman during the pleasure of the magistrates.

Strangers made free paid 20s.; and one 15s.

Festo S. Matth. 1585, 27 Eliz. James Clarke elected mayor the second time. Freemen, 18.

Sept. 29. The town clerk and common serjeant were further sworn; viz. the clerk for the safe keeping of the records and evidences of the town, and the serjeant for his attendance.

Feb. 25, 28 Eliz. At a common hall, the draught of the assurance of the land in Ratcliffe, sold to George Burbadge, was read, and liked of.

March 18. At a common hall, agreed by the twenty-four and forty-eight to lend money till Christmas next, towards paying 300l. which the town is indebted for the Grange, &c.

April 22, 1586. At a common hall, agreed the twenty-four to pay 16d., the forty-eight 8d. each; and the rest to be levied of the inhabitants, for the four post-horses; for which allowed 26s. 8d. each.

The second payment of the subsidy was assessed Sept. 19; the gross and total sum whereof is 20l.

Strangers made free for market-days paid 20s. fine, and for scot and lot, yearly, 2s.

[Here ends the Hall-book beginning 10 Eliz. There is an omission of one year, 28 Eliz. between this book and the next.—During several foregoing mayoralties, the chief acts of the common hall, designed to be lasting orders, were transcribed into a large red book, called "The Town Book of Acts," out of which several extracts have been made under their regular dates.]

The Council's letter, recommending those citizens and burgesses who were chose the last time. Dated at Windsor, Sept. 19, 1586. Directed to William Turpin, sheriff of Leicestershire [3].

James Ellis was elected mayor on St. Matthew's day 1586; and to him was directed the following letter from Roger Bromley, Oct. 4, 1586: "If the knights of the shire shall not be allowed in the next election; I desire to understand whether you mean in like sort to continue your burgesses accordingly, as the Council's letters do require [3]."

Oct. 13. A return of Henry Skipwith and Thomas Johnson to be burgesses of parliament [3].

Oct. 20. A person charged with saying, that Babynton, which suffered, was an honest man, &c. [3]

Feb. 10. The letter of the Queen's Council, for keeping Lent; and articles to be observed by the justices for the same purpose [3].

March 9. Recognizances of several butchers and innkeepers not to kill or dress flesh, nor suffer it to be eaten during Lent [3].

March 13. Recognizances taken for abstinence from flesh during Lent of tiplers, brewers, &c. [3]

At a common hall, May 2, 1587, for obtaining 400l. which is by covenant to be paid to Mr. Francis Hastings the 12th of May next, for the reversion of one moiety of the Grange, which he hath procured from her Majesty, it was agreed as followeth; viz. Henry Byddel lent 50l.; Mr. Morton, 50l.; Mr. James Ellys, mayor, 30l.; Mr. William Noryce, 20l.; Mr. Thomas Clarke and Mr. Robert Heyrick, 160l.

July 13. William Stapleford gave a bond of 20l. for faithful discharge of his office of a broger for a year.

Ult' Martii. A note of implements in that moiety of the Grange belonging to the Corporation of Leicester, now in occupation of John Coye, and by him sold to the Corporation [3].

Accounts of discourse about Merlin's prophecies relating to the Queen and kingdom, &c. [3]

Further extracts out of the next Book belonging to the common hall of the borough of Leicester.

29 Eliz. 1587, William Ludlam mayor.—Mr. John Tatam and Mr. James Clark chosen, according to the statute, for that he is a butcher and an innkeeper.—Candles, 3½d. per pound, and afterwards 4d. Ale at 4d. the gallon, and 1d. a quart as sold by tiplers.—

Peck, Desiderata Curiosa, Book II. Ch. IV.   [2] Harl. MSS. 474.   [3] Carte, MS. from the Files in the Town-clerk's chamber.

No ſtranger to be made free (if he be of any trade) under 6l. fine.

Whereas it was agreed, at a common hall in the ſecond mayoralty of Mr. John Tatam, March 14, 20 Eliz. that the mayor, and ſuch as have been ſo, ſhall wear ſcarlet on Chriſtmas-day, New-year's-day, Twelfth-day, Eaſter-day, Whitſunday, and on the days next after Chriſtmas, Eaſter, and Whitſunday; alſo at the fairs ſuch as ſhall be then appointed: It is now ordered, that they ſhall wear it alſo on the Queen's day to the ſermon, and at the aſſize to meet the judges, on pain of 10s.

Livery gowns ordered for the 4 ſerjeants next year.

Ordered, that woollen and linen cloth be ſold not in the women's market, but only in the drapers', on pain of 6s. 8d.

March 1, John Underwood choſen mace-bearer, in room of Thomas Worſhippe deceaſed.

May 8, 1588. Agreed to keep four poſt-horſes as uſual; and there is allowed for each horſe 26s. 8d.; in the whole 5l. 6s. 8d. Towards which each of the twenty-four is to pay 16d., and of the forty-eight 8d., and the reſt to be levied of the commoners of the town.—The like order for many years.

Agreed that the twenty-four pay each 10s. yearly towards the preacher's ſtipend, and the forty-eight 5s. beſides the benevolence that each will give more; and alſo the commonalty.

May 17. " Mem. the town of Leiceſter was charged with 40 ſoldiers, footmen, which were preſt & ſet forthe, readye funnyſhed with arms and muny given, under the leading of George Villers, eſq." Of theſe 40 ſoldiers, 8 were furniſhed with muſkets, 18 with calyvers, and 14 with corſlets and pikes.

Towards the furniture of theſe 40 ſoldiers, who were to be ready on five days' warning, the twenty-four to pay 13 . 4d. the forty-eight 6s. 8d. each, and the commoners to be tax.d.

Queen Elizabeth, in the 30th year of her reign, by her charter under the great ſeal of England and the dutchy of Lancaſter, did incorporate the ſaid town; and to conſiſt of a mayor, 24 aldermen, and 48 burgeſſes of the inhabitants of Leiceſter, and to be called by the name of " The mayor and burgeſſes of the town of Leiceſter;" and doth enable them to purchaſe and ſell lands by that name, and to ſue or be ſued by that name in any court or place (non obſtante the ſtatute of mortmain): And that one of the 24 aldermen ſhall, yearly, be choſen mayor on St. Matthew's day, in the Guildhall, by the greater of the twenty-four and the forty-eight; Mr. William Ludlam then to continue mayor until St. Matthew's day: And granteth, that the mayor and burgeſſes, and their ſucceſſors, ſhall have, hold, and enjoy all liberties, juriſdictions, concurrence of pleas, cuſtoms, and power to hold pleas and other things, in ſuch manner and form as hath been heretofore uſed within the ſaid town; and that the mayor and burgeſſes ſhall hold and enjoy all profits, commodities, and hereditaments whatſoever, in ſuch manner as any former Corporation there have had and enjoyed: And if any mayor die in the time of his mayoralty, the two companies of the twenty-four and forty-eight, or the greater number, to meet within ſix days after, and make choice of one of the twenty-four to be mayor in his place: And by the ſame charter, hath given and granted to the ſaid mayor and burgeſſes, and their ſucceſſors, that the weekday ſhambles, and many other lands in fee-farm, at the yearly rent of 137l. 13s. 7d. ob. q. with a clauſe of diſtreſs, and nomine penæ of 10l. if it be unpaid 40 days; and nomine penæ of 20l. if it be unpaid 80 days; and another nomine penæ, if it be unpaid ſix months (with divers non obſtantes); and a letter of attorney to Mr. Perkins and Mr. Archer to give poſſeſſion.

Aug. 8, 1588. Mr. Sacheverel, the now preacher for this town, and confrater of Wigſton's Hoſpital, ſhall have for this year 13l. 6s. 8d. paid by the chamberlains, who are to receive of the twenty-four 5s. each, and of the forty-eight 2s. 6d. and tax the com-

moners; but preſently, upon applica ion of ſir Edward Haſtings, it was agreed that he ſhould have 20l.

30 Eliz. 1588, George Noryce mayor. Freemen, 20. Candles at 3d. per pound: ale as before.

In this year, the memorable æra of the defeat of the Spaniſh Armada, Thomas Skeffington, eſq. of Belgrave, then high ſheriff for this county, ſummoned together all perſons between the ages of 19 and 50 (to the number of 12 530) able to bear arms; 2000 of the prime of which were ſent to Tilbury camp; the reſt were ſent home, furniſhed with various miſſile weapons, and directed to rendezvous on the firſt news of the Spaniards ſetting foot on Engliſh ground. After the defeat of that mighty armament, the Queen went to St. Paul's, to return thanks to Almighty God; and every where there were general rejoicings. George Noryce, mayor of Leiceſter, entertained in the moſt ſumptuous manner all the firſt nobility and gentry of the county at his hall; among which were, Henry earl of Huntingdon, lord lieutenant of the county; Walter Haſtings, his brother, of Kirby in this county, eſq. who was a major-general, and commanded the choſen Leiceſterſhire men who made a part of Tilbury camp; Thomas Skeffington, eſq. high ſheriff; and many others of note.

Feb. 21. The recorder declared, there was obtained of her Majeſty the confirmation of a new charter and corporation; the fee-farm of all her Majeſty's lands, ſometime belonging to the four colleges in Leiceſter; and the leaſe in reverſion of the whole Grange called the Newark Grange.

Towards paying for the lands purchaſed in the South Fields of Mr. Wightman, the twenty-four lend 40s. each, and the forty-eight 20s., for ſix months.

A letter, dated at London, March 10, 1589, ſubſcribed Francis Walſingham, directed to the mayor and his brethren, and the reſt of the town of Leiceſter; wherein, highly commending Mr. Sacheverel, whom he had made confrater of Wigſton's Hoſpital, he ſays, " The living being ſmall, ſhould be by yourſelves ſupplied in ſuch liberal ſort, as you before relieved one Pelfant that was preacher among you; on whom you beſtowed above 40l. by the year, beſides ſuch other maintenance as he had elſewhere, &c." [1]

Mr. Sacheverel's ſtipend ſettled at 20l. per annum, March 13; and afterwards, April 14, it was, at requeſt of the earl of Huntingdon, made 30l. per annum, ſo long as he ſhould continue preacher of Leiceſter; which was confirmed to him by writing under the town ſeal.

31 Eliz. 1589, John Hynde mayor. Freemen, 26.

December. An account of debts owing by the town of Leiceſter. Total, 925l. 10s. [1]

21 Jan. The common hall deſired of the mayor, Mr. John Hynde, that all the lands and tenements given by her Majeſty's letters patent might remain to the uſe of the mayor and burgeſſes, according to the Queen's grant; that the town might be put in poſſeſſion of them all; and that none of them be ſold but by conſent of a common hall: And ſay that they are grieved, in that Mr. Noryce, late mayor, ſet the town-ſeal without conſent of a hall; and in that the commiſſioners had bought and ſold parcel of the ſaid lands and tenements among themſelves without their conſent.

Jan. 23. The twenty-four agreed, that every alderman of a ward ſhall have a deputy appointed by the mayor, with conſent of the alderman.

Feb. 6. Richard Parkyns, in a letter to the mayor, ſtates Mr. Edmonds's demand for his leaſe 266l. 13s. 4d.

Feb. 11. At a common hall, concerning the buying of a leaſe from Mr. Edmonds, ſervant to ſir Francis Walſingham, knight, chancellor of the dutchy; all parties aſſembled were ſatisfied with the bargain of the lands and tenements aſſured unto Mr. George Tatam by the commiſſioners, in lieu of his moiety of his leaſe, which he and Mr. Harvye held together of her Majeſty.

On Tueſday, March 2, before the mayor, juſtices, and aldermen, the books of the four Jews were, according to the antient cuſtom of this town, affaired.

[1] Carte, MS. from the Files in the Town-clerk's chamber.

May

May 31, the Queen's almoner sent to the mayor, for the fines and forfeitures of persons for killing and eating flesh in Lent, to be disposed of by him as the Queen's alms [1].

June 17. Notes taken touching the closes in the Frith, parcel of the Newark Grange of Leicester [1].

An indenture of lease demised to sir Richard Sacheverel, knight, and the lady Anne his wife, of the Grange and premisses, &c. in question; and, after the death of Sacheverel, in the occupation of his executors; and this recital is contained in an indenture m e under the duchy seal, March 1, 3 Edw. VI. to one Layton, for 31 years from Easter last, paying 30l. 18s. 5d.; which William Layton assigned over his interest to Henry Pachet, son and heir of William Pachet lord Pachet of Beaudesert; the said Henry Pachet assigns his estate in the premisses to William Twynshed, of London, gent.; from him to one Robert Harrye. And the lease of Richard Sacheverel endured till Michaelmas, 1 Eliz.; which was made by the Dean and chapter of the Blessed Virgin Mary of the Newark, for term of 31 years; during which lease none of the lessees aforesaid intermeddled with the possession of the premisses.—Nota, that when King Henry VIII. disforested the Friths, the Dean and chapter of the Newark shewed forth their charter to the officers of the King for their common of pasture in the said Frith, to the value of 24 beasts and more, and six mares and a stone-horse; in consideration of which common, the King granted to the said college, to be taken in, a certain ground called Braunston pasture: And after the said pasture being purchased by the tenants of the said college, the other tenants thereof finding themselves grieved therewith, order was taken by the King, and Dean and chapter, that the said Dean and chapter should have to themselves the said closes; and the other tenants had allotted to them the residue of the said pasture, containing 120 acres; which close has been ever since occupied by the tenants thereof, by lease from the Prince, without claim of the closes belonging to the Grange [1].

A petition to the earl of Huntingdon, desiring him to qualify the charge which they sustained with 40 armed men; and now they were charged for four score, whereof their accustomed charge never exceeded 10, saving once 20. Shewing also, that certain inhabitants, to avoid the charge of the town, and the service of her Majesty, had procured themselves the livery of certain gentlemen; and that a saltpetre-maker threatened to throw down their mudwalls (being the common fencing of the town), which would be a thousand marks damage, &c. [1]

[N. B. In August, there used annually to be two named to be put in election for mayor.]

Sept. 21, 32 Eliz. 1590, John Tatam mayor. Candles, 4d. per pound. The absenters from common halls are to have no votes in any business; and the twenty-four to pay 12d. and the forty-eight 6d. each, without leave of the mayor.

Oct. 29, 32 Eliz. A note taken of writings touching the Granges, sent to the recorder at London; viz. the lease of the Grange made to Francis Hastings, esq. and William Worship, &c.; an assignment from Mr. Temple to Mr. Hastings of the same; a lease of the close in the forest from Mr. Temple to Cater and Somerfyld; an assignment of the lease from Mr. Hastings to the mayor and burgesses, &c. &c. [1]

Ordered, 20 Nov. 33 Eliz. that no kiln be used in this town, that standeth near any housing, on the pain of 40s.

March 26, 1591. Ordered, that no one decay or pull down the town-wall by getting stones, except by licence of common hall, on pain of 20s.

It was agreed, that the parish of St. Peter shall be united to All Saints [but those of St. Martin's parish were against it; whence arose some dispute.]

A letter of Henry earl of Huntingdon, complaining that 14l. of the moiety of the salary due to Mr. Sacheverel at Lady-day was not yet paid, &c. Aug. 3, 1591 [1].

Several papers relating to a bargain of Mr. George Tatam and Mr. Thomas Clarke of 600l.; giving account of indentures about houses and lands sealed and delivered to several persons [1].

A dispute about the Castle-mills, between Richard Grey and Nicholas Walker [1].

Mention is made of an obligation of 1200l. made by the mayor and burgesses to Mr. George Tatam and Mr. Thomas Clarke, for the sealing such bargains as they shall pass at any time within four years of the 20l. land, for the payment of 600l. of the town's debt. Dated Sept. 4. [1]

33 Eliz. 1591, Ralph Chettel mayor. Being a baker and common brewer, two persons were joined with him, according to the statute for assizing victuals. —Freemen, 10. Candles, 4¼d.

A taxation for the fourth, fifteenth, and tenth, in the several wards, &c.; in which very few were taxed so much as 12d.; but Mr. John Thurdburne was taxed 2s.; Mr. Pottel, 2s. 6d.; Mr. Thomas Cotton, 5s.; Mr. Francis Belgrave, 2s. [1]

Oct. 16. A letter of Henry earl of Huntingdon to the mayor and his brethren, complaining of the unkindness of many in the town to their preacher; and desires the mayor, &c. to take care to pay him the stipend promised, &c. [1]

1592, June 2. The earl of Huntingdon ordered the mayor, that, on his receipt of the coal-money from Mr. Roe, he should deliver 70l. of it to John Clerk, to be employed by him in setting the poor at work about clothing, and to lease the looms of Henry Bradgate to John Clerk.

July 28. At a common hall, agreed that Archer shall have a lease [of the Bailiwick, I think] for twenty-one years from Michaelmas next; paying 4l. per annum for the first ten years, and 5l. for the other eleven years, over and above the Queen's rent; and that he shall, presently after the confirmation of the said lease, make a perfect rental of all his Bailiwick, and deliver the same to Mr. Mayor, &c. to be surveyed.

July 29. John Knight, tanner, said to Mr. Hynde [an alderman], "There is never a just man of the Bench amongst you all;" for which the said Knight was by the mayor committed to ward in the hall.

A petition was drawn up to the Queen, complaining of the abuse of her Majesty's late grant to the Corporation, to the oppression of the poor, and enriching of some private persons by indirect means. This seems to be drawn up by Tuster and Layton; and it said, that one of the best of the twenty-four offered them 40s. to make it, and said that he would procure 500 hands to it. Hereupon, it was ordered, that whosoever should be found guilty of doing so should be dismissed the company, and disfranchised.

Sept. 4, the Corporation gave a bond of 400l. to Nicholas Elcock senior, of London, to pay him 200l. Sept. 6, 1593, and another bond to pay 36l. for interest of the 200l.; viz. 18l. Sept. 6, 1592, and the other 18l. Sept. 6, 1593. These were delivered Nov. 29, 33 Eliz. to William Ward, for the use of the said Nicholas Elcock; and then William Ward delivered the lease heretofore made to the said Nicholas of the Grange, &c.; and the same was cancelled [1].

34 Eliz. 1592, John Stanford mayor. Freemen, 22. Ale under the sieve at 2¼d. the gallon; candles, 4d. The mayor's fee, by this year's accompts, was 13l. 6s. 8d.; Richard Parkins, esq. the recorder, 4l.; the town-clerk's wages, 1l. 6s. 8d.; and Mr. James Clark's charges (one of the burgesses in parliament), 6l. 6s.

Oct. 20. At a meeting of the mayor and several aldermen, agreed that a bond shall be made to Mr. Ellcock, of London, from the mayor and burgesses, under the common seal, for payment of the 200l. owing to him, and the interest of the same, viz. 18l. per annum so long as the 200l. is unpaid; and thereupon the lease lately made to him of the Grange for ten years to be called in and cancelled, so as thereby

[1] Carte, MS. from the Files in the Town-clerk's chamber.

the

the rent of the Grange may be employed for the ufe of the town, and paying of the preacher.

Oct. 22, 1592. Delivered to Mr. George Tatam, at his going to London, (among other writings) articles drawn by the recorder, of the Frith and Braunfton paftures, and an order out of the Duchy court, termino Michaelis, 32 & 33 Eliz. for poffeffion of the clofes, &c.

Nov. 19. It was agreed, that Robert Eyrycke, glover, being gone from Leicefter to live at Mountforell, fhall not keep fhop, buy or fell in the town, but only as a ftranger, on Saturday market and fair-days.

Dec. 20. Letters of Richard Parkyns, about a difference between fir Edward Haftings, knight, and the town of Leicefter. In one, he fays " the cuftoms of the Duchy were confirmed by act of parliament."

Mr. Richard Parkyns, troubled at the factions in town, was inclined to refign his recorderfhip, and the earl of Huntingdon recommended Mr. Humphrey Purefoy ; but, peace and concord being reftored, he was induced to continue recorder.

Thomas Heneage, chancellor of the Duchy, wrote to the mayor, bailiffs, and burgeffes, Jan. 8, 1592, wherein he propofes ; viz. that, " leaving the choice of both the burgeffes to me, as heretofore it hath been to my predeceffors, I fhall make choice of two fuch burgeffes as fhall be without all exceptions," &c.

March 17. The ferjeants to have gowns this year.

Agreed, that no one dwelling out of Leicefter, though free of the faid town, fhall ufe his trade there on week-days, but only on Saturday markets and fair-days.

5 July, 1593. Agreed, that Mr. Thomas Clarke fhall have for term of life St. John's, with the appurtenances, paying the Queen's rent, to make a wool-hall thereof, at his own charge ; and he promifes to leave the fame to the ufe of the Corporation.

28 July. Whereas Henry earl of Huntingdon ordered that the money employed by him formerly to buy coals for the poor in Leicefter fhall be for cloathing, and for coals alfo ; and the mayor and burgeffes being willing that it fhould be all for cloathing, they agree that the twenty-four fhall give 5s. and the forty-eight 2s. 6d. apiece, for the chamberlains to provide coals, and fell them, in winter, at 5d. a hundred, to the working poor, and the poor indeed. The chamberlains are to give a juft account ; and the gain arifing to remain to the ftock for increafe thereof.

Friday, July 28, 34 Eliz. At a hall, for agreement with Richard Archer for his travel for four years in obtaining their fee-farm ; and in confideration that, by his diligence and knowledge, the particular contained in the grant of the Queen to the town was found out, which no other perfon was then able to perform ; being a bailey and collector, &c. ; and that he fhall endeavour to deliver poffeffion of all the lands and tenements which the Corporation holds in fee-farm of the Queen, to his utmoft knowledge of the particular, &c. ; it is agreed, that the faid Richard Archer fhall have to him, his heirs and affigns for ever, all thofe lands and tenements which are already affured to him in fee-farm under the common feal of Leicefter ; and in confideration that he releafes to the Corporation all the refidue of the lands and tenements to him promifed in fee-farm, he, his heirs, executors, and adminiftrators, are difcharged againft the Corporation of and for 100l. by him received, with the intereft and arrears of it, for evermore ; alfo he fhall have a leafe of all the reft of the lands and tenements, parcel of his Bailiwick, to be made for 21 years from Michaelmas next, paying during the firft ten years, over and above the Queen's rent, 4l. ; and during the refidue of the term, 5l. : And whereas the faid Archer hath, by grant of the Corporation, two yard land in the South Field of Leicefter, the Corporation, at any time within fix years, may exchange or buy the faid two yard land, at a rate adjudged by four indifferent men.

Sept. 18. At a meeting of the mayor and others, fealed to Thomas Cave, efq. an indenture of fee-farm of Sythefton miln, and a cottage, with a horfe-miln, in the town of Sythefton, and a piece of meadow ; rent, per annum, 3l. 6s. 8d. ; and alfo of a meffuage and tenement in Hungerton, rent, per annum, 30s. N. B. The fine of thefe parcels is 115l. 2s. parcel of the bargain of Mr. Tatam and Mr. Thomas Clarke of 20l. per annum, in paying of 600l. of the town's debt.

Sept. 21, 1593, 35 Eliz. *Robert Heyrick* mayor. Freemen, 41.—Agreed, that the twenty-four pay weekly 2s. and the forty-eight 12d. apiece, towards the charge of the vifited ; and to Oct. 19 : and the commons to be taxed according to their abilities.

Jan. 24. The letter being read, and alfo one from Mr. Tamworth and Mr. Brockas, in the common hall ; Mr. Tamworth and Mr. Brockas were rejected ; as alfo the propofal of the chancellor of the Duchy ; and there were chofen, Mr. John Stanford mayor, who will bear his own charge ; and Mr. James Clarke, who is to have his charge.

April 6, 1594. Agreed, that whofoever difclofes any fpeeches, fecrets, or matters, out of the common hall, or at any common hall hereafter, to any perfon whatfoever, fhall forfeit, to the ufe of the town, 5l.

Robert Heyrick, glover, now dwelling at Mountforell, now continues his freedom by the yearly payment of 2s. payable half yearly.

Aug. 19. Agreed that the twenty-four fhall pay 10s. and the forty-eight 5s. apiece, towards the firft and fecond fifteenth and tenth ; and the commons to be taxed according to their ability.

Sept. 21, 1594, 36 Eliz. *George Tatam* chofen mayor.

Chriftopher Sutton, for his abfence this day and other times, and difobedience to the mayor, fined 5l.

Ale under the fieve, 3½d. ; pale ale, ⁴½d. the gallon ; candles, 3d. per pound.

Nov. 9. Agreed, that every freeman ufing his trade elfewhere, and doth not return home nightly to his houfe in Leicefter, fhall pay, weekly, double in every payment to all charges, watch and ward, &c. ; and if they do not return home, and continue in the town as an inhabitant ought, before the Conception of our Lady next, they fhall pay, for every week they fo continue out afterwards, 40s. a-week, to the ufe of the vifited and poor people.

Jan. 11. Agreed, that Mr. Mayor take up 100l. at intereft, for redeeming the North mylns ; the Corporation to be bound, and the intereft to be paid by the twenty-four and forty-eight, after the rate of 2s., and 12d. &c. Item, the mayor to buy the wind-miln in the South Field (the purchafe whereof is 20l.), upon the town's bond.

Jan. 24. Agreed between the mayor, his brethren, and John Willne bailiff of Leicefter, that the four ferjeants fhall attend on the mayor, as of old times hath been ufed ; and to have ufual fees and allowances.

Certain perfons petitioned to have certain indentures to be kept among the records of the town till the death of a perfon ; and it was granted.

This year the plague raged in Leicefter. The accompts fay, " Paid charges in making ready at Hallows church for the judges to hold the affize in, becaufe the other part of the town was infected with the ficknefs.

" Given to fir Edward Haftings, knight, as followeth ; two loaves of refined fugar (19 lb. 2 oz.), 24s. ; pepper (3 oz.), 6s. ; ginger (1 oz.), 1s. 4d. ; cinnamon (2 oz.), 4s. ; currants (12 lb.), 5s. ; raifins (12 lb.), 3s. 8d. ; pruens (12 lb.), 5s. ; 1 lb. of bifcuits, 1 lb. of carraways, and 1 lb. of comforts, 2l. 11s. 4d.

" Given to the lord Anderfon, chief juftice of England ; one bottle of white wine, 1s. 4d. ; one bottle of claret, 1s. 4d. ; one bottle of fack, 2s. ; and 1 lb. of fugar, 1s. 4d.—In toto, 6s."

March 14. The intereft of the 100l. which was 8l. now agreed to be but half paid by the company ; the reft out of the receipts of the town.

April 16, 1595. Agreed, that the mayor and burgeffes fhall appoint two of the four ferjeants, who fhall be kept at the charge of the town, and fhall attend on the mayor and town bufinefs ; and arreft people, and be attorneys in the town court, as has been ufed by the bailiff's ferjeants; and the bailiff to choofe the other two ferjeants, to attend him, arreft people, and be attorneys, and kept at his charge, &c.: And the town, every fourth year, to give each of the bailiff's two ferjeants a gown-cloth, for their attendance on the mayor; and the town and bailiff each to pay their ferjeants' wages, &c.

July 10. Robert Roberts, of the twenty-four, being charged, before Mr. Mayor and his brethren, with having carnal knowledge of widow Dawfon, was difcharged from the company till he clear himfelf of the faid crime.

Sept. 21, 1595, 37 Eliz. *William Yates* chofen mayor.

Chriftopher Sutton was chofen chamberlain; but abfented himfelf as living in the Bifhop's fee, and was fined 5*l.* Freemen, 23.

The toll of horfes was let for 20*s. per annum.*

March 5, 38 Eliz. Agreed, that all the common lanes and common places taken in within the remembrance of man fhall be laid open again, and that all lanes that be ftraitened fhall be enlarged again, before Michaelmas next; and they to be done by fix of the antients of the twenty-four and forty-eight.

April 21, 1596. Ordered, that no mayor (after his mayoralty is expired) fhall keep in his cuftody any record of the town's, or any letters which concern the Corporation; but to be among the records in the town-hall.

The clofe in the Frith, near the Foreft of Leicefter, let for 21 years for 20*l.* fine, and 10*l. per annum.*

May 19. Chriftopher Sutton put out of the company of forty-eight, and disfranchifed, becaufe not refident in the liberty of this town, and refufes to pay fuch duties as a freeman and one of the company ought; likewife Robert Carter, for refufing to come to common halls, and pay the duties of a freeman, and one of the faid company.

James Pawlmer was releafed from the company of forty-eight, becaufe gone to live out of the town; yet he may continue his freedom, by the yearly payment of 12*d.* being demanded, or lofe his freedom.

Agreed, that the twenty-four pay 2*s.* and the forty-eight 12*d.* apiece, towards mending the ways near the North bridge and Abbey-gate; and collection to be made among the inhabitants.

Ale under the fieve at 3½*d.*; ftale ale at 4*d.* the gallon; candles, 3*d. per* pound.

Hugh Haroulde, a freeman, removing to Kibworth, is allowed to continue his freedom, to trade on market-days and fairs, for 2*s. per annum.*

Sept. 21, 1596, 38 Eliz. *William Morton* mayor. Freemen, 18.—Ale under the fieve, 5*d.*; ftale ale, 6*d.* the gallon; candles, 3½*d. per* pound.

Jan. 21, 39 Eliz. John Clarke had a leafe of the toll of horfes for 21 years, from Michaelmas 1559; paying 8*l.* fine, and 20*s.* rent *per annum.*

Lent 20*l.* for a year to the wife of Thomas Clark, in refpect that fhe keeps many poor children at work in knitting of jerfey. The town bore the intereft.

March 30, 1597. Agreed, that the lane near Cow-lane, leading into Burgefs meadow, be inclofed.

June 19. It was agreed, that Mr. Thomas Chapman fhall be made a free burgefs, and afterwards one of the forty-eight, and then to fine for the chamberlainfhip, and then to be made a mayor's brother; fo his fine be for his freedom 5*l.*: all which was done next day.

Sept. 21, 1597, 39 Eliz. *Thomas Nixe* mayor. Being a fifhmonger, two perfons were appointed with him for the affizing of victuals. Freemen, 12.

George Parkyns, eldeft fon of Mr. Parkyns the recorder, and John Stanford junior, eldeft fon of Mr. John Stanford fenior, chofen burgeffes of the parliament.

Oct. 21. Agreed, that no mayor hereafter fhall receive any of the town's money, but the chamberlains only, who fhall yearly make accompt thereof.

Every alderman in his ward fhall appoint his conftable to command that two, or one at leaft, of every houfhold, fhall come to the fermons weekly, on pain of 6*d.* for every default.

The ftewards of the fair fhall yearly make their accompt to the mayor, and pay the overplus to the chamberlains, for the ufe of the town.

The mayors fhall, yearly, anfwer the overplus of the fifteenths' and poft-horfes' money to the town, if there be any.

This year a poor unfortunate woman was hanged for being old. " Paid, for the charges of meat and drink of old Mother Cooke, being kept in the hall five days, at the fuit of Mr. Edward Saunders, upon fufpicion of witchcraft, who was afterwards removed to the county gaol, and was for the fame arraigned, condemned, and hanged; 2*s.* 6*d.*". [Mafter Edward Saunders deferved hanging the moft.]

Nov. 18, 40 Eliz. Ale under the fieve, 6*d.*; ftale ale, 7*d. per* gallon; candles, 4*d. per* pound.

At the fame time, agreed that the beaft-market fhall be kept in the lane called the Cow-lane, Cank-ftreet, and Lofeby-lane, and not in Saturday market.

The order renewed of Oct. 21, 39 Eliz. for attending fermons on the Fridays and other days of the week; the defaulter to pay 4*d.*

John Underwood the mace-bearer fhall have, every third year, a gown-cloth given him.

No ftranger of any trade fhall be made free under 5*l.* nor fuffered to ufe his trade till he be free.

By a letter of the earl of Huntingdon's, dated April 29, 1598, it appears, that of 500 trained foldiers charged on the county, the town found 40, whereof there were 12 culivers, 4 mufkets, 11 bows and arrows, 8 corflets and pikes, and 5 bills. The Queen ordered the bows and arrows and bills to be refufed, and fupplied with mufkets.

May 3. The letter being read; towards the charge, agreed that the twenty-four pay 6*s.* 8*d.* and the forty-eight 3*s.* 4*d.* each, and the inhabitants to be taxed according to ability. The town-armour to be marked with a cinquefoil, and delivered from chamberlain to chamberlain, by inventory indented.

Sept. 21, 40 Eliz. *Thomas Clarke* mayor; and two perfons were then nominated for choice of the mayor for the next year: and Mr. Edward Newcome being excufed this year from being mayor, gave 40*l.* bond, to pay to the town 20*l.* if he fhould refufe to ferve the next year.—Freemen, 22.

Nov. 24. Ale under the fieve, at 4*d. per* gallon for a fortnight; afterwards, 3*d.* Stale ale, 5*d. per* gallon for a fortnight; afterwards, 4*d.* Candles, 4*d. per* pound.

Agreed, that the companies attending the mayor at common halls, affize feffions, and fairs, fhall wear gowns, on pain to the twenty-four of 12*d.* and forty-eight 6*d.* each.

It appears that, in this year, the commonalty of Leicefter were called upon to pay a portion of the town's debt incurred by the Corporation purchafes, and law expences; towards which the aldermen paid 58*l.*; the forty-eight (common council), 39*l.* 15*s.* 6*d.*; and the commonalty, 20*l.* 11*s.* 4*d.*

Wheat was this year at 9*s.* a bufhel.

May 6, 1599. Agreed, that Mr. John Wilne, the Queen's bailiff of this borough, fhould be made a mayor's brother.

Queen Elizabeth, by her charter, dated June 1, the 41ft year of her reign, doth grant, that the borough of Leicefter fhall be a free borough of itfelf; and that the burgeffes thereof, and their fucceffors, fhall be a body politic and corporate, confifting of a mayor, two bailiffs, and burgeffes, of the borough of Leicefter; and by that name fhall purchafe lands in fee and perpetuity, and goods, chattels, and other things; and to fell, leafe, grant, and affign, lands, tenements, and hereditaments, goods and chattels; and to plead, and be impleaded, in any Court or Courts, in all actions, fuits, and demands: And that the mayor, bailiffs, and burgeffes aforefaid, fhall have a common feal for the caufes and bufineffes to be done; which feal they may alter and change at their pleafure: And that the mayor and aldermen, or the greater part of them, fhall have power, from time to time, to make, ordain, and conftitute, fuch reafonable laws and orders as to them fhall feem good, profitable, honeft, and neceffary, for the good government of the bur-

geffes,

geffes, artificers, and inhabitants, of the borough aforefaid; and to declare how and in what manner the mayor, aldermen, bailiffs, and burgeffes, artificers, and inhabitants of the borough aforefaid, fhould behave themfelves in their offices, trades, and bufineffes, within the borough and limits thereof; and alfo for the further benefit, and government of the faid borough, and of victualing thereof; and for the difpofing and letting of their lands: And that the faid mayor and aldermen, and their fucceffors, fhall ordain fuch penalties and punifhments, by imprifonment or fine, or both of them, againft the delinquents, as to the faid mayor and aldermen, or the greater part of them, fhall feem meet; and granteth power to levy the faid fines, fo that the faid ordinances, imprifonments, and fines, be not contrary to the laws of the land; and maketh *Thomas Clarke* then prefent mayor till St. Matthew next, and 24 others, prefent aldermen; and they to continue aldermen during their lives, unlefs in the mean time they be removed for their ill government or ill behaviour; and maketh *Thomas Chettle* and *James Andrew* the firft bailiffs, and fo to continue until St. Matthew next, if they fo long live; and nameth 48 others of the company of the forty-eight during their lives, unlefs they be removed by their ill government or ill behaviour: And that, yearly, at St. Matthew the Apoftle, the mayor, aldermen, and forty-eight, or the greater part of them, fhall affemble themfelves together in the Guildhall, or any other convenient place within the faid borough, to be appointed at their difcretion, and there fhall continue until they, or the greater part of them affembled, fhall choofe one of the faid aldermen to be their mayor, and two of the burgeffes to be their bailiffs, for the year following; and that the mayor and bailiffs elected, before they do execute their offices, muft take their oaths, upon St. Martlemas day, before the laft mayor, and, in his abfence, before fome of the aldermen which fhall be there prefent, at the Guildhall, or other place, &c. to execute his office well and truly in all things; and that, if the mayor die, or be removed from his office, or not behave himfelf well in his office, that then they fhall choofe another in his place within fourteen days, and fo *toties quoties*, &c.; and that the bailiffs are removeable by the mayor and aldermen, or the greater part of them, if they behave not themfelves well; and if the bailiffs, or either of them, do die or be removed, then a new one to be chofen within fourteen days, *ut fupra*; and if any of the aldermen die or be removed (they being removeable, if they do not behave themfelves well in their places, at the pleafures of the mayor and aldermen, or the greater part of them), that then the mayor and refidue of the aldermen, or the greater part of them, within convenient time, fhall choofe another of the burgeffes to be alderman in his place, who fhall have the faid office *tam diu quam fe bene gefferit*, and he is to be fworn to perform his office; and if any of the forty-eight die, or mifbehave themfelves, that then the mayor and aldermen, or the greater part of them, within convenient time, fhall affemble themfelves, and the greater part of them fo affembled to choofe another in his place, and to fwear him to perform his place and office: And makes Mr. *Parkins* the prefent recorder for life; and, after his deceafe or renewal, the mayor and aldermen, or the greater number of them affembled, to choofe another, expert in the law, to be recorder, and fo *toties quoties*; and he to take an oath to perform his office: And that they fhall have a fteward, expert in the law; Mr. *Thomas Ward* to be prefent fteward of the fame borough; and, after his deceafe or removal, the mayor and aldermen, or the greater number of them affembled, to choofe another, expert in the law, to be fteward of the fame borough; and he to be fworn to execute his faid office by himfelf or his deputy: And that they fhall have an honeft and difcreet man to be town clerk, common clerk, and prothonotary of the faid borough; *William Dethicke* to

be prefent town clerk for life; and, after his deceafe, the mayor and aldermen, or the greater number of them affembled, to choofe another, and he to hold it *tam diu quam fe bene gefferit*; and he to be fworn before the mayor well and truly to execute his office: And that there fhall be five ferjeants at mace to execute all proclamations, precepts, proceffes, and other bufineffes to them appertaining, to be chofen by the mayor and aldermen, or the greater part of them affembled for that purpofe, and fhall be attendant upon the mayor and bailiffs, and fhall be fworn before the mayor and aldermen, or the greater part of them; and that they fhall carry maces of gold or filver, with the arms of the Kingdom engraven upon them; and that they fhall carry them before the mayor within the faid borough and precincts thereof: And that the mayor and burgeffes, and their fucceffors, may hold a court upon Monday every week, or oftener if need be, at the Guildhall, or any other convenient place within the faid borough, before the mayor, recorder, bailiffs, and fteward, or one of them; and gives them power to hold plea of all actions of trefpafs, *quare vi & armis*, otherwife actions of the cafe, debts, accompts, covenants, deceipts, detinue of charters and chattels, and other contracts whatfoever, happening within the faid borough, in fuch manner as hath been there ufed; and if they will implead any man for any freehold, that then the plaintiff fhall procure a writ of right patent, directed to the mayor and bailiffs, whereupon the court may proceed; and that the ferjeants at mace fhall execute all proceffes of the faid court as fhall be fit, and as hath been ufed in other the like places: And the mayor, recorder, and four aldermen which have been laft mayors, fhall be juftices of the peace, and fhall execute the places and offices of juftices of the peace; and gives them, or any three of them, whereof the mayor and recorder to be two, power to enquire, hear and determine, of all offences, as hath been heretofore ufed within the faid borough, or as any of the juftices of any county may do, fo that they do not proceed to the determination of any murder or felony, or any other matter concerning lofs of life or member, without fpecial command from the Queen, her heirs or fucceffors; and grants to them view of frankpledge of all the inhabitants of, and refiants within, the faid borough, to be holden twice by year, to be holden before the mayor, bailiffs, and fteward of the faid borough, or any of them: And that no foreigner fhall buy or fell any wares or merchandize within the faid borough in grofs, but only in the times of fairs and markets, without fpecial licences of the mayor, bailiffs, and burgeffes of the faid borough, for the time being.—— The charter then proceeds to define the right of the mayor, bailiffs, and burgeffes, to a jurifdiction [1] over the Bifhop's Fee, the parifhes of St. Mary and St. Leonard, and the Newark, with a faving of all rights to thofe who may be interefted. It appears alfo by this grant, that much damage had been done in the town by malt-kilns being erected within it; it therefore orders, that no granary of that fort fhould be erected hereafter to be ufed, but what was thirty yards from any building, under the penalty of 6s. 8d. for every time it was ufed. For the better relief of the poor of the faid place, it grants a market for wool, yarn, and worfted, and other commodities, on certain days heretofore ufed and appointed; and all fines, amercements, tolls, &c. were to be ufed to the fervice and maintenance of the poor within the borough aforefaid. It concludes with reinftating them in all their lands, hereditaments, grants, charters, &c. But the original charter fhall here be copied.

" Regina omnibus ad quos, &c. falutem. Cum burgus nofter de Leycefter, in comitatu noftro Leyceftrie, fit burgus valdè antiquus et populofus, et ab antiquis temporibus fuit burgus incorporatus, inhabitantefque inde et predeceffores fui diverfas libertates, franchefia, privilegia, et immunitates hactenus habuerunt et tenuerunt, tam ratione diverfarum prefcriptionum et confuetudinum in eodem

---

[1] The Judges have lately given an opinion that the Corporation has only a concurrent power with the County Juftices.

burgo à tempore cujus contrario memoria hominum non exiftit ufitatarum, quam ex donationibus et conceffionibus diverforum progenitorum noftrorum quondam regum Anglie; que quidem conceffiones eifdem inhabitantibus non per unum nomen corporationis, fed per varia et diverfa nomina facta fuerunt, prout in diverfis cartis et literis patentibus diverforum progenitorum noftrorum inde preanteà factis et conceffis plenius apparet: Cumque dilecti fubditi noftri major et burgenfes predicti burgi noftri de Leicefter nobis humillimè fupplicaverunt, quatenus nos eifdem majori et burgenfibus gratiam et munificentiam noftram regiam in hâc parte graciosè exhibere et extendere velimus; quodque nos, pro meliori gubernatione, regimine, et melioratione ejufdem burgi, dictos majorem et burgenfes ejufdem burgi in aliud corpus corporatum et politicum, per nomen " Majoris, ballivorum, et burgenfium burgi de Leicefter," per literas noftras patentes, ratificare, confirmare, facere, conftituere, redigere, feu creare de novo dignaremur, cum additione et augmentatione quarundam libertatum pro bono publico ejufdem burgi, prout nobis melius videbitur expedire. Nos igitur, meliorationem ejufdem burgi graciosè affectantes, ac volentes quod de cetero in perpetuum in eodem burgo continuò habeatur unus certus et indubitatus modus de et pro cuftodiâ pacis et bono regimine ac gubernatione populi ibidem, et quod burgus predictus de cetero in perpetuum fit et remaneat burgus pacis et quiet', ad formidinem et terrorem malorum, et in premium bonorum, et quod pax noftra ceteraque facta jufticie ibidem abfque ulteriori dilatione ferventur; fperantefque quod fi burgenfes ejufdem burgi et fucceffores fui ampliori ex conceffione noftrâ gaudere poterunt honores, libertates, et privilegia, tunc ad fervicia que poterint nobis ac heredibus et fucceforibus noftris impendend' et exhibend' fpecialius fortiufque fentiant fe obligatos: De gratiâ noftrâ fpeciali, et ex certâ fcientiâ et mero motu noftris, voluimus, ordinavimus, conftituimus, et conceffimus, ac per prefentes, pro nobis, heredibus et fucceforibus noftris, volumus, ordinamus, conftituimus, declaramus, et concedimus, quod dictus burgus de Leicefter, in dicto comitatu noftro Leyceftrie, de cetero fit et erit liber burgus de fe, et quod burgenfes burgi illius et fucceffores fui de cetero in perpetuum fint et erunt, vigore prefentium, unum corpus corporatum et politicum, in re, facto, et nomine, et communitas perpetua, de uno majore, duobus ballivis, et burgenfibus, per nomen " Majoris, ballivorum, et burgenfium burgi de Leycefter," et eos, per nomen " Majoris, ballivorum, et burgenfium burgi de Leicefter," unum corpus corporatum et politicum, in re, facto, et nomine, realiter et ad plenum, pro nobis, heredibus et fucceforibus noftris, erigimus, facimus, ordinamus, conftituimus, confirmamus, et declaramus per prefentes; et quod per idem nomen habeant fucceffionem perpetuam; et quod ipfi per nomen " Majoris, ballivorum, et burgenfium burgi de Leicefter" fint et erunt, perpetuis futuris temporibus, perfone habiles et in lege capaces ad habend', perquirend', recipiend', et poffidend' terras, tenementa, libertates, privilegia, jurifdictiones, franchefia, et hereditamenta, cujufcumque generis, nature, vel fpeciei fuerint, fibi et fucceforibus fuis, in feodo et perpetuitate; et etiam bona et catalla, et quafcumque alias res, cujufcunque generis, nature, vel fpeciei fuerint; necnon ad dand', concedend', dimittend', et affignand' terras, tenementa, et hereditamenta, bona et catalla, ac omnia et fingula alia facta et res faciend' et exequend', per nomen predictum; et quod per idem nomen " Majoris, ballivorum, et burgenfium burgi de Leicefter," placitare et implacitari, refpondere et refponderi, defendere et defendi, valeant et poffint, in quibufcumque curiis, placeis, et locis, et coram quibufcumque judicibus et jufticiariis, ac aliis perfonis et officiariis noftris, ac heredum et fucceforum noftrorum, in omnibus fectis, querelis, placitis, caufis, materiis, et demandis quibufcumque, cujufcumque fint generis, nature, feu fpeciei, eifdem modo et formâ, prout alii ligei noftri hujus regni noftri Anglie,

perfone habiles et in lege capaces placitare et implacitari, refpondere et refponderi, defendere et defendi; ac habere, perquirere, recipere, poffidere, dare, concedere, et dimittere, valeant et poffint; et quod major, ballivi, et burgenfes predicti burgi de Leiceftrie, et fucceffores fui, habeant in perpetuum commune figillum, pro caufis et negociis fuis et fucceforum fuorum quibufcumque agend' ferviturum; et quod benè liceat et licebit eifdem majori, ballivis, et burgenfibus, et fucceforibus fuis, figillum illum ad libitum fuum, de tempore in tempus, frangere, mutare, et de novo facere, prout eis melius fieri et fore videbitur. Et ulterius volumus, ac per prefentes, pro nobis, heredibus et fucceforibus noftris, concedimus et ordinamus, quod de cetero in perpetuum fit et erit infra burgum predictum unus de magis probiorum et difcreciorum burgenfium burgi predicti, in formâ inferius in hiis prefentibus mencionatâ, eligendi, qui erit et nominabitur " Major" burgi predicti; quodque fimiliter fint et erunt infra eundem burgum duo probi et difcreti burgenfes mencionati eligendi, qui erunt et nominabuntur " Ballivi" burgi predicti. Ac eciam volumus, ac per prefentes, pro nobis, heredibus et fucceforibus noftris, concedimus et ordinamus, quod de cetero fint et erunt infra burgum predictum, de tempore in tempus, viginti quatuor probi et difcreti viri, inhabitantes et commorantes infra eundem burgum, qui erunt et vocabuntur " Aldermanni" burgi predicti; et quod major burgi predicti pro tempore exiftens, et fucceffores fui, de tempore in tempus, reputabitur fore et effe unus de predicto numero viginti quatuor aldermannorum ejufdem burgi; ac eciam quod de cetero fint et erint infra predictum burgum, de tempore in tempus, quadraginta et octo alii probi et difcreti viri inhabitantes et commorantes infra eundem burgum, qui erunt et vulgariter nuncupabuntur " The Company of eighte and fortie." Et volumus, ac per prefentes, pro nobis, heredibus et fucceforibus noftris, concedimus, quod predicti quadraginta octo burgenfes, vulgariter vocati " The Company of eighte and fortie," erunt et vocabuntur " Commune Confilium Burgi" predicti, et erunt de tempore in tempus affiftentes et auxiliantes majori et aldermannis dicti burgi de Leiceftriâ predictis pro tempore exiftentibus, in omnibus caufis et materiis burgum predictum tangentibus feu concernentibus. Et ulterius volumus, ac per prefentes, pro nobis, heredibus et fucceforibus noftris, concedimus prefatis majori, ballivis, et burgenfibus burgi predicti, et fucceforibus fuis, quod major et aldermanni ejufdem burgi, et fucceffores fui pro tempore exiftentes, vel major pars eorumdem, habeant et habebunt plenam poteftatem et auctoritatem condendi, conftituendi, ordinandi, et faciendi, de tempore in tempus, hujufmodi leges, ftatuta, et ordinaciones rationabilia quecumque, que eis bona, falubria, utilia, honefta, et neceffaria, juxta eorum fanas difcreciones fore videbuntur, pro bono regimine et gubernacione burgenfium, artificum, et inhabitantium burgi predicti pro tempore exiftentium; ac pro declaracione quoquomodo et ordinacione predictorum majoris, aldermanni, ballivi, et burgenfium, artifices, inhabitantes, et refidentes burgi predicti, in officio, miniftris, et negociis fuis, infra burgum illum ac limites ejufdem, pro tempore exiftentes, fefe habebunt, ac gerent et utentur, ac aliter, pro ulteriori bono et publicâ utilitate et regimine burgi illius, ac victualicione ejufdem burgi; ac eciam pro meliori prefervacione, gubernacione, difpoficione, locacione, et dimiffione terrarum, tenementorum, poffeffionum, revencionum, et hereditamentorum, prefatis majori, ballivis, et burgenfibus, et fucceforibus fuis, dat', conceff', affignat', five confirmat', aut in pofterum dand', concedend', five affignand', ac res et caufas quafcumque burgi predicti, aut ftatum, jus, et intereffe ejufdem burgi tangentes, feu quoquomodo concernentes; et quod dicti major et aldermanni et fucceffores fui, vel major pars eorundem pro tempore exiftentium, quociefcunque hujufmodi leges, ftatuta, et ordinaciones, condiderint, fecerint, et ordinaverint, et ftabilierint in formâ predictâ, hujufmodi

modi et tales racionabiles penas, penalitates, et puniciones, per imprifonamentum corporis, vel per fines et amerciamenta, vel per eorum utrumque, erga et fuper omnes delinquentes contra hujufmodi leges, ftatuta, et ordinaciones, five eorum aliquod five aliqua, imponere et affidere poffint, quales et que eifdem majori et aldermannis ejufdem burgi, vel majori parti eorumdem pro tempore exiftentium, rationabilia et requifita fore videbuntur ; ac eadem fines et amerciamenta levare ac habere poffint et valeant, abfque impedimento noftri, heredum et fucceflorum noftrorum ; que omnia et fingula leges, ftatuta, et ordinaciones, fic ut prefertur faciend', obfervari volumus, fub penis in eifdem continendis ; ita tamen quod leges, ftatuta, ordinaciones, imprifonamenta, fines, et amerciamenta hujufmodi, non fint repugnantes nec contraria legibus, ftatutis, confuetudinibus, five juribus regni noftri Anglie. Et, pro meliori executione earumdem conceffionum noftrarum in hâc parte, affignavimus, conftituimus, nominavimus, et fecimus, ac per prefentes, pro nobis, heredibus et fucceffioribus, affignamus, nominamus, conftituimus, et facimus, dilectum nobis Thomam Clarke, modò majorem burgi predicti, fore et effe primum et modernum majorem burgi predicti ; volentes quod idem Thomas Clarke in officio majoris ejufdem burgi erit et continuabit à confectione prefencium ufque ad diem fefti Sancti Matthei Apoftoli proximè futurum, et de eodem fefto quoufque alius aldermannus burgi predicti ad officium illud prefectus et juratus fuerit, juxta ordinaciones et conftituciones in prefentibus inferius expreffas et declaratas, fi idem Thomas Clarke tamdiu vixerit. Affignavimus etiam, nominavimus, conftituimus, et fecimus, ac per prefentes, pro nobis, heredibus et fucceffioribus noftris, affignamus, nominamus, conftituimus, et facimus, dilectos nobis Thomam Chettell, modò aldermannum burgi predicti, et Jacobum Andrewe, modò unum de quadraginta octo burgenfibus ejufdem burgi, fore et effe duos primos et modernos ballivos burgi predicti, continuandos in eodem officio ufque ad predictam diem fefti Sancti Matthei Apoftoli proximè futurum, et de eodem fefto quoufque duo alii de burgenfibus burgi predicti prefecti et jurati erunt juxta ordinaciones et conftituciones in prefentibus expreffas et declaratas, fi idem Thomas Chettell et Jacobus Andrew tamdiu vixerint. Affignavimus eciam, nominavimus, conftituimus, et fecimus, ac per prefentes, pro nobis, heredibus et fucceffioribus noftris, affignamus, nominamus, conftituimus, et facimus, predictum Thomam Clarke, modò majorem burgi predicti, ac etiam dilectos nobis Willielmum Norrice, Jacobum Clarke, Johannem Stanford, Georgium Tatam, Robertum Heirick, Willielmum Morton, Jacobum Ellis, Willielmum Ludlam, Radulphum Chettell, Willielmum Yates, Thomam Nixe, Edwardum Newcome, Robertum Gillot, Willielmum Rowe, Hugonem Hunter, Johannem Mabbs, Francifcum Watts, predictum Thomam Chettell unum ballivorum burgi predicti, Thomam Manby, Lebbeum Chamberleyn, Willielmum Warde, Thomam Chapman, et Johannem Freake, modò aldermannos burgi predicti, fore et effe viginti et quatuor primos et modernos aldermannos burgi predicti, continuandos in eodem officio aldermanni ejufdem burgi durantibus vitis fuis, nifi interim pro malâ gubernacione feu malè fe gerend' in eâ parte ab officio illo amoti fuerint. Affignavimus eciam, nominavimus, conftituimus, et fecimus, ac per prefentes, pro nobis, heredibus et fucceffioribus noftris, affignamus, nominamus, conftituimus, et facimus, dilectos nobis Georgium Brooke, Thomam Heirick, Richardum Archer, Willielmum Biggs, Valentinum Wells, Richardum Barftall, Thomam Hunt, Robertum Woolley, Johannem Bennett, Johannem Woodford, Robertum Atton, Michaelem Thornton, Richardum Stanford, predictum Jacobum Andrewe (unum ballivorum ejufdem burgi), Arthurum Tatam, Henricum Halpeny, Willielmum Stanley, Johannem Spencer, Reginaldum Faufit, Hugonem Marfhall, Johannem Brighte, Antonium Webfter, Thomam Pate, Johannem Lawnder, Criftoferum Ne-

Vol. I.

dam, Thomam Taylor, Criftoferum Hallifield, Johannem Eyrick, Bartholomeum Middleton, Henricum Penyngton, Willielmum Okes, Wiatum Fowler, Willielmum Vickars, Thomam Paynter, Johannem Pare, Robertum Crofby, Georgium Greene, Edmundum Abney, Radulphum Orton, Thomam Stanford, Robertum Johnfon, Johannem Buggs, Nicholaum Gillott, Willielmum Jee, Richardum Normande, Thomam Yonge, Radulphum Chettell, et Johannem Hynde, fore et effe quadraginta octo primos et modernos burgenfes, vulgaritèr vocatos "The Company of eighte and fortie," ejufdem burgi, continuandos in eodem officio durantibus vitis fuis, nifi interim pro malâ gubernacione feu malè fe gerend' in eâ parte, aut aliquâ aliâ causâ racionabili ab officio illo amoti fuerint. Et ulterius volumus, ac per prefentes, pro nobis, heredibus et fucceffioribus noftris, concedimus prefatis majori, ballivis, et burgenfibus burgi predicti, et fucceffioribus fuis, quod major et aldermanni et predicti quadraginta octo burgenfium ejufdem burgi, et fucceffores fui pro tempore exiftentes, five major pars eorumdem, de tempore in tempus, perpetuis futuris temporibus, poteftatem et auctoritatem habeant et habebunt annuatim, quolibet anno, in die fefto Sancti Matthei Apoftoli, femet vel eorum majorem partem affembland' in Guihaldâ burgi predicti, five in alio loco conveniente infra burgum predictum juxta eorum difcreciones limitando et affignando, ac ibidem continuand' quoufque ipfi vel eorum major pars ibidem adtunc affemblat' elegerunt vel nominaverunt unum aldermannorum burgi predicti effe major pro anno fequenti, in formâ fequenti eligend' et nominand'; et quod eligere et nominare ibidem valeant et poffint antequam ab inde recefferunt unum aldermannorum burgi predicti, qui erit major burgi predicti pro uno anno integro tunc proximè fequente ; quodque ille, poftquam fic ut prefertur electus et nominatus fuerit in majoratum burgi predicti, antequam ad officium illum exequend' admittatur, facramentum corporale fuper fancta Dei Evangelia annuatim, in die fefti Sancti Michaelis Archangeli tunc proximè fequente, coram majore ultimo predeceffore fuo, ac in ejus abfenciâ coram hujufmodi predictis aldermannis et ceteris burgenfibus burgi predicti qui tunc prefentes fuerint in Guihaldâ burgi predicti, aut in alio loco conveniente infra burgum predictum juxta eorum difcreciones limitand' et affignand', ad officium illum rectè, benè, et fideliter, in omnibus officiis illis tangentibus exequend' preftabit ; et, quod poft hujufmodi facramentum fic preftitum, officium majoris burgi predicti ufque ad diem feftum Sancti Matthei Apoftoli tunc proximè fequente fufcipiat, et ulterius quoufque aliis de predictis aldermannis burgi predicti debitis modo et formâ in majoratum burgi predicti electus, prefectus, et juratus fuerit, exequi debeat, valeat, et poffit. Et ulterius volumus, ac per prefentes, pro nobis, heredibus et fucceffioribus noftris, concedimus prefatis majori, ballivis, et burgenfibus burgi predicti, et fucceffioribus fuis, quod major et aldermanni burgi predicti, et fucceffores fui, vel major pars eorumdem pro tempore exiftentium, de tempore in tempus, perpetuis futuris temporibus, poteftatem et auctoritatem habeant et habebunt, annuatim, quolibet anno, in fefto Sancti Matthei Apoftoli, femet vel eorum majorem partem affembland' in Guihaldâ burgi predicti, five in alio loco conveniente infra predictum burgum juxta eorum difcreciones limitand' et affignand', et ibidem continuand' quoufque ipfi ficut prefertur affemblati elegerint vel nominaverint duos burgenfes burgi predicti fore et effe ballivi pro anno fequente, in formâ fequente eligend' et nominand'; et quod eligere et nominare ibidem valeant et poffint, antequam abinde recefferint, duos de burgenfibus ejufdem burgi, qui extunc erunt ballivi burgi predicti pro uno anno integro tunc proximè fequente; quodque illi, poftquam fic ut prefertur electi et nominati fuerint in ballivos burgi predicti, antequam ad officium illud exequend' admittantur, facramenta corporalia fuper fancta Dei Evangelia annuatim, in die fefti Sancti Michaelis Archangeli tunc proximè fequenti, coram majore burgi

burgi prediĉti, aut in abfenciâ diĉti majoris coram ballivis ultimis predeceſſoribus ſuis, aut uno eorumdem ballivorum, in preſenciâ hujuſmodi prediĉtorum aldermannorum et prediĉtorum quadraginta et oĉto burgenſium burgi prediĉti pro tempore exiſtentium, et ceterorum burgenſium burgi prediĉti qui tunc preſentes fuerint in Guihaldâ burgi prediĉti, aut in alio loco conveniente infra burgum prediĉtum juxta eorum diſcreciones limitand' et aſſignand', ad officium illud reĉtè, benè, et fideliter, in omnibus officiis illis tangentibus exequend' preſtabunt; et, quod poſt hujuſmodi ſacramentum ſic preſtitum, officium ballivi burgi prediĉti uſque ad feſtum Sanĉti Matthei Apoſtoli tunc proximè ſequentem ſuſcipiat, et ulterius quouſque alii de prediĉtis burgenſibus burgi prediĉti, debito modo et formâ, in ballivos burgi prediĉti, eleĉti, prefeĉti, et jurati fuerunt, exequi debeant, valeant, et poſſint. Et ulterius volumus, ac per preſentes, pro nobis, heredibus et ſucceſſoribus noſtris, concedimus prefatis majori, ballivis, et burgenſibus burgi prediĉti, et ſucceſſoribus ſuis, quod ſi contigerit majorem burgi prediĉti aliquo tempore in poſterum infra unum annum poſtquam ad officium majoris burgi prediĉti, ut prefertur, prefeĉtus et juratus fuerit, obire, vel ab officio ſuo amoveri, vel ſi contigerit eundem majorem ſe non benè gerere in officio illo, quod tunc et toties benè liceat et licebit aldermannis et quadraginta oĉto burgenſibus, vulgariter vocat' "The Company of eighte and fortie," burgi prediĉti, pro tempore exiſtentibus, vel majori parti eorumdem, infra quatuordecim dies proximè ſubſequentes ipſius majoris mortem ſive amocionem, aſſemblare in Guihaldâ burgi prediĉti, ſivè in alio loco conveniente infra burgum prediĉtum; quodque ſuperinde benè liceat et licebit prediĉtis aldermannis et quadraginta oĉto burgenſibus burgi prediĉti pro tempore exiſtentibus, et ſucceſſoribus ſuis, vel majori parti eorumdem ſic aſſemblatis, eligere, nominare, et preficere unum alium probum et idoneum virum de prediĉtis aldermannis burgi prediĉti, in majoratum et pro majore burgi prediĉti, in loco ipſius ſic mortui vel ab officio ſuo amoti, et quod ille in officio majoritatis ſic eleĉtus et prefeĉtus ſacramentum corporale in formâ prediĉtâ prius preſtand' officium illud habeat et exerceat durante reſiduo ejuſdem anni, et quouſque alius aldermannus burgi prediĉti ad officium illud eleĉtus et juratus fuerit, et ſic tociens quociens caſus ſic acciderit; et ſi contigerit ballivos burgi prediĉti, vel eorum aliquem, obire vel ab officio ſuo ballivi burgi prediĉti amoveri, quoſquidem ballivos, et eorum alterum ſe non benè gerentem in officio ſuo prediĉto, amobiles et amobilari eſſe volumus ad beneplacitum majoris et aldermannorum burgi prediĉti pro tempore exiſtentium, vel majorem partem eorumdem, quod tunc et totiens benè liceat et licebit majori et aldermannis burgi prediĉti pro tempore exiſtentibus, vel majori parti eorundem, infra quatuordecim dies proximè poſtquam prediĉti ballivi vel ballivus ſic obierint vel obierit, aut ab officio ſuo prediĉto amoti fuerint vel fuerit, in Guihaldâ burgi prediĉti, ſive in alio loco convenienti infra burgum prediĉtum, aſſemblare; quodque ſuperinde benè liceat et licebit prediĉtis majori et aldermannis, burgi prediĉti pro tempore exiſtentibus, et ſucceſſoribus ſuis, vel majori parti eorundem pro tempore exiſten' ſic aſſemblat', eligere, nominare, et preficere unum vel duos de burgenſibus burgi prediĉti, in loco ſive locis ipſius ballivi vel ballivorum ſic mortui vel mortuorum, aut ab officio ſuo amoti vel amotorum, eligere et preficere; et quod ille ſive illi ſic ut prefertur eleĉti et prefeĉti officium illum ſive officia illa habeat et exerceat, habeant et exerceant, durante reſiduo ejuſdem anni, et quouſque alius ſive alii de burgenſibus burgi prediĉti ad officium illud ballivi vel ballivorum ejuſdem burgi eleĉtus et juratus fuerit, eleĉti et jurati fuerint, ſacramento corporali in formâ prediĉtâ prius preſtando, et ſic totiens quotiens caſus ſic acciderit. Et ſi aliquis vel aliqui de aldermannis burgi prediĉti obierit vel obierint, vel ab officio ſuo amotus fuerit vel fuerint, quos ſe non benè gerentes in officio ſuo amobiles eſſe vo-

lumus ad beneplacitum majoris et aldermannorum ejuſdem burgi pro tempore exiſtentium, vel majoris partis eorumdem pro tempore exiſtentium, quod tunc et totiens benè liceat et licebit majori et reſiduis aldermannis burgi prediĉti pro tempore exiſtentibus, vel majori parte eorundem, in tempore conveniente poſtquam prediĉtus aldermannus vel aldermanni obierit vel obierint, aut ab officio ſuo prediĉto amoti fuerit vel fuerint, in Guihaldâ burgi prediĉti, ſive in alio loco conveniente infra burgum prediĉtum aſſemblare; quodque ſuperinde benè liceat et licebit prediĉtis majori et reſiduis aldermannis ejuſdem burgi pro tempore exiſtentibus, vel majori parte eorundem ſic aſſemblat', eligere, nominare, et preficere unum vel plures de burgenſibus burgi prediĉti in locum ſive loca ipſius aldermanni vel ipſorum aldermannorum ſic mortui vel mortuorum, aut ab officio ſuo amoti vel amotorum, eligere et preficere; et quod ille ſive illi, ſic ut prefertur eleĉt' et prefeĉt', officium illud ſive officia illa habeat et exerceat, habeant et exerceant, quamdiu ſe benè geſſerit vel geſſerint in eodem officio, ſacramento corporali coram majore et reſiduis aldermannis burgi prediĉti, vel eorum majore parte, de officio illo in omnibus officiis illud tangentibus exequend' prius preſtando, et ſic totiens quotiens caſus ſic acciderit. Et ſi contigerit aliquem vel aliquos de quadraginta oĉto burgenſibus, vulgariter vocat' "The Company or eighte and fortie," obire vel ab officio ſuo amoveri, quos ſe non benè gerentes in officio ſuo amobiles eſſe volumus ad beneplacitum majoris et aldermannorum ejuſdem burgi pro tempore exiſtentium, vel majoris partis eorundem pro tempore exiſtentium, quod tunc totiens benè liceat et licebit majori et aldermannis burgi prediĉti pro tempore exiſtentibus, vel majori parti eorundem, in tempore conveniente poſtquam aliquis vel aliqui prediĉtorum quadraginta oĉto burgenſium obierit vel obierint, aut ab officio ſuo prediĉto amot' fuerint vel fuerint, in Guihaldâ burgi prediĉti, ſive in alio loco conveniente infra burgum prediĉtum aſſemblare; quodque ſuperinde benè liceat et licebit prefatis majori et aldermannis burgi prediĉti pro tempore exiſtentibus, vel majori parte eorundem ſic aſſemblatis, eligere, nominare, et preficere unum vel plurimos de burgenſibus burgi prediĉti in locum ſive loca ipſius burgenſis vel ipſorum burgenſium, vulgariter vocatorum "The Company of eighte and fortie," ſic mortui vel mortuorum, aut ab officio ſuo amoti vel amotorum, eligere et preficere; et quod ille ſive illi, ſic ut prefertur eleĉtus et prefeĉtus, eleĉti et prefeĉti, officium illud ſive officia illa habeat et exerceat, habeant et exerceant, quamdiu ſe benè geſſerit vel geſſerint in eodem officio, ſacramento corporali coram majore et aldermannis burgi prediĉti pro tempore exiſtentibus, vel eorum majore parte, de officio illo in omnibus officiis illud tangentibus exequend' prius preſtand'. Et ulterius volumus, ac per preſentes, pro nobis, heredibus et ſucceſſoribus noſtris, concedimus prefatis majori, ballivis, et burgenſibus burgi prediĉti, et ſucceſſoribus ſuis, quod ipſi et ſucceſſores ſui habeant in perpetuum unum virum probum et diſcretum, in legibus hujus regni noſtri Anglie eruditum, in formâ inferius expreſſâ eligendum et nominandum, qui erit et vocabitur "Recordator" burgi prediĉti; et aſſignavimus, conſtituimus, et fecimus, ac per preſentes, pro nobis, heredibus et ſucceſſoribus noſtris, aſſignamus, nominamus, conſtituimus, et facimus, dileĉtum noſtrum Ricardum Parkyns armigerum, fore et eſſe primum et modernum recordatorem burgi prediĉti, continuandum in officio prediĉto durante vitâ ſua naturali; et quod idem Ricardus Parkyns, antequam ad execucionem officii ſui prediĉti proceſſerit, ſacramentum corporale ſuper ſanĉta Dei Evangelia, coram majore burgi prediĉti ad officium illud recordatoris burgi prediĉti fideliter in omnibus officium illud tangentibus exequend' preſtabit; quodque poſt mortem ſive amocionem prediĉti Ricardi Parkins, major et aldermanni ejuſdem burgi pro tempore exiſtentium, vel major pars eorumdem pro tempore exiſtentium, in tempore conveniente, unum virum probum et diſcretum in legibus Anglie eruditum, de tempore in tempus, totiens quotiens

quotiens eis necessarium fore videbitur, in recordatorem burgi predicti eligere, nominare, et preficere valeant et possint; quodque ille qui in officium recordatoris burgi predicti, sic ut prefertur, post mortem sive amocionem dicti Ricardi Parkyns electus, prefectus, et nominatus fuerit, officium illud recordatoris burgi predicti habere, exercere, et gaudere possit et valeat, sacramento corporali pro officio predicto fideliter exequend' prius ut prefertur prestand', durante beneplacito majoris et aldermannorum burgi predicti pro tempore existentibus, vel majoris partis eorumdem. Et ulterius volumus, ac per presentes, pro nobis, heredibus et successoribus nostris, concedimus prefatis majori, ballivis, et burgensibus burgi predicti, et successoribus suis, quod ipsi et successores sui habeant in burgo predicto in perpetuum unum virum probum et discretum, in legibus hujus regni Anglie eruditum, in formâ superius expressâ eligend' et nominand', qui erit et vocabitur " Senescallus" burgi predicti; et assignavimus, constituimus, et fecimus, ac per presentes, pro nobis, heredibus et successoribus nostris, assignamus, nominamus, constituimus, et facimus, dilectum nostrum Thomam Warde, generosum, fore et esse primum et modernum senescallum burgi predicti, continuandum in eodem officio quamdiù se bene gesserit in eodem officio; quodque idem Thomas Warde officium illud senescalli burgi predicti, per se vel per sufficientem deputatum suum aut deputatos suos sufficientes, habere, exercere, et gaudere possit et valeat; et quod idem Thomas Warde et deputati sui, antequam ad execucionem officii sui predicti processerit sive processerint, sacramentum corporale super sancta Dei Evangelia, coram majore burgi predicti, ad officium illud fideliter in omnibus officiis illis tangentibus exequend' prestabit et prestabunt; quodque post mortem sive amocionem predicti Thome Warde, major et aldermanni ejusdem burgi pro tempore existentes, vel major pars eorumdem, in tempore convenienti unum virum probum et discretum in legibus Anglie eruditum, de tempore in tempus, totiens quotiens eis necessarium fore videbitur, in senescallum burgi predicti eligere, nominare, et preficere valeant et possint; quodque ille qui in officio senescalli burgi predicti, sic ut prefertur post mortem sive amotionem dicti Thome Warde electus, prefectus, et nominatus fuerit, officium illum senescalli burgi predicti habere, exercere, et gaudere possit et valeat, per seipsum, vel per sufficientem deputatum suum, sacramento corporali pro officio predicto fideliter exequend' prius ut prefertur prestand', durante beneplacito majoris et aldermannorum burgi predicti pro tempore existentium. Et ulterius volumus, ac per presentes, pro nobis, heredibus et successoribus nostris, concedimus prefatis majori, ballivis, et burgensibus burgi predicti, et successoribus suis, quod erit in burgo predicto unus probus homo et discretus, in formâ inferius expressâ eligendus et nominandus, qui erit & vocabitur " Communis Clericus et Prothonotarius" burgi predicti; quodque communis clericus sic ut prefertur electus et nominatus, antequam ad officium illud exequend' admittatur, sacramentum corporale coram majore burgi predicti pro tempore existente, ad officium illud communis clerici burgi predicti recte, bene, et fideliter, in omnibus officium illud tangentibus exequend' prestabit; et quod post sacramentum predictum sic prestitum, officium communis clerici burgi predicti exerceat in burgo predicto; ac assignavimus, nominavimus, constituimus, ac per presentes, pro nobis, heredibus & successoribus nostris, assignamus, nominamus, constituimus, & facimus, dilectum nobis Willielmum Dethick, generosum, fore et esse primum et modernum communem clericum burgi predicti; volentes quod idem Willielmus Dethick in eodem officio erit et continuabit durante vitâ naturali ejusdem Willielmi Dethick; ac volumus quod idem Willielmus Dethick, antequam ad executionem officii predicti admittatur, sacramentum corporale coram majore burgi predicti ad officium illud recte, bene, et fideliter exequend' prestabit; quodque major et aldermanni burgi predicti pro tempore existentes, vel major pars eorun-

dem, immediatè post mortem predicti Willielmi Dethick, unum probum hominem et discretum, de tempore in tempus, communem clericum sive prothonotarium burgi predicti eligere, preficere, & nominare possint et valeant; quodque ille qui in communem clericum sive prothonotarium burgi predicti, sic ut prefertur electus, nominatus, prefectus, & juratus fuerit, officium communis clerici burgi predicti habere, gaudere, et exercere possit et valeat, quamdiu se bene gesserit in eodem. Et ulterius volumus, ac per presentes, pro nobis, heredibus & successoribus nostris, concedimus prefatis majori, ballivis, et burgensibus burgi predicti, et successoribus suis, quod de cetero in perpetuum sint et erint in burgo predicto quinque officiarios, qui erunt & vocabuntur " Servientes ad clavam" in curiâ burgi predicti deservituros, ac pro proclamatione, arrestatione, et executione processuum, mandatorum, & aliorum negotiorum ad officium servientis ad clavam in burgo predicto, et limitibus, bundis, et procinctis ejusdem pertinentibus, de tempore in tempus, exequend' et peragend'; qui quidem servientes ad clavas appunctuati, nominati, et electi erunt per predictos majorem et aldermannos burgi predicti, vel per majorem partem eorumdem, totiens quotiens predictis majori et aldermannis conveniens et necessarium videbitur, et erunt attendentes de tempore in tempus super majorem et ballivos burgi predicti pro tempore existentes; quodque predicti servientes ad clavas, sic ut prefertur eligendi et nominandi, ad officia sua predicta bene et fideliter exercend' debito modo jurati sint et erint coram majore et aldermannis burgi predicti, vel majore parte eorundem pro tempore existentibus, quorum majorem pro tempore existentem unum esse volumus; et, quod post hujusmodi sacramentum sic prestitum, officium illud durante beneplacito majoris et aldermannorum burgi predicti, sive majoris partis eorumdem, quorum majorem pro tempore existentem unum esse volumus, exequi et exercere debean, valeant, et possint. Et ulterius volumus et ordinamus, et per presentes, pro nobis, heredibus et successoribus nostris, concedimus prefatis majori, ballivis et burgensibus burgi predicti, et successoribus suis, quod predicti servientes ad clavas in burgo predicto deputandi clavas deauratis vel argenteas et signo armorum hujus regni Anglie sculpatas et ornatas, ubique infra dictum burgum de Leicester, suburbia, libertates et procinctus ejusdem, coram majore burgi predicti pro tempore existente, portabunt et gerent. Et volumus, ac per presentes, pro nobis, heredibus et successoribus nostris, concedimus prefatis majori, ballivis, et burgensibus burgi predicti, et successoribus suis, quod ipsi et successores sui de cetero in perpetuum habeant et teneant, ac habere et tenere valeant et possint, in Guihaldâ ejusdem burgi, sive in alio loco conveniente infra burgum predictum, unam curiam de recordo, in die Lune in quâlibet septimana, vel sepius ad eorum libitum, coram majore, recordatore, ballivis, et seneschallis ejusdem burgi, aut uno eorum pro tempore existente, tenend'; et quod in curiâ illâ tenere possint, per querelam in eadem curiâ levandam, omnia et omnimodo placita, querelas, et actiones, de quibuscumque transgressionibus, vi et armis, seu aliter, in contemptum nostri, heredum et successorum nostrorum, factis sive faciendis, ac de omnibus et omnimodis placitis super casum, debitis, compotis, conventionibus, deceptionibus, detentionibus cartarum, scriptorum, munimentorum, et catallorum, captionibus et detentionibus averiarum et catallorum, et aliis contractibus ex quibuscumque causis sive rebus, infra burgum predictum, limites ac procinctos ejusdem, emergentibus sive contingentibus, in talibus hujusmodi et consimilibus, ac in tam amplis modo et formâ, prout perantea in eodem burgo consuetum et usitatum fuit; et quod quoties aliqua persona, sive alique persone quecumque, aliquam aliam personam, sive alias personas quascumque, terras, tenementa, redditus, sive hereditamenta, infra burgum predictum, limites et procinctas ejusdem, possidend' sive tenend', possident' sive tenent', de eisdem terris, tene-

tenementis, redditibus, et hereditamentis, implacitare voluerit feu voluerint, toties ipfe vel ipfi fic implacitare volens five volentes breve noftrum de recto patent' in curiâ noftra cancellarie Anglie emanentem prefatis majori et ballivis burgi predicti dirigendum profequetur, fuper quo quidem brevi in curiâ predictâ, coram majore, recordatore, et ballivis burgi predicti, et fenefcallo ejufdem burgi, aut uno eorumdem pro tempore exiftentium, ipfe vel ipfi, fic ut prefertur implacitare volens five volentes, faciet five facient poteftationem fuam ad fequend' querelam fuam fuper brevi predicto factam, in naturâ brevis affife, hove diffeifine, mortis anteceffioris, attincture, aut in naturâ alicujus alterius actionis five brevis cujufcumque ad communem legem, prout materia et cafus exigit; et quod hujufmodi placita, querele, et actiones, tam reales quam perfonales et mixte, ibidem audientur et determinabuntur, coram majore, recordatore, ballivis, et fenefcallo burgi predicti, aut uno eorum pro tempore exiftentium, in Guihaldâ burgi predicti, vel in alio loco conveniente infra burgum predictum, per tales et confimiles proceffus et modus, fecundùm legem et confuetudinem regni noftri Anglie, pro qual' et prout legi noftre confonum fuerit, ac in tam amplis modo et formâ, prout in aliquâ aliâ curiâ de recordo in aliquo alio burgo aut villâ incorporatâ infra hoc regnum Anglie ufitatum et confuetum eft, aut fieri poteft aut debet, ac in eifdem confimilibus ac in tam amplis modo et formâ prout antehâc in eodem burgo ufitatum et confuetum fuit. Et volumus, ac pro nobis, heredibus et fucceffioribus noftris, per prefentes concedimus et ordinamus, quod fervientes ad clavas burgi predicti pro tempore exiftentes omnia jurata, pannellas, inquifitiones, attachiamenta, precepta, mandata, warrantas, judicia, proceffus, et alia quecumque neceffaria faciend', caufas predictas, aut alias caufas quafcumque burgum predictum tangentes five concernentes infra burgum predictum et libertates ejufdem, faciant et exequantur, prout eis confonum fuerit, juxta legis exigentiam, ac prout in confimili cafu ufitatum eft, aut fieri debeat, in aliquâ aliâ curiâ de recordo in aliquo alio burgo aut villâ incorporatâ infra hoc regnum Anglie. Conceffimus infuper, et pro nobis, heredibus et fucceffioribus noftris, per prefentes concedimus prefatis majori, ballivis et burgenfibus burgi predicti, et fucceffioribus fuis, quod major, recordator, et quatuor aldermannorum ejufdem burgi qui ultimò fuerunt majores ejufdem burgi, durante tempore quo ipfi in officio illo fore contigerint, fint jufticiarii noftri, ac quilibet eorum fit jufticiarius noftri, et heredum et fucceffiorum noftrorum, tam ad pacem in eodem burgo ac libertate et procinctibus ejufdem confervandum, quam ad ftatuta de vagabundis, artificium, et laboratorum, ponderum et menfurarum, infra burgum predictum, ac libertates et procinctus ejufdem, confervand', corrigend', et cuftodiri feu corrigi faciend' et exiquend'; ac quod iidem major, recordator, et quatuor aldermanni predicti burgi, vel aliqui tres eorum, quorum majorem et recordatorem burgi predicti pro tempore exiftentes duos effe volumus, omnia et fingula tranfgreffiones, offenfas, defecta, res, materias, et articulos, que ad officium jufticiarii pacis infra burgum predictum, libertates et procinctus ejufdem pertinentes faciend', inquirere, audire, peragere, et terminare poffint et valeant in perpetuum, in tam amplis et confimilibus modo et formâ prout preantea in eodem burgo ufitatum et confuetum fuit, adeo plenè et integrè, ac in tam amplis modo et formâ, ficut aliqui alii jufticiariorum pacis noftrorum, ac heredum et fucceffiorum noftrorum, in aliquo comitatu infra regnum noftrum Anglie, per leges et ftatuta ejufdem regni noftri Anglie, inquirere, audire, feu determinare poffint feu poterint; ita tamen quod predicti major, recordator, et aldermanni ejufdem burgi pro tempore exiftentes, vel fucceffores fui, ad determinationem alicujus murdredi five felonie, aut alicujus alie materie tangent' amiffionem vite vel membrorum, infra burgum predictum, aut liberates vel procinctus ejufdem, abfque fpeciali mandato noftri, heredum

vel fucceffiorum noftrorum, quoquomodo in pofterum non procedant. Et ulterius volumus, ac per prefentes, pro nobis, heredibus et fucceffioribus noftris, concedimus prefatis majori, ballivis, et burgenfibus dicti burgi de Leiceftriâ, et fucceffioribus fuis, quod habeant, teneant, et gaudeant, ac habere, tenere, et gaudere poffint et valeant, infra dictum burgum de Leiceftriâ, vifum francplegii de omnibus et fingulis inhabitantibus et refidentibus infra eundem burgum de Leiceftriâ, ac infra limites, procinctus, et jurifdictiones ejufdem burgi, ac omnia que ad vifum francplegii pertinent feu fpectare poffint vel debent, bis per annum tenendum, videlicet, unâ vice infra menfem Pafche, et aliâ vice infra menfem Sancti Michaelis, coram majore burgi predicti pro tempore exiftente, vel recordatore five fenefcallo ejufdem burgi pro tempore exiftente, fingulis annis tenendum in eifdem, hujufmodi et confimilibus modo et formâ prout preantea in eodem burgo predicto legitimè ufitatum et confuetum fuit. Et ulterius volumus, ac per prefentes, de uberiori gratiâ noftrâ fpeciali, ac ex certâ fcientiâ et mero motu noftris, concedimus prefatis majori, ballivis, et burgenfibus burgi de Leiceftriâ predicti, et fucceffioribus fuis, quod nullus mercator, aut aliquis alius qui non fit liber homo ac burgenfis ejufdem burgi, aliquod commercium habeat, vel eodem utatur, cum aliquo mercatore, aut aliquâ aliâ perfonâ, aut emat, aut vendat, committet, five diftrahat, aut emptioni vel venditioni exponat, aliter quam in groffo, aliquas merchamdizas, merces, aut mercimonia quecunque, infra dictum burgum de Leiceftriâ, fuburbia, limites, five procinctus ejufdem, cuiquam mercatori, aut aliqui perfone cuicunque, nifi tantummodo in tempore nundini et ferie ibidem in eodem burgo de tempore in tempus tenend', abfque fpeciali licenciâ majoris, ballivorum, et burgenfium ejufdem burgi pro tempore exiftentium in eâ parte prius habitâ et obtentâ. Et ulterius, pro meliore regimine et gubernatione predicti burgi noftri de Leiceftriâ, ac omnium et fingulorum burgenfium, inhabitantium, commorantium, et refidentium infra eundem burgum, volumus et concedimus, quod omnia et fingula domus, edificia, meffuagia, terre, tenementa, et hereditamenta quecunque, fcituat', jacent', vel exiftent', tam infra parochiam Sancte Margarete, vulgariter vocatam *The Bifhop's Fee*, in predicto burgo de Leiceftriâ, quam infra parochias Sancte Marie, Sancti Leonardi, et Le Newark, in eodem burgo de Leiceftriâ, per quodcunque aliud nomen vel alia nomina vocantur five nominantur, necnon omnes burgenfes, inhabitantes, commorantes, et refidentes in eifdem parochiis et locis, five in eorum aliquâ, pro tempore et de tempore in tempus exiftentes, de cetero in perpetuum fint, erunt, et reputabuntur fore fub regimine, poteftate, gubernatione, jurifdictione, correctione, et coercione majoris, ballivorum, et burgenfium burgi de Leiceftriâ predicti et fucceffiorum fuorum; et quod major, ballivi, et burgenfes burgi de Leiceftriâ predicti, et fucceffores fui, deinceps in perpetuum habeant, gaudeant, et utantur omnibus et fingulis eifdem et confimilibus juribus, libertatibus, preheminenciis, et jurifdictionibus, in omnibus et fingulis eifdem parochiis Sancte Margarete, Sancte Marie, Sancti Leonardi, et Le Newark, qualia et que ac in tam amplis modo et formâ prout iidem major, ballivi, et burgenfes, virtute harum literarum noftrarum patentium, aut aliorum progenitorum noftrorum, habere, uti, et gaudere poffint aut debent in predicto burgo de Leiceftriâ, aut in aliquo membro, parte, vel parcellâ ejufdem burgi; ita tamen quod hec prefens conceffio noftra non fit ad prejudicium noftri, heredum aut fucceffiorum noftrorum; falvis etiam omnibus et fingulis corporibus corporatis et politicis, ac aliis perfonis quibufcunque, ac alii perfone cuicunque, omnibus juribus, libertatibus, preheminenciis, et jurifdictionibus quibufcunque, al' quam predictis majori, ballivis, et burgenfibus ut prefertur conceffis, que ipfi aut eorum aliquis jure et legitime habuerunt et gavifi fuerunt ante confectionem et tempore confectionis harum literarum noftrarum patentium, in tam amplis modo

et

et formâ prout fi he litere noftre patentes nunquam habite vel facte fuiffent. Cumque hos informamur quod quamplurimum detrimentum et magna pericula et inconvenientia infra predictum burgum noftrum de Leicefter quotidie exiftunt, ad terrorem burgenfium et inhabitantium ibidem, ratione quod quedam perfone, reipublice et ftatus burgi predicti penitùs immemores, ac commodum fuum proprium avidè refpicientes et molientes, edificaverunt et conftruxerunt quafdam fornaces granorum, Anglicè vocat' *Mault killnes*, pro hordeo et alio grano ibidem operando et exarando, in diverfis partibus ejufdem burgi, ubi eedem fornaces valdè incommodè et periculose fituantur, ad magnum periculum incendii, et combuftionis domorum, edificiorum, bonorum, et catallorum, infra eundem burgum fituatorum et exiftentium : Nos igitur, valdè cupientes remedium tempeftivum in hâc parte providere, volumus, conceffimus, et ordinavimus, et per prefentes, pro nobis, heredibus et fucceffuribus noftris, volumus, concedimus, et ordinamus, quod nulla fornax granarum, Anglicè *Mault kilne*, de cetero edificetur aut conftruatur, aut in aliquâ parte predicti burgi de Leicefter utatur, nifi eadem fornax granorum diftet et fituatur triginta ulnas ad minus ab omnibus ftructuris et edificiis vicinorum ibidem inhabitantium et commorantium, fub penâ forisfacture fex folidorum octo denariorum, forisfaciend' prefatis majori, ballivis, et burgenfibus, per quemlibet perfonam offendentem in premiffis, toties quoties aliqua talia offenfa fieri contigerit. Et ulterius, pro majore relevamine, fuftentatione, et manutentione pauperum et infirmorum hominum et mulierum infra eundem burgum de Leicefter inhabitantium et commorantium, volumus, ac per prefentes, pro nobis, heredibus et fucceffuribus noftris, concedimus prefatis majori, ballivis, et burgenfibus burgi de Leicefter predicti, et fucceffuribus fuis, quod iidem major, ballivi, et burgenfes, et fucceffores fui, habeant et teneant, ac habere et tenere valeant et poffint in perpetuum, unum mercatum lanarum in dicto burgo de Leicefter, Anglicè vocatum *A Wool Market*, pro vendicione et emptione lane, fili lanei, et foraginis, fimul cum omnibus proficuis, commoditatibus, emolumentis, et liberis confuetudinibus, ad hujufmodi mercatum accidentibus, emergentibus, contingentibus, pertinentibus, et fpectantibus, nifi mercatum illud fit ad nocumentum vicinorum mercatorum vel alicujus eorum ; et quod bene licuerit et licitum erit unicuique fubdito noftro, heredum vel fuccefforum noftrorum, ad libitum et voluntatem fuam, emere infra dictum burgum de Leicefter quaflibet lanas, fila lanea, et foragines, adductas vel adducendas in dicto burgo de Leicefter, diebus et temporibus conftitutis et affuetis, quibus ferie, nundine, et mercata, five eorum aliquod, ibidem tenebitur vel cuftodietur ; et poftea dictas lanas, fila lanea, five foragines, five earumdem aliquas, in dicto burgo Leicefter, five alibi infra regnum noftrum Anglie, vel infra aliqua alia dominia noftra, iterum vendere, vel aliter et aliquem alium ufum convertere in proprium fuum commodum et emolumentum, ftatuto de anno domini Edwardi nuper regis Anglie Sexti quinto, aut aliquo alio ftatuto, actu, ordinatione, prefcriptione, confuetudine, five aliquâ aliâ re, materiâ, vel causâ quacumque, in contrarium inde non obftante. Et infuper volumus et precipimus, pro nobis, heredibus et fucceffuribus noftris, quod omnia et fingula eadem tolneta, ftallagia, piccagia, fines, amerciamenta, et omnia et fingula alia proficua, commoditates, libere confuetudines, et emolumenta, provenientia, accidentia, emergentia, contingentia, pertinentia, five fpectantia dicto mercato lanario, capiantur, difponentur, et convertentur, ad opus, ufum, commodum, et proficuum pauperum et infirmorum virorum et mulierum infra burgum de Leicefter predictum. Et ulterius, de uberiori gratiâ noftrâ fpeciali, ac ex certâ fcientiâ et mero motu noftris, dedimus, coffceffimus, et confirmavimus, ac per prefentes, pro nobis, heredibus et fucceffuribus noftris, damus,

concedimus, et confirmamus prefatis majori, ballivis, et bugenfibus burgi de Leicefter predicti, et fucceffuribus fuis, omnia et fingula maneria, meffuagia, terras, tenementa, et hereditamenta, libertates, liberas confuetudines, privilegia, franchefias, immunitates, exemptiones, quietantias, et jurifdictiones quecunque, que predicti major, ballivi, et burgenfes burgi de Leicefter predicti, aut que major et burgenfes ejufdem burgi de Leicefter, aut burgenfes ejufdem burgi, per quecunque homina five per quodcunque nomen incorporationis, vel per quamcunque incorporationem, vel pretextu cujufcunque incorporationis, antehac jure et legitimè habuerunt, tenuerunt, ufi vel gavifi fuerunt, aut habere, tenere, uti vel gaudere debuerunt, aut que infra burgum predictum, fuburbia, limites, aut procinctus ejufdem, antehac legitimè habita, tent', ufitat' vel gavis' fuerunt, ratione five pretextu aliquarum chartarum aut literarum patentium per nos aut per aliquem progenitorum noftrorum, quoquo modo antehac factarum, confirmatarum, vel conceffarum, feu quocunque alio legali modo, jure, confuetudine, ufu, prefcriptione, five titulo, antehac legitimè ufitato, habito, et confueto ; habendum et gaudendum eifdem majori, ballivis, et burgenfibus, et fuccefforibus fuis in perpetuum ; reddendo inde annuatim nobis, heredibus et fuccefforibus noftris, talia, hujufmodi, et confimilia redditus, fervicia, denariorum fummas, et demandas, que proinde nobis, heredibus et fuccefforibus noftris, perantea debita, foluta, et de jure confueta fuerunt. Volumus etiam et concedimus prefatis majori, ballivis, & burgenfibus burgi predicti, et fuccefforibus fuis, quod habeant, teneant, utantur, et gaudeant, ac plenè habere, tenere, uti, et gaudere poffint et valeant in perpetuum, omnes libertates, liberas confuetudines, privilegia, authoritates, et quietantias predictas, fecundùm tenorem et effectum harum literarum noftrarum patentium, fine occafione vel impedimento noftri, heredum vel fuccefforum noftrorum quorumcunque ; nolentes quod iidem major, ballivi, et burgenfes burgi predicti, vel eorum aliquis, five aliqui burgenfes burgi predicti, ratione premifforum, five eorum alicujus, per nos, vel per heredes noftros, jufticiarios, vicecomites, efcaetores, aut alios ballivos five miniftros noftros, heredum feu fucceforum noftrorum quorumcunque, inde occafionentur, moleftentur, vexentur, feu graventur, moleftetur, occafionetur, vexetur, aut gravetur in aliquo, feu perturbetur. Volumus etiam, &c. abfque fine in Hanaperio, &c. eo quod expreffa mentio, &c. In cujus rei, &c. Tefte Rege, apud Weftmonafterium, primo die Junii. Per Breve de privato figillo, &c." [1]

June 21, 1599. Three foldiers (viz. two with mufkets, and one pike, having fwords, daggers, blue coats lined with yellow cotton, and blue and yellow ribbon) were fent to Afhby de la Zouch, to the earl of Huntingdon, to join the country foldiers (being 100 in all) to go into Ireland.

Sept. 24. Thomas Warde, fteward of the court, made free for a pottle of wine.

The Queen's clerk of the market, coming and examining the meafures and weights, had 20s. reward.

41 Eliz. *Edward Newcome* mayor. Freemen, 49.

Quarter Seffions to be held, without dinner kept by the mayor ; only he fhall dine the recorder.

Sept. 29. Agreed, that the glovers of the town fhall weigh no wool at their houfes, but only in the wool-hall, on pain of 6d. 8d. ; and there fell it.

Oct. 24. Agreed, that all wool brought to this borough to be fold fhall be weighed at the wool-hall, on pain of 3s. 4d. for every ftone, &c.

Oct. 26. Agreed, that all freemen (being tradefmen) fhall, before St. Thomas's next, come and dwell within the liberties of the borough, or be disfranchifed for ever.

Item, that no butcher of the county fhall bring flefh to fell, without the hide, fell, fkin, and tallow, of the fame, on pain of 6s. 8d. to the chamber of Leicefter.

[1] Rot. Pat. 41 Eliz. 1599, pars 1.

Ale under the fieve, 3*d.*; ftale ale, 4*d.* the gallon. Candles, 4¼*d. per* pound.

The fine for not wearing fcarlet gowns on days appointed altered from 10*s.* to 2*s.* 6*d.* for each default; and agreed, that they who ought to wear fcarlet fhall then wear caps (if then it rain not), upon the like pain of 2*s.* 6*d.* for each default.

The two companies, at every meeting at common halls, affize, feffions, and fairs, fhall wear gowns and caps; the twenty-four on pain of 12*d.*, the forty-eight 6*d.* each.

Dec. 17. John Underwood, mace-bearer, being dead, there was chofen in his room *Clement Charde.*

Ordained, that no one fhall fet up to be a common brewer but by licence from the mayor and aldermen, on pain of 40*s.*

Jan. 2. 42 Eliz. At a common hall, agreed that the commiffioners for fale of lands fhall meet, within eight days, at the town-hall, and confer how to raife 200*l.* for fetting the poor at work, and pay the town debts, on pain of 20*s.* for each making default.

Jan. 6. On Sunday, at a meeting of the twenty-four, agreed that the mayor proceed in fuit (for maintenance of our charter) in reftraint of foreign glovers from traffick in this borough.

Jan. 9. Agreed to fue forth procefs againft the glovers of the country, which had been difcharged from traffick in our market.

Jan. 15. At a meeting of the mayor, recorder, and twenty-four, agreed that John Wilne, gent. bailiff of Leicefter, and Thomas Ward, the now fteward, fhall have their feveral offices affured to them for their lives by grants under the common feal.

Feb. 15. A letter from George earl of Huntingdon being read, wherein fignifying that 100 footmen were charged on Leicefterfhire, he requires the town to furnifh fix; Mr. Mayor and others rode to the earl, and obtained a releafe of three: fo as thereby the faid burgh and the new liberties thereof were charged only with three foldiers; viz. a pike, a mufket, a calyver.

Feb. 22. At a meeting of the mayor's brethren, a bond of 200*l.* was fealed, and delivered to John Wilne, gent. bailiff of the burgh, and alderman, under the town-feal, for the quiet enjoyment of his office for life; and alfo a patent to Thomas Warde, gent. fteward of the court, and one of the aldermen, in confideration of 6*l.* 13*s.* 4*d.* for the enjoyment of his office for life.

Mem. that the faid Thomas Warde doth promife not to fell or affign over the faid office to any perfon but whom the mayor and aldermen agree to.

March 19. At a common hall, agreed that John Woodford, baker, be high conftable of this borough for the year following, according to ftatute 35 Eliz.

Alfo to continue keeping four poft-horfes; and allowed for each horfe 26*s.* 8*d.*; whereof the twenty-four to pay 16*d.* each, and the forty-eight 8*d.*; and the commons to be taxed.

Thomas Wallis, gent. deputy to the Queen's clerk of the market, April 3, examining the ftandards of the town, and finding them juft, had 10*s.* reward.

At a common hall, agreed that foreign tradefmen fhall be reftrained from traffick within our town; yet foreign tanners and fellmongers, upon confideration for their income and yearly penfion, and the tanner bringing half as much tanned leather to be fold in our leather-hall, and the fellmonger half as much wool to our wool-hall, weekly, to be fold there as they buy in our market, may buy of our freemen butchers on Saturday market only, and not of any ftranger, (fair-days only excepted) on pain for every offence of 6*s.* 8*d.*

N. B. Lands mentioned in Marckham's leafe are faid to be parcel of the town-wall and ditch of the town of Leicefter.

Item, agreed that the two laft fifteenths and tenths be taxed as they have been; viz. the twenty-four 10*s.*, and forty-eight 5*s.* apiece; and the commoners to be taxed and affeffed.

May 1. Mr. Gyllot and Mr. Rowe put in election for the choice of mayor for the year to come.

Here are many orders about foreign glovers.

At a common hall, July 25, agreed that the whole ftock of money for coals be beftowed in coals for the poor, and that the coals be laid at the town-hall; and if any remain unfold at the year's end, the fucceeding chamberlains fhall receive them, by weight, at 6*d.* the hundred; and this on forfeiture of 5*l.*

Certain perfons were appointed to compound with country tradefmen for liberty of our market, fo as none be compounded with under 10*s.* fine, and, quarterly, 5*s.* at leaft.

Aug. 14. It was agreed, by Mr. Mayor and fome others, that Chriftopher Alifander and Henry Watts fhall have the keeping of the wool-hall; and each to be bound with fureties to the Corporation in 2*l.* apiece for their honeft behaviour; taking, for every draught upon fale, one halfpenny, fo as it be not above a todd; and for every draught of wool left with them, on truft, before fale, one farthing.

Francis Belgrave gave two fwans to the borough, going at the Newark milnes, in lieu of a fine due from him.

Number of freemen this year, 34.

Sept. 21, there was chofen mayor *Robert Gillot.*

It is agreed that, hereafter, fifteenths fhall be taxed by the parifhes, every man according to his abilities; and fo all other taxations hereafter to be taxed according to mens' abilities.

Sept. 20, Mr. W. Rowe and Mr. James Ellyce in election for choice of the mayor for the year to come.

At a common hall, Oct. 7, agreed, that the act made in the mayoralty of Mr. William Ludlam, for coming to fermons in the week-day, be put in execution; and fuch as make default, forfeit 12*d.*; and thofe that haunt ale-houfes in fermon-time forfeit, for every default, 12*d.* apiece, and the alehoufe-keeper 3*s.* 4*d.*: ftrangers in their travail only excepted.

Alfo, agreed that there fhall be a cage prefently made, and to be fet up in the place called the Barrel Crofs, or near thereabouts.

Ale under the fieve at 4*d.* the gallon; and ftale ale, a wine quart, at 1*d.* how ftrong foever it be: and fo in 1601.

Certain perfons took the fines of the forfeitures of butchers of the country that do not bring their hides, tallow, fkins, and fells, of fuch *bowlks* as they bring to our market to fell for the year enfuing, paying 40*s.*: the payment to be quarterly.

The earl of Huntingdon, by letter, charged fix perfons named by him to furnifh a foldier.

Jan. 16, 43 Eliz. At a common hall, it was agreed that the town fhall be at half the charge of the faid foldier, to be fent into Ireland; to be paid by the chamberlains, notwithftanding the faid letter.

[It appears that the town, about this time, had a fuit with Mr. Lifter, about the clofes in the Frith near the Foreft of Leicefter, parcel of the Grange called Newark Grange.]

March 6. At a common hall, Thomas Cotton, gent. fhall be accepted a free burgefs of Leicefter; and granted, that he fhall not bear any office in this borough without his own confent.

John Heyrick is releafed 40*s.* of his fine of 5*l.* for redemption of the chamberlainfhip, and fhall pay only 3*l.*

Freemen, 26.

Sept. 21, 1601, *William Rowe* chofen mayor.

Sept. 29. Agreed, that Edmund Hunt fhall drefs the town armour, and have 20*s. per annum*; and have leather found by the town for the fame.

Oct. 20, 44 Eliz. At a common hall, for the parliament to be held Oct. 27, there were chofen burgeffes *George Belgrave*, efq. and *William Heyrick*, efq.

Alfo it is agreed that every alderman keep in his houfe two leather buckets, and the forty-eight one apiece, at their own charge, and the able commoners one apiece; and every alderman look to his ward for performance hereof.

For choice of the mayor for the year to come, Mr. James Ellyce and Mr. Hunter.

Nov. 20. Agreed, that the owner or landlord of

any

any tenement repair the pavement againſt the ſame, on pain of 6s. 8d. [This is one of the earlieſt inſtances of any charges reſpecting the pavement.]

Agreed, that every landlord taking a ſtranger to be his tenant ſhall give bond to the Corporation, that they ſhall not be chargeable to the town, or elſe to diſcharge them, on pain of 40s.

Item, at every of the common gates there ſhall be a ladder and a hook remaining, for danger of fire; to be made ready by the chamberlains.

Item, the Cow Paſture let from this day till a fortnight before Lady-day, for 40s.

Item, every alderman to cauſe ſearch to be made in his ward in the ale-houſes for tipling in ſermon and ſervice time, and preſent the offenders to the mayor.

Dec. 16. At a common hall, a letter read from Hugh Atwell, parſon of St. Tew in Cornwall; by which it appears, that he gave 3l. to Leiceſter, to ſet the poor at work.

Mr. Ralph Chettel, one of the aldermen, deceaſed, gave 5l. to be yearly beſtowed in coals for the uſe of the poor; which is ordered to be ſo employed for ever.

Dec. 18. At a common hall, a compoſition being propoſed with Mr. Liſter about the cloſes, it was agreed to give him 60l. or more; but not above 100 marks.

May 28. At a common hall, agreed that the coal money (which is 17l. 10s.) be made up 20l.; and that John Clarke, one of the ſerjeants at mace, lay at the town-hall 63 quarters before Michaelmas next, and to ſerve the poor for 6d. the hundred; and on Low Sunday ſhall pay back the coal-money to the chamberlains, and 40s. for uſe of the hall, balance, and weights.

Aug. 26. Mr. Pilkington was made free, paid 10s., and was choſen of the forty-eight, and fined for the redemption of the chamberlainſhip 40s.; and then was preſently made a mayor's brother.

Sept. 21, choſen mayor Jacob Ellice. Freemen, 27.

The wayts, becauſe they cannot agree together, are now diſmiſſed from being the town wayts.

Candles affized at 4¼d. per pound.

Nov. 26, 45 Eliz. There was delivered to Mr. Mayor twelve ſilver ſpoons, which Mr. William Heyrick, of London, gave to the town in lieu of 10s. for his freedom.

Jan. 28. At a common hall, agreed that George Ridgeley and his company (being five in all) be, upon his good behaviour, admitted the town wayts, and have their wages, quarterly, of the twenty-four 6d. apiece; and of the forty-eight, quarterly, 3d. apiece; and of the other inhabitants what they of their kindneſs will give.

Mem. On Saturday, March 26, 1603, was proclaimed, in open market in Leiceſter, by the mayor and his brethren, the death of the Queen's Majeſty (who died on Wedneſday night, March 24), and the King of Scots proclaimed.

Mem. that, at the requeſt of Mr. Mayor, Henry Haſtings, eſq. ſon and heir apparent of ſir Edward Haſtings, knt. did read the proclamation to the publiſher thereof, both in the open market at Gainſborough chamber, at the High Croſs, in the preſence of Mr. Mayor and divers of his brethren, and many gentlemen of the county of Leiceſter.

Another proclamation, ſent by the lords from London, was publiſhed on Saturday, April 2, by the mayor, lord Haſtings, and high ſheriff, &c.; and was read by the lord Haſtings.

JAMES I.

May 9, 1 Jac. Mr. William Stanley, in open court, took the oaths of a mayor's brother, &c.; and thereupon, according to antient cuſtom, was called by Mr. Mayor to the bench, and for that preſent was ſet next to Mr. Mayor during the ſaid court.

Mem. Mr. Thomas Cotton, gent. deceaſed, gave 5l. for coals; ſo that the ſum of the ſtock for coals now is 27l. The chamberlains are to ſerve the poor with coals, on Wedneſdays and Fridays, at 6d. the hundred; and on the 4th of May are to pay 40s. over and above the ſaid 27l. for uſe of the coal-houſe,

ſcales and weights: ſo the whole ſum they are to pay is 29l.

Item, agreed that the twenty-four ſhall give 4d. apiece, and the forty-eight 2d. apiece, to repair the North bridge.

Agreed, that every houſeholder repair the pavement belonging to their houſes, and paint the ſtreetſide of their houſes: if they have not ability to do it, they are to be relieved by their landlords.

June 10. [It being expected that the Queen and Prince would come to Leiceſter in their way to London;] at a common hall, it was thought fit to give a preſent to her Majeſty, and another to the Prince: and it was agreed to take up 40l. to that uſe, without any taxation.

Sunday, June 19. At a meeting of the aldermen, it was agreed that the mayor, and ſix of the antient brethren which have been mayors, ſhall meet the Queen on horſeback; and the chief mace-bearer to ride, and the reſt of the twenty-four to go on foot, and the other ſerjeants.

The preſent appointed; firſt, one ſtanding cup, with a cover of ſilver double gilt, to be given the Queen's Majeſty; and one other like cup, with a cover of ſilver double gilt, to be given to the Prince.

Mem. On Thurſday, June 23, Queen Anne and Prince Henry came from Aſhby de la Zouch (from the earl of Huntingdon's) to Leiceſter, and lay that night at ſir William Skipwith's houſe; and the Princeſs, the King's daughter, came to Leiceſter on Wedneſday night next before, and lay at Mr. Pilkington's houſe: and the Queen, Prince, and Princeſs, went from Leiceſter on Friday, June 24, to Dingley, ſir Thomas Griffin's houſe.

Mem. That Mr. Mayor and his company received the Queen beyond the Weſt bridge; viz. between the ſaid bridge and the corner as far as the old liberties go, ſtanding along by the Freer wall ſide, where Mr. Mayor preſented to her the bigger and fairer of the ſaid cups, and to the Prince the other cup; and did preſent the Princeſs at her lodging with wine and ſugar, whom, upon Wedneſday night, he met, and conducted to her lodging.

Mem. That there was no oration made to the Queen; for that the recorder, who for that purpoſe came that Thurſday morning from Boucy, fell ſick at Leiceſter, where he remained ſick till Sunday next after, and then went home ſick.

Fees paid to the King's officers attending her Majeſty:

To the gentleman uſher, 40s.; yeoman uſher, 20s.; litterman, 20s.; porter, 10s.; trumpeters, 40s.; the groom of the chamber, 20s.; yeoman of the ſtirrup, 20s.; footman, 20s.; herbengers, 20s.; the Queen's whey-maker, 13s. 4d. Summa totalis, 11l. 3s. 4d.

Mem. That Richard Parkyns, eſq. died at Boney, July 3.

July 4. At a meeting of the twenty-four, it was agreed to make an aſſeſſment towards the relief of the people commanded to keep their houſes on ſuſpicion of the ſickneſs, and towards relief of perſons in the town gaol; viz. that the twenty-four pay each 4d. per week, and the forty-eight 2d., and the beſt commoners 1d.; and to be weekly collected by the alderman and conſtable of every ward, and paid to the mayor every Friday; and they that refuſe to pay to be committed till they pay.

Mr. Ellis, mayor, releaſed Henry Palmer from the company of forty-eight; for that his maſter Mr. Francis Preſgrave (notary and regiſter for the archdeaconry of Leiceſter) told Mr. Mayor, if he would not releaſe him from being of that company, then he muſt diſcharge him of his ſervice and office he holdeth under the ſaid Francis, and would retain ſome other to ſupply his place; and ſaid, that the Biſhop of Lincoln (at his being at Leiceſter to meet the Queen and Prince) was greatly offended with him, for that the ſaid Henry did not then attend in the Biſhop's livery.

At a meeting of the aldermen, July 8, John Stanford, of Barkby, eſq. was choſen recorder, and admitted July 11.

Aug.

Aug. 4. At a meeting of the aldermen, Mr. Chriſtopher Tamworth exhibited a patent of the ſtewardſhip of the court of Leiceſter, granted to him by ſir John Forteſcue, knt. chancellor of the Durchy of Lancaſter; and requeſted the mayor not to ſeal or allow any writs except they come from him.

The controverſy about this matter is by Mr. Tamworth left for a time to Mr. Recorder, to be adviſed whether the title of the ſaid Mr. Tamworth under the Durchy ſeal, or the title of the town under the great ſe l o England, be beſt.

Freemen, 27.

Michaelmas day, 1603, Mr. *Hugh Hunter* mayor.

Agreed, that George Ridgley and his company (being the town wayts) ſhall have, for their wages, of the twenty-four 8*d.*, and of the forty-eight 4*d.* apiece, quarterly, and of the commonalty as hath been uſed.

Ale under the ſieve 3*d.*, and ſtale ale at 4*d.* the gallon; candles, 3*d.* the pound.

Nov. 25. At a common hall, agreed to give Mr. John Stanford, our recorder, 6*l.* 13*s.* 4*d.* yearly, for his fee of recorderſhip. He died Dec. 1, 1603.

On Monday, Dec. 12, a privy ſeal was ſerved on Mr. Mavor, by Mr. Tamworth, about the ſtewardſhip.

Dec. 14. At a meeting of the aldermen, Mr. Serjeant *Nicolls* was choſen recorder.

Agreed to give William Dethicke, their clerk, a gown, at the town's charge.

Dec. 28. At a common hall: Whereas Mr. Tamworth hath ſerved a privy ſeal, or injunction, on Mr. Mavor, to ſuffer the ſaid Mr. Tamworth to enjoy the office of ſtewardſhip, or elſe to appear in the Duchy chamber this next term to anſwer the ſame; it is now agreed, that Mr. Mavor ſhall anſwer the ſame according to our counſel, and the direction of our recorder.

[N. B. Some were appointed touching the incloſure of the South Fields, &c.]

Feb. 20. Henry Palmer made one of the forty-eight.

Feb. 28. Mr. Auguſtine Nicolls, ſerjeant at law, was ſworn recorder.

March 1. At a common hall, there were choſen, for burgeſſes of the parliament to be held March 19, ſir Henry Beaumont, de Gracedieu, knight, and ſir William Skipwith, knight.

Mem. that, before theſe two were choſen burgeſſes for the town, they were made freemen; ſir Henry in Mr. Ellis's mayoralty, and ſir William this year; and paid 6*l.* apiece for their freedom.

May 2, 2 Jac. At a common hall, agreed that the 20 nobles heretofore allowed to Mr. Ellis, late mayor (over and beſides the old fee), ſhall not be allowed neither to him, nor any other mayor hereafter.

Alſo, it is agreed to allow Mr. Morton 13*s.* 4*d.* of the 26*s.* 8*d.* he beſtowed in repairing of the High Croſs againſt her Majeſty's coming to Leiceſter with the Prince.

[The chamberlains' order to receive the ſtock of money for coals of the late chamberlains, 29*l.*; and of the executors of Mr. Rowe, 5*l.*; and of the executors of Mr. Thomas Clarke, 5*l.*; given to that uſe: ſo the whole ſtock is 39*l.* And they are to provide Cole Overton coals, and ſell to the poor at 6*d.* *per* hundred; and muſt pay, for the uſe of the coal-houſe, &c. 40*s.*, May 4; and to buy no coals in the town, or coming to the town.]

June 15. At a common hall, agreed that, upon default of coming to the town-hall, or not coming at the hour appointed, they ſhall forfeit, the twenty-four 6*d.*, and the forty-eight 3*d.* apiece, although they come afterwards; and none to come in their cloaks, upon the pains aforeſaid.

Freemen, 29.

Sept. 29, 1604, Mr. *Thomas Chettle* mayor.

Oct. 12. Commiſſioners being appointed for ſettling and letting lands, &c.; ordered, that none of the ſaid commiſſioners ſhall be takers of any thing to be let, neither for themſelves or others, but by the conſent of a common hall.

Jan. 18. Agreed, at a common hall, that what townſmen ſoever or other ſhall put into the Cow Paſture or South Fields any more beaſts or ſheep than they ought, either by their freedom or otherwiſe, ſhall forfeit to the chamber of the town, for every beaſt, 2*s.*; and the farmers of the Grange, for every ſheep, 6*d.*; and that none that keep teams (except the farmers) ſhall put their draught horſes into the meadows or South Fields of Leiceſter at any time in the year, upon pain of 2*s.* for every horſe, &c.

In this year the Corporation of Leiceſter had a renewal and confirmation of their charter [1]; which coſt them 376*l.* 10*s.*

March 17. At a meeting of aldermen, agreed to give Henry now earl of Huntingdon, againſt the funeral of George late earl of Huntingdon, a preſent; viz. ſix fat wethers; and to be preſently ſent to his lordſhip at Aſhby de la Zouch.

King James, by his letters patent, dated April 17, 1605, reciting that Queen Elizabeth, by her letters patent, dated the 1ſt of June, in the 41ſt year of her reign, did give power to the mayor and aldermen, or the greater part of them, to make reaſonable laws for the preſervation, government, diſpoſing, ſetting, and letting, of the lands of the ſaid Corporation; doth, by theſe letters patent, grant to the mayor, bailiffs, and burgeſſes, and their ſucceſſors, that the mayor and aldermen, and 24 of the antienteſt of the company of the forty-eight, or the greater part of them, ſhall have power and authority to make laws for the better preſervation, government, diſpoſing, ſetting, and letting, of the lands or tenements; and that all and every act and order for the making of any writing, inſtrument, or deed, containing any grant, demiſe, conveyance, or aſſurance, of any of the lands or tenements, or for or concerning the diſpoſing of any of the rents, revenues, or annuities, whereupon the common ſeal is to be put; that all ſuch grants, leaſes, or aſſurances, unleſs they be in the preſence, or with the conſent, of the ſaid mayor and aldermen, and 24 of the antienteſt of the ſaid forty-eight, ſhall be void: and that the common ſeal of the borough aforeſaid ſhall not be put to any deed, grant, or aſſurance, but by the conſent, and in the preſence, of the ſaid mayor and aldermen, and 24 of the antienteſt of the company of the forty-eight, or of the major part of them; with a ſtrict command of the performance of this his Majeſty's laſt ordinance, upon pain that every offender contrary to the ſaid order ſhall undergo ſuch pains, forfeitures, and impriſonments, as by the laws or ſtatutes of the land may be inflicted upon contemners of his Majeſty's royal command: And further granted to the ſaid mayor, bailiffs, and burgeſſes, and their ſucceſſors, to hold in the Guildhall, or in any other convenient place in the ſaid borough, a court of record, upon Monday weekly, or oftener, before the mayor, recorder, and aldermen, or any three of them, whereof the mayor to be one; and giveth them power to hold plea of all actions of treſpaſs *vi & armis* or otherwiſe, and all manner of actions of the caſe, debt, account, covenant, detinue; of charters, writings, minnuments, or chattels, taking and detaining of cattle, and other contracts, of what cauſes whatſoever ariſing within the ſaid borough, in ſuch and in as large and ample manner and form as hath been uſed in the ſaid borough; and giveth them power, upon a writ of right patent, to hold plea of any real action within the ſaid court, and to award ſuch proceſs upon every ſuch action, as well real as perſonal, as is awardable by the common law, or is uſed in any other borough or town corporate, *(non obſtante* the former or any other letters patent, or any uſe, cuſtom, preſcription, or other thing to the contrary); ſaving to the King all and ſingular perquiſites, profits, iſſues, fines, amerciaments, pains, and forfeitures (after Edmond's leaſe), ariſing or to be ſet in the ſaid court of record; of which ſaid perquiſites, profits, &c. the ſaid mayor, bailiffs, and burgeſſes,

---

[1] Records in the Lord Treaſurer's Remembrancer's office. 7 Pars Original. 3 Jac. I. Rot. 46.

are

are to yield account before the auditor, and to pay all which belongeth to the King to the particular receiver of the Dutchy of Lancaster, reserving to themselves the accustomed fees; and further reciting a former patent made to John Wilne of the bailiwick of the said borough, to hold at the King's pleasure; and another patent, made to Christopher Tanworth, of the stewardship, to hold also at the King's pleasure; determineth his will and grant to the said mayor, bailiffs, and burgesses, and their successors; and ordaineth, that the mayor and aldermen of the said borough, and their successors, or the major part of them, whereof the mayor to be one, shall have power and authority in full court to name, chuse, appoint, admit, and swear, one sufficient and fit person, to be steward or clerk of the said borough, and such or so many sufficient and fit persons to be bailiff or bailiffs of the said borough, and keeper of the gaol there; and also such or so many attorneys and bailiffs, and other inferior officers and ministers of the court aforesaid; and the clerk of the peace within the said borough to be attendant, as well within the court aforesaid, as elsewhere within the said borough, as often as need shall be requisite, as the mayor and aldermen, or the major part of them, shall think necessary, and hath been used within the said borough or court; and that the said steward, bailiff, and other officers, shall take such fees for the executing of their offices as of antient time hath been lawfully taken; with proviso, that the mayor, bailiffs, and burgesses, and their successors, or their deputies, shall yearly make account, to the auditor of the premisses, of all the fines, amerciaments, pains, forfeitures, profits, and revenues, of the town and borough aforesaid, and shall pay all that belongeth to the King to the particular receiver thereof, saving and reserving to themselves the accustomed fees: And further, for the better maintaining of the privileges of the Duchy within the said borough and honour of Leicester, the mayor for the time being, upon Monday next after Martlemas day in winter, take his oath, before the steward of Leicester, at the Castle of Leicester, betwixt the hours of ten and eleven of the clock in the forenoon; and he shall well and truly observe, keep, and perform, all and singular antient customs, jurisdictions, privileges, and pre-eminences, of the Duchy of Lancaster, within the said borough of Leicester, for and during the time of his mayoralty, to his knowledge and skill: And reciting, that whereas the said late Queen Elizabeth, by her said letters patent, hath, for the better relief of the poor of the said town, granted unto the said mayor, bailiffs, and burgesses, and their successors, that they shall, for ever hereafter, hold one wool-market, for the buying and selling of wool, thread, and yarn, with all profits and commodities to the said market belonging, but no certain day therein limited for the holding of the said market; it is granted, that the said mayor, bailiffs, and burgesses, and their successors, shall hold the said wool-market within the said borough every Wednesday and Saturday, at their pleasures: It is granted to the said mayor, bailiffs, and burgesses, that the mayor and aldermen, and justices of the peace, or the major part of them, whereof the mayor to be one, shall and may punish whores, bawds, harlots, and common scolds, there dwelling, as well by presentment of twelve men, as by other means which to them shall seem most fit, as heretofore hath been used within the said borough: And further grants and confirms unto them all the same liberties, immunities, exemptions, jurisdictions, lands, tenements, and hereditaments, which the said mayor, bailiffs, and burgesses, or the mayor and burgesses of the borough and town of Leicester, by whatsoever name incorporate, did ever lawfully hold and enjoy, or might have held and enjoyed, as well within the liberties as without, through the whole realm, by an estate of inheritance, any non-use, or abuser or misuser, notwithstanding; rendering to the King, his heirs and successors, all such rents as have been usually paid, or ought to be paid, for the same: And therefore wills and ordains that the

mayor, bailiffs, and burgesses, and their successors, shall hold the said liberties, authorities, jurisdictions, and privileges, without let or hindrance of the said King, his heirs or successors, or of the justices, sheriffs, bailiffs, or other ministers of the King, his heirs or successors; forbidding that the mayor, bailiffs, and burgesses, or any of them, by reason of the premisses, be hindered or disturbed by us, our heirs or successors, or by our justices, &c.; and also granting that neither the said mayor, bailiffs, and burgesses, or their successors, or any of them, for the not using, abusing, or misusing, of any of the liberties, franchises, or jurisdictions, of the said borough, at any time before the date hereof, shall be molested, troubled, or caused to answer, by any of the justices or officers aforesaid. [See the charter of 7 Jac. I.]

Sept. 4, 1605, 3 Jac. [The yard lands were set at 6l. 13s. 4d. apiece, with a fine.]

Ralph Chettel's licence for drawing wine in Leicester was confirmed, and his fine taxed 20s.; and his rent, 4l. per annum. The like licence was granted to William Ive and George Rowe, on the same terms.

Sept. 29, Mr. *Robert Heyrick*, mayor, sworn. Freemen, 32.

Sir Henry Hastings, being tenant to the Castle mills, would not have the North mills nor Newark mills to have any grinding of malt or other corn, but to his sufferance: [hereupon the said sir Henry commenced a suit.]

Oct. ult. At a common hall, in room of sir Henry Beaumont, of Gracedieu, deceased, there was chosen for a burgess sir William Heyrick, knt.

Dec. 11. At a common hall; ordered, that every country butcher that brings flesh to this market to sell, and doth not bring his hides, skins, fells, and tallow, shall forfeit each time 6s. 8d.

Dec. 13. At a meeting of the aldermen, upon the death of Clement Charde, mace-bearer, there was chosen in his room Richard Beswicke, gent.; and Henry Palmer, notary publick, promised to give bond that the said mace-bearer should truly pay to the chamberlains all such sums as he, by reason of his office, shall receive for the use of the Corporation.

Mr. Robert Heyrick, mayor, Jan. 22, bought, for the use of the parlour at the town-hall, a pair of tongues, 14d.; a pair of bellows, 16d.

25 June, 4 Jac. At a common hall, it is agreed that the mayor for the time being shall have to his own use the docket-money.

Item, agreed that the mace-bearer shall now have a gown given him, and so every third year (a livery gown), at the town's charge.

In this year the expences of the toll-charter were 109l. 8s. 10d.

Aug. 13. It is agreed that Mr. Jesson Clarke, stipendiary minister of the parish church of St. Mary in Leicester, shall be tenant to the town of the Easter book, or dues, of St. Mary's parish, and of the tithe-pigs and chrisoms, as Richard Normond had them; and shall also have the mortuaries, from Michaelmas next, from year to year, upon his honest behaviour, during the town's pleasure, not exacting any tithes in other sort than heretofore they have been paid at Easter; paying yearly to the town, upon Tuesday in Easter week, 40s.; and shall also pay, from henceforth, the 2s. per annum which is due of the vicarage of St. Nicholas in Leicester.

Sept. 29, 1606, 4 Jac. *Lebbeus Chamberlin* mayor. Freemen, 17.

Jan. 30, 4 Jac. At a common hall, it is agreed that none of either of the two companies shall be compelled to pay towards any plays, but such of them as shall be then present at the said plays (the players of the King, Queen, Prince, or of any lord of the privy council, excepted): to these they are to pay according to the antient custom, having warning by the mace-bearer to be at every such play.

March 20. At a common hall, agreed that no land, from henceforth, be let in fee-farm, but only by lease for 21 years.

Also, agreed that the chamberlains that hereafter shall be shall collect all the town's rents whatsoever, and fhall have, yearly, for their pains, 20 nobles a-year, with their old fee ; and all arreirage or . . . . rents any of them fhall upon their accompts bring in . . . . to be ftopt upon their faid fee.

Alfo, agreed that if at any time any of the twenty-four come to a common hall in their cloaks, they fhall forfeit 12d. apiece ; and any of the forty-eight, for like offence, 6d. apiece.

Aug. 14, 5 Jac. At a common hall, agreed that no perfon fhall winnow any corn within any of the ftreets within this borough, on pain of 5s. for every default, to be paid by the owner of the corn or grain, to the ufe of the chamber of the town ; and for default of payment thereof to the chamberlains, the offender to be committed to ward, there to remain till he pay the fame.

Item, agreed to give to the earl of Huntingdon and his countefs, and the countefs of Derby, a tierce of claret wine, and four gallons of fack, and two fugar-loaves of fix or feven pounds apiece.

In 1607, 7l. 17s. 6d. of charges were incurred in fuppreffing of unruly people who affembled to lay open inclofed grounds [1] ; and a further charge of 10l. 10 . was paid for two barrels of gunpowder for the ufe of the town, by the command of the lord lieutenant the earl of Huntingdon, to compel the people of Leicefter to defift from fuch practices. But this was no way effectual ; for another charge occurs of 15l. 15s. expended by the mayor and Mr. Gilliot, and others, who went to Cottefbach to quell an unlawful affembly there and in the neighbourhood, who were deftroying the fences of inclofed grounds. By the command of the lord lieutenant, a gibbet was fet upon the Corn-wall in Leicefter, to deter the people from affembling on thofe accounts ; which was torn down by the mob. This brought down on Mr. Mayor and Mr. Robert Erick the anger of the earl of Huntingdon, who caufed them to be confined in their own houfes, for not preventing or fuffering the gibbet to be taken down without his warrant.

A charge of 3l. 19s. 9d. occurs alfo this year, being the expences of Chamberlain Walker, who was fent to London with letters to Mr. Recorder, concerning the imprifoning Mr. Mayor and Mr. Erick. What the iffue of this was does not appear ; but the Corporation was defirous to appeafe the earl's wrath ; for a Mr. Hunter was fent, by the appointment of the mayor and his brethren, to Afhby de la Zouch, to prefent a gelding to the younger countefs of Huntingdon for her ufe, as a token of their contrition. The gelding was not received by the countefs ; for we find that it was kept there twelve weeks at the Corporation's expence, in hopes that time would have favoured their offer.

Sept. 29, 1607, 5 Jac. *Thomas Jackfon* mayor. Freemen, 25.

Ale under the fieve at 3½d. the gallon, and candles at 3d. the pound.

Agreed, that the mace-bearer fhall have a gown this year, and henceforth a gown-cloth every third year, at the town's charge ; and the other ferjeants to have gown cloths given them, according to the order heretofore made in Mr. George Tatam's mayoralty. [Which is every fourth year.]

It is further agreed, that henceforth no ftranger fhall be made a freeman under the fum of 10l. upon pain of the chamberlains that do admit any under that fum to forfeit fo much out of their own purfes as they abate of the fame fum of 10l.

[N. B. Here ends the writing of William Dethick, town-clerk ; but he ftill continued being mentioned among the officers, Sept. 21, 1608.]

Sept. 29, 1608, 6 Jac. *Jacob Andrewe* mayor. Freemen, 31.

At a meeting of the aldermen (not dated), it is ordered that Roger Halfeilde fhall be the clerk to the mayor of this borough, and clerk of the peace of the faid borough, during the pleafure of the faid mayor

and aldermen, fo long as the faid Roger fhall well demean and carry himfelf in the faid office ; and that the faid Roger fhall give fuch a fum of money to the faid town for the faid office, as Mr. James Andrew, now mayor, Mr. Robert Heyrick, &c. fhall think meet, and affefs ; and, upon the conditions aforefaid, the faid Roger Halfeild is at this meeting chofen to the faid office, and fworn to execute it.

An expence of 107l. 6s. was occafioned in a fuit about the tolls taken in Leicefter ; and 96l. 9s. 9d. was paid in Hilary Term concerning the charter, which in March 1609 was ready for the great feal of England ; but the lord chancellor would not fuffer the great feal to pafs, becaufe he difcovered a claufe which empowered the mayors to choofe a deputy. Great intereft was made to obtain the lord chancellor's confent ; which proved ineffectual : it was therefore drawn anew, leaving out that claufe. The expence then 109l. 5s. 8d.

" Paid, for mulberry trees [2] commanded to be bought and fet in divers counties in the realm, by letters from the lords of his Majefty's privy council, 1l. 10s. 6d."

Sept. 29, 1609, 7 Jac. *Thomas Parker* mayor. Freemen, 32.—The recorder was not prefent at the election of this mayor.—This year the Plague raged in Leicefter.—Sir Thomas White's arms were ordered and put up in the town-hall this year.

Feb. 19, 7 Jac. At a meeting of the twenty-four, and 24 of the eldeft of the forty-eight. Whereas Henry earl of Huntingdon hath offered the mafter or wardenfhip of the Hofpital in the Newark of Leicefter to the town of Leicefter, paying the fame fum to his Honour as his lordfhip did give and pay to William Fowkes, late mafter of the faid Hofpital ; it is at this meeting agreed, that the town of Leicefter fhall have and take the faid mafter and wardenfhip, and give that fum of money to the faid earl as he paid to the faid William Fowkes ; and to have the patent made in the name of the mayor of Leicefter for the time being, and fo fucceffively.

March 28, 1610. At a common hall, agreed that the fee of 13l. 6s. 8d. due to the mafter of the Hofpital in the Newark of Leicefter, fhall yearly come and be to the ufe of the chamber of the town of Leicefter ; and as the poor in the houfe fhall die, one other poor perfon of the town fhall be chofen to fupply that room, which perfon fhall be chofen by the mayor and twenty-four, or greater part of them ; and the poor of every parifh to be placed one parifh after another ; and fpecial regard be had of the parifhes where moft poor are.

In this year the following renewal of the charter [3] was obtained from King James.

" Rex omnibus ad quos, &c. falutem. Cum prechariffima foror noftra domina Elizabetha, nuper regina Anglie, per quafdam literas fuas patentes fub magno figillo fuo Anglie confectas, gerentes datum apud Weftmonafterium, primo die Junii, anno regni fui quadragefimo primo, inter alia, voluerit & concefferit majori, ballivis, & burgenfibus burgi de Leiceftriâ & fucceff oribus fuis, quod major & aldermanni ejufdem burgi, & fucceffores fui pro tempore exiftentes, vel major pars eorundem, haberent plenam poteftatem & auctoritatem condendi, conftituendi, ordinandi, & faciendi, de tempore in tempus, hujufmodi leges, ftatuta, & ordinationes rationabilia quecumque, que eis bona, falubria, utilia, honefta, & neceffaria, juxta eorum fanas difcretiones, fore viderentur, pro meliori prefervatione, gubernatione, difpofitione, locatione, & dimiffione terrarum, tenementorum, poffeffionum, revencionum, & hereditamentorum, prefatis majori, ballivis, & burgenfibus, & fucceff oribus fuis, antetunc dat', conceff', affignat', five confirmat', aut adtunc in pofterum dand', concedend', five affignand', prout per eafdem literas patentes inter alia plenius liquet & apparet. Sciatis tamen quod nos, publicum bonum & emolumentum burgi predicti gra-

---

[1] " Infurrection in Leiceftershire, Northamptonfhire, &c. in 1607." See Wharton's Almanack for 1667, in Chronological Events.
[2] " In my time there has not been lefs than ten or twelve large mulberry-trees cut down in Leicefter : probably fome of thofe fet at that time." Throfby.   [3] See p. 418.

tiosè affectantes, & humilem petitionem nunc majoris, ballivi, & burgensium burgi predicti; de gratiâ nostrâ speciali, ac ex certâ scientiâ & mero motu nostris, volumus, ac per presentes, pro nobis, heredibus & successoribus nostris, concedimus prefatis majori, ballivis, & burgensibus burgi de Leicestriâ predicti, & successoribus suis; ac etiam, pro nobis, heredibus & successoribus nostris, ordinamus perpetuis futuris temporibus, quod major, aldermanni, & viginti quatuor de senioribus de quadraginta octo burgensibus burgi predicti, vocati "The Company of eighte and fortie," & successores sui, aut major pars eorundem majoris, aldermannorum, & viginti quatuor de senioribus de quadraginta octo burgensibus ejusdem burgi, vocatis "The Company of eighte and fortie," de tempore in tempus, in perpetuum habeant & habebunt plenam potestatem & auctoritatem condendi, constituendi, ordinandi, & faciendi, de tempore in tempus, hujusmodi leges, statuta, & ordinationes rationabilia quecunque, que eis aut eorum majori parti bona, salubria, utilia, honesta, & necessaria, juxta eorum sanas discretiones, fore videbuntur, pro meliore preservatione, dispositione, gubernacione, locatione, & dimissione, terrarum, tenementorum, possessionum, revencionum, & hereditamentorum, prefatis majori, ballivis, & burgensibus burgi predicti, & successoribus suis, antehac dat', concess', assignat', seu confirmat', aut in posterum dand', concedend', sive assignand', predictis literis patentibus, aut aliquibus aliis literis patentibus, aut aliquo usu, prescriptione, aut aliquâ aliâ re, causâ, vel materiâ quâcunque, in contrarium inde in aliquo non obstante. Et ulterius volumus, ac pro nobis, heredibus & successoribus nostris, de gratiâ nostrâ speciali, ac ex certâ scientiâ & mero motu nostris, per presentes statuimus, ordinamus, & concedimus prefatis majori, ballivis, & burgensibus, & successoribus suis, quod quelibet actus, ordinatio, sive constitutio in posterum facienda vel agreanda per predictos majorem, aldermannos, & viginti quatuor de senioribus de quadraginta octo burgensibus burgi predicti, vocatis "The Company of eighte and forty," aut majorem partem eorundem, ut supradictum est, pro & concernens confectionem aliquorum scriptorum, instrumentorum, sive factorum, continentium aliquam concessionem, dimissionem, locationem, conveianciam, assuranciam, aut dispositionem, aliquarum terrarum, tenementorum, sive hereditamentorum, parcellarum possessionum ejusdem burgi, aut pro sive concernens dispositionem reddituum, revencionum, & annuitatum quarumcunque, eisdem majori, ballivis, & burgensibus, spectantium sive pertinentium, quibus quidem scriptis, factis, sive instrumentis concessionum, dimissionum, locationum, conveianciarum, conventionum, assuranciarum, sive dispositionum, commune sigillum dicti burgi appendi aut effigi necessarium fuerit per leges hujus regni nostri Anglie, quod tunc & toties, ac in omnibus hujusmodi casibus, omnes & singuli hujusmodi actus, concessiones, dimissiones, locationes, conveiancie, & assurancie, nisi sint per assensum & consensum & in presentiâ predictorum majoris, aldermannorum, & viginti quatuor de senioribus quadraginta octo burgensium vocat' "The Companie of the eighte and forty," burgi predicti pro tempore existentium, vel majoris partis eorundem, ut supradictum est, vacuè & nullius effectûs erunt ad onerandum vel ligandum dictos majorem, ballivos, & burgenses ejusdem burgi, vel successores suos; & quod commune sigillum burgi predicti dictis actis concessionibus, dimissionibus, locationibus, conveianceis, assuranceis, dispositionibus, scriptis, instrumentis, ac factis, vel eorum aliquibus vel alicui, non erit appensum aut affixum, nisi per assensum & consensum & in presenciâ predictorum majoris, aldermannorum, & viginti quatuor de senioribus de predictis quadraginta octo burgensibus burgi predicti pro tempore existentibus, aut majoris partis eorundem, ut supradictum est. Et ulterius volumus, ac per presentes, pro nobis, heredibus & successoribus nostris, firmiter precipimus & mandamus prefatis majori, ballivis, & burgensibus burgi predicti, & successoribus suis, quod ipsi & eorum quilibet, de tempore in tempus in perpetuum, benè, firmiter, & inviolabiliter observabunt & perimplebunt hanc nostram

ultimam ordinationem & concessionem in omnibus, secundùm veram intentiónem ejusdem; & quod omnes persone offendentes & delinquentes contra formam & effectum ejusdem ordinationum & concessionum incurrent & subibunt tales penas, penalitates, forisfacturas, & imprisonamenta, qualia per aliquas leges & statuta hujus regni nostri Anglie infligi & imponi possint versus contemptores & neglectores mandati nostri regalis in eâ parte. Et ulterius volumus, ac per presentes, pro nobis, heredibus & successoribus nostris, concedimus prefatis majori, ballivis, & burgensibus burgi predicti, & successoribus suis, quod ipsi et successores sui de cetero in perpetuum habeant & teneant, ac habere & tenere valeant & possint, in Guildhall ejusdem burgi, sive in aliquo alio loco conveniente infra burgum predictum, unam curiam de recordo, in die Lune in quâlibet septimanâ, vel sepius ad eorum libitum, coram majore, recordatore, & aldermannis burgi predicti pro tempore existentibus, vel aliquibus tribus eorum, quorum majorem burgi predicti pro tempore existentem unum esse volumus; & quod in curiâ illâ tenere possint, per querelam in eâdem curiâ levandam, omnia & omnimoda placita, querelas, & actiones, de quibuscunque transgressionibus vi & armis, seu aliter, in contemptu nostri, heredum vel successorum nostrorum, facta seu facienda, ac de omnibus & omnimodis placitis super casum, debitis, compotibus, conventionibus, detentionibus cartarum, scriptorum, munimentorum, & catallorum, captionibus & detentionibus aver' & catallorum, & aliorum contractuum, ex quibuscumque causis sive rebus, infra burgum predictum, limites & precinctus ejusdem, emergentibus sive contingentibus, in talibus, hujusmodi, & consimilibus ac in tam amplis modo & formâ, prout perantea in eodem burgo consuetum & usitatum fuit; & quod quoties aliqua persona sive alique persone quecunque aliquam aliam personam sive personas quascumque, terras, tenementa, redditus, sive hereditamenta, infra burgum predictum, limites & precinctus ejusdem, possidentes sive tenentes, de eisdem terris, tenementis, redditibus, & hereditamentis, implacitare voluerit seu voluerint, toties ipse vel ipsi fic implacitare volens seu volentes breve nostrum de recto patentem è curiâ nostrâ Cancellarie Anglie emanentem, prefatis majori, recordatori, & aldermannis burgi predicti dirigendum prosequantur; super quo quidem brevi, in curiâ predictâ, coram majore, recordatore, & aldermannis burgi predicti, aut aliquibus tribus eorum, quorum majorem burgi predicti pro tempore existentem unum esse volumus, ipse vel ipsi, fic ut prefertur implacitare volens sive volentes, faciet five facient protestationem suam ad sequendum querelam suam super breve predictum factam, in naturâ brevis assise, nove disseisine, mortis antecessoris, attincture, aut in naturâ alicujus alterius actionis sive brevis cujuscunque ad communem legem, prout materia & casus exigit; & quod hujusmodi placita, querele, & actiones, tam reales quam personales & mixte, ibidem audientur & determinabantur, coram majore, recordatore, & aldermannis burgi predicti, aut aliquibus tribus eorum, quorum majorem burgi predicti pro tempore existentem unum esse volumus, in predictâ curiâ tenendâ in Guildhall burgi predicti, vel in aliquo alio loco convenienti infra burgum predictum, per tales & consimiles processus & modos, secundùm legem & consuetudinem regni nostri Anglie, pro qual' & prout legi nostre consonan' fuerit, ac in tam amplis modo & formâ, prout in aliquâ aliâ curiâ de recordo in aliquo alio burgo aut villâ incorporatâ infra hoc regnum Anglie usitatum aut consuetum est, aut fieri potest aut debet, predictis literis patentibus dictæ nuper regine Elizabethe hic prerecitatis, aut aliquibus aliis literis patentibus, aut aliquo usu, consuetudine, prescriptione, aut aliquâ aliâ re, causâ, vel materiâ, in contrarium inde factâ in aliquo non obstante; salvis semper nobis, heredibus & successoribus nostris in perpetuum, ut in jure ducatûs nostri Lancastrie, omnibus & singulis perquisitionibus, proficuis, exitibus, finibus, amerciamentis, penis, & forisfacturis, de tempore in tempus, annuatim in perpetuum, post finem dimissionis antehac inde inter alia factam cuidam Thome Edmonds, generoso, emergentibus, crescentibus, five provenientibus, in curiâ predictâ de recordo, vel por-

timoto

timoto curie burgi predicti & aliis curiis noftris, ut in jure ducatûs noftri Lancaftrie, infra burgum predictum tent' vel tenend', folvend' annuatim nobis, heredibus & fuccefforibus noftris, ut in jure ducatûs noftri Lancaftrie; de quibus perquifitionibus, proficuis, exitibus, finibus, amerciamentis, penis, & forisfacturis predictis, major, ballivi, & burgenfes, & eorum fucceffores, annuatim coram auditoribus premifforum pro tempore exiftentibus, juftum & fidelem compotum reddent, & de omni eo quod ad nos, heredes vel fuccefforus noftros, inde pertinet, in jure ducatûs noftri Lancaftrie predicti, benè & fideliter folvent & fatisfacient ad manus particularis receptoris noftri, heredum vel fuccefforum noftrorum dicti ducatûs noftri Lancaftrie pro tempore exiftentis, omnibus & fingulis vadiis, feodis, & allocationibus, per nos aut progenitores noftros inde antehac allocatis, aut de jure confuetis, predictorum majoris, ballivorum, & burgenfium, & eorum fuccefforum, in cuftodiâ fuâ femper refervatis & deductis, per auditorem noftrum, heredum & fuccefforum noftrorum, inde ibidem annuatim allocandis in perpetuum vifu prefencium. Ac ulterius, cum nos, per literas noftras patentes fub figillo ducatûs noftri Lancaftrie, gerentes datum apud palacium noftrum Weftmonafterii, fexto die Junii, anno regni noftri Anglie, Francie, & Hibernie primo, & Scotie tricefimo fexto, per advifamentum & confenfum confilii noftri ducatûs noftri Lancaftrie, dederimus & concefferimus dilecto fubdito noftro Johanni Willne, alias Willis, officium ballivi dominii five manerii noftri Leiceftrie, ac ville noftre Leiceftrie, in comitatu noftro Leiceftrie, ac ipfum Johannem Wilne, alias Willis, ballivum dominii five manerii noftri predicti, ac ville predicte, fecimus, ordinavimus, & conftituimus, per eafdem literas noftras patentes, habendum, occupandum, exercendum, & gaudendum officium predictum, prefato Johanni Wilne, alias Willis, per fe vel per fufficientem deputatum fuum, five deputatos fuos fufficientes, durante beneplacito noftro, cum vadiis & feodo quatuor librarum per annum, una cum omnibus aliis feodis, vadiis, commoditatibus, & advantagiis dicto officio ab antiquo debitis & confuetis, percipiendis annuatim, de exitibus, proficuis, & reventionibus dicti dominii five manerii noftri, ac dicte ville Leiceftrie, provenientibus five crefcendis, tam per manus fuas proprias, quam per manus receptoris particularis ibidem pro tempore exiftentis, ad fefta ibidem ufualia, per equales porciones, in tam amplis modo & formâ prout predictus Johannes Wilne, alias Willis, aut aliquis alius five aliqui alii officiarii predicti, habens five exercens, habentes five exercentes, unquam legitimè habuit vel percepit, habuerunt vel perceperunt, in & pro exercitio ejufdem, prout per eafdem literas patentes pleniùs liquet; quod quidem beneplacitum noftrum per prefentes determinamus & determinari volumus in perpetuum: Ac cum nos etiam, per literas noftras patentes fub figillo ducatûs noftri Lancaftrie, gerentes datum apud palacium noftrum Weftmonafterii, undecimo die Julii, anno regni noftri Anglie, Francie, & Hibernie primo, & Scotie tricefimo fexto, per advifamentum & confenfum confilii noftri ducatûs noftri Lancaftrie, dederimus & concefferimus dilecto fubdito noftro Chriftofero Tamworthe, armigero, officium fenefcalli ville noftre Leiceftrie, in comitatu noftro Leiceftrie, alias dictum officium clerici vocati " The Towne Clerke" ejufdem ville noftre, ac ipfum Chriftoferum Tamworthe fenefcallum noftrum ville noftre Leiceftrie predicte ac clericum ejufdem ville ordinavimus, fecimus, & conftituimus per eafdem literas noftras patentes, habendum, tenendum, gaudendum, occupandum, et exercendum officium predictum prefato Chriftofero Tamworthe, per fe vel per fufficientem deputatum fuum, five deputatos fuos fufficientes, durante beneplacito noftro, una cum omnibus et fingulis vadiis, feodis, proficuis, commoditatibus, advantagiis, et emolumentis dicto officio pertinentibus five fpectantibus, habendum et percipiendum, annuatim eadem feoda et vadia eidem Chriftofero Tamworth, durante beneplacito noftro, de exitibus, proficuis, et reventionibus Honoris noftri

Leiceftrie, prout per eafdem literas patentes pleniùs liquet et apparet; quod quidem beneplacitum noftrum per prefentes determinamus et determinari volumus in perpetuum: Sciatis quod nos, de uberiori gratiâ noftrâ fpeciali, ac ex certâ fcientiâ et mero motu noftris, volumus, et per prefentes, pro nobis, heredibus et fuccefforibus noftris, concedimus prefatis majori, ballivis, et burgenfibus burgi predicti, et fuccefforibus fuis, ac etiam ordinamus, quod major et aldermanni burgi predicti, et fucceffores fui pro tempore exiftentes, vel major pars eorum, quorum majorem pro tempore exiftentem unum effe volumus, habeant et habebunt de tempore in tempus in pofterum in perpetuum, poteftatem et auctoritatem, in plenâ curiâ burgi predicti, nominare, eligere, appunctuare, admittere, et jurare, unum fufficientem et idoneum perfonam fore et effe fenefcallum five clericum burgi predicti, ac tot et tantos fufficientes et idoneos perfonas fore et effe ballivum et ballivos ville noftre Leiceftrie predicte, et cuftodem et cuftodes gaole noftre pro burgo predicto; necnon tot et tantos attornatos, fubballivos, et alios inferiores officiarios et miniftros curie predicte, ac clericum pacis noftre infra burgum predictum, fore et effe attendentes, tam in curiâ predictâ, quam alibi infra burgum predictum, limites et precinctus predictos, tocies quocies eorum prefencia, minifteria, et fervitia requifita fuerint, quot prefatis majori et aldermannis burgi predicti pro tempore exiftentibus, vel majori parti eorundem, quorum majorem burgi predicti pro tempore exiftentem unum effe volumus, eligendos, nominandos, appunctuandos, et jurandos videbuntur neceffarios, ac quot et quantos in eodem burgo aut curiâ predictâ antehac ufitati et confueti fuerunt; et quod predicti fenefcallus five clericus burgi predicti, ballivus et ballivi, cuftos gaole, attornati, fubballivi, clericus pacis, et omnes alii predicti officiarii et miniftri, fic ut prefertur eligendi, nominandi, et jurandi, exequentes et fungentes aliquo officio aut minifterio in vel ratione curie predicte, five occafione aliquorum premifforum, circa adminiftrationem vel executionem juftitie infra burgum predictum, libertates et precinctus ejufdem, habeant et percipiant, et eorum quilibet habeat & percipiat deinceps in perpetuum, talia et hujufmodi rationabilia et legalia vadia, feoda, et regarda, de et pro executione minifterii five officii predicti, que ab antiquo legitimè habuerunt et perceperunt, vel percepi debuerunt: Provifo femper, quod predicti major, ballivi, et burgenfes burgi predicti, et fuccefores fui pro tempore exiftentes, five deputati fui, de exitibus, finibus, amerciamentis, penis, forisfacturis, proficuis, et reventionibus ville five burgi noftri Leiceftrie predicti, provenientibus, emergentibus, five crefcentibus, annuatim, nobis, heredibus et fuccefforibus noftris, juftum et fidele computum redderint five reddant, coram auditore premifforum pro tempore exiftente, et de omni eo quod ad nos, heredes et fucceffores noftros, inde pertinet feu pertinere poterit et debetur nobis, heredibus vel fuccefforibus noftris, annuatim, benè et fideliter refpondeant et fatisfaciant, ad manus particularis receptoris noftri, heredum vel fuccefforum noftrorum, eorundem premifforum pro tempore exiftentium, prout fieri folebat, et ut juftum eft, omnibus et fingulis vadiis, feodis, proficuis, advantagiis, et allocationibus, per nos aut aliquem progenitorum noftrorum, annuatim antehac legitimè allocatis, pro exercitio dicti officii ballivi domini et ville Leiceftrie predicte, predictis majori, ballivis, et burgenfibus, et eorum fuccefforibus, in cuftodiâ fuâ femper refervatis et deductis, allocandis per auditorem noftrum, heredum et fuccefforum noftrorum, inde ibidem pro tempore exiftentium annuatim, vifu prefentium. Et ulterius, pro prefervatione et manutentione aliquarum confuetudinum, privilegiorum, jurifdictionum, et preheminenciarum ducatûs noftri Lancaftrie infra burgum noftrum Leiceftrie, ad Honorem noftram Leiceftrie, parcellam antiqui ducatûs noftri Lancaftrie, in comitatu noftro Leiceftrie, performand', concedimus, ac per prefentes, pro nobis, heredibus et fuccefforibus noftris, ordinamus, quod major burgi noftri Leiceftrie

trie

trie prædicti, de tempore in tempus in perpetuum, super diem Lunæ proximè post festum Sancti Martini in hieme, Anglicè communiter vocatam " The Monday after Martilmas daye," annuatim pro tempore existente, venerit in aulam castri nostri Leicestrie, in comitatu nostro Leicestrie, propè dictum burgum nostrum Leicestrie; et adtunc et ibidem, inter horas nonam et undecimam ante meridiem cujuslibet eorum dierum Lunæ proximè post quodlibet festum Sancti Martini in hieme, sacramentum corporale super Evangelia coram senescallo nostro Honoris nostri Leicestrie prædicti pro tempore existente præstabit, benè et fideliter ad observandum et performandum omnes et singulas antiquas consuetudines, jurisdictiones, privilegia, et preheminentia ducatûs nostri Lancastriæ infra burgum nostrum Leicestrie prædictum, pro et durante tempore tunc majoratûs suæ, secundum optimam notitiam et scientiam suam. Et cum dicta domina Elizabetha, nuper regina Angliæ, per easdem literas suas patentes prementionatas, pro majore relevamine et sustentatione pauperum et infirmorum hominum et mulierum infra eundem burgum de Leicestriâ inhabitantium et commorantium, voluerit et concesserit præfatis majori, ballivis, et burgensibus prædicti burgi de Leicestriâ et successoribus suis, quod iidem major, ballivi, et burgenses, et successores sui, haberent et tenerent, ac habere et tenere valerent et possent in perpetuum, infra burgum prædictum, unum mercatum lanarum in dicto burgo de Leicestriâ, Anglicè vocatam *A Wool Market*, pro venditione et emptione lanæ, fili, et foraginis, simul cum omnibus proficuis, commoditatibus, emolumentis, et liberis consuetudinibus, ad hujusmodi mercatum accidentibus, emergentibus, pertinentibus, et spectantibus; et cum in eisdem literis patentibus nullum certum tempus sive dies pro custodiâ mercati lanarum prædicti appunctuabatur, limitabatur, et specificabatur; sciatis quod nos, tam pro pleno supplemento defectûs illius in mercatu prædictâ in eâ parte, quam pro meliore relevamine et sustentatione pauperum inhabitantium ejusdem burgi, et limitum et precinctuum ejusdem, de gratiâ nostrâ speciali, ac ex certâ scientiâ et mero motu nostris, volumus et eisdem majori, ballivis, et burgensibus, et successoribus suis, per præsentes concedimus, quod iidem major, ballivi, et burgenses, et successores sui, liberè, benè, et quietè habeant et teneant, ac habere et tenere valeant et possint, in dicto burgo Leicestrie, prædictum mercatum lanarum, Anglicè vocatam *The Wool Market*, pro emptione et venditione lanæ, fili, et foraginis, quibuslibet diebus Mercurii et Sabbati in quâlibet septimanâ per annum, perpetuis futuris temporibus, ad beneplacitum eorundem majoris, ballivorum, et burgensium, et successorum suorum in perpetuum. Et ulterius, de uberiori gratiâ nostrâ speciali, ac ex certâ scientiâ et mero motu nostris, ordinamus, ac pro nobis, heredibus et successoribus nostris, per præsentes damus et concedimus, præfatis majori, ballivis, et burgensibus burgi Leicestrie prædicti, et successoribus suis, plenam potestatem, auctoritatem, et jurisdictionem, quod iidem major et aldermanni, justiciarii pacis burgi prædicti, et major pars eorundem (quorum majorem pro tempore existentem unum esse volumus) habeant et exerceant, habere et exercere valeant et possint, infra burgum prædictum, ac libertates et precinctus ejusdem in perpetuum, punitionem et correctionem omnium et singulorum scortorum, meretricium, lenonum, et communium rixatorum, Anglicè vocat' *Scolds*, ibidem commorantium et inhabitantium sive delinquentium, tam per veredictum et presentationem duodecim proborum et legalium hominum burgi prædicti pro tempore existentium, quam aliis viis, mediis, et modis, quibus eis magis expediens fore videbitur, prout antehac in eodem burgo usitatum et consuetum fuit. Et ulterius, de ampliori gratiâ nostrâ speciali, ac ex certâ scientiâ et mero motu nostris, pro nobis, heredibus et successoribus nostris, concedimus, et per præsentes confirmamus præfatis majori, ballivis, et burgensibus burgi de Leicestriâ prædicti, et successoribus suis, omnes et omnimodas easdem hujusmodi et consimiles

libertates, et franches', immunitates, exemptiones, quietant', consuetudines, jurisdictiones, terras, tenementa, et hereditamenta, que major, ballivi, et burgenses burgi de Leicestriâ prædicti, aut que major et burgenses burgi vel ville de Leicestriâ prædicti, aut eorum aliquis vel aliqui, per quecumque nomina, sive per quodcumque nomen, vel per quamcumque incorporationem, vel pretextu cujuscunque incorporationis, unquam antehac legitimè habuerunt, tenuerunt, usi vel gavisi fuerunt, aut habere, tenere, uti vel gaudere potuerunt aut debuerunt, habuit, tenuit, usus vel gavisus fuit, aut habere, tenere, uti vel gaudere potuit vel debuit, tam infra burgum Leicestrie prædictum, limites vel precinctus ejusdem, quam alibi infra totum regnum nostrum Angliæ, eis et successoribus suis in perpetuum, de statu hereditario, ratione vel pretextu aliquarum cartarum aut literarum patentium aliquorum progenitorum sive antecessorum nostrorum, quoquomodo antehac fact', confirmat', vel concess', sive quocunque alio legali modo, jure, titulo, consuetudine, sive præscriptione antehac habit', usitat', seu confirmat', aliquo nonusu, abusu, sive misusu, concernente præmissa, aliquo tempore antehac commisso, facto, præmisso, sive perpetrato, in aliquo non obstante; reddend' tamen et solvend' inde nobis, heredibus et successoribus nostris, talia, eadem, et hujusmodi annuales redditus et denariorum summas, qualia et que, et taliter et tali modo, ut pro eisdem antehac reddiderunt et solvere consueverunt, seu de jure debuerunt: Quare volumus, et per præsentes, pro nobis, heredibus et successoribus nostris, firmiter injungendo precipimus, quod prædicti major, ballivi, et burgenses burgi prædicti, et successores sui, habeant, teneant, utantur, et gaudeant, ac habere, tenere, uti, et gaudere valeant et possint in perpetuum, omnes libertates, auctoritates, jurisdictiones, franches', et quietanc' prædict', secundùm tenorem et effectum harum literarum nostrarum patentium, ac in tam amplis modo et formâ, prout antehac ratione alicujus doni, carte, sive concessionis aliquorum progenitorum sive antecessorum nostrorum, aut alicujus usûs, consuetudinis, sive præscriptionis, usi seu gavisi fuerunt, aut uti et gaudere debent seu possint, sine occasione sive impedimento nostro, heredum sive successorum nostrorum, justiciariorum, vicecomitum, sive aliorum ballivorum sive ministrorum nostrorum, heredum et successorum nostrorum quorumcunque; nolentes quod iidem major, ballivi, et burgenses burgi prædicti, vel eorum aliquis vel aliqui, ratione præmissorum, sive eorum alicujus, per nos, vel per heredes vel successores nostros, justiciarios, vicecomites, aut alios ballivos sive ministros nostros, heredum vel successorum nostrorum quorumcunque, inde occasionentur, molestentur, vexentur, seu graventur, seu in aliquo perturbentur; volentes, ac per præsentes firmiter mandantes et precipientes, tam thesaurario, cancellario, et baronibus Scaccarii nostri Westmonasterii, ac aliis justiciariis et officiariis nostris, ac heredum et successorum nostrorum, et attornato et solicitario nostro generali pro tempore existentibus, quam cancellario et attornato nostro ducatûs nostri Lancastriæ, et auditoribus, receptoribus, et supervisoribus nostris generalibus pro tempore existentibus, ac omnibus aliis officiariis et ministris nostris ejusdem ducatûs nostri Lancastriæ, et eorum cuilibet, et omnibus aliis officiariis et ministris nostris quibuscunque, de tempore in tempus in perpetuum in futuro, quod nec ipsi, nec eorum aliquis sive aliqui, aliquod aliud breve sive summonitionem de Quo warranto, seu aliquod aliud breve, brevia, vel processus nostros quoscunque, versus majorem, ballivos, et burgenses burgi prædicti, vel eorum aliquem vel aliquos, pro aliquibus causis, rebus, materiis, offensis, clameis, aut usurpationibus, aut eorum aliquo, per ipsos sive eorum aliquos debitis, clamatis, attemptat', usitatis, habitis, seu usurpatis, ante diem confectionis præsentium prosequatur vel continuatur, prosequantur aut continuantur, aut prosequi aut continuari facient aut causabunt, seu eorum aliquis faciet vel causabit; volentes etiam quod iidem major, ballivi, et burgenses burgi prædicti, vel eorum aliquis vel aliqui, per aliquos vel aliquem jufticiarios, officiarios, vel miniftros prediétos, in aut pro debito, ufu, clameo, nonufu, vel abufu aliquarum libertatum, franchefiarum, aut jurifdiétionum burgi prediéti, fuburbiorum et precinétuum ejufdem, ante diem confeétionis harum literarum noftrarum patentium, minimè moleftentur aut impediantur, aut ad ea vel eorum aliquod refpondere quovifmodo compellantur. Volumus etiam, ac per prefentes, pro nobis', heredibus et fucceforibus noftris, concedimus prefatis majori, ballivis, et burgenfibus burgi de Leiceftriâ prediéti, et fucceforibus fuis, quod ipfi prefati major, ballivi, et burgenfes burgi prediéti, et fucceflores fui, habeant et habebunt has literas noftras patentes tam fub magno figillo noftro Anglie, quam fub figillo ducatûs noftri Lancaftrie, debito modo faétas et figillatas, abfque fine feu feodo magno vel parvo nobis, in Hanaperio noftro feu alibi, ad ufum noftrum proínde quoquomodo reddend', folvend', feu faciend' ; eo quod, &c. In cujus rei, &c. Tefte Rege, apud Weftmonafterium, 17° die Aprilis,

Per breve de privato figillo, &c." [1]

May 19, 1610, 8 Jac. At a common hall, Henry Riche, efq. fecond fon of the lord Riche, was chofen burgefs of parliament, inftead of fir William Skipworth, deceafed.

Mem. That Aug. 24 was received the firft 40*l.* of the gift of fir Thomas White, knt. from the city of Coventry ; and on the 24th of September next after let forth to feveral perfons, to hold the faid fums of 10*l.* apiece for nine years, beginning the 10th of March laft ; and they to fet the poor on work in knitting and fpinning of jerfey, and weaving bonelace, and fuch like work fit for young children.

Aug. ult. At a common hall, agreed that the chamberlains for the time being fhall pay, yearly, to Mr. Thomas Hunt, under ufher of the free fchool, 20*s.* towards his better maintenance, during the pleafure of the companies of twenty-four and forty-eight, or the greater part of them.

Freemen, 21.

Sept. 29, 1610, 8 Jac. *John Mabbes* mayor.

Paid the charges about fuch perfons as have been vifited by the plague [2], befides divers taxations to the charges of the mayor and the twenty-four and the forty-eight, 23*l.* 6*s.* 11*d.*

Freemen, 14.

Sept. 29, 1611, 9 Jac. *John Freake* mayor.

" At Lent affizes at Leicefter, 10 Jac. I. the cafe was, one William Haynes had in the night-time digged up the feveral graves of three men and one woman, and took the winding-fheets from the dead bodies, and buried the bodies again [3]. And for the rarenefs and ftrangenefs of the faét, being *furtum inauditum*, all the Judges of Serjeants Inn in Fleet-ftreet met to advife about it. And they all refolved, that the property of the fheets muft be in fomebody, viz. the executor or adminiftrator of the dead party, or they who had property in them when the dead body was firft wrapped therewith ; for the dead body is not capable of any property. But, if apparel be put on a boy, it is efteemed a gift in law, for the boy hath capacity to take it : but a dead body, being but a lifelefs lump, or *cadaver*, hath no capacity ; but it is beftowed on the body for the reverence towards it, and to exprefs the hope of refurreétion. And then, when a man hath property in any thing (as the executor or adminiftrator, or fome other once had in the fheets), he cannot be divefted of that property till it be legally vefted in another who hath capacity to take it. And according to this refolution, Haynes was indiéted at the next affizes for the feveral takings of thefe fheets. And the firft indiétment was for petty larceny, for which he was whipped : and, after he was indiéted for the felonious taking the other three fheets, and found guilty, and had clergy allowed him ; and, being burned in the hand, efcaped the fentence of death for that notorious and uncouth felony [4]."

July 17, 10 Jac. At a common hall, agreed to fend to London, to provide a fair ftanding cup, with a cover of filver and gilt, worth 30*l.* or thereabouts, to give to King James, at his coming to Leicefter the 27th Auguft next ; and alfo to have the town's great mace mended and gilded, and to have the King's arms of new fet upon the top of the faid bafe.

Item, alfo agreed that Mr. Mayor, Mr. Robert Heyrick, and the three Juftices, fhall affefs the twenty-four at 24*l.*, and the commoners in town according to their abilities, towards buying the plate and mending the mace, and for fees which are to be given to the King's officers, and other charges then to be laid forth. The forty-eight (among themfelves) have agreed to give 24*l.*

July 27. At a common hall, it is now agreed to provide two ftanding cups, with covers of filver gilt, one for the King, and the other for the Prince, worth 30*l.*

Ordered, that every houfeholder, upon notice given by the alderman and conftable of the ward, forthwith caufe the ftreet before his door to be paved, on pain of 40*s.*

It is agreed, that the twenty-four, fuch as have been mayors, provide themfelves to ride in fcarlet, with horfe and foot-cloth, to meet and attend the King, on pain of 10*l.* ; and the reft of the twenty-four to provide themfelves with gowns, citizenfafhion, garded with fquare backs, to be likewife ready to attend the King on foot, on pain of 10*l.*

Item, agreed that every of the forty-eight fhall, for like attendance, provide a fair black fuit of apparel, black gowns, and ruff bands, on pain of 5*l.* againft the King's coming on the 28th of Auguft next.

Mem. On Tuefday, Aug. 28, both companies met accordingly at the town hall, and thence went, two and two, together to St. Sunday's Bridge foot, fomething on the fide Southward ; and between the faid bridge and the little bridge called Frogmire Bridge, did Mr. Mayor and the faid companies receive the King and Prince ; where Mr. Mayor, upon his knee, delivered the mace to the King, and he prefently delivered to Mr. Mayor again. Thereupon Mr. John Wincoll, the town's counfellor, made an oration in Latin, which was pleafing both to the King and Prince. Then Mr. Mayor prefented one ftanding cup to the King, and the other to the Prince. This done, the mayor took his horfe, and, bare-headed, carried the town-mace before the King ; viz. Henry earl of Huntingdon, lord lieutenant of this county, carried the fword next before the King ; Mr. Mayor next, before the faid earl, accompanied with the gentlemen ufhers, with the King's two great maces ; and fo before them our mayor's brethren, in fcarlet, fuch as had been mayors, and the reft ; and alfo the forty-eight attended the King and Prince to the court-gates ; viz. to the faid earl's houfe in Leicefter.

Among the charges of this year, is one for repairing the ftreets againft the coming of the King and Prince, in their progrefs to Leicefter, 26*l.* 3*s.* 7½*d.* Another was for a filver cup and cover, prefented to the King Aug. 18, 1612, 20*l.* 5*s.* 1*d.* ; another for the value of a filver and gilt cup, prefented to the Prince by the mayor, 13*l.* 4*s.* Fees to the King's officers, 34*l.* 6*s.*

Freemen, 49.

Sept. 29, 1612, 10 Jac. *William Morton* mayor.

Nov. 20. At a common hall, agreed to grant licence to Thomas Buckfton to draw wine, during the pleafure of the mayor, bailiffs, and burgeffes, paying for the fame 4*l.* till Michaelmas next. The like to Mr. John Mabbes.

Dec. 1, 1612, 10 Jac. Sir Auguftine Nicolls, knt. being made one of the Juftices of Common Pleas, the twenty-four met, and chofe Mr. Francis Harvey, of Northampton, a Bencher of the Middle Temple, to be recorder ; and it is agreed, that he

---

[1] Vicefima Pars Patent' de anno regni Regis Jacobi, Anglie, &c. feptimo.

[2] In the Parifh Regifters of St. Nicholas and St. Martin are feveral particulars relative to this plague ; which will be printed hereafter under thofe refpeétive parifhes.

[3] Coke, 3 Inftit. 10 Jac. I.   [4] Staveley's Hiftory of Churches, p. 272.

fhall

shall have for his fee, yearly, 5l.; and at every affizes, towards his charge, 20s.; and the town to
bear and pay his charge at his coming to Leicester
at all times about the town's business. Agreed to
write to Mr. Justice Nicolls, to desire him to acquaint
Mr. Recorder elected with this our order for his fee
and other charges, in regard to the town is now poor,
and indebted, and that our recorders in time past
have only had 4l. fee *per annum*, and less.

Among the charges this year, one is for the carrying a letter to Kibworth to the county justices, to
forbid them to call any of the Bishop's-fee men
thither, 1s.

Dec. 14, 10 Jac. In full court, Mr. Francis
Harvey was sworn recorder.

Freemen, 31.

Sept. 29, 1613, 11 Jac. *Thomas Manbye* mayor.

In this year, John Stamford and his deputies were
authorized to issue his Majesty's Farthing Tokens
for the counties of Leicester and Rutland.

At this period also it was noticed, that " the hosiers of Leicester are constreyned by some officers of
Blackwell-hall to paie 2d. in every score of
stockens for hallage, unlesse they will bringe theire
stockens to the hall, there to be solde. They are
alsoe at composition with the duke of Linox for ul-
nage, and paie yearely to the duke's collectors for
the same. That there may be a restreynt for erectinge
of new cottages and takinge of inmates, as well in
Leicester as in other villages that are not market-
towns.—The burgesses of Darby or Nottingham are
about the like for their towns."

April 2, 1614, 12 Jac. At a common hall, there
were chosen sir Henry Rich, knight, and sir Francis
Leigh, knight, one of the masters of request, to be
burgesses for the parliament to be holden April 5 next.

Aug. 18. The King, in his progress, came this
night to Leicester, to the earl of Huntingdon's house,
and there lay.

Mr. Mayor and his brethren, and the forty-eight,
attended the King at the said earl's house, and there
received him, where Mr. John Wincoll made a
speech in Latin unto his Majesty at the court gates,
where the King sat in his coach, and heard the same
very pleasingly; and his Highness did much commend
the said speech, and gave Mr. Wincoll his hand to
kiss; and from the court-gates Mr. Mayor carried
the mace, before the King, up into the presence
chamber.

Freemen, 28.

Sept. 29, 1614, 12 Jac. *John Bennet* mayor.

Freemen, 22.

Sept. 29, 1615, 13 Jac. *William Ive* mayor. Candles 5d. *per* pound.

Nov. 1, 1615. Whereas the lord Cavendish hath
given to the Corporation of Leicester 100l. in consideration that the town pay yearly 6l. to such charitable uses as shall be set down at the discretion of
the mayor and his brethren; it is agreed, that a yard
land shall be assured to his Honour, for sure payment of the same. Hereupon 20 poor freemen were
nominated to receive 6s. apiece, to buy them coals.

If it were not well attested, posterity would scarcely
believe that *nine* poor women were executed as *witches*[1]
at Leicester, July 18, 1616.

Sept. 29, *Thomas Ericke* mayor. Freemen, 26.

Aug. 8, 1617. At a meeting of the twenty-four,
and 24 of the forty-eight, agreed to give to the earl
of Huntingdon, against the King's coming to Ashby,
one yoke of fat oxen, worth 13l. 6s. 8d. or 14l.

Sept. 29, *Roland Pewsey* mayor. Freemen, 13.

Paid lord Spencer, by Mr. Woodland, the first
payment for the land in the South Fields, which was
purchased of him this year for 40l.

By letters patent, dated March 25, 1617, King
James made the borough of Leicester a staple town
for the buying and selling of wool and wool fells;
and hath, by the same charter, given them power to
take conusance of statutes.

Sept. 29, 1618, 16 Jac. *Nicholas Gilliott* mayor.

Candles at 4¼d. *per* pound. Ale under the sieve,
3d. the gallon.—Freemen, 27.

The Corporation recovered this year, of the
bailiff of North Allerton in the county of York,
charge in a suit of law in the Duchy chamber, for
taking toll of a freeman of the borough of Leicester.

The heir of the good sir Thomas White was
treated by Mr. Mayor with sugar and wine, at the
expence of 3s. 4d. And in the same account,
" Paid, for a broad arrow given to Mr. Auditor
Fanshaw, at the audit holden at the Castle of Leicester, for the rent of the Butt Close, 6d."

On the 23d of September, 1619, the Borough of
Leicester was visited, in due form, by Sampson Leonard and Augustine Vincent, heralds.

Sept. 29, *John Heyrick* mayor. Freemen, 14.

Sept. 29, 1620, 18 Jac. *John Pare* mayor.

Jan. 8. At a common hall, there were chosen sir
Richard Morison and sir William Heyrick, knights,
to be burgesses for parliament.

Feb. 12, 1620. At a meeting of the twenty-four,
Mr. Nicholas Bolyvant was chosen town-clerk and
clerk of the peace for this borough, during the pleasure of the mayor and his brethren, and for so long
as he shall demean himself well in their judgment;
and upon condition that he perform such other covenants as they, or the greater part of them, shall
think fit. The said Nicholas Bolyvant was admitted
and sworn a freeman Feb. 19; and also to the said office.

Freemen, 14.

Sept. 29, 1621, 19 Jac. *Jacob Andrew* mayor.
Ale, 3d. a gallon. Candles, 3¼d. *per* pound.

Mem. Presently after the death of Mr. Wylne,
late bailiff of the borough, a letter was sent to
acquaint the earl of Huntingdon, it being his turn to
nominate the next to that office; whereupon he nominated Robert Wright, gent.; and thereupon, at a
meeting of the twenty-four, March 7, 1621, Mr.
Robert Wright was chosen, admitted, and sworn to
be bailiff, and keeper of the gaol of the said borough;
to enjoy the same offices, with all fees and profits
thereto belonging, for the term of his life: this
being the first turn of his Honour's nomination of
the said bailiff, and keeper of the gaol of the said
borough.

" I, A. B. shall and will, from henceforth, well
and truly exercise the office and offices of the bailiff
of this borough and town of Leicester, and of the
keeper of the gaol of the said borough; and shall
not, nor will not, deal corruptly or unjustly in the
said offices, or either of them; nor shall or will receive or take, directly or indirectly, by any colour,
means, or device whatsoever, any manner of fee or
reward of any person or persons for the impanneling
or returning of any inquest, jury, or tales, in his
Majesty's Court of Record of this borough of Leicester, more than the due fees as are allowed and appointed for the same by the law and statutes of this
realm; nor shall, for any money or other reward,
nor for any hatred or malice, or for any love or affection, or otherwise, make any partial return of
any jury or inquest; or shall refuse or neglect to execute any writ or process that shall be duly directed to
me by the mayor or justices of this town, or by any
others that have or shall have authority to direct any
process to me; nor shall, directly or indirectly, by
any colour, means, or device whatsoever, take any
fees, or any other reward or recompence, for executing any writ or process, or for doing of any execution, more than the due fees that shall be allowed
unto me by the laws and statutes of this realm for
doing and executing the same; but shall, truly and
indifferently, and with all convenient speed, impannel
all juries, and execute and return all such writs, process, and executions, as shall be directed unto me,
and shall appertain to me to do, by virtue of the said
office or offices of bailiff of this borough, or keeper
of the said gaol; and the said office and offices, in
all things appertaining thereunto, to the uttermost of
my power shall and will faithfully and uprightly exe-

[1] Six others were imprisoned as witches, of whom one died in the gaol, and the other five were set at liberty. See under
Husbands Bosworth, vol. II. p. *471.

cute, during the time that I ſhall remain in the ſaid office or offices : So help me God."

Freemen, 20.

Sept. 29, 1622, 20 Jac. *John Hynde* mayor.

King James, by charter, dated June 26, hath given and granted to the mayor, bailiffs, and burgeſſes, of the ſaid borough, licence for the purchaſing of lands, tenements, or hereditaments, to the yearly value of 200*l.*; ſo as the fame be not holden of the King, his heirs and ſucceſſors, *in capite*, or of the King or any other in knight's ſervice, the ſtatute of mortmain notwithſtanding.

Freemen, 13.

Sept. 29, 1623, 21 Jac. *Jacob Ellis* mayor. Ale, 3*d. per* gallon. Candles, 3½*d. per* pound.

A petition was ſigned by a number of inhabitants to the Corporation, to have the Cow Paſture enlarged for their benefit ; but it was rejected.

Nov. 28, 1623. At a common hall, agreed that all that have been ſtewards of the fair ſhall account to the mayor before Candlemas ; and that the like be done hereafter, on pain of 40*s.* for every offence.

Jan. 16. At a common hall, ſir Humphrey May, knt. chancellor of the Duchy of Lancaſter, and William Ive, of Leiceſter, gent. were choſen burgeſſes.

Freemen, 38.

Sept. 29, 1624, 22 Jac. *William Ludlam* mayor.

In this year, 14*s.* 10*d.* was charged for watching to keep Londoners out of the town during the plague there.

Oct. 24, 1624. At a meeting of the twenty-four, Francis Harvey, late recorder, certifying that he was made a Judge of the Common Pleas, Thomas Chapman, eſq. was choſen recorder ; who in open court, Oct. 25, was ſworn. [See here the form of the oath [1].]

Mem. By virtue of a warrant from Henry earl of Huntingdon, lord lieutenant of this county, 20 men of this borough were impreſſed, and ſent to Aſhby Nov. 24, 1624 ; and on Dec. 7, ten men more were ſent to Loughborough, and ten more to the Caſtle in Leiceſter ; and 10*l.* in money, for coats and conductors' allowance, ſoldiers' pay, &c.

Mem. Wedneſday, March 30, 1625, Henry lord Grey of Groby came, and acquainted the mayor, &c. that King James was dead, March 28, &c. Whereupon Prince Charles was proclaimed ; Mr. Thomas Chapman, recorder, reading it to the publiſher, Mr. Robert Wright, gent. bailiff of the borough, at the door of the Guildhall, the High Croſs, at the Gainſborow chamber, and at Barril Croſs, in the preſence of the mayor, divers of his brethren, the lord Grey, and other gentlemen.

CHARLES I.

April 3, 1625. Sir Henry Shirley, knight and baronet, high ſheriff, deſired Mr. Mayor's company the day following, to proclaim King Charles ; at which time they proclaimed him at the High Croſs, and then at the Gainſborow chamber ; at which time the high ſheriff himſelf read the proclamation.

May 3. At a common hall, ſir Humphrey May, knight, chancellor of the Duchy of Lancaſter, and ſir George Haſtings, knight, were choſen to be burgeſſes of Parliament.

A meeting of Mr. Mayor, and divers of his brethren, with the preachers and miniſters of God's word, here undernamed, July 15, 1625 ; Mr. William Ludlam, mayor ; Mr. James Andrew, Nicholas Gilliot, James Ellis. The preachers ; Mr. Sacheverell, Mr. William Rudyard, Mr. Edward Blount, Mr. Thomas Holmes, Mr. John Bonnet, Mr. Francis Higinſon. It is thought fit that there ſhall be a collection made in every ſeveral pariſh church upon every Wedneſday during the time of the public faſt ; and a note to be delivered every week to Mr. Mayor of the ſame collections : the money to remain in the churchwardens' hands till it be called for.

It is alſo agreed, that there ſhall be public prayers and divine ſervice at every church in the town, to begin betwixt eight and nine of the clock in the forenoon, and at two in the afternoon ; and that there ſhall be one ſermon at one church only every Wedneſday, according to his Majeſty's late proclamation, and book of orders. And that for that day all trading be forborne, and no frequenting of taverns or ale-houſes be uſed ; and that there be two, at the leaſt, appointed in every pariſh to look to ſuch diſorders.

July 22, 1625. At a common hall, ſir Humphrey May being returned as a burgeſs for Lancaſter, as well as this place, and chooſing to ſerve for Lancaſter ; at his requeſt, his kinſman, Mr. Thomas Fermin, was firſt choſe a freeman of this borough, and afterwards burgeſs of Parliament, in ſir Humphrey May's ſtead.

July 25, 1625. At a meeting of Mr. Mayor, Mr. Recorder, and twenty-four, it is agreed, that the Wedneſday exerciſe of faſting, praying, and preaching, be held at every ſeveral pariſh church ; and that no bell ſhall be rung for ſermon at any church, in regard of the heat of the weather, and the danger of the time.

And it is agreed, that the peſt-houſes ſhall be cleared of the tenants preſently, and repaired, and made fit for the preſent uſe by the chamberlains.

Item, it is agreed that no inhabitant ſhall lodge any perſon coming from London, or other place infected with the plague, without conſent of Mr. Mayor, or the alderman of the ward ; neither ſhall receive or ſend for any wares from London, or other place infected, without the like conſent : and that this order be proclaimed through the town, and continue till other order be taken therein.

Mem. That divers diſobedient perſons, which received wares from London contrary to this order, were bounden with ſureties to the next ſeſſions, and to be of good behaviour in the mean time.

The watchmen (with Mr. Mayor's allowance) authorized to relieve poor travellers with neceſſary food ; and that to be paid by the chamberlains.

Freemen this year, 19.

Sept. 29, 1625, *William Ive* mayor. Freemen, 12.

Jan. 13. Sir Humphrey May, knight, chancellor of the Duchy, and ſir George Haſtings, were at a common hall choſen burgeſſes of Parliament for this borough.

Freemen, 16.

Sept. 21, 1626, 2 Car. elected *Gilbert Fawſit* mayor.

Daniel Mureſin, for that he cannot write, is by moſt voices diſcharged from being chamberlain hereafter, paying 10*l.* for a fine. Thomas Chapman, upon the like reaſons, is alſo diſcharged from being chamberlain hereafter, paying for his fine 5*l.*

A petition of the mayor, bailiffs, and burgeſſes of Leiceſter, againſt incloſure of the Foreſt.

A commiſſion to ſeveral perſons for a loan ; viz. to Henry earl of Huntingdon, William earl of Exeter, Henry earl of Holland, Henry lord Grey, ſir John Coke, knight, a ſecretary of ſtate, ſir John Savile, knight, the mayor of Leiceſter for the time being, ſir Thomas Hayſilrigge, ſir Henry Skipwith, knights and baronets, ſir Henry Haſtings and ſir William Faunt, knights ; enjoining them, or any two or more of them, to call before them ſuch perſons within the borough of Leiceſter as their inſtructions ſhould direct, &c. Dated Oct. 11, 2 Car. I.

A letter from the council, directing the commiſſioners to accept the ſums demanded of perſons, without preſſing them to ſubſcribe their names ; but ſo bind ſuch perſons as, being appointed, refuſe to be collectors of the loan, to anſwer their contempt at the council board.

Sept. 21, 1627, *Francis Churchman* elected mayor. Freemen, 24.

Sept. 21, 1628, *William Biller* mayor. Freemen, 18. Bollivan clerk there.

1629, *Roger Coates* mayor. Freemen, 22.

1630, *Thomas Smith* mayor. Freemen, 20.

The following letter, dated " Leiceſter, 16th of November 1630," was addreſſed " To the right

honourable

honourable Henry lord Loughborowe, lord leiuftent of the county of Leicefter. Theis humbly prefent.

"Right Honorable; We had well hoped that thofe meffingers which weere fent to wayte upon your Honour would have given your Honour a fatisfyinge anfwear; but, perceaving the contrarie, both by theire relation, and your Honour's fecond letter of the 13th of this prefent November (according to your Honour's defire and direction therein), we have fummoned both the Companies, and all the other Subfidie-men within this Borough; upon whofe appearance, both your Honour's letters were openly read unto them; and theire generall anfweare is, that they will be rédie to give your Honour theire anfwears therein when it fhall pleafe your Honour to call them thereunto. So that wee cannot fatisfve your Honour's expectation with any generall or groffe fome of money; but humbly defire your honourable favour to this poore Corporation in this beehalfe. And fo, gevinge your Honour all humble thanks for your good care of us herein, with our humble fervice remembred, wee take our leaves.

Your Honour's to be commanded,

Thomas Smith, mayor.   John Parr.
Nicholas Gilliott.   John Hynde.
John Heyricke.   Francis Churchman '."

1631, *John Norrice* mayor. Freemen, 11.—By a payment this year, it appears that the plague was at Loughborough; for there is a charge of 13*l*. 10*s*. "to keep Loughborough people forth of the town."

1632, *Nicholas Gilliott* mayor. Freemen, 22.

1633, *Hugh Watts* mayor. Freemen, 27.

"Charges of gifts prefented to the King and Queen at their coming to Leicefter, with the fees and gratuities given to their Highnefies officers and fervants, &c. 201*l*. 1*s*. 4*d*." [2]

1634, *William Ive* mayor. Freemen, 28.

Agreed to give the earl of Huntingdon and his countefs, and the countefs of Derby, a tierce of claret wine, and 4 gallons of fack, and 2 fugar loaves of 6 or 7 lb apiece.

By a letter from the lords of the council to the fheriff of Leicefterfhire, Aug. 12, 1635, this county was directed to provide 4500*l*. for the fitting out of a fhip of 450 tons burthen, and 180 men [3].

1635, *Ralph Tompfon* mayor. Freemen, 28.

N. B. The laft mention of Bollivan's being common clerk was in 1628; and this year, viz. 1635, Richard Martin fubfcribes himfelf common clerk.

Dec. 23, 1635. At a meeting of Mr. Mayor and his brethren, Richard Martin, efq. counfellor at law, was elected to be the town-clerk and clerk of the peace of this borough; and was then fworn a freeman, and took the oath, &c.

Henry Harold, a ftranger, was made free at a common hall; and, 9th of March, was chofen ferjeant at mace, and one of the attorneys of the court; and paid for his freedom 5*l*.

Aug. 6, 1636. Ludovicus Prince Palfgrave of the Rhine dined at the Angel in Leicefter, coming from King Charles, who was then at Tutbury, to go to Honebye [4], where the Queen then lay; and the mayor, recorder, and moft of the twenty-four, went thither, and prefented to him a banquet, prefently after the meat was taken from his table, which coft 23*l*. and fomething more; and three gallons of canary, three gallons of claret, and three gallons of white wine; which was very kindly accepted of by the Prince.

Agreed to take the mafterfhip of the Hofpital, and give to the earl of Huntingdon that fum of money as he paid to Mr. Fowkes, late mafter thereof.

September 21, 1636, *Richard Inge* mayor. Freemen, 28.

In his year is a charge of 6*l*. 11*s*. 6*d*. for the making up 200*l*. for the fhip-money.

Sept. 29. At the common hall, ordered that the old chamberlains for the year paft fhall pay and lay out all charges and fees which are due for the town to pay till this Michaelmas day be ended; and from and after this day the new chamberlains are to pay and difburfe all payments, and not for any payments which are payable upon this Michaelmas day, or

before: and fo the fame order to be continued in this Corporation for ever hereafter.

This year the parlour belonging to the Guildhall, with the chamber gallery, evidence houfe, and other rooms adjoining unto the fame, were newly erected, at the charge of the common chamber.

September 1637, *Daniel Murfyn* mayor. Freemen, 22.

September 1638, *John Hinde* mayor fecond time. Freemen, 19.

April 6, 1639. Eleven men were impreffed out of this borough for the King's fervice againft the Scots; and went, April 8, to Loughborough, &c.

June 14. The Corporation gave a bond of 400*l*. to Ralph Holme and Mary his wife, and Edward Goodridge her fon, for payment of 200*l*. to them on June 19, 1653, in the South porch of St. Martin's church in Leicefter, in confideration of 100*l*. at the time of fealing the bond, paid to the ufe of the Corporation.

September 1639, *John Norrice* mayor. Richard Martin, common clerk.

"Paid the fufferers by fire at Glen, 6*l*. 13*s*. 4*d*." [5]

March 23. At a meeting of Mr. Mayor and his brethren, Edward Palmer, gent. was chofen town-clerk and clerk of the peace for the fame borough, by general confent; and took the oaths.

March 27, 1640, 16 Car. I. At a common hall, Symon Every, of Egginton in the county of Derby, efq. and Thomas Cooke, of Gray's Inn, London, efq. were chofen freemen, and burgeffes of Parliament for this borough.

By virtue of a warrant of the deputy lieutenants for this county of Leicefter, May 28, 1640, 24 of the trained bands for this borough were fent to Loughborough, for his Majefty's fervice againft the Scots; and others going with them to Loughborough were there impreffed.

Aug. 12, 1640. At a meeting of Mr. Mayor and his brethren, William Palmer was elected to be of the forty-eight; but, refufing the oath of the forty-eight, time was given him till the next meeting to confider thereof; at which meeting he refufing to take the faid oath, was confined to the hall, where he continued two days and two nights; but afterwards, viz. 21ft of that month, he took the accuftomed oath.

By warrant from Henry earl of Huntingdon, Sept. 1, 1640, all the trained bands of this borough went to Loughborough with their complete arms; and continued there till the 11th of that month, when they were difcharged by his Majefty's proclamation.

Freemen in mayoralty of Mr. J. Norrice, 18.

Sept. 1640, *William Stanley* mayor. Freemen, 25.

Edwardus Johnfon, electus in officio camerarii pro communitate, recufans officium illud, ponetur in mifericordiâ 20*l*.—& folvebat.

Oct. 23, 1640. At a common hall, Thomas lord Grey, fon and heir of Henry earl of Stamford, was chofen freeman; and the faid Thomas lord Grey, and Thomas Cooke, of Gray's Inn, efq. were chofen burgeffes of Parliament.

May 21, 1641, 17 Car. I. At a common hall, it was agreed that Mr. John Angel, the town lecturer, fhall have 10*l*. *per annum* given out of the town-ftock, fo long as by the two companies of twenty-four and forty-eight fhall be thought fit, for his pains-taking in the Wednefday lecture, to be paid at Midfummer and St. Thomas.

September 1641, *Thomas Rudiarde* mayor.—Freemen, 26.

Oct. 18, 1641, *John Beeby* was chofen bailiff of this borough, at a meeting of the mayor and his brethren; and on the 25th of the faid month was fworn.

"Paid the fufferers by fire at Hinckley, 6*l*. 13*s*. 4*d*.; and 8*l*. to the inhabitants of Thurmafton and Burftale, being vifited by ficknefs." The charges for the year, in watching to keep the ficknefs from Leicefter which prevailed at Thurmafton, Birftal, Whetftone, and Oakham, were 46*l*. 8*s*. 7*d*. There is in thefe accounts an article with no fum fet down: "Paid for locks and chains at the gates and bridges;" (probably to prevent contagion.)

---

[1] Carte's MSS. in the Bodleian Library, F F F. No 13, &c.
[3] Harl. MSS. 1842.   [4] Holmby.

[2] Corporation accounts.
[5] Corporation accounts.

About this time began the important ſtruggles in the ſeventeenth century; but what more particularly relates to Leiceſter and its vicinity has been detailed at large in the Appendix to vol. III. pp. 17, & ſeqq.

By Biſhop Sancroft, we learn that the King was at Leiceſter the 22d, 23d, 24th, and 25th of July, 1642; and, by the payments of Mr. Robert Heyrick, church-warden of St. Martin's for the year 1642, it appears, by the following items, that the King attended divine ſervice at that church when at Leiceſter.

" Item, given to Mr. White, the counteſs of Devon's gentleman, for ſetting up the King's throne in our church, 5s.

" Item, paid to Norman, for flowers and herbs to ſtraw the church at the King's coming, 1s. 8d.

" Item, paid to Knowles, for ſix burdens of ruſhes for the church at the King's coming, 2s."

The Counteſs then lived at Leiceſter Abbey, which had been in a great meaſure re-built; and probably there was no perſon in or about Leiceſter at that time ſo proper to fix the throne for the recep-tion of the royal gueſt in the church as the counteſs's gentleman. Againſt theſe articles there is no month, or day of the month, entered in the pariſh book.

In the accounts for this year, there are an unuſual number of payments for days' work done in the church. They include payments from April 1642 to April 1643. Mr. Rudyard the mayor was choſen in September 1641, and ſerved till September 1642; ſo that, in this particular, Biſhop Sancroft's account of the King being at Leiceſter in July for four days, the payment of the Corporation to Prince Charles, &c. in Mr. Rudyard's mayoralty, and the pariſh books, all perfectly agree.

Prince Charles was preſented by the Corporation with 50l.; but it does not appear why this money was given.

There is alſo a charge of 29l. 15s. " Paid to his Majeſty's officers, at his firſt coming to town, as fees."

" This day came letters from Nottingham, Aſhby, and Leiceſter, intimating that many troopers and ca-valiers have done and do much hurt in thoſe towns; that in Leiceſter they have ſearched all the town, both box and cheſt, but have taken nothing but arms and ammunition, leaving them not ſo much as a fork or ſtaff to defend themſelves; deſiring ſpeedy forces might be ſent for the relief and aſſiſtance of thoſe towns and counties; which was ordered ac-cordingly [1]."

Two letters, the one from King Charles, the other from Prince Rupert [2], on September 6 and 7, 1642, have been already printed in vol. III. p. 31.

Sept. 1642, *Richard Ludlam* mayor. Freemen, 13.

Lord Cavendiſh gave to the Corporation 100l. to buy 6l. a-year to charitable uſes.

Sept. 1643, *William Ward* mayor. Freemen, 9.

In this year's accounts an article occurs, which is rather extraordinary;

" Paid, for wine and ſugar given to the Receiver of the King, Queen, and Prince's revenue, 5s. 1d."

William Billers mayor. Freemen, 16.

Nov. 22, 1644. At a meeting of the mayor and his brethren, it is ordered that the Biſhop's Fee be annexed to Mr. Thompſon's ward; and that Mr. Thompſon ſhall be alderman thereof alſo.

Mem. Upon Saturday morning in Whitſun week, being the laſt day of May 1645, the King's Majeſty, with his army, did enter Leiceſter, and took it by ſtorm, having laid ſiege before it three days before; at which time the town was much plundered, and Mr. Mayor's mace, and divers of the town ſeals, taken away by the unruly ſoldiers.

Mem. On the 18th of June next following, the town of Leiceſter was regained by the Parliament army under ſir Thomas Fairfax, general of the ſaid forces.

Aug. 22, 1645, 21 Car. I. At a common hall, agreed that a new mace be bought, about the ſize of the old mace, and as near to the price as conve-niently may be; the charge of the mace to be de-frayed out of the chamber of the town; and that two chamberlains' ſtaves be provided, with ſilver and gilt

boſſes, engraven with the town's arms, according or near the faſhion of the former ſtaves, at the diſcre-tion of the chamberlains.

It is alſo agreed, that a common ſeal for the Cor-poration, a ſeal of office, and the mayor's ſeal, ac-cording to the former ſeals lately uſed for the town, and taken away alſo at the taking the town, be pro-vided at the town charge.

In the payments this year are ſome things curious; which prove that the Corporation was plundered of all their regalia and valuable moveables. Even their charter they were ſtripped of by the conquerors; who, it could not be expected, would ſhew them much fa-vour, their leading men being exceedingly active par-tizans againſt the King, the mayor Mr. Billers, and ſome of the leading aldermen, being upon the com-mittee who ſat in Leiceſter to ſequeſter property, ſend out ſcouring parties for intelligence, and give information to Parliament of the tranſactions of the armies, &c. in theſe parts.

" Paid to . . . . to redeem the town charters, being ſeized when the King's forces took the town, ...

Paid, for the ſtatute ſeal, to a ſoldier, 5s.

Paid for two ſeals; the common ſeal braſs, the mayor's ſeal ſilver, 1l. 9s.

Paid for the new mace, being ſilver and gilt, 24l. 6s. 6d.

Paid to ſundry workmen, for taking down divers houſes near the South gate, 3l. 3s.

Paid, to . . . . poor people . . . . apiece to buy the wood, being the rent of 40 acres in the Foreſt of Lei-ceſter, 10l."

Sept. 1645, *Edmund Cradock* mayor. Freemen 19.

Oct. 24. At a common hall, Mr. John Beeby is choſen clerk of the ſtatutes for this borough till May 1 next.

Nov. 17. At a common hall, Peter Temple, eſq. was choſen a freeman; and, by virtue of the King's writ to the high ſheriff of Leiceſterſhire, and the high ſheriff's precept (inſtead of Thomas Cook, eſq. lately elected one of the burgeſſes for the ſaid bo-rough, and ſythence, by judgment of the Houſe of Commons, is adjudged incapable to ſit any longer there as a member of the ſame during this preſent Parliament), Peter Temple, of Temple Hall, co. Leic. eſq. was choſen burgeſs of the ſaid Parliament.

March 13. At a meeting of the mayor and his brethren, Edward Palmer, town-clerk, in regard of offences by him committed both to the governor and the committee for this garriſon, and for the ſame having been by them confined, whereby the buſineſs of this Corporation ſuffers great detriment; and to make his peace appearing unfeaſible, the company diſcharge him of his ſaid office, and declare the place void.

Hugh Aſton, gent. was elected town-clerk the day and year above ſaid; and took the oaths April 24.

July 28. " The humble petition of the well-affected tradeſmen of Leiceſter was this day read. Ordered, that an ordinance be brought in, for grant-ing a public benevolence for relief of Leiceſter, by taking the voluntary contributions of the well-affected people in all the counties, except the Weſtern Aſſociation. That 500 muſkets and furni-ture be furniſhed, out of the public ſtores, for the ſer-vice of the town of Leiceſter. And that 1500l. be charged upon the ordinance for ſale of delinquent's eſtates, to be paid in its courſe, after all other aſſign-ments already paſſed upon that ordinance, and em-ployed towards the providing of horſe, ſaddles, and piſtols, for the ſervice of the town of Leiceſter [3]."

Aug. 25, 1646. At a meeting of the mayor and his brethren, Thomas Welden, mace-bearer, having given offence to the governor and committee for this garriſon; and by them being reſtrained from execu-ting the ſaid office, &c. the company diſcharge him of the ſaid office, &c.

Mr. William Mawſon was elected to be me-bearer, during the pleaſure of the company.

Sept. 1646, *Daniel Abney*, gent. mayor. Free-men, 30.—Southgate ward; the whole ſtreet was de-moliſhed, in theſe times of war, Oct. 2, 1646.

---

[1] A true and perfect Diurnal of the Meſſages in Parliament from Nottingham, Aſhby, and Leiceſter, Sept. 6, 1642.
[2] Their ſignatures are here given in Plate XXXIII.
[3] Journals of the Houſe of Commons, vol. IV. p. 221.

Juriers Oath, p. 377.

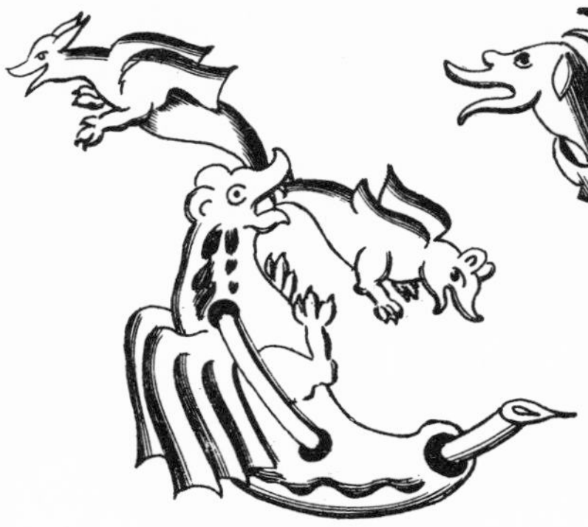

Chamberlain's Oath, p. 377.

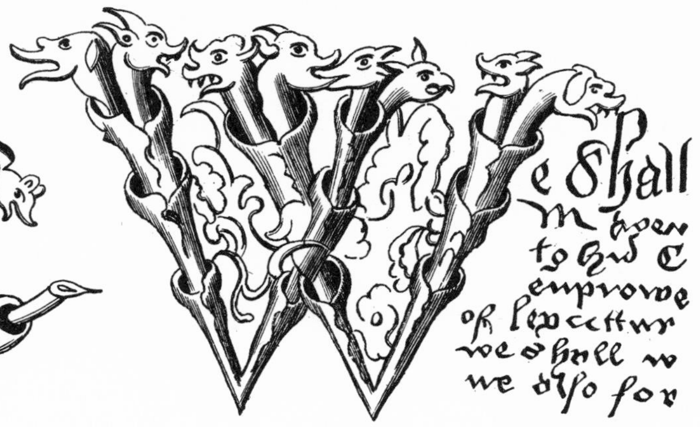

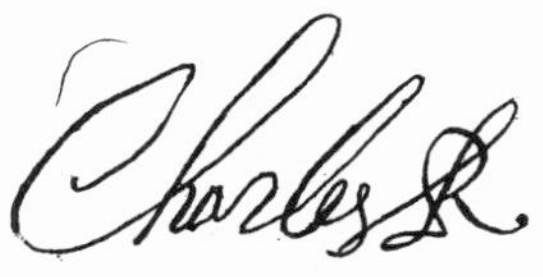

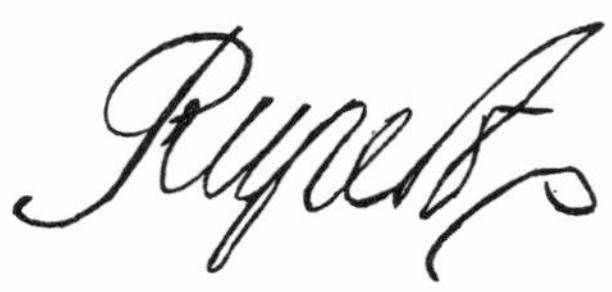

LEICESTER TOKENS.

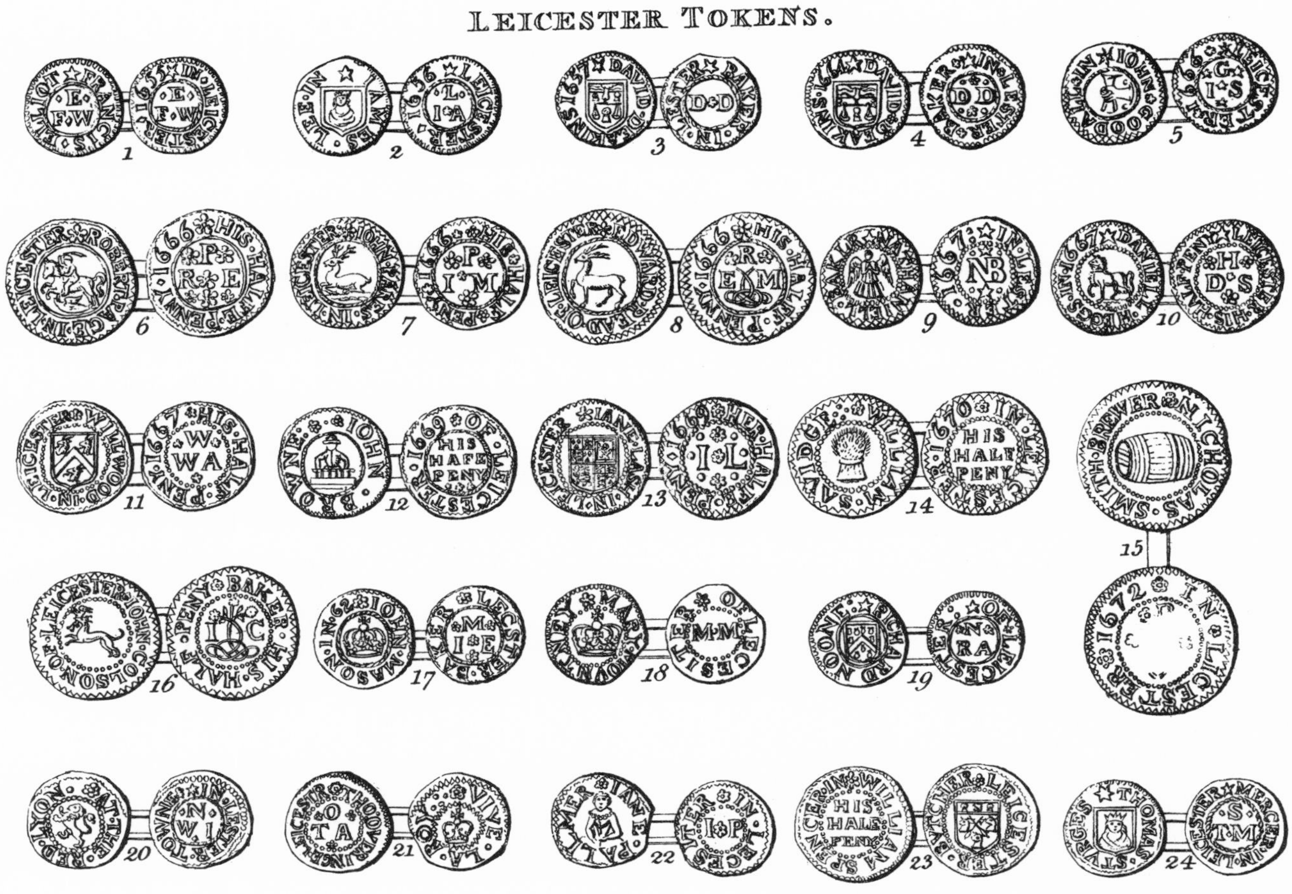

Fig. 27. p. 464.

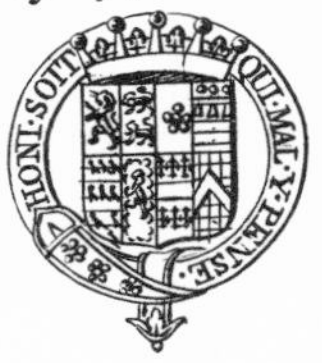

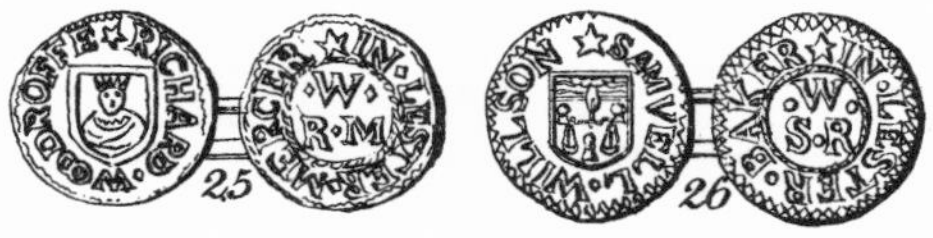

28

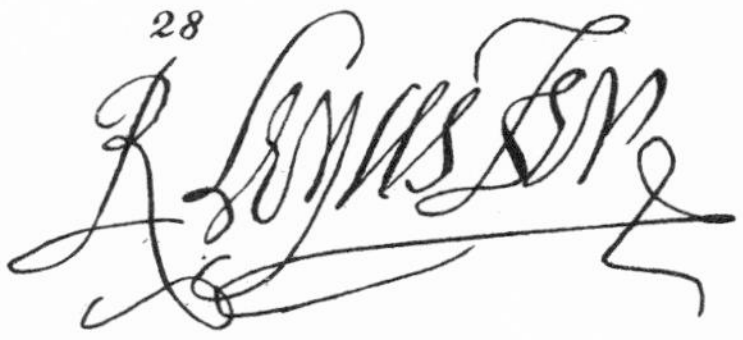

Fig. 29. p. 464.

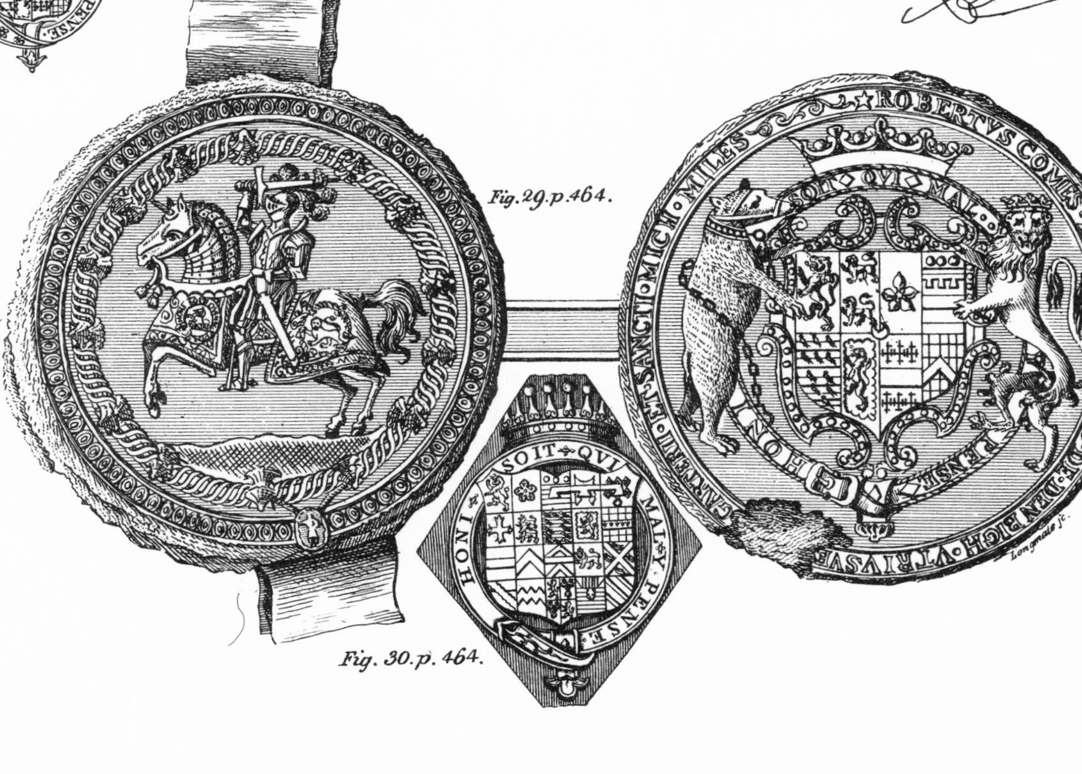

Fig. 30. p. 464.

Beft beer and ale affized at 3½d. the gallon, and candles 4½d. per pound.

Dec. 2. At a meeting of the twenty-four, agreed that Mr. Hugh Afton, town-clerk, fhall be clerk of the ftatutes for this borough, and fhall give fecurity to fave the town from damage; and, 27 July 1647, he put in 1000l. fecurity truly to difcharge the faid office, &c.

Dec. 17. At a common hall, agreed that all who live, and ufe any trade, within the borough, and be called to be made free, and refufe to become freemen, fhall be taxed double to all taxes made within this borough, in regard they refufe to bear office or do fervice in the Corporation, as well thofe that be free-born as others; and that if any refufe to become freemen that ufe *chapmandry* abroad, being thereto called, that notice be fent to all places of their dealing, that they are not to have any benefit as freemen of this Corporation.

April 23, 1647. At a meeting of the mayor and his brethren, William Palmer, cordwainer, chofe a ferjeant at mace, in room of Edward Newcome, who is placed in the new hofpital.

Sept. 1647, *Thomas Blunt* mayor. Freemen, 29.

" Received fines for tithes of Danet's Hall, Weftcotes, &c. 120l."

Sept. 29. Ten pounds, out of the town-ftock, fent to Loughborough, for the vifited people there.

Oct. 8. At a meeting of the mayor and juftices, it is ordered that no maltfter, or other perfon, buy any barley to convert into malt for three months next till 12 o'clock in the day, that tradefmen and others may firft make their neceffary provifion; and then no perfon fhall buy barley to convert into malt but only fuch as fhall be allowed by the mayor and juftices; and they to buy fuch quantities as the mayor and juftices appoint, and that for themfelves, not others: And that they fhall fell again to the poor, requefting the fame, fuch quantity of barley as they need for their weekly ufe (each quantity not exceeding a ftrike), at the fame rate as they paid for it *bona fide*: And each maltfter fo buying barley fhall, till further order, bring into the market fome reafonable proportion of malt or corn, as the mayor and juftices think fit, and fell it at reafonable prices; and fuch as refufe to abide their order to be put down from malting till further order.

Nov. 22. Orders to be obferved by the fchoolmafter and fcholars of the Free-fchool. [Of this valuable foundation a particular account will be given hereafter.]

Jan. 14. At a meeting of the mayor and his brethren, agreed that no freeman by purchafe fhall have a licence to keep a victualing-houfe without confent of the company of twenty-four.

Feb. 14. William Palmer, for mifdemeanors and abufes, difmiffed; and Thomas Godeby, cordwainer, chofe ferjeant at mace in his ftead.

Feb. 25. At a common hall. Whereas ufually two feffions only have been kept; ordered that four be kept, or three at leaft; and that the mayor be allowed, out of the chamber of the town, for every feffions dinner, 1l. 6s. 8d. if he keep three feffions; but he is to have no allowance at all if he keep but two.

Sept. 1648, 24 Car. I. *William Stanley* mayor. Freemen, 24.

" 6l. 12s. was given to the fufferers by fire at Lutterworth."

About the time of the King's death, the enemies to the Eftablifhed Church made a practice of taking jack-affes into the churches of Leicefter; and led them to the fonts, in ridicule of the Church baptifm. This audacious practice created much wrath in the town: feveral battles were fought at the churchdoors in confequence; but the liberty-men in general prevailed. No wonder, in times like thofe we are noticing, that fuch indecencies fhould be practifed. The multitude have often ftruggled to effect a change; but they have not always bettered their condition by it.

Sept. 1649, *William Speechley* mayor. Freemen, 8.

" Received of Mr. Churchman, by Alexander Baker, being money given for the ufe of the poor of this Corporation by divers well-affected (difaffected to the King), after the ftorming of the town, 200l.

" Paid, for taking down the King's Arms, . . . (No fum mentioned. There would probably be help enough to take them down, without pay, after the King was dead.)

" Paid the clerk to the commiffioners that came down to furvey and enquire after the King's revenue, 10s."

Sept. 1650, *John Somerfield* mayor. Freemen, 12.

In his time there was a fire at Burton Overy. Towards the loffes the fufferers fuftained, the Corporation paid 6l. 13s. 4d. But a more remarkable payment occurs: " Paid for wine, and the minifters' dinners, that kept the Fridays' lectures and days of humiliation, 4l. 1s. 8d.; and for charges for minifters on the Lord's days and Wednefdays, fince Mr. Angel and Mr. Price left the town." Thefe were, moft probably, the King's friends, or thofe, amongft many others, who favoured not the King's death, ufurpation, and tyranny that followed.

Sept. 29. Ordered, that it be referred to Mr. Mayor and the juftices, to confider what fhall be given to Mr. Garland for his great affiftance about the purchafe of the great houfe.

Mr. Ing, one of the fenior aldermen, for abfenting himfelf from the Corporation, was difcharged.

Sept. 1651, *Alexander Baker* mayor. Freemen, 17. This year all began to be wrote in Englifh.

Sept. 1652, *William Billers* mayor. Freemen, 24.

Dec. 22. Thomas Goadbye was chofen macebearer, during pleafure.

Sept. 1653, *Edmund Johnfon* mayor. Freemen, 14.

James Winftanley, efq. recorder.

The common clerk laft year was Hugh Afton, who then died; but this year, Abel Coles.

Sept. 29. Ordered, that 5l. be given out of the chamber of the town to the inhabitants of Cropfon, who had great lofs by fire.

A terrible fire broke out at Lutterworth. Towards the lofs, the Corporation paid 10l.

It is fomewhat fingular to remark what a number of fires there happened in the county about this time.

In the four fucceeding years, there was a fire at Hinckley; towards the loffes fuftained thereby they paid 5l. One at Asfordby, 5l. Another at Wimefwould, they paid 3l. 19s. 10d. At Desford there was one; to the fufferers there they paid 10l. And one at Ratby, 3l. 6s. 8d.

June 2. Abel Coles, gent. was chofen town-clerk and clerk of the peace for this borough, during the pleafure of the mayor and aldermen.

July 7. At a common hall, ordered that Mr. Abel Coles, town-clerk, be clerk of the ftatutes, he giving fecurity to difcharge the town from any damage by his neglect, &c.

July 12. At a common hall, fir Arthur Haflerigge, of Nofeley, bart. and William Stanley, gent. alderman of this borough, were chofen burgeffes of Parliament.

Sept. 1654, *Richard Ludlam* [1] mayor. Freemen, 29.

---

[1] " This gentleman ferved during the troubles in a civil and military capacity, and has been noticed by every writer who particularized the tranfactions of the times in this diftrict; a man whom we muft imagine had abilities fuperior to his brethren in office, which the times called forth into action. By Captain Symonds's account of the fiege, he lived near the Weft Bridge; and by the accounts which I have of the various profeffions of the mayors of Leicefter, he was a chandler, as I have noticed above; and, I rather think, a flater and plafterer alfo. The firft of this name that occurs in the lift of mayors was a William Ludlam, who ferved the office in 1587. Another William, probably his fon, ferved in 1624; whofe fon, moft likely, was this Richard, who ferved in 1642 and 1654. There was a Thomas Ludlam about this time in Leicefter, in the building line alfo, whofe name I have to an inftrument in the year 1633; who was appointed, with fome others, to make an eftimate of part of the materials of the Caftle, and of the neceffary repairs of another part of that building; but, whether a brother or not, it is not certain. But thus much is certain; that the late Mr. Alderman Edmund Ludlam, of refpectable memory, and the late Rev. Mr. William Ludlam his relation, were of this family, and probably from this quondam captain and leading magiftrate of Leicefter. It feems that no portion of his abilities has been diminifhed in paffing from him to his defcendants." Throfby, p. 127.

Jan. 5. At a meeting of the mayor and aldermen, it is agreed that John Beeby, gent. (for several misdemeanours, offences, and miscarriages, by him lately committed against the Corporation) shall no longer continue the ministerial office in the court of record of this borough, in returning the process of the same court; and it is ordered, that all process of the same court henceforth be directed to the chief serjeant at mace, or his deputy, till further order.

1655. At a meeting of the mayor and aldermen, ordered, that if any freeman of this borough shall carry wares to any country town within the county of Leicester (except market-towns, on fair or market-days), and expose them to sale, he shall forfeit, to the use of the poor of the said borough, 20s. for every offence, to be levied by distress, by warrant of the mayor.

In this year there was collected in the town of Leicester, for the relief of the poor Protestants in Piedmont, at St. Martin's, 12l. 7s. 8d.; at St. Margaret's, 4l. 5s. 7d.; at St. Mary's, 2l. 19s. 4d.; at All Saints, 3l. 18s.; at St. Nicholas's, 1l. 5s. 6d.; and at St. Leonard's, 10s.

Sept. 1655, *George Martin* mayor. Freemen, 13. Bailiff, Mr. John Beeby, gent. &c.; and so again in 1656.

Money was so scarce about this time, that principal traders of towns passed tokens for the use of themselves and neighbours. The date of the earliest known to have been issued at Leicester is 1655; and the latest in 1672; under which later year a description will be given of those which are engraved in Plate XXXIII.

April 18, 1656. An account is entered, of Mr. Haynes's gift or exhibition to two scholars in Lincoln college in Oxford.

Sept. 1656, *Edward Billers* mayor. Freemen, 31. May 11. Orders made at a visitation of the free-school by Edward Billers, mayor; Mr. Richard Lee, master of Wigston's Hospital; and Mr. William Syms, brother of the said Hospital. [Of this fee hereafter]

Jan. 21. Philip Mann the elder chosen master of the house of correction.

April 8, 1657. Agreed, that the three Bibles given by Mr. Haynes's will, and the sermon appointed to be preached at the time of the defeat of the Spanish Armada in 1588, be speedily put in execution according to the will.

Sept. 1657, *Edmund Cradock* mayor. Freemen, 26. Bailiffs, Mr. Thomas Henshaw and Anthony Curtis.

Oct. 16. At a meeting of the mayor and aldermen, William Major, gent. is chosen and admitted bailiff and keeper of the gaol, for term of life, according to the nomination of Theophilus earl of Huntingdon, being his second turn of nomination. He was sworn Oct. 19. But the said company protest against these things mentioned in the nomination of the said earl and countess; viz. his liberty "to execute the said office by his sufficient deputy," and the word "appurtenances."

April 16, 1658. At a court of aldermen. In obedience of a writ of his Highness the Lord Protector, issuing out of his Highness's Court of Upper Bench at Westminster, dated Feb. 12 last past, to the mayor, recorder, and aldermen, of the borough of Leicester, directed: It is now ordered, that Edward Palmer, gent. some time clerk of the peace of the said borough, shall be restored to the said place and office, with all things thereto belonging.

Sept. 14. Jacob Bauthumley admitted serjeant at mace, during pleasure.

Sept. 1658, *Samuel Wanley* mayor; who died Nov. 17, 1658. Bailiffs, William Franke and William Callis.

Nov. 18. Such as had been mayors agreed that Mr. Richard Ludlam, the senior justice, should be as a deputy mayor till the election of a new one; and should have the mace carried after him, lying upon the mace-bearer's arm.

Friday, Nov. 19. Both companies appearing at the funeral, according to invitation, the funeral proceeded thus:

The two serjeants at mace, having their maces covered with black tiffany, went before the corpse;

Mrs. Wanley being led by her son, and attended by the town-clerk. And divers mourners followed the corpse; and after them the aldermen, gentry, and forty-eight.

The body being interred, Mrs. Wanley attended as before, returned to the mayoress's seat, it being hung with mournings; and the great mace was carried into and laid down in the mayor's seat, it being likewise hung in mourning, Mr. Ludlam sitting alone in the next seat to it; and, sermon being ended, was carried after Mr. Ludlam to his house, and lodged there; and Mrs. Wanley returned to her own house, attended as before.

The Lord's day, Nov. 21, Mr. Ludlam went to church, attended by the mace-bearer, where he sat as on Friday before, the mace lying as before. Mrs. Wanley, attended by the town-clerk and mourners, went to church, and sat in the mayoress's seat, it still continuing covered with black.

Monday, Nov. 22. After a short speech made by Mr. Ludlam, the companies went to election by ticket; and the two great numbers happening to be even, they broke up till one o'clock in the afternoon, at which time they chose Mr. *William Franke* to be mayor, and swore him immediately; who invited them to his house, and gave them a very free welcome.

At the common hall, Nov. 22, 1658, it was agreed that Mrs. Wanley, late mayoress, shall have the fourth part of one year's allowance, formerly paid and allowed to the mayor yearly, in regard of the great trouble and charge she hath been already put to.

Freemen made in the year of Mr. Wanley and Mr. Franke, 30.

Jan. 3. At a common hall, sir Arthur Hesilrigge, bart. and William Stanley, gent. an alderman of this borough, were chosen burgesses to serve in the Parliament, Jan. 27.

Feb. 18. Richard Parsons was chosen master of the house of correction, in room of Philip Mann, deceased, during pleasure; and shall have the usual wages of 20 nobles *per annum*, paid quarterly.

Richard Noon, John Birkhead, and Matthew Coultman, of the forty-eight, have failed in their estates and credits, and compounded for inconsiderable sums, and yet kept their places in the said company, without desiring to be dismissed; which this company judges to be not only a miscarriage and misbehaviour, but a dishonour to the rest of the members. It is ordered, that they be dismissed.

Sept. 1659, *John Clay* mayor. Freemen, 30. Bailiffs, Mr. Robert Ericke and George Abney.

March 15. At a common hall, John Grey, esq. and Thomas Armeston, of Burbage, esq. were chosen freemen; and, by virtue of a writ of the keepers of the liberty of England, by authority of Parliament, to the sheriff of the county of Leicester, and a precept of the said sheriff to the bailiff of this borough directed, they were also chosen burgesses for the parliament ensuing.

In a former portion of these extracts (see p. 377) Mr. Carte has transcribed several oaths of office. He has here added some others.

The Oath of the COMMON COUNCIL, or FORTY-EIGHT MEN.

"You shall be obedient to the mayor in all his lawful commands and summons touching the business and state of this borough of Leicester. The secrets and council of the body politick of this borough you shall not reveal to the hurt or prejudice, to your knowledge. You shall give your attendance on the mayor for the time being of this borough of Leicester, at the fairs, common halls, and other meetings, upon lawful summons. You shall decently and conveniently apparel yourself, according to your place and calling. You shall not utter nor disclose any speeches or secrets that shall be had or made at any common hall, or other meeting, to the hurt of any man, or of the said borough. But shall justly and truly counsel, do, and execute, all things appertaining unto your office, as one of the burgesses of the common council of the said borough, during the time thereof. So help you God."

The

The Oath of the Justices of Peace.

" You shall swear that, as a Justice of the Peace within the Borough of Leicester, in articles concerning the same, you do equal right to the poor and to the rich, after your best cunning, learning, and power, and after the laws and customs of this realm and statutes thereof made; and you shall not be of counsel with any quarrel hanging before you. And that you hold your sessions as usual, after the form of the statutes thereof made. And the issues, fines, and amerciaments, that shall happen to be made, and forfeitures which shall fall before you, you shall cause to be entered, without concealing or embezzling, and truly send them to the King's Exchequer. You shall not let   gift or other cause, but well and truly you shall do your office of justice of the peace in that behalf; and you shall take nothing for your office of justice of the peace to be done, but of the King, and fees accustomed and limited by the statutes. And you shall not direct, or cause to be directed, any warrant by you to be made, but you shall direct them to the ordinary officers of the said Borough, or other indifferent persons in that behalf, to do execution there. So help you God."

The Steward's Oath.

" You, A. B. shall be true and faithful to our Sovereign Lord the King, his heirs and lawful successors; and shall, faithfully, justly, and uprightly, execute the office of Steward of the Court of Record of our Sovereign Lord the King within the Borough of Leicester aforesaid, in all things belonging to the same. You shall do equally and indifferently to all men, without favour, affection, or partiality; and all the lawful customs, privileges, liberties, and jurisdiction, of this Borough, you shall, by your best skill, learning, knowledge, and advice, in all things maintain, defend, and preserve. The lawful counsel and secrets of this Borough you shall not disclose nor reveal, to the hurt or prejudice thereof. So help you God."

The Coroner's Oath.

" You shall swear that you will well and truly serve our Sovereign Lord the King's Majesty and all his liege people, in the offices of Coroners of this Borough of Leicester; and herein you shall diligently do and accomplish all and every thing and things appertaining to your offices, after the best of your power, wit, skill, and ability, both for the King's profit, and good of the inhabitants within the said Borough, taking only such fees as are allowed you by the laws and statutes of this realm, and no otherwise. So help you God."

The Oath of the Common Clerk of the Borough of Leicester.

" You, A. B. shall a true and faithful Common Clerk of the Peace be unto the Corporation of this Borough of Leicester, and the said office shall faithfully serve and execute. The charters, deeds, evidences, and records, of the said Borough, which be or shall be committed to your keeping, you shall safely keep for the behoof of the same Borough. The secrets and lawful counsels of the body politick of the said Borough you shall not disclose nor reveal to the hurt or prejudice thereof, to your knowledge. You shall be obedient and ready, at the commandment of the Mayor and his successors, for the Town business, and in all other things. The said office of a Common Clerk of the said Borough you shall faithfully, uprightly, and honestly execute, in all duties appertaining thereto, to the best of your skill and knowledge. So help you God."

The Oath of the Five Serjeants at Mace for the Borough of Leicester.

" I, A. B. shall not use nor execute the office of Serjeant at Mace of this Borough of Leicester, and Attorney of the Court of Record within the said Borough, corruptly, during the time I shall remain therein. I shall truly serve and execute all such pro-

cess and warrants as shall come to my hands by reason of my office (if possibly I can or may), and true return thereof shall make, or cause to be made; and the said offices shall execute uprightly, truly, and faithfully, in all things appertaining thereto, during the time thereof, to the best of my power and skill. So help me God."

The Oath of every Freeman of Leicester, being of any Trade or Occupation.

" You shall swear, that to our Sovereign Lord the King, and his heirs and successors, you shall bear faith and true allegiance. You shall also be obedient and faithful to the Mayor and ministers of this Borough of Leicester. The franchises, liberties, and lawful customs thereof, you shall maintain, and this Borough keep harmless, so far forth as in you lieth. You shall be contributary to all manner of charges within this Borough; as summons, watches, contributions, taxes, tallages, lot and scot, and all other charges, bearing the part as a Freeman ought to do, whether you dwell within this Borough or in any other place, so long as you shall claim the freedom of the said Borough. You shall not take any apprentice but according to the law in that case provided; the indenture of which apprentice you shall cause to be made by the Common Clerk of the same Borough, and shall them enroll before the mayor for the time being, according to the custom of the said Borough. You shall also keep the King's Majesty's peace in your own person so far forth as in you is. (You shall know no gathering conventicles, nor conspiracies made against the peace of our Sovereign Lord the King, but you shall warn the mayor or other officers thereof, or else let it to your power.) And also the lawful customs, liberties, and franchises of this Borough, you shall, to your power, keep and maintain, so far forth as in you lieth; and the lawful secrets and counsels of the body politick of this Borough you shall not disclose nor reveal to the hurt or prejudice thereof. All these points and articles you shall well and truly keep, according to the laws and lawful customs of this borough. So help you God."

The Oath of the Stewards and Wardens of the Occupations.

" You shall swear truly to observe and keep, and of your and every of your parts cause to be observed and kept, all the good and lawful rules, ordinances, and constitutions, contained and specified within this your Ordinal, so far forth as in you is, and by the laws of this realm you ought. You shall truly, without partiality, collect and gather up, or cause to be collected and gathered up, all and every such fine, pains, penalties, forfeitures, and sums of money whatsoever, that shall be forfeited, payable, or due, by any of you, or any of your Occupation, or by any other person or persons whatsoever, by reason or force of this your Ordinal; and thereof shall, at the end of your year, make and yield up, in writing, a just and true account to all the rest of your said Occupation, or to the most part of them that shall to that purpose assemble together; and shall also, truly, without fraud or delay, yearly, and at the end of your year, or at the furthest within one month before the Chamberlains of the said Borough of Leicester shall make their accounts, pay or cause to be paid to the said chamberlains of the town, and to the use of the town, the just moiety or one-half of all the said fines, pains, penalties, forfeitures, and sums of money, as shall come to your hands by force of the said office. These and all other things belonging to your said office and offices, you and every of you shall well and truly perform, to the best of your power and skill. So help you God."

The Oath of the Well Reeves.

" A. B. and A. D. You shall faithfully and diligently execute the office of a Well Reeve of your said ward for the year ensuing, and cause the said wells to be kept in good and sufficient repair, for the benefit of the neighbourhood, and service and use of the Corporation; and fhall do and execute all other things belonging to your faid office, fo long as you or either of you fhall continue in the fame, truly and juftly, according to the beft of your powers, knowledge, and abilities. So help you God."

The Oath of a PINDER.

" You fhall fwear that you will well and truly execute the office of a Pinder, or Hayward, within the South Fields of Leicefter, and the liberties thereof; and you fhall prefent all pound breaches that fhall be made within the fame, and all waifs and ftrays you fhall take and be anfwerable for the fame; and all other things belonging to your faid office you fhall do and perform, to the beft of your power, knowledge, fkill, and ability. So help you God."

The Oath of fuch BUTCHERS as are free for Market-days only.

" You fhall fwear you will well and truly keep and obferve all and every the particulars expreffed in the 7th and 8th branches of the Butchers' Ordinal of this Borough, and do and perform all other matters and things as in any fort concern the good orders and rules of the faid trade to the beft of your knowledge, fkill, and ability. So help you God."

The Oath of the COUNTRY BAKERS.

" You fhall fwear you fhall well and truly obferve and keep all and every thing contained in the three branches in the Bakers' Ordinal, and which concerns the Bakers of the Country; and do and perform all other matters and things as in any fort concern the good orders and rules of the faid trade, fo far forth as concerns you, to the beft of your knowledge, fkill, and ability. So help you God."

By indenture, May 26, 12 Charles II. his Majefty's Attorney General of the Duchy of Lancafter fold to the Mayor, &c. of the Borough of Leicefter, the Mill under the Caftle of Leicefter, with the holmes adjoining; the fifhing of the Soar, from a place called Morehead unto the North Mill, and the appurtenances thereunto belonging, referving an annual rent to the King of 17*l.*, for 610*l.*

It appears, by the Corporation accounts, that, on the Reftoration, they expended, at the proclaiming Charles the Second King, whofe father's arms had been torn from the walls of churches in Leicefter with the moft indignant fury, and whofe memory they had branded with the vileft epithets, 11*l.* 19*s.* 7*d.*; and on the day of general thankfgiving for his Majefty's happy Reftoration to the Crown of his anceftors, which they acknowledged had been defpoiled by lawlefs tyranny, 9*l.* 13*s.* 1*d.* They, who had been the foremoft to rob him of his dignity, and lay his fceptre at the feet of ufurpers, now prefented him with 300*l.*; and expended 19*l.* 13*s.* 7*d.* to procure the fum in gold. Three aldermen and the two chamberlains, who went to prefent it to his Majefty, were accompanied by their ferjeants at mace, with their fhining emblems of office, attired at the expence of 45*l.*; on which occafion they expended 17*l.* 12*s.* 5*d.*

" In this year, there was a double return of members to ferve in Parliament for this Borough. Thofe returned were, John Grey, of London, efq. and William Hartopp, of Rotherby, efq.; and fir John Pretyman and fir William Hartopp, knights."

The preceding article is from the MS Collections of Mr. Carte; who has preferved fome interefting particulars relative to this fubject.

" In feveral Hall-books I have met with the following account of members chofen for the town.

17 Edw. IV. Jan. 12. There were elected Peers Curtes by the commons, and John Wigfon by the mayor and his brethren. The Parliament began the 17th of January, and was diffolved the 25th of February following.

22 Edw. IV. On Friday before the Epiphany were elected Peers Curtes, mayor, by the commons, and John Roberts by the mayor's brethren.

1 Ric. III. Jan. 12. Elected John Roberts, mayor, by the mayor's brethren, and Peers Curtes by the commonalty. The Parliament began Jan. 13.

4 Hen. VII. Dec. 22. Elected Peter Curteys and Roger Wigfon. The Parliament began Jan. 13.

7 Hen. VII. Aug. 23. Elected Peter Curteys by the commons, and Robert Croft by the mayor and his brethren. The Parliament began Oct. 17.

19 Hen. VII. die Jovis prox' ante feftum Nativitatis Domini. Elected Robert Orton by the commons, and William Wygfton junior by the mayor and his brethren.

14 Hen. VIII. On Tuefday before the Annunciation elected William Bolte, mayor, by the commons, and Roger Wygfton by the mayor's brethren.

" I have met with no more elections of Parliament men till 1 Mary.

" As to the electors, obferve, 1. That the government of the town being antiently lodged in 24 perfons, ftyled ' The mayor and his brethren,' thefe feparately made choice of one of the members of Parliament, and the commonalty of the town chofe the other. This diftinct choice lafted a good while in King Henry the Eighth's reign; but I cannot tell the precife time when they began to choofe jointly. 2. That the commons concerned in the election of their members were all the inhabitants of the town, whether freemen or others, till 4 Hen. VII. when the King, by the advice of his counfel of the Dutchy, to prevent the diforders which frequently happened in the election of mayor, burgeffes of parliament, and making affeffments, ordered the mayor and 24 comburgeffes to call unto them only 48, whom they fhould judge to be the wifeft and graveft of the commonalty, upon thefe occafions. And at the next election of annual officers, Sept. 21, 5 Hen. VII. the commons at large infifting upon their antient privilege in a tumultuous manner, the King in Parliament that year ordained, that the mayor and his brethren fhould, from time to time, choofe 48 of the moft difcreet inhabitants of the town, who, with the mayor and his brethren, or more part of them, fhould make yearly election of all the mayors and other officers of the faid borough, and their election fhould be good, &c.

" N. B. The election of Parliament-men is not expreffly mentioned in this act; neverthelefs all elections of them were, in fact, made agreeable to the tenor of it till the Reftoration of King Charles II. when fir John Pretyman made intereft with the Commons at large; and, upon a hearing in the Houfe of Commons, was admitted to be duly elected in virtue of their votes.

" The right of election is vefted in the freemen at large, not receiving alms, and in the inhabitants paying fcot and lot, not being perfons certificated from other places. The number of electors is now (1712) fuppofed to be about 2000. [The electors for the county are about 5000.]

" As to the perfons elected, it is obfervable, that of old they were always inhabitants and members of the Borough; the firft inftance which I have met of any country gentleman's election being in the firft Parliament of Queen Mary, when William Faunt and Thomas Farnham, efqrs. were chofen.

" When fuch as were not freemen purpofed to ftand as candidates to be chofen members of Parliament, they commonly purchafed their freedom before-hand to qualify themfelves. So at leaft fir Henry Beaumont, of Gracedieu, and fir William Skipwith, knts. that were chofen 1 Jac. I. paid 6*l.* each for their freedom."

Aug. 7, 1660. Richard Parfons, gaoler for the Borough, was agreed to be admitted a ferjeant at mace, in place of John Tyrlington, who is hereby difcharged.

The following letter, dated Leicefter, 4 September, 1660, was addreffed to Henry earl of Huntingdon:

" Right Honorable, The lowe condition of this Corporation of Leicefter wee prefume your Lordfhipp may have heard of; yet it is our great defire to expreffe our duty unto our moft gracious Kinge to the utmoft wee can, and in all things to fignifye our loyalty to his facred Majeftie; which wee hope our Recorder will declare on our behalfe; who, with fome others of this Corporation, are appointed to deliver unto his Majeftie a prefent of 300*l.* value, with a furrender of a fee-farme rent of 17*l. per annum*; which

was

was heretofore purchafed by the Corporation, beinge iffueing out of their own lands. It is now our humble fuite to your Lordſhipp, you will favour this Corporation foe much as to vouchſafe your Lordſhipp's preſence att the delivringe of this preſent, and to gaine it and us a good acceptance with his Majeſtie, which wee know well may bee done by your Lordſhip's favour, and may bee as well accepted as greater preſents from greater and richer Corporations. Wee have great hope, and are well aſſured, that your Lordſhipp will not onely graunt us this fuite; but alſo that your Lordſhipp will continue thoſe favours which your anceſtors have always borne to this Corporation. Wee humbly begg your Lordſhipp's pardon for this great boldnes; and ſhall ever remain your Lordſhipp's humble ſervants,

John Clay, mayor.
William Stanley.
Richard Ludlam [1]."

September 1660, 12 Car. II. *Daniel Abney* major. Ballivus, *Willielmus Major.* Freemen, 45.
[Now they begin to uſe Latin again in their titles.]
Oct. 24. At a meeting of the mayor and aldermen, agreed that Mr. Edward Palmer, town-clerk, ſhall be clerk of the ſtatutes for this Borough, he giving fecurity to ſave the town harmleſs. He was ſworn Jan. 7; and the ſeal was delivered to him.
Sept. 1661, 13 Car. II. *Francis Noble* mayor. Freemen, 20.—N. B. *James Winſtanley* was recorder Sept. 21.
A Mr. Wood received 2*s.* being the arrears of rent for the Butt-cloſe, the price of two broad arrows.
Sept. 12, 1662. At a meeting of the mayor and his brethren, Robert Harding, eſq. is choſen recorder (and was ſworn a freeman), upon ſurrender of James Winſtanley, late recorder.
Sept. 1662, 14 Car. II. *Daniel Deakin* mayor. Freemen, 17. A fire at Grantham happened in his time. Towards the ſufferers' loſs, the Corporation contributed 10*l.*
1663, *Thomas Blunt* and *Richard Palmer* mayors. Freemen, 34.
Walter Hood, a ſtranger, made free July 1, 1664. His fine 20*l.* [Note; he was the firſt that paid ſo much.] John Pares, Sept. 28, paid 15*l.*
Sept. 1664, *William Callis* mayor. Freemen, 16.
N. B. Edward Palmer ſubſcribes as town-clerk to laſt year; but now, Johannes Huckle comis clericus.
James Duke of York, Lord High Admiral of England, and brother to the King, was entertained at Leiceſter by the Body Corporate, at the expence of 16*l.* 3*s.* 10*d.*—" Paid to the Duke of York's trumpeters, pages, coachmen, &c. 4*l.* 15*s.*"
Wiliiam Callis was an apothecary, who was honoured with this Princely viſit.
In this year Charles II. granted a new charter to Leiceſter, ratifying and confirming thoſe of his predeceſſors. This varies but little from thoſe before recited. The preamble, as uſual, ſets forth, that " the borough of Leiceſter being an antient borough, &c." which had many antient privileges, grants, immunities, and preſcriptions, from Kings, and other noble perſonages, prior to its being incorporated; it ſays, therefore, " We, for the better governing of that town, do grant, ratify, and confirm, all former acts of our progenitors that they, the inhabitants of that place, may enjoy *quot, quanta, qualia,* as they had done under the letters patent of our predeceſſor Edward the Fourth, under the great ſeal of England, or likewiſe what they had under Queen Elizabeth, &c. &c." In ſtrong terms, it requires all officers acting in this Corporate Body to take the oath of ſupremacy. But hear the charter:
" Rex omnibus ad quos, &c. ſalutem. Cum burgus noſter de Leiceſtriâ, in comitatu noſtro de Leiceſtriâ, ſit burgus antiquus & populoſus, & per quamplurima ſecula jam retroacta fuerit corporacio five corpus corporatum & politicum: Cumque major, ballivi, & burgenſes burgi de Leiceſtriâ predicti, diverſas libertates, privilegia, francheſias, conſuetu-

dines, poteſtates, immunitates, preheminencias, terras, tenementa, poſſeſſiones, & alia hereditamenta, habuerunt, tenuerunt, exercuerunt, uſi & gaviſi fuerunt, ac modo habent, tenent, utuntur, & gaudent; ac cum eiſdem, tam vigore & virtute diverſarum cartarum, literarum patentium, conceſſionum, et confirmationum, per diverſos progenitores noſtros reges et reginas hujus regni noſtri Anglie antehac factarum, conceſſarum, ratificatarum, et confirmatarum, quam ratione et pretextu diverſarum laudabilium et antiquarum preſcriptionum in eodem burgo uſitatarum et approbatarum, imbuti et dotati fuerunt et exiſtunt: Cumque dilecti ſubditi noſtri modò major, ballivi, et burgenſes burgi de Leiceſtriâ, in comitatu noſtro Leiceſtrie predicto, nobis humillimè ſupplicaverunt, quatenus nos, pro melioratione et meliore regimine burgi illius, gratiam et munificentiam noſtram regiam eiſdem majori, ballivis, et burgenſibus, in ratificatione et confirmatione corporis corporati predicti, et antiquarum libertatum et privilegiorum ejuſdem burgi, gratioſè exhibere et extendere velimus: Sciatis igitur, quod nos, meliorationem burgi predicti et proſperam conditionem populi noſtri ibidem gratioſe affectantes, ac volentes quod major, ballivi, et burgenſes burgi illius poteſtatibus et privilegiis convenientibus, tam pro debitâ correctione et emendatione malorum et inconvenienciarum, quam pro bono regimine et gubernatione ejuſdem burgi, armentur et induentur; de gratiâ noſtrâ ſpeciali, ac ex certâ ſcientiâ et mero motu noſtris, volumus, ac per preſentes, pro nobis, heredibus et ſucceſſoribus noſtris, damus, concedimus, confirmamus, ratificamus, et approbamus, majori, ballivis, et burgenſibus burgi predicti, et ſucceſſoribus ſuis, omnia et omnimoda meſſuagia, molendina, terras, tenementa, decimas, prata, paſcua, paſturas, communias, coronatores, eſcaetores, curias de recordo, cognitiones placitorum, bona et catalla felonum et fugitivorum, felonum de ſe et in exigendo poſitorum, deodanda, waviatas, extrahuras, mercata, ferias, nundinas, tolneta, theolonia, ſtallagia, taxationes, fines, redemptiones, exitus, amerciamenta, foriſfacturas, perquiſitas curie, gaolas, libertates, et tot, tanta, talia eadem hujuſmodi et conſimilia libertates, francheſias, immunitates, exemptiones, privilegia, quietancias, juriſdictiones, vaſta, vadua, funda, commoditates, proficua, emolumenta, et hereditamenta quecumque, quot, quanta, qualia, et que, per cartam five literas patentes predeceſſoris noſtri domini Edwardi Quarti nuper regis Anglie, ſub magno ſigillo ſuo Anglie, gerentes datum apud Woodſtock, viceſimo quarto die Auguſti, anno regni ſui quarto, aut que per literas patentes incliti predeceſſoris noſtri domine Elizabethe nuper regine Anglie, ſub magno ſigillo ſuo Anglie, gerentes datum apud Weſtmonaſterium primo die Junii, anno regni ſui quadrageſimo primo, conceſſ' five mentionat' fore conceſſ', five que major, ballivi, et burgenſes ejuſdem burgi, vel predeceſſores ſui, per quecunque nomina five per quodcunque nomen, vel quamcunque incorporationem, vel pretextu cujuſcunque nominis vel incorporationis, antehac legitimè habuerunt, tenuerunt, uſi vel gaviſi fuerunt, ſeu occupaverunt, aut habere, tenere, uti, vel gaudere debuerunt, aut modò habent, tenent, utuntur, et gaudent five occupant, ſibi et ſucceſſoribus ſuis, ratione vel pretextu cartarum five literarum patentium predictarum, ſeu earum alterius, vel aliquarum aliarum cartarum, conceſſionum, aut literarum patentium, per aliquem progenitorem vel anteceſſorem noſtrorum nuper regum vel reginarum Anglie, quoquomodo antehac fact', conceſſ', five confirmat', aut quocunque alio legali modo, jure, ſeu titulo, conſuetudine, uſu, five preſcriptione, antehac legitimè uſitat', habit', five conſuet', licet eadem aut eorum aliquod vel aliqua foriſfacta vel deperdita fuerunt aut ſint, ac licet eadem vel eorum aliquod malè uſa vel non uſa, abuſa, vel diſcontinuata fuerint vel fuerit; habend', tenend', et gaudend', prefatis majori, ballivis, et burgenſibus burgi de Leiceſtriâ predictâ, et ſucceſſoribus ſuis in perpetuum, ac reddend' et ſolvend' proinde annuatim

[1] Carte's MSS. in the Bodleian Library, F F F. No 13, &c.

nobis,

nobis, heredibus et fuccefforibus noftris, tot, tanta, talia, hujufmodi, et confimilia feoda, firmas, redditus, fervicia, denariorum fummas, et demanda quecunque, quot, quanta, qualia, et que, antehac pro eifdem reddi feu folvi confueverunt, feu reddere aut folvi debuerunt: Quare volumus, ac per prefentes, pro nobis, heredibus et fuccefforibus noftris, firmiter injungendo precipimus, quod predicti major, ballivi, et burgenfes burgi predicti, et fucceffores fui, habeant, teneant, utanrur, et gaudeant, ac habere, tenere, uti, et gaudere valeant et poffint in perpetuum, omnes libertates, authoritates, jurifdictiones, franchefias, exemptiones, immunitates, quietantias, et hereditamenta predicta, fecundùm tenorem et effectum harum literarum noftrarum patentium, ac predictarum aliarum literarum patentium fuperiùs in prefentibus mentionat', fine occafione vel impedimento noftri, heredum vel fuccefforum noftrorum, vicecomitum, efcaetorum, ballivorum, officiariorum, vel miniftrorum noftrorum, heredum vel fuccefforum noftrorum quorumcunque; nolentes quod iidem major, ballivi, et burgenfes burgi predicti, aut eorum aliquis vel aliqui, ratione premifforum feu eorum alicujus, per nos, vel per heredes vel fucceffores noftros, jufticiarios, vicecomites, ballivos, vel miniftros noftros, heredum vel fuccefforum noftrorum quofcunque, inde occafionentur, moleftantur, graventur, feu in aliquo perturbentur; volentes, ac per prefentes mandantes et precipientes, tam jufticiariis ad placita coram nobis tenenda affignatis, et thefaurario, cancellario, et baronibus Scaccarii noftri apud Weftmonafterium, et aliis jufticiariis noftris, heredum et fuccefforum noftrorum, quam attornato et folicitatori noftro generali pro tempore exiftentibus, et eorum cuilibet ac omnibus aliis officiariis et miniftris noftris, heredum et fuccefforum noftrorum quibufcunque, quod nec ipfi, nec eorum aliquis vel aliqui, aliquod breve five fummonitionem vel diftrictionem de quo warranto, five aliquod aliud breve, brevia, vel proceffus noftra quecunque, verfus prefatos majorem, ballivos, et burgenfes burgi predicti, aut eorum aliquem vel aliquos, pro aliquibus caufis, rebus, materiis, vel offenfis, aut eorum aliquo, clamatis, ufitatis, acceptatis, feu habitis, ante diem confectionis prefentium, profequantur aut continuantur, aut profequi aut continuari facient feu caufabunt, aut eorum aliquis faciet feu caufabit; volentes etiam quod major, ballivi, et burgenfes ejufdem burgi, aut eorum aliqui vel aliquis, per aliquem vel aliquos jufticiarios, officiarios, vel miniftros predictos, in aut pro debito ufu five clameo aliquarum aliarum libertatum, franchefiarum, aut jurifdictionum, infra burgum predictum, libertates, franchefias, limites et precinctus ejufdem, ante diem confectionis harum literarum noftrarum patentium, minimè moleftentur aut impediantur, aut ad ea vel eorum aliquod vel aliqua refpondere compellantur, non obftante non recitando vel malè aut non rectè recitando literas patentes predictas, vel datum earum, et non obftante malè nominando vel malè recitando aut non nominando aut non recitando predicta meffuagia, molendina, terras, tenementa, decimas, prata, pafcua, pafturas, et cetera premiffa fuperiùs per prefentes preconceff', aut mentionat' fore conceff' feu confirmat', feu aliquam inde partem five parcellam; et non obftante non inveniend' officium five officia, inquifitionem five inquifitiones premifforum, fuperiùs per prefentes preconceff', aut mentionat' fore conceff', aut alicujus inde partis five parcelle, per que titulus nofter invenire debuit ante confectionem harum literarum noftrarum patentium; et non obftante malè recitando, malè nominando, aut non recitando, aliquam dimiffionem five conceffionem de premiffis, vel de aliquâ inde parte vel parcellâ, de recordo vel non de recordo, vel aliter qualitercunque antehac fact' exiftent'; et non obftante malè nominando aut non nominando aliquam villam, hamelettam, parochiam, locum, vel comitatum, in quibus premiffa aut aliqua inde pars vel parcella exiftunt vel exiftit; et non obftante quod de nominibus tenentium, firmariorum, five occupatorum meffuagiorum, molendina-

rum, tenementorum, decimarum, vel hereditamentorum predictorum, feu aliquorum premifforum, vel alicujus inde partis vel parcelle, aliqua vera, plena, aut certa non fit mentio; et non obftante aliquibus mifprifionibus vel defectionibus de certitudine vel computatione aut declaratione veri annui valoris premifforum, vel alicujus inde partis vel parcelle, aut annualis redditûs refervati de, in, et fuper premiffa, vel de, in, et fuper aliquam inde parcellam in hiis literis noftris patentibus expreffam et contentam; et non obftante ftatuto in Parliamento domini Henrici nuper regis Angliæ Sexti antecefforis noftri, anno regni fui decimo octavo, facto et edito; et non obftante aliquibus aliis defectubus in nominando, aut non nominando, aut malè nominando, naturam, genera, fpecies, quantitates, aut qualitates premifforum, vel alicujus inde parcelle. Provifo femper, et volumus, ac per prefentes, pro nobis, heredibus et fuccefforibus noftris, ordinamus et firmiter injungendo precipimus, quod major, ballivi, burgenfes, recordator, communis clericus, et omnes alii officiarii et miniftri burgi predicti, et eorum deputati, necnon omnes jufticiarii ad pacem noftram, heredum et fuccefforum noftrorum, infra burgum predictum, virtute aut fecundùm tenorem prefentium, aut aliquarum aliarum literarum patentium five cartarum antehac factarum, in pofterum nominando, eligendo, feu conftituendo, antequam ipfi ad executionem five exercitium officii vel officiorum, loci vel locorum, cui vel quibus refpective in pofterum nominati, electi, five conftituti fuerint admittantur, aut aliqualiter in eâ parte intromittant, feu eorum aliquis refpective intromittat, tam facramentam corporale communiter vocatum *The Oath of Obedience*, quam facramentum corporale communiter vocatum *The Oath of Supremacy*, fuper facrofanctis Dei Evangeliis preftabunt, et quilibet eorum preftabit, coram tali perfonâ, five talibus perfonis, quales et que ad hujufmodi facramenta dandum et preftandum per legem et ftatuta hujus regni noftri Angliæ ad prefens appunctuantur et defignantur, aut in pofterum appunctuati vel defignati fuerint vel fuerit. Et ulteriùs volumus, et intentionem noftram regiam declaramus, quod nullus recordator, fenefchallus, folicitator, vel communis clericus burgi predicti, de cetero eligendus feu conftituendus, intromittat in hujufmodi officio five officiis, feu eorum aliquo, antequam ipfi refpective approbati fuerint vel fuerit per nos, heredes vel fucceffores noftros, aliquo in prefentibus contento, aut aliquâ aliâ caufâ vel materiâ quâcunque in contrarium inde in aliquo non obftante; eo quod expreffa mentio, &c. In cujus rei, &c. Tefte Rege, apud Weftmonafterium, vicefimo die Januarii. Per ipfum Regem '."

Sept. 1665, 17 Car. II. *William Alfop* mayor. Freemen, 18.

Some heavy fines were laid upon two inhabitants for refufing to ferve on the company of forty-eight. One was Mr. Edward Billars, and the other Mr. William Warburton, who paid each 33l. 6s. 8d. as a fine of 100 marks, impofed (as it is called) for the contempt of not ferving on the forty-eight.

Sept. 1666, 18 Car. II. *Edmund Townfend* mayor. Freemen, 23.

The terrible fire that happened at Loughborough [2] Oct. 5, 1666, called forth an unufual fum for accidents of that fort. "Paid, towards their prefent relief, 15l." What they contributed afterwards does not appear.

"Paid, for the repairs of Bow bridge, 15l. 12s."

At the fame time St. Auftin's well was repaired, at the expence of 2l. 14s. 8d.

A tax alfo was paid for the "town lands" to the royal aid, 72l. 13s.

Sept. 1667, 19 Car. II. *William Southwell* mayor. Freemen, 16.

Sept. 1668, 20 Car. II. *Thomas Overing* mayor. Freemen, 25.

Sept. 1669, 21 Car. II. *Andrew Freeman* mayor. Freemen, 27.

"Received, for the fines for the tithes of Danet's Hall, Weftcotes, &c. 190l."

---

[1] Vicefima Pars Patentium de anno regni Regis Caroli Secundi fexto decimo.

[2] See vol. III. p. 894.

Sept. 1670, 22 Car. II. *William Dean* [1] mayor. Freemen, 26.

Sept. 1671, 23 Car. II. *Alexander Baker* mayor. Freemen, 18.

1672, *John Clay* (fecond time) mayor. Freemen, 12.

The earlieft token that has been traced, iffued by a Leicefter tradefman, is in 1655; the lateft in 1672. Between thofe dates 26 have fallen under our infpection, which are here engraved in Plate XXXIII.

Francis Eliot, 1655.
James Lee, 1656.
David Deakins, 1657.
Another of his, 1664.
John Goodall, 1664.
Robert Page, 1666.
John Pares, 1666.
Edward Read, 1666.
Nathaniel Baker, 1667.
Daniel Heggs, 1667.
William Wood, 1667.
John Browne, 1669.
Jane Lafh, 1669.
William Savidge, 1670.
N. Smith, 1672.
John Colfon.
John Mafon.
Mary Mountney.
Richard Noone.
J. W. N. at the Red Lyon.
Thomas Overing.
Jane Palmer.
William Spencer.
Thomas Sturges.
Richard Woodroffe.
S. Wilfon.

1673, *Robert Hartfhorn* mayor. Freemen, 18.

1674, *Francis Noble* [2] (fecond time) mayor. Freemen, 16.

1675, *George Becket* mayor. Freemen, 6.

1676, *Edmund Sutton* [3] mayor. Freemen, 21.

1677, *William Alfop* mayor. Freemen, 19.

1678, *Philip Abney* mayor. *Robert Harding*, miles, recordator. Ballivus, *William Major*, generofus, &c. Senefcalli, *Edmund Sutton*, ald', *John Norris*, ald', *Walter Hood*.

At a common hall, Oct. 8. Whereas Henry Dyfon, gent. did, upon Sunday laft, being Oct. 6, ftop Mr. Mayor, as he was going to his parifh church of St. Mary in Leicefter, and caufed the ferjeants and mace-bearer (after an unufual manner) to ftoop their maces, and alfo when they came to the church-door; and would not fuffer the great mace to be fet up in the cafe where it ufually did hang: It is ordered, that, if Mr. Dyfon fhall ever hereafter offer the like affront, Mr. Mayor fhall confult with perfons learned in the law, in what manner the Town may proceed to vindicate their antient rights and privileges.

Ordered, that Mr. Wakeman, head-fchoolmafter of the free fchool, on condition that he voluntarily refign the place of head-fchoolmafter, fhall have given him, by the Corporation, 45*l.*

Nov. 12. At a meeting of Mr. Mayor and his brethren, it is ordered: In regard a damnable plot has been carried on by the Papifts, a watch be appointed nightly; the aldermen taking it in their turns, and likewife a conftable, every night, and two of the forty-eight.

Jan. 3. At a common hall, Mr. William Thomas is elected head-fchoolmafter of the free fchool in this Borough.

Aug. 5, 1679, 30 Car. II. Mr. John Wilkins chofen of the company of twenty-four.

1679, *John Roberts* mayor. Sir *Robert Harding* recorder.

March 12. The parifh of St. Mary petitioning this Hall to grant them fome money, towards payment of 20*l.* to Mrs. Lacy, who hath offered to fettle upon the vicars of St. Mary's, for ever, the houfe late in occupation of Mr. Jofeph Bond, vicar of the faid parifh: It is ordered, that the faid parifhioners fhall have 5*l.* paid them, out of the chamber of the town, to the faid ufe.

At the requeft, and by the complaints, of the common council and freemen of the Borough, a law was enacted, in Auguft 1680, in conformity and confirmation of one made in the reign of James I. that if any perfon, being a non-freeman of the borough, " fhall at any time exercife any trade, myftery, occupation, or craft, within the liberties or precincts thereof, contrary to the antient ufage and cuftoms of the faid Borough, he fhall, for every offence, forfeit the fum of 20*s.* to the mayor, bailiffs, and burgeffes, to be recovered by action of debt, bill, or plaint, in any of His Majefty's Courts of Record, to be levied by diftrefs of the goods of the offenders."—Mem. This law was exhibited to fir Thomas Raymond, knight, and fir Thomas Street, knight, juftices of affize; and fully approved by them, and allowed. In witnefs whereof, the faid juftices thereto fet their hands and feals, in the prefence of two witneffes.

Sept. 9, 1680. At a meeting of the mayor and commiffioners, it is ordered, that the prefent owner or occupier of the vicarage-houfe belonging to the parifh of St. Martin fhall pay, yearly, for a chamber they now hold, which is part of the Town-hall, and is now ufed with the faid vicarage-houfe, the fum of 2*s.* 6*d.* during the pleafure of the Corporation.

1680, 32 Car. II. *John Goodball* mayor. *Nathan Wrighte*, arm', recorder.

Nov. 26. At a meeting of the twenty-four, it is ordered, that all the aldermen that have been or fhall be mayors fhall attend Mr. Mayor for the time being in their fcarlet gowns to wait on the judge at every affize; and the juftices of peace of the Borough to fit with the judges and Mr. Mayor, upon delivering the gaol, in their fcarlet gowns.

It is alfo ordered, that for the future all elections of members to be chofen of either company fhall be elected by tickets only.

May 30, 1681. At a common hall, it is ordered that an engine be bought, for the ufe of the Corporation in cafe of fire, with the monies fubfcribed by the feveral perfons of both companies, and what elfe fhall be collected and fubfcribed by the inhabitants.

Aug. 16. At a meeting of the twenty-four, Mr. William Brown is chofen folicitor for the Corporation during pleafure.

Sept. 7. At a common hall, it is ordered, that if any freeman of this borough be difturbed in paying toll in any place where they ought not to pay, by virtue of the patents granted to the Corporation, fuch perfon bringing his action, &c. and be put to charges to try the right of the Corporation, fhall be repaid by the Corporation out of the chamber of the town.

1681, *George Bent* mayor.

Whit-Monday, 1682, 34 Car. II. At a common hall. Whereas feveral members were appointed to view the fix widows almfwomens' houfes of the college of St. John the Baptift, within the faid

---

[1] This man was exceedingly unpopular in his time; on whom the following lines were written, which I have heard from the mouths of fome old people even at this diftant day:

" Dean, Dean, and double Dean, the child that is to bear,
May curfe the time that ever Dean was mayor;
For cutting of the ftrike, and felling the town land,
And putting the money into fquinting Pollard's hand."

Pollard, I have been told, was a chamberlain, and ran away with the money which had been received for the fale of fome Corporation property. One houfe fold was " a tenement in Holy Rood lane," now Town Hall lane.

[2] Great murmurings prevailed in Leicefter in his time, among the freemen of the borough, againft the farmers who rented the land in St. Mary's field. Throfby.—See vol. IV. p. 347.

[3] A little article occurs in his year for mending St. Anthony's bridge in Sanvey gate. One that ftood there, I apprehend, before the Town-ditch was filled up. Throfby.

Borough, &c. the faid members conceive it more fit the faid fix poor widows be removed up into the chamber, there being more conveniences for them than the houfes they now dwell in can be made to have, without very great charge: It is therefore ordered, that the little rooms in the faid chamber be fpeedily made fit for them to be removed up thereunto.

1682, 34 Car. II. *William Southwell* mayor.

1683, 35 Car. II. *Andrew Freeman* mayor.

Nov. 23. Ordered, that the under-ftewards of fairs fhall, in their own perfons, without deputing any other perfon, collect the moneys due from all perfons ftanding in the fairs, &c. for ufe of the chamber of the town, upon penalty of 13*s.* 4*d.* for every neglect, for the ufe of the chamber of the Corporation, &c.

Jan. 15. At a meeting of the twenty-four, John Major, efq. barrifter at law, is chofen fteward of the Court of Record, in the place of Thomas Staveley, efq. lately deceafed.

March 26, 1684. At a meeting of the twenty-four, Daniel Keene, M. A. late of Jefus college in Cambridge, is chofen head-ufher of the fchool, to be placed therein at or before Whitfuntide next, and therein to continue during pleafure, &c.

Sept. 25. At a common hall, it is agreed that the charters and liberties fhall be furrendered unto his gracious Majefty.

Thefe accounts occur refpecting the charter:

" Paid charges to Mr. Mayor and aldermen to London, to renew the charter, 20*l.*

" Paid Mr. Brown, town folicitor, his charges about the charter, 180*l.*"

1684, 36 Car. II. *Thomas Ludlam* mayor [1].

JAMES II.

Feb. 6, 1684, King Charles II. died; and King James was proclaimed here, Feb. 14, by the high fheriff and Corporation, attending in their formalities.

King James's fpeech to the Parliament May 22, 1685, and on Argyle's landing; and, May 30, upon fettling his revenue, are entered in the Town Books.

June 12, 1685, 1 Jac. II. At a common hall (the charter being furrendered), it is ordered, that every member of both companies fhall come to all meetings appointed by Mr. Mayor, at the Town-hall or elfewhere, in decent gowns and habits, their apparel being either black, or near thereunto, upon pain of forty fhillings, to be levied upon every one offending.

It is alfo agreed, that if any perfon neglect to appear upon fummons, or on days appointed to meet without fummons, and cannot fhew juft caufe of abfence to Mr. Mayor and his brethren, he fhall forfeit, if an alderman, 2*s.*; and a common-councilman, 1*s.* And if any do not appear at any meeting of commiffioners appointed by Mr. Mayor (without his leave), he fhall forfeit, if an alderman, 2*s.* 6*d.*; if a common-council-man, 1*s.* 6*d.*

It is alfo agreed, that every one neglecting to appear in his gown, at the Town-hall or elfewhere, as Mr. Mayor appoints, fhall forfeit, if an alderman, 4*s.*; and a common-council-man, 2*s.* 6*d.*

21 and 22 June, 1685, the mayor, &c. in confideration of 130*l.* fold unto Lawrence Carter, gent. the Mill, &c. and feveral fifhings of the Soar, from a place called Morehead unto a certain bridge called Weft-bridge, lying over the faid river; paying yearly to the King, for the faid premifes, the referved rent of 17*l.* per annum.

And the mayor, &c. as far as by law they be enabled, grant to the faid Lawrence Carter free leave and liberty, at his own expence, not only to make cifterns within the High Crofs, in the Borough of Leicefter, for the holding and furnifhing with water fuch pipes as he fhall lay down in the faid Borough, Bifhop's Fee, Newark and Caftle of Leicefter, or in any of them.

1685, *Walter Hood* mayor. *Theophilus* comes *Huntingdon*, recordator. *Nathan Wrighte*, deput' record'. [N. B. The chamberlains are here ftyled *ballivi*.]

Bill of Fare at Mr. Hood's Mayor's Feaft.

" FIRST COURSE.

The firft Table in the Hall.
The firft mefs.
A coller of brawn.
A difh of fifh.
Venifon pafty.
Choyne and turkey.
Ham and pulletts.
Mince pyes.
Grand fallett.
Roft geefe.
Venifon pafty.
Tongues and udders.
  The fecond Mefs.
Boare's head.
A difh of fifh.
Choyne and turkeys.
Boyld venifon.
Mince pyes.
Grand fallett.
Roft geefe.
Venifon pafty.
Tongues and udders.
  The third Mefs.
A coller of brawn.
A difh of fifh.
Choyne and turkeys.
Boyld fowle.
Grand fallett.
Mince pyes.
Roft geefe.
Venifon pafty.
Tongues and udders.
The fecond Table in the Hall.
  The firft Mefs.
A coller of brawn.
A difh of fifh.
Choyne and turkey.
A venifon pafty.
Roft geefe.
Grand fallett.
Mince pyes.
Ham and pulletts.
Tongues and udders.
  The fecond Mefs.
A difh of fifh.

Choyne and turkeys.
Venifon pafty.
Roft geefe.
Grand fallett.
Mince pyes.
Tongues and udders.
Boyld fowl.
  The firft Table in the Parlour.
  The firft Mefs.
A coller of brawn.
A difh of fifh.
Venifon pafty.
Choyne and turkeys.
Grand fallett.
Mince pyes.
Roft geefe.
Ham and pulletts.
Tongues and udders.
Grand fallett.
A difh of fifh.
A venifon pafty.
  The fecond Table in the Parlour.
A coller of brawn.
A difh of fifh.
Choyne and turkey.
Venifon pafty.
Roft geefe.
Grand fallett.
Ham and pulletts.
Mince pyes.
A difh of fifh.
Tongues and udders.
The Table in the Chamber.
A difh of fifh.
Choyne and turkeys.
Venifon pafty.
Ham and pulletts.
Grand fallett.
Roft geefe.
Mince pyes.
A difh of fifh.
Grand fallett.
Venifon pafty.
Tongues and udders.

" SECOND COURSE.

For the long Table.
  The firft Mefs.
A difh of wild fowl.
A difh of lobbftars.
A difh of pulletts.
Sturgeon.
Collard pigg.
Ducks.
Ham and tongues.
Tarts.
Rabbetts.
Cufterds.
  The fecond Mefs.
Wild fowl.
Sturgeon.
Collerd beef.
Cold pye.
Pulletts.
Warden and puffs.
Ham and tongues.
Rabbetts.
Cufterds.
  The third Mefs.
Pulletts.
Wardens and puffs.

Collerd pigg.
Rabbetts.
Ducks.
Cufterds.
  The fecond Table.
  The firft Mefs.
A difh of wild fowl.
Lobbfters.
Pulletts.
Wardens and puffs.
Sturgeon.
Ham and tongues.
Tarts.
Rabbetts.
Cufterds.
Collerd pigg.
  The fecond Mefs.
Ducks.
Sturgeon.
Pulletts.
Wardens and puffs.
Rabbetts.
Tongues.
Tarts.

[1] " Mr. Newton, vicar of St. Martin's church, this year preached a fermon before an amazing concourfe of people, who moftly attended there to fee an unfortunate woman at divine fervice, prior to her being burnt alive for killing her hufband at Ibftock, in this county." Throfby.

The firſt Table in the Parlour.
The firſt Meſs.
Wild fowl.
Lobbſters.
Pulletts.
Wardens and puffs.
Cold pye.
Sturgeon.
Tarts.
Collerd beefe.
Rabbetts.
Cuſterds.
Collerd pigg.
The ſecond Table.
Wild fowl.
Sturgeon.
Pulletts.

Wardens and puffs.
Ham and tongues.
Tarts.
Tongues.
Ducks.
Collerd pigg.
The Chamber.
Ducks.
Wardens and puffs.
Pulletts.
Tongues.
Collerd pigg.
Tarts.
Collerd beef.
Rabbetts.
Cuſterds.
Pulletts.
Tongues."

Whit-Monday 1686, 2 Jac. II. At a common hall, it is agreed that there ſhall be a ſcavenger appointed for carrying dirt ſwept up from the doors of the inhabitants of this Borough; and to agree with him is left to all the ſenior aldermen, or major part of them.

1686, 2 Jac. II. *Francis Ward* mayor.

1687, 3 Jac. II. *Joſeph Cradock* mayor. Iidem recordator & deput' record'.

March 13, 1687, 4 Jac. II. At a meeting of the mayor and aldermen [there were choſen 11 aldermen and 16 common-council-men alſo], Mr. John Oneby bailiff, Mr. John Creſſwell town-clerk, Mr. Vollentine Houſe town-ſolicitor.

1688, 4 Jac. II. *William Bentley* mayor. Iidem recordator & deput' record'.

James II. iſſued a proclamation for reſtoring antient charters, liberties, rights, and franchiſes, when he was threatened with an invaſion. In conſequence all that had been ſurrendered (which were many) were reſtored; " putting them (it ſays) in the ſame condition, ſtate, and plight, they were in at the time of ſuch deeds of ſurrender."

Mr. Major was bailiff at the ſurrender; but refuſed to re-aſſume his office when it was reſtored.

" A Proclamation for reſtoreing Corporations to their antient Charters, Liberties, Rights, and Franchiſes.

" Whereas wee are informed that ſeverall deeds of ſurrender, which have been lately made, by ſeverall corporations and bodyes corporate of and in our cityes and townes, within our kingdome of England and dominion of Wales, of their charters, franchiſes, and priviledges, are not yet recorded or enrolled; and that upon the proceedings and rules for judgement which have been lately had upon the *Quo Warrantos*, or informations in nature of a *Quo Warranto*, judgements are not yet entered upon record; whereupon notwithſtanding new charters have been granted in the reigne of our late deare Brother, and in our reigne; which ſaid deeds, being not enrolled or recorded, do not amount unto, or in law make, any ſurrender of the charters, franchiſes, or liberties, therein mentioned; and ſuch of the ſaid corporations or bodyes politique, againſt which rules for judgements have been made, in the life-time of our late deare Brother or ſince, in our Court of King's Bench, but no judgements entered upon record, are not diſcorporate or diſſolved; and that it is in our power to leave ſuch corporations in the ſame eſtate and condition they were in, and to diſcharge all further proceedings and effects that may be of ſuch rules for judgements and deeds of ſurrender: We doe hereby publiſh and declare, that, upon due ſearch and examination made, we have ſatisfaction that the deeds of ſurrender made by the corporations and bodyes politique of the ſaid cities and townes, except the corporations following; that is to ſay, Thetford, Nottingham, Bridgwater, Ludlow, Bewdley, Beverley, Tewkeſbury, Exeter, Doncaſter, Colcheſter, Wincheſter, Launceſton, Liſkerd, Plimpton, Tregoney, Plymouth, Dunwich, St. Ives, Fowey, Eaſt Looe, Camelford, Weſt Looe, Tintegall, Penryn, Truro, Bodmyn, Hadleigh, Leſtwythell, and Saltaſh, are not inrolled or recorded in any of our courts;

and that though rules for judgements have paſſed, upon informations in nature of a *Quo Warranto*, againſt the corporations and bodies politique of ſeveral cities and townes in our ſaid kingdome and dominion, yet no judgements have been or are entered upon record upon any ſuch informations, except againſt the cities of London, Cheſter, Calne, St. Ives, Pool, York, Thaxted, Llanghour, and Malmeſbury. And wee, of our meere grace and favour, being reſolved to reſtore and put all our cities, townes, and burroughs, in England and Wales, and alſo our town of Barwick upon Tweed, into the ſame ſtate and condition they were and was in our late deare Brother's reigne, before any deed of ſurrender was made of their charters or franchiſes, or procedings againſt them, or the corporations or bodies politique in or of the ſaid cities, townes, or burroughes, upon any *Quo Warrantos*, or informations in nature of a *Quo Warranto*, had; wee do hereby therefore publiſh, declare, direct, and require, that the ſaid corporations and bodies politique and corporate of all the ſaid cities, townes, and burroughs, whoſe deeds of ſurrender are not inrolled, nor judgements entered againſt them as aforeſaid, and the mayors, bailiffs, ſheriffs, aldermen, common-councilmen, aſſiſtants, recorders, town-clerks, magiſtrates, miniſters, officers, freemen, and all and every others the members of or in every of them reſpectively, upon the publication of this our proclamation, take on them and proceed to act as a corporation or body politique; and, where places are vacant by death or otherwiſe, to make elections, conſtitute and fill up the ſame, notwithſtanding the uſual dayes and times of elections by the antient charters and conſtitutions ſhall happen to be paſt; and to doe, execute, and perform, all and every matter and thing as they lawfully might and ought to have done, if noe ſuch deeds of ſurrender, rules for judgement, or other proceedings, upon any ſuch *Quo Warrantos* or informations, had been had or made: And, for the better effecting our ſaid intention, we have, by order made by us in council, and under our ſign manual, and we do alſoe by this our proclamation, made with the advice of our ſaid council, diſcharge, remove, and diſmiſs, all and every perſon and perſons of and from all offices and places of mayors, bailiffs, ſheriffs, aldermen, common-council-men, aſſiſtants, recorder, towne-clerk, and all and every office and place which they or any of them have or clayme only by charter, patent, or grant, from our deare Brother, or from ourſelf, ſince the dates of the reſpective deeds of ſurrender or rules for judgement, except ſuch corporations whoſe deeds of ſurrender are inrolled, or againſt whom judgement is entered; and that all and every ſuch perſon and perſons deliver up into the hands and cuſtody of the ſaid perſons hereby appoynted and intended to act and execute the ſaid offices and places, all and every the charters, records, bookes, evidences, and matters, concerning the ſaid reſpective corporations: And wee do hereby further publiſh and declare, that wee have cauſed all and every the ſaid deeds of ſurrender which can be found to be delivered and put into the hands of our Attorney Generall, to be by him cancelled, and returned to the corporations and bodies politique of the reſpective cities and townes whom they concern; and have alſo given to our ſaid Attorney authority, and do hereby warrant and command him, not only not to proceed or enter judgement upon the ſaid *Quo Warrantos*, or informations in nature of a *Quo Warranto*, or any of them, but to enter upon the reſpective records *Noli Proſequi's* and legall diſcharges thereof: And wee doe hereby publiſh and declare our further grace and favour to the ſaid cities, corporations, and burroughs, at any time hereafter, by any further act, to grant, confirm, or reſtore unto them, all their charters, liberties, franchiſes, and priviledges, that, at the reſpective times of ſuch deeds of ſurrender or rules for judgement made or given, they held or enjoyed; and in order to the perfecting our ſaid gracious intentions, wee doe hereby likewiſe publiſh and declare our royal will and pleaſure, as for and concerning the reſtoreing

to

to fuch of our cities, corporations, and burroughes, within our faid kingdome and dominion, which have made deeds of furrender, or have had judgement given againft them, which furrenders and judgements are entered of record; that our Chancellor, Attorney General, and Solicitor General, without fees to any officer or officers whatfoever, upon application to them made, fhall, and they are hereby required to, prepare and paffe charters, inftruments, grants, and letters patent, for the incorporateing, regranting, confirming, and reftoreing, to all and every the faid cities, corporations, and burroughs, their refpective charters, liberties, rights, franchifes, and priviledges, and for reftoreing the refpective mayors, bailiffs, recorders, fheriffs, towne-clerks, aldermen, common-council-men, affiftants, officers, magiftrates, minifters, and freemen, as were of fuch cities, corporations, or borroughs, at the time of fuch deeds of furrender or judgements refpectively given or had, and for the putting them into the fame ftate, condition, and plight, they were in at the times of fuch deeds of furrender or judgements made or given. And whereas diverfe burroughs that were not heretofore corporations have, fince the year one thoufand fix hundred feaventy-nine, had charters of incorporation granted and paffed unto them, wee hereby further expreffe and declare our royal pleafure to determine and annul the faid laft-mentioned charters and corporations; and to that end we have, in purfuance to the power referved in the faid charters, by our order in councill, and under our figne manuall, removed and difcharged, and wee doe alfoe by this our proclamation, made with the advice of our faid councill, remove and difcharge, all and every perfon of or in the faid laft-mentioned corporations of and from all offices and places of mayors, bailiffs, recorders, fheriffs, aldermen, common-councill-men, affiftants, and of and from all and every other office and place from which we have power referved by the faid charters refpectively to remove or difcharge them: And wee do hereby promife and declare, that wee will do and confent to all fuch acts, matters, and things, as fhall be neceffary to render thefe our gracious intentions and purpofes effectual, it being our intention to call a parliament as foon as the general difturbance of our kingdome by the intended invafion will admitt thereof. Given at our Court at Whitehall, the feventeenth day of October. By the King[1]."

Oct. 20, 1688. At a common hall [Mr. Thomas Ludlam is ftyled mayor, and many aldermen are changed; and then] Mr. William Bentley, chofen mayor for the year enfuing, took the ufual oaths of the Corporation, the oath of allegiance and fupremacy, the oath mentioned in the Act for regulating Corporations, and fubfcribed the Declaration for renouncing the Covenants.

Mr. Ludlam, Mr. Hood, Mr. Ward, Mr. Cradock, chofen juftices of the peace for the year enfuing.

It is agreed at this meeting, that thofe perfons as have been mayors fhall have their precedency according to their places of feniority of mayoralty.

Dec. 27. At a common hall, it is agreed that the companies of twenty-four and forty-eight fhall yearly appear, Dec. 27, at the hall, without fummons, and wait on the mayor, in their gowns, to hear a fermon at All Saints church, or in the Hofpital of St. John's chamber, to extend their charity to the poor widows. The abfenters to fend to chamberlains; elfe to pay, if of the twenty-four, 12d.; if of the forty-eight, 6d.

Dec. 18. At a meeting of the twenty-four, Mr. Thomas Palmer is elected bailiff in the place of Mr. William Major, who refufed to execute the faid office, and abfolutely declined the fame.

WILLIAM AND MARY.

April 24, 1689. At a meeting of the twenty-four,

Thomas Noble, gent. attorney at law, is chofen to be the Corporation folicitor during pleafure.

William Higgs is elected, in room of William Orton, deceafed, mace-bearer of this Corporation during pleafure.

Giles Coker is elected library-keeper for the faid Corporation during pleafure, in the place the faid William Higgs lately enjoyed.

1689, 1 William and Mary, *John Bent* mayor. *Nathan Wrighte* recorder.

In this year, 160l. was paid for fines for the tithes of Danet's Hall, Weftcotes, &c.

Oct. 11. At a common hall, Mr. John Kilby is chofen head-ufher of the free-fchool, in room of Mr. Daniel Keen, deceafed, during pleafure of the Corporation.

1690, 2 William and Mary, *John Goodhall* mayor.

July 9, 1691. At a common hall. Whereas divers perfons elected into the common council have refufed the place, or neglected to take the oaths, &c.; it is ordained and enacted, by Mr. Mayor and aldermen, with the advice of the common council, that fuch fo neglecting or refufing fhall forfeit the fum of 100 marks, or fuch greater or leffer fum as fhall feem meet to the mayor and aldermen to impofe upon them, to be levied on their goods and chattels, or to be recovered by action of debt, bill, or plaint, in any of their Majefty's courts of record.

May 26. At a meeting of the twenty-four, it is agreed, by all the aldermen prefent, and the reft abfent upon notice given, or fo many as then fhall think fit, fhall meet at the Town-hall upon the Friday next after St. Matthew's day, and fo yearly, to take account of the bonds in the Charter-houfe, and of other matters and things they fhall think fit to infpect done that year.

1691, 3 William and Mary, *George Becket* mayor.

Aug. 18, 1692. At a common hall, upon the death of Mr. George Becket late mayor, Mr. *John Wilkins* is elected in his room, and fworn.

" Paid Mr. Wilkins, mayor, for 940 yards of new-caft leaden pipes, 142l. 4s."[2]

1692, 4 William and Mary, *John Brookfby* mayor.

Dec. 27. At a meeting of the twenty-four, Robert Tyrlington was elected mace-bearer, in room of William Higgs deceafed, during pleafure.

1693, 5 William and Mary, *Edmund Johnfon* mayor. *Nathan Wrighte*, Serviens ad legem, recordator.

June 27, 1694. At a meeting of the twenty-four, Samuel Wilcocks was chofen library-keeper during pleafure, and no longer.

1694, 6 William and Mary, *Thomas Palmer* mayor.

March 25, 1695. At a meeting of the aldermen, Edward Jevon, gent. was elected to be town-clerk, and took his oath.

Sept. 12. At a meeting of the aldermen, Jofeph Kilby was elected to be library-keeper during pleafure.

1695, 7 William III. *John Pares* mayor.

Jan. 24. At a meeting of the twenty-four, it is ordered that this Corporation will join with the reft of the Corporations in a fuit againft the City of Coventry, for an account of Sir Thomas White's charity given to the faid Corporations.

May 22, 1696. At a common hall, ordered that two perfons be fent to London to folicit for fome new money, for the ufe of the poor of this Corporation, for fmall money.

A petition was alfo figned, and the common feal affixed, to the Lords' Committees for managing the government, for 6000l. in new money, to be exchanged for clipt money.

June 9, 1698. At a common hall, ordered that Mr. John Wilkins fhall repair the pipes that are laid from the conduit in the fields to the conduit in the town, at the charge of the Corporation, and maintain the common decay that fhall happen to the faid

---

[1] Nona pars paten' de anno regni Regis Jacobi Secundi Quarto.

[2] " The leaden pipes found fo frequently acrofs the ftreets, and in the yards of the houfes in the South part of the town, are accounted for by this item of expenditure. Wilkins was a clock-maker. In the year 1791, I faw two lengths of thefe pipes taken up by the workmen betwixt the High Crofs and the Peacock, when that ftreet was begun to be paved after the modern fafhion. The water-works were where the pump is, at the end of the new buildings, below the Peacock." Throfby.

pipes,

pipes, for 5s. *per annum*, at his own charge; and that Mr. John Wilkins fhall mend the conduit in the field at the charge of the Corporation.

Aug. 27, 1696, 8 Will. III. At a common hall, ordered that Mr. George Bent junior fhall have a leafe of the Foreft-land given by King Charles I. for 21 years, and not to plough the laft feven years, under the yearly rent of 14l.; to begin from the end of the laft leafe.

1696, 8 Will. III. *John Roberts* mayor. *Nathan Wrighte*, ferviens ad legem, recordator.

March 31, 1697. At a common hall, ordered that Mr. John Wilkins fhall have 40l. and deliver up both the engines, and leave the water-courfes and the conduit in good repair, to the Corporation; and, if there be any want of repairs in the faid engines, Mr. Wilkins to allow it out of the 40l.

Aug. 9. At a common hall, ordered that the town-clerk fhall take but 6s. 8d. for a copy of the charter.

Sept. 1. At a meeting, Laurence Carter junior, efq. was chofen recorder of this Corporation.

1697, 9 Will. III. *Henry Pate* mayor. *Laurence Carter* junior recordator.

Oct. 22. At a common hall, ordered that an account of the toll of the feveral fairs be brought in, and filed upon the file of the mayors for the future.

Ordered alfo, that all the ten pounds that fhall be remaining in the old chamberlains' hands fhall be paid into the hands of the new chamberlains at and before St. Thomas's day next enfuing, upon the forfeiture of 5l. to be paid by the chamberlains fo neglecting, and to be paid into the chamber of the town; and all chamberlains fucceffively fhall obferve the order of payment abovefaid, under the like penalty.

It is likewife ordered, that what moneys fhall be expended by this Corporation upon any public accounts fhall be laid out with the members of this hall, they felling as cheap as other tradefmen.

It is likewife ordered, that the mayor for the time being, and the alderman of every ward, fhall call to their affiftance the conftables of every ward a month before Lady-day feffions, and walk the feveral wards of this Borough, to fee how the ftreets are kept in repair; and to caufe the conftables to take an account, in writing, of the perfons that make neglect; and to give them notice to repair their doors, or elfe to be prefented the next following feffions.

March 10. Whereas Mr. John Roberts, late mayor of Leicefter, did bind feveral perfons as apprentices, [viz. John Townefend of Aylefton, and Henry Bowler and Mary Cradock, in September 1697, for feven years, but their indentures to commence in 1693 and 1694;] ordered, that the faid Mr. Roberts hath forfeited the 20 marks payable out of the Gofling clofe, for binding the abovefaid perfons in manner abovefaid; and that the faid 20 marks be ftopped out of his falary.

April 1698. At a common hall, ordered that what money Mr. Noble, folicitor for this Corporation, fhall pay or lay down towards the charges of a patent for the poor of the Hofpital of the Holy Trinity in the Newark, fhall be repaid him by the Corporation.

Ordered, that 5l. fhall be allowed towards the charge of carrying on the fuit againft Coventry about fir Thomas White's will.

July 5. At a common hall, ordered that a common hall fhall be called within ten days after the new mayor is fworn; and then the book for binding apprentices, and making freemen, for the preceding year, fhall be publicly read, to fee what perfons are bound, and freemen made, contrary to the former orders, for the forfeiture of 13l. 6s. 8d. paid out of the Gofling clofe, which fhall, by order of the faid hall, be ftopped by the chamberlains; and if nothing appear to the contrary, it fhall be paid to the faid mayor.

Ordered, that Mr. Nidd's gift of 32l. *per annum* to the poor of Mountforell be henceforth paid to the church-wardens and chapel-wardens of Mountforell jointly; and that they fhall call to their affiftance

Vol. I.

four of the feniors of the faid town, whereof two of the North end, and two of the South end, to fee the faid money paid according to the will of Mr. Nidd.

1698, 10 Will. III. *John Cracroft* mayor.

Jan. 13. At a common hall, ordered that a petition be fent up to the Houfe of Commons againft making the river Derwent, co. Derby, navigable.

Q. Whether this hall will confent that the town of Harborough fhall have a new fair?

Refolved in the negative, *nemine contradicente*.

Ordered, that a letter be fent to the earl of Stamford, to return his Lordfhip thanks.

March 31, 1699. Ordered, that [certain perfons] fhall view what incroachments are made in the South Fields by any of the tenants of the Corporation, and what grafs-ground is converted into tillage, contrary to their leafes; and to report the fame to the next common hall; and what controverfies are among any of the faid tenants the faid commiffioners are to endeavour a reconciliation.

July 11. At a common hall, Mr. John Goodal was difmiffed from his future attendance as alderman.

Sept. 21. Ordered, that Mr. John Ludlam, being chofen chamberlain for the year enfuing, according to the cuftom of the Borough, by Mr. Samuel Woodland, mayor elect, and refufing to ferve the faid office, fhall pay for his fine 11l. to be paid into the hands of the chamberlains.

1699, 11 Will. III. *Samuel Woodland* mayor.

1700, 12 Will. III. *John Abney* mayor.

Nov. 12. At a meeting of the commiffioners, agreed that the houfe belonging to this Corporation, called *The Lords Place*, with the appurtenances, be fold for 500l.; and the purchafer to take all incumbrances of leafes whatfoever.

April 13, 1701. At a common hall, agreed that this Corporation will join with the reft of the Corporations, and bear their proportionable charges, in an appeal to be brought before the Houfe of Lords about Coventry lands.

June 20, 1701. At a common hall, ordered that the arrears of Mrs. Elizabeth Ward's gift, being 20s. *per annum*, fhall be demanded of Mr. William Ruding; which gift is 3l. *per annum*, payable out of Duck-holme clofe, now in his poffeffion; and, for want of payment of the faid arrears, he fhall be fued at common hall.

1701, 13 Will. III. *Richard Townefend* mayor. Chamberlains, John Pares, Francis Lewin. Communis clericus Edward Jevon, generofus.

Sept. 29. At a common hall, ordered that 18l. being received by Mr. Noble of Mr. Acham, all charges expended by this Corporation towards getting and receiving that money fhall be deducted thereout, and the remainder to be diftributed to the poor, according to the gift.

Ordered, that a bond be given from the Corporation to the overfeers of the poor of St. Mary for 10l. being the gift of Mr. Lacy and Mr. Sherman; there being a bond formerly given for the fame, and loft.

Ordered, that Mr. Bennet's and Mr. Ward's gift fhall henceforth be paid according to the donor's gift.

King William III. died March 8, 1701-2; and Queen Anne was proclaimed.

ANNE.

March 16, 1701-2, 1 Anne. At a common hall, Mr. Jofeph Hardy was elected head-ufher, to fucceed Mr. Kilby, in the free-fchool.

Ordered, that Mr. Chamberlain Lewin fhall receive into his hands, for the ufe of the Corporation, the lottery-money from Mr. Watts; and no intereft to be paid for it till the Corporation makes ufe of it.

May 25, 1702. At a common hall; ordered, according to a former order, that every perfon neglecting to appear at any meeting upon fummons, or days which they are appointed to meet without fummons, and have not fpareing; every alderman fhall forfeit 2s. and every common-council-man 1s. according to the faid order.

Aug. 28. At a meeting of the commiffioners, [they] agreed to fell to Simon Barwell, gent. the

great

great houfe called *The Lords Place*, with all the gardens, orchards, and appurtenances, for 400*l*.; to hold to him and his heirs for ever.

Sept. 18. At a meeting, Mr. John Boley was elected town-clerk, in room of Mr. Jevon deceafed; & *tunc juratus*.

1702, 1 Anne, *Edmund Cradock* mayor. Chamberlains, Thomas Hemfly, John Smally.

Nov. 7. At a common hall, Eleanor Headly, Sarah Ward, Springthorp-Joyce Legit, widows, were chofen to have Mr. Bent's gift in St. John's Hofpital; and are to take preference as they were elected.

Feb. 3. At a common hall, ordered that an entry and claim be forthwith made into part of the land (in name of the whole) lying within the liberties of Enderby, being the lands of Mr. John Bent, given by his will to the Corporation for the benefit of four widows in St. John's Hofpital, in order to fulfil the donor's will, and affert the rights of the Corporation; and that a letter of attorney be made, under the common feal, to the town-clerk, to make the faid entry and claim, in name of the Corporation; and the Corporation to fave him harmlefs.

It is ordered, that the houfes in St. John's Hofpital be made fit, as foon as they can, for the four widows; and that what charges they coft fhall be paid out of the rents of Enderby lands, given by Mr. John Bent for maintenance of the faid widows, before fuch time as any thing be allowed to the faid widows.

March 5. At a common hall, the leafe for 21 years, to commence from Lady-day next, of the lands at Enderby given by Mr. John Bent, at the rent of 24*l*. *per annum*, was fealed.

March 31, 1703. At a meeting of the twenty-four, Mr. Bowers, fteward to the earl of Huntingdon, by order of the faid earl, nominated Simon Barwell, gent. to be fteward of this Corporation, according to a deed made by the Corporation to Henry earl of Huntingdon in the reign of King James I.; and the faid Simon Barwell was elected.

July 12. At a common hall, ordered that all the members of this hall attend here to-morrow morning, at eight o'clock, in order to meet the right hon. the earl of Denbigh, lord lieutenant of the county of Leicefter. Ordered, that fuch and fo much wine and bifcuit, and other things neceffary for a handfome treat fit for the faid lord Denbigh, be provided, as Mr. Mayor fhall think proper, according to the company that appears; to be paid for out of the chamber of the town.

1703, 2 Anne, *Richard Wefton* mayor. Chamberlains, Charles Tufley, John Cooper.

Oct. 8. At a common hall, ordered that the great mace be new-gilded with gold; and that the chamberlains pay for doing the fame.

Nov. 26. Ordered, that Mr. Noble, the town folicitor, bring an action againft the town of Bedford, for exacting toll of Mr. Thomas Ayres and Mr. George Bent for their cattle, notwithftanding they fhewed them the copy of the charter.

Ordered, that the chamberlains forthwith put into repair the chambers over the Eaft gate, to make them fit for a tenant to live in.

Jan. 28. Ordered, *nemine contradicente*, that Mr. Boley, the town-clerk, for his extraordinary care and pains taken for the benefit of the Corporation, fhall have a gratuity of 20*l*.; to be forthwith paid by the prefent chamberlains.

March 6. At a common hall, ordered that every mayor fhall, twice in the year, viz. the firft hall after his election, and the firft hall after Lady-day, caufe all the heads and titles of fir Thomas White's and Mr. Heyrick's bonds to be publicly read, that the hall may judge of fuch as ought to renew their fecurity, and fuch as ought to pay in the faid money; and then the mayor for the time being fhall forthwith give notice to all fuch perfons [of what is ordered]; and if, after fuch notice given, any neglect to renew their fecurity, or pay in their money, according to fuch order, by the fpace of two months, then the mayor fhall caufe fuch perfons to be profecuted at law by

the folicitor: And it is ordered, that if any mayor fhall neglect to perform this order, he fhall, for every neglect or breach of this order, forfeit and pay, to the ufe of the bailiffs and burgeffes of Leicefter, 5*l*. to be recovered by due order of law.

It is ordered, that the mayor for the time being fhall, in all things, fo far as in him lieth, put in execution, obferve, and keep, all fuch orders as hereafter fhall be made in this hall; upon pain of his neglect (upon notice given to him by this hall to put the fame in execution) to forfeit and pay 10*l*. to the then chamberlains, or to be ftopped out of his falary.

March 31, 1704. At a common hall, ordered that the town-clerk, taking with him one alderman and two common-council-men, one being of the firft 24, and one of the laft 24 of the forty-eight, fhall have liberty, from time to time, to go into the charter-houfe, and infpect the writings there, and put them into order, that they may be more readily found, and the town better know how their title ftands in the lands they now enjoy, and whether they be not wronged of other lands and tenements which it is fuppofed belong to them.

It is ordered, that Thomas Wall, of Belgrave, millwright, fhall have a leafe of the North mills, late in poffeffion of John Townefend, from Lady-day laft, for 21 years, paying yearly 26*l*.

June 1. At a common hall, ordered that Mr. John Boley, town-clerk, fhall be made free without paying any fine.

Jnne 5. At a common hall, ordered that the orders now read concerning the four widows at St. John's Hofpital, &c. be kept by them; and that 6*d*. a-week be by the town paid to a keeper, to look to them in their illnefs; and the keeper to make them a fire in the morning, and then clean the public room, every day. Widow Armfton to be the firft keeper; and that the chamberlains make the fpare-room below ftairs fit for the keeper to lay in.

Ordered, that the Corporation fhall, as ufual, make a prefent of wine to the earl of Stamford, and a treat for him when in this town, according to the difcretion of Mr. Mayor.

Ordered, that the Queen's arms be frefh drawn, and the coats of arms in the Gainfborough; and that the earl of Denbigh's arms be put up there.

1704, 3 Anne, *Thomas Ayres* mayor. Chamberlains, John Denfhin, William Goadby.

1705, 4 Anne, *Thomas Hartfhorn* mayor. Chamberlains, John Pratt, Robert Winfield.

Dec. 18. At a common hall, ordered that Mr. Hartfhorn prefent mayor, Mr. R. Townefend, Mr. Edmund Cradock, Mr. Richard Wefton, and Mr. Thomas Ayres, attend (at the meeting of the Corporations of Nottingham, Northampton, and Warwick), and treat with Coventry, at fuch place as fhall be agreed on.

Feb. 6, 1705-6, the Houfe of Commons determined that the right of election for the Borough of Leicefter was in the freemen not receiving alms, and in the inhabitants paying fcot and lot; but perfons living in the Borough by certificate, not having gained a fettlement, by renting 10*l*. a-year, or ferving in an annual office, are not entitled (by paying fcot and lot) to vote.

May 12, 1706. At a common hall, ordered that widow Buyers fhall have the Willoughby lands for 21 years at the old rent, paying a guinea in hand, and to plough five acres the three firft years, &c.

June 18. Ordered, that on the 27th of this month, being a day of thankfgiving for the victories in Brabant, &c. Mr. Mayor fhall make fuch an entertainment at the Gainfborough as is fuitable to the occafion.

Aug. 13. At a common hall, ordered that Mr. Fox fhall have the rent of St. Mary's church-yard till the end of Mr. Wilkins's leafe; and after that, the ufe and benefit of the church-yard fo long as this hall fhall think fit.

Aug. 26. At a common hall, a draught of the fettlement of the charity given by fir Thomas White was read, and approved of.

1706, 5 Anne, *George Bent* mayor. Chamberlains, Matthew Jud, William Hammonds.

Oct. 8. At a common hall, ordered that Nicholas Swingler and John Yates be bellmen, to go nightly through the Borough, from ten at night till fix in the morning, to be removeable at pleasure of the mayor for the time being; and that the Corporation provide bells; and that each of the bellmen have a coat, the price not to exceed 4s. *per* yard, and a small badge of silver, with the town arms, on the sleeve of each coat, and two staves: the said bells, coats, badges, and staves, to be taken away, and bellmen removed, by the mayor and justices for the time being, or more part of them, upon any misdemeanour.

Dec. 5. Ordered, that the 31st instant, being a thankfgiving-day for the battle of Ramillies, a hogfhead of ale be given; and so much ale, and kidds for bonfires, at the Gainsborough, as Mr. Mayor thinks fit.

April 1, 1707. At a meeting, William Handy was unanimously chosen mace-bearer, and sworn, in place of Mr. Turlington deceased; John Blifs chosen ferjeant, in place of William Handy.

At Leicester, in 1707, was a free school, in which 24 boys were taught.

Sept. 21, *John Lualam* was elected mayor; Roger Lee, William Topp, chamberlains.

Sept. 21, 1708, *Johannes Ludlam* amotus; *Jacobus Annis* electus major. Camerarii, Edward Palmer pro com', Francis Coltman pro majore.

Flefh-tafters, two butchers; fearchers and fealers of leather, a tanner fealer, two cordwainers, one currier, and one fadler; triers of tallow, two butchers, two chandlers, two fellmongers.

"Received of Mr. Robert Sherwin, purfuant to agreement made at Lutterworth between the Corporation and the City of Coventry, concerning fir Thomas White's gift, for which city he paid, as their agent, 200*l*., and for the interest money 3*l*. 5s., and for a year's rent of fir Thomas White's land, according to agreement."—[" Mem. This 200*l*. was repaid to Coventry in 1719, by order of the Court of Chancery. E. L."]

Feb. 11. Ordered feveral perfons to affift the town-clerk, and infpect the old files and papers in his chamber, and fet them at rights.

Ordered the old filver falt to be exchanged for two wax filver candlefticks, a pair of filver fnuffers and ftand; and what they come to more to be paid by the chamberlains.

March 23. The twenty-four chofe Jofeph Abell to be common crier, in room of John Ogden deceafed; and George Befton beadle, in room of Thomas Oliver, who was turned out; to continue during pleafure.

April 8, 1709. Articles were fealed between Mary Coy and John Coy her fon, and the Corporation, for a half yard and half a quarter of a yard land in Houghton, in confideration of 160*l*.; whereof 20*l*. now paid, and 140*l*. to be paid at the confirming the title, of which 120*l*. is due to Mrs. Elizabeth Brown, upon a mortgage which fhe hath of the premiffes; and the Corporation this day gave her a bond for it.

May 27. At a common hall, ordered the chamberlain to prepare a handfome entertainment for the Bifhop [Dr. Wake]; and that the aldermen who have been mayors meet him at the town-hall, in fcarlet, on Friday next, at five o'clock, P. M.—Ordered, that the late beadle be allowed 20s. for his coat, to be paid by 2s. *per* week; and Joan Oyder was allowed 10s.

June 10. Ordered a new Queen's arms to be erected over the Weft gate.

Item, that Mr. Fox, vicar of St. Mary's, fhall be tenant of St. Mary's church-yard, paying yearly for the fame 10s., and enjoy it during pleafure of the mayor; and that the 3s. 4d. charged on him for the Eafter book, and other dues of the parifh of St. Mary, be not for the future *fupered*, but that he pay the fame. Item, ordered that Mr. Fox be paid by the chamberlains 13s. 4d. over and above the 10*l*. already granted him during the pleafure of the hall.

June 13. Ordered, that the Conduit be taken down, and re-built.

June 20. Ordered, that the charge of re-building the Conduit be defrayed by the chamberlains; and that the founder's name and other ornaments, lately upon the old, be put upon the new one.

The chamberlains were ordered to pay to the grand jury that ferved the laft feffions 20s. for their extraordinary charges.

Sept. 21, *Edward Hood* elected mayor; Humphrey Chapman, Thomas Ayre, chamberlains.

Oct. 6. Several ordered to meet, and confider what is proper to be done in order to the inclofing the South Fields, according to a former order for inclofing the fame.

Nov. 22. The order made 8 Jac. I. for cleanfing the ftreets, was ordered to be duly executed; and that the cryer forthwith proclaim the faid order through the whole town.

Dec. 16. The chamberlains were ordered to pay 5*l*. to William Harris, late one of the forty-eight, he being reduced low in his eftate.

Several perfons were ordered to be fued, at the charge of the Corporation, for ufing their trades within the Borough, not being free.

Dec. 27. Ordered, that all thofe of the twenty-four and forty-eight that do not pay, or refufe to pay, all and every fine and fines already due, or that fhall become due, for not attending at common halls on days of fummons, or fuch days on which they are to appear without fummons, fhall, from time to time, be fued for the fame, as the fame fhall become due, at the charge of the Corporation.

Jan. 31, 1709-10. Ordered, that fuch members of the twenty-four as do not appear at the hall to go to the church with Mr. Mayor on St. John's day fhall forfeit for each neglect 2s. apiece, unlefs they fend 1s. to the mayor for the ufe of the poor of St. John's Hofpital; the forty-eight for like neglect to forfeit 1s., unlefs he or they fo abfent fend 6d. for the like ufe.

March 3. Mary Cook, widow, took a leafe of two clofes, called Freak's grounds, for 21 years, from March 25, 1710, paying 30*l*. *per annum* rent, &c. when grazed; but 60*l*. *per annum*, for the firft three years, when fhe is to plough them.

Ordered, papers to be put up at the Gates and High Crofs, and left at the Coffee-houfe, giving notice that the Bend-houfe meadows, South Field lands, Gofling clofes, and the houfe and ground in the Senvey gate, are to be let at the next meeting of the commiffioners.

March 29, 1710. At a meeting of the commiffioners, Robert Lord took the fheep-penns for fix years, from Candlemas laft, paying yearly 16*l*. and the parifh levies, and keeping the penns in repair, and making the pavement good where broken up during the faid term.

John Smalley took a piece of ground where a houfe ftood formerly, and a garden belonging to it, on the South fide of Senvey gate, next the houfe of Chriftopher Law, on the Eaft fide, to hold it, from Ladyday laft, for 41 years, paying yearly 6s. 8d. and building a houfe on it, with brick and other materials, as good as Chriftopher Law's is, and leave it in good repair, and paying all taxes.

Item, by 25 out of 36 prefent, it was voted that the South Fields fhall be let in fix farms, to be ufed as heretofore, to the beft bidder, as foon as conveniently they can be.—Mr. John Ludlam and Mr. Thomas Helmfley protefted againft this order.

April 5. Edward Broughton took the lands lying up to the Swans windmill, abutting to the Sick, and next the caufeway leading from the Pinfold to Wigfton, along by the hedge-fide; and five lands, lying together, by the hedge againft Mr. Carter's windmill, to dig the fame for making brick, from Michaelmas next, for 21 years, paying yearly 25s. for every acre, and proportionably for lefs than an acre; and he is to level the fame at the end of the term, and pay all taxes and levies; and he is to hold the four acres which he has a leafe of at the fame rent *per* acre as the farmers fhall give for their farms, &c.

George Bent fenior, draper, took the farm called Four yard lands, in St. Mary's fields, now in poffeffion of Mr. John Abney, to hold it for 21 years, from Michaelmas next, paying yearly 48*l.* and all taxes and levies.

Mr. William Southwell junior took the Grange and Farm, reputed four yard-land, in St. Mary's field (except fix acres fet to Mr. Edward Broughton), to hold for 21 years, from Michaelmas next, paying 52*l. per annum,* and all taxes and levies.

Thomas Hall, tinman, took the Grange yard, barn, and land, in St. Mary's field, reputed three yard land, then in poffeffion of Henry Coulfon (except five lands next the hedge, by Mr. Carter's windmill, being about one acre and a half), to hold for 21 years, from Michaelmas next; to pay 39*l. per. annum,* and all taxes and levies.

John Prat took three yard-land, then in his poffeffion, to hold for 21 years, from Michaelmas next, paying 36*l. per annum,* and all taxes and levies.

Thomas Ward, innholder, took three yard-land, then in his poffeffion, to hold for 21 years, from Michaelmas next, paying 36*l. per annum,* and all taxes and levies.

Robert Winfield and William Wells took the clofe, now divided into four parts, called the Gofling clofes, then in Mr. Townefend's poffeffion, to hold for 21 years, from Michaelmas next; to pay 24*l. per annum,* and all taxes and levies.

Mr. Edmund Johnfon took the farm, reputed three yard-land and a half, in the poffeffion of Mr. John Wilkins, to hold it 21 years, from Michaelmas next, paying 42*l. per annum,* and all taxes and levies.

May 3. An addrefs was fealed, to be prefented by fir George Beaumont to the Queen.

June 16. The commiffioners fet to Jofeph How, taylor, three clofes or meadows lying behind the Swanns mill, late in poffeffion of Edmund Johnfon, to hold from 25th March laft, for 21 years, paying 15*l. per annum.*

Aug. 25. A common hall ordered, that John Haftings, fon of Robert Haftings, of Countefthorpe, on his petition, fhould be bound apprentice to Samuel Jacome, fellmonger, and that his indentures fhould bear date from March 25, 1707; it appearing to the hall, that the faid apprentice had lived with and ferved his mafter from that time as an apprentice.

The tenants mentioned above, neglecting to appear and feal their leafes, as they were appointed to do this day, they were ordered to be fued at law, unlefs they fhould appear at the next common hall.

William Breen, miller, was ordered to be profecuted at law for a tithe of 18*s.* payable out of the mills he holds, due to the Corporation.

Aug. 31. Mr. Winfield, Mr. Wells, Jofeph How, and Mr. George Bent, fealed their leafes.

Sept. 21, *Thomas Bradley* elected mayor; John Newton, John Ayre, chamberlains.

Sept. 22. At a meeting of the twenty-four, Mr. James Annis, one of the aldermen, being charged with fpeaking feveral unmannerly and reproachful words to Mr. Edward Hood, mayor, and feveral aldermen then prefent, at the White Hart in this Borough; the faid Mr. Annis did, at this meeting, publicly acknowledge himfelf in a fault for the fame, and declared that he was very forry for what he had faid.

Oct. 23. At a hall, a releafe was fealed (Mr. Newford of Carleton) of lands in Houghton fuper Montem.

Nov. 3. Mr. Lord's leafe for the fheep-penns was fealed.

Jan. 17, 1710-11, Mr. Pratt and Mr. Smalley's leafes were fealed; and Wall's leafe for one acre and a half of land, whereon his windmill ftands, for 14 years and a half, ending at Lady-day 1721.

Ordered, that from Lady-day next the town-clerk for the time being fhall be allowed 10*s. per annum,* and no more, for pen, ink, wax, paper, and parchment, for the town's ufe.

Aug. 23, 1711. The commiffioners ordered certain perfons to enquire the value of Mr. Ruding's fmall tithes, which he holds by leafe of the Corporation, expiring at Michaelmas next, and other fmall

tithes of the Corporation, and make report to the commiffioners at the next meeting.

Sept. 7. The commiffioners, not liking the report made to them, ordered the fame to be further deliberated on.

The aldermen of the wards agreed, that they fhould return a particular account of the diftribution of the charitable gifts given by King Charles I., the duke of Devonfhire, Mr. Haines, and widow Offiter, within a fortnight after they have difpofed of the fame, to the mayor for the time being.

Sept. 21, *Edmund Johnfon* elected mayor; Thomas Gamble, Thomas Lewin, chamberlains.

Several chofen to be chamberlains were fined; viz. Thomas Willows, 10*l.*; Robert Low, 11*l.*; Robert Headly, 14*l.*

Jan. 15, 1711-12. A common hall ordered the chamberlains to give and pay to Thomas Roberts 12*l.* for making a furvey of the Corporation.

John Franklin, one of the ferjeants (being unfit for bufinefs), had 2*s. per* week paid him.

Feb. 22. A hall abated 4*l.* of the fine laid on Robert Headly for not ferving as chamberlain; fo he paid only 10*l.*

The farmers petitioning to have the taxes for the South Fields abated, their petition was rejected.

June 17, 1712. A common hall ordered an addrefs to the Queen, for communicating to her people the terms of the general peace.

Thomas Oliver, once fervant to the Corporation, had 12*d. per* week allowed him.

The roof of St. Mary's chancel ordered to be repaired.

Aug. 27. The re-grant of fir Thomas White's eftate to Coventry was fealed.

Sept. 21, *John Cooper* elected mayor; Edward Bracebridge, Thomas Ludlam, chamberlains.

Sept. 26. At a meeting of the twenty-four; there being 400*l.* of fir Thomas White's eftate come from Coventry to this Borough, to be put out, in fifty pounds, to eight young men, of good name and fame, freemen; at this meeting it was refolved, that none of the companies of twenty-four or forty-eight fhall have any of it for this time; but that afterwards, as the further charity comes, one half fhall be put out to thofe of the body that fhall petition for the fame, and the other half to freemen that are not of the body politick, giving good fecurity for the fame: And that all and every perfon who fhall have any of the fifty pounds fhall, at his own charge, take the advice of the recorder for the time being, or fome other counfel learned in the law, as the mayor and aldermen for the time being fhall approve, that fuch fecurities may be by him or them advifed on: And that no perfon fhall be capable of taking this 50*l.* that has 10*l.* either of fir Thomas White's or Mr. Heyrick's money, unlefs he refign the faid 10*l.*: And that all bonds or other fecurities, to be given for any of the fifty pounds, fhall be fealed and executed in a court of aldermen. The perfons to whom at this time the fifty pounds were granted were, John Roberts, William Noon, hatter, Richard Jervis, Richard Denfhire, John Page, fmith, Samuel Miles, Tobias Pickering, and William Sutton.

Oct. 10. At this hall, ordered *(nemine contradicente)* that there fhall be, yearly, paid by the chamberlains, to the mayor for the time being, 20*l.* over and above the 40*l.* now paid by the chamberlains; and to begin this additional payment to Mr. John Cooper, prefent mayor.

Likewife ordered, that there fhall be added to the four nobles, now the town-clerk's falary, fo much as fhall make his yearly falary full 5*l.* during pleafure, by quarterly payments, to begin from Michaelmas laft.

Nov. 28. At a hall; it being propofed, whether John Lee, eldeft fon of Mr. Roger Lee, fhall have his freedom, his father not having of fome time after his birth taken his freedom, by omiffion of the officers not calling him to take it as ufual, and the faid Mr. Roger Lee not being fenfible of the inconvenience of neglecting it; and, in confideration of the faid Mr. Lee's faithful fervice to the Corporation, it was carried in the affirmative by a great majority.

At

At the fame hall, it was ordered that 13s. 4d. ſhould be added to the 6s. 8d. quarterly to the beadle, during pleaſure, to make his pay 4l. per annum.

Ordered alſo, that hereafter the chamberlains ſhall not ſtop the 20s. from the mace-bearer once in three years, as lately they have done.

Jan. 16, 1712-13. At this hall a bond was ſealed to William Bromley, eſq. and other truſtees of ſir Thomas White's lands, for 405l. 4s. 2d. that the ſame ſhall be let out according to the deeds of truſt and decrees of Chancery; which bond was ſigned and perfected Feb. 2.

New ſchedules were this day (Jan. 16) put to Twiggs Pilgrim's leaſes, wherein ſome of the ſtalls, &c. in Saturday Market, are raiſed, to help Mr. Pilgrim to pay the taxes to the church and poor of St. Martin's pariſh from Michaelmas laſt, during the reſidue of his leaſe.

Mr. George Bent was abated out of his rent 20s. a year, in conſideration of the loſs of ground belonging to his farm, which Mr. Broughton holds.

Feb. 2. The hall ordered the chamberlains to take the rent of Mr. Towneſend, upon his promiſe not to ſow the land dug, that is now unſown, in Horſe-fair cloſe, nor to plough or dig the ſame again during his leaſe.

Ordered, that the High Croſs ſhall be cleared and kept from rubs, and cleared weekly by the beadle; and benches made by the chamberlains for people to ſit on.

Feb. 9. The hall ordered George Bent to ſue the mayor of Derby, and ſuch as were concerned in taking his heifer on pretence of toll for cattle paſſing through the ſaid borough; and the charges of the ſuit to be paid by the chamberlains.

As to Mr. Botham's gift out of the Parrot, it was ordered that the rent ſhould be received by the chamberlains on Thurſday before Eaſter, and Thurſday before Chriſtmas.

The tithes of Danet's Hall, Weſtcotes, and St. Mary's, are ordered to be let to the preſent tenants, upon paying the rents they paid before, and double rent according to the fines heretofore paid.

May 6, 1713. The hall ordered the chamberlains to pay to Ruth, widow of Ralph Houghton, of Houghton on the Hill (upon her, and St. John Houghton her ſon, ſealing a grant and releaſe to the Corporation of their right in and to the garden on the back ſide of St. John's Hoſpital as now divided), the ſum of 50s.

The Addreſs to the Queen, on concluſion of the Peace, was ſealed.

The twenty-four ordered the chamberlains to pay James Ludlam 1s. 6d. per week from Midſummer next; and he being incapable of ſerving as underſchoolmaſter, they choſe Thomas Adcock, of Belgrave, in his place.

July 3. The hall ordered Mr. Chamberlain Ludlam to provide 100 yards of good white ribband, to be made into cockades, for the two companies, officers, clergy, &c.

Aug. 13. The hall ordered that 1s. in the pound be allowed Mr. Harte, auditor of the Duchy rents, out of the Tutbury money, being 66l. 13s. 4d. payable to the old Hoſpital, ſo long as he ſhall pay the ſaid 66l. 13s. 4d. without any trouble or charge to the Corporation.

The hall ordered that the chamberlains ſhall pay Mr. Thomas Wright, of Coventry, ſolicitor for ſir Thomas White's charity, his bill of charges; and alſo give him fifty guineas, as a preſent, for his extraordinary care and pains in the ſaid cauſe.

Ten pounds allowed towards the Town plate at the horſe-race.

Sept. 21, *Arthur Noone* elected mayor; John Guthridge, William Page, chamberlains.

Sept. 25. The hall ordered Robert Clayton, late apprentice to Joſeph Richmond, to be made free; it appearing that he ſerved five years, and bought out the two laſt.

The hall ordered, that 15l. ſhall be paid by the chamberlains to Mr. John Cooper, late mayor, for

the extraordinary charges he hath been at by relieving poor travelling ſoldiers, upon the diſbanding the army.

Ordered, that to the 3l. the town's free gift to the under-ſchoolmaſter, ſhall be added 5l. per annum, to make it 40s. a quarter, to be paid by the chamberlains till further order.

Ordered, that 10l. per annum ſhall be added to Mr. Carte's allowance of 20l. per annum, to be paid quarterly by the chamberlains, during pleaſure.

Sept. 29. At this hall, all former orders, for fining the aldermen and common council for not attending, are confirmed.

Nov. 5. At this hall, Mr. Watts's leaſe of the tithe herbage of his eſtate at Danet's hall was ſealed, for 21 years from Michaelmas 1713; rent 4l. per annum. Dated 6th of May laſt; and ſigned by Mr. Cooper, late mayor.

Elias Wallins and John Bellamy's leaſes were ſealed for Mrs. Town's eſtate, for 21 years from Lady-day 1714, and ſigned by Arthur Noon, preſent mayor.

Mr. Ruding's likewiſe ſealed, for the tithe herbage of his eſtate at Weſtcotes, for 21 years from Lady-day 1713; dated May 6 laſt, ſigned by Mr. Cooper.

Reſolved *(nemine contradicente),* that 2s. 6d. per week be allowed to William Harris, ſlater, late one of the forty-eight, he being reduced to very great poverty.

Ordered, that 10s. per annum ſhall be allowed to each of the four ſerjeants, over and above what their yearly ſalary now is, during pleaſure.

Jan. 24, 1713-14. At a meeting of the mayor and his brethren that have been mayors, Mr. Thomas, late head-ſchoolmaſter, being dead; after a diſpute, it was reſolved, that it appears by antient precedents, that the right of election of ſchoolmaſters for the free-ſchool is in the mayor, and the aldermen his brethren that have been mayors; and not in the mayor, aldermen, and common council. Whereupon,

Jan. 25, Mr. John Clayton was choſen headſchoolmaſter, to continue *quamdiu ſe bene geſſerit,* if the maſter of Wigſton's Hoſpital thereto conſent. And N. B. Mr. Hardwick, maſter of the Hoſpital, by letter, dated Grimſthorp, Feb. 18, 1713, ſignified his approbation of the choice of Mr. Clayton, directed to Mr. Arthur Noone; which came to hand Feb. 25.

Here is an account of Gunnerby lands; out of which 6s. 8d. ſhould be yearly paid to the Corporation by Mr. Perkins of Grantham. Which lands were heretofore ſold by Mr. Kelham.

Feb. 15. The commiſſioners ſet to farm, to Auguſtin Heyford, the cottage and back-ſide in his occupation, next to the ground of Mr. Towneſend on the South and Weſt, and Thomas Garret on the Eaſt, to hold them, from Lady-day next, for 21 years, paying the rent of 25s. half yearly, by equal portions, and to pay all taxes, dues, and levies, and to leave them in good repair, and not ſet the ſame without licence; and to ſeal a leaſe upon theſe terms on demand.

On the like terms and conditions they ſet the cottage and back-ſide adjoining to the foregoing for 21 years to Thomas Garret, cordwainer. They alſo ſet to Samuel Brown the ſhop under the Gainſborough, in his and late in Daniel Dann's poſſeſſion, for the rent of 15s. per annum; and to Thomas Smith, cordwainer, the ſhop in his and late Simon Richford's poſſeſſion, for 20s. per annum, for 21 years from Lady-day next, under the like conditions as Auguſtin Heyford.

March 8. The hall ordered the chamberlains to pay to Mr. Hickes, miniſter of All Saints, 10l. per annum, by half-yearly payments, whereof the firſt to be made at Michaelmas next; and this to continue during pleaſure, and no longer.

April 6, 1714. A hall abated 40s. per annum in Mr. Johnſon's leaſe, on the account of land belonging to Wall's windmill, brick-kilns, and Mr. Wilkins.

The hall ordered the chamberlains to pay 20l. towards the two new bells at St. Margaret's.

Ordered, that the two rows of shops and sheds in the Saturday market shall be pulled down, and one good row of double shops built; and certain commissioners were appointed to agree by the great with workmen, &c.

April 29. The commissioners set the two corner shops under the balcony at the Gainsborough, from March 25 last, for 21 years, each of them for 30s. *per annum*, payable half yearly; viz. that next the pump and cobler's shop to William Spencer, and the other to John Hose.

The twenty-four chose Edward Sutton mace-bearer, in room of William Handy deceased; and they chose John Brookes, a serjeant, to be keeper of the bridewell.

May 14. The mayor, and his brethren that had been mayors, chose Mr. Samuel Elly (*nemine contra-dicente*) head-usher of the school, in room of Joseph Hardy, who died April 21, 1714.—N. B. Mr. Elly died June 18, 1734.

July 12. The hall ordered, that Mr. John Ludlam should be paid 30s. by the chamberlains, for two pigs of lead taken from his father by the town of Derby for toll.

John Ducket, ironmonger, took the two stables in Saturday market by Harris's house, from Michaelmas next, for seven years, for 50s. *per annum*.

Several were disfranchised (that they might be witnesses for the Corporation), and were restored to their places soon after.

Queen Anne died Aug. 1, 1714.

GEORGE I.

Aug. 3, King George was proclaimed; and the hall ordered wine and ale, &c. for the entertainment of the gentlemen and company.

Sept. . . The hall ordered the King's arms to be painted, and set up over the North gate.

Sept. 10. Mr. William Bunney's hearing failing him, that he could not hear the business transacted in the hall, was, on his petition to the twenty-four, dismissed the company.

Sept. 21. *John Pares* elected mayor; Richard Whitman, Richard Jordan, chamberlains.

In 1714-15, there happened at Leicester, and in many other places, a remarkable tempest, which has been ever since called *Bird's wind*, from a gentleman of that name being then a candidate for the honour of serving in Parliament for this county [1].

Oct. 11. At a hall, an address to King George I. sealed, congratulating his accession to the throne; and an order made, that on Wednesday October 20, being the King's coronation day, both companies should meet in the morning, and go with the mayor to church; and return to the hall, and then walk to the White Hart to an ordinary; and the Corporation to allow a bottle of wine between two of all such as have tickets, and as much ale as necessary; and so much ale and wine at the Gainsborough at night as Mr. Mayor shall think fit; with bonfires, and other demonstrations of joy.

Oct. 15. The hall ordered the badges on the arms of the crier and beadle to be renewed, and the town plate to be beaten out, sodered, and repaired.

Nov. 30. The hall ordered, that the chamberlains shall pay 10l. yearly, by quarterly payments, to Mr. John Kilbie, vicar of St. Margaret's, during pleasure; and to commence from Michaelmas last. Also, that they pay to the grand jury 20s. for their extraordinary pains in walking the town to view the streets.

Jan. 17, 1714-15. Thursday next being the day appointed for thanksgiving for the King's accession, the hall ordered near the same solemnities as on Oct. 20.

Feb. 21. The hall ordered, that for the future

the allowances to the mayor annually, for relief given to soldiers or other travellers, or any other charities whatever, shall be 15s. and no more.

April 5, 1715. The balance of the accounts of the last year's chamberlains was 190l. 7s. 6¾d.; which they were to pay to the present chamberlains.

The commissioners ordered, that Martin Hartop and his heirs shall pay yearly at Michaelmas 5s. and no more, for the ground he hath taken from the sheep-penns, and whereon he built part of his lease for 900 years.

Mr. Boley and his wife being both ill, the hall ordered 5l. to be paid for their better support.

April 8. The commissioners ordered, that a new row of shops shall be built where the shoemakers' shops (now pulled down) stood; and that the ground there be paved with a good row of pavement down the middle, and a pavement of three yards from the shops, with a channel on each side the middle row.

Item, that the shops next the shambles shall be repaired, and made as uniform as they can; and certain persons were appointed to settle the length, width, and height, of the shops, and agree with the workmen.

June 25. The mayor and twenty-four agreed, that Mr. Mayor shall lay out 40s. for the burial of Mr. John Boley, late town-clerk; and at the same time chose Thomas Jordaine, gent. to be town-clerk in his room.

July 4. The commissioners agreed that Mr. Cook's lease of Freake's land shall be assigned to Mr. Nutt for the remainder of the term.

July 28. The commissioners ordered, that the old shops standing on the back-side of the shambles be pulled down, and re-built.

Sept. 19. The commissioners set the new row of shops for 21 years from Michaelmas next; the tenants to pay parish duties; repair, and not sell the shops to any without consent of the Corporation; viz.

	£.	s.	d.	
Nº 20, for	1	12	6	to John Pares, mayor.
1,	1	12	6	Josiah Nutt, tanner.
23,	1	5	0	Thomas Johnson, baker.
11,	2	0	0	John Willows, sherman.
12,	1	5	0	J. Taylor, baker.
17,	1	5	0	John Johnson, leather-dresser.
18,	1	5	0	J. Wilson, baker.
19,	1	15	0	James Norris, woolcomber.
21,				Mr. Noon.
22,	1	15	0	John Buckerfield, glover.
25,	1	5	0	Nicholas Swingler, slater.
24,	1	15	0	J. Stubs, glover.
32,	1	15	0	Robert Shilton, taylor.
16,	1	5	0	Charles Tuffley, baker.
9,	1	5	0	Robert Almey, sherman.
14,	1	5	0	John Stubbs.
26,	1	5	0	Joseph Mitcher, hosier.
29,	1	5	0	Jonadas Tylecoat, baker.

Sept. 21, 1715, *Francis Lewin* elected mayor; Simon Martin, Benjamin Guthridge, chamberlains.

Sept. 27. The commissioners agreed that the four corner shops Nº 1, 11, 20, and 33, shall be let at 1l. 12s. 6d. *per annum*; and that the corner shop, Nº 10, be let for 1l. 7s. 6d. *per annum*; and all the front shops on both sides at 1l. 5s.; and the back shops at 1l. *per annum*.

	£.	s.	d.	
Nº 10, for	1	7	6	to Clement Stretton, shoemaker.
13,	1	5	0	John Hose, milliner.
30,	1	5	0	Richard Fauset.
4,	1	0	0	Geo. Hartshorn, cordwainer.
33,	1	12	6	Henry Smith, baker.
28,	1	5	0	Thomas Green, labourer.
31,	1	5	0	Thomas Poyner, carpenter.
5,	1	0	0	David Dudley, tanner.

[1] " On the credit of my aged mother (who was born in the first year of the eighteenth century, and died in 1797, at the advanced age of 97), I give the following: A Mrs. Dickman, going from St. Margaret's church, was blown from the foot causeway into the Town-ditch in Church-gate; and another lady was saved from being blown over the West bridge into the river by two men: hoops were in general use at that time. She informed me further, that the leads on some of the churches were torn up; and that many of the people left the churches in the middle of divine service, expecting every minute the destruction of the steeples." Throsby.—In vol. IV. p. 104, Mr. Macaulay applies the epithet of *Bird's wind* to the storm of 1703.

Oct.

Oct. 10. The hall ordered, that Mr. John Abney shall have yearly 10l. paid him for preaching at St. Nicholas, to commence from Michaelmas last.

Ordered, that when and as often as any framework-knitters, inhabiting within this Corporation, being freemen, are sued by the company of framework-knitters of London, upon account of their binding or making free any apprentice before the Mayor, the Corporation, at their charge, shall defend the said prosecution; and that Mr. Noble, the solicitor, defend the action now brought against Thomas Derbyshire and William Brown, freemen of this Borough, and framework-knitters; and if the company of framework-knitters, London, shall not prosecute their action so as to bring the same to trial, Mr. Noble to bring actions for the recovery of the costs. And the said Derbyshire and Brown shall give 100l. bond not to agree with the company of London in any manner relating to the said actions, without consent of the Corporation. And all persons sued are to do the same.

Nov. 22. The hall ordered, that his grace the duke of Rutland, lord lieutenant of this county, shall be met by the whole company, in their formalities, in the Belgrave gate, and wait upon him to his inn.

Feb. 6, 1715-16. The hall chose flesh-tasters, sealers of leather, and of hides and tallow, fish-tasters, and ale-tasters; and ordered, that the auditors and these officers, for the future, shall be appointed the first hall after the mayor's feast.

April 16, 1716. The commissioners set to Samuel Blockfome, gardener, a cottage or tenement in Senvey gate, late in possession of widow Dennis, for seven years, from Lady-day last, for 15s. per annum. He to put and keep it in repair; and pay taxes, except the King's.

April 27. The hall ordered, that the shoemakers' shops be taken down, and set upon brick pillars.

The same day, the commissioners ordered that John Davenport, of Bushby, have a lease for 21 years of the land there, under the same rents and covenants as in his former lease.

May 7. The commissioners set to Robert Lord the sheep-penns, and places used for that purpose, for seven years, if he so long lived, from Feb. 2 last, under the rent of 17l. per annum, payable half-yearly; and also a place called Coker's kitchen, under the same rent, in consideration of his repairing it, and leaving it so. They also set to Mr. Richard Townefend the house and close in the horse-fair called Stanley's house and close, from Lady-day next, for 21 years, he paying 12l. per annum, and all taxes and dues, except the King's tax; and not to plough or dig the close, or let the same, without consent of the Corporation; and to put the house, and leave it, in good repair. And what buildings he erects he may take away, or satisfaction is to be made him by the Corporation.

May 25. The hall ordered, that the chamberlains for the time being take care to have the two engines played once a quarter, on pain of 20s. a quarter; and that they employ such persons as they see convenient, whereof the beadle and cryer to be two; and to pay such persons 5s. for their trouble every quarter or time when they are played. The first time to be within two days before or after Midsummer next, and so two days before or after each other quarter-day.

July 23. The hall ordered, that the new sheds to be built be arched.

Samuel Blockfome was released from his agreement for the house in Senvey gate.

Ordered, that no chamberlains' accounts shall for the future be passed without receipts on the bills, and the money actually paid.

Ordered, that no taxes shall be allowed to any person without they bring a receipt for the same.

Sept. 17. At a hall, several leases of the new shops were sealed.

Sept. 21, *William Goadby* elected mayor; Augustin Heafford, Thomas Orme, chamberlains.

Oct. 12. The hall ordered a bond to be given to the executors of Mr. Thomas Ayre, deceased, for the 20l. left by his will to St. John's Hospital, which was sealed Oct. 19.

Oct. 19. The hall ordered the aldermen who have wards each to take his constable, and on Wednesday next view the several streets, lanes, and causeways, in their several wards, that are out of repair; and enquire which of them are to be repaired by the Corporation, and which by other people.

Nov. 7. The hall gave alderman Johnson liberty to assign his lease of his farm in St. Mary's field to his brother Joseph Johnson.

Nov. 7. The commissioners set to John Dawson a cottage in Senvey gate for one year from St. Thomas next; he to pay 4l. and all taxes except the King's.

Feb. 1, 1716-17. At a hall: Upon the dispute of repairing the pavement against the Parrot under Mr. Noble's garden-wall, it is agreed, the Corporation shall repair that part, provided Mr. Noble repair at the same time the pavement from thence to the end of the Friers; and that the pavement, so far as the Corporation agrees to repair, be measured.

Feb. 15. It is the opinion of this hall, that the narrow pavement from the Corn-wall by the pillory to the grand pavement towards the Saracen's head doth belong to the Corporation; and resolved, that the sheep-penns taken from that pavement to the Dolphin-house be set down again, that the Corporation may have the benefit thereof as heretofore.

March 1. The commissioners resolved, that whatever stalls in the middle pavement are taken, none shall be tilted. Also, that every stall that is six feet long shall pay 10s. and every stall that is more than six feet shall pay 2s. 6d. the foot above the 10s. per annum.

Item, resolved that the standings under the new buildings against the Corn-wall, from pillar to pillar, be marked No 1, 2, 3, 4, 5, 6, 7, 8, 9; and that the standing under one building to be marked No 1, and the standing to be marked No 9, be let at 20s. per annum; and the other standings, from pillar to pillar, under each building, be let at 15s. per annum.

Richard Griffin took the shop marked No 14 at the same rate as John Stubbs had the same, for the remainder of his term.

Augustin Heafford took the sheep-penns, and places used for that purpose, with the place called Coker's kitchen, from Candlemas last, for 21 years, under the rent of 20l. per annum, payable at two equal payments.

March 27, 1716-17. The commissioners set to Thomas Ayre, gent. the close garden or orchard lying in All Saints parish, from Lady-day last, for 21 years, at the rent of 6l. 10s. to be paid at two equal payments; and he to pay all taxes, and repair the fences, and to leave at the said term as many growing fruit-trees as are now in the said orchard.

May 27. Ordered, that the tenant of Allexton land have a new lease for 21 years, from the expiration of the former, on the same terms and covenants.

July 29. The hall ordered 5l. for relief of the poor sufferers by fire at Oundle.

Ordered, that the four serjeants at mace be paid 15s. apiece every quarter for their salary during pleasure, instead of the salary which they now have; they providing themselves good and handsome apparel of cloth black, or near that colour; the first payment to be at Michaelmas next.

Aug. 9. Two leases, one of Stanley's lands to Mr. Townefend, and the other of an orchard in All Saints parish to Mr. Thomas Ayre, for 21 years from Lady-day last, sealed.

Sept. 16. The commissioners set to John Billers, tobacconist, the shop under the Gainsborough which Jonas Davy of Mountforell had, at the same rate.

Sept. 21, *Thomas Helmesley* elected mayor; Richard Roberts, Robert Reynolds, chamberlains.

Sept. 27. The hall ordered, that Mr. Adcock, under-usher of the school, shall live in the new house in Senvey gate during pleasure, paying yearly 1s.; he is to put it in repair, and keep it so, and pay all taxes.

The commissioners the same day set to Augustin Heaford,

Heaford, carpenter, the ftable in Saturday market, late John Ducket's (the leafe to expire at the fame time as his leafe for the fheep-penns), at the rent of 25s. per annum. He is to keep it in repair, and pay all taxes except the King's.

Oct. 11. The hall ordered the chamberlains, with aldermen of wards, with fome others, to view all the ftreets and pavements; and report, in writing, to the next hall, what are to be repaired by the Corporation, together with dimenfion, and how bounden. This order was renewed Nov. 25.

Nov. 25. At a hall, fealed a bond for fir Thomas White's 423l. 13s. 9d.

Dec. 13. The commiffioners fet to Thomas Hall, innholder, the clofe called the Foreft clofe, now in leafe to Mr. George Bent, from Lady-day next for 21 years, at the rent of 18l. for the firft year, and 19l. afterwards, to be paid March 25 yearly; the firft payment to be at his entering.

Dec. 20. The aldermen ordered, that the 50l. of fir Thomas White's charity now to be difpofed of be difpofed by balloting and petition.

Feb. 14, 1717-18. The order of April 5, 1715, relating to Dr. Hartop's building, his houfe on Cornwall, is by this hall declared void. Mr. Sutton (mace-bearer) was allowed 2s. 6d. per week during his illnefs.

Feb. 14. The commiffioners ordered, that Mr. John Watts, or fuch perfon as the lord lieutenant or his deputies fhall appoint, fhall have a leafe of that which adjoins to the Magazine which belongs to this Corporation, for 21 years from Michaelmas laft, for 40s. per annum, paying all arrears from the death of Mr. Mawfon till laft Michaelmas, after the rent of 20s. per annum, and to pay all taxes, and leave all in repair at the end of the term.

April 9, 1718. The commiffioners ordered that Mr. Robert Lord have liberty to build on the town ground that part of his houfe called the Wheat-fheaf, on the Corn-wall fide, even with Dr. Hartop's houfe, and not exceeding four feet and a half at the end next Mrs. Woodland's; and that he have a leafe of it for 500 years, at 20s. per annum.

The court of aldermen chofe John Armfton to be keeper of the Bridewell, in room of John Brooks deceafed. They alfo chofe Ebenezer Beafley to be mace-bearer, in room of Edward Sutton deceafed.

Alfo ordered, that for the future, for every 10l. bond, the town-clerk fhall take but 7s. 6d. and 6d. for the mace-bearer; and for every 50l. bond 9s. and 1s. for the mace-bearer; and fo the fame for renewing.

June 2. The hall ordered workmen to repair the town gaol.

Sept. 5. The hall ordered, that for the future, at the hunting feaft, which is yearly on Eafter Monday, the twenty-four, in their formalities, attend Mr. Mayor into the field, if the weather permit, according to the antient cuftom; and what entertainment fhall be given that day fhall be at the charge of the mayor only, upon forfeiture of 20l. the late additional falary.

Ordered alfo, that when fir Thomas White's and Mr. Heyrick's bonds are turned over, according to order of hall, what money or bonds fhall be in the late mayor's hands, fuch money or bonds fhall be immediately paid to the prefent mayor, upon forfeiture of 20l. by the late mayor.

Sept. 21, *Charles Tuffley* elected mayor; Henry Smith, John Payne, chamberlains.

Sept. 26. The hall ordered, that fuch perfons as fhall hereafter come before the mayor to bind any apprentice, he fhall be obliged to come to the town court, and there make oath, that fuch apprentice is to be an actual menial fervant, for the term of feven years, to the trade or occupation mentioned in the indenture, before fuch apprentice fhall be bound. And that every perfon that fhall hereafter claim his freedom, he fhall firft acquaint Mr. Mayor with his claim; and Mr. Mayor, at the next hall, acquaint the members therewith, to the intent that no perfon fhall have his freedom but fuch as are legally entitled to the fame; and if any Mayor fhall act contrary to this order, he fhall forfeit 20l.

Whereas Mr. Thomas Lambert, one of the aldermen, had reflected on Mr. Mayor and the court of aldermen, upon difmiffing fome late members from the forty-eight; upon his fubmiffion, he was forgiven his offence, by a court of aldermen, this day.

Oct. 13. The hall repealed the order, made September 26, about binding apprentices, and making freemen.

Jan. 21, 1718-19. Mr. Southwell had liberty to affign his leafe of four yard-land to Mr. Thomas Willows for the remainder of his term.

" In March, on a Thurfday night, about eight o'clock, there was feen a meteor in the air, which appeared like a ball of fire, and feemed to fall to the earth, being very furprifing to all that faw it [1]."

May 27, 1719. The hall ordered, that Mr. Hartop have a leafe of the ground he has built on, belonging to the town, on the Corn-wall, for 21 years, at the yearly rent of 5s.

Aug. 3. The balance of the late chamberlain's accounts was 292l. 5s. 10½d.

Sept. 21, *John Ludlam* elected mayor; Samuel Simpfon, Edward Hawkins, chamberlains.

Nov. 16. The hall ordered Mr. Henley [2], of Melton, fhall have fuch books out of the Library as he has occafion for; Mr. Mayor taking a note for the returning the fame.

Jan. 13, 1719-20. It is the opinion of this hall, that the pavement without the Eaft gate, againft Mr. Hood's door and William Wright's door, which is out of repair, ought to be repaired by them.

Sept. 21, 1720, *Robert Winfield* being elected mayor, was found dying, and *Edward Hood* fucceeded; John Earp, Gabriel Newton, chamberlains.

Sept. 21, 1721, *William Hammond* elected mayor; Edward Noon, George Bent, chamberlains.

Sept. 21, 1722, *Humphrey Chapman* elected mayor; William Lewin, Jofeph Bunney, chamberlains.

Paid to fufferers by fire at Wellingborough 15l.

" A Ball
at the Caftle in Leicefter,
on the 28th day of November 1722,
Thomas Hodgfon mafter.
No admittance after four o'clock."

Sept. 21, 1723, *Thomas Ayre* elected mayor; Henry Payne, Richard Goodhall, chamberlains.

June 12, 1724, at 2 p. m. an awful cloud, charged with lightning and inceffant thunder, difcharged itfelf over Leicefter, to the great terror of the inhabitants, who expected nothing lefs than the final diffolution of all things. It was as dark between the flafhes of lightning as night—birds, beaft, and man, were equally terrified. The hail-ftones, which fell in amazing quantities, meafured fome of them fix inches round; and lay in great quantities five hours after the ftorm. The ripening fruits of the earth were moftly deftroyed.

Sept. 21. *Thomas Lambert* elected mayor; William Cook, Thomas Bafs, chamberlains.

Paid the fufferers by fire at Cofby, 10l.; and to thofe by another at Rearfby, 3l.

Sept. 21, 1725, *Thomas Ludlam* elected mayor; Thomas Johnfon, William Lee, chamberlains.

Sept. 21, 1726, *John Guthridge* elected mayor; John Willows, William Brufhfield, chamberlains.

GEORGE II.

Sept. 21, 1727, *William Page* elected mayor; Jofhua Goodrich, Edmund Ludlam, chamberlains.

Sept. 21, 1728, *Simon Martin* elected mayor; John Noon, Edward Bates, chamberlains.

Paid to the fufferers by fire at Hinckley, 50l.

---

[1] Book of Mayors.

[2] Afterwards the celebrated Orator Henley; of whom fee vol. II. p. 259. At the time of this loan, he was mafter of Melton fchool, and was preparing for his " Oratio habita in Scholâ Meltonienfi, ad Comitia Cleri calata, Maii 16, 1720, per Alumnum iftius Ludi primarium. Auctore Johanne Henley, A. M. Gymnafii Præfecto;" 1720.

Sept.

Sept. 21, 1729, *Richard Roberts* elected mayor; John Cartwright, Robert Winfield, chamberlains.

Sept. 21, 1730, *Henry Smith* elected mayor; William Noon, Joseph Newton, chamberlains.

Sept. 21, 1731, *Edward Hawkins* elected mayor; Samuel Miles, Samuel Belton, chamberlains.

Sept. 21, 1732, *Gabriel Newton* elected mayor; John Brown, Edmund Johnson, chamberlains.

Sept. 21, 1733, *George Bent* elected mayor; Edward Vesey, Thomas Ludlam, chamberlains.

Sept. 21, 1734, *Richard Goodhall* elected mayor; Richard Ogden, Thomas Phipps, chamberlains.

Sept. 21, 1735, *Samuel Simpson* elected mayor; Saul Broadhurst, William Helmsley, chamberlains.

Sept. 21, 1736, *William Brushfield* elected mayor; Joseph Denshire, William Burstall, chamberlains.

In this year an ineffectual attempt was made to procure a navigation.

Paid, for the expences of soliciting to obtain a navigation in Parliament, 60*l.* 10*s.* 4*d.*

Sept. 21, 1737, *William Lee* elected mayor; Thomas Topp, John Winter, chamberlains.

Paid, on account of the treasonable papers, 42*l.* 11*s.* 6*d.* [1]

Sept. 21, 1738, *Thomas Bass* elected mayor; John Smalley, Edward Harris, chamberlains.

Sept. 21, 1739, *Edmund Ludlam* [2] elected mayor; Thomas Martin, William Watton, chamberlains.

Sept. 21, 1740, *Edward Bates* elected mayor; Samuel Simpson, Robert Lee, chamberlains.

Sept. 21, 1741, *John Cartwright* elected mayor; Robert Hall, Joss Taylor, chamberlains.

Sept. 21, 1742, *Samuel Miles* elected mayor; Richard Denshire, William Brabson, chamberlains.

August 18, at Leicester, about eight in the evening, there happened a violent storm of hail and rain, attended with terrible thunder and lightning, which lasted two hours. Pieces of five inches in length, and hail-stones two inches in circumference, fell; which killed some hundreds of birds, that were found next morning in the gardens within the town. The streets were so flooded, that scarcely one house in ten but had its first floor filled with such quantities of water, that the people were obliged to carry it out in pails; and some cellars were overflowed six feet deep, whereby several of the inhabitants sustained great damage. Many waggon-loads of ice were to be seen the Saturday morning following. Those who had been at sea, and saw this storm, compared it to the breaking of water-spouts coming down in streams. This happened on a race-day; and, it is believed, the first year of the races being changed from the Abbey meadow to St. Mary's field.

Sept. 21, 1743, *Samuel Belton* elected mayor; Thomas Chapman, Joseph Hall, chamberlains.

Sept. 21, 1744, *Thomas Ayre* elected mayor; James Sismey, John Hammond, chamberlains.

The rebellion in this year occasioned many and frequent alarms in Leicester [3].

Sept. 21, 1745, *Joseph Denshire* elected mayor; William Higginson, Robert Belton, chamberlains.

Sept. 21, 1746, *Thomas Topp* was elected mayor; Nicholas Throsby, John Westley, chamberlains.

Sept. 21, 1747, *John Smalley* elected mayor; Samuel Brown, Samuel Oliver, chamberlains.

Sept. 21, 1748, *Robert Hall* was elected mayor; Henry Guthridge, Richard Beal, chamberlains.

Sept. 30, the devisees of the Mills, &c. named by the will of Thomas Carter, sold to Jane Flower, for the sum of 270*l.* the purchase made of the Corporation by Mr. Carter in 1685, subject to the annual reserved rent belonging to the Crown.

In this year a bill was framed for establishing a regular watch, cleansing the streets, maintaining the wells and pumps in the streets, and lighting the town with lamps; but it did not pass into an act.

About the beginning of the year 1749, efforts were made to restrain non-freemen from enjoying the privileges of exercising their trades, &c. in Leicester, except on market and fair-days, according to former usage [4].

Sept. 21, 1749, *Thomas Phipps* elected mayor; Anthony Ward, John Wigley, chamberlains.

Sept.

---

[1] "The business of an election about this period had so inflamed some of the incendiaries of this town, as to paste up against the walls of several public places treasonable papers of a very atrocious nature; and the two contending parties shewed great zeal in discovering the offenders to be of the contrary interest to themselves. Men, women, and children, took an active part in the contention; invectives of the most horrid kind were thrown out against each other without the least reserve. In short, things were carried to such a height, that a Mr. Norton, a lawyer, a man of fair character, with some others, were by the Corporation's friends suspected to be the authors (though they sent an early account of the treasonable papers to Government), and were taken before the magistrates of the Borough. When under examination, to the astonishment of every beholder, Mr. Norton faltered in his reply, became speechless, and died without a groan, Feb. 1, 1738." Throsby.

[2] By this gentleman many of the items of public expences were communicated to Mr. Throsby.

[3] "When the rebels were at Derby, this town was thinned of more than half its inhabitants. Warm and threatening partizans in the cause of their king, while Charles was at a distance, appeared in arms at mock fights in the Castle-yard; but, when his army arrived at Derby, they deserted the parade, and sneaked away with the aged, the women, and the children, to seek asylums under the humble roofs of neighbouring villages. Those who were left at home were some of them busied in depositing their valuables in the earth, and others in roasting and boiling to accommodate the unwelcome guests, on their hourly expected arrival—scouring parties, messengers on foot and on horseback, were sent to bring intelligence of their approach. Sometimes they were at Loughborough, sometimes at Rothley, and sometimes near Leicester. Frightened servants, who were kept at home with some masters of families, were in convulsions, at the idea of being defiled and murdered by the rebel army. The mayor was surrounded by a few of his brethren (who had resolution to stay at home) and his servants, all in continual fear; while some, who favoured the old cause, prayed fervently in secret for the success of the Prince's arms. In this state were things at Leicester, when news was brought that the little army of the Pretender was hastening back towards Scotland, and the duke of Cumberland in forwardness to attack him: which he did, soon after, at Culloden, with success; but, alas! some say, without mercy." Throsby.

[4] "One Green, a watchmaker, made no little stand against the Corporation laws and charters in this particular. I have not less than 60 quarto pages in MS. of the transactions. The following abridgement contains sufficient on that head. It shews also that the charter given by King John, p. 97, is the first charter known to be granted to the burgesses of Leicester. One Stubbs, a glover, resisting the bye-law of the Corporation, which was made to exclude non-freemen of the Borough from exercising trades within their jurisdiction, occasioned a case to be drawn up, and laid before sir John Strange and sir Dudley Rider, in 1749; which case stated, that it appeared, by the first charter extant, that of King John, in the first year of his reign, that the burgesses of Leicester had certain privileges granted them, particularly that of being free from tolls throughout England. It stated also that, time immemorial, non-freemen were not suffered to exercise their trades and callings within the liberties of the Borough, excepting on market and fair-days. Further, that the charter of Elizabeth, granted in the 41st year of her reign, empowered the Corporation to make bye-laws for the regulating the antient usage of the town with respect to trades, offices, and business, ordaining such penalties and fines, in cases of non-compliance, as they should think fit, so as they were not made contrary to the law of the land. The mayor and aldermen, in September 1681, made a bye-law, in consideration of some efforts being made by non-freemen to exercise their trades within the limits of the Borough contrary to antient usage; reciting, that the freemen were liable to serve many town offices, which subjected them to loss of time and expences, for which they ought to have some encouragement and privileges above those of strangers. It further recited, that at a common hall, holden in the Borough in the 8th year of King James I. it was ordained, that every person selling articles openly within the limits of the Borough, non-freemen, excepting on market and fair-days, should forfeit 40*s.* for every month wherein he should offend; but, notwithstanding, persons had notoriously offended against the said bye-law and antient customs: It was therefore enacted, by a bye-law, at the request of the common council, that if any person or persons, not being freemen, should at any time exercise their trades and callings contrary to antient usage, he or they should forfeit 20*s.* to the mayor, bailiffs, &c. of the Borough, "to be recovered by action of debt, bill, or plaint, in any of his Majesty's Courts of Record, or to be levied by distress." The said bye-law was approved and allowed by the judges of assize next held at Leicester after the making thereof. After this, it appears that no non-freeman ever attempted to offend against this bye-law till the year 1730, when

Sept. 21, 1750, *Thomas Martin* elected mayor; Clement Streeton, Joseph Chambers, chamberlains.

On the last day of September, a severe shock of an earthquake was felt in Leicester and its vicinity, which created a general alarm. It happened about half after twelve at noon, and was perceived generally in the county, in most parts of Lincolnshire, and part of Northamptonshire. The houses tottered, plates and glasses fell from the shelves, and slates, tiles, and some chimnies, fell from the houses; but, happily, no greater mischief was done. In some churches, where service was not over (it being on a Sunday), the people ran from their devotions in the utmost consternation. The shock was attended with a rumbling noise [1]."

Sept. 21, 1751, *Samuel Simpson* elected mayor; Joseph Treen, John Norton, chamberlains.

Sept. 21, 1752, *Richard Denshire* elected mayor; Richard Roberts, John Miles, chamberlains.

At the assizes for this county, which ended the 18th of August 1753, the rev. Mr. Hubbard received sentence of death, for robbing Mrs. Burbage of Melton. On the day the robbery was committed, he dined with Mrs. Burbage at Oakham, whom he followed at a distance some miles towards home; he then, disguising himself with a cloak and visor, rode up to her, and ordered her to deliver her money, which she complying with he rode off; but he was detected by Mrs. Burbage having a knowledge of his horse. In consideration of his function he was transported.

Sept. 21, 1753, *Thomas Chapman* elected mayor; Hamlet Clark, John Fisher, chamberlains.

A violent contest, fraught with mischief, happened at this time for members to serve in Parliament for Leicester, called *Mitford's opposition*; when the attempt to inclose the South Fields was a pretence, at least, for the destruction of private as well as public property that ensued [2].

Sept. 21, 1754, *William Lee* elected mayor; William Orton, John Cartwright, chamberlains.

Sept. 21, 1755, *James Sismey* elected mayor; William Clark, Thomas Streeton, chamberlains.

In the Spring of 1756, Count Beauville, with about 30 French officers, who were taken prisoners prior to the declaration of war, were sent to Leicester, where they remained till they were exchanged in October 1757. During their stay at Leicester, it was computed that they expended 9000l. some of them being gentlemen of the first rank in France. For their genteel behaviour, they were much esteemed by the inhabitants of Leicester; and they mingled in all polite assemblies with, as it were, a native agreeableness.

June 14, 1756, in Leicester, between the hours of 8 and 10, there was a remarkable heavy shower of rain, attended with incessant claps of thunder, and very alarming lightning, which was followed with a heavy hail-storm, during which was seen a ball of fire, which divided into particles, and vanished without doing any damage.

September 21, 1756, *Edmund Ludlam* elected mayor; John Gamble, Cornelius Norton, chamberlains.

September 21, 1757, *Joseph Hall* elected mayor; William Holmes, John-Cox Brown, chamberlains.

Wheat was sold in Leicester market, in this year, for 9s. a strike; and, in consequence of the high price of corn, the people grew tumultuous. In this town they forced the corn from the inns into the market, but offered no injury to the person of any one. At Mountsorell a mob destroyed a bolting-mill, from whence they went to Sileby and Loughborough, and likewise destroyed the bolting-mills in those places. In other parts of the country disturbances of the like kind happened.

Sept. 21, 1758, *Robert Belton* elected mayor; Samuel Jordan, John Ward, chamberlains.

September 21, 1759, *Nicholas Throsby* elected mayor; Thomas Astle, Benjamin Sutton, chamberlains.

England this year was alarmed by a threatened invasion from France.

At a common hall, held Nov. 23, 1759, the mayor was empowered to subscribe 100l. for the laudable purpose of aiding government during the war, by giving large bounties for able-bodied men to serve in the fleets and armies. A spirited address was printed to the friends of government on this occasion, to urge them to join the Corporation in this laudable measure; which was followed by a large subscription from individuals.

The mayor was also empowered to give a grand banquet at the 'Change to the duke of Grafton, and the officers of the Suffolk militia, which then lay at Leicester, officered by the first characters in that county. It was then considered the most elegant and costly treat ever given by the Corporation, and one of the most inebriating. Mr. Mayor at night was assisted by the duke down stairs; and the duke, soon after, was assisted to his carriage by the town servants, there not being a soul left in the room capable of affording help to enfeebled limbs: field officers and aldermen, captains and common-council-men, were perfectly at rest—all were levelled by the mighty power of wine [3].

Sept. 21, 1760, *John Westley* elected mayor; James Cooper, William Mason, chamberlains.

Stubbs above-mentioned refused to buy his freedom, and traded in defiance of the bye-law. The Corporation therefore commenced an action of debt in the year 1730, upon the bye-law of 1681. The cause being at issue upon *nil debet*, the same was tried. It coming out upon evidence that foreigners and non-freemen were always permitted to use and exercise their trades and occupations within the said Borough, as well as the freemen thereof, upon market-days and fair-days, the plaintiffs were nonsuited. The question to sir Dudley Rider and sir John Strange in 1749 was thus: "If the Corporation should commence an action upon the case, upon the said customs, with an exception of fair-days and market-days (as the custom truly is), against any person not being free of the said Borough, for using and exercising any trade within the said Borough on those days that are neither market-days or fair-days there; if the defendant should give the plaintiffs notice to produce at the trial of the cause the said bye-laws, which are founded on a custom, without any exception of market-days and fair-days, and the bye-laws should be produced, what effect would the bye-laws (they being Corporate acts) have upon the trial, they shewing a different custom than that which will be declared upon. Will that evidence nonsuit the plaintiffs, although the custom declared upon should be fully proved, beyond any doubt, to be as laid in the declaration; and is it adviseable, upon the circumstances of this case, for the Corporation to commence and try such action for supporting the said custom?"—" I am of opinion that the above-mentioned mistake of the custom in the introduction to the bye-laws will not be conclusive to the Corporation, but that they may be allowed to prove the custom by antient witnesses; and if they do prove it, they ought not to be nonsuited on account of the description in the bye-law, which is only more extensive than the true custom, but really contains nothing that is contradictory to the custom. I think, therefore, it is adviseable for the Corporation to try the action proposed for the supporting their custom. J. STRANGE, April 10, 1749."—" The production of the bye-law, though it would be of some weight, yet it is but evidence, I think, not sufficient to overturn a custom fully proved by other evidence; therefore, it may be adviseable for the Corporation to commence a new action on the foot of the custom, as it can be clearly proved by witnesses. D. RYDER, 29 April, 1749."

" I know not in what manner the trial ended, if there were any; but some time afterwards Green the watchmaker and others set the bye-laws at defiance; and from that time to this the Borough has been and is open to all descriptions of men, excepting publicans." Throsby.

[1] See under Stanford, vol. IV. p. 354.   [2] See vol. IV. p. 347.   [3] Throsby.

GEORGE III.

On the 25th of October, 1760[1], his prefent Majefty began his aufpicious reign.

Sept. 21, 1761, *Samuel Brown* elected mayor; John Cooper, John Poynton, chamberlains.

Sept. 21, 1762, *Samuel Oliver* elected mayor; Tyringham Palmer, William Stephens, chamberlains.

Sept. 21, 1763, *Henry Guthridge* elected mayor; James Bates, Robert Peach, chamberlains.

Sept. 21, 1764, *Richard Beal* elected mayor; John Pocklington, Samuel Woodford, chamberlains.

Sept. 21, 1765, *Joseph Chambers* elected mayor; Richard-Robert Drake, John Gregory, chamberlains.

Sept. 21, 1766, *John Fisher* elected mayor; John Coleman, Joseph Johnson, chamberlains.

In the Corporation charter of King James it is expreffed, that on Monday after Martinmas-day the newly-elected mayor fhall attend at the great hall of the Caftle, and take an oath, " before our fenefchall," that he fhall perform well and faithfully all and every antient cuftom, jurifdiction, privilege, and preheminence, of the Duchy of Lancafter, within the Borough of Leicefter, being a part or parcel of the antient Duchy of Lancafter, according to the beft of his knowledge. It was a cuftom, before Mr. Fifher's time, to flope the great mace when Mr. Mayor and his attendants arrived at a certain place within the precincts of the Caftle, which was omitted when *he* went to take the oath; in confequence, the Conftable of the Caftle, or his Deputy, refufed him admittance. This was at the eve of an election, which was conducted with much party heat. However, fince this happened, Mr. Mayor goes in private to the Caftle, without ceremony, to comply with the requifition of the charter.

Provifions having arifen to a great price, by forestalling and other evil practices, the common people at Hinckley affembled in a riotous manner, and upon the road leading thither they ftopped fome waggon-loads of cheefe, and diftributed their contents among the mob, to the amount of 87*l.* And in about three weeks after, being the laft day of September 1766, a great riot on the fame account happened in Leicefter. Mr. Pridmore, of Market Harborough, lodged a confiderable quantity of cheefe at a warehoufe at the Blue Bell inn, contrary to the advice of the magiftrates, and was imprudent enough to take it away before the fair. Accordingly, a waggon-load was fent thence about one o'clock; but the poor, upon an alarm being given, ftopped the waggon, and diftributed the cheefe among the mob before the magiftrates could be acquainted with the riot. The mob by this time was become extremely numerous; and proceeded to Mr. Pridmore's warehoufe, which they broke open, and began to give away the cheefe before the juftices arrived. The whole town was now alarmed—the magiftrates expoftulated with the incenfed multitude, but to little effect. At length the drum was ordered to beat to arms (the militia being in Leicefter), and the foldiers were foon in order

upon the fpot, headed by Mr. Mortimer, one of their officers. With their bayonets fixed, they with difficulty cleared the ftreets; but notwithftanding this, and the riot act being read, the people refufed to difperfe, and behaved unruly at fome little diftance from the foldiers. Then the magiftrates ordered all the cheefe that was in the market-place to be removed to the 'Change, under a ftrong guard; and promifed that the cheefe fhould be fold at 3*d. per* pound. Upon this, the mob emptied in a fhort time all the warehoufes and inns, where it had been lodged for fale, and huckfters' fhops alfo of the cheefe, and took it to the 'Change. Towards the evening, the foldiers being difmiffed, the mob collected again, and grew more tumultuous than before, and fearched every waggon which came into Leicefter that night. They were now no lefs in number than 4000, and feized almoft every thing in their way. The drums were again ordered to beat to arms; and there feemed confufion on the face of every one. Here a lawlefs mob, joined by numbers from the neighbouring villages; and there the foldiers running with their arms to join the main body, who were marching towards the waggons. Peaceable people, with the magiftrates, procured torches lighted; but the lights were almoft as inftantly ftruck out by the mob. In the end, however, the foldiers protected and fecured the waggons; and the next day fome of the rioters were caft into prifon. But the mob affembled again, and broke all the gaol windows. Some of thefe rioters alfo were fecured in prifon; and, to prevent a refcue, a captain's guard of 100 men, with 15 rounds of powder and ball, ftood to guard the prifon, where they continued all night. The mob, after this fpirited conduct, difperfed. In feveral other places in the county there were riots about the fame time. At Hinckley two principals in this riot were refcued, when in cuftody of fome conftables, by the mob there; but, on a troop of dragoons, and a party of the militia of the county, marching to the affiftance of the civil power, fome of the rioters were taken, and brought, under a ftrong guard, to prifon, where they were for a time fecured in the dungeon, loaded with irons. Afterward feveral other rioters were taken up, and lodged in prifon. At Sheepfhed, it was with difficulty fome rioters were taken who had been concerned in defperate outrages. Thefe rioters were tried in the fucceeding March, 1767; when, in confideration of their long imprifonment, their punifhment was but inconfiderable: fome were fined in fmall fums, and others were imprifoned for a certain portion of time. Thus ended, by the fpirited behaviour of thofe in power, one of the moft alarming tumults which has been known in thefe parts.

Sept. 21, 1767, *William Holmes* elected mayor; John Lewin, Henry Watchorn, chamberlains.

In his mayoralty was a violent conteft; in which the Hon. Booth Grey and Colonel Coote were chofen to reprefent this place in Parliament, in oppofition to Mr. Darker and Mr. Palmer. This conteft lafted 14 days[2].

---

[1] " In this year a fhocking murder was committed on the body of an old foldier, a pedlar, by a young man and his wife of the name of Cherry, who the preceding night flept in the fame room at a common lodging-houfe in Church-gate, oppofite to the Butt Clofe. It appeared that they from neceffity, by their own account, intended only to rob him; but the old man, being ftrong and powerful, overcame the young man, who, to difengage himfelf, murdered him with two of the poor pedlar's own knives; the woman affifting, they ftabbed him to the heart. They were hanged together, near the place where they committed the murder. The woman had been well educated, and perfifted in her innocence. When they were pinioning her arms in the gaol the morning of the execution, fhe fainted away; but, recovering, fhe with fortitude, and feemingly innocent compofure, faid, " My God died to appeafe a multitude, and why fhould I repine." Throfby.

[2] " Since this election an innocent holiday has been gradually dwindling into difufe. It had long before been cuftomary, on Eafter Monday, for the mayor and his brethren, in their fcarlet gowns, attended by their proper officers in form, to go to a certain clofe, called *Black-Annis's-Bower Clofe* (fee vol. III. p. 1051), parcel of, or bordering upon, Leicefter Foreft, to fee the diverfion of hunting, or, rather, the trailing of a cat before a pack of hounds: a cuftom, perhaps, originating out of a claim to the royalty of the Foreft. Hither, on a fair-day, reforted the young and old, and thofe of all denominations. In the greateft harmony the Spring was welcomed. The morning was fpent in various amufements and athletic exercifes, till a dead cat, about noon, was prepared by annifeed water, for commencing the mock hunting of the hare. In about half an hour after the cat had been trailed at the tail of an horfe over the grounds, in zigzag directions, the hounds were directed to the fpot where the cat had been trailed from. Here the hounds gave tongue, in glorious concert. The people from the various eminences, who had placed themfelves to behold the fight, with fhouts of rapture, gave applaufe; the horfemen, dafhing after the hounds through foul paffages and over fences, were emulous for taking the lead of their fellows. It was a fcene, upon the whole, of joy; the governing and the governed, in the habits of freedom, enjoying together an innocent and recreating amufement, ferving to unite them in bonds of mutual friendfhip, rather than to embitter their days with difcord and difunion. As the cat had been trailed to the mayor's door, through fome of the principal ftreets, confequently the dogs and horfemen followed. After the hunt was over, the mayor gave a handfome treat to his friends. In this manner the day ended." Throfby.

Sept. 21, 1768, *John Wesley* elected mayor; but he dying, *John Gamble* was chosen; William Brown, William Simpson, chamberlains.

Sept. 21, 1769, *Joseph Chambers* elected mayor; John Hartall, Thomas Phipps, chamberlains.

Sept. 21, 1770, *James Cooper* elected mayor; John Clark, Samuel Topp, chamberlains.

Sept. 21, 1771, *John Cartwright* elected mayor; William Taylor, Thomas Barwell, chamberlains.

At the general quarter sessions of the peace, held at Leicester Castle in the spring of 1772, a woman, deaf and dumb, gave evidence by signs against the father of her bastard child, to the satisfaction of a crowded court.

June 27, a terrible storm of hail and rain, attended with thunder and lightning, did much damage in Leicester to chimneys and roofs of houses. At Wistow, several large elms were split from the top to the bottom, and some were torn up by the roots.

In July, a fire broke out in the night-time at the Lion and Lamb inn, which totally destroyed three bays of buildings, and greatly damaged some others.

Sept. 21, 1772, *Robert Peach* elected mayor; Edward Price, William Oldham, chamberlains.

The manufacturers of stockings in Leicester, and the villages adjacent, hearing some unfavourable reports respecting a stocking-frame which had been made by an ingenious mechanic, assembled on Monday March 15, 1773, for the purpose of destroying it; it being supposed so to expedite their business, that might occasion numbers of them to be unemployed. But, though the report was groundless, they dared even to force themselves into the 'Change, where it had been lodged by the order of the mayor; took it thence, and carried it in triumph round the town, and at last destroyed it, and dispersed without further mischief. The conduct of Mr. Peach, then mayor, and Mr. Simpson and Mr. Good, proprietors of the frame, was highly applauded by the inhabitants of Leicester in general on this occasion, in endeavouring, by gentle means, to convince the stocking-makers of the impropriety of their conduct.

Sept. 21, 1773, *Richard-Roberts Drake* elected mayor; James Bishop, James Oldham, chamberlains.

Sept. 21, 1774, *Samuel Oliver* elected mayor; Sampson Chapman, John Parsons, chamberlains.

Sept. 21, 1775, *Joseph Johnson* elected mayor; William Astle, Hamlett Clark, chamberlains.

Sept. 21, 1776, *Samuel Jordan* elected mayor; Edward Sutton, Robert Dickinson, chamberlains.

Sept. 21, 1777, *John Coleman* elected mayor; Joseph Neale, Thomas Bass Oliver, chamberlains.

A remarkable trial took place in August 1778. Francis Soules, a French teacher in Leicester, was indicted for the murder of John Fenton, who lost his life in the amiable office of preventing, as he thought, the murder of his own brother [1].

Sept. 21, 1778, *John Pocklington* elected mayor; John Eames, Thomas Lockwood, chamberlains.

Sept. 21, 1779, *John Gregory* elected mayor; Joseph Burbage, John Mansfield, chamberlains.

Sept. 21, 1780, *Henry Watchorn* elected mayor; Benjamin Gregory, Thomas Cristy, chamberlains.

A fire at the Lion and Lamb, in December, burnt six tons of hay, and the building it was in.

Sept. 21, 1781, *Thomas Barwell* elected mayor; James Willey, Thomas Jeffcut, chamberlains.

Sept. 21, 1782, *James Bishop* elected mayor; William Bellamy, William Bishop, chamberlains.

Cockmuckhill houses were taken down, and alms-houses in their stead built, lower down the Belgrave-gate, by subscription.

Aug. 18, 1583. About 9 at night, a ball of fire, with a long train, was seen passing over Leicester, apparently about 40 yards above the houses, in a direction North and South-west. It was seen in other parts of the kingdom; and some affirmed it was accompanied by the shock of an earthquake.

Sept. 21, 1783, *William Oldham* elected mayor; Edward Harris, John-Bass Oliver, chamberlains.

In February 1784, there was a grand masquerade on the river, near the Bath gardens, during a hard frost. The gentlemen performers attracted an amazing concourse of people, and afforded much pleasantry in their masques. Fahrenheit's thermometer was, Dec. 26, sunk to 39 degrees; which is eleven lower than the freezing point, and eight lower than it is in most winters.

The abolition of throwing at cocks on Shrove Tuesday was begun, and nearly effected, in Mr. Oldham's mayoralty.

Sept. 21, 1784, *Joseph Chambers* elected mayor; Abel Webster, William Watts, chamberlains.

This gentleman's third mayoralty. A thing very unusual in so large a corporate body.

Mail-coaches first came to Leicester July 26, 1785.

Sept. 21, 1785, *John Parsons* elected mayor; but he dying, *Robert Peach* succeeded; James Mallet, J. P. Allamand, chamberlains.

Sept. 21, 1786, *Hamlett Clark* elected mayor; John Slater, John Saywell, chamberlains.

Sept. 21, 1787, *Robert Dickinson* elected mayor; James Cook, Thomas Peach, chamberlains.

A riotous mob assembled, in consequence of an attempt to introduce into Leicester a spinning machine, Nov. 30, 1787. The people assembled for the purpose of destroying it. They searched many houses where they thought any part of it was concealed; and at length broke into Mr. Wetston's house in North-gate-street in the night-time, and destroyed his furniture, stock in trade, and trading utensils, as being a principal (as the mob conceived) in introducing into the town a piece of mechanism that would eventually rob them of that labour which supplied their wants.

This year the inhabitants began to tax themselves (without applying for an Act of Parliament) with the expence of paving the streets after the London fashion.

Sept. 21, 1788, *Henry Watchorn* elected mayor; Edmund Swinfen, William Parsons, chamberlains.

Sept. 21, 1789, *John Dalby* elected mayor; Thomas Chatwin, Edward Marston, chamberlains.

The election this year for representatives to serve in Parliament for the Borough was carried on with warmth and intemperance; which was opportunely stopped by withdrawing a candidate on each side. The gentlemen who retired to prevent further mischief, and an intolerable growing expence, were Mr. Montelieu and Mr. Halled.

Sept. 21, 1790, *John Eames* elected mayor; John Freer (who dying, was succeeded by Joseph Johnson), Thomas Wright, chamberlains.

A rigid examination into the weights and measures used in this town, was a popular act of this magistrate.

---

[1] " Soules and James, the brother of the unfortunate John, were playing together at billiards at the Dolphin inn; a quarrel arose about 6s.; violent words passed, in which Soules conceived himself reflected upon by Mr. Fenton, and in consequence borrowed, or purchased, a brace of pistols, with which he soon returned to the billiard-room, and challenged Fenton to fight, laying one down on the table. Mr. F. hastily took it up, and ran down stairs with it for the purpose of informing the mayor of the transactions, thinking his life in danger. Soules immediately followed to find him, went once or twice to his mother's house, the Green Dragon in the market-place, and enquired after him. John, the young man who was killed, was sitting with company in the house; and, knowing the business in some measure that Soules was upon, seized the Frenchman by the hams, and was endeavouring to thrust him out of the house, when Soules, pulling out a pistol from his pocket, shot him in the neck; of which wounds he died next day. The trial was before Mr. Justice Ashurst. Soules's counsel pleaded, that in the prisoner was no malice *propense*, and requested to have the verdict, if it affected his life, made special; to which the Court consented. The Judge, after summing up the evidence, put the following questions to the jury: 1. Do the jury agree to the representations given by the evidence touching the facts at the billiard-table? *Agreed.*—2. Did the prisoner fire the pistol designedly, or did it go off by accident? *Designedly.*—3. Did the prisoner go to the Green Dragon only to recover his property (the pistol), or with an intent to excite James Fenton to fight a duel, or to do him some mischief? *He went there with a design only to recover his property.* The next assizes following, by the Judges' opinion, it appeared that he was guilty of murder; but a special messenger also appeared, at the same time, with his Majesty's pardon." Throsby.—An epitaph on Fenton will be found under the parish of St. Martin.

Sept. 21, 1791, *Joseph Neal* elected mayor; Thomas Read, Samuel Clark, chamberlains.

May 19, 1792, a number of diforderly perfons met in the market-place in the evening; and, becaufe they could not lower the price of butchers' meat, they lowered the butchers' ftalls, by throwing them down; after which they amufed themfelves by breaking every individual butcher's windows in the town.

Sept. 21, 1792, *Joseph Burbidge* elected mayor; William Firmadge, Sam. Towndrow, chamberlains.

Sept. 21, 1793, *John Mansfield* elected mayor; John Stevenson, Mark Oliver, chamberlains.

Sept. 21, 1794, *Benjamin Gregory* elected mayor; John Reynolds, John Walker, chamberlains.

Sept. 21, 1795, *William Dabbs* elected mayor; Thomas Copfon, David Harris, chamberlains.

Sept. 21, 1796, *Hamlett Clark* (fecond time) elected mayor; Will. Hall, James Cort, chamberlains.

Sept. 21, 1797, *Thomas Jeffcutt* elected mayor; Michael Miles, Robert Walker, chamberlains.

Sept. 21, 1798, *William Bellamy* elected mayor; John Gregory, Charles Sanfome, chamberlains.

Sept. 21, 1799, *William Bifhop* elected mayor; John Jackfon, Francis Burgefs, chamberlains.

Sept. 21, 1800, *John Saywell* elected mayor; Thomas Sutton, Thomas Miller, chamberlains.

Sept. 21, 1801, *Thomas Peach* elected mayor; Robert Johnfon, Jofeph Dalby, chamberlains.

Sept. 21, 1802, *John Slater* elected mayor; James Mallett, James Bankart, chamberlains.

Sept. 21, 1803, *Hamlett Clark* (third time) elected mayor; John Sarfon, Ifaac Lovell, chamberlains.

Sept. 21, 1804, *Edmund Swinfen* elected mayor; William Heard, William Sultzer, chamberlains.

Sept. 21, 1805, *William Parfons* elected mayor; George Ireland, John Davenport, chamberlains.

Sept. 21, 1806, *Joseph Johnson* elected mayor; Thomas Yates, John Adams, chamberlains.

BAILIFFS OF LEICESTER.

37 Hen. III. Roger de Ordener.

16 Edw. I. Tho. de Ryder and Will. de Gracna.

8 Hen. V. Henry Forfter was then Bailiff.

24 Hen. VI. Richard Hotoft and Thomas Meryng, efquires. Their deputies then were, William Braunfton and Alexander Villers.

31 Hen. VI. Richard Hotoft continued Bailiff; and William Hynde was his deputy.

3 Edw. IV. Peter Curtes was Bailiff, and fo continued in 17 Edw. IV. and for feveral years afterward; for he, or one of the fame name, was Mayor of the town in 22 Edw. IV.; and was a member of parliament for the town in 17 and 22 Edw. IV., and again 1 Ric. III., and 4 and 7 Hen. VII.

14 Hen. VII. Robert Orton was Bailiff; and fo continued 7 Hen. VIII.

23 Hen. VIII. Thomas Cattelyn was then Bailiff; and alfo in 28 Hen. VIII.

1 Edw. VI. Thomas Danet was Bailiff.

March 11, 6 Edw. VI. at a common hall, it was agreed to fend Mr. Boughton, vicar of St. Martin's, to London, to try (among other things) to get the Bailiwick of Leicefter in fee-farm to the town. And it feems that they did obtain a grant of it for fome time; for in the fame year, June 20, an order was made at a common hall, that the Bailiwick fhould remain to one of the Mayor's brethren who had not been Mayor, to occupy every man in his order upon the bench; and that if any of the twenty-four in his courfe fhould refufe it, he fhould pay 40s. or be committed. And accordingly, on the laft of November that year, Mr. Overend promifed to pay 40s. to the Chamberlains, on Jan. 20 next, for his refufal of the Bailiwick; and fo alfo Nov. 29, 1 Mary, Mr. Smith promifed to pay 40s. for the like refufal.

6 Eliz. William Reynolds and Thomas Fowler were Bailiffs.

7 Eliz. William Reynolds and John Tatam.

8 Eliz. William Norys and Thomas Newcombe.

9 Eliz. James Clarke and Thomas Newcombe.

10 Eliz. Nicholas Englyfhe and T. Newcombe.

Vol. I.

11 Eliz. William Shingleton; and again 12 Eliz.

Some time after this, it feems that Mr. John Danet got a patent for the Bailiwick; for July 22, 21 Eliz. it being agreed, at a common hall, to purchafe the Bailiwick for the ufe of the town, Mr. John Stanford bought Mr. John Danet's patent, and fold it to the town for 4l. befides his charges; and the Town was to enter on it at Michaelmas.

June 24, 36 Eliz. John Wilne, *alias* Willes, being then Bailiff, it was agreed, between him and the Mayor and his brethren, that the four ferjeants fhould attend on the Mayor as of old time was ufed. And May 6, 1599, he is ftyled the Queen's Bailiff, and was made a Mayor's brother; and Jan. 15, 1599, the company of twenty-four affured his office to him for his life, by a bond of 200l. under the common feal. But in the firft year of King James he thought fit to procure a patent from him for the faid office; which was granted to him June 6, *durante beneplacito*. He died in 1621.

An indenture, made Dec. 20, 7 Jac. witneffeth, that whereas king James, by patents under the great feal of England and the feal of the Duchy, dated 17 April, 7 Jac. granted to the mayor, bailiffs, and burgeffes of Leicefter, power to elect a fufficient perfon to be fteward or town-clerk, and fo many fit perfons to be bailiff or bailiffs of Leicefter, and keeper or keepers of his gaol; and they to have fuch reafonable fees as of antient time they have had: The mayor, bailiffs, and burgeffes, in performance of certain agreements, grant unto Henry earl of Huntingdon, and the heirs male of his body lawfully begotten, that they, as often as occafion requires, may, every firft term, nominate a fit perfon to be fteward of the faid Borough; and that the mayor, bailiffs, and burgeffes, will elect and admit the perfon fo nominated within ten days after he is fo nominated to be fteward of the town for his life: And that, at the third, fifth, feventh, and ninth avoidance, the prefent avoidance being counted for the firft, and from thenceforth at every fuch other term, the faid earl, and heirs male of his body, may nominate a fit perfon to be fteward; which perfon fo nominated the mayor, bailiffs, and burgeffes, fhall admit to be fteward for life within ten days after fuch nomination, as long as the faid earl, or any heir male of his body, as fhall be living; faving to the mayor, bailiffs, and burgeffes, the nomination, &c. of the fecond, fourth, fixth, eighth, and tenth ftewards, and fo in every fuch other turn. In like manner, the mayor, &c. grant to the faid earl, and the heirs male of his body, to nominate to the mayor, &c. any fit perfon to be bailiff of the faid town, and keeper of the gaol, for the fecond turn thereof, accounting this prefent turn to be the firft; and fo after the fecond turn for the fourth, fixth, eighth, and tenth, and every fuch other turn, fo long as he, or any heir male of his body, fhall be living; and that the faid mayor, &c. will elect and admit the perfon and perfons fo nominated within ten days after to be bailiff and keeper of the faid gaol for his life; faving to the mayor, bailiffs, and burgeffes, the nomination and appointment of the bailiff and keeper of the gaol for this prefent avoidance, as the firft time, and fo for the third, fifth, feventh, ninth, and eleventh turns, and every fuch other turn for ever, &c. The mayor, bailiffs, and burgeffes, gave to the faid earl a bond of 1000l. for performance of the conditions in the indenture.

On the death of Mr. Wilne, notice was given to the earl of Huntingdon, it being his turn to nominate the next to this office; and, upon his nomination,

March 7, 1621-2, Robert Wright was, by the company of twenty-four, chofen, admitted, and fworn, to be Bailiff, and Keeper of the Gaol, &c. for his life.

Oct. 18, 1641, John Beeby was chofen Bailiff, and fworn Oct. 25; but he being guilty of feveral mifdemeanours, the return of proceffes was taken from him Jan. 5, 1654-5; and it was ordered, that the proceffes of the Court of Record of the Borough fhould be directed to the chief ferjeant at mace, or his deputy, till further order. Neverthelefs he continued Bailiff in 1656.

Oct.

Oct. 14, 1645. Mr. John Beeby, at a common hall, was chosen Clerk of the Statutes till May 1 next.

Sept. 1657, Thomas Henshaw and Anthony Curtis were Bailiffs.

Oct. 16, 1657, at a meeting of the Mayor and Aldermen, William Major, gent. was chosen and admitted Bailiff and Keeper of the Gaol for term of life, according to the nomination of Theophilus earl of Huntingdon. He was sworn Oct. 19; but the company protested against some words in the nomination, viz. " liberty to execute the said office by his sufficient deputy," and the word " appurtenance."

Sept. 21, 1658, William Franks and William Calles are said to be Bailiffs.

Sept. 21, 1659, Robert Erick and George Abney.

1660, William Major resumed his office; which he continued to execute till the new charter of Jac. II.

In 1685, in virtue of the said new charter, among other alterations made in the Corporation, the Chamberlains were called Bailiffs.

The following royal mandate was copied by Dr. Farmer, in the year 1760, from the original.

" JAMES R.—Trusty and well-beloved, we greet you well. Whereas we have, by our Order in Council, thought fit to remove John Roberts, John Goodall, Thomas Ludlam, Walter Hood, Francis Ward, Gabriel Hill, Samuel Robinson, Samuel Woodland, Henry Pate, William Springthorpe, and John Crecroft, from being Aldermen of that our Borough of Leicester; Samuel Martin, Thomas Tompson, David Clay, Thomas Drake, Godfrey Borundell, George Steares, John Hardy, John Burdett, Thomas Ayres, Nicholas Allsop, Richard Mason, George Crofts, Henry Dann, John Pollard, Edward Wagstaffe, and John Roberts junior, from being Common-council-men; William Major senior from being Bailiff, John Hackles from being Town-clerk, and William Brown from being Town-solicitor of the said Borough : We have thought fit hereby to will and require you forthwith to elect and admit our trusty and well-beloved William Bentley, John Bent, John Brooksby, William Sheares, Edmund Johnson, Matthew Symonds, Richard Mason, Robert Lord, Jonathan Coleman, Henry Treene, and William Warberton, to be Aldermen; Thomas Wallings, John Kerby, Joseph Dudley, William Walker, Francis Churchman, William Harris, Tobiah Marshall, John Hevitt, John Cooke, John Hughes, John Buxtone senior, Robert Page senior, John Davy, William Page, Robert Langton, and John Warburton, to be Common-council-men ; John Oneby to be Bailiff, John Creswell to be Town-clerk, and Valentine House to be Town-solicitor, of our said Borough, in the room of the persons above mentioned, without administering unto them any oath or oaths, but the usual oath for the execution of their respective places, with which we are pleased to dispense in this behalf; and for so doing this shall be your warrant : And so we bid you farewell. Given at our Court at Whitehall, the 27th day of February 1687-8, in the fourth year of our reign.

By his Majesty's command, SUNDERLAND, P.
To our trusty and well-beloved the Mayor, Aldermen, and Corporation, of our Borough of Leicester, in our County of Leicester."

March 13, 1687-8, John Oneby, by virtue of the new charter, and the above order, was chosen Bailiff.

On revocation of that charter, Mr. Major was restored : but he declined to act ; and thereupon,

Dec. 18, 1688, Thomas Palmer, gent. was elected. He died Aug. 18, 1723.

Aug. 26, 1723, Leonard Piddock, gent. was unanimously elected Bailiff of the Borough and Town of Leicester, and Keeper of the Gaol there; and he made Thomas Herrick his deputy. He died in 1744.

Sept. 25, 1744, Thomas Herrick [1], gent. was unanimously chosen Bailiff of this Borough, and Keeper of the Gaol there, in the room of Leonard Piddock.

Jan. 12, 1767, John Kirkland, of Loughborough, in the county of Leicester, gent. was unanimously elected Bailiff of the said Borough and Town of Lei-

cester, and Keeper of the Gaol there (which places were then vacant by the death of Thomas Herrick, gent. who died Dec. 10, 1766, aged 73, and was buried at St. Martin's [2].)

Sept. 26, 1771, Samuel Topp, esq. was unanimously elected Bailiff of the Borough and Town of Leicester, and Keeper of the Gaol there, in the room of John Kirkland, gent. deceased. He resigned 1779.

March 15, 1779, Edward Dawson, gent. was unanimously elected Bailiff of the Borough and Town of Leicester, and Keeper of the Gaol there, vacant by resignation. He is still Bailiff, 1807.

RECORDERS.

They seem to be first constituted by the charter of 4 Edward IV. The first whose name we meet with is,

16 Hen. VII. Thomas Jakys, who so continued till 1 Hen. VIII.; when, Dec. 20, Ralph Swyllyngton was made free, and admitted to be one of the coburgesses ; but not to be charged with any office, nor be liable to be summoned by the mayor but at his own pleasure. He died 16 Hen. VIII.

16 Hen. VIII. Thomas Broksby, alias Broxby, was chosen in his room, and continued Recorder till 27 Hen. VIII. inclusive.

28 Hen. VIII. John Baymond; continued till 33 Hen. VIII.; when Edward Gryffyn succeeded ; and was Recorder till 3 Edw. VI. inclusive.

4 Edw. VI. John Beaumont succeeded him; and was " Magister Rotulorum Curiæ Cancellarii Domini Regis, & Recordator Leicestriæ," 5 Edw. VI.

6 Edw. VI. John Hunt.

1 Mar. John Hunt is blotted out; and in his stead is inserted Francis Fernham [3], Recorder. He was chosen burgess of parliament March 16, 1 Mar.; and again 26 Oct. 1 & 2 Phil. & Mar. ; and continued Recorder Sept. 21, 3 & 4 Phil. & Mar.

3 & 4 Phil. & Mar. May 7, Francis Gyffon was chosen Recorder ; and was so in September, 4 & 5 Phil. & Mar. ; in which year Robert Bream, Breham, or Braham, about Christmas, became Recorder; and, Jan. 11, was chosen burgess of parliament ; and so also 2 Dec. 5 Eliz.; and again 17 April, 14 Eliz.

July 18, 17 Eliz. Richard Parkins was sworn Recorder. He had a scarlet gown voted for him, at the charge of the town, 21 Eliz. Sept. 21 ; and (applying himself to reading and digesting the records of the town) had a chamber fitted up and furnished for him to lye at, &c. in the Town-hall, when he came to the town.—This Mr. Parkins, a revered man in his time for learning and judgment, purchased the entire manor of Boney in Nottinghamshire, which still continues with his posterity.—In 1592, " troubled at the factions in the Town of Leicester," he wished to resign his office ; but peace and concord being restored, was induced to continue Recorder (see p. 407.)—In the next year, several persons were charged with plucking wool off the backs of sheep; the North mills were redeemed, with other houses and lands (money being then at 10 per cent. interest) ; and Mr. George Tatham, for 15l. to be paid him, and Mr. Thomas for 15l. to be paid him, agreed to surrender up to the Town the lands and tenements in their book, of 20l., and the obligation they have of the Town ; and the said book and bond to be canceled.—Oct. 29, 1593, a letter occurs, from Mr. Robert Heyrick, then mayor for the second time, to Thomas Cave, esq. high sheriff, complaining of the deficiency of the contributions of the country for relief of the visited ; shewing, that, unless the contributions came in more duly, he should be forced to complain to the Queen's Council, or to set the poor people at liberty to seek for better maintenance. Other letters to the same purpose—500 or 600 poor that yet stand clear, cannot live without relief, or going into the country. Out of 21 houses visited, 35 persons have died ; afterward 46 houses visited, and dead 87 ; and many letters to the justices of the county for weekly contributions.—In December, a letter to the Earl of Huntingdon acquaints him, that Dr. Steward and Dr. Chippingdale proceeded in their suit, against the inhabitants of Leicester, about

[1] See p. 454.　　　[2] Where see his epitaph.

[3] Of him, and his respectable family, see vol. III. p. 103.

grinding

grinding corn and multure at the Caftle mills, contrary to Dr. Chippendale's promife made to the Earl, of referring it. Another letter, Feb. 5, 1593-4, ftates " fome new houfes are infeated towards the South end of the town; whereby I fhall hardly bring the Judge to fit at the Caftle, but be forced to lodge them at Mr. Stanford's, and have them fit at our Town-hall."

June 23, 1603, being Thurfday, Queen Anne and Prince Henry came from Afhby-de-la-Zouch to Leicefter; and that morning the Recorder came from his family refidence at Boney, in order to have made a fpeech to them; but was prevented to do fo by falling fick here, where he continued till Sunday, and then went home fick.

He died July 3; and a monument[1] on the North wall of Boney church thus perpetuates his memory:

" Here lyeth Richard Parkins, efquire, juftice of peace and quorum in the county of Nott. and recorder of the towns of Leicefter and Nott. and an ancient utter barrifter in the Inner Temple; who married and took to wife Elizabeth Barlowe, then a widow, late wife of one Humfrey Barlowe, of Stoke, in the county of Darby, efq. deceafed, being the eldeft daughter of Aden Beresford, of Fenne Bentlye, in the county of Darby, efq. deceafed; by whom the faid Richard had 8 children, viz. 4 fons and 4 daughters; that is to fay, fir George Parkins, knight, his fon and heir, Adrian Parkins, John Parkins, Aden Parkins, Fraunces, Anne, Elizab. Margaret; and died the 3d day of July, 1603. Upon whofe foul, &c."

July 8, 1603, John Stanford[2], of Barkby, efq. was chofen to be Recorder; and Nov. 25 it was agreed, at a common hall, to allow him' 6l. 13s. 4d. per annum as his fee: but he died foon after, viz. Dec. 1.

Whereupon, Dec. 14, Auguftin Nicolls[3], ferjeant at law, was chofen in his place by the aldermen, and was fworn Feb. 28 following. He was knighted in 1607, and made a Judge of the Common Pleas 1612.

Dec. 1, 1612, Francis Harvey, of Northampton, a bencher of the Middle Temple, was chofen; and it was ordered, that he fhould be paid yearly 5l. for his fee as Recorder, and at every affizes 20s. towards his charges; and that the town fhould bear his charges at his coming to Leicefter, at all times, about the town's bufinefs. And Mr. Juftice Nicolls was fent to acquaint him with this order; and acquaint him that the town was then poor, and that the Recorders formerly had only 4l. per annum, and lefs. In 1624, he was made a judge of the Common Pleas; of which he gave notice to the town in October.

Oct. 24, 1624, Thomas Chapman[4], efq. was chofen, and continued Recorder in 1652.

1653, James Winftanley, efq. was Recorder; and, refufing to conform, furrendered in 1662, when Robert Harding, efq. was chofen, Sept. 12. He was afterwards knighted; and continued Recorder in 1679.

1680, Nathan Wrighte[5], efq. On furrender of the charter, 1684, Theophilus earl of Huntingdon was Recorder, and Nathan Wrighte Deputy Recorder. But the charter being reftored in 1688, Nathan Wrighte became Recorder again; and was made ferjeant in 1693; and continued Recorder till 1697.

Sept. 1, 1697, Laurence Carter junior, efq. (fon of Laurence Carter, efq. of the Newark[6]) was chofen Recorder; called to be ferjeant April 30, 1724; knighted May 4, 1724; and October 16,

1726, made a baron of the Exchequer. He was of a refpeatable family of that name in Leicefter, whofe defcendants ftill rank in the firft clafs of its inhabitants. This gentleman (being a barrifter at law, and a near relation of a worthy perfon, who is mentioned in p. 438 as a projeator or great encourager of the fcheme for conveying water by pipes to the houfes of the inhabitants of Leicefter) was fixed on, almoft unanimoufly, to fucceed Nathan Wrighte in the Recorderfhip of this Borough in 1696, in which office he continued till 1729. He was thrice chofen reprefentative for the Town; and refigned that honourable ftation on being appointed one of the Barons of the Court of Exchequer. He died in 1744, at the age of 73. Baron Carter refided within the Newark, Leicefter, in the dwelling afterward occupied by Mr. Coltman, a manufaaturer, on the fite of which ftood the beautiful collegiate church[7].

William Wrighte, efq. (a younger fon of fir Nathan Wrighte, late lord keeper) was eleated in 1729. He refigned in 1763; and died at Envill in Staffordfhire June 4, 1765. æt. 71[8].

1763, Robert Bakewell[9], efq.; removed by a court of aldermen in 1766.

William Burleton, efq. LL.D. of the Univerfity of Oxford 1754, was chofen Recorder in 1766. He was in the commiffion of the peace for the county of Leicefter, and major of the Militia on its firft eftablifhment. In 1785, he was alfo eleated recorder of Shaftefbury; and died Nov. 1, 1786, aged 66[10].

Feb. 8, 1787, Edmund Wigley[11], of the Middle Temple, London, efq. was unanimoufly eleated Recorder, in the place of William Burleton, efq. deceafed.

Feb. 14, 1798, John Vaughan, efq. of the Temple, London, barrifter at law, was unanimoufly eleated Recorder, in the room of Edmund Wigley, efq. (whofe refignation of that office was accepted.) He is now (1807) a ferjeant at law, and continues Recorder of Leicefter.

SENESCHALS; or Stewards of the Court[12].

The firft of thefe whom we have met with is Thomas Ward, who in 1599 is ftyled Steward of the Court; and, Sept. 4 in that year, was made free for a pottle of wine, and foon after was chofen to be an alderman; and Feb 22, 1599 1600, at a meeting of the mayor's brethren, had a patent delivered to him, in confideration of 6l. 13s. 4d. for the enjoyment of his office for term of his life: And he promifed not to fell or affign over the faid office to any perfon but whom the mayor and aldermen agree to.

Chriftopher Tamworth[13], in 1603, Auguft 4, exhibited a patent from fir John Fortefcue, knt. chancellor of the Duchy of Lancafter, for the Stewardfhip, the validity of which the Corporation difputed; whereupon they were, Dec. 28, ferved with a privy feal, or injunation, to fuffer him to enjoy the office, or to appear next term in the Duchy chamber to anfwer the fame: which laft it was agreed the mayor fhould do. But, upon the King's grant of a new charter, 1609, he was eftablifhed in his office. He made his will April 28, 1624, in which he made feveral bequefts for pious and charitable ufes, which was proved Sept. 26 the fame year.

John Oneby, efq. of Hinckley (of whom an account will be given under the hiftory of that town) is the next that we meet with as Senefchal.

[1] This monument, on which are the kneeling effigies of Mr. Parkins and his wife, with their eight children, is engraved in Thoroton's Nottinghamfhire; as is alfo the monument of Humfrey Barlow, efq. the former hufband of Mrs. Parkins; pp. 46, 47.

[2] See the Pedigree of his Family under Barkby, vol. III. p. 81.

[3] See farther particulars of fir Auguftin Nicolls, and a Pedigree of his Family, under Halfted, vol. III. p. 480.

[4] See under Foxton in vol. II p. 564.

[5] Of this eminent perfon, who was afterwards Lord Keeper, fee fome memoirs, with a portrait, vol. III. p. 216.

[6] Who died in 1710, æt. 69, as recorded on his epitaph, vol. I. p. 318. See alfo the fon's epitaph, p. 319.

[7] " A man, whom the Baron on a circuit condemned to die, efcaped from the cart, by the affiftance of the multitude, going to the place of execution; and afterwards fettled at Leicefter, near the Baron, in the houfe, or rather in a houfe upon the fite of that, occupied by Mr. Wheatley, in Red-crofs-ftreet. The man, I am told, made an ufeful member of fociety, lived money, and died in peace." Throfby.

[8] See vol. III. p 218; and his epitaph, ibid. p. 1134.

[9] See an account of him under Swebfton, vol. III. p. 1037.

[10] Mr. Burleton was buried at St. Margaret's in Leicefter, where fee his epitaph. He poffeffed confiderable property at Wyken in this county, where further particulars of him will be given.

[11] See the Pedigree of this Family in vol. III. p. 788.

[12] See the Charter of 1609, 7 James I. p. 420.

[13] Of whom, and of his charities, fee under Halfted, vol. III. p. 476.

Thomas

Thomas Staveley [1] fucceeded him. He died Jan. 2, 1683 ; and was buried at St. Mary's, an. æt. 57.

John Major, barrifter, was chofen in his room, Jan. 15, 1683-4; and thereupon prefented to the Corporation two great filver candlefticks.

Simon Barwell, attorney, was nominated by the earl of Huntingdon, March 31, 1703, and elected. He died June 24, 1720, and was buried at St. Martin's church July 6.

William Wrighte was elected July 3, 1720, and fworn July 8. He made Mr. Richard Hill his deputy ; and in 1729 was appointed Recorder; fee p. 453.

He was fucceeded by Norrice Cradock, gent. Jan. 11, 1729.

Norice Cradock, efq. Steward of the Court of Record of this Borough, was removed from his office of Steward Jan. 21, 1765; and died foon after [2].

William Tilley, gent. attorney at law, was unanimoufly elected Steward of the Court of Record of the faid Borough in 1765. He was alfo coroner for the county ; and died in 1797.

March 15, 1797, Henry Dalby, gent. attorney at law, was unanimoufly elected Steward of the Court of Record of this Borough, in the room of Mr. William Tilley, deceafed. He is the prefent Steward (1807.)

TOWN CLERKS;
antiently ftyled "THE MAYOR'S CLERKS."

22 Edw. IV. Thomas Lynalls, the Mayor's Clerk, was made free ; and Robert Gaddifby was the Mayor's Clerk in 12 Hen. VIII.

William Deathick feems to have been chofen, or admitted to his office, the laft of February, 1571-2; for then his hand-writing begins in the Hall-book. He at firft wrote his name Deadyck, but after 17 Eliz. Deathyck, and in 20 Eliz. Dethyck, and fo continued for the future. He feems to have been the moft careful perfon that ever had been in his office ; and therefore, for his encouragement, 14 Eliz. April 14, it was agreed, that no apprentice fhould be bound within the liberties of Leicefter but by indenture made by the Mayor's Clerk ; for each pair of which he fhould have 16 d. to be fealed and recorded before the Mayor by his Clerk ; and he to have of the mafter 4 d. And on Sept. 21, 14 Eliz. it was agreed, that the Chamberlains fhould pay the Mayor's Clerk four nobles per annum more wages than ever had been paid before. And whereas formerly he had ufed to have but 2d. for the fwearing of freemen, in 17 Eliz. he was allowed 6d.; and, 29 April that year, for the better maintenance of the Mayor's Clerk, it was ordered, that every one chofen to be of the twenty-four fhould give him 12d. for adminiftering the oath, and recording their names ; and every one chofen to be of the forty-eight to pay him 6d.; and every one made free of any occupation by force of their ordinal to give him 6d. for the oath, and recording their names. And Dec. 14, 1603, at a meeting of the aldermen, it was agreed to give William Dethick, their Clerk, a gown at the town's charge. He was alive Sept. 21, 1608; but, foon after,

Roger Halfeilde was, at a meeting of the Aldermen, chofen to be Clerk to the Mayor, and Clerk of the Peace, fo long as he fhould demean himfelf well in his office, upon condition that he fhould give fuch a fum of money to the town for the faid offices as Mr. James Andrew then Mayor, Mr. Robert Heyrick, &c. fhould think meet.

Nicholas Bolyvant was chofen Feb. 12, 1620-1, at a meeting of the twenty-four, to be Town-clerk and Clerk of the Peace during their pleafure, for fo long as he fhould demean himfelf well in their judgement, and upon condition that he fhould perform fuch other covenants as they, or the greater part of them, fhould think fit; and, Feb. 19, he was admitted and fworn a freeman, and to the faid office. He was buried Dec. 17, 1635, at St. Martin's.

Richard Martin, efq. counfellor at law, Dec. 23, 1635, was chofen to fucceed him ; and the fame day was fworn a freeman, and took the oath of his office. He was buried Feb. 20, 1639-40, at St. Martin's.

Edward Palmer, gent. was elected March 23 following, and took the oaths. In 1645-6, he gave great offence to the governor and committee of the garrifon then in Leicefter, for which they confined him, whereby the bufinefs of the Corporation fuffered detriment ; and, there being no profpect of making his peace, the mayor and his brethren, March 13, declared his place void ; and

Hugh Afton, gent. was the fame day elected, and took the oaths required April 24, 1646; and Dec. 2, he was made Clerk of the Statutes; and July 27, 1647, he gave 1000l. fecurity truly to difcharge the faid office. He died in 1652.

Abel Coles officiated in the place 1653; and June 2, 1654, he was chofen to be Town Clerk and Clerk of the Peace during pleafure ; and July 7, at a common hall, was ordered to be Clerk of the Statutes, he giving fecurity to fave the town from any damage that might arife by his neglect, &c.

Edward Palmer, in virtue of a writ from the Upper Bench at Weftminfter, dated Feb. 12, was reftored to his office of Clerk of the Peace April 16, 1658; and Oct. 24, 1660, was chofen to be Clerk of the Statutes, he giving fecurity to fave the town harmlefs ; and June 7 following he was fworn, and the feal delivered to him. He died Feb. 27, 1663-4.

John Huckle was elected March 15, 1663-4.

John Creffwell, March 13, 1687-8, in virtue of the new charter, was chofen; but, that being recalled, John Huckle was reftored. He was buried at St. Martin's, March 10, 1694.

Edward Jevon, March 25, 1695, was elected, and fworn. Aug. 19, 1697, an order was made, that the Town-clerk fhould take but 6s. 8d. for a copy of the charter.

John Boley, Sept. 1, 1702, was elected in room of Mr. Jevon deceafed, and fworn.—Jan. 2, 1703-4, he had a gratuity of 20l. paid him by the Chamberlains, for his extraordinary care and pains taken for the benefit of the Corporation; and March 3, 1704-5, it was ordered, that, taking with him one alderman and two common-council-men, he fhould have liberty, from time to time, to go into the charter-houfe, and infpect the writings there, and put them into order, that they might be more readily found, and the Town better know how their title ftands in the lands they now enjoy, and whether they be not wronged of other lands and tenements which it is fuppofed belong to them; and June 1, 1704, at a common hall, he was ordered to be made free without paying any fine. Mr. Boley died in 1715 ; and was fucceeded by

Thomas Jordaine, gent. who was unanimoufly chofen Town-clerk June 15, 1715. He died June 9, 1745, aged 63 ; and his widow (who was daughter of Thomas Noble, efq.) May 5, 1788 [3].

Sept. 27, 1745, Thomas Herrick, gent. was chofen Town-clerk, in the room of Thomas Jordaine, gent. deceafed. He refigned in 1764; and died in 1766 [4].

Oct. 5, 1764, John Heyrick [5], gent. was unanimoufly elected Town-clerk of this Borough, in the room of Mr. Thomas Herrick.—If this truly worthy character, whom I am proud to call my Friend, were not ftill living, the prefent paragraph would be very confiderably extended.

Feb. 10, 1791, William Heyrick, gent. was unanimoufly elected Town-clerk of this Borough, in the room of John Heyrick, gent. his father, who had refigned that office. He is the prefent Town-clerk, 1807.

---

[1] See memoirs, and fine portraits of him and his lady, vol. II. p. 677 ; and his epitaph, vol. I. p. 318.
[2] See the Pedigree of his Family, vol. III. p. 1149. He had his Chriftian name from his mother Katharine Norrice, the "only daughter of John Norrice, gent. ;" who in his tomb at St. Mary's is ftyled "late mafter of the family of the Norrices;" fee vol. I. p. 315. [3] See their epitaphs at St. Mary's, vol. I. p. 319. [4] See p. 452.
[5] See feveral curious particulars of Alderman Robert Herrick (the immediate anceftor of the Town-clerk), and of feveral other members of this family, in vol. I. pp. 340—345; and in vol. II. p. 615—634, where the Family Pedigree is given. See alfo vol. III. pp. 148—169.

MEMBERS of PARLIAMENT for the COUNTY of LEICESTER.

⁎ Where no Place of Meeting is mentioned in this Lift, it is to be underftood that *Weftminfter* is meant.

EDWARD I.

Anno regni 23. Parliament held at Weftminfter. Robert de Wyvill, John de Dungevill.

25. London. Robert de Meynill, William Burdet.
26. York. John de Aunger, Robert Poutrell.
28. John de Mandevill, John de Folvile.
29. Lincoln. John de Aungervile, John de Folvile.
30. Robert Moutrell, John de Folvile.
33. John de Aungervile, Robert Poutrell.
34. Council at Weftminfter. John de Aungervile.
35. Carlifle. William Marmion, Richard de Perers.

EDWARD II.

1. Northampton. John de Aungervile, William Marmion.
2. Henry de Erdington, Richard de Egebafton.
4. London. Richard de Perers, John de Bakepuiz.
5. Richard de Perers, John de Bakepuiz.
6. John de Folvile, Alan Talbot.
6. John de Aungervile, John de Folvile.
7. William Braˑefon, Henry de Nottingham.
8. York. William Truffell, John de Houby.
8. York. Robert de Wiverell, Ralph de Secchevile.
9. Council at Weftminfter. Ralph de Folvile, Richard de Egebafton.
10. Council at Lincoln. Richard de Egebafton, Ralph de Folvile.
12. Robert de Folvile, John de Olney.
12. York. Hen. de Nottingham, Rob. de Gaddefby.
15. Hugh de Preftwold, Richard de Egebafton.
16. York. Robert de Gaddefby, William Flamvile.
17. Ralph de Sacchevile, Nicholas Payne.
18. London. Robert Burdett, Roger la Zouch.
19. Ralph Beler, Roger Belane.

EDWARD III.

1. Lincoln. Roger de Belgrave, Robert de Saddington.
2. Northampton. Robert Burdett, William Moton.
2. New Sarum. Ralph de Secchevile, Jordan de Garthorpe ¹.
2. York. Ralph de Secchevile, Robert de Waltham.
2. Northampton. Rob. Burdett, Robert de Sadington.
2. York. Rob. de Gaddefby, Rob. de Sadington.
2. John Talbot, Simon Pakeman.
3. New Sarum. Ralph de Secchevile, Jordan de Garthorpe.
4. Robert Burdett, Richard de Egebafton.
4. Winchefter. William Moton, Robert Burdett.
5. Roger la Zouch, William de Staunton.
6. Philip de Folvile, Alan Talbot.
6. Richard Egebafton, Ralph Secchevill.
6. York. Alan Talbot, John de Knighton.
8. Richard de Egebafton, Hugh Turvile.
8. York. John de Knighton, Simon Pakeman.
9. York. William de Moton, William de Bredon.
10. William de Bredon, Hugh de Turvile.
11. William Moton, Hugh de Turvile.
11. Council at Weftminfter. Roger le Zouch, William Moton.
11. Hugh de Turvile, Roger de Belgrave.
12. Council at Northampton. William Moton, Nicholas Charnels.
12. Ralph de Folvile, John de Elvey.
13. William Moton, Robert de Waltham.
14. Richard de Egebafton.
14. John de Boivile, Thomas de Whellefburgh.
14. Ralph de Secchevile, William de Keythorp.
14. William de Nevill, Ralph Mallory.
15. John le Waleys, Nicholas Charnels.
17. William Moton.
17. Ralph de Secchevile, Nicholas Payn.
18. Thomas Charnels, John Hackluyt.
18. New Sarum. Robert Burdett, Roger le Zouch.
20. Simon Pakeman, Robert de Kegworth.

21. John le Waleys, Simon Pakeman.
22. Roger le Waleys, Robert de Gaddefby.
24. John Paynell, John de Leare.
26. William de Bredon, Geffrey de Villiers.
26. Council at Weftminfter. Robert de Wyleby.
27. Council at Weftminfter. Thomas Malefours.
28. Thomas Malefours, John Paynel.
29. Nicholas Charnels, Thomas Malefours.
31. John Paynell, Thomas Malefours.
31. Thomas Malefours, Matthew de Folvile.
34. Thomas de Chaworth, John Charnels.
34. Philip Nevill, John Talbot.
36. John Talbot, William Flamvile.
37. Robert de Herle, Roger de Belers.
38. Ralph de Haftings, Simon Pakeman.
39. William Flamvile, Simon Pakeman.
42. John Talbot, Simon Pakeman.
43. John Talbot, Thomas de Ondeby.
45. William Flamvile, Thomas Walfh.
45. Council at Winchefter. William Flamvile.
46. John de Berkeley, William de Burgh.
47. John Talbot, Robert Digby.
50. James Beler, William Flamvile.
50. William Flamvile chivaler, James Beler chivaler.
51. Iidem.

RICHARD II.

1. John Beler chivaler, William Flamvile chivaler.
2. Gloucefter. Edmund de Appleby, Thomas de Erdington chivaler.
2. Thomas Walfhe chivaler, Roger Perwich.
3. John Fauconer chivaler, John Burdett.
4. Thomas Walfhe chivaler, Laurence Hauberk.
5. Wm. Flamvile chivaler, Tho. Walfhe chivaler.
6. John Nevill chivaler, Roger Perwich.
6. Thomas Walfhe chivaler, John Fauconer chivaler.
7. James de Beler chivaler, Robert de Langham.
7. New Sarum. Edmund de Appleby chivaler, William Flamvile chivaler.
8. Thomas Walfhe chivaler, John Fauconer chivaler.
9. John Fauconer chivaler, John Calveley chivaler.
10. William Flamvile chivaler, Thomas Walfhe chivaler.
11. Iidem.
12. Cambridge. William Flamvile chivaler, Richard Perwich.
13. Tho. Walfhe chivaler, Tho. Burdett chivaler.
14. Robert Langham, Thomas Walfhe chivaler.
15. Thomas Walfhe chivaler, William Flamvile.
16. Hugh Shirley chivaler, Robert Harrington chivaler.
17. Tho. Walfhe chivaler, Rob. Harrington chivaler.
18. Thomas Walfhe chivaler, Nicholas Coleman.
20. Thomas Walfhe chivaler, Edmund Bugge.
21. John Calveley chivaler, Henry de Nevill chivaler.

HENRY IV.

1. Tho. Maureward chivaler, Tho. Maundevill.
2. Gloucefter. John Nevill chivaler, Thomas Derby.
4. Winchefter. Henry Nevill, knt. John Berkley, knt.
5. Edmund Bugge, William de Brokefby.
6. Coventry. John Berkeley chivaler, Robert Vere.
8. John Nevile chivaler, Henry Nevile chivaler.
9. Gloucefter. John Blacket, Robert Sherard.
11. John Blakett, Bartholomew Brokefby.
12. John Berkeley, Thomas Maureward.

HENRY V.

1. James Belers, William Belgrave.
2. Leicefter. John Blacket, Thomas Afhby.
2. John Beler, Richard Hotoft.
8. Ralph Shirley, James Beler.
8. John Blaket, Robert Sherard.
9. William Truffell chivaler, Laurence Berkley.

¹ In 1328, the Sheriff of Leicefterfhire was directed to pay, to Ralph de Sachevile and Jordan de Garthorp, 9*l*. 12*s*. for their expences in attending Parliament for 24 days. Rot. Parl. vol. II. p. 441.

HENRY VI.

1. Robert Moton chivaler, Bartholomew Brokeſby.
2. Thomas Fouleherſt, John Boivile.
3. Bartholomew Brokeſby, Baldwin Bagge.
4. Leiceſter. Baldwin Bagge, John Boivile.
5. Bartholomew Brokeſby, John Boivile.
8. Bartholomew Brokeſby, Everard Digby.
9. Laurence Berkley, knt. Thomas Foulchurſt.
13. John Boivile, John Beler.
15. Richard Hotoft de Humberſton, Thomas Aſteley de Rawſton.
20. Thomas Palmer, Richard Neel.
25. Richard Hotoft, Thomas Staunton.
27. Thomas Everingham, Thomas Palmer.
28. Richard Hotoft, William Feldyng.
29. John Belers, Robert Staunton.
31. Reading. Thomas Evingham, John Boivile.
33. Laurence Haſtings, Thomas Palmer.
38. William Feldyng, eſq. John Whatton, eſq.

EDWARD IV.

7. Thomas Palmer, Robert Staunton.
12. William Truſſell, Robert Berkley.
17. William Truſſell, William Moton, eſq.

EDWARD VI.

1. Edward lord Haſtings—Sir Ambroſe Cave, knt.
6. The ſame—The ſame.

MARY.

1. Rob. Strelley, eſq. infirmus—Tho. Haſtings, eſq.
1. Oxford. Sir T. Haſtings, knt.—Hen. Pool, eſq.

PHILIP and MARY.

1 & 2. Sir Tho. Haſtings, knt.—Geo. Turpin, eſq.
2 & 3. . . . .—William Skeffington, eſq.
4 & 5. George Vincent, eſq.—George Sherard, eſq.

ELIZABETH.

1. William Stokes, eſq.—Francis Cave, eſq.
5. Nicholas Beaumont, eſq.—George Turpin, eſq.
13. Francis Haſtings, eſq.—Adrian Stokes, eſq.
14. Sir George Turpin, knt.—Nicholas Beaumont, eſq.
27. Francis Haſtings, eſq.—Sir Geo. Haſtings, knt.
28. The ſame—The ſame.
31. Henry Beaumont, eſq.—William Turpin, eſq.
35. Sir Francis Haſtings, knt.—Thomas Skeffington, eſq.
39. Sir Edward Haſtings, knt.—Sir Francis Haſtings, knt.
43. Henry Haſtings, eſq.—William Skipwith, eſq.

JAMES I.

1. Sir Geo. Villiers, kt.—Sir Tho. Beaumont, kt.
12. Sir Tho. Haſtings, kt.—Sir Tho. Heſilrige, kt.
18. Sir Tho. Beaumont [1], knt.—Sir Henry Haſtings, knt.
21. Sir Thomas Heſilrige, bart.—The ſame.

CHARLES I.

1625 Ferdinando lord Haſtings—Sir Wolſtan Dixie, bart.
1626 Sir Henry Haſtings, knt.—Fran. Stareſmore, eſq. [2]
1628 Ferdinando lord Haſtings—Sir Edward Hartopp, bart.
1640 (April) Sir Arthur Heſilrige, bart.—Henry lord Grey of Ruthin.
1640 (November) The ſame—Henry Smith, eſq.
1643 (November) Henry Danvers, eſq. on the lord Grey's becoming earl of Kent.

INTERREGNUM.

1654 (September) Thomas Beaumont, eſq.—Thomas Pochin, eſq.
1656 (September) Thomas Beaumont, of Stoughton Grange, eſq.—Francis Hacker, of Okeham, co. Rutland, eſq.—William Quarles, of Enderby, eſq.—And Thomas Pochin, of Barkby Thorpe, eſq.
1658-9 (January) Sir Thomas Beaumont, bart.—Francis Hacker, eſq.

CHARLES II.

1660 Thomas Merry, eſq.—Matthew Babington, eſq.
1661 John lord Ros—George Faunt, eſq. afterwards knighted.
1678-9 The ſame—Bennet lord Sherard [3].
May 1679 Sir John Hartopp [4], bart. on lord Ros's being called to the houſe of peers as baron Manners of Haddon.
Aug. 1679 lord Sherard—Sir John Hartopp, bart.
1680-1 Lord Sherard—Sir John Hartopp [5], bart.

JAMES II.

1685 Hon. John Verney—Sir John Hartopp, bart.

WILLIAM and MARY.

1688-9 Sir Thomas Halford, bart.—The ſame.
1690 Sir Thomas Heſilrige, bart.—The ſame.
1695 George Aſhby, eſq.—Hon. John Verney.
1698 John Wilkins, eſq.—The ſame.
1701 John lord Ros—Bennet lord Sherard.
1702 Hon. John Verney—John Wilkins, eſq.
1705 The ſame—The ſame.
1707 Thomas Aſhby, eſq. inſtead of Verney, dead.
1708 Sir Gilbert Pickering, bart.—Sir Jeffery Palmer, bart.
1710 John marquis of Granby—The ſame.
1711 Sir Thomas Cave, bart. on the marquis of Granby's becoming duke of Rutland.
1713 The ſame—Thomas lord viſcount Tamworth.

[1] On complaint to the Houſe againſt ſir Alexander Cave, then Sheriff, this return was amended ; and ſir George Haſtings took his ſeat in the room of ſir Thomas Beaumont. Journals, vol. I. p. 516.

[2] A petition of ſir Henry Haſtings againſt ſir Thomas Hartopp, the Sheriff, for miſconduct at this election, was preſented to the Houſe, March 25, 1626 ; and the Sheriff was reprimanded by the Speaker, May 4. See Journals, vol. I. pp. 841. 855.

[3] A petition was preſented againſt this election, March 26, 1679, by Robert Johnſon and others, on behalf of ſir John Hartopp ; but the Houſe decided, April 15, in favour of the Sitting Members. See Journals, vol. IX. pp. 577. 596.

[4] A petition againſt this election was preſented, May 9, 1679, by Henry Rayſon, John Seagrave, and John Edwin, gentlemen, on behalf of themſelves and other Freeholders (ibid. p. 616.) ; but the Parliament was diſſolved in leſs than three weeks.

[5] On the 24th of February, in the Caſtle at Leiceſter, the writ for electing the Knights for that Shire being read, the freeholders did unanimouſly chooſe their old members, Benet lord Sherard, and ſir John Hartopp baronet, their repreſentatives to ſerve in the approaching Parliament to meet at Oxford. And after their ſaid choice, the freeholders preſented the following Addreſs to them ; which was audibly read in the Court by the Sheriff, as followeth : " We, the Freeholders of the County of Leiceſter, having choſen you to be our Repreſentatives in the two laſt Parliaments, being highly ſenſible of the care you have taken to ſecure his Majeſty's royal perſon, the Proteſtant Religion, our Liberties and Properties ; as alſo your endeavours further to diſcover and proſecute the horrid Popiſh Plot ſpread over the Realm of England, and others of his Majeſty's dominions ; with your zealous promoting an happy union of all good Proteſtants in this land, not only by good and wholeſome laws for that end, but by repealing thoſe which were deſtructive to it ; and eſpecially for your perſiſting in the excluſion of James Duke of York, and all other Popiſh ſucceſſors, from inheriting the Imperial Crown of England, which we eſteem the only ſecurity under God of his Majeſty's Perſon and Dominions ; likewiſe your vindicating our fundamental right of petitioning his Majeſty for frequent fitting of Parliaments, by your particular marks of diſpleaſure laid upon the oppoſers of it. For all which, and other good laws you were about to make, we give you our moſt hearty thanks. And having now again unanimouſly choſen you for the enſuing Parliament, if you ſhall continue the proſecution of the afore-mentioned abſolutely neceſſary things, we ſhall ſtand by you with our lives and fortunes." Proteſtant Mercury, March 2, 1680-1.

" Harborough, March 2. We had no oppoſition at all in our County againſt ſir John Hartopp ; for we were ſo unanimous and hearty in our choice, that ſir John was not only without any charge at his election, but the expence of his journey hither, and back again to London, was likewiſe diſcharged by the Freeholders : but as ſir John came back to this town, a certain debauched fellow (ſaid to be backed and ſet on by ſome others), who had been drinking hard with ſome gentlemen all Sunday afternoon, and all the night, after ſir John was come into the town, came out with his man, ſwearing and curſing at ſir John ; and when a neighbour of our town rebuked him, the villain diſcharged a piſtol with a brace of bullets at him, which miſſed his head very narrowly, ſwearing—That all the Fanaticks ſhould be ſent to the devil with bullets ere long."—Smith's Proteſtant Intelligencer, March 10, 1680-1.

GEORGE

GEORGE I.

1714 Sir Thomas Cave, bart.—Sir Jeffrey Palmer, bart.
1719 Lord William Manners, on the death of sir Thomas Cave.
1722 The same—Edmund Morris, esq.

GEORGE II.

1727 The same—Sir Clobery Noel, bart.
1733 Ambrose Phillipps, esq. on the death of sir Clobery Noel.
1734 Edward Smith, esq.—Ambrose Phillipps, esq.
1737-8 Harry lord Grey, on the death of Phillipps.
1739 Heneage lord Guernsey, on the lord Grey's becoming earl of Stamford.
1741 Sir Thomas Cave, bart.—Edward Smith, esq.
1747 Edward Smith, esq.—Wrightson Mundy, esq.
1754 The same—Sir Thomas Palmer, bart.

GEORGE III.

1761 Edward Smith, esq.—Sir Thomas Palmer, bart.
1762 Sir Thomas Cave, bart. on death of Smith.

1765 Sir John Palmer, bart. on the death of his father.
1768 Sir Thomas Cave, bart.—Sir John Palmer, bart.
1774 Hon. Thomas Noel.—The same.
1775 John Peach Hungerford, esq. on Mr. Noel's becoming lord viscount Weymouth.
1780 The same—William Pochin, esq.
1784 The same—The same.
1790 Sir Thomas Cave, bart.—The same.
1792 Penn Asheton Curzon, esq. on the death of sir Thomas Cave.
1796 William Pochin, esq.—Penn Asheton Curzon, esq.
1797 George Anthony Legh Keck, esq. on the death of Curzon.
1798 Sir Edmond Cradock-Hartopp, Bart. on the death of Pochin.
1802 George Anthony Legh Keck, esq.—Sir Edmond Cradock-Hartopp, bart.
1806 The same—Lord Robert Manners.
1807 The same—The same.

MEMBERS OF PARLIAMENT FOR THE BOROUGH OF LEICESTER.

EDWARD I.

23. Ralph Norman, Robert de Scarnford.
28. John de Knythtecote, Roger de Glenne.
28. Lincoln. Richard Donnington, Roger de Glenne.
30. London. Ralph Tewe.
33. Richard Soning, Nicholas de Glenne.
34. Henry Palmer, Hugh de Mercer.
35. Carlisle. Ralph Norman, Henry de Carleton.

EDWARD II.

1. Northampton. William Lyndrych, William le Palmer.
2. Henry de Erdington, Richard de Eggalbaston.
4. William de Lyndrych, Peter de Kent.
5. London. William de Lyndrych, Robert de Leycestre.
6. William Clowne, Richard Leverych.
6. Robert Hereward, Nicholas Mercer.
7. Roger de Glenne, John Stocton.
8. William de Benham, Simon de Lyndrych.
8. York. Roger de Pickering, William le Palmer.
12. William de Palmer junior, Thomas Fox.
12. York. Henry Palmer, John Derby.
15. John Derby, Geffrey Staunton.
16. York. Ralph de Burton, Walter Busseby.
19. William Reddington, William Jolly.

EDWARD III.

1. Lincoln. John Fitz-Henry de Leicester, John Geryn.
2. Northampton. Richard Claver, John Geryn.
2. New Sarum. John de Glenne, William Petlyng.
4. Richard de Boynington, Robert de Gryndon.
4. Winchester. John de Leverych, Thomas Dawbenny.
6. Henry Merlyn, Richard de Donnington.
6. } York. { John Leverych, John Fitz-Henry.
7. } York. { Richard Foxton, Richard Clerk.
9. John Leverych, John Querndon.
9. Lincoln. William de Rodington, William le Palmer.
11. Richard de Donnington, Richard Leycester.
11. Richard de Donnington, John Martyn.
11. Council at Westminster. William Warin, Richard de Walcote, Robert le Porter, Robert de Foston.
12. Richard de Donnington, John Quorndon.
12. Council at Northampton. Richard de Donnington, John Turney.
12. York. William Palmer, Thomas Fox.
12. Northampton. John Harding, Robert Bonyng.
13. William Warryn, Thomas Fitz-Robert.
14. Nicholas Radding, William Fitz-Richard.
14. Richard Walcote, William Brad.
14. Ralph Burton, John Blake.
15. John le Clerk, William Donnington.
17. Walter Busseby, William Reddington.
20. Richard Walcoat, William Dunstable.
21. Richard Beby, Alan Sutton.
22. John Recenour, William Wakefield.

¹ See before in this volume, p. 369.

24. }
25. } William Dunstable, Thomas Beby.
28. John Martin, John de Hodynges.
29. William Dunstable, Thomas Beby.
31. John de Petlyng, Thomas de Crom.
34. Thomas Beby, Roger Belgrave.
34. Roger Knighton, Thomas Beby.
36. Richard Knighton, William Burton.
37. John Peterburgh, Roger Kilby.
39. William Tabb, John Stafford.
42. Walter Lynd, Roger de Belgrave.
43. William Burton, William Atte-grene.
45. William Taillard, Richard de Knighton.
45. Council at Winchester. William Taillard.
46. William Atte-grene, Roger Beby.
47. John Stafford, John Peterburgh.
50. Henry de Petlyng, Henry de Clipston.

RICHARD II.

2. William Huntedon, John Stafford.
2. Gloucester. William Humberston, William de Thornton.
3. John Chapman, Andrew Glasewright.
4. John de Stafford, William Ferrour.
5. John Sherote, Richard Boyes.
6. Stephen Chambre, Robert Norton.
7. Roger Belgrave, Richard Braunston.
7. New Sarum. John Stafford, Thomas Wakefield.
8. Geffrey Clark, John Fode.
11. Geffrey de Okham, William de Morton.
12. Cambridge. John Fitz-John Cook, Geffrey Clark.
15. Geffrey Okham, Henry Beby.
20. Thomas Wakefield, Roger Humberston.

HENRY IV.

1. William Bispham, John Churche.
2. John London, Peter Clerke.
8. John Donnington, Roger Goldsmith.
11. John Church, Robert Ernington.
12. Ralph Humberston, Robert Ennington.

HENRY V.

1. Thomas Denton, Ralph Bracy.
2. Leicester¹ (April 30). John Clench, John How.
2. Henry Foster, Robert Ennington.
3. *Cedula amissa.*
7. Gloucester. John Donnington, Roger Goldsmith.
8. John Chirche, John Pykewell.
9. Henry Foster, John Nightyngale.

HENRY VI.

1. John Heket, Henry Salter.
2. John Church, Ralph Brasier.
3. Thomas Walgrave, John Loughburgh.
4. Leicester² (Feb. 18). Ralph Brasier, Thomas Wardgrave.
6. John Church, William Newby.
8. William Newby, John Reynolds.
9. John Pykewell, Adam Kady.

² Ibid. p. 371.

11. William

11. William Pacy, John Loughburgh.
13. John Church, William Pomerey.
15. Cambridge. John Reynold, Thomas Herbert.
20. Thomas Burton, William Newby.
25. Cambridge. Thomas Burton, Adam Rady.
27. William Newby, William Stringer.
28. William Grantham, Adam Rady.
29. Richard Fifher, Thomas Grene.
31. Reading. Will. Wymondefwold, Will. Clerk.
33. Thomas Dalton, William Wigfton.
38. Thomas Green, Robert Shilling.

EDWARD IV.

1. Thomas Grene, John Roberts.
7. Robert Sherringham, John Roberts.
12. Robert Wigfton, John Robardes.
17. Peter Curteys, John Wigfton.
22. Peter Curteys mayor, John Robartes.

[The Writs, Indentures, and Returns, from 17 Edward IV. to 1 Edward VI. are all loft throughout England, except one imperfect Bundle of 33 Henry VIII. However, fix of Leicefter Town in that interval are fupplied, in p. 456, from entries in the Town-books by the Rev. Samuel Carte.]

RICHARD III.

1. John Roberts mayor, Peter Curteys.

HENRY VII.

4. Peter Curteys, Roger Wigfton.
7. Peter Curteys, Robert Croft.
19. Robert Orton, William Wigfton junior.

HENRY VIII.

14. London. William Bolte mayor, Roger Wigfton.
21. At London. . . . .

EDWARD VI.

1. George Swillington, efq. Ralph Skinner, gent.
6. George Swillington, efq. Robert Cotton, gent.

MARY.

1. William Faunt, efq. Thomas Farnham, efq.
1. Oxford, April 22. Francis Farnham recorder, Thomas Jenkinfon mercer.

PHILIP AND MARY.

1 & 2. Oct. 26. Francis Farnham recorder, Hugh Afton.
2 & 3. Francis Farnham.
4 & 5. Robert Breham recorder, Maurice Tyrryll.

ELIZABETH.

1. John Haftings, Robert Breham.
5. Robert Breham, efq. Thomas Brokefby, efq.
13. Thomas Cave, efq. Stephen Hales, efq.
14. Robert Breham, gent. John Stanford, gent.
27. Henry Skipwith, efq. Thomas Johnfon, efq.
28. Henry Skipwith, Thomas Johnfon.
31. John Chippendale, Robert Heyrick.
35. John Stanford, efq. James Clark, efq.
39. George Parkyns, John Stanford junior.
43. George Belgrave, efq. William Heyrick, efq.

JAMES I.

1603. Sir Henry Skipwith, knt. Sir Henry Beaumont, knt.
1605. Sir William Heyrick, knt. on the death of Beaumont.
1610. Sir Henry Rich, knt. on the death of Skipwith.
1614. Sir Francis Leigh, knt. Sir Henry Rich, knt.
1620. Sir Richard Morrifon, knt. Sir William Heyrick, knt.
1621. Sir Humphrey May, knt. William Ive, gent.

CHARLES I.

1625. Sir George Haftings, knt. Sir Humphry May, knt.—Thomas Jermyn, in place of May, who ferved for Lancafter.
1625. Sir Humphrey May, knt. Sir George Haftings, knt.

1628. Sir Humphrey May, knt. Sir John Stanhope, knt.
1640. Simon Every, efq. Thomas Cook, of Gray's Inn, efq.
Nov. 1641. Thomas lord Grey of Groby, Thomas Cook, efq.
1645. Peter Temple, efq. in room of Cook ; who was expelled Sept. 30.

INTERREGNUM.

1654. Sir Arthur Hefilrige, bart. William Stanley, gent. alderman.
1656 (September). The fame.
1658-9 (Jan. 3). The fame.

CHARLES II.

1660. John Grey, efq. Thomas Armfton, efq.
1661. A double return. By the one, John Grey, efq. and Sir William Hartopp, knt. were returned. By the other, Sir William Hartopp, knt. and Sir John Pretyman, knt. and bart. ' The Houfe determined, July 17, that Sir John Pretyman was duly elected.
1678.
1679. } Oxford. { John Grey, efq.
1681.   { Sir Henry Beaumont, knt.

JAMES II.

1685. Sir H. Beaumont, bart. Tho. Babington, efq.

WILLIAM AND MARY.

1688. Lawrence Carter, Thomas Babington, efqrs.
1690. Sir Edward Abney, knt. Lawrence Carter, efq.

WILLIAM III.

1695. Sir Edward Abney, knt. Archdale Palmer, efq.
1698. } Sir William Villiers, bart.
1700. } Laurence Carter junior, efq.
1701. Laurence Carter junior, efq. James Winftanley, efq.

ANNE.

1702.
1705.
1707. { Sir George Beaumont, bart.
1708. { James Winftanley, efq.
1710.
1713.

GEORGE I.

1714. Sir George Beaumont, bart. James Winftanley, efq.
1719. George Noble, efq. on the death of Winftanley.
1722. Sir Laurence Carter, knt. fir George Beaumont, knt.
1726. Thomas Boothby-Skrymfher, efq. on fir Laurence Carter's being made a baron of the Exchequer ².

GEORGE II.

1727. } Sir George Beaumont, bart.
1734. } George Wrighte, efq.
1741.
1747. } George Wrighte, James Wigley, efqrs
1754.

GEORGE III.

1761. George Wrighte, James Wigley, efqrs.
1765. Ant. James Keck, efq. on death of Wigley.
1766. John Darker, efq. on death of Wrighte.
1768. Hon. Booth Grey, Colonel Eyre Coote.
1774. } Hon. Booth Grey, John Darker, efq.
1780. }
1784. Shukburgh Afhby, efq. on death of Darker.
1784. John Macnamara, Charles Lorraine Smith, efqrs.
1790. Tho. Boothby Parkyns³, Sam. Smith, efqrs.
1796. Lord Rancliffe, Samuel Smith, efq.
1800, Thomas Babington, efq. on death of Lord Rancliffe.
1802. } Samuel Smith, efq.
1806. } Thomas Babington, efq.
1807. }

' See vol. III. p. 329.   ² See vol. I. p. 319.
3 Colonel Parkyns, who in 1795 was created Lord Rancliffe, vacated his feat in that year, on a military promotion; but was unanimoufly re-elected.

Lift of all the SHERIFFS [1], to whom the feveral Kings of England, from time to time, committed the Counties of Leicefter and Warwick (for thofe two Counties formerly went under one charge, from HENRY the Second's time, until the 9th of Queen ELIZABETH) continued down to the prefent year 1807.

HENRY II.

1 Geffry Clinton.
2 Robert Fitz-Hugh.
3 Robert Fitz-Hugh.
4 William de Bello-campo, and Robert Fitz-Hardulph.
5 Bertram de Bulmer, and Ralph Baffet.
6 Ralph Baffet.
7 William Baffet, for Ralph his brother.
8 Robert Fitz-Geffrey, and William Baffet.
9 William Baffet.
10 Randolph Glanvill, and William Baffet.
11 William Baffet.
12 William Baffet.
13 William Baffet.
14 Bertram de Verdon.
15 Bertram de Verdon.
16 Bertram de Verdon.
17 Bertram de Verdon.
18 Bertram de Verdon.
19 Bertram de Verdon.
20 Bertram de Verdon.
21 Bertram de Verdon.
22 Bertram de Verdon.
23 Bertram de Verdon.
24 Randolph de Glanvill, and Bertram de Verdon.
25 Randolph de Glanvill, Bertram de Verdon, Arnulph de Barton, and Adam Aldelega.
26 Randolph de Glanvill, Adam de Audley, Bertram de Verdon, and Arnulph de Barton.
27 Arnulph de Barton.
28 Randolph de Glanvill, Bertram de Verdon.
29 Randolph de Glanvill, and Michael Belet.
30 Michael Belet.
31 Michael Belet.

RICHARD I.

1 Michael Belet [2].
2 Hugh Bifhop of Coventry.
3 Hugh Bardolph, and Hugh Clarke.
4 Hugh Bifhop of Coventry, Gilbert de Segrave, and Reginald Baffet.
5 Reginald Baffet.
6 Reginald Baffet, and Gilbert Segrave.
7 Reginald Baffet, William Aubein, and Gilbert Segrave.
8 Reginald Baffet.
9 Reginald Baffet, William Aubein, and Gilbert Segrave.
10 Robert de Harecourt.

JOHN.

1 Reginald Baffet.
2 Robert Harecourt.
3 Robert Harecourt, and Godfrey de Lega.
4 William de Cantelupe, and Robert de Poyer.
5 Robert de Poyer.
6 Hugh Chaucombe.
7 Hugh Chaucombe.
8 Hugh Chaucombe.
9 Hugh Chaucombe.
10 Robert Roppefle.
11 Robert Roppefle.
12 William de Cantelupe, and Robert de Poyer.
13 Robert de Poyer.
14 Robert de Poyer.
15 Robert de Poyer.
16 . . . .
17 Robert de Poyer.

HENRY III.

1 . . . .
2 William de Cantelupe, and Philip de Kniton.
3 Philip de Kniton.
4 Philip de Kniton.
5 William de Cantelupe, William de Luditon.
6 William de Luditon.
7 William de Luditon.
8 John Ruffel, and John Winterborne.
9 Robert Lupus.
10 Robert Lupus.
11 Robert Lupus.
12 William Stuteville, and William Afcellis.
13 William Afcellis.
14 Stephen de Segrave, and William Edmonds.
15 William Edmonds.
16 William Edmonds.
17 Stephen de Segrave, and John de Ripariis.
18 Ralph Bray.
19 Ralph Fitz-Nichol, and Ralph Brewedon.
20 Ralph and William de Erleg.
21 William de Lucy.
22 William de Lucy.
23 Hugh Pollier, and Philip Afcett.
24 Hugh Pollier.
25 Idem.
26 Idem.
27 Idem.
28 Idem.
29 Idem.
30 Idem.
31 Idem.
32 Baldwin Paunton.
33 Idem.
34 Philip Marmion.
35 Idem.
36 Idem.
37 William Maunfel.
38 Idem.
39 Idem.

40 William Maunfel.
41 Alan Swinford.
42 Ankitel Martivaus.
43 Idem.
44 William Bagot.
45 Idem.
46 Sir Henry Mirdac.
47 William Bagot.
48 Idem.
49 Idem.
50 Idem.
51 Idem.
52 Idem.
53 Idem.
54 Idem.
55 Idem.
56 W. Moretyen, and William Bagot.

EDWARD I.

1 William Mortimer.
2 Idem.
3 Idem.
4 William Hameline.
5 Idem.
6 Idem.
7 Thomas de Hafele, and Robert Verdon.
8 Robert Verdon, and Ofbert Bereford.
9 Iidem.
10 Iidem.
11 Iidem.
12 Iidem.
13 Robert Verdon, Ofbert Bereford, and Thomas Farendon.
14 Iidem.
15 Thomas Farendon, and Foulk Lucy.
16 Foulk Lucy.
17 William Bonville.
18 Idem.
19 Stephen Rabuz of Kilworth.
20 Idem.
21 Stephen Rabuz, and William de Caftello.
22 William de Caftello.
23 Idem.
24 Idem.
25 Idem.
26 Idem.
27 John Broughton.
28 Idem.
29 Philip Gayton.
30 Idem.
31 John Deane, and Richard Herchus.
32 Iidem.
33 Iidem.
34 Richard Whitnere.
35 Idem.

EDWARD II.

1 John Dene, and Geffrey Segrave.
2 Richard Herthull.
3 Idem.
4 John Dene.
5 Idem.
6 John Olney.

7 John Olney.
8 William Truffell.
9 Idem.
10 Walter Beauchamp.
11 Walter Beauchamp, and William Neville.
12 Ralph Beler.
13 William Neville.
14 Thomas le Rous.
15 Idem.
16 . . . .
17 Henry Nottingham, Robert Morin, and Oliver Walleis.
18 Iidem.
19 Iidem.

EDWARD III.

1 Roger Aylefbury.
2 Thomas Blancfort.
3 Robert Burdet.
4 Robert Burdet, and Roger de la Zouch.
5 Roger Aylefbury.
6 Idem.
7 Henry Hockley, and Roger de la Zouch.
8 Roger de la Zouch.
9 Idem.
10 Idem.
11 Idem.
12 Idem.
13 Idem.
14 Idem.
15 William Peito.
16 Robert Bereford.
17 John Walleis.
18 Idem.
19 Thomas Beauchamp, Earl of Warwick [3].
20 Idem.
21 Idem.
22 Idem.
23 Idem.
24 Idem.
25 Idem.
26 Idem.
27 Idem.
28 Idem.
29 Idem.
30 Idem.
31 Idem.
32 Idem.
33 Idem.
34 Idem.
35 Idem.
36 Idem.
37 Idem.
38 Idem.
39 Idem.
40 Idem.
41 Thomas Beauchamp.
42 Idem.
43 Idem.
44 John Peach.
45 William Catesby.
46 Richard Herthull.
47 Roger Hillary.
48 John Boivile.
49 John Burdet.
50 William Breton.
51 Richard Herthull.

[1] There is fome (not confiderable) difference between this Lift and that printed by Dr. Fuller in his "Worthies of England;" to ufe whofe words, "I will neither condemn his, nor commend my own; but leave both to the examination of others."

[2] An action was brought, 1 Ric. I. by Roger de Limecote againft the Sheriff of Leicefterfhire, for difpoffeffing him of two knights' fees.

[3] "De Officio Vicecomitis Warr' & Leyc', Commiffio Comiti Warwick, ad terminum vite exercendum per deputatum fuum pro quo refpondere velit." Trin. Record. 18 Edw. III.—"De Ricardo de Stonleye admiffo in Officium Subvicecomitis Warr' & Leyc'." Mich. Record. 19 Edw. III.

RICHARD II.

1 Roger Perewich.
2 Sir John Bermingham.
3 William Flamvile, of Aston Flamvile.
4 Thomas Raleigh.
5 Thomas Bermingham.
6 William Bagot.
7 Idem.
8 John Bermingham.
9 Sir John Calveleigh.
10 John Parker, of Olney.
11 Richard Ashby.
12 William Flamvile.
13 Adomar Litchfield.
14 Robert Harington.
15 John Mallory, of Swinford.
16 Thomas Wodeford, of Sproxton.
17 Thomas Ondeby, of Oadby.
18 Robert Vere.
19 Henry Nevill.
20 Robert Goushull.
21 John Eynesford.
22 Adomar Litchfield.

HENRY IV.

1 Sir John Berkeley[1], of Wymondham, Kt.
2 Sir Henry Nevill, Kt.
3 Sir Alured Truffell, Kt.
4 John Blaket, of Noseley, Esq.
5 Idem.
6 Sir John Berkeley, Kt.
7 Thomas Lucy.
8 John Pare.
9 Sir Henry Nevill, Kt.
10 William Brokesby.
11 Robert Castell.
12 Bartholom. Brokesby.

HENRY V.

1 Thomas Crew, Esq.
2 Sir Rich. Hastings, Knt.
3 Sir Thomas Burdet, of Newton-Burdet, Kt.
4 John Malory.
5 William Bishopeston.
6 John Salveyn.
7 Bartholom. Brokesby.
8 Thomas Maureward, of Cold Overton, Esq.

HENRY VI.

1 Sir Rich. Hastings, Kt.
2 Humphrey Stafford, of Grafton, Esq.
3 John Malory.
4 Richard Clodesale.
5 Sir Rich. Hastings, Kt.
6 Thomas Stanley.
7 William Peyto.
8 Nicholas Rugley.
9 Humphrey Stafford.
10 Sir W. Mountfort, Kt.
11 Sir Rich. Hastings, Kt.
12 Thomas Foulethurst.
13 Thomas Ardington.
14 William Lucy.
15 Sir William Peyto, Kt.
16 Robert Ardern.
17 Sir Humphrey Stafford, of Grafton, Knt.
18 Lawrence Berkeley.
19 Thomas Ashby, of Lowesby, Esq.
20 William Mountford.
21 William Bermingham, and Lawrence Sherard, Esq.
22 Lawrence Sherard.
23 Robert Harcourt, of Market Bosworth.
24 Sir Tho. Erdington, of Burrow, Knt.
25 Thomas Everingham.
26 Thomas Porter and Will. Purefoy, Esqrs.
27 William Purefoy, of Fenny Drayton, Esq.
28 William Lucy.
29 William Mountford.
30 Sir Robert Moton, of Peckleton, Knt.
31 Sir William Bermingham, Kt.
32 Sir Laurence Hastings, of Kirby, Knt.
33 Thomas Berkley.
34 William Hastings.
35 Thomas Walsh, of Wanlip, Esq.
36 Thomas Maston, Esq.
37 Henry Filongley, Esq.
38 Sir Edmund Mountford.

EDWARD IV.

1 Thomas Ferrers, Esq.
2 John Grevill, Esq.
3 Idem.
4 Sir W. Harcourt, Kt.
5 John Hugford, Esq.
6 Thomas Throkmorton, Esq.
7 Ralph Woodford, of Knipton.
8 Sir Edw. Raleigh, Kt.
9 Sir Thomas Ferrers.
10 Sir John Grevill, Kt.
11 Sir Simon Mountford.
12 William Moton, of Peckleton, Esq.
13 John Hugford, Esq.[2]
14 Sir John Grevill, Kt.
15 William Lucy, Esq.
16 Sir Will. Truffell, Kt.
17 John Branfitz.
18 Sir John Grevill, Kt.
19 Thomas Poultney, of Misterton, Esq.
20 Richard Boughton, of Lawford, co. Warw.
21 Thomas Cocksey.
22 Everard Feilding, of Newnham, Esq.

RICHARD III.

1 Thomas Entwifell.
2 Humphrey Beaufort.
3 Richard Broughton.
4 Robert Throkmorton.

HENRY VII.

1 John Digby, Esq.
2 Henry Lisle.
3 Robert Throgmorton, Esq.
4 Sir William Lucy, Kt.
5 Thos. Brereton, Esq.
6 John Villers, of Brokesby, Esq.
7 Robert Throgmorton, Esq.
8 Sir Thomas Poultney, of Misterton, Knt.
9 Sir Ralph Shirley, of Staunton Harold, Kt.
10 John Villers, Esq.
11 Sir Edward Raleigh, Knt.
12 Will. Brokesby, Esq.
13 Thomas Nevill, Esq.
14 Sir Richard Pudsey, Knt.
15 John Villers, Esq.
16 Thomas Hesilrige, of Noseley, Esq.
17 Edwd. Belknap, Esq.
18 Nich. Malory, Esq.
19 Henry Lisle.
20 Nicholas Brome, Esq.
21 Sir Henry Willoughby, Kt.
22 Sir Edw. Raleigh, Kt.
23 Thomas Truffell, Esq.
24 Will. Skeffington, of Skeffington, Esq.

HENRY VIII.

1 Simon Digby, Esq.
2 Sir John Afton, Kt.
3 Maurice Berkeley, Esq.
4 William Turpin, of Knaptoft, Esq.
5 Sir Edw. Ferrers, Kt.
6 Sir John Digby, Kt.
7 Sir Will. Skeffington.
8 Sir Maurice Berkeley.
9 Simon Digby, Esq.
10 Sir Edw. Ferrers, Knt.
11 Sir Hen. Willoughby.
12 Everard Digby, Esq.
13 Sir Will. Skeffington.
14 William Browne, Esq.
15 Edwd. Conway, Esq.
16 Sir Thomas Lucy, Kt.
17 Sir Hen. Willoughby.
18 Sir Geo. Throgmorton.
19 Sir Tho. Poultney, of Misterton, Knt.
20 Roger Ratcliffe, Kt.
21 Richard Perney, Esq.
22 Christoph. Villers, Esq.
23 Sir John Villers, Kt.
24 John Harrington, Esq.
25 John Audley, Esq.
26 Reginald Digby, Esq.
27 Will. Boughton, Esq.
28 Walter Smith, Esq.
29 Sir John Villers, Kt.
30 Thomas Nevill, Esq.
31 John Digby, Esq.
32 Richard Catesby, Esq.
33 Roger Wigston, Esq.
34 Sir Foulk Grevill, Kt.
35 Sir Geo. Throgmorton.
36 Reginald Digby, Esq.
37 Sir Rich. Catesby, Kt.
38 Francis Poultney and William Lee, Esqrs.

EDWARD VI.

1 Sir Foulk Grevill, Kt.
2 Sir Ambrose Cave, Kt.
3 Sir Rich. Munnay, Kt.
4 Sir Edw. Grevill, Kt.
5 William Wigston, Esq.
6 Sir Thos. Nevill, Kt.

PHILIP and MARY.

Ph. M.
1   Sir Rob. Throgmorton, Kt.
1   2 Sir Tho. Hastings.
2   3 Sir Ed. Grevill, Kt.
3   4 Fran. Shirley, Esq.
4   5 Sir Fran. Wigston.
5   6 Brian Cave, Esq.

ELIZABETH.

1 Thomas Lucy, Esq.
2 William Skeffington, Esq.
3 Sir Thos. Nevill, Kt.
4 Sir Rich. Verney, Kt.
5 John Fisher, Esq.
6 William Devereux, Esq.
7 Sir George Turpin, of Knaptoft, Knt.
8 Francis Smith, of Ashby Folvile, Esq.

[Here the Two Counties were divided; and have ever since had separate Sheriffs.]

[1] "De onerando Johannem de Berkeley, Vicecomitem, de Auro Regine in manum Regis capto." Mich. Record. 2 Hen. IV. Rot. 19.

[2] Governor of Warwick castle, steward of the town, and surveyor of the parks and chaces in that county. He died in 1495; and was buried in the collegiate church of St. Mary in Warwick. See his Epitaph, and a Pedigree of the Hugford family, in Mr. Gough's Sepulchral Monuments, vol. II. p. 326.

SHERIFFS OF LEICESTERSHIRE ONLY.

ELIZABETH.
9 George Sherard, of Stapleford, Efq.
10 Henry Poole, Efq.
11 Brian Cave, of Ingarfby, Efq.
12 Sir James Harington.
13 Sir George Haftings, Knt.
14 Francis Haftings, Efq.
15 Edward Leigh, of Shawell, Efq.
16 Sir George Turpin, of Knaptoft, Knt.
17 Roger Villiers, of Brokefby, Efq.
18 Thomas Skeffington, Efq.
19 Nicholas Beaumont, of Cole Orton, Efq.
20 Thomas Afhby, of Quenby, Efq.
21 Thomas Cave, of Stanford Hall, Efq.
22 Francis Haftings, Efq,
23 George Purefoy, of Drayton, Efq.
24 Brian Cave, of Ingarfby, Efq.
25 Andrew Noel, of Great Dalby, Efq.
26 Henry Turvile, of Afton Flamvile, Efq.
27 William Turpin, of Knaptoft, Efq.
28 Anthony Faunt, of Fofton, Efq.
29 William Cave, of Pickwell, Efq.
30 Thomas Skeffington, of Belgrave, Efq.
31 Edward Turvile, of Thurlefton, Efq.
32 George Purefoy, of Fenny Drayton, Efq.
33 George Villiers, of Brokefby, Efq.
34 Thomas Cave, of Stanford Hall, Efq.
35 William Turpin, of Knaptoft, Efq.
36 Henry Beaumont, of Cole Orton, Efq.
37 William Cave, of Pickwell, Efq.
38 Henry Cave, of Barrow, Efq.
39 William Skipwith, of Cotes, Efq.
40 William Digby, of Welby, Efq.
41 Thomas Skeffington, of Skeffington, Efq.
42 Roger Smith, of Withcote, Efq.
43 George Afhby, of Quenby, Efq.
44 Thomas Humphreys, of Swebfton, Efq.

JAMES I.
1 Sir William Faunt, of Fofton, Knt.
2 William Noel, of Wellefborough, Efq.
3 Sir Bafil Brooke, of Lubbenham, Knt.
4 Sir Thomas Nevile, of Holt, Knt.
5 Sir Henry Haftings, of Leicefter, Knt.
6 William Villiers, of Brokefby, Efq.
7 John Plumbe, of Marfton, Efq.
8 Sir Thomas Beaumont, of Cole-Orton, Knt.
9 Sir Brian Cave, of Ingarfby, Knt.
10 Sir Thomas Hefilrige, of Nofeley, Knt.
11 Thomas Staveley, of Langton, Efq.
12 Sir Wolftan Dixie, of Bofworth, Knt.
13 Sir William Faunt, of Fofton, Knt.
14 Sir William Halford, of Welham, Knt.
15 Edward Hartopp, of Buckminfter, Efq.
16 William Jerveis, of Peatling, Efq. died June 9, 1618.
   Sir William Roberts[1], of Sutton Cheynell, Knt.
   appointed for the remainder of the year.
17 John Cave, of Pickwell, Efq.
18 Sir Alexander Cave, of Bagrave, Knt.
19 Richard Halford, of Wiftow, Efq.
20 George Bennet, of Welby, Efq.

21 Sir John Bale, of Carleton, Knt.
22 Sir Henry Shirley, of Staunton Harold, Knt.

CHARLES I.
1 Sir Thomas Hartopp, of Burton Lazars, Knt.
2 N. Lacy, of Melton Mowbray, Efq.
3 George Afhby, of Quenby, Efq.
4 Sir Erafmus de la Fontaine, of Kirkby Beler, Knt.
5 William Wollafton, of Shenton, Efq.
6 John Bainbridge, of Lockington, Efq.
7 Gregory Brokefby, of Birftall, Efq.
8 John St. John, of Cold Overton, Efq.
9 Sir Thomas Burton, of Stokerfton, Bart.
10 Francis Saunders, of Shangton, Efq.
11 John Poultney, of Mifterton, Efq.
12 Sir Henry Skipwith, of Cotes, Bart.
13 Sir Richard Roberts, of Thorp Langton, Knt.
14 John Whatton, of the Newark, Leicefter, Efq.
15 William Halford, of Welham, Efq.
16 John Pate, of Sifonby, Efq.
17 Archdale Palmer, of Wanlip, Efq. ; difplaced by the King[2].
18 Henry Haftings, Efq. fecond fon of the Earl of Huntingdon, appointed by the King July 16, 1642.
19 Peter Temple[3], Efq. appointed by the Parliament, Dec. 30, 1643.
20 Sir John Pate[4], of Sifonby, Bart. appointed by the King; and Arthur Staveley, of Weft Langton, Efq. by the Parliament[5], Feb. 13; 1644-5[6].
21 John Stafford, Efq. Oct. 25, 1645.
22 William Hewett[7], of Great Stretton, Efq. Dec. 1, 1646.
23 George Pochin[8], of Barkby, Efq. Nov. 17, 1647.
24 William Bainbridge[9], of Lockington, Efq. Nov. 23, 1648.

CHARLES II.
1 Arthur Staveley[10], of Weft Langton, Efq. Nov. 7, 1649.
2 William Noel, of Kirkby Malory, Efq.
3 Sir Thomas Cave junior, of Stanford, Knt.
4 Mark Hyland, of Calthorpe, Efq. difcharged; and in his room Abel Burton, of Keythorpe, Efq. who was alfo difcharged; and in his room William Quarles, Efq.
5 John Pretyman[11], of Horninghold, Efq. Nov. 10, 1653.
6 Archdale Palmer[12], of Wanlip, Efq. November 1654.
7 Henry Smith[13], Efq. November 1655.
8 William Bradgate[13], of Little Peatling, Efq. November 1656.
9 Richard Bennett[13], of Welby, Efq. 1657.
10 Henry Hudfon[13], of Melton Mowbray, Efq. 1658.
11 George Faunt[14], of Fofton, Efq. 1659.
12 Richard Roberts, of Thorpe Langton, Efq.
13 Sir Wolftan Dixie, of Market Bofworth, Bart.
14 Sir Thomas Halford, of Wiftow, Bart.
15 Thomas Caldecote, of Calthorpe, Efq.
16 . . . . 1664.
17 Sir Edward Smith, of Edmondthorpe, Bart.

[1] Knighted at Belvoir, Aug. 6, 1619.
[2] Aug. 23, 1642, a Committee was appointed by the Houfe of Commons, to confider of the King's difplacing and new-placing Sheriffs of Counties. Journals, vol. II. p. 734.—Nov. 21. The proper officers were enjoined, not to make out any commiffion or patent for electing of Sheriffs, or *dedimus poteftatem* for fwearing of Sheriffs, or writs for difcharge of old Sheriffs, unlefs by order of the Houfe. Ibid. p. 857.—" The king nominated fheriffs; but they were not allowed by the parliament to be fworn, as not being recommended by the judges; and becaufe they were uniformly difaffected to the parliament, and the prefent good of the ftate." England's Memorable Accident, Tuefday, Nov. 22, 1642.—Dec. 1. The Houfe ordered copies to be fent in of the new commiffions to the new Sheriffs folely nominated by his Majefty. Journals, vol. II. p. 870.
[3] Journals, vol. III. p. 354.—Aug. 2, 1644, he had a difpenfation from that part of his oath which relates to not ftirring out of the county; and Sept 24, had liberty granted him to come to London. Ibid. pp. 576. 638.
[4] He raifed the *poffe comitatus* for the king againft the parliament. Journals, vol. III. p. 650.
[5] Nov. 13, 1644. The feveral members for counties were directed to nominate three perfons fit for fheriff for each county; of whom one to be elected by the Houfe. Journals, vol. III. p. 694.
[6] Journals, vol. IV. p. 47.   [7] Ibid. p. 732.   [8] Ibid. vol. V. p. 360.   [9] Ibid. vol. VI. p. 85.
[10] Ibid. p. 319. He had liberty, Jan. 28, 1649-50, to go out of the county upon his urgent affairs, as his occafions fhould require. Ibid. p. 350.
[11] Ibid. vol. VII. p. 548. He was afterwards of Lodington; where fee an account of him, vol. III. p. 329.
[12] " Bis vicecomes." See his and his fon's epitaphs at Wanlip, vol. III. p 1099.   [13] Nominated by the lord protector.
[14] Ordered into cuftody Feb. 7, and difcharged Feb. 22. Journals, vol. VII. pp. 836. 848.

18 George

18 George Afhby, of Quenby, Efq.
19 Thomas Boothby, of Tooley Park, Efq.
20 Sir Thomas Beaumont, of Stoughton Grange, Bart.
21 Thomas Pochin, of Barkby, Efq.
22 Sir John Hartopp, of Freathfby, Bart.
23 Sir William Wael, Knt.
24 William Wollafton, of Shenton, Efq.
   William Franke, of the Newark, Efq.
26 William Boothby, of Marfton, Efq.
27 William Cole, of Laughton, Efq.
28 Walter Ruding, of Weftcotes, Efq.
29 Thomas Babington, of Rothley Temple, Efq.
30 Richard Browne, of Burrow, Efq.
31 St. John Bennet, of Welby, Efq.
32 Jeremiah Dove, Efq.
33 Richard Roberts, of Thorpe Langton, Efq.
34 John Wilfon, of Keythorpe, Efq.
35 Samuel Cotton, Efq.
36 John [1] Wilfon, Efq.

JAMES II.

1 Thomas Wilfon [2], Efq.
2 Sir Thomas Hefilrige, of Nofeley, Bart.
3 William Palmer, Efq.
4 George Afhby, of Quenby, Efq.

WILLIAM and MARY.

1 William Whaley, of Norton, Efq.
2 George Moreton, Efq.
3 Matthew Symonds, Efq.
4 St. John Bennet, of Welby, Efq.
5 John Wilkins, of Raunfton, Efq.
6 George Pochin, of Barkby, Efq.
7 Richard Cheflyn, of Langley, Efq.
8 Ifaac Wollafton, of Shenton, Efq.
9 Nathanael Gold, Efq.
10 John Bainbridge, of Lockington, Efq.
11 Thomas Skeffington, of Skeffington, Efq.
12 George Hewett, of Great Stretton, Efq.
13 Thomas Charnell, of Snarefton, Efq.

ANNE.

1 James Armfton, of Burbach, Efq.
2 Sir Edward Wigley, of Scraptoft, Knt.
3 Sir Gilbert Pickering, of Langton, Bart.
4 Charles Morris, of Lodington, Efq.
5 Clifton Packe, of Preftwould, Efq.
6 Thomas Boothby, of Marfton, Efq.
7 William Hartopp, of Little Dalby, Efq.
8 George Burton, of Stokerfton, Efq.
9 Thomas Pochin, of Barkby, Efq.
10 Henry Tate, of Ulvefcroft, Efq.
11 Thomas Grefley, of Nether Seile, Efq.
12 Francis Mundy, of Ofbafton, Efq.

GEORGE I.

1 Sir John Meres, of Kirkby Beler, Knt.
2 Sir Robert Hefilrige, of Nofeley, Bart.
3 Sir Clobery Noel, of Kirkby Malory, Bart.
4 Thomas Smith, of Gaddefby, Efq.
5 John Bakewell fenior, of Normanton, Efq.
6 William Hewett, of Great Stretton, Efq.
7 Jofeph Danvers, of Swithland, Efq.
8 Thomas Hartopp, of Quorndon, Efq.
9 Francis Edwards, of Welham, Efq.
10 Richard Smith, of Enderby, Efq.
11 John Bletfoe, Efq.
12 Edward Dawfon, of Long Whatton, Efq.
13 Sir Wolftan Dixie, of Market Bofworth, Bart.

GEORGE II.

1 George Moore, of Appleby, Efq.
2 John Symonds, Efq.
3 William Wells, of Burbach, Efq.
4 Richard Greene, of Rollefton, Efq.
5 William Bainbridge, of Lockington, Efq.
6 Waring Afhby, of Quenby, Efq.
7 Edmond Cradock, of Leicefter, Efq.
8 Robert Wilfon, of Keythorpe, Efq.

9 Charles Bofville, of Ulvefcroft, Efq.
10 Timothy St. Nicholas, of Burbach, Efq.
11 John Payne, of Dunton Baffet, Efq.
12 John Turner, Efq.
13 William Newland, Efq.
14 Peter Wyche, of Godeby Marwood, Efq.
15 John Wright, of Lubbenham, Efq.
16 James Wilfon, of Keythorpe, Efq.
17 John Ayre, of Gaddefby, Efq.
18 Thomas Marriott, of Asfordby, Efq.
19 Edmund Morris, of Lodington, Efq.
20 John Grundy, of Little Wigfton, Efq.
21 James Winftanley, of Braunfton, Efq.
22 Philip Bainbridge, of Lockington, Efq.
23 Thomas Babington, of Rothley Temple, Efq.
24 Samuel Phillipps, of Garendon, Efq.
25 Thomas Boothby junior, of Marfton, Efq.
26 William Herrick, of Beaumanor, Efq.
27 John Edwin, of Bagrave, Efq.
28 Sir John Danvers, of Swithland, Bart.
29 William Pochin, of Barkby, Efq.
30 Jonathan Grundy, of Newhall Park, Efq.
31 Shukburgh Afhby, of Blaby, Efq.
32 Edward Palmer, of Withcote, Efq.
33 Sir William Halford, of Wiftow, Bart.

GEORGE III.

1 Sir George Beaumont, of Cole Orton, Bart.
2 Calverley Bewicke, of Hallaton, Efq.
3 Edward-William Hartopp, of Little Dalby, Efq.
4 John Wefton, of Godeby, Efq.
5 A. Saunders, of Stoke Golding, Efq.
6 Charles-James Packe, of Preftwould, Efq.
7 Jofeph Cradock, of Gumley, Efq.
8 Edward Dawfon, of Long Whatton, Efq.
9 Sir Charles Halford, of Wiftow, Bart.
10 Charles Hefilrige, of Nofeley, Efq.
11 Lebbeus Humfrey, of Kibworth, Efq.
12 John-Peach Hungerford, of Dingley, co. Northampton, Efq.
13 William-Shalcrofs Mafon, of Burton on the Wolds, Efq.
14 Clement Winftanley, of Braunfton, Efq.
15 John Simpfon, of Laund Abbey, Efq.
16 Robert Haymes, of Glen, Efq.
17 Robert Abney, of Lindley, Efq.
18 William Hurft, of Hinckley, Efq.
19 Charles Morris, of Lodington, Efq.
20 Sir Thomas Cave, of Stanford, Bart.; on his death, in June, Thomas Babington, of Rothley Temple, Efq. for the remainder of the year.
21 Edmond Cradock-Hartopp, of Newbold, Efq.
22 Sir John Palmer, of Carleton Curlieu, Bart.
23 Charles Lorraine-Smith, of Enderby, Efq.
24 Charles-Grave Hudfon, of Wanlip, Efq.
25 William Vann, of Belgrave, Efq.
26 William Herrick, of Beaumanor, Efq.
27 John Goodacre, of Little Afhby, Efq.
28 John Clarke, of Great Wigfton, Efq.
29 Jofias Cockfhutt, of Ofbafton, Efq.
30 Edward Hartopp-Wigley, of Little Dalby, Efq.
31 John Frewen-Turner, of Cold Overton, Efq.
32 Richard-Spooner Jaques, of Burbach, Efq.
33 John Noon, of Burton on the Wolds, Efq.
34 George Moore, of Appleby, Efq.
35 Edward Muxloe, of Pickwell, Efq.
36 James Richards, of Afhby de la Zouch, Efq.
37 Samuel-Bracebridge Abney, of Lindley, Efq.
38 René Payne, of Dunton Baffet, Efq.
39 Henry Greene, of Rollefton, Efq.
40 Edward Manners, of Godeby-Marwood, Efq.
41 Thomas March-Phillipps, of Garendon, Efq.
42 John Pares, of the Newark, Leicefter, Efq.
43 James Vann, of Belgrave, Efq.
44 Henry Otway, of Stanford Hall, Efq.
45 George Payne, of Dunton Baffet, Efq.
46 F. W. Woolafton, of Shenton, Efq.
47 Edward Dawfon, of Whatton Houfe, Efq.

---

[1] *Thomas* Wilfon, in the Gazette of Nov. 24, 1684; but *John* in a fubfequent Gazette, Jan. 8, 1684-5.
[2] Gazette, Nov. 30, 1685.

ARCHDEACONS of LEICESTER[1].

This Dignity confifts only in the perquifites of its office; and pays now to the Bifhop, for exercifing of ecclefiaftical jurifdiction, annually, 22*l*. The amount of the Firft Fruits is 87*l*. 19*s*. 2*d*.

Ralph is the firft Archdeacon whom I find noticed. He was inftituted by Bifhop Remigius in 1092.

Godfrey fucceeded about 1100. The next was Walter, who held it about 1120.

Robert de Querceto, or Chefneto, was from this dignity made Bifhop of Lincoln in 1147[2]. He appeared frequently in arms during the contefts between King Stephen and Matilda[3]. In Stow's Survey of London, he is called Robert de Curars[4].

Hugh[5] held it 1151; as did

Baldric de Sigillo, 1158 and 1189[6].

Roger[7] de Rolvefton, 1191. In 1194, he was concerned in regulating certain matters at York. Epiftola Cæleftini Papæ contra Gaufridum Ebor. Archiepifcopum. Haimoni decano Lincolnie & Rogero archidiacono Leiceftrie, &c.[8]; and was one of the delegates appointed to arbitrate between Abp. Hubert and the Monks of Chriftchurch, about the founding of a College of Canons at Lambeth[9]. He was made Dean of Lincoln 1195. Hoveden gives a relation of the appearance, in a dieam, of Hugo Bp. of Lincoln to Dean Roger, fifteen days after the death of that prelate.

William about 1199; fo that he was in the *fede vacante*. Burton, p. 96; but was foon gone.

C. *fede vacante* alfo, about 1207; Burton, pp. 98, 248, 278. He is omitted by Willis.

Reginald occurs in 1211.

Raymond de Bleis in 1212, 1214, and 1222; and William Glamdi[10], 1226 and 1228.

The celebrated Robert Groffetefte[11], who refigned it in 1231 for the archdeaconry of Chefter; and was made Bp. of Lincoln in 1230.

William de Drayton, collated 1231.

John de Bafing, or Bafingftoke[12], where he was born, the famous Author of that name, was firft of Oxford, then went to feveral foreign univerfities[13]; occurs Archdeacon of Leicefter 1238; Archdeacon of Chefter 1247, and held it with that of Leicefter, though this was not agreeable to canon.

Solomon fucceeded in 1252; and held it in 1254.

Roger de Saxenherft about 1274. He died in 1294.

Roger de Martival[14], S. T. P. fon of fir Anketin de Martival, was collated Jan. 16, 1294. He and his father founded the college of Nofeley[15] in this county in 1273. He was Archdeacon of Huntingdon 1288, and Chancellor of Oxford; occurs Archdeacon Jan. 10, 1307[16]; and was made Dean of Lincoln in 1310; Bp. of Salifbury 1315; and died March 14, 1329.

Raymond de Fargis; admitted Prebendary of Ketton 1308[17]; inftituted Archdeacon Oct. 31, 1310. In his time the following fingular requeft was made to the Clergy of this Diocefe:

" Litera Epifcopi, pro aliquo fubfidio fibi conceffo.

" Henricus[18], permiffione divinâ, Lincolnienfis epifcopus, dilectis in Chrifti filiis, clero archidiaconatûs

Leyceftrenfis, noftre diœcefis, ac fingulis perfonis ejufdem, falutem, cum abundantiâ gratie, & benedictione Salvatoris. Nuper vobis (pro diverfis negotiis, ex parte noftrâ, vobis exponendis apud Leyceftriam convocatis, & expofitâ inter cetera vobis in communi per dilectos filios magiftros Richardum de Stratton, canonicum ecclefie noftre Lincolnienfis, & Johannem de Aylefton, rectorem ecclefie de Denton, nuncios noftros ad vos deftinatos, indigentiâ nobis (abfque culpâ noftrâ) notorie imminente; iidem magifter Richardus & Johannes vos (ex parte noftrâ) humiliter requifiverunt & rogârunt, ut noftre indigentie hujufmodi fubvenire dignaremini (cum ad hoc fubfit manifefta & rationabilis caufa, que vos latere nequit) de aliquo auxilio moderato; & vos qui tunc prefentes extitiftis, pro majori parte, oftendentes fingillatim vos in hâc nobis benevolos, ad impendendum nobis moderatum auxilium hujufmodi, & paratos, ficùt dicti nuncii nobis retulerunt (de quo grates vobis referimus quas valemus): Propter tamen abfentiam quamplurium ejufdem cleri, qui tunc non interfuerant, vos eifdem nunciis noftris iterum dare refponfum in communi non decere afferuiftis, dictis abfentibus inconfultis: Nos igitur, conjicientes & prefumentes (ex premiffis) veftre benevolentie exuberantiam non minùs fervere nos erga quam ceterorum noftre diœcefis, qui (fue gratie) nobis fubvenire longiflue, tam liberaliter concefferunt; veftram caritatem exoramus, quatenus veftrum gratum refponfum ad premiffa dilectis nobis magiftris Hugoni de Walmesford, & . . . . . Officiali Archidiaconi Leyceftrenfis, vel uni eorum, nomine noftro; ita quòd (fi non in communi hoc volueritis) finguli veftrûm fingulariter dare velitis; ac voluntatem veftram (quoad premiffa in omnibus) eifdem, vel eorum uni, dignemini plenitèr intimare, ut fic de zelo veftro erga nos certiùs inftrui valeamus. Diu & feliciter in Domino vobis & veftrûm fingulis falus vigeat, & augmentum crefcat gratie falutaris. Datum apud Lafford, pridie calendar' Januarii, anno Domini millefimo trecentefimo vicefimo quarto[19]."

Dominus Reymundus Sancte Marie, nove dioc' cardinalis, fuit archidiaconus Leyc' 10 kal' Maii, 1340[20]. This Raymond died in 1346.

Henry de Chaddefden, Archdeacon of Stow 1338; admitted Archdeacon March 14, 1346; prebendary of Saudiacre, Lichfield cathedral, Aug. 10, 1350[21]; and was prebendary of St. Martin's, Lincoln, which he exchanged for a portion of Waddefden church, Bucks[22]. He died in 1354; and was buried in St. Paul's cathedral, with this infcription:

" Orate pro anima Henrici de Chaddefden, Archidiaconi Leiceftriæ, qui quidem Henricus obiit 8° Maii, 1354."

In 1355, a patent paffed for the founding a chantry, confifting of a warden and two chaplains, in the church of Chaddefden, co. Derby, for the foul of Henry Chaddefden, late Archdeacon of Leicefter[23].

---

[1] " This Archdeaconry contains 200 parifhes, out of which were ejected by the parliament fequeftrators, in 1641 and afterwards, 58 minifters; and in 1662, by the Bartholomew act, 32 or thereabouts. All the firft fet were exemplarily good, fucceeded by many of a different caft, as players, broken attornies, &c.; yet, in lefs than 20 years, when thefe were to be turned out, they were all of the firft water." Sir T. Cave, MS.

[2] See an account of his benefactions in Stukeley, Palæogr. N° ii. p. 112.

[3] Lyttelton's Life of Henry II. 8vo. vol. II. p. 142. [4] Edit. 1638, p. 824.

[5] He gave to the Church Library at Lincoln four MSS. which ftill remain there. In one of them, called " Decreta Gratiani, & Hegefygas," is written, " Ex dono Hugonis archidiaconi Leyceftrie." Haimo the Chancellor had then the care of the Library.   [6] Appendix to vol. I. p. 133.   [7] Willis, p. 112, calls him *Robert*.

[8] Vide Scriptores poft Bedam, Hoveden, fol. 427. b.; 458. a.; 462. b.

[9] Hiftory of that Parifh, p. 16.   [10] See Appendix to vol. I. p. 93.

[11] To the merits of this excellent Prelate ample juftice has been done, in his Life by the late Rev. Dr. Pegge.

[12] A fhort account of this learned man may be feen in Dr. Pegge's Life of Groffetefte.

[13] Tanner, Bibliotheca Britannica, p. 430. See alfo Fabricius, Cod. Apoc. vol. III. p. 516.

[14] Not Martiwall, as in Oughton, Ordo Judic. vol. II. p. 92.   [15] See vol. II. p. 739.

[16] Reg. Haymo de Hethe, Epifc. Roff. fol. 110.   [17] Browne Willis, Survey, vol. II. p. 191.

[18] Of Henry de Burgerfh, Bifhop of Lincoln 1320—1343, fee Willis, vol. II. p. 52. He was alfo lord chancellor and lord treafurer. He was a covetous man, a great oppofer of the king, and an inftrument of his depofition.

[19] Oughton, Ordo Judiciorum, vol. II. p. 7. Act. VII.; ex Regift. Burgh. Mem. fub Tit. Mem. fol. 136.

[20] Reg. Burwefh.   [21] Willis, vol. I. p. 460.

[22] Willis, vol. II. p. 217. His benefactions may be feen in Dugdale's Hiftory of St. Paul's, p. 35.

[23] Tanner's Notitia, fol. 236. in notis.

William Donne [1], LL. D. was collated May 12, 1354; and in 1373 received from the Knights Hofpitallers of Rothley 2l. 13s. 4d. as an annual rent, pro jurifdictione infra parochiam de Rotheley [2].

On Dr. Donne's quitting this archdeaconry [3], the King granted it to

John de Bottlefham, 1385. He was admitted prebendary of Crackpole, St. Mary, Oct. 4, 1386 [4]; of Milton Eccles, Jan. 18, 1389 [5]; and of Brampton Jan. 15, 1393 [6].

The Pope thinking proper to confer this archdeaconry on Porcelinus de Urfinis, a Cardinal Prieft, Bottlefham gave up his pretenfions, and obtained a prebend at York; was made in 1410 Bifhop of Rochefter; and was alfo Mafter of St. Peter's college, Cambridge.

Porcelinus held this archdeaconry till 1392; when, being difplaced,

John Elvet was admitted to it, on the King's donation, Aug. 4, 1392. He was admitted prebendary of Ewithington, Hereford, June 11, 1395; of South Newbald, York, Dec. 5, 1395; and of Leighton Bifard in 1400 [7]. He died in 1404, being then a prebendary alfo of Sarum and Lincoln.

Richard Elvet fucceeded; and in 1408 a matter in difpute concerning jurifdiction, between him and Philip de Repyngdon Bp. of Lincoln, was referred to arbitration [8]. Oct. 9, 1424, he exchanged a prebend in the church of Lincoln with John Leghburne, rector of Seggesfelde, co. Durham [9]. The time of his death does not appear; but he was fucceeded by

Thomas Barnefley, who had been prebendary of St. Margaret's 1421. He was alfo dean of the college of Stoke Clare, co. Suffolk, the ftatutes of which he formed [10], and where he was buried. He held that dignity 40 years, as he did this till his death in 1454; when

Richard Ewen is faid to be collated to it, Aug. 14, 1454. He was removed to the archdeaconry of Lincoln in 1455; and was fucceeded by

William Wytham, LL. D. who had been archdeacon of Stow in 1454. He died July 16, 1472; and was buried in Wells cathedral, where he was dean, with this epitaph, long fince defaced:

Infignis legum doctor, decus atque decanus
Ecclefiæ gemma; cujus hic una fuit,
Altera Leiftrenfis fimul archidiaconus illuc
Willielmus Witham nobilis hic recubat.
Dapfilis ac hilaris fuit hofpitio, miferorum
Solamen, culto juftitiæ requies.
Juftorum Sp . . . . bonitatis tutor, et auctor
Pacis, confilii fons, pugil ecclefiæ.
Hunc mors eripuit vitam tribuens morienti
Umbra mi . . . . at mors modo vita mort
Anno milleno C. quater LX duodeno
In fetodeno clauditur hic tumulo."

Roger Rotheram, LL. D. fucceeded in 1472, in which year he occurs alfo as archdeacon of Rochefter, which he probably then refigned, though Mr. Le Neve places his inftalment not till Nov. 11, 1475. He was alfo prebendary of St. Margaret, Leicefter; and died at Rochefter in 1477. His fucceffor,

John Moreton, LL. D. was inftalled by proxy (as Rotheram had been) Jan. 3, 1477. He was archdeacon alfo of Huntingdon, Derby, and Norfolk, and Mafter of the Rolls. He was next year made Bifhop of Ely; and fucceeded by

Richard Lavendyr, admitted likewife by his proxy, Oct. 5, 1485. He was chancellor and commiffary to John bifhop of Rochefter, Oct. 17, 1478, as appears by the will of Thomas Marchant. He was rector of Hungat Epifcopi, and patronift of Alvefton, ult. Sept. 1486; and died in 1504. He was buried in the chancel of St. Peter and St. Paul's church in

the town of Bucks, where he was prebendary, and had an infcription on his grave-ftone, long fince defaced. His fucceffor was

William Sparke, M. A. collated March 18, 1507. He was of Cambridge, but incorporated M. A. at Oxford December 1512 [11]; and was fucceeded by

Henry Wilcocks, inftalled May 1, 1515. He proceeded LL. D. in 1500; and was Principal of the Civil Law School in St. Edmund's parifh, Oxford, and deputy to William Warham, Mafter of the Rolls [12]. He died in 1518, being alfo prebendary of Croperdy; and was fucceeded by

Richard Mawdley, or Mawdlen, M. A. inftalled May 29, 1518. He took the degree of B. D. July 17, 1529. He was Vicar-general to Bifhop Smith; and was a zealous preacher againft the Lutherans. He died in 1530, being alfo prebendary of Tame.

Feb. 16, 1520, a commiffion was iffued to Mafter Richard Brokyfby, in decretis bacaulareo, and Richard Parker clerk, to vifit the clergy and people (clerum & populum) of the archdeaconry of Leicefter [13].

Stephen Gardiner, D. C. L. 1520; mafter of Trinity hall, Cambridge, 1525; archdeacon of Norwich 1529; and of Leicefter, in which latter he was inftalled March 31, 1531: but he kept it not long, being made Bifhop of Winchefter the fame year. Though he fubfcribed to all the alterations in Religion under king Edward VI. he was ftill regarded as a fecret enemy to the Reformation; and in 1547 was imprifoned in the Fleet, and in 1548 in the Tower; and foon after, Feb. 14, 1549-50, was deprived of his bifhoprick. On the acceffion of queen Mary, he was reftored to his bifhoprick; made lord chancellor; and became, in fact, prime minifter. He was diftinguifhed for his extenfive learning, infinuating addrefs, and profound policy; the mafter-piece of which was the treaty of marriage betwixt Philip and Mary, which was an effectual bar to the ambitious defigns of Philip. His religious principles appear to have been more flexible than his political, which were invariably fixed to his own intereft. He was a perfecutor of thofe tenets to which he had fubfcribed, and in defence of which he had written. He was author of a treatife "De Verâ Obedientiâ;" had a great hand in the famous book, intituled, " The Erudition of a Chriftian Man;" wrote an "Apology for Holy Water," &c. [14]; and died Nov. 12, 1555, æt. 72.

Edward Fox, S. T. P. provoft of King's college, Cambridge, was inftalled Sept. 27, 1531; made Bifhop of Hereford in 1535 [15]. He was the author of " Libri de verâ differentiâ Regal. Poteftatis & Ecclefiafticæ;" and died in 1538.

Peter Ichell, Thomas Trys, and Robert Wingfield, were appointed, by the King's writ, Jan. 30, 1534-5, to take the ecclefiaftical furvey of the county of Leicefter.

Edmund Bonner, LL. D. inftalled Oct. 17, 1535. He was baftard fon of George Savage, parfon of Davenham in Chefhire, bafe fon to fir John Savage junior, of Clifton, co. Ceftr, Edmund's mother was Elizabeth Frodfham, firft married to one Edmund Bonner, a fawyer with Mr. Armingham, who had other children by her afterwards, and dwelt at Potter's Henley, co. Worcefter [16]. Edmund Bonner (afterwards Bifhop of London), fat in the Convocation, as Archdeacon of Leicefter, in 1536, when the Clergy infcribed the inftrument of King Henry's divorce from Queen Catharine; of whom Fuller thus writes: " As for Edmund Bonner, Archdeacon of Leicefter, prefent, and active in this Convocation, I may fay, Bonner was no Bonner YET, but a perfect Cromwellift, and as forward as any to promote his defigns [17]."

[1] 12 May, 1354, Magifter Will' Donne, LL. D. collatus fuit ad archidiac' Leyc' per mortem Mag' Henrici Chaddefden. Reg. Sywell, fol. 312.   [2] Burton, p. 236.   [3] " Archidiaconatus Leyceftr' vacat' 1 Sept', 1385." Reg. Buckingham.   [4] Willis, vol. II. p. 172.   [5] Ibid. p. 220.   [6] Ibid. vol. I. p. 152.   [7] Ibid. vol. I. p. 162; vol. II. p. 204.   [8] " Commiffio d'ni archiep'i Mag' Joh'i Elmere, LL. D. & Joh'i Southam archidiacono Oxon. directa, ad cognofcend' & procedend' in quadam caufâ appellationis, occafione jurifdictionis archidiaconi Leyceftr', inter d'num Richardum Elvet archidiaconum Leyceftrie in eccl' Lyncoln' partem appellantem ex unâ, & ven' patrem d'num Phil' Lyncoln' ep'um, partem appellantem ex alterâ. Dat' apud Lameheth, 8° die Novembris, 1408." Reg. Arundel, pars 1. fol. 150. a.   [9] Reg. Chicheley, fol. 249.   [10] Britannia Antiqua & Nova, vol. V. p. 292.   [11] Wood, Athen. Oxon. vol. I.; Fafti, p. 19.   [12] Wood's Fafti, vol. I. p. 124; Wood, Athen. Oxon. vol. I.; Fafti, p. 2.   [13] Reg. Wareham, fol. 289.   [14] Granger, vol. I. pp. 136. 160.   [15] Willis, vol. I. p. 520.   [16] Sir Peter Leycefter, p. 233.   [17] Church Hiftory, book V. p. 208.

William

William More, B. D. who had been confecrated Suffragan Bifhop of Colchefter Oct. 20, 1536, was inftalled Sept. 4, 1539. He was prebendary of Gerendale in the church of York; and held the priory of Walden (where Audley Inn now ftands) *in commendam*, but furrendered it in 1539; obtained a penfion and this archdeaconry Oct. 20, 1540; and was fucceeded by

Thomas Robertfon, S. T. P. who was born at or in the neighbourhood of Wakefield in Yorkfhire; and was at firft of Queen's college, Oxford; afterwards of Magdalen college, where he obtained a fellowfhip, and was mafter of the adjoining fchool, his character being that of a correct grammarian. He greatly exceeded his predeceffors in the education of his pupils; added *Quæ genus* to Lilly's Grammar; and was the author of feveral grammatical works. In 1539, he was treafurer of the church of Salifbury. It is faid the congregation of Regents were fupplicated by him, for admiffion to the reading of the Sentences, being then efteemed *Flos & decus Oxonii*. In 1540, by the intereft of Langford Bp. of Lincoln, he obtained the archdeaconry of Leicefter; was collated Feb. 19, and inftalled March 5. He had been rector of St. Laud's church at Sherrington, Bucks; was in Convocation July 7, 1540; and one of the Committee appointed to enquire into the validity of King Henry the Eighth's marriage with Anne of Cleves [1]. In 1546, he was inftituted vicar of Wakefield; on which he refigned his treafurerfhip; and in 1549 he was named among thofe who were appointed by king Edward VI. to compofe the Church Liturgy. In July 1558, he obtained the deanery of Durham; and Queen Mary, who greatly refpected him for his learning, would have nominated him to a bifhoprick, which he modeftly refufed. On Queen Elizabeth's acceffion to the Crown, he was forced to refign the deanery of Durham, to make room for Dr. Robert Horne's reftoration. He refigned the archdeaconry of Leicefter, to avoid the difgrace of an ejection; and though a bitter adverfary to reformation, was overlooked, as fome thought, on account of his lamenefs; but Willis [2] fays he was taken into cuftody. He is mentioned by Strype [3], in "Lifts of the names of Popifh Recufants, late Dignitaries of the Church." "Dr. Robinfon (or Robertfon, Archdeacon of Leicefter, and) late Dean of Durham, is excufed by his lamenefs: one thought to do much hurt in Yorkfhire [4]." On Horn's promotion to the fee of Winchefter, Dr. Robertfon might have been reftored to his deanery, if he would have taken the oath of fupremacy; but he refufed. What afterwards became of him, our authorities are filent [5].

This dignity lay void till Dec. 24, 1560; when

Richard Barber, LL. D. (who had been inftalled Archdeacon of Bedford [6]) was inftalled here. "Mr. Richard Barber, Chancellor to the Reverend Father in God Nicholas, by the grace of God, Bifhop of Lincoln, is now Archdeacon of Leicefter, and hath the jurifdiction of the faid archdeaconry, and dwelleth at Lincoln. July 28, 1563 [7]." Dr. Barber fubfcribed in Convocation, Feb. 5, 1562, to the Thirty-nine Articles of Religion [8]; elected warden of All Souls college, Oxford, April 10, 1565, and refigned Oct. 25, 1571; was one of the Bifhop of Lincoln's commiffioners in vifiting Baliol college, March 4, 1565 [9]. He died in 1588, and was buried at Yoxall, co. Stafford, where he was rector, with this infcription:

"Here lyeth the body of Richard Barber, Doctor of Laws, born in this county; fometime fellow, after elected warden, of All Souls in Oxon, April 10, 1565, which he refigned Oct. 25, 1571; whence he retired to his parfonage at Yoxhall, and there died, Feb. 15, 1589."

Hugh Blythe, D. D. fucceeded. He had been elected to King's college, Cambridge, 1559; was rector of Appleby in this county; fchoolmafter of Eton about 1572; in which year, Aug. 23, he obtained a canonry of Windfor. He was inftalled archdeacon May 13, 1589; refigned in 1591; and died in 1610.

Robert Johnfon, fon of Maurice Johnfon, alderman of Stamford, who took the degree of M. A. at Cambridge; and was incorporated at Oxford Feb. 20, 1564-4. He was afterwards B. D. and twice made Prebendary of Rochefter, which he twice refigned. He was inftalled a Prebendary of Norwich 1570; obtained the rectory of North Luffenham, Rutland, 1571; a canonry of Windfor 1572; and was inftalled archdeacon of Leicefter July 27, 1591, being then an honorary fellow of Jefus college, Oxford [10]. Whilft Mr. Johnfon was archdeacon, a man was tried at Leicefter, at the Lent affizes 1 Jac. I. for digging up dead folks, and ftealing their winding fheets [11]. He was the founder of an Hofpital [12] and a Free-fchool at Oakham, and of a Free-fchool at Uppingham; and is mentioned as a benefactor to Sidney college in Cambridge [13]; gave four exhibitions to Clare Hall [14]; the fame number to St. John's college [15]; the fame number to Emanuel, with a preference to fuch as were brought up in the fchools of Oakham or Uppingham [16]; the fame number to Sidney [17]. He died in July 1625; and, as appears by the Regifter of the parifh of North Luffenham, was buried there on the 24th. On a fmall brafs, fixed on a ftone in the chancel floor of that church, is infcribed,

"Robart Johnfon, Bachelor of Divinitie, a painful preacher, parfon of North Luffenham,
had a godlie care of Religion, and a charitable minde to the poore.
He erected a faire free Grammar-fchoole in Okeham.
He erected a faire free Grammar-fchoole in Uppingham.
He appointed to each of his fchooles a fchoolemafter and an ufher,
He erected the Hofpitalle of Chrifte in Okeham.
He erected the Hofpitalle of Chrifte in Uppingham.
He procured for them a corporation and a mortmain of fower hundred marks,
Whereby well-difpofed people maie give unto them as God fhall move their hartes.
He bought landes of Quene Elizabeth towardes the maintenance of them.
He provided place in each of the Hofpitalles for xxiiii poore people.
He recovered, bought, and procured, the olde Hofpitalle of William Dalby in Okeham,
and caufed it to be renewed, eftablifhed, and confirmed,
which before was found to be confifcate and concealed,
wherein divers poore people he releaved.
He was alfo beneficiall to the towne of North Luffenham,
and alfo to the towne of Stamforde, where he was born of worfhipful parents.
It is the grace of God to give a man a wife harte, to laie up his treafure in heaven.
Theis be good fruites and effectes of a juftifieing faith, and of a trew profeffion of religion,
and a good example to all others to be benefactors to theis and fuch like good works;
that fo they may glorifie God, and leave a bleffed remembrance behinde them,
to the comfort and profite of all pofteritie.
All the glorie, honor, praife, and thankes, be unto God for evermore, Amen.
Sic luceat lux veftra. Let youre light fo fhine."

[1] Ecclefiaftical Memoria's, vol. I. pp. 359. 361; Wood, Athen. Oxon. vol. I. p. 135; Magn. Brit. Antiq. & Nov. vol. VI. p. 359; Tanner, Biblioth. Britann. p. 635.   [2] Vol. I. p. 213.
[3] Annals. vol. I. c. xxiv.   [4] Ibid. p. 244.   [5] Hutchinfon's Hiftory of Durham, vol. I. p. 142.
[6] Wood, Athen. Oxon. vol. I. p. 694.   [7] Harl. MSS. 595.   [8] Strype's Annals, vol. I. p. 290.   [9] Savage's Baliol, p. 70.
[10] Wood, Ather. Oxon. Fafti, vol. I. p. 94; Le Neve, pp. 164. 226. 383; Bridges, Northamptonfhire, vol. II. p. 566; Willis, vol. II. pp. 114. 523. 543.   [11] See before, p. 424.
[12] See Ordinances of the Hofpital, in Magna Britannia Antiqua & Nova, vol. V. p. 593. An account of his benefactions may be feen in Survey of Stamford, p. 66.
[13] Fuller's Hiftory, p. 154.   [14] Carter's Hiftory, p. 53.   [15] Ibid. p. 249.   [16] Ibid. p. 353.   [17] Ibid. p. 375.

Richard Pilkington [1], S. T. P. collated Aug. 16, 1625. He died in September 1631, and was buried at Hambledon, co. Bucks, where he was rector, without any monument; and succeeded by

William Warr, who paid First Fruits for it Oct. 14, 1631; to whom succeeded

Henry Ferne, S. T. P. rector of Medborne in this county 1639, and master of Trinity college, Cambridge [2]. On his b ing made Dean of Ely [3],

Robert Hitch [4], S. T. P. afterwards Dean of York, succeeded, June 18, 1661, and was installed July 13, 1661. He was present in the Convocation that passed the Book of Common Prayer, and signed it Dec. 20, 1661 [5]. He resigned this archdeaconry next year, in exchange for that of East Riding in the church of York, with

Clement Bretton [6], S. T. P. who was installed Sept. 7, 1662. He was fellow of Sidney college in Cambridge [7], and rector of Langton in this county [8]. He died in 1669, and was buried at Uppingham, without any inscription. He was succeeded by

William Outram [9], S. T. P. installed July 30, 1669, on the death of Breton. He published five Sermons, on Faith, Providence, and other subjects, 8vo, 1680; Twenty Sermons preached on several Occasions, 8vo, 1697. He died Aug. 23, 1679; and was buried in Westminster Abbey, with this inscription:

" Prope jacet
GULIELMUS OUTRAM, S. T. P.
ex agro Derbiensi collegiorum apud
Cantabrigienses S. & individuae Trinitatis &
Christi focius, hujus ecclesiae canonicus &
Leycestrie Archidiaconus, Theologus
confummatus & omnibus numeris abfolutus;
Scriptor nervofus & accuratus; concionator
egregius & affiduus; primo in agro
Lincoln', poftea Londini, & tandem apud
S. Margaretam Weftmon', ubi confecit
poftremum vitae fuae curfum magna
cum laude nec minori fructu: Sed in
tantis laboribus & animi contentione dum
facrarum literarum & Sanctorum Patrum
ftudio ardebat, ut in renum dolores
inciderit; quibus diu afflictus, & tandem
fractus, aequiffimo animo e vita difceffit,
Augufti 23°, anno Domini MDCLXXIX,
poftquam impleverat annum
quinquagefimum quartum."

On the base:
" Poft longum religiofae fenectutis decurfum annorum,
etiam 42° viduitatem, hic requiefcit JANE uxor
Gul' Outram, S. T. P. propter votam optimo femper
confilio inftitutam, pietatem erga Deum,
fidem erga amicos, charitatem erga egenos,
coelo dilecta, chara multis, omnibus infignis,
defunctis ad honorem vivis ad exemplum.
Ob. 4° die Octobris, 1721."

Francis Meres [10], M. A. fucceeded, being collated Sept. 10, and installed Nov. 3, 1679. He was rector of Misterton 1666, and of Lutterworth 1678; died Aug. 27, 1683, aet. 77; and was buried at Misterton [11].

Byrom Eaton [12], S. T. P. was collated Sept. 3, and installed Sept. 5, 1683. He died in 1703; and was buried at Newnham Courtney, near Oxford, where he was rector, without any monument; and was succeeded by

John Rogers, M. A. collated Nov. 29, 1703. He died in 1715 [13].

David Trimnell, M. A. (brother to the Bp. of Winchester) fucceeded, being collated May 17, 1715. He was born May 20, 1675 [14]. Dr. Trimnell is mentioned, in the History of Lambeth Palace [15], as chaplain to Abp. Wake. He feems to have been in the fame office under Dr. Wake whilst Bishop of Lincoln, as he was poffeffed of thefe benefices in the difpofal of the prelates of that fee; the rectory of Stoke Hammond in Bucks; the prebends of Tarenton 1710, and Caftor 1712, in the church of Lincoln; and the archdeaconry of Leicester May 17, 1715, which was a few months before his Patron's tranflation to Canterbury; by whom he was prefented, in 1718, to the prebend of Kelfey, and alfo to the precentorfhip in Lincoln cathedral, probably an option at the confecration of Bishop Gibfon. Dr. Trimnell publifhed an Affize Sermon, 8vo, 1714; Text, Rom. xiii. 4.

On a flat stone in Lincoln cathedral, near the West door, is this infcription:
" Sacred to the memory of
the Rev. David Trimnell, S. T. P.
rector of Stoke in Bucks 48 years,
prebendary of Caftor 48 years,
archdeacon of Leicester 41 years,
and precentor of this church, and
prebendary of Kildefley, 38 years;
who died May 28, 1756, aged 81 years."

John Taylor, LL. D. collated June 1756, on the death of Dr. Trimnell. He was of Chrift Church, Oxford; M. A. 1742; B. and D. D. 1752. He obtained the archdeaconry of Bedford in 1744; and was alfo prebendary of Aylefbury, which he exchanged, April 28, 1747, for the rectory of St. Mary Aldermary, London; which he held till the time of his death in 1772. He publifhed a Sermon, preached at the Confecration of Bifhops John Thomas, Lifle, and Trevor; Phil. ii. 15.16.4to, preached April 1, 1744.

James Bickham, M. A. fellow of Emanuel college, Cambridge, was prefented by that Society, in 1761, to the rectory of Loughborough. He died Dec. 23, 1785 [16].

Andrew Burnaby, D. D. elected into Weftminfter college in 1748, but removed from that fchool; was of Queen's college, Cambridge; instituted vicar of Greenwich 1769; and collated to the archdeaconry of Leicester in 1786. Of this venerable and refpectable Divine (who ftill does honour to the fituation he fo ably fills) fome account has been already given under Bagrave [17]. He has fince printed, for the ufe of particular friends, a very fmall impreffion of " Journal of a Tour to Corfica in the year 1766. By the Rev. A. Burnaby, D. D. at that time Chaplain to the Britifh Factory at Leghorn. With a Series of original Letters from General Paoli to the Author, referring to the principal Events which have taken place in that Ifland, from 1766 to 1802. With explanatory Notes. 1804." He has alfo publifhed, in 1805, an octavo volume of " Occafional Sermons and Charges," moft of which had before appeared in feparate and detached publications; a form in which they were likely to be preferved only in the collections of the curious; but they will now make a part of every well-chofen Theological Library. The volume contains XVIII Sermons, delivered at various places, and chiefly on public occafions, between the years 1764 and 1782; Four Charges to the Archdeaconry of Leicester; a Petition from the Clergy of that Archdeaconry (propofed, but not accepted) on the Slave Trade, 1788; and a Letter to the Clergy on the fame Subject, 1792.

---

[1] Wood, Athen. Oxon. vol. I. p. 647.   [2] See Kennett's Hiftorical Regifter, pp. 231. 293. 481. 584. 585. 643. 644. 655. 668.
[3] He was afterwards bifhop of Chefter. See memoirs of him in vol. II. p. 723.
[4] See of him in Kennett's Regifter, pp. 376. 467. 474. 565.   [5] Ex Origine; and Wilkins, Concil. vol. IV. p. 568.
[6] See Kennett's Hiftorical Regifter, pp. 224. 251. 322. 330. 737.   [7] Walker's Sufferings, Part II. p. 203.
[8] See more of him in vol. II. p. 666.   [9] Kennett's Hiftorical Regifter, p. 843.   [10] Ibid. pp. 384. 385.
[11] See his epitaph, vol. IV. p. 315.   [12] Kennett's Hiftorical Regifter, p. 220; Wood, Athen. Oxon. vol. II. p. 136.
[13] See a full account of him, as confrater of Wigfton's Hofpital, p. 502.
[14] Dr. Denne, from the perfonal information of Archdeacon Trimnell.   [15] Appendix, p. 22.
[16] See an account of him, and his epitaph, vol. III. pp. 900. 902.   [17] See vol. III. p. 288.

for digging up dead folks, and stealing their winding sheets[1].

Richard Pilkington, descended of an antient family in Lancashire, was, at 17 years of age, sent to Cambridge till M.A. and, retiring to Queen's college, Oxford, was incorporated in that degree 1599, and in 1600 was B.D. and seven years after D.D. He was collated to this archdeaconry Aug. 16, 1625, being then vice-rector of Hambleton, in Bucks. He preached and wrote against the Papists; and was buried at Hambleton, in the middle of September 1631, at which time there was the most dreadful storm of wind, thunder, and lightning, that was ever known in those parts. He has no monument; and was succeeded by

William Warr, who paid First Fruits for it Oct. 14, 1631; to whom succeeded

Henry Ferne, S.T.P. rector of Medborne in this county 1639, and master of Trinity college, Cambridge[2]. On his being made Dean of Ely[3],

Robert Hitch[4], S.T.P. afterwards Dean of York, succeeded, June 18, 1661, and was installed July 13, 1661. He was present in the Convocation that passed the Book of Common Prayer, and signed it Dec. 20, 1661[5]. He resigned this archdeaconry next year, in exchange for that of East Riding in the church of York, with

Clement Bretton[6], S.T.P. who was installed Sept. 7, 1662. He was fellow of Sidney college in Cambridge[7], and rector of Langton in this county[8]. He died in 1669, and was buried at Uppingham, without any inscription. He was succeeded by

William Outram[9], S.T.P. installed July 30, 1669, on the death of Breton. He published five Sermons, on Faith, Providence, and other subjects, 8vo, 1680; Twenty Sermons preached on several Occasions, 8vo, 1697. He died Aug. 23, 1679; and was buried in Westminster Abbey, with this inscription:

" Propè jacet
GULIELMUS OUTRAM, S.T.P.
ex agro Derbiensi collegiorum apud
Cantabrigienses S. & individuæ Trinitatis &
Christi socius, hujus ecclesiæ canonicus &
Leycestrie Archidiaconus, Theologus
consummatus & omnibus numeris absolutus;
Scriptor nervosus & accuratus; concionator
egregius & assiduus; primò in agro
Lincoln', postea Londini, et tandem apud
S. Margaretam Westmon', ubi confecit
postremum vitæ suæ cursum magnâ
cum laude nec minori fructu: Sed in
tantis laboribus & animi contentione dum
sacrarum literarum & Sanctorum Patrum
studio ardebat, ut in renum dolores
inciderit; quibus diu afflictus, & tandem
fractus, æquissimo animo è vita discessit,
Augusti 23o, anno Domini MDCLXXIX,
postquam impleverat annum
quinquagesimum quartum."

On the base:

" Post longum religiosæ senectutis decursum annorum,
etiam 42o viduitatem, hic requiescit JANE uxor
Gul' Outram, S.T.P. propter votam optimo semper
consilio institutam, pietate erga Deum,
fidem erga amicos, charitatem erga egenos,
cœlo dilecta, chara multis, omnibus insignis,
defunctis ad honorem vivis ad exemplum.
Ob 4o die Octobris, 1721."

Francis Meres[10], M.A. succeeded, being collated Sept. 10, and installed Nov. 3, 1679. He was rector of Misterton 1666, and of Lutterworth 1678; died Aug. 27, 1683, æt. 77; and was buried at Misterton[11].

Byrom Eaton[12], S.T.P. was collated Sept. 3, and installed Sept. 5, 1683. He died in 1703; and was buried at Newnham Courtney, near Oxford, where he was rector, without any monument; and was succeeded by

John Rogers, M.A. collated Nov. 29, 1703. He died in 1715[13].

David Trimnell, M.A. (brother to the Bishop of Winchester) succeeded, being collated May 17, 1715. He was born May 20, 1675[14]. Dr. Trimnell is mentioned, in the History of Lambeth Palace[15], as chaplain to Abp. Wake. He seems to have been in the same office under Dr. Wake whilst Bishop of Lincoln, as he was possessed of these benefices in the disposal of the prelates of that see; the rectory of Stoke Hammond in Bucks; the prebends of Tarenton 1710, and Castor 1712, in the church of Lincoln; and the archdeaconry of Leicester May 17, 1715, which was a few months before his Patron's translation to Canterbury; by whom he was presented, in 1718, to the prebend of Kelsey, and also to the precentorship in Lincoln cathedral, probably an option at the consecration of Bishop Gibson. Dr. Trimnell published an Assize Sermon, 8vo, 1714; Text, Rom. xiii. 4.

On a flat stone in Lincoln cathedral, near the West door, is this inscription:

" Sacred to the memory of
the Rev. David Trimnell, S.T.P.
rector of Stoke in Bucks 48 years,
prebendary of Castor 48 years,
archdeacon of Leicester 41 years,
and precentor of this church, and
prebendary of Kildesley, 38 years;
who died May 28, 1756, aged 81 years."

John Taylor, LL.D. collated June 1756, on the death of Dr. Trimnell. He was of Christ Church, Oxford; M.A. 1742; B. and D.D. 1752. He obtained the archdeaconry of Bedford in 1744; and was also prebendary of Aylesbury, which he exchanged, April 28, 1747, for the rectory of St. Mary Aldermary, London; which he held till the time of his death, in 1772. He published a Sermon, preached at the Consecration of Bishops John Thomas, Lisle, and Trevor; Phil. ii. 15, 16. 4to, preached April 1, 1744.

James Bickham, M.A. fellow of Emanuel college, Cambridge, was presented by that Society, in 1761, to the rectory of Loughborough. He died Dec. 23, 1785[16].

Andrew Burnaby, D.D. elected into Westminster college in 1748, but removed from that school; was of Queen's college, Cambridge; instituted vicar of Greenwich 1769; and collated to the archdeaconry of Leicester in 1786. Of this venerable and respectable Divine (who still does honour to the situation he so ably fills) some account has been already given under Bagrave[17]. He has since printed, for the use of particular friends, a very small impression of " Journal of a Tour to Corsica in the year 1766. By the Rev. A. Burnaby, D.D. at that time Chaplain to the British Factory at Leghorn. With a Series of original Letters from General Paoli to the Author, referring to the principal Events which have taken place in that Island, from 1766 to 1802. With explanatory Notes. 1804." He has also published, in 1805, an octavo volume of " Occasional Sermons and Charges," most of which had before appeared in separate and detached publications; a form in which they were likely to be preserved only in the collections of the curious; but they will now make a part of every well-chosen Theological Library. The volume contains XVIII Sermons, delivered at various places, and chiefly on public occasions, between the years 1764 and 1782; Four Charges to the Archdeaconry of Leicester; a Petition from the Clergy of that Archdeaconry (proposed, but not accepted) on the Slave Trade, 1788; and a Letter to the Clergy on the same Subject, 1792.

[1] See before, p. 424.
[2] See Kennett's Historical Register, pp. 231. 293. 481. 584. 585. 643. 644. 655. 668.
[3] He was afterwards bishop of Chester. See memoirs of him in vol. II. p. 723.
[4] See of him in Kennett's Register, pp. 376. 467. 474. 565.   [5] Ex Origine; and Wilkins, Concil. vol. IV. p. 568.
[6] See Kennett's Historical Register, pp. 224. 251. 322. 330. 737.   [7] Walker's Sufferings, Part II. p 203.
[8] See more of him in vol. II. p. 666.   [9] Kennett's Historical Register, p. 843.   [10] Ibid. pp. 384. 385.
[11] See his epitaph, vol. IV. p. 315.   [12] Kennett's Historical Register, p. 220; Wood, Athen. Oxon. vol. II. p. 136.
[13] See a full account of him, as confrater of Wigston's Hospital, p. 502.
[14] Dr. Denne, from the personal information of Archdeacon Trimnell.   [15] Appendix, p. 22.
[16] See an account of him, and his epitaph, vol. III. pp. 900. 902.   [17] See vol. III. p. 288.

BOOK of DIRECTIONS to the MAYOR of LEICESTER, 1758; communicated by Mr. BICKERSTAFFE.

	£.	s.	d.
To Robert Belton, efq. mayor, for his year's falary, payable at Lady-day and Michaelmas - - -	60	0	0
To him more, payable half-yearly, viz. Lady-day and Michaelmas - -	13	6	8
To him more, as mafter of the hofpital of the Holy Trinity in the Newark, on All Saints day and Whitfunday - -	13	6	8
To him more, out of the rent of the Gofling clofes - - -	13	6	8
To William Wrighte, efq. recorder, for his falary, at Lady-day and Michaelmas	10	0	0
To the Town-clerk, for his fees as clerk of the peace, at Michaelmas only -	0	6	8
To him more, for his year's falary, by quarterly payments - - -	5	0	0
To him more, for certifying the Coroner's inqueft at Michaelmas only -	1	0	0
To the Town-clerk and Mace-bearer, upon All Saints day and Whit-Monday, being an antient gift of the Town, to be divided between them - -	5	6	8
To the Mace-bearer, to be paid quarterly	3	13	4
More, by order of Hall - -	1	0	0
More, for burning of pipes -	0	3	0
To the Keeper of the houfe of correction, to be paid quarterly - -	1	13	4
To the four Serjeants at Mace, to be paid each of them quarterly, by order of Hall, to keep them from going about with their Chriftmas-box, during pleafure	1	0	0
To the Cryer for his wages, to be paid quarterly - - -	1	6	8
More for fweeping the Town-hall and Gainfborough - - -	0	6	8
To the Cryer and Beadle, on St. Thomas's day, to keep them from going about with their Chriftmas-box -	0	4	0
To the Beadle for fweeping the Market and Barrell-crofs, quarterly - -	4	0	0
More for weeding and keeping clean the Town-hall yard, Eaft-gates, &c. -	2	0	0
To John Veafey, library-keeper, for his annual falary, paid quarterly -	3	0	0
To the Waits, for their year's falary, to be paid quarterly - - -	6	13	4
To the Sexton of St. Martin's, for ringing the bell on St. Matthew's day -	0	1	0
To the Rev. Mr. Haynes, as lecturer, his year's ftipend, payable quarterly, the firft on St. Thomas's day - -	20	0	0
More, Corporation gift during pleafure	10	0	0
More, Mr. Stanley's gift, as vicar of St. Martin's - - -	1	10	0
To the Rev. Mr. Andrewes, head fchoolmafter, being the Town's free gift during pleafure - - -	16	0	0
To the Mafter of Wigfton's Hofpital, the earl of Huntingdon's gift to the head fchoolmafter - - -	10	0	0
To the Head Ufher, being the gift of Queen Elizabeth, to be received of the auditor at Michaelmas, to whom you pay for portage 5d. and for a quietus 3d.; which 8d. you muft ftop with the head ufher when you pay him - -	10	0	0
To him more, being the Town's free gift during pleafure - -	5	0	0
More, the Town's free gift during pleafure - - -	3	0	0
More, the gift of Mr. Norris, to be paid half-yearly out of a clofe in the Abbey Gate, paid by Mr. Hammond -	3	6	8
More, the gift of Mrs. Dorothy Baker, to teach poor fcholars to write -	0	10	0
More, the gift of Mr. Stanley -	0	13	4
More, the gift of Mr. Thomas Gilbert	1	10	0
To the Under Ufher of the School, the gift of Mr. Clarke out of the water laggs - - -	1	0	0

Vol. I.

	£.	s.	d.
The gift of fir Ralph Rawlett, out of the manor of Thedingworth, lately paid by fir Thomas Cave, now paid by Mr...... of Harborough, to be paid half-yearly -	3	6	8
More, gift of the Town during pleafure	3	0	0
More, ditto - - -	5	0	0
More, the gift of Mrs. Margaret Hobby	0	12	0
More, the gift of Mr. Stanley -	0	6	8
More, the gift of Mr. Thomas Gilbert	0	10	0
More, the gift of Mrs. Baker, to teach poor children to write - -	0	10	0
To the vicar of St. Margaret's, being the Town's free gift during pleafure -	10	0	0
To the vicar of All Saints, the like -	10	0	0
To the vicar of St. Nicholas, the like	10	0	0
To the vicar of St. Mary, the like -	10	0	0
To him, out of the water laggs, payable at Midfummer - -	0	2	0
To the organift of St. Martin's during pleafure - - -	10	0	0

CHARITABLE GIFTS.

The gift of Mr. John and William Stanley:

	£.	s.	d.
To the vicar of St. Martin's -	1	10	0
To the head fchoolmafter -	1	0	0
To the head ufher - -	0	13	4
To the under ufher - -	0	6	8
To widows and maids 12d. a piece, to be difpofed by the Mayor - -	0	10	0
To the old Hofpital, Mr. Wm. Stanley's	1	0	0
	5	0	0

The gift of Mr. Thomas Gilbert:

	£.	s.	d.
To the head fchoolmafter -	3	0	0
To the head ufher - -	1	10	0
To the under ufher - -	0	10	0
	5	0	0

The gift of Mr. Hugh Botham, payable out of the houfes in Lofeby-lane, formerly the fign of the Parrot, now Mr. Jofeph Cradock fenior:

	£.	s.	d.
The parifh of St. Martin's -	0	13	4
St. Margaret - - -	0	13	4
St. Mary - - -	0	13	4
	2	0	0

The gift of Chriftopher Tamworth, efq. payable out of the land at Whetftone:

	£.	s.	d.
To the vicar of St. Martin's, for reading week-days prayers - -	7	5	0
To the clerk of St. Martin's, for ringing the bell - - -	0	10	0
	7	15	0

The gift of Mr. Haynes, out of Allexton lands:

	£.	s.	d.
To be paid for Bibles - -	1	0	0
To two fcholars, ftudents in Lincoln college, Oxford - - -	6	0	0
For preaching a fermon, about the beginning of Auguft, in commemoration of the deliverance from the Spanifh Armada	1		0
To the poor of the Corporation at Midfummer (this is part of the wood-money); tenants pay the taxes - -	5	0	0
To the fchoolmafter at Thruffington -	6	0	0
	19	0	0

	£.	s.	d.
Mr. Bennett and Mr. Ward's gift to the poor yearly - -	1	0	0

Mr. Robert Heyrick's gift:

	£.	s.	d.
To 20 widows of St. Martin's parifh, 1s. each	1	0	0
To 20 others in the other parifhes, as the mayor and aldermen think fit -	1	0	0
	2	0	0

Mr.

Mr. Ives' gift, out of a house and meadow in St. Mary's parish:

	£.	s.	d.
To buy eight gowns - -	4	0	0
To the poor of the Old Hospital -	5	12	0
To the poor of the New Hospital -	0	8	0

Every Friday in clean Lent 13s. 4d. in bread for six weeks. These poor to have it weekly: St. Martin's, 20s.; St. Margaret's, 20s.; St. Mary's, 20s.; All Saints, 12s.; St. Nicholas, 8s. - - 4 0 0

14 0 0

Mr. Ives' gift to the poor of the Old Hospital the first week in clean Lent - 1 0 0
Mr. Elkington's gift, payable on St. Thomas's day:

	£.	s.	d.
To the poor of St. Martin's parish -	2	0	0
To the poor of Lutterworth -	2	10	0
To the Town-clerk -	0	10	0

5 0 0

The gift of John Poultney, esq. out of the manor of Cotes Devile:

Payable on St. Thomas's day to St. Martin's parish - - - 2 10 0
To St. Margaret - - 2 10 0
To St. Mary - - - 2 10 0
All Saints - - - 1 12 6
St. Nicholas - - - 0 17 6

Taxes to be deducted if paid. 10 0 0

The gift of sir William Courteen and gentlemen of the Lottery, 4l. 16s.; payable half-yearly on New Year's day and Whitsunday:

To the parish of St. Martin's -	0	10	8
St. Margaret's - -	0	10	8
St. Mary - - -	0	10	8
All Saints - - -	0	9	4
St. Nicholas - - -	0	6	8

2 8 0

The countess of Devonshire's gift, Monday before Easter:

Payable to St. Martin's parish -	0	9	0
St. Margaret's - -	0	9	0
St. Mary's - - -	0	9	0
All Saints - - -	0	7	0
St. Nicholas - - -	0	6	0
St. Leonard's - - -	1	0	0

3 0 0

The gift of Mr. John Norris, out of lands at Willoughby Waterless:

To St. Martin's parish - -	1	7	4
St. Margaret's - -	1	7	4
St. Mary's - - -	1	7	4
All Saints - - -	1	2	0
St. Nicholas - - -	0	16	0
The Old Hospital - -	1	13	4
St. John's Hospital - -	0	6	8

8 0 0

The gift of Mr. Acham, paid now by Edward Southwell, esq. of Wisbeach, 9l.; to be distributed to the poor of the several parishes underwritten on the last Sunday in every other month; to begin in November; then January, March, May, July, and September; 30s. to be given in every one of these months in wheaten bread:

St. Martin's - - -	0	7	0
St. Margaret's - -	0	7	0
St. Mary's - - -	0	7	0
All Saints - - -	0	5	6
St. Nicholas - - -	0	3	6

1 10 0

The gift of widow Ossiter to the poor of the Corporation, to buy coals, payable the 8th of June - - - 6 0 0
The gift of the earl of Devonshire to the poor of the Corporation, viz. to 20 freemen to buy coals, to be paid to the mayor in July - - 6 0 0
The gift of Mr. Moreton, out of the Tippets, paid to the mayor by Mr. Nathaniel Simpson:

To six widows of St. John's, to buy coals, at 3s. each - - - 0 18 0
To seven poor housekeepers, at 6s. each 2 2 0

3 0 0

The gift of King Charles the First, of ever blessed memory, being the rent of the Forest Closes, in the occupation of John Brewing - - - 18 0 0
Land-tax, at 4s. in the pound, deducted 2 8 8

15 11 4

Distributed by the aldermen of the several wards:

With widow Ossiter's - -	6	0	0
Earl of Devonshire's - -	6	0	0
Mr. Moreton's - -	2	2	0
Mr. Haynes's - - -	5	0	0

(Called Wood-money.) 19 2 0

The gift of widow Hobby:

To the poor of the Old Hospital -	0	2	6
To the poor of the New Hospital -	0	2	0
To the widows of St. John's -	0	0	6
To the poor of St. Martin's -	0	2	0
To the poor of St. Mary's -	0	2	0
To the under usher as before-mentioned	0	12	0

1 1 0

The gift of Mr. Nidd, out of lands at Busby, 32l. This is paid to Mr. Mayor, and by him to the overseers of Mountsorell.

Chamberlains are to pay,
To the Bailiff of the Borough of Leicester, for certain rents due to his Majesty from the Corporation, if demanded - 10 16 0
To the Company of Taylors - 0 1 8
A chief rent to Merton college in Oxford 0 1 3
To the Bailiff of the Augmentation at Michaelmas (this has been demanded by Mr. Finnis, and 4d. for an acquittance) - 0 7 0
To the parish of St. Mary's yearly, for the interest of 10l. said to be the gift of Mr. Sherman (not to be paid without orders) 0 12 0
The excise for the Corporation plate, 60l. 0s. 8d. - - - 1 10 0

Paid to the poor of the Hospital of the Holy Trinity. The weekly pay is 2l. 15s. 8d.

You are to pay them about Easter for wood and coal-money 7 0 0
For drover's money, half at Midsummer and Ash Wednesday - 1 12 9
For repairs in the Spring, which you are to see laid out to the best advantage - 4 0 0
For lamp, livery, halfpenny, and sixpenny money - - - 19 1 8
To Mr. Pocklington, for reading prayers yearly - - - 5 0 0
Mr. Hesilrige's gift, to be paid half-yearly, one half to the poor of the Hospital, and the other half to the poor of the Corporation - - - 1 4 0
Mr. Hythe's gift - - 0 3 0
Mr. Julius Billers's gift, to be paid on Good Friday 5 12 0
Mrs. Ward's gift to the common box there 0 10 0
More, her gift to Alias Women, not having the pay of the house - - 0 10 0

Mr.

	£.	s.	d.
Mr. Taylor's gift for oatmeal. This has been lately paid by Mr. Samuel Heyrick from Bourden in rent; but you must not pay it unless you receive it -	2	0	0
To the widows of St. John's, to buy coals	0	7	6
More on St. Thomas's day -	0	2	0
Mr. Robert Heyrick's gift, to be paid to Trinity Hospital out of the Fryers; that is to say, 12d. to each - -	5	12	0
You receive this of Mr. Richard Garle. There being now but 90 people in the house, he will pay but 12d. to each, which is - -	4	10	0
Andrew Noel, esq. and Mr. William Sutton, their gift to the Old Hospital and St. John's, out of lands at Enderby in the occupation of Robert Goddard. This received and paid by Mr. Mayor -	15	0	0

Mr. Ward's gift out of the Duck Holmes, paid by Mr. Ruding:

	£.	s.	d.
To the widows of St. John's, to buy gowns for three of them yearly -	1	10	0
To coals for all of them - -	0	10	0
To two women in the Old Hospital -	0	10	0
To the common box, mentioned before	0	10	0
	3	0	0

Mr. Twickden's gift out of Rawlett's Close in Braunston Gate:

	£.	s.	d.
To the widows of St. John's, to buy gowns for three of them yearly -	1	10	0
To buy coals for all of them -	0	10	0
	2	0	0

Other Payments to the Hospital and St. John's:

	£.	s.	d.
Mr. Sutton's interest of 20l. to the Old Hospital - -	0	16	0
Mr. Staveley's gift, if not paid by Mr. Staveley to the foremen -	1	0	0
Mr. Topp's gift - -	1	0	0
Mr. William Weightman's gift -	0	5	0
Mr. George Bent senior -	0	5	0
Mr. Ayre's gift to the poor of St. John's living above stairs, on Michaelmas day -	1	0	0
Mr. Alderman John Ludlam, to the poor of St. John's - -	2	10	0
Mr. Alderman George Bent, to St. John's, out of Sadler's house -	2	10	0

Mr. Alderman Thomas Ludlam, to St. John's Hospital:

	£.	s.	d.
Paid as follows: viz. for a sermon -	1	0	0
To a nurse 12d. a week -	2	12	0
Amongst the other poor there -	0	8	0
	4	0	0

	£.	s.	d.
Mr. Alderman Thomas Ludlam's gift to the Corporation, to put out one boy apprentice yearly for seven years -	8	0	0

And then another sum of 8l. to be paid for each boy to put out at the end of his apprenticeship, if he has behaved well, towards his setting-up.

	£.	s.	d.
Mr. Garland's gift to St. Mary's parish	0	5	0
The Rental -	947	17	0
The Book of Charities -	507	5	0
	440	12	0

A List of CAUSEWAYS *which are to be repaired at the Charge of the Corporation, in and near the* BOROUGH *of* LEICESTER.

In Mr. Brushfield's Ward.

Under the East Gates, the causeway at Barrel-cross, from the Channel at East Gates up to the pump by Mr. Sismey's house, and no further.

In Mr. Marten's Ward, viz. Nicholas parish.

From four yards and a half, all the length of the front of John Wilkes's house, at the Rose and Crown, to each channel, and to the point of the causeway Westward, the West Bridge, the West Gates, the Watering Place; from the West end of Elias Wailin's house, formerly Robert Dunn's; and Captain Atkinson, now rented by John Fisher, and in possession of Thomas Holyland, at the Red Cow, to Braunston Gate Bridge; from the Bridge over against the Bow Bridge to the corner of the stonewall; and the North side to the West Bridge, as by order of Hall, 14 Dec. 1744; the causeway between Dunn's corner and West Bridge.

In Mr. Simpson's Ward, viz. from the South Gates to the Horsepool.

Under the South Gates, the middle causeway leading from the Little Bridge into the South Fields, being three yards from the Great Stone to the house.

In Mr. Smalley's Ward, viz. from the High Cross to the North Gate, Bond Street, and Back Lanes.

Under the North Gates, the causeway in the Back Lanes over against Mr. Cradock's garden, and over against the Meeting-house, the lane leading into the Butt Close.

In Mr. Phipps's Ward, viz. Senvey Gate and Church Gate.

All the grand causeway from the channel of Mr. Swan's house to St. Margaret's Church, and so to the Coal-hill.

In Mr. Lee's Ward, viz. from the North Gates to Great Bridge.

From the Little Bridge to the Round Stone, halfway over the Great Bridge, all the grand causeway, a wall in Frogmire Lane, and a bridge leading into the Pasture.

In Mr. Ludlam's Ward, viz. Silver Street and Loseby Lane.

Before the Town Hall, from the West end of St. Martin's church-yard, on the South side, to King's house, formerly Huffin's, about 59 yards.

In Mr. Newton's Ward, viz. Saturday Market.

From the West side of the Gitty, leading from the Corn Wall below the Lion and Dolphin to the Horse Fair, the pavement being about 100 yards.

The pavement from the Turnstile at the Horse Fair to Augustine Heaford's channel, 15 yards.

The grand pavement from the White Swan to the King's Head, now the sign of the Crown, being about 62 yards; and the middle pavement from the North corner of the Pinfold to the Corn Wall, being 25 yards.

And from Joseph Goodwin's house about 7 yards.

The grand pavement of the Corn Wall from the gutter against the Lion and Dolphin.

All the pavement from the Corn Wall to Mr. Whatton's ground.

A causeway leading from the George Inn sign-post up against Mr. Noble's gates, now Mr. Garle, about 38 yards in length, and three yards wide.

Mr. Miles's Ward, viz. Belgrave Gate.

The Spittle-house causeway; also the Bridge and grand causeway up to the end of the Crabtree Close, and the foot-causeway by the wall to Crabtree Close.

The new causeway, beginning at Mr. Pares' Close corner, and all the grand causeway up near the Common, and the grand causeway against the Cock Muckhill, being 100 yards in length.

Also the grand causeway in Humberstone Gate.

Mr. Ayres' Ward, viz. Gallowtree Gate.

The causeway from the Toll-gate to the corner of Mr. Robert Hall's wall; from thence both grand and foot causeway to the gutter and channel that runs into the Horsepool.

A causeway extending itself from the house lately known by the Wheat-sheaf, within nine yards and a half of William Hall's house, at the Three Crowns.

The Coal-hill, from the Gutter to the Stocks, extending from the channel on the West end of Humberstone Gate, on the East 10 yards and a half.

The upper end of the Coal-hill from the White Hart sign-post to the end of the building within six yards all the way.

NOBILITY

NOBILITY in LEICESTERSHIRE, 1681.
(From the Heraldic Visitation.)

George Duke of Bucks—	Garenton House—	West Goscote Hundred.
Arthur Earl of Kent—	Burbage—	Sparkenhoe.
John Earl of Rutland—	Belvoir Castle—	Framland.
	Bagworth Park—	Sparkenhoe.
	Aylston—	Guthlaxton.
	Croxton Park—	East Goscote.
	Bottesford—	Framlamd.
Theophilus Earl of Huntingdon—	Ashby de la Zouch—	West Goscote.
	Donington Park—	West Goscote.
Thomas Earl of Stamford—	Bradgate House—	West Goscote.
	Groby—	Sparkenhoe.
Robert Earl of Cardigan—	Staunton Brudenell—	Gartre.
Robert Lord Ferrers—	Staunton Harold—	West Goscote.
	Rakedale—	East Goscote.
Francis Lord Carrington—	Ashby Folvile.	East Goscote.

IRISH NOBILITY.

Thomas Viscount Beaumont, of Swords in Ireland, at Cole Orton, West Goscote Hundred.
Bennet Lord Sherard, of Leitrim in Ireland, at Stapleford, Framland Hundred.

A List of the DEPUTY LIEUTENANTS in the County of LEICESTER in 1681.

Lord Beaumont.
Lord Sherard.
Anchitell Grey, Esq.
Philip Sherard, Esq.
Sir Wolston Dixie, Bart.
Sir Henry Hudson, Bart.
Richard Lister, Esq.
Beaumont Dixie, Esq.
Sir Henry Beaumont.
Sir William Hartopp.

John Cooke, Esq.
Thomas Babington, Esq.
Charles Cocken, Esq.
Thomas Boothby, Esq.
Samuel Cotton, Esq.

These underwritten were not resident in the County.

Sir William Hartopp.
George Faunt, Esq.
Thomas Merry, Esq.

The Names of the Officers of the Three Troops of Horse.

Lord Roos, Captain.
Richard Lister junior, Lieutenant.
Richard Brudenell, Gent. Cornet.
Richard Mawson, Gent. Quartermaster.

Lord Beaumont, Captain.
John Wilkins, Esq. Lieutenant.

. . . . Cornet.
Matthew Halford, Gent. Quartermaster.

Lord Sherard, Captain.
John Hacket, Esq. Lieutenant.
George Williams, Gent. Cornet.
Edward Bunnis, Gent. Quartermaster.

Names of the Officers of Foot in the Six Companies.

Richard Lister, Esq. Colonel.
Peter Sargiant, Gent. Captain-lieutenant.
Richard Rollefton, Gent. Ensign.

Wolston Dixie, Esq. Lieutenant-colonel.
Henry Dudley, Gent. Lieutenant.
George Bent, Gent. Ensign.

William Cole, Esq. Major.
Robert Johnson, Gent. Lieutenant.
Thomas Bennington, Gent. Ensign.

James Harrison, Esq. Captain.
Thomas Freer, Gent. Lieutenant.
Thomas Lydall, Gent. Ensign.

Henry Farnham, Esq. Captain.
Thomas Bennet, Gent. Lieutenant.
Thomas Wright, Gent. Ensign.

Timothy Hemsley, Esq. Captain.
Thomas Lilly, Gent. Lieutenant.
Richard Swan, Gent. Ensign.

St. LEONARD near Leicester.

C. R.

A Brief to collect money to repair the Church of St. Leonard, near the Borough of Leicester.
Sessions held 7 Jan. 163..

The steeple hath been heretofore a fair square steeple; but the foundation not being good, for that it was made of soft mouldering stone, it so happened that the said steeple was, by a most violent tempest of wind, blown down; so that with the fall the middle aile, and North side of the church, were so shaken and decayed in the main timber, that it cannot be long upheld. Charge, 510l. [1]

[1] From a printed copy of the original Brief.

WIGSTON'S, or THE NEW HOSPITAL (Plate XXXV.)

This is the Hofpital which in Mr. Burton, and in the Catalogue of Religious Houfes in the Monafticon, is called *St. Urfula's*, it having originally been endowed as a chantry for two priefts in the collegiate church of our Lady in the Newark, in honour of the Virgin Mary, St. Catharine, and St. Urfula; and owed its foundation to the benevolence of *William Wigfton*, a merchant of the Staple of Calais, who was chofen mayor of Leicefter in 1499, and again in 1510; and who, May 16, 1511, in conjunction with *Thomas Wigfton* clerk, *Roger Wigfton* [1], and *William Colte* [or *Bolte*], obtained the king's licence for that purpofe, as has already been noticed under the Hiftory of that College [2]; where the letters patent of king Henry VIII. are alfo given at large [3]; and as will more fully appear by the following document:

"This indenture quadripartite, made Jan. 20, 1512-13, 4 Hen. VIII. between *William Wigfton* the younger, merchant of the Staple of Calys, of the firft part; *John Yonge*, dean of the new collegiate church of our Lady of Leicefter, of the fecond part; and *Richard Pexall*, abbot of the monaftery of *our Lady in the Meadows of Leicefter* aforefaid, and the convent of the fame, of the third part; and *Richard Gyllot*, mayor of the town of Leicefter, and burgefs of the fame, on the fourth part. Whereas the faid William Wigfton, by the fpecial agreement and licence of the faid dean and canons, at his proper cofts and charges, hath newly builded and erected a manfion-place, and inclofed the fame manfion with a garden thereto adjoining, within the precinct and walls of the faid College, for the manfion-place of and for two chantry priefts, by him, with God's grace, to be founded within the fame College, to the honour of Almighty God, our Bleffed Lady, Saint Urfula, and Saint Catharine; which manfion and garden being fet between the manfion-place and garden of Mr. Thomas Wigfton, now one of the prebendaries of the faid College, of the prebend called *The Thirteen Prebends*, on the Eaft part, and the Caftle-way on the Weft part, and extendeth from the church-yard of the faid College on the South unto the garden of the Rood-houfe on the North part: And, for the foundation of the aforefaid chantry and chantry priefts, the aforefaid William Wigfton hath obtained the letters patent of our forefaid Sovereign Lord the King, to the aforefaid William Wigfton, Thomas Wigfton, and William Fifher. And whereas the fame William Wigfton, by the fpecial licence, agreement, and confent, of the aforefaid dean and canons, hath newly erected, made, and edified, in the honour of Almighty God, our Bleffed Lady, Saint Urfula, and Saint Catharine, a new chapel, inclofed with coftly works wrought and made of laten, fixed and laid betwixt two pillars in the body of the church of the aforefaid College, on the North fide; to the ufe and intent that the aforefaid chantry priefts and their fucceffors fhall there daily, perpetually, minifter divine fervice, as chantry priefts of the chantry of the faid William Wigfton the younger, according to fuch ordinances and ftatutes as the fame William Wigfton, or the aforefaid Thomas, Roger, and William, or the executors of them, or the over-liver of them, fhall make, by the confent of the faid dean and chapter by his or their writing to be fealed with his or their feal: It is now covenanted, granted, and agreed between the faid parties, and every of them, in manner following, that is to fay: Firft, the faid dean and canons, and their fucceffors, fhall fuffer the faid chantry priefts and their fucceffors for ever thereafter to minifter divine fervice in the fame newly-erected laten chapel, without difturbance of the faid

dean or canons, or of any other, according to the aforefaid ordinances. For which and other purpofes William Wigfton granted to the dean and canons, and their fucceffors, the manor of Chefter, in the county of Northampton, and all his lands and tenements in Chefter aforefaid, Archefter, Little Chefter, Chefter by the Water, and Irtlyngburgh, and alfo two meffuages and two yard-lands in Swannington, in the county of Leicefter, to the yearly value of 20*l.* above all charges: And the dean and canons engage to grant to the faid chantry priefts an annuity of 14*l. per annum*; i. e. to either of them 7*l. per annum*, payable, quarterly, at Candlemas, May-day, Lammas, and All Saints. Alfo they engage, yearly, on 26th of January, to keep a folemn obit, with Dirige and mafs on the morrow, with fong, and bells to be rung, for the good eftate of the faid William Wigfton junior during his life, and for his foul after his death, in like manner as they do in other folemn obits; at which they who are prefent are to have as followeth; viz. the dean, 2*s.*; every canon, 12*d.*; every vicar, 6*d.*; every chief clerk, 6*d.*; each of the faid chantry priefts, 6*d.*; and other chantry priefts of the faid College, 4*d.*; each chorifter, 3*d.*; and the verge-bearer, 3*d.*: And if any of the faid canons or other minifters be out of town of Leicefter, he is to have as if prefent; but if in town, and yet abfent, to have nothing. The dean and canons alfo engage, at the time of Dirige and mafs of the faid obit, to find four wax tapers, fuch as they find at other obits, to burn at the hearfe of the faid William; and alfo to pay on the day of the faid obit, yearly, as follows; viz. to the mayor of Leicefter, and his brethren and minifters of the faid town, reforting to the faid obit, and offering there at the mafs, and faying at the door of the faid new laten chapel, before they depart out of the faid College, the Pfalm *De profundis*, for the foul of the faid William Wigfton, 3*s.*; to be applied as followeth; viz. to the mayor, 8*d.*; and to every fix of his moft antient brethren, 4*d.*; to the mayor's ferjeant, 2*d.*; and to the mayor's clerk, 2*d.*; and the bellman, to make relation and notice throughout the town the day and time of the faid obit, as he doth at other fpecial obits, 2*d.*: And alfo the dean and canons, yearly, to diftribute among the poor people, on the day of the faid obit, 2*s.* in money; and, yearly, to caufe 24 penny tapers of wax to be made, and fet upon the candlefticks of the faid new laten chapel; and that the fame be made and renewed twice in the year; i. e. at the feaft of Eafter and All Saints; and they fhall be lighted by the clerk of the College or deputy at the eight principal feafts folemnized in the faid College, and all the feafts of our Lady, and in the feaft of St. Catharine [4] and St. Urfula, in time of high mafs and *Magnificat*: And the dean, yearly, to pay the clerk, for lighting and doing out the tapers, 16*d.*; i. e. each quarter 4*d.*; and the dean and canons to pay, yearly, for fcowering the faid laten chapel, 4*d.*; and to find for the two chantry priefts bread, wine, wax candle for their mafs; and to keep and repair the ornaments which William Wigfton gave to the chapel, &c. (as mentioned particularly in p. 335.) For which agreements and grants, William Wigfton paid to the faid dean and canons, the day of the date of thefe prefents, 100 marks fterling: And further it was agreed, that the dean and canons pay to the provoft of the faid College 6*s.* 3*d. per annum*, for his pains in the premiffes; for which William Wigfton paid the faid dean and canons ten marks over and above the other gifts."

---

[1] Roger Wigfton, "defcended from a family of the Wigftons in Leicefter, divers whereof were merchants of the Staple," was a lawyer, and fteward to the priory of Pinley in Warwickfhire; where, at the time of the diffolution, Margaret Wigfton was priorefs. He was lord of the manor of Wolfton in Warwickfhire; high fheriff 33 Hen. VIII.; for feveral years in the commiffion of the peace; and, by his will, dated 34 Hen. VIII. he left his body to be buried in Wolfton church. Dugdale's Warwickfhire, vol. I. p. 37; vol. II. p. 822. His fon William afterwards obtained a grant of the fite of the priory of Pinley. See p. 476.   [2] See before, p. 334.   [3] See the Appendix to vol. I. p. 112.   [4] The 25th of November.

Vol. I.   [6 F]   " *Northampton*'.

" *Northampton*'.—Territorium vel Rentale manerii de Chefter by the Water, & terrarum parcell' manerii prediȼti, faȼtum vicefimo die Septembris, anno regni Regis Henricus Oȼtavi quarto, per Willielmum Roberts de Wollafton, Thomam Roberts, Ricardum Smith, & alios.

Per fitum manerii infra metas ejufdem, & prediȼtarum terrarum arabilium vocatarum Chefter borough, continentium xx acras; & alie parcelle infra metas ejufdem, vocate Eft croft, continentis alias xx acras, vocatus in toto duas virgatas & plura, cum unâ parvâ parcellâ prati adjacente. Sunt modò in tenurâ diȼti Willielmi Roberts & Willielmi Fifher, & reddunt per annum in toto   1 16 8

Item ibidem quoddam pratum vocatum Chefterton Holme, in tenurâ diȼti Willielmi Roberts & Willielmi Fifher, & reddit per annum   –   –   –   –   1 10 0

Item ibidem claufum prati, vocatum Chefterton Sugg, in tenurâ diȼti Willielmi Fifher, & reddit per annum   –   –   1 6 8

Item ibidem trefdecim virgatas terre arabilis, jacentes in campis de Archefter."

But the bounty of William Wygfton did not ftop here. He very foon enlarged his original plan; and, on the 10th of June 1513, affociating with him his two brothers, obtained letters patent from King Henry VIII. for the founding and endowing a perpetual Hofpital within the town of Leicefter; and, in confequence, compiled a fuitable code of laws and regulations[1]; and provided for its endowment with divers manor and lands; direȼting, that, at the expiration of the term which he had granted to the chantry in the collegiate church of the Newark, there fhould be in the Hofpital, befides the 12 poor men and 12 women (if the revenue would thereunto extend) a Mafter and three Confraters: but at firft there was a Mafter and one Confrater only, and fo it ftill continues.

It appears, however, that Mr. Wigfton did not live to carry his benevolence into effeȼt; for it is ftated in the Aȼt of Parliament of 18 Elizabeth, that " he did not accomplifh the fame during his life[2];" but that the then furviving truftees (whom he had made his executors) obtained, on the 13th of July in the fame year, the king's letters patent for the fame purpofe[3]; and on the 10th of November following had a further confirmation of the fame grant, with permiffion to purchafe, for the ufe of the faid Hofpital, manors, lands, and tenements, of the yearly value of 23*l. ultra reprifas*[4].

Feb. 1, 1516-17, " Rex affignavit Rogerum Wygfton receptorem fuum generalem omnium maneriorum, &c. que fuerunt alicujus heredis infra etatem in cuftodiâ fuâ exiftentium, ac percipiendi xxlĩ. per annum & xxs̃. pro portagio cujuflibet centum librarum, ad vitam[5]."

The Hofpital having been ereȼted within the parifh of St. Martin; an indenture was made, between *Richard Pekefall*, abbot, with his convent, and fir *Nicholas Wagftaffe*, vicar of St. Martin's, and fir *William Fyfhar*, mafter, and fir *John Thorpe*, confrater of the Hofpital, and the 24 poor people; whereby it was agreed, that the vicar fhall adminifter the facraments to the faid poor, and vifit them, as they do their other parifhioners, when there is need, and bury their bodies in the church-yard when dead: That the faid poor fhall be exempted from paying tithes, either predial or perfonal: That the abbot and vicar fhall permit the mafter and confrater to celebrate divine fervice in the chapel, and not compel them to be prefent at divine fervice in St. Martin's church or church-yard, or to adminifter the facraments to the parifhioners, or to fwear obedience to them: That at the death of any of the poor no mortuary fhall be demanded; but the mafter and confrater fhall pay mortuaries. It was alfo agreed, that, inftead of tithes, oblations, and other parochial rites due from the faid poor, the mafter fhall, every Eafter eve, before noon, pay

6s. 8d. on the high altar of St. Martin's church, to be divided equally between the abbot and the vicar; and, in cafe of failure or negleȼt, fhall forfeit 13s. 4d. to be divided between the abbot and vicar. And the parties above-named confented that they fhould be compelled to the obfervation of the premiffes by the bifhop of Lincoln, or his commiffary. Dated July 10, 1520, 12 Hen. VIII. Which compofition was ratified by William bifhop of Lincoln July 12. 1520; who alfo granted licence to have and adminifter the Eucharift in the chapel of the Hofpital, provided it were without detriment to the parifh church.

June 1, 1520, the mafter, confrater, and poor of this Hofpital, obtained a leafe for 100 years, renewable for ever, of a large garden abutting in St. Francis lane, the property of the Grey Friers[6].

Feb. 12, 1521-2, new letters patent were obtained from the king, in the following ample terms:

" Henricus Oȼtavus, Dei gratiâ, Anglie & Francie Rex, fidei defenfor, & dominus Hibernie; omnibus ad quos prefentes litere pervenerint, falutem. Sciatis quod cum nos, decimo die Junii, anno regni noftri quinto, per literas noftras patentes, concefferimus & licentiam dederimus, pro nobis & heredibus noftris, quantum in nobis fuit, dileȼtis nobis Willielmo Wigfton de Leiceftriâ juniori, mercatori Stapule Califie, Thome Wigfton clerico, Rogero Wigfton, & Willielmo Fifher clerico, & eorum cuilibet, heredibus & executoribus fuis, quod ipfi aut eorum aliquis, heredes aut executores fui, aut eorum aliquis vel aliqui, quoddam Hofpitale perpetuum, de duobus capellanis perpetuis, & de duodecim pauperibus perpetuis, in villâ Leiceftrie, in comitatu Leiceftrie, fingulis diebus, pro falubri ftatu noftro & Katherine regine Anglie confortis noftre dum vixerimus, & pro animabus noftris cum ab hâc luce migraverimus, necnon pro bono ftatu prediȼti Willielmi Wigfton dum vixerit, & pro ejus animâ cum ab hâc luce migraverit, & pro animabus patris & progenitorum fuorum, & pro animabus patris & progenitorum fuorum, & aliorum amicorum & benefaȼtorum ejufdem Willielmi Wigfton, & pro animabus omnium fidelium defunȼtorum, juxta ordinationes & ftatuta ipforum Willielmi Wigfton, Thome, Rogeri, & Willielmi Fifher, aut eorum aliquorum, feu eorum heredum vel executorum eorum, vel eorum alicujus, in eâ parte fiendas, in perpetuum celebraturis, facere, fundare, creare, erigere, & ftabilire poffet & poffent, perpetuis futuris temporibus duratura; & quod Hofpitale prediȼtum, cum fundatum, creatum, ereȼtum, & ftabilitum foret, Hofpitale Willielmi Wigfton de Leiceftriâ in perpetuum nuncuparetur; & quod capellani & pauperes prediȼti Hofpitalis, cum Hofpitale prediȼtum fic fundatum, creatum, & ftabilitum foret, & fucceffores fui, Capellani & pauperes Hofpitalis illius, fint unum corpus corporatum in re, jure, et nomine, haberentque fucceffionem perpetuam, ac forent perfone apte, habiles, & capaces in lege; & quod capellani & pauperes Hofpitalis prediȼti pro tempore exiftentes, & fucceffores fui capellani & pauperes Hofpitalis illius, per nomen et fub nomine Capellanorum et pauperum Willielmi Wigfton in villâ Leiceftrie, in comitatu Leiceftrie, placitare et implacitari, refpondere et refponderi, profequi et defendere poffent, in quibufcunque curiis noftris, heredum et fuccefforum noftrorum, et aliorum quorumcunque, in omnibus et omnimodis et quibufcunque aȼtionibus, feȼtis, querelis, et caufis realibus et perfonalibus, cujufcunque generis forent vel nature, coram quibufcunque juftitiariis et judicibus fpiritualibus ac temporalibus, ac aliis perfonis quibufcunque; & quod iidem capellani & pauperes, & fucceffores fui, haberent commune figillum pro negotiis Hofpitalis prediȼti agendum. Et ulterius concefferimus, & licentiam dederimus, pro nobis & heredibus noftris, per literas noftras prediȼtas, prefatis Willielmo, Thome, Rogero, & Willielmo, & eorum cuilibet, executoribus fuis & eorum cuilibet, ac quibufcunque aliis perfonis, & cuicunque alio perfone, quod ipfi, vel eorum aliquis vel aliqui, maneria, terras, & tenementa, vel redditus in perpetuum, ad annuum valorem quadraginta marcarum ultra omnia onera & reprifas, licet de nobis tenentur in

---

[1] See p. 474.   [2] See p. 484.   [3] Pat. 5 Hen. VIII.   [4] Pat. 6 Hen. VIII.
[5]   [6] See the Infpeximus Deed in p. 476.

capite vel per fervicium militare vel aliter, aut de aliquo alio, dare poffent & poffet & concedere capellanis & pauperibus Hofpitalis predicti pro tempore exiftentibus, cum Hofpitale predictum fic factum, fundatum, creatum, erectum, & ftabilitum foret, & fuccefforibus fuis in perpetuum; habendum & tenendum predicta maneria, terras, tenementa, & redditus, cum fuis pertinentiis, ad eundem annuum valorem quadraginta marcarum, eifdem capellanis & pauperibus, & fuccefforibus fuis in perpetuum, juxta ordinationes predictorum Willielmi, Thome, Rogeri, & Willielmi, vel executorum fuorum, vel aliquorum feu eorum alicujus, inde fiendas; & eifdem capellanis & pauperibus, & fuccefforibus fuis, quod ipfi & fucceffores fui eadem maneria, terras, & tenementa, cum pertinentiis, prefatis Willielmo, Thome, Rogero, & Willielmo, & executotibus fuis, feu eorum aliquo vel aliquibus, feu aliquibus aliis perfonis, vel aliquo alio perfone, recipere, gaudere, & optinere poffent & tenere, predictis capellanis & pauperibus Hofpitalis illius, & fuccefforibus fuis in perpetuum, juxta eandem ordinationem, ut premittitur, fiend', ficut predictum eft, tenore prefentium, fimiliter licentiam dederimus & conceffremus fpecialem, abfque impetitione, moleftia, impedimento, vel perturbatione noftri, vel heredum noftrorum, jufticiariorum, efchaetorum, vicecomitum, coronatorum, ballivorum, feu miniftrorum noftrorum vel heredum noftrorum quorumcunque, & abfque fine vel feodo in cancellaria noftra feu in hanaperio cancellarie noftre aut alibi qualitercunque, ad opus noftrum vel heredum noftrorum inde faciend', reddend', aut folvend', & abfque aliquo brevi de ad quod dampnum, five de aliquibus aliis literis patentibus feu mandatis, & abfque aliqua inquifitione fuper aliquo brevi de ad quod dampnum, five de aliquibus aliis literis patentibus feu mandatis noftris, vel heredum noftrorum, in ea parte habend' perfequend', impetrand', feu capiend', aut in cancellariam noftram, heredum vel fuccefforum noftrorum, feu alibi retornand', ftatuto de terris & tenementis ad manum mortuam non ponend' edito, aut aliquo alio ftatuto, actu, ordinatione, provifione, inde in contrarium facto, ordinato, five provifo, non obftante. Sciatis etiam quod cum nos, decimo die Novembris, anno regni noftri fexto, per alias literas noftras patentes, meliorationem Hofpitalis predicti, necnon fuftentationem eorundem capellanorum & pauperum augmentare plurimum affectantes, prefatas literas noftras patentes, ac omnia & fingula in eifdem contenta, predictis Willielmo, Thome, Rogero, et Willielmo, et cuicunque alio, per eafdem conceffas, ratas et rata, grata et gratas habentes, de uberiori gratia noftra, et fpeciali et mero motu noftris, ac pro diverfis aliis confiderationibus nos fpecialiter moventibus, conceffremus, ac etiam licentiam dederimus, per literas noftras predictas, pro nobis et heredibus noftris predictis, quantum in nobis fuit, prefatis Willielmo Wigfton, Thome Wigfton clerico, Rogero Wigfton, et Willielmo Fifher clerico, et eorum cuilibet, et executoribus fuis et eorum cuilibet, et quibufcunque aliis perfonis et cuicunque alio perfone, quod ipfi, vel eorum aliquis vel aliqui, dominia, maneria, terras, tenementa, redditus, reverfiones, fervicia, et hereditamenta quecunque, aut alias poffeffiones quafcunque, cum pertinentiis, ad annuum valorem viginti et trium librarum ultra omnia onera et reprifas, licet de nobis tenentur in capite, vel per fervitium militare, vel aliter, aut aliquo alio modo, dare, concedere, legare, et affignare poffent et poffet, ultra et fuper maneria, terras, et tenementa, ad annuum valorem dictarum quadraginta marcarum, que virtute conceffionis et licentie noftre in dictis aliis literis noftris patentibus fpecificate dicto Hofpitali, capellanis et pauperibus pro tempore exiftentibus, et fuccefforibus fuis, in perpetuum dare et concedere contingerint; habendum et tenendum dicta dominia, maneria, terras, tenementa, redditus, reverfiones, fervicia, hereditamenta, et poffeffiones, ad eundem annuum valorem viginti et trium librarum, ultra et fupra dicta maneria, terras et tenementa ad annuum valorem quadraginta marcarum, eifdem capellanis & pauperibus, et fuccefforibus fuis in perpetuum, concedend', juxta ordinationes predictorum Willielmi, Thome, Rogeri, et Willielmi, feu executorum fuorum, vel aliquorum five alicujus eorum, inde faciendas; et quod ipfi et

fucceffores fui eadem omnia et fingula dominia et maneria, terras, tenementa, redditus, reverfiones, fervicia, hereditamenta, et poffeffiones, a prefatis Willielmo, Thoma, Rogero, et Wiliielmo, et executoribus fuis, eorum aliquo vel aliquibus, feu aliquibus aliis perfonis, vel aliqua alia perfona, recipere, acquirere, gaudere, et optinere poffent, et tenere; habend' et tenend' capellanis et pauperibus predictis, et fuccefforibus fuis in perpetuum, juxta eafdem ordinationes, permittatur fiend'. Et fimiliter, tenore predictarum literarum noftrarum, licentiam dederimus fpecialem et conceffremus prefatis Willielmo, Thome, Rogero, et Willielmo, quod ipfi, aut eorum aliquis, aut executores vel affignati fui, aut eorum aliquis vel aliqui, optineat vel optineant, ac habere et optinere poffent, tam predictas literas noftras patentes, quam omnia et omnimoda brevia ac literas regias executorias et confirmatorias in hac parte de tempore in tempus fienda et exequend', fine impedimento five impetitione, contradictione, feu gravamine noftri, vel heredum aut fuccefforum noftrorum, jufticiariorum, vicecomitum, ballivorum, feu aliorum miniftrorum noftrorum quorumcunque, & abfque fine vel feodo in cancellaria noftra, feu in hanaperio cancellarie noftre, aut alibi qualitercunque, ad opus noftrum vel heredum noftrorum inde faciend', reddend', folvend', taxand', imponend', feu capiend', & abfque aliquo brevi de ad quod dampnum, five aliquibus aliis literis patentibus feu mandatis noftris, & abfque aliqua inquifitione feu aliquo brevi de ad quod dampnum, five de aliquibus aliis literis patentibus feu mandatis noftris, vel heredum noftrorum, in hac parte habend', impetrand', profequend', feu capiend', aut in cancellariam noftram, heredum vel fuccefforum noftrorum, feu alibi, retornand'; & quod cuftos five clericus hanaperii predicti, aut ejus deputatus ibidem pro tempore exiftens, erit inde quietus, & in computo fuo ad Scaccarium noftrum, & heredum vel fuccefforum noftrorum reddend', exonerati exiftent in perpetuum, ftatuto de terris & tenementis ad manum mortuam non ponendis, aut aliquibus aliis ftatutis, actubus, ordinationibus, provifionibus, reftrictionibus, five mandatis noftris inde in contrarium factis, editis, ordinatis, five provifis, aut aliqua alia caufa, re, vel materia quacunque in aliquo non obftante, prout in literis noftris plenius continetur: Nos, nolentes conceffiones & licentias noftras predictas effectum debitum mancipari, conceffimus & licentiam dedimus, pro nobis & heredibus noftris, prefatis Willielmo Wigfton, Thome Wigfton, Rogero Wigfton, & Willielmo Fifher, & eorum cuilibet, quod ipfi & eorum quilibet manerium de Caftel Carlton, cum pertinentiis, in comitatu Lincolnie; & viginta fex meffuagia, fex tofta, quadraginta acras terre, centum acras prati, quinquaginta acras pafture, triginta acras bofci, & quadraginta folidatos & novem denaratos, & unum obolum redditus, cum pertinentiis, in Caftel Carlton, & advocationem libere capelle de Caftel Carlton, que de nobis tenentur per fidelitatem & redditum octo denariorum, & que ad valorem viginti & duarum librarum extenduntur per annum, prout per quandam inquifitionem coram Johanne Topecliffe armigero, efchaetore noftro in comitatu predicto, de mandato noftro captum, & in cancellariam noftram retornatum, eft compertum; necnon manerium de Swannington, cum pertinentiis, ac duodecim meffuagia, decem tofta, viginti acras terre, centum acras prati, ducentas acras pafture, centum acras bofci, & fexdecim folidatos redditus, cum pertinentiis, in Swannington predicto, Sybfton, Raunfton, Ibftoke, Hatherne, & Arbery; ac unum meffuagium, quatuor crofta, centum per viginti & quatuor acras terre, viginti acras prati, viginti acras pafture, cum pertinentiis, in Cawdwell & Wickham, in comitatu Leiceftrie; ac etiam tria meffuagia, & quatuor claufuras continentes triginta acras pafture, in villa & fuburbiis Leiceftrie, unde unum meffuagium jacet in le Southgate, & alia duo meffuagia jacent in le Canke juxta meffuagium Roberti Harward, & una de predictis quatuor claufuris jacet in Hangman lane, & alia de eifdem juxta Humberftone gate, & tertia ejufdem juxta Barkelane, & quarta juxta Gellfhall lane; & unum ortum, quondam tria gardina, juxta Cow lane, per terram Roberti Orton, & duos folidatos

datos redditûs, cum pertinentiis, exeuntes de quodam tenemento Thome Greene in Southgate ; necnon unum meſſuagium, quadraginta acras terre, decem acras prati, duodecim acras paſture, & decem ſolidatos redditûs, cum pertinentiis, in Oadeby, in comitatu predicto ; & tria meſſuagia, duas virgatas & dimidiam terre, duodecim acras prati, & viginti acras paſture, cum pertinentiis, in Kylnecote & Walton, in comitatu predicto, que de nobis tenentur ut de ducatu noſtro Lancaſtrie, & que ad annuum valorem decem & octo librarum extenduntur per annum, prout per quandam aliam inquiſitionem, coram Johanne Peyto armigero, nuper eſchaetore noſtro in comitatu Leiceſtrie predicte, de mandato noſtro captam, & in cancellariam noſtram retornatam, eſt compertum, dare & concedere poſſent vel poſſet dilectis nobis in Chriſto Willielmo Fiſher & Johanni Thorpe, capellanis Hoſpitalis Willielmi Wigſton de Leiceſtriâ, in comitatu Leiceſtrie, & pauperibus ejuſdem Hoſpitalis ; habend' & tenend' eis & ſucceſſoribus ſuis, capellanis & pauperibus Hoſpitalis predicti in perpetuum, in partem quadraginta & novem librarum, treſdecim ſolidorum, & quatuor denariorum, dictorum tenementorum & reddituum predictorum ; & eiſdem Willielmo Fiſher & Johanni Thorpe, capellanis Hoſpitalis predicti, & pauperibus ejuſdem, quod ipſi manerium & cetera premiſſa, cum pertinentiis, à prefatis Willielmo Wigſton, Thomâ Wigſton, Rogero Wigſton, & Willielmo Fiſher, ſeu eorum aliquo vel aliquibus, recipere poſſint & tenere, ſibi & ſucceſſoribus ſuis, ſicut predictum eſt, ſimiliter licentiam dedimus ſpecialem, ſtatuto predicto non obſtante ; nolentes quod prefati Willielmus Wigſton, Thomas Wigſton, Rogerus Wigſton, Willielmus Fiſher, heredes vel executores ſui, aut prefatus Willielmus Fiſher & Johannes Thorpe, capellani Hoſpitalis predicti, aut pauperes ejuſdem, vel ſucceſſores ſui, ratione premiſſorum, per nos vel heredes noſtros, juſticiarios, eſcaetores, vicecomites, aut alios ballivos vel miniſtros noſtros, ſeu heredum noſtrorum, quodcunque futuris temporibus inde occaſionentur, moleſtantur, impetantur, inquietantur, perturbentur in aliquo, ſeu graventur ; ſalvis tamen nobis & heredibus noſtris ſerviciis inde debitis & conſuetis. In cujus rei teſtimonium, has literas noſtras fieri fecimus patentes. Teſte meipſo, apud Weſtmonaſterium, duodecimo die Februarii, anno regni noſtri tertio decimo."

The ſtatutes which were compiled by the Founder are in Latin, and very long ; nor have I a complete copy of them ; but, by what remains, it appears that it was the intention of Mr. Wigſton that both the maſter and confrater ſhould be *ſeculares, non religioſi*. He directs alſo, that, after the deceaſe of himſelf, and his two brothers *Thomas* and *Roger*, upon any vacancy of the maſter or confrater, the dean and chapter of the collegiate church of *The Newark* ſhould have power to chooſe and put into the vacant place a fit perſon for one fortnight ; which if they neglected to do in that fortnight's ſpace, then the mayor of Leiceſter for the time being, with the four juſtices of peace of the ſaid town, or at leaſt with the two ſenior juſtices, ſhould have the power, for the next following fortnight, to name, admit, and put, a fit perſon into the place vacant ; and in caſe of their neglect, the like power was granted to the abbot for the next fourteen days ; and in caſe of his neglect, it reverted to the dean and chapter of the Newark again for another fortnight, and then to the mayor and juſtices, and to the abbot, ſucceſſively, till the place ſhould be filled. It was alſo ordered, that the maſter and confrater ſhould conſtantly reſide within the precincts of the Hoſpital ; and not be abſent above 40 days in a year, unleſs upon the affairs of the Hoſpital, without leave of one of the canons of the Newark ; with this proviſo, that the maſter and confrater ſhould never both be abſent at the ſame time one whole day and night. The founder allowed the maſter to have one benefice out of the town of Leiceſter, provided that he conſtantly reſided in the Hoſpital ; but confined the confrater to his preferment in the Hoſpital, ſo that if he had any other benefice, with cure or without cure, or any farm or promotion whatſoever, he ſhould be deprived and expelled immediately. He alſo ordained, that all fines and profits ariſing from letting the lands and

tenements ſhould be applied to the uſe of the Hoſpital ; and that, if either the maſter or confrater ſhould retain any of the ſaid profits to their own uſe, he ſhould be expelled, &c. Theſe, with other ſtatutes relating to the maſter, confrater, 12 men and 12 women, were confirmed by John biſhop of Lincoln ; and by Richard Mawdely, archdeacon of Leiceſter.

Mr. Rogers, who was confrater here in 1697, and archdeacon of Leiceſter in 1704, having contended againſt Mr. Carte, then vicar of St. Martin's, that Wigſton's Hoſpital was no part of that pariſh, and having forbid ſuch perſons as lived within the precincts of the Hoſpital, although no members of the Hoſpital, to pay any parochial due, either to the vicar or officers of the pariſh ; " I think it proper to obſerve," ſays Mr. Carte, " that William Wigſton, in his foundation charter, ſays he had built it ' ſupra quandam terram meam infra villam Leyceſtrie, juxta cemiterium eccleſie parochialis Sancti Martini ex parte occidentali, & infra limites ejuſdem parochie.' And John biſhop of Lincoln, in his confirmation of the ſtatutes of William Wigſton, dated at Buckden, ultimo Sept. 1522, deſcribes it to be ' Hoſpitale conſtructum infra parochiam Sancti Martini de Leiceſtriâ.' So likewiſe Richard Mawdely, S. T. B. archdeacon of Leiceſter, in his confirmation of the Statutes, dated at Leiceſter April 13, 1525, calls it, ' Hoſpitale pauperum infra parochiam Sancti Martini, Leiceſtrie.' And in the compoſition made between the abbot of Leiceſter, and the vicar of St. Martin, and the maſter of the Hoſpital, it is ſaid to be founded ' infra parochiam eccleſie parochialis Sancti Martini, Leiceſtrie ;' and the ſaid vicar is bound, by himſelf or deputy, to viſit and miniſter the Sacrament and ſacramentals to all the poor men and women in the Hoſpital, ' prout aliis ſuis ibidem parochianis & filiis ſpiritualiis facient ;' dated July 10, 1520.'

By a copy of an inſtrument, or Inſpeximus, remaining in the Court of Exchequer, bearing " Teſte, Thomâ duce Norfolc', theſaurario Anglie, apud Weſtmonaſterium, 29 Octobris, 23 Hen. VIII." it appears that *William Hopton*, eſq. ſon and heir of *John* Hopton, eſq. formerly held of the king, *in capite*, the third part of the manor of Caſtel Carleton, with the third part of the advowſon of the church there, by ſervice of the third part of a knight's fee, &c. &c. The chaplains and poor men of Wigſton's Hoſpital in Leiceſter 19 Hen. VIII. appearing in the Exchequer, ſhewed that *Arthur Hopton*, eſq. was ſeiſed of that third part, and alſo two other parts of the manor of Caſtel Carleton, in the county of Lincoln, in demeſne, as of fee ; and that *William Wigſton* (in virtue of the king's letters patent for founding an Hoſpital, &c.) having the ſaid manor, with the appurtenances, ſettled for his uſe, by a recovery, did, by writing, 1 March, 11 Henry VIII. ſettle on them the ſaid manor, with the appurtenances, in Caſtel Carleton, Great Carleton, and Little Carleton, co. Lincoln ; and alſo the manor of Swannington, and 12 meſſuages, 10 tofts, 20 yard-lands, 100 acres of meadow, 200 acres of paſture, 100 acres of wood, and 16s. rent, in Swannington, Sybſon, Raunſton, Ibſtock, Hathern, and Arbery ; and one meſſuage, four crofts, 124 acres of land, 20 acres of meadow, 20 acres of paſture, in Cawdewell and Wykeham, co. Leic. ; and three meſſuages, four cloſes, containing 30 acres of paſture, in Leiceſter and its ſuburbs ; one garden, formerly three gardens, juxta Cow-lane, and 2s. rent of the houſe of Thomas Grene, in Southgate ; alſo one meſſuage, 40 acres of land, 10 of meadow, 12 acres of paſture, and 10s. rent, in Ondeby ; and three meſſuages, two yard-lands and a half, 12 acres of meadow, and 20 of paſture, in Kymcote and Walton, co. Leic. ; all which amounted to the yearly value of 49l. 13s. 4d. And they ſaid, that the manor of Caſtel Carleton, with its appurtenances, viz. 26 meſſuages, 6 tofts, 40 acres of land, 100 acres of meadow, 40 acres of paſture, 30 acres of wood, 100 acres of mariſh, and 40s. 9d. ob. rent, in Caſtel Carleton, Great Carleton, Little Carleton, in the county of Lincoln, beyond repriſals, are worth 22l. per annum, and no more ; and the manor of Swannington,

with

with its appurtenances there, and in Sybfton, Raunfton, Ibftock, Hathern, and Arbery, and the meffuages, lands, and tenements, in Cawdewell and
Wyken, and town and fuburb of Leicefter, and Ondeby and Kymcote, and Walton, in the county of
Leicefter, beyond reprifals, are worth but 18*l. per
annum* [1].

In 1539, a furvey of this Hofpital was made by
the king's commiffioners; the refult of which will appear in the following account, remaining in the Augmentation office:

" Hofpitale Sancte Urfule, ex fundatione Willielmi Wigfton, in cemiterio Sancti Martini, infra
villam Leyceftrie, valet in firmâ,

Omnium terrarum & tenementorum, tam liberorum
quam cuftumariorum tenentium ac ad voluntatem, in
Carleton, in comitatu Lincolnie, folvend' ad feftum
Annunciationis Beate Marie Virginis & Sancti Martini
equaliter, prout particulariter per Rentale inde factum & renovatum apparet, per annum xxviili. iiid. ob.

Omnium terrarum & tenementorum, tam liberorum
quam cuftumariorum tenentium ac ad voluntatem, in
Swanyngton, Hatherne, Gnypton, Raunfton, Yp-
ftoke, & Harbere, in comitatibus Warr' & Leic', folvend' ad fefta predicta, prout particulariter, &c.
xxiiili. ixs. iiid. qª.

Diverfarum aliarum terrarum & tenementorum in
Burton fuper Trent, dimiff' diverfis perfonis per indenturas, folvend' ad feftum Michaelis tantùm, prout
particulariter, &c. xs.

Omnium terrarum & tenementorum in villâ Leiceftrie, Odebye, Wygfton, Bowdoen, Norton, Lyn-
cot, & Walcot, in comitatu Leiceftrie, folvend' ad
fefta Annunciationis Beate Marie & Sancti Martini
Apoftoli equaliter, prout, &c. xxili. xviis. ixd. ob.

Omnium terrarum & tenementorum in Bottisforth, in
predict' comitatu Leiceftrie, folvend' ad fefta predicta
equaliter, per annum, prout, &c xxli. xviiid. ob.

Unius domûs elimozynarii, cum quatuor cameris &
fuis pertinentiis ibidem, valet per annum xiiis. iiii.

Inde ᵡᵡxviili. xviiis. ob. qª.

Reprif', viz. in

Redditubus refolutis diverfis perfonis fequentibus; viz.

Domino Regi, ut Ducatui fuo Lancaftrie, iiiis.

Comiti Rutlandie iid.

Eidem Domino Regi, ad manus vicecomitis Leiceftrie, exeunt' de tenemento in tenurâ Thome Houfe, xiid.

Gardiano ecclefie parochialis de Bottysford, xiid.

Prefato comiti Rutlandie, exeunt' de tenemento
in tenurâ Johannis Lambe, viiid.

Eidem comiti, exeunt' de tenemento in Barefton
Petri Dyxon, q̃. lb. piperis, appreciat' ad iis.

Prefato Domino Regi, ad manus vicecomitis Leiceftrie, exeunt' de predicto tenemento, xiid.

Vicecomiti Lincolnie, pro fecta curie relaxand', viiid.

Eidem Domino Regi, ut ducatui fuo Lancaftrie,
exeunt' de certis terris in Swannyngton, xxviis. iiiid.

Ducatui Lancaftrie predicto xd.

Eidem Domino Regi, ut in jure nuper prioratûs five
Hofpitalis Sancti Johannis Jerufalem in Angliâ, ad manerium fuum de Hether, iid.

Vicecomiti Lincolnie, pro fecta relaxand', iiiid.

Eidem vicecomiti, pro fecta curie in Carleton, viiid.

Nuper abbati de Pratis, Leiceftrie, exeunt' de tenemento in Braunfton gate, xiis.

Eidem nuper monafterio de Pratis, Leiceftrie, exeunt' de certis terris vocatis Grone land, in le Weft
field, in Suburbiis Leiceftrie, xiid.

Decano Beate Marie juxta Caftrum Leiceftrie xiid.

Gilde Sancte Margarete Leiceftrie vid.

Collegio Novi Operis Leiceftrie xvid. ob.

Johanni Ruding, exeunt' de uno tenemento in villâ
Leiceftrie, in tenurâ Henrici Stampforde, vs.

Thome Catlyn iiiid.

Ducatui Lancaftrie xvid.

Eidem ducatui iiiis.

Eidem, exeunt' de tenemento vocato Canke, ixd.

Eidem, exeunt' de alio tenemento in Southgate, ixd.

Eidem, exeunt' de uno claufo in Mylfton lane, vs.

Eidem, exeunt' de uno claufo in Normandy, xiid.

Eidem ducatui, exeunt' de uno claufo in Humberfton, xviid. ob.

Heredibus domini Broke, exeunt' de uno tenemento in Kymett, xixd. ob.

In toto, per annum, iiiili. iiis. iiiid. ob.

Stipendio Walteri Browne, gardiani Hofpitalis five
domûs oratorii predicti, per annum viiili.

Stipendio Thome Thorpe, clerici, divina fervicia
infra capellam ejufdem Hofpitalis, celebrantis, per
annum vili.

Denariis folutis prefatis Waltero Browne & Thome
Thorpe per dotes, fcilicet ex dono fundatoris, durante vitâ eorum naturali, cuilibet eorum ad xls. per
annum, in toto iiiili.

Stipendio Ricardi Wylcocks & Nicholai Lubbenham, clericorum, divina fervicia infra capellam predictam celebrantium, cuilibet eorum ad cvis. viiid.
per annum, in toto xli. xiiis. iiiid.

Denariis folutis xii pauperibus viris & xii pauperibus mulieribus infra Hofpitium predictum degentibus,
ad xvs. iiiid. per feptimanam inter eos dividend';
viz. cuilibet viro per feptimanam viiid. cuilibet mu-
lieri ix mulierum predictarum viid. & tribus aliis re-
fiduis viiid. ; in toto, juxta ratam predictam, per annum, xxxixli. xiiis.

Confimilibus denariis annualiter folutis pro novâ
vefturâ xii illorum pauperum, per annum xxxixs. xd.

Denariis folutis pro carbonibus & focalibus inter
predictos pauperes annualiter expendendis, per annum xliiis.

Feodo Thome Lyttylbury, fenefcalli omnium terrarum & poffeffionum domini de Carleton, per annum
vis. viiid.

Feodo Harberti Thornedyke, baliivi ibidem, per
annum xvis. viiid.

Feodo Petri Dyxton, ballivi ballivatûs de Bottis-
ford, per annum xiiis. iiiid.

Denariis folutis Edwardo Beamont, ballivo ballivatûs de Swannyngton, Burton, & Horningho, in comitatu Staffordie, per annum vis. viiid.

Confimilibus denariis folutis Johanni Beamonte
armigero, fenefchallo ibidem, per annum xs.

Denariis folutis pro cuftubus & expenfis fenefchalli
ibidem, per annum vs.

Denariis annualiter folutis pro fectâ curie relaxand'
ad dominum curie per annum iis.

Denariis annualiter folutis vicario Sancti Martini,
pro decimis ordinatis per compofitionem, per annum
vis. viiid.

Denariis folutis pro pane & vino ac cerâ & oleo
infra capellam Hofpitalis predicti annualiter expend',
per annum xs.

Denariis folutis anniverfariis fundatoris & parentum fuorum in ecclefiâ parochiali Sancti Martini,
cum expenfis campanarum ibidem, per annum xiis.

Denariis folutis pro fale farinâ pro pauperibus predictis annualiter expend', per annum xiiis. iiiid.

Denariis folutis pro expenfa for', cum reparationibus, per annum xs.

Annuitate Agnetis Dawkins vidue, annualiter re-
cipiendâ, tam extra quoddam tenementum in Walton ad
xis. per annum, quam extra alium tenementum in Kymcote ad xiiis. per annum, que tenet per literas patentes ut parcellam dotis, fcilicet, per annum xxiiis.

Annuitate Willielmi Wigfton armigeri, & Johannis Haywar generofi, conceffâ per literas patentes,
pro termino vite, fcilicet, per annum xxvis. viiid.

Decimis Domino Regi annualiter inde folutis iiiili.
iiis. viiid.

Et remanet clarè per annum is. viid.

" The faid chauntry was founded by William Wygfton the younger, under the lycens of our Sovereign
Lord the King that now ys, to th'entente to find one
warden, three prefts, and twenty-four poor people,
continually to pray for th'eftate of the faid king, and
for the founders of the fame, within the faid Hofpital, whereof one of the faid four prefts to fing dyvyne
fervice within the parifh church of St. Martyn there,
for certain years not yet finifhed; and, after thofe
years expired, to celebrate within the faid Hofpital, yf
the revenues and profytts of the fame would fuffyce;
which feid warden and prefts, with the poor men, be

---

[1] Extracted from the original Record in the Court of Exchequer.

all there refident, in good order and eftate, according to their foundation. And there hath been no lands nor tenements to the fame belonging fold fince the time before lymited; and an inventory of the ornements thereto appertaining hereafter doth appear. And all the faid rooms be full, and none void."

The two chantry priefts in 1539 were, John Hardy and Humfrey Gyliot [1].

In 1540, the following deed occurs:

" Henricus Octavus, Dei gratiâ, Anglie & Francie rex, fidei defenfor, dominus Hibernie, & in terrâ fupremum caput Anglicane Ecclefie. Omnibus ad quos prefentes litere pervenerint, falutem. Infpeximus, inter recorda & irrotulamenta Curie Augmentationum Reventionum Corone noftre, quoddam decretum per Cancellarium & Concilium Curie predicte factum, in hec verba: " Memorandum, quod Termino Sancti Michaelis, videlicet, 29° die Novembris, anno regni regis Henrici Octavi 30°, Willielmus Fifher capellanus, Johannes Thorpe capellanus, & duodecim pauperes viri Hofpitalis Willielmi Wigfton junioris Leiceftrie, venerunt in Curiam dicti domini regis Augmentationum Reventionum Corone fue, & protulerunt ibidem quandam indenturam fub figillo conventuali Fratrum Minorum ville Leiceftrie predicte factam & figillatam, & petunt illam allocari, cujus quidem indenture tenor fequitur, in hec verba : ' Hec indentura, facta 20° die menfis Julii, anno regni regis Henrici Octavi poft Conqueftum Anglie 12°, inter fratrem Alanum Bell, gardianum & conventum domûs fratrum Minorum ville Leiceftrie ex parte unâ, & dominum Willielmum Fifher & dominum Johannem Thorpe capellanos, & duodecim pauperes viros Hofpitalis Willielmi Wigfton junioris Leiceftrie ex parte alterâ, teftatur, quod predicti gardianus & conventus, ex confenfu & beneplacito reverendi patris fratris Ricardi Brinckley, theologie doctoris, ejufdem ordinis minifterii provincialis & capituli provincialis, concefferunt, tradiderunt, & ad firmam dimiferunt, predictis domino Willielmo Fifher & domino Johanni Thorpe capellanis, & pauperibus Hofpitalis predicti, & fuccefforibus fuis, unum gardinum jacentem infra limites ejufdem domûs fratrum Minorum, juxta venellam vocatam *Saint Francis lane* ex parte Boreali, & extendit fe ab eâdem venellâ juxta Auftrum in latitudine LXXXV pedes per ftandardum, & longitudine ab Orientali parte ufque ad Occidentem CXV pedes; habend' & tenend' predictum gardinum, cum fuis pertinentiis, prefatis capellanis & pauperibus, & fuccefforibus fuis, à die confectionis prefentium, ufque ad terminum centum annorum, & fic deinde de centum annis in centum annos in perpetuum; reddend' inde prefatis gardiano & conventui, & fuccefforibus fuis, in puram elemofinam, annuatim, quatuor folidos bone & legalis monete Anglie, folvend' eifdem omnino ad feftum Pafche, vel infra quatuordecim dies proximè fequentes fine ulteriori morâ. Et fi contingat predictam fummam quatuor folidorum à retro fore poft aliquod feftum quo folvi debeat, in parte vel in toto, & unum menfem extunc, benè licebit predictos gardianum & conventum, & fuccefforesfuos, in predictum gardinum, cum fuis pertinentiis, diftringere, & diftrictiones fic captas & ibidem inventas afportare, abducere, effugare, & penes fe retinere, quoufque de totâ predictâ fummâ, cum omnibus inde arreragiis, fuerit fatisfactum. Et fi contingat dictam fummam à retro fore in parte vel in toto per unum dimidium anni poft feftum quo folvi debeat, extunc licebit prefatos gardianum & fuccefforesfuos in predictum gardinum, cum pertinentiis fuis, reentrare ut in ftatu priftino; & predictos dominum Willielmum Fifher, & fuum confratrem, & pauperes predictos, & fuccefores, totaliter expellere licebit, hâc indenturâ non obftante. Et

predicti gardianus & conventus, & fuccefores fui, predictum gardinum, cum pertinentiis, predictis capellanis & fuccefforibus fuis Hofpitalis predicti warantizabunt & defendent. In cujus rei teftimonium, tam figillum commune gardiani & conventûs predicti, quam figillum capellanorum & pauperum predictorum, alternatim appofuerunt. Datum Leiceftrie, die & anno predictis.' Et ego vero predictus Ricardus Brinckley, minifter provincialis antedictus, ex confenfu & affenfu provincialis capituli, in fidem & teftimonium omnium & fingulorum premifforum, figillum meum appofui." Et quia, per debitam examinationem in hâc parte factam, & hic videtur Curie predicte indenturam predictam factam & figillatam fuiffe bonâ fide, & abfque covinâ, fraude, feu dolo, ideò indentura illa, ac omnia & fingula in eadem contenta & fpecificata, per Cancellarium & Concilium Curie predicte allocatur; provifo tamen quod fi in pofterum debito modo probatum fuerit coram Cancellario & Conciliio Curie predicte pro tempore exiftentibus, quod predicti Willielmus Fifher & Johannes Thorpe capellani, & XII pauperes viri Hofpitalis predicti, indenturam predictam in formâ predictâ habere & gaudere non debeant, quod tunc & deinceps hoc prefens decretum vacuum fit ac nullius vigoris in lege, aliquo claufo five articulo in eodem contento in contrarium inde non obftante." Nos autem tenorem decreti predicti, ad requifitionem predictorum Willielmi Fifher & Johannis Thorpe capellanorum, ac duodecim pauperum virorum Hofpitalis predicti, duximus exemplificandum per prefentes. In cujus rei teftimonium, has literas noftras fieri fecimus patentes. Tefte, Ricardo Rich, milite. Apud Weftmonafterium, 7° die Septembris, anno regni noftri 30°."

In 1545, *William Wigfton* [2], of Wolfton in the county of Warwick, obtained from king Henry VIII. a grant of the fite of the priory of Pinley, in that county [3].

In an account of Wigfton's Hofpital, taken in 1547, it is ftated to be worth,

" In firmâ, &c. LXXXXVIIĨ. XVIIIS. IXd. ob. q[a].
Reprif' inde LXXXIIIIĨ. VIIIS. IId. ob.
Remanet clarè per annum LVS. VIId. q[a]."

On the 13th of February 1551-2, king Edward VI. reciting the two grants of his royal Father, of Jan. 10, 1513, and Feb. 12, 1521-2, thus confirms them.

" Edwardus Sextus, Dei gratiâ, Anglie, Francie, & Hibernie Rex, fidei defenfor, & in terra ecclefie Anglicane, &c. & Hibernie fupremum caput. Omnibus ad quos prefentes litere pervenerint, falutem. Infpeximus literas patentes domini Henrici nuper Regis Anglie Octavi, patris noftri percariffimi, factas in hec verba, ' Henricus Octavus,' &c. [as in p. 472.] Nos autem literas predictas, ac omnia & fingula in eifdem contenta rata habentes & grata, ea, pro nobis & heredibus noftris, quantum in nobis eft, acceptamus & approbamus, ac nobis unus capellanis & pauperibus Hofpitalis predicti, & fuccefforibus fuis, ratificamus & confirmavimus, prout litere predicte in fe confionabiliter teftantur. In cujus rei teftimonium, has literas noftras fieri fecimus patentes. Tefte meipfo, apud Weftmonafterium, decimo octavo die Februarii, anno regni noftri fexto. F. BEAUMONT."

John Herault, fometime mafter of this Hofpital (in a letter which Mr. Carte faw), fays that Queen Mary alfo granted letters of confirmation of the Founder's gift; but no fuch confirmation has occurred in our refearches.

At the requeft of Henry earl of Huntingdon, a generous benefactor to the town of Leicefter [4], Queen Elizabeth gave authority to the faid earl and others to make ftatutes and ordinances for the government of the Hofpital; which were accordingly thus framed:

" Whereas our Sovereign Lady Elizabeth, by the

---

[1] See p. 337.

[2] This William was fon of Roger (p. 471); and nephew of our Founder. He was in the commiffion of the peace and efcheator towards the latter end of the reign of king Henry VIII.; fheriff 5 Edw. VI.; knighted 2 & 3 Phil. & Mar.; died Sept. 27, 1577, and was buried in the chancel of Wolfton church. His fon Roger, who was then 40 years old, dying afterwards without iffue male, the manor of Wolfton defcended to his two daughters; by one of whom, Sufanna, it was brought in marriage to Nicholas Wentworth, efq. Dugdale's Warwickfhire, vol. II. p. 802.   [3] 1 Pars Original. 36 Hen. VIII. Rot. 99.

[4] On his picture in the Town-hall (fee p. 353) his benefactions are thus recorded: " This noble peere gave an hundred marks a year for ever to fundrie godlie ufes, and thirtie pounds to a publique preacher for the whole towne of Leifter; ten pounds to the chief fchoolmafter their, ten pounds to four poore fchollers, and twenty nobles a year to the poore of Wigfton's Hofpital in Leifter; befides many bookes for a librari, and a ftock of twentie poundes to provide coles at the beft hand for the general good of the poore; and fundrie other greate favours which he did for this Corporation."

grac-

grace of God, Queen of England, France, and Ireland, defender of the faith, &c. by her letters patent, bearing date the 7th day of May, in the 14th year of her reign, hath, amongst other things, given authority unto us, Henry earl of Huntingdon; Ralph Sadler, knight, chancellor of her Majesty's Duchy of Lancaster; and George Bromley, esq. attorney general of the said Duchy, and to the survivors of us, to make ordinances, rules, and statutes, for the good government of the Hospital of William Wigston in Leicester, in the county of Leicester; and hath, in the said letters patent, commanded that the now two chaplains and poor folk of that Hospital, and their successors, shall for ever hereafter behave themselves, be conversant together, and be chosen, according to the rules and statutes by us, or the survivors of us, to be made, and put in writing under our seals, or the seals of the survivors of us, as by the same letters patent more at large appeareth: We the aforesaid Henry, Ralph, and George, to accomplish her Highness's pleasure and commandment in this behalf; having also considered the statutes heretofore made concerning the said Hospital by William Wigston the younger, late of Leicester aforesaid, merchant of the Staple, deceased, founder of the said Hospital, and finding some defects in the same, do make, constitute, and ordain, these statutes, rules, and ordinances following, to be accepted, reputed, taken, and obeyed, as the only and sufficient statutes, rules, and ordinances, made, decreed, and ordained, by the authority aforesaid, for the government of the said Hospital, and the possessions thereof, and of the said chaplains and poor folk, and their successors for ever; and the same statutes, rules, and ordinances, we ordain, make, and establish, in manner and form following; that is to say: First, that the Hospital now called ' William Wigston's Hospital in Leicester' aforesaid, be for ever hereafter called by the name of *William Wigston's Hospital in the Town of Leicester, of the Foundation of the same William*; and do not, at any time hereafter, bear the name of any fancied Saint, or other superstitious name: Also, when the said Hospital is incorporate by the name of ' The chaplains and poor folk of the Hospital of William Wigston, in the Town of Leicester, of the Foundation of the same William,' as by the said letters patent of our Sovereign Lady the Queen's Majesty that now is doth appear, we ordain, establish, and declare, that, in respect of order and distinction of degree, the one of the said chaplains shall, in common speech, and for the better understanding of the true meaning of these ordinances, but not by way of any alteration of the name whereby they are, together with the poor folk of the same Hospital, incorporate by the said letters patent, be called the *Master*, and the other chaplain the *Brother*, of the same Hospital; and that, in all the places of these ordinances where the Master of the said Hospital, or the Master, is spoken of, the same is meant and intended of the office or promotion within the said Hospital which Thomas Sampson now occupieth or enjoyeth; and that in all places of the said ordinances when the Brother of the said Hospital is spoken of, the same is meant and intended of the office or promotion within the said Hospital which one Geffrey Jonson now occupieth or enjoyeth.

Item, that the said Thomas Sampson, now master of the said Hospital, shall enjoy and possess that office or promotion during his natural life, according to the purport and true meaning of these ordinances; and that, after his decease, or other avoidance of the same office or promotion, the same office or promotion may and shall be conferred, given, and granted, by the Queen's Majesty, her heirs and successors, by letters patent under her and their Highnes' seal of the Duchy of Lancaster, for term of life of such person to whom the same shall be so conferred, granted, or given, only by advice of the chancellor and counsel of the said Duchy, and without any warrant by bill assigned; and that the person to whom such letters patent shall be so made shall, by force of the same letters patent, immediately after he hath made such corporal oath for the good government of the said

Hospital as hereafter in these ordinances is appointed, be in actual and real possession of the said office or promotion of master, without any putting in possession, or other ceremony or circumstance in that behalf, to be used.: And we ordain and appoint, that no person shall be capable of the said office or promotion last above mentioned, unless he be a man learned, and admitted into one of the Ecclesiastical orders now established within the Church of England.

Item, that at what time soever hereafter the said office or promotion of the master shall be void, either by death, resignation, deprivation, or otherwise, that then such person as then shall occupy or enjoy the office or promotion of the brother of the said Hospital shall, within 14 days next after such avoidance, signify the same unto the Chancellor of the Duchy of Lancaster for the time being, to the end the same may be conferred, given, or granted, as is aforesaid, with all convenient speed.

Item, that the master of the said Hospital, at such time as he receiveth the patent of his said office, shall, in the Court of the Duchy of Lancaster, if it be in the Term-time, or otherwise before the Chancellor of the Duchy for the time being, or, in his absence, before the Attorney of the same Court, receive a solemn oath, to become a good and profitable master of the said Hospital, and to procure the profit and commodity of the same, and of the incorporation thereof, by all lawful means, to the uttermost of his power; and to govern and order the said Hospital, and all the members thereof, and all the possessions, goods, revenues, and other things belonging to the same, according to the purport and true meaning of these ordinances.

Item, that the master of the said Hospital for the time being shall have committed to his faithfulness and discretion full and whole authority to receive, disburse, administer, and keep, according to these ordinances, all the rents, revenues, goods, and chattels, moveable and immoveable, and other profits whatsoever, which do now belong, or shall hereafter belong, to the said Hospital, or the incorporation thereof, or to be received or levied upon, or by reason of, the possessions belonging, or which hereafter shall belong, to the said Hospital, or upon or by reason of any part or parcel thereof; and that he shall have full, sole, and perfect authority to conclude for the making of leases, and for all other improvements, profits, and commodities, to be lawfully raised, had, or obtained, of, in, or upon, the lands, tenements, hereditaments, and possessions, belonging, or which hereafter shall belong, to the said Hospital, or of, in, or upon, any part or parcel thereof.

Item, that the said chaplains and poor folks, or their successors, or any of them, by what name or names soever they be called or incorporate, shall not, at any time hereafter, alien, convey, assure, or devise, or cause to be aliened, conveyed, assured, or devised, any manors, lands, tenements, rents, tithes, or hereditaments, which now are, or hereafter shall be, parcel of the possessions of the said Hospital, unless it be by leasing or granting the same, or any parcel thereof, only for one and twenty years or under, and not above, or for one, two, or three lives, and not above, and upon which leases and grants such and as much rent or rents or more as hath been most commonly paid for the thing or things so leased or granted, within the space of twenty years next before such lease or grant shall be reserved to the leasers or granters thereof, and their successors, and yearly payable to the use and behoof of the incorporation of the said Hospital, according to such reservation, and according to the purport and true meaning of these ordinances, during the continuance of the same leases or grants, the same estate, conveyances, and assurances, so to be made for years or lives, to be made only of such effect, and in such manner and form, as bishops being seised of any lands or tenements of any estate of inheritance in the right of their churches or bishopricks were, by the statute made in the thirty-second year of the reign of the late king of famous memory, King Henry VIII. limited

mited and authorized to make leafes, and not other-wife; and that all alienations, conveyances, and af-furances, leafes, eftates, or in-trufts, hereafter to be made, conveyed, or affured, of any the manors, lands, tenements, rents, tithes, or hereditaments, which now are, or hereafter fhall be, parcel of the poffeffions of the faid Hofpital, other than fuch leafes and grants as are before in this article appointed, to be made as is aforefaid, fhall be utterly void and of non-effect.

Item, that the mafter of the faid Hofpital for the time being fhall convert and employ all manner of improvements of rents, profits of wood-fales, and all other fums of money arifing, or hereafter to be levied, of, in, or upon, any lands, tenements, or heredi-taments, now belonging, or which hereafter fhall be-long, to the faid Hofpital, other than fuch fines as fhall be reafonably taken for leafes hereafter to be made, to the only ufe, profit, and commodity, of the faid Hofpital, and the incorporation thereof, accord-ing to the purport and true meaning of thefe ordi-nances, if the fame be not difpofed to other ufes, or appointed to other purpofes by thefe ordinances; which faid fines for leafes it fhall be lawful for the mafter of the Hofpital for the time being to take and convert to his own proper ufe, and to the increafe of his living there.

Item, the mafter of the faid Hofpital, hereafter at any time to be made, fhall, at his firft entry into that office, receive, by inventory, at the delivery of the brother of the faid Hofpital, and in the prefence of two of the elder poor men of the fame Hofpital, all the plate, houfehold ftuff, and other furniture, to the fame Hofpital and to the mafter's houfe there be-longing, the which plate, houfehold ftuff, and fur-niture, the fame mafter fhall ufe and occupy only within that houfe which is appointed to him within the fame Hofpital. He fhall alfo, from time to time, repair and amend the fame furniture when it is in decay, and buy fuch new as he, from time to time, fhall think neceffary, at the coft and charge of the faid Hofpital. All which faid plate, ftuff, and fur-niture, he fhall keep faithfully in an inventory tripar-tite; one part whereof, figned with the hand of the brother of the fame Hofpital, fhall remain with the mafter himfelf; and another part whereof, figned with the mafter's own hand, fhall remain with the faid brother; and the third part, figned alfo with the hands of the faid mafter and brother, fhall remain in the Court of the Duchy of Lancafter, amongft the records of the fame Court. And that at all times, and from time to time, whenfoever the faid office or promotion of the mafter of the faid Hofpital fhall be vacant, either by death, deprivation, refignation, or otherwife, then it fhall be lawful for the mafter of the faid Hofpital which fhall be made and appointed next after fuch avoidance to demand the fame plate, houfehold ftuff, and other furniture, of the laft mafter of the faid Hofpital, if he be then living; and if he be dead, then of his executors or adminiftra-tors, executor or adminiftrator, or of any other per-fon or perfons in whofe cuftody or poffeffion any of the fame plate, houfehold ftuff, or furniture, fhall be; and to fue for the fame if it be denied, or not de-livered according to fuch demand, by bill, in the faid Court of the Duchy; upon which the Chancellor and Counfel of the fame Court fhall have authority to hear and determine the fame matter, according to that they fhall think confonant to right and equity.

Item, that it fhall not be lawful either for the mafter or for the brother of the faid Hofpital to grant to any perfon or perfons any of his or their faid offices or promotions within the faid Hofpital, nor to refign or give up the fame, elfewhere or otherwife than into the hands of the Queen's Majefty, her heirs or fucceffors, before the Chancellor and Counfel of the faid Duchy, in fuch manner and form as leafes or letters patent under the feal of the faid Duchy are ufed to be furrendered or given up.

Item, that, for the better order of the remembrance or reckoning of the yearly charges, receipts, and ex-pences of the faid Hofpital, the mafter there do, every year, from time to time, make a perfect book of the faid receipts and expences, the contents of which book and books fo to be made fhall always begin at the 1ft day of November, and end at the laft day of October following; which book fo made up he fhall, before the laft day of December next fol-lowing that day at which the fame book fhould end as is aforefaid, prefent and fhew to fome fuch perfon or perfons as the Chancellor of the Duchy for the time being fhall appoint to be auditor or auditors for that purpofe; and thereupon the fame auditor or auditors fhall take the account of the faid mafter for the charges and expences aforefaid; which account being finifhed, as well the faid auditors, as alfo the then mafter and the then brother of the faid Hofpital, fhall fign that book with fubfcription of their hands; whereupon the faid mafter fhall lay up that book, thus figned, in a cheft ftanding in the chamber of the faid Hofpital, now ufed or appointed for the keep-ing of the evidences of the faid Hofpital, there to be kept, with the reft of the books of accounts, locked under two divers locks of fundry wards, with keys for the fame, the one of which keys fhall remain in the keeping of the mafter, the other in the keeping of the brother; and that the mafter fhall or may give the auditor or auditors, at every audit, 6s. 8d.; of which reward to the auditor or auditors, and alfo for parchment, paper, ink, and writing of the accounts, and for a dinner or fupper to be made to the auditor or auditors, if the mafter fhall think good, the charge of the fame dinner or fupper not exceeding the fum of 10s., the mafter fhall have due allowance of, upon his faid account, to be retained in his own hands, of the rents and revenues of the faid Hofpital.

Item, that all the money which fhall be found to remain in the hands of the mafter at every fuch ac-count fhall be by the faid mafter laid up in fome ftrong cheft, thenceforth to be prepared, and fet in the lodging of the mafter within the faid Hofpital; and that every fum and fums fo by him put in, and the days when it is laid in, fhall be noted in a book with his own hands, which book fhall always be kept in the cheft laft mentioned; out of which cheft it fhall be lawful for the mafter, from time to time, to take out fuch fums of money as he fhall think good, to be employed about the affairs of the Hofpital. He fhall alfo note, with his own hand, the fum fo taken out, and the day of taking it out, in a bill indented tripartite; one part whereof fhall remain in the keep-ing of the mafter, the other part in the keeping of the brother, the third part to be always kept in the faid cheft laft mentioned; to the end that at the next audit he may give a juft account of the money fo taken out, together with other receipts of that year for which he doth account; and the faid cheft laft mentioned fhall have two feveral locks, the wards whereof fhall be diverfe the one from the other, with two keys for the fame; and the one of the fame keys fhall be in the keeping of the mafter, and the other in the keeping of the brother. And we do alfo or-dain, that the common feal of the faid Hofpital fhall be always fafely kept in the cheft laft mentioned; which feal fhall for ever hereafter be engraven with the arms of the faid William Wigfton the Founder only; having thefe words engraven about the faid arms in one circle, *Sigillum Hofpitalis Gulielmi Wigfton*; and in another circle thereof thefe words, *Date Eli-mofinam, & ecce omnia munda funt vobis.*

Item, that all and every mafter hereafter to be made, at his firft entry into that office, fhall and may require of his next predeceffor, if he be living, or of his executors or adminiftrators, executor or admini-ftrator, if he be dead, the accounts of all receipts and expences had and made by his laft predeceffor at any time fince the fame predeceffor made his laft ac-count of the receipts and expences concerning the faid Hofpital as is aforefaid; and if the fame predeceffor (if he be living, or his executors or adminiftators, executor or adminiftrator, if he be dead) refufe to make fuch account, or, having made fuch account, do not within forty days after fuch account pay, or caufe to be paid, to the faid mafter to whom fuch ac-count was made, or to his fucceffors, fuch fum or fums

of

of money as shall, upon the same account, be found to be due and payable by the same accountant or accountants, that then it shall be lawful as well for the master of the said Hospital for the time being to sue for remedy in that behalf in the said Court of the Duchy, as also for the Chancellor and Counsel of the same Court for the time being, upon such suit, to hear and determine the same matter and controversy, according as shall seem to them to stand with right and equity.

Item, that whensoever hereafter it shall come to pass, either by such frugal ordering of the revenues of the said Hospital as the master shall use, or by the gifts or bequests of any other person or persons, that the treasure or money, being the goods of the said Hospital, and to be kept in the said chest as is aforesaid, do amount to the sum of 100*l*. of lawful English money and upwards, then it shall be lawful for the master to employ and bestow that sum of money which shall from time to time be more than the 100*l*. according to his discretion, in relieving of some poor of the town of Leicester, or upon the amendment of highways about Leicester, or in doing of any act or acts profitable either to the said Hospital, or to the incorporation thereof, or to the poor there, or to the said town of Leicester, or the inhabitants thereof; so that the said matter do, at every audit, bring, in writing, the true manner of bestowing of the said sum or sums, signed with the hands of them which received the same money at his hands to any such purpose.

Item, that the master shall, once in every seven years, survey all the lands, tenements, hereditaments, and other possessions, to the said Hospital belonging; he shall procure perfect Rentals and Terriers to be made of them, and shall keep the same safely with the other Evidences of the same Hospital. He shall not only do and maintain all manner of reparations in any wise concerning the said Hospital; but also shall travel about the affairs and businesses of the same Hospital, as the necessity of them shall require, or send the brother or some other man about the same; and his and their necessary expences at which he and they are or shall be, in these and like charges and businesses, shall be borne of the revenues of the said Hospital, and be allowed upon the accompt to be made as is aforesaid.

Item, that the master shall receive yearly, of the revenues of the said Hospital, the sum of 10*l*. of lawful money of England, for his yearly stipend, to be paid, and retained in his own hands, of the rents and revenues of the said Hospital, at four times in the year; that is to say, at the feast of the Nativity of our Lord God, the Annunciation of St. Mary the Virgin, the Nativity of St. John the Baptist, and the feast of St. Michael the Archangel, by even portions; and shall and may also receive and have, yearly, 7*s*. of yearly rent, out of the lands and tenements appointed for the maintenance of the Grammar-school there, together with such meadowing and leye as the master there hath heretofore used to have; and that he shall have at his pleasure, use, and occupy, so long as he enjoyeth that office, for his dwelling-house, the four rooms, built of stone, adjoining to the lodging of the poor there, together with the house, hall, kitchen, buttery, cellar, lofts, and the little court and back-yard thereunto belonging, now used for the lodgings and house of the master, with all other the gardens and houses there, now in the occupying of the master, which do lie between the church called St. Martin's and the High-street; the garden also called Francis garden, the yard thereunto belonging, with the stable and housing standing there, with all easements thereto now belonging. He shall also have authority to make provision for himself and his family upon the rents, issues, and revenues, of the possessions belonging to the said Hospital, as well of sufficient fuel of wood and coals, of oatmeal, salt, and candles, as also of sufficient provision for the finding of two geldings, and no more, of the rents and revenues of the said Hospital. He shall also have authority, at his discretion, either to entertain in the

said Hospital, or to present in the town of Leicester, such strangers, and especially such of the kindred and name of the Founder, as he shall think needful, so that the charge of such entertainment and presents do not exceed the yearly value of 40*s*.; and thereof he shall also have allowance upon his said accompt.

Item, that the master shall not take any other thing or things belonging to the said Hospital, more than is appointed by these ordinances, to his own proper use, or to the use or behoof of any other person or persons. He shall not spoil, waste, nor consume the goods, nor outrageously spoil the woods or underwoods belonging to the said Hospital; but faithfully keep and order them, according to these ordinances, and to the best commodity of the said Hospital, and of the incorporation thereof, and the members of the same. And if the master shall at any time be found to do the contrary, then, upon complaint made in that behalf in the said Court of the Duchy, it shall be lawful for the Chancellor and Counsel of that Court for the time being, not only to compel such master, for misbehaving himself in wasting, spoiling, or consuming (if he be then living, or his executors or administrators, executor or administrator, if he be dead), to make full satisfaction of all that is by him turned to his proper use, or to any other use, or wasted, spoiled, or consumed, contrary to the true meaning of these ordinances; but also to take order, according to these ordinances, for or concerning the reformation of the said misbehaviours or offences, and for or concerning the expulsion or other correction of the said master so misbehaving himself, or for or concerning any the same matters or causes: And for these or the like purposes, we do ordain, that the Chancellor and Counsel of the said Duchy for the time being shall have authority, from time to time, to visit the said Hospital, or to grant out letters patent of commission, under the seal of the said Duchy, to such persons as the said Chancellor and Counsel shall nominate or appoint for the visiting of the said Hospital, as often as need shall require; which visitors so to be appointed shall have authority to examine the faults, transgressions, and misbehaviours, of the said master and brother, or either of them, or of the poor folk of the said Hospital, or any of them, and thereof to make certificate to the said Chancellor and Counsel for the time being, to the end that reformation may be therein had as occasion requireth; and the said Chancellor and Counsel shall, upon such certificate, or upon any other good and lawful information, have authority, by some of these ordinances, not only to reform and correct such faults, transgressions, and misbehaviours, whereof they shall be so certified or informed, either by checking and disallowing of the offender or offenders in some part of his, her, or their ordinary wages or allowance, which should be due within one year after such certificate or information shall be had, or otherwise by any reasonable means as to their discretions shall seem most convenient; but also, from time to time, to take order that the said Hospital, and the incorporation thereof, and all the members of the same, and all and singular the possessions, revenues, and goods, belonging to the said Hospital, be governed and used according to these ordinances, and to the best commodity of the said Hospital, and of the incorporation thereof; and further, to expound and declare the true meaning of these ordinances, and every or any of them, where they are in any point doubtful; likewise to deprive the master and brother of the same Hospital, or either of them, upon good and just cause duly proved against them, or either of them, either for wilful and unmeasurable wasting, spoiling, or consuming, of any the lands, tenements, possessions, or goods, belonging to the said Hospital, by reason of unprofitable and outrageous leases or wood-sales, or otherwise; or for placing any poor within the said Hospital for any bribe or reward; or else for corrupt religion, heresy, perjury, adultery, fornication, unseemly frequenting and haunting of taverns and alehouses, or for any other notorious crime, indecent behaviour, exercise, or condition, whereby notorious

slander

flander or reproof towards the faid Hofpital, or the government thereof, fhall or may juftly arife, and whereof the fame mafter or brother fo to be deprived hath before that time had mention from the Chancellor of the Duchy for the time being, or by any vifitors appointed to vifit the faid Hofpital as is aforefaid, and hath not, upon fuch motion, reformed himfelf in that behalf.

Item, that he and they which fhall, from time to time, hereafter be chofen to that office or promotion of one of the chaplains within the faid Hofpital which is by thefe ordinances called the Brother, and which office or promotion the faid Jeffrey Jonfon now hath or occupieth, fhall be a man learned, of found judgement in the Chriftian religion; fuch one alfo as is admitted into the orders of a prieft or deacon, and allowed to be a preacher of the word of God: And that at all times from henceforth, and from time to time, the office or promotion of the brother fhall be conferred by letters patent under the feal of the faid Duchy, in fuch form and manner as before is appointed for the making of the mafter.

Item, that the brother fhall receive a corporal oath, after his letters patent obtained, and before his firft entering into his faid promotion or office; which oath fhall be adminiftred to him by the mafter, before the poor people in the faid Hofpital, and fhall be of this effect; to wit, that he fhall be a diligent minifter of the Hofpital, a true and obedient brother to the mafter, in furthering all his lawful doings concerning the government of the faid Hofpital, and doing thofe things which do appertain to the office of the brother, as they be appointed by thefe ordinances.

Item, that the brother fhall, from time to time, diligently inftruct the poor folk of the faid Hofpital, and ufe all diligence in teaching them to recite in Englifh, and alfo to know and underftand, the Ten Commandments of Almighty God, the Lord's Prayer, the Articles of the Chriftian Faith as they be expreffed in the Common Creed which is called the fymbol of the Apoftles; to have fuch underftanding as is neceffary for good Chriftians touching the nature and ufe of the Sacraments of Chrift, and to live holily as good Chriftians ought to do. He fhall diligently vifit, inftruct, and comfort them when they are fick; and fhall rebuke and reprove all manner of evil which he fhall fee amongft them, feeking by all means to reform it; and if any of the faid poor folk be fo wilful that they do refufe to be inftructed, reproved, and reformed by him as is aforefaid, he fhall declare the fame to the mafter, who fhall punifh that evil perfon according to the ordinances hereafter fpecified. The brother alfo fhall, either by himfelf, or by fome fuch order as he fhall take with the confent of the mafter, fee that all the poor people of the Hofpital do, every Dominical day and week-day, go to the church called St. Martin's, to morning and evening prayer; to hear alfo the fermons there made, and to receive the holy communion, adminiftered there according to an ordinance hereafter in this book fpecified: Neverthelefs, the brother, upon urgent caufe, with the confent of the mafter, fhall or may fay, or caufe to be faid, the morning and evening prayer on the days aforefaid in the chapel belonging unto and being within the faid Hofpital. The brother alfo fhall fay, every day, at feven of the clock in the evening, the prayers now ufed in the faid Hofpital, in which are recited the Ten Commandments of Almighty God, the Articles of the Chriftian Faith, the Lord's Prayer, with a Prayer for the Queen's Majefty and the Realm; which prayers fhall be pronounced fo diftinctly, that all the whole number of the poor folk may pronounce and pray the fame with the minifter.

Item, that the brother fhall receive yearly, of the revenues of the Hofpital, by the hands of the mafter, the fum of 20 marks for his wages; that is, of the old penfion accuftomed to be paid to the brother, 8l., and of the penfion ufed to be paid to a finging prieft, 5l. 6s. 8d.; and alfo, out of the lands and tenements appointed for the maintenance of the Gram-

mar-fchool there, 5s. yearly, as heretofore hath been ufed, and out of fuch manors, lands, tenements, and rents, as it fhall pleafe the faid earl of Huntingdon to affure and convey to the faid chaplains and poor folk, and their fucceffors, fuch yearly rent and ftipend as it fhall pleafe the faid earl; by his writing figned with his hand, and fealed with his feal, to limit and appoint for that purpofe. And that of all the faid fums of money fo to be yearly paid by the faid mafter to the faid brother the mafter, fhall have allowance upon his accompt, to be made as is aforefaid. The brother alfo fhall have for his dwellinghoufe the fame which joineth on the South to the great back gate of the faid Hofpital, on the Weft upon the High-ftreet in Leicefter aforefaid, with all houfes, yards, and gardens thereunto belonging, and that without paying any yearly rent for the fame; from the which houfe the brother fhall always have and ufe a paffage to be made through the wall of his back-yard into the yard next unto the houfe and lodging of the poor people; which faid houfe appointed to the brother fhall be repaired, fo oft as need fhall require, with flate and great timber, at the coft and charges of the Hofpital, as the mafter fhall appoint it; of which charge of reparations the mafter fhall have allowance upon his accompt. The brother fhall poffefs and occupy that houfe for himfelf only and his family to dwell in; he fhall not let nor fell the fame, nor any parcel thereof, to any perfon, but occupy it himfelf; and that fo long as he enjoyeth the office of the brother, and no longer: if he do not dwell in it himfelf, or if he do let it, or any part of it, to any perfon, it fhall be lawful for the mafter to take the whole houfe into his hands, and to fell and let the fame to the ufe of the Hofpital.

Item, the brother fhall not be abfent any one whole day from the Hofpital, and from his office and charge there, unlefs it be by the leave of the mafter firft obtained; and the brother having fuch leave of abfence fhall procure and provide fome fuch minifter as the mafter fhall like of, to difcharge his office during the time of his abfence. Such times alfo for his abfence fhall be by the mafter allowed of, and none other: in which times the mafter himfelf fhall be prefent at the Hofpital; fo that both of them at once fhall not at any time be abfent from the faid Hofpital one whole day. The brother fhall not take any other ecclefiaftical living with cure, while he enjoyeth this office. If he do take any fuch, at his firft taking poffeffion thereof, he fhall lofe the faid office or promotion of the brother, and ftand deprived thereof *ipfo facto*, and of all commodities thereto belonging.

Item, that when the office of the brother doth, by death, deprivation, refignation, or otherwife, become void, the mafter for the time being fhall, within 14 days next after any fuch avoidance, fignify the fame to the Chancellor of the Duchy for the time being, to the end the fame office or promotion of the brother may be granted in convenient time as is aforefaid; and the brother fo departing from the faid office fhall deliver, or caufe to be delivered, fuch keys and writings as are committed to his cuftody to the keeping of two of the elder or difcreeteft poor men of the faid Hofpital, who fhall fafely keep the fame until another do enter into that office of the brother, to whom they fhall deliver the faid keys and writings, immediately after that he hath taken the oath to him by the mafter adminiftered as is before ordained.

Item, that if the brother do break any of thefe ordinances which do concern him and his office, it fhall be lawful for the mafter to punifh his tranfgreffion, by fubtracting for a time fome part of his ftipend appointed to him; and if the tranfgreffions be fuch as do deferve greater correction, the mafter fhall declare the fame to the Chancellor and Counfel of the faid Duchy, who fhall have authority to proceed and do for the correction and for order of the faid brother in fuch manner and form as by thefe ordinances may be done for the correction of the mafter.

Or-

ORDINANCES CONCERNING THE POOR FOLK OF THE HOSPITAL.

Also we ordain and establish, that there shall be twelve poor men kept always within the said Hospital, according to the foundation of it, and also twelve poor women, as there be at this present; and when the place of any of the poor there doth become void, by death, resignation, expulsion, or otherwise, according to the tenor of these ordinances, there shall be chosen, and put into the place or places so void, some other poor person, such as is either very aged, decrepid, blind, lame, or maimed, or that wanteth natural wit. And that none be admitted for a poor person within the same Hospital which hath of himself or herself whereon to live, or else friends that be able and willing to keep them. Respect also shall be had, as near as may be, that the person and persons so to be admitted be of good fame and name, and in no wise to be married. And that the poor persons to be placed in the said Hospital, according to these ordinances, shall enjoy their said place during their lives, so that they be such and do live so as is appointed by these ordinances.

Item, that when at any time hereafter any place or places of any of the poor there shall be void, by any such means as is aforesaid, the master shall put another in the same place or places within the space of 21 days next after such avoidance; which if he neglect to do, then it shall be lawful for the brother to appoint some one, of such condition as is before mentioned, and to put him, her, or them, into the place or places void, within the space of 14 days next after the expiring of the same 21 days. And if the brother do not the same within the space of the same 14 days, then it shall be lawful for the Mayor of Leicester for the time being to put into the same place or places another or others of such condition as is appointed by these ordinances. And we ordain, that the weekly wages which should have been paid to any poor person of the said Hospital, as well which shall decease (8d. for his or their funeral so deceasing being deducted), as also which shall be expelled or displaced out of the said Hospital according to these ordinances, shall, during the time that the place remaineth void, be put by the master into one of the boxes of the poor appointed by these ordinances; or, in absence of the master, by the brother, until some other be placed in the room that is void.

Item, that every poor person, at his or her first entry, shall receive a corporal oath, the master administering the same, in which he or they shall swear to be true to the Hospital, and not to reveal to any others which be not of the said Hospital any thing which may be prejudicial to the same; that he or she shall be obedient to the master, and in his absence to the brother, in all his and their good and lawful commandments; and also that he or she shall open and make known to the master, or in his absence to the brother, all that which he or she shall, from time to time, know that may turn to the detriment of the said Hospital; and shall likewise reveal to the master, or in his absence to the brother, or to the lawful visitor or visitors of the same Hospital for the time being, all other disorders concerning the said Hospital, or any member thereof, whereof he or she shall be examined by the said master, or in his absence by the brother, or by any such lawful visitor or visitors.

Item, that none shall be chosen, or put into the said Hospital, which hath any of the diseases hereafter named; that is to say, the leprosy, the French pox, the falling sickness, or any such other foul and loathsome disease as shall annoy the residue of the poor folk. And that if it shall fortune hereafter any of the poor folk of the said Hospital to be infected with any of such diseases, that then the person and persons so infected shall be removed out of the said Hospital without delay, either to some lesser house, or some such other place as he or she or they, or his, her, or their friends can provide for him, her, or them, so infected; and that every person so removed shall, during his or her life, receive, by the week, of the said Hospital, 8d. if the person so removed be a man,

and a woman 7d.; and none other to be chosen into his or her place so removed until he or she departeth this life, or resigneth over the place, or committeth some such crime for which he or she is by these ordinances to be expelled.

Item, that if, by descent or gift, there do fall or come to any of the poor folk of the said Hospital any estate of inheritance of and in any lands or tenements or hereditaments, being of the clear yearly rent of 40s. or any moveable goods to the value of 20l. that then every such poor person shall by the master be put out of the Hospital, and another put into his or her place.

Item, that the poor person or persons which shall at any time hereafter be admitted into the said Hospital as is aforesaid shall be taken of such as have been inhabiting within the said town of Leicester, if there may be found among them any such as these ordinances do appoint fit for that place. If there be none such, it shall be lawful to take any such out of those towns where the lands or possessions of the said Hospital do lay, or elsewhere, so that the person or persons so to be taken be not of any other sort and condition than is appointed by these ordinances.

Item, that each one of the twelve poor men shall have, at the appointment of the master, a several chamber in the lower part of the Hospital, as now is used; and that every one of them do lay alone in his own chamber every night; and that none of them do lay or lodge any night out of his own chamber, either in the town of Leicester or elsewhere; nor shall absent himself from the Hospital the space of one whole day, but by the licence of the master, or in his absence of the brother. If any do otherwise lodge, or be otherwise absent, for the first fault he shall lose his stipend or wages appointed for one week; and for the second offence, he shall lose his stipend for four weeks; which sums of money shall be every Friday, by the master, put into the boxes made and set for the poor; and for the third offence, the master shall expel and put him out of the Hospital for ever. The said twelve poor men shall also have that kitchen which is at the end of their lodging, to make them fire in it, to warm them, to dress their meat, and to eat it there, either together or severally, as they shall think good; to which kitchen the poor women of the said Hospital, other than such as are permitted by these ordinances, shall have no access.

Item, that of the said twelve poor women before appointed three of them shall be called the keepers, and they shall be chosen and appointed by the master, and shall be such as have strength and skill apt to be keepers, and shall have charge of the keeping of all the other poor men and women, according as is appointed by these ordinances. And further we ordain, that the other nine of the said poor women shall, every of them, have her chamber alone to herself, in the higher part of the said Hospital, as now is used; and in the same chambers they shall severally lodge each of them alone every night. And that none of the said twelve poor women shall be absent from the Hospital any one night or whole day, but by the licence of the master, or in his absence of the brother; if they be otherwise absent, they shall be punished so as is already appointed for the absence of the men. The women also shall have the kitchen which is at the end of their lodging, for their only use, to have their fire in it, to warm them, to dress their meat, and to eat their meat in it, either together or severally, as they shall think good; to which kitchen the poor men shall have no access.

Item, that two of the strongest poor women shall be the keepers of the twelve poor men; and that each of them shall have the keeping of six men, as the chambers of the men do stand in order, so as one of the same women shall be keeper of the men which lodge on the East side, and the other of the men which lodge on the West side, in such sort as by the master shall be appointed. And that the other third woman, to be appointed by the master, shall be the keeper of all the said nine poor women; and she shall keep the kitchen appointed for the women, and

shall

shall have one of the chambers next adjoining to the said kitchen for her several chamber. The two keepers of the men shall keep the kitchen appointed for the men, and have for their lodging that one chamber which joineth to the said kitchen; each one of them lying there alone in a several bed.

Item, that these three keepers shall always diligently attend and wait upon these poor men and women which are committed to their charge, keeping them at all times as they ought to be kept, and serving them in all things which they have need of as they ought to be served. They shall make the beds of the weak, lame, and blind; they shall keep all their chambers clean; they shall prepare and dress all their meat and get their drink; they shall wash their clothes, make their fires in their kitchens; at due and convenient seasons light their lamp, and keep it burning the time appointed; and they shall keep not only the kitchens, but also all other places to which the poor men and poor women do resort, swept and clean from all filth, and from every thing which may breed any evil or unwholesome air. They shall also have delivered unto them, by inventory indented, one part of which shall remain with the master, the other with the keepers, all such stuff and implements as doth belong to the kitchen of the poor people, and all such other houshold stuff, goods, and implements, belonging to the said Hospital, as shall be committed to their charge and custody; all which they shall safely keep, according to the trust committed to them. And when any of those things do by wearing decay, they shall signify the same to the master, that, on the charge and cost of the Hospital, it may either be repaired or new bought for it, as he shall think good. They shall faithfully use, without waste, to the best profit of the Hospital, and commodity of the poor there, the wood, coal, salt, oatmeal, and such like things, which are committed to their keeping and disposition. They shall also see that the apparel and the goods of every one of the poor be clean, and safely kept within the several chambers of those poor to whom such apparel or goods do belong. They shall help the lame, sick, and weak, off and on with their clothes, when they do go to bed, and arise from it. When any of the poor committed to their charge is sick, they shall diligently serve and help them to provide such things for them as they are able to get, watch with them in the night, and do in all things as good keepers ought to do. The keepers shall neither ask nor receive any thing of any of the poor people for any service that they do towards them. The keepers shall also receive, at the master's hands, weekly, every Friday, the wages of all the poor committed to their keeping, and deliver over, without delay, to every one of the said poor, his or her due portion; and if any of the said poor, for want of wit, sight, or health, cannot dispose or bestow his or her portions to or for his or her necessary provision, then the keeper or keepers of such poor person or persons so being unable to make their own provision, shall, at the commandment of the master there for the time being, be bound to bestow the same portion or portions, weekly, to the most commodity of such person or persons so being unable as is aforesaid. When any of the said poor people do die, the keepers shall wind [1] him and them, and prepare them to the grave. If any of the keepers be found faulty touching any of the premises, it shall be lawful for the master to punish her by expulsion or otherwise, reasonable as the fault shall in his discretion seem to deserve.

Item, that the woman appointed to keep the nine poor women shall shut every night, and open every morning, that door which openeth and goeth into the lodging of the women. The two keepers appointed for the men shall likewise shut every night, and open every morning, the doors of the Hospital; and from the first day of April until the last day of September they shall open the doors at six of the clock in the morning, and shall shut them all at eight, or one half

hour after eight, of the clock at night; from the first day of October until the last day of March the keepers shall open the doors at seven of the clock in the morning, and shut them at seven of the clock at night, or within one half hour after seven. From the times that the doors are appointed to be opened by these ordinances, none of all the doors shall be opened at any time for any cause, unless the master, or in his absence the brother, doth command it. The two keepers of the men shall keep the keys of the doors all the day, and especially all and every night, safely; they shall not deliver them out of their custody to any body but to the master, or in his absence to the brother, when he shall call for them. If the said keepers, or any of them, do open the doors at any other times or hours than as is before appointed, or do let into or out of the said Hospital any body at other hours than the doors are appointed by these ordinances to stand open, they shall be punished by the master with expulsion, or otherwise reasonably by his discretion, according to the quality of the fault.

Item, that if any of the keepers do fall so sick that she is not able to do her duty in her office, then the master, or in his absence the brother, shall appoint one of the nine women, which is strongest, to supply the place of the keeper that is sick during her sickness; and the new keeper shall have the weekly wages which belongeth to her that was so removed for sickness, and she so removed the weekly wages which belonged to the new keeper before she was put into that office. And if the sick woman do so recover health and strength that she be able to do the office of the keeper as she was, she shall be by the master restored to her old office, and the other woman to her place also again. But if none of the nine women be able to do that business, then the master shall put some other woman, where he can, which is both able and willing to take the pain, and put her in that office; and then shall the sick woman have her allowance of 7d. a-week, and be removed out of the Hospital, to abide for the time where she can till she have recovered her health, and be able to serve as before, or else till the place of some other of the poor women do become void by death, or by some other lawful means; and then the master shall again receive the said woman so removed as is aforesaid unto a room or place within the same Hospital. And to the end these three keepers may diligently attend upon their offices, we do ordain, that they, nor any of them, shall at any time be absent one hour from the Hospital but by the licence of the master, or in his absence of the brother, unless their absence be by occasion of necessary provision to be made touching some such thing as pertaineth to their charge within the Hospital; if they be otherwise absent, they shall be punished by expulsion, or otherwise reasonably, according to the quality of the fault, by the discretion of the master.

Item, that all the twelve poor men and twelve poor women shall be under the government of the master, and in his absence of the brother. They shall reverence and obey the master, and in his absence the brother, in all their godly, honest, and lawful commandments; if they do otherwise, they shall be punished by withdrawing of their wages, by the discretion of the master; and if they be incorrigible, then the master shall have power to displace them from their homes within the same Hospital.

Item, that every one of the said twelve men and twelve women, at their first entry into the said Hospital, shall be examined by the master or the brother of their faith and religion, to the end that, if they be well instructed, they may be not only confirmed therein, but trained to further increase of knowledge; or that, their ignorance being known, they may be the rather charged to be diligent to learn. And, that the brother, according to the special care and charge to him committed in that behalf, may be the more ready and diligent always to instruct them; and the said poor folk, for their part, shall shew themselves willing to learn; they shall also,

[1] Winding-sheet; now shroud of woollen.

at all such times as any public prayer appointed to be said or used is said or celebrated in that church which is called St. Martin's, within the said town of Leicester, resort to the same church, to hear and pray with the congregation there present the morning and evening prayer; to hear the sermons which are made there; to receive there also the holy Communion at times convenient, unless the master do appoint the same to be done by the brother in the chapel belonging to the said Hospital, in the church of St. Martin's aforesaid. The poor folk shall all sit together in those two seats which are appointed now for them; the men on the North side, and the women on the South side, of the West door of the same church. They shall also be all present every day, at seven of the clock in the evening, at the prayers made amongst them in the Hospital. None of all the poor men or women shall, at any of these prayers or sermons, be absent, but shall be and continue at them from the beginning to the ending. If any of them, without licence of the master or brother, be absent, or do not continue as is aforesaid, the brother shall signify the same to the master, to the end they may be punished or ordered by the master according to these ordinances. And as these twelve men and twelve women are thus to be trained in learning of godliness, so shall they endeavour themselves to live godly; they, nor any of them, shall be swearers nor cursed speakers, nor drunkards, nor haunters of taverns nor alehouses; they shall not commit adultery nor fornication, neither use any filthy or ungodly talk; they shall be no pickers nor stealers, nor liars, tell-talers, brawlers, chiders, quarrel-pickers, fighters, railers, slanderers, common beggars, dicers, carders, table-players, bowlers, or users of any such unthrifty and unlawful games; they shall be no hunters, hawkers, neither keepers of dogs nor hawks within or without the Hospital; but shall live godly, lovingly, and quietly, among themselves, towards all other persons lowly and humble; applying themselves to some such labour as they be able to do. If any of them do the contrary hereof, or offend any point in this article contained, they shall be punished by withdrawing their wages for a time, by the discretion of the master; and if they shall seem incorrigible, or otherwise the fault be very heinous, the master shall in such case displace them out of their rooms within the said Hospital.

Item, the master shall pay to every one of the twelve poor men, and to every of the three keepers, weekly, on the Friday in every week, 8d.; and to every one of the nine poor women, weekly, the same day, 7d. And between the 1st of November and the 20th of December the master shall, yearly, buy so much frize as shall make gowns for twelve of the poor people, only so that the twelve men shall have gowns one year, and the twelve women shall have gowns the other year following: the frize shall be bought, and the gowns made, at the cost and charge of the Hospital. Every poor man and woman shall, on the breast or sleeve of their gown, have and wear this letter, W. The master shall likewise, of the cost and charge of the Hospital, provide, yearly, for the twelve poor men, eight loads of wood, and four loads of coals; and for the poor women, seven loads of wood, and three loads of coals, to be burned and spent only for their necessity in their several kitchens within the Hospital. Also the master shall yearly provide sufficient oil for their lamps, to burn from the beginning of October until the end of February; also sufficient oatmeal and salt, to be occupied in both their kitchens, with brooms, and such other necessary furniture for their houses and kitchens as he shall think necessary. And if any of the poor men and women shall be so sick and impotent, that he or she be not able to go abroad to labour, or to gather for his or her necessary sustenance, nor have any friends by whose benevolence they may be relieved, then it shall be lawful for the master to make some allowance, at the charges of the Hospital, for fire, and such other necessaries as the said master shall think needful for that sick or impotent man or woman during the time of his or her sickness or impotence.

VOL. I.

Item, that the master shall always hereafter provide some convenient house wherein the keepers shall wash the clothes of the poor men and women, and such kind of fuel for that purpose, as pease-straw, and such like, as now they use, at the charges of the Hospital. He shall also cause the keepers to refresh all the beds of the poor men and women with fresh straw twice every year; that is, in March and October. He shall likewise take, or cause to be taken, a view, once every year, of the beds of the twelve men and twelve women; and if he do find any that is unfurnished of that which is necessary, and doth understand that the same poor body so unfurnished hath, neither of himself, nor can have by labour or help of friends, any thing to supply that want, or, for folly or frowardness, will not provide for his or her necessity in that behalf, the master shall cause some necessary supply to be provided; and either levy the sum laid out for it upon the weekly wages of the poor for whom the provision is so made, or of the revenues of the Hospital, at his discretion.

Item, that none of the poor men shall go into the lodging of the women, nor any of the women (the keepers only excepted) into the lodging of the men. The poor men shall not suffer any strange women to come into the chambers of any of the twelve men; the poor women shall not suffer any strange men to come into the chamber of any of the women, unless they have two or one of the keepers with them all the time of their abode there. Whoso doth the contrary, shall be punished, by the discretion of the master, as in case of other offences is in these ordinances limited. And if any of the said twelve men or twelve women do contract marriage after their entry into the Hospital, the master shall put the persons contracted out of the Hospital, and put some such other meet person into their rooms and places as are by these ordinances appointed.

Item, that there shall be set two boxes, the one in the lodging of the women, the other in the lodging of the men, to receive such alms as God shall move them to give which do resort to the said Hospital. Every box shall have two locks of divers wards, with two keys for the same; one of which keys shall remain in the keeping of the elder poor men, the other in the keeping of the brother. The said boxes shall be opened twice every year, about the end of March and of September; and the money found in them shall be equally divided among the twelve men and twelve women, by the oversight of the master, and in his absence of the brother.

Item, that when any of the twelve men or twelve women so die, they shall make no testament concerning their moveable goods, to bequeath the same to any body, but shall leave all that they have in money and moveable goods to the use of the Hospital, which the keepers shall see safely kept and delivered to the master; and if any make any testament thereof, the same, for so much as it is contrary to these ordinances, shall be void. And if the keepers, or any of them, do either themselves embezzle any of the same goods, or suffer any other person to embezzle or convey the same away, and do not declare the same to the master, the keeper or keepers so offending, or concealing the fault, shall not only make full recompence for the things so taken away, but shall be put out of the said Hospital for ever. The goods which were the poor person's deceased, so delivered to the master, he shall have authority to give some part thereof to the keeper which kept the poor person so deceased since the time of his or her sickness; the residue he shall take, dispose, or sell, to those of the Hospital; and of all the money by him received upon any such sale, he shall make accompt at every audit, as by these ordinances he ought to do of other revenues of the Hospital.

Item, that all such sums of money as shall be due as penalties for breaking of any of these ordinances shall be, by the master, put into the boxes of the poor people, to be distributed equally among them all at the opening of the same boxes as is before ordained. And whensoever the master shall, by virtue of these ordinances, expel any of the said poor men or women for

any

any crime, the party expelled fhall never be admitted into the faid Hofpital again.

Item, that the mafter, or by his appointment the brother, fhall, every year to come hereafter, read the ftatutes pertaining to the office and duties of the keepers and poor people, in the hearing of all the faid poor people, about the fealts of Eafter and St. Michael.

Item, that all and every fuch legacies, compofitions, difpenfations, and licences, as have been heretofore made or granted to the corporation of the faid Hofpital by any perfon or perfons, or by any body politick, by what name or names foever the fame was incorporate, or by what name or names foever fuch grants, legacies, compofitions, difpenfations, or licences, grant, legacy, compofition, difpenfation, or licence, were or was made, the fame not being contrary to the laws of the realm now in force, fhall be good, and remain in force, according to the intent and true meaning thereof.

Item, that if, upon any affurances or gifts made by any perfon or perfons, body or bodies politic, of any lands, tenements, or hereditaments, or any money or goods, to the faid Hofpital, or the incorporation thereof, at any time fince the feaft of St. Michael the Archangel, in the year of our Lord God one thoufand five hundred feventy and two, or at any time from thenceforth to be made, there fhall be any declaration made, in writing, by the party fo giving or affuring, or by any other, by his, her, or their affent, to what ufe, intent, or purpofe, it is meant or intended that the fame affurance or gift fhould be, that then the writing and writings as well concerning the fame gift or affurance, as alfo concerning the ufe and intent thereof, fhall remain and be kept with the Evidences of the faid Hofpital. And that the intent and ufe fo declared concerning any things fo given, if the fame be not repugnant to the laws of this realm, or derogatory to thefe ordinances, or any of them, fhall be of like validity and force, to all intents and purpofes, as thefe ordinances are and ought to be.

Provided always, that any thing in thefe ordinances, or any of them contained, fhall not in any wife extend to alter the incorporation made and declared concerning the faid Hofpital by the faid letters patent of our Sovereign Lady the Queen's Majefty that now is; but that the fame incorporation, and the name thereof, fhall continue and be in fuch manner and form as by the fame letters patent is limited and declared, any thing in thefe ordinances or any of them contained, or any other thing whatfoever, to the contrary thereof, in any wife notwithftanding.

H. HUNTINGDON.
R. SADLER.
G. BROMLEY."

The ftatutes being thus made, the following act of parliament for confirming them was obtained:

" In the Parliament held at Weftmynfter, the 8th day of February, in the 18th yeare of the raigne of Queene Elizabeth, &c.

" Whereas, aboute the beginninge of the raigne of the Queene's Matie moft noble Father, of famous memory, Kinge Henry the Eight, one William Wigfton, of the towne of Leicefter, marchant of the Staple, of charitable and good difpofition, meaninge to releive in thofe partes the poore people, did goe about to found and ftablifh for ever one Hofpital in the faid towne of Leicefter: and for that he did not accomplifhe the fame duringe his life; his executors, for that purpofe, by letters patent under the greate feale of England, dated the 13th day of July, in the 5th yeare of the raigne of the faid late kinge, obtained lycence of the fame kinge to found and erect the faid Hofpital, to confift of two perpetuall chaplaines and twelve poor men for ever, to be called by the name of ' The Hofpital of William Wigfton of Leicefter' for ever; and further did incorporate the fame, by the name of ' Chaplaines and Poore of the faid Hofpirall:' And allfoe the faid late kinge did licenfe the fame executors to purchafe landes and tenements of the annuall vallue of 40 markes, and to amortiffe the fame to the faid chaplaines and poore, towardes their maine-

tynance for ever, as by the faid letters patent more plainly may appeare, by vertue whereof the fame Hofpitall was founded: And whereas, after that our Soveraigne Lady the Queene's Matie that now is, goeinge aboute not onely to confirme the faid foundation, but allfoe to increaffe the fame of her vertuous difpofition, by her Highnes' letters patent, under the greate feale of England, dated the 7th day of May, in the 14th yeare of her Highnes' raigne, did further graunt and confirme, to the nowe chaplaines and poore of the faid Hofpitall, that the fame fhould remaine in full and reall beinge for ever of two chaplaines and twelve poore people: And further, that as well the faid chaplaines as poore for the tyme beinge, as they that fhould be chaplaines and poore people of the faid Hofpitall for ever from thenceforth, fhould be elected, ruled, ordered, and governed, by fuch orders, rules, and ftattutes, as the right honorable Henry earle of Huntingdon, Ralph Sadler, knight, chancellor of the Duchy of Lancafter, and George Bromley, efquire, her Highnes' attorney general of the faid Duchy of Lancafter, or the furvivors of them, fhould after that time make, in wrytinge, and to be fealed as well with her Highnes' Duchie feale, as with the feverall feales of the faid earle, chancellor, and attorney, or the furvivors of them: And alfoe did, of her Highnes' further liberality, graunte divers lands, tenements, liberties, franchices, to the faid chaplaines and poore people, as in her Highnes' faid letters patent more planely doth or may appeare: For conformation and eftablifhment whereof; be it enacted and ordained, by our faid Soveraigne Lady the Queene, the Lordes fpirituall and temporall, and the Commons, in this prefent Parliament affembled, and by the authority of the fame, that the faid letters patent of our faid Soveraigne Lady the Queene, and all and every the grauntes, articles, claufes, provifions, authorityes, jurifdictions, and ordinances, therein fpecified and graunted, and all and fingular the ordinances made, or hereafter to be made, by the faid earl of Huntingdon, fir Ralph Sadler, knight, and George Bromley, or the furvivors of them, accordinge to the tenor of the faid letters patent of our faid Soveraigne the Queene, fhall ftand, remaine, and be good, avaleable, and effectuall in the lawe, to all intente and purpofes, accordinge to the purporte, true intent, and meanynge of the fame letters patent of our faid Soveraigne Lady the Queene; faving to all and every perfon and perfons, boddies pollitique and corporate, theire heires and fucceffors, and to the heires and fucceffors of every of them, other than our faid Soveraigne Lady the Queene, her heires and fucceffors, all fuch right, title, ufe, prefent intereft, reverfion, remaynder, entry, condition, rente, covenante, commons, profitts, commodityes, and hereditaments whatfoever, which they, or any of them, might, could, or ought to have, if this act had never beene had or made."

To this act is annexed the certificate of Anthony Mafon, clerk of the parliaments, dated March 22, 1576-6, that it is a true copy.

The following document, particularizing the benefactions of the earl of Huntingdon, is copied from the original enrolment in the high Court of Chancery:

" Whereas our Sovereign Lady Elizabeth, by the grace of God, Queen of England, France, and Ireland, defender of the faith, &c. hath, by her Highnefs's letters patent, bearing date May 17, in the 14th year of her reign, given power and licence to all and every perfon and perfons that will to give lands, tenements, or any other hereditaments, to the chaplains and the poor of ' The Hofpital of William Wigfton in the town of Leicefter, of the foundation of the faid William Wigfton,' and to their fucceffors; and alfo hath given power and licence to the faid chaplains and poor to receive and enjoy the faid gifts fo given to them and their fucceffors for ever, as by the faid letters patent more at large doth appear. And further; whereas, by authority aforefaid, among other ordinances concerning the faid Hofpital, it is ordained, that it fhall be lawful to any perfon that giveth any thing in manner and form abovefaid to declare, by writing under his hand and feal, the

ufe

ufe or ufes, purpofe and purpofes, for which he giveth any fuch gifts to the faid chaplains and poor, and to their fucceffors; and that the fame his declaration, by writing fo made, fhall be of as good force and value, to bind and charge the faid chaplains and poor, and their fucceffors, in refpect to the thing, things, and gifts fo given, to the fame ufe, ufes, and purpofes, to which it is or fhall be fo given, appointed, or declared to be ufed or beftowed, as any other ordinance is or fhall be, which is or fhall be made by authority aforefaid, or any thing touching the fame Hofpital, fo long as they the faid chaplains and poor, and their fucceffors, do or fhall poffefs and enjoy the fame gift or gifts: And whereas I, Henry earl of Huntingdon, lord Haftings, Hungerford, Boutreaux, Mollens, and Moyles, knight of the moft honourable order of the Garter, Lord High Prefident of the Queen's Majefty's Council eftablifhed in the North parts, minding not only the bettering of the eftate of the faid chaplains and poor, and their fucceffors, but alfo the good and diligent information of the inhabitants of the town and fhire of Leicefter in the true knowledge of God and Chriftian religion, have, by my deed indented bipartite, bearing date the 11th day of October, in the 18th year of the reign of our Sovereign Lady Elizabeth the Queen's Majefty, given and granted unto the faid chaplains and poor of the faid Hofpital of William Wigfton in the faid town of Leicefter, of the foundation of the faid William Wigfton, and to their fucceffors for ever, one yearly rent-charge of 32*l*. 13*s*. 4*d*. of lawful Englifh money, iffuing out and forth of one clofe commonly called *The Afh Clofe*, and out and forth of one meadow near thereunto adjoining, late parcel of the poffeffion of the late diffolved monaftery of St. Mary in the Meadows of Leicefter, near to the faid town of Leicefter, in the county of Leicefter, now or late in the tenure or occupation of William Bradgate, or of his affigns; and alfo one other yearly rent-charge of 24*l*. of lawful Englifh money, iffuing out and forth of one clofe called *Pynder's Clofe*, and of a certain meadow or certain parcels of meadow ground belonging to the faid clofe called *Pynder's Clofe*, or demifed, or let with the fame for one entire rent, now or late in the tenure of one Richard Stanford, or of his affigns, and late parcel of the poffeffion of the faid late diffolved monaftery of St. Mary; and alfo all that my annual and yearly rent-charge of 10*l*. of lawful Englifh money, with the appurtenances, iffuing and going out of all thofe lands, tenements, and hereditaments, now or late in the tenure or occupation of Phillip Freeke, or of his affigns, and late parcel of the poffeffions of the faid late diffolved monaftery of St. Mary, as further by my faid deed indented bipartite it doth and may appear: All which faid rents, fo by me granted by my faid deed indented bipartite, do amount in the whole to the total yearly fum of 66*l*. 13*s*. 4*d*. I the faid earl do now, by thefe prefents, declare my meaning and intent, in what fort and to what ufe and purpofe my mind is, to have the faid yearly rent by me granted to be beftowed and employed for ever; that is to fay; Firft, that the one of the faid chaplains, called the mafter of the Hofpital, and his fucceffors, or his fufficient deputy or deputies by him or his fucceffors for the time being lawfully appointed, fhall yearly for ever receive the faid yearly rents by me granted, when the fame fhall be due by my aforefaid grant; and fhall alfo pay and difburfe the fame yearly as enfueth; that is to fay, that he the faid mafter and his fucceffors fhall yearly pay, or caufe to be paid, to the fchoolmafter of the Free-fchool in Leicefter, and his fucceffors for ever, the fum of 10*l*. of lawful money, parcel of the faid yearly rent by me granted, at the feaft of the Annunciation of our Lady St. Mary the Virgin, and St. Michael the Archangel, by even portions; and fhall alfo yearly pay to the other chaplain of the faid Hofpital, who is by the aforefaid ordinances named to be the brother, the fum of 30*l*. parcel alfo of the faid yearly rent by me granted, at two times in the year; that is to fay, at the feaft of the Annunciation of the Virgin Mary, and St. Michael the Archangel, yearly,

by even portions, on thefe conditions following; firft, that the faid brother and his fucceffors fhall and do fuffer his other fellow-chaplain, called the mafter of the Hofpital, and his fucceffors, quietly to occupy, enjoy, and have, to the proper ufe of the faid mafter and his fucceffors, all that leafe for term of years yet to come of the tithe corn of the South Fields by Leicefter, with all commodities and profits thereunto belonging, which was given jointly to the faid chaplains by the laft will and teftament of Agnes Wigfton, late wife of William Wigfton, founder of the faid Hofpital: And if the faid other chaplain called the brother and his fucceffors fhall or do not fuffer the faid mafter and his fucceffors quietly to enjoy the faid leafe and commodities aforefaid during the term of years expreffed in the faid leafe, then I will, that the other brother called the mafter and his fucceffors fhall pay to the faid brother and his fucceffors yearly, during the faid term, but only the fum of 20*l*. of lawful money, parcel of the faid yearly rents by me granted; and the other 10*l*. parcel of the faid 30*l*. I will that the faid mafter and his fucceffors do yearly receive and retain in his and their own hands to his and their own proper ufes, for his and their better maintenance and increafe of living in the faid Hofpital, during all fuch time as he fhall be letted by the other chaplain or his fucceffors to receive and take the profits and commodities of the faid leafe during the faid term; and after the term, the faid chaplain and his fucceffors to have yearly 30*l*. parcel of the fum aforefaid, in manner and form above fpecified. Secondly, I will that the faid brother and his fucceffors, to whom the faid ftipend of 30*l*. or 20*l*. fhall in manner and form aforefaid be paid, fhall be a continual refident preacher in the town of Leicefter; and that he and they, and his fucceffors, fhall preach in the church called St. Martin's, in Leicefter aforefaid, every Sunday in the year, except that he or they be fick, or that the faid church fhall be occupied upon any of thofe days by any other preacher; and alfo, that he and they do preach every Wednefday and Friday, or upon two other days, every week, in the faid church of St. Martin's, at fuch hours as the mafter of the Hofpital and his fucceffors fhall appoint, unlefs upon any of thofe Sundays or other days the place be by fome other preacher fupplied, or that he fhall be letted by ficknefs, or other lawful caufe againft his will: Alfo I will, that the faid mafter of the faid Hofpital and his fucceffors do and fhall yearly pay the fum of 10*l*. of lawful money, towards the finding of certain fcholars which do or fhall fet their mind and apply themfelves to the earneft ftudy of Divinity, and to become preachers of the Gofpel of Chrift in the Church of England; which faid fum fhall be in this form following beftowed; which is, I will, that unto two fcholars, fuch as I the faid earl during my life do or fhall name or appoint, of which one of them to be fcholar and ftudent in the Univerfity of Cambridge, the other a fcholar and ftudent in the Univerfity of Oxford, to either fcholar 3*l*. yearly, at the Annunciation of the Virgin Mary, and St. Michael, by even portions; which faid exhibitions the faid mafter fhall pay; and every of the faid fcholars fo ftanding fhall only enjoy the fame for five years, and no longer: Alfo I will, that the mafter and his fucceffors fhall pay, for ever, unto other two fcholars, born in the town of Leicefter, or Leicefterfhire, fuch as have but poor parents, and apt to learn, and fhall be thought meet to become preachers of the Gofpel, and able to be taught of the fchoolmafter of Leicefter in fome of the forms which are appointed to be at his teaching in the fchool of Leicefter; whofe parents or friends will faithfully promife that the fame their children fhall, by their good wills, follow their ftudies in all knowledge meet for preachers of the Gofpel, and that the faid children fhall be kept and found as fcholars of the fchool of Leicefter, and to be ordered and governed there by fuch orders and rules as are for that fchool appointed; to either of the faid two fcholars, or to their parents to be beftowed upon them or to their ufes, the fum of forty fhillings by the year, at the aforefaid two feafts, by even portions; which faid exhi-

exhibition of forty fhillings to every of the faid two poor fcholars fhall only be paid to any one fcholar fo learning in the fchool of Leicefter for the fpace of five years only, and no longer: And I will, that at the end of the faid five years the one of thefe two fcholars fhall go to Cambridge, the other to Oxford, there to ftudy; and, being in the faid Univerfities, fhall either of them have the exhibition of 3l. for fuch time, and in like manner and form, and upon like conditions and confiderations, as fuch fcholar as is or fhall be in the Univerfities of Oxford or Cambridge as is before faid fhall have and obferve: And I the faid earl do ordain and will, and my mind is, that continually for ever there fhall be two fcholars at the faid Univerfities, and two other fcholars at the faid fchool of Leicefter, to have the aforefaid ftipends, amounting in all to 10l. yearly, paid to them by the mafter of the faid Hofpital in Leicefter and his fucceffors for ever, for like times, and in like fort, order, and conditions, and for the fame confiderations, as are before expreffed and appointed for the faid payment and order of the faid fcholars and their ftudies; fo that for ever hereafter there fhall be two fcholars in the two Univerfities, and two fcholars in the fchool of Leicefter, which fhall yearly have and receive the aforenamed exhibition towards their finding at the hands of the mafter of the Hofpital aforefaid and his fucceffors for ever: And further, I do order and appoint, that if the room of any of the faid fcholars fhall be vacant at any time, either by the end of five years appointed for any fcholar to have any fuch exhibition, or by death, or by departure from learning and ftudy before limited, or for any other reafonable caufe, then I the faid earl, during my life, to have the nomination and placing of every fcholar in the room or rooms fo void; and after my death, my mind is, and I do order, that the faid mafter and brother of the faid Hofpital, and their fucceffors, fhall have the nomination and placing of every of the faid fcholars to receive any of the faid exhibitions in form aforefaid: And if they the faid chaplains cannot agree in the placing and naming of any fcholars in any of the faid rooms, then I ordain, that the one of them, with the affent of the mayor of the faid town of Leicefter for the time being, fhall for that time have the nomination and placing of the fcholar to be appointed to the room of a fcholar then fo void; and if the faid two chaplains, or one of them with the affent of the faid mayor, fhall not, within one month next after every avoidance of the room of any of the aforefaid fcholars for any caufe, name, place, and appoint, one other fcholar in the fame place, according to the true intent above fpecified, that then I will, and do ordain, that my heirs fhall, at every fuch avoidance, and for every fuch default, name and appoint the fcholar or fcholars then to be placed, fo the fame nomination and placing be had and executed within one month next after the default of the faid two chaplains. I will alfo, and ordain, that the faid mafter of the faid Hofpital for the time being and his fucceffors do, for ever hereafter, yearly employ and beftow the fum of 6l. 13s. 4d. either in money upon the 24 poor people of the aforefaid Hofpital, to be equally divided amongft them, or elfe to buy and give 12 gowns of frize yearly to thefe 12 poor folk of the fame Hofpital which are not provided for, but want liveries every other year; fo that, by this gift of mine yearly, together with that which is already allowed by the ordinance of the Founder of the faid Hofpital, every one of the 24 poor people fhall have one livery: And I will, that the faid mafter of the Hofpital and his fucceffors, every year, at the audit in which he maketh the accompt of the revenues of the Hofpital, do fhew, in writing, unto the auditor appointed, the true and faithful diftribution and payment of all the portions above mentioned, according to this my order and declaration. And I do further order and declare, that the mafter of the faid Hofpital

and his fucceffors, for and in confideration of their travel, care, and diligence to be ufed herein, fhall, towards the increafe of his living, take and keep to his and their ufes all the refidue of the faid yearly rents by me granted, which fhall remain after the fums and ftipends before appointed fhall be paid as is before faid, the which faid refidue doth and will amount yearly to the fum of 10l.; fo that the mafter and his fucceffors for the time being fhall do his endeavour and diligence to the due execution to this my ordinance, intent, and declaration; or if he make any wilful default therein in any year, by the judgement of the vifitor of the faid Hofpital, then I will, for that year he fhall lofe the benefit of the fum of 10l. and fhall beftow the fame upon the poor of the faid Hofpital, as fhall be limited and appointed by the vifitor of the faid Hofpital for the time being, for that year's profits only when fuch default fhall be in the faid mafter. In witnefs whereof, I the faid earl to this my prefent writing have fet my feal, given the 11th day of October, in the 18th year of the reign of our Sovereign Lady Queen Elizabeth, by the grace of God, Queen of England, France, and Ireland, defender of the faith, &c. H. HUNTINGDON.

Capt' & recognit' coram me Will' Cordell milite, magiftro Rotulorum curie cancellarie domine regine, decimo fexto die Novembris, anno regni dicte domine regine decimo nono, in Ædibus de le Rolles.
WILLIAM CORDELL.
Irrot' in dorfo clauf' cancellar' infrafcripte domine regine, decimo nono die Novembris, anno regni dicte domine Elizabethe regine decimo nono, per W. Ballard & Jo. Wythers, deputatos clericos irrotulamentorum."

Elizabeth [1] wife of *John Whatton,* efq. of the Newark, appears to have been the next benefactor to this Hofpital, by adding to it two fmall houfes [2]; which her death, in 1638, prevented her from endowing. But her charitable intentions were directed to be carried into effect by her hufband, as appears by the following extract from his laft will:

"Item, I give, to be iffuing out of my clofe or garden called *The Shire-hall Clofe,* in Leicefter aforefaid, the fum of 7l. yearly for ever, to be paid into the hands of the mayor, bailiffs, and burgeffes, of the borough of Leicefter for the time being, at the 25th day of March, and 29th day of September, by equal portions, to be by the faid mayor and juftices diftributed as is hereafter expreffed (that is to fay); 7l. yearly for ever for the maintenance of one poor widow placed, or to be placed, in one of the two houfes in the New Hofpital in Leicefter, called *Wigfton's Hofpital,* which two houfes Elizabeth my late wife, deceafed, did build there, with the confent of the then mafter of the faid Hofpital; and I defire, the other houfe of thofe two houfes may be for her to lay her fuel in, or other neceffaries; the money to be paid to the faid widow by 2s. 6d. a week, or 10s. a month, at the difcretion of the faid mayor and juftices; and the other 10s. refidue of the 7l. I defire one-half of it may be given to the mafter of the faid Hofpital, defiring his countenance and affiftance that the poor widow be not wronged, and the other half of the 10s. to be for the mayor and juftices to drink in wine together. The widow to be placed in the faid houfe, after it is empty or void, to be chofen by Katherine my now wife, during her natural life, and afterwards by the faid mayor and juftices for the time being, within two months next after the faid houfe fhall be at any time empty or void; and in the mean time, during that vacancy, I will, the faid 2s. 6d. a week fhall be given amongft the other women then dwelling in the faid Hofpital: And if it fhould happen that default fhould be made of payment of the faid 7l. out of the faid Shire-hall clofe, by the fpace of one whole year or more, then I do give the deeds and evidences belonging to the fame to the mayor, bailiffs, and burgeffes, and their fucceffors for ever,

---

[1] Daughter of Alderman Robert Herrick; and wife firft of Robert Orpwood, who died in 1609, and afterward of John Whatton. See vol. II. **p. 617.**
[2] She was alfo at the expence of building the Conduit in the Market-place.

for the feveral ufes aforefaid : And if it fhall happen that fuch a widow cannot be allowed of or fuffered to live in the faid houfe, then my will is, that 6*l.* of the faid 7*l.* fhall be by the faid mayor and juftices of the faid borough beftowed for the maintenance of one poor widow in fome other place ; and the other 20*s.* I will, fhall be given to ten poor widows within the faid borough, the 20th day of December every year[1]."

In 1656, *John Goodman* and *William Sherman* were appointed commiffioners for vifiting Wigfton's Hofpital ; who made the following report of their lands :

In *Leicefterfhire.*

Odeby. Mr. John Wigfall held two yard and a half land for three lives, paying yearly 1*l.* 10*s.* and two capons, or 2*s.* and the carriage of a load of coals ; but the land is computed worth 7*l. per annum* a yard land.

Great Wigfton. William Lewis held three yard land and fome clofes for three lives, for 4*l. per annum,* two capons, or 2*s.* and carriage of a load of coals ; but the land is worth 9*l. per annum* a yard land, and the clofes 2*l.* [In the margin 35*l. per annum.*]

Thomas Jackfon held one meffuage, three quarters of a yard land, and a little croft, for three lives, for 1*l.* 4*s. per annum,* and two capons, or 2*s.* ; the carriage of a load of coals. The three-quarters of a yard land is worth 6*l. per annum,* and the little clofe 10*s. per annum.* His fine was 20*l.*

William Brabftone held one meffuage and half a yard land for three lives, for 16*s. per annum,* two capons, or 2*s.* and carriage of half a load of coals. The half-yard land is worth 4*l.* 10*s.*

William Boulter held one meffuage, with a little croft, and quarter of a yard land, with common for two cows and ten fheep, for three lives, paying 2*s. per annum* ; the quarter of a yard land being worth 2*l.* 5*s.* befides the meffuage and croft.

Thomas Lowe held one yard land for three lives, paying yearly 2*l.* and two capons, or 2*s.* and the carriage of a load of coals ; the land being worth 9*l. per annum.*

Barkefton. Mr. Henry Dixon held five oxgangs and a half for three lives, at 4*l. per annum* ; the land being worth 3*l. per annum* an oxgang. His fine was 50*l.*

Kimcote. John Blockley held a meffuage and half-yard land for three lives, paying 15*s. per annum* ; but it is worth 3*l. per annum.* His fine was 15*l.*

Walton by Kimcote. John Blockley held one meffuage and half-yard land meadow and pafture for three lives, at 1*l. per annum,* the meffuage and land being worth 5*l.* His fine 15*l.*

Humphrey Wormlaton held one meffuage and one yard and a half land for three lives, at 1*l.* 4*s.* ; the one yard and a half land being worth 10*l.* 10*s.*

Bottesford. Thomas Bennet held two oxgangs for three lives, at 3*l.* 6*s. per annum* ; the land being worth 4*l. per annum* the oxgang. And by another leafe held one meffuage and three-quarters of an oxgang for three lives, paying 10*s. per annum* ; it is worth 4*l.* the oxgang.

Robert Orfon held two oxgangs for three lives, at 2*l. per annum* ; the land being worth 4*l.* the oxgang.

John Sumner held one houfe and clofe and four oxgangs for three lives, at 5*l. per annum* ; the land being worth 4*l.* the oxgang. His fine 140*l.*

Anthony Vincent held one oxgang for three lives, at the rent of 1*l.* ; it is worth 4*l.* the oxgang.

Richard Tutbury held a cottage, and common pafture for two beafts and a half and ten fheep, for three lives, paying 8*s. per annum,* and 4*s.* chief rent to a Bede-houfe in Bottesford.

John Clifton held a cottage, with the appurtenances, for three lives, paying yearly 10*s.*

William Northley held a houfe, without leafe, paying yearly 5*s.*

George North held a cottage, two cow paftures, and a follower, ten fheep common, without leafe, paying yearly 6*s.*

William Leeton held a houfe and back-fide ; which,

with the houfe, was burnt. The houfe is rebuilt, and he pays yearly 1*l.* 4*s.*

Robert Peeke held a houfe and two cow paftures, without leafe, paying yearly 6*s.* 8*d.*

Redmyle. Dorothy Dalliwater held one arable land and nine leas of pafture for three lives, paying yearly 2*s.*

Norton. Edward Beaumont held a houfe, and a clofe of three acres and a half, for three lives, paying yearly 13*s.* 4*d.* His fine was 5*l.*

Mrs. Sufan Whalley widow, and Mr. William Whalley, held two houfes and two farms, containing four yards and a half land, for three lives, paying 6*l.* 3*s.* 4*d.*—[Since the letting the faid leafes, the lordfhip is inclofed, and the Hofpital land laid out in the worft place of the lordfhip. N. B. There were 24 yard lands belonging to the whole lordfhip of Norton ; and there belonged to every yard land fix cow paftures, and common for forty fheep, &c.]

Belvoir. John Quelch held one cottage-houfe (burnt, and not re-edified), with a clofe of two acres and a half of arable, and three acres and a rood of leys, with common in the lanes for one horfe and two beafts, for three lives, paying 8*s.* 6*d. per annum.*

Bredon on the Hill. Sampfon Burrough held one meffuage, 22 acres and a half of land, and leazes, and four little clofes of pafture, and one clofe called Burrough hill, with a meffuage in the faid clofe, for three lives, paying yearly 2*l.* 18*s.* and two capons. His fine was between 50*l.* and 60*l.*

Thomas Turner held one cottage, a back yard, and a croft joining to it, with fome arable land, meadows, and pafture, containing about half an acre, for three lives, paying yearly 8*s.* His fine was 12*l.*

Hatherne. William Lowley held one meffuage, two yard lands of meadow and pafture, for three lives, paying yearly 1*l.*

John Throne held one meffuage and four yard lands of ground, and a little parcel of a clofe, for three lives, paying yearly 4*l.* 6*s.* 8*d.*

John Savage held one meffuage and two yard lands of ground for three lives, paying yearly 2*l.* Fine, 10*l.*

Thomas Newbold held one meffuage, 52 acres, and fome other parcels, for three lives, paying yearly 1*l.* 10*s.* and two capons, or 2*s.*

Raunfton. William Jaquis held one cottage or meffuage, with half-yard land and two clofes, viz. *Mofell clofe* and *Channel-end clofe,* for three lives, paying yearly 8*s.*

Swannington. The lord Beaumont, by leafe, dated Nov. 10, 1566, held the whole manor of Swannington for 99 years, paying yearly 25*l.* ; but now pays 35*l.* But the fub-tenants to the lord Beaumont pretend to be immediate tenants to the Hofpital, by leafes made by Mr. Job Grey and Mr. Chillingworth ; viz.

Henry Roe held one meffuage or cottage and three clofes ; viz. *Daunes clofe, Bradley clofe, Cuckoo Gap clofe,* for three lives, paying yearly 6*s.* 4*d.* And by another leafe held two clofes, viz. *Meller's clofe* and *Newell's clofe,* for 21 years, from March 12, 23 Car. 1. paying yearly 6*s.* 8*d.*

Edward Muglefton held one meffuage, and a little clofe adjoining, and 36 acres of arable, and a clofe called *Over Baugh croft,* and a little clofe called *Land Bed clofe* and *Bradley clofe,* alfo a little clofe called *Towns-end,* alias *Depdalle,* for three lives, paying yearly 2*l.* and the carriage of a load of coals.

Francis Baly, *alias* Mafon, held one meffuage, and *Mantle clofe,* and *Breach clofe,* and *Heath clofe,* for three lives, paying yearly 5*s.* and the carriage of a load of coals.

Edward Bifhop held one meffuage, a back-fide, four clofes, and four acres of arable, for three lives, paying yearly 10*s.*

Henry Leatherland held one meffuage and one cottage, with clofe thereto belonging, viz. *Taubit wood, Pollard brook, Bettem Broad acre, Hackett's croft, Hall meadow, Home clofe,* and *Pepfhyan clofe,* and

---

[1] Taken by Mr. Carte out of a bundle of papers penès T. Palmer, gent. in which there is the requeft of the mayor and juftices for the admittance of Elizabeth Becket, widow, into the houfes built by Mrs. Whatton, dated 20 Sept. 168:, fubfcribed by John Goodall mayor, &c.

Heath clofe, with the arable land in three fields thereto belonging, for three lives; paying yearly 5*l.* and the carriage of two loads of coals.

Thomas Barrodale held one meffuage or manor-houfe, with a clofe called *Carryag breach*, and *Wormwood hole clofe*, and *New clofe*, for three lives, paying yearly 6*l.* and two capons.

The rents of the fub-tenants of the lands in Swannington come to 14*l.* 16*s.*; which, I fuppofe, is comprehended in the lord Beaumont's rent.

Wikeham and *Cawdwell.* Jervas Day held a manor or hall-place, with its appurtenances, for three lives, paying yearly 6*l.* 13*s.* 4*d.*

Leicefter. Mrs. Lucy Dannet held parcel of the Hofpital land, meadow, and pafture, lying in the Weft field, *alias* Bromkinthorpe field, near Leicefter, containing 48 acres, with common and appurtenances, for three lives, paying yearly 3*l.* The fine was 60*l.* N. B. This land is to let to under-tenants, fome for 8*s.* and fome for 16*s.* the acre *per annum.*

Mary Wood held a houfe, with a back-fide, containing about 20 yards of ground, for three lives, paying yearly 10*s.* The fine was 13*s.* 4*d.*

William Sanders held a houfe and little yard belonging to the Hofpital for three lives, paying yearly 10*s.* His fine was 12*l.*

Henry Howard held a garden-place, containing three roods, for 21 years, from May 12, 1636, paying yearly 1*l.* His fine was 9*l.*

Thomas Palmer held two fmall orchards or gardens, from April 17, 1638, for 21 years, paying yearly 4*s.* His fine was 40*s.*

Mr. Richard Coleman held a garden, or orchard, from April 1, 1654, for 21 years, paying yearly 1*l.* befides 4*s.* yearly given to the poor. His fine was 5*l.*

John Payne held a houfe, without leafe, paying yearly 12*s.*

Annis Griffin held one meffuage or tenement, from 1650, for 21 years, paying yearly 12*s.*

Mr. Richard Ing held a clofe in the Horfe-fair leys, containing 60 yards in breadth, and 80 in length, for three lives, paying yearly 1*l.*

Mr. John Wadland held Humberftone's clofe, containing one acre; Sandby clofe, containing half an acre; Barkby lane clofe, half an acre; and one acre of meadow in Ailfton meadow, from 1640, for 21 years, paying yearly, for Humberfton's clofe, 30*s.*; for Barkby-lane clofe, 10*s.*; for Sand-pit clofe, 10*s.*; and for the acre in Ailfton meadow, 10*s.* In all, 3*l.*

Abrey Symkyn pays 10*s. per annum.*

John Burbage, no leafe; but pays 13*s.* 4*d. per ann.*

Thomas Woolafton has no leafe; but pays 13*s.* 4*d.*

Lincolnfhire Tenants.

Denton. Mr. William Welby held one houfe and lands in the open fields for three lives, paying yearly 2*l.* His fine was 15*l.*

Fawfon. Mr. William Vincent held a meffuage, and four oxgangs and a half of land, meadow and pafture, for three lives, paying yearly 2*l.*

Thomas Lovet held the manor-houfe of Fawfon, and four oxgangs and a half, for three lives, paying yearly 2*l.*

Allington. Thomas Lovet, or Mrs. Peete, paid for lands there 4*l.*

Harlaxton. Sir Daniel Delyve held lands there for three lives, at 1*l.* 4*s. per annum*; which he fet out to under-tenants for 39*l.* 7*s.* 4*d. per annum.* His fine was 210*l.*

Caftle Carleton. Mr. Nicholas Thornedicke, by leafe, dated Sept. 29, 6 Eliz. held the whole manor of Caftle Carleton for 99 years, paying yearly 27*l.* 3*s.* 7½*d.* But, 12 Jac. I. Mr. Thornedicke, of his free will, for better relief of the poor of the Hofpital, granted a rent of 10*l.* 8*s.* out of the faid manor.

Staffordfhire.

Horningloe. Thomas Clarke, of Horningloe, in the parifh of Burton upon Trent, held one meffuage, and a farm containing 50 acres and 3 roods, for three lives, paying yearly 3*l.* 6*s.* 8*d.* His fine was 20*l.*

Total, 157*l.* 16*s.* 11½*d.*

June 19, 1656, Thomas Wadland, of the Newark, Leicefter, gent. fworn; faith, that it appears, by decree of Chancery, made Nov. 27, 22 Car. I. that the Hofpital had antiently two yard and a half lands in Brankingfthorpe, in the parifh of St. Mary's Leicefter, which was in leafe to Mr. John Danet and his anceftors; and that the faid lordfhip being long fince inclofed, there was fet out to the Hofpital 50 acres; and that, by decree in the Exchequer 3 Car. I. upon difafforefting the Foreft of Leicefter, there were 25 acres in the Foreft allowed to Mr. Danet, in lieu of 15 yard lands in Brankingfthorpe, the two and a half yard lands held by the faid Mr. Danet being part of the faid 15 yard lands; and that he never heard that any part of the faid 25 acres is fet out for the faid Hofpital.

Some depofitions taken Nov. 4, 1656.

There was about 40 acres of land in poffeffion of Mr. Danet, and another plot of ground, called *Ryplot*, of about ten acres, and two little clofes containing about five acres.

Sept. 8. By feveral, it appeared that there was paid weekly to each of the poor men, 16*d.*; and, whilft the South field tithes belonged to the Hofpital, they ufed to have 4*d.* a week more.

Joan Taylor, one of the poor, fays fhe has been in the houfe 24 years; and when fhe came firft the poor women received but 11*d.* a week each, till Dr. Clarke augmented 3*d.* a week apiece.

The following titles were taken by Mr. Carte from a bundle of papers in poffeffion of Mr. T. Palmer:

A Rental of the lands in 1561, 1562, out of which the fchoolmafter is paid.

Two furveys of the Hofpital lands at Norton.

Two inventories of the goods of the Hofpital.

A Terrier of the Hofpital lands in Belvoir, Denton, and Harlefton.

An account of the lands at Harlaxton.

The title of Wigfton's Hofpital to the South Field tithes, and a note of writings relating thereto, delivered to Mr. Clarke by Mr. Thomas Wadland.

Nov. 18, 1656, on the humble petition of the Mayor, Bailiffs, and Burgeffes of Leicefter, to the Houfe of Commons; it was ordered, that Mr. Stanley do bring in a Bill, to the purpofe mentioned in their Petition, touching the Hofpital of Leicefter [1]. The Bill was prepared November 29; read the firft time Dec. 2; a fecond time Dec. 9, and referred to a Committee; who were directed alfo to confider the Petition of Richard Lee, Mafter of Wigfton's Hofpital, with that of William Simms, Public Lecturer of the Borough of Leicefter, and Confrater of Wigfton's Hofpital [2]. The Bill was reported Feb. 6, 1656-7, and feveral new Governors added [3]. It was read the third time Feb. 16; and ordered " to be offered to his Highnefs the Lord Protector for his confent [4];" which was given, by the Protector in perfon, June 9, 1657 [5].

The title of it is, " An Act for the fettling and regulating of the Hofpital called Wigfton's Hofpital, in the Borough of Leicefter, and eftablifhing of the Government thereof;" and an attefted copy of it is here given:

" Whereas one William Wigfton, deceafed, who was heretofore Mayor of the Borough of Leicefter, in the county of Leicefter, heretofore, in or about the fifth year of Henry the Eighth, late King of England, by licence of the faid king, founded an Hofpital in the faid Borough, now commonly called *Wigfton's Hofpital*, confifting of two chaplains and twenty-four poor people: And the late Queen Elizabeth, for the prefervation of the faid charitable ufe, re-founded the faid Hofpital, and incorporated the fame by the name of " The Chaplains and Poor of the Hofpital of William Wigfton, in the Town of Leicefter, of the Foundation of the faid William;" and divers orders were confirmed by Act of Parliament concerning the ordering of the faid Hofpital, the faid Hofpital being endowed by the faid founder of divers manors and lands, which, according to a

---

[1] Journals of the Commons, vol. VII. p. 456.   [2] Ibid. p. 466.   [3] Ibid. p. 487.   [4] Ibid. p. 492.   [5] Ibid. p. 552.

true

true and full value, are worth above 1200*l.* by the year, and a very confiderable part thereof employed to the relief of the poor : Be it enacted, by his Highnefs the Lord Protector of the Commonwealth of England, Scotland, and Ireland, and by the prefent Parliament affembled, and by the authority of the fame, that the faid Hofpital is hereby, and for ever hereafter fhall be, incorporated, to all intents and purpofes, by the name or names of ' The Chaplains and Poor of the Hofpital of William Wigfton, in the Borough of Leicefter :' And be it enacted, by the authority aforefaid, that, for the government and regulation of the faid Hofpital, there fhall be a perpetual fucceffion of perfons of piety, and known integrity, to be truftees and governors thereof; who fhall keep and ufe a common feal for the faid Hofpital in the cheft appointed for that purpofe, ftanding in the Evidence chamber thereof ; which cheft fhall have two locks, with feveral wards and keys, one key whereof fhall be always in the cuftody of the mayor of the Borough of Leicefter, and the other of the mafter of the faid Hofpital, or his confrater, and fhall not be opened but in the prefence of eight or more of the faid governors : And be it further enacted, by the authority aforefaid, that the mayor of Leicefter for the time being, Edward Whalley efquire, fir Chriftopher Pack knight, alderman of the City of London, Thomas Beaumont, Francis Hacker, William Quarles, Thomas Pochen, Thomas Hafelrigg, Thomas Charnells, William Purefoy, Henry Smith, Henry Markham, efquires ; William Stanley, Richard Ludlam, Edmund Cradock, Edward Johnfon, Edward Billers, Anthony Major, Alexander Baker, Samuel Wanley, Robert Hicklin, gentlemen, and Richard Lee, clerk, be, and are hereby, conftituted and appointed the firft truftees and governors of the faid Hofpital, to all intents and purpofes ; which faid truftees and their fucceffors, before they enter upon the execution of the truft and powers by this Act vefted in them, fhall, before two juftices of the peace, take an oath, which faid juftices are hereby authorized and empowered to adminifter the fame, in thefe words : " You fhall fwear to be true and faithful in the execution of the office of truftee and governor of the Hofpital of William Wigfton in Leicefter ; and that you will not, by yourfelf, or any other in truft for you, or to your benefit, take any leafe or leafes of the faid Hofpital, but will, to your beft fkill, knowledge, and power, impartially perform the truft committed to you, and procure the profit and commodity of the Hofpital by all lawful means :" And when and fo often as it fhall happen that any of the faid truftees and governors fhall die, thofe that furvive, or the greater number, fhall and are hereby authorized to elect other fit perfons, men of piety, known integrity and ability, to be joined with them, fo as the number may be always fifteen to continue a fucceffion : And be it further enacted, by the authority aforefaid, that the faid truftees and governors, and their fucceffors, or the greater number of them, fhall and may make fuch byelaws and ordinances as they fhall judge convenient and neceffary for the better government of the faid Hofpital, to have equal force with any ftatutes or conftitutions heretofore made for the fame ; and fhall and may meet as often as they fhall judge it convenient for the good of the faid Hofpital : And they, and their fucceffors, by the names of the truftees and governors of the chaplains and poor of the Hofpital of William Wigfton in Leicefter, or the greater number of them, fhall and may purchafe any lands or tenements to the only benefit and advantage of the fame : And they or their fucceffors, or the greater part of them, and no other, fhall or may demife or leafe the manors, lands, and tenements, which now are or hereafter fhall be belonging to the faid Hofpital, under their common feal, fo as the fame exceed not the term of one and twenty years in poffeffion, and not in reverfion, upon reafonable improved rents, and not upon fines, any law, ftatute, or cuftom, to the contrary in any wife notwithftanding : Provided always, and be it further enacted, by the authority aforefaid, that none of the manors, lands, or tenements, be-

longing to the faid Hofpital, fhall be demifed or fet in grofs to any perfon or perfons whatfoever, but that the prefent occupiers of the refpective manors, lands, or tenements, fhall be admitted immediate tenants of the Hofpital, fo as they fhall give a full value of the fame, to the beft advantage of the faid Hofpital : And it is hereby further enacted, by the authority aforefaid, that as well the faid Hofpital, as alfo all the manors, meffuages, lands, tenements, rents, and hereditaments, with their appurtenances whatfoever, belonging to or parcel of the poffeffions of the faid Hofpital, fhall be and are hereby vefted, fettled, and eftablifhed, in and upon the faid truftees and governors, and their fucceffors, for the ufe and benefit of the chaplains and poor of the faid Hofpital and their fucceffors for ever : And be it further enacted, by the authority aforefaid, that all and every perfon and perfons whatfoever that now have or fhall have any feal or feals, deeds, evidences, books, or other goods, of and belonging to the faid Hofpital, fhall forthwith deliver the fame unto the faid truftees and governors, or the greater number of them : And be it further enacted, by the authority aforefaid, that the faid truftees and governors, and their fucceffors, or the greater number of them, fhall pay, or caufe to be paid, yearly, to the mafter of the faid Hofpital, and his fucceffors, the fum of forty pounds, in full difcharge of all other demands and dues to him as mafter of the fame, to be a falary for performance of the duty of his place, and to be paid quarterly, at the four ufual days of payment ; and the faid truftees and governors, and their fucceffors, fhall in like manner pay, or caufe to be paid, to the confrater of the faid Hofpital, yearly, the fum of forty and three pounds, as it is already fettled upon him : And be it further enacted, by authority aforefaid, that the truftees and governors of the faid Hofpital, and their fucceffors, fhall and are hereby authorized, upon the improvement of the revenues of the faid Hofpital, to enlarge the buildings thereof, and increafe the falaries of the mafter and his confrater, and the number and maintenance of the poor that are or fhall be therein placed, and for fuch other pious, charitable, and good ufes, as are limited, conftituted, and appointed, by certain orders and rules eftablifhed in the fourteenth year of the reign of Queen Elizabeth, and by all and every fuch bye-founders and benefactors as are or fhall be directed, limited, or appointed, refpectively ; provided always, that the refpective falaries to the mafter and his confrater appointed in this Act fhall not be conftrued to take from them their dwellings in the faid Hofpital, according to the ftatutes : And for the better execution of the feveral trufts in this Act mentioned and ordained, be it further enacted, by the authority aforefaid, that the faid truftees and governors, and their fucceffors, or the greater number of them, fhall appoint the mafter or confrater of the faid Hofpital for the time being, fo as the faid mafter or confrater be always refident in the faid Hofpital, and not one of the truftees or governors thereof, to receive the rents of the faid Hofpital, and defray the charges and difburfements thereof, according to fuch rules and directions as he fhall from time to time receive from the truftees or governors, and their fucceffors, or the greater number of them ; which faid mafter or confrater fhall keep a true and perfect regifter of the receipts, difburfements, acts and doings, relating to the faid Hofpital ; and fhall, once in every year (that is to fay, the firft Tuefday in April), make a true and juft account thereof to the truftees and governors, and their fucceffors, or the greater number of them, which fhall be kept in a book fairly written for that purpofe ; and being approved of and fubfcribed by the truftees and governors, or the greater number of them, fhall be put into the cheft, and remain with the public feal and evidences therein belonging to the faid Hofpital ; which faid mafter or confrater fhall have allowed to him, for his pains herein, fuch additional falary as the faid truftees and governors, and their fucceffors, or the greater number of them, fhall appoint, fo as the fame exceeds not the fum of 6*l.* 13*s.* 4*d.* : And it is further enacted,

by

by the authority aforefaid, that the faid truftees and governors, and their fucceffors, or the greater number of them, fhall at all times hereafter have the full power and authority of electing, placing, and upon juft caufe of the difplacing, of the poor of the faid Hofpital, and alfo of the difplacing of the mafter and his confrater, who are the chaplains in this Act named, for fcandal and mifdemeanours by them, or either of them, done or committed: Saving to his Highnefs the Lord Protector, and his fucceffors, the donations of the places of the mafter and brother of the faid Hofpital, called by the names of the chaplains of the fame, fo often as they fhall become void by death, refignation, or deprivation; which chaplains fhall be able minifters of the Gofpel, and men of godly life and converfation; and before they are admitted into their refpective places, the truftees and governors of the faid Hofpital fhall, and they are hereby empowered to, adminifter an oath unto them, in thefe words following, that is to fay; ' You fhall fwear to be true and faithful in the execution of the office of   in Leicefter; and that you will not, by yourfelf, or any other in truft for you, or to your benefit, take any leafe or leafes of the faid Hofpital, but will, to your beft fkill, knowledge, and power, impartially perform the truft committed to you, and fhall procure the profit and commodity of the Hofpital by all lawful means.'
Examined, Feb. 18, 1657, *by Samuel Horneby.*"

A warrant occurs, dated July 19, 1661, from Charles lord Seymour of Trowbridge, Chancellor of the Duchy, to Mr. John Angel, clerk, and Robert Tyringham, gentleman, to be auditors of the Hofpital accompts.

A leafe, dated Oct. 6, 1663, made to William Henworth, of Burton upon Trent, in the county of Stafford, butcher, his executors, adminiftrators, and affigns, of a meadow-ground called Braffingcote Hurft, *alias* Briffingcote Hurft, in the parifh of Burton upon Trent, containing about 30 acres. late in tenure of Daniel Brown; *habend'* to the faid William Henworth, his heirs, &c. for the lives of Robert Brown, William Brown, and Anne Brown, being three of the children of Daniel Brown, of Burton upon Trent, clothier; the faid Robert Brown being of the age of ten years, William of three years, and Anne of fifteen years. *Reddend'*, yearly, at the mafter's houfe, 10*l.* at Lady-day and Michaelmas, and one couple of fat capons, or 2*s.* in money, at Michaelmas, with claufe of re-entry if the rent be unpaid for 20 days, &c. Worth, *per annum,* 30*l.*

A leafe, dated Oct. 8, 1663, made to Dorothy wife of Thomas Mollibarre, her executors, adminiftrators, and affigns, of one meffuage or tenement, and one farm, confifting of divers clofes, lands, arable, meadow, and pafture, in Horningloe, co. Stafford, and three acres of meadow, called the Trent meadow, in Horningloe, in the parifh of Burton upon Trent, in tenure of Sarah Clarke and Thomas Seale (except all timber-trees); *habend'* to Dorothy wife of Thomas Mollibarre and her affigns, during the lives of the faid Dorothy wife of the faid Thomas Mollibarre, and Dorothy Seale and Mary Seale, being two of the children of Thomas Seale, of Horningloe, yeoman; Dorothy Seale being of the age of ten years, and Mary Seale of the age of fix years. Rent, 3*l.* 6*s.* 8*d.* *per annum,* at Michaelmas and Lady-day; with claufe of re-entry at 20 days, &c. Worth, *per annum,* 20*l.*

A leafe, dated Sept. 15, 1664, was made to William Vincent, of Creaton, co. Northampton, gent. of a meffuage, with the homeftead, and four oxgangs, and the half of one oxgang, in Fofton, co. Lincoln (except all timber-trees); *habend'* to the faid William Vincent of Creaton and his heirs, for the lives of himfelf, and William Vincent of Great Sheepy, father of William Vincent of Creaton, and of William Vincent the youngeft, being the eldeft fon and heir apparent of William Vincent of Creaton; the faid William Vincent the youngeft being of the age of half a year. Rent, 2*l.* 10*s.* *per annum,* payable at Michaelmas and Lady-day, at the mafter's houfe; and a claufe of re-entry for want of payment at 40 days. Worth, *per annum,* 18*l.*

A leafe, dated Aug. 2, 1672, made to Robert Archer, gent. and his affigns, of one meffuage or tenement, with the home-clofe, orchard, and back-fide adjoining, in Hungry Harbury, in tenure of Thomas Cox the elder, of Hungry Harbury, and one yard land in Hungry Harbury, co. Warwick, in tenure of Thomas Cox fenior (except all timber-trees); *habend'* to Robert Archer and his heirs and affigns, for the lives of Thomas Cox fenior, Richard Cox and Thomas Cox junior, fons of Thomas Cox fenior; Richard Cox being 21, and Thomas Cox 15, years of age. The rent 30*s.* *per annum,* at Lady-day and Michaelmas; with claufe of re-entry at 20 days for non-payment, and a covenant from the chaplains and poor, at any time within five years (if Mr. Richard Clarke fhould fo long live and continue mafter, &c.), at the requeft and charges of Robert Archer, to make a new leafe to Mr. Archer; for, in a leafe of this houfe and yard-land, made heretofore to Thomas Cox, a Terrier is annexed to that leafe.

A leafe, dated Sept. 4, 1673, made to William Welby, efq. of one meffuage in Denton, co. Lincoln; and of one clofe adjoining to the faid meffuage, on the North fide thereof, and of three oxgangs and a half of land, arable, meadow, and pafture, in Denton, particularly mentioned in a Terrier annexed to the leafe (except all timber-trees, &c.); *habend'* to William Welby and his heirs, for the lives of William Leiveffey of Allington, &c.

A leafe, dated Aug. 28, 1679, made to Richard Grant, gent. of a capital meffuage, and feven oxgangs of land, leys, meadow, pafture, and common, *cum pertinentiis,* in Allington, in tenure of Thomas Marryot, and of a cottage, *cum pertinentiis,* in Allington, in tenure of John Day (all trees of oak, afh, and elm, and other timber-trees, with liberty to fall, cut down, and carry away the fame, always excepted); *habend'* to Richard Grant and his heirs, for the life of the faid Richard Grant, and Thomas Trefham, only fon of William Trefham, of Bottesford, gent.; and of Thomas Sills, eldeft fon of Richard Sills, of Bottesford, yeoman (Thomas Trefham being about 27, and Thomas Sills about 15 or 16 years old.) *Reddend',* yearly, at the mafter's houfe, 4*l.* 10*s.* at Michaelmas and Lady-day, and alfo one couple of fat capons, or 2*s.* in money; and one couple of fat hens, or 12*d.* in money, at Lady-day; with claufe of re-entry for non-payment at 30 days. Worth, *per annum,* 4*l.*

A leafe, dated March 29, 1682, made to Maurice Dalton, Thomas Fifher, and Robert Cowles, of the capital manfion or manor-houfe in Fofton, co. Lincoln, in tenure of Thomas Lovett, and four oxgangs and a half of arable land, meadow and pafture, to the faid capital meffuage, manor, or manfion-houfe belonging, in Fofton, in tenure of Thomas Lovett (except all timber-trees); *habend'* to the faid Maurice Dalton, Thomas Fifher, and Robert Cowles, and their heirs, for the lives of Thomas Lovett, party to this deed, and of William Lovett brother to the faid Thomas, and of Thomas Welby, gent. youngeft fon of William Welby, late of Denton, co. Lincoln, efq. deceafed. *Reddend',* yearly, 3*l.* 8*s.* at Michaelmas and Lady-day. Provided that if the leffees fhould not duly pay rent, and truly obferve the covenants, then the leafe to be void. Worth, *per annum,* 18*l.*

A leafe, dated Sept. 14, 1682, made to Nathaniel Garthwaite fenior, of Grantham, co. Lincoln, of a meffuage, with the homeftead thereto adjoining, and feveral clofes, plots, and parcels of arable land, leys, meadow, pafture, and greenfward ground, being 64 acres and a half, in Harlexton, co. Lincoln, and all other their lands and hereditaments in Harlexton (except all trees of oak, afh, and elm, and other timber-trees); *habend'* to Nathaniel Garthwaite fenior and his heirs, for the lives of Mary wife of Nathaniel Garthwaite fenior, and of Nathaniel Garthwaite junior, fon and heir apparent of Nathaniel Garthwaite fenior, and of Edward Garthwaite fecond fon of Nathaniel Garthwaite fenior, under the yearly rent of 5*l.* payable at Michaelmas and Lady-day. Worth, *per annum,* 40*l.*

The

The Reckoning and Accompt of Edward Palmer, made to John Pike, Clerk, Master of the Hospital of William Wigston in the Town of Leicester, of the Foundation of the same William, of all the Rents and Revenues of the said Hospital, due at Michaelmas 1686, and Lady-day 1687, and of all Monies received by the Accomptant for the said Hospital at and after Michaelmas 1686, until Michaelmas 1687, and of all the Accomptant's Disbursements for the said Hospital, as followeth; (this Accompt not comprising any of the Rents received for Michaelmas 1687.)—Of which the Accomptant dischargeth himself as followeth:

The CHARGE.

Received of	£.	s.	d.
Allington.—Mr. Richard Grant –	4	10	0
Capon and Hen money – –	0	3	0
Belvoir.—The earl of Rutland –	1	9	8½
Barkston.—Mr. Dixon – –	5	0	0
Bottesford.—Thomas North. His year's rent is 6s.; but he is arrear for the whole year.			
Samuel Hardy, formerly widow Tutbury	0	8	0
William Leighton – – –	1	4	0
John Clifton – – –	0	6	0
Robert Cragg, formerly —— Somerby	0	6	8
Thomas Orson – –	2	5	0
Thomas Bennett – –	4	0	0
Thomas Bennett and widow Somner, for North leys, house, and three quarters of an oxgang of land – –	0	12	6
Richard Sills – – –	4	12	6
Francis Somner, formerly Eleanor Somner widow – – –	1	7	6
Katherine Vincent – –	1	5	0
Bowden.—Mr. Richard Bucknall –	3	0	0
More, an arrear cast up at the last accompt	1	10	0
Capon money – – –	0	2	0
Bredon.—Hannah Burrough –	5	0	0
Capon money – – –	0	2	0
Thomas Turner – –	0	10	0
Burton super Trent.—Thomas Newton	10	0	0
Capon money – – –	0	2	0
Castle Carlton.—Mrs. Jackson. Her year's rent is 41l.; but she is arrear for the whole year.			
Denton.—Mr. William Welby –	2	10	0
Foston.—Mr. William Vincent –	2	10	0
Thomas Lovett – –	6	0	0
Harlaxton.—Mr. Nathaniel Garthwait –	5	0	0
Hathern.—Thomas Bowley – –	1	0	0
Capon money – – –	0	2	0
John Savage – – –	2	5	0
Capon money – – –	0	2	0
John Throne – – –	4	10	0
Capon money – – –	0	2	0
Nicholas Low – –	1	10	0
Horningloe.—Thomas Seale –	3	6	8
Hungry Harbury.—Mrs. Archer –	1	10	0
Anne Mills, widow. Her year's rent is 1l. 10s.; but she is arrear for two years, ending at Lady-day 1687.			
Ibstock.—Thomas Pagett – –	0	15	0
Kimcote.—William Carter –	0	17	6
Capon money – – –	0	2	0
Leicester.—Mr. Lawrence Carter –	8	4	0
William Inge, esq. –	1	10	0
Chamberlains of Leicester.			
George Boyer – – –	0	18	0
Thomas Fawset, formerly Roger Taylor	1	0	0
John Hewett – –	0	12	6
Margaret Worrall, widow –	0	15	0
Mr. John Newton, formerly John Duckett	0	3	6
Elizabeth Hartthorn – –	0	19	0
Ann Burbage – –	0	18	0
More, for an arrear cast up at the last accompt – – –	0	18	0
Benjamin Tapper. His year's rent is 5s.; but he is arrear for Lady-day 1687; so the Accomptant chargeth himself with	0	2	6
More, for an arrear cast up at the last accompt – – –	0	2	6
Mr. Edward Palmer – –	3	0	0
Elizabeth Wood – –	0	13	4
The earl of Devon – –	56	13	4
Mrs. Elizabeth Coleman, relict of Mr. Richard Coleman – –	1	6	0
Thomas Paine – –	0	15	0

VOL. I.

The DISCHARGE.

	£.	s.	d.
The weekly pay of 24 poor folk, at 3l. per week, for 52 weeks, doth amount in the whole to –	156	0	0
The Accomptant's [the Master's] stipend	20	0	0
For his usual allowance for keeping two geldings, with provender, straw, groom's wages, shoeing, and other requisites	10	0	0
For his usual allowance for salt, candles, wood, coals, and travelling charges	4	0	0
For his stipend out of the school lands –	0	7	0
For the Confrater's foundation stipend	13	6	0
For his stipend out of the earl of Huntingdon's gift – –	30	0	0
For his stipend out of the School lands	0	5	0
The head-schoolmaster, for his exhibition	20	0	0
Paid the usher for his allowance –	1	0	0
Paid the two University scholars for their exhibitions – – –	6	0	0
Paid the two Grammar-scholars for their exhibitions – –	4	0	0
The vicar of St. Martin's, for his exhibition	0	6	0
Paid the poor folk for their exhibition, out of the earl of Huntingdon's gift, out of the Abbey meadow –	6	13	0
Bread and wine for two Sacraments –	0	14	0
Paid the poor folk, to buy them fuel –	3	13	0
Paid, for the pit price of 23 loads of coals, with the carter's usual allowance for drink and dinners; John Russell having brought one this year that he should have brought the last; so there is one load in arrear – –	9	6	0
Paid for chiefs payable out of the Hospital lands in the collection of the bailiffs of Leicester	0	14	3
Paid the chamberlains of Leicester, for chiefs in their collection –	0	1	10½
Paid the earl of Rutland, for chiefs payable out of Neathouse meadow –	0	0	4½
Paid him more, for chiefs of several Hospital lands lying near Belvoir Castle	0	9	8
Paid Mr. Herrick, for rent of Francis garden – –	0	4	0
Paid Mr. Cradock, for cloth for 12 womens' gowns – – –	9	0	0
Paid, for making them up	1	4	0
Paid the keepers, for salt, two scuttles, a wash-sieve, a ladle, and for sweeping chimnies – – –	0	10	0
Paid William Anderson, gardener, upon his two bills, for 17 days work of himself in the great garden and little garden, and for two days work of a weeder, and half a day of another labourer, and for old hats to nail up the trees – – –	1	2	0
Paid Anthony Gilbert, for helping the gardener half a day – –	0	0	6
Paid Hester Boylston, for weeding two days	0	0	6
Paid Cecily Skeffington, for drink for the gardener – –	0	1	0
Paid Henry Hitchcock, for three dwarf pear-trees and seven cherry-trees for the Master's garden – –	0	12	0
Paid Mr. John Warberton, for nails for the trees – –	0	1	0
Paid Ann Ward, for nine strikes of grits	2	4	0
Paid Elias Hartall, slater and chandler, upon his two bills for slaters work done at the Hospital and Confrater's house, and for materials, and for three dozen and one pound of candles –	4	14	0
Paid John Beaumont, carpenter, upon his two bills for the work of himself and servants			

CHARGE *continued.*

	£.	s.	d.
Norton.—Mrs. Elizabeth Beaumont. Her year's rent is 13s. 4d.; but she is in arrear for Lady-day 1687; so the Accomptant chargeth himself with	0	6	8
Mr. Stanhope Whalley	10	0	0
Mr. William Whalley	10	0	0
Odeby.—Mr. John Noone, for Mawson's farm	2	15	0
Redmile.—Widow Dalliwater	0	2	0
Raunston.—Elizabeth Jaques, widow	1	10	0
Swannington and *Snibson.*—Sir William Villiers	70	8	0
Nether Seale.—Reginald Newbold	2	10	0
Capon money	0	2	0
Walton.—Jonathan Blockley	1	5	6
Anne Wormeleighton	1	10	0
Wykeham.—Mr. Nichols	7	0	0
Wigston.—Thomas Law, for his part of Law's Farm	1	0	0
Capon money	0	2	0
John Noone, for his part of Law's farm	1	0	0
William Brabson. His year's rent is 16s.; but he is in arrear for Lady-day 1687; so the Accomptant chargeth himself with	0	8	0
Capon money	0	2	0
Widow Lewis	4	4	0
Capon money	0	2	0
William Bolter	0	4	0
Dionis Jackson	1	4	0
Capon money	0	2	0
The Accomptant received more, of the goods of Dannet Pollard deceased	2	15	0
More, for the goods of Edward Palmer deceased	0	10	0
More, for the goods of John King deceased	2	2	0
More, for the goods of Francis Croft deceased	2	0	0
More, for the goods of Thomas Chapman deceased	0	14	0
More of Elias Hartill, for some plaister which he bought, which were left of some work done at the Hospital	0	1	0
Of Mr. Ward, for 20 loads of stones	1	11	0
Remaining in the Accomptant's hands, upon the foot of his last accompt	49	2	2
The Charge is	333	1	0½

DISCHARGE *continued.*

	£.	s.	d.
servants about repairing the Master's house, the Confrater's house, and Hospital stable, and for boards, planks, and splenting for that stable	2	5	0
Cecily Skeffington, for drink for the slaters	0	4	0
Paid for two loads of straw	1	2	0
Paid Richard Skelson, upon his two bills for smith's ware and work	1	17	4
Paid for hearth-money for the chimnies in the Master's lodging, and in the Hospital kitchens and wash-house	0	16	0
More, for the twelve poor men's chimnies for two years, to Michaelmas 1686	2	8	0
More, for those twelve chimnies at Lady-day 1687	0	12	0
More, for three half-years ending at Lady-day 1687, for four chimnies in Mr. Raynor's house	0	12	0
Paid William Hall, for glaziers' work	0	16	0
Paid John Hewett, for coopers' work	0	5	8
Paid Thomas Brown, for a sack of lime	0	2	0
Paid, for crying the house wedges	0	0	2
Paid Mr. Thomas Palmer, vintner, for six quarts and one pint of claret, and two quarts of sack, for the entertainment of the Bishop of Peterborough and his attendants at the Hospital	0	11	7
Paid, for the charge of the several funerals of Dannett Pollard, Edward Palmer, John King, Francis Crofts, and Thomas Chapman, and the appraiser's usual allowance	2	4	5
Paid Cornelius Jones, for the work of himself and his servants, for making a wall belonging to the Hospital	1	10	5
Paid Anthony Gilbert, for removing stones out of Mr. Orton's yard to a cart, which carried them to that wall	0	1	0
Paid Mr. William Orton, for six loads of stones for that wall	0	12	0
Paid Mr. John Hare, for a load of straw for that wall	0	11	0
Paid John Harris, upon his bill for carriage	0	11	0
For several letters sent and received about the Hospital affairs	0	3	0
For drawing and ingrossing the several accompts of this year	1	10	0
For the Auditor's allowance and entertainment at the accompt	0	16	0
The Discharge is	325	19	9
Remains in the Accomptant's hands	7	1	3½
	333	1	0½

A RENTAL OF THE LANDS OF WIGSTON'S HOSPITAL, 1687.

Tenants.	Yearly Rent 1661. £. s. d.			Advance.	£. s. d.			£. s. d.			
Allington.—Mr. Peete	4	0	0	1680	4	10	0				
Barkston.—Mr. Dixon	4	0	0	1665	5	0	0				
Bottesford.—George North	0	6	0								
Richard Tutbury	0	8	0								
William Leighton	1	4	0								
John Clifton	0	6	0								
Robert Peeke	0	6	8								
Robert Orson	2	0	0	1676	2	5	0				
Thomas Bennet	3	11	0	1672	4	0	0				
John Sumner	5	0	0	1672 { Richard Sills	4	12	6				
				{ John Sumner	1	7	6				
Francis Vincent	1	0	0	1673	1	5	0				
William Northley	0	5	0	1680	0	12	6				
Bowden.—Richard Bucknall	3	0	0								
Bredon.—Sampson Burroughs	2	18	0	1665	5	0	0				
Thomas Turner	0	8	0	1672	0	10	0				
Burton super Trent.—Daniel Brown	6	13	4	1664	10	0	0				
Castle Carleton.—Mr. Allington	37	11	8	1664	40	0	0	1685	41	0	0
Denton.—John Livesley	2	0	0	1671	2	10	0				
Foston.—William Vincent	2	0	0	1665	2	10	0				
Thomas Lovet	2	8	0	1683	3	0	0				
Harlaxton.—Lady Delyve	1	4	0	1683	5	0	0				
Hathern.—Anthony Croson	1	0	0								
John Savage	2	5	0								

John

Tenants.	Yearly Rent 1661.			Advance.										
	£.	s.	d.		£.	s.	d.		£.	s.	d.			
John Throne - - -	4	10	0											
Nicholas Lowe - - -				1663 - -	1	0	0	1668 =	1	10	0			
Horningloe.—Widow Clarke -	3	6	8											
Kimcote.—John Blockley -	0	15	0	1679 - -	0	17	6							
Leicefter.—Mrs. Dannet -	3	0	0	1677 - -	8	4	0							
Edward Bracebridge, Edward Palmer, for the Mafter's houfe -	3	0	0											
Mr. Inge - - -	1	0	0	1677 - -	1	10	0							
Chamberlains of Leicefter, for Freake's land - - -	10	0	0											
Anne Griffin - - -	0	12	0	1671 - -	0	18	0							
Robert Bates (Norris Taylor) -	1	0	0											
Henry Heyward (Thomas Norris) -	1	0	0											
Richard Simpkin (Herrick) -	0	10	0	1683 - -	0	12	6							
John Burbage - -	0	13	4	1674 - -	0	18	0							
William Sanders -	0	10	0	1679 - -	0	15	0							
John Cooper (Tupper) - -	0	5	0											
Francis Immins - -	0	5	0	1664 - -	0	3	6							
Widow Wood - -	0	10	0	1674 - -	0	13	4							
Countefs of Devon - -	56	13	4											
Mr. Coleman - -	1	0	0	1676 - -	1	6	0							
John Pain - - -	0	12	0	1677 - -	0	15	0							
Norton.—Mrs. Whalley -	2	16	8	1663 - -	10	0	0							
Mr. Whalley - -	3	6	8	1663 - -	10	0	0							
Thomas Beaumont -	0	13	4											
Odeby.—Widow Wigfall -	2	0	0	1663 - -	2	15	0							
Redmile.—Widow Dalliwater -	0	2	0											
Swannington.—Lady Beaumont -	35	0	0	1663 - -	60	0	0	1669 -	70	8	0			
Walton.—John Blockley -	1	0	0	1677 - -	1	5	6							
Humphrey Wormleighton -	1	4	0	1676 - -	1	10	0							
Wykeham and *Cawdewell.*—Mr. Nichols	6	13	4	1676 - -	7	0	0							
Wigston.—Thomas Law -	2	0	0											
William Brabfon - -	0	16	0											
Jane Jackfon - -	1	4	0											
William Lewis - -	4	0	0	1680 - -	4	4	0							
William Bolter - -	0	2	0	1676 - -	0	4	0							

ADDENDA.—Capon Money.

	£.	s.	d.		£.	s.	d.		£.	s.	d.
Belvoir—Earl of Rutland -	0	18	6	1680 - -	1	9	8½				
Hungry Harbury.—1664, Thomas Cox	1	0	0	1668 - -	1	10	0				
Edward Mills - - -	1	0	0	1668 - -	1	10	0				
Ibftock.—1664, Richard Willimot -	0	5	0	} 1679 Thomas Paget	0	15	0				
William Maffey - - -	0	5	0								
Leicefter.—Robert Hartfhorn -	0	13	4	1674 - -	0	19	0				
Raunfton.—1665, Jofeph Jaques -	1	0	0	1669 - -	1	5	0	1683 -	1	10	0
Nether Seale.—1665, Thomas Newbold	2	10	0								

Swannington.—A delph of coals, 1666, 18*l.*; 1667, 10*l.*; 1668, 7*l.*; 1669, 6*l.* &c.

N. B. Capon-money is paid moft at Michaelmas, once a year, viz. 16 of them; and only Bredon at Lady-day. He mentions 17, who paid each 2*s.* for Capon-money.

ANNUAL PAYMENTS MADE OUT OF THE REVENUES OF WIGSTON'S HOSPITAL.

	£.	s.	d.		£.	s.	d.
To the poor 1661 (note, one Chefter had 8*d.* a week allowed him); and then the payment weekly was - -	1	14	8	Which in fifty-two weeks was -	100	10	8
1662, the weekly pay was -	2	6	0	Which in fifty-two weeks makes -	119	12	0
1668, ------------- -	2	10	0	------------------------- -	130	0	0
1674, ------------- -	2	14	0	------------------------- -	140	8	0
1677, ------------- -	2	18	0	------------------------- -	150	16	0
1681, ------------- -	3	0	0	------------------------- -	156	0	0

Of the earl of Huntingdon's gift, annually, 6*l.* 13*s.* 4*d.* for gowns, oatmeal, coals; to buy fuel, 3*l.* 13*s.* 4*d.*

	£.	s.	d.		£.	s.	d.
To the Mafter, for his ftipend -	20	0	0	To the ufher - -	1	0	0
For his ufual allowance, for keeping two geldings, provender, ftraw, groom's wages, &c. - -	10	0	0	To two Univerfity fcholars -	6	0	0
				To two School fcholars - -	4	0	0
His allowance for falt, candles, wood, coals, and travelling charges -	4	0	0	Chief Rents payable,			
				To the bailiffs of Leicefter -	0	14	3
His ftipend out of the fchool lands -	0	7	0	To the chamberlains of Leicefter -	0	1	10½
To the Confrater, his ftipend -	13	6	8	To the earl of Rutland, for Neat-houfe meadow - -	0	0	4½
The earl of Huntingdon's gift -	30	0	0	For lands near Belvoir - -	0	9	8
His ftipend out of the fchool lands -	0	5	0	To Mr. Heyrick, for the rent of Francis garden - -	0	4	0
To the vicar of St. Martin's -	0	6	8				
To the head-fchoolmafter -	20	0	0				

CHIEFS PAYABLE OUT OF THE HOSPITAL LANDS.

	£.	s.	d.
To the King, for the lordſhip of Carleton	o	o	8
To the Duchy of Lancaſter, for the lordſhip of Swannington	1	7	8
To the Auditor, for the Exchequer fee for the ſame	o	1	4
For a *Quietus eſt*	o	o	4
To the houſe of St. John's in Heyther, for a cottage in Swannington	o	3	o
To Bottisford church, for a light there out of the land at Bottisford	o	1	o
To the bailiff of Bever, for Caſtle-ward	o	1	o
To the bailiff of Bottisford, for Burſton's houſe	o	o	8
Pyper's cloſe	o	o	2
To the lord of Belvoir, for the great houſe at Barſton, a pound of pepper	o	2	2
To the conſtable of Bever, for a chief	o	o	4½
For certain fines of Courts, and other expences	o	o	6
For a houſe and land in Walton, to the chantry of Clipſton	o	o	6
To Henry Over, for the ſame houſe	o	o	7
To the lord Brook, for a houſe in Kimcote	o	1	6
To John Bloue, of Walton, for ground	o	o	1
To Mr. Turvile, for land held by Heyrick	o	o	1½

In Leiceſter.	£.	s.	d.
To the King, for a houſe in South gate	o	o	6
For two acres	o	o	3
For two houſes in the Cank	o	o	6
For a cloſe in Hangman-lane	o	5	o
For a cloſe in Barkby-lane	o	1	o
For a cloſe in St. Peter's pariſh	o	o	8
For a houſe in the Abbey-ſtreet	o	4	o
To the Abbey, for land in the Weſt field	o	1	o
To St. Mary's cloſe, for a houſe in the South gate	o	o	6
And for two hens	o	o	3
To the Newark, for a cloſe in St. Peter's pariſh aforeſaid	o	o	4½
To the ſaid College, for a piece of ground taken into the ſaid cloſe	o	1	o
To the Grey Friers, for St. Francis garden	o	4	o
To Mr. Purfrey, a houſe in the High-ſtreet	o	5	o
To St. Margaret's gild, for a cloſe in Normandy, held by William Alyſander	o	o	6
In ſome other papers there is,			
For a cloſe in Humberſton gate	o	1	4½
For the ſame, to Corpus Chriſti gild	o	1	8
To St. Margaret's gild	o	o	6

Note.—In the time of Edward VI. the lamp-money ceaſed to be paid.

A leaſe occurs, dated Oct. 12, 1663, made to Edward Palmer ſenior, gent. of one cloſe of paſture, called Humberſtone gate cloſe, containing three acres, in the pariſh of St. Margaret, near the Borough of Leiceſter, in tenure of Edward Palmer ſenior, lying next the land of Edward Palmer ſenior towards the Weſt part; one plot of ground, called Sandpit-lane cloſe, in the pariſh of St. Margaret, next the land of Thomas Blunt, eſq. mayor of Leiceſter, towards the North, and the land of Robert Green towards the South; and one other cloſe, called Barkby-lane cloſe, in the pariſh of St. Margaret, in tenure of Jane Springthorp, widow; and of one plot of meadow, containing one acre, in a certain meadow, called Borrowſy meadow, *alias* Neathouſe meadow, in the pariſh of St. Mary, Leiceſter, and of Aileſton, or one of them, in tenure of Edward Palmer ſenior. *Habend'* to the ſaid Edward Palmer, for the lives of Edward Palmer junior, gent. Thomas Palmer, and Jane Palmer, children of the ſaid Edward Palmer ſenior. Rent, *per annum*, 3l. at Lady-day and Michaelmas; and a clauſe of re-entry for non-payment 30 days, if no ſufficient diſtreſs be upon the land. Worth, *per annum*, 6l.—Aug. 26, 1686, this leaſe was ſurrendered, and a new leaſe granted to *Edward Palmer* ſenior, gent. of the ſame lands (except as in the former leaſe is excepted); *habend'* to Edward Palmer ſenior, his heirs and aſſigns, during the lives of his ſon Thomas Palmer, gent. Edward Palmer junior, ſon and heir apparent of the ſaid Thomas Palmer, and grandchild of the ſaid Edward Palmer ſenior, and of Richard Goodal, one of the ſons of John Goodal, gent. and the life of the longeſt liver of them; Edward Palmer junior being nine years, and Richard Goodal ſeven years of age. Rent as before.

A leaſe, dated Aug. 28, 1673, made to Elizabeth Wood, of a cottage or tenement in the Borough of Leiceſter, without the South gate, in tenure of Elizabeth Wood; *habend'* to the ſaid Elizabeth Wood, her heirs and aſſigns, for the lives of the ſaid Elizabeth Wood, and of John Wood, brother of the ſaid Elizabeth Wood, and of Sarah Wood, ſiſter of the ſaid Elizabeth Wood. Rent, *per annum*, 13s. 4d. at Michaelmas and Lady-day; and a clauſe of re-entry on non-payment at 20 days. Worth 1l. 10s. *per annum*.

A leaſe, dated Jan. 28, 1675, made to Richard Coleman, of one garden, or orchard, in the pariſh of St. Martin, in the Borough of Leiceſter, in tenure of Richard Coleman; *habend'* to the ſaid Richard Coleman, his executors, adminiſtrators, and aſſigns, from Michaelmas laſt paſt, for 21 years. Rent, *per annum*, 26s. at Lady-day and Michaelmas, and 4s. more to the poor on Trinity Sunday; with clauſe of re-entry for non-payment 21 days. Worth, *per annum*, 2l.

A leaſe, dated Aug. 14, 1676, made to Thomas Payne, barber, of one cottage, or tenement, in the Borough of Leiceſter, in a certain ſtreet called the Cank-ſtreet, *alias* the Cank-well ſtreet, over-againſt the backward part of the White Lion, in tenure of Thomas Payne; *habend'* to the ſaid Thomas Payne, and his heirs and aſſigns, for the lives of the ſaid Thomas Payne and Elizabeth his wife, and Thomas Payne the younger, ſon of the ſaid Thomas Payne the elder. Rent, *per annum*, 15s. at Michaelmas and Lady-day; with clauſe of re-entry for non-payment at 30 days. Worth, *per annum*, 1l. 10s.

A leaſe, dated April 15, 1682, made to Nicholas Smith, of a little piece of ground, with a barn thereupon built, in the Borough of Leiceſter, in or near a ſtreet called Redcroſs-ſtreet, in tenure of Nicholas Smith; *habend'* to the ſaid Nicholas Smith, his executors, adminiſtrators, and aſſigns; from 25 March laſt paſt, for 21 years. Rent, *per annum*, 5s. at Michaelmas and Lady-day; with clauſe of re-entry for non-payment of rent at 20 days. Worth, *per ann.* 15s.

The counteſs of Devon pays to the Hoſpital two annuities, or yearly rents, amounting to 56l. 13s. 4d. Theſe were of the gift of the earl of Huntingdon; and the two chaplains have each of them part thereof, and the poor people have the reſt.

Robert Hartſhorn is tenant at will of a meſſuage, with the appurtenances, in the Biſhop's Fee, near the Borough of Leiceſter; rent 19s. at Michaelmas and Lady-day. Worth, *per annum*, 1l. 10s.

—— Burbage is tenant at will of a houſe and croft in the ſaid Biſhop's Fee; rent 18s. payable at Michaelmas and Lady-day. Worth 1l. 5s. *per annum*.

A leaſe, dated Nov. 28, 1684, made to Margaret Palmer, widow, of the manor of Caſtle Carleton, co. Lincoln, and all the meſſuages, cottages, lands, tenements, meadow and fen grounds thereto belonging, in Great Carleton, Little Carleton, Caſtle Carleton, Dalby, and Southkeſton (except all timber-trees, other than for neceſſary reparations); *habend'* to the ſaid Margaret Palmer, and her heirs and aſſigns, for the lives of Elizabeth Jackſon, Thomas Jackſon, gent. and Edward Sawyer; the ſaid Elizabeth Jackſon being of the age of 50 years, Thomas Jackſon 24 years, and Edward Sawyer 13 years. Rent, *per annum*, 41l. Worth, *per annum*, 80l.

The

Fig. 1. WIGSTON'S HOSPITAL, E.

Vol. I. Pl. XXXIV. p. 495.

Fig. 4.

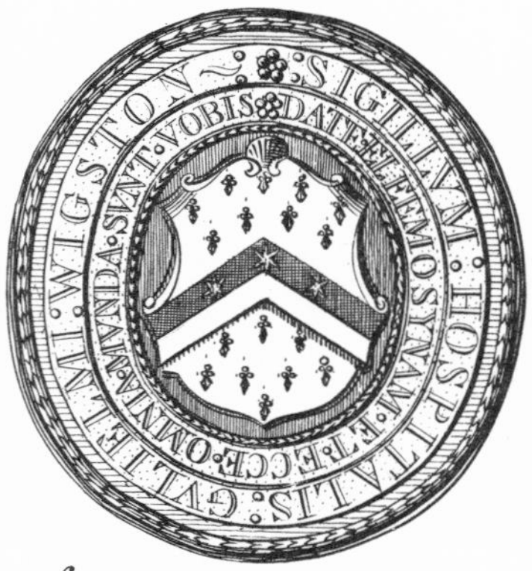

Fig. 2.

Fig. 5.

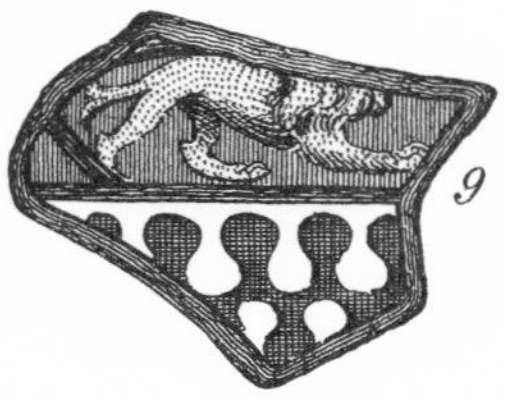

6

7

8

9

Fig. 3.

10

20

Fig. 19

18

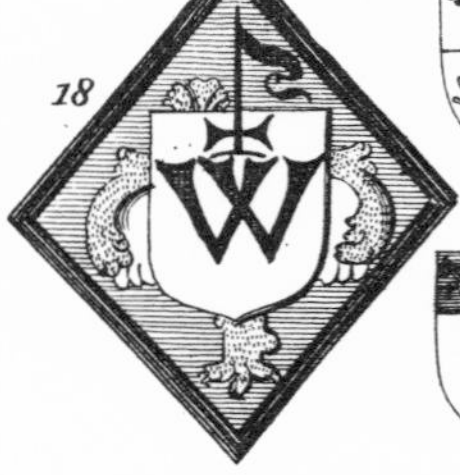

21

17

22

23

11  maioris

St apule 12

13 Calicie

q̄ va̅t m̄ta chrtate 15

14 ũdatoris et ro

En illa te̅ pore cũ us 16

24

25

Longmate del. et fo. 1795.

The CHAPEL (fee Plate XXXIV. fig. 1.)

of this Hofpital was originally a beautiful little Gothic building; the ftalls, fcreen, and loft, of oak, neatly finifhed. On the outfide, the great South window, very noble, is between two rich canopies; fig. 2.

On a tablet, fupported by two angels, over the door of entrance, are the Founder's arms, Ermine, on a chevron Sable, three eftoiles Or, fig. 3.; infcribed,

" Hoc Ædificium,
à Gulielmo Wigfton conditum,
extructum erat ad A. D. 1515;
refectum & adauctum A. D. 1730,
Joh. Jackfon Magiftro."

The Founder's arms are alfo on the common feal of the Hofpital, fig. 4.; and on a fmaller feal, which was occafionally ufed for leafes, fig. 5.

The pulpit is at the South end of the chapel, clofe to the window.

The Communion-table is very plain, covered with a green cloth, but not railed round.

The South window originally contained much fine painted glafs; which in 1760 was greatly defaced; but fo lately as 1790 feveral fragments remained; among which were,

The Founder's arms, as in fig. 6.

Semé of trefoils Or, a lion rampant Argent; fig. 7.

In a ftar quaterfoil, Sable, a fleur de lis Argent; between four crofs crofflets; fig. 8.

Argent, a fefs nebulé Azure; fig. 9.

A griffin holding a pendant flag; fig. 10.

Two figures praying to the Virgin.

On five feparate lights (fig. 11—15.):
majoris . . . . . Stapule . . . . Califie . . . .
Fundatoris et . . . ro . . . . Sua mera charitate.

In the Weft window, in 1790, were the Four Evangelifts, nearly entire; one of them with a book; in which appeared, " In illo tempore cũ . . . ua;" fig. 16.

In the fame window, well preferved, was the rebus of *Wigfton*, with a merchant's mark; fig. 17, 18.

In the Eaft window were originally the Twelve Apoftles, of whom in 1790 were feveral remains; particularly St. Peter, diftinguifhable by the cock.

In the fame window, on a fmall glafs circle, over an eagle with expanded wings, " Sit laus Deo."

Such was the ftate of the chapel in 1790. On a review in 1807, I find that the whole has been lately repaired. The Eaft and Weft windows, I am forry to fay, have been blocked up; and the fine old South window re-placed by a modern one, in which only five fmall pieces of the painted glafs are retained. The fmall gallery has alfo been plaftered over and white-wafhed. The whole, however, ftill looks very neat.

MONUMENTAL INSCRIPTIONS.

On the brafs felvage of a grave-ftone on the floor, round a very neat figure in brafs, fig. 19:

" Hic requiefcit corpus Domini Will'mi Fylsher, primi magiftri huj' Hofpitalis, quod creatu' fuit per licenciam regiam, et anno gracie 1473, per viru celeberimu' mercatorem o'm'nu Will' Wigfton, fautorem facerdotu et pauperu benefactorem, et quater Stapule Califie majorem; et ppter ejus meritum preftet fibi Deus eternum premium. Amen." [1]

On each fide of his head, " Refpice finem."

Under his figure, " Hoc totu mihi fupeft fepulcru."

On a narrow white marble, below the altar:

" Hic jacet Ceci
lia, filia' [2] . . . . armig', que
obiit anno Domini MCCCLXXVIII,
cujus a'i'e mifereatur Deus, Amen."

On the Weft wall:

Arms: Argent, a crofs botoné between four efcalops Sable, fig. 20. Alfo: Quarterly, 1. and 4. Argent, three boars' heads Sable, couped Gules, *Johnfon*; 2. and 3. . . . . a lion rampant regardant . . . . ; a crefcent for difference, fig. 21.

" Præco & confrater poft annos fexque decemque
Galfridus Johnfon relligione pius.
Prole quater geminâ poft fata fuperftite; fatis
Succubuit; ftrati terra fit ifta loco.
Anno 1585;
Sumptibus Brigittæ uxoris, & Roberti fratris ejus."

On the fame wall, near the above (now gone [3]):

" Memoriæ & honori Thomæ Sampfon, Theologi;
Hierarchæ Romanæ, Papaliumque Rituum
Hoftis acerrimi;
Sinceritatis Evangelicæ Affertoris conftantiffimi;
hujus Hofpitalis per xxi annos Cuftodis fidelis;
de Republicâ Chriftianâ optimè meriti;
Patri chariffimo hoc Monumentum pofuerunt
Johannes & Nathanael Filii."

On the South wall:

Arms: Argent, on a bend Gules, between three pellets, as many fwans of the field; on a finifter canton Azure, a demi-ram faliant Argent, debruifed with a baton; in chief two fleurs de lis Or, *Clarke*; impaling, Or, on a crofs Azure, five pheons of the field; *Harrifon*, fig. 22.

Clarke fingle, fig. 23; and *Harrifon* fingle, fig. 24.

" P. M. S.
Parum tacende, nec premende pulveris
cæco cubili; gratiâ (Clarki [4]) tuâ
vocalis, ecce! paries fio, geftiens
pium tibi nomen eloqui perenniùs.
in te uno defideratiffima quæque amifimus,
Theologum quam fcientiffimum,
nec loquentem tamen, fed viventem magna;
Civem, vicinum, amicum, ope, confilio, fide,
nemini non utilem.
Porro, quodcunque tibi contigit lateritium,
cum Cæfare, marmoreum reliquifti.
Hoc fenfit Hertingfordburienfis pagus;
hoc Templum ibidem, hoc ædes rectoriæ,
hoc & homines fenfêre;
nec fenfit minus hoc ipfum Ptochotrophium:
cui ornando, augendo, in omnibus
beneaciendo, operam impendifti maximam.
Cum te omnes plorent, tum omnium maximè
chariffima conjux Anna, ex inclytâ Harrifonorum,
de Balls [5] apud Hertfordienfes familiâ oriunda:
quæ, memoriæ ergô, quam colit fanctiffimè,
è marmore me indicem fecit.
Obiit 19 Octob. ann. Sal. rep. 1684, ætat. 52."

On flat-ftones:

1. " Here lieth the body of William Rogers, only fon of John Rogers, Archdeacon of Leicefter, and Confrater of this Hofpital, and Sarah his wife. He departed this life May 3, 1701, in the 11th year of his age."

2. On a fmall brafs plate:

" Here lieth the body of the reverend and learned Mr. John Jackfon, Mafter of this Hofpital 34 years. He died May 12, 1763, aged 77 years."

3. A fmall flat ftone, in memory of " Elizabeth Jackfon," and a mural tablet over it, againft the South wall, with the following infcription:

" Underneath lieth interred the body of Elizabeth, the virtuous wife [6] of the Rev. John Jackfon, Mafter of this Hofpital. She died Dec. 28, 1760, aged 73 years. Near hereto lie the bodies of four of their children, who died infants."

4. " Sacred to the memory of Mr. John Jackfon, fon of the rev. Mr. John Jackfon, Mafter of this Hofpital; who departed this life October 4, 1769, aged 52."

---

[1] See Sepulchral Monuments of Great Britain, vol. II. p. 259.   [2] Probably a daughter of William Wigfton the Founder.
[3] Preferved in Wood's Hift. & Antiq. Univ. Oxon. lib. ii. p. 254.   [4] Richard Clarke, M. A. See p. 497.
[5] Balls, near Hertford, defcended to the prefent earl of Leicefter, whofe grandmother Audrey was daughter and heir of Edward Harrifon, efq. of Balls.
[6] They had been married 48 years; and had twelve children, of whom four furvived them; John, whofe death in 1769 is recorded above. The eldeft of three daughters married Mr. John Green, of Leeds, merchant; the fecond, Mr. Bellam, furgeon, of Leeds; the third, Elizabeth, Mr. Abbot, of Shilton.

MASTERS OF WIGSTON'S HOSPITAL.

1. William Fyfher, the firft mafter, is joined with William, Thomas, and Roger Wigfton, in the patents for the founding of the Hofpital in 1513. He procured from the Grey Friers the grant of St. Francis's garden, paying 4s. a year, 21 July, 1521; and Nov. 29, 1539, appeared in the Court of Augmentations, to have the faid grant allowed and ratified. It is probable that he died the next year [1]; for,

2. Walter Brown is mentioned as Warden of the Hofpital by the commiffioners of furvey in 1540. He was buried Jan. 10, 1560-1.

3. Nicholas Harwar fucceeded, and died in 1567; for

4. Thomas Sampfon gave up the accompts, partly for Mr. Harwar, and partly for himfelf, in 1567 and 1568.—This Mr. Sampfon was born about 1517; and, after an academical education at Oxford, became a ftudent of the municipal law in the Temple; but, renouncing the errors of Popery, he entered into holy orders under the patronage of Abp. Cranmer and Bp. Ridley; and in 1551 obtained the rectory of Allhallows, Bread-ftreet, where he was famous as a Preacher. In 1552, he obtained the deanery of Chichefter; but in the next year, on the acceffion of Queen Mary, he was oufted from both his preferments; and, having been charged with collecting money in the Metropolis for the ufe of fuch fcholars in the Univerfities as were " haters of the Roman Catholic Religion," he was compelled (with his wife, a niece of Bp. Latimer) to quit the kingdom, and take refuge at Strafburgh, where he became a profound Divine. When Queen Elizabeth afcended the Throne, returning to England, he became a frequent Preacher, both in London and in the Northern counties. In 1560, the Queen defigned for him the Bifhoprick of Norwich; which he declined, from a diflike to the Hierarchy and Church Ceremonies. At the latter end of that year, he was allowed by the Univerfity of Oxford (on his particular fupplication) to take the degree of B. D. though he had taken no preceding degree there. In November 1561, being then recently inftalled Dean of Chrift Church, he fupplicated that he might be allowed to preach, within the limits of the Univerfity, in a Doctoral habit; which, though thought unreafonable, was granted, as he was a Dean, but only to continue till the following Act. After this, he ufually preached every other Sunday at St. Mary's; " till (fays Wood) being too fevere a Calvinift, if not worfe, to govern fuch a noted College as Chrift Church (for he was an enemy to organs, ornaments of the church, clerical veftments, the fquare cap, he always wearing the round one); he was at length, after a great many admonitions from authority to conform, and entreaties from certain Bifhops fo to do, removed from his Deanery, by the fentence of Matthew Abp. of Canterbury, in 1564." He obtained the Mafterfhip of Wigfton's Hofpital in 1567; and the prebend of St. Pancras in St. Paul's cathedral 1570. Continuing his fame as a Preacher, he obtained, by the Queen's licence, the office of Theological Lecturer in Whittington college, London; but, before he had enjoyed that fituation quite fix years, he was afflicted with the palfy; after which he retired to Leicefter, where he paffed the remainder of his days in preaching and writing; and died April 9, 1589, æt. 72. He was buried in the chapel of his Hofpital [1]; with an infcription to his memory by his fons John and Nathaniel Sampfon [2]. His publications were, " Letter to the Profeffors of Chrift's Gofpel in the Parifh of Allhallows in Bread-ftreet, London;" printed at Strafburgh, 1550, 8vo; " A Warning to take heed of Fowler's Pfalter, 1578," 8vo; " Brief Collec-

tions of the Church, and Ceremonies thereof, 1581," 8vo. In that year alfo he publifhed " Two Sermons, the firft of Repentance, the other of the Lord's Supper," written by his Friend John Bradford, with other things of that Author. After his death alfo appeared his " Prayers and Meditations Apoftolique, gathered and framed out of the Epiftles of the Apoftles, &c. 1592," 16° [3].

5. Nathaniel Sampfon, fon of the laft mafter, was appointed confrater in 1585; and in 1589 fucceeded his father as mafter of this Hofpital. He died in 1611, and was buried Sept. 21.

6. John Herault, efq. who appears to have been a native of France, was the next mafter. Mr. Carte mentions a letter from " ..... de Saint Sauveur," dated London, July 20, 1612, to Mr. Thomas Sacheverell, confrater of the Hofpital of William Wigfton in Leicefter. By another, not directed nor dated, but fubfcribed " de Saint Sauveur," it feems that he had a conteft with his predeceffor's executors. In it he fays, " The chiefeft ground of the adverfe parties is, that when Thomas Sampfon came to be mafter, he found all the Hofpital land forfeited to the Queen, which is a moft abominable lie; and the letters patent which he obtained were rather for his own benefit, than for the profit of the houfe; for his predeceffors did afore him, both in king Edward and alfo in queen Mary's time, obtain letters for confirmation of the Founder's gift, and therefore needeth no other formality; but, forafmuch as he faw that he was accountable for the fines unto the houfe, he therefore charged that article to his own proper ufe."

Mr. Herault was fucceeded, in 1620, by

7. Samuel Clarke, D. D. fecond fon of Edward Clarke, or Clerke, of Willoughby in Warwickfhire (a manor antiently belonging to the Hofpital of St. John in Oxford; and afterward to Magdalen college in that Univerfity, under whom the Clerkes have for three centuries been tenants.) Of this family feveral were of no fmall eminence. Henry, elder brother to our Mafter, was a ferjeant at law; and they were related to the Clerkes of Wolfton, the refidence of the Wigftons [4].

Samuel Clarke was of Magdalen college, Oxford; where he took the degree of D. D. as a grand compounder June 13, 1616, being at that time chaplain to Prince Charles [5]. He obtained the rectory of St. Peter's, Northampton, with the chapelries of Kingfthorpe and Upton annexed, 1608; and the rectory of Winwick in that county 1614.—He wrote a letter to the confrater, Nov. 8, 1633, about a fuit againft fir Thomas Beaumont. In another letter, he acquaints him that he was admitted one of the chaplains of the Prince. But he was a very bad man; for (on his conduct being called to an account), in 1640, it was made to appear that he had 10l. for placing Jeremy Fynnys in the Hofpital (befides what he received for his clothes and goods at his death); that he had alfo 10l. for admitting George Chefter; and that his wife had 10l. for placing Dorothy Everard there; and that Mr. Robinfon paid him 6l. 13s. 4d. for his mother's admittance, &c. Mr. Carte quotes the following papers in proof of the above affertion:

A note of the fines and bribes taken by Dr. Clarke. The particulars were proved before the referees at Leicefter, Jan. 15, 1640.

The fines mentioned between 1620 and 1638 amount in all to 1681l. 6s. 8d.; befides above 1000l. received of the rents of the South Field tithes in Leicefter, of which he never allowed any thing to the poor, or made any account; and 40l. in wood fold at Caftle Carleton.

---

[1] See the epitaphs of Fifher and Sampfon, p. 495.

[2] From whom, it is fuppofed, defcended Thomas Sampfon, a pretender to Poetry, author of " Fortune's Fafhion, pourtrayed in the Troubles of Lady Elizabeth Grey, Wife of Edward IV. 1613," 4to, dedicated to Henry Pilkington, of Gaddefby.

[3] Wood, Athen. Oxon. vol. I. p. 238.

[4] See p. 471; Dugdale, Warwickfhire, vol. I. pp. 37. 281; and Bridges, Northamptonfhire, vol. I. pp. 446. 601. 605.

[5] Wood mentions him conjointly with a relative, another Samuel Clerke, Minifter of St. Bennet Fink, London, born at Wolfton Oct. 10, 1599, who was afterwards a fevere Calvinift, and a fcribbling plagiary; as his works (moftly the Lives of Prefbyterian Divines) fhew; a Catalogue of which may be feen in one of his Books, intituled, " The Lives of fundry eminent Perfons in this latter Age, in two Parts; 1. Of Divines; 2. Of Nobility, &c. 1683," folio; before which is a canting narrative of his own life. He died at Ifleworth, Dec. 25, 1682.—Wood, Athen. Oxon.; Fafti, vol. I. p. 202.

By

By letter, dated Kingſthorpe, June 24, Dr. Clarke owns the taking ſome of the Hoſpital goods away; but promiſes to allow for them in his accounts.

8. William Chillingworth, clerk, M. A. was his ſucceſſor; whoſe patent was dated 10 March, 16 Car. I. empowering him to receive the like profits, &c. as Nathaniel Sampſon, Thomas Sampſon, John Herault, or Samuel Clarke, or any other maſter of Wigſton's Hoſpital, did or might receive. The hiſtory of this bright ornament of Chriſtianity is too well known to need being even mentioned here, were it not to relate a circumſtance his biographers have overlooked. He became chancellor of Saliſbury and maſter of Wigſton's Hoſpital about 1638; "both which," ſays Wood, "and perhaps other preferments, he kept to his dying day." It appears, however, that he was ſequeſtered from the maſterſhip of Wigſton's Hoſpital 8 Jan. 1643-4, on being taken with the forces in arms againſt the Parliament at Arundel caſtle; an event which he did not ſurvive many days, as he died on or about the 30th of the ſame month, in his 42d year, at the Epiſcopal Palace at Chicheſter. The Preſbyterian party were unwilling at firſt to allow him Chriſtian burial[1]; but afterwards conſented that he ſhould be buried by *thoſe of his own perſuaſion*; which was accordingly performed in the Cathedral church, moſt of the Royal party in that city attending his body to the grave; and on a neat mural monument on the South ſide of the cloiſters of that Cathedral is the following epitaph:

" *Virtuti ſacrum.*
Spe certiſſimâ reſurrectionis
hic reducem expectat animam
GULIELMUS CHILLINGWORTH, A. M.
Oxonii natus & educatus,
Collegii S. Trinitatis
Socius, decus & gloria;
omni literarum genere celeberrimus;
Eccleſiæ Anglicanæ adverſus Romanam
propugnator invictiſſimus;
Eccleſiæ Saliſburienſis cancellarius
digniſſimus.
Sepultus Januar. menſe A. D. 1643-4,
ſub hoc marmore requieſcit;
nec ſentit damna ſepulchri."

9. John Meredith, who had been created D. D. Nov. 1, 1642, and was at that time fellow of Eton College, had been preſented to the rectory of Stanford Rivers, Eſſex, in 1641; but was deprived of that valuable living, by an ordinance of Parliament, May 6, 1643. He was chaplain to the earl of Newburgh, Chancellor of the Duchy of Lancaſter, who, by patent, under the Duchy ſeal, dated Feb. 3, 1643-4, gave him this maſterſhip. But the Parliament would not permit him to enjoy it; for, after the ſequeſtration of Chillingworth, they directed this maſterſhip to be diſpoſed of to the benefit and advantage of Mr. Job Grey, miniſter, brother to the earl of Kent; and on the 6th of March, 1643-4, finding by their Journals that the Chancellor of the Duchy had not complied with their order, he was peremptorily commanded ſo to do. On the 11th of April, the following entry occurs:

" Whereas John Meredith, doctor in divinity, was, for divers miſdemeanours, &c. ſequeſtered from the Church of Stamford Rivers in Eſſex, by judgment of the Houſe of Peers, May 6, 1643; notwithſtanding, ſince he is preferred to be governor of the Hoſpital of Leiceſter: It is ordered, that he be forthwith ſequeſtered from being governor of the ſaid Hoſpital; and that Job Grey, clerk, ſhall ſupply the government of the ſaid Hoſpital; and ſhall have for his pains all houſes, lodgings, rents, revenues, and benefits whatſoever belonging thereunto, until further order be taken by this Houſe[2]."

This paſſed on, however, without any farther notice, till the year 1646, when

10. Job Grey was intruded by the Parliament;

his patent bearing date that year, April 16. He had been a priſoner to the Royaliſts in 1645; and was exchanged, by order of Parliament, June 13, for ſir William Riddall, knight. He continued maſter till the beginning of 1650.

11. Richard Lee was in poſſeſſion in 1650 and 1651; for which he accounted in a letter of his, dated at Hatfield, July 19, 1661, directed to Mr. Stanley and Mr. Cradock, wherein he ſpeaks of " ſeveral evidences, which he delivered in the Hoſpital chapel to them and their fellow truſtees; and prays them to conſult the two attorneys their brethren in that forced truſt, that the evidences may be delivered to Dr. Meredith, the maſter of the Hoſpital, to whom (ſays he) I had the honour to reſign the place upon noble terms," &c.

At the Reſtoration, Dr. Meredith was reſtored to his fellowſhip and to this Hoſpital; elected warden of All Souls; and made provoſt of Eton. He was a perſon of a very generous ſpirit, and very bountiful to the poor, to whom he left a yearly ſtipend at his death, which happened July 18, 1665. By his laſt will, dated Jan. 24, 1664, and proved November 21, 1665, he forgave what ſums of money ſhould be due to him at his death upon account of Wigſton's Hoſpital. This benefaction is noticed in the following epitaph, on a black marble, againſt the wall of the chapel in All Souls College[3]:

Arms: Argent, a lion rampant Sable, gorged with a collar, and chain thereto affixed, reflexing over his back, Or; Plate XXXIV. fig. 25.

" M. S.
JOHANNES MEREDITH,
S. S. Theologiæ Profeſſor, hujus Collegii Cuſtos,
Ætonenſis etiam Præpoſitus,
necnon Ptochodochii Wigſtonienſis apud Leiceſtriam
Magiſter; quas provincias ſic adminiſtrabat quaſi
ſingulis impenderetur:
ut neque hic fidem, illic curam, iſtic demum
ſolertiam deſiderares.
Ita in hoc Collegio ſe geſſit,
ut pateret eum ſcire quali & quanto viro ſuccederet.
Ita in Regali verſabatur,
ut munere juxta & Patrono auguſtiſſimis perquam
dignus exiſteret,
cui anceps utrobique incubuit labor,
Ætonæ, ut viros efficeret; Oxoniæ, ut viros regeret.
Ita Ptochodochio præfuit,
ut non (ſicuti vulgò factum) pauperes alio etiamnum
indigere cogeret,
(confecti inedia corporis ſaginatum caput)
at è contra,
publicos reditus privati diſpendio liberaliter admodum,
hoc eſt ſuo more auxerat.
Vir ſi quis alius,
miſerorum ara, pauperum ærarium:
blandis moribus, quanquam & antiquis,
proſperis æquè adverſis rebus, par ſibi & conſtans,
fortunæ utriuſque victor.
Quo non alter magis
aut Deum pietate, aut Principem fide, aut univerſos
benevolentia coluerit.
Tandem gloriæ & annorum ſatur,
hoc in ſacello quod à ſitu vindicavit, et marmoreum
effecerat, magno ſuo, & nimium fatali climacterico,
vitâ defunctus,
carnis exuvias depoſuit:
XVII cal. Aug. an. MDCLXV."

12. Richard Clarke, M. A. had his patent Aug. 4, 1665. He was a very good man, and kind maſter of the Hoſpital. He died Oct. 19, 1684, at Leiceſter, and was buried Oct. 24. See his epitaph, p. 495.

Mr. Carte notices ſeveral letters from Mr. Richard Clarke to Mr. Edward Palmer; by which it appears that he lived at Iſleworth in Middleſex.

13. John Pyke, M. A. obtained his patent Nov. 1, 1684. See his year's accompts, p. 491.

14. Robert Hardwick[4] ſucceeded; and died in

---

[1] A ſpecimen of the effects of outrageous bigotry, and a Jeſuitical apology for the groſſeſt inhumanity, may be found in Cheynell's " Chillingworth's Noviſſima;" which Mr. Locke, in a letter to Anthony Collins, eſq. in p. 262 of a Collection of ſeveral Pieces, juſtly calls " one of *the moſt villainous* books that ever was printed."

[2] Journals of the Houſe of Commons, vol. III. p. 456.

[3] See Gutch's Hiſtory of the Colleges and Halls, p. 295.

[4] Of Sidney Suſſex college, Cambridge; B. A. 1672; M. A. 1676.

1717-18. " In his time, one of the poor men of Wig-ſton's Hoſpital made a will, and therein bequeathed a Note (given to him for money and intereſt), ſigned by Thomas Noble the elder, eſq. to Rebecca Warner, paying ſomething out of it, the reſidue to her own uſe; and made her executrix. He dies; Mr. Hard-wick, the Maſter of the Hoſpital, entered a caveat againſt any proof of the will. This was conteſted, upon this footing; that one of the orders among the new Statutes of the Hoſpital provides, that, when any of the poor men or women die, they ſhall not make any will concerning their moveable goods, but ſhall leave what they die poſſeſſed of in money or goods to the uſe of the ſaid Hoſpital; which the Keeper (i. e. Nurſe) ſhall take and deliver over to the Maſter, who is empowered to reward the ſaid Keeper for nurſing and attending the deceaſed in his illneſs, and put the remainder to the accompt of the Hoſ-pital. It was objected, firſt, in bar to the demand of the Maſter of the Hoſpital, that this Note could not be compriſed within the meaning of this ordinance. Secondly, that the Note being ſubject to the Ordi-nary's authority, it could not as ſuch be left to the Hoſpital; and if ſo, it muſt be put in ſuit by the executor or adminiſtrator *cum teſtamento annexo*. [Mr. George Newel, a Lambeth LL. B. Chancellor of Lincoln, and Official of Leiceſter, granted admini-ſtration of the Note to Mr. Simon Barwell, Steward of the ſaid Hoſpital.] A third objection was, that, by another ordinance of the Hoſpital, if any of the poor ſhould acquire the value of 20l. he ſhould be diſplaced; therefore, this being 20l. and more, the Hoſpital had no more right to it now the man was dead, than when he was alive. Upon hearing the cauſe, Mr. Nowel gave ſentence in favour of the Hoſpital.—This ſentence ſeems a diſcouragement to the above ordi-nance, diſplacing a poor man; becauſe the more ſuch a one dies poſſeſſed of, the better for the Hoſpital; who therefore may connive at the increaſe of his goods, that the corporate emolument may be the more advantageous [1]."

15. Samuel Clarke, D. D. rector of St. James's, Weſtminſter, ſucceeded March 7, 1717-18. The life of this truly amiable man, like that of his prede-ceſſor Chillingworth, is ſo univerſally known, that I need not detail it here. But a conciſe character of him, by the late Rev. Dr. Salter, is worth tranſcribing:

" Samuel Clarke, D. D. Rector of St. James', Weſtminſter: in *each* ſeveral part of uſeful knowledge and critical learning, *perhaps* without a ſuperior; in *all* united, *certainly* without an equal: in his *Works*, the beſt *defender* of Religion; in his *practice*, the greateſt *ornament* to it: in his *converſation*, communicative; and in an uncommon manner inſtructive: in his *preaching* and *writings*, ſtrong, clear, and calm: in his *life*, high in the eſ-teem of the *wiſe*, the *good*, and the *great*: in his *death*, lamented by every friend to *learning*, *truth*, and *virtue*. He died in the fifty-fourth year of his age, May 17, MDCCXXIX."

16. John Jackſon, the confrater, ſucceeded him.

He was the eldeſt ſon of the rev. John Jackſon (firſt rector of Senſey near Thirſk, and afterwards rector of Roſſington, and vicar of Doncaſter in Yorkſhire); born at Senſey in that county April 4, 1686; and educated at Doncaſter ſchool, under the famous Dr. Bland (afterwards dean of Durham, and provoſt of Eton); who, obſerving his proficiency, often left the inſtruction of the younger ſcholars to his care. Thus accompliſhed, he was entered of Jeſus College [2], Cambridge, towards the end of 1702; and from his reſidence at Midſummer following proſecuted the aca-demical ſtudies with diligence, and learned Hebrew under the celebrated Orientaliſt Simon Ockley. He proceeded B. A. at the uſual period; and, leaving the Univerſity in 1707, was appointed tutor to the children of Mr. Simpſon, at Renſhaw in Derbyſhire. In the mean time, the rectory of Roſſington having been reſerved from the death of his father for him, by the Corporation of Doncaſter [3], he took deacon's orders in 1708; and in 1710 was ordained prieſt, and entered into the full poſſeſſion of that rectory. But, the parſonage-houſe being gone to decay, he boarded at Doncaſter; and in 1712, married Elizabeth daughter of John Cowley, eſq. collector of Excite there. On this marriage, he entirely re-built the par-ſonage-houſe at Roſſington, and went to reſide in it. He commenced author in 1714, by publiſhing three anonymous letters in defence of Dr. Samuel Clarke's " Scripture Doctrine of the Trinity." He was not at that time perſonally acquainted with Dr. Clarke; but met with him ſoon after at Lynn Regis in Norfolk. Mr. Tonſon the bookſeller intending, in 1726, to publiſh a Bible, with paraphraſe and notes by ſeveral hands, applied to him, by Dr. Clarke, to undertake the comment upon the Prophets, propoſing a hand-ſome gratuity; but he declined the offer, and the ſame year engaged in the cauſe of his friend againſt Dr. Waterland [4]. In the ſame year alſo there paſſed ſe-veral letters between him and Mr. Whiſton, on the ſubject of Infant Baptiſm. In 1718, he went to Cam-bridge to take his degree of M. A.; but, finding ſuch an oppoſition raiſed againſt it as he was unable to re-move, he deſiſted from the purſuit [5]. Preſently after his return, he received a conſolatory letter from Dr. Clarke, who alſo procured for him this Confraterſhip [6], to which he was preſented in 1719 by lord Lechmere, in whoſe gift it was as then Chancellor of the Duchy of Lancaſter, and to whom Dr. Clarke had been the year before indebted for the Maſterſhip. On this promotion Mr. Jackſon left Roſſington; and, remo-ving to Leiceſter, took out a licence, May 30, 1720, from his dioceſan, Dr. Gibſon biſhop of Lincoln, to qualify him, as confrater, to be the afternoon preacher or lecturer of St. Martin's church; but he conſtantly viſited his flock at Roſſington for two or three months every year during his life. In 1721, and the following year, ſeveral preſentments were lodged againſt him in the Biſhop's Court, as alſo in that of Dr. Trimnel archdeacon of Leiceſter, for preaching erro-neous doctrines [7]; but he ſo ſtrenuouſly vindicated him-ſelf, as to defeat the proſecutions [8]. Yet, after the caſe

of

---

[1] Sir T. Cave, MS.   [2] This, I ſuppoſe, led the executors to give, unaſked, his large collection of New Teſtaments to that College, which they had before eſtimated to be worth 100l.

[3] The Corporation might do ill or well on this occaſion, in reſerving their living for a minor, as it ſhould happen; how-ever, againſt his death, they ſold the next turn for 800l. and with the money paved the long ſtreet of their town, that forms part of the great North road.

[4] Nine treatiſes by Mr. Jackſon on this controverſy, from 1716 to 1738, are enumerated in the Supplementary Volume [vol. VI. part 2.] of the Biographia Britannica, 1766, p. 107.

[5] Dr. Clarke, in a letter to him on the occaſion, writes thus: " It is of great ſervice to the Jacobite cauſe, to diſcourage ſuch perſons as you are. I ſhall particularly thank the then Chancellor and Dean Sherlock for being of a better ſpirit."

[6] This office is held (for life) by patent from the Chancellor of the Duchy of Lancaſter, and was particularly acceptable to Mr. Jackſon, as it requires no ſubſcription to any Article of Religion. His predeceſſor Chillingworth had (for a time) refuſed to ſubſcribe. Neal, in his Hiſtory of the Puritans, vol. III. chap. ii. p. 101, 8vo, ſays, " Chillingworth was perſuaded to ſubſcribe for the two preferments he before mentioned [viz. the chancellorſhip of Sarum, and the maſterſhip of Wigſton's Hoſpital.] Both theſe are held by patent, and require no ſubſcription." But Chillingworth was not chancellor of the dioceſe, but of the church of Sarum; which ſtill undoubtedly requires ſubſcription, as much as any ſimple prebendal ſtall in a cathedral.

[7] Complaint was made to Biſhop Gibſon that Mr. Jackſon did not read the Athanaſian Creed in the Chapel of the Hoſpital; to which Mr. Jackſon replied, " that the Chapel was not in the Biſhop's juriſdiction; and that the Statutes of this Houſe di-rected the Apoſtles' Creed to be read, and no other."

[8] The following notes reſpecting Mr. Jackſon's Sermons are from Mr. Carte's hand-writing: " Oct. 30, 1720, Mr. Jackſon, in his Sermon [upon Matth. xv. 6. as I was informed], did, in expreſs terms, aſſert, that giving worſhip [to an object] where God had not commanded it, was the only true and proper notion of idolatry. He alſo inſtanced in ſeveral traditions among the Jews, which he aſſerted to be within the intent of the cenſure of traditions contained in the text; and then ſpecified ſeveral traditions in the Church of Rome, as parallel or agreeable to what he had quoted from the Jews; and, amongſt the reſt, he particularly mentioned the impoſition of rites, ceremonies, &c. and forcing articles of doctrines upon men's conſciences; and,

after

of the Arian fubfcription was publifhed by Dr. Water-land, he refolved, with Dr. Clarke, never to fubfcribe the Articles any more; by which refolution he loft, about 1724, the hopes of a prebend of Salifbury, which bifhop Hoadly refufed to give him without fuch fub-fcription [1]. The Bifhop's denial was more remarkable, as he had fo often intimated his own diflike of all fub-fcriptions. However, he had been prefented by fir John Fryer to the private prebend of Wherwell in Hampfhire, where no fuch qualification was requifite. In 1723, Mr. Jackfon publifhed " The Duty of Sub-jects towards their Governors; a Sermon preached before the Hon. Charles Churchill's Regiment of Dragoons, at their Camp near Leicefter, Auguft 1723;" and in 1728, " The Duty of a Chriftian fet forth and explained in feveral Practical Difcourfes, being an Expofition of the Lord's Prayer; to which is added, a Difcourfe on the Sacrament of the Lord's Supper, for the Ufe of Families." On the death of Dr. Clarke, in May 1729, Mr. Jackfon fucceeded, by the prefentation of the duke of Rutland, then chan-cellor of the Duchy of Lancafter, to the mafterfhip of this Hofpital; which office he held till his death. He repaired and made feveral additions to the mafter's houfe; repaired the Hofpital, and by degrees aug-mented the ftipend of the poor to 3s. a-week.

In 1730, an extraordinary difpute arofe between Mr. Jackfon and Mr. Carte, refpecting the Trinity, which was conducted with an acrimony that difgraces the profeffors of Religion. Mr. Carte was a rigid Trinitarian, and Mr. Jackfon publicly profeffed the Unitarian fyftem. In the eftablifhment of Wigfton's

Hofpital, the confrater is enjoined to preach a fer-mon at St. Martin's church every Sunday in the year, and alfo every Wednefday and Friday (or two other days every week), at fuch times as the mafter of the Hofpital fhall appoint, unlefs the church fhall be oc-cupied by any other preacher, or he be letted by fick-nefs [2]. Mr. Carte, with a manlinefs and zeal that became his function, held out to the people a picture of a dying Saviour, and a God in a Ghoftly Com-forter. Mr. Jackfon, with as much zeal, and great claffical knowledge, but with lefs temperance, and in defiance of that Eftablifhment which he had engaged to defend at his ordination, boldly afferted the doc-trine of *One only God.* For a time the church was crowded to hear thefe zealous difputants: they each had their partizans. One Sunday the churchwardens, in the midft of Mr. Jackfon's difcourfe, bad him leave the pulpit. Another Sunday the fexton was placed to prevent his going into the pulpit; till at length, the people growing weary of the difpute, the feats in the church were left almoft without hearers. The bickerings ended with an appeal to the Duchy Court, refpecting the claims of the one, and the privi-leges of the other; and, like moft difputes of this kind, each party found themfelves involved in confiderable expences, and neither of them was much a gainer [3].

In the fame year, 1730, Mr. Jackfon publifhed " A Defence of Human Liberty, in Anfwer to the principal Arguments which have been alledged againft it, and particularly to Cato's Letters on that Subject, &c. The fecond Edition; to which is added, A Vindication of Human Liberty, in anfwer to a Differtation on Liberty

after an harangue againft thefe practices, declared this practice much worfe when ufed by men who owned themfelves fallible, and affumed not the vain pretence of infallibility: fpoke againft authority in matters of faith, as within the condemnation or cenfure in the text."—" Nov. 6, the Confrater preached at All Saints church, in the morning. His difcourfe was on the At-tribute of Mercy; and, on difcourfing on thofe objects of it, Penitent Sinners, the fubftance of his doctrine was, that propor-tionable repentance alone was fufficient to entitle them to it, without any fatisfaction of a Redeemer: neither was it neceffary at all, from the Attribute of Juftice, that any expiatory facrifice fhould be offered. I cannot charge my memory with parti-cular words and phrafes whereby he expreffed himfelf, but this was the purport of his doctrine. He faid fome things, which I prefume to be very heterodox, concerning the eternity of Hell torments.—" Jan. 15, 1720-21, Mr. Jackfon, in his Sermon [upon Jeremiah xxiii. 24. *Do not I fill Heaven and Earth*], defcribed God as pervading all material fubftances and others, and therefore incapable of local motion, and without figure. He afferted, that he pervaded the extramundane places; and, in my apprehenfions, confounded his effence or nature with that of fpace; or at leaft I do not remember that he attempted to diftinguifh them. He afterwards faid, that the appearances of God, as mentioned in the Old Teftament, were only the appearances of an Angel, who came from him, and fpoke in his name—which Angel he afterwards exprefsly afferted to be our Saviour; and taking occafion, from the text, to fpeak of the practice of the Papifts in worfhiping Saints and Angels, he faid, that, in fo doing, they not only gave religious worfhip where God had not commanded, but even where he had forbade it; in which he afferted the true notion of idolatry to confift. He took notice that Saints and Angels were confined to certain places, and could not hear prayers that were made to them; which he defcribed could be done only by God, and fuch to whom he fhould reveal it."—" February 5, 1720-21, Mr. Jackfon, preaching on Micah vi. 6, 7, 8, made it his bufinefs to magnify morality in an extraordinary manner, and depreciate all rites and ordinances, even thofe inftituted by God himfelf, both in time of the Law and of the Gofpel; the frequenting of the Public Worfhip, the two Sacraments, Baptifm and the Lord's Supper, &c. And though it cannot, I think, be denied but that each of his fentences might be explained in a fenfe agreeable to truth, yet the general tenor of his difcourfe tended to leffen people's regard to the Public Worfhip and the Sacraments of the Gofpel, and to make them rely on their moral virtues for falvation."—" March 26, 1721, at the Affize, preaching on Genefis xviii. 25, *Shall not the Judge of all the world do right,* he afferted that it was unlawful for the magiftrate or legiflative power to make any law in matters of religion to fupprefs any opinion, though never fo abfurd; and, excepting the Papifts from any toleration, faid that Popery totally deftroyed Chriftianity."

[1] See a letter of Mr. Jackfon's on this occafion, Biog. Brit. ubi fupra, p. 108.

[2] By the Earl of Huntingdon's injunction (fee p. 485), the Confrater was only to preach at fuch times as the pulpit fhould be vacant, he having no power to thruft out the vicar. But on the 1ft of November, 1730, Mr. Jackfon being then mafter of the Hofpital, and intending to officiate in the place and at the defire of Mr. Hacket the confrater, Mr. Carte (then vicar), without fending Mr. Jackfon notice, fet the facriftan at the bottom of the pulpit-ftairs to refufe him admittance to the pulpit, alledging he would preach himfelf; which he did, having firft of all thus publicly affronted Mr. Jackfon. Mr. Hacket, then confrater, admonifhed as fuch on that occafion, by a thrice repeated citation directed by the churchwardens, when Jackfon was ftopped at the pulpit-ftairs, " Mr. Philip Hacket, come and do your office." Mr. Jackfon immediately removed the fermon from Sunday to Friday, alledging he had a power to do fo by the Earl of Huntingdon's deed. Some of the parifhioners on this filed a bill (which is always in the nature of a petition) againft him in the Duchy Court. This appears by the following entry in the accompt-books of the churchwardens of St. Martin's: " July 1, 1730. It is agreed at this meeting, that if the prefent churchwardens, or their fucceffors, fhall be put to any expence on the account of the fuit that has been fome time depending between Mr. John Jackfon, mafter of Wigfton's Hofpital, and them, the fame expence fhall be allowed them in their accompts with the parifh."—The Chancellor, Oct. 23, 1731, decreed the fermon fhould be on Sunday, according to the former ufage; but difmiffed the other complaints in the bill. " In a meeting of the parifh of St. Martin's, Leicefter, Mr. Mayor being prefent, this 2d of November, 1731, it is refolved, that the thanks of this parifh be given to the Right Honourable the Earl of Huntingdon, for his generous protection of the faid parifh, by efpoufing their caufe, in the matter of their complaint to the Chancellor of the Duchy, againft the mafter and confrater of Wigfton's Hofpital, who were craftily endeavouring to defeat and pervert the defigns of his noble Anceftor's benefactions; and for his pious and honourable interpofition, by his counfel, at the hearing of the faid caufe, to make it effectual for the Chriftian purpofes as it was intended, to promote the glory of God, the edification of the county in general, and the inftruction of this parifh in particular, in the true doctrine of Chriftianity, and principles of the Church of England. And it is further ordered, that the churchwardens do appoint others, or go down with the fame. Edward Hawkins, Gabriel Newton, Samuel Brown, Churchwardens."—The fubftance of the account was taken by the late Rev. William Ludlam from a copy of the bill (or petition) filed againft Jackfon; Jackfon's anfwer, and the duke of Rutland's determination. The original papers relative to thefe proceedings, with the ftatutes of the Hofpital, the act of parliament confirming the fame, the earl of Huntingdon's deed of gift, and the deed declaring the ufes, are now in the Evidence-room of the Hofpital, with innumerable leafes (for lives) of lands belonging to the fame, terriers, &c.

[3] Mr. Jackfon lived to fee fome of thofe who figned the petition, and were moft violent againft him, fo reduced, as to be glad of a place among the poor in Wigfton's Hofpital; which with a true Chriftian temper he beftowed upon them without hefitating, or reproaching them for their former behaviour.

and Neceffity, written by Anthony Collins, Efq."
8vo. And in that and the following year he publifhed four tracts in defence of human reafon, occafioned by bifhop Gibfon's " Second Paftoral Letter."
In 1731, he attacked Tindal's " Chriftianity as old
as the Creation ;" in 1733, he publifhed an anfwer
to " Things divine and fupernatural, conceived by
Analogy with Things natural and human," a work
attributed to bifhop Brown, of Cork ; in 1734,
" The Exiftence and Unity of God proved from his
Nature and Attributes, &c. To which is added an
Appendix, wherein is confidered the Ground and
Obligations of Morality," which led him into a controverfy with Mr. William Law and other writers ;
in 1735, " A Differtation on Matter and Spirit, with
fome Remarks on a Book, intituled, An Enquiry
into the Nature of the human Soul," [by Mr. Bax-
ter] ; and in 1736, " A Narrative of the Cafe of the
Rev. Mr. Jackfon's being refufed the Sacrament of
the Lord's Supper at Bath ;" which had been done,
in a very public manner, by Dr. Coney[1]. In 1742, he
had an epiftolary debate with his friend William Whifton, concerning the order and times of the high priefts.
In 1744, he publifhed " An Addrefs to the Deifts[2] ;
being a Proof of Revealed Religion from Miracles
and Prophefies, in anfwer to a Book, intituled, The
Refurrection of Jefus confidered by a Moral Philofo-
pher," 8vo ; and in 1745 entered the lifts againft Mr.
Warburton, in " The Belief of a future State proved
to be a fundamental Article of the Religion of the
Hebrews, and held by the Philofophers ; the Heathen Theology explained, and the Time of Job ;
with Remarks on Mr. Lardner's fifth Volume, &c.
1745," 8vo. On this production Mr. Warburton
not unpleafantly remarked, " that all its objections,
even to the very blunders, had been long ago obviated or anfwered. But I would recommend," he
fays, " Mr. Jackfon's pamphlet to the reader's pe-
rufal, as a fpecimen of that illuftrious Band in which
he has thought fit to enlift ; and which indeed would
have been imperfect without this Anfwerer General ;
and, after having written againft the Enquiry into the
Nature of the Human Soul, does me too much honour to be overlooked." Mr. Jackfon either publifhed a fecond part of his " Belief of a future State,"
or added an Appendix to his former part, " occafioned by fome fevere reflections on the author and
his writings, contained in the fecond part of Mr
Warburton's Remarks," which appeared in 1746.
Mr. Warburton, in March 1747, replied, in a Preface to Mr. Towne's " Critical Enquiry into the
Opinions and Practice of the ancient Philofophers,
&c." Mr. Jackfon immediately purfued the fubject,
in " A further Defence of the antient Philofophers,
againft the Mifreprefentations of a Critical Enquiry,
prefaced by Mr. Warburton, 1747 ;" and by " A
Treatife on the Improvement made in the Art of
Criticifm, collected out of the Writings of a celebrated Hypercritic ; by Philocriticus Cantabrigienfis,
1748." Mr. Warburton having made fome remarks
on this treatife, the controverfy clofed by " A Defence of a late Pamphlet, called A Treatife on the
Improvement made in the Art of Criticifm, being an
Anfwer to fome Remarks made upon it, 1749."
Soon after the controverfy between Mr. Jackfon and
Mr. Warburton, who knew not each other's perfon,
chance brought them together in the little parlour
behind Mr. Whifton the bookfeller's fhop. They

looked ftedfaftly at each other. Mr. Jackfon, paffing
through the fhop, afked whom it was he had juft
met. Being told that it was Warburton, he anfwered, " I thought it was fome fuch fellow !" Warburton, in like manner, afked who Jackfon was ; and replied, " I thought it was fome fuch blockhead !" This
anecdote was communicated by the Rev. Dr. Owen.
Mr. Jackfon's next work was, " Remarks on Dr. Middleton's free Enquiry into the miraculous Power fuppofed to have fubfifted in the Chriftian Church after
the Days of the Apoftles." From this time he does
not appear to have publifhed any thing till his laft
and capital work, " Chronological Antiquities ; or,
the Antiquities and Chronology of the moft antient
Kingdoms, from the Creation of the World, for the
Space of 5000 Years, &c. To which are added
proper Indexes[3], 1752," 3 vols. 4to. He afterwards
made many collections and preparations for printing
an edition of the New Teftament in Greek, with
Scholia in the fame language ; and would have inferted all the various readings, had not the infirmities
of age, which he felt fome years before his death,
prevented him from finifhing the defign[4]. His bodily ftrength declining, and the faculties of his mind
gradually decreafing (of which he feemed but too fenfible), he became incapable of clofe application to
ftudy[5] ; but retained his thirft after knowledge till his
death, which happened at Leicefter, on Afcenfion-
day, May 12, 1763. By his wife, who died three years
before him[6], he had twelve children ; of whom one
fon and three daughters were living in 1764.—The following hints of Mr. Jackfon's character were given me
by the late Rev. William Ludlam, who was acquainted
with him from the year 1750: " He always feemed to
me rather a man of induftry than genius ; at leaft fuch
genius as is neceffary to reconcile the inconfiftent accounts of antient writers, and make out a clear fyftem of antient Chronology. He certainly took all
that he has faid about hieroglyphics and metterics
from Warburton ; but fo totally forgot or overlooked it (as was his cuftom on other occafions), that
he verily thought it all his own ; nor did he underftand any of the Eaftern languages, except a little
Hebrew. He was much offended at Dr. Coney (and
would have been at any one) for faying that he denied
the Divinity of the Son. But then he would not on
any account give the Son the appellation of *felf-
exiftent, neceffarily-exiftent,* &c. or any of thofe me-
taphyfical titles. His being fo early a defender of
Dr. Clarke, and his political zeal for the Hanover
family, got him his preferment ; and his earlieft writings, efpecially his ' Plea for Human Reafon,' appear to have been his beft."
17. William Rawftorne, M. A. of St. John's College, Cambridge, 1763 ; rector of Badiworth near
Doncafter. He died Aug. 24, 1790, in his 80th year.
18. Folliott-Herbert-Walker Cornewall, fellow of
St. John's college, Cambridge ; B. A. 1777 ; M. A.
and Chaplain to the Houfe of Commons[7], 1780 ; and
Canon of Windfor April 10, 1784. He was prefented
to this Hofpital[8] Aug. 2, 1790 ; and refigned it in
1793, on being promoted to the deanery of Canterbury. He was made Bifhop of Briftol March 18,
1797 ; and tranflated to Hereford in 1802.
19. John Selwyn, of Pembroke college, Oxford,
B. C. L. 1780 ; rector of Ludgerfhall, Wilts ; was
prefented to this Hofpital in January 1793 ; and is
the prefent Mafter, 1807.

---

[1] The particulars were given at the time in Gent. Mag. vol. V. p. 617.

[2] In 1758, Mr. Jackfon abfurdly complained, in a letter to Dr. Birch, that out of 500 copies which Mr. Knapton had
printed of his " Addrefs to the Deifts," 150 were unfold through Mr. Knapton's negligence.

[3] In a quarter of a fheet of " Additions to this work, is an anfwer to a note printed at the end of a new edition of the firft
volume of " The Divine Legation."

[4] An account of the materials he had collected for this intended edition, with notes containing alterations, corrections, and
additions to his Chronology, are inferted in an Appendix to " Memoirs of the Life and Writings of the late Rev. Mr. John
Jackfon, &c. London, 1764, by Dr. Sutton, of Leicefter," 8vo ; whence, and from the Anecdotes of Bowyer, this account
is principally extracted. There are many particulars alfo relating to him in Whifton's Life of Clarke.

[5] He had publifhed thirty-fix feparate books and pamphlets. And in " The Old Whig," N° 33 and N° 39 were his productions. He was editor alfo of " Novatiani Prefbyteri Opera quæ extant omnia, poft Jacobi Pamelii Brugenfis recenfionem,
ad antiquiores editiones caftigata, & à multis mendis expurgata, 1728," 4to. [6] See their epitaphs in p. 495.

[7] He publifhed, in 1782, a Sermon preached before the Houfe of Commons on the 30th of January, from Pfalm cx. 15 ;
and in 1798 (as Bifhop of Briftol), a Faft Sermon before the Houfe of Lords.

[8] Mr. Cornewall's ufual refidence was then at Delbury, near Ludlow, Shropfhire.

CONFRATERS.

CONFRATERS.

1. John Thorpe, named in the founder's ſtatutes. In the return of the Commiſſioners, 31 Hen. VIII. we find a *Thomas* Thorpe. They might be different perſons.

2. Peter Wood.

3. Geoffrey Johnſon was confrater at the making the new ſtatutes in 1572. He was buried Sept. 25, 1585. See his epitaph, p. 495.—" The firſt lecturer which we have met with in the Town of Leiceſter, was this Mr. Johnſon. March 13, 1584, a common hall agreed, that the twenty-four and forty-eight ſhould give ſome yearly portion or ſalary to the ſaid Mr. Johnſon the preacher, towards his better maintenance, together with other inhabitants of the town. N. B. That Henry earl of Huntingdon ſettled 30l. a year on the confrater of Wigſton's Hoſpital, to preach in St. Martin's church on Sunday, Wedneſday, and Friday, or two other week-days. But before this, Nov. 22, 1567, it was agreed, that the lecture on Wedneſday and Friday ſhould begin at ſeven o'clock in the forenoon, and end at eight. But the lecture was began ſtill before this ; for, Feb. 20, 1561-2, it was ordered, that there be of every houſe one at every ſermon on Wedneſday and Friday [1], on pain that every houſe-holder making default forfeit 4d. Which order was renewed Nov. 18, 1575, and the penalty made 12d.; and Nov. 21, 1578, ordered, that no perſon reſort to any inn on Wedneſday, Friday, and in time of ſermon or divine ſervice, on pain of 12d. May 8, 1588, agreed that the twenty-four pay each 10s. yearly towards the preacher's ſtipend, and the forty-eight 5s. beſides the benevolence that each will give more, and alſo the commonalty. Oct. 21, 1596, ordered, that one of every houſehold come to the ſermons weekly, on pain of 6d. for every default. The order was renewed Nov. 18, 1598, and the penalty made 4d.; and Oct. 7, 1600, the foregoing orders were enforced [2]."

4. Nathaniel Sampſon was appointed confrater in 1585 ; and was advanced to be maſter in 1589.

5. Thomas Sacheverell ſucceeded in 1589 ; and on the 31ſt of Auguſt it was agreed, that Mr. Sacheverell ſhould that year have 13l. 6s. 8d. paid by the chamberlains, who were to receive of the twenty-four 5s. each, and of the forty-eight 2s. 6d. and tax the commoners. But ſir Francis Walſingham, who had made him confrater, in a letter dated at London, March 10, 1589-90, directed to the mayor and his brethren, and the reſt of the town, complained of their not giving due encouragement to Mr. Sacheverell, whereas they had allowed to Mr. Pelſant, their former preacher, above 40l. *per annum*, beſides what other maintenance he had elſewhere ; and ſir Edward Haſtings alſo being of opinion that what they had as yet done for him was not ſufficient, it was agreed, that Mr. Sacheverell's ſtipend ſhould be ſettled at 20l.; and afterwards, April 14, at the requeſt of the earl of Huntingdon, made 30l.; which was confirmed to him, by Town-ſeal, as long as he ſhould continue Preacher of Leiceſter. In 1590, he married Mary daughter of Alderman Robert Heyrick ; and continued in the joint office of Confrater and Lecturer, with much credit, till his death. He was buried at St. Martin's, Dec. 1, 1626; and the following epitaph for him is preſerved in Bancroft's Poems:

" Who dare prophane thee, noble, rare Divine,
Thou mighty workman in the ſacred mine !
Behold this hand thus deep engraves thy praiſe,
Whoſe mind thou didſt with emulation raiſe.
One line ſhall thy reproachers all confute,
Thoſe beaſts diſlik'd that could not reach thy fruit !"

See ſeveral letters of Mr. Sacheverell [3], which ſhew him to have been a man of ſound ſenſe and great public ſpirit, in vol. I. pp. 341—345; and vol. II. p. 628.

6. John Angel, a native of Glouceſterſhire, was entered at Magdalen Hall, Oxford, about 1610. Taking orders, and his degrees in Arts, " he became a frequent and painful Preacher [4];" was appointed Confrater in 1626; and continued ſeveral years Lecturer at St. Martin's, in high eſteem amongſt the Puritans, till 1634; when " the Dean of the Arches ſuſpended one Mr. Angel att Leiceſter; who hath continued a Lecturer in that great town for theſe divers years, without any licence at all to preach, yet took liberty enough. I doubt this violence hath crackt his brains ; and do therefore uſe him the more tenderly, becauſe I ſee the hand of God hath overtaken him [5]."

Mr. Angel married Alice daughter of Francis Oliver. She died April 17, 1631 ; and was buried at St. Martin's, Leiceſter [6]. Bancroft thus celebrates her, by way of epitaph, in his Poems.

" *Angel* in name, and *Angel* like in life,
Save that ſhe was a mortal, and a wife :
Theſe bonds diſcharg'd, advanc'd this perfect wife
To *Angel's* ſingle and immortal life ! '

May 21, 1641, it was agreed, that Mr. John Angel, the Town-lecturer, ſhould have 30l. *per annum*, given out of the Town ſtock, ſo long as the two Companies think fit, for his pains-taking in the Wedneſday lecture, to be paid at Midſummer and Chriſtmas.

June 13, 1645, it was agreed, by the lords and commons in parliament, that John Angel, miniſter, confrater of Wigſton's Hoſpital, and then a priſoner at Leiceſter, ſhould be exchanged for Davies Ambroſe, D. D.; and Mr. Job Grey for ſir William Riddall, knt. [7]

June 17, 1646, the following proviſion was made for Mr. Angel in particular, and for the other Miniſters of Leiceſter [8]: " Whereas there are five pariſh churches in the town of Leiceſter, in the county of Leiceſter, and the maintenance to them all belonging is worth but 83l. 6s. 8d. or thereabouts ; for that divers of the ſaid churches may be conveniently united, and a competent maintenance thereby the better advanced for the encouragement of an able Miniſtry in the ſaid town : It is therefore ordered, that the members of parliament that ſerve for the ſaid county be deſired to conſider how the ſaid churches may with the beſt convenience be united, and to certify the ſame to this Committee : And whereas Mr. Angel, a godly, learned, and orthodox Divine, of whoſe deſerts this Committee have received large teſtimony, is Lecturer there : It is ordered, by virtue of an order of both houſes of parliament, of the 2d of May laſt, that the yearly ſum of 80l. be paid, out of the profits of the impropriate rectory of Melton in the ſaid county, ſequeſtered from Henry Hudſon, eſq. delinquent ; and out of the impropriate rectory of Great Eaſton, in the ſaid county, ſequeſtered from ſir Lewis Watſon, delinquent ; and out of the profits of the impropriate rectory of Garthorpe, in the ſaid

[1] " One Mr. William Hughes, of the Univerſity of Cambridge, who had obtained to be Lady Margaret's preacher, became a preacher at Leiceſter ; where his doctrine giving great offence, the inhabitants made a complaint to the Univerſity, deſiring to be releaſed of him ; whereupon a grace was granted to Dr. Whitgift (then Regius Profeſſor), May 31, 1567, that he ſhould be ſent to Leiceſter, about the ſcandal given by their preacher." Biog. Brit. vol. VI. p. 4234.

[2] Mr. Carte, MS. from the Records of the Corporation.

[3] Joſeph Sacheverell, gent. was buried at St. Martin's in 1636; and Elizabeth Sacheverell, widow, in 1640.

[4] Wood, Athen. Oxon. II. 190. [5] From a MS Certificate of Abp. Laud to the King, 1634, concerning the ſtate of his Dioceſe.

[6] Frances, one of her ſiſters, was wife, firſt, of Robert Miller, alderman of Leiceſter ; afterward of Gamaliel Carre, rector of Stanſted in Eſſex ; and died April 25, 1632. [7] Journals of the Houſe of Commons, vol. IV. p. 174.

[8] Mr. —— Higginſon, who had been educated at Emanuel College, Cambridge, proceeding M. A. was afterward parſon of one of the five churches in Leiceſter, where he continued for ſome years, till he was deprived for nonconformity ; but ſuch were his talents for the pulpit, that, after his ſuſpenſion, the Town obtained liberty from Biſhop Williams to chooſe him for their Lecturer, and maintained him by their voluntary contributions, till Laud being at the head of church affairs, he was articled againſt in the High Commiſſion, and expected every hour a ſentence of perpetual impriſonment. This induced him to accept of an invitation, in 1628-9, to accompany the firſt ſettlers to New England, where he arrived in June 1629, and was elected teacher to the new colony ; but not being able to bear the fatigues of a new ſettlement, he fell into a hectick, and died in the following winter, at the age of 43. Neal's Hiſtory of the Puritans, vol. II. p. 205.

county,

county, fequeftered from fir Lewis Watfon; to and for increafe of the maintenance of the faid Mr. Angell, for and during the continuance of his faid fervice and miniftry in the faid town: And that the yearly fum of 50l. be paid out of the profits of the premiffes for the increafe of the maintenance of fuch perfon and perfons as fhall fucceed the faid Mr. Angell in the faid fervice: And that the further fum of 100l. be paid and allowed, out of the faid profits, to and for increafe of the maintenance of fuch other Minifters as fhall be appointed to officiate in the faid town, the faid churches being united as aforefaid."

" July 30. Whereas this Committee, by virtue of an order of both houfes of parliament of the 2d of May laft, have, by their order of the 17th of June laft, ordered, that the yearly fum of 80l. fhould be paid, out of the profits of the impropriate rectory of Melton, in the county of Leicefter, fequeftered from Henry Hudfon, efq. delinquent; and out of the impropriate rectory of Great Eafton, in the faid county, fequeftered from the faid fir Lewis Watfon, delinquent: and out of the profits of the impropriate rectory of Garthorpe, in the faid county, fequeftered from the faid fir Lewis Watfon; to and for increafe of the maintenance of Mr. Angel, a godly, learned, and orthodox Divine, for and during the continuance of his fervice and miniftry in the town of Leicefter, in the faid county, and fuch other Minifters as fhould officiate in the faid town: For that it is now attefted that the faid Henry Hudfon hath compounded for his delinquency, whereby the fequeftration of the faid rectory of Melton is difcharged: It is ordered, that the faid former order be difcharged; and, in lieu thereof, the faid fum of 90l. be paid, according to the purport of the faid order, out of the impropriate rectory of Sifonby, in the faid county, fequeftered from fir John Keate, delinquent, and out of the faid impropriate rectories of Great Eafton and Garthorpe, in the faid county, fequeftered from fir Lewis Watfon, delinquent. And the fequeftrators of the premiffes are required to pay the fame accordingly, at fuch times and feafons of the year as the fame fhall grow due and payable [1]."

About the year 1650, Mr. Angel compiled the Catalogue of the Public Library at Leicefter [2]. In the following year, declining to take the Engagement demanded by the Independents, he was difmiffed from the Confraterfhip; but was foon after appointed, by the Company of Mercers in London, to preach the Lecture founded at Grantham by the will of Elizabeth Vifcountefs Campden in 1642; and, fettling at that place, " he fhone as a burning light, until God tranflated him to fhine above as a ftar for ever [3]." In September 1654, he was appointed an Affiftant to the Commiffioners of Lincolnfhire for the ejection of fcandalous and ignorant Minifters and Schoolmafters [4]. He died at Grantham in 1655; and was buried in that church [5], June 6, attended to the grave by many Divines of the neighbourhood, where a large oration of mortality and in praife of the defunct was delivered by Lawrence Sarfon, B. D. of Emanuel College, Cambridge. Before he fell fick, he was feveral times heard to fay, that it was his great defire to live to fee the conclufion of the year 1660, hinting that he was very confident that there would be great revolutions in the kingdom of England. " As his name was *Angel*, fo he was a man indeed of evangelical underftanding and holinefs, a burning and fhining light, &c. [6]" It is not known that he publifhed any works in his life-time; but there were pofthumoufly printed, 1. " The right Government of the Thoughts; or, a

Difcovery of all vain, unprofitable, idle, and wicked Thoughts, &c. 1659," 8vo. 2. " Four Sermons; 1. and 2. The right ordering of the Converfation, two Sermons on Pfalm i. laft verfe; 3. Funeral Sermon at the Burial of John Lord D'arcy, of Afton in Yorkfhire, 27 Aug. 1636, Pf. xxxix. 5.; 4. Preparations to the Communion, 1 Cor. xi. 28; 1659," 8vo [7]. Another John Angel clerk, probably his fon, has been noticed in p. 490.

7. William Symmes fucceeded Mr. Angel; but was deprived before 1662, being intruded by the ufurped powers, and a Nonconformift. In the act paffed in 1657, he is called " Public Lecturer of the Borough of Leicefter." He died Aug. 9, 1669, æt. 67, and was buried at St. Martin's church, where he is ftyled " Minifter Jefu Chrifti; & Evangelii in hoc templo concionator."

7. Thomas Peftell junior; afterwards rector of Markfield in this county. See vol. III. p. 930.

8. John Newton. He refigned, and removed into Gloucefterfhire in 1697.

9. John Rogers; who took the degree of M. A. March 22, 1672, being then of St. John's college, Oxford [8]. He was chaplain to lord Berkeley. Mr. * * * *, a clergyman (who was examined upon the trial of Ford lord Grey for debauching lady Henrietta Berkeley), depofed, that he was told by Mr. Rogers, lord Berkeley's chaplain, that Charnock was the man who took lady Henrietta away [9]. Mr. Rogers was prefented by George earl of Berkeley to the rectory of Segrave in 1681 [10]. The manor and rectory of Segrave were purchafed by him of lord and lady Berkeley, March 9, 1684, for fix hundred pounds and *ten ginneys* [11]; and in 1686, in his turn, he prefented the Rev. George Berkeley, M. A. to the rectory. By a licence from the Commiffary and Official of the Archdeaconry of Leicefter, dated May 27, 1690, he was directed, as patron, to repair the chancel of the church of Segrave, and to fell the lead which covered the roof to defray part of the expence [12]. His patent of appointment to the Archdeaconry of Leicefter is dated Nov. 29, 1703 [13]. Whilft he was confrater, he had nearly loft his life in an attempt to part two of the brethren who were fighting, one of whom drew a dagger, and made a blow at him with it [14]. The dagger is ftill preferved in the family. Mr. Rogers married Sarah Wilfhere, by whom he had a fon John, who died young [15]; and a daughter Sarah, married to Walter Ruding, efq. of Weftcotes; to whom, in 1704, he conveyed the advowfon of Segrave [16]. Mr. Rogers refigned the confraterfhip in 1713; and died May 17, 1715, æt. 67. His only publications were two Sermons [17]; Jonah, i. 6. preached before the Trinity-houfe, on the 30th of May, at the election of their Mafter, 1681, 4to; Pfalm xxvii. 6. Thankfgiving, 4to, 1702. He furnifhed Bifhop Gibfon with many particulars of the county of Leicefter [18]. Sarah his widow (to whom probably the next turn had been referved) prefented to the rectory of Segrave in 1715; and died Jan. 27, 1722, æt. 65. They were both buried at St. Mary's, in Leicefter [19].

10. In 1713, on the refignation of Archdeacon Rogers, George Anderfon, M. A. rector of Lutterworth [20], was appointed by the following patent:

" Anna, Dei gratiâ, Magne Britannie, Francie, & Hibernie Regina, fidei defenfor, &c. Omnibus ad quos, &c. Sciatis quod nos, per advifamentum & confenfum Cancellarii & Concilii noftri Ducatûs noftri Lancaftrie, dedimus & conceffimus, ac per prefentes, pro nobis, heredibus & fucceffioribus noftris,

damus

[1] From the original Minute-books of the Committee of Sequeftrations, preferved in the Bodleian Library.
[2] See p. 505. [3] T. B. in the Preface to " The right Government of the Thoughts," &c.
[4] Scobell's Acts and Ordinances, p. 342.
[5] " 1656, June 6, Mr. John Angel, minifter of God's word, buried." Parifh Regifter of Grantham.
[6] Thomas Cafe, in his Preface to " The Morning Exercife, or more fhort Notices."
[7] Wood, Athen. Oxon. vol. II. p. 691. [8] Lift of Graduates. [9] State Trials, vol. III. p. 526.
[10] See vol. III. p. 414. [11] Conveyance penès Walter Ruding, efq. [12] Orig. penès Rev. Rogers Ruding.
[13] Orig. penès Walter Ruding. Le Neve, p. 526, fays he was inftalled December 1704.
[14] From the information of the late Mr. Ruding. [15] See his epitaph, p. 495. [16] Orig. penès Walter Ruding.
[17] Cooke's Preacher's Affiftant. [18] Britifh Topography, vol. I. p. 514.
[19] See their epitaphs, with that of their only daughter, p. 317. [20] See vol. IV. p. 265.

damus & concedimus Georgio Anderſon clerico, & in artibus magiſtro, penſionem ſive ſalarium quam vel quod Petrus Wood, Galfridus Johnſon, Nathaniel Sampſon, Thomas Sacheverell, Johannes Angel, Thomas Peſtell, Johannes Newton, ac Johannes Rogers, clerici, ſucceſſivè nuper habuerunt, ſeu eorum aliquis nuper habuit, in domo eleemoſynariâ vocatâ *Wigſton's Alms-houſe*, in villâ ſive burgo noſtro Leiceſtrie, in comitatu noſtro Leiceſtrie, ac locum ſive promotionem fratris ſeu confratris in domo eleemoſynariâ prediĉtâ; parcellâ Ducatûs noſtri Lancaſtrie, prediĉti, in diĉto comitatu Leiceſtrie; habend' prefato Georgio Anderſon, durante vitâ naturali ipſius Georgii Anderſon, ſerviend' & faciend' in domo prediĉtâ prout prediĉti Petrus Wood, Galfridus Johnſon, Nathaniel Sampſon, Thomas Sacheverell, Johannes Angel, Thomas Peſtel, Johannes Newton, ac prediĉtus Johannes Rogers, fecerunt, ſeu eorum aliquis fecit, aut licitè facere debuit, ac percipiend' annuatim penſionem ac ſalarium prediĉt' per manus receptorum particularium noſtri & ſucceſſorum noſtrorum poſſeſſionum noſtrarum in diĉto comitatu noſtro Leiceſtrie, in jure ducatûs noſtri Lancaſtrie, in tam amplis modo & formâ prout prefati Petrus Wood, Galfridus Johnſon, Nathaniel Sampſon, Thomas Sampſon, Johannes Angel, Thomas Peſtell, Johannes Newton, aut prefatus Johannes Rogers, nuper habuerunt aut perciperunt, ſeu eorum aliquis nuper habuit ſive percepit. Proviſo ſemper quod he litere noſtre patentes irrotulentur, infra III menſes jam proximè & immediatè ſequentes, coram auditore noſtro premiſſorum pro tempore exiſtente; alioquin vacue ſint, & pro nihilo habeantur in lege. In cujus rei teſtimonium, has literas noſtras fieri fecimus patentes. Datum apud Palatium noſtrum Weſtmonaſterii, ſub ſigillo ducatûs noſtri Lancaſtrie prediĉti, 2° Decembris, anno regni 12°.

" Irrotulat' in officio auditoris ducatûs Lancaſtrie in partibus Borealibus, 10° Decembris, anno regni 12°, anno Domini 1713.

W. BELLAMY, Auditor."

His Patent for preaching at the Old Hoſpital.

" Anna, &c. [ut ſupra, uſque ad] . . . . concedimus dileĉto nobis Georgio Anderſon clerico, & in artibus magiſtro, annuam penſionem, annuitatem, ſive annualem ſtipendium decem librarum, ad concionandum, & predicandum verbum Dei, purè & ſincerè, tam in domo oratorum infra clauſuram nuper Collegii Novi Operis Leiceſtrie, quam in villâ ſive burgo Leiceſtrie, parcellâ diĉtâ ducatûs noſtri Lancaſtrie, in comitatu noſtro Leiceſtrie; habendum, gaudendum, & percipiendum, diĉtam annuam annuitatem, ſive annualem ſtipendium x librarum, prefato Georgio Anderſon clerico, durante beneplacito noſtro, percipiendum annuatim diĉtum ſtipendium x librarum de exitibus, proficuis, & revencionibus diĉti nuper Collegii Novi Operis Leiceſtrie prediĉte provenientibus & creſcentibus, per manus receptorum noſtrorum particulariter ejuſdem nuper Collegii pro tempore exiſtentibus, ac heredum & ſucceſſorum noſtrorum, ad feſta Paſche & Sanĉti Michaelis Archangeli, per equales porciones. Proviſo ſemper quod prediĉtus Georgius Anderſon

habebit & gaudebit vel percipiet diĉtam annuam penſionem, annuitatem, ſive annualem ſtipendium x librarum, durante tempore quo prediĉtus Georgius Anderſon concionabit, tam infra domum oratorum prediĉtum, quam infra villam ſive burgum noſtrum Leiceſtrie prediĉte, & non diutiùs. Proviſo etiam quod he litere noſtre patentes irrotulentur, &c. ut ſupra. Dat' 2° Decembris, anno regni 12°.

" Irrotulat' in officio auditoris ducatûs Lancaſtrie in partibus Auſtralibus, 9° Decembris, anno regni 12°, A. D. 1713. THOMAS TURNER, Auditor."

In 1717, Mr. Anderſon reſigned to his brother,

11. Robert Anderſon; who was then ſickly; and, dying May 17, 1717, was buried in the chapel of the Hoſpital, May 19.

12. John Jackſon, reĉtor of Roſſington, B. A. ſucceeded; and was made maſter in 1729. See p. 498.

13. Philip Hacker, reĉtor of South Croxton [1], ſucceeded in 1729; and died April 17, 1735.

14. William Tiffin, a very worthy, modeſt clergyman, 1735. He was author of a Treatiſe on Swift Writing; *i. e.* Short Hand [2]; but it never got on.

" Currant verba licet manus eſt vel ocior illis
     Nondum lingua ſuum dextra peregit opus [3]."

Mr. Tiffin was a Norfolk man, recommended to Mr. Jackſon, maſter of the Hoſpital, by Mr. Pyle of Lynn Regis, and made confrater at the inſtance of Mr. Jackſon; whom he aſſiſted in his various collations of the New Teſtament [4]. The place was particularly acceptable to Mr. Tiffin, as not requiring ſubſcription to the Articles, to which, it ſeems, he had ſome objection. He died in December 1759; and was buried in the croſs aile of St. Martin's church, under the ſteeple. A braſs plate, with a Latin inſcription written by Mr. Jackſon, was put upon his grave; but, a new tenant ſucceeding, the plate was taken away. Being unwilling to ſubſcribe, he had no other preferment.

15. Thomas Ludlam, of St. John's college, Cambridge; B. A. 1748; M. A. 1757; ſucceeded in 1760; and is the preſent confrater (1807.) He is alſo reĉtor of Foſton. Mr. Ludlam is brother to the very eminent mathematician, the Rev. William Ludlam [5]; and is himſelf a writer of conſiderable merit; as appears by his " Four Eſſays, on the ordinary and extraordinary Operations of the Holy Spirit; on the Application of Experience to Religion; and on Enthuſiaſm and Fanaticiſm. To which is prefixed, a preliminary Diſſertation, on the Nature of clear Ideas, and the Advantage of diſtinĉt Knowledge [6]. In theſe Eſſays, the Nature of the Opinions maintained, the Juſtneſs of the Reaſoning employed, and the Propriety of the Language adopted in the Scripture Charaĉters of the Rev. Thomas Robinſon [7], are fully conſidered, 1797," 8vo. Theſe were followed by " Six Eſſays upon Theological, to which are added Two upon Moral Subjeĉts, 1799 [8]."

The Confrater of Wigſton's Hoſpital preaches four times in a year in the chapel of the Old Hoſpital in the Newark; for which he has an augmentation to his ſtipend, by patent from the Duchy of Lancaſter during pleaſure [9].

---

[1] See vol. III. p. 237.

[2] Mr. Tiffin publiſhed " Propoſals for printing, by Subſcription, a Help to the Art of Swift Writing: Being an Alphabet chiefly contrived for that Purpoſe, eaſy to learn, and correſponding in its Elements to the ſeveral diſtinguiſhable Articulations of the Engliſh Tongue, with as great Exaĉtneſs (eſpecially in the Conſonants) as the Author could attain, conſiſtent with Swiftneſs of Writing, and Facility of Learning. To which are added, Suitable Rules and Expedients of joining Letters and abridging Words; ſome of which may be praĉtiſed with Advantage in any other Alphabet, and moſt of them invented by the Author, William Tiffin, Chaplain of Wigſton's Hoſpital in Leiceſter. With an Appendix, containing Charaĉters and Inſtructions for the Uſe of a larger Set of Vowels, wherein a Philoſophical Exaĉtneſs is further purſued." The ſpecimen conſiſts of eight heroic verſes (of ten ſyllables each) taken in ſucceſſion from a noted Engliſh Poet; wherein no charaĉter is employed but what is purely alphabetical; nothing is omitted but what every writer will find to be natural and convenient to omit, when he underſtands the charaĉter, and writes in haſte; nothing but what may all be inſerted in its proper place without confuſion. The price to ſubſcribers is 2s. 6d. paid at the time of ſubſcribing, and 2s. 6d. more upon the delivery of the work: whoever ſubſcribes for ſix ſhall have a ſeventh gratis. To non-ſubſcribers the author will ſell none under 7s. 6d. Subſcriptions are taken in by Meſſrs. Oſborne at Gray's Inn, Noon in Cheapſide, Knapton in St. Paul's church-yard, Whiſton and Reeve in Fleet-ſtreet, Dodſley in Pall-Mall, Fletcher in Oxford, Thurlbourn in Cambridge, and Leake at Bath. [3] Martial, xiv. 208.

[4] See the teſtimony of Wetſtein to this purpoſe, p. 510. [5] Who has been noticed under St. Mary's, p. 318.

[6] " A ſtronger evidence of a clear, ſound, and diſcriminating underſtanding than appears in theſe Eſſays we have not often obſerved. The purity of the language is equal to its preciſion; and both are throughout well worthy of a ſcholar, and a man of ſtrong ſenſe." Britiſh Critic, vol. XI. p. 404. [7] The preſent vicar of St. Mary's; of whom ſee p. 311.

[8] " A pamphlet which ſhews that Mr. Ludlam is a man of refleĉtion; and it is calculated to lead the mind to a diſcriminating and right way of thinking." Monthly Review, New Series, vol. XXIX. p. 383. [9] See p. 347.

The furname of WIGSTON was originally derived from one of the two townfhips of that name in this county. The earlieft whom I have found mentioned is *William Wigfton* [1], who was mayor of Leicefter in 1448; again in 1459; and a burgefs in parliament for the town of Leicefter in 1455.

Roger Wigfton was thrice mayor of Leicefter, 1465, 1472, and 1487 [2]; and burgefs in parliament for the town in 1488. He held, under the abbot and convent of St. Mary de Pratis, a tenement in Braunfton gate, paying annually one hen, and two pence [3].

John Wigfton was mayor in 1469; burgefs in parliament for the town in 1477; and mayor again in 1480 [4]. He purchafed from John Belgrave the tenement fituate on the Weft fide of St. Martin's churchyard, where afterwards the Hofpital was built [5]; and for this tenement he paid an annual acknowledgement of two capons to the abbot and convent of St. Mary de Pratis [6].

Thomas Wigfton, merchant of the Staple of Calais, died in 1502; and his wife Elizabeth in 1503. They were both buried at Belgrave, under a tomb which has long been demolifhed [7].

William Wigfton the elder is faid, in the moft antient Hall-book of the Corporation of Leicefter now extant, to be " the fon and heir and executor of Roger Wigfton, efq. [8]" He was thrice mayor, 1498, 1511, and 1520 [9]; and had three fons, William, Thomas, and Roger [10].

William Wigfton junior, the Founder of the Hofpital, was a merchant of the Staple; burgefs in parliament for the town of Leicefter in 1504; and mayor

in 1510 [11]. He died in 1513 [12]; and was buried in the chapel of the chantry which he had founded in the collegiate church of the Newark. The houfe which he built for the two chantry priefts in the Newark is ftill ftanding, with his arms over the portal.

Agnes Wigfton his widow (by whom he left no iffue), by her laft will, gave to the mafter and confrater the leafe of the tithe corn of the South field of Leicefter, the term of which was not expired in 1576 [13].

Thomas, the next brother to William, was in holy orders, and a prebendary of St. Mary's in the Newark; where he died, and was buried.

" On the fide of the church ly 3 Wigeftons, greate benefactors to the College; one of them was a prebendary there, and made the Free Grammar Schole [14]."

Roger Wigfton, the third brother, who was a burgefs in parliament for the town of Leicefter in 1523, and fheriff in 1541, has been noticed in p. 471; and his fon *William* in p. 476.

Sir *Francis* Wigfton, fheriff of Warwickfhire and Leicefterfhire in 1557, is the laft of the name that occurs in either of thofe counties. He is fuppofed to have died young, and unmarried; as the property at Wolfton and Pinley priory in Warwickfhire, on the death of Roger, paffed to two daughters and coheirs [15].

In the courfe of my refearches into the hiftory of this family, I have met with none of the fame name, except *John* Wigfton, efq. of Trent Park, near Barnet; to whom I am obliged for the communication of fome of the above dates; but whofe relationfhip to the Founder of the Hofpital I have not been able to trace.

---

[1] See before, p. 373.   [2] See p. 388.   [3] See pp. 375. 376. 382.   [4] See pp. 376. 379.
[5] Charyte's Rentale, fol. lxxxviii.   [6] Appendix to vol. I. p. 78.   [7] See vol. III. p. 182.
[8] See Appendix to vol. I. p. 78.   [9] See pp. 384. 388. 389.   [10] See p. 471.   [11] See p. 388.
[12] See p. 472.   [13] See p. 485.   [14] Leland, Itinerary, vol. I. p. 17.   [15] See p. 476.

PEDIGREE of WIGSTON of LEICESTER.

William Wigfton, mayor of Leicefter in 1448 and 1459, and burgefs in parliament for the town in 1455.=....

Roger Wigfton, mayor of Leicefter in 1465. 1472, and 1487; and burgefs in parliament for the town in 1488.=....

1. John Wigfton, mayor of Leicefter in 1469 and 1480; and burgefs in=....   2. Richard Wigfton, fteward of parliament for the town in 1477.   St. John's guild at Leicefter 1477.

Thomas Wigfton, efq. of Belgrave; died 1502.=Elizabeth....; died at Belgrave 1503.

William Wigfton the elder, efq. mayor of Leicefter in 1498, 1511, and 1520.=....

1. William Wigfton the younger, efq. burgefs in par-=Agnes   2. Thomas Wigfton, pre-=....   3. Roger Wigfton, bur-=....
liament for the town of Leicefter in 1504, mayor ....;   bendary of the collegiate   gefs in parliament for
in 1510; founder of a chantry in the collegiate   furvived   church of St. Mary in   the town of Leicefter
church of St. Mary in the Newark, and of the   her huf-   the Newark; living in   in 1523; fheriff in
Hofpital which bears his name; died 1513, f. p.   band.   1516.   1541.

William Wigfton, of Wolfton, co. Warwick, fheriff 1551; died Sept. 19, 1576.=....

Sir Francis Wigfton, fheriff   Sufanna, daughter and coheir; married to Nicholas   Another daughter.
1557; died f. p.   Wentworth, efq. owner of Wolfton in right of his wife.

PEDIGREE of SHERMAN, of the NEWARK, LEICESTER.

Thomas Sherman, of Yaxley, co. Suffolk.=.... daughter of .... Waller, of Wartham, co. Suffolk.

1. Thomas=....dau.   2. Richard;   3. John.   5. William Sher-=Faith, dau. of   6. Frances.   A daughter, married
Sherman.   of....   died f. p.   4. Henry.   man, grocer and   Henry de Lany,   7. Jacob.   to .... Lockwood.
  Yaxley,   merchant, of   of Cratfeild,   8. Bartholomew.
  of Suffolk.   London.   co. Suffolk.   9. Anthony.

1. Thomas=....dau. of   Elizabeth,   Anne, married to   2. John Sher-=Anne, dau. of   3. Richard   4. Owen;
Sherman,   Thwaites,   married   .... Browne,   man, of the   William Cave.   Sherman,   died f. p.
of Yaxley.   of Herding,   ... Browne,   brother of the   Newark,   clerk.
  co. Norfolk.   yeoman.   other Browne.   Leicefter.

Thomas   Faith, m.   1. Wm. Sherman, fon=Mary d.   2. Tho-   Eleanor,   Jane.   5. Wm.;   Marga-   Faith, m.
Sherman,   Henry   and heir, æt. 31 in   of....   mas, of   wi. of Geo.   Milicent.   died   ret, wife   ... Bel-
fon and   Heming,   1619; a benefactor to   Lafcel-   Prentis,   Jermin, of   Elizabeth.   f. p.   of ...   lard, of
heir   of the   the Town Library   les, of   co. Suff.   co. Notts.   Anne.   Duch, of   Yorkfh.;
1619.   Newark.   (fee p. 506.)   Notts.   æt. 18.   Kent.   died at
                                                                 Ipfwich.

John Sherman, fon and heir 1619.   Anne, æt. 2 in 1619.

THE

THE TOWN LIBRARY,

is fituated on the North fide of Wigfton's Hofpital; and joins the hall formerly belonging to St. George's guild, and which is now the Guildhall of the Borough.

The room which contains the Library is ornamented with two portraits, which in 1790 were thus defcribed by Mr. Bickerftaffe:

"Here enframed is the figure of St. Hierome, in a fcarlet cap and gown, his name prefixed, a candle burning low, left fore-finger end refting on a fcull; a pen and ink, a time-piece, and "Surgite, venite ad judicium;" right hand fupporting his contemplative head.

"Over the door of the Library, within a black clofe cap edged with flowered white, with a plain fair tippet not two inches below the collar, like the modern ornament of boys, appears with whifkers thus announced: "M. S. Thomas Hayne [1], qui inter eruditos & optimos nominari meruit, Thruffingtoná hujus agr. Leiceftrienfis oriundus, in coll. Linc. apud Oxoni A. M. patriam & hanc villam pecuniá & redditibus quotannis in egenos erogandá devinxit: & præter multa piæ libertatibus teftimonia paffim collata, Bibliothecam hanc fupellectile libraria munificè adornavit. Diem obiit Julii 27, an. Chr. 1645, ætat. 64."

The Library in 1790 contained 948 books; and the more curious mifcellaneous articles which occurred to the refearches of Mr. Bickerftaffe were,

An Hebrew book in Syriac characters, curioufly written on paper, bordered with gold.

Walton's Polyglott, 6 vols.; with Caftelli Lexicon, 2 vols.

The New Teftament, tranflated into the Indian language; *Cambridge*, 1671.

A valuable edition of Erpenius's Arabic Grammar.

And an Arabic MS. with many leaves torn out by ignorant vifitors.

The MSS. were then only five; viz.

1. "Biblia Sacra, Latinè."

2. "Novum Teftamentum Græcè;" commonly called the *Codex Leiceftrenfis.*

3. A Latin Bible, including Apocrypha and New Teftament. It has a Prologus of two leaves and a quarter, and after the index "W. Stanlay, alio noïe Walue, fcripfit." At the end, "Edwardus Dei grã rex Angl', &c." It is bound in leather, and ornamented with the Royal arms.

4. "Pfalmi Davidis."

5. On facred fubjects; the title wanting.

From the fame attentive obferver I had feveral other particulars; which are fuperfeded by the following very ample details, tranfcribed by the late Mr. Richard Wefton, from an authentic document, intituled, "A Booke made and provided to preferve the memoriall, and to eternize and immortalize the names, of fuch good men who heretofore have bine, or hereafter fhall and will be, benefactors to this Publique Librarie: Hoping that this may be a fpeculative and exemplarie motive to ftirr up and incite many others to add fomthing to this good worke: And all to the glorie of Almightie God, the helpe and benefitt of Minifters and Scholers; the folace and recreation of well-willers to Learning; and, finally, to the everlafting fame, honour, and renowne, of this Corporation. Anno Domini 1644.

"We that are nam'd and lifted in this Booke,
As coadjutors to fo good a caufe,
For theife our Workes do not defire or looke
To gett a vaine and popular applaufe.

Nor do we come of Merit-mongers breed,
That found their trumpets to be prais'd of men;
Nor yet doe fpring from any Popifh feed, [Heaven:
Which thinke good workes alone may gaine

But what we doe, we doe to magnifie
The facred name of the Omnipotent;
And that our workes our fincere faith may trie,
No other thinges or by refpect 's are meant.

Let Momus then, and all impoftum'd tongues,
Forbear to barke, when any good is wrought;
And let them vent their bafe malignant fonges
On fuch defignes which of themfelves are nought;
And ftill we wifh that more new Freuds may give
More Bookes and Prefents to this Trefurie,
That fo their names recorded here may live
In honor, fame, and immortalitie.

But bleft be God, who laid the corner-ftonn,
And was cheife Founder of this houfe of ftore;
He mov'd mens' minds, and fo did fett them on
T' improve this worke, which was infirme before.

Come therefore, come, Students of ech degree,
Come when you pleafe, and vifit this our Mufe;
All frendes to lerning may hither welcome be,
And read fuch bookes as they affect and choofe."

An Account of the Foundation.

"This Librarie was erected and builded, at the onely coft and charges of the Corporation of Leicefter, att the motion, and by the approbation, of the Reverend Father in God John Lord Bifhop of Lincolne, and by the profecution of Mr. John Angell, publique lecturer for the fayd Burrough of Leicefter. The Building whereof was begun in the time of the mairolty of Mr. John Norrice, anno Domini 1632, Thomas Somerfeild and Richard Ludlam being chamberlins; and finifhed in the fecond time of the mairolty of Mr. Nicholas Gilljot, anno 1633, Thomas Burfnall and Alexander Baker being chamberlins."

A Catalogue of the Names of its Benefactors, together with their Donations.

"Henry Earle of Huntingdon, Lord Prefident of York, gave many bookes heretofore, which then weare placed in the parifh church of St. Martin in Leicefter, for the help and benefit of Minifters and Scholers. But, upon the building and foundation of this Librarie, and by the confent and approbation of thaforfayd Lord Bifhop of Lincoln, all thofe bookes which weare of the donation of the fayd earl of Huntindon, and many other bookes given then by former Benefactors, weare removed and placed in this Library, for the better furnifhing thereof.

"The aforefayd Reverend Father in God John Lord Bp. of Lincolne gave, towards the furnifhing of this Librarye with bookes, the fomm of tenn poundes.

"Ther was a generall and voluntarie collection in and throughout the Corporation of this Burrough of Leicefter, for the raifing of a fomme of money, to be beftowed in bookes for the better furnifhing of this Librarye; whereupon many gave willingly and bountefully. Infomuch, that the totall of the fomme collected did arife to a great quantitie and proportion, and was beftowed in bookes, according to the intent and mind of the Corporation, and doners thereof.

"A general collection was likewife made in every Deanary in this County of Leicefter, amongft the Minifters and Clergie, to raife money for the aforfayd ufe; wherein the Minifters fhewed their good and great refpect to fo good a worke, and gave liberally in mony, and fome in bookes. The feveral fommes collected in every Deanary are hereunto fubfcribed; videlicet,

			£.	s.	d.
In Framland Deanarie	—	—	6	15	0
In Gudlaxton	—	—	—	12	15	0
In Sparkenhoe	-	—	—	7	5	10
In Gartrie	—	—	18	5	0
In Gofcote	—	—	7	13	4
Iu Akeley	—	—	1	10	0
			54	4	2

"Mr. Anthony Cade [2], vicar of Billefdon in the countie of Leicefter, gave twelve worthy bookes to

---

[1] Of Mr. Hayne an account has been already given, under his native town, vol. III. p. 459.　　[2] Of whom fee vol. II. p. 436.

this

this Librarie, with his name fet and fubfcribed at the beginning of every one of the fayd bookes. The names of the authors of his bookes are thefe following:

Suarez Comment. 4 vols. fol.
Grego. de Valen. 2 vols. fol.
Arias, Vetus & Nov. Teſt. 1 vol. fol.
Grego. 3 vols. fol.
Gefneri Bibliotheca, 1 vol. fol.
Azorii Inſt. 1 vol. fol.——12 vols. fol.

" Sir Arthur Hefelrigg [1], of Nofeley in the county of Leicefter, gave thirteen bookes in folio, being the works of that famous Divine, Alphonfus Toſtatus Biſhop of Abulence.

Of which thirteen books, four of them are Commentaries upon the Five Bookes of Mofes.

One a Commentary upon the Books of Joſhua, Judith, and Ruth.

Two are a Comment upon the Book of the Kings.
One upon the Booke of the Chronicles.
Four upon the Evangeliſt Matthew.
And one Index of all the faid workes of Toſtatus.

" Mr. John Whatton, of the Burrough of Leicefter, efquire, gave to this Library five great and large bookes in folio, intituled,

Concilia Generalia & Provincialia, per Birrium. 5 vols.

" John Evans, of the Citty of London, gentleman, for the greate love, zeale, and affection, which he had for the advancement of learning, but efpecially in the ſtudy and practice of Divinitie, gave ten worthy bookes towards the furniſhing of this Library, though he was altogether unknowne and unacquainted in theife parts, having a care of the publique and wunderfull good of the kingdome. The names and titles of the books are fubfcribed; videlicet,

Balduini Cafus Confcientiæ.
Davenantius Determin. quarundam Queſtionum.
Lorini Comment. in 3 vols. fol. upon David's Pfalmes, divided into three Quinquagenes.
Lorinus in Acta Apoſtolorum.
Lorinus in Jacobum & Judam.
Lorinus in Ecclefiaften.
Helvici Theatrum Hiſtoricum.
Clavis Regia ; Authore Sayro.

" Mr. Thomas Rudiard, an alderman and maior of this Burrough of Leicefter, gave three bookes in folio ; being

The Workes of that famous Divine, Mr. William Perkins, in the Univerſitie of Cambridge.

" Mr. Richard Ludlam, an alderman, and maior of this Burrough, gave three large bookes in folio ;

The Theological Works of that famous Divine, Hieronimus Zanchius.

" James Andrew junior, of the Burrough of Leicefter, gentleman, gave to and for the ufe of this Librarie twelve bookes, eleven whereof are the workes of that learned writer, Johannes Henricus Alſtedius. And the other intituled, A general View of Papiſtrie, written by Andrew Willett.

" Mr. John Poultney, of Miſterton in the countie of Leicefter, efquire, gave, towards the better furniſhing of this Librarie with ufeful and neceſſarie books, five pounds.

" Simon Craftes, of the Burrough of Leicefter, innholder, gave heretofore four good books, written in the Engliſh tongue, for the good and benefitt of the volger and not fo well learned fort of people.

One being the Sermons of Mr. John Calvin upon the Book of Job.
One a Commentarie upon St. Matthew, written by Mr. Time.
One a Commentarie upon the Epiſtles to the Corinthians and Epheſians, written by the fayd Mr. Time.
And the other, a Commentarie of Luther upon the Galatians.

" Chriſtopher Bardfey, of this Burrough of Lei-

cefter, gentleman, gave the whole Books of Actes and Monuments, commonly called

The Book of Martyrs, written by that good and famous Divine, Mr. John Fox.

" Mr. William Watkins, fomtime vicar of the pariſh of St. Martin in this Burrough of Leicefter, gave a very worthye booke, entituled,

The Survey of Chriſte's Sufferinges, written by Thomas Bilfon, fomtime Bp. of Wincheſter.

" Mr. John Angell, fometime head and chiefe fchoolemaſter of the Free-fchoole in this Burrough of Leicefter, gave two bookes in folio.

The one being the Workes of Plotinus, about and concerning Queſtions in Philofophie.
The other being the Workes of C. Suetonius Tranquillus ; with the reſt of the fmall Romane Hiſtorians, in folio.

" Elizabeth Bonnet, the relict and executrix of Mr. John Bonnet, fomtime vicar of the pariſh of Saint Marye in this Burrough of Leicefter, gave to this Librarye a worthye booke, entituled,

A Commentarie upon the whole Booke of Judges, written and penned by the Reverend Divine Mr. Richard Rogers, Preacher of God's word att Wetherfeild in Eſſex.

" Mr. John Glover [2], Parfon of Laughton in this county of Leicefter, gave to this Library an excellent booke, entituled,

A Commentarie upon the Twelve fmaler and leſſer Prophetts, written and fett forth per Francifcum Riberam.

" Mr. William Stanley, an alderman, and fomtime maior of this Corporation, gave, towards the furniſhing of this Librarye with bookes, one very learned booke, entituled,

The Miſterie of Iniquitie, firſt fett forth by Phillip Morney, Knight, and after Engliſhed by Samfon Lennard.
And alfo the Workes of that learned Divine Jofeph Hall, Doctor in Divinitie, and Deane of Worceſter.

" Mr. Francis Higginfon [3], a Reverend Divine, and fomtime Preacher of God's word att the pariſh of Saint Nicholas in this Burrough of Leicefter, gave divers bookes for and towards the better furniſhing of this Library ; videlicet,

Oecolampadius in omnes Prophetas & Job.
Strigelius in omnes Pfalmos.
Sarcerius in Epiſtolas Dominicales.
Sarcerius in Evangelia Dominicalia.

" The Lady Beaumonte, who heretofore did live att the towne called Cole-orton in this county of Leicefter, gave, for the ufe of this Library, three large bookes in folio, entituled,

Difputationes Roberti Bellarmini.

" Mr. Francis Belgrave, fometime an inhabitant in this Borough of Leicefter, gave, for the ufe of this Librarie, a very antient and learned booke, in folio, intituled,

Speculum Aureum ; or, a Commentary upon the Ten Commandements, written and penned by Anthony Oburger, in a very large and learned Methode.

" Mr. Francis Nedham [4], a Reverend Divine, and fomtime parfon and rector of Rotherby in this county of Leicefter, gave, for the better improvement of this Librarie, a very large and learned book in folio, intituled, Marloreti Expofitio Novi Teſtamenti Catholiac Ecclefiaſtica.

" Mr. William Sherman [5], of the Newark, near Leicefter, efquire, gave forty ſhillings towards the furniſhing of this Library.

" Mr. Thomas Hayne [6], of the Cittie of London, Maſter of Artes, but borne att Thruſſington in this county of Leicefter, was a prime benefactor to this Librarie ; who, for the love and zeale he had for

---

[1] See before, vol. II. p. 743.
[2] Of whom fee before, p. 501.
[3] See before, p. 505.
[4] This name may be added to the rectors of Laughton, in vol. II. p. 696.
[5] See vol. III. pp. 268. 399.
[6] See the Pedigree of his Family, p. 504.

the advancement of learning, and affection he had to this Librarie, being *witeinles* [1] *limitted* of his native countrie, and for the better improvement thereof (it being but in its minoritie, and then unfinished), gave, by his laft will and teftament, unto this place,

" All his books in his own Librarie (except fome few [2]), amounting to the number of fix hundreth and above, being worthy books, both divine and morall.

" And alfo many antient and modern Chronicles and Hiftories.

" Books of Philofophie and Poetrie.

" Dictionaries of divers forts; many Schoole-bookes; and divers other Tractates and Treatifes, of which divers weare fett forth, penned, and putt into print, by the fayd Thomas Hayne, with the addition of his name to the fame books: All which here offer themfelves ready to releafe men's feveral affections. Moreover, many other legacies and annuities, as well for the relief of the poor, and other pious ufes, were given, bequeathed, and confirmed, by his fayd laft will and teftament.

" Trevor Williams, of Langriby caftle, in the county of Monmouth, barronett, for the better fur-nifhing of this Library with books, gave fourty fhil-lings; with which was bought,

Dr. Whitaker's Workes.
The Sixt and Eight Booke of Hooker's Eccle-fiaftical Politie.
And Scultetus his Exercitationes.

" William Billers, gent. one of the aldermen of this Borough of Leicefter, hath given one great Bible for the ufe and benefitt of this Library.

" Thomas Browne, of this Borough of Leicefter, gent. for the beautifying and adorneing of this Li-brary, and for the benefitt of Schoilers, gave one great Mappe, being a Defcription of the whole World.

" Mr. Richard Lee, Mafter of Wigfton's Hofpitall, for the better furnifhing of this Library, hath given Annotations upon all the New Teftament.

" George Tirwhitt, of the Burrough of Leicefter, gent. towards the furnifhing of this Library, gave two books; the one entituled,

Doctor Taylor's Sermons.
The other, The Italian Convert.

" William Heyricke [3] the younger, of Beaumannor, in the county of Leicefter, efq. for the better fur-nifhing of this Library, gave eight bookes; viz.

A Pifgah Sight of Paleftine, in folio.
Harmonicon Cœlefte; or, the Cœleftiall Har-mony of the vifible World; folio.
Pyrotechnia; or, a Difcourfe of Artificial Fire Workes; folio.
Antiquitatum Romanorum; 4to.
Curfus Theologicus; 4to.
Chriftian Aftrology; 4to.
Euclide's Elements; 4to.
Trignonometrie; or, the Manner of calculating the Sides and Angles of Triangles.

" Captain William Billers, of London, gent. gave, for the better furnifhing of this Library, one booke, in folio, entituled,

Burton's Melancholy; and alfo
One great Bible, with marginal notes.
And one little Bible for a Minifter when he goeth to preach.

" Mr. Richard Richardfon, head fchoolmafter in the Free grammar-fchoole in Leicefter, gave to this Library one ufeful and neceffary Booke, entituled,

Cotton's Concordance of Ould and New Teftament.

" John Turvyle, of Normanton Turvile in the county of Leicefter, efquire, gave to this Library three excellent bookes; viz.

Dr. Hammond's Annotations on all the New Teftament.

The Hiftorie of the World, by Sir Walter Ralegh, Knight, and
The General Hiftorie of Spaine.

" William Ward the younger, of the Burrough of Leicefter, mercer, gave to this Library two bookes, viz.
The General Hiftorie of the Turkes; and
The unmafking of a Maffe-monger; and
A Diffuafive trom the Errours of the Tyme; both bound together."

The preceding Benefactions are undated; and, probably, were all beftowed before the regular and well-digefted Catalogue of this Library was taken by Mr. Angel, the learned confrater of Wigfton's Hof-pital; which, by the favour of the Rev. Rogers Ru-ding, I have now before me, in the fmall but neat hand-writing of Mr. Angel, whofe mottoes to it are,
" Qualis cujufcunque animi affectus, talis eft homo."
" Ubi amor, ibi oculus."

The Books are by him catalogued in claffes; in which Theology has by much the largeft fhare. In that clafs are feveral Bibles; of which the principal are,
Hutteri Biblia, ufque ad Ruth; *Noreberg.* 1539.
Novum Teft. Græcè, Stephani, *Paris,* 1550.
Vetus Teftamentum, cum var. Lect. *Francof.* 1597.
Biblia Junii, Tremellii, & Bezæ; *Hannov.* 1624.
Septuaginta, cum Nov. Teft. Græco-Latinè, 3 vols. *Paris,* 1638.
Tindal's and Cranmer's Bibles.
Teftamentum Novum, *Rheims,* 1582.
——————————— Heb. & Lat.; *Paris,* 1584.
——————————— Græc. & Lat. *Lubini,* 1614.
Two Miffals.
Several valuable Concordances and Lexicons.

The *Libri Hiftorici, Libri Oratorii & Poetici,* and *Libri Philofophici, Medici, Grammaticales, & Mathe-matici,* contain feveral good books, and 56 volumes of " Divers and mifcellaneous Treatifes," bound toge-ther; the whole then confifting of 876 articles.

Mr. Angel, of whom an account has been already given in p. 501, removed from Leicefter foon after he had completed this Catalogue; but the entries in the Library-book are thus continued:

" Mr. John Angell, a moft famous and reverend Divine, Publique Lecturer for the Burrough of Lei-cefter, for many yeares together Confrater of Wig-fton's Hofpitall, now called The New Hofpitall, was a fpeciall and liberall benefactor and well-wifher to this Librarie; and did not onely excite and ftirr up many, both Divines and Gentlemen, to offer and extend their guiftes to this TREASURY, but was a pattern and example himfelf, to doe that which he perfuaded others to doe; and gave above twenty worthy bookes, as well Commentaries, as alfo other works of divers Divines, very ufeful and neceffary for this Librarie.

" 1666. Thomas Bodle, of Markfeild in the countye of Leicefter, gentleman, gave to this Li-brarye one ancient booke in folio, being
The Workes of John Whitgift, Dr. of Divinitie.

" 1667. William Bale [4], of Humberfton, in com' Leceft', gentleman, for the better furnifhinge of this Librarye, gave two bookes; one antient Bible, in folio; and another Booke in quarto, being the Worke of Mr. John Angell, late Publique Lecturer of this Burrough, entituled, The right Government of our Thoughts; as alfo Four Sermons by the fame author.

" Francis Elliott, of the Burrough of Leicefter, ironmonger, for the better furnifhing of this Li-brarye, gave two antient large books in folio, being
The Worke of B. Rombolt about the Civil Law.
As alfo one other book in folio; the famoufe and antient Hiftorie of Aurelius Tacitus.

" Henry Wilkinfon, Doctor in Divinity, and late Principall of Magdalen Hall [5] in Oxford, gave
Mr. Hilderfham's Works, folio; viz.

[1] So Mr. Wefton's tranfcript.   [2] He gave a few books to the Library at Weftminfter. See vol. III. p. 459.
[3] This was the eldeft fon of fir William Heyrick; who had imbibed a tafte for literature, under the tuition of Mr. Chrif-topher Wren, at St. John's College in Oxford. See vol. III. p. 156.   [4] Ibid. p. 276.
[5] Dr. Wilkinfon received that appointment Aug. 12, 1648; and was removed in 1662 for Non-conformity. He built the Library at Magdalen Hall, and gave to it feveral Prefbyterian books, and Roman coins; and procured others from gentlemen and fcholars that had been of that Hall. He died at Great Cornard, near Sudbury, Suffolk, in 1690, æt. 74, and was buried in Milding church in that neighbourhood. Gutch, Colleges and Halls, pp. 685. 687.

Lectures on the fifty-firft Pfalme, and on the fourth Chapter of John.

" William Elliott, of the Burrough of Leicefter, iremonger, for the better furnifhinge of this Librarye, gave three bookes; viz.

Sion's Profpect; beinge the Workes of Mr. Robert Moffom, quondam in Coll. S. T. C.

As alfoe two other bookes; one entituled, The Governor, 12 C. three books.

The other, The Life of the noble and eloquent Marcus Aurelius.

" David Stoakes, D. D. fellow of Eaton colledge near Windfor, gave three bookes for the better furnifhinge of this Librarye; viz. one entituled,

A Paraphraftical Explication of the Twelve Minor Prophets, in 4to.

The fecond beinge a Direction for Private Devotion and Retirement, in 4to.

The third a Treatife, beinge Two Sermons preached at Hertford; the other in Eaton colledge: Being all his owne Workes.

" 1668. Sir Thomas Dolman, knt. for the better furnifhing of this Library, gave

The Workes of St. Chryfoftome, compleat, in eight fair volumes of Sir H. Savile's edition.

" Mr. Thomas Stanhope, Minifter of St. Margarett, Leicefter, gave fix bookes to this Library; viz.

1. Bifhop Andrewes' Sermons, in a large folio.
2. One great Latine Bible; a Manufcript [1].
3. Rogers, in 4to; entituled, The Faith and Doctrine of the Church of England, expreft in the Thirty-nine Articles.
4. Riverus his Obfervations and Cures in Phificke, in 4to.
5. Dr. Hammond's Chriftian Obligations to Peace and Charity, in 4to; with Nine other Sermons.

And Bifhop Hall's Practicall Cafes of Confcience refolved, in 8vo.

Since thefe he hath given one booke more, confifting of Four Sermons preacht by himfelfe in Leicefter on feveral occafions.

As alfo a Treatife of Worldly Politye, Morall Evidence, and Chriftian Wifdom, or Herle his Tripos.

" 1669. Lazarus Seaman [2], D. D. fometime Vice-chancelor of Cambridge, and Mafter of Peter houfe, out of his love to this Corporation (being the place of his nativitye), for the advance of learninge, and the further enlarginge this Librarye, gave eleven worthy bookes, as follow; viz.

Imprimis, four Hebrew Concordances of the Bible, in folio.

Item, Dr. Mayer's Comentaryes upon the ould Teftament; 4 vols. folio.

Item, Ruiz de Predeftatione } 2 vols. folio.
—— de Prudentia }

Item, Pifcator in Novum Teft.; a large 4to.

" 1672. The above-mentioned Doctor gave the Biblia Polyglotta, in fix large volumes, in folio.

" As alfoe Dr. Mayer's Commentaryes on the New Teftament, unto the Epiftle of St. James, in two volumes in folio.

" 1670. Mr. Jofeph Birkhead, Mafter of Arts in both Univerfityes, and fome time head-fcholemafter in Leicefter, gave to this Library

The Hiftory of Venice (being a tranflation), folio.

" Mr. John Wilkins, of this Burrough, for the better furnifhinge this Librarye, gave thefe bookes;

Johannes de Imola, 2 vols. in folio.

Dyni Muxellani, in 4to.

With two or three other leffer Treatifes, in 4to.

" William Kinns [3], rector of Swithland, gave one worthy booke; viz.

Marlorett's Commentary on the New Teftament.

" 1674. Two Manufcripts of Foraine Nations [not here].

One New Teftament, printed in the Language of the New Englifh Nations.

As alfo an Egiptian Hierogliphicke; with a China Almanack.

" 1676. Mr. Cave, rector of Cold Overton, gave one book; A Relation of the Kinge's Entertainment by the States of Holland in feverall Places.

" 1677. Mr. Cadwallader Jones [4], rector of Rearfby, gave
Dr. Taylor's Life of the Holy Jefus; and
Dr. Cave's Lives of the Apoftles, in folio.

He gave alfo Dr. Cave's Lives of the Primitive Fathers, in folio.

" Dr. Humphry Babington [5], Vice-mafter of Trinity college in Cambridge, gave to this Library's ufe;
S. Chryfoftomi Opera, Gr. & Lat.; 10 vols. fol.
Capellus in Nov. Teftamentum; fol.
Sylveftr. Sguropuli Concilii Florentini Hiftoria, Gr. & Lat.; fol. 1660.
Launoii Epiftolae omnes; fol. Cantabr. 1689.

" 1679. Jonathan Callis, of this Burrough, (his widow) gave to this Library,
Itinerarium totius Sacrae Scripturae; or, the Travels of the Holy Patriarchs, Prophets, Kings, our Saviour Jefus Chrift, and the Apoftles.

" Thomas Holbech, D. D. fometime Vice-chancellour of Cambridge, and Mafter of Emanuel colledge, out of his love to this Corporation, gave two worthy bookes; being The Works of Sebaftianus Barra; viz. his Commentaria in Concordiam & Hiftoriam Evangelicam, in 4 tomes and 2 volumes.

" 1695. John Newton, vicar of St. Martin's, and confrater of Wigfton's Hofpital [6], gave
Baldus's Repertorium Confiliorum, folio.

" 1696. The moft Reverend Father in God Thomas Lord Archbifhop of Canterbury gave to this Library
Dr. Caftell's Lexicon on the Polyglott, 2 vols. fol.

" June 22, 1699.
" Samuel Barnard, of Coggefhall in Effex:
Nos Patriam fugimus, nos dulcia linquimus arva. VIRG.
[What Mr. Barnard's benefaction was, does not appear.]

" 1701. Thomas Seagrave [7], rector of Leir, kinfman to Mr. Thomas Hayne, benefactor to this Library and Corporation, gave three books; viz.
1. Lightfoot's Horae Hebraicae, in Chorographiam Terrae Ifraeliticae, & in Evangelium S. Matthaei; 4to, Cantab. 1658.
2. Seldeni de Diis Syris Syntagmata duo, cum Additamentis Andr. Bey; 8vo, Amftel. 1680.
3. Chriftoph. Cartwright's Electa Thurgumico-Rabbinica, in Exodum; 8vo, Londini, 1658.

" 1702. Edward Millington (Proto-auctionarius) gave to this Library,
Marcus Antoninus; publifhed by George Stanhope, D. D. 1697.

" 1705. The Reverend Mr. Robert Cotes, rector of Burbach in Leicefterfhire, gave to this Library,
The Hiftory of the Civil Wars of England, 3 vols. fol. by Edward Earl of Clarendon; 1702.
Sir Thomas Craig's Right of the Succeffion to the Kingdom of England, againft Parfons the Jefuit, alias Doleman, in Englifh; 1703.

" 1713. Matthew Simons, of this Burrough, efq. gave
Papal Ufurpation and Perfecution; fol. tome I.
Quo teneam vultus mutantem Protea nodo?
Nam facinus quos inquinat aequat.

" Mr. Humfry Wanley, fon of the Reverend Nath. Wanley [8], vicar of Trinity church in Coventry, gave,
Antonini Iter Britanniarum Commentariis illuftratum Thomas Gale, S. T. P. nuper Decani Ebor. Opus pofthumum revifit, auxit, edidit, R. G. Acceffit Anonymi Ravennatis Britanniae Chorographia. Ed. Lond. 1709, 4to.

" Mr. Samuel Carte, vicar of the church of St. Martin in Leicefter, gave
Two Tables of the Bifhopricks in England and Wales. One hung up in a frame; the other joined with notes explaining it in Latin.

" Mr. Richard Ludlam [9], M. B. gave to this Library 84 books, as by a Catalogue on clafs No 5.

" The Rev. Mr. John Wightman, of Desford, gave Pool's Synopfis Criticorum, in five volumes.

[1] See p. 505.   [2] See fome memoirs of him under Rotherby, vol. III. p. 398, where he is by miftake called *Laurence*.   [3] This name may be added to the rectors of Swithland, vol. III. p. 1051.   [4] See vol. III. p. 392.   [5] Son of Adrian Babington, rector of Coffington. He was joint founder of the Hofpital at Burrow. See vol. III. pp. 68. 965.   [6] See p. 502.   [7] See vol. IV. p. 244.   [8] Ibid. p. 273.   [9] See his epitaph at St. Mary's, vol. I. p. 318.

" 1743.

"1743. The Rev. Mr. John Harryman, rector of Peckleton, by his last will, bequeathed to this Library:

Folio.
Episcopii Opera; 2 vols. Amst. 1650. Rot. 1665.
Irenæus, Gr. & Lat. Ed. Grabe. Oxon. 1702.
Cypriani Opera. Ed. Fell. Amst. 1700.
Ayliff. Par. Juris Canon. Angl. Lond. 1700.
Johann. Forbesii Opera; 2 vols. Amst. 1703.
M. A. De Dominis de Republicâ Ecclesiasticâ. Heid. 1618.
Herodotus, Gr. & Lat. Lond. 1679.
Scapulæ Lexicon. Amst. Blaeuw. & Elz. 1652.
Lightfoot's Works. London, 1684.
Clemens Alexandrinus, G. L. Lutetiæ, 1629.
Biblia Interlin. cum Nov. Test. Montani. 1619.
Gregorii Astronomiæ Elementa. Oxon. 1702.
Euripides, ed. Josh. Barnes. Cant. 1694.
Du Pin, Ecclesiastical History; 7 vols.
Dawson, of the Origin of Laws. 1694.
Justini Martyris Opera, Gr. & Lat. Colon. 1686.
Limborch Theologia Christiana. Amst. 1700.
Stone's Construction and Uses of Mathematical Instruments. 1723.
Kersey's Algebra, with Halley's Lectures. London, 1717.

Quarto.
Crellii Ethica, cum Catech. Polon. Cosmop. 1681.
Motte's Abridgment of Philosophical Transactions, 1701—1720; 2 vols.
Reid and Gray's Ditto, 1721—1732; 2 vols. figured 6. 7.
Beveregii Codex Canonum Ecclesiæ Prim. vindicatus. 1678.
Du Pin, de antiquâ Ecclesiæ Disciplinâ. Colon. Agr. 1691.
Ignatii & Barnabæ Epist. Ed. Is. Vossius. 1646.
Dav. Blondelli Apologia pro Sententiâ Hieronymi. Amst. 1646.
Beveregii Institutiones Chronologicæ. 1669.
Polycarpi & Ignatii Epist. Ed. Usserii, 1644.

Octavo.
Grotius de Jure Belli & Pacis, notis Gronovii, Amst. 1689.
Clementis ad Corinthios Ep. duæ, Gr. Lat. Ed. Wotton. Cant. 1718.

12mo.
Outramus de Sacrificiis. Amst. 1688.
Buxtorfi Synogoga Judaica. Bas. 1641.
Vincentius Lerinensis. Colon. 1613."

In the year 1802, the late Mr. Richard Weston (from whose MSS. I have taken the foregoing extracts) announced an intention of publishing "An Account of the Foundation of the Town Library of Leicester; with the Names of its Benefactors, from its Institution to the last, the Rev. Mr. Harryman, in 1743; a Catalogue of the Books and MSS. contained in it; its present neglected Condition, and a Plan for improving and enlarging it;" but, from the want of sufficient encouragement, and from, I am sorry to say, the *res angustæ domi*, was never able to complete his publication.

Mr. Weston thus proceeds: "This Library has met with very extraordinary fate; and it is with regret I mention it, that I have now described the last Benefactor. A period of 59 years without the addition of a single book to it—nor any notice taken of it, except that, soon after that time, I remember several of the books were fresh bound, and some repaired, under the direction of Mr. Tiffin.

"Within about seven years too after that period, five gentlemen of eminence in the literary way, who lived adjoining to it, published the following volumes:

"Thomas Carte, esq. son of the Rev. Samuel Carte, vicar of St. Martin's; History of England, 4 vols. fol. 1747.

"Rev. John Jackson, Master of Wigston's Hospital; Chronology, 3 vols. 4to. 1750.

"Rev. William Tiffin, Confrater of Wigston's Hospital; a Treatise on Short Hand, 4to, 1751.

"John-Gilbert Cooper, esq.; The Life of Socrates; 8vo. Letters concerning Taste; 8vo.

"Notwithstanding all these gentlemen lived in or near the Church-yard, not one of their Works were deposited in it; nor, on a strict examination of the donations, and the Catalogue, can I find a single book from any of the Authors, either of the Town or County, though so many have been produced within the last century. And though the Librarian, Jacob Bauthumley, in the year 1676, wrote 'An Historical Relation of the Persecution of the Church,' with a Dedication to the Mayor, Aldermen, &c. of the Corporation, complimenting them on their 'pious devotion to Religion and Learning,' yet the work is not to be found; nor any mention of it in the Catalogue taken in 1773.

"Great depredations have been committed on several of the Books.

"A MS. Bible, written in the time of Edward the First, on vellum, the first letters of each chapter of which are illuminated with light sky-blue and red alternately, has some leaves cut out at the beginning, and above 200 of the bottom margin cut out, even into the writing; and seem to have been of no use to any body except to a book-binder as bands for binding. One of the covers also is torn off with the chain. This MS. was the gift of Mr. Thomas Stanhope, minister of St. Margaret, Leicester, and written by William Stanlay[1]; and is very well worth examining, the writing being remarkably neat and uniform, and the ink remains of a beautiful black, although written as above.

"The Plates in the Anatomy of Plants, &c. by Malpighius, and two volumes of the Philosophical Transactions, are many of them torn, and some missing.

"Purchas's Travels, in five volumes in folio, have not one quarter of the work remaining; and many others of the most valuable works are much damaged, especially a book in one of the Oriental languages.

"Gesner's History of Plants, folio, missing, which was there in 1772, as I then copied his life from it; and many more I expect, when they are searched for.

"The chains affixed to most of the books cause great damage to the binding, and ought to be taken off.

"The Library has remained in this supine, neglected condition, getting worse every year; many of the books being much dirtied lately, the last time it was white-washed; and in 1793, at Mr. Mansfield's feast, part of the company dining there, some hundreds of the books were removed from their places, and have lain in a confused state ever since, without being restored to their proper places.

"In 1796, I presented to Mr. Clarke, then mayor, hints for improving it; but it still remains in the same state; and the motive of publishing this account is, to shew its present condition, and to stir up an emulation in the inhabitants of the Town and County, particularly those of the Town, to improve and increase it by a collection of modern books, to make it of more general utility. Public Libraries are of such benefit to mankind, that it is unnecessary to enlarge on their usefulness; and when one has been established, it is to be lamented that it is not encouraged and improved, especially in this enlightened age.

"Having fairly explained the condition in which it is, I shall beg leave to offer to the publick my plan for improving it. The Catalogue, being printed, will give information of the books it contains.

"As soon as this Work is printed, I propose to put 50 copies of it into the hands of some of the Booksellers of the Town and County[2]; and the profit arising from

[1] See before, p. 505.

[2] It is much to be regretted that Mr. Weston did not live to give effect to his benevolent intentions.—This very useful Writer, who died at Leicester, Oct. 20, 1806, in his 74th year, had formerly been a thread hosier in that town; and was author of several valuable publications, as will appear from the following list, communicated by himself not long before his death: 1. "Tracts on Agriculture and Gardening; with a Chronological Catalogue of Authors, from the Year 1480 to 1773," 1769, 8vo. 2. Second edition, enlarged, 1773. 3. "Gardener's Pocket Calendar," 1774, 18mo. 4. 5. Second edition, 17..; third edition, 1783.

from the fale to be applied for the ufe of the Library, with twenty volumes which I have publifhed, and a few others; and fhould hope, that *every Author now living* will follow this example: and if the Relations of the Deceafed would do the fame, a large number of books would foon be collected. And when fuch a plan is once really begun to be put into execution, there is no doubt but that, in this fcientific and enlightened age, the Nobility, Gentry, and Clergy of the county, would contribute either in books or money, efpecially if it be once properly fet on foot in the Town."

The *Codex Leiceftrenfis* (fo long and fo juftly the pride of this Library) was fent to Oxford, in 1671, by the efpecial permiffion of a Common Hall[1] of the Borough of Leicefter, for the ufe of Dr. Mill[2]; whofe collation of it is thus noticed by Wetftein, in his Prolegomena, p 53:

"Codex Leiceftrenfis, totum N. T. complectens, quem Thomas Hayne, Magifter Artium, natus Thruffingtoni, vico comitatûs Leiceftrienfis, dedit anno 1669[3], Bibliothecæ urbis Leiceftriæ. Eft feculi xiv in foliis tum membranaceis tum chartaceis temere permiftis fcriptus. Incipit à Matth. xviii. 5. Deficit ab Act. x. 45. ad xiv. 17; à Judæ 7 ad finem; ab Apoc. xxi. 1. ad finem libri. Ejus Collationem edidit Jo. Millius, fed ita ut & plurima omiferit, & multa perperam notaverit, & uti fufpicor frequenter Lincolnienfem pro Leiceftrienfi pofuerit. Epiftolæ ad Hebræos præfigit partem prologi Euthaliani, qui eft apud Millium anonymus ex Oecumenico. In hoc codice hiftoria adulteræ non reperitur fuo loco Jo. viii. (quod Millius affirmat, Prol. 1506) fed ad finem capitis Lucæ xxi. Hiftoria verò de fudore fanguineo Chrifti ex Luc. xxii. 43. 44. tranfpofita eft poft Matthæi xxvi 39. Poft Evangelia fequuntur Epif-

tolæ Paulinæ; deinde Acta, &c. Titulum Evangeliorum habet fingularem, ἐκ τῶ καζα Μάρκον Εὐαζγελία, ἐκ τῶ καζα Λϡκᾶν Εὐαζγελία, ἐκ τῶ καζα Ἰωάννην Εὐαζγελία. Multò autem accuratiùs hunc codicem contulerunt Jo. Jakfon & Gulielmus Tiffin, cujus variantes lectiones margini editionis Oxonienfis in octavo adfcripfit Rev. Gee, paftor apud Leiceftrienfes, quod exemplar cum Rev. Cæfar De Miffy fibi comparâffet, mecum liberaliter communicavit anno 1748. Huic codici gemellus ac fimilis eft Parif. 6. quem fupra defcripfi n. 13. Alterutro etiam aut utroque ufus eft Erafmus, qui inde lectiones fingulares in Annotationibus producit. Vid. in Marc. iii. 14. & 16.; iv. 21. 30. 40.; v. 33.; vi. 3.; viii. 11. 26.; ix. 11.; xiv. 36. 41.; Luc. xviii. 7.; Jo. vii. 26.; xi. 47.; Act. xiv. 19. Præcipuè vero notandum, hunc codicem ex verfione Latinâ interpolatum fuiffe: infcriptiones Epiftolarum Pauli Latinos fequuntur, ordo verborum idem eft ac in Latinis. Confenfum cum codice Cantabrigienfi etiam Millius obfervavit. Vide Marc. ii. 14.; Luc. xvi. 21.; xix. 37.; xx. 47.; xxiii. 29.; Jo. iv. 43.; v. 9. 19.; vi. 23. 24.; vii. 31.; viii. 24.; ix. 4.; xiii. 5.; xiv. 17.; xvi. 18.; quod & Bengelius faffus eft, in Introd. p. 415, fcribens ' in Evangeliftis Latinizare Leiceftrienfem.' Idem poterat affirmare de Epiftolis. Vid. Rom. v. 18.; viii. 38.; xiv. 23.; xv. 23.; xvi. 9.; 1 Cor. i. 15.; 2 Cor. vi. 15.; xii. 19.; καζέναν]ι Θεῷ. 1 Tim. vi. 19."

April 24, 1689, Giles Coker was elected Library-keeper, in the room of William Higgs, promoted to be mace-bearer. Mr. Coker died in or before the month of October in the fame year.

June 27, 1694, Samuel Wilcocks was chofen Library-keeper.

1783. 6 Fourth edition, in 12mo, 1787. 7. " Gardener's and Planter's Calendar; containing the Method of raifing Timber Trees, Fruit Trees, and Quick for Hedges; with Directions for Farming, and managng a Garden, every Month in the Year," 1773, 12mo. 8. Second edition. 9, 10, 11, 12. " The Univerfal Botanift," 4 vols. 8vo, 20 copper-plates, 1770, 1773. 13. " The Englifh Flora, defcribng 4000 Plants cultivated in the Nurferies." 1778, 8vo. 14. Supplement to ditto, 1780. 15. Treatife on Alabafter, 8 vols. 179... 16. " The Leiceftr Directory," 1794. 12mo. 17. With Supplements. 18. " The Gentleman and Lady's Gardener," in 8vo (for Mr. Edmades, feedfman). 1774. 19. " Ellis's Gardener's Calendar," 1774, 12mo (for Mr. Richardfon. bookfeller). (Printed of the above Work 21,000) 20 " The Nurferyna and Seedfmen's Catalogue of Trees, Shrubs, Plants, and Seeds, fold by them," 1774— 785, 12mo —To this ingenious Writer the Gentlemans Magazine was alfo indebted for feveral ufeful and entertaining articles; particularly ' A Catalogu of various Gardeners' Catalogues publifhed in ths Kingdom," vol. LXXIV. p. 1103; vol. LXXV. pp. 34, 1133. " Directions for managing Strawberries in Summer." vol. LXXV. pp. 504, 611; " The Natural Hiftory of Tobacco; the different Ufes to which it is applied; its native Place of Growth; Introduction into Europe, and into this Country; and Method of cultivating it in England," vol. LXXVI. p. 195. " A Review of the principal Authors on Horticulture and Botany," ibid. 097; " Critical Remarks on Botanical Writers, written in 1802," vol. LXXVII. p. 518 —Many others are the Works of which Mr. Wefton had formed more than the outline; and which, at various times, he propofed to give to the publick. Among thefe was one for which he iffued Propofals in 1800, under the title of " Leiceftriana; or, A Collection of Fugitive Pieces, in Verfe and Profe, arrange in Chronological Order." For this Work he had formed a large collection, " having found many amongft the papers of an Uncle then lately deceafed, who was curious in preferving literary curiofities." He had alfo nearly all Mr. Rozell's Works, and feveral of Mr Bickerftaffe's. In the fame year he announced as preparing for the prefs, and nearly completed, to be publifhed by fubfcription, in 8vo. in three or four numbers, " A Botanical Dictionary, explaining the Words in the Writings of Linnæu, particularly in the Genera and Species Plantarum, and Syftema Vegetabilium; with their Derivation from the Greek and latin; the Greek written alfo in Englifh Letters. With about Twenty Copper Plates, for explaining the Linnæan Syftem. On Two Copper Plates will be expl ined the Genders of 1344 Genera of Plants, by their Terminations. The reft of the Plants are already engraved." At the fame time he advertifed as alfo preparing for the prefs, " The Literary Hiftory of Leiceflerfhire; containing an Account of the Authors, Natives or Refidents of the Town or County; a Catalogue of their Works; and a Collection of Fugitive Pieces, from the Year 1500 to 1801, arranged in Chronological Order, with Anecdotes relating to the Authors, and Extracts from their Works. To which are added, an Account of the Foundation of the Town Library, &c. (fee p. 509.)—" As there is no Work extant in which there is a general account of the ingenius and learned which the Town and County have produced, I flatter myfelf that fuch a publication will not be unacceptable to the publick. As many valuable fugitive pieces have been printed in a detached manner, and are with difficulty found; thefe I have been collecting for feveral years, with many in manufcript, as this is not intended as a Catalogue of Books only; and flatter myfelf the collection will be found more numerous and entertaining than could have been expected. This has been increafed by a large number of a gentleman deceafed, curious in preferving fuch things. The Addreffes from Candidates at fome of the late Elections to the Electors, worthy of notice, will alfo be inferted, and remarkable epitaphs. With this plan, I have inferted the names of feveral Authors, and fome of their Works. The living ones I intend applying to by letter, or in perfon. As to the deceafed, I fhall think myfelf obliged to the furvivors of the family, or any perfons who will be fo kind as to give me information of their works, or any anecdotes relating to them." In 1805, he publifhed Propofals for " The Natural Hiftory of Strawberries, defcribing above Seventy Species and Varieties, their native Places of Growth, and Introduction into England; with the modern Improvements in their Cultivation, to have a regular Succeffion of Fruit in every Month of the Year. Embellifhed with Ten Copper Plates, explaining the Fructification of the Flower; the Leaves, Flowers, and Fruit of their natural Size and Colour, with a Steam-Flue and Water-Flue for Forcing them. To be printed in fmall 8vo, in Five Numbers." He had alfo prepared for the prefs, a fmall " Treatife on the Management of Fifh and Fifh Ponds, tranflated from the French; with Additions adapted to this Country."—But none of thefe Propofals have been carried into effect.

[1] Dr. Farmer, who cites " the Book of the Catalogue," obferves that it is there called " a *Greek* MS. of the *Latin* Teftament."

[2] In Mr. Jackfon's copy of Kufter's New Teftament, 1712, many of the MSS. of Dr. Mill are collated anew, and feveral MSS. added which Dr. Mill did not fee; almoft all the various readings of all the moft antient Chriftian Writers are added, &c. and many thoufand errors of Dr. Mill's edition are corrected. In a fheet or two of paper, prefixed to the Book itfelf, is a fuller account: " In hoc exemplari excufo N. T. habentur omnes variæ Lectiones Cod. MS. Leiceftrienfis, poft Millium denuò cum diligentiâ collati."—MS. Cod. Leic. eft Fol. ut dicunt, partim membranaceus, partim chartaceus. Scriptus fuit feculo poft natum Chriftum decimo tertio, quatenus conftat ex Charact. ex iftius Seculi à Montfaucon defcripto, qui clarè congruunt cum Charactere MS. Leic. Vide Palæograph. Græc. in cap. viii. lib. 4. p. 320.

[3] A miftake, probably, of Wetftein, for 1649, the year in which Mr. Hayne died.

The

The FREE GRAMMAR SCHOOL.

"The moſt antient mention," ſays Mr. Carte, "that I have met with of any School in Leiceſter is in a deed without date, whereby Robert Fitz-John, of Whitwick, granted to Adam le Sage, of Torp, formerly rector of the ſchools in Leiceſter, and to his heirs or aſſigns, certain lands in the field of Rotebi; to which were witneſſes, ſir Peter ſon of Roger, John ſon of the ſame, knights; John de Aneſti, John de Lumchamp, William Bate of Groby, &c. [Q. Whether the firſt of theſe witneſſes be not the ſame with Peter ſon of Roger, who was the firſt mayor of Leiceſter in 1246, and ſo continued till 1256 incluſively?]

"The next mention that I find made of a ſchool here is, that a biſhop of Carliſle had given land for the maintaining a free-ſchool in the pariſh of St. Margaret. This biſhop I take to have been John Penny, who was abbot of Leiceſter, afterwards biſhop of Carliſle, and lies buried in St. Margaret's church. This land, it is ſaid, Mr. John Beaumont about 1541 (at which time he was recorder, and a commiſſioner) ſold away; but by what authority doth not appear. Certain it is, the Corporation was diſſatisfied with what he had done; and therefore, March 11, 6 Edw. VI. at a common hall, they reſolved to endeavour the recovery of it; and for that and ſome other purpoſes ſent Mr. Robert Boughton, vicar of St. Martin's, to London, whoſe charges were borne, half by the town, and half by the pariſh of St. Margaret: but what progreſs he made in the matter I find not; only the event ſhews that this attempt proved abortive, and it is poſſible that the death of King Edward VI. might occaſion them to deſiſt from proſecution of the matter.

"The origin of the Free-ſchool is, by all perſons whom I have diſcourſed with about it, computed to have been in 1573; which is an error in itſelf, and an occaſion of other errors; and therefore I ſhall deliver my opinion, and then mention ſome of the circumſtances on which it is founded.

"My opinion is, that Thomas Wigſton, prebendary of the church of Newark, brother of the famous William Wigſton, founded the ſchool in the place where the ſchool-houſe now ſtands, and that he endowed it with lands; which, together with the guardianſhip or overſight of the ſchool, he entruſted with the maſter and confrater of his brother's Hoſpital, charging them to pay 10l. a-year to the maſter of the ſchool; and that thus it continued till the augmentation and new eſtabliſhing of it about 1573. The circumſtances upon which my opinion is grounded are as follows: 1. Leland aſſerts that Thomas Wigſton made the Free-ſchool in Leiceſter[1]. 2. John Pott, ſchoolmaſter of Leiceſter, is ſaid to be one of the fugitives that were gone beyond ſea, contrary to the Statute 13 Eliz. 3. I have ſeen, among other papers concerning the New Hoſpital, a rental of lands in 1561 and 1562, out of which the ſchoolmaſter is paid. 4. It was agreed, at a common hall, June 30, 1564, that one of the bells of St. Peter's church ſhould be ſold, to repair the School-houſe. All which was before the ſuppoſed foundation of the Free-ſchool, and confirms what I have ſuggeſted. And hence we learn how it comes to paſs that the Maſter and Confrater of Wigſton's Hoſpital are ſo much concerned in the viſitation and government of the School, though Queen Elizabeth in her grant takes no notice of them, but only of the Mayor, &c. Hence alſo we may obſerve how erroneouſly the 20l. a-year, which is paid by the Hoſpital to the Schoolmaſter, is all of it called the earl of Huntingdon's gift; whereas the earl, by his deed, gave only a rent-charge of 10l. a-year; and the other 10l. ariſes from the lands entruſted to the Hoſpital for maintenance of the School, &c.

"April 7, 15 Eliz. the queen, in conſideration of 35l. having granted to the mayor and co-burgeſſes of Leiceſter the materials of the decayed church of St. Peter[2]; they, according to their obligation, ſet about building a ſchool-houſe anew (which I ſuppoſe was on the ſame ground as the former) becauſe I find no account of the purchaſe of the ſite of it, and finiſhed it the next year; and at the ſame time they erected a new houſe at the North end of the ſchool-houſe for the head ſchoolmaſter to dwell in, and thereto laid all the backſide that lately was in the occupation of Johnſon, a maſon, reſerving to themſelves the rent of 20s. a-year[3]. For defraying theſe and ſome other charges, they laid themſelves, the twenty-four at 2s. and the forty-eight at 1s. each, May 7, 16 Eliz.

"The ſchool is ſituated on the Eaſt ſide of the High-croſs ſtreet, over againſt the Blue-boar-lane, and is ſeparated from the County Gaol by Free-ſchool lane. The building is a rugged pile of foreſt-ſtone, interſperſed with ſome pieces of wrought free-ſtone, lying in all directions. It is covered with ſlate. The upper room is aſſigned to the maſter, and the lower or ground-room to the two uſhers, whereof the upper teaches the Latin grammar, and the under-uſher Engliſh, all which have their ſalaries out of the benefactions[4]."

The ſtone in the left tablet in front is of modern erection, and has the following names of benefactors:

		£.	s.	d.
Queen Elizabeth, *per annum*	—	10	0	0
Henry earl of Huntingdon	—	20	0	0
Sir William Wigſton	— —	10	0	0
Sir Ralph Rawlett	— —	3	6	8
Mr. William Norrice	— —	3	6	8
Mr. James Ellis ſenior	— —	1	6	8
Mr. James Ellis junior	— —	3	0	0
Mr. John Stanly	— —	2	0	0
Mr. Thomas Gilbert	— —	5	0	0
Mrs. Dorothy Baker	— —	1	0	0
Mr. Robert Heyrick	— —	0	13	4
Mr. Thomas Clarke	— —	1	0	0
Mrs. Margaret Hobby	— —	0	12	0
Mr. Thomas Haine	— —	0	6	0

Mr. Tobias Heyrick (not on the tablet), 6s. 8d.

"Another tablet on the right has the national arms in the middle, and town cinquefoil on the left; at top a bull's head; date on the right ſide of the national arms, 1574. On the right, at bottom, in a circlet, 'Walter Rawlet' only in words. On the left, at bottom, ſeemingly a bare or uncovered head of a perſon unknown."

"Queen Elizabeth gave an annuity of 10l. *per annum* for maintenance of the head-uſher in the School, to be received of the Auditors for the Honour of Leiceſter, at Michaelmas and Lady-day.—This is now paid at Michaelmas only; but is uſually paid quarterly to the uſher.

Henry earl of Huntingdon gave 10l. *per annum* to the head-maſter of the School, to be paid by the Corporation out of certain grounds which they purchaſed of Mr. Freak, due at Michaelmas and Lady-day, and to be paid to the maſter of the New Hoſpital; which is done once in the year, at Michaelmas; and the maſter of the Hoſpital pays it to the maſter of the School at Michaelmas and Lady-day. Alſo, 10l. *per annum* more is paid him out of the chamber of the Town at the ſame times during pleaſure.

The ſame noble earl, Oct. 11, 18 Eliz. gave an annuity of 40s. apiece to two poor ſcholars in the School, and 3l. apiece to two at the Univerſity, which none of them were to enjoy above five years.

Sir Ralph Rawlett gave, out of his manor of Thedingworth, an annuity of 3l. 6s. 8d. for the under-uſher of the School, due at Michaelmas and Lady-day.—Theſe lands were purchaſed by Serjeant Newdigate; and the annuity is paid by his heirs. The Town pays the under-uſher quarterly.

Mr. William Norrice, once one of the aldermen, gave an annuity of 3l. 6s. 8d. for the head-uſher, payable out of a cloſe in the Abbey-gate. This is uſually paid to the head-uſher at Michaelmas and Lady-day. The ſaid uſher was enjoined by Mr. Norrice to bring ten of his ſcholars to the houſe of the ſaid Mr. Norrice by North-gate upon the ſecond

---

[1] See before, p. 502.   [2] See before, p. 399.   [3] See before, p. 400.   [4] Carte, MS.

Tuesday after Trinity Sunday in the forenoon, and there to sing the 113th Pfalm.

Mr. Robert Heyrick, once alderman, gave an annuity of 13s. 4d. *per annum* for the under-usher, payable out of his lands in Leicester, at Michaelmas only. This is paid out of the Grey Friers by the heirs of the said Robert Heyrick.

Mr. Tobias Heyrick, son and heir of the aforesaid Robert Heyrick, added to the said annuity 6s. 8d. for the same use, paid by his heirs at Michaelmas only.

Mr. Thomas Clarke, alderman, gave an annuity of 20s. for the under-usher, payable out of a piece of ground adjoining to the Soar, called *The Water Laggs*, at Michaelmas and Lady-day. This is paid to the usher by the chamberlains.

Margaret Hobby, widow, gave 12s. annuity for the under-usher, payable out of a house in the South gate. It is usually paid by the tenant to the usher. Item, there is paid out of the said house yearly, for the use of the poor, 12d. The said house was, in 1712, in the tenure of widow Owin.

Mrs. Dorothy Baker gave a sum of money to the Corporation, in trust, that they should yearly give to the ushers of the said School 10s. apiece, that each of them should teach their scholars to write.

Mr. James Ellis senior, an alderman, gave 26s. 8d. yearly out of a house in the parish of All Saints, in tenure of William Noone senior, baker, for the head usher [1]."

"The masters' salaries, &c. are; the head master, 40l. a-year, a house, with entrance-money from half a guinea to a guinea; the first usher, 24l. a-year, with a small garden-ground, entrance from a crown upwards; the second usher, 19l. 16s. with a house during pleasure, set at four guineas a-year, and no entrance-money. Scanty appointments for liberal education, but respectable in the reign of the foundress [2]."

By the Corporation-books it appears that the master of Wigston's Hospital had originally the power of recommending, if not the appointment, of the master and ushers; but this right has for nearly a whole century been exercised by the mayor and senior aldermen; sanctioned, however, by the testimonials of learned public characters, which are always a better ground of choice than private opinion.

To those who know that the founder of Wigston's Hospital was a principal founder also of the Free-school, it will not appear strange that the master of that Hospital should have been originally intrusted with some sort of superintendance of this seminary; which should, properly, be visited by the master and confrater; and Mr. Jackson, the last master who resided in Leicester, was a punctual attendant at the stated periods, accompanied generally by the Clergy of the respective parish-churches, and the Mayor of the Town [3], &c. But the master of Wigston's Hospital, in the present times, being no longer a resident, his visiting the School once a year would be only an useless intrusion.

Within the last dozen years there have not been more than about 50 boys, nor less than about 30.

The following charge occurs in the records of the Corporation:

"A. D. 1618, paid 9th Dec. to watchmen, for watching the School when the scholars were so unruly as to shut out their master, 4s. 3d."

Thomas Horne, M. A. of Magdalen Hall, Oxford, 1624, was schoolmaster at London, Leicester, Tunbridge, and at length at Eton, where he succeeded N. Grey; and continuing till his death, Aug. 22, 1654, was buried in the College chapel, Aug. 24 [4].

"1627, Mr. John Angel master. He was offered 20l. in 1636, if he would resign."

"1647, Nov. 22. Certain orders were made, at a common hall, to be observed by the schoolmaster and scholars of the Free-school.

"1648, Mr. Coleman, under-usher, was discharged the School by the *mayor and justices*, after being twenty years under-usher.

"1649, Mr. Millis was proposed for master by Mr. Lee; who afterwards wrote to Mr. Bahemeny, that his brother might supply his place.

"1651, Mr. Wood, master, from Croydon. Agreed, at a *common hall*, that if Mr. Wood would come to the Free-school, and be approved by the *mayor and visitors*, he should have the School.—Joseph Bickland, under-usher, it appears, was made by the master of the Hospital; and it was asserted by him, that it is the undoubted power of his place to present a schoolmaster.

"1662, Mr. David Thomas, head master, *recommended* by Mr. Meredith, warden of All Souls, and master of the Hospital.

"1667, Mr. Nathaniel Ball, master, recommended by Dr. Busby, at the *mayor's* request.

1670, Joseph Birkhead, M. A. head-schoolmaster, was a benefactor to the Town Library [5].

"1671, Mr. Wells was invited by the mayor and seniors to take the School.

"William Davy, under-usher, to hold during pleasure of the *mayor and aldermen who have been mayors.*

"1678, Mr. William Thomas, master, elected by a common hall; and his election confirmed by patent, dated Sept. 10, 1680. He continued to be the head-master for 34 years; was 28 years vicar of All Souls; and died Dec. 6, 1713.

"1684, Daniel Keene, M. A. of Jesus college, Cambridge, usher, by the *twenty-four*.

"1689, Mr. Kilby, head-usher, at a common hall.

"March 16, 1701-2, Joseph Hardy was elected to succeed Mr. Kilby as head-usher.

On the death of Mr. Thomas, the Rev. John Clayton, some time vicar of St. Nicholas, was elected head-master in 1713.

"Sept. 25, 1713, at a common hall, 3l. (the Town's free gift to the under-master) was increased to 8l.

"May 14, 1714, Samuel Elly chosen head-usher, in room of Mr. Hardy, who died April 21, 1714. Mr. Elly died June 18, 1734.

"Sept. 27, 1717, Mr. Adcocks, under-usher of the School, was allowed to live in a new house in Senvey gate, at an annual rent of one shilling [6]."

Rev. Gerrard Andrewes, M. A. succeeded Mr. Clayton as head-master of the Free-school in 1739; obtained the vicarage of St. Nicholas in 1757; resigned the school in 1762; and died in 1764. Of this gentleman a particular account, with a Pedigree of his family, and some particulars of the Free-school whilst under his direction, has been given in vol. III. p. 456; but, since that page was printed, the venerable Bp. of London (Dr. Beilby Porteus) has done himself great honour, by presenting, unsolicited, the valuable rectory of St. James, Westminster, to the Rev. Dr. Gerrard Andrewes, the very meritorious son of the late excellent schoolmaster.

The Rev. John Davenport, vicar of St. Nicholas, was elected head-master April 29, 1762; and died Feb. 6, 1769.

The Rev. James Pigott, M. A. was elected head-master Feb. 14, 1769; and resigned in 1799; when

The Rev. Samuel Heyrick, M. A. was elected; who resigned in 1802; and is now rector of Brampton in Northamptonshire.

On Mr. Heyrick's resignation, some of the inhabitants of the Town, who were dissatisfied with the mode of education, as being purely classical, remonstrated against the election of a classical master; but, after much newspaper altercation, application being made to counsel for an opinion, it was found that the charter would allow no other than a regularly-educated member of either of the Universities to be elected, and that the education given must be principally classical. Of course their remonstrance was withdrawn.

The present head-master, elected in 1802, is the Rev. Henry St. John Bullen, M. A. of Trinity college, Cambridge, and rector of Tuddenham, Suffolk.

The second master is the Rev. R. Davies, B. D. of Queen's college, Oxford, and vicar of Welton, co. Northampton, and of Llanwnog, co. Montgomery.

---

[1] Carte, MS.   [2] Bickerstaffe, MS.   [3] See Throsby, p. 366.   [4] Wood, Athen. Oxon. vol. II. p. 106.
[5] See p. 508.   [6] Thus far the extracts from the Corporation Books.

ACCOUNT

ACCOUNT OF PAYMENTS DUE TO THE MASTER AND USHERS OF THE FREE-SCHOOL.

HEAD-MASTER.	£.	s.	d.	
Free gift of Corporation -	16	0	0	⎫ Thefe fums
Do. by order Feb. 24, 1797	30	0	0	⎪ paid by the
Mr. Stanley's gift -	1	0	0	⎬ chamber-
Mr. Gilbert's do. -	3	0	0	⎭ lain.
Lord Huntingdon's do. -	10	0	0	⎫ Thefe paid
Wigfton's do. - -	10	0	0	⎬ by Mr.
	—			Pares, as
	70	0	0	agent to the
	—			mafter of
				Wigfton's
				Hofpital.

HEAD USHER.			
Mr. Norris's gift -	3	6	8
Mrs. Dorothy Baker's do. -	0	10	0
Mr. Stanley's do. -	0	13	4
Mr. Gilbert's do. -	1	10	0
Free gift of Corporation -	8	0	0

Thefe fums paid by the chamberlain.

Paid by the Receiver of the rents for the Duchy of Lancafter:

Queen Elizabeth's gift, 10l.; deducting poundage and fees, 17s. 6d. -	9	2	6

Paid by the chamberlain:

Rent of garden, in the occupation of Abell -	2	12	6

Paid by Mr. Pares, as agent to the mafter of Wigfton's Hofpital:

Wigfton's gift - -	1	0	0

	26	15	0

UNDER USHER.			
Mr. Clark's gift -	1	0	0
Mr. Ralph Rowlett's do. -	3	6	8
Mrs. Hobby's do. - -	0	12	0
Mr. Stanley's do. - -	0	6	8
Mr. Gilbert's do. - -	0	10	0
Mrs. Baker's do. - -	0	10	0
Free gift of Corporation -	3	0	0
Ditto - - -	5	0	0
Ditto - - -	5	0	0

Thefe fums paid by the chamberlains.

Paid by Mr. Pares, as proprietor of the houfe:

Heyrick's gift, iffuing out of a houfe in the Friar-lane	1	0	0

Paid by the chamberlain:

Rent of a houfe in the Sanvey gate - -	6	6	0

	26	11	4

	£.	s.	d.
Payments to the Head-mafter -	70	0	0
Head Ufher -	26	15	0
Under Ufher -	26	11	4
	123	6	4

CHARITY SCHOOLS IN LEICESTER.

" The firft of thefe was begun by Mr. Stephenfon; and continued by his daughter Mrs. Lydia Stephenfon, who died in 1720; and after by another daughter, Mrs. Allen. In this fchool are 24 boys, clothed in grey, having coats, caps, bands, ftockings, and fhoes [and in 1717 began to have fhirts alfo given them, which continued only one year]; but neither waiftcoats nor breeches. From 1711 to 1717 about 29 were apprenticed from this fchool. The mafter who teaches them has 8l. per annum[1]."

Matthew Simons, efq. about 1714, left 10l. 4s. for cloathing twelve boys; 1l. 16s. to buy them Bibles; and 4l. a-year for teaching them: they are taught by the under ufher of the Free-fchool[2].

In 1720, twenty poor boys, belonging to the town of Leicefter at large, were taught and clothed at the charge of the Regiftrar; and ten poor girls taught and cloathed at the expence of the Commiffary[2].

" Another fchool was founded by Walter Ruding, efq. about 1710, at firft for 12 boys, but in 1717 for 16, to be chofen out of any parifh. They are found wholly in cloathing; and their outward garment is blue. The mafter is allowed 6l. per annum; and is required to teach them to read and write, and alfo arithmetic as far as the Rule of Three; for which he receives 10s. for each boy, when he goes to be apprenticed, over and above his conftant falary. At Chriftmas Mr. Ruding gives the mafter, his fon, and the boys, a feaft; for which he allows 12d. each boy, and 12d. for the mafter. In about three or four years [this was written in 1717], fix of thefe boys have been apprenticed; for which purpofe Mr. Ruding gave with each boy 5l.[3]"

" Under the care of Mr. Holbetch, by the charity of an unknown perfon, are ten boys, of St. Margaret's parifh, to whom are given coats, caps, fhirts, bands, fhoes, ftockings, and buckles, and proper books, particularly Common Prayer-books. John Borma the mafter, who teaches them, has 50s. and a coat. If their parents fet them out to be apprentices, and they behave themfelves well during their apprenticefhip, each of them, at his coming out of his time, has 5l. given him to begin the world.—N. B. Thefe ten boys began to be taken care of about Midfummer 1716. If their parents can fpare them, they may be taught gratis by the under ufher of the Free-fchool; and therefore the gentleman takes care only for the inftruction and good government of them on Sundays, when they are ftrictly bound to attend the mafter whom he provides for them, by whom they are taught to read, catechized, and conducted to church, &c.[3]"

St. Margaret's Charity-school.

In the year 1806 was erected, by the unparalleled exertions of the Rev. R. Davies, curate of St. Margaret's, on a piece of ground commonly called *The Butt Clofe*[4], in Church-gate, a fpacious building, containing two rooms, each competent to accommodate fifty children; one for boys, the other for girls; together with a houfe at each end for the refidence of the mafter and miftrefs. The expence of the building was defrayed by the voluntary contributions of the parifhioners; to which Mrs. Harris, a lady diftinguifhed for her benefactions to the Charities of Leicefter, gave 100l.; and at her death bequeathed the intereft of 100l. more for its fupport. In this School 100 children are annually taught reading, writing, and accompts; the entire expence of which, together with the cloathing, is fupported by voluntary fubfcription.

Shambles[5], or Green-coat School.

The place now occupied by the charity-boys belonging to the fchool founded by Alderman Gabriel Newton (who in his life-time had built a fchool at the North-eaft corner of St. Nicholas's church-yard)

---

[1] Carte, MS. [2] Magna Britannia, Leicefterfhire, p. 1393. [3] Carte, MS.

[4] The Butt Clofe, which was purchafed from fir Nigel Grefley, has lately been ufed as a wood-yard; but was formerly given by Queen Elizabeth to the freemen of Leicefter, for the purpofe of public fports, and efpecially archery; whence, from the butts, or fhooting marks, it received the name. Walk through Leicefter, 1804, p. 20.

[5] Thefe Shambles, built in 1682, at the expence of 55l. for the ufe of the Town butchers on the week-day markets, were but for a fhort time ufed for that purpofe. The other Shambles, a regular-formed building, which ftood in the Market-place, having been found to be of no ufe except on the Saturday, were taken down in 1746, at the erection of the Exchange. The Gainfborough, and fome wretched fmall buildings which were taken down about the fame time, were miferably inconvenient.

was

was originally the Shambles. It is fituate near St. Nicholas church, facing the Jewry-wall; and on the front of it is infcribed,

"This Charity-fchool for 35 Boys was founded by the Corporation, as Truftees in the late Alderman Gabriel Newton's [1] will, anno 1785."

The boys are cloathed in green, with red collars on their coats, a black cap, and are allowed a half-penny roll for breakfaft; they are taught reading, writing, arithmetic, and pfalmody [2], and apprenticed with 5l. They have two mafters, one at a falary of 30l. and the other 10l. per annum; the latter teaches them to fing, at ftated times, and attends them to church, with the other mafter, on Sundays, Wednef-days, and Fridays [3].

St. Mary's School.

On a line of ftone in the front of this edifice, which ftands near the church, is infcribed: "A Cha-rity-fchool, founded and fupported by voluntary fub-fcriptions, erected 1785;" principally by the in-habitants and congregation at that church; towards which the preacher, the Rev. Mr. Robinfon, may be juftly faid to have done much. On the door a flit, infcribed, "For the benefit of this Charity-fchool." On a tablet without: "This building, which contains two feparate fchools, and a dwelling-houfe for the mafter's family, was erected by volun-tary fubfcriptions in the year 1785, for the religious education of the children of the poor in this parifh, who fhall be recommended by the annual fubfcribers."

Two ftatues, a boy and a girl, properly habited, ftand in niches over the door, thus underwritten: "Thefe figures were erected at the joint expence of John Johnfon and John Horton, efqrs. London; both natives of Leicefter. By the kindnefs of our bene-factors, we are here inftructed in the Holy Scriptures, which are able to make us wife unto falvation."

In this fchool 45 boys and 35 girls are educated, not only in reading, &c. but in religious duties; and the girls, moreover, in habits of induftry. The children are clothed in light brown, kept exceedingly orderly and clean, and are frequently attended, or rather fuperintended, by their benefactors. A mafter and miftrefs refide. The falary of the former is 39l. and the latter 15l. a-year. It coft building 600l. [4]

St. Martin's School.

This alfo is a fchool for the education of the chil-dren of the poor belonging to the parifh, built and fupported by voluntary fubfcription. The building (which is, doubtlefs, one of the prettieft ornaments, as a public edifice, in the town) was erected in the year 1791, at the expence of 950l. It educates 35 boys, and 30 girls; and ftands in Friar-lane, on a healthful fpot. Here refide a mafter and a miftrefs, in genteel apartments; the former on a falary of 30l. and the latter 20l. a-year. The former is indulged by the committee to educate with his boys fix fcho-lars, for his better maintenance, who are not upon the eftablifhment.

An annual fermon is preached, refpectively, for the benefit of St. Mary's and St. Martin's fchools. At prefent they are each without a permanency: it is devoutly to be wifhed [5].

There is a Sunday-fchool for each of the Churches of the Eftablifhed Religion.

There is alfo a large daily free-fchool, by fubfcrip-tion, for 20 boys and 20 girls, of any denomination be-longing to the Prefbyterian or Great Meeting; and a Sunday-fchool alfo for 80 fcholars.

At the Independent Chapel is a Sunday-fchool.

The General Baptifts have a large Sunday-fchool, at their Meeting in Friar-lane, carried on upon Mr. Lancafter's improved plan of education.

ANTIENT PAINTED GLASS.

In the hall and kitchen of the houfe of Mr. Stephens, in High Crofs-ftreet, on a long range of lights, is a regular feries of antient paintings on glafs, as delineated, in 1790, at my requeft, by Mr. Throfby; con-taining, among other things, the figures of four Saints, and the Seven Sacraments of the Church of Rome [6].

Plate XXXVI.
1. St. Margaret.
2. St. Chriftopher.
3. St. Katharine.
4. St. George.
[A cypher [7] of W. R. accompanies this figure.]
5. The Annunciation.
6. The Birth of Jefus.
7. The Wife Men's Offering.
8. The Prefentation of Jefus in the Temple.
9. The Refurrection.
10. The Afcenfion.
11. The Transfiguration.
12. The Holy Euchariſt.

Plate XXXVII.
13. The Affumption.
14. Part of the fame.
15. Marriage.
16. Baptifm.
17. Confirmation.
18. Holy Orders.
19. Penance.
20. Extreme Unction.
21. Vifiting the Sick.
22. Burial of the Dead.
23. The Trinity.
24. Prifoner releafed.
25. Relieving the Hungry and Thirfty.
26. Clothing the Naked.
27. Creft of Town Arms.
28. The Town Arms.

---

[1] In this fchool, Mr. Newton in his life-time had 35 boys clothed in green, with green caps, and fair bands, an halfpenny coarfe roll each for breakfaft, taught reading, writing, and accompts; and apprenticed with 5l. And he intended at his death to provide 5l. to enable them, after their fervice, to launch into bufinefs; but was fo croffed, maligned, and perfecuted, by an ungrateful tribe, that after a few years he broke his charity here, though he promifed to do fomething that way by will, and got me to make propofals to thofe diftant communities who enjoy his charitable eftablifhments. Lincoln difregarded our tender—they were filent; and Mr. Newton would not fuffer me to repeat my application, faying they were forry dogs, and cared not for their poor. He declared, if he had not been maltreated here in his native place, he intended to have en-dowed it with his whole fortune. It is computed that he left lands and money to the amount of 16,000l. for charitable ufes. His executors, inftead of enforcing the will, by an over-caution fearched for his neareft relation; and met with a Richard Walker, a pauper, a member of Trinity Hofpital here. Him they produced to Chancery; and acknowledged, though on difputable grounds, as firft of kin. I found out the man, and drew up his pretenfions; but he, inftead of accepting of a pecuniary prefent, and affifting them to pafs a fine, got advice and fupport, to embarrafs them feveral years. But the will emerged at laft in its full force in every refpect." W. Bickerstaffe.

[2] The Founder's will particularly directs that they fhall be "inftructed in toning and pfalmody."

[3] Throfby, p. 372.   [4] Ibid.   [5] Throfby, p. 373.

[6] 1. Baptifm (marked 16); 2. Confirmation (17); 3. Penance (19); 4. The Holy Euchariſt (12); 5. Extreme Unction (20); 6. Holy Orders (18); 7. Marriage (15).

[7] The initials probably of the artift; which may affift in afcertaining the age of the workmanfhip.

Throfby del.1788.　　　　　　　　　　　　　　　Rowe ſc.

This Figure & part of 13. are cover'd by a wall.

LEICESTER INFIRMARY.

The hiftory of this moft excellent Inftitution will with great propriety be prefaced by the Addrefs to which it owed its origin; Dr. Watts, the firft projeftor [1] of the Infirmary, having recommended his benevolent plan in language the moft forcible and convincing:

"The great utility of the laborious poor, thofe fupporters of fociety, upon whom the wealth, upon whom the profperity, upon whom the defence, upon whom the very exiftence of the Nation, doth fo manifeftly and mainly depend. The but too obvioufly difgraceful and fatal neglect of them. The leaving them to the vexatious and diftrefsful confequences of the various deplorable accidents and diftempers to which they are fo liable; or, what is ftill far worfe, a prey to thofe ignorant, thofe interefted, to thofe enterprifing, to thofe utterly unfeeling, intruders upon the Faculty, and depredators upon property and life, who in this Nation (though fo happy in its Laws and Government) fo grievoufly abound. The natural and alarming confequences of fuch unnatural and evident neglect; a numerous fickly, maimed, languifhing, and burthenfome poor; a weakly offspring; and population decreafing from this, at leaft as much as from any other fingle caufe. The improbability, not to fay impoffibility, of having them taken care of fpeedily, effectually, comfortably, and cheaply, at home. But the Minifter of each parifh, and the Gentlemen of the Faculty, can beft tell, and let every honeft and experienced one teftify, the frequent confequences in fufferance, and at length in expence, of even the commoneft accidents, whether contufions, or the flighteft puncture or cut; efpecially in depraved habits, in bad fituations, and unfavourable feafons; through want of proper, or under (what is ftill worfe) improper care: what foul ulcers, and even foul bones, and ftiff joints, thence proceed. Thofe gentlemen can alfo beft tell, what complicated and radicated diftempers arife from, that univerfal one amongft the poor, worms; or from, that almoft as univerfal one, intermittents, fuperinduced, amongft other caufes, thereby; degenerating into putrid fevers; bringing on jaundice, dropfy, afthma; or terminating in deep-feated abfceffes: whence a languifhing, hopelefs life, and a premature death. Here is no exaggeration; but the too daily experience, alas! affording but too full and melancholy evidence of thefe.

"Any perfon, who at all adverts to the ftate of the laborious poor, cannot but obferve how few have houfes fit for a bed of ficknefs, how very few can be attended properly in their habitations, fuch as they are; being fometimes at great diftance from each other, vaftly further from the profeffors of Phyfic and Surgery, which muft make the charge of medicine and attendance utterly infupportable to them; whence, either left to themfelves, or falling into unfkilful and difhoneft hands, they become objects of the moft complicated mifery and diftrefs. The fecondary inducements arife from the manifeft and manifold advantages of the many Eftablifhments of this kind, which have in various Counties already taken place: advantages, fuch to the fick and maimed poor as are indeed not to be had by even perfons of fortune in their private families. Thofe admitted are not only accommodated with every thing neceffary or proper for them in their refpective conditions; but have fuch conftant and regular attendance of perfons thoroughly verfed in every branch of Phyfic; fuch well-infpected drugs, fuch appropriate medicines, fuch

[1] His philanthropic endeavours were, fo early as 1766, thus celebrated by the Rev. Mr. Morton, a Northamptonfhire Divine:

" WAFT, ye frolic Winds! away
Cowardly Fear, your proper prey:
Secure in fuch a theme, the Bard
Laughs at each felfifh low regard.
The meaneft of the Mufes' train,
Wifhing a Pindar's power in vain,
Dares in fo good a caufe defy
Contempt's rude tongue, and Cenfure's baleful eye.

" When roll'd the deep-mouth'd Bard along,
The tide of dithyrambick fong,
While all the echoing world around
The double mount reflects the found;
What was the elevating deed
Crown'd with this immortal meed
Did feats of ftrength or fkill well done,
On the athletic dufty plain,
The race by Theron or by Hiero won
Engrofs th' inimitable ftrain?
Inftant breaking from his chain,
Nobly fung the Theban Swan,
The Patriot, Legiflator, Friend of Man:
WATTS! could I equal Pindar's lays,
As equal is thy worth, equal fhould be thy praife.

" Ambition! execrable name!
Back to the Hell, from whence you came:
Perifh the wreath, tho' all the Nine
Confpire th' ill-fated flowers to twine,
Perifh the Bard, who ftrives, in Virtue's fpite,
To deck the foes of Man, the fiends of night,
With ornaments the Mufes meant to grace
The' friends, the guardian angels of the human race.

" This wife, benevolent defign,
Envy, tho' ever bafely prone
To damn the nobleft projects not her own,
Dares not openly malign.
Hardly in fecret undermine.
Prejudice, whofe jaundic'd fight
With her own yellow tinges fair and white,
Is forc'd to fay fhe fees aright.
Ridicule forbears his jeft;
Goodnefs, like Truth, will ftand his teft.
Avarice with feeming warmth muft now expand
The long-contracted heart and hand:
Mifcreants like thefe muft now controul
Their native narrownefs of foul;
Mifcreants like thefe muft feign they feel,
Too feeble to oppofe concurrent hearty zeal.

" Mufe! tell each churlifh harden'd elf,
Who feels for none befides himfelf;

Whofe heart has never learnt to glow
' At others good, or melt at others woe;'
Tell them, that the liberal Arts
Have never civiliz'd their better parts:
Nor could—the heart that's made of rock
Is ftill companion to a head,
Made of thickier, heavier lead,
That Culture's every art will mock:
Incapable of being grac'd,
Either with fentiment or tafte,
Nor Mufe nor Grace can work on fuch a block.
Mufe! tell the churls, that, vers'd in Nature's fchool,
You ever found a churl a blockhead and a fool.

" Gods! fhall a wretch, infulting common fenfe,
Make to Nobility pretence,
Who wants humanity:
Lefs than a Man a Noble muft he be!
In vain his head a mitre wears,
Whofe heart no human imprefs bears;
Lefs than a Lay-plebeian he!
Titles nor coronets impart
The patent of a noble heart.
Not Granby's high illuftrious birth;
Not Granby's courage, proves the man of worth:
Was not a Granby, like the truly brave,
Tho' pleas'd to conquer, better pleas'd to fave.

" The wounds of Poverty to heal,
Which oft the undeferving feel;
To fave her, in a dangerous hour,
From an Empirick's fatal power;
To make to her thofe bleffings known,
Enjoy'd before by Wealth alone;
While Affiduity and Art,
With Tendernefs, act each their part,
To mitigate the boiling ire
Of Fever's unremitting fire.
To make the pale and quiv'ring lip
The Soul-recalling cordial fip;
To ftop th' involuntary groan,
Extorted by the tort'ring ftone,
Bid Bloom and Vigour once more feek
The feeble limb and faded cheek;
To make the lame ' his crutch forego,
And leap exulting like the roe;'
To eafe th' ideal widow's fear,
Prevent the future orphan's tear;
And thus by pious alms conduce
To private good and public ufe.
Say ye of fentimental kind,
Is it not luxury of mind

such exact diet, such experienced nurses and assistants; such convenience of external applications, as of hot and cold baths, pumpings, sweating-chairs, and other collateral aids; that it must be an happy combination of circumstances, indeed, under which persons of wealth and distinction themselves can be so assisted.

" The advantages to the community in prompt relief, speedy and radical cures, whereby so very many are kept from being long a load alike to society and themselves; which advantages are so very conspicuous, where men with minds open to conviction attend duly thereto; and result indeed so immediately from the above, that it would be impertinent to specify them here. The result of a proper enquiry into the state of the sick and maimed poor, how very greatly they stand in need of, and how very highly they deserve, better care; the result of an inquiry into the nature and obligations of our duty to them, and therein to the universal Lord: The result of an enquiry into the manner wherein the most consolotary, the most efficacious, the most endearing, at the same time the least expensive assistance, can be given, will, I doubt not, be, that a Public Infirmary, not only in this, but in every County, is required. Whether the voice of the most œconomical polity, the voice of reason, of humanity, of religion, be heard, each loudly declareth, that the most adequate relief of the distressed, to the disburdening the parishes, to the credit of the nation, to the credit of this Province, to the credit of each individual Subscriber, to the endearing the rich to the poor; to the glory of that unspeakable great and good Being, who delighteth in mercy, and to the obtaining that mercy pronounced upon the merciful, of which not only the Nation in general, but each individual, so very greatly standeth in need.

" Much more might certainly be added concerning the expediency and necessity of an institution in every view agreeable to the dignity of the County, and for the public good. But the lives and limbs of those tillers of our fields, by the sweat of whose brow we break bread; the lives and limbs of those soldiers and sailors, who are at once the intrepid assertors of our liberty, and that of mankind; the ease and relief of our compatriots and comprovincials, of those our fellow-sufferers who have truly the post of honour in this life of manly trial here below, and are heirs of the same sure and immortal hope: Motives these so exceedingly interesting and important, the great characteristic of the Nation so prevalent also and diffused, that it would be an insult to enlarge. Only be it permitted to add, that I write in the fullest and most experimental persuasion of the necessity of what I have undertaken to recommend; that I nevertheless most heartily wish the affair was in abler hands; that I am too well acquainted with my station to presume, and with the rights of mankind, whatever were my station, to pretend to dictate, in a manner of so general and weighty concern.

" If, either in virtue of any personal experience, or of the materials which I have collected, or of the assistance wherewith I am favoured, I can in any shape serve the community, and that (I hope evidently) without any the least interested intent, I shall have a great additional cause to bless and praise that good God, under whom I submit this to all to whom it any way relateth, and principally to those who in their exalted station may, through the divine influence, best promote and bring it speedily to good effect. I would hope, that it will not appear assuming or presumptuous in me, that, in the humble duties of mine, I endeavour thus to render myself an useful (being very truly an affectionate) servant of the Community in general, and of my native County in particular.   W. WATTS, M. D."

Dr. Watts, whose family resided at Danet's Hall near Leicester, was educated for a Physician; and afterwards entered into holy orders, but obtained no considerable preferment in the Church. With a slender fortune he lived usefully; and died, an honour to his family and friends, Dec. 17, 1786, aged 61 [1].

More rich, exalted, and refin'd,
Than sense, than wealth, the world can give?
And does there such a worldling live,
Who would not, for this pleasure's sake,
A friend of the unrighteous Mammon make,
Could you admit the cruel curse,
With your worst foe his heart; you cannot wish him worse.

" This is the truly Golden use of pelf,
The loan the universal Lord
Deigns to own, and to reward
As lent unto himself:
These the first fruits that sanctify the whole,
Of a dead mass the vital soul.
Should, ye Benevolent, in evil day,
Should Riches take their wings, and fly away,
Tho' thus by virtuous Violence bound to stay:
Hence will Reflection's conscious power
Strike out the most enliv'ning ray,
To chear that sad and gloomy hour.
Should Riches stay—Disease and Pain assail;
These, when Physic's power shall fail,
These will make your sickly bed,
These support your drooping head,
These the cordial influence shed,
As grateful and refreshing found,
As dews distilling on the thirsty ground.
And when Death, who summons all,
Shall give the rich the common call;
These, ere your Spirit breaks away
From its frail tenement of clay,
At Heav'n's Tribunal shall appear,
To plead your cause, and prove your ablest patron there.

" Hail, Charity! whom Pity bore
Unto Humanity in days of yore.
No sooner true Religion came,
Than to the venerable dame
Her beauty and her worth was known;
Strait she adopts her for her own,
And christens her Benevolence.
Now thro' her lore to full perfection grown,
Her matchless merit to proclaim,
And give her just pre-eminence;
She owns her of more worth possess'd,
Than the two Sisters * she had given birth,   * Faith and Hope.
And nourish'd at her breast,
Tho' they were Heav'nly-born—she sprang from earth.
'Tis her's, on Nature's noblest plan,
In sympathetic bands to bind
The universal human kind,
Making a Brother of the Man:

Her heart still prompt at wretchedness to grieve,
And her hand still extended to relieve;
The doing good her sole employ,
Her meat and drink, and only joy.
Nature's dissolution past,
When her two Sisters shall have breath'd their last,
She, snatch'd from Earth's annihilated frame,
Shall gain that Heaven from whence they came;
And dwell for ever with the blest above,
In happiness as boundless as her love.
Oh Britain! Oh my Country! need I tell,
That 'tis with thee this Fair delights to dwell,
Where she beholds Love's labour thrive so well:
While in this her dear retreat
She sees her thousand structures rise,
Grandly useful, simply great;
Not Heaven's own structures shine more fair in Heaven's
own eyes.

" Britain! 'tis to her you owe
All the good that you enjoy;
'Tis thro' her, you do not know
Any ill that would destroy.
Cherish the precious guest, nor drive her hence;
Not your own rocks or fleets so sure defence.
Then may, O Watts, thy plan of perfect love,
Like the stirr'd waters' circles still expand,
O'er district and o'er district move,
Till it encompass all the land.
So, Britain! give your Patroness to plead
A good against each guilty deed.
So may she hide the multitude of crimes
Born in these flagitious times;
So may the vengeful ministers of death
Harmless, tho' furious, fit at her command;
Black Pestilence restrain his blasting breath,
Pale Famine hold his blighting hand.
So may no elements, in earth's dark womb,
Be e'er permitted to engage
With sulphureous devouring rage,
Your living Sons and Cities to entomb;
But Industry, with chearful smiles,
Reap the reward of all her toils;
While laugh your Vales with golden grain,
And Commerce whitens all the liquid plain.
Still more than conquerors in foreign wars,
So may you triumph still o'er feudal jars;
Still see your sails to willing winds unfurl'd,
Ride o'er the willing waves, and rule the watery world."

[1] See his epitaph at Medbourne, in vol. II. p. 723.

The

The Infirmary ftands within the limits of St. Mary's parifh, at the extremity of the Southern part of the Town, on the fite of the old chapel of St. Sepulchre; and is reprefented in Plate XXXII. in two points of view. It is erected upon a plan, which, for its convenience and utility, received the approbation of the great Howard, whofe experience and obfervation qualified him for a competent judge; and is calculated to admit, exclufive of the fever ward, 54 patients, without reftriction to county or nation; and was opened in 1771 for the reception of patients, fick and lame, from any country. The building is plain and neat, with two wings, fronted by a garden, the entrance to which is ornamented with a very handfome iron gate, the gift of the late truly benevolent Shukburgh Afhby, efq. of Quenby.

A two-handed pump on the back near the houfe forces water to the top of the Infirmary into a refervoir, containing 60 hogfheads, which fupplies every ward. Another pump in the wafh-houfe fupplies the bath.

The following are fome of the names of the noblemen and gentlemen who were the earlieft and chief benefactors to the Infirmary: Shukburgh Afhby, efq. 300*l.*; Jofeph Cradock, efq. of Leicefter, 100*l.*; fir Wolftan Dixie, bart. 100*l.*; John Darker, efq. 300*l.*; Charles Jennens, efq. 100*l.*; Anthony James Keck, efq. 300*l.* and 500*l.* left to him by his mother to be difpofed of to charitable ufes; fir John Palmer, bart. 300*l.*; Charles-James Packe, efq. 100*l.*; fir George Robinfon, 100*l.* — Annual fums: Jofeph Bunney, efq. 10*l.* 10*s.*; fir Thomas Cave, bart. 10*l.* 10*s.*; Jofeph Cradock, efq. of Gumley, 10*l.* 10*s.*; right hon. the earl of Denbigh, 21*l.*; right hon. the countefs of Denbigh, 10*l.* 10*s.*; right hon. the earl of Huntingdon, 20*l.*; Charles Jennens, efq. 10*l.* 10*s.*; his grace the duke of Montague, 20*l.*; right hon. lady Maynard, 10*l.* 10*s.*; Samuel Phillipps, efq. 10*l.* 10*s.* and a gift of 50*l.*; Henry Palmer, 10*l.* 10*s.*; right hon. the earl of Stamford, 20*l.*; right hon. lord vifcount Wentworth, 15*l.* 15*s.*; Mrs. M. Wigley, 10*l.* 10*s.*; and Mrs. Anne Wigley, 50*l.* and 2*l.* 2*s. per annum*, &c.

The Officers appointed at or foon after the eftablifhment of this Houfe were; Prefident, his Grace the Duke of Montague; Vice-prefidents, the Earls of Huntingdon, Stamford, and Harborough; Lords Vifcount Wentworth and Maynard[1]; Vifitor, the Right Rev. the Lord Bifhop of Lincoln; Phyficians, Drs. Vaughan and Arnold; Treafurer, Jofeph Bunney, Efq.; Auditors, Samuel Oliver and Henry Coleman, Efquires.

The furgeons of Leicefter attend in weekly rotation.

The following ftatutes and rules for the government of the Infirmary were compiled by Dr. Vaughan; who received the thanks of the firft general meeting of the fubfcribers in terms the moft flattering and honourable.

I. The building known by the name of the Infirmary, with the clofe and garden adjoining, fhall be vefted, as a truft, in a certain number of gentlemen, conformable to the directions of the late Lord Chancellor Yorke; who fhall likewife be governors of the fame.

II. All fubfcribers of two guineas or more annually fhall be governors during payment; and all benefactors of 50*l.* or more, at one time, fhall be alfo governors during life.

III. From the lift of governors fhall be chofen the following great officers, who are to remain fo for life, or as long as they continue fubfcribers; a prefident, vice-prefident, and a vifitor; to whofe infpection every tranfaction refpecting the Infirmary fhall at all times be open: and each of whom fhall be empowered to call a fpecial meeting, fo often as to them fhall appear neceffary; obferving the form directed in the 15th ftatute.

IV. A general board of governors fhall be held at four ftated times every year; viz. on the Thurfday preceding the 24th of June, which is to be confidered as the principal annual meeting; on the Thurfdays preceding the 29th of September, the 25th of December, and the 25th of March; or oftener on fpecial occafions.

V. The power of making and repealing laws, and of electing or removing officers, fhall be vefted in the general board only.

VI. There fhall be a weekly committee, or board of governors, confifting of five at leaft, who are to meet every Tuefday, by 11 o'clock, at the Infirmary.

VII. At the general board held next before Midfummer, a treafurer fhall be annually chofen out of the governors, who fhall give fecurity, to fuch perfons as the general board fhall appoint, for the due accounting for all fuch money as he fhall receive for the ufe of the Infirmary; and fhall pay all fuch bills as are ordered by the general or weekly board, fuch order being firft figned by the fecretary.

VIII. The treafurer, at every weekly board, is to take the chair; or, in his abfence, a chairman fhall be appointed by the members then prefent; who fhall have a cafting vote. And at every general board the proceedings of the former, and at every weekly board the proceedings of the laft weekly board, fhall be read over; and all laws and orders made at one general board fhall be in force until the next general board, but no longer, unlefs confirmed by two-thirds of the governors prefent at fuch fubfequent general board; and all orders of the weekly committee are to continue in force till repealed by fome fubfequent weekly or general board.

IX. The proceedings of every board fhall be fairly regiftered, and figned by the chairman.

X. At the general board held next before Midfummer, two auditors fhall be chofen from the governors, to infpect and audit the accompts of the Infirmary, and to report, from time to time, to the general board; and at the end of every year, viz. at Midfummer, fhall draw out the accompts of the charity, calling to their aid fuch affiftance as may be neceffary. They fhall alfo ftate the number of patients received and difcharged in the year, and give an abftract of the proceedings of the governors, and fhall report the fame to the general board.

XI. One or more of the contributors refiding in town fhall be appointed, in the order they ftand in the alphabetical lift, at every weekly board, to vifit the houfe once every day for the enfuing week, each of which, in cafe of ficknefs or neceffary avocation, may appoint another contributor to be his deputy. When vifiting, they fhall enquire whether the rules concerning officers, fervants, and patients, have been obferved; whether prayers have been duly read; whether the patients and fervants have been guilty of fwearing, drunkennefs, or any immorality or indecency; whether the provifions are good, and whether they have been carried out of the houfe, or brought into the patients, clandeftinely; and they are to enter what they think proper to be obferved in a book provided for that purpofe, and fhall attend the next weekly board.

XII. An apothecary, fecretary, and matron, fhall be appointed by the general board, and fuch nurfes and fervants as are neceffary to attend the Infirmary, after the firft appointment by the weekly board.

XIII. An apothecary fhall from time to time infpect the fhop, and fee that the medicines are properly compounded, and good in their kind, who fhall be called the vifiting apothecary.

XIV. The weekly board fhall infpect the obfervations of the houfe vifitors, regulate all matters relating to the admiffion and difcharge of patients (fubjecting neverthelefs the admiffion of them to the determination of the phyficians, who are the only judges how far the cafe of a patient renders him proper for an in or out-patient, or whether he fhould be admitted a patient in any refpect); they fhall enquire into the conduct of officers and fervants, examine and pafs accompts, order payments, execute the orders of the general board, and prepare fuch matters as are proper to be laid before the fame.

XV. When a vacancy fhall happen in any of the offices, or in the place of apothecary, fecretary, or matron, the weekly board fhall fummon a general board to fill up the vacancy, unlefs the ftated general board fhall happen at a convenient diftance of time; and, till fuch election be made, the weekly board

[1] See p. 522.

fhall

fhall appoint a perfon or perfons to act in the vacant office.

XVI. The weekly board, feven members being prefent, fhall have power to fummon a general board, upon any fpecial occafion, giving public notice, fourteen days at the leaft, and fpecifying the bufinefs to be tranfacted at fuch meeting in the Leicefter Journal.

XVII. All elections, if contefted, fhall be by ballot, and all queftions decided by a majority of votes prefent, which fhall be taken by ballot if required; but no fubfcriber fhall have a vote at any general board, unlefs he has fubfcribed one year, and paid his fecond year's fubfcription.

XVIII. All fubfcriptions for the current year fhall be paid as foon as may be after the year commences; and all fubfcriptions entered before Michaelmas fhall be deemed to commence at the preceding Midfummer; and all fubfequent fubfcriptions are to commence from the quarter-day preceding the time of fubfcribing, unlefs the fubfcriber defires otherwife.

XIX. The fecretary fhall fend a monitory letter to all perfons whofe fubfcriptions are three months in arrears, to prevent further delay of payment; all fubfcriptions being fuppofed to continue, unlefs the fubfcriber orders the contrary by letter.

XX. No phyfician, furgeon, treafurer, or auditor, fhall receive any reward, falary, or gratuity, from the Infirmary for his fervice.

XXI. No patient, or perfon related to the Infirmary, fhall at any time prefume, on pain of expulfion, to give or take from any tradefman, patient, fervant, ftranger, or other perfon whatfoever, any fee, reward, or gratuity, directly or indirectly, for any fervice done, or to be done, on account of the Infirmary.

XXII. A Table of Rules and Orders relating to the conduct of patients and fervants fhall be hung up in each ward, and publicly read over every Wednefday morning by a perfon to be appointed by the matron.

XXIII. An inventory of all the houfhold goods and furniture belonging to the Infirmary fhall be kept by the fecretary, and a copy thereof by the matron; and once every year, at fome convenient time, before the ftated board in June, the auditors fhall caufe a frefh inventory to be made, and compared with that of the preceding year, as well as with the account of what has been purchafed fince; and, as often as any thing be wanted, it fhall be immediately notified by the matron to the vifitor of the week.

XXIV. The method of dealing with tradefmen in general fhall be to publifh an account of the provifions and goods wanted, for fuch as are willing to furnifh the fame to bring their propofals, fealed up, to the fecretary, at a day fixed, in order that the next weekly board may determine which fhall be accepted.

XXV. The appointment of the particular diet of the patients fhall be under the regulation of their refpective phyfician or furgeon; and no other provifions or liquors fhall be brought into the houfe to them, on any pretence whatfoever.

XXVI. A poor's box or boxes fhall be fet up in fome convenient place or places, to each of which there fhall be two locks; one key to be kept by the treafurer, and the other as the weekly board fhall direct; and the money therein collected applied to the ufe of the Infirmary.

XXVII. The matron and fervants fhall be ready to attend the vifitor in the board-room; and when the vifitor enters the wards, the matron and fervants are to withdraw, and the patients to ftand by their refpective beds.

XXVIII. All deeds, evidences, and writing, relative to the Infirmary, or, where the originals cannot be obtained, attefted copies thereof, fhall be preferved in a cheft provided for that purpofe, and fecured by three locks; and the keys fhall be kept by fuch perfons as fhall be appointed by the general board held at Midfummer.

XXIX. No repeal, addition, or alteration, in any of the ftatutes fhall take place, excepting at the quarterly meeting of the governors in June, 21 or more being prefent, two-thirds of which muft vote for fuch repeal, addition, or alteration.

Rules for the admiffion and difcharge of Patients.

I. The patients fhall be admitted and difcharged every Tuefday, by the committee, between the hours of 11 and 1 o'clock; and none fhall be admitted after 12, except on fome extraordinary occafions, as the committee will be then adjourned.

II. If, by accident, or fome unforefeen caufe, a fufficient number of governors do not meet on the day of appointment for the admiffion of patients, the phyfician and furgeon of the week fhall then difcharge fuch patients as are ready to be difcharged, and admit fuch patients as fhall then offer themfelves and be approved of.

III. The head or other officer for the time being of any body corporate, townfhip, parifh, or fociety, fubfcribing to the Infirmary, fhall have the fame power of recommending patients with a fubfcriber of equal value.

IV. Every fubfcriber fhall have the power of deputing another fubfcriber to recommend patients in his abfence, obferving the form directed in the Supplement.

V. No patient fhall be admitted but by the recommendation of a fubfcriber or benefactor, unlefs in cafes which admit of no delay; in which cafes the apothecary and matron may receive patients, giving immediate notice to the phyfician and furgeon of the week.

VI. No fubfcriber's recommendation fhall be accepted whilft his fubfcription is in arrear; nor any governor's vote permitted, until his fubfcription and arrears are paid.

VII. Every fubfcriber of a guinea annually, or benefactor of 10 guineas, fhall have a power of recommending either three out-patients annually, or one in-patient.

VIII. Every fubfcriber of 20 guineas at any one time, or two guineas annually, fhall have the privilege of recommending two in-patients and two out-patients annually, having no more than one in-patient in the houfe at a time; and fo in proportion for every increafed fubfcription, up to five guineas *per annum*.

IX. Every fubfcriber of five guineas *per annum*, or 100l. in benefaction, fhall have the power of fending any number of patients annually; but fhall not have more than two at any one time in the houfe.

X. No perfons fhall be admitted who are able to fubfift themfelves, and pay for their cure; and no one fhall be admitted, or fuffered to remain as an in-patient, who is capable of receiving equal benefit as an out-patient.

XI. An alphabetical lift of all fubfcribers in arrear fhall be made out by the fecretary, and laid before the chairman of the committee at the end of every quarter, that he may immediately refer to any perfon's name whofe fubfcription is unpaid.

XII. No domeftic fervant, or other, fhall merely on that account be excluded the benefit of the Infirmary, but it fhall be left to the determination of the committee, how far the fervant recommended is or is not a proper object; which committee will alfo confider, that it is contrary to the intention of this charity to relieve thofe who are able to pay for relief; and it is reafonable to fuppofe, that all mafters (whether fubfcribers or not) who are in affluent circumftances, and have hitherto been accuftomed to pay for their fervants, will not defire them to be relieved at the public expence, to the detriment of more neceffitous objects, and to the difadvantage of the furgeons who give their attendance gratis.

XIII. A letter figned by the chairman, and counterfigned by the fecretary, fhall be fent to every fubfcriber recommending a patient, to fignify that the perfon recommended is admitted, poftponed, or rejected; and the like notice fhall be given to the fubfcriber or benefactor when a patient is difcharged.

XIV. Thofe who recommend patients from diftant places are defired to fend a fhort ftate of the cafe, drawn up by fome phyfician, furgeon, or apothecary (poft-paid); to which an anfwer fhall be returned, whether, and when, they fhall be admitted; but the

committee

committee is at full liberty to reject such patients, if the case appears to have been misreprefented; nor will any answer be sent to a letter of which the postage or carriage is not paid.

XV. When there shall be want of room in the Infirmary for the admission of such as are properly recommended, and qualified to be in-patients, the preference, in cases of equal exigency, shall be given,

1. To those who live at the greatest distance.

2. To those recommended by such subscribers and benefactors as have not recommended any in-patients within the year. And,

3. To those recommended by the largest contributors.

XVI. Patients properly recommended and qualified, who cannot be admitted for want of room in the Infirmary, shall be entered in the books as in-patients, and received into the house, before any other in equal necessity, upon the first vacancy; and in the mean time shall be treated as out-patients.

XXVII. One bed in each ward shall be reserved, as a provision for such accidents as require immediate relief, and for such medical cases as will admit of no delay.

XVIII. No soldier shall be admitted an in-patient until his officer has engaged to pay his subsistence-money to the committee, during such time as he shall continue there; except a soldier on furlough, when there is no officer at hand to engage for him.

XIX. All such as are admitted into the Infirmary, and in two months receive no benefit, shall of course be discharged; unless the physicians and surgeons certify to the committee, that there is a probability of a cure, or of considerable relief.

XX. No woman big with child; no child under six years of age, except in extraordinary cases, as fractures, or where cutting for the stone, or any other operation, is required; no persons disordered in their senses, suspected to have the small-pox, itch, or other infectious distemper, or that are apprehended to be in a dying condition, or incurable, be admitted as in-patients; or, if inadvertently admitted, be suffered to continue.

XXI. The several patients shall be enjoined to desire that public prayers may be offered for them during their illness, and return public thanks, in their respective places of worship, upon their recovery.

XXII. It is expected that any person, parish, or society, who shall recommend a patient, do take care that he comes with a change of linen; cleanliness, as far as is consistent with circumstances, being necessary to be carefully observed.

R U L E S   A N D   R E G U L A T I O N S.

I. The physician, with the surgeon whose turn it is to attend, shall meet at the Infirmary every Friday morning at ten o'clock, and consult upon such cases as may require it; after which they will prescribe for such out-patients as they had ordered on the preceding Tuesday then to attend them, and will give a list to the apothecary of such patients as are proper to be discharged the Saturday following; they are also to visit their respective patients, at such other times as they judge necessary, or shall have notice of such necessity from the apothecary.

II. The physicians shall be constantly referred to in all difficult and mixed cases by the surgeons, and shall jointly consult with him; but no internal medicine shall be administered by the surgeons, or dispensed to them by the house apothecary, but by the direction of the physician, unless on casualties, when patients are suddenly brought into the Infirmary, or where a chirurgical case instantly requires the administration of internal medicines, and at a time when the physician cannot conveniently be consulted.

Rules for the Surgeons.

I. The surgeons shall attend by weekly rotation every Tuesday morning, from 11 to 12 o'clock; that is, during the time the physician continues to admit the patients.

II. Each surgeon, during the time of his attendance, shall dress those daily that require it; appointing a certain hour in the forenoon for the attendance

of the out-patients at the Infirmary; and no out-patient shall be dressed who is not at the Infirmary by that hour.

III. No amputation, or any other principal operation, shall be performed in the Infirmary, without a previous consultation of the physician, and all the surgeons belonging to it, except on some sudden accident, the physician and other surgeons being out of town.

IV. Each surgeon shall be allowed to introduce any number of articled apprentices or pupils, first giving in their names to the quarterly or special board, and having them entered in their minutes, with permission to attend at the Infirmary; but no pupils or apprentices are to dress the patients, but under the direction of one of the surgeons; nor are the surgeons to suffer such pupils or apprentices to perform any operation, except bleeding, cutting an issue, making a seaton, or drawing a tooth.

V. None shall be admitted, except the physicians and his pupils, the surgeons' apprentices and pupils, with the apothecary and his apprentice, to see either the great operations, or common proceedings of the surgeons, without their approbation.

VI. Each surgeon, whose business or indisposition shall oblige him to be absent, shall engage some one of the other surgeons to inspect the proceedings, that the patients may not be left to the sole management of the pupils and apprentices.

VII. The surgeons appointed to attend the Infirmary shall have the same privileges with a subscriber of two guineas per annum.

Rules for the Apothecary.

I. The apothecary shall fix two tickets on each patient's bed; one specifying the name of the patient, together with that of the physician or surgeon, or both, if the cure be partly medical, and partly chirurgical, and the other the diet according to the prescription of the physician; and he shall take care that the cases so fixed exactly correspond with the physician's book, and shall give a list to the matron thereof on each prescribing day.

II. He shall keep a diet-book of the number of patients on each diet, according to the expences in the book of the physician.

III. He shall make a report, to the weekly board or committee, of any patients who shall have been received into the Infirmary during the foregoing week; and shall deliver a list of such patients as have been in the Infirmary two months.

IV. He shall go into the wards every morning, and enquire into the respective state of the patients' healths; whether the medicines prescribed have been taken, what effect they have had; and shall make a report of whatever may be necessary to the physician.

V. An account of the number of beds, which become vacant in each ward, shall be delivered by him at the weekly board, with a list of the patients received into the house in the foregoing week, and of such patients as have been in the house two months.

VI. He shall dispense no medicines without the direction of the physician, except in cases of necessity, when they cannot be consulted.

VII. He shall not suffer any apothecary, or others, to inspect the physician's book, or Pharmacopœia, without leave first obtained from the physician himself.

VIII. There shall be a committee appointed, whenever the general board shall judge it convenient, to buy drugs for the use of the Infirmary; and till such time the apothecary shall provide what is necessary, by the direction of the physician; and he shall deliver to the weekly board an account of what drugs and medicines are expended, and shall bring in a bill of the expence once every month.

IX. On a supposition any medicine shall be wanted for immediate use, the apothecary shall pay ready money for such medicine; and if any apothecary in the town should, from a deficiency of any particular medicine, desire a supply from the Infirmary for his immediate use, such apothecary shall in like manner pay ready money for it; but no borrowing or lending of drugs shall on any pretence be admitted.

X. The

X. The apothecary shall never be absent when the physician and surgeons are to attend, and shall always leave notice with the matron where he is to be found; and in case of sickness, or other necessary avocation, he shall depute another apothecary, who shall be approved by the physician, to officiate in his place.

XI. The salary of the house-apothecary shall be 25*l.* a-year, with a gratuity of 5*l.* a-year, provided he stays 12 months complete, and behaves to the satisfaction of the governors, but not else. He shall have his diet, washing, and lodging, at the Infirmary; and shall also have the privilege of taking a pupil, and money for his instruction, provided such pupil resides out of the Infirmary: the apothecary shall also have the liberty of taking an apprentice, to be maintained at the expence of the charity, but not without the particular favour and appointment of the governors, assembled at a general or special board; nor shall the apothecary ever be permitted to have both an apprentice and pupil at the same time.

XII. Whenever the apothecary shall chuse to quit his place, he shall give three months notice, at a quarterly meeting, of such his intention.

XIII. The house-apothecary shall not administer any medicines, nor act in his profession, out of the Infirmary.

Rules for the Matron.

I. The matron shall take care of the houshold goods and furniture according to the inventory, and be ready to give an account thereof when required.

II. She shall visit the wards and offices every day, and shall take care that the chambers, beds, cloths, linen, and all things within the Infirmary, be kept clean.

III. She shall weigh and measure the provisions and other necessaries which are brought to the Infirmary, and shall keep a daily account of them in the check-book, and lay it before the weekly committee every Tuesday; and shall never suffer any of the provisions, utensils, or goods, to be carried out of the house.

IV. She shall keep a diet-book, by which the number of patients on each diet may be known.

V. She shall cause the names of the patients in each ward to be called over every morning and evening, and enter into the house-visitor's book the names of those who are absent, and shall suffer no in-patient to go further than the gravel-walk without leave.

VI. She shall take care of the keys of the doors, and see they be always locked by nine in the evening from Michaelmas to Lady-day, and at ten in the evening from Lady-day to Michaelmas.

VII. She shall see that the nurses, servants, and patients, do observe the rules of the house, and do their duty; and, in case of misbehaviour or neglect, acquaint the weekly board or house-visitors thereof.

Rules for the Secretary.

I. The secretary shall attend every weekly, quarterly, and special board, to minute down and register all proceedings; and he shall be always ready to produce the books and accompts of the society, fairly written.

II. He shall enter, in a Register to be kept for the purpose, the names of the in-patients and of the out-patients, the parish or township they belong to, their age and distemper, when admitted, when discharged, and in what state.

III. He shall give notice, in writing, every Saturday preceding the commencement of the attendance, to the surgeon whose turn it is to visit the sick; as also to the house-visitor, who is to visit the following week.

IV. He shall not presume to divulge the proceedings of the governors, or report any thing which may be said in relation to tradesmen, and others, under pain of immediate dismission.

Rules for the Porter.

I. The porter shall carefully attend the gate, and shall suffer no in-patient to go out without leave; and he shall inform the matron of every stranger who comes into the Infirmary.

II. He shall obey the orders of the physicians, surgeon, and apothecary, pound in the great mortar, and do the labouring work of the house, when ordered by the apothecary or matron; and shall never be absent on any business whatsoever, without giving the matron notice, that the laboratory-man, or one of the patients, may be appointed to attend the door during his absence.

Rule for the Messenger and Laboratory-man.

A strong lad shall be hired as an assistant in the laboratory, and to go occasionally on errands, and to do such other business in the house as the apothecary or matron may require.

Rules for the Nurses and Servants.

I. The nurses shall clean their respective wards by seven in the morning, from the 1st of April to the 1st of October; and before eight, from the 1st of October to the 1st of April.

II. The nurses and servants shall obey the house-apothecary as their master, and the matron as their mistress; and shall behave with tenderness to the patients, and with civility and respect to strangers.

III. All persons concerned as servants in the house shall be free from the burden of children, and the care of a family.

Rules for the In-patients.

I. No patient shall go out of the Infirmary without leave from the physician or surgeon, first signified to the matron, or lie out of the house on any account whatsoever, on pain of expulsion.

II. No men-patients shall go into the women's ward, nor any women-patients into the men's, or be permitted to go into any ward but their own, without leave of the matron.

III. No in-patient shall sit up after eight o'clock in the winter, or after nine o'clock in the summer, unless the matron should on any particular occasion direct otherwise; and every one, unless such as are ordered to the contrary by the physician and surgeon, shall rise by seven in the summer, and by eight in the winter.

IV. There shall be no swearing, cursing, rude or indecent behaviour, on pain of expulsion after the first admonition.

V. No patient shall presume to play at cards, dice, or any other game, on any account whatsoever, within the limits of the Infirmary; nor to smoak any where within doors, without leave from the physician or surgeon first signified to the matron.

VI. Such patients as are able shall be employed in nursing the other patients, washing and ironing the linen, cleaning the wards, and such other service as the matron shall require; the apothecary being first asked, whether such employment is likely to interfere with the medicines prescribed.

VII. Such in-patients as are able are expected to attend divine service in the Infirmary on Sundays, and at all times when it shall be administered; and no stranger or others shall be permitted to see the Infirmary on that day, nor shall the patients be visited without special leave of the matron (which she is not to grant but on extraordinary occasions), viz. to the friends of those patients who live at a great distance, and cannot conveniently come on any other day.

VIII. None who shall have been discharged for irregularity shall be admitted again as patients of the Infirmary, on any recommendation whatsoever, unless some very extraordinary case, or where they have met with an accident which requires immediate assistance.

IX. These rules for the patients, and those for the nurses, shall be read every Monday evening, after the admission of the new patients, by the apothecary in the men's ward, and by the matron in the women's ward.

Rules for the Out-patients.

I. The out-patients shall be assisted with advice and medicines; and be in no other respect chargeable to the society, except occasionally for trusses, which are to be returned, and in the article of cloth, proper for straight or laced stockings, which shall be made

up

up for them, under the direction of the furgeons, by fome of the in-patients, provided they are not capable of doing it properly for themfelves.

II. No frefh medicines fhall be given them until they deliver to the apothecary, his pupil or apprentice, the phials or gallipots, and fuch medicines as they have not taken.

III. They fhall attend exactly at eleven o'clock every Friday, and at fuch other times as fhall be appointed by the phyfician and furgeons; and if they abfent themfelves twice together, without a reafonable caufe, allowed to be fo by their phyfician or furgeon, they fhall be difcharged for non-attendance.

IV. No out-patient fhall prefume to loiter about the Infirmary, or ftreets adjacent, but come immediately to the place appointed to receive them; nor are they to beg any where in the town, on pain of being difcharged for mifbehaviour.

Printed Notice to be given to every Out-patient.
Leicefter Infirmary.

You are ordered to attend
at the Infirmary every Friday, at 11 o'clock precifely, and no other time, unlefs fomething extraordinary feems to render the phyfician's more frequent advice neceffary; in which cafe you muft firft apply to the houfe apothecary.—Take notice, that if you twice neglect attending your phyfician on the day and at the hour appointed, without particular leave from him, you will be difcharged for non-attendance, and not admitted on a future occafion.

N. B. All the out-patients are ordered to bring back every week to the apothecary, his pupil, or apprentice, whatever medicines they have left, together with the bottles, phials, gallipots, and the truffes, they receive from him. Whoever neglects this order will have no more medicines.

Such of the out-patients as are under the care of the furgeons are to attend at the Infirmary at the hour appointed by their furgeon.

Directions for the Houfe-vifitor.

I. The Infirmary is to be vifited by the houfe-vifitor once every day, for the week after his appointment; when he is to walk through the wards, with a white wand in his hand, that he may be known to be the houfe-vifitor; and as foon as he enters the wards the nurfes are to withdraw, and the patients to ftand by the fides of their refpective beds.

II. He fhall then enquire whether the apothecary, matron, nurfes, and fervants, have behaved agreeably to the rules of the fociety; particularly whether the patients have been duly attended, and their medicines difpenfed to them without delay; whether any thing has been carried out of or brought into the Infirmary clandeftinely by the friends of the patients, or by any of the fervants; as well as any other queftions he may think neceffary.

III. He fhall view the meat and provifions brought into the houfe, and fee that the malt-liquor is found, and in every refpect proper for the family.

IV. On his return from vifiting the wards, the apothecary, matron, nurfes, and fervants, fhall be ready to attend him in the governor's room, to anfwer all his queftions, and execute his orders; and whatever he thinks obfervable fhall be entered either by himfelf or by the apothecary, and figned by him, in a book provided for that purpofe, which is to be examined every week by the committee.

Directions for the Chairman and the Committee.

I. To nominate the chairman of the day in the abfence of the treafurer, who, when prefent, is always chairman, conformable to the ftatutes.

II. To enter the names of the governors then prefent in the minute-book.

III. To read the minutes of the laft committee, which are to be figned by the chairman.

IV. To read the entries in the vifitor's book, and appoint a new one for the enfuing week.

V. If the laft Monday in the month, to read the

bills, and order them to be paid, being firft approved by the committee.

VI. To difcharge fuch patients as are judged proper to go out of the houfe; and to inform thofe who are cured, that it is expected they return thanks the Sunday following, at their refpective places of worfhip, giving them printed notes, filled up by the fecretary for that purpofe; and alfo directing them to return thanks to their phyfician, furgeons, and recommenders.

VII. To continue fuch patients as are not now difcharged, and have ftood on the book two months fince their admiffion (or fince laft continued), and to fend for them into the committee-room [unlefs by their indifpofition they are prevented], and to hear from their own mouths what benefit they have received, or are likely to receive by a continuance in the Infirmary.

VIII. To admit fuch patients as appear, on examination, to be proper; charging the in-patients to obferve the rules of the Infirmary, which will be read to them in their wards; to conform to the directions of their phyfician or furgeon; to obey the matron; to receive no provifions or medicines from any one out of the houfe, nor to give any money or gratuity whatfoever to the nurfes or other fervants; and to acquaint them, that the confequence of their mifbehaviour, in any of thefe refpects, will be a difcharge for irregularity, by which they will be rendered incapable of a future admiffion.

IX. To report new fubfcriptions, benefactions, or legacies, deaths of fubfcribers, and fubfcriptions withdrawn, &c.

X. To examine and pay the apothecary, and matron's incident expences, and to make up and balance the treafurer's accompts.

XI. To fee what former orders, either of a general court or weekly board, remain to be executed, and whether any new orders are proper to be made, relating to the ordinary expences, government, or conduct of the Infirmary, and of the officers, fervants, and patients, belonging to it.

XII. To read the minutes of the day, and adjourn the committee.

The method by which the Auditors may examine the Butcher's and Baker's monthly bills, to fee that the confumption of bread and meat does not exceed the ftated allowance:

Each of the patients on common diet is allowed four pounds of meat in every week, and thofe on low diet two pounds, including the butcher's meat allowed to make their broth. Thofe on dry diet are likewife allowed two pounds weekly each, though they have no broth. They who are on milk-diet are allowed no meat, except on the day of their admiffion, when all patients coming from the country have an allowance for both after their journey.

From hence the following method of calculation may be eftablifhed; viz. to double the fum of low and dry diets, to add four [1] times the number of common diets, and divide the fum by feven, the quotient will then fhew the number of pounds of butcher's meat allowed for the patients, exclufive of their ufual allowance on the day of their admiffion.

In examining the butcher's bills for the family, obferve that they are to be kept diftinct from thofe of meat bought for the patients; and as the daily allowance for each fervant is not to exceed a pound of meat, if the number of days in any given time are multiplied by the whole number of fervants, the product will be the number of pounds allowed them during that time.

Each patient is allowed a loaf a day, weighing 15 ounces, the whole number of diets therefore in any given time (found by adding the fums of all the four different diets together) is the fame with the whole number of 15 ounce-loaves, which ought to be brought to the Infirmary during that time, for the ufe of the in-patients.

---

[1] By the number of diets is here meant, the amount of the daily number of patients on each kind of diet, as regiftered in the diet-book, and fummed up at the end of each month, or other time for which they are audited, being equivalent to fo many patients' diets for one day, or fo many diets for one perfon.

A Table

A Table of Diet.—Common Diet.

Sunday and Thurſday. Breakfaſt, a pint of water-gruel or milk-pottage; dinner, eight ounces of roaſt or boiled beef, mutton, or veal; ſupper, a pint of broth.

Monday. Breakfaſt, the ſame as on Sunday and Thurſday; dinner, a pint of rice milk, or 12 ounces of baked pudding; ſupper, two ounces of cheeſe or butter.

Tueſday and Saturday. Breakfaſt, a pint of panada, or milk-pottage; dinner, a pint of broth, four ounces of boiled mutton or beef, and eight ounces of roots; ſupper, a pint of broth.

Wedneſday. A pint of milk-pottage or water-gruel; dinner, baked pudding, or twelve ounces of boiled roots; ſupper, a pint of broth or milk-pottage.

Friday. Breakfaſt, a pint of water-gruel; dinner, baked pudding, or a pint of rice-milk; ſupper, two ounces of cheeſe or butter.

Low Diet.

Sunday and Thurſday. Breakfaſt, a pint of milk-pottage or water-gruel; dinner, two ounces of boiled beef, mutton, or veal, with a pint of broth; ſupper, a pint of water-gruel or broth.

Monday. Breakfaſt, a pint of water-gruel; dinner, a pint of rice-milk; ſupper, a pint of broth or panada.

Tueſday and Saturday. Breakfaſt, a pint of milk-pottage; dinner, two ounces of boiled mutton, with a pint of broth; ſupper, a pint of water-gruel or milk-pottage.

Wedneſday. Breakfaſt, a pint of panada or milk-pottage; dinner, eight ounces of bread-pudding boiled, or roots; ſupper, two ounces of cheeſe or butter.

Friday. Breakfaſt, a pint of water-gruel; dinner, roots boiled, bread-putting, or a pint of rice-milk; ſupper, two ounces of cheeſe or butter.

Milk Diet.

Sunday, Tueſday, Thurſday, and Saturday. Breakfaſt, a pint of milk-pottage; dinner, a pint of rice-milk, or haſty-pudding, or boiled bread-pudding; ſupper, a pint of milk-pottage.

Monday. Breakfaſt, a pint of water-gruel; dinner, baked rice, or bread-pudding; ſupper, a pint of milk-pottage or boiled milk.

Friday. Breakfaſt, a pint of panada; dinner, a pint of rice-milk; ſupper, a pint of boiled milk; bread ſufficient, without waſte; drink, three pints each day, one part whereof to be milk, and two water.

Dry Diet.

Sunday and Thurſday. Breakfaſt, two ounces of cheeſe or butter; dinner, half a pound of mutton, veal, or beef, with roots; ſupper, two ounces of cheeſe or butter.

Monday and Friday. Breakfaſt, two ounces of cheeſe or butter; dinner, rice-pudding; ſupper, two ounces of cheeſe or butter.

Wedneſday. Breakfaſt, two ounces of cheeſe or butter; dinner, baked bread, or rice-pudding; ſupper, two ounces of cheeſe or butter.

Tueſday and Saturday. Breakfaſt, two ounces of cheeſe or butter; dinner, ſix ounces of mutton, veal, or beef, with roots; ſupper, two ounces of cheeſe or butter; bread or ſea-biſcuit, without waſte; beer half a pint every day.

Leiceſter Infirmary, July 5, 1771.

Ordered, That the thanks of this meeting be given to Dr. Vaughan, by ſir Thomas Cave, chairman, for the great care and trouble he has taken in compiling and digeſting the rules for the good government of the Infirmary, in the following manner:

"Dr. Vaughan—Sir, it is the unanimous requeſt of all the ſubſcribers now preſent, that you will accept their grateful thanks, for the great care and trouble you have taken in compiling and digeſting the Book of Rules and Orders for the good government and diſcipline of the Infirmary of this County, which has this day been univerſally approved of."

Ordered, That the above be printed in the Leiceſter newſpaper, and alſo annexed to the ſaid Rules and Orders; which are alſo to be printed.

Ordered, That the thanks of the ſubſcribers be given to the Rev. Dr. Watts, by Sir Thomas Cave, chairman, in the following manner:

"Dr. Watts—The general meeting of the ſubſcribers to the Leiceſter Infirmary, this day aſſembled, being ſenſible of the great benefit and emolument ariſing to this County, from your original plan and propoſal for ſuch an eſtabliſhment, do unanimouſly and gratefully beg your acceptance of their thanks on that account; and, as a further teſtimony of their regard for you, have elected you a governor."

Ordered, That the above be printed in the Leiceſter paper, and alſo prefixed to each copy of the ſaid Rules and Orders.

On Wedneſday, Sept. 11, 1771, being the day appointed for opening the Leiceſter Infirmary, about half-paſt ten in the forenoon, the Governors, attended by the Biſhop of Lincoln, formed a proceſſion to St. Martin's church; upon their entrance into which, a grand overture was played; and, during intervals in the Church ſervice, ſeveral ſelect pieces were performed from the Meſſiah, by the moſt capital performers from London, and other parts of the kingdom. After which, the Biſhop of Lincoln preached a ſuitable ſermon on the occaſion, from St. Mark, chap. i. and the former part of the 34th verſe; "And he healed many that were ſick of divers diſeaſes." The ſervice concluded with the Coronation Anthem. Divine ſervice being ended, the Biſhop, attended by the Governors, and an amazing number of decent ſpectators, went to the Infirmary, which they opened with great ſolemnity, and admitted therein one patient. From the Infirmary the gentlemen returned to the Three Cranes, and the ladies to the Three Crowns, where genteel ordinaries were provided for them. The collection at the church-doors, which was made by lady Robinſon, and the lady of Anthony James Keck, eſq. amounted, including the admiſſion tickets, to 233*l*. 14*s*. 10¼*d*.

In the evening, there was a grand concert at the New Aſſembly-room, to the moſt brilliant company that had ever met there on any former occaſion. The firſt violin was played by Mr. Fiſher, the hautboy ſolos by Mr. Fiſcher, and the ſongs by Mr. Vernon and Mrs. Barthelemon, attended by a large band of gentlemen performers, and the band of muſic belonging to the Blues. The whole was conducted by Joſeph Cradock, eſq. and the Rev. Mr. Jenner. The admittance tickets into the concert amounted to 98*l*. 10*s*.—On this occaſion Mr. Garrick very kindly engaged the performers at a light expence, and made an offer of any muſick-books from Drury Lane.

In 1773, Lord Maynard was invited to take the office of a Vice-preſident, by the following official letter:

"For the Lord Maynard.

"The regard your Lordſhip has ſhewn to the humane eſtabliſhment of the Leiceſter Infirmary, demands the moſt grateful acknowledgments of the Governors of that Inſtitution; and I have the orders of their general anniverſary meeting, this day, to convey their thanks to your Lordſhip for all favours conferred on them. It is their unanimous requeſt, that your Lordſhip will do them the honour to be one of their Vice-preſidents, being the only method in their power of expreſſing their grateful ſenſe of your Lordſhip's goodneſs. I am,

Your Lordſhip's moſt obedient
and humble ſervant,

Leiceſter, June 17, 1773.   THO. CAVE, Chairman."

Lord Maynard's Anſwer.

"Sir—I received the favour of your obliging letter by the laſt poſt; and beg I may be permitted to aſſure you and the other gentlemen, Governors of the Leiceſter Infirmary, of the high ſenſe I entertain of the honour they intend me in making me one of the Vice-preſidents. Such an honour I can by no means refuſe; and yet, totally unable as I am of attending any of the meetings, I feel myſelf very unwilling to prevent that office being filled by one whoſe attendance might be of uſe to the Society; therefore beg they will diſpoſe of me as they ſhall judge moſt likely

to

to be of fervice to the Inftitution. Give me leave to trouble you to make my beft compliments to the Go-vernors at your next meeting; and to fubfcribe myfelf, Sir, your moft obedient humble fervant, *Eafton Lodge, June 23, 1773.* MAYNARD."

The Governors of the Infirmary, in the moft fpi-rited manner, continued the anniverfaries for the be-nefit of the Inftitution; particularly in 1774, in which year, previous to the meeting, the publick were thus pathetically addreffed by Mr. Cradock:

" Moft ages have borne fome charaéteriftic mark of their excellence and attainments. It is the peculiar happinefs of the prefent, to be equally diftinguifhed for its progrefs in the Arts, as for its rapid advance-ments in the duties of Humanity. The many public Buildings which have of late years been erected, are living monuments of the vaft improvements that have been made in modern Architecture; and the various purpofes for which they have been applied, as well as the known utility which has been received from them, have alike evinced, that Charity has gone hand in hand with Magnificence. So many Hofpitals are now interfperfed through the whole kingdom, that there is fcarce any part of the wretched who do not in fome degree feel their good effects; but this fpe-cies (of which we now give an account) feems to be the moft highly entitled to our attention and regard; for it is founded on the foundeft principles of poli-tical wifdom as well as piety—is addreffed to thofe who, from their very occupations, muft experience the utmoft rigours of inclement elements—who breathe as it were difeafe from the inftruments they ufe, and the materials they employ—to thofe who, in the hand of Providence, are the bulwarks and fe-curity of our national welfare. And where can relief be fo readily fupplied as in Public Infirmaries? The patients receive every requifite help, the moft able advice, the moft proper medicines, and in a manner which the rich can rarely experience even in their own houfes. In fhort, what do they not experience, but the moft effectual means towards the accomplifh-ment of the beft end?

" In the infancy of this Charity, a prejudice pre-vailed (and where has it not?) that trials of fkill were to be made, and that the torture of the patient was the experience of the Phyfician. The prejudice is as ill-founded as it is illiberal; and has only been pro-pagated by thofe who wifhed for fome fpecious pre-tence for with-holding their fubfcriptions. This, like moft other prejudices, carries the height of ab-furdity on the very face of it: for what is it but in other words to fay, that the fkilful affemble to defeat their own art; and a fet of gentlemen are employed, at a vaft expence, to erect a Charity, to deftroy the very purpofes of its inftitution?

" The Poor, who have hitherto benefited by this Charity, have not proved themfelves unworthy of the care that has been fhewn for them; and we have reafon to hope that they will ever moft thankfully exprefs their fenfe of gratitude for the aid they have received in this merciful afylum, as they are now fully convinced of its ufe and efficacy.

" Of the continuance of fuch bleffings, little more need be faid, than that the Charity (as it was firft founded) is ftill fupported by men of character and integrity; who will watch with affiduity and care the good work they have begun, and enfure (as far as human power can enfure) that the fame care and af-fiduity fhall be tranfmitted to pofterity, of which them-felves are fuch eminent examples.

" Such is the nature of that Charity we fo ftrongly recommend; a Charity beneficial to individuals, and moft ufeful to the Publick: for, though the good man would, in every age, from the generous impulfe of his own heart, in fome degree fupply the want of fuch eftablifhments, by ' cafting his bread upon the

waters,' yet he has now the happier confolation to re-flect, that, under the judicious regulation of them, he gives *that* ' bread to the *hungry*.' "

At the Anniverfary of 1774, the new organ at St. Martin's (which had been then juft completed by Mr. Snetzler, and paid for by a liberal fubfcription of the nobility and gentry in the neighbourhood) was opened to a brilliant and refpectable affembly; and the following Occafional Ode [1], written by Mr. Cra-dock, and fet to mufick by Dr. Boyce, Compofer to his Majefty, was performed:

AIR. Mr. NORRIS.
Lo! on the thorny bed of care
    The trembling victim lies,
Deep funk his eye-balls with defpair,
    What friendly hand his wants fupplies?

CHORUS.
Deplore his fate to woes confign'd,
Deplore the fate of human-kind.

RECITATIVE. MISS DAVIES.
Forbear to murmur at Heav'n's high decree,
Nor fwell the bulk of human mifery.

AIR. MISS DAVIES.
Think not in vain the pitying tear
    To thoughtlefs man was giv'n;
Sweet as the morn. its dews appear,
    A balmy incenfe in the fight of Heav'n.

DUET. Mr. NORRIS and Mr. CHAMPNESS.
Here fhall foft Charity repair,
    And break the bonds of Grief,
Smooth the flinty couch of Care;
    Man to man muft bring relief.

RECITATIVE accompanied. Mifs DAVIES.
Why lingers then the generous flame?
Awake an high enraptur'd ftrain,
Breathe louder yet—nor yet refrain—
Again—repeat—and yet again—

FULL CHORUS.
To hail the Work the full-voic'd Choir we raife,
And all unite to fing Jehovah's praife.

So great and excellent was the band of muficians on this day, that a capital London performer ob-ferved, that if the great Handel had been living, and prefent on the occafion, he would have declared, that then was the firft time his *Te Deum* was per-formed agreeable to the fublimity of his conception. For the accommodation of the band, a temporary loft was erected, reaching nearly half way along the nave; and the performers were honoured with the affiftance of the Earl of Sandwich upon the kettle-drums. Befides moft of the Nobility and Gentry of thefe parts, who were of the auditory, was Omai, the famed native of Otaheite.

Much commendation is due to a worthy native of St. Martin's parifh, who, poffeffed of intereft, kindly made ufe of it, on this occafion, to have the organ infpected, in almoft every ftage of its building, by the moft qualified perfons; as appears by the fol-lowing letter of thanks from the fubfcribers and pa-rifhioners affembled in veftry, Oct. 27, 1774:

" To Jofeph Cradock, efq. of Gumley.

" Sir—When fo many perfons of the firft rank, as well as the moft eminent muficians, affembled at our late Oratorio, have expreffed their entire approbation of the new organ built under your directions; it would be very ungrateful, either in the parifhioners or fubfcribers, not to acknowledge their obligation to you. They are fenfible this noble inftrument [2] owes much of its perfection to your fuperintendency, as well as the fkill of Mr. Snetzler. Your diftinguifhed tafte for mufic, poetry, and polite learning, have made you juftly admired; but it is the application of

---

[1] It was performed at Hinchinbroke, under the direction of Joah Bates, efq.; afterwards at Covent Garden Theatre, under the direction of the late Mr. Linley; fince that time again at Leicefter, when Madame Mara fung the principal air; and dif-ferent parts of it have been continually introduced into Mifcellaneous Performances at feveral Cathedrals. The Mufick of the Duet only is printed (with permiffion) by the late Mr. Afhley, after Dr. Boyce's Anthems.

[2] It has three fets of keys, from F in alt to GG. The ftops in the great organ are, two open and a ftop diapafon, prin-cipal, 12th, 15th, fes-quialtra, cornet, clarion, trumpet. Choir organ, two diapafons, principal, 15th, flute, baffoon. Swell, two diapafons, principal, cornet, hautboy, trumpet.

thefe talents to the glory of God and the good of mankind (of both which you have lately given a noble example) that makes you univerfally efteemed. We are directed, both by the fubfcribers and parifhioners in veftry affembled, to return you their fincere thanks, for thus enabling them to have the fervice of the Church performed in a manner worthy of the occafion.

"We beg leave to fubfcribe ourfelves, with the greateft refpect, your moft humble fervants,

WILLIAM CARTE, } Churchwardens
EDWARD PRICE, } of
WILLIAM WATTS, } St. Martin's, Leicefter."

The whole expence of this capital organ, including every incidental charge, was 600*l*.

At the Anniverfary of 1775, Mr. Cradock's Ode was repeated; and the Sermon was preached by the Rev. Dr. Parry, of Market Harborough.

An additional wing was ordered to be added to the building, for Lunatics, June 16, 1781. This meafure was ftrongly recommended by Dr. Vaughan; and a legacy of 1000*l*. was left for that purpofe by Mrs. Topp. The building, which was completed in confequence, is large and elegant; but deftroys the fymmetry; though it lies back, at the South-weft end of the Infirmary, from the fide of the general erection, and looks to the opening of the Raw-dykes at a moderate diftance.

Other bequefts, for the fpecific purpofe of its being opened, were afterwards received, one of which was left by Mrs. Anne Wigley, amounting to 200*l*. For feveral years, however, the want of a fufficient fund prevented the good intention from taking effect.

In September 1788 the Bifhop of Lincoln preached at St. Martin's, at the Infirmary meeting; and fignified his Majefty's gracious intention of giving to that charity, from the fale of Thurnby eftates, which belonged to the Whatton family, 2000*l*. three per cent. Confols, with intereft from the year 1782. At that meeting, it appeared that there had been received, by legacies, benefactions, fubfcriptions, &c. &c. fince its opening, the fum of 23,548*l*. 14*s*. 9*d*.; out of which fum there then remained 379*l*. 13*s*. 8½*d*. And that there had been cured, in-patients 3384, out-patients 1320; in all 4704. In-patients relieved 399, out-patients 401; in all 800: which make together, cured and relieved, 5504.

At a Special Meeting of the Governors of this Inftitution, Lord Vifcount Wentworth in the Chair, "The Committee of Enquiry, who were appointed Sept. 18, 1792, and appear to have fat for 19 days, delivered a very interefting Report on the ftate of the Charity.

"The Governors therefore defire, in this public manner, to exprefs their thanks to the Gentlemen who attended that Committee, for their laudable exertions, in examining with peculiar exactnefs the various articles of receipt and expenditure belonging to the Infirmary, and propofing œconomical arrangements for the improvement of its finances. They acknowledge their obligations likewife to the Phyficians, for their attention to the interefts of the Charity; and for the offer they have made in their Report, to adopt fuch regulations in the Medical department as are likely to diminifh the expence. The Governors can have no doubt but that folid and permanent advantages will refult from the inveftigation which has taken place, and the adoption of the fyftem which has been recommended.

"They feel a peculiar pleafure in affuring the publick, that, upon reviewing the management of the Charity for ten years, at two different periods, though the expence has increafed, a proportionate increafe of benefit has been received. It appears alfo, upon a comparifon of this Infirmary with 17 others in different parts of the kingdom, that it has provided for its patients with as much œconomy as fimilar inftitutions have, upon an average. As the numbers to whom its affiftance has extended have increafed, its income has been of late years fcarcely fufficient for its fupport; but the Committee have given good reafon to expect a gradual augmentation in its receipts. It will not be forgotten that, notwithftanding its funded property, its welfare and continuance muft principally depend upon annual fubfcriptions.

"Among other objects of enquiry, the Committee have turned their attention to the propofed Lunatic Afylum. Upon this fubject, Dr. Arnold has come forward with a liberality which entitles him to the public thanks. In a feparate Report, he has ftated what additions, alterations, and furniture, may be neceffary to prepare the Building adjoining to the Infirmary for the reception of Lunatic Patients. He has made calculations of the expence likely to be incurred by opening and fupporting fuch an Inftitution, and promifed that he will moft willingly and cordially undertake its management. The prefent finances of the Infirmary will not admit of any addition to its expenditure; but the Governors hope, that the bounty of the Publick will foon enable them to open the Afylum. They therefore propofe a fubfcription for this particular intent; the amount of which will afcertain on what terms, and in what number, infane patients may be received. They do not prefume that the Charity can be carried to its full extent at the firft; but judge it expedient to begin upon a fmall fcale, which may be extended in proportion as their plan meets with approbation and fupport. The following Addrefs, prepared by the Committee, is accordingly adopted:

"LEICESTER LUNATIC ASYLUM.

"The Governors of the Infirmary, convinced that very extenfive benefits will refult from the opening of a Lunatic Afylum, for which a feparate Building has been erected fome years, earneftly recommend that Inftitution to the attention and bounty of the Publick. They cannot believe that, when liberal provifion is made in the County of Leicefter for fuch of the poor as are under the preffure of other difeafes, thofe will continue to be deftitute of public affiftance, who are afflicted by the fevereft malady incident to human nature. The Governors are already in poffeffion of certain funds, appropriated by the Donors to this particular Charity; but thefe are barely adequate to the expence that muft be incurred by preparing the prefent Building for the accommodation of only half the number of patients which it is capable of receiving. They are ftill deftitute of an annual income for the fupport of the houfe; and are therefore under the neceffity of foliciting fubfcriptions for the purpofes of this Charity; nor can they take any meafures for its eftablifhment, on the fmalleft fcale, till they can reckon upon a clear receipt of 100*l*. *per annum*. Subfcriptions are received by Mr. Mansfield, in Leicefter. Thofe who intend to promote the charitable Inftitution here propofed, will moft effentially ferve its interefts by an early contribution, in order that the Governors may be enabled to complete the neceffary alterations in the courfe of the enfuing fummer."

A Sermon preached before the Governors of the Leicefter Infirmary, Sept. 16, 1794, by R. Horfman, A. B. was publifhed in 1794, in 4to; and in that year the following Addrefs was publifhed:

"The prefent age has confeffedly been diftinguifhed by its liberal exertions for the alleviation of human mifery; and, among the various charitable Inftitutions which are the ornament of our Country, Infirmaries, for the cure of the fick and lame in a ftate of indigence, have obtained the moft decided proof of public approbation.

"But the health of the body, however important, is not the fole object of our Hofpitals; they furnifh inftruction for the foul. The poor are here required to worfhip God, and confider their obligations to him; the facred Scriptures are regularly read, and expounded among them; and exhortations, reproofs, or confolations, are adminiftered, according to their different cafes.

"The utility of thefe Inftitutions has now appeared, not merely from fpeculation, but from a long fource of experience. Objections and prejudices which prevailed againft them at firft have gradually fubfided; and not only the very liberal contributions by which they

they are maintained, but the numerous and importunate applications of the poor to gain admiffion, demonftrate the very high refpect in which they are held.

" The Governors of the Leicefter Infirmary contemplate with peculiar pleafure the exertions which have been made for the fupport and extenfion of this Charity; and yet it cannot be concealed, that the Expenditure has uniformly exceeded the ftated Income; the deficiency having been fupplied by cafual Benefactions and Legacies.

" This deficiency lately amounted to fo large a fum, that it was thought neceffary to inftitute a Special Committee, to enquire into its caufes, and the means by which it might hereafter be obviated. Great advantage has been derived from the labours of that Committee. The œconomical arrangements propofed are now adopted, from which the moft beneficial confequences are expected; and a pleafing hope is entertained, that, by liberal Subfcriptions and Donations, this Inftitution will be raifed to a degree of profperity, which need no longer fear embarraffment, or inconvenient limitation.

" It is, in an efpecial degree, neceffary to call the attention of the Charitable to the important object now in contemplation, the opening of an Afylum for that moft helplefs and pitiable clafs of mortals, poor Lunatics.

" That the effects of Infanity are moft deplorable, few need be told. Every fpecies of it produces a ftate of diftrefs and degradation, peculiarly humiliating to human nature. In general, the grand concerns of the Soul can no longer be attended to, nor any further preparation made for Eternity. Surrounding friends deeply partake of the calamity, and, in addition to the feelings which the prefent ftate of the Lunatic muft excite, are fubject to the alarming apprehenfion of thofe common effects of mental derangement, outrage to themfelves or others, or the fuicide of the unhappy fufferer.

" The Legacies and Donations of a few generous individuals have enabled the Governors to enter upon a plan of preparing the Building, which has for many years been erected for the reception and relief of fuch miferable objects; and it is hoped, that the Inftitution will now meet with that degree of encouragement, which its importance appears to demand.

" The Afylum is capable of receiving twenty patients, but it cannot be opened upon fo large a fcale at prefent. It is prefumed, however, that the Charity is now competent to fupport a fmaller number, from each of whom a weekly payment, as in the fimilar Inftitutions at York and Manchefter, may be expected; and nothing can prevent or delay the full advantage which this Inftitution is capable of producing, but a want of that benevolence, in which the inhabitants of this Country have rarely been found deficient.

" The Governors feel themfelves under peculiar obligations to thofe Clergymen, and other Minifters of Religion, who have been the foremoft to promote the intereft of thefe united Charities, by acceding to the plan of preaching annually for their benefit; and it is prefumed, that the reft of their brethren will foon follow this laudable example, when they underftand how much their exertions are wanted."

In the Report of 1801, the Governors fay, that " they are under the neceffity of ftating, that, through the increafed expence of every article of life, they are not able to continue their plan upon fo large a fcale as they have done for fome years paft. They have long lamented that their permanent income has not been adequate to the full fupport of the Houfe.

" By the œconomical arrangements which have been made, they entertained the hope of preventing all embarraffments, or inconvenient limitation; but in that expectation they are difappointed, through the peculiar preffure of the prefent times.

" They had gone fo far beyond their Annual Receipts, by endeavouring to give to this benevolent Inftitution its full effect, in the admiffion of as many patients as poffible, that they were in the year 1796 obliged, though reluctantly, to come to the refolution of reducing the number of beds from 54 to 40; and have fince been obliged, by the fame caufe, to continue this reduction, till laft year; during a period when the unparalleled diftreffes of the poor, compelled greater numbers than ordinary to apply to this Charity for that medical aid, for which many of them had been accuftomed to have recourfe to the Faculty in their feveral neighbourhoods, and to pay from their own refources. Thefe applications have been annually increafing with the increafing mifery which gave occafion to them; and are now become fo numerous, that the Governors, no longer able to refift a diftrefs fo grievous and fo preffing, have, with a confidence which they are perfuaded will not deceive them, prefumed upon the public benevolence; and, though ftill too confined in their income, have ventured to enlarge the extent of their Charity: well affured, that when the friends of humanity fhall be made fenfible how much, at the prefent moment, their affiftance is wanted, they will bring it with that promptnefs and alacrity, for which this age is diftinguifhed above all which have preceded, and Englifhmen above all other Nations.

" In this confidence they have yielded to the feelings, which the fight of fo much mifery as weekly prefents itfelf to the view, and folicits the commiferation of their Committees, could not fail to produce; and have reftored to fuffering humanity fome of thofe beds, which for the laft five years have remained unoccupied and ufelefs.

" Laft Midfummer they increafed the number of beds from 40 to 46: and though the unfavourable appearance of their finances, at the quarterly meeting in March following, led them again to reduce them to 40; yet, re-animated by fome recent fymptoms of improvement, and trufting to the fuccefs of their *intended preffing application to the publick*, they have agreed, at the prefent annual meeting, to venture on an immediate addition of 10 beds, and to increafe the number to 50.

" In order to do this, they have ventured to borrow money upon intereft of their Treafurer; who has cheerfully confented to accommodate them till the public benevolence, on which they have thus prefumed, and on which they confidently rely, fhall enable them to repay the debt, and to fupport, without borrowing, this beneficial extenfion of their Charity, fo imperioufly demanded by the unexampled diftrefs of that ufeful branch of the community, the labouring and induftrious poor.

" The cafe is preffing, the want of relief is urgent; and to the humane and good it will not be reprefented in vain. Diftrefs will excite a generous fympathy, and its call will be heard by the County at large; which will come forward, without hefitation or delay, to make frefh efforts in aid of this noble Inftitution, and to extend its fphere of beneficence, by adding many a liberal name to the honourable lift of its annual Subfcribers and Benefactors.

" Were the Clergy, and other Minifters of Religion, in their refpective places, to make it, as it ought to be, a general caufe, and ftrenuoufly recommend its fupport to their congregations, the moft effectual affiftance might be expected from their united influence. Much advantage has already been derived from the Collections which have been made in various places of worfhip; and, were fuch Collections general throughout the County, and annually repeated, the Infirmary might foon be raifed to that degree of profperity, as no longer to fear embarraffment, or refufe its aid to any of the fick or lame in a ftate of indigence. It is prefumed that the Preachers of Chriftianity, the Divine Author of which both taught and exemplified the duty of going about doing good, will not refufe their zealous exertions, when they are informed what extenfive benefits they may procure to their fellow-creatures in diftrefs."

In 1802, " The Governors add their thanks for the very public-fpirited exertions of the Clergy; who have, by their Sermons in behalf of the Infirmary and Lunatic Afylum, enriched their funds with the fum of 1287*l*. 6*s*. 4*d*. part of which fum has been laid

out

out in neceffary repairs and improvements of the Infirmary; part expended in defraying the increafed expence of thefe Charities above the amount of the Annual Subfcriptions; and part in purchafe of ftock for the improvement of their permanent annual income: And they beg leave to remark, that they place great confidence in the continued exertions of this philanthropic fpirit of the Clergy, by which they are enabled to contribute fo effential an affiftance to thefe important Charities."

1803.—" The Special Report of the Committee of Enquiry, which was publifhed in the latter end of the year 1802, gives a favourable reprefentation of the refult of its refearches; and affords a pleafing view of the ftate and profpeft of the Infirmary and Lunatic Afylum, in confequence of the late, as well as of the expected future, exertions of the Clergy, and of the Publick in general; which there appears reafon to hope will rather increafe than diminifh. The fame number of 50 beds are therefore to be continued in ufe, for the reception of as many patients; as we agree with that Committee, that, *whatever may have been the difficulties with which the Charity has had occafion to ftruggle, there is no juft ground for alarm:* and the fum to be paid weekly for each patient in the Lunatic Afylum is henceforth reduced from 10 to 8s. per week.

" We cannot be too grateful to the Clergy for thofe effectual exertions to which thefe Charities are fo greatly indebted, and to a continuance of which they muft look for much of their future profperity: fince the benefit of their Sermons is not only immediately great, but may be expected to reach much farther than the Collections made at the time; they will keep up through the County a lively intereft in favour of the Inftitution, and be the probable means of adding to its finances frefh Subfcriptions, Legacies, and Benefactions."

1804.—" The Governors have the fatisfaction to inform the Publick, that the finances both of the Infirmary and of the Lunatic Afylum are rather in an improving ftate; and they are perfuaded that the fame benevolent aids of Church Collections, increafing annual Subfcriptions, and occafional Legacies and Donations, which have lately been fo feafonably granted, will continue to fupport them. In this perfuafion they have ventured to increafe the number of beds in ufe from 50 to 54.

" The amount of Stock in the Three per Cent. Bank Annuities of the Infirmary is 9533l. 6s. 8d.; and of the Lunatic Afylum, 666l. 13s. 4d.

" That much of the profperity of thefe Charities depends upon their good internal government, and œconomical management, cannot be doubted: nor can it be doubted, that a ftrict attention to thefe things can alone be kept up by the exact attendance and infpection of the Houfe Vifitors, and the diligent care of Weekly Committees. The watchfulnefs of thefe fhould never be remitted. That it has been too much fo of late years is greatly to be lamented; and it is earneftly requefted, that the inconveniences arifing from this remiffnefs of the Governors refiding in the Town, and its vicinity, may for the future be remedied, by a punctual and exact performance of the duties of the Houfe Vifitor, and by full and unfailing Committees."

The Report of 1806 concludes with ftill brighter profpects:

" The Governors of the Leicefter Infirmary contemplate with pleafure the exertions which have been made for the fupport and extenfion of this Charity. Among other liberal benefactions, they gratefully acknowledge the kindnefs of the Rev. Thomas Gifborne, and J. H. Browne, efq. executors of the late Ifaac Hawkins, efq.; who, out of the property bequeathed to them by that gentleman, have appropriated a large fum to the funds of the Infirmary; in confequence of which, the number of beds has been increafed to fifty-four: and yet they are under the neceffity of ftating, that they ftill labour under confiderable difficulties, through the increafed expence of every article of life, and that their permanent in-

come is not adequate to the full fupport of the houfe. It is hoped that this reprefentation will induce the Gentlemen of the County to come forward, without hefitation or delay, to make frefh efforts in aid of this noble Inftitution, and to extend its fphere of beneficence, by adding many a liberal name to the honourable lift of its annual Subfcribers and Benefactors.

" The Inftitution is greatly indebted to the Clergy, and other Minifters of Religion, for their effectual exertions. From the collections made fome years ago in the different places of worfhip throughout the county, no lefs a fum than 1287l. 6s. 8d. was received in one year, by which the difficulties then felt were removed; and by a fimilar effort made within this laft year a very large fum, amounting to 687l. 4s. 11d., has already (June 24) been collected, to which fomething more probably ftill remains to be added. The Governors avail themfelves of this opportunity to exprefs their grateful acknowledgements to the Lord Bifhop of the Diocefe, who fo kindly condefcended to their requeft that he would ufe his influence with his Clergy; and to the Clergy, and other Minifters of Religion, who have fo honourably and fo fuccefsfully exerted themfelves to relieve the very preffing neceffities of this excellent Inftitution.

" To the General Infirmary for the fick and the lame, has been lately added another Charitable Inftitution, equally important and beneficial. An Afylum, in a feparate building, has been opened for the reception of that moft helplefs and pitiable clafs of mortals, *poor* Lunatics; but it is much to be lamented, that it has not yet received that degree of encouragement which might have been expected, and without which it cannot be carried to that extent of utility for which it is calculated.

" That the effects of Infanity are moft deplorable, few need be told. Every fpecies of it produces a ftate of diftrefs and degradation peculiarly humiliating to human nature: in general, the grand concerns of the foul can no longer be attended to, nor any further preparations be made for Eternity. Surrounding friends deeply partake of the calamity; and, in addition to the feelings which the prefent ftate of the Lunatic muft excite, are fubject to the alarming apprehenfion of thofe common effects of mental derangement, outrage to themfelves or others, or the fuicide of the unhappy fufferer.

" The Afylum is capable of receiving twenty patients; but, for *want of an adequate fund from Donations and Annual Subfcriptions,* it is at prefent opened upon a more contracted fcale, and can receive only fourteen, for each of whom the Governors will be obliged to demand 8s. weekly, till fuch time as the bounty of the Publick fhall have fufficiently increafed their refources. They flatter themfelves, however, that they fhall foon be enabled gradually to augment the number of patients, and to reduce the weekly demand for each, as was done in the fimilar inftitutions at York and Manchefter. Thefe are improvements, which will give the full advantage this Charity is capable of producing; and nothing can prevent or delay them, but a want of that benevolence in which the inhabitants of this County have rarely been deficient.

" But the Governors of thefe Charities are folicitous not only to augment their pecuniary refources, but to improve and turn to the beft account thofe which they already poffefs. They wifh that the internal government may be maintained with the ftricteft attention to œconomy, good order, morality, and piety: but they are aware that fuch a fyftem, however directed by their ftatutes, cannot long be practically adhered to, without the conftant attendance and careful infpection of the Houfe Vifitors and Weekly Committees. With much concern they obferve a remiffnefs in thefe refpects, and a neglect of thefe important duties. And therefore they take this method of earneftly requefting the Gentlemen of the Town and its vicinity to devote fome portion of their time, as well as their money, to the improvements of thefe Charities, and watch over them with conftant folicitude, to prevent or correct the introduction of any wafte or abufe in any one of their departments.

" Anniverfary

"Anniverfary Meeting, Sept. 19, 1806;
Lord Vifcount Wentworth, V. P. in the Chair.

"Refolved, That an Extra Report be printed; conveying the grateful acknowledgements of the Governors to the Lord Bifhop of the Diocefe, for ufing his influence with the Clergy; and to the Clergy, and other Minifters of Religion, who have fo honourably and fuccefsfully exerted themfelves to relieve the very preffing neceffity of this excellent Inftitution. That to this Report be fubjoined an Alphabetical Lift of the various Contributions made in the different Parifhes in the County; and that a copy be fent to every Preacher. WENTWORTH, Chairman."

The Report was accordingly printed; and it appears that the total fum collected was 1003*l.* 4*s.* 6*d.*

The Officers enumerated in the Report of 1806 were, Prefident, Earl of Stamford and Warrington; Vice-prefidents, Earls of Cardigan, Ferrers, Moira, and Lord Vifcount Wentworth; Vifitor, the Right Rev. George Lord Bifhop of Lincoln; Treafurer, John Mansfield, Efq.; Auditors, Mr. Robert Clarke and Mr. J. B. Oliver; Phyficians, Dr. Arnold and Dr. W. W. Arnold; Surgeons, Mr. Peake and Mr. Paget; Chaplain [1], Rev. Mr. Robinfon; Houfe Surgeon and Apothecary, Mr. John Bridges; Secretary, Mr. John Throfby; Matron, Mrs Robinfon.

Abftract of the Accompts, from the opening of the Infirmary, Sept. 22, 1771, to June 24, 1806.

RECEIPTS.

	£.	s.	d.
By fubfcriptions, dividends on ftock, fee-farm rents, &c.	34,218	17	5½
By benefactions and legacies	7,910	3	6
By Collections at Anniverfary Meetings	5,958	1	6¾
By articles fold	487	6	9
By poors' boxes	118	9	2½
Balance due to the Treafurer	301	5	4
	48,994	3	9¾

PAYMENTS.

	£.	s.	d.
Expended, as by former Accompts	47,001	12	6¾
Ditto this year, as by the Accompt	1,992	11	3
	48,994	3	9¾

Return of the Patients of the Leicefter Infirmary, for the year ending June 24, 1806.

IN-PATIENTS.

Remaining on the Books, June 24, 1805	41
Admitted fince	447
Total	448
Of which were difcharged, cured	307
relieved	32
at their own requeft	0
Died	22
made Out-patients	67
Improper	0
Remaining in the Houfe	55
on the Books waiting for vacancies	5
Total	448

Of thefe, 44 were fudden accidents requiring immediate afftance, and without recommendation.

OUT-PATIENTS.

Remained on the Books, June 24, 1805	103
Admitted fince	1,266
Total	1,369
Of which were cured	701
relieved	4
Died	10
made In-patients	4
fuccefsfully inoculated for Vaccine Pox	540
Remaining on the Books	110
	1,369

General Return of In and Out-Patients fince the opening of the Infirmary, Sept. 22, 1771, to June 24, 1806.

Difcharged In-patients, cured	8,147
Out-Patients, ditto	7,481
Total cured	15,898
Difcharged In-Patients, relieved	1,138
Out-Patients, ditto	1,128
Total relieved	2,266

LUNATIC ASYLUM ACCOMPTS, TO JUNE 24, 1806.

RECEIPTS.

	£.	s.	d.
Balance due to the Afylum laft year	451	14	7
By receipt of one year's dividend on 666*l.* 13*s.* 4*d.* Confols	20	0	0
Annual Subfcriptions	109	4	0
Received for Patients' Board	169	8	0
One year's Short Annuities	100	0	0
Legacy	100	0	0
	950	6	7

PAYMENTS.

	£.	s.	d.
Repairs and Alterations	10	0	11
Furniture	6	14	7
Drugs	7	8	0
Coals	11	16	5
Servants' Wages	39	9	6
Apothecaries' Incidentals	7	10	8
Board of Patients, Servants, &c.	374	8	0
Coals, &c. from the Infirmary	7	2	0
Stamp for a Legacy	10	0	0
Balance due to the Afylum	475	16	6
	950	6	7

Return of Patients of the Lunatic Afylum, from June 24, 1805, to June 24, 1806.

Remained in the Houfe laft June	14
Admitted fince	10
	42
Difcharged, cured	4
relieved	5
Died	1
Remain in the Houfe	14
	24

*** Mr. Howard, in his Account of the principal Lazarettos in Europe, &c. 1789, p. 160, fays, "The ground floors of the County Infirmary at Leicefter are brick; the upper floors rough tarras; and none of the windows being open, the wards were very clofe. The under fafhes are not moveable." To the latter part of thefe fuggeftions a proper attention has been paid, under the judicious direction of John Johnfon, efq. an eminent architect in London, and a native of this town [2].

[1] Mrs. Dorothy Afhby (afterward Mrs. Middleton) gave 50*l.* for the efpecial purpofe of eftablifhing a falary for a Clergyman.
[2] See p. 528.

The CONSANGUINITARIUM (fee Plate XXXV.)

is a handfome ftone-building, confifting of five houfes, in Southgate-ftreet, near the Water-houfe pump, partly fcreened by four neat dwelling-houfes which bound the ftreet, erected by John Johnfon, efq. of London, on the fpot where he was born. Each dwelling has a room on the ground-floor, and a chamber over it: the rooms are neat and convenient; and the windows glazed with beautiful ftained glafs. To each inhabitant is regularly given a printed copy of the following Rules and Orders:

" I. The CONSANGUINITARIUM being an Afylum for fuch relatives as are, through age or infirmities, incapable of procuring a comfortable refidence and fupport for themfelves; the inhabitants of each dwelling will be paid the fum of 5s. every week, and yearly receive one ton of coals; except that, out of fuch fum of 5s. will be referved 6d. each week, or more fhould the fame be required, for the purpofes hereafter mentioned.

II. That each inhabitant fhall, on admiffion, bring one new, or very good feather-bed, one bolfter, one pillow, two pair of fheets, two blankets, a new coverlet, and curtains for the bed; four chairs, one table, good utenfils for cooking and other purpofes, the whole not to be under the value of 5l.; all of which fhall be left on the premifes at the time of the death of him or her, in each habitation, for the benefit of the furviving inhabitants, who are to be at the expence of the decent burial of the deceafed.

III. No inhabitant to keep either dog, cat, fowls, or rabbits, nor any other animal that may be a nuifance; nor to carry on any bufinefs in his or her dwelling that may render the fame unfeemly.

IV. No inhabitant to be allowed to keep any inmate, or any vifitor to fleep with him or her, on pain of difmiffion.

V. No wafhing of clothes to take place, otherwife than in the wafh-houfe; nor any flop to be thrown in the paffage; or dirt, or duft, or refufe of any kind, in any other place than in the brick receptacle, built in the yard or garden. For the firft offence againft any of the foregoing reftrictions, to forfeit 6d.; for the fecond, and every other, 1s.—N.B. The wafhing-day of No. 1, to be on Monday; No. 2, on Tuefday; No. 3, on Wednefday; No. 4, on Thurfday; No. 5, on Friday. The wafh-houfe to be left clean.

VI. Each inhabitant, in turn, to keep the lawn, paffage, drying-yard, and walks to the entrance, gate, &c. clean, and in good order, for a week, beginning with the firft inhabited dwelling, on pain of difmiffion.

VII. Each inhabitant to lock the entrance-gate at going out, or returning; nor to be from home, or have vifitors at their dwellings, at a later hour than ten o'clock in the evening in the fummer, and nine in the winter; on the forfeiture of 6d. each time, in either cafe.

VIII. No child or children to be admitted into the lawn, on any account.

IX. The rain-water not to be ufed for any other purpofe than that of wafhing, under the forfeiture of 6d. for each offence.

X. In cafe of ficknefs, the females to attend on each other, by turn, and alfo on the males, or be difmiffed.—N.B. The coals to be delivered on the outfide the railing of the entrance, and to be carried to the feveral places appropriated by the male inhabitants, or at their expence.

XI. Each inhabitant to be accountable for the reparations, painting, white-wafhing, &c. of his or her feparate dwelling and coal-houfe.—N.B. The repairs of the other offices and things, and keeping the fhrubbery, &c. in condition, to be at the joint expence of the whole—[It is expected, that each inhabitant do keep the garden belonging to his or her dwelling in good order;]—and the 6d. per week is retained for the feveral purpofes before mentioned. Such of the inhabitants as fcreen others from the forfeits againft the offences mentioned, fhall be liable to the fame forfeits, if in any way made known to the Truftee Vifitors appointed to infpect into the good order of the Houfe.

XII. It is prefumed that every kind of good order and decorum among the inhabitants of the Confanguinitarium will exift; that they will be neat and clean in their apartments and drefs; vie with each other in acts of friendly affiftance to their refident relatives; that they will alfo duly attend public worfhip, at fuch place as is moft congenial to their confcience, and give praife to the Great Author of the Univerfe, for enabling and permitting the Founder of thefe dwellings to have the pleafure of giving the comforts they afford to them. But fhould any be fo loft to themfelves, as to fow ftrife and difcord, or by abufive words or actions render the meek-minded unhappy, they will be removed for ever from their places of refidence.—N.B. When the expence of the general reparations is afcertained, each inhabitant will have an equal divifion of the remaining fum of the 6d. per week. Then, out of each inhabitant's fum fo divided will be taken any expence that has been paid by the Truft for the repairs, &c. of his or her feparate dwelling. The forfeits for offences that have been committed will alfo be given annually to thofe who are found moft deferving."

This comfortable refuge for his diftreffed relations, which was finifhed in 1792, was defigned and named by, and erected at the expence of, the above-named Mr. Johnfon; who, by a deed enrolled in Chancery, charged an eftate which he then had at Lubbenham with the payment of 70l. a year for the fupport of the Charity.

The philanthropic Founder is well known by the many fubftantial public and private edifices of which he has been the Architect; particularly at Chelmsford [1] in Effex, where the Stone Bridge, County Hall, Church, and a very large Prifon, were built from his defigns, and under his direction, as Architect and Surveyor of the County [2]; an office which he has ably filled nearly 26 years.

---

[1] Among the feveral public buildings which have been defigned and erected by Mr. Johnfon, may be more efpecially mentioned:

MIDDLESEX.
Earl of Gallaway's houfe, Charles-ftreet, St. James's-fquare.
Lord Middleton's, Portman-fquare.
The Hon. Charles Greville's, ditto.
Earl of Hardwicke's, Cavendifh-ftreet, Portland place.
William Udney's, efq. ditto.
Bifhop of Offory's, Harley-ftreet.
John Pybus's, efq. ditto.
Sir Hugh Palifer's, Pall Mall.
Sir John Anderfon's, bart. Mill-hill.

ESSEX.
Terling-place, John Strutt's, efq.
Langford-grove, N. Weftcombe's, efq.
Colonel Tyrell's, Hatfield.
John Judd's, efq. Broomfield.
Major Carr's, Stroud-green.
John Crabb's, efq. Torrile's Hall.
The Rev. John Bramftone-Stane's, Willingale.
The Rev. Henry Bate-Dudley's, Bradwell juxta Mare.

SUFFOLK.
Woolverfton Hall, William Berners, efq.

Benhall, Sir William Rufh.
Noblemen's and Gentlemen's Club-rooms, Newmarket.

NORTHAMPTONSHIRE.
Carlton Houfe, Sir John Palmer, bart.
James Fremeaux, efq. Kingfthorpe.
Colonel Money's, Pisford.

LEICESTERSHIRE.
Hotel, Leicefter; fee p. 532.
Town Gaol, ditto; fee p. 531.
Whatton Hall, Edward Dawfon, efq.; fee vol. III. p. 1101.

GLAMORGANSHIRE.
Gnoll Caftle, Sir Herbert Mackworth, bart.
Clafmount, John Morris, efq.

DEVONSHIRE.
Killerton Hall, Sir Thomas Dyke Ackland, bart.
Sadborough Houfe, William Bragge, efq.

SURREY.
Wimbledon Church.

SUSSEX.
The Seat of Charles Beauclerk, efq.

[2] At the Quarter Seffions held at Chelmsford in January 1792, the Shire Houfe Committee made their final Report: " That that public ftructure had been completed in the moft perfect and elegant manner, with a faving of near 2000l under the original eftimate; and recommended the eminent fervices of their Surveyor to the confideration of the Court, for fome mark of their approbation. On which it was moved by Mr. Bate Dudley, and feconded by Mr. Kynafton, ' That the thanks of the County Quarter Seffions be given by the Chairman to John Johnfon, efq.; and alfo that a piece of plate of the value of one hundred guineas (with a fuitable infcription thereon) be purchafed out of the furplus money raifed under the Act of Parliament for building a New Shire Houfe, and prefented to the faid John Johnfon, efq. as a public teftimony of his integrity and profeffional abilities, in the execution of the faid Shire Houfe, as Architect and Surveyor of the County of Effex.' The whole Bench expreffed their concurrent opinion of the acknowledged merit of their Surveyor. The motion was of courfe agreed to; and the Chairman, in a very complimentary addrefs, delivered the thanks of the Court to Mr. Johnfon; who returned his acknowledgements to the Court in the handfomeft manner. And a Committee was appointed, to purchafe the plate accordingly." Chelmsford Chronicle, Jan. 13, 1792.

Elevation of Four Houses, Built by the Founder of the CONSANGUINITARIUM, being the Place of his Birth.

CONSANGUINITARIUM.

John Johnson Esq.　　　　　*contributes this Plate.*

LEICESTER HUMANE SOCIETY.

The following benevolent plan was fuggefted in 1805, in a letter to the Mayor of Leicefter:

"Sir—We the underfigned, the Phyficians and Clergy of the Town, refpectfully requeft that you will call a meeting of fuch inhabitants as may approve of the inftitution of a Humane Society in Leicefter, in order to confider of the beft mode of carrying the plan into effect.

H. S. J. BULLEN.	RICHARD DAVIES.
W. W. ARNOLD.	THOMAS ROBINSON.
EDW. ALEXANDER.	WILLIAM MANDELL.
WM. WARD.	J. ANDERSON.
E. T. VAUGHAN.	WILLIAM HAYTON."
THOMAS ARNOLD.	

"In confequence of the above refpectable requifition, I appoint a Meeting to be held at the 'Change, at eleven o'clock, on Wednefday Sept. 4, 1805.
EDMUND SWINFEN, Mayor."

A general meeting was accordingly held, when the bufinefs was thus opened by the Rev. H. S. J. Bullen:

"Mr. Mayor, and Gentlemen—The purport of this Meeting is, to eftablifh, upon a refpectable fcale, a Society upon the principles of the Royal Humane Society; an Inftitution fo replete with good, that it is unneceffary for me to expatiate upon the ufefulnefs of it. Suffice it to fay, that, in the fhort period of 30 years fince its firft eftablifhment, 3000 perfons have been reftored to Society, to their Families, and the State.

"Gentlemen, need I inform you that the riches of a country are its population, and that the life of a citizen is one of the deareft poffeffions we have to protect? Upon this ground, therefore, the wifdom and policy of the meafure are evident. But, there is a ftill higher order of fentiment, that cannot fail of actuating your breafts; which is, the duty as it ftands in a moral view. It is the bounden obligation of every good man, efpecially in this age, prodigal as it is of human life, to be as inftrumental as poffible in preferving the lives of his fellow-men. The Humane Society eminently prefents the means of exercifing this virtue: it feems, indeed, as if Providence intended it as a peculiar bleffing, to counteract the deftructive inventions which War is fure to encourage.

"And here I would fuggeft to thofe who are not of the medical profeffion, that the Refufcitative Procefs, though generally applied to cafes of drowning, is equally applicable to cafes of fufpenfion by rope, fmothering, fuffocation, intenfe cold, immoderate dofes of opium, intoxication, and accidents by lightning; in fhort, to almoft every fpecies of death, where the mifchief has gone no farther than merely to the obftruction of the organs, without any danger to thofe organs themfelves.

"Gentlemen, with regard to the local motives which fhould induce us to further this Inftitution, you are aware that the great increafe of inland navigation has made the poffibilities of accidents more frequent, and, of confequence, our obligation to obviate them more impofing. It is a melancholy truth, that of thofe inftances which have already occurred of drowning, in many cafes death might have been prevented by the timely affiftance of a medical man, aided by the proper co-operation of the publick. But, as the cafe now ftands, there is nothing but ignorance, prejudice, and ill-treatment of a body; enough of itfelf to extinguifh the vital fpark, if it were ever fo vivid. To overcome thefe prejudices, and to correct this ignorance, is the province of this benevolent Inftitution.

"I am convinced, Gentlemen, that I need not adduce further arguments to perfuade you to come forward, and, by your generous aid, refcue many a victim from death, and many a family from tears. Under this conviction, I commit the fubject to abler hands; affured that the caufe of Humanity, if ever fo indifferently pleaded, will not have been pleaded in vain before fo enlightened an Audience."

The refult of the meeting was, an unanimous refolution, to commence a fubfcription, for eftablifhing a Humane Society, on the plan of that which has fo long been fuccefsfully eftablifhed in London; Dr. Hawes, the Treafurer of that benevolent Inftitution, with the philanthropy for which he is fo eminently diftinguifhed, having affifted in its promotion, and countenanced it with his patronage.

THE PRISONS AT LEICESTER

have lately been re-built on fo improved a plan, that it is pleafant to contraft their former ftate, as defcribed by the benevolent Mr. Howard [1] in 1782, with their prefent improved appearance.

COUNTY GAOL.

Gaoler, Samuel Jordan, 1773; William Jordan, 1782. Salary, none.

Fees, for debtors or felons, 15s. 4d. Tranfports; if only one, 8s.; if more than one, 7s. each.

Licence. Beer, to deputy.

Allowance, to debtors and felons, a fourpenny loaf every other day; weight, once, 2 lb. 8 oz.; twice, 3 lb. 5 oz.

Garnifh; debtors, 4s.; felons, 3s.

Number in 1773, Nov. 26, 16 debtors— 3 felons, &c.

1774, April 4,	16	11
1775, Jan. 3,	15	7
—— Nov. 11,	17	2
1776, Oct. 29,	17	5
1779, Mar. 27,	23	10
1782, May 2,	20	5

Chaplain, Rev. James Pigott; duty, Sunday; falary, 30l.—Surgeon, Mr. Maule; falary, 15l. for debtors and felons.

For mafter's fide 9 or 10 rooms. Day-room common. The fide ward, *the cellar*, is a dungeon, 29½ feet by 9, and 6 feet 8 inches high, down 7 fteps, and damp [2]; two windows; the largeft about 15 inches fquare. Felons' day and night rooms are dungeons, from five to feven fteps under ground. They fleep on thick mats on the floor; which, if cribs and coverlets were added, would be better than ftraw. The whole clofe and offenfive. Court fmall, 36 feet by 17 feet four inches. No chapel.

Two rooms lately built for an Infirmary; but the Gaol is not convenient or healthy.

In 1774, three debtors and a felon died of the fmall-pox. Of that difeafe, I was informed, few ever recover in this Gaol. The Caftle-hill is near the Shire-hall, and is a fine fpot for air and water [3]. Claufes of the act againft the ufe of fpirituous liquors painted on the fame board with the table of fees. The act for preferving the health of prifoners not hung up. Here, as in many other places, is an

[1] "The mention of a character fo widely expanding beyond the cuftomary fphere of human actions irrefiftibly arrefts the attention of the heart that glows with admiration at ftriking examples of virtue, and of the head that feels intereft in tracing the motives which influence the conduct of men." Walk through Leicefter, p. 30.

[2] This feems to be the "low moift dungeon" that was complained of by a debtor in the gaol, in his letter, 13 Nov. 1690, fent to Mofes Pitt, a prifoner in the Fleet; who printed it, with other letters from prifoners, in his "Cry of the Oppreffed, 1691." By this, and one or two more of the letters in that little tract, it appears that fome inconveniences which I obferved in gaols, and have fet down in my remarks, are of long ftanding. [3] See Plate XXIV. p. 363; and Pl. XXVIII. p. 326.

ufelefs

uſeleſs *tub*, inſtead of a *bath*, for cleanlineſs and health [1].

An inſcription on a board fixed over the gate, " No money to be aſked for by turnkeys, or priſoners, for garniſh, or any other pretence whatever."

In this County they make an annual collection by a kind of voluntary brief. The Gentlemen of the Grand Jury recommend it to the Clergy; moſt of whom promote the collection in their reſpective pariſhes. The thanks of the Grand Jury to 48 Clergymen by name were inſerted in the Leiceſter Journal of Feb. 16, 1775, for the ſatisfaction of thoſe gentlemen and other contributors. There is a table of the ſums received from each pariſh; and a liſt of debtors cloathed or diſcharged; and an account of the expenditure of the remainder in feeding and warming all the priſoners in the inclement ſeaſon.

The collections in 1774 amounted to 74*l.* I find in 1776 the accounts were kept, and the application of the money chiefly directed, by John Simpſon, eſq. of Leiceſter. I wiſh every County would imitate this exemplary benevolence; and I wiſh every County that does ſo, a ſteward equally faithful and aſſiduous. I am ſorry to find the collection fall ſhort. It amounted, in 1779, only to 12*l.* 5*s.* 6*d.*; in 1780, to 6*l.* 1*s.* 9*d.*; and in 1781, to 3*l.* 18*s.*

" *Leiceſterſhire*. A TABLE of FEES to be taken by the Keeper of this Gaol. *s. d.*

	s.	d.
For lodging of every priſoner *per* week —	2	4
For Gaol-fees for diſcharge of every priſoner	13	4
For the Turnkey — — —	2	0
For the copy of every warrant or commitment	1	0
For ſigning the certificate in order to obtain a *ſuperſedeas* — — — — —	1	0

Thomas à Becket Seſſions, July 10, 1759.

We whoſe names are hereunto ſubſcribed, his Majeſty's Juſtices of the Peace in and for the County of Leiceſter, do hereby allow of the above fees to be taken. W. WRIGHTE, CH. HUTCHINSON. J. DANVERS, W. CANT.

We, the Judges of Aſſize for the County of Leiceſter, have reviewed, and do hereby confirm, the above Table of Fees. Given under our hands, this 17th day of Auguſt, 1759. T. PARKER, JA. HEWITT. The above is a true copy of the original [2]."

On a ſubſequent viſit, Oct. 25, 1787, Mr. Howard adds, " The debtors' ſick ward is ſtill a *dungeon*; their beds are on bedſteads; but the felons have only the County allowance of mats in their damp dungeons. One ſmall court for debtors and felons. Keeper's ſalary, 200*l.*; out of which he is to give each priſoner three pints of ſmall beer a day. The Gaol now clean and quiet. Garniſh aboliſhed.— Debtors, 15; felons, &c. 14 [3]."

COUNTY BRIDEWELL. Three rooms below for men; five above for women; one of theſe not uſed, becauſe not ſecure: no chimneys. Court not ſafe for priſoners to be allowed the uſe of it. Allowance *now*, twopennyworth of bread a day, after a month's confinement. Clauſes againſt ſpirituous liquors not hung up. There was painted on a board, " By order of the Court, at Eaſter Seſſions 1778, that there ſhall be no ale or beer brought into this Priſon on a Sunday, nor after ſeven o'clock in the evening on a week-day."—In a former edition I ſuggeſted, that if a wall were built with brick, inſtead of the clay-wall, there would be no need of a chain and log to ſecure the priſoners in the Court. The apartments alſo would be more airy; and men and women might be ſeparated, if the narrow Court were enlarged from the orchard, which was let to the keeper for 6*l.* a year. At my laſt viſit, I found the Court enlarged,

and a wall built; but there is not a proper ſeparation of men and women. The priſoners now are without the chain. The priſon is white-waſhed once a year, and kept remarkably neat and clean. The priſoners do not lie on the floors; but, very properly, their mats are on cribs or bedſteads. Keeper a woolcomber; his ſalary 21*l.* He pays window-tax 14*s.*

1775, Jan. 3, Priſoners	3	1779, Mar. 27,	6
1776, Oct. 29,	2	1782, May 2,	2

Committed from Eaſter Seſſions 1779 to 1780, 48 [4]."

The COUNTY-GAOL (ſee Plate XXVIII. p. 326) was re-built in 1791, at an expence of 6000*l.* which was raiſed by a County-rate; and without looks like what it ſhould be; it has a priſon-like appearance. The architect, Mr. George Moneypenny, has ſhewn his knowledge of grand deſign, bordering on the terrific. In the elevation, the Cap of Liberty, the Roman Faſces, and his own name ſo large and conſpicuous on the front, have been ſubjects of animadverſion; and the following " Impromptu on ſeeing the Cap of Liberty on the new Building," appeared in the Leiceſter Journal:

" It needs no ſymbol ſure to tell,
No tale from claſſic lore,
That he who enters here to dwell,
Leaves Freedom at the door."

" This Priſon, to which the *County Bridewell* is now added, was erected, on the ſite of the old Gaol, five years after the benevolent Howard laſt v ſited Leiceſter. It is built with ſolitary cells, after the plan recommended by that celebrated Philanthropiſt; and was firſt inhabited [5] in 1793. It has four airy Court-yards, with water in every one, and a day-room to each. The Court for debtors is 74 feet by 32, and the day-room 29 feet by 13½; for thoſe on the Maſter's ſide there are ten rooms, to which the keeper furniſhes beds at 2*s.* 4*d. per* week for a ſingle bed; and if two ſleep together, 1*s.* 6*d.* a week each. Common-ſide debtors have a free-ward, with ten good-ſized ſleeping-rooms, to which they furniſh their own beds.

One room is ſet apart for an Infirmary.

Clauſes of the Act againſt the uſe of Spirituous Liquors painted on the ſame board as the Table of Fees. The Act for preſerving the health of the priſoners not hung up. No firing allowed. Thoſe priſoners who work receive all their earnings, but no County allowance of bread. Six debtors and two criminals were weaving ſtockings, and one making ſhoes, at my viſit in 1803. Here, as in many other gaols, is an uſeleſs *tub*, and two cold baths never uſed.

Gaoler, John Simons. Salary, 130*l.* out of which he allows every priſoner a quart of ſmall-beer daily.

Fees; ſee Table [as in the preceding column.] Beſides which the Under-ſheriff takes a fee of 6*s.* 8*d.* for his *liberate*.

Garniſh. None, on any pretence whatever.

Chaplain, Rev. Mr. Anderſon. Duty; Prayers four days, Sermon on Sunday. Salary, 60*l.*

Surgeon, Mr. Maule. Salary, 15*l.* for debtors and felons.

Number of Debtors,

1800, March 28, . . 18	1803, Aug. 23, . . . 12
1802, Jan. 27, ... 4	1805, Sept. 26, . . . 8

Allowance. One pound ſix ounces of bread ſent from the bakers every other day, in loaves weight 2 lb. 12 oz. each; and one quart of ſmall-beer daily.

Mr. Gregory informed me no collection had been made for ſeveral years; that from 1795 to 1803 the whole amount collected was only 5*l.* 1*s.* 6*d.*; and that the balance remaining in his hands was 32*l.* 6*s.* 11*d.* [6]"

---

[1] " In many priſons I have mentioned that there is *no bath*, though baths are ordered in all gaols in the ' Act for preſerving the health of priſoners.' I would here alſo remind gentlemen, that when baths are provided in compliance with the Act, if they be not made convenient, ſo that felons in their irons may commodiouſly uſe them; and if there is no allowance for ſoap and *towels*; theſe priſoners will receive little or no benefit from them, and will never bathe but when actually compelled."

[2] Mr. Howard's State of the Priſons in England and Wales, third edition, 1784, p. 313.

[3] Mr. Howard's Account of the principal Lazarettos in Europe, &c. 1789, p. 160. [4] Mr. Howard on Priſons, p. 315.

[5] " It may be obſerved as an example of ſudden viciſſitude, that the builder of this fabrick became, as a debtor, its firſt inhabitant." Walk through Leiceſter, p. 30.

[6] Mr. Neild's Account of Priſons for Debtors in England, Scotland, and Wales, p. 247.

TOWN AND COUNTY GAOL.

" Gaoler, Henry Coulſon, 1776; Samuel Jordan, 1779; William Jordan, 1782.

Salary, none ; he pays 3l. rent.

Fees, debtors and felons, 15s. 4d.

Tranſports, 10l. each.

Licence. Beer, to deputy.

Allowance to debtors and felons, 2d. a day each in bread (viz. May 1782, 1 lb. 11 oz.)

Garniſh ; debtors, 4s. 6d. ; felons, 2s. 6d.

1774, April 4, 5 debtors—5 felons, &c.

1775, Jan. 3,	1	2
—— Nov. 21,	1	0
1776, Oct. 29,	1	2
1779, Mar. 27,	3	2
1782, May 2,	2	3

Chaplain, none.

Surgeon, Mr. Maule ; no ſalary, makes a bill.

A common day-room, 12 feet by 9 : two rooms above, for ſuch as pay. Down five ſteps is a dungeon for men-felons ; another for women ; another for common-ſide debtors. This Gaol is too cloſe, and is never white-waſhed : it has a Court with plenty of water, and yet the ſewers are very offenſive. Neither clauſes againſt ſpirituous liquors, nor the act for preſerving the health of priſoners, are hung up ; but there is now (1782) a table of fees.

" Borough of Leiceſter, in the County of Leiceſter. A Table of Fees to be taken by the Keeper of his Majeſty's Gaol for the ſaid Borough.

	£.	s.	d.
For lodging every priſoner per week ——	0	2	4
For a room of every perſon who finds his own bed per week —— —— ——	0	1	0
For the Gaol, for the diſcharge of any priſoner —— —— —— ——	0	13	4
For the turnkey —— ——	0	2	0
A room called the Debtors' room, if they find their own bed to pay —— ——	0	0	0
For the copy of every warrant or commitment —— —— —— ——	0	1	0
For ſigning a certificate in order to obtain a ſuperſedeas —— —— ——	0	1	0
At the delivery of every declaration ——	0	1	0
Attending upon every priſoner to give bail, ſpecial bail, habeas, or any thing neceſſary to go out of gaol, for every mile travelling —— —— ——	0	1	0

" Michaelmas Seſſions, 1776. We whoſe names are hereunto ſubſcribed, three of his Majeſty's Juſtices of the Peace for the Borough of Leiceſter aforeſaid, do hereby allow the above fees to be taken (the 13s. 4d. above to the gaoler and the 2s. to the turnkey where the priſoner againſt whom no bill of indictment ſhall be found by the Grand Jury, and who, on his or her trial, ſhall be acquitted, or who ſhall be diſcharged by proclamation for want of proſecution, only excepted.)

WILL. BURLETON, Recorder,
ROB. PEACH, JOS. JOHNSON."

" We the Judges of Aſſize for the Borough of Leiceſter aforeſaid have reviewed, and do hereby confirm, the above Table of Fees. Given under our hands this 22d day of March, 1777.

G. NARES, S. S. SMYTHE.

" This is a true copy of the original."

At my laſt viſit, William Slack, one of the felons, had received his Majeſty's free pardon (April 9) ; and was " ordered to be ſet at liberty," ſigned Shelburne ; but, for the fees of the ſecretary of ſtate (1l. 7s. 6d.) and clerk of aſſize (1l. 1s.), the pardoned criminal was ſtill in priſon [1]."

October 25, 1787, Mr. Howard adds, " No alteration. The felons complained of illneſs contracted by lying on the damp brick-floor with only a mat. Keeper no ſalary. The magiſtrates continue his licence for beer.

Debtor, 1 ; Felon, 1 [2]."

LEICESTER TOWN BRIDEWELL, at the laſt viſitation of Mr. Howard, was in the Town Gaol, down five ſteps ; two ſmall rooms for men, and two for women. Keeper's ſalary amounted to 5l.

1776, Oct. 29,	
1779, Mar. 27,	} No Priſoners [3].
1782, May 2,	

In 1792, in taking down the old Gaol for the erection of the preſent edifice, incorporated with the walls of the cells, were diſcovered the remains of the Chapel of St. John [4], ſuppoſed to have been deſtroyed during the conteſts between king Henry the Second and his ſon.

The new Gaol was deſigned by Mr. Johnſon, the benevolent Founder of the Conſanguinitarium [5]; and its appearance forms an agreeable contraſt to the County Priſon. See a ſmall view in Plate XXVIII. p. 326.

On the front of it is inſcribed,

" TOWN GAOL, AND HOUSE OF CORRECTION."

Over which are the Arms of the Town, with the Creſt.

" On each ſide of the Gaol is a narrow ſlip of ground, partitioned off by open iron paliſades, and divided into Courts for the different claſſes of priſoners.

The Court-yard for debtors is 32 feet by 16, with a day-room, 13 feet by 12, and up-ſtairs eight lodging-rooms ; to which if the debtor brings his own bed he pays nothing ; the Keeper furniſhes a ſingle bed at 2s. 4d. per week ; and if two ſleep together, 1s. 9d. each.

The Chapel, which is in the centre of the priſon, is very ſmall ; and there is no proper ſeparation of the priſoners.

Gaoler, Welborn Owſton. Salary, 37l. 10s.

Fees, 15s. 4d. beſides which the Under-ſheriff demands 6s. 8d. for his liberate. Garniſh. None.

Chaplain, Rev. Thomas Robinſon. Duty, Prayers and Sermon once a month. Salary, 10l.

Surgeon, Mr. Maule. Salary, none ; makes a bill.

Number of Debtors,

1800, March 28, . . . 2		1803, Aug. 23, . . . 5
1802, Feb. 2, ... 1		1805, Sept. 26, . . . 4

Allowance. 22 ounces of bread per day each.

No Rules and Orders.

Neither the Act for preſervation of health, nor clauſes againſt ſpirituous liquors, hung up.

No priſoner who is permitted to work receives the County allowance of bread ; but ſome of them pay one or two ſhillings per week for that indulgence.

A room is ſet apart for an Infirmary.

A bath, which has never been uſed ; ſeldom viſited. The Priſon is clean ; and there is water in every Court.

There was formerly a Table of Fees, ſigned by three Magiſtrates for the Borough, and confirmed by Judges of Aſſize [fee col. 1.] ; but there has been none hung up in the Priſon theſe many years.

The Town Bridewell adjoins the Gaol [6]."

BRUNSWICK SQUARE,

of which I have now before me a beautiful Plan deſigned in 1792 by Mr. Johnſon, was intended to have been formed on the ſite of The Horſe Fair (Johnſon's Garden), an extenſive plot of ground, at that time the property of the Corporation of Leiceſter. In the area of the Square was to have been St. Margaret's Chapel ; on two of the ſides, beautiful ſtreets, to be named, George-ſtreet and Charlotte-ſtreet, after their preſent Majeſties. A Royal Terrace would have filled the ſide looking towards the London road ; and a new Town-hall, opening into Millſtone-lane, was to have filled the fourth ſide. Had this plan taken effect, it would have been creditable to the Town ; in which no place can be put in competition, either for public convenience, or a diſplay of corporate magnificence and civic grandeur.

[1] Mr. Howard on Priſons, p. 316. [2] Mr. Howard on Lazarettos, p. 160. [3] Mr. Howard on Priſons, p. 317.
[4] See a particular account of theſe diſcoveries, p. 326 : and an engraving of the antient Arch in Plate XXVIII. p. 326.
[5] See p. 528. [6] Mr. Neild on Priſons for Debtors, p. 250.

STREETS, LANES, &c.

Abbey Gate. An indifferent paſſage in St. Leonard's pariſh, leading from Sunday-bridge to the Abbey. At the Abbey end ſtands Counteſs's Hoſpital; at the other end ſtood St. Leonard's church.

Northgate-ſtreet is underſtood to take in all that open way extending from the North gate to Sunday-bridge, formerly Sanvis-bridge: ſome extend it to the Croſs. The beſt buildings ſtand near the Bridge.

High-Croſs-ſtreet extends from North gate to Red-croſs-ſtreet end. In that portion between the North gate and the Croſs ſtand the Town and County priſons, King Richard's houſe, Free-ſchool, and All Saints church. Here alſo ſtood St. John's chapel or church, and St. Peter's. That portion from the Croſs to Peacock-lane has been called *St. Martin's-ſtreet*, and *Croſs-ſtreet*. This ſtreet is a medley of good and bad buildings. At the end of this ſtreet the name of *High Croſs* is ſtill given to a plain Doric pillar, which, till the year 1773 (when it was in ſo ruinous a ſtate as to be dangerous, and an annoyance[1] to the paſſage in the ſtreet it ſtood in), formed one of the ſupporters of a light Temple-looking building of the ſame name, which has been engraved in Plate XXXI. and noticed in p. 354, which ſerved as a ſhelter to the country people, who here hold a ſmall market on Wedneſdays and Fridays for the ſale of butter, eggs, &c. Here the members of parliament are proclaimed. Here alſo may be ſeen, on Michaelmas-day, the groteſque ceremony of the poor men of Trinity Hoſpital, arrayed like antient knights, having ruſty helmets on their heads, and breaſt-plates faſtened over their black tabards, proclaiming the fair[2].

Southgate-ſtreet is now underſtood to extend from Red-Croſs-ſtreet to the Infirmary, or Horſe-pool-end, an open place, where formerly ſtood a chapel. That portion of this paſſage which extends from Red-Croſs-ſtreet end to the South gate was formerly called, very properly, Caſtle-ſtreet; but in the late rage for altering the names of ſtreets, &c. in Leiceſter, one of the moſt narrow entrances of the town, leading from this ſtreet, has been honoured with the name of *Caſtle-ſtreet*: before, properly, called *St. Mary's Church-lane*. The buildings in general are tolerable. Here ſtands the Magazine, the entrance into the Newark. The above-named ſtreets, together, form a line from North to South, the extremity of the Town, each way, about a mile and half in length: they formerly conſtituted the high road from the North of England to the Metropolis.

Paſſages of any conſequence from this main road, beginning Northwardly, are,

Wood gate, an opening leading to Aſhby-de-la Zouch. A few houſes only on the right hand.

Senvy gate; ſo called, it is ſuppoſed, *quaſi ſancta via*, becauſe there uſed to be general annual proceſſions made through this ſtreet to St. Margaret's church on Whitſun-Monday, &c. It has been alſo called *le Skeith*; and is a broad way leading to St. Margaret's church. This has no buildings of conſequence. Oppoſite to it is

Soar-lane, near the North gate, alias *Walker-lane*; which leads to the river. A few houſes ſtand on the left, and the Quakers' Meeting-houſe.

Elbow-lane is ſituate near the North gate.

St. John's (or *Bridewell-lane*) and *Bull's-lane* are ſituate oppoſite each other, near the Town-gaol.

St. Peter's-lane is a few paces nearer the Croſs.

Blue-Boar-lane (of old *The Mayor's-hall-lane*, 1 Ric. III.) lies oppoſite the Free-ſchool; and *Free-ſchool-lane* at the end of the ſchool.

High-ſtreet commences near the Croſs, and leads to Coal-hill, or Round-hill, through the Eaſt gate.

This ſtreet is not ſo wide as many of the ſtreets; but it is in general better built. In it appears conſpicuous a lofty hexagon turret, whoſe top is glazed for the purpoſe of a proſpect ſeat. It bears on the inſide marks of conſiderable antiquity, and is a remain of the manſion of Henry earl of Huntingdon, called *Lord's Place*[3]. It has a winding ſtaircaſe of ſtone, with a ſmall apartment on each ſtory; and is now modernized with an outward coating of brick.

The Swine's-market (ſo called 15 Hen. VIII.), a narrow ſtreet at the Eaſt end of High-ſtreet, was formerly called *Parchment-lane*: it might now, with ſome propriety, be called *Market-ſtreet*, as it leads to the market, and the Pig-market is removed.

Shambles-ſtreet (called *Apulgate* 1 Ric. III.), oppoſite, was, till lately, called *Shambles-lane*. It leads to Weſt-bridge.

Thornton-lane, and *Town-Hall-lane*, lie oppoſite to each other; below which are *Peacock-lane* and *Red-croſs-ſtreet*. Theſe are all narrow paſſages.

Bakehouſe-lane, and *St. Mary's Church-lane*, alias *Caſtle-ſtreet*, lie nearer the South gate, a few paces from each other. *Friar-lane*, and *Millſtone-lane*, are ſituate, the former on the North ſide, and the latter on the South ſide, of South gate.

Hangman's-lane, a little farther on, now called *Horſe-fair-ſtreet*, is a paſſage made up on each ſide with dirt walls, a few little dwellings, a malt-office, and a large wool-warehouſe.

Green's-lane, lower down, leads to Swan's mill.

Another principal paſſage of the Town lies nearly parallel to that above deſcribed. It commences at the St. Margaret's church end of Sanvis gate, and extends to the London road above the town.

The firſt portion of this, called *Church-gate*, alias *Goſwell-gate*, extends from St. Margaret's church to the Coal-hill. It is in general indifferently built, but ſpacious.

Archdeacon's-lane, and *Bull's-lane*, lead from Church-gate. *Butt's Cloſe* is alſo ſituated here.

The other portion, called *Golltree-gate*, *Galtree-gate*, or *Gallowtree-gate* (becauſe leading to the gallows), and *Gartre-gate* (as leading to Gartre hundred), extends from Coal-hill to the end of the Town, near the Three Crowns Inn. Here are the principal inns.

From the main paſſage at the Coal-hill, branch out *Belgrave-gate* and *Humberſtone-gate*, two very open ſtreets. The former is well built, and leads to Loughborough; in it ſtands the Roman milliary.

Humberſtone-gate, part of the manor antiently poſſeſſed by the Biſhops of Lincoln, and ſtill called *Biſhop's Fee*, leads to Uppingham; in it are ſome very good houſes, and others very indifferent. A great nuiſance, St. Margaret's workhouſe, ſtands at the nether end of it, in the middle path-way.

The Roundle, now called *The Round-hill*, *Coal-hill*, or *Haymarket*, for it has all theſe names, is an opening on which ſtands the old Aſſembly-room, a building of private property, formerly uſed on public occaſions for concerts, &c. and as a play-houſe. Under part of it is a machine for weighing coals, &c. The houſes ſituate on it were parcel of St. Margaret's gild. On their Eaſt ſide ſtood *Barehill Croſs*, alias *Barrel Croſs*.

Silver-ſtreet, in a line almoſt parallel to High-ſtreet, leads from the Town-hall to the Eaſt gate. It was formerly called *The ſtreet on the back-ſide of the Lion*; becauſe, where now is the ſign of the King's Arms, there was formerly the ſign of the Lion, till about 1670. It was alſo called *The old Sheep-market* (1 Ric. III.), *Church-gate*, and *St. Martin's Church-gate*[4], *Kyr-gate*, *Kyrk-lane*, *Lychyrs-lane*, *Chyrch-lane*; *Vicus calidus*, or *Hot-ſtreet*. Silver-ſtreet

---

[1] In anſwer to ſome objections which had been made to this removal, an intelligent friend obſerves, " that the trade and commerce of Leiceſter when the Croſs was taken down was great. What was it in 1576? Could the Croſs have been repaired, which I queſtion, the annoyance could not have been removed. The Corporation were not actuated by the ſordid motives which have been aſcribed to them; but by the beſt, i. e. the good of the Town, in the ſafety of the inhabitants."

[2] Walk through Leiceſter, p. 29.

[3] July 27, 1569, John Eaton, of Raunſton, gent. and Ralph Eaton, of Leiceſter, gent. for 100l. ſold to *Henry* earl of *Huntingdon* their capital meſſuage or tenement, called *Reynold's dwelling-houſe*, ſituate in a ſtreet called *High-ſtreet*, or *The Swine's Market*, and all buildings, &c. about the ſaid capital meſſuage, with all yards, gardens, courts, &c. Near this place was found the curious old Pipe, with a coat of arms on it, as engraved in Plate XXXII. p. 380.

[4] The *Church-gate* above-mentioned, *St. Martin's Church-gate*, *Kyr-gate*, *Kyrk-lane*, &c. ſeems to be the lane from the end of Silver-ſtreet, viz. from Mr. Bent's corner to the High-ſtreet; and is called *The Church-lane unto the High-ſtreet* in 1 Ric. III.

is narrow, but in it are fome good dwellings. St. Martin's church ftands at the Weft end.

Cank-ftreet leads from New-ftreet, near St. Martin's church, to what has been lately named *Cheapfide*; an open way, which may be confidered a portion of the Market-place, below the Conduit.

New-ftreet, leading to St. Martin's church Northwardly, was built on part of the Gray Friars. It is a bad paffage, with fome good dwellings.

Applegate-ftreet and *Bridge-ftreet* (the latter a name given lately to a paffage, which contains about two houfes on each fide, leading to Weft-bridge) form an elbow. Thefe, and the lanes and avenues about them, ftand upon the fite of the Roman city, in general but indifferently built; but this portion of the town is honourable and venerable, from years, and its antiquarian treafures. Applegate-ftreet, which leads to the church of St. Nicholas, will not be paffed without intereft by thofe who recollect that on this fpot, where the ground rifes in a gentle afcent from the river, the legions of Rome eftablifhed their town; and we are now arrived at an object which brings them more forcibly to remembrance, a maffy arched wall, commonly termed, from its bounding the quarter antiently inhabited by the Jews, the *Jewry Wall*. This ruin, defcribed and engraved in vol. I. p. 7, will afford to curious and learned obfervers a valuable fpecimen of the mode of building practifed by the Romans; but the ufes for which it was defigned will, moft probably, for ever elude their refearches [1]. The adjoining church of St. Nicholas is a fmall edifice of very rude, and confequently very antient, conftruction. The area, Eaftward of the church-yard, is called *Holy Bones* [2].

Lofeby-lane, now the *Pig-market*, a fhort ftreet leading to Cank-ftreet, contains two or three good houfes.

St. James's Square, a name given to a little opening at the upper end of the Market-place, without the leaft propriety, might be now altered, with much propriety, to *Rozzel's-fquare*, in honour of the Poet of that name. His conduct implied this language, " Here will I dwell, for I have a delight therein."

Other lanes, &c. there are, of inferior note, befides thofe that occafionally change their names with the whim of the inhabitants.

Among thefe, the MSS. of Mr. Carte take notice of *St. Francis-lane*, between Wigfton's Hofpital and the Grey Friers.

From the Nag's Head to Mr. Bent's corner, *St. Martin's-lane*, *Holyrood-lane*.

Soper's-lane, the back lane running parallel to the Swine's-market.

Dead-man's-lane; of old, *Dead-lane*, 1 Ric. III.

Little-bridge, alias *Frogmere-bridge*.

The paffage from The George to Horfe-fair leas is called *Double-gate-lane* in widow Brown's writings.

THE MARKET PLACE

is rather fmall for the abundance of bufinefs which is tranfacted there on a market-day; but the market abounds with every fpecies of good living. For an inland town, it is remarkably well ferved with fifh; and the butchery is the delight of ftrangers. Here have been repeatedly fhewn many extraordinary fine fheep, from the feed of the moft capital graziers and breeders in the neighbourhood. The buildings which furround the Market-place have of late years been confiderably improved; the low fheds have been removed, and capital dwellings raifed up in their room, ornamental, and calculated for extenfive bufineffes.

The EXCHANGE [3] (fee Plate XXVIII. p. 326.) was built in the year 1747, to ferve the purpofes of the Shambles [4] and Gainfborough. The former was a building of confiderable ornament to the Town; the latter, a place fet apart for the adminiftration of juftice. The upper rooms of the Exchange (as noticed in p. 354) are ftill ufed by the magiftrates on certain days; but the lower room was only a fhort time ufed by the butchers; and is now almoft ufelefs.

The CONDUIT,

which ftands in the Market-place, is an octagon heavy building, intended as an ornamental fcreen to cover a large leaden ciftern. It was erected in 1612, and rebuilt in 1709. The conduit-water, which is brought in pipes from a confiderable diftance, is ufed for all choice purpofes; and is much efteemed for its purity of flavour. It is drawn from a fpring, about three quarters of a mile from this building, in St. Margaret's Field; which fpring is covered with a ftone-building, to fecure it from injury and filth. The inhabitants in the Market-place and ftreets adjacent have alfo, by fubfcription, made a large refervoir near the Conduit, to preferve the wafte or overflowing water, to be ready in cafe of an accident by fire.

ASSEMBLY ROOMS, AND HOTEL.

That ingenuity of improvement, not only in the conveniences, but the recreations of life, which has lately advanced fo rapidly, as well in the provincial towns as in the capital, led the inhabitants of Leicefter into a plan for the erection of new edifices appropriated to the purpofes of public amufement. The confiderable buildings, which in this place arreft the ftranger's eye, were accordingly erected by John Johnfon, efq. architect, on fubfcription fhares. The front of the Hotel, which name it bears, having been originally defigned for that purpofe, may, from the grandeur of its windows, its ftatues, baffo relievo, and other decorations, be juftly confidered as the firft modern architectural ornament of the Town.

A room, whofe fpacious dimenfions (being 75 feet by 33, and 30 feet high) and elegant decorations adapt it in a diftinguifhed manner for fcenes of numerous and polifhed fociety, is appropriated to the ufe of the public balls. The entrance is in the centre of the fide wall, over which is a fpacious orcheftra, projecting a fmall way into the room. It is of a femi-circular plan, domed, and carried back over the landing of the ftairs: the accefs to it is by a back ftaircafe. The ceiling of the room is arched, and formed into compartments; three of which are large circles, decorated with the allegorical paintings of Aurora, Urania, and Luna. At each end is a chimney, over which is a painting, in a compartment, of an aerial figure in a dancing attitude: there are alfo two others, in compartments, on the fide wall. On each fide the chimneys are niches, in which are beautiful figures, from the models of Bacon. Mr. Johnfon employed Mr. Ramfey Reinagle to execute the Paintings, who has done great juftice to his appointment; but they have fuffered much from the damp, for want of fire. Befide the eight beautiful luftres, branches of lights are held by four ftatues from the defigns of Bacon. Mr. Roffi, R. A. was employed (partly on account of his mother being a native of Leicefter, but much more fo from his fuperior merit as an Artift) to execute the two figures in the front of the building (Comic and Lyric Mufes), and the bas reliefs between the windows.

Uniting under the fame roof every convenience for the gratification of tafte, and the amufement of the mind, a coffee-room handfomely furnifhed, and fupplied with all the London papers, affords the

[1] Walk through Leicefter, p. 79.
[2] Ibid. p. 83.
[3] Mr. Bakewell publifhed, 1745—1747, from drawings by Taylor, Three Views at Leicefter. 1. The Exchange. 2. South-eaft View of the Saturday's Market; taken from the Corn Market. 3. North-weft Profpect of the Corn Market.
[4] See p. 513.

gentlemen

gentlemen of the town and country, as well as the ftranger, to whom its door is open, an agreeable and commodious refort; while on the oppofite fide a fpacious bookfeller's fhop, under the management of Mr. Combe, the very intelligent as well as attentive proprietor, furnifhes the literary enquirer with a feries of all the new publications.

Adjoining the Hotel, a fmall Theatre, built alfo by Mr. Johnfon, neatly and commodioufly fitted up, nearly on the plan of the London houfes, furnifhes the inhabitants of Leicefter with a more complete difplay of the dramatic art than they had before enjoyed, and has been the means of gratifying them by the talents of feveral performers of the firft-rate excellence. The popular pieces of the London ftage are here every feafon reprefented in a manner pleafing to the town, and honourable to the manager[1].

A View of the Affembly Houfe, capitally engraved by J. Walker, infcribed, "To his Grace the Duke of Rutland, Lord Lieutenant of the County of Leicefter; and to the other Noblemen and Gentlemen of the County and Town, Contributors to the Building of the Hotel and Affembly Rooms;" was publifhed in 1800 by Mr. Johnfon; and, by his permiffion, is copied in Plate XXXV. as an accompaniment to his *Confanguinitarium.*

POPULATION, TAKEN FROM THE PARISH REGISTERS, &c.

On this important fubjeft, I fhall begin by referring to the Differtation on Domefday, already given in vol. I. p. xlviii; where the number of families in this county is pretty accurately fixed to have been about 6820, amounting, on an average of five to each family, to 34,000.

Sir Matthew Hale, in his "Origination of Mankind," p. 234, after a careful furvey of Gloucefterfhire, comparing Domefday and the ftate of that county at the time he wrote, concludes that the inhabitants were increafed *twenty* times in 600 years; an error into which that great Writer has fallen, by taking no more than the number of perfons actually mentioned in Domefday Book; not confidering that only the heads of families are there noticed, and that each family would contain, on an average, at leaft five perfons; which will reduce the increafe to *four* times inftead of *twenty*. With this too accords the actual ftate of Leicefterfhire; which, from 34,000, was in 1790 fuppofed to have increafed to 85,000; but in 1800 was found, to a certainty, to be not lefs than 130,000.

To apply this to the Town of Leicefter, where in the time of the Norman Conqueror there were only 322 houfes, and it may be fuppofed the inhabitants did not much exceed 1600; the prefent increafe, from the introduction principally of a very confiderable manufacture, is in a *tenfold* degree.

In 1564, the number of families in the Town of Leicefter, as officially returned to the Archdeacon, was only 338; namely, in All Saints, 27; St. Leonard's, 32; St. Margaret's, 164 (exclufive of 17 in the chapelry of Knighton); St. Martin's, 160; St. Mary's, 120; St. Nicholas, 22; St. Peter's, 27.

Mr. Throfby's remarks on this important fubject, from the Parifh Regifters, &c. are worth preferving:

"The firft ftatement in the following table is the average of a year in five, at progreffive periods, including the four next fucceeding years after each date; in the divifion of each, fractions are not regarded.

St. Mary's, St. Nicholas's, and All Saints Regifters, are not much to be depended on before the year 1600. St. Martin's is very clear fo early as 1558; and St. Margaret's in 1615; confequently the births and burials at that time are given under the head 1600; and St. Leonard's not till lately. The Regifter of that parifh has been fometimes kept with the officiating minifter of All Saints; but latterly with the minifter of St. Margaret's.

	1558.	1600.	1650.	1700.	1750.	1787.
St. MARY's—Births - - -	—	26	19	26	70	120
Burials - - - -	—	18	14	24	73	112
St. NICHOLAS—Births - -	—	6	10	13	13	23
Burials - -	—	6	7	9	16	16
St. LEONARD's—Births - -	—		·			12
Burials - -	—					9
ALL SAINTS—Births - - - -	—	23	24	24	44	86
Burials - - -	—	24	15	21	50	88
St. MARTIN's—Births - -	41	38	46	62	56	73
Burials - -	38	35	35	53	71	77
St. MARGARET's—Births -	—	38	35	53	56	139 .
Burials -	—	30	37	40	83	117

By this table it appears that there were baptized, annually, at the parifh churches, taken collectively in Leicefter, about the year 1600, adding 6 for St. Leonard's, - - - - - - 137

At the prefent period, on an average of five years, - - - - - 453

Increafe - 316

Burials at the former period - 119
At the prefent period - - 419

Increafe - 300

To the Rev. Mr. Carte's ftatement of the families and fouls in Leicefter in 1712, have been added that taken in 1785, and one taken by Mr. Throfby, in which the dwellings are given from the levy-books of the poor, with the addition of fome not rated. In St. Mary's parifh ftatement, the Newark and Caftle View are included. The ftatement in 1785 is liable to objections refpecting the number of fouls, as they were afcertained by queftions put to the heads of families, many of whom replied with irony, others grew angry, and would not reply at all, and fome evaded anfwers. Calculating five to a family, is perhaps nearer than any other given number; but the reader may judge for himfelf refpecting the number of fouls in Leicefter in 1792, from the following Table, whether his opinion be 4½, 5, 5½, or any other number, to a family.

	Mr. Carte's, 1712.		1785.		1792.		
	Families.	Souls.	Families.	Souls.	Dwellings.	Families.	Souls.
All Saints - - -	220	1100	501	2428	470	551	2755
St. Margaret's -	380	1900	756	3296	800	850	4250
St. Martin's - -	350	1750	524	2620	533	565	2825
St. Mary's - - -	250	1250	668	3090	604	687	3435
St. Nicholas - -	90	450	180	900	138	187	935
St. Leonard's not noticed.			97	450	90	95	475
	1290	6450	2726	12,784	2635	2935	14,675

The following Table will fhew the wonderful increafe in the population of Leicefter fince 1680, when the manufactory of hofe was there eftablifhed. It is taken to fhew the progreffive increafe, at ftated periods, from the burials of the parifhes, collectively, by Dr. Price's calculation, that one in 30 die every year. The firft column commences in 1558, nearly 400 years after the Town was deftroyed; but, as St. Martin's Regifter alone begins fo early, the reft are given in that column from an average ftatement of the increafe of fucceeding years. The reader fhould obferve that this ftatement does not include the Diffenters, who bury at their refpective places of worfhip.

		Deaths.	Families.	Souls.
In	1558	100	600	3000
	1600	116	696	3480
	1650	111	666	3330
	1700	151	906	4530
	1750	301	1806	9030
	1787	419	2514	12,570

To the 12,570 fouls fuppofed to be at prefent in Leicefter (1792), taken from the deaths of all the parifhes, being an average of 1787, 1788, 1789, 1790, and 1791, if we add fifty burials, to have been on an average in a year, in that time, at the Diffenting places of worfhip, it will give an addition of 300 families and 1500 fouls, making the number of fouls, in all, 14,070."

Such were the remarks of an attentive obferver in 1792. By the Return, however, made to Parliament in 1800, it appears that the preceding calculation was much too fmall; the number of inhabited houfes at that period being 3205; of uninhabited, 15.

The families were 3668, confifting of 7921 males, and 9032 females; in all, 16,933. Of thefe 499 were chiefly employed in agriculture, and 11,330 in trade, manufactures, &c.

[1] Walk through Leicefter, p. 129.

EARLS OF LEICESTER; *Continued from p. 250.*

By the affiftance of my very learned friend the late Rev. Sambrook Ruffell, an ample and valuable account has been given, in a former part of this volume, of the Earls of Leicefter of the Saxon and the Norman race. I fhall now refume the fubject.

The Earldom of Warwick, which had become extinct on the death of Edward Plantagenet in 1499, was revived by King Edward VI. in 1547, in the perfon of John fecond fon of Edmund Dudley [1], by Elizabeth Grey, an immediate defcendant from Margaret daughter of Richard Beauchamp earl of Warwick. In 1551 he was elevated to the title of duke of Northumberland; but was beheaded, Aug. 18, 1553, for endeavouring to fettle the crown upon the lady Jane Grey, to whom he had married his fon Guilford Dudley [2].

The attainder of the Dudley family was foon after reverfed by queen Mary; and the title of earl of Warwick again conferred on Ambrofe the third fon, whofe hiftory appears in the following epitaph, which is placed in our Lady's chapel, adjoining to the collegiate church at Warwick, at the head of the monument of Richard Beauchamp:

" Heare under this tombe lieth the corps of the lord Ambrofe Duddely; who, after the deceafe of his elder brethren without iffue, was fonne and heir to John duke of Northumberlande, to whom Q. Elizabeth, in the firft yeare of her reigne, gave the mannour of Kibworth Beauchamp in the county of Lyc', to be held by the fervice of being pantler to the kings and quenes of this realme at their coronations; which office and manor his faid father and other his anceftors earles of War. helde. In the fecond yeare of her reigne the faid quene gave him the office of mayfter of the ordinaunce. In the 4th yeare of her fayd reigne fhe created him baron Lifle, and erle of Warwick. In the fame yeare fhe made him her livetenant generall in Normandy; and duringe the tyme of his fervice there he was chofen knt. of the noble order of the Garter. In the twelveth yere of her reigne the faid erle, and Edward l'd Clinton, l. admerall of England, were made livetenantes generall jointctely and feverally of her Ma'ties army in the North partes. In the thirtenth yeare of her reigne the fayd quene beftowed on him the office of chief butler of England; and in the xvth yeare of her reigne he was fworne of her prevye counfell. Who departinge this lief without iffue the xxith day of February, 158. at Bedford howfe neare the City of London, from whence, as himfelf defired, his corps was conveyed, and interred in this place, neare his brother Robert e. of Ley. and others his noble anceftors; which was accomplifhed by his laft and wel beloved wiefe the lady Anne countefs of Warr.; who, in further teftimony of her faythful love towardes him, beftowed this monument as a remembrance of him."

The figure of earl Ambrofe is lying on a mat rolled up, and is in plated armour; his hair fhort and curled, and his beard long; at his feet a muzzled bear.

On the North fide are thefe arms and infcriptions:

Or, a lion rampant queué furchée Vert; *Dudley*, with a crefcent of difference; impaling a chevron between three ftags' heads; *Whorwood*.

" The fayd lord Ambrofe Duddeley maried to his firft wiefe Anne dowghter and coheir of William Whorwood efquier, atterney general to kinge Henry the Eygthe."

2. *Dudley*; impaling a faltire; in chief three efcalops. *Taylboys.*

" The faid lord Ambrofe maried to his fecond wief Elizabeth dowghter of fir Gilbert Taylboys knight, fifter and fole heir of George lord Taylboys."

3. *Dudley*; impaling *Baffet.*

" The faid Ambrofe, after he was erl of Warwik, maried to his third wife the lady Ann eldeft daughter to Francis Rufel erle of Bedford, k't of the Garter."

On the North fide.

1. *Dudley*; impaling *Bramfhot.*

" John Duddeley efqr. fecond fonne to John l. Duddeley, and knight of the Garter, maried Elizabeth dowghter and heir of John Bramfhot efq. and had iffue Edmond Duddeley."

2. *Dudley*; impaling *L'Ifle.*

" Edmund Duddeley efqr. one of the prive counfell to k. Henrie 7. married Elizab. fifter and fole heir of John Grey vifcou't Lifle, defcended as heir of the eldeft do. and coheir of Ric. Beachamp e. of Warr. and Elizab. his wief do. and heir of the l. Berkeley, and heir of the l. Lifle and Tyes, and had iffue Jo. duke of Northumb'."

3 *Dudley*; impaling *Guilford.*

" John duke of Northumberland, erle of Warr. vicount Lifle, and knight of the Garter, maried Jane da' and heir of fir Edward Guildeford knight, and Eleanor his wief, fifter and coheir to Thomas l. Lawarre; and had iffue the fayd l. Ambrofe."

At the feet is a fhield with 32 quarterings, under a coronet, fupported by a goat and a lion collared [3].

ROBERT DUDLEY, fifth fon of the duke of Northumberland, experienced from queen Elizabeth an ample fhare of favour. On the 5th of June 1563, he obtained a grant, to himfelf and his heirs, of the caftle and manor of Kenilworth; a noble domain, " to the value of four and twenty pounds and better [4]," which he confiderably improved; the charges he beftowed on the caftle, parks, and chafe, amounting to 60,000l. [5]

Sept. 28, 1564, he was created baron of Denbigh [6]; and the next day earl of Leicefter.

In 1571, he procured from Henry Fitz-Alan earl of Arundel an affignment of the Wardenfhip of New Foreft, which had been granted to his anceftors in 6 Edward III.; and obtained liberty to found an Hofpital in Warwick, for the relief of poor and indigent people; which Hofpital might purchafe lands in England not exceeding the yearly value of 200l. that were not holden of the queen immediately by knight's fervice in chief, or elfe by knight's fervice not in chief [7].

In 1575, he had the honour of entertaining his Royal Miftrefs for 19 days. Of the particulars of this fumptuous treat, a minute detail was publifhed at the time by Robert Laneham; and alfo in " The Princely Pleafures at Kenelworth Caftle, by George Gafcoigne;" both of which have been very lately re-printed in the " Progreffes of Queen Elizabeth."

The three following letters, written a fhort time before the earl of Leicefter was honoured with the Royal vifit, afford a good fpecimen of that Nobleman's epiftolary correfpondence [8]:

[1] This Edmund Dudley, the fecond fon of John lord Dudley, of Dudley caftle, co. Stafford, was a ftudent in Oxford about 1478; then ftudied in Gray's Inn, Holborn: and, for his fingular prudence, was made of the privy council to Henry VII. in 1486, being then but 24 years of age. Obferving the king to be of a frugal difpofition, he in 1506 projected the exaction of forfeitures for tranfgreffions under the penal ftatutes, affifted by fir Richard Emfon (another lawyer), fon of a fieve-maker of Towcefter in Northamptonfhire; whence they grew fo hated, that guards were forced to attend them in the ftreets. In 19 Hen. VII. he was Speaker of the Houfe of Commons; and in 22 Hen. VII. obtained the ftewardfhip of the Rape of Haftings in Suffex. Henry VII. dying, his fucceffor Henry VIII. iffued his fpecial warrant for his execution, being then a prifoner in the Tower of London; and, in order to pleafe the people, he loft his head on Tower Hill Aug. 28, 1510. He was author of a juridical book, called *Arbor Reipublicæ*, which fome time was preferved in the Cotton Library as a great curiofity. He left feveral children; the eldeft of whom was John, earl of Warwick and duke of Northumberland.

[2] See vol. III. p. 670.   [3] Gough's Defcription of the Beauchamp Chapel, 1804, pp. 28—31.

[4] Holinfhed, vol. III. p. 1207.   [5] Dugdale, Warwickfhire, vol. I. p. 249.

[6] It is noticed by Mr. Camden, that a new church was built at Denbigh, " tùm Domini fui Roberti Comitis Leiceftrenfis, tùm collectitiâ plurimorum per Angliam pecuniâ."   [7] 13 Eliz. c. 17. 1570.

[8] Sir Robert Naunton, fpeaking of the earl of Leicefter's letters and writings, which fhould beft fet him off, fays, " I never faw a ftyle or phrafe more feeming religious, and fuller of the ftreams of devotion, then they were." *Fragmenta Regalia*, p. 25.— Many of the earl's letters to Gilbert earl of Shrewfbury are preferved among the very curious " Unpublifhed Talbot Papers " in the College of Arms. Among thefe are, Apologies for fending for lord Talbot to Court, March 13, 1570-1; a patent of high ftewardfhip of all his lands, as a token of friendfhip; from the Court, May 26, 1571. A wifh to relinquifh his troublefome office of Deputy High Marfhal; and complaining that his conduct had been mifreprefented with refpect to certain manors in Oxfordfhire; July 5. Treachery of Circar, one of Shr wfbury's chaplains, and Howartn, another clergyman; he calls them " devilifh Divines;" Jan. 30, 1571-2. Profeffions of exceffive friendfhip; Feb. 3. The Queen's favour to the Countefs of Shrewfbury, June 7, 1575. Dr. Mey's fuit for a bifhoprick fuccefsful; mifconduct of Rolfton, a fervant of Shrewfbury's at Sheffield, Dec. 4, 1576. Compliments, and affurances of the Queen's favour, Jan. 18, 1580-1. Befeeching the earl of Shrewfbury to permit lord Talbot to remain at the Court; Nonfuch, April 19, 1585. Had prefented his very fat ftag to the Queen; Greenwich, April 27 (year not mentioned); &c. &c. &c.

"My L. Wher at your late being here, I conferred with you about the nomination of such as should be put into the graunt for her Matie touching *Concealed Wards*, &c. your L. then named old Mr. Walker; and I named my friend Mr. Townyshend [1] this berer, whom your L. did well allow of: I have synce talkyd with him; and ys at my requeſt very well contented to uſe his name, and take any frendly peanes for me: and as he is every way a very ſuffycient man, ſo have I had ſundry ways very good proofe, as well thereof, as of his dyſcretion and judgement in hys doings, beſyde thoſe I have thought good to ſend to your L. to talk withall; and to lett him underſtand your pleaſſure touching this matter, yf ther be any thing that you ſhall think good to impart, bycauſe he ys to joyne with him that you appoint for the ſaid ſervyce.

"I have to thank your L. alſo very hartely, perceiving by Hen. Hawthorn that your L. is pleſed to help me that I may have ſome ſtone toward the making a lytle banquett-houſe in my garden. Yf yt pleaſe your L. to lett him know your further mynde touching the ſame, the pleaſſure wil be great you doe me, and I wyll [be] reddy [to] the beſt of my power to requyte. And ſo comytting your L. to the Almighty, the 17th of May [1575],

Your L. veary frend, R. LEYCESTER.

To my very good L. the L. Burley, high Treaſorer of England, &c."

"My L. Hit hath pleaſed her Matie to ſigne the book of Concealed Wardes as hit was ſent by your L. Fayne wold her Matie have yt but during my lyfe; which, as I told her Matie, being only a caſuall thing, I wold by no meanes deal withall; neither could I yet tell what benyfytt wold or ſhould grow to me. Sure I was, yf any ſhould, her Majeſties perſon was beſt and ſureſt. Now being done as it ys, I have thought good to ſend it to your L. that you will ſee aſſurances made from ſuch as are named grantees to us, which I referre to your L. beſt dyſcretion, as alſo what you ſhall think meete to conſider of, for the uſe of their names, as for ſuch as ſhall follow her ſewte. For which cauſe I have ſent Joh. Dudley to attend your L.; and what order your L. ſhall think beſt, I wyll aſſent unto it. Or whether you wyll make your profe firſt agenſt the next terme, to ſee what they will deſerve. All which I referre to your L. And ſo comyttyng your L. to the Almighty, doe byd you for this time farewell. In haſt, this Tueſday morning, [June 21]

Your L. aſſured, R. LEYCESTER.

To the right honorable my very good L. the Lord High Treaſorer of England."

"My good L. The great expectation I had of your being here before this tyme, hath cauſed me to be more ſylent to you then ells I had been; but finding your coming yet doubtfull (albeyt I hope Kenelworth [2] ſhall not myſſe you), I will lett your L. underſtand ſuch newes as we have, which ys only and chefely of her Majeſties good health, which, God be thanked, ys as good as I have long known yt; and for her lyking of this houſe [3], I aſſure yourL. I think ſhe never came to place in her lyfe ſhe lyked better, or commended more; and ſynce her comyng hither, as oft as wether ſerves, ſhe has not been within-dores. The howſe lykes her well, and her owen lodgings ſpecyally. She thinks her coſt well beſtowed, ſhe ſayth, yf it had been five times as much: but I wold her Majeſty wold beſtowe but half as much more, and then I think ſhe ſhould have as pleaſant and as comodyus a howſe as any in England. I am ſorry your L. ys not here to ſe yt. Even by and by her Majeſty ys going to the Foreſt, to kill ſome bucks with her bowe, as ſhe hath done in the Park this morning. God be thanked,

ſhe is very merry. But at her firſt coming, being a mervelous hott day-at her coming hither, not one drop of good drink for her, ſo ill was ſhe provyded for, notwithſtanding her oft telling of her coming hither; but we were fayn to ſend to London with bottells, to Kenelworth, to divers other places where ale was. Her own here was ſuch, as there was no man able to drink it; yt had been as good to have drank malmſey; and yet was it laid in about three dayes before her Majeſty came. Hit did put her very farr out of temper, and almoſt all the company beſide ſo: for none of us all was able to drink either bere or ale here. Synce, by chance, we have found drink for her to her lykyng, and ſhe is well agayn: but I feared greatly, two or three dayes, ſome ſickneſs to have fallen by reaſon of this drynk. God be thanked, ſhe is now perfect well and merry; and I think, upon Thurſday come ſe'nnight, will take her journey towards Kenelworth, whear I pray God ſhe may lyke all things no worſe than ſhe hath done here: I hope the better by the good newes. For the graunt of her Majeſty touching the Concealed Wards, &c. as I have to thank your L. for the friendly dealings, ſo will I be no whit the leſs thankfull than I have promiſed; and therof your L. aſſure yourſelf, though it pleaſe you to refer it to my conſideration. It ſhall be even as I offered your L. at firſt, and ſo ſhall your own dealers be the doers as myne. And as I know your L. charge to be as myne, and as your place required, ſo wold it did lye in me, or may lye in me, to help to better yt; as you ſhall ſone find, when the occaſion ſhall offer, that I will deal no leſs, but more earneſtly than for myſelf; for ſo I may do; and what your L. ſhall impart unto me at any time for the accompliſhment hereof, ye ſhall ſe how willingly and carefully I will deal in yt. And ſo wiſhing you good health, and alway well to do, with my moſt hearty commendations, will byd your L. farewell. In ſome haſt, reddy to ryde, this Tueſday toward evening, [June 28]

Your aſſured friend, R. LEYCESTER.

Her Majeſty has ſigned my other book alſo; but no years after death.

To the right honourable my very good L. the Lord Burley, L. Treſorer of England, &c." [4]

Another letter on a different ſubject ſhall be given.

"Coſen Daviſon; The cauſe that of late I have not written to you is, for that ſince Duke Caſimire is coming hither, I have bene allwayes almoſte in his companye, and otherwiſe ſo buſied in her Maties affayres, that, I aſſure you, I have had no leyſure to wryte. The Duke is a very wellcome man hither, and well lyked of bothe of her Matie and of all other ſortes here, and hathe bene greatley entreteigned and feaſted allmoſte every daye; eſpecially the Londoners have bothe feaſted him, and given him a fayre preſent, a chayne and plate, in the whole to the value of 2000 crownes. Her Matie lodgeth him, and provydeth his dyet on her coſte, in Somerſett howſe. She hathe made him knighte of the ordre, and giveth him in preſents in the whole to the value of 3000 crownes. As he is lyked here, ſo he lyketh his enterteignment, and taketh in very good parte the greate courteſſie he findeth. He miſlyketh the States harde dealing wth him for the paye for his ſervices, and is grieved to heare howe his men daylye conſume and waſte for want thereoff; wch he taketh to hurte him ſo neare, as that I feare he will either not return thither, or not remaine there, to be ſo dealt wth any longer. Of the Prince he giveth good ſpeaches. But of theſe thinges I thincke Mr. Secretaryes do advertyſe you more at large. Another thinge I have to lett you undreſtand, wch is this: We are informed here of newe contentious quarrells lately ariſen amongſt o^r Engliſhe gentlemen and ſouldiours

---

[1] Q. Sir Henry Townſhend, Juſtice of Cheſter, &c. who (it is believed) has a monument at Ludlow, and was father of Hayward Townſhend, author of the Hiſtorical Collections.

[2] His own houſe, given him by the Queen; ſee p. 535. A view of it is engraved in Queen Elizabeth's Progreſſes; and alſo in Britton and Brayley's Beauties of England, juſt publiſhed.

[3] It is not very certain at which of the royal houſes the Queen was then reſident. Probably at Grafton; as ſhe paſſed through Northamptonſhire; and meſſengers we e diſpatched for ale both to London and Kenelworth.

[4] Harl. MS. 6992. 3. 5. 6. See the ſignature and ſeal engraved in Plate XXXIII. 27, 28. The earl of Leiceſter's great ſeal, in the ſame Plate, fig. 29, is copied from a fine impreſſion on wax, communicated in 1793 by Craven Ord, eſq. His arms alſo, as knight of the Garter, with 16 quarterings, from painted glaſs in an old houſe at Iſlington, are copied in the ſame Plate, from Gent. Mag. vol. LXII. p. 121.

there;

there; wch we all here muche miſlyke, and are ſorry to heare that o^r Nation, having gotten ſome reputation by their valour, ſhould again loſe their credit by quarreling, and confirme the badde opinion had of them for their lyke mutinous dealinges in Holland heretofore. I earneſtley pray and requyre you to looke into the matter, and by all the good meanes you can to endeavo^r to appeaſe and compoſe it, and to keape them in ordre and quyet; and, to ſhewe that the authors and cauſers of ſuche broyles may knowe how litel credit they are lyke to wynne by it here, I pray you in any wyſe to enforme yo^rſelfe throughlye of the whole matter, and to certefye hither under good teſtimonye and proofe what you fynde, and whome, to be in faulte, that, when they retourn hither, they may be dealt with as they deſerve. I have written to the Prince of Orange, praying his Excell. to enquyre of the matter, and as he ſyndeth cauſe bothe to puniſhe there, and to certefye hither, aſſuring him that he ſhall thereupon fynde howe litle we lyke here of ſuche dealinges. I ſend you the l'res incloſed, wch you may deliver or keepe as you ſhall ſee cauſe. I have written alſo to Mr. Norriſs and to cap^tain Morgan touching the ſame, and do ſend you the l'res incloſed. In any wiſe, I pray you, uſe all goode meanes to quyet the matter, and certefye throughlye hither what you fynde in it. The Q. Matie and all here, thanked be God, are well. Thus, wth my harty commendations, fare ye well. From the Court, the xii^th of Febr. 1578. Yo^r very loving frende and couſen,

R. LEYCESTER [1].

To my very loving frende and couſen Mr. Daviſon, Ambaſſador reſident for the Q. Matie in the Lowe Countryes."

In 1581, the earl of Leiceſter, who bore ſuch a ſway in thoſe days, thought it no ſmall policy to court Thomas Cartwright , whom Camden calls *inter Puritanos anteſignanus*, his party in this realm being ſo conſiderable ; inſomuch, that he made him maſter of the Hoſpital then newly by him founded at Warwick [3].

In June 1584, he was ſplendidly entertained in the Town of Leiceſter [4].

His letter to the Burgeſſes of Andover, in that year, is remarkable, and not unentertaining :

" After my heartie commendations. Whereas it hath pleaſed her Majeſty to appoint a Parliament to be preſentlie called : Being ſteward of your towne, I make bould heartile to pray you that you would give me the nomination of one of your burgeſſes for the ſame ; and yf, mynding to avoyde the chardges of allowance for the other burgeſſe, you meane to name anie that is not of your towne, yf you will beſtow the nomination of the other burgeſſe alſo upon me, I will thank you for it, and will both appoynt a ſufficient man, and ſee you diſcharged of all charges in that behaulſe. And ſo praying your ſpeedie anſwere herein, I thus bid you right hartilie farewell. From the Courte, the 12th of October, 1584.

Your loving frende, R. LEYCESTER.

Yf you will ſend me your election with a blank, I will put in the names.

To my very loving friends the bayliefes, aldermen, and the reſt of the town of Andover."

The particularities of this great Nobleman's life and actions being recorded at large in ſeveral books and treatiſes, I ſhall forbear any further remarks upon him here ; only that he had great honours, employments, and advantages ; but went off the ſtage with no applauſe at all, as he was univerſally allowed to be the moſt ambitious, inſolent, corrupt, and wicked perſon of his age. One of the laſt important events of his life was his attending the Queen at Tilbury, at the memorable period of the threatened invaſion, in

Auguſt 1588 ; ſoon after which, in his return to Kenilworth, he was taken ill of a fever [5], at Cornbury Park in Oxfordſhire, of which he died on the 4th of September following. His corpſe was removed to Warwick, and interred in the Beauchamp chapel ; where, on the North ſide, is a handſome monument, of four Corinthian pillars, ſupporting an entablature, under which is an arch, over the figures of an earl in his coronet, plated armour and mantle, and of his counteſs in her coronet and mantle of Ermine, on a table of marble, incloſed with iron rails.

On a tablet within the arch is this inſcription :

" Deo Viventium S.

Spe certâ reſurgendi in Chriſto hic ſitus eſt illuſtriſſimus Robertus Dudleyus, Johannis ducis Northumbriæ, comitis Warwici, vicecomitis Inſulæ, &c. filius quintus, comes Leceſtriæ, baro Denbighiæ, ordinis tum S. Georgii tum S. Michaelis eques auratus, reginæ Elizabethæ (apud quam ſingulari gratiâ florebat) hippocomus regiæ auræ, ſubinde ſeneſchallus, ab intimis conſiliis ; foreſtarum, parcorum, chacearum, &c. citra Trentam ſummus juſticiarius, exercitûs Anglici a dictâ reginâ Eliz. miſſi in Belgio ab anno M D LXXXV. ad annum M D LXXXVII. locum tenens & capitaneus generalis, Provinciarum Confederatarum ibidem gubernator generalis & præfectus, regnique Angliæ locumtenens contra Philippum II. Hiſpanum numeroſâ claſſe et exercitu Angliam M D LXXXVII. die IV° Septembris ; optimo et chariſſimo marito mœſtiſſimo uxor Leticia, Franciſci Knolles ordinis S. Georgii equitis aurati, et regiæ theſaurarii, filia, amoris et conjugalis fidei ergô poſuit."

Within the arch are ſixteen flags with arms.

For his iſſue, it is hitherto uncertain whether he left any legitimate or not [6]; his lawful and true marriage with his ſecond wife, the lady Douglas Howard, daughter to William lord Howard of Effingham, and widow of John lord Sheffield, being dubious, in regard it came in queſtion after his death, and at length adjudged not lawful.

By his laſt will, dated at Middleburgh in Zeland, Aug. 1, 1587, being at that time general of the Engliſh auxiliaries in the United Provinces, he gave Kenilworth to Ambroſe earl of Warwick, his brother, for life ; and the inheritance to ſir Robert Dudley, knight, whom he then thought not proper to ſtyle his lawful ſon, having openly married Lettice, daughter of ſir Francis Knollys, knight of the Garter, and treaſurer of the houſhold to Queen Elizabeth, and widow of Walter earl of Eſſex, in the life-time of the lady Douglas, and by her had a ſon ; but he died young ; for whom, near the altar in the South wall of the Beauchamp chapel, is placed an altar tomb, with his figure in the coat and mantle of a child, and a cap with a double row of pearls on his head, on a cuſhion, and a bear chained at his feet. In the front is this inſcription, in capitals :

" Here reſteth the body of the noble impe Robert of Duddely Baron of Denbigh, ſonne of Robert Erle of Leyceſter, nephew and heire unto Ambroſe Earle of Warwick, brethren, both ſonnes of the mighty Prince John late Duke of Northumberland, that was coſin and keire to Sir John Grey vicount Liſle, nephew and heir unto the Lady Margaret Counteſſe of Shrewſbury, the eldeſt daughter and coheire of the noble Earl of Warr' Sir Richard Beauchamp here interred ; a child of great parentage, but of farre greater hope and towardneſs, taken from this tranſitory unto everlaſting life, in his tender age, at Wanſted in Eſſex, on Sunday the 19th of July, in the yeare of our Lord God 1584, being the XXVIth year of the happy raine of the moſt virtuous and godly Princeſſe Quene Elizabeth. And in this place layd up among his noble aunceſtors, in aſſured hope of the general reſurrection."

On the back of this tomb are the arms of Dudley; and the quarters, and the ſloping moulding of the tomb, are charged with ragged ſtaves.

It is remarkable that though the earl of Leiceſter continued in the Queen's favour all his life, he was no ſooner dead than ſhe ſeized all his eſtates, and cauſed them to be ſold at a public ſale, for the payment of money which ſhe had lent him [7]; and certain it is that his widow encountered, after his deceaſe, many ſerious difficulties.

In 1589, ſhe was re-married to ſir Chriſtopher Blount [8], gentleman of the horſe to queen Elizabeth, and knighted by lord Willoughby of Ereſby in Flanders. He was with his ſon-in-law lord Eſſex in the

---

[1] Harl. MSS. N° 285. 3. p. 75.

[2] See an account of this man in Walton's Life of Hooker. See alſo Beloe's Anecdotes of Literature.

[3] Dugdale, Warwickſhire, vol. I. p. 443.   [4] See before, p. 403.

[5] Some ſuſpected he died of poiſon ; and reported that his wife ſerved him as he had ſerved others. There is a print and account of this earl in Holland's Heroologia (for the contents of which rare book ſee Cenſuria Literaria, vol. I. p. 305) ; where is alſo a print of his brother Ambroſe earl of Warwick.

[6] Of his firſt lady, by whom he had no iſſue, and who died ſuſpiciouſly before he was ennobled, ſee a note in p. 545.

[7] Sir Richard Baker, in one place, ſays, " This Earl was an exquiſite Stateſman for his own ends;" in another, " That he was in ſo great favour with the Queen, that ſome thought ſhe meant to marry him ; yet when he dy'd, his goods were ſold at an outcry, to make payment of the debts he ow'd her."

[8] See Birch's Elizabeth, vol. I. p. 56.

expedition

expedition to Cadiz, and had a command there; was elected in 1597 M. P. for Staffordshire [1]; wounded in Effex's infurrection, taken prifoner, tried, condemned, and beheaded [2].

The following particulars relative to the earl of Leicefter's property are curious.

" A noate whatt Legafyes weare given by my L. of Lecefter, and delivered by my Ladye, beinge excequetrixe.

To hir Matie a chaine of great pearle of xii hundred powndes price, befide the jewell my ladye added unto itt. It was delivered to the L. chauncellor Hatton for hir Maties ufe.

To the Earl of Warwick,
To the L. treaforer Burghley, } all jewells.
To the L. chauncellor Hatton,
To divers others jewells alfo, nott now remembred."

" A remembraunce, to fhewe howe my Ladye hathe bynne ridde of hir jewells.

" The firfte yeare fir Chriftopher Blunte was married, he foulde manye greate jewells; and hathe continewed the fame courfe almofte every yeare fince.

" Three yeares pafte was foulde unto the earle of Effex a greate chaine of pearle, a fayer table diamonde, and a pointed rubye, for the wch fir Chriftopher Blunte receaved three thoufande poundes.

" The Counteffe of Northumberland boughte twoe fayer pendentt pearle.

" Att my Ladyes lafte beinge att London, was foulde twoe fayer collors, and other jewells of pearles and ftones.

" Hir Matie had twoe fayer pearles and a jewell of opales made fafte to the feales of a lettre.

" Att fir Chriftopher Blunte his lafte unhappye coming to London [3], he broughte a clocke of diamonds, a greate table diamonde, and one other fayer jewell of diamonds the befte my Ladye had left hir. How he beftowed them, God knoweth.

" My Ladye hathe given heartofore att feverale times divers jewells, for offices of kindnes don for hir by reafon of hir manye trobles.

" It is well knowne my Ladye hathe payed of my L. of Lecefter's debtts, at the leafte, fyftye thowfande pounds.

" All thefe confidered, my Ladyes ftore of jewells muft needes be fmale."

" Landes and Leafes.
" A noate whatt f^r Chriftopher Blunte foulde outt of my ladye of Lecefter's livinge.

" Item, a leafe in Kentt, for the wch he receaved eyther eyghte or tenn thowfande pounde.

" A leafe for fiftye years of Grafton pafturs, worthe fower hundred pownds yearlye above the rentt.

" The lordfhippe of Benington, wherein fhe had an eftate for terme of life, bettre worthe then three hundred powndes a yeare.

" The inheritaunce of Wanftead, bettre worthe then three hundred powndes a yeare.

" Divers other thinges alfo, percell of hir jointure by the olde earle of Effexe, hathe he choptte and chaunged awaye; fo as hir eftate of livinge is farre worfe then itt hathe bynne.

" Hir jointure alfo from my L. of Lecefter is extended [4], out of the wch fhe payethe three hundred powndes yearely to hir Matie; wch is contrarye to equitye, the heyre having lande of inheritaunce fufficient to difcharge debtts to hir Matie [5]."

Among the Harleian Rolls, D. 35. are,
" An Inventorie of all the goods and chattels of Robert late Earl of Leicefter, at Leicefter Houfe, at the time of his deceafe, 3197l. 14s. 2d.

At Wanfted, taken 14 Nov. 1588, 1119l. 6s. 6d.
At Kenellworth, 2684l. 4s. 1d.
Leafes held by him, 14,314l. 6s. 8d.

Debts owing by the Earl, 53,120l. 8s. 5d.
Debts owing to the Earl of Leicefter, 2196l. 10s.
Goods removed from Kenellworth to Langley, and from Langley to London, 111l. 8s. 8d.
Jewells, 446l. 4s.
Ready money, &c.
Sum total of the Inventorye, 24,777l. 10s. 9d.
Rental of the Earl of Leicefter's lands.
Copy of the Earl of Leicefter's will.
Various Inventories and calculations concerning the real and perfonal eftates of the Earl of Leicefter [6]."

The Earl of Leicefter's widow furvived to a good old age; and was buried in the Beauchamp chapel at Warwick; where, on the wall above the monument of her hufband, hangs a wooden tablet, with this infcription:

" UPON THE DEATH OF THE EXCELLENT AND PIOUS [7]
LADY LETTICE COUNTESSE OF LEICESTER, WHO
DYED UPON CHRISTMASS DAY IN THE MORNING. 1634.

I.

Look on this vault, and fearch it well,
Much treafure in it lately fell.
We are all rob'd, and all do fay
Our wealth was carried this-away;
And, that the theft might ne'er be found,
'Tis buried clofely under ground:
Yet if you gently ftir the mould,
There all our loffe you may behold.
There you may fee that face, that hand,
Which once was faireft in the land.
She that in her younger yeares
Match'd with two great Englifh peers;
She that did fupplye the warrs
With thunder, and the court with ftarrs;
She that in her youth had bene
Darling to the Maiden Quene,
Till fhe was content to quitt
Her favour for her favouritt.

II.

Whofe gould thread when fhe faw fpunn,
And the death of her brave fonne,
Thought it fafeft to retyre
From all care and vaine defire,
To a private countrie cell,
Where fhe fpent her days fo well,
That to her the better fort
Came, as to an holy court;
And the poor y^t lived neare,
Dearth nor famine could not feare.
Whilft fhe liv'd, fhe lived thus;
Till that God, difpleas'd with us,
Suffrid her at laft to fall,
Not from him, but from us all:
And becaufe fhe tooke delight
Chrift's poore members to invite,
He fully now requites her love,
And fends his Angels from above,
That did to Heaven her foule convey
To folemnize his owne birth-day.
GERVAS CLIFTON [8]."

" Lettice countefs of Leicefter, Eue. and Effex, vifcountefs Hereford, baronefs of Denbigh, and Ferrars of Chartley, fifter to William lord Knolles of Greys, vifcount Wallingford, and earl of Banbury, knight of the Garter, had the happinefs to fee living the grandchildren of her grandchildren, as is declared in her ftem at the manor of Drayton [9]."

SIR ROBERT DUDLEY, the earl of Leicefter's fon by the lady Douglas, was educated under fir Thomas Chaloner, the accomplifhed governor of Prince Henry; and diftinguifhed his youth by martial atchievements, and by ufeful difcoveries in the Weft Indies [10]. Notwithftanding his father's character of

[1] Birch's Elizabeth, vol. II. p. 362.   [2] Ibid. p. 493.
[3] This evidently alludes to fir Chriftopher's engagement in the infurrection of his fon-in-law Effex, for which he fuffered death.
[4] See Shaw's Staffordfhire, vol. II. p. 8.   [5] Harl. MSS. N° 304. p. 88. a. b.
[6] Mr. Ayfcough's Catalogue of Charters in the Britifh Mufeum.
[7] Not very pious, if there is any credit due to the reported caufe of lord Leicefter's death; fee p. 537.
[8] Dugdale, Warwickfhire, vol. I. p. 448. This Gervafe Clifton, who feems by this to have had fome talents for poetry, was probably of the baronet's family.   [9] Plot's Staffordfhire, p. 328. See alfo Shaw's Staffordfhire, vol. II. p. 8.
[10] Anthony Wood fays, " The duke was a complete gentleman, an exact feaman, a good navigator, an excellent architect, mathematician, phyfician, chemift, and what not? He was a handfome, perfonable man, tall of ftature, red haired, and of admirable comport; and, above all, noted for riding the great horfe, for tilting, and for his being the firft of all that taught a dog to fit, to catch partridges."

him

him in his will, he did not account himself illegitimate [1]; for, soon after the death of queen Elizabeth, having married Alice eldest daughter to sir Thomas Leigh, of Stoneley, co. Warwick; and considering that, in case he made good his legitimacy, not only a good title to the earldom of Leicester, but also to many good lordships, manors, and lands, would accrue unto him; he obtained a commission out of the archbishop's court of audience, to examine witnesses to prove his father's marriage with the lady Douglas his mother. But, this being opposed by the lady Lettice, dowager of the earl, and the business being heard and examined in the Star-chamber [2], sentence was given against the earl's marriage with the lady Douglas, though the matters and circumstances deposed were very pertinent and home to the business; but the credit of the witnesses was suspected.

Upon this, sir Robert Dudley conceived such discontent, that he resolved to quit the realm; and for that purpose obtained licence for three years to travel into Italy. But, he being gone, his adversaries procured a special privy seal to be sent after him, to command his return; whereunto he not obeying, his lands were seized by force of the Statute of Fugitives, of which Kenilworth castle, his chief seat, was part. But it was not long after, that prince Henry, affecting this castle as one of the most noble and magnificent things in the Midland part of the kingdom, made overture, by agents, to sir Robert Dudley, to purchase his title to it; and thereupon agreement was made, and, in consideration of 14,500l. to be paid within a year, deeds were sealed, and fines levied, settling the inheritance thereof, with some other lands, upon the prince and his heirs. But the prince died not long after; so that there was not above 3000l. ever paid, and to a merchant also that broke; so that it never came to the hands of sir Robert. But prince Charles, as heir to his brother, held the possession thereof; and, in 1622, obtained a special act of parliament to enable the lady Alice, wife to sir Robert, because she had a jointure therein, to alienate all her right to him as if she had been a *feme feule*; which she did, in consideration of 4000l. assigned to her out of the Exchequer, and certain other annual payments [3]. On sir Robert's departure out of England, he took with him (as is credibly reported) a beautiful young lady, the daughter of sir Robert Southwell, in the habit of a page, whom, it is said, he married in Italy; and, seating himself in the territories of the duke of Tuscany, had, by reason of his singular and excellent endowments, very great esteem in all those parts. And, his fame spreading into Germany, he had, by grant from the emperor Ferdinand II. the title of Duke conferred on him, 1620, to be used by him and his heirs throughout all the dominions of the Sacred Empire; whereupon he was generally called Duke of Northumberland; as also after him was Charles his eldest son by the daughter of sir Robert Southwell. Farther, as a testimony of the great esteem which he there had, the great duke of Tuscany [4] allowed him a yearly stipend of 1000l. sterling; and the daughters by the wife he took thither were all married to several Princes of the Empire. At his abode in Florence he built a noble palace in that city; but, dying at a palace of the duke of Florence's, not far off, in or about the year 1650, his body was first laid in the nunnery at Boldrone, to be removed to the church of St. Pancrace in Florence, where he had erected a noble monument for that wife, with purpose to be there interred himself. Several sons he also left there, but of their fortunes I can give no farther account.

But for his lady Alice, which he left in England, and the five daughters that he had by her; two of his daughters, Alice and Douglas, died unmarried: Katharine was married to sir Richard Leveson, knight of the Bath; Frances to sir Gilbert Kniveton; and Anne to sir Richard Holborn, solicitor general to king Charles I. And, for the lady Alice, she received the said sum of 4000l. payable from the Exchequer. But of her annuity, or yearly payments, there was a great arrear at the beginning of the Civil Wars; for the receipt whereof there being but little hope, and considering that her husband sir Robert, then alive, had the title of a Duke in those foreign parts where he did reside, and representing the same to king Charles I. she obtained a grant under the great seal of England, bearing date at Oxford, 20 Car. I. of the title of a Dutchess during her life, and that her daughters should have place and precedence as children of a person of that degree. And this lady Alice was that dutchess Dudley that lived for many years in the parish of St. Giles in the Fields, and died Jan. 22, 1669, at her house near that church; in which the following inscription was set up, though her corpse was conveyed to Stoneley, her native town:

" Alice Duchess Duddeley;
a lady of a vast charitable mind, and who did many
good deeds to this parish. She died anno 1669; third daughter
of Sir Thomas Leigh, of Stoneley in Warwickshire, Knt.
and Bart. Her mother was Katharine daughter to Sir
John Spencer, of Wormleighton, Knt. and great-
grandfather to the Earl of Sunderland. The foresaid Sir
Thomas Leigh had, by the said Katharine, John
Leigh, Knt. who was the father of the Lord
Leigh Baron of Stoneley [1]."

In the church at Stoneley also an elegant monument was erected, with her effigies, and this inscription:

" H. S. E.
Domina Alicia Dudlea, Thomæ Leigh Mil. & Bar. filia natu secunda Rob. Dudlei Equ. Aurati (Rob. Comitis Leic. filii, titulo Ducis à Sereniss. Ferdin. II°. Germ. Emp. ob eximia merita ornati) nuper defuncti relicta: ac in gradum Ducissæ per illustrem nuper Regem Car. I. evecta: Cui filias hasce; scil. Aliciam Douglassam, Francescam Gilb. Kniveton Equ. Aur. uxorem, Annam Rob. Holburne Equ. etiam Aur. Linc' Hospit. socio enuptam, jamdudum defunctas; ac Katherinam Ric. Levefon prænob. Ord. Baln. Militis relictam (modò superstitem) peperit. Quæ quidem Ducissa, pietate & charitate excellens, huic de Stoneley, necnon singulis de Manceter, Leke Wotton, Ashow, Kenilworth, & Kirby Monachorum (in hoc agro Warwic.) Ecclesiis xxli. annuas in vicariarum earundem egenarum perpetuam augmentationem; eisdemque, & insuper de Bidford in dicto com', Acton in com' Midd', S. Alban in com' Hertf', Patshull in com' North'ton, S. Egid' in Suburbio Civit' London', vasa diversa argentea, pretii non exilis, dudùm contulit; dictæque S. Egidii Ecclefiæ in novam ejusdem structuram multùm deponens, campanam maximam, ac Rectori ibidem perpetuò mansionem habilem vivens comparavit; moriens verò in redemptionem Christianorum ab Infidelibus captivorum cli. annuas: Xenodochio infra dictam S. Egidii parochiam ccccli.; in pauperum puerorum opificibus quæstuariis allocationem ccli. Indigentibus dictorum de Stoneley, Kenilworth, Leke Wotton, Ashow, Bedford, & Patshull, necnon de Lichborow & Blakesly in agro Northampt', parochianis cli. ibid. annuas; plurimaque aliorum pauperibus & egenis ultimo testamento legavit. Diem obiit xxii Jan. anno ab Incarn. Dei MDCLXVIII, ætatis suæ xc°."

On the same monument with her mother:
" H. S. E.
D'na Alicia Dudlæa, filia natu maxima
prænob. Aliciæ Dudleæ;
quæ ante nuptias moriens xxiii Maii,
anno Domini MDCXXI°,
lautum patrimonium in pietatis operibus disponendum dictæ matri charitative legavit."

The venerable dutchess being a person of great piety, prudence, temperance, and thrift, she became enabled and disposed to do many extraordinary acts of piety and charity, both in her life-time and at her death; of some of which, for the exemplariness thereof, I will take the liberty here to give a brief inventory.

She gave 100l. to the re-building of the church of St. Giles, with rich hangings for the East end of the chancel; hanging of green velvet for the back of the altar; a carpet of green velvet, with a deep gold fringe, and a cover of cambrick thereto, edged with rich bone-lace. Also, one other altar-cloth of damask, and two cushions richly embroidered with gold; and two service-books, with bosses of silver; and a large Turkey carpet for the altar, to cover it on ordinary days. Also, a rich screen of carved work, to sever the chancel from the church; also a fair organ, with a case richly guilt; very costly hand-

---

[1] Dr. Campbell has discussed this point in the Biographia Britannica.   [2] Gervase Holles's account of this affair is curious.
[3] Dugdale, Warwickshire, vol. I. p. 250.
[4] "It was the House of Medici, those patrons of learning and talents, who fostered this enterprising spirit; and who were amply rewarded for their munificence, by his projecting the free port of Leghorn." See more of him in Park's edition of the Royal and Noble Authors, vol. V. p. 335.   [5] Dugdale, Warwickshire, vol. I. p. 261.

fome rails, to guard the altar of the Lord's table from prophane abufes; communion plate of all forts, in filver and gilt, as large and rich as any in the City and fuburbs; a pavement for the chancel, of black and white marble; the great bells, with frames for all the reft, new-caft at her own charges[1]. Alfo, to the churches of Stoneley, Leek-Wotton, Manceter, Afhow, Kenelworth, and Monks Kirby, all in co. Warwick, 20l. per annum to each of them, for the augmentation of their poor refpective vicarages.

Alfo, to every of thofe churches, as alfo to thofe at Bitford, Acton, Patfhull, and St. Alban's, certain pieces of communion plate, very rich.

Alfo, a fair houfe and garden, near the church of St. Giles, for the parfons to dwell in; with a ftipend yearly to the fexton there, to toll the great bell as prifoners pafs to execution at Tyburn, and to ring it out after execution.

Alfo, great fums towards the repair of Litchfield cathedral, and St. Sepulchre's church, London.

Alfo, 100l. per annum, for ever, towards the redemption of Chriftian captives from the Turks.

Alfo, 400l. to purchafe lands for the Hofpital fituate near St. Giles; and 200l. to purchafe lands of 10l. per annum value, for putting out poor children of that parifh apprentices.

Alfo, to the poor of Stoneley, Kenilworth, Leck-Wotton, Afhow, Bitford, Patfhull, Lichborow, and Blakefly, 100l.

Alfo, 50l. to be diftributed, at her funeral, to the poor of St. Giles.

Alfo, to 90 poor widows (fhe being fo many years old), to each of them a gown of black cloth, with a large holland kerchief, to attend her hearfe at her funeral (which was on March 16, 1669), befides 12d. apiece for their dinners that day.

Alfo, 5l. to every parifh, for their poor, where her corpfe fhould reft, in her paffage from London to Stoneley in Warwickfhire, where fhe was buried, under a noble monument by her erected in her lifetime; and to every poor body on the road, 6d. Alfo, to the poor of Stoneley, to be diftributed at her funeral, 50l. To the poor of the parifhes of Blakefly, Patfhull, and Lichborow, 10l. to be fo diftributed.

On a marble monument fixed to the wall under the Eaft window of the Beauchamp chapel:
" To the memory of the Lady
Katherine (late wife of Sir Richard Levefon of Trentham, in the county of Staff. K't of the Bath), one of the daughters and coheirs of Sir Rob. Dudley, Kn't, fon to Rob. late earl of Leicefter, by Alicia his wife, daughter of Sir Tho. Leigh, of Stonley, Kn't and Bar't (created Dutchefs Dudley by K. Charles I. in regard that her faid hufband, leaving this realme, had the title of a Duke confer'd upon him by Ferdinand II. Emp'r of Germany) w'ch hon'bl' Lady taking notice of thefe tombes of her noble anceftors being much blemifht by confuming Time, but more by the rude hands of impious people, were in danger of utter ruine by the decay of this Chapell, if not timely prevented; did in her life-time give fifty pounds for its fpeedy repair. And by her laft will and teftament, bearing date xviii° Dec. 1673, bequeath forty pounds per annum, iffuing out of her manor of Foxley, in the county of Northampton, for its perpetual fupport and prefervation of thefe Monuments in their proper ftate; the furplufage to be for the poor brethren of her grandfather's Hofpitall in this Borough, appointing William Dugdale, of Blythe Hall in this County, Efq. (who reprefented to her the neceffity of this good worke) and his heirs, together with the Mayor of Warwick for the time being, to be her truftees therein."

And now, having feen the fates and fortunes of the DUDLEYS, we muft look for the fucceeding earls of Leicefter in the SIDNEYS, of Penfhurft Place, Kent, a line connected with them by marriage.

Sir Henry Sidney, fon of fir William Sidney[2], knt. had livery of the manors of Penfhurft and Yensfield in 1553, on the death of his father. He was highly efteemed by king Edward VI. with whom he had been bred from his infancy, and brought up in the court as a companion to him; at whofe acceffion he was knighted, and made gentleman of his privy chamber, and in the third year of his reign fent ambaffador into France, though not fully 21 years old. He was afterwards elected knight of the Garter, was of the privy council, and four times made lord juftice of Ireland, and thrice deputy for that realm, which is much indebted to him for the wife and prudent regulations he made, and the public works he effected during his government there. Having in his paffage by water from Ludlow in Wales, of which principality he was then prefident, taken cold, he died, after a few days ficknefs, at the Bifhop's palace at Worcefter, May 5, 1586, aged almoft 57 years; whence his body was, by the queen's order, conveyed with great folemnity, according to his degree, to Penfhurft, where it was interred; but his heart was carried back to Ludlow, and buried there. By the lady Mary, eldeft daughter of John Dudley duke of Northumberland, who died on Aug. 9 next enfuing his deceafe, and lies buried at Penfhurft, he had iffue three fons; fir Philip, fir Robert, and fir Thomas Sidney, knights; and one furviving daughter, Mary, a lady of learning and genius, and an author[3]. " She was married in 1570 to Henry earl of Pembroke, whom fhe furvived 20 years. The countefs died, at a very advanced age, in Alderfgate-ftreet, London, Sept. 25, 1621; and was buried in the cathedral church of Salifbury, without any monument to her memory; the want of which, however, is amply compenfated by the well-known epitaph compofed for her by Ben Jonfon, a tribute that never has been exceeded in the records of monumental praife[4]:
" Underneath this marble herfe
Lies the fubject of all verfe,
Sidney's fifter, Pembroke's mother;
Death, ere thou haft fuch another,
Learn'd and fair, and good as fhe,
Time fhall throw his dart at thee."

Sir Philip Sidney, the eldeft fon, was born, as is fuppofed, at Penfhurft, Nov. 24, 1554; and, had he not been cut off fo foon, would moft likely have proved one of the greateft worthies that England had ever feen, as well for his learning as his other extraordinary qualities. Camden, in his Britannia, ftyles him " the great glory of his Country, the great hopes of mankind, the moft lively pattern of virtue, and the darling of the learned world." Being made governor of Flufhing in Zeland, he went over into Flanders with the forces fent to affift the States; and, encountering the Spaniards near Zutphen in Guilderland, Sept. 22, 1586, was there mortally wounded in the thigh, and died October 16 following, at Arnheim, aged 34, not many months after his father. His corpfe was brought over to England, and interred with great honour[5] above the

[1] Dugdale, Warwickfhire, vol. I. p. 261.

[2] Sir William Sidney (defcended from William Sidney, who came from Anjou with king Henry III.) had in the reign of king Henry VIII. acquired great reputation in his profeffion, as a foldier; and in 1514, commanded the right wing of the army under the earl of Surrey at the battle of Flodden field, when he was made a knight banneret. He was chamberlain, and afterwards fteward to prince Edward before his acceffion to the crown; after which, he was one of the gentlemen of that king's bedchamber. He died in 1553; and by Anne his wife, daughter and heir of Hugh Pakenham, left fir Henry Sidney, knt. his fon and heir; and four daughters; Frances (founder of Sidney-Suffex college, Cambridge), married to Thomas Ratcliff earl of Suffex; Anne, to fir William Fitzwilliam, knight; Mary, to fir William Dormer, knight; and Lucy, to fir James Harington, knight, whence comes the prefent fir John Harington, bart. He was buried at Penfhurft; where, on the South fide of the South chancel, is a fine old monument of ftone, under which is an altar tomb of grey marble; and on the wall above it is a plate of brafs, infcribed,

Here lyeth fir William Sydney, knight and bannerer, fometyme chamberlen, and after fteward to the moft mighte and famous prynce kynge Edward the VIth, in the tyme of his being prynce, and the firfte of that name, being lord of the manner of Penfhurfte, who dyed the Xth day of February, in the XXX yere of our Lord God M fyve hundred fiftie and three. On whofe foul Jhefu have mercy.

[3] See Ballard. [4] Park's Edition of the Royal and Noble Authors, vol. II. p. 191; &c. &c.

[5] The fplendid funeral proceffion of this illuftrious Hero was engraved in 1587, from drawings by Thomas Lant, in a roll more than 38 feet in length, and containing 144 figures. A fine copy of it, formerly belonging to the earl of Leicefter, was poffeffed by Mr. Thorpe, who has amply defcribed it in his " Cuftumale Roffenfe," p. 142; and his account of it is alfo given in Queen Elizabeth's Progreffes.

choir

choir in St. Paul's church, London, with no small lamentation, not only of the queen and court, but of the nation in general. He left issue, by Frances his wife [1], daughter and heir of sir Francis Walsingham, secretary of state, an only daughter, named Elizabeth, who afterwards married Roger earl of Rutland. It does not appear by Dugdale's History of St. Paul's that any monument was placed there for sir Philip Sidney; but in Popham's " Elogia Sepulchralia" is the following inscription to his memory :

" Philippus Sidneius, Miles,
Henrico patre natus, viro nobili,
qui ter Hiberniæ prorex,
complures annos præses Walliæ,
& à consiliis Elizabethæ Reginæ fuit :
matre nobiliore, filiâ Ducis Northumbriæ;
istâ bonis literis domi forisque,
ad omnum humanitatem, prudentiam, virtutem,
excultus & informatus,
ut insigni legatione,
antequam vicesimum primum ætatis annum implevisset,
ad Rodolphum Imperatorem honoratissimè sit perfunctus :
ac nisi immaturâ morte præreptus esset,
dum adversus hostes fortius quàm cautius
in Belgio pugnam iniens patriem defendit,
ei ornamentum commodumque majusquam pater
allaturus fuisset.
Filiam duxit illius, quorum sub hoc marmore,
beatam expectans resurrectionem,
corpore quiescit.
Ex eâ genuit unicam filiam Elizabetham,
cohæredem jure sanguinis,
cum Huntingdoniæ Comitissâ,
Comiti Warwici & Leicestriæ;
vixit annos 32. Obiit 16 Octob. ann. 1586."

Sir *Robert* Sidney, knt. the next brother and heir, succeeded to his estates; and in 1589 was appointed governor likewise of Flushing. In 1594 he was sent ambassador into France, and in 1598 was joined in command with sir Francis Vere over those English auxiliaries then sent against the Spaniards. On king James's accession to the throne (having in vain sought a peerage in the reign of queen Elizabeth, whose œconomy of honours is well known), he was, by letters patent, dated May 13, 1603, advanced to the dignity of a baron of this realm, by the title of lord Sidney of Penshurst in Kent. July 24 that year, being the day of the king's coronation, he was made lord chamberlain to the queen; and May 4, 1605, created viscount L'Isle; July 7, 1617, was installed knight of the Garter; and, in farther consideration of his services, on Aug. 2, next year, he was dignified with the title of earl of Leicester, the ceremony of his creation being performed in the hall of the bishop's palace at Salisbury. He was also of the council to the lord president of Wales, and of the privy council to king James; and dying at Penshurst, July 13, 1626, was buried in that church. He was twice married; first, to Barbara daughter and heir to John Gamage, of Coytie, co. Glamorgan, esq. by whom he had issue three sons; sir William Sidney, knt. who died unmarried; Henry, who died an infant; and sir Robert, made knight of the Bath at the creation of Henry prince of Wales; and eight daughters.

Sir *Robert* Sidney, knight of the Bath, the only surviving son and successor, was, whilst viscount L'Isle, in his father's life-time, chosen one of the knights to serve in that Parliament which met in the 18th year of king James I. and one of the knights for Monmouthshire in the 21st year of that reign, as also in the 1st of king Charles I; and the year after succeeded his father as earl of Leicester. He was by king James several times sent ambassador to the king of Denmark, the States of Germany, and the Court of France [2]; and, on the removal of the earl of Strafford, was nominated lord lieutenant of Ireland, though he never went over thither. He died at Penshurst, Nov. 2, 1677, aged 82 years all but one month; and, having married Dorothy, eldest daughter of Henry Percy earl of Northumberland, had issue by her six sons, and eight daughters. Of the sons who survived him to maturity, Philip was his successor; Algernon was the zealous Republican, who was beheaded

on Tower-hill Dec. 7, 1683, æt. 66, for being concerned in the Rye-house plot; and Robert, the third son, died at Penshurst in 1668. Henry [3], the youngest surviving son, was, April 9, 1689, created baron of Milton and viscount Sidney of the isle of Shepey; and April 25, 1694, advanced to the title of earl of Romney. He was master of the ordnance, constable of the Tower, and warden of the Cinque Ports; and died, unmarried, April 8, 1704.—Macky says, " He was the great wheel on which the Revolution rolled." Swift adds, " He had not a wheel to turn a mouse." Macky : " Of great honour and honesty, with a moderate capacity." Swift : " Of none at all."

The eldest son, *Philip*, succeeded to the titles and estate; and lived, in great honour and esteem, to a good old age, departing this life at London, March 6, 1698. He married Catharine daughter of William Cecil earl of Salisbury, who died in 1658, by whom he had Robert his successor, and two daughters.

Sir *Robert Sidney*, knight, his son and heir, was called up by writ to the house of peers [4], as baron *Sidney*, in his father's life-time, July 11, 1689; and succeeded as earl of Leicester in 1697. He died Nov. 10, 1702, aged 52, and was buried at Penshurst, having had, by Elizabeth his wife, daughter of John Egerton earl of Bridgewater (who died in 1709, and lies buried there), 15 children, of whom nine died young, and four sons and two daughters survived him. Of the former, Philip, the second son, was his successor; John, the fourth son, was afterwards earl of Leicester; Thomas, the sixth son, was a colonel of dragoons; and Joceline, the seventh son, was afterwards earl of Leicester.

In the church at Penshurst, on the North side, on the upper part of a fine monument of white marble, are seven Cherubims heads placed semicircular, over which are the following names :

| William Sidney. | Charles Sidney. | Henry Sidney. | The 1st child. | Dorothy Sidney. | Harry Sidney. | Henrietta Sidney. |

Beneath is an urn supported by two angels, and these inscriptions on tablets of black marble :

" Robert Sidney, the eldest son; he had wit, judgment, and beauty, to so great a degree, that dayly increas'd the surprising admiration of all that knew him. He died 1680, in the 6th year of his age."

" Frances Sidney, the fourth daughter, in all respects a perfect copy of her eldest brother; so that she was all that could be wished. She died in 1692, in the 6th year of her age."

" To the dear memory of Robert Sidney, earl of Leicester, viscount Lisle, baron Sidney of Penshurst. 4th earl of his family. He married the lady Elizabeth Egerton, daughter to the earl of Bridgewater, with whom he lived 30 happy years, had 15 children, of which 9 dy'd young, whose figures are plac'd here; Robert, the eldest son, the 3d and 6th daughters, buried in this place. 6 surviv'd him, whereof 4 were sons, and two daughters. His person was gracefull and beautifull, his mind truly noble and great; of a quick wit, good judgment, a sweet temper, and pleasing conversation; he had an honest heart, a gratefull and generous spirit, and upon all occasions ever strictly just and good; a faithfull friend, the best of husbands, a most kind and tender father, a true lover of the interest of his Country, and the Church of England. He died the 53d year of his age, the 10th of November, 1702, and was buried under this monument; which, in true affection to his lov'd memory, is erected by his disconsolate afflicted wife."

" To the memory of Elizabeth countess of Leicester, the happy and only wife of her dear-lov'd Robert earl of Leicester, whose death she survived seven tedious years, having lost in him her better life. The affection and solicitude for her children, which was constantly very great for all, forced her a little into the world, and, not wholly giving up herself to what was most agreeable to her, lulling herself [5] in her infinite sorrow : the great desire of her life was to make a good wife and a good mother, and did so. She died, in the 57th year of her age, 1709, and is buried under here, in the same vault with her dear lord.

" These inscriptions are here plac'd by her own directions [6]."

Philip, the eldest surviving son, above mentioned, succeeded his father as earl of Leicester; and married Anne eldest daughter and coheir of sir Robert Reeves, of Suffolk, bart. by whom he had one son and one daughter, who both died infants. He died July 24, 1705, and was buried in Penshurst church; on which the titles and estate devolved to his next brother,

---

[1] Who was twice re-married; first to the earl of Essex, the unhappy favourite of queen Elizabeth; and afterwards to Richard Bourk, earl of Clanrickard and St. Alban's.

[2] See lord Clarendon's character of him.   [3] See his character in Burnet's History of his own Times.

[4] The writ was addressed " Roberto Sydney de Penshurst Chivalier;" and he was seated on the Barons' bench, in his father's barony, next to the lord Chandos. Journals of the House of Lords, vol. XIV. p. 274.

[5] This is written in the same plaintive spirit as her father John earl of Bridgewater, in his epitaph, speaks of her mother, Elizabeth, the virtuous daughter of William duke of Newcastle. See Censura Literaria, vol. II. p. 260.

[6] Thorpe's Regiftrum Roffenfe, pp. 917—919.

John earl of Leicester, who was appointed one of the lords of the king's bedchamber, and in 1717 warden of the Cinque Ports, and conſtable of Dover caſtle; after which he was made a knight of the Bath, captain of the yeomen of the guards, and lord lieutenant of the county of Kent. In 1732 he was ſworn of the privy council, and at the ſame time conſtable of the Tower of London. He was a man of moſt eaſy and engaging manners; and, though he had led the life of a courtier and man of faſhion, his heart abounded with a thouſand amiable traits [i]. He died unmarried, Sept. 27, 1737, and was buried at Penſhurſt. On which (Thomas, the third and next ſurviving ſon of Robert earl of Leiceſter, having died Jan. 27, 1729, without male iſſue, leaving by Mary his wife [2], youngeſt daughter and coheir of ſir Robert Reeves, bart. only two daughters and coheirs, of whom hereafter); the titles and eſtate devolved to

Joceline, the fourth ſurviving ſon of Robert earl of Leiceſter. He was a man of eccentric and doubtful character, and ſuppoſed to have had a touch of infanity. In 1717 he married Elizabeth daughter and heir of —— Thomas, of Glamorganſhire, eſq.; but died, without lawful iſſue, on July 7, 1743; being the laſt heir male of this noble family, in whom the title of earl of Leiceſter expired.

On the South ſide of Penſhurſt church, on a handſome monument of white marble, is a pyramid of black, with the arms and quarterings of the *Sidney* family, and this motto, *Quo fata vocant*; and on the baſe of the monument are the following inſcriptions:

"To the memory of the moſt noble lord Philip Sidney, the fifth earl of Leiceſter, viſcount Liſle, and lord Sidney of Penſhurſt, ſon and heir of Robert the fourth earl of Leiceſter here interred, who was ſon and heir of Philip earl of Leiceſter, ſon and heir of Robert earl of Leiceſter, ſon and heir of ſir Robert Sidney, knight, created earl of Leiceſter by king James the Firſt; which laſt-named Robert earl of Leiceſter was nephew and heir [3] of Ambroſe Dudley and Robert Dudley, brethren, earls of Warwick and of Leiceſter, ſons of the high and mighty prince John Dudley duke of Northumberland, whoſe grandſon and heir the ſaid earl Robert Sidney was after the deaths of his ſaid uncles, his aunt Catharine counteſs of Huntington, and his niece Elizabeth counteſs of Rutland, who all died without iſſue; which duke of Northumberland was ſon and heir of Elizabeth Grey viſcounteſs Liſle, daughter and ſole heir of Edward Grey and Elizabeth Talbot his wife, created baron Liſle, to them and the heirs of their bodies iſſuing for ever [4], by patent the 15th of Edward the Fourth. Philip the fifth earl of Leiceſter married Ann eldeſt daughter and coheir of ſir Robert Reeves, of Thwaits, in the county of Suffolk, bart. by whom he had a ſon and one daughter, who all died in the firſt year of their ages; and his lordſhip departing this life on the 24th of July, 1705, was ſucceeded by John his brother and heir.

John, the ſixth earl of Leiceſter, was couſin and heir of Henry Sidney earl of Romney, and one of the lords of the bedchamber, and lord warden of the Cinque Ports, and governor of Dover caſtle, and choſe one of the knights companions of the moſt honourable order of the Bath, in the reign of king George the Firſt; and under king George the Second, he was captain of the yeomen of the guard, conſtable of the Tower of London, lord lieutenant of the county of Kent, and one of his Majeſty's moſt honourable privy council; who deceaſing unmarried on the 27th of September, 1737, his nieces Mary and Elizabeth Sidney, daughters and heirs of his brother the honourable Thomas Sidney, third ſurviving ſon of Robert the fourth earl of Leiceſter, became his joint heirs, and legal repreſentatives.

Thomas Sidney, their father, married Mary the youngeſt daughter, and, after the death of her ſiſter Anne counteſs of Leiceſter without iſſue, ſole heir, of ſir Robert Reeves, bart.; which Thomas dying on the 27th of January, 1728-9, was here interred; as was alſo the ſaid Mary his widow.

Joceline, the ſeventh earl of Leiceſter, youngeſt brother and heir male of earl John, died without iſſue on the 7th of July, 1743, and alſo lyes here interred with his brethren, in whom the title of earl of Leiceſter expired: So that the aforeſaid Mary and Elizabeth, his nieces, are his heirs, and alſo the only heirs of their noble Anceſtors above-mentioned; of whom Mary the eldeſt is the wife of ſir Brownlow Sherard, of Lopthorp in Lincolnſhire, bart.; and Elizabeth, of William Perry, of Turville Park in Bucks, eſq.; who erected this monument in the year 1743."

Joceline earl of Leiceſter had, by indenture of bargain and ſale in 1738, ſuffered a common recovery of the manor of Penſhurſt, &c. &c. to the uſe of him and his heirs and aſſigns for ever; upon which, ſir Brownlow Sherrard, bart. and dame Mary his wife, and William Perry, eſq. and Elizabeth his wife

(which Mary and Elizabeth were the daughters and coheirs of colonel Thomas Sidney, third ſurviving ſon of Robert earl of Leiceſter, and next elder brother of the ſaid Joceline) inſiſted that the ſaid Joceline earl of Leiceſter was only tenant for life in theſe premiſes by virtue of deeds of ſettlement of all the ſaid premiſes, dated the 13th and 14th of December, 1700, whereby the ſame were, after ſeveral limitations long ſince ſpent, limited *to the uſe* of the ſaid Joceline for life, with remainder to the uſe of his firſt and other ſons in *tail male*, with remainder to the uſe of Robert earl of Leiceſter his father, and the heirs of his body, and for want of ſuch iſſue *to the uſe of the right heirs* of the ſaid Robert for ever. And that the ſaid Joceline, by ſuffering ſuch recovery, had forfeited his life eſtate, and, having no lawful iſſue, the ſaid dame Mary and Elizabeth, as heirs of the body and heirs general of the ſaid Robert earl of Leiceſter, were entitled to the next eſtates in remainder created by the above ſettlement, expectant on the ſaid eſtate for life of Joceline, and therefore that they and their huſbands were entitled to take advantage of ſuch forfeiture; and thereupon, in November 1739, they ſerved ejectments on the ſeveral tenants of theſe eſtates, and commenced a ſuit in Chancery for the recovery of them, during the litigation of which Joceline earl of Leiceſter died, in 1743, without iſſue, having by his will, dated June 29, 1743, deviſed all his eſtates whatſoever to Anne Sidney, his natural daughter, and to the heirs of her body, with remainder to the duke of Bridgewater, and the heirs of John late earl of Bridgewater; and in November following the ſaid Anne Sidney, then an infant, by her guardians, exhibited a bill in Chancery againſt ſir Brownlow Sherard and William Perry, eſq.; inſiſting that earl Joceline was tenant in tail by the former ſettlement, and by the ſaid recovery was ſeiſed in fee ſimple, and claimed the ſaid eſtates under his will as above recited. After great litigation in the ſaid court, the ſuit being at iſſue, was tried at the bar of the Court of King's Bench April 23, 1745; when, after a long hearing, the jury found a ſpecial verdict, wherein the infanity of the earl, before inſiſted on by ſir Brownlow Sherrard and Mr. Perry, was not touched on, but remained ſtill to be controverted; and as both parties found theſe ſuits at law very expenſive, and that it would be many years before they would be decided; and the guardians of Anne Sidney [5] foreſeeing, if the will was ſet aſide, ſhe would be deſtitute of maintenance: For theſe reaſons, they agreed to compromiſe this diſpute; and they agreed that ſir Brownlow Sherrard and Mary his wife, and William Perry, eſq. and Elizabeth his wife, ſhould enjoy all the manors and eſtates whatſoever of the ſaid earl in the county of Kent, free from any demand from the ſaid Anne Sidney, and that *one moiety* of the ſame ſhould be ſettled *in truſtees* for the uſe of dame Mary Sherrard, and the heirs of her body, with remainder to her and her heirs, and the *other moiety in truſtees* for the uſe of Elizabeth Perry, in like manner, as *tenants in common*, and not as joint tenants; each moiety to be ſubject to the ſum of 5000l. for the uſe of the ſaid Anne Sidney, who was likewiſe to enjoy the earl's eſtate in Glamorganſhire, according to his will, ſubject to ſuch eſtate as Elizabeth counteſs of Leiceſter had therein. All which was confirmed by parliament in 1747; after which, ſir Brownlow Sherrard and Mary his wife, and William Perry, eſq. and Elizabeth his wife, remained poſſeſſed, *as tenants in common*, of the manors of Penſhurſt, &c. &c. Sir Brownlow Sherrard died in November 1748, without iſſue, after which his widow poſſeſſed this moiety of theſe eſtates, and on March 28, 1752, had the king's ſign manual that ſhe and her iſſue ſhould uſe the name of *Sidney*, and the coat armour of Robert late earl of Leiceſter, deceaſed.

Mary Sidney lady Sherrard died without iſſue in 1758; and by her will, dated June 3, 1757, bequeathed her whole intereſt in theſe eſtates to Anne widow of ſir William Yonge, baronet, and knight of the Bath, daughter and coheir of Thomas lord Howard

---

[1] From private information.

[2] Who was afterwards re-married to John Shepherd, eſq. of Campſey Aſh, Suffolk; and died May 3, 1726.

[3] This is taking for granted Robert Dudley's illegitimacy; which is not very generally believed.

[4] If this is correct, Mrs. Perry had ſome grounds for claiming the barony of L'Iſle; ſee p. 543.

[5] I have been informed that this lady (ſee p. 543) received 20,000l. as a compenſation.

of

of Effingham, for her life, remainder to her fon fir George Yonge, of Efcot, co. Devon, bart. and his heirs for ever. They in the year 1770 joined in the fale of the undivided moiety of the Sidney eftate above-mentioned to Mrs. Elizabeth Perry, of Penfhurft-place; and in the fale of the divided moiety as above-mentioned (except the advowfons of Lyghe and Cowden) to Richard Allnutt, efq. wine-merchant of London; who on part of it, called South-park, in the parifh of Penfhurft, built himfelf a feat for his refidence[1], whofe fon continues the prefent poffeffor of thefe eftates.—At Penfhurft is ftill one of the few remaining *heronries* in England[2]. Vertue's bird's-eye view of Penfhurft Place, in Hafted's Kent[3], is very curious. Dr. Ducarel had a lift of the pictures in this fine old manfion, which is now in Mr. Gough's poffeffion.

William Perry, of Turville-park, co. Bucks, efq. who married Elizabeth the other daughter and coheir of colonel Thomas Sidney, as above related, refided at Penfhurft-place, which he repaired and beautified, enriching it with a good collection of pictures, which he had purchafed in his travels through Italy. On March 4, 1752, he procured the king's fign manual, that the iffue of himfelf and Elizabeth his wife, granddaughter and heir of Robert late earl of Leicefter, deceafed, might ufe and enjoy the name of *Sidney* only, and bear and ufe the coat armour of the faid late earl. He died in 1757, having had iffue, by Elizabeth his wife, two fons; William, who died an infant at Turville[4]; and Algernon-Perry Sidney, who died unmarried in September 1768, and five daughters; Mary, Jane, and Anne, who died unmarried; Elizabeth, the 2d daughter, married Bifhe Shelley, efq. whofe fon John took the name of *Sidney* in 1783, as heir and devifee to Mrs. Perry. This gentleman, who is now owner of and refident at Penfhurft, was for fome time in the 7th regiment of dragoons; and afterwards married a daughter of the late fir Henry Hunloke, bart. and fifter to the prefent fir Thomas-W. Hunloke, who counterclaimed the barony of Roos, againft lady Henry Fitzgerald, in right of the marriage of his anceftor fir Henry with Catharine only daughter and heirefs of Francis Tyrwhitt[5]. Frances, the 5th daughter, married Mr. Poictiers, fince deceafed, by whom fhe has iffue. Mr. Perry left Elizabeth his wife furviving, who poffeffed the other divided moiety of thefe eftates allotted to her in the divifion of them; and in 1770 purchafed of lady Yonge, and fir George Yonge her fon, the undivided moiety of the reft of them mentioned above, fo that fhe was the entire poffeffor of the manors of Penfhurft, &c.; and refided till her death, in 1783, at Penfhurft-place, a fine old manfion[6] ftanding at the South-weft corner of the park, which is ftill, though greatly

diminifhed, of no fmall extent. An advertifement has juft appeared, offering on leafe part of Penfhurft-park lands, to be divided into farms.

Thomas Coke, of Holkham, co. Norfolk, efq. was elected May 27, and inftalled June 17, 1725, a knight of the Bath; was created Baron Lovel, of Minfter Lovel, co. Oxford, May 28, 1728; was appointed Joint Poftmafter General[7] in June 1733, which office he retained till his death (April 20, 1759); and was created Vifcount Coke of Holkham, and Earl of Leicefter, May 9, 1744. He married, July 2, 1718, Lady Margaret Tufton (fourth daughter of Thomas fixth Earl of Thanet), to whom King George II. was pleafed to confirm the antient barony of De Clifford. Their iffue was only one fon, Edward Vifcount Coke, who married Mary youngeft daughter of John duke of Argyll, but died without iffue Aug. 31, 1753. (Lady Mary ftill furvives.) On the Earl's death, all his titles became extinct; and the reprefentation of his family (his two brothers and eldeft fifter having alfo died f. p.) devolved on Wenman Roberts, of Longford, co. Derby, efq. fon of his youngeft fifter Anne, by Philip Roberts, major in the 2d troop of Horfe Guards; which Wenman Roberts in 1773 affumed the name of Coke; and by his fecond wife Elizabeth Denton, of Hilfdon, Bucks, was father of Thomas-William Coke, of Holkham, efq. now member for the county of Norfolk; who, by a fifter of Lord Sherborne, has three daughters; the eldeft married the late vifcount Andover; and, fecondly, captain Digby of the Navy.

In 1781, the title of earl of Leicefter, and the family eftates, were claimed by Mr. *John Sidney*, as fon of Joceline the laft earl[8]; and a Trial at Bar was had, Feb. 11, 1782, on a writ of right, and proceedings before the grand affize, in the Court of Common Pleas at Weftminfter, between " John Sidney earl of Leicefter, vifcount Lifle, and baron Sidney of Penfhurft in Kent, demandant, and Elizabeth Perry, widow, tenant," on Monday the 11th day of February, 1782, for Penfhurft place, park, and premifes, in the county of Kent; before lord chief juftice Loughborough, Mr. juftice Gould, Mr. juftice Nares, and Mr. juftice Heath[9].

The barony of L'Ifle was unfuccefsfully claimed by Mrs. Perry in June 1782.

The title of " Earl of the County of Leicefter" was conferred by patent, May 18, 1784, on George Townshend, Baron de Ferrars of Chartley, Baron Bourchier, Louvaine, Baffet, and Compton, the prefent Earl, who is lineally defcended both from the Saxon and Norman earls of Leicefter, and alfo from the Sidneys late earls. His Lordfhip is alfo Prefident of the Society of Antiquaries; and, Sept. 14, 1807, fucceeded his father in the title of Marquis Townfhend.

---

[1] Of which a view is given in Hafted's Kent, vol. I. p. 409.   [2] See Charlotte Smith's fine Sonnet on Penfhurft.

[3] Vol. I. pp. 408—417; whence much of this account of the Sidneys is extracted. This Place, which had been engraved in 1747, and had long been fuppofed to be loft, was luckily recollected by Dr. Ducarel to have been depofited in a particular cabinet at Penfhurft, to which he referred; and where it was found by Mrs. Perry, who prefented it to Mr Hafted.

[4] On a noble mural monument in Turville church: " In this vault are depofited, 1740, William Sidney, fon and heir to William Perry, efq. and Elizabeth his wife, grand-daughter, and coheir with her only fifter Mary, to fir Robert Sidney, knt. fummoned to Parliament i William and Mary, who was afterwards earl of Leicefter by defcent; and alfo coheir to Ambrofe and Robert the late famous earls of Warwick and Leicefter, both fons of John Sutton de Dudley late duke of Northumberland." Langley's Defborough, p. 393.   [5] See the Pedigree of Manners, under Belvoir, vol. II. p. 68.

[6] See fome account of it in King on Antient Caftles; and the lines regarding it in *The Wizard*, vol. II. of Cenfuria Literari a

[7] See in Gent. Mag. vol. XXIII. pp. 493. 537. an account of two threatening letters fent to him.   [8] Ibid. vol. LI. p. 45.

[9] By this Trial, which, " with the Speeches and Arguments of the Counfel and Judges," was publifhed in 1782, it appears that earl Joceline and his countefs, about the year 1722 or 1723, were feparated, and fo continued till his death in 1737. He was only tenant for life. The demand fuppofes him tenant in fee: and, as if feifed in fee, he made a will (which was produced on the Trial) in 1743, devifing the eftate to a natural daughter, Anne Sidney (afterwards Mrs. Streatfield, of Chidingftone, Kent), in fee. Mrs. Perry was his furviving niece, to whom and her fifter [the late lady Sherrard] his eftates defcended, and with them he joined in a deed to raife money in 1742, declaring that at that time he had no male iffue. He died in 1743. The demandant ftates, that he was born in 1738. Yet, allowing his legitimacy, which was not contefted, the tenant has the greater right, claiming as heir-general of the firft fettler (Robert earl of Leicefter) in 1700, which was incontrovertibly proved. And on the equitable maxim, *In æquali jure melior eft conditio poffidentis*; and earl Jocelyn having devifed away his eftate by a will, duly executed; the grand affize had no difficulty in finding their verdict (as the Court directed) for the tenant, agreeing that " Elizabeth Perry has the beft right to hold the premifes and appurtenances mentioned to her and her heirs." Thus Mr. Sidney, though he loft the eftate, gained a nominal peerage; the fhadow, but not the fubftance.—The cafe, as to the legal privilege of legitimacy, appears to have been exactly fimilar in point of law to that of the earls of Banbury. But the fate of Mr. Sidney was peculiarly hard. He was the reputed fon of a farmer; but was undoubtedly fon of the countefs of Leicefter, and confequently, *in foro juris*, of the earl, being born not only in wedlock, but when (though they had been many years feparated) there was no divorce between the parties; which on the Trial feems to have been admitted on both fides. It is not at all wonderful that the earl of Leicefter fhould have paffed him by unnoticed; but, ftrange to fay, he was equally neglected by his mother, who died when he was young. He was brought up in the neighbourhood of Penfhurft; articled to an obfcure attorney; practifed fome time in that profeffion; and was not long fince living in Weft Kent.

PEDIGREE of DUDLEY, and of SIDNEY, EARLS of LEICESTER.

Elizabeth, daughter and heir of—Richard Beauchamp, earl of War-=Ifabella, daughter and heir of
Thomas lord Berkeley ; firft wife. | wick and Albemarle, died 1452.   Thomas de Defpenfer.

Maud, daughter of =John Talbot, earl of Shrewfbury,=1. Margaret ; | 2. Eleanor, married to Thomas lord Ros.
fir Thomas Ne- | flain in France, July 7, 1453, | fecond wife. | 3. Elizabeth, married to George Nevil, lord
vill ; firft wife. | æt. 85. | Latimer.

John Talbot, earl of   John Talbot, created baron and vifcount L'Ifle ;=Joan, daughter and heir
Snrewfbury, died 1466.   flain, with his father, 1453. | of Thomas Chedder.

Thomas Talbot, vifcount L'Ifle, married Margaret   Elizabeth Tal-=Sir Edward Grey, knt. fecond fon of Edward lord
daughter of William earl of Pembroke ; but was   bot, heir to | Ferrers of Groby ; created baron L'Ifle 1476 ;
killed at Wotton under Edge 1471, f. p.   her brother. | and vifcount 1483 ; died 1500.

John Grey,=Muriel, dau. of   Elizabeth Grey,=Edmund Dudley, fon of John (fecond fon of John lord Dudley¹, of
vifc. L'Ifle,   Thomas duke   heir to her | Dudley caftle, co. Stafford, K. G. privy counfellor to Henry VII.) by
d. 1504, f. p.   of Norfolk.   brother. | Elizabeth daughter and coheir of John Bramfhott, efq. of Hampfhire.

1. John Dudley, created earl of Warwick, and=Jane, daughter and heir of   Several other
duke of Northumberland 1551; beheaded 1553. | fir Edward Guilford, knt.   children.

1. Henry Dudley, who died	Anne,=Douglas=5. Robert=Lettice,	6. Guilford	1. Ma-=Sir Henry	2. Catharine, m.
at the fiege of Bologne.	d. of fir Howard, Dudley, dau. of	Dudley,	ry, Sidney,	to Henry earl
2. John Dudley, who had	John dau. of created fir	beheaded	K. G. died	of Hunting-
the title of earl of Warwick	Rob- William earl of Francis	with his	(fon of fir 1586.	don ; fee vol.
in his father's life-time.	fart, lord Leicefter Knolles³,	1586.	William	III. p. 608.
3. Ambrofe Dudley, re-	knt. ; Howard 1565: di. married	wife Jane	Sidney⁴, . 3 Margaret.
ftored to the title of earl of	d. f. p. of Ef- in 1588 ; 1578 ;	Grey, 1553.	knight 4. Temperance.
Warwick 1562 ; married,	1560, fingham ; and was	7. Henry Dud-	banneret) 5. Another Ca-
1. Anne, daughter and	at Cum- 2d wife . buried at	ley, flain at	lord pre- tharine.
coheirefs of Wm. Whor-	ner, War-	St. Quin-	fident of
wood ; 2. Elizabeth, dau.	Berks¹, wick.	tin, 1557.	Wales.
of fir Gilbert, and fifter and	1ft w.	8. Charles Dud-	
heir of George lord Tailbois;		ley, died young.	
3. Anne, daughter of Francis	Alice Leigh, created=Robert Dudley, born=Elizabeth Southwell, Robert Dud-
earl of Bedford ; died in	duchefs Dudley for	1674, declared illegi- fecond wife, in the ley, bu. at War-
1589, without iffue ; and	life in 1645 ; died	timate, died 1649⁵. life-time of the firft. wick 1584.
was buried at Warwick.	in 1673, æt. 90;	
4. . . . Dudley, died young.	firft wife.	Catharine, d. after 1673. = Sir Richard Levefon. Charles Dudley.

1. Sir Phi-=Frances, d. and	Barbara, dau.=2. Sir Robert Sidney, kt. created lord Sid-=1626, Sa-	3. Sir	1. Margaret,
lip Sidney,	heir to fir Fra. and heirefs of	ney of Penfhurft in Kent, by patent dated rah, wid°	Thomas died an in-
d. Oct. 16,	Walfingham ; John Gam-	May 13, 1603; vifcount L'Ifle, by patent, of fir T.	Sidney. fant April
1586, aged	re-mar. Robert mage, of Gla-	dated May 4, 1605 ; and earl of Leicef- Smith, of	10, 1558.
33.	earl of Effex. morganfhire,	ter, by patent, dated Aug. 2, 1618 ; to Bilborough,	2. Mary, m.
	efq ; d. 1621 ;	hold to the faid Robert, and his heirs- da. and heir	Henry earl
Elizabeth, d. and heir, m. to	firft wife.	male for ever; he was alfo K. G. ; of W. Blount;	of Pembroke;
Roger earl of Rutland⁶; d. f. p.		died July 13, 1626. 2d wife.	died 1621.

1. Sir William Sid-	3. Sir Robert Sid-=1618, Dorothy,	1. Mary⁷, m. to fir Robert Wroth,	5. Bridget, d. 1579.
ney, died unma. ;	ney, K. B. fe- d. of Henry Per-	of Durance, Middlefex.	6. Alice, died 1579.
bur. at St. Paul's.	cond earl ; died cy, earl of North-	2. Catharine, m. fir Lewis Manfel⁸.	7. Barbara, married to
2. Henry Sidney,	Nov. 2, 1677, umberland, died	3. Elizabeth, died unmarried 1605.	Thos. Smith¹⁰, efq.
died an infant.	æt. 82. Aug. 19, 1659.	4. Philippa, m. to fir John Hobart⁹.	8. Vere, d. young 1606.

Philip Sidney,=1645, Catharine,	2. Algernon Sidney, beheaded	1. Dorothy, married to Henry earl of	2. Lucie,=Sir John Pelham, bart.¹²
third earl ;	dau. of William	Dec. 7, 1683.	Sunderland¹¹.	
died March 6,	Cecil, earl of Sa-	3. Robert Sidney, died unmar-	3. Anne, married to Rev. Jofeph Cart, M. A.	Thomas lord=Elizabeth
1697-8, aged	lifbury; fhe died	ried 1668.	4. Mary, died young, 1648.	Pelham.	Jones.
upwards of 80.	Aug. 18, 1652,	4. Henry, created baron of Mil-	5. Diana, died 1670.	
	aged 24.	ton and vifc. Sidney 1689 ;	6. Ifabella, m. Philip vifc. Strangford, of Ireland¹³.	Elizabeth,=Charles vifc.
		earl of Romney 1694 ; died	7. Frances, 1651.	died 1711.	Townfhend,
		April 8, 1704, unm. æt. 63.	8. Elizabeth, died 1650.		died 1738.

Robert Sidney, called to the houfe of peers as baron=Elizabeth, dau. of John	1. Dorothy, married 2. Elizabeth,	Charles vifc.=Audrey
L'Ifle 1689 ; fucceeded as fourth earl in 1697-8 ;	Egerton, earl of Bridge-	to Thomas Cheke, died young.	Townfhend,	Harri-
died Nov. 10, 1702, æt. 53.	water, died 1709, æt. 63.	efq. of Pirgo.	died 1764.	fon.

1. Robert	2. Philip=Anne, d. &	4. John	6. Colonel=Mary,	7. Jofceline=Eliz. dau.	1.	6. Eliz. m. fir Har-	George vifc.=
Sidney,	Sidney, coheir of fir	Sidney,	Thomas d. and	Sidney, 7th & heir of	2. Dorothy,	court Mafters, kt.	Townfhend,
3. William	5th earl, R. Reeves, 6th earl,	di. July	Sidney¹⁴, finally	earl, m. in . . . Tho-	3. Henrietta,	alderman of Lon-	created mar-
Sidney,	di. July of Thwaites, died	24, 1705.	died Jan. heir of	1716; fepa- mas, of	4. Elizabeth,	don, d. f. p. Mar.	quis Townf-
5. Charles	24, 1705. co. Suffolk; fingle		27, fir Ro-	rated Glamor-	5.	13, 1727-8.	hend ; died
Sidney,	re-m. to J. 1737,		1728-9, bert	1722-3 ; ganfhire,	all died	7. Catharine, ma.	1807.
and	Shepherd, of aged		aged 49. Reeves.	d. July 6, died	young.	Wm. Baber, of
8. Henry	Campfey Afh, 57.			1743. about		the Inner Tem-	George,
Sidney,	Suffolk, efq.			1751.		ple, efq. and died	created earl
all d. young.	d. May 3, 1726.					1722.	of Leicefter
							1784, now
One fon, and one	1. Mary, =Sir Brownlow	2. Elizabeth,=William Perry, efq. of Turville	John Sidney (born	marquis
daughter, both	died June Sherrard, of Lop-	died at her	Park, Bucks, obtained the king's	in 1738, claimed	Townfhend.
died infants.	3, 1757, thorpe. c. Linc.	houfe in	licence, March 4, 1752, to ufe	the Penfhurft	
	f. p. bart. died f. p.	Berkeley-	the name and arms of Sidney ;	eftate¹⁵.	George, by courtefy
	Nov. 1748.	fqu. 1783.	died in 1757.		earl of Leicefter
					(fee p. 545).

1. William-	2. Algernon-Perry Sidney,	1. Mary, 3. Jane, 4. Anne,	2. Eliza-=Bifhe Shel-	5. Frances, married
Sidney Perry,	efq. died at Penfhurft-	all died unmarried.	beth.	ley, efq.	. . . . Poictiers, and
died an infant.	place in Sept. 1768.				left iffue.

John Shelley, efq. took the name of *Sidney* 1783, as heir and devifee to Mrs. Perry.

¹ This defcent is difputed. See Biographia Britannica, and Dugdale's Warwickfhire. Dugdale feems to have changed his mind in favour of the
defcent between the time of his Warwickfhire and his Baronage.

[See p. 545 for the other Notes on this Pedigree.]

A GE-

A GENEALOGICAL TABLE of the Defcent of the Family of DE FERRARS.

From

The Saxon Earls of Leicester.

Algar, feventh earl of Leicefter, died 1059.

|

Lucia, only furviving fifter and heir to Morcar and Edwin, earls of Leicefter, m. Ranulph de Mefchines, earl of Chefter.

|

Ranulph, fecond earl of Chefter, died 1153.

|

Hugh, third earl of Chefter, died 1181.

|

Agnes, fifter and coheir to Ranulph, laft earl of Chefter, married William de Ferrars, earl of Ferrars and Derby.

|

The Norman Earls of Leicester.

Robert Bellomont, earl of Leicefter, died 1118.

|

Robert, fecond earl of Leicefter, died 1168.

|

Robert, third earl of Leicefter, baron of Groby and Hinckley, and lord fteward of England.

|

Margaret, fifter and coheir to Robert laft earl of Leicefter married Saier de Quincey, earl of Winchefter.

|

Roger Quincey, earl of Winchefter, died without male iffue.

|

William earl of Ferrars and Derby,═Margaret, eldeft daughter and coheir
Baron of Tutbury and Chartley. │ of Roger earl of Winchefter.

Robert earl of Ferrars and Derby, loft his eftate in the civil wars, temp. Henry III.; died 1278.

|

John, firft baron of Chartley.

|

Robert, fecond baron of Chartley.

|

John, third baron of Chartley.

|

Robert, fourth baron of Chartley.

|

Edmund, fifth baron of Chartley.

|

William, fixth baron of Chartley.

|

Anne, fole daughter and heir, married Walter Devereux, baron of Chartley, in right of his wife.

|

John Devereux, baron of Chartley.

|

Walter, created vifcount Hereford.

|

Sir Richard Devereux, died in his father's life-time.

|

Walter, created earl of Effex.

|

Robert, fecond earl of Effex.

|

Dorothy, fifter and coheir to Robert, third earl of Effex, married fir Henry Shirley.

|

Sir Robert Shirley, bart.

|

Robert baron of Chartley, created earl Ferrers.

|

William de Ferrars, fecond fon, firft baron of Groby.

|

William, fecond baron of Groby.

|

Henry, third baron of Groby

|

William, fourth baron of Groby.

|

Henry, fifth baron of Groby.

|

William, fixth baron of Groby.

|

Thomas, fecond fon and heir male, lord of Tamworth.

|

Sir Thomas Ferrars, knight.

|

Sir John Ferrars, knight.

|

Sir John Ferrars, knight.

|

Sir Humphry Ferrars, knight

|

Sir John Ferrars, knight.

|

Sir Humphry Ferrars, knight.

|

Sir John Ferrars, knight.

|

Sir Humphry Ferrars; knight.

|

John Ferrars, of Tamworth, efq.

|

Sir Humphry Ferrars, knt. died in his father's life-time.

Robert Shirley, eldeft fon, died in his father's life-time.═Anne Ferrars, heir to her grandfather.

Elizabeth Shirley, baronefs de Ferrars, &c. married James Compton, earl of Northampton.

|

Charlotte Compton, baronefs de Ferrars, &c. married George Townfhend (the late marquis Townfhend.)

|

George Townfhend, baron de Ferrars, &c. created earl of Leicefter 24 Geo. III. 18 May, 1784; and now, 1807, marquis Townfhend.

|

George Ferrars, eldeft fon, by courtefy earl of Leicefter, born Dec. 13, 1778; married, May 1807, mifs D. Gardner, an heirefs.

*** Notes on the Sidney Pedigree, *continued from p. 544.*

[2] Dugdale (Bar. II. 222.) mentions the death of the firft of thefe ladies (which happened before her hufband was ennobled) at one Mr. Fofter's houfe at Cumner near Oxford, by a fall down ftairs, *as 'twas faid.* But the character of Mr. Fofter ftands not clear of the imputation of having been acceffary to her murder. A chamber is fhewn in the ruined manfion, which adjoins the church-yard at Cumner, called the Dudley chamber, where this lady was faid to have been murdered, and afterwards thrown down ftairs to make it appear that her death was accidental. She was buried at Cumner; but her body was afterwards removed to St. Mary's church in Oxford. Dr. Babington, lord Robert Dudley's chaplain, preaching her funeral fermon at the fecond interment, recommended to the memory of his audience the virtuous lady *fo piteoufly murdered.* See Afhmole's Berkfhire; Gervafe Holles's Memoirs of the Holles family; and Reflections on the Augmentation of the Englifh Peerage, p. 89.

[3] Widow of Walter Devereux, earl of Effex. She married, 3dly, 1589, fir Chriftopher Blount, kt.; and died Dec. 25, 1634.

[4] Of whom fee p. 540. He died May 5, 1586, aged 57. See Holland's Heroologia. Moft beautiful portraits of him and his wife are at Penfhurft. See an account of the Sidney family in the Kentifh Regifter, 1793, vol. I. pp. 143. 181.

[5] Called duke of Northumberland; and was probably legitimate. See p. 539.

[6] See vol. II. p. 67; and Memoirs of James's Peers.   [7] An authorefs. See Ballard, &c. Ben Jonfon's Epigrams, &c.

[8] Anceftor to the late lord Manfel.   [9] Anceftor to the earl of Bucks.

[10] Created vifcount Strangford.   [11] Re-married, 1652, to Robert Smythe, efq. of Bounds, Kent.

[12] Whence is defcended John-Thomas Townfhend, now vifcount Sydney, lord Sydney, and baron Sydney of Chifelhurft in Kent.; as well as the marquis Townfhend, who is Earl of Leicefter.

[13] Whence comes Percy Smythe, now vifcount Strangford; a young man of genius, and a poet.

[14] He had a natural fon, who bore the name of Sidney, and died near five years ago at his eftate at Bolington, Hants, f. p. m.

[15] See p. 543.

CHANCELLORS of the DUTCHY of LANCASTER, from the firſt Creation of the DUKEDOM [1].

Temp.

Edw. I. Ralph de Ergham, clerk, biſhop of Sarum.

Ric. II. Thomas de Thelwall, clerk.

Hen. IV. John Wateringe, clerk.
Thomas Harby, clerk.
John Springthorpe, clerk.
Sir William Burgoyne, Knt.

Hen. V. John Woodhouſe, Eſq.

Hen. VI. William Troutbecke, Eſq.
Walter Sherington, clerk.

Edw. IV. William Threſham.
Richard Fowler, Serviens & Conſiliarius Scaccarii.
John Gay, Eſq.
Thomas Thevington, Eſq. dileƈtus Serviens & Conſiliarius Scaccarii.

Ric. III. Thomas Metcalfe, dileƈtus Serviens & Conſiliarius.

Hen. VII. Sir Reginald Bray, Miles pro corpore.
Sir John Mordant, Knt.
Sir Richard Empſon, Knt.

Hen. VIII. Sir Henry Marney, Knt. Serviens & Conſiliarius.
Sir Richard Wingfield, Miles pro corpore.
Sir Thomas More, dileƈtus & fidelis Conſiliarius.
Sir William Fitzurban, Knt.
William Earl of Southampton, Treaſurer of the Houſhold.
Sir John Gage, Comptroller of the Houſhold.

Edw. VI. Sir William Paget, Knight of the Garter, afterwards Baron Beaudeſert; was buried in Lichfield cathedral, where his monument was deſtroyed in the civil wars. He was, as may be collected from his epitaph, Secretary and Privy Counſellor to Henry VIII. and conſtituted by his will Counſellor and Adjutant to Edward VI. during his minority; to whom he was alſo Comptroller of the Houſhold, and by him created Baron, and Knight of the Garter, and by Queen Mary lord privy ſeal.
Sir John Gage, Knight, Vice-chamberlain of the Houſhold, and Captain of the Guard.

1553 Sir Robert Rocheſter, Knt. Comptroller of the Houſhold, died 1557; and was ſucceeded by his nephew,

1557 Sir Edward de Waldegrave, Knt. Maſter of the Great Wardrobe. On the acceſſion of Queen Elizabeth, he was committed to the Tower, where he died Sept. 4, 1561.

1563 Sir Ambroſe Cave, Knt. 1563; died 1568 [2].

1568 Sir Ralph Sadleir, " eques notæ virtutis." In right of his ſituation as Chancellor of the Dutchy, Sir Ralph Sadleir, Nov. 11, 1584, claimed the privilege of nominating the two burgeſſes in parliament for the Town of Leiceſter; and was allowed to name one of them [3]. He died March 24, 1587, in his 80th year, after having been a privy counſellor 41 years; and poſſeſſed, at the time of his death, 22 manors, with ſeveral advowſons, and other large grants of land.

1588 Sir Francis Walſingham, Knt. died April 6, 1590; and was buried in St. Paul's cathedral [4].

1590 Sir Thomas Heneage, Knt. Vice-chamberlain of the Houſhold.

1597 Sir Robert Cecil, Knt. Chancellor of the Dutchy, and Keeper of the Privy Seal; reſigned 1599, on becoming Maſter of the Court of Wards. He was created Baron Cecil May 13, 1603; Viſcount Cranbourn, Auguſt 20, that year; Earl of Saliſbury, May 4, 1605; and died May 24, 1614.

1599 Sir John Forteſcue, Knt. He was alſo Maſter of the Wardrobe to Queen Elizabeth, and Chancellor of the Exchequer; but, on the acceſſion of King James, retained only the Chancellorſhip of the Dutchy. He died Dec. 23, 1607.

1607 Sir Thomas Parry, Knt. died 1616.

1616 John Dackombe, Eſq.; knighted 1616.
Sir Humphrey May, Knt. [5] occurs as Chancellor in 1625. He obtained in 1629 the reverſion of the office of Maſter of the Rolls; but died, before it became vacant, June 9, 1630.

1627 Sir Edward Barret; created Lord Newburgh 1627. Dying ſ. p. the title became extinƈt.

1647 William Lenthall, Speaker of the Houſe of Commons, was made Chancellor [6] of the Dutchy, then worth about 4000l. a-year.

1660 Francis [7] Lord Seymour (third ſon of Edward Lord Beauchamp, ſon and heir to Edward earl of Hertford). He had been advanced to the dignity of Baron Seymour of Troubridge, 19 Feb. 1640-1; was appointed Chancellor of the Dutchy June 1, 1660; and died July 12, 1664.

1672 Sir Robert Carr, Knt. and Bart. Feb. 14.

1680 Sir Thomas Ingram, Knt. Feb. 14.

1688 Robert Lord Willoughby of Ereſby.

1697 Thomas Earl of Stamford [8].

1702 Sir John Leveſon Gower, Bart. (afterward Lord Gower.)

1706 James Earl of Derby, June 10.

1710 William Lord Berkeley of Stratton.

1714 Heneage Earl of Aylesford, Oƈt. 12.

1716 Richard Earl of Scarborough, March 6. He reſigned May 8, 1717.

1717 Nicholas Lechmere, Eſq. (afterward Lord Lechmere) for life, June 12.

1727 John Duke of Rutland, July 17.

1736 George Earl of Cholmondeley, May.

1743 Richard Lord Edgecumbe, Dec. 22.

1758 Thomas Hay Viſcount Dupplin (afterward Earl of Kinnoul), Jan. 24.

1762 James Smith Lord Strange, Dec. 15.

1771 Thomas Lord Hyde (afterward Earl of Clarendon), June 14.

1782 John Lord Aſhburton, March 27.

1783 Edward Earl of Derby, Aug. 29.

—— Thomas Earl of Clarendon, Dec. 31.

1786 Charles Lord Hawkeſbury (now Earl of Liverpool), Sept. 9.

1803 Thomas Lord Pelham (now Earl of Chicheſter), Nov. 9.

1804 Henry Lord Mulgrave, Oƈt. 6.

1805 Robert Earl of Buckinghamſhire.

1805 Dudley Lord Harrowby, July 10.

1806 Edward Earl of Derby, Feb. 22.

1807 The Right Hon. Spencer Perceval appointed Chancellor of the Dutchy of Lancaſter March 30. He is alſo Chancellor of the Exchequer.

---

[1] There is a Court at Weſtminſter, called *The Dutchy Court of Lancaſter*, where all cauſes any way relating to the revenue of the Dutchy of Lancaſter are tried. Another branch of the ſame Court is eſtabliſhed at Preſton in Lancaſhire, called *The Court of the County Palatine of Lancaſter*, for the ſame purpoſes in that county as the other is in Weſtminſter. Theſe Courts were ereƈted by King Henry IV. after his having depoſed King Richard II.; when, poſſeſſing the Dutchy of Lancaſter in right of his mother, he imagined his claim to it better than that to the Throne, and therefore ſeparated it from the Crown, and ereƈted theſe Courts for its uſe. The Chief Judge of theſe Courts is the Chancellor, under whom are a ſet of inferior officers in each Court for the conduƈting of buſineſs.—See Prynne's 4th Inſtitute, for diſtinƈtion between *Dutchy* of Lancaſter and Crown.

[2] See an account of his family, vol. IV. p. 351; and his epitaph, p. 357.

[3] See before, p. 404. At this eleƈtion the members eleƈted promiſed to bear their own charges.

[4] " Triennium Cancellarius Ducatûs Lancaſtriæ." Popham, Elogia Sepulchralia, p. 311.

[5] See ſome account of him in vol. III. p. 169; and hereafter under Sutton Cheynell.

[6] Sir Thomas Bedingfield, knight, ſometime Attorney-general to the Dutchy of Lancaſter, and afterwards one of the Juſtices of the Court of Common Pleas (which offices he laid down after the murder of his Royal Maſter), died March 24, 1660, æt. 68; and Thomas Bedingfield, eſq. died Steward of the Dutchy in 1665.

[7] In a former page miſcalled *Charles*.

[8] Of whom ſee vol. III. p. 683.

DISSENTING PLACES OF WORSHIP.

The PRESBYTERIAN, or GREAT MEETING HOUSE, built in 1708 for the use of a congregation which was first established in 1680, is situated near the Butt Close, in St. Margaret's parish. It forms a square, nearly in the centre of the Meeting-house yard, built of brick, and is by far the largest, including every other denomination, in the Town. The congregation are genteel and numerous; several of the first families of the Town being Presbyterians. The seats are calculated for the accommodation of 800 persons. An organ was erected here in 1800, a valuable advantage to the choir, who form a musical society, cultivated with great care, and justly celebrated for its excellence. This place has a burial-ground.

With much pleasure I here repeat a tribute which in another place[1] has been paid to the memory of the Rev. Hugh Worthington, M. A. who died at the age of 86, Oct. 29, 1797, after having been 56 years the much-respected pastor of this Dissenting Congregation[2]. His literary abilities and benevolence of character were well known; and his loss sincerely lamented by his numerous congregation, who revered him as a minister, and loved him as their friend. A life prolonged beyond its utility was the greatest trial he feared; but this was graciously superseded. The Lord's day previous to his death he exerted himself in prayer; and, strenuous to his duty to the last, he spent the few remaining days in advising, admonishing, and exhorting those around him to be stedfast in duty; that, though he was leaving them, they would soon meet again, where friendship would reign in much higher perfection, and separation take place no more. He lay some hours without motion, and at last expired so easy, that his departure was scarcely perceptible to those around him. He might have done as Addison and Beattie did before him,—challenge the Infidel to come and see how a Christian could die. He printed a Sermon on the Fast, 1752; another on the Death of J. Dawson, 1757; and in 1785 an octavo volume of " Discourses on various Subjects, Evangelical and Practical;" composed with the best design; that of edifying his flock, and impressing their minds with a deep sense of the nature and obligations of Christian piety, and the moral duties of human life[3].

On a marble slab in the Meeting-house is the following epitaph:

" To the memory
of the Rev. Hugh Worthington,
who died Oct. 16, 1797, aged 86,
pastor of this church 56 years.

To the reverence due to superior talents unceasingly exerted to enlighten and improve mankind, he was peculiarly entitled. The affectionate warmth of his attachment as a *friend* will leave an indelible impression on the minds of his near connexions. The value of his public and private services, as a *Christian minister*, manifested by the rational fervour of his devotion, the uncommon energy of his addresses, and his assiduous attention to the other pastoral duties, can alone be properly estimated (as these will long be gratefully remembered) by this Congregation. To his exemplary conduct in all the intercourses of social life, the inhabitants of this Town and Society at large will bear respectful testimony.

May the eloquence of the Tomb still edify the survivors of him, whose living example, alas! can no longer stimulate to a virtuous emulation."

The Rev. Mr. Jacomb, who succeeded Mr. Worthington as minister here, has since resigned; and has been succeeded by the Rev. Charles Berry, the present minister.

Opposite the Great Meeting is a Meeting-house newly erected by a Society of INDEPENDENTS. A gallery is now erecting in this Meeting-house on both sides of it, which, with one at the end erected before, is supposed to make it capable of containing near 800

persons. The Rev. Thomas Cave, M. A. is the present minister.

In a lane not far from St. Nicholas' church, called Harvey-lane, is the Meeting-house of the PARTICULAR CALVINISTIC BAPTISTS, which is capable of containing 500 persons; with a large vestry. The Rev. Robert Hall[4], M. A. is the present minister.

The Meeting-house of the GENERAL BAPTISTS is situate in Friar-lane, and has a respectable appearance without; but it stands in a yard, screened by buildings. The present minister is Mr. John Deacon. On a tablet on the outside:

' This Edifice,
appropriated to the public worship of Almighty God,
and the Preaching of the Gospel of Christ,
was erected by the GENERAL BAPTISTS,
assisted by others of their Protestant Brethren,
MDCCLXXXV."

Each of these Baptist Meetings has a burial-ground.

In Archdeacon lane is a Meeting-house for another Society of General Baptists; Mr. Thomas Stevenson is the present minister.

In *Woman's-lane* (formerly called *St. Peter's-lane*) is another Meeting-house, erected in 1803 by a society calling themselves EPISCOPALIAN BAPTISTS[5]. This is called *Ebenezer Chapel.* Mr. Horne late minister.

The small CATHOLIC CHAPEL is built in a lane now called Causeway-lane, but formerly St. John's, leading to the Town-gaol, the site of St. John's chapel. It is secluded from observation, being situated behind the house of the officiating priest, and is a neat miniature representation of the peculiar decorations with which the members of that religion adorn the places where they offer up their public devotions. Their priest is the Rev. Mr. Chapel, a gentleman of education, and suavity of manners; but he makes no proselytes. It is believed that not a family or individual have been added to this small congregation in the space of fifty years. I rather think several have seceded in that space of time[6].

The QUAKERS MEETING-HOUSE, rather obscurely situated, near the North gate, is a small, but neat place of worship. The Quakers in Leicester and the neighbourhood are not numerous, though the founder of this sect, George Fox, began his career in this county. A burial-ground is attached to this place. I think the Quakers here retain more of the original simplicity of dress and manners than in any other place I have seen[7].

MILLSTONE-LANE MEETING-HOUSE, or that under the denomination of Mr. Wesley's connexion, was lately built; towards the expence of which the inhabitants of the town in general were solicited. This also is a square building; the front of brick, ornamented with stone. The building occupied before by these people stood on the same site, and was used originally by strolling players. This congregation is numerous. These being upon the itinerant plan, the minister is changed every year, or every two years at the farthest.

In Granby-street, near the London road, is a large chapel, called *Hephzibah Chapel*, belonging to the new Methodists, who are seceders from the connexion as established by the late Rev. John Wesley. These have no regular minister; but are frequently changing from one place to another.

In Free-school-lane is a small Meeting-house for the followers of the late Rev. Jeremiah Learnhoult Garrett; who has not yet a successor.

A Society of SANDEMONIANS is statedly held in a room in Town-hall-lane. No regular preacher.

A Society of HUNTINGTONIANS statedly hold a meeting in a large room in Bond-street. They have no preacher; but read Huntington's works.

A Society of SWEDENBORGIANS have a small meeting in Sanvey-gate.

[1] See Gent. Mag. vol. LXVII. p. 985.
[2] He had before been Pastor of the congregation at Newington Green; and Librarian in Redcross-street.
[3] Another Hugh Worthington, son of the preceding, is a celebrated Preacher at Salters' hall in London; and published " A Sermon, delivered on Wednesday the 6th of May, 1789, at the Meeting-house in the Old Jewry, London, to the Supporters of a new Academical Institution among Protestant Dissenters;" containing many pertinent and judicious observations; and a public retractation of an opinion which he once entertained, that it was unadvisable to educate Divinity and Lay Students together in one house.   [4] Of whom see under Arnsby, in vol. IV. pp. 12, 417.
[5] Walk through Leicester, p. 25.   [6] Throsby, p. 381.
[7] Many of the young females, followers of the Rev. Mr. Robinson, at St. Mary's church, are imitators of the dress, if not of the primitiveness and simplicity, of the Quakers. Throsby, p. 381.

PEDIGREE

PEDIGREE of BAGHOTT, of LEICESTER, 1619.

Arms: Ermine, on a bend three eagles difplayed . . . . . . ; in chief a martlet ; impaling, Vert, a chevron between three eagles difplayed Or, crowned . . . . . a buck's head cabofhed Sable. Creft, a buck's head cabofhed Sable, between the horns a greyhound currant Argent, collared Or.

Thomas Baghott, alias dominus Badger.══Alice . . . . .

William Baghott, of Hall-place in Prefbury, co. Gloucefter.══Alice, daughter of John Martine, of Chalkeley, co. Glouc.

1. William Baghott. 2. Richard══Mary, daughter of Richard Barrow. 3. George Baghott, of Prefbury.══Rofe, daughter of . . . Perfon, of London. 4. Giles Baghott. 5. Edward Baghott. 6. Charles Baghott. Eleanor, mar. Jo. Staines.

Anne. William Baghott.

1. Edmund══Katherine, daughter of fir Richard Hide[1], of Blagrave, co. Berks. knt. Baghott, of Prefbury. 2. Thomas Baghott, of the Court, knt. alias Badger, living fingle 1619. 3. William══Winifrid, daughter of . . . . Rayman. Baghott. 4. Charles Baghott, of the town of Leicefter, married Sufan, da. of . . . . Fineux, of Coventry, relict[2] of fir Thomas Cave, of Bagrave, kt. 1619. 5. Richard Baghott. 1. Elizabeth, married fir Richard White, of Hampfhire, knt. 2. Margaret, married Francis White, of Fyfield, Berks. 3. Anne. 4. Frances.

1. Francis Baghott. 2. Richard Baghott. 3. Thomas Baghott.

[1] Knighted at Royfton April 15, 1604.
[2] Q. if not *firft* the wife of Baghott ? or the widow of an *earlier* fir Thomas Cave ? See vol. III. p. 290.

PEDIGREE of PACE, of LEICESTER, 1619.

Hugh Houghton, of Houghton.══ . . . .

Alice, daughter and heir.══William Cobley.

Margaret, daughter and heir.══John Pace.

1. John Pace, of Leicefter, temp. Edw. IV.══Alice, daughter of Richard Read. 2. Thomas Pace.══Elizabeth, dau. of . . . . Southborne, of Hampfhire.

Alice Pace.

PEDIGREE of TURNER, of LEICESTER, 1619.

Richard Turner, of Sutton Colfield, co. Warwick, counfellor at law, of the Inner Temple.══Mary, daughter of . . . . Mafterfon, of Chefhire, and fifter and coheir of John Mafterfon.

William Turner, of Sutton Colfield.══Margaret, daughter of Chriftopher Bretton.

Joyce.══Edward Hume, of Marfton Truffel, co. Northampton. 1. Edward Turner, of Leicefter.══Joyce, daughter of Lerbeus Chamberlayne, of Leicefter. 2. Richard Turner. 3. John Turner.══ . . .

1. William Turner, aged 8, 1619. 2. Edward Turner, aged 2. 1. Elizabeth. 2. Frances. 1. John Turner.══ . . . daughter of George Bathurft, of Kent ? 2. Richard Turner.

PEDIGREE of WINCOLL, of LEICESTER, 1619.

John Wincoll, of Waldingfield, co. Suffolk.══ . . . . daughter of . . . . Gidam, of Burt, co. Suffolk.

1. John Wincoll, marr. the da. of . . . Groome, of Pattelfden, Suffolk; died f. p. 2. Roger Wincoll, of Waldingfield. 3. William Wincoll, of══Anne, da. of Jo. Gordon, of Waldingfield. Langham, co. Suffolk.══ . . . . . dau. of Robert Vaghen; d. f. p. 1 . . . m. to . . . Cage, of Beere, in Suffolk. 2. Alice.══ . . . . . . Spencer.

1. Anne, daughter and coheir, married to fir Leonard Hollyday, lord mayor of London in 1605; after to fir Henry Mountagu, lord chief juftice of England 1616; lord high treasurer 1620; created baron Kimbolton and vifcount Mandeville the fame year; duke of Manchefter 1625; died in November 1642. 2. Margaret, da. and coheir, mar. John Spencer, of Barford, c. Suff. Sir John Spencer, alderman of London; lord mayor in 1594.

1. Roger══ . . . da. of . . . Bantock, of Hicham, Suffolk. Wincoll. 2. John Wincoll. 5. William Wincoll. 6. Richard Wincoll. 3. Robert══Anne, dau. of Wincoll, ... of Caxton, co. Cambr. Wincoll, of London. 4. Thomas══Sufan, d. of . . . Madocke, of Ipfwich. Wincoll, 7. John Wincoll, of Leicefter, counfellor, of the Middle Temple, London.══Anne, da. of John Dover, of Gloucefter. Mary, married to Thomas Hudfon, of London.

Elizabeth. John Wincoll, of Waldingfield, 1619.══ . . . . daughter of . . . Chaplyn, of Lindfey, Suffolk. Mary Wincoll. Thomas Wincoll, 1619. Roger Wincoll, æt. 15, 1619.

PLATES in Addition to the TOWN of LEICESTER.

For the Lift of Plates in GUTHLAXTON HUNDRED, fee p. 424.

DIRECTIONS TO THE BINDER.

Title and Dedication ; B to 4 E ; Pedigree of FIELDING ; 4 F to 5 P ; LEICESTER TOWN, 4 Z to 7 B.

NICHOLS and SON, Printers, Red Lion Paffage, Fleet Street.

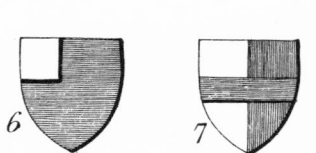

6   7   8

Fig. 4.

Fig. 5. p. 553.

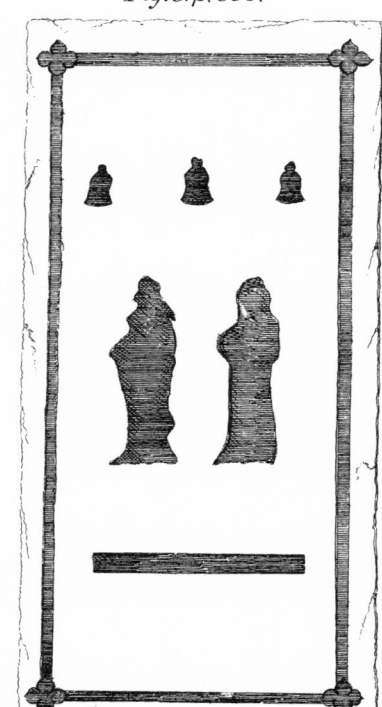

Fig. 10. p. 557.

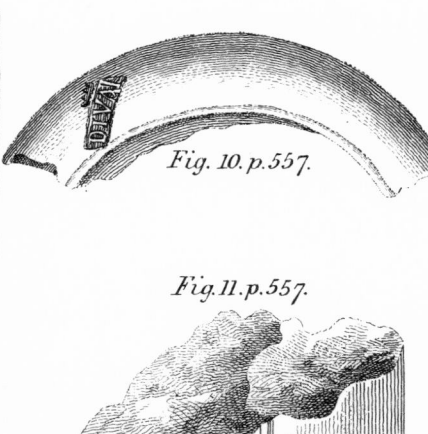

Fig. 11. p. 557.

Fig. 9.   p. 557.

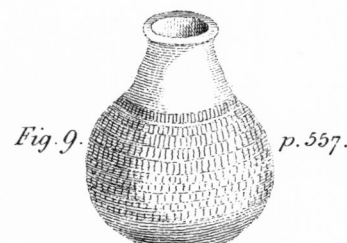

Longmate sc.

Fig. 12, *North Bridge or S.t Sunday's Bridge,* erected in 1796. p. 557.

PAROCHIAL HISTORY OF LEICESTER *continued.*

ALL SAINTS

includes the antient parish of St. Michael, and the greater part, if not the whole, of St. Clement; to which, in 1584, St. Peter's was also added.

The united parishes contain within their limits the County and Town Gaols, as delineated in a former part of this volume, Plate XXVIII. p. 326; and described in pp. 529—532. They are both situated in High Cross street.

Of St. *Michael's* and St. *Peter's* churches before the union, some account has been given in p. 327; of St. *Clement's,* p. 328.

A lease occurs from *John-Harlexton* of Leicester, to *John Seyton* and another, of a messuage in *Le Skeyth,* alias *Senvey gate,* in the parish of All Saints, Leicester; dated Friday in Pentecost week, 5 Edw. IV.

Georgius Belgrave, de Belgrave, in com' Leic', armiger, et Maria uxor mea, pro 8*l.* dedimus, Roberto Newcom de Leic', bell-founder, totum messuagium nostrum in parochiâ Omnium Sanctorum in Leic', situatum inter tenementum prefati Roberti Newcom ex parte Australi, et tenementum Thome Brygas ex parte Boreali; et abuttat versus ecclesiam Omnium Sanctorum ex parte Orientali, et ve-

The **CHURCH** (see before, Plate XXIV. p. 303.) projecting on the West and into High Cross street, consists of a low embattled tower (in which are five bells), a good chancel, nave, and two ailes; and, though not large, is convenient and handsome; and is well-paved.

The pillars and arches which support the roof of the nave are plain, and rather low.

On the North side of All Saints church, in the third window from the West, in the nave, which overlooks the leads, is the inscription,[2] represented in Plate XXXVIII. fig. 1. 2. 3.

No. 1. intersects the middle light.

The next or right-hand light in the said window has the couple of lines in No. 2. near each other, and parallel, included in an irregular sphere of glass, that just contains them.

No. 3. a single word, in the left-hand light of the first window from the chancel, in the same wall, and parallel with the other literary window.

A fire-place was formerly in the belfry, about three yards from the ground-floor. Its frame remains, opposite a door-passage; which, before it was blocked up, communicated with the stairs that lead to the steeple. The chamber-beams occupied holes in the walls, large and deep, which were filled up before the year 1790. The ground-floor[3] of the belfry was of equal extent with the room above, from 12 to 14 feet; from East to West, 24 feet.

The font is old and circular; see fig. 4.

Mr. Burton found these arms in the church of All Saints; Pl. XXIV. p. 303.

1. Gules, three lions passant guardant in pale Or. *England.*

2. Gules, three lions passant guardant in pale Or, a bend Azure. *De Monmouth.*

3. Gules, three lions passant guardant in pale Or, a label of France. *Edmund Crouchback* earl of *Lancaster.*

4. Gules, a cinquefoil Ermine. Earl and Abbey of *Leicester.*

nellam vocatam *Clement lane* ex parte Occidentali, &c. Dat' 1° Martii, 31 Hen. VIII.

In 1564, there were 66 families in All Saints, and 27 in St. Peter's.

	£.	s.	d.
Money raised for the poor, within the year ending at Easter 1776, —	594	15	8
Expended in county rates, &c. —	141	15	6
—————— on the poor, — —	457	2	2
Rent of workhouse[1] and habitations,	8	10	8
Expended in litigations, — —	15	16	2
Money raised for 1783, — —	550	11	5
—————————— 1784, — —	661	10	2
—————————— 1785, — —	528	12	10
Medium of these three years, —	580	4	10
————— of county expences, —	20	12	4
————— of expences not relating to the poor; repairs of the church, roads, &c.	0	0	0
————— of nett annual expences, —	559	12	6
————— of attending on magistrates,	0	0	0
————— of entertainments at meetings,	0	11	3
————— of law expences, — —	11	19	7
————— of setting the poor to work,	0	9	0

The Return made to Parliament in 1786, in answer to an enquiry respecting the charitable donations in this parish, may be seen in vol. I. p. 117.

5. Gules, a lion rampant queué fitché Argent. *Mountfort* earl of *Leicester.*

6. Gules, a fess between six cross crosslets Or. *Beauchamp.*

7. Gules, a lion rampant Argent. *Mowbray.*

8. Or, a maunch Gules. *Hastings* earl of *Huntingdon.*

9. Argent, a maunch Sable. *Hastings* earl of *Pembroke.*

10. Gules, seven mascles voided and conjoined Or. *Quincy.*

11. Azure, a bend between six mullets Argent. *Hoby.*

12. Azure, a pale between six mullets Argent. *Hoby.*

13. Azure, three water-bougets Argent, on a chief Gules, three annulets Or.

And these in St. Leonard's church:

14. Gules, a lion rampant Argent. *Mowbray.*

15. Gules, seven mascles voided and conjoined Or. *Quincy.*

16. Sable, three fishes naiant Argent. *Fisher.*

In the Matriculus of 1220, the churches of *All Saints,* St. *Clement,* St. *Michael,* and St. *Peter,* are all described to be under the patronage of the Abbot of *Leicester,* who held them *in proprios usus ab antiquo;* and of St. Clement, it is thus noticed, *vix sufficit ad sustentationem capellani*[4].

In the Roll of 1344, St. *Clement's* is wholly omitted; but the churches of *All Saints,* St. *Michael,* and St. *Peter,* are each charged 7s. 6¼d. for procurations; and the Abbot of *Leicester* had a pension of one shilling from each. St. Peter's paid 1s. 4d. for Peter-pence; the other churches nothing.

In 1534, the procurations and synodals for *All Saints* are 9s. 11d.; for St. *Peter's* no charge is entered.

In 1650, the vicarage was returned worth 50l. a-year; and the incumbent weak, and a Pluralitan.

In an original roll, dated July 4, 1664, signed *Matthew Hale,* and on the title " Exonerationes

---

[1] The workhouse at that time contained 55 persons.

[2] The first line (of which one word is reversed) is probably " Oluuer Bankar;" the second, which makes two on the glass, is " Rose Bynson," and " Luys Blakstyn" (a compound similar to *Bens-kin, Manakin, Wai-kin*); the third is clearly " niabs."

[3] Most probably, a vestry, poorly accommodated with one sorry window South-west, and *that* perhaps darkened with stained glass: it might be a dormitory, or recess suitable to early matins, or vespers. The vestry at present is a boarded inclosure, open at top, at the North corner of the church, by the belfry. W. B.

[4] See the Introductory Volume, p. lv.

Decimarum," I find this entry: "Vicar of All Saints, 8s. 4d."

In the king's books the vicarage of St. Peter's is stated to be worth, in all its tithes, with a manse, garden, and other annual profits, 2l. 8s.; and All Saints, in all its vicarial dues, both from great and small tithes, *una cum exit' mans'*, 4l. 8s. 5d.

The clear yearly value is stated to be 15l. 12s.

The archidiaconal procurations are, 8s. 6d.

At the West end, near the North door, is placed an old chest, with rings and hinges of uncommon strength, containing the churchwardens' accompts for a considerable number of years, and the originals of the following instruments relative to the union of the churches.

1. The institution of William Rudierd, clerk, to the vicarage of All Saints, on the presentation of the Queen, by John Whitgift, Archbishop of Canterbury, the see of Lincoln being then vacant, dated at Lambeth, 22 May, A. D. 1584, & nostre translationis anno 1°. (Johannes Incent, Registrarius, &c.)

" Johannes, providentiâ divinâ, Cantuariensis archiepiscopus, totius Anglie primas et metropolitanus, ad infrascripta auctoritate Parliamenti Anglie ultimè fulcitus. Dilecto nobis in Christo Willielmo Ruddierd, clerico, vicario ecclesie parochialis Sancti Petri infra villam Leicestrie, dioc' Lincoln', salutem et gratiam. Meritis tue probitatis inducimur ut te spiritualibus favoribus et gratiis prosequamur. Hinc est quod cum nobis pro parte tuâ fuerit jampridem expositum, quod vicaria ecclesie parochialis Sancti Petri predicti, quam in presenti obtines, fuerit et sit, in suis fructibus, oblationibus, et proventionibus, perquam exiles, ut puta ad summam duntaxat XLV solidorum; si vicaria ecclesie parochialis Omnium Sanctorum infra eandem villam ac ejusdem dioc' per te jam obtenta, que etiam eidem ecclesie Sancti Petri contermina et contigua infra unius milliaris spatium constituta est, cujus etiam fructus, oblationes, et proventiones, communi valuatione, summam quatuor librarum per annum non excedunt, uniretur, annecteretur, et incorporaretur, ex hoc commoditati tue plurimùm consuleretur; ac proinde nobis humiliter supplicâsti desiderio tuo in hâc parte clementer prospicere: Nos igitur, tam dictorum beneficiorum proximitatem et contiguitatem, quam fructuum et proventuum eorundem exilitatem et exiguitatem attendentes, tuis in hâc parte supplicationibus favorabiliter inclinati, dictam vicariam ecclesie parochialis Omnium Sanctorum, cum suis juribus et pertinentiis universis, eidem vicarie ecclesie parochialis Sancti Petri, durante tempore incumbentie tue in eâdem ecclesiâ, auctoritate quâ in hâc parte fulcimur, unimus, annectimus, et incorporamus; ita quod benè liceat tibi, prefato Willielmo Ruddierd, dictam vicariam ecclesie parochialis Sancti Petri, una cum dictâ vicariâ ecclesie parochialis Omnium Sanctorum, unius tantummodò beneficii nomine, insimul quoad vixeris retinere, illarumque redditus, fructus, et proventus, in tuos et ecclesiarum predictarum usus et utilitatem convertere, diocesani loci aut cujusvis alterius licentiâ super hoc minimè requisitâ; constitutionibus, ordinationibus, decretis, sive legibus, aut ceteris quibuscunque in contrarium editis, in aliquo non obstante. Proviso tamen quod dicta vicaria ecclesie parochialis Omnium Sanctorum debitis propterea non fraudetur obsequiis, et animarum cura in eâdem nullatenus negligatur, sed ejusdem congruè supportentur onera debita et consueta. Volumus autem ut he litere tibi non proficiantur, nisi per literas patentes Regie Majestatis debitè fuerint confirmate. Datum sub sigillo ad Facultates, 17° die mensis Maii, A. D. 1584, et nostre translationis anno primo."

To this is annexed a confirmation under the great seal, in the name of the Queen, in the same form of words as above used, dated at Westminster, 21° Maii, 26° regni. This serving for the union of the two parishes during the life of Mr. Rudyard only; in order to the perpetual union of them, the following petition was made:

" Villa Leicestr'. To all Christian people to whom this presente wrytinge shall come, the maior and burgesses of the town of Leicester, in the county of Leicester, and also William Rudyarde, clerk, vicare perpetual of the said parish of St. Peter's in the said town of Leicester, and of the parish of All Saints in the same town, send greeting in the Lord God everlasting. Whereas the parish church of the said parish of St. Peter's in Leicester aforesaid was many years past utterly decayed, the church and vicaridge house thereof taken down, and nothing thereof remaining, and while it was standing had but the portion of five pounds yerely to the utmost value belonging unto ytt, for the indifferent mayntenance of a mynyster to serve the cure there; and the said parish church of All Saints in the aforesaid town of Leicester, being next thereunto adjoyning, hath also very small mayntenance, being but of the yearly value of eight pounds at the most, the which church of All Saints ys a very fayr, convenyent, and large church, and much cost thereof of late bestowed, whereby yt ys able to receyve the inhabitants of both the said parishes, as ys manifest to the wholl town, where they often doe frequent themselves, to the heyringe of the preaching of God's most holye worde: In consideration whereof, we the said maior and burgesses of the said town of Leicester, and also I the said William Rudyarde, clerk, vycar perpetual of both the said parishes, have, and by these presents doo give our full, wholl, perfect, and absolute consents and assents, that the said two parishes may be unyted and annexed together into one only church and parish, by the name of 'The parish church of All Saints in Leicester,' according to the statute in that case made and provided. In wytnes whereof, wee the aforesaid maior and burgesses of the town of Leicester have hereunto set our common seal of the same town; and also I the said William Rudyarde, clerk, vycar of both the said parishes, have hereunto sette my seal and subscribed my name. Dated att the town of Leicester aforesaid, the 2d day of February, in the year of the raigne of our sovereign lady Elizabeth the two and thirtieth."

Under this is written:

"And I William [1], by God's permission, Bushop of Lincoln, in consideration of the smalnes of the lyvings of the vicarage of St. Peter's and All Saints in the town of Leicester, and other causes before mentioned, do think it meet and convenient that the said two parishes of St. Peter's and All Saints should be united into one only church and parish, by the name of the parish church of All Saints in Leicester; and in witnes whereof have hereunto set mie hand and seale, 18 Nov. A. D. 1590."

The Queen also signified her consent, by her letters patent following:

" Elizabetha, Dei gratiâ, Anglie, Francie, et Hibernie Regina, fidei defensor, &c. Omnibus ad quos presentes litere pervenerint salutem. Sciatis quod nos, de gratiâ nostrâ speciali, ac ex certâ scientiâ et mero motu nostris, necnon ad humilem petitionem dilectorum subditorum nostrorum, Willielmi Rudyarde, clerici, vicarii perpetui vicariarum ecclesiarum parochialium Sancti Petri et Omnium Sanctorum ville nostre Leicestr', majoris et comburgensium ville predicte, et parochianorum infra parochiam Sancti Petri predicti commorantium et degentium, unioni, incorporationi, et consolidationi vicariarum ecclesie parochialis Sancti Petri predicti, cum suis juribus et pertinentiis universis, nostri juris patronat' existen', vicarie perpetue ecclesie parochialis Omnium Sanctorum, et nostri similiter juris patronat', per reverendum in Christo patrem Lincolnie episcopum, ejus loci ordinarium, fiend', sponte et gratiosè, regalem nostrum consensum pariter et assensum damus et concedimus per presentes; eo quod expressa mencio de certitudine premissorum, sive eorum alicujus, aut de aliis donis sive concessionibus per nos, seu per aliquem progenitorum nostrorum, prefatis Willielmo Rudyarde,

[1] William Wickham, Bishop of Lincoln 1584; translated to Winchester 1595.

majori

majori et comburgensibus ville predicte, et parochianis infra parochiam Sancti Petri predicti commorantibus et degentibus, sive eorum alicui, ante hec tempora factis in presentibus minimè factis existit', aut aliquo statuto, actu, ordinatione, provisione, proclamatione, sive restrictione, in contrarium inde antehac hic fact', edit', ordinat', seu provision', aut aliquâ aliâ re, causâ, vel materiâ quâcunque in aliquo non obstante. In cujus rei testimonium, has literas nostras fieri fecimus patentes. Teste meipsa, apud Westm', 15° die Junii, anno regni nostri 36°.

Per literas de privato sigillo, &c. MARBURYE."

" Willielmus, permissione divinâ, Lincolnie episcopus, universis et singulis Christi fidelibus presentes literas nostras testimoniales visuris, lecturis, vel audituris, et quos infrascripta tangunt seu tangere poterint quomodolibet in futuro, salutem in Domino sempiternam, ac fidem indubiam presentibus adhiberi. Ad universitatis vestre notitiam deducimus, et deduci volumus per presentes, quod oblata nobis nuper, tam ex parte dilecti nobis in Christo Willielmi Rudiard, clerici, vicarii perpetui vicarie perpetue ecclesie parochialis Sancti Petri ville Leicestrie, et dioc' nostre Lincolnie, quam ex parte dilectorum nobis in Christo majoris et comburgensium ville Leicestrie, necnon parochianorum et inhabitantium parochie Omnium Sanctorum infra dictam Leicestrie villam et nostram Lincolnie dioces' etiam existen', peticio continebat, quod cum fructus, redditus, et proventus vicarie perpetue ecclesie paroch' Sancti Petri predicti adeo tenues et exiles sint et existunt, silicet, valorem annuum quadraginta quinque solidorum legalis monete Anglie non exceden', prout in libris primitiarum excellentissime principis domine nostre Regine existimantur et taxantur, ut ad congruam sustentationem vicarii ibidem pro tempore existen', et aliorum onerum eidem incumbent' supportationem minimè sufficiant, nec sufficere possint quomodolibet in futurum ; cumque dicta ecclesia Sancti Petri predicti diruta sit et destructa, ac in usus prophanos conversa, ut nullus jam locus ad divina officia celebrand' et sacramenta ministrand' sit relictus ; cumque insuper in parochiâ Sancti Petri predicti domicilia perpauca sint, et inhabitantes sive parochiani non multi, necnon vicaria perpetua et parochia Omnium Sanctorum ejusdem ville et dioces' adeo vicina et prorsus contigua, videlicet, non ultra unum miliar' Anglicanum ab invicem distant', ut inhabitantes parochie Sancti Petri predicti ad eandem ecclesiam Omnium Sanctorum, ad divina audiend' et sacramenta participand', non minus commodè et sine difficultate de tempore in tempus accidere possint, quam ad ecclesiam Sancti Petri predicti, si diruta et distructa non fuisset ; cumque preterea vicarie perpetue ecclesie parochialis Omnium Sanctorum predicte fructus, redditus, et proventus adeo tenues et exiles existunt, ut ad congruam sustentationem vicarii ibidem, et supportationem aliorum onerum eidem vicarie incumbentium non sufficiant, et ecclesia parochialis Omnium Sanctorum sit bene reparata, spaciosa, ac omnium parochianorum tam vicarie Sancti Petri quam etiam inhabitantium ejusdem parochie Omnium Sanctorum commodè capax existit ; quare nobis fuit humiliter supplicatum quatenus dictam vicariam perpetuam ecclesie parochialis Sancti Petri, cum suis juribus et pertinentiis universis, prefate vicarie perpetue ecclesie parochialis Omnium Sanctorum, ob causas predictas et alias nobis expositas, imperpetuum unire, annectere, incorporare, et consolidare, curamque et regimen animarum parochianorum dicte parochie Sancti Petri vicario perpetuo ecclesie parochialis Omnium Sanctorum predicte in Domino committere, ceteraque peragere et perimplere que in hâc parte necessaria fuerint, seu quomodolibet requisita vel opportuna, auctoritate nostrâ ordinariâ graciosè dignaremur : Nos igitur, tam ex facti notorietate, debitâque inquisitione in eâ parte habitâ et factâ, quam ex aliis nonnullis legitimis documentis coram nobis exhibitis, ac per nos previâ diligenti examinacione debitè consideratis, premissa nobis suggesta veritate fulciri intelligentes, causasque

unionis, annectionis, incorporationis, et consolidationis hujusmodi justas et rationi consonas fuisse et esse censentes, ideò supplicationibus predictis favorabiliter annuentes (vocatis primitùs coram nobis omnibus et singulis qui de jure in hâc parte fuerunt evocandi) eandem vicariam perpetuam ecclesie parochialis Sancti Petri, cum suis juribus et pertinentiis universis, memorate vicarie perpetue ecclesie parochialis Omnium Sanctorum, de et cum expresso consensu et assensu serenissime in Christo principis Domine nostre Domine Elizabethe, Dei gratiâ, Anglie, Francie, et Hibernie Regine, fidei defensoris, &c. vere et indubitate, tam pred' vicarie perpetue Sancti Petri ville Leic', quam vicarie Omnium Sanctorum ibidem patrone, ut per literas suas patentes magno Anglie sigillo munitas, &c. patentibusque annexis, pleniùs liquet ; necnon prefati Willielmi Rudyard, clerici, eorundem moderni incumbentis, ac omnium et singulorum interesse in hâc parte habentium, auctoritate nostrâ ordinariâ imperpetuum unimus, annectimus, incorporamus, et consolidamus, curam et regimen animarum parochianorum Sancti Petri predicti vicario Omnium Sanctorum predicto, ejusque successoribus in eâdem vicariâ pro tempore existentibus, adjecimus, dictamque vicariam perpetuam ecclesie parochialis Sancti Petri predicti et vicariam perpetuam ecclesie parochialis Omnium Sanctorum memorate unum beneficium efficimus, per nomen ' Vicarie perpetue Omnium Sanctorum una cum vicariâ perpetuâ Sancti Petri eidem annexâ,' ex nunc perpetuis futuris temporibus nuncupari, ac per unitam personam idoneam, per nos et successores nostros, vel loci ordinarium pro tempore existentem, de tempore et in tempus admittend' et instituend', possideri volumus et decernimus ; ita ut benè liceat et licebit prefato Willielmo Rudyard, clerico, vicario moderno ecclesie Omnium Sanctorum predicte, suisque successoribus, eandem vicariam Omnium Sanctorum una cum dictâ vicariâ Sancti Petri eidem annexâ, unius tantum beneficii nomine, perpetuis futuris temporibus ad omnes quoscunque juris effectus exinde sequi valen', habere, retinere, et possidere, fructusque, redditus, et proventus, decimas, oblationes, et alia quecunque jura et emolumenta, tam dicte vicarie perpetue Omnium Sanctorum quam memorate vicarie perpetue Sancti Petri (debitis congruis et consuetis earundem supportatis oneribus) habere, retinere, et percipere, ac in eorum proprios usus convertere et applicare, ordinationibus ecclesiasticis quibus nos derogare possumus non obstantibus quibuscunque ; reservatis tamen illustrissime domine nostre Regine predicte, heredibus et successoribus suis, primis fructubus, perpetuis decimis, utriusque vicarie memorat', aliisque omnibus et singulis oneribus consuetis ab eis seu earum alterâ exeuntibus et hactenus solvi consuetis, necnon nobis et successoribus nostris, meisque et suis ministris archidiaconi Leicestrie pro tempore existentis, procurationibus, synodalibus, aliisque juribus et emolumentis de jure vel consuetudine debitis seu debendis per incumbentem in ecclesiis sive vicariis annexis et consolidatis, seu earum alterâ, pro tempore existentibus, hactenus respectivè consuetis, in tam amplis modo et formâ ac si predicta unio, incorporatio, et consolidatio, omninò facta non fuisset ; omnibus juribus nostris episcopalibus, et ecclesie nostre cathedralis Beate Marie Lincolnie consuetudinibus, dignitate, et honore, in omnibus semper salvis. In quorum omnium et singulorum premissorum fidem et testimonium, nos prefati Willielmus permissione divinâ Lincolnie episcopus, et Willielmus Rudyard, vicarius prenominatus, sigilla nostra quibus in similibus utimur presentibus apposuimus. Datum apud Buckden, decimo septimo die mensis Junii, anno Domini millesimo quingentesimo nonagesimo quarto, regnique felicissime predicte domine nostre domine serenissime Elizabethe, Dei gratiâ, Anglie, Francie, et Hibernie Regine, fidei defensoris, &c. 36°, ac nostre consecrationis decimo."

In 1636, an exemplification of the foregoing instruments was obtained from the Bishop of Lincoln, in the following terms:

" Uni-

" Universis et singulis Christi fidelibus ad quos presentes litere nostre testimoniales pervenerint, seu quos infrascripta tangunt vel tangere poterint quomodolibet in futuro. Nos Johannes [1], providentiâ divinâ, Lincolnie episcopus, salutem in Domino sempiternam, ac fidem indubiam presentibus adhiberi. Sciatis quod, scrutato Registro nostro apud Lincolniam fideliter custodito, in libro institutionum tempore domini Willielmi Wickham, quondam episcopi Lincolnie, inter alia ibidem registrata compertum est prout sequitur ; viz.

" Junii 1594 decimo septimo, reverendus pater dominus episcopus predictus, vicarius Sancti Petri Leicestrie, vicarius Omnium Sanctorum ibidem, de et cum consensu serenissime principis domine nostre Elizabethe regine, &c. earundem patrone, Willielmi Rudyard, clerici, incumbentis moderni in eisdem, majoris et comburgensium ville Leicestrie, et parochianorum utriusque ecclesie etiam id petentium, &c. vinxit, annexit, et consolidavit, prout per litteras suas inde factas pleniùs liquet, sub verborum tenore sequentium :

" Willielmus, permissione divinâ," &c. (as in p. 550, to " decimo," above.)

" In quorum omnium et singulorum premissorum fidem, robur, et testimonium, has literas nostras testimoniales exinde fieri, ac sigillo vicarii nostri in spiritualibus generalis, quo in hâc parte utimur, communiri et corroborari fecimus. Datum Lincolnie, vicesimo septimo die Septembris, anno Domini millesimo sexcentesimo tricesimo sexto.

FRAN. CARRE, Notarius Publicus.
THO. HIRST, Surrogatus."

Yearly donations to the poor :

New Year's Day.

Sir William Curteen [2], and gentlemen of the lottery, in four-penny bread, ordered and paid for by the chamberlains of the borough, 9s. 4d.

The last Sunday in every other month, beginning January, Mr. Acham's, in four-penny bread, paid by the same, 5s. 6d.

Candlemas.

Mr. Robert Heyrick's, in four-penny bread, ordered and paid for by the mayor, of which 4s. goes to St. John's Hospital, 1l.

Every Friday in Lent.

Mr. William Ive's, in two-penny bread, to be fetched from St. Martin's church, and distributed to twelve poor persons, 2s.

March 21.

Mr. Joseph Wright's, of ten pairs of women's shoes, at 2s. 6d. a pair ; two pairs of which, to the widows of St. John's Hospital, paid by Mr. Daniel Woodland, out of a piece of ground called Colt-

man's, now or late in the possession of the said Mr. Woodland, to be disposed of by the overseers, 1l. 5s.

Thursday before Easter.

The Countess of Devonshire's, 7s.
Mr. John Norris's, 1l. 7s. 6d.
The two last received of the chamberlains.

The second division, or half, of the tablet :

Good Friday.

Out of ground, late Alderman Annis's, called Hickling's land, paid by Mr. Daniel Woodland, and distributed to the poor, 6s. 8d.

Thursday before Whitsunday.

Sir William Courteen's, in four-penny bread, as first mentioned, 9s. 4d.

St. Bartholomew.

Mr. William Norrice's, out of ground in Soarlane, in tenure of John Noon, viz. to the minister, churchwardens, clerk, and sexton, 4d. each, and the rest to forty poor people of this parish, 4d. each, 1l. 5s.

Christmas.

John Poultney's, esq. paid by the chamberlains of this borough, 1l. 12s. 6d. ; out of which, land-tax is deducted.

Mr. Robert Heyrick's, to poor widows, at the discretion of the mayor for the time being, 40s. for the whole town.

For repairs of the church, an annuity of 3s. 4d. issuing out of land in Northgate-street, paid by Mr. Brothers.

Mr. Simons's, of 6d. every other Sunday, delivered in penny bread.

Samuel Howe, } Churchwardens,
Thomas Walker, } Anno Domini 1785.

John Saunders, of All Saints parish, tanner, by will, dated . . . . gave two annuities to the parish of All Saints ; viz. one to be given in bread yearly, on Friday next before Easter, to the poor of the said parish, 6s. 8d. payable, by the heirs of the said John Saunders, out of a ground in the said parish ; the other, 3s. 4d. towards the repair of the parish church of All Saints, payable yearly out of a tenement in the said parish, in tenure of William Robinson, chandler, who married one of the heirs of the said John Saunders.

Extracts from the Register :

" William Graham and Catharine Macaulay, both of this parish, were married by licence in this church, 14 day of Nov. 1778, by T. Haines, in presence of Thomas Arnold [3] and Eliz. Arnold."

Thomas Newcomb [4], bell-founder, who cast the six great bells of St. Margaret's, was buried in this church, May 20, 1594.

VICARS.	PATRONS.
William the chaplain, 1221.	
Nicholas de Leycester, 1249.	} Abbot and convent of St. Mary de Pratis.
Henry de Kynston, 1278.	
Robert de Barnesby, 1286.	
Thomas Walsh, 1534 [5].	
William Rudierd, May 22, 1584.	
William Thomas [6], 1685.	
Philip Hacket died May 18, 1735, aged 52.	} The King.
John Makepeace, Aug. 1740 ; died Feb. 17, 1745-6.	
Thomas Haines [7], B.A. March 18, 1745-6 ; died 1786.	
Joseph Gregory [8], B.A. 1786 ; died Feb. 26, 1802.	
Edward-Thomas Vaughan, M.A. 1802.	

[1] John Williams, Bishop of Lincoln 1621 ; translated to York 1642.
[2] See Henry Stubbe's Justification of War against the Netherlands, p. 69. line 8.
[3] Dr. Thomas Arnold, a native and inhabitant of Leicester, was educated in Scotland, and his wife was sister to Mr. William Graham. Mrs. Macaulay (the celebrated Republican Historian) resided at the Doctor's, as his wife's visitor, in All Saints parish.
[4] March 20, 1520, Thomas Newcomb of Leicester, an earlier bell-founder, wills to be buried in All Saints church in Leicester, and gives legacies to Robert and Edward Newcomb his sons, and Jane his daughter ; proved Aug. 25, 1520. The vestiges of his tomb are still visible ; see p. 554. There was still an earlier bell-founder in the family ; see p. 549.
[5] John Ward was at that time vicar of St. Peter's.
[6] He was head-master of the free-school in this town 34 years ; died Dec. 6, 1713 ; and was buried in the chancel.
[7] Vicar also of St. Martin's.   [8] Vicar also of St. Martin's.

MONUMENTAL INSCRIPTIONS.

On tablets against the North wall of the chancel:
Arms: Sable, on a fess wavy, between three demi-lions rampant Or; a crescent for difference; Plate XXIV. fig. 17.
"This monument is erected to the memory of Matthew Simons, esq. sometime high sheriff of this county, who, for many years before his death, by his known integrity, humility, and charity, did acquire a just esteem and veneration. He gave many generous legacies; as also a sum of 98*l.* 18*s.* 10*d.* to charitable uses, yearly for ever; which said sum is yearly paid by his heir and executor John Simons, esq. to whom he gave the remainder of his estate: and from whom (though much artifice was used) nothing could withdraw his affections. He departed this life June the 19th, anno Domini 1714, ætat. 84."

Arms: Azure, à canton Argent; Pl. XXXVIII. fig. 6.
" Near this place lies interred
the body of Mr. John Clarke,
late a worthy citizen of London.
His estate (not inconsiderable),
acquired by great industry,
he bequeathed with equal piety to the Corporation,
for the relief of widows and
children of poor clergymen.
He departed this life Oct. 31,
in the year of our Lord 1732.
This monument was erected,
at the expence of the above-mentioned Corporation,
in grateful remembrance of so liberal a benefactor."

Against the South wall:
" In memory of Mrs. Elizabeth Watchorn,
who died the 18th day of December, 1800,
aged 62 years."

"In memory of John Mason, surgeon, of this Borough,
one of the three sons of William and Jane Mason,
both deceased.
He departed this life the 25th day of August, 1795,
in the 56th year of his age."

" In memory of John,
son of Thomas Watchorn and Ann his wife;
he died May 1, 1800, aged 25 years.
Also of Thomas Watchorn, gent.
who died July 27, 1806, aged 56 years."

" In memory of John Watchorn, gent.
who died Nov. 25, 1795, aged 74 years;
also of Ann his wife,
daughter of John and Ann Lambert,
who died March 21, 1770, aged 46 years."

" Near this place lies the mortal part of
William Dickins, gent.
He died Jan. 14, 1804, in the 75th year of his age.
Ann, the wife of the above William Dickins, gent.
died April 1, 1805, in the 74th year of her age."

On flat stones in the chancel:
" Under this stone
lyeth the body of John Norrice, gent.
the last male of the family of the Norrices.
He left behind him only one daughter;
and died, in the 59th year of his age, July the 29th,
anno Dom. 1700."

Arms: Ermine, a saltire . . . . .; a crescent for difference; Plate XXIV. fig. 18.
" Sub hoc saxo depositæ
sunt reliquiæ Gulielmi Thomas, A. M. scholæ publicæ hujus burgi per. xxxiv annos archididascali, huic parochiæ xxviii annos sedulò invigilavit. Maturus cœlo feliciter in Christo obdormivit Dec. 6, 1713.
Incorruptam cujus erga omnes

fidem nudamque veritatem,
egenis charitatem, Deo
pietatem, meritò mirentur
præsentes, imitentur posteri."

" Here lyes the body of the Rev. Mr. John Makepeace, vicar of this parish,
who departed this life Feb. 17, 1745-6,
in the 39th year of his age."

"Here lyeth interred the body of Mr. Philip Hackett,
who was rector of South Croxton,
in the county of Leicester,
confrater of Wigston's Hospital,
and vicar of this parish;
who departed this life the 18th day of May,
A. D. 1735, in the 72d year of his age.
Jane his wife was buried here
May 12, 1747, aged 76."

Elizabeth, wife of James Palmer, gent. Aug. 6, 1675, aged 30.
Lucy, daughter of John Minston, Jan. 13, 1752, aged 63.
Hannah, wife of Hugh Jordan, Aug. 16, 1727, aged 82.
Richard Jordan, Jan. 18, 1728, aged 42.
Mrs. Emma Hill, wife of Robert Hill, Sept. 14, 1726, aged 54.
William Armston, May 1, 1702, aged 64.
Anne Thorp, daughter of William and Mary Thorp, Nov. 13, 1773, aged 70.
Dorothy Twells, daughter of Robert Twells, Jan. 22, 1750, aged 35.
William Brown, May 1, 1783, aged 62. Also Jane Brown his wife, July 1, 1783, aged 75.

On a large wooden framed tablet, hung in the pew next the Mayor's, on the South:
Arms: Per pale, Argent and Gules, a fess Azure; Pl. XXXVIII. fig. 7.
" In this church-yard doth lye the corps
Of William Norrice dead and gone;
Whose grave from all the rest is knowne
By finding out *the greatest stone* [1]:
A homely tomb, yet grac'd with fame
Of worthy works which he hath done:
A monument which he did choose,
Before his houre-glass was runn.
Thrice fifteen groats he did bestow,
Which yearly ever shall renew,
And to be given to All Saints' poore,
On the feast-day of Barthol'mew:
O happy All Saints, that hath bredd
Such Saints on earth to feed thy poore;
Let Saints in Heaven and earth below
Give prayses to the Lord therefore.
Five marks he gave unto the schoole,
An annuall stipend for to bee;
And that it shall be yearly payd
To the second master of the three.
Twice was he grac'd with serving twice
The office of the maioraltye.
Three wives he had, and had his will
To be entomb'd amongst them three:
But Death, the end of flesh and blood,
Did wound to death the good old man.
Though ninety-six years liv'd on earth,
Yet was his life in length a spann.
He departed this life January the 8th, 1615."

In the nave, on flat stones:
The tomb of Thomas Newcomb, marked by the *bells*, still remains, robbed of its brasses, near the pulpit stairs; Plate XXXVIII. fig. 5.
Thomas Topott, March 23, 1698-9, aged 44.
John, son of Thomas Topott, Dec. 16, 1716, aged 29.
Thomas Leeson, Feb. 17, 1767, aged 63.
Charles Roberts, son of Samuel and Ann Roberts, Sept. 29, 1790, aged 10 months.

[1] A piece of rough forest granite, two feet by one foot and a half (perhaps not half a hundred weight), without inscription, now nearly level with the surface of the ground. It is about fourteen feet from the chancel's outward wall.

Sarah Lawrence, Sept. 1, 1739, aged 49.

Rose, wife of John Smith, Aug. 18, 1755, aged 78.

John Smith, March 17, 1768, aged 86.

Anne, the wife of John Watchorn junior, March 21, 1770, aged 47.

John Watchorn, 1795.

Mary, wife of John Watchorn, Nov. 12, 1738, aged 38.

John Watchorn, Aug. 1, 1742, aged 55.

In one of the West windows is a small modern painting, which represents Jesus Christ surrounded with a Glory, and pointing with his left hand to a label, on which is written, *See that ye love one another*. On a cloud which descends nearly to the bottom of the Glory are figures of Cherubim.

Below is a figure of the Virgin to the knees, with a Glory round the head ; then appears a drapery, and under it an Angel, blowing a trumpet.

Beneath is this inscription:

" Under this glass painting
lies interred the body of John Langton.
He died May 13, 1743, aged 13."

At the West end of the church, on mural stones:
" Near this place lieth interred the body of
John Brewin,
who departed this life Jan. 27, 1762,
in the 57th year of his age.
Near this place also lieth the body of Anne,
the wife of John Brewin,
who departed this life January the 2d, 1766,
in the 62d year of her age."

" Near this place is interred the body of
Mr. Simeon Brewin,
who died suddenly, at Press in Scotland,
June 3, 1782, in the 50th year of his age."

" Near this place is interred the body of Elizabeth,
the wife of Mr. Simeon Brewin,
who died Aug. 5, 1786, in the 51st year of her age."

" Near this place is interred the body of
Mary, the wife of Mr. Robert Brewin,
who died May 29, 1784, in the 42d year of her age."

" Near this place is interred the body of Elizabeth,
the wife of Mr. William Chamberlin,
and daughter of John and Anne Brewin,
who died June 28, 1791,
in the 57th year of her age."

" Near this place lie the remains of Edward Eagle,
late of the city of Coventry,
who died January the 10th, 1804,
in the 61st year of his age."

" Near this place lie the remains of William Ward,
who departed this life the 8th day of November, 1784,
aged 80 years.
Also of Mary, the wife of William Ward ;
she died Jan. 31, 1783, aged 75 years.
Likewise of John,
son of the above William and Mary Ward ;
he died August the 4th, 1773,
in the 33d year of his age "

" Near this place lie the remains of Deborah,
the wife of Edward Eagle, of the city of Coventry,
and daughter of
William and Mary Ward of this Borough ;
she departed this life the 19th day of September, 1783,
in the 36th year of her age.
She was——
What a wife should be."

" Williamson Platt, son of Joshua Platt,
Alice, the wife of Joshua Platt, supervisor of Excise,
was buried here May 13, 1735, aged 11 months.
with her three infant sons (viz.),

Williamson, William, and Joshua,
lie buried near this stone ;
she died Nov. 21, 1737, aged 38 years.
Her husband, children, and acquaintance,
mourn her absence."

"Here lieth interred the body of Elizabeth Hitchcock,
the wife of Benjamin Hitchcock ;
she deceased the 25th day of August, 1763,
aged 66 years.
Here lieth interred the body of Benjamin Hitchcock,
who died on the 19th day of June, 1782,
aged 84 years."

" Near this place lie the remains of Edward Webb,
who died June 9, 1799, aged 51 years."

On flat stones at the West end :

" Depositum Johannis Langton,
qui obiit 13 die Maii,
an. $\begin{cases} \text{Dom. 1743,} \\ \text{ætatis 13."} \end{cases}$

Sarah Ward, Aug. 2, 1772, aged 26.

In the North aile, on flat stones :
Rev. Robert Heaton, M. A. March 19, 1784, aged 29.

Samuel Pratt, Nov. 15, 1742, aged 10 months.

Robert Brown, June 27, 1744, aged 56.

John Hastings, April 16, 1746, aged 55.

In the South aile, on flat stones :
Jane, widow of Mr. William Mason, Oct. 27, 1770, aged 69. Also Elizabeth Mason, daughter of Mr. Henry Coulson, Jan. 11, 1772, aged 72.

Frances, relict of Joshua Bracebridge, Dec. 21, 1763, aged 62.

John Pratt, Sept. 29, 1719, aged 60.

Robert Warburton, Feb. 15, 1740, aged 78.

William Johnson, March 4, 1742, aged 32.

In this church was formerly a stone thus inscribed :
" Here lyeth interred the body of Joseph Wright,
a gardener; who changed this life for a better,
March 20, 1678-9.
My Mother Earth, though mystically curst,
Hath me, her son, most bountifully nurst ;
For all my pains, and seed on her I sow'd,
A blessed crop she has on me bestow'd ;
Out of which store that I of her received,
My painfull wantfull brethren I relieved.
And though this Mother I full well did love,
I better lov'd my Father that's above :
My Mother feeds my body for a space,
My soul for aye beholds my Father's face."

In the church-yard.

On the South-east side of an altar-tomb, near the South-east angle of the church:
" In memory of Gabriel Newton, gentleman,
one of the aldermen, and once mayor of the
Borough of Leicester, who died the 26th of October,
1762, aged 78 years [1]. By his first wife,
Elizabeth daughter of Mr. Alderman Wells,
he had several children, which all died in their
minority. By his second wife, Mary
daughter of George Bent, gentleman, he had
George Newton, who died the 8th of March, 1746,
in the 18th year of his age. By his last wife,
Eleanor daughter of John Bakewell, gent.
of Normington on the Heath, he had no issue."

On the North-west side of the same tomb :
" Mr. Alderman Newton, in his life-time, by
deeds of trust, charged several of his estates
with the payment of 26 pounds annually for
ever to the following towns, for cloathing and
educating poor children therein ; viz. to

---

[1] " Leicester, Oct. 28, 1762. Tuesday died Alderman Gabriel Newton, in the 79th year of his age. He was mayor of this Corporation in the year 1732. The greatest part of his fortune is left in trust to the Corporation, for educating children of poor housekeepers. In this town, 35 ; at Ashby de la Zouch, 25 ; at Earl Shilton, 20 ; at Northampton, St. Neots, Hertford, Huntingdon, Bedford, and Buckingham, each 25. It is computed that he has left, in lands and money for supporting this charity, to the value of 14,000l. and upwards ; most of which he settled in his life-time, in pursuance of the Mortmain act. And last night his corpse was interred in All Saints church-yard. The funeral was attended by eight Clergymen, the Mayor, Aldermen, Town-Clerk, and Chamberlains, in their formalities, &c. The great mace, covered with black crape, was carried before the Mayor ; the four Serjeants with their maces, and other Officers, following." London Evening Post, Nov. 4, 1762.

HERTFORD;

HERTFORD, BEDFORD [1], BUCKINGHAM, ST. NEOT'S, NORTHAMPTON, and ASHBY DE LA ZOUCH; and also 20 pounds 16 shillings yearly for ever to EARL SHILTON; and by his last will directed 3250 pounds to be raised out of his personal estate, for supporting a charity of the same kind in Leicester."

Near this monument are others for William and Anne Wells, and some of their children.

" Here lie the earthly remains of Mary Worrall, wife of John-Hunt Worrall, who resigned this transitory life, in hopes of eternal life, May 26, 1753, in the 29th year of his age."

" In memory of Dyer Simpson, late a Citizen of London, and eldest son of John and Elizabeth Simpson, late of this town. He departed this life Oct. 23, 1761, aged 24 years."

Arms: Per bend nebulé, Or and Sable, a lion rampant counterchanged. Crest, on a mural coronet Argent, a demi-lion guardant, per pale undée Or and Sable, holding in his paw a sword erect of the first, hilted of the second. Pl. XXXVIII. fig. 8.

On the top of an altar-tomb near the street, on the South side of the church:
" To the memory of John Simpson, esq. late one of his Majesty's justices of the peace, and receiver general of the land-tax for this county, who died Nov. 29, 1758, aged 60."

On the North side:
" Here lieth the body of Abstinence Poughfer, esq. who died the 5th day of September, 1741, aged 62 years."

On the South side:
" Here lieth the body of Martha Poughfer, the wife of Abstinence Poughfer, esq. who died Dec. 23, 1734, aged 52 years."

On the West side:
" Mary Simpson, daughter of Abstinence Poughfer, esq. and widow of John Simpson, esq. died the 28th of February, 1774, aged 68 years.
Thou most esteem'd, most honour'd, most rever'd, Accept this tribute to your merit due; Nor blame me if, by each fond tie endear'd, I bring again your virtues into view.
This awful scene your mem'ry shall restore, Here oft' for thee the silent tear be shed; Belov'd, till gratitude can feel no more, And mourn'd, till filial piety be dead."

Joseph Marshall died Dec. 10, 1779, aged 79.
Anne Marshall died May 2, 1789, aged 77.
Elizabeth Black, 20 March, 1764, aged 47.
Davis Black, 9 Dec. 1796, aged 80.

Fig. 9. in Plate XXXVIII. represents a Roman urn, of red clay, in the possession of the Rev. James Pigott, found at the depth of nine feet, in digging for the foundation of the new County Gaol.

Fig. 10. is a fragment of Roman pottery, found in the Town-ditch in 1793; the original of which, if whole, would form a circle within of nine inches and a half.

Fig. 11. is the fragment of a wrought stone, found at the same time and place.

Fig. 12. shews the North Bridge, commonly called *St. Sunday's Bridge*, an elegant stone structure, finished in the summer of 1796; the old Bridge having been nearly destroyed by a great flood in February 1795. " When viewed from the Abbey Meadows below, this Bridge forms, with the trees and slopes beyond it, a very pleasing scene. Its three arches are small segments of a larger circle. At the foot of this Bridge, in an area inclosed by a low wall, and distinguished by a few scattered grave-stones, the church-yard of St. Leonard's (p. 321) meets the eye [2]."

SAINT MARGARET'S.

This parish is very extensive, but consists entirely of Suburbs; amongst which are the Belgrave [3] and Humberston [4] gates [5].

Simon filius Joh'is le Lond nihil capit per assisam suam versus Helewisam filiam Thome, & Willielmum de Knaptoft & Aliciam uxorem ejus, de uno messuagio, unâ rodâ terre, unâ rodâ prati, tribus solidis redditûs, et redditûs sex gallarum, in Suburbio Leicestrie; quia suburbium extra Australem portam Leicestrie, ubi predictum tenementum est, pertinet ad libertatem Leicestrie Burgi, et ibi non placitatur tale breve [6].

[1] " Bedford, Oct. 4, 1757. Last Sunday, 25 poor children of the town, who was cloathed and educated by Gabriel Newton, one of the aldermen of the town of Leicester, went in procession to St. Paul's church in the above town, with their worthy donor before them, where was a great congregation; and an anthem was by the children, &c. sung in the organ-gallery. After which the donor, &c. had a decent entertainment, at a place appointed for their reception."

[2] Walk through Leicester, p. 44.

[3] See p. 532. In this street (leading to Loughborough), which is of considerable extent, is placed the famous *Milliare* which has been amply described in p. clv.; " an object which exhibits a curious instance of the civilization introduced by the Roman arms into this Island; for the erection of marks to denote the distance from place to place is an accommodation, at least to the travelling stranger, which unpolished Nations never devised; and which the inhabitants of Britain never generally enjoyed from the final departure of the Roman legions till the last century, when mile-stones were again erected along our principal turnpike-roads. The situation in which this stone is at present placed has often been thought improper; for it is undoubtedly exposed to injuries from the wantonness of play; and is so little conspicuous from its place in the obelisk, that nothing appears necessarily to attract the attention of the stranger. A situation more private, though not wholly so, would be more proper; such a one as the garden of the Infirmary would afford: it would there have all the publicity the curious could wish, and all the security the Antiquary could desire. —The visitor, continuing his walk along this street, which, as he probably will know, is on the great road from the Metropolis to the North-west part of the kingdom, arrives at a scene of busy traffick. Here, among numbers of newly-erected dwellings (proofs of the increasing population of the Town), is the public and principal wharf on the navigable Canal, near which is an iron foundery. This Canal (see p. clxvii.) was formed, in consequence of a bill passed in 1791, for the purpose of opening a communication with the Loughborough canal, and through that, with the various navigations, united to the Trent." Walk through Leicester, pp. 8—11.

[4] See p. 532. This street, which, passing by a range of new and handsome buildings, leads to Uppingham, is part of the manor possessed by the Bishops of Lincoln in the twelfth century, and is still called *The Bishop's Fee*. [See p. 567.]

[5] I cannot better describe the boundaries than in the quaint, but accurate description given me by the late Mr. Bickerstaff: " St. Margaret's consists entirely of Suburbs. It reaches from near St. Sunday's Bridge, on the North side of the street, All Saints *ex adverso*; and it parallels with it through the Sanby Gate, or Sancta via Gate, as it leads to St. Margaret's church; thence bending by an acute angle to the Church Gate, its Liberty; thence entering the Coal Hill, it branches into the Belgrave Gate and Humberston Gate; but, passing through the Coal Hill and Gallow Tree Gate, it still claims the off-side the street. Being now opposite St. Martin's side, it still continues, by house or field, till it takes in a groupe of houses, from the Hangman's Lane fronting the Magazine, to the Mill-stone Lane near the South Gate, a mile in extent, here opposite St. Mary's side of the street. From the North Gate, the continuation, under the title of North Gate Street, to St. Sunday's Bridge, is at least a quarter of a mile, besides the branches immediately on the opposite end of St. Sunday's Bridge towards the fields, which constitute St. Leonard's parish, and are called, that which runs W. W. by S. the " Wood Gate;" that on the N. N. by E. the " Abbey Gate," leading to the Abbey, whose brick wall begins near its extremity."

[6] Roper, MS.; ex Placitis apud Leicest. 44 Hen. III. coram Joh'e de Verdon & Gilberto de Preston, in Receptu Scaccarii, Rot. 5.

Juratores

Juratores presentant quod suburbium Leicestrie extra Portam Orientalem solebat respondere coram justiciariis & escaetoribus cum toto hundredo de Gartre. Jam XL annis elapsis subtractum est in libertatem burgi de Leicestrie (exceptâ parte Episcopi Lincolnie) per Will'um de Dingele, quondam ballivum comitis Leicestrie. Nil, &c. [1]

Cantia. Rex scripsit Recluse de Hakinton, quia illa pre ceteris novit jura et libertates pertinentes ad senescalciam Anglie ratione comitatûs Leicestrie; volens per illam super hiis pleniùs certiorari [2].

In 4 Edw. II. [1311] Richard de Glen demised to Richard de Pochewell a messuage and orchard in Belegrave gate, at an annual rent of one shilling. Testibus; Johanne Alsis majore Leicestrie, Willielmo de Basseby ballivo; and many others.

In 1387, Richard de Burgh, Roger Millyn, John Unly, and Nicholas o' the Ile of Leicester, conveyed to Thomas de Boseworthe the half of a toft of land in the Eastern Suburb of Leicester. Testibus; Willielmo Brone, tunc majore Leycestrie; Johanne Colchester, tunc ballivo; and many others. Dat' apud Leyc', die Lune, in Festo Nativitatis Sancti Johannis Baptiste, anno Ricardi Secundi post Conquestum secundo. See the four seals, Plate XLI. fig. 1—4.

The mayor and commonalty of Leicester set, for 12*d. per annum,* for twelve years, to *Ramelyth Beryngton,* taylor, a piece of land lying in the parish of St. Margaret, in *le Walker Croftes,* between the land of St. Margaret's gild and the land of St. John Leyc'. Dated Sept. 10, 4 Edw. IV.; John Reynolds then being mayor, Peter Curtis bailiff, &c.

The mayor and commonalty of Leicester, for 60 years, at 30*s. per annum,* let to *John Whitewell* two tenements, lying together " in foro porcorum Leyc', inter molendinum equinum domini regis ex parte orientali et tenementum Everardi Feldyng ex parte occidentali, &c." Dated Sept. 27, 15 Edw. IV.; John Roberds then mayor, Peter Curtis bailiff.

Ricardus Elkesley, nuper de Leycestriâ, capellanus, gave to the mayor, chamberlains, and commonalty of Leicester, a messuage in Belgrave-gate, extending thence to Barkby-lane; to the intent, that the chamberlains should expend 28*l.* for celebrating his obit in St. Margaret's church on the 11th of August, paying the vicar 3*d.* &c. Dated Festo Inventionis Sancte Crucis, 18 Edw. IV.; John Reynolds then being mayor, and John Bayhawe vicar of St. Margaret's church.

" Nos Johannes Pomerey abbas monasterii Beate Marie de Pratis, Leyc', et Walterus Pomerey de Leyc', dedimus Johanni German de Leyc', wright, Agneti uxori ejus, &c. unum messuagium cum gardino in parochiâ Sancte Margarete, in suburbio boreali ville Leyc', inter tenementum predicti Walteri ex parte boreali et tenementum magistri domûs Sancti Leonardi Leyc' ex parte australi, et extendit se à viâ regiâ usque ad aquam de Sore; et predictum gardinum continet in latitudine in superiori parte versus orientem XIX virgatas in parte, et XXVII virgatas in parte; et per aquam de Sore continet in latitudine XXIX virgatas, &c. Hiis testibus; Willielmo Newby majore ville Leycestrie, Willielmo Braunston, Alexandro Villers, deputatis, Ricardo Hotoft et Thomâ Meryng armigeris, ballivis ejusdem ville, &c. Dat' apud Leyc', Sept. 23, 24 Hen. VI."

John German, &c. granted the said house and garden to John Bellers of Leicester, Robert Barker, &c. Hiis testibus; Ricardo Gillot tunc majore ville Leicestrie, Petro Curtes ballivo ejusdem, &c. Dat' Aprilis 10°, 8 Edw. IV.

John Bellers granted the same to Hugh Thomson, Grisogono Spenser, and Robert Barker of Leicester. Testibus; Ricardo Gillot majore ville Leicestrie, Roberto Orton ballivo ejusdem, &c. Dat' Sept. 22°, 14 Hen. VII.

John Bellers, with consent of the forenamed feoffees, settled the same on his wife. Testibus;

Ricardo Reynold majore ville Leicestrie, Roberto Orton ballivo ejusdem, &c. Dat' Aprilis 20°, 21 Hen. VII.—He confirmed the same again. Testibus; Johanne Ware majore ville Leicestrie, Roberto Orton ballivo, &c. Dat' penult' Feb', 22 Hen. VII.

The feoffees grant it to Henry Fysher and Margaret his wife, Feb. 11, 4 Hen. VIII.

Henry Fysher of Canterbury and his wife sold it to John Bereye, of Leicester, carrier, June 9, 21 Hen. VIII. In a deed for the purpose, dated June 11, 21 Hen. VIII. Roger Gillot then being mayor, the messuage and garden are said to be situate " inter tenementum quondam Walteri Pomerey, nuper Johannis Charyte, ex parte boreali, et tenementum nuper magistri domûs Sancti Leonardi Leicestrie ex parte australi."

John Berege and Margaret his wife granted the same to their son John Berege and Alice his wife. Testibus; Rogero Gillot tunc majore, 13°, Maii, 29 Hen. VIII.

Ego Hugo Whalley concessi Nicholao Reynold de Leicestriâ generoso unum messuagium scituat' in *le Swyne market* inter tenementa Johannis Sherrard voc' *le George* ex parte Orientali, et tenementum domini regis ex parte Occidentali; et extendit se à dicto vico versus Boream usque quandam venellam, &c. *Soper's lane.* Dat' 15 Julii, 31 Hen. VIII.

In 1564, there were 164 families in St. Margaret's, and 17 in Knighton.

In an indenture dated 1702, Mrs. Brown's house and yard is said to be situated between Frier-lane on the North, and Millstone-lane on the South, and Double-gate-lane towards the East, &c. [3]

The workhouse of this parish was thus described in 1724:

" The person who had the chief management of this workhouse tells me, that, before the building of the parish houses in 1714, they paid above 30*l. per annum* rent for the poor, and that the whole charge on the poor was about 300*l. per annum;* for defraying which, they levied 4*s.* in the pound rent. For building the houses, they borrowed 240*l.* and reduced their levies from 4*s.* to 3*s.* 4*d.*; by which levies so reduced, they paid off the 240*l.* in five years. About 1720, the poor began to increase again; so that there was little or no further abatement in their levies. In 1723, they borrowed 200*l.* for making alterations and additional buildings to the parish-houses built 1714; as a working-room, a kitchen, cellar, a pump, and other conveniences, for turning them into a workhouse, which, he believes, will save the parish two-thirds of their former levies. Before the setting up the workhouse, the weekly payments to the poor were 3*l.* 5*s.* or thereabouts, besides by-bills, as they are called, which often amounted to 1*l.* or 1*l.* 10*s.* more; but since then, he supposes that 1*s.* 4*d.* in the pound will defray their charge; nevertheless they at present levy more, in order to pay off the 200*l.* which they borrowed. The salary of the master, the number of the poor in the workhouse, and orders of management, are much the same as in St. Martin's parish, saving that they trust the master himself to buy the provisions. They have bought about 11 ton of coals, to serve the house for the year current, and allow two strike of malt for a hogshead of beer; and the poor have hot meat three times a week [4]."

In 1764 an act was passed, for dividing and inclosing three several common and open fields, lying within the parish of St. Margaret, near the Borough of Leicester, called *Saint Margaret's Fields,* distinguished or known by the several names of *The Conduit Field, Middle Field,* and *The Nether Field,* and estimated and computed to contain together about 34 yard lands, besides four yard lands or thereabouts of glebe-land, and also certain meadows or pieces of lammas-ground adjoining or lying near to the said common and open fields, and called by the several names of *The Abbey Meadow, Dent's*

---

[1] Roper, MS.; ex Placitis apud Leicest. 44 Hen. III. coram Joh'e de Verdon & Gilberto de Preston, in Receptu Scaccarii, Rot. 13.
[2] Vide Claus. de anno 49 Hen. III. in Turri. Lond'.
[3] Carte, MS.; extract. è chartis quibusdem penès Joh. Haslock.
[4] Account of Workhouses, 1724, p. 146.

Meadow,

Meadow, *Palmer's Leroe*[1], and *Valentine's Leroe*. In this act, lord *William Manners* is described as lord of the manor of the said three common and open fields called *Saint Margaret's Fields*, and also as seised of 18 yard lands or thereabouts within the same fields, part of the said 34 yard lands; and the Reverend *Andrew Burnaby*, clerk, prebendary of St. Margaret in Leicester, in Lincoln, in right of his said prebend, as seised of the perpetual advowson, right of patronage and presentation of, in, and to, the vicarage church of St. Margaret, and of all the tithes in kind of corn, grain, hay, wool, and lamb, arising and issuing out of the said three common and open fields and meadows, and also of the said four yard lands of glebe-lands lying dispersed in the said common and open fields; which said tithes and glebe-land were held by *Ambrose Saunders*, late of Stoke Golding, in the said county of Leicester, but now of Haselbeech, in the county of Northampton, esquire, under a lease for three lives from the said Andrew Burnaby; yet nevertheless as to the said four yard lands of glebe-land in trust for *Mary Needham*, spinster: And lord William Manners, the Rev. Andrew Burnaby, Ambrose Saunders, esq. together with the Mayor, bailiffs, and burgesses of the Borough of Leicester, *George Coulton* the elder, clerk, *Richard Hill*, *John Willows*, *Joseph Cradock*, *Alice Loe*, and others, were then owners and proprietors of all the lands and grounds within the same fields; and the inhabitants within the said parish of St. Margaret, who pay levies and taxes to the said parish, though they have not any lands in the said fields, had, time immemorial, enjoyed a right of common over and upon the said open fields and Dent's meadow, jointly with the proprietors thereof respectively, from the open tide, or the time the harvest in the said fields is got in, until the 11th day of December in every year. An allotment to be made in the first place to those entitled under the prebendary to the four yard lands of glebe; and then a plot to be set out, for the use of the inhabitants of the parish paying taxes and levies (exclusive of the proprietors of the open fields), equivalent to their right of common, and to be vested in the churchwardens and overseers of the poor, and by them to be annually let or disposed of on Easter Tuesday, and the profits to be applied as the majority at the parish-meeting should annually direct; and the residue of the land to be proportionably divided. The allotment in lieu of one quarter of a yard land, held by the mayor, bailiffs, and burgesses, for the use of the Old Hospital on the Newark, to be paid without expence to the charity. A yearly rent to be allotted to the lessee of the glebe for the term of his lease, and in reversion to the prebendary, of 110*l.* out of the common fields; another rent of 50*s.* out of Dent's Meadow, and 15*s.* out of Palmer's Leroc in lieu of all tithes and compensation for corn grain, hay, wool, and lamb, and other tithes whatsoever. Provision is made for preserving for general use a conduit in the fields, which for time immemorial had been in the mayor, bailiffs, and burgesses of Leicester, situated in a close in the tenure of Mr. James Bishop of the Three Crowns Inn; and for preserving the post roads from Loughborough, through Leicester, to Harborough, and from Uppingham to Leicester.

Money raised for the poor, within the year ending at Easter 1776, —	*£.*	*s.*	*d.*
	721	5	9
Expended in county rates, &c. —	57	0	0
———— on the poor, — —	683	2	2
Rent of workhouse[2] and habitations,	20	1	1
Expended in litigations, — —	23	15	1
Money raised for 1783, — —	612	14	10
———— 1784, — —	778	8	1
———— 1785, — —	658	18	8
Medium of these three years, —	683	7	2
———— of county expences, —	31	13	4
———— of expences not relating to the poor; repairs of the church, roads, &c.	0	0	0
———— of nett annual expences, —	651	13	10

	£.	*s.*	*d.*
Medium of attending on magistrates,	0	0	0
———— of entertainments at meetings,	0	16	9
———— of law expences, — —	23	9	10
———— of setting the poor to work,	1	6	6

The Return made to Parliament in 1786, in answer to an enquiry respecting the charitable donations in this parish, may be seen in vol. I. p. 122.

On a tablet in the church:

" DONATIONS to the poor of this Parish.

" Mr. Robert Heyrick, late an alderman of Leicester, gave 40*s. per annum* for ever, to be paid into the hands of the mayor and justices of Leicester, to be by them distributed on St. Thomas's day, to 40 poor widows of the said Borough, 1*s.* each, 20 whereof to be of St. Martin's parish; the rest to be at the discretion of the mayor and justices. This gift began in 1618. The same Mr. Heyrick gave also by his last will 5*l. per annum* to be distributed at Candlemas, by the mayor and justices of the Borough of Leicester, amongst the poor of their several parishes, St. Leonard's included; which sum being delivered in bread by the mayor and justices to the minister and churchwardens of every several parish, they to distribute the same. This also began in 1618.

Elizabeth countess of Devon gave 50*l.* wherewith was purchased land of the yearly value of 3*l.*; of which 3*l.* twenty shillings to be given to the poor of the parish of St. Leonard's; the other forty shillings to be paid yearly, by the mayor and justices of the Borough of Leicester, to the minister and churchwardens, or overseers of the poor of the several parishes in Leicester, upon Thursday before Easter-day, and by them to be distributed at discretion. This gift began in 1628.

A house given at Loughborough; the yearly rent, now 28*l. per annum*, to be paid to the overseers of the poor of St. Margaret, 5*l.* of which to be given to the minister; the rest to be given to the poor of the said parish, half at Michaelmas, the other at Lady-day.

Gave by Hugh Botham, gent. deceased, 6*s.* 8*d.* to be paid to the minister and churchwardens, either three days before Christmas, or three days before Easter-day, to be by them distributed to the poor of the said parish, at their discretion.

By order of a common hall held for the Borough of Leicester, the chamberlains are to deliver to the ministers and churchwardens of St. Margaret's, either three days before New Year's day, or three days before Whit-Sunday, in bread 10*s.* 8*d.*

Mr. Barrage gave 1*l.* yearly for ever, to be paid out of the rents and profits of an orchard, now the property of Mr. Thomas Yates, in Belgrave-gate.

Catharine, wife of Samuel Holmes, gave by her last will 30 chaldron of pit coals, to be paid out of the rents and profits arising from the house now occupied by Thomas Wheatley, known by the sign of the Black Lion, Belgrave-gate; the said coals to be distributed by the owner or occupier, with the overseers of St. Margaret's, amongst the people dwelling in the Cock-muck-hill houses, upon Christmas-day, five chaldrons each, yearly for ever.

John Bass, esq. gave by his last will 5*l.* to be laid out in pit-coal, and given to the poor of St. Margaret's, the day before Christmas, for ever."

Over the Poor-houses:

" The Corporation of Leicester, and Thomas Chamberlain of the same place, gent. gave 50*l.* each to remove the six poors' houses, called *The Cock-muck-hill*, out of Belgrave-gate upon this spot. The residue of the money (which amounted to . . . . .[3]) was raised by a voluntary subscription of the parishioners.—Mrs. Catharine Holmes gave 500 weight of coals to the occupier of each house on St. Thomas's day yearly for ever. This donation was charged upon a house in Belgrave-gate, now the property of Mr. *Thomas Wheatly*; who has paid a certain sum of money into the hands of the parish-officers of St. Margaret's; and they have en-

---

¹ Sic. Sed Q. *lewe* from *leuca*?   ² This workhouse in 1776 was capable of accommodating 80 persons.   ³ The sum is left blank.

gaged, in behalf of the parish, that the said coals shall in future be provided by them."

" The following rules and orders are to be strictly observed by the inhabitants of these houses.

" If any of them behave disorderly, or use any ill language to the churchwardens and overseers (who are invested with the appointment of these places), for the first offence will be severely reprimanded, and for the second will be expelled the premises by a majority of the parish officers, and be incapacitated from enjoying any privilege or emo-

lument as may arise from the charity; and they are strictly prohibited from taking in any lodgers or inmates. When any of the windows are broken, the occupiers shall repair them at their own expence. On neglecting so to do, when called upon, the parish officers will give directions to have them made good, and the charge of so doing will be stopped off their yearly coals.

" John Brewin and Mark Oliver, churchwardens.

" Robert Clarke, J. P. Allamand, Collwell Langdon, and Edward Swann, overseers. Anno 1782."

The CHURCH (Plates XXXIX. XL. and XLI.)

consists of a lofty tower, three spacious ailes, and a chancel, answering the nave, all which are leaded.

" St. Margarete's is thereby the fairest paroche chirch of Leircester, wher ons was cathedrale chirch, and therby the bisshop of Lincoln had a palace, wherof a litle yet standith. John Peny, first abbate of Leircester, then bisshop of Bangor and Cairluel, is here buried in an alabaster tumbe. This Penny made the new bricke workes of Leicester abby, and much of the brick walles[1]."

This church may still deserve the character of being " the fairest parish-church in Leicester[2]."

This structure is rendered venerable by its tower (36 yards high), whose battlements, pinacles, and trefoil-work, with the niche, or tabernacle, on the corner of the South wall of the church, would have even shewn it to have been the work of the æra of the regular gothic, had not its date been confirmed by the Register of Bishop Alnwyke, fol. 48 : " Commissio domini episcopi ad levandum le Smoke-farthen, alias dict' Lincoln farthing, à nostris archidiaconatûs nostri subditis, ad utilitatem nostre matricis ecclesie Lincolnie cathedralis, sponse nostre, convertendum dict' Smoke farthings, concedentur ad constructionem campanilis ecclesie prebendalis Sancte Margarete, Leycestr', A. D. 1444[3]."

Under the tower is a deep well.

Both within and without the church there are still visible marks remaining of this grand repair ; and, what is particularly remarkable, the Gothic arches on the two sides of the nave are not uniform.

From the tower[4], a ring of ten large bells, well known for their excellence, sounds its frequent peals of harmony along the meadow and river below.

On eight of the bells[5] are these inscriptions:

I. A[braham] R[udhall]. 1711.

II. Prosperity to all our Benefactors. 1711.

III. Crede, resipisce, disce mori. 1633.

IV. Jhesu Nazarene, Rex Judeorum, fili Dei, miserere mei, 1633.

V. Morte beata nihil beatius. 1633.

VI. Statutum est omnibus semel mori. 1633.

VII. Feare God, obaie the King. George Palmer. 1633.

VIII. Cum sono, si non vis adire,
nunquam ad Preces capias ire. 1633.

Originally there were but six, placed there by Hugh Watts, once mayor of Leicester; to which two were added in 1633; and two more in 1741, by William Fortrey, esq. of Norton by Galby, who was the patron and director of the founder, Thomas Eayre of Kettering, and paid the whole charge of the new bells, and a great part of that of new hanging the old ones[6].

The inside of the church is handsome ; the nave and side ailes are supported by gothic arches, whose beauty and symmetry are not concealed by awkward galleries.

In the chancel, on each side of the high altar, is a large niche, beautifully carved, and formerly, no doubt, as beautifully painted.

In that on the North side, as the tradition goes, stood the image of the Blessed Virgin Mary. At her feet Robert Bossu earl of Leicester (who built part of this church), kneeling, and praying to her : whose figure being yet entire, for the oddness and singularity, is here annexed, Plate XLI. fig. 5. The rim of his cap and belt have so natural an appearance of iron and its rust, that the deception will not yield to the closest inspection. He is recumbent, and rests his head upon his left hand, partly inserted under his cap ; his sheathed sword under him, the hilt towards his head ; one heel, his right, the only one in sight, upwards, or he could not have been contained in the bottom of the niche; his back to the East ; his head to the South ; on the left side of the communion-table in the approach. He is 20 inches long.

In that on the South side stood the image of St. Margaret. At her feet a lion couchant ; fig. 6.

Near the altar, on the left, is a loop-hole, or confessionary, opening into the vestry.

In the first window on the left, on entering the chancel from the church, is " St. Amb."

The opposite or South-east window has a groupe of human figures, strangely collected, and stuck together, all very plump[7].

The present altar-piece is lofty ; formed of good carving and wainscot. In the middle a large painting of Cherubim, the Commandments, Creed, and Pater-noster, set off with pilasters and other ornaments ; all which are preserved from dust with large curtains of scarlet.

[1] Leland's Itinerary, vol. I. p. 18.
[2] " It is to be observed of this, and the other churches in this place, that the entrance is by a descent of several steps ; a circumstance proving incontestibly that the ground without has been considerably raised, since no reason could induce the founders of these sacred edifices to sink the floors beyond the natural level ; nor is the surface of the church-yards alone, higher than the floors of the churches ; so caused by the continued interment of the dead : but the general level of the pavements of the streets is also higher ; from which it must be inferred, that the ground on which the present houses are built has been every where raised, and that very considerably." Walk through Leicester, pp. 16, 17. [3] Cowel, sub titulo Smoke-farthings.
[4] This tower gives a noble appearance to Leicester, from the Abbey Meadows and Birstall hill; and is a fine lofty pile of strength, symmetry, and beauty.
[5] " The antient six bells at St. Margaret's, cast by the famous Watts, are increased to ten, which are almost the best peal of that number in the kingdom. There is an anecdote of the first of these six bells not a little extraordinary, as well as true, which I picked up by tradition when a boy, and enquired afterwards into its validity : When the metal and moulds of the bells were preparing, and almost finished for casting, the son would have his father go to London, to hear the best-toned tenor he could before they put-to the final hand. The father went up accordingly at the son's request ; who set to work, without loss of time, immediately after his father's departure. He cast the great bell, which did not completely please him ; he re-cast it ; and, finding it had every qualification he wished for, he then wrote to his father in town, to come upon a certain day in the following week ; nay, even a certain hour. The father could not make out what his son meant by being so particular ; however, he obeyed him. The son, upon casting a second tenor which so fully answered all his wishes and expectations, set to work to hang it ; and, at the critical minute the father was to approach the town of Leicester on his return, this inimitable great bell was ringing, to the no small joy of the father, who cried also ; for he guessed, and knew, what the younger Watts had done at, and contrived, as there could be no such bell in existence at the time he left his foundery : (the ninth, which is now in St. Margaret's steeple, being equally as finetoned ; nay, some say better). These six hindmost bells were cast about 1629. The two trebles in the present ten were cast by Mr. Eayre of Kettering, one of the first of this occupation in his time, and a person of great ingenuity, as well as property. About 1741, the peal of ten were made complete." This note is by the late Reverend Philip Hackett.
[6] See under Norton by Galby, vol. II. p. 733.
[7] See a rough sketch of these figures in the Leicestershire Collections, Bibl. Top. Brit. No. L. Plate XXI. p. *486.

On

Schnebbelie del. Oct.ʳ 22 1790.

R. Basire Sc.

Fig. 1.

Fig. 5.

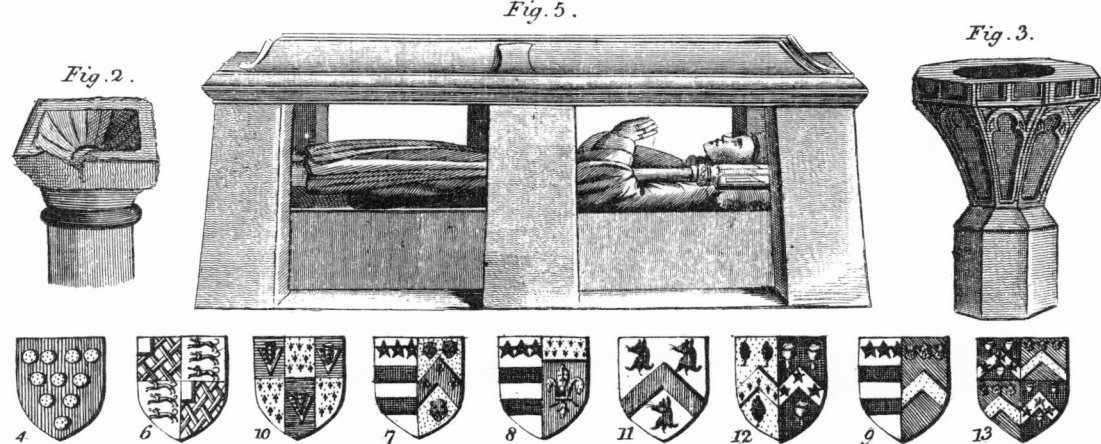

Fig. 2.

Fig. 3.

4   6   10   7   8   11   12   9   13

Edw. Blore del.

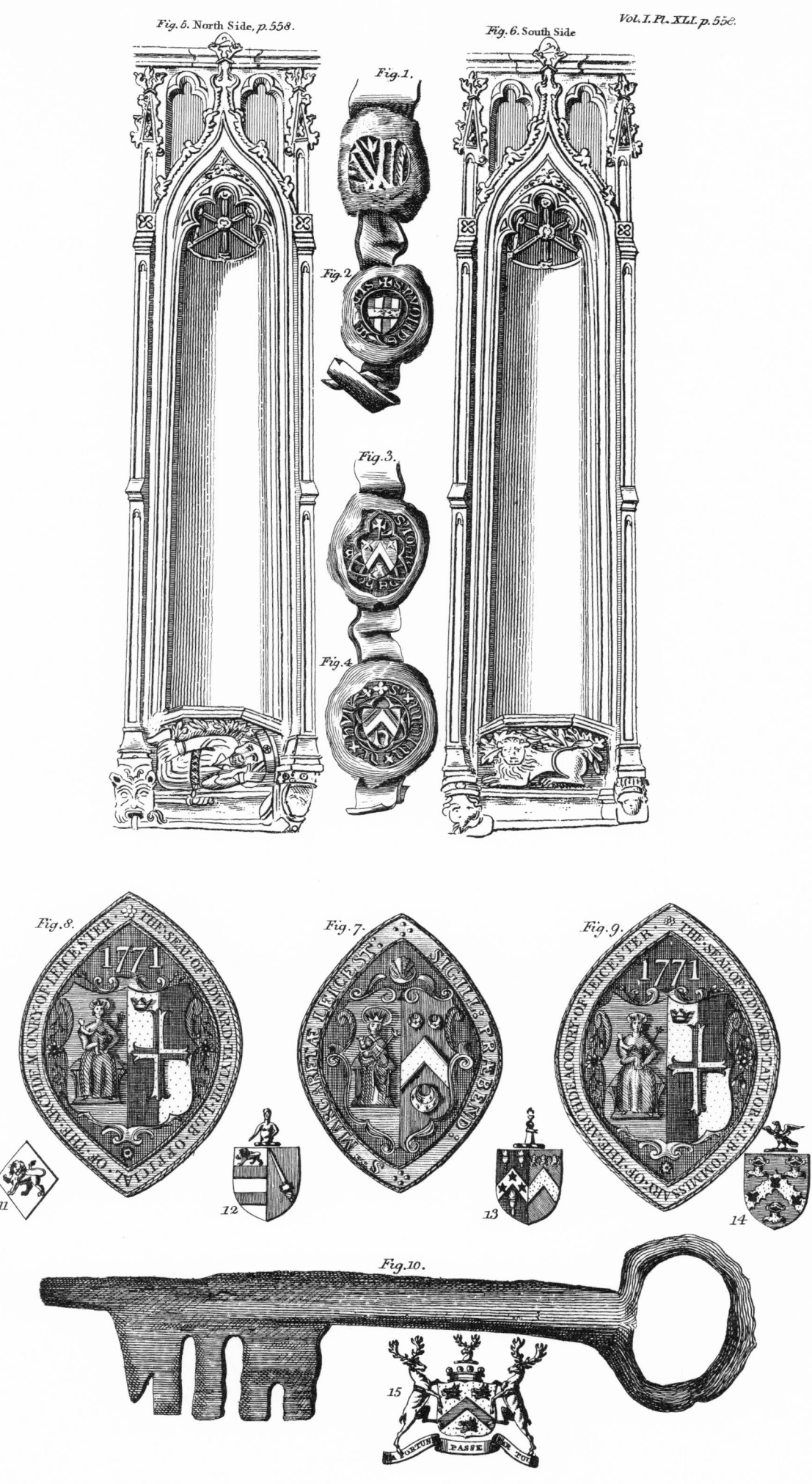

Fig. 5. North Side. p. 558.

Fig. 6. South Side

Fig. 1.

Fig. 2.

Fig. 3.

Fig. 4.

Fig. 8.

Fig. 7.

Fig. 9.

11

12

13

14

Fig. 10.

15

On the South side remain three fine stone-seats and a piscina, Plate XXXIX. fig. 1.

Another piscina is in the South aile; fig. 2.

The font is given in fig. 3.

On the roof of the nave is carved the bust of a man, with two other smaller heads standing under it; and along a beam runs an inscription somewhat to this purpose:

Theis are iman bothe that theis
That janglythe in tyme of god serbiss
Loke how bright our howse and praty.
In wyth my silltwas by me holde.

Mr. Burton notices only one coat of arms here: Gules, ten bezants, *Zouch*; fig. 4.

Under Mr. Charles Horton, late master of the society of singers here, the barbarous custom of rustic psalmody in these parts gave way to a more cultivated taste; and the parishioners, with a laudable spirit, have erected, by subscription among themselves, a handsome organ, which was finished in 1773; the charge for erecting which, and placing it in the church, was 409l. 17s. 8½d.

The church is also ornamented by an elegant brass chandelier, with twelve branches above, and twelve below, pendent from the roof of the nave, and opposite the reading-desk; the gift of John Bass, esq. in 1754.

When all the other churches in Leicester were settled upon the Abbot and his monks, *in proprios usus*, this escaped, as not belonging to the Earl, but to the Bishops of Lincoln, who annexed it as a prebend to the Cathedral of Lincoln.

The right of presentation is vested in the person holding the prebend; and the parish, with the neighbouring dependant parish of Knighton, is exempted from the jurisdiction of the Archdeacon of Leicester.

In the Matriculus of 1220, St. Margaret's church is described to be under the patronage of the Bishop of *Lincoln*, and as a prebend of that Cathedral [1].

The endowment of the vicarage is here given, from an attested copy taken in 1736.

" Ordinatio vicarie ecclesie Sancte Margarette Leicestrie, 1276.

" Walterus de Bornington presbyter, presentatus per magistrum Rogerum archidiaconum Leycestrie, prebendarium Sancte Margarette de eâdem, ad vicariam dicte prebende per nos ordinandam, que in portionibus subscriptis ordinata existit, factâ prius inquisitione per decanum et capitulum Lincolnie; per quam acceptum est, et etiam ad ipsam est admissus 14 calendarum Aprilis, anno 19°, et cum honore residendi in ipsâ perpetuus vicarius canonicè institutus in eâdem, juratâque episcopo canonicâ obedientiâ in formâ consuetâ, scriptum fuit decano et capitulo quod ipsum, &c.

" Est autem forma ordinationis vicarie talis:

" Ordinamus autem vicariam dicte prebende in omnibus oblationibus in pecuniâ que ad ecclesiam pertinent ordinandam, cum oblatione candelarum in die Purificationis, et aliis oblationibus que in candelis et cereis in purificationibus, et cum corporibus presentibus diversis vicibus obvenerint ad eandem; necnon pane altaris, et ovis, et in sex marcis annuis per manus prebendarii vicario qui pro tempore fuerit solvendis ibidem terminis subscriptis; (viz.) in festo Sancti Michaelis duabus marcis, in festo Pasche duabus marcis, et in festo Beati Petri ad Vincula duabus marcis, una cum terrâ dicte ecclesie appropriatâ que jacet in Lethepol croftis, quam exnunc dicte vicarie, et item cum omnimodis proventibus altaris capelle de Knighton, que ad dictam ecclesiam pertinet, salvis prebendario decimis lane, agnorum, et vivis mortuariis pro defunctis. Injungimus autem prebendario, quod de manso competenti, ab omni seculari servitio libero, et hâc vice sufficienter edificato, citra festum Sancti Michaelis vicario provideat memorato. Deserviet verò vicarius per se, cum

socio sacerdote, diacono, et clerico ecclesie Beate Marie Margarette presentato, et capelle de Knighton per idoneum sacerdotem sumptibus suis; eö excepto, quòd diacono et clerico ultra consuetas oblationes, in duplicibus festis, et in diebus dominicis, et in corporibus presentibus pro quibus fuerint oblationes, nihil ministrabit. Inveniet merus vicarius totum luminare in cancello, tam ad libros quam ad altare; videlicet, novem cereos ad magnum altare super herliis in festis consuetis, et duos cereos supra altare furos, et alios duos processionales, et unam lampadem in cancello. Libros et ornamenta ecclesie sustinebit et reparabit, et locricibus vestimentorum. Stipendia ministrabit, ac extraordinaria onera pro suâ ratâ agnoscet; et nihil aliud preter officium divinum requiretur ab ipso. Prebendarius verò omnia alia onera ordinaria et extraordinaria pro suâ ratâ agnoscet et sustentabit.

" Instantiâ magistri Rogeri de Saxenhirst, prebendarii ecclesie Sancte Margarette Leicestrie, et Roberti de Hereby vicarii ejusdem ecclesie Sancte Margarette, et consensu capituli ecclesie Lincolnie precedentibus, 4 non' Julii, anno Domini 1284, apud Ulfescroft, mutata fuit ordinatio dicte vicarie in hoc; quod vicarius qui pro tempore fuerit omnimodam decimam curtilagiorum habebit, in recompensationem sex marcarum annuarum quas percipere consuevit à prebendario prenotato, et habuit dictus vicarius super hoc literam patentem sub hâc formâ:

" Universis, &c. Oliverus, &c. Noverit universitas vestra quod nos literas bone memorie quondam domini Ricardi predecessoris nostri, in mediocri super ordinatione vicarie in ecclesiâ prebendali Sancte Margarette Leicestrie, inspeximus sub hâc formâ:

" Ricardus, miseratione divina, Lincolnie episcopus, dilectis in Christo filiis Olivero decano et capitulo Lincolnie salutem, gratiam, et benedictionem. Quod dilectum in Christo filium Walterum de Bornington presbyterum ad vicariam prebendalis ecclesie Sancte Margarette Leicestrie, in subscriptis portionibus per nostram ordinationem consistentem admisimus, ipsumque cum onere personaliter residendi in eâ perpetuum vicarium canonicè instituimus in eâdem. Vobis mandamus quatenus corporalem possessionem dicte vicarie prefato Waltero tanquam vicario habere faciatis in formâ prenotatâ. Ordinamus antem," &c. [ut supra ex aliâ parte rotuli de verbo ad verbum.] Verumque suggerentibus nobis dilectis in Christo filiis magistro Rogero de Saxenhirst archidiacono Leicestrie, prebendarioque ecclesie Sancte Margarette predicte, ac magistro Roberto de Kerby diacono, per nos ad eandem vicariam de novo admisso, quod tam prebendario quam vicario, certis de causis, expediret non modicum decimas croftorum seu curtilagiorum dicte vicarie, in recompensationem dictarum sex marcarum annuarum, assignari, et ipsum prebendarium ab onere presentationis hujus relevari, quod et per nos fieri eorum uterque cum instantiâ postulavit: Nos, ponderatis oneribus ponderandis in hoc facto, prefatas decimas croftorum et curtilagiorum totius parochie ecclesie predicte, sive de leguminibus, sive de quibuscunque aliis qualitercunque proveniant, prefate vicarie de cetero assignamus, et auctoritate pontificali ordinamus; et de dictâ peractione annuâ sex marcarum, de utriusque partis assensu expresso, prebendarium imperpetuum pro se et suis successoribus exoneramus et absolvimus antedictum. In cujus rei testimonium, sigillum nostrum presentibus est appensum. Datum apud Ulfescroft, 4° non' Julii, anno Domini 1284°, et Pontificatûs nostri quinto [2]."

Jan. 20, 1428. Robert Bytham, rector of Norton Twycross in this county, had leave from his patrons, the prior and convent of Belvoir, to exchange with sir William Gilbert, vicar of St. Margaret's [3].

Christian, wife of *Richard Grenville*, in Henry the Sixth's time, by her will (in Latin), orders her

---

[1] See the Introductory Volume, p. lv.

[2] E Rotulis domini Ricardi Gravesend, quondam Lincolnie episcopi, qui cepit preesse ecclesie Cathedrali Beate Marie Virginis Lincolnie, anno Domini 1258.

[3] Mr. Peck, from the MSS. at Belvoir.

body to be buried in St. Mary's chapel, within the prebendal church of St. Margaret at Leicester [1].

In the time of Henry VII. *Church Ales* were very frequent. When they made collections for poor, or for church repairs, a kind of treat was given.

A. D. 1498. Received at the Church Ale, on the Sunday next before the Assumption, 17*s*. 5*d*.; and on the Assumption, 2*s*. 7½*d*.

Paid, for bread and flesh for the Church Ale, 4*s*.

Ditto, on our Lady Day Assumption, 2*d*.

Received, at the Church Ale holden of St. Bartholomew's eve, 38*s*. 1*d*.

Paid, for powder, beef, and cheese, 10*d*.

1513. They had a calf cost 2*s*. 4*d*. and three calves' heads and a ewe cost 8*d*.

In 1525, a calf cost 3*s*. 8*d*.; and for their breakfasts, three calves' heads and two plucks, &c. dressing, fire, and other things, 4*d*.

In 1534, the value of the prebend of St. Margaret's, then held by *Master Doctor Dudley*, was 33*l*. The Vicar Choral of Lincoln had from the church an annual payment of 2*l*.

The stipend of Thomas Nelson, vicar, was 17*l*.; and the King had an annual payment of 2*s*. 10½*d*.

In the Visitation of Dr. John White, Bishop of Lincoln, under the authority of a mandate from Cardinal Pole, it is thus, *inter alia*, reported: " Thomas More in Ecclesiâ parochiali Divi Martini Leicestrie, ac post etiam in Ecclesiâ Dive Margarete, xxi° die Aprilis 1556, coram nobis comparuit, et multas Hereses defendit; dicens inter cetera: " This is my faith, that in the Sacrament of the Altar is not the body of Christ; no more than if I myself should give one a piece of bread, and say, Take, eat, this is my body; meaning my own body within my doublet." Unde sententia contra ipsum lata. Scriptum est ad Dominem Regem et Reginam: Et per Breve *De Heretico comburendo*, apud Leicester predict', mense Junii fuit combustus [2]."

The following extracts from the Churchwardens' Accompts were made by Mr. Peck in 1729:

	£.	s.	d.
1553. Rec'd, at the Obit of sir Rich. Helkyslers — — — —	0	0	3
Rec'd, at the Obit of Christo. Jennison — — — —	0	3	4
For mending the Pyx — —	0	0	3
For payntyng the Awter-clothes	0	2	2
For two Crosses — — —	0	12	6
For payntyng the Rode — —	0	2	10
For II Crosse-staves, and payntyng the same — — —	0	0	8
For mending the Canape —	0	0	2
For the Crosse-cloths — —	0	3	0
For making St. John's Aultar —	0	0	10
For making owr Lady Aultar —	0	3	0
For payntyng the II Aultar-clothys	0	2	11
For watchyng the Sepulture —	0	0	8
For a Cope — — — —	0	13	4
For the Pascale and Judas —	0	0	12
For Stone to the Aultar — —	0	0	4
For Chayns to the Sencers, and skowryng — — — —	0	0	10
For a Chrysmatory — —	0	2	4
For a Cope — — — —	3	5	0
For III Banner-clothes — —	0	1	4
For sawyng, makyng, and paynting x Banner-polys, and II that Mr. Conyesbie had — —	0	3	0
For a Patten to the Chales —	0	11	3
For mendyng the Skons —	0	0	6
1554. Paid, for Tythe of Willows —	0	1	0
For Waforus on Pawm Sonday —	0	0	1
For Freng for a Streymar that Master Fleychar gaf — —	0	2	0
For a Manwell [Manual] —	0	3	0
For makyng Serch for the Chales	0	2	4
For Parrs and a Surples —	0	10	0

	£.	s.	d.
1555. Rec'd, for *Lyncoln Farthyngs* of [the hamlet of] Knighton] [3]	0	0	4½
Paid for setting up the Pulpet —	0	0	2
For a Key for the Kofar of the Qweyar — — — —	0	0	2
For the Rode Mary and John —	0	1	8
For payntyng the Rode Marie and John, and Sent Margarett's Crowne — — —	0	2	6
For settyng up the Images —	0	0	8
For Cord to the Orgeyns —	0	0	1
For II Antiphonals — —	0	2	0
For makyng II Surples of II Albis	0	0	4
For a Hally-water-stock —	0	3	6
For another — — — —	0	3	0
1557. Rec'd of Saunders' sister for hir Legacy — — — —	0	1	0
Paid for mendyng the Crosse —	0	0	4
For xvi yards of new Clowth for the Roode — — —	0	9	4
For peynting the same — —	0	3	0
1558. For ryngyng the Bells wheyn Q. Eliz. was proclaymed Quene —	0	0	8
Rec'd for the Obit of Mrs. Heysylryge — — —	0	2	0
Rec'd of Rob. Ynsley, for a white alabaster stone — — —	0	3	4
Rec'd for Lingcollne Farthyngs —	0	1	4
1559. For taking down the Angels —	0	0	8
1561. Rec'd for Peynted Cloth —	0	8	0
Paid to Father Clerke — —	0	3	4
For wrytyng of the Com'andements	0	4	0
Paid to the Organ Pleaer —	0	3	4
Rec'd for a Staffe that aperteyned to the Roode-lofte — —	0	13	11
Rec'd for the Haly-loffe —	0	2	0
1564. Paid to the Vyset Folks [4] —	0	18	10
Sold, Brase Stuff — —	0	15	0
One Cope — — —	1	0	0
Baner-cloths and other Stuff	0	6	8
St. Hugh's Cote, and others	0	6	8
3 Vestments and 1 Cope	6	13	4
1565. For mendyng of the Balyes of the Orgaynes — — — —	0	0	2
For kepyng the Organ halfe a yere, at the com'andement of Mr. Mayor and the whole People	0	2	0
For takyng down of the Roode-lofte	0	0	8
For Bred and Wyne for II Com'unions — — — — —	0	0	2
For vii yardes of grene Say for my Lorde's Seate — —	0	9	4
Paid to Sir Peter Stryngham, for kepyng of the Booke — —	0	0	6
For a quart of Maumsye on Good Friday — — — —	0	0	6
Rec'd for the Holy-water Stoke	0	0	8
1566. Paid to Syr Rich. Cusenrate, for kepyng the Booke — —	0	0	6
1567. Layd forthe for the Egle [Lectern, forsan] — — —	4	19	3
For one day's work for the Organs	0	0	8
1568. Rec'd for the Chales —	4	13	4

This yere, 1568, Mr. John Lounde (being Prebendary) was mayd also Vycar of the same. And the sayd Lounde mayd, the same year, the chymbney within the kitchyng, and the valt in the halle, and repayryd the howse, wch was so ruynous that a man cold not lye dry therein: yet cold he recover nothyng for delapydations, because the Vicar had playd a ...... part. And in the same yere, he, with consent of his lovyng parishioners, dyd extyrpe and pull downe all monuments of superstytyone owt of the said prebendall church. I pray God so kepe ytt.

	£.	s.	d.
1568. Paid for skowryng the Egle —	0	0	4
For carryyng the Supplycac'on to Loughborowe, to my Lord of Loughborowe, &c. — —	0	1	10

[1] Collins's Peerage, 1768, vol. VI. p. 37.
[2] Fox's Martyrs, vol. III. p. 632; and Strype's Ecclesiastical Memorials, vol. III. Appendix, p. 165; from the Lincoln Register.
[3] This article often occurs.   [4] This article occurs often the same year, and relates to the poor visited with the Plague.

To

	£.	s.	d.
To Tho. Grene, for his peanstakyng — — — —	0	6	8
For the copy of the Declaration at London — — — —	0	2	0
Gyven to my Lord of Loughborow's Butler and Porter —	0	1	6
For a Samon gyven to my Lord of Loughborow — — —	0	13	8
Paid for the Com'union Coppe —	4	8	0
1569. Rec'd for the red Velvet Coveryng	1	2	1
Rec'd for the Organ's Casse —	0	10	0
Rec'd for the Organ Pypes —	1	8	1

	£.	s.	d.
Rec'd for part of the Organ Casse	0	7	6
1570. Rec'd of Mr. Lounde, for carvyd. Boards — — — —	0	0	4
Rec'd of Mr. Newzamm, for the Eagle — — — —	5	0	0
1572. Paid to the Parit. for warning the Dean of Lyncoln's Visitation	0	0	4
Paid to the Vicar, for tythes of the Wyllowes standing in the Cow-pasture — — —	0	1	2
1573. Paid to the Vicar, for his Offering every Sunday — — —		.....	[1]

The PREBEND of ST. MARGARET,

consists of the impropriation and advowson of St. Margaret's parish in the town of Leicester, where antiently stood the episcopal see of Leicester.

The value of the prebend in 1534 was 27l. 6s. 3d.

The following Prebendaries have been successively Proprietors and Patrons of this Church.

John de Winton, 1236.

Roger de Saxenhirst, Archdeacon of Leicester about 1274, and Prebendary in 1276, presented Walter de Bornington to the vicarage.

Roger de Martival (afterwards Bishop of Salisbury), being collated in 1294 to this prebend and the archdeaconry of Leicester, accepted the archdeaconry, but quitted the prebend.

John Maunsell, collated to it 2 cal. Julii, 1295, occurs in 1301 and 1325.

Adam de Limbergh died possessed of it 1339, and was succeeded by

Comenges, a Roman Cardinal, 1339; who held it 1343.

John de Edyngton, 12 cal. Jan. 1349; he exchanged it, 13 cal. Nov. 1366, with

John de Appelby, Prebendary of Chamberleyneswode in the church of St. Paul, London; who held it 1380.

Thomas Brightwell, Dean of Leicester college; on whose death, in 1390,

Thomas Bennet[2], LL. D. succeeded, being installed Nov. 21, 1390.

Richard Younge, LL. B. was installed July 18, 1391. In 1399, he was made Bishop of Bangor.

Thomas More was presented to it by the King, June 23, 1399; and died 1421, being Dean of St. Paul's cathedral, London, where he was buried, without any inscription to his memory.

Thomas Barnesley was collated 1421, on More's death; and quitted it, being Archdeacon of Leicester.

Reginald Kentwode held it 1437. He died 1441, being Dean also of London; and was buried by his predecessor Dean More, without any monument.

John Walpole died in May 1445, possessed of it.

William Biconell succeeded 1445, and died 1477. His successor was

John Wardhall, LL. D. collated Nov. 7, 1477, on Biconell's death.

Roger Rotherham, Archdeacon of Rochester, was collated July 17, 1472, and quitted it the same year.

John Blackhall, M. A. succeeded, being installed Nov. 14, 1472.

Geffry Simeon quitted it, 1485, for the Chancellorship of Lincoln.

Simon Stallworth was collated Aug. 11, 1485, on Simeon's resignation.

Robert Momey was collated March 18, 1492, on Stallworth's quitting it the same year.

John Cotteler was collated March 28, 1492, on the resignation of Momey. He was also Treasurer.

Robert Moine was Prebendary in 1501.

Richard Dudley, M. A. was collated March 30, 1507, on Cotteler's resignation.

Henry Morgan, LL. D. was presented by the King, with the consent of the Bishop; and was collated June 7, 1536, on Dudley's death. He was preferred to the see of St. David's 1554; and deprived by Queen Elizabeth 1559.

Thomas Todde held it about 1559.

John Londe, LL. B. was installed into it April 20, 1560; as was

John Robinson, Precentor, installed July 9, 1581. He died in 1597, and was buried at Somersham, co. Huntingdon, where he was rector.

George Eland, afterwards Chancellor of Lincoln, enjoyed it March 8, 1603-4. He resigned it 1605.

Richard Clayton, S. T. P. Master of St. John's college, Cambridge, was collated to it Jan. 22, 1605-6. He died in 1612, being also Dean of Peterborough, and Archdeacon of Lincoln.

Thomas Turner, S. T. B. rector of Stokehammond, Bucks, succeeded, being installed Aug. 23, 1612. He was afterward Dean of Canterbury; and died Oct. 8, 1672, aged 81.

John Walcot, M. A. was installed into it July 26, 1618, on Turner's resignation. He died about 1660, being rector of Keyston, co. Huntingdon.

Nathanael Ward was installed Oct. 20, 1660; and died possessed of it 1668.

Edward Boteler, M. A. installed Oct. 12, 1668, on Ward's death. He died in 1670, and was buried at Wintringham, co. Lincoln, where he was rector. His successor was

Nicholas Stratford[3], S. T. P. installed April 7, 1670. He was made Bishop of Chester in 1689, and succeeded by

John Gostling, M. A. installed Oct. 26, 1689. He was chaplain to his Majesty, one of the priests of the Royal Chapel, subdean of St. Paul's, a minor canon of the cathedrals of Canterbury and London, rector of All Saints Hope, and vicar of Littlebourn, in Kent. He died July 17, 1733.

Thomas Geary, M. A. 1733.

Andrew Burnaby[4], M. A. 1737; Prebendary and Vicar. He was also rector of Asfordby.

Robert Burnaby, LL. B. younger brother to the Archdeacon; died April 2, 1807.

—— Palmer, 1807; the present Prebendary, 1810.

The style of office is, " Prebendary of the prebendal church of Saint Margaret in Leicester, founded in the cathedral church of the Blessed Virgin Mary in Lincoln."

[The names of the Vicars of St. Margaret's may be seen under the description of Knighton, vol. IV. p. 238; to which may be added,

Robert de Horeby, 1280.]

ST. MARGARET'S GUILD.

" In this church," says Mr. Carte, " was founded St. Margaret's guild, for which I have seen a memorandum of a patent granted 16 Ric. II. This

---

[1] " Extract. è veteri Compotu Guardianorum Ecclesie B. Margaretæ, penès virum Reverendum Johannes Kilby, ejusdem ecclesiæ vicariam A. D. 1729, per me, F. Peck."

[2] "Penult' die Oct', 1390, dominus episcopus Lincolnie contulit mag'ro Bennet, presbytero, Curie Cantuariensis officiali, prebendam Sancte Margarette Leicestrie, per mortem magistri Thome de Bryghtwell, decani ecclesie Collegii novi Beate Marie." Reg. Bokyngham.

[3] See some account of him in vol. IV. p. 239.

[4] See vol. III. p. 17. His son, Dr. Andrew Burnaby, is the present Archdeacon of Leicester; and vicar of Greenwich.

guild was rich, and used to join with Corpus Christi guild in defraying the public charges[1]."

" Gilda Sancte Margarete, in villâ Leicestrie, valet in redditibus et firmâ omnium terrarum et tenementorum predicte gilde pertinentibus, scituatis et existentibus in villâ Leicestrie, prout &c.

	£.	s.	d.
	19	10	1½

Firmâ annuali ejusdem gilde, simul cum duobus cameris ibidem, que ii capellani predicte gilde modò inhabitant, ac gardino cum pomario, valuatis in toto per annum — — — — 1 0 0

| | 20 | 10 | 1½ |

Reprise; viz.
Redditus resoluti diversis personis sequentibus:
Domino Regi, ut ducatûs sui Lancastrie, exeunt' de certis terris in Belgrave gate — — — — — — 1 10 9½
Eidem, exeunt' de diversis tenementis in North gate — — — — 0 6 8
Eidem, exeunt' de ii peciis terre in Towne ditche — — — — — 0 0 6
Custodi Castelle ibidem, ut parcella ducatûs predicti — — — 0 1 4
Waltero Grossyn, de unâ peciâ terre in Belgrave gate — — — 0 1 8
Collegio Beate Marie ibidem — 0 0 4

Et magistro Nethermyll, exeunt' de unâ peciâ terre in Belgrave gate predictâ 0 0 9

In toto per annum — 2 0 11½
Feodum ballivi sive collectoris redditûs ibidem, per annum — — 1 0 0

Stipendium duorum capellanorum ibidem, cuilibet eorum ad 106s. 8d. per annum — — — — 10 13 4
Et remanet clarè per annum — 6 18 10

The said gild was founded by king Richard the Second, and incorporated in the name of two *custodes* or masters of the same gelde; and to th'entente to find two priests, to celebrate divine service within the said church of St. Margaret, and to pray for the founder's souls; and there hath been no land sold synce the tyme before I my ted; and the inventory, &c."

In another account I find,
Gilda Sancte Margarete valet in redd' et firm' — — — — 20 10 1½
Repris' inde — — — 13 6 3
Et remanet clarè per annum — 6 18 10½

All the lands belonging to the gilds of Corpus Christi and of St. Margaret's in Leicester were purchased from king Edward VI. by *Robert Cuteler*, esq. afterwards sir *Robert*, and chief justice of the king's bench[2].

MONUMENTAL INSCRIPTIONS.

At the upper end of the North aile is an alabaster altar monument of *John Penny*, LL.D. abbot of *Leicester*, Bishop of *Bangor* 1504, and of *Carlisle* 1509. He died, at the end of the year 1519, or the beginning of the year 1520, on a visit at Leicester abbey; where it is supposed that he was buried; and that, on the suppression of that monastery, his monument was removed to this church, to which he had been a special benefactor.

This tomb[3], the work of no inferior artist, still remains in good preservation; and is represented in Plate XXXIX. fig. 5.

Wyrley's Notes, in the College of Arms, preserve an epitaph, on a mural monument, to the memory of *John Middleton*, mayor of Leicester in 1578, who died in 1588.
Arms: Quarterly, 1. and 4. . . . . . fretty . . . . . and a canton; 2. and 3. . . . . . three hounds currant in pale Or; fig. 6.

In the chancel.
On mural monuments on the North side:
" In memory of Francis Nedham, gent.
who died September the 16th, 1786, aged 71 years;
and of Elizabeth his wife,
the daughter of Thomas Stanley, gent.
who died September the 19th, 1802, aged 79 years."

Arms: Party per fess, Argent and Ermine, a pale counterchanged; three pheons' heads Argent. Crest, upon a chapeau Gules, turned up Ermine, a pheon's head Or, between two wings Argent. *Nutt*; fig. 10.
" Near to this place
lie interred the remains of
William Nutt, esq.
late of Hornsey-lane in the county of Middlesex,
and son of Josiah and Dorothy Nutt,
of this place.
He was a father to the fatherless—
the widow and orphan felt his bounty.
He was frugal in his own expences,
that he might have the heartfelt
satisfaction of relieving others.

None could more lament his death
than his relations;
which happened on the 16th of October, 1788,
in the 64th year of his age."

On the South side, on a neat marble tablet:
" Near to this place lie the remains
of Mrs. Mary Nutt, wife of Mr. James Nutt
of this place,
who departed this life July 28, 1790,
aged 43 years.
She was a most affectionate wife,
a tender mother, and a sincere friend.
She stretched out her hand to the poor—
yea, she reached out her hand to the needy."

On flat stones:
" Here lieth interred the body of Hellen Pares,
the wife of Thomas Pares,
and daughter of Mr. Thomas Peak of Loddington,
who departed this life October the 16th, 1706,
aged 25 years.
Here also lieth the body of John the son of
Thomas and Hellen Pares,
who departed this life October 10th, 1706.
Here lies also the body of Dorothy,
the second wife of Thomas Pares,
and daughter of Mr. John Wilford of Gadsby,
who departed this life the 23d day of October, 1717,
aged 24 years.
Also John, the son of Thomas Pares
by Dorothy his wife,
died Oct. 30, 1715, aged 14 days."

" Here lieth interred the body of Mr. John Pares,
one of the aldermen, and once mayor, of this Borough,
who departed this life the 6th of September, 1712,
aged 77 years.
Here also lieth interred the body of
Mary the wife of John Pares, gent.
who departed this life February the 1st, 1728,
in the 92d year of her age."

" Here lies the body of Elizabeth
the wife of Mr. Thomas Pares,

---

[1] There used formerly to be a solemn procession from the collegiate church of St. Mary de Castro to that of St. Margaret, every Whit-Monday, in which the image of the Virgin Mary was carried under a canopy borne by four persons, with a minstrel, harp, or other musick, and twelve persons representing the twelve Apostles, each of whom had the name of the Apostle whom he represented written on parchment fixed on his bonnet; and fourteen persons bearing banners, with the virgins in the parish attending. When they came to St. Margaret's, among other oblations there were two pairs of gloves, whereof one is said to be for God, the other for St. Thomas of India. A similar procession was, on the same day, made from St. Martin's church to St. Margaret's; viz. the image of St. Martin was carried thither, with twelve persons representing the Apostles, and twelve banners, &c.; but no musick, or any canopy carried over St. Martin. And the like procession, Mr. Carte thought, was made from all the other churches in the town; but the records of them are lost. These annual processions occasioned a very broad street leading from the North Gate to this Church to be called *Sonvey*, or *Sancta via*.

[2] See under Beby, in vol. III. p. 169.

[3] See a more particular description of it under Leicester Abbey, p. 263.

and

and daughter of Mr. John Newton of Leicester,
who departed this life July 17, 1727, aged 32 years.
Also John and Anne,
son and daughter of the above-named Thomas Pares
and Elizabeth his wife.

He } died { June 17, 1727, } aged { 8 years.
She } { July 24, 1761, } { 38 years."

" Here lies interred the body of Anne
the wife of John Gwyer,
and daughter of Isaac Woollaston, esq.
of Loseby in this county,
who departed this life the 18th day of November, 1786,
aged 33 years."

" Here lieth interred the body of John Pares, gent.
one of the aldermen, and once mayor, of this Borough,
and senior of the 72 members of
this antient Corporation.
He departed this life Dec. 25, 1739, aged 74.
Here also lieth interred the body of
Mary the wife of the said John Pares, gent.
and daughter of John Orme,
of Shopnall hall in Staffordshire, gent.
She departed this life February 24, 1722, aged 49."

" Here lies the body of Deborah,
late wife of Nathaniel Norris,
daughter of Mr. John Potter, citizen of London,
and grand-daughter of Dr. John Boylston,
late rector of Bosworth.
Her piety and devotion, her charity and goodness,
her humanity and modesty,
her pleasing and innocent conversation,
as also her obliging demeanour to all sorts of people,
made her a great ornament to her sex,
and a good example to all such women as
desire to excel in virtue.
She departed this life Sept. 15, 1711, aged 32.
In the same grave lies Rebecca the daughter of
Nathaniel Norris by the said Dorothy his wife;
she died the 22d of September, 1711, aged 9 days.
Near this place lies the body of Deborah
their eldest daughter,
who died the 1st of April, 1711, aged 12 months.
As also of Rebecca Walker, late wife of Treen Walker,
of Draycut in the county of Warwick, gent.
daughter of John Shuckbrough,
of Burbury in the same county, esq.
by Anne his wife, and great-grandmother
to the last-mentioned Deborah.
She died Sept. 1, 1711, aged 92."

" Hic jacet Anna, uxor Edvardi Wigley, M. D.
quæ cum indole eximiâ, et fide erga Deum insigni, virtutum omnium feraci, innuptam ex-
ornâsset vitam : ne quid tam charæ superis
animæ deesset, omnem conjugii vicem, pietate
et studio in suos, paucis heu! annis [pro sorte
humanâ] explevit, obiit 1 Maii, A.D. 1731.
Devenit maritus, A.D. 1751."

" Here lieth interred the body of William Collins,
late of this Borough, gent.
who departed this life the 21st day of September, 1760,
in the 37th year of his age."

" Here lieth interred the body of William Gray,
citizen of London,
who departed this life the 22d day of August, 1762,
aged 64 years."

" On the 21st of November, 1796,
the body of Mary wife of Thomas Rickards of Leicester,
and daughter of David and Sarah Nutt
of Kidlington, Oxfordshire,
was consigned to mingle with its kindred clay
in this place,
inspired with humble confidence of divine acceptance.
She resigned her soul on the 13th of November, 1796,
aged 31 years.
William-Ascough Rickards, their son,
was born May the 6th; died August 11;
and was buried here August the 14th, 1787."

" In memory of Edward Davie, gent.
and Anne his wife.

He } died { Aug. 22, } 1763, aged { 56.
She } { June 20, } { 52."

Elizabeth, wife of William Goadby, Feb. 17, 1698,
aged 27.
William Goadby, Dec. 21, 1718, aged 48.
Thomas Joyce died September 1716, aged 75.
William Goadby, Feb. 11, 1717, aged 72.
Joyce Margetson, Feb. 24, 1731, aged 20.
William Foster, gent. March 19, 1757, aged 69.
Dorothy, wife of Josiah Nutt, Nov. 20, 1757,
aged 72.
William, son of James and Mary Nutt, Feb. 11,
1772, in his infancy.
James Nutt, April 17, 1775, aged 9 months.
James, son of James and Mary Nutt, Jan. 12,
1781, aged 1 year and 9 months.
Mary, wife of Abel Webster, May 11, 1784,
aged 39.
Abel Webster, Dec. 6, 1794, aged 54.

In the nave:
On flat stones:
" Here lieth the body of William Burleton,
of Wykin in this county,
doctor of laws, and barrister,
in the commission of the peace for this
and several other Counties,
and for more than 20 years Recorder
of this antient Borough.
Having acquitted himself with great reputation
in his professional, as well as in his social
and domestic character;
he died, much lamented, Nov. 12, 1786, aged 64."

Arms: In a lozenge, a lion passant guardant;
Plate XLI. fig. 11.

" Here lie the bodies of Elizabeth and Jane Tonson,
daughters of James Tonson and Jane his wife,
who was daughter of Benjamin Billers and
Jane his wife.

Elizabeth } died { Nov. 19, } 1718, } aged { 25.
Jane } { Nov. 29, } { 30."

Georgius Billers[1], generosus, Dec. 16, 1702, aged 42.
Jane his wife, July 8, 1738, aged 70. (This is on
a small brass let into the stone.)
William and Benjamin, sons of the above; Wil-
liam, Dec. 20, 1660; Benjamin, Feb. 3, 1669.
John, son of John Billers, March 26, 1694,
aged 5 months.
Mary, daughter of John Billers, May 15, 1695,
aged 8 months.
Joseph, son of John Billers, Jan. 18, 1698, aged
11 months.
Elizabeth Coulton, daughter of George and Eliza-
beth Coulton, and grand-daughter of Mr. Benjamin
Billers, March 3, 1713, aged 12.
George Coulton, son of George Coulton, late of
Osgathorpe, gent. Oct. 19, 1719, aged 51.
Elizabeth his wife, Jan. 31, 1744, aged 77.
Rev. George Coulton, Dec. 19, 1772, aged 68.
Petty Coulton, his son, 1772, aged 2.
Mary Wilson, relict of Thomas Wilson, gent.
March 18, 1745, aged 62.
John Davies, gent. Feb. 20, 1755, aged 18.
Mary, the wife of John Davies, Nov. 4, 1772,
aged 67.
Elizabeth Davies, daughter of John Davies,
April 6, 1769, aged 30.
Thomas Stanley, Jan. 8, 1756, aged 65.
John Oldfield, gent. Sept. 16, 1805, aged 66.

In the North aile.
On mural tablets:
" Inter mortis exuvias
hic propè jacet Maria Kilbye,
Johannis Kilbye hujus ecclesiæ vicarii uxor
non immeritò charissima;
liberos indulgenter dilexit;
dum amor, obsequium,

---

[1] See vol. III. p. 188, under the History of Birstall.

fides,

fides, delicias illam conjugis fecere.
Pertæsa vitæ, non timida mori,
pietatis speique plena feliciori,
vitam dolosam reliquit,
vicesimo quarto die Februarii,
anno ætatis 55, Salutis 1720."

" In the memory of Elizabeth,
the wife of Henry Temple, gent.
who died July 18, 1799, aged 24 years.
Also Elizabeth their daughter died May 13, 1799,
aged 15 months."

" Near this place are deposited the remains of
Theophilus Holmes,
who died Sept. 23, 1785, aged 34 years."

" Near this place are deposited the remains of
William Cooke, gent.
who departed this life the 19th day of June, 1784,
in the 81st year of his age.
Also of Martha, wife of William Cooke, gent.
who departed this life the 27th day of August, 1773,
in the 80th year of her age."

" Here lieth the body of James Sloane,
of Gough-square in the city of London, gentleman ;
who departed this life May 19, 1754, aged 54 years.
And also Susanna his wife, who died the 18th of
December 1755, aged 52 years."

Arms : Argent, two bars Gules ; in chief a lion
passant guardant of the second ; a crescent for difference : Impaling, Gules, a sword in bend Or ; over
it a demi-negro proper.   Plate XLI. fig. 12.
" In memory of Katharine, wife of the
Reverend Robert Burnaby, LL.B.
many years vicar and prebendary of this church,
rector of Wanlip, and an acting magistrate
for this County.
She was the only daughter of the late
Thomas Jee, esq. of this town ;
and died March 22, 1795, in the 54th year of her age.
Also in memory of Robert Burnaby,
attorney at law, their second son,
who died April 12, 1795,
in the 29th year of his age.
Also of Andrew, Sarah, Andrew, Katharine,
and Katharine,
their children, who died in their infancy.
The Reverend Robert Burnaby, LL.B.
died April 2, 1807, in the 69th year of his age."

On flat stones :
" Near this place lieth Thomas Bocherton, gent.
and Frances his wife."

John Cogan, surgeon, March 4, 1763, aged 36.
Arthur Richards, gent. Oct. 17, 1774, aged 43.
Joseph Smith, June 2, 1737, aged 46.
Sarah Holmes, wife of William Holmes, May 26,
1752, aged 35.
William Holmes, March 28, 1770, aged 56.
Henry, son of Thomas Palmer, May 29, 1744,
aged 7.
Agnes, the wife of Thomas Palmer, Aug. 19, 1757,
aged 47.
Ellis Shipley, Sept. 6, 1775, aged 73.
Elizabeth, wife of Ellis Shipley, Sept. 27, 1761,
aged 57.
Dorothy Armston, widow of Joseph Smith, and
relict of John Armston, March 27, 1742, aged 58.

On mural tablets at the West end of the North
aile :
Anne, daughter of William and Edith Capp,
July 31, 1771, in her infancy.
Edith, the wife of William Capp, June 6, 1782,
aged 44.

John, son of Anthony and Esther Topham, Jan. 7,
1770, aged 26.
Anthony, son of Anthony and Esther Topham,
Sept. 28, 1780, aged 40.
Esther, wife of Anthony Topham, Feb. 28, 1780,
aged 70.
Anthony Topham, Jan. 3, 1788, aged 86.

In the South aile, on mural tablets.

On an atchievement :
Argent, two bars, and in chief three mullets Sable, pierced of the field ; impaling, Or, on a chevron, between three leopards' faces Gules, three trefoils Argent.   Crest, a demi-hound, couped Sable,
collared Argent.   *Major* ; Plate XXXIX. fig. 7.

On a monument under this atchievement :
Major ; impaling, Gules, a fleur de lis Or, and
a chief Ermine ; fig. 8.
" Mariæ uxoris Antonii Major [1], generosi,
quod in terris reliquum est, vicino requi-
escit pulvere, pientissimæ, viz. animæ non
indignum domicilium ; quod ut meliori po-
tiretur, libentissimè resignavit, quarto die
Septembris, anno Domini 1649, ætatis
suæ 26.
" *Maria Major.*"
Anagramma,
" *Jam Ira Amor* [2]."
Now Anger's chang'd to Love ; now Death, which is
The Wage of Sin, becomes the way to bliss.
See what the soveraigne vertue of Christ's blood
Can do, make Crosses Crownes, and Poyson food."

On a slate in the South-east aile :
" Hic jacet corpus Thomæ Major . . . .
Major et Janæ uxor ejus, filia Gulielmi
Farmer, ... juxta hoc monumentum
. . . . . . [*The rest obliterated.*]
On a white stone, with the arms of *Major* (fig. 7.) :
" Sub hoc saxo deposita sunt corpora Joannis
Major, generosi, et Janæ uxoris ejus.   Ille
obiit 12 die Aprilis, anno Dom. 1661, ætatis
suæ 60.   Hæc 11 die Aprilis, anno Dom.
1676, ætatis suæ 78."
Round the margin :
" Here lieth interr'd the bodie of Willam Farmer,
. . . ." [*The rest obliterated.*]
On another atchievement :
Major ; impaling, Vert, a chevron, and in chief
three escalops Or ; fig. 9.
On a flat stone :
" Joh'es Major, Joh'is filius . . . ."
On a brass plate let into the stone :
" . . . . Siste, Viator.
. . . . Legas, ne lugeas, quæso.   Hic
Susanna Major, relicta Johan. Major, armi-
geri, ad pedes viri sui charissimi jacet, quem
vivum et mortuum observandum novit ; annos viduitatis egit tres ; et tandem vitâ hac
fragili prudenter piè et religiosè consummatâ
in vitam sempiternam migravit, decimo nono
die Martii, anno Dom. 1705, ætatis 28."
Under the above :
" Formâ magnus ; nomine
major ; maximus jure.
. . . è scalâ nitidis scandit
. . . . . och superis
. . . . . ite nitidis."

" Here lieth interred the body of John Newton senior,
who departed this life the 15th of December, 1739,
in the 67th year of his age.

[1] Extracts from St. Margaret's Register :

1628. Thomas Major, filius Johannis Major gen', bapt. fuit 4º die Januarii.
1696. John, son of John Major, esq. baptized Jan. 4.
1698. Jane, daughter of John Major, esq. baptized May 9.
1718. John, son of John Major, esq. born June 21, baptized July 7.

1649. Mary wife of Anthony Major, Feb. 21.
1661. John Major senior, April 14.
1677. Antonius Major, verè pius et generosus, sepultus 19º Januarii.
1679. Gabriel Major, Evangelii Minister, sepultus 29º Junii.
1716. Mr. John Major and Mrs. Catharine Byrd, marr. Oct. 8.

[2] Though anagrams are commonly elaborate trifles, yet there is a singular and edifying quaintness in the sententious import of the above, especially when collated with the English paraphrase that attends it.   W. B.
Also

Also Elizabeth his wife departed this life
Jan. 17, 1747, aged 85 years."

" Here lieth interred the body of John Newton junior,
who departed this life the 18th day of May, 1742,
in the 46th year of his age."

" Here lie interred the bodies of
John and William Newton,
sons of John Newton junior by Mary his wife.
William departed this life May the 18th, 1749,
in the 22d year of his age;
John died July the 30th, 1749, aged 30 years."

" In memory of James Bishop,
one of the aldermen of this Borough,
who served the office of mayor in the year 1782,
and died Aug. 18, 1803, in the 79th year of his age.
Also of Hannah his wife, who died June 15, 1797,
in the 78th year of her age."

" To the memory of Mrs. Sarah Bishop,
wife of Mr. William Bishop,
who died the 23d day of September, 1787,
in the 32d year of her age."

" To the memory of John-Peter Allemand,
who died Jan. 19, 1789, aged 45 years."

" In a vault near this place are deposited
the remains of Mr. Samuel Miles,
late of this Borough.
He departed this life the 9th day of June,
in the year of our Lord 1798,
and in the 54th year of his age.
In the same vault are deposited six of his children."

Arms : Argent, a chevron between three foxes'
heads, erased Gules; fig. 11.
" Sacred to the memory of John Fox, surgeon.
His conduct in domestic life endeared him
to his family; and his professional merit
gained him the esteem of all with whom
his practice connected him.
He departed this life July 5, 1787,
aged 59 years.
Also near this place are deposited the
remains of Jane Fox, one of the daughters
of the above John Fox.　She departed
this life Nov. 6, 1785, aged 26 years."

On flat stones :
William Stretton, Nov. 20, 1691, aged 65.
Richard Mansfield, Nov. 27, 1699, aged 29.
Robert, son of Robert Norton, Jan. 30, 1723.
William Borrows, Sept. 9, 1726, aged 59.
Mr. Robert Norton, Feb. 1, 1737, aged 47.
Jane, wife of John Berridge, Dec. 21, 1737,
aged 37.
George Blaksley, June 29, 1739, aged 69.
Hannah, the wife of Samuel Hutchinson, June 18,
1741, aged 50.
Matthew Linwood, Feb. 28, 1783, aged 56.
Samuel Markland, March 12, 1805, aged 46.

Under the organ-loft :
" William, son of the Rev. William Sparrow, M. A.
vicar of Diseworth, and Sarah his wife,
born Dec. 12, 1777, died July 12, 1788."

" Anthony Ward, June 21, 1765, aged 65.
Also the body of Anne, wife of Henry Ward,
Sept. 21, 1779, aged 40.
She was a good Christian, a sincere companion,
and met with calm intrepidity the stroke of Death.

To thee my gently drooping head I bend;
Thy sigh, my husband, and thy tear, my friend;
On thee I muse, and in thy hast'ning sun,
See life expiring ere 'tis well begun.
The Angels call—they call me from above,
And bid me hasten to the realms of love;
My soul with transport hears the happy doom;
I come, ye gentle Messengers, I come."

" Mary, daughter of Robert Bree, M. D.
and Elizabeth his wife,
died Nov. 26, 1792, aged 2 years."

On a monument against the South-west wall :
" Near this place are deposited the remains of
Elizabeth the wife of John Miles,

one of the aldermen of this Borough,
and daughter of the late John Hickman,
of Tinkwood Hall in Cheshire, gent.
She died Jan. 30, 1772, in the 57th year of her age.
She was an amiable pattern of
conjugal virtues, and of maternal
tenderness.　How great then the loss
of her surviving son and husband!"

At the West end of the church :
" D. O. M.
Here lie the remains of Mr. John Farmer, attorney at law, solicitor of this Corporation,
whose integrity in his profession, humanity of
temper, easiness of address, and extensive charity, gained the hearts of all who knew him
alive, and drew tears from their eyes when
dead; but from none more abundant and sincere, than his afflicted wife Isabella, daughter
and coheir of Thomas Levinge, of Shepey, esq.
who, at her own costs and charges, inclosed
this ground [1], and erected this monument, a
token of her conjugal love, and a resting-place
for herself and family.　He departed this life
the 17th day of June, in the year of our Lord
1737, aged 54 years."

" Here also lie the remains of Isabella, wife of the
said John Farmer, of Leicester, gent. and daughter of the late Thomas Levinge, of Shepey in
the county of Leicester, esq.
She departed this life Nov. 16, anno Domini 1764.
Here also is interred Isabella Burrell,
daughter of the above John and Isabel Farmer.
She departed this life June 28, 1755, aged 27.

Mortal, gaze on!　Still as you gaze,
Let this be your instruction;
That, like a plant, God did you raise;
Earth was your chief production.
One blooming plant lies wither'd here,
Admir'd by all who'd seen her:
Death cropt its stem, by God's command,
To grace our dear Redeemer."

" To the memory of William Farmer,
son of John Farmer by Isabella his wife.
He died Nov. 17, 1758, aged 26 years.
Here rests benevolence in manly youth,
Complacent manners, and ingenuous truth;
With filial piety and social join'd
Unshaken constancy, to fate resign'd :
If to his share some human errors fell,
Ask your own breast where does perfection dwell?"

" Here lyeth the body of Mary Miles,
wife of alderman Miles,
and daughter of John Pares, gent.
She departed this life July 24, 1759, aged 67."

In the church, under the tower :
" Here lieth interred the body of Jane,
the daughter of Anthony Ward by Alice his wife,
who departed this life the 7th day of May, 1757,
in the 13th year of her age.
Hark, from the tombs a doleful sound;
My ear, attend the cry:
You living men, come view the ground
Where you must shortly lie.
Princess, this clay must be your bed,
In spite of all your towers:
The tall, the wise, the reverend head,
Must lie as low as ours."

At the West end, against the tower :
" Sacred to the memory of John Mansfield, esq.
who died Sept. 24, 1798, aged 59.

If feelings just, which unconstrain'd expand
With genuine ardour warm from Nature's hand;
A heart that glow'd each selfish thought above,
With social kindness, and parental love;
A public spirit, lib'ral, unconfin'd,
The World his circle, and his friends Mankind;
If such may justly claim the hallow'd tear,
Let faithful Memory drop the tribute here."

A public

" In memory of Elizabeth Cotchett,
daughter of Thomas and Elizabeth Cotchett;
she died Nov. 25, 1793,
aged 5 years and 4 months."

On atchievements:
1. Or, a chevron Ermine, between three olive-leaves Vert, *Hesilrige*; impaling, Sable, on a chev-ron between three lamps Argent, fire Or, three mullets Sable; *Farmer*; Plate XXXIX. fig. 12.

2. Quarterly: 1. and 4. *Farmer*; 2. and 3. Vert, a chevron Or; in chief three escalop-shells; *Levinge*. Crest, a cubit arm couped proper, holding a lamp as before. Plate XLI. fig. 13.

3. *Farmer;* impaling *Levinge.* Pl.XXXIX.fig.13.

In the church-yard.

A splendid monument, adorned on the North and South sides with military trophies, beautifully carved in slate, and containing at the West end the following inscription, is hastening rapidly to decay:

Arms: Argent, a chevron between three boars' heads erased Azure. Crest, on a wreath, a stag's head couped proper. Supporters, two stags of the last. Motto, *La Fortune passe par tout.* Pl. XLI. fig. 14.

" Here are deposited, by his express desire, the remains of the Right Honourable
ANDREW Lord ROLLO, a Scots peer, who betaking himself, though late, to
a military life, soon became distinguished by the exertion of every talent which
constitutes the spirited commander, the humane officer, and compleat gentleman.
As lieutenant-colonel-commandant, he embarked with the 22d regiment
in the year 1756 for North America, from whence, after a series of the
severest and most dangerous services, in the year 1761, as brigadier-general,
he was detached by General Amherst, to reduce the island of Dominique,
with 700 men, which he happily effected.
He soon after shared in the siege of Martinique, where he lost his
only son, a youth of the most promising hopes, who had served the
Generals Amherst and Monkton as brigade-major. He afterwards landed
at the Havannah, where he served at the head of a brigade, till within
ten days of the reduction of Port Moro, when the pressure of present duty,
the fatigues of past services, a broken constitution, and the importunity of
his General and Physicians, obliged him to retire. He died at Leicester [1]
the 2d of June, 1765, in the 61st year of his age, on his way to Bristol, where
he had been advised to go for the recovery of his health."

On altar-tombs:
" Here lieth the body of James Annis,
one of the aldermen of this Borough,
and once mayor.
He died the 18th day of October, 1719, aged 69.
Here lieth the body of Martha,
the wife of James Annis, one of the aldermen of
this Borough, and once mayor.
She died Nov. 5, 1719, aged 46.
Here lieth the body of James Annis, gent. their son,
who departed this life Aug. 2, 1733, aged 28."

" In certain hopes of a happy resurrection,
here are deposited the remains of Catherine,
daughter of John and Mary Palmer,
who, after supporting a long and painful decline
with patience, resignation, and Christian fortitude,
departed this life April 20, 1778, aged 26.
Early thy life of pilgrimage is run,
Thy business on this earthly stage is done.
Stern Death, who levels all that's form'd of clay,
Of thy fair blossoms made an easy prey:
Easy indeed; for like a lamb you went,
And full as innocent your life was spent.
Content and thankfulness, those gifts divine,
With meekness, mildness, patience, all were thine;
Strict filial duties were thy constant guide,
For in such virtues was thy only pride.
Death, whose grim aspect frightens each degree,
Had yet no terrors that could frighten thee:
E'en Death itself left on thy face a smile,
Expressive of, ' Farewell, my friends, awhile!'
What shall we say, if Heaven's to thee not kind?
What must become of us who stay behind?
All doubts forbear; thou'rt now at peace and rest,
And with thy kindred Saints supremely blest.
Reader, whoe'er thou art, to die prepare;
To live hereafter be thy constant care."

On upright stones:
" Here lieth the body of John Roberts, gent.
twice mayor of this Borough.
He died April 17, 1705, aged 75;
and Elizabeth his wife died Nov. 14, 1696, aged 71."

" William Heaford departed this life June 9, 1723,
in the 19th year of his age.
In swimming I my pleasure oft have sought:
By sinking, I to sudden death was brought.
*Oh! that they were wise, that they would consider
their latter end!*"

" Here lieth interred the body of William Spencer,
who departed this life the 2d of March,
in the year of our Lord 1763,
in the 47th year of his age.
Farewell, my friends of every kind:
Imprint this lesson on your mind;
In time you all must sleep in dust,
Until the rising of the just.
Dear wife, prepare 'gainst that great day!"

" In memory of John Bass, esq.
who departed this life Nov. 8, 1764, aged 69."

" In memory of Alice Newbery.
She died Feb. 13, 1777, aged 61 years."

" In sure and certain hope of a happy resurrection,
lie the remains of Martha,
wife of John Dalby of this parish.
She departed this life on the 29th of August, 1781,
aged 41 years.
Being early instructed in the true principles
of Religion,
she did not depend on her own perfections,
but on the merits and redemption of a blessed Saviour,
for a joyful and happy resurrection.
Also two of their children, Mary and Samuel,
who both died in their infancy."

On an elegant marble monument:
" John, Ann, and Mary-Ann,
children of John and Mary Mansfield,
died in their infancy.
Sacred to the memory of Mary Mansfield,
wife of John Mansfield, gent.
She died Oct. 31, 1787, aged 43 years."

" Near this stone are deposited the remains of
John Brooke, esq.
of Withybrooke, in the county of Warwick;
who, during the period of life allotted to him
by Providence,
acquired much various and useful knowledge;
united great elegance of manners with
a correct and discriminating taste;
and was deservedly esteemed by those who knew him.
He maintained a long, but ineffectual struggle
with the infirmities of a feeble constitution;
and at length died in this Borough, May 14, 1795,
in the 36th year of his age.
This stone is placed to perpetuate his memory by
one of his surviving friends."

[1] At the Three Crowns Inn, then kept by Mr. James Bishop.

A grave-

A grave-stone of curious workmanship [1], by Mr. William Firmadge of Leicester, is thus inscribed:

" In memory of Elizabeth, wife of John Ireland,
who died March 26, 1804, aged 83 years.
In hopes of a joyful resurrection,
here rest the remains of John Ireland,
who departed this life Sept. 7, 1776, aged 60."

" Here lieth the body of Mr. Robert Newton,
attorney at law ;
who married the 4th daughter of George Ashley, esq.
deceased, and had by her 4 sons and 9 daughters.
He died Feb. 1, 1737, aged 47."

" Here lie the remains of Mary Tansley, who,
after living 40 years in the service of William Cooke,
of this parish, gent. departed this life
the 2d of May, 1784, in the 61st year of her age.
The memory of the just is blessed."

" In memory of Samuel Oliver, esq.
one of the aldermen, and twice mayor, of this Borough.

He died June 19, 1787, aged 72 years.
Margaret Oliver died Aug. 15, 1764, aged 48:
Thomas-Bass Oliver, gent.
son of the late Samuel Oliver and Margaret,
died June 13, 1790, aged 40."

In Plate XLI. are given three Official Seals.

The Seal of the Prebendary of St. Margaret's ; containing the Arms of the See of *Lincoln*; impaling, Quarterly, Or and Sable, a cross moline quarterly countercharged. *Taylor*; fig. 7.

The Seal of Edward Taylor, LL. B. Official of the Archdeaconry of Leicester 1771 ; fig. 8.

The Seal of the same Gentleman as Commissary of the Archdeaconry 1771 ; fig. 9.

Both these contain the Arms of the See of *Lincoln*; impaling, Gules, a chevron Or, between three crescents Ermine ; *Geary*.

Fig. 10. represents an old Key, found in digging a grave in St. Margaret's church-yard in November 1793.

The BISHOP'S FEE.

The antient Lords of Leicester were the Earls of Mercia and the Bishops [2].

Remigius de Fescamp Bishop of *Lincoln*, at the time of the general survey, in 1066, held ten plough-lands in Leicester. He had five ploughs in demesne; and a mill and a half of ten shillings and eight pence value ; and two churches, of the value of fifteen shillings ; and seventeen burgesses, who paid thirty-two pence yearly. From one part of the land in the Suburbs *(extra murum)* he had five shillings and four pence ; and three villans, with a priest and twelve bordars, had four ploughs. He had also twenty acres of meadow [3].

In an Inquisition taken in 1279, this district is thus noticed :

" Leicestrie Suburbium, extra Portam Orientalem in hundredo de Gartre. Episcopus Lincolnie tenet in dictó suburbio duas carucatas terre de domino rege in eleemosynâ, et habet regale, & mensuram panis et cervisie, et mensuram villenagii.

Willielmus Touke octavas virgatas terre, de quibus sex tenentur de heredibus Wintonie et heredes de rege in capite ; et alie due virgate terre de Abbate Leicestrie, et ipse de comite Leicestrie, et comes de rege. Et non dat scutagium.

Et Thomas Coste in quinque virgatas terre de predicto Episcopo, et episcopus de rege in eleemosynâ.

Et sunt in dicto Suburbio viginti messuagia ; tenentur de Episcopo Lincolnie, et episcopus de rege in eleemosynam [4]."

In the subsidies of 1416 and 1445, the district called *The Suburbs of Leicester*, in *the Hundred of Gartre*, was assessed at 1*l.* 16*s.*

" The manor which the Bishops had lay in the Suburbs on the East side of the town in the parish of St. Margaret, and in Knighton, containing of old 32 houses and two churches. It is still called *The Bishop's Fee, and remains out of the jurisdiction of the town, though attempts were made in the reigns of Edward VI. and Queen Elizabeth to have it united to, and reduced under, the government of it ; but without effect* [5]. The Bishops made the parsonage of St. Margaret a prebend of *Lincoln*; and the manor remained in them in 1138, as appears by a bull of Pope Innocent III. [6] dated 4 cal. of May in that year, confirming it to Alexander the then Bishop and his successors. But it was very soon after this tranferred to the Earl of *Leicester*, in exchange for the manor of Westcotes, and other lands in Estfordeby and Segrave, under the title of the manor of Cuihinton, or Knighton (as appears by Mon. Angl. vol. II. p. 315) ; and by *Robert Bossu*, founder of the abbey, was given to the monks there ; and does now belong to the Duke of *Devonshire*. The rest of the Town and Suburbs belonged to the Earl of Mercia before the Conquest [7]."

A case was argued in the Court of King's Bench, May 19, 1789, *Blankley* against *Winstanley* and *Burnaby*, on an action of trespass and false imprisonment against the defendants, who were justices of the peace for the County of Leicester, " for causing the plaintiff to be apprehended and sent to the house of correction by virtue of a warrant issued by them, they not having any jurisdiction over *The Bishop's Fee* in the said county, inasmuch as it is within and under the exclusive jurisdiction of the magistrates of the Borough of Leicester, and not under the jurisdiction of the justices of the County. Plea, *Not guilty*." A special verdict had been found on this case at the preceding assizes for the County of Leicester ; which stated the Borough of Leicester to be an antient Borough and body corporate, &c. ; and, after citing several of the charters, stated the trespass to have been committed within the parish of St. Margaret, commonly called *The Bishop's Fee*, &c. The point on which the question turned was, " Whether the charter of Elizabeth, referring to former charters, has granted an exclusive jurisdiction to the Borough Magistrates over *The Bishop's Fee*, or only a concurrent jurisdiction with the County Justices?" By the determination of the Court for the defendants, the jurisdiction of course becomes concurrent [8].

In Nº 22. of Decrees, &c. of Queen Elizabeth, Trin. 26 Eliz. fol. 53. b. the Queen's manor of Leicester is called *The Bishop's Fee*.

" Henricus Harington, miles, tenet manerium de Bishop's Fee, alias manerium Leicestrie, de rege, ut de honore de Hampton-court [9]."

In 1613 sir *Richard Morison* was cited, to shew by what title he held the manor called *The Bishop's Fee* [10].

There are several places in or about the town which are out of the franchises or liberties of it ; viz. the Castle and Newark toward the South-west, the Bishop's Fee on the East, Abbey-gate and Wood-gate beyond the North bridges, and Braunston-gate, *alias* Bruntingsthorp, on the West side of the town.

---

[1] The prominent figure on this stone is Death presenting a globe to a sick man in bed.

[2] By the Bishops, is meant the Bishop of Lincoln for the time being. At the time of the Domesday Survey, Remigius de Fescamp, the then Bishop, held ten carucates of land in Leicester, with two churches, and other large possessions ; among which, he had land " extra murum, tres bordarii, cum presbytero, et 12 bordarii." The Archbishop of York had two houses at th t time in Leicester (with several carucates of land in Gartre Hundred), the abbey of Coventry ten, the abbey of Croyland three ; Hugo de Grentesmainell had two churches, and nearly 200 houses ; and many individuals and townships were owners of houses here.

[3] " Episcopus Lincolniensis tenet in Ledecestre 10 carucatas terræ. In dominico habet ibi 5 carucas ; et molinum et dimidium de 10 solidis et 8 denariis ; et 2 ecclesias de 15 solidis ; et 17 burgenses, 32 denarios per annum reddentes. De unâ parte terræ extra murum habet 5 solidos et 4 denarios ; et 3 villani, cum presbytero et 12 bordarii, habent 6 carucas. Ibi 30 acræ prati." Domesday, fol. 230. b. 2.

[4] Inq. 7 Edw. I.   [5] This, I am told, is ill-founded. The Bishop's Fee was always in some measure subject to the Borough magistrates.

[6] Mon. Angl. vol. III. p. 269.   [7] Carte, MS.

[8] See the whole case in Durnford and East's Reports, Easter Term, 1789, p. 279.

[9] Esch. 7 Jac. I.   [10] Trin. Rec. 10 Jac. I. Rot. 173.

SAINT MARTIN'S.

The statistical particulars in this page are extracted from the late Sir Frederick Morton Eden's valuable Publication " On the State of the Poor."

" St. *Michael's* consists entirely of buildings. In 1792, it contained 565 inhabited houses, and about 2825 souls. 520 houses pay the window-tax: very few are exempted, as the parish is situated in the centre of the town, and principally consists of good houses. The land-tax is about 10*d.* in the pound.

A considerable manufacture of worsted stockings is carried on here. Stocking-weavers earn from 7*s.* to 1*l.* 1*s.* a-week; wool-combers, from 9*s.* to 12*s.* a-week; worsted-spinners, from 4*d.* to 8*d.* a-day; agricultural labourers at present (1795) receive 1*s.* 6*d.* a-day, with victuals.

The prices of provisions in 1795 were, beef, 4½*d.* the pound; mutton, 5*d.*; veal, 4½*d.*; butter, 10½*d.* or 1*s.* the pound; bread, 1lb. 11oz. for 6*d.*; milk, 1¼*d.* the quart, short measure.

In the town of Leicester there are now (1792) 143 public-houses; of which, 40 are inns; and 14 Friendly Societies, of which 3 are in this parish: almost all have had their rules confirmed by the magistrates. These institutions are much liked here, and are increasing in number very rapidly.

The poor of this parish are farmed by a man who receives from the parish 14*l.* a-week, or 728*l.* a-year. There are 42 persons (principally old women and children) at present under his care: some out-poor receive 4*l.* 11*s.* a-week. The farmer is a stocking-manufacturer, and employs the poor in spinning worsted, &c.: they work, in the summer, from 6 o'clock in the morning till 8 at night; and, in winter, from 7 in the morning till 9 at night; the time of meals excepted. The house is not well situated, nor aired in the best manner, but appears to be kept very clean: the beds are of flocks, and much infested with bugs. A woman teaches the children to read and spin. In cases of bastardy, the farmer does not take care of such as were not chargeable, or not born before his agreement with the parish. His agreement is renewed annually.

Table of Diet in the Poor-house.

	Breakfast.	*Dinner.*	*Supper.*
Sunday—	Milk-pottage, or gruel.	Broth, meat, and vegetables.	Bread, cheese, and Beer.
Monday—	Broth and bread.	Cold meat, vegetables, and beer.	Ditto.
Tuesday—	As Sunday.	As Sunday.	Ditto.
Wednesday—	As Monday.	As Monday.	Ditto.
Thursday—	As Sunday.	As Sunday.	Ditto.
Friday—	As Monday.	As Monday.	Ditto.
Saturday—	Milk-pottage.	Bread, cheese, and beer.	Ditto.

About 16*l.* a-year, from different donations, are annually distributed among the poor of this parish. There are in Leicester five Hospitals, in which there are usually about 200 poor.

The war has had no other effect upon the manufacturers of this town than by taking off a great number of hands: several soldiers' families of course became burdensome.

The manufactures of Leicester are sent to different parts of the kingdom, and to America.

Baptisms, Burials, and Marriages, in St. Martin's parish [1].

	Baptisms.			Burials.			
	Males.	Fema.	Total.	Males.	Fema.	Total.	Marr.
1680 [2]	—	—	54	—	—	63	—
1685	—	—	53	38	29	67	—
1690	—	—	62	15	19	34	—
1691	—	—	54	27	18	45	—
1692	—	—	55	20	21	41	—
1693	—	—	56	17	24	41	—
1694	—	—	53	21	19	40	—
1695	—	—	44	34	31	65	—
1696	—	—	56	30	21	51	—
1697	—	—	44	14	28	42	—
1698	—	—	46	23	20	43	—
1699	—	—	58	17	19	36	—
1700	—	—	62	32	21	53	—
1720	30	25	55	39	26	65	—
1740	28	29	57	29	27	56	—

Baptisms, from 1680 to 1700 inclusive, } 590—Yearly average, $53\frac{7}{11}$.

Ditto, from 1775 to 1794 inclusive, } 1629—Yearly average, $81\frac{9}{20}$.

Burials, from 1680 to 1700 inclusive, } 491—Yearly average, $47\frac{7}{11}$.

Ditto, from 1775 to 1794 inclusive, } 1422—Yearly average, $71\frac{2}{20}$.

Money for repairing bridges, &c. called Borough rates, is paid out of the poor's rates: it was generally about 70*l. per annum;* but now amounts to 200*l.* and upwards, in consequence of the floods last winter having carried away several bridges."

[1] Every parish in the town supports its own poor separately. The rates in the other parishes, it is said, are on an average nearly similar to those in this parish; some are a little higher, and some a little lower.—The following is an account, given by a wool-comber, of his earnings and expences. He is 50 years old; has a wife and two sons, the eldest 13, the youngest 9 years of age:

	£.	s.	d.
The man earns on an average 9*s.* a-week; annually	23	8	0
The oldest boy serves a bricklayer; he earns about 4*s.* 6*d.* a-week in winter, and 2*s.* a-week in summer, upon an average 3*s.* 6*d.* a-week; annually	8	9	0
The woman earns, by spinning and seaming stockings, 1*s.* 6*d.* a-week; annually — —	3	18	0
Total earnings of the family — —	35	15	0
In bread, 3*s.* a-week before the present scarcity; at present 7*s.* a-week: the former sum amounts annually to — — — — —	7	16	0

		£.	s.	d.
10 lb. of butcher's meat weekly, at 3*d.* the lb.	}	6	10	0
Potatoes and vegetables, 1*s.* 6*d.* weekly -		3	18	0
Milk, 2*d.* a-day — — —		3	1	4
Ale and beer, about 1*s.* 6*d.* weekly —	} Annually.	3	18	0
Butter, 2lb. weekly, at 9*d.* the lb. —		3	18	0
Cheese, 3½ lb. weekly, at 6*d.* the lb. —		4	11	0
Tea, sugar, &c. weekly about 1*s.* 6*d.* —		3	18	0
Clothes and fuel, estimated at — — —		6	0	0
House-rent — — — —		3	18	0
Total annual expences —		47	8	4
Deduct earnings —		35	15	0
Deficiency —		11	13	4

This account, it is probable, is erroneous in some particulars; for the man has not lately received any assistance from the parish. He stated his various expences with every appearance of veracity. That he does not earn more than 9*s.* a-week, in a place where wages are high, is easily accounted for; he often spends two or three days in the week in an ale-house, lamenting the hardness of the times. Some inferences may be drawn from this account respecting the proportion of the different kinds of food used by people of this description in manufacturing towns. The improvidence of the family is glaring: not a sixpence is laid by to provide against sickness or old age; and it is probable, that the temporary incapacity arising from the one, or the inevitable effects of the other, will ultimately throw them on the parish.—F. M. E. *August,* 1795.

[2] It appears, from an old parish book, that in the year 1677 a rate of 1½*d.* in the pound was raised for the maintenance of the poor. Houses in this parish are usually assessed at about two-thirds of the net rent.

EXTRACTS, taken by Mr. CARTE and Mr. THROSBY, from the CHURCHWARDENS ACCOMPTS.

ANNO 1489.

Rec' pro oblatione in die Dedicationis 4s. 8d.

   Assumptionis B. Marie 3s. 4d.

   Omnium Sanctorum 5s. 5d.

   Nativitatis Domini 7s.

   Paschæ 12s. 8d.

N. B. On the same days, besides the oblations, they had also gathering for the church works.

See the book in 1499; and in 1512 it is expressed, " ad opus fabricæ ecclesiæ."

See the years 1493, 1495, 1506, 1571, 1577.

Et tunc (scil' ad Nativitatem Domini) parochiani concesserunt sedibus faciendis in navi ecclesiæ, quâlibet die Dominicâ, quilibet secundùm pietatem suam, viz. 2s. 1d. ob. quª. ut habetur in libro inde scripto. Here follows an account of the sums collected every Lord's-day from Christmas till Midsummer. And in the following year,

Solut' Thomæ Walker campanistæ, pro suo quarterio, 10d.; and so quarterly.

Solut' Johanni Nicoll carpentario, pro sedibus 10s. & 10s. & 10s. & 13s. 4d.; and so the following years.

Tegulario, pro emendatione capellæ Beatæ Annæ, 17d.

Willielmo Wells, pro cerâ ad altum Crucifixum in navi ecclesiæ, 2s. 10d.

Pro 6 libris Calendariorum ad Natale Domini 6d.

Pro funiculo pro stellâ 1d. ob.

Paid for three ells of cloth to make a rochet for the clerk, and making, 2s. 1d. ob.

1490, 1491.

Paid for two load of clay, to mend between the Vestry and St. Anne's chapel, and workmanship, 12d.

Paid to a man to keep the church, in the vacation of a clerk, for four weeks, 2s.

Mr. Mayor's pew made.

Paid for making St. George's candlestick 2s. 2d.

For painting the Vestry and St. Anne's chapel 6s. 10d.

1492.

Paid to the players on New-year's day at even in the church 6d.

For mending the silver candlestick 20d.

For keeping the Sepulchre and . . . . the long altar 8d. to the clerk.

For a key for the torch coffer 2d.

1493.

At Christmas, they paid, for holly and ivy, ob. 1493; 1d. 1494; 2d. 1495; and so other years.

They spent 13 pounds of candles in the church 13d. 1495; 14d. ob. 1498.

They spent 15 pounds of tallow candles 20d. 1521.

In Henry Seventh's time they had often church ales; but they seem to be left off in Henry Eighth's time.

1495.

At Easter, for the rood-light 20d.

At the procession to St. Margaret's on Whitmonday, they received yearly 6d. 1495.

The treat in 1495 was,

In bread 6d.; 1513, 16d.

In ale 11d.; 1498, 20d.; 1515, 18d.

Flesh 9d.

N. B. For many years there was constantly a calf.

1498.

Received of the church ale the first day, i. e. on Sunday next after the Assumption, 17s. 5d.

Item, on our Lady's Assumption 2s. 7d. ob.

Paid for bread to the church ale, and flesh, 4s.

Item, bread on our Lady day Assumption 2d.

Received of the church ale holden of St. Bartholomew's even 38s. 1d.

In 1499, they had at the church ale powdered beef 2s. and cheese 10d.

There were 12 Apostles, 14 banner bearers, and 4 that bear up the canopy, each allowed 1d. for their labour, 1523; but other years they used to be feasted, and nothing given them. They had musick went before the Mary, sometimes a harp, for which paid 4d. 1507; 2d. 1523; a minstrel 2d. 1515.

With these virgins went in procession; spent on them 3d. 1518.

N. B. The Apostles names were wrote on parchment, for which paid 4d. 1499. They used to spend, in points 1d.; tucking-strings and whipcord 2d.; gloves, 2 pair, 2d. which, 1505, are said to be for God and St. Thomas of India[1], but there were three pair for two ladds and St. Thomas of India 1515.

1507.

Paid for a day's work, mending all the red copes of silk, 4d.

Item, a day's work, mending the red suit of velvet, 4d.

Item, two days work, mending the Trinity banner and the great streamer of silk, 10d.

1512.

In 1513, a calf 2s. 4d.; three calves heads and a yew 8d.

In 1525, a calf, &c. 3s. 8d.; and for the breakfast three calves' heads and two plucks.

Id. and half a calf 9d. &c. &c.

Dressing, fire, and other things, 4d.

In 1513, spice 1d. ob. and at other times.

1544.

For burials with bells paid, for three bells 8d.; four bells 20d.; five bells 5s. 4d. In 1550 it was 3s. 4d.; 1555, it was 5s. 4d. again.

At obits, whether of the gilde or others, was paid, for three bells 8d.; four bells 20d.; five bells 4s.

Item, for the burial of sir Robert Cowper, five bells 5s. 4d.

Received, for my lord Huntingdon's obit of a garden given to the town, of Edmund Couper, 2s. 4d.

Paid sir William Boroughs quarterly for the clock and chimes 8d.

Robert Sexton, quarterly, 2s. 8d.

Francis Clarke, quarterly, 1s. 4d.; 1546, 2s.

For keeping the clock and chimes, Thomas Skipton, quarterly, 8s. 4d. 1553; 2s. 2d. for ringing the day bell.

Paid to Robert Gouldsmith, for mending a chalice belonging to St. George's chapel, and a pix, 1s. 4d.

For the two-pound candle for the lanthorn in the church 2d. ob.

To Robert Crofte, for a day's work at the storehouse, 5d.

To the plumber, for a day's work on our Lady's chapel, 7d.

For the procession at St. Margaret's on Whitmonday, to the vicar, priests, and clerks, 1s. 1d.

For bread and ale that day 1s.

To the sumners at St. Margaret's for the offering 8d.

For other charges at the procession on Whit-monday 10s.

Paid on Palm Sunday to the Prophete . . . . and for ale at the reading the passh'on 2d.

Paid to two poor women for scouring the eagle of brass, the candlestick, and holy-water stop, 1s. 10d. ob.

[1] The Saxon Chronicle, speaking of Alfred, in the year 883, p. 86: " And eac on Indea to S'te Thome and to S'te Bartholomee." " He also sent offerings into India to St. Thomas and St. Bartholomew." And William of Malmesbury, p. 24, lib. II. " Eleemosynis intentus [Alfredus] privilegia ecclesiarum, sicut pater statuerat, roboravit: & trans mare Thomam, & ad Sanctum Thomam in Indiam, multa munera misit." The conversion of India by St. Thomas may be found in any ecclesiastical history. The Christians of St. Thomas are noted in modern travels into India. See those of Paulus Venetus (13th century), p. 406, edit. Basil. 1537, folio, where lib. III. cap. 27, is intituled, " De civitate in quâ corpus Divi Thomæ sepultum est." This city is in Malabar.

1545.

Paid for this church book, bought at London the 14th day of February, anno Dom. 1544, 4s. 8d.[1]

Palm Sunday, the account was delivered to the succeeding churchwarden, Richard Raynford, who had a transfer of 9s. 6d. More owing to the church the same day, for the bells, as appeareth on the side of this leaf 37s. 4d. More owing to the church by Henry Maybley, for a Sepulchre light 10s.

Paid to the ringers at the obit for my lord of Huntingdon, and the belman 12d.

Paid for three quarts of claret wine that was given to my Lord Judge's chaplain 9d.

A quart of malmsey wine cost 4d.

Paid to the ringers for king Henry the Eighth 12d.

A gallon of wine for my lord of Lincoln's chancellor, when he preached at St. Martin's, cost 12d.

Paid for four pounds of wax and . . . . weke for a torch, and making the same, 2s. 6d.

Paid to Danyell, for mending the vestments, 2s. 8d.

Paid for a yard of green silk, and ten skains of thread, 7d.

Paid for charcoal on Easter even 2d.

Paid for mending certain things belonging to the procession, which was needful to be done, 12d.

Paid for bread and ale on Whit-monday 12d.

Paid to the sumner at St. Margaret's, for the offering, 8d.

1545.

In the year 1545, the church, and particularly the nave, was repaired: six load of freestone from the Freers, at 18s. per load. Then paid chief workmen 7d. per day; ordinary labourers 4d. per diem.

Annual obits in the church of St. Martin:

Of the gylde: Mr. Parsons . . . . . 5 bells.
Mr. Lyle 4
Mr. Hurste 4
Mr. Davers 3
Mr. Baylie's 4
Mr. Whytwell's . . . 3
Mr. Swyk's 3

Other obits: Mr. Wymeswold . . 4
West 5
John Wygston . . . 5
Thomas Drake . . . 4
Richard Fenes 4
Cloughe 5

N. B. The last mention of these obits is in the 2 Edw. VI.; and I do not find that they were renewed in queen Mary's time.

Charge to the poor:

Nothing in 1544—1546; 1547, 3l. 2s. ob. when several tabernacles, &c. were sold in 1 Edw. VI.; and then nothing till 1551, 5 Edw. VI.; given to the poor at Christmas 20s.; and to the prisoners 2s. 8d.; 1552, 6 Edw. VI. to the poor 3s. 4d.; 1553, nothing.

It appears that there is not a constant account in this book of the charge of the poor.

The first time of the vicars of St. Martin's being present at the churchwardens accounts (which I find) is 1546; 3 Edw. VI. 1549; and then he is mentioned after several others, some few following, and so 1550 and 1553.

Those who are named before the vicar are said to be masters of the said parish 1551, 1552.

The account of Richard Boynsforde and Henry Mabley, churchwardens of St. Martin's in Leicester, made on Palm Sunday, the 18th of April, in the year of our Lord God 1546, before Mr. Cotton, then mayor of the town of Leicester, Mr. Gyllot, Mr. Reynolds, Mr. Wood, Mr. May, Mr. Vicars, and others, in our Lady's choir within the same church.

The parcels of the goods that was sold forth the church of St. Martin's the 20th day of March,

[1546-7,] in the first year of the reign of Edward the Sixth, by the grace of God, &c.

Item, Received of Mr. Mayre for old gere 5d.

Item, Received of Mr. Tayllor for one vest and an albe 12d.

Item, Received of Mr. Damport for two vestments 6s. 8d.

Item, Received of Mr. Cotton for two hangings for the high altar of white damask and purple velvet 33s.

Item, Received of Mr. Vycker for an old vest of green 2s. 2d.

Item, Received of Mr. Manbe for altar-cloths 12s.

Item, Received of the same for an organ case 3s.

Item, Received of Mr. Damport for altar-cloths 3s.

Item, Received of the same for altar-cloth of red velvet and white damask 17s.

Item, Received of Richard Davy for two vestments of blue velvet 29s.

Item, Received of the same for two yellow copes 13s.

Item, Received of the same for a blue velvet cope 18s.

Item, Received of Mr. Manby for three white copes 17s.

Item, Sold to Mr. Reynold one canopy 20s.

Item, Sold to the same one vestment red 6s. 8d.

Item, Sold to Mr. Cotton one pall of blue velvet 13s. 4d.

Item, Sold to Thomas Hallam one green cope of Brydgs sattin, and an altar-cloth of the same, 10s.

Item, Willim Odam for the rood light 7s. 8d.

Paid to Robert Sexton and his fellow, for taking down tabernacles and images, 22d.

Another tabernacle cost 4d. taking down.

Receipts of fasting days:

Rec' on St. Ch . . . . . . and at Easter, of the parishioners at God's borde 15s. 3d. ob.; Item, at St. Margaret's church at Whitsuntide 2s. 2d.; Item, at Midsummer quarter 5s. 9d.; Item, at Michaelmas 5s. 6d.; Item, at Christmas 6s. 2d.—34s. 10½d.

Item, Received of Mr. Tallamore, then mayor of Coventry, the 11th day of August, for certain plate sold to him, as appeareth by his particular bill thereof, 24l. 5s. 10d.[2]

Item, Received of the Chamberlain, as appeareth by obligation, 20s.

Item, Paid in expences, two days at Coventry, when we sold the plate there, for our horses and ourselves, 3s. 4d.

Item, for a load of lime 3s. a load of sand 4d.[3]

1547.

Mem. That Symon Nyx and Thomas Hallam, churchwardens, William Manby, and John Eyryk, Hew Barlow, and William Bladvyn, then hath sold these parcels following, by the commandment of Mr. Mayor and his brethren, according to the King's Injunctions, in the year of our Lord 1546, and the first year of the reign of Edward the Sixth:

First, sold seven cloths that hung before the rood-loft, price 3s. 8d.

Sold to Nicholis Eyrike a tabernacle 2s. 8d. Other tabernacles in the account were sold for 1s.; two for 5s.; another for 3s.

Sold to Henry Mayblay the horse that the George rode on, price 12d.

A hundred and a quarter and seven pound of iron was sold for 6s. 2¼d.

Two other tabernacles were sold for 1s. each; and one for 3s. 4d.

A man of Stoughton Grange bought as much alabaster as came to 1s. 8d.; and another man as much as came to 10d.

Sold to Jhon Eyryke the organ chamber 8s. 6d.

Sold to Symon Nyx the florth and the vente that the George stood on 3s.

Four hundred and a quarter of brass was sold for 19s. per cwt. to one man; and three hundred weight

---

[1] This folio volume contains 773 pages of writing paper, bound in rough calf, with strong brass clasps.
[2] A very considerable sum in those days.
[3] The former now is nearly as many pounds, and the latter nearly as many shillings.

and

and three quarters was sold to another at the same price; and one hundred to William Taylor.

Sold to Rychard Raynford the Sepulchre light, weighing three score and 15 pounds, at 3½d. a lb, 21s. 10½d.

Sold to Mr. Newcome 100 pounds weight of the organ pipes 16s.

Eight pound of wax at 3½d. the lb.

And so all the whole that is already sold cometh to 13l. 2s. 2½d.

Goods sold forth of the church of St. Martin's.

An old press 6d.; a vest and a robe 12d.; 2 vestments 6s. 8d.; an old vest 2s. 2d.; altar cloths 2s.; an organ case 3s.; 2 yellow copes 10s.; 3 white copes 12s.; 2 hangings for the high altar of white damask and purple velvet 34s.; altar cloth of red velvet and white damask 17s.; a grene cope of Bruges sattyn and an altar-cloth of the same 9s.; a pall of blew velvet 13s. 4d.; the rood-light 7s. 8d.

For a pottle of wine paid 6d. and so 1 and 2 Philip and Mary.

In the year 1569 this is expressed thus: viz. Received of the young people for the church work 9s. ob.

Received of the housholders for the whole year for their church works 47s. 6d.

N. B. By comparing the accompts 1544 and 1548, 2 Edw. VI. it appears that what was received for church works were offerings made at Easter, Midsummer, Michaelmas, and Christmas. Servant men and children paid to them as well as housholders, as appears by the accompt for 1570.

Item, Paid for an Homily for sir William the parish priest 12d.

For five bells, and lying in the church, 12s.

The sexton's wife, for washing church cloths, had yearly 3s. 4d. viz. 1545 and 1546, &c.

The glazier's fee at Easter 1s. 8d.

Charge at Easter:

To the Prophete, and for ale on Palm Sunday 2d.; for a strike of charcoal on Easter even 2d.; to Robert Sexton, for scouring the church stuff at Easter 20d.—2s.

Charge at Whitsuntide:

For paper, pins, and points, at Whitsuntide, 3d.; for bread and ale, stakes in the church. 14d.; for cost and charges of all the rest, and procession, 11s. 1d.; to the sumners on Whit-monday 8d.; to the priests of our church, of the offerings, 6d.—13s.

April 13, 1548, 2 Edw. VI.

Item, Paid to the King's Majesty 3s. 4d.

Received on Christmas day and Easter day, for church work 13s. 5d.

Item, St. Margaret's on Whit-monday 10d.

Item, for the church work at Midsummer 4s. 5d.

at Michaelmas 4s. 1d.

at Christmas 3s. 1d.

In other years different sums.

Paid to sir William, the parish priest, for washing of his surplice 3d.

Paid to the sexton, for scouring the candlesticks 21d.

For a surplice cloth for sir William 6s. and for making the same 20d.

To Agnes, sexton, for washing church cloths 20d. half yearly.

For a key to the treasure-house door 2s. 4d.

For a door in our Lady's quire 10d.

For 2 pound of candles for Christmas day 5d.

For the holy lofe the fourth day of March 3d.; and so also for 1st March and the 18th March, and on Palm Sunday, and Good Friday.

For writing new of the church book for christenings, weddings, and buryings 6s. 8d.

2 Edw. VI. the charges on Whit-monday mentioned, but none in 3 Edw. VI. 1549, nor till 1 Mary, when 12 banners were bought again, &c. and mentioned till 1561.

N. B. The usual time for the churchwardens to give up their accompts was Palm Sunday; and, 3 Edw. VI. on Good Friday.

Lincoln farthings paid to the churchwarden's in queen Mary's reign, but not after.

1549, 3 Edw. VI.

Sir William Bradley was then vicar.

In this year the foot-stools of the tabernacle sold for 2s.

Paid for ringing the day-bell half yearly 3s. 4d.

Paid for making a surplice for Ralph Clarke, 4d.

For the Paraphrase of Erasmus 10s.

For 2 chains and nails for the Bible 5d.

For giving the holy loaf three Sundays 9d.

For taking down the rood-loft 10d.

In that year the church was white limed all over.

In the accounts 1550, 4 Edw. VI.:

Rec' for Mr. Wood's burial in the church 6s. 8d.

For a cieling over St. Dunstan's altar 16d.

For a cieling over St. Katherine's altar 12d.

For the table that stood at St. Katherine's altar 12d.

For the holy water stoke 16d..

3 catch corp bells, at 26s. per hundred.

Paid for work in the new quire, June 5, ...

To Ralph Clarke for keeping the Register book 20d.

To the glazier, his half year was 20s.

For mending the baudricks 12d.

For four days work about the store-house 2s. 3d.

Given to the poor at Christmas 20s.

A hundred of iron was sold for 13s.; and the "catche coppe bells" for 25s. per cwt.; a canopy and a green vestment was sold for 26s. 7d.; a green cope of Bruges sattin sold for 9s.

A book of service for the church cost 4s. 8d.

1551, 5 Edw. VI.

Received for the table in the Rood chapel 5s.

For the table in our Lady chapel 6s. 8d.

Of Thomas Wart for the vente over St. George altar 2s. 8d.

For a painted cloth and chapel cloth 16d.

The least catch cope bell was sold for 27s. 11d.; and two other bells were sold for 3l. 11s. 8d.

For two candlesticks, two holy water stocks, and six little bells, 37s. 6d.

For timber left of the new quire 3s. 4d.

Received for the post horse 26s. 9d. And further on in this year's account 8d. is paid for grass for a post horse; and 3s. 5d. for grass for the same in Beaumont Leys [1].

Paid for knolling the lecture bell yearly 2s. This was paid some years before.

For two persons, a week's work, for taking down the altar in our Lady's quire 4s. 9d.

For cutting down the quire 8d.

For painting the rood-loft 40s.

Lent to the parish priest, sir William, of the church money, 13s. 4d.

1552, 6 Edw. VI.

There was received for a press 23s. 4d.; and for a crown of wood covered with silver, and a knot of copper, 3l. 6s. 8d.

There was paid for a minister helping the vicar on a Sunday 3s. 4d.; and for one officiating during his absence in London 5s.

Given to St. Nicholas, for keeping Mr. Boughton the vicar to serve in the church April 5th, 3s. 4d.

To Mr. Boughton, for making a bill at the visitation, 4d.

For Mr. Boughton's dinner at the visitation 12d.

To St. Nicholas, for helping Mr. Boughton at Whitsuntide, 2s.

To St. Nicholas, for serving whilst the vicar was at London, 5s. &c.

To the preacher 5s.

Paid for a pound of candles (about Christmas) 4d.

For setting up the lecterne on the pulpit 8d.

For matts to be about the table 2s.

1553, 7 Edw. VI.

Received of Nicholas Gaussun, of Nottingham, for two copes, one vestment, and two tenakyles of

[1] A horse was then kept, at the expence of the parish, for general use.

cloth

cloth of tesshew, one vestment, and two tenakyles of cloth of silver, and two copes and one vestment of blue velvet, 18*l.*

Received of Richard Dare, for a corporas case and eight shets, one towel, one altar-cloth, and the rowd coat 38*s.* 4*d.*

A vestment of blue velvet was sold for 10*s.*

Received of Nicholas, goldsmith, for two shirts that was for St. Nicholas, and a hold [an old] towell, 3*s.* 4*d.*

Received of Richard Hewis, for corporas case, and St. Martin's cowte, and a towell of diaper work, 2*s.* 8*d.*

Received of John Wryght for 14 banner cloths 4*s.*

For the priest's wages 26*s.* 8*d.*

Of Mr. Mayor towards the priest's wages 13*s.* 11*d.*

Paid for a book of Preaffrasys [Paraphrases] 7*s.*

For two Psalters for the clerk's use 20*d.*

For the new service 5*s.*

For a book concerning the Rebels, that was read in the church, 16*d.*

For the two lectarynes of yerne 6*s.*

To Mr. Boughton, for the priest's wages, 26*s.* 8*d.*

For making two ratchetts for the clocke 6*d.*

N. B. Several payments were this year made for timber and work at the church-house. Q. whether that was not the vicarage-house, and was repaired by the churchwardens?

1554.

On Palm Sunday, the churchwardens accompts were passed before the Mayor and others, as usual, being the first year of the reign of Mary I. In which account are several things bought in for the use of the church upon the old Religion.

Among the receipts of this account are the value of some trees, which most likely stood in or about the church-yard, some ash and some elm.

1 March. The vicar not named in the account.

Received for an old black vestment and tunicle 10*d.*

Payments to sir Richard for his wages at Easter 30*s.*

For two copes and a vestment of blew velvet 20*s.*

For the brazen lectory 20*s.*

To the commissioners, for two priests 3*s.* 4*d.*

For the church bill for the collectors 6*s.*

For a rood coat 20*d.*

For three corporas cases 12*d.*

For 12 banner cloths 2*s.*

For a white sattin cope 10*s.*

To sir Richard, for his wages 30*s.* at Midsummer.

For a sacring bell 8*d.*

To the Queen's commissioners, for the cope of tissue that were sold 8*l.*

Payments. To the sexton, for setting up the altar, and mending the church cloths 12*d.*

For nine yards and a half of say, for Mr. Mayor's seat and Mrs. Mayoress, 10*s.* 3*d.* ob.

For a red skyn for the same 6*d.*

For red nails for the same 2*s.*

To sir William Burrows, for a Psalter, a Processioner, a Manual, and a Cowcher, 6*s.* 8*d.*

To sir William Burrows, for packthread and canvas for the organs, 4*d.*

For mending the organs, for glew, nails, leather, packthread, and weights of lead to lay upon the organs 6*s.*

For two candlesticks for the altar 2*s.*

For a Manual, to wed, chrysten, and bury withall, 3*s.* 4*d.*

For a Mass-book and a Cowcher 10*s.*

For a grayl to sing in the church on 10*s.*

For dressing and harnesing St. George's harness 6*s.* 8*d.*

To Syngylton for a cross 20*s.*

For carrying the altar stone from Mr. Mayor's house to the church 4*d.*

Many days work and stones about the altar.

For one yard and a quarter of red sey to cover the canopy and the Sacrament 17*d.*

For a pyx for the Sacrament 2*s.* 6*d.*

For painting the church and dressing the altar 9*s.*

For a vestment and an albe, and all belonging thereto, 13*s.* 4*d.*

For 4 yards of sey cloth for the high altar 2*s.* 4*d.*

Gatherers for the Sepulchre light are here mentioned; and so 1555, and 1 and 2 Philip and Mary.

Near the signature of the churchwardens are the names of " John Busshe and William Rechardson, appointed gatherers for the Sepulchre light."

1555.

The preamble in this year runs thus, after mentioning the year of our Lord, " in the first and second year of the reigns of our sovereign lord and lady Philip and Mary, by the grace of God, of England, France, Naples, Jerusalem, and Ireland, King and Queen, defender of the Faith."

Received for Sepulchre light 4*s.*; and at another time 7*s.* 8*d.*

For 5 bells at the burial of Mr. Ovende 5*s.* 4*d.*

For his lying in the church 6*s.* 8*d.*

More at his 7th day for bells 2*s.* 4*d.*

At the obit of Mr. Clough of the chamberlains 2*s.* 4*d.*

Of Mrs. Ovende for 3 torches 6*d.*

Payments. For holy water stock 5*s.*

For painting the Pascal stock 14*d.*

Item, for the pyx 4*d.*

For oyl and cream, and mending the chrysmatory 12*d.*

For the priest's wages for Midsummer quarter 33*s.* 4*d.*

For the offering that lackyd at St. Margaret's at Whitsunday, and drink there for the engyns, 12*d.*

To sir William Hobbs 33*s.* 4*d.*

To Francis Swynsworth, for singing 6*s.* 8*d.*

To Richard Lylling, for playing on the organs 5*s.*

For the Pascal stock and a hair cloth 8*d.*

For a pattern of a chalice 11*s.* 3*d.*

To Richard Mason, for making the altar in our Lady's chapel 18*d.*

For a pattern of the chalice 16*d.*

For a cross and censers 5*s.* 4*d.*

For timber, and for making the Sepulchre, 5*s.*

For the Sepulchre light 4*s.*

For painting the Sepulchre, and a cloth for our Lady's altar, 22*d.*

Some banners cost 3*s.*; and the offering at St. Margaret's, and drink there for the attendants, cost 12*d.*

A pottel of wine given to Mr. Doctor when he preached 6*d.*

For a cross and sauters 5*s.* 3*d.*

Duties received of the vicarage from Easter last until Michaelmas last past:

Received for 20 crysoms 5*s.*; for 14 pigs 5*s.* 10*d.*; for other offerings 12*s.* 2*d.*—Sum 23*s.*

1556, 2 and 3 Philip and Mary.

Received in Lincoln farthings 2*s.* &c.

Received at burial of Mr. Gyllot, for 5 bells 5*s.* 4*d.*; for his grave 6*s.* 8*d.*; for waste of the torches 20*d.*

Paid for two banner poles 15*d.*

To the three shepherds at Whitsuntide 6*d.*

For ale and cakes at St. Margaret's 18*d.*

For scouring the eagle 16*d.*

For mending a hole in the Rood chapel . . . .

For making the seats in Trinity chapel 18*d.*

For 2 boards and nails for the collectors' seats 6*d.*

For two dinners, &c. at the Visitation, 12*d.*

For nine copper dishes for the rood-loft 9*s.*

1557, 4 and 5 Philip and Mary.

Received at Easter for tithing and church works 14*s.* 4*d.*

In Lincoln farthings at Whitsuntide 3*s.* 10*d.* ob.

These are mentioned in 2 and 3 Philip and Mary, viz. 2*s.* 4*d.*; and 5 and 6 Philip and Mary, 1510, all the gatherings for the altars 11*s.* 11*d.* ob.

Paid for making the Rood Mary and John 13*s.* 4*d.*

For three gallons of ale, and 4*d.* in cakes at St. Margaret's, 19*d.*

For bearing of the cross and banners 14*d.*

Paid for a lock for the font 2*d.*

This year were appointed two gatherers for the Sepulchre light, and two for the Rood light.

1558,

1558, 5 and 6 Philip and Mary.

Received in Lincoln farthings 2s. 11d.

Paid for charges of the procession to St. Margaret's 3s.; at the same time for other offerings of the altars 2s. 2d.; and (to 1560) for ale and cakes at the same time 10d.

The gathering for the altars came to 11s. 11½d.

For a strike of charcoal for hallowed fire 5d.; and so 1560.

N. B. Two pounds of candles at Christmas generally used.

Paid for men to remove the ladder to Corpus Christi hall, for light to burn by the Rood, ...

The making the Rood Mary and John cost 13s. 4d.

Three gallons of ale, and 4d. in cakes, at St. Margaret's, cost 19d.

Paid for the bearing the cross and banners 13d.

The gilding the Rood Mary and John cost 1s. 10d. More was paid for gilding the Rood Mary and John.

1559.

Received in Lincoln farthings 2s. 2d.

Received for the morrice dance of children 3s.

The charge at St. Margaret's cost 3s.

A strike of charcoal 5d.

A hide of leather 4s. 8d.

Eleven ells of holland for two surplices cost only 9s. 8d. and 8d. making.

Ale for the ringers, when the Queen's Grace was proclaimed 8d.

Paid for drink for 4 men at taking down the altar stones . . . .

For a Bible and Paraphrase 3s. 4d.

For a Service Book 5s. 4d.

For three Psalters 5s. 10d.

For an Injunction Book 4d.

For a Processioner 2d.

1560.

Received of Bafforthe for the lord and the lady 21d. ob.

Received for Lincoln farthings 2s. 2d. ob.

Paid for 2 matts, 8 yards of length, for the table 12d.

For a matt for the choir 6d.

For a pound of candles 3d.

For half pound of wax candles 6d.

The offering at St. Margaret's cost 2s. 2d.

Paid to the players for their pains 7d.

1561.

Received for a sale of vestments 42s. 6d.

For banner cloths 2s.

For the Rood-loft 12s.

Several other things were then sold.

Received for certain stuff lent to the players of Foston 6d.

Paid for bird-lime 4d.

Paid for a beam to be laid on the high roof fetched from the Freers, 15s.

To the mason for his work on Good Friday and Easter even 14d. ob.

For a table for the Comandments and a Kalendar 16d.

For a frame to the Commandments 14d. ob.

For taking down the great beam, and setting up seats in Mr. Mayor's chapel, 4s.

For mending both the choir doors 4d.

For fetching the seats from St. Peter's, and making the collectors' seats, 5s. 4d.

A red skin and garnish nails for Mr. Mayor's seat 12d. (Many seats were set up this year.)

For mending the priest's surplice, and mending the clerk's surplice 14d.

For a dinner bestowed on the clerks that keep the choir at Christmas 6s. 8d.

1563.-

Richard Rabynson and John Wyllens account, 5 Eliz. April 14.

Paid for pulling down the organ chamber 2s.

For making the Communion-table frame 3s. 4d.

For a Communion book 3s.

For the Communion at Easter, 3 quarts of malmsey and 9 quarts of claret wine, 4s. 6d.

To Mr. Fisher, of Warwick, for a pension going

out of the church of St. Martin's, being due to the Queen, 40s.

To Mr. Gotes, for the tenths of St. Martin's, 12s. 4d.

Paid to the ringers on Black Monday, at the commandment of master Mayor, 12d.

Here is a special charge for mending the church windows, and repairing the leads after " the tempaste;" the window cost 1s. 3d. ob.; and the nails for nailing down the lead 18d.

About this time there are frequent charges for bird-lime, and sometimes for gunpowder, to kill the starlings about the church.

Ordered, that for the future nothing shall be allowed for visitation dinners, nor writing the accompts. But this was not observed, as appears by the accompt next year.

Memorandum. Henry Parke, of Leicester, barbour, by will, gave to the church of St. Martin's 3s. 4d. yearly, out of an house at the Cankwell, occupied by Thomas Pyokere, after the death of his wife, viz. Ellen, now wife of William Walker.

1564. Palm Sunday, March 26.
John Wyllne and Richard Parker.

Received of Robert Johnson, for the rent of St. Peter's church-yard this year, 5s.

For 29 lb. of brass 6s.

Paid for mending the little pulpit and the seats 8d.

For new books for the Leterne 1d. ob.

For a book of Homilies 3s. 4d.

Prayers 8d.

For a pound of candles at Christmas 3d.

For a day's work about my lord's seat [the earl of Huntingdon] 10d. &c.

For matts for my lord's chapel 3s. 4d.

For 5 yards of broad green . . . . . , a yard and ¼ of narrow green for my lord's seat 6s. 2d.

1564-5.
Richard Parker and John Stanford, 7 Eliz.

Received of Mr. English, for burying his wife in the church, and the great bell 10s. 4d.

(Here is first mentioned one bill of funerals.)

For 5 bells, and burying in church 12s. (ergò for the great bell 20d.)

For a cope and two albys 26s. 10d.

For 4 towels 9s.

For a nobe 4s. 8d. &c.

For timber of the rood-loft 12s.

Paid for lime and stone, and working about Mr. Mayor's seat, 8d.

For removing timber out of Mr. Venholde's chapel.

8 Eliz. 1565-6.

Paid Mr. Vicar, for a service-book 8s.

For making 2 inventories out of the Register book 12d.

For four quarts of malmsey at the Communion 2s.

1566-7.

Received for the organ pipes and the case of all things thereto belonging, 5l.

Paid for putting out the imageries out of the pulpit 3s.

To Mr. Brown, vicar, for certain arrears of tenths and subsidies, as appears by his bill, 5l.

Mem. A chalice, weighing 15 ounces and ¼, sold at 5s. 4d. per oz. amounting to 4l. 4s. 4d.; and bought a communion cup and cover, double gilt, weighing 21½ ounces, at 6s. per oz. 6l. 9s.

1567-8.

Paid for mending the church stiles, for nails when the minister's seat was turned, 4d.

For work about the seats where the minister and clerk sit 20d.

For a candlestick to hang upon the pulpit 3d.

For scouring the eagle 8d.

1568-9.

Received of Mr. Norris for the eagle 4l. 18s.

Paid for setting the seats in St. George's chapel 3s. &c.

Paid Mr. Commissary, when we were suspended for lacking a bill, and to his officers, 23d.

Received

Received March 8, A. D. 1569, for the parish of St. Martin's, for christenings and weddings 18s. 6d.

Item, the same day, received of the parish of St. Nicholas 2s. 8d.

Item, received of William Shipton, for the parish of St. Margaret's 3s. 4d.

Which 24s. 6d. was delivered the same day to the poor.

N. B. At the end of the accounts this year is this memorandum:

1569-70.
Received for 3 pieces of timber and a grave-stone 5s. 6d.

A stone of the cross, lead, and iron of the same.

Paid for carrying the stones and rammel away where the cross stood 8d.

1571.
Received of Thomas Friers, for the tops of the ashes in the church-yard 6s.

Paid for taking down things over the font 12d.

Paid for taking down the petyshons [partitions] about the chancel 20d.

Paid for cutting down the images heads in the church 20d.

Paid for cutting down a board over the font 14d.

Paid for taking down the angels' wings . . . .

Paid for mending the North church porch and the chamber over it 2s. 4d.

Paid for the churchwardens and the four sworn-men's dinners at the visitation 2s. 5d.—N. B. These sworn-men are mentioned in former years.

Mem. An act was made by Mr. Mayor and his brethren, that if any of the 24, or their wives, at death, have the great bell, to pay but 5s.; of the 48, or their wives, at death, have the great bell, to pay but 3s. 4d.; of the best commoners 2s.; middle commoners 12d.

Item, it is agreed by Mr. Mayor and his brethren, that if any be elected and refuse to be churchwardens he shall pay, for the first time, 10s. and the money to be for the use of the church.

Paid to Bodyly the sexton, for going through the parish, and one with him, to make an Easter-book, and paper for the same, 8d.

The church work, or rather the levy on the parishioners for the church, in this year, came to 51s. 9d. about an average sum at that time.

By the accompts about this time it appears that 10s. a year was given to the repairs of the church by one John Davie; and 3s. 4d. to the parish also by Henry Peake, annually.

1573.
Paid to Mr. Allen for the tops of the ashes in the church-yard 6s.

Paid for mending the block-house door 6d.

For making the cover over the font 4s.

For cutting the pillar next Mr. Mayor's seat 16d.

For three pounds of lead, to set fast the hook over the font, 3d.

Here is a copy of the last will of Henry Perke, of Leicester, painter, dated Oct. 25, 1557, by which he bequeaths to Alice Pelton, after his own and wife's decease, his tenement at Cankwell; she, her heirs and assigns, paying yearly out of the same to the church of St. Martin's, 3s. 4d. to be prayed with all his friends, and all Christian souls.

Received for the cover that did hang at the font 18d.

Received of Mr. Mayor, &c. Feb. 10, 53s. 4d. towards payment of certain arrears that our church was indebted to the Queen's Majesty, being part of a legacy that was given by Mr. Thomas Turner, of London, deceased, to the maintaining the preaching of the Gospel of Christ.

Paid for painting the dial of the clock house, for the four sworn-men's dinner at the visitation, and of one of the church-masters, 2s. 6d.

1574.
Received of William Pelton for his house at Cankwell 3s. 4d.

N. B. This is the first time of receipt of this legacy.

Paid Ralph Clerk for keeping the Register-book 2s. N. B. This is mentioned in some former years.

1575, 1576.
Paid for an hour-glass 4d. (This first mentioned here.)

N. B. For several years the clerk, for writing a copy out of the Register at Michaelmas, was paid 18d. or 12d.; and Mr. Gotes 6d. for setting his hand to the same.

1577, 1578, 1579, 1580, and 1581.
Paid for the Ten Commandments 9d.

For one bench in my lord's seat, and mending other seats in the church, 22d.; mentioned also 1582.

In 1579 there was only one churchwarden.

1582, 1583, 1584, and 1585.
Paid for the vicar's and sworn-men's dinners 3s. 6d.; so also 1587, 1588, &c.

For five yards of green seys for Mrs. Mayoress's seat 7s. 6d.; for trimming the same 1s. 3d.

It is agreed by the parish, that if any of the children of Mr. Mayor's brethren or their wives die, if they have any bells they shall pay according to custom; and if they have not the bells, they shall pay for the burial of every child 12d.; every one of the 48 for their children 6d.; and every one of the best commoners for their children 4d. if they be buried in the church-yard.

The clock and chimes were costly in repairs about this time; and in 1586 the "forr bell" was re-cast, towards which the mayor and nine of the aldermen paid 6s. 8d. each; and twenty-one of the common council paid 3s. 4d. The whole sum of the receipts on the occasion 11l. 18s. 6¼d. The casting cost only 5l.; metal and incidental charges 10l. 11s. 8d.

1587.
The mayor's brethren's seat made this year.

Paid for two planks, and two shelves in the library, 2s. 6d.

1588, 1589.
Paid to the ringers on St. Hugh's day 8d.

For a book, called the New Catechism, 16d.

1590.
Received of Mrs. Heyrick, for all the bells, and lying in the church for her husband, 12s.

Paid on Palm Sunday for bread and wine, more than was gathered, 10d.; and so at other times, 1592.

The causeways were paved to the church doors this year.

1591, 33 Eliz.
Paid to particular poor persons 6d. and 8d. apiece, because they did not gather in the church.

Paid to the Spittle-house folk, because they did not gather in the church, 6d.

The Sacrament used to be received monthly (as appears from the years 1591 and 1592), and so successively till this present.

1592.
Paid to a man, who had the Queen's broad seal, that did not gather in the church 8d.

N. B. It appears the Eucharist was oft received this year, by frequent mention of what the churchwardens laid down for wine more than was given at church; but next year they received more at Easter than spent; and at other times, and after, sometimes more, sometimes less.

1593.
Paid for two mats for the forms at the communion table 8d.; and for seven mats for the new seats 20d.

Wine to the Communion, Nov. 17, 8s.; bread 4d.

For washing, painting, and gilding the Queen's arms, 5l. 11s. 8d.

1594.
It appears by the accompts at this time that there was a library within the belfry of the church.

Paid for whiting the library wall in the belfry 16d.

N. B. The seats of the 48 were this year made.

Paid

Paid for making the partition in St. George's chapel 8*d*.

For serge to trim Mr. Mayor's seat and Mr. Clark's seat 5*s*. 4*d*.

For a red skin 10*d*.

For 19 hundred garnishing nails 12*d*.

1595.

Received seven books that were chained in the church, and given by Simon Crafts.

Paid for binding the seven books 5*s*.

Paid for a Prayer-book to John Walker, for the Queene, 8*d*.

N. B. The leads of the church were cast this year; the mayor's brethren and Mr. Cotton paying 3*s*. 4*d*. each, 2*l*.; and 32 of the 48 paid 20*d*. each, 36*s*. 8*d*.

It appears also, that for any great jobs done in the church, the mayor and corporation contributed largely.

The re-casting the leads of the church came, in this year, to 6*l*. 12*s*. 7*d*. towards which half was raised by the aldermen and common council.

1596.

The churchwarden Richard " Folliare" is written Richard " Folzer, churchmaster."

A levy was made this year for the communion plate, viz. of twelve of the mayor's brethren, and two gentlemen, 50*s*.; of 19 of the 48, 31*s*. 8*d*.; of the commoners 19*s*. 6*d*.

1597.

Here begins, and continues in the following years, an account of the particular receipts and payments at the Communions; and it was received 17 times this year. The receipts were between 1*s*. 2*d*. and 6*s*. The charge of bread and wine between 1*s*. 10*d*. and 7*s*.

A churchwarden refusing to serve his second year paid for a fine 5*s*.

1598, 40 Eliz.

Paid for painting the Communion-place and church, 80 yards, 26*s*. 8*d*.

For three yards of great wire to make a sun-dial, with which Mr. Belgrave made to set the dial by at the end of the New Hospital, 12*d*.

For ledging the seats in the Communion-place 2*s*.

The Acts and Monuments, or Book of Martyrs, given by Mr. Barsey.

1599, 41 Eliz.

Received for the burial of Mrs. Renouls in the chapel called Mr. Renouls' chapel 10*s*.

It is ordered, that whosoever shall hereafter refuse to be churchwarden shall pay 13*s*. 4*d*.

1600.

This year the overseers for collecting for the poor, being four, are named, and so the following years, according to the Statute.

1601, 43 Eliz.

Mr. Holmes, April 13, had what was gathered at the Communion after the bread and wine was paid for. Wine was now at 14*d*. the quart, and used at Communions from two to eight quarts.

Mr. Mayor's seat new trimmed.

1602.

It is agreed, that whoever refuses to be churchwarden shall pay for his fine 20*s*.

Paid for mending of Sir Edward's[1] and my Lady's seat several sums.

Paid to Mr. Holmes (the minister) for keeping the Register-book for a year and three quarters 5*s*. 10*d*.

Paid more to him for Lady-day quarter last 10*d*. for keeping the same book.

1603.

Paid Mr. Holmes for keeping the Register-book 3*s*. 4*d*.; so also 1604, &c.

At the Communion were used four quarts of wine, and three and a quarter, and once eight quarts.

Total of payments in 1603, on the church account, 8*l*. 17*s*.

1604.

Paid to the ringers when her Majesty was in this town 2*s*. 4*d*.

Paid for mending Sir Henry Hastings's[2] seat 6*d*.

For mending the long seat in the Communion-place, and for mending other seats 12*d*.

Here first mentioned Jewel against Harding, and a book of Canons; and four sidesmen first named, the same as the sworn-men.

1605.

Received of Mr. Bramley for his seat 6*s*. 8*d*.

Paid for a sheet of parchment to copy the Register-book 6*d*.

For carrying it to Huntingdon 2*s*. 6*d*.

For the registrer's fee there 2*s*. 6*d*.

To Mr. Holmes for keeping the Register-book 4*s*.; so 1608.

For half a yard and an ell of green kersey for a cushion for the pulpit 3*s*.

For a red skin and a white skin for the same 18*d*.

For one pound and a half of feathers, fringe, and crewel, for the same, 4*d*.

The mayor and his brethren's seats new made 5*l*. 16*s*. 1*d*.

1607.

Received of Mr. Robert Heyrick for a gravestone, which must not go forth never out of the church, 10*s*.

The steeple was mended this year.

Paid for painting of the church 3*l*. 8*s*. 8*d*.

The bells new hung; the leads mended.

Paid for lime and sand, and mending the church wall, which was broken down by the great wind, 4*s*. 10*d*.

1608, 1609, 1610.

Paid for taking seats in Reynolds' chapel 14*d*.

To the prisoners when they did not beg the town 4*s*.

The church-yard paved, church whited, leads new cast, &c.

Mem. Richard Elkington, of Shawell, by will, dated May 29, 1607, gave to the mayor, bailiff, and burgesses of Leicester 50*l*. to be lent on St. Andrew's day, payable at St. Thomas, to five tradesmen of Lutterworth 10*l*. each, at the rate of 5*l*. per cent. for one year, and so for ever. Of the use money, being 50*s*. 35*s*. is to be between the 21st and 25th of December distributed by the parson and churchwardens of Lutterworth to the poor there; 5*s*. for the town-clerk for entering orders and making bonds; and 9*s*. for the artificers charges in coming to Leicester. He also gave other 50*l*. to the said mayor, bailiff, and burgesses, to be lent in like manner to five such artificers of Leicester as the minister or vicar and churchwardens of St. Martin's shall nominate on St. Andrew's day, who are to receive it on St. Thomas's day, &c. Of the 50*s*. use, 40*s*. between December the 21st and 25th, to be distributed by the vicar and churchwardens among the poor; and the other 10*s*. to be for the town-clerk for orders and bonds.

1611.

The second bell cast.

Received 40*s*. by Mr. Elkington's will.

Paid for a spring latch and a pair of hinges for Mr. Holmes's seat 2*s*.

Paid 12*d* a week towards the prisoners great part of this year. Relief granted also next year.

Paid for making two tables of the old Communion-table 3*s*.

For removing Mr. Holmes's seat 12*d*. &c.

An apprentice was set forth by the parish.

Paid Mr. Holmes for writing the christenings, weddings,

---

[1] Sir Edward Hastings, of the Abbey Gate.

[2] Sir Henry Hastings, of Kirby.

weddings, and burials, 2s. (besides 12d. a quarter for keeping the Register.)

Thomas Winbie, chosen by Mr. Holmes, minister, to be churchwarden. There was a division about the choice.

1612.

Received of the money gathered in the church for the Grecian bishop 5s. 8d.

Paid to the sexton, for burying the poor visited people, by Mr. Mayor's appointment, 3s. 4d.

Paid for being presented for not having a flagon and tablet in the church for marriages 6s. 4d.

Paid for cieling for Mr. Holmes's seat 8s.

For iron work for Mr. Holmes's seat 3s. 6d.

It is agreed, that if any bells be rung for a burial, the sexton not having the consent of one of the churchwardens, he shall be dismissed his office for the first default; and if the churchwardens have knowledge, and take not sufficient security, they shall pay for the ringing themselves.

1613.

It is agreed that the churchwardens shall not bring in any decays of any cessment but such as the parish shall allow of.

Agreed, that there shall be no bells rung at any marriage, except they pay to the churchwardens 2s. 6d. presently upon the bells ringing, and then only to have three peals at the most; and if they have more, to pay 2s. for every peal.

Mr. Thomas Manly, mayor, gave to the church a pewter flagon.

Paid to six ringers, for ringing three days, when the King and Prince was here, 18s. 6d.

Work done about my lord's[1] seat 4s.

1614.

N. B. The inventories for several years were carried to Bugden.

Paid for a book of Jewel's Works 24s.

1615.

Paid to the ringers when his Majesty came to Leicester 13d.

1616.

Paid to the prisoners in some former years, and this, monthly, 2s. 8d.; and so in following years.

1617.

Received for a gravestone for Mr. Stafford Watts, carried out of the church into the library, 19s. 8d.

It is agreed, that no gravestone shall be removed in the church to set any man's name on, but first they shall agree with the churchwarden for the same. And also, that if the sexton shall ring at any time when any nobleman cometh to town, he must have 2s. 6d. from the churchwardens, if he have nothing sent him from the . . . . . where they lie. And that also, he shall not ring at any other time without the consent of the churchwardens.

Robert Mylner paid for his fine 30s.

It is agreed, that the sexton shall have for his wages, yearly, 26s. 8d. (before it was 20s.)

1619.

Paid for painting and sizing Mr. Holmes's seat 5s.

To the ringers at the earl of Huntingdon's coming 2s. 6d.

1620.

Lord Chamberlain's coming 2s. 6d.

Mrs. Alice Morton gave to the church, for the pulpit, a bear-colour velvet cushion stuffed with down.

1621.

Paid to five ringers for ringing three days at the earl of Huntingdon's coming to town 7s. 6d.

Given this year by Mrs. Elizabeth Ward a silver gilt cup, weight 8 ounces and a half and one eighth.

1622.

Paid for divers parcels of timber for the Communion-place 27s. 6d. &c.

For ringing to prayers every Sabbath and Holydays 3s.

Note. In preceding years, John Byerly, being clerk, wrote the accompts; and was allowed, yearly, 3s. 4d.; but he being dead, this year, Mr. Holmes (minister) wrote them, and had 3s. 4d.

1623.

Paid for 50 yards of matting about the Communion-place 26s.

For a bolt and a stock-lock for the chancel 2s.

For mending the compass cieling in the Communion-place, &c. 3s.

For mending the seat-bottoms in the Communion-place, with the benches, 3s. 2d.

For mending the seat below the churchwardens' seat 10d.

For a piece of dufftails, and eight yards of benching for the new seats, 12s. 8d.

For blanks for the churchwardens' seat, and the seat by the font, 4s. 2d.

For making the gates into the chancel 8l.

For taking down the lead when the chancel was mended 12d.

To four ringers for ringing a twelvemonth 20s.

For whiting the chancel 13s. (this is blotted out.)

Charge of the seats where the 48 sit 54s. 9d.

For charges to Dr. Lamb, and at London, about the great seat, 3l. 16s.

1624.

Received of the tax made for repair of the church 45l. 3s.

Here are receipts for three gravestones, each 22s. apiece; one 15s.; and one 10s.

Paid for ringing at the Prince's coming home 7s. 6d.

For ringing for the Judge 12d. (the first time mentioned).

For four ringers' yearly wages 20s.; and so in following years.

Received for fines taken of victuallers for breaking the assize 3l. 4s. 2d.

Fines taken of two drunk 20d.; of another 12d.

It is agreed, that no church officer shall be hereafter privileged of any taxes or payments for the church or bells, or any other payments for the church, in respect of their offices.

1625.

Paid for ringing when the proclamation was published for banishing Jesuits 2s. 6d.

2s. 6d. was paid for ringing when the French Ambassador came to Leicester.

For ringing at the first and second time proclaiming the King 5s.

For the seats in the belfry, which hold 40 several people, 2l. 7s. 1d.

Received for fines of victuallers 4l. 13s. 8d.

For . . . . 4l. 5s.

1626.

Paid for paving and heightening the seats 16s. 6d. and 12s.

The seats mended and garnished, &c.

Paid for a letter from the Bishop concerning the plague 6d.

For ringing on the coronation-day 2s. 6d.

Received of the fines of victuallers 3l. 16s.

Received of swearers 8s.

Money collected in this church sundry days for sundry poor people is 29l. 15s. 6d.; the money given upon fast days 21l. 9s. 7d. ob. which was paid to Mr. Mayor, for the buying corn for the poor.

1627.

Paid for ringing at the earl of Devonshire's coming to the Abbey 2s. 6d.

There were also charges for ringing when the countess of Huntingdon was at the Angel, and when the earl of Devonshire and the Chancellor were at the Abbey.

Paid for raising the seats behind the churchwardens' seat several sums.

[1] The Earl of Huntingdon.

Mem.

Mem. Alice Chattel, widow, of the parish of St. Martin's, Aug. 13, 37 Eliz. enfeoffed Robert Heyrick, ironmonger, Ralph Chattel, baker, Thomas Sacheverell, clerk, Nathaniel Sampson, clerk, and others, in a close of the parish of St. Margaret's, for her own use during life, and then 2s. yearly for the 12 poor women of William Wigston's hospital, and the rest for the poor of St. Martin's parish, that are honest, and have most need. Now all the feoffees being dead, except George Brooks, he, by deed, 19 April, 1628, enfeoffed others, viz. Richard Inge, &c.; which deed, with others, lie in the long chest in the church. This close was by the former feoffees leased for 16 years, the lease ending at Lady-day, 1638, and is in possession of Richard Deacon, chandler.

1628.

Paid for taking up a gravestone under the Hospital seats, and laying down the tiles, and lime and sand, 16d.

For Communion-table carpet-cloth 4l. 3s. 1d.

For a new cover for the pulpit 21s. 6d.

For a pulpit cloth of velvet, and cushion of the same, 16l. 18s. 8d.

For a case of green cotton for the velvet cushion 3s. 8d.

Note. These two sums for the velvet cushion and case were disallowed at passing the accompts.

1629.

Paid Mr. Holmes, for keeping the Register-book, 2s. and 4s.; and 1630, 4s. 6d.

1630.

This year, Mr. Holmes, minister, is mentioned the first among the persons present at the account.

Paid for mending Mr. Holmes's door, lock, and key, 1s.

For ringing at the Earl [of Huntingdon]'s coming to dwell in the town 2s. 6d.

For work about Mr. Holmes's seat 10s. 6d.

For painting Mr. Holmes's seat 3s.

Received for fines of victuallers 9l. 1s. 2d.

Two fines for churchwardens, each 30s.

In this year there is a charge for a prayer for the Queen's being with child.

There are also charges for ringing when the Countess [of Devon] came to the Abbey, and for the Earl of Exeter; also for the Governor of Scotland.

The steeple was pointed down by William Hastwell, and other expences occurred, which made the rate amount to 110l. and upwards.

1631.

A new frame made for the bells.

The steeple-top mended.

Received of sir Thomas Hartup, for sitting in the new seat the time that he hath been here, 20s.

1632.

Paid for making a door where the scholars sit 8d.

For mending the velvet cushion 9d.

It is agreed, that no bells be rung between nine of the clock and four of the clock in the night; if they be rung, the sexton shall forfeit his quarter's wages.

1633.

George Martin, churchwarden, paid for bells, and burial of his child, 12s.

Received of widow Chattel's gift, for three half years rent out of the Close, 24s.; and other years the like.

Received of the Lady Billers, for a seat, 5s.

Received of Mr. Rydings, for a seat, 5s.; so 1634.

March 24, 1633, it was agreed, that the Lord Keeper's propositions shall be answered unto, according to the articles sent down by his Honour.

1634.

Paid for warning the parishioners to meet . . . . . the Library 6d.

Paid for taking down the seats in chancel 2s. 9d.

Paid two masons for eight days work about the chancel 17s.

VOL. I.

For twenty loads of earth and sand for the chancel 12s.

Given Mr. Newton a quart of sack 14d.; and so to others.

Paid for a sequestration from the Archbishop of Canterbury [Dr. Laud,] &c. 6s. 8d.; three journies of the churchwardens to London.

Paid for drawing a petition to the Lord Keeper 3s. 4d.

1635.

Paid to the apparitor, for summoning us several times to appear at Court, about the Communion-place, 18d.

For whiting the church and porches 3l. 1s. 6d.

For painting the king's arms, porches, and pillars, 3l. 7s. 2d. &c.

Paid Edmund Cradock, for charges, being excommunicated, about buying the surplice, 7s. 8d.

Paid Moses Andrew, &c. for taking away the two rows of seats in the church, against the King's coming, 4s.

For two loads of rushes, and mowing them, against the King's coming, 20d.; the carriage of them cost 3s. More was paid for boughs and rushes.

For taking away the mayor's brethren's seats against the King's coming 2s. 6d.

Paid the King's officers, for fees for the floor where the King sate, 4s.

To eight ringers, whilst the King staid in Leicester, 15s.

For flowers for the King's cushion 4d.

For setting down the mayor's brethren's seats 12s.

For stuff to make a hood for Mr. Angel, against the Archbishop's visitation, and making it, 20s.

To the ringers, at the Archbishop's visitation, 11s. 6d.

For horse-hire to Harborough, and charges there, to certify the Court that the loft was taken down 3s. 6d.

To the ringers when our minister came 12d.

For a piece of wood used about the loft setting up 10s.

N. B. It seems that they attempted to set up a gallery, and were forced to take it down again; and after set it up again.

Paid for setting up the loft again 36s.

For painting the dial and bottom of the loft 22s.

Paid Mr. Recorder, for his counsel and pains to my Lord Keeper, and to his man, for writings concerning a new minister, 3l. 2s.

In this account also is a charge for a Mr. Hall (supposed to have been a clergyman) assisting Mr. Holmes.

Dec. 21, 1635, it was agreed, that the churchwardens for the time being, during the residency of Mr. Walter Wattkin, now vicar of the said parish, and two others of the parish joined with them at their nomination, whereof one to be of the 24, and the other of the 48, shall tax and raise by way of levy 20l. to be paid by 5l. a quarter, to the said vicar; and so to take an acquittance for every several payment.

1636.

This agreement was again confirmed Oct. 2, 1636.

1637.

The particulars of the account not mentioned.

1638.

Paid to Mr. Walter Wattkin (vicar), due to him at his going away, 5l. 4s. 10d.

Paid to Read and Cockle (the clerk), for carrying away the rails and forms, and placing them every Sabbath-day, a whole year, 6s.

1639.

To Robert Gilloit, for writing to the Lord Keeper in behalf of the parish for a vicar, 10d.

To Mr. Wattkin, for keeping the Register, 4s.

For keeping the loft a whole year 4s.

For bread and beer at the perambulation 3s. 6d.

For points ribbons given to the children at the same time 3s. 8d.

[7 K] Paid

Paid for rushes for the church at Whitsuntide 2s.

To the officers in court, June 19, being summoned to take down the seats 2s. 5d.

Paid in court, July 11, when we gave in our terral of glebe land, 3s. 6d.

For a quart of wine and biscuits, given to our vicar at his coming, 1s. 6d.

Gave to Mr. Kins a quart of wine, when we went a perambulation, 1s. 4d.

Being summoned to meet sir John Lamb, about our seats taking down, 1s.

Paid for taking off part of the seats at the chancel gates 6s. 6d.

For a stander to set the dish on at the Communion 3s.

For mending the benches in the old Communion-place 6d.

Given in wine to several ministers that preached 14s. 7d.

Thomas Stringer chosen by the parish, } church-
Anthony Gilber chosen by the vicar, } wardens.

Mem. May 30, 1639, William Knowles was chosen sexton, according to the antient custom, by the most voices of the parish.

1640.

Paid for ringing Bow bell when Cockle lay sick 6d.

To the ringers when peace was concluded in Scotland 2s.

For mending the seats in the old chancel 1s. 4d.

Given the ringers, when the knights of the shire were chosen, 3s. 6d.

Laid out for Cockle (the clerk) when he died 2s.

1641.

Paid for fastening the book that Mr. Stokes gave to the church 4d.

For matting the old chancel 7s.

More for matting the chancel 7s.

For two pieces of benching in the old chancel, and other work there, 15s.

For pegs for the 48 men's hats 1s. 8d.

In this year the Lord Keeper came to town.

There is also a charge for a matt " for the Countesse her seat." By this the countess of Devon probably had a seat in this church.

1642.

Received for swearing 10s. 4d.

Paid for mending Mr. Inge's seat 7s.

For Mr. Oneby's seat and boards 1l. 5s. 3d.

For Mr. Angel's seat 14s.

Mem. Aug. 15, 1642, Thomas Griffin was then chosen clerk of the parish of St. Martin's, Leicester, by the free and full consent of Mr. Thomas White, then vicar, and most of the parish then and there present.

1643.

Given to Mr. White and Mr. Angel two quarts of sack 2s. 8d.; the like Nov. 30, being fast-day, July 27.

To Mr. White, Dec. 28, being fast-day, a quart of sack, 1s. 4d.; the like June 25, Feb. 22.

For taking down the bell-frame 15s. 8d.

Given to several, by Mr. White's note, for flowers and herbs to strew the church at the King's coming, 1s. 8d.

For rushes 2s.

The things provided in the church this year when the King came, are noticed in p. 428. By these accounts we find, that King Charles the First, with his court, honoured this church twice, by attending the public service of Almighty God, in 1635, and in 1643.

1644.

April 23. At this meeting William Knowles, sexton, was put out of his office, for getting a bastard child on Margaret Weston, having a wife of his own; and Thomas Todd was chosen sexton, according to the antient custom, by the most voices of the parish present, May 30, 1644.

Received the annual gift of Mr. Heyrick 1l.

The gift of Mr. Geyrie 1l.

The annual gift of the countess of Devon 9s.

Paid for parchment, and engrossing the vow and covenant, and entering the names of those that took it.

For mending benches and seats in the Communion-place 1s. 6d.

For engrossing the National Covenant 3s. 6d. &c.

In this year's account there is a charge for ringing on the discovery of the " London plot;" and on account of Lord Grey's coming to town.

1645.

April 16. Mr. Grace refusing to assure the parish of his continuance, Mr. Thomas Palmer, of London, was elected minister in the room of Mr. Grace, and Mr. Angel desired to acquaint him with the vote.

In this accompt is a receipt of 6s. 8d. for burying a soldier who was wounded at the siege of Leicester; and a charge for mending the locks of church doors, broken by the King's army.

Paid William Hastwell, mason, for taking down the steps leading to the Communion-table, appointed to be taken down by an ordinance of the Lords and Commons in Parliament; and for laying down many graves which were taken up at the burying of divers great officers of the King's army, which was slain at the storming of this town, 3l. 17s.

Another bill Hastwell was paid 7s. for taking down the holy-water font.

Received for charitable uses at Communions, besides what was plundered and distributed, 5l. 12s. 3d.

Thus far out of the first volume of the Churchwardens Accompts.

N. B. The parish allowed Mrs. Holmes 10s. a quarter, viz. 40s. a year, for several years.

Q. Whether this was not the vicar Mr. Holmes's widow?

Extracted from out of the second volume of Accompts.

1645. What was received at the Communions on April 13, and May 11, being about 30s. was taken out of the poor men's box by the soldiers at the taking of Leicester.

Paid for mending the little aile in the chancel 7s. 3d.

For a bason to be used at baptism 5s.

For a standard to bear the same 15s.

For laying the same in marble colour 5s.

Here is a memorandum that Carver is behind for rent of his house, four years and upwards, 4l. 3s.

1646.

Jan. 8, it was ordered, that the churchwardens take of Mr. John Bryan his house, late in the occupation of Mr. John Prat, and see the same put in repair for the use of Mr. Thomas Daffy, at the charge of the parish; and that they advance what rent they can on the vicarage-house towards payment of Mr. Bryant's rent.

May 20, the churchwardens set the vicar's house to Mld. Hebb for 40s. a year, allowing repairs out of the rent.

Whereas the parishioners had voluntarily subscribed towards the maintenance of a minister several sums amounting to 50l.; which being thought too little, it was agreed, March 15, 1646, that 13 persons should be chosen, the major part of whom shall add to the same subscriptions, in way of tax, such sums as they think fit, to make up the full sum of 80l. for the said minister, with Tamworth's exhibition, besides the other parochial duties, which sums the inhabitants engaged to pay; but this engagement was to continue only till Michaelmas. A tax was made accordingly; and, April 11, 1647, unanimously agreed to; and that the like sum be yearly raised, as long as Mr. Daffy should continue minister of the parish.

Received of Thomas Doctor (or Carter) for a house in the Abbey-Gate, given by widow Ossiter, lately deceased, being an annuity for the poor of St. Martin's parish, 20s.

At

At this time (1646) there were great changes of the parish ministers.

Paid, the 7th of May, to the ringers, when New-worke was surrendered up unto Parliament, 2s. 6d.

Paid to the ringers when the Lords and Commons and Judges were at Leicester 4s.

Paid to the ringers, Jan. 22, 1646, when the Lords and Commons came unto Leicester, by the appointment of the committee, 6s.

Paid to the ringers, when his Excellency came to Leicester, 2s. 6d. Was it Cromwell, or Fairfax?

Paid to the ringers when the King came unto Leicester 3s.

1647.

Mem. The Sacrament was received but three times this year, viz. April 5, Aug. 23, 1646, and Easter-day 1647.

Paid for a Directory, and a Psalm-book, 3s. 4d.

For a cushion for the pulpit 1l. 12s. 9d.

To Mr. Daffy, Sept. 24, 1646, by consent of the parish 20s.

For ringing at his election by the parish 3s.

To the ringers when the King came to Leicester 3s.

In this year the minister's tax fell short.

In the list of names taxed to support the vicar appears a *Captaine Hamden.*

A Thomas Griffen was paid 5s. for *redeeming* the Register-book.

1648.

March 27. There being three quarters of the assessment for Mr. Daffy raised, and it coming to but 45l. 7s. 6d. so that 7l. 8s. 5d. was behind unpaid by several persons; it is ordered, that, if upon demand the said arrears are denied, the churchwardens shall pay the 7l. 8s. 5d.; and what is denied, and the deniers, be raised in the next tax for the church duties, and be distrained for in case of refusal.

It was then also agreed, that Mr. Thomas Daffy, our vicar, if he will stay, shall have his allowance for the year ensuing, according to the former agreement.

N. B. In the churchwardens accompts, after the particulars of taxes, there is an account of receipts in groats from several persons in 1646, 1l. 11s. 10d. in 1648, 2l. 1s. 1d.

1647. Received of Mr. Whatton, for his seat in the parish, 20s.; and so 1649, 1650.

Received of Thomas Carver, for a house, being the gift of widow Ossiter, for the use of the poor of St. Martin's, 20s.

N. B. The Communion received eleven times.

Paid for a Scotch declaration 6d.

For a League and Covenant, with a frame, and an Ordinance, 3s. 9d.

To Thomas Griffin, for collecting Mr. Daffy's money, 20s.

1648, March 6, it is ordered, that Mr. William Frank shall pay to Mr. Price, minister, the remainder of his Christmas quarter, till it can be collected up (I suppose this was 1648-9).

Paid June 22, 1648, for summoning the parish to the choice of a minister, 2s.

Paid Mr. Daffy, by the parish's order, April 25, 1648, as the full of his due, 9l. 4s.

N. B. The parish seem to have chosen Mr. Herring, of Coventry, for minister, whom they sent to, and he seems to refuse them.

Paid July 28, 1648, for wine, ale, and tobacco, at our first meeting Mr. Price, 9s. 2d.

Aug. 21, at the second meeting Mr. Price, 12s. 9d.

Paid Sept. 3, to Thomas Griffin, for his charges to get ministers to preach, 2l. 10s.

Lost by clipped money 6s.

Paid Mr. Wanley, for repairs of Mr. Bryan's house, which was rent, 7l. 10s.

For work done at Mr. Price's house 1l. 13s. 2d.

Sept. 14, for carriage of two loads of Mr. Price's goods, and thirteen packets, 9l. 10s. 6d.

For making a seat for Mr. Price, and for timber, 1l. 6s. 6d.

For timber and work at Mr. Price's house 5s. 8d.

Dec. 21, to Thomas Gryffin, for collecting Michaelmas quarter for Mr. Price, 7s. 6d.

March 5, for a tax for Mr. Bryan's house 1s. 6d.

Paid Mr. Price, to make up his Michaelmas and Thomas quarterage, 10l. 2s. 6d.

Paid Mr. Edward Palmer, for drawing writings between Mr. Daffy and the parish, and Mr. Price and the parish, 13s. 6d.

Here are charges for ringing at the victory over the Scots; for good tidings from Wales; on the day of thanksgiving for regaining of Leicester; and for a victory over the Enemy at Willoughby, by the Committee's appointment.

1649.

March 27. At this meeting, John Newton is chosen clerk of the parish during his good demeanour; and 13 persons were chosen for Mr. Price's tax for this whole year; and this tax was to be paid within a month after quarter day.

Received of Mr. Sherman, for his liberty in church, 5s.

Of Mr. Thomas Wadland, for his liberty in church, 5s.; so 1650, &c.

Of Mr. George Palmer, for a piece of ground in Margaret's parish, 10s.; so 1650, 1651.

Of Thomas Carver, for a house in Abbey Gate, 10s.; so to 1666.

Aug. 27. It is agreed, that the churchwardens shall pay to Mr. Price 4l. for the last two quarters; and for the future Mr. Price is contented to proceed according to the former order made at a meeting concerning Mr. Tamworth's gift for the prayers at St. Martin's parish.

1650.

April 16. Accompts of Robert Cotes.

Paid to John Newton, for a book for Mr. Price's quarterage, 8d. (Note. This was also paid in April 1649; and so other years.)

To Mr. Bryan, of Coventry, for Lady-day half year's rent for Mr. Price's house, May 11, 2l. 10s.

To Mr. Price, to make up Lady-day quarter, 3l.

Paid three months tax for Mr. Price's house 2l. 6s.; and so at other times.

To John Newton, for collecting Mr. Price's quarterage, 1l. 10s.; for his year's wages 10s.; for keeping the Register-book 4s.

1651, May 7. Accompts.

Received of George Smith, for a stone belonging to the font, 7s.

Of Mr. Hugh Watts, for his liberty of the church, 10s.; and so for him and others, 1651, 1653.

Paid for casting the third bell, and charges in court, 11l. 11s. 10d.

For washing down the King's arms in the church 6s.

May 7. Mr. Price sent in his bill of demand for 22l. in arrears, whereof there is 20s. in John Newton's hands; and 3l. for Mr. Tamworth's prayers; and 30s. to discount for a quarter for Tamworth's prayers; so there is due to him 16l. 10s. to be paid by the present churchwardens at or before Midsummer next.

In this year a mat is charged for lady Hungate's seat; and a charge for destroying the King's arms.

Several charges appear about this time for procuring ministers to preach.

Between 1640 and 1650 there were five vicars.

1651-2.

March 19. Agreed, that Mr. Richard Pike be presented to the Committee for Reformation of the Universities, to be minister of the parish of St. Martin's, in Leicester; and that Mr. Mayor signify, by his letters, to the Committee, and the lord Grey, and sir Arthur Haslerigge, our election of the said Mr. Pike.

1652.

1652.

April 20. Accompts of Francis Vable.

Paid for a quart of sack when Mr. Blant preached 1s. 8d.

The parish charge for ministers officiating among us, from Easter to Michaelmas 1651, 8l. 3s. 1d. &c. &c.

Paid John Newton, for summoning the parish about electing a new minister, 1s.

To John Newton, for summoning the parish, and stating the accompts with him and the parish upon his removal, 1s.

To John Newton, for going to Mr. Pike, to acquaint him with his being elected vicar, 10d.

To Mrs. Holmes her whole year's salary, ended March 25, 1652, allowed her by the parish for her life, 2l.

Paid to the ringers for the 18th of June, being the day of regaining the town, 4s.; and 2s. 6d. at general Cromwell's passing by, Aug. 25; and upon the news of beating the Scots, 3s. 4d.; and for ringing on the thanksgiving day, on that account, by lord Grey's order.

In this accompt also are many charges in procuring clergymen to preach on the Lord's day, while they had no stated minister.

1653.

Accompts, April 12.

Received of Mr. Billington, for the ground in the chancel, 6s. 8d.

Of John Newton, for the grass in the church-yard, 2s. 6d.

N. B. For several years they used to ring June 18, for regaining of Leicester, and allowed for it, 4s.

Paid to John Newton, for giving warning to the parish of a meeting, June 17, 8d.

To John Newton, for his whole year's wages, 10s.

Mem. Mrs. Holmes, of the New Hospital, buried Jan. 28, 1652-3, to whom the parish allowed 40s. per annum.

Paid for ten quarts of sack 20s.

April 12, it was agreed, that for the future no tax should be made for church or poor by any officer without public notice given to the parish.

April 22, agreed, that the ringers shall demand but 6s. upon the death of any parishioner who has the bells; and that the sexton shall demand but 3s. for ringing the bell and making a grave in the church, chancel, or chapel; and for such as are buried in the church-yard with a coffin 18d. and without a coffin 9d.

It was agreed also, that such seats in the church which are usually taken up by persons in no other parish, and refuse to pay any church duties, shall be locked up until they submit to such payments for the church as shall be judged reasonable, and they are to have notice thereof.

May 23. Mr. Churchwarden Curtise is to desire Mr. Dixie, of Cadeby, to preach one Sabbath; and to signify the desire of the parish to choose him for their minister.

Agreed, that Mr. Curtise provide for the morning sermon on the Lord's-day for a month, the parish being content to allow 10s. a day.

Oct. 20. Mr. Christopher Wright chosen minister; the parish engaging to pay him so much as will make up Mr. Tamworth's exhibition 80l. per annum, payable quarterly, the first payment Dec. 25 next; and Mr. Wright to have the vicarage-house, and 3l. per annum more to provide him an habitation, or if he let the parish have the vicarage-house he is to have 5l. for a house.

N. B. There was a vacancy of the vicarage from Midsummer 1651 till Michaelmas 1653.

It is agreed, that the 30s. per annum given by Mr. John Stanley, and 20s. per annum given by Mr. James Ellis, to the minister of this parish, towards making the said 80l. per annum; and all other parochial and accidental duties and emoluments Mr. Wright is to have over and above the 80l. per annum. Every particular person to be engaged for so much as he subscribes for.

1654.

April 4. Accompts of Anthony Curtise.

Received of the gentlemen in the new market 1l. 2s. 8d. (This is for seats in the church; viz. Mr. Whatton 10s. Mr. Watts 6s. 8d. Mr. Thomas Wadland 5s. William Frier 1s.)

Paid to Dr. Bryan, for rent for Mr. Price's house, 5l.

To John Newton, for collecting Mr. Wright's quarter, 7s. 6d.

For making his quarterly book 6d.

Oct. 20. Agreed, that the lands of such as inhabit in the parish shall be chargeable to the poor, after the rate of 1d. in the pound; 1d. for setting the poor on work; 2d. for the relief of the impotent; and 3d. to put forth apprentices.

1655.

April 7. Accompts of William Warburton.

Paid Mr. Wright, towards payment of his house rent, 5l.

To John Newton, for his year's wages, 2l.

To Thomas Todd, for his year's wages, 2l. 14s.

To Francis Motley, for his year's wages, 10s.

Feb. 29. The overseers and churchwardens placed Margaret Hopkins in a cottage or tenement in the church-yard, which, with two other cottages thereto adjoining, was bequeathed to us by Hugh Lewis, late of this parish, for three widows, during their lives, &c. paying the chief or fee farm rent to the town.

1656.

April 8. Accompts of Nich . . . . . .

Paid Francis Motley, for looking to the clock this year, 10s.

To John Newton, his wages as clerk, 10s.

Oct. 5. Agreed, that the churchwardens weekly pay to Mr. William Barton 20s. so as he perform all the offices of a minister in the said parish, and administer the Sacrament of the Lord's Supper monthly.

Feb. 20. Agreed, that this order be in force for raising 20s. a week for Mr. William Barton from Dec. 22 past to March 25 next.

1657.

March 31. Accompts of John Turvile.

It was at this meeting agreed, that a quarter's tax for the poor shall be collected by John Newton, towards payment of Mr. William Barton, our present minister, according to a former order.

Several others, besides Mr. Barton, officiated as ministers.

Sept. 1. Agreed, that the ring of bells be made into six tuneable bells; the treble and tenor to be cast into three bells tuneable under the other three, and the fourth bell that now is, to be made a tuneable tenor, without casting, &c.

1658.

April 13. Accompts of Alexander Cote.

Then the two bells being cast in three bells by Mr. Norris, of Stamford, it seems they were disliked, whereupon,

Aug. 31, it was agreed with Mr. George Oldfield, of Nottingham, to cast the six bells into six new tuneable bells, &c. for 50l.

1659.

Accompts of James Ludlam.

Thomas Rudyard became tenant to the parish in room of Mr. George Palmer; the rent for a close 10s. per annum.

1660.

April 18. Accompts of Stephen Lincoln.

Paid for ringing, June 18, 5s. (ergo the rejoicing for recovery of Leicester lasted till 1660).

1661.

May 3. Accompts of William Alsop.

Paid for ringing, when the King came to London, May 31, 5s.

For painting the King's arms, and mayor's seat, 6l. 13s. 4d.

Feb.

Feb. 4. Agreed, that the font of stone formerly belonging to the church shall be set up in the antient place, and that the other now standing near the desk be taken down.

Agreed with John Hall and William Hall, for keeping plumbing the leads, and glazing the windows, to pay them yearly, 5l.

At a parish meeting, the new font, fashioned and placed agreeable with the Puritanic times, was ordered to be taken down, and the old stone one to be erected where it formerly stood.

1662.
April 8. William Southwell.

Paid for a Common Prayer Book, and binding Bishop Hall's Works, belonging to the church, 17s. 6d.

Paid widow Smith, for the font-stone, being the price her husband paid for it, 7s.

Mem. The last account for bells alone is 1652.

For bells and grave in 1653.

Once bells in 1655 and 1656.

July 15. Edward Read was nominated and elected parish clerk, in the presence of Mr. William Barton, vicar, in room of John Newton, who lately resigned the said office; and that he shall have the 30s. per annum allowed to his predecessors for collecting the vicar's quarterage, with all other profits belonging to the said office.

There was delivered into his custody at the same time, one pulpit cushion, one hour-glass, two great Bibles, one new and the other old, one Common Prayer Book, one Testament with a case, for the use of the clerk, &c. &c.

July 28. Four sidesmen or assistants were chosen by order of the Ecclesiastical Court (which had not been done from the time of the war); and so till 1666; then omitted till 1671; and then left off.

On his Majesty's coronation day, and on the public day of thanksgiving, the 29th of May, there was much ringing, and additional pay.

1663.
April 21. Accompts of Samuel Wanly.

Received of the gentry in the New Market towards repair of the church, in consideration of their seats, 9s.

Paid for fees at the Ecclesiastical Court, &c. 13s. 8d.

June 30. Agreed, that the churchwardens shall set up the chimes at the parish charge, and also a quarter clock to go upon the five least bells.

1664.
April 12. Accompts of William Deane.

Paid for a pint of sack, given to Mr. Angel when he drew up the bill of presentment, 11d.

Paid for railing the seats in the middle aile 14s.

Spent on the witnesses which came in about Mr. Barlory chancel 3s. 2d.

June 27. Agreed, that Francis Motley, for making a tuneable pair of chimes, shall have 12l. 4s.; and for keeping them yearly, 20s. with the materials of the old chimes now in the vestry.

Aug. 29. The churchwardens may lay a quarter's tax for paying unto Francis Motley for the chimes, and out of it to pay 3l. to Mr. Barton for his pains in tuning the chimes; and they shall appoint six honest able men to be standing ringers, who shall receive 4s. per annum apiece for ringing and chiming on Sundays, holydays, and other days, as the churchwardens shall appoint, for giving convenient notice to the parishioners for preparation to come to church.

1665.
March 28. Accompts of George Bent and John Huckle, for 1664.

Paid to Thomas Todd, for dressing the church against the Bishop's visitation, 8d.

Paid Mr. Burton, by order of the parish, 3l.

April 10. William Cockle is chosen sexton upon his good behaviour.

1666.
Accompt of William Newton.

Paid for bread and drink upon the people and parson, when he went upon perambulation, 6s.

VOL. I.

To the young people, in points, 2s. 6d.

Paid to Richard Sheenes, for a new table chancellor, 14s. 6d.

Paid for two visitation dinners 1l. 10s.

Paid for setting a little tree in the church-yard, given by Robert Hartshorn, 3d.

1667.
April 9. Accompts of William Ward.

Agreed, that the collection at every Sacrament defray the charge of bread and wine, and the overplus given to the poor; if the money collected be not sufficient, the rest to be paid by the churchwardens.

March 11. Mem. That the piece of ground in St. Margaret's parish, given to this parish, is in length between the two end walls 87 yards, and in breadth from the four trees to the West of widow Biggs her close 17 yards and a half.

1667-8.
Accompts for 1667.

Paid for painting the Commandments 1l. 8s.

March 24. Agreed, that the 24s. per annum, hitherto allowed for chiming the bells on the Sabbathday, shall be allowed no longer; and that the bells shall be chimed notwithstanding by the sexton. Also, it is further agreed, that the 2s. 2d. formerly allowed to the minister, clerk, and sexton, for the burying of such poor that have collection, or their children, shall be taken off and paid no longer, but that the said officers shall do the same freely.

1669.
April 20. Accompts for 1668, of John Mabbie.

Paid Mr. William Barton 2l. 10s.

Paid Mr. Levit, proctor, by bill, 2l. 2s. 2d.

For work about the catechising seat for boys 2s. 8d.

Paid Mr. Read, for writing out of the Register of the christenings, burials, and marriages, that was delivered to the Bishop, 20s.

Paid to the Women of the New Hospitals, due out of Joseph Wright's lands, 2s.

For ringing at the bishop's visitation 8s.

For matting the loft, 58 yards, at 6d. per yard. 1l. 9s.

6s. paid for the orders to hang in the loft.

Agreed, that the parish will not allow above 10s. for any visitation dinner hereafter.

Ordered, that the churchwardens for the year ensuing shall pay Mr. Barton, minister, 50s.

July 2. Ordered, that all lands within the parish of St. Martin's shall be taxed a penny in the pound to the church and poor.

Jan. 25. Michael Benshaw is chosen clerk of this parish; and it is agreed that widow Read shall enjoy all the profit of the clerk's place till Lady-day next.

1670.
April 5. Accompts for 1669, of John Hall.

Aug. 5. Agreed that Mr. Bliss have 65l. to mend the spire of the steeple.

Oct. 3. Ordered, that the churchwardens provide a hood for Mr. William Barton, at the charge of the parish, and so to be kept for the use of the parish.

Dec. 29. Ordered, that the churchwardens pay Mr. Barton, our present vicar, 50s. towards repair of his house.

Agreed, that all parish children should be clothed in blue cloth, and if any officer or person shall use any other colour, it shall be at their own proper cost and charges.

In this year the steeple was repaired, part taken down, at the expence of 65l.

1671.
April 25. Accompts of John Goodal and William Elliot for 1670.

Paid Mr. Barton 2l. 10s.

Paid Mr. Barton, towards repair of his house, 2l. 10s.

Ordered, that whereas there is 20s. due to the poor of this parish out of a house in the Abbey-Gate, and 10s. out of a close near St. Margaret's church, and 3s. 4d. out of a house near Cankwell,

and

and the monies collected at sacraments; all which used to be brought to the Churchwardens Accompt, to defray the expence of the church: It is now ordered for the future, that the said monies shall all be paid to the overseers of this parish, and by them to the poor, and brought to the collector's accompts.

It is also ordered, that for the future no monies shall be paid to the sexton or any other for ringing at the Assizes.

It is ordered, that the new churchwardens shall pay to Mr. Barton 50s. for his King's rent; and so 1672, 1673, &c.

Aug. 2. Four sidesmen chosen; and agreed, that 15s. be allowed for each visitation dinner.

Jan. 10. Ordered, that the collectors shall pay to Mr. Barton 40s. towards repair of his house.

1672.
July 4. Accompts for 1671, of Thomas Bellamy.

Ordered, that the churchwardens shall pay Mr. Barton for the repairs of his house 3l.

Jan. 14. Ordered, upon request of Mr. William Barton, on the behalf of his son, that the church-wardens shall give his 40s. out of the parish money.

Sept. 25. Joseph Wright is to pay 15s. yearly for part of a close in St. Margaret's parish.

1673.
April. Accompts for 1672 of Francis Ward.

Ordered, that the churchwardens cause to be written upon the church walls the fees agreed to be paid to the clerk and sexton, which are this day ordered to be paid as followeth:

The sexton, for ringing the calling, and passing, and sermon bells, and making the grave in the church, chancel, or chapel, 3s.; in the church-yard, with a coffin 18d. without a coffin, 9d.

The clerk shall have for the burial of any person in the church, chancel, or chapel, and the registring thereof, 2s.; for the burial in the church-yard, with a coffin, and the registering thereof, 12d.; for the burial in the church-yard, without a coffin, and registering thereof, 6d.; for the christening and registering of any child, and the churching of the woman, 6d.

It is ordered also, that the collectors pay Mr. Barton 50s. upon his request this day to the parish.

It is also ordered, that the clerk and sexton shall not demand the fees for burial of any person until the third day after the burial, unless strangers are concerned in the payment of them.

1674.
April 21. Accompt of William Bentley, &c. for 1673.

1675.
April 6. Accompts of Robert Spence for 1674.

Received, for a piece of a grave-stone, 3s.

Paid Mr. Barton, for writing a copy of the registers, 6s.

Paid Mr. Stephens, and the Apparitor, for a terrier of the vicarage-house and church-yard, 4s.

Feb. 29. Agreed, that for the future the taxes shall be levied upon land as well as by estimation of personal estates.

1676.
April 27. Accompts of William Holmes.

Paid William Billing, for his help in making return to the Archbishop's and Bishop's letters, 2s. 6d.

Aug. 7. Agreed, that the Master of Wigston's Hospital may make and continue seats for the people of the said Hospital, from the great South door to the West end of the church, and for setting down rails for the defence and ornament of the said Hospital at the Southgate wall next the Hospital, and for taking down that part of the wall.

1677.
May 10. Accompts for 1676 of Walter Hood.

Nov. 6. Agreed that a tax be laid on lands and houses and grounds in this parish at the rate of $1\frac{1}{2}d$. in the pound, collecting the third part of the rent for repairs and other charges thereof, and personal estates to be adjudged by estimation of the parish meeting, and this for the poor.

Jan. 3. Agreed that Mr. Barton should have 40s. as a free gift for his present occasion.

1678.
May 15. Accompts for 1677, of John Bent.

1679.
June 6. Accompts for 1678, of Edmund Hood.

Paid Mr. Barton, for writing the Register, 6s.

Paid Michael Banshaw, for gathering Mr. Barton and Mr. Newton's money this year, 30s.

Paid for two acts for burying in woollen 1s.

Paid for removing the schoolmaster's seat 4s.

Paid for Mr. Newton's Visitation dinner 2s.

1680.
May 19. Accompts for 1679, of Edmund Malson.

Paid at the Bishop's Visitation, for Mr. Newton's dinner, the sidesmen, and other charges, 17s. 10d.

Paid fees for the sequestrations 1l. 3s. 2d.

Paid John Coleman, for the sequestration, 2l.

For ringing when the earl of Rutland came to town the sessions after twelfth day 10s.

For work and wood about the vicarage house, &c. 1l. 4s. 6d.

To the ringers, for one quarter's chiming on Sundays before sermon, 6s.

For wood to burn plaister for the vicarage house 10s. 7d.

For glazing at the vicarage house 5s. 6d. &c. &c.

1681.
May 19. Accompts for 1680, of Edward Billers.

Paid for cloth for the clerk's gown 1l. 4s. 6d.

For trimming and making it 4s. 8d.

For 45 yards of rails and banisters for the Aldermen, and 48 men's seats, at 17d. the yard, 3l. 3s. 9d.

For the King's arms over the mace-case 2l.

1682.
May 24. Accompts for 1681, of Samuel Robinson.

Paid for chiming 14s. 6d.

Mr. William Warburton paid 50s. fine for not serving churchwarden; and so likewise Mr. William Orton; so likewise Mr. Thomas Ludlam; and Mr. William Shears paid 4l.

Mr. Thomas Simpson paid a fine of 40s. for not serving collector for the poor.

1683.
May 9. Accompt of G. Stears and S. Woodland, for 1682.

Paid for paving the street by the church 4s. 10d.

Paid for perambulation 8s. $10\frac{1}{2}d$., and more 11s. 10d.

April 10. Whereas there is a demand of arrears of tenths for 1660, 1662, and 1677; agreed that if Mr. Newton, vicar of the parish, cannot produce the acquittances for those years from the executors of Mr. Barton, or otherwise, toward payment of the same, then the churchwardens shall pay such charges as he is put to concerning the same.

It was then agreed, that William Cockle shall be no longer sexton of the parish; and that the present vicar, Mr. Newton, and the churchwardens, do take care of a fit person for that place.

1684.
Account of Samuel Woodland, &c. for 1683.

Paid at Visitations 3s.; and 2s. for Mr. Newton's dinners, 5s.

Paid Mr. Newton for writing the Register 6s. 8d. and so other years.

Agreed, that William Cockle shall have 20s. toward putting him into the Hospital.

Paid Francis Hooke, for his Majesty's declaration for the times when his Majesty touches for healing.

1685.
Accompts of William Sprix and H. Pate, for 1684.

At the procession on Holy Thursday 16s.

Given in points 1s. 6d.

For making the bounds 1s.

Paid for ringing, when the charter was surrendered 3s. 6d.

Paid Mr. Newton for visitation dinner 2s. 6d. and so afterwards.

Paid

Paid John Silby his quarter's wages 14s.

Paid for painting the pulpit and seats 1l. 5s.

Paid Mr. Stephens, for enlarging the seats, being the fees of the Court 1l. 5s.

1686.

Accompt of Henry Pate, and Thomas Ward, for 1685.

Paid for a standish, pens, ink, and sandbox, for the vestry, 2s.

For bread, ale, and tobacco, at the procession, 1l. 3s.

For chiming the bells this year 1l. 4s.

For ringing when the news came of Rebels routed 10s.; of Monmouth and Greys being taken 10s.

Paid for painting and whiting in and without the church 28l. 10s. 4d.

Several payments about the king's picture.

May 12. It is agreed that Mr. Craycroft shall carry in the charge for the first half year of churchwarden, and Mr. Abney the other half year; and to have two new ones chosen every Easter Tuesday for the future.

Agreed that the churchwardens shall make a search at the registers, which seats in the church are licensed, and to whom, whether appropriated to the parsons or houses. It is also agreed, that no seats be licensed to any persons without the consent of a parish meeting.

Aug. 4. It is agreed that 5s. a quarter shall be allowed to the Sexton and his assistants for chiming the bells on the Sabbath days. Agreed also that John Sylby shall have but 10 days pay for making of the bank in the church yard, next the Hospital.

Agreed also, that Mrs. Hargrave have leave to erect a loft before the North door, with the chancellor's and minister's consent.

King Charles the First's picture, now over the Consistory Court, was painted by a Mr. Rowley, charge 10l.

1686-7.

Feb. 1. Agreed that a licence be taken out of the court, in the churchwardens' names, for Mrs. Hargraves erecting of the loft before the North door, and that the licence be paid for at the charge of the parish.

Agreed, that Thomas Cartwright's bill for making the altar in St. Martin's church, and the table therein placed, and other work, be referred to the judgment of Robert Scampton, joiner, and he to set the price of the whole.

1687.

Accompt of Mr. Craycroft and Mr. Abney for 1686.

March 29. Agreed that a new clock shall be made at the charge of the parish.

April 27. Paid for keeping the crowd out at confirmation 4s.

For ringing at the Bishop's coming to town 2s.

Paid for two pair of large candlesticks for the church 1l.

Aug. 17. Agreed, that George Hill, of Ousen, have 15l. to mend the lower steeple, according to an agreement made with him.

1688.

Aug. 16. Collected for the French Protestants 15l. 17s. 5d.

Received for the old clock 20s. of Mr. Wilkin.

Paid for ale, bread, and tobacco, on Holy Thursday 19s.

For points 18d. marking the bounds 1s.

Paid for a cloth gown for Michael Banshaw 1l. 15s.

Paid for a new hearsecloth 1l. 10s.

1689.

April 2. Agreed, that at the perambulation there shall not be expended above 8s.

May 6. Accompts of John Burdet and Joseph Wilkins, for 1688.

Paid upon Ascension-day for ale and bread 13s. 6d.; points 18d.

For marking the bounds 12d.

For ringing at the restoring of the old charter, Oct. 20, 6s.

Paid November the last for ringing for the Princess Ann, 5s. 6d.

July 1. Agreed that the bells be all new hung.

July 11. Collected for Irish Protestants 26l.

Jan. 8. John Silby voted out of the sexton's place, and Richard Yates chosen sexton.

May 14. Accompts of John Burdet.

May 9. Paid for making the bounds, points, and ale 8s.

1690.

June 16. Collected upon the second brief for Irish Protestants 13l. 12s. 9½d.

1691.

May Accompts for 1690 of George Croft.

May 9. Agreed, that whoever refuses to pay to the church, shall pay the church levies proportionable to the poor.

1692.

Accompts of Robert Hobson, and Thomas Simpson for 1691.

Paid for points, ale, and bread at perambulation, 11s.

For making the bounds 12d.

May 4. Agreed, that Henry Cotton, and his son, repair the tower and staircase; and they are to be allowed 2s. 8d. apiece for each day they work; and we to provide our own labourers, and pay them, and employ what other workmen we think convenient.

1693.

Accompts of Thomas Simpson, and Richard Townshend, for 1692.

Paid for gilding the Weather-cock 1l. 4s.

1694.

May 16. Accompt of Richard Townshend, and R. Weston, for 1693.

1695.

May 9. Accompt of Richard Weston, and Thomas Hartshorn for 1694.

Paid for tolling at the Queen's interment 2s.

For 12 yards of fine Holland 3l. for making of a surplice 7s. 6d.

Oct. 4. Collected for French Protestants 8l. 4s.

1696.

June 18. Accompt of Thomas Hartshorn, and G. Bent for 1695.

Paid for a large Bible ruled for the church 4l.

Paid for ringing on the King's birth day, and the King coming through Leicester the same day 5s.

For ringing November 5th, 10s.

Paid Michael Banshaw and Josiah Payne their year's salary 2s. 6d.

Paid for Common Prayer Book for the church 12s. 6d.

Paid Mr. Newton for copying the Register 6s. 8d.

Dec. 15. Agreed or consented that Mr. Hopkin Thomas, of Barkby, should be vicar of St. Martin's.

Agreed to remove the organ.

1697.

April 18. Agreed that the churchwardens shall take off the two locks of the seat formerly called Mr. Inge's seat, lately set on by order of Mr. Inge; and by order of Mr. G. Bent, late churchwarden; and if any controversy arise, the parish shall bear them harmless.

Accompt of G. Bent, and Thomas Topp, for 1696.

Paid for trimming for Joseph Payne's gown 6s. 5d.

Paid the ringers when Mr. Thomas was chosen 5s.

June 30. Agreed, that a petition be drawn to the Bishop concerning two seats, one called Mr. Stephens's, the other Mr. Inge's seat, which are now in dispute with the parish.

Agreed, that a bottle of wine be given to any minister for preaching during the present vacancy.

Also, Agreed, that Mr. John Newton, minister, shall be allowed 6s. 8d. for keeping the register, which Mr. Bent, late churchwarden, should have paid him.

1698.

1698.

June 22. Accompt of Thomas Topp, and Thomas Worall, for 1697.

Paid Mr. Thomas, for his visitation dinner 2s. 6d.

Paid for two day's work of five men to clean the church against the Bishop's visitation, 8s. 6d.

Paid two men, for keeping the chancel at the Bishop's visitation, 2s.

Paid for victuals and drink when Mr. Pool took induction 7s. 2d.

Paid the ringers on that occasion 5s.

Paid to Mr. Martin the minister, upon Mr. Pool's induction as was allowed at a parish meeting, for reading prayers, 2l.

Paid to the ringers, when Mr. Wood took possession of the place, 5s.

Agreed, that the organ be removed at the parish charge, within one month.

Jan. 4. Agreed, that whereas there has been 30s. allowed to the clerk of the parish annually for collecting of the vicar's contribution and dues, that the said 30s. shall be at the discretion of the said vicar, therewith to employ either the clerk, or such other person as he shall think more fit.

Agreed also, that Richard Yates, sexton, shall have 10s. a year, from the date hereof, for cleansing the church-yard and about the church such excrements and nastiness as shall be found, and to take care the same be prevented for the future, by getting such persons punished as shall be found guilty of such offences.

1699.

Accompt of Thomas Worral and Thomas Hemsley, for 1698.

May 3. Agreed, upon complaint and request of Mr. Samuel Heyrick, clerk, of Mr. Noble, and Henry Hitchcocks, that the Freears shall be taxed at no higher value than after 25l. per annum, the rest being given to charitable uses.

1700.

July 1. Accompt of Thomas Helmesley and R. Foxton, for 1699.

Paid for 13 yards of holland, at 5s. per yard, for a surplice, 3l. 5s. ;

For making thread, &c. 7s. 6d.

For a looking-glass for the vestry 4s.

Collected for relief of the Vaudois 22l. 13s. 7d.

July 1. Agreed, that the fifth bell, being cracked, shall be new cast.

Agreed, that William Noone, of Nottingham, shall have 20s. per cwt. for casting it, tuneable to the rest, and as near the same weight as may be, he allowing 10d. per lb. for what it wants, and we 12d. for what it weighs more. The parish to be at charge to carry it to Nottingham; and he to return it, and recast it if not tuneable, or if cracked in a year.

July. Collected for Redemption of Captives 5l. 6s. 6d.

June 4. Agreed, between All Saints parish and this, that John Dalloway shall pay to church and poor in All Saints parish, for his garden there, during his lease, after the rate of 18s. per annum, and he and his successors shall pay 12d. yearly for church and poor to the said parish, viz. 2d. every quarter to the poor, and 4d. to the church, which make 12d. per annum, for part of a barn which he renteth of Thomas Worral, and no more, provided it be not made a dwelling-house.

1701.

July 7. It is agreed at this meeting, that the Rev. Mr. Carte, vicar of St. Martin's, in the borough of Leicester, shall have 5l. per annum, paid half yearly by the churchwardens for the time being, beginning at Lady-day last, for the paying his rent, over and above the rent of the vicarage-house belonging to the parish.

May 19. 50s. given to H. Valentine, for playing on the organ, for a year ending at May-day last.

Aug. 13. Agreed, that the fifth bell be new cast by Mr. Noone, of Nottingham.

1702.

June 19. Agreed, that 5l. be given to H. Valentine, for playing the organ, for a year ending at Lady-day last, and the like sum yearly for the future.

June 26. Ordered, that new chimes be made.

Oct. 6. The tenor bell being cracked, ordered to be sawn, which cost 1l. 4s.

1703.

July 5. Ordered, that 3s. 4d. be spent every parish meeting, and to be allowed in the collector's accompts.

1704.

April 17. Agreed with Mr. Noone, of Nottingham, to cast the tenor bell; and, memorandum, the bell being taken down weighed 19cwt. 1qr. 16lbs.

Paid for wine in the year 1703, 7l. 11s. 6d.

Paid for casting the tenor bell, 1704, 26l. 8s.

For wine, 1704, 6l. 7s. 6d.

Paid for a Form of Prayer, for a thanksgiving after the great storm, 1s.

1705.

For a draught for the loft, 1l. 1s. 6d.

To Mr. Stephens, and the official, for a licence 6l. Austin Heyford's bell 44l. 2s. 6d.

To German Pegg, and John Oswin, for wainscots, 31l. 11s. 10d.

Aug. 7. It was agreed, that a gallery be built, to extend from the schoolmaster's seat, and to join to the third pillar which stands in the first seat next the aile.

The victories of the duke of Marlborough created much ringing.

1706.

April 5. The vacant seats in church and gallery ordered to be disposed of to those persons who are not otherwise provided for, at the discretion of the churchwardens, according to their payments to the church and poor.

April 5. Agreed, that the seat next the reading desk be locked, and kept for women strangers, christenings, and churchings.

Oct. 4. Agreed, that two women shall have 6d. per day for looking after a certain number of seats; and that the two sextons shall have 5s. per quarter added for looking after such seats as they are appointed for.

Paid for taking a Papish priest, and expences, 3s. 6d.

1707.

May 8. The Quakers refusing to pay any thing to church levies, it is agreed, that they shall be charged so much more to the poor's tax, as will balance what they ought to pay to the church.

Aug. 5. Agreed, that the churchwardens shall repair the chancel windows at the cost of the parish.

Much ringing for good news from abroad.

1708.

Jan. 4. It was agreed, that the collectors shall pay the weekly bill at the church on every Friday morning betwixt 9 and 10, unless it be a holy-day or fair day; and that the sexton toll the bell at the time, and be allowed 10d. per day, and such poor as do not appear within that time with their badge (unless sick or lame, or other reasonable let approved by the collector), are to forfeit that week's collection.

April 28. To prevent the charge of locking and unlocking the seats, ordered, the churchwardens to cause keys to be made, and given to the persons placed in these seats.

1709.

Aug. 22. The seat called Mr. Whatton's seat, granted to the use of Mr. Carter and his family; and the South chancel ordered to be repaired.

Sep. 27. Agreed, that the churchwardens shall try the title with Mr. Stephen for Mr. Whatton's seat.

1709-10.

1709-10.
Feb. 20.   John Dyson chose organist.

1710.
March 30.   Agreed, that the churchwardens shall shew to Mr. Stephen what books he designs to peruse relating to the dispute about the seat, if the counsel think fit; otherwise not.

Mrs. Elizabeth Coats gave a silver communion-cup and cover, weight 18 oz. 10 dwts.

Jan. 5.   Agreed, that the poor who will not wear the badges shall have their collection stopped; the badges are **M. P.** in blue cloth.

Feb. 23.   Agreed, that John Dyson shall have 5*l.* yearly, for playing on the organ.

This year the piece of ground near St. Margaret's church, given by Widow Chetle 37 Elizabeth, was let to Henry Garet for 21 years, ending at Lady-day 1732, for 25*s. per annum.*

1711.
Jan. 15.   Agreed to allow Mr. Roger Lee 20s. *per annum,* to look after and repair the clock and chimes.

July 4.   Agreed, that if any of the poor appear without the badge, he is to forfeit for every default a week's collection; and if the collector pay any defaulter, it shall not be allowed in his accompt.

Aug. 23.   Agreed, that the churchwardens for the time being put the chancel into repair, at the expence of the parish, out of respect to Mr. Carte, the present vicar, to whom the said repairs belong.

At this parish meeting Mrs. Alice Barnes, widow of Mr. John Barnes, of London, daughter of Mr. Edward Billers, formerly of this parish, presented two silver flagons, the one 46 oz. 2 dwts. the other 46oz. 9dwts. for the use of the parish of St. Martin, at the Holy Eucharist. And ordered, that the two pewter flagons be forthwith melted down, and the value of the pewter applied to the repairs of the church.

1712.
May 14.   Agreed, that the churchwardens shall forthwith cause to be pallisadoed the two arches of the great chancel, to render it more convenient for the Bishop to confirm children in.

July 11.   Agreed, that all shops in the Saturday market which pay rent to the Corporation shall pay taxes to the church and poor.

1713.
July 23.   Agreed, that a skylight shall be made in the roof opposite to the pulpit, for a better light, at the request of Mr. Archdeacon Rogers.

1714.
Nov. 28.   Paid the ringers when Mr. Carte was inducted.

Paid Mr. Willows, for charges in going to Hilmington, in Norfolk, 2*l.* 5*s.*

1715.
Jan. 12.   Agreed, that Mark Anthony Dallow repair and mend the organ (as here mentioned), for which he is to have 50*l.*

1716.
July 20.   Mr. Dallow having fully performed his agreement, and added two stops, and other work not mentioned in the agreement; it was ordered, that the churchwardens pay him the 50*l.* and 20*l.* over and above.

April 3.   Mr. Edmund Cradock, to be excused from being overseer of the poor, paid a fine of 20*s.* and spent 5*s.* at the meeting.

1717.
April 23.   Agreed, that Mr. John Dyson, present organist, shall have 10*l. per annum* during pleasure.

1718.
April 20.   Agreed, that the churchwardens shall cause the staircase leading up the steeple to be repaired.

1719.
September 4.   Agreed with Benjamin Garland and Mr. John Brothers for an altar to be set up in the chancel; viz. Mr. Brothers to have 25*l.* and Mr. Garland 10*l.*; and Mr. Brothers is to have 5*l.* more if he perform his work to the liking of the parish.

This year the altar-piece cost 40*l.*

1720.
Jan. 13.   The churchwardens and overseers ordered to purchase a piece of ground in the parish, and build a house on it for the poor, which they did of Timothy Sampter, in Mill-stone-lane.

1721.
Jan. 3.   My son Samuel[1] made declaration, that he would not put the parish to any charge about the prosecution of Mr. Jackson, &c. on the presentments of the churchwardens.

1722.
June 13.   Agreed, that workmen be employed to take down the weathercock, that it may be made useful, to turn with the wind.

June 27.   Agreed with John Jones and John Tompson, masons, to give them 20*l.* to put the weathercock in order, and point and repair the spire.

1723.
June 4.   The churchwardens ordered to provide a house, or hand engine, to extinguish fire.

1724.
An order came from the Bishop of Lincoln for new-pewing the church, and building the North gallery uniform with the South gallery built in 1705.

In April this year, the inhabitants of St. Martin's determined to convert their parish houses into a workhouse, by joining two of the lower apartments into one, for a working-room, and fitting up two others for a kitchen, cellar, &c. and furnishing them[2].

In the year 1730, Mr. Needham, who lived in the church-yard, obtained leave from the parish to make the gravel-walk, and plant it with trees at his own expence.

In 1737, it was agreed, that part of the spire should be taken down, i. e. two feet below the first window, at the expence of 126*l.*; an enormous expence, if compared with the rebuilding St. Mary's spire lately. Moreover, the builder, whose name was Jackson, tricked the parish out of a full yard of its height[3].

[1] Samuel Carte, esq. afterwards an eminent solicitor in Chancery, and an able Ecclesiastical Antiquary.

[2] In about six months after this alteration, the state of this workhouse was thus described: "They first made choice of a master, who has the immediate care of the poor, to keep them in order, and employ them in such work as they are capable of, and see that their food is duly prepared, and given to them, &c. He has two apartments assigned to him, his diet and washing, and 12*l.* a year salary. The parish overseers buy all things necessary for the house, and the poor in it. For their cloathing, they buy whole pieces of woollen and linen; which, when cut out, is made up into cloaths, by such of the poor as are capable of it. The overseers, about once a month, send in five strike of malt, which the master brews at once into good drink; and every Saturday the overseers buy a sufficient quantity of wholesome meat, and send it to the master. If any of the poor fall sick, a proper provision is made for them, and some of their fellow-poor is appointed to attend them. They are all confined within the precincts of the house, and are not to go out of it without leave of the master; if any of them have employment abroad, they are obliged to return in a due hour; and whoever employs them, agrees with the master for the wages, and pays them to him; which, together with the product of the labours of the rest, he delivers to the overseers every Friday in the evening, who take the accounts from the master; and adds, out of the parish-stock, what is wanting for making provision for the following week. The general method for employing them, besides what is above-mentioned, is in spinning jersey: such as cannot spin are set to knit stockings for the rest; and one is appointed to teach children to read. The time of working is twelve hours in the day, winter and summer. The number of the poor is 28, viz. 16 old, and 12 under 8 years of age. The product of their labours, one week with another, is about 14*s.* the charge of maintaining them weekly is 2*l.* that is, about 1*l.* 6*s.* above their labour. The charge of maintaining the poor used to be about 250 or 300*l.* a year. The charge this year, in cloathing the poor, upon placing them in the workhouse, and buying utensils, &c. is much greater than can be in future years; and yet the overseer assures me, that he is sure the parish will even this year save 100*l.* The children have a form placed for them in the alley, before the seat of the parish officers, to sit upon on Sundays; but there is no particular place as yet assigned to the elder poor at church." *History of Workhouses, Oct.* 10, 1724.

[3] Throsby's Leicester, 1791. p. 262.

PEDIGREE of STEPHENS, of LEICESTER.

Arms : Per chevron Azure and Argent, in chief two falcons rising Or. Crest, a demi-eagle, wings expanded Or. (See the Monument of Stephens, in Plate XLII.)

Henry Stephens, of Frocester, co. Gloucester; buried in the church of=..... daughter and heir of Edward Lugg, of St. Peter's at Frocester. Will dated Jan. 9, proved March 16, 1552. | the county of Hereford; died before 1552.

Edward Stephens, esq. eldest son and heir. He purchased the manor of Easting-=Jane, daughter of Richard Fowler, of Many ton, co. Gloucester, of Henry lord Stafford 1573; died Oct. 22, 1587, aged about | Stonehouse, co. Gloucester, gent. other 64; buried at Eastington. Will dated Aug. 13, proved Nov. 27, 1587, by his | died Aug. 5, 1587, aged about 63, chil- brother-in-law William Fowler, gent. and his son Richard. | and was buried at Eastington. dren.

1. Richard Stephens, of Eastington aforesaid, esq. eldest son and heir, buried there Dec. 24, 1599; married, and left issue.
2. James Stephens, of Eastington, esq. died 19, and buried 24 Feb. 1594, at Eastington; marr. and had issue.

3. Thomas Stephens, of Over Lypiate, in the parish of Stroud,=Elizabeth, daughter Three co. Gloucester, esq.; attorney-general to prince Henry and | and coheir of John daugh- king Charles the First; sometime reader at the Middle Tem- | Stone, of Over Ly- ters. ple, London; died at Lypiate, April 26, 1613, æt. 55; bu- | piate, esq. and sis- ried in Stroud church, where is the monument in the an- | ter to Wm. Stone; nexed Plate. Will dated March 8, 1612, codicil in April, | was executrix to her and proved Nov. 24, 1613, by his wife Elizabeth. | husband 1613.

1. Edward=Anne, dau. of Stephens, | sir Thos. Crewe, of Little | of Stene, co. Sodbury, | Northampton, co. Glou- | knt. serjeant at cester, esq. | law, and sister a minor in | to the first lord 1590; died | Crewe, of Stene. about 1670.

Sir Thomas Stephens, of=Catharine, dau. of William Sodbury, co. Glouces- | Coombes, of Stratford- ter, kt.; living 1681. | upon-Avon, co. Warwick.

2. John Stephens, of Over Lypiate; a bencher of the Middle Temple; had four wives, and left issue; d. 4, and buried at Stroud Aug. 12, 1679, aged about 76.

3. Nathaniel=Elizabeth, Stephens, | daughter, of Horton | and at and Cheri- | length sole ton, both co. | heir of Ro- Gloucester, | bert Ty- esq.; died | ringham[1], about 1640, | of Weston- æt. about 30. | upon-Fa- | vell, co. | Northamp- | ton, and of | Barkby, co. | Leicester, | esq.

Eliza-=Samuel Codrington, of Dodington, Other beth, | co. Gloucester, esq. born July 31, chil- died | 1599. Will dated June 11, 1674; dren. 1687. | proved by Elizabeth his relict and | executrix Nov. 13, 1676.

Samuel=Jane, daughter of John Codrington, of Codring- | Codrington and Didmarton, co. Glouces- ton, | ter, esq. by Anne his second wife, eldest 2d son. | daughter and coheir of Nathaniel Still, of | Hutton, co. Somerset, esq. son of John | Still, of Durley, co. Somerset, bishop of | Bath and Wells.

Elizabeth, third daugh-=Edmund Rowe. possessed ter and coheir, died in | the right of the advowson childbed, at Doding- | of Linson, co. Devon. ton, in April 1677.

1. Edward=Mary, daugh- Stephens, | ter of John of Alder- | Raynsford, of ley, Hor- | Staverton, c. ton and | Northamp- Cheriton, | ton, and of all co. | Wolfhamcote, Glouces- | co. Warwick, ter, esq.; | esq. elder bro- and of the | ther to sir Ri- Middle | chard Rayns- Temple, | ford, kt. lord barrister | chief justice at law; | of the King's bapt. | Bench. July 25, 1633; liv- ing in 1682.

Isabel, 4th=2. Tyringham Ste-=Milicent, 4th dau. daughter | phens, of the Cas- | of William Inge, of George | tle, near the Bo- | of Thorpe Con- Rayson, of | rough of Leices- | stantine, co. Staf- the Bo- | ter, archdeacon | ford, esq. by Eli- rough of | of Leicester, | zabeth his 2d wife, Leicester, | born 16, and | daughter and heir esq. died | bapt. at St. Mar- | of Thos. Tunsted, about | tin's, Leicester, | of Tunsted, co. 1668; | May 29, 1635; | Derby, esq. bapt. first wife. | buried at St. | Feb. 23, 1646; | Mary's, Leicester, | buried at St. Ma- | June 21, 1710. | ry's, Leicester, | | Nov. 23, 1721; | | second wife.

Elizabeth, only dau. and=Benjamin Michell, of heir, born at Dodington | Sea Side, in the parish aforesaid, Mar. 31, 1677; | of Branscombe, and of married at Windon, co. | Slade, in the parish Somerset, Oct. 1699; | of Salcomb Regis, co. died March 11, 1760; | Devon, gent. born in buried at Salcomb. | April 1676; di. Apr. 1, | 1751; bur. at Salcomb.

Elizabeth, only daughter, and=John Heard, some at length heir, born 1, and | time of Bridgewa- bapt. at Branscomb afore- | ter, co. Somerset, said, Aug. 21, 1705; mar- | afterwards of Lon- ried at Salcomb June 11, | don, gent. born at 1726; died Sept. 22, 1778; | Bridgewater, May and buried in the cemetery | 30, 1698; died at of St. George, Bloomsbury, | Richmond, c. Sur- co. Middlesex, the 26th of | rey, 24, and there the same month. | bur. June 27, 1759.

1. Tyringham Stephens, born and baptized at St. Mary's, Leicester, April 30, 1672; died unmarried; buried at St. Mary's, June 6, 1710.
2. Walter Stephens, bo. Feb. 27, 1675; died s. p.
3. Thomas Stephens, an officer in the army, born Dec. 10, 1677; bapt. at St. Mary's, Jan. 2, 1677-8; died s.p.

4. Rev. Nathaniel=Ellis, d. of Stephens, rector | P. Deane, of Alphamstone, | of Har- c. Essex, born 3, | wich afore- and bapt. at St. | said, gent.; Mary's, July 22, | mar. there 1697; buried at | May 5, Harwich, co. Es- | 1709; sex, April 28, | died Aug. 1730. | 18, 1762; | buried at | Harwich.

5. Richard Stephens, born 2, bapt. at St. Mary's, Leicester, Nov. 5, 1684; mar- ried, but died s.p.; buried at Leicester in 1745.
6. Charles Stephens, born the 12th, and bapt. at St. Mary's, Sept. 30, 1686; buried there April 8, 1687.

Jane, æt. 8, 1681.
Milicent, ætat. 9 months, 1681.
Other da's, 1681.

Sir Isaac Heard, knt. Garter Principal King of Arms, gentleman usher of the most honourable military order of the Bath, and Brunswick Herald, born at St. Mary Ottery, co. Devon, Dec. 10, 1730; appointed Bluemantle pursuivant of Arms Dec. 5, 1759; Lancaster herald July 3, 1761; Norroy king of Arms Oct. 18, 1774; Clarenceux March 16, 1780; and Garter May 1, 1784; knighted at a chapter of the most noble order of the Garter, at St. James's, June 2, 1786; living 1810.

1. Tyringham Stephens, esq. a commissioner in the Victualling Office, born March 20, 1713; died unmarried, Feb. 18, 1768; buried at Harwich aforesaid. Administration of his effects granted to his brother Philip, Jan. 17, 1769.
2. Nathaniel Stephens, esq. captain of the Lively man of war, born Oct. 13, 1721; died unmarried, at Fort St. David's in the East Indies, March 23, 1747.
3. Sir Philip Stephens, of St. Faith's and Horsford, co. Norfolk, and of Fulham, co. Middlesex, born at Bures, co. Essex, Oct. 11, 1723; representative in parliament for the borough of Sandwich; late, and for many years secretary to the Admiralty; created a baronet of Great Britain, to him and his heirs male, in default to his nephew Stephens Howe, esq. and his heirs male, by patent, bearing date March 17, 1795; one of the lords commission- ers of the Admiralty; died s. p. Nov. 20, 1809, and was buried at Fulham.

1. Ellis, born Feb. 22, 1709; died Aug. 4, 1710.
3. Grace, born Aug. 5, 1719; died unmarried, Mar. 14, 1783; buried at Harwich.

2. Milicent,=William Howe, of Mistley born Feb. | Thorne, co. Essex, gent. 11, 1715; | (son of Leonard Howe, of married | Wickham Brook, co. Suf- at Wester- | folk, gent. by Elizabeth field, co. | his wife, daughter of ..... Suffolk; | Nunn, of Bury St. Ed- living in | mund's, co. Suffolk, esq. 1795. | counsellor at law); died | in 1766, and was buried | at Ipswich, co. Suffolk.

1. William Howe, esq. captain of the Montreal frigate, born July 31, 1739; died unmarried, Jan. 31, 1765; buried at Gib- raltar.
2. Tyringham Howe, esq. a post captain in the Royal Navy, born Jan. 23, 1748; married, but died without issue, June 14, 1783; buried at Thames Dit- ton, co. Surrey.
3. Nathaniel Howe, born July 6, 1741; died young.

4. Philip Howe, of Havant, c. Hants, esq. a captain of marines, born March 18, 1750; married Mary- Anne, daughter of ..... Tongue, of Gibraltar, gent.
5. Stephens Howe, esq. born at Har- wich, March 10, 1759; M. P. for Yarmouth; colonel of the duke of York's, or 5th West India regi- ment; and brigadier-general of his majesty's forces in the West Indies; late aid-du-camp to the king; died unmarried.

1. Grace, born Oct. 11, 1737; died young.
2. Grace, born July 18, 1752; living 1795, unmarried.
4. Ellis-Cornelia, bo. July 24, 1743; died in June 1792, unmarried; buried at Brompton, co. Kent.

Thomas Wilkinson,=3 Milicent, esq. a captain in | bo. Aug. 18, the Royal Navy; | 1745; re- died, in February | mar. in Sept. 1777, on board | 1783, to Ga- the Pearl frigate, | briel Mat- on his voyage | thias, of from New York | Scotland-yd. to Antigua, aged | co. Middle- 43; first husband. | sex, esq. She | buried at St. | Martin's in | the Fields.

Philip Wilkinson, esq. captain of his majesty's frigate Her- | Grace, born April 24, 1772; died unmarried, Feb. 13, 1793; mione, born at Harwich, Dec. 1770; living 1795, unmarried. | buried at St. Martin's in the Fields, co. Middlesex.

[1] See the Pedigree of Tyringham, of Barkby, p. 407.

PEDIGREE of MILES, of LEICESTER.

Arms: Azure, on a chevron engrailed, between three knights helmets Or, as many mill-rinds Sable. Crest, an eagle rising Erminois, collared, chained and charged on the breast with a mill-rind Sable. Plate XLI. fig. 15.

Richard Miles.═

Francis Miles, died 1626.   Ralph Miles.═Mary.   Thomas Miles, living 1633.

Ralph Miles, died 1689.═Mary Stevenson.

Robert Miles.   Ralph Miles.   William Miles, died 1714.═Elizabeth Ward.   George Miles.

Samuel Miles, died 1762.═Mary, daughter of John Pares, of Leicester.   Joseph Miles.   Thomas Miles.

John Miles, died 1773.═Elizabeth, daughter of John Hickman, of Tinkwood in Cheshire.

Samuel Miles, died 1798.═Justina, daughter of Roger Dutton, of Cheshire.   George-Hickman Miles, died a minor.

John Miles, LL. B. of Willoughby Waterless.═Eleanor, daughter of Thomas Lomas, of Leicester.   Elizabeth.═Clement Leigh, M. A. of Newcastle-under-Lyne, c. Stafford.   George Miles.   Samuel Miles, F.S.A.   Roger Miles.   Thomas Miles.   Anne.   Several other children, died young.

Samuel-Thomas Miles.   John-Henry Miles.

PEDIGREE of GREGORY, of ASHOVER, DERBYSHIRE; and of ST. MARTIN'S, LEICESTER.

John Gregory, of Pyllesley and Overton, purchased the last 1601.═Elizabeth.

Richard Gregory.═Ellen, daughter of .... Moore, of Dronfield, and sister to Robert; married 1658.

John Gregory, buried 1691.   John Gregory, born 1659; died 1688.   Richard Gregory, born 1660; died 1688.═Elizabeth, daughter of William Gilsthorpe, of Whatton, co. Nottingham; died 1688.

John Gregory,═Sarah, daughter of Giles Cowley, of Ashover.   Elizabeth, bapt. Jan. 1683; buried March following.   Ellen, bapt. 1687; buried 1688.
bapt. 1685.

John Gregory, of Overton, born 1799.═Sarah, daughter of : .... Murray, a West-country woman.   Richard Gregory, born 1705.   William Gregory, bapt. 1708.═

George Gregory, of Ashover.   Sarah, of Ashover.

Richard Gregory, died 1789.═Mary, daughter of John Cockayne, of Kayside, Ashover.   John Gregory, esq. alderman of Leicester, and printer of the Leicester Journal; died at the Adelphi tavern, London, Mar. 22, 1789.═   Sarah, wife of Edward Terry, an officer of excise.   Anne.   Richard Gregory, of Botsdale, co. Suffolk, surgeon.   Frances.

John Gregory.

1. John Gregory, printer of the Leicester Journal, died s. p. 1806.   2. Joseph Gregory, M. A. vicar of St. Martin's and All Saints, Leicester, died 1802.═Elizabeth, daughter of Thomas Vowe, of Hallaton, esq.   Fanny, dead.═John Price, editor of the Leicester Journal, 1810.

1. Thomas-Vowe Gregory, printer, at Leicester; living 1810.   2. John Gregory; 3. Joseph Gregory; living 1810.   Mary.   Fanny-Gregory Price.   Peter-Lea-Gregory Price.   Sophia-Penfold Price.   John-Edward Price.   Charles-Henry-Shaddeus Price.   Felix-Frederic Price.   Orderic-Elfrida Price.

Writings of Richard Gregory. Collected by the Rev. Dr. Pegge, from the Originals in the possession of Adam Wolley, esq. 1792.

Sans date. Robert, son of sir Robert de Wylneby, grants to Allan, son of Ralph Fat, of Overton, the service of William, son of John Gregory, of Wymond, for all that land which said William formerly held of him (Robert de Wylneby grantor) in territory of Overton, which half acre of land lying between a toft which said William formerly held, and the moor, &c. to hold to him, except *men of Religion and Jews*, for a pound of cummin, and 2s. of silver, at three times in the year. Witness, sir Walter de Rybyf, Ralph de Rerysby, Geoff. de Dethea, Geoffr. de Monasteriis (Musters), Hen. de Knottingham, Rob. de Butterley, &c.

Sans date. Robert also grants to the same an oxgang of land, with a toft and croft, &c. which David le Smiltes formerly held in Overton, with a place of land called the *Syward Parroc*, to hold to grantee and theirs, or whomsoever he should assign, except *men of Religion and Jews*, paying yearly 3s. of silver, at twice. Witness, same.

Sans date. Robert, son of William son of John de Overton, grants to Simon, son of Nicholas Catigon, of Overton, a croft in *villa* of Overton called the *Calve Croft*, to hold of the chief lord of the fee, paying to the lord services due, and to grantor a penny of silver. Witness, William de Wynnefeld, Hen. de Cnottingham, William son of Hen. of the Green, Richard son of William, Gilbert son of Robert, William son of Henry, Richard de Laffordia, clerk, &c.

21 Edw. I. Same grants to Simon de Cadigan, of Overton, and his heirs, all the land and tenements, with the toft and croft, and houses thereon erected, which he had in the territory of Overton, with the rents, escheats, wards, reliefs, and all *privamentis* (privileges) within the said land, to hold of chief lords, &c. to him and theirs, &c. paying yearly to chief lord 2s. and one pound of cummin, at twice. Witness, John Deyncurt, Robert Ribuf, Simon de Reresbi, Walter de Oraston, Hen. de Cnottingham, Reginald de Holmes, Gilbert son of Dobin, William son of Henry, Ralph son of William, &c.

24 Edw. I. Symon Cadigan, of Essover, grants to Richard Cadigan, of Clatercotis, his brother, and his heirs and assigns, an oxgang of land, with toft and croft, and which Richard Fat formerly held in Overton; also a piece of land called the *Syward Parroc*, &c. to hold of chief lord, &c. to him, heirs, and assigns, except *men of Religion and Jews*, paying to the lord 3s. at twice. Witness, Symon de Rerysby, William de Wynefeld, William of the Green, Ralph son of Robert, John of the Holmes, Robert la Warde, Robert the Clerk, &c.

16 Edw. II. Johanna, formerly wife of Simon son of Godfrey del Stabbyng in the Soke of Essover, in her viduity, releases, &c. to William le Hunte, of Overton, Richard le Hunte their brother, and John le Hunte their heirs and assigns, her claim in all the lands, &c. which the aforesaid William, Richard, John, had of the gift and feoffment of Simon her husband, and of her gift and feoffment, in territory of Overton, in soke of Essover. Witness, sir Adam de Rerisby, knt. Ralph de Rerisby, Walter de Oggaston, Robert de Wynnefeld, &c.

18 Edw. II. Hauuisa, formerly wife of Godfrey del Stubbyng, de Essover, in her viduity, grants to William le Hunte, of Essover, and Richard his brother, one messuage and one oxgang of land in Overton, in the fee of Essover, which were formerly Hugh le Hewer's, to hold of lords of the fee. Witness, sir Adam de Rerisby, Ralph de Rerisby, Robert de Wynnefeld, Robert de Ubbestoft, Robert de Stubbyng, Robert de Pres, &c.

20 Edw. II. John le Hunt, of Essover, granted and released to Richard le Hunt his brother, his heirs and assigns, all his right in two messuages, two oxgangs of land, and two places of land, one called *Calve Croft*, with appurtenances, in Essover, as by the deed, which John son of Richard Cadigan, of Essover, thereof made to them, more fully appeared. Witness, Robert de Wynnefeld, of Essover, Robert de Ubbestoft, of the same, Ralphe de Cryche, Robert de le Stubbyng, Pet. de Allen, &c.

40 Edw. III. Ralphe Hunt, of Treedon, son of Richard Hunt, of Ashover, released to John Hunt his son all his right in all his lands and tenements, meadows, woods, and common of pasture, which were the said Richard Hunt's his father in Overton, in the parish of Ashover. Witness, sir Thomas, rector of the church of Ashover, Roger de Wynfeld, John son of Simon de Ashover, John Hunt son of William Hunt, John of the Marsh, &c.

39 Eliz. 1597. William Hunte, of Overton, parish of Ashover, co. Derby, yeoman, in consideration of 260l. paid him by Robert Dakyn, of Chelmarton, in the said county, yeoman, granted to Robert, his heirs and assigns, all that capital messuage or tenement, with appurtenances, in Overton aforesaid, then or late in the occupation of said Robert and Margaret Hunte his

(grantor's)

(grantor's) mother, and their assigns, and also all other the messuages, cottages, lands, tenements, meadows, feedings, pastures, woods, underwoods, rents, reversions, services, moors, marshes, &c. lying in Overton aforesaid, and in Mylnedowne, within the parish and county aforesaid, or elsewhere in the said county of Derby, to hold to said Robert Dakyn, his heirs and assigns, to the only proper use and behoof of said Robert Dakyn, his heirs and assigns for ever. General warranty against said William, his heirs and assigns.

43 Eliz. 1601. Robert Dakyn, of Chelmarton, co. Derby, gent. granted to John Gregory, of Pythesley, in said county, yeoman, his heirs and assigns, all said premises mentioned in last deed, to hold to said John Gregory, his heirs and assigns, for ever. Dakyn warrants the same to the said Gregory, his heirs and assigns, against said Robert Dakyn and his heirs; and against Adam Hunt, deceased, and his heirs; and against William Hunt, son and heir of said Adam, and his heirs; and against Arthur Hunt, Ralph Hunt, and Edward Hunt, brother of said William Hunt, and their heirs. Witness, Roger Dicken, Francis Burton, and Thomas Northege.

24 Car. I. Indenture between Richard Hodgkinson and John Farneworth, of Ashover, co. Derby, yeoman, on one part, and John Gregory, of Ashover aforesaid, yeoman, of the other part; reciting, that sir Thomas Reresbye, late of Friburgh, in the county of York, knt. by his indenture, bearing date 16 April, 17th year of late king James, &c. did demise unto sir Francis Wortley, knt. and bart. sir Robert Mounson, knt. Anthony Mounson, esq. and to one Thomas Lewis, gent. all those several manors or lordships of Ashover, Reresby, and Babington, alias Cossehall, with their and every of their rights whatsoever, situate in Ashover aforesaid, and to the said manors, or either of them, belonging, for the term of 2000 years, on special trust; and to the intent and purpose nevertheless, amongst other things, that the rents and profits of the said manors and premises should be for the maintenance of the younger children of the said sir Thomas Reresbye, and for raising of portions of 1500l. apiece for his two daughters, viz. Bridget, who was afterwards married to one Isaac Scott, gent. and Mary, who was afterwards married to one Robert Steward, esq.; and that since which time, the estate, interest, and term of years of them, the said sir Francis Wortley, &c. was by good assurance of, in, and to the said manor called Babington, alias Cossehall, with the rights thereof, vested and settled in them the said Richard Hodgkinson and John, for all the residue of 2000 years then unexpired. It was witnessed, that the said Richard Hodgkinson and John Farneworth, in consideration of 97l. 4s. 4d. to them in hand then paid by the said John Gregory, did grant and sell unto him the said John Gregory all those two closes called the *Doelayes*, one other close called *Half Acre*, lying beyond the Hay, formerly parcel of a farm called *Dick Lant Farm*; and also, all those two lands lying in Middlefield, one dole lying in the White Gangs, or land lying in the Stoney Acre, one parcel of land lying in the Stores, two lands in the Gate Lands, four butts lying in a close of George Hodgkinson, formerly parcel of a farm called the *Raven's Nest*; all which premises lying in Ashover aforesaid, and in the occupation of John Gregory, George Cowlishaw, William Henstock, and George Hodgkinson; and all that seventh part (the whole being divided into seven equal parts) of all chief rents and waste grounds; and of all mines, and royalties, that are parcel of the said manor called Babington, alias Cossehall; to hold unto the said John Gregory, his heirs and assigns, during the term of the said 2000 years then unexpired.

Richard Gregory's title to an estate at Overton, and abstract of some of his other writings.

15 Hen. VI. Richard Barat grants to Edmund de Trafford and William Perpont, knts. John de Huntingdon, clerk, John de Heyton, and Ralph de Calcroft, chaplain, all his goods and chattels, as well live as dead, which he then had in the county of Derby. Witness, Richard Calcroft, Thomas Swalowe, William Marshall, Thomas Hewgate, Richard Coke, and others.

3 Hen. VIII. Thomas Hountte and Jone his wife, of Overton, yeoman, granted and sold lands and tenements, called the *Harpper's Pynghylls*, and the *Hollmedowe*, in the parish of Ashover aforesaid, to Thomas Babington, of Dethick, within the parish and county aforesaid, esq. for a certain sum of money paid by the hands of the said Thomas Babington. Witness, George Jackson, Rauffe Donstone, John Woodhouse, &c.

1597. Margaret Hunt, of Overton, widow, late wife of Adam Hunt, deceased. Robert Dakyn, of Chelmarton, co. Derby, yeoman.

43 Eliz. A bond of Robert Dakyn, of Chelmarton, gent. to John Gregory, of Pythesley, near Ensor, co. Derby, yeoman, for 700l. on performance of covenant between Dakyn and Gregory.

1682. Article between William Gilthorpe, of Whatton, co. Nottingham, gent. and John Gregory, of Overton, gent. relating to a marriage between Richard Gregory, son of John, and Elizabeth daughter of William, whose portion was 300l. and John was to give his son half of his goods and chattels, to be divided by Thomas Sharpe, of Barneby in the Willows, George Shaw, of Spittlefields, parish of Chesterfield, and William Cockayne, of Matlock, gents. or any two of them.

4 Jac. II. Richard Gregory, by will, proved 1688, leaves guardianship of his two children John and Ellen, to his wife, then to his father and mother Ellen Gregory.—N. B. John Gregory then lived at Overton, and married Sarah Cowley.

PEDIGREE of STEPHENS[1], of St. Martin's, Leicester.

Thomas Stephens, of Leicester.══Hannah, daughter of Francis and Abigail Ward, of Leicester, bapt. Dec. 19, 1679; buried at St. Martin's Jan. 16, 1767.

1. John Stephens, born Jan. 10, and bapt. Feb. 5, 1707; died Nov. 15, 1782; buried at St. Martin's Nov. 21 following.══Elizabeth, d. of John Barfoot, of Evington, born Aug. 14, 1714; d. Aug. 30, 1782; buried at St. Martin's Sept. 4 following.

2. Thomas Stephens, born July 1, 1710.══Hannah, dau. of ...... Garratt.

3. Francis born Oct. 5, 1712; died in November following.

1. Elizabeth, born June 11, 1706; married ...... Mears, of Leicester; died s. p.
2. Hannah, born Dec. 19, 1743; married .... Cape, of London.

3. Mary,══Laurence Read, of Leicester. bo. Oct. 4, 1716.
1. William Read.
2. Thomas Read. ✝
3. Lawrence Read.

4. Anne.══... Badily, of Dadley, co. Stafford.
Elizabeth, married, and had issue.

John Badily, died s. p.   Elizabeth, living unmarried.

1. William Stephens, born Nov. 11, bapt. Dec. 11, 1733.
2. Thomas Stephens, born Aug. 2, bapt. Sept. 3, 1740.
3. Joseph Stephens, died in his infancy.
1. Mary, born Nov. 26, bapt. Dec. 26, 1735.
2. Elizabeth, born Mar. 7, bapt. April 3, 1738.══Thomas Lockwood, of Leicester.
3. Sarah, born Feb. 11, bapt. Aug. 5, 1746.
4. Anne, born Feb. 15, bapt. March 12, 1743; married Robert Kirkwall, of Cosby.

1. Thomas Lockwood.   2. George Lockwood.   1. Elizabeth.   2. Mary.══...... Joice, of Leicester, ✝ who died a young man.

1. John Stephens, born Dec. 12, 1733; died Mar. 7, 1808; buried at St. Martin's, s. p.
2. Thomas Stephens, born May 14, 1735; died Jan. 29, 1790, in Leadenhall-str. London, s. p.══Anne, daughter of ..... Dell, merchant at Hull, c. York.
3. William Stephens, born Oct. 8, 1737; died Feb. 16, 1760, s. p.
4. Richard Stephens, of St. Martin's, Leicester, born June 28, 1745; married July 20, 1774.══Alice, dau. of John Lettice, vicar of Boscate, c. Northampton, born Sept. 22, 1744.
Sarah, born Sept. 24, 1739; died Nov. 1739.

1. John Stephens, born May 23, 1775, in St. Martin's, Leicester.══Maria, daughter of Walter Ruding, of Westcotes; m. Sept. 30, 1800, at St. Mary's, Leicester.
2. Richard Stephens, of Brasenose College, Oxford, born March 29, 1785, in St. Martin's, Leicester.
1. Elizabeth, born Oct. 25, 1776, in St. Martin's, Leicester.
2. Alice, born Aug. 12, 1778; died Feb. 14, 1780; buried at St. Martin's, Leicester.
3. Anne, bo. June 27, 1780.
4. Maria, born Jan. 9, 1782.
5. Alice, born Nov. 11, 1783.

1. John Stephens, born July 1, 1802, in St. Michael's, Bassishaw; died July 18, 1802; buried at St. Mary's Aldermanbury, London.
2. John-Ruding Stephens, born July 12, 1803; bapt. Nov. 26 following, at Hackney, Middlesex.
3. Richard-Ruding Stephens, born Dec. 19, 1807; bapt. Dec. 27, 1808, at Hackney.
1. Maria, born July 4, 1801; bapt. Aug. 4 following, at St. Mary-le-bonne, London.
2. Elizabeth-Ruding, born Jan 7, 1805; bapt. April 9 following, at Hackney.
3. Sarah-Ruding, born Oct. 10, 1806; bapt. Jan. 26, 1807, at Hackney.

[1] Communicated by Mr. Richard Stephens, of Brasenose College, Oxford; with the following Remark: "I have adopted no date which cannot be proved by parish registers."

EASTINGTON.

Tomb of EDWARD STEPHENS Efquire
and JOAN his WIFE, 1587.

Baptisms, burials, marriages, and poors' rate, in this parish, continued from p. 568.

Years.	Baptisms.			Burials.			Mar.	Net amount of poors' rate.			Total disbursem.ts, including balances in officers' hands.			Rate in the pound.	
	Ma.	Fem.	Total.	Ma.	Fem.	Total.		£.	s.	d.	£.	s.	d.	s.	d.
1760	28	24	52	46	59	105	—	736	18	8	737	12	7	—	—
1775	43	43	86	24	38	62	27	714	9	0½	808	4	1	3	0
1776	48	42	90	42	42	84	31	735	19	4	736	6	7	3	0
1777	37	48	85	28	30	58	27	744	1	3	715	6	2	3	0
1778	31	43	74	29	43	72	25	693	9	8¼	740	16	5	3	9
1779	36	47	83	33	46	79	28	897	3	11	937	5	7	3	6
1780	37	43	80	31	34	65	32	971	13	9	1110	12	4½	3	9
1781	46	51	97	51	16	107	29	962	17	7	1018	15	7	3	9
1782	35	39	74	22	48	70	41	926	14	3	967	18	8	3	9
1783	45	47	92	38	38	76	—	889	16	5	1008	15	8	3	5
1784	52	36	88	35	39	74	—	931	1	10	1003	17	3	3	7
1785	40	42	82	35	38	73	—	980	16	9	1027	14	5	3	9
1786	35	47	82	40	45	85	—	983	18	7	1083	3	6	3	3
1787	40	42	82	28	31	59	—	870	5	8¼	1012	3	10	3	5
1788	44	35	79	41	53	94	—	919	7	1	1012	15	4	3	6
1789	44	29	73	35	42	77	—	950	14	8	1132	14	8	3	9
1790	34	43	77	34	36	70	—	1028	1	3	1109	2	8	3	10
1791	42	37	79	38	31	69	—	955	7	10	1106	6	4	3	6
1792	30	32	62	46	39	85	—	963	17	9	1119	5	1	3	6
1793	32	40	72	23	40	63	—	923	2	10	1015	16	6	3	4
1794	43	45	90	—	—	—	—	1109	14	6	1301	3	11	4	0
1795	—	—	—	—	—	—	—							5	5

Extracts from the Registers, &c.

"Parish book of St. Martin's, 1576, February the 5th day:

" Thomas Tilsye and Ursula Russel were maryed; and because the sayde Thomas was and is naturally deafe, and also dumbe, so that the order of the forme of mariage used usually amongst others which can heare and speake, could not for his parte be observed. After the approbation had from Thomas the bishoppe of Lincolne, John Chippendale, doctor in lawe, and commissarye, as also of Mr. Richard Davye, then mayor of the towne of Leicester, with others of his brethren, with the rest of the parishe; the said Thomas, for the expressing of his minde instead of words, of his owne accorde used these signes; first he embraced her with his armes, and took her by the hande, putt a ringe upon her finger, and layed his hande upon his hearte, and then upon her hearte; and held up his hands toward heaven; and to shewe his continuance to dwell with her to his lyves ende, he did it by closing of his eyes with his hands, and digginge out of the earth with his foote, and pullinge as though he would ring a bell, with diverse other signes approved."

" 1590. Thomas Sacheverell [the confrater] and Mary Eyricke married.

" 1599, July 22. William Rowditch and Agnes Hyndeman were married.

" 1635, June 30. Mary, daughter of Mr. John Oneby, by Emmet his wife, was baptised.

" 1636, March 1. Joseph Sacheverell, gentleman, [son of the confrater] was buried.

" 1637, March 23. John, the son of John Onebie, Esq. counsellor at lawe, by Emmet his wife, was baptised.

" 1638, May 2. Abigale, the daughter of William Staveley, was buried.

" 1649, July 2. Mrs. Elizabeth Sacheverell, widow [of Thomas], was buried.

" 1650, Sept. 5. George Curtis, bell-founder, buried.

" 1655, Aug. 20. Sicilla, daughter of Richard Yates, baptised.

" Queen Elizabeth's reign; baptisms.—1559, 26; 1560, 42; 1561, 41; 1562, 51; 1563, 37; 1564, 48; 1565, 44; 1566, 37; 1567, 40; 1568, 43; 1569, 41; 1570, 42; 1571, 36; 1572, 41; 1573, 42; 1598, 30; 1599, 31; 1600, 45; 1601, 29; 1602, 34.

" King James's reign; baptisms.—1604, 41; 1605, 32; 1606, 40; 1607, 45; 1608, 50; 1609, 45; 1610, 37; 1611, 38; 1612, 37; 1613, 41;

1614, 32; 1615, 37; 1616, 43; 1617, 39; 1618, 38; 1622, 40; 1623, 28; 1624, 51.

" King Charles I.; baptisms.—1635, 54; 1636, 41; 1637, 51; 1638, 43; 1639, 46; 1640, 49; 1641, 50; 1642, 62; 1643, 52; 1644, 34; 1645, 22; 1646, 33; 1647, 26; 1648, 23; 1649, 52; 1650, 44."—" Caroli Regis 24⁰, vivat vivat," ceases in 1648, though usually at the dates of the preceding years in the baptisms.

" Queen Elizabeth's reign; marriages.—1559, 22; 1560, 9; 1561, 16; 1562, 13; 1563, 15; 1564, 11; 1565, 12; 1566, 8; 1567, 15; 1568, 12; 1569, 1570, 14; 1571, 9; 1572, 9; 1573, 13; 1574, 10."

After 1592 comes "1599, 8; 1600, 8; 1601, 12; 1602, 6."

" King James I.; marriages.—1604, 17; 1605, 19; 1606, 14; 1607, 9; 1608, 10; 1609, 10; 1610, 8; 1611, 11; 1612, 22; 1613, 16; 1614, 19; 1615, 19; 1616, 16; 1617, 18; 1618, 18; 1619, 13; 1620, 9; 1621, 7; 1622, 11; 1623, 10; 1624, 6."

" King Charles I.; marriages.—1635, 10; 1636, 19; 1637, 15; 1638, 8; 1639, 9; 1640, 16; 1641, 19; 1642, 8; 1643, 8; 1644, only January and February, and Caroli Regis 20⁰, vivat vivat." Here ensues a blank till 1649.

" In Queen Elizabeth's reign; burials.—1559, 57; 1560, 37; 1561, 39; 1562, 23; 1563, 24; 1564, 41; this year, May 11, the daughter of William Righlye, buried of the pest; same day, Bagalie's sonne, of the pest. 25th, Awfray, daughter of Richard Bagalie, of the pest. June, 3d day of the same year, Richard Baglye, of the pest. 9th, William, sonne of Richard Jackson, of the pest;" these are all the pest burials at St. Martin's through this year mentioned. From the first of her reign to the end of 1562, there is a register of the number of bells used at the funerals, not less than three, and five seems to be the whole power of the steeple; I suppose the fees, either to sexton or master, rose with the number of bells. Most are without bells, though a single bell, as now, might announce the funeral.

" 1565, 36." After April 13, 1566, the register says, " the rest is wanting from the 13th day of April, reginæ 8, anno Dom. 1566, as may appeare in the old book."

" 1567, 29; 1568, 46; 1570, 37; 1571, 27; 1572, 30; 1573, 19." Five bells used five times in 1587, and five bells once in 1588, Feb. 2, no other number.

" 1599, 24; 1600, 22; 1601, 32; 1602, 35."

" King James's reign.—1604, 30; 1605, 52; 1606, 26; 1607, 44; 1608, 31; 1609, 42; 1610, 82; a cross on the left margin, " the sickness began

gan, plague, 21st of August;" " 1611, 128; 1612, 39; 1613, 25; 1614, 34; 1615, 60; 1616, 41; 1617, 39; 1618, 37; 1619, 28; 1620, 25; 1621, 43; 1622, 27; 1623, 37; 1624, 24."

" In the reign of King Charles I.; burials.— 1635, 45; 1636; 1637, 23; 1638, 54; 1639, 77; 1640, 43; 1641, 45; 1642, 54; 1643, 48;" here ends vivat vivat. The register ends, and a blank ensues after April 27, 1644, till April 27, 1649, and then no vivat vivat.

" 1650, 44; 1651, 52; 1652, 40." The register ends, *ne plus ultra*, 1653, with October 1, " Thomas Ward, clerke, was buried."

" Richard Elkinton, of Shawell[1], yeoman, May 29, 1607, bequeathed to the mayor, bailiffs, and burgesses of Leicester 50*l*. to lend to five poor artificers or tradesmen of Leicester, such as the vicar and churchwardens of this parish nominate, on St. Andrew's day, yearly; to be paid them on St. Thomas's day; upon proper security for re-payment, with use, after the rate of 5*l. per cent*.; and of the use, 40*s*. to be distributed by the vicar and churchwardens of this parish, between the 21st and 25th of December, among the poor of this parish, and the other 10*s*. to be to the town clerk, for entering the orders, and making the bonds."

In St. Martin's parish, between Midsummer and St. Thomas's day 1793 only 18 persons died, of whom three were widows, whose ages (added together) make 266 years. The average deaths in the parish, at that period, were supposed to be about 80.

A lectureship was founded in this parish in the seventeenth century; and a parish workhouse established early in the eighteenth century[2].

In a deed 6 Edw. VI. there is mentioned *Parchment-lane*[3], in the parish of St. Martin's. The Horse and Trumpet was then called the Angel; and was sold for 26*l*. 13*s*. 4*d*. by John Cressey, glover, to John Stanford, butcher, 4 and 5 Philip and Mary.

" Clement Charde, mercer, & Dorothea uxor ejus. Noveritis quod nos pro vi*l*. x*s*. tradidisse Thomæ Cotton, generoso, gardinam, continentem dimidiam acram, jacentem inter terram Henrici Harrington, militis, quondam Henrici comitis Huntingdon, ex parte Orientali & terram predicti Thomæ Cotton, quondam Georgii Turpin, militis, ex parte Occidentali, & extendit se a venellâ vocatâ *Dead Lane*, in parte Australi, usque terram prædicti Thomæ Cotton, quondam Georgii Turpyn, militis, versus Borealem. Dat. 38 Eliz. 6 Feb."

A tenement, called *Talbot's House*, and three acres of land in Leicester, were let to Edmund Froste, by queen Elizabeth, 1584[4].

A tenement lying in Leicester town, with a croft there, called *The Isle of the Fenn*, were let to Robert Newcome, by lease from the Crown, 1587[5].

	£.	s.	d.
Money raised for the poor, within the year ending at Easter 1776, —	735	19	4
Expended in county rates, &c.	109	11	10
———— on the poor,	620	5	5
Rent of workhouse and habitations,	11	6	5
Expended in litigations —	13	1	7
Money raised for 1783, —	889	1	11
——————— for 1784, —	931	1	11
——————— for 1785, —	981	7	0
Medium of these three years,	933	16	11
———— of county expences,	40	14	4
———— of expences not relating to the poor; repairs of the church, roads, &c.	0	0	0
———— of net annual expences,	893	2	7
———— of attending on magistrates,	0	0	0
———— of entertainments at meetings,	0	14	6
———— of law expences, —	19	9	10
———— of setting the poor to work,	1	10	4

The CHURCH (Plate XLIII).

The latitude of St. Martin's church (which stands nearly in the centre of the town) is 52° 38'; and the difference between the meridian of this and the Observatory at Greenwich is 4' 35" to the West.

The church is very ancient; one of the largest, and esteemed the principal church in the county.

The materials, particularly on the North side, appear to have been taken from an old ruin, probably from a portion of the Town-wall, which, at the Conquest, lay in massy heaps.

At what period it was re-built after the destruction[6] of Leicester in the reign of king Henry the Second, cannot be accurately stated; but it then consisted only of a handsome spire[7], spacious chancel, and two ailes. A considerable addition (of a third aile) was some time after[8] made to it all along the South side; when the outer wall being taken down, on nearly the same ground whereon it stood was erected that remarkable light range of clustered columns which now support the roof, partly hidden by a gallery. On each side of this aile are some curious roof-supporters.

" The chancel is 18 yards and a half long, and is 7 yards and 20 iches wide, within the walls. This," says Mr. Carte, " I observe, because I find the following memorandum in Charyte's Rentale: " Cancella Sancti Martini ædificata fuit A. D. 1409, tempore Ricardi Rotheley abbatis, & constabat xxxiv*l*."

---

[1] See vol. IV. p. 258.

[2] The following account of it is from a letter dated Oct. 10, 1724: " In April last, St. Martin's parish determined to convert their parish houses into a workhouse, by joining the lower apartments into one, for a working-room, and fitting up two others for a kitchen, a cellar, &c. and furnishing them. They first made choice of a master, who has the immediate care of the poor, to keep them in order, and employ them in such work as they are capable of, and see that their food is duly prepared and given to them, &c. He has two apartments assigned to him, his diet and washing, and 12*l*. a year salary. The parish overseers buy all things necessary for the house, and the poor in it. For their cloathing, they buy whole pieces of woollen and linen; which, when cut out, is made up into cloaths, by such of the poor as are capable of it. The overseers, about once a month, send in five strike of malt, which the master brews at once into good drink; and every Saturday the overseers buy for them a sufficient quantity of wholesome meat, and send it to the master. If any of the poor fall sick, a proper provision is made for them, and some of their fellow-poor are appointed to attend them. They are all confined within the precincts of the house, and are not to go out of it without leave of the master; if any of them have employment abroad, they are obliged to return in a due hour; and whoever employs them, agrees with the master for their wages, and pays them to him; which, together with the product of the labour of the rest, he delivers to the overseers every Friday in the evening, who then take the accounts from the master; and add out of the parish stock, what is wanting for making provision for the following week. The general method for employing them, besides what is above mentioned, is in spinning jersey: such as cannot spin are set to knit stockings for the rest, and one is appointed to teach the children to read. The time of working is twelve hours in the day, winter and summer. The number of the poor is 28, viz. 16 old, and 12 under 8 years of age. The product of their labours, one week with another, is about 14*s*. the charge of maintaining them weekly is about 2*l*. that is, about 1*l*. 6*s*. above their labour. The charge of maintaining the poor used to be about 250 or 300*l*. a year. The charge this year, in cloathing the poor, upon placing them in the workhouse, and buying utensils, &c. is much greater than can be in future years; and yet the overseer assures me, that he is confident the parish will even this year save 100*l*. The children have a form placed in the alley, before the seat of the parish officers, to sit upon on Sundays; but there is no particular place as yet assigned to the elder poor at church." This workhouse is still kept up, though not precisely in the manner here described; and in 1776 contained 90 persons.

[3] Now the Swine-market.   [4] Leases in the Augmentation-office.   [5] Ibid.

[6] Before that event, Mr. Throsby supposes " that the church, and even some of the streets, stood in a different position."

[7] " As the addition of spires to sacred edifices was not introduced into England from the East till the beginning of the reign of Henry the Third, the date must be fixed between the two intervening centuries; and, if the spire was built with the church, not very early after the introduction of that ornament of our churches, as the handsome, solid form of St. Martin's bespeaks considerable practice and expertness in the art." Walk through Leicester, p. 133.

[8] " Somewhat like this was formerly done in Greece and Asia Minor, to the old Greek parallelogram temples. The external colonade was walled up, and pillars substituted to the original side walls; and so became a church, or nave, a body, with two ailes or wings." G. A.

T. Pratten del. et fc. 1792.

Fig. 1.

2   3   4   5

Fig. 15.

6   7   8

16

Fig. 13.

Fig. 19.

12

17

41

20

18

Fig. 14.

23   35   21   39   40

24   25   29

26   27

28   30

37   37

32   34

33   36

Fig. 11.

Fig. 10.

Fig. 9.

22   38

In the chancel (which is the property of the king, and is rented by the vicar) are three stalls, with flat arches, all of equal height, and filled up.

The Fox preaching to the Geese, in the great window of the North cross aile in this church, as standing there June 29, 1730, is engraved, from a drawing by Mr. Peck, in Plate XLIII. fig. 1. Under it is written, " Testis est mihi Deus, quam cupiam vos omnes visceribus meis."

Mr. Burton, in 1622, describes these arms in the church, Plate XLIII. fig. 2—8:

In the North-east window:

Gules, a cinquefoil Ermine. The coat of the old *Earls of Leicester*, and of the *Abbey*.

Quarterly, Argent and Gules. *Soulney.*

Argent, gutté de sang in saltire Gules.

Azure, a plain cross Argent. *Aylesbury.*

In the North-west window:

Gules, three lions passant guardant Or. *England.*

The same, debruised in the bend Azure. *Henry* earl of *Lancaster* and *Derby.*

The same, with a label of three points of France. Earl of *Lancaster.*

In the Matriculus of 1220, St. Martin's is noticed among the churches under the patronage of the abbot and convent of *St. Mary de Pratis,* who held it to their own use *ab antiquo* [1].

In Pope Nicholas's taxation, about 1290, this church was thus valued:

" Ecclesia Sancti Martini xi marc'.

" Vicaria ejusdem vii marc'.

" Æstimatio obventionum Sanctæ Crucis in eâdem ecclesiâ x marc'."

In 1344, this church paid 7s. 6¾d. for procurations; was valued at 11 marks; and paid 1s. 4d. for Peter-pence.

Charyte, in his Rentale [2], treating of the profits which the Abbey of Leicester received, says,

" Ecclesia Sancti Martini respondet communibus annis circa xxi*l.* Solebat reddere xxxvi*l.* xl*l.* vel quaterviginti decem libras; scilicet, ut in anno Domini mcccxlviii; nam circa illum annum Domini Pixis vocat' reddebat x*l.* xi*l.* vel xii*l.* & quandoque xxx*l.* & ultra; Pes Thomæ Lancastriæ respondebat vi*l.* xs.; Alta Crux reddebat xi*l.*; Pes Crucis reddebat x*l.* xii*l.* vel xiii*l.*"

As to the vicarage, Charyte [3] says, " Ordinatio ejus per Hugonem episcopum facta est, ut vicarius ecclesie Sancti Martini habeat ad vestitum suum ii marcas de portionibus altaris, per manum abbatis Leicestrie solvenda; & legata usque ad vid.; & quolibet die solemni id. Habebit victum suum in abbathiâ in omnibus ut canonicus, & diaconus suus sicut major serviens in abbathiâ; & unam dimidiam marce pro stipendio. Præterea habebit panem ad garcionem suum qui ei serviet. Abbas providebit ei mansum competentem, & sustinebit onera ecclesie debita & consueta."

After this, there were several compositions, or agreements, made between the abbot and the vicar for his better subsistence. And whereas he had no certain house belonging to him, he was allowed 8s. *per annum* to provide himself an habitation, till William Charyte, being prior of the abbey, Jan. 1, 1457, purchased from William Wystow, of Great Petelyng, a messuage, with the appurtenances, situate between the tenement lately of Roger Belgrave on the South, and the tenement of Corpus Christi Chantry on the North side, which is said to be worth 16s. a year. Whereupon William Charyte says, " Modò vicarius habet mansum honestum & appropriatum, & iis. quâlibet septimanâ per manus procuratoris, & vid. in die Omnium Sanctorum, vid. in die Nativitatis Domini, vid. in die Paschæ, & vid. in die Dedicationis, per manus subcellarii. Item habet omnes decimas minutas, omnes denarios Romanos, & omnia oblata ad Crucem in Vigiliâ Paschatis, & in Die."

" Vicarius Sancti Martini dictos denarios [Sancti Petri] colligit, & eos ad proprios usus conservat. Et nos pro ipso dictos denarios archidiacono persolvimus.

" Abbas solvit,

" Ecclesie Sancti Martini, Leyc', ixs. xd. ob. qᵃ.;

" Ecclesie Sancte Marie, ixs. xd. ob. qᵃ.;

" Ecclesie Sancti Leonardi, ixs. xd. ob. qᵃ.;

" pro procurationibus, synodalibus, & de-" nariis Sancti Petri [4]."

In 1534, the vicarage was valued at 6*l.* 13s. 4d. and 10s. was paid *duobus clericis parochianis* [5].

Whatever the profits were that belonged to the Abbey, they were vested in the Crown upon the Dissolution, and by it were transferred to the vicar for the annual rent of 5*l.* whereof 3*l.* still vests in the Crown, and the other 2*l.* *per annum* has been paid to several proprietors successively since the purchase of them from the Crown in king Charles the Second's time. The 3*l.* still resting in the Crown ssrves to quit the 3*l.* pension which by the Crown is payable to the vicar.

In 1650, the vicarage was returned worth 50*l.* a year; and the minister as sufficient.

The parsonage house of St. Martin's was an humble building for modern times. It was let by Mr. Haines for 40s. a year, and was situate between the town library and the dwelling-house of the master of Wigston's hospital; against the South-west door of the church. The house was taken down, and the ground consecrated as an additional burying ground, about the year 1760. The vicar has in lieu an handsome annual allowance.

There was formerly a Well at the end of the church-yard wall, by the Town-hall, now covered. We read of Chapel wells; this was, no doubt, the Church well.

In the new South aile of this church were two chapels; one of them at the East end, called Our Lady's chapel, or choir, where the Consistory Court is now held; the other at the West end, called St. George's chapel.

In the early parts of the churchwardens accompts, which, to the credit of the parish, are now well preserved, are some particulars of charges for repairing these chapels. In one place, in the payments for 1544, " Payd to the plumar for a dais worc on our Lady Chappell;" and, a few years after, is a charge for work done in St. George's chapel, where stood St. George's horse harnessed in the church splendour of those times.

The riding of the George was one of the principal solemnities in this town, as may appear by the express mention of it in an order made at a common hall, 17 Edward IV. which enjoins all inhabitants summoned to attend the mayor to ride against the king (so it is expessed), or for riding the George, or any other thing, to the pleasure of the mayor, and worship of the town.

14 Henry VII. it was ordered, that every one of the 48 should pay towards the upholding St. George's guild; they who have been chamberlains, 6d.; and such as had not been so, 4d. yearly at least: and 15 Henry VIII. the masters of the gild having neglected the riding of the George, an order was made, enjoining them to do it according to antient custom, between St. George's day and Whitsunday, on pain of forfeiting 5*l.*

The like solemn procession was made from St. Martin's church to St. Margaret's, on Whit Monday, by the vicar, priests and clerks, and the parishioners, as there was from St. Mary's; viz. the image of St. Martin was carried thither, attended by twelve persons with banners, representing the twelve Apostles, each person having the name of the Apostle whom he represented inscribed on parchment. But there was no music, or any canopy carried over St. Martin.

---

[1] See vol. I. p. lv.   [2] Fol. 88, seu 97 col. 1.   [3] Ibid. col. 2.

[4] Fol. 207, seu 215, col. 2.   [5] See vol. 1. p. lxxxii.

In this church was founded also Corpus Christi guild, which was the chief guild in the town, and contributed largely to the public charges [1] ; *e. g.* in the purchase of charters, &c. ; and the masters of it had great interest in the government of the town ; having power, with the mayor, to levy penalties on the mayor's brethren for their misdemeanors ; and, upon the mayor's neglect they were empowered to levy them upon him.

A licence was granted for founding a chantry in St. Martin's church, 13 Edward III. 16 Richard II. and 2 Henry IV. There belonged to the church, besides the vicar, four chantry priests ; and, upon a vacancy of any of them, the masters of the guilds and two churchwardens, with the senior chaplain of the chantry, presented a fit person to the abbot of Leicester, who instituted and inducted him.

The hall belonging to St. George's guild, and the four houses belonging to the chantry priests, were all situated at the West end of St. Martin's church.

The hall is now occupied as the Town-hall ; of which see an account in p. 353.

The house belonging to Mr. Steevens, containing, in two spacious rooms, a long range of lights, adorned with the painted glass engraved in Plates XXXVI. XXXVII. p. 514. is supposed to have belonged to the chantry of Corpus Christi.

There were also three altars in the church before the Dissolution : the High Altar, St. Dunstan's, and St. Catharine's ; and, probably, the two last stood, one in what is now called Heyrick's chancel, and the other near the entrance into the Vestry.

Leading to the high altar was a fine range of steps, which were taken down in 1645, under the authority of an Ordinance of both Houses of Parliament.

In the Churchwardens Accompts, are many curious entries respecting the sale of what were deemed superstitious articles at the period of the Reformation ; of their being reinstated in the short reign of Queen Mary ; and their subsequent removal in that of Queen Elizabeth.

On the suppression of Colleges and Chantries, in 1537, the following return was made :

Cantaria Corporis Christi, in villâ Leicestriæ, valet in

Redditibus & firmâ terrarum & cotagiorum infra Leicestriam, predictæ cantariæ pertinentibus, per annum, prout, &c.   xviii*l*. xvii*s*.

Firmâ diversorum aliorum tenementorum, cotagiorum, & gardinarum ibidem, dimiss' diversis per-indenturas, prout, &c.   —   —   —   xix*s*. viii*d*.

Redditibus assisæ diversorum liberorum tenentium ibidem, prout, &c. vi*l*. xiiii*s*. xi*d*. q.

Firmâ mansionis cum gardino eidem pertinente, per annum, scituato ex occidentale parte ecclesiæ Beatæ Mariæ ibidem, valuat'   —   —   — x*s*.

xxvi*l*. xix*d*. qª.

Reprisis ; viz. in redditibus resolutis diversis personis sequentibus ; viz.

Domino Regi, pro diversis provisoriis redditibus exeuntibus de diversis tenementis prædictis, ut Ducatûs sui Lancastriæ   —   —   vii*s*. x*d*. ob.

Willielmo Swede generoso, exeunt' de terris in Southfelde   —   xii*d*.

Præfato Domino Regi, ut Ducatûs sui Lancastriæ prædicti   xii*s*. ix*d*. ob.

Pro diversis aliis parvis redditibus eidem Domino Regi, ut in jure nuper Monasterii Leicestriæ   —   vii*s*.

Diversis aliis personis   xii*s*. v*d*.

In toto, prout per Rentale prædictum renovatum   —   —   —   xli*s*. i*d*.

Vacatione diversorum tenementorum ibidem, per annum   —   —   xvii*s*. viii*d*.

Stipendio Henrici Grymys, capellani divina servicia infra ecclesiam ibidem celebrantis, per annum   —   cvi*s*. viii*d*.

Stipendio Johannis Foster, capellani ibidem, per annum   —   cvi*s*. viii*d*.

Obitibus & elemozinariis ibidem annualiter expendend', per annum   xliii*s*. ii*d*.

Feodo seneschalli sive ballivi ibidem, per annum   —   —   —   xx*s*.

Denariis solutis pro vino, cerâ, & lucernis, tam pro prædictis duobus capellanis v*s*. vi*d*., quam pro uno alio capellano celebrante missam vocatam *Jhesus masse* iiii*s*., infra ecclesiam prædictam annualiter expendend', per annum   ix*s*. vi*d*.

Reparationibus super dicta tenementa ibidem annualiter factis, per annum   viii*s*. xi*d*.

Et remanet clarè per annum   xviii*l*. vii*s*.[2]
viii*l*. xiiii*s*. vii*d*. qª.

" The said chauntry was founded by William Humberston, and John Ive the younger, under the lycens of king Edward III. to th'entente to find iiii priests, to celebrate divine service within the parish church of St. Martin in Leicester, and to pray for the founders' souls ; in which parish is 500 houselyng people, and no more priests but only the vicar, whose stipend or lyvyng ys so sore decayed, that he ys not able to fynde any other priest to serve there ; so that, without the help of the said chantry priests, many of the said parishioners in time of sickness shall be like to perish, withowte the rites of the church ; also the churchwardens, with eleven other housemen [housholders] of the said parish, hath the presentation and election of the same ; and at this present time there are but two of the said four priests singing, for that the rents of the same are so far in decay and loss of rent than they have been heretofore.

"And there hath been no lands sold, &c. ; and an inventory, &c." [3]

The five following paragraphs are from the MSS. of the late Rev. William Bickerstaffe :

"Under the South-west gallery stairs in this church is a triple frame of oaken seats, like compass chairs, the pommels human heads. The first head, or pommel, a crown or coronet next the stairs, on the left to the sitter ; the second, or right pommel from that, a sort of cap highly and broadly edged round ; the third from the stairs a plain head uncapped, or worn or broken off ; the fourth head broken off entirely ; as you face it, the first of the three seats on the left, the only one that turns up, has a moveable sitting-board, through which is a hole wide enough for a very thick wand, more than an inch and half deep ; on the reverse, or under, the figure strong in alto relievo of a dragon, or flying serpent, with long talons and expanded wings, colour black-leaden, over two human skulls, at the ends of a curve passing through the scalps ; a sight horrid enough to make a little human sensibility shudder ! The monster rests upon the lower part of its tail, tied or turned over towards its extremity ; one paw only with four nails ; two nails much below these, as belonging to the not appearing extremity of the other paw. This frame, which formerly stood on the East side of the South-east door, facing the great walk in the church-yard, over which the church commands the street, the soldiers of King Charles I. might set on fire with menaces when they forcibly entered to check the enemy on the church, who made no small havock of the passing Loyalists. Thus we may account for the burnt appearance of the fore-part of the right hand supporter or foot of the well-timbered cathedræ ; or they might fix to

[1] March 12, 31 Hen. VIII. the king having granted to the mayor and common burgesses and inhabitants of Leicester two fairs annually, besides their two antient fairs, towards the charges of the letters patents under the seal of the Dutchy of Lancaster, the masters and wardens, and stewards of the guild of Corpus Christi, and the guild of St. Margaret in Leicester, in name of all the brotherhood, gave out of the said guilds 20*l*. that is, out of each 10*l*.
[2] There is a trifling error in the total ; but the several items accord with Mr. Carte's MS.
[3] Certificate of Colleges and Chantries, in the Augmentation Office.

the chair one of the noxious assailants, and burn to intimidate the rest. Though I will not deny but some peaceable workmen might fire it carelessly; yet I had rather, encouraging the miraculous and historically interesting incident, incline to the former account [1].

"At the East end of the South aile, and over the Consistory Court, is a portrait of King Charles I. a copy of the picture at the title-page of most editions of Εἰκὼν Βασιλικὴ. Its frame is seven feet and a half from side to side, and about the same in height [2].

"In 1705, there were spacious galleries erected in this church for young people, there being before that time only a loft at the West end of it, called the Scholars' Loft; and the church was handsomely pewed about 1726.

"In the nave are two chandeliers with orbs and branches each; that nearest the reading-desk the gift of Alderman Gabriel Newton, at the desire of his wife Elizabeth [Wells]; whose base was a sensible obstruction to the reader, till the said nave was underdrawn or ceiled, and that with elegance, at 80l. expence; the other given at the same time by the Corporation.

"A superb clock with two dials, South-east and North-west, repeating the quarters by four musical strokes at each: the mechanism within is an agreeable object, through the glazier's art. Mr. Arnold, now of Leicester (1790), who prepossessed the parish in his favour, by sounding the steeple harmony of eight delightful bells, and whose genius takes no small range in several departments, has since given farther proofs of his abilities, in two additional bells and chime." [There are now ten light bells.]

At the East end of the nave was formerly a small organ, which, in 1754, was repaired and ornamented with a new case, and placed at the West end of the same aile. This alteration being inadequate to the wishes of the parishioners, some attempts were ineffectually made to obtain a new one, till in 1773 a spirited subscription [3] was begun by the Corporation of Leicester and several individuals of the parish, aided by the warm efforts of the then churchwarden, Mr. William Cart; and the present organ was accordingly opened, in 1774, at the musical meeting described under the Infirmary, p. 523 [4].

The following articles were extracted by Mr. Carte from the churchwardens' accompts of St. Martin's:

"1633. There were propositions made to the parish, after the death of Mr. Holmes, by the Lord Keeper (I suppose about settling a revenue for the vicar), which occasioned three or four journeys to London for the churchwardens, 1634, to manage the treaty, but it seems not to have taken effect; only a voluntary augmentation was made by the parish to the next and following incumbents.

"The minister (so far as appears) used to be sent by the Lord Keeper, &c.; but the parish concerned themselves to chuse one in 1646, 1649, 1651, 1652, 1653, 1696, 1697. The parish wrote to the Lord Keeper for one, 1639. They chose several, who refused to accept of it, viz. Mr. Thomas Palmer, of London, 1646; Mr. Herring, of Coventry, 1649; Mr. Richard Pike, 1651-2; Mr. Dixie, of Cadeby, 1653.

"At the ministers' first coming they used to pay the ringers, 1635, 1646; to treat him with wine and biscuit, 1639; with ale, &c. 1649, 1698. They paid the charge of bringing his goods, 1649.

"As for his rights and income, &c. A terrar was made, 1639, 1675. The vicarage-house was repaired by the parish, 1553, 1670, 1671, 1672, 1680; was taken into the churchwardens' hands; and the parish took a house, Dr. Bryan's, for the minister, paid his rent, repairs, and taxes, 1646, 1649. 1653, allowed 5l. per annum for a house, and 1654.

Profits: his wages 26s. 8d. quarterly, 1553; 30s. quarterly, 1554; 33s. 4d. quarterly, 1555; chrysomes 20, 5s.; 14 pigs, 5s. 10d.; other offerings, 12s. 2d. from Easter till Michaelmas 1555.

"In 1636, given by the parish, 20l. per annum.

"In 1646, Tamworth's exhibition made up 80l. per annum, raised by a tax, with all other duties; payable within a month after quarter-day, 1649, 1653.

"1656, 20s. weekly; for which a tax raised, 1657.

"Monies given him at several times, 1672.

"The King's rent paid by the parish 1562, 1573; allowed towards it, 50s. 1669, 1671, &c.

"Tenths paid by the parish, 1562, 1566.

"The minister's seat turned, 1567; mended, 1611, 1630; removed, 1611; sealed, 1612; painted and sised, 1619, 1630; made, 1649.

"Chancel repaired by the churchwardens in 1633.

"The minister sent his note to the churchwarden, to allow money to poor people, 1644.

"The parish paid for supply of the place in the absence of the vicar, 1552.

"Given to the minister, by Mr. John Stanley, 30s. per annum; by Mr. James Ellis, 20s. per annum; by Mr. Tamworth, 20 nobles.

"They used to give the minister a quart of sack every fast-day, 1643."

"1705. At the bottom of the Brief for All Saints church in Oxford, was an advertisement, signifying a design of publishing the present state of parish churches, and desiring an answer to several queries, whereupon I made the return following [5]:

"The present state of the vicarage of St. Martin:

"1. The parish is situated in the heart of the town, and has no field belonging to it.

The church, before the Reformation, was appropriated to the abbot of St. Mary de Pratis, Leicester, who had it in proprios usus ab antiquo.

2. The profits now belonging to the vicar are, first, a pension from the Crown (the antient salary of the abbot I suppose)

2. A composition for the poor of Wigston's Hospital, erected in the same parish in the time of Henry VIII.

	£.	s.	d.
	3	0	0
	0	6	8

---

[1] "There is a like triple frame in the chancel of St. Mary's, on the left of the pulpit stairs, and close to them. The left seat, as that of St. Martin's, turns up, and is decorated underneath with clusters of grapes; the semicircle ex adverso, i.e. under the seat of the first compass chair, over a tree well stemmed, well branched, and well clustered with berries or grapes. There is also a double compass chair on each side of the chancel door at St. Margaret's." W. B.

[2] "The parish books are silent about the time and artist; but, as it leans towards, and is close to, the Consistory or spiritual court, it is supposed to have been executed at their expence, as their triumph and trophy, who fell with him their patron, and whom their gratitude has revived on canvas their tutelar saint. But where is Archbishop Laud, their champion and martyr? There is room for him over his master, and even by his side, locus est & pluribus umbris: what a marvellous change! He, whom in his life-time in 1645 the very women bore arms against to keep him out of this town, is now in quiet possession of that church whose doors he broke open to subdue the annoyance from the leads, as appears by an entry in the parish-book, thus: ' Paid Francis Morley for mending the locks of the church-doores, broke by the King's army, three shillings." W. B.—This picture was painted by a Mr. Rowley, some time about the year 1686: the charge of painting, &c. amounted to 10l. And I am rather inclined to think that the parish, and not the Spiritual Court, were at the expence of procuring it. J. S. H.

[3] "The Committee appointed to conduct a subscription for erecting a new organ in St. Martin's church, humbly presume to solicit the assistance of the gentlemen of the county of Leicester, now in London, and all others who wish to see so laudable an undertaking speedily carried into execution. The agreeable situation of the above church, its lofty and spacious middle aile, with an organ at the West end of it, worth 500l. (the sum intended to be laid out), and the variety of elegant seats it contains, it is hoped will be pleasing circumstances to the numerous and polite company which resort to Leicester, at the Anniversary Meeting of the Governors of the County Infirmary. The subscription for the above purpose was opened on the 30th of December last, and now amounts to 438l.—Sir John Palmer, bart. and Thomas Cave, esq. have been pleased to add ten guineas each to the above subscription." Advertisement in January 1773.

[4] "In contemplating the inside of this church," says an elegant female writer, " it is curious to draw a brief parallel between its present plain but handsome appearance, and its Catholic magnificence, before the zeal of the Reformation, justly excited, but intemperate in its direction, had, during its career against Romish absurdities, destroyed almost every trace of ornament in our churches. And whilst we survey its present few decorations, its brass chandeliers depending from the elegant cieling of the nave, the beautiful oak Corinthian pillars of its altar-piece, which is ornamented with a picture of the Ascension, by Francesco Vanni (the gift of sir William Skeffington, bart.), and its excellent organ, we can scarcely forbear lamenting the violence with which the magnificent range of steps was torn from its high altar, then hung with draperies of white damask and purple velvet." Walk through Leicester, pp. 134, 135. [5] Notitia Parochialis, in the MS Library at Lambeth, No. 673.

3. Gathered yearly, of Easter offerings, about — — 0 12 0
4. Christopher Tamworth, in time of
James I. and Charles I. gave the vicar
yearly 20 nobles, to read prayers twice
every work day in the year — 6 13 4
5. John Stanly, by will, about 1650,
gave to the vicar, yearly — 1 10 0
6. By a medium of ten years last,
there were yearly christened 56, and buried 50, the due for each 1s. — 5 6 0
7. Marriages afford yearly about 2 5 0
————————
19 13 0

Payments annually issuing out of the vicarage:
To the archdeacon, for procurations,
synodals, and two acquittances 0 9 2¾
To the Crown, at Christmas, for rents,
with the acquittal — — 0 13 8
To the Crown, at Michaelmas 5 0 0
This 5l. I suppose became payable by
agreement at the Reformation in lieu
of the profits of the rectory; but those
profits, whatever they were, are now
quite lost, nothing being here paid as
due but what is before mentioned. Of
this 5l. 40s. is sold out of the Crown,
and is now enjoyed by the lady Apsley;
the other 3l. rests in the Crown, to
quit the 3l. due to the vicar from the
Crown; but the fees for a debenture
6s. 8d. and acquittances 6d. is a charge of 0 7 2
Much business forces me to hire one
to read prayers on week-days; for which
I allow — — — 10 0 0
————————
16 10 0¾

Which being deducted from the profits,
8. There rests clear profit to me 3 2 11¼
Whatsoever is paid more than this is voluntary.
9. Henry earl of Huntingdon, president of York,
gave several books, which were placed in the church
of St. Martin's. This stock was increased by other
benefactors; and in 1632 and 1633, upon the motion of John then lord Bishop of Lincoln, this Corporation erected a convenient room at the West end
of the church-yard, in which the said books were
placed, and considerable additions have been made
to them by subsequent benefactors [1].

There is no occasion to answer the rest of the que-
ries. SAMUEL CARTE, minister of the said parish.
WALTER WELLS, } churchwardens."
WILLIAM FOSTER, }

" In May 1709, the Bishop proposing certain queries relating to the parish, they were answered thus:

1. There are 416 families, in which there are
1984 persons; of which there are 235 Dissenters,
viz. four Papists, 191 Independents or Presbyterians, 35 Quakers, and five Anabaptists.
2. There is one meeting of Anabaptists; the persons who teach in it are —— Treen and Thomas Davye, of Leicester, and Zachary Stanton, of Belgrave.
They seldom meet except on Sundays; and then
sometimes once, and sometimes twice. Their numbers are various; but, upon great concourse from
neighbouring towns, are said to be about 150.
3. Within the parish several poor women teach
children to spell, and two men teach to read, write,
and cast accompts; whereof one, Mr. Thickpenny,
has a license; the other, Nathan Tyler, is an Independent, and I suppose has none.
4. No charity-school has been set up in this parish.
5. There is within this parish an hospital called
the New, or W. Wigston's Hospital, of which Mr.
Archdeacon is confrater, and can give a full account.
6. No lands or tenements have been given for repairs of the church.
7. No abuses or frauds in relation to these establishments.
8. I baptized Sarah Child Feb. 23, 1707-8, who
was then 24 years of age, and was not baptized before, because educated by her father and mother,
who were both Quakers.
9. I do not know that any who come to church
are unbaptized; but several that have been baptized
are not confirmed.
10. Of 1749 persons who are not professed Dissenters there are 1157 above 16 years of age; and of
these I reckon that about 150 received the Lord's
Supper at Easter last.
11. Mr. Watts is removed into St. Mary's parish.

"In 1705, an account was taken and given to me,
that there were then in the parish 65 Independents
or Presbyterians; six Anabaptists; 13 Quakers; and
two Papists. In all, 86. But this account comprehended only those of ripe age.

1709, May 23 and 24, a more exact account was
taken of all men, women, and children; and by it
there appears to be in the parish 416 families, in
which there are 1984 souls, whereof there are 235
Dissenters in 53 families, viz.

191 Independents or Presbyterians, in 42 families.
35 Quakers, in eight families.
5 Anabaptists, in two families.
4 Papists, in one family.
So that of persons not professing themselves Dissenters there are 363 families, and 1749 souls, whereof
1157 are above 16 years of age."

" A Terrar of the houses, lands, goods, rights,
and perquisites, belonging to the church, vicar,
clerk, and sexton, of the parish of St. Martin in
Leicester 1714:

" 1. The vicarage house is timber pained, and is
covered with slate. The rooms belonging to it are,
" On the first floor, 1. a kitchen, boarded; 2. a
very little parlour, boarded, under which is a little
cellar, with an earthen floor; 3. a wash-house,
paved with pebbles.
" In the second floor there is a space at the top of
the stairs, and two chambers floored with plaster.
" The garden or homestall is twenty and one
yards long, and four yards and a half broad at the
upper end. Its front is to the church-yard on the
East; on the North is Town-hall; on the South is
Wigston's Hospital; and on the West is the back
buildings of the Nag's Head inn.
" 2. No glebe land except the church-yard.
" 3. It is supposed that all manner of tithes are
due to the vicar, partly in right of his vicarage, and
partly in right of the rectory, which he holds of
the Crown, by payment of 5l. per annum, but no
manner of tithes are paid, or hath been paid for
upwards of 60 years.
" At the erecting of William Wigston's Hospital
there was a composition made between the abbot
of Leicester as parson and the vicar on one part, and
the master and confrater of the Hospital on the
other part, whereby the poor of the said Hospital
are exempted from payment of tithes, offerings, and
mortuaries, &c. in lieu thereof, whereof there is
payable by the master of the Hospital, or his deputy, the sum of 6s. 8d. yearly, on Easter eve, on
the high altar of the church, before noon, on forfeiture of 13s. 4d. more; which agreement was confirmed by William lord bishop of Lincoln, the 10th
of July, A. D. 1520, as appears by a copy thereof
(in a book) at the end of William Wigston's statutes, in a book in the custody of the mayor of
Leicester; but where the original is, whether in the
Bishop's Registry, or in the Court of the Duchy of
Lancaster, or among the writings belonging to the
Hospital, or the Augmentation Office, we know not.
" The Easter offerings are 6d. for each person
from whom due.
" The surplice fees are, for a chrysom and churching, 1s.; for marriage by licence 5s. by banns 2s.
6d. each person who lives in the parish; so that if
both parties are of the parish they pay 5s. for publishing banns, 6d. usually given to the clerk; for a
burial in the church-yard 1s. in the church 2s. in
the chancel 2s. 6d. and for the ground in the chancel 10s.
" Mortuaries were antiently due; for, in the composition of Wigston's Hospital, the mortuaries of

[1] See a particular account of this Town Library in p. 505.

the master and confrater are expressly reserved, but have not been paid, time out of mind.

" 5. Pensions charged on the vicarage are, 13s. 4d. for tenths, now extinct; 5l. to the Crown, at Michaelmas, in lieu of the rectory, whereof 40s. is now enjoyed by Peter Apsley, esq. and the remaining 3l. continues in the Crown, to quit a pension of 3l. due to the vicar from the Crown; 7s. 6¼d. to the archdeacon, for procurations at Easter, and 1s. for synodals at Michaelmas.

" 6. For the furniture of the church, chancel, &c. here is the communion table, with a blue carpet; a diaper table cloth; a napkin; a silver chalice, weighing 10 ounces 12 pennyweights; and a patten, four ounces seven pennyweights, without any inscription; two pewter flaggons; a pewter platter, inscribed thus; " This belongeth to St. Martin's church, Leicester, A. D'ni 1677;" two pewter dishes to collect the offerings in.

" For the pulpit, a purple cloth, with a gold fringe and a cushion of the same; an old plain cushion; two brass candlesticks; four pewter candlesticks; a great Bible; one Common Prayer Book for the minister, another for the mayor, and a third for the judges, or other honourable person; a Book of Homilies; Jewell's Defence of the Apology; and Erasmus's Paraphrase on the New Testament; a pewter bason, used at the font and in private baptisms; ten forms, used at communions; a chest for public writings; three surplices; two hoods for the minister; an organ; six bells in the steeple; with a clock and a set of chimes. In the vestry, a wainscot chair, a table, a looking-glass, a chamber-pot, a press with two cloths, two hearse cloths.

" 7. No lands or money in stock for the repair of the church or utensils.

" 8. The parish repair the church and churchyard fence.

" 9. It is the vicar's right to nominate the clerk, but the parish choose the sexton.

" The clerk's wages are, for attending the parish business per annum, 40s.; for every burial in the church, chapel, or chancel, 2s.; in the churchyard, with a coffin, 1s.; without a coffin, 6d.; for every marriage, 1s.; for every baptism, 6d.

" The sexton's wages are from the parish per annum, 56s.

" Mr. John Stanley gave 30s. yearly to the vicar; Mr. Christopher Tamworth gave money, wherewith was purchased land to the value of 7l. per annum in Whetstone, 20 nobles whereof he granted to the vicar to read prayers twice every day in the week.

" And the clerk receives 10s. yearly for ringing the bell, and his attendance. These are paid by the chamberlain of the Borough."

The mayor and aldermen, with the town clerk, in their formalities, attend divine service in St. Martin's church on the three grand festival-days. The whole corporation on St. Matthew's day (when the mayor and other corporation officers are chosen); on the Monday after St. Martin (the mayor's feast day); and on the Sunday after St. John's day, when a sermon is preached for the benefit of the widows in St. John's Hospital. The Judges of Assize also attend divine service here; and the Bishop's and Archdeacon's Visitations, and the Ecclesiastical Courts, are held in this church [1].

From the tablet on the South-east wall of the church:

Donations to the poor of this parish.

*1. The gentlemen of the Lottery, and sir William Curtun's [Courten's], in 4d. bread, to be given on New Year's-day and Whitsunday, 1l. 1s. 4d.

2. Mr. Robert Heyrick's, in 4d. bread, on Candlemas-day, 1l.

*3. Mr. Anthony Ackham's, in 4d bread, on the last Sunday in every other month, beginning at January, 2l. 2s.

*4. Mr. Ives, in 4d. bread, every Friday in Lent.

The six following gifts are distributed in money on Lady-day:

*5. The Countess of Devon, 9s.
*6. Mr. Norris's, 1l. 7s. 4d.
*7. Mrs. Hobby's, 2s.
8. Mrs. Ossiter's, 18s.
9. Mr. Garland's, 3s. 4d.
10. Mrs. Ward's, 1l. 5s.
Total of the Lady-day money, 4l. 4s. 8d.

The three next are given away with the money that is collected for the poor housekeepers against Christmas:

*11. John Poutney's, esq. [Poultney's,] 2l. 4s. 7¼d.
*12. Mr. Botham's, 13s. 4d.
*13. Mr. Elkinton's, 2l.
Total of the Christmas money, 4l. 17s. 11¼d.

14. Mr. Heyrick's, distributed by the mayor of this Borough, to twenty widows, 1l.

15. Mr. Topp's, at the discretion of the minister and churchwardens of this parish for the time being, to apprentice a boy to a master able to learn him a trade, 8l.

16. Mr. Bent's, to twelve poor women who attend divine service on Sunday, one penny loaf each.

*17. Mr. Garland's, in bread, on St. Luke's day, 5s.
Of whom received:

Those marked thus *, of the chamberlains of this Borough.

No. 2, the mayor; No. 8, Mr. Burgess in the Abbey-gate; No. 9, Mrs. Garland; No. 10, Mr. Theophilus Holmes; No. 15, the vicar of this parish; No. 16, the tenant of a bakehouse in Silver-street. Thomas Christy, } churchwardens, James Oldham, } 1776.

VICARS.	PATRONS.
William Capellanus, 1220.	
Richard de Melton, 12 . . .	
John de Beverle, 1265.	
Rudde Roleg, 1279.	
Roger de Cosyngton, 1411.	Abbot and convent of St. Mary de Pratis.
Henry Whytche, had licence to preach, Dec. 17, 1420.	
Nicholas Wagstaffe, 1520.	
William Bradeley, 1534.	
Robert Boughton, 1552.	
Nicholas Lubbenham [2], 1556.	
Thomas Sacheverell [3], 1614; died in November 1626.	
William Holmes, 1626; died 1633.	
James Andrews, M. A. 1633; died 1638.	The King.
Walter Watkins [5], 1638; resigned.	
Thomas White, M. A. by resignation, June 22, 1638 [4].	
Thomas Palmer, of London, April 16, 1646.	
Mr. Herring, of Coventry, 1649.	
Mr. Richard Pike, 1651-2.	Appointed by the Parish.
Mr. Dixie, of Cadeby.	

[1] In the early part of the reign of Henry VIII. the ecclesiastical courts were held in the parish church of Saint Mary juxta Castrum; but, since the Reformation, they have generally been held in St. Martin's church. J. S. H.   [2] Rymer, vol. XV. p. 242.
[3] Confrater of Wigston's Hospital, where see an account of him, p. 501. And see his Pedigree, vol. III. p. 220.
[4] Pat. 14 Car. I.
[5] In some instrument, which I very well remember to have seen, bearing date in July 1638, Mr. Watkins is described as vicar of St. Martin's in Leicester. J. S. H.

<table>
<tr><td>VICARS.</td><td>PATRONS.</td></tr>
</table>

VICARS.

William Barton[1], 1656.
John Newton[2], M. A. 1679; resigned 1697.
Richard Wood[3], 1697, sequestered 1700.
Samuel Carte[4], M. A. sequestrator, April 8, 1700.
Humfrey Clayton[5], resigned 1702.
William Thomas[6], 1702; died in 1713.
Samuel Carte, M. A. 1713; died April 16, 1740.
Gustavus Broughton, M. A. presented April 1740.
Thomas Haines[7], B. A. inducted Sept. 1753; died in 1786.
Joseph Gregory[7], B. A. 1786; died 1802.
Edward-Thomas Vaughan[7], M.A. 1802 (present vicar 1811.)

PATRONS.

The King.

MONUMENTAL INSCRIPTIONS.

The three oldest monuments now remaining in this church are,

In the small South aile, towards the gallery stairs, on a large flat stone, is a tall cross, with a chalice on its side (fig. 9); and an inscription almost vanished, but on which Mr. Bickerstaffe decyphered somewhat like

" . . . . . Carbemaker bece'b . . . . Amen."

In the great chancel the brasses have been torn away from the slab shewn in fig. 10, on which was a kneeling figure, with a canopy over his head; on each side of him a small kneeling figure; at the top a sort of chair of state; and at the four corners shields of arms. It is not easy to say whether it was for an Ecclesiastic, or a Civil Magistrate.

Round about a gravestone at the lower end of the choir, the effigies of a woman, with two escocheons, but defaced, fig. 11 (and partly hid by a pew):

" Orate pro anima Elizabeth nuper ux. Rich. Reginold, de Leyc. mercatoris Stapule Calisie, que quidem Elizabeth filia Joh'i Curzon, de . . . shall, armig. & que obiit . . Aug. anno D'ni millesimo CCCCC°XXX°; cujus anime propitietur Deus. Amen."

On the North wall, on a brass plate[8]:

Arms; . . . . a fess; in chief three lozenges. Crest, a bull's head couped, fig. 12.

" Here under lieth interred the body of Walter Aston, esq. born at Longdon in Staffordshire, who had to wife Joyce, the daughter of —— Nason, gent. of Rowingstone in Warwickshire, by whom he had issue five sons, viz. Edward, Thomas, Simon, and Walter; and three daughters, Joyce, Anne, and Katherine; who departed this life the 30th day of March, anno Domini 1638, and being aged . . years."

Near the aforesaid place, against the side of this, between the great chancel and the choir, are these arms in colours: Quarterly, 1. Argent, on a saltire Azure, five water-bougets Or; *Sacheverell*. 2. Gules, a stork Argent, ducally gorged Or; *Langford*. 3. Argent, a lion rampant Sable, crowned Or; *Burnell*. 4. Gules, three lozenges in pale Argent; *Neale*. 5. Sable, a lion rampant Argent; *Verdun*. 6. Argent, three squirrels Gules, playing upon bagpipes proper; *Matherley*; (fig. 13).

At the bottom of the arms, on a label, is written,

" SACHEVERELL HIS ARMES[9]."

---

[1] Rector also of Cadeby; where see an account of him, vol. IV. p. 575.—He possessed considerable poetical abilities, and published some hymns. A complaint was once preferred against him in the Ecclesiastical Court, charging him with neglecting to read the Common Prayer in the manner prescribed by law; but the then churchwarden and others making certificate to the contrary, the information does not appear to have been prosecuted. J. S. H.

[2] Of Clare Hall, Cambridge, where he took the degree of M. A. 1662. He published, in 1684, a Sermon, on burning a woman for poisoning her husband, 4to. He was confrater of Wigston's Hospital (see p. 502); resigned this vicarage in 1697, and went into Gloucestershire.

[3] " Gulielmus Foster, Legum Doctor, Archidiaconatûs Leicestriensis Commisarius & Officialis legitimè constitutus; dilecto nobis in Christo Samueli Carte, clerico, artium magistro, curato ecclesiæ Sancti Martini, infr burgum Leicestriæ, salutem in Domino. Cum, ut accepimus, vicariam ecclesiæ parochialis Sancti Martini Leicestriæ prædictæ, per cessionem Richardi Wood, clerici, ultimi incumbentis ibidem fore vacantem, & in divinis desolatam pariter & derelictam; ex officiq nostro volentes indemnitati dictæ ecclesiæ plenè consulere; nos, ut conemur omnes & singulos fructus, decimas, oblationes, & proventus, ad dictam vicariam spectantes & pertinentes, & à tempore vacationis ejusdem obvenientes, sequestravimus, prout per presentes sequestrationes; & tibi sequestrationi nostræ custodiam committimus & mandamus, quatenus dictos fructus, decimas, oblationes, proventus, ac alia jura & emolumenta ecclesiastica quæcunque ad dictam ecclesiam spectantes, & per nos, ut præmittitur, sequestros, & à tempore vacationis ejusdem obvenientes, colligis & colligi facias, & dictæ ecclesiæ in divinis & sacris quibuscunque deservire facias; teque præfatum Samuelem Carte sequestratorem omnium & singulorum jurium ecclesiasticorum & emolumentorum ad dictam ecclesiam Sancri Martini nominamas, ordinamus, deputamus, & constituimus, per præsentes. In cujus rei testimonium, sigillum officii nostri præsentibus apponi fecimus. Datum 8° die mensis Aprilis, anno Domini 1700. TYRINGHAM STEPHENS, Registrarius."

[4] Mr. Carte published two Sermons, in 1694 and 1705; " Tabula Chronologica Archiepiscopatuum & Episcopatuum in *Anglia* & *Walliâ*, ortus, divisiones, translationes, &c. breviter exhibens; una cum indice alphabetico nominum, quibus apud authores insigniuntur; concinnata per Sam. Carte, Vic. S. Martini, Leicestr. & explicatæ per eundem," folio, without date. Part of a letter of his to Mr. Humphrey Wanley, dated Aug. 7. 1710, concerning a tesselated pavement found about 1670, near All Saints church in Leicester, with a drawing of it by B. Garland, is in the Philosophical Transactions, No. 331, p. 324. And his account of that town, in answer to some queries by Browne Willis, esq. (from a MS. in the Bodleian Library) is printed in the Bibliotheca Topographica Britannica.—His assistance to Dr. Willis is gratefully acknowledged in the Preface to the second volume of " Mitred Abbeys;" and to him Dr. Stukeley inscribes his plan of Roman Leicester, plate 92 of his Itinerary, vol. I.—He is said in Letsome's " Preacher's Assistant" to have been vicar of *St. Mary's*, and in Philosophical Transactions is miscalled vicar of *St. Margaret's*. Of the last of these misnomers he has himself taken notice of in one of his MSS. which was shewn by Mr. Cole to Dr. Farmer; and the other was a mistake. He was vicar of *St. Martin's*; and the time of his death, with some traits of his character, will appear from the inscription page 597. This gentleman occasionally presided as official surrogate in the Archdeaconry Court, and was a zealous advocate for the doctrine of the Holy Trinity.

[5] " Johannes Rogers, clericus, A. M. Archidiaconatûs Leicestriæ Archidiaconus, & Georgius Newell, in Legibus Baccalaureus, Archidiaconatûs Leicestriæ Officialis legitimè constitutus, universis & singulis rectoribus, vicariis, curatis, capellanis, clericis & ministris quibuscunque, in & per totum Archidiaconatum Leicestriæ prædictum ubiliquet constitutis, salutem. Cum reverendus in Christo pater & dominus, dominus Gulielmus, permissione divinâ, Lincolniæ episcopus, dilectum sibi in Christo Samuelem Carte, clericum, in artibus magistrum, ad vicariam Sancti Martini, in villâ Leicestriæ, in archidiaconatu Leicestriæ, Lincolniæ diocesi & jurisdictionis, legitimè vacantem, eâ ratione quod Humfredus Clayton, clericus, ultimus incumbens ibidem. legere neglexit matutinas & vespertinas orationes & preces, nec declaravit assensum & consensum suum adinde secundùm statutum in eâ parte factum editum & provisum, ac proinde ipso facto deprivatus existit; & idso (uti asserabatur) ad præsentationem dominæ nostræ Annæ, Dei gratiâ, Magnæ Britanniæ, Franciæ, & Hiberniæ reginæ, pleno jure spectantem, legitimè presentatus extitit; ipsumque vicarium ejusdem vicariæ, ac in & de eâdem, cum suis juribus, membris, & pertinentiis universis, instituerit & investiverit, prout in mandato nobis directo plenius liquet & apparet: Vobis igitur confidimus & discretionem committimus, & firmiter injungendo mandamus, quoties eundem Samuelem Carte, seu procuratorem suum legitimum, ejus nomine, & pro eo, in realem, actualem, & corporalem possessionem dictæ vicariæ, juriumque & pertinentium suorum universorum inducatis, seu induci faciatis cum effectu, sub pœnâ juris. Et quod in præmissis feceritis nos, aut surrogatum nostrum, in vel citra mensem jam proximè futurum, debitè certificatis. Datum Leicestriæ, sub sigillo quo in hâc parte utimur, vicesimo septimo die mensis Novembris, anno Domini millesimo septingentesimo duodecimo. R. STEPHENS, Registrarius Deputatus."
See some brief memoirs of Mr Carte in p. 598.

[6] Vicar also of All Saints in Leicester.   [7] These three gentlemen have all held also the vicarage of All Saints.

[8] This was copied at the Heralds' Visitation in 1682; but is not now remaining.

[9] This was copied at the same time, and is still preserved.

On

On the West arch of the chancel gate, in canonicals, in a small niche, kneeling, with a book before him (fig. 14):

" *James Andrewe.*
Anagram.
Reede I was man.
Deo & posteritati sacrum.

Sub hoc arcu, marmor, cui titul' " Andreas fui [1]," contegit Jacobum Andrewe, verè Andream, Leicestriâ oriund', Cantabrigiæ Artium Magister, ingenuus, probus, pius, ultra biennium conjugatus, prolem non suscepit, ast naturâ piè imitatus privignis suis, aliisque, munificentior vixit, piéque obdormivit,

die 4° } Augusti, { 1604 natus,
die 5° } { 1638 obiit.

Hæc dilectionis pignora ei reponit Margareta conjux ejus charissima.   Laus Deo."

A very curious monument, about the middle of the North-west wall, close to the arch, has the busts of John Whatton[2] and his two wives (fig. 15). On this tomb are the following coats, fig. 16—18 :

1. Azure, three hedgehogs passant Or; *Whatton.*

2. *Whatton*; impaling, Argent, a fess Vair Or and Gules ; *Heyrick.*

3. *Whatton*; impaling, Argent, ten torteauxes, 4, 3, 2, 1 ; over all, a label of three points; *Babington.*

Mr. Whatton has whiskers on his upper lip, and a picked chin beard, his own hair. The second has her hair curled, but flat, like his at top, beads round the neck. The first wife has an handkerchief, with a rose-tie on the stomach, head-covering like a capuchin. The breasts of both are covered. This monument is thus inscribed :

" John Whatton, of the Newark, neare Leicester, an Esquire of the Body of the late King Charles, Justice of Peace for the county of Leicester.

His first wife was Elizabeth Orpwood, widow, daughter of Mr. Robert Heyrick, alderman of this town. His second wife was Katherine, daughter of Thomas Babington, of Temple Rodeley, esq.; and by her only he had children, viz. three sons, John, William, and Thomas, and three daughters, Katherine, Mary, and Sence.   He died Feb. 16, 1656; in memory of whom his dear surviving wife erected this monument.

" Thus stands the triumph of Death's dart,
That in him wounded many a heart.
His children's tears, his sad wife's groanes,
The widows' and the orphans' moanes.
His friends' complaints that laid him here,
Best spake his proper character.
So good, so just, so gracious, that
All did admire, none imitate.
Virtues heap'd up in him did lie
All open by humility.

He shunn'd in public streams to swim,
He sought not honour, it found him.
Though balls of gold lay in his race,
They could not slack his holy pace,
Which if sometimes he stoop'd to take,
'Twas chiefly for the needy's sake.
To schisme he never did incline,
Yet was a compleat Lay Divine,
Whilst Scripture was his doctrine laid,
His holy life the use he made,
A stranger's life i' th' world he spent,
Till to his glorious home he went;
Where now to him the freedom's given,
To be a denizen of Heaven."

On a neat mural monument on the North side of the North aile ; fig. 19 :

Arms : Argent, on a chevron Azure, three garbs Or ; impaling, Azure, on a fess Gules, three hurts between six bezants. Crest, an Indian prince surrendering his sword ; over which crest the Corporation arms appear ; fig. 20.

" P. M. S.
Elizabethæ & Mariæ, uxorum
Gabrielis Newton, aldermanni, & hujus municipii
olim præfecti.

Eliz. } filia { Guil. Wells, ald. & Annæ } uxoris
Maria } erat { Geo. Bent, gen. & Aliciæ } ejus.

Obiit { Illa May 7, 1725, } ætatis suæ { 35.
{ Hæc Aprilis 1, 1737, } { 47.

Et Aliciæ filiæ unicæ, natæ & denatæ anno 1733."

Near the chancel, on a flat stone, on the North side:

" Underneath lyes the body of
Mrs. Martha Sansom, relict of Arnold Sansom, esq.
and only sister of lieutenant-colonel Thomas Fowke,
born at Hartenfordbury Park the 1st of May, 1690.
She was lineally descended from the Fowkes
of Staffordshire.

" This stone can only tell, in a few words, what would require a history to relate ; her charity, good-nature, and excellent parts. She had by Nature what others scarce attain by Art and Application ; and from the age of sixteen composed several pieces of poetry on different subjects, which, for their beautiful turn of thought and strength of imagination, have not only met with the approbation, but the admiration of the good, the learned, and the witty.

Friend ! whoe'er thou art, wish her soul at rest, who, when living, wished well to the whole world.
Obiit 17th February, 1735-6."

At the steps of the altar :
" The remains of Samuel Carte[3], M. A.
many years vicar of this parish.
He was a person of great learning,
exemplary

---

[1] These words were engraved on a flat stone on the floor.

[2] In 1637, Mr. Whatton was resident in Leicester ; and at that time had a sister Collier, who had then two sons, one of them an apprentice in London.   The following letter from this gentleman is here printed from the original :

" GOOD SIR,   *Raunston, the 2d of August,* 1639.

" I receaved your letter, and should have bene verie glad to have had your company at the assizes ; which, if I had known of your being in towne, I should have sent to desire it ; but yt seemeth you had other occasions hindered your cominge. For the other business you write of, yt is indeed likely that I shall marrye a young daughter (in comparison to my yeares) of Mr. Babington's, being betweene five and sixe-and-twentye yeares old : yet of a dossen or more that were motioned to me, both knight's daughters, and knight's and barronet's daughters, and some of greater birth, and others of verie good fashion and quality, before I pitched upon this gentlewoman, and divers since, there hath not bene above two above the age of this, but divers of them younger. I did not hastely resolve on this, but with good considerations, and the approbation and verie good likeing of a verie worthy Divine, and did thinke that, all things wayed well, she would be the fittest of any that I heard of, and so I thinke still, of others that have been motioned since ; she is commended to be verie meeke, humble, and one that will be suteable to my conditions, which I am assured of by a neer freind of mine that hath bene in house with her from her birth ; and she hath made as great shew in her words and carriage to me and others that she can affect me, and will carrie herselfe in such a loveing manner as is fitting as I can desire ; which indeed I have bene doubtfull of whomesoever I should much withall in respect of my age ; but, if I doe marry at all, I must make a hazard, and this waye is as likely a waye to prove well as any I can goe, for greater hopes I cannot have ; and that was it which I aymed at rather than greatness of birth, friends, or portion, she being one that feareth God, and is of verye good report. I see, to live unmarried will be a verie uncomfortable life for me, which I have had sad experience of since my wife died ; and having, I hope, performed those things for her which were fitting, both in her life, at her death, and since, yt is neither unlawful nor discommendable for me to marrye againe, which indeed she on her death-bed did wish and desire. I did seeke to God for his blessing and direction in this business, of so great wayght to me ; and I hope his blessing will goe along with me, and make it good and comfortable both for soule and bodye. And thus, good Sir, giveing you thankes for the love and good you write, you have and wish to me, I take leave, and rest your verie loveing kinsman; JOHN WHATTON."

" To the right worshipful his verie loveing unkle sir William Heiricke, knight, at his house in Beaumanor.   Present these."

[3] The Rev. Samuel Carte (some of whose publications have been mentioned in p. 596) was son of Thomas Carte, clothier, of Coventry, where he was born Oct. 21, 1652, and was instructed in grammar-learning in the free-school there. He became a member of Magdalen College, Oxford, in 1669 ; and was matriculated at the same time into the University, where he took the degree of Arts, that of B. A. 1672 ; M. A. 1675. In the Oxford Catalogue of Graduates his name is spelt *Chart,* though in the Matriculus it is spelt right. He received deacon's orders from the Bishop of Lichfield and Coventry, at Eccleshall, Sept. 21, 1673 ; priest's from the Bishop of London, at St. James's chapel, June 10, 1677 ; was collated by the Bishop of Litchfield and Coventry to the prebend

exemplary life and conversation, strict piety,
sound judgment, orthodox principles,
and a zealous and *able*[1] defender of the doctrine
of the Holy Trinity.
He died April 16, 1740, in the 87th year of his age,
in full assurance of a joyful resurrection.
" Near this place lie interred Ann, wife, and
Elizabeth, daughter, of the said Samuel Carte.
" Here lieth the body of Sarah Carte,
who died March 6, 1773, in the 72d year of her age."

Next to Mr. Carte's:

" Sacred to memory.
Under this stone lies buried
Mrs. Hill, widow of Mr. Hill, lately deceased,
and daughter of the Rev. Mr. Alfounder,
rector of Thurcaston, in this county.
She was trained up from her youth
with her venerable father,
in a thorough knowledge
of the Holy Scriptures.
Her excellent endowments of mind and body,
and her extraordinary goodness towards all,
made her universally esteemed,
ever ready in all the duties of her family,
aa a wife and mother, sister and friend.
She had few her equals,
chearful in her conversation,
courteous in her behaviour,
a pattern of beneficence, in all its branches.
Her soul thus adorned with heavenly graces,
she resigned to heaven,
and her body to the grave,
waiting for a joyful resurrection, to life eternal.
She was born at Thurcaston, Aug. 16, 1683;
she died at Leicester Oct. 18, 1754, aged 71,
much beloved and much lamented."

Against the South-east wall:
" Near this place lies interred George,
the only son of Gabriel Newton, gent. by Mary his wife,
daughter of George Bent, gent.
He departed this life 8th of March, 1746,
in the 18th year of his age;
to whose memory his affectionate
and disconsolate father erected this monument,
and with a pious intention cloathed 35 poor boys[2],
and put them out to trades at his own expence,
settling 3,250*l.* by his last will,
for a perpetual support of the charity,
and for carefully instructing them
in toning and psalmody,
which you may see more pathetically described
2 Chron. 5. 13.
and for educating them rightly in
the principles of our most holy and divine religion;
for, as Denham says,
" All human wisdom to divine is folly,
This truth the wisest man made melancholy,
That man's the greatest monster, without doubt,
Who is a wolf within and sheep without."

On a neat tablet on the North side of the altar:
" In mournful and most affectionate remembrance
of the late Elizabeth-Anne Vaughan, wife of
Edward-Thomas Vaughan, vicar of this parish,
who died in child-bed, January 16, 1808,
aged 26 years.

Reader!
let this early grave remind you to lose no time in
preparing for death: let the salvation of *Jesus
Christ* be the one object of your desire and pursuit;
seek it with all diligence; but, seek it as the free
gift of *God*: seek it in self-abhorrence, but in the
constant and lively exercise of repentance, faith,
hope, love, meekness, and every Christian grace;
so shall you resemble the beloved person whose
earthly remains lie here.
" For if we believe that *Jesus* died, and rose
again; even so, them also which sleep in Jesus,
will *God* bring with him."
1 Thessalonians, iv. 14 v.

On a handsome and lofty monument on the
North wall:
" Near this place lieth the
body of
John Westley, Alderman,
and twice Mayor of this Borough,
who departed this life in his
second Mayoralty
IV February, A. D. MDCCLXIX.
aged LXVII."

Just within the South-east gate, on the floor:
" Here lies the body of Mary, the daughter of
Francis Breton, late of Teton in Northamptonshire,
esq. and of Mary his wife, who was buried the
22d of May, anno Dom. 1662."

At the South-west end, on the floor (now so
broken and defaced as to be illegible):
" Samuel Marshall, here interred,
departed Dec. 26, 1671.

" Stroakes not so sharpe, nor many, squar'd a stone
For him, as serv'd to couch him under one;
Nor stroakes did polish halfe so well the tombe,
As the bright soul of him that's to it come."

On the West wall:
" In memory
of the Rev. Mr. John Harryman,
M. A. rector of Peckleton,
in this county,
of a most extensive learning,
in his own profession eminent,
not aspiring after more preferment,
of much greater deserving,
possessed of many shining qualities,
which his modesty would have concealed.
His life was private, yet pub-
lickly useful, and suitable to his most
Holy Function. He departed this life
June 13, A. D. 1743, ætatis 60 years."

of Tachbrook in the cathedral church of Litchfield, into which he was installed Sept. 30, 1682. He was presented by sir John Bridgman, of Castle Bromwich, to the vicarage of Clifton upon Dunmore, to which he was instituted March 26, 1684, and inducted March 28, where he lived till 1691; when, for the better education of his children, he became master of the free-school at Coventry; collated by the Bishop of Litchfield and Coventry to the vicarage of Dunchurch, in the county of Warwick, July 2, 1697, inducted July 30; presented by the Lord Chancellor to the rectory of Eastwell, in the county of Leicester, instituted Jan. 7, and inducted Jan. 21, 1698-9; and in the beginning of 1700 he was presented to the vicarage of St. Martin's in Leicester; which depending on voluntary contributions, he held it without institution till the year 1712, when a person surreptitiously obtained from the Lord Chancellor a presentation to it; but was deterred by the affections of the parishioners from prosecuting it; and Mr. Carte was again presented to it, instituted Nov. 21, and inducted Nov. 28, 1712. This latter living Dr. Kippis (in the Biographia Britannica) erroneously supposes that he resigned at the accession of king George the First, as it has been said that he assisted the celebrated Jeremiah Collier, in preaching to a Nonconforming Congregation in Broad-street, London. It was not, however, the vicar of St. Martin's, but his son Thomas Carte, the Historian, who was the occasional assistant to Mr. Collier.—Mr. Samuel Carte continued at Leicester till his death. A high, but I believe very just, character is given of him in the inscription printed above.—Of his three son, Samuel, the eldest, was an eminent solicitor in Chancery; Thomas, the second, was well known as an eminent Historian; and the third, John, was many years vicar of Hinckley. A full account of them may be seen in the Anecdotes of Mr. Bowyer; and of John, in particular, under the History of Hinckley, in this work, vol. IV. p. 744. The titles of his printed Sermons are, 1. " A Dissuasive from Murmuring, London, 1694," 4to; 2. " The Cure of Self-conceit, London, 1705," 4to. His " Tabula Chronologica, &c." was re-printed in Lord Somers's Tracts, first collection, vol. IV. p. 344. His " History of the Town of Leicester" is incorporated in the First Volume of this Work. See p. 596.

[1] This word is an interlineation on the stone.
[2] The school built by Gabriel Newton in his life-time stood in the South-east corner of St. Nicholas's church-yard. This school was rebuilt in the year 1808. It was probably founded for 35 boys; but the stated number is now increased to 80, who are supported (i. e. cloathed and educated) out of the funds raised by the bounty of Alderman Newton. J. S. H.—On this subject see further under the parish of St. Nicholas.

Near the West door of the church is a monument to the memory of John Stephens and Elizabeth his wife, both of whom died in 1782.

On the same side of the church is a plain marble tablet, in memory of John Stephens[1], who died in 1808, aged 75.

Opposite to the South-east door, and on the South wall of the chancel, is an elegant sarcophagus monument, with the following inscripton :

" To the memory of Richard Stephens [2], of this town, and Alice his wife, daughter of John Lettice, B. A. rector of Strixton, in the county of Northampton, this tribute of pious affection, respect and gratitude, is placed by their sons and daughters.
A. S. ob. Sep. 18, 1809, ætat. 64.
R. S. ob. Aug. 11, 1810, ætat. 65."
" *The memory of the just is blessed.* Proverbs."

On the East-east-by-South side, on a wall tablet:
" Juxta
conditur quod reliquum est
Thomæ Haines,
Omnium Sanctorum in annos quadraginta,
hujus ecclesiæ in triginta & amplius
vicarii.
Et hominem & ministrum Christi
Contemplator !
In omni vitâ suo officio fungi conatus est.
Obiit ann. Dom. 1786, ætatis suæ 65[3]."

On a flat stone :
" To the memory of William Bentley[4], who departed this life the 10th of January, 1784, aged 83 years.

" When I lie buried in the dust,
My flesh shall be thy care ;
These with'ring limbs with thee I trust,
To raise them strong and fair.

" To the memory of Mary Bentley,
the wife of William Bentley,
who departed this life
the 25th day of May, 1759, aged 50 years.
His son William Bentley laid down this stone."

On a tablet on the South-south-east wall :
Arms : Ermine, a griffin segreant, within a border engrailed Azure ; fig. 21.
" H. S. E.
Richardus Walker [5], armig.
Vir sæculi planè antiqui,
priscæque Virtutis ;
Negotiis solers, & rerum prudens ;
Moribus comis, idem & integer ;
Et hac nostrâ vitâ apprimè dignus,
Æternâ adeò dignior.
E vivis decessit 19° kal' Septem.
Anno { Redemptionis 1781 ;
{ ætatis 65.
Optimo Parenti
Johannes, filius minor,
Ex ex semisse hæres,
Animi in se verè paterni memor,
Hoc qualecunque officii sui monumentum
Mœrens posuit."

On one of the pillars :
Arms : Azure, on a chevron Argent, between three lamps burning Or, a leopard's face between two estoiles Azure ; *Farmer* ; fig. 22.
" Sacred to the memory of

Mrs. Elizabeth Farmer,
who departed this life
July 25th, 1766, aged 61 years.
" Also of
Thomas Farmer, gent.
who departed this life
Jan. 5th, 1771, aged 62 years.
" And of William Farmer, gent.
who departed this life
Oct. 8th, 1790, aged 76 years."

Near the upper end, on a gravestone :
" The remains of Daniell Morfiun, gent.
one of the aldermen, and once mayor of the
Borough of Leicester,
aged 88, and changed October the 4th, 1660."

Close to the aforesaid gravestone was another (now removed), with the effigies of a man and woman ; round about them,
" Here lieth the body of William Ive, esq.
and Jane his wife, which William departed this life
the 31 of October, anno Dom. 1641,
which Jane departed the 16 day of May, 1638.
His age 68 ; her age 73."

Under the communion table still remains :
" Hic sepultum jacet corpus Amie Browne, uxor Thomæ Browne, generosi, ætatis suæ 23, A.D. 1661."

On three gravestones [6] in the North corner :
1. " Here lieth the body of John Whatton, esq. whose age was 70 years."

2. " Here lieth the body of Mrs. Catherine Whatton, the wife of John Whatton, esq.
She departed this life the 14 day of July,
in the year of our Lord 1673, her age 39."

3. " Here lieth Milicent, daughter of Tiringham Stephens by Milicent his wife,
daughter of William Inge, of Thorp Constantine,
in the county of Stafford, who departed this life
the 20 of February, anno Domini 1674."

On a flat stone [7] in the middle :
" William, the son of Bartholomew Cradock, of Farndon in Northamptonshire, died Feb. 24, 1661."

Near the lower end :
" Here lieth the body of William Franke, esq. once mayor of this Borough, and once high sheriff of the county of Leicester. He had to his first wife Alice, the daughter of Richard Ludlam, twice mayor of this Borough, who departed this life Jan. 20, 1661, and lieth here interred. He had to his second wife Alice, the daughter of Gilbert Armstrong, of Rempston, in com. Nottingham, esq. by whom he left one son, viz. William, obiit March 29, anno Domini 1679, ætatis 67."

At the lower end of the chancel [8], on a gravestone :
" Hic jacet Gulielmus Heaward, gener. quondam hujus curiæ procurator, qui obiit 17° Aug. 1661."

Near the aforesaid :
" Here lies the body of Francis, the son of Francis Breton, late of Teton in Northamptonshire, esq. and of Mary his wife, who was buried the 16th day of January, anno Dom. 1663."

In the chancel :
" Here lyeth interred Captain John Cochran, who served in the Navy and Army

---

[1] John, son of John and Elizabeth Stephens, was never married ; but constantly resided with his younger brother Richard, with whom he was in partnership.

[2] The town of Leicester lost, in Mr. Richard Stephens, an able and zealous promoter of its interests and its prosperity. He was the first, and an active commissioner of the property-tax, which honourable, though odious office, he discharged with fidelity to his king and his country : no private feeling, nor private friendship, made him swerve from that line of conduct which his conscience dictated. His knowledge of inland navigation was very extensive : he was unanimously elected chairman both of the committee and of the half-yearly meetings of the proprietors of the Leicester navigation. Upon every public occasion, which called forth the liberality of the inhabitants of the town, he was always conspicuous. His subscriptions and donation to the Infirmary, to the Humane Society, to the relief of the poor, to the assembly-rooms, and theatre, &c. &c. will bear sufficient testimony.

[3] This gentleman acquired an ample fortune in the banking line ; and to young men in business, whom he found steady, he was exceedingly useful.

[4] The above epitaph was composed by the late Rev. Mr. Gregory, vicar of this parish. J. S. H.

[5] See his wife's epitaph at Little Stretton, vol. III. p. 738.

[6] These, it is believed, are now covered over with basses, forms, &c. &c. J. S. H.   [7] This is supposed to have been taken up.

[8] Several stones have evidently been taken up ; and as I cannot find this or the two that follow, I apprehend they are removed. J. S. H.

in the reign of Queen Anne, George I. and II.
upwards of 50 years.
He departed this life May 19, 1756,
aged 66 years.
" And Charlotte Cochran his wife, aged 66 years."

" Here lieth the body of Mr. Richard Hill,
attorney at law. He was beloved in his family,
respected by his acquaintance, deservedly gained the
character of a fair and skilful practitioner in his
own profession, and of a prudent and honest man in all
his dealings. He died Dec. 1, 1739, aged 59, in
full hope, through Christ's merits, of a joyful
resurrection to life eternal."

" Here lyeth the body of Mr. Samuel Woodland,
alderman, and once mayor of this Borough,
who departed this life Aug. 29, 1712, aged 66 years.
" Also the body of Mary Woodland his second wife,
who died Feb. 18, 1732, aged 68 years.
" Also the body of John Woodland,
son of the said Samuel and Mary Woodland,
who died March 31, 1728, aged 37 years.
" Here lyeth interred the body of Mary Woodland,
the wife of Samuel Woodland, who was the
eldest daughter of Thomas Cradock, of Farndon,
in the county of Northampton, gent.
who departed this life for a better Dec. 26, 1679.
" Samuel, the eldest son of Samuel Woodland
by Mary his second wife, departed this life
Aug. 24, 1689, being the 7th year of his age.
" Edward the second son departed this life
Sept. 17, 1689, being the 2d year of his age.
" Matilda the second daughter departed this life
the 12th of June, 1690, being the 1st year of her age.
" Mary their eldest daughter departed this life
the 31st day of August, 1697, being the 12th year
of her age."

" Here lyeth interred the body of Elizabeth,
wife of Thomas Fisher, gent. of Repton, in the
county of Derby, and daughter of
Mr. Samuel Woodland by Mary his wife,
who died the 8th of June, 1735, aged 37."

" William, son of the late
Rev. William Bainbrigge, and grandson
to William Bainbrigge, of
Hugglecoate Grange, in this
county, esq. deceased, was born
the 29th of December, 1782, at
Fort St. George in the East Indies,
and departed this life, at Leicester,
the 10 day of January, 1787."

" Near this place are deposited the
remains of John Gregory [1], late
alderman, and once mayor of this
Borough. He passed through life with
integrity and honour, respected by
all who knew him ; and died at
the Adelphi Hotel, London, March
22, 1789, in the prosecution of a
public good, the navigation and
commerce of the Town of Leicester,
ætat. 62.

" Also of Frances, relict
of Thomas Gregory, who died
11th April, 1795, aged 71 years."

Close to the preceding :
" To the memory of
the Rev. Joseph Gregory,
16 years vicar of Saint Martin's
and All Saints, Leicester.
He died 26th February, 1802,

aged 40 years.
" Haud facile emergunt, quorum virtutibus obstat
Res angusta domi !" Juv."

In the middle chancel, on a mural tablet:
Arms : Or, semée of crosslets Gules, and three
boars' heads erased Sable ; Cradock, fig. 23.
" P. M. S.
Edmundi Cradock [2], gen.
& Mariæ uxoris ejus.
Obiit { ille Aug. 26, 1716, æt. 76.
{ illa Feb. 20, 1725, æt. 68.
Quicquid horum mortale fuit,
Felicis spe resurrectionis,
Propè hunc murum reconditur.
Tu interim eis semper memor,
Hora enira dum non cogites
Extrema veniat dies."

On the floor :
" Here lies the body of Elizabeth Cradock,
daughter of Alderman Johnson, of the
Borough of Leicester, and wife to Edmund Cradock,
who died in July 1731, aged 49 years.
" Near this place is likewise interred Anna Maria,
daughter of the said Edmund Cradock, which
died in October 1741, in the 25th year of his age.
" Samuel Cradock, the son of the abovementioned
Edmund and Elizabeth, who died the
31st of October, 1746, in the 23d year of his age,
is buried under this stone."

On a mural tablet (Arms as above) :
" Here lie deposited
the remains of
Joseph Cradock,
who was born
the 17th of Nov. 1689,
and died
the 20th of April, 1759.
" Enough that Virtue fill'd the space between,
Prov'd by the end of being to have been. Pope."

A Latin epitaph in this church on a brass plate for
Mr. Tiffin, confrater of Wigston's Hospital, who
died in December 1754, has been removed to make
way for a modern tomb [3].

About the walls of the East, North, and South
sides of a chapel at the East end of the North aile,
commonly called The Heyrick's chancel, are several
inscriptions :

1. On an upright slate in the North-west recess, on
its North-west-by-East side :
" Here lieth buried the bodie of John Heyricke, of this parish, who
departed this life the 2d of Aprill, 1589, being about the age of 76. He
did marry Marie, the daughter of John Bond, of Wardend, in the
county of Warwicke, esq. who lived with the said Marie in one
house full fifty-two years, and in all that tyme never buried man, woman,
nor childe, though they were sometimes 20 in houshold. He had yssue
by the said Marie fiue sons and seuen daughters, viz. Robert, Nicholas,
Thomas, John, and William ; and daughters Ursula, Agnes,
Marie, Elizabeth, Ellen, Christian, and Alice. The said
John was mayor of this town in the year 1559, and again in
1572. The said Marie departed this life the 8th of December,
1611, beinge of the age of 97 yeares [4]. She did see before her
departure, of her children, and children's children, and their
children, to the number [5] of 142."

2. The next upright slate adjoining on the right :
" Here lyeth the body of Robert Heyrick, ironmonger, and
alderman of Leicester, who had been thrise maior thereof.
He was eldest son to John Heyrick and Marie ; and had
2 sons and 9 daughters by one wife, with whom he liued
51 yeares.
At his death he gaue 16 pounds 10 shillings a yeare to
good uses.

---

[1] See the Pedigree of Gregory, p. 587.
[2] See the Pedigree of Cradock, vol. III. p. 1149.
[4] Of this venerable Matron an excellent portrait has been given in vol. II. p. 622. Her autograph also, with those of several of her descendants, may be seen in the same volume, p. 612 ; and a copious account of her descendants, with an ample Pedigree, pp. 615—636.
[3] See p. 503.
[5] See these enumerated (to the number of 143) in vol. II. p. 616.

he lived 78 yeares; and after dyed very godly, the 14th of June, in the yeare 1618.

All flesh is grasse; both yonge and old must die;
And so we passe to judgment by and by."

3. On the next upright slate:

Arms: Vert, a fess between three boars' heads couped in chief, and in base three crosses pattée, 2 and 1, Argent; *Orpwood*; impaling *Herrick*; fig. 24.

"Here lyeth buried the bodie of Robert Orpwood, citisen and gooldsmith of London, born in Abingdon, in the county of Berks. He departed this life the 23 of August, in anno D'ni 1609. Hee did marry with Elizabeth Heyricke, the daughter of Robert Heyricke, of this parishe, and one of the Aldermen of this Incorporation."

4. On another upright slate:

"Hic jacet Elizabetha, uxor Roberti Orpwood generosi predicti, defuncti, necnon Johannis Whatton, corporis regiæ majestatis armigeri relicti, quæ migravit in æternitatem decimo septimo Augusti, anno Domini 1638, ætatis suæ 64. A speciall benefactrix, and of sacred memory in this corporation; wherein if any parallel her..."

On the North wall there is a fair monument, with the arms and crest of *Heyrick* (the inscription not now legible) for sir William Heyrick[1], knight; who married Joan, daughter of Richard May, of Mayfield in Sussex, esq. by whom he had seven sons and five daughters, and died March 2, A. D. 1652, æt. 96.

On the floor:
"Sir William Heyrick was here buried March 8, 1652."

On another mural tablet:
"M. S.
G. HEYRICK.
Si stirps honesta, si stirpe mens nobilior,
si excelsum ingenium, candidique mores,
castis excultissimi literis;
si ipsæ prorsus litera,
si mira linguæ suavitas, si corporis decor,
si impavida virtus, illibata probitas,
fidiq. pectoris integra constantia,
fortunæ vicibus frangenda nullis,
eximi acerbo meruere letho;
Vixisses semper, & quidem semper vivis;
ultra Musarum marmorumque vires,
& supervacuos tumuli honores
(fraterni amoris pignus inutile)
vivit vigetq.;
Fati nescia pars melior tui,
ad nativa scilicet sydera
lubens recessit,
negatum terris petitura cœlo,
ubi solum poterat,
pietatis præmium pariter & incrementum.
Obiit 11 Jan. 1696-7, ætat. suæ 32.
Desideratissimo fratri, G. H.
hoc sepulchrale marmor
posuit mœstissimus superstes,
S. HEYRICK."

On the same wall:

Arms: *Herrick*; impaling, Argent, on a chief Gules, a lion passant guardant Or, crowned of the last; *Noble*; fig. 25.

"Here lies interred Martha, the [first] wife of Thomas Herrick, of this Borough, gentleman, who was the younger daughter of Thomas Noble, of the same Borough, esq. She departed this life 17th May, 1723, aged 24."

Against the North wall:

Arms: Azure, on a fess Or, between six bezants three hurts; *Bent*; fig. 26.

"Here lieth interred the
body of George Bent, gent.
twice mayor of this Burrough,
who departed this life the 24th of June,
Anno { Domini 1709.
{ ætatis suæ 75.
"Here also lieth interred
the body of William Bent,
son of the abovenamed George Bent,
who departed this life the 16th of August,
Anno { Domini 1707.
{ ætatis suæ 46.
"Also Elizabeth, the wife of
William Bent, gent.
who departed this life
Sept. 30, 1725, aged 59 years."

Arms; *Bent*; impaling, Per bend sinister Ermine and Argent, a lion rampant Sable, fig. 27.
"Near this place lieth interred George Bent, gent. late of this parish, aged 67. He died Jan. 13, 1730.
"Also George Bent his son,
late one of the aldermen, and once
mayor of this Borough, died the 20th
May 1736, aged 48.
"Also Alice, the wife of George
Bent, Gent. departed this life the
6th day of April, 1737, aged 70 years."

Against the South wall, at the lower end:
"Siste, viator.
Ecce tibi
depositum Mariæ uxoris Francisci Noble,
gen. honore prætorio bis decorati. En matrona
pietate nullisque non ornata virtutibus; &, inter
decora sui sexûs meritò numeranda, cum marito anno 36 suavissimè convixit; tandem verò,
matura cœlo, valedixit viro; & abiit, non obiit,
15 Aug. 1675, ætatis 62."

Near the aforesaid place:
"Here lieth interred the body of Armestrong,
daughter of Gilbert Armstrong,
of the county of Nottingham,
esq. who died June 11, 1669."

"Jane, wife of Simon Barwell, gent. died A. D. 1703."

On the South side of the said chapel:
"Here lieth the body of Francis Noble, gent.
who was twice mayor of this Burrough of Leicester,
and departed this life the 13th day of December,
anno Domini 1689, ætat. suæ 78."

On a flat stone in the North aile:
Arms: 1. *Herrick*; impaling, Paly of six, Argent and Azure, on a chief Gules, a lion passant reguardant Or; *Bakewell*; fig. 28.
"Here lies interred Katherine, the wife of Thomas Herrick, of this Borough, gentleman, and daughter of Robert Bakewell, of Swepston in this county, gentleman, deceased, by Ruth his wife. She departed this life March 26, 1730, aged 23."

The five which follow were transcribed by Mr. Carte from the floor of the same chapel, but are not now to be found:

1. On an old blue stone, stript of its brasses:
"James Andrews, twice mayor of Leicester, who died A. D. 1627, æt. 75."

2. "Robert, son of Robert Hickling, gent. who died April 28, A. D. 1687, æt. 28."

[1] Good portraits of sir William Heyrick and his Lady, with a particular history of their branch of this antient family, may be seen in vol. III. p. 152; to which may be added the following anecdote, preserved by Mr. Samuel Clarke, pastor of the church of Christ in Bennet Finch, London, in a publication dated "from my Study in Threadneedle-street, this 20th of November 1656:" The lady Herrick living at her house in Leicestershire in the time of our late wars, there came one to her, and told her, that, if she staid in her house, a party of the King's soldiers would come presently, and take her away prisoner. She thanked him, and retired herself to seek unto God by prayer for direction, and was encouraged to stay. Presently after came another, with the same message, importunately desiring her to absent herself. She thanked him also; and again retired unto prayer, and was still encouraged. Then came a third messenger, from justice Babington; and she, as before, sought to God for direction; but found her former confidence abated: yea, the more she prayed, the more her heart failed her. Whereupon she left her house; and immediately came in a troop of soldiers, which searched all the house for her. This she told my reverend friend Master White." It appears that his reverend friend Master White lived in Leicestershire. This was probably Mr. Thomas White, the vicar of St. Martin's (see p. 595).—In the same publication Mr. Clarke gives a wonderful account of a miller that was murdered at Lutterworth.

3. " Mary, daughter of sir William Herrick, of Beaumanor, who died Sept. 20, A. D. 1628, æt. 20."

4. " Thomas, the only son of Francis Noble, who died Dec. 6, A. D. 1655, æt. 3."

5. " Elizabeth, daughter of Gilbert Armstrong, of Rempston, in the county of Nottingham, esq. who died June 11, A. D. 1669."

In St. Mary's chapel, where now the Consistory is, there are, on the floor, the following inscriptions, covered with a range of new seats:

1. " Nicholas Lisle, gent. of Palmers in the Isle of Wight, who died March 28, A. D. 1711, æt. 28."

2. " Andrew Freeman, son of Henry Freeman, of London, gent. who died June 1, 1680."

3. " Elizabeth, daughter of Edward Palmer, of Leicester, gent. late wife of Thomas Newdigate, of Hawton, in the county of Nottingham, esq. third son of sir Richard Newdigate, bart. She died June 10, 1712."

4. " Edward Palmer, gent. who died July 14, 1687, æt. 74; as also Anne, wife of Thomas, son of the said Edward Palmer, who died May 28, A. D. . . . . . æt. 26; and also Henry, son of the said Edward Palmer, who died Dec. 16, 1692."

On a tablet on the North wall of the South chancel:
" Near this place lie
the remains of Samuel Simpson [1],
alderman, and once mayor of this Borough.
He died the 14th day of May, 1788,.
aged 77 years.
" Elizabeth, his wife
died May 6, 1795,
aged 77 years.
" William Simpson, son of the above
Samuel and Elizabeth, died August 10, 1798,
aged 41 years."

By the South gate of the chancel, without, is this elegant, truly poetical, and pathetic epitaph, said to be written by her brother the Rev. Mr. Lettice:
" Here lieth the body of Mary Lettice,
who departed this life June 11, 1770, aged 34 years.
Now, should this tomb the stranger's step arrest,
The virtues of its tenant to proclaim,
He'd judge the eulogy by flatt'ry drest,
Or ostentation catching at a name.
Then silent rest her unambitious tomb:
She needs no fame sepulchral praises breath:
Affection drops its tribute in their room,
And her own conscience twines th' immortal wreath."

" Sacred to the memory of Edward Hodges,
who departed this life,
on the 18th of January, 1801,
aged 60 years;
and of Martha his wife,
who died on the 22d of April, 1789,
aged 45 years.
" Also three of their children,
who died infants."

On a tablet over the vestry door:
" In memory of
John Throsby [2],
who was born in 1740,
and died February 3rd, 1803.

He was 32 years Parish-clerk;
of a peaceful disposition,
lived respected; and died an humble
Member of the Church of Christ."

On the South side of the vestry:
" Mr William Lee,
alderman, and twice mayor
of this Borough,
died August 1, 1759, aged 68.
He married Penelope, daughter of the
Rev. Mr. Goode, rector of Weldon, in
the county of Northampton; and she
dying without issue, he married Ann,
daughter of Mr. John Ludlam, alderman
of Leicester, and by her had issue Mary Lee,
who died March 27, 1766, aged 37;
and the Rev. Mr. John Lee, rector
of Burton Overy, in this county, and who,
from filial piety and fraternal affection
ordered this tribute of respect
to be paid to their memory."

" Here lieth Mary, the wife
of Arden Elsmere, gent. who
departed this life the first day of
August, in the year of our Lord 1712, aged 46.
" Here also lieth the abovenamed
Arden Elsmere, gent.
who departed this life the fourth day
of Sept. in the year of our Lord 1714, aged 47."

Arms: *Herrick;* impaling, Gules, two bars; a chief Or, three crosses pattée Gules; *Winstanley;* fig. 29.

" Near to this place lie the remains of Elizabeth, wife of Thomas Herrick, of this Borough, gent. and daughter of James Winstanley, late of Braunston, in this county, esq. who departed this life the 10th day of January, 1757, aged 49 years."

" To the memory of Thomas Herrick, gent. A good father, a good friend, and a good citizen. Ob. 10th Dec. 1766, æt. 73 years."

On a flat stone in the North aile:
Arms: Gules, three chevrons Vairè; *Turvile;* impaling *Bent;* fig. 30.
" Anne Turvile, wife of Richard Turvile, gent. and second daughter of William Bent, gent. died May 1, 1718, in the 27th year of her age."

On a flat stone in the North aile:
Arms of *Barwell,* between his two wives, Argent, three martlets between two bars Gules; impaling, 1. *Newton;* 2. *Major;* fig. 31.
" Here lieth interred the body of Simon Barwell, late of the Borough of Leicester, gent. who departed this life 24th June, 1720, aged 57 years; who married for his first wife Jane, the daughter of William Major, late of the same Borough, gent.; and for his second, Anne, the widow of Babington Bradley, late of the same Borough, M. D. and daughter of Robert Newton, of the city of London, grocer, by whom he had issue one only daughter, viz. Anne.
" Here also lieth Anne, the wife of the said Simon Barwell, who died 4th May, 1723, aged 47."

The following arms were on a monument in the South aile, which is now not to be found:
Barwell, on an escocheon of pretence . . . a cross moline . . . . on a canton a gauntlet . . . . . for *Topp;* fig. 32.

---

[1] This gentleman was profoundly skilled in the Hebrew language.
[2] Mr. Throsby, for whom I had a very sincere regard, died in his 66th year, after a lingering illness, which he supported with patient fortitude and pious resignation. He was a man of strong natural genius; and, during the vicissitudes of a life remarkably chequered, rendered himself conspicuous as a draughtsman and topographer. He attempted many expedients for the maintenance of a numerous family, few of which answered his purpose; and his last days would have been shaded with penury and disappointment, but for the assistance of those friends who knew his worth, and justly appreciated him as a man of honesty, integrity, and merit. His publications were, " The Memoirs of the Town and County of Leicester, 1777," 6 vols. 12mo. 2. " Select Views in Leicestershire, from original Drawings, 1789," 4to. 3. " A Supplementary Volume to the Leicestershire Views, containing a Series of Excursions in the Year 1790, to the Villages and Places of Note in the County, 1790," 4to. 4. " The History and Antiquities of the antient Town of Leicester, 1791," 4to. 5. " Letter to the Earl of Leicester, on the Roman Cloaca, or Sewer, at Leicester; with some Thoughts on the Jewry Wall, 1793," 8vo. 6. " Thoughts on the Provincial Corps raised, and now raising, in Support of the British Constitution at this aweful Period, by a Private in the Leicestershire, 1795," 8vo. 7. " Thoroton's History of Nottinghamshire, re-published with large Additions, and embellished with Picturesque and Select Views of Seats of the Nobility and Gentry, Towns, Villages, Churches, and Ruins, 1797," 3 vols. 4to. See an epitaph on his father, p. 604.

At

At the upper end of the choir, on a gravestone:
" Hic etiam Robertus Hickling, fil. Roberti Hickling, gen. & Susanna uxor ejus, filia Johannis Herick, gen. ob. 28 April. 1667, æt. suæ 28."

In St. George's chapel:

Arms: Argent, a chevron between three cross molines Gules; *Cheselden;* impaling, a chevron between three leopards' faces; fig. 33.
" George Cheselden, M. D.
who died 6th March, 1736."

On another tomb, not now remaining, were these arms: *Cheselden;* impaling, a lion rampant . . . . . . debruised with a bend; fig. 34.

On a tablet on the wall of the small South aile:
" In this porch, near several of his
sons, one of whom, named Charles, died
August 5, 1770, aged 35 years, are
deposited the remains of
Philip Hackett, gent.
son of the late Rev. Philip Hackett,
rector of South Croxton, vicar of All
Saints, and confrater of Wigston's Hospital;
he practised many years as a proctor in
the Ecclesiastical Court of the Archdeaconry of Leicester [1]; and departed this
life on the 16th day of August, in the 63d
year of his age, and that of Christ 1770.
If the tender husband, the kind
parent, the liberal benefactor, the friend
of the poor, and the best of masters; if the
strictest fidelity and humanity, the most
inviolable attachment to friendship, and
the truest regard to the rights of society,
acquire the attention due to so amiable
a pattern; the deceased will never die,
whilst the gratitude of contemporaries
exists, and posterity is mindful
of good examples.
" Also are deposited the remains of
Thomas Hackett, gent. a proctor of the
Spiritual Court, son of the above
Philip Hackett, gent.
deceased Aug. 7, 1781, aged 41 years."

At the upper end of the South aile:
Arms: the sun in splendour; *Dyson;* fig. 35.
" Hic jacet corpus . . . . . Ra. Dison, gen. . . . . . .
18º die Octobris, anno D'ni 166 . . . ætatis 51."

On a gravestone lying at the South door, in 1683:
Arms as before.
" Hic jacet corpus Radulphi Dison, gen. qui
ob. s'c'do die Novembris, anno D'ni 1675."

Near the middle of the South aile:
" Here lyeth the body of Andrew Freeman, son of
Henry Freeman, of London, gent. who departed
this life the 2d day of June, anno 1680."

In the South aile, and contiguous to the Consistory Court:
" Near this place lie interred the remains of
Joseph Cleadon, apparitor,
who departed this life June the 8th, 1786,
in the 70th year of his age.
" A wit's a feather, and a chief's a rod,
An honest man's the noblest work of God."

" Near this place lie interred
the remains of Mr. Joseph Simpson,
who died Jan. 28, 1787, aged 76 years.
" Also the remains of Mrs. Deborah Woodcock
his sister, who died Feb. 20, 1779, aged 70 years."

" In memory of Henry Gutheridge, gent. one of
the aldermen, and once mayor of this Borough. He
departed this life Feb. 14, 1775, in the 62d year of
his age."

" To the memory of Mary, the wife of William
Capp, and daughter of Thomas and Margaret Fo-
den, of Congleton in Cheshire, who departed this
life the 7th day of August, 1786, aged 35 years."

" Near this place
are interred the remains of
Mr. James Willey,
one of the aldermen of this Borough,
who departed this life 3d October, 1802,
in the 73d year of his age."

" To the memory of
John Gamble, esq.
alderman, and once mayor of this
Corporation,
who died at Buxton, aged 69,
23d September, 1789.
This monument, as a tribute
of gratitude to a deceased friend, was
erected by Henry Watchorn, esq. of the
Newark, Leicester."

" Sacred to the memory of
Henry Carrick [2], gent.
who died 9th January, 1809,
aged 65 years."

On a brass plate near the window at the West end
of the South aile:
" P. M. S.
Mariæ,
Johannis Ward uxoris dilectissimæ;
Reverendi Johannis Newton,
hujus ecclesiæ quondam pastoris,
filiæ charissimæ;
quæ 26 die Maii, A. D'ni 1716, æt. 41,
vitam meliorem obtinuit."

" In memory of Samuel Brown, gent. one of the
aldermen, and once mayor of this Borough. He
died the 10th day of June, 1784, aged 72 years."

" To the memory of
Mrs. Mary Brown, relict of Samuel Brown, gent.
who died the 21st day of September, 1785,
aged 47 years."

" Near this place are buried,
Susanna Dowley, sen.
Susannah Dowley, jun.
Mary, the wife of Benjamin Dowley,
and two of their children."

Under the organ-loft:
" Near this place lieth the body of
Elizabeth, the wife of Thomas Lockwood,
and daughter of Mr. Thomas Stephens.
She departed this life the 3d day of September, 1784,
in the 47th year of her age."

" Near this place lie the remains of John Stephens, who departed this life the 15th day of Nov.
1782, aged 74 years.
" Also the remains of Elizabeth his wife, who
died the 30th day of August, 1782, aged 68."

" Near this place are deposited the remains of
Thomas Marshall, who departed this life on the 24th
day of January, 1737, in the 39th year of his age.
" Likewise the remains of Elizabeth his wife,
who departed this life on the 22d day of January,
1776, aged 71 years."

" Near this place are deposited the remains of Richard Earle, esq. who departed this life the 19th of
December, 1775, aged 73 years.
" Likewise the remains of Elizabeth his wife, who
departed this life the 4th day of April, 1740, aged
31 years."

" Sacred to the memory of
Edward Mortimore, gent.
lieutenant and adjutant of the Leicestershire militia.
He departed this life March 30, 1779, aged 44.

[1] He was parish clerk of this parish upwards of 30 years, and was killed by a fall from his horse. The above inscription on his monument was written by Mr. Bickerstaffe.
[2] This gentleman taught school at Leicester for nearly half a century.

" Also

" Also of Mary, relict of
Edward Mortimore, gent.
She departed this life
the 20th of January, 1782, aged 34.
" Susanna Mortimore, (daughter of the above)
died Feb. 6, 1780, aged 2 years."

On a small neat tablet, on the wall of the South aile:
" In memory of
Mary, the wife of Caleb Lowdham, gent.
She died May 27, 1785,
in the 40th year of her age."

On a North pillar, on a neat tablet of white marble:
" To the memory of Susanna Pepin,
who died Oct. 29, 1790, aged 30 years."

In the nave:
" In hopes of a joyful immortality,
are deposited near this place
the earthly remains of
William Oswin, late of this Borough,
who died Sept. 7, 1786,
in the 53d year of his age."

Near the pulpit:
" In memory of
Mrs. Martha Vowe,
daughter of Mr. Richard Vowe,
late of this place;
a lady remarkable for the constancy
of her devotions, and the sincerity of
her friendships.
She died 6th January, 1804,
in the 75th year of her age.
Farewell! dear friend, till we do meet again!"

In the North aile:
" Sacred to the memory of
Sarah Read,
wife of
Mr. Alderman Read,
and daughter of
Captain David Haldane, of Auchterander,
in the county of Perth, Scotland.
She died November 16th, 1809,
aged 59.
" How lov'd, how valued once avails thee not,
To whom related, or by whom begot;
A heap of dust alone remains of thee,
'Tis all thou art, and all the proud shall be."

Near to the foregoing:
Arms: Argent, a chevron between three crosslets
fitchée Sable; fig. 36.
" Ensign Samuel Davenport,
of the Hon. Colonel William Handasyde's
regiment of foot, son to
George Davenport, of
Calveley, in the county of Chester, esq.
He died Dec. 22, 1741, aged 23 years."

On a pillar at the end of the North aile:
Arms: ..... two chevrons ..... between three
flies erect, fig. 37.
" Near this place is interred the body of
Thomas Phipps,
who in the first year of this [the eighteenth] century
entered into life in this county,
and continued in the same till his death in the year
1768.
While he lived,
he made it his chief concern to live usefully,
and to die not without having been serviceable.
In the year 1750 he was advanced to the dignity of
the Mayoralty of this Borough,
which high office he served with
distinguished reputation.
He maintained the highest reverence and unreserved

confidence in God; to which,
as he himself oftentimes piously acknowledged,
he owed his own success, and that of his family.
He in general enjoyed a chearful
temper of mind, and a good constitution of body;
the one the natural result of his integrity,
and the other of his temperance.
After a most painful illness,
which he bore with true Christian fortitude,
he quitted this mortal life, in full assurance
of a glorious resurrection to life eternal.
" Also, near this place is interred the body of
Ann Phipps, the wife of Thomas Phipps,
who departed this life Jan. 10, 1786, aged 89 years."

On a South pillar near the chancel (Plate XLIV.):

" In memory of   " Also of
Mr. John Johnson,   Frances his wife
late of this parish,   who died Oct. 19,
who died Jan. 25, 1780,   1776,
aged 72.   aged 69.
Honour thy father and mother [1]."

On the opposite pillar:
" Nicholas Throsby was born in the year 1699;
was chosen mayor of this Borough in 1759;
and died A. D. 1782 [2].
Religion taught him to look towards the
peaceful regions of Eternity; the prospect of which,
when compared with this fleeting, uncertain, and
momentary existence, he found full of consolation."

Arms: Or, a pile Sable; on a canton Azure, a saltire engrailed Argent; *Goodall*; fig. 38.
" Near this place lyeth the
bodys of John Goodall, late
of ys Borough, and twice mayor
of the same. He died 8th Aug.
1724, aged 84; and of Sarah his
wife, the daughter of Abraham
Roe, citizen of London, by whom
he had 7 sons and 4 daughters."

In the church-yard:
On four stones set against a tomb in the church-
yard, the four stones lying against the middle of each
side of the tomb, with the arms of the Town:
" Here lieth Edward Seamer, who departed this
life the 1 day of Septemb. ....."

" In memory of Elizabeth Brett.
The rageing sea, by a fierce tyd,
Swept her away, and so she dy'd,
the fifth day of June,
Anno { Domini 1704.
      { ætatis suæ 28."

" Here lies the body of Mary,
the wife of John Marston,
who died the 17th day of Sept. 1760,
in the fifty-ninth year of her age.
Reader, permit some short suspence to grieve,
One silent tear to flow, one sigh to heave;
Whilst her dear memory wakes my hope I smart,
And her fresh image wrings my aching heart."

" In memory of John Lambert, senior,
who departed this life the
30th day of July, 1760, aged 61 years [3].
" Also Ann his wife
died April 11th, 1765, aged 70 years."

" Here lyeth interred the
body of William Page, senior,
who departed this life Dec. 18, 1762,
in the 52d year of his age.
His wearysome nights are turned to joyful dayes."

[1] This monument does equal credit to the worthy designer, the son of the deceased, the charitable founder of the *Consanguinitarium* (see p. 528); and to the artist, the late John Bacon, esq. R. A.
[2] Father to the intelligent communicator of many particulars in this History, of whom see p. 602. Martha his second wife, died
Oct. 6, 1797. She had been, for several years prior to her death, the oldest person in Leicester, and retained her memory to nearly
the last hour of her existence; since about the year 1750 she had enjoyed, in general, a good state of health; and walked in the
garden the preceding week, and to church the latter end of last year. Through life she lived abstemiously, and would frequently
tell her grandchildren to rise from table with an appetite. She was born in the first year of the eighteenth century; and consequently lived in the reigns of William III. Anne, and the Three Georges.
[3] He was County Gaoler; and, in his profession, a man of great humanity.

" To

IN S.ͭ MARTINS CHURCH, LEICESTER.

In Memory
of
M.ͬ John Johnson
late of this Parish.
who Died
25 January 1780.
Aged 72
also
Frances his Wife
who Died
October 29.ᵗ 1776.
Aged 69.

HONOUR THY FATHER and MOTHER

" To the memory of Elizabeth Middleton,
who departed this life the 13th of September, 1775,
aged 37 years.

Blest with discernment and a peaceful mind,
In hope she liv'd, an after-bliss to find:
On earth, to heaven she made her humble way ;
Religion taught her there to fix her stay.
Happy are they who make that wish'd-for shore,
Where pleasures reign when Death and Time's no
        more."

" Enquiring mortal, whoe'er thou art,
        ponder here on an incident
        which highly concerns
        all the progeny of Adam.
Near this place lieth the body of JOHN FENTON [1],
        who fell by violence May 17, 1778,
        and remains a sad example of the
        incompetency of Juridical institutions
        to punish a Murderer!
He left, to mourn his untimely fate,
a mother, a widow, and two children.
        These, but not these alone,
        are greatly injured ;
Personal security received a mortal wound
when vengeance was averted from his assassin
by the sophistical refiners of natural justice [2].
        Obiit anno ætatis suæ 32."

" Here lieth the body of Elizabeth,
the third daughter of Thomas Ayscough, by Anne
his wife, who died June the 27th, 1747, aged 23."

" Here lie the remains of Anthonina Greatorex,
who was born Oct. 2, 1762, and died July 20, 1767.
        Harmonious soul! took'st thou offence,
        At discords here, and fled'st from hence?
        Or, in thy sacred raptures, hear
        The music of Heaven's warbling sphere?
        Then mounted straight where Angels sing,
        And Love does dance on ev'ry string."

" Here rests her head upon the lap of earth
        Hannah Grundy,
        daughter of Charles and Sarah Grundy,
late of Carlton, near Market Bosworth in this county.
 She came up and was cut down like a flower,
on the 13th day of January, in the 20th year of her age,
        in the year of our Lord 1788."

" To the memory of Ann, the wife of
William Hudson, who departed this life
        Oct. 9, 1790, aged 34 years.
" Also two of their sons, who died in their infancy."

" To the memory of Nathaniel Eames, who
died the 23d day of February, 1791, aged 45 years.
Reclin'd at rest beneath this humble stone,
Are the poor, shrunk, but dear remains of one,
With merit humble, and with virtue fair,
With knowledge modest, and with wit sincere ;
Upright in all the social calls of life,
To friend, to daughter, sister, and to wife.
So just the disposition of his soul,
Nature left Reason nothing to controul.
Firm, pious, patient, affable of mind,
Happy in life, and yet in death resign'd."

" In memory of John Ball,
who departed this life Feb. 22, 1800,
aged 81. She lived servant in one
family 65 years, serving faithfully grandfather,
        father, and son.
Well done, good and faithful servant !"

" Thomas Taylor died Jan. 28, 1769, aged 83."

" John Cartwright (mayor in 1771)
        died April 26, 1783, aged 66."

" James Page, gent. died April 1, 1797, in the 66th
        year of his age."

On a white stone near the small South door :
        " In memory of Moses Wing,
who departed this life the 11th day of June, 1785,
        aged 24 years.
How little they who think aught great below ;
All our ambitions Death defeats, but one ;
And that it crowns !"

" To the memory of
Isabel Blick, relict of William Blick,
of Walcot, and daughter of the Rev. John Wightman,
        late rector of Desford, in this county.
She died 8th of June, 1783, aged 74."

" In memory of John Withers Bryan,
who died August 5th, 1790, aged 42 years.
        Reader !
the sigh which thou dost heave
at the recollection of this Man,
eloquently speaks his virtues,
        and thy sensibility.

No farther seek his merits to disclose,
        Or draw his frailties from their dread abode ;
There they alike in trembling hope repose,
        The bosom of his Father and his God."

" To the memory of Robert Raven,
who departed this life July 8, 1778, aged 32 years.
        Long time afflicted sore I lay,
        Under the hand of God ;
        Till he was pleased to take away,
        The scourges of his rod.
        Then cease, dear wife, to mourn for me,
        Tho' human Nature's frail ;
        Dry up your tears, alas! for why ?
        They nothing can avail !
        But place your trust in CHRIST on high,
        On him alone depend ;
        For he'll the widow's wants supply,
        And be the orphan's friend !"

" To the memory of Joseph Cave,
who departed this life Feb. 27, 1782, aged 30 years.
Also Thomas, son of Joseph and Ruth Cave,
        he died October 27, 1781, aged 1 year.
        Why do we mourn departing friends,
        Or shrink at Death's alarms ;
        'Tis but the voice that Jesus sends,
        To call them to his arms.
        Are we not trav'lling upwards too,
        As fast as Time can move ?
        Nor would we wish the hours more slow,
        To keep us from our love."

" Sacred to the memory of Mary, the wife of
        John Reynolds, who
departed this life April 18, 1806, aged 47 years.
Inconstant earth! why do not mortals cease,
To build their hopes upon so short a lease !
Uncertain term! whose lease but just begun,
Tells never when it ends 'till it be done ;
We doat upon thy smiles, not knowing why,
And while we but prepare to live, we die !
We spring like flow'rs, and for a day delight,
At morn we flourish, and we fade at night !"

In 1784, in digging a grave under the steeple, in
the space between the nave and the chancel of this
church, several scuttles-full of cattle-bones, horns,
and jaw-bones of the herd, came to light, the teeth
in many instances entire, five feet deep from the
surface, and a foot deep in bones, with an appearance of a lateral continuation. Some months before,
a few yards distant South of the above discovery,
near the steeple or belfry door, were met with (in
making a grave, within a foot of the surface, continuing on all sides, as well as through the cut, and
not terminating with it) a vast quantity of very large
pebbles, wedged or heaped together, without inter-

[1] Written by Mr. Charles Rozzel, a schoolmaster in Leicester ; whose epitaph is given in p. 320. Fenton was killed in his
own house by François Soulés, a French teacher. The jury, by the direction of the judge, returned a special verdict, grounded
on the plea that he went to the house in search of his property (a pistol which Fenton had taken from him). This plea was not
allowed by the twelve judges ; but Soulés afterwards received his Majesty's pardon. See Gent. Mag. vol. XLVIII. p. 47.
[2] " The above inscription gave considerable offence, as it was considered as reflecting on the court before which Soulés was
arraigned ; and the Spiritual Court ordered the stone to be removed ; but this order was never executed." J. S. H.

stices of earth or mortar. Foundations, well set in mortar, have likewise sometimes occurred to the present sexton, within the precincts of this church. About a quarter of a mile on the West of this church, at the place called "Holy Bones," a few yards from St. Nicholas's church easterly, many like bones of victims have at times been discovered [2].

P. 320. In St. Mary's church-yard:
"Joseph and Sarah Horton.
Joseph Horton, died 25th Feb. 1769, aged 50.
Sarah died 19th March, 1763, aged 52 years.

Death can't disjoin, whom Christ hath join'd in love,
Life leads to Death, and Death to Life above;
In Heaven's a happier place, frail things disguise;
Live well, a gem in future Life the prize."

P. 560, note [1], *read* Collins's Peerage, 1769, vol. V. p. 240.

P. 596, l. 2. Mr. Newton was M. A. in 1662. On a small freestone tablet in the chancel of St. Nicholas's church, Gloucester:

Arms: Argent, on a chevron Azure, three garbs Or; *Newton*; impaling, Per chevron, Sable and Argent, three elephants' heads erased counterchanged; *Saunders*; fig. 39.
"Hic jacet
R. Vir Johannes Newton, A. M.
Ecclesiæ Anglicanæ Presbyter,
Olim
Aulæ de Clare apud Cantab. Socius,
et Ecclesiæ S'ti Martini apud Leicestrienses vicarius;
Deinde
Ecclesiæ Cathedralis Glocestriensis Prebendarius,
et Ecclesiæ Taynton in agro Gloc. Rector
dignissimus.
Vir
(dum vixit)
erga Deum pius, erga homines benevolus & beneficus;
Amicus fidus, vicinus utilis & innoctuus,
Pastor sedulus;
Maritus & pater amantissimus, & suis charissimus:
Qui demùm, LXXIII annorum pondere

variisque infirmitatibus gravatus,
desideratus obiit
Sept. xx, MDCCXI."

On a grave-stone in the chancel:
Arms as on the monument.
"Johannes Newton ob. Sep. 21 [3], 1711.
Juditha, ux. Johannis Newton,
Ob. Jun. 1, 1715."

At Tormarton, in Gloucestershire:
"Here lie the remains of
ELIZABETH HEYRICK [4],
wife of SAMUEL HEYRICK,
of the Borough of Leicester, gent.
who departed this life
the 17th day of October, 1753,
in the 53d year of her age."

In the chancel at Measham, near Ashby-de-la-Zouch:
"Here lieth the body of William Hill, of Measham, in the county of Derby, gent. who departed this life in the 66th year of his age, A. D. 1692. He left one daughter, Elizabeth, who married Robert Phillips, of Newton-in-the-Thistles, in the county of Warwick, esq. He also left two sons, Richard and William. Richard married Mary, the eldest daughter of the Rev. Mr. Alfounder, rector of Thurcaston, in the county of Leicester. The said Richard departed this life the first day of December, 1739, in the 59th year of his age; and his body lies interred in the chancel of the parish church of St. Martin, in the Borough of Leicester. He left one daughter and one son, to wit, Mary and Richard, now living in Leicester.
"Here also lieth the body of William Hill, the brother of the said Richard Hill, deceased, who departed this life the 16th day of September, 17 ... in the 67th year of his age."

Of the soldiers slain in the market-place at Leicester, 24 were buried under St. Martin's communion table. This appears (says Mr. Bickerstaffe) from an old book, near a foot long, and perhaps almost as thick, in the late vicar Mr. Gregory's possession, and containing some other *memorabilia*.

⁎ P. 568, line 4, for *St. Michael's*, read *St. Martin's.*

Since p. 596 was printed, I have met with a very old copy of the epitaph on Elizabeth Reynolds, wife of John Curzon, of [Crox]all, who died Aug. [23,] 1521, which is there said to be " in Reynolds' chapel," and bore these arms : Argent, a chevron Ermine, between three cross crosslets Gules; fig. 40.

The same MS. preserves also, " from a gravestone in the *Library*," (probably the present Consistory Court) :
" George Pilkinton, of Stanton,
in com. Derby, ob. 31 Oct. 1598 ;"
on which were the following arms: Quarterly, 1 and 4, Argent, a cross patonce, voided Gules; *Pilkington;* 2, ... fretty ......; a canton Ermine; 3, on a fess three mullets; impaling *Babington;* fig. 41.
2. *Pilkington* as above; impaling, Or, fretty Azure; *Willoughby of Risby;* fig. 42.
3. *Pilkington* as above; impaling *Basset of Blore* (vol. IV. p. 893) ; fig. 43.

....daughter of Hugh Willoughby,	Edmund Pilkington, of Staunton	Margaret, daughter of John Babington of Dethick ; second wife.
of Risby, co. Derby; first wife.	le Dale, Derbyshire.	

1. Edmund Pilkington.=Katherine, sister of William Bassett, of Blore, co. Stafford.		2. Robert Pilkington.

Dorothy, sister of Thomas Poutrell, of Derbyshire; first wife.	1. George Pilkington.=Mary, daughter of William Gibson, of Kent, temp. Hen. VIII. ; second wife.	2. Jeremiah Pilkington, of Staunton, twin with his brother George.	Katherine, died unmarried.

1. George Pilkington, of Barston ; died Oct. 31, 1598.	Frances, daughter of .. Miles, of Coventry.	2. Edward Pilkington, of Staunton, c.Derby, and Worthington, co. Leicester.	Mildred, daughter and heir of Walter Morgan, of Leyton, Essex.	3. Thomas.	Gertrude, married Gawen Phillips, of Swainton.	Hugh Pilkington, of Stanton; died s. p.

George Pilkington, 1619.	Susan, married Thomas Humfrey, esq. of Swebston, who was high sheriff in 1602, and knighted in 1603 ; see vol. III. p. 1036.	Mary, m. ... Armstrong, of Grenthby, c. Lincoln.	[See vol. III. p. 650.]

[2] See before, in vol. I. p. ⁎5.
[3] On the monument it is Sept. 20; and on the stone Sept. 21.
[4] This lady (daughter of John Cooper, gent. and widow of William Tyers, of Queenborough, gent.) was the mother of my truly respectable friend the late Town Clerk of Leicester, who still enjoys a green old age in honourable retirement from the fatigues of public life. His son (William Heyrick, esq.) succeeded him as Town Clerk in 1791 ; and still enjoys that office.

Additions

Additions to the PEDIGREE of STEPHENS, of St. Martin's, Leicester, p. 588.

Richard Stephens;=Alice, daughter of John Lettice [1], B. A. vicar of Bozeate, and
died Aug. 11, 1810. | rector of Strixton, co. Northampton; died Sept. 18, 1809.

1. John =Maria, daugh- | Elizabeth, married=Samuel Bankart, | 2. Richard Stephens, B. A. 1806; M. A. 1809; elected
Stephens. | ter of Walter | April 11, 1809, | of St. Mary's. | fellow of Brasenose College, Oxon, June 29, 1810;
| Ruding, esq. | at St. Martin's. | | ordained deacon Dec. 23, 1810.

Agnes-Alice, born at Hackney, | Samuel-Stephens Bankart, born Jan. 19, 1810;
Middlesex, Sept. 14, 1810. | baptized at St. Mary's July following.

P. 514. The house in the High Cross-street, lately in the possession of Mr. Stephens, containing the painted windows, which are peculiarly interesting to an Antiquary, being perfectly unique in their kind, has devolved by will, upon his youngest son, the Rev. Richard Stephens, M. A. and fellow of Brasenose College, Oxford.

The partiality which has, generally, been shewn by natives of the county of Leicester for the University of Cambridge, in preference to that of Oxford, has partly arisen from the proximity of the two counties of Leicester and Cambridge, and partly from the facility of conveyance from the one to the other; but more than all, from the ignorance of the greater advantages, which natives of this county enjoy in the University of Oxford, than they do in the sister University, where no benefits are peculiar to this county. Though the following list of benefactions embraces a wider field, than the map of the county of Leicester presents, they may not be the less acceptable; because, if they are not all peculiar to this county, they still may be within its reach.

Merton College.—There are twenty-four fellowships belonging to this college, to which those candidates are eligible who are born within the diocese in which the college possesses estates. The living of Kibworth Beauchamp, and other land in the county of Leicester, belonging to that society, the natives of that county are of course eligible to the fellowships of that college.

John Willyott, D. D. chancellor of Exeter, gave exhibitions in 1380, for the maintenance of twelve portionistæ, called postmasters, which are open to the University at large. John Chamber increased them to 14; but directed that his two additional exhibitioners should be elected from Eton College.

Exeter College.—Sir William Petre, in 1565, founded eight fellowships, to which those candidates are eligible who are born in those counties in which his heirs should have lands or possessions. So great a latitude being allowed for the eligibility of candidates, it is probable that some of the founder's descendants at least do possess lands in this county.

Oriel College.—William Smyth, Bishop of Lincoln, in 1507, purchased lands for the maintenance of one fellow, successively to be chosen out of the diocese of Lincoln. The ten original fellowships of Adam de Brome appear to be open to the University in general.

Lincoln College.—Thomas Rotheram, Bishop of Lincoln, augmented the number of fellows to 12; and ordained that the rector and 12 fellows should, according to the place of their nativities, be thus ordered; viz. all to be born within the dioceses of Lincoln, York, and Wells, so that from the last there be but one. As for the 11 (from whom the rector is always to be elected), eight of them are to be of the diocese of Lincoln, and four of those eight to be of the county.

Thomas Hayne, of the parish of Christ-church in London, some time a student in this college, gave 12l. yearly, for the maintenance of two scholars, to be chosen by the mayor, recorder, and three senior aldermen of Leicester, from those descended of his father Robert Hayne, or his uncle John Musson, wherever educated. In defect of such. then they are to be chosen out of the freeschool at Leicester, or Melton in that county, &c. Given by will Sept. 28, 1640.

All Souls College.—Archbishop Chicheley, the founder of the college, created 40 fellowships for the natives of the counties within the province of Canterbury; but with this provision, that those of his alliance should be first regarded.

Brasenose College.—Edward Darby, Archdeacon of Stow, in the county of Lincoln, founded a fellowship for one born in the said archdeaconry; or in defect of one there, then from the county of Leicester; and if not there also, from the county of Northampton; and if there neither, from the county of Oxford; or, in defect of such person, one born in the diocese of Lincoln.

Settled 29th May, 1537.

It was covenanted by indenture, bearing date July 3, 1522, between the College, John Port, serjeant at law, and John Hales, esq. one of Williamson's executors, that, with the sum of 200l. paid by Hales, lands should be purchased of the annual value of 9l. for the maintenance of two scholars or fellows, born in the city, or in the county palatine of Chester, of the name, cousenage, or lineage of John Williamson or John Port. The family of Miles, of St. Martin's, Leicester, and the family of Fenwicke, of Hallaton, in this county, can trace their pedigree to the founders of these two fellowships.

William Hulme, in 1691, gave lands in trust to certain persons mentioned in his will, and their successors, for the maintenance of four exhibitioners, for the space of four years, to commence from the time of taking the degree of B. A. with preference to the natives of Lancashire; but in defect of such to any county. They are to be nominated by the warden of Manchester, the rector of Prestwich, and the rector of Bury, for the time being. These exhibitions have been augmented to the number of 15, at the value of 100l. and 10l. for books per ann. each.

Trinity College.—Sir Thomas Pope, in 1554, founded 12 fellowships and 12 scholarships, for the benefit of the natives of his manors. In defect of such, the scholars who succeed to the fellowships are to be chosen from any county in England, with the limitation that no more than two persons of the same county be admitted fellows at the same time. N. B. It seldom happens that there is any claimant from the manors of the founder.

Wadham College.—In Wadham College there are 15 fellows and 15 scholars. The scholars from the fellows to be chosen are to be three of the county of Somerset, three of Essex, and the rest of any other county of Great Britain.

Worcester College.—George Clark, D. C. L. endowed six fellowships and three scholarships. The scholars are to be born of English parents, within the provinces of Canterbury and York [2].

[1] John Lettice, D. D. late fellow of Sidney Sussex College, Cambridge; vicar of Peesmarsh, in the county of Sussex; prebendary of the cathedral of Chichester; and chaplain to the present marquis of Douglass (the son of this clergyman), informs me, that his father, who was of Sidney Sussex College, did not proceed farther than to the degree of B. A. The Graduate-book of the University of Cambridge also bears the same evidence. R. S.
[2] These extracts are chiefly taken from Gutch's Antony à Wood, Chalmers' History of the Colleges, and Churton's Lives of the Founders of Brasenose College. R. S.

ST. NICHOLAS.

ST. NICHOLAS.

This church has little to boast of in respect of architecture: its walls are immoderately thick, the pillars and arches that support the roof are heavy, and consequently an impediment to the preacher.

The tower and the South-west entrance of the church bear very evident marks of the remains of very early Saxon architecture, almost bordering upon the Norman æra. See Plate XLV.

The steeple, being in a very dilapidated state, was taken down about ten years ago; and the poverty of the parish (with the consent of the Bishop) has not suffered it to be rebuilt [1].

The bells are the oldest in Leicester. The inscriptions are,

1st bell, " Goldfield. Nazarenus Rex 1656."
2d, " Henry Smith, Richard Hunt, churchwardens, 1710. God save his church."
3d, " Sonus iste 1617. Celorum Christe [2]."

Mr. Samuel Carte noticed in the Archiepiscopal Register at Lambeth an article relative to the taking away one of the bells from St. Nicholas's church in 1321, and the date of the cross the same year; with a memorandum of a distant cross [3].

There is in this church a modern raised font.

The chancel is used as a vestry; and a chapel at the East end of the South aile is now the site of the altar.

There were formerly three ailes; but about the year 1697, that towards the North was taken down in consequence of its ruinous state.

In 1650, the only return made was, " the same man that hath St. Martin's."

The parish is small [4], and formerly unable to maintain a preacher; for which reason it was usually held by the vicar of St. Martin's; but of late years, by the beneficence of Queen Anne, the liberality of the Corporation, and the contribution of the parishioners, it is regularly provided with a separate vicar.

Much praise is due to the present vicar, the Rev. John Anderson, for having secured, by a fence, the holy and consecrated ground of this church-yard from a nuisance, offensive both to feeling and decorum. It used to be the resort of idle boys, who amused themselves with defacing the sepulchral stones, and committing other depredations.

	£.	s.	d.
Money raised for the poor, within the year ending at Easter 1776, —	164	16	7
Expended in county rates, &c. —	10	5	0
————— on the poor, — —	154	13	10
Rent of workhouse and habitations, —	8	6	6
Expended in litigations, — —	1	1	0
Money raised for 1783, — —	172	7	3
——————— 1784, — —	167	15	3
——————— 1785, — —	161	4	5
Medium of these three years, —	167	2	4
————— of county expences, —	10	4	0
————— of expences not relating to the poor; repairs of the church, roads, &c.	0	0	0

	£.	s.	d.
Medium of nett annual expences, —	156	18	4
————— of attending on magistrates,	0	0	0
————— of entertainments at meetings,	1	8	2
————— of law expences, — —	4	0	4
————— of setting the poor to work,	0	0	0

Benefactions to the poor:

Mr. Equon gave to the poor of this parish, every last week in May, 3s. 6d. in bread, yearly, for ever.

Item, Sir William Cotton, knight, gave to the poor of this parish, every Thursday before Whitsunday, in bread, 6s. 8d. yearly, for ever.

Item, Mr. Equon gave to the poor of this parish in bread, every last week in July, 3s. 6d. yearly, for ever.

Item, Mr. Smart gave to the poor of this parish in bread, every 14th of August, two penny loaves, yearly, for ever.

Item, Mr. Norris gave to the poor in money, every June, yearly, for ever, the sum of 16s. to be received of the town chamberlain.

Item, Mr. Equon gave to the poor of this parish, every last week in September, in bread, 3s. 6d. yearly, for ever.

Item, Sir William Cotton, knight, gave to the poor of this parish in bread, every New Year's-day, 6s. 8d. yearly, for ever.

Item, Mr. Equon gave to the poor of this parish, every last week in November, in bread, 3s. 6d. yearly, for ever.

Item, Mr. Equon gave to the poor of this parish, every last week in January, in bread, 3s. 6d. yearly, for ever.

Item, Mr. Heyrick gave to the poor of this parish, every Candlemss day, 13s. 4d. in bread, yearly, for ever.

Item, Mr. Equon gave to the poor of this parish, every last week in March, in bread, 3s. 6d. yearly, for ever.

Item, the right honourable the earl of Devonshire gave to the poor of this parish, every Thursday before Easter, 6s. yearly, for ever, to be received of the town chamberlain.

Item, Mr. Inge gave to the poor of this parish, every Friday in Lent, eight two-penny loaves, yearly, for ever.

Item, Mr. Francis Palmer gave to the poor of this parish, every Lady-day, the sum of 10s. yearly, ever, to be paid by Mr. Hill.

1781, Miss Elizabeth Clark, of Peatling, daughter of the late Mr. Henry Clark, hosier, of this borough, gave £.50. to the poor of this parish; to which was added £.5. by the parishioners, which bought £.100. in the three per cents, in order that the poor might have an annual income at Christmas of £.3. for ever.

All the aforesaid benefactors' gifts are to be disposed of by the overseers of the poor for the time being; only Mr. Equon's gift by the churchwardens.

VICARS.

William Capellanus, 1221.
Nicholas, 1236.
William de Barwe, 1263.
John Guidynes [5], died 154...
Stephen Johnsone, 154...

PATRONS.

} Abbot and Convent of Leicester.

---

[1] " The tower belonging to the steeple is now covered over with a good roof, and ornamented with four pinnacles, one at each angle, with an iron spindle rising from the centre of the roof, which supports a weathercock.—That venerable monument of antiquity, Jewry Wall, is now also protected from the inadvertence of passengers, and the insults of boys, by a substantial railing." J. S. H.
[2] Imperfect. Perhaps, " Celorum Christe, placeat tibi, Rex, sonus iste."
[3] MS Letter to Sir T. Cave, Sept. 9, 1756.
[4] See p. 609.
[5] Reg. Chicheley, archiep. Cantuar', sede Lincoln' vacante, p. 282. 2.

John

ST. NICHOLAS, N.W.

JEWRY WALL.

To the Right Rev.ᵈ **WILLIAM BENNET,** D.D. **LORD BISHOP OF** *CLOYNE,* this Plate is respectfully inscribed by his *Lordship's much obliged & very obedient Serᵗ.* *J. Nichols.*

Thomas Jesson, died June 21, 1614.
John Angel [1], died June 6, 1655.
Josiah Bond, 1664.
John Clayton, B. A. 1720.
Thomas Sanderson, M. A. presented Nov. 1739. } The Crown.
Joseph Juxon [2], M. A. died 1757.
Gerrard Andrewes [3], 1757; died in 1764.
John Davenport [4], 1764; died Feb. 6, 1769.
James Pigott [5], M. A. 1769; resigned in 1788.
John Anderson, Nov. 1788; present vicar, 1811.

Mr. Burton describes the following arms in the church of St. Nicholas.
1. Or, a maunch Gules; *Hastings.*
2. Or, a lion rampant Azure; *Percy.*
3. Gules, two bezants; *Zouch.*
4. Gules, two bezants; a quarter Ermine.
5. Gules, a chevron between ten crosslets formy Argent. *Berkley.*
6. Barruly, Or and Gules. *Fitzalan.*
7. Argent, two bars, and a canton Gules; *Bois.*

8. Gules seven mascles voided Or, a label of three points Azure, charged with nine horse shoes, Argent; *Ferrers.*
10. Azure, a chevron ermine embattled above between three cross crosslets fitchè, Or.
11. Within a Garter, the atchievment of the Earl of *Shrewsbury.*
** For the account of this and the other Parishes in the Town of Leicester, as given in " Charyte's Rentale," see the Appendix to vol. 1. p. 113.

MONUMENTAL INSCRIPTIONS.

In the vestry, on an old stone:
" Here lieth the body of Thomas Jesson, sometime vicar, with Eales his wife, &c.
" *Jesu Fili Dei miserere mei.*"

On a white stone, round the ledge of which is an older inscription:
" Orate p' a'i'ab's Thome Copley, & Johan'e ...... qui ob' ..... Mo ... ii."

---

[1] See some memoirs of Mr. Angel in the Town History, pp. 502 and 512.—Mr. Throsby mentions having seen an account of an annual gift of 5*l.* to the preacher of this church, left by will, and gives also the following quotation from the Parish Books: " Memorandum—It was agreed upon the 17th day of July, in the yeare of our Lord 1664, betweene Mr. Bonde, minister of St. Maryes, in the borough of Leicester, and the parishioners of St. Nicholas parish, in the same borough, that the said Mr. Bond shall come once every fortnight, on the Sabbath day, and read divine service, according to the Canons of the Church of England; and that the said Mr. Bond, either by himselfe or sufficient preacher, preach one sermon every month in the yeare, in the parish church of St. Nicholas." Beside this, he was conditioned to administer the sacrament, and do all other duties of a parish minister; for which he was to have all the tithes and dues which were usually paid to their late vicar, Mr. John Angel.

[2] Rector also of Eastwell, Twyford, and Hungarton; and chaplain to the earl of Derby. He died in 1757. Abigail his wife died Jan. 14, 1774, aged 66.

[3] " He was a gentleman much esteemed as a Divine and a Scholar. Under his tuition the free-school was a seminary of great repute; not only the sons of the first families, in these parts, were placed under his care, but numbers from much greater distances also received the rudiments of an education that does honour to his abilities. Dr. Farmer, not to mention many more of literary fame, was his scholar. Chearful in his deportment, and destitute of tyranny, his school was a scene of lively obedience. Beloved by the boys for his free and gentle treatment, his precepts were readily received, and the task dispatched with alacrity. As a divine, he alike captivated in the desk and pulpit. He read with an energy just and influencing; taught with a conciseness pertinently persuasive, and intelligible to a general auditory, and was long considered as one of the brightest ornaments of the clerical profession." J. T.—See memoirs of him p. 512; his epitaph, p. 610; and for the pedigree of his family, vol III p 456.

[4] He was elected head master of the Free school April 29, 1762. See p. 512, of the Town History. Mr. William Davenport, the eldest son of this gentleman, was a very excellent scholar; and, having had the good fortune to be noticed by Dr. Johnson, was, by his recommendation, apprenticed to William Strahan, esq. his Majesty's Printer; and, for his knowledge in Greek and Latin, obtained, for a short time before his death, an annuity of 30*l.* bequeathed by my late worthy friend and partner, Mr. Bowyer, for the purpose of encouraging the study of the learned languages among the succeeding race of Printers. This young man died Jan. 2, 1792.

[5] Vicar of Great Wigston, see p. 320.—At the time he was about to resign the small vicarage of St Nicholas, my poor friend the Reverend William Bickerstaffe (of whom see p. 320) cast many " a longing look" at the old church; and some of the characteristic Letters he then wrote shall be here given:

" To the Right Honourable Edward Lord Thurlow, Lord High Chancellor of Great Britain.
" My Lord, *Leicester, August* 10, 1786.

"By the advice of Mr. Macnamara, a Representative of Leicester, I am instructed to appeal to your Lordship's humanity, to grant me a gracious hearing, by a private address. At fifty-eight years of age, permit a poor Curate, unsupported by private property, to detain your attention a few moments. From 1750 I have been Usher at the Free Grammar school here, with an appointment of 19*l.* 16*s.* a year; seven years Curate of St. Mary's, my native parish, in this Borough; then six years Curate at St. Martin's with All Saints, lately bestowed by your Lordship on Mr. Gregory of this place; and now an opportunity occurs to your Lordship, to give me an occasion to pray for my Benefactor, and those that are dear to him, during my life. 'Tis this; a dispensation is expected every day, by the Head Master of the School where I serve, the Rev. Mr. Pigott, Vicar of Great Wigston in this county, to connect a fresh acquisition in Lincolnshire with it; and he urges your Lordship's Petitioner to try for the living of St. Nicholas here, which he must relinquish. It is simply 35*l.* a year; but, as this Corporation grants an annual aid to each living in Leicester, of 10*l.* a year, St. Nicholas, joined to my School, might render me comfortable for life, and prevent the uncertainty of a Curacy, and the hard necessity, at any time of life, of being harassed, in all weathers, by a distant cure. My Lord, if this freedom is disgusting, impute it to the sympathising heart of the generous Macnamara, who prompted me to it in these words, speaking of your Lordship: ' Indeed, I feel too forcibly my obligations to press further, or trespass more at present upon his Lordship; but, as you are a native of Leicester, and a freeman, I conceive it my duty to hint to you, that an application immediately from yourself, stating your situation exactly, as you have done to me, may have the desired effect, as his Lordship's great abilities can only be equalled by his humanity and benevolence.' May the all-mighty, all-present, and all-merciful God direct your Lordship, on this and all occasions, to do His pleasure; and protect you from all dangers, which may threaten soul, body, or estate; is the hearty prayer of " Your Lordship's humble suppliant, WM. BICKERSTAFFE."

" For the Rev. Dr. Farmer, Master of Emanuel College, Cambridge.
" I think, if Dr. Farmer would undertake my cause, through means usually at hand with men of eminence, I might, by Divine Providence, find the Lord Chancellor disposed to serve me. This living is so immediately tenable with my school, and compatible with an additional curacy, such as Ayleston, which I have, that I cannot forbear troubling your Reverence to take up arms in my cause, and declare, 'Old neighbour, old playfellow, *inveniam viam, aut faciam.*'—My school is but 19*l.* 16*s.* a year. I have no other certain tenure at present. I served Mr. Simmonds seven years at St. Mary's, and Mr. Haines six at St. Martin's with All Saints. These have vanished with their Vicars; and if I had not Ayleston, I might be harassed with a distant cure, to the discomfort of my life, and the prejudice of my health, at a time when more ease and leisure seem necessary.—I presume Mr. Secretary Pitt, the Representative of Cambridge University, and even the Chancellor of the same, with a crowd of other great personages, have eyes, ears, and hearts, at the service of its late Vice-chancellor, and yet Master of Emanuel."—To another friend Mr. Bickerstaffe writes, " At 58 years of age, having more inclination to a church-living than a wife, I applied to my old neighbour and playfellow, Dr. Farmer, to procure me St. Nicholas parish here; and my application was so well-timed, as to get the business into the hands of Mr. Pitt, their University-representative, by the kind service of the Vice-chancellor, who at the same time attended to him the University-address to the King. Dr. Farmer informed me, that this Chancellor was his particular friend; and that, if St. Nicholas's was pre-engaged, I was put in the way of church-preferment. The living is yet undisposed of; the Lord Chancellor is, or lately was, at Buxton; and I remain uninformed of any thing further: there is no room to expect a smile of favour till the gout is more civil! It seems like a Chancery-suit. The present Chancellor is said to be a leisurely gentleman in these matters. He keeps livings in suspense. This may be designed to accumulate an aid, to pay for the seals and the induction.—Swift says, ' Lord Treasurer, for once be quick!' Should you tell the Chancellor, ' it would suit *him,* and that *I* say it,' it might cost me the loss of his slow favours. At *my* age, I could tell *him,* with strict propriety, *Bis dat, qui citò.*"

Letters to the same purport were addressed to Mr. Macnamara and Mr. Hungerford. To the latter he says, " Mr. Keck and yourself solicited lord Denbigh in my behalf for St. Mary's; and I hope I have not forfeited your favour since."

Round the ledge of another old stone :
" ..... Bakeden ..... anno ....."

On the West side of the pulpit :
"Thomas Rickards, died March 9, 1804, aged 39 years.
Here also lieth Mary Ayscough, who died Sept.
30th, 1805, in the 80th year of her age."

On flat stones in the North aile :
" Here lies the body of William Deane, gent.
heretofore mayor of this Corporation.
He departed this life Sept. 4, 1693, aged 70.
And here also lieth the body of Grace his second wife,
who departed this life Aug. 29, 1713, aged 80."

" Here lieth the body of Susannah Deane, widow,
relict of Jane Deane, clerk. She was daughter
of sir John Harpur, of Cawke, in the
county of Derby, bart. She departed this life Sept.
20, 1706, in the 53d year of her age.
In the same grave, or near it,
lie the body of two of his children,
James and Dorothea.
He died Nov. 28, 1685, aged about 6 years ;
and she died March 22, 1696, aged 19 years."

In piam gratamque parentum memoriam
hunc posuit lapidem Gulielmus Deane,
utriusque Offordi rectoris, com. Hants, 1716."

" Here lieth the body of Captain Thomas Mawson,
who served King Charles I. of blessed memory,
and also his sacred majesty Charles II.
He departed this life the 11 April, 1678, aged 64."

Near the altar :
" Here was interred the body of
Gerrard Andrewes, clerk, M. A.
late vicar of this parish, and many
years master of the free-school.
He departed this life
the 29th day of February, 1764,
in the 60th year of his age."

" Near this place lies his mother
Mrs. Frances Andrewes.
She died in May 1751, aged 82 ;
and his sister,
Mrs. Elizabeth Fenn,
died the 4th day of February, 1760,
aged 65 years.
On his left hand lie the remains
of his daughter Isabella.
She departed this life
the 28th day of January, 1760,
in the 9th year of her age ;
and of his son,
Francis-Henry Andrewes,
who died Sept. 20, 1756,
in the 5th year of his age.
Beneath is interred the body of
Mrs. Isabella Andrewes,
relict of the late
Rev. Gerrard Andrewes.
She died March 10, 1788,
in the 70th year of her age."

In the vestry :
" Here lie interred the remains of
Anne Clayton, daughter of the
Rev. John Clayton, once vicar of this parish.
She died March 14, 1784,
in the 63d year of her age."

" Beneath this stone
are deposited the remains of John Freestone Wilson
(formerly of Doughty-street, London),
who departed this life at Leicester,
16th May, 1810, aged 32,
and to whose memory this stone is placed here by
his afflicted and disconsolate father."

" Here lies the body of William Sutton,

who departed this life June 13, 1736,
in the 45th year of his age."

In the North aile :
" Here lies the body of Joseph Newton, sen.
one of the aldermen of this Borough.
He departed this life Dec. 31, 1759, in the
78th year of his age.
He was a worthy, pious, and honest man."

On a neat monument :
" In memory of Mary Slack,
daughter of James and Lucy Slack,
who died Feb. 1, 1794, aged 14 years.
Sleep on, thou fair, and wait Th' Almighty's will ;
Then rise unchang'd and be an Angel still."

In the church-yard :

Rev. William Clayton, rector of Ravenstone, in
the county of Derby, and vicar of Anstey near Coventry, in the county of Warwick, died April 27,
1799, aged 75.

"Here are deposited the remains of Hamlett Clarke[1],
one of the aldermen of this Borough.
He departed this life May 29, 1772, aged 58 years.
Elizabeth his wife, died Sept. 23, 1784, aged 70 years.
Elizabeth their daughter, died April 10, 1782, aged 34.
Sarah (another daughter) died April 5, 1766, aged 16.
Elizabeth, Mary, and William, died infants."
Grace Hartshorn (another of their daughters, and
wife of W. Hartshorn), March 27, 1773, aged 30.
Jane Baxter (another of their daughters, and wife
of William Baxter), died June 16, 1785, aged 45.
Alice, wife of James Liquorice, of Elstor, died
Jan. 15, 1725-6, aged 91.
Anne Hubbard, wife of John Hubbard, died May
4, 1735, aged 38.
{ John Slater, died Feb. 17, 1734, aged 78.
{ Elizabeth Slater, died March 7, 1744-5, aged 80.
Eliz. wife of John Slack, Dec. 15, 1775, aged 73.
Alderman John Denshire, died in 1725, aged 73.
Richard Marler, died Jan. 14, 1726, aged 50.
Edward Goodess, died Dec. 6, 1764, aged 59.
Dorcas Goodess, died Oct. 20, 1805.
{ Robert Langton, died July 27, 1770, aged 55.
{ Elizabeth Langton, died Jan. 10, 1784, aged 73.
Elizabeth, second wife of William Hartshorn,
and daughter of William and Anne Woodward, of
Burton Overy, died April 4, 1789, aged 36,
Benjamin Hurst, died Aug. 31, 1745, aged 48.
Hannah Hurst, died May 20, 1737.
Mary Hurst (second wife), June 14, 1753, aged 55.
Robert Guy, senior, died Oct. 18, 1733, aged 54.
Alice Guy, died Jan. 28, 1794, aged 71.
Robert Guy, died April 22, 1784, aged 69.
William Guy, died April 16, 1777, aged 57.
Mary Guy, died April 9, 1772, aged 44.
John Parsons, died March 10, 1777, aged 53.
Anne Burgess, died May 7, 1781, aged 66.
John Keightley, died April 8, 1790, aged 3.
Elizabeth, his wife, died Dec. 28, 1801, aged 71.
Mary Willson, died Dec. 16, 1803, aged 80.
John and Elizabeth, children of William and
Ann Keightley. John, died May 1, 1788, aged 5 ;
Elizabeth, died Nov. 25, 1788, aged 9 months.
Elizabeth, the wife of Henry Brown, died June
25, 1743, aged 65.

The Charity-school founded by Alderman Newton
in his life-time, at the North-east corner of the
church-yard, on the site of the antient Shambles,
has been already noticed, amongst the other Public
Schools[2], in p. 514.—It was re-built by the Corporation of Leicester in 1808, and enlarged for the
reception of eighty boys.

[1] This gentleman was married at Mowsley.
[2] Where see some sensible remarks on Mr. Newton's Will, by the late Rev. William Bickerstaffe: See also, in p. 598, an epitaph
placed by the Alderman in St. Martin's church to the memory of his only son.

Abstract

Abstract of the late Mr. Alderman GABRIEL NEWTON's [1] Trust Deed for establishing Schools [2].

15 March, 1760. By indenture of bargain and sale of this date, inrolled in the Court of Chancery, and made between Gabriel Newton, of the Borough of Leicester, gent. (one of the aldermen of the said Borough) of the one part; and Nicholas Throsby, Esq. mayor of the borough of Leicester, and the bailiffs and burgesses of the said borough, of the other part; reciting, that it had pleased God to endow the said Gabriel Newton with a plentiful fortune, but to take away his only son, whereby he was left childless; and therefore the said Gabriel Newton being desirous of settling great part of his substance to charitable uses, and having it much at heart to establish such a charity as might be most conducive to the general good of mankind; from a long series of reflection and observation of life, the said Gabriel Newton had sufficient reason to conclude that a religious education of children would, of all others, be the most extensive branch of charity, as its salutary effects might possibly operate in some degree to the latest posterity; for, if children whose parents were not able to bear the expence of putting them to school, and either totally negligent or not capable of instructing them at home, were, by the beneficence of others, taught to read and write, and therewith, for a series of years, obliged daily and duly to attend and join in the service of the Church, might it not reasonably be hoped that they were in the most likely way to receive such impressions of religion as might some time work together for their future happiness, as well as be a means to improve their condition in this present life, and that such children so educated (with the assistance of God's grace), becoming men of truly virtuous and Christian lives, might possibly, by their shining example in the deportment of themselves and the prudent government and pious instruction of their families, so effectually implant amongst their children, servants, and neighbours, such principles of religion and virtue as might happily derive to future generations inestimable blessings:

And also reciting, that the said Gabriel Newton was desirous of promoting the due reading of the Creed of St. Athanasius, as thereinafter mentioned, which he looked upon as the completest body of Divinity ever composed since the time of the Apostles, and a full answer to all heretical objections to the doctrine and tenets of the Church of England; concurring with Dr. Waterland in his History of that Creed, who deemed the minister or parishioners of any place, who did not receive and read the same as directed by the rubrick of the Church of England, to be lukewarm Christians:

It is witnessed, that the said Gabriel Newton to the intent to carry his said design in execution, and to the intent to settle and assure the messuages, cottages, closes, lands, tenements, tithes, and hereditaments thereinafter mentioned, to the several uses, intents, and purposes thereinafter expressed and declared of and concerning the same; and, in consideration of five shillings to him paid by the said mayor, bailiffs, and burgesses, did grant, bargain, sell, alien and confirm unto the said Nicholas Throsby, the said mayor, and the said bailiffs and burgesses, their successors and assigns,

Certain estates at Barwell, Earl Shilton, Bushby, and Stretton, all in the county of Leicester; to hold unto the said Nicholas Throsby the said mayor, and the said bailiffs and burgesses, their successors and assigns for the time being for ever, to the only proper use and behoof of the said Nicholas Throsby the said mayor, and the said bailiffs and burgesses, their successors and assigns for the time being for ever, upon the several trusts, intents, and purposes, and subject to the several provisoes or conditions thereinafter expressed; to wit:

Upon trust, that the said mayor, bailiffs, and burgesses, their successors and assigns for the time being [2], should, by and out of the rents, issues, and profits of the said granted premises, after deduction of all necessary outgoings thereout, for taxes, repairs, quit-rents, or otherwise, yearly for ever pay, or cause to be paid, unto the several mayors, or chief officers, bailiffs, and burgesses, of the several boroughs or corporations, their successors or assigns for the time being, after mentioned, and to the several resident ministers, whether rector, vicar, or curate, churchwardens and overseers of the poor, of the several parishes and hamlets after mentioned, the several yearly sums of money after expressed; viz.

	£.	s.	d.
To the mayor, or other chief officer, bailiffs, and burgesses of the borough or corporation of Bedford, in the county of Bedford - - - - - - - -	26	0	0
To the mayor, or other chief officer, bailiffs, and burgesses of the borough or corporation of Buckingham, in the county of Bucks - - - - - -	26	0	0
To the mayor, or other chief officer, bailiffs, and burgesses of the borough or corporation of Hertford, in the county of Hertford - - - - -	26	0	0
To the mayor, or other chief officer, bailiffs, and burgesses of the borough or corporation of Huntingdon, in the county of Huntingdon - - - - -	26	0	0
To the resident minister as aforesaid, churchwarden and overseers of the poor, of the parish of Ashby de la Zouch, in the said county of Leicester, for the time being - - - - - - - - -	26	0	0

[1] "Gabriel Newton was the son of reputable parents in Leicester, where, by marriage chiefly, he procured a considerable fortune. He was bred to the combing line; and afterwards was master of a capital inn, the Horse and Trumpet, near the High Cross, which he quitted, and lived afterwards in the line and character of a gentleman. He had three wives, but only one child, a son, who lived nearly to the age of manhood; after whose death, he turned his thoughts to the laudable purpose of being serviceable to posterity. His projects, in the way of charity, were many; and his opponents, who were always ready to thwart his schemes, not a few. His temper might not be even at the decline of life; but those who had neither abilities nor inclination to do good might have humoured his inclination without the least injury to themselves. He once offered to re-build the South front of St. Martin's Church, if the Churchwardens would indulge him with a sitting in it, to his mind, for the charity boys. He likewise offered to re-build the Old Hospital, if the Corporation would consent to his boys occupying a certain place on the Town's premises; and many other praise-worthy schemes he would have executed, had he not been opposed by those in power. He was chosen Mayor in 1732. He was a regular attendant on divine service, daily; and was at times rude to the Clergyman if he ever omitted the performance of the Church-service, particularly the Athanasian Creed on the days appointed for it to be read: even the ringing of the prayer-bell he attended to with critical exactness: Mr. Philip Hackett, the then parish clerk, and he, fought once in the belfry, about Mr. Hackett's boy being irregular in ringing the bell. He broke his cane over the clerk's head, for which the clerk kicked him down the stairs. If he ever found a man indelicately turned against the church wall, he was sure to receive a blow from the Alderman's cane." Throsby's Leicester, p. 188.

[2] "Leicester, March 23, 1808. The Corporation of Leicester, having now the satisfaction to find themselves sanctioned by the opinion of Counsel, in extending the Charities of the late Mr. Alderman Newton, hereby give notice, that they are about to appropriate to the establishment of Schools in Leicester, and some other Towns in Leicestershire, the large accumulation of rents, which have been invested in the funds, pending the repeated litigations of the heir at law, and subsequently, till Time has barred his claim. For the School at Leicester there is wanted a master, well qualified to teach reading, writing, and arithmetic. There will be a considerable number of boys under his tuition, inclusive of those now in the School which was established out of the personal estate of Alderman Newton, the present master of which is about to retire. Any person who can produce satisfactory testimonials of his abilities and habits of teaching, as well as of his moral and religious character, may leave written applications at the Town Clerk's Office. None need apply who does not answer this description, as a liberal salary will be given to secure a master well qualified for the situation.—Sanctioned also in carrying into execution the ulterior trusts reposed in them by the Alderman's will, the Corporation give notice, that they are about to appropriate the surplus rents of his estates, and of the accumulation thereof arising from the investments made pending the litigation of the heir at law, and subsequently, till Time has at length barred his claims, in apprenticing poor boys of the Town of Leicester. The trust-deeds define the objects of this charity to be, 'Poor boys of indigent and necessitous parents of the Established Church of England, and inhabitants of the Town of Leicester, not receiving relief from the poor rates. Persons answering the above description may apply at the offices of Thomas Wrighte, esq. Mayor; or Mr. William Heyrick, Town-clerk." Copied from a Public Advertisement in the Leicester Journal.

To

To the resident minister, churchwardens and overseers of the poor of the parish of St. Neot's, in the said county of Huntingdon - - - - - - - - 26 0 0

To the resident minister, churchwardens and overseers of the poor of the parish of Barwell, in the said county of Leicester, for the time being - - 20 16 0

To the resident minister, churchwardens and overseers of the poor of the hamlet of Earl Shilton, in the said county of Leicester, for the time being 20 16 0

To be by the said several mayors, or other chief officers, bailiffs, and burgesses of the said boroughs or corporations last mentioned, respectively for the time being, and by the said ministers, churchwardens, and overseers of the poor of the said parishes and hamlets of Ashby de la Zouch, St. Neot's, Barwell, and Earl Shilton, respectively, applied, disposed of, and appropriated, towards the cloathing, schooling, and educating of 25 boys, of indigent or necessitous parents of the Established Church of England, in each of the said towns, parishes, and hamlets respectively, without any regard to particular parishes in the said boroughs or corporations, where there are more parishes than one, all the parishes in such borough or corporation, respectively, being to receive the benefit thereof as if only one parish ; as should, by such mayors, or other chief officer, bailiffs, and burgesses, and such minister, churchwarden, and overseers of the poor respectively, be deemed proper objects of such charity (save and except in the said parish of Barwell, and in the said hamlet of Earl Shilton, in which places there were to be but 20 boys only), under the restrictions and regulations after mentioned : viz.

The boys to be taken and chosen from the age of seven years inclusive, to the age of 14 years inclusive ; (to wit,) none under the age of seven years, nor above the age of fourteen years ; each boy to be allowed annually, or once in 15 months, or once in 18 months, as the said last-mentioned trustees shall think proper, a green cloth coat, waistcoat, and breeches, not under 20d. per yard, one shirt of flaxen cloth, not under 13d. per yard, and such stockings and caps, and other apparel, to be bought out of each of the said several annual sums, as the said Gabriel Newton had usually allowed for some time past, in some or one of the said towns, boroughs, parishes, or hamlets ; and the residue then remaining out of each annual sum to be yearly paid to a proper master, to be chosen as after mentioned, to teach and instruct such a number of boys as before mentioned, in each of the said boroughs, towns, parishes, and hamlets respectively, reading, writing, and arithmetic, and singing of Psalms, and toning the responses in and during divine service, in the several parish churches and chapels in the said boroughs, towns, parishes, and hamlets, respectively, where only one parish church or chapel ; and, where there are more than one, in such parish church or chapel as the said trustees for the application of the said annual sums respectively, for the time being, should think proper ; such master and boys, in each borough, town, parish, or hamlet, respectively, to be nominated and chosen by the mayor, bailiffs, and burgesses for the time being in each borough or corporation, respectively, assembled at their common hall there, or the major part of the same body then present ; and by the resident minister, whether rector, vicar, or curate, churchwardens, and overseers of the poor in such parishes or hamlets respectively, or the major part of them ; in which election, the mayor, or other chief officer, in each corporation, respectively, for the time being, and the resident minister as aforesaid, in each parish and hamlet, respectively, to have the casting vote, when the electors were equally divided (subject nevertheless to such inspection, visitation, and regulation, as after mentioned). Provided always, and it was the true intent and meaning of the said Gabriel Newton, and of those presents, that no boy or boys should be admitted to receive the benefit of the above donation, if the parent or parents of such boy or boys for the time being should receive any collection or benefit from the levies raised in such town, borough, parish, or hamlet, respectively, for the maintenance of the poor there. Provided also, and it was the true intent and meaning of the said Gabriel Newton, and of those presents, and the said Gabriel Newton did thereby declare, that no town, or parish, hamlet, or place, should receive any benefit from the said donations, where the said creed of St. Athanasius used in the Rubrick of the Church of England, was not publicly read, in the church, chapel, or place used for divine service, in such town, parish, hamlet, or place, on the days appointed in the said Rubrick for that purpose; and where the boys should not be permitted to tone the responses in divine service, as before directed :

Provided further, that if the rector, vicar, or curate, of any town, parish, hamlet, or place, that for the time being should happen to enjoy the benefit of the said donation, should, at any time thenafter, neglect or refuse to read the said Creed of St. Athanasius in divine service, as directed by the said Rubrick of the Church of England ; or if the said boys should not be permitted to tone the responses in divine service as before directed ; that then, and in either of the said cases, and when and as often as it should so happen, it should and might be lawful to and for the said mayor, bailiffs, and burgesses of the borough of Leicester aforesaid, for the time being, assembled at their common hall in the same borough, or the major part of the members of the same body then present, to take away the benefit of the said donation from such nonconforming town, parish, hamlet, or place ; and pay and apply the money usually paid to such town, parish, hamlet, or place, to and for the benefit of the like number of boys in any other town, parish, hamlet, or place, in the same County that the said nonconforming place or places should or might be situate, or in any other town, parish, hamlet, or place, not then enjoying the benefit thereof, for the time being, in the manner, and under the same regulations and restrictions, as aforesaid, as the said mayor, bailiffs, and burgesses of the borough of Leicester aforesaid, for the time being, assembled at their common hall as aforesaid, or the major part of the same body then present, shall think fit (save, except, and unless the said Creed should at any time thereafter, by King, Queen, or Parliament, be abrogated or abolished out of, and not used in, the Rubrick of the Church of England, which abolition, in the opinion of the said Gabriel Newton, would be a greater blow to the Church and State than taking off the head of the Royal Martyr King Charles the First, that then the omitting reading the said Creed as aforesaid should not be deemed a forfeiture of the said donation.) Which said mayor, bailiffs, and burgesses of the borough of Leicester aforesaid, for the time being, assembled at their common hall in manner aforesaid, were thereby appointed the proper judges, to determine whether the said Creed should be, or for the time being had been properly, read or not read, or whether the said toning of the responses had or had not been used, so as to entitle any town, parish, hamlet, or place, to enjoy or subject them to be deprived of the benefit of the said donation, according to the true intent and meaning of those presents. Provided also, and it was the true intent and meaning of those presents, and the said Gabriel Newton did thereby impower the said mayor, bailiffs, and burgesses, of the borough of Leicester aforesaid, and their successors for the time being, or the major part of them, assembled at their common hall, from time to time, and when and as often as they should think fit, to elect and appoint one or more person or persons, as steward, treasurer, or secretary, to the said charity, to receive the rents of the said granted premises, and do all other matters relative thereto, and to keep the accompts of the fund thereby created for carrying on and supporting the said charity, and to receive and pay the several appointments thereof; and also, by such steward,

steward, treasurer, or secretary, or otherwise, when and as often as the said mayor, bailiffs, and burgesses of the borough of Leicester aforesaid, assembled as aforesaid, should think fit, to visit the several towns, parishes, hamlets, and places, that should for the time being receive the benefit of the said donation, and inspect into the accompts of the several trustees thereby appointed for the disposition thereof, and to regulate the application of the same, according to the true intent and meaning of the said indenture ; and also to pay and allow unto such stewards, treasurers, or secretaries, out of the said fund, his or their necessary charges and expences, and all other charges and expences attending such visitation ; and such yearly stipend or salary for his or their trouble as they the said mayor, bailiffs, and burgesses of the borough of Leicester aforesaid, for the time being, or the major part of them, assembled as aforesaid, should think proper ; such steward rendering an accompt to them when and as often as they should think proper ; with power for the said mayor, bailiffs, and burgesses of the borough of Leicester aforesaid, for the time being, or the major part of them, assembled as aforesaid, such stewards, treasurers, or secretaries, to remove, and other or others in his or their stead to appoint, when and as often as they, or the major part of them, assembled as aforesaid, shall see occasion. Provided further, and it was the true intent and meaning of the said Gabriel Newton, and of the said indenture, that in case the funds thereby created for the establishing, and supporting the said charities for the time being, should not be sufficient, after deduction of all necessary outgoings as aforesaid, to pay to the several towns, parishes, hamlets, and places before mentioned, the several annual sums before expressed ; that then it should and might be lawful to and for the said mayor, bailiffs,

and burgesses of the borough of Leicester aforesaid, for the time being, assembled as aforesaid, or the major part of the same body then present, from time to time, and at any time thereafter, to lessen the number of such towns, parishes, hamlets, or places, as they should think fit ; and, so, on the contrary, if the same funds for the time being, by any improvement thereof, should happen to be more than sufficient for the purposes aforesaid, it should be lawful for them, the same mayor, bailiffs, and burgesses assembled as aforesaid, to increase the number of towns, parishes, hamlets, and places, and add such as they should think proper, in the same manner, for the like purposes, under and subject to the like restrictions and regulations as before directed, so as the said charity or donation of the said Gabriel Newton might be as extensive as possible.

Provided always, and it was the true intent and meaning of the said Gabriel Newton, and of the said indenture, that it should be lawful for the said mayor, bailiffs, and burgesses of the borough of Leicester aforesaid, for the time being, or the major part of them assembled as aforesaid, from time to time thereafter, and when and as often as they should think fit, to remove the said charity or donation from any town, parish, hamlet, or place, that should for the time being receive the benefit thereof, where the same should be abused, or the regulations before directed not be complied with, according to the true intent and meaning of the said indenture ; or for any other just and reasonable cause ; and pay, apply, and dispose of the same, to and for the benefit of any other town, parish, hamlet, or place, as they the said mayor, bailiffs, and burgesses of the borough of Leicester aforesaid, for the time being, or the major part of them, assembled as aforesaid, should think proper [1].

[1] In consequence of the increased funds of this charity, the following correspondence took place on the establishment of one of these Schools in the County.

" To the Mayor, Aldermen, and Common Council of the Borough of Leicester. *January* 1, 1809.

" We the minister, churchwarden, and principal inhabitants of the parish of Hinckley,—desirous of establishing a free-school under the will of the late Alderman Gabriel Newton,—Petition and solicit you to grant us such a pecuniary aid and assistance from the fund given by the said Gabriel Newton, for the furtherance of cloathing and educating of the industrious poor children as you in your discretion may think fit. Signed, H. E. HOLLAND, Minister ; JOHN WARD, THOMAS SANSOME, Churchwardens ; &c. &c."

" GENTLEMEN, [" To the Minister and Churchwardens of Hinckley.] " *Leicester, January* 24, 1809.

" The Corporation of Leicester are possessed of certain estates in Leicestershire, under a deed of trust made by Mr. Gabriel Newton, formerly an alderman of Leicester, for the purpose of paying certain annual sums, specified in the deed, to several towns therein mentioned, towards cloathing and educating a certain number of children at each of those places ; with a provision that, in case the rents should at any time become more than adequate to the support of the schools at such places, this Corporation, as his trustees, should have power to extend the charity to *other* towns. It is with great satisfaction that the Corporation (after many years of tedious litigation with the Alderman's heir at law) find themselves enabled to perform the gratifying part of their duty. The increase of the rents, added to the dividends arising from the sums which accumulated during the time the suits with the heir at law were pending, and which were invested from time to time, and now remain in the funds, will afford the means of granting 26*l.* per annum to five places besides those specifically mentioned in the trust deed, and besides a sum which they have appropriated to a school at Leicester. Under these circumstances, and having reason to believe that the town of Hinckley is one in which the donation may be made very useful, I am directed to acquaint you, that they intend to grant 26*l. per annum* to that parish, commencing at Lady-day next, provided the conditions mentioned in the trust-deed be complied with, and that the minister and principal inhabitants will use their best endeavours to procure voluntary contributions in aid of it. The trustees are not authorized to give a larger sum. As it is not sufficient of itself to establish a school upon the plan settled by the donor, they think it right to require *an assurance* that exertions will be made by the parishioners, so as to render it as beneficial as possible ; and they doubt not but that you and the more opulent inhabitants of your town will gladly promote an object so desirable. The principal conditions which the donor himself has annexed to the gift are the following : It is to be applied " towards the cloathing, schooling, and educating of 25 boys of indigent or necessitous parents of the Established Church of England in each town, between the ages of seven and 14 years ; each boy to be allowed, annually, or once in 15 months, or once in 18 months (as the trustees may think proper), a green cloth coat, waistcoat, and breeches, not under 20*d. per* yard, a flaxen shirt not under 13*d. per* yard, and such stockings, caps, and other apparel, as Mr. Newton in his life-time had usually allowed. To be taught reading, writing, and arithmetic, singing of psalms, and toning the responses in the parish church. No boy whose parents receive parochial relief is to be admitted ; nor is any parish to have the donation where the Creed of Saint Athanasius shall not be read in the Church on the days appointed in the rubric." If the parishioners of Hinckley accept the donation upon the terms above stated, an abstract of the material parts of the trust-deed will be hereafter sent for their better guidance ; and it now only remains for me to request the favour of a speedy answer, and which I shall take the earliest opportunity of laying before the Corporation. W. HEYRICK, Town-clerk."

" SIR, [" To William Heyrick, esq. Town-clerk.] " *Hinckley, Aug.* 29, 1809.

" A few days ago, at a meeting of the parishioners of this place, reference was had to a letter received from you so long since as January last, respecting the late Mr. Alderman Newton's charity. We are deputed by that meeting to notify to you, that the annuity of 26*l.* will be gladly accepted, and met with an adequate sum, to fulfil the intentions of the said charity. We are desired to give an assurance to that effect ; also to ask you for any further necessary information on the subject.

" We are, Sir, your obedient servants, JOHN WARD, JOHN BLAKESLEY, Churchwardens."

" GENTLEMEN, [" To Messrs. Ward and Blakesley, Churchwardens, Hinckley.] " *Leicester, July* 7, 1810.

" Owing to the answers from several other parishes to which the Corporation, as Trustees of the late Mr. Alderman Newton's charities, had made offers for establishing schools, similar to that made to Hinckley, not having been received ; the Committee, to whom the management of the affairs of those charities are confided, did not meet until the 3d instant, when I laid before them your letter of the 29th of August last, by which it appears that the parishioners of Hinckley are desirous of receiving the annuity of 26*l.* upon the terms mentioned in my letter of the 24th of January, 1809. At this meeting I received the directions of the Committee, to inform you, that I am ordered to pay the annuity to your parish from Lady-day last, in case the school is already established, or shall be established by Michaelmas next ; and that, if it should not be established by that time, the payment shall commence from Lady-day next, if the school be then established. I inclose an abstract of the trust-deed [p. 611], which shews fully the conditions annexed by the donor to the grant, and which I need scarcely observe, the Corporation, as Trustees, are bound to see complied with. I am not aware that you will need any further information from me than my letter of the 24th of January and the trust-deed will afford ; but if you do, I beg you will make no hesitation in applying to me for it. W. HEYRICK, Town-clerk.

September 22, 1810. Whereas the Town of Hinckley having obtained the late Mr. Alderman Newton's donation, " towards the cloathing, schooling, and educating of twenty-five boys, of indigent or necessitous parents, of the Established Church of England, between the ages of seven and fourteen years ;" any person belonging to the said parish (not receiving parochial relief) who wished to have the benefit of the above charity, were requested to apply to the minister or churchwardens.—In course the establishment immediately took place ; and 25 boys were cloathed at Hinckley in March 1811.

PEDIGREE of STANTON and PICKERING, of LANGTON, continued from vol. II. p. 384.

Arms of *Stanton:* Vairè, Argent and Sable, a canton Gules.—Arms of *Pickering:* Ermine, a lion rampant, crowned Or.
Arms of *Ord:* Sable, three salmon hauriant in fess Argent, Crest, an elk's head Or.—Plate XLV. fig. 12, 13.

Sir Francis Stanton, of Birchmore, Woburn, Bedfordshire; living 1634.=Elizabeth; died 1630, æt. 66.

Sir Gilbert Pickering, knt.; died 1613.=Elizabeth Hazard, of Boun.

Sir John Pickering, of Tichmarsh, knt.; died 1617.=Susannah, daughter of sir Erasmus Dryden.

PEDIGREE of BYRD, of CLEYBROOK.

William Byrd[3], esq. a counsellor at law, purchased Cleybrook Hall about 1670; and died there soon after 1700.=Frances, his widow, buried at Cleybrook, April 22, 1710.

PEDIGREE

PEDIGREE of DILLINGHAM of BEDFORDSHIRE; and ORD; continued from that of NOBLE of RERESBY and LEICESTER, in vol. III. p. 461.

Arms of Dillingham: Argent, ten fleurs de lis, 4, 3, 2, 1, Sable. Plate XLV. fig. 14.—Arms of Ord; see p. 614.

[Pedigree chart of the Dillingham and Ord families, arranged as a genealogical tree. Principal entries include:]

Thomas Dillingham, rector of Barnwell All Saints, co. Northampton, 1618; died the same year.

Thomas Dillingham, living at Over Dean[1], co. Bedford, in 1600.

1. William Dillingham, M. A. senior fellow of Emanuel College; elected master in 1653; vice-chancellor 1659 and 1661; died in 1662.

2. Thomas Dillingham[2], rector of Barnwell All Saints 1658; died April 23, 1702, æt. 72.

2. Theophilus Dillingham[5], born at Over Deane 1602; master of Clare Hall, Cambridge, 1654; rector of Otford Cluny, Huntingdonshire; prebendary of Ulskelf, in the cathedral of York, 1661; archdeacon of Bedford 1667 (in which year he published "Articles of Visitation"); died Sept. 3, 1678.

Elizabeth, daughter of Thos. Paske, D.D. some time master of Clare Hall, and prebendary of York.

1. John Dillingham[3], D.D. born 1600; died æt. 90.

Grace; died 1693, æt. 90.

1. John Dillingham, died s.p. 1694, æt. 72.
2. Oliver Dillingham, died s.p. 1698, æt. 74, leaving his property to his relation Benjamin Boswell.

Anne, married Thomas Allen, of Bridgewater, esq.

Thomas Dillingham, born at Great Hadham, Herts; fellow of Clare Hall; died Dec. 19, 1722, æt. 60.

John Ord.=Jane, daughter of Ralph Bowes, by ... Errington.

John Ord, died=Ann Preston, died 1689; first wife. John Ord.=Anne, daughter of Michael Hutchinson, of Leeds; second wife.

Robert Ord, esq. chief baron in Scotland; resigned 1775; died 17...

Mary, da. of Ord, nel.

James=Anna-Petronella, da. of sir Roger Ellison, of ... Orgil, of Jamaica.

Harry Ord=Anne, d. of of the King's Fra. HutchRemembrancer's Office, esq.; died 1746; buried at Hampstead.

1. Thomas=Anne BaOrd. con, of Hackney.

Mary, daughter of Samuel Norman of Henley, Oxon, esq.

John Ord, D.D. living at Formham, Suffolk, 1:11

1. Rev. John, rector of Wheathampsted, Herts; died April 16, 1811.

Anne, dau. of Thomas Cocksedge, of Bury, esq.

John-Thomas Ord.

1. Anne, born 1747; died 1767, aged 20.
2. Jemima, born 1748; married Thos.-Charles Bigge, of Little Benton, c. Northumberland; died .....; and left issue.

4. Robert Ord, born 1766; died in India.

1. Susanna, born April 30, 1789.
2. Jemima, born July 17, 1791.
3. Frances-Anne, born Jan. 23, 1796.

1. Susanna, born 1750; died unmarried 1769.
2. Susanna, born 1753; died aged about 16 years.
3. Charlotte, born 1756; died unmarried.

[Prose notes, left and lower columns:]

1. "The family of Dillingham appears to have been very numerous in the parish of Dean; but no record of his birth appears in the Register." Lysons's Bedfordshire, p. 73.

2. "Francis Dillingham, born at Dean, and bred Fellow in Christ College in Cambridge, was an excellent Linguist and Disputant. My Father was present in the Bachillor's Schools, when a Greek Act was kept, between him and William Alabaster, of Trinity College, to their mutual commendation: a disputation so famous that it served for an æra, or epoch, for the Scholars in that age, thence to date their seniority." Fuller's Worthies, Bedfordshire.

"Qui doctus .... quoque vel ....
Vixit & ingenui, conditur hoc Tumulo.
Franciscus Dillingham, Rector hujus Ecclesiæ, quondam Socius Coll. Christi Cantab.; Academiæ Taxator; unus ex Translatoribus Sac. Bibl. Hebr. & Oratoribus in Publicis Comitiis; Græcâ Baccalaureatâs. Obiit Feb. 24, an. Dni 1625."

3. Epitaphs in the church of Barnwell All Saints:
1. "Thomas Dillingham, A. M. Rector of this church 44 years; died Sept. 23, anno Dom. 1702, ætat. suæ 72. A good man, and faithful pastor of Christ's church."
2. "Here lyeth interred Mrs. Frances Dillingham, the widow of Mr. Thomas Dillingham, rector of this parish. She was buried July the 7th, 1716, in the 76th year of her age.
Many weeping eyes were at this grave,
who had been cured by her care and skill."

3. "Sacred to the memory of Mr. Thomas Dillingham, A. M. and worthy rector of this parish;
an ingenious, learned, charitable, and pious man.
He was the son of an excellent and pious father,
William Dillingham, Doctor of Divinity,
Master of Emanuel College in Cambridge,
And Vice-chancellor of that University;
whose father was also a worthy man,
and rector of this parish many years. He married
Eliz. Pickering, daughter of Major Gilbert Pickering,
grand-daughter of sir Gilbert Pickering, of
Tichmarsh, bart., by whom he had issue
William, Elizabeth, and Ann Dillingham,
Anno Domini 1704, he died, much lamented,
in the 46th year of his age;
and was buried here, by his entirely affectionate
and much afflicted widow, who erects this
small monument to his honoured memory."

[Latin column, right:]

Johannes etiam & Oliveri filiorum.
Johannes pater, honestâ familiâ in hâc villâ oriundus, obiit, anno ætatis 70, Domini 1670.
Gratia relicta, & in mortem viduata, in bonâ canitie expiravit, anno ætatis 90, Christi 1693.
Johannes filius primogenitus, bis matrimonio conjunctus, liberis necnon orbatus, improles decessit, anno æt. 72, Domini 1694.
Oliverus postremò, cum annis 74 penè compleverat, inuaptus, patribus occubuit 1698.
Hic Magister Oliverus, affinem Thomam Boswell, filium Benjamini Boswell,
Londinensis, ex asse hæredem & executorem suâ ac fraternâ, sponte cooptavit.
In cujus gratitudinem hoc erexit memoriale."

4. One of these ladies married a Mr. King, whose son (Thomas King, esq.) was living in 1797.

5. The Masters of Emanuel College and Clare Hall had each of them Verses in the Gratulatory Poems of 1660.
In St. Edmund's church, Cambridge:
"Hic jacet Theophilus Dillingham, filius Thomæ, natus Over Deane, in com. Bedfordiæ, ejusdemque Archidiaconus, & Præfectus Aulæ de Clare; denatus Cantabrigiæ Nov. 22, 1678, annoque ætatis suæ 76. Hic jacet etiam Thomas Dillingham, A. M. filius natu maximus prædicti Theophili & Elizabethæ suæ uxoris, ejusdem Collegii Socius; natus fuit Hadham Magnâ, in com. Hartfordiæ; ob. 19° Decembris, anno Domini 1722, ætatis suæ 60."

"Aug. 4, 1660.—Dr. Thomas Paske, who had been elected master of Clare Hall in 1610, being ejected in 1640, was succeeded by Dr. Ralph Cudworth, and he by Dr. Theophilus Dillingham in 1654; who having married a daughter of the said Dr. Paske, the Doctor being very old, quitted his right of restitution to his said son in law, who accordingly was re-admitted 1660."—"Jan. 26, 1661. Theophilus Dillingham, D. D. was collated to the prebend of Ulfskelf, in the church of York, void by the resignation of Thomas Paske, D. D. He was master of Clare Hall, Cambridge; installed Archdeacon of Bedford, Sept. 3, 1667; and died in 1678. Dr. Dillingham had married the daughter of Dr. Paske; and, by his double resignation, came now to the prebend of York and the mastership of Clare Hall, having been in possession of that headship from 1654, and now, by Paske's resignation, and the fellows' reelection, was re-admitted in 1660." Kennett's Register, pp. 222, &c.
4. See p. 614.

7. Buried at Barnet, Herts. Her epitaph, written by Dr. Paley:
"Hanc Tabulam, M. S. optimæ Parentis Annæ Ord, quæ obiit 4° Aprilis, A.D. 1794, anno ætatis 82, per 38 Vidua, Joh: Ord, Ah! quantulum pietatis judicium, mœrens posuit."

PEDIGREE

PEDIGREE of NOBLE, of RERESBY and LEICESTER; enlarged from vol. III. p. 461.

(Enlarged from a MS. communicated by the Rev. MARK NOBLE[1], F. A. S. Lond. and Edinb. and rector of Barning in Kent.)

William Noble, gent.=Elizabeth, sister and coheir of John Kebell, of Reresby. She had half the estate; the
of Thrussington. | other part went to .... Orton, who married the other sister and coheir of Mr. Kebell.

George Noble, gent. of Reresby. He purchased the other part of the estate of=Catharine, daugh- | Thomas No-=.... daughter
the Kebells, which part was come to the family of Faunt: ever after the | ter of Henry | ble, gent. or | of William
Nobles, as representatives of the Kebells, yearly received from the Spital- | Hoode, of Bos- | Thrussing- | Webster, of
house, an hospital standing at the end of Belgrave-gate in Leicester, twelve | ton. | ton. | Rushington.
chickens, to acknowledge that their ancestors the Kebells had given the
ground upon which it had been built.

Thomas Noble,=Frances, daugh- | George, | Agnes, ma. Thos. Watts, | Eliza-=Rev. Thomas Sa- | William, | George=Elizabeth,
of Reresby, | ter of Robert | died | of Grimston, c. Linc. | beth; | cheverell, vicar | died s. p. | Noble, | dau. of ...
gent. born in | Heyrick, esq. | s. p. | Margaret, mar. William | 2d wife; | of St. Martin's, | | of | Kenning,
1564; died | M. P. alder- | | Watts, of Radcliffe. | marr. | Leicester, and | | Thrus- | of co. Not-
July 10, 1625. | man, & thrice | | Mary, married Richard | about | confrater of Wig- | | sington. | tingham.
| mayor of Lei- | | Watts, of Cason, co. | 1619; | ston's Hospital[4]; | |
| cester. | | Bedford. | d. 1640. | died in 1626. | .... Noble[3], and other children.

George Noble,=Elizabeth, daugh- | Thomas, | Rev. William Noble, | Francis[4] Noble, gent.=Mary.... | Robert, born | Catharine,
of Reresby, | ter of Rev. Ed- | born in | born 1611; rector | born 1612; mayor | died Aug. | 1613. | bo. 1607.
gent. born | ward Barwell, | 1608. | of Blockley, and | of Leicester 1661 | 15, 1675, | Joseph, born | Margaret,
1605; living | rector of Keg- | | vicar of Queenbo- | and 1674; died | aged 62 | 1616. | bo. 1618.
in 1652. | worth. | | rough; died Feb. | Dec. 13, 1689, | (see p. 601).
| | | 6, 1644; buried at | aged 78;
| | | Purley, all c. Berks. | (see p. | Thomas, died Dec. 6, | Mary.=William Major.
| | | | 601.) | 1655, æt. 3 (see p. 602).

Thomas Noble, of Reres-= | Frances. | Elizabeth. | 1. William Major. | 1. Mary.
by, gent. born 1631; | Susanna[5]. | Catharine. | 2. John Major. | 2. Anne.
living 1670. | Margaret. | Anne. | 3. Francis Major. | 3. Jane.

Mary, wi-=Thomas Noble, Esq.=Margaret, eldest daugh- | George Noble,=Anne, | ...... = | Eliza-=Rev. Man- | 2. Margaret,
dow of ... | M. P. for Leicester | ter of sir William Keyte, | esq. of Lei- | da. of | | beth, | sel Court- | died Sept.
Harvey, of | 1719; he resided in | bart. of Everton, co. | cester. | .... | | died | man[6], | 15, 1680,
c. Lincoln. | that borough; died | Gloucester, by Eliza- | | Brew- | George=Ca- | Aug. | co. North- | aged 10.
| May 3, 1730, aged | beth, sister and at length | | ster. | Noble, tha- | 25, | ampton; | 3. Barbara,
| 74. | heir of the hon. Fr. | | | of Lei- rine, | 1698. | died Feb. | died July
| | Coventry, 2d son of lord | | | cester. living, | | 1, 1704, | 3, 1738,
| | keeper Coventry, died | | | a wi- | | aged 43. | aged 50.
| | Mar. 7, 1710-11, æt. 47. | | | dow,
| | | | | some years
| | William, died a minor, and unmarried. | | after 1766.

Thomas Noble, esq. killed | Mary, born=Thomas | Martha,=Thomas Her- | George Noble, | Susan-=William Dilling- | Anne,
by a fall from his horse | 1694; died | Jordain, | first | rick, esq. | of Swansea, | nah, | ham, of Red Lion | marr.
in the town of Reresby | May 5, 1788, | esq. town- | wife, | town-clerk | a wine mer- | died | square, a very emi- | Rev.
Feb. 8, 1743, aged 48; | s. p. She | clerk of | died s. p. | of Leicester | chant, died | 1789, | nent apothecary; | ....
dying unmarried, he de- | devised her | Leicester | Nov. 17, | in 1745; | s. p. | æt. 92. | died 1733. | White,
vised his estates to Ro- | property to | 1715; died | 1723, | resigned the | Christopher Noble, | | | of
gers Ruding, esq. of | her relation | June 9, | æt. 24. | office 1764; | esq. of Leicester, | | [See p. 615.] | Suf-
Westcotes. | Christopher | 1745, æt. | | died 1766, | a wine merchant; | | | folk.
| Noble, esq. | 63. | | aged 65. | died May 8, 1793.

[1] " I have found no less than eleven coats of arms belonging to the different families of Noble, six of which are evidently only different bearings derived from one, i. e. those of Devonshire dispersed into other Counties. The Nobles of Leicestershire have a very different coat; it is, Quarterly, 1st, Argent, on a chief Gules a lion passant Or, for Noble; 2d, Barry, nebulé, Argent and Gules, on a canton a crescent Or; Kebell, or Keeble; 3d, Argent, on a bend Sable, five bezants; Palmer; 4th, Gules, a chevron Ermine, between three eagles displayed Or; Eaton. For a crest, an eagle displayed proper. Plate XLV. fig. 15.
" The Nobles of Leicestershire have been a numerous and genteel family for some centuries. The Baronetage, under the article CAVE, says, that a Noble, of Stowford in Leicestershire, married the daughter of Christopher Cave, esq. who died in 1495, the ancestor of the baronets of that surname. Mr. Lodge, Somerset Herald, remarks, that the account in the Baronetage of the Caves is long, but very inaccurate. I suppose it is erroneous in this instance, because Stowford is not in Leicestershire, but in the county of Devon. Is it not, therefore, very probable, that one of the Nobles, having married a lady in Leicestershire, who was an heiress, went into that county, and settled there. Though the arms are very different, yet I have no doubt that the Nobles of Leicestershire descend from a cadet of those of Devon, long before the present distinctions of houses were invented, when we know that different branches of the same family took different bearings.
" Though not allied to the Nobles of Leicestershire, yet my father Mr. William-Heatly Noble was intimately acquainted with the late Mr. George Noble, of Swansea; and I have corresponded with his brother the last Christopher Noble, esq. From him and Mr. Heyrick, of Leicester, two very judicious gentlemen, I received much information relative to the last descents in this pedigree.— The direct line is now extinct in the name from want of heirs male; but in Leicestershire there are various families, as branches of these Nobles of Reresby. One of these, I suppose, was the very respectable and Rev. Thomas Noble, incumbent of Wolvey in Warwickshire. He kept for some years an academy at Leicester Grange; and died at Hinckley March 10, 1784. M. N."
[2] His first wife (whom he married in 1590, and who was living in 1616) was Mary, another of the daughters of Robert Heyrick, esq. (See their Pedigree, vol. III. p. 220.)
[3] Probably Henry, the first rector of Frolesworth of this family, who was born in 1652.
[4] Mr. Francis Noble was a woollen-draper by trade. He had a niece, who married a Mr. Watson, whom she survived. J. S. H.
[5] This Susanna died about the year 1671. One of her sisters (I do not know which) married a Mr. Watts, by whom she had a daughter, named Elizabeth. J. S. H.
[6] See their epitaph in Brydges's History of Northamptonshire, vol. II. p. 30.

PEDIGREE of NOBLE, of FROLESWORTH. (See p. 616.)

Rev. Henry Noble, of Emanuel College, Cambridge; B. A. 1676; rector of Frolesworth 1679; M. A. 1681;=Margaret ....;
purchased the advowson 1700 (George Noble and Joseph Noble, gents. trustees[1]); died 1722, æt. 70. | bur. Sept. 24, 1717.

| Jane, bapt. Jan. 11, 1681. | Richard Noble[2], bapt. Jan. 10, 1686. | Rev. Anthony Noble, of St. John's=Dorothea Smith; buried May 18, 1796. College, Cambridge; rector of Frolesworth 1723; died Dec. 1, 1738, æt. 51. | Mary, bapt. April 13, 1691. | Henry Noble, bapt. Sept. 28, 1698; buried March 8, 1718. |

Rev. Henry-Lovell Noble[3], of St. John's College, Cambridge; M. A. 1764;=Jane Newbold, died
rector of Frolesworth the same year; died Nov. 8, 1788, æt. 51. | March 4, 1807.

| Rev. Samuel-George Noble, educated at the Char-=Margaret, daugh-ter-house; of Sidney Sussex College, Cambridge; ter of Thos. Lam-B. A. 1789; rector of Frolesworth 1790; mar-bert, esq. of Mal-ried Oct. 6, 1794; living 1810. ton, co. York. | Elizabeth-New-=Rev. William Babington, bold Noble; rector of Cossington married 1784; 1787; living 1811. living 1811. | Jane-Maria, born April 4, 1771; buried Nov. 9, 1792. |

[See vol. III. p. 965.]

| 1. Samuel-Lambert Noble, born Aug. 26, 1795. | 2. Henry-Thomas Noble, born Oct. 15, 1796. | 3. George Noble, born Dec. 13, 1799. | 4. Charles-William Noble, born Aug. 12, 1803. | 5. Edmund-New-bold Noble, born Oct. 15, 1805; died Apr. 21, 1806. | 6. Sidney Noble, born Nov. 4, 1806; died Dec. 4, 1806. | 1. Margaretta, born Sept. 11, 1796. 2. Maria, born Sept. 27, 1800. | 3. Rebecca-Jane, bo. Nov. 12, 1801. 4. Eliz.-Berdmore, born Aug. 4, 1804. 5. Isabella-Frances, born Nov. 21, 1807. |

[1] The names of Joseph (who died Feb. 15, 1711, æt. 47; and Anne his wife died Dec. 12, 1755, æt. 94; see vol. II. p. 385.) and George Noble occur among the benefactors at Waltham.—George Noble, of Waltham (probably brother to Henry, rector of Thurleston in 1679), died March 19, 1725, æt. 66; and Mary his wife, died May 5, 1713, æt. 51.—Their son, George Noble (one of that happy class of beings whom Charles the Second used to talk of, viz. between a Justice of Peace and Chief Constable) died Feb. 2, 1777, æt. 77; and left his property to Joseph Noble, esq. of Melton, woollen-draper and banker, who died Nov. 6, 1792, aged 68, and gave a handsome legacy to the present rector of Frolesworth. He was buried at Melton (see vol. II. p. 254).

[2] There was one Richard Noble, a clergyman, who lived at Stoke, in the county of Northampton. I am not certain of the abovementioned Richard being the one to whom I refer; but I have reason to believe that this Clergyman was related (at least intimately connected) with the above family. J. S. H.

[3] Originally of All Souls, Oxon, where he graduated B. A.; and took an M. A. degree at Cambridge.

ROMAN ANTIQUITIES.

Nearly adjoining to the Church of St. Nicholas is a famous remnant of Roman Antiquity, the JEWRY WALL; which has been very copiously described in the former Part of this Volume, pp. 7, & seqq. where three different Views of it are given; one of which shews its relative situation to the Church of St. Nicholas, evidently built in great measure from Roman bricks, which had previously formed a part of the Jewry Wall. Another small View of the Wall is here given in Plate XLV. In pages 9—12, will also be found a particular description of the several Mosaic pavements and other remnants of Roman grandeur. Several other discoveries have since been made; of which the late Mr. Throsby, who was resident on the spot, very diligently marked the progress.

In 1788, on digging a well near St. Nicholas's Church, was found among the rubbish, at the depth of 24 feet[4], one of the finest copper coin[5] ever discovered in Leicester; which is now in the collection of Mr. Fowke, of Elmesthorpe, near Hinckley. Obverse, a fine bust of the Emperor; round his head,

"MAXIMIANVS . NOB . C. S."

Reverse, a figure representing DEUS GENIUS, standing before a lighted altar[6]. Round it,

"GENIO . POPVLI . ROMANI . I . C."

Four other Coins, found still more recently, are here given in Plate XLV.; namely,

Fig. 17. a coin of Nero, found in Belgrave Gate. This coin, in a perfect state, reads as follows:

Obverse, round his laureated head,

"NERO . CAESAR . AVG . P . MAX . TR . P . P. P.;" i. e. *pontifex* MAXI*mus* TR*ibunitiæ* *potestatis pater patriæ.*

Reverse, "GENIO . AVGVSTI . S. C." The Genius is represented standing before an altar; in its right hand a *patera*, in its left a *cornucopiæ*[7].

Fig. 18. is a coin of Hadrian, but in a lamentably defective state[8], found in High-street, in digging for the foundation of the King's Arms Inn. A perfect copy of this coin, engraved by Gesner, has on the Obverse, "HADRIANVS . AVG . COS . III . P . P."

Reverse, "FORTVNAE . REDVCI . S . C.;" struck, it seems, on his safe return to Rome, from one or other of his visits to the remoter provinces of the empire.

Fig. 19. was found near the West Bridge:

Obverse, "DIVA . FAVSTINA."

Reverse, "AVGVSTA........S. C."

Faustina Senior, represented on this very perfect coin, holds in her right hand a *Palladium* or *Victoriola*, and in her left a *Hasta prora*, "s. c." *Senatus Consultu*[9].

[4] Five feet lower was found the plain Roman pavement described in p. 12.

[5] This coin has been engraved in a former part of this Volume, Plate III.

[6] See Occo & Mediob. Numism. Imp. Rom. fol. Mediol. A. D. 1683, p. 90.

[7] Occo & Mediob. *ubi supra.*—There is a fine engraving of a very similar coin of Nero in Musel's Numismata, tom. II. among his engravings of the coins of Nero, No. 5. It reads on the obverse, NERO . CLAVD . CAESAR . AVG . GER . P . MAX . T . R . P . IMP . P . P. And on the reverse, GENIO . AVGVSTI . S . C.

[8] " This may be one of the many common coins struck in honour of that emperor, to commemorate his coming [ADVENT] into some or other of the departments or provinces, or countries in subjection to the Roman empire, at his time very many. The coins of this class are very numerous, and generally exhibit on their obverses this emperor's head, sometimes laureated; at other times not, with the simple inscription, HADRIANVS . AVG. to which is added, not unfrequently, COS . III . P . P. *i. e.* CONsul *tertium*, a third time, and *Pater Patriæ*, Father of his Country. On the reverses of them, two figures at full-length joining hands, very often an altar between them, and the appearance of a sacrifice, in solemnization of his *advent*, and the usual legend ADVENTVS . AVG . with s. c. Most frequently the Emperor's *advent* to the honoured country or province of his empire is particularly specified on these coins thus: ADVENTVS . AVG . HISPANIAE . GALLIAE . BYTHINIAE . ITALIAE . IVDAEAE . AFRICAE . MAVRITANIAE . &c. with or without an altar between the two upright full-length figures. There is a little variation on some of these *advent* coins of Hadrian, it being sometimes ADVENTVS, in the nominative, and at others in the dative, ADVENTVI . AVG . ARABIAE . SICILIAE . MACEDONIAE . &c. with and without the s. c. or the altar between the two figures joining hands.—The state of the above coin of Hadrian is so deplorable that it may be described as one of his *advent* coins to any of all the countries above-mentioned, or any other Roman province; on which there was not originally either an altar or the letters s . c. of which I cannot perceive the smallest vestige. The curious may be referred to the " Numismata of J. J. Gesner," a standard, scarce, and valuable work, rarely to be seen entire, in folio, Tigari, 1738, and to his coins of Hadrian. For my own opinion is, that the coin, fig. 18, is finely and more correctly engraven, in the " Numismata Antiqua à Jacobo Musellio collecta & edita Veronæ, 1702," in three volumes in folio, tom. II. among his coins of Hadrian, tab. LXXII. No. 2. To enable your readers to judge for themselves, I shall transcribe the legend on his engraving. Obverse, around Hadrian's head, HADRIANVS . AVG . COS . III . P . P.; and on the reverse, FELICITAS . AVG. The figure standing upright, joining hands with the other, which I take for that of the emperor, in his other hand, drooping down, holds a *caduceus* that reaches above his shoulder, of which there seems to be in the engraving (fig. 18) something that may be conceived to be a vestige of the remains of the *caduceus*." I owe this explanation to my good friend the Rev. Dr. Calder.

[9] Of this coin of Faustina Senior there is a fine engraving in Musel *ut supra*. See also, Numism. Imp. Rom. ut supra, Occ. Mediob.

Fig. 20. is a Colonial coin of Philippus Senior; and the true reading on the Obverse is as follows:

" ΑΥΤΟΚ . ΚΜΑ . ΙΟΥΑ . ΦΙΛΙΠΠΟC . CEB."

Reverse, " ΑΝΤΙΟΧΕΩΝ . ΜΗΤΡ . ΚΟΛΩΝ ."

On the head, the usual symbol of Antioch, are the Greek letters Δ and E, and the Latin letters s and c. Musel's Latin description is, *Imperator Caesar Marcus Julius Philippus Augustus. Antiochensium Metropolis Colonia Caput velatum et turritum in vertice Aries*[1]. The Greek letters on the Reverse, with the head of Antioch as usually represented on its coins, Δ E, denote the words Δημαρχικης Εξουσιας *Tribunitiæ potestatis*, i. e. Tribunitial Power, and the Roman letters s. c. *Senatus Consultu*, which I think the Colony of Antioch only was permitted to put on their money.

The principal Collector of Roman Coins at Leicester in the middle of the Eighteenth Century was Mr. Thomas Lee, a silversmith, who died in 1776, æt. 76. He had made a large collection of coins; and had, through life, made Antiquity his chief study. He mingled but little with the world, and cared as little about its concerns. He was extremely shy, and particularly modest. He would neither hear nor utter an expression of levity; notwithstanding he was agreeably familiar with his acquaintance. His memory was retentive even on the verge of the grave. His peculiarities, were of that kind which rather called forth the smile of pleasure than the frown of disgust. After his death, the greater part of his collection (amongst which were some early Saxon coins) was sold by auction in London. Some of them, however, came into the possession of Mr. George Buckley, of Thornton; out of which Mr. Throsby selected a sufficient number to form a Plate in his " History of Leicester." Mr John Coltman[2] also, at a period somewhat later, made a large and valuable collection of Roman coins; from which Mr. Throsby gave a second Plate[3]. To the labours of Mr. Throsby, I am principally indebted for the following particulars:

" In February 1793, as some workmen were employed in removing the earth from a piece of ground nearly an equal distance between the Jewry Wall and the River, they discovered, at the depth of about five feet, some very large blocks of free-stone, half a ton weight; which being removed, it was discovered that they had been placed over a kind of tunnel, two feet over and four deep, made of the same kind of materials and built on the same principles as the Wall. The bottom of this tunnel is of freestone, like the blocks which cover it. The commencement of it (so far as is known) is in a cellar of Mr. S. Roberts's house, near the South end of the Wall; and continues, with a considerable descent, in a right line, North-westwardly to the river.

" In emptying this tunnel of its contents (for it was completely glutted up) I found that it contained light earthy particles on the surface, somewhat

heavier lower, at the bottom gravelly, the whole blended with broken pottery, in general of a singular construction; besides which, a few bones of animals were found therein, in a petrifying state, and a fragment or two of glass vessels; the bottom of one of which was layered with silver. Hence it seems apparent that this subterraneous passage was originally the *Cloaca*, or common Sewer, of the Roman town." [See the form of it in Plate XLVI. fig. 1.]

" Among the fragments of pottery which I selected from this store-house of antiquarian treasure, I was agreeably surprized to find some Roman characters impressed in relievo very legible. [In the mass which is grouped in *Fig.* 2. these characters are given to shew the size of the labels, and the formation of the letters.] In one or two instances, however, the contrary is the case, to me at least: these I will first notice. On the rim of a portion of a vessel made of white clay are several characters, doubly impressed, with a rude instrument. This fragment is represented with a label (marked *Fig. a.* 2). I need not observe that the letters c o are legible enough; the others call for investigation. The vessel originally was made shallow: its circumference, near the rim, about 27 inches, the breadth of the rim, which forms a half circle, two inches; it is layered within with a kind of grit, or small pebble, and bears the marks of fire. Might not this vessel be a censer used in sacrifice, called by the Romans *Thuribulum?* The other illegible characters (marked *Fig. b.*) are on the bottom of a vessel made of beautiful red clay. I guess that these all remain but one: they are copied in *Fig. c.*

" The legible characters are impressed chiefly on the bottoms of vessels of red clay, fashioned like a wine glass which is narrow at the bottom and broad at top. These were probably cups used in libations, with emperors' or consuls' names impressed thereon. One has MACRINI, probably the emperor Opillius Macrinus, who reigned 218 years after Christ. Another has ALBINVS; the third ALBVSA. Part of a bottom has only the ending of a name, TOR or IOR. If TOR, it might stand for, or rather be the ending of, CLAVD. FVSCVS SALINATOR, who flourished after Christ's nativity 118 years. The o and R are very plain. If IOR, there can be no ascertaining for whom it stood, as it doubtless, in that case, stands part of the word IVNIOR of which there were Emperors and Consuls many between the years 319 and 541. A part of two other impressions, found near, but without the sewer, bear these characters respectively, CICVR and MARINH on a sort of composition stone.

" Partly adjoining it, and nearly of a level with the covering stones, was discovered a floor of extraordinary formation : it consisted of mortar, small pebbles, and pounded brick or tile, of each about an equal portion. I have preserved a piece of it, as a singular curiosity : it shews strongly the simplicity and art-

---

[1] " Musel quotes, as his authorities for the justness of his engraving of this coin, M. Theup. p. 740, and Vaillant, in Colon. p. 157. I have examined both his authorities, and find his references correct and satisfactory." *Dr. Calder.*

[2] " By the death of Mr. Coltman, which happened Feb. 15, 1808, in his 81st year, the Town of Leicester lost one of its principal literary ornaments, and society was deprived of a most valuable member, whether we consider him as a scholar of profound learning, as an Antiquary of considerable research, or as a man and a Christian, distinguished by his simplicity, his candour, his humanity, his love of truth, and his attachment to the genuine principles of civil and religious freedom. Nature had cast him in no ordinary mould, and given him no common talents. He was a striking instance of the elevation and triumph of native genius above the adventitious circumstances of fortune and of situation. Himself engaged in trade, and placed in a town more remarkable for its manufactures than for its learning, he might have trod the common path of thousands, who have lived, grown rich, and died, forgotten. Such men are necessary to maintain the state of the world ; but of such men Mr. Coltman was not one. Not assimilating with the maxims or the spirit of trade, he neither followed the one, nor imbibed the other. Hence, when his Warehouse required his presence, he was more frequently to be found in his Study, raised above this world by a contemplation of the Works of Nature and of Providence, or by a perusal of the writings of the Poets and Orators of Greece and Rome. Absorbed in speculations and disquisitions, which, whilst they exercised all the high powers of his mind, afforded to him a pure and unmixed delight, his spirit could not stoop to the petty cares, anxieties, and forms, of ordinary men. His circumstances were easy, and riches were never the objects of his desire. He was therefore but little known ; and was generally looked upon as a man of an eccentric character, destitute of the knowledge of common life. But if to live be to exercise the faculties of thought and of reason, and to employ all the intellectual powers with which we are endowed, and not merely to eat and to drink and to labour, then indeed he knew how to live in a superior degree to most of his contemporaries ; for few men were ever blessed with so clear a perception and so exquisite a relish of the sublime and beautiful, or with so much time and leisure to indulge his favourite taste to the latest period of a long life. The study of the antient Classicks, and of the Antiquities of his Country, were so much his favourite objects, as to justify a hope that he may have left behind him some writings on these subjects in a state to be given to the world. To those who knew him best, this slight tribute of respect from one who honoured him when living, and laments him now that he is no more, will not be unacceptable, and to those who knew him not, it will convey a faint sketch of one of the " most ingenious, unassuming, and amiable of mankind." Gent. Mag. vol. LXXVIII. p. 181.—To Mr. Coltman I was indebted for an original Heraldic MS. by Mr. Burton, as acknowledged in the Preface to Vol. I. p. viii.

[3] See his quarto History of Leicester, pp. 388—393; and his " Letter to the Earl of Leicester, on the recent Discovery of the *Cloaca,* or Sewer, 1793," 8vo, *passim.*

lessness

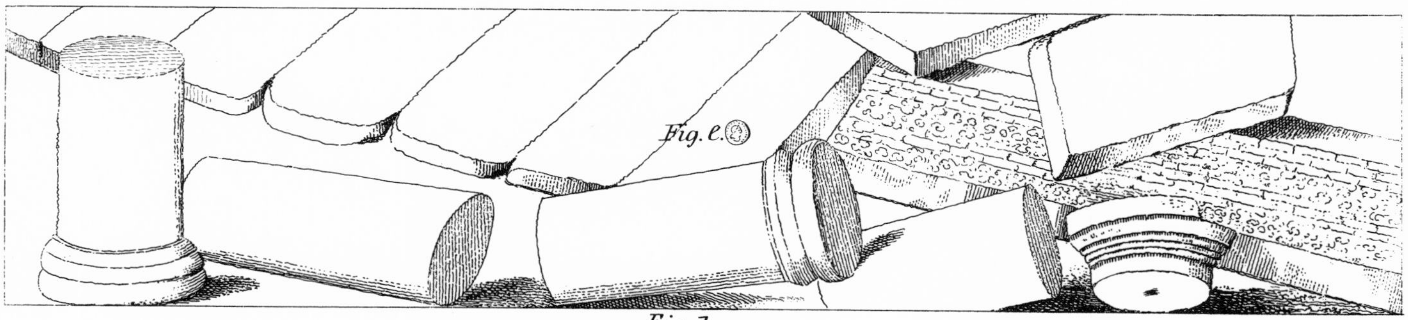

Fig. 2.

Vol. I. Pl. XLVI. p. 448.

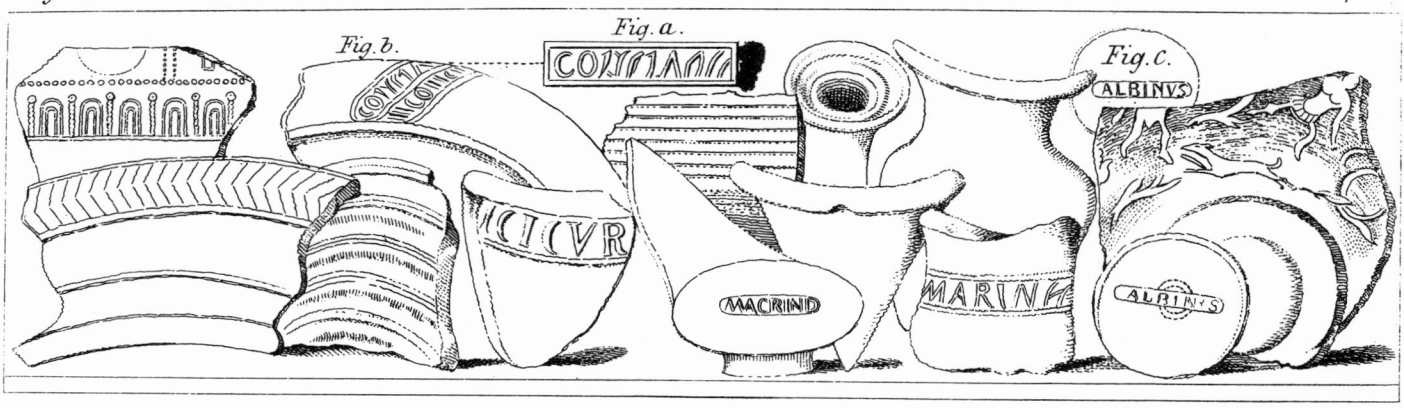

Fig. b.

Fig. a.

COMMANA

Fig. c.

ALBINVS

ININININI

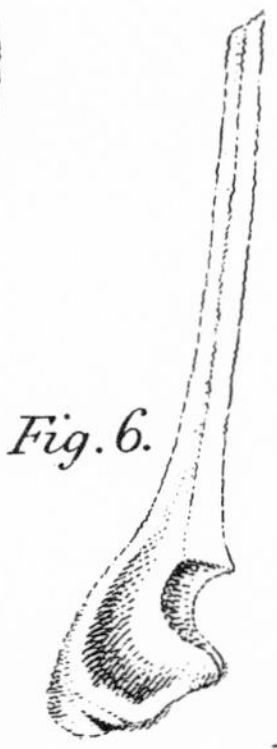

XCICVR

MACRIND

MARINA

ALBINS

VIIAO

Fig. e.

Fig. 1.

Fig. 3.

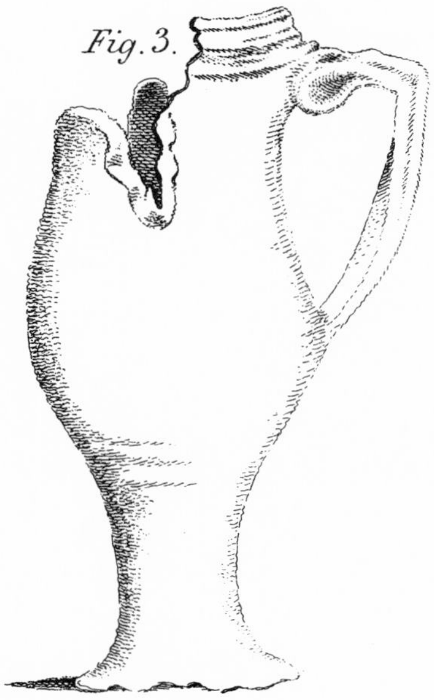

Fig. 4.

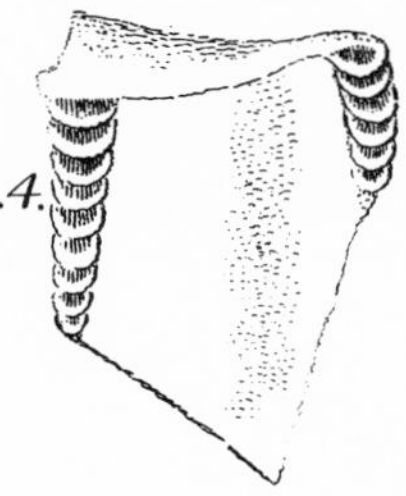

Fig. 7.

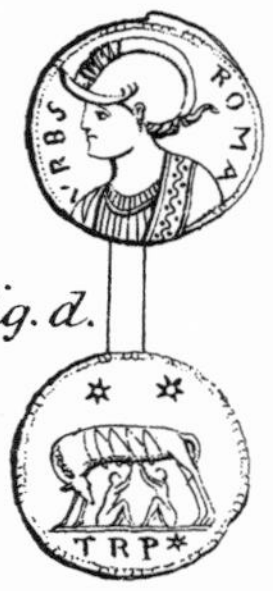

Fig. d.

URBS ROMA

TRP

Fig. 6.

Fig. 5.

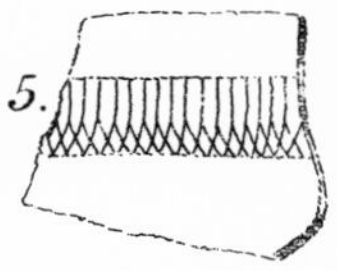

Fig. 8.

IMPCAESNERTRAIANOOPTIMOAVGERGDAC

Fig. f.

PMTRPCOS VIPP SPQR

Fig. 9.

Fig. 10.

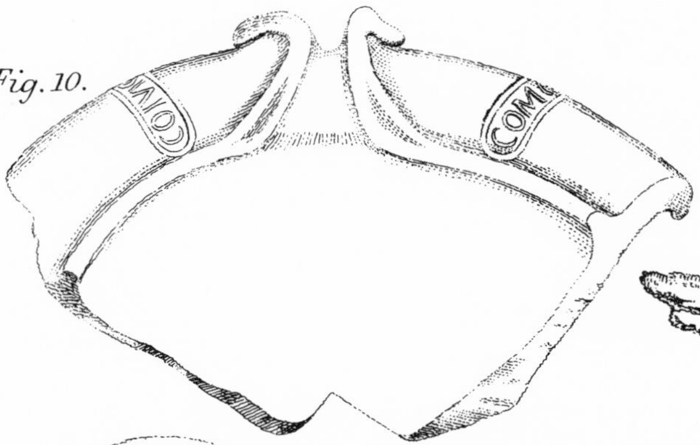

COMG

COMG

Fig. 12.

Fig. 13.

Fig. 11.

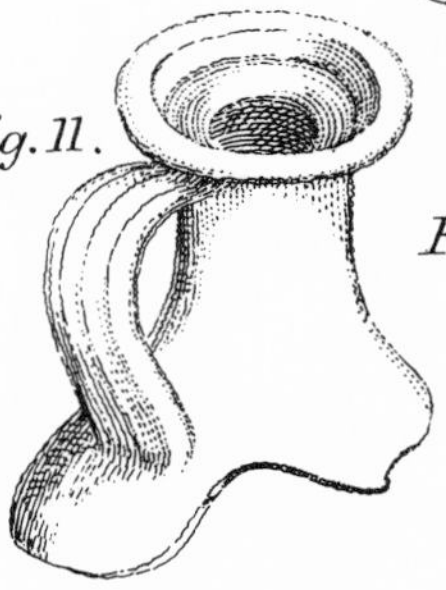

Fig. 15.

Fig. 14.

Fig. 16.

Longmate jc.

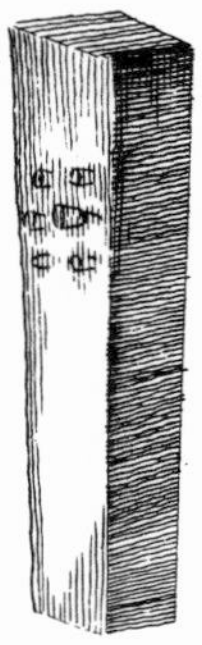

Thoresby pinx.   W. & J. Walker sculp.

ST. MARY LEICESTER,

Representing its Spire as it appeared after it was split by Lightning
July 10.th 1783 .

lessness of the age when it was formed. Dare we say that this was a labour of the inhabitants of this Island prior to the invasion of the Romans?

" The copper coin shewn in *Fig. d.* was shoveled from the top of one of the covering stones of the sewer *(Fig. e.)*, and was in high preservation. The legend of VRBS ROMA, and the galeated head of Rome on the Obverse, and the wolf, with the twins of Romulus and Remus on the Reverse, are commonly ascribed to Constantine the Great. The T. R. P. on the Exergue is the mint-mark, TR*everis* P*ercusse*. (Subauditur Moneta Trevas.)

Fig. f. on the same Plate was found, in August 1793, near the site of St. Peter's church, in the part below the Freeschool; and Mr. Throsby believed it to be the only gold coin ever found in Leicester. It was taken from the earth by a workman who was lowering the foot passage in the street; and was in the highest perfection; and is inscribed,

Obverse, " IMP*eratori* CAES*ari* NERV*œ* TRAIANO OPTIMO AVG*usto* GER*manico* DAC*ico*."

Reverse, " P*ontifici* M*aximo* TR*ibunitiœ* P*otestatis* COS. *i. e.* CONS*uli* VI. P*atri* P*atriœ* *senatus* P. Q. *populusque* R*omanus*."

Another coin, of inferior metal, nearly the size of the former, was found at the same time with the stones which have the inscriptions CICVR and MAR*T*NH; but Time had so defaced it, that the head was scarcely visible. On the reverse scarcely any thing was distinguishable, to make it differ, in appearance, from a lump of base metal injured by rust.

" To attempt a description of all the fragments of pottery would be vain; the variety is manifold both with respect to colour and formation. It is remarkable that none of the pieces, except one, are glazed, but those made of red clay: the exception is a small piece of thin black pottery delicately veined. When I compare this little beauty to many others which seem artless in their formation, their original use mysterious, and bearing about them no characteristic but clumsy strength; I am sometimes apt to conceive they, respectively, were in use at very distant periods. One piece of red clay has a rude representation of hunting: two figures appear in Roman military dresses; one pretty perfect.

" The glazed pottery has suffered nothing from time; many of the other it has much injured. Besides numbers of pieces which seemed formed for culinary purposes, there are a variety of different sized heads of vessels, of white clay, with thick short handles to the necks; on the whole not unlike the top of candlesticks.

" Figs. 4, 5, are singular pieces of pottery.

" Fig. 6, is the bone of an animal in a petrifying state.

" Figs. 7, 8, are representations of vessels, formed from fragments of pottery, to shew other original formations.—All these were found within the sewer.

" I shall now advert to other things, which form a part of this extraordinary discovery.

" Within the space of a yard of this antient sewer lay the base of two columns; and two shafts, each above a yard long, girth nearly a yard and three fourths; none of these lay below the blocks of stone which covered the shore. About the same time, but at the distance of thirty yards from these, was discovered, on a bed of fine red clay, at the depth of 12 feet, a capital of a column, made of the same sort of stone as the base and columns, and corresponding in every particular with them. I have put all the members of one column together in my garden. This, now it is erected, shews that it was originally hewn behind, to fit some rugged building, probably of Forest stone[1]. This column corresponds exactly with no order; it is of a purple hue. I observed that, in the centre of the shaft, where there had been originally a piece of square iron to hold the joints

together, that which remained of the iron was reduced to a rusty scale or mould. Near these columns lay two amazing strong foundations of a considerable building, made of Forest stone and grout; the extraordinary floor mentioned above joined to one of them.

" The workmen of Mr. Thomas Lomas, of this place, having been employed in the April following, in removing a portion of the earth which was formerly the Grey-Friars (the burial-place of Richard III.) for the purpose of making some additional buildings to his house there; they found, at the depth of two yards, a fragment of a Roman pavement formed of a variety of coloured squares, very small, but destitute of design. This discovery was, almost immediately, succeeded by that of an extraordinary formed vessel of stone, shallow, but in other respects like an apothecary's common sized mortar. It had several projections without, seemingly for strength; within, its circumference about four feet. Near the pavement were found many pieces of pottery, and part of a Roman tile, ornamented with parallel lines at equal distances.

" These pieces of pottery correspond exactly, in every particular, with those found in the sewer; and one of them *(Fig. 9.)* deserves more than ordinary notice. It is part of a large vessel of fine red clay, glazed, with a variety of devices and figures thereon, in relievo, on the outside; many of the ornaments agree exactly with the hunting piece noted above, but it is considerably larger. On one compartment is a figure like a mastiff dog, running; another represents a man in a Roman dress, in an attitude like dancing, with something like a snake in each hand, forming a half circle over his head with their tails; but these figures are so rude that I may be wrong in my conjecture. Under the man's feet is a hare hastily running. The next compartment, among other devices, shews a hound in full cry.

" One piece of pottery is exactly like that which I have already noticed as a censer, layered within with grit and small pebble. It is shewn in fig. 10. This, being a more perfect fragment, has a kind of outlet upon the rim, for pouring forth its contents, which rather staggers me in my opinion of these vessels. It is probable that they were *paterœ*, or goblets, used to catch the blood of the victim in sacrifice, which was afterwards poured upon the altar. This has two impressed inscriptions from the same instrument; and has, like the other, co, very legible at the beginning, followed by an aukward formed M, and a c, or o. When the characters are decyphered, we, perhaps, may have a juster knowledge of their use.

" Fig. 11. appears to be the top of a sort of bottle, of white clay, of which many were found in the sewer.

" These things, there can be no doubt, are of the age of those found within the sewer. That with figures, taken as a picture, is of superior excellence.

" The *Bone*, fig. 12. was dug from a grave in St. Martin's church; it appears to have been the broken bone of some person never properly set, or set by some bungler in his profession; in either case *Dame Nature* seems to have performed wonders.

Fig. 13. is a small urn, and Fig. 14. a leaden coffin[2], found in 1783, in digging for gravel in Mr. Hardy's farm-yard in Humberstone Gate.

Fig. 15. was found subsequently near the same spot. This probably Roman brick is three inches thick, and was originally 16 inches long, but a part now is broken off.

Fig. 16. is a small urn, found in 1811, at Sproxton in this county, containing exactly 100 silver coins; which was presented, by the Rev. William Mounsey, vicar of Sproxton, to his Grace the Duke of Rutland[3].

***In Plate XLVII. is given Mr. Throsby's View of St. Mary's Church at Leicester, as it appeared after the violent Storm of July 10, 1783.

---

[1] " Charnwood Forest, about nine miles from Leicester, presents some picturesque scenery of the rock which workmen say will not chisel into form. All the old foundations, so frequently discovered in Leicester, in the old part of the town, many of which take directions quite across the present streets, are made wholly of this durable rock."

[2] See Mr. Bickerstaffe's very accurate account of the contents of this Coffin in the former part of this Volume, p. 5*.—It appears that on the Coffin was placed a Bason, and round it six Urns, only one of which was perfect, nor was any thing within them.

[3] See the Additions to Sproxton, in Framland Hundred.

Of the Origin, Progress, and Present State of the Manufacture of Frame-worked Stockings.

" The manufacture of Hose has been the chief mean of the prosperity of LEICESTER. It has diffused, with a bountiful hand, amongst its inhabitants, riches and population. In this branch of commerce Leicester has no competitor of consequence but NOTTINGHAM. These places together form one grand machine, whose movement, at this time (A. D. 1792) is smooth and rapid, furnishing employment for 20,000!—This astonishing statement will be easily credited when the various branches employed in the manufactory are enumerated, viz. hosiers, stocking-makers, woolcombers, dyers, framesmiths, comb-makers, winders, sizers, seamers, spinners, bobbiners, sinker-makers, stocking-needle makers, &c. &c.—In Leicester there are upwards of seventy manufacturers called Hosiers, who, it is computed, employ 3000 frames, i. e. including the wrought goods they individually purchase. Out of the 14,000 souls in Leicester[1], 6000, it is conjectured, are employed or depend on one branch or other of this great business.

" The Rev. Mr. Ross, of Leicester, gave the publick, through the channel of the Leicester Journal, about the year 1788 an account of the first stocking-maker in Leicester. He says, " In the year 1680, *Alsop*, a Northamptonshire man, came to Leicester, and resided in the parish of All-Saints, at or near the North-gate-way, where he followed the occupation of stocking-making, being the only person of that trade in Leicester. His first apprentice was Samuel Parker, and with Samuel Parker was Samuel Wright, a man well known here by many who are now living. The same Samuel Wright, in the latter period of his life, kept a potter's shop near the High-cross, and died in the year 1768. About 30 years prior to his death, Wright communicated the above account to a person who is at this time alive, resident in Leicester.

" The family of *Poughfer*, in Leicester, was one of the first that made any great progress in the stocking business. It was the practice of hosiers, on the first establishment of the business in this place, to send their hose for sale on a horse in panniers. So great was the dislike, or rather prejudice of the lower orders of the people to the hose wrought in a frame, on account of the knitters, that when the business was about to be established, we are told, that the frames were set up in cellars, from the streets, and other secret places, where they were worked by night as well as day; a frame, in consequence, served two men.

" Deering, whose History of the Town of Nottingham was published in 1751, says, after enumerating the towns where the stocking business flourished the most; ' of all these none comes in competition with Leicester for quantity of goods; but even this very town, though it may boast of its large concerns, yet must confess that its best goods are made at Nottingham.' At this time (1792) most of the silk and fine hose continue to be made at that place, and the more ordinary at Leicester[2]."

As Dr. Deering's account of the origin of this useful art is the most circumstantial that has yet appeared, I shall here transcribe it:

" The inventor of the stocking-frame was one Mr. William Lee, M. A. of St. John's College in Cambridge, born at Woodborough, a village in Nottinghamshire, about seven miles from the town of Nottingham. He was heir to a pretty freehold estate; of whom the traditional story says: That he was deeply in love with a young townswoman of his, whom he courted for a wife; but she, whenever he went to visit her, seemed always more mindful of her knitting, than the addresses of her admirer; this slight created such an aversion in Mr. Lee, against knitting by hand, that he determined to contrive a machine, that should turn out work enough to render the common knitting a gainless employment: accordingly he set about it, and having an excellent mechanical head, he brought his design to bear in the year 1589; after he had worked a while, he taught his brother and several relations to work under him. Having for some years practised this his new art, at Calverton, a village about five miles from Nottingham; either himself or his brother James worked before queen Elizabeth, in order to shew an experiment of this kind of workmanship, offering at the same time this discovery of his to his countrymen, who instead of accepting the offer, despised him, and discouraged his invention: being thus discountenanced by his native country, and soon after invited over to France, with promise of great rewards, privileges, and honour, by king Henry IV. he embraced the seeming fair opportunity, and went himself, with nine workmen his servants, and as many frames, to the city of Roan, in Normandy; where they wrought with so great applause from the French, that in all likelihood the trade was to have been settled in that country for ever, had not the sudden murder of that monarch disappointed Mr. Lee of his expected grant of privilege, and the succeeding intestine troubles of that kingdom delayed his renewed suit, and at last frustrated all his hopes, at which, seized with grief, he ended his life at Paris. After his death, seven of his workmen (being left to shift for themselves) returned with their frames to England, two only remaining behind.

" These seven, with one Aston[3], who had been an apprentice to Mr. Lee, and by him was before left at home, and who also added something to his master's invention, did lay the foundation of this manufacture in England; and in the space of fifty years, this art was so improved, and the number of able workmen become so great; that the heads among them thought it necessary for the better regulating their members, and keeping this valuable business from spreading abroad, to petition Oliver Cromwell, to constitute them a body corporate, which however, for what reason I cannot tell, they did not obtain at that time. Their petition is wrote in the language of the time, but with so much strength, and giving so good an account of the usefulness and public advantage of this manufacture, that it deserves perpetuating, wherefore I have given it a place[4].

" King Charles II. after the Restoration granted them at last a charter[5]; by which their jurisdiction extended to ten miles round London.

" In process of time, when the trade spread farther into the country, they also in proportion stretched their authority and established commissioners in the several principal towns in the county where this trade was exercised; there they held courts, at which they obliged the country framework knitters to bind and make free, &c. whereby they (for many years) drew great sums of money, till some person, of more spirit than others, in Nottingham brought their authority in question; and a trial ensuing, the company was cast. Since that time the stocking manufacture has continued entirely open in the country.

---

[1] The Return of the Population in Leicester in 1801, was 16,933 (see p. 534) : in 1811 it was 23,146.
[2] Throsby's History of Leicester, 1792, p. 401.
[3] This Aston was some time a miller at Thoroton, near which place he was born. Thoroton, p. 297.
[4] See this Petition in the Appendix to Deering's Nottingham, p. 301—308.
[5] " The Fraternity of Stocking-weavers was incorporated by letters patent of the fifteenth of Charles the Second, 19 Aug. 1663, by the name of the Master, Wardens, Assistants, and Society of the Art and Mystery of Framework-knitters, in the Cities of London and Westminster, the Kingdom of England, and Dominion of Wales. This Company consists of a master, two wardens, eighteen assistants, and fifty-eight liverymen, whose fine for the livery is ten pounds. They have a small, but convenient hall, in Redcross-street, to dispatch their affairs in." Maitland's History of London, p. 1245.—Their arms are, a Stocking-frame proper. Motto, SPEED, STRENGTH, AND TRUTH, UNITED. See Plate XLV. fig. 16.

" Nor

" Nor did these large sums do the company any service as a body; for, as they got the money illegally, so they spent it as lavishly, and instead of growing rich, the company became very poor; and many of their heads, having got a taste of high living and neglecting their business also dwindled to nothing. To which add, that within these thirty years last past [this was written in 1751] the merchants and hosiers in London, finding they could be fitted from the country with as good work at a cheaper rate than the London framework-knitters could afford; the bulk of that trade has since shifted from thence, and the chief dependance they had left was upon what is called *Fashion work*, it being for many years the mode to wear stockings of the same colour of the cloaths; and this also being by degrees left off, what remains now in London, does hardly deserve the name of trade.

" There are, besides the capital of England, ten towns in the country where this manufacture is carried on: viz. in Nottinghamshire, Nottingham and Mansfield; in Leicestershire, Leicester, Mount-Sorrel, Loughborough, Hinckley, and Ashby-de-la-Zouch; in Northamptonshire, Towcester; in Surrey, Godliman; in Derbyshire, Derby [1].

" Of all these none comes in competition with Leicester for quantity of goods; but even this very town, though it may boast of its large concerns, yet must confess, that its best goods are made at Nottingham, where by far the greatest part of the richest and most valuable commodity, whether of silk, cotton, thread, or worsted, is wrought; and it seems this so profitable employment, as it were by a magnetical force, is in the height of its improved state drawn towards the place of its birth, in order to make it ample amends for deserting it in its infancy [2]."

The principal trade of the town is that of making stockings, of which alderman Cowper, the chief manager of it in 1712, gave this account: That 20,000 todd of wool is wrought up yearly in the manufacture of hose, which employs in the town and country about 1,000 hands, to sort, comb, and dye; 6,000 to spin, double, and throw; 6,000

to weave, seam, and dress up; and that the improvement amounts to six times the value of the wool in the lowest sort of hose, and above that in the fine sort [3].

" A very lucrative branch of the frame business was established at Leicester by the late Mr. *Whiteman*, called *Machine pieces*; which displayed a wonderful variety of colours and forms. Some of his workmen, it is said, have earned on this fancy-work nearly 2l. 2s. *per* week, when the ordinary stocking-makers could scarcely gain, by hard labour, one fourth of the sum [4]."

" The manufactory of stockings in the Town and County of Leicester is the largest in the world; besides worsted wove hose, which are the staple article of the place, a great variety of cotton hose are now made, which from their cheapness obtain a sale in this and most other countries [5]."

A stocking-frame was introduced in *Hinckley* so early as 1640, by Mr. *William Iliff*; whose immediate descendant Mr. Joseph Iliff, after having carried on the manufacture there with much reputation for more than half a century, died universally respected, March 5, 1795, at the age of 76 [6].

Of the same family (the son of Mr. Iliff's only sister) is John Green, esq. of Hinckley; than whom few men have carried on the profession with more ability, or with more success. He was also for some years a very diligent and active Captain of the Hinckley Volunteers; and is now (1811) Lieutenant-colonel of one of the four regiments of the Leicestershire Local Militia.

In 1778, the number of frames in Hinckley were 864; which furnished employment for 2585 persons; and from that period the increase has been very great; as that town stands, as taken in May 1811, agreeable to the act 51 George III. for taking an account of the population of Great Britain, 1126 houses, occupied by 1244 families, which contained 2872 males, 3186 females; total of inhabitants 6058. And at the same time 1550 stocking-frames were found at work in the parish of Hinckley.

[1] Mr. Hutton, the Historian of Derby, p. 190, speaking of the invention of the Stocking-frame, says, " The art was founded in revenge, and revenge in love. In process of time the machine found its way into Derby, and promised to become a staple trade; but the silk-mill being introduced, and the wages tempting, it was foretold, " that the hosiery would stagnate." The event verified the prediction; and *frames* are not more numerous than they were seventy years ago. There were (in 1791) about 150 in the place."

[2] " There are at this time (1751) in Nottingham fifty manufacturers, employers of frames, or as they are commonly called putters out, who all trade directly to London, besides those who can only deal with Leicester: both together occupy 3000 frames, of which upwards of 1200 are employed in Nottingham, and the rest in the villages about, who buy their provisions and other necessaries in this town: upon the just mentioned frames entirely depends, the masters, 3000 workmen, and a considerable number of winders, sizers and seamers; woolcombers, frame-smiths, setters up, sinkermakers, stocking-needle makers, not reckoning those trades who in part get their livelihood by this manufacture, as joyners, turners, &c, in the whole upwards of 4000." Deering, pp. 99—101. See also, in his Appendix, p. 364, a more particular description of the stocking-frame, with two copper-plates, and also one plate of the different constituent parts of this curious machine. See Evelyn on Medals, p. 163.

Prefixed to a Poem published, by T. Baldwin, at Hinckley, 1776, and addressed, by Moses Ford, of that place, to the Gentlemen Hosiers, Frame-work-knitters, Framesmiths, &c. &c. of the several counties of Leicester, Nottingham, Derby, &c. on the rise, progress, and present state of the ingenious art of frame-work-knitting, is the following historical note: " The English and French have greatly contested the honour of the invention of the Stocking-frame; but whatever pretensions the French may claim to this invention, it was certainly invented by William Lee, of St. John's College, Cambridge, in the year 1589: but it does not appear that Mr. Lee ever received any hint, from any person whatever, relative to this great invention; but according to tradition, Mr. Lee paid his addresses to a young lady of great beauty and fortune, and one day he surprized her in a grove, knitting a fine silk stocking; and it was in this grove that the young lady gave Mr. Lee an absolute refusal of her hand, which so offended Mr. Lee, that he declared, he would invent a machine that should be a means of spoiling the knitters trade; so that it seems either love or revenge was the first moving cause to this great invention. However, soon after Mr. Lee had completed the stocking-frame, he petitioned Queen Elizabeth for her royal encouragement, but this petition was rejected; therefore, despairing of success in his own country, he went to France, and applied to Lewis the Thirteenth, for his royal encouragement and protection. Accordingly Mr. Lee continued at his court for some time, and the French King was so pleased with the ingenious art of frame-work-knitting, that he had a frame made of silver, for his own use, and he really learned the art of frame-work-knitting himself; and the said silver frame is kept in Paris, as one of the greatest curiosities in France. After the King had set the royal example, most of the French nobles learned it; but Lewis the Thirteenth, as a greater encouragement, issued out an order, that all persons that were willing to serve an apprenticeship to learn this art, should be allowed to wear a sword, which honour no other mechanic is permitted to do in France. In consequence of this order such numbers learnt it, that it is said there were several thousand of frame-work-knitters in Paris. Some few years after, Mr. Lee received an invitation to return to his native country, which he accepted; and soon after the art of frame-work-knitting became famous in England, and Charles the First, with a great many of his nobles, learned it; and it is said, that, as Mr. Lee had gained so much honour both at home and abroad by this invention, his former lover nobly gave him her hand, and crowned his wishes and ingenuity with her person."—I quote this paragraph as a matter of curiosity, without vouching for its historical exactness.

[3] Letter from the Rev. Samuel Carte to Browne Willis, esq. in 1712. [4] Throsby's History of Leicester, 1792, p. 401.
[5] Walk through Leicester, 1804, p. 147; where " a full account of this manufactory in all its branches" is announced as " ready for the press;" but this, I believe, has not yet been published. [6] See vol. IV. p. 691.

MAYORS AND CHAMBERLAINS OF LEICESTER; continued from p. 451.

Sept. 21, 1807, *Thomas Wright* elected mayor; Thomas Bryan, Thomas Cook, chamberlains.

Sept. 21, 1808, *Samuel Clarke* elected mayor; William Thompson, James Burbidge, chamberlains.

Sept. 21, 1809, *William Firmadge* elected mayor;

Charles Coleman, Thomas Marston, chamberlains.

Sept. 21, 1810, *David Harris* elected mayor; H. Wood, W. Hill, chamberlains.

Sept. 21, 1811, *John Stevenson* elected mayor; Mansfield Gregory, —— Higginson, chamberlains.

HONOUR OF LEICESTER.

THIS Honour appears to have been created by the following grant from king John, in the first year of his reign, to Robert (Fitzparnell) the fourth Norman earl of Leicester, who then enjoyed not only the antient possessions of the earldom derived from the earl of Mellent, but also the baronies of Hinckley and Groby, and other large possessions of his maternal ancestor Hugo de Grentesmainell:

"Johannes, Dei gratiâ, &c. Sciatis quod concedimus, volumus, & precipimus, quod Robertus comes Leicestrie & heredes sui post eum habeant & teneant, de nobis & heredibus nostris, omnes terras suas & feoda sua, cum omnibus libertatibus & liberis consuetudinibus suis, benè & in pacè, & honorificè, liberè, & quietè de sectis schirarum & hundredorum, & auxilio . vicecomitum, sive capiatur' per hydatas terre, sive per carucatas, & de pecuniâ dandâ pro murdro & latrocinio, & de denario ad francumplegium pertinentibus; & preterea concedimus eis Tol & The'am, & Infengenthef, & Soch & Sach, & quietanciam de Dominicis suis per Dominica nostra de Pontagio, Passagio, Thelonio, Pedagio, Pa'agio, Stallagio, Tallagio, Geldis & Danegeld', Blodwite, Fithwite, Operationibus Castellorum, Murorum, Pontium,. Parcorum, Fossatorum, Calcearum & Domorum; & quod habeant liberam Chaceam, &c. &c."

The abovenamed earl of Leicester died without issue, in the sixth year of king John, leaving his two sisters coheiresses to his great estates; viz. Amicia wife of Simon de Montfort, and Margaret wife of Saiher de Quincy, between whom the earl's estates were divided; and Simon de Montfort had a moiety of the Honour of Leicester, with the Barony of Hinckley, and was created earl of Leicester. The partition was thus confirmed by king John, in the eighth year of his reign.

"Johannes, &c. Sciatis nos concessisse & presenti cartâ confirmâsse partionem factam coram nobis & baronibus nostris per Simonem de Montforti comitem de Leycestrie, & Saiherum de Quenci comitem Wintonie, de omnibus terris & honoribus que fuerunt comitis Roberti Leycestrie die quo obiit, cum omnibus pertinentiis· suis, ita scilicet quod tota medietas illarum terrarum & honorum in dominiis & feodis & omnibus aliis rebus & locis remanet uni illorum comitum, & altera medietas alteri. Salvis predicto comiti Simoni tertio denario comitatûs Leicestrie & senescalcia nostra, ita etiam quod xx librate terre de parte comitis Simonis remanebunt prefato comiti Saihero, preter partem suam quousque similiter deliberavit eidem comiti Saihero rationabilem partem suam de terrâ que fuit prenominati comitis Roberti in Normanniâ, &c."

Simon earl of Leicester left two sons, Simon and Almaric; the former was earl of Montfort in France, and resigned the title of Leicester, with its possessions, to his brother. The instrument of disclaimer is set forth in the Appendix to the First Part of this Volume, p. 41.

Simon, the younger son, who in consequence succeeded to the earldom of Leicester, was slain in the battle of Evesham (1265); and he was afterwards attainted, and his lands were seized.

King Henry the Third immediately gave the inheritance of the earldom of Leicester to his youngest son Edmund; and it afterwards became, and remains to this day, parcel of the Duchy of Lancaster. This point is stated in the Appendix to this Volume, page 41, where many other grants and charters are set forth concerning the Honour of Leicester; and in page 48 of such Appendix, all the towns in the county of Leicester, which are within the Honour of Leicester, and jurisdiction· of the Duchy of Lancaster, are enumerated.

At this day a Steward, and Bailiff for the Honour are appointed by the Duchy of Lancaster, as well as a Constable of the Castle of Leicester.

A Court of Pleas is held at the Castle, from three weeks to three weeks, before the Steward, who also holds views of frank-pledge at the Castle, and various other places within the Honour; and all replevins on distresses taken within the Honour are granted by the Steward instead of the Sheriff; also the execution of all process within the Honour of right belongs to the Bailiff of the Honour; but, for convenience, the Bailiff allows the Sheriff to enter the Honour on making a compensation for the profits.

The Mayor of Leicester is required by charter personally to appear in the Court of Pleas for the Honour on Monday next after St. Martin in the winter, and there take an oath " well and faithfully to observe and perform all and singular the ancient customs, jurisdictions, privileges, and pre-eminences, of the Duchy of Lancaster, within the Borough of Leicester, during his mayoralty."

The men and tenants of the said Honour have time immemorial been free, quit, and exempt from payment of toll for all their goods and things, in and throughout the realm of England, and had been so time immemorial. King Henry IV. granted his letters mandatory, under the Great Seal of England, at the town of Leicester, the 24th day of May, in the 4th year of his reign, in hæc verba:

"Henricus, Dei gratiâ, Rex Anglie & Francie & d'nus Hibernie, universis & singulis vicecomitibus, majoribus, ballivis, constabulariis, ministris, ac aliis fidelibus & subditis suis, tam infra libertates quam extra, ad quos presentes littere pervenerint, salutem. Cum, secundum consuetudinem in regno nostro Anglie hactenus optentum & approbatum, homines & tenentes Honoris de Leycestr', à tempore quo non extat memoria, quieti esse consueverint, a presentatione theolonei, pontagii, picagii, muragii, panagii, stallagii, passagii, lastagii, & cariagii, pro bonis & rebus suis, per totum regnum nostrum; vobis & cuilibet vestrum præcipimus, firmiter injungentes, quod omnes & singulos homines & tenentes Honoris predicti de hujusmodo theoloneo, pontagio, picagio, muragio, panagio, stallagio, passagio, lastagio, & cariagio, vobis seu alicui vestrûm, pro bonis & rebus suis, præstand' quietos esse permittatis juxta consuetudinem supradictam, & prout ipsi inde quieti esse debent, ipsique & antecessores homines & tenentes Honoris predicti à tempore predicto hactenùs rationabiliter quieti esse consueverunt. Test. meipso apud Villam Leycestrie, 24 die Maii, anno regni nostri quarto. Wymbysh."

King Edward VI. granted his letters mandatory, tested at Westminster, the 28th day of November, in the first year of his reign, in the same words as the former.

The men and tenants of the said honour of Leicester have accordingly all along used and enjoyed the aforesaid privileges and liberties of all places in England, without any hindrance or molestation, upon producing a certificate under the hand and seal of the Steward of the Honour, or his deputy, signifying that the bearer is a tenant or inhabitant within the Honour.

The antient form of certificate, which is still used, is as follows:

"To all and singular sheriffs, bailiffs, toll-gatherers, and other officers, ministers, and subjects of our sovereign lord the King, to whom in this case it shall appertain: Whereas, by divers of the King's majesty's most noble progenitors, kings and queens of the kingdom of England. (amongst sundry other privileges, protections, and liberties, given, granted, and confirmed unto the Duchy of Lancaster), it is given, granted, and by acts of parliament confirmed, that as well the officers as the tenants inhabiting and resident of and in the said Duchy, and every of them, shall be freed, acquitted, and discharged, of and from all theolonage, pannage, pontage, passage, . lastage, tollage, carriage, pessage, pickage, and terriage, for his and their goods, cattle, chattels, merchandize, and wares, by and through the whole realm of England, in all and singular markets, fairs, towns,

towns, and places, as well within liberties as without (except in towns and places being of the same Duchy); and that neither they nor any of them, nor their or any of their goods, cattle, chattels, factors, or servants, shall be distrained, exacted, molested, or impeached in the premises by any person or persons whomsoever (except as before excepted), upon pain to forfeit to our said sovereign lord the King, his heirs and successors, the sum of one hundred pounds, and to the parties aggrieved their damages besides; Now know ye, that I, Thomas Pares the younger, esquire, Steward of the Honour of Leicester, parcel of the said Duchy, do hereby certify, that A. B. the bearer hereof, is one of his Majesty's tenants, and inhabits and resides at S. in the county of Leicester, within the said Honour, parcel of the said Duchy, and is therefore intitled to the privileges, protections, and liberties aforesaid. Given under my hand and seal, &c."

The like priority and exemption is enjoyed by the burgesses of the Borough of Leicester, which is parcel of the Honour, on producing a certificate under the hand and seal of the Mayor.

The form of the certificate, as granted by the corporation of Leicester to a burgess in the mayoralty of Edmund Cradock, 1657, is this:

" To all Christian people to whom this present writinge shall come. The maior, bailiffs, and burgesses, of the burrough of Leicester, in the county of Leicester, send greetinge in our Lord God everlastinge. Know yee, that whereas, as well by letters pattents of Kinge John, sometimes Kinge of England, &c. bearinge date the sixe and twentyeth day of December, in the first yeare of his raigne; as also by divers other grauuts, statutes, and acts of parliament, of Edward the Third, Henry the Fourth, Henry the Fifth, Henry the Sixth, Edward the Fourth, Henry the Seaventh, sometymes also kings of England; and also by divers other grauuts, confirmations, statutes, and concessions, of Henry the Eighth, Edward the Sixth, also sometymes late kings of England, and of the lady Elizabeth, sometymes queene of England, and of the late King James; it is graunted, enacted, appoynted, established, and confirmed, that all and singuler tenents of the Honour of Leicester, holden of the Dutchy of Lancaster, and more especially the maior and burgesses of the burrough of Leicester, shall have, enjoy, and use (amongst other things) their liberties, priviledges, and immunities following, that is to say, that they shall be quitt of all and all manner of toles, pannages, passages, lastages, stallages, pessages, pitchages, terrages, murages, carriages, and stannages, whatsoever, in and thorough the realme of England, as well by sea as by land, for all their goods and merchandizes whatsoever, without any molestation, as by the said letters pattents, grauuts, statutes, and confirmations, remayninge upon record, more at large it doth appeare. And because many from tyme to tyme (as it is said) doe clayme the said liberties, priviledges, and immunities aforesaid, which are not of the company of burgesses of the borough of Leicester aforesaid, nor ought to be quitt from such toles and payments: Know yee therefore now moreover, that wee the said maior, bayliffes, and burgesses, to you and every of you, by tenor of theis presents, doe certifye that William Newton, vintner, is one of the burgesses of the burrough of Leicester aforesaid, and that the said privileges and immunities, by force of the said grauuts and confirmations, freely and quietly hee ought to haue and enjoy; wee therefore again instantly by theis presents doe desire and require that the said William Newton, and every other burgesse of the said burrough of Leicester, freely and quietly you will suffer to goe and returne with their goods and merchandizes whatsoever, without any of your letts or molestations, or without takinge or clayminge of them, or any of them, any tole, pannage, passage, lastage, stallage, pessage, pitchage, terrage, murage, carriage, and stanage, contrary to the liberties and immunities aforesaid,

and for you and every of your more full satisfaction herein, that the said William Newton is one of the burgesses of the said burrough of Leicester as aforesaid, wee make you theis and our letters testimoniall; and for the better strengtheninge and confirminge thereof, wee have hereunto put our common seale of the burrough of Leicester aforesaid, dated at the Guildhall of the said burrough of Leicester, the tenth day of March, in the year of our Lord, one thousand sixe hundred fifty and seaven.

ABEL COLES, common clerk here.
EDM. CRADOCK, maior."

In the 11th year of queen Anne a cause was tried between George Bent, gent. (one of the men of Leicester) plaintiff, and Thomas Gisbourne, esq. mayor of Derby, and Isaac Barker, his toll-gatherer, defendants, in an action of trover, for one heifer taken by defendants at Derby for non-payment of toll; which cause, by consent of all parties, was tried at Nottingham, and the plaintiff succeeded therein; but the action being in trover, the point then in question does not appear.

In another cause, tried in 1743, between Thomas Ayre the younger, plaintiff, and John Hornbuckle, esq. mayor of Bedford, and John Marchant his toll-gatherer, defendants, the following arguments were urged in the plaintiff's brief:

Mr. Ayre the plaintiff lives at Leicester, and is, and for several years past hath been, a very considerable grazier, and a freeman of the town of Leicester, and as such entitled to the aforesaid liberties and privileges; and it being necessary for him to take his cattle to divers fairs and markets in order to sell them; therefore, that they might pass and re-pass unmolested upon account of toll, he obtained a certificate, dated the 25th of March, 1737, under the hand of William Brushfield, then mayor of Leicester, and under the common seal of the said town of Leicester, signifying that he the said Mr. Ayre was a freeman of Leicester, and as such was entitled to the aforesaid liberties and privileges; and Mr. Ayre hath, subsequent to such certificate, taken his cattle to a great many fairs and markets, which have always been permitted to pass and re-pass toll-free, without any hindrance or molestation whatsoever, upon producing the said certificate, until the instance now in question.

Mr. Ayre the plaintiff sent a drove of cattle to a fair held at Bedford the 8th of December, 1743; and having about ten or twelve of them undisposed of, thought proper to send them to Newport Pagnell in the county of Bucks; and it being necessary for them to pass over the bridge over the river Ouze at Bedford, in their road to Newport aforesaid, that they might pass over the bridge unmolested, delivered his certificate to defendant Hornbuckle, then mayor of the town of Bedford, for his perusal and satisfaction that he the said Mr. Ayre was entitled to the said liberties and privileges; but Hornbuckle, after he had kept the certificate some time for his perusal, returned it, with answer that he should order the cattle to be stopped upon refusal of payment of toll for them; and on the next day, being the 9th of December, as plaintiff's servant was driving the cattle over the said bridge, defendant Marchant stopped them, and would not permit them to pass over without toll paid for them, although the plaintiff's said certificate was then produced to him; but, after some dispute, let them all pass except the two steers in question, which he still stopped for the toll of the whole drove; and after some more time spent in disputing about the toll, the residue of the drove being gone over the bridge along the road, plaintiff's servant was obliged to leave the said two steers to the pleasure of Marchant, and in his custody upon or near to the said bridge, in order to follow and take care of the others which were gone along the road. That Marchant, after having kept the said two steers for about an hour upon or near to the said bridge, impounded them; therefore plaintiff brought this action to obtain a satisfaction for his damages."

The plaintiff obtained a verdict.

HONOUR

HONOUR OF WINTON.

THIS Honour was originally part of the Honour of Leicester, and the reason of its obtaining that name appears to have been as follows: Saier de Quincy, who married Margaret, one of the two sisters and coheiresses of Robert (Fitz Parnell) earl of Leicester, and had, in her right, half of the earldom of Leicester, was created earl of Winchester; to which earl succeeded Roger de Quincy his son, who obtained a grant from king Henry the Third, in the 36th year of his reign, of all the liberties named in the charter, which king John made to the earl of Leicester, of the Honour of Leicester, "ita quod idem Rogerus et heredes sui de cætero ita plene et integre prædictis libertatibus utantur et gaudeant in medietate prædicti Honoris ac si totus Honor ille in manu sua existeret." This grant may be termed the creation of the Honour of Winchester. Earl Roger died in 1264; and an inquisition was taken about that time, which particularly describes the knight's fees which appertained to the Honour.

Earl Roger leaving three daughters his heirs, viz. Margaret the wife of William de Ferrars earl of Derby, Elizabeth married to Alexander Comyn, earl of Buchan in Scotland, and Ellen to Alan le Zouch, the inheritance of the Honour of Winton was divided between them; and that part which Margaret de Ferrers had, she gave to her second son William de Ferrars, with the possessions of the barony of Grooby, together with the perquisites of the court of the Honour of Winton.

King Edward the Fourth, in the 13th year of his reign, ratified and confirmed by inspeximus to sir John Bourchier, knt. and Elizabeth his wife, kinswoman and heir of Roger de Quincy earl of Winton, the charters which were granted by king John to the earl of Leicester, and by king Henry to the earl of Winton.

The abovenamed Elizabeth Bourchier was the grand-daughter and sole heir of William de Ferrars of Grooby, and had been previously married to sir Edward Grey; to her issue by whom this Honour descended, with the barony of Groby, and now belongs to George-Harry Grey, earl of Stamford and Warrington.

The courts for the Honour continue to be held regularly at Leicester, and Nun-Eaton; as well as occasionally at Syston, and other manors belonging to the Honour.

At the Easter court at Leicester, according to antient custom, a shilling is brought into the court-room in a sack-bag across a cowl-staff borne on two men's shoulders, when a scuffle ensues, and the man who can first get possession of the bag has the shilling.

ECCLESIASTICAL JURISDICTION—LEICESTERSHIRE.

Leicester is situated in the diocese of Lincoln and province of Canterbury; it was once a bishop's see, but is now governed by an archdeacon, who exercises jurisdiction over the whole of the county (with the exception of the peculiars hereafter mentioned).—The jurisdiction of the archdeaconry is inhibited once in three years by the lord bishop of the diocese, who holds his triennial visitation once in the above period.—The court of the archdeacon's official is held in the South aile of the parish church of St. Martin in Leicester.

There are several peculiar jurisdictions within the County.

The Peculiar of *St. Margaret in Leicester* is a prebendal one; it is founded in the Cathedral Church of the Blessed Virgin Mary in Lincoln, and extends over the parish of Saint Margaret, and the chapelry of Knighton, which lies contiguous to Leicester[1]. A Prebendary exercises spiritual cognizance over this exempt district, and holds his court in the church of Saint Margaret; in which court, he has the power of proving wills, granting administrations, marriage licences, &c.—The patronage of St. Margaret is also vested in the Prebendary.—The rev. John Palmer, B. A. is the present Prebendary. See the Prebendal Seal, with those of the Commissary and Official, in Plate XLI. figs. 7, 8, 9, p. 558. Another Official Seal is given in Plate XLIX. fig. 5.

The Peculiar of *Rothley*[2] is exempt from the general ecclesiastical jurisdiction: this peculiar, extends over the villages of Rothley, Wikeham, Gaddesby, Keam (two or three houses in which I believe, are subject to the archdeacon's power), Grimstone, Wartnaby, Caldwell; it also includes certain parts of Somerby, South Croxton, Mountsorrel, Baresby, and Saxulby; but the churches and chapels belonging to these latter villages and town are in the archdeaconry.—The rev. Thomas Robinson, M. A. (vicar of St. Mary in Leicester) is the present commissary of this peculiar: he holds his court in the parish church of Rothley.

The Peculiar of *Groby*[3] includes the villages of Ratby, Groby, Botcheston, Newtown Linford, Glenfield (the church of which is supposed to be in the archdeaconry), and Swithland: parts of Ansty, Cropston, and Stanton under Bardon, are also in this peculiar. The Rev. Robert Martin of Ansty is the present commissary of this jurisdiction.

The Peculiar of *Evington*[4] is governed by a commissary, who holds his court in the church at Evington: rev. Mr. Sherrard Coleman is the present commissary.

In a State of the Archdeaconry of Leicester 1564, *Bowden Magna* is mentioned among the Peculiars, as an Impropriation belonging to Christ Chu. Oxford[5].

The venerable and highly-esteemed vicar of Greenwich (Dr. Burnaby) is the present Archdeacon of Leicester: he holds his visitation twice in every year.

CANAL FROM LEICESTER TO MARKET HARBOROUGH.

An act of parliament having been obtained, for varying the line of communication of the intended Canal from Leicester to the River Nen (see p. clxviii.); the work, which had been for some time suspended, was renewed with great industry; and the *Leicestershire and Northamptonshire Union Canal* is now completed as far as Market Harborough.

Nov. 20, 1810, at the Half-yearly General Meeting of the Proprietors of this Canal, held at the Bell inn, Leicester, Richard Gresley, esq. in the chair, a very favourable report from the Committee was read; stating the great increase of tonnages, since the opening of the Canal to Harborough, and the evident advantages which will accrue from the intended line from that place to Stamford; and it was unanimously resolved, to give, collectively and individually, the most strenuous support to that undertaking. It was also unanimously resolved, that the Chairman of the Committee, and two other members, be deputed to present to Joseph Cradock, esq. a gilt cup, as a tribute of the said Company's respect for the uniform attention he has shewn on every occasion to the said Company and its interests; and to convey the high sense which the Company entertain of Mr. Cradock's assistance, during the progress, and to the opening of the said Canal to Market Harborough.

A Plan of the immense Reservoir of this Canal, near Gumley and Saddington, surveyed by J. Varley, junior, in 1797, is here given in Plate XLVIII. at the expence of the worthy Chairman.

The Seals of three of the Leicestershire Canal Companies[6] are here given, in Plate XLIX.

---

[1] See p. 561.   [2] Of the Peculiar of Rothley, see vol. III. p. 953; and also the Seal of the Commissary, p. 961, Plate CXXX
[3] See more particulars of the Peculiar of Groby, vol. IV. 632.   [4] See further particulars of the Peculiar of Evington, vol. II. 559.
[5] See vol. II. p. 475.   [6] Ashby de la Zouch, Loughborough, and Melton Mowbray.

DOMESDAY

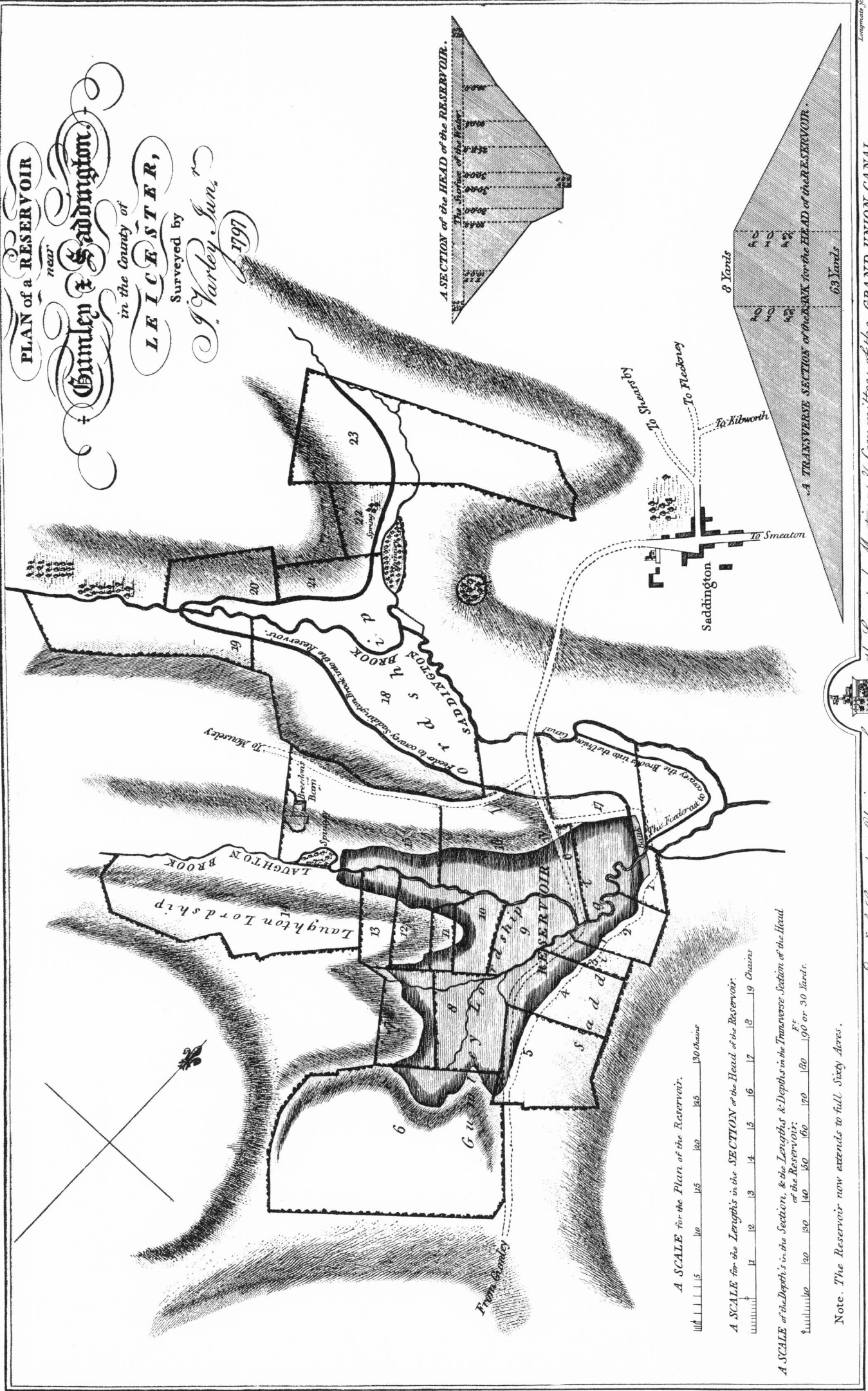

PLAN of a RESERVOIR near Grimley & Saddington in the County of LEICESTER, Surveyed by J. Varley Jun. 1797

A SECTION of the HEAD of the RESERVOIR.

A TRANSVERSE SECTION of the BANK for the HEAD of the RESERVOIR.

8 Yards

63 Yards

Longmate fc.

To Shearsby

To Fleckney

To Kibworth

To Smeaton

Saddington

SADDINGTON BROOK

LAUGHTON BROOK

Laughton Lordship

Grimley Lordship

RESERVOIR

Breedon's Barn

To Mowsley

From Grimley

A SCALE for the Plan of the Reservoir.

A SCALE for the Lengths in the SECTION of the Head of the Reservoir.

A SCALE of the Depths in the Section, & the Lengths & Depths in the Transverse Section of the Head of the Reservoir.

Note. The Reservoir now extends to full Sixty Acres.

To JOSEPH CRADOCK Esq.r of Gumley, Chairman of the General Meetings & Committees of the GRAND UNION CANAL, much obliged & faithful Friend & Servant J. Nichols. this Plan is respectfully inscribed by his

Throsby pinx.   *Millar sculp.*

TRINITY HOSPITAL,

as it appeared in 1790.

Fig. 1.

Fig. 2.

ASHBY DE LA ZOUCH CANAL COMPANY

NE TENTES AUT PERFICE

HAY. SC.

MDCCXCIV

TENDIMUS IN LATIUM.

Fig. 3.

THE
SEAL OF THE
COMPANY
OF THE
PROPRIETORS
OF THE
NAVIGATION
FROM THE RIVER
TRENT TO THE
TOWN OF
LOUGHBOROUGH.
MDCCLXXVI.

J. Webster del.

Fig. 4.

Fig. 5.

Longmate del. et sc.

DOMESDAY BOOK.

The four following articles in Domesday I have not been able to appropriate.

Twelve ploughlands in *Cliborne*, which in the time of king Edward had employed ten ploughs, and were valued at forty shillings, were worth sixty shillings at the general survey, when they were held by Robert de Veci. In the demesne were three ploughs and six bondmen ; and ten villans, with six socmen and six bordars and one foreigner, had five ploughs. There were sixteen acres of meadow[1]. Robert de Veci had three houses in the borough of Leicester, with sac and soc belonging to Cliborne[2].

Nine ploughlands all but one yard land in *Elvestone*, which in the reign of the Confessor had been valued at twenty shillings, were worth thirty shillings at the general survey, when they were held by Hugo de Grentemaisnell. The land was equal to six ploughs. Thirteen socmen, with one villan and two bordars, had four ploughs. There were twenty acres of meadow[3].

Four ploughlands in *Plotelei*, which in the time of king Edward had been held by Leuric, employed four ploughs, and were valued at ten shillings, were worth thirty shillings at the general survey, when they were held by Robert, one of the homagers of the earl of Mellent. Two ploughs were then in the demesne, and two bondmen ; and four villans, with one bordar, had one plough. There were two acres of meadow[4].

At the general survey *Nigell* held three waste ploughlands in *Windesers* under Henry de Ferieres. In the time of king Edward this land was held freely by Aluric, and employed two ploughs[5].

ADDITIONS AND CORRECTIONS.

In the *List of Baronets*, p. xlvii*. *add thus :*

" In the chancel of Combe Flory church, Somersetshire, a mural monument of white and Sienna marble is thus inscribed :

" Sacred to the memory of Alexander Malet, M. A. rector of this parish, and of Maiden Newton in the county of Dorset ; and a prebendary of the church of Gloucester ; whose exemplary virtues added dignity to his profession, and lustre to the antient family from whom he was descended. He was a kind husband, an affectionate parent, and a cordial friend. To his surviving acquaintance his death is an inestimable loss ; to himself the commencement of an endless felicity. He died Sept. 19, 1775, aged 71." Arms : Azure, three escallops Or, *Malet* ; impaling, Argent, on a bend Sable, three annulets Or, *St. Lo*[6].—" This gentleman's preferments all together produced 700*l.* a year. He had two sons and three daughters ; 1. Charles, who under the patronage of Mr. Boddam, when governor of Bombay, in about 26 years acquired not quite 100,000*l.* and has purchased an estate in Somersetshire, which an eminent attorney, who married one of his sisters, looked out for him. Another sister was the wife of colonel Dunsey, of the third regiment of guards, and aid de camp to the king, who died at St. Domingo, Feb. 1794. (Gent. Mag. vol. LXIV. p. 279.) Her other sister is believed to be unmarried : and his younger brother was named Alexander." R. G.

P. 321. 1307, 1 Edw. II. by writ ad quod dampnum, Thomas duke of Lancaster was allowed, &c. to give 3 messuages, 4 acres and 1 rood of land with xxii*s.* to the hospital of St. Leonard.

1322-3, 16 Edw. II. a grant of Simon de Montford, earl of Leicester, of 7*l.* 9*s.* 1*d.* was confirmed.

1 Edw. III. 1327. Philip Danet was permitted to give 3 messuages and 5 virgates and a half of land.

P. 294. The ring here mentioned was not found in the Abbey meadow, but, in a field on the other (the South) side Leicester, called St. Mary's field.

P. 324. A pension of 10*s.* was payable to the Bishop of Lincoln, from the Hospital of St. John, at Leicester, at Michaelmas.

P. 329. A Lease from John Whestones, dean of the college of Newarke within Leycester, and the chaplains of the same, to Robert Browne, of Leycester, carpenter, of a messuage within the North gate of Leycester, for 41 years, without any rent for the first three years, and afterwards at a rent of 2*s.* a year. Dated Sept. 22, 4 Hen. VIII.[7] See the Seal, Plate XLIX. fig. 4.

P. 348. After the dissolution of the College, Mr. William Fowkes was master of this hospital ; and of him, Henry earl of Huntingdon purchased the wardenship, who, in 1609, 7 Jac. I. offered it to the town of Leicester, upon condition that they would pay the earl for it as much as he gave to the said William Fowkes, which was agreed to at a meeting of the twenty-four aldermen, and twenty-four of the seniors of the company of 48, Feb. 19, 1609-10. Soon after which, the king, at the request of the said earl, issued out his letters patent, whereby he changed the name of " St. Mary," to that of " The Holy Trinity of the Newark[8]," and appointed the mayor of Leicester for the time being to be the master or warden of it, whose fee is £.13. 6*s.* 8*d.* ; and he enters on this office on the Friday after he is chosen mayor. The town chamberlains take care to receive the annual payment from the dutchy, and on Friday every week pay to the poor people their allowance, &c. Upon the dissolution, many of the possessions belonging to this College were granted to Thomas Fisher, alias Hawkins, esq. of Warwick ; but whether he or some other had the houses in the Newark, says Mr. Carte, does not appear. An additional view of Trinity Hospital is given in Pl. XLIX.

P. 436. Feb. 21, 1684-5, John Broadhurst, a button-maker in the Borough of *Leicester*, confined in the gaol there on information of setting fire to three houses, and publishing a scandalous and horrid libel against the Government, broke out of gaol ; and a reward was offered by the mayor for his apprehension[9].

P. 447. A worthy and respectable Octogenarian Friend has favoured me with the following remarks : " I well remember this storm. It happened on the evening of one of the race nights. I was very young ; but permitted by my parents to go to the ball with some ladies at their house. The thunder and lightning were so tremendous as to prevent the ball being opened for more than an hour after the company were assembled ; and I recollect my mother saying, that some of the coachmen observed, " they drove devils, and not ladies." That the first floors in many houses were filled with water, and the cellars overflowed, I believe to be true. But that many waggon loads of ice were to be seen on the *Saturday morning following* I do absolutely contradict ; for, being at that time on the spot, and an inquisitive boy of the age of 10, at the freeschool, then in a flourishing state, I must have heard, and most probably been a witness of so extraordinary (not to say, in the month of August, almost miraculous) a sight. J. H."

P. 561. col. 2. l. 58. *r.* " John Palmer, B. A."

P. 568. l. 4. *for* " St. Michael's," *r.* " St. Martin's."

P. 596. l. 2. *for* 1679, read 1662. Some further corrections and additions to this parish in p. 606.

---

[1] " Robertus de Veci tenet 12 carucatas terre in Cliborne. Tempore Regis Edwardi erant ibi 10 carucæ. In dominico fuit 3 carucæ & 6 servi ; & 10 villani, cum 6 sochmannis, & 6 bordariis, & 1 panigenâ, habent 5 carucas. Ibi 16 acræ prati. Valuit 40 solidos ; modò 60 solidos." Domesday, fol. 234. a. 1.

[2] " Robertus de Veci habet 3 domos cum sacâ & socâ pertinentes at Cleiborne." Ibid. fol. 230. a. 1.

[3] " Hugo de Grentemaisnel tenet in Elvestone 9 carucatas terræ, unâ virgatâ minus. Terra est 6 carucarum. Ibi 13 sochmanni, cum 2 villani & 2 bordarii, habent 4 carucas. Ibi 20 acræ prati. Valuit 20 solidos ; modò 30 solidos." Ibid. fol. 232. a. 1.

[4] " Robertus tenet de co[mite de Mellent] in Plotelei 4 carucatas terræ. Ibi fuerunt 4 carucæ. Nunc in dominico 2 carucæ & 2 servi ; & 4 villani, cum 1 bordario, habent 6 carucam. Ibi 2 acræ prati. Valuit 10 solidos ; modò 30 solidos. Leuric tenuit." Ibid. fol. 237. a. 2.

[5] " Nigellus tenet de H[enrici de Fereires] in Windesers 3 carucatas terræ vastas. Tempore Regis Edwardi erant ibi 2 carucæ. Aluric liberè tenuit." Ibid. fol. 233. b. 1.

[6] Collinson's Somerset, vol. III. p. 248.

[7] From the original, in the possession of Tho. Sharpe, esq. of Coventry.

[8] Newark Hospitalis Fundatio, 4 Pars Original. 12 Jac. I. Rot. 76.

[9] Gazette, Feb. 26, 1684-5.

BRIEF INDEX to the SECOND PART of the FIRST VOLUME; to be enlarged hereafter.

END OF THE FIRST VOLUME.

JOHN NICHOLS and SON, Printers, Red Lion Passage, Fleet Street, London.—*Nov.* 28, 1811.

APPENDIX, N° XVII. LEICESTER ABBEY.

RENTALE NOVUM GENERALE MONASTERII B. MARIE DE PRATIS LEYCESTRIE,

meritò inscriptum ab authore, MEMORIALE FRATRIS WILL'I CHARYTE Prioris ibidem,

Qui hunc librum incredibili labore compofuit, fuáque manu defcripfit.

Opus tantum aggreffus anno MCCCCLXXVII, & regis Edwardi Quarti XVII.

Nam & propriâ manu fcripfiffe apparet XXV codices five rotulos materiis diverfos,
quorum ultimum fcripfit A. D. MDII, ætatis fuæ LXXXI, & poft ingreffum fuum in religionem LXIII.

Omnia tam accurato methodo congefta ut nihil poffit clarius exprimere
perfectiffimi adminiftratoris & œconomi imaginem.

" Has facras ædes pietas conftruxit avorum,
Quas fucceffores devaftant more luporum."

[Liber Gulielmi Laud, Archiepifcopi Cantuar', & Cancellarii Univerfitatis Oxon', 1635'.]

GULIELMUS CHARYTE, Prior monafterii augufti & amœni B. Mariæ de Pratis Leyceftriæ, chartas omnes atque codices ad dictum monafterium pertinentes fummâ curâ excuffit perlegitque, & exindè librum ingentem compofuit, quem infcripfit *Rentale novum generale monafterii B. Marie de Pratis Leyceftrie.* Opus hoc eximium inchoavit anno Domini CIↃCDLXXVII°, regis Edwardi IVᵗⁱ XVII°, & ad exitum perduxit A. D. CIↃDII°, ætatis fuæ LXXXI°, à monafticæ vitæ habitu fufcepto LXIII°; cujus exemplar, ab auctore ipfo maximam partem exaratum, in Bibliothecâ Bodlejanâ, beneficio maximi præfulis & fanctiffimi martyris Gulielmi Laudi, jam exftat. Quod fanè rerum Anglicarum fcriptoribus, aliifque rei antiquariæ ftudiofis, magno ufui effe poteft. Nam auctor erat (ut cuilibet librum evolventi conftabit) vir probus, fapiens, fagax, diligens, & qui complura in monafterium benignè contulit. Unde mirari fubeat nihil apud Lelandum, Baleum, Pitfeumve, de eo memoratum occurrere; aut demùm apud Gulielmum Burtonum, agri Leyceftrenfis defcriptorem luculentiffimum.   T. HEARNE."

1. Hiftoria fundationis, & progenies fundatoris[2].

MEMORANDUM quod Robertus comes Mellenti, veniens in Angliam cum Willielmo duce Normannie, adeptus confulatum Leyceftrie ex dono dicti ducis & conqueftoris Anglie, deftructâ prius civitate Leiceftriâ, cum caftello & ecclefiâ infra caftellum, tempore predicti conqueftoris, re-edificavit ipfam ecclefiam Sancte Marie infra caftellum, ftatuens ibidem XII canonicos feculares & unum decanum, conferens iifdem & approprians omnes ecclefias Leiceftrie preter ecclefiam Sancte Margarete, que non erat fue ditionis, eo quod fuit & eft prebenda ecclefie Lincolnienfis, cum quinque carucatis terre, ex parte boreali civitatis, & aliis poffeffionibus in ipfâ civitate, & cum omnibus ecclefiis de focis de Schepefheved & Halfo, & pluribus aliis ecclefiis, redditibus, & poffeffionibus.

Ipfo quoque Roberto defuncto, fucceffit ei Robertus le Cocrea, filius & heres ejufdem; &, de confilio domini Alexandri tunc epifcopi Lincolnie, & aliorum difcretorum, fundavit abbathiam iftam de Pratis Leiceftrie; transferens poffeffiones & prebendas dicte ecclefie Sancte Marie de Caftro, cum omnibus aliis redditibus & poffeffionibus fuis, in ufum canonicorum iftius abbathie; largiens & approprians eifdem, tam per fe quàm per fuos, plures alias ecclefias, redditus, & poffeffiones, cum unâ carucatâ terre in Leiceftriâ jacente ad cuneos[3] monete, cum prato adjacente ufque Narfike, & aliis pertinentiis fuis. Qui quidem Robertus, de confenfu Amicie uxoris fue, fumpfit in abbathiâ iftâ habitum noftre religionis; vivens juftè & fanctè quindecim annis & amplius. Ipfa quoque Amicia uxor fua fanctamonialis apud Eton eft effecta.

Ifto Roberto fundatore noftro defuncto, fucceffit ei in hereditatem Robertus filius ejus, & vocabatur Robertus as Blanche meyns; qui Robertus accepit in uxorem Petronillam filiam Hugonis de Granmenyl, cum honore de Hynkelee, & aliis poffeffionibus ipfius Hugonis, quas habuit in Angliâ; et extunc primò honor de Hynkelee eft conjunctus comitatu Leyceftrie. Et ex dictâ Petronillâ genuit tres filios & duas filias; fcilicet Robertum, qui vocabatur Robertus filius Petronille, ad differentiam predictorum; & qui fucceffit patri fuo in hereditatem, fed nullum habuit heredem de fe genitum; & Willielmum leprofum, fecundum fi-

lium; et Galfridum epifcopum Sancte Andree in Scotiâ, tertium filium; & Amiciam primogenitam filiam, & Margaretam juniorem.

Illo quoque Roberto as Blanche meyns in redeundo de Terrâ Sanctâ defuncto, & apud Duraz in partibus tranfmarinis fepulto, fucceffit ei predictus Robertus filius fuus & heres, vocatus filius Petronille, in hereditatem. Ipfo quoque fine herede defuncto, divifa eft hereditas[4] inter predictas forores, Amiciam & Margaretam, eo quod dicti duo fratres fui fuerant jam defuncti. Et Amicia defponfata fuit domino Simoni de Monteforti, patri illius Simonis, qui moriebatur apud Evefham; et Margareta defponfata fuit Sayero de Quincy. Et facti funt duo comitatus, fcilicet de Leicefter & Wyncefter, de comitatu Leyceftrie prius integrè exiftente.

2. Adhuc de fundatione, & progenie fundatoris[5].

Robertus comes Mellenti venit cum Willielmo (Conqueftore) in Angliam; cui Roberto datus eft comitatus Leiceftrenfis. Ifte Robertus reedificavit ecclefiam Sancte Marie de caftro Leiceftrenfi; & pofuit in eadem canonicos feculares, & reftituit eis terras, poffeffiones, & ecclefias.

Robertus Boffu, filius ejufdem Roberti de Mellent, de confenfu Alexandri epifcopi Lincolnienfis, anno Gratie MCXLIII, fundavit monafterium Beate Marie de Pratis Leiceftrie, in honorem Affumptionis ejufdem gloriofe Virginis; & de ecclefiis, terris, & poffeffionibus antedictorum canonicorum fecularium, cum multis aliis fupererogatis, tam ecclefiis, aliifque poffeffionibus & redditibus, luculenter dotavit, & eas in ufum canonicorum regularium transformavit; qui etiam in eodem monafterio, de confenfu Amicie uxoris fue, canonicus regularis factus eft, & annis XV in habitu regulari ibidem Chrifto militans, canonicus vitam finiens, obdormivit in pace, in latere ibidem chori dextro fepultus, fcilicet anno Gratie MCLXVII.

Ifte Robertus fundavit abbathiam de Gerondonâ, monachorum; & monafterium fanctimonialium de Etonâ, in quo Amicia uxor ejufdem Roberti, ex mutuo affenfu viri fui, facta eft fanctimonialis, de refiduo vite fue Deo ferviens. Unde ipfe factus eft canonicus regularis, & illa fanctamonialis.

---

[1] Now (1796) in the Bodleian Library, marked H. 72. Several extracts from it will occur among the charters here given; and for a fuller account of it, fee hereafter, p. 61.

[2] Dugdale, Mon. Angl. vol. II. p. 312; from Charyte's Rentale, fol. clxxxviii. a.   [3] The fite of the Mint.

[4] See the deed of partition, under the Hiftory of Leicefter, p. 100.

[5] Dugdale, ibid. ex Chron. MS. Hen. Knyghton, in Bibl. Cotton. lib. ii. cap. 2.

3. De fundatione & dotatione ejufdem [1].

IN nomine Sancte & Individue Trinitatis : notum fit omnibus fancte Dei ecclefie filiis, prefentibus & futuris, quatenus ab Incarnatione Domini anno MCVII, regnante Henrico rege Anglorum, Robertus comes Mellenti confulatum Leiceftrie adeptus, ibi in honorem fancte Dei genitricis Marie, & Omnium Sanctorum veneratione, pro animâ Willielmi regis Anglie, expugnatoris Anglorum, ejufque uxoris Matildis regine, & eorum filii Willielmi Secundi regis; atque futuram memoriam anime Henrici regis & ejus uxoris regine Matildis Secunde, & pro eorum liberis; & pro animâ Rogeri de Bellomonte, & ejus uxoris Adeline, & pro feipfo & fuâ uxore Elizabethâ, & eorum filiis; & pro animâ fratris fui Henrici comitis; & pro animâ Albrede fororis fue, abbatiffe; & pro animabus omnium Henrici regis & aliorum predeceſſorum & fidelium defunctorum, ecclefiam reedificavit, in quâ canonicos & decanum, & eorum capitulum, conceffu regis Henrici & Roberti epifcopi Lincolnienfis ecclefie canonicè difpofuit; ad quorum victum ftatuit omnia que eadem ecclefia antiquitùs habuerat, in terris, & omnibus fuis confuetudinibus reconformatis eifdem in dedicatione ipfius ecclefie per Robertum epifcopum Lincolnienfem. Preter hec donavit eidem ecclefie ad pontem de North quinque carucatas terre, & octo manfiones hominum; & in aliâ parte civitatis tres virgatas terre, & tres bovatas terre. Et idem, de fuo proprio redditu civitatis Legreceftrie, fex libratas per annum, & extra civitatem Legeceftrie ecclefiam Omnium Sanctorum, & ecclefiam Beati Petri, & ecclefiam Sancti Martini, que Radulfus Pincerna dedit predicte ecclefie in augmentum prebende; & ecclefiam de Lileburnâ, cum terris & decimis omnibus eidem ecclefie pertinentibus, & fexaginta folidos per annum de redditibus Lileburne. Et Radulfus Pincerna dedit predicte ecclefie Sancte Marie triginta folidos per annum in Blingeffet & in Tormedeftunâ. Robertus comes Mellenti donavit Sancte Marie tres carucatas terre, & unam virgatam terre; & molendinum de ponte North ad veftitum infirmorum in cuftodiâ canonicorum commendavit. Et in Burtonâ Ifabella comitiſſa . . . . [*Abhinc recordum laceratur.*]

4. Hiftoria de terrarum donationibus [2].

Habemus, ex dono fundatoris noftri, in primâ fundatione hujus monafterii, omnes prebendas & poffeffiones, que fuerunt canonicorum fecularium ecclefie Sancte Marie infra caftellum; fcilicet, ecclefiam Sancte Marie, cum totâ poffeffione in parochiâ fuâ, cum terris & pafcuis & pratis, & omnibus aliis pertinentiis fuis, cum omnibus libertatibus quas Robertus comes Mellenti pater fuus predicte ecclefie ante conceſſerat. Item quinque virgatas terre extra portam de North, & octo manfiones hominum; et in aliâ parte civitatis tres virgatas terre, & tres bovatas terre; & de redditibus Leyceftrie fex libras per annum. Ecclefias quoque omnes Leiceftrie, tam infra muros quàm extra, que funt fue ditionis, cum domibus & manfuris, cum terris & pratis, & omnibus pertinentiis fuis. Item ecclefiam de Lilburnâ, cum terris & decimis & omnibus pertinentiis fuis; & LXs. per annum de redditibus ejufdem ville. Item in Thurmodeftonâ tres carucatas terre & unam virgatam terre. Item unam virgatam terre, ex dono Ifabelle matris fue, in Burtonâ. Item in Segrave fex carucatas & tres bovatas [3] terre; & manerium de Asfordeby totum & integrum, cum molendinis, &c. Hec omnia predicta fuerunt poffeffiones canonicorum predictorum ecclefie Sancte Marie infra caftellum, ficut patet in primâ, fecundâ, & tertiâ cartâ Roberti comitis Mellenti.

Et preter hoc dedit nobis fundator nofter, apud pontem de North, carucatam terre que jacebat olim ad cuneos monete, & cenfum & domos quos Gilbertus decanus tenebat de eo ad portam de Suth; & decimam pullorum de fuâ equariâ; & molendinum quod fuit epifcopi, & quicquid ad ipfum molendinum per-

tinet; & quicquid Ofbertus capellanus de ipfo tenebat in focâ de Schepifhed, & in focâ de Halfo, omnes fcilicet ecclefias de utraque focâ; cum ecclefiâ de Sygrefham, que de parochiâ de Brachaleiâ effe cognofcitur, cum terris & decimis, & omnibus pertinentiis fuis; & decimam denariorum fuorum de utrâque focâ, & de pannagio [4].

Item ecclefiam de Ildefley, que eft in Berchefirâ, cum terris & decimis, &c.

Item conceffit nobis, quod ubicunque in foreftis fuis ad proprios ufus ligna fumpferit, ibi & nos cum tribus carectis [5] cotidiè ad ignem noftrum liberè ligna fumamus. Et ubicunque tempore paftionis fui dominici porci fuerint, ibi & nos dominicos porcos noftros liberè & fine pannagio habeamus.

He funt ecclefie & poffeffiones omnes, quas fundator nofter dedit nobis in cartâ originali fundationis iftius abbathie.

Item, in eadem cartâ, confirmavit omnes donationes, quas homines totius terre fue nobis fecerunt; fcilicet, ecclefiam de Thurnby, ex dono Radulphi Pincerne, cum terris, decimis, &c. Et, ex dono Roberti Pincerne filii fui, ecclefiam de Thedyngworth. Et, ex dono Ernaldi de Bofco, ecclefiam de Cliftonâ, & ecclefiam de Thorp juxta Melton, cum terris, decimis, &c. & unam marcatam redditûs in Leiceftria. Et, ex dono Rogeri de Watevil, ecclefiam de Bulkyntonâ, cum terris, decimis, & omnibus pertinentiis fuis; & dimidiam hidam terre in Brankotâ; & pratum quod fuit de Weftonâ de dominio. Et, ex dono Sewardi Pitefridi, terram quam de ipfo tenebat in Bruntingfthorp. Has terras & ecclefias, poffeffiones, & redditus, voluit & firmiter conftituit, ut nos liberè, quietè, & honorificè teneamus ab omni fervicio & exactione feculari erga ipfum & heredes fuos, &c. ut in eadem cartâ, datâ circa annum Domini MCXXXVII.

Item habemus, ex dono fundatoris noftri, ecclefiam de Cofby, que pertinet ad ecclefiam Sci Auguftini de Leycefter. Item ecclefiam de Aldeby [6]; & fic ecclefiam de Wefton [7]. Item totam Stoctonam, preter feodum Radulphi Friday, cum molendino de Belgrave. Item duas virgatas terre apud portam de Weft. Item manerium de Pynflad, cum quatuor virgatis terre ibidem. Item totum manerium de Knyton, cum molendino & pertineniis fuis. Item tria millia anguillarum & xxxi. ftreyling apud Nun-Eyton. Item unam virgatam terre in Whatton, &c. ut in cartâ; in quâ carta fic fcribitur: " Ego Robertus comes Leyc' remifi & quietum clamavi abbati & conventui Leyceftrie omnem actionem & demandam, quam habui verſùs eofdem & eorum homines, liberos & villanos, ac terras fuas fuper vifum franciplegii ubique in dominio noftro; & quod cartis fuis de libertatibus per reges Anglie eifdem conceſſis liberè ac pacificè poffint uti," &c. ut in cartâ. Item habemus vs. vid. liberi redditûs in Brunthonfthorpe de uno crofto & unâ bovatâ terre de terris Thome Walche.

5. Carta Stephani regis.

Stephanus, rex Anglie, &c. Sciatis me conceffiffe Roberto comiti Leyceftrie fundare ecclefiam Sancte Marie, &c. & ibi conftituere abbatem, &c. Et concedo Deo & Beate Marie, & Ricardo abbati & canonicis regularibus, &c. omnes donationes quas Robertus comes Leyceftrie dedit, conceffit, vel adquifivit, five adquifierit, feu que deinceps eis dabuntur in eleemofinam. Inprimis concedo, &c. ut in cartâ originali fundatoris noftri, ufque huc. Item, ex dono Walerani comitis de Mellent, xx miras falis in Wiche de Wireceftrefirâ. Ex dono Ranulfi comitis Ceftrie, duas carucatas terre in Rolejâ, que vocatur Hanecheftoft, cum prato adjacente, &c. Has donationes terras, &c. que eifdem canonicis pertinent, liberas & quietas concedo ab omni expeditione infra Angliam, &c. et omni fervicio feculari, &c. Et volo & firmiter precipio, ut prefata ecclefia & canonici benè & pacificè, liberè & quietè teneant, & libertatem curie fue

---

[1] Dugdale, Mon. Angl. vol. II. p. 312; ex Cart. Antiq. CC. n. 23. 1107. Vide etiam Cart. Antiq. CC. n. 21.
[2] Ibid. p. 308; from Charyte's Rentale, fol. i. b. fol. ii. a.   [3] As much land as an ox can till in a year, 28 acres.
[4] Wafte of woods and hedge-row that cattle feed on; alfo money given for it in forefts.   [5] Three cart-loads.
[6] Afterwards transferred to Eudeby. See under that parifh.   [7] Whetftone is ftill a chapelry to Lade by.

habeant, cum facâ & foca, tol & team, & infangene-theof, & omnibus aliis confuetudinibus, &c. in nemore & plano, &c. ficut aliqua ecclefia totiûs terre mee de eleemofinâ meâ meliùs & quietiùs & honorificentiùs tenet, &c. ut in cartâ.

6. Carta Amicie comitiffe [1].

Habuimus quondam in Everley certas terras ex do-ho Amicie comitiffe, uxoris fundatoris noftri, quas terras nos dedimus & per cartam noftram conceffimus Ade de Afton ad perpetuam firmam, reddendo nobis annuatim v marcas; quas terras per longum tempus, cum unâ carectâ â ligni cotidiè in forellâ Leyc', re-nunciavimus Dño Henrico duci Lancaftrie, pro appro-priatione ecclefiarum Hungarton & Humbrefton, ex fumptibus fuis propriis factâ, ficut patet in cartâ.

Mem' quod abbas & convenıus Leyc', pro quibuf-cunque decimis in futuro concedend' pro temporalibus in Everley, erga dominum regem & heredes fuos ex-onerati & quieti exiftunt in perpetuum, per placitum in quo 11ſ. v111ď. exarctantur per predictos de abbate Leyc' pro medietate unus decime pro temporalibus in Everley, anno regni regis Henrici Sexti x1°, ut in dicto placito, quod eft in libro placitorum.

Habuimus quondam, ex dono Amicie comitiffe Leyc', 1111 libratas terre in Everley, fcil' nonam par-tem ejufdem ville, &c. ad fuftentationem fratrum de infirmitorio, &c. ut patet in primâ cartâ.

Habemus confirmationem Roberti fundatoris noftri, & Roberti filii ejus, pro eifdem quatuor libratis terre in Everle, ut in cartâ fecundâ.

7. Robertus comes Leyc' univerfis fancte matris ecclefie filiis & fidelibus falurem. Sciatis quod volo & precipio Roberto filio meo, &c. ut excambiat terram de Cnictintone cum abbate Leyceftrie'. Teftibus; Turftino abbate de Gerondon', Robto priore de Kine-leworth, Robto capellano, Wiłło Baffett, Robto de Croft, Rogero de Crauford, Anfchetillo Mallore [2].

8. Carta Roberti filii fundatoris noftri.

Habemus confirmationem Roberti filii fundatoris noftri, per cartam fuam, de omnibus donationibus quas pater fuus & homines fui nobis dederunt in cartâ originali fundationis; & de omnibus donationibus quas ipfi dederunt nobis per alias cartas fuas; ut, ex dono fundatoris noftri, manerium de Knytonâ, cum molendinis & pertinentiis fuis, &c. Ex dono Amicie comitiffe, quatuor libras in Everley. Item, ex dono Ernaldi de Bofco, ecclefias de Thorp, Evyntonâ, & Humberfton, &c. Item locum de Stokingforth, & xLſ. in Welton, ex dono & confirmatione fundatoris; & cenfum domorum quas tenuit Godewinus Bena, fcilicet, 1vſ. in Leyceftriâ; & terram quam Jocelinus Marefcallus dedit predicte ecclefie, fcilicet, v effarta [3] de North, nemoris fui, & feptum ante capellam. Et, ex dono Gaufridi de Turvillâ, illam terram que dici-tur Netlebede; et, ex dono Willielmi de Alnejâ, unam carucatam terre, fcilicet Aneftaneflaya, cum om-nibus effartis que in circuitu ejus funt, & cum parte nemoris, &c. Et, ex dono fundatoris, ecclefiam de Aldeby, totam Stoctonam, & molendinum de Bel-grave, &c. ut in cartâ.

Item habemus, ex dono ejufdem Roberti filii fun-datoris noftri, fingulis annis, unum cervum die Affump-tionis Beate Marie, & alium cervum in Nativitate Dei genitricis Marie; & licentiam pifcandi in magno vivario fuo de Groby quatuor diebus per annum; fcilicet, vigiliâ Purificationis Beate Marie, Annuncia-tionis Beate Marie, Affumptionis Beate Marie, & Na-tivitatis ejufdem.

Item habemus, ex dono ejufdem Roberti, pafturam de Desforth ad decem vaccas, cum exitu earum de duobus annis, cum duabus acris terre in alnetâ, & defuper inter viam & terram quam magifter Radul-phus de Wolfcroft tenuit, ut in cartâ.

9. Carta Roberti filii Petronille.

Habemus confirmationem Roberti filii Petronille, per cartam fuam, de omnibus donationibus nomina-tim, quas avus fuus, & pater fuus, & homines fui nobis dederunt, ut in cartâ fuâ primâ.

Item habemus, ex dono ejufdem Roberti filii Petro-nille, pafturam inter duas vias in defenfo [4] Leiceftrie; fcilicet inter viam de Groby, & inter viam de Anfty, ad averia [5] noftra pafcenda, & unam carectatam ligni cotidiè in foreftâ Leicestrie, ut in cartâ.

Item habemus, ex dono ejufdem Roberti, viginti quatuor virgatas terre in villâ de Anfty, & quatuor cotarios [6], cum toftis fuis, ut in cartâ.

Item habemus, ex dono ejufdem Roberti, terras de Farnigo & Sygrefham; fcilicet, Weftcot, cum omni-bus pertinentiis fuis, quas Robertus comes avus fuus dedit ecclefie Lincolnie, in efcambium pro manerio de Knyton, &c. Has autem terras dedit nobis pro terris noftris de Asforby & Segrave, quas affenfu noftro de-dit ecclefie Lincolnienfi, pro pace refervandâ in perpe-tuum inter ipfam ecclefiam Lincoln', &c. ut in cartâ.

Item habemus, ex dono Simonis de Monteforti, quandam placeam bofci vocatam Donelond, in efcam-bium pro quietâ clamatione predicte pafture in de-fenfo Leyc', & unius culture in eodem defenfo vocato Mikeldal, & unius carecte cotidiè in foreftâ de dua-bus carectis, &c. Item habemus, ex dono ejufdem Simonis, quandam placeam terre & bofci verfûs Anfty, vocatam Ofulveſhawe, &c. cum omnibus angulis bofci & terre, &c. Item, ex dono ejufdem Simonis, unam placeam terre quam Willielmus de Belgrave quondam tenuit, &c. ut in cartâ.

10. Carta Roberti filii Radulphi, de ecclefiis de Cnipe-ton & Areftone [7].

Univerfis fancti Dei ecclefie fidelibus, Robertus filius Radulfi falutem. Notum fit univerfitati veftre, quod ego Robertus, pro animâ patris mei & matris mee, & pro animâ Aveline conjugis mee, & Willielmi fratris mei, & pro animabus parentum & amicorum meorum in perpetuum, conceffi & dedi ecclefie Sancte Marie de Legreceftria, & canonicis regulariter ibidem Deo fervientibus, ecclefiam de Cnipeton, & ecclefiam de Areftonâ, cum terris & decimis & manfuris, & om-nibus pertinentiis, & hoc conceffu Willielmi filii & heredis mei, & Roberti filii mei, & Gervafii filii mei; ita tamen quod idem Gervafius teneat de predictâ ec-clefiâ Sancte Marie de Legreceftriâ prenominatas ec-clefias liberè & quietè quamdiu vixerit. Volo autem & firmiter conftituo, ut predicta ecclefia Sancte Marie & canonici has prenominatas ecclefias benè & in pace, liberè & quietè & honorificè teneant, cum omnibus libertatibus & liberis confuetudinibus que ad eafdem ecclefias pertinent, & cum omni libertate & commu-nitate pafture utriufque ville. Hiis teftibus; Roberto Lincolnie epifcopo; Roberto comite Legreceftrie, Roberto de Croft, Ivone de Harcurt, Willielmo Baffet; magiftro Edmundo, magiftro Pernardo, Willielmo capellano, Hugone de Blabi; Gumfredo prefbitero; Gervafio filio Turgis, Roberto filio Suani, Walcellino, Johanne & Willielmo fcriptoribus, Hugone de Bede-ferd, Abei filio ejus, Willielmo Difpenfatore, Rogero, Johanne, Petro, famulis abbatis.

11. Carta Petronille comitiffe.

Habemus confirmationem Petronille comitiffe, de omnibus donationibus quas dedit nobis Robertus co-mes filius ejus. Item habemus, ex dono ejus, totum pratum fuum de Thurmodefton, vocatum Belloholm; & domos fuas in Leyceftriâ, cum terrâ & gardino ul-tra pontem de Weft, que fuerunt Hugonis clerici, &c. ut in cartâ primâ.

12. Carta Saeri de Quyncy.

Habemus, ex dono Saeri de Quincy, fex libratas redditûs in Brakley & Halfo, pro feifinâ factâ fibi de octo libratis redditûs in fuburbio Leyceftrie, quas ha-buimus de feodo Lincolnienfis epifcopi, &c. ut in cartâ.

Habemus, ex dono Saeri de Quincy, cum affenfu & confenfu Margarete comitiffe fue, omnia que funt in carta fequente, ufque ad conceffionem unius cervi, ut in cartâ in Schepiſhed tertiâ.

[1] Charyte's Rentale, fol. ii. b. and fol. lvii.   [2] Cotton MSS. Plut. IV. F. p. 62, 63.
[3] Ground cleared of fhrubs.   [4] Ground fenced in.   [5] Cattle or oxen, or horfes ufed for the plough.
[6] Tenants in focage.   [7] Dugdale, Mon. Angl. p. 315; ex autographo in Officio Armorum.

13. Carta Margarete de Quincy.

Habemus confirmationem Margarete de Quincy, de omnibus donationibus quas antecessores sui, comites Leyceftrie, nobis fecerunt, ut patet in cartâ fuâ: et per illam cartam dedit nobis unam virgatam terre in Schepished, cum tofto & crofto & molendino de Schepished, cum omnibus pertinentiis fuis, &c. & cum alnetâ adjacente, & cum totâ multurâ de Schepished & Hathern, & cum multurâ proprie domûs fue de Schepished ; & cum omni commodo, &c. ita quod nec illa nec heredes fui aliquod molendinum infra territorium de Schepished feu Hathern unquam faceret in pofterum. Item, per eandem cartam, conceffit nobis houfebote & haybote ad domos noftras in Schepished, & meremium ad earum fuftentationem & molendini noftri in foreftâ fuâ de Charnwood, & bofco fuo de Schepished, ubicunque quoties opus fuerit, &c. Ifta preterea dedit nobis, fpecialiter in recompenfationem LX s. pro decimis Leiceftrie ad ipfam pertinentibus, & in recompenfatione denariorum decimarum reddituum de utraque focâ, &c. quos antiquitùs percipere folebamus ad fcaccarium de Leyceftriâ, quos remifimus ei & heredibus, fub tali conditione ; falvâ nobis totâ decimâ de pannagio, & venditione nemoris utriufque foce. Item conceffit nobis unum cervum in die Nativitatis Beate Marie in Charnwood. Item conceffit nobis ut homines & tenentes noftri de Brakley, Sygresham, Weftcote, Halfo, Farnigo, Wefton, Clifton, Bulkinton, Brankot, Bernangul, Sow, Merfton, Stocton, Lokyngton, Schepished, Hemyngton, Whatton, Anfty, Thurmafton, Clenfeld, & Burton, & in omnibus locis, terris, & poffeffionibus, in feodo fuo conftitutis, liberi fint & quieti ab omni fervitio feculari, exactione & demandâ, fectâ curie, vifu franciplegii, & forinfeco fervitio, &c. ut in cartâ.

14. Carta Rogeri de Quincy [1].

Habemus cartam Rogeri de Quincy, de quietâ clamatione omnium ecclefiarum noftrarum & fecte curiarum pro nobis & hominibus noftris in feodo fuo conftitutis. Habemus cartam predicti Rogeri fuper quietâ clamatione de vifu franciplegii & fectâ curie pro nobis & hominibus noftris & tenentibus fuis; fcilicet, de Brakley, Sygresham, &c. ut in cartâ predicte Margarete Quincy. Item conceffit nobis, per eandem cartam, houfebote & haybote &c. ut in cartâ Margarete Quincy, &c.

Rogerus de Quincy, comes Wintonie, &c. dilecto & fideli fuo domino R. Chamburleyn, fenefcallo fuo, falutem. Mandamus vobis, firmiter precipientes, quatinus ponatis abbatem & conventum Leyceftrie in feyfinam plenam de houfebote & haybote in Schepished, & de meremio ad emendationem & fuftentationem molendini fui de Schepished, & de vifu franciplegii, &c. ut in cartâ.

Habemus cartam ejufdem de duabus carectis, & in qualibet carectâ duos equos ad tractandum ligna ad ignem in foreftâ, &c. ut in cartâ.

Habemus cartam ejufdem de quatuor carectatis bofci, à fefto Annunciationis ufque ad feftum Sancti Michaelis, &c. ut in cartâ.

Habemus quietam clamationem ejufdem de ftabilâ quam exigebat à nobis & tenentibus noftris de Anfty, ut in cartâ. Habemus confirmationem ejufdem Rogeri comitis de omnibus donationibus que funt in cartâ Margarete comitiffe matris fue, ut in cartâ.

Habemus, ex dono ejufdem, totam decimam omnium venditionum bofcorum fuorum de Acle, & de Wyffeley, &c. per manus venditorum & receptorum earundem venditionum, quicunque pro tempore fuerint, percipiendum, &c. ut in cartâ.

Habemus, ex dono ejufdem, dexterum humerum cujuflibet fere capte in parco fuo de Acle, ut in cartâ.

Habemus, ex dono ejufdem, licentiam ad edificandum & conftruendum boveriam & bercariam in territorio noftro de Stanton, & licentiam habendi liberum introitum & exitum, cum averiis noftris, ad pafturam communem forefte fue, &c. ut in cartâ.

Habemus, ex dono ejufdem, unam virgatam terre in Whefton, quam Ricardus Kyrke tenuit, & communiam liberam ad animalia noftra propria pafcenda omnimoda, per totam foreftam Leyceftrie, in proparte fuâ ejufdem forefte in bofco, plano, &c. ut in cartâ.

Habemus, ex dono ejufdem, x s. per annum apud Schevifby, a priore de Chakombe, & III s. IIII d. apud Hemyngton, de heredibus Hugonis de Derby, & particibus fuis, pro quietâ clamatione pifcationis in vivario de Groby quater per annum, &c. ut in cartâ.

Habemus, ex dono ejufdem, homagium & fervicium Helie de Lynfey, & Alicie uxoris ejus, de quatuor virgatis terre in Thurmafton, ut in cartâ.

15. Carta Simonis de Monteforti.

Habemus confirmationem Simonis de Monteforti, de omnibus rebus quas dederunt nobis predeceffores fui, ut in cartâ.

Habemus, ex dono ejufdem Simonis, in defenfo Leyceftrie, juxta abbathiam, pafturam fufficientem ad centum & viginti averia, in efcambium pafture in predicto defenfo, inter viam que vadit à Leyceftriâ ufque Groby, & viam que vadit à Leyceftriâ ufque Anfty, &c.

Habemus cartam ejufdem in efcambio de Mukeldale, & pafturis predictis, & unâ carectâ ligni pro Donelond & Ofulveshaw, & aliis, ut fequitur in cartâ Roberti filii Petronille.

Habemus, ex perquifito abbatis & conventûs ut dicitur, & ex dono & feoffamento Simonis de Monteforti, trecentas acras terre & bofci, fimiliter cum pertinentiis, contiguas trefcentis acris predictis in foreftâ noftrâ, que appellatur defenfa, juxta Leyceftriam, &c. que videlicet acre omnes jacent à via de Anfty ufque ad Dalfyke in tranfverfo, & à Dalfyke ultra Storkyshull, &c. ufque ad Oldfeld in tranfverfo fuper fettam à Cropfton, &c. & ab Oldfeld per campum de Belgrave, &c. Item dedit nobis totum Cleyheges, cum vefliturâ, &c. ut in cartâ.

16. Carta Alani la Zouche [2].

Habemus confirmationem Alani la Zouche, de omnibus donationibus quas anteceffores ejus comites Leiceftrie & Wintonie nobis fecerunt, ficut patet in cartâ octavâ & nonâ in Schepished.

17. Univerfis, &c.

Johes Comyn, filius dni Alex' comitis de Bouhan, falutem. Noverit, &c. me, pro falute anime mee, &c. conceffiffe, &c. Deo & ecclefie Beate Marie de Pratis Leiceftrie, & canonicis regularibus, &c. quandam placeam terr' annexe terre dictor' canonicorum juxta locum eorum de Horfepol, ex dono Alexandri patris mei, continent' IV acras, reddendo XVIII denar' per ann.' Teftibus ; dnis Rado de Lafcelles, Roberto le Walleys, Johanne filio Petri, militibus ; Joh' de Anefty, Rob' carectario de Dad', Johanne de Infirmatorio de Leyceftr', Willielmo de Soleby de Dad' [3].

18. Carta Ernaldi primi de Bofco.

Habemus, ex dono Ernaldi primi de Bofco, ecclefiam de Cliftonâ, cum capellis de Woverâ & de Rokeby ; ecclefiam de Thorpe juxta Melton ; ecclefias quoque de Humberftone & de Evyngtone.

19. Carta Ernaldi fecundi de Bofco.

Habemus, ex dono Ernaldi fecundi de Bofco, confirmationem de predictis ecclefiis. Et preterea concedit & confirmat nobis ecclefiam de Bulkyngtonâ, cum duabus virgatis terre, & omnibus pertinentiis fuis, &c. Item confirmationem duarum virgatarum terre in Branktonâ, & fex virgatarum terre in eadem, pratum de dominio de Wefton, molendinum de Brankot, cum terrâ & prato & vivario de Crafwell, & omnibus pertinentiis fuis. Item conceffit ut homines canonicorum habeant communem pafturam, cum hominibus fuis, ficuti unquam melius habuerunt tempore Henrici regis fenioris, &c.

---

[1] Dugdale, Mon. Angl. vol. II. p. 310; from Charyte's Rentale, fol. iii. a.   [2] Ibid. fol. iii. b.
[3] P. Le Neve, MS. ex autographo in Armorio Collegio Armor. London, 1714.

I

20. Carta Ernaldi tertii de Bosco.

Habemus, ex dono Ernaldi tertii de Bosco, confirmationem de omnibus que Ernaldus de Bosco avus suus & Ernaldus pater suus nobis dederunt.

Preterea habemus, ex dono ejus, unam bovatam terre in Thorp-Ernald, cum tofto & crofto, & communem pasturam ad sexies viginti oves, & decem acras prati in loco qui vocatur Redinwalde.

21. Carta Ernaldi quarti de Bosco.

Universis Christi fidelibus Ernaldus de Bosco salutem in Domino. Noveritis quod ego confirmavi omnes donationes & concessiones quas Ernaldus de Bosco atavus meus, & Ernaldus de Bosco avus meus, & Ernaldus de Bosco pater meus, dederunt Deo & ecclesie Sancte Marie de Pratis Leycestrie, & canonicis regularibus ibidem Deo servientibus.

Ecclesiam de Cliftonâ, cum capellis de Wovere & de Rokebi, & omnibus pertinentiis suis.

Ecclesias quoque similiter de Evinton & de Humberstone, & ecclesiam de Bulkinton, cum duabus virgatis terre.

Item unam carucatam terre in Bernangall, illam scil' terram quam Henricus de Merston aliquando de Ernaldo de Bosco avo meo tenuit.

Item duas virgatas terre in Bramcote, que fuerunt Ranulfi, & pratum quod fuit de dominico de Weston.

Item sex virgatas terre in Bramcote, quas habuerit de dono Galfridi L'abbe.

Item molendinum de Bramcotâ, cum terrâ & prato, & vivario, scil' Cressewelle, & cum omnibus ad ipsum molendinum pertinentibus.

Et concessi ut homines predictorum canonicorum habeant communem pasturam cum omnibus meis ubicunque sicut unquam majus habuerunt tempore regis Henrici senioris, secundum cartarum predecessorum meorum tenorem.

Item ecclesiam de Thorpe Ernald juxta Melton, cum terris & toftis & croftis, cum situ bercarie eorum, & omnibus pertinentiis suis, cum decem acris prati in loco qui dicitur Redinwalde, inter pratum quod fuit Alicie Bassett & pratum de dominico meo; & communem pasturam ad sexies viginti oves.

Preterea dedi, pro salute anime mee, & Johanne uxoris mee, & omnium predecessorum meorum & successorum meorum, ad honorem dicte ecclesie de Thorpe, ut sepedicte canonici in perpetuum habeant decem averia, scil' VIII boves & duas vaccas, in propriâ pasturâ meâ, cum propriis averiis meis, ubicunque pascantur, &c. absque aliquâ demandâ, &c. salvâ mihi & heredibus meis unâ librâ piperis per annum ad festum Sancti Botulfi solvend' pro bovatâ terre quam Radulphus clericus tenuit.

Et confecta fuit hec carta anno Domini MCCXL, ciclo lunari currente per sex. Hiis testibus; dño Rogeri de Quincy, comite Winton', & constabulario Scotie; Thomâ de Esteleye, Serlone de Sancto Andreâ, Johanne de Herci, & Ricõ rectore de Thurkeliston; Rado de Orrabi; magistro de Meleford; Wilto Grinâ, & Wilto fil' Willi de Keleby; Henrico de Lilleburne; Simone clerico de Oseliston; & multis aliis [1].

22. Carta regis Henrici Secundi, donatorum concessiones recitans & confirmans [2].

Henricus, rex Anglie, dux Normannie & Aquitanie, & comes Andegavie, archiepiscopis, &c. salutem. Sciatis me concessisse, & in perpetuam eleemosinam confirmâsse, Deo & ecclesie Sancte Marie de Prato Leicestrie, & canonicis regularibus ibidem Deo servientibus, quicquid Robertus comes Leircestrie eis dedit, vel daturus est, in terris & ecclesiis, & decimis, & omnibus aliis rebus; & quicquid alii eis rationabiliter dederunt vel daturi sunt.

Ex dono videlicet predicti comitis Roberti Leicestr', ipsum locum in quo abbatia fundata est.

Ecclesiam Sancte Marie de Castello Leicestr', cum omnibus prebendis & possessionibus ejusdem ecclesie;

& cum omnibus pertinentiis suis, sicut Robertus comes Mellend predicte ecclesie olim concesserat; & ceteras omnes ecclesias Leicestrie.

Et ecclesiam de Coffebi, que pertinet ad ecclesiam Sancti Augustini de Leicester, cum omnibus rebus predicte ecclesie pertinentibus.

Et extra portam de Nort de Leicestre, sex carucatas terre & dimidiam, cum illâ que olim jacebat ad cuneos monete, & octo mansiones.

Extra portam de West, septem virgatas terre & unam bovatam.

De reddtibus Leicestrie sex libras per annum, & omnes domos quas Gubertus decanus tenebat ad portam de Suth.

Et decimam pullorum de equariâ comitis.

Et totum molendinum juxta abbatiam, cum socâ & prato adjacentibus.

Et ecclesiam de Lilleburne, & XL s. de redditibus ejusdem ville.

Et ecclesiam de Sepenhevâ, & omnes ecclesias de eâdem socâ; & decimam denariorum de redditibus; & decimam de pasnagio in eâdem socâ.

Et ecclesiam de Brackele, cum capellis de Halfo & de Sigresham, cum omnibus pertinentiis suis; & cum decimis denariorum de redditibus de Brackele, & de socâ de Halfo.

Et ecclesiam de Farningehou, cum pertinentiis suis.

Et in Turmodestone tres carucatas terre & tres virgatas terre.

Et in Burtone unam virgatam terre.

Et totum manerium de Aisfordeby, cum ecclesiâ, & cum molendino, & cum omnibus pertinentiis suis.

In Sedgrave, sex carucatas & tres bovatas terre.

Et ecclesias de Knapetoft & Ernesby, & de Turneby; & de Teingworth, & de Stantonâ, & de Ilmesdon, & de Hildeslai in Berkesirâ, cum omnibus pertinentiis suis.

Et locum de Stokkiford, cum nemore & terrâ adjacente, sicut comes Leicestr' eam escambiavit Willielmo de Novo Mercato pro Witewich.

Et de Ricardo Mallorie & de heredibus suis quadraginta solidos pro terrâ de Weltone & de Trop.

Et quatuor solidos in Leicestriâ de domibus Godwini Bena; et sex exsarta de dono Jocelini Marescalli.

Ex dono Willielmi de Aunciâ, unam carucatam terre, que vocatur Anestaneslaya.

Ex dono Gaufridi de Turvillâ, terram que vocatur Netlebed.

Ex dono Avicie comitisse, quatuor libratas terre in Everleys; scilicet nonam partem ejusdem ville, cum pertinentiis suis.

Ex dono Ernaldi de Bosco, ecclesiam de Cliftonâ, cum capellis de Rokeby & de Wovere; & ecclesiam de Torp, cum capellâ de Brantingby; & ecclesias de Evintonâ & de Humberstan.

Ex dono Willielmi de Novo Mercato & Rogeri de Bordeni, ecclesiam de Langeton, cum capellis de Torp & Turlingtone.

Ex dono Ranulfi comitis Cestrie, ecclesiam de Barwâ, cum capellâ de Querendone; cum terris, decimis, & omnibus pertinentiis suis; & cum illâ carucatâ terre quam idem comes de suo dominio in Barewâ & in Querendonâ accrevit eidem ecclesie.

Ex dono Roberti comitis de Warewich, ecclesiam de Norburch, cum capellâ de Hounecote; & cum omnibus pertinentiis suis.

Ex dono Gaufridi de Dalby, unum pratum in Segefwold.

Ex dono Rogeri de Watervillâ, ecclesiam de Bulkyntone, cum capellis & omnibus pertinentiis suis; & sex virgatas terre in Bramcotâ.

Et, ex dono Roberti fratris ejusdem Rogeri, molendinum ejusdem ville, cum terra & prato adjacente.

Ex dono Willielmi Avenel, villam Conkersberiam totam, cum molendinis; & clivam ex alterâ parte aque, & viginti acras terre in campo de Haddonâ.

Et ecclesiam de Adestoke, cum una carucatâ terre in eâdem villâ.

Ex dono Henrici Tuschet, unam virgatam terre in Assevellâ.

---

[1] Roper, MS. ex libro de Placitus 31 Edw. I. penes Oliverum St. John; fol. 217.

[2] Peck, MSS. 4937, fol. 184; ex Cart. 10 Edw. III. m. 2, n. 1. per Inspex. Vide etiam Cart. 11 Edw. II. n. 10.

Q

Ex dono Hugonis de Divâ & Helewifie uxoris ejus, duas partes decime garbarum de dominio de Gaham.

Item, ex dono Roberti comitis Leiceſtrie, molendinum de Belegravâ; & villam de Stoctonâ totam, preter terram Radulphi Fridai.

Ex dono Roberti de Syfrewaſt, medietatem ecclefie de Ceſtreſham.

Ex dono Willielmi Triket, ecclefiam de Sharnebrok.

Ex dono Ricardi filii Walonis, ecclefiam de Eindonâ.

Ex dono Willielmi Barre, ecclefiam de Billinges.

Ex dono Willielmi de Sifrewaſt, ecclefiam de Billeſdone, cum capellis de Rolveſtone & de Gouteby, & omnibus aliis pertinentiis fuis.

Ex dono Thome Sorell, ecclefias de Thorentonâ & de Sigreſham.

Ex dono Roberti comitis Leiceſtrie, ecclefiam de Aldeby, cum capellâ de Whetſtan, & omnibus aliis pertinentiis fuis.

Ex dono Willielmi de Lodbrok, ecclefiam de Blaby, cum capellâ de Torp, & omnibus aliis pertinentiis fuis.

Ex dono Roberti Rabaz, ecclefiam de Kivelingworthe.

Ex dono Roberti de Barefworth & Rogeri Cute filii ejus, ecclefiam de Barefworth, cum pertinentiis fuis; & unam carucatam terre in eâdem villâ.

Ex dono Rogeri Sampfon, unam virgatam terre in Barefworthe.

Ex dono Reginaldi de Muflei, duas virgatas terre in Muflei.

Ex dono Radulfi de Martivall, filii Ricardi Martivall, unam virgatam terre in Humberſtan.

Ex dono Roberti de Burtonâ, unam virgatam terre in Nortonâ.

Ex dono Walteri le Poher, ecclefias de Barkeby & de Hungertonâ, cum capellis & omnibus aliis pertinentiis fuis.

Ex dono Willielmi de Evermue, ecclefiam de Eitonâ.

Ex dono Roberti Arabi, ecclefiam de Eſtwellâ.

Ex dono Roberti filii Radulphi, ecclefiam de Hareſtan & de Kniptonâ.

Ex dono Roberti, filii Roberti, filii Col, ecclefiam de Yolgrave, cum capellis, terris, decimis, & omnibus aliis pertinentiis fuis.

Item, ex dono ipfius Roberti, ecclefiam de Bitmeſwellâ.

Ex dono Hugonis de Ardenâ, ecclefiam de Croddeworth, & ermitagium & nemus de Berewode, cum molendinis & omnibus aliis pertinentiis fuis.

Ex dono Gaufridi de Croft, unam carucatam terre in Sutton.

Ex dono Roberti de Croft, unam carucatam terre in Stoke.

Ex dono Radulphi de Turvillâ, ecclefiam de Croft.

Ex dono Ofberti de Lementonâ, unam bovatam terre in Sugkebergâ.

Ex dono Ricardi l'Abbe, ecclefiam de Anlep, & fex virgatas terre in eâdem villâ.

Item, ex dono ejufdem Ricardi, & Ricardi filii Philippi, unam carucatam terre in Empyngham.

Ex dono Roberti comitis, locum de Pineflade.

Ex dono Willielmi de Kileby, tres virgatas terre in Kileby.

Ex dono Godefridi Patroc, quinque virgatas terre in Bitmeſwellâ.

Ex dono Willielmi de Kereby, unam carucatam terre in Theingworth.

Ex dono Radulfi Pincerne, ecclefiam de Theingworth, cum pertinentiis fuis.

Ex dono Willielmi de Loncaſtre, totum manerium de Cokerham, cum ecclefiâ ejufdem ville, cum capellâ de Elhale, & cum omnibus aliis pertinentiis & libertatibus fuis, ficut carte predicti Willielmi teſtantur.

Ex dono Radulfi de Queneburch, ecclefiam ejufdem ville, cum terris, decimis, & omnibus aliis pertinentiis fuis.

Ex dono Ricardi l'Abbe, unam virgatam terre in Lilleburnâ.

Ex dono Galfridi de Dalby, tres virgatas terre in eâdem villâ.

Ex dono Roberti de Cotis, unam virgatam terre in Foxtonâ.

Quare volumus & firmiter precipimus, quod prefati canonici has predictas terras & tenementa teneant & habeant benè & in pacè, liberè & quietè & honorificè, cum omnibus libertatibus & liberis confuetudinibus prefatis terris pertinentibus, ficut carte donatoru teſtantur. Hiis teſtibus; Rogero archiep' Ebor'; Roberto Lincoln' epifc'; Nigello Helienfi epifc'; Thomâ cancellario; Roberto comite Leiceſtrie; Reginaldo comite Cornubie; Ricardo de Humez, conſtabulario; Henrico de Effex, conſtabulario; Ricardo de Lucy, Warino filio Geroldi. Apud Doveram.

23. Carta Henrici II. conceſſa abbatie Sancte Marie de Legeceſtriâ de Prato [1].

Henricus, rex Anglie, dux Normannie & Aquitanie, & comes Andegavie, archiepifcopis, epifcopis, abbatibus, comitibus, baronibus, ballivis, miniſtris, & omnibus fidelibus fuis Francie & Anglie, falutem. Sciatis me recepiſſe in meâ propriâ manu & cuſtodiâ & protectione (ficut unam de propriis meis eleemofinis) ecclefiam Sce Marie Leiceſtr' de Prato, cum omnibus pertinentiis fuis. Quare volo & firmitèr precipio, quòd canonici in predictâ ecclefiâ Deo fervientes omnia tenementa fua teneant benè & in pace, liberè & quietè, integrè, plenariè, & honorificè, in bofco & in plano, pratis & pafcuis, aquis & marifcis, in pifcariis, in toftis & croftis, in viis & femitis, & in omnibus locis, tam in burgo quàm extra burgum, libera & quieta de geldis & danegeldis, & auxiliis & wapentachiis, & hundredis & fhiris, & tenêmannetale, & murdris, & fcutagiis, & aſſifis & fummonitionibus, & de omnibus placitis & querelis, & occafionibus & confuetudinibus, & de omni terreno fervicio & feculari exactione, cum focâ & facâ, & tol & theam, & infangenethef, & omnibus aliis confuetudinibus & libertatibus. Et volo, ut predicti canonici & homines fui habeant falvum conductum meum, & fint liberi & quieti à paſſagio & pontagio, & theloneo & ſtallagio, per omnes civitates meas & burgos; & vendant & emant liberè & quietè. Et volo ut fint quieti à traverfo per omnes portus noſtros. Et fi quis versùs domum illam aliquid de poſſeſſionibus ejus clamaverit, prohibeo ne pro aliquo refpondeant, nec in placitum ponantur, nifi per me, & in prefentiâ meâ. Teſtibus; Thomâ cancellario, Philippo epifcopo Baioc', Rico de Humez, Man' de Bifet. Apud Rothom'.

24. Charta Ricardi I. conceſſa abbatie Sancte Marie Legreceſtrenfi prato, in comitatu Leiceſtrie [2].

Ricardus, Dei gratiâ, &c. Sciatis nos recepiſſe, &c. [ut fuprà]. Teſtibus; B. Cantuar' archiepo, H. Dunelm' epo, W. de Longo Campo cancellario ñro & Elyen' electo, Robto de Wileſt; octavo die Novembris; apud Weſtm'.

25. Carta regis Johannis, donatorum conceſſiones recitans & confirmans [3].

JOHANNES, Dei gratia, &c. Sciatis nos conceſfiſſe, & prefenti cartâ noſtrâ confirmâſſe, in liberam, quietam, & perpetuam eleemofinam, Deo & ecclefie Sancte Marie de Prato Leic', & canonicis regulariter ibidem Deo fervientibus, ex dono Roberti comitis Leirc'; fundatoris ejufdem ecclefie, totum manerium de Cnithtintone, quod eis dedit, cum molendino & aliis pertinentiis & omnibus libertatibus fuis, exceptis burgenfibus infra muros Leirc' & citra ad idem feodum pertinentibus; & exceptis terris fervientum fuorum; fcilicet, Roberti Bacheler, & Willielmi Oggeri, & Willielmi filii Godefridi, in perpetuam eleemofinam, liberam & quietam ab omni exactione & fervicio feculari; ita quod heredes fui acquietabunt hanc eleemofinam erga dominum epifcopum Linc' de fervicio unius militis, quod ei debent pro x libratis terre, quas tenuerunt in predicto manerio, fcilicet Weſtcote, cum omnibus pertinentiis fuis, quas Robertus comes, avus ejufdem comitis, dederat ecclefie Linc' in efcambium pro predicto manerio de Cnithtintone & Suburbio Leirc', cum pertinentiis fuis; quas etiam terras prefatus comes filius Petronille, aſſenfu predicti

---

[1] Cartæ Antiquæ ex Turre London. X. n. 19. inter Harl. MSS. 84. fol. 271. b. [2] Ibid. n. 20. fol. 272. a.
[3] Dugdale, Mon. Angl. vol. II. p. 315; ex Cart. 6 Johannis, n. 44.

epif-

epifcopi & capituli Linc', dedit predicte ecclefie & canonicis Leirc', pro terris fuis de Esfordeby & de Segrave, cum pertinentiis fuis, quas affenfu eorundem canonicorum dedit ecclefie Linc', pro pace refor-mandâ inter ipfum & ecclefiam Linc', fuper predicto manerio de Cnithtintone & Suburbio Leic', cum pertinentiis fuis; in quo manerio & fuburbio conceffit predicte ecclefie & canonicis Leirc', quicquid in eis habent. Preterea conceffimus & confirmavimus eifdem canonicis Leirc', in liberam, quietam, & perpetuam eleemofinam, ex dono predicti comitis filii Petronille, cum corpore fuo, xxiiii virgatas terre in Anefty, cum hominibus & aliis pertinentiis fuis, & quatuor cotariis, cum toftis fuis, in eâdem villâ; & pafturam inter duas vias in defenfo Leirc', fcilicet, inter viam de Groby & viam de Anefty, ad averia fua pafcenda; & i carectatam ligni cotidiè in foreftâ Leirc', in perpetuum, ad focum domûs infirmarie canonicorum Leirc', cum aliis tribus carectatis fuis, quas ex donatione avi fui prius habuit, ficut carte predictorum donatorum, quas inde habent, rationabiliter teftantur. Quare volumus, &c. Dat. per manum J. de Well', apud Wigorn', xxiiii die Marcii, anno, &c. vi°.

26. Charta Henrici III. pro canonicis Sancte Marie de Prato Leiceftrie, five abbatie canonicorum Leiceftrie, in agro Leiceftrenfi [1].

Henricus, Dei gratiâ, rex Anglie, dominus Hibernie, dux Aquitanie, Normannie, & comes Andegovie, &c. Sciatis nos recepiffe, &c. [ut fupra]. Si quis, &c. prohibemus ne pro aliquo refpondeant, nec in placitum ponantur, nifi coram nobis, vel coram capitali jufticiario noftro, aut per preceptum noftrum. Hiis teftibus; Euftacio London' epo, Petro Winton', Jocel' Bathon', Rico Sarum, epis; Huberto de Burgo, comite Kancie, juftic'; Rado filio Nicholai, Rico de Argentein, Henrico de Capellâ, & aliis. Dat' per manum Radi Ciceftr' epi, venerabilis patris noftri cancellarii, apud Weftm', xvi° die Martii, anno regni nri vi°.

27. Charta regis Edwardi I. de liberâ warennâ in omnibus terris dominicis domini abbatis & conventûs in com' Leic' [2].

Rex archiepifcopis, &c. falutem. Sciatis nos conceffiffe, & hâc cartâ noftrâ confirmâffe, dilectis nobis in Chrifto abbati & conventui beate Marie de Leiceftr', quòd ipfi & fucceffores fui in perpetuum habeant liberam warennam in omnibus dominicis terris fuis de Leiceftr', Stofton, Thurmefton, Barkeby, Queniburgh, Lokyngton, Bitmefwell, Borefworth, & Pinflade, in comitatu Leiceftr', dumtamen terre ille non fint infra metas forefte noftre; ita quod nullus intret terras illas, ad fugandum in eis, vel aliquid captandum quod ad warennam pertinet, fine licentiâ domini abbatis & conventûs, vel fuccefforum fuorum, fuper forisfacturam noftram x librarum. Hiis teftibus; venerabilibus patribus, A. Dunelm', W. Coventr' & Lichf', epifcopis; Guidone de Bello Campo, comite Warw'; Adomaro de Valenciâ, Hugone le Defpenfer, Roberto de Monte Alto, Willo Martyn, Rogero de Mortuo Mari, Johe de Moun, & aliis. Dat' per manum noftram, apud Kenilworth, fecundo die Junii.

Rex precepit ad inftantiam Agnetis de la Crace, domicelle regine.

28. Infpeximus regis Edwardi Secundi, confirmationem Thome comitis Lancaftrie, de diverfis diverforum hominum, recitans & confirmans.

Rex omnibus, &c. falutem. Infpeximus quoddam fcriptum, quod dilectus confanguineus & fidelis nofter Thomas comes Lancaftrie fecit dilectis nobis in Chrifto abbati & conventui de Leiceftr', in hec verba. Conceffionem & confirmationem quas Ernaldus de Bofco fecit abbati & conventui de Leiceftr', de omnibus donationibus & conceffionibus, quas Ernaldus

de Bofco avus ipfius Ernaldi, & Ernaldus pater ejufdem Ernaldi, fecerunt predictis canonicis, de ecclefiâ de Clifton, &c. [ut fupra, p. 57.]

Conceffionem etiam quam idem Ernaldus de Bofco fecit canonicis prediclis, de omnibus terris & tenementis, cum omnibus pertinentiis fuis, que fuerunt Radulphi de Arrabi in Wibetoft & in Omechifton.

Habendas dictis canonicis quietè & folutè de omnibus curiis, fectis, releviis, vifibus franciplegii, &c.

Tefte rege, apud Ebor', vi° die Novembris [3].

29. A fire Seignr le Roy & fon confeil pent fes chapelleyns l'abbe & covent de Leyc', q come ils eient del doun Robt jadiz counte de Leyceftr' lur fundour, & del doun & confirmement autres countes de Leyc', divfes chofes dont eaux & lur pdeceffours ont eftee feifiz tant q'l temps q le honr de Leyc' deveynt en la meyn nre feignr le roy p la forfete fire Thomas jadiz counte de Lanc'; c'eft a faver, vi livres de añuele rente iffantz de la rente de Leyc', a prendre chefcun an pmy la meyn le refceviour de Leyc' a la Pafch' & la Seint Michel, p oweles portions; & une charettee de bufche chefcun jour l'an, a prendre del boys de Leyc'; & touz lur demeynes porcs a pefczer en temps de peftzon en la defenfe de Leyc', fantz doner pafnage; & une pcele de tre & de boys q'il lur doune fire Simon jadiz counte de Leyc', & une autre pcele de bois q'il ont del doun fire Robt jadis counte de Leyc'; a enoffer les, & enclore, & faire les garder p lur gentz, & faire lur pfit de eaux a mieux q'il verront pour lur avantages, come plus pleinemet eft contenuz en les chartres des ditz countes, lefquels il ont preftres a monftrer; des queux chofes ore de novel funt ouhtez & defturbez p les miniftres nre dit feignr le roy, en deshitance de eaux & lur maifon. Pleife a nre dit feignr & fon confeil comander al gardeyn de Leyc', & fes autres miniftres illoec, p fes briefs, q fes ditz chapelleyns peuffent aver & ufer les chofes avantdites dont il funt defturbez, & totes autres chofes comprifes en lur chartres dont il ont eftee feifiz; & dont il doutent eftre defturbez p malice en temps a venir.

Oftendant cartas fuas, & inquiratur veritas facti p certos fideles ad hoc affignandos; &, inquificoe retornatâ, fiat jufticia [4].

30. A fire Seignr le Roi prient fes chapelleyns, abbe & covent de Leyceftre, qe come le park de Baggeworth, femblement ove le manere, ove toutz les aportenances, q'eft en la mayne nre feigneur le roi, foit dedeynz la paroche de la eglife de Thornton, laqele ils unt en ppres ufes, et de quele park, enfemblement od le maner, les ditz abbe & covent ount eu en tout maner de difme tut temps, auxi bien de harace come de altre, taun qe al temps qe le ditz park & manere vindrent en la mayn nre feignure le roi. Pleife a nre feigneur le roi commander, qe la difme de fon harace q'eft dedeinz le dit park de Baggeworth, & dedeinz la paroche de lur dit efglife de Thornton, lour foit livere, auxi bien del temps paffe nre feigneur le roi, come del temps a venir. Et plefe a nre feigneur le roi comaunder au treforer & as barons de l'Efcheker, q'ils alowent la difme de l'avaundite harace fire feigneur le roi au gardeyn de mefme la harace.

Affignentur per breve de cancellar' aliqui fideles, ad inquirend' in prefenciâ cuftodis predictarum forisfcurar' in com' Leic', fi parcus de Baggeworth fit infra procinctum paroch' ecclefie de Thornton, & fi abbas & conventus Leic', rectores ejufdem ecclefie, & eor' predeceffores, antequam manerium de Bagworth cum dicto parco devenerunt ad manus dñi regis, femper habuerunt & perceperunt decimas haracii ibidem; &, retornata dca inquif' in canc', fi compertum fuerat ita effe, tunc fiat ei jufticia [5].

31. Confirmatio regis Edwardi Tertii diverfarum cartarum [6].

Rex archiepifcopis, &c. falutem. Infpeximus

---

[1] Peck MSS. 4937, fol. 188: ex Cartis Antiquis in Turre London. A. n. 28; vel ex Harl. MSS. 84. fol. 9.
[2] Peck, ibid. fol. 191; ex Cart. 29 Edw. I. n. 27.
[4] Rot. Parl. vol. I. p. 388.   [5] Ibid. p. 434.
[3] Peck, ibid. fol. 195; ex Pat. 12 Edw. II. parte 1. m. 18.
[6] Peck, MSS. 4937, fol. 146; ex Clauf. 10 Edw. III.

cartam

cartam quam dominus Henricus, quondam rex Anglie, fecit Deo & ecclefie S. Marie de Prato Leiceft', & canonicis regularibus ibidem Deo fervientibus, in hec verba : " Henricus, rex Anglie, dux Normannie," &c. prout fupra, p. 58.

Infpeximus aliam cartam domini Henrici, quondam regis Anglie, in hec verba: " Henricus, Dei gratiâ, regis Anglie, dominus Hibernie," &c. prout fupra in Protectione, p. 58.

Infpeximus aliam cartam domini Edwardi, regis Anglie, in hec verba; " Rex," &c. [prout fupra; Julii 2, 29 Edw. I.]

32. R. dilco fibi in Xpo abbi beate Marie de Pratis Leic', faltm. Quia in ultimo parliamento ñro ordinatum fuit, q̃d denarii de decimâ & quintadecimâ nobis in eodem parliamento p cõitatem regni ñri Angl' conceff' ,pvenientes in aliquâ eccl:â cathedrali, vel monafterio, in quolibet comitatu, ubi melius cuftodi poffent, ponerentur & ibidem ,p expenfis guerras ñras contingentibus falvò cuftodirentur : Per q̃d mandavimus dilc̃is & fidelibus ñris Hugoni de Preftwold & Rogero de Belgrave, quos ad d̃cas decimam & quintamdecimam in com' Leiceft' colligend' affignavimus, q̃d ões denarii de eifdem decimâ & quintâdecimâ in d̃c̃o com' ,pvenientes, in abb̃â v̄râ p̃d̃câ ,p fecuriori cuftod' reponi faciant : Et ideò vobis mandamus, quòd p̃fatis collectoribus q̃dam domum congruam & fortem in eâdem abbatiâ, ubi denarii p̃d̃ci fecurius poterunt cuftodiri, lib̃ari faciatis, & ipfos collectores lib̃um ingreffum & egreffum ad eandem ,p voluntate fuâ h̃ere pmittatis; ita q̃d ipfi nobis de denariis illis refpondere valeant, cùm ipfos fup̃ hoc fecimus p̃muniri. Et hoc ficut de vobis confidemus, & nos & v̄ra indempnia s̃vare volũitis, nullatenùs omittatis. T. R. apud Weftm', xiii die Octobris [1].

33. Licentia regis Edwardi Tertii abbati, quòd non teneatur venire ad parliamentum [2].

Rex omnibus ad quos, &c. falutem. Supplicavit nobis dilectus nobis in Chrifto abbas de Leyceftriâ, ut cùm abbatia fua predicta per Robertum Fitz Robert de Melan, dudum comitem Leyceftrie, fundata fuiffet in puram & perpetuam eleemofinam, & advocatus five patronatus ejufdem ad manus domini Henrici, quondam regis Anglie, per forisfacturam Simonis de Mountforti, tunc comitis Leyceftrie & patroni ejufdem, devenerit, idemque abbas aliqua terras feu tenementa de nobis per baroniam feu alio modo non tenet, per quod ad parliamenta feu confilia noftra venire teneatur, nec aliquis predecefforum fuorum ante XLIX annum dicti proavi noftri poft forisfacturam predicti Simonis (quo anno omnes abbates & priores regni noftri Anglie ad parliamentum ejufdem proavi noftri tunc tentum voluntariè fummoniti fuerunt) fummonitus extiterit. Velimus ipfum abbatem de hujufmodi adventu ad parliamentum facere exonerari. Et quia, vifis cartis & confirmationibus de terris & tenementis eidem abbatie datis & conceffis in rotulis cancellarie noftre irrotulatis, compertum eft quòd dicta abbathia per predictum Robertum Fitz Robert de Melan, tunc comitem Leyceftrie, fundata erat in puram & perpetuam eleemofinam, & non invenitur in rotulis predictis quòd predictus abbas aliquas terras feu tenementa de nobis tenet per baroniam, feu aliquo alio fervitio, nec quòd predeceffores fui abbates loci predicti ad aliqua parliamenta progenitorum noftrorum ante predictum XLIX annum dicti proavi noftri aut poftmodum continuè, fed vicibus interpolatis, fummoniti fuerunt. Nolentes ipfum abbatem indebitè fic vexari, conceffimus, pro nobis & heredibus, quòd idem abbas & fucceffores fui de veniendo ad parliamenta & confilia noftra vel heredum noftrorum de cetero quieti fint & exonerati in perpetuum; ita femper quòd dictus abbas & fucceffores fui in procuratores ad hujufmodi parliamenta & confilia pro clerum mittendos confentiant, &, ut moris eft, ex-

penfis contribuant eorundem. In cujus, &c. Tefte rege, apud Weftm', xv° die Feb'.

Per petitionem de parliamento.

34. A Roi ñre t̃s fovain S̃r, fupplient t̃s humblement voz poṽes & continuelx orators les noirs chanons de l'ordre de Seint Auftyn, q̃ come c̃teins des ditz chanons fueront a vous ore tarde a Leyceftre, reherceant, coment toutz auts religioufes avoient a eux appropriez places & colleges honeftes & neceffaries deinz ṽre uniṽfite d'Oxenford, p grauntes, ordinances, & licences de voz t̃s nobles ,pgenitors, pur continuer lour ftudie illoeq̃s en les Efcoles, a l'encrefte de fcience & v̄tue, al fupportacion de Seinte Efglife & la Foie Chriftiene, forfpris voz ditz Oratours, queux font defolatz de foil ou place deinz la dite uniṽfite pur eux edifier pur lour ftudie, en graunde anientiffment de eux. Et fur ceo, t̃s gracious S̃r, l'Evefq̃ d'Exceftre avoit en cõmandement dept vous d'enquerer s'il fuift afcun lieu ou foil de.nz la dite uniṽfite a vendre, quelle fuift competent pour faire une covenable place pour l'eftudie des ditz fupplientz : et fur cella le dit Evefq̃ eft enfourme, q̃ font trois mees & quatre tofts a vendre, affiz fur Candiche jouft les moynes de Durefme, dehors les mures du dite uniṽfite, queux font del value annuel de quatre marcz out' les reprifes, & le foil des ditz mees & toftes eft covenable & covenable au̇iel place pur les dit fuppliantz, come avant eft dit, ovefq̃ ceo q'ils pourront avoir ṽre g̃cious s̃rie & focour en cefte ptie. Plefe a ṽre roial majefte, a la reṽence de Dieu, & ñre dame, & de Seint John de Bridelyngton, qi jadis fuift du dit ordre, q'ils achatent en ṽre noun les mees & toftes fuis ditz de les poffeffours d'icelles; &, qant ils ount les achatez, q'ils p ṽre licence & g̃ce efpecial purront doner les ditz mees & toftes folonc ṽre advis & ordinance as ditz fuppliantz & lour fucceffours, ou a afcun de eux, a toutz jours, pour faire une mefon competent pour lour ftudie, & de prier pour vous come pour lour Foundour ppetuelment. Et ceo fanz fyn ou fee a paier a ṽre oeps, l'eftatut des t̃res & tefitz a donerz a mortmain fait a contre non obftant, pour Dieu, & en oevre de charite. Confiderant, t̃s gracious S̃r, q̃ fi les ditz fuppliantz p̃ront avoir p ṽre g̃cious ordinance les ditz mees & toftes, ils vorront a lour coftages ordeiner pour la edificacion & novel conftruction du dite mefon [3].

35. Patentes regis Edwardi Quarti, de inquirendo an cenobium beate Marie de Pratis exoneratum eft de corrodiis, concedendis ad requifitionem regis? quibus explicatur, ex cujus fundatione ipfa domus eft; quomodo, per rebellionem Simonis de Monteforti, ejufdem patronatus ad manus regias pervenit (ubi plurima paffim de genealogiis ejufdem comitis & regis Edwardi Quarti); & quibus tamen pauperibus, quamvis domus hec corrodiis non eft onerandum, ex complacentiâ abbatum ad rogatus regum, corrodia aliquando conceffa fuerunt; ac etiam de quibus rebus eo tempore corrodia eadem conftituerint [4].

Rex dilectis & fidelibus fuis Willielmo Sutton, magiftro de Burton Sci Lazari Jerufalem in Angliâ; Ricardo Neel, uni fervientium noftrorum ad legem; Johanni Pulteneye, armigero; & Roberto Staunton; falutem. Monftravit nobis Johannes abbas monafterii beate Marie Leiceftrie, ut, cùm monafterium predictum fit de fundatione Roberti Melan, quondam comitis Leiceftrie, fundatum ante tempus memorie; & non de fundatione noftri, nec aliquorum progenitorum noftrorum regum Anglie; qui quidem Robertus Melan dictum monafterium fundavit, tenendum in puram & perpetuam eleemofinam; quod quidem monafterium quidam Ricardus, abbas monafterii illius, predeceffor predicti nunc abbatis, tenuit quietum & exoneratum de omnibus & fingulis corrodiis & fuftentationibus, concedendis ad requifitionem, rogatum, feu defiderium, alicujus regis Anglie, tempore pacis, tempore regis Edwardi Secundi, nobilis pro-

---

[1] Rot. Parl. vol. II. p. 451 ; ex Rot. Clauf. 18 Edw. III. p. 2. m. 11.
[2] Peck, MSS. 4937, fol. 147; ex Pat. 26 Edw. III. pars 1. m. 22.
[3] Rot. Parl. vol. IV. p. 159.   [4] Peck, MSS. 4937, fol. 157; ex Pat. 5 Edw. IV. parte 2. m. 35.

genitoris

gènitôris noftri; patronatus cujus monafterii ad manus Henrici Tertii, filii regis Johannis, nobilis progenitoris noftri, devenerit, per forisfacturam Simonis Mountefort, nuper comitis Leiceftrie, & patroni monafterii predicti, confanguinei & heredis predicti Roberti Melan, viz. filii Anne, fororis Roberti, filii Roberti Blaunchmaynes, filii Roberti Boffu, filii dicti Roberti Melan; pro eo quòd dictus Simon, apud Evefham in com' Wigorn', levaverit guerram erga dictum regem Henricum Tertium, quarto die Augufti, anno regni fui XLIX°, & ibidem interfectus fuit in campo; & de prefato rege Henrico Tertio patronatus dicti monafterii regi Edwardo Primo defcenderit, ut filio & heredi dicti regis Henrici Tertii; & de eodem rege Edwardo dictus patronatus regi Edwardo Secundo defcenderit, ut filio & heredi dicti regis Edwardi, filii regis Henrici; & de eodem rege Edwardo Secundo dictus patronatus regi Edwardo Tertio defcenderit, ut filio & heredi dicti regis Edwardi Secundi; & de prefato rege Edwardo Tertio predictus patronatus regi Ricardo Secundo defcenderit, ut confanguineo & heredi prefati regis Edwardi Tertii, filio principis Edwardi, filii dicti regis Edwardi Tertii; & de prefato rege Ricardo patronatus dicti monafterii nobis defcenderit, ut confanguineo & heredi dicti regis Ricardi, filio Ricardi, filii Anne, fororis Edwardi, filie Philippe, filie Lionelli, fratris Edwardi, patris prefati regis Ricardi. Et antedictus Ricardus abbas & omnes predeceffores predicti nunc abbatis tenuerunt, & de jure tenere debuerunt, dictum monafterium quietum & exoneratum de quocunque corrodio five fuftentatione habendo & percipiendo in vel de monafterio predicto, conceffo, five de jure concedendo, alicui perfone, ad defiderium, mandatum, five rogatum, aliquorum progenitorum noftrorum regum Anglie, feu aliquorum aliorum, à tempore cujus contrarii memoriâ hominum non exiftente, ufque ad tempus quod predictus abbas dicti monafterii & ejufdem loci tunc conventus, ad fpecialem inftantiam & rogatum, & pro fingulari complacentiâ progenitoris noftri regis Edwardi Tertii, & non de aliquo jure, concefferunt cuidam Johanni de la Sale talem fuftentationem, percipiendam in eâdem domo fuâ, pro termino vite fue, qualem Willielmus Puyllover habuit & percepit in eâdem domo dum vixerit; qui quidem Willielmus, omnibus diebus vite fue (dum fervire potuit), ferviens in dicto monafterio fuerat, & in fenectute fuâ, eâ confideratione, habuit competentem fuftentationem conceffam fibi in eâdem domo pro termino vite fue, viz. quâlibet die annuatim unum album panem de paftu *nuce* [1] conventualis, & unum panem de nigro paftu, & unam lagenam cervifie . . . .[2] feu melioris; & fervicium pro coquinâ (prout aliquis unus liberorum fuorum fervientium adtunc deferviebatur), & unam robam annuatim de fectâ liberorum fervientium fuorum ad feftum Natalis Domini, vel x s. argenti pro eâdem; & unam cameram in abbatiâ predictâ; & hec omnia abfque rogatu aut mandato alicujus progenitorum noftrorum regum Anglie; &, poft dictum conceffum eidem Johanni de la Sale, dictus nobilis progenitor rex Edwardus Tertius, per literas fuas patentes datas apud Wigorn', VIII° die Januarii, anno regni fui tertio, recitans dictam conceffionem fic factam ad fuam requifitionem, volens indempnitatem dictorum nunc abbatis & conventûs ex eâ parte, concefferit, pro fe & heredibus fuis, quòd dicta conceffio, fic gratiosè facta ad requifitionem fuam, non cederet in dampnum feu prejudicium illorum feu fuccefforum fuorum, vel domûs fue predicte, nec exnunc traheretur in confequentiam; vel quòd ipfi, feu fucceffores fui, vigore ejufdem conceffionis, aliquo tempore fequente, effent onerati de aliquâ ejufmodi fuftentatione erga ipfum vel heredes fuos; prout in dictis literis plenius continetur. Quibus non obftantibus, poft mortem dicti Johannis de la Sale, aliàs dicti Johannis atte Hall, Thomas Thedingworth, ad rogatum predicti regis Edwardi Tertii, habuit & percepit tale corrodium five fuftentationem in monafterio predicto. Et, poft eun-

dem Thomam, quidam Robertus Sadeller habuit & percepit tale corrodium five fuftentationem, &c. Tefte rege, apud Weftm', XVIII° die Julii.

36. Advocatio ecclefie de Eydon conceffa Paulo abbi de Leic' & fuccefforibus fuis per Ricum Wale, fil' Henrici, per finem levat' apud Weftm', à die Pafch' in xv dies, anno 4° Johis regis.
Finis apud Weftm', à die Pafche in xv dies, 4 Hen. III. inter Ricum Wale, fil' Henrici, per', & Willm abbem de Leic' deforc', de advocat' ecclie de Eyndon effe jus ipfius abbis & ecclie fue Sce Marie Leyc'[3].

37. Robertus abbas Sce Marie de Prato de Legrecefter concedit Salamoni capellano iconomo Hofpitalis de Brackele, & fuccefforibus ejus, habere ecclefiam intra fepta curie ejufdem hofpitalis & fepulturam, &c.; & ecclefia fit ab omni fubjectione quieta, &c. Teftibus (inter alios), Robto capellano noftro de Brackele [4].

38. Pro Rege.

De Rotulis jufticiariorum fuorum, per diverfa loca.
Mandatum eft abbati de Leyceftriâ, quòd, omnibus dilationibus & occafionibus poftpofitis, habeat coram, &c. in craftino Claufi Pafche, omnes Rotulos in abbathiâ fuâ refidentes, de placitis que fuerunt coram Stephano de Segrave, quondam jufticiario, &c. tam in banco quàm in itinere, per diverfos comitatus, &c. Et habeat breve.
Eodem modo mandatum eft priori de Kenilworth[5].

39. De Patrono.

Juratores dicunt, quòd Edmundus, frater regis, comes Leiceftrie, obiit feifitus de advocatione Abbathie Leiceftrenfis [6].

40. De terris abbatis & conventûs apud Burftall, ex dono Robertifilii Robertide Burftall [7].

Juratores dicunt, quòd non eft ad dampnum domini regis, nec aliorum, licèt dominus rex concedat Roberto filio Roberti de Burftall, quòd ipfe XXIIII acras prati, cum pertinentiis, in Burftall, in com' Leic', dare poffit abbati beate Marie de Leiceftriâ. Et dicunt, quòd predictus Robertus tenet eafdem terras, cum aliis tenementis, de quodam Johanne de Burton, per fervitium x marcarum per annum.

41. De molendino de Anefty, ex dono Ricardi de Bricheley [8].

Juratores dicunt, quòd non eft ad dampnum domini regis, nec aliorum, fi dominus rex concedat Ricardo de Bricheley, quòd ipfe molendinum in Anefty, in com' Leic', dare poffit & affignare abbati & conventui beate Marie de Leiceftriâ; & quòd tenetur de Willielmo de Ferrariis, per fervitium id. per annum; & quòd dictus Ricardus de Bricheley terras alias non habet, nifi v s. redditûs, cum pertin', in Leiceftriâ.

42. Licentia regis Edwardi II. Antonio epifcopo Dunelm', ut ipfe XXIIII acras terre & XL acras pafture, cum pertinentiis, in Ratby, dare poffit abbati & conventui beate Marie de Pratis[9].

Rex omnibus ad quos, &c. falutem. Licèt de communi confilio regni noftri, &c. per finem tamen quem dilectus nobis in Chrifto abbas Leiceftrie fecit nobifcum, conceffimus & licentiam dedimus, pro nobis & heredibus noftris, quantum in nobis eft, venerabili patri Antonio epifcopo Dunelmenfi, quòd ipfe quatuor-viginti acras terre & quadraginta acras pafture, cum pertinentiis, in Rotby, dare poffit & affignare prefatis abbati & conventui ejufdem loci, habend' & tenend' fibi & fuccefforibus fuis in perpetuum; & eidem abbati & conventui, quòd ipfi predictas terram & pafturam, cum pertinentiis, à prefato epifcopo recipere poffint & tenere fibi & fuccefforibus fuis in

---

[1] Sic. F. *n'ro*; *paftus* fignifying a *meal*. Du Cange, in voce.
[2] Deeft verbum. F. P.
[3] Bridges, MS.
[4] Ibid.
[5] Ex Memor. 42 Hen. III. Rot. 12. b.
[6] Peck, MSS. 4937. fol. 189; ex Efch. 25 Edw. I. N° 51. Leic.
[7] Peck, ibid, fol. 190; ex Inq. ad quod dampn. 29 Edw. I. N° 92. Leic.
[8] Peck, ibid. fol. 192; ex Inq. ad quod dampn. 34 Edw. I. p. 204. Leic.
[9] Peck, ibid.; fol. 193; ex Pat. 4 Edw. II. pars 2. m. 15.

R

perpetuum;

perpetuum; & eidem abbati & conventui, ficut predictum eft, tenore prefentium licentiam dedimus fpecialem; nolentes quòd predictus epifcopus vel heredes
fui, aut prefati abbas & conventus vel fucceffores
fui, ratione ftatuti predicti, per nos vel heredes noftros inde occafionentur in aliquo feu graventur;
falvis tamen capitalibus dominis feodi illius ferviciis
inde debitis & confuetis. In cujus, &c. Tefte rege,
apud Berwick fuper Tweede, xx° die Februarii.
Per finem decem marcarum.

43. De terris ex dono Willielmi Aunfelys & Ricardi
Whileby, in villâ de Abbey-gate juxta Leic' [1].

Juratores dicunt, quòd non eft ad dampnum, &c. fi
rex concedat Willielmo de Aunfelys, de Thorpe Ernald, quòd ipfe tria meffuagia, cum pertinentiis, in
l'Abbe-gate juxta Leic'; & Ricardo de Whileby,
clerico, quòd ipfe unum meffuagium in eâdem villâ;
dare poffint abbati de Leic'; & quòd antedicta tria
meffuagia tenentur in capite de ipfo abbate per fervitium vid. per annum, & duarum appar' ad vifum
franciplegii; & unum meffuagium tenetur de ipfo abbate per fervicium iid. Et quòd remanebunt [antedi-
dicto Willielmo] (ultra donationem) unum meffuagium, & unam virgatam terre in Cofby; & tenentur
in capite de ipfo abbate per fervitium xiis. & duarum
appar'. Et [antedicto Ricardo] cs. redditûs in Leic',
que tenentur de ipfo comite per fervitium i redditûs.

44. Commiffio Mag' Tho' de Bray, canonico Lincoln' directa, in negotio inter parochiam Sci Nicolai
in Leiceftria ex unâ parte, & abbatem & conventum
B. Marie Leyceftr', in negotio moto fuper carentiâ
unius vicarii, qui, ut dicitur, ad prefentationem ipforum
abbatis conventûfque per loci dioecefanum confuevit
admitti, defervitur eccl' antedict'; & fuper afpor-
tatione unius campane, librorum, veftimentorum, &
aliorum, ab ecclefiâ Sci Nicolai predicti facta, ut pre-
tenditur, per eofdem. Dat' apud Northampton, 2
kal. Aprilis, 1321 [2].

45. De cantariâ in ecclefiâ beate Marie de Pratis,
ex fundatione Johannis de Tours [3].

Juratores dicunt, quòd non eft ad dampnum, &c.
fi rex concedat Johanni de Tours, quòd ipfe unum
meffuagium, duo tofta, quater-viginti & octo acras
terre, & quinque acras prati & dimidiam, cum pertinentiis, in Burftall, Leiceftre, & Staunton juxta Bardon, in com' Leic', dare poffit abbati de Leiceftre,
ad inveniendum quendam capellanum; & quòd unum
meffuagium, xl acre terre, & due acre prati & dimidia, in Burftall, & x libre terre & redditûs in eâdem
villâ (que Robertus Burftall tenuit), & due acre
prati, cum pertinentiis, in Leiceftre, tenentur de domino rege, ut de honore Leiceftre, faciendo fectam
de tribus feptimanis in tres; & quòd duo tofta, &
quater-viginti & octo acre terre, & dimidia acra prati,
in Stanton juxta Bardon, tenentur de priore de
Charley per fervicium unius efparverii forinfeci, fol-
vendum ad feftum Sci Martini in hieme; & quòd duo
tofta, & xl acre terre, & dimidia acra terre & prati
in Staunton, tenentur de predicto priore per fervicium
predictum.

46. Breve regis Edwardi Tertii vicecomiti Leiceftrie,
ut abbati de Leiceftre quandam parcellam bofci in
Halliwellhagh juxta Loughborough, emptam ab
Henrico de Bello Monte, habere faciat, rebellione
ejufdem Henrici non obftante.

Rex vicecomiti Leiceftrie falutem. Quia acceffimus
per inquifitionem, quam per dilectos & fideles noftros
Willielmum Herle, Robertum Gaddefbye, & Rogerum
Belgrave, fieri fecimus, quod dilectus nobis in Chrifto
abbas de Leiceftr' quandam parcellam bofci in Halli-

wellhaghe juxta Loughtebourghe, de Henrico de
Bello Monte (diu antequam idem Henricus contra
nos in rebellionem proniffet, viz. die Lune in craftino
Dominice in mediâ Quadragefimâ, anno regni noftri
fecundo) emit; & xxviii libratas, pro quibus dictus bof-
cus emptus fuit, plenariè folvit prefato Henrico in
manerio de Loughteburghe; & quod predictam parcellam bofci continet in fe circiter duos acras; & quod
idem abbas partem inde vendidit & abduxit eadem
feifinâ; & quod quedam pars dicte parcelle capta fuit
in manum noftram per rebellionem dicti Henrici, &,
fimul cum aliis terris & tenementis fuis, in manu
noftrâ fic exiftit ex caufa predictâ: Vobis mandamus, &c. [4]

47. De terris abbatis apud Shepefheved, in com' Leic',
ex dono Johannis de Spondon, vicarii de Lokinton,
& Willielmi de Winelleston, vicarii de Shepevefhed [5].

Juratores dicunt, quod non eft ad dampnum domini
regis, nec aliorum, licet dominus rex concedat Johanni
de Spondon, vicario ecclefie de Lokinton [in com'
Leic'], & Willielmo de Wivellefton, vicario ecclefie
de Shepefheved, quod ipfi unum meffuagium, unum
toftum, & duas virgatas terre, cum pertinentiis, in Shepefheved, dare poffint abbati de Leiceftria, in parte
fatisfactionis viginti marcatarum terre & redditûs per
annum. Et dicunt, quod predicta meffuagium, toftum, & due virgate terre, tenentur de Matildâ de Holand, per fervitium vs. per annum; et quod remanebunt eifdem Willielmo & Johanni lx acre terre, cum
pertinentiis, in Shepefheved, que tenentur de predictâ
Matildâ de Holand per fervicium faciendi fectam, &c.

48. De terris abbatis apud Skeftington, in com' Leic',
ex dono Johannis de Spondon & W. de Afton [6].

Juratores dicunt quod non eft ad dampnum domini
regis, nec aliorum, fi dominus rex concedat Johanni
de Spondon & W. de Afton, quod ipfi tria meffuagia, fex virgatas terre, fex acras prati, x acras
pafture, x folidatos redditûs, cum pertinentiis, in
Skeftington, dare poffint abbati de Leiceftriâ, in partem fatisfactionis xx marcarum terre, quas dominus
rex eis dedit; et quod tenentur de Willielmo Gofce-
lyne per fervicium fex folidorum & octo denariorum
per annum; et quod remanebunt, ultra donationem
predictam, in Lokington, duo meffuagia, due virgate
terre, & xx acre prati, que tenentur de abbate per
fervicium unius grani piperis.

49. De terris abbatis in Lobefthorp, ex dono Willielmi la Zouche nuper decani [modò archiepifcopi]
Eboracenfis, & Rogeri la Zouche militis [7].

Juratores dicunt, quòd non eft ad dampnum domini
regis, nec aliorum, fi dominus rex concedat Willielmo
la Zouche, nuper decano ecclefie beati Petri Ebor',
& Rogero la Zouche militi, quòd ipfi fex meffuagia,
feptem virgatas terre & dimidiam, duas acras prati,
quatuor acras pafture, cum pertinentiis, in Lobefthorp, in com' Leic', dare poffint abbati beate Marie
de Leiceftriâ; quod quidem manerium tenetur per fe,
de predicto Willielmo, per fervicium quarte partis
unius feodi militis.

50. Licentia regis Edwardi Tertii Simoni de Iflep,
archiepifcopo Cantuarie, ut diverfas terras & tenementa, in com' Leic', dare poffit abbati & conventui
B. Marie de Pratis, ad quandam cantariam in ecclefiâ eorum conventuali inveniendum & fuftentan-
dum in perpetuum [8].

Juratores dicunt, quod non eft ad dampnum, fi rex
concedat magiftro Simoni de Iflep, archiepifcopo Cantuarie, quod ipfe vii meffuagia, iiii tofta, ii caru-
tatas terre, & v virgatas terre, ii acras prati, & xiiii
folidatas redditûs, cum pertinentiis, in Babbegrave,

---

[1] Peck, MSS. 4937; ex Inq. ad quod dampn. 5 Edw. II. N° 659. Leic.
[2] Regifter of Archbifhop Reynolds, fol. 89. b.
[3] Peck, MSS. 4937, fol. 142; ex Inq. ad quod dampn. 17 Edw. II. N° 129. Leic.
[4] Peck, ibid.; fol. 147; ex Clauf. 3 Edw. III. m. 18.
[5] Peck, ibid. fol. 144; ex Inq. ad quod dampn. 8 Edw. III. N° 36. Leic.
[6] Peck, ibid. fol. 145; ex Inq. ad quod dampn. 11 Edw. III. N° 56. Leic.
[7] Peck, ibid.; ex Inq. ad quod dampn. 23 Edw. III. pars 2. N° 3.
[8] Peck, ibid. fol. 145; ex Inq. ad quod dampn. 26 Edw. III. Leic. N° 39.

Stocton,

Stocton, Cosseby, & Thorp juxta Northburgh, & manerium de Ingwardby, cum pertinentiis, que de nobis non tenentur (exceptis xii messuagiis, xii virgatis terre, & xi denarratis redditûs in eodem manerio) ; & advocationem ecclesie de Wilughbye; & que quidem messuagia, tofta, terra, pratum, & manerium, sic danda & assignanda, valent per annum viii libras & xvi denaratas, dare possit abbati de Leicester; & quod ii messuagia, iiii tofta, & ii carucate terre de supradictis, que sunt in Babbegrave, tenentur de Willielmo la Zouch, per servicium vi s. per annum; & quod ii messuagia, & ii virgate terre, ii acre prati, & xiii solidate redditûs, de supradictis tenementis, in Stocton & Cosseby, tententur de abbate predicto, per servicium ii s. per annum, & sectam ad curiam suam de Stocton ; et quod iii messuagia, & iii virgate terre, que sunt in Cosseby & Thorp, tenentur de abbate, per servicium vii s. per annum; & manerium de Ingwardby tenetur de Johanne de Grey de Codnore, per servitium militare.

51. Licentia regis [1].

Rex omnibus ad quos, &c. salutem. Sciatis quod, cum per literas nostras patentes, de gratiâ nostrâ speciali, concesserimus & licentiam dederimus, pro nobis & heredibus nostris, quantum in nobis fuit, venerabili in Christo patri nunc archiepiscopo Cantuarie (sub nomine magistri Simonis de Islep) quod ipse x libratas terre vel redditûs per annum (que de nobis non tenentur in capite) dare possit & assignare quibuscunque religiosis vellet infra regnum nostrum Anglie existentibus, ad quandam cantariam inde (juxta ordinationes ipsius Simonis) inveniendum & sustentandum ; habendas & tenendas dictis religiosis & successoribus suis, ad dictam cantariam inveniendum & sustentandum in perpetuum ; & eisdem religiosis, quod ipsi dictas x libratas terre vel redditûs annui a prefato Simone recipere possint & tenere sibi & successoribus suis in perpetuum, sicut predictum est, similiter licentiam dederimus specialem, statuto de terris & tenementis ad manum mortuam non ponendis edito non obstante, prout in literis predictis plenius continetur : Nos (volentes concessionem predictam nostram effectui debito mancipari) concessimus & licentiam dedimus, pro nobis & heredibus nostris, quantum in nobis est, eidem archiepiscopo, quod ipse vii messuagia, &c. que quidem messuagia, &c. sic danda & assignanda valent per annum viii libras & xvi denaratas, juxta verum valorem eorundem (sicut per inquisitionem inde per dilectum nobis Johannem de Windesore, escaetorem nostrum in com' Leic', de mandato nostro captam, & in cancellariâ nostrâ retornatam, est compertum) dare possit & assignare dilectis nobis in Christo abbati & conventui de Leicester ; habendas & tenendas sibi & successoribus suis in perpetuum, in plenam satisfactionem x librarum, & terrarum & reddituum predictorum, ad quandam cantariam, juxta ordinationem ipsius archiepiscopi, inveniendum & sustentandum in perpetuum ; & eisdem abbati & conventui, quod ipsi messuagia, &c. cum pertinentiis (exceptis prout supra exceptis), & advocationem predictam, a prefato archiepiscopo recipere possint & tenere sibi & successoribus suis in perpetuum, sicut predictum est, tenore presentium, similiter licentiam dedimus specialem, statuto predicto non obstante ; nolentes quod predictus archiepiscopus per nos vel heredes nostro inde occasionetur in aliquo seu gravetur ; salvis tamen capitalibus dominis feodorum illorum serviciis inde debitis & consuetis. In cujus, &c. Teste rege, apud Westm', xxiii die Maii.

Pro xl s. solutis in hanaperio de incremento ultra plenam satisfactionem.

52. De cantariâ fundatâ per dominum Simonem Cant' archiep', in monasterio Beate Marie de Pratis, apud Leicestr' [2].

Universis sancte matris ecclesie filiis hanc cartam suspecturis, Simon de Islep, permissione divinâ Cant' archiepiscopus, totius Anglie primas, & apostolice sedis legatus, salutem in Domino sempiternam. Cum dominus Edwardus illustris rex Anglie & Francie, & dominus Hibernie, nobis concesserit, & per cartam suam licenciam dederit, sub nomine Simonis de Islep, quod possumus dare & assignare x libratas terre vel redditûs per annum, que de ipso dno rege non tenentur in capite, quibuscunque religiosis voluerimus infra regnum Anglie existentibus, ad quandam cantariam juxta ordinationem nostram inveniendum & sustinendam : Sciatis nos, pro salute nostrâ & animarum omnium fidelium defunctorum, dedisse, concessisse, & hâc presenti cartâ nostrâ confirmâsse, abbati & conventui ecclesie Beate Marie de Pratis Leycestrie, ii messuag', iiii tofta, ii carucatas, & v virgatas terre, ii acras prati, & xiiii solidatas redditûs, cum pertinentiis, in Babbegrave, Stocton, Cosseby ; advocationem ecclesie de Willoughby ; & manerium de Ingwardeby, cum pertinent', exceptis xii messuag', xii virgatis terre, & xi denaratis redditûs, cum pertinentiis, in eodem manerio, quod quidem manerium tenetur de domino Johanne de Grey de Codnore in capite ; & etiam i messuag' & i virgat' terre, cum pertinent', in Thorp juxta Northburgh, que habui de dono Galfridi de la Launde, in partem satisfactionis predictorum x libratar' terre vel redditûs, juxta extentam inde in cancellariâ dicti domini regis retornatam & allocatam, ad inveniendum & sustentandum unam cantariam, viz. unam missam p unum diem in septimanâ p unum canonicorum eccl' predict' in eâdem ecclesiâ pro animabus omnium fidelium defunctorum perpetuò celebrand'; habend' & tenend' prefato abbati & conventui, & eorum successoribus in perpetuum, faciendo inde capitalibus dnis feodi servicia debita & consueta. In cujus rei testimonium, sigillum nostrum presentibus apposuimus. Hiis testibus ; domino Willo Mottoun, domino Rog' de la Zouch, domino Ric' de Shelton, militibus ; Galfrido Vilers, Johanne Felelenle de Rerisby, Johanne de Sadynton, Johanne Eyric, Ric' de Stretton ; & multis aliis. Dat' apud Ingwardeby, v die mensis Junii, & regni regis Edwardi Tertii post Conquestum vicesimo sexto.

53. Licentia regis Edwardi Tertii, Simoni Pakeman, Thome de Roppele, clerico, & Ricardo de Leicestr', ut manerium & ecclesiam de Kirkeby Mallore, & diversas terras & redditus, & ecclesiam de Bytmeswell, &c. dare possint abbati & conventui de Leic' [3].

Juratores dicunt, quod non est ad dampnum, si rex concedat Simoni Pakeman de Kereby, Thome de Roppele [4], clerico, & Ricardo de Leicestr', quod ipsi manerium de Kirkeby Mallore, cum pertinentiis, & advocationem ecclesie ejusdem ville de Kirkeby ; necnon vii messuagia, unum molendinum, v virgatas terre, x acras prati, lxii solidatas & unam denaratam redditûs, & duas libras cumini, cum pertinentiis, in Bitmeswell, in com' Leic', & advocationem ecclesie ejusdem manerii, dare possint abbati & conventui Beate Marie de Pratis. Et dicunt, quod tenentur de Willo duce Bavarr' & Matildâ uxore ejus, & heredibus ejusdem Matildis, ut de honore Leic'; viz. manerium & advocatio per servicium medietatis feodi unius militis ; & messuagia, molendinum, terre, pratum, & redditus, &c. in Bitmeswell tenentur per servicium quarte partis unius feodi militis. Et remanebunt, ultra donationem, prefatis Simoni & Thome, e libras terre & redditûs, viz. apud Kereby, Braundeston, & Wykyngston, in com' Leic' ; & tenentur, de predicto duce & Matildâ uxore ejus, per servicium feodorum duorum militum.

54. Licentia regis [5].

Rex omnibus ad quos, &c. salutem. Licet, &c. Volentes tamen, ob specialem affectionem quam ad dilectos nobis in Christo abbatem & conventum ecclesie Beate Marie de Pratis Leicestr' gerimus & habemus, concessimus & licentiam dedimus, pro nobis & heredibus nostris, quantum in nobis est, Simoni Pakeman de Kereby, Thome de Roppele clerico, &

[1] Pat. 26 Edw. III.
[2] Register of Archbishop Islep, fol. 169. a. b inter Addenda.
[3] Peck, MSS. 4937, fol. 151: ex Inq. 35 Edw. III. n. 22.
[4] In alio exemplo, "Appleby." The Ropeley family had property at Appleby. See an inscription under the history of that parish.
[5] Pat. 35 Edw. III. pars 3. m. 28.

Ricardo

Ricardo de Leicefter, quod ipfi, manerium de Kirkeby Mallore, cum pertinentiis, & advocationem ejufdem ville de Kirkeby; necnon VII meffuagia, &c. in Bytmefwell (que tenentur de honore Leiceftr' ut dicitur), dare poffint & affignare predictis abbati & conventui, habendas & tenendas fibi & fucceffioribus fuis, de honore predicto, per fervicia inde debita & confueta in perpetuum; & eifdem abbati & conventui, quod ipfi predicta manerium, advocationem, meffuagia, molendinum, terram, pratum, & redditus, cum pertinentiis, a prefatis Simone, Thomâ & Ricardo, recipere poffint & tenere, fibi & fucceffioribus fuis, de honore predicto, per fervicia inde debita & confueta in perpetuum, ficut predictum eft, tenore prefentium, fimiliter licentiam dedimus fpecialem: ftatuto predicto non obftante; nolentes quod predicti Simon, Thomas, & Ricardus, vel heredes fui, aut prefati abbas & conventus, feu fucceffores fui, ratione ftatuti predicti, per nos vel heredes aut miniftros noftros quofcunque moleftentur in aliquo feu graventur; falvis tamen capitalibus dominis feodorum illorum ferviciis inde debitis & confuetis. In cujus, &c.

Tefte rege, apud Weftm'.

55. Licentia regis Ricardi II, Johanni Oxcliff, Johanni Coiton, Johanni Twywell, Johanni Anfty, Ricardo Gamefton, Roberto of the Halle, & Ricardo Barwe, quod ipfi diverfas terra & tenementa in Cokerham, Leicefter, Humberftan, Burftall, Barkeby, & Lokyngton, dare poffint abbati & conventui de Leiceftr' [1].

Juratores dicunt, quod non eft ad dampnum, fi rex concedat Johanni Twywell, Johanni Anfty, & aliis, quod ipfi VI meffuagia, XVI cotagia, III virgatas, unam bovatam, unam acram, & unam rodam terre, octo acras prati, XXIII folidatas, & IIII denarios redditûs, & redditum unius libre cumini, cum pertinentiis, in Leiceftriâ & fuburbio ejufdem ville, Humberfton, Burftall, Barkeby, & Lokyngton, dare poffint abbati & conventui Beate Marie de Pratis Leiceftr'.

56. Licentia regis [2].

Rex omnibus ad quos, &c. falutem. Sciatis quod, cum nos nuper conceffierimus & licentiam dederimus, pro nobis & fucceffioribus noftris, quantum in nobis fuit, dilectis nobis in Chrifto abbati & conventui domûs Leiceftrie, que de fundatione progenitorum noftrorum exiftit, quod ipfi terras & tenementa ad valorem XX marcarum per annum, tam de feodo fuo proprio quam alieno (exceptis terris & tenementis que de nobis tenentur in capite), adquirere poffint, habendas & tenendas fibi & fucceffioribus in perpetuum, ftatuto de terris & tenementis ad manum mortuam non ponendis edito non obftante, prout in breve noftro continetur: Nos (volentes conceffionem noftram predictam effectui debito mancipari) conceffimus & licentiam dedimus, pro nobis & heredibus noftris, quantum in nobis eft, Johanni Oxcliff & Johanni Coiton, quod ipfi unum meffuagium, XII acras terre, & IIII acras prati, cum pertinentiis, in Cokerham; & Johanni Twywell, vicario ecclefie de Lokyngton, Johanni Anfty, Ricardo Gamefton, Robert of the Halle, & Ricardo Barwe, quod ipfi VI meffuagia, XV cotagia, III virgatas, unam bovatam, unam acram, & unam rodam terre, VIII acras prati, XXIII folidatas & IIIId. redditûs, & redditum unius libre cumini, cum pertinentis, in Leiceftr' & fuburbio ejufdem ville, Humberfton, Burftall, Barkeby, & Lokyngton (que quidem meffuagia, cotagia, terre, pratum, & redditus, de nobis non tenentur) dare poffint & affignare prefatis abbati & conventui, habendas & tenendas fibi & fucceffioribus fuis in perpetuum, in plenam fatisfactionem dictarum XX marcarum terrarum & tenementorum predictorum in perpetuum; falvis tamen capitalibus dominis feodi illius ferviciis inde debitis & confuetis in perpetuum.

Tefte rege, apud Beverlac, VII die Septembris.

57. Breve regis Ricardi Secundi Egidio Jurdan de Lughtburg, ut decimas de Woodhoufe, infra parochiam de Barwe fuper Sore, in com' Leic', ab eo detentas, abbati beate Marie de Pratis reftitui faciat, fub periculo quod incumbit [3].

Rex Egidio Jurdan de Lughtburghe falutem. Clamore plurium laborante noftris eft auribus intimatum, quòd tu, regiam majeftatem non verendo, nec juftitie equitatem ponderando, dilectos nobis in Chrifto abbatem & conventum beate Marie de Pratis juxta Leyceftriam de decimis, oblationibus, proventibus, & obventionibus hameletti fui de Woodhoufe, infra fines & limites ecclefie parochialis ipforum abbatis & conventûs de Barwe fuper Sore, in com' Leic' exiftentes (quam quidem ecclefiam iidem abbas & conventus & predeceffores fui in proprios ufus à tempore quo non extat memoria obtinuerunt), ex folâ auctoritate & temerariâ voluntate tuâ, abfque aliquo juris proceffu, violentèr expellere & fpoliare prefumpfifti; decimas, oblationes, proventus, & obventiones predictos penès te, per tempora non modica, contra juftitiam & fanam confcientiam, & voluntatem ipforum abbatis & conventûs, maligno propofito adhuc temerè detinendo & nequitèr occupando: Nos igitur, de oppreffione Sce ecclefie gravitèr commoti, & indempnitati noftrî & abbatie predicte (que de fundatione progenitorum noftrorum, quondam regum Anglie, & noftro patronatu, exiftit), quatenùs cum juftitiâ poterimus, profpicere volentes in hâc parte, ut tenemur, nè (quod abfit!) abbatiam predictam, amiffione jurium fuorum, periculis fubjacere, aut injuriarum & expenfarum profluviis contingat fatigari; tibi, fub gravi forisfacturâ noftrâ, precipimus, diftrictiùs quo poffumus injungentes, quòd eifdem abbati & conventui hujufmodi decimas, oblationes, proventus, & obventiones, fic fpoliatos & detentos, &, ex auctoritate tuâ, abfque juris proceffu occupatos (aut verum valorem eorundem, fi non exftent), citra Quindenam Sci Hilarii proximè futuri, liberari & reftitui facias, fub periculo quod incumbit. Et, fi caufa nobilis fubfuerit quare id ad mandatum noftrum facere non debeas, tunc in propriâ perfonâ tuâ fis coram nobis in cancellariâ noftrâ in Quindenâ predictâ, ubicunque tunc fueris, caufam illam ibidem coram nobis oftenfurum; facturum & recepturum quod per nos confideratum fuerit in hâc parte, ubi tibi & prefatis abbati & conventui in premiffis debitum juftitie complementum equo libramine fieri volumus & exhiberi. Tefte rege, apud Ebor', XX die Decembris. Per ipfum regem.

58. Concordia inter Johannem Lichf' & Covent' epifcopum, & Philippum abbatem beate Marie de Pratis, de divisâ & bundâ territoriorum fuorum ex utrâque parte rivi de Trent in villis de Sallowe & Lokyngton adjacentium [4].

Hec indentura, facta inter venerabilem patrem Johannem, Dei gratiâ, Coventrie & Lichfeilde epifcopum, ex parte unâ; & Philippum, abbatem ecclefie beate Marie de Pratis, & conventum ejufdem loci, ex alterâ; teftatur, quòd cùm dictus epifcopus teneat & feifitus fit de manerio de Sallowe, cum pertinentiis, in com' Derb' (de quo manerio idem epifcopus & predeceffores fui feifiti fuerunt & tenuerunt ut de jure epifcopatûs fui), quòd quidem manerium eft adjacens cuidam rivo, qui vocatur Trent; & predicti abbas & conventus & predeceffores fui (ut de jure ecclefie fue beate Marie de Pratis Leiceftr') tenent & tenuerunt manerium de Lokyngton, cum pertinentiis, in com' Leic', adjacens eidem rivo; cujus quidem rivi curfus, à tempore quo extat memoria, extitit divifa & bunda ibidem inter comitatus & maneria predicta; & etiam predictus nunc epifcopus habeat & teneat unam parcellam terre, vocatam Sandholme, in predictâ villâ de Lokyngton, adjacentem predicto rivo, de predictis abbate & conventu, per fervicium III folidatarum annuatim folvendarum; & nunc tardè dictus rivus reliquit antiquum curfum fuum, & cepit novum curfum per medium dicte terre de Sandholme; dicti abbas &

[1] Peck, MSS. 4937, fol. 152; ex Efch. 16 Ric. II. parte 2. n. 86.
[2] Pat. 16 Ric. II. pars 2. m. 6.   [3] Peck, MSS. 4937, fol. 153; ex Clauf. 19 Ric. II. m. 12.
[4] Peck, MSS. 4937, fol. 153; ex Pat. 4 Hen. IV. pars I. m. 14. per infpex.

conventus

conventus, unanimi affenfu & confenfu, per prefentes
concefferunt & confirmaverunt, pro fe & fuccefforibus
fuis, quòd predictus epifcopus & fucceffores fui totam illam partem dicte terre de Sandholme, nunc jacentem ultra dictum rivum de Trent versùs predictum
manerium de Sallowe, habeant & teneant quietè, &
abfque reclamatione dictorum abbatis & conventûs
vel fuccefforum fuorum, in perpetuum; & jam tardè
dicti abbas & conventus in alteram partem dicte terre
de Sandholme, nunc jacentem ultra rivum dictum de
Trent versùs dictum manerium de Lokyngton, ex conceffione dicti epifcopi, intraverunt & feifiti fuerunt;
quam quidem partem, fimul cum omnibus aliis terris
ejufdem epifcopi ibidem, tunc jacentem ultra dictum
rivum versùs predictam villam de Lokyngton, prefatus epifcopus predictis abbati & conventui & fuccefforibus fuis conceffit, confirmavit, & per prefentes
relaxavit; habendam & tenendam eifdem abbati &
conventui & fuccefforibus fuis, quietè & abfque reclamatione predicti epifcopi & fuccefforum in perpetuum. Et infuper, tam predictus epifcopus pro
fe & fuccefforibus fuis, quàm predicti abbas & conventus pro fe & fuccefforibus fuis, concefferunt, quòd
dictus rivus de Trent, modo & formâ quibus tenet
curfum fuum tempore confectionis prefentium, erit
divifa & bunda in perpetuum inter terras predicti epifcopi, per iftam concordiam, versùs Sallowe remanentes; & terras predictorum abbatis & conventûs,
per eandem concordiam, remanentes versùs Lokyngton; abfque hoc, quòd dictus epifcopus vel fuccefores fui in futurum clamabunt aliquam partem terre
ultra dictum rivum versùs Lokyngton; & fimilitèr
abfque hoc, quòd dicti abbas & conventus vel fuc-
cefiores fui clamabunt aliquam partem terre ultra
dictum rivum versùs dictum manerium de Sallowe in
perpetuum. Et ulteriùs, iidem abbas & conventus
per prefentes remiferunt, relaxaverunt, & de fe &
fuccefforibus fuis quietas clamaverunt, prefato epifcopo & fuccefforibus fuis, dictas tres folidatas redditûs, & omnia alia fervicia de predictâ terrâ de Sandholme fibi debita. Ac etiam concordatum eft per
prefentes inter partes predictas, quòd tam predictus
epifcopus & fucceffores fui, quàm predicti abbas &
conventus & fucceffores fui, & quilibet eorum, ex
parte fuâ de Trent, ponere poffint pilas, & figere pa-
las, & plantare arbores, pro defenfione & falvatione
terrarum fuarum, rationabilitèr, ad manutenendum &
cuftodiendum dictum rivum in fuo curfu quem nunc
tenet, abfque perturbatione aliquali in perpetuum.
In cujus rei teftimonium, partes predicte prefentibus
indenturis alternatim figilla fua appofuerunt. Data
tertio die Junii, anno Domini MCCCCII, & regni
regis Henrici Quarti poft Conqueftum tertio.

59. Philippus, eps, &c. Ricardo abbati, &c. Cùm
dilecta in Chrifto filia Ifolda N. pompas feculi & mun-
dane converfationis illecebras volens, ut afferit, in
eterni thefauri divitias commutare, in quandam domum
infra cemeterium ecclefie parochialis beati Petri Leyceftrie, juxta ecclefiam fituatam, ubi perpetuam vitam
committere fuam ad id perelegit fpiritualem manfionem
recludi defideret firmitèr & proponat, & fic fub vitâ
anachoriticâ, fpretis mundi blanditiis, Creatorem fuum
valeat liberiùs contemplari: Nos, ejufdem Ifolde in
hâc parte devotionem & falubre propofitum in Domino
commendantes, ac de veftris circumfpectione, fidelitate, & puritate conftante plenam in Dño fiduciam
obtinentes, ad examinandum propofitum mentem communem dicte Ifolde, & fi vos eam in propofito & in-
tentione hujufmodi perfeverantem inveneritis ftabilem
& conftantem, ac aliàs ad hoc habilem, idoneam, &
nullatenùs vacillantem, fuper quibus veftram con-
ftantiam oneramus, & nichil in hâc parte obvenerit de
canonicis inftitutis ad recludendam ipfam Ifoldam, ut
prefertur votum quod eft promiffum, faciend', admittend', & eidem impendend' habitum in hâc parte con-
gruum cum officio confueto, & ad expedend' omnia
alia & fingula que circa hujufmodi officium de jure
feu confuetudine quomodolibet requiruntur, vobis tenore prefentium committimus vices noftras; mandantes quatenus de toto proceffu veftro in hoc habendo
nos, expedito negotio, certificatis literis veftris patentibus, habentes hunc tenorem. Dat', &c. [1]

60. De cantariâ in Collegio Novi Operis.
Thomas Langley, eps Dunelmenfis, dedit nobis
patronatum cujufdam cantarie duorum capellanorum
in Novo Collegio Leyc'; qui quidem eps fuit executor
teftamenti dni Johis ducis Lancaftr'; fcil', ex ejus voluntate, & de terris ipfius, fundavit predictam cantariam [2].

61. Compofitio inter archiepifcopum Cantuar' & decanum & capitulum Lincolnie.
Univerfis fancte matris ecclefie filiis, &c. Bonifacius,
miferatione divinâ, archiepifcopus Cantuarienf', &c.
Poft magnas lites & varias, tandem fub hâc formâ
concordatum eft; videlicet, quòd quoties in futurum
fedem Linc' per mortem vel ceffionem epifcopi, &c. vacare contigerit, decanus & capitulum, &c. Item dictus
decanus, vel ejus gerens vices, toto tempore vacationis,
liberè exercebit jurifdictionem epifcopalem in ecclefiâ
Linc', tam in canonicis quàm in clericis & beneficiis,
&c. & in domibus religiofis que funt de patronatu
Linc', ecclefie videlicet Eynefham & Dorcheftr', &c.
Item vifitabit decanus Linc' jure epifcopali in fingulis
archidiaconatibus duo monafteria, exceptis monafteriis
que funt de patronatu domini regis, & non plura, &c. ut
in dictâ compofitione, que eft in VI libro Chartwary;
unde benè patet, quòd monafterium iftud non debet
decanus Linc' vifitare tempore vacationis, quia eft de
patronatu domini regis: Veruntamen, ratione hujus
compofitionis, voluit magifter Johannes Makworthe,
tunc decanus Linc', iftud monafterium vifitaffe; fcil',
tempore fratris W. Sadyngton abbatis; qui ipfum decanum inhibuit, per Ricardum Taylard generofum
fuum, extra portas monafterii; qui dictus decanus
eas portas omninò voluit ingredi. Qui ore inhibitus
receffit, & cum fuis in villam ivit; & fic deinceps vifitare ceffavit [3].

62. Memorandum, quòd, anno Dñi MCCCCXXXIX°,
in die Pafche, dnus Johannes Bayford, capellanus
magiftri Roberti Matfeyn, magiftri Sci Leonardi, recepit duos fervientes predicti magiftri ad facramentum
Euchariftie & communionis in eâdem capellâ, in magnum prejudicium abbatis & conventûs Leyceftrie, &c.
Super quod gravamen dictus abbas petit judicium
fieri côram magiftro Johanne Wardale, tunc commif-
fario epifcopi Lincoln'; qui quidem commiffarius ci-
tari fecit predictum Johannem Bayford ad comparend',
&c. Et, quia predictus Johannes Bayford, nec aliquis alius prò fe, aliqua privilegia oftendere voluit,
quorum autoritate infra dictam capellam facramenta
miniftrare potuit, dictus commiffarius, contra dictum
Johannem judicialitèr procedens, talem ei injunxit
penitentiam; fcilicet, quòd, die Dominicâ fequenti,
in ecclefiâ Sci Leonardi ad proceffionem incederet,
nudus pedes & caput, & fine camifiâ, inter crucem &
chorum, portans in manibus unum cereum trium librarum; &, ingreffâ proceffione, ipfe ftaret in medio
chori dicendo feptem pfalmos, &c. ut in rotulo Johannis Schepifhed de officio facrifte & fabrice [4].

63. Antiloquium Rotuli cujufdam omnibus vicinis
ecclefiis conventualibus miffi, ad earum preces pro
animabus benefactorum, &c. exorandum [5].
Univerfis Chrifti fidelibus, & crucis Chrifti amicis,
Johannes, permiffione divinâ, abbas monafterii beate
Marie de Pratis Leyceftrie, & ejufdem loci conventus,
ordinis Sci Auguftini, Lincoln' diocefis, falutem &
letis gaudere diebus, cum falubri memoriâ memo-
rari noviffima uraniaque regni agalmata fcandere poft
laborem. Quoniam, exigente primi parentis pre-
varicatione, prolis pofteritas, ab immortalitatis amœ-
nitate, in hanc erumnofam & lugubrem laboris dolo-
rifque dejecta convallem, corruptionis mortalitatem
cogitur induere; & in tantâ pofitus tenebrarum den-
fitate, utrùm amore vel odio fi dignus fit, non con-
ceditur fibi fcire; &, licèt tempus gratie nobis at-
tribuatur ad enervationem concupifcentie & virtutum
exercitium, ut à ftatu turbinis ad quietem patrie ten-
damus; ipfa tamen peccata levia, que ex neceffitate
indiès proveniunt, fecum cremalia ferunt, & in terrâ
terre globus inclufus nequaquam ulteriùs cuiquam
fufficit fubvenire: ingens eft igitur caritatis officium,
devotaque fanitatis cogitatio, ut hiis, quos exutos
corpore futurum feculum jam fufcepituros, piis pro-
curemus facramentorum remediis & devotis rationum

---

[1] Harl. MSS. 2179 fol. 79.
[2] Cotton MSS. Vitellius F. XVII. fol. xv. a.
[3] Charyte's Rentale, fol. lxxxv. a.
[4] Ibid. fol. xciv. b. xcv. a.
[5] Peck, MSS. 4937, fol. 155; ex Cod. MS. penès amicum Leiceftrenfem, Feb. 24, 1733, fol. 65. b.

suffragiis

suffragiis subvenire; que quidem magna, ex miserantis Dei munere, solatia dinoscantur esse vivorum, & juvamina defunctorum. Quia igitur, *pro se laborat qui pro aliis orat*, & oratio ejus in suum sinum convertitur; auras vestre pietatis lacrimosâ prece pulsamus, quatenùs pro animabus defunctorum nostrorum (quorum nomina vobis transmittimus scripta) orationum suffragia, absolutionum remedia, & oblationum solatia, caritatis intuitu, salubriter impendatis; & Johanni Parre, hujus legationis bajulo (ne deficiat in viâ victus) beneficia cum favore benevolo dignemini exhibere; scientes, quòd, quicquid à vobis petimus pro nostris fieri, pro vestris in casu consimili volumus obligari. Felicitèr valeat universitas vestra, Creatori omnium continuè placitura! Dat' in domo nostrâ capitulari Leycestrie, xx° die Octobris, MCCCCLVIII.

64. Omnibus Christi fidelibus ad quos hoc presens scriptum pervenerit, Johannes, divinâ permissione, epus Bang', ac abbas monasterii Sce Marie de Pratis juxta Leicestriam & ejusdem loci conventus, salutem in Domino sempiternam. Noveritis nos prefatum abbatem & conventum, unanimi assensu & consensu, ac assensu nostro, pro diversis pecuniarum summis nobis fideliter per Thomam Stoke, de Elsforde, in com' Stafford', armigerum, solutis; de quibus predicti abbas & conventus per presens concedunt se fore soluturos; necnon pro diversimodis terris & tenementis ipsius Thome in Okethorpe, in com' Derbie, per eundem Thomam nobis & successoribus nostris preanteà concessis, que gratantèr collatus est, concessisse, & hoc presenti scripto nostro confirmâsse, prefato Thome, heredibus & assignatis suis, patronatum & advocacionem ecclesie parochialis & rectorie de Boresworth, cum pertinentiis, in com' Leic'; necnon presentationem ad eandem, quodcunque & quotiescunque per vacationem contingerit; habend' & tenend' predict' patronatum, advocationem, & presentationem ecclesie & rectorie predict', cum suis pertinentiis, prefato Thome, heredibus & assignatis suis, ad eorum opus & usum proprium in perpetuum, absque contradictione, impetitione, sive disturbatione nostrâ, sive successorum nostrorum. Et nos prefati abbas & successores nostri eosdem patronatum, advocationem, & presentationem, cum pertinentiis predictis, prefato Thome Stoke, heredibus, & assignatis suis, contra omnes gentes warantizabimus & adquietabimus, & per presens defendemus; salvo tamen nobis abbati & conventui, & successoribus nostris, & domino nostro predict', annualem pensionem trium librarum & unam petram cere exeunt' de predictâ ecclesiâ sive rectoriâ per rectorem sive incumbentem ecclesie sive rectorie predict', nobis ab antiquo debitam & annuatim solutam. In cujus rei testimonium, presenti scripto nostro, ex nostro unanimi consensu, sigillum nostrum commune apposuimus [1]. Dat', &c.

65. Noverint universi per presentes nos Ricardum permissione divinâ abbatem monasterii Beate Marie de Pratis Leycestrie recepisse & habuisse, die confectionis presentium, de Willielmo Calvert juniore, XLI libras, XIII solidos, & IV denarios legalis monete Anglie, pro firmâ manerii & dominii mei de Cokerham, pro termino Nativitatis Sci Johannis Baptiste ultimè preterito ante datum presentium. De quibus quidem XLI libris, XIII solidos, & IV denariis, fatemur nos fore solutos den' quod Willielmus inde esse quietus per presentes. In cujus rei testimonium presentibus sigillum apposuimus. Data XIV° die Julii, anno regni regis Henrici octavi VII°, per me Ricardum abbatem Leic' [2].

66. A nre seygnur le roy prie Gilbert del Bed, de sicum il ad este son sumeter vint anz e plus, e en tens de guere dela la meer e de ca en garnestures dys ans, e puis fu pris ore en la dereyne demure nostre seygnur le roy en Escoce en auffre des Escotz qe il ne peut sei mesmes deformes ben eyder, qe il le voille si lui plest graunter sa lettre a akune mesun de Religiun, que ne soit charge de autre par le roi pur sun vivere aver, sicum il set sa grace a autres qe li unt si lungement servy.

Responsio. Nominet aliquem locum Religiosum non oneratum per regem; & rex scribet pro eo, &c.

Postea idem Gilbertus venit, & nominavit loca; scilicet, Bardeney vel Leicestriam [3].

67. Omnes iste ecclesie subscripte, scil' XXXV, collate nobis fuerunt ad appropriandum nobis; de quibus alique nobis appropriate sunt, & alique adhuc non sunt appropriate. Et omnes iste ecclesie, tam appropriate quàm non appropriate, confirmate sunt per papas; scil', Eugenium, Alexandrum, Urbanum, & Innocentium, & quedam per alios papas.

Item confirmate sunt per reges; scil', per Stephanum, Henricum secundum, Edwardum primum, & Henricum septimum.

Item confirmate sunt per diversos episcopos [4].

Ecclesia Sce Marie juxta castrum, cum capellâ Sci Sepulchri.
Ecclesia Sci Martini.
Ecclesia Sci Nicholai.
Ecclesia Sci Petri.
Ecclesia Omnium Sanctorum.
Ecclesia Sci Leonardi.
Ecclesia Sci Michaelis.
Ecclesia Sci Clementis, ubi jam sunt Fratres Predicatores.
Ecclesia Sci Augustini, cum capellâ de Cosby.

{ Hec omnia sunt ex dono fundatoris nostri.

Ecclesia de Thurnby, cum capellâ de Stanton, ex dono Radi Pincerne.
Ecclesia de Evington, ex dono Jordani Humett.
Ecclesia de Humberston, ex dono Ernoldi I. de Bosco.
Ecclesia de Hungarton, cum capellâ de Yngwarby, ex dono Willi Sifrewast.
Ecclesia de Barkby, cum capellâ de Hamilton, ex dono Willmi Poer.
Ecclesia de Queniboro, ex dono Radi de Queniboro.
Ecclesia de Thorp Ernold, cum capellâ de Brentby, ex dono Ernoldi primi de Bosco.
Ecclesia de Eytonâ, ex dono Willi de Evermu.
Ecclesia de Lokynton, cum capellis de Hemyngton & Diseworth, ex dono fundatoris nostri.
Ecclesia de Baro, cum capellâ de Querndon, ex dono Ranulfi comitis Cestrie.
Ecclesia de Thornton, cum capellâ de Bagworth, ex dono Thome Sorell, & consensu fundatoris nostri.
Ecclesia de Enderby, aliàs vocat' Aldeneby, cum capellâ de Whefton, ex dono fundatoris nostri.
Ecclesia de Cosby, que quondam erat capella Sci Augustini Leic', ex dono fundatoris nostri.
Ecclesia de Bittefwell, ex dono Roberti Coll.
Ecclesia de Schepished, ex dono fundatoris nostri.
Ecclesia de Lilburn, ex dono fundatoris nostri.
Ecclesia de Brakley, cum capellâ Sci Johis ibidem, & cum capellâ de Halfo, ex dono fundatoris nostri.
Ecclesia de Scharnebroke, in comitatu Bedfordie.
Ecclesia de Cestresham, in comitatu Buckinghamie, cum capellis Sci Leonardi & Ilvamstede, ex dono Willi Sifrewast.
Ecclesia de Clyfton, in com' Warwyche, cum capell' de Wover & Neuton, ex dono Ernoldi I. de Bosco.
Ecclesia de Crudworth, cum capellâ de Berwod, ex dono Hugonis de Ardenâ.
Ecclesia de Bulkington, cum capellâ de Brankote, ex dono Rogeri de Watervyle.
Ecclesia de Yolgrave, in comitatu Derbie, cum capellis de Medulton, Elton, Cratton, & Wynster, ex dono Roberti Coll.
Ecclesia de Cokerham, in comitatu Lancastrie, cum capellis de Elhale & Thurneham, ex dono Willi de Lancastriâ.

Memorandum, quòd habemus libertatem & licentiam papalem convertendi omnes ecclesias subscriptas in proprios usus nostros; scil', ecclesiam de Bosworth, ecclesias de North Kilworth & East Kilworth, de Blaby, Croft, Eyton, Estwell, Hathurn, Whatton, Dixley, Knaptoft, Harston, Segrave, Norboro, Hungarton, Claycotys, Sigresham, Farnyngho, Billing, Ildesley, Ilmydon, Anlep.

Item habemus libertatem regis ad convertend' ecclesiam de Kirkby Malory in proprios usus; similitèr & ecclesiam de Stoke.

Ecclesie appropriate in numero sunt XXXV; capelle XXXII. Ecclesie licentiate ad appropriationem, ut supra, & nondum appropriate, XXV.

Mem', quòd tempore preterito potuit respondere cuilibet canonico istius monasterii, una ecclesia, una capella, unum molendinum dominicale, & aliud molendinum decimale.

---

[1] The date [which was between 1504 and 1509] is left out in the transcript.   [2] Cart. Ant. Harl. 44. f. 23.
[3] Rot. Parl. vol. I. p. 156; 30 Edw. I. 1302.   [4] Cotton MSS. Vitellius F. XVII.

RENTALE NOVUM FRATRIS W. CHARYTE.

I. Genealogia Fundatorum [1].

II. Chartæ Fundatorum & Benefactorum [2].

III. Chartæ regalium confirmationum & gratiarum [3].

IV. Regiftrum amplum, exactiffimum, villarum & locorum, numero CLXXI; in quibus omnibus monafterii poffeffiones & redditus omnes ordine alphabetico, & fingula que eo fpectant, defcribuntur; viz.

  1. Terrarum acquifitiones & evidentiæ.

  2. Ecclefiarum advocationes.

  3. De decimis, penfionibus, & portionibus.

  4. Redditus veteres, novi, aucti, diminuti, deperditi, ex comparatione Rentalium veterum, le Pyn (1254), Geryn (1341), Bathe (1408), & novi hujus (1477), &c.

  5. Ordinationes vicariarum & capellarum antiquæ & recentes; & ecclefiarum appropriationes, procurationes, fynodales, denarii Sci Petri, &c.

6. Compofitiones reales, chirographa.

7. Privilegia, franciplegii curiarum, warenniæ, homagii, & fines communes, relevii, maritagii, villanorum, heriottorum, weif & ftray, &c.

8. Confuetudines fingulorum maneriorum, & fines communes.

9. Papales confirmationes, indulgentiæ, inhibitiones, conceffiones, brevia, examinationes, &c.

10. Cardinalium, archiepifcoporum, & epifcoporum, ordinationes, ratificationes & adjudicationes, &c.

11. Notariorum publicorum inftrumenta.

12. Placita in curiis regiis coram jufticiariis, finales concordie, inquifitiones quo warranto, &c.

13. Beneficia collata per abbates.

14. Nobiles & milites qui apud eos religionem ingreffi, facti funt canonici, &c.

Tabula omnium villarum & locorum que fcribuntur in ifto Rentali [4]; & ftant in ordine fecundùm modum alphabeti, ficut hìc patet. Et in omnibus iftis villis & locis aut habemus redditum voluntarium feu liberum, feu penfionem, portionem, vel decimas.

Anfty,	—	fol. viii	Ernefby,	— —	lvi	NORTHAMPTON,	*cxiii
Anlep,	— —	xi	Efiwell,	— —	lvii	Nowfely,	—	*cxiii
Adeftok (Bucks),	—	xi	Effewell (Rutland),		lvii	Nuneyton (Warw.),	*cxiv
Aldeby,	— —	xi	Evyngton,	——	lvii	Oldfeld & Longwong,	cxiv
Apulby,	— —	xi	Evenley (Northt.),	—	lvii	Okethorpe (Derb.),	cxiv
Asforby,	— —	xi	Everley (Wilts),	—	lvii	Othorpe (Northt.),	cxiv
Bagworth,	—	xi	Faryngo (Northt.),		lviii	Oudeby,	— —	cxv
Baggrave,	— —	xi	Fleckney,	—	lviii	Peccum (Derb.),	cxv—cxix
Barkeby,	— —	xii	Foxton,	— —	lviii	Pynflad,	— —	cxx
Baroo,	— —	xiv	Fryfby,	—	lix	Quenby,	— —	cxx
Baryfby,	— —	xvi	Gadfby,	—	lix	Queniboro,	— —	cxx
Belgrave,	— —	xvi	Gaham (Nottingh.),		lix	Querndon,	—	cxxii
Bernangul (Warw.),	xvi	Garadon,	—	lix	Rerefby,	— —	cxxiii
Berwode (Warw.),	xvii	Godby juxta Billefdon,	lx	Ryton (Warw.),	—	cxxiii
Bewmaner,	—	xix	Groby,	— —	lx	Rodely,	— —	cxxiii
Bewmont Wood,	—	xix	Halfo (Northt.),	—	lx	Rokeby (Warw.),	cxxiii
Billing (Northt.),	—	xix	Hamilton.	—	lx	Rolfton,	— —	cxxiii
Byllefdon,	—	xix	Harborough,	—	lx	Rotby, feu Lowndrefhey,	cxxiv
Bytefwell,	—	xxi	Harfton & Cnipton,	—	lxi	Scalforth,	— —	cxxiv
Bitulfden (Bucks),	—	xxii	Hathurn,	— —	lxi	Shakerfton,	—	cxxiv
Blaby,	— —	xiii	Hemyngton,	—	lxi	Scharnbroke (Bedf.),	cxxiv
Borefworth,	—	xxiv	Hertythorn & Schorthafuls (Derb.),		Schene (Surrey),	—	cxxv
Benington (Linc.),	xxv			lxi	Schepefhead,	—	cxxvi
Botulfton (Bofton, Linc.),	xxv	Holme (Warw.),	—	lxii	Schevifby,	—	cxxviii
Brakley (Northt.),	—	xxvi	Holmer (Warw.),	—	lxii	Shucboro (Warw.),	cxxviii
Brancote (Warw.),	xxviii	Horfpoll,	—	lxii	Shelton & Anfty (Warw.),	cxxviii
Braunfton juxta Glenfield,	xxix	Howes,	— —	lxiii	Scraptoft,	—	cxxviii
Brenteby,	—	xxix	Howton,	— —	lxiv	Segrave,	— —	cxxix
Bryculfworth (Northt.),	xxix	Humberfton,	—	lxiv	Skeyfington,	—	cxxix
Brokefby,	—	xxx	Hungarton,	——	lxv	Sygrefham (Northt.),	cxxix
Bromwych (Warw.),	—	xxx	Ingwarby,	— —	lxvi	Sow (Warw.),	—	cxxx
Bulkington (Warw.),	xxx	Ilmefdon (Warw.),		lxvii	Sowrdrop (Bedf.),	cxxx
Burftall,	— —	xxxi	Kayham,	—	lxviii	Standeford,	—	cxxx
Burton Overy,	—	xxxiii	Kelyngworth Rabaz,	lxviii	Stanton juxta Bagworth,	cxxx
Bufby,	—	xxxiv	Keyrby juxta Braunfton,	lxviii	Stoke,	— —	cxxxi
Camefton (Bedf.),	xxxiv	Kylby,	— —	lxviii	Stokyngforth (Warw.),	cxxxi
Cateby,	—	xxxiv	Kyrkby Mallory,	—	lxix	Stocton,	—	cxxxi
Charley & Ulvefcroft,	xxxiv	Kyrby Bellars,	—	lxxxi	Stretton Magna,	—	cxxxiv
Chefsham (Bucks),	xxxv	Knaptoft,	—	lxxxiii	Sutton juxta Croft,	cxxxiv
Cley-cotys (Northt.)	xxxvii	Knyton,	—	lxxxiii	Theddyngworth,	cxxxv
Clenfelde,	—	xxxvii	Langton,	—	lxxxv	Thornton,	—	cxxxvi
Clifton (Warw.),	xxxvii	Lawton,	—	lxxxv	Thorp Barkby,	cxxxviii
Cokerham (Lanc.),	xxxix	LEYCESTRIA,	lxxxvi—civ	—— Ernald,	cxxxix
Cokerfonde abbey (Lanc.),	xlvi	Leyr,	—	civ	—— Lilburn (Cat-thorp),	cxl
Cofby,	—	xlvii	Lilburn (Northt.),	—	cv	—— juxta Cofby,	cxli
Cofyngton,	—	xlviii	Lokynton,	—	cvi	Thurkafton,	— —	cxli
Craft,	— —	xlviii	LONDON,	—	cix	Thurneby,	— —	clxi
Croxton South,	—	xlviii	Lowndershey (req. Rotby),	cx	Thurmedefton,	—	clxi
Croxton Abbey,	—	l	Loufby,	— —	cx	Walton juxta Kimcote,	cxlv
Curdworth (Warw.),	li	Melton,	— —	cx	Welton (Northt.),	cxlvi
Wygynhill juxta Curdworth,	li	Merfton (Warw.),	—	cx	Wefton (Warw.),	—	cxlvi
Dalby Parva, & fuper Wolds,	lii	Mynworth (Warw.),	—	cx	Whatton,	— —	cxlvi
Desforth,	—	liii	Montforrel,	—	cxi	Whefton,	— —	cxlvi
Dyfworth,	—	liii	Mowfeley,	—	cxii	Wybtoft (Warw.),	cxlvii
Dyxley,	— —	liii	Newhay (Warw.)	—	cxii	Wyfordby,	— —	cxlvii
Dunton (Warw.),	liv	Newbold-Folvil,	—	cxiii	Wygefton,	— —	cxlvii
Eyton,	—	lv	Newton juxta Swebfton,	cxiii	Wylugbby Waterlefs,	cxlviii
Eydon (Northt.),	lv	Newton-Clifton (War.),	*cxiii	Wodhows,	— —	cxlviii
Endreby,	— —	lv	Narboro,	— —	*cxiii	Wover (Brounfover, Warw.), cxlix
Empyngham (Rutland),	lvi	Norton (Tugby),	—	*cxiii	Wygynhill (Warw.),	cxlix

[1] The pedigree of the Bellomonts has been already given, p. 98; and of the Montforts, p. 212.   [2] See thefe, p. 53—58.
[3] See p. 58—61.   [4] Such places as are in Leicefterfhire are printed in Italics. To the others the county is here added.

1. Ordo inquirendi & fcrutandi evidentias noſtras, pro aliquâ re, vel materiâ, vel redditu, ſi ſit in lite. Per fratrem W. Charyte.

Mem', quòd ſi aliquis fratrum noſtrorum temporibus futuris voluerit inquirere vel fcrutare ad inveniend' & ad habend' evidentias neceſſarias & fufficientes ad defendend', fortificand', cognofcend', vel ad demonſtrand', quale jus habemus de tali redditu vel materiâ modò in lite, vel ſi illa materia erit in diſcordiâ erit in futuro; primò oportet ut ipſe frater ſciat benè & promptè vertere duos libros, fcil', primum Regiſtrum de le Chartwary ſic vocatum, & novum Rentale fratris Wilłi Charyte, cum aliis libris & rentalibus hìc fubfcriptis. Tunc inquirat ſi ſint alique carte de illâ materiâ vel re jam in lite in prediſtis duobus libris de le Chartwary, & hoc poteſt valdè apertè ſcire per Rentale prediſt' W. Charyte. Tunc inquirat utrùm ille carte ſint confirmate per papas, reges, vel epifcopos. Poſteà inquirat & videat Rentalia iſta; fcil', Rotulum de Pyn, Rentale Geryn, Rentale fratris W. Joħis Hynkley, Wilłi Wyxton, Rentale domini Gilberti Abbatis [1], Rotulos de compotis celarariorum, Rotulos Curiales, Matriculum epifcopi, & librum de Placitis. Tunc inquirat utrùm illa materia anteà unquam fuit in lite vel in placito; & ſi ſic, tunc inquirat & videat ſi ſint aliqua placita de illâ materiâ, vel finales concordie, fententie definitive, feu compofitiones vel fententie date coram judicibus ordinariis, &c. Et pro penfionibus reſtorum, vicariorum, & pro portionibus ecclefiarum, & pro jure patronatûs earum, & pro capellis earundem, & quomodo ipſe capelle debent deſervire per capellanos fuos; pro omnibus iſtis requirat & videat Matriculum epifcopi. Et pro penfionibus reſtorum & vicariorum, & portionibus ecclefiarum, vide taxationes decimarum, & fententias definitivas datas coram judicibus ordinariis. Et pro penfionibus vicariorum, videat ordinationes eorum. Tunc omnino & pro omnibus aliis requirat follicitè quanto temporis habuimus poſſeſſionem illius rei, & quando & quo anno ultimo habuimus poſſeſſionem illius rei; quod quanto tardius tanto melius. Et pro omnibus prediſtis ſemper provideat hunc prediſtum Rentale fratris Wilłi [2].

2. Mem', quòd ſi quis voluit fcrutare veritatem, & cognofcere certitudinalitèr quomodo firme ecclefiarum noſtrarum & terrarum dominicalium, & confuetudines tenentium, & omnium reddituum noſtrorum receptus, decreverunt, ab anno Domini M°ccc°xxxv° ufque ad annum Domini Mᵐccccᵐ ſeptuageſimum, vel ab anno regis Edwardi Tertii ixᵒ ufque ad annum regis Edwardi Quarti ixᵐ, debet fcrutare & videre Rentalia fratris W. Geryn & fratris Galfridi, & taxationes ecclefiarum, & rotulos celarariorum ante peſtilentiam, & rotulos de Hemᵍ, & Rentale fratris W. Charyte; & in iſtis Rotulis inveniet certitudinalitèr valorem dominicalium maneriorum, firmariorum, & omnium reddituum noſtrorum, prediſto anno regis Edwardi III. Tunc videat & fcrutetur Rentalia moderna, fcil', ad annum regis Edwardi Quarti ixᵐ, &c.; illic inveniet valorem dominicalium maneriorum, &c. ut tunc. Hoc faſto, tunc poterit cognofcere quomodo prediſte firme, &c. degenerent [3].

3. Mem', quòd omnes iſte carte duplicantur; fcil', Carta Henrici III. regis, de licentiâ perquirendi Parcum noſtrum & le Stokyng de Simone de Monteforte.

Carta confirmationis Ed. II. omnium poſſeſſionum noſtrarum.

Carta Ed. III. de licentiâ đno Roberto Bird, pro cantariâ in Queniboro.

Item, carta Ed. III. de appropriatione ecclefiarum de Hungarton & Humburſton.

Item, carta Ed. III. pro manerio de Yngwarby.

Item, carta Ed. III. de non inveniendo ad parliamentum.

Item, carta Ed. III. de licentiâ adquirendi manerium Simonis de Seynvil de Lokyngton.

Item, carta de warennâ in omnibus dominicis noſtris terris in Leyc', Stoſton, Thurmaſton, Queniboro, Lokyngton, &c. ut in cartis.

Item, carta ejufdem, de licentiâ vacationis abbathie.

Item, carta Edwardi III, ad appropriand' ecclefiam de Kyrkby Malore.

Item, carta Ric. II. regis, de confirmatione carte regis Ed. III. de licentiâ vacationis abbathie Leyc' [4].

Item, carta H. IV. regis, de quietâ clamatione & reconceſſione manerii de Cokeram, & de manfione aliquorum canonicorum ibidem, & de confirmatione quiete clamationis & remiſſionis eorundem, faſt' per dominam Philippam de Conor, duciſſam Hibernie, &c.

4. Mem', quòd iſta non confirmantur per cartam confirmationis alicujus regis; fcil', Glenfeld, Croxton, Briculfworth, Mynworth, Merſton, Kyrkby Bellers, Newbold, Hamilton, Thurmaſton, Okethorpe, Gaddyſby, Shakerſton, Belgrave, Cofyngton, Howes, & Stretton.

Iſta tantùm confirmantur per cartam confirmationis regis Henrici VII; fcil', Boſton, Thorpbarkby, Nowſley, Odeby, Mountforel, & Barifby [5].

5. Privilegia Apoſtolica [6].

Eugenius III. Papa, MCXLVIII, conceſſit, quòd nullus petat decimas de laboribus noſtris, vel de novalibus quos propriis manibus colimus, five de nutrimentis animalium noſtrorum. Item quòd nullus quilibet furreptione, aut injuſtitiâ, feu violentiâ, p̄ponatur in eleſtionem, ſi quem fratres cum confilio vel fratrum pars confilii fanioris providerint eligendum. Sepulturam ipſius loci vel monaſterii liberam eſſe decernimus, ut eorum qui illic fepeliri deliberaverint donationi extreme voluntatis, ſi forte excommunicati vel interdiſti ſint non obſtante, falvâ cum juſtitiâ interdiſtâ ecclefie. Item quòd nos poſſimus eligere facerdotes de fratribus noſtris ad ecclefias noſtras, & eos epifcopis prefentare, quibus, ſi idonei fuerint, eis curam ecclefiarum committant.

Lucius III. Papa conceſſit, MCLXXXI, quòd nullus ſine causâ rationabili & manifeſtâ in nos vel ecclefiam noſtram fententiam excommunicationis feu interdiſti audeat promulgare.

Urbani III. confirmatio MCLXXXVI, fupér hiis que inſtitute fuerunt ab Alexandro [7] ēpo & fundatore noſtro.

Confirmatio Celeſtini III. Pape, MCLXXXXI, fuper amicabilem compofitionem inter nos & priorem de Trentham, de ecclefiâ de Brakley.

Confirmatio Innocentii IV. fuper omnibus poſſeſſionibus ñris, & fpecialitèr fuper ecclefiis de Cokeram & de Yolgrave.

Alexander IV. Papa, MCCLX, conceſſit, quòd nulli ecclefiaſtico perfone liceat indebitas & injuſtas exaſtiones in ecclefiam noſtram exercere. Item quando commune interdiſtum terre fuerit, liceat nobis, clauſis januis, exclufis excommunicatis interdiſtifve, pulfatis tintinnabulis, fuppreſsâ voce, in ecclefiâ noſtrâ divina officia celebrare. Item quòd liberè liceat nobis, clericos five laicos, liberos & abfolutos, de feſto fugientes, ad converfionem fufcipere, & in ñro collegio retinere. Conceſſit etiam, ut nemini liceat ecclefias noſtras indebitis & inconfuetis exonerationibus vel injuſtitie gravaminibus fatigare.

Honorius IV. Papa conceſſit, ne aliquis, ratione cujufcunque prave confuetudinis, animalia noſtra vel bona capiat aut vadiari prefumat. Item quòd liceat nobis uti privilegiis & indulgentiis noſtris, dummodo non ſit nobis per prefcriptionem aliàs derogatum.

Nicholaus IV. Papa conceſſit, quòd quilibet abbas hujus monaſterii liberè & licitè poſſit in capite uti pilio, conſtitutione vel confuetudine non obſtantibus.

Celeſtinus V. Papa conceſſit, quòd non licet contra privilegia apoſtolica interdicere vel excommunicare.

Gregorius XI. Papa conceſſit privilegium de licentiâ comedendi laſticinia in tempore Adventûs Domini. Item de licentiâ celebrandi miſſam in die. Item de IIII cantariis. Item de licentiâ habendi altare portabile.

---

[1] i. e. "Rentale W. Charyte." [2] From the firſt fpare leaf at the beginning of Charyte's Rentale.
[3] Ibid. fol. ccxv. a. [4] Ibid. fol. ccxi. b. [5] Ibid. from a fpare leaf at the beginning.
[6] Ib. fol. clxxxiv. a. b. clxxv. a; compared with the Regiſtrum Breve, Cotton MSS. Vitellius F. XVII. fol. 1. a. b.
[7] Alexander biſhop of Lincoln 1123—1147; and lord chancellor.

Item licentiam de ufu caligarum & fotularium. Item licentiam pro deodatis noſtris. Item bullam Gregorii Pape pro habitâ noſtrâ declaratoriâ.

Bonifacius VIII. Papa, de dimiſſione eccleſiarum noſtrarum ad firmam, licentiâ ordinarii non acceptâ.

Clemens V. Papa prohibebat, quòd alienatio cujuſcunque beneficii vel poſſeſſionum non debet fieri ſine communi aſſenſu totius capituli, vel ſanioris partis capituli.

6. Procurationes, ſynodalia, & denarii Sċi Petri [1].

Notandum, quòd nos ſolvimus procurationes pro omnibus eccleſiis noſtris quas in proprios uſus habemus, niſi pro eccleſiâ de Baro, pro quâ ſolus vicarius ſolvit, &c.

Et omnes vicarii noſtri de archidiaconatu Leyceſtr' ſolvunt ſynodalia, preter vicarios de Hungerton & Humburſton, pro quibus nos ſolvimus ex ordinatione epiſcopi.

Et omnes colligunt denarios Sċi Petri, & eos archidiacono ſolvunt, preter vicarios de Evyngton & Thurnby, ubi parochiani, ex antiquâ conſuetudine, colligunt & ſolvunt archidiacono dictos denarios; & preter vicarium Sċi Martini, qui dictos denarios colligit, & eos ad proprios uſus conſervat; & nos pro ipſo dictos denarios archidiacono perſolvimus.

Item nos colligimus denarios Sċi Petri in parochiâ Sċi Leonardi; & eos archidiacono ſolvimus. Denarios Sċi Petri in parochiâ Sċe Marie nullus adhuc ibi collegit.

7. Iſti ſubſcripti tenentur nobis in pipere, cumino, roſis, cirotecis, flectis, & calcaribus, ſicut patet per cartas [2].

De acubus & zinſeber' [3].

Anlip. Dominus ville redd' iſi. piperis.

Bulkynton. W. Orchard redd' 1 par cirotecarum.

Botulſton. Heres de Gerun redd' iſi. piperis, & iſi. cumini.

Burſtal. Heres Walſche redd' 1 par cirotecarum.

Humberſton. Ricardus Hotoft redd' iſi. cumini, 1 par cirotecarum, & 1 par pendent' glovys, & roſam.

Kyrkby Malory. Wiltus Warde redd' 1 roſam & 1 par cirotecarum.

Dñs Ferrers de Chartley redd' iſi. piperis.

Thomas Corbeyt de Sibefdon redd' iſi. piperis.

Joħes Molton redd' 1 roſam & 1 granum piperis.

Joħes Roxton redd' 1 par cirotecarum & duo para calcariorum.

Kylby. Elena de Kylby redd' unum acum.

Bytyſwell. Joħes Dowis redd' iſi. cumini.

Leyceſtria. Parochia Sċi *Martini.*

Joħes Wyxton redd' 1 flyche.

Thomas Swyft redd' 1 roſam.

Parochia Sċe *Marie.*

Joħes Edwyn redd' 1 par cirotecarum.

Wiltus de Pâtre Regis 1 roſam.

Wiltus de Engho redd' 1 flectam, ut patet per cartas.

Parochia *Omnium Sanctorum.*

Joħes Hewſon redd' 1 par cirotecarum.

Brunkyſthorp. Alexander P'peynt redd' iſi. cumini.

Joħes Anſty, pro domo juxta portum auſtralem, 1 par cirotecarum.

Parochia Sċi *Nicholai.*

Joħes Baker redd' 1 par cirotecarum, ſicut patet per cartas.

Lokyngton. Wiltus Pollard redd' iſi. cumini.

Rogerus Roby redd' iſi. cumini.

Mynworth. Heres Joħis Philyp redd' 1 roſam.

Mowſley. Joħes Emlyn redd' iſi. piperis.

Thorp-Norboro. Robtus Croft redd' di. li. cumini.

Wiltus Seyr redd' iſi. piperis & iſi. cumini.

Thurmaſton. Joħes Draper redd' 1 flectam & 11 raſyns zynſeberi.

Prior de *Scben* redd' 1 roſam.

Joħes Belgrave redd' octavam partem unius libre piperis, & 1 flectam.

Eps Lincoln' redd' 1 quarentenam piperis.

Ric' Hotoft redd' 1 quarent' piperis, & 1 flectam.

Dominus de Northfolk redd' 1 flectam & 1 roſam.

8. Summa pecuniarum quam habemus de Novo Collegio Leyc', &c. [4]

Habemus de eodem collegio, pro ingreſſu & egreſſu in capellam ſuam Sċi Leonardi, x ſ.

Item 11 ſ. 11 capones, 1111 gallinas, pro tenemento quondam Joħis Sedwax, in Belgrave-gate.

Item pro tenemento Chapman de Hope, x11 d. & 11 gallinas, in parochiâ Omnium Sanctorum.

Item pro tenemento quondam domini Willi Crownſby, v1 d. & 11 gallinas, in eâdem parochiâ.

Item pro uno tofto ſuper ſtagnum molendini borealis x11 d. in eâdem parochiâ.

Item pro hoſpitio ex oppoſito porte occidentali, & iſto ubi pira ſolebant creſcere, 1x d. & gallinam in parochiâ Sċi Nichi.

Summâ, xv ſ. 1111 d. 11 capones, & 1x gallinas; pretium unius caponis 111 d.; pretium unius galline 1 d. ob. Summa, x1x d. ob. pro caponibus & gallinis. Summa totalis, xv1 ſ. x1 d. ob.

Summa pecuniarum quam Novum Collegium Leyc' habet annuatim de nobis.

Habet dictum collegium, pro le Backhows, 111 ſ. v111 gallinas, & 1 gallum.

Item, pro tenemento juxta, 11 ſ. 1111 gallinas.

Item, pro tenemento ex eâdem parte vie, quondam Thome Bodyngton, 111 d. & 1 gallinam.

Item, pro tenemento in vico boreali, quondam Thome Okthorp, 11 ſ. & 11 capones.

Item, pro tenemento in cemeterio Sċi Martini, x11 d.

Non ibunt hecque tria,
Niſi dicuntur Ave Maria.

William Charyte.

Item clamant habere, de uno tenemento in vico boreali, quondam Waleſſe, unum caponem, & hoc injuſtè ut ſupponitur.

Summa, x111 ſ. 1111 d. 111 capones, x111 gallinas, & unum gallum; pret' 1 caponem 1111 d. pret' 1 gallinam 1 d. ob. pret' gall' 1 d.

Summa totalis, x ſ. v111 d. ob.

Et ſic reſtat nobis v1 ſ. 1111 d.

7. Peccum [5].

Recept' agnorum & vellerum, anno Dñi MCCCXXVI°.

De Yolgrave, xxxv agni; vellera xl111.

De Wynſter, xxx111 agni; vellera lx111.

De Eltonâ, agni xxx11; vellera lxxv1.

De Crattonâ, xxxv1; vellera lx111.

De Smerhul, 11; vellera xx11.

De Mydultun, xl111; vellera XXx1111.

De Birchover, v1; vellera xx1x.

De Lyes, x11; vellera xxxv.

De Stantonâ, xx; vellera lxv.

De Haddonâ, v111; vellera xv1.

Summa agnorum, XXXv11. Summa vellerum, 1111 c. per majus centum, & xxv1. Ponder', XX & v11 petras.

10. Omnes indenture iſtius monaſterii, de diverſis officiis ſcilicet, & univerſis firmis, molendinis, & tenementis, tam dictis, ad firmam, M°CCCCLXXVII°. [6]

Indentura pro firmâ de Bagworth, locata ad firmam pro 1111 li.

Indentura de Barkby, locat' ad firmam pro lxv1 ſ. v111 d.

Indentura de Baro, v111 li. pro decimis.

Indentura pro dominicis ibidem, 1111 ſ. 1111 d.

Indentura de Bylſden, pro dominicis, xl ſ.

Indentura de Bytſwell; v1 li. x111 ſ. 1111 d. pro decimis.

Indentura de Boſton, pro principali hoſpitio, xx ſ. cum reparatione.

Indentura de Bulkyngton, xv11 li.

Indentura de Chefsham, x1111 li. v1 ſ. v111 d.

Indentura de Clifton, xxv1 ſ. v111 d.

Indentura de Defworth, lx ſ.

Indentura de Faringo, manerium regis, lxxx1 ſ.

Indentura de Horſpoll, redd' in granis.

[1] Charyte's Rentale, fol. ccvii. b.
[3] Ginger; *zinziber* Latin; *gingero* Italian. Johnſon's Dictionary. And ſee Miller's Dictionary, *ad verbum.*
[4] Charyte's Rentale, fol. ccxix. b.
[2] Ibid. fol. ccxiv. b. ccxv. a.
[5] Ibid. from a ſpare leaf at the beginning.
[6] Ibid.

Indentura

Indentura de Lilburn, viii li. vi s. viii d.
Indentura de Lokynton, ix li. vi s. viii d. pro decimis.
Indentura de Sarfunheyd in London, viii li. xiii s. iiii d.
Indentura pro alio tenemento ibidem, xl s.
Indentura de Mowfley, lx s. ix d.
Indentura de Oldfeld, v marc'.
Indentura de Othorp, iiii li.
Indentura de Medoplek, &c.
Indentura de Evinton, lxvi s. viii d.
Indentura de Mydulton, lxvi s. viii d.
Indentura de Querndon, viii li.
Indentura de Schepifhed, viii li. x s. pro decimis.
Indentura de Thedyngworth, xi li. iii s. iiii d.
Indentura pro Bylfden, vi li. xiii s. iiii d. pro decimis.
Indentura pro Brakley, xviii li. vi s. viii d.
Indentura pro decimis ibidem, xxvi s. viii d.
Indentura alterius tenementi, xx s. cum reparatione, ad terminum vite.
Indentura de Burftall, xl s.
Indentura de Clifton, vii li. vi s. viii d. pro decimis.
Indentura de Cofby, xiiii li. xiii s. iiii d.
Indentura de Eyton, cvi s. viii d.
Indentura de Hartfhorn & Shorthafuls, xxvi s. viii d.
Indentura de Kyrkbe Malory, liii s. iiii d.
Indentura de Lowndurfhey, lxxiii s. iiii d.
Indentura ibidem pro dominicis, xl li.
Indentura pro tenementis juxta, xxv s. viii d.
Indentura pro hofpicio Abbatis ibidem, xvi s.
Indentura de Newton, viii li.
Indentura de Okthorpe, xxviii s. viii d.
Indentura pro decimâ de le ore in parco redd', ficut patet per indenturam ibidem.
Indentura de Stanton, xxvi s. viii d.
Indentura de Wynfter, xxxiii s. iiii d.
Indentura de Quenyboro, redd' in granis.
Indentura de Scharnbroke, xv li. vi s. viii d.
Indentura pro dominicis ibidem, xl s.
Indentura de Thornton, v li.
Indentura de Thorp Ernold, viii li. pro decimis.
Indentura de Whetfton, viii li. xiii s. iiii d.
Indentura de Woodhows, iiii li.
Indentura pro decimis de Thorp Ernold, xl s.
Indentura pro decimis de Whetfton, xl s.
Indentura de Wover, viii li.

11. Indenture molendinorum eodem anno [1].

Indentura de molendino Abbathie, ix s.
Indentura de molendino Belgrave, viii li.
Indentura de Lokyngton molendino, xl s.
Indentura de molendino de Schepyfhed, lx s.
Indentura de molendino de Anfty, xxxiiii s. iiii d.
Indentura de molendino de Brancot, liii s. iiii d.
Indentura de molendino in Parco, xl s.

12. De indenturis diverforum officiariorum predicto anno [2].

Indentura prioris, facta de ponderatione omnium jocalium in ifto monafterio, & de valore eorum, & de pretio.
Indentura precentoris, de omnibus libris fibi traditis per precentorem fibi immediatè precedentem.
Indentura precentoris, de omnibus libris traditis per ipfum quibufcunque fratribus, &c.
Indentura fubcantoris, de omnibus libris qui funt in fuâ cuftodiâ.
Indenture facrifte & fubfacrifte, thefaurarii, eleemofinarii, firmarii, celararii, magiftri grangie, fubcellararii, hofpitiarii, capellani, camerarii, abbatis pincerne, butterie, & taberni, & celarii, & pantrie.
Omnes ifte indenture facte fuerunt intra officiarios egredientes & officiarios ingredientes.

13. Indenture Grangii abbatis, Porte Occ', Stouton, Midoplek, & Yngwarby, de catallis, & de libris & veftimentis, &c. in capellâ, & de fubtellectibus dimiff' in manerio ibidem per abbatem & conventum [3].

Omnes ifte indenture facte fuerunt inter celararium egredientem & celararium ingredientem, & inter eorum ballivos.

14. Indenture capellani facte fuerunt inter capellanum & camerarium abbatis, de omnibus que fuerunt in le wardrop abbatis; & inter capellanum & pincernam de omnibus que fuerunt in provituario, butteriâ, celario, & in taberno; & inter ipfum & pantlarium de omnibus qui fuerunt in pantriâ.

Omnes ifte indenture femper habeantur & bene cuftodiantur, & nullo modo oblivifcantur.

Scripte & compilate per fratrem W. Charyte, in exemplum aliorum futurorum [4].

15. Penfiones vicariorum, & termini folutionis [5].

Vicarius de Bulkynton redd' xxvi s. viii d. Term' Annunc'.
Vicarius de Barkby redd' xx s. Term' Annunc'.
Vicarius de Endurby redd' vi s. viii d. in augmentatione. Term' Sci J. Bapt'.
Vicarius de Lokyngton redd' liii s. iiii d. Term' Martini & Pafch'.
Vicarius de Bytfwell redd' iii s. iiii d. in augment'.
Vicarius de Schepifhed redd' xxvi s. viii d. Term' Mich' & Pafch'.
Vicarius de Thedyngworth redd' xiii s. iiii d. Term' Mich'.
Vicarius de Thornton redd' liii s. iiii d. in augmentatione. Term' Mich' & Pafch'.
Vicarius de Quenyburgh redd' xxxiii s. iiii d. in augmentatione. Term' Mich' & Pafch'.
Vicarius de Thurnby redd' xxx s. in augmentatione. Term' Mich' & Pafch'.
Summa, xiiii li. vi s. viii d.

Omnes ifti vicarii quondam folverunt penfiones.
Vicarius Sci Petri Leyc' reddebat v marcas.
Vicarius Omnium Sanctorum v marcas.
Vicarius Sancti Nicholai vi marcas.
Vicarius de Baro xl s.
Vicarius de Clifton iiii marcas.
Vicarius de Chefham xx s.
Vicarius de Thorp Ernold iiii s.

16. Penfiones Rectorum, & termini folutionis [6].

Rector de Kylingworth Abbas redd' liii s. iiii d. Terminis Mich' & Pafch'.
Rector de Bofworth redd' lx s. & iii s. iiii d. facrifte.
Rector de Faringho redd' liii s. iiii d. Term' Annuntiationis.
Rector de Hathern redd' xl s. & iiii s. facrifte. Term' Mich' & Pafch'.
Rector de Blaby redd' lx s. & iiii s. facrifte. Term' Sci Johis Baptifte.
Rector de Craft redd' xl s. & iiii s. facrifte. Term' Mich', Purif', & Pentec'.
Rector de Whatton redd' xx s. Term' Mich'.
Rector de Barkby redd' xx s. Term' Mich'. Quondam reddebat xl s.
Rector de Cleycotys redd' xx s. Term' Nativ' Dñi.
Rector de Dyxley, modò abbas de Garadon, redd' xiiii s. term' Annunc' & Mich', ut patet per compofitionem inter ipfum & nos.
Rector de Sygrefham redd' vi s. viii d. Term' Mich'.
Rector de Harefton redd' v s. & iiii s. facrifte. Term' Annunc'.
Rector de Wyxfton redd' xxvi s. viii d.
Rector de Eftwell redd' xiii s. iiii d. & iiii s. facrifte. Term' Annunc'.
Summa, xiiii li. xv s. viii d.

Rector de Rokeby quondam reddebat xl s.; modò redd' xx s.

17. Ifti fuerunt milites & canonici abathie Leyceft'; fcil', dñs Robertus Boffu, comes Leyc', fundator nofter, miles & canonicus; dñs Wills de Novo Mercato, miles, & canonicus nofter; dñs Stefanus Segrave, miles, & canonicus nofter; dñs Gaufridus Craft, miles, & canonicus nofter; dñs Rogerus Aungervyle, miles, & canonicus nofter [7].—Stephanus Segrave, miles & canonicus, nuper dedit nobis in diverfis locis diverfas particulas terre & redditûs, & magnam fummam pecunie ad negotia noftra; pro quibus permiffum fuit [8].

---

[1] From a fpare leaf at the beginning of Charyte's Rentale.
[5] Ibid. fol. clxi. a.　[6] Ibid. fol. clxi. b.　[7] Ibid. fol. ccxv. a.
[2] Ibid.　[3] Ibid.　[4] Ibid.
[8] Cotton MSS. Vitellius F. XVII.

18. Nomina

18. Nomina eorum qui dederunt nobis certas terras, &c. cum corporibus fuis [1].

Mem', quòd omnes fubfcripti dederunt nobis certas terras & tenementa, cum corporibus fuis, ut patet inferiùs.

Robertus Boffu, comes Leyc', & fundator hujus abbathie, dedit nobis, cum corpore fuo, die quâ habitum religionis fumpfit, totam Stoctonam, & molendinum de Belgrave, cum fuis pertinentiis, &c.

Robertus, filius Petronille & tertius fundator nofter, dedit nobis, cum corpore fuo, viginti-quatuor virgatas terre, & IIII cotagia, cum fuis pertinentiis, in villâ de Anfty.

Petronilla comitiffa, mater predicti Roberti, dedit nobis, cum corpore fuo, totum pratum fuum in Thurmafton, quod vocatur Belleholme, & domos fuas in Suburbio Leyc' extra portam de Weft, que fuerunt Hugonis Clerici.

Henricus de Onlip dedit nobis, cum corpore fuo, in territorio de Thurmafton, IIII virgatas terre.

Helias de Lyndefcy & Alicia uxor ejus dederunt nobis, cum corporibus fuis, IIII virgatas terre in territorio de Thurmafton.

Witts de Dynâ dedit nobis, cum corpore fuo, die quâ habitum noftre religionis fumpfit, unam virgatam terre & dim' in Blaby; & homagium & fervicium Henrici de Reygate & Wilti filii Henrici.

Walterus Gerun dedit nobis, cum corpore fuo, terram fuam in villâ fuâ Sci Botulphi, juxta magnum vicum ufque mare, &c.; & homagia & fervicia multorum; ut pleniùs patet in cartâ XVI [2].

Aliz de Temple dedit nobis, cum corpore fuo, dimid' virgatam terre in territorio de Bernangul.

Wittus de Altâ Villâ dedit nobis, cum corpore fuo, unam virgatam terre, cum pertinentiis fuis, in Clenfeld.

Henricus, filius Fulconis de Merfton, dedit nobis, cum corpore fuo, IIII virgatas terre in Merfton; & pro hâc donatione recepimus eum in canonicum, & uxorem ejus in fororem.

Witts de Folvillâ dedit nobis, cum corpore fuo, molendinum fuum de Newbold, cum omni fequelâ domorum ejufdem ville, & unum lutinum adjacentem predicto molendino, & unum toftum.

Ricardus de Morvill, conftabularius regis Scotie, dedit nobis x s. annuos de quâdam dimidiâ carucatâ in Bangelane (pro quibus x s. percepimus modò de priore Sci Andree apud Northampton), eo quòd corpus Malcolmi fratris fui, per Alexandrum de Sco Martino interfecti, fepultum eft in cemeterio noftro.

Radulphus de Araby dedit nobis, cum corpore fuo, tertiam partem de Wybtoft, & unam virgatam terre in Stretton, quam Rogerus Torr tenuit.

Robertus de Burtonâ legavit in extremis, cum corpore fuo, nobis, unam virgatam terre in Nortonâ, cum pertinentiis fuis; quam quidem virgatam terre poftea nos dedimus Hugoni de Burton, in efcambium pro unâ culturâ in Bylfdon, que vocatur Byffopefcroft, & redditu II s. per annum.

Robertus, filius Roberti le Sweyn de Clifton, dedit nobis, cum corpore fuo, unam bovatam terre in territorio de Clifton, quam Robertus pater fuus fibi dedit.

Rogerus Pepyn de Leyc' dedit nobis, cum corpore fuo, ad luminare ecclefie, illud toftum quod Robertus Faber tenuit de ipfo in parochiâ Sci Michaelis.

Ranulphus Portarius dedit nobis, cum corpore fuo, totam illam terram quam habuit de Roberto filio Witti filio Aufredi de Bruntyngfthorp, fcil', manerium noftrum ad portam occidentalem.

Hugo de Seis, vel Saxo, dedit nobis, cum corpore fuo, redditum II s. per annum de molendino fuo in villâ fuâ de Broxby.

Gaufridus pater Roberti de Craft dedit nobis certas terras in Sutton, quando fe in canonicum reddidit, ficut patet in primâ cartâ de Kenelworth.

Wittus de Evermo dedit nobis, cum corpore fuo, ecclefiam de Eyton, cum certis terris & tenementis.

Reginaldus Baffet dedit nobis, cum corpore fuo, XVIII virgatas terre & unam bovatam, cum pertinentiis fuis, in Lokyngton.

19. Hìc pauca recordantur de multis bonis domini Witti Clowne, abbatis, tempore prelacie fue.

Hic emit redditus & fervicia ad valorem decem marcarum per annum pro conventu.

Porte nove monafterii cum muris edificate fuerunt tempore fuo.

Item aula abbatis, que conftabat xxxix li. & ultra.

Item cancella de Brakley, que conftabat xxxiii li. & ultra.

Item manerium de Kyrkby Malory, cum advocatione ecclefie, perquifitum fuit tempore ejufdem abbatis, qui folvebat pro mortizatione & reparatione ejufdem manerii cc marcas & ultra.

Item manerium de Yngwarby perquifitum fuit tempore ejufdem abbatis.

Item de bofco noftro factum fuit pretium.

Item perquifivit cartam regis, ut, tempore vacationis, prior & conventus de temporalibus bonis plenam & liberam adminiftrationem habent, &c. reddendo ei, fi vacaverit per quatuor menfes vel per minus temporis, IIII marcas, &c. per ratam; ubi anteà folverunt c marcas fi vacaverit per duos menfes vel per minus tempus, & pro quolibet alio menfe fequente L marcas, fi tanto tempore vacaverit.

Item Edwardus rex Tertius conceffit eidem abbati habere nundinas vel feriam pro leporariis [2], & aliis canibus cujufcunque conditionis effent, emendis & vendendis, &c. ut in Cronicis Henrici Knyton [3].

Item perquifivit cartam regis Edwardi Tertii, de non veniendo ad parliamentum.

Item perquifivit aliam cartam ejufdem regis, de non folvendo cupam vel palfridum poft deceffum alicujus abbatis.

Item dominus rex, & princeps filius ejus, & plures domini regni Anglie cum eo, retenti erant fub annuâ pencoe leporariorum.

Item ipfe ordinavit cantarias conventûs.

Et mutavit ufum nigrarum botarum in nigris caligis cum nigris fotularibus.

Item, preter hec predicta, multa alia fecit & perquifivit, ficut patet perfcrutanti evidentias noftras.

20. Mem', quòd pulpitum in refectorio, pictura capelle Sce Marie, celatoria totius chori & corporis ecclefie, & depinctio ejufdem, tabula fuper altare Sce Marie, crux de argento cum Johanne & Mariâ, pictura Crucifixi, Marie & Johannis, cum multis aliis. Omnia ifta facta fuerunt per fratrem W. Geryn [4].

21. Mem', quòd pauca hìc memorantur de multis bonis dni Philippi abbatis, collata per fratrem W. Charyte.

Primò perquifivit nobis ccxLv li. per annum de proventubus prioratûs de Ware, ex dono regis Henrici Quarti, & anno ejufdem regis primo; & habuimus eas in pacificâ poffeffione ufque ad tempus regis Henrici Quinti.

Item perquifivit nobis cartam de licentiâ perquirendi terras ad valorem cli. per annum.

Item perquifivit nobis cartam de quietâ clamatione manfionum canonicorum apud Cokeram, & hoc per magnum laborem & expenfas diverfas.

Item perquifivit nobis cartam regis Henrici Quarti, de corrodio non habendo in monafterio noftro.

Item de fine habito inter nos & dominum de Beamont & priorem de Bermundefey, pro decimis de Woodhous [5], que materia longo tempore fuit in lite; tamen recuperavit contra eos. Unde perquifivit cartam regis de confirmatione hujus finis, &c.

Item quomodo finivit materiam inter nos & epm Covent' & Lich' pro Sandholme [6], que fuit materia valdè difficillima, onerofa, & fumptuofa. Indè adquifivit cartam regis de confirmatione hujus finis, &c.

Item quomodo tranfmutavit cantariam Roberti Byrde de villâ de Quenyboro ad abbathiam Leyc'.

Item perquifivit nobis cartam regis Henrici Quarti, de confirmatione omnium poffeffionum noftrarum, &c.

Item perquifivit nobis notabile tranfcriptum bullarum fummorum pontificum, archiepifcoporum, & epifcoporum, de confirmatione omnium poffeffionum

[1] Charyte's Rentale, fol. iiii. b. v. a. b.
[2] Greyhounds.—In a charter of king Henry II. to the priory of Wikes in Effex, (Dugd. Mon. Angl. II. 283.) we find, " Concedo eis duos leporarios & quatuor bracatos ad leporem capiendum in noftrâ foreftâ de Effex."
[3] See the Hiftory of Leicefter, p. 262.   [4] Charyte's Rentale, fol. ccxiv. b.   [5] See before, p 63.   [6] See p. 64.

noftrarum;

noftrarum; valdè notabile eft. Et, preter hoc, multa alia fecit & perquifivit, ficut patet fcrutanti evidentias noftras.

Item perquifivit cartam regis Henrici Quarti, quòd nullus provifor feu captor regis merchatur feodum noftrum; nec bladum, beftias, vel cariagia capiat, &c. [1]

22. Mem', quòd hec verba contenta funt in indenturâ inter abbatem Leyc' & ejufdem loci conventum ex unâ parte, & Bartholomeum Brokefby, &c. ex alterâ parte; fcilicet, quòd abbas monafterii predicti qui pro tempore fuerit celebrabit, vel faciet alium canonicum ejufdem monafterii, vel honeftum capellanum fecularem, fumptibus ejufdem monafterii, celebrare miffam pro animâ Johanne Beauchamp, ad altare Sci Johannis Baptifte & beati Auguftini, ex parte auftrali ejufdem monafterii, vel alibi fi id ibidem commodò fieri non poterit, orando & mentionem vel memoriam in eâdem mifsâ pro & de animâ dicte Johanne fpecialitèr & nominatìm faciendo. Concedunt etiam predicti abbas & conventus, quòd iidem canonici admittendi vel profitendi jurabunt fuper fancta evangelia quòd dictam celebrationem & memoriam hujufmodi formâ & modo predictis faciend' pro poffe fuo fuftentabunt in perpetuum. Et infuper predicti abbas & conventus concedunt predicto Bartholomeo, &c. cs. nomine pene, quandocunque continget dicti abbas & conventus, &c. in celebratione & memoriis, modo & formâ predict', faciend', legitimo impedimento ceffante, per tres menfes ceffarent, ut in indenturâ [2].

23. Mem', quòd anno Domini MCCCCLXXXII°, in die Perpetue & Felicitatis, abbas & conventus in domo capitulari convenerunt, & communi affenfu & confenfu ftatuerunt & ordinari fecerunt, ut cotidie in mifsâ capitulari fpecialis fiat memoria pro fratre Willo Charyte, pro beneficiis eidem conventui & monafterio diverfimodè collatis per eundem; fic quòd celebrans dictam miffam, fi de Sanctis aut de Dominicâ fuerit, capiat collectam, "Deus qui caritatis fub uno p dñm." Si verò pro defunctis celebret, dicta collecta erit fexta in meridiem, additis iftis terminis, "famulo tuo." Huic etiam ordinationi addiderunt dicti abbas & conventus quòd idem Wills obitum fuum fpecialem cum William Afton fingulis annis celebratum cum fpeciali memoriâ ad Placebo, Dirige, & Mifsâ. Item ordinatum eft, quòd poft mortem dicti Willi cotidie ad miffam capitularem fiet memoria pro ipfo in collectâ, fcil', "Deus, cùm proprium," additis terminis, "famulo tuo."

Et, ut mentes fingulorum fratrum ad dictam ordinationem perimplendam excitentur, pauca ejufdem beneficia, de multis collecta, modò hìc recitantur.

Primò idem Willus contulit XLli. ad perquirend' terras & tenementa ad capellam beate Marie, pro exibicione puerorum & aliorum eodem provenientium eodem die Perpetue & Felicitatis.

Item poftea emit unum molendinum ventriticum apud Stouton, quod conftabat XXli. valens per annum XLs.

Item emit in eâdem villâ II meffuagia & II virgatas terre, que conftabant XIIIIli. valent' per annum XVIs.

Item emit certas terras & tenementa in Hungarton & Baggrave, que conftabant VIli. valent' per annum XIIIIs. IIIId.

Item dedit conventui X libras in communi ciftâ cuftodiendas, ut, cum defecerit fin habitualis ftipendii folutio ex parte celararii vel camerarii, folveretur eifdem de dictâ fummâ debitis temporibus.

Item contulit C marcas officio celararii, pro catallis emendis ad juftand' ad pafturas de Ingwarby.

Item contulit XLli. officio fubcelararii, eidem deliberandas cum neceffe fuerit.

Item dedit terras & tenementa ad valorem per annum X marcarum.

Item dedit calicem de auro, & ymaginem Sce Marie deauratam [3].

24. Mem', quòd frater W. de Malvernâ abbas habuit licentiam communi figillo firmatam, quòd, inftallatione fuâ habitâ, domus Leyc' tenebatur diverfis creditoribus in fummâ duarum millium & fexaginta marcarum, Xs. VId. Dat' die Martis proximâ poft feftum Omnium Sanctorum, anno Domini M°cc°XCI [4].

25. Mem' quòd die Annunciationis beate Marie, anno Domini M°ccc°, fumma falfarum in abbathiâ Leyceftrie argenteorum fuit XXI; fumma difcorum argenteorum, XLIII; de quibus dominus abbas habet unum duodenam & VIII falfaria; & XXXI difci & XIII falfaria liberati fuerunt ad coquinam [5].

26. Mem', quòd cancella Sci Martini edificata fuit anno Domini M°cccc°IX°, tempore Rici Rotheley abbatis; & conftabat XXXIIIIli. Et cancella de Cokeram edificata fuit anno Domini M°cccc°XLII°, tempore domini Johis Pomerey abbatis [6].

27. Nota, quòd ifta verba inveniuntur inter evidentias domini de Aftley:

" Abbas Leyceftr' habet manerium de Yngwardby, cum pertinentiis, perquifit' de Rogero Angervyle, milite. Et tres virgate terre, cum meff' in Bufsheby, cum pratis & pafturis, & tres virgate terre, affignantur cuidam cantarie ibidem.

" Item dominus de Aftley habet in Wylloby Waterlays unam virgatam terre vocat' Canteray, & VI denaratos redditûs, cum advocatione ecclefie ejufdem, dicto manerio pertinent'.

" Item Willus Danet tenet in eâdem de dicto domino 4 virgatas terre, cum V meffuagiis dicto manerio pertinent', reddendo annuatim dicto domino de Afteley Vd. & dim' libram piperis; pro quibus dictus dnus de Afteley faciet fervicia pro quantitate. Et fciend', quòd totum predictum manerium tenetur de domino de Grey de Codenor pro uno feodo militis."

Et notandum, quòd 12 virgate terre & 2 denaratus redditûs, cum pertin', in Wylloby Waterleys, cum advocatione ecclefie ejufdem ville, pertinent manerio de Yngwarby, ficut patet in cartis noftris de Yngwarby, & omnibus aliis evidentiis noftris.

Et notandum, quòd III virgate terre quas habuimus in Bufsby vendite fuerunt, ficut patet in rotul' Johannis de Thorp & Radulfi de Grifley celarariorum, cujus dat' eft anno Domini MCCCLXXI [7].

28. Pateat univerfis per prefentes, me Johem Grey, dñm de Codenore & de Yngwarby, recepiffe de dno Willo de Afteley milite VIIs. pro relevio terrarum & tenementorum, cum advocatione ecclefie de Wylleby Watles in comitatu Leyc', que quondam fuerunt Radi de Angervyle militis, pro portione unius feodi militis manerii de Yngwarby, quod eft in manibus abbatis Leyc'; videlicet, VIs. VIIId. pro quintâdecimâ parte unius feodi militis, & IIIId. ultra, fecundum confilium & ordinationem predictorum domini Willi & Abbatis; de quibus quidem predictis VIIs. fateor me effe pacatum, & dictum dominum Willm in formâ predictâ fore quietum per prefentes. In cujus rei teftimonium, prefentibus figillum meum appofui. Dat' apud Evyngton, die Martis proximâ poft Claufum Pafce, anno regni Ricardi II. poft Conqueftum IX°. [8]

29. Mem', quòd Edwardus rex quartus, cum confenfu & affenfu domini Johannis Schepifhed abbatis Leyc', & ejufdem loci conventûs, pofuit quandam palum fuper terram $\left\{ \begin{array}{l} \text{ipfius [9]} \\ \text{noftram} \end{array} \right\}$ inter bofcum vocat' Bewmontwod & Stokkyng, fuper quandam pafturam vocat' Calverhey, ad faciend' five applicand' fibi novum parcum; volens & percipiens, pro fe & fuccefforibus fuis, quòd liceat dictis abbati & conventui, quotiens & quando voluerint, fuccidere & auferre tam arbores prope dictam palam crefcentes, quam infra dictam palam, in ipfâ terrâ que dictorum abbatis & conventûs fuiffe dinofcitur, ut patet in bundis in dicto monafterio habitis [10].

[1] Charyte's Rentale, fol. ccxiv. a.
[2] Ibid. from the firft fpare leaf at the beginning.
[3] Ibid. fol. ccxix. a.   [4] Ibid. fol. ccxix. b.
[5] Ibid. fol. ccxix. b.   [6] Ibid. fol. ccxiv. b.
[7] From the firft fpare leaf.   [8] Ib. fol. i.   [9] Sic in Orig.   [10] Charyte's Rentale, from the fi.ft fpare leaf.
SCHENE.

30. Schéne. Compofitiones.

Habuimus & tenuimus de abbate Sci Ebrulphi & éjufdem loci conventûs, ad perpetuam firmam, omnes decimas garbarum dominici comitis Leyc' apud Leyc', & decimas garbarum dominicarum de Kereby, & Kyreby, & de Thorpernold, per annuam firmam octo marcarum, ut patet per primam compofitionem inter ipfos & nos, &c.

Item, per eandem compofitionem, habuimus ab eifdem abbate & conventu decimas garbarum de dominico de Stowton pro firmâ xxxiiis. iiiid.

Item, decimas garbarum de dominico de Evington, pro firmâ xs.

Item, decimas garbarum de Humberfton, de dominico, pro firmâ xiiis.

Mem', quòd pro omnibus prediétis decimis, cum decimis de Wyxton, per iftam primam compofitionem, folvimus prediéto abbati & conventui de Sco Ebrulpho xlī.

Habuimus, ab eifdem abbate & conventu, decimas affartorum de Stathay & Hothay, etiam affartorum faétorum & faciendorum in bofcis de Thornton & Bagworth, per eandem compofitionem. Et etiam decimas cujufdam loci qui vocatur Schadhay. Item, ut in eâdem compofitione, quòd pro fingulis virgatis terre in diétis locis annuatim perfolvamus xiiiid.

Habemus, per aliam compofitionem, ab eifdem abbate & conventu, decimas dominicarum garbarum de dominicis de Wykengefton, folvendo eis annuatim pro eifdem decimis vis.

Mem', quòd nos recuperavimus omnes iftas decimas de abbate de Sco Ebrulpho per fententiam diffinitivam, ficut patet in Rentali fratris W. Charyte.

Habuimus, per ultimam compofitionem, inter diétum abbatem & conventum & nos, ad perpetuam firmam, omnes decimas garbarum dominici comitis Leyc' apud Leyc', de Porâ de Sowth & de Wheft, pro annuâ firmâ xxs. viiiid.

Item habuimus, per eandem compofitionem, decimas garbarum de Branfton & Keyrby, pro iiilī. xiiis. iiiid. per annum.

Item habuimus decimas garbarum de Thorpernold, ab eifdem, pro iiilī. per annum, per eandem compofitionem.

Item habuimus, per aliam compofitionem, de eifdem, decimas garbarum de Evyngton, pro xlvis. viiid. per annum.

Item habuimus, per eandem compofitionem, de eifdem, decimas garbarum de Humburfton, pro xxs. per annum.

Mem, quòd pro omnibus prediétis decimis, cum decimis de Wykengefton, per iftam ultimam compofitionem, folvimus annuatim xiiilī. vis. viiid.

Habuimus, per aliam compofitionem, ab eifdem, omnes decimas provenientes de bofco noftro in defenfo Leyc', pro annuâ firmâ xiiis. iiiid.

Mem', quòd cùm varie contentiones fuiffent exorte inter abbatem Leyc' & abbatem de Sco Ebrulpho fuper quibufdam decimis, &c.; tandem materia diétarum contentionum fic conquievit; videlicet, quòd prediéti abbas & conventus de Sco Ebrulpho concefferunt abbati Leyc', &c. omnes decimas, tam majores quàm minores, de terris affartatis & affartandis infra limites fubfcriptos, ut patet in compofitione, &c.; ita videlicet, quòd prefati religiofi de Leyc' pro decimis fingularum virgatarum terre infra limites ufque Thornton & Bagworth, &c. perfolvant xiiiid.

Item dimiferunt ad firmam perpetuam omnimodas decimas, tam majores quàm minores, de omnibus terris novitèr affartatis & in futurum affartandis infra dom' de Enderby; falvis diétis abbati & conventui de Sco Ebrulpho decimis minutis de vi cotagiis infra dominicum de Enderby.

Item dimiferunt nobis ad firmam omnimodas decimas provenientes de Doveland, & omnes decimas provenientes de quodam loco qui vocatur Affartum Simonis Danet fub defenfo Leyc'; item omnes decimas de locis vocatis Culleferland, Edwynerop, & Stokkyng, dimiferunt abbas & conventus Leyc'; falvâ tamen decimâ venditionis bofci, herbagii, pannagii, & venationis, in omnibus locis prediétis, excepto bofco de Doneland, eifdem religiofis de Sco Ebrulpho.

Mem', quòd abbas & conventus Sci Ebrulphi percipient totam decimam garbarum venditionis bofci, & totam decimam pannagii porcorum extraneorum de Bagworth & Thornton; falvâ totâ decimâ pannagii abbatis & conventûs Leyc' de porcis parochianorum de Thornton, & medietate decime de porcis parochianorum de Bagworth.

Mem', quòd jam folvimus priori de Schen, pro omnibus decimis prediétis, tam majoribus quàm minoribus, per novam compofitionem faétam inter ipfum & nos, xiilī. per annum, ad feftum Michaelis & Annunciationis, vel ipfâ menfe, fub penâ perditionis xs. toties quoties, &c. ut in libro de Chartwary [1].

31. London. Dona diverforum, ficut patet per cartas.

Habemus ibi, ex conceffione, venditione, & dimiffione, Radulphi fratris quondam domini Willi de Langley clerici, Hugonis le Chaundeler, Johis de Stratford, & Johis de Eure, executores teftamenti prediéti Willi defunéti, virtute & poteftate feu auétoritate executionis teftamenti in pleno Huftingo London', die Lune, in Oétab' Sce Trinitatis, de omnibus placitis, anno regni regis Edwardi filii regis Edwardi quinto, leéti & irrotulati, illud tenementum, cum domibus, celariis, fchopis & celariis, fuperedificatis, & omnibus aliis pertinentibus fuis, quod eft in parochiâ Sanéti Sepulchri extra Newgat in fuburbio London'; quod quidem tenementum, cum medietate cujufdem fontis, fitum eft in latitudine inter cemeterium ecclefie prediéte & tenementum quod prediétus dominus W. legavit ad quandam cantariam indè faciend' ex parte Orientali, & tenementum Gerardi le Barber & tenementum Prioriffe de Haliwell ex parte Occidentali; & extendit fe in longitudine à vico regio qui ducit de Newgate ufque ad pontem de Holburn versùs Auftrum, &c. Pro iftâ conceffione, venditione, & prefentis carte confirmatione, dedimus prediétis executoribus quandam fummam pecunie, ficut patet in cartâ xiia.

Mem', quòd Edwardus rex filius regis Edwardi dedit nobis licentiam ad mortizand' prediét' ten', domus, &c. ut patet in cartâ; fcil', un' meff' & duas fhopas juxta ecclefiam Sci Sepulchri extra Newgat, & xiiii fhopas in Cock-lane; & xxs. de i meff' vocat' Renedere. & xxs. de meff' in Weft Smythfield juxta le Pool, &c. ut in cartâ Edwardi regis.

Habemus, ex quietâ clamatione, remiffione, & relaxatione fratris Thome, magiftri hofpitalis Sci Egidii extra barram veteris Templi London', & ejufdem hofpitalis fratrum & priorum, totum jus fuum & clameum quod habuerunt, &c. in omnibus terris & tenementis que habuimus de dono & feoffamento Radulphi fratris domini Willi de Langley, aut in redditibus indè provenientibus, &c.; falvo, &c. annuo redditu quem percipiunt annuatim de illâ terrâ, &c.

Habemus remiffionem & quietam clamationem Humfridi prioris ecclefie Sce Marie de Suwerk, & ejufdem loci conventûs, de iiis. annui redditûs, quos folebamus eis reddere pro quâdam terrâ in Smithfield.

Habemus, ex dono Hugonis le Fraunceys & Dionife uxoris ejus, tenementum fuum quod habuit in civitate London' & extra, fcil', capitale meffuagium fuum, cum omnibus pertinentiis fuis, in parochiâ Sci Sepulchri extra portam de Newgate; redd' indè annuatim ut patet in cartâ xxva.

Habemus, ex dono Johis de Woburn, xiiis. annui redditûs, quos ipfe folebat recipere de prediéto tenemento Hugonis le Fraunceys.

Habemus, ex conceffione & confirmatione Warini de Neapoi', prioris hofpitalis Ierofolomit' in Angliâ, cum conceffu fratrum capituli, totam terram fuam de Smithefeld, quam emerunt de Thomâ Tornato, redd' eis annuatim iis. & i libram incenfi; &, ex conceffione eorum, terram ufque forum equorum, que habet xxiiii pedes in latitudine, redd' eis annuatim vid.

Mem', quòd nos conceffimus, dimifimus, & per cartam noftram confirmavimus, Criftine filie Radulphi Fabri de Newgath, London', totam terram noftram, cum domibus fuperedificatis, quam habuimus de dono Hugonis Francifci piftoris, in parochiâ Sci Sepulcri extra Newgat, que jacet intra cemeterium Sci Sepulcri & terram que fuit Gilberti le Horfmeg'e, &c. habend' & tenend' fibi & heredibus fuis, redd' nobis annuatim xxis.

Modò magifter & fratres hofpit' Sci Bartholomei de Smethefeld habent prediétum, & redd' nobis xxs.

Mem', quòd magifter & fratres hofpitalis Sēi Bartholomei· de Smethefeld tenent unum tenementum, cum pertinentiis fuis, de feodo noftro, in parochiâ Sēi Sepulcri extra Newgat, quod vocatur Renedere, ex parte boreali ejufdem ecclefie, unde obligantur nobis, per cartam fuam, in quodam redditu fervicii. xx s̄. per annum; & licebit nobis, per eandem cartam, diftringere pro predicto redditu in illis duobus tenementis fuis, inter dictum tenementum quod vocatur Reneder & cemeterium dicte ecclefie fituatis, quam in eodem tenemento quod vocatur le Renedere, pro voluntate noftrâ.

Mem', quòd Henricus de Calabre recepit de nobis, fibi & heredibus, molendinum noftrum, quod vocatur Algodfmilne, in parochiâ de Stebenheth, in Eldeford, cum omnibus pertinentiis fuis, in aquis, ftagnis, foffatis, pratis, pafcuis, & pafturis, viis & femitis; habend' fibi & heredibus, &c. reddend' nobis annuatim duas marcas, & capitali domino x s̄.

Mem', quòd Johes de Honilane, civis London', recepit de nobis, fibi & heredibus fuis, molendinum noftrum quod vocatur Algodfmilne, in parochiâ de Stebenheth, quod fitum eft Anglicè atte Eldeford, cum prato adjacente, & aliis fuis pertinentiis; fcil', aquis, ftagnis, pifcariis, &c. redd' inde nobis annuatim xx s̄. & capitali dno x s̄.

Mem', quòd Johes Bukonite conceffit & confirmavit Waltero Carpentario de Smethefeld terram quam nos per cartam noftram ei confirmavimus, que jacet juxta Chykenlane, que continet in longitudine lv pedes de pedibus Sēi Pauli, juxta venellam que vocatur Chykynlane, in latitudine ufque Orientem xxvii pedes & dim', & in capite Occident' xxvii de eifdem pedibus; habend' & tenend' fibi & heredibus fuis, reddend' nobis annuatim xii d.

Habemus, ex dono Petri de Southampton, dicti de la Hull, & Agnetis de la Hull uxoris ejus, viii s̄. annui redditûs, recipiend' de tenemento quod fitum eft in Cokkyflane, & extendit fe juxta januam fuam ufque ad tenementum Johis Moritii, &c. Et poffumus diftringere pro predicto redditu, quando neceffe fuerit, tam in toto tenemento quod ipfi tenent de nobis in parochiâ predictâ juxta cemeterium Sēi Sepulcri, quàm in tenemento fupradicto.

Tenentes ad voluntatem.

Eleanor Bredon tenet unum cotagium & unam cameram annexam Sarfonhed; & redd' xx s̄.

Wills Strette tenet Sarfonhed per indenturam; & redd' viii l̄. xiii s̄. iiii d.

Johes Rutt ten' tenementum juxta Sarfonhed per indenturam, & redd' xxvi s̄. viii d.

Ricardus Burftal tenet tenementum juxta, & redd' l s̄.

Wills Mynt tenet i mess' in Smythefeld, & redd' liii s̄. iiii d. Duo fuerunt cotagia ibidem, que quondam reddiderunt nobis xx s̄.

Modò predictus Wills Mynt emit de nobis predicta meffuagium & ii cotagia pro c marcis; pro quibus adquifivimus nobis in comitatu Leyc' certas terras & tenementa ad majorem valorem in proficuis.

Thomas Littelton, unus juftitiarius domini regis de Banco, tenet hofpitium dicti abbatis per indenturam, ad terminum xl annorum à fefto Pafche, anno regni regis Edwardi Quarti xiii°, ufque ad predictum terminum, reddend' nobis annuatim xvi s̄. Et fi contingat predictum redditum à retro fuerit, in parte vel in toto, &c. liceat nobis diftringere in predicto meffuagio. Et fi à retro fuerit per dimidium anni, folverit nobis nomine pene xl d. & fic toties quoties. Et poffumus diftringere in predicto meffuagio pro predict' xl d. ficut pro redditu. Et fi predictus redditus à retro fuerit per unum annum, &c. licebit nobis intrare in predictum meffuagium, & illud in priftino ftatu poffidere, &c. Et predicti Thomas vel executores fui non dimittere terminum fuum alicui fine licentiâ & voluntate noftrâ.

Summa xvii l̄. xix s̄. iiii d.

Tenentes liberi.

Magifter hofpitii Sēi Bartholomei, pro uno tenemento vocat' Renedere, redd' liberè xx s̄.

Summa totalis, xviii l̄. xix s̄. iiii d.

Refolutiones; fcil',

Magifter Sēi Egidii London', pro tenemento juxta Sarfonhed, quondam Johis Faytt, xx s̄.

Monialibus de Clerkenwell, pro le Sarfonheyd, xiii s̄ iiii d.

Hofpitali Sēi Johis Jerlm, pro tenemento in Smethefeld vocato Blakyates, ii s̄.; & pro i librâ incenfi viii d. pro eodem tenemento. Et eodem, pro tenemento juxta Chickenlane ufque forum equorum, vi d.

Ecclefie Sēi Sepulcri London', pro quâdam pendulâ ultra cemeterium in hofpitio de Sarfonheyd, ii s̄.

Summa, xlv s̄. ii d. [1]

32. Habemus, ex dono Ricardi de Morvill, conftabularii regis Scotie, redditum x s̄. fingulis annis, quem canonici de Drieburk nobis annuatim ad feftum Sēi Michaelis perfolvent in perpetuum pro quâdam terrâ, fcil', pro dim' carucatâ in Bangelane, quam Alexander de Sēo Martino dedit predicto Ricardo in concordiâ pro interfectione Malcolmi de Morvillâ fratris fui, cujus corpus in cemeterio canonicorum de Leyc' fepultum eft.

Mem', quòd cum controverfia orta fuerit inter abbatem & conventum Leyc' & abbatem de Drieburk pro redditu x s̄. per annum, tandem lis fic conquievit, quòd abbas & conventus de Drieburk perfolvent de cetero abbati & conventui Leyc' v s̄ quos eis affignaverunt de redditu fuo apud Northampton, quos canonici de Sēo Jacobo de Northampton canonicis de Leyc' annuatim perfolvent, de redditu xxxiii s̄. iiii d. quos canonici de Dryeburk pro ecclefiâ de Bofiat perfolvere tenentur.

Habemus cartam abbatis & conventûs de Dryeburk, directam ad abbatem & conventum de Sēo Jacobo de Northampton, pro folutione v s̄. annuatim in his verbis: " Univerfitati noftre notum facimus, quòd ex conventionê quâdam inter nos & abbatem & conventum de Leyc' factâ, fuper dim' carucatâ terre in Pangelane, eidem abbati & conventui v s̄. pro dictâ terrâ fingulis annis ad Purificationem beate Marie in perpetuum folvere tenemur. Quocirca vobis mandamus & fupplicamus, quatenùs loco noftro prefatis abbati & conventui Leyc' memorat' v s̄. ad predictum terminum perfolvatis, de redditu quem nobis debetur pro ecclefiâ de Bofyath."

Habuimus modò de priore Sēi Andree Northampt' v s̄. annui redditûs, quos folebamus recipere de abbate & conventu Sēi Jacobi de Northampt' [2].

Mem', quòd canonici de Drieburk concefferunt canonicis Sēi Jacobi extra Northt' ecclefiam fuam de Bofyath, &c. reddendo annuatim eis duas marcas & dim'; quas quidem duas marcas & dim' abbas de Drieburk & conventus affignaverunt predictis abbati & conventui Sēi Jacobi extra Northt' folvere annuatim priori & conventui Sēi Andree de Northampt'; falvâ ex utrâque parte conventione inter eos priùs factâ, ut in conventionibus que funt in libro de Chartwary.

33. Habemus capellam de Halfo, ex dono fundatoris noftri, cum decimis garbarum & feni, &c. que confuevit habere capellanum refidentem per matricem ecclefiam de Brakley. Et fciendum, quòd inhabitantes dicte hamelette de Halfo tenentur ad reparationem ejufdem capelle; & nos exoneramur à reparatione ejus, ut patet in concordiâ inter dominum Johem Lovell & abbatem Leyc', apud Northampton, in craftino Apoftolorum Petri & Pauli, cujus dat' eft anno Domini m°ccc° nonagefimo viii°, & regis Ricardi II. xxi°; ubi abbas proteftatus eft, pro fe & fuccefforibus fuis, quòd nec ipfi nec predeceffores fui aut fucceffores fui non tenebantur nec tenentur ad reparationes dicte capelle, ex aliquo pacto, vel compofitione aliquâ, feu debito aliquo. Tamen, ad fpecialem rogatum ejufdem domini Johannis, cum proteftatione publicâ, quòd hujufmodi factum predicti abbatis non procederet in jus aliquid vel clameum dictis inhabitantibus, feu in prejudicium dicti abbatis, conceffit predictus abbas, pro hâc vice tantùm, fe velle tectum cancelli dicte capelle & feneftras competenter emendare. Et, pro iftâ conceffione, predictus dominus Lovell conceffit ad predictam reparationem vi bonas arbores quercinas accipiend' in filvâ fuâ de Bagworth, & xl s̄. in pecunia, ficut patet in dictâ concordiâ in Rotulo Pynchebek, que eft in libro Parliamenti [3].

[1] Charyte's Rentale, fol. cix. a. b. cx. a.   [2] Ibid. fol. cxiii.   [3] Ibid. fol. lx. b.

34. Confuetudines Tenentium [1].

He funt ville in quibus tenentes noftri confueverunt facere nobis diverfa opera vocat' *Lovebenys* [2], & alia certa fervicia, per confuetudinem villarum, prout hic patet in villis fubfequentibus.

Et primò notandum eft generalitèr, quòd omnes tenentes noftri & firmarii confueverunt folvere domino abbati ingreffum fecundùm quod potuerint convenire cum ipfo.

Anfty. Notandum, quòd quelibet virgata terre de xxiiii virgatis ibidem folebat reddere ante peftilentiam marchetam, & i diem meffionis in autumpno cum duobus hominibus, vel ii diebus cum uno homine; & unum diem cariagii cum ii hominibus. Modo reddit tantum cariagium i die cum ii hominibus, vel i hominem, &c. & fectam curie.

Bagworth. Tenentes ibidem folebant reddere pannagium, marchetam, ... gallinas, & fectam curie.

Barkeby. Tenens i bovate terre ad voluntatem dedit ii gallinas; falcavit per unum diem; dedit auxilium & marchetam pro filiâ. De arboribus & pull' axiftul' per confuetudinem regiam; & debet harriotam & fectam curie. Alitèr ut funt in le Pyn & Gerin.

Bernangul. Tenentes ibi ad voluntatem dant auxilium, marchetam, & hariot', & fectam curie.

Baro. Quilibet cotarius de x folvebat ii gallinas ad Natale, & xx ova, metebat per ii dies, & fecit pratum molendini, & fectam curie. Alitèr ut fuprà in Baro, & ut in le Pyn & Geryn.

Bytfwell. Tenens unam virgatam terre folebat metere in autumpno cum i homine per duos dies, & folvere marchetam de filiâ fuâ maritandâ, & fectam curie. Alio modo ut in le Pyn.

Bofworth. Tenens i virgatam terre dat auxilium; falcat per duos dies ad croftum noftrum, & fectam curie; & dat i hariot'; & per Rotul' le Pyn dat marchet'.

Brakley. He funt confuetudines diebus comitis Leyc'; fcil', quelibet virgata reddidit auxilium; ad feft' Michaelis tres maturas, tres falcationes tempore feminationis, tres levationes, & cariagium feni ad domum comitis; tres fanalationes, & tres meffiones bladi in autumpno. He funt confuetudines ex voluntate abbatis. Quelibet virgata reddit xiiſ. & eft libera de omni fervicio preter franciplegium. Pretereà quelibet virgata reddit xiiiſ. iiiid. & hariot', falvâ marchetâ modò.

Branket. Tenentes ibi debent auxilium, marchetam, hariotam, & franciplegium.

Clerfeld. Tenentes ibi folebant operari per i diem in autumpno, & folvere marchetam & fectam curie.

Clifton. Tenentes ibi folebant falcare per ii dies ad cibum noftrum.

Cokeram. Omnes tenentes de Cokeram operant; dant gallinas; dant *plow-filver* per tenuras fuas, ficut patet in matriculo rentali fratris W. Charyte.

Crudworth. Fuerunt ibi iii tenentes, quorum quilibet tenuit unam quartam partem unius virgate, & meffuit cum uno homine per ii dies; & fecerunt fenum per i diem ad cibum domini abbatis.

Alius tenuit . . . . & fecit fimilitèr.

Unus cotarius operabat cum i homine per i diem, ficut habetur in cartâ quam habemus, cujus dat' eft anno Dni m°cc°lxvii.

Faringo. Tenens i virgate falcabit totum pratum abbatis cum vicinis fuis; levabit, cariabit ad croftum fuum; fed abbas dabit falci unum panem, & omnibus vicinis unam ovem; & operabit in autumpno ad croftum fuum per ii dies, & tertiâ die ad croftum abbatis, & cariabit per i diem ad croftum fuum, & ad feftum Sci Matthei arabit unam acram, & feminabit cum femine abbatis quod ipfe triturabit & mundabit, & harabit ad croftum fuum, & in quibus arabit per i diem, & farculabit per i diem. Et fi abbas voluit ponere eos ad operandum a fefto Pent' ufque ad feftum Michaelis, unaqueque virgata inveniet i hominem per totam feptimanam preter diem Sabbati, & tunc quieti erunt de xxd. ad feftum Michaelis. Et dabit auxilium, pannagium de porcis fuis, five fint in bofco five domi;

& dabunt marchetam pro filiis & filiabus, & franciplegium & hariotam. Alitèr ut fuprà in Faringo & in le Pyn.

[3] *Kyrkby Malore.* Notandum, quòd tenens i virgate terre folebat falcare, levare, & cariare pratum noftrum dominicum cum vicinis fuis, & arare cum caruis fuis femel in yemali tempore, & femel in Quadragefimâ; & tunc femel in die habuerunt prandium de domino. Et coterelli folebant tuffare in grangiâ, & furcare fenum ibidem ad carectam. Et ad magnum Rederop tenentes folebant invenire ii homines in autumpno ad cibum domini. Et quelibet dim' virgata terre folebat reddere ii gallinas, & i wodhenne, & x ova, & unum panem frumenti pretii iid. Et omnes coterelli folebant reddere woodhenne & v ova. Et ix coterelli rectoris eodem modo reddebant. Summa gallinarum fylveftrium xxxiii. Summa gallinarum de redditu xxii. Summa panum ix, pret' xviiid. Summa ovorum ccxx, pret' xiid. Summa operum ix carucarum per ii dies tempore feminali, pret' xiiſ. per diem viiid. Summa operum lxi mefforum in autumpno pret' . . . . Alitèr ut fuprà in Kyrkeby Malory.

Modò omnes tenentes noftri ibidem, tam liberi quàm voluntarii, cotarii, & tres tenentes rectoris, quilibet eorum folvit gallinam; & omnes predicti, preter tenentes voluntarios, operantur, fcil' metendo, vel dant iid.

Lokyngton. Quelibet virgata de feodo Baffet falcabit per i diem, & dabuntur eis omnibus iiiid. ad potandum; & levabit per i diem fenum ad croftum fuum; & cariabit ii carectatas feni, & metet per iii dies fine cibo, & quarto die omnes ad cibum noftrum. Et, fi neceffariè fuerit, quelibet virgata metet cum cibo fine mercede per i diem. Ad feftum Sci Michis dant auxilium. In hieme arabunt fine cibo per i diem; & hariabunt per i diem cum cibo. Tenentes arabunt & hariabunt, & fimilitèr in Quadragefimâ. Quilibet eorum dabit i gallinam ad Natale, & ad Pafcha v ova. In eftate farcalabunt per ii dies fine cibo, & tertio die cum cibo. Dabunt pro filiabus marchetam; & de ceteris ut ruftici, fequentes curiam & placitum apud Leyc', & franciplegium. Coterelli dabunt auxilium ad feftum Michaelis. Alio modo ut in le Pyn. Modò ut fuprà in Lokynton.

Nowfeley. Tenens ibi folebat reddere iii gallinas & i panem ad Natale, & dant auxilium.

Peccum. Yolgrave. Tenens (fc. liber) viii acras & dim' reddit iiii dies operis, & debet auxilium ad feftum Michaelis, & dabit marchetam.

Conkyfbyry. Quilibet tenens xii acras & dim' debet metere in autumpno duobus diebus fine cibo, & tertio ad cibum abbatis; debet falcare fenum per ii dies, & levare fenum per i diem, & farculare per i diem, & auxilia dare ad voluntatem abbatis. Alitèr ut fuprà in Pecco.

Quenyboro. Quelibet bovata reddit ii gallinas ad Natale, & xx ova ad Pafcha, & auxilium. Arabit per iii dies fi habeat carucam propriam, vel per i diem fi affociatus fuerit hominibus domini. Hariabit in hieme & in Quadragefimâ per i diem. Sarculabit per i diem; metet per iii dies, duobus ad cibum fuum, tertio ad cibum abbatis. Faciat fenum per i diem; dabit auxilium, & dabit marchetam.

[4] *Querndon.* Quilibet tenens i virgatam terre reddit 3 gallinas, 30 ova; & metet per ii dies, & falcat per i diem, & levat fenum & folvit merchetam.

Shepifhed. Quilibet cotarius de . . . . . levabit fenum per i diem fine cibo, metet per ii dies fine cibo, tertio die ad cibum abbatis. Non metet alicubi pro mercede donec metatur bladum abbatis. Ad Natale ii gallinas, & folvet marchetam.

Sygrefham. Quelibet virgata debet auxilium & franciplegium, & hariotam.

Stoke. Quelibet virgata debet auxilium & franciplegium; & manentes in toftis venient ad vif' noftrum.

Stocton. Quilibet tenens i virgatam operabitur à fefto Michaelis ufque ad feftum Sancte Margarete, quâlibet feptimanâ ii diebus; & à die Sancte Mar-

---

[1] Charyte's Rentale, fol. ccxvi. a.
[2] Or free boons.
[3] Charyte's Rentale, fol. ccxvi. b.
[4] Ibid. fol. ccxvi. b.

garete ufqué ad feftum Michaelis, quâlibet feptimanâ iv diebus. Arabit in hieme per 1 diem, & in Quadragefimâ per 1 diem. Falcabit totum pratum fine cibo; levabit, cariabit, tuffabit in operibus dierum fuorum. Et metet fimilitèr terram ad parcarium cum totâ familiâ fine cibo. Et ad Witheacre fimilitèr cum totâ familiâ cariabit in operibus dierum fuorum. Si neceffe fuerit, ad metend', cariand' cum prece, faciet ad cibum noftrum in operibus dierum. Faciet autem 1 cariagium per annum extra comitatum, fi neceffe fuerit, ad cuftum [1] fuum, vel redimet illud cariagium ad voluntatem fuperioris fui. Cùm autem cariaverit in autumpno bladum, duo virgate facient 1 carectam, unà ante prandium, alius poft prandium; & tunc habebunt unam garbam inter eos ad vifum, & liberationem frumenti cujufcunque generis bladi. Ad feftum Sancti Michaelis dabit auxilium, fi quod habet. Nec poteft vendere pullum equi mafculum fine licentiâ fui fuperioris, nec movere fraxinum, nec vendere vel pirum vel pomarium, nec aliquod genus nemoris preter falices vel falnicos. Et dabit marchetam, &c. Quilibet cotarius operabitur per iii dies, & dabit auxilium ad feftum Michaelis. Secundùm Rentale Geryn, quelibet virgata dedit ii gallinas; & fic quedam cotagia. Refpice Rentalia le Pyn & Geryn quomodo ifte confuetudines mutantur.

Sutton. Quilibet tenens 1 virgatam arabit per ii dies, hariabit per ii dies, cariabit per 1 diem, metet per ii dies ad cuftum fuum, & tertio die ad cibum noftrum. Et dabit marchetam, & auxilium, & hariotam.

Thedingworth. Quelibet virgata dabit iii gallinas & 1 gallum ad Natale, & xx ova ad Pafcham, & marchetam, & hariotam, &c.

Thurneby. Quilibet tenens 1 virgatam dabit auxilium, marchetam, & 1 gallum & ii gallinas; & non operatur. Alitèr ut fuprà in le Pyn.

Thurmaſton. Hec funt confuetudines tenentium xiii virgatarum terre quas fundator nofter nobis dedit ibidem. Omnes arabunt cum iv optimis carucis ad cibum abbatis. Queque virgata falcabit unâ die ufque ad nonam, & quelibet habebit obolum, & tunc habere quantum falcans poterit fuper dorfum fuum levare cum falce fine auxilio alicujus. Et metent ii diebus in autumno, uno die ad cibum abbatis, alio ad cibum fuum, quelibet virgata cum duobus hominibus. Quelibet virgata farculabit per 1 diem ad cibum abbatis, & hariabit femel in anno, five in hieme, five in Quadragefimâ, ad voluntatem celararii. Dabunt auxilium, & marchetam, & gallinas, &c. ficut confuetudinarii. Alitèr ut fuprà in le Pyn & Geryn.

35. Notandum, quòd he funt ville in quibus jam invenitur per Rotulos curiales quòd ibi antea habuimus weyfe & ftreyfe; fcil', Vicus Abbathie, Lowton, Mowfley, Stouton, Thurnby, Kylby, Burton Overey, Hungarton, Thurmaſton, Croxton, Barkby, Queniboro, Stoke, Cofyngton, Schepifhed, Whatton, Lokyngton, Baro, Querndon, Thorp juxta Cofby, Blaby, Sutton, Bofworth, Thedyngworth, Bittefwell, Bulkyngton, Bernangul, Brankote, Wybtoft, Stoke, Humburfton, Faringo, Sygrefham, Brakley, Medoplek, Conkyfbery, Curdworth, Cofby, Berwode.

In aliis villis non invenitur per Rentalia quòd habuimus weyfe & ftreyfe; tamen fortè tam eft quia cafus non acciderit; fed apud Anfty multoties cafus accidit, ut benè cognofcitur; tamen non habuimus; fed ballivus domini de Groby fepè attachiare prefumat per homines Anftie. Ideò confulendum, &c. [2]

36. He funt ville in quibus tenentes noftri folebant dare abbati hariotas [3].

Brakley folebat dare duas hariotas, ficut patet in diverfis rotulis curialibus, per conventiones factas inter celararium & tenentes.

Faringo. Poft obitum viri tenentis terram, uxor fua confuevit dare bovem unum, vel melius averium vel catallum, & tenere terram in vitâ fuâ. Poft obitum uxoris, filius convenire confuevit prout meliùs potuit. Item, fi aliquis tenens ad voluntatem recefferit à dominico, dabit bovem, vel melius averium vel catallum.

Mem', quòd Willus Mawntel & heredes fui dabunt vis. viiid. nomine unius hariote quolibet principio x annorum, ficut patet per indenturas.

Sygrefham. Quilibet tenens ibidem ad voluntatem domini dabit domino in quolibet receffu feu deceffu fuo optimum animal.

Thedyngworth. Mem', quòd quilibet tenens ibidem ad voluntatem domini dabit domino in quolibet receffu vel deceffu fuo fecundum animal fuum.

Bofworth, Cofby. Quilibet tenens in iftis villis ad voluntatem domini dabit domino in receffu fuo, vel poft mortem, unam hariotam.

Sutton, Blaby. Quilibet tenens in iftis villis ad voluntatem domini dabit domino poft mortem, & etiam in receffu, unam hariotam.

Brankote. Sciend', quòd quilibet tenens hujus dominii, tam liberè quàm voluntariè, dabit domino, in quolibet receffu vel deceffu fuo, optimum animal fuum, nomine hariote.

Bulkyngton, Bernangul. Quilibet tenens in iftis ii villis dat hariotam, &c. eodem modo ut in Brankot.

Wybtoft: Quilibet tenens ad voluntatem domini ibidem, recedens & difcedens, dabit domino unam hariotam.

Thurmaſton. Quilibet tenens ad voluntatem domini dabit domino poft mortem animal fecundum.

Barkeby. Quilibet tenens ibidem ad voluntatem domini dabit domino poft mortem animal fecundum.

Kyrkby Malore. Si aliquis tenens ibi ad voluntatem domini obierit, dabit domino fecundum animal; &, fi animal non habuerit, dabit domino optimam rem de rebus fuis mobilibus.

Horfpol. Quere de Stanton.

Stanton. Si aliquis tenens ibidem obierit, dabit domino unam hariotam, fcil', optimum animal.

Stocton & Cofyngton folebant dare hariotas, ut apparet in Geryn, in fine rentalis finium.

Peccum, Yolgrave, Conkyfbyry, Stanton, Wynſter, & Medoplek. Sciend', quòd omnes tenentes noftri ad voluntatem domini in predictis villis, poft mortem eorum, dabunt domino fecundum melius animal, nomine hariote, quilibet in receffu eorum.

Cokeram. Si aliquis tenens ibidem obierit, dabit domino fecundum animal.

Berwode, Curdworth, & Mynworth. Si aliquis tenens ibidem ad voluntatem domini recefferit vel obierit, dabit domino melius animal nomine hariote, ficut tenentes liberi; & firmarius poft mortem [4].

37. De vifu franciplegii & curiis baronibus [5].

Habemus vifum franciplegii de omnibus tenentibus noftris in villis fubfequentibus; fcilicet, in Vico Abbathie; de Brunthyngthorp; de tenentibus facrifte inter magnum parietem borealem & parcum de Anfty; de Thoroton; de Bagworth; de Stanton; de Horfpol & Clenfeld. Et in omnibus iftis villis habemus weyf & ftreyf, & omnia ad vifum pertinentia. Et in quibufdam de iftis villis poffumus habere vifum noftrum, & ad placitum noftrum mutare locum.

Item habemus vifum franciplegii de omnibus tenentibus noftris manentibus in villis fubfequentibus; fcil', in Stowton, Flekney, Nowfeley, Kylby, & Burton Overy, Humburfton, Thurnby, Hungarton, Knyton, Yngwarby. Et in quibufdam de iftis villis habemus weyfe, ftreyfe, &c. Et in illis poffumus habere vifum noftrum ad placitum, prout in Yngwarby, &c.

Item habemus vifum franciplegii de omnibus noftris tenentibus in Thurmaſton, Croxton, Quenyboro, Barkby, Thorp-Barkby, Hows, Kyrkby Bellers, & Gaddefby. Et in quibufdam de villis iftis habemus weyfe & ftreyfe, & poffumus habere vifum.

Item habemus vifum franciplegii de omnibus tenentibus noftris in Schepifhed, in Whatton, &c.

Item habemus vifum franciplegii de omnibus tenentibus noftris utriufqne feodi in Lokyngton, & omnia ad vifum pertinentia, &c. ut fuprà.

Item habemus vifum franciplegii de omnibus te-

---

[1] i. e. *ad proprias expenfas.* Idem nempe valet quod vox Anglica & Cambro-Britannica *coft.* T. Hearne, MS.
[2] Charyte's Rentale, fol. ccxviii.   [3] Ibid. fol. ccxvii. a. b.   [4] Ibid. fol. ccxviii. b.   [5] Ibid.

nentibus noftris de Baro & Querndon, & omnia ad vifum provenientia; fcilicet, in Cofby, Blaby, Thorp juxta Norboro, Enderby, Sutton, Bofworth, Thedyngworth, &c. Et poffumus mutare locum visûs franciplegii ad libitum noftrum.

Item habemus vifum franciplegii de omnibus tenentibus noftris de Bythfwell, & omnia ad vifum pertinentia, &c.

Item habemus vifum franciplegii de omnibus tenentibus noftris manentibus in villis fubfequentibus ad libitum noftrum, & omnia ad vifum pertinentia; fcilicet, in Bulkyngton, Brankote, Bernangul, Wybtoft, Stoke, Clifton, & Wover. Et poffumus habere weyfe & ftreyfe, & vifum noftrum ad placitum noftrum, ut fuprà.

Item habemus vifum franciplegii de omnibus tenentibus noftris manentibus in villis fubfcriptis; fcilicet, in Brakley, Sygrefham, Halfo, & Faringo. Habemus in prediétis villis weyfe & ftreyfe, & omnia ad vifum pertinentia. Et poffumus habere vifum noftrum in quâlibet iftarum villarum ad eleétionem noftram.

Item habemus vifum franciplegii de omnibus tenentibus noftris manentibus in Crudworth & Mynworth; & weyfe & ftreyfe, & omnia ad vifum pertinentia in eifdem villis. Et poffumus limitare vifum noftrum effend' nunc in unâ earum, nunc in aliâ, ad voluntatem noftram.

Item habemus vifum franciplegii de omnibus tenentibus noftris manentibus in Mydoplek, Yolgrave, & Conkyfbyry; & weyfe & ftreyfe, & omnia ad vifum pertinentia, in eifdem villis; & locum visûs poffumus affignare ut volumus.

Item habemus vifum franciplegii de omnibus tenentibus noftris manentibus in Cokeram.

Mem', quòd abbas Leyc' refignavit in manus comitis Leyc' vifum franciplegii de hominibus fuis infra muros Leyc', & extra portum borealem ufque ad pontem borealem, falvâ facriftariâ inter magnum pontem borealem & parvum pontem, &c.

Item folebamus habere curiam baronis in Kyrkby Malory, Yngwarby, Lawton, Burftal, Chefham, & Mowfley.

36. De Nativis.

He funt ville in quibus infra breve nativos habuimus, ficut patet in Rotulis noftris curialibus, in quibus curiis prefentatum fuit ubi tunc manferunt diverfi nativi noftri [1].

Brakley. Hugo Howlowth, nativus domini, tunc ibidem manfit.

Brankot. Thomas Taylur, tunc morans apud Cleybrok, nativus domini; Thomas Pyne, morans apud Cowntre; Joħes Style, morans apud Brankot.

Crudworth. Stephanus Kene, morans apud Northampton'.

Faryngo. Wilħus Ruffell, morans apud Abbethorp; Joħes Lenys, morans apud Tame.

Kyrkby Malor'. Katerina de Lotrynham, morans apud Lobenham.

Yngwarby. Henricus Pert', morans apud Ketingā; Joħes Port', morans apud Frifby vel Wyginfton.

Leyceftria. Joħes Amifon plaftrar'.
Filius ejus Wilħus.
At' ejus frater minor eft Nicholaus.
A...clus ejus morans apud Alderwas in com' Staffordie.

Lawton. Joħes Grant, morans ibidem; Wilħus Wygyn, morans apud Harboro.

Quenyboro. Wilħus Margery, morans apud Whatburgh in comitatu Leyc', vel Tylton; Agnes Margery, morans apud Coventre.

Sigrefham. Johanna Page, morans ibidem.

Sutton. Joħes Mydwynter; habuit filios & unam filiam; inquire, &c.

Sygrefham. Mem', quòd Wilħs Parkar defponfavit Matildam filiam Wilħi Gorale de Sygrefham, nativam domini, fine licentiâ domini. Et Joħes Lane fponfavit Matildam fororem ejufdem fine licentiâ. Et Walterus Chery defponfavit Johannam fororem prediétarum fine licentiâ. Et dominus Wilħus Capellanus, frater earundem, recepit ordines fine licentiâ domini.

Thurmaston. Robertus Blakebert, aliàs vocat' Hamulton, morans apud Odby vel Belton; Joħes Ha-

multon, morans apud Belton; Agnes Cartwryt, morans apud Baro.

Thurnby. Joħes Amyfon, morans ibidem; Robertus Gervas, morans apud Stok juxta Heham; Wilħus Amyfon moratur in comitatu Stafford'.

Wybtoft. Thomas Harn, morans apud Cowntre.

37. Notandum, quòd habemus liberam warennam in omnibus locis fubfequentibus; fcilicet, in omnibus terris noftris dominicalibus de Leyc', Stokton, Thurmafton, Barkeby, Quenyboro, Lokynton, Bytefwell, Bofworth, Pynflade, Yngwarby, Faringo, Sygrefham, Cotes, Conkyfbyry, Mydoplek, Clyfton, Bulkynton, Bramcote; ita quòd nullus intret terras noftras ad fugandum in eis, vel ad capiendum quod ad warennam pertinet, fine licentiâ noftrâ, fuper forisfaéturam decem librarum [2].

38. Rentale de omnibus caponibus, gallinis, & gallis, liberis & voluntariis, nobis pertinentibus, prout tenentes nobis reddere confueverunt. Item & de ovis [3].

Bagworth. Robertus Ratclife tenet i meff', i toftum, & i virgatam terre. Indè reddere folebant iii gallinas.

Barkby. Joħes Powr, pro i meff', iii qrt' terre, i gallinam & i gallum.

Joħes Page, pro i meff' & i virgat' terre, ii gallinas & i gallum.

Wilħus Jonfon, pro ii meff', i virgat' terre, & i qᵃrt' terre, ii gallinas & ii gallos.—Summa ix.

Liberi tenentes. Wilħus Stevens, pro i meff' & i virgatâ terre, v gallinas & i gallum.—Summa totalis x v.

Burftall. Notandum, quòd iii meff', ii virgate terre & dim', folebant reddere x gallinas. Inde J. Steyn pro i meff' & i virgat' terre folvit iiii gallinas; W. Damyfell pro confimil' iiii gallinas; W. Sybefdon pro i meff' & dim' virgat' terre ii gallinas. Modò terre dividuntur inter tres tenentes noftros; quorum J. Boffe folvit ii gallinas, T. Lenton iiii; J. Hanfon iiii gallinas.

Cokeram. Omnes tenentes folvunt gallinas, ut fupra.

Endurby. Rogerus Wodwyt tenet i virgatam terre, & redd' vi capones.

Kyrkby Malore. Notandum, quòd quelibet dimidia virgata terre folebat reddere ii gallinas & i wodheyne, & v ova. Et ix cotrelli reétoris fimiliter reddiderunt. Summa gallinarum filveftrium folebat effe xxxiii. Summa gallinarum de redditu folebant effe xxxii.

Modò omnes tenentes noftri, & iii cotarii reétoris, quilibet eorum folvit i gallinam.

Summa, v galline, ii galli, & i wodcoke.

Liberi tenentes. Wilħus Warde, pro i meff' & xv acris terre, ii gallinas.

Joħes Roxton, pro i meff' & dimidiâ virgatâ terre, ii capones ret'.

Joħes Molton, pro i meff' & iii acris terre, i gallinam.—Summa, xvi galline.

Joħes Dynys, pro iii meff', dim' virgat' & iiii acris terre, ii gallinas & i gallinam filveftrem.

Summa, ii capon', v galline, & i gallum filveftre.—Summa totalis, ii capones, xx galline, & i gallum filveftre.

Lawton. Unum meffuagium, i virgata terre, & un' quart', folebant reddere viii gallinas; modò in tenurâ.

LEYCESTRIA. Notandum, quòd omnes tenentes de Leyc' ad voluntatem, tam infra quàm extra in fuburbanis, folebant reddere gallinas. Modò foli tenentes de Vico Abbathie folvunt gallinas.

Ifti funt liberi tenentes de totâ Leyc', qui folvunt capones, gallos, vel gallinas.

Infra Pontem, liberi tenentes.

Camerarii Leyc', pro i tenemento ibidem, ii gallinas & i gallum.

Robertus Bull, pro ten' fuo, i gallinam.

Joħes Bawdweyn, pro ten' i gallinam.

Camerarii Leyc', pro alio ten' ibi, i gallum, i gallinam, & i wodecoke.

Johanna Charyte, pro ten' ex oppofito, iiii gallin; modò in dominico.

Summa, v galline, ii galli, & i wodcoke.

Parochia *Omnium Sanétorum.*

Magifter Hofpitii Sanéti Leonardi, pro i tofto, ii gallin' ret'.

---

[1] In this title, as referred to in the Introductory Volume, p. xlv. taken from an imperfeét copy, the attentive reader will perceive fome material correétions. It is now given from Charyte's Rentale, fol. ccxviii. [2] Ibid. [3] Ibid. fol. clviii. b.

X Joħes

Joħes Glover, pro ɪ cotag', ɪ gallinam.
Wiłłs Baro, pro ten', ɪɪ gallinas.
Hugo Bull, pro ɪ ten', ɪɪ gallinas ret'.
Joħes Gaddeſby, pro ɪ ten', ɪɪ gallinas & ɪ gall' ret'.
Dñs W. Bedal, pro ɪ ten', ɪ gallinam.
Joħes Glover, pro ɪ ten', ɪ gallinam & ɪ gallum.
Joħes Howſon, pro ɪɪ ten', ɪɪ gallinas, ɪ gallum, & ɪ wodecoke, & ɪ par cirotecarum.
Wiłłs Stonſby, pro ɪ ten', ɪɪ gallinas.
Joħes Smyth de Swydlond, pro ten', ɪɪ capones.
Joħes Bawdwyn, pro ſhopâ, ɪɪ capones.
Idem, pro ten' ſuo, ɪɪɪ capones.
Joħes Gadeſby, pro gardino in Vico fullonum, ɪɪ gallinas & ɪ gall' ret'.
Summa, v capones, xvɪɪɪ galline, ɪɪɪɪ galli, & ɪ wodecoke.
Parochia *Sancte Margarete.*
Skeyth. Roƀtus Newark, pro ten' ibi, vɪ gallinas.
Summa patet.
Belgrave-gate.
Canonici Novi Operis Leyc', pro ten' ibi, ɪɪ capones & ɪɪɪɪ gallinas.
Wiłłus Campe, modò Gilda Sc̄e Margarete, pro ten' quondam Niċħi Fyſcher, ɪɪ gallin'.
Joħes Blankemy, pro ten', ɪɪɪɪ gallinas.
Summa, ɪɪ capones, x galline.
Parochia *Sancti Michaelis.*
De miniſtris regis, pro ɪ gardino, ɪ caponem ret'.
Parochia *Sancti Petri.*
Matilda Dalahey, pro ɪ gardino, ɪɪ capones ret'.
Thomas Grene, pro domo ſuâ, ɪɪ capones.
Wiłłs Hore, pro ten' ſuper cornerium, ɪɪ capones.
Summa, vɪ capones.
Parochia *Sancti Martini.*
Joħes Wyxton, pro ten' in cemeterio ejuſdem ecclefie, ɪɪ capones.
Henricus Keyſteyn, pro ten' in Loſeby-lane, ɪɪɪ gallinas ret'.
Joħes Dreyt, pro ten' in Schepyſmarkeyt, ɪɪ capones.
Joħes Moke, pro ten' in le Parchement-lane, ɪɪ gallinas.
Joħes Wyxton, pro ten' in Foro Sabbati, ɪ capon' & ɪ flectam.—Summa, v capones & v galline.
Parochia *Sancti Nicholai.*
Thomas Lynſey, pro ten' ibidem, ɪɪ capones.
Parochia *Sancte Marie.*
Joħes Robert, pro ten' juxta Portam Auſtralem, ɪ caponem.
Petrus Curtes, pro ten' juxta, ɪɪɪ capones.
Thomas Whytakur, pro medietate ten', ɪ caponem.
Rogerus Botall, pro alterâ medietate dicti ten', ɪ caponem.
Wiłłs Hor', pro ten', ɪ caponem.
Summa, ɪɪ capones.
Extra Portam Orientalem.
Bruntyngyſthorp. Roƀtus Borear, pro ten' nuper J. Kegworth, ɪɪ gallinas.
Roƀtus Stanton, pro ten', ɪɪ gallinas.
Roƀtus Bruar, pro ten' in *Brawnſtongat*, ɪ gallinam.
Joħes Holt, pro ten' juxta, ɪ gallinam.
Roƀtus Aſhby, pro certis ten' ibi, ɪ caponem & ɪɪɪ gallinas, ɪ libram cumini.
Rogerus Wyxton, pro ɪ crofto ibi, ɪ gallinam & ɪɪđ.
Summa, unus capo, & x galline.
Lokynton. Quelibet virgata de feodo Baſſet dabit ɪ gallinam & v ova.
Merſton. Joħes Hardwyck, pro ɪɪ meſſ' & ɪɪ virgatis terre, ɪɪ gallinas.
Nowſeley. Tenens ibi ſolebat reddere ɪɪɪ gallinas.
Queniboro. Quelibet bovata ſolebat reddere ɪɪ gallinas & xx ova.
Querndon. Tenens ɪ virgate ſolebat reddere ɪɪɪ gallinas & xxx ova.
Summa virgatarum ɪɪ; ſumma gallinarum vɪ.
Schepiſhed. Quilibet cotarius de ɪx ſolebat reddere ɪɪ gallinas.
Thedyngworth. Quelibet dim' virgata terre ſolebat reddere ɪ gallum & ɪ gallinam.

Summa dimid' virgatarum terre vɪɪ; ſumma gallorum & gallinarum xɪɪɪɪ.
Thurmaſton. Omnes tenentes noſtri de Northorp in Thurmaſton ſolvunt gallinas; & unus cotarius ſimiliter de Thurmaſton.
Joħes Aly de Northorp, pro ɪ meſſ', ɪɪɪɪ virgatis terre, ɪ gallinam.
Robertus Lambarte, pro ɪ meſſ' & ɪ virgat' terre, ɪ gallinam.
Joħes Dreyton, pro ɪɪ meſſ' & ɪɪɪ virgatis terre, ɪɪɪɪ gallinas.
Joħes Tirlyngton, pro ɪ meſſ' & ɪɪ virgatis terre, ɪɪ gallinas.
Wiłłus Schankton, pro ɪ meſſ' & ɪɪ virgatis terre & ɪ acrâ, ɪɪɪɪ galline.
Roƀtus Reynold, pro ɪ meſſ', ɪɪ virgatis terre & dimid', ɪɪɪ galline.
Ricardus Gybſon, pro ɪ meſſ', ɪ virgat' terre & dim', ɪɪ galline.
Wiłłs Skeythe, pro ɪ cotagio in Thurmaſton, ɪ gallina.—Summa, xvɪɪɪ galline.
Thurnby. Quelibet virgata terre de Thurnby ſolebat reddere ɪ gallinam & ɪɪ gallinas.
Summa virgatarum v; ſumma gallorum & gallinarum xv.—Summa virgatarum xxx; ſumma gall' xx/ɪɪɪ.
Stocton. Quelibet virgata ſolebat reddere ɪ gallinam. Item diverſi cotarii ibidem ſolebant reddere gallinam.
Thornton. Quilibet cotarius de tribus cotariis ibidem reddit ɪɪ gallinas.—Summa, vɪ galline.

39. Edmundus, illuſtris regis Anglie filius, dedit nobis duos damos pro uno cervo in Aſſumptione beate Marie Virginis [1].

40. Reſponſiones operum cuſtumariorum, & valores diverſarum conſuetudinum villanagiorum & tenentium noſtrorum, cum multis aliis proficuis & incrementis que habuimus ſupradicto anno regis Edwardi, &c. & poſtea de decremento & diminutione eorundem reddituum.
Summa tenentium qui dederunt domino auxilium fuerunt cɪɪ, preter Stocton, quorum quilibet dedit auxilium ſecundùm quantitatem & numerum averiorum ſuorum; ſcil', pro bove ɪɪɪđ. pro vaccâ ɪɪɪđ. pro v bidentibus ɪɪɪđ. pro v porcis ɪɪɪđ. Et quia numerus averiorum eſt incertus, tamen quia centum & duo ſunt virgate terre, pro quibus earum tenentes dederunt domino auxilium, ſcil', quilibet tenens unam virgatam de predictis ſecundùm eſtimationem habuit ad minus v caballa, ɪɪ vaccas, v porcellos, & v bidentes, pro quibus ſolvit auxilium, ſcil' ɪɪ ſ̃. ſecundùm rationem. Omnes iſti greges reſponderunt ad minus vɪ marcas; & modò in predictis villis nullum gregem habemus, tamen ſolvimus regi decimas pro eiſdem.
Stocton reddebat xxxlɪ̃. xɪɪ ſ̃. & ſic taxatur; modò xvɪɪ lɪ̃. x ſ̃.
Conſuetudines tenentium & cuſtumariorum, ut opera dierum, galline, auxilia, ingreſſus, lufbenes panes, & ova, reſponderunt xᴌv liƀ. ad minus; modò nihil habemus ibidem.
Eccleſia Sc̄i Martini Leyc' reddebat ᴌxvɪ liƀ.; modò redd' xxɪ libras; & ſic per ſingulas eccleſias.
Baro, altaragium reſpondebat xxɪ liƀ. ante peſtilentiam; modò circa ɪɪɪɪ liƀ. [2]

41. Redemptio carnis & ſanguinis.
Wiłłus filius Hugonis tenet dim' virgatam terre de eodem Timotheo ad voluntatem dñi ſui, & facit auxilium & redemptionem carnis & ſanguinis pro filiis & filiabus ſuis ad voluntatem dicti Timothei, & reddit per annum eidem Timotheo vɪɪɪ ſ̃. in Rotulo de tempore Edw. I. qui nunc eſt in manibus Thome Cotton in titulo de Kinebolton, ſimiliter in titulo de Coninton, ſimiliter in Magnâ Geddyng. Hugo Burgenſis tenet ɪ meſſuagium de Roberto Eſt pro ɪɪɪɪ ſ̃. ad terminum vite; ſed predictus Henricus Abraham dat auxilium ad feſtum Sc̄i Michaelis ad voluntatem prioris, & facit redemptionem pro carne ſuâ & pueris ſuis maritandis, & redemptionem pro pueris ſuis maritandis ad voluntatem domini prioris [3].

---

[1] Cotton MSS. Vitellius F. XVII.   [2] Ibid.   [3] James's MSS. in Bibl. Bod.

42. Excerpta

42. Excerpta ex quodam brevi Regiſtro Abbathiæ de Leiceſtriâ, in cuſtodiâ Thômæ Cotton, baronetti; ac etiam ex quodam Regiſtro Abbathiæ de Leic', remanente in Bibliothecâ communi Academiæ Oxon'.

Bernanguil infra parochiam de Bulkynton eſt.

Habemus in Bernangul, ex dono Henrici filii Fulconis de Merſtonâ, poſtea canonici noſtri, ſicut patet in cartâ primâ de cartis de Bernangul, IIII virgatas terre de feodo domini Ernoldi de Boſco, domini ſui; redd' inde ſibi & heredibus ſuis, pro omni ſervitio, II ſ.

Habemus confirmationem & donationem Henrici de Merſton de predictis IIII virgatis terre, ſolvend' annuatim domino ſuo Ernoldo de Boſco XVIII d̃. &c.

Habemus confirmationem predictarum terrarum per dominum feodi, ſcil' Ernoldum de Boſco, ſicut in cartâ primâ; & confirmationem Joħis de Merſton, filii Henrici; & confirmationem regis Henrici II.

Memorandum, quòd abbas conventuſque Leic' conceſſerunt Guidoni militi, domino de Bernangul, quòd ipſe & heredes ſui poſſint habere cantariam capelle in curiâ ipſius de Bernangul ſite; ſalvo in omnibus jure matricis eccleſie de Bulkyngton & ejuſdem eccleſie vicarii in perpetuum. Capellanus, in eâdem capellâ celebraturus, antequam in omnia celebret, in ſcriptis ſacroſanctis jurabit coram prefate eccleſie vicario de indempnitate matricis eccleſie predicte obſervandâ, & fidelitate ipſi vicario preſtandâ, &c. ut in compoſitione.

Decime garbarum & feni pertinent ad matricem eccleſiam de Bulkyngton ex dono Rogeri de Watervile; & redd' cum Bulkyngton circa XLIII ſ. IIII d̃.

Habemus ibidem decimam paſture & boſci in parco. Modò decima de parco reſpondet VI ſ. VIII d̃. [1]

Habemus ibidem weyſe & ſtreyſe.

Berwode. Hugo de Ardenâ dedit nobis manerium de Berwode, unum meſſuagium, unum molendinum, duas carucatas terre, LX acras prati, LX acras paſture, CCC acras boſci, & X ſ. cum pertin', in Crudworth; & advocationem eccleſie de Crudworth, cum pertin'.

Item Thomas de Ardenâ & Wilłus de Ardenâ dederunt nobis certas parcellas terre & boſci in Berwode & Crudworth. Firmarius ibidem pro decimis & redditibus noſtris reddebat XXli. modò XVIli.

Habemus in Berwode, ex dono Hugonis de Ardenâ, cum conſenſu & aſſenſu fratrum ſuorum, ſcil' Oſbini & Henrici, & ex confirmatione regis Henrici Secundi, locum de Berwodâ, cum exartis & pratis, & omnibus pertinentiis ſuis in boſco & in plano; & totam illam partem nemoris ſui que eſt inter filum aque de Ebroc & filum aque de Tamâ, cum inſulâ de Wycheſholme, uſque ad diviſas de Erdinton; & cum pannagio & omnibus libertatibus; ita quòd infra prenominatas diviſas faciamus omnia aiſiamenta, &c.

Item habemus confirmationem predicti Hugonis de omnibus predictis, cum homagio & ſervicio Alani de Bromwych de tenemento quod de ipſo tenet infra predictas diviſas, ſcil' de XII d̃. terre, homag' & ſervic'.

Item habemus, de dono ejuſdem Hugonis, pannagium quietum, & omnes libertates noſtras; ita quòd nullus heredum vel hominum ſuorum infra predictas diviſas, ſine voluntate noſtrâ, aliquid de nemore noſtro capiat, quia ipſe vult quòd homines ſui habeant aiſiamenta ſua in nemore ſuo quod ibi habet.

Item habemus confirmationem regis Henrici Secundi, & confirmationes Wiłłi comitis Warrwyck & Walerani comitis ejuſdem de omnibus predictis.

Habemus, de dono Thome de Ardenâ, illam partem terre ſue, cum nemore, que eſt in longitudine à gibboſâ quercu ſtante in acrâ canonicorum Leic' juxta veterem Ebroc, &c. ut in cartâ.

Item totum illum locum terre, cum nemore, que deſcendit ab antiquo Ebroc juxta Hulſmo uſque ad terram Wiłłi filii Galfridi de Minworth, & duas particulas terre, quarum una eſt inter viam Denhee & Aldmanſleye, & altera meta in longitudine inter januam de Mugehale & terram Nicholai de Munworth, & altera particula inter terram Hen' de Munworth, &c.

Item habemus cartam Walerani com' Warw'; in quâ cartâ predictus comes dedit Orm de Wyginghulle ad claudend' & infoſſand' V acras terre in foreſtâ ſuâ; illas, ſcilicet, quas tenet de Thomâ de Ardenâ.

Item conceſſit eidem Orm, ad claudend' & infoſſand' totam Humuageſholme inter Tame & Ebroc, & unum manſum apud Fenniford juxta cemeterium canonicorum

de Berwod ſuper ripam de Tame, ad menſuram unius acre terre, quod ſepèdictus Orm tenet de canonicis.

Habemus, ex dono Thome de Ardenâ, totam illam terram quam Orm de Wychinghull de ipſo tenuit, &c.

Item habemus confirmationem Thome de Ardenâ, filii Thome de Ardenâ, de omnibus donationibus, &c.

Item per eandem cartam dedit nobis predictus Thomas communam nemoris ſui, ad terras noſtras ſepiendas.

Mem', quòd abbas Leyc' tenet locum de Berwode, cum pertinentiis, in puram & perpetuam eleemoſinam, & non per ſervicium militare, de omnibus auxiliis regum & primogenitis ſuis faciend' milit' quietam, &c.

Habemus, ex conceſſione & quietâ clamatione Thome, filii Alani de Bromwych, communem paſturam infra ſepes de Blakſtanes de Berwode; & nos providemus ei heiſam quandam ad capiend' clauſturam infra predictas ſepes de Blakſtanes, per viſum foreſtarii noſtri, ad claudend' terram ſuam, &c.

Mem', quòd, anno regni regis Edwardi III. poſt conqueſtum 33°, Joħes de Ardenâ petiit versùs abbatem de Leyc' unum meſſ', unum molendinum, duas carucatas terre, LX acras prati, LX acras paſture, CCC acras boſci, & X ſ. redditûs, cum pertin', in Cruddeworth, quos Wiłłus de Ardenâ, chevalier, conſanguineus predicti Joħis, cujus heres ipſe eſt, dimiſit Roberto quondam abbati Leic' & ſucceſſoribus ſuis, ad inventionem duos canonicos apud Berwodhall, divina celebrantes in capellâ beate Marie, pro animâ ipſius Wiłłi, & animabus ſucceſſorum & heredum ejuſdem, &c. ut patet in placito. Que omnia predictus abbas Leyc' recuperavit contra predictum Johannem de Ardenâ in eodem placito, &c.

Extenta manerii de Berwode.

Manerium de Berwode in parochiâ de Crudworth eſt, quod habuimus ex dono Hugonis de Ardenâ, &c. ut ſupra, cum decimis garbarum, feni, pannagii, &c.; ubi quondam habuimus capellam pertinentem ad matricem eccleſiam de Crudworth. Eſt ubi modò aula, cum canonicis, cantuariis, cœnaculis, piſtrinâ, reſtrinâ, clibano, & granario, &c.

Eſt ibidem unum orreum, ad imponend' grana, de IIII bays. Eſt ibi aliud orreum, pro feno, de III bays.

Eſt ibi una vaccaria, de VI bays.

Eſt ibi una antiqua domus, quondam cottagium, extra curiam, de III bays, que valent per ann' XX ſ.

Eſſent ibi, ut patet ſupra, II carucate terre, LX acre prati, LX acre paſture, CCC acre boſci.

Mem', quòd Thomas de Bromwych non debet habere aliqua eſtoveria in boſco de Berwode, niſi ſolummodo mortuum boſcum ad ignem ſuum dominicum, ſicut patet in antiquis placitis, &c.

Item Alanus de Bromwych tenet medietatem inſule que vocatur Hawycheſholme, redd' XII d̃. &c.

[Sequuntur particule plures de eâdem extentâ.]

Item & ibi boſcus, in quo arbores noſtre ſunt omnes ſecundùm bundas & metas ibidem. Paſtura ejuſdem communis eſt. Fere ſunt comitis Warwychie.

Habemus ibi weyf & ſtreyf in omnibus in boſco & in plano, &c. Item ſunt ibi duo tauri, XLVII vacce de noſtris tradit' firmario noſtro ad firmam [2].

Brancote. Robertus Watervile dedit nobis ibidem molendinum; & Gaufridus l'Abbe dedit nobis VI virgatas terre.—Redditus reddebat LVIII ſ. IIII d̃. Molendinum reddebat V marcas & dim'; modò LIII ſ. IIII d̃.

Habemus ibidem decimas garbarum, feni, & boſci, &c. pertin' ad matricem eccleſiam de Bulkyngton.

Habemus ibidem, pro decimâ feni de quâlibet virgatâ terre, VI d̃. Summa virgatarum VIII.

Habemus ibidem, ex dono Gaufridi l'Abbe, & ex confirmatione Ernoldi de Boſco, & ex confirmatione regis Henrici Secundi, VI virgatas terre liberas ab omni ſervitio ſeculari, & dim' carucatam terre in Rowlawâ. Et ibidem Gaufridus habuit, ex dono Rogeri de Watervillâ, in ſochâ de Weſtonâ, III hidas terre per ſervicium quarte partis unius militis.

Item habemus molendinum de Brancote, cum terrâ & prato, & omnibus ad ipſum molendinum pertin', ex dono Roberti de Watervillâ, cum conſenſu domini ſui Roberti com' Leyc', fundatoris noſtri, de cujus feodo eſt,

---

[1] Charyte's Rentale, fol. xvi. a.

[2] Ibid. fol xvii.

Habemus,

Habemus, ex conceſſione & confirmatione Ernoldi de Boſco, & ex confirmatione Ernoldi de Boſco atavi ſui, molendinum de Brancote, cum terrâ & prato, & vivario, ſcil' Creſſwell, & cum omnibus ad ipſum molendinum pertin', quod Robertus Watervill, avunculus ſuus, nobis dedit, ut in cartâ, &c.

Item iidem Ernoldi conceſſerunt per eaſdem cartas, ut homines canonicorum teneant communem paſturam cum hominibus ſuis, ſicuti unquam meliùs habuerunt tempore Henrici regis ſenioris, ac deindè.

Mem', quòd Wills Lucas de Brancote fecit homagium domino Joĥi Pomerey, abbati Leyc', die Dominicâ poſt feſtum Aſſumptionis beate Marie, in clauſtro ibidem; preſentibus fratre Wilĺo Charyte priore, fratre W. Cartre, & aliis, anno regni regis Edwardi quarti x°; & eodem tempore ſolvebat abbati IIIs. IIIId. Et Joĥes Lucas fecit homagium domino abbati in magnâ aulâ die Dominicâ prox' ante feſtum Sc̄i Gregorii Pape, anno Domini MCCCXLII.

Si aliquis ibidem tenens receſſerit vel obierit, dabit domino abbati unam hariotam. Et ſolebant tenentes ibi dare auxilium & marchetam. Habemus ibi weyfe & ſtreyfe, &c.—[Sequitur de quamplurimis aliis conceſſionibus ibidem per diverſos, quorum tenorem non dignum cenſui annotare.]

Habemus in Brancote, ex dono Roberti fratris Rogeri de Watervillâ, ſedem molendini que antiquitùs fuerat in eâdem, cum terrâ & prato adjacente, &c. ut in cartâ primâ Roberti filii fundatoris noſtri [1].

Habemus in *Bulkyngton* eccleſiam, ex dono Rogeri de Watervillâ, cum conſenſu & aſſenſu Roberti comitis Leiceſtrie, fundatoris noſtri, & domini ſui, & Amicie comitiſſe, & confirmatione Ernoldi de Boſco, cum duabus virgatis terre, que dicuntur gleba eccleſie, cum terris, decimis, &c. [Sequuntur alie diverſe minute conceſſiones, quas, brevitatis causâ, omiſi.]

Habemus in Bulkyngton eccleſiam in propriis uſibus, cum duabus virgatis terre, ex dono Rogeri de Watervile, cum capellis de Bernangul, Weſton, Ryton, Merſton, Shelton, Anſty, & Brancote, & cum decimis garbarum, feni, & boſci, &c. Et percipimus de vicario ibidem annuatim, nomine penſionis, XXVIs. ſicut patet in ordinatione vicarii ibidem faĉâ per Robertum de Boſco, archidiacono Coventr', ſede vacante, de voluntate & aſſenſu Oſberti abbatis, & conventûs Leyc', in hiis verbis : " Vicaria de Bulkyngton in hoc conſiſtit, quòd quicunque vicarius perpetuus in eccleſiâ ibidem exiſterit, totum altaragium & omnes obventiones & decimas minores totius parochie, unà cum novem acris terre, quas Ricardus capellanus de prediĉis abbate & conventu ad ſummam tenuit, & cum honeſto manſo & orreo poſſidebit."—Redd' indè annuatim prediĉo abbati & conventui XXVIs. VIIId.

Habemus franciplegium ibi de omnibus tenentibus noſtris, cum omnibus libertatibus ad eam pertinent'. Ad quem veniunt tenentes noſtri de Brancote, de Bernangull, de Merſton, de Wybtoft, & Stoke, & ſolvent ad commune fyn, ſcil', tenentes de Brankote IIIIs.; de Bernangull XIIs.; de Wybtoft IIIs. VId. (ſolebant ſolvere IIIIs.); de Stoke XIId. Et dant hariotam in receſſu, & poſt mortem. Habemus ibi weyf & ſtreyf, &c. ut patet per inquiſitionem [2].

Bulkyngton reddebat XXX li.; modò XV li.

Redditus XXVI marce. Decima redditùs XXXIIIIs. VIIId. Augment' vicar' XXs. Reparatio cancelli, &c. preter caſualia.

Clyfton. Ernoldus de Boſco primus dedit nobis eccleſiam de Clyftonâ, cum capellis de Woverâ & de Rokby, que prius fuit prebenda de caſtello Leyc'; & III virgatas terre; & redditum Vs. VId. per annum.

Mem', quòd Thomas Truan, Robertus de la Beauveiſme, & Thomas de Landâ, dederunt, &c. abbati de Leyc' & conventui, pro ſe & hominibus ſuis de Clyfton, totum pratum quod vocatur Flexdames, quod extendit in longitudine de ponte uſque in Preſtewell-ſiche, & in latitudine de foſſato uſque in aquam que vocatur Avene, pro decimis feni quas ipſi abbas & conventus exigebant ab ipſis & hominibus ſuis ratione eccleſie de Clyfton; habend', &c. ut in cartâ.

Habemus eccleſiam de Clyfton in proprios uſus, cum penſione IIII marcarum de vicario ibidem, cum capellâ de Wover, cum decimis garbarum & feni.

Et pro decimis feni habemus totum pratum quod vocatur Honedlonmedowe, quod eſtimatur ad VIII careĉatas, que valent communibus annis Xs.

Habemus ibidem decimas feni de hadys & leyes.

Clifton reddebat XXXV marcas; decima XXXIIIs. Modò reddit VIII li. Indè x li. XXXXIIIIs. IIIId.; procurat' ſynod'. Reparationes cancelli & reĉorie, &c.

Crudworth. Hugo de Ardenâ dedit nobis eccleſiam ibidem, cum decimis garbarum, feni, & boſci, & dim' virgatam terre & duo jugera de dominico ſuo ; &, ex dono Cecelie ſororis ſue, unam acram de ſuo dominico; &, preter hec, decimas ſuas tam de molendino quàm in pannagio & in ceteris rebus ſuis, &c.

Item habemus, ex dono Thome de Ardenâ, decem acras & dim' de boſco ſuo de Crudworth; redd' ſibi & heredibus ſuis VId. per annum, &c.

Mem', quòd nec Henricus de Caſtello de Bromwych, nec aliquis heredum ſuorum, debet attachiare aliquem gurgitem aque de Tame, tangentem pratum quod vocatur Wychelleſhoĺme, niſi de voluntate & conſenſu abbatis & conventûs Leyc', &c.

Habemus quietam clamationem ejuſdem Henrici de Caſtello de illâ terrâ, quam pater ſuus Alanus tenuit, que vocatur Haunge, ad le Blakſtons juxta Berwod, quam Adam Bromwych nobis antea dedit, & cartâ ſuâ confirmavit.

Habemus in Crudworth eccleſiam in propriis uſibus, cum decimis garbarum, feni, boſci, & pannagii, &c. Et vicaria ibidem, ſecundùm ordinationem factam ab antiquo, conſiſtit in tofto quod fuit Aldithe Winter, & in majoribus & in minoribus decimis ville de Dunton, & toto altaragio parochie de Crudworth, & decimis feni ; exceptis Edmedwe & dominico noſtro de Berwode, & exceptis decimis feni de Bromwych & Wyginhull.—Decima reddebat X marcas; modò redditur cum firmâ redditùs [3].

Dunton. Mem', quòd nos conceſſimus, &c. Willo de Bracebrugge & heredibus ſuis, pro homagio & ſervicio ſuo, terram noſtram in villâ de Dunton, cum omnibus pertinentiis ſuis ; illam, ſcilicet, que eſt inter diviſas Holĕm veteris & veterem foveam que eſt inter brueram, & terram que antiquitùs exculta fuit versùs orientem, & versùs auſtrum à viâ que deſcendit de Colle de Crudworth versùs Sanfard uſque ad quercum propinquiorem prediĉe terre, que quercus eſt in latere Bruelli diĉi Matthei, &c. Redd' nobis per annum IIs.

Habemus ibi decimam garbarum & feni, &c. pertin' ad matricem eccleſiam de Crudworth; quam, ſcilicet, decimam vicarius recepit, cum toto altaragio, &c. [4]

Holm. Habemus in Holme, ex dono Roberti filii Fulconis de Holm, dimidiam virgatam terre, cum tofto & crofto.

Habemus ibidem, ex dono Radulphi le Enfaunt de Newton, domum & toftum, cum pertin'; & quatuor acras terre in campis de Holm ſecundùm metas & bundas, ſecundùm cartam ejuſdem Radulphi; & per eandem cartam poſſumus habere duo animalia in heyâ.

Habemus, ex dono Roberti filii Roberti de Holm, duos ſolidatos terre, quos Radus le Enfaunt ſolebat ei reddere pro IIII acris terre & unâ rodâ prati, cum I meſſuagio.

Habemus ibidem, ex dono Roberti domini de Holm, duas rodas prati juxta Newdych.

Habemus ibidem, ex dono Humfridi de Newton, dimidiam virgatam terre, cum tofto & crofto in eâdem.

Habemus ibidem, per compoſitionem inter nos & abbatem de Rouceſtr', duas rodas terre, cum pertin', in quodam loco qui vocatur Centelemedwe juxta pratum noſtrum, in eſcambium pro aliis duabus rodis terre jacent' in quodam loco qui vocatur Neweburgyng, & communem paſturam ad decem groſſa animalia quamdiu c̄oralabunt in heyâ & alibi, ſecundùm tenuram carte Roberti filii Roberti de Holm, & XL bidentes in campis ſuis de Holm & pratis ejuſdem ville, tam in wareĉ' quàm alibi, per totum annum, poſt fenum & blad' levat' & aſportat', ſicut in compoſitione.

Willus Harpar tenet omnia prediĉa. Reddebat XXs. preter omnimodas decimas; modò reddit XIIIs. IIIId.

Habemus ibi decimam garbarum & feni pertinent' ad eccleſiam de Clifton, ſicut in antiquis Rentalibus.

Et habemus ibi unam placeam prati, pro decimâ feni, quod eſt in Meriolm; & decimam de molendino, ſicut patet in Rentali le Pyn [5].

---

[1] Charyte's Rentale, fol. xxviii.   [2] Ib. fol. xxx.   [3] Ibid. fol. xxxvii.   [4] Ibid. fol. liv.   [5] Ibid. fol. lxii. a. b.

Habemus in *Holmer* [1], ex dono Henrici de Rokeby, totam terram quam Ric' de Camvillâ dedit ei in villâ de Holmer, cum omnibus pertinentiis suis, in villâ & extra, in bosco, pratis, &c. ut in cartâ de Chesham.

Hanc donationem dedit nobis pro concordiâ factâ inter nos in curiâ domini regis de advocatione ecclesie capelle de Rokeby, & istam donationem debet nobis warantizare, &c. Redd' xviii s. pro predictâ advocatione, sicut patet in finali concordiâ.

Habemus redditum xx s. in Holmer, per cartam nostram factam Rogero de Messenden clerico de terrâ nostrâ, in quâ feoffavimus eum pro homagio & servitio suo, reddend' nobis annuatim xviii s.

Habemus finalem concordiam inter nos & predictum Henricum de Rokby pro predictis advocatione & terrâ in Holmer, in cujus fine sic scribitur : " Et predictus Henricus & heredes ejus warantizabunt, acquietabunt, & defendent, quandam virgatam terre, cum pertin', ipsi abbati & successoribus suis, contra omnes gentes, ut puram & perpetuam eleemosinam suam. Postea preceptum fuit vicecomiti, quòd scire faceret predictum Ran' quòd esset coram rege in crastino Purificationis beate Marie, ubicunque, &c. ostens' ei quòd sciret dicere quare predictam virgatam terre, cum pertinentiis, predicto abbati & successoribus suis, & ecclesie sue predicte, ut predictum est, warantizare, adquietare, & defendere, non deberet. Et ipse non venit. Et vicecomes mandavit, quòd scire fecit ei per Henricum de Beston in Rokeby & Alanum de Stoke, primò considerand' quare predictus Ran' distr' quondam abbati & successoribus suis & ecclesie sue predicte predictam virgatam terre, cum pertin', &c. Et preceptum est vicecomiti, quòd distr' predictum Ran' ad warantizand', acquietand', & defendend', predictum abbatem, secundùm formam finis predicti quando ab eodem fuerit requisitum." Istud irrotulamentum invenietur in Rotulis regis de Hengman de termino Sci Hillarii, anno regis Edwardi xviii°.

Mem', quòd Gilbertus de Grantingthorp, thesaurarius abbatis Leyc', recepit de Thomâ Missenden pro terrâ quam idem tenet de abbate Leyc' in Holmer xviii s. ut patet in computo dicti Gilberti, anno Dñi millo ccc° decimo, tempore dñi Willi Malverne abbatis, & anno regis Edwardi xxiii.

Item Rogerus de Leyc', thes' abbatis, recepit de Thomâ Messenden pro terrâ quam idem tenet de domino abbate Leyc' in Holmer xviii s. ut patet in computo dicti Rogeri, anno Dñi millo ccc°xi.

Item idem Rogerus de Leyc' recepit de Thomâ Messenden pro terrâ quam tenet de domino abbate Leyc' in Holmer xviii s. ut in computo dicti Rogeri, anno Dñi millo cccxiii. pro arreragiis anni precedentis.

Item Wilfus Geryn, thesaurarius abbatis Leyc', recepit de Thomâ Messenden, per manus Roberti, pro arreragiis duorum annorum ult' precedent' xxxvi s. ut patet in computo predicti Willi, anno Dñi millo ccc°xviii°. Item recepit de Holmer xviii s. ut patet in quodam computo, anno Dñi mil° cccxxiii, tempore dni Rici Tourse abbatis.

Item mem', quòd abbas Leyc' condonavit Thome Myssenden, tenenti suo in Holmer, diversa arreragia, ut patet in quâdam acquit' que sequitur : " Noverint universi per presentes, quòd nos frater Ricardus, permissione divinâ, abbas ecclesie Sce Marie de Pratis Leyc', remisimus & pardonavimus Thome de Messenden, tenenti nostro de Holmer, omnia arreragia cujusdam annui redditûs xviii s. in quibus nobis tenetur, usque ad diem confectionis presentium ; ita quòd amodò nobis & successoribus nostris dictum redditum pro terrâ & ten' que de nobis tenet in Holmer fideliter solvat terminis consuetis. In cujus rei testimonium, sigillum nrm presentibus est appositum. Dat' Leyc', die Jovis prox' ante festum Sci Michis Archangeli, anno regis Edwardi Tertii à conquestu tertio, & tempore dñi Rici Tourse abbatis."

Item Rogerus de Leyc', thes' abbatis Leyc', recepit de redditu de Holmer vi s. in parte solutionis arrer' iiii annorum precedentium, ut patet in computo ejusdem Rogeri, anno Dñi millo ccc°xxvii°, tempore domini Rici Rodley abbatis.

Dñs Johes Browes tenet unum messuagium & unam virgatam terre, & unum boscum, quondam Willi Messenden, juxta Holmere-heth ; reddend' inde per annum xviii s. ad tres anni terminos, anno regni regis Henrici secundi post Conquestum primo.

De terrâ Willi Mussenden.

Wills Capon tenet unum campum, cum aquâ voc' le Brech, continent' viii acras.

Johes Dunesmore tenet de eodem unum campum voc' Argentesfelde, & i toftum voc' Argentecroft, cont' similitèr viii acras.

Johes Baldewyn tenet iii croftos, inde i vocat' Oldfelde, & ii al' voc' Hechynges, continent' ix acras.

Et Johes Brewise, dñs terrarum predictarum, non percipiet de terris predictis per annum nisi ad val' xx s.

Prior de Burcestr' tenet i unum toftum & boscum ubi Wills de Mussenden manebat, & ii campos, inde i voc' Dichefeld, & alter voc' Homefelde, continent' xx acras terre, & plus.—Abbatissa de Burnham petit sectam curie pro dictis terris.

Mem', quòd Wills Inngisby habuit custodiam heredis Henrici de Rokeby usque ad legitimam etatem ejus pro terris in Holmer, quas ipse Henricus dedit abbati & conventui de Leyc', que sunt de feodo ejus, ut in cartâ primâ in Rokby.

Holmer reddebat xviii s.; modò reddit ii d. [2]

Habemus in *Merston* decimas garbarum, feni, & bosci, &c. pertin' ad matricem ecclesiam de Bulkynton ; & percipimus fenum decimale de cumulis ibi, quod valet communibus annis x s.

Habemus ibidem, ex dono Henrici filii Fulconis de Merstonâ, quatuor virgatas terre, quas dederat Alicie uxori sue in dotem, cum hominibus & omnibus eidem terre pertinentibus.

Redditus redd' ibidem xiii s. ii d. & ii gallinas.

Decima pertinet ad ecclesiam de Bulkyngton, ex dono Hugonis de Ardenâ, & redd' circa lx s.

Et mem', quòd, istâ donatione factâ, recepimus eum in canonicum, & uxorem suam in sororem, ut in cartâ primâ. Et est predicta terra de feodo Andrei de Estote, & libera de omnibus nisi de tanto forinseco servicio quantum pertinet ad octavam partem unius militis, sicut patet ex confirmatione Philippi, Thome, & Thome de Estleyâ, &c. [3]

Mynworth. Decima pertinet ad ecclesiam de Bulkyngton, ex dono Rogeri Waterville, & redd' xxx s.

Wills de Ardenâ dedit nobis servicium Simonis filii Nicholai, & xii d. annuatim redd' de toto tenemento suo ibidem. Item Adam filius Nicholai dedit nobis unum toftum ibidem. Jordanus filius Henrici dedit nobis vi d. liberè exeunt' de tenemento Ricardi filii Ade ibidem. Reddit' redditûs x s. ix d. [4]—[Sequuntur diverse alie minute particule in Mynworth.]

Newhay. Mem', quòd Henricus de Lilburn & heredes sui reddebant annuatim Stefano de Segrave & heredibus suis x s. pro xxx acris terre quas de predicto Stefano & heredibus suis tenebant in Newhay.

Habemus, ex dono & confirmatione Stefani de Segrave, homagium & totum servicium Henrici de Lilburn & heredum suorum, quod sibi facere solebant de bosco de Newhay, cum pertinentiis suis, inde sibi reddere solebant xiii s. iiii d.

Prior de Erdbury tenet de nobis terram de Newhay, & redd' xiii s. iiii d. cum Stokyngforth [5].

Newton. Habemus ibidem decimam garbarum & feni pertinentem ad matricem ecclesiam de Clifton.

Habemus ibidem, ex dono Bertrami de Newton, unum toftum quod se extendit in latitudine inter toftum quod fuit Ernaldi Broun & terram que fuit Coleys ; ita quidem quòd predictum toftum se extendit in longitudine sex viginti pedum ; redd' sibi annuatim & heredibus suis iiii d.

Habemus ibidem orreum dominicalem & croftum, que reddunt cum firmâ ibidem. Habemus ibi, ex quietâ clamatione Marie filie Bertrami, relaxationem iiii denariorum redditûs, quos solebamus ei annuatim solvere pro quâdam quantitate terre in quâ situm est orreum nostrum, in villâ de Newton. Et mem', quòd parochiani nostri de Newton dederunt nobis quoddam pratum pro decimâ feni quod vocatur Wafford, à viis

---

[1] A manor in Buckinghamshire. See the History of Leicester Abbey, p. 279.
[2] Charyte's Rentale, fol. lxii. b. lxiii. a.   [3] Ibid. fol. cx.   [4] Ibid.   [5] Ibid. fol. cxiii. b.
positis

positis usque ad aquam que vocatur Avene. Habemus ibi decimas feni de hadys & leys; &, pro decimâ feni, III placeas prati, quarum una jacet ad vadum de Newton, alia jacet ad id vadum, scil' juxta pontem; alia jacet in Meyryham. Et fenum inde proveniens estimatur ad VIII carectatas, valens communibus annis VIIIđ.—Habemus ibidem decimam de molendino vocat' Cutulmylne, q̃ redd' per ann' IIIs̄. IIIIđ. Mem', quòd decima hujus molendini recuperata fuit per sententiam dat' coram judicibus ordinariis in ecclesiâ beate Marie de Arcubus London', ultimo die mensis Julii, anno Domini MCCCCLII. Decima redditûs reddebat xvIlī. modò vIIIlī. [1]

Nuneyton reddebat III M. anguillarum & xxx streylynges, & postea xs̄. pro certis anguillis. Modò reddit MI. anguillarum & xxx streylynges [2].

Rokeby. Habuimus, ex dono Ernoldi de Bosco, advocationem ecclesie de Rokeby, ex confirmatione regis Henrici II. que solebat esse capella de Clifton, modò tantùm presentamus nominatum ad episcopum. Et habemus homagium & servicium de heredibus Henrici de Rokeby. Rector de Rokeby habet totam decimam de ecclesiâ ibidem, & solvit xxs̄. pro procuratione.

Mem', quòd causa que vertebatur inter Hen' de Rokeby & Paulum abbatem Leyc', in curiâ dni regis, super advocatione ecclesie de Rokeby, hoc modo finita est; scil', quòd dictus H. juri q̃d sibi competere asserebat renunciavit, & in predictâ curiâ recognovit eam esse capellam matricis ecclesie de Clifton, &c.; tamen dictus abbas pro se & conventu suo concessit prenominato Hen' & heredibus suis, pro homagio suo & servicio, ut liceat eis in perpetuum, post mortem Simonis decani, clericum eligere, & abbati & conventui presentare, cui eam concedent, si fuerit idoneus, pro xxs̄. annuatim, nomine firme, ipsis solvend', &c.; ita quòd predicti H. & heredes sui plegii erunt de predicto redditu: & clericus qui predictam capellam tenebit singulis annis percipiet cisma de matrice ecclesiâ.

Mem', quòd anno regni regis Henrici filii regis Johannis v°, facta fuit finalis concordia in curiâ domini regis, apud Coventr', inter Willm abbatem Leyc' & Hen' de Rokeby, de advocatione capelle de Rokeby; unde predictus abbas recognovit advocationem predicte capelle esse jus ipsius H.; ita quòd idem H. & ejus heredes liberabunt idoneum clericum ipsi abbati & successoribus suis, quem ipse abbas & successores sui presentabunt episcopo loci; & qui clericus reddet annuatim abbati & conventui Leyc' antiquam & debitam pensionem quam predicta ecclesia de Leyc' percipere consuevit. Et pro istâ advocatione dedit nobis predictus H. totam terram suam quam habuit in villâ de Holmer.

Mem', quòd causa annue pensionis xxs̄. verteretur in consistorio episcopali Lichf', hecque acta fuit inter abbatem Leyc' & dominum Petrum de Bilneye rectorem ecclesie de Rokeby, &c.: tandem illa annua pensio xxs̄. recuperata fuit per sententiam diffinitivam & latam coram diversis judicibus ordinariis, sicut patet in quibusdam instrumentis publicò super hoc confectis.

Item mem', quòd eadem pensio annua xxs̄. recuperata fuit per placitum in curiâ domini regis à dno Johe Stone, personâ ecclesie parochialis de Rokeby, anno Edwardi regis quarti v°; & in curiâ epi per sententiam diffinitivam, ut in libro placitorum [3].

Ryton. Decima garbarum & feni pertinet ad ecclesiam de Bulkyngton, ex dono Rogeri de Watervile [4].

Schelton & *Ansty*, ex dono Rogeri Watervile; que quondam fuerunt capelle de Bulkyngton. Prior de Coventry habet totam decimam; & reddit nobis xs̄. per annum per compositionem [5].

Schuckboro. Osbertus de Lemyngton dedit nobis dim' virgatam terre ibidem, quam nos dedimus Thome, filio Oliveri de Schuckboro. Redd' nobis annuatim ixs̄. liberè [6].

Sowe. Habemus ibi visum franciplegii, sicut patet in inquisitione factâ per regem; & debet sectam. Reddebat IIs̄. modò vIIIđ. [7]

Habemus in *Stokyngforth*, ex dono Willi de Novo Mercato, & ex confirmatione regis Henrici II. cum assensu Roberti comitis Leyc', locum de Stokyngforth, cum totâ illâ terrâ quam predictus Robertus comes dedit ei in escambium pro Wytewyck.

Habemus in Stokyngforth, ex dono Gaufridi de Turvillâ, capellam de Stokyngforth, & quicquid Gaufridus heremita de feodo suo, tam in bosco quàm in plano, &c. à magno bosco suo usque ad dimnetum ex parte aquilonari, & ex aliâ parte per magnam viam usque ad divisam terre Hugonis de Hardreshull, &c. [8]

Stephanus de Segrave dedit nobis ibidem boscum de Newhay; & redd' per annum xIIIs̄. IIIIđ.

Modò dedimus priori de Erdbury locum de Stokyngforth, cum bosco de Newhay.

Mem', quòd eodem die & anno Ricardus abbas Leyc' & ejusdem loci conventus concesserunt per cartam, &c. Willo Botillar, Willo Babyngton, Thome Warner, & Johi Catby, qui statum habuerunt in manerio de Stokyngforth, quòd ipsi dare, concedere, & assignare, poterint Johi priori de Erdbury, &c. predictum manerium, cum pertin'; salvis abbati & conventui de Leyc' fidelitate & securitate de LxIIIs̄. IIIIđ. nomine relevii.

Shelton reddebat unam libram piperis; modò II libras.

Weston. Decima garbarum, feni, & bosci, pertinet ad ecclesiam de Bulkyngton, ex dono Rogeri Watervile.

Wovere. Ernoldus primus de Bosco dedit nobis capellam de Wovere, cum decimis garbarum & feni, cum unâ virgatâ terre & I messuagio, pertinent' ad matricem ecclesiam de Clyfton.

Reddebat xxIs̄.; modò reddit cum firmâ.

Decima reddebat xIIIIlī.; modò vIIIlī.

Mem', quòd capella de Brownswovre est dependens matrici ecclesie de Clifton, & non est ecclesia parochialis per se. Est tamen ibidem sepultura & baptisterium; & hoc concessum fuit specialitèr per abbatem Leyc' propter locorum distanciam, & fluvii de Avene discrimina, &c. ut in inquisitione [9].

Wybtoft. Radus Araby dedit nobis in Wybtoft vII messuagia, x crofta, v virgatas terre & dim', I molendinum.

Omnes tenentes nostri de Wybtoft debent venire ad visum franc' nostrum de Bulkyngton, & solvere ad communem syn. Si aliquis tenens ibi recesserit vel obierit, dabit domino abbati unam hariotam. Omnes debent solvere ingressum domino abbati sicut quod possint finire cum ipso.

Habemus ibi weyfe & streyfe, &c.

Habemus ibi visum franciplegii, sicut patet in le Chartwary per inquisitionem factam per regem.—Reddebat vIlī. xvIIs̄. vIIIđ.; modò reddit IIIIlī. xIIIIs̄. [10]

Wyginhull juxta Crudworth. Mem', quòd cum lis esset mota inter abbatem Leyc' & rectorem de Sutton pro certis decimis provenientibus de Ix virgatis terre in Wyginhull, quarum sex sunt de feodo com' de Warewyck ad ecclesiam de Sutton pertin', & tres sunt de feodo Thome de Ardenâ ad ecclesiam de Crudworth pertin'; &, quia difficilis fuit separatio feodorum; tandem judices, auctoritate apostolicâ, pronunciaverunt duas partes garbarum predictarum novem virgatarum ecclesie de Sutton solvi debere, tertiam partem ecclesie de Crudworth.

Statuerunt insuper, ut manentes in sex virgatis terre de feodo com' Warw' visitent matricem ecclesiam de Sutton in die Assumptionis beate Marie & Pasche, & ibidem eodem die communicent, & confessiones in Quadragesimâ & in extremis à capellano de Sutton recipiant, & mortui ibidem sepeliantur, & omnes minutas decimas omni tempore eidem ecclesie persolvent. Et quia remoti sunt à matrice ecclesiâ, nec sine gravi detrimento assiduè eam adire possunt, omnes alias obventiones & oblationes à predictis hominibus provenientes capellanus in ecclesiâ de Crudworth ministrens percipiet, qui ipsis spiritualia ministret in ecclesiâ de Crudworth, cùm opus fuerit.

Item capellanus de Sutton IIIđ. die Pasche solvat ecclesie de Crudworth ad thus emend'. Omnes quidem manentes in tribus virgatis de feodo Thome de Ardenâ in omnibus obventionibus & oblationibus matrici ecclesie de Crudworth respondebant, &c. [11]

---

[1] Charyte's Rentale, fol. cxiii.
[3] Charyte's Rentale, fol. cxxiii.
[7] Ibid. fol. cxxx. [8] Ibid. fol. cxxxi.
[2] Cotton MSS. Vitellius F. XVII. fol. 28. a.
[4] Ibid. fol. ccxiii. [5] Ibid. fol. ccxxviii. [6] Ibid.
[9] Ibid. fol. cxlix. [10] Ibid. fol. cxlvii. [11] Ibid. fol. cxlix.

43. Taxatio

43. Taxatio fpiritualium bonorum & temporalium abbatis & conventûs Leyc', per Oliverum Linc' epüm, anno Dñi millo cc° nonagefimo-fecundo ¹.

Abbas Leyc' habet ecclefias, portiones, & penfiones, in decanat' fubfcriptis; videlicet,

Gudlakfton.
- Portio in ecclefiâ de Wiluby, vis. viiid. } Decima viiid.
- Ecclefia de Coffeby, xii marc' — xvis.
- ——— Bitmifwell, viii marc' — xs. viiid.
- ——— Enderby, xxiiii marc' — xxxiis.
- Penf' in vicar' ejufdem, vis. viiid. — viiid.
- Porcio in ecclefia de Clenefeld, v marc' vis. viiid.

Gofcote.
- Humburfton, xxv marc' — ii marc', di.
- Ecclef' de Barkeby, cum penf', xxxv marc', } xlvis. viiid.
- Penf' prioris de Trentham in eadem, viii marc', di. } xis. iiiid.
- Penf' in vicar' ejufdem, xxs. — iis.
- Ecclef' de Queniburg, cum penf', xxiiii marc', } xxxiis.
- Penf' ejufdem vicar', ii marc', di. — iiis. iiiid.
- Ecclef' de Hungton, xxxv marc' xxiiis. iiiid.

Gertre.
- Ecclef' de Thedyngworth, xv marc' — xxs.
- Penf' in vicar' ejufdem, i marc' — xvid.
- Ecclef' de Thyrneby, xxvii marc' — xxxvis.
- Penf' in vicar' ejufdem, xxxs. — iiis.
- Ecclef' de Evynton, xx marc' — xxvis. viiid.
- Ecclef' de Billifdon, xxiiii marc' — xxxiis.
- Portio in ecclefiâ de Borefworth, i marc' — xvid.

Akele.
- Ecclef' de Lokynton, xxiiii marc' — xxxiis.
- Penf' in vicar' ejufdem, iiii marc' — vs. iiiid.
- Ecclef' de Schepifhed, xii marc' — xvis.
- Penfio in vicar' ejufdem, ii marc' — iis. viiid.
- Penf' in eccl' de Dixeley di. marc' — viiid.
- Ecclef' de Barowe, cum penf' xl marc', liiis. iiiid.

Sparkenhou.
- Ecclef' de Thornton, xxiiii marc' — xxxiis.
- Penf' in vicar' ejufdem, xxvis. viiid. iiis. viiid.

Leyceftr'.
- Ecclef' Sci Leonardi, ls. — — vs.
- ——— Sce Marie de Caftro, xii marc' — xvis.
- ——— Sci Martini, xi marc' — xxiiiis. viiid.
- Obventiones Sce crucis in eadem x marc', xiiis. iiiid.

Framelond.
- Ecclef' de Eyton, xii marc' — xvis.
- ——— de Thorpernold, xv marc' — xxs.

Summa, cc͞xx͞iiijlî. vis. viiid. — xxvlî. viiid.
Et fumma ccccxxxv marc', vis. viiid.
Summa iiiid. ad marcam pro fpiritualibus apud Linc', vilî. vs. iid.
Summa obol' ad marc', pro fpiritualibus apud Linc', xvs. viiid. ob. q̃.
Item ibidem, pro temporalibus, xs. id.
Item apud Eynefham, pro fpiritualibus & temporalibus, vs. vd. ob. q̃.
Item apud Burton, pro fpiritualibus & temporalibus, xvid. ob.
Item apud Coventr', pro fpiritualibus & temporalibus, iis. vid. ob. q̃.
Summa omnium obolorum xxxvs. iid. ob. q̃.
Summa quadrant' ad marc' folvend' locis predictis, xviis. vid. q̃.

Abbas de Leyceftr' habet temporalia in decanat' fubfcriptis; videlicet,

Leyceftr', xxviiilî. viiid. ob.		lvis. id.
Gartre, xliiilî. xs. viiid.		iiiilî. viis. id.
Gofcote, xliilî. xviiis. viiid.		iiiilî. vs. xd. ob.
Framelond, lviiis. vid.		vs. xd. q̃.
Akele, ixlî. xviiis. viiid.		xixs. ixd. q̃.
Sparkenhou, vilî. xvis.		
Gudlakfton, xxiilî. xixs. ixd.		xlvs. xid. ob. q̃.
Hoyland, iiiilî.		viiis.
Roteland, viiis.		ixd. ob.
Summa, clxilî. xs. q̃.		

Summa quatuor denar' ad marc', folvend' apud Linc' pro temporalibus, iiiilî. ixd.

Coventr'.
- Eccl' de Clifton, xxv marc' — xxxiiis. iiiid.
- ——— Bulkyngton, xxvi marc' xxxiiis. viiid.
- ——— Crudworth, vii marc', di. —
- Summa, lviii marc', di. — lxxviiis.
- Berewode, in temporalibus, xxvs. — iis. vid.
- Item apud Stokyfotth, i caruc', xvs. — xviiid.
- Summa, xls. — iiiis.

Peccur'.
- Eccl' de Yolgrave, xxx marc' — iii marc'.
- Item, pro Meduplot, lxviiis. — vis. ixd. ob. q̃.
- Summa, xxiiilî. viiid. — xlvis. ixd. ob. q̃.

¹ From a Cotton MS. Nero D. X.

- Eccl' de Cokeram, xxvi marc' — xxxiiiis. viiid.
- Sacrifta Lich' percepit in eodem x marc'.
- Ecclef' de Scharnebrok, xx marc' — ii marc'.
- Penf' archidiacono Bedeford in eadem xxs. — iis.
- Ibidem, in temporalibus, iid. — q̃
- Ecclef' de Lilburn, x marc' — i marc'.
- Ibidem, in temporalibus, lxs. — v: s.
- Ecclef' de Chefham, pro medietate, xxx marc', } iii marc'.
- Ibidem, in temporalibus, xxxs. vd. ob. — iis. ob.
- Ecclef' de Brackele, xxxvi marc' — xlviis.
- Idem habet in Sirefham & Faringho xviiilî. xxd. } xxxvis. iid.
- Apud Eynefham.
- Summa xxiiiilî. xiis. iiiid. ob. } viiilî. xvs. iid. ob.
- Summa, iiii den' ad marcam apud Eynefham xliiiis.
- Item, pro ob' de librâ, iiis. viiid.
- Summa decimar' ibidem, pro ii terminis, viiilî. xvs. xid.
- Summa iiiid. ad marc' pro archidiac' Leyc', lxis. ixd.
- Summa quadrant' ad lî. de omnibus fpiritualibus, viis. ixd.
- Summa quadrant' ad marc' xis. viiid. q̃.
- Summa totalis decime lvlî. xvis. viiid.

Taxatio bonorum temporalium abbatis Leyc' in decanat' fubfcript'.

- Abbas Leyc' habet redd' in villâ Leyc' iiiilî. iiiis. iiiid. } viiis. vd. q̃.
- Idem habet de fccrio dñi comitis Leyc' vilî. — xiis.
- Idem habet, de redd' pitancie conventûs, lxvis. id. ob. } vis. viid. q̃.
- Cuftos fabrice ecclefie, vis. xid. ob. — viiid. ob.
- Sacrifta habet in Leyc' lxs. xid. ob. — vis. id. q̃.
- Abbas habet in vico abbatis, de terrâ abbie, iilî. vis. iiiid. } xxiis. iid ob.
- Summa, xxviiilî. viiid. ob. — lvis. ob. q̃.

Gertr'.
- Abbas Leyc' habet in Nowfeley reddit' xxiiiis. } iis. iiiid. ob. q̃.
- Idem in Burton Noveray redd' & heriett' xxis. } iis. id. q̃.
- Idem in Billifdon terram, iiis. viid. } iiiid. q̃.
- Item de fructibus gregum & animalium, xvs. xd. } xixd.
- Idem in Stocton terr', redd', pratum, molend', cur', & relev', xxxlî. xiis. viiid. lxis. iiiid. q̃.
- Idem de fruct' gregum & animalium liiis. iid. } vs. iiiid. ob. q̃.
- Idem in Thedyngworth, cum rec' ecclefie, rec' penfionum, gallinarum, & ovorum, lxvis. id. ob. q̃. } vis. id. ob.
- Idem in Foxton redd' iiiis. vid. — vd. ob.
- Idem in Moufeley, Borefworth, Pynflade, terr', redd', rel', lxxiiiis. — viis. iiiid. ob. q̃.
- Summa, xliiilî. xs. viiid ob. q̃. iiiilî. viis. id.

Gofcote.
- Abbas habet in Hungton redd' xls. — iiiis.
- Idem in Gaddefby iis. — iid. ob.
- Idem habet in Barnefby & Croxton lxvis. iiiid. } vis. viiid. ob.
- Idem in Dalby Hofpit' & Segrave, xxiiis. } iis. iiiid. ob.
- Idem in Asfordeby, cum prato, xxs. — iis.
- Idem [epus habet] ii molend' aquatic', valent' iiii lî. — Epus folvit decimam.
- Idem in Belgrave terr', prat', molend', vilî. xviiis. } xiiis. ixd. ob.
- Idem habet molend' de Newbolt viiis. ixd. ob.
- Idem in Thurm' terr', redd', cur', rel', xvlî. xiiid. } xxxs. id. ob.
- Item in Humburfton redd' & her' lviis. iiiid. } vs. viiid. ob. q̃.
- Item in Barkby & Thorp terr', prat', redd', xxxviiis. } iiis. ixd. ob.
- Item de fruct' gregum & animalium xxxixs. iid. } iiiis. xid.
- Item in Queniburg terr' & redd' xs. — xiid.
- Item in Cofynton xls. — iiiis.
- Item habet in Stokkynge terr' & redd' lxs. } vis.
- Et de fruct' gregum & animalium, xxxvs. viiid. } iiis. vid. ob.
- Summa xliiis. xviiis. viiid.
- Summa decime, iiiilî. viis. xd. obol', & ultra.

² Sic Orig.

Abbas

Framland.
- Abbas habet in Scalford redd' xiii s.   xvii d. q̃.
- Idem in Wylfordeby pratum valet } iiii s. vi d.   v d. ob.
- Idem in Kirkeby Melton xxx s.   iii s.
- Idem in Thorpernald, cum facriſtâ, x s.   xii d.
- Summa, lviii s. vi d.   vi s. x d. q̃.

Akele.
- Abbas habet in Lokynton terr', redd', mol', rel', vi li. xv s. } xiii s. vi d.
- Et fruct' gregum & animalium, xli s. iiii d. } iiii s. ob.
- Idem in Barowe & Shepeſhed, terr' & fruct' animal', xxi s. iiii d. } ii s. ob.
- Summa, ix li. xvii s. viii d.

Spark'.
- Abbas Leyc' habet in Stanton juxta Berdon, Kyrkeby Mallor', & Shaçton, redd' vii. iii s. iiii d. } x s. iiii d.
- De fruct' gregum & animalium, xxxii s. viii d. } iii s. iiii d. q̃.

Geuth'.
- Abbas habet in Outheby redd' v s. xi d. ob. viii d.
- Idem in Waleton xxxvi s. viii d.   iii s. viii d.
- Idem in Schevefby, ad pitanciam conventûs, x s. } xii d.
- Idem in Kileby redd' xl s.   iiii s.
- Idem in Leyre xv s.   xviii d.
- Idem in Blaby xxxvii s. vii d.   iii s. ix d.
- Idem in Wheſton redd', terr', xxxii s. xi d. } iii s. iiii d. ob.
- De fruct' gregum & animalium ibidem xii s. } xiiii d. ob.
- Idem in Thorp juxta Northburg viii s. iiii d.   x d.
- Idem in Wybetoft allocatur pro ii capellis vii. ix s. vi d. } xii s. ii d.
- Idem in Bitmiſwell terr', cum rec' ecclefie, lxxiii s. iiii d. } vii s. iiii d.
- Idem in Coſſebv terr', redd', & fruct' gregum & animalium, lxv s. } vi s. vi d.
- Idem in Clenefelde, cum opere, xii s. ii d. } xiiii d. ob.
- Item in Desford ii s.   ii d. ob.
- Idem in Bruntyngeſthorp, terr' & prat', cum fruct' greg' & animal', iiii li. xx s. ix d. ob. } ix s. i d.
- Mem', quòd taxatum fuit poſtea ad x li. ii s. viii d.
- Summa, xxii li. xix s. ix d.

Summa decimarum xlvi s. q̃. minus.

- Rotelande. Idem abbas habet in Aſſewell & Empyngham redd' viii s. } ix d. ob.

- Holand. Idem habet in villâ Sci Botulphi redd' iiii li. } viii s.
- Summa, iiii li. viii s.   viii s. ix d. ob.

- Clapham. Abbas habet in Cheſham redd' xxx s. v d. ob. } iii s. ob.
- Burnham. Idem in Shernebrok ii d.   q̃.

- Brackel. Idem abbas habet in Sireſham & Faringho cur', redd', prat', & cur' ac rel', xviii li. xx d. } xxxvi s. ii d.
- Haddon. Idem habet in Lilborn lx s.   vi s.
- Summa xxii li. xii s. iiii d. ob.   xlv s. ii d. ob. q̃.

Idem abbas habet apud Berewode i caruc' terr', valet xvi s. pratum iiii s. molendinum v s.   ii s. vi d.
Item apud Stockford i caruc' terr' valet xv s. xviii d.
Summa, xl s.   iiii s.

Idem abbas habet in Pecco apud Mudueplec terr', prat', redd', val' lxviii s.   vi s. ix d. ob. q̃.
Item apud Cokirham xxvii s.   ii s. viii d. ob.
Item apud London' redd' xl s.   iiii s.
Item in Everle, ad pietanc' conventûs, iiii marc' v s.
Modò abbas exhoneratur de prediçtis v s. per placitum.
Summa, ix li. viii s. iiii d.   xviii s. vi d. q̃.
Summa totius decime temporal' xix li. xiii s. iv d.

Abbas de Leyc' habet le Medewplek, in decanatu de Alto Pecco duas bovatas terre que valent per annum xiiii s.
Et habet ibidem de reddit' aſſiſſ' per annum xx s.
Et habet ibidem de molendin' per annum x s.
Et habet ibidem de placitis & perquifitis per annum ii s.
Et habet ibidem de minerâ per annum ii s.
Et habet ibidem de profeçtis ſtauri per ann' i marc'.
Et habet ibidem de prato per annum vi s. viii d.

---

44. Summa totalis omnium receptuum cujuſlibet ville vel loci hic fubfequitur nobis pertinent', mccclxxvii [1].

Anſty redd' xv li. ix s. vi d.
Anlep, v s. vi d. i li. piperis.
Apulby, vi d.
Bagworth, iiii li. x s.
Baggrave, iiii l. iii s. iiii d. preter grana.
Barkeby, viii li. ix s. viii d. ob. q̃. x gallos, v gallinas, preter grana.
Baryſby, xiiii s. viii d.
Baro, xv li. communibus annis, preter lanam, mortuaria, & decimas prati.
Belgrave, cum molendinis, redd' viii li. xvi s. viii d.
Bernangul, xix s. preter decimam garbarum.
Berwod, xvi li.
Byllſdon, viii li. xv s. iiii d.
Bytſwell, xiii li. xv s.
Bitulſden, vi s. viii d.
Blaby, iii li. xiiii s. vi d.
Boſworth, c s. x d.
Botulſton, lxxvi s. vii d. ob. / *Bonyngton*, vi quart' ſal' ret'.
Brakley, xvii li. vii s. ix d.
Brankkot, ix s. vii d. preter grana.
Braunſton, xvi s.
Brentby, decima redd' xl s.
Bryculſworth, iiii s.
Bulkyngton redd' xviii li. ii s. viii d. ob. & par cirotecarum.
Burſtall, vi li. x d.
Burton Overy, xii s. iiii d.
Buſby, decimas inter grana.
Cateby, iii s. iiii d.; &, poſt deceſſum magri Lathbury, ut ſupra.

Charley, ...
Cheſham, xiii li. vi s. viii d.
Cleycotys, xx s. & homagium.
Cleynfeld, xiii s. x d.
Clifton, viii li. xviii s. iiii d.
Cokeram, xx/iiii li. lxvi s. viii d.
Cofeby, xii li. vi s. iiii d.
Cofyngton, xxiiii s. iiii d.
Craft, xl s. & i petram cere.
Croxton, xxxix s. ob. q̃.
Croxton Abbey, xxii s.
Crudworth redd' cum Berwode, ſcil' xv s.
Dalby, viii s. ret'.
Desforth, iiii s.
Dyſworth, lx s.
Dyxley, xiiii s.
Eyton, c s.
Empyngham, v s. ret'.
Endreby redd' viii s. vi d. vi capones, dim' petram cere, preter grana & fenum.
Erneſby, xii d. ret'.
Eſtwell, xiii s. iiii d. & unam petram cere.
Evyngton, xxii s. viii d. preter grana.
Everley, xiii s. iiii d. ret'.
Faryngo, xii li. viii s. x d.
Fleckney, xxx s.
Foxton, iiii s. vi d.
Fryſby, ii s.
Gadeſby, ii s. vi d.
Garadon, xxvi s. & xiiii s. pro Dixley.
Halſo, iiii s. preter granum.

Hamilton, vii s. x d. preter grana & fenum.
Harboro, xx s.
Harſton, vi s. & i petram cere.
Hathurn, xl s. & i petram cere.
Hemyngton, vi li. iii s. x d.
Hertyſhorn, xxiiii s. iiii d.
Holme, xiii s. iiii d.
Holmer, xviii s. ret'.
Horſpol! redd' inter grana.
Hows, vii s. x d.
Howton, v s. vi d.
Humburſton, vii s. iiii d. i li. cumini, ii paria cirotecarum, preter grana.
Hungarton, v li. preter grana.
Ingwarby valet l li.
Kenelworth, liii s. iiii d.
Keyrby, xii s.
Kylby, xxx s.
Kyrkby Malore, ii li. xxii d. preter grana, xvi gall', & alia fervitia.
Kyrkby Beller, xxvi s. ob. Inde ret' vii s. ob.
Knaptoft, pratum q̃ vocatur Cotyngham Medow.
Knyton redd' xxiiii li. ix d. Inde ret' vii s. vii d.
Lawton, lxxvi s. ob.
Leyceſtr', cum decimis, redd' ciii li. xii s. xi d. ob. lvii gallinas, [galline ad voluntatem xxxvi] xxvii capones libere, ii paria cirotecarum, & i li. cumini.
Leyr, xvi s. ob. Inde ret' ix s. x d.
Lilburn, ix li. ii s. viii d.

[1] Charyte's Rentale, fol. clviii. a. b.

Lowderſhey,

Lowndersbey, LXXIII s. IIII d.

Lokyngton, L li. XII s. II li. cumini, preter provent' de omnibus.

London, XIII li. XIX s. IIII d.

Melton, III s. IIII d.

Merston, XIIII s. II d. II gallinas, preter grana & fenum.

Mynworth, IIII s. V d. ob. redd' cum Berwod.

Montsorell, VIII s. VI d.

Mowsley, VI li. VI d. ob. preter dim' li. piperis.

Newbold, XIIII d.

Newhay, XIII s. IIII d. redd' cum Stokyngforth.

Newton Clifton, VI li. XIII s. IIII d.

Newton juxta Swepston, XI s. ret'.

Northampton, V s.

Nowseley, XIII s. VIII d.

Nuneyton, III mill' anguillarum, & XXX sterlyngas.

Octhorp, XXVI s. VIII d.

Odeby, XXXIX s. VII d. ob.

Oldfeld & Longwong, XLV s. IIII d.

Othorp, IIII marcas.

Peccum. ⎰ *Yolgrave,* LVII s. V d. ob. q. preter decimam garbarum, & preter proventum manerii, scil' omnium agnorum, lane, plumbi, &c.
Elton, IIII li. V s. I d.
Mydulton, LXXI s. II d. ob.
Wynster, XLIII s. IIII d.
Stanton, LXXV s. VI d.
Byrchover, XIII s. X d.
Lyes Stanton, IX s.
Hertull, II s. & VI carect' feni. ⎱ preter dec' lane.

Peccum. ⎰ *Nether Haddon,* IIII s. IIII d.
Smerhul & Gratton, vicarius habet totam.
Conkysbyry, IIII li. VI s. VI d. preter proventum minere. ⎱

Pynslad, III s. IIII d. preter certas virgatas terre in tenurâ firmarii de Mowsley.

Quenby, redd' inter grana.

Quenyboro, LXIII s. VIII d. preter decimas garbarum & feni.

Querndon, X li. XI s. VIII d. preter lanam, mortuaria, &c.

Reresby, XXIX s. VI d.

Ryton, dec' redd' cum Bulkyngton.

Rodely, XII d. ret'.

Rolston, IIII li.

Scalforth, III s. IIII d.

Schakerston, V s.

Scharnbrok, XI li. VI s. VIII d.

Schepeshead, XIIII li. preter decimam bosci, &c.

Schetheby, X s.

Schukboro, IX s. ret' VII s.

Scraptoft, XX s. cum Ansty.

Segrave, XX s.

Skefyngton, XXX s.

Sygresham, VI li. III s. VIII d. ob. q.

Sow, VIII d.

Stanton, XXIIII s. VIII d. preter decimas garbarum & feni.

Stocton redd' XXII li. III s. II d. ob. preter decimas garbarum, & preter provent' manerii, scil', omn' agnorum, lane, & granorum, &c.

Stokyngforth redd' L s.; & XIII s. IIII d. pro Newhay, ut supra.

Stretton, I li. piperis.

Sutton, XLIII s. II d.

Thedyngworth, XIIII li. IX s. VI d. & IIII gallinas.

Thornton, IIII li. II s. V d.

Thorp-Barkby, XVIII s. X d. preter decimas garbarum & feni.

Thorp-Ernold, X li.

Thorp-Lilburn, II s. ret'.

Thorp-Norboro, XX s. IX d. & I li. piperis, I li. cumini, & dim' part' decimarum garbarum & feni.

Thurkaston, XXII d.

Thurnby, LVII s. IIII d. X gallinas, V gallos, preter decimas garbarum & feni.

Thurmaston, XIII li. VIII s. II d. ob. XVIII gallinas, preter decimas garbarum & feni.

Walton, XVIII s.

Weston, II s. preter decimam molendini. Decima redd' cum Bulkyngton.

Whatton, XXXII s. IIII d.

Wheston, IX li. III s. IIII d.

Wybtoft, IIII li. XVII s. VI d.

Wyforby, redd' cum firmâ de Thorp-Ernold.

Wygeston, XXVI s. VIII d.

Wyloby Waterles, XXVI s. VIII d.

Wodhaws redd' III li. & IIII s. pro Braxleykar, preter decimas agnorum, lane, mortuorum, & oblacionum, &c.

Wover redd' VIII li.

Summa, VII^c LXXII li. XV s. VIII d. q.

45. RESOLUTIONES [1].

Dño Pape VII s. per annum, & II d. pro acquietanciâ.

Ansty. Dño de Groby, pro molendino ibidem.

Barkeby. Archidiacono Leyc', pro procuratione, VII s. VI d. ob. q. Priori de Trentham C XIII s. IIII d. per compositionem. Dño de Ros VI s. pro auxilio vicecomitis & wardâ castri de Bealver.

Bewmont Wode. Magistro de Dalby, pro Sandepittis juxta Calverhey, II s.

Bernangull. Dño le Sowche, pro unâ virgatâ terre ibi, XVIII d.

Bilsdon. Archidiacono Leyc', pro procuratione, VII s. VII d. ob. q. Et vicario ibidem LIII s. IIII d. per ordinationem R. epi Linc' de decimâ capelle de Godeby sol'. Et eidem XL s. pro augmentatione ad voluntatem, solv' per firmarium nostrum de Rolston.

Bytswell. Archidiacono Leyc' VII s. VI d. ob. q. Vicario ibi XX s. de redditu illius ville pro augmentatione ad voluntatem nostram, ultra pensionem, scil' XX s. quam nobis annuatim reddere solebat.

Boresworth. Ad wardam castri de Rokyngham, III d. per tenent'.

Brakley. Archidiacono Northamptonie, pro procuratione, VII s. LIII s. ob. q. Vicario, per compositionem ex antiquo, c s. Et XLVI s. VIII d. eidem vicario ex novo, ultra predict' c s. pro augmentatione suâ. Item duo quarteria ordei, duas carectatas feni, I carectatam straminis.

Brankot. Dño de Sowche unam quartrenam cumini pro ayfiamento in quâdam viâ.

Braunston. Priori de Schene XL s. & ultra pro quâdam portione ibidem.

Brenteby. Vicario ibidem XX s. pro augmentatione suâ XLVI s. VIII d.

Bulkyngton. Archidiacono Coventr', pro procuratione, VII s. VI d. ob. q. Dño le Sowche III d. pro terris Wytynt ibidem.

Burstall. Domino de War IX d. pro I cotagio ibidem.

Busby. Priori de Schene, pro II garbis unius virgate terre ibi. Summa denariorum molendini in summâ porticnis quam habemus in Slawton.

Chesham. Archidiacono Bugkyng', pro procuratione III s. X d. pro medietate ecclesie. Et capellano deservienti capellam de Yneshamstede quinque quarteria frumenti de granariâ nostrâ.

Clifton. Archidiacono Richemond, pro procuratione, VII s. VII d. ob. q.

Cokeram. Decano Eborac', ut in Queniboro.

Dño regi VI s. VIII d. pro libertate omnium articulorum visûs franciplegii, &c. Eidem I d. ob.

Dño regi II s.

Priori de Lancastr', pro decimâ de Thurun, prout possumus concordare secum. Et eidem priori unam libram incensi. Totum per firmarium.

Cosby. Archidiacono Leyc', pro procuratione VII s. VI d. ob. q. Dño duci Lanc' pro sectis curie, secundùm quedam Rentalia, II s. Vicario ibi ad voluntatem nostram.

Crudworth. Archidiacono Coventr' VII s. VII d. ob. q. Et vicario X s. ad voluntatem nostram.

Dalby. Heredibus Ricardi filii Willi de Dalby, XII d. pro terris nostris in Dalby.

Enderby. Archidiacono Leyc' VII s. VI d. ob. q.

Godeby. Vicario de Bilsdon LIII s. IIII d. totam decimam feni, & totum toftum, quorum medietas ex antiquo nobis pertinuit.

Evyngton. Priori de Schene, pro decimis garbarum dominicalium ibi, XLVI s. VIII d.

Archidiacono Leyc', pro procuratione, VII s. VI d. ob. q.

Eyton. Archidiacono Leyc', pro procuratione, VII s. VI d. ob. q.

Hertyshorn & Schorthasuls. Johi Yrlond III s. VI d. pro certis terris ibidem; & ad curiam de Grisley pro shreyvetothe X d.

Humberston. Episcopo Linc', pro ecclesiâ ibi, LXX s. Priori de Schene, pro decimis dominicorum ibi, XX s. Archidiacono Leyc', pro procuratione, VII s. VI d. ob. q. Et eidem pro synod' III s. VI d. Et domino de Grey, pro sectâ curie apud Evyngton, XVIII d.

Hungarton. Episcopo Linc', pro ecclesiâ ibi, XX s. Archidiacono Leyc', pro procuratione, VII s. VI d. ob. q. Et eidem pro synod' III s. VI d. Abbati de Wolton XVI d. pro domo in quâ Ric' Ibatson manet. Vicario, pro augmentatione, ad voluntatem nostram, pro Yngwarby, XIII s. IIII d.

Ingwarby. Priori de Schene, pro portione, II s. Capellano ibi IIII marcas, & ad mensam nostram. Dño

[1] Charyte's Rentale, fol. cxlix. b.—cli. a.

duci

duci Lancaſtr', pro communi fyn, vɪđ. quos jamdudum tenentes noſtri de Ingwarby folverunt.

Keyrby. Priori de Schene, pro quâdam portione ibi,
xxxɪɪɪs. ɪɪɪɪđ.

Kyrkby Mallory. Comiti Leyc', pro feɕâ curie, ɪɪs.

Knaptoft. Dño ejufdem ville, pro ɪɪɪɪ acris prati ibi
vocat' Cotyñ-Hāmedwe, dɪ̄. lɪ̄. piperis per firmarium.

Lawton. Comiti Oxon' xxs.

Lilburn. Archidiacono North' vɪɪs. vɪđ.

Leyceſtr'. Priori de Schene, pro decimis garbarum
dominicarum comitis Leyc' apud portam de South &
de Weſt, xxvɪs. vɪɪɪđ. Archidiacono Leyc', pro
ecclefiâ Sɕi Martini, ɪxs. xđ. ob̄. q̄.

Eidem, pro ecclefiâ Sɕe Marie, ɪxs. xđ. ob̄. q̄.

Eidem, pro ecclefiâ Sɕi Leonardi, ɪxs. xđ. ob̄. q̄.

Capellano Sɕi Leonardi xɪɪɪ marcas, & ad menfam
noſtram.

Ecclefie Sɕi Leonardi vs. pro Crâforthe-medwe.

Comiti Leyc', pro terris Janitoris in Weſtgate-felde,
vɪs. vɪɪɪđ.

Eidem, pro pifcariâ in Sorâ à molendino boreali
ufque ad pontem borealem, vɪs. vɪɪɪđ.

Eidem, pro domo Fylyngley juxta·ecclefiam Sɕe
Crucis, xvđ. ɪɪ gall'.

Eidem, pro domo quondam Bugden, nunc in tenurâ Johis Holdernis, xɪɪđ.

Eidem, pro peciâ terre in Northmylne-lane, xvđ.;
fed jam ceſſat illa folutio, quia rex illam peciam habet.

Eidem, pro tenemento fuper Frogmerbanke, ɪɪs.

Eidem, pro tenementis in Humburſtone-gate, vɪɪđ.
ob̄. per camerarium.

Eidem pro tenemento juxta, jam in tenurâ Johis
Cartewrighte, xɪɪɪɪs.

Eidem, pro tenemento nunc in tenurâ Wilłi De-
thyk, xɪđ. Et ɪɪɪđ. pro ɪɪ gall'.

Eidem, pro tenemento in Seyvoy-gate, xvɪɪɪđ.

Eidem, pro tenemento in vico porcorum, quondam
Nakerer, ɪɪs. Et Johi Janitori ɪɪ gall'.

Abb̄i de Myryvale, pro domo quondam Adlyn, xɪɪđ.

Canonicis ecclefie Sɕe Marie juxta caſtrum, pro
Crâforde-medwe, xɪɪđ.

Eifdem, pro prato vocat' Heyrdcroft, vɪđ.

Eifdem, pro domo quondam Bugden, xɪɪđ.

Johi Danet, pro medietate unius tenementi infra
portam occidentalem, quondam Johis Nakerer, ɪɪs.
ɪɪɪđ.; & ɪɪ gall', ficut patet in cartâ dñi ducis Lanc'.

Magiſtro Sɕi Leonardi, pro le Benkhows, ɪɪɪs.
vɪɪɪ gallin'.

Eidem, pro domo juxta, ɪɪs. ɪɪɪɪ gallin'.

Eidem, pro domo quondam Thome Bodyngton,
modò in tenurâ Wilłi Scharp, ɪɪs. ɪđ. & ɪ gallin'.

Magiſtro Sɕi Johis Leyc', pro domo in quâ Johes
Plumer manet in vico boreali, ɪɪs. ut dicitur.

Eidem, pro domo quondam in cimiterio Sɕe Crucis,
xɪɪđ. per antiqua Rentalia.

Dño regi, pro ɪ meſſ' & xɪ fchopis in foro Sabbati,
xxvɪs. vɪɪɪđ. & ɪɪɪs. ad terminum certum.

Procuratori noſtro Sɕi Martini xɪɪs. ɪɪɪɪđ. pro falario fuo. Item ɪɪs. in feſtis principalibus. Item
ɪɪɪɪs. pro camerâ fuâ.

Item prepofitis ecclefie ɪɪɪɪs. pro ſtramine in redditu
de le ſtourhows.

Item vicario Sɕi Martini ɪɪs. in feptimanâ, &c.

Item ɪɪ clericis ibidem ɪɪɪɪs. ɪɪɪɪđ. per annum.

Item pulfatoribus, fcil' ɪɪ clericis & aliis pulfantibus,
per annum, ɪɪɪɪs. ɪxđ.

Lokyngton. Archidiacono Leyc', pro procuratione,
vɪɪs. vɪđ. ob̄. q̄.

Comiti Leyc', pro manerio ibidem, xxs.

Eidem, pro feɕâ curie pro eodem manerio, ɪɪs.

London. Magiſtro Sɕi Egidii, pro tenemento vocat'
Sarfonheyd extra Newgate, vɪs. vɪɪɪđ.

Eidem pro tenemento juxta, quondam Johis Faytt, xxs.

Monialibus de Clerkenwell, pro le Sarfonheyd,
xɪɪɪs. ɪɪɪɪđ.

Hofpitali Sɕi Johis Jerufalem, pro tenemento in
Smethefelde vocat' Blackyates, ɪɪs.

Eidem, pro eodem tenemento, unam libram incenfi, vel vɪɪɪđ.

Eidem, pro tenemento juxta Chikynlane ufque forum equorum, vɪđ.

Ecclefie Sɕi Sepulchri, pro quâdam pendulâ ultra
cimiterium in hofpitio de Sarfonheyd, ɪɪs.

6

Mowſley. Dño regi, pro feɕis curie ad Gartere-
hyll, ɪɪɪɪs. xđ. per firmarium noſtrum.

Caſtello Northamptonie ɪɪs. vɪɪđ.

Abbati de Sulbi ɪɪɪs. pro ɪ meſſ' & ɪ virgatâ terre.

Okethorpe. Dño regi, pro feɕis curie, ɪɪs. per tenentem.

Peccum. Ecclefie Lychefeld, pro ecclefiâ de Yolgrave, vɪlɪ̄. xɪɪɪs. ɪɪɪɪđ.

Archidiacono Derbie, pro procuratione ejufdem
ecclefie, vɪɪs. vɪđ. ob̄. q̄.

Priori de Lenton, pro ɪɪ garbis decimarum, cum
pertin', in Midoplec, apud Kankefbyri, ɪɪɪs.

Vicario ibidem decimam garbarum & feni, cum
orreo, xlɪ̄.

De Elton, que valent per annum v marcas, ɪxs.

Item eidem decimam garbarum & feni, cum orreo,
xlɪ̄. de Wynſter, que valent per annum xxxɪɪɪs. ɪɪɪɪđ.

Item eidem decimam garbarum & feni de Smerhull,
que valent per annum xs.

Item habemus ɪ cotagium, quod redderet nobis
per annum ɪɪɪs.

Item habemus totam decimam garbarum & feni de
Gratton, que valent per annum xls.

Summa totalis penfionis vicarii vɪɪɪlɪ̄. ɪɪs.

Dño de Mydulton, pro paſturâ arietum noſtrorum
in Mydulton morâ, ɪɪɪɪs.

Summa totalis, xvlɪ̄. ɪxs. xđ. ob̄. q̄.

Queniboro. Ecclefie Eborac', pro ecclefiâ de Queniboro, lɪɪɪs. ɪɪɪɪđ. fol' per firmarium de Cokyrham.

Archidiacono Leyc', pro procuratione, vɪɪs. vɪđ.
ob̄. q̄.

Capellano cantarie lxɪɪs. ɪɪɪɪđ. de redditu in Queniboro. Item xxs. de Segrave. Item xxs. à celerario
abbathie.

Summa cɪɪs. vɪɪɪɪd. fol' annuatim capellano cantarie.

Dño ville, pro unâ bovatâ terre, ɪɪđ. ob̄.

Summa totalis, vɪɪlɪ̄. xɪɪɪs. ɪɪɪɪđ. ob̄. q̄.

Rerſby. Dño de Norfolk xvɪɪɪđ. Johi Ribull,
pro uno crofto, ɪɪs. vɪđ.

Rolſton. Vicario de Bilfdon xs. per firmarium ad
voluntatem noſtram.

Scharnbrok. Ecclefie Lincoln', pro ecclefiâ de
Scharnbrok, cs.

Vicario ibidem xxs. pro augmentatione, ad velun-
tatem noſtram.

Archidiacono Bedfordie, pro annuâ penfione ejufdem ecclefie, xxs.

Eidem, pro procuratione ejufdem ecclefie, vɪɪs. vɪđ.

Summa totalis, vɪɪlɪ̄. vɪɪs. vɪđ.

Schepiſheyd. Archidiacono Leyc', pro procuratione,
vɪɪs. vɪđ. ob̄. q̄. Dño de Lovel, pro tenemento in
tenurâ Nicholai Cofby; ɪɪs. per tenentem.

Quilibet tenens abbatis Leyc', de parte dotis comitis de Bowhan, dabit ɪ gallinam.

Dño de Haſtyngs, pro tenemento quod vocatur
Froſtland, in tenurâ Simonis Bayly, vɪđ.

Segrave. Capellano cantarie de Queniboro xxs.
ut fupra.

Skeyfyngton. .... *(No entry.)*

Stanton. Dño de Groby, pro unâ virgatâ terre &
dim', xɪɪđ. Et, pro feɕâ curie, ɪđ. per tenentem.

Stoɕon. Priori de Schene, pro duabus partibus de-
cimarum garbarum de dominicis noſtris ibi & Johis
Friday, & pro duabus garbis unius virgate terre in
Buffeby, xls.

Capellano ibi xɪɪɪɪs. de decimâ feni ibi. Vicario
ibi ɪɪs. De decimâ molendinorum ventritici & aquatici pertinentium nobis.

Dño de Martas pro ɪɪ virgatis terre, quondam
Thome Warknaby, xɪɪđ. & dɪ̄. lɪ̄. piperis.

Dño de Suthwyk, pro uno cotagio & dim' virgatâ
terre, quondam Johis Becket, ɪɪɪs.

Ecclefia de Stowton, ad lumen fepulchri, pro ɪ cotagio & vɪ acris terre quondam Johis Atkin, ɪlɪ̄. per
tenentem.

Thedyngworth. Archidiacono Leyc', pro procuratione, vɪɪs. vɪđ. ob̄. q̄.

Thornton. Archidiacono Leyc', pro procuratione,
vɪɪs. vɪđ. ob̄. q̄.

Vicario ibi, pro augmentatione fuâ, ultra penfionem,
fcil' ɪɪɪɪ marc', quam nobis annuatim reddere folebat,
lxs.

Dño de Bagworth, pro German's Clofe, ɪɪɪs. ɪɪɪɪđ.
Thorp Ernald.

Thorp Ernald. Priori de Schene, pro 11 partibus decimarum garbarum de dominico Ernoldi de Bofco, LX ſ.

Archidiacono Leyc' VII ſ. VI đ. oƀ. q̃.

Vicario ibi XLVI ſ. VIII đ. de decimâ de Brentby, ut ſupra, preter penſionem, fcil' IIII ſ. quam nobis annuatim reddere ſolebat.

Dño ville, pro I bovatâ terre & ex x acris prati, I li. piperis.

Thorp Norboro. Dño de Norboro I li. piperis & I li. cumini.

Et đno de Frolefworth III đ.

Et quondam priori Sci Hoſpitalis Jeruſalem III đ.

Thurmudeſton. Roberto Kyng & Joħi Pyll, heredibus Joħis Draper, pro I tofto, III rodis terre, I rod' & dim' prati, &c. quondam Wilti Blakberd, IIII ſ.

Collegio Sci Martini Oxon', pro unâ dimidiâ acrâ prati jacent' in prato de Thurmaſton ſub Anlep, per tenentem.

46. Capelle firme & arreregia ante peſtilentiam.

Cokeram ſolebat reddere vel ſolvere ante peſtilentiam L li.

Yolgrave ſolebat reddere x vel XII li.

Decima de Haddon x ſ. anno Dñi MCCCXXX.

Elton ſolebat ſolvere VI li. XIII ſ. IIII vel x li.

Mydulton, VIIII li. vel x li. XIIII ſ. IIII đ.

Wynſter, VIII li. vel XII li. XIII ſ. IIII đ.

Stanton, VI li. vel x li. VII ſ.

Byrchover, VI li. VI ſ. VIII đ. vel VI li.

Lyes, L ſ. XLVIII ſ. IIII đ. vel LIII ſ. IIII đ.

Smerhul, VI ſ. VIII đ. VIII ſ. vel XIII ſ. IIII đ.

2 Summa L li. VIII ſ.

Brakley, XL li. LIII li. vel LVI li. XIII ſ. IIII đ.

Scharnebroke, XXIII li. vel XXVIII li.

Cheſham, XXIIII li. vel XXVI li. XIII ſ. IIII đ.

Lilleburne, XIIII li. XIII ſ. IIII đ. vel XVI li.

Berewod, x li.

Crudworth, x marc'.

Bulkyngton, XXX li. XXXII li. XL li. vel XLVIII li.

Wover, XX li. anno Dñi M° CCCXLII.

Newton, VII li. XI li. VI ſ. vel XVI li.

Ciiſton, VII li. Item XVI li.

Faringo, dominicalia v li. x li. vel XII li.

Baro, altaragium, XIIII li. VI ſ. VIII đ. XX vel XXI li.

Eyton, XXI li. in diverſis Rotulis.

Thorp Ernald, VII li. Item XX li. de claro.

Thedyngworth, XVI li.

Goadeby, IIII li. VI li. vel XI li.

Lokyngton, decima XX li.

Lokyngton & Hemyngton, XXX li. XLIIII li. vel XLV li.

Porta Occidentalis ſolebat ſolvere ad Grangiam.

Porta Auſtralis ſolebat ſolvere ad Grangiam.

Baro ad Grangiam.

Querndon ad Grangiam.

Mountforel ad Grangiam.

Queniboro, Barkby, Hungarton, Ingwarby, Billeſdon, Rolſton, Thurnby, Stotton, Evyngton, Humburſton, Coſby, Wheſton, Endurby, Thurnley, Bagworth, Stowton, Horſpol, Schepyſhed, Byttelwell, Pynſlade, Skeyffyngton, Mowſeley, Herteſhorne, Eccleſia Sci Martini Leyc', ut ſupra, ſolverunt ad Grangiam.

Eccleſia de Baro ſolvebat ut ſupra.

Wodhows, XX marc', ut patet in Rentali Geryn.

Omnes alie capelle, firme, & maneria, tunc temporis reſpondebant inter grana; ſcil',

Grangia Abbathie ſolebat ſolvere vel reddere ad Grangiam.

Burſtall ſolebat reddere ad Grangiam lane XXIIII ſac' ſol' vendi; pretium I ſac' x marc', &c. ut in Rotulo fratris Galfridi Sallow, cujus dat' eſt circa annum Dñi MCCCLV, & regis Edwardi Tertii XXIX.

Pretium unius ſacci communibus annis illo tempore VII li. VIII li. vel IX li.

Anno Dñi MCCXIIII.
- Dyſworth reddebat VI li. XIII ſ. IIII đ.
- Thorp Parva reddebat v li.
- Bagworth & Thornton, XXI li. VIII ſ. VIII đ.
- Item XXVI li.

Thurnby. Archidiacono Leyc', pro procuratione, VII ſ. VI đ. oƀ. q̃.

Vicario ibi IIII marcas in pecuniâ, & III ſ. VI đ. pro ſynodalibus jam ex novo, & in granis ad voluntatem noſtram, ultra penſionem, ſcil' XXX ſ. quam nobis annuatim reddere ſolebat.

Whetſton. Archidiacono Leyc', ut ſupra in Endurby.

Vicario ibidem XIII ſ. IIII đ. ultra penſionem, ſcil' VI ſ. VIII đ. quam nobis annuatim reddere ſolebat.

Wodhows. Heredibus Wilti filii Gerardi, pro ſitu orrei noſtri, ſecundùm aliqua Rentalia, IIII đ. Tamen recuperantur per aſſiſam ſecundùm Rotula Rogeri Pynchebeke.

Summa totalis omnium reſolutionum CIII li. piperis, I li. cumini, & I quatren' II li. incenſi, I li. cere, XX galline, VII quarteria frumenti, II quarteria ordei, & II careċtate feni, & una careċtata de ſtramine.

Wygeſton. Priori de Schene, pro decimis duarum garbarum de dominico de Wygeſton, VI ſ.

(Peſtilentia fuit anno Domini M° CCCXLVI°.) [1]

MCCCXXV.	Thornton, XXVI li. XIII ſ. IIII đ.
	Piſcaria de Burſtal XX đ. tunc primò.
MCCCII.	Porta Auſtralis, XV li. VI ſ. VIII đ. Poſtea XVI li.
	Bagworth, VI li. XIII ſ. IIII đ.
	Faringo, pro blado, IX li. XII ſ. Item XII li. de dominicis.
MCCCVII.	Thornton, XX li.
	Faryngho, XII li. VI ſ. VIII đ. pro blado vendit' de dominicis.
MCCCXLVII	Brakley, XL li.
poſt peſt'.	Scharnbrok, XXVIII li.
MCCCXXXIIII.	Molendinum dominicum Abbathie fullonum, XXVI ſ. VIII đ.
MCCCXV.	Thorp Norboro, VI li. XIII ſ. IIII đ
	Wylloby Waterles, XX ſ.
MCCCXXXIIII.	Piſcaria de Burſtal, XX đ.
	Evenley, XIII ſ. IIII đ.
	Molendinum dominicum Abbathie fullonum, XIIII ſ. IIII đ.
MCCCXLII.	Peccum, Yolgrave, XII li.
	IIII ſodar' plumbi pro decimâ; lane cc li.
	Decima lini & canabi in prato in Baro & Barkby.
MCCCXIII.	Hemyngton, XXIIII li.
MCCCXXX.	Decima de Haddon, in prato, x ſ.
MCCCXC.	Vicarius Sci Petri VII ſ. VI đ. oƀ. q̃.
	Vicarius Omnium Sanċtorum VII ſ. VI đ. oƀ. q̃.
	Vicarius Sci Leonardi VII ſ. VI đ. oƀ. q̃.
	Cheſham, XXVII li. XIII ſ. IIII đ.
	Altaragium de Baro x li. XIII ſ. IIII đ.
	Molendinum de Belgrave XL ſ.
MCCCVI° vel IX°.	Molendinum de Schepiſhed VI li. x ſ.
	Molendinum de Brankot IIII li.
MCCCLXVIII.	Brentby, VII li. VI ſ. VIII đ. poſt peſtilentiam.
MCCCVI.	Baro, altaragium, XVII li. III ſ. VIII đ.
	Molendinum de Belgrave III li. XIII ſ. IIII đ.

Decima feni terrarum dominicarum de Evyngton reddebat XVI li.

Schepiſheyd, XXII li. XIX ſ.

Baro pro ſe, ſine altaragio & capellis, XIIII li.

Butyſwell, deduċtis è decimis XVI li, XVIII ſ.

Bylleſdon, de claro, XIX li. XIIII ſ.

Barkby, XXXII li. XVI ſ.

Wheſton, XXV li. XII ſ.

Coſby, cum capellâ de Thorp, XVII li. de claro.

Stokton, XVII li. XVI ſ.

Evyngton, XVII li. de claro.

Clyfton, cum capellis, XLIII li.

Queniboro de claro, deduċtis è decimis XXVIII li. XIX ſ.

Capella de Stanton, de claro, VIII li.

Porta Occidentalis, deduċtis è decimis, blada decimalia IX li. v ſ.

---

[1] Charyte's Rentale, fol. clxx. b. clxxi. a.

[2] This total does not exactly agree with the particulars; but it is not eaſy to ſay which was the exaċt ſum intended to be reckoned, many of the ſums being additions or correċtions in the margin of the original.

47. Capelle

47. Capelle & firme, & refponfiones in granis, annis communibus, modernis diebus, anno Dñi MCCCCLXXVII [1].

Clifton.
Frumentum, IV quart', vel V.
Siligo, X quart', vel XI.
Ordeum, XXVII quart'.
Pife, XV quart'.
Avene, IIII quart', vel V.

Newton.
Frumentum, VI quart', vel VII.
Siligo, II vel III modios.
Ordeum, VII quart', vel VIII.
Pife, VII quart', vel VIII.
Avene, I quart',

Wover.
Frument', VII quart'.
Siligo, I quart'.
Ordeum, XXIIII quart'.
Pife, XXIIII quart'.
Avene, dim' quart'.

Lilburn.
Frumentum, V quart'.
Siligo, III quart'.
Ordeum, XXX quart'.
Pife, XX quart'.
Avene, VI quart'.

Brakley.
Frumentum, III vel IIII quart'.
Siligo, III quart'.
Ordeum, XXX quart'.
Pife, XX quart'.
Avene, dim' quart'.

Alfo.
Frumentum, III quart'.
Siligo, III vel IIII quart'.
Ordeum, XX quart'.
Pife, VI vel VII quart'.
Avene, IIII vel V quart'.

Scharnbroke.
Frumentum, V quart'.
Siligo, III quart'.
Ordeum, $\frac{XX}{IIII}$ quart', & XX vel $\frac{XX}{V}$.
Pife, II quart'.
Avene, II quart'.

Chesfham.
Frumentum, LX quart'.
Siligo, ...
Ordeum, V quart'.
Pife, II quart'.
Avene, XLV quart'.

Crudworth, Mynworth, Wygingyl.
Frumentum, I quart'.
Siligo, VIII quart'.
Ordeum, V quart'.
Pife, II quart'.
Avene, VIII quart'.

Stoĉton, de decimis.
Frumentum, VIII quart'.
Siligo, II quart'.
Ordeum, XXV quart'.
Pife, XXIIII quart'.
Avene, IIII quart'.

Stoĉton, de dominicis.
Frumentum, XVI quart'.
Siligo, III quart'.
Ordeum, $\frac{XX}{III}$ quart'.
Pife, $\frac{XX}{III}$ quart'.
Avene, II quart'.

Stanton.
Frumentum, III vel IIII quart'.
Siligo, I quart'.
Ordeum, XXIIII quart'.
Pife, XVI quart'.
Avene, X quart'.

Cofby.
Frumentum, VIII quart'.
Siligo, VI quart'.
Ordeum, $\frac{XX}{III}$ quart'.
Pife, XX quart'.
Avene, III quart'.

Hemyngton.
Frumentum, IIII quart'.
Siligo, VI quart'.
Ordeum, XXX quart'.
Pife, XX quart'.
Avene, V quart'.

Montforel.
Frumentum, VI mod'.
Siligo, VI mod'.
Ordeum, V quart'.
Pife, IIII quart'.
Avene, un' quart'.

Wodhows.
Frument', VI quart'; quondam X.
Siligo, un' quart'.
Ordeum, XII quart'.
Pife, XII quart'.
Avene, III quart'.

Brentby.
Frumentum, V quart'.
Siligo, I quart'.
Ordeum, XXX quart'.
Avene, V vel VI quart'.
Pife, XV quart'.

Thorp Ernolde.
Frumentum, XI vel XII quart'.
Siligo, II vel III quart'.
Ordeum, XX quart'.
Avene, I quart', vel II.
Pife, XXX quart'.

Eyton.
Frumentum, VI quart'.
Siligo, XXIIII quart'.
Ordeum, XVIII quart'.
Avene, III quart'.
Pife, VIII quart'.

Bulkyngton, cum membris.
Frumentum, III quart', vel IIII.
Siligo, III quart'.
Ordeum, XVI quart'.
Avene, IIII quart'.
Pife, XII quart'.

Brancot.
Frumentum, VII quart'.
Siligo, II quart'.
Ordeum, VII quart'.
Avene, II quart'.
Pife, IIII quart'.

Bernangul.
Frumentum, un' quart'.
Siligo, dim' quart'.
Ordeum, VII quart'.
Pife, IIII quart'.
Avene, IIII quart'.

Merfton.
Frumentum, II quart'.
Siligo, II quart'.
Ordeum, X X quart'.
Avene, IIII quart'.
Pife, VIII quart'.

Wefton.
Frumentum, un' quart', vel II.
Siligo, un' quart', vel II.
Ordeum, VII vel VIII quart'.
Avene, III quart'.
Pife, VI quart'.

Ryton.
Frumentum, un' quart'.
Siligo, un' quart', vel II.
Ordeum, III quart'.
Avene, III quart'.
Pife, VI quart'.

Summa frumenti X quart', vel XII.
Summa filiginis X quart', vel XI.
Summa ordei VI quart', vel VII.
Summa avenarum XX quart'.
Summa pifarum XL quart'.

Bagworth.
Frumentum, III quart', vel VI.
Siligo, II quart', vel III.
Ordeum, XVIII quart', vel XX.
Avene, III quart', vel IIII.
Pife, XVIII quart', vel XX.

Thornton.
Frumentum, III quart', vel VI.
Siligo, II quart', vel III.
Ordeum, XVIII quart', vel XX.
Avene, III quart', vel III.
Pife, XVIII quart', vel XX.

Bilfdon, de dominicis.
Frumentum, V quart'.
Siligo, I quart'.
Ordeum, XXVIII quart'.
Avene, I quart'.
Pife, XXX quart'.

Lokyngton, de dominicis.
Frumentum, V quart'.
Siligo, XX quart'.
Ordeum, XL quart'.
Avene, X quart'.
Pife, XXIIII quart'.

Mowfley.
Frumentum, X quart'.
Siligo, III quart'.
Ordeum, XXXV vel XL quart'.
Avene, un' quart', vel II.
Pife, XVI quart'.

Shepifhed, de dominicis.
Frumentum, VIII quart'.
Siligo, VI quart'.
Ordeum, XXXVI quart'.
Avene, un' quart', vel II.
Pife, XVI quart'.

Othorp.
Frumentum, VI quart'.
Siligo, XVIII quart'.
Ordeum, XVIII quart'.
Avene, II quart'.
Pife, XVI quart'.

Queniboro, de dominicis.
Frumentum, X quart'.
Siligo, XX quart'.
Ordeum, L quart'.
Pife, XXX quart'.
Avene, VI quart'.

Queniboro, de decimis.
Frumentum, X quart'.
Siligo, XX quart'.
Ordeum, XL quart'.
Pife, XL quart'.
Avene, II quart'.

Difworth.
Frumentum, II quart'.
Siligo, un' quart'.
Ordeum, XX quart'.
Avene, dim' quart'.
Pife, VIII vel IX quart'.

Evyngton.
Frumentum, VII quart'.
Siligo, II quart'.
Ordeum, XXVI quart'.
Pife, XXVI quart'.
Avene, I quart'.

. . . .
Frumentum, X quart'.
Siligo, XX quart'.
Ordeum, XXXIIII quart'.
Pife, XX quart'.
Avene, VI quart'.

Godby, Rolfton, Braunfton, Keyrby.
Frumentum, ... ⎫
Siligo, ... ⎪ *No entry.*
Ordeum, ... ⎬
Avene, ... ⎪
Pife, ... ⎭

[1] Charyte's Rentale, fol. clxxi. b. clxxii. a.

48. Capelle

48. Capelle & firme, & refponfiones earum in granis receptis circa annos Domini ut hìc fequitur.

Grangia Abbatis.

Anno Dñi M°ccc°xciii.	Anno Dñi M°ccc°xcix.	Anno Dñi M°cccc°i.	Anno Dñi M°ccccLxx°.
Frumentum, $\frac{xx}{iiii}$ & iiii quart'.	xviii quart'.	xxxii quart' & dim'.	L quart', $\frac{xx}{iii}$ vel $\frac{xx}{iiii}$.
Siligo, xLvi quart'.	xxv quart'.	xii quart'.	xv, xvi, vel xx quart'.
Ordeum, $\frac{xx}{viii}$ & viii quart'.	$\frac{xx}{vii}$ xv quart'.	$\frac{xx}{vi}$ & v quart'.	$\frac{xx}{viii}$ quart', $\frac{xx}{x}$, vel $\frac{xx}{xv}$.
Avene, xxxvi quart'.	xxiiii quart'.	viii quart'.	xvii quart', vel xviii.
Pife, $\frac{xx}{vi}$ & x quart'.	$\frac{xx}{iiii}$ & xix quart'.	$\frac{xx}{vi}$ & v quart'.	$\frac{xx}{vi}$ quart'.

Bagworth & Thornton.

Frumentum, xii quart'.	xvi quart'.	xi quart'.
Ordeum, Lxxii quart'.	$\frac{xx}{iii}$ v quart'.	L quart'.
Avene, vi quart'.	xii quart'.	xvi quart'.
Pife, Lx quart'.	L quart'.	Liii quart'.
Siligo, nil habet.	ii quart'.	ii quart'.

Barkby, de decimis tantùm.	De decimis & dominicis.	Barkby, de decimis.	
Frumentum, xvii quart'.	xxxi quart' & dim'.	xiii quart' & dim'.	xiii quart'.
Siligo, iiii quart' & dim'.	xxii quart'.	ix quart'.	xiiii quart'.
Ordeum, Lxvi quart'.	$\frac{xx}{iiii}$ xv quart'.	Lxvii quart'.	$\frac{xx}{iiii}$ quart' & x.
Avene, ...	xv quart'.	vi quart' & dim'.	xviii quart'.
Pife, xiii quart'.	xLi quart' & dim'.	xv quart'.	xL quart'.

Barkby, de dominicis.	De decimis & dominicis.	Barkby, de decimis.	Barkby, de dominicis.
Frumentum, ii quart'.	xxviii & dim' quart'.	xxxvi quart'.	xiiii quart'.
Siligo, iiii quart'.	xiiii quart'.	xxv quart'.	vi quart'.
Ordeum, xxvii quart'.	$\frac{xx}{vi}$ quart'.	$\frac{xx}{vii}$ vi quart'.	L quart'.
Avene, i quart'.		vi quart'.	iiii quart'.
Pife, xxxi quart'.		$\frac{xx}{v}$ xv quart'.	xxx quart'.

Baroo.		Baroo, de decimis.	
Frumentum, xv quart'.	xv quart'.	xv quart'.	Frument', viii quart', vel ix.
Ordeum, xxx quart'.	xL quart'.	xL quart'.	Siligo, un' quart', vel ii.
Pife, xv quart'.	xx quart'.	xx quart'.	Ordeum, xxxvi quart'.

Baroo, de dominicis.

Frumentum, vi quart'.
Siligo, iiii vel v quart'.
Ordeum, xL quart'.
Pife, xL quart'.
Avene, ii modii, vel iii.

Decima de Berwode.

Frumentum, iii quart'.	
Siligo, x quart'.	x quart'.
Ordeum, xi quart' & dim'.	ix quart'.
Avene, vi quart' & dim'.	iiii quart' & dim'.
Pife, iii quart'.	xix quart'.

Bytfwell.

Frumentum, xii quart'.	xii quart'.	vi quart'.
Siligo, ...	. . . .	iiii vel v quart'.
Ordeum, xxx quart'.	xxx quart'.	xL quart', vel xxi.
Pife, xii quart'.	xii quart'.	xx quart'.
Avene, ...	. . . .	iiii quart'.

Chefham. Refponfio granorum anno regni regis Hen. VI. xxiii°, ficut patet in computo Johis Dryfeld, firmarii ibidem; fcil' Lx quart' frumenti, xLix quart' ordei, Lxv quart' avenarum, un' quart' & dim' pifarum.

Eyton.

Siligo, xx quart'.	xxv quart'.	xx quart'.

Thorp Ernold, vel Erlfthorp, decima.			Thorp Ernold, decima.
Frumentum, xx quart'.	xxi quart'.	xx quart'.	xvii quart'.
Siligo, ...	. . . .	. . . .	v quart'.
Ordeum, xL quart'.	xLvi quart'.	Lii quart'.	xL quart'.
Avene, viii quart'.	xii quart'.	xii quart'.	iii quart'.
Pife, xxxii quart'.	xxxii quart'.	xxxii quart'.	xxxiii quart'.

Dominica.

Frumentum, xx quart'.
Siligo, ii quart'.
Ordeum, xx quart'.
Avene, i quart'.
Pife, xxx quart'.

Lokyngton,

Lokyngton, de decima.

Frumentum, xv quart'.	xvii quart'.	xii quart'.	iiii quart'.
Siligo, x quart'.	xiii quart' & dim'.	vii quart'.	viii quart'.
Ordeum, $\frac{xx}{v}$ xviii quart', dim'.	$\frac{xx}{iiii}$ xiii quart'.	vi quart' & dim'.	xliiii quart'.
Pife, lxiii quart', dim'.	xxiii quart'.	xxxi quart'.	xxiiii quart'.
Avene, ...	iiii quart' & dim'.	iii quart'.	iiii quart'.

Nunc, *Lokyngton* de dominicis, frumenti x quart', filiginis xx quart', ordei xl quart', pifarum xxiiii quart', avenarum x quart'.

Porta Auſtralis.

Frumentum, ii quart' & dim'.	iiii quart' & dim'.	ii quart'.	iii quart'.
Siligo, dim' quart'.	un' quart'.	un' quart'.	ii quart'.
Ordeum, l quart'.	xxxv quart'.	xxxiiii quart'.	xx quart'.
Avene, un' quart'.	un' quart'.	. . . .	un' quart'.
Pife, xxviii quart'.	xvi quart'.	xxxi quart' & dim'.	x quart'.

Porta Occidentalis.

Frumentum, xv quart'.	xi quart'.	x quart'.	xii quart'.
Siligo, xiii quart'.	xi quart'.	xviii quart'.	viii quart'.
Ordeum, $\frac{xx}{v}$ x quart'.	$\frac{xx}{iiii}$ xviii quart'.	$\frac{xx}{v}$ quart' & dim'.	l quart'.
Avene, viii quart' & dim'.	vii quart' & dim'.	xi quart'.	x quart'.
Pife, xxxviii quart'.	xliiii & dim'.	xxx quart'.	xl quart'.

Peccum. Midoplek, dominicis redd'.   Tolgrave, decima.

Frumentum, xxiii quart'.	xv quart'.	xxiii quart'.	v vel vi quart'.
Ordeum, xvii quart' & dim'.	xii quart' & dim'.	ix quart'.	ix vel x quart'.
Avene, $\frac{xx}{v}$ xiiii quart'.	lx quart'.	$\frac{xx}{iiii}$ i quart' & dim'.	vi vel vii quart'.
Pife, v quart'.	nil hoc anno.	xviii quart'.	

Queniboro.

Frumentum, x quart'.	x quart'.	xv quart'.	xi quart' vel x (modernis diebus.)
Siligo, xv quart'.	xv quart'.	xv quart'.	x quart', vel xx.
Ordeum, xl quart'.	xl quart'.	xl quart'.	xxxii quart', vel xxxiiii.
Pife, xxv quart'.	xxv quart'.	xx quart'.	xx quart'.
Avene, ...	. . . .	. . . .	vi quart'.

Querndon.

Frumentum, i quart' & dim'.	v quart'.	v quart'.	vi quart'.
Siligo, vii quart' & dim'.	xxiii quart'.	xxiii quart'	xv vel xvi quart'.
Ordeum, xxx quart'.	xxxv quart'.	xxxv quart'.	xxx quart'.
Pife, xxiiii quart'.	xxiii quart'.	xxvi quart'.	xv quart'.
Avene, nil.	iiii quart'.	iiii quart'.	xxx quart'.

Schepiſheyd.

Frumentum, iii quart'.	xxiii quart'.	xxiii quart'.	vi quart', vel vii.
Siligo, ii quart'.	. . . .	. . . .	v vel vi quart'.
Ordeum, $\frac{xx}{v}$ quart'.	lxvi quart'.	lxvi quart'.	xliiii quart'.
Avene, x quart'.	. . . .	. . . .	iiii quart'.
Pife, $\frac{xx}{iiii}$ quart'.	xxxi quart'.	. . . .	xxiiii quart'.

Stoĉton. de decimâ.   De dominicis eodem anno.   De decimis.   De dominicis.   De decimis.

Frumentum, viii quart'.	iiii quart'.	xi quart' & dim'.	xvi quart' & dim'.	vii quart'.
Siligo, i quart'.	xviii quart' & dim'.	liii quart'.	viii quart' & dim'.	ii quart'.
Ordeum, lxi quart' & dim'.	$\frac{xx}{vi}$ quart'.	xxvii quart'.	$\frac{xx}{v}$ ix quart' & dim'.	xxv quart'.
Pife, xxx quart'.	$\frac{xx}{iiii}$ & ii quart'.	iiii quart'.	xxix quart'.	xxvi quart'.
Avene, ...	. . . .	. . . .	. . . .	i quart'.

Stoĉton, de decimis & dominicis.   De dominicis.

Frumentum, xli quart'.	xxxiii quart' & dim'.	xxv quart' & dim'.	xvi quart'.
Siligo, viii quart'.	xiii quart' & dim'.	xix quart' & dim'.	iii quart'.
Ordeum, ccx quart'.	$\frac{xx}{vii}$ iiii quart'.	$\frac{xx}{viii}$ vi quart'.	$\frac{xx}{iii}$ quart'.
Avene, i quart' & dim'.	. . . .	ii quart'.	ii quart'.
Pife, de decimâ, i quart' & dim'.	$\frac{xx}{vii}$ xiiii quart'.	lxv quart'.	$\frac{xx}{iii}$ quart'.

Schorthaſuls, de firmario recept'.

Frumentum, ii quart'.	iiii quart'.	ii quart'.
Siligo, iii quart'.	ii quart' & dim'.	ii quart'.
Ordeum, vel drag', xi quart' & dim'.	iiii quart' & dim'.	iiii quart'.
Avene, i quart'.	ii quart'.	iiii quart'.
Pife, iii quart'.	viii quart'.	x quart'.

Thedyngworth,

Thedyngworth.

Frumentum, XLIII quart' & dim'.	XIII quart'.	XXII quart'.	XVIII quart'.
Siligo, IIII quart'.	VII quart'.	. . . .	I quart' & dim'.
Ordeum, XLVII quart' & dim'.	XXVI quart'.	LXVIII quart'.	LIIII quart'.
Avene, ...	I quart'.	. . . .	I quart'.
Pife, I taff'.	IIII quart' & dim'.	XXVIII quart'.	$\overset{xx}{III}$ quart'.

Thurnby & Bufby.

Frumentum, x quart'.	XIII quart' & dim'.	VI quart'.	VIII quart'.
Ordeum, XLIII quart'.	LI quart'.	XXIV quart'.	XXX quart'.
Pife, XXXV quart'.	LVIII quart'.	LIV quart'.	XXII quart'.
Siligo, ...	Dim' quart'.	Dim' quart'.	III quart'.
Avene, ...	. . . .	I quart'.	II quart'.

Whefton.

Frumentum, x quart'.	VIII quart'.	VIII quart'.	x quart'.
Siligo, IV quart'.	II quart'.	II quart'.	VIII quart'.
Ordeum, XXXIV quart'.	XXX quart'.	XXX quart'.	$\overset{xx}{IIII}$ quart'.
Pife, x quart'.	Pife expenduntur per bidentes; ideo nil habet.	x quart'.	XXX quart'.
Avene, ...		. . . .	VIII quart'.

Billefdon.

Frumentum, XXII quart'.	XXII quart'.	xx quart'.	VII quart'.
Ordeum, XXXII quart'.	XXXII quart'.	XXXII quart'.	XXXVI quart'.
Avene, VIII quart'.	VIII quart'.	VIII quart'.	II quart'.
Pife, VIII quart'.	VIII quart'.	VIII quart'.	XXX quart'.
Siligo, ...	. . . .	. . . .	II quart'.

Endurby.

Frumentum, IIII quart' & dim'.	IIII quart' & dim'.	III quart'.	XII quart'.
Siligo, II quart'.	II quart' & dim'.	II quart'.	VIII quart'.
Ordeum, XL quart' & dim'.	XLVI quart' & dim'.	XXXIII quart' & dim'.	XL quart'.
Pife, LXIIII quart'.	XXXVII quart'.	LXVIII quart'.	XXX quart'.
Avene, nil.	III quart'.	II quart'.	v quart'.

Horfpoll.

Frumentum, III quart'.	III quart'.	III quart'.	
Ordeum, VIII quart'.	VIII quart'.	VIII quart'.	
Avene, v quart'.	v quart'.	v quart'.	
Pife, III quart'.	III quart'.	III quart'.	

Humburfton.

Frumentum, XII quart'.	IX quart'.	VII quart' & dim'.	XVI quart'.
Ordeum, XL quart' & dim'.	LII quart'.	XXI quart'.	XXXIIII vel XL quart'.
Siligo, nil.	II quart'.	I eftr'.	III quart'.
Avene, I quart'.	II quart' & dim'.	Nil.	II vel III quart'.
Pife, XLVII quart'.	XLIII quart'.	L quart' & dim'.	XXXIII vel XL quart'.

Hungarton.

Frumentum, XXI quart'.	L quart' & dim'.	xv quart' & dim'.	XVI quart'.
Ordeum, XLI quart' & dim'.	XLIX quart'.	XXXIIII quart' & dim'.	XXXIIII quart'.
Pife, $\overset{xx}{v}$ IIII quart'.	XXXIIII quart'.	XL quart'.	XXXVI quart'.
Avene, nil.	Nil.	IIII quart'.	II vel III quart'.

Ingwarby.

Frumentum, XL quart'.	XXI quart'.	XVIII quart' & dim'.	XXX quart'.
Siligo, nil.	Nil.	III quart'.	III quart'.
Ordeum, LII quart'.	L quart'.	LV quart'.	$\overset{xx}{III}$ x quart'.
Avene, nil.	v quart'.	IIII quart' & dim'.	IIII quart'.
Pife, LXII quart' & dim'.	XLV quart'.	XLIIII quart' & dim'.	XL quart'.

Summa omnium rec' quart' frumenti, rec' anno M°CCC, LXIII; pret' unius quart' VI s. VIII d.
Summa omnium quart' filiginis XXVIII; pret' unius quart' IIIs. IIII d.
Summa omnium quart' ordei hoc anno mil' LI quart'.
Summa omnium quart' avenarum LIIII.
Summa omnium quart' pifarum CCCXV.
Summa omnium bladorum mil' VCCCXLIIII quart' prediĉlo anno.
Summa argenti diĉlorum bladorum, CC$\overset{xx}{IIII}$xVIII li. VIII s. IIII d. ob.
Summa omnium bladorum rec' anno Domini M°CCC nonagefimo IIII°, CXXII quart'.
Summa totalis expenf' hoc anno III mil' VCC XXV quart'.
Mem', de XVIII quart' & dim' frumenti rec' hoc anno à molendino de Belgrave, & de II quart' & dim' de bladis mixtis, & de VIII quart' de brafio.
Summa omnium quart' bladorum mixtorum rec' de molendino de Belgrave hoc anno XXXI quart' & dim'.

49. " Habemus

49. " Habemus in *Evyngton* ecclefiam & rectoriam in proprios ufus, cum decimis garbarum & feni, &c. ex dono Arnoldi de Bofco & Jordani de Humeth, & ex confirmatione regis Henrici II. ut patet in matriculo, in hiis verbis:

' Ecclefie de Evyngton patronus abbas Leyc', habens eam in proprios ufus ex conceffione H. nunc epi Linc'. Vicarius Wittus capellanus, inftitutus, &c. percipiens nomine vicarie fue omnes proventus altaris & redditum terre pertinentes ad ecclefiam, & decimam bladi de unâ carucatâ terre. Monachi Sci Ebrulfi percipiunt duas partes decimarum garbarum [fcil', de IIII acris terre, ficut patet in extentis manerii de Evyngton], ex dono Johis de Humet;' unde folvimus ei annuatim XLVI ş. VIII đ."

Decima garbarum reddebat XVII li. modò IIII li. X ş.

Habemus ibidem, pro decimâ feni de villatâ de Evyngton, X ş. per annum; fcil', de quâlibet virgatâ terre VI đ.

Summa virgatarum terre XX; fumma denariorum X ş.

Mem', quòd folebamus habere XX ş. per annum, & decimas pafture trium claufarum in campis ibidem; quarum una modò eft in tenurâ Petri Yrmogyar de Leyc'; & redd' đno de Grey V li; nobis pro decimâ VI ş VIII đ. & vicario III ş. IIII đ. Alia eft in tenurâ Roberti Schedingham; & redd' đno IIII li. & nobis pro decimâ nil. Alia eft in tenurâ Rici Watts; & reddit đno LX ş. & nobis pro decimâ nil. Ideò confulendum eft cum confilio dicti abbatis.

Habemus ibidem decimam molendini ventritici & aquatici đni Grey de Evyngton.

Habemus ibidem IIII ş. per annum, homagium & relevium, de heredibus Ricardi Hotoft de Humberfton, pro unâ virgatâ terre & quâdam parte tofti, quas nos dedimus, & per cartam noftram confirmavimus, Alano de Lindifeiâ pro homagio & fervicio fuo, quondam in tenurâ Johis Evyngton, poftea Radulphi Brafyar de Leyc'. Et dicta placea tofti extendit fe à tofto quod fuit Rogeri Wolf in longitudine XII perticas ufque orientem, & in latitudine octo perticas.

Mem', quòd abbas & conventus Leyc' concefferunt Johi de Humet & heredibus, quòd clericum ydoneum quem nobis prefentabunt in fratrem & canonicum recipiemus.

Habemus, de domino de Evyngton, pro decimâ dominicarum pratorum fuorum, IIII pecias prati, videlicet, inter parcum & villam de Evyngton ex parte boreali gurgitis ibidem; & II pecias prati ex parte auftrali dicti gurgitis inter parcum & villam predict'; IIII pecias prati ex parte occidentali parci ab Evyngton inter parcum & Leyceftr' ex parte boreali dicti gurgitis.

Item habemus in perpetuum unam placeam prati ex parte orientali gurgitis vocati Evyngton-brook, que quidem placea prati vocatur Jenkynnes Pafture, que quidem paftura tenebit in latitudine in fine auftrali juxta gutturam ufque borealem VIII perticas, quarum quelibet pertica tenebit in certo VIII pedes in ftandardum; que quidem paftura affignatur abbati & fucceflforibus fuis in perpetuum pro decimâ pratorum predicti Johannis de Evyngton.

Item habemus de đno Grey de Evyngton in perpetuum XXII perticatas, quarum quelibet pertica continet VIII pedes; apud Gondonfty VI perticas infimul jacentes, & III perticas infimul jacentes, & alias III perticas infimul in le Netherfty, & IIII perticas apud Golbdonfty-ford ex utrâque parte le forth, & II perticas abutt' fuper eandem forth, IIII perticas in le Hetherfty defuper vallum predictum.

Mem', quòd cùm queftio vertebatur inter abbatem Leyc' & W. vicarium de Evyngton, fuper decimis provenientibus de molendino de eâdem, lis in hoc modum conquievit, videlicet, quòd dominus W. vicarius renunciaverit in jure coram prioribus de Nehnham & Caldewell, & decano Bedford', omni juri fuo, fi quod habuerit, vel habere potuit, pro capiend' decimas de dicto molendino, &c. [1]

50. Ecclefie de *Foxton* patronus prior de Daventr'. Habemus eam in proprios ufus, ficut patet in matriculo epifcopi.

Habemus in Foxton II bovatas terre ex dono Roberti Côtes & Helewyfe uxoris ejus, & ex confirmatione regis Henrici II.

Inde dedimus, & per cartam noftram confirmavimus, Rogero filio Ade de Foxton, & heredibus fuis, pro homagio & fervicio fuo, unam dimidiam bovatam terre, excepto tofto, reddendo nobis annuatim XVIII đ. Sed utrùm feoffavimus aliquem vel aliquos in alterâ bovatâ & dimidiâ predict', non habemus in fcriptis. Et apparet per Rentalia, quòd quidam Ada de Sadyngton & Rogerus Heron habuerunt feoffamenta ñra, quòd multis annis occupaverint dict' bovatam & dimidiam terre, reddend' nobis III ş. per annum; & quo titulo occupaverint jam nefcimus.

Ricardus Tolyns nobis reddit II ş. VI đ. ficut patet per cartas fuas proprias, demonftratas fratri W. Charyte & Willo Lylle de Leyc', in abbathiâ de Leyc', Sabbato ante feftum Sci Auguftini Anglorum, anno regni regis Henrici VII. XV° [2].

51. *Flekney* capella de Wefton eft, habens capellanum refidentem, & folvit fynodalia, & habet omnia integra parochialia, ut matrix ecclefia, ficut patet in matriculo epifcopi.

Habemus in Flekney III meffuagia, III virgatas terre, cum pertinentiis fuis, ex dono & confirmatione Willi de Afton & Roberti of the All, que ipfi habuerunt ex dono & feoffamento Roberti filii Willi de Mowfley, prius habitâ licentiâ đni regis Edwardi Tertii & aliorum quorum intereft.

Habemus ibidem fitum cujufdam molendini ventritici, cum toto circuitu dicti molendini, ex quietâ clamatione đni Johis rectoris ecclefie de Wylughby. Willis Ruffel tenet I meff', unum croftum magnum, & III virgatas terre, & reddit XXX ş. & fectam curie ad Stanton [3].

52. Secundùm matriculum epifcopi, ecclefie de *Langeton* patronus eft abbas Leyc'; perfona G. nepos quondam legati, inftitutus per eundem; & habet capellas Thorp & Thyrlington, habentes capellanos refidentes per matricem ecclefiam. Idem abbas percipit de eâdem ecclefiâ dimid' marc' ab antiquo. Item habet capellam Langeton, que confuevit deferviri III diebus in ebdomatâ per matricem ecclefiam. Monachi Sci Ebrulfi percipiunt ibi duas partes decimarum garbarum de dominico H. de Breybrok & Rofti de Langton.

Habemus ecclefiam de Langetonâ, cum terris, decimis, & omnibus pertinentiis fuis, &c. ex dono Willi de Novo Mercato, & cum affenfu domini fui Roberti comitis Leyc'.

Habemus confirmationem & ratificationem Roberti comitis Leyc'.

Habemus confirmationem & ratificationem Roberti comitis Leyc' de donatione ecclefie de Langetonâ, quam fecit nobis Willis de Novo Mercato, & poftea Regin' de Berdon'.

Habemus confirmationem & conceffionem Criftine filie Gore, de donatione ecclefie de Langtonâ, quam W. de Novo Mercato, avus fuus, nobis fecit; unde firmitèr conftituit, ut nos teneremus & poffideremus dictam ecclefiam, cum omnibus libertatibus & pertinentiis fuis.

Habemus confirmationem Hugonis epi Linc', de ecclefiâ Langtone, ficut predeceffor fuus Robertus eps figilli atteftatione confirmavit.

Habemus advocationem ex dono Willi de Novo Mercato, & ex confirmatione fundatoris noftri. Et recepimus de rectore ibidem VI ş. VIII đ. per annum nomine penfionis.

Nota placitum inter antiqua placita, que funt in Rentali Geryn, pro advocatione ecclefie de Langeton.

Teftimonium magiftri Rogeri Rolvift' de VI ş. VIII đ. pro annuâ penfione ecclefie de Langton [4].

53. Ecclefie de *Lawton* patronus comes Wyntonie. Monachi Sci Ebrulfi percipiunt II partes decimarum garbarum de dominicis Thome Malefme. Modò Gregorii de Formue, & G. de Graunforde.

Habemus, ex dono, conceffione, & confirmatione, Willi Ken & Roberti of the All, omnia tenementa,

[1] Charyte's Rentale, fol. lvii. a, b.
[3] Ibid. fol. lviii. b.
[2] Ibid. fol. lviii. b. lix. a.
[4] Ibid. fol. lxxxv. b.

redditus, proviſiones, & ſervicia, cum pertinentiis ſuis, in villis de Lawton, Mouſeley,, Flekney, & Knaptoft, p̄t' excepta ; que quidem terras & tenementa, redditus, &c. ipſi habuerunt ex dono & feoffamento Roberti filii Willi de Mouſeley ; habend' & tenend', &c. ut in cartâ xvᵃ apud Mowſley.—Mem', quòd Edwardus Tertius, rex Anglie, dedit licentiam magiſtro Willo Ken & Robto of the Hall, quòd ipſi poſſint omnia terras, tenementa, redditus, reverſiones, & ſervicia ſua, cum pertin' ſuis, in villis de Lawton, Mowſley, Flekney, & Knaptoft, exceptis pre-exceptis, affirmare abbati & conventui de Leyc'.

Mem', quòd dñs Joĥes de Ver, comes Oxon', capitalis dñs de Lawton, dedit licentiam Willo de Aſton & Roberto of the Halle, quòd ipſi poſſint aſſignare abbati & conventui Leyc' x meſſ', x virgat' terre, unum molendinum, cum pertinentiis ſuis, in Lawton, que de ipſo tenentur, & que dicti W. & Robertus habuerunt ex dono & feoffamento Roberti de Moſeley, &c. ſalvo ſibi & heredibus ſuis rationabili relevio xx s. poſt mortem vel ceſſionem cujuſlibet abbatis [1].

55. Secundùm matriculum ep̄i, patronus ecclefie de *Nowſley* abbas Sci Ebrulfi.

Habemus in Nowſley, ex dono Willi de Martival, & cum aſſenſu Roberti comitis Leyc', quod in preſentiâ ejus factum fuit, duas virgatas terre. Confirmatur per Henricum VII. & Henricum VIII.

Mem', quòd cùm Radus de Martiwaſt & Sara uxor Ricardi filii ſui debent canonicis regularibus Leyc' xIIII marc', & infra ſtatutum terminum eis reddere non potuerunt, dederunt eiſdem canonicis duas virgatas terre in Nowſley.

Willus Syſſon tenet ibi unum tenementum, unum toftum, & duas virgatas terre ; & reddit xIIII s. & III gallinas, & ſectam curie de Stowton, & commune fyne vIIId.—Solebat tenens ibi dare I panem ad natale Domini, & auxilium [2].

56. Eccleſie de *Scraptoft* patronus prior Coventrie ; perſona Petrus inſtitutus per W. quondam Linc' ep̄m, ſolvens priori I marc' annuatim. Idem prior retinet decimas de dominico ſuo ibidem ab antiquo.

Habemus de eccleſiâ de Scraptoft, que quondam fuit capella de Humburſton, per manus prioris de Coventr', per viam compoſitionis inter ipſum & nos, annuatim x s.—Habemus ab eodem priore de Coventre, pro capellis de Schelton & Anſty, que quondam pertinebant ad matricem eccleſiam de Bulkinton, ſicut patet in cartâ Sci Thome Cantuar' archiepiſcopi, ſcilicet per viam compoſitionis, x s.

Mem', quòd in cauſâ que vertebatur inter nos & priorem de Coventre & ejuſdem loci conventum ſuper eccleſiâ de Scraptoft, & de capellis de Anſty & Schelton, hoc modo communi aſſenſu & amicabili concordiâ compoſitum eſt ; videlicet, quòd nos relinqueremus totum jus quod habuimus in predictis eccleſiâ & capellis. Et ſic habemus annuatim x s. de eccleſiâ de Scraptoft, & x s. pro capellâ de Schelton ; ſumma xx s. quos quidem xx s. magiſter fabrice abbathie Leyc' percipit, & in perpetuum percipiet, apud Scraptoft, per manum prioris & conventûs de Coventr' qui pro tempore fuerint, ad duos anni terminos, ſcil' ad feſt' Paſche & Michaelis equaliter [3].

57. Habemus in *Stoke*, ex dono Roberti de Craft, & confirmatione Amicie de Sapcote & Roberti de Campaniâ militis, unam carucatam terre, cum omnibus pertinentiis ſuis, in eſcambium pro molendino de Sapcote, quod predictus Robertus de Craft nobis antea dedit. Et mem', quòd quidam Willus de Stoke implacitavit nos de totâ dictâ carucatâ terre, cum pertin'. Et pro quietâ clamatione trium virgatarum de predictâ carucatâ terre dedimus ei quartam, pro homagio & ſervicio ſuo, reddend' nobis annuatim xvIIId. Et jam reddit nobis annuatim II s. Et jam eſt tā. Cùm quidam J. Low, qui dictam virgatam terre perquiſivit, caſu, ex defectu ejus & negligentiâ, totum tenementum noſtrum incendio ignis ibidem deſtructum fuit, ipſo Joĥe non habente unde nobis recompenſaret, obligavit ſe & heredes ſuos, ut patet in cartâ, ad augmentand' antiquum redditum (ſcil' xvIIId.) plus

annuatim per vId. Et ſic jam reddit II s.—Joĥes Lowe tenet unum meſſuagium, unam virgatam terre liberè, quondam Robti Stoke ; & redd' II s. & fect' hominum.

Willus Horne tenet I meſſ', unum croftum, III virgatas terre, & redd' xxvII s. ſectam curie, cōe fyn ; & veniet ad viſum franc' nr̄m de Bulkyngton, & ſolvet ad cōe fyn xII d.

Habemus ibi viſum franc', ſicut patet per inquiſitionem quandam in Chartwary, in tenurâ fratris Willi Charyte.

Mem', quòd heredes W. Baſſet de Sapcote & heredes Hugonis de Campaniâ defendent tenentes nunc manentes in duabus carucatis terre in Stoke & Sutton de feodo ſuo ab omni forinſeco ſervicio, ſicut patet in cartâ vel feoffamento [4].

58. *Kylby* eſt de parochiâ eccleſie de *Wyſtow*, ſicut ſcribitur in matriculo epiſcopi.

Habemus in Kylby, ex dono W. de Kylby, ad perpetuam firmam, unam virgatam terre, ſcil' illam virgatam terre quam Ecbetha vidua tenuit, cum tofto ad eandem virgatam pertinente, & cum medietate tofti unius quam prefato tofto accrevit juxta illud ad partem occidentem ; & quatuor acras terre quas eis accrevit de dominico ſuo, duabus ſcil' ſuper Hon & duabus contra Loundinſes, cum prato quod vocatur Inſula atantron, &c.

Habemus ibidem, ex dono Willi de Kyleby, & ex confirmatione regis Henrici II. &c. III virgatas terre, quarum duas Hugo Preſbiter tenuit, & unam quam Edwardus Preſbiter tenuit ; ſcil' illam quam Editha vidua tenuit, cum tofto ad eandem virgatam pertinente, & cum medietate tofti unius.

Habemus ibi, ex dono Willi de Kylby, unam acram terre in campis de Kylby, cum pertinentiis, que vocatur Forland, & dimidiam acram in Turnedale, & II rodas in Forte Medwe.

Habemus, ex dono Elie fratris W. de Kilby, dimidiam acram terre, cum pertinentiis, in campo de Kylby, que jacet in Turnedale, juxta culturam dñi.

Mem', quòd Willus de Kyleby conceſſit per cartam ſuam, quòd haya ſua de Kyleby in tres divideretur, ſalvâ culturâ in Haleburgh, & una pars ſibi remaneret, & heredibus ſuis, ad paſcend' averia ſua ; due alie partes remanerent Roberto filio Edwardi & heredibus ſuis, & ceteris hominibus abbatis ejuſdem ville, & hominibus ſuis de Kyleby, ad paſcenda averia ſua. Et in iſtâ cartâ vel compoſitione idem W. dedit predicto Roberto & heredibus ſuis, cum aſſenſu abbatis, I rodam in toftis juxta Hamelandam ejuſdem Roberti, & dim' rodam de dominico ſuo ſuper Malne, in eſcambium pro prato ejuſdem Roberti in Abbethurme & Gutulmeſholm, &c.

Habemus confirmationem iſtius carte per Robertum filium Thome de Maydewel, & confirmationem illius carte per Elizabetham & Leciam filias Roberti clerici de Kyleby ; ſed ubi in primâ cartâ non habentur niſi IIII acre, ipſi habent vI acras.

Habemus quietam clamationem Ricardi filii Willi clerici de Kyleby de toto jure ſuo & clameo quod habuit in duabus virgatis terre in Kyleby, & duobus toftis, ſcil' adjacentibus juxta toftum Radulphi Doleman, cum pratis, paſcuis, &c. exceptis tribus acris terre, & unâ rodâ prati in Barkykhul, & paſturâ unius bovis, & unâ placiâ, &c. quas pater ſuus dedit Elene ſorori ſue pro unâ acu annui redditûs.

Habemus ibi, ex dono predicti Ricardi, ſervitium unius acûs redditûs, quam Elena ſibi reddere conſuevit pro tribus acris terre & I rodâ.

Willus Watt⁹ tenet I meſſuagium, III virgatas terre, I croftum. Reddit xxx s. ſectam curie ad Stoughton. Et habemus ibi weyfe & ſtreyfe, &c.

Mem', quòd nos feoffavimus Robertum filium Edwardi de Kyleby & heredes ſuos in unâ virgatâ terre in Kyleby, cum pertinentiis, &c. Reddit nobis annuatim II s. vIIId. pro omni ſervitio, &c. ut in cartâ lxxxIx inter cartas feoffamentorum Kyrkeb'.

Mem', quòd preceptum fuit ſeiſire in manus domini quandam peciam terre vocat' The Beak, quam magiſter de Saynſdewe tenet per ſervitium ad inveniend' unum capellanum ibidem quotidie celebrare, & per ſervitium xIId. annui redditûs, &c. ut in rotulo curiali, cujus dat' eſt anno regni Ricardi regis xᵒ [5].

[1] Charyte's Rentale, fol. lxxxv. b. lxxvi. a.   [2] Ibid. fol. cxiii. a.   [3] Ibid. fol. cxxviii. b.   [4] Ibid. fol. cxxxi.   [5] Ibid fol. lxviii. b.

59. Collectanea ad ecclesiam de Thurneby & capellam de Stoughton in agro Leyceftrenfi fpectantia, ex Rentali Novo Generali à Gulielmo Charitee confecto, et in Bibliothecâ Bodleianâ adfervato, in gratiam domini Georgii Beaumont, baronetti, à Thomâ Hearne, A. M. fideliter excerpta ac defcripta, xı° kal. Sextileis, cıↃↃ ᴅ ᴄᴄ ᴠ ᴠ ıııı°. [1]

Thurnby. Habemus ibidem ecclefiam & rectoriam, cum decimis garbarum & feni, lini & canabi, in proprios ufus, ex dono Radulphi Pincerne, & ex confirmatione regis Henrici II. &c. & confirmatione fundatoris noftri, cum capellâ de Stowton, cum terrâ fubfcriptâ ; que quidem terra pertinet ad ecclefiam. Unde matriculus epifcopi : " Ecclefie de Thurnby patronus abbas Leiceftrie, habens eam in proprios ufus ab antiquo ; & habet capellam Stowton, habentem capellanum refidentem per matricem ecclefiam. Vicarius inftitutus per H. epifcopum Linc'." Et folvit nobis annuatim xxx folidos nomine penfionis [2], ficut patet in ordinatione factâ per Hugonem fecundum ecclefie Linc' epifcopum, in hiis verbis : " Vicarius de Thurnby habebit totum altaragium, nomine vicarie fue, in eâdem ; & folvet abbati & conventui Leyc' xxx folidos per annum. Refpondebit etiam de fynodalibus ; & habebit etiam focium capellanum." Et memorandum, quòd ifta penfio xxx folidorum recuperata fuit coram judice ordinario, die Sabbati proximo poft feftum fancte Agathe Virginis, a° Dñi ᴍᴄᴄʟııı°.

Tenentes ad voluntatem.

Johannes Whyth tenet 1 meffuagium, 1 croftum, 11 virgatas terre ; & reddit xxıı folidos, ıııı gallinas, & 11 gallos.

Willielmus Palmer tenet 1 meffuagium & 1 virgatam terre ; & reddit xı ʃ. ıı gallinas, & 1 gallum.

Thomas Palmer tenet 1 meffuagium, 1 croftum, 11 virgatas terre ; & reddit xx ʃ. ıııı gallinas, & 11 gallos.

Habemus ibidem orreum xl ı̄. cum orto quod vocatur Barnyarde ; in propriis manibus eft.

Summa virgatarum terre v. Summa redditûs ʟııı folidi, x galline, & v galli.

Omnes tenentes noftri de Thurnby debent venire ad vifum francum noftrum de Stocton ; & folvunt ad commune fyn xıı ᵭ. Et omnes facient finem cum domino abbate in ingreffu tenementorum fuorum eo modo quo poterunt convenire.

Require confuetudines tenentium in fine libri.

Habemus ibi weyfe & ftreyf.

Habemus ibidem decimam garbarum & feni, que reddunt inter grana ; fed fenum cariatur ad grangiam de Stowton ; & quandoque venditur pro ııı ʃ. ıııı ᵭ. quod non plus valet.

Habemus ibidem unum pratum vocatum Thurnby Grene, affignatum nobis pro decimâ feni. Ac etiam omnes tenentes de Thurnby ex antiquo folebant reddere nobis 11 ʃ. pro decimâ feni ultra pratum predictum. Et memorandum, quòd, licèt ex antiquo folebat reddi decima garbarum in villis de Thurnby & Bufby ad oftia orreorum, tamen modò concedunt, pro fe & fuis in perpetuum, pro confuetudine, reddere totam decimam garbarum in campis fuper terris in tenuris fuis.

Summa totalis, ʟᴠıı ʃ. x galline, & v galli.

Refolutiones ; fcilicet,

Archidiacono Leyc', pro procuratione, ᴠıı ʃ. ᴠı ᵭ. ob. q̄.

Vicario ibidem ıııı marc' in pecuniâ ; & in granis ad voluntatem noftram ultra penfionem xxx ʃ. quam nobis annuatim reddere folebat.

Decima refpondet xıııı lı̄. ; modò ᴠı lı̄. xıııı ʃ. ıııı ᵭ. in granis [3].

Item in eâdem cartâ [originali *Fundator nofter*] confirmat omnes donationes quas homines totius terre fue nobis fecerunt ; fcilicet, ecclefiam de Thurnby, ex dono Radulphi Pincerne, cum terris, decimis, &c. [4]

Habemus confirmationem Edwardi III. de omnibus poffeffionibus noftris, & hoc nominatìm per propria vocabula, cum claufulâ licet, ut patet per cartam fuam ; per quam cartam conceffit nobis habere warennam in omnibus dominicis terris noftris de Leyceftriâ, Stocton, & Thurmafton, &c. [5]

Stocton [6]. Habemus capellam in Stocton, ex dono Radulphi Pincerne, & ex confirmatione regis Henrici II. &c. cum confirmatione fundatoris noftri, pertinentem ad matricem ecclefiam de Thurnby. Et debet habere capellanum refidentem. Et nos habemus decimam garbarum & feni ; fed monachi Sci Ebrulfi percipiunt duas partes garbarum ex antiquo, ficut patet in matriculo epifcopi in hiis verbis : " Ecclefie de Thurnby patronus abbas Leyc', & habet capellam Stocton, habentem capellanum refidentem per matricem ecclefiam. Monachi Sci Ebrulfi percipiunt ibi duas partes decimarum garbarum de dominico abbatis Leyc' & Johannis Friday," &c. pro quibus nos jam folvimus annuatim priori de Schene xxxıı ʃ. ıııı ᵭ.

Decima garbarum reddit inter grana.

Habemus ibidem pro decimâ feni xıııı ʃ. per annum ; fed, fecundùm antiqua Rentalia, habebamus pro decimâ feni totum Bromhill, quod continet xıı acras ; nunc dividitur inter tenentes noftros. Et memorandum, quòd quelibet virgata terre in Stowton reddit pro decimâ feni ıııı ᵭ.

Summa virgatarum xʟıı. Summa denariorum xıııı ʃ.

Habemus ibidem decimam de molendinis, fcilicet ventritico & equino, fcilicet 11 folidos.

Tenores cartarum fundatoris noftri & aliorum benefactorum noftrorum in Stowton.

Habemus totam Stoctonam, ex dono fundatoris noftri, & ex confirmatione regis Henrici II. cum corpore fuo, preter feodum Radulphi Friday, & terram quam idem Radulphus calumniatur in câdem villâ, quam (fcilicet villam) dedit nobis eodem die quo habitum noftre religionis fumpfit, ut patet in cartâ fuâ primâ de Stoctonâ.

Habemus ibi, ex dono Rogeri Hufbond de Stocton, 11 acras terre in efcambium pro aliis certis terris noftris quas nos dedimus ei, ut patet in cartâ noftrâ.

Memorandum, quòd parochiani de Stocton moverunt materiam contra vicarium de Thurnby in curiâ de Stanforth pro exibicione unius diaconi in ecclefiâ de Stocton ; pro quâ materiâ data eft fententia diffinitiva contra predictos parochianos in curiâ de arcubus Londonie, prout, patet in compotis fratris Johannis Ratclif fexto & feptimo.

Habemus ibidem, per conventionem factam inter nos & Radulphum Friday & homines fuos, ᴠı acras & dimidiam, cum prato in duabus culturis que vocantur Helmpittis Furlong & les longas Rodas, in efcambium pro ᴠı acris & dimidiâ, cum prato de dominico noftro versùs meridiem, fub villâ de Stocton juxta viam, &c. ut in conventione in fecundo libro Chartwary.

Habemus ibi, ex dono Radulphi Friday, quatuor feliones jacentes inter vivarium noftrum & regiam viam que ducit de Stretton apud Leyceftriam ex auftrali parte dicti vivarii, in efcambium pro v felionibus terre noftre fuper Broc-furlong, fimiliter jacentibus, &c. ut in cartâ fecundi libri Chartwary, & inter feoffamenta.

Memorandum, quòd prefentatum fuit in curiâ dñi abbatis, tentâ apud Stowton, v° die Octobris, anno regni Henrici Quinti ᴠıı°, quòd Johannes Hotoft, armiger, tenet 1 meffuagium & 1 virgatam terre in Stowton, que perquifivit de Margaretâ Derlynge, que reddunt abbati Leyc' v folidos per annum. Item quòd tenet 1 meffuagium & ᴠııı acras terre, que perquifivit à Thomâ Burton, que reddunt ııı ʃ. per annum. Item quòd idem Johannes tenet ıııı acras terre, quas perquifivit de Thomâ Hankoc, & reddunt xᴠı ᵭ. quadrantem. Et quòd idem Johannes Hotoft, Robertus Tyllot, & Johanna [7] Zarowdale, tenent conjunctìm 1 meffuagium & [8] v virgatas terre in Stowton ; que quidem meffuagium & terra nuper fuerunt

---

[1] Thefe extracts, as far as relate to Thurnby and Stoughton, are here given from the MS. of Mr. Hearne, who had carefully digefted it under the title, and for the purpofe, above expreffed, and with the fhort prefatory notice already printed in p. 53.

[2] " Nota taxationem decimarum & fententias diffinitivas pro primâ penfione," in margine, eâdem manu, fed diffimili atramento. T. H.   [3] Charyte's Rentale, fol. cxli. b.   [4] Ibid. fol. ii. a.

[5] Ibid. fol. v. b.   [6] Ibid. fol. cxxxi. b. & feqq.   [7] Vel Yarowdale.

[8] Imprimis fuit ᴠıı ; fed literas numerales ıı eadem, ut videtur, erafit manus. T. H.

Thoma

Thome Fryday, &, poft deceffum fuum, Amicie uxoris fue, &c.; poft cujus obitum dicta meffuagium & terra particulariter acciderunt jure hereditario Magote, Amicie, & Johanne, filiabus predictorum Thome Friday & Amicie uxoris ejus. Et predicta Magota cepit in virum quendam Thomam Newman. Et predicta Amicia cepit in virum quendam Thomam Hanford. Et predicta Johanna cepit in virum quendam Robertum Zarowdale. Que quidem filie coheredes funt predictorum meffuagii & terrarum; que quidem meffuagium & terra reddere folebant 11ṡ. ficut patet in finali concordiâ. Et etiam dicta meffuagium & terra debent fectam curie de Stowton de tribus feptimanis in tres feptimanas, ex conceffione Radulphi Fryday, antecefforis predicti Thome Fryday, ficut patet in Rotulis de Pyn & Geryn, & in Rotulis de Habemus [1]; & facit homagium, ficut patet in tribus Rotulis de Habemus [1]. Et memorandum, quòd Radulphus Fryday, & heredes fui poft eum, tenuerunt v virgatas terre, viii toftos, per fervicium 11ṡ. per annum de abbate Leyc', ficut patet in finali concordiâ, fi benè & clarè intelligatur. Et Robertus comes, fundator nofter, dedit ei v virgatas terre in Stocton, cum toftis fuis, ficut patet in cartâ fuâ; & debet fectam pro eis, ut patet fuprâ.

Habemus ibidem duo tofta & vi acras terre, cum pertinentiis, quondam Johannis Brafyar, recuperata per breve de Ceffavit, anno regni regis Henrici VI. poft conqueftum xviii°; que tofta & acre terre tenebantur de nobis per fervicium 11ṡ. ob. per annum; quorum vi acre, cum pertinentiis, jam funt in tenurâ Thome Yonge, ballivi; & ex duobus toftis factum eft unum meffuagium, & nunc eft in tenurâ ejufdem Thome Yonge, ballivi.

Habemus ibi, de perquifito fratris Johannis Pomerey, abbatis, omnia illas terras & tenementa, redditus & fervicia, cum pertinentiis, &c. que Willielmus Stowton habuit in villâ & in campis de Stowton; fcilicet, unum meffuagium, unam virgatam terre, iiii pafturas, &c. que tenebantur de nobis per fervicium 1 libre piperis per annum; pro quibus dictus abbas folvit dicto Willielmo xxl̄i. Et habemus predicta omnia ex dono & feoffamento Ricardi Reynold, Jacobi Howton, & Henrici Enfworth, ficut patet in cartâ fextâ fecundi libri de Chartwary.

Habemus ibi, de perquifito abbatis & conventûs, omnia terras & tenementa, prata, pafcua, &c. que Thomas Warde habuit in villâ & in campis de Stowton; fcilicet, 1 virgatam terre, 1 meffuagium, & v pafturas, pro quibus folvimus dicto Thome viiid̄. que antea tenebantur de nobis per fervicium xxd̄. & que habemus ex dono & feoffamento Willielmi Frifby, Johannis Habraham, & Henrici Enfworth, ficut patet in cartâ duodecimâ fecundi libri de Chartwary.

Habemus ibi, ut in cartâ decimâ-tertiâ fecundi libri de Chartwary, de perquifito abbatis & conventûs, & ex feoffamento Ricardi Nell & Roberti Curtes capellani, 1 meffuagium, 1 cotagium, 11 virgatas terre, v acras prati, & 1 acram pafture, que ipfi Ricardus & Robertus prius habuerunt ex dono & feoffamento Johannis Beket & Margarete uxoris fue; pro quibus folvimus dictis Johanni Beket & Margarete uxori ejus xiiil̄i. viṡ. viiid̄. & ultra. Et que virgate terre, meffuagium, &c. tenebantur de nobis per fervicium duarum librarum piperis per annum, &c. Et memorandum, quòd Johannes Beket tenuit predictum cotagium & unam dim' virgatam terre de tribus predictis virgatis terre de Suthwyk per fervicium 11ṡ. per annum, quos nos jam folvimus eidem domino annuatim pro predicto cotagio & dimidiâ virgatâ terre.

Mem', quòd illud meffuagium, virgate terre, &c. quondam Johannis Beleth & Margarete uxoris fue, recuperata fuerunt per placitum in curiâ domini regis apud Weftmonafterium coram Roberto Danby & fociis fuis jufticiariis domini regis de banco, de termino Mich', anno regni regis Edwardi Quarti poft conqueftum primo, &c. ut in libro placitorum.

Habemus ibi, de perquifito abbatis & conventûs, & ex dono & feoffamento Johannis Atkyne de Stowton, unum cotagium, vi acras terre, 1 pafturam, in villâ & campis de Stowton, pro quibus folvimus dicto Johanni iiii marcas, iii folidos, iiii denarios, modò in tenurâ Roberti Newton; & illud cotagium, cum predictis vi acris & pafturâ, oneratur annuatim cum 1 librâ cere ad lumen fepulchri.

Habemus ibi, de perquifito fratris Willi Charyte, 1 toftum, 1 meffuagium, & 11 virgatas terre, quondam Thome de Warkanaby, que tenentur de abbate Leyc' per fervicium [2] . . 11d̄. per annum.

Parcelle liberi redditûs, per diverfos donatores & feoffatores nobis collate, & annuatim reddite.

Habemus ibidem, de dono Ricardi de [3] Satrino, homagium & fervicium Radulphi filii Hugonis, carpentarii, quod debet pro uno tofto, cum uno meffuagio & unâ acrâ terre, videlicet, dimidiâ acrâ fuper Woldfurlong, & dimidiâ acrâ fuper montem ufque in pratum domini ville, & uno buto fuper Wakerifhul, unde folebat predictus Radulphus reddere facriftarie beate Marie de Prato Leyc' xiid̄. per annum.

Habemus ibidem, ex dono predicti Ricardi de [4] Sartrino, per aliam cartam, xiid̄. per annum, folvendos per manus Walteri filii Radulphi, nepotis fui, & heredum fuorum, pro terrâ quam dedit eis in Stocton.

Conceffimus, & per cartam noftram confirmavimus, Ricardo filio Walteri de Stocton, & heredibus fuis, illud toftum extra portam noftram, fcilicet, quod fuit Arneburch, cum pertinentiis fuis. Reddit nobis annuatim xviiid̄. & 11 gallinas pro omni fervicio, &c. ut in primâ cartâ inter feoffamenta.

Conceffimus, & per cartam noftram confirmavimus, Johanni Flori de Stocton, & heredibus fuis, pro homagio & fervicio fuo, duas virgatas terre in Stocton, cum omnibus pertinentiis fuis. Reddit nobis annuatim duas libras piperis pro omni fervicio. Et ipfe J. Flori in capitulo noftro, tactis facrofanctis [5], juravit, quòd verax & fidelis ecclefie noftre exiftet ubique in omnibus, &c. Iftas 11 virgatas terre jam habemus per emptionem à Johanne Beket, & recuperatas per placitum, &c. ut fuprâ, ut in cartâ tertiâ inter feoffamenta.

Conceffimus, & per cartam noftram confirmavimus, Amicie filie Ketilbu, & heredibus fuis, unam virgatam terre in Stocton. Reddit nobis annuatim viṡ. viiid̄. Iftam virgatam terre tenet modò Johannes [6] Ganult; & pro iftâ conceffit & confirmare quietè clamavit nobis totum jus & clameum quod habuit inmittendi quinque averia fua & 1 equum in pafturam, ubicunque averia noftra depafcerentur, & demandam unius quarterii frumenti, &c. ut in cartâ.

Habemus ibidem xxd̄. per annum ex heredibus Thome filii Willielmi Edyth de Stowton, exeuntes ex quartâ parte unius dimidie virgate terre in Stocton, & quartâ parte unius meffuagii, que ipfe habuit ex dono Alicie filie Walteri Hemerey, &c. ut patet in cartâ quintâ. Ifta eft quarta pars illius virgate terre quam J. [7] Gamult tenet.

Conceffimus, & per cartam noftram confirmavimus, Johanni Dawe, & heredibus fuis, quendam fitum five montem molendini ventritici, cum foffâ ejufdem montis, & fex pedibus terre in latitudine, [8] circumdatam totam foffam illam in Stocton, cum unâ rodâ terre ibidem jacente inter viam vocatam Derbye-wey ex parte auftrali, & terrâ domini de Suthwyk ex parte boreali, & extendit fe à viâ regiâ vocatâ Thurnby-wey ex parte orientali ufque viam vocatam Derby-wey. Reddit nobis annuatim xiid̄.

Modò habemus illud molendinum ex perquifitione fratris Willi Charyte, quod conftabat ei xxl̄i. Reddit xlṡ. per annum.

Ad curiam tentam apud Stowton, die Lune proximâ poft feftum Sci Leonardi, anno regni Henrici Quarti feptimo, duodecim jurati, videlicet, Rogerus Prior, Johannes Symfon, Johannes Bole [9], Johannes Elyot, Johannes Lewen, Johannes Peek, Johannes Tokeby, Johannes Ley, Robertus Smyth de Hungurton, Willielmus Man, Willielmus Bacheler, & Willielmus Palmer, dicunt fuper facramentum fuum, quòd Johannes Hotoft tenet de domino abbate Leyc' certas

---

[1] Sic. [2] Hujus fummæ prima pars detrita eft; fed x fuiffe videtur. T. H. [3] Infra, Sartrino.
[4] Vide paulò fupra. [5] Adde evangeliis.
[6] Vide paulò infra, ubi Gamult fcribitur. [7] Supra Gamult. [8] In MS. circumdat. compendiofè. T. H. [9] Q. Bole?

terras

terras & tenementa in Stowton, quondam Willielmi Hotoft patris fui, reddendo inde annuatim per annum xiid. retro v annis fummam v s.

Item dicunt, quòd idem Johannes tenet i meffuagium & i virgatam terre, quondam Margarete Darlyng; & reddit per annum v s. retro ii annis fummam x s.

Item, quòd idem Johannes tenet iii acras terre, quondam Thome Hancok, & reddit per annum xvid. quadrantem, retro iiii annis fummam v s. v d.

Memorandum, quòd Radulphus Fryday dedit Margerie, filie fue, ii virgatas terre, reddendo fibi annuatim xii d. & dim' li. piperis; que quidem ii virgate terre priùs tente fuerunt de abbate Leyc' per fervicium xiid. per annum; & que quidem ii virgate poftea fuerunt Johannis Warknaby, de quo frater W. Charyte perquifivit dictas ii virgatas terre. Reddit domino Marcas xii d. & dim' li. piperis.

Tenentes ad voluntatem.

Thomas Yonge, ballivus nofter, cuftodit ibidem manerium noftrum, cum pertinentiis fuis, videlicet, ortis, claufuris, pomario, vivario, columbari, cum terris dominicalibus continentibus ccxiii acras terre per majus centum; & cum granis & fenis de dominicis & decimalibus; & cum incremento & proficuo cc ovium, cum vaccis, equabus, fuilibus, & cum exitubus earum, &c. que omnia hìc non arentantur, neque extenduntur, quòd in propriis manibus noftris funt; tamen valent nobis per annum, ut dicitur, fecundùm eftimationem ultra reprifas.

Memorandum, quòd ballivus de Stocton folet reportare ad abbathiam Leyc' de decimâ garbarum de Stowton & Evyngton $\frac{xx}{iii}$ [1] quarteria ordei, xx quarteria frumenti, vi quarteria filiginis, $\frac{xx}{iiii}$ quarteria pifarum.

Terre dominicales refponderunt xvi li. xv s. modò refpondent viii li.

Decima refpondet xvii li. modò iiii li. x s.

Summa terrarum dominicarum in culturâ in omnibus campis.

Memorandum, quòd funt in dominico ccxiii acre per majus centum, quas abbas & conventus colunt in omnibus campis preter le Neweclos, quondam in culturâ, que eftimatur ad octo acras; videlicet, in campo boreali versùs Thurnby $\frac{xx}{v}$ acras, videlicet, $\frac{xx}{iiii}$ infra foffam, & xx acras extra foffam; & in campo orientali vocato Longwong in unâ culturâ inter Kafpergate & Longbygate, & continet in fe xviii acras; & vii rode infimilitèr jacentes, buttantes in Longbygate; & v rode infimilitèr jacentes, buttantes fimilitèr into Longbygate; & v acre jacentes fuper Medewynterftykkes; & v acre extendunt fe juxta Longbygate; & v acre, que fe extendunt à fine ville, buttantes fuper Longbygate; & viii acre fubtus villâ ex parte auftrali; & xvi acre in unâ claufurâ vocata The Wyndyard. Item in campo auftrali fuper le Brokfurlong viii acre juxta Brymmilfyke; & in culturâ vocatâ Nicolfwong v acre; & $\frac{xx}{iiii}$ acre infimilitèr jacentes in unâ culturâ inter Smalthorngate & Knyton-more.

Prata dominicalia in Howton-more.

Memorandum, quòd abbas Leyc' habet pratum dominicale in Howton-more, quod cariatur apud Stocton manerium domini ibidem, videlicet, una pecia prati apud le Netherforth, vocati Galbyforth, quod continet in fe per eftimationem duas carectas feni. Item alia eft pecia prati apud le Overforth, vocati Bullokkesforth, & continet in fe unam carectam feni. Item una pecia prati vocati le Bayly Medewe, & continet in fe unam carectam feni. Item una pecia prati vocati Bandilands, quod continet in fe iiii carectas feni. Item alia pecia prati vocati Schulfyke, & continet in fe iii carectas feni. Item alia pecia prati vocati Watmore, & continet in fe quafi unam carectam feni. Item alia pecia prati vocati Stucfold, & continet in fe unam carectam & dimidiam feni. Item alia [2] prati vocati Pyndermedew, & continet in fe unum parvum cok feni. Item alia eft pecia prati aggregati de cheviciis felionibus, vocati Hewedefmedewe, & continet in fe v carectas feni.

Memorandum, quòd habemus decimam garbarum & feni de xii felionibus, & de omnibus pratis noftris & hominum noftrorum in morâ de Howton fitis, &c. ficut patet per fententiam diffinitivam dictam coram judicibus

ordinariis, &c. Acta anno ab Incarnatione Domini m°cc° tricefimo-nono, &c. ut in compofitione que eft in fecundo libro de Chartwary versùs finem libri.

Prata abbatis Leyc' in Howton-more inter tenentes.

In Sykkedole viii acre & dim'.
In Whynedoles viii acre & i roda.
In Efterdoles x acre.
In Teneacras v acre & dim'.
In Newdole vii rode.
In Bromhyll vii acre.
In More-hedde ix acre & i roda.
In Galbyfcroft ii rode.
Item in unâ peciâ prati ibi, annis communibus, ii carecte feni.
In aliâ peciâ prati i carecta.
In Holmefyke ii acre.
Super Hylmarehaw xiii feliones. Item eft ibi una pecia terre, que vocatur Corona Abbatis, continens xi feliones. Item eft ibi alia pecia, que vocatur Galbefirth, continens xi feliones. Iftas xxxiiii feliones tenet tota villa de Howton, & reddit v s.

Pratum de Howton-more divifum inter tenentes noftros, prout modò dividuntur inter eos.

Robertus Bayly tenet ibi unam peciam prati vocat' Bullokysforthe, continentem iii carectas.
Item idem tenet unam peciam prati vocati Heydefmedow, continentem v carectas.
Matilda Batte tenet vii rodas & ii pecias prati, continentes iii carectas feni.
Willielmus Philip tenet iii acras. Johannes Dorman tenet iii acras. Johannes Batte tenet iii acras. Johannes Palmer tenet xiii rodas & dim'. Alyn Bolfener tenet iii acras & dim'. Willielmus Segrave tenet x rodas. Johannes Beton tenet v acras & ii rodas. Willielmus Waren tenet iii rodas. Thomas Swan tenet x rodas. Johannes Orlande tenet unam peciam prati, vocati Bandlandys, continentem xix rodas. Rogerus Elyot tenet iiii acras & i rodam. Robertus Sawnderfon tenet vi acras & dim' rodam. Item unam peciam prati, vocati Bullokyforth, continentem iiii carectas. Item idem tenet i rodam. Thomas Bayly tenet xv rodas & dim'. Henricus Walker tenet ix rodas. Tenentes de Howton tenent certas pecias terre, ut fupra in Howton.

Item claufure funt infra manerium, fcilicet, Okley, Wyndeyarde, Hardmydo, Newclofe, & Flokmydo. Ifte claufure funt extra manerium, fcilicet, Sowthefeld, Northemedo.

Tenentes ad voluntatem.

Robertus Bayle tenet i meffuagium, i croftum, ii virgatas terre & i quarteriam, xii pafturas; & reddit xxviis.
Matilda Bate tenet i meffuagium, i virgatam terre, quondam W. Stowton, iiii pafturas; & reddit xiii s. iiii d.
Eadem Matilda tenet i toftum, i virgatam terre, viii pafturas; & reddit xi s.
Willielmus Philyp tenet i meffuagium, i virgatam terre & dim', vi pafturas; & reddit xv s. iiii d.
Johannes Dorman tenet i meffuagium, ii virgatas terre, vi pafturas; & reddit ii s.
Johannes Bate tenet i meffuagium & dim' virgatam terre & plus, & iiii pafturas; & reddit vii s.
Johannes Palmer tenet i meffuagium, i croftum, ii virgatas terre, viii pafturas; & reddit xxiii s. iiii d.
Alyn Bolfhen tenet i meffuagium, ii virgatas terre, viii pafturas; & reddit xx s.
Thomas Yonge, ballivus, tenet i meffuagium, iii quarterias terre, iii pafturas; & reddit vi s. iiii d.
Willielmus Segrave tenet i meffuagium, i virgatam terre, v pafturas; & reddit ix s.
Johannes Beton tenet i meffuagium, iii virgatas terre, xii pafturas; & reddit xxxvi s. viii d.
Johannes Newton tenet i cotagium, & i quarteriam terre, i pafturam; & reddit iiii s. & unam libram cere ad lumen fepulchri.
Willielmus Waren tenet i meffuagium & dim' virgatam terre, ii pafturas; & reddit vi s.
Johannes Orlande tenet i meffuagium, i croftum, iii virgatas terre, xii pafturas; & reddit xxx s.

---

[1] Id eft, *fexaginta*; quod & de fequentibus notandum. T. H.   [2] Deeft vox *pecia*.

2

Thomas

Thomas Swan tenet 1 meſſuagium, 1 virgatam terre & dim', vi paſturas; & reddit xviii s.

Rogerus Elyot tenet 1 meſſuagium, 1 croftum, iii virgatas terre, & xii paſturas; & reddit xxx s.

Robertus Sawnderſon tenet 1 meſſuagium, ii virgatas terre & 1 quarteriam, ix acras terre, xii paſturas; & reddit xxxi s.

Thomas Bayly tenet 1 meſſuagium, 1 croftum, ii virgatas terre, x paſturas; & reddit xxiiii s.

Henricus Walkar tenet 1 cotagium, & 1 quarteriam terre, 1 paſturam; & reddit iiii s.

Willielmus Grenam tenet 1 meſſuagium, 1 virgatam terre, iiii paſturas; & reddit xii s.

Thomas Lewen tenet 1 toftum, dimidiam virgatam terre, & ii paſturas; & reddit vi s.

Johannes Wedyrbon tenet 1 cotagium; & reddit ii s.

Willielmus Filip tenet 1 meſſuagium, 1 toftum, ii virgatas terre; & reddit xvii s.

Johannes Sybulley tenet molendinum; & reddit xl s.

Summa redditûs voluntarii, cum molend', xixlī. xvi s.

Summa omnium virgatarum xxxiiii, & una quarteria.

Summa omnium virgatar' in totâ villâ xlviii & dim'.

Memorandum, quòd quælibet virgata ſolebat reddere ii gallinas. Sic & cotarii; & facere certa opera, ut patet in fine libri. Et ſolebat dare hariotas, ſicut patet in Rotulis de Releviis, Wardis, &c.

Tenentes liberi.

Dominus Johannes Barre, miles, tenet viii toftâ & v virgatas terre, quondam Radulphi Friday; & reddit ii s. &c. ut patet in finali concordiâ.

Johannes Gamul tenet 1 meſſuagium, 1 virgatam terre, quondam Thome Lewen; & reddit v s. iii d. liberè. Remanet, ſicut patet per Rotulam Curialem.

Thomas Lewen tenet 1 meſſuagium & 1 virgatam terre, quondam Willi Gaylard; & reddit liberè iiii s.

Henricus Colfox tenet 1 toftum & 1 quarteriam terre, quondam Radulphi Friday; & reddit iiii d. ob.

[1] Dominus Johannes Barre, miles, tenet 1 meſſuagium, 1 virgatam terre, quondam Margarete Darlyng. Reddit v s.

Idem Johannes Barre tenet 1 toftum, viii acras terre, quondam Thome Burton, poſtea Johannis Hotoft; & reddit iii s.; ſolebat reddere iiii s.

Idem Johannes Barre tenet 1 capitale meſſuagium, quondam Johannis Hotoft; & reddit xii d. [Et iiii acras terre, quondam Thome Hancok; & reddit xvi d. q̃. Idem tenet v virgatas terre & viii tofta. Reddit ii s.] [2]

Summa liberi redditûs xviii s. vii d. ob.

Reſolutiones; ſcilicet, priori de Schene xl s. Domino de Suthewyk iii s. Sepulchro Domini 1 lib. cere. Item dno Marcas xii d. & dim' libram piperis.

Habemus in Stoâon viſum francum de omnibus tenentibus noſtris illius manerii, tam de liberis tenentibus quàm voluntariis, cum omnibus libertatibus ad eum pertinentibus, ad quem venient omnes tenentes noſtri de Hungurton, de Babgrave [3], de Yngwarby, de Humburſton, de Nowſeley, de Burton, de Kylby, de Knyton, de Thurnby, & Flekney.

Et ſolvunt ad commune ſyn omnes tenentes noſtri de Stowton xi s. viii d.

Summa totalis xxiii lī. iii s. ii d. ob. cum decimis feni, molendinorum, & communi ſyn.

Habemus quietam clamationem Rogeri Quincy, comitis Wyntonienſis, de omni demandâ, ſeâtâ curie, & de toto jure quod habuit ſuper viſu franco, &c. que à nobis vel tenentibus noſtris in feodo ſuo exigebat, &c.

Memorandum, quòd ſunt ibi ii virgate terre, nuper Johannis Browne, jure Agnetis uxoris ſue, filie Johannis Warknaby; quarum unam Thomas Warknaby de Warknaby modò tenet; & Margareta Synder de Stoâon tenet aliam. Modò habemus eas duas virgatas terre per acquiſitionem fratris W. Charyte.

Omnes tenentes noſtri de Stoâon debent ſolvere ingreſſum domino abbati ſecundùm quod poſſunt finire cum ipſo.

Habemus in Stoâon liberam piſcatiam in [4] ſtangno, & liberam warennam.

Et habemus liberam warennam in omnibus terris noſtris ibidem.

Omnes clauſure noſtre ibidem foſſis ſeparabiles nobis ſunt omni tempore anni.

Require terrarium breve de terris dominicalibus, & aliud de terris Edeke in terrario fratris W. Charyte.

Habemus ibi weyf & ſtreyf, &c.

Memorandum, quòd ſolebamus habere ibidem unum gregem, ſcilicet, cc & dim' ovium.

Stokton reſpondit xxvi lī. xiiii s. Modò reddit xvii lī. xi s. [5]

Reſolutiones.

Stoâon. Priori de Schene, pro duabus partibus decimarum de dominicis noſtris ibi & Johannis Friday, & pro duabus garbis unius virg' terre in Buſſeby, xl s.

Capellano ibi, xiiii s. de decimâ feni ibi.

Vicario ibi, ii s. de decimâ molendinorum ventritici & equini, pertinentium nobis.

Domino de Marcas, pro ii virgatis terre quondam Thome Warknaby, xii d. & dim' libram piperis.

Domino de Suthwyk, pro uno cotagio & dimidiâ virgatâ terre, quondam Johannis Beket, iii s.

Eccleſie de Stowton, ad lumen ſepulchri, pro 1 cotagio & vi acris terre, quondam Johannis Atkyn, 1 libram cere per tenentes.

Thurnby. Archidiacono Leyc', pro procuratione, vii s. vi d. ob. q̃. [6]

Vicario ibi, iiii marc' in pecuniâ, & iii s. vi d. pro ſynodalibus jam in novo; & in granis ad voluntatem noſtram. Ultra penſionem, ſcilicet xxx s. quam annuatim reddere ſolebat.

Stokton reddit xviii lī. xiiii s. vii d. ob.

Thurnby reddit liii s. x gallinas, & v gallos. [7]

Stoâon reddit xxii lī. iii s. ii d. ob. preter decimam garbarum, & preter proventus manerii, ſcilicet, ovium, agnorum, lane, granorum, &c.

Thurnby lvii s. iiii d. x gallinas, v gallos, preter decimam garbarum & feni [8].

Thurnby. Quælibet virgata terre de Thurnby ſolebat reddere 1 gallum & ii gallinas.—Summa virgatarum v. Summa gallorum & gallinarum xv.

Stoâon. Quælibet virgata terre ſolebat reddere ii gallinas.—Summa virgat' xxx. Summa gallinar' $\frac{xx}{iii}$.

Item diverſi cotarii ibidem ſolebant reddere gallinam [9].

Molendina de *Stowton*, unum ad ventum, aliud aquaticum, reſponderunt iiii lī. [anno Domini cɔɔcccxçi° [10].]

Decima molendini de Stowton ventritici reddit xii d.

Decima molendini de Stowton equini, xii d. [11]

Decima molendini de *Thurnby* [12].

Vicarius de *Thurnby* reddit xxx s. in augmentationem, terminis Mich' & Paſch' [13].

Stoâon. Quælibet virgata dat ibi per annum iiii d. Summa virgatarum . . . . [14]. Summa denariorum xiiii s. Et, ſecundùm antiqua Rentalia, habuimus pro decimâ feni unam placeam prati vocati Bromhyl, quod continet xii acras; jam illud dividitur inter tenentes noſtros [15].

---

[1] " *Modò dominus de Marcas*" ſupra lineam ab eâdem manu, diverſo atramento. T. H.

[2] Voces uncis incluſæ ab auâore additæ ſunt poſt liberi redditûs ſummam integram colleâam. T. H.

[3] Alibi *Baggrave* ſcribitur.   [4] Ita MS. pro *ſtagno.*   [5] Charyte's Rentale, fol. cxxxi. & ſeqq.

[6] Ibid. fol. cli. a.   [7] Ibid. fol. clvi. ſub titulo *Rotulæ de Pyn.*

[8] Ibid. fol. clviii. ſub hoc titulo: *Summæ totales omnium receptuum cujuſlibet villæ vel loci hîc ſubſequentes, nobis pertinentes.*

[9] Ibid. fol. clix. b. ſub hoc titulo: *Rentale de omnibus caponibus, gallinis, & gallis, liberis & voluntariis, nobis pertinentibus, prout tenentes nobis reddere ſolebant. Item de ovis.*

[10] Ibid. fol. clx. b. ſub titulo *Molendina Dominicalia,* ex Rotulâ le Pyn.   [11] Ibid. ſub titulo *Decima Molendinorum.*

[12] Summa non conſtat; uti nec de aliis quibuſdam molendinis, quorum in Rentali mentio faâa eſt; neque de molendino in hâc parochiâ, ſub *molendinorum* titulo, quicquam dixit auâor. T. H.

[13] Ibid. fol. clxi. a. ſub titulo *Penſiones Vicariorum.*

[14] Deeſt numerus virgatarum; ſed eſt ſpatium. Lege XLII. T. H.   [15] Ibid. fol. clvii. a. ſub titulo *Decima Feni. Thurnby.*

Thurnby [1]. Habemus ibi unum pratum voca um Thurnby-gren, affignatum nobis pro decimâ feni; ac etiam confuevimus habere 11ʃ. de villatâ ultra predictum pratum ex antiquo. Et fenum inde proveniens eftimatur ad 111 carectas ad dim', pret' 11ʃ. 1111d̄.

Anno Domini MCCCLXXXX. *Stoɛ̃on*, de decimis & dominicis; frumentum, XLI quarteria, &c. [ut fupra] [2].

Stokton folebat reddere & folvere ante peftilentiam XVIIlī. XVIʃ. [3]

Stoɛ̃on, de decimis. Frumentum, VIII quarteria, &c. [ut fupra.] [4]

Stoɛ̃on reddit XIʃ. VIIId̄.; folebat reddere, cum membris, XIIIIʃ. VIIId̄.

Thurnby reddit XIId̄. [5]

Stoɛ̃on. Johannes Gamul tenet 1 meffuagium & 1 virgatam terre, quondam Thome Lewen. Reddit Vʃ. 1111d̄. rem'.

Thomas Lewen tenet 1 meffuagium & 1 virgatam quondam Willielmi Gaylard. Reddit 1111ʃ.

Radulphus Friday tenet 1 toftum & 1 quartronam terre, quondam Ricardi Fryday. Reddit 1111d̄. ob̃.

Dominus Johannes Barre, miles, tenet 1 meffuagium & 1 virgatam terre, quondam Margarete Darlyng. Reddit Vʃ.

Idem dominus Johannes tenet 1 toftum & VIII acras terre, quondam Thome Burton, poftea Johannis Hotoft. Reddit 111ʃ. homagium.

Idem dominus Johannes tenet capitale meffuagium [& VI virgatas terre, quondam Thome Fryday, que folebant reddere 11ʃ. & fectam curie hom'.

Idem dominus tenet 1111 acras terre, quondam Thome Hancok; & reddit XVId̄. q̃. [6]]

Sunt ibi 11 virgate terre, quondam Joħis Browne, jure Agnetis uxoris fue, filie Johannis Warknaby; quarum unam Thomas Warknaby de Warknaby modò tenet; & Margareta Pynder tenet aliam: que tenentur de abbate Leyc' per acquifitionem fratris W. Charyte. Summa levatorum XVIIʃ. VIId̄. ob̃. [7]

Arreragia.

Apud *Stowton*, VIʃ. 111d̄. ob̃. Indè recuperati per fratrem W. Charite XIXd̄. ob̃. Item confuetudines tenentium ibi, ut in le Pyn Regiftro.

Thurnby, 11ʃ. pro decimâ feni, ultra pratum affignatum pro decimâ, & [8] galline [9].

Arreragia penfionum vicariorum.
De vicario de Thurnby XXXʃ. [10]

Arreragia eorum qui debent adventum vel fectam ad curias noftras, & non faciunt; fcilicet, tenentes noftri, &c. Heres domini Johannis Barre, militis, pro VII virgatis terre & dim' in Stowton. Tenentes noftri de Humburfton, de Nowfley, de Knyton, de Flekney, debent fectam ad vifum noftrum de Stowton, & non faciunt [11].

Inter privilegia pontificum confirmationis Urbani III. meminit anno Gratie cɪɔcɪxxx°, quâ totam Stoctonam, & quicquid donavit comes Leyceftrie corroboravit [12].

Hundredum de *Gartre* [13].

Stoughton. Habemus in Stoughton totam villam, preter feodum Radulphi Friday, ex dono fundatoris noftri, cum corpore fuo, de quo cepit habitum canonici inter nos. Et colimus ibi in culturis prout jacent in diverfis locis, ficut pleniùs continetur in libro terrarum de dominicis confecto.

Et, preter predictas terras in Stoughton, habemus VI culturas terre in Houghton-more, que fcribuntur in dicto libro, & que pertinent ad Stoughton. Et tam nos quàm tenentes noftri de Stoughton habemus ibidem prata, & aliquam eorum terram arabilem. Et habemus ibi ecclefiam de Stoughton, que eft capella matricis dicte de Thurneby, cujus decimas percipimus in villâ de Stoughton. Et habemus pro decimâ feni totum Bromhil, quod continet XII acras.

Tenentes in villenagio.

Juliana Hemri tenet 1 meffuagium integrum, & 1 virgatam terre continentem XXIIII acras, & prati; & reddit XIIʃ. 11 g. [14]

Rogerus Aftel tenet 1 meffuagium, & 1 virgatam terre continentem ut fuprà, & 1 prati; & reddit XIIIʃ. VId̄. 11 g.

Johannes de Thorpe tenet 1 meffuagium, & 1 virgatam terre continentem ut fuprà, & prati; & reddit XXʃ. 11 g.

Adelina Pertre, pro 1 meffuagio, & 1 virgatâ terre continente ut fuprà, & prati; & reddit XIIʃ. 11 g.

Rogerus Palmer tenet 1 meffuagium integrum, & dimidiam virgatam continentem XII acras prati; & reddit VIIʃ. 1 g.

· Rogerus Owyn tenet 1 meffuagium, & 1 virgatam terre continentem XXIIII acras, & prati; & reddit XIIʃ. 11 g.

Rogerus filius Henrici tenet 1 meffuagium, & 1 virgatam terre continentem ut fuprà, & prati; & reddit XIIʃ. 11 g.

Hugo Howeman tenet 1 meffuagium, & 1 virgatam terre continentem ut fuprà; & reddit XIIʃ. 11 g.

Rogerus de Barkeby tenet medietatem 1 meffuagii, & dimidiam virgatam continentem XII acras, & 1 acram terre, cum paftura ad animalia, & prati; & reddit IXʃ. VIIId̄. 1 g.

Willielmus de Frefiby tenet 1 meffuagium, & 1 virgatam terre continentem XXIIII acras, & prati; & reddit XIIʃ. 11 g.

Inecta Odard tenet 1 meffuagium, & 1 virgatam terre continentem ut fuprà, & prati; & reddit XIIʃ. 11 g.

Johannes Odard tenet 1 meffuagium, & 1 virgatam continentem ut fuprà, & V rodas prati; & reddit XIIIIʃ. 1d̄. 11 g.

Robertus Howfone tenet 1 meffuagium, & 1 virgatam terre continentem ut fuprà, & prati; & reddit XIIʃ. 11 g.

Robertus Makeles tenet 1 meffuagium, & 1 virgatam terre continentem ut fuprà, & prati; & reddit XIIʃ. 11 g. Idem Robertus tenet commune furnum; & reddit 1111ʃ.

Alicia Gerneys tenet 1 meffuagium, & 1 virgatam terre continentem ut fuprà, & prati; & reddit XIIʃ. 11 g.

Rogerus Ston tenet 1 meffuagium, & 1 virgatam terre continentem ut fuprà, & prati; & reddit XIIʃ. 11 g.

Willielmus de Anfty tenet 1 meffuagium, & 1 virgatam terre continentem ut fuprà, & prati; & reddit XIIʃ. 11 g.

Robertus de Hemyngton tenet 1 meffuagium, & 1 virgatam terre continentem ut fuprà, & prati; & reddit XIIʃ. 11 g.

Johannes Hobbefone tenet 1 meffuagium, & 1 virgatam terre continentem ut fuprà, & prati; & reddit XIIʃ. 11 g.

Radulphus Rogerfone tenet 1 meffuagium, & 1 virgatam terre continentem ut fuprà, & prati; & reddit XIIʃ. 11 g.

Rogerus Sire tenet 1 meffuagium & 1 virgatam terre continentem ut fuprà, & prati; & reddit XIIʃ. 11 g. Idem Rogerus tenet dim' rodam pro toftebote. Idem Rogerus tenet aliud furnum commune & reddit Vʃ.

Willielmus Jonfone tenet 1 meffuagium, & 1 virgatam terre continentem ut fuprà, & dim' rod', & prati; & reddit XIIʃ. 11d̄. 11 g.

Johannes Homma tenet 1 meffuagium, & 1 virgatam terre continentem ut fuprà, & 111 rodas & dim' terre pro toftebote prati; & reddit XIIIʃ. 1d̄. 11 g.

Eleanora Owyn tenet 1 meffuagium, & 1 virgatam terre continentem ut fuprà, & prati; & reddit 11ʃ. 11 g.

Matilda Makeles tenet 1 meffuagium, & 1 virgatam terre continentem ut fuprà, & prati; & reddit XIIʃ. 11 g.

Willielmus Jonfone tenet 1 meffuagium, & 1 virgatam terre cont' XII acras, & prati; & reddit XIIʃ. 1 g.

---

[1] Charyte's Rentale, fol. clxvii. b. fub titulo *Decima Feni.*   [2] Ibid. fol. clxix. b. Vide fupra, p. 90.
[3] Ibid. fol. clxxi. a. fub titulo *Capelle, Firme, & Maneria, ante peftilentiam.* [Peftilentia fuit anno cɪɔccxlvi°.] Vide p. 90.
[4] Ibid. fol. clxxi. b.   [5] Ibid. fol. clxxii b. fub titulo *Communes Fines per annum.*
[6] Uncis inclufa, poft levatorum rationem fubductam ab auctore addita. T. H.
[7] Ibid. fol. clxxxi. a. fub titulo *Novum Rentale de liberis Redditibus tantùm.*   [8] Forfan *gallinas.*
[9] Ibid. fol. clxxxiii. a. fub titulo *Arreragia collecta & aggregata per fratrem W. Charyte ex diverfis Rentalibus novis & antiquis.*
[10] Ibid. fol. clxxxiii. a.   [11] Ibid. fol. clxxxiii. b.   [12] Ibid. fol. clxxxv. b.
[13] Ex Rentali de *Geyn*, apud Rentale de Charyte, fol. cxciv. & feqq.   [14] i. e. *gallos*, ut opinor. T. H.

Thomas

Thomas Houthehul tenet I meffuagium, & I virgatam terre continentem XXIIII acras, & prati; & reddit XII ſ. II g. Summa virgatarum terrarum XXVIII & dim'.—Summa denariorum iftius redditûs XVI lī. XVII ſ. VI đ. oƀ. q̃. Summa g. LIII.

Et memorandum, quòd II virgate antiquitùs in villenagio arentate funt in manu noſtrâ, preter certas acras perpoſt arentatas; de quibus poſt fiet mentio.

Et ſciendum, quòd predicti tenentes facient villanas confuetudines, ut in redemptione carnis & fanguinis, callagiis ¹, & aliis operationibus cotidiè cum furcis & flagellis, & omnibus aliis conditionibus villanis, abbati & fucceſſoribus fuis ad voluntatem fuam in perpetuum.

Et ſciendum, quòd, fecundùm primam taxationem villanorum tempore Henrici abbatis, operatio cujuſlibet virgate terre, fine redditu & auxilio, valet per annum XII ſ. III đ.; &, fecundùm taxationem fecundam feptem nativorum, factam coram eodem abbate H. poſt Pafcham, anno Domini cIↃCCLV°, operatio cujuſlibet virgate terre, fine redditu & auxilio, valet per annum IX ſ. V đ.

Tenentes terrarum de novo arrentatarum.
Rogerus le Palmer tenet dim' acram ad placitum XI đ.
Rogerus Henrifon III acras & III rodas ad placitum; & reddit V ſ. IX đ.
Hugo Howeman tenet II acras & dim' ad placitum; & reddit IIII ſ. VII đ.
Willielmus de Frefsby tenet II acras ad placitum; & reddit III ſ. IIII đ.
Rogerus Ston tenet VI acras ad placitum; & reddit IX đ.
Johannes Hobefone tenet I acram ad placitum; & reddit XX đ.
Radulphus Rogerfon tenet I acram, II rodas & dim' ad placitum; & reddit II ſ. XI đ.
Rogerus Sire tenet V rodas ad placitum; & reddit XV đ.
Summa acrarum XVIII acre, II rode & dim'.
Summa denariorum iftius redditûs XXIX ſ. V đ.

Cotarii, tenentes terram antiquam preter virgatas predictas.
Thomas Heryng tenet I cotam, I acram & dimid' terre, & de nová terrâ III rodas, ad placitum; & reddit V ſ. IX đ.
Robertus Scheperd tenet VI acras, I rodam, nove terre, ad placitum; & reddit XII ſ. VI đ.
Willielmus Attpertre tenet dimidiam acram nove terre nunc ² in ma. A. Mich. XLI. ad placitum; & reddit XII đ.
Thomas Attpertre tenet I cotam & II acras terre, cum paſturis & bonis, ad placitum; & reddit IX ſ. III đ.
Nicholaus de Queniburgh tenet I cotagium ad placitum; & reddit II ſ. VI đ.
Johannes Coberd tenet I cotagium, IIII acras, II rodas & dimidiam terre, ad placitum; & reddit XII ſ. I đ.
Johannes Outhehill tenet I cotam, & III acras terre, & VIII acras & dimidiam nove terre, ad placitum; & reddit XX ſ. VI đ.
Willielmus de Digby tenet I cotagium, & V rodas terre, & II rodas nove terre, cum paſturâ I animalis, ad placitum; & reddit VI ſ.
Rogerus le Smyth tenet I cotam & III acras terre, cum paſturâ I animalis, & dimidiâ acrâ terre de efcambio ad placitum; & reddit VIII ſ. I đ.
Et ſciendum, quòd II acre quas tenebat funt in manu domini; & habet predictam dimidiam acram in efcambium, pro tanto apud Barkeby.
Robertus de Queneby tenet I cotagium ad placitum; & reddit III ſ. IIII đ. II g.
Henricus Glover tenet I cotagium ad placitum; & reddit III ſ. IIII đ. II g.
Willielmus Bolle tenet I cotagium, III acras terre, cum paſturâ I animalis, ad placitum; & reddit VII ſ. VII đ.
Stephanus le Swon tenet I cotam, & I acram, III rodas & dim' terre, ad placitum; & reddit IIII ſ. IIII đ. oƀ.
Willielmus Concefone tenet I cotagium, & I acram terre, cum paſturâ I animalis, ad placitum; & reddit V ſ. I đ.

Ricardus Attpertre tenet I cotagium ad placitum, & reddit IIII ſ.
Juliana de Barton tenet I cotagium ad placitum; & reddit III ſ. VI đ.
Johannes Candel tenet I cotagium & III acras, II rodas & dim' nove terre, ad placitum; & reddit VI ſ. VI đ. oƀ.
Inetta Owyn tenet I cotam, I acram, II rodas & dim' terre, ad placitum; & reddit V ſ. II g.
Johes Nicol tenet I cotagium, I acram terre, cum paſturâ I animalis, ad placitum; & reddit IIII ſ. III đ. q̃.
Johannes Henrifon tenet I acram & dim' terre ad placitum; & reddit II ſ. VI đ.
Johannes Bolley tenet III acras & dim' terre ad placitum; & reddit V ſ. X đ.
Willielmus Kyng tenet I cotam ad placitum; & reddit IIII ſ.
Johannes Flory tenet I toftum, quod Johes Dikoun quondam tenuit ad placitum; & reddit XVIII đ. oƀ. q̃.
Idem Johannes tenet I placeam, ubi columbare fuum fituatur, ad terminum vite; & reddit VI đ.
Idem Johannes tenet quandam terram, que tradita fuit Johanni Flory & Matilde uxori ejus, ad terminum vite illorum trium; & reddit II ſ.
Summa acrarum antique terre XXIX acre, I roda, & dim'. Summa acrarum nove terre XIX acre, III rode. Summa denariorum VII lī. III đ. X đ. quorum XII đ. vacat. Summa g. iſtorum. Cote VIII. Summa omnium g. LXI.
Sciendum, quòd predicti ³ cotagerii operantur per III dies, & omnes dabunt auxilium fecundùm quantitatem averiorum; fcilicet, pro bove III đ.; pro vaccâ III đ.; pro caballo III đ.; pro quinque bidentibus III đ.

Liberè tenentes.
Thomas Friday, fucceſſor in hereditate tenentis Radulphi Friday, tenet de nobis III virgatas terre, cum V toftis, per cirographum levatum in curiâ đni regis, anno regni ejuſdem IIII°, unde placitum fuit inter ipfum Radulphum & Paulum abbatem in eâdem curiâ de quinque virgatis terre & VIII toftis. Et dictus Radulphus remifit predicto abbati & fucceſſoribus fuis totum jus fuum quod habuit in II virgatis terre & III toftis. Et idem Radulphus conceſſit fe tenere predictas III virgatas terre, cum quinque toftis, pro fervicio fecte ad curiam predicti abbatis de tribus feptimanis in tres feptimanas; & reddit II ſ.
Idem Thomas tenere debuit de nobis in ⁴ Strectoun II virgatas, quarum I dedimus Johanni filio Radulphi Friday, & quam Rogerus Cor quondam tenuit, & poſt eum Alanus Eyrik; & alteram tenuit Henricus Eyrik, & reddit I libram piperis Henrico regi.
Et ſciendum, quòd iſtas II virgatas tenent Robertus Eyrik filius predicti Alani, & alii plures, per particulas; de quibus particulis & nominibus tenentium fit mentio in libro fcripto de tenentibus dominicarum terrarum.—Summa II ſ. oƀ. q̃.
Sequela virgate terre & tofti quam Walterus Hemerey quondam tenuit, unde percipiebamus dim' marc'.
Thomas filius Willielmi Edyth tenet medietatem dicti tofti, & dimidiam virgatam terre predicte; & reddit III ſ. IIII đ.
Thomas Hufbonde tenet quartam partem dicti tofti, & quartam partem dicte virgate terre; & reddit XX đ.

	Summa XX đ.
Thomas le Warde tenet III acras & II rodas terre, VI đ. oƀ. q̃.	
Amicia Ingrith tenet dim' acram, I đ.	
Thomas Edyth fenior tenet dimidiam acram; & reddit de quartâ parte dicte virgate, que fe extendit ad VI acras, I đ.	
Thomas filius W. Edith tenet III rodas; & reddit I đ. oƀ.	
Willielmus Chaumberleyn tenet I rodam & dim'; & reddit oƀ. q̃.	
Johannes Hufbonde tenet I rodam & dim', & II rodas prati, & quartam partem tofti predicti, & quartam partem pafture; & reddit IX đ.	

Summa acrarum iſtius virgate. Summa, dim' marc'.

¹ Forfan *tallagiis.*
³ Potiùs *cotarii.*
² Sic in MS.; forfan, *in manibus ad feſtum Michaelis* XLI. T. H.
⁴ Alibi *Stretton.*

6

Johannes

Johannes Flory tenet II virgatas terre; & reddit modò Rogerus Coke II libras piperis ad nat' H. regis.

De terrâ quondam Edeke.

Amicia Ingrith tenet tertiam partem unius tofti, in quâ edificatur folare domûs fue, cum celario, juxta domum Johannis Flori; & reddit pro dictâ placeâ, in quâ fieri debet diftrictio, IIIIđ.

Johannes Flory tenet II partes dicti tofti juxta dictum folare dicte Amicie, & I acram terre fuper le Woldelong; & reddit VIIIđ.

Amicia Ingryth tenet III acras, & II rodas & dim' terre, partem illarum IIII acrarum quas tenuit Symon de Ingwardby, & III placeas prati, & quartam partem communis pafture, & I virgatam terre; & reddit IIš. IXđ. ob. q.

Johannes Flori, filius Henrici Flori, tenet I rodam & dim', partem illarum IIII acrarum quas tenuit Symon de Ingwardby; & reddit Iđ.

Thomas Flori, filius H. Flori, tenet II acras & III rodas terre, quas Ricardus de Newton tenuit; & reddit XVIIđ. ob. q.

Thomas Baldewyn, qui alio nomine vocatur Thomas le Warde, tenet I meffuagium & VII acras terre; & reddit IIIIđ. ob. Hom' rel'.

Johannes Baldewyn tenet VI rodas & dim' terre, quas ¹ dicti emit de Nicholao de Fryfeby; & reddit Iđ. ob.

Summa acrarum XVI acre, & I roda & dim'. Summa denariorum VIš. ob.; inde facrifta percipit XIXđ.

Habemus ibi I molendinum ad ventum, & I aquaticum; & reddit per annum . . . .

Item de diverfis tenentibus, pro VI culturis in Houghton-more, preter pratum ibidem quod cariatur apud Stoughton, & preter decimam bladi dictarum culturarum que cariatur apud Stoughton, que funt de dominico & parochiâ de Stoughton & Billefdon

Duo homines de Houghton tenent indè XIIII acras; & redd' } IXš. IIIIđ.

Summa totalis iftius redditûs XXVIIš. XIIIš. XIđ.

Tyrneby. Habemus ecclefiam de Thyrneby, ex dono Radulphi Pincerne, & confirmatione fundatoris noftri, cum capellâ de Stocton, & cum terrâ fubfcriptâ, & eam tenentibus, cum villenagio; que quidem terra, cum manfis, pertinet ad ecclefiam.

Decime garbarum collecte ibidem.

Et percipimus de vicariâ, nomine penfionis, annuatim XXXš.

Et habemus ibi pratum pro decimâ feni, & IIš. de villatis & decimâ feni per totum de Buffeby.

Willielmus Amifone tenet I meffuagium, & I virgatam terre continentem . . . . .²; & reddit I marcam, III g.

Idem tenet I placeam à parte boreali grangie noftre, longitudinis dicte grangie, & latitudinis XVIII pedes, & non arentatam.

Willielmus Jonefone tenet I meffuagium, & I virgatam continentem . . . . . .³; & reddit I marcam, III g.

Idem tenet quandam placeam terre ubi fuit via versùs pofticum rectorie; & reddit VIđ.

Ricardus Amifon tenet I meffuagium, & I virgatam terre continentem . . . . .; & reddit I marcam, III g.

Johannes Gerneys tenet I meffuagium, & I virgatam terre continentem . . . . .; & reddit I marcam, III g.

Nicholaus Hichefone tenet I meffuagium, & I virgatam terre continentem . . . . . .; & reddit I marcam, III g.

Cum uno tofto quod Rogerus filius Hugonis quondam tenuit, & folebat reddere VIđ.

Cum uno tofto quod Galfridus filius Athelyne quondam tenuit, & folebat reddere IXđ.

Summa iftius redditûs, preter redditum II toftorum predictorum, LXVIIš. IIđ. ⁴

Notandum, quòd nos folvimus procurationes pro omnibus ecclefiis noftris, quas in proprios ufus habemus, nifi pro ecclefiâ de Baro, pro quâ folus vicarius folvit procurationes & fynodalia. Item folvit denarios Sci Petri pro Baro, Querndon, Montforel, & Wodhows. Tamen nos colligimus denarios Sci Petri in Wodhows ex antiquâ confuetudine; & eos nobis retinemus. Et omnes vicarii noftri de archidiaconatu Leyc' folvunt fynodalia preter vicarios de Hungarton & Humburfton, pro quibus nos folvimus ex ordinatione epifcopi. Et omnes colligunt denarios Sci Petri, & eos archidiacono folvunt, preter vicarios de Evyngton & *Thurnby,* ubi parochiani ex antiquâ confuetudine colligunt & folvunt archidiacono dictos denarios; & preter vicarium Sci Martini, &c.

Procurationes.

Evyngton, VIIš. VIđ. ob. q.
Thurnby, VIIš. VIđ. ob. q.

Synodalia & denarii Sci Petri.

Evyngton. Vicarius fynodalia IIIš. VIđ.
Parochiani denarios Sci Petri XVIIIđ.
Thurnby. Vicarius fynodalia IIIš. VIđ.
Parochiani de Thurnby denarios Sci Petri XXđ.
Parochiani de Stowton XVIIIđ. ⁵

Confuetudines Tenentium. [Vide fupra, p. 75.]

Stocton folebat dare hariotas, ut apparet in Geryn, in fine Rentalis fui ⁶.

Item habemus vifum franciplegii de omnibus tenentibus noftris manentibus in villis fubfequentibus; fcilicet, in *Stowton, Thurnby,* &c. Et in quibufdam de iftis villis habemus weyfe & ftreyfe. Et in illis poffumus habere vifum noftrum ad placitum, preter in Yngwarby, &c. ⁷

Notandum, quòd hec funt ville in quibus jam invenitur per Rotulos Curiales, quòd antea habuimus weyfe & ftreyfe, &c.; fcilicet, *Stocton, Thurnby,* &c. ⁸

Hec funt ville in quibus infra breve nativos habuimus, ficut patet in Rotulis noftris curialibus; in quibus curiis prefentatum fuit, ubi tunc manferunt diverfi nativi noftri.

Thurnby. Johannes Amyfon morans ibidem. Robertus Gervas morans apud Stok juxta Hekam. Willielmus Amyfon moratur in comitatu Stafford ⁹.

Notandum, quòd habemus liberam warennam in omnibus terris noftris dominicis de Leyceftriâ, *Stocton, Thurmafton, Barkeby,* &c. ¹⁰

Mentio omnium beneficiorum que conventui & monafterio beate Marie de Pratis contulit Guil' Charitee; in quibus & fequentia in Stoughton memorantur: *Inde poftea emit unum molendinum ventriticum apud Stowton, quod conftabat XXlĩ. valens per annum XLš. Item emit in eâdem villâ II meffuagia & II virgatas terre, que conftabant XIIIIlĩ. valentia per annum XVIš.* ¹¹

---

¹ Sic in MS. perperàm. *Emit,* ni fallor, in *tenuit* eft mutandum, & pro *dicti* viri alicujus nomen reponi debet. T. H.
² Defunt acræ. ³ Acrarum numerus defideratur; & fic in fequentibus. T. H.
⁴ Hactenus ex Rentali de Geryn.
⁵ Charyte's Rentale, fol. ccvii. b. fub titulo *Procurationes, Synodalia, & Denarii Sancti Petri.*
⁶ Ibid. fol. ccix. b. fub hoc titulo: *Hec funt villæ, in quibus tenentes noftri folebant dare domino abbati hariotas.*
⁷ Ibid. fol. ccx. a. fub titulo *De Vifu Franciplegii & Curiis Baronis.* ⁸ Ibid.
⁹ Ibid. fol. ccx. b. ¹⁰ Ibid. ¹¹ Ibid. fol. ccxi. a.

REGISTRUM LIBRORUM MONASTERII BEATE MARIE DE PRATIS LEYCESTRIE,

renovatum tempore fratris W. Charyte, hìc precentoris [1].

Contenta hujus Regiftri fequentis, prout fequuntur in ordine.

Primò, tabula facta per fratrem Willum Charyte de nominibus omnium doctorum Auctorum, five compilatorum, quorum libri, volumina, tractatus, &c. notantur in ifto Regiftro. Deindè omnes Biblie pertinentes huic monafterio; poftea libri Biblie gloffate cum diverfis Doctoribus in eifdem. Deindè quatuor Doctores Ecclefie, fcil' Auguftinus, &c.; tunc alii diverfi Doctores, Auctores, & Compilatores, ficut ftant in ordine. Poftea Hiftorialia, Cronicalia, Vite Sanctorum, Epiftole & Omelie doctorum. Tunc Summe, Penitentialia, Sermones, Volumina, Concordancie, Conftitutiones, Specula, Teftamenta Prophetarum, Elucidaria, Proverbia, Yfagoge Philofophorum, Refponfa Philippi Secundi; cum multis aliis. Tunc libri de Grammaticâ, de Poetriâ, de Sophiftriâ, de Logicâ, de Philofophiâ, de Arithmeticâ, de Muficâ, de Geometriâ, de Aftronomiâ, de Inftrumentis, de Phificâ Naturali. Tunc libri de Jure Civili, & de Jure Canonico. Tunc Regiftrum de omnibus libris qui funt in librariâ & fcriptoriâ, prout dividuntur in 9 ftallis. Tunc Regiftrum omnium librorum in choro, in capellâ, in firmariâ, & apud Yngwardby, prout dividuntur intra conventum. Ultimò, Regiftrum diverforum librorum & rotulorum concernentium Evidentias noftras, ut patet in fine hujus Regiftri.

Tabula de nominibus Doctorum & aliorum Auctorum, prout fequuntur in ordine, quorum libri, volumina, vel tractatus, notantur in ifto Regiftro fequente, facta per fratrem Willum Charite.

Biblie, defect' & ufit'.
Each book of the Old Teftament gloffed.
Evangelia gloffata.
Auguftinus.
— ad Julianum comitem.
— de vifitacõe infirmorum.
— de vitâ clericorum.
— ad Cirillum.
Ambrofius.
Ieronimus.
Gregorius.
Bernardus.
Hugo de Viennâ [2] fuper Evangelia dominicalia.
Hugo de Sto Victore [3].
Ricardus de Sancto Victore.
Beda.
Chryfoftomus.
Yno (or Yvo [4]).
Odo [5].
Origines fuper Exodo & Levitico.
Haymo [6].
Damafcenus [7].
Seneca de clementiâ—beneficiis—epiftolæ ad Lucilium—de paupertate —liber orationum ethicarum--de quæftionibus (naturalibus)—de remediis fortunæ—de morali, epiftola ad Paulum--proverbia--de honeftâ vitâ.
Anfelmus.
Boecius.
Bonaventura [8].
Yfidorus.
Willus de Montibus [9].
Johes de Rupell' [10].
Cafiiodorus.
Dionifius.
Alexander Necham [11].
Innocentius ⎫
Leo ⎬ papæ.
Bafilius.
Rabanus [12].
Petrus Colenfis [13].
——— Blefenfis [14].
——— de Auriolo [15].
——— Lumbardus [16].
——— Comeftor [17].

[1] " Regiftrum hoc compofitum fuit per Willielmum Charyte, qui vixit anno 1492. Scriptus autem hic liber ad annum octavum regis Henrici Septimi, ut patet fol. 139°." MS. Laud. 1415. 75. in the Bodleian Library.—In the year 1482, the library of the abbey of Leicefter contained eight large ftalls, which were filled with books, fays Mr. Warton, Differtation, II. p. 82, as referred to in this catalogue.

[2] His " Lecturæ fuper librum Sapientiæ & Canticorum," Cat. MSS. Angliæ, Bibl. Bodl. 2220 *; " fuper Pentateuchum, Jofue, Judices, Ruth, Jeremiam, Ezekielem, Apocalypfen; Balliol, 302—3—4. 383; Merton, 617, 618, 619. 21; feventeen volumes of his Comments on the Old Teftament at Exeter College, 817; his " Seminarium Predicationis," ib. 818; " Commentarium fuper Evangelium Joh'is, & Pfalmos 24 priores" Oriel, 903; on Luke and John, All Souls, 1434; on Ifaiah, Pembroke college, Cambridge, 1998; Paul's epiftles, 1971. 1974. 2073. 2138. " Hugonis de Viennâ Lecturæ fuper librum Jobi; 3. ejufdem " Lecturæ fuper Cantica Canticorum." Bodl. 2220. 2.

[3] A celebrated divine, and voluminous writer, of the fourteenth century; and a cardinal. " De Sacramentis Chriftianæ Fidei, partes 18, Bibl. Bodl. 646; " de feptem Sacramentis ecclefiafticis," ib. 787. 1074. 1103. 1169. 1209. 1749. 1891. 2005. 2434. 2556. 2885; " de arrhâ animæ," ib. 794. 1109. 1184. 1430. 1888. 1924. 3897; mifcellaneous, ib. 801. 823. 973, 974. 999. 1096. 1167. 1209. 1209. 1249. 1273. 1275. 1512. 1550. 1842. 1872. 2601. 2661. 2989. 3609; on Ecclefiaftes, 6641; and Lamentations of Jeremiah, 2411.

[4] Ivo Camotenfis, a native of Beavais, and bifhop of Chartres, a great enforcer of the difcipline of the church, died 1116; canonized 1576. His works, confifting of decrees, epiftles, homilies, and a chronicle, were publifhed by father Gouchet in 1647.

[5] Dupin, among the writers of the tenth century, notices at p. 51. Odo abbat of Cluny: and at p. 64. archbifhop Odo: the former is probably the perfon alluded to, as he compofed feveral treatifes: " De 12 Patriarchis," Bibl. Bodl. 1081; " Sermones," 1109; " Tractatus exceptionum qui continet originem & difcretionem artium, fitumque terrarum, & fummam hiftoriarum, diftinctus in 14 libros," of which four books were printed, ib. 1150; " De gradibus & perfectione charitatis," ib. 1205; " Tractatus fuper pfalmos, & de ftatu interioris hominis, & de contemplatione qui infcribitur Liber Benjamin," ib. 1801; " liber dictus Benjamin minor," ib. 1888; " de tabernaculo fœderis," ib. 1900; " de fcientiâ & difciplinâ," ib. 1978; " Tractatus ad literam de ædificiis templi in Ezekiele," ib. 2415; " de Trinitate, ib. 3614; " Teftamenta 12 patriarcharum," Merton, 709. [6] A relation and contemporary of Bede, and a writer on the Old Teftament. Tanner, Bibl. Brit. p. 385.

[7] Johannes, one of the fathers in the eighth century.

[8] He was a Francifcan frier of Tufcany, made a cardinal by Pope Gregory for his many theological writings, and died in 1274.

[9] Royal MSS. 1900. 8 C. VII. 16. " Gulielmi de Montibus de Pœnitentiâ tractatus." Willielmus de Montibus; Cotton MS. Vefpafian, D. XIII. 2. " Speculum pœnitentis editum à Magiftro Gulielmo de Montibus, cancellario Lincoln'." 5. Idem " de Confeffione." Vefp. E. X. 6. " Tropi in theologicâ facultate à Magiftro Willielmo, Lincolnienfis ecclefiæ cancellario, collecti. 10. " Numerale Willielmi de Monte Nicholfi ecclefiæ Lincolniæ. Liber Mifcellaneus, præfertim de rebus theologicis." Cat. MSS. Angl. Bodl. 3825. 5. Guil. de Montibus, aliàs Leycefter, " Diftinctiones Theologiæ." " Willielmus de Montibus de errorum eliminatione," Bodl. 1273; " Diftributiones," ib. 2318; and in 2723. are " Poftillæ feu collectæ ex auditis fuper pfalmos in fcholâ W. de Montibus."

[10] Qu. John de Rupe Sciffa, a grey frier, noticed by Dupin, cent. xiv. 80, who wrote upon the Revelation, &c.? Royal MS. 14. C. IV. 2. " Johannis de Rupellâ Summa de Animâ & Viribus ejus." Cat. MSS. Angl. Bodl. 4051. 10. " Jo. de Rupellâ de decem præceptis." [11] Of him fee Tanner, Bibliotheca Britannica, p. 538—541. An Oxonian. See Wood's Annals of Oxford Univerfity by Gutch, I. p. 189. [12] Maurus, archbifhop of Mentz, a famous writer in the ninth century.

[13] Qu. Peter of Colle, of the order of Friers Minors, who wrote a treatife of the authority of a council, commentaries upon the fentences, and fome fermons? Dupin, xv Cent. p. 105.

[14] He was a native of France, and ftudied the civil law and divinity; was invited to England by Henry II. who made him his fecretary, in which office he was continued under queen Eleanor and Richard I.; he was made archdeacon of Bath about 1175; archdeacon of London 1198, archdeacon of Canterbury, dean of Wolverhampton, prebendary of Sarum and St. Paul's. He died after 1205, and was buried at Bath. His works were printed at Mentz in 1603 in quarto; Cologne, 1618, folio; and with an appendix, 1624, octavo; Paris, 1677. 1519; his continuation of Ingulfus' Hiftory, Ox. 1684, folio; a Chronicle of Peterborough in heroic verfe, at the defire of Henry abbot of Croyland, MS. Cotton Claud. A. V; " Carmen de ftellâ magos ducente", in Leonine verfe, MS. Bodl. Laud B. 163. " Duæ epiftolæ ad Henricum II. Angliæ regem," Bibl. Bodl. 643; " de amicitiâ & charitate," ib. 1343; " epiftolæ," ib. 2017. 2009. 2671; " de vitâ S. Job," ib. 2025; " Commentarium fuper Job," ib. 2206; " lectiones fuper Job," ib. 2302. 2327; " Compendium libri Job, cui præfixa eft epiftola ad Henricum II." ib. 2323; " de utilitatibus tribulationis," ib. 2689. He is faid to have firft ufed the term *tranfubftantiation.* Tanner, Bib. Brit. p. 105. Of the writings of Peter of Blois there is a copious detail in Dupin, xii Cent. pp. 158—166. The concluding paragraph gives an account of the different editions of his works.

[15] Or de Aureolis, or de Aureolo; by whom there is in the Bodleian Library, 2231, a tract " de decem præceptis" at Baliol college; " fuper duos libros fententiarum," at Merton, 480. 579. 710; " Compendium literalis fenfus Sanctæ Scripturæ" at New college, 978; " Augment. omnium librorum totius Sanctæ Scripturæ" at Bene't college, Cambridge, 1517, " Epitome totius bibliæ."

[16] Born in Lombardy, bifhop of Paris 1160, died 1164, called " Mafter of the Sentences" from four books of Sentences written by him. A long account of Peter Lombard in Dupin, xii Cent. p. 191. & feqq.

[17] Chancellor of the Univerfity of Paris, died 1198; a fcholaftic writer. Petrus Comeftor, Claudius, E. I. 17. " Explanatio Vifionum Danielis ad literam, fecundùm Magiftrum Petrum Comeftorem." 18. " Verbum abbreviatum Magiftri Petri, primùm cantoris Parifienfis, poftea novitii Longipontii, in quo novitius fepultus eft." Noticed by Dupin, xii Cent. p. 176.

* All the references to MS Libraries are numbered according to the " Catalogus Manufcriptorum Angliæ, Oxon. 1697," fol.

Petrus

Petrus Remigius ¹.
——— de Carentefiâ.
——— Olfonfis ².
Thomas Alquinus ³.
Tho. Bradwordyne ⁴.
Gandanus mar. R. magn ⁵.
Armachanus ⁶.
Lincoln.
Wodeford contra Wyclyf de facramento altaris ⁷.
Johes Waldeby ⁸.
Egidius ⁹.
Parifienfis de verbo abbreviato ¹⁰—de prebendis—

HISTORIALIA.

Jofephus de antiquitatibus, & de bello Jud'.
Freculphus ¹⁴.
Hiftoriale fcolafticum W. Frumentyn per fe cum albo ¹⁵.

de fide & legibus—fermones.
Nichius Trivet, expof' fuper rem angeli, & fuper officio miffe jacet in choro—de expofitione miffe 2 —meditationes Stephani abbis Trivet fuper Rē Angl' ¹¹—expof' fuper Boec. de cofolatione.
Hildebertus ¹².
Nichius de Lirâ ¹³.
Wyclif.

Hiftoriale fcolafticum Alani de Ybeftoke ¹⁶ in fub-albâ.
Egidius ¹⁷ de rege pio.
Darius Frigius ¹⁸, inter volumina.

Petrus Conmeftor ¹⁹.
Rabanus fuper Judith ²⁰.
Alexandri epiftolæ ad Ariftotelem de mirabilibus Indie ²¹.
Hiftoriale Evangelicum,

CRONICALIA.

Orofius de geftis Romanorum.
Hiftoria evangelica & apoftolica in eodem.
Egefippus de excidio Jud'.
Beda de geftis Anglorum.
Julius Solinus.
Petrus Alphonfus ²⁴.
Carolus Magnus ²⁵.
Cronica Leyc' ²⁶.
Cornelius ad Aiprium de bello Trojano ²⁷.
Trogus Pompeius de mundi ornamentis .

verfùs Ricardum Barre.
Eufebius.
Itinerarium Clementis ²².
Galfridus de hiftoriâ Britonum ²³.

Ovidius de mirabilibus mundi ²⁹.
Bellum Trojanum per Guidonem de Columpnâ ³⁰.
Alanus de planctu naturæ³¹.
Cronicale abbreviatum per Thomam de Ripley ³².
Cronica Martini ³³.
Giraldus de inftructione principis ³⁴.
Ranulphus Ceftrenfis in fua Polycronica ³⁵.
Johannis Gower Cronica ³⁶.
Vigetius de re militari.

¹ Remigii "expofitio nominum Hebraicorum." Bibl. Bodl. 1573. 2228. 3497. Dupin, ix Cent. p. 174, notices Remigius, a monk of St. Germans of Auxerre, as being very learned in profane fciences, but who employed himfelf more profitably in expounding the Scriptures.

² Petrus Alphonfus, a Spanifh Jew, who formerly bore the name of Mofes. Dupin, xii Cent. p. 170. Royal MSS. 15 C. II. 9. "Petri Alphonfi Dialogus contra Judæos." "Petri Alphonfus Judaifmus five Dialogus de capitibus Chriftianæ religionis contra Judæos & Saracenos, inter Petrum tunc converfum ad religionem Chriftianam & quendam Moyfen. Illum de facro fonte levavit Alphonfus, rex Hifpaniæ, die natali S. Petri, anno C. 1106; unde illi utrumque nomen. Otho A. XV. 2. Bodl. 1353.

³ Qu. Tho. Aquinas. ⁴ Fellow of Merton College, Oxford; and archbifhop of Canterbury. Bibliotheca Britannica, p. 120. His great work was "De Caufâ Dei," againft Pelagius.

⁵ Henricus Gandavus wrote "Summa" & "Quodlibeta," Balliol, 186, 187; Oriel, 883; "Quæftiones" & "Summa quæftionum theologicarum," Baliol, 574—5. Henry Goethals, commonly called Henry of Gaunt, archdeacon of Tournay. Dupin, xiii Cent. p. 75; who notices his "Sum of Divinity" and "Quodlibetick Queftions".

⁶ Richardus Armachanus was a native of Ireland, fellow of Baliol College, and chancellor of Oxford; primate of Ireland; and a controverfial writer in the fourteenth century. Wood's Hift. vol. III. p. 54. 85. App. 21. Annals, vol. I. 405. Richard Fitz-Ralph, arch-bifhop of Armagh. Dupin, xiv Cent. pp. 70, 71. 118.

⁷ William Wodeford was an Irifh Francifcan, who wrote againft Wicliffe. Bibliotheca Britannica, p. 784. MS. Bodl. 3629. Cat. MSS Angl. Leland faw in the library of Queen's College, Cambridge, "Defenforium Gul. Wodeford contra Armachanum." His comment on Boetius is in Bibl. Bodl. 2150.

⁸ A Yorkfhire man and Auguftine monk, who alfo wrote againft Wicliffe; and was by Richard II. made archbifhop of Dublin, as was his brother Robert, and alfo archbifhop of York. Bibliotheca Britannica, p. 745.

⁹ Ægidius Romanus, or Giles of Rome, archbifhop of Bourges. Dupin, xiv Cent. p. 54. He was a native of Rome, a pupil of Thomas Aquinas, eminent among the fchoolmen by the name of Doctor fundatiffimus (which we may tranflate the well-bottomed Doctor); and an archbifhop, flourifhed about the year 1280, and wrote a Latin tract in three books "de regimine principum," or the art of government, for the ufe of Philip le Hardi, fon of Louis king of France, early tranflated into Hebrew, French, Italian, and Englifh; and printed at Rome, 1482; and at Venice, 1498. An Oxonian. Annals, 210.

¹⁰ "Verbum abbreviatum Magiftri Petri, primùm cantoris Parifienfis, poftea novitii Longipontis," is among Dr. James's MSS. at Oxford. Cat. MSS. Angl. pars I. p. 260. a. See note (¹⁶), p. 101.

¹¹ Nicholas Trivet was a great writer of divinity, as well as of Englifh Hiftory; but, as to thefe pieces, "expof' fuper rem Angeli," and "Meditat. fuper Rem Anglic'," probably one and the fame treatife, whatever be the fubject, no work of either denomination is mentioned by Tanner, ibid. p. 722; perhaps it was part of his book "de Officio Miffæ," or fome other theological work. Qu. if it does mean his "flores fuper regulam beati Auguftini," Bibl. Bodl. Cat. MSS. Angl. 3609?

¹² Hildebert, archbifhop of Tours, noticed by Mofheim, xi Cent. ch. 11. near the end; 8° edit. vol. II. p. 316. He was a theological writer. He is called in the Oxford and Cambridge MS Catalogues "epifcopus Cenomanenfis."

¹³ A Jew, converted to a Francifcan, and a great gloffator, died in 1349.

¹⁴ Bifhop of Lifieux, author of a Chronicle in two parts. To him Rabanus Maurus infcribed his Comments on Genefis.

¹⁵ Alba is a word of the lower empire for pearls; and may here fignify, that thefe books were emboffed with precious ftones? but then what is fub alba? or have thefe terms any relation to the colour of the binding? (Perhaps, however, alba and fub-alba may not have any reference to the books or manufcripts; and may mean that the donors of thefe manufcripts prefented alfo, the one a veftment called the alba, and the other fub-alba. S. D.) Frumenteyn and Ybeftoke were probably canons of the houfe. Ibftock is the name of a town in this county; and Robert Furmenteyn was abbot here in 1244.

¹⁶ A native of Ibftock. ¹⁷ See notes (¹) and (³¹), p. 105. ¹⁸ Dares Phrygius, the well-known fictitious writer of the Trojan war.

¹⁹ See before, p. 101, note (¹⁷). He wrote "Hiftoria Scholaftica," abridged by W. Hunter, an Englifhman.

²⁰ Rabanus Maurus, archbifhop of Mentz in the ninth century, died in 856, a voluminous commentator on the Bible, and theological writer. ²¹ A well-known monkifh fiction. ²² Qu Clement, monk of Lanthoni? though no fuch title appears among his works, Tanner, Bibliotheca Britannica, 183; nor the Penitentiale hereafter mentioned. ²³ Qu. Monumuthenfis?

²⁴ Petrus Alphonfus wrote "de lege Chriftianâ, Judaicâ, & Saracenorum, per modum dialogi." Bibl. Bodl. MS. Laud. Cat. MSS. Angl. 1353; and other pieces againft the Jews. Ib. 2659. ²⁵ Under the title of Carolus Magnus, in the MS libraries, is the Life of Charlemagne by Eginhard; Bibl. Bodl. 837. 1302; befides French or Romance lives of him. ²⁶ Moft probably Knighton's.

²⁷ Qu the fame as Dares Phrygius, whofe hiftory of the Trojan war has been abfurdly afcribed to Cornelius Nepos?

²⁸ For ornamentis we fhould read originibus, which is the title of fome copies of Juftin, the abbreviator of Trogus Pompeius.

²⁹ It is not unlikely Ovid's books of Metamorphofes are referred to in this article. Mirabilia mundi was a common title among the monkifh plagiaries.

³⁰ Guido de Colonnâ was a Sicilian in the fuite of Edward I. when he returned from the Croifade, and wrote a Chronicle. He lived, fays Mr. Warton, (Hiftory of Englifh Poetry, II. 90.) when the mode of fabling by blending Gothic extravagances in Grecian ftory was at its height, and gave romantic additions to the plain and credible facts invented by Dictys and Dares, who, by mifreprefenting or enlarging Homer, falfified the Trojan Story. Lydgate tranflated into Englifh verfe, and Gower copied largely from, Colonna's "Hiftoria Trojana," which was printed at Oxford, 1480, 4to, and at Strafburgh, 1486, and 1489.

³¹ Alanus de Infulis wrote "de planctu naturæ contra fodomiæ vitium." Tanner, Bibliotheca Britannica, p. 16.

³² No fuch Chronicler mentioned by Tanner. ³³ Qu. Martinus Polonus, who wrote a chronicle, and died in 1279? Martinus in Chronicis, Tiberius A. VIII. 1. "Chronica Martini, domini papæ pœnitentiarii & capellani, de geftis fummorum pontificum & imperatorum;" alfo Caligula A. XVI. and Galba E. XI.; 4. "cum continuatione A. D. 1391."

³⁴ Giraldus Cambrenfis, enumerating this in the Catalogue of his works in Wharton's Angl. Sac. II. 446, fays of it: "toties promiffus, fere inter primos inchoatus, inter ultimos autem propalatus, diu nimium claufus & fopitus quando tute prodire poffit plurimis annorum curriculis tempus expectans liberalitèr quidem & non lividè legenti labor fua quoque laude non indignus." Yet I do not find it mentioned in Tanner.

³⁵ Ranulphus Higdenus Ceftrenfis, author of a chronicle printed among Gale's Hift. Angl. Scriptores, Ox. 1696.

³⁶ Chronicon tripartitum Ric. II. lib. 3. Tanner, Bibliotheca Britannica, p. 336. His "Confeffio amantis," the only one of his three great works which has yet been printed, is pronounced by Mr. Warton, II. 9, "no unpleafing mifcellany of thofe fhorter tales which delighted the readers of the middle age," and feems to have been borrowed from the Chronicle of Godfrey of Viterbo. It commences with the creation of the world, and is brought down to the year 1186.

Vitæ Sanctorum; require infra in fuis locis.
Epiftolæ doctorum [1].
Thomas Cantuarenfis in epiftolis fuis.
Epiftolæ Algor [2] ad dnum

Johem.
Epiftolæ Alexandri Magni.
Epiftolæ Urbani papæ.
Epiftolæ Ariftotelis [3].
Epiftolæ Gwydonis miffivæ.

Require iftas epiftolas infra in Epiftolis Doctorum.

OMELIA.

Eufebii; require infra in Omeliis Doctorum.

SUMME.

Johannes Bronuard [4] in Summâ.
Althini in Summâ.
Bartholomæus de proprietatibus [5].

Ochinus de facramento altaris [6].
Wilfus de Sancto amore [7].
Alcoran Machameti.
Afforifmi Urfonis [8].

Require omnes predictos infra in Summis Doctorum.

PENITENTIALIA.

Ricardus Chabnam [9].
Magifter Alanus [10].

Robertus canonicus de Plumpton.

Johannes Beleth [11].
Clemens Lantone [12].
Bartholomæus [13].
Raymundus [14].

Chérubyn de Confeffione [...]
Holkott [15].
Mounteftrell Baccalarius in Januenfi [16].

Require predictos infra in Penitentialiis Doctorum.

SERMONES.

Armachanus in Sermonibus [17].
Babianus in Sermonibus [18].
Cefarius [19].
Alredus.
Johannes archiepifcopus [20].
Bafilius.
Gadifby [21].
Gorlim [22].

Bromyard [23].
Henricus Stretforde [24].
Wilfus de Anlep [25].
Marbodus [26].
Ulgerus papa [27].
Mag. Johannes Felton [28].
Abvile Wyclyf.
Dñs Ricardus de Bury [29].
Lathbury fuper tomos [30].

Require omnes iftas infra in Sermonibus & voluminibus Doctorum.

SPECULA.

Alredus de caritate [31].　　Johannes Beleth [32].

[1] Under this title are included Epiftles of the Greek and Latin fathers; " Epiftolæ variæ variorum," Bibl. Bodl. 1012; " Epiftolæ multum ornatæ & rhetoricæ," ib. 1162; " Epiftolæ decretales, circiter 180, maximè Alexandri papæ III. ad varios, Angliæ præfertim, epifcopos & abbates variis de rebus miffæ," ib. 2452; " Epiftolæ Arnulphi epifcopi Lexovienfis, fome not in the printed edition of his works," ib. 2482.

[2] Qu. Alger, deacon of Leige and monk of Cluny? who flourifhed in the twelfth century; though noticed by Dupin among the authors of the eleventh century, p. 19. & feq. becaufe the principal treatife written by him was that whereby he refutes the *errors* which Lanfrank and Guitmond have oppofed concerning the doctrine of tranfubftantiation.

[3] Ariftotle moft famous philofofre
His epiftles to Alexander fent.
Occleve's MS. tranflation of Cafulis' " liber moralis de ludo fcaccorum." It is pretended by myftic writers, that Ariftotle in his old age reviewed his books, and digefted his philofophy into one fyftem, or body, which he fent in the form of an epiftle to Alexander. This fuppofititious tract goes alfo by the name of " Secretum Secretorum," and was in part tranflated by Lydgate. Warton, II. 9. 41.

[4] Tanner notices " *Brunyordus Gulielmus*, Dominicanus, qui fcripfit *Summam* Theologiæ," Bibl. Britan. p. 132.

[5] Bartholomew Glanville was a Francifcan frier of Suffolk. His principal work is " de proprietatibus rerum," in nineteen books, compiled from Ariftotle, Plautus, and Pliny, and frequently printed in Germany. Tanner, Bibl. Britan. p. 326. Whether he was author of a " Penitenciale," I have not found.

[6] This piece does not occur in any of the MS libraries.

[7] He was anfwered by archbifhop Peckham " de paupertate Chrifti." Tanner, Bibl. Britan. p. 585. k.

[8] " Aphorifmi Urfonis" occur in the Bodleian Library, Cat. MSS. Ang. 1638. 1754; and his " Aphorifmi medicinales," ibid. 2597.

[9] *Thomæ* de Chabaham " Quodlibetica" in Univerfity College, Oxford. Ib. 119. His tract " de pœnitentiâ & officiis ecclefiafticis," in which he is ftyled fubdeacon of Sarum. Oriel College. Ib. 869. Tho. de Chebham " Summa de Penitenciâ." Trinity College, Cambridge. Ib. 399. [10] See note ([31]) in page 102.

[11] Tanner, Bibliotheca Britannnica, p. 93, mentions his " Rationale de divinis officiis."

[12] Clemens Lantonienfis' " explanatio fuper alas Cherubin & Seraphin." Bodl. Cat. Ib. 2312, " Collectarium. Ib. 2333, " a book made of the four Gofpelles by Clemens, a prieft of the church of Lantony, in twelve parts;" " Concordia Evangeliftarum" in 12 books; " Commentaria in quatuor Evangelia," in four books. Ib. 2553. He is called *prior* in an effay on the Cherubim's wings. Ib. 3650, " venerabilis prior Lantoniæ, nomine Clemens & opere, vir fingularis religionis & climatæ fcientiæ, præclarus in fuo luxit tempore inter illuftres viros Angliæ." Leland, Collect. I. p. 278. He retired from Lanthony in Gloucefterfhire to Lantoney in Wales, that he might purfue his favourite ftudies with lefs interruption, and died of a paralytic ftroke. Ib. II. 89. Tanner, Bibl. Britan. p. 185.

[13] Qu. *Brixienfis*, who commented on the Decretals, &c.

[14] Qu. de Pennaforte, chaplain to Pope Gregory IX, another commentator on the Decretals.

[15] Robert Holkott, a celebrated Dominican of Northampton, who died of the plague in 1399. Bibl. Britan. p. 407. Bibl. Bodl. 2241. [16] Jacobus Januenfis wrote an " opus quadragefimale" on the Gofpels. MS. Bodl. 2693. Qu. if this was a commentator thereon? " Tabula Januenfis in facram Scripturam." Publ. lib. Camb. 2188.

[17] See before, note ([6]), p. 102. His fermons are in the Bodleian library, 1926; and, among them, thirteen, " quorum primus factus eft ad populum in aulâ epifcopi Londinienfis, 1356, quarta Dominica adventûs." Harl. MS. 1900. " Sermo domini archiepifcopi Armachani Anglicè;" fol. 6. fee a long account of it. He lived in 1357.

[18] In the library of Mr. Theyer (Cat. MSS. Angl. 6489.) are " Petri Babionis fermones 70;" and, 6491, " Sermones aliquot Babionis;" and, 6534, " 73 fermones plerique per Babionem."

[19] Qu. bifhop of Arles in the fixth century? His fermons " de Pafchate," and homilies to the monks, are in Trinity College, Cambridge. Cat. MSS. Ang. 176. 464. Sidney 713. Peterh. 1776.

[20] Qu. archbifhop Peckham? whofe " Sermones Dominicales" are mentioned, ibid. p. 584. An Oxonian. See Annals, vol. I. p. 212. [21] Probably a native of the village of that name in this county; but he is not mentioned by Tanner.

[22] Qu. Gorhm for Nicholas Gorham? a native of Gorham in the county of Herts, who ftudied at Merton College, Oxford, and at Paris, where he died, having been made a doctor of the Sorbonne and provincial of the Dominican order in France. He wrote a number of Sermons, Diftinctions, and other theological pieces. Tanner, Bibl. Britan. p. 333.

[23] Qu. Joannes Bromeardus, or John Bromyard? mentioned in Bibl. Britan. p. 129. John Broomyard's " Summa predicantium" is in Oriel college library. Cat. MSS. Ang. 862. See before, note ([4]).

[24] The name of Stretforde does not occur in Bibl. Britan. Sermons by John Stratford archbifhop of Canterbury are mentioned there, p. 696. [25] Wanlip, near Leicefter, was formerly called *Anlepe*.

[26] Claudius A. VI. 4. " Marbodi epifcopi ad ancillam Chrifti Epiftola parænetica." Vitellius A. XII. 21. " Marbodi Verfus de Laude Caftitatis & de Diffuafione mundanæ Cupiditatis." He was bifhop of Rennes, whofe poems and letters are noticed by Dupin, cent. xii. p. 150.

[27] Ulger, bifhop of Angiers, fent a letter to pope Innocent II. on behalf of the abbey of St. Mary at Roe, &c. Dupin, xii. cent. p. 172. [28] A celebrated preacher of Magdalen College, Oxford. Bibl. Britan. p. 277.

[29] Ricardus de Bury, bifhop of Durham in 1333, firft founder of a public library at Oxford in his college called Durham college. Brit. Top. II. 120. See Gutch's Annals, vol. II. pars 2. p. 910. Sermons are not among his writings in Tanner, p. 57. [30] A Francifcan of Reading. Bibl. Britan. p. 469.

[31] Alredus Rievallenfis wrote feveral theological works, &c. " de amicitiâ fpirituali de vinculo perfectionis," &c.; and may have written " de caritate" alfo. St. Ælred, or St. Æthelred, abbot of Revefby. Dupin, xii Cent. 173. Among his works is noticed a treatife, called " The Mirror of Charity," divided into three books; with an abridgement of that treatife. Bifhop Tanner, however, afcribes " de vinculo perfectionis" to Ælred abbot of Wardon in Bedfordfhire. Bibl. Britan. p. 267.

[32] See before, note ([11]).

Gerardus

Gerardus in Speculo [1].
Johannes Hampole [2].
Walterus Hylton [3].
Require predictos infra in Speculis Doctorum.

Frater Vincentius in Speculo [4].

Petrus Helyas [25].
Kylwardby [26].
Emerus.
Claudianus [27].
Quere omnes istos libros infra in Grammaticâ.

Egidius de Aragoniâ, de modo fignandi.
Mag. W. Kokeke.
Tho. de Hannayâ [28].

ELUCIDARIUM.

Terencii.
Nicholaus Bolarde [5] inter volumina.
Ranulphus Ceftrenfis [6].

Willielmus de Alunia.
Robertus abbas in Yfidoro.
Benedictus Abbas in Bernardo.

POETRIA.

Claudianus Magnus.
Lucanus.
Ovidius in multis.
Horatius.
Marcianus.
Virgilius.
Marbodus.
Galfridus Anglicus [29].

Alanus [30].
Fulgentius [31].
Yfopus.
Socrates [31].
Macrobius.
Penelope Ulyffi.
Sompnus Scipionis.

PROVERBIA.

Ufpionis.
Wiltus cantor Linc' [7].
Proverbia Ricardi regis [8] Anglorum ftrenuiffimi & Ufpionis.
Require infra in Proverbiis.

Quirinus Philofophus [9].
Secundus Philofophus [10] in refponfis fuis.
Quere infra in Yfagogis Philofophorum.

RHETORICA.

Tullius in multis.
Thomas de Capuâ.
Guido.
Galfridus Anglicus [33].
Quere infra in Rhetoricâ.

Macrobius.
Plato.
Boetius.

GRAMMATICA.

Januenfis in fuo catholico [11].
Hugucio [12].
Papias [13].
Brito [14].
Johes de Garlandiâ [15].
Liber primus Alexandri [16].
Cato [17].
Arrianus [18].
Liber Urbani.
Marbodus [19].

Boycius [20] de modo fignandi.
Donatus.
Rogerus Bacon in fummâ fuâ Grammatice.
Remigius [21].
Ludolphus in floribus [22].
Colores Waleys [23].
Magifter Ofbernus [24].
Yfidorus in ethimologiis.
Prifcianus.

SOPHISTICA.

Ric. Feyrbrighe [34].

LOGICA.

Sutton [35].
Dunns.
Alyngton [36].

Frater Egidius.
Johannes Wyclyf [37].
Occham [38].

---

[1] Giraldus Cambrenfis wrote two pieces under that title. Bibl. Britan. p. 321.

[2] *John* Hampol is not noticed by Tanner; who in Bibl. Britan. gives an account of Richardus Hampolus.

[3] A Carthufian monk of Shene, and canon of Thurgarton. *Speculum* is not among his works in Tanner, Bibl. Britan. 425.

[4] Vincentius Bellovacenfis, a Dominican of Burgundy in the thirteenth century, wrote a " Speculum" in four parts. Dupin, XIII Cent. p. 66. He undertook in the reign of St. Louis, who was at the expence of it, a fort of encyclopædia of fcience, in a great work intituled " The Mirror."

[5] He does not feem the fame with Nicolaus *Bollar* in Bibl. Britan. p. 110.   [6] Higden. See note ([35]), p. 102.

[7] Probably William de Montibus, *cancellarius* Lincolniæ. See note ([8]), p. 101.

[8] I did not find thefe Proverbs mentioned in Bibl. Britan. Are they the rhymes which are noticed by Lord Orford among the Royal and Noble Authors? Hoveden charges him with begging rhymes of the French poets.

[9] In Bibl. Bodl. 2004. are " Quirini fapientis verba. Huc pertinet narratio de duobus negotiatoribus."

[10] In the Bodleian Library (50) are " Secundi Philofophi Sententiæ ad Hadriannum," Greek, 1748; " Secundi philofophi Sententiæ Lat." 2067. " De Secundo philofopho, qui omni tempore filentium fervavit. Interrogata Adriani ad eundem, ejufque refponfio: vocantur autem Secundi problemata."   [11] Diftinctiones & Allegoriæ. Bodl. 1419. 1807. 2214. " Excerpta Leylandi ex Prifciano, Januenfi, Alexandro, & Ebrardo." Ibid. 2538.

[12] " Huiccii Pifani dictionarium Latinum." Bodl. 1344. 2582.—248. " Huguitionis Pifani Derivationes magnæ, five dictionarium etymologicum." " Magnæ Derivationes fecundùm Huguitionem, alphabetico ordine compofitæ;" in Caius college library, 1037. " Dictionarium Huguitionis," Peterhoufe library, 1664.

[13] Papias was a grammarian, who wrote a Latin Dictionary in alphabetical order.

[14] Gul. Brito, a Francifcan, who died in 1356, wrote a Lexicon, or Vocabulary, of the Bible, which Leland fays was common in the univerfity. Archbifhop Peckham in the ordinance of Merton College, Oxford, directs to be found " libros Papie & Hugulionis cum Summa Britonis." Tanner, Bibl. Britan. p. 128.

[15] Johannes Garlandius, an eminent grammarian and poet in the eleventh century. Bibl. Brit. p. 309.

[16] Alexander Grammaticus occurs in the library at Durham. He wrote thirty-four volumes of various works, and was reckoned a very fkilful man in imitating Hoffman.

[17] A work grounded on a poem " de moribus" by Cato, cited by Aulus Gellius, xi. 2. but written between the reign of Nero and Valentianus III. Whoever was the author, this metrical fyftem of ethics had attained the higheft degree of eftimation in the barbarous ages. Warton, II. 166, 167.   [18] Qu. the commentator on Epictetus ?

[19] See before, note ([6]), p. 103.   [20] David Boyfus occurs in Bibl. Britan. p. 118; but no fuch work is attributed to him as " De modo fignandi." It is more probable that *Boethius* is here meant.

[21] Qu. Remigius, bifhop of Lyons in the fixth century, a commentator on the Bible ? " Remigii expofitio in artem primam Donati." Bibl. Bodl. 3582. " Donatus cum expofitione Remigii", Caius college library Camb. 1045. " Remigius fuper Phocam grammaticum." Bibl. Theyer, 6389. See note ([1]), p. 102.

[22] Qu. Ludolphus, a Carthufian, and a theological writer in the fourteenth century.

[23] " Joannis Guallenfis Floriloquium & communiloquium." Bibl. Theyer, 6383. " Floriloquium philofophorum Jo. Walenfis," Corpus Chrifti College, Cambridge, 1563; " Manipulus florum quem inchoavit Jo. Gualenfis, qui floruit 1260;" Peterhoufe 1745. Tanner, Bibl. Britan. 749, gives no *Thomas* Waleys, but John. Qu. fhould we for *Colores* read *Flores*, or *Collationes*, as his " Summa Collationum" is in Bibl. Bodl. 2684.

[24] Precentor of Canterbury, a very learned man in times of great ignorance in the eleventh century. Among other writings, is one " de vocum confonantiis." Tanner, Bibl. Britan. p. 563.

[25] " Excerpta è Prifciano ordine alphabetico, juxta expofitionem Petri Heliæ;" Bibl. Bodl. 2088. " P. H. fuper Prifcian. ;" " Quæftiones P. H. de conftructionibus;" Trinity College, 1041-2. " De fpeciebus conftructionis;" Merton, 776.

[26] Qu. Robert Kylwardby, archbifhop of Canterbury, who wrote fome grammatical pieces? Bibl. Britan. p. 455. " Rob. Kylwardeby fuper libros Prifciani de Conftructione;" Merton, 768. He ftudied at Oxford. Gutch's Annals, vol. I. 212. 221. 305.

[27] In Afhmole's Mufeum are two copies of " Proverbia Alexandri, Pamphilii, Getæ, Claudiani Magni, Perfii, Ovidii, Virgilii," and other poets. Whether thefe are grammatical or other extracts may be doubted. " Liber Claudiani" occurs in the catalogue of Peterhoufe, 1687. " Claudianus minor" among If. Voffius' MSS. 2664. may be oppofed to " Claudius magnus" in our poetical article.   [28] Of him fee Bibl. Brit. p. 376.

[29] Galfridus Anglicus is Galfridus de Vinefalvo, or Vinefauf, who wrote " de arte dicendi, de novâ poetriâ, de loquendi artificio, de modo & arte dictandi," on the culture of trees and keeping of fruits, and the expedition of Richard I. into the Holy Land; which laft was printed in the " Gefta Dei per Francos, and in Gale's " Hift. Angl. Scriptores, Ox. 1687. II. 247. Tanner, Bibl. Britan. 736.   [30] Alanus, bp. of Autun, and Alanus de Lynne & de Theokefbury, were theological writers; but not mentioned as poets.   [31] Fulgentius Planciades was a writer of mythology.

[32] Socrates " de morte contemnendâ" is a Latin MS. Bodl. 4054. When *Socrates* is reckoned among *poets* who may not be?

[33] See before, note ([29]).   [34] Richard Feribrige was a fophift of Oxford about 1360; author of " Confequentiarum regulæ," publifhed with notes by Alexander Sermoneta, Matthew Campagna, and Gaetano de Tierni, Venice, 1511, 4to. Tanner, Bibl. Brit. p. 278.   [35] At Merton, 605, " Quodlibeta Tho. Sutton."

[36] In the Bodleian Library, 1699, is " Tractatus generum nominum per Magiftrum Robertum Allington." Oriel 887. " Rob. Alington, Theolog. prof. in prædicamenta." In Worcefter library, 898, " Alyngton fuper prædicamenta & anteprædicamenta."   [37] Among Wiclif's writings, Bibl. Britan. 768, are " Quæftiones logicales."

[38] William Occham's logical writings occur, Bibl. Britan. p 554.

Sanctus Thomas. Burley Linc' [1]. Kylwardby [2]. Hermes [15]. Orich. Tebyth [16].
Quere infra in Logicâ. Archelaüs [17]. W. Rede [20].
Rogerus Bacon, prefatius Capianus.
Meſſallak [18].

PHILOSOPHIA.

Thomas Aquinas in multis. Antonius.
Egidius [3]. Petrus de Alvernâ [4].
Burley [1]. Ayt W. de Conchis [5].

INSTRUMENTA.

Magnum } aſtrolabium. fratre Thomâ Halo.
Minus } Stellarium [21] per fratrem
Spera de auricalco. W. Charite.
Raius per fratrem W. Quedam viridis tabula [22]

ARITHMETICA. MUSICA. GEOMETRIA.
Boetius. Boetius. Euclid.

Charite de auricalco. ad cognoſcend' literam
Duotrianguli per eundem, Dominicalem.
& trigonometer dat. à

ASTRONOMIA.

Hermannus [6]. Alkabucius [10].
Epiſtola Meſſale de mo- Alexander. Trocula [11].

PHISICA NATURALIS.

tibus planetarum [7]. Philonius.
Sophar de pluviis. Sortes. Roſa medicinæ [23]. Johannicius [29].
Alphadhog filius Zeel in Ypocrates [12]. Johannes Bokkedene [24]. Galienus [30].
auguriis ſtellicis. Robertus Groſthed [13] [de Theophilus [25]. Egidius [31].
Omer benalſthargum Ti- pronoſticatione aëris]. Phalaretus [26]. Yſaac [31].
beriadis, de judiciis na- Hayly [14]. Nictis. Johannes de Sancto A-
tivitatum [8]. Zael [15]. Mr Gilbertus Anglicus [27]. mando [33].
Tholomeus de almageſt. Johannes pchorie. Rogerus major & minor [28]. Giraldus.
Albumazar [9]. Almageſtus.

[1] Walter Burley, another learned Scotiſt, as well as Occham. Ibid. p. 141. Both Oxonians. Annals, ut supra, 406.

[2] See note ([26]), p. 104.   [3] Qu. Ægidius Romanus " de Eſſe & Eſſentia." Baliol, 268. 449.

[4] " Petri Alveres, or de Alverniâ, è Soc. Jeſu comment. in Ariſtotelis libros de generatione & animâ;" Bibl. Bodl. 2162.——"in libros metaphyſicos Ariſtotelis; ibid. 2366. 2444; on other pieces of Ariſtotle, Baliol, 28. 429. 449; Merton, 741. 742; Peterhouſe, 1702. 1706.

[5] " Secunda Phyſica Will. de Conchis;" Caius college, 1151. " Dialogus W. de Conchis;" Peterhouſe, 1706. " Philo-ſophia Willielmi de Conchis, aliàs Shelles;" Corpus Chriſti College, Oxford, 1562. " Philoſophiæ Compendium;" Univerſity college, 6 App. Bodl. 1602. 1705. 2596. 3565. 3623. 4056. See alſo ib. 1708.

[6] " Hermannus de aſtrolabio," Caius college, 1154; " Hermannus Contractus de aſtrolabiis," Theyer, 6625.

[7] " Meſſahalæ epiſtola de ecliptibus Lunæ, &c;" Bodl. 1030. 1098 :—" de proprietatibus ſtellarum," " libellus interpre-tationum," 1648; other pieces, 1795. 1808. 1829. 2272. 2354. 3338. 3466. 6561; alſo in the Aſhmolean Muſeum.

[8] " Liber Aomar filii Alfragani de nativitatibus," among ſir Henry Digby's MSS. in the Bodleian library, 1795. " Liber Aomaris Aburfariari de nativitatibus & interrogationibus." Bodl. 2354.

9 A great Arabian aſtrologer, called Almaſor in the catalogue of Peterborough library. Gunton, p. 187. See Bodl. 1673. 3338. Peterhouſe, 1712-16.

[10] Alkabitii " Introductorium ad Aſtronomiam judicialem." MS. Savile. More Bodl. 1848. 3466.

[11] Can this be " Troſula," of which there were two, major and minor. Bodl. 1463. 2696. 3541. It was a work of Eros, an antient phyſician treating on the diſeaſes of women, is alſo called " Trotula mulierum," and has been printed.

[12] Hippocrates.

[13] In Dr. Pegge's enumeration of biſhop Groſſeteſte's publiſhed works, p. 279, is one " de impreſſione aëris;" Leland (Collect. III. 21.) ſaw in the library at Peterhouſe, Cambridge, " Lincolnienſis de impreſſionibus aëris ;" and in the liſt of inedited works is another tract with a like title, a different piece from the printed one, which in another place is called " de aëris in-temperantia prognoſtica." This laſt is probably meant in this Catalogue. See Annals, ut ſupra, 406.

[14] A famous Arabic aſtronomer and commentator on Galen in the eleventh century which produced ſo many celebrated Arabian phyſicians. Haly, called Abbas, was likewiſe an eminent phyſician of this period, and called Galen's Ape. Warton, I. 440. His treatiſe on Judicial Aſtronomy is among ſir H. Saville's MSS. Bibl. Bodl. His comment on Ptolomy's Quadripartitum, Digby, 1715.

[15] " Ars Judiciaria ſecundùm 9 Judices; Alkindum, Zaelem, Albumazar, Meſſehalla, Dorotheum, Jergem, Ariſtotelem, Abennaret, Homar." MS. Savile. More by Zael, Bodl. 561. 1795. 2354. " Liber Judiciorum Zaelis." Bodl. 1148. " Introductorium," Aſhmole, 6721.—Zahel, or Zael, or Zeel Bebiz, was an Arabian writer, who diſtinguiſhed himſelf by his writings, " de temporum ſignificationibus in judiciis," & " de electionibus," publiſhed by Nicholas Pruenel with Firmicus and others at Baſle, 1533. Hofman.

[16] Triſmegiſtus, the myſtic philoſopher, whoſe ſpurious writings occur in monaſtic libraries.

[17] The like obſervation applies to this philoſopher.

[18] Meſſehalla " de nativitatibus." MS. Saville, Bibl. Bodl. " Theoria," Aſhm. 6734. Sir Thomas Browne (Vulgar Errors, Book IV. c. 12.) of the difference of dating the climacterical year ſays, " Haly, Meſſahalaeh, Ganivetus, & Guido Bonatus, begin it ab horâ quæſtionis." Arzahel Meſſalak, whoſe works were printed at Venice 1493, flouriſhed about 1080 in Spain, and wrote about the obliquity of the Zodiac, in which he remarks that the greateſt declination of the Sun in his time was 23.34 degrees. Hofman.

[19] Thebit, " de proportionibus;"—" de figurâ Catha;"—" Tractatus patris." See Leland, Coll. IV. 35. " Thebit filii Corred in motum acceſſionis & receſſionis." MS Saville.

[20] William Rede, or Reade, was a very learned fellow of Merton College, Oxford, where he built and furniſhed the library; on the wall of which was painted his portrait; and many of his mathematical inſtruments were preſerved there, when Harriſon wrote his Deſcription of Britain, prefixed to Holinſhed's Chronicle. His " aſtronomical tables," calculated for the meridian of Oxford, were followed by others for that of Cambridge by John Holbrook; but he wrote alſo on divinity-ſubjects, and was promoted in 1369 to the ſee of Chicheſter, where he died in 1375; and was buried before the high altar of his cathedral at Selſey. Tanner, Bibl. Britan. p. 618. Leland mentions another Rede, who wrote a medical tract, which, ſays he, " neſcio quid magiæ ſpirabat." Tanner, Bibl. Britan. v. Gladeſaunt. Phyſic and Aſtrology went together.

[21] Stellarium. Qu. a Catalogue of the then-diſcovered ſtars? or a Map repreſenting their relative poſitions in the ſky, and the courſes of the planets? In Bibliotheca Britannica, article Botonerius, p. 115, " Verificacio omnium Stellarum fixarum pro anno MCCCXL. Hunc ille libellum, inſtante Falſtafio, contexuit—varia Aſtronomica, &c.; ſcilicet, ſtellas verificatas pro anno Chriſti MCCCCXL, ad inſtanciam Johannis Falſtoff; & duas tabulas de ſtellis fixis."

[22] To the calendars in our books of Common Prayer is almoſt always annexed a table, either for finding, or explicitly de-noting, the dominical letter for a certain number of years; and ſuch a table, as it is believed, was generally prefixed to the antient liturgies and miſſals, as alſo to old almanacks; and theſe were of different colours, agreeably to the taſte of the il-luminator. In ſome old almanacks and diaries, which Mr. Gough poſſeſſes, are theſe coloured tables.

[23] This was written by John Gatiſden, or Gaddeſden, fellow of Merton College, about 1320, the moſt celebrated phyſician of his age in England. This his principal work, divided into five books, was printed at Paris, 1492. Leland calls it " opus luculentum juxta ac eruditum." Tanner, Bibl. Britan. p. 312. Warton, I. 443. Freind and Aikin's Hiſtory of Phyſic. " Roſa Medicinæ," Bibl. Bodl. 2059. 2463. 3619. His " Hiſtoria aurea," ib. 2469.

[24] Neither Bokkedene nor Bokedene occur in Bibliotheca Britannica. His library was purchaſed for Leiceſter abbey.

[25] " Theophilus de uriris." Bodl. 261. 1252. 1355. 2753; Aſhmol. 7751.

[26] Philaretus " de pulſibus." Bibl. Bodl. 1251. 1355. 2753; " de urinâ," New college, 1130.

[27] Of Gilbertus Anglicus, ſee Bibl. Britan. p. 317. His popular compendium of the medical art, Leland ſays, was much ſtudied by many " ad quæſtum properantes."

[28] Rogerina major & minor are mentioned among Roger Bacon's works, Bibl. Britan. 64.

[29] Johannitii " Iſagoge ad Galeni technon," Bodl. 1252.; " Gloſſæ in Aphoriſmos," ib. 1709; " Iſagoge ad micro-technum Galeni," ib. 2753.   [30] Galen.

[31] Joannes Ægidius, or de Sancto Ægidio, a native of St. Albans in the thirteenth century, ſtudied at Paris, became phyſician to Philip king of France, and a celebrated Dominican preacher, the firſt Engliſhman of that order. He attended biſhop Groſſeteſte on his death-bed, 1253. Matthew Paris. He was an Oxonian; ſee Wood's Annals, by Gutch, vol. I. p. 210.

[32] Honain ben Iſhac tranſlated Galen's Aphoriſms and other pieces into Arabic. Herbelot, p. 209.

[33] " Joh. de Sco Amando de baſibus medicinæ," Bodl. 1761; " Aureolæ," 2696.

Salernus [1].
Mr Bartholomeus [2].
Mr Petrus Hifpanus [3].
Magifter Poncius.
Nicholas Rypon [4].
Lucianus.
Platearius [5].
Conftantinus [6].
Magifter Maurus [7].
Walterus [8] Agelinus.
Reginaldus de Aronte.

Peffulanus [9].
Johes Meffue [10].
Avicenna.
Avôys [11].
Lanfrancus [12] Garrio.
Alexander [13] de Aileflon.
Mr Mattheus Platearius.
Macer [14].
Plato.
Johannes Baytley.

Require iftas infra in Phificâ Naturali.

JUS CIVILE.

Magna Charta in parvo
volumine 2 fo & pᵍᵍᵘ.
Digeft' inforciat'.

Bartholomæus fuper cafum
codicis.
Summa Azonis [15] inftitut'.

Require infra in Jure Civili.

JUS CANONICUM.

DECRETA.

Decreta Alexandri.   Decreta Yvonis.

DECRETALIA.

Cardinal' Geffelyn.
Andrew fuper Sext' [16].
Johannes Andrew [16].
Wiltus & Galfridus fuper
Clement'.
Raymundus [17] Gaufridius.
Johannes Cardinal.
Summa Azonis [18].
Archus in rofario.
Martinus.
Bartholomæus [19].
Johannes Antonius [20].
Innocentius Hoftienfis [21].
Wiltus in Speculo [22].
Galfridus de Duranti [22].
Egidius [23].
Hugo fuper decreta [24].
Barnardus.
Petrus in Lecturâ.
Johannes in addicõibus.
Willielmus Duratis [22].
Gratianus [25].

Johes Novellus; require in-
fra in Jure Canonico.
Radulphus fuper Leviti-
co [26].
Quere ibidem in Levitico.
Valerius [27].   Quere in
Canticâ Canticorum.
Sibilla Merlyn.
Metodius [28] & beatus Blafius.
Quere in pphis.
Johannes Humaunde de
compofitione Goliæ, &
Evangelium Nicodemi [29].
Quere in Evangeliftis.
Cantor Parifius. Quere in
Auguftino ad Cirillum [30].
Decretum Lucilii, & Lu-
cilius. Quere in Jero-
nimo de Cenâ Divinâ.
Paulus, in revelat' vifionis
fuæ. Quere in Hugone
fuper regula cancella-

---

[1] Qu. Rich. Salernitanus, whofe tract " de urinis" is in the Bodleian Library, ib. 3541.

[2] " Tractatus de regimine fanitatis fecundùm Bartholomæum," Bodl. 1632. 2006; " Practica Medicinæ," 2462.

[3] Petri Hifpani " Summularium paf. in Græc. trad. per Max. Planudem," Bodl. 76; Caius college, 978; " In phyfio-
gnomiam Ariftotetlis," Peterhoufe, 1716; " Thefaurus pauperum," Bibl. Pub. Cantab. 2329.

[4] Not mentioned in Bibl. Britan. Nicholas de Ferneham was an eminent practitioner, phyfician to king Henry III. and afterwards bifhop of Durham, where he died in 1241. Matthew Paris; and Tanner's Notitia, p. 277. An Oxonian. See
Annals, vol. I. 167.

[5] " Platearii liber de fimplici medicinâ. Bodl. 7770;" " Gloffæ Antidorii Nicolai," ibid. 1748.

[6] " Conftantinus Afer, a monk of Caffino in Italy, was one of the Saracen phyficians who brought medicine into Europe,
and formed the Salernitan fchool, chiefly by tranflating various Arabian and Grecian medical books into Latin. He was born at
Carthage; and learned grammar, logic, geography, arithmetic, aftronomy, and natural philofophy, of the Chaldees, Arabians,
Perfians, Saracens, Egyptians, and Indians, in the fchool of Bagdad. Being thus completely accomplifhed in thefe fciences,
after thirty-nine years' ftudy, he returned into Africa, where an attempt was formed againft his life. Conftantine, having
fortunately difcovered this defign, privately took fhip, and came to Salerno in Italy, where he lurked fome time in difguife;
but he was recognifed by the caliph's brother, then at Salerno, who recommended him as a fcholar, univerfally fkilled
in the learning of all nations, to the notice of Robert duke of Normandy. Robert entertained him with the higheft marks of
refpect; and Conftantine, by the advice of his patron, retired to the monaftery of Caffino, where, being kindly received by the
abbot Defiderius, he tranflated in that learned fociety the books abovementioned, moft of which he firft imported into Europe.
Thefe verfions are faid to be ftill extant. He flourifhed about 1086. Petr. Diacon. de vir. illuftr. Monaft. Caffin. cap. xxiii.
He is mentioned by Chaucer in the Merchant's Tale, V. 1326, p. 71, Urry's edition:
    And lectaries had he there full fine,
    Soche as the curfid monk *Dan Conftantine*
    Hath written in his book " de Coïtu."
The title of this book is " de Coïtu, quibus profit aut obfit, quibus medicaminibus & alimentis acuatur impediaturve". Inter
Op. Bafil. 1536. fol. Warton's Hiftory of Poetry, I. 441. This was in Peter-houfe library, Cambridge. Lel. Coll. III. 24.

[7] Qu. Rabanus Maurus beforementioned.

[8] " Walteri fumma de urinis;" Bodl. 1301.

[9] Or *Mons Paffulanus*, fome phyfician of Montpelier.

[10] " Omnes libri fupradicti, quondam Johannis Bokedene, medici, funt de perquifitione domini W. Sadyngton." This note
is in the original Catalogue.

[11] Averroes. As the Afiatic fchools decayed by the indolence of the caliphs, Averroes was one of thofe philofophers who
adorned the Moorifh fchools erected in Africa and Spain. He was born at Cordoua of an antient Arabic family, was a profeffor
of the univerfity of Morocco, wrote a commentary on all Ariftotle's works, died about the year 1169, and was ftyled the moft
Peripatetic of all the Arabian writers. Warton, I. 441.

[12] " Chirurgia minor Lanfranci." New College, 1135.

[13] Qu. Alexander Trallianus " de re medicâ," lib. 12, &c. Caius college, Cambridge, 933. 977.

[14] The poem " de virtutibus herbarum," under the name of Macer, now extant, was written by Odo, or Odobourne,
a phyfician of the dark ages. Warton, II. 167.

[15] Azo was a learned civilian of Bologna, who died in 1200, and whofe Epitome of Civil Law,' and Comments on the Di-
gefts, are ftill much ufed. Hoffman's Lexicon.

[16] " Jo. Andreæ Summa fuper lib. Decretalium, Bodl. 851; " Novellæ fuper eofdem," ibid. 2447. 2503.

[17] Qu. Raymundus de Pennaforte, an eminent civilian. Bodl. 670. 675. 1012. 1483.

[18] See Appendix to Oxford College MSS.   [19] Glanville beforementioned.

[20] Qu. " Antonius de fex principiis," Bodl. 6564.

[21] " Gloffa Hoftienfis fuper Decretalia," New College, 1199; " Hoftienfis in lectura fuper Decretales Gregorii," " Lectura
Hoftienfis fuper Conftitutiones Innocentianas," Caius college, 905. " Hoftienfis de pœnitentiis & remiffionibus." Ib. 1101.
" Canones pœnitentiales fecundùm Hoftienfem." Ibid. 1170.

[22] " Speculum Juris Cannonici ac repertorium vocatum Summa Summarum." Pembroke hall, Cambridge, 2060. This
Speculum, called alfo " Speculum Judiciale," was the work of Durandus, or Durantes. (Durham cath. MS. 266-7.) " Reper-
torium Magiftri Willielmi Durandi." (Worcefter Cathedral, MS. 786.) " Repertorium in lib. hift. Decretal." (Hereford
Cathedral, 1680.) He was author of the " Rationale Divinorum Officiorum." (Ib. 804.)

[23] Ægidius Bonomenfis, an eminent civilian. His " ordo judiciarius," Trinity College, 549; Caius, 914, 915, 916. 933.

[24] Hugo Cardinalis Hoftienfis, commonly called de S. Victore, commented on the Pfalms and New Teftament. Or fee
before, note (3), p. 101.

[25] A very old copy of this MS. remains in the Church Library at Lincoln. See note (6), p. 107.

[26] " Radulphus Flaviacenfis monachi Benedictini explanatio fuper Leviticum, libris 20." Bodl. 2127; All Souls, 1413;
Trinity College, Oxford, 1954; Trinity College, Cambridge, 285. 389; Corpus Chrifti College, Cambridge, 1424; Peterhoufe, 1904; Bibl. Pub. Cant. 2206. In a copy at Pembroke it is noticed that he wrote on almoft all the books of the Old
and New Teftaments, and is to be diftinguifhed from Radulphus Niger, who was an hiftorical writer, though confounded with
him in the Index to the MSS. in the Cambridge libraries, where Numbers 2911. 284. 1594. 2004. belong to Niger.

[27] Qu. " epift. ad Rufinum de uxore non ducendâ." Bodl. 1668. 1748. 1767.

[28] Methodius was bifhop of Olympus, Patara, and Tyre, and wrote in Greek, Queftions on Genefis, Bodl. 2016; Hymns
to the Virgin, Bodl. 76. 234. 2500. Jerom tranflated fome of his works; and fome were printed by Allatius. His tract " de
fine feculi & revelationis," Rom. 1656, may be a prophetic piece.

[29] " Evangelium Nicodemi de paffione & refurrectione Chrifti" is in the Bodleian library, 1113. Other copies there bear
the title of " Gefta Salvatoris."

[30] " B. Auguftini epiftola ad Cyrillum de obitu S. Hieronymi, prefbyteri, cum refponfis." Bodl. 778. In Nᵒ 1220. it is
" de *magnificentiâ* Hieronymi;" and in 1390. " de *laude* Hieronymi."

rum Linc' ibidem.
Johannes Holden. Quere in Hugone de Confci-entiâ '.
Thomas abbas de Urfellis².
Quere in Damafceno.
Robertus abbas.
Helpicius & Paftafius ³. Require in Yfidoro.
Beatus Sextus in Dionifio require.
Raymundus in Alexandro require.

Johannes Waldeby in Linc' require.
W. Lincoln' cancellarius. Require in W. de Montibus ⁴.
W. de Sčo Amore.
W. Norton.
W. Antifiorenfis.
W. de Anler.
W. de Alverniâ.
W. in Speculo.
W. Durantis.
W. de Conchis.

Conftitutiones, paĉta, Ottonis, & Stephani Cantuarenfis, & Ottobonis.
Johannis papæ benedictiones provinciales.
Johannes de Bofco.
Paffio Chrifti in Gallico ⁵.
Bellum Trojanum in Gallico ⁵.
Liber de Drian & Madok in Gallico ⁵.
Hiftoriæ de Bibliâ in Gallico ⁵.

Beviz de Hampton.
Lumen legum in Gallico.
Manuale.
Gefta Alexandri Magni.
Liber de Maundeville.
Liber de Gallico—2 fo. Liber de Gallico, 2 fo. manuell.
Gefta Alexandri Magni. 2 fo. de Stheo.

Many books are referred to fome other arrangements; many have only 2 folia. The firft words of fome given; and, after all our enquiries, many of the writers here enumerated muft remain as unknown as they are uninterefting; and perhaps pofterity has very little reafon to regret the lofs of the Library of Leicefter Abbey ⁶.

MISSALIA.
Regiftrum omnium librorum in choro, in capellis, in infirmariâ, & apud Ingwarby.

8 Miffalia abbreviata.
5 Pfalteria abbreviata.
Pfalterium.

The abbot had others in his chapel; Antiphonaria, gradale, proceffionale, portiferium, pfalterium juvenale; as had alfo the prior, fubprior, frater W. Charite, John Grene, W. Eyton, fr. Stephanus, Tho. Yngewardby, W. Stowton celerarius, T. Pynder, Joh. Whytley, fubcelerarius, John Nores, J. Talis, J. Peny ⁷, J. Hornyngewold, W. Fofbrok, W. Chaunce, Joh. Garby, J. Twyforth, T. Browhton, W. Frawnceys, fr. Nich', Ric' Palet; who appear to have been the whole of the monks in 1477.

Altars enumerated are the High Altar, thofe of the Virgin, Trinity, St. Gabriel, Stephen, Michael, Leonard, Andrew, Katharine, Anne, Auguftine.

In the choir were a Martirologium,
3 Collectaria,
Vetus ⎱ Ordinale.
Novum ⎰

Ante capellam S. Auguftini.
Portiforium notatum.

In pulpito.
Magna Legenda in duobus voluminibus.
Item liber Parliamenti, cum expofitione rᵉ beati Auguftini p M. Trivet, & cum conftitutionibus Benedicti & conftitutionibus Ottonis, & aliis.
5 lib' collationum per fratrem W. Charite.
Item liber de certis collect', & longâ letaniâ.
Item una rotula de longâ letaniâ.
2 Gradalia abbreviata.
Liber lectionum diebus omnibus.
Magnum antiphonarium.
Unum portiferium catenatum.
Pupilla oculi catenata.
Liber de 9 lectionibus per fratrem W. Charite.
Liber de hymnis & antiphonis abbreviatus in certis feftis.
Cantica organica.

1 liber de canticis organicis per fratrem W. Prefton.
Another by W. Charite.
Kyrieleyfon vocat' Zouglons.
Another canticus organicus by the fame.

In the Infirmary.
A miffal; 2 portiforia.
1 falterium; 2 gradalia.
1 Quaternus de fervicio Corporis Xᵗⁱ.

At Ingwardby.
A miffal, antiphonar, portiforium, and manuale graduale.
Martiro'oges.

LIBRI ET ROTULÆ EVIDENCIARUM NOSTRARUM, VALDE NECESSARII.
The Chartulary.
Vetus Chartularium.
Second Chartulary, compofed by W. Charite.
Liber Placitorum; diverfa placita, condemnationes contra vicarios noftros.
Compofitiones, corrodia, cum recitat' fratris Galfridi Salow.
Liber de terris dominicalibus, in quo continentur " Terraria de terris noftris dominicalibus, & aliis terris in diverfis locis & villis.

RENTALIA.
One called *Rotula de Pyn*, 1254.
" Habemus," about 1224.
Another, 1258. Another, 1267. Another, 1294.
Two others ⎱ about the fame time.
Two others ⎰
Another called *Geryn*, with antient pleas.
Another called *Bathe*, on paper; and two others in the fame book; with four Rentals " de Leyceftriâ "
The Novum Rentale by W. Charite; account of all the advowfons, penfions, portions of mills, and tithes of mills, &c. In princ', " Habemus ex dono fundatoris;" t Tho. Wylfon.
Another New Rental by W. Charite.
Ordered by the abbot and convent, that all thefe rentals be kept " in uno loco pro eifdem concernent' ad cuftodiend' limitato."
One roll of all who hold lands.

¹ " Hugo de Confcientiâ." Bodl. 1716.
² Qu. Theobaldus de Urfinis, archbifhop of Panormus. Leland, Coll. III. 21.
³ " Helpericus de arte Calculatoriâ," and " Pafchafius epifcopus, epiftola ad Leonem papam de ratione Pafchæ," occur in the Bodleian Library, 2372. Helpericus " de computo ecclefiaftico," Trinity College, Cambridge, 395; " de temporibus," Salifbury Cathedral, 1017; " Computus" (Wagftaffe MS. 3482.)
⁴ See before, p. 101, note (⁸). ⁵ Thefe and other books are improperly claffed under Decretalia.
⁶ Bifhop Repyndon, who was abbot here, gave to his church of Lincoln a book called Peter de Aureolis (a breviary of the Bible) after the death of one of his prebendaries: which book is now in the Britifh Mufeum. MSS. Reg. 8 G. fol. 111. Warton, I. Differtation II. p. 80. The newer library of Lincoln cathedral, built by dean Honeywood at the clofe of the laft century, has fuperfeded the ufe of the older, fo that the few MSS. left in it were in total diforder when I vifited it, 1791. Among thefe, however, were fome which had been given by Hugh archdeacon of Leycefter about 1151, when Haimo Chancellor of Lincoln had the care of the library. On two of thefe (" Hegefippus," and " Decreta Gratiani") was written, " Ex dono Hugonis archid. Leyceftr'."—Mr. Warton's obfervation on the royal library at Paris in the beginning of the fourteenth century (I. Diff. II. b 2.) will apply to this of Leicefter abbey. " There were only four claffics in the royal library. Thefe were one copy of Cicero, Ovid, Lucan, and Boethius. The reft were chiefly books of devotion, which included but few of the fathers; many treatifes of aftrology, geometry, chiromancy, and medicine, originally written in Arabic, and tranflated into Latin and French: pandects, chronicles, and romances. This collection was principally made by Charles the Fifth, who began his reign in 1365. This monarch was paffionately fond of reading, and it was the fafhion to fend him prefents of books from every part of the kingdom of France." ⁷ He was afterwards abbot.

Many

Many Rentals of Leicefter, very good; one dated 4 Hen. IV.; others of John Bathe, T. Wyxton, W. Wyxton, John Sadyngton, W. Charite. All to be well kept.

A rental of William Extildefham.

There are alfo 23 rolls written by the hands of brother William Charyte.

LIBRI, QUOS PROPRIA MANU SCRIPSIT ET COMPILAVIT FRATER W. CHARITE.

Hugo de Vienna.

Libri evangeliftarum & epiftolarum feftis principalibus.

Five books of Collations.

Troporium in miffali ad altare S. Stephani.

The New Rental; quē librū ipe cōpilavit & fibi fecit.

The book called Char-wary.

A book of demefne lands.

Cantica organica.

Words in the Bible.

Names of our founders and their gifts.

Quatuor libri fpecialitèr ordinati pro curiis ñris, in quibus funt diverfa

rentalia & evidenciæ fu-per jure habendi vifum franciplegii, & tenendi curias ñras.

Breve opufculum per quod aliquis poteft planè cog-nofcere quomodo red-ditus noftri decreverunt à tempore Edwardi re-gis III. ufque ad tempus 8 Hen. VII.

Account of alienations; from the former.

2 Antiphones.

1 Gradale.

2 Proceffionals.

Hymns, Gofpels, &c.

Item notavit Gradale & Antiphonarium fratris Johis Ratclyf.

LIBRI QUOS FRATER WILL'M'S CHARITE SCRIBI FECIT, VEL PROPRIA MANU NO-TAVIT.

Novum Rentale; Liber de terris dominicalibus.

2 rolls de liberis redditibus.

3 of names of tenants and homage tenants.

3 of jewels belonging to the abbey, and their weight.

4 de notabilibus, extracted by him from various books.

Others on Bible words.

Names of founders, lands, and other rolls.

In all 24 rolls.

BOUGHT AND PURCHASED BY HIM.

Liber vocatus Brounnard.

Boetius de confolatione.

Parabole Salomonis.

Metaphyfica.

Logica.

Manuale puerorum.

" De Arte componendi Sermonem."

Lucanus.

Ovidius de Faftis.

———— de Arte amandi.

Claudian.

Penelope Ulyffi.

Macrobius de fomnio Sci-pionis

Anteclaudianus.

Horologium Sapientie.

Pupilla oculi.

Vita Efopi fabulatoris.

And various other, in Me-taphyfics, Logic, Di-vinity, and Law.

From this Catalogue it feems to be rather doubtful, whether in the library of this religious houfe there might be any one complete collection of all the Holy Scriptures. Suppofing *Biblie*, in the firft article, to have included both the Old and the New Teftaments [1], it was a tome *defective* and *worn*, (*defect' & ufitat'*). The fecond confifted of each book of the Old Tefta-ment only; and the third of the Gofpels, without any mention of the Acts of the Apoftles, of the Epiftles, or of the Apocalypfe. There is, however, a feparate mention of " Actus Aptor' glofſ'," " Apocalypf' glofſ'," " Epie Pauli [2] glofſ'," " Epie Canonice;" and among the laft occurs the " Canticus Canticorum." Perhaps there might be fome of thefe Auguftine monks, to whom the divine oracles in the learned languages would have been of little ufe; and yet to thefe was not indulged a tranflation in Englifh, there being in the Confiftorial Acts at Rochefter the minutes of a rigid procefs againft the *precentor* of the priory of that ca-thedral for retaining an Englifh Teftament in dif-obedience to the general injunction of Cardinal Wolfey to deliver up thefe prohibited books to the bifhops of the refpective diocefes.

Knighton, a canon of St. Mary le Pre, has, to his own difgrace, recorded his bitter condemnation of the tranflation made by his contemporary Wicliff (X Scr. col. 2644.): " Chrift intrufted his Gofpel," fays that ecclefiaftic, " to the clergy and doctors of the church, to minifter it to the laity, and weaker fort, according to their exigences and feveral occafions: but this Mafter John Wicliff, by tranflating it, has made it vulgar, and has laid it more open to the laity, and even to women, who can read, than it ufed to be to the moft learned of the clergy, and thofe of the beft underftanding; and thus the Gofpel Jewel, the Evangelical feaft, is thrown about, and trodden under feet of fwine." Such language, as an ingenious and learned Divine has juftly obferved, was looked upon as good reafoning by the clergy of that day, who faw not with what fatire it was edged againft themfelves [3].

" A. 1528, Jan. 15. In palatio Roffenf', coram ipfo reverendo patre, comparuit perfonalitèr Dr. Will. Mafelde, monachus & precentor in ecclef' Caftr' Roffenf', notatus, quod, poft publicationem factam in civitate predictâ quòd unufquifque fancta Dei Evan-gelia in idioma noftrum tranflata apud fe fervand' ei-dem reverendo patri inferrent, & traderent, fub pœnis in literis reverendi patris cardinalis contentis, idem Wiltus hujufmodi libros poft tempus per eundē rev' patrē limitat' apud fe fervavit & retinuit," &c.

---

[1] There is very little reafon to doubt that *Biblia* was a general name for MS copies of both Teftaments, as well as for printed ones afterwards, from the firft publication to the prefent time.

[2] No other of the Epiftles in the New Teftament occur, fave thofe of St. Paul.

[3] Gilpin's Life of Wicliff, p. 39.

APPENDIX, Nº XVIII. NEWARK HOSPITAL and CHURCH.

1. Rex, &c. Sciatis, quòd, de gratiâ noftrâ fpeciali, conceffimus & licentiam dedimus, pro nobis & heredibus noftris, quantum in nobis eft, dilecto confanguineo & fideli noftro Henrico comiti Lancaftrie, quòd ipfe in quâdam placeâ fuâ in Leiceftriâ, continente in fe quatuor acras terre, quoddam hofpitale in honorē Dei & beate Marie Virginis de novo fundare; & quoddam oratorium ac domos pro morâ & inhabitatione unius magiftri & quorundam capellanorum, per ipfum comitem vel heredes fuos in hofpitali predicto conftituendorum, conftruere; ac quatuor carucatas terre, cum pertinentiis, in eâdem villâ; necnon advocationem ecclefie de Irceftre in com' Northampt'; que quidem placea, terra, & advocatio tenentur de nobis in capite, ut dicitur, dare poffit & affignare prefatis magiftro & capellanis; habenda & tenenda fibi & fucceffioribus fuis pro fuftentatione fuâ & pauperum in eodem hofpitali, fecundùm difpofitionem ipfius comitis vel heredum fuorum, recipiendorum in liberam, puram, & perpetuam eleemofinam in perpetuum. Et eifdem magiftro & capellanis, quòd ipfi terram predictam, cum pertinentiis, & advocationem illam à prefato comite recipere, & ecclefiam illam appropriare, & eam appropriatam in proprios ufus tenere poffint fibi & fucceffioribus fuis in liberam, puram, & perpetuam eleemofinam, pro fuftentatione fuâ & pauperum predictorum in perpetuum, ficut predictum eft, tenore prefentium fimiliter licentiam dedimus fpecialem; ftatuto de terris & tenementis ad manum mortuam non ponendis edito non obftante, &c. In cujus, &c. Tefte rege, apud Wodeftoke, fecundo die Aprilis[1].

2. Bulla Clementis VI. Papæ univerfis directa, & relaxatio pœnitentiæ vifitantium hofpitale pauperum: Quod, ficut accepimus, quondam Henricus comes Lancaftriâ, in villâ de Leiceftriâ, Linc' dioc', ad honorem Dei & fuftentationem pauperum Chrifti, pro fuâ & parentum fuorum animarum falute, fundavit & de bonis fuis ditavit ecclefiam, pro certo capellanorum numero in eis conftituendo, perpetuò Altiffimo fervitur' ibidem; in quâ etiam tam ipfe quàm dilectus filius nobilis vir Henricus comes Lancaftrie, dicti Henrici filius, relicto loco fepulture progenitorum fuorum & aliorum de regali profapiâ defcendentium, fepulturas fuas elegiffe dicuntur. Dat. Avincon. 3 id. Aprilis pont. noftri anno 7º [2].

3. Indulgentia XL dierum conceffa omnibus vifitantibus ecclefiam hofpitalis Leiceftrie per VIII dies immediatè precedentes feftum Sci Michis Archangeli; & XXX dierum fingulis annuatim dictam ecclefiam vifitantibus. Dat' apud Maghefeld, 1350[3].

4. Rex omnibus ad quos, &c. falutem. Sciatis, quòd ob fpecialem affectionem, quam ad perfonam dilecti confanguinei & fidelis noftri Henrici ducis Lancaftrie gerimus & habemus, & ob fenfum gratuiti obfequii nobis per ipfum ducem pluriès laudabilitèr impenfi, de gratiâ noftrâ fpeciali conceffimus & licentiam dedimus, pro nobis & heredibus noftris, quantum in nobis eft, eidem duci, quòd ipfe maneria de Inglefham, Wolafton, Kynemeresford, & Cheddeworth, cum pertinentiis, & advocationes ecclefiarum de Thorpe-Edmere, Wymondham, Hegham-Ferrars, Raundes, & Prefton (que de nobis tenentur in capite ut dicitur) dare poffit & affignare dilectis nobis in Chrifto magiftro, five cuftodi, & capellanis hofpitalis Annunciationis beate Marie Virginis Leiceftr', quod Henricus nuper comes Lanc', pater predicti ducis, fundavit ibidem; habendas & tenendas fibi & fucceffioribus fuis, de nobis & heredibus noftris, per fervicia inde debita & confueta, in perpetuum. Et eifdem magiftro, five cuftodi, & capellanis, quòd ipfi maneria predicta, cum pertinentiis, & advocationes illas, à prefato duce recipere, & ecclefias illas appropriare, & eas appropriatas in proprios ufus tenere poffint fibi & fucceffioribus fuis, de nobis & heredibus noftris, per fervicia predicta, in perpetuum, tenore prefentium, fimiliter licentiam dedimus fpecialem. Tefte rege apud Weftm', 4º die Martii. Per breve de privato figillo [4].

5. Cefte endenture faite parentre les nobles hoīe monfieur Henri duc de Lancaftre, counte de Derbye, de Nicole, & de Leiceftre, fenefcall d'Engleterr, d'une part; & les dean & chanoygnes de l'Eglife collegiale de l'Annunciation de noftre Dame de Leiceftre, d'autre part; tefmoigne, come le dit duc eft done & graunte, & p fon fait conferme, du conge noftre feigneur le roi, as ditz dean & chanoynges & lours fucceffoures, mil livres de annuele rente, a prendre perpetuelment, as termes de Seint Michel & Pafques, per oueles portions, des manoirs, feigneuries, demefnes; manoir de Kinges-fomborne, en le counté de Southampton, ove les membres dycel, deux centz livres; des manoirs de Gymingham, Tunftede, Methewold, & Thetford, ove les appertenaunces, en le counte de Norfolk, quatre livres; & des feigneuries & demefnes terres de Kedwelly, Carnwaltham, Ifkemyn, Ugmore, & Morgannock, ove les appurtenaunces, en Gales, quater centz livres; fur tiele condicion, qi fi la dite rente foit ariere a nul des termes fus-ditz, qi bien life as ditz dean & chanons & lour fucceffours entre mefmes les manoirs, feigneuries, & demeifnes terres, pour les arrerages de mefme la rente annuele de mil' livres, deftriner, & les diftreffez retenir tanqz gree lour foit fait des ditz arrerages pleinement, ficome en le dit fait eft contenu plus au pleyn. Qe les ditz dean & chanoignes voillent & grauntent, pur eux & lour fucceffours, qi s'ils eient, tiegnent, & peifiblement enjoient, les manoirs de Inglefham, Wolftanton, Kynemersford, Chedworth, & Harindon, ove toux les appurtanaunces, & les avouefons des efglifes de Thorp-Edmere, Wymondham, Hegham-Ferrers, Raundes, Prefton, & Haryndon, queux il ont & teignent de la foundation & droit de lour dite efglife, de doun & graunte le duc, & conge noftre feigneur le roi, & auctorite du pape fur ce fairz, faunz nul empefchement & fanyces; & les ditz dean & chanoignes ou nul de lour fucceffours foient empledey, & par tien plee ou ea afcune manere ouftey des ditz manoirs & avoufons, ou de nul parcel d'icels, par le dit duc, ou per nul de fes heirs, en temps a venir, qi adonques le paiement dez avantditz mille livres annueles ceffe de tout. Et le dit duc voel & graunte, pour lui & feis heirs, q fi le dit dean & chanoignes, ou nul de lour fucceffours, foient empeifchex ou empledez, & le dit duc & fes heirs ne les garantont ne defendent point, en cas q'ils vouchent ou foient pour nul autre vouchey a garanter, ou autrement foient ouftey des ditz manoirs & aureteus, ou de nul parcel d'icels, ou del fyte ou la dite efglife eft foundue, ou de nul place environ, ou de nulles terres, prees, aftures, boys, molins, cours de eawe, ou de nulles autres eifementz queux Henri nadgaires counte de Lancaftre, piere le dit duc (qi heir il eft) dona & granta as gardein & chapeleins de la place ou mefme l' eglife eft ore foundue au temps qi la dite efglife eftoit hofpitale & foundue par le dit counte, & les queux fort ore uniez & annexez as ditz dean & chanoignes & leur fucceffours, en les fufditz mil' livres annueles a prendre perpetuelment des manoirs, feigneuries, & demeifnes terres fufditz & ovefqz ceo foient le dit duc & ces heirs chargey devers les ditz dean & chanoignes & lour fucceffours, en ceo cas des arrerages de mefmes les mil' livres annueles de tout le temps puis la date du graunte faitz

---

[1] Dugdale, Mon. Angl. vol. II. p. 468; ex Pat. 4 Edw. III. p. 1. m. 36.
[2] Reg. Iflip, archiep. Cant. f. 24. a.   [3] Ibid. f. 34. b.   [4] Pat. 29 Edw. III. p. 1. m. 22.

as ditz dean & chanoignes & lour fucceffours de les mil' lieures annueles fufditz; & qi bien life as ditz dean & chanoignes & lour fucceffours, pour celles arrerages, en les ditz manoirs, feigneuries, & demeifnes terres deftreindre; & les diftreffes detenir tanqz gree lour foit faite de mefmes celles arrerages, fans nulle diftourbance au contraditz du dit duc, au de nul de fes heirs en temps a venir. En tefmoignaunce de queles chofes, a l'une partie de cefte endenture le dit duc, & a l'autre partie les ditz dean & chanoignes, entrechangleablement ont mys lour feale. Don en le mefon du chapitre des ditz dean & chanoignes a Leiceftre, le xii jour de Juyn, l'an de Grace mil troiz centz cinquante fifme; & du regne le roi Edward Tierz puis le conqueft d' Engleterre trientifme, & de Fraunce dys & feptifme [1].

6. Rex omnibus ad quos, &c. falutem. Sciatis, quòd, cùm bone memorie Henricus nuper comes Lancaftrie defunctus, colore licentie noftre fibi, de quodam hofpitali in honorem Annunciationis beate Marie in villâ Leiceftrie fundandi facte, dictum hofpitale in fuburbiis Leiceftrie predicte fundâffet, & cuftodem & capellanos in eodem hofpitali conftituit, pro fuftentatione eorundem, ac pauperum infirmorum, clericorum, & mulierum, in dicto hofpitali commorantium, in quandam placeam terre continentem quatuor acras, cum pertinentiis, in fuburbio predicto, in quo dictum hofpitale conftructum exiftit; ac etiam quatuor acras, cum pertin', in eodem fuburbio; que quidem terre & hofpitale in cartâ noftrâ de licentiâ, ac etiam in cartâ ipfius comitis, in villâ predictâ effe fpecificantur; ac duas placeas terre & prati, Clofe-medowe & Mary-medowe nuncupatas, viginti acras in fe continentes ibidem, tanquam dictis quatuor carucatis terre pertinentes & annexas, colore donationis & affignationis predictarum, occupârunt; idemque comes communam pafture in parco fuo de Leiceftriâ, vocat' le Fryth, prefatis cuftodi & capellanis & fuccefforibus fuis, ad viginti & fex boves five vaccas, & fex equos, quolibet tempore anni, & etiam communam pafture ad omnimoda animalia fua in forinfecis bofcis fuis de Leiceftriâ, menfibus porcis in defenfo pofitis exceptis, necnon duas carectatas bofci percipiendas fingulis feptimanis in bofcis predictis, abfque licentiâ noftrâ dediffet & affignâffet; terras, prata, pafturas, parcos, & bofcos predicta de nobis, ut parcella honoris Leiceftrie, in capite tenentur; cujus honoris reverfio ad nos & heredes noftros, fi Edmundus nuper comes Lancaftrie, avus predicti ducis, cujus heres ipfe eft, fine herede de corpore fuo exeunte obiiffet, fpectat, ut dicitur: Ac dilectus confanguineus & fidelis nofter Henricus dominus Lancaftrie, filius & heres dicti Henrici comitis, poft mortem ejufdem, quoddam molendinum aquaticum vocat' le New-milne, cum pertinentiis, in fuburbio ville predicte, fimul cum ftagno & aquâ predictis, que de nobis tenentur in capite, ut parcella honoris predicti, cuftodi & capellanis hofpitalis predictis, tenend' fibi & fuccefforibus fuis, de ipfo duce & heredibus fuis, in liberam, puram, & perpetuam eleemofinam; necnon reverfionem manerii de Chedworth, in comitatu Glouceftrie, &c.; ac cuftos & capellani hofpitalis predicti duas acras prati, cum pertin', in fuburbio predicto, & tenuit de predicto duce per fervicia predicta; & prefatus dux conefferit prefatis decano & canonicis & fuccefforibus fuis predictas duas carectatas bofci, percipiendas fingulis feptimanis; necnon quinque damas de pinguedine & decem de forinfecâ, percipiendas fingulis feptimanis in chafeâ de Leiceftriâ, que de nobis tenentur in capite, ut parcella honoris predicti. Jamque iidem decanus & canonici, metuentes fibi & fuccefforibus fuis, tam pro eo quòd dictum hofpitale in primariâ fundatione, ac dicta ecclefia in erectione eorundem, ac poftmodùm per fingulas licentias noftras in hâc parte factas, ac donationes, conceffiones, & perquifita hujufmodi; ac etiam dicte quatuor acre terre & quatuor carucate terre, dictis cuftodi & capellanis in fundatione dicti hofpitalis fic dati & conceffi in dictâ villâ Leiceftrie, pretendantur exiftere, cùm reverâ in dicto fuburbio exftiterint.

Conceffimus etiam, & licentiam dedimus, pro nobis & heredibus noftris predictis, quantum in nobis eft, eidem duci, quòd ipfe duas venellas in fuburbio dicte ville Leiceftrie, quarum una fe extendit à magno ftrato vocat' Southgate ufque ripam vocat' Sore, & altera fe extendit à portâ gardini caftri Leic' ufque venellam vocat' Newmilne-lane; ac etiam quandam placeam, que eft parcella caftri predicti, continentem duas acras terre & dim', juxta venellam vocat' Newmilne-lane; ac etiam quandam placeam, que eft caftri predicti, continentem duas acras terre & dim', juxta venellas predictas, cum pertinentiis, manfo & ecclefie ipforum decani & canonicorum contiguas, que quidem venella & placea de nobis tenentur in capite, ut parcella honoris predicti, ut dicitur, dare poffit & affignare eifdem decano & canonicis; habend' & tenend' fibi & fuccefforibus fuis, de prefato duce & heredibus fuis, in liberam, puram, & perpetuam eleemofinam, in elargationem manfi & ecclefie fuorum predictorum in perpetuum; & eifdem decano & canonicis, quòd ipfi venellas & placeam predictas, cum pertinentiis, à prefato duce recipere, & eas includere, &c. Tefte rege, apud Weftm', xxixº die Novembris. Per breve de privato figillo [2].

7. Rex univerfis & fingulis vicecomitibus, majoribus, ballivis, miniftris, ac aliis fidelibus & fubditis fuis, tam infra libertates quàm extra, ad quos, &c. falutem. Sciatis, quòd cùm Henricus quondam dux Lancaftrie, avus nofter, quandam ecclefiam collegiatam apud Leiceftriam, in honorem Annunciationis beate Marie, ac quafdam domos, muros, & edificia, pro claufurâ ecclefie & collegii predictorum, & inhabitatione canonicorum, clericorum, & infirmorum, ibidem degentium, in vitâ fuâ conftruere inchoâffet; ac chariffimus pater nofter Johannes, nuper dux Lancaftrie, hujufmodi opera per dictum avum noftrum in hâc parte fic inchoata, juxta piam intentionem ejufdem avi noftri, poftmodum falubritèr complere & perficere defiderâffet, ut accepimus: Nos, piam intentionem & laudabile propofitum ipforum avi & patris noftrorum in hâc parte meritò commendantes; volenterfque opera predicta ad finem, quòd in premiis eorundem participes effici valeamus, potiùs accelerari; affignavimus dilectos nobis Johannem de Byngham, Robertum Skyllington, Johannem Hornynghold, & Thomam Whytebred, conjunctim & divifim, ad conducendum & providendum in fingulis locis, infra libertates & extra, cementarios, carpentarios, & alios operarios quofcunque, ufque ad numerum viginti & quatuor, pro operationibus predictis; & ad eofdem cementarios, carpentarios, & operarios, in hujufmodi artificiis operari confuetos, ponendos ibidem ad vadia eis in hâc parte rationabilitèr folvendos moraturos; necnon ad maeremium & petram, & alia pro eifdem operationibus neceffaria, pro denariis indè promptè folvendis capienda, cariagiis noftris operariis pro aliis operationibus noftris conductis, & in eifdem exiftentibus, ac feodo ecclefie duntaxat excepto. Et ideò vobis mandamus, quòd eifdem Johanni, Roberto, Johanni, & Thome, & eorum cuilibet, in premiffis faciendis & explendis intendentes fitis, confulentes, & auxiliantes, quoties & quando per ipfos, feu eorum aliquem, ex parte noftrâ fueritis requifiti. In cujus, &c. Tefte rege, apud Weftm', xxviº Martii [3].

8. Rex archiepifcopis, &c. falutem. Sciatis, quòd, cùm nos nuper per literas noftras patentes, de gratiâ noftrâ fpeciali, conefferimus, pro nobis & heredibus noftris, quantum in nobis fuit, dilectis nobis in Chrifto decano & canonicis ecclefie nove collegiate beate Marie Leiceftr', quòd ipfe & fucceffores fui, quamdiu rebellio rebellium in partibus Wallie duraverit, & iidem decanus & canonici & fucceffores fui de perceptione exituum & proficuum ecclefiarum, maneriorum, terrarum, & poffeffionum fuorum, in partibus illis exftiterint per rebelles noftros predictos impediti, effent quieti de auxiliis ad primogenitos filios regum maritandos, & de omnibus auxiliis regum, necnon contributionibus & talliagiis que ab ipfis ratione ter-

---

[1] Clauf. 30 Edw. III. m. 32. dorfo.
[2] Pat. 34 Edw. III. pars 3. m. 13.
[3] Dugdale, Monafticon, vol. III. p. 139; ex Pat. 1 Hen. IV. part 6. m. 15.

rarum,

rarum, tenementorum, reddituum, aut bonorum, feu catallorum fuorum, que tunc habuerunt, vel extunc effent habituri, per nos vel heredes noftros, aut ballivos vel miniftros noftros vel heredum noftrorum quorumcunque, ad opus noftrum vel ipforum heredum noftrorum exigi deberent, feu poffent, durante termino fupradicto; & quòd, quandocunque clerus regni noftri Anglie, aut Cantuarienfis provincie per fe, aut Eboracenfis provincie per fe, decimam feu aliam quotam de bonis fuis fpiritualibus & ecclefiafticis, vel communitas com' regni noftri Anglie, aut cives vel burgenfes civium vel burgorum predictorum comitatuum, decimam, quintam-decimam, vel aliam quotam feu taxam quemcunque, de bonis feu temporalibus fuis vel mobilibus, aut terris, tenementis, feu redditibus fuis, nobis vel heredibus noftris qualitercunque conceffiffent, feu nos vel heredes noftri dominica noftra per Angliam feciffemus talliari, aut dominus fummus pontifex qui pro tempore foret decimam feu quotam aliam clero regni Anglie aut Cantuarienfis vel Eboracenfis provinciarum predictarum impofuiffet, & eam vel aliquam partem ejufdem nobis vel heredibus noftris conceffiffet, ecclefie & beneficia ipfis decano & canonicis appropriate & appropriande, terre, tenementa, redditus, & bona & catalla ipforum decani & canonicorum, & fucceftorum quorumcunque, ad opus noftrum vel heredum noftrorum, durante termino predicto, non taxarentur, affidarentur, vel talliarentur, nec iidem decanus & canonici, vel eorum fucceffores, in terris, tenementis, feu bonis fuis predictis, hiis occafionibus diftringerentur, moleftarentur in aliquo, feu graventur, fed de decimis, quintifdecimis, & aliis quotis & talliagiis hujufmodi, dicto termino durante, effent quieti; &, fi contigerit fuper homines com' dicti regni noftri Anglie, vel alienis eorundem comitatuum aut aliorum locorum ipfius regni, feu ipforum terras, poffeffiones, vel bona, aliquas pecunie fummas pro munitione & apparatibus hominum ad arma, hobilar', fagittar', feu predictorum quorumcunque pro obfequio noftro vel heredum noftrorum extunc eligendorum, & in hujufmodi obfequio ad quafcunque partes, & ex quâcunque caufâ. Ac infuper conceffimus, pro nobis & heredibus noftris, prefato decano & canonicis, quòd ipfi & fucceffores fui, & omnes homines fui, durante termino predicto, quieti effent de theolonio, homagio, pontagio, kaiagio, muragio, paffagio, paagio, leftagio, ftallagio, tallagio, cariagio, pefagio, barbicariagio, terragio, fcotto & geldo, hidagio, & de operationibus caftrorum, parcorum, & pontium, claufuris, & domorum regalium edificatione & reparatione, necnon de fectis comitatuum, hundredorum, & wapentachiorum, & de vifu franciplegii, ac de murdro, & de communi mifericordiâ quando contigerit, videlicet com' coram vel aliquibus jufticiariis noftris, vel heredum noftrorum, de banco vel itinerantibus, feu aliis jufticiariis quibufcunque, in mifericordiam noftram vel ipforum heredum noftrorum incidere, & de omni aliâ hujufmodi confuetudine per totum regnum & poteftatem noftram. Et concedimus eidem decano & eifdem canonicis, & fucceftoribus fuis, vifum franciplegii, letam, & landays, & quicquid ad hujufmodi letam & vifum pertinet, de omnibus tenentibus & refidentibus infra fitum & precinctum, portus & muros ejufdem collegii, in perpetuum; ac etiam retorna & executiones omnimodorum brevium, preceptorum, & attachiamentorum, tam de placitis corone quàm de aliis placitis quibufcunque, tam in prefentiâ noftrâ & heredum noftrorum & fucceftorum noftrorum, quàm in abfentiâ noftrâ & illorum, infra fitum, precinctum, & portum, & muros predictos; ita quòd nullus vicecomes, ballivus, nec alius minifter quicunque, fe intromittat nec intret infra fitum, precinctum, portus, & muros predictos, pro aliquo recapio, nec executione alicujus brevis, precepti, feu attachiamenti faciendi, nifi in defectu miniftrorum collegii fupradicti, eo quòd parcella predicti fitûs eft infra vifum noftrum de Caftlewarde de Leiceftrie, &c. Dat' XIII° die Julii [1].

9. Rex omnibus ad quos, &c. falutem. Sciatis, quòd, cùm Ricardus nuper rex Anglie, fecundus poft

Conqueftum, per literas fuas patentes, de gratiâ fuâ fpeciali, & pro eo quòd dilecti fui in Chrifto decanus & canonici ecclefie collegiate beate Marie de Leiceftriâ per Henricum nuper ducem Lancaftrie, defunctum, fundati exfterint ad orandum fpecialiter, tam pro regibus & reginis Anglie vivis & defunctis, ac progenitoribus & heredibus ipfius regis, & pro duce & anteceffioribus fuis, conceffit, pro fe & heredibus fuis, quantum in ipfo fuit, eifdem decano & canonicis, quòd ipfi terras & redditus, ad valorem quadraginta librarum per annum, adquirere, & eos fic adquifitos habere & tenere poffint fibi & fucceftoribus fuis in perpetuum, in augmentatione dicte ecclefie & divini fervicii in eâdem: conceffimus & licentiam dedimus, quantum in nobis eft, Thome Quenby, Thome Maundeville, & Willo Almanbury, clericis, quòd ipfi duo meffuagia & duo tofta, cum pertinentiis, in Leiceftriâ, in fuburbio ejufdem, &c. dare poffint & affignare predictis decano & canonicis, & fucceftoribus fuis, &c. Tefte rege, apud Weftm', xi° die Januarii [2].

10. Rex archiepifcopis, &c. falutem. Sciatis, quòd, cùm nos, reducentes in devote confiderationis examen profufa Chrifti beneficia, quibus ex folâ miferationis dulcedine in opportunitatibus nos pervenit, &c.; quandam ecclefiam, Novam Collegiatam beate Marie Leiceftrie vulgariter nuncupatam, per illuftriffimum principem Henricum nuper ducem Lancaftrie, progenitorem noftrum, opere fumptuofo, de uno decano & canonicis fecularibus, ac aliis miniftris, ibidem perpetuò divinis obfequiis vocaturis, in honore Annunciationis gloriofe & intaminate Virginis Marie, fundatam, diverfis libertatibus, franchefiis, privilegiis, quietanciis, & immunitatibus, amplificatam; decernentes, ut, quò liberiùs privilegiati exfterint, eô meliùs, devotiùs, & quietiùs, Deo valeant famulari; de gratiâ noftrâ fpeciali, dedimus & conceffimus, pro nobis & heredibus noftris, magiftro Willo Walfeby, uni capellanorum noftrorum, nunc decano collegii predicti, & ejufdem loci canonicis & fucceftoribus fuis in perpetuum, quòd ipfi & fucceffores fui in perpetuum fint quieti de auxiliis ad primogenitas filias regum maritandas, & omnibus auxiliis regum, necnon contributionibus & talliagiis, que ab ipfis, ratione terrarum & tenementorum, reddituum, aut bonorum, feu catallorum fuorum, que nunc habent, vel nunc funt habituri, per nos vel heredes noftros, &c. [3]

11. 1424, 3 die Augufti, in prioratu de Landâ admifit dnus Henricum Rofe capellanum ad feptimam prebendam infra novâm ecclefiam collegiatam beate Marie Leiceftrie, Linc' dicec. ad prefentationem domine Katarine regine Anglie, matris regis Anglie & Francie, filie Caroli regis Francie & dni Hibernie, vere ipfius prebende patrone [4].

12. Intimatio facta decano & capitulo collegii beate Marie Leyc', de vacatione vicarie de Higham-Ferrers.

Johannes, permiffione divinâ, Cantuarienfis archiepifcopus, totius Anglie primas, & Apoftolice fedis legatus, venerabilibus viris decano & capitulo ecclefie collegiate beate Marie de Leiceftriâ falutem, gratiam, & benedictionem. Cùm, per liberam refignationem magiftri Willielmi More, nuper magiftri collegii noftri de Higham-Ferrers, Linc' dicec', noftre fundationis, ac vicarii ibidem, dicta vicaria vacet in prefenti: nos vacationem hujufmodi, juxta formam cujufdam compofitionis nuper inter bone memorie dnum Henricum Chichele, ultimum & immediatum predeceffforem noftrum ex unâ & vos parte ex alterâ in hâc parte inite, vobis intimamus; rogantes quatenùs magiftrum Ricardum Whyte ad dictam vicariam venerabili confratri noftro dno Willo, Dei gratiâ, Lincolnienfi epifcopo, juxta effectum dicte compofitionis, actualiter prefentare velitis. Dat' in manerio noftro de Lambeth, 20 die menfis Februarii, A. D. 1443, & noftre tranflationis anno primo [5].

13. Rex omnibus ad quos, &c. falutem. Sciatis, quòd, cùm nos, reducentes in devote confiderationis

[1] Cart. 8 Hen. IV. N° 2. [2] Pat. 9 Hen. IV. pars i. m. 17. [3] Clauf. 1 Hen. VI. N° 11.
[4] Reg. Chicheley, archiep. Cant. fol. 243. a. b. [5] Reg. Stafford, archiep. Cant. fol. 8. b.

examen

examen profusa Chrifti beneficia, quibus ex folâ miferationis fue dulcedine in opportunitatibus nos pervenit, à variis licèt immeritos liberando periculis, & dextrâ fuâ potenti contra adverfariorum impetus cum victoriofis fucceffibus magnificè defendendo, ac aliàs in tribulationibus quibus plurimùm involuti fuimus, cùm infperatâ fuper fufione remediorum, confolandi quidem, tot & tantarum gratiarum, mifericordiffimo largitori, qui, cùm fit Dominus omnium, caducis non indiget rebus noftris, quomodo retribuere debeamus penitùs ignoramus; effufam igitur circa nos fuam magnificentiam devotiffimè contemplantes, ac fibi propter hoc facrificium cordis noftri, ne redeamus oblivifci retributiones ejus, qui fic in bonis noftrum defiderium adimplet, humiliter offerentes, adque gloriam fui nominis, & perpetuam dictarum gratiarum memoriam, ecclefiam noftram, Ecclefiam novam collegiatam beate Marie Leiceftrie vulgariter nuncupatam, de uno decano & canonicis fecularibus, vicariis, & aliis miniftris, ibidem perpetuò divinis obfequiis vocaturis, in honore Annunciationis gloriofe & intemerate Virginis Marie fundatam, diverfis libertatibus & privilegiis amplificandi; difcernentes, ut, quò meliùs privilegiati dotati fui ftabiliti exiftunt, eò quietiùs & devotiùs Deo valeant famulari; de gratiâ noftrâ fpeciali, & ex certâ fcientiâ & mero motu noftris, dedimus & conceffimus, & per prefentes damus & concedimus, dilecto nobis in Chrifto Willo Chauntre, uni capellanorum noftrorum, nunc decano collegie five ecclefie predicte, & canonicis, quòd ipfe nunc decanus & canonici & fucceffores fui fint de cetero unum corpus corporatum & nomine; ac ipfos decanum & canonicos ejufdem ecclefie noftre nove collegiate beate Marie Leiceftrie perpetuis temporibus duraturos corporamus, & ipfos unum corpus creamus, facimus, & ftabilimus, ipfofque pro uno corpore declaramus, acceptamus, & approbamus, necnon pro uno corpore tenentur; & quòd ipfi habeant fucceffionem perpetuam; & quòd ipfi & fucceffores fui perfone habiles & in lege capaces, ad perquirend', recipiend', & acceptand', terras, tenementa, redditus, reverfiones, & fervicia, libertates, franchefias, privilegia, & immunitates, ac alias poffeffiones quafcunque, fibi & fucceffioribus fuis habend' & tenend',& poffidend' in feodo & perpetuitate; & quòd habeant figillum commune pro rebus & negotiis ipfos decanos & canonicos & fucceffiones fuas tangentibus deferviturum; & quòd ipfi & fucceffores fui per nomen decani & canonicorum ecclefie noftre nove collegiate beate Marie Leiceftrie placitari poffint & implacitari, ac perfequi omnimodas caufas, querelas, actiones reales, perfonales, & mixtas, cujufcunque generis fuerint vel nature, ac libertates & franchefias calumpniare, necnon refpondere & refponderi, ac defendere fe fub nomine predicto, in eifdem caufis, querelis, & actionibus, ad quodcunque aliud proficuo & jure dicte ecclefie noftre nove collegiate beate Marie Leiceftrie facere coram judicibus ecclefiafticis & fecularibus, tam coram nobis quàm coram quibufcunque jufticiariis, in quibufcunque curiis & placeis noftris & heredum noftrorum in aliis curiis quibufcunque. Et ulteriùs, de uberiori gratiâ noftrâ, conceffimus & licentiam dedimus, pro nobis & heredibus noftris, quantum in nobis eft, quibufcunque perfonis, feu cujufcunque perfone, regni noftri Anglie, aliquas terras, tenementa, redditus, reverfiones, & fervicia feodorum militum, aut advocationes ecclefiarum, eifdem decano & canonicis ecclefie noftre nove collegiate beate Marie Leiceftrie predicte pro tempore exiftentibus, dare, concedere, affignare, feu legare, volentibus aut volenti, quòd ipfe perfone, feu ipfa perfona, terras, tenementa, redditus, reverfiones, & fervicia feodorum militum, cum pertinentiis; ac etiam advocationes ecclefie ufque ad valorem c s. per annum, tam de illis que de nobis vel heredibus noftris tenentur in capite, vel aliquo alio modo, aut de aliis perfonis quibufcunque, prefatis decano & canonicis ejufdem ecclefie noftre nove collegiate beate Marie predicte, qui nunc funt, & qui pro tempore erunt, dare, concedere, affignare, feu legare poffit, feu poffint; habend' & tenend' eifdem decano & canonicis & fucceffioribus fuis, in auxilium fuftentationis & fupportationis onerum eidem ecclefie incumbentium, in perpetuum, &c.; et eifdem decano & canonicis & fucceffioribus fuis, quòd ipfi hujufmodi terras, tenementa, redditus, reverfiones, & fervicia feodorum militum, cum fuis pertinentiis, ac advocationes ecclefiarum predictarum, ufque ad valorem predictum, de perfonis aut perfonâ predictis, de tempore in tempus recipere; & advocationes & ecclefias illas eifdem decano & canonicis annexare, unire, & appropriare, & eas fic annexatas, unitas, & appropriatas, in proprios ufus fuos, &c. [1]

14. Ricardus, &c. revendo in Xpo patri Johanni, cadem grâ, Lincoln' epo, aut, ejus in abfenciâ, vicario fuo genali, falutem. Ad duodecimã pbendam in libera capella ñrâ five ecclîa collegiatâ Novi Operis beate Marie infra villam ñram Leiceftrie jam vacantẽ, & ad ñram donacõem racõe ducatûs noftr' Lancaftrie fpectant', p mortem Jacobi Letes capellani, ultimi incumbentis ejufdm, dilectum fervientem ñrum Laurencium Squier capellanũ vobis pfentamus, intuitu caritatis rogantes quatenus eundem Laurencm ad pbendam pdictã admittatis, ipfumq inftituatis in eâdem, cum fuis juribs & ptin' univfis, ceteraque peragere que ѵro in hâc pte incumbunt officio paftorali dignemur cum favore. In cujus, &c. anno 2° [2].

15. Henricus, Dei gratiâ, rex Anglie & Francie, & dominus Hibernie, omnibus ad quos prefentes litere pervenerint falutem. Sciatis, quòd nos, de gratiâ noftrâ fpeciali, ac de certâ fcientiâ & mero motu noftris, conceffimus & licentiam dedimus, ac per prefentes concedimus & licentiam damus, pro nobis & heredibus noftris, quantum in nobis eft, dilectis nobis Willo Wigfton de Leiceftriâ juniori, mercatori ftapule, Thome Wigfton clerico, Rogero Wigfton, & Willo Colte, quòd ipfi, vel eorum aliquis, executores aut affignati fui, feu eorum aliquis vel aliqui, ad laudem Dei & Domini cultûs augmentationem, quandam cantariam perpetuam de duobus capellanis, divina ad altare beate Marie Virginis, Sanctorumque Urfule & Katharine Virginum & Martyrum, infra ecclefiam collegiatam beate Marie Novi Operis Leiceftrie, in comitatu Leiceftrie, pro falubri ftatu noftro, & Katharine regine Anglie confortis noftre precariffime, dum vixerimus, & pro animis noftris cùm à luce migraverimus; necnon pro bono ftatu dicti Willi Wigfton dum vitam gerit in humanis, & pro animâ cum prefentis vite curfum terminaverit, ac etiam pro animis omnium parentum & benefactorum ejufdem Willi Wigfton, juxta ordinationem ejufdem Willi, feu prefatorum Thome, Rogeri, & Willi, vel executorum aut affignatorum fuorum, vel alicujus aut aliquorum eorum diutiùs viventium, in hâc parte fact' vel in pofterum faciend' in perpetuum celebraturo, facere, fundare, & creare, & ftabilire poffint & valeant, poffitque & valeat, perpetuis futuris temporibus duraturam; & quòd cantaria illa, cùm fic facta, fundata, erecta, creata, & ftabilita fuerit, "Cantaria Willi Wigfton in ecclefiâ collegiatâ beate Marie Novi Operis Leic' in com' Leic." perpetuò nuncupetur; & quòd capellani dicte cantarie fint unum corpus corporatum in re & nomine, habeantque fucceffionem perpetuam, & quòd fint habiles & capaces in lege; & quòd capellani ejufdem cantarie, & fucceffores fui, per nomen & fub nomine "capellanorum cantarie Willi Wigfton in ecclefiâ collegiatâ beate Marie Novi Operis Leic." placita poffint implacitari, necnon omnimodas actiones, querelas, & caufas reales, perfonales, & mixtas, cujufcunque generis fuerint & nature, quibufcunque jufticiariis, judicibus fpiritualibus & temporalibus, feu aliis perfonis quibufcunque, perfequi, ac in eifdem refpondere, ac eos defendere poffint & valeant, prout & in eodem modo quo ceteri ligei noftri, perfone habiles & capaces, infra regnum noftrum Anglie facere & agere poffint; aliquo ftatuto, actu, ordinatione, permiffione, five reftrictione, in contrarium fact', edit', ordinat', five provif', aut aliquâ aliâ re, caufâ, feu materiâ quâcunque non obftante, & hoc abfque fine feu feodo magno, nobis vel heredibus noftris in hanaperio cancellarie noftre, feu alibi ad opus noftrum aliqualiter folvend' feu faciend'. In cujus rei teftimonium, has literas noftras fieri fecimus patentes. Tefte meipfo, apud Weftmonafterium, fexto-decimo die Maii, anno regni noftri tertio [3].

[1] Pat. 19 Edw. IV. pars 1.   [2] Harl. MSS. 433. p. 71. a. p. 185. b.
[3] From the original in the Rolls Chapel, inter Priv. Sigill. & Bill. affignat. temp. Hen. VIII.

4

APPENDIX, N° XIX.

EXTRACTS from CHARYTE's Rentale, relative to divers CHURCHES in LEICESTER;

Parochia *Omnium Sanctorum*. Patronus hujus ecclefie abbas Leyc'. Vicarius ibidem inftitutus per epifcopum Linc'. Penfio vicario quondam fuit vi marc'. Clericus parochialis eligendus eft & ordinandus per abbatem Leyc'. Ordinatio vicarii per Hugonem epifcopum patet in Chartwary [1].

Habemus, de perquifito fratris W. Charyte, & ex dono & feoffamento Willielmi Wyftow de Petelyng Magna, unum meffuagium, cum pertinentiis, fituatum inter tenementum quondam Rogeri Belgrave, ex parte auftrali, & tenementum cantarie Corporis Chrifti ex parte boreali; &c. [2]

Parochia Sce *Margarete*. Patronus hujus ecclefie dns Lincoln', ut patet in Matriculo epifcopi, his verbis : ' Ecclefie Sce Margarete extra muros, patronus dominus Lincoln'; & eft prebenda Lincoln'. [3] '

Memorandum, quòd quandocunque aliquis de quatuor capellanis cantarie Sci *Martini* recefferit, feu aliquo modo vacaverit, tunc magiftri gildarum & duo prepofiti dicte ecclefie, cum feniore capellano cantarie predicte, capellanum idoneum ejus loco abbati Leiceftrie prefentabunt, qui abfque difficultate eum admittet & inftituet, & in poffeffionem dicte cantarie inducet corporalem, &c. nihil ab ipfo petens vel recipiens [4].

Mem', quòd quatuor capellani de cantariâ ibidem debent uti amictubs in dictâ ecclefiâ quum divinis interfuerint, &c. Et omnes & finguli capellani ad dictam cantariam in futuro admittend' in fuâ admiffione jurabunt coram abbate Leyc', vel alio per ipfum affignato, tactis per ipfos facrofanctis Dei evangeliis, fe quafdam ordinationes & ftatuta quatenùs eos concernunt fideliter obfervaturos, prout in fundatione ejufdem cantarie pleniùs continetur [5].

Habemus ibi, ex dono fratris T. de Bretford, magiftri hofpitalis Sci Johannis Leiceftr', & ejufdem loci fratrum & fororum, unam placeam terre, cum pertinentiis, de tenemento fuo juxta cemeterium ecclefie Sce *Trinitatis* Leiceftrie à parte orientali; que quidem terra jacet juxta cemeterium ecclefie antedicte ex unâ parte, & terram dicti hofpitalis ex alterâ, &c.

Habemus redditum fubfcriptum, ex donis diverforum benefactorum noftrorum, ut patet in cartis eorum.

Canonici Novi Collegii, pro ten' quondam Thome Charyte, videlicet, pro quâdam placeâ terre fuper quâ fituantur parvum ftudium, latina, pars coquine, & alterius domûs official'. Et jacet fuper cornerium ufque le kanke. Et reddit xiid. liberè.

Iidem canonici, pro ten' cum gardino juxta fcalam auftralem, reddunt viis. per compofitionem.

Ricardus Operarius, pro duabus cameris ibidem, juxta . . . . . . [6], reddit iiis. Dominus Hugo Procurator, pro duabus cameris, redd' iiiis.

Prepofiti ecclefie, pro le Storhows, iiiis.

Johannes Wyxton, pro tenementis quondam Johis Belgrave, ex parte occidentali ecclefie, refpondet liberè xiid. ii capon'.

Idem Johannes Wyxton, pro tenemento ad fcalam ecclefie, quondam predicti Johannis Belgrave, refpondet liberè ixd.

Capellani cantarie ibidem, pro diverfis tenementis que de nobis liberè tenent, refpondent viiis. videlicet, pro uno novo meffuagio in cemeterio predicto ad fcalam occidentalem, ficut itur versùs Altam Crucem, ubi quondam fuerunt duo tenementa, reddunt per annum iiis. ubi jam cantaria edificata eft.

Iidem capellani tenent de nobis liberè ii fhopas in Crift-chyrch lane, jacent' inter ten' predictum & ten' noftrum quod Johes Barbur de nobis tenet, & redd' per annum iiis.

Iidem capellani tenent de nobis liberè unum meffuagium ex parte boreali fcale ecclefie juxta arctam viam quâ itur ad furnum domini comitis à finiftris; & redd' per ann' iis. liberè; ubi quondam fuerunt tria tenementa; que tenementa Symon de Cameiâ, Alicia Barnefby, & Johes Turvey, quondam tenuerunt de nobis liberè. Summa viiis. [7]

Parochia Sci *Martini*. Patronus hujus ecclefie abbas Leyceftr', habens eam in proprios ufus. Vicarius ibidem inftitutus per epifcopum; penfio ejus ab antiquo v marce. Prefbyteri cantarie debent facere juramentum & fidelitatem abbati Leiceftrie pro indemnitate ecclefie.

Ordinatio ejus per Hugonem epifcopum facta eft, ut vicarius in ecclia Sancti Martini habeat ad veftitum fuum ii marc' de porcionibus altaris, per manum abbatis Leyceftr' folvend', & legata ufque ad vid. & quolibet die folenni id. Habebit victum fuum in abbathiâ in omnibus ut canonicus, & diaconus fuus ficut major ferviens in abbathiâ; & unam dimidiam marcam pro ftipendio. Preterea habebit panem ad garcionem fuum qui ei ferviet. Abbas providebit ei manfum competentem, & fuftinebit onera ecclefie debita & confueta.

Alia conventio inter abbatem & W. vicarium Sci Martini, quod dictus vicarius percipiet viii marcas per manus abbatis, & pro omnibus oblationibus fuis per annum vs. & panem altaris, excepto pane benedicto ad Pafca. Et recipiet decimas parochie, tam de animalibus quàm de ortis & virgultis, & ova ad Pafca. Ecclefia percipiet principale legatum, vicarius fecundum & fua privata, &c. ut in rotulo rubro [8].

Item ordinatum fuit per abbatem & conventum Leyc', cum confenfu dni Thome de Rondes, tunc vicarii Sci Martini Leyc', quòd ipfe T. effet contentus in omnibus pro xxiid. pro ftipendio fuo fingulis ebdomatibus per ann', A. D. MCCCXXVIII; & fic contentus fuit per totam vitam fuam.

Modò vicarius habet manfum honeftum & appropriatum, & iis. quâlibet feptimanâ per manus procuratoris; & vid. in die Omnium Sanctorum, vid. in die Nativitatis Dni, vid. in die Pafce, & vid. in die Dedicationis, per manus fubcellararii. Item habet omnes decimas minutas, omnes denarios Romanos, & omnia oblata ad crucem in vigiliâ Pafcatis & in die; & fic eft contentus, &c. funt omnes vicarii ante ipfum fuerunt contenti per multos annos preteritos.

Vicarius tenet unum meffuagium, quod jam vocatur *vicaria*, per adquifitionem fratris Willi Charyte quondam prioris; quod reddere folebat per annum xvis.

Memorandum, quòd anno Dni MCCCCLVII, primo die menfis Januarii, frater Willielmus Charyte, prior, perquifivit quandam manfionem, quam vicarius Sci Martini nunc inhabitat, eâ conditione, quòd octo folidi liberi redditûs de cantariâ ibidem, cum ceteris adquifitis, per eundem priorem effent affignati conventui in perpetuum, ad duo dat' pro filo emendo; qui quidem octo folidi longo tempore antea allocati fuerunt vicario ibidem pro manfione fuâ, quia ante hoc tempus vicarius Sci Martini nunquam habuit certam manfionem vel propriam [9].

Ecclefia Sancti Martini reddit communibus annis circa xxi li.; folebat reddere xxxvi li. xl li. vel $\frac{xx}{iiii}$x li.; fcil', ut in anno Domini MCCCXLVIII; nam circa illum annum Domini pixis dominicalis reddebat xl li. xl li. vel xii li. & quandocunque xxx li. & ultra.

Pes Thome Lancaftrie refpondebat vi li. xs.

Alta Crux reddebat xi li.

Pes Crucis [10] reddebat xl li. xl li. vel xii li.

Abbas

[1] Charyte's Rentale, fol. lxxxix. a.   [2] Ibid. fol. xci. In the margin of the original is written " Manfio vicarii."

[3] Charyte's Rentale, fol. xcvi. b.   [4] Ibid. fol. xcvi. b.   [5] Ibid. fol. xcvii. a.   [6] Sic in Orig.

[7] Ibid. fol. xcvii. a. b.   [8] Ibid. fol. xcvii. b.   [9] Ibid. fol. xcvii. b. & xcviii. a.

[10] This evidently alludes to the offerings made by thofe who on Good Friday had crept on their faces to the foot of the crofs, of which ceremony there is the underwritten account in Hutchinfon's Hiftory of Durham, vol. II. p. 240. " The Paffion. Within the church of Durham, upon Good Friday, there was a moft folemn fervice ; in which two of the eldeft monks took a large beautiful crucifix, all of gold, laying it upon a velvet cufhion, having St. Cuthbert's arms upon it, embroidered with gold, bringing it betwixt them upon the faid cufhion to the loweft fteps in the choir, and there betwixt them held the faid picture of

our

Abbas folvit archidiacono Leiceſtrie, pro procurationibus, fynodalibus, & denariis Sci Petri, ecclefie Sci Martini, Leyc', ixꝛ. xđ. oƀ. q¹. ²

Vicarius Sancti Martini dictos denarios [Sancti Petri] colligit, & eos ad proprios ufus confervat; & nos pro ipfo dictos denarios archidiacono perfolvimus ³.

Refolutiones.

Item vicario Sci Martini iiꝛ. in feptimanâ, &c. ut fupra. Item duobus clericis ibidem ivꝛ. ivđ. per annum. Item pulfatoribus, octo clericis, & aliis pulfantibus, ivꝛ. ix đ. ⁴

Parochia Sancti *Nicholai*. Patronus hujus ecclefie abbas Leyceſtrie; &, fecundùm Matriculum, habens eam in proprios ufus ab antiquo.

Vicarius ibidem inſtitutus per epifcopum. Ordinatio ejus per Hugonem epifcopum patet in le Chartwary. Penfio ejus ab antiquo vi marc'. Clericus illius ecclefie eligendus eſt, & ordinandus, & removendus per abbatem. Habemus ibidem plures reditus nobis collatos ex diverfis benefactoribus noſtris.

Simon *Broke*, pro uno tenemento juxta communem aulam ville Leyceſtr', refpondet viiiꝛ.

Elizabet' *Chandeler*, pro uno gardino extracto ex iiii gardinis tenement' predictor' extendente fe in longitudine ad hofpitium de Leonard', in quo eadem Elizabet' manet, ex parte occidentali hofpitii predicti ufque locum vocatum *Holybonys* verfùs ecclefiam Sci Nicholai; & refpondet vꝛ. ad voluntatem ⁵.

ADDITIONS and CORRECTIONS.

P. xii. In the lift of Plates add,
14.⎫ Two Plates of the monument of Edmund
15.⎭ Crouchback Earl of Leiceſter, p. 222.

In the Tranſlation of Domefday, and in the Effay:

P. iii. l. 42. r. " Two *ploughs* are in demefne."
Ibid. l. 68. r. " One *plough*."
P. iv. l. 45. 55. r. " *plough* ;" l. 52. " *ploughs*."
P. v. l. 43. 45. r. " *ploughs*" and " *plough*."

P. xiii. l. 21. *Heletone* fhould undoubtedly be *Beletone*, though the original has an *H* by miſtake of the fcribe ; and a like inſtance occurs, p. xvii. l. 26. where *Holesford* fhould be *Botesford*.

P. xvi. l. 36. r. " *three* ploughlands.

P. xxvii l. ult. r. " *three* fhillings."

P. xli. note 1. it is faid, " There are frequent inſtances of lands being fituated in one parifh, which are now rated in the books of another; to the parfon or impropriator of which the tithes of thofe lands are alfo paid. In the maps of counties we often fee large portions of land laying in one, and belonging to another county." A learned Barriſter fuggeſts that this is not accurately expreffed. Though parcels of land belonging to one parifh may lie intermixed with, or furrounded by, the lands of another parifh, they cannot properly be faid to lie in the latter. They are to all intents and purpofes parts of the firſt. So of land feparated from the main body of the county, as a part of Worceſterſhire ; part of Wilts furrounded by Berks.

P. xlv. note 13. l. 2. r. " in rotulis noſtris curialibus, in quibus curiis prefentatum fuit, &c."

Ibid. note 18. r. " before high *Heaven*."

P. xlix. note 8. l. ult. r. " valet l marcas."

P. xcix. l. 6. r. " in penfione x marcarum."

Ibid. l. 54. r. " penfio xlviꝛ. viiiđ."

Pp. 97. 129. " Sciant, &c. quod nos Radulphus abbas Sci Jacobi [in Northampton] dedimus, conceffimus, &c. Martinio de Montorie, burgenfi Northampton', pro xl marcis, domum illam, cum pertinentibus, que fuit Schola Judeorum Northampton', unà cum domibus illis dirutis ante ingreffum ejufdem Schole ; & etiam domos illas que fuerunt Sarre de London Judee, quos domos, &c. habuimus ex conceff' Edwardi regis Anglie, regis Henrici primogenito ; reddend' inde nobis annuatim xꝛ." ⁶

P. 263. In the Cotton MSS. is preferved an article, in old Englifh, intituled, " Breves expofitiones decem mandatorum fecundùm magiſtrum Philippum [Repindon] quondam abbatem de Leyceſtriâ;" beginning, " A Deo gratias in eternum. Amen ;" and ending thus : " Expliciunt mandata Chriſti fecundum magiſtrum Philippum quondam abbatem de Leyceſtriâ. Deo gratias. Amen ⁷."

P. 264. " Ordinationes pro gubernatione monaſterii Beate Marie de Pratis," are preferved in the MS

Library of the Archbifhop of Canterbury at Lambeth ⁸.

P. 272. note, l. 4. r. " as they ſtood," &c.

P. 274. l. 57. r. " *Amyfworth* ;" l. 62. " *Hamfwell*."

P. 283. The abbot of Leiceſter held in Farninghoe the fourth part of a knight's fee of *Elen Zouch*, who held the fame of the king.

P. 294. It has juſtly been lamented, that no drawing has been preferved, nor any defcription given of the ſtyle of the building, of Leiceſter Abbey ; that only excepted which is given at the top of Plate XVII. fig. a. But fir *William Manners*, owner of the fite of Leiceſter abbey, having lately let the grounds within the walls of that place to a gardener, and alfo converted a portion of the Countefs of Devon's manfion into a dwelling for him, and the remains of the ruin having in confequence been much explored, feveral foundations of the original Abbey have been difcovered ; with the leaden feal to a bull of Pope Alexander III. engraved under the portrait of Cardinal Wolfey in Plate XVII. The ſtyle of the windows may alfo now be afcertained. Amidſt a quantity of rubbifh which had obvioufly been buried at the building of the late manfion, Mr. Throfby defcried, March 13, 1797, many fragments of the windows ; and, by a nice infpection, and putting the mutilated parts of fome of them together, they form the figure engraved in Plate XVII. fig. b. Two or three other fragments, like that in fig. c. (2½ inches round) lay among the rubbifh abovementioned. And many fragments like fig. d. (4 inches round) were found within the walls of that part of the building lately pulled down, all evidently from the old Abbey.

An ornamented niche from the Abbey-wall, which undoubtedly once held an image of the Virgin Mary, is alfo fhewn in fig. e ; and in fig. f. the door-way, with the blank fhield, noticed in p. 293.

Ibid. Six acres of freehold meadow-land in the Abbey Meadow were advertized for fale, in March 1798, being then let to Mr. *James Hardy*, tenant at will, at £25. a year.

P. 330. In 1379, the rectory of Cranefley in Northamptonfhire was appropriated to the collegiate church of the Newark ⁹ ; and the dean and canons continued regularly to prefent an incumbent to that vicarage till 1530, when Thomas Harryfon was prefented by *Francis Cave*, *Roger Gyllot*, &c. under a grant from the members of the collegiate church ¹⁰.

Ibid. The canons of Leiceſter held one knight's fee at Wollaſton in 1427 ¹¹.

P. 331. William Walefby was, in 1434, a canon of Hereford, and prebendary of Morton Parva ; which he exchanged, in 1437, for the rectory of Church Langton ; and in 1440 again exchanged his rectory for a canonry and prebend at Hereford.

---

our Saviour, fitting on either fide of it : and there one of the faid monks rofe, and went a pretty fpace from it, fitting down upon his knees, with his fhoes put off, crept upon his knees unto the faid crofs, and kiffed it ; and after him the other monk did fo likewife."—The offerings under the denomination of *pes crucis*, at the church of St. Martin's in Leiceſter, were at that time very large ; and as large were the receipts *per* year by means of the cheſt or box termed *pixis dominicalis*. But, according to Ecton, in Liber Valorum, the clear yearly value of the vicarage was, at the beginning of this century, only £9. 13s. 7¼d. And from whom has the modern vicar the diet of a canon for himfelf, the allowance of provifion and of pence for his deacon or curate, and a loaf for his fervant, to make him as contented with his ſtation as his predeceffors were faid to be while the abbot and his canons poffeffed the appropriation ? S. D. ² *Charyte's Rentale*, fol. cxlii. a. ³ Ibid. fol. ccvii. b.

⁴ Ibid. fol. cxlii. b. ⁵ Ibid. fol. xcviii. b. ⁶ *Bridges*, MSS. vol. E. p. 432. ⁷ Vefpatian A. XXIII. p. 107—115. ⁸ Reg. Courtney, archiep. Cant. fol. 138. b. ⁹ Pat. 3 Ric. II. p. 2. m. 32. ¹⁰ *Bridges*, vol. II. p. 21. ¹¹ Inq. 6 Hen. VI. at Walineford, before Thomas Powis and Popley, collectors of the fubfidy out of the knights fees.

PLATES INTENDED FOR THE THIRD AND FOURTH VOLUMES;

WITH SUCH OTHERS AS MAY OCCUR IN THE COURSE OF PRINTING.

⁎ Almoſt all the following Plates are already engraved; and may be ſeen, by any Gentleman who will do the Author of this Hiſtory the Honour of calling on him, at Cicero's Head, in Red Lion Paſſage, Fleet-ſtreet.

Frontiſpiece by LONGMATE.
Map of EAST GOSCOTE HUNDRED.
Allexton Church, Portrait of R. Blount, Seals, &c.
Asfordby Church, Town Crofs, Painted Glafs, &c.
Aſhby-Folvile Church, and Woodford Monuments.
Barkby Church, Hall, Arms, &c.
Barrow Church, Hoſpital, and Monuments, with the Portrait of Biſhop Beveridge.
Barrow Foſſils.
Mountforrel and Quorn Churches, Old Crofs, &c.
View of Mountforrel, and the New Town Crofs.
Monuments of the Farnham Family at Quorn.
Woodhouſe Church, School, Arms, &c.
Monuments, Antiquities, &c. from Woodhouſe, &c.
Antient and Modern Views of Beaumanor.
Portraits of Sir William Herrick and his Lady.
Accurate Plan of Charnwood Foreſt.
Three Picturefque Views in the Foreſt.
Beby Church, and Monument of Villiers.
Belgrave, Burſtall, and Thurmaſton Churches.
Brokeſby Church and Monuments.
Portrait and Monument of Sir Nathan Wrighte.
Coſſington Church, Parſonage, and Monuments.
South Croxton and Great Dalby Churches, &c.
Dalby on the Woulds Church, Monuments, &c.
Friſby Church, Monuments, &c.
Hoby, Hoton, and Humberſtone Churches.
Hungarton Church, Bagrave Hall, Arms, &c.
View of Quenby Hall.
Laund Abbey, Lord Cromwell's Monument, &c.
Lodington and Lofeby Churches, Arms, &c.
Preſtwould Church and Monuments.
Three other Monuments at Preſtwould.
Queniborough Church and Monuments.
The old Manſion-houſe at Ragdale.
Ragdale Church, with the Modern Houſe.
Radcliffe on the Wreke Church and Monument.
Rereſby and Rotherby Churches.
Saxulby Church and Monuments.
Segrave and Sileby Churches.
Skeffington Hall.
———— Church, and the Hall-houfe.
Monuments at Skeffington.
Syſton and Thruſſington Churches, &c.
Tilton Church and Monuments.
Twyford and Thorpe-Sachvile Churches.
Tugby and Eaſt Norton Churches, &c.
Walton and Wymeſwould Churches, &c.

Map of WEST GOSCOTE HUNDRED.
Various Views of Aſhby Caſtle.
Aſhby Church, Coins found on Aſhby Would, &c.
Blackfordby Chapel.
Two Views of Belton, with Lady Roeſia Verdun.
Two Views of Bradgate Houfe, complete, and in Ruins.
Two other Views of Bradgate in its preſent ſtate, &c.
Three Picturefque Views in Bradgate Park.
Bredon, Staunton, and Worthington Churches.
Monuments at Bredon and Staunton Harold.
Three Picturefque Views of Bredon Hill.
Modern View of Staunton Harold.
Another View, from the Park, at a Diſtance.
Fac Simile of a Letter from King Charles I.
Cole-orton Church, Hoſpital, Monument, &c.
Diſeworth and Diſhley Churches, &c.
Old Manſion, and other Views, at Caſtle Donington.
Caſtle Donington Church, Caſtle, and Hoſpital.
Two Plates of Monuments at Caſtle Donington.
View of Garendon Hall.

Temple of Venus, and fine Pyramid, in the Park.
Garendon Monks and Seals.
Two Views of Gracedieu, with Nun, Seals, &c
Hathern Church, Monuments, &c.
Kegworth and Walton Iſley Churches.
A Nun of Langley, Arms, &c.
Lockington and Hemington Churches, &c.
Lockington Hall, View of Hemington, &c.
Loughborough Church, Rectory, &c.
Braſs Monuments, &c. at Loughborough.
Houſes of Mrs. Tate, Mr. Hyde, and Mr. Whatton.
Views of Three Bridges, all near Loughborough.
Oſgathorpe Church and School.
Packington and Snibſton Churches.
Ravenſton Church, Hoſpital, &c.
Rodeley Temple, Rodeley Church, &c.
The Will of Bartholomew Kingſton, from his Tomb.
Other Monuments in Rodeley Church.
Two Views of Gaddeſby, Monuments, &c.
Caldwell, Grimſton, Keame, and Wartnaby Churches.
Seile Church, Hall, Monuments, &c.
Shepeſhed Church and Monuments.
Snareſton Church.
Stretton Church, Hall, Monuments, &c.
Swebſton Church, Monuments, &c.
Swithland Church, Monuments, &c.
Thurcaſton and Anſtey Churches, &c.
Portrait of Biſhop Latimer.
Ulveſcroft Abbey, an Eremite Monk and Nun.
Another View of Ulveſcroft, with Seals, &c.
Wanlip Church, Monuments, and Arms.
Whatton Church, Arms, and Seals.
Whitwick Church, Monuments, and Arms.

Map of GUTHLAXTON HUNDRED.
Ten Plates of the Legend of St. Guthlac.
Arnſby and Great and Little Aſhby Churches.
Aylſtone Church, and Lubbeſthorpe Ruins.
Monument of William Heathcot.
Bittefwell Church, Monument, &c.
Blaby and Counteſsthorpe Churches, &c.
Broughton Aſtley Church.
Bruntingthorpe Church and Rectory.
Catthorpe Church.
Cleybrook Church, Antiquities, &c.
Wibtoft and Little Wigſton Chapels.
Dr. Stukeley's View of Bennonis.
Antient and Modern High Crofs.
Cofby, Cotteſbach, and Dunton Baſſet Churches.
Foſton Church, Monuments, &c.
Frolefworth Church, &c.
Gilmorton Church, and Seal.
North and South Kilworth Churches.
Knaptoft Church, Manor-houfe, &c.
Mouſley and Shearſby Churches.
Leir Church, &c.
Lutterworth Church and Monuments.
Braſs Figures, &c. from Lutterworth Church.
Miſterton Church, and Monuments of the Poultneys.
Oadby Church and Stalls.
Seals of the Hardreſhull Family, &c.
Great Peatling Church and Monuments.
Little Peatling Church and Monument.
Shawell Church, Round Hill, Dow Bridge, &c.
Stanford Church, and Stanford Hall.
Braſs Plates of the Family of Cave at Stanford.
The Churches at Wigſton Two-Steeples.
Funeral Reliques found in the Barrows at Wigſton.
Willoughby Waterleſs Church.

Map

Map of SPARKENHOE HUNDRED.
Appleby Free-fchool.
Appleby Church, Religious Houfe, &c.
Monuments, &c. from Appleby Church.
Afton Flamvile and Burbach Churches.
View of Burbach Houfe, Monuments, &c.
St. Peter, and other Painted Glafs, from Burbach.
Barwell Church, Monuments, Shenton's Tree, &c.
Stapleton and Potters Marfton Churches, Hall, &c.
Market Bofworth Church, Hall, &c.
Portrait of Richard III. and his Queen, Seals, &c.
Accurate Plan of Bofworth Field, and various Curi-
ofities found near the Site of the Battle.
Barlefton, Carleton, Shenton Churches, Ofbafton Hall.
Shenfton and Sutton Halls, Cadeby Church, &c.
Congefton and Croft Churches, Arms, &c.
Desford Church, Monument, &c.
Drayton (Fenny) Church and Monument.
Elmefthorpe Church and Arms.
Enderby and Whetftone Churches.
Glenfield Church, Monument, &c.
Braunfton Church, Hall, &c.
Braunfton, Kirby Muxloe Churches, and Kirby Ruin.
Two Views of Groby, and one of Steward Hays.
Hether Church and Monument.
Two Views of Higham Church, &c.
Lindley Old Chapel, &c.
Portraits of William and Robert Burton.
View of the Modern Houfe at Lindley.
Ground-plan of Hinckley.
Hinckley, Stoke, and Dadlington Churches, &c.
Two other Views of Hinckley Church.
Monuments, Antiquities, &c. at Hinckley.

Map of the Country Five Miles round Hinckley.
View of Leicefter Grange, near Hinckley.
Portraits of Cleveland, Onebye, &c.
A Plate of Natural Hiftory from Hinckley.
Monks of Hinckley Priory and Mountgrace.
Ibftock and Hugglefcote Churches; Dunnington, &c.
Kirkby Malory and Earl's Shilton Churches.
Lord Wentworth's Houfe, Monuments at Kirkby.
Markfield Church, and Two Picturefque Views.
Nailfton Church, Barton in Fabis, and Normanton.
Narborough and Newbold Verdon Churches.
Portrait of Bifhop Crew.
Norton Church.
Portrait of the Rev. William Whifton.
Orton on the Hill Church, Hall, &c.
Monuments from Orton Church.
Gopfal Chapel; Twycrofs Church, Monuments, &c.
Elevation of Gopfal Houfe.
Peckleton Church, Monuments, &c.
Ratby and Newton-Linford Churches, &c.
Sapcote, Shakerfton, and Sharnford Churches.
Shepey and Ratcliff-Culey Churches.
Shepey Foffiis.
Sibbefton Church, Stalls, Monuments, &c.
Stony-Staunton Church, Saxon Door-way, &c.
Thornton and Bagworth Churches, Bardon, &c.
Thurlefton Church.
Two other Views of Thurlefton Church.
Monuments from Thurlefton Church.
Witherley, *Manduessedum*, &c.
Weftcotes, and Danet's Hall, both near Leicefter.
Arms to illuftrate the Pedigree of Ruding.
Portrait of Sir Walter Raleigh.

PLATES INTENDED FOR THE GENERAL HISTORY OF THE TOWN;
IN ADDITION TO THOSE ALREADY PUBLISHED.

A fmall View of the Town of Leicefter.
Font, Monuments, &c. in All Saints Church.
St. Margaret's Church, Monuments, &c.
Two fine Niches at the Altar of St. Margaret's Church.
St. Nicholas's Church, with the old Roman Wall, &c.

Wigfton's Hofpital, Monuments, Glafs, &c.
Portrait and Seals of Robert Dudley Earl of Leicefter.
Painted Glafs from Mr. Stephens's Houfe.
Traders Tokens iffued in the Town of Leicefter.
Plan of Modern Leicefter,

DIRECTIONS TO THE BINDER, 1798.

In GARTRE HUNDRED, Vol. II. Part II. TITLE and DEDICATION; 5 S—5 X, X 2, X 3;
5 Y—6 D 1, 2, 3, 4; 6 E—7 Y, 1, 2, 3, 4; 7 Z—10 T; Appendix, N n—P p.

Sheets now given in Addition to Vol. I; to be placed (for the prefent) at the End of Gartre Hundred.

[*T t t*]—[4 *I*]; then follows a fingle leaf marked (by miftake) [6 *K*]; then [4 *L*]—[4 *Y*]; and APPENDIX,
P—*G g*.

*** A farther Continuation of Vol. I. will be given with the Hundred of EAST GOSCOTE (in which a confiderable progrefs is already made at the prefs) and alfo with each fucceeding HUNDRED.

An APPENDIX of ADDITIONS and CORRECTIONS.

VOLUME I.

₊ The Reader is requested to notice the Additions and Corrections in the Appendix to Vol. I. Part I.
p. 48 ; in p. 625 of Vol. I. Part II.; and also in the Appendix to Vol. I. Part II. p. 114.

THE Portrait of my much-valued Precursor WILLIAM BURTON (given with Sparkenhoe Hundred, see vol. IV. p. 651.) is to be placed as a FRONTISPIECE to vol. I. Part I.

Vol. I. p. ix. Preface. *add to note.* Bassano's copy of Burton's " Leicestershire," was purchased by the late William Latham, esq. F. R. S. and F. S. A.

P. iii. Domesday, col. 2, l. 6. *read,* In *Seglebi* are two ploughlands and two oxgangs, and ten acres of meadow.

P. vii. l. i. *for* p. 232, *read* p. 231.

P. xi. col. 2, l. 3 from bottom *read, four* bordars.

P. xxix. col. 2, l. 22. The words, " The value is unknown," belong to preceding paragraph, *Prestwald.*

P. xxxvii. col. 2, l. 53. *add note.* See Rev. Samuel Denne, in the Archæologia, vol. VIII. p. 218.

P. xli. col. 2, l. 48, *read* capacity.

P. xlvi. *add:* Names of the Nobility, Gentry, and others, in the County of Leicester, who contributed to the Defence of this Country at the time of the threatened SPANISH INVASION in 1588 : £.

	£.
Frauncis Beomount, armiger, 24 Aprilis,	25
John Stanford, gracier, 29 Aprilis,	25
Richard Paramor, armiger, sexto die Maii,	25
Valentyne Hartopp, gen. 11 die Maii,	25
Bryan Cave, armiger, 12 die Maii,	25
Richard Walker, 14 die Maii,	25
Robert Brookesby, armiger, 16 die Maii,	25
Richard Evington, 25 die Maii,	25
Frauncis Smithe, armiger, 27 die Maii,	25
Ralphe Whaley, gen. eodem,	25
George Ashebye, armiger, 28 die Maii,	25
William Digby, armiger, 10 die Junii,	25
John Tomworth, armiger, 12 Junii,	25
Edwarde Turvile, armiger, 14 Junii,	25
William Blunt, armiger, 16 Junii,	25
Edward Pell, 16 die Junii,	25
Stephen Rogers, gen. 20 Junii,	25
Frauncis Sherard, armiger, 24 Junii,	25
Edward Pate, armiger, 28 Junii,	25
William Lawe, gen. quarto Julii,	25
Mawrice Barklie, arm. 14 Julii,	25
Erasmus Smithe, 9 August,	25
Robert Hasilwoode, 2 Septembris,	25
William Roberts, 6 Septembris,	25
John Elkington, 8 Septembris,	25
John Copeland, 10 Septembris,	25
Basil Brooke, eodem,	25
Roberte Kilbie, eodem,	25
Michaell Cosen, 19 Septembris,	25
Edmunde Temple, 25 Septembris,	25
Nicholas Perpointe, 27 Septembris,	25
Thomas-Walronde, 28 Septembris,	25
John Plumbe, 29 Septembris,	25
Richard Brocke, 12 Octobris,	25
Richard Kestyn, the 23	25
John Grever, 25 Octobris,	25
William Johnson, 27 Octobris,	25
John None, 28 Octobris,	25
Thomas Lanye, 30 Octobris,	25
Jane Bowes, widow, 3 Novembris,	25
William Coke, 14 Novembris,	25

P. [xlviii.] In the " Nomina Villarum," col. 1, l. 32. *for* Segrave, *read* Belgrave.

P. [xlvii.] " Testa de Nevill."—The Copy of this Record published by Parliament has furnished some various readings.—Col. 1, l. 3. *for* De Overton, *read* In Overton.—L. 17. *for* Nevill, *read* Deivile. —L. 23. *for* 3 caruc', *read* 4 caruc'—L. 26. *read* Brandiston.—L. 28. *read* Berscaldeby.—Col. 2, l. 40. *for* Picard', *read* Ricard'.—L. 46. *for* Bourt, *read* Bourc'.

P. xlviii. col. 1, l. 37. *read* Edimshove.—L. 41. and 59. *read* Bescaldeby.—L. 65. *read* Bourc'— Col. 2, l. 6. *for* alio, *read* alio.—L. 63. *for* destendit, *read* descendit.

P. xlix. l. 28. *for* Restold, *read* Rescold.—L. 38. *for* vicariã, *read* vacariã.—L. 53. *read* quolibet.— Col. 2, l. 3. *read* Cortingstorp.—L. 42. *read* Berscaldeby.—L. 3 from bottom, *read* Redmild.

P. l. col. 1, l. 23. *read* Chawrcis.—Col. 2, l. 5. and 10. *read* Picwell.—L. 11 and 12 should be transposed.—L. 65. *for* Lorre, *read* Loire.—L. 2 from bottom, *read* Ada.

P. li. col. 1, l. 12. *for* Breauce, *read* Breante.— L. 47 and 52. *for* Warg', *read* Waig'.—L. 2 from bottom, *for* Ervit, *read* Ervic'.—Col. 2, l. 6. *read* Brenugthũrst.—L. 14. *for* Odmell, *read* Odinell'.— L. 36 and 44. *read* Chaurces.—L. 63. *for* Gremvill, *read* Greinvill.

P. lii. col. 1, l. 32. *read* 110s. 6d.—L. 61. *read* dnacõi.—L. 65 and 66. *read* Levinton.—L. 67. *read* Cubinton. L. 75. *read* Sckeitesclive.—L. 76. *read* p'tin'. — Col. 2. l. 8. *read* Gresel.—L. 9. *read* Mittun.—L. 17. *read* Suarkeston.—L. 53. *read* Sf'tton.

P. liii. col. 1, l. 4. *read* Kanvill.—L. 49. *read* Bendeng.—L. 73. *read* Stakethirne.—L. 2 from bottom, *read* Muschet.—Col. 2, l. 4. *read* Wulfricheston.—L. 17. *read* Touney.

P. liv. col. 2, l. 7. *read* Bracy.—L. 26. *read* Shetesclive.—Between l. 38 and l. 39. *insert,* In Cuntusthorp unum feodum quod Henr' de Lodbroc ten' de Thomâ de Arders, et ipse de p̃dic' com'.—In Rottel' 1 feodum quod Thom' Arden ten' de eodem com'.

P. lv. " Matriculus," col. 2, l. 22, and 31. for antestante, *read* auctoritate.—L. 26. *read* Helnestowe. —L. 29. *read* pro XVII sol'.—Note 2, l. 24. *read* canonized.

P. lviii. col. 2, l. penult. *read* Cortlyngstog.—L. ult. *read* pro quintâ parte. Persona IIII portionum R. de Verdon, &c.

P. lix. col. 1, l. 4. *read* Cortlinstog.—L. 19. *for* Donynton, *read* Bonynton.—L. 48. *read* de Bello Capite.—L. 49. *add note on* Radi. Rather Ranulfi ; see Pegge's Beauchief Abbey, pp. 13. 219.—L. 52. *add note on* Petri ad Vincula'. Lammas, or 1st of August.

P. lx. col. 1, l. 13. *read* Bernysby.—Col. 2, l. 49. *read* sive ecclesia in eodem feodo.

P. lxxiii. l. 13. *for* Amington, *read* Donington.— L. 18. *for* pro, *read* quia.

P. lxxvi. col. 2. l. 4 from bottom, *for* Buñiintun, *read* Duñintun.

P. lxxxiii. col. 2, l. 5. *read* Subseneschallo.

P. lxxxiv. In a benevolence granted to king Henry VIII. upon commission to all the counties in 1544, Leicestershire gave 629l. 14s. [1]

P. lxxxv. under Hallertone, the name of the hamlet should be read " Hallertone Blastone."

P. lxxxvi. The Press is misarranged : Waltone should have no hamlet ; Whytwick should have the hamlets of Thrinkstone and Swannyton.—L. ult. Mistertone should have the hamlet of Walcote instead of Mistertone.

---

[1] Strype, Eccl. Mem. I. Append. p. 333.

P. lxxxix. l. 37. *for* Sadington, *read Dadl*ington.

P. xci. col. 1, l. 50. *for* Foston, *read* Stotton.—Col. 2, l. 15. *for* Halsoe, *read* Haliok.—L. 16. *for* Langston, *read* Laughton. Q ?—L. 20. *read* Eston cum Socâ.—L. 47. *for* Mousley, *read* Nousley.

P. xcix. col. 1, l. 3. *read* 10 marc'.—L. 5. *read* Ecclesiarum.—L. 48. *read* 46s. 8d.

P. ci. col. 1, l. 30. " De Serjantiis." *add note on* Duston : " Dudston, co. Warwick."

Ibid. In the Itinerary of Leicester, 27 Hen. III. in the Archives of the Tower of London, the Manor of *Piddlesey* in Leicestershire is said to have been held by one Henry Angage, " per Serjantiam capiendi lupos," as the inquisition delivers it. I have not been able to discover in what part of the county the manor of *Piddlesey* is situated.

P. ciii. col. 1, l. 46. *for* Fouche, *read* Zouche.—Col. 2, l. 9 from bottom, *for* Baston, *read* Bozon.—L. 8 from bottom, *read* Rohaut.

P. cxix. col. 1, l. 8 from bottom, *read* Laugton.—L. 7 from bottom, *read* virgate.—Col. 2, l. 8 from bottom, *read* Graunford.

P. cxxiv. col. 2, l. 25. *read* Redding.—Head-line, *read* libro de Love*l*.

P. cxxxviii. col. 1, l. 16. staple, *i. e.* steeple.—L. 43, *for* mydle, *read* needle.—Col. 2, l. 44. chef-fats, *i. e.* cheese-vats.

P. cxxxix. l. 65. *for* 1152, *read* 1552.

P. cxliv. col. 1, l. 51. *for* Stathern, *read* Hathern.—Col. 2, l. 10, *for* Burton, *read* Barton.

P. cxlv. Sir Charles Asgill has fee-farm rents in Belton, Long Whatton, Hathern, Thringston, Sheepshead, Osgathorpe, Coleorton, Gracedieu, Wilson, Isley Walton, Castle Donington, Cossington, Belgrave. See other fee-farm rents under Billesdon.

P. cxlvi. col. 1, l. 5. *read* Tooley Park.

P. cli. col. 2, l. 2. *for* 1640, *read* 1630.

P. cxci to ccviii. The Natural History of the Vale of Belvoir, by the Rev. George Crabbe, B. D. [given with vol. IV.] is to be here introduced.

P. [42]. " Benefactions." Under Woodhouse, William Rawlins, the year should be 1696. The Trustee, Mr. Heane, not Kaines.

P. 18. In Genealogy of Saxon Earls of Leicester : Ralph de Gernoniis earl of Chester died 1156, not 1155.—*Add* Hawise, 4th daughter of Hugh Cyvelioc, married to Robert de Quincy; and had issue Margaret, only daughter, married first to John de Lacy earl of Lincoln, afterwards to Walter Marshall earl of Pembroke.—See the Pedigrees of the Twelve Competitors for the Crown of Scotland, in vol. IV pp. 448, 449.

P. 21. Genealogy of Grentesmainell, second descent, *read* William de Geroiis. See Appendix, p. 13.

P. 25. col. 1, l. 35. *read* nuncupatory devise just before.

P. 59. notes, l. 1. *read* Statutes of Clarendon.

P. 64. col. 2, l. 10 from bottom, *read* but that.

P. 94. col. 2, l. 9. *read* Flemings.

P. 98. Genealogy of the Bellomonts, eighth descent: It was Simon the Bald, *father* of Simon earl of Leicester, who married Amicia. See p. 99.—Notes, l. 15. *read* probably nearly *of* the same age.

P. 100. col. 1, l. 17 from bottom, *for* pactionem, *read* partitionem.—L. 16 from bottom, *for* nostris *read* meis.—L. 12 from bottom, *for* tota, *read* una. The above errors are in Madox; but are corrected from a MS. of Mr. Roper; who adds the remainder of the Record.—Col. 2, l. 42. *read* Ranulph Blundeville earl of Chester.

P. 104. col. 2, l. 36. *for* son, *read* daughter.

P. 105. col. 1, l. 29. *read* hostis.—L. 45. *read* comes.

P. 146. col. 1, l. 32. *omit* his.

P. 151. notes, l. 34. and p. 163. col. 2, l. 40. pro *de* men, *i. e. probi homines,* see note [4], p. 150.

P. 165. notes, l. 2. *read* Henry's daughter Beatrice, see p. 167.

P. 169. col. 1, l. 6 from bottom. Q. if right? Hugh le Bigot was warden of the Tower of London; see p. 151. *n.*

Ibid. Notes, l. 1. *for* Manuel, *read* Mansel.

P. 178. col. 1, l. 22. *after daughter, add* Alianora; see p. 167.—Col. 2, l. 48. *for* G. *read* Geoffry.

P. 182. col. 1. l. 40. *add note on* warden : " Richard de Gray; see p. 184."

P. 187. col. 2, l. 20. *add note on* "Arundel," "The heir of William de Fortibus ; see p. 151."

P. 188. col. 2, l. 19 from bottom, *for* William, *read* Walter de Cantelupe; see p. 204. *n.*

P. 197. notes, l. 17. *add note on* earl of Leicester: " This was Bossu ; see p. 17."

P. 199. col. 2, l. 17. *add note on* Carnis-privio: " This is oddly expressed ; but it means the time of Lent."

P. 205. col. 2, l. 33. *for* Hereford, *read* Hertford; see p. 137.

P. 210. col. 1, l. 6. Shireburne castle is mentioned p. 151, *n.*

P. 212. The patient industry of Mr. Joseph Strutt having considerably enlarged and corrected the Montfort Pedigree, his copy of it is here inserted :

PEDIGREE of MONTFORT EARL of LEICESTER.

Robert king of France, died 1031.=

Union of the Bellomonts and Montforts.

Robert Blanchmaines,=Petronilla. third of the Bellomonts earls of Leicester.

Almaric, a base son, builder of Montfort, in France.=

Simon de Montfort, earl of Evreux=Bertha, daughter and heir of Richard in right of his wife. | earl of Evreux, and constable.

Simon de Montfort II. surnamed=1. Amicia; married into the the Bald; count of Rochfort and Evreux.
(His wife is omitted in Pedigree, p. 212, and placed to his son: hence much confusion. But page 90 compared with 99 will set all right.)

1. Amicia; married into the Montfort family (though not, as in Pedigree, p. 212, to the *earl of Leicester,* the first : she was his mother.) *In the Pedigree, p. 212, this lady is joined with her son in the matrimonial line; and at p. 259 she is made the daughter of her brother Fitz-Parnell.*

2. Margaret ; married Sayer de Quincey. *At p. 259, this lady is called the daughter of Fitz-Parnell: but was his sister.*

1. William de Britolio.
3. Roger, bishop elect.
4. William?

2. Robert Fitz-=Loretta ; Parnell; left died a no issue. (He nun. was the fourth and last Bellomont.)

Here the earldom of Leicester was parted.

1. Amauri. *See more respect-*
2. Guy*. *ing these, pp.*
3. Robert. 104. 212.

4. Simon II. de Montfort the Younger ;=Alianor, daughter earl of Leicester ; slain at Evesham : | of king John, &c. the hero of 100 pages in volume I.

Amicia.
Laura.
Perronelle.

1. Sir Henry de Montfort, slain with his father at Evesham.
2. Sir Simon, defeated at Kenilworth by Edward Longshanks. Assisted in slaying sir Henry D'Almaine, son of the king of the Romans, at Viterbo ; and died a vagabond.

3. Guy, *earl of Tuscany ;* with his brother Simon's aid, slew the son of the king of the Romans. [*Not the earl of Bigorre ; who was his uncle ; see above.*]

4. Richard, accompanied his mother to France after the battle of Evesham.

5. Almaric, an ecclesiastic; stripped of his dignity after the battle of Evesham.

Eleanor,=Llewellin, prince of Wales

* *This Guy was earl of Bigorre : and not the Guy who slew the king of the Romans : the Pedigree, p. 212, blends the two.*

P. 220.

P. 220. col. 1, l. 25. *add note on* Ranulfus: "This must be Ranulfus de Gernoniis the fourth earl: because Ranulph was his father. See p. 219."—Col. 2, l. 5. *for* Robert, *read* Roger; see p. 98.—L. 11 from bottom, *for* unum, *read* unde.—L. 10 from bottom, *fill up the blank with* rectum.—L. 7 from bottom, *read* comite Salisbure; Humfrido de Bohun, dapifero; J. filio Gilberti; R. de Hum', constabulario; Guarino filio Ger'; Roberto de Curcy, dapifero; Manasseto Bysset, dapifero; Philippo de Columbe, ex parte comitis. Ranulphi, Will' com' Lincoln'; &c. as in l. 4 from bottom.

P. 221. col. 1, l. 7. *add note on* bp. of Romania: "John Bishop of Bologna; see pp. 132, 133."

P. 224. col. 1. l. 47. *for* Marchers, *read* Marches. —L. 62. *read* banners.—Notes, l. 2. *for* 1304, *read* 1262.—Ibid. *read in* Plate XIII. figs. 1 and 2.

P. 226. col. 1, l. 1. *for* Mary, *read* Maud.

P. 229. col. 1, l. 8. qu.? *for* twenty, *read* forty pounds; see Appendix, p. 26; and preceding page, 228.—L. 11 from bottom, *read* Syruse.—Col. 2, l. 3. *read* Otho duke of Brunswick.

P. 237. col. 1, l. 3. *add note on* Huntingdon: " This is Northampton, p. 247. col. 1, l. 15. qu.?"

P. 238. col. 2, l. 6 from bottom, *for* John king of Castile, *read* Henry Transtamare; see p. 242, 243. The duke's daughter Philippa married *John* of Portugal.

P. 239. notes, l. 18. qu. *for* three children, *read* four? see p. 243.

P. 243. col. 1, l. 2. qu.? Henry prince of Asturias is called John, p. 238.

P. 245. col. 2, l. 25 from bottom, *read* earl of Huntingdon.

P. 247. col. 2, l. 35. *add note on* earl of Nottingham: "Q? Norfolk? see p. 246."

In the APPENDIX to the early Earls of Leicester.

P. 5. In head-line, *after* High Steward of England, *correct thus* (See p. 20.)

P. 9. col. 1, l. 9. *for* Robert Bellomont, earl of Leicester, *read* Le Bossu, earl of Leicester; see p. 48.—L. 19 from bottom, *add note on* Augustus III. —Q.? Augustus II. as Phil.-Augustus III. did not commence his reign till 1226.

P. 10. l. 4. *for* Henry IV. *read* Henry III.

P. 11. l. 18. *add note on* Robertum comitem Leicestriæ. " Robert de Bellomonte; see p. 23."— L. 55. *add note on* Roberti: " Le Bossu; see p. 48."

P. 12. Agreement between the Earls of Chester, &c. *Add note on* Chester: " This was Ranulph de Gernoniis; but the page referred to does not shew this. See p. 26."

P. 15. col. 2, l. 36. Carta confirmationis. This was Blanchmaine's charter.

P. 26. col. 2, l. 42. *for* 33, *read* 34 Edw. III.

P. 32. col. 2, l. 42. *for* gardium, *read* gardino.

P. 33. l. 5. *read* Ranulphus de Blundeville comes Cestriæ, ob. 16 Hen. III.

P. 47. col. 2, l. 41. *for* Bardon-park, *read* Barne-park.

P. 48. The accurate Reader is requested to notice some Additions and Corrections inserted in this page.—In col. 2. l. 4. *for* p. 39, *read* p. 59.

P. 50. col. 1, l. 31. *for* 16, *read* ib.; col. 2, l. 26. *for* 86, *read* ib. l. 51. *for* 22, *read* 20.

P. 51. col. 1, l. 4. *read* App. p. 18.—L. 42. *for* 26. *read* 27.—Col. 2, l. 1. *for* William, *read* Walter.—Col. 3, l. 4 from bottom, *for* 26, *read* 27.

VOLUME I. PART II.

P. 256. col. 1, l. 42. *add note on* " duke of Ireland:" Who this duke was appears at p. 281, *n.*; and see p. 368.

P. 258. col. 1, l. 32. *add note on* " letters." See before, pp. cxlii. cxliii.

P. 259. col. 1, l. 40. Mr. Strutt has pointed out to me, that Mr. Staveley appears to have fallen into a double error here, in making Simon Montfort earl of Leicester marry Amicia, the elder *daughter* and co-heiress of Robert Fitz-Parnell. 1st. Amicia was *sister* to Robert Fitz-Parnell, being daughter of Earl Blanchmaines; see pp. 90. 98. 212. And 2dly, it was not Simon earl of Leicester, that married Amicia; but Simon the Bald, count of Evreux. From them descended Simon I. de Montfort earl of Leicester; who married Alice de Montmorency; see pp. 102, 103, 104; and the Pedigree, in the preceding page, 118.

P. 260. col. 1, l. 47. A charter of Richard I. should have been noticed here. See Appendix, p. 58.— Col. 2, l. 33. *for* p. 455, *read* 255.

P. 261. note [20]. *for* p. 62, *read* p. 61.

P. 262. col. 2, l. 7. *for* Edward I. *read* Edw. III.—Note [11], *for* p. 68, *read* p. 71.

P. 264. note [9], *for* p. 70, *read* 68.

P. 274. col. 2, l. 15 from bottom, *for* Dingesworth, *read* Amysworth.—L. 10 from bottom, *for* Gamswett, *read* Hamswell.—Note [10], *for* seal of this abbey, *read* of Leicester college.

P. 275. note [22], *for* p. 266, *read* 268.

P. 278. notes, l. penult. *for* before, *read* hereafter (in vol. II.)

P. 281. note [11], *for* John, *read* Robert de Vere.

P. 282. col. 2, l. 15. *for* p. 266, *read* 267.

P. 303. *add to note* [6], and Appendix, p. 80.

P. 306. col. 2, l. 36. *for* od, *read* on.

P. 311. *add to* Vicars of St. Mary de Castro, William Croftes, M. A. Oct. 8, 1638, by lapse.

Ibid. l. ult. The Rev. Thomas Robinson, Vicar of St. Mary's, died March 24, 1813, in his 64th year. He was seized with an apoplectic fit whilst shaving, after which he never spoke. Mr. Robinson was as much distinguished for his zeal and ability in performing his pastoral duties, as for his piety, benevolence, and virtues, in private life. On the morning of Sunday, March 21, he visited the different gaols as Chaplain, and in the evening delivered an animated and eloquent discourse from James v. 9. "Behold the Judge standeth before the door." The 7th of March was the 39th anniversary of his ministry in Leicester. He had been Vicar of St. Mary's 34 years, and, as an *Evangelical Minister*, had long classed among the most popular Preachers of the age. The different public charities (of many of which he was the founder) have in him lost one of their warmest friends and most able advocates, and the town of Leicester will have just reason to regret his death.—An immense concourse of spectators attended his interment, which took place on March 29th. 14 Clergymen preceded the funeral procession, and every avenue to the church was crowded to excess; but, notwithstanding the great pressure, the strictest solemnity and silence prevailed throughout the whole ceremony [1].—Mr. Robinson was formerly Fellow of Trinity College, Cambridge, B. A. 1772; M. A. 1775. Besides the works, already noticed in p. 311, he published, " The Christian System unfolded; or Essays on the Doctrines and Duties of Christianity," 3 vols.: " Prophecies on the Messiah;" a Visitation Sermon, published by request; and " A Sermon, preached in London, 1808, before the Society for Missions to Africa and the East, promoted by Members of the Established Church," &c.—An elegant monument, by Bacon, will shortly be erected to the memory of Mr. Robinson in St. Mary's church.

P. 312. col. 1, l. 13. A view of St. Mary's Church, as it appeared after the violent storm of July 10, 1783, is given in Plate XLVII. p. 619.

P. 318. col. 1, l. 12. *for* of the first, *read* Or.

Ibid. *Add to note*[3]: " The Rev. William Ludlam left two sons. The eldest, Thomas Ludlam, esq. died at Sierra Leone, July 25, 1810, on board the Crocodile frigate, in the 35th year of his age. He had been appointed by his Majesty a Commissioner for special purposes on that Coast. The premature death of this excellent young man was not only a subject of sincere lamentation to his numerous friends, but was in some degree a national loss. Inheriting no small portion of his father's natural talent for scientific pursuits, and cultivated by a sound classical education, his first views in life were turned to the liberal profession of a Printer; and in that capacity I gladly bear testimony to the excellence of his conduct during a regular apprenticeship. Gentle and unassuming in his manners, and industrious in his habits of business, his conduct gave general satisfaction both to his equals and his superiors. Soon after the expiration of his apprenticeship, an opportunity occurred, which was thought favourable both to his health and future fortune, of entering into the service of the Sierra Leone Company; and in that infant Colony he was for some time one of the Council, and at length became Governor. On the Colony being taken into the hands of the Administration, a new Governor was appointed by the Crown; but Mr. Ludlam obtained an especial commission, with power to visit such parts of the coast of Africa as might be thought useful to the interests of Great Britain and the general cause of Humanity; a commission for which, by his mild conciliatory manners, and by the experience acquired during a long residence at Sierra Leone, he was most eminently qualified. But his bodily strength was not equal to the task he had undertaken; and he fell a victim to disease, originally arising from a weak constitution; but with the pleasing consolation, both to himself and his surviving friends, that his life, though not a long one, was wholly passed in endeavours to be useful to all mankind.—The following tribute of respect (inscribed on his monument by his affectionate mother) was the joint production of the late Henry Thornton, esq. M. P. for Southwark, Thomas Babington, esq. M. P. for Leicester, and Zachary Macaulay, esq.:

" Sacred to the memory of Thomas Ludlam, esq. during many years Governor of Sierra Leone, and afterwards one of his Majesty's Commissioners for examining into the state of the British Settlements on the Coast of Africa, for the pur-

pose of rendering them subservient to the civilization of that continent.—To his zeal in the pursuit of this object he fell a victim on the 25th of June, 1810, aged 34 years.—In the execution of the important and arduous services to which he was called, he manifested superior talents and intelligence, singular moderation and firmness, unshaken integrity, and a disinterestedness and modesty which adorned all his other qualities.—His unwearied and judicious labours to promote the best interests of the natives of Africa, will not be forgotten by the friends of that deeply-injured race, and entitle him to a distinguished place among their benefactors. His life was short; but in that short life he did much for God and man.—The foundation of all his virtues, was a stedfast faith in the Gospel of Jesus Christ. This impelled him to engage in occupations which promised extensive usefulness, supported him under various difficulties and dangers, consoled him in seasons of sickness, and cheered him in the hour of death.—His widowed mother has erected this monument as a token of gratitude to God for having vouchsafed to her the gift of such a son, whose filial piety was most exemplary; who, while he lived, was a blessing and comfort to her declining years, and whom she humbly hopes again to meet at the resurrection of the just.' "

Mr. William Ludlam, youngest son of the Rev. William Ludlam, died April 1, 1813. He was in the high path of professional eminence, and deservedly esteemed in public and private life, as a very able, honourable, and upright man. He left an aged mother, and a widow and young family, to lament his loss.

Ibid. note [4]. Baron Carter died a batchelor, and left his estate to his brother Thomas Carter.

P. 329. col. 1, l. 9 from bottom, *for* Clement III. *read* Clement VI.; see Appendix, p. 109.—Col. 2, l. 11 from bottom, *add note on* Symon: " Or might he not have been the Simon Simeon, who at p. 231, is mentioned as the Duke's testator?—Note [14], *for* p. 219, *read* p. 229.

P. 329. St. Mary's College held the church of Bradford in Yorkshire, given by the duke of Lancaster temp. Hen. III.

P. 331. col. 1, l. 25. *add note on* " clerks:" " See Appendix, p. 111."—L. 45. This must be an error respecting John of Gaunt. His body was not interred in the Newark, but in St. Paul's, London. See p. 240.—Col. 2, l. 24 from bottom. William Walesby was a canon and prebendary of Morton Parva in the church of Hereford 1434, which he exchanged for the rectory of Church Langton in 1437; which he again exchanged for his canonry and prebend at Hereford in 1440. See vol. II. p. 666.

P. 332. col. 1, l. 3. Is there not an error here, respecting Margaret of Anjou? King Henry the Fifth's queen was Catharine of France.

P. 338. col. 2, l. 14. Dean Robert Boune, was summoned to convocation the year before the dissolution, 1 Edw. VI.—Note [3]. *for* p. 303, *read* p. 330.

P. 339. note [4], *for* where, *read* were.

P. 349. notes, l. 6. *for* p. 347, *read* 351.

ceeds to enforce and apply them to the cases of his hearers. Intelligible in his illustrations, forcible in his applications, and animated in his exhortations, there is no portion of his audience, however different as to intellectual attainments, uninformed or unimproved. While he fills the rich with good things, the poor are not sent empty away. Bred in the good old school, he knows that no sermon is properly concluded, edifying though it prove to the believer, without admonishing the unbeliever and alarming the transgressor. Here he is great. His ' life,' as Gregory Nazianzen said of Basil, being ' lightning,' and his word thunder, his remonstrances, and his admonitions are delivered with the energy of apostolic eloquence. If there be any fault in his voice, it is its sounding loudness, the tremendous clapping, rather than the tempered rolling, of the thunder. Admirable is his animation. Though somewhat advanced in years, and not exempt from the inroads of age, no sooner is he in the pulpit than he becomes the new man; ' renews his strength,' and, as it were, ' mounts upward !' His eyes beam with the light of life; his soul gives motion to his frame; and, as he draws near the end of his Sermon, he seems rising from the pulpit to glory. Sensible of the influence of his conduct on others, and perhaps from higher views, Mr. Robinson takes part in the Psalmody of his congregation. ' I can testify,' declares Augustus Toplady, in his Short Memorials of himself, ' by sweet and repeated experience, that singing is an ordinance of God, and a means of grace. Lord !' he adds, ' fit my soul to bear a part in that song, for ever new, which the elect angels, and saints made perfect in glory, are now singing before the Throne and before the Lamb.' Excepting some few notes of heads, which he now and then looks to, Mr. Robinson preaches extempore. If he brings with him the skeleton of his discourse, he trusts for its living substance to the breath which can breathe on the dry bones of this earth ! Some of his pulpit prayers are also delivered extemporary, with great judiciousness, and true efficaciousness. Having mentioned his use of head-notes in preaching, I must glance at a circumstance connected with them. Whenever his voice fails, which, notwithstanding its powerfulness, it is found to do, this failure is particularly perceptible when, as his sight is not now good, he lowers his head towards his cushion, in order to peruse his notes. These notes are contained between the leaves of his large Pulpit Bible. What, however, are defects like this, spots in the sun, when we look at the merits of such a man? His appearance is venerably fine; his dressing, as well as his preaching, being quite of the old school. It might seem superfluous to add, what yet it may be right to add, that the people flock to his church. He also is a great popular preacher, and he also is a good parish priest. Leicester ought to be thankful for, I must not say proud of, the present Vicar of St. Mary."

P. 350.

P. 350. col. 2, l. 37. *for* Ware, *read* Ward.

P. 351. col. 1, l. 49. *Margaret* Sherman is called *Anne* in p. 348, col. 2.

P. 357. note [7]. *for* p. 310, *read* 300.

P. 358. col. 1, l. 32. *read* David earl of Huntingdon.

P. 359. col. 2, l. 4 and 11. Mr. Strutt observes, "These two Simon Montforts are not the same. The one, l. 4, is Simon the Bald; father of the lower one, who was created Earl of Leicester. See pp. 90." 98, 99.—L. 29. *add note on* "Montfort," See Appendix, p. 38.—L. 30. *for* ton, *read* tun.

P. 361. col. 2, l. 14. *read* Pope Innocent IV.; see p. 122.—L. 36. *read* libertatibus.—Notes, l. 6. *read* town*s*.

P. 362. col. 1, l. 40. *for* Robert, &c. *read* Richard de Clare, earl of Gloucester and Her*t*ford.—Col. 2, l. 37. *for* nephew, *read* son.—L. 46. *for* Hereford, *read* Her*t*ford.—L. 69. *omit the words* " brother to the."

P. 363. col. 1, l. 20 from bottom. It was not to his wife; but to lady Mortimer; see p. 208.—Col. 2, l. 18. *read* Her*t*ford.

P. 364. col. 2, l. 19. *for* Margaret, *read* Alice: see pp. 222. 225.

P. 366. col. 2, l. 6. This was William de la Pole duke of Suffolk. The paragraph should be carried forward to the year 1450: see p. 373; and Rapin, *sub anno.* There was no duke of Suffolk till 1448. —Note [4] should be united to note [5].

P. 367. col. 1, l. 26. *add note on* "plague," See the parallel passage, p. 231.

P. 369. col. 1, l. 18. *for* Triseley, *read* Friseley; see p. 297.—Col. 2, l. 34. *read* Beaufor*t*.

P. 370. col. 2, l. 36. *read* Edmond.

P. 371. col. 1, l. 50. *read*, in which year Sir John Oldcastle, lord Cobham, was hanged.

P. 373. col. 1. l. 24. *for* ab, *read* ob.—L. 33. An event respecting this duke of Suffolk, is antedated, and by mistake placed in p. 366; see above.

P. 374. col. 1, l. 4. *read* Rober*t*s.

P. 376. col. 1, l. 45. *Edward* Digby is called *Everard* p. 373.

P. 377. col. 1, l. 7. *transpose,* and *read,* " and Peter Curteis, bailiff."

P. 379. notes, l. 3. *read* commonalty.

P. 387. col. 2, l. 47. *for* Seyton, *read* Layton; see p. 296.

P. 393. col. 1, l. 1. *point thus* Richard, Roger, and Robert Taverner, gents. See pp. 286, 287.

P. 397. col. 1, l. 49. *for* Jacob, *read* James Clarke. This and similar errors have arisen from the name being entered in Latin, *Jacobus.*

P. 403. col. 2, l. 24. *add note on* earl of Leicester; see p. 537.—L. 27. *add note on* Countys of Huntingdon: " Catharine; see p. 544."

P. 415. col. 2, l. 52. *for* Rege, *read* Reginâ.

P. 417. col. 1, l. 39. *for* Jacob, *read* James Ellice.

P. 420. col. 1, l. 6 and p. 425. col. 2, l. 31. *for* Jacob, *read* James Andrewe.

P. 426. col. 1, l. 14. *for* Jacob, *read* James Ellis. —Col. 2, l. 12. Fermyn is printed Jermyn in p. 438; And *Jermyn* is probably right.

P. 427. col. 1, l. 24. *for* Parr, *read* Pare.

P. 429. col. 2, l. 38. *add,* I am obliged to my good friend the Rev. Robert Watts, Librarian of Sion College, for extracts from a MS. in folio in Sion College Library, intituled in the Catalogue, " Acts of the Committee for plundered Ministers in the years 1650, 1651," relating to the following towns, Leicester, Knighton, Belgrave, Orton on the Hill, Foston, and Hinckley; which I shall introduce in the Additions to those respective places.

" *Jan.* 28th, 1651.

" Leicester.—Upon the peticon of the Maior and Justices of the Borough of Leicester, in the County of Leicester; setting forth, that there are five antient parish churches in the said Borough, and the maintenance belonging to them is not one hundred pounds a yeare; and praying this Committee,

for a competent additionall maintenance to be setled upon able Ministers sutable to the numerousnes and pouerty of the people there; and upon due consideracon of the great usefulnes of able Ministers in such populous places, whereby the Gospell may be the better propagated; It is resoלved by the Committee, that the yearly sume of twenty-foure pounds ten shillings, going out of the Prebend of Margaret's in Leicester, and soe much more as will make the said twenty-foure pounds ten shillings a yeare the yearly sume of two hundred pounds, be granted and paid by the Trustees for maintenance of Ministers out of the said Prebend, and other the accrewing rents and revenues in them vested, for increase of maintenance to such godly and able Ministers, as shall officiate in the said Churches within the said Towne, and be approued by this Committee. And it is ordered, that the Maior and Common Councill of Leicester be desired to consider how the same may be fitly distributed among such Ministers; And whether any of the said Churches may not conveniently be united, and to certify the same to this Committee with all convenient speed, that such union may be thereupon made by authority of Parliament, and the said augmentacon of two hundred pounds a yeare may be setled accordingly.

JOHN BOURCHIER. PHIL. SKYPPON.
M. OLDISWORTH. R. BREWSTER."
WM. MASHAM.
" *March* 24th, 1651.

" Leicester.—Whereas this Committee, the 28th of January last, directed the trustees for maintenance of Ministers to grant and pay for an augmentacon to the severall Churches within the said Burrough of Leicester the yearly sume of two hundred pounds; and this day apporconed the sume as followeth : *viz.* to the Minister of Martin's, sixty pounds a yeare; to the Minister of Margaret's, 50*l.* a yeare; to the Minister of Mary's, 50*l.* a yeare; and to the Minister of All Saints, 40*l.* a yeare. And whereas, this Committee have this day receiued good and satisfactory testimony from the Lord Grey, Member of Parliament, of the piety and ability of Mr. William Sims, Minister of the said Martin's: It is now ordered by this Committee, that the said Trustees doe pay the said yearly sume of sixty pounds to the said Mr Sims, from time to time, out of the accrewing rents and revenues in them uested.

M. OLDISWORTH. RIC. DARLEY.
RI. ALDWORTH. WAL. STRICKLAND [1]."
J. DAUERS.

P. 432. col. 2, l. 2. *read* Wigs*t*on.

P. 435. col. 2, l. 9. *for* Joseph, *read* Josiah Bond. see pp. 308. 311. 314.

P. 441. col. 2, l. 23 from bottom, *read* yearly.

P. 442. col. 2, l. 9. *read* widow Ossiter.

P. 444. col. 2, l. 30. *read* Mrs. Mary Cook's lease; see p. 441.

P. 450. col. 1, l. 24. François Soules was killed at Paris by the mob, Aug. 9, 1792. He was one of the persons employed by the Court of France for various purposes. His first effort was a Translation of Mr. Burke's pamphlet on the French Revolution, which he rendered with very little depreciation of its elegance. After that time he wrote several small pieces against the Revolution; and had been so often at Coblentz, that he was stigmatized by the name of " The Coblentz Writer."

Ibid. col. 1, l. 8 from bottom. W. Oldham, esq. who served the office of mayor in 1783, died March 24, 1814, in his 74th year.

Ibid. col. 2, l. 13. Mr. Alderman John Eames, of Leicester, died Feb. 25, 1811. He served the office of Mayor in 1790, and his magistracy was distinguished by a degree of independence and public spirit, never excelled, and seldom equalled. During his mayoralty, a thorough investigation took place throughout the town in weights and measures, and more than a waggon load of the latter were publicly cut up in the market place by the town servants.

[1] " Acts of the Committee for Plundered Ministers," in Sion College Library.

P. 450. col. 2, l. 15. *add,* "On Tuesday last, being Shrove Tuesday, an unfortunate accident happened at Leicester. —— Ward, a schoolmaster, having got upon the top of a part of the old Town-wall, near the Newark-gate, in order to see the *ancient,* but ridiculous custom of the WHIPPING TOMS, one of the large stones of the parapet wall gave way, and fell with him, by which he was so much bruised, that he died that night."—Aris's Birmingham Gazette, Monday, Feb. 26, 1787.

P. 451. col. 1, l. 1. Mr. Alderman Joseph Burbidge died Sept. 15, 1807, in his 59th year. He served the office of mayor in 1792, and discharged his public duties with integrity and independence.

Ibid. l. 27. Mrs. Parsons, relict of Mr. Alderman Parsons, died April 23, 1811, in her 82d year.

Ibid. Mr. Alderman Samuel Clarke, died at Leicester Feb. 14, 1812. He served the office of mayor in 1808.

Ibid. l. 38. *add,* The Mayors and Chamberlains of Leicester, from 1807 to 1811, are given in p. 621.

1812, Sept. 21. John Fox, esq. elected mayor; James Rawson, William Forester, chamberlains.

1813, Sept. 21. William Walker, esq. [since knighted] elected mayor; Mr. W. Howcutt, Mr. R. W. Wood, chamberlains.

1814, Sept. 21. Michael Miles, esq. elected mayor; J. Higginson, jun. and R. Kinton, gents. chamberlains.

Obituary of respectable Individuals of Leicester:

Mr. Alderman Watts died Nov. 28, 1803, in his 76th year. Early in life he quitted the tillage of the field for the field of glory; and, during the American war, was sent to Canada, in which province he remained 12 years, and was engaged in several pitched battles; was at the taking of Quebec, and in the field when the gallant General Wolfe fell. On his return to this country he took a public-house, and, by perseverance and industry as a brewer, acquired handsome property with strict honour and integrity. His widow died August 3, 1806.

Mrs. Linwood died at Leicester, Dec. 28, 1804. During the course of a long life she performed the various duties of a Christian with exemplary piety, and in the exercise of practical benevolence. The genuine purity of her mind, the active kindness of her disposition, and the warm philanthropy of her heart, had long endeared her to a large domestic circle, and to a numerous acquaintance. She was mother of the incomparably-ingenious Artist whose performances in needle-work have been so justly and universally admired; see p. 123.

Mr. Alderman Price died Jan. 10, 1807, in his 84th year. Courteous in disposition, warm in affection, and ardent in friendship; the great object of his life was usefulness; and the grand spring of all his actions religion.

Mr. John Ireland, printer, of Leicester, died April 17, 1810; he was strictly independent in his principles, of great probity, and much esteemed.

Anne Barlow died at the Red Cow, in Belgrave Gate, Leicester, in her 96th year, Nov. 8, 1810. She was left a widow with seven children in the reign of George II.; was a stout woman, seldom ill, but blind for the last ten years.

The Rev. Obadiah Clayton died in the Borough Gaol, in which he was confined for debt, Nov. 29, 1810, aged 37.—His history is eventful and affecting. He was entered of Magdalen-college, Cambridge, in 1790, under the best auspices, and was remarkable for his good conduct during his residence there; soon after he left the University, however, symptoms of a deranged state of mind made their appearance: these never ceased, at intervals, to recur, and were the sole cause of the irregularities which afterwards took place in his character. Being appointed usher of Giggleswick school in Yorkshire, he continued to acquit himself there with considerable credit to himself and satisfaction to the publick, till his former malady returning in a slight degree, he left home and came to Leicestershire, and was employed as curate at Segrave in that county. Still, however, the rambling disposition continuing, he gave up this employment, and, coming to Leicester, resided at a public-house in High-street, where the debt was contracted for which he was arrested. That there was much to be pitied in the case of this unfortunate man, is apparent, from the conduct of the Trustees of the School; for, from the time of his commitment to the day of his death, they continued to allow him a guinea every week; and during his illness ordered that he might be supplied with any additional expenditure, which his medical attendants deemed requisite. From the nature of his disorder, his friends thought that he could not with safety be liberated: indeed he has often been heard to say himself, that Leicester Gaol was to him an asylum, where the galling idea of confinement was unceasingly removed by the humane attentions of Mr. Owston and family. During his last illness, he evinced a mind deeply imbued with religious impressions. As a scholar, he was far above mediocrity; and as a man, possessed the strictest integrity and accuracy in his dealings, whenever he was in perfect possession of his intellects. On the whole, Christian charity will drop a tear upon his tomb, and emphatically say with our Poet:

" No farther seek his merits to disclose."

His remains were interred with decent solemnity, and attended by four of the Clergy of Leicester.

Mr. Alderman Benjamin Sutton died Dec. 7, 1810, in his 81st year.

Thomas Browne, gent. died aged 90, Dec. 22, 1808. He was formerly an eminent hosier at Leicester, but had retired from business many years, with independence acquired with honour and integrity.

Mr. Charles Measures died at Leicester in his 21st year, Feb. 18, 1811. He served his apprenticeship in the office of " The Leicester Journal" with fidelity; succeeded to the confidential department, as principal superintendant; and was followed to his grave with every mark of sympathizing regret from his relatives, and several of the profession, of which he was an able and upright member.

Mrs. Simpson died at Leicester about May 1811, aged 95. She lived in three kings' reigns, and had 60 sons, grandsons, and great-grandsons, serving his Majesty.

George-Davies Harley, gent. died at Leicester Oct. 28, 1811. He was a poet of some eminence, and a comedian of much provincial celebrity; esteemed as an independent, and honourable man.

Thomas Buxton, esq. late banker at Leicester, died at Camberwell, Dec. 26, 1811.

T. Paget, esq. of the Newark, died Jan. 24, 1814, Though upwards of 80, his faculties were not impaired. He deservedly claimed rank with Mr. Bakewell, as a promoter of the breed of Cattle.

George Noble, esq. of Leicester, died at Clifton, April 9, 1814, in his 48th year.

Mr. Francis Brown, a builder, at Leicester, who had realized considerable property, died in 1814.

Mr. Alderman Richard Beale died in 1814.

Mr. John Moore, of London, died at Leicester, in Dec. 1814, or Jan. 1815, aged 70. He arrived, with a view of ending his days with his two sons and son-in-law, resident at Leicester. On leaving the coach he appeared severely indisposed, and expired in about four hours. Mr. Raikes, of Gloucester, has generally been considered as the first person who engaged in the praiseworthy undertaking of establishing Sunday-schools, in 1784; but it is known that Mr. Moore devoted his Sundays to the instruction of the poor children of Leicester, in reading and writing, so far back as 1778. He had a turn for Literature, and had devoted his leisure hours to the composition of various religious tracts, which he had made arrangements for revising and completing in his retirement.

P. 452. col. 1, l. 29. *read* Cracroft.

P. 454. l. ult. *add to* Town Clerks: Sept. 20, 1813, Thomas Burbidge, gent. on resignation of Mr. William Heyrick.

P. 457.

P. 457. col. 2, l. 4. John Peach Hungerford, esq. of Dingley, died at Clifton, near Bristol, in his 90th year, June 3, 1809. He was a deputy-lieutenant, and for 15 years an honourable, independent, and able representative of the County of Leicester in Parliament, to which he was first elected in 1775, after one of the severest contests ever remembered. The public character of Mr. Hungerford fully justified the assertion of one of his friends upon that memorable occasion, which we select as a just tribute to his memory: "What I have known of Mr. Hungerford, during the 20 years I have lived in his near neighbourhood, has inclined me to recommend him, on this occasion, as a gentleman of independent fortune and public spirit; a liberal benefactor to the necessitous and deserving of his fellow-creatures, without distinction of parties; a man of strict integrity and honour; a true friend to the illustrious Royal Family now on the Throne; and a well-wisher to the civil and religious liberties of his fellow subjects; a gentleman of spirit and abilities to distinguish himself, to do honour to his constituents, and to serve his Country and Parliament, and who will not be afraid or ashamed either to vote or speak there with a freedom becoming a British senator and an honest man." He bequeathed an immense property (supposed to be at least 14,000l. a year) to the son of the Rev. Edward Holditch, rector of Burton Overy, a youth (at Mr. Hungerford's death) of eight years old.—Mr. Hungerford had encouraged one of his dependents to compile an ample History of the *Hungerford Family*; which I have seen, completed; and which I might have called my own, had I chosen to risque the expence of publication.

Ibid. col. 2, l. 21. *add to* Members of Parliament: 1812. The same.—The same.

P. 458. l. ult. *add*, 1812. The same.—The same.

P. 462. l. ult. *add to* Sheriffs.
51. R. Norman, of Melton Mowbray, esq.
52. R. Cheslyn, of Langley, esq.
53. R. Hames, of Great Glen, esq.
54. J. H. Franks, of Misterton, esq.

P. 466*. l. ult. Dr. Burnaby died March 9, 1812, in his 80th year. The purest integrity and benevolence of heart, the most unaffected urbanity of manners, and a lively and ardent zeal for his holy profession, were conspicuous among the many public and private virtues which adorned this truly excellent man and venerable Divine. His Sermons and Charges are excellent compositions, as well in a literary point of view, as in their able support of our present religious establishment; and in his Travels, which have reached a third edition, he relates what he saw, with great fidelity. His latest publication was, "The Sin and Danger of Schism, considered in a Charge (intended to be) delivered to the Clergy of the archdeaconry of Leicester, at the summer visitation in 1811," 8vo. (See Gent. Mag. vol. LXXXI. part ii. page 149.)—On March 16, 1812, ten days after the decease of her venerable husband, died, aged 76, Mrs. Burnaby, daughter and heiress of John Edwyn, esq. of Bagrave. In the performance of the most extensive charities, and of every Christian duty, towards her fellow creatures, she most cordially co-operated, for more than 40 years, with her beloved husband; and their mutual and earnest desire that they might not long be separated by death, was granted them by the mercy of their Creator. —Dr. Burnaby was succeeded in the Archdeaconry of Leicester by

THOMAS PARKINSON, D. D. rector of Kegworth (see vol. III. p. 856); and who had for some time previously held the Archdeaconry of Huntingdon.

P. 471. John Wigston, esq. of Trent park, Herts, (a descendant of the founder of Wigston's Hospital) died Nov. 21, 1810.

P. 504. col. 2, l. 3. William Wigston was mayor twice; see pp. 384 and 388; and 471.

P. 505. col. 2, l. 25. *for* 1632, *read* 1631.

P. 512. col. 2, l. 26. *read* All Saints.

P. 517. col. 1, l. 51. Henry Coleman, esq. one of the deputy-lieutenants of the County, and many years an extensive manufacturer in the hosiery business, died at Leicester, March 16, 1794.—He had attended, the same morning, in his usual good state of health, with his family, at St. Margaret's church, and being indisposed during the service, he retired to the adjacent house of Mr. Burnaby, the rector, where, in about two hours, he expired by apoplexy. No man, as well in public as in private life, being more deservedly and more universally esteemed, his unexpected loss has proved extremely severe and afflicting to his family, and the extensive circle of his friends. The distinguished urbanity of his manners, the affability of his disposition, and the uprightness of his character, his public spirit, and his domestic virtues, united to render him a valuable and useful citizen.

P. 524. col. 1, l. 19. *for* added, *read* made.

P. 527. The following correspondence deserves to be perpetuated:

"*To the Governors of the Leicester Infirmary.*
"Gentlemen, *Leicester, Feb.* 1, 1813.
"I have had the pleasure of paying into the hands of the Treasurer of the Infirmary, one hundred and fifty-five pounds, for the particular purpose of increasing the funded property of that noble Institution; and that the annual interest arising therefrom may be expended for its use. I have the honour to be, Gentlemen, your obedient, &c. MARY LINWOOD."

"*To Miss Linwood.*
"Madam, *Feb.* 2, 1813.
"The amount of the sums received from the Exhibition of your much-admired Works has been paid to our Treasurer; and we embrace the earliest opportunity of acknowledging in this public manner, the very liberal part you have taken in coming to the aid of this Charity. According to your intention, the donation of 150l. shall be added to the funded property of the Infirmary, and its annual interest only shall be applied to the recurring necessities of our Institution. With every sentiment of regard, I am for myself and the Governors at large, Madam, your obedient servant, W. W. ARNOLD, Chairman."

P. 528. l. ult. John Johnson, esq. died at Leicester (the place of his nativity) Aug. 27, 1814. This venerable and worthy man left Leicester in early life, possessing little more than strong natural abilities; which soon found their way in the Metropolis; and ultimately brought him into distinguished notice in his profession.

P. 531. note 4. *read* Plate XXIII. p. 302.

P. 532. col. 2, l. 42. "The noble stone face of the County Gaol extends 120 feet in front of the street, and near to it is the Free-school. The gaoler's house is at one corner; and the turnkey's lodge, which adjoins it, leads both to the men-felons' court-yard, and likewise, by a passage, to that of the debtors.

"It was first inhabited in 1793, and has four airy court-yards, with water in all; and a day-room each. The court for debtors is 74 feet by 32, and the day-room 29 feet by 13 feet 6 inches. For those on the master's-side there are ten rooms, which the keeper supplies with beds at 2s. 4d. weekly for a single bed; and if two sleep together, 1s. 6d. a week each. Common-side debtors have a free ward, with ten good-sized sleeping-rooms over the men-felons' cells, to which they furnish their own beds. One room is set apart for an infirmary, 30 feet by 16, with opposite windows, and a fire-place.

"The men-felons' court-yard is 59 feet by 30, with a day or common mess-room, 23 feet by 13, which has a fire-place, a large table, and benches to sit on. They have also four sleeping-cells on the ground floor, each 8 feet by 4 feet 11; one cell of double the size, for convicts under sentence of death, which is likewise occasionally used for refractory prisoners; and, at the back of these, and separated by a narrow passage, are five other cells, of equal dimensions. The cells upon the ground floor are boarded, but much out of repair, and dirty. Several of them had ashes heaped up in the corners. The

The felons, for bedding, have two straw mats and two blankets each.

" One side of the court-yard is occupied by a room with a cold bath; and another adjoining, for prisoners to undress in, with a boiler for warm water.

" Behind these buildings is another court-yard for less-atrocious felons, 38 feet square; a day or mess-room (fitted up as above) 18 feet 4 inches by 11 feet 9; an infirmary-room 16 feet square over it; and on the ground-floor are five sleeping-cells, exactly similar to those already mentioned.

" Women felons have a court-yard, a day-room, an infirmary, and three sleeping-cells; another room having a cold bath, and one adjoining it, with a boiler, like those before described. The women's bath had not been used, nor is there any water to supply it.

" The chapel is a square building in the centre of the prison; and has at each corner a door of entrance for the respective classes, who are seated in the area, separated from each other by partitions 6 feet 6 inches high.

" Over the rooms that contain the bath are two spacious infirmaries, 30 feet each by 16, with large opposite casement windows, and fire-places: but some of the infirmary windows have been injudiciously stopped up. These rooms open into the gallery of the chapel, which is partitioned off for the sick. The chapel is open to the top, with a large sky-light, and fan sash-window.

" The cells of this gaol have boarded floors, with arched roofs, and are fitted up with three mats and two blankets each. The door-ways, being only 22 inches wide, are both too narrow to admit the introduction of a bedstead, and too few in number for so populous a prison; so that two prisoners are generally locked up in each cell, affording a space of 2 feet 5 inches only for each prisoner. The court-yards here are not kept clean: I found grass growing between the flag-stones: but they are well supplied with water, and the sewers are not offensive. The keeper [Christopher Musson] appears humane; and the prison is as clean as its present construction will admit. It is much to be regretted, however, that the plan originally proposed by so able an architect was not adopted. There would then have been no cells on a ground-floor, which are incommodious, unhealthy, and insecure [1]."

" *The County Bridewell.*

" Keeper, Daniel Lambert; now William Phillips.—Salary 52l. 10s. He is also allowed mops, brooms, pails, soap, and every requisite for prison cleanliness.

" Chaplain, none: but at my visit in 1807, the keeper told me his prisoners regularly attended prayers three times a week; and also prayers and sermon on Sundays, in the chapel of the county gaol.

" Surgeon, Mr. Maule[2]; now Mr. Ludlam[3]. Makes a bill.

" Number of prisoners,

1803, Aug. 23,   7.   1807, July 30,   17.
1805, Sept. 26, 15.   1809, Aug. 22,   17.

" Allowance, one pound six ounces of bread *per* day, sent in loaves of 2 lb. 12 oz. every other day from the baker's; and one pint of small beer daily.

" Remarks.—This *New Bridewell*, first inhabited in 1804, is situate in Freeschool-lane, and adjoins to the County Gaol; in the wall of which there is a door of communication for the prisoners, who go thither, as above noticed, to the chapel; where the sexes are properly placed in separate divisions, out of sight of each other.

" Here are two court-yards, for the men and women, with dust-pens to receive ashes, which in the County Gaol are much wanted. To each court-yard there is a day-room.

" A reception-room is provided, for prisoners to be examined by the surgeon, previous to their admission into the interior of the prison. In the centre of the men's court is a small detached building, which contains a bath. Their sleeping-cells are nine, all on the ground-floor; and each 8 feet by 5, with arched roofs and boarded floors. They are all supplied with two straw mattresses; lighted by an iron grating above each door, having an inside shutter; and all opening into the court-yard, in which there are two convenient sewers.

" The women's court is of the same size as the former, and has four sleeping-cells attached to it on the ground-floor, fitted up in the same manner as those for the men. Three other such cells are also building (1809) on the women's side, and over them a large work-room. The sewers are all judiciously placed, and not offensive.

" Above stairs are two rooms, set apart as infirmaries, which have each a large iron-grated and glazed window, with a fire-place. Also two large work-rooms, with similar windows, spinning-wheels, stocking-frames, &c.

" Those prisoners who work for themselves, and are not committed for hard labour, pay to the keeper 2s. 6d. in the pound out of their earnings; and such have no county allowance of food. Those committed for hard labour, and who can earn more than 10s. per week, have the overplus for themselves.

" Prisoners discharged from hence are sent away pennyless. At least, therefore, it is hoped that they are dismissed in a morning.

" Here are no books provided for the visiting magistrates to enter their remarks; a deficiency, which it would be highly useful to supply.

" Neither the Act for preserving the Health of Prisoners, nor the Clauses against Spirituous Liquors, are hung up.—The keeper shewed me a bottle of gin, which he had taken from a person who was bringing it into the prison.

" At my visit to the *Old County Bridewell*, in 1803, the keeper of it was the celebrated Mr. Daniel Lambert[4], who afterwards exhibited himself for

[1] Neild, on Prisons, 4to, 1812, p. 334.

[2] Mr. John Maule, surgeon, the oldest member of the profession in Leicester, died Jan. 18, 1808, aged 64, deservedly esteemed as an able practitioner, a kind father, and a sincere friend.

[3] See p. 120.

[4] " Mr. Daniel Lambert was born on the 13th of March, 1770, in the parish of St. Margaret, at Leicester. From the extraordinary bulk to which Mr. Lambert attained, the reader may naturally be disposed to enquire, whether his parents were persons of remarkable dimensions? This was not the case, nor were any of his family inclined to corpulence, excepting an uncle and an aunt on the father's side, who were both very heavy. The former died during the infancy of Lambert, in the capacity of game-keeper to the earl of Stamford, to whose predecessor his father had been huntsman in early life. The family of Mr. Lambert, senior, consisted, besides Daniel, of another son, who died young, and two daughters, who are still living, and both women of the common size. The habits of the subject of this memoir were not, in any respect, different from those of other young persons, till the age of 14. Even at an early age he was strongly attached to the sports of the field. This, however, was only the natural effect of a very obvious cause, aided, probably, by an innate propensity to those diversions. We have already mentioned the profession of his father and uncle, and have yet to observe, that his maternal grandfather was a great cock-fighter. Born and bred among horses, dogs, and cocks, and all the other appendages of sporting, in the pursuit of which he was encouraged even in his childhood, it cannot be a matter of wonder that he should be passionately fond of all those exercises and amusements which are comprehended under the denomination of field sports. About the year 1793, when Mr. Lambert weighed 32 stone, he had occasion to visit Woolwich, in company with the keeper of the county-gaol of Leicester. As the tide did not serve to bring them up to London, he walked from Woolwich to the Metropolis, with much less apparent fatigue than several middle-sized men who were of the party. Such were the feelings of Mr. Lambert, that no longer than four years previous to his death he abhorred the very idea of exhibiting himself. Though he lived exceedingly retired at Leicester, the fame of his uncommon corpulence had spread over the adjacent country to such a degree, that he frequently found himself not a little incommoded by the curiosity of the people, which it was impossible to repress, and which they were continually devizing the means of gratifying, in spite of his reluctance. A gentleman travelling through Leicester conceived a desire to see this extraordinary phænomenon; but, being at a loss for a pretext to introduce himself to Mr. Lambert, he first took care to enquire what were his particular propensities; being informed that he was a great cocker, the traveller thought himself sure of success. He accordingly went to his house, knocked at the door, and enquired for Mr. Lambert; the servant said he was at home, but that he never saw strangers. " Let him know,"

the gratification of the metropolis. He is said to have weighed in 1805, 49 stone 12 lbs. (or 698 lbs.), which exceeds, by nearly 90 lbs. the corpulency of Mr. Edward Bright, of Maldon, in the county of Essex [1]. Some few years since, Lambert is said to have been very active; and, considering his bulk, was of singular vivacity in the year 1807.

" In 1805, I found at Leicester both a new prison and a new keeper. The sedentary habits of Mr. Lambert, we are told, rendered him so much attached to his late employ, that it was with reluctance he heard the business of the Bridewell was to be transferred to the County Gaol; and himself obliged, like some other great men, to retire upon a pension.

" Mr. Lambert, it seems, had an invincible objection to have his weight ascertained. It was at length, however, effected by the following contrivance: Going one day to Loughborough, the carriage that conveyed him was designedly drawn over a weighing engine; and thus, to his great vexation, he was informed of the fact, which he had so assiduously wished to avoid.

" His brief historian, in a vein of irony, observes, ' that had this fat man studied a thousand years, he could not have thought of a *profession* better calculated to suit his constitutional propensity to ease.' It is hoped that the wit and humour of the above shrewd remark outweigh its scrupulous conformity to matter of fact; and yet even gaolers, possibly, like the pilot Palinurus of antient times, may now and then be found nodding on tne post of duty. To name instances might be deemed sarcastic, or invidious.

"A tolerably executed etching of Mr. Lambert has been in circulation. He died in June 1809. *Obruit mole sud;* and his weight then was 52 stone 11 lbs. (or 739 lbs.)! He is spoken of as a humane, benevolent man [2]."

P. 533. col. 2, l. 13. Mr. William Rozzel, died in 1813. He was upwards of twenty years master of St. Martin's school, an inoffensive and very honest man, known as the author of an " English Grammar in Verse," and of some other tracts. He was brother of Charles Rozzel, the *Leicester Bard*, noticed in p. 320.

P. 535. notes, l. 8. *read* Reipublicæ.

P. 537. col. 2. *add note on* widow : " Anne Robsart; see pp. 544 and 545 *n.*"

P. 539. col. 1, l. 21 from bottom, *read* by Elizabeth daughter of Sir Robert Southwell.

P. 541. col. 1, l. 20 from bottom, *after* " daughters," *add,* and, secondly to Sarah Smith, by whom he left no issue.

P. 543. l. ult. George second Marquis Townshend, and first Earl of the County of Leicester, died at his house at Richmond, July 27, 1811. His lordship was a great Genealogist, on which subject his Library was amply furnished, as well in foreign works, as in those of our own country. This Library was sold by Messrs. Leigh and Sotheby, in May 1812, and produced about 5,700*l.* His lordship left the antient family estates at Rainham, and elsewhere, in Norfolk, to his second son, lord Charles. He was succeeded in his titles by his eldest son, George, now third Marquis Townshend, and second Earl of Leicester [3].

P. 544. *correct,* daughters of Robert Sidney

know," replied the curious gentleman, " that I called about some cocks." Lambert, who chanced to be in a situation to overhear what passed, immediately rejoined, " Tell the gentleman that I am a *shy cock.*" On another occasion, a gentleman from Nottingham was extremely importunate to see him, pretending that he had a particular favour to ask; after considerable hesitation, Mr. Lambert directed him to be admitted: on being introduced, he said, he wished to enquire the pedigree of a certain mare. " Oh! if that is all," said Mr. Lambert, perceiving from his manner the real nature of his errand, " she was got by *Impertinence* out of *Curiosity.*" Finding, at length, that he must either submit to be a close prisoner in his own house, or endure all the inconvenience, without receiving the profits of an exhibition, Mr. Lambert wisely strove to overcome the repugnance, and determined to visit the Metropolis for that purpose. As it was impossible to procure a carriage large enough to admit him, he had a vehicle constructed expressly to carry him to London, where he arrived, for the twenty-second time, in the spring of 1806, and fixed his residence in Piccadilly. His apartments there had more the air of a place of fashionable resort than an exhibition; and as long as the town continued full, he was visited by a great deal of the best company. The dread he felt coming to London, lest he should be exposed to indignity and insult from the curiosity of some of his visitors, was soon removed by the politeness and attention which he universally experienced. There was not a gentleman in town, from his own county, but went to see him, not merely gazing at him as a spectacle, but treating him in the most friendly and soothing manner, which, he declared, was too deeply impressed upon his mind ever to be forgotten. Many of his visitors seemed incapable of gratifying their curiosity to its full extent, and called again and again to behold what an immense magnitude the human figure is capable of attaining; one gentleman, a banker in the City, jocosely observed, that he had fairly had a pound's worth.—Mr. Lambert died at Stamford June 21, 1809. He travelled from Huntingdon thither in the early part of the week, intending to receive the visits of the curious who might attend the then ensuing races. On the preceding evening he sent a message to the office of the Stamford Mercury, requesting that, " as the Mountain could not wait upon Mahomet, Mahomet would go to the Mountain;" or, in other words, that the Printer would call upon him, and receive an order for executing some hand-bills, announcing Mr. Lambert's arrival, and his desire to see company. The orders he gave upon that occasion were delivered without any presentiment that they were to be his last, and with his usual cheerfulness. He was in bed, one of large dimensions—(" Ossa upon Olympus, and Pelion upon Ossa")—fatigued with his journey; but anxious that the bills might be quickly printed, in order to his seeing company next morning. Before nine o'clock on that morning, however, he was a corpse! Nature had endured all the trespass she could admit : the poor man's corpulency had constantly increased, until, at the time we have mentioned, the clogged machinery of life stood still, and this prodigy of Mammon was numbered with the dead! He was in his 40th year; and upon being weighed, within a few days, by the famous Caledonian balance (in the possession of Mr. King, of Ipswich), was found to be 52 stone 11 lbs. in weight (14 lbs. to the stone), which is 10 stone 11 lbs. more than the great Mr. Bright, of Maldon, ever weighed. He had apartments at Mr. Berridge's, the Waggon and Horses, in St. Martin's, on the ground floor—for he had been long incapable of walking up stairs. His coffin, in which there was great difficulty in placing him, was six feet four inches long, four feet four inches wide, and two feet four inches deep : the immense substance of his legs made it necessarily almost a square case, consisting of 112 superficial feet of elm, built upon two axle-trees and four clog-wheels; and upon these the remains of the poor man were rolled into his grave, in the new burial-ground at the back of St. Martin's church. A regular descent was made, by cutting away the earth slopingly for some distance. The window and wall of the room in which he lay were taken down, to allow his exit. Having been extricated from the lodging in which he died, his remains were drawn by eight men with ropes into the burial ground : into the church it was not possible to take him. As might be expected of such a corpse, in a very few hours after death almost all identity of feature was lost; and, though he was buried in eight-and-forty hours, his remains had been kept quite as long as was prudent. A large concourse attended his funeral; and in the course of the day many hundred persons from the neighbourhood visited the grave.—Mr. Lambert was an intelligent and pleasant companion; and, notwithstanding his extreme corpulence, his body and limbs are said to have borne a very exact proportion to each other. In his youth he was an excellent swimmer; and he was for many years celebrated in the sporting world as a great breeder and feeder of cocks. He was also famous for his dogs; some of which were sold at Tattersall's a short time ago, at prices which proved the estimation in which Mr. Lambert was held by sportsmen of the first eminence. Extraordinary as it may appear, it is true, that he had his greyhounds with him at Stamford when he died, and intended to have taken the diversion of coursing in the season!—that is, he meant to have been taken in his carriage to an open part of the country, where he might have seen his dogs pursue the game. It is said that Stamford was the last place at which he meant to exhibit himself for a price.—He had a sister living at Leicester, who attended his funeral.—Very little money would be requisite for the erection of a rude and durable monument to his memory; and as the grave of Lambert will always be one of *the Lions* of Stamford, we trust a subscription will be promoted for the purpose. The good people of Leicester, perhaps, would contribute something to honour the memory of their townsman." Gent. Mag. vol. LXXIX. pp. 681, 682.

Since the above article appeared in the Magazine, a worthy Friend, in a letter dated Oct. 31, 1814, has observed to me,

" The burial-place of Mr. Daniel Lambert, in St. Martin's church-yard at Stamford, was, as you say, one of the *Lions* to be seen by strangers; and, as a testimony of respect, a very neat stone is thus inscribed: " In remembrance of that Prodigy in Nature, Daniel Lambert, a native of Leicester, who was possessed of an exalted and convivial mind, and in personal greatness he had no competitor. He measured three feet one inch round the leg; nine feet four inches round the body; and weighed 52 stone 11 lb. (14 lb. to the stone). He departed this life on the 21st of June, 1809, aged 39 years. As a testimony of respect, this stone is erected by his friends in Leicester."

On an urn at the top of the stone, " *Altus in animo, in corpore maximus.*"

[1] From the well-known print of Mr. Bright (engraved by McArdell, after a painting by Osborne), it appears that he died on the 10th of November, 1750, aged 29 years; and weighed, while living, 43 stone 7 pounds, which amount to 609 pounds.

[2] Neild, on Prisons, p. 338.

[3] Collins's Peerage, by sir Egerton Brydges, bart. vol. II. p. 618.

and Elizabeth Egerton, thus: 4. Frances. 5. Elizabeth.

P. 545. Pedigree of de Ferrars. Saxon Earls, 5th descent. John le Scot was the last earl: in him the title became extinct, not in Ranulf. See pp. 18 and 219.—Note [4], *for* he, *read* Sir Henry Sydney, died May 5, 1586.

P. 547. note [3]. The younger Rev. Hugh Worthington died July 26, 1813, æt. 61, after having been 40 years minister of the congregation of Protestant Dissenters meeting at Salters Hall. See a very ample and interesting account of him in Gent. Mag. vol. LXXXIII. part ii. pp. 188—190. 455. 579. Mr. Worthington bequeathed all his property to Miss Eliza Price.

P. 552. Mr. Hickes was *minister* of All Saints, 1713; see "Annals," p. 443.

Ibid. . . . . . . Thirlby was vicar in 17. . .

P. 554. col. 1, l. 2 from bottom, *strike out* "aged 11 months."

P. 556. col. 1, l. 21. Brone mayor; qu.? as it appears that Richard Braunston was mayor in 1387 and 1388.—L. 28. *for* Ramelyth, *read* Ranulph.—L. 30. *for* Walker, *read* Water.—Col. 2, l. 9. *for* Bereye, *read* Berege.

P. 557. col. 1, l. 24 from bottom, *read* Leroe.

P. 558. col 2, l. 14. *for* 1741, *r.* 1714; see p. 443.

P. 559. col. 1, l. 30. The original appropriation was to St. Mary de Castro by this earl's father, Robert de Bellomont I. See p. 22.

P. 561. col. 2, l. 14 from bottom, *read* John Palmer, qu. B. A.—L. 5 from bottom, Hereby; see p. 569.

P. 563. col. 1, l. 37. *for* Dorothy, *read* Deborah.

P. 567. *add note on* Bishop's Fee; see p. 14, *n.* and 17.—Col. 1, l. 28. *add note on* murum: see pp. iv. and v.—Col. 2, l. 41. qu.? Cnichteton. Q. as to this. See vol. IV. p. 235.

P. 568. col. 1, l. 1. *for* St. Michael's, *read* St. Martin's.

P. 569. col. 1, l. 19. *read* campanistæ.

P. 578. col. 2, l. 4 from bottom, *for* Carter, *read* Carver.

P. 584. col. 1, l. 4 from bottom, Henry Valentine, sometime Organist of St. Martin's, Leicester, had a merry way of acting Punch as in a puppet-show. At other times he would twist his face into a strange variety of postures; he had his crying face, his laughing face, his gruff face, his base viol head face, and many others hugely mimical, all which I have many times seen him perform here.—SAM. CARTE.

P. 585. col. 1, l. 16. *add note on* Chettle: "Alice Chattel; see p. 577."

P. 592. col. 1, l. 23. *read* Stephens.

P. 595. Mr. Brown occurs vicar of St. Martin's, 1566-7; see p. 573.—Note [3], *read* pp. 501, 589.—*Add to note* [5], "See Churchwarden's Accompts," p. 577.

P. 596. l. 1. *add* Christopher Wright, vicar, 1653.—L. 2. John Newton, M. A. 1662, not 1679; see p. 606.—Col. 1, l. 19. Elizabeth Reginold, qu.? if not Reynolds; see p. 606.—Col. 2, l. 8. *read* four sons.—Notes, l. 5, *add note on* "Sermon:" "See p. 436 n."—See Mr. Newton's epitaph, p. 606.

P. 596. The Rev. J. Davies, late curate of St. Martin's, died at Great Harborough, co. Warwick, Dec. 11, 1814.

P. 598. notes, l. 14. *add note on* "Chancery:" "See p. 585 n."—L. 19. *read* See vol. *II.* p. 677.

P. 599. col. 2, l. 14 from bottom, *correct pointing thus:* William. Obiit, &c.

P. 600. col. 1, l. 6. *add note on* Hill: "He was deputy seneschal; see p. 454."—Col. 2, l. 16. *read* enim.—L. 25, *read* her age.

P. 601. col. 2, l. 42. qu.? Alice Armstrong.

P. 603. *add to note* [2]. Henry Carrick was upwards of half a century conductor of an extensive seminary at Leicester. In his professional capacity he was greatly esteemed; in society, he was a well-informed, pleasant companion; and in his general deportment a man of strict probity and honour.

P. 605. col. 1, l. 11. *for* She, *read* He.

P. 609. l. 9. The Rev. James Pigott died Dec. 28, 1812. See hereafter, under Additions to Wigston, p. 144.—L. 10. The Rev. John Anderson died Feb. 3, 1813. See hereafter, under Additions to Wanlip, p. 141.—Mr. Anderson was succeeded in the vicarage of St. Nicholas, by the Rev. Richard Davies.—Note [5], *read*, "Vicar of Great Wigston. See vol. IV. p. 383."

P. 621. col. 1, l. 38. of Alderman John Cooper, see p. 442.

P. 621. A MS. of Mr. Carte supplies the following particulars:

"The Jersey and Stocking Trade.

"Mr. William Topp, who keeps the seals of aulnage, gave me the account following, *viz.*

"The first duty upon stockings is after the rate of 1*d. per* score.

"Persons who travel abroad with stockings agree to pay an annual rate, which does not amount to more than one third of the real duty.

"The aulnage upon stockings from Lady-day 1707 to Lady-day 1708:

"Paid for seals, 87*l.* 7*s.* 10*d.*

"Paid by composition of those who travel 4*l.* 14*s.*

"85*l.* 7*s.* 10*d.* amounts to 20,494 pence, or scores of stockings, which is 34,156 dozen and 8 stockings.

"4*l.* 14*s.* is 94 shillings or dozens of stockings; but if that be but the third part of the real duty, it is paid for 282 dozen."

P. 624. col. 2, l. 10 from bottom, the following inscription is on the cup:

"A Tribute of Respect
from the Union Canal Company
to Joseph Cradock, Esquire,
19 November 1810."

P. 625. The reader is requested to notice the Additions and Corrections in this page.—Col. 1, l. 46. *for* duke, *read* earl.—For Corrections on the Notes in this page, see p. 29 of General Index to Vol. I. article Domesday.

P. 626. col. 1, l. 21. *for* 442, *read* 449.

APPENDIX, p. 57, note [1], *read* Placitis.

P. 58. col. 2, l. 17 from bottom, *read* Leic'.

P. 61. col. 2, l. 44. *read* Roberti filii Roberti de Burstall.

P. 77. col. 1, l. 18 from bottom, qu.? *read* Avunculus.

P. 92. col. 2, l. 20. *for* Weston, *read* Wistow.—L. 34. *read* Stouton.—L. 3 from bottom, *read* Forniüe.

P. 99. col. 2, l. 49. *for* Cor, *read* Tor.

P. 112. col. 2, l. 34. *for* Domini, *read* divini.

P. 113. col. 1, l. 27. amictuбs, qu? amestibus.

P. 311. *add to vicars of* St. Mary: Rev. George Berkeley Mitchell, 1813.

VOLUME II.

FRAMLAND HUNDRED.

THE General Map of the County is to be placed as a Frontispiece to Volume II. Part I.

P. 4. John Notzel died at Wolsthorpe Aug. 31, 1810, aged 77. He was a native of Switzerland, and particularly known for having saved the life of the great Marquis of Granby; who ever after, as well as the rest of the Rutland family, evinced the greatest esteem and friendship for him. He carried the standard at the funeral of the Duke of Rutland in Nov. 1787, who died Lord Lieutenant of Ireland.

P. 8. col. 2, l. 33. Sir William Manners has bought all Lord Moira's Manors, and the paramountship, in Framland Hundred.

P. 23. col. 1, l. 34. I was favoured with the following note, relative to the situation of Belvoir Castle:

"Burton places Belvoir Castle in Lincolnshire. Throsby has observed, that in my Map it is placed in Leicestershire. My reason is this: When I had the management of the survey, I went to Belvoir Castle, while the old Duke lived. Mr. Thoroton, who married one of his daughters by Mrs. Drake, then lived at the Castle, and superintended the Duke's affairs, being a very sensible, intelligent, and genteel man. I asked him whether the Castle was in Leicestershire or Lincolnshire. He replied, they believed it was in Leicestershire. I begged the favour of his reasons; and he said, it paid taxes and levies in Leicestershire. The stables at the bottom of the hill, he believed to be in Lincolnshire. With this authority I was perfectly satisfied. I do not know where you have placed the Castle, and I thought this account might possibly be not unacceptable to you.

Your most obedient servant, J. Prior."

P. 43. In 1532, Thomas earl of Rutland gave to king Henry VIII. as a New-year's Gift, 6l. 13s. 4d.

P. 47. col. 1, l. 26. The following curious "Note of the Funeral of Edward [Third] Earl of Rutland," is copied from the Gentleman's Magazine, volume LXXXIII. part i.:

"The body of Edward Erle of Rutland was brought from London to the Castle of Belvoir, and layd in the Chappell there, upon Satterday being the xiij of May, 1587. W'ch Chappell was hangd all with black and garnished with armes, and his body laid upon a bord of a good hight, with a great pawle of black velvett garnished with armes. And upon the pawle was layd his cote armore, sword, tardge, helmett, and creaste, with fowre banneroyles of every corner, his banner and standerd, in the Chappell, where he remayned till the day of the funerall. And in the said Castle of Belvoir, the hall was hangd with black and garnished with armes. Likewise the great chamber was hanged with black, and garnished also, and in it a cloth of estate of black velvett with chayne and quisheyne of the same.

"Then p'parac'on being made for the day of the funerall, the corpes remayned till that day, w'ch was appointed to be at a P'ish Church, being thre myles of, called Botesworth, w'ch Church was hangd all with black and garnished with armes; and in the body of the said Church a stately hearse made, being xxiiij fete high, xviii foote longe, and xij foote brode, all hangd with blacke velvett fringd with silk and garnished with a greate sorte of armes, and two hundred pensills sett upon it, and a rayle round about the hearse conteyninge xxiiij foote every way covered all with blacke, and upon the vj mayne pillors of the herse was sett divers goodly armes with crownes of gould upon them, and upon the toppe of all fower arms joyned together and a crowne over all. Then was there sett within the rayle and without the herse a stole against the mid-

dest of the said herse for the L. Chiefe Murner, with a carpett and a quisheyne of black velvett. And then of ether side of the herse was sett fower stoles, carpette, and quishenes of black cloth, for the residew of the Murners. And within the Chauncell there was made a vaute, wherein his corpse was to be layd upon the right hand of his father's tombe. And upon Munday being the xv of May, 1587, the said body was conveyed from the Castle of Belvoir to the Church of Botesworth in most solempne and honourable manner, as followeth:

"First, there was appointed to go before to conduct the company two porters with ther staves. Then followed them fiftie poore men in black gownes. After them came all my L.'s yeomen and gromes, to the number of a hundreth and fiftie. Then came the standerd, caryed by Mr. George Villars of Leycestershier, esq. And under it fowerscore gentlemen all in black clokes, his L.'s howsehould servaunts on horsebacke. After them eight Chapleynes in ther degrees, with there gownes and hodes. Then followed them his Steward, Tresurer, and Controwler, with ther white staves. Then followed them the great Banner of Armes, w'ch was caryed by Sir Andrewe Nowell, Knight. And under it went all the Gentlemen of the countrey in mourning gownes and hodes, to the number of forty or fiftie, their horses covered with fyne black all saving their eyes. Then followed them my L. Rose and Sir Thomas Stanhopp, with all my L.'s children. Then followed the Harrolds with their ceremonye. The first was Winzar, w'ch caryed the helmett and creast with my L.'s cote armore upon his backe, presenting my L.'s owne ha rold. Next after him came Chester, who caryed the sword. The next after him Richmond, who caryed his tardge. And then came Garter King at Armes, who caryed my L.'s coate armore upon a staffe of hight; so that all the Harrolds, saving Winzar onely, ware the Quenes Ma'tyes coote armore upon ther backs. Then followed a Gentleman Usher. And after him came the Chariott wherin his body was layd, the Chariott covered with black velvett with armes upon it, w'ch chariott was drawen with fower great horse covered all with blacke saving their eyes, and upon his a pawle of blacke velvett garnished with armes. Then was ther fower Knights appointed for the gard of the body, who was appointed to ryde by every corner of the chariott; as, Sir John Berryne, Sir Edward Dymocke, Sir Anthony Tharold, and Sir William Hollis. Then was fower bannerroyles caryed by fower gentlemen of good accompt upon every corner of the chariott, who were these, Mr. Phillip Constable, Mr. Raphe Crathorne, Mr. Raphe Babethorpe, and Mr. Marmaduke Grimstone[1]. And then went there of both sydes the chariott, the foote men in blacke velvet. Then folowed the Horse of estait, led by the Gentleman of the Horse. Then folowed him a Gentleman Husher. And then after him my L. him selfe, beinge Cheife Mourner, alone. Then after his L'p folowed eight Mourners, two by two, w'ch were these, Mr. Roger Manners and Mr. John Manners, Sir Thomas Manners, Sir Thomas Siscell, Sir Jarvis Clifton, Sir Francis Willowghbie, Sir Robert Constable, and Sir George Chaworth. Then folowed all the Servinge men, to the number of two hundreth, beinge all in blacke.

"And thus he was conveyed from the Castle of Belvoir to the Churche of Bootesforth. And so sone as he lighted in the Churche yeard all his gentlemen went before into the Church, savinge a dosen, w'ch was appointed to carie the corpes into the Churche; w'ch they did. The corps being caried in, then came the fower asistans and went upon the

---

[1] The MS. here is continued, apparently by a different hand.

corners

corners with the fower banneroyles, and so brought it to the hearse, and layd it there upon a bord, beinge a gieat height; and then the fower asistans beinge placed within the corners of the herse, and the fower bannerroyles without the corners of the reales, where they remayned till the bodie was caried to the voate.

"Then the Chiefe Mourner, folowinge the bodie, had his trayne borne by one of his gentlemen hushers; and aboute the midest of the end of the herse there was a stoole and a quisheine of blacke velvet, w'ch was layd for him to kneel downe upon. The eight Mourners attendinge upon him came within the reale, where there places were made redie, kneled downe, carpitts and quishens beinge layd for them, all of black. Then was the gentleman of the bannerroyles appointed everie of them to stand in the corner of the reales w'ch invironed the hearse. And then at the far syde of the herse was appointed Mr. Villars to stand with the standerd. And soe against Sir Andrewe Nowell with the banner. Then the Harolds layd downe the coate armoure, the sword and tardge, with the helmit and crest, upon the powle which layd upon the bodie till such tyme as they were offered, w'ch was after the Sermon.

"And at such tyme as the Sermon was done, w'ch was made by the Bushope of Lincolne, who was in m'wrninge attyre also, then the Harolds made rome for the offringe; and when it was fully made, came they all to the Cheife L. Mourner, and he arose and folawed, the Harolds goinge before him, and all the rest of the murners folowinge of him, went up and offered for the deade, and so came backe to his place. So when the Harolds came againe before him, he went upp alone, and offered for him selfe; and then the rest of the Murners, being brought two by two, went up and offered for themselves. And then after the Murners had offered for themselves, and come to their places, then Garter went and toke of the coat armoure, and brought it to Mr. Roger Manners and Mr. John Manners, and went before them with the rest of the Harolds and offered it to the Church, beinge layde upon the Com'n Table, brought them backe to there places. Then he went to the herse and fetcht the sword, and delivered it to Sir Thomas Manners, and to Sir Thomas Siscell; the Harolds goinge before them, they went up and offered it likewise. And then they went up and fetcht the tardge and delivered it to Sir Jarvis Clifton and Sir Francis Willowghbie, the Harolds going before them, went up and offered likewise. And when they were come to there places, then they went and fetcht the helmit and crest, w'ch was offered by Sir Robert Constable and Sir George Chaworth in like maner. Then the Harolds fetcht Sir Andrew Nowell, who offered the banner in like sort. And then after him they fetcht Mr. Villars, who offered the standard likewise. And then the Harolds sett two of the assistaunce Sir Edward Dimocke and Sir Anthonie Tharold, who offered for them selves. And then they went for the other two, Sir Will'm Hollis and Sir John Berne, who did offer for them selves. And then the Harolds fetcht Sir Andrew Nowell and Mr. Villars, who offered for them selves. And then went up my Lord Rose with Sir Thomas Stanhope, and all my L. children. Aud after them went upp the Steward, Tre'rer, and Controller.

"And, after the offringe, my L. with all the cheife gent' went away, saving such as was appointed to attend upon the officers, and to se his body layd within the voate p'pared for him.

"And after his body was layd in the voate, all the officers broke there staves with many a weeping eye.

"So that this was the end of the Funerall of this noble man. And all the company brought to the Castle of Beluior, where they were nobly entertayned; and six of his Chapleynes appointed to se the Poore releved with drink, meat, and money, beinge in number thre or fower thowsand."

P. 66. His Grace the Duke of Rutland married April 22, 1799, Lady Elizabeth Howard, daughter of Frederick earl of Carlisle, K. G. and has had issue, Lady Carolina, born May 25th 1800, died Dec. 1804; Lady Elizabeth, born January 1802; a son, who died in a few days, 1807; and another son, born 1813, who died 1814.

Ibid. The visit of the Prince Regent to *Belvoir Castle* was an event so highly flattering to the Owner of that noble Mansion, and to the County at large, that I make no apology for shortly detailing the whole of the Royal Progress.

1813. *Dec.* 27. The Prince Regent left town at 7 in the evening, intending to proceed to Hatfield, on his way to Belvoir Castle. The fog, however, was so dense in the metropolis, and for several miles round, that he was induced to return. Lord Lowther was in one carriage with the Prince, and Gen. Turner in a second. They had not got further than about a mile from Tottenham-court-road, when an outrider was thrown off into a ditch.

Dec. 28. At half past 12, His Royal Highness again set off on his tour; and visited the Marquis of Salisbury's seat at Hatfield, where he slept that night.

Dec. 29. His Royal Highness proceeded on his journey, and reached Apthorpe, the seat of the Earl of Westmoreland, where he spent the day. At eight the Prince sat down to a sumptuous entertainment, at which were present the Duke of Rutland, Marquis of Exeter, Earls of Lonsdale, Cardigan, Winchelsea, and Carysfort, Sir S. and Mr. Fludyer, &c.

Dec. 30. His Royal Highness passed through Stamford at 4 in the afternoon, and was met at Bridge Casterton by the Earl of Lonsdale's carriage. His Royal Highness dined at the Earl's seat at Cottesmore with a large party. There were at his Lordship's the Marquis of Exeter, the Earls of Winchelsea and Westmorland, Visc. Lowther, Lord Robert Manners, Sir Gerard Noel, Gen. Grosvenor, Mr. Croker, &c. The Prince continued at Cottesmore till Sunday Jan. 2, rode out every day, and was in excellent health and spirits.—His Royal Highness received during his stay an Address from the Corporation of Stamford, on the present prosperous state of affairs, presented to him by a Deputation from the Body Corporate.

1814. *Jan.* 2. His Royal Highness the Prince Regent left Cottesmore; and arrived at Belvoir Castle the same day. The Duke of Rutland's tenants and yeomen of the County went out four miles to meet the Prince, and formed a procession in advance to the Castle. The number of persons assembled between Denton and the seat of his Grace the Duke of Rutland was immense. It consisted of horse and foot, with females of interesting appearance, conducted by brothers, mothers, and family connexions, wearing their best rustic attire, while others of higher rank in society appeared in more fashionable garb. They came with the design of drawing the Prince's carriage up the hill to the Castle, as a testimony of loyalty and respect. It was difficult to prevent the completion of their wishes, which was, however, denied, under the impression that accidents might have happened, injurious to the good folks themselves.—The Prince was received by his Grace of Rutland amidst a royal salute from cannon on the battlements of the Castle. A shout of joy made by the spectators increased the sound of the ordnance; at the same time the royal standard was proudly displayed on the Staunton tower. The Duke of Rutland received the Prince Regent at the door of the Castle, but the key of Staunton tower, made of gold, and of exquisite workmanship, was delivered to the illustrious guest in the drawing-room, soon after his arrival, on a cushion of crimson velvet, by the Rev. Dr. Staunton [1], by etiquette of the following order: —The chief strong-hold of the Castle is an out-work defence called Staunton tower; the command of which is held by the family of that name, in the manor of Staunton, by tenure of castle-guard, by

---

[1] See an account of Dr. Staunton, and of the Staunton family, as connected with Belvoir Castle, in vol. IV. p. 687.

which

which they were anciently required to appear with soldiers for the defence of this strong post, in case of danger; or, if required, to be called upon by the lord of the Castle. It has been the custom, when any of the Royal Family honoured Belvoir Castle with their presence, for the chief of the Staunton family personally to appear and present the key of the strong-hold to such distinguished personage. This ceremony was performed by the Rev. Doctor, by virtue of his tenure, with an appropriate speech, to which the Prince Regent returned a most gracious reply.

Jan. 4. The day of festivity on occasion of the baptism of the infant Marquis, was also the birth-day of the Duke, and was ushered in and marked accordingly. His Royal Highness rode again round the domains, and the Duke of York took the diversion of shooting. The infant was baptised at 6 o'clock in the evening, by the Archbishop of Canterbury, in the great gallery, in the presence of the whole of the nobility and gentry at the Castle, by the name of George John Frederick; the sponsors were the Prince Regent and the Duke of York; and the Duchess Dowager of Rutland, Proxy for the Queen. The noble party soon after sat down to dinner. The health of the Infant Heir to the House of Rutland was drank at the proposal of the Prince. The Duke of Rutland returned thanks to the distinguished visitor with great feeling; and his Royal Highness in reply assured the noble Lord that he should never forget the respectful manner in which he had been received at Belvoir Castle. The noble host then gave the health of the Prince, which was received with enthusiasm, and succeeded by a dignified reply. Mr. Douglas, the Duke's butler, entertained the tenantry with an oval cistern of punch containing 50 gallons.

Jan. 5. A deputation from the Corporation of Leicester, consisting of William Walker, esq. mayor, the Recorder (Mr. Serjeant Vaughan), the four Magistrates, the Town-clerk, and the Chamberlains, attended by the Mace-bearer, and other servants of the Corporation, waited on the Prince Regent, with an Address. The deputation was ushered into his Grace's splendid and magnificent library. The apartment selected to receive the Address in was the long gallery, which had been recently fitted up for the reception of his Royal Highness in a style of elegance, splendour, and magnificence, perhaps not to be surpassed in Europe. His Grace the Duke of Rutland did the Corporation the honour of acting as Master of the Ceremonies, and introduced the deputation to his Royal Highness. The band of the Leicestershire militia, arranged on the staircase and at the entrance of the gallery, played "God save the King," as the deputation passed. The Address[1] was delivered by the Mayor into the hands of the Recorder, by whom it was spoken to his Royal Highness, with a dignified respect and attention, and in a tone of manly feeling most suitable to the occasion, and evidently producing an impression on the countenance of his Royal Highness most marked and gratifying. The Prince Regent immediately read his Answer[2], with a degree of spirit, and with a grace and affability peculiarly characteristic of His Royal Highness, which fascinated all those in whose presence it was delivered. His Royal Highness then conferred the honour of knighthood on the Mayor (now Sir William Walker), who kissed his Royal Highness's hand.

His Royal Highness also received an Address of congratulation on the auspicious state of public affairs, from the Corporation of Grantham; and both deputations afterwards partook of a handsome dinner provided by the Duke.

Jan. 7. His Royal Highness the Prince Regent, accompanied by the Duke of York, left Belvoir at two o'clock, for Burleigh, the seat of the Earl of Winchelsea, a few miles distant. The distinguished personages took leave of the noble Rutland family, evidently affected by the handsome manner in which they had been treated, expressing at the same time their high regard for the welfare of the family. Previously to leaving the Castle, the Prince Regent named one of the towers "The Regent Tower," in remembrance of his visit; and was pleased to signify his pleasure that a bust of himself should be placed in the centre.

[1] " To His Royal Highness George Prince of Wales, Regent of the United Kingdom of Great Britain and Ireland.

" May it please your Royal Highness,

"We his Majesty's dutiful and loyal subjects, the Mayor, Bailiffs, and Burgesses of the Borough of Leicester, animated by the liveliest affection and devotion to your Royal Highness's Person and Government, desire permission to approach your Royal Highness, and to lay at your feet our cordial congratulations on the happy and glorious change, which by the wisdom of your Royal Highness's councils, and by the exertions and example of this country, has been wrought in the state of Europe.

" It seemed good to Divine Providence, in whose hands are the issues of life and death, and the fate of contending Empires, by a great calamity, the continuation of which, we, in common with every class of his Majesty's subjects, deeply deplore, to call your Royal Highness to the Government of these Kingdoms in a season of difficulty and danger unexampled. When Spain and Portugal, surprized by the treachery of France, were struggling for their existence as independent kingdoms. When the weaker States, ensnared by the arts, or enslaved by the arms of France, and the more powerful nations and empires on the continent of Europe, after being despoiled of their fairest provinces, were constrained to support the colossal power of the enemy in his further schemes of aggression and aggrandizement. At such a crisis, when our alliances were broken, our trade declining, our commerce with the ports of Europe interdicted, your Royal Highness, by assuming the reins of Government, and by a steady and determined perseverance in councils the most enlightened, happily laid the foundation of those brilliant victories which have terminated in the deliverance of Europe, and in fixing on the firmest basis the welfare and prosperity of these dominions.

" We contemplate with gratitude to the Supreme Disposer of events these transcendent blessings.—In the Peninsula the sword of the Tyrant broken after a series of the most splendid atchievements under Field Marshal the Marquis of Wellington.—The humiliation and expulsion of the French arms from the states of the German Empire. and their integrity and independence vindicated.—The Confederation of the Rhine dissolved.—The Hereditary Dominions of our beloved Sovereign in the Electorate of Hanover restored. The United Provinces of Holland delivered from the galling yoke of France.—Our Trade revived.—Our Commerce extended, and our antient alliances renewed and cemented by ties the most binding and affectionate.

" We fervently implore the Almighty to continue to inspire your Royal Highness's councils with the same wisdom, energy, and moderation, by which they have been uniformly guided.—And we humbly trust that your Royal Highness is reserved to the high and grateful privilege of extinguishing the flames of war, of binding up the bleeding wounds of Europe, and of pouring into them the healing balm of an honourable and lasting peace.

" We beg your Royal Highness to permit us to add, that we have found a peculiar pleasure on this occasion of addressing your Royal Highness, when you have condescended to participate in the joy of a Noble House, always famed for its loyalty, on an event so calculated to increase its happiness, and to perpetuate that attachment to the House of Brunswick by which it has ever been distinguished.   " Signed, by the unanimous order of a Common Hall,   THOMAS BURBIDGE, Town-clerk."

[2] Answer.

" I thank you for this dutiful and affectionate Address, which it is highly gratifying to me to receive at this place, the residence of a Family distinguished, as you have justly described it, for its loyalty, and for its steady attachment to the House of Brunswick.

" I accept, with the liveliest satisfaction, your congratulations on the great change which has been produced in the state of public affairs at home and abroad, and especially on the unexampled career of victory, which, through the favour of Divine Providence, has attended the arms of his Majesty, and those of his Allies.

" Never was heroic perseverance in a good cause more eminently rewarded, nor injustice and oppression more signally punished than by the expulsion of the Enemy from the Peninsula of Spain and Portugal, and the deliverance of the greater part of Europe from the yoke and domineering influence of the Ruler of France.

" We may now cherish a well-founded hope that by a continuance of the exertions, which have led to these most important events, the independence of the Continent will be ultimately established on a solid and permanent foundation.

" It is (you may be assured) my ardent and invariable wish, that by a due combination of moderation and energy, the Government of this Country may at all times be administered in a manner congenial to the generous and high-spirited character of his Majesty's people, and I entertain the most perfect confidence, that, animated by the experience of what has been effected by their own fortitude and example during this momentous contest, they will remain determined to spare no efforts, and to withhold no sacrifices which may still be found necessary for the purpose of bringing it to a satisfactory conclusion, by a secure and honourable peace."

Jan. 10. His Royal Highness and suite arrived at Buckden Palace, the residence of Dr. Tomline[1], bishop of Lincoln, where a sumptuous dinner was provided, and where he slept that night.

Jan. 11. At half-past ten, his Royal Highness and suite left Buckden Palace, and arrived in the afternoon at Carleton House.

The Duke of Rutland has since had the misfortune to lose this young hope of his noble House, the child dying June 15, 1814, aged 10 months.

P. 67. Cole's MSS. Vol. VII. p. 180. b. contains an account of the Family of *Manners Duke of Rutland;* beginning thus : " 1281, 9 Edw. I. *Henricus de Manerio*[2] tenet in Theversham de *Baldwin de Manerio,* de feodo Eliensi, med. feod. militis, & similiter per 18 partem feod. mil. & facit scutagium." &c.

Bringing it down to 3 Edw. III. in this page, and then referring to another of his volumes, *viz.* XXXVI. p. 139. Pedigree and alliances of Chester of Cokenhatch, Herts, relates to the Rutland family, pp. 179, 180, 181, &c. same vol. begins with, Henry Manners, earl of Rutland, who died 1563.

P. 90. Mr. William Prince, surgeon, died at Bottesford early in 1811, aged 68.

P. 142. Esther, relict of the Rev. Thomas Frewen Turner, died Oct. 6, 1803, aged 81.

Ibid. Mary Frewen, daughter of the Rev. Thomas F. died at Brickwall House, Northiam, in 1811.

P. 144. col. 2, l. 26. James Phelps, esq. of Coston house, a magistrate and one of the deputy-lieutenants of the county, died in 1814.

P. 149. Rev. Samuel Herbert, D. D. rector of Croxton Kyriel and Folkston sinecure, co. York, died Dec. 5, 1813, at Grantham, aged 65; and was succeeded by the Rev. George Crabbe (see p. 131).

P. 159. Pedigree of Hartopp, last descent :

The hon. Juliana Hartopp-Wigley, wife of Edward Hartopp-Wigley, esq. of Little Dalby, died May 20, 1807, aged 47. She was daughter of George fourth lord Carberry, who married Juliana, third daughter of Baptist fourth earl of Gainsborough. Her ladyship fell a martyr to the measles, which she caught through an unintermitted attention on the sick bed of a deservedly favourite son. Her remains were interred in the family vault at Dalby. The funeral retinue, superbly decorated with the escocheons of the family, attracted at Leicester the attention of an immense concourse of spectators.

Edward Hartopp-Wigley, esq. husband of the above, died June 28, 1808.

Miss Hartopp, his only daughter, died at Bath, June 13, 1804, in her 21st year.

The son, Edward Hartopp, esq. was married at Clifton, by special licence, June 18, 1808, to Anna-Eleonora, eldest daughter of sir Bourchier Wray, bart. of Tawstock-house, Devon. He died in Grosvenor-square, after a short illness, aged 30, Feb. 5, 1813.— To enumerate his virtues would be superfluous : his excellencies were of that unobtrusive kind which attract not the admiration of strangers, but which will remain indelibly engraved on the hearts of all who knew him. In performing the duties of husband, father, and friend, few equalled and none surpassed him. Actively benevolent, he was the friend of man ; and, if a life of undeviating rectitude may claim so glorious an appellation, " the friend, too, of his God."

P. 162. Mr. John Leadbeater died at Little Dalby, Dec. 31, 1813, advanced in age.

P. 180. *add to rectors of* Edmondthorpe :

Charles-Augustus Steuart, M. A. inst. 1804. .... Surtees, who resigned in 1811.

Charles Swan, M. A. 1811. Mr. Swan is also rector of Bedlington, co. Rutland.

P. 188. col. 2, l. 43. Garthorpe has since been purchased of lord Sondes, by sir William Manners, bart. the present owner, 1814.

P. 195. l. 3 from bottom. Edward Manners, esq. died at Godeby hall, in his 67th year, Feb. 19, 1811.

P. 203. note[3]. See Vol. III. p. 918, for a material correction in this note.

P. 213. *add to rectors of* Harby : Rev. Thomas Norris, M. A. 1804.

P. 229. Rev. Thomas Hornsley, of Kirkby Beler, died in 1812.

P. 229. *add to perpetual curates of* Kirkby Beler : Rev. John Noble, 1813. He is also vicar of Frisby.

P. 237. The Rev. William Peters, prebendary of Lincoln, and rector of Knipton, &c. died at Brasted-place, Kent, March 20, 1814. He was a very eminent and ingenious painter, and a Royal Academician, but resigned that honour, and relinquished the pencil many years, except as an amusement, or for the gratification of his friends. His Resurrection of a Family, Spirit of a Child, and other pieces, are esteemed among the choice works of British art. A good engraving of the ruins of the old church at Wolsthorp, as it appeared in 1792, from a drawing by Mr. Peters, is given in vol. II. p. 83. He married a niece of the late Dr. Turton, the bulk of whose great fortune has descended to the second son of Mr. Peters.

P. 243. col. 1, l. 19. *for* John, *read* Thomas Mowbray, &c.

P. 250. Mrs. Elizabeth Caldecott, wife of Samuel Caldecott, of Melton Mowbray, died Feb. 15, 1804, in her 38th year. See an account of her and her family in Gent. Mag. vol. LXXIV. p 279.

Ibid. Edward Stokes, gent. died at Melton Mowbray, May 10, 1805, in his 69th year. He practised as an attorney, with ability, success, and integrity, more than 40 years ; and was also one of the coroners for the county, which office he resigned, on the appointment of Mr. Thomas Clarke his son-in-law.

Ibid. Mrs. Reeve died at Melton Mowbray, in her 91st year, Dec. 28, 1808. She was relict of William Reeve, esq. and grandmother of the late earl of Harborough.

P. 254. Mr. Wyrley, in 1603, found the following epitaphs in Melton Mowbray church :

On a grave-stone in the chancel :

" Of your charitie prey for the soule of John Wode, sometymes merchant of the staple of Calis, and Margery his wyfe, which John deceased 28 March, 1510, and the said Margerie the . . . .

On another :

" Orate pro animâ Aliciæ Wode, viduæ, quondam uxoris Richardi Wode, de Notyngham, merchant, quæ ob. 29 Oct. 1483."

In an aile, about a fair tomb :

" Pauperum fautor, Dominique cultor,
Transigens annos decies novenos, hic jacet,
Vitam fragilem relinquens astra petivit."

Over, upon the wall :

Arms : Argent, three ʒ's Sable. Crest, a bird volant ; but, looking backwards, under that, is,

" Edverdus Pate de Ekettilbie, ar. et Katherina uxor ejus, sub hoc tumulo inhumantur ; qui quidem Edverdus ob. Apr. 19, 1597. Katherina vero Sept. 29, 1593. Et habuerunt liberos undecim : Henricum, Elizabetham, Edmundum, Doritheam, Henricum, Johannem, Mariam, Annam, Ursulam, Margaretam, et Franciscum."

On a grave-stone :

" Here lieth burried the bodie of Henry Gulstonn, gent. which maried Elizabeth Chancy, the eldest daughter of Clement Chancy, esq. who had

---

[1] " The Rev. George Pretyman, D. D. of a very antient family in the county of Suffolk, and well known as the tutor and friend of Mr. Pitt, was promoted to the see of Lincoln early in the year 1787. In June 1803, Marmaduke Tomline, of Riby Grove, in the county of Lincoln, esq. died, and left him a considerable estate, consisting of the whole parish of Riby, and a handsome mansion-house, upon condition that he should change his name to Tomline, which accordingly he did. Mr. Tomline had scarcely any acquaintance with the Bishop, and therefore this bequest is to be attributed to general respect for his Lordship's character.". Clutterbuck's Herts (speedily to be published), vol. I. p. 300.

[2] This is a curious explanation of the name.

yssue

yssue xi sonnes and viii daughters. In the praise and glory of God, he being of the age of 46 yeares, deceased 17 Nov. 1592."

On another grave-stone: ·

Arms: *Chauncy*: .... three foxes .... between two flanches Or, on each flanch an anchor Sable.

" Hic jacet Clemens Chancy, alias Gyles, ar. et Elizabetha uxor ejus, ob. 8 Sept. anno 1578, qui filiu' unu' habueru' et 3 filias."

On another grave-stone:

" Maria Chantler, uxor Rogeri Chantler, Artium Magistri, Meltoniensis, filiaque Clementis Chauncy, alias Gyles, de Melton, sub hoc lapide inhumatur. Ob. 12 Junii, 1585."

On another grave-stone:

" Of your charity pray for the soules of Mr. Berthelmew Brokisby, esq. and Elizabeth his wyfe, which Berthelmew deceased 12 May, anno 1543." Under are seven children.

On a grave-stone in the body of the church:

" Hic jacent Thomas Hartope, de Burton, qui ob. 29 Martii, anno ..... Habuit filios Gulielmum, Valentinum, Richardum, et unicam filiam Johannam."

P. 282. col. 2, l. 14. *for* 1329, *read* 1399.

P. 292. My excellent friend Mr. Crabbe has resigned Muston, on being presented, in 1814, to the rectory of Trowbridge in Wiltshire.—Of this elegant and sensible Poet, see " Literary Anecdotes of the Eighteenth Century," vol. VIII. pp. 90, 122.— Mr. Crabbe lost his amiable wife in October 1813.

P. 305. The present worthy vicar of Saltby, in a letter to the Editor of the Gentleman's Magazine, Dec. 13, 1813, says, " In the parish of Saltby, containing 213 inhabitants, there had not been, in the beginning of October last, a death for more than two years; the scale of mortality being there not one in 400 annually. From this circumstance, my curiosity led me to look into the Register for the last ten years, by which it appears there were 23 deaths only (a period of 20 years will give more), and one half of these were upwards of 70 years of age, or infants; hence it is clear, on a rough calculation, that latterly only one in 90 has died annually ; yet so insensible are the inhabitants of this blessing, that they would smile at any intimation of the sort seriously advanced. Nor are there any remarkable instances of longevity to found any theory upon: one arrived to the age of 87, another to 92. And what may be equally worthy of remark, is, that there has not been a Wedding in the Parish for more than four years."

P. 319. col. 2, l. 13 from bottom, Mrs. Elizabeth Dickinson, daughter of William Scott, esq. of Market Overton, aged nearly 90, in May 1812.

Ibid. col. 2, l. 11 from bottom. Edward Cheselden, esq. a gentleman of great benevolence and hospitality, died Oct. 10, 1804. He was many years receiver-general of this county; one of the deputy-lieutenants; and in the commission of the peace. During the American war he served as major in the Leicestershire militia, and in the late war as lieutenant-colonel; both which situations he filled with credit to himself and honour to the county.

P. 320. *Vicars of* Somerby: *for* Heuson, *read* Henson.

P. 336. col. 1, l. 54. The death of my generous patron, Robert fourth earl of Harborough, is noticed vol. III. p. 525. He was succeeded by his only son Philip fifth earl of Huntingdon, who married in 1791 Eleanor, daughter of the hon. John Monckton, of Fineshade, in Northamptonshire (cousin to viscount Galway), by whom he had issue: 1. Lucy-Eleanor, born May 20, 1792; 2. Anna-Maria, born 1794; 3. Sophia, born 1795, married in 1812 to the eldest son of sir Thomas Whichcote, bart. of Aswarby-house, co. Lincoln; 4. Philip, born Aug. 26, 1797; 5. A daughter, born 1799; 6. A daughter, born 1802. His lordship died Dec. 9, 1807; and was succeeded by his only son, Philip, present and sixth earl of Harborough.

P. 385. *add to note* 8: " Dr. Sparke has since met with well-merited preferment. He was promoted

to the deanry of Bristol 1803, in which year he took the degree of D. D. He published a " Concio ad Clerum," 1807; was elected Bishop of Chester 1810; and translated to Ely in 1813. This benevolent Prelate has frequently been invited to advocate the cause of Public Charities; and has pleaded for them with singular ability and success. Among the single Sermons of his which have been printed, are, 1. " On the 30th of January 1810, before the House of Lords;" 2. " At the Foundling Hospital, 1810;" 3. " For the Royal Humane Society, 1814."

P. 393. *add to vicars of* Withcote: Rev. Joseph Cragg, 1808 ; *vice* Coulton, dec.

P. 397. Mr. Robert Hickling, of Wyfordby, died Nov. 28, 1811, aged 79. He was chief constable of Framland Hundred upwards of 40 years.

P. 406. Dr. James Wood, rector of Wyfordby, died at Bath, Dec. 27, 1814, æt. 65.

GARTRE HUNDRED.

P. 431. col. 2, l. 41. Mr. Colman, of Harborough, has in his possession a Subsidy Roll of the Hundred of Gartre, temp. Car. 1.

P. 435. Mr. Nicholas Joyce, surgeon, of Billesdon, died April 12, 1807, in his 77th year.

P. 443. col. 2, l. 34 from bottom. The Rev. Henry Greene, M. A. died at his seat at Rolleston, Sept. 13, 1797. He was rector of Little Burstead and Laingdon cum Basildon, Essex, and in the commission of the peace for the county of Leicester; and was succeeded in his property at Rolleston by his son, Henry Greene, esq. who served the office of sheriff for Leicestershire 1799, and died March 13, 1801.

P. 449. col. 1, l. 43. John Owsley, esq. died at Hallaton, at a very advanced age, Nov..... 1808.

P. 464. col. 2, l. 41. Mr. John Ward died at Husbands Bosworth, March 13, 1814, in his 90th year.

Ibid. Maria-Hariott, eldest daughter of P. A. La Fargue, esq. died at Husbands Bosworth, of a decline, June 21, 1814, aged 16. She survived her brother but three months.

P. 467. Of an elegant Brooch found near Husbands Bosworth, see hereafter.

P. 468. Rev. Samuel Rogers died July 29, 1790. See Censura Literaria, vol. V. p. 110.

Ibid. Rev. Richard Pearce, rector of Husbands Bosworth, died Jan. 3, 1814, aged 55.

Ibid. *add to the rectors of* Husbands Bosworth: Rev. William West Green, Vice-principal of Magdalen Hall, Oxford, 1813.

P. 496. Penford Goodhall, gent. formerly of Ingersby, died at Market Harborough in 1814.

Ibid. Mr. C. Heygate, surgeon and apothecary, died at Market Harborough Feb. 19, 1811. The cheerfulness of temper and urbanity of manners, which this truly worthy young man possessed, together with the assiduous attention which he paid to the duties of his profession, will long endear his memory to a numerous circle of friends. His remains were interred in the family vault at Husbands Bosworth. See Pedigree of Heygate, in vol. IV. p. 628.

Ibid. Henry Coleman, esq. died at Market Harborough, in his 60th year, May 9, 1813.

P. 501. col. 2, l. 14. Mr. William Harrod, son of the schoolmaster, has published a History of his native Town of Market Harborough; and had previously published Histories of Stamford and Mansfield, in both which places he for some time resided as a printer and bookseller, as he now does at Harborough.

P. 529. The Rev. William Brown died at Burrow, in his 86th year, April 17, 1814. He was 54 years rector of that place, and was also rector of Loseby, and in the commission of the peace. He was an upright magistrate, an honest man, and unremittingly and religiously attentive to the accurate discharge of his clerical duties.

P. 534. *add to rectors of* Burton Overy: ..... Holditch, who resigned in 1811. Rev. Thomas Thorpe, M. A. 1811.

Ibid. Mr. Judd, of Burton Overy, died July 19, 1810. He was high constable of Gartre Hundred nearly 52 years.

P. 534

P. 534. Mrs. Lee, relict of the late Rev. John Lee, M. A. rector of Burton Overy, died at Leicester, Sept. 16, 1807, aged 70.

P. 543. col. 2, l. 50. *for* 1724, *read* 1636.

P. 555. *add to rectors of* Cranhoe: Rev. Thomas Chilton Lambton Young, M. A. 1809.

P. 556. col. 1, l. 44. *for* p. 298, *read* p. 290.

P. 559. *add to vicars of* Evington: Rev. . . . . . . Allanson, 1808; *vice* Coulton, deceased.

P. 577. Rev. Nathaniel North, vicar of Great Glen, died at Winchester 1814. He was also vicar of Bisbrooke, co. Rutland, and of Aswarsby, co. Lincoln.

P. 591. l. 17. Rev. George Gordon resigned the rectory of Gumley 1807. He was afterwards dean of Exeter, and is now dean of Lincoln.

Ibid. *add to rectors of* Gumley: Rev. Frederick Apthorp, M. A. 1807. He married a niece of the lady of Dr. Tomline, the present bishop of Lincoln; who gave him a prebend in his cathedral, and collated him to the rectory of Bicker, in that county, and afterwards to the vicarage of Gumley.

P. 604. Rev. William Fenwicke, son of the Rev. John F. rector of Hallaton, died at Tugby in 1803. He was of St. John's college, Cambridge, B. A. 1788.

P. 610. The Rev. Jethro Inwood, vicar of Horninghold, died at Tugby, April 26, 1814. He was also curate of Tugby and Norton.

P. 613. Rev. Richard Coulton, M. A. died June 16, 1808. He was rector and patron of Houghton, to which he was inducted on his own presentation in 1773; vicar of Evington, to which he was presented by Bishop Green in 1769, on the resignation of his father, who died in 1772; and also vicar of Withcote, and perpetual curate of Ouston 1792, to these he was presented by Sir John Palmer, bart.

Ibid. *add to rectors of* Houghton: Rev. James Sherard Coleman, 1808.

P. 641. The Rev. James Norman, rector of Kibworth, died Dec. 20, 1811.

Ibid. *add to the rectors of* Kibworth: Rev. James Beresford, M. A. 1812, a gentleman of great celebrity in the literary world; author of " The Miseries of Human Life," &c. &c.

P. 669, *n.* 20. Mr. John Kendal, of Thorpe Langton, died May 26, 1804, aged nearly 73.

P. 717. col. 1, l. 16 from bottom, *for* Dr. Christopher, *read* Dr. Charles Mason.

P. 749. col. 1, l. 42. Bridget 4th daughter of the late Sir Arthur Haselrige, bart. died in St. Martin's, Stamford Baron, in 1813, aged 74; a constant and most liberal friend to the poor.

P. 756. Lieut. Hesilrige, 58th regiment, second son of the late Grey Hesilrige, esq. of Noseley-hall, died Oct. 18, 1814, in the wreck of a transport-ship, bound to America.

P. 761. Mr. Cole, a respectable grazier and an amiable man, died at Ouston, March 23, 1813.

P. 763. *add to perpetual curates of* Ouston: Rev. Joseph Cragg, 1808; *vice* Coulton, deceased.

P. 771. The Rev. William Brereton, rector of Pickwell, died January 4, 1812, aged 86. He was formerly of King's College, Cambridge, B. A. 1749; M. A. 1753.

P. 784. Isaac Carter, esq. died at Scraptoft in July 1804. He was formerly an eminent attorney at Leicester; from which profession he had for some years retired, and was deservedly esteemed.

John-Edward Carter, esq. died at Scraptoft-hall, in his 60th year, June 8, 1813. He was lieutenant-colonel commandant of the Leicester division of local militia, and formerly a solicitor in Leicester, of extensive practice, and high character in his profession. He was a man of great benevolence and mildness of manners; and died rich in the blessings of the poor, and the regrets of his family and friends.

P. 797. col. 2, l. 45. My kind friend Mr. John Tailby, of Slawston, died on 5th Jan. 1815, the day which completed his 56th year. His proper description was that of an independent English yeoman, farming a paternal estate. His father, John Tailby, dying June 25, 1781, æt. 53, " bequeathed to his son a good name," and the family property; both of which the son assiduously cultivated. The Writer of this heartfelt tribute to his memory well knew and justly appreciated his merits. Their acquaintance commenced at an early period of this " History," in which the assistance afforded by Mr. Tailby would scarcely be credited by those who were not perfectly acquainted with him. The pains he took, and the journeys he made, to contribute all that was in his power to the correctness and improvement of this Work may be extensively traced in the parishes more particularly surrounding Slawston. His patience of investigation was, indeed, unwearied. Though a plain, unlettered man, he wrote an excellent hand; and soon acquired the habit of delineating coat-armour in the churches which he visited, and several of which he re-visited, for the express purpose of comparing the proof-sheets on the spot. In November 1799, as an apology for not having been more expeditious in returning some proof-sheets, he says; " The weather has, until the last week, been in general very wet; the waters frequently out and deep; the roads (pasticularly our clayey cross-roads) intolerably bad, more so than ever I knew before; days short; wheat-seed time late, and, when commenced, lingering, slow, and tedious. But notwithstanding these impediments, I have, after three separate days-ride, visited Skeffington, Tilton, Twyford, Tugby, and East Norton, Churches; and trust that I have made the necessary corrections and additions in each Parish."

A few of his articles it may be sufficient to specify. His Description of Burrow-hill is printed in vol. II. p. 525; of a Cross on a stone in the wall of his relation Mr. Warner's house at Cranhoe, p. 554; his Statistical Account of Medbourne, p. 716; of Slawston, p. 797; his Account of Gartre Bush, p. 791; of Tilton, vol. III. p. 469; of an Oak Chair at Lubbenham, p. 539; of Kirby-Muxloe Ruins, vol. IV. p. 625; of the Bridge, and Monument of Mrs. Edwards and her father, at Welham, p. 1047. The Pedigree of the Family of Kendall of Thornton (vol. IV. p. 385)—a Family which includes in one of its branches the Mother of Dean Swift—was materially improved by Mr. Tailby, whose paternal grandfather is therein described " as worthy a yeoman;" and where, in a note, I had the satisfaction of thus noticing my friend John Tailby: " to whose diligence and attention I have been considerably indebted in the progress of these volumes. And I cheerfully embrace this opportunity of expressing my admiration at the skill which this self-taught Genius has acquired in decyphering old Registers, in transcribing obscure Epitaphs, and blazoning Coat Armour; and of thanking him thus publicly for the readiness which he has at all times shewn in assisting my researches."

Unfortunately, the latter years of Mr. Tailby were embittered by disease; but, in the paroxysms of bodily disorder, his mind continued firm, and he consoled himself by the perusal of such books as his own small library, or the kindness of the neighbouring Clergy (many of whom knew and esteemed him) could supply.

January 13, 1810, he thus describes himself: " For the last six weeks I have been quite laid up, so as not to be able, for the first month thereof, to walk across the house without personal assistance; and my left hand has been violently in pain, and so swelled, and entirely useless, that I could not cut my food, dress or undress myself—or mend or make a pen, even to this day. It is now nearly free from pain, but quite helpless;" and adds, " Though I have felt a deal of very acute pain during this long-continued fit, yet, I thank God, my right hand has never been so bad but what I could use my pen, which I consider as a very great blessing; and have (except the first three or fours days) enjoyed very good health during the whole six weeks; and my appetite has through the whole time been good (except as before). I have called in no medical advice, as in my former fits of the gout I never found scarcely any benefit therefrom. I have had an exceedingly good nurse, Mrs.

Mrs. Tailby, who has spared no pains in waiting upon and assisting me, in and with all things that were in her power; and to her very kind attendance, the efforts of Nature, assisted by the merciful blessing of God, do I attribute my present convalescence; and to a continuance of those mercies do I speedily hope for a total removal of pain and swelling from my limbs, and an entire re-establishment of strength. Another blessing I must not forget to mention.

"To pass the inactive and painful hours away with some degree of ease, I have been kindly supplied with pleasing and valuable books (especially Paley's Works) by the goodness of the Rev. Mr. Dance, of Medbourn, and the Rev. Mr. Fenwicke, of Hallaton."

In July 1810; "I have been highly gratified with the Gothic Specimens from Lavenham, which you was so good as to lend me; and I have lately had, from a neighbouring Clergyman, the reading of two volumes of Chalmers's ' History of the University of Oxford;' and it was quite a treat to me. It pleased me much to see ' Nichols's History of Leicestershire,' &c. so frequently referred to. I think the whole a pleasing and instructive book on the subject. In a few days I am to have, from the same gentleman, ' Dugdale's Monasticon,' the receipt of which I anticipate with pleasure as a double treat."

In October 1810, he says, "I am now reading ' Dugdale's Monasticon;' it is a pleasing and instructive book to all lovers of Antiquity. I have just read Mr. Miller's 'Account of Ely Cathedral and Monastic Buildings;' from which I gained some farther knowledge of Antient Architecture, and derived much satisfaction.—I have lately also had the favour of the reading of the last edition of ' Milner's Winchester;' from which I have obtained much information and amusement, during my confinement to the chimney-corner."

On the last day of the year 1813, he says, "I am just recovering from a severe fit of the rheumatic gout, which again attacked me at the beginning of this month so violently in the right hand, knee, and foot, that I could not walk across the house without personal support and assistance, nor feed myself, or write a word, for ten days; and, though in part recovered, I am still lame, and fingers swelled, stiff, and clumsy. In short, I am quite an invalid (although, thank God, I enjoy through his mercy tolerably good health). Always at home : except now and then taking a ride on my pony an hour or so round my closes, which are all contiguous to my dwelling, I have not been so far from home as Harborough (six miles) but once this nearly three years. Sometimes, in fine weather, I venture to a neighbouring village, a mile distant; for the frequency of this complaint has left (in my best state) such a numbness, stiffness, and callosity in my joints, as makes it nearly as painful and fatiguing to ride on horseback as to go on foot··················At the latter end of October, Mr. Blore paid me a friendly visit for four or five days; and made me the valuable present of his ' History of Rutland.' During his stay, he deciphered, translated, and took abstracts from, some very old and almost obliterated Latin deeds in the old Court-hand, relating to my small paternal estate at Slawston; which I prize much, as the estate has been in our family of Tailby (then spelled Tayleby) nearly 200 years. Since then, Mr. Blore has had the goodness to send, and present me with, his ' Account of the Public Schools, Hospitals, and other Charitable Foundations, in the Borough of Stanford, in the Counties of Lincoln and Rutland,' a well-written and well-intentioned publication. Many hidden things are brought to light, and many secret affairs are made manifest, which are not much to the credit of the present *should-be* Managers."

To these particulars I need scarcely add, that Mr. Tailby was a valuable man, and a worthy member of society; and his letters shew that he was a good Christian. He had been for several years married to a very excellent and affectionate woman, who survives him, but has no children.

VOL. I. PART II.

P. 799. "Mr. William Hodgkin, a respectable grazier, died at Slawston, Aug. 6, 1806, aged 76. It appears, by authentic records, that the family of *Hodgkin* hath lived in Slawston ever since 12 Henry VIII. (see vol. II. p. 799); and, farther, the Register of that parish has an entry of the same family in the year 1559, when it first commences; and the name and same family is continued to 1806 in as regular a way as Registers generally are.—His son, Mr. William Hodgkin died also at Slawston, Jan 6, 1807, aged 34. By the death of this person the name of Hodgkin is become extinct in Slawston; nor are there any of the same name and family living any where else, that the writer of this article knows of.

J. TAILBY."

P. 807. James Brudenell, earl of Cardigan, Baron Brudenell of Dean, co. Northampton, died Feb. 24, 1811, in his 86th year. His Lordship held the places of Privy Purse to his Majesty, and Governor of Windsor Castle. He first married Lady Anne Legge, sister to the second Earl of Dartmouth; and, secondly, Lady Elizabeth Waldegrave, sister to the fourth Earl of Waldegrave. Dying without male issue, he was succeeded in his title and estates by his nephew, Robert Brudenell, esq. one of the Equerries to the Queen.

P. 828. *add to vicars of* Thedingworth : Rev. ..... Cooke 1810, *vice* Cave, deceased.

P. 846. *add to vicars of* Thurnby: Rev. J. Allinson, of Packington; inst. 1804.

P. 871. col. 1, l. 31. Sarah countess of Denbigh and Desmond died at Brighton, Oct. 2, 1814, in her 74th year. She was the widow of the late Basil Feilding, sixth earl, grandfather of the present earl, a minor. Her ladyship was the youngest daughter of Edward Farnham, esq. of Quorndon, co. Leicester. She was born Oct. 25, 1741; and married May 3, 1769, to Sir Charles Halford, bart. who died without issue in 1780. She was married, secondly, July 21, 1783, to the late earl of Denbigh: and by his lordship's death, July 14, 1800, was again left a widow. — Lady Denbigh bequeathed 600*l*. for placing a monument in Quorn church to the memory of her father; and, after giving legacies to some particular friends and faithful domestics, devised the rest of her personal property, with 50 acres of land at Lutterworth, to Edward Farnham, esq. her youngest and only surviving brother, and to his wife and children. Her remains were deposited at Wistow, with those of her first husband, under whose will, the lordship of Wistow with its appurtenances (now worth between three and four thousand pounds a year) devolves to sir *Henry Halford*, bart. The paternal name of this deservedly eminent Physician was *Vaughan*; descended from the Vaughans of Brecknockshire in Wales. He changed his name, by his Majesty's permission under his sign-manual, for that of *Halford*, in respect to the memory of his maternal cousin, sir Charles Halford (whose fortune he now inherits), the last of a series of Baronets of remarkable Loyalty in Leicestershire, of whom an ample account is given in volume II. Sir Henry Halford married Elizabeth-Barbara, fourth daughter of John tenth lord St. John of Bletso; and has issue a daughter, Louisa, born March 18, 1796; and a son, Henry, born April 22, 1797.

Ibid. note [1]. The Honourable Augusta Vaughan, wife of Mr. Serjeant Vaughan, died in Montague-place, Jan. 20, 1813. She was the second daughter of Lord St. John of Bletsoe.

P. 872. l. ult. The Rev. Thomas Willows died at Leicester, June 25, 1813, aged 54.

Add to vicars of Wistow: Rev. Henry Kebbel, D.C.L. 1813.

P. 888. *Correct Pedigree :* Rev. Samuel Chambers, rector of Higham, died Feb. 18, 1788. Anna-Maria died 1743, æt. 9. Matilda, married to *William* King, gent.

P. 893, col. 1, l. 8. for *James*, read *George-Anthony-Legh Keck.*

VOLUME III.

EAST GOSCOTE HUNDRED.

P. 16. Mrs. Green, relict of Thomas Green, esq. formerly a captain in the Leicestershire Militia, died at Asfordby, July 7, 1810, aged 80.

P. 51. Mrs. Mary Pochin died July 21, 1804, in her 75th year. She was only sister of W. Pochin, esq. M. P. who left her for life all his Leicestershire estates, which, after her death, descended to Charles-William Pochin, esq. of Rotherby, eldest son of the late Thomas Pochin, esq. of Loughborough, and grandson of Thomas Pochin, M. D. who was first cousin to the late knight of the shire.

Ibid. Frances Pochin, only sister of Charles William Pochin, esq. died at Loughborough, Nov. 4, 1806, aged 27.

P. 94. Charles-Small Pybus, late M. P. for Dover, and one of the Lords of the Treasury, died unmarried, in Great George-street, Sept. 5, 1810. In 1800, he published a poem, intituled "The Sovereign, addressed to his Imperial Majesty of all the Russias;" superbly printed, with his own portrait prefixed; of which a copy magnificently bound was sent over to Russia. [The Hero, as almost immediately afterwards appeared, was unfortunately selected. See Gent. Mag. vol. LXX. p. 854.]

P. 101. col. 2, l. 29. Hugo Meynell, senior, esq. died Dec. 14, 1808, aged 71 (see a full account of him in Gent. Mag. vol. LXXVIII. pp. 1134. 1186); and his widow, Mrs. Mary Meynell, in Charles-street, Berkeley-square, aged 77, Dec. 10, 1814.

P. 102. col. 2. Miss Meynell, eldest daughter of the late Hugo Meynell, esq. of Quorndon, and grand-daughter of the viscountess Irwin, of Temple-Newsome, died October 28, 1806, aged 20.

P. 109. Barnard, second son of S. J. Hyde, esq. of Quorndon, died January 7, 1814.

P. 115. A large addition was made to the church-yard at Woodhouse about 1808, and consecrated by Dr. Tomline, Bishop of Lincoln; and the church has since been entirely new pewed.

One of the two bells at Woodhouse having long been cracked, they were both taken down in September 1813, and replaced with three new ones.

Ibid. Mr. John Patchet, a worthy farmer, died at Woodhouse, aged 84, Dec. 24, 1809.

P. 148. Richard Dyott, esq. died July 7, 1813. See Gent. Mag. vol. LXXXIII. part ii. pp. 92. 198.

P. 176. col. 2. add, James Vann, esq. of Belgrave, died Oct 30, 1812, aged 65. This gentleman, who was the youngest and last of four brothers, is supposed to have died worth more than 100,000l. principally acquired in the hosiery business at Leicester; and the bulk of it, with the exception of a few legacies, is bequeathed to a distant relation. William, the elder brother, was high-sheriff of the county in 1785, and died April 20, 1794, æt. 66. Mr. James Vann served that office in 1803. He married a daughter of the Rev. John Clayton, rector of Belgrave, who survived him, but had no issue. The three elder brothers died unmarried.

P. 182. "March 5th, 1650.

"Belgrave—Whereas the Committee for Plundered Ministers, the 12th of March, 1648, granted the yearely rent of thirty pounds reserued to the Bpp. of Coventrey and Leichfeild out of the impropriate Rectory of Belgrave, in the County of Leicester, over and above the present stipend of twelve pounds, for increase of the maintenance of Mr. William Kinnes, Minister there; This Committee, being certified that the said Mr. Kinnes is a godly and orthodox divine, doe order that the yearely sume of thirty pounds be continued to the said Mr. Kinnes; And

the Trustees for maintenance of Ministers are to pay the same accordingly; provided that such money as is due out of the said rectory for pious and charitable uses bee first paid.   JO. BOURCHIER[1]."

P. 182. The following was copied by Mr. Wyrley, from a tomb in the chancel of Belgrave church, about 1603:

"Arms: *Grenewood*: .... a (chevron) between three saltires Gules.

"Here under resteth the body of James Grenewood, lately of Belgrave, and clerk of the peace in Leycestershire. Ob. 29 Januarii, 1558. Dirige eum in semitâ rectâ."

P. 195. Brooksby. Rev. Thomas Orton died March 1, 1804. He was presented to Brooksby in 1755, and to the rectory of Reresby 1791, in which last preferment he succeeded his father, and was the fifth successive rector of the name of Orton.

Ibid. *add to rectors of* Brooksby: Rev. Thomas Gardner, B. A. 1804.

P. 228. Francis Goude, gent. died at Cossington in his 79th year, Feb. 23, 1811.

Ibid. Mrs. Rachel Marshall, widow of captain W. Marshall, late of Cossington, and sister of the late Richard Wyatt, esq of Hornchurch, formerly governor of the East India Company's settlement of Bencoolen in the Island of Sumatra, died at Romford, in Essex, March 24, 1814, aged 84.

P. 229. Mrs. Fisher, mother of the Rev. Mr. Fisher of Cossington, died at Ashby-de-la-Zouch, March 6, 1806, in her 77th year.

P. 234. To the Letters of the Rev. Philip Hacket, in this and some of the subsequent pages, I shall add another extract or two, characteristic of that gentleman's accuracy and pleasantry.

" DEAR SIR,   *March* 30, 1799.

" If I understand you right, you wish to have a little of my assistance upon the present state of South Croxton, &c.— I am far from supposing any thing of mine would much contribute to illustrate your performance; to which, however, I wish the utmost success and honour. I have lately been busied with a new inclosure, and almost making new the old parsonage-house, totally at my own expence. The lumber of this last part of the work has sadly deranged my papers; and whether I can recover some relating to my observations on such subjects as the above, is uncertain at present. Perhaps, however, I may be able to mark some things from my memory, that may be totally left to your judgment of approbation or rejection, to make what use of them you think proper, or none at all.

"I think the pedigree of Hackett is a little out of place, and something erroneous. We came from Pentorry to Abkettleby by a marriage with one of the coheiresses of Danvers of Thrussington, and not of Shackerston, though they had estates there, and probably lived there before. The Hacketts had been founder's-kin of Winchester and New College for generations.—I don't mind the postage. My living is worth nearly 200l. *per annum*; Patron, the duke of Rutland.—Should be glad likewise to be informed how long at the utmost you can possibly wait for any thing from me, which, notwithstanding all this parade, I am afraid will be worth but little of your notice or recording. I am always very busy, at the same time irresolute, like one moving in a circle; so advance but little. I certainly was calculated never to cut a figure—except, like *Erskine*, not in writing, it might possibly have been in talking; which, I think, is the chief *forte* of that gentleman.

---

[1] Acts of the Committee for Plundered Ministers in Sion College Library.

" I

"I was in town about five years since; and, though almost lost in your great and populous *village* for a fortnight, most of my old acquaintance being out of the way (a melancholy circumstance!) I never did stumble on Red Lion Passage.

"I am now in my 70th year, and never had an hour's illness in my life; and nearly enjoy myself as well as at 30.—I see *Thomas*, at the head of *our Pedigree*, aged 97. It is not impossible that one of the *last* may come almost up to the *first*. *Sic placeat Deo.*—The celebrated Mr. Dibdin exhibits tonight at Leicester, being the only night he has to spare, as he announces to the publick, between this and the 5th of October, from the West of England; when he returns, and opens Sans Souci, Leicester-square, as he says, under the auspices of the Lord Chamberlain. I mean to be there; ticket 3s.—I am, Sir, your sincere friend, and very humble servant,
                            PHILIP HACKET."

P. 238. note [2]. On the subject of the Bell-ringing at Hoby, mentioned in this note, and again in p. 458, Mr. Hacket thus wrote:

"DEAR SIR,   *June* 1, 1799.

"No mention in the award by the commissioners for the inclosure of Thrussington, I have been lately informed, is distinctly made, to what use the rent is to be applied. Your inserting this account in your History will undoubtedly keep it alive in memory of many persons, and cause it to be talked of. The laudable custom of the Bell-ringing, which is amusing to that side of the country, may be kept up, or dropt, by the interested designs of certain individuals, to the great disappointment of a country long used to a *memento*; and in a moral and Christian sense it may be, as it happens, *to the hearer*, to be of use as a *memento mori*, as well as a *temporary one*.

"At the Archdeacon's Visitation at Leicester I saw Mr. ———, the present rector of ———; and asked him questions about the bell-ringing, whether it was constantly performed.—'It is, both winter and summer.'—'Who is it supported by? or who pays the ringer, or slave under the rope?'—'The parish.'—'Then, if the parish refuse to pay, the bell ceases, and the purposes of the Ladies are defeated.' —'What Ladies?'—'The Danvers,' says I, 'my relations, from whence I sprung. Are there not four or five acres of land somewhere, probably lying in Thrussington lordship? and who receives the rent?' —'The said land, on the inclosure of Thrussington, was laid out as near to me, close to the ring fence of Hoby Field, as possible.'—'Who receives the rent?'—'I do.'—'As an augmentation to your living! However, pay the poor bell-ringer well for his trouble; and give the remainder to the poor; for if the parishioners think you are personally a gainer, the bell will be discontinued, and the country disappointed of their usual memorandum.—The Historian of Leicestershire, by my agency, will record it. You will be talked of more than the bell; and be called upon to continue so laudable a custom.—He called me out from dinner after this; but apologized for the intrusion; for he did not dine with us. (He belongs to Melton Visitation). —'Mr. Hacket, I would not have it mentioned in the History: I don't consent to it.'—'Whether you do or no, it must be. I have sent up a true statement of the bequest; and I know that Mr. N. is a punctual and accurate Historian, as well as Antiquary. *Nescit vox missa reverti.*'—So we parted.

"I must now put an end to my commentaries, which will sufficiently tire all patience. I have no time to transcribe; for I am now writing on my *piano fortè*, which instrument has been my old hack, or second wife, for more than 40 long years; which often regales me, for I scarce know what low-spiritedness is one moment of my life. I hope you will be able to make out my scrawl, which I wrote precipitately yesterday and this morning. Make what use you please of it, or none at all;

and believe me to be your sincere well-wisher, and very humble servant, to command,   P. HACKET."

P. 237. l. 29. Rev. Philip Hacket died March 27, 1801. An account of him, extracted from this work, is given in Gent. Mag. for that year, p. 568. His widow unfortunately lost her life, at Osgathorpe, March 13, 1814, from being dreadfully burnt the evening before by her cloaths catching fire.

Ibid. *add to rectors of* South Croxton: Rev. William Wilkinson, 1801: rector also of Folksworth, co. Huntingdon, 1807.

P. 243. The Rev. Thomas Lumley the younger, died December 1, 1805, at Great Dalby, aged 72.

P. 262. Mr. Wyrley, in 1603, noticed the following epitaphs at Frisby:

"On a grave-stone:

"Here lieth the body of John Sharp, of Frisby in the county of Leic', gent. Ob. 9 Junii, 1578."

"On a stone for a child:

"Hic jacet Bartholomeus Brokesby, quonda' fil' Barthofomei Brokesby, arm. qui obiit 10 Martii, aº 1466."

P. 267. Mr. Wyrley gives these epitaphs at Hoby:

"Hic jacet Anthonius Cate de Hobie in com' Leye', generosus, qui ob. 2 die mensis Apr. aº 1589."

"They say his wife was Mary, daughter of . . . . Digby, of Welby. They had issue George-Anthony, who died young, and Saundera a daughter."

"On a grave-stone:

"Hic jacet Joh'es . . . . arm. qui ob. 27 Jun. aº 1476, et Eliz. uror ejus qᵉ ob. . . . . . ."

"They say this epitaph is for John Beler [1]."

P. 284. note 5. The Rev. George Ashby, B. D. died June 12, 1808, in his 84th year. See an account of him in Nichols's "Literary Anecdotes."

P. 288. col. 2, l. 8. April 8, 1731, John Edwin, esq. son of the late Sir John Edwin, was married to Miss Bradshaigh, daughter of Roger Bradshaigh, esq. M. P. for Wigan; and, the same day, Roger Bradshaigh, esq. was married to Miss Bellingham, of Preston in Lancashire.

Ibid. col. 2, l. 50. Dr. Burnaby died March 9, 1812. See before p. 122.

P. 340. col. 1. l. 28. Lady Fowke, relict of Sir Thomas Fowke, knight, and one of the co-heiresses of sir Isaac Wollaston, bart. died at Loseby-hall, Nov. 25, 1803.

P. 347. *add to rectors of* Loseby: Rev. William Wilkinson, 1814. He is rector also of South Croxton.

P. 359. col. 1. The antient epitaphs to the Nele family, in Prestwould church, are thus given, by Mr. Wyrley, in 1603:

"Hic jacent Rich'us Peel, militis, ac d'nus de Prestwouldia, et Isabella uror ejus, qui ob. 15 Junii, 1478."

"Hic jacent Ric'us Peel, unus justicior' d'ni regis de com'uni banco, et Isabella uror ejus, quæ Isabella ob. 23 Maii, aº 1496."

Thus there appear to have been two inscriptions; the former of which, noticed by Burton (see p. 359, col. 1, l. 42), is now gone. The latter inscription still remains.

P. 360. col. 1, l. 17 from bottom. Mr. Wyrley gives the following epitaph, "about an old tomb, where two women seem to lye:

"Hic jacent An'a Peel et Margeria Peel . . . . quonda' d'ni . . ; . . . . . . choli et d'ni et Margeriæ uroris suæ nup' d'na de Kenthorpe, qᵃ quidem Margeria ab hac luce migrabit ultimo Dec. 1518, et dicta An'a . . . ."

P. 362. Packe Pedigree. Francis Stratford, esq. of Merevale Hall, Warwickshire, was married to Miss Packe, Feb. 18, 1728-9.

P. 377. The Rev. Henry Woodcock, vicar of Barkby, has favoured me with a Plate of Sepulchral Relicks, and also with the following particulars:

"The Figures Nº 1 to 14. represent the things

[1] See vol. III. p. 265. col. t. l. 49.

found

found in a bed of dry sand about 4 feet beneath the surface in Queneborow Field, on a flat plain in the West of the Town, in a close about 500 yards, from where the public highways intersect each other, and where I, and many of the inhabitants of Queneborow, well remember a very long rampart, like the side of an encampment, between the inclosure of the field, in a direction North and South, very nigh, if not exactly, over the spot. Of these Nᵒ 1, 2, and 3, are the remains of brass vessels, very thin and finely polished. One of them, Nᵒ 2, about eight inches in diameter, seems much to resemble that which was found at Ash in Kent, as given in vol. III. Pl. XLII. Nᵒ 4, and was probably cased with wood, for the purpose perhaps of carrying dry wheat; and if it must have a name, I should call it a *frumentarium*; and, guided by Mr. Douglas's opinion as to the other, consider it, and the other contents of this grave, as Saxon remains of the eighth century. It is remarkable, that the circles in the bottom of this vessel are exactly such as are used (ornamentally I suppose) by braziers of the present day. I know not what to say of the very elegant little glass vessel, Nᵒ 4. I am doubtful whether the lachrymatory *of glass* was in use at that period. The authority of the Psalmist, Ps. lvi. 8. " Put my tears into thy bottle," leaves no doubt as to the very antient use of such vessels; but whether of glass, leather, or pottery, does not appear. I recollect to have read of a bottle, like ours, found in Hindostan, not many years back, supposed to have contained *sacred oil for sacrifices*; and I give you this hint to be improved upon by your well-informed Antiquarian Friends. Nᵒ 5. is a very fine earthen vase, 6⅜ inches at the top, and 8 inches diameter in the widest part: it has been glazed within, and holds exactly two quarts ale measure. The cap to it, Nᵒ 6 a. and 6 b. is of iron, and seems to have been studded [1]. The vase, Nᵒ 7, is of coarser materials, and holds about ¼ of a pint. Nᵒ 8, 9 a, 9 b, 10, are remains of brass or copper buckles, such as fasten on armour; and Nᵒ 11, is a piece of cloth, apparently coarse linen or hempen, found in one of them. Nᵒ 12, 13, are the parts of a long and very broad iron sword; and Nᵒ 14, part of a spear-head of the same metal. These are all from this grave.—Nᵒ 15, 16, are spear-heads found a few years prior to the above, in a ridge of sand in Queneborow, next to Barkby Field, and I have no doubt were left there by Prince Rupert's army, encamped on that spot during the siege of Leicester, in Cromwell's wars; and therefore of no antiquity compared with the others; and Nᵒ 17. a small vase (Roman I believe), discovered with many others in getting gravel some years ago at Knaptoft, upon an estate belonging to his Grace the Duke of Rutland. H. W."

P. 382. l. ult. The Rev. Griffith Gardiner, B. A. of Chelsea, vicar of Radcliffe-on-the-Wreke, 1784, died of a paralytic stroke Dec. 12, 1813.

P. 386. Mr. Wyrley, in 1603, says:

" In Ragdale, where Mr. Shirley has a house, in the little chapel there, on a grave-stone:

" 𝖧𝗂𝖼 𝗃𝖺𝖼𝖾𝗍 𝖳𝗁𝗈𝗆'𝗌 𝖠𝗅𝗒𝗇 𝖾𝗍 𝖩𝗈𝗁𝖺𝗇'𝖺 𝗎𝗑𝗈𝗋 𝖾𝗃𝗎𝗌, 𝗊𝗎𝗂 𝖳𝗁𝗈𝗆'𝗌 𝗈𝖻. 4 𝖩𝗎𝗅𝗂𝗂, 𝖺ᵒ 1468, 𝖾𝗍 𝖩𝗈𝗁𝖺𝗇𝗇𝖺 𝗎𝗑. 𝖾𝗃𝗎𝗌 𝗈𝖻. 3 𝖬𝖺𝗂𝗂, 𝖺ᵒ 1464."

" On another grave-stone:

" 𝖧𝗂𝖼 𝗃𝖺𝖼𝖾𝗍 𝖶𝗂𝗅𝗅'𝗌 𝖬𝖾𝗒𝗌𝗎𝗇, 𝗊𝗎𝗂 𝗈𝖻. 5 𝖬𝖺𝗂𝗂, 1496."

P. 391. Mr. Riley, an eminent grazier, died at Reresby, March 28, 1814, aged 70.

P. 392. Reresby. Rev. Thomas Orton died Mar. 6, 1804.

Ibid. *add to rectors of* Reresby: Rev. Edward Morgan, 1804. He was the eldest son of the Rev. N. Morgan, master of the grammar-school, Bath, and died Nov. 1, 1812.

P. 394. Mr. Richard Sacheverell, late one of the attendants at the British Museum, died Feb. 14,

1810, in his 65th year. He was a native of Oxford, and descended of a good family in Derbyshire; although, from the slender means of his mother, he was apprenticed to a book-binder. He was a man of a quiet, grave deportment; of a virtuous life; charitable, almost beyond the extent of a very limited income; and of inflexible integrity. The death of such a man, though he moved in humble life, was a loss to society.

P. 404. col. 1, l. 5. Robert Brokesby was grandfather to Mr. Robert Brokesby, of Shouldby, living 1603, aged 78.

Ibid. col. 1. l. ult. Another copy of this epitaph, taken by Mr. Wyrley in 1603, reads thus:

" 𝖧𝗂𝖼 𝗃𝖺𝖼𝖾𝗍 𝖶𝗂𝗅𝗅'𝗆𝗎𝗌 𝖡𝗋𝗈𝗄𝗌𝖻𝗒, 𝖺𝗋𝗆. 𝗊𝗎𝗈𝗇𝖽𝖺𝗆 𝖽'𝗇'𝗌 𝖽𝖾 𝖲𝗒𝗐𝗈𝗅𝖽𝖾𝖻𝗒, 𝖺𝖼 𝖾𝗍𝗂𝖺𝗆 𝗉𝖺𝗍𝗋𝗈𝗇𝗎𝗌 𝗂𝗌𝗍𝗂𝗎𝗌 𝖾𝖼𝖼𝗅'𝗂𝖾, 𝗊𝗎𝗂 𝗈𝖻𝗂𝗂𝗍 𝗉 𝖲𝖾𝗉𝗍. . . . . 𝖺𝗇ᵒ 𝖣𝗈𝗆. 1505, 𝖾𝗍 𝖽𝗂𝖼𝗍𝖺 𝖤𝗅𝗂𝗓𝖺𝖻𝖾𝗍𝗁. 𝗈𝖻. 𝗑𝗑𝗏 𝖩𝖺𝗇𝗎𝖺𝗋𝗂𝗂, 1523."

P. 405. In 1671, a very curious Volume was published, by a retainer of the *Englefield* family of Shoulby, under the title of " The Accomplisht Cook, or the Art and Mystery of Cookery. Wherein the whole Art is revealed in a more easie and perfect Method, than hath been publisht in any Language. Expert and ready Wayes for the Dressing of all Sorts of Flesh, Fowl, and Fish, with variety of Sauces proper for each of them; and how to raise all manner of Pastes; the best Directions for all sorts of Kickshaws; also the tearms of Carving and Sewing. An exact account of all Dishes for all Seasons of the Year, with other A la mode Curiosities. The Third Edition, with large Additions throughout the whole Work; besides two hundred Figures of several Forms for all manner of bake't Meats, (either Flesh or Fish) as Pyes, Tarts, Custards, Chessecakes, and Florentines, placed in Tables, and directed to the Pages they appertain to. Approved by the fifty-five Years Experience and Industry of Robert May, in his Attendance on several Persons of great Honour. London, Printed by J. Winter, for Nath. Brooke, at the Angel in Cornhill neer the Royal Exchange, 1671."

To this Volume, containing nearly 500 pages, is prefixed Robert May's Portrait, and these Verses:

" What! wouldst thou view but in one face
All hospitalitie, the race
Of those that for the Gusto stand,
Whose tables a whole Ark comand
Of Nature's plentie, wouldst thou see
This sight, peruse May's booke, 'tis hee [2]."

The Work is inscribed,

" To the Right Honourable my Lord Montague, my Lord Lumley, and my Lord Dormer; and to the Right Worshipful Sir Kenelme Digby; so well known to this nation for their admired hospitalities.

" Right Honourable, and Right Worshipful,

" He is an alien, a meer stranger in England, that hath not been acquainted with your generous housekeepings; for my own part, my more particular tyes of service to you, my honoured Lords, have built me up to the height of this experience, for which this Book now at last dares appear to the world: those times which I attended upon your Honours were those golden days of peace and hospitality, when you enjoyed your own, so as to entertain and relieve others.

" Right Honourable, and Right Worshipful, I have not only been an eye-witness, but interested by my attendance; so as that I may justly acknowledge those triumphs and magnificent trophies of Cookery that have adorned your tables; nor can I but confess to the world, except I should be guilty of the highest ingratitude, that the onely structure of this my Art and Knowledge, I owed to your costs, generous and inimitable expences, thus not onely I have derived my experience, but your Countrey hath reapt the plenty of your humanity and charitable bounties.

" Right Honourable, and Right Worshipful, Hospitality, which was once a relique of the gentry, and a known

---

[1] " The iron instrument Nᵒ 6, could never be intended as the cover to the earthen vase Nᵒ 5.—" Q. if a rest for a tilting-spear. B. L."—By Douglas's " Nenia Britannica," it appears be the *umbo* of a shield; similar to one engraved under Bagrave, vol. III. p. 289. Plate XLII. fig. 2.

[2] " The Author of " The School of Instruction for the Offices of the Mouth," flourished at the same time with May. He exceeded all his contemporaries in folding of napkins. See the prints in his book, which exhibit them under a great variety of forms. This practice continued for many years. It seems to have required almost as much time as dressing an elegant dinner."· GRANGER.

cognizance

Sepulchral Relicks found at Queneborow, &c.

Longmate del.et sculp.

cognizance to all ancient houses, hath lost her title through the unhappy and cruel disturbances of these times, she is now reposing of her lately so allarum'd head on your beds of honour: in the mean space, that our English World may know the Mæcenas's and Patrons of this generous Art, I have exposed this Volume to the publick, under the tuition of your names; at whose feet I prostrate these endeavours, and shall for ever remain your most humbly devoted servant,   ROBERT MAY.

" *From Sholeby in Leicestershire, September 29, 1664.*"

A Preface, addressed " To the Master Cooks, and to such young Practitioners of the Art of Cookery, to whom this Book may be useful," is followed by " A short Narrative of some Passages of the Author's Life," signed **W. W.**

" For the better knowledge of the worth of this Book, though it be not usual, the Author being living, it will not be amiss to acquaint the reader with a brief account of some passages of his Life, as also what eminent persons (renowned for their good house-keeping) whom he hath served throughout the whole series of his life; for, as the growth of the children argueth the strength of the parents, so doth the judgment and abilities of the Artist conduce to the making and goodness of the Work : now that such great knowledge in this so commendable Art was not gained but by long experience, practice, and converse with the most ablest men in their times, the Reader in this brief Narrative may be informed by what steps and degrees he ascended to the same.

" He was born in the year of our Lord 1588. His father being one of the ablest cooks in his time, and his first Tutor in the knowledge or practice of cookery; under whom having attained to some perfection in that art, the old Lady Dormer sent him over into France, where he continued five years, being in the family of a noble Peer, and first President of Paris; where he gained not only the French Tongue, but also bettered his knowledg in his cookery : and returning again into England, was bound apprentice in London to Mr. Arthur Hollinsworth in Newgate Market, one of the ablest workmen in London, cook to the Grocers Hall and Star-Chamber. His apprenticeship being out, the Lady Dormer sent for him to be her cook under his father (who then served that honourable Lady), where were four cooks more, such noble houses were then kept, the glory of that, and the shame of this present age ; then were those golden days wherein were practised the triumphs and trophies of cookery; then was hospitality esteemed, neighbourhood preserved, the poor cherished, and God honoured ; then was religion less talkt on, and more practised ; then was atheism and schism less in fashion ; and then did men strive to be good, rather than to seem so.   Here he continued till the Lady Dormer died, and then went again to London, and served the Lord Castlehaven, after that the Lord Lumley, that great lover and knower of art, who wanted no knowledge in the discerning this mistery; next the Lord Montague in Sussex; and at the beginning of these wars, the Countess of Kent; then Mr. Nevel of Chrissen-Temple in Essex, whose Ancestors the Smiths (of whom he is descended) were the greatest maintainers of hospitality in all those parts; nor doth the present Mr. Nevill degenerate from their laudable examples. Divers other persons of like esteem and quality hath he served, as the Lord Rivers, Mr. John Ashburnham of the Bed-Chamber, Dr. Steed in Kent, Sir Thomas Stiles, of Drury-Lane in London, Sir Marmaduke Constable in Yorkshire, Sir Charles Lucas ; and lastly the Right Honourable the Lady Englefield, where he now liveth."

Then is given a whimsical account of " Triumphs and Trophies in Cookery, to be used at Festival Times, at Twelfth Day, &c.; followed by two Copies of Verses, signed James Perry and John Town, on their " loving Friend, Mr. Robert May, his incomparable Book of Cookery." After " The most exact, or à la Mode Ways of Carving and Sewing," are given " Bills of Fare for every Season in the Year; also how to set forth the Meat in order for that service; as it was before Hospitality left this Nation."—The Work is *adorned* with two hundred engravings on wood, as patterns for tarts, mincepies, cheese-cakes, forms of fishes, &c. &c.

P. 414.   The Rev. Robert-Acklom Ingram was the eldest son of the Rev. Robert Ingram, late vicar of Wormingford and Boxted[1]; and received the

chief part of his early education under the care of the late Mr. Grimwood and the present Dr. Grimwood, who were successively masters of the very respectable school at Dedham, Essex.   At the University he took the degree of B. A. and was senior wrangler in 1784; M. A. 1789; was moderator in 1790; B. D. in 1794; and was presented to the rectory of Segrave in 1802.   The retired situations in which most of his curtailed life was spent, at the time that they now forbid a lengthened memoir, furnish just cause for regret that so much virtue, aided by considerable talent, had not a more extensive field allotted for its exercise.   His unwearied exertions in the " labour of love," both within and without the limits of his profession, sufficiently well known to his particular friends, will be best attested to the world by the following list of his principal publications.   " A Sermon, preached at St. James's Colchester, for the Benefit of the Charity School, 1788."   " The Necessity of introducing Divinity into the regular Course of Academical Studies considered; and other Regulations suggested for the Improvement of the present Mode of Education at the University of Cambridge, 1792."   " Select Questions and Answers on the Knowledge and Practice of the Christian Religion, compiled for the Use of a Sunday School."   " Select Portions of Psalms from different Versions: to which are added, a few occasional Hymns."   " An Enquiry into the present Condition of the Lower Classes, and the Means of improving it, 1797."   " A Sermon preached at St. James's, Colchester, for the Benefit of the Sunday Schools, 1797." " A Sermon, preached at Wormingford and Boxted, to persuade the Congregations to form themselves into Military Associations for the Defence of the Country, 1798."   " A Syllabus, or Abstract of a System of Political Philosophy; to which is prefixed A Dissertation recommending that the Study of Political Œconomy be encouraged in our Universities, and that a Course of Public Lectures be delivered on that Subject, 1799."   " Parochial Beneficence, a Sermon, preached at Boxted, for the Benefit of a School of Industry, 1800."   " An Essay on the Importance of Schools of Industry and Religious Instruction, in which the Necessity of promoting the good Education of poor Girls is particularly considered, 1800."   " Causes of the Increase of Methodism and Dissension, 1807."   " Disquisitions on Population ; in which the principles of Mr. Malthus's Essay are examined and refuted, 1808."   The above writings will also serve to manifest the very firm attachment of their Author to the best interests of Church and State; an attachment, however, which neither precluded him, on the one hand, from the exercise of the most exemplary candour towards those who differed from him; nor, on the other, from suggesting such corrections, precautions, and improvements, as appeared to him at once suitable to the exigencies of the times, and conducive to the future benefit of an Establishment which he revered and valued.   His death surprized him, at the age of 47, after an illness of only a few days, whilst occupied in fresh schemes of public utility, Feb. 5, 1809.   He left a widow and three infant children.

Robert Ingram, M. A. father of the rector of Segrave, died at Segrave, Aug. 3, 1804.   See a long account of this learned and worthy Divine in the Gentleman's Magazine, vol. LXXIV. pp. 882—884.

Catharine, relict of the Rev. Robert Ingram, vicar of Wormingford and Boxted, Essex, and mother of the above Rev. Robert-Acklom Ingram, died at Kegworth, March 27, 1809, having nearly completed her 82d year.

Mr. Ingram was succeeded at Segrave by the Rev. Robert Gutch, M. A. second son of the Rev. John Gutch, registrar of the University of Oxford.

P. 421.   William King, esq. of Sileby, formerly captain in the Leicestershire Militia, second son of Thomas King, esq. died June 2, 1810, aged 37.

[1] See Gent. Mag. for September 1804.

P. 439. col. 1, l. ult. The estate of Sir William Skeffington, at Skeffington (consisting of the manor, or reputed manor of Skeffington, with its royalties and appurtenances; the mansion-house called Skeffington-Hall; and about 100 acres of land) was offered for sale July 5, 1814, at Leicester; and was bought by the Rev. . . . . Bright, of Northamptonshire, who now resides there.

P. 440. On the 12th of July and eight following days, the valuable Collection of Pictures (described in pp. 440, 441) was sold by auction at Skeffington-Hall; and on July 25 and 26, the Books were sold.

P. 450. Catharine Josepha, Lady Skeffington, died, at the residence of Sir William Skeffington, bart. Beaumont-street, Devonshire-place, after a lingering indisposition of five years, in her 69th year, July 26, 1811. Few minds were more liberally endowed by nature, or more highly embellished by cultivation. As a wife, a mother, and a friend, few ever surpassed her.

Ibid. Sir William Skeffington, bart. died in Charles-street, Berkeley-square, Jan. 26, 1815; and was buried at Paddington, Feb. 6. He was born June 24, 1742; and served in the First regiment of Foot-guards for 25 years. He was appointed one of the Esquires to his Royal Highness Prince Frederick, Duke of York, at the installation of the Knights of the most honourable Order of the Bath in 1772; he was a deputy-lieutenant for the county of Leicester; and was elected F. S. A. in 1793. At the important crisis of 1794, sir William was colonel of the Leicestershire Yeomanry Cavalry, which was the first regiment of yeomanry that was completed, and made its returns to Government. Sir William Skeffington was distinguished, in private society, for the urbanity of his manners; and in public life, the duties of his station were upheld by ardour, and maintained with firmness. He is succeeded in the title by his only son, now sir Lumley St. George Skeffington, bart. a gentleman well known both in the literary and fashionable world; of whom a biographical memoir may be seen in the new edition of the "Biographia Dramatica," by Mr. Stephen Jones.

P. 455. The Rev. John-Dawes Ross, vicar of Syston, died in 1814; and was succeeded by the Rev. E. Morgan, M. A. curate of St. Mary's, Leicester.

P. 469. My venerable friend William Hutton, esq. the Historian of Birmingham, &c. in a letter written in 1815, says "You mention a hill called Robin-o'-tiptoe, in the parish of Tilton. Upon the summit is a Fortification, of an oblong square, which I take to be Danish, containing about one acre. There is one Tree within the Camp, in a state of great decay; probably not less than a thousand years old: from this I apprehend, the Hill took its name of Robin-o'-tiptoe. I have lately purchased the Hill."

P. 474. For various particulars relative to the Digby family, see the Fourth Volume of the new edition of Hutchins's "Dorsetshire," pp. 133—136.

P. 484. add to vicars of Tugby: Rev. Benjamin Drury, assistant master of Eton school, instituted 1810.

P. 494. add to vicars of Twyford: Rev. George Osborn, 1809, vice Clarke, deceased.

P. 499. add to rectors of Walton on the Woulds: Rev. Philip Laycock Story; vice his father.

P. 505. Edward James died at Wimeswould, in his 84th year, in January 1807. He had received two premiums from the Leicester Agricultural Society; one for supporting his numerous family, by his indefatigable industry, without becoming burthensome to the parish; and the other for long servitude in the family of Mr. William Burrows, of Wimeswould. He maintained, through life, an unexceptionable character for honesty, industry, and piety; and was carried to the grave by six of his grandsons.

P. 506. Rev. Thomas Wightman of Wimeswould, a truly conscientious faithful minister; and in every respect a worthy, amiable man, died Dec. 26, 1812.

P. 509. Sir Henry Sacheverell, of Morley in Derbyshire, married Dorothy Danvers, of Cullworth in Northamptonshire, a descendant of lord Say and Sele, by which marriage his issue and theirs became a-kin to William of Wykeham, and enjoyed the privileges of the said founder's kinsmen, as did the issue of sir Henry's grandson, Ambrose Sacheverell, of Ballscot in Oxfordshire, namely, Erasmus and James Sacheverell; as did also that of their sister Margaret by her husband Dr. William Oldys, parson of Addesbury in Oxfordshire, who had three sons, or more, bred up at New College, Oxford, upon the privilege of founder's kinsmen[1]. W. Oldys[2].

P. 521. col. 2, l. 12. for Edmund, read Edward Smith, esq.

WEST GOSCOTE HUNDRED.

P. 561. The Portrait of the Right Hon. Francis Rawdon, Earl of Moira, from the charming pencil of Sir Joshua Reynolds, is intended as a FRONTISPIECE to Vol. III. Part II. (West Goscote); in which Hundred, Donington Park, his Lordship's chief seat, is situated.—(See p. 139.)

P. 605. col. 2. Theophilus earl of Huntingdon was married, May 8, 1690, in king Henry the Seventh's chapel, to his second wife Frances, daughter and sole heir to Francis Leveson, of Trentham, co. Stafford, esq. son and heir to Richard Fowler, of Harnage Grange, co. Salop, esq. and adopted heir to sir Richard Leveson, Knight of the Bath, which lady was widow to Thomas viscount Killmorey, of the kingdom of Ireland, and mother to Robert now lord viscount Killmorey. By her this earl had issue, 1. Ann-Jaqueline, born in London May 1, 1691. 2. Alice, born at Donington, Jan. . . , 1691, and died the same day; and buried at Ashby. 3. Frances, born at Donington Jan. 8, 1694. 4. Theophilus, born at Donington Nov. 12, 1696. 5. Katherine-Marie, born at Donington Feb. 13, 1697. 6. Ferdinando, born at Donington Oct. 22, 1699. 7. Margaret, born at Donington Feb. 15, 1700.

The preceding, and also the following fragment, appear to have been written by this noble Earl:

" . . . . . for a licence to go to St. Germain's for such a time as the Queen (the King being then in the Low Countries) should permit. In return to which I received a letter from that earl that I should repair forthwith to London; upon which, and for some other reasons, I immediately went to town, and on May . . . 1692, I went to Whitehall, to the Secretary's office; where, being examined before the Cabinet Council, I was dismissed that time. But the next morning I was taken into custody by a serjeant at arms, and the following night committed to the Tower for high treason; Robert lord Lucas being then governor of that place. And though there was no information of any treason sworn against me, yet I was detained near four months prisoner, and then released only on bail, and was not discharged till Michaelmas term—that the House of Peers, taking notice of the oppression, I was discharged of my recognizance. After this I made my residence at Donington as formerly; and think myself happy in that retirement.— . . . . At that time the French drew down their fleet to La Hogue, with a great number of troops, having intentions to make a descent on England, though prevented by an engagement at sea, wherein they received considerable loss."

P. 606. Elizabeth countess-dowager of Moira, and Baroness Hungerford in her own right, died at Moira-house, Dublin, April 12, 1808, in her 76th year. "The illustrious birth, the superior en-

[1] Founders' Kinsmen at New College.
[2] There was one sir Henry Sacheverell made knight banneret by king Henry VIII. in his expedition to Guyenne in France, in the former part of his reign. See Lord Herbert's Life of that King. W. Oldys, Norroy.

dowments,

dowments, the admirable qualities of head as well as heart, which so peculiarly distinguished the late Countess-dowager of Moira, demand a more ample delineation than my limits will allow. But it is no adulatory language to say that she was truly an ornament to her sex, to the exalted sphere in which she moved, to Ireland, which, though not her native country, she most truly loved, and indeed to that enlightened period of society in which it was her lot to have been born. She was uncommonly gifted: great powers of memory, great quickness of intellect, and a peculiarly easy yet splendid elocution, with which she adorned whatever subject she touched upon, whether the mere passing events of the day, the various topicks of literature, or those useful arts by which the community is benefited, and the resources of a nation enlarged. Her acquaintance with such branches of knowledge was by no means limited or superficial; on the contrary, some learned Societies have borne respectful testimony to her acquirements in this particular, and to the real utility which flowed from the productions of her active and discerning genius. She was married to the late Earl of Moira in Feb. 1752, and resided in Dublin, or the North of Ireland (with the exception one year in France), for the long period of 56 years. Let those who remember what Moira-house was in the earlier days of that period, when she led and reflected a grace upon every beneficial fashion; when she cultivated the fine arts; when she rendered her house the favourite spot where every person of genius or talents in Dublin, or who visited Dublin, loved most to resort to:—let such persons say whether Moira-house, and its most illustrious Lady, as well as its truly noble and beneficent Lord, deserve not every panegyrick that gratitude can bestow. She was the last in a direct line of the great name of Hastings — the last!! a word which, when so applied, every liberal Nature will dwell upon with melancholy sensations, even to enthusiasm — such are, perhaps, the universal feelings of mankind in favour of exalted birth, which a vain-glorious philosophy never can eradicate, that when a race of Nobility, distinguished by the length of years during which they wore their honours uninterrupted, is finally terminated, the extinction of such a family is regarded, not without a generous sympathy; but when the tomb closes on a Noble Matron, the representative of a great House, with whose history the best and perhaps most inspiring images of our earliest days are associated, and herself not inferior to any in that history, it is scarcely possible even for a stranger not to hang over such a tomb without every emotion of sorrow, of regret, and of veneration. Such sentiments may ill accord with a frivolous and, in some respects, a selfish age. Be it so—yet this age, even under the influence of a more than iron war and much bigotry, has not lost " all its original brightness," but retains much of its good old virtues undiminished. It possesses domestic charity at least; and those who know how to appreciate charity will learn to venerate the memory of the good Countess of Moira, for in truth she may be said to have been charity itself. Never did there exist in the human bosom a more feeling heart, a disposition more sympathizing with, or more truly alive to, the miseries of her fellow-creatures. Many respectable emigrants from France at this day, who in her have lost their best benefactress, and the poor, the unhappy, and the forlorn, who during her long and valuable life were rendered less so, of this can bear the most ample testimony. She had a strong resemblance, in many respects, to her ancestors: a lofty spirit, magnificence of disposition, untired hospitality — altogether she was a lady of other times; and when she mingled with society more than her increased infirmities would of late years allow, few persons ever beheld her without something of more heroic days passing in indistinct yet splendid array before the imagination. In the reception of persons of the first distinction at her house, there was an air, a dignity, which will hardly be equalled, and never can be surpassed. But the noble manner, the imposing ceremonial of life, leave but slight vestiges for remembrance, compared to those intrinsic and domestic virtues which give to the female sex their truest ornament. In all the private relations of life she was, to the utmost, valuable. Her maternal duties she fulfilled with the enlightened spirit, and more perhaps than the sensibility of a Cornelia. They could only be equalled by the unceasing assiduity, the soothing tenderness, the sweet and pious and filial regards, which accompanied her to her last hour — but sorrow is sacred, and the writer forbears. He can only add, that this imperfect tribute is the product of an hasty and anxious moment, the effusions of gratitude, resting indeed upon the basis of truth, but no exact delineation of Lady Moira's character. The style is warm, for it flows from the heart; and who that knew her could write of Lady Moira in a style which was inert and grovelling? Ireland will long have cause to regret — she cultivated her best interests — to the gentry she displayed an example of attachment to this country which they might well have imitated—to the peasantry of all descriptions she was a guardian friend — to every illiberal party distinction, whether arising from a false zeal for the State or Religion, she was an unprejudiced, enlightened opponent. From the contemplation of such a character it is indeed not easy to withdraw."

P. 606. The Hon. John Theophilus Rawdon, youngest son of the late Countess of Moira, died at Vienna, May 5, 1808 [1].

Ibid. To what has been stated in this page, I may now be allowed to add, that Lord Moira, choosing a military life, served in America, where he distinguished himself in several engagements, as Lieutenant-colonel, particularly at the battle fought near Camden, August 16, 1780, when the British forces gained a complete victory. Earl Cornwallis, who commanded the British army, makes very honourable mention of his Lordship's courage and ability on that occasion, not only in the public thanks which he gave to the officers and soldiers after the battle, but likewise in his dispatches to government. On his return home he was created an English Peer, by the title of Lord Rawdon, March 5, 1783; and, in 1789, succeeded to the estates of his uncle Francis earl of Huntingdon. He has since taken an active part in public life; and has had several military commands of importance. He has uniformly possessed the confidence of his Royal Highness the Prince Regent; and frequently taken a conspicuous and useful part in the business of the House of Lords; among which his name will always stand recorded for his benevolent and persevering exertions on the Debtor and Creditor Bill. His Lordship was promoted to the rank of Colonel in the army, Nov. 20, 1782, and the command of the 105th regiment of foot, and one of the aides-de-camp to his Majesty. He was promoted a Major-general in 1793; Commander in chief in Scotland 1805; Constable of the Tower 1806; and Master-general of the ordnance 1806-7. His Lordship was invested with the Order of the Garter in June 1812; and in December had the important and honourable appointment of Governor General of India. His Lordship married, July 12, 1804, Flora Muir Campbell, in her own right countess of Loudon, by whom he has issue: 1. Flora-Elizabeth, born 1806; 2. a son, born Feb. 20, 1807, died an infant; 3. George-Augustus-Francis, lord Rawdon, born Feb. 4, 1808; 4. a daughter, born Sept. 1, 1809; 5. a daughter, born April 15, 1810.—His Lordship's proper titles are, Baron Hastings, Hungerford, Newmarch, Botreaux, Molins, and Moels; also Lord Rawdon, of Rawdon, in the county of York; Earl of Moira in Ireland.

P. 614. *add,* A mineral water, of a very salubrious nature, has been discovered on Ashby-Woulds.

---

[1] Gent. Mag. vol. LXXVIII. pp. 463. 651.

New

New warm and cold baths have, in consequence, been erected, and it is expected, that they will become a place of great resort.

A new village has been built by the Earl of Moira (by name *Moira Town*), near his Lordship's iron foundry, coal-works, &c. upon Ashby Woulds. It consists of 50 houses, built with stone; it is said that 50 more houses are to be built in this new village, in the parish of Ashby-de-la-Zouch.

P. 617. Mr. J. Dinwoodie, English and Mathematical Schoolmaster at Ashby-de-la-Zouch, died in 1812. He was a native of Scotland, educated at Dumfries, and about eight years ago, on the extension of the uses of that antient and wealthy endowment, was selected from eleven other candidates, and nominated by the Earl of Moira to the appointment, then first created. To the acquirements and unwearied application of Mr. D. the institution owes much of its present high character; accidental circumstances having till lately deprived it of the advantages of a classical master (now, however, happily supplied by Rev. R. W. Lloyd, Fellow of St. John's college, Cambridge). The Trustees, to perpetuate their sense of Mr. D.'s extraordinary merits, have ordered a monument to be erected to his memory.

Ibid. Mr. S. Webster, solicitor, of Ashby-de-la-Zouch, died December 17, 1812, in his 54th year.

P. 625. col. 2, l. 8 from bottom, *add to the epitaphs at* Ashby-de-la-Zouch:

In the chancel:

" In memory of the Rev. John Prior, B. D. vicar of this parish, and of Packington, and master of the grammar-school in this town. He died October 15, 1803, aged 74. Also of Anne his wife, who died July 20, 1774, aged 43."

On a tomb erected on the South of the tower:

" In a vault underneath lie interred the remains of Ellis Shipley Pestell, esq. late of this place, Solicitor; who died on the 2d day of April 1809, in the 63d year of his age. A gentleman of great benevolence, most pleasing manners, address, and of superior acquirements in polite literature: he was beloved by an extensive circle of valuable friends; and earned and retained the esteem of his numerous Clients, by his professional knowledge, zeal, and activity in their service.—Also of his father and mother, Charles and Jane Pestell; the former of whom (for many years a Solicitor of eminence in this place) died on the 2d day of August 1783, aged 62, and the latter on the 18th day of November, 1786, aged 68 years."

P. 632. col. 1, l. 80. *add* John Brinsley, a nonconformist Divine, was born at Ashby-de-la-Zouch, in Leicestershire, in 1600. His father was also a divine of the puritan kind, and master of the school at Ashby. The noted astrologer William Lilly, was at his school in 1613. His mother was sister to Bishop Hall. After being educated by his father, he was admitted of Emanuel College, Cambridge, at the age of thirteen and a half. Having resided there three or four years, he attended his uncle Hall, then dean of Worcester, as his amanuensis, to the synod of Dort, and after his return, resumed his studies at Cambridge, and being elected scholar of the house, resided there until he took his degrees. When ordained, he preached first at Preston, near Chelmsford, then at Somerleyton in Suffolk, and lastly was called to Yarmouth, on the election of the township, but his principles being objected to by Dr. Harsnet, bishop of Norwich, he could only preach on the week days at a country village adjoining, whither the people of Yarmouth followed him, until the township applied to the king for his licence for Mr. Brinsley to preach in Yarmouth. This being granted by his majesty, he remained there until the restoration, when he was ejected with his numerous brethren, who refused the terms of conformity. Although a man of moderate sentiments, he appears to have been inflexible in the points which divided so large a body of clergymen from the church, and is said to

have refused considerable preferment to induce him to remain in it. He is praised by his biographer for piety, and extensive learning in theology. He died Jan. 22, 1665. He wrote several treatises enumerated by Calamy, none of which, we believe, are now much known. He had a son, Robert, who was ejected from the university, and afterwards studied and took his degree of M. D. at Leyden, and practised at Yarmouth[1].

P. 647. *add to rectors of* Belton:
Rev. Charles Sandby, 1807.
Rev. J. Eddowes, 1810.
Rev. Francis Harris, vicar of Belton, died 1814.

P. 661. col. 1, l. 14. *for* earl of Leicester, *read* Winton.

P. 702. Mr. John Smith, of Newbold-Saucey, a worthy farmer and grazier, died in 1812.

P. 717. Mrs. Eliz.-Rose Jolliffe, wife of Hylton Jolliffe, M. P. for Petersham, died at Rakedale Jan. 13, 1809, aged 24. The remains of this very amiable young lady were interred on the 25th, in the family-vault at Bredon.

P. 747. Thomas Cheslyn, esq. of Diseworth, died Jan. 21, 1814, in his 78th year. He was the youngest and last surviving of 21 children of the late Robert and Cave Cheslyn, of Langley Priory, and father of the late high sheriff for Leicestershire.

P. 756. col. 1, l. 65. Mrs. Mary Lowdham died 1788, not 1778.

P. 779. Thomas Fisher, esq. several years owner of Caldicote-hall, co. Warwick, died at Castle Donington, aged 84, May 9, 1810.

Ibid. Mr. Charles Best died in 1810, at Donington Park Hall, aged 51. He was one of the oldest domesticks in Lord Moira's establishments; he attended him when Lord Rawdon, in the American War, and was with him when his Lordship distinguished himself so conspicuously; he was likewise taken prisoner with him by the Count de Grasse, when on their return. The Americans artfully endeavoured to have his Lordship delivered over to them, but the Count, being acquainted of the sacrifice they purposed committing, refused to acquiesce; and to that cause must we attribute the Earl's friendship to the unfortunate exiles of that country.

Ibid. Mrs. Penelope Hearson; late wife of William Hearson, gent. died at Castle Donington, Sept. 30, 1809. She supported herself with exemplary fortitude under a severe indisposition for 15 days, without any kind of nutriment, solid or liquid.

P. 782. l. 15. Rev. Joseph Collier died at Castle Donington in May 1807, in his 81st year.

Ibid. *add to vicars of* Castle Donington:
Rev. J. Dalby, 1807.

Ibid. The Rev. T. W. Paterson died at Castle Donington, in his 43d year, Aug. 18, 1812. He was for many years minister of the independent congregations of Ashby-de-la-Zouch and Bardon. The Gospel which he had faithfully preached was his support under a long and painful affliction; to his numerous family the loss is irreparable, and his virtues will long remain in the recollection of all who have been honoured with his friendship.

P. 844. Mr. Marriot, who for more than thirty years kept a house at Hathern for the reception of insane patients, died in 1814.

P. 858. Mrs. Clifford, relict of John Clifford, esq. of Kegworth, co. Leicester, died at Sileby, aged 74, Sept. 11, 1814.

P. 895. Robert Steevens, gent. died at Loughborough in his 94th year, Dec. 21, 1808, much respected by his friends as a truly honest man, and a chearful companion. He was the last surviving son of William Steevens, of Quorndon, gent. and uncle to the present Dr. Steevens, whose family have resided at Quorndon, and possessed a considerable property there, for near a century and a half. See the Quorndon Registers, vol. III. p. 102.

Ibid. Mr. John Farrow died at Loughborough, in his 69th year, December 23, 1809, much

---

[1] Chalmers's Biographical Dictionary, vol. VII.

respected.

respected. He was one of Mr. Bakewell's earliest followers in the improvement of the breed of sheep, from whose original ideas he never departed.

P. 895. Henry Cropper, esq. formerly an eminent attorney at Loughborough, died June 8, 1812, in his 80th year.

Ibid. John Burkitt, gent. died at Loughborough, at an advanced age, January 15, 1814.

Ibid. Mr. William Adams died at Loughborough, in his 70th year, Feb. 26, 1814. He was a very worthy, inoffensive man, who for many years carried on the profession of a bookseller with unblemished reputation.

P. 899. Nicholas Buckley, esq. of Normanton-hill, near Loughborough, one of the oldest and most eminent breeders of the new Leicestershire sheep, died June 20, 1814.

P. 901. Mr. Wyrley, in 1603, noticed the following epitaph on a tomb in the body of Loughborough church:

"Hic jacet Gilb'tus Mering, generosus, qui ob. 15 Febr. 1481."

P. 911. Mrs. Sarah Bennet, of Woodthorpe, died March 27, 1804, aged 70, of a cancer in her breast; having lived and died in the same house where her ancestors had resided for more than a century and a half; and, as was the then custom of the manor, only paying a new year's gift of a couple of fowls annually to the Herrick family for the house and land they occupied. She was hospitable, and of a cheerful disposition; had never travelled 20 miles from home; had a natural turn for poetry, and was fond of reading. Her way of life was very singular; and, by strict œconomy she amassed a handsome property, which devolved to her nephew and nieces.

P. 954. The whole-sheet Pedigree of Babington, (with which I have been favoured by the Rev. Matthew-Drake Babington) given with this Volume, is to be inserted between pages 954 and 955 of Volume III.

P. 1029. *add to the* Chambers Pedigree: Rev. Charles Chambers, rector of South Kilworth, married Mary Peterson, and had issue: James-Peterson Chambers, Samuel, Maria, Judith-Martha, Charles-William, Catherine, Matilda, and Joseph-Thomas.

P. 1038. Dr. Gery, rector of Swebston and Stoney Stanton, and in the commission of the peace of Leicestershire, died, at an advanced age, August 9, 1722.

P. 1048. *add to note* [4]. The relict of Mr. John Throsby died at Leicester, Oct. 7, 1813.

P. 1051. The Rev. John Llwyd died at his rectory, Swithland, March 16, 1814, in his 77th year. He had been nearly 53 years rector.

P. 1073. My early and very kind Patron the late Bishop Hurd, died May 28, 1808; and I have since endeavoured to do justice to his memory in another publication: see full particulars of his Life and Writings, in the "Literary Anecdotes of the Eighteenth Century," article HURD, General Index, vol. VII.

P. 1096. col. 2, l. 6 from bottom, Sir Charles Grave Hudson married, secondly, Jan. 13, 1806, the eldest daughter of the late Peter Holford, esq. one of the Masters in Chancery, with 50,000*l*.; and died at his seat at Wanlip, in his 84th year, Oct. 24, 1813.

P. 1098. l. ult. Rev. Robert Burnaby, LL. B. rector of Wanlip, died April 2, 1807. He was in the commission of the peace for the county of Leicester.

Add to rectors of Wanlip: Rev. John Anderson, 1807.—He died Feb. 3, 1813, at Wanlip, after a long and afflicting illness, aged 59. He was presented to the rectory of that parish 1807, vicar of St. Nicholas, Leicester, and chaplain to the County-gaol. He was a sound and orthodox minister of the Church of England, both with respect to its discipline and doctrine; and distinguished himself, throughout life, by his Christian benevolence and amiable attention to the charities of domestic life; his good-nature, and unoffending and unassuming manners, having endeared him to all to whom his modest merit was known.

Rev. Henry Barnes, of Dunchurch, 1813.

P. 1126. William Averne, gent. a liberal benefactor to the poor, died at Thringston in 1814.

P. 1127. l. 1. *for* Stapleford, *read* Stapleton.

P. 1138. col. 1, l. 33. *for* earl of Shaftesbury, *read* Shrewsbury.

P. 1148. Mrs. Anne Mason died at Ipswich, Jan. 10, 1806, aged 73.

Ibid. Emma-Mason Morris was married June 2, 1808, to the Rev. Thomas Leigh, M. A. rector of St. Magnus, London Bridge, and of Wickham Bishop, Essex.

APPENDIX. P. 69. col. 2, l. 32. *for* Leesthorpe, *read* Stapleford.

Ib. l. 34. *for* Stapleford, *read* Staunton Harold.

P. 70. col. 3. *read* Grey, lady Katharine, 673.

P. 71. col. 2. *read* Hurd, Bp. 1059.—Mershden, John de, 1059.—Palmer of Wanlip, pedigree, 1101. Roby pedigree, 784.—Shuttlewood, John, 938.—Staunton pedigree, 704.

VOLUME IV.

GUTHLAXTON HUNDRED.

I have great pleasure in being able to introduce, as a FRONTISPIECE to GUTHLAXTON Hundred, an excellent Portrait of my very kind and much-respected Friend, RICHARD FARMER, D. D. Master of Emanuel College, Cambridge, and Principal Librarian of that University; painted by G. Romney, at the request of the College; and engraved by J. Jones.—See a memoir of him in vol. IV. p. 943.

P. 31. Rev. Thomas Manners died in the New Road, Mary-le-bonne, in 1812. He was rector of Ayleston and Willoughby, co. Lincoln, second son of the late Lord William Manners, and uncle to the present Sir William Manners, bart. He was B.A. of Merton-college, Oxford; was presented by the Duke of Rutland in 1755 to the Rectory of Ayleston; and in 1760 took the degree of B. C. L. to enable him to hold (by dispensation) the rectory of Silk Willoughby. He had held Ayleston more than 57 years, and Willoughby more than 52.

P. 61. The Rev. Thomas Greaves died Aug. 21, 1806, in his 71st year. He was rector of Broughton-Astley, and in the commission of the peace for the county of Leicester; a tender husband, kind father, good master, an upright magistrate, and much regretted.—His relict died at Cossington, aged 75, Nov. 25, 1811.

P. 63. Epitaphs in Sutton meeting-house yard:
" Rev. Robert Gilbert, pastor of Sutton, died Dec. 17, 1742, in his 27th year."
" Rev. Clayton-Mordaunt Cracherode, pastor of Sutton, died Nov. 22, 1807, aged 49."
These Epitaphs are given at length in Gent. Mag. vol. LXXXI. p. 424.

P. 64. Thomas Horneby, exonerated of an accompt of the outgoings and profits of the king's rent called *Princecourt,* to the amount of four marks a year and upwards, 3 Hen. IV. [1]

P. 79. Pedigree of Caldecote, last descent, *for* Rev. William Damer, *read* Rev. Thomas James, D. D.

P. 103. Mrs. Sarah Wells, widow, died at Little Claybrook, in 1814, aged 92.

P. 104. Thomas-Edward Dicey, of Claybrook-hall, was married, Nov. 10, 1814, to Anne-Mary, youngest daughter of James Stephen, esq. M.P.

P. 105. Mr. Thomas Blockley, sen. a respectable farmer and grazier, died at Great Claybrook, in 1814, in his 76th year.

P. 119. Richard Warner, esq. of Ullesthorpe, died in June 1804. He possessed a very superior understanding, well cultivated by an extensive and judicious course of reading, together with strict integrity of heart, a disposition truly amiable, and all the graces of the Christian life. For many years he devoted the leisure hours of Sunday to the instruction of poor children in Scriptural knowledge; and his active benevolence was conspicuous on all occasions; with which his truly Christian faith enabled him to meet death without dismay, after sustaining a lingering illness with exemplary fortitude.

P. 124. col. 2. Jonathan Grundy, esq. eldest son of the late Jonathan Grundy, of Wigston Parva, died October 29, 1803, aged 59, at the Lightwoods, co. Stafford.

P. 150. Rev. Robert Marriott, LL. D. rector of Cottesbach 1767, and of Gilmorton 1787, died at Cottesbach, aged 67, July 18, 1808.
Ibid. *after* Pedigree of Bent, *read* See p. 144.

P. 154. To the intended Cardinal college at Oxford, it was proposed to impropriate the parsonages of Dunton Basset, Foston, Scalford, and Rakedale[2].

P. 172. " *May* 7th, 1651.
" Fosston.—Whereas this Committee is certified

that the living of Fosston, in the County of Leicester, is not worth aboue fifty pounds a yeare, and Mr. Charles Asforby, Minister there, having approued himselfe to this Committee, It is ordered by this Committee, that the yearely sume of thirty poundes be graunted by the Trustees to the said Mr. Asforby, for increase of his mainteñnce, to comence from the 25th of March last. And the Trustees for mainteñnce of Ministers are to pay the same accordingly, out of the accruing rents and revenues in them vested. " HUM. EDWARDES.   THO. CHALONER.
EDM. ASHE.   AUG. SKYNNER[3]."
M. OLDSWORTH.

Ibid. col. 2, l. 19. *correct thus :* The present value in the King's books of the rectory of Foston is 14*l.* 2*s.* 3½*d.*

P. 194. *add to the rectors of* Gilmorton : Rev. John Brewin, 1808, *vice* Marriott, deceased.

P. 206. Joseph Thomas Chambers, midshipman R. N. and youngest son of Rev. Charles Chambers of S. Kilworth, died Oct. 21, 1812, aged 16.

P. 206. James Harryman Holmes, esq. captain in the Leicestershire Militia, son of the Rev. Mr. Holmes, of Normanton, Notts, died at Woburn, on his route from his regiment into Leicestershire, May 7, 1810. He had lately married the eldest daughter of the Rev. Charles Chambers.

P. 210. I am indebted to the Rev. Mr. Ridge, for the following " Extracts from the Churchwardens Accompt Book, for Kimcote and Walton;" in the possession of Mr. J. Lucas, surgeon, of Kimcote, who is of a very old family resident there :

For the year 1606.—Thomas Cave for the rector, and John Sturges for the parish, churchwardens.

In Thomas Cave's Accompt :

	£.	s.	d.
For bread and wine for the communions	0	6	2
For repairing the church, mending the seats, &c. various items.			

In John Sturges' accompt—the same year :

	£.	s.	d.
For bread and wine, the 12th of August	0	2	1
For bread and wine for the communion	0	1	4
For mending the church gate - - -	0	0	6
To Lane, for mending the fore bell -	0	2	0
To Lane the carpenter, in parte of payment, for mending the seats, &c.	0	3	6
To exhibiting the copy of the Register	0	1	0
For a book bought at Leicester - - -	0	2	0
For paving the church - - - - -	0	1	10
For tiles for the same work - - -	0	3	0
For the communion, Jan. 4 - - - -	0	2	7
For the communion, March 29 - - -	0	2	8

1607. Thos. Elliott and Thos. Coton, churchwardens.

In the accompt of Thomas Coton :
Various items for timber, &c. for the church.

	£.	s.	d.
For wine for the communion - - -	0	2	0
For wine at another communion -	0	2	0
For bread and wine at Easter - - -	0	2	7

In the accompt of Thos. Elliott, for the same year :

	£.	s.	d.
For lead for the North isle of the church	8	3	4
For the communion at Easter - - -	0	4	4

1608. Thos. Cooke and Thos. Tod, churchwardens.

In the accompt of Thomas Cooke :

	£.	s.	d.
For bread and wine for one communion	0	4	5
For another communion - - - - -	0	4	6
Paid for the pewter flagon - - - -	0	8	2
Give for bread and wine, for Knaptoft	0	2	0
For the communion at Easter - - -	0	9	0

Various items for repairs of the church, &c.

In the accompts of Thomas Tod :

	£.	s.	d.
For bread and wine at one communion	0	5	5

Memorandum. That (beside diverse of Knaptoft Fee, as appeareth upon the aforewritten accompt of Thomas Cooke) there remain due to the parish, and yet are unpaid, and are to be collected by the

churchwardens

---

churchwardens succeeding, to the parishe's use, these sums following:

First, for the two levies aforesaid, due by
Richard Burdett - - - - - - - - 0 4 8
Item, the half-year's rent of the year
1608, for Sweetlad's house - - - - - 0 1 3
Item, the year's rent of anno 1608, for
Hardiman's house - - - - - - - 0 2 6
And of Thomas Cooke upon his ac-
count as aforesaid - - - - - - - 0 0 1¼

1609. Thos. Hall and Foulke Button, churchwardens.

In the accompt of Foulke Button:
Paid for bread and wine at the commu-
nion after Midsummer - - - - - - 0 2 6
For the communion after Christmas - 0 3 4
In the accompt of Thomas Hall:
For the communion for Michaelmas - 0 3 7
For the communion for Palm Sunday - 0 3 8
Provision for communion, Easter-day - 0 5 10

Memorandum. That the rent of the church-meddow in the year 1610 was collected by Valentine Blockley, by the permission of Richard Putt and of Robert Dash, being then churchwardens, and the same rent of 40s. was bestowed in scouring and cleansing the brook there, and by him to be accounted for at the pleasure of the parishioners.

1610. Rich. Putt and Robt. Dash, churchwardens.

In the accompt of Robert Dash:
Item, for the communion on Palm Sunday 0 2 8
In the accompt of Richard Putt:
Item, for the communion, July 29 - - 0 3 7
Item, for the communion, Sept. 30 - 0 4 3
Item, for the communion, Dec. 29 - - 0 4 2
Item, for the communion at Easter - 0 6 11

1611 and 1612. William Wolfe and Henry Hartshorne, churchwardens.

Anno 1612, Aug. 13. An action was commenced, by consent of the parishioners, by William Wolfe and Henry Harteshorne, then churchwardens, by way of presentment at the Lord Bishop's visitation then held at Harborowe, against Robert Wormlaughton, of Walton, refusing to pay the levies at that time challenged by the said churchwardens, so many of them as were then due; to which presentment he pleading himself not bound to pay them; the said churchwardens averred the presentment, and thereupon proceeded in the tryal of that action. The account of the charges of which suit hereafter followeth.

To all Mayors, Sheriffs, Bailiffs, Constables, and other his Majesty's Officers, to whom it may apply:

Forasmuch as complaint hath been made unto us, that this Sunday morning, being the 7th of this instant November, about one of the clock, his Majesty's packet of letters was intercepted, and forcibly taken from the postboy, by four horsemen, in scarlet coloured coates or cloakes, having pistols by their sides, and some of these horses being gray, and bay coloured, which was done and executed between Stone and Lichfield, to the great prejudice of his Majesty's affairs in these unquiet times in Ireland. These are, in his Majesty's name, straitly to charge and command you, and every of you, that forthwith you cause diligent search to be made for the offenders aforesaid; that you stay, and cause to be examined, all suspicious persons, and that you be careful to send this hue and cry up and down, and especially towards Tamworth, and so Eastward forward, that his Majesty and the State may perceive that the service of the K. and the Commonwealth is not neglected. Thereof fail not at your peril. Given under the hands and seals of the said City of Lichfield, this seventh day of November, 1641.
To Whittington.

Tamworth.   JOHN BARNES, bailiff.
(L. S.)   Polesworth.   RICH. DYOT.
Grindon.
Hinkley.   And so forward.   (L. S.)

This hue and cry was brought to Kimcott by Tho. Dun, of Morton, on Wednesday morning, Nov. 20,

about 7 o'clock; and presently it was sent to Thorp, by Richard Dash, and search made diligently.

The Protestation ordered in Parliament, 5to Maii, 1641, was taken and subscribed in the parish church of Kimcott, on Sunday the 12th of September, 1641, according to the directions therewith published, by those whose names are underwritten.

Georgius Teonge, rector ibidem.
[Signed also by 52 of his neighbours.]
These Protestations were taken: G. Teonge, rector ibi.
Thom. Button; Edward Marsden; Richard Dash.

P. 211. Rev. John Wootton died at Kimcote, Oct. 12, 1810, aged 64. He was formerly master of the Grammar School at Tuxford, Notts. and curate of Kimcote.

Ibid. The Rev. Robert Miller, B. C. L. rector of Kimcote, died Nov. 14, 1810, in his 72d year. He was also vicar of St. Nicholas, Warwick, and chaplain to the earl of Warwick.

P. 223. *In the memoir of* Bp. Watson, l. 12, *add*, F. R. S. 1709.

P. 230. col. 1, l. 31. *for* Mary Noone, &c. *read* Anne Noone, widow, daughter of John Burdett, died Sept. 26. 1717, aged 84.

P. 238. "*Novemb.* 13, 1650.

"Knyghton.—Whereas the Committee for Plundered Ministers have formerly graunted unto Mr. John Dutton, Minister of Knighton, in com. Lecester, the yearely sume of five and twenty pounds reserved to the Prebendary of Lincolne out of the impropriate rectory of Knighton aforesaid, for the increase of his maintenance, this Committee being certified by Justices of Peace that the said living is worth but five pounds *per annum*, and the said Mr. Dutton having approved himselfe to this Committee by good certificats from approved Ministers, to be a man deserving the same; It is ordered by this Committee, and they doe thinke fitt to continue the same augmentacon unto the said Mr. Dutton. And the Trustees for maintenance of Ministers are to allow and pay the said sume to the said Mr. Dutton yearely, out of the rents and profitts of the said rectory as it shal be due and payable, provided that such sumes of money as are due and payable out of the said rectory, and the said rectorie stands charged with, for pious and charitable uses, be first paid.
FRANCIS ROUS [1]."

P. 243. The Rev. George Mason, upwards of forty years rector of Leire, died there in January 1808, in his 76th year.

P. 245. Lady Grantham, who is erroneously stated to have died in 1788, is still alive.

Ibid. Elizabeth, 7th countess of Kent, died 1651.

P. 260. col. 1. Mr. Robert-Bell Wheeler, of Old Town, Stratford upon Avon, will accept my best acknowledgments, for a transcript with which he has favoured me, of the Certificate of Chantries in the Counties of Warwick and Leicester, from an original Survey which he possesses, and which probably belonged formerly to the Augmentation-office, where there is now no copy of it among the Records. The whole of it is, however, already interspersed in the various parishes, described in these Volumes, from a transcript made by the Rev. Samuel Carte early in the Eighteenth Century, and said by him to be then in the Augmentation-office.

P. 265. The Honourable and now Very Reverend Henry Ryder obtained a Canonry of Windsor in 1808; and in 1812 the Deanery of Wells; and has frequently distinguished himself as an animated Preacher on public occasions.

P. 325. Mr. John Waldron, grazier, died at Oadby, aged 80, January 28, 1814. See a character of him in the Gentleman's Magazine, vol. LXXXIV. part i. p. 301.

P. 334. Anne Jervis, relict of the late Rev. W. Jervis of Lutterworth, and mother of Charles Jervis, esq. of Stoney Stanton, and of Hinckley, died at Stanton Oct. 21, 1814.

---

[1] "Acts of the Committee for Plundered Ministers," in Sion College Library.

P. 340.

P. 340. Rev. Edward Sherrier, minister of Shawell, died March 3, 1731.

P. 341. col. 1, l. 4 from bottom, *Add to the Account of Sir Edward Leigh's Books:*

" 6. The Saints encouragement in evil times ; or, observations concerning the Martyrs in general. London, 1648, 51," 8vo.

P. 344. To the children of sir Robert Wilmot, of Chaddesden, bart. *add,* Robert-Roberts, born 1799; Henry-Sacheverell, born 1801; Richard-Coke, born 1802; Maria; Mead; John; Willett; and Edmund.

Ibid. Edward-Sacheverell Wilmot, rector of Langley, co. Derby, was educated at Rugby school, from whence he was removed to St. John's College, Cambridge, 1784, where he took the degree of B.A. 1788; M.A. 1791. He died in 1809.

Ibid. Julia, the first wife of sir Robert Wilmot, of Osbaston, died in 1788. By this lady the baronet had issue two sons and a daughter; Robert (who married Anne Horton, and has two sons and a daughter); William; and Elizabeth.—By the second lady sir Robert has Mary-Anne; Charles-Foley; and other children.

Ibid. My benevolent and highly-esteemed friend John Wilmot, esq. having taken the name of *Eardley,* by royal license, in 1811 ; I shall briefly enumerate his descendants :

Frances, daughter of Samuel Sainthill, co. Surrey; marr. April 20, 1776 ; first wife.	John Eardley-Wilmot, of Berkswell, co. Warwick, esq. born in April 1749.	Sarah-Anne, dau. of col. Anthony Haslam ; second wife.

John-Eardley, born 1783.	Eliz.-Emma, da. of C.-H. Parry, M. D. of Bath.	Fanny. Maria-Emma.	Ara-bel-la.	John Holt, ma. jun. Rev. Guy of Bryan, rector of S. Totten-ham, co. Derby.	Selina, ma.	Anne, and Percival, di. infants.

Emma, born 1809.	John-Eard-ley, born 1810.	Fred.-Marow, born 1812.	Edw.-Revell, 1814.	John-Wilmot, born 1814.

Ibid. Gen. Blomefield (now sir Thomas Blomefield, bart.) has a son, William-Thomas, born Mar. 6, 1791.

P. 378. col. 1, l. 29. Fig. 4. Or, three chevrons Gules, are the arms of Clare earl of Gloucester.

P. 382. Thomas Irvin, gent. died at Great Wigston, in his 87th year, Jan. 13, 1814.

P. 383. Rev. James Pigott died at Great Wigston, Dec. 28, 1812, aged 74. He was educated in the Grammar-school of Christ's Hospital, London, and at Pembroke-college, Cambridge; B.A. 1758; M.A. 1761; in which year he was presented by the Governors of Christ's Hospital to the vicarage of Great Wigston (which he held for more than half a century). He published one Sermon, intituled, "The Age of Methuselah, and the House of Mourning, Gen. v. 27, 1762," 4to; and was presented in 1769 to the vicarage of St. Nicholas in Leicester, which he resigned in 1778. He was also elected head-master of the free-grammar-school at Leicester in 1769, which he resigned in 1799.—His first wife died at Aldershot-lodge, Surrey, Oct. 17, 1809, aged 61.—His son-in-law, John-Freestone Wilson, esq. son of Mr. Wilson, of Doughty-street, London, died at Leicester, in the prime of life, May 15, 1810.

Ibid. *add to the rectors of* Great Wigston : Rev. W. H. Walker, B.A. 1813.

Ibid. note [8], *for* M.A. 1578, *read* 1758.

P. 393. H. N. Gamble, esq. died in 1814, at Willoughby Waterless.

P. 394. The third volume of the new edition of Hutchins's " History of Dorsetshire" enables me to make the following additions to the Pedigree of Fielding: Sarah, wife of lieut. Edmund Fielding, was buried at East Stour, co. Dorset, April 18, 1718. —*Correct the account of the children of* lieut. Edmund and Sarah Fielding thus : Henry Fielding, the Novelist, was born in 1707.—Sarah was born Nov. 8, and baptized Nov. 23, 1710, at East Stour.— Anne, born June 1, bapt. June 22, 1713; buried at East Stour Aug. 6, 1716.—Beatrice, bapt. July 29, 1714.—Edmund, bapt. April 22, 1716.

P. 396. col. 2, l. 7. *read* P. 107.

P. 402. James Hall, esq. died in Bloomsbury place, July 14, 1809, in his 40th year. He was surveyor to St. Bartholomew's Hospital, and to the Sun Fire-office, &c. &c. ; a gentleman of the most amiable manners, and of great professional abilities. He was the third (and last surviving) son of Henry Hall, esq. who for many years was Principal Clerk to the Commissioners of Sewers, Lamps, and Pavements for the City of London, and also Surveyor to the Sun Fire office. He was of an antient family, long seated at Asfordby in Leicestershire, and collaterally related to the pious and learned Bishop Hall.

P. 416. col. 2, l. 46. *for* P. 1110, *read* P. 1120.

P. 423. *read* Belgrave of Preston pedigree, 207. —Gore pedigree, 128.—Hutchinson, Dr. Charles, memoirs of, 134.—*For* James, Charles, *read* Jenner, Charles.—Jenner, C. memoirs of, 135.—Maidwell, John, memoirs of, 134.—Mason, Maydwell, epitaph, 400.

SPARKENHOE HUNDRED.

It is with the utmost pleasure that I present to my Readers, as a FRONTISPIECE to this HUNDRED, a Portrait of the noble Owner of Bradgate Park, the inheritor of the antient Barony of Groby, the friend of human-kind—the benevolent and noble Peer, GEORGE-HARRY GREY, Earl of Stamford and Warrington, &c. &c. from a Plate inscribed to his Lordship's virtues by the ROYAL HUMANE SOCIETY OF LONDON; an Institution sacred to Philanthropy, and of which this noble Earl has for many years been the highly-valued President. The Portrait is copied from a mezzotinto after a Painting by Romney.

Part II. P. viii. col. 1, l. 12. *for* Coleman, Henry, esq. Leicester, *read* Market Harborough.

Ibid. *add to* Subscribers :

Brydges, Sir Samuel Egerton, Bart. K. J. M. P.

Bagster, Mr. Samuel, Bookseller, Strand.

Haggard, William-Henry, esq. Park-st. Westminst.

Lisle, Rev. Dr.

Long, Edward-Beeston, esq. Hampton Lodge, near Farnham.

Power, John, esq. Atherstone.

Ray, Robert, esq. F. S. A. Gower-street.

P. 418. col. 1. l. 53. Mrs. Frances Charnock died at Bath, December 3, 1808 ; and her husband, John Charnock, esq. July 16, 1809, aged 87.

P. 425. l. 4. It is here stated, on the (generally accurate) authority of the Rev. S. Carte, " that the High Sheriff of Leicestershire pays annually to the earl of Stamford 10*l.* for licence to come into the Hundred of Sparkenhoe, to execute any part of his office." On this a professional gentleman at Leicester, of great respectability, says, " No such payment is made, or was, I believe, ever before heard of ; I have served the office of under-sheriff myself, and seen it executed several times ; and have also inquired of most of the practisers here who have served it ; and all say the same thing. What could give rise to the idea I cannot conceive, unless by some blunder respecting a payment made by the Sheriff to the Steward of the Honor of Leicester, for the liberty of executing process within the *Duchy of Lancaster,* which, you know, includes or extends over considerable portions of the County, and I believe, more or less, all the Hundreds ; which payment used to be 8*l.* till lately, when it was raised to, I believe, about 20*l.* If you can devise any means of rectifying this mistake, I, and all I have talked with, hope and trust you will ; as otherwise it may possibly some time or other produce mischief, besides, at all events, now operating against the credit of the work itself ; to preserve which there is no one of your subscribers more anxious than,

Yours, &c. C. LOWDHAM."

P. 441. note [5], *for* " Middleton Cheyney, *Bucks,*" *read* " Middleton Cheney, *Northamptonshire.*"

Ibid. It may be worth referring the reader to what Mr. Whiston says, in his Memoirs of his Life and Writings, p. 17, of the School which Sir John Moore erected at Appleby, near Norton, Leicestershire.

shire, and of what *his* Father contributed toward bringing it about.

P. 443. Pedigree of Moore.—George Moore, esq. of Appleby, died June 11, 1813, aged 71.

Ibid. Susan, wife of George Moore, jun. and only daughter of John Drummond, esq. died at Snareston Lodge, after a few days' illness, in her 21st year, April 7, 1813.

Ibid. Rev. John Moore died at Appleby, Dec. 26, 1814, aged 66. He was of most engaging manners and most benevolent mind. He lived almost adored by the poor, beloved by his friends, and respected by all: correct in his religious faith, and exact in its duties, his piety was practical, and the first wish of his heart was to make mankind better and happier. The loss of no private individual can be more deeply felt or more sincerely lamented.

P. 453. Martha, youngest daughter of sir Edward Cradock Hartopp, bart. died July 8, 1812; and was buried at Aston Flamvile, on the 15th.

P. 466. Mr. Jonah Clarke, a very worthy man, died at Burbach, aged 85, in 1805. See a character of him in Gent. Mag. LXXV. 188.

P. 475. Pedigree of ONEBY, of Barwell, continued.

Judith Chester, died before 1709; first wife. = Robert Oneby, born 1665; died Feb. 1, 1720-1; married, secondly, Susannah Webb, who died July 2, 1743; leaving one son, Robert Oneby, of Lowdham, who died June 16, 1753.

1. Elizabeth, living 1719; married Robert Ryder, of Nuneaton, died s. p.
2. Robert, born 1690; ⎫
3. John, born 1695; ⎬ all died young.
4. Mary, born 1696; ⎪
6. Mary, born 1698; ⎪
7. Mary, born 1699; ⎭

5. Anthony Oneby, born 1697; died intestate, in September 1727. = Jane Major, administered to her husband's effects, Nov. 7, 1727; died in 1767.

1. Susannah, born 1724; will made July 14, proved Aug. 1, 1772. She devised one moiety of her freeholds to her sister, the other to the relations of her mother: but, not having passed a fine, her intentions were defeated, and her sister succeeded as heir at law.

3. Jane, born 1727; married, Aug. 16, 1749, to Wm. Frith; 2dly, 17.., to John Ailway, of Watford, surgeon (whose will was proved May 13, 1793). She died Oct. 6, 1812; and devised the manor of Barwell, and her other estates there, to Charles Kilby, of Watford, M. D.

2. Robert Oneby, born Feb. 24, 1725; died 1726.

P. 477. Mr. T. Bonsar, of Barwell, late of Coates, breeder, whose integrity and private judgment had made him greatly respected, died at his sister's at Broughton Sulney, in 1814, aged 76.

P. 478. note [6], *for* B. A. 1774, *read* 1747.—Note [9], *for* He was of New College, Oxford, M. A. 1773, *read* Rev. Simon Adams was of All Souls College, B. C. L. July 8, 1752.

P. 489. l. 2. *for* Deeds from the Chartulary of Coventry *Abbey,* read *Priory.* The "Abbatia" of Domesday Book led to the error.

P. 500. l. 2. Anthony Blackwall is said to have died 1726; but in p. 510, he died April 8, 1730. The latter is right, for he did not resign Clapham till June 1729.

P. 502. Mr. Wyrley in 1603 noticed the following epitaph at Bosworth:

"Hic jacet Maria Blount, quondam uxor Walteri Blount de Blount's Hall in com. Staff. filia et hæres Joh'is Sutton de Osbaston in com. Leic. arm. quæ quidem Maria ob. 11° Maii a° d'ni . . . . ."

P. 507. Pedigree of Dixie, last descent: Sir Beaumont Dixie, bart. died at Market Bosworth July 20, 1814, being only a few days arrived from France, where he had been a prisoner many years, having been brought up in the Royal Navy.

Ibid. Mrs. Margaret Dixie, relict of the late Rev. Beaumont Dixie, of St. Peter's, Derby, died July 11, 1810, in the presence of six of her children. On the 18th she was attended to the grave by two sons, four daughters, and eight grand-children.

P. 546. Mr. John Swinfen, father of the late Mr. John Swinfen of Leicester, died at Market Bosworth, in his 80th year, Feb. 12, 1810.

P. 554. col. 2, l. 19 from the bottom. Having requested Mr. Hutton's permission to re-publish his

interesting Account of the Battle of Bosworth Field, illustrated by some Engravings from the "History of Leicestershire;" and having asked whether he had any additions to make; my venerable Friend, in a very kind Answer, says,

"I paid a visit in July 1807 to Bosworth Field; but found so great an alteration since I saw it in 1788, that I was totally lost. The manor had been inclosed; the fences were grown up; and my prospect impeded. King Richard's Well, which figures in our Histories, was nearly obliterated; the swamp where he fell become firm land; and the rivulet proceeding from it, lost in an under-drain; so that future inspection is cut off. I wished to sleep in the room, at the Three Tuns, in Atherstone, that was the last in which Henry the Seventh slept prior to the battle; but was not permitted."

In a subsequent Letter, he adds,

"I have no other remarks to make upon my last visit to Bosworth Field, than those already communicated to you, but am pleased with your Additions to it. I cannot tell by what mistake the wood came to be 4 or 500 acres (see p. 554.): nor can I now call to mind what I conjectured it to be; so make it 4 or 5 acres, or any other number you may think more correct."

Thus far the original Historian of Bosworth Field; whose apprehensions, however, that the famous Well where Richard quenched his thirst will sink into oblivion, I am happy to observe, are totally done away, by the recent exertions of my profoundly-learned Friend, the Rev. Dr. Parr; by whose indefatigability, intelligence, and erudition, the site of this memorable spot will be handed down to the latest posterity.

In a Letter dated "Hatton, Sept. 13, 1813," which I here use by his express permission, Dr. Parr says,

"As to Bosworth Field, six or seven years ago I explored it, and I found Dick's Well, out of which the tradition is that Richard drank during the Battle. It was in dirty, mossy ground, and seemed to me in danger of being destroyed by the cattle. I therefore bestirred myself to have it preserved, and to ascertain the owner. The Bishop of Down spoke to the Archbishop of Armagh, who said that the ground was not his. I then found it not to be Mrs. Pochin's. Last year I traced it to a person to whom it had been bequeathed by Dr. Taylor, formerly Rector of Bosworth. I went to the spot, accompanied by the Rev. Mr. Lynes, of Kirkby-Malory. The grounds had been drained. We dug in two or three places without effect. I then applied to a neighbouring Farmer, a good intelligent fellow. He told me his family had drawn water from it for six or seven years, and that he would conduct me to the very place. I desired him to describe the signs. He said, there were some large stones, and some square wood, which went round the Well at the top. We dug, and found things as he had described them; and, having ascertained the very spot, we rolled in the stones, and covered them with earth. Now Lord Wentworth, and some other Gentlemen, mean to fence the place with some strong stones, and to put a large stone over it with the following inscription; and you may tell the story if you please.

S. PARR."

AQUA . EX . HOC . PVTEO . HAVSTA
SITIM . SEDAVIT
RICARDVS . TERTIVS . REX . ANGLIAE
CVM . HENRICO . COMITE . DE . RICHMONDIA
ACERRIME . ATQVE . INFENSISSIME . PRAELIANS
ET . VITA . PARITER . AC . SCEPTRO
ANTE . NOCTEM . CARITVRVS
II . KAL . SEPT . A . D . MCCCCLXXXV.

P. 557. Of a Halberd or Pike supposed from Bosworth Field, see hereafter, p. 149.

P. 568. In pedigree of Ruding, notes, col. 1, l. 3. *after* " and in this county they do not appear in the Heralds' Books," *should follow* " until the time of Henry VIII."

Ibid. col. 2. l. 7. *read* " Watercrofte."

P. 569. Mrs. Sarah Ruding, daughter of Rogers Ruding and Anne Skrymsher, died at Warwick June 14, 1813, in her 67th year, deeply lamented by all who knew her. To the poor of Warwick and its vicinity, she was eminently kind and charitable.

Ibid. The Rev. Rogers Ruding, in 1812, circulated " Proposals for publishing by Subscription, Annals of the Coinage of Britain and its Dependencies: from the earliest Period of authentic History, to the End of the Fiftieth Year of His present Majesty, King George III.

" That the Art of Coinage," he says, " in this Kingdom, has long been extremely defective, hardly requires any proof. The barbarity of the workmanship is evident, from the slightest inspection: and the constant disappearance of the Money, in a short time after it has been issued from the Mint, irrefragably proves, that the principles on which it is constructed are not less imperfect in the execution. To trace the progress of the Errors in our Coinage, from the earliest times down to the present, and to offer to the consideration of the Publick a theory less liable to objection than that which has hitherto been acted upon, are the main objects of this work, which will form Three Volumes in Quarto, of which only 300 Copies will be printed. On account of the limited number, the price will be Ten Guineas for the common Paper, and Fifteen for the large, of which no more will be printed than are subscribed for."

For the illustration and embellishment of these Volumes, the Society of Antiquaries have permitted the Plates of Mr. Folkes's Work on Coins to be used. I heartily wish success to a work of such sterling merit; and shall only observe, that the Publick at large have to regret that worth and talents like those of Mr. Ruding should be confined to the precincts of a small sequestered village.

P. 574. add to note 3. " June 2, 1668. Whereas William Barton, of Leicester, hath promised very suddenly to tender the Amendments of his Psalms to the view and perusal of the Company, in such manner and form as he will thereby be concluded, so as to make no further alteration of them, and thereupon has moved the Table, to furnish him with ten pounds, for his present occasions, upon his bill, under his hand and seal, for repayment thereof within three months:—Ordered, that the said Mr. Barton shall have the said sum of ten pounds lent unto him by this Company for three months, according to his desire."—Court Books, D. 140. a.

P. 605. Mr. Richard Garner, of Elmesthorpe, a person of very extraordinary bulk, died December 11, 1813, aged 73, and was buried at Barwell.

P. 614. add to rectors of Glenfield: Rev. George Winstanley, 1813.

P. 628. Mrs. Heygate, relict of Thomas Heygate, esq. of Husbands Bosworth, died Sept. 19, 1807.

P. *633. See a continuation of one branch of the Ferrers, from Edward Ferrers of Groby (a younger son of William lord Ferrers of Groby, who died in 1445), in Clutterbuck's " History of Hertfordshire," vol. I. p. 360.

P. 676. col. 1, l. 28. Thomas Sansome, esq. married, in November 1814, the relict of the late William Brown, esq. of Hinckley.

P. 677. June 12, 1806, Dr. Tomline, the Bishop of the Diocese, confirmed in the parish church of Hinckley 566 persons.

P. 685.   *June 13th,* 1651.

" Hinkley.—Whereas this Committee is certified that the living of Hinkley, in the county of Leicester, is worth but 20*l.* a yeare, by reason whereof they are destitute of a minister: It is ordered by this Committee, that the yearly sume of fifty pounds be graunted by the Trustees for maintenance of Ministers, to such a godly and able preacher as shall be appointed to officiate there, and be approued by this Committee, for increase of his maintenance, to commence from the 25th of March last, which the said

Trustees are to pay accordingly out of the accrewing rents and revenues in them vested.

JO. BOURCHIER.   ROB. BREWSTER.
NATHANIEL HALLOWES.   M. OLDISWORTH."
THO. LISTER.

" *March* 24th, 1651-2.

Hinkley.—Whereas this Committee, the 13th of June last, directed the Trustees for maintenance of Ministers to graunt and pay for an augmentacon to such godly and able preacher as should officiate in the church of Hinkley, in the county of Leicester, the yearly sume of fifty pounds: It is now ordered by this Committee that the said augmentacon be paid to Mr. Thomas Eyre, minister there, to commence from the 29th of Sept. last: And the said Trustees are to continue payment thereof from time to time out of the accrewing rents and revenues in them vested.

JAMES CHALONER.   R. ALDWORTH.
R. BREWSTER.   RICH. DARLEY[1]."
GILBERT MILLINGTON.

P. 687. Mr. Luke Wright, of Hinckley, died Jan. 5, 1811, aged 63. He formerly took a very active part in instructing the Church choir; and though by no means eminent as a performer, knew well the theory of musick. As a composer he was not below mediocrity; he never published any of his productions, yet they seldom failed, when performed, to give satisfaction to an audience. His anthems, as well as his other pieces, are written strictly according to the rules of composition, and evidently prove, that he possessed ingenuity and fertility of imagination.

P. 687. Mr. Nathaniel Kemp, of Hinckley, died Jan. 15, 1811, in his 92d year. He was baptized Dec. 22, 1719, by the Rev. William Bilby, of the Presbyterian persuasion of that place, before the present meeting-house was built.

Ibid. Mr. John Shipman, of Hinckley, died March 9, 1812, in his 80th year; a man of the most active benevolence.

Ibid. Mr. Thomas Baldwin died at Hinckley Jan. 27, 1813. He was well known by the appellation of " The Old Doctor," on account of his skill in that virulent pest of humanity, the small-pox; many thousands having been inoculated by him, in the course of the last thirty years, with unexampled success; till on the introduction of the Jennerian system, which in a great measure superseding his former practice, his intelligent mind, after duly investigating the subject, led him to adopt the Vaccine mode, in which he shone equally conspicuous. Few men can boast of that equanimity of temper which he possessed; no change of circumstances or situation appeared to elate or to distress him. His mind was comprehensive, his memory retentive, and, by his coolness and deliberation in argument, but few excelled him. He was a great politician, having been a reader of diurnal prints for upwards of half a century. The principles which he uniformly avowed and supported, were of the old Whig school: he used frequently to observe, " that our excellent Constitution, in its pristine purity, was one of the greatest efforts of human ingenuity." He also distinguished himself on several other occasions; and in 1776 published a poem on the rise, progress, and present state of the ingenious art of frame-work-knitting, as mentioned in vol. I. p. 621.

P. 687. Mr. Matthew Bloxam, an eminent surgeon and apothecary, of Hinckley, died April 15, 1814, aged 70. He had been long in a very extensive practice, and much celebrated as a successful accoucheur in that neighbourhood. His disposition was open and honest. Such a man could have no real enemies, and he had many sincere friends; many to whom the plain sincerity of his manners were the best recommendation. He will long be affectionately remembered at Hinckley.

P. 688. The Rev. Matthew Brown was presented, by the dean and chapter of Westminster, to the vi-

" Acts of the Committee for Plundered Ministers," in Sion College Library.

carage

carage of Hinckley with Stoke and Dadlington annexed, on the resignation of, and in exchange with Rev. Dr. Staunton for the rectory of Elton-super-Montem, Nottinghamshire; and inducted Sept. 5, 1812, by H. E. Holland, curate, in the presence of John Ward, churchwarden.

P. 689. *add to note* [3]. William Brown, esq. was a well-known firm adherent to the principles of our Constitution in Church and State; was highly esteemed, and deservedly looked up to as a public man, by his neighbourhood; and in him public institution and private merit have lost a sincere friend, for he was equally ready to extend a liberal hand to the former as a friendly one to the deserving and industrious character. He died very rich, and devised £.500. to the Infirmary at Leicester.

P. 689. Mr. John Bass, brother to W. Bass, the ingenious self-taught painter recorded in this page, died at Hinckley, June 4, 1810.

P. 690. col. 2, l. 42. The following epitaph has been placed on a white marble monument on the North wall of the chancel in Hinckley church:

" Beneath are deposited the remains of Elizabeth, youngest daughter of the late George Hicks, esq. M. D. of St. James's, Westminster. She died in this place on the 1st of Dec. 1811, of a rapid decline on her way from Edgerston, in Roxburghshire to Bristol, in the 34th year of her age. This stone is intended only to mark the place of her interment; the hearts of all who knew her are the tablets upon which her virtues are inscribed."

P. 695. col. 2, l. 2. The title of Mr. White's sermon was, " Unlimited Confidence not to be placed in the best of Princes. A Sermon preached at Hinckley in Leicestershire, Nov. 5, 1760, on occasion of the sudden and much-lamented Death of his late Most excellent Majesty King George the Second, who departed this life October the 25th, 1760, in the 77th year of his age, and the 34th of his reign. By Nathaniel White." 30 pp. 8vo.

P. 697. Rev. A. Underhill, priest of the Catholic Chapel at Hinckley, died in 1814.

P. 702. col. 1, l. 43. Mr. Thomas Robinson, one of the lords of the manor of Hinckley, and feoffee of both Feoffments, died June 14, 1808.

P. 702. col. 1, l. 44. Mr. Robert Tompson died at Hinckley, at the advanced age of 87, Sept. 17, 1814. He was an honest and worthy man, and much respected by those who knew him.—In politics he was a staunch Whig of the old school. In religion he was a zealous and consistent Protestant Dissenter of the Presbyterian persuasion, of which congregation in that town he was a valuable member, whose interest, harmony, and prosperity he was at all times solicitous to promote: he was, however, no bigot, but esteemed good men of all parties, whom he appreciated rather for their actions than their sentiments. It is pleasing to remark, that his remains were followed to the grave by many highly respectable persons of different denominations, who met together to pay a last tribute of respect to an aged and valuable friend. He had been declining for some years, and was fully aware of the awful event which was to take him from this life, and place him in the silent, peaceful grave; " where the wicked cease from troubling, and where the weary are at rest." He survived his sister Mrs. Bond, only two months. He had been one of the trustees of the Great Feoffment in Hinckley for more than half a century, being admitted to that situation in 1760.

Ibid. col. 1, l. 45. The Great Feoffment in Hinckley.—Thomas Sansome, grocer, and Thomas Sansome, esq. surviving trustees, Dec. 12, 1814, admitted Thomas Short, hosier, John Ward, gent. John Hill, surgeon, John Blakesley, gent. Robert Chessher, esq. Thomas Bray, hosier, George Woodcock, hosier, Thomas Needham, dyer, Robert Milligan, gent. and George Holland, hosier.

P. 703. col. 2, l. 43. The Lesser Feoffment.—The only surviving trustee, Jan. 2, 1813, Thomas Sansome, esq. admitted John Ward, gent. Thomas Short, jun. hosier, Thomas Needham, jun. hosier, Henry Blakesley, son of John Blakesley, gent. Joseph Bray, son of Thomas Bray, hosier, and John Hill, surgeon.

P. 704. Benefactions to Hinckley continued:

In 1810, the minister and churchwardens obtained for the town of Hinckley the late Mr. Alderman Newton's, of Leicester, donation of 26l. towards cloathing, schooling, and educating 25 boys of indigent or necessitous parents, of the Established Church, between the ages of seven and 14 years; which not being sufficient of itself, the trustees of the Great Feoffment annually receive the above sum, and clothe and educate the children agreeably to the intentions of the donor [2].

Add, Richard-Spooner Jacques, esq. died at Sketchley, Jan. 30, 1811. This gentleman was the posthumous son of Richard Jacques, of Sketchley, and Elizabeth his relict, and baptized at Hinckley, April 26, 1743. He was a disciple of the old school, and consequently an enemy to all modern innovations under the name of improvements, many of which he thought were little calculated for the benefit of the community at large. This was decidedly his opinion in regard to the system of modern agriculture. He was a steady friend to his King and Country. In the year 1792, he served the office of high sheriff for the county of Leicester. Having received a classical education, and being fond of reading, he was often an entertaining companion. Cheerful himself, he communicated that cheerfulness to others. By frugality and care he increased his patrimonial inheritance to a large amount; and did not forget to leave something handsome for charitable uses.—Mr. Jacques was never married, though partial to the society of the fair sex.

Extract of Mr. Jacques's will, dated July 3, 1803. He died Jan. 30, 1811. Will proved April 27, 1811, in the Prerogative Court of the Archbishop of Canterbury.

" I give and bequeath to the vicar and to the churchwardens and overseers of the poor of the parish of Hinckley, the sum of one hundred pounds, to be placed out at interest in the public funds, in the names of such vicar, and the churchwardens and overseers, and two respectable inhabitants of the said parish. And that the clear interest, dividends, and produce, shall for ever be paid and laid out by the vicar, and by the churchwardens and overseers for the time being of the said parish, in manner following, (that is to say;) ten shillings and sixpence shall be paid out of the interest and dividends of the said sum of one hundred pounds to the resident minister of the said parish, for preaching a sermon on Christmas Day annually for ever. And that the remainder shall be laid out in six-penny loaves to be given to such poor persons belonging to the parish as shall attend the preaching of such sermon. And if the number of poor persons attending in the said parish shall not be sufficient on receiving one six-penny loaf, to exhaust the residue of the interest and dividends of the one hundred pounds, then I direct as many more six-penny loaves may be given to each poor person so attending as aforesaid, as the residue of the said interest and dividends will admit. And I do direct the last mentioned sum of one hundred pounds, to be paid at the end of twelve months after my decease."

" Received Feb. 20, 1812, the sum of ninety pounds in payment of the legacy above mentioned, having first allowed or paid ten pounds for the duty thereon. J. Staunton, Vicar.

John Ward, } Churchwardens.
Geo. Holland, }

J. Hollingsworth, } Overseers.
R. Weightman, }

" April 1, 1812, For the above 90l. 100l. stock in the Navy five per Cent. Annuities was transferred to John Staunton, LL. D. Vicar, John Ward, John

[2] For particulars of this establishment at Hinckley, and abstract of the trust deed, see under St. Nicholas, Leicester, I. 611—613.

Hol-

Hollingsworth, and Thomas Sansome, all of Hinckley, esqrs.; only four names being allowed to be entered in one stock account."

The original extract from the will and receipt for the 100*l.* stock, were put into the parish chest, by *John Ward*, churchwarden, Hinckley, 1812.

Mr. Jacques also left 100*l.* to each of the parishes of Burbach and Wolvey; and 200*l.* to the Leicester Infirmary.

P. 709. Pedigree of Iliffe, add, George Iliffe, son of John and Christian Iliffe, died Jan. 31, 1812, in the 89th year of his age. He was the last survivor of four brothers and a sister, rather remarkable instances of longevity in one family: Mr. Joseph Iliffe died March 4, 1795, aged 76; George Iliffe, Jan. 31, 1812, aged 89; John Iliffe, Aug. 7, 1799, aged 74; William Iliffe, March 12, 1792, aged 64; Mary Green, Feb. 18, 1792, aged 71.—George Iliffe was the oldest inhabitant of Hinckley. He had been churchwarden in 1755; and formerly kept the Star inn, in that town, where an assembly-room was built for him before the death of king George II.

P. 709. Anne Iliffe, relict of Joseph Iliffe, died at Hinckley in her 89th year, April 12, 1813. She was the fourth daughter of William Scott, esq. of Market Overton, Rutland; and was married Feb. 6, 1755. A gentlewoman by birth, she was a sincere Christian from inclination and conviction; and had very deservedly acquired the general esteem of all who had the happiness of her acquaintance. She was buried, on the 17th, in a vault in the churchyard, where the remains of her husband had been deposited; and the funeral was marked with that degree of respect to which the many virtues of this venerable matron so eminently entitled her. Besides the relations who attended as mourners, the Rev. M. Brown, vicar of Hinckley, with the Rev. Jerome Dyke and the Rev. George Mettam, rectors of Aston Flamvile and Barwell, two adjoining parishes, joined the solemn procession; six of the principal inhabitants of Hinckley walked as pall-bearers; and a large concourse of neighbours thronged to pay the last sad tribute of respect to departed worth.

The following epitaph has been placed on the same stone with that of her husband (see p. 691, col. 2, l. 14 from bottom):

" His widow, Mrs. *Anne Iliffe,* daughter of Wm. Scott, esq. of Market Overton, after a long life of exemplary piety, died April 12, 1813, aged 89."

[The death of Mrs. Dickinson, an elder sister, is recorded in p. 131.]

Ibid. Mrs. Mary Argyll died at Stoke Golding, May 16, 1814, aged 76. The merits of this worthy woman should not be buried in obscurity. She was for more than 60 years the most faithful servant, and sincerely attached friend, of Mr. and Mrs. Iliffe, of Hinckley; most warmly partaking in all the joys and sorrows of her excellent master and mistress; and among their numerous friends and acquaintance, as highly valued as she was generally known. Yet this intimacy never caused her for a moment to forget her rank in society; and she continued to fulfil the humble duties of her station, highly to the satisfaction of her honoured mistress, till her own strength failed her; after which she resided with her as a humble, faithful friend, (in which light she had been very long considered,) till her mistress's death in the spring of 1813 (see the preceding paragraph). She then retired to her own native village, and died in the bosom of her brother's family, among whom she has distributed her hard-earned savings, gained in a service of two thirds of a century wholly passed in one family. Farewell, thou kind-hearted woman! The writer of this embalms thy memory with a tear; for, from lisping infancy to maturer age, thy hand was always ready to aid and befriend him.

" *Well done, thou good and faithful servant; enter thou into the joy of thy Lord !*"

P. 709. Pedigree. Mary, 2d daughter of John Nichols and Martha Green, was married, at Islington, Dec. 3, 1814, to John Morgan, esq. of Highbury-place.

Ibid. l. 6 from bottom, *add*, William-Bowyer Ni-

chols died Jan. 25, and Eliza his infant sister May 1, 1811. Another son, Charles-Bowyer Nichols, born March 1, 1812, died May 20 following.

Ibid. A daughter, Mary-Anne-Iliffe Nichols, born April 5, 1813; and a son, Bowyer-Edward Nichols, born October 28, 1814.

P. 710. Miss Sarah Ward, printer, Hinckley, has a curious and very antient oak bedstead, much gilt and ornamented, with various pannelled compartments, neatly painted with emblematic devices, and Latin mottos in capital letters conspicuously introduced in each piece. On the outside of the top, among several other decorations not described, are arms: Sable, three mullets Gules, on a chevron Or, three stags' heads caboshed, Or.—Sable, an eagle displayed, Or.—Sable, a phœnix Or.—&c. A description of the different representations, with the Latin mottos faithfully transcribed, and translated, is given in the " History of Hinckley," 2d ed. 1813, p. 753; and also in Gent. Mag. 1811, LXXXI. part ii. p. 416.

P. 711. Thomas Perkins, who married Mary Applebee, died Oct. 21, 1812.

P. 717. Mrs. Miles, relict of Mr. George Miles, died at Stoke Golding, aged 80, April 21, 1811.

P. 721. col. 2. line 23. Daniel Preston, esq. of Wykin Hall, died March 15, 1814, aged 56.

P. 725. Rev. Robert Parr, rector of Heigham, died in May 1812. This gentleman was formerly fellow of Magdalen college, Oxford, rector of Heigham, co. Norfolk, and of Kirkley, in Suffolk. His first preferment was the vicarage of Modbury, in Devonshire, to which he was presented by Dr. Southernwood, fellow of Eton college, an old friend of his father; and was successor in that vicarage to the father of the late sir George Baker, bart. He had afterwards the rectory of St. Lawrence in Norwich; which he resigned, about 1803, for that of Heigham. In 1801, he sold a considerable estate, called the Brockeys, in the parish of Barwell, co. Leicester, which had been in his family for several generations. He was first cousin to my very worthy and profoundly-learned friend Dr. Samuel Parr.

Ibid. The following character of Sarah-Anne Wynne, daughter of Rev. Dr. Parr, is copied from Gent. Mag. LXXX. part ii. p. 92. The brilliancy of her imagery in conversation and writing; the readiness, gaiety, and fertility of her wit; the acuteness of her observations upon men and things; and the variety of her knowledge upon the most familiar and most profound subjects; were very extraordinary. They who lived with her in the closest intimacy were again and again struck with admiration at the rapidity, ease, vivacity, and elegance of her epistolary compositions: whether upon lively or serious topics, they were always adapted to the occasion; they were always free from the slightest taint of affected phraseology and foreign idiom; they were always distinguished by a peculiar felicity and originality of conception and expression; and the genius displayed in them would most undoubtedly have placed the writer in the very highest class of her female contemporaries, if she had employed her pen upon any work with a deliberate view to publication. Her reading in the most approved authors, both French and English, was diversified and extensive; her memory was prompt and correct; and her judgment, upon all questions of taste and literature, morality and religion, evidently marked the powers with which she had been gifted by Nature, and the advantages which she had enjoyed for cultivating those powers under the direction of her enlightened parents, and in the society of learned and ingenious men, to which she had access from her earliest infancy. With becoming resignation to the will of Heaven she endured a long and painful illness, which had been brought upon her by the pressure of domestic sorrow on a constitution naturally weak. Her virtues as a friend, a child, a wife, and a mother, were most exemplary; and her piety, being sincere, rational, and habitual, gave additional value to the great faculties of her understanding, and the generous feelings of her heart."

P. 748.

T. Bass delin.   J. Basire sculp.

MR JOHN WARD,

HINCKLEY.

Ætat. 45. March 8, 1810.

London: Published by Nichols, Son and Bentley, Red Lion Passage, Fleet Street. 1811.

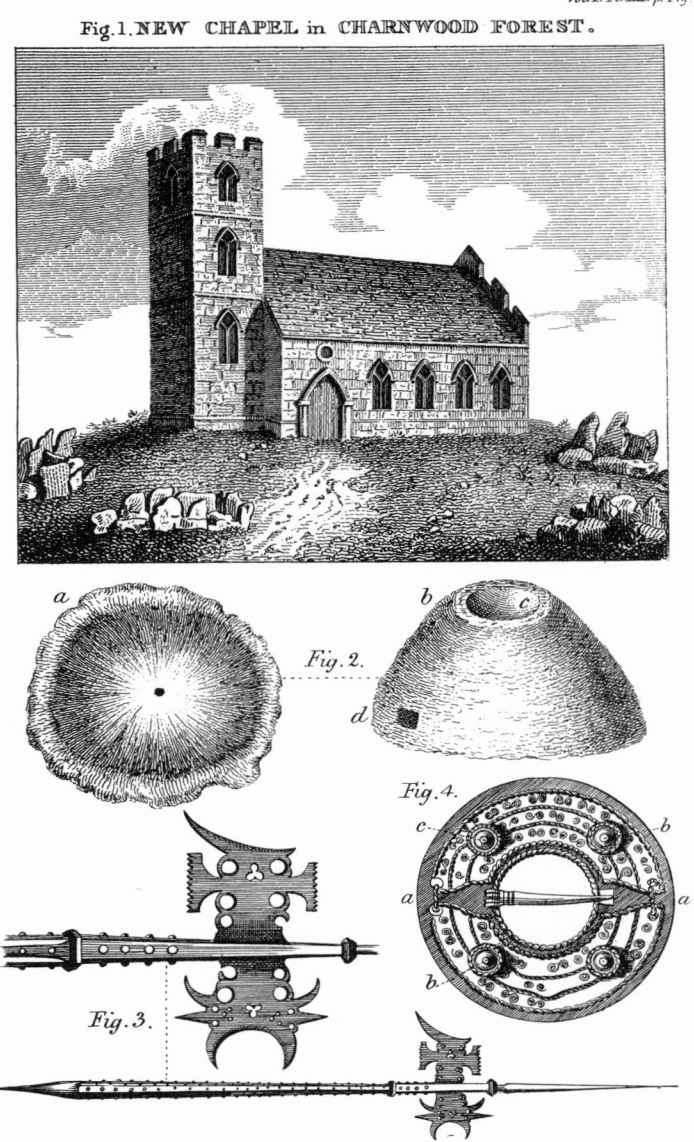

Vol. I. Pl. LII. p. 149.

Fig. 1. NEW CHAPEL in CHARNWOOD FOREST.

Fig. 2.

Fig. 3.

Fig. 4.

P. 748. col. 2, l. 36. I had great pleasure in prefixing the following brief Dedication to a second Edition of " The History of Hinckley."

" To Mr. John Ward.

" DEAR SIR,   *March* 8, 1813.

" Recollecting that the former Edition of ' The History of Hinckley' was inscribed to my worthy Friend the late Mr. John Robinson, as ' a hearty Well-wisher to the prosperity of his Native Town,' I cannot be at one moment's loss for a similar name to prefix to the present Re-publication. You are not only a ' Well-wisher' to your ' Native Town,' but have shewn yourself a warm and disinterested Promoter of its best interests; and from your being a resident at Hinckley, I have been well acquainted with many demonstrations of your attachment to the principles of our excellent Constitution both in Church and State. Of your accuracy in Heraldic and Antiquarian research, and of the prompt and very able assistance you have given in the improvement and correction of the following sheets, I can thankfully add the testimony of, Dear Sir, your greatly obliged and faithful servant,   J. NICHOLS."

Mr. Ward was born March 8, 1765; and received his education under his father Mr. William Ward, who was for more than 30 years master of the free-school at Hinckley; author of " The Scripture Spelling Book, 1762;" and was the first who established a printing-press at Hinckley in 1773. He carried on the business of a bookseller in that town for many years; and died Oct. 21, 1791, aged 60, where several of his children are respectably settled; and one of his family is now the printer and bookseller of the place. The subject of this memoir was for several years engaged in the business of a hosier, carried on with reputation and success, from which he retired in 1809; and is resident in his native place very much respected. A Pedigree of his family may be seen in vol. IV. p. 710; and a good Portrait of him is herewith given, (see Pl. LI.) engraved in 1813, by Mr. James Basire, from a miniature painted in 1810 by Mr. Thomas Bass. Many of the prints have been distributed among his friends.

P. 760. The Rev. Spencer Madan, D.D. bishop of Peterborough, died Nov. 8, 1813. See an account and character of him in Gent. Mag. vol. LXXXIII. part ii. pp. 509, 703. LXXXIV. part. ii. p. 99.

P. 766. col. 2, l. 32. *add the following Epitaph,* from the church of Chipping Barnet in Hertfordshire:

" Here lieth interred the body of William Noell, of Kirkby Malory, in the county of Leicester, esq. He marryed Frances, the eldest daughter, and one of the coheires of Richard Cresheld, late one of the Justices of the Common Pleas, and departed this life the first of March, anno Dom. 1654, aged about 55 years."

P. 769. A labourer named Robinson died at Kirkby Malory early in 1811, aged 107.

P. 770. Mary viscountess Wentworth died at Kirkby Malory, June 29, 1814.

P. 771. l. penult. *read* William Pares, LL. B. December 1786, rector of Narborough, co. Leicester, and vicar of Ockbrook, co. Derby, and Selston, co. Nottingham.

P. 781. col. 2, l. 12 from bottom. *add to the account of* LEICESTER FOREST. The following is transcribed from " A Booke of Offices, as well of his Ma'tye's Courtes of Records, as of his Howse-holde, the Cowncells of Yorke, Wales, and the Marches, his Ma'tie's Townes of Warr, Castles, Bullwarkes, and Fortresses, the Parks, Howses, Forrests, and Chases, with the Fee belonging to euery particular Officer: made perfect according to the Tyme of 1617."

" Leycester.——" Com' Leicestriæ.

		£.	s.	d.
Duchy Lanc'.—Constable and porter of the castle, fee		3	0	8
Forester and keeper of the chase, fee		3	0	8
Keeper of Thewaight, alias Walker-ship, within the chase of Leycester, fee		2	10	4
Keeper of *Barne Parke,* parcel of the chase, fee		2	5	6

VOL. I. PART II.

Keeper of *Hartley Ward,* within the said chase, fee

		£.	s.	d.
Keeper of *Hartley Ward,* within the said chase, fee		2	5	6
Tholowe.—Keeper of the parke, fee		2	5	6
Hinkley Parke.—Keeper of the woods, fee		2	10	4
Birdnest.—Keeper of the house and lodge, fee		3	0	8
Abbotts Parke.—Keeper of the woods, fee		1	16	8
Keeper of the parke, fee		3	0	8
Paler of y^t fee	and th'erbage.	0	13	4

Sum' com' Leycest' -   22   9   2."

P. 782. col. 2, l. 5 from bottom, J. E. Carter, esq. died 1813; see before, p. 132.

P. 792. At the moment this sheet was preparing for the press, Feb. 14, 1815, a worthy Friend informs me, that the Commissioners for the inclosure of Charnwood Forest have so nearly completed their labours, that the whole will be ready for cultivation this Spring. My Friend has also favoured me with an accurate view of a New Chapel (*see Plate* LII. *fig.* 1.) which has been built by subscription in the Forest, not far from Charley, on the side of a rock, as appears in the view; the church-yard being a complete rocky ground. The Bishop is to consecrate it next Summer. There are, and will be, about 220 acres of land set out in the Forest, for the endowment of this and any other Chapel that may be deemed expedient. That already built is in Lord Stamford's Peculiar, in the parish of Newtown Linford. The appointment is in six of the Lords of the Forest; *viz.* Earls of Stamford and Moira, Edward-March Phillipps, esq. William Herrick, esq. the Rev. Thomas Bosvile, and Edward Dawson, esq.

The Rev. William Mounsey, the worthy Vicar of Sproxton and Saltby, has favoured me with the following communication:

" The two stones *a* and *b,* wrought and formed for some particular use, of which a rough sketch is given *(see fig.* 2.) were lately found at Garthorpe upon a bed of gravel six or seven feet below the surface. He leaves it to the Antiquary to explain their use—in what age—or whether commonly found, or scarce. For the present let them be called a *Handmill.* The nether millstone *a* is not much unlike a platter or large shallow dish, with a shelved off edge, in some places chipped, in others broke down. The bottom is not quite flat, but gently rises to the center (like a fish-plate) which is perforated apparently for the purpose of a spindle; weight 31 pounds, diameter 16 inches. The upper millstone *b,* resembling in shape the bottom part of a cone or sugar loaf, is extremely perfect, and was found in its proper place upon the other, which it exactly fits. At the top *c* is an aperture or *hopper,* 5 inches in diameter, contracting as it descends, and may hold three pints. Greatest diameter 12 inches, least 7, and perpendicular height 6 inches, weight 33 pounds. Near about the situation of *d* is a square hole, which communicates with the bottom of the *hopper,* or that in the center, where there is a bed cut, evidently for a frame of iron work, which may have perished, and by the wearing down on that side by natural pressure, we may be somewhat countenanced in an opinion of the handle having been fixed there. The stone (not met with in this country) is of a dirty white coarse grit, and may be taken for a rough composition of beat sand and mortar; and though it has not the least resemblance to millstones now in use, yet appears not ill calculated for the grinding of corn.   W. MOUNSEY."

Mr. Fowke, of Elmesthorpe, has also communicated the following article:

" As many of your Readers may be gratified with a description of what is curious or antique from or near to Bosworth field, you will herewith receive a drawing of a Halberd or Pike *(fig.* 3.) found recently in the roof of an old house at Stapleton, which is supposed to have been preserved by the antient family of *Dawes* in that place. It is upwards of 9 feet in length, the shaft of oak, banded on four sides with iron, and studded with brass nails between every band; the shaft is surmounted with two wings of iron cut into rude open work, which terminates from the knob above the wings to a square taper point of about two and a half feet in length. It is shod with sharp iron to be occasionally rested in the ground. Stapleton being situate adjoining Radmore plain [1], the field of battle, I have not the least doubt, it has been preserved as a rare relick of that memorable period, as it bears evident marks of other times [2]. RICHARD FOWKE."

The 4th article in the same Plate, found near Husbands Bosworth, was thus illustrated in 1800, by Mr. Tailby, in the Gent. Mag. vol. LXX.:

" The subject is a large and rich *broche* or *buckle*, which was found five or six years ago, with some human bones, in digging for gravel, somewhere between Husbands Bosworth (co. Leiceter) and Welford (co. Northampton); but in which Lordship, I know not. However, I inclose a correct drawing of the same, coloured as it now appears *(see fig.* 4). But, as the colours cannot be shewn in your plate, I will subjoin a faithful description of the whole for the satisfaction of your Antiquarian friends.—It appears to have been found in (or very near) the route of the hasty retreat of part of King Charles the First's army to Leicester, after its defeat in Naseby field, June 14, 1645. Whether it belonged to some of the officers or suite of that ill-fated monarch or not, I dare not determine; but I am inclined to think it to be of a much earlier date. The under part of the *broche* consists of one entire circular thin plate of silver, its diameter $2\frac{1}{4}$ inches, with a circular hole in its centre $\frac{7}{8}$ of an inch in diameter. On this plate lie two nearly semicircular moveable thin plates of pure gold, each $\frac{1}{2}$ inch wide, fastened together, and to the silver plate by a single gold wire passing through them at *a a*. Each of these gold plates is environed with a double twisted wire of the same. Each semicircular plate is circularly divided into three divisions or compartments by a single gold wire laid upon the same. Each compartment is overlaid with notched wire (which I have endeavoured to represent by dotting) of the same metal, and in the same forms, as shewn in the drawing. At nearly equal distances upon these plates are four gold sockets, two on each plate, placed in a kind of wreath of double-twisted wire of the same metal, in each of which is studded a pearl about the size of a white pea; and in the crown of each pearl is set a ruby about the size of a common pin's head; one of which (that just below the point of the tongue of the buckle) is gone, the other three remain bright and sparkling; but the pearls have quite lost their lustre, and are somewhat corroded by lying in the earth, and now appear of a dead white, inclining to a light brown. The rubies, which I have marked *b b*, have a flat surface; but that marked *c* is rose-cut, as probably was that in the opposite angle, which is now wanting. The buckle and tongue are of silver, the rim of which appears to be of twisted wire, but is not so, being only cast in that form (which I believe, is called *cable* silver), the under surface being flat, and falls within the gold plates upon the inner projecting part of the under silver plate. The upper part of this plate is much tarnished, especially the outer and inner projecting extremities, which appear as dark in colour as is shewn in the drawing. The buckle and under side of this plate, are of a brighter colour but rather dull. The gold belonging to this curious *broche* weighs 4 penny-weights, and the silver 5 penny-weights and 12 grains. J. TAILBY."

P. 800. The Rev. Richard Williams, rector of Markfield, observes:—" I herewith send you a copy of the deaths that have occurred in my parish of Markfield, from January to the end of March in the year 1813:—One only under twelve months.—Two only under 5 years.—Six deaths under 24 years.—Ten, aged 60, 61, 74, 75, 77, 79, 80, 81, 82, 83.—In the year 1812, 64 deaths.—Population about 560 souls.—Births about 40. If, Sir, you think this proof of good nursing and kind maternal attention worth your observation it is at your service."

P. 816. l. ult. Rev. William Brown, the venerable rector of Burrow, who was presented to Narborough in 1810, died in 1814 (see p. 129); and was succeeded by the Rev. Isaac Crouch, M. A.

P. 837. Mr. Gough, in a Letter dated June 9, 1801, says: " Having lately visited the chapel at STEAN, in Northamptonshire; of the monuments in which your lamented Correspondent Mr. Henn gave so full an account, in Gent. Mag. vol. LX. pp. 420, 493, (see it in vol. IV. p. 838.) and Mr. Ayscough, vol. LVI. p. 933. from a MS. in the British Museum, before that part of Bridges's History was published; I have not much to add to either.

The inscription in the blank of the Bible is:
" Biblia hæc SSta,
cum venerandæ Ecclesiæ Anglicanæ
Liturgia reformata
olim ab ipsomet Carolo II. augustissimo
Britan' Monarcha quocies divinis
interfuit officiis diligentius versata
in
ædium har' sacrario ceu et pietatis suæ
in Deum ter Opt. Max. gratique serenissimum
erga Regem animi monumentum perpetuo
conservando
gentisque suæ posteris summi
Numinis cultui vacari liberis
sedulo perlegenda
D. D. D. qui heic lucem hanc primo adspexit vere
reverendus in Christo pater
D. D. Nathaniel Crewe,
olim Oxoniensis, hodie vero Dunelmensis
episcopus,
idemque excellentissimæ dicti regis majestati ab
intimioribus sacris
anno Christianor' 1674."

" It is the folio edition printed by Feilde, at Cambridge, 1660, having in the frontispiece Solomon on his throne of lions. On the cover is the crown over two Cs conjoined, for *Carolus à Carolo;* and on the edge the rose and crown. The Common Prayer is the London edition. In it is the autograph of the Bishop. The books, cushions, &c. are kept in a wainscot chest, which, standing on the stone floor, contracts damp and mould.

" The chapel has a large West window over a small door; an aile of two arches on clustered columns. A screen divides it from that part where the monuments are, which were crowded with the furniture of the farm-houses then under repair. This Mr. Bridges calls the North aile, built to answer the South, and used only as a place of burial, vol. I. p. 198. The covering for the pulpit, the communion-table, and the arm-chair, all of crimson velvet, are remaining in a very torn and ragged state. Mr. Henn could not have expected a *font* if he had recollected this was a private family chapel, though called in Ecton a *rectory*, and joined with Hinton, the rector or curate of which officiates in it once a month during the summer months, for which, I am informed, 20*l.* is paid; a benefaction of Bp. Crewe.

" All that remains of the old mansion-house on the South side of the chapel is the kitchen, which, with the contiguous large farm-house, from the road has the appearance of a considerable mansion. In it is one large lofty parlour, used as a dairy during the repair, in which are, a portrait of Charles I. and another of a lady holding a lamb in her right arm, and in her left hand a book; Hogarth's prints of Hudibras and Marriage à-la-mode; and the Luxemburg gallery.

---

[1] See Mr. Pridden's Plan of Bosworth Field, in vol. IV. p. 556.
[2] Baker's Chronicle says, " The battle king Richard led himself, which consisted of a thousand bill-men, empaled with two thousand pikes, &c. &c."

" The

LEA-GRANGE
Estate
1815.

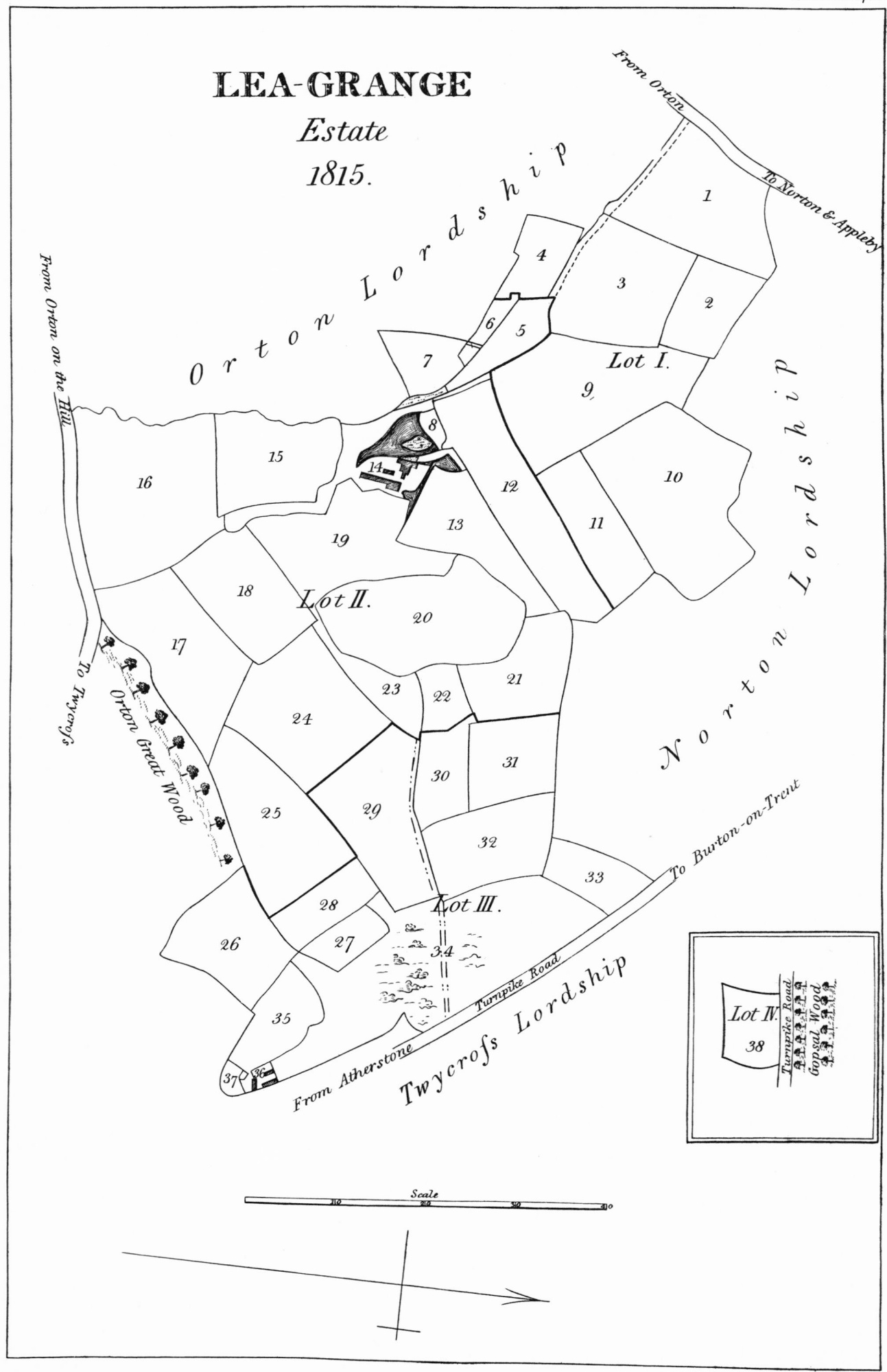

Scale

" The present tenant of the farm is Mr. Smith, of Charlton.

" Over the chapel West door,

" HOLINES BECOMETH THINE HOWSE, O LORD!"
and in the pediment above a shield inscribed,

. UILT BY

T. C.

162..

probably Serjeant Crewe, who died 1633, and married Temperance Bray, who died 1619.

" In the spandrils of the South door the arms of *Crewe*, and three eagles' legs[1], *Bray*, by whom the manor of Hinton and Stean came to Crewe.

" There are so many gilded vine-leaves and bunches of grapes about the monuments, that I suspect Polxyena's [Governor Thicknesse's] story, in Gent. Mag. vol. LVI. p. 450. [see vol. IV. p. 837.]

" The oldest monument is that of Sir Thomas Crewe, serjeant at law, and speaker of the House of Commons 21 James I. and 1 Charles I. who died 1633, aged 66. His figure, in a serjeant's gown, lies on a tomb, resting his head on his right hand, and holding in his left a roll; and by him is his wife Temperance, daughter of Reginald Bray, esq. who died 1619, aged 38. Next below this are the monuments of Thomas Lord Crewe, and his wife, Mary Townsend, his grandson, and John Lord Crewe, his son 1679, and his wife, Jemimah Waldegrave; of Penelope, daughter of Sir Philip Frowde, knt. wife of the Bishop, who died 1699, aged 44; of the bishop himself 1721, aged 38, and of his second wife, Dorothy, daughter of Sir William Forster, knt. who died 1715, aged 42.

" On the opposite side, a monument for the serjeant's third daughter, Temperance, wife of John Brown, esq. who died 1634, aged 25, representing her rising out of the tomb; made by John and Mathias, sons of Gerard Christmas; of whom see Walpole's Anecdotes, vol. II. p. 38. 4to."

P. 840. Sydney Wortley died Nov. 11, 1727.

P. 851*. Mr. Thomas Ball, late of Norton by Twycross, died at Leicester May 3, 1810. He was a highly-respected character, and at 93, could read the smallest print without glasses, and retained his faculties unimpaired till his last moments.

P. 850.   " *June* 13th, 1651.

" Orton-on-the-Hill.—Whereas the Committee for Plundered Ministers, the 2d of July 1647, graunted the yearly sume of forty-two poundes reserved to the Bishop of Oxon out of the impropriate rectory of Orton-on-the-Hill, in the County of Leicester, for increase of maintenance to the Minister of the parish church of Orton-on-the-Hill aforesaid; And whereas Mr. Thomas Hill is by order of the said Committee for Plundered Ministers of the 22d of April, 1651, appointed to officiate in the said church, whose maintenance is certified to bee but twenty-five poundes a yeare; It is ordered by this Committee, that the yearly sume of forty-two pounds bee continued and paid to the said Mr. Hill, who is approued by this Committee, for increase of his maintenance, to commence from the said 22d of April. And the Trustees for maintenance of Ministers are to pay the same accordingly.

JO. BOURCHIER.   M. OLDISWORTH.
PET. TEMPLE.   NAT. HALLOWES[2]."
THO. ALEIN.

P. 850. The following inscription is on a neat white marble monument against the North wall in the church of Orton-on-the-Hill, in memory of the late truly pious, charitable, and good-disposed wife of Rev. Joseph Phillimore.

" Near this stone lie the remains of Mary, wife of the Rev. Joseph Phillimore, Vicar of this Parish; second daughter of John Machin, of Kensington, Middlesex, esq. Born August 12th, 1751. Married January 5th, 1775. Died February 2d, 1810.

Blessed are the pure in heart, for they shall see God."

In the church yard, on a tomb-stone to the memory of the late Edward Brown, that once-admired fine tenor-singer (see Barr Chapel, in Shaw's History of Staffordshire, vol. II. page 106, &c.) is the following inscription:

" In memory of Edward Brown, Professor of Musick, who departed this life February 19, 1811, in his 62d year:

Lord, tune my heart within my breast,
    And frame it to thy holy will,
And let thy Spirit within me rest,
    Which may my soul with comfort fill."

" In memory of Mary wife of Edward Brown, who died July 1, 1786, aged 35 years; also of Elizabeth, daughter of Edward and Mary Brown, who died February 7th, 1800, aged 21 years."

Edward Brown lived respected by numerous friends and acquaintance; possessed an excellent disposition; and was zealously attached to the Established Church; he was an amateur in musick, and in the practice of instructing the choirs of Leicestershire, and the adjoining counties.

At Orton-on-the-Hill there is a wake kept annually on the Sunday previous to September 4, or St. Bartholomew O. S.

P. 850. The Rev. William Churchill died in June 1804, at Orton-on-the-Hill. This gentleman was the youngest brother of the Poet, and was educated at Westminster school, at the same standing with Lloyd, Bonnel Thornton, Christopher Smart, and other contemporary sons of Genius. Mr. Churchill's modesty was unequalled; and he would have continued an humble curate to the grave, if his uncle, the late Bishop of St. Asaph, had not rewarded his merit with the living of Orton. Besides other valuable publications, he left a life and comment on the writings of his brother Charles, with notes explanatory of those political passages, and personages likely to grow obsolete. These have been principally incorporated in an edition of the Poet's works, lately published in two octavo volumes. Mr. Churchill was an excellent scholar, a man of merit and probity, and often benevolent to his own prejudice. He was beloved by all his acquaintance, and, while genius and literature are cherished, will live in the remembrance of all who possess a knowledge of his character.

P. 853*. At the Bean Hills, Richard Inge, esq. in 1811, built a handsome hall for his family-residence.

P. 864. A Particular for the sale of *Lea Grange*, in January 1815, gives so minute a description of this antient possession of the Abbey of Merevale, that I am induced to insert it, accompanied by a Plan of the Estate. (see Pl. LIII.)

" Lea Grange is a freehold estate, situate in or near the Parishes of Merevale, Twycross, and Orton-on-the-Hill, in the County of Leicester; and comprises an antient messuage, several cottages, and extensive farm-buildings, and nearly 320 acres of land, adjoining the turnpike road leading from Atherstone to Burton-on-Trent, distant about five miles from the former, and 14 from the latter of those places, and within a short distance from Tamworth.

Numbers on Plan.	Descriptions.	Quantities.		
	LOT I.			
1.	Blower's Lane Croft and Little Orton Close - - - - - - - - - -	12	3	29
2.	Oak Tree Close - - - - - -	5	2	15
3.	Clay Close - - - - - - - -	11	3	12
4.	Flat Close - - - - - - - -	3	3	34
9.	Barn Close, with Barn therein -	18	1	30
10.	Over Fox Nook - - - - - -	15	3	13
11.	Nether Fox Nook - - - - -	8	0	6
		76	2	19

This Lot to be subject to a Right of Way to Lot II. as marked on the Plan.

---

[1] The same arms impaled by Crewe are on six almshouses at the North end of Brackley, founded by the Serjeant, and augmented by the Bishop.

[2] " Acts of the Committee for Plundered Ministers," in Sion College Library.

LOT II.

5. Bull's Meadow - - - - - -	3	1	9
6. Croft, with Cottage, &c. - - -	1	0	25
7. Intake *(in the Parish of Orton)* -	3	3	13
8. Bull's Pingle - - - - - - -	0	1	15
12. Norton Meadow - - - - - -	11	3	30
13. Calves Croft - - - - - - -	7	3	22
14. Messuage, Yards, Gardens, Moat, &c.	8	3	33
15. Little Rachel - - - - - - -	9	2	7
16. Big Rachel - - - - - - -	19	1	14
17. Hill Meadow - - - - - -	11	3	39
18. Old Clover - - - - - - -	10	0	25
19. Mowing Park - - - - - -	12	0	14
20. High Park - - - - - - -	14	1	31
21. Near Beadman's Close - - - -	7	0	33
22. High Park Flat - - - - - -	2	2	29
23. Pen Close - - - - - - - -	3	2	11
24. Near Foggy Close - - - - -	14	0	10
25. Far Ditto - - - - - - -	12	0	38
	154	**2**	**38**

This Lot to have Rights of Way over
Lots I. and III. as shewn in the Plan.

LOT III.

26. Ash Croft - - - - - - -	8	1	27
27. Far Green's Close - - - - -	2	3	10
28. Green's Close - - - - - - -	4	0	3
29. Bontree Close - - - - - -	12	1	3
30. Rushy Close - - - - - -	4	2	27
31. Middle Beadman's Close - - -	6	2	0
32. Far Ditto - - - - - - - -	8	2	37
33. Hobley's Close - - - - - -	4	0	27
34. Shepherd's Close, Horse Close, and Crofts - - - - - - - - -	26	2	26
35. Twycross Meadow - - - - -	4	3	20
36. Cottages and Gardens - - - -	0	1	15
37. Garden Croft - - - - - -	0	1	36
	83	**3**	**31**

This Lot to be subject to a Right of
Way to Lot II. as marked on the Plan.

LOT IV.

38. Holyheath Close, near Gopsal Wood *(in the parish of Norton)* - - - -	3	2	10
Contained in the whole,	**318**	**3**	**18**

" Lea Grange is subject to Land Tax of 21*l.* 8*s.* 4*d.* *per annum*, and to a yearly payment of 5*s.* 6*d.* to the Parson of Merevale; which Outgoings are to be apportioned per acre."

P. 873. Peckleton: The Rev. William Wood died Jan. 26, 1814, aged 69.

Ibid. *Add to vicars*: Rev. John-Mawbey Cooper, 1814.

P. 889*. col. 2, l. 40. Mrs. Margaret Choyce died May 3, 1704, aged 106. See an account of her great-grandchild Dorothy Buckley hereafter, p. 144. *n.* —L. 44. *read* Thompson.

P. 900. Mr. Joseph Smith, an opulent grazier, of Sapcote, died March 24, 1808, in his 54th year. His skill in musick and an uncommonly fine voice, uniformly and regularly exerted in aid of the Public Worship of the Established Church, to which he was zealously attached, contributed to render the Sapcote choir, for many years, one of the most respectable in the county. In consequence of a paralytic seizure he had been for some months deprived of the use of his right leg and hand; but he bore his affliction with the patience and resignation of a Christian.

P. 921. In the Particular published for the sale of *Sherman's Lodge*, April 15, 1812, the property is described, as consisting of a good farm house, standing on rising ground, with suitable barns, stables and outhouses, orchard, fold, and garden, and 255 acres, 3 roods, and 21 perches of land including the site on which the buildings stand, a considerable part of which land is meadow and pasture, and the remainder arable; the whole entirely compact, and divided into convenient inclosures; with a sprinkling of forest trees, and convenient ponds for watering cattle. This property, it is added, possesses rural and interesting views, both within itself and over the surrounding country, including *Bradgate Park*, the property of the earl of Stamford, *Marchfield*, *Charley Forest*, and other adjacent rising lands, interspersed with villages and churches at proper intervals, which enrich and complete the landscape. The ground in general lies well for drainage; and the situation is particularly eligible for carrying off and conveying the produce to market, it being within two miles of *Leicester*, to which there is a turnpike road running through the South-east extremity of the estate from Groby. The whole is extra-parochial and tithe-free, and moderately assessed to the land-tax; and the dwelling-house placed on an eligible and convenient part of the estate.

P. 947. notes, l. 21. The *jeu d'esprit* was more probably written by Mr. George Steevens.

P. 958. col. 2, l. 26. Benjamin Bennet, a Dissenting minister of considerable note in the beginning of the last century, was born at Whellesburgh in Leicestershire, in 1674. He was educated at the neighbouring freeschool of Market Bosworth. After going through a course of theological studies, he was first settled at a meeting house erected in 1710 on Temple Farm, the place of his nativity, from which he was called to succeed Dr. Gilpin at Newcastle upon Tyne, where he continued until his death, Sept. 1, 1726, exercising his ministerial functions with success and popularity, and acquiring a high character among his brethren for his talents and piety. He wrote several books: 1. " A Memorial of the Reformation," 1721, 8vo, an historical sketch of that event, full of prejudice against the church of England. 2. " A Defence" of the same, 1723, 8vo. 3. " Discourses on Popery," 1714, 8vo. 4. " Irenicum, or a review of some late controversies about the Trinity, &c." 1722, 8vo. Of this work one of his biographers says, that " like many other good men, he was not aware of the pernicious effects of Arianism, and entertained a more favourable idea of the sentiments of some of the dissenting ministers than they deserved. The general principles of the book are good, but not suitably applied." 5. " Sermons on the Inspiration of the Holy Scriptures." But his most popular work, and which has gone through many editions, is his " Christian Oratory," which the biographer just quoted calls the " Dissenters' Whole Duty of Man." Job Orton, a very eminent divine among the dissenters, appears by one of his letters, to have read this book at least ten times [1].

P. 971. Anne, wife of Mr. Job Farmer, died at Stoney Stanton, Feb. 12, 1810, aged 72. She had been early under the instruction of the Rev. John Bold; and was an almost faultless pattern of piety, virtue, industry, and every good work. £.100 of Mr. Bold's savings (at 5*l. per annum*) set her and her husband up in a little farm, which they managed so well as to provide for, and set up in farms four children, who never went to bed, or rose from it, without performing their devotions. None ever asked relief from her in vain. She was diligent in attending the sick; and in her whole life was but once at Leicester, and two or three times to see her sister at Sapcote, not two miles from her own residence.

P. 972. Stoney-Stanton; Dr. Nicholls died at his rectory house, Stoney-Stanton, Oct. 11, 1814, in his 72d year. By the death of this worthy Divine, the cause of true Religion, and of the Church of England in particular, has been deprived of a most valuable friend and advocate; and all the poor with whom he was in the remotest degree connected have sustained a severe loss.

Ibid. *add to the rectors of* Stoney Stanton: Rev. Mr. Doyle, son of sir John Doyle, instituted 1815.

[1] Chalmers's Biographical Dictionary; compiled from the Protestant Dissenters' Magazine; vol. V. Bogue and Bennet's History of Dissenters, vol. III. Orton's Letters to Stedman, vol. I.

P. 975.

P. 975. note, l. ult. *for* 1732, *read* 1703.

P. 1001. The following article occurs in the Parliamentary Records:

"A nostre Seigñr le Roy & a son Counsail monstrent Gregori de Normanton, Gregori Broun, Henri le Mey, William Roger, Richard Roger, Robert Roger, Henr' Roger, William de Snarkyston, Roger fiz Richard, Robert fiz Roger, William Henk, Robert Cok, Geffrey le Fowere, Henr' de Catebi, & Simound Henr', & altris, qe come le vescounte de Leycestr' avoit en comandement, q̃ touz ceux q̃ de une trespas feat a gent nostre Seigñr le Roy en Normanton fussent troves coupablis en du maner, prendreyt & en p̃soun mettereyt. Par colour de quele maundement, & verdist d'un enqueste illux p̃se, les avauntdistis Gregori, & les altris nent coupablis, ove ceux q̃ coupe aveient, prist & en prisoun mist, & uncore les detient a tort : Dount y priunt a nostre Seigñr le Roi & a son diste Consayl, qe de sa dreiturele Seignurie plese pite de eux prendre, & lur deliveraunce comaunder, issint q̃ eux ne seiunt puniz pur altri trespas.

"Mandeñr Vic' Leyc' qd̃ si ita est, tunc eos sine ditone delibari [1]."

P. 998. Mrs. Elizabeth Trotter died at Chater House, early in 1813. Her mind, highly gifted by nature, and improved by cultivation, was associated with the most amiable qualities of the heart.

P. 1007. Prefixed to a small impression (of 30 copies only) of a new edition of the History of Witherley and *Manduessedum*, printed in 1813, for private use, is the following brief Dedication:

"To John Newdigate-Ludford, Esq. D. C. L.

"Dear Sir, *Feb.* 15, 1813.

"In presenting to the publick a small impression of the History of Witherley, I have almost imperceptibly been led to enlarge it by some copious Extracts from our late learned Friend Mr. Bartlett's "History of the *Manduessedum Romanorum*," first printed in 4to, 1791, and now (by a fatal accident) become exceeding scarce. The task, however, has been much facilitated, by the suggestions and communications received in repeated visits at your hospitable mansion, and the frequent correspondence with which you have indulged me. This Portion, therefore, of my "History" can to no one be so properly inscribed as to yourself; and I hope you will accept it as an acknowledgement of sincere regard and respect.—You will be pleased, I am sure, to observe, that, in consequence of our last joint Perambulation of the old Roman Camp, I have been favoured by Mr. Thompson with an accurate Plan and Description of its present state, and with several additional particulars relative to the parish of Witherley. I am, dear Sir,

"Your greatly obliged and faithful servant, J. NICHOLS."

P. 1008. *Witherley* lordship was inclosed about 1700, by articles of agreement between the Proprietors and Henry Grove, rector; and the award is at Lindley Hall.

	A.	R.	P.
The land which paid composition for tithes was near	718	0	23
The mill meadow, a modus	5	1	0
A croft near Witherley Bridge belonging to Mr. Thomson, a modus	0	3	0
Glebe land	61	1	5
Total of the lordship, except a few cottagers' gardens	785	1	28

So that 60l. a year in lieu of tithes was laid upon — — — 718 0 23

But in the year 1810, the present rector, to exonerate the land tax, sold, from the glebe, to Mr. John Chapman of Atherstone,

	A.	R.	P.
The Mithe close	4	1	31
The Mithe meadow	8	1	5
Total	12	2	36

For the residue he gave up to the church, the two Mill Nooks, the Mill Lane, and two cottagers' houses with the gardens thereunto belonging, contiguous to the rectorial house, viz.

	A.	R.	P.
The two Mill Nooks	5	1	35
Two cottagers' houses with the gardens	0	1	1½
Total	5	2	36½

Which makes the land which now pays composition for tithes	725	0	22½
And the glebe land is now but	54	1	5½

The tithe was about 20d. per acre: but, a few years before the late rector's death, he set aside the agreement, and laid 60l. a year upon Witherley, and 40l. upon Atterton, in addition to what was settled. Witherley now pays from six to ten shillings *per* acre for tithe, and Atterton in proportion. The value of the living, some time after the inclosure, was about 200l. a year; now it is about 600l.

The resident Proprietors, in February 1813, were *Ralph Thompson, John Wilson, James* and *John Goodman.* There were then also a great many Out Town Proprietors.

Witherley and Atterton join in the church and constable levies, Witherley paying two thirds, and Atterton one third; but each maintains their own poor.

A whimsical occurrence took place here, Sept. 2, 1782, upon the finishing the new octagon tower to the Old Priory Church at Atherstone. One of the workmen came to the church, which has an octagon spire, ornamented with knobs at every angle; and, with a rope which he threw over every third knob, he drew himself up to the next, and so on to the top which is 52 yards from the ground, taking two bell-ropes with him. He took off the weathercook, and sent it about the town, to collect ale, &c. He then drew up a bottle, and drank there. He also hung down by his buckles from the hooks upon the cross-bar under the weathercock. After staying up some time, he tied the bell-ropes together in a noose round the iron bar, and let himself down again. On releasing the ropes, he drew out one of the knobs; fortunately for him, he did not go up by that angle.

P. 1009. l. 12. Rev. J. Roberts is also rector of Wolverton, co. Warwick.

P. 1009. col. 1, l. 20. In the year 1743 there were but four bells at Witherley, and the fourth was cracked, upon which Mr. Farmer of Witherley, being a great ringer, wished it to be re-cast into two smaller ones, to make five of them; but Mr. King opposed him, wanting it to be recast of the same size, and not to alter the number of them. The contention running high, Mrs. Beet, a near neighbour, said to Mr. King, "If I had your fortune, I would turn Mr. Farmer's red waistcoat wrong side outwards;" but after being at law for some time, Mr. King [2] gave it up, and it was cast into two. R. THOMPSON.

---

[1] Rot. Parl. 15 & 16 Edw. II. 1321-2. Vol. I. p. 359.

[2] This gentleman, grandfather to Mr. Thompson by his mother's side, was the last resident of his family at Atterton; but he left it, and retired to his estate at Stoke Golding, where he died in January 1757, aged 78. His daughter Dorothy Buckley, who died at Thornton, Jan. 22, 1813, in the 87th year of her age, was the relict of George Buckley, gent. She was endowed with a very strong memory, which she retained to her last; had a taste for Poetry, and composed many pieces, which she distributed amongst her friends. Her remains were interred in the North aile of Ratby church, in the same vault with her great-grandmother Mrs. Margaret Choyce, who died May 3, 1704, aged 106 years. (See vol. IV. p. 889*.) A Funeral Sermon was preached there, Jan. 31, 1813, by the Rev. Mr. Martin, from Rev. xiv. 13; and on Feb. 7, another at Thornton, by the Rev. Mr. Wood, from Amos iv. 12; and the following inscription is intended to be put on her monument: "She was a meek woman, a tender mother, a dutiful wife, always ready to relieve a neighbour in want, and deeply lamented by her only surviving son, William Buckley."

John King, esq. now resident at Leicester, is a grandson of Mr. King of Atterton.

On the five bells are these inscriptions:

1. " OMNIA FIANT AD GLORIAM DEI. THO. EAYRE FECIT. RICHARD FARMER, C. W. 1744."

2. " OMNIA FIANT AD GLORIAM DEI. GLORIA DEO SOLI. THO. EAYRE FECIT, 1744."

3. " BE YT KNOWNE TO ALL THAT DOTH ME SEE ; THAT NEWCOMBE OF LEICESTER MADE MEE. 1609."

4. " I. H. S. NAZARENVS REX IVDEORVM FILI DEI MISERERE MEI, 1619."

5. " IESVS NAZARENVS REX IVDEORVM."

The fifth bell sounds A. It has no date upon it.

Witherley is rather remarkable for longevity : there were living there, in February 1813, six poor men, who were each of them 80 years of age, and one woman 91.

P. 1018. col. 2. At Ansley Hall, is a drawing of Kenilworth Castle when compleat, reduced in 1716, by Mr. Henry Beighton of Griff, from an old drawing belonging to the Earl of Denbigh, taken about 1620.

P. 1019. BRET'S HALL.

" In the parish of *Ansley* there is a place though but of mean consideration, yet noted in the common maps by the name of *Bret's Hall*, from a family of that name, sometime owners thereof."

The following information respecting that family has been communicated by William Hamper, esq. of Birmingham ; who transcribed it from the original, a Scrap of Paper in an ancient hand, probably of the time of Henry VII. or VIII. amongst Mr. Chetwynd's MSS. in the possession of the Right Hon. Charles-Chetwynd Talbot, Earl Talbot, A. D. 1812.

" M^d y^t Henrycus brette wedud ye detur Alyc' of Ryc' salle & heyr

& by henr' had well' brette wedud syssyll ye dotur of Nycolas of Calten' & he had a son' by her ye hett well brett & his fadur dyud wen he was but

iij her' of Age & wen he com to hys Age he send for is re'tts and brout doun a fyene y' a pond And yen y' was a grette troubull he fell in ye lond

And yen he wentte to the Kyngns warres

And y^t wyll y^e fyne passud A Genust hym

And wed y^e dotur Elysabet of Wyll Freeman And by hyr he had a son y^t hett Wyll Brett."

Indorsed in a later hand,

" Descent of Brett of Brettes hall co. War."

When reduced into Pedigree, will stand thus:

Henry Brett.=Alice, daughter and heir of Richard Salle.

William Brett.=Cecily, daughter of Nicholas de Calten, [qu. de Colton, co Stafford ?]

William Brett, aged 3 years=Elizabeth, daughter of at his father's death. William Freeman.

William Brett.

" The first of this family was *William ;* unto whom William de Hardreshull (lord of Ansley in Henry the Third's time) gave certain lands here; from which William descended another *William,* unto whom the Bishop of the Diocese, in 34 Edward III. granted licence to have divine service celebrated, for the space of two years, in a private oratory here. But from these Brets, who possessed it till the beginning of Henry IV.'s time (which is above 200 years), it came to *Nicholas Palmer,* of Stanton, in com. Leicester, and by the daughters and coheirs of *William* Palmer to · · · · · · *Harecourt* and *William Pouchin ;* which William Pouchin, in 37 Henry VIII. passed away his interest to *John Purefey,* it being then reputed a manor ; whereupon, in 14 Elizabeth, partition was made betwixt the said *John* and *George*

Harecourt ; to which John Purefey succeeded *Michael,* who sold his part thereof to *John White,* of Busby in Leicestershire.—In this family it continued till the 15th of December, 1658, when *Thomas* White the elder and *Ellen* his wife, and *Thomas* White the younger, passed it by indenture, bearing similar date, with other hereditaments, to *William Thornton* of Manceter ; and in Hilary term, 1658-9, a fine was levied of one messuage, two cottages, three gardens, two orchards, 20 acres of land, 10 acres of meadow, 100 acres of pasture, seven acres of wood, and common of pasture for all cattle in Bret's Hall, Ansley, Hartshill, and Stockingford ; wherein William Thornton aforesaid was plaintiff, and Thomas White the elder, and Ellen his wife, and Thomas White the younger, and Francis Bacon, clerk, and Barbara his wife, deforcients. The said William Thornton, on the 3d of April, 13 Charles II. and A. D. 1661, conveyed it to *John Stratford,* esq. of Horston Grange, in the parish of Nun-Eaton ; whose descendant *Francis Stratford,* late of Merevale, esq. on the 10th of October, 6 Geo. II. A. D. 1732, exchanged it for a spring wood, called Hoare Park, in the hamlet of Bentley and parish of Shustoke, and in consideration of 180*l.* with the late *John Ludford,* esq. whose son *John* is now (1815) possessor of it.

The site, as well as most of the demesnes, are inclosed in the park at Ansley Hall. Part of the dwelling-house, and the oratory above noticed, were standing at the time it was purchased by the late Mr. Ludford : it was surrounded by a moat, which now remains, though divided into two parts ; the sides of the N. E. part of which were raised, and the whole enlarged some years ago, and carried round an adjacent piece of land, so as to form a complete island ; in the centre of which stands a Chinese temple, built A. D. 1767, from the 2d figure in plate VI. of Sir William Chambers's Chinese Designs ; and in a cell underneath is erected the monument of the Purefoys ; a drawing whereof is engraved in Dugdale's History of Caldecote [1], fig. 4 ; and which was pulled down and thrown away into the church-yard when the church was repaired about 1766 ; from whence it was removed in 1778, in order to be preserved in its present situation.

The South-west part of the moat still retains its proper name, and about 17 yards West of it is a well of very good spring water, $3\frac{1}{2}$ yards deep, which is always full to the top, and in wet weather runs over. The house and oratory were pulled down about the year 1750, and the stones of the oratory removed into the old gardens of Ansley Hall, where in a small dale they were formed into a cell for an hermitage, and at present remain so.

Mr. T. Warton, the celebrated Poet Laureat, wrote the annexed copy of verses [2] there in April 1758:

" Beneath this stoney roof reclin'd,
I sooth to peace my pensive mind ;
And while, to shade my lowly cave,
Embowering trees their umbrage wave ;
And while the maple dish is mine,
The beechen cup unstain'd with wine,
I scorn the gay licentious crowd,
Nor heed the toys that deck the proud.

Within my limits lone and still,
The blackbird sings in artless trill :
Fast by my couch, congenial guest,
The wren has built her mossy nest ;

[1] Ex autog. penès W. Sheldon, ar.

[2] " These verses, as printed in the Fourth Volume, p. 1044, are taken from an altered copy, published by Mr. Warton himself, with other Poems, in 12mo, London, 1777.—The facts are as follows : Mr. Warton was tutor to the last Earl and late Marquis of Donegall, of Trinity College, and as such visited Ansley Hall in the Easter vacation 1758, when he wrote and left these verses in the cell. He never saw Ansley Hall after that time above once, if ever, and that the following year. Lord Donegall leaving Oxford in 1759, or thereabouts, came of age in 1760 ; and of course all connexions between Mr. Warton and Ansley Hall ceased. The two poems are now before the publick ; and let them be the judges whether the natural and local simplicity of the original, written upon the spot, with all the objects around him, and on the spur of the moment, is not preferable to the stiff and affected style of the altered copy published by the finished Poet, afterwards Poet Laureat, certainly above 18, if not nearer 20 years after he had ceased visiting Ansley Hall, and of course forgot all the *locality* of the poem. And as the copy he has given the publick is very different from the original, having little or no resemblance (except in the first and last words, and *first verse,* and this is even mutilated, and the word " eo-genial," in the second verse, which he still retained), I verily believe he wrote this entirely from memory, without a scrap of the original poem in his possession, though he knew I was resident at Oxford at the very time, and could have furnished him with a copy at any time, as I always carried it in my *port-feuille,* and he knew the original, in his own hand-writing (which I still have safe at Ansley Hall) was in the hands of the late Miss Juliana Ludford, carefully preserved." J. N. L.

From

From social scenes, by nature wise,
To lurk with innocence she flies;
Here hopes in safe repose to dwell,
Nor aught suspects the sylvan cell.

At morn and eve I take my round,
To mark how blows my flowery mound;
And every budding primrose count,
That trimly paints my blooming mount;
Or o'er the sculptures quaint and rude,
Which deck my gloomy solitude,
I teach in many a wreath to stray
Fantastic ivy's gadding spray.

While such pure joys retirement wait,
Who but would smile at guilty state;
Who but would wish his holy lot
In calm Oblivion's thoughtful grot?
Who but would cast his pomp away,
To take my staff and mantle grey;
And to the world's tumultuous stage
Prefer the peaceful Hermitage?　　　T. W."

MONWODE.

" This lying on the West side of 𝔄𝔫𝔰𝔩𝔢𝔶, and in the same parish, had heretofore the reputation of a mannour; for by that name, did sir *John de Hardreshull* call it in 39 Edw. III. at which time he settled it[1] with 𝔄𝔫𝔰𝔩𝔢𝔶 and 𝔥𝔞𝔯𝔡𝔯𝔢𝔰𝔥𝔲𝔩 in the hands of certain feoffees: and so by records of later time hath it often been termed: but as it was originally a member of 𝔄𝔫𝔰𝔩𝔢𝔶, so is it now deemed to be; no part (that I know) retaining the name, but a piece of waste ground lying on the utmost skirt thereof, called 𝔐𝔬𝔫𝔴𝔬𝔡𝔢 𝔏𝔢𝔢."

[Though, as Sir William Dugdale observes, there is no part of Ansley retains the name of Monwode, except Monwode Lee, yet this is owing more to the lands being vested in one family for a number of years, and conveyed with other parts of Ansley, than for want of vestiges of the antient manor; both the Hadreshulls and Colepeppers being styled lords of the manor of Monwode; and Nature seems to have left a boundary to the manor, when Tradition is silent; a direct line drawn North from Ansley-mill to Hoare-park, cutting off a corner of the parish of Ansley, containing about 400 acres, and bounded nearly all round by lanes, which probably was the whole of the manor. Within this boundary are two places, which, from their names, appear to have been capital mansions, the one now destroyed called the Moat-house, and the moat of which still remains on the South side of Monwode Lea, a short way after you enter it from Ansley church; and the other, now called the Old-house, with two pieces of land adjacent, called the Great and Little Paddock. And here it is observable, that either our ancestors frequently changed their mansions; or capital houses were much more numerous formerly; as within the parish of Ansley, besides these two and Bret's Hall, there are no less than three others which appear to have been such, *viz.* the manor house of Ansley, situate at the church-end; a house called New Hall, situate upon the Colliery; and the present capital mansion of Ansley Hall.]

It is mentioned above in the account of the manor and parish, copied from Sir William Dugdale's Warwickshire, that this place is joined with Hartshill in the Conqueror's survey; upon which it is to be observed, that the constable of Ansley, chosen annually the day after Christmas-day, at the manor house of Ansley, by the parishioners, is also the constable of Hartshill; from which it appears, that the constablewick is a more antient division than manors or parishes.

The manor is valued in Domesday at 100 shillings, being a knight's fee; and is now, including the value of the woods and mines, not far off 3000*l.* There are about 50 acres of woodland still preserved in different parts of the parish as spring wood; but most of the hedge-rows abound with oak and ash,

to the growth of which the soil seems naturally adapted, and which occasions the forest appearance above mentioned. The rest of the land is mostly arable, though there are some good upland meadows and pastures, but very little of what the graziers call prime-land (except about 50 acres in the manor of Bret's Hall); it bears very good crops of wheat and oats; but is not so favourable to barley, being naturally strong land inclinable to a marley clay.

About half a mile from the North-east side of Ansley-hall is an extensive mine of coals, which in this parish consists of upwards of 200 acres; but the vein continues into Nun Eaton South and Oldbury North; and for many miles both ways to the borders of Staffordshire, and beyond the city of Coventry: they have been severally worked for many years, and supply all this country with coals. Upon the East or Basset side of the coal runs a vein of iron stone, which was worked formerly, but not of late years; and a few hundred yards from the South or deep side of the coal, and on the South-west side of Ansley-hall, lies a vein of lime-stone, which likewise accompanies the coal into the neighbouring parishes; the manor of Ansley being in this place the narrowest, and not far exceeding half a mile in breadth. The lime is used not only in building, but also as a manure for the land, to which, being applied in sufficient quantities, it is a beneficial improvement. The coal-pits are from 38 to 88 yards deep; and the lime-pits about 15 yards. At Ansley-hall, which is situated between the two delfs of coal and lime (though the miners have conjectured there might be coal under it at a very great depth), there are several wells of excellent water at 33 feet; and what is very remarkable, at the new house about half a mile West of it, a well was sunk, and no water could be found till they got to 80 feet deep; and at a cottage between the two houses, the cottager, a collier, attempting to sink a well, nearly ruined himself, and was obliged to give up the pursuit, not having come to water at the depth of the new house well, and the damp preventing him proceeding farther; and what renders this still more remarkable, there is at an old farm-house, not above 100 yards of the new house, a draw-well of good water not exceeding three yards deep; and the spring of which is so strong, that it frequently runs over the top. About the year 1750, the late John Ludford, esq. enclosed a small piece of ground for a park, which he afterwards enlarged to 100 acres, the present size, containing the site, demesnes, and part of the manor of Bret's Hall, and also part of the parish of Nun Eaton; in this has frequently occurred the circumstance mentioned by Dr. Plot, in his History of Staffordshire, ch. VII. p. 258, *viz.* " Fawns cast with their lower jaws so short that they cannot suck; and so consequently all die; all of which are white, as if white was an imperfection in animals, as well as in plants." Dr. Plot is certainly right in his conjecture, that they are all white which are born so imperfect; and it is further observable, they are always buck fawns; they have been brought home alive, and tried to be sustained with cows milk, but without success; but the Doctor is certainly mistaken in his idea of white being an imperfection in deer, because there are many milk-white deer in this park; and it has been observed, both in the bucks and does, that they are larger and fatter deer when killed than any other colours.

Two other circumstances in Natural History which have happened at this place may not be unworthy of observation: *viz.* In the year 1781 an ewe sheep yeaned one ram-lamb; and in about eight or ten days after, which was the 3d of April, she again yeaned two lambs, *viz.* one ewe and one ram. The first-yeaned lamb and the ewe lamb were left with her, and the youngest ram-lamb was taken from her and reared a kade; the ewe-lamb died in four or five days, the other lamb being too strong, and taking all the ewe's milk from it; the ram-

[1] Ed. Dugdale, 1656, p. 790; and ed. Thomas, vol. II. p. 1098.

lamb

lamb, which was reared a kade, was killed on the 21st of December, 1785, as a wether (after being sheared four times), and weighed 111 pounds when dressed.—On Monday May 17, 1784, three rearing cow-calves about three months old got into a drying-yard, where there was a yew-hedge (out of the croft into which they were turned to grass by a gate being left open), and, as is supposed, eat very plentifully of the yew; they were suckled as usual in the afternoon; and the next morning, *viz.* Tuesday, the 18th of May, two were found quite dead; and the third dying, to which they gave a few spoonfuls of oil, and it did not live half an hour after. They were opened and skinned, and their entrails thrown upon a muck-hill, where the dogs got to them; and a Dane-dog went out with the servants and horses, and was seen to drink at a spring, soon after which he was seen to leap up at the horse's nose as if to catch a fly from it, which he had frequently used to do, and dropped down dead immediately; upon bringing him dead home, being much alarmed for the safety of a favourite blood-hound, and not then having been informed of the other dog dying immediately after drinking, some sweet oil it was thought might relieve him, and a common drenching-horn full was accordingly given him, in about five minutes after which he died much in the same way as the other dog before. Many other dogs had eaten of the same entrails, but none else received any hurt, particularly two pointers, who were seen to eat voraciously of them, one of which is still living, and the other died of old age in January, 1790. The method which rendered yew innoxious to them was, the moment the effect of liquid was perceived on the death of the other two dogs, they were tied up, and kept without water or any liquid for 24 hours; and this seems to prove that yew is innoxious to the stomach unless thrown into a fermentation by liquids drank after it. The yew-leaves quite green were found both in the entrails of the calves and the dogs killed by it; and they were perforated through with small holes, which certainly occasioned their death.

The torrent or rivulet, mentioned by Dugdale, rises in the most Northern corner of the parish; from whence it runs in a South direction to a pool called Wagstaffe's pool, where it unites with another small stream, which bounds part of the North-west side; and from thence runs in almost a direct line North-west for nearly two miles to Ansley-mill, which it works; and from thence turns again Southwards, and forms not only the South-west boundary of this part of the parish and manor, but also of the two hundreds of Hemlingford and Knightlow. Upon the entrance of Arley, it is united with another small brook, which rises at Nuthurst Heath, and forms likewise this boundary line between the two parishes and hundreds. There are several other small brooks in the parish, one of which rises near the new park above mentioned, and runs East till it joins a third, which rises on the other side of Nuthurst Heath, and forms the South bounds on this side. At the junction of these two streams (as well as at a small distance up a short brook, which falls into the Millbrook before it enters Arley), there are still remaining cinders of iron stone, from which it appears there antiently has been two small smithies at these places for the melting of the iron stone, though no other tradition of them remains. A little lower on this stream a fourth joins it, which rises not far from Ansley-hall, and forms the South and East bounds between this manor and the manor of Stockingford, in the parish of Nun Eaton; to which place these united streams continue their course, and fall into the Anker. A fifth rises in Bret's Hall wood, and continues its course to Nun Eaton, but in a different direction. A sixth rises on the North-east side the colliery, and forms the bounds between here and Oldbury and Hartshill; this also runs to Nun Eaton

(but in another course the greatest part of the way), being first joined by the Bret's Hall brook, and then by the Nuthurst Heath brook, within half a mile of the junction with the Anker. A seventh stream rises at Birchley Heath, and forms the bounds between Ansley and Bentley North-west till it enters the parish of Over Whitacre, through which it runs, and unites with the Bourne, near Whitacre Furnace End.

P. 1025. The Rev. F. Bichley Astley, M. A. rector of Manningford Abbots, Wiltshire, third son of F. D. Astley, esq. of Everley-house, in the same county, and Mary-Anne, youngest daughter of John Newdigate-Ludford, esq. D. C. L. of Ansley Hall, were married at Ansley, July 19, 1813.

P. 1026. *Atterton* lordship was inclosed by articles of agreement between the Proprietors and Henry Grove, rector; *viz.* Charles Jennens, esq. Robert Charnels, Mr. John King[1], and John Geary, and a map and survey was taken by Mr. Henry Beighton in 1728, now in the possession of Captain Weaver, when the allotments were as follow:

				Tithe *per ann.*		
	A.	R.	P.	£.	s.	d.
Charles Jennens, esq.	189	3	15	18	0	3
Robert Charnels,	53	0	32	5	4	6
Mr. John King	135	0	17	14	0	6
John Weaver	63	1	35	6	15	10
Elizabeth and Thomas Harris	94	0	10	9	14	1
John Geary,	61	3	29	6	4	10
Titheable land	597	2	18	60	0	0 Total
Glebe —	16	3	24			tithe.

Total of the lordship 614 2 2

And by the award in the possession of the present proprietors, dated April 25, 1729, it was agreed that the rate tithe was set upon the inclosure in lieu and full satisfaction of all tithes and tenths of corn, grain, and hay, and all other tithes and tenths both predial, personal, and mixed, also in lieu and full satisfaction of all oblations, obventions, and other payments, except Easter book mortuaries and surplice fees.

P. 1031. For the annexed Plan of the site of Manduessedum (see Pl. LIV.) and the remarks which accompany it, I am indebted to Ralph Thompson, esq. of Witherley Bridge; who says, " I have lately purchased of the honourable *Charles Finch* that part of Manduessedum (called in the writings *Offal Bank*) North of the Watling Street, and also *Offal Close*; and it appears from the writings, dated the 23d of November 1717, that *Charles Jennens*, of Gopsal, esq. purchased, of *Thomas Hodgkinson*, of Slearston, and then of Sysham, in the county of Northampton, tanner, son and heir of *John* Hodgkinson, then late of Mancetter, in the county of Warwick, tanner, deceased, the above lands, with other property in Witherley.

" The remainder of the estate is purchased by Messrs. *Willson, Goodman, Nuttall,* and *Baker.*

" Content of that part of Manduessedum South of the Watling Street, including A. R. P. the cottager's gardens - - - - - - 3 0 11

" The North side - - - - - - 2 3 4

" The Watling Street through the above 0 1 29

" Total of Manduessedum - - - - 6 1 4

" Mean length, - - - - - - - 627 feet.

" Mean breadth, - - - - - - 438

" The above is the survey of the level surface, not including the slope, which is about 33 feet, and is very perfect on that part of Manduessedum North of the Watling Street: but on the South side the plough has almost obliterated it, except at the South-east end, where I have frequently observed in a dry time the grass was burnt up for some breadth across it,

---

[1] About the year 1600 a branch of this antient family, which had resided at Witherley for several centuries, possessed the Hall orchard in that lordship. See vol. IV. Part II. p. 1008; also note [5], p. 984.
The following memorandum occurs during the period of the Civil War in 1642:
" Received of John King, of Atterton, a brown bay horse for the public service, value 5l. Peter Temple."

more

more than on any other part: and, in September 1804, I informed *Thomas Cowper Hincks,* esq. the proprietor of this part of Manduessedum; who ordered a man to dig into it; and at the depth of four feet he found a causeway leading towards Manceter. Also in the year 1796 or 1797, as some workmen were making a sawpit at the North corner, they found a brass coin, which I gave to Mr. Hincks. I do not remember what the inscription was; but it is still, I believe, in his possession. There were also some antient kinds of pottery dug up, a specimen of which I have by me.

" In the Furlongs a road has been discovered leading towards Manceter. About 70 years ago that part of Manduessedum North of the Watling Street was gardened, and a great number of coins were dug up; also a brass plate, containing four curious seals, was dug up in one of the cottager's gardens, and an antient spur.

" I have lately purchased, from the executors of the late Mr. *Dudley Baxter,* the Furlongs; and it appears from the writings, that *William Burleton,* late of Fonthill Gifford, in the county of Wilts, but then of Handley, in the county of Dorset, esq. eldest son and heir at law of *William* Burleton, late of Donhead St. Mary, in the said county of Wilts, esq. deceased, in 1791, sold to Mr. Dudley Baxter the remainder, in four pieces, called the Furlong, Second Furlong, Roundhill, and Barnes's Meadow; and also the tithes of the lands of Manceter belonging to the vicarages of Stoneley, Ashow, Kellingworth, Manceter, and Monk's Kirby.

" At the latter end of December 1812, in making a ditch on the North-east side of Manduessedum, now called Oufort Bank, we discovered at the depth of two feet, some large red and white free-stones, and other large rough stones: they probably were to denote the bounds of the two parishes, or are some remains of Manduessedum; there did not appear to be any mortar upon them. Also about the same time, in making some soughs in the Broad close to drain the land, at the depth of four feet were discovered a road from Manduessedum; it appears to be a continuation of the road above described. There were also dug up some fragments of antient pottery.
R. Thompson."

It appears from family writings, that the *Thompson* family have resided there for several centuries. On the first leaf of the Register, *John* the son of *John Thompson* was baptized April 21, 1572; and a *Ralph* Thompson, who resided there in 1595, was a proprietor of lands in the common fields of Witherley: viz. Moore Field, Middle Field, Mithe Field, and of the cow pasture called Witherley Mithe: he also occupied land in the liberty of Manceter (spelt at that time *Manceyter,* and now usually *Mancetter)* in a field called the Bottom Field, which he rented of Basil Fielding, of Paddox Newnham, in the county of Warwick, esq.

After Ralph, who died in 1640, the next residents in succession were

Thomas, the son of Ralph, bapt. April 22, 1610.
Ralph, the son of Thomas, bapt. Aug. 15, 1641.
Samuel, the son of Ralph, bapt. Sept. 23, 1686.

John Thompson, an eminent mathematician and philosopher, son of *Samuel* and *Dorothy,* was born here March 1, 1721-2. When a child, he used to sit by his mother, a literary woman, and a great reader of the Scriptures; and he, probably, imbibed from her that early taste for books, which was afterwards the cause of his future acquirements. After having received the first rudiments of his education at Atherstone school, his genius for mathematical studies soon discovered itself, and he applied very closely,

to what few Mathematical Books he was acquainted with; which were purchased by his mother, against his father's consent; so that he was obliged to steal a little time, when he could, which was generally in the night; his father wishing him to attend his own occupation, the Farming and Grazing business, to which the son had a great aversion; so that he laboured under very great difficulties, to procure books, and time to peruse them; and though there were but few writers upon mathematical subjects at that time, and the road to scientific pursuits very intricate, yet under every disadvantage, by the strength of his own genius, having no master to instruct him, he soon made extraordinary advances in algebra, geometry, plain and spherical trigonometry, land surveying, &c. &c. He had also made great proficiency in Music, and took a survey of every branch relating to that science, such as the doctrine sounds, the description of musical instruments, &c.; and was an excellent performer on the violin, and other instruments: and used to say that a true genius surmounted all difficulties. He had made this progress very early in life, which attracted the notice of two very eminent mathematicians, Mr. Henry Beighton of Griff, and Mr. Anthony Thacker[1], of Chilvers Coton, near Nuneaton, who were so fond of his company that they frequently held periodical meetings to discourse upon mathematical and philosophical subjects; and with the latter of these gentlemen he further extended his knowledge, and afterwards assisted him in writing,

A new Method of solving Geometrical Problems, A Complete Treatise of Spherical Trigonometry," and " A Collection of Spherical Problems," &c. His knowledge in astronomy, and the various branches of the mathematics, he made subservient to practical purposes, making theory and practice go hand in hand, a specimen of which is well worth recording. On the inclosure of Atherstone common fields, in 1765, it was agreed that the small cottagers should have their claims laid out together in one piece of land, on which some of the most eminent surveyors and commissioners at that time were employed, who laid it out in the form of two trapezia (now called *The Cottager's Piece),* which was to contain just 100 acres. The cottagers, being desirous of having it examined, requested Mr. Thompson to re-survey it, and he found they had laid out near three acres too much; on which he proposed it for a prize question in the Gentleman's Diary for that year (being the first that was proposed for that work), which exercised the abilities of some of its ablest contributors, as may be seen from the answers in the following year, which gave great satisfaction. The variety of subjects he wrote upon, in the mathematical, philosophical, and astronomical sciences, which appeared in Heath's Palladium[2], Martin's Magazines, the Ladies and Gentleman's Diaries, &c. &c. bespeak his great abilities: he made many improvements in the plain table, and other mathematical and philosophical instruments. His method of surveying land was entirely original, and his curious inventions in that art are very numerous, as appears from a manuscript treatise written upon that subject; he has also left manuscripts upon arithmetic, algebra, geometry, plain and spherical trigonometry, conic sections, fluctions, &c. &c. His conspicuous talents in these august sciences received additional lustre, from the milder virtues of domestic life, and the amiable qualities of a Christian. He was candid in his judgment, uniform and blameless in his manners; always communicative, and totally disinterested. His qualifications were tempered with a vein of gaiety, which neither his abstracted speculations nor his infirmities were able to impair. He had naturally a

---

[1] He was appointed to teach the mathematics at Birmingham free-school in the year 1740, which was but of short duratiom; for he was seised with a violent fever, which baffled the art of the physicians, and died in March 1741. He composed the mathematical parts of the Ladies Diary for his friend Mr. Beighton for some years before Mr. Beighton's death. He also printed Proposals for publishing a Miscellany of Mathematics, in three volumes, 8vo, but he only lived to finish the first volume. Dr. Hutton laments that, after many fruitless endeavours to procure proper materials for memoirs of the early compilers of the Ladies Diary, he was obliged to relinquish that favourite design. Diarian Miscellany, vol. I.

[2] Heath, who would hardly ascribe merit to any one, said (Palladium, 1762), " This solution is by a curious and careful computor, who always commanded our esteem."

strong healthy constitution; but, being too fond of a studious life, it brought on the rheumatism; and for some years, he complained of a numbness in his limbs, which ended in a dropsy, of which he died Feb. 25, 1783. The editors of the Leicester Journal for March 29 following, after enumerating very highly his qualifications, conclude with these words: "Bosworth may boast of her Simpson, Burbach of her Cotes, &c. and Witherley bridge will long be noted as the residence of a Thompson."—He married Elizabeth, eldest daughter of John King, of Stoke Golding, near Hinckley, gent. a woman of an amiable disposition, and of great virtue and piety, an affectionate wife, and a tender mother, whose exemplary life will long be affectionately recollected. She died Dec. 16, 1799, aged 74. They had three sons; *John, Ralph,* and *Samuel.*

John died June 24, 1777, aged 24.

Ralph married *Ann,* daughter of William Lole, of Barnacle, gentleman, by whom he has a son and a daughter, John and Elizabeth.

Samuel the third son is living, with his brother.

P. 1034. col. 1, l. 5 from bottom. *Thomas-Cowper Hincks,* esq. the son and heir of John Hincks, esq. of Chester, and of the late Mrs. Hincks, is now (1813) the largest proprietor in Manceter lordship.

P. 1035. col. 2. line 11. *Ridge Lane.*

"To the West is a lane called Ridge-lane, in which are some houses that do not belong to the manor of Oldbury." Ridge-lane has no more to do with the manor or hamlet of Oldbury than that of St. Dunstan's in the East. Ridge-lane is the continuation of the antient road from the Cross of the Hand, about a quarter of a mile above Ansley church, leading over Birchley-heath, from Ansley to Atherstone, and what I apprehend to be the antient Birchley-street, described above, p. 1035, col. a. par. 3. l. 28. It is flanked, leading from Ansley on the left or North-west side, all the way from Birchley-heath to Atherstone Out Woods (where it terminates), by Bentley Park, and Monk's Park, the property of Dugdale Stratford Dugdale, esq. a large wood of 200 or 300 acres, and the greatest remaining part of the antient Arden in Warwickshire.

The White Hart alehouse, now through ignorance tranformed from the White Stag into a White Human Heart, or rather the heart upon a pack of cards, instead of the antient Forest sign, which obtains all along the Watling-street from Barnet to Atherstone, is situate at the end of another lane or highway, about a mile or more in length, commencing at the Sun alehouse in Ansley, near the North gate of Ansley Park, and running in a direct line from South to North, about a quarter of a mile through Ansley, where it is called Bounds-lane, not half a mile through the hamlet of Oldbury, to a gate near to which a house has been built within a very few years, where it assumes the name of Piper-lane, and continues another quarter of a mile, to the above house. This place, which consists of several more houses, for what reason is unknown, assumes to itself the privilege of a village, and holds a wake as such annually on the Sunday after St. James the Apostle, 25th July. From the gate in Piper-lane to the gate into Bentley park, a very few yards beyond the White Hart, the parish and manor also of Manceter comes up, and joins Ansley as in vol. IV. p. 1033, col. 2. par. 8. l. 3. The land on the West side is the property of *John Newdigate Ludford,* esq. and on the East the property of *Dugdale Stratford Dugdale,* esq.

Ridge-lane wake is held upon the Sunday three weeks before Ansley wake, which is the Sunday after 15th August, though it ought to be after the 10th, the church of Ansley being dedicated to St. Laurence; and as, upon enquiry, it is found that no wake is held at Manceter, probably this may be the remains of the antient Manceter wake, which church is dedicated to St. Peter. J. N. L.

P. 1038. col. 1. l. 33. *Stafford-Squire Baxter,* esq. of Gray's-inn, died March 22, 1812; and his well-selected Library was sold by auction by Mess. King and Lochée, May 25, 1812, and seven following days

His brother, *Dudley Baxter,* esq. died Dec. 27, 1811; and his Library was sold by auction.

P. 1041. col. 1, l. 40. *read* Kynnesman.

P. 1042. col. 1, l. 2. *for* 373, *read* 272.—L. 6. *read* Humphrey Banas*ter.*

P. 1043. col. 2, l. 9 from bottom, *read* P. 859.

P. 1048. col. 1, l. 46. Mrs. Sarah Heyrick died on the 17th, not on the 10th, of November, 1811.

P. 1051. *read* Grey, Thomas lord, letter of 634*.

P. 1052. *read* Herdwike, of Lindley, pedigree, 643.

P. 123. *add to Sheriffs :*

55. Edward Farnham, of Quorndon, esq.

P. 519. Rev. Samuel Deacon, junior, died March 19, 1812, aged 98.

⁎⁎⁎ When the Memoirs of Mr. Robinson, in p. 119 of these Additions, were printing, I had not seen the very appropriate and elegant "Character, exhibited in the Speech of Robert Hall, M. A. at the Annual Meeting of the Leicester Auxiliary Bible Society, April 1813." And I cannot now forbear to extract from it a sentence or two highly creditable to the Speaker, as well to his deceased Friend.

"Though I have had the honour of a personal acquaintance with Mr. Robinson for upwards of thirty years, it is comparatively but of late that I had an opportunity of contemplating him more nearly. While placed at a distance, I admired him as one of the remote luminaries which adorn the hemishere; I certainly perceived him to be a star of the first magnitude: but no sooner was I stationed on the spot, than I became sensible of the lustre of his beams, felt the force of his attraction, and recognised in him the sun and centre of the system. His merit was not of that kind which attracts most admiration at a distance; it was so genuine and solid, that it grew in estimation the more closely it was inspected. It is possible some men may have extended their influence to a wider circle, and moved in a more extended sphere. But where influence is diffused beyond a certain limit, it becomes attenuated in proportion to its diffusion; it operates with an energy less intense. Mr. Robinson completely filled as large a sphere of personal agency, as is, perhaps, possible to an individual. He left no part of it unoccupied, no interstices unsupplied; and spread himself through it with an energy, in which there was nohing irregular, nothing defective, nothing redundant. ......The hearers of Mr. Robinson were too much occupied by the subjects he presented to their attention to waste a thought on the speaker; this occupied a second place in the order of their reflections; but when it did occur, it assumed the character, not of superficial admiration, but of profound attachment. Their feelings towards him were not those of persons gratified, but benefited; and they listened to his instructions, not as a source of amusement, but as a spring of living water. There never was a settled pastor, probably, who had formed a juster conception of the true end of preaching, who pursued it more steadily, or attained it to a greater extent. He preached immortal truth with a most extraordinary simplicity, perspicuity, and energy, in a style adapted to all capacities, equally removed from vulgarity and affected refinement; and the tribute paid to his exertions consisted not in loud applauses, it was of a higher order; it consisted of penitential sighs, holy resolutions, a determination of the whole soul for God, and such impressions on the spirits of men, as will form the line of separation betwixt the happy and the miserable to all eternity...... Though he had reached that period of life which constitutes old age, it was a *cruda viridisque senectus.* His age had impaired little or nothing of his vigour; its chief effect was that of imparting additional dignity to his countenance, and weight to his character. He fell like a noble tree, after two or three strokes, with all his sap and verdure, with extended boughs and rich foliage, while thousands were reposing under his shadow and partaking of his fruits. Seldom has death gained a richer spoil than in the extinction of the earthly existence of this admirable man."

Feb. 14, 1815.—*Laus Deo.*

R. Thompson's Land

Oufort Close

Glebe Land

R. THOMPSON'S LAND

Barn Close

Manduefsedum

now called Oufort-Bank

Mr Thompson's Land

Cottages

Cottages

Manduefsedum

now called Castle Bank

Mr Hincks's Land

Thos Cowper Hincks Esqr

Broad Close

Back Lane

Toll-gate

Mr Goodman's Land

The Leys

The Furlongs

Watling Street

R. THOMPSON'S LAND

The Furlongs

Witherley

Ralph Thompson

Witherley Bridge

River Anker

MAP
and Survey of
Manduefsedum
with part of the Fields
Adjoining
made in October 1812.

RALPH THOMPSON,
of Witherley.

Scale 44 Yards in an Inch

Chains

Lithomite Jr. M. Alanzano Stºsworsleh Esqr.

Manduefsedum is denotted by the Dotted Line.

ABSTRACT of Answers and Returns to the Population Act of 51 George III. 1811.

COUNTY OF LEICESTER. ——— HUNDREDS.	PARISH, TOWNSHIP, OR EXTRA-PAROCHIAL PLACE.	HOUSES.				OCCUPATIONS.			PERSONS.		
		Inhabited.	By how many Families occupied.	Building.	Uninhabited.	Families chiefly employed in Agriculture.	Families chiefly employed in Trade, Manufactures, or Handicraft.	All other Families not comprised in the Two preceding Classes.	Males.	Females.	Total of Persons.
FRAMLAND.											
Ab-Kettleby a	Parish — —	31	31	—	2	28	3	—	74	68	142
Barkstone	Ditto — —	52	53	—	—	38	14	1	146	159	305
Belvoir b	Extra-Paroch.	2	3	—	—	—	2	1	46	50	96
Bottesford with Normanton	Parish — —	184	200	—	5	97	70	33	411	480	891
Branston	Ditto — —	47	48	—	1	52	15	1	115	121	236
Broughton, Nether	Ditto — —	78	78	—	2	40	30	8	171	196	367
Buckminster c	Ditto — —	61	63	1	1	40	17	6	180	150	330
Burton-Lazars	Ditto — —	40	41	1	3	33	8	—	100	112	212
Claxton, Long, alias Clawson	Ditto — —	134	137	1	5	85	36	16	296	331	627
Cold-Overton d	Ditto — —	18	18	—	—	16	2	—	47	49	96
Coston	Ditto — —	27	27	—	—	7	4	16	82	70	152
Croxton-Kyrial	Ditto — —	90	115	—	—	21	88	6	228	243	471
Dalby, Little	Ditto — —	28	28	—	1	25	1	2	78	77	155
Eastwell	Ditto — —	22	22	—	—	19	2	1	62	52	114
Eaton	Ditto — —	51	61	1	3	50	11	—	128	141	269
Edmondthorpe	Ditto — —	32	34	—	1	19	3	12	75	83	158
Freeby e	Chapelry —	22	22	1	—	22	—	—	54	57	111
Garthorpe	Parish — —	17	18	1	1	16	2	—	60	47	107
Godeby-Marwood	Ditto — —	36	39	—	1	24	5	10	70	98	168
Harby	Ditto — —	75	77	—	2	57	12	8	177	187	364
Harston	Ditto — —	31	39	—	—	34	3	2	62	89	151
Holwell a	Township —	20	20	1	—	19	1	—	42	53	95
Hose	Parish — —	55	58	—	—	34	13	11	147	149	296
Kirby-Belers	Ditto — —	36	41	1	1	36	5	—	107	89	196
Knipton	Ditto — —	48	59	—	—	38	13	8	134	143	277
Melton-Mowbray e	Ditto — —	411	447	—	11	72	261	114	994	1,151	2,145
Muston	Ditto — —	45	46	—	—	36	9	1	109	117	226
Plungar	Ditto — —	41	41	—	—	38	3	—	92	99	191
Redmile	Ditto — —	66	68	1	1	10	16	42	161	167	328
Saltby	Ditto — —	37	39	—	1	32	3	4	107	106	213
Saxby	Ditto — —	26	29	—	1	27	1	1	58	73	131
Scalford	Ditto — —	78	87	—	—	74	13	—'	173	198	371
Sewstern c	Chapelry —	52	57	—	—	49	8	—	130	136	266
Somerby d	Parish — —	76	78	—	1	39	26	13	154	179	333
Sproxton	Ditto — —	64	64	1	—	41	18	5	150	160	310
Stapleford	Ditto — —	31	31	—	—	31	—	—	80	82	162
Stathern	Ditto — —	86	88	1	3	71	16	1	170	202	372
Stonesby	Ditto — —	38	40	—	2	33	7	—	100	94	194
Sysonby	Ditto — —	11	12	—	—	11	—	1	24	24	48
Thorpe-Arnold	Ditto — —	19	19	—	—	19	—	—	46	42	88
Waltham-on-the-Woulds	Ditto — —	93	94	—	—	62	32	—	238	274	512
Welby e	Township —	8	8	—	—	3	—	—	37	39	76
Withcote d	Parish — —	8	8	—	—	8	—	—	25	25	50
Wyfordby with Brentingby	Ditto — —	20	20	—	—	20	—	—	51	46	97
Wymondham	Ditto — —	80	87	—	1	60	25	2	232	205	437
		2,527	2,695	11	50	1,571	798	326	6,223	6,713	12,936
GARTRE.											
Bagrave f	Liberty — —	1	1	—	—	—	—	1	7	11	18
Billesdon g	Parish — —	121	126	1	5	58	66	2	264	270	534
Blaston	Ditto — —	12	13	—	2	13	—	—	36	22	58
Bowden, Magna h	Ditto — —	196	203	—	7	56	110	37	377	449	826
Bringhurst i	Ditto — —	16	19	—	1	7	11	1	44	50	94
Burrow	Ditto — —	28	34	—	1	27	5	2	74	64	138
Burton-Overy	Ditto — —	86	86	—	7	40	35	11	198	188	386
Bushby j	Township —	16	16	—	—	8	8	—	29	42	71
Carlton-Curlieu k	Parish — —	8	8	1	—	7	—	1	21	23	44
Cranhoe	Ditto — —	21	24	—	—	24	—	—	44	53	97
Drayton i	Township —	29	29	—	3	24	5	—	63	66	129
Easton Magna i	Ditto — —	114	129	—	2	69	57	3	250	264	514
Evington	Parish — —	49	52	—	—	32	15	5	109	113	222
Fleckney	Ditto — —	77	78	—	—	17	54	7	185	188	373
Foxton	Ditto — —	82	96	—	1	20	33	43	175	190	365
Frisby l	Chapelry —	8	8	—	2	—	8	—	10	11	21
Galby l	Parish — —	21	21	—	—	14	4	3	47	61	108
Glen Magna m	Ditto — —	118	133	—	5	42	81	10	342	309	651
Glooston	Ditto — —	29	30	—	—	26	3	1	73	62	135
Godeby g	Chapelry —	18	20	—	1	20	—	—	41	46	87
Gumley	Parish — —	55	56	—	1	18	11	27	127	134	261
Hallaton	Ditto — —	147	147	—	4	52	91	4	278	320	598
Holy Oaks-Lodge n	Lordship —	1	1	—	—	1	—	—	2	2	4
Holt and Bradley o	Chapelry —	9	9	—	1	8	—	1	17	31	48
	Carried forwd	1,262	1,339	2	43	583	597	159	2,813	2,969	5,782

a Holwell is in Ab-Kettleby Parish. ——— b Partly in Lincolnshire (Soke of Grantham). ——— c Sewstern is in Buckminster parish. ——— d Cold-Overton, Somerby, and Withcote, form a detached portion of this Hundred, to the Southward. ——— e Freeby and Welby are in Melton-Mowbray parish. ——— f In Hungerton parish (East-Goscote Hundred). ——— g Godeby and Rolleston are in Billesdon parish. ——— h Market-Harborough is in Bowden parish. ——— i Drayton and Easton Magna are in Bringhurst parish. ——— j Bushby and Stoughton are in Thurnby parish. ——— k Illston-on-the-Hill is partly in the parish of Carlton-Curlieu, partly in the parish of Norton. Stretton Parva is in the parish of Norton. ——— l Frisby is in Galby parish. ——— m Stretton Magna is in Glen Magna parish. ——— n In Dry-Stoke parish, Rutlandshire (Wrangdike Hundred). ——— o Holt and Bradley are in Medbourne parish.

COUNTY OF LEICESTER. —— HUNDREDS.	PARISH, TOWNSHIP, OR EXTRA-PAROCHIAL PLACE.	HOUSES. Inhabited.	By how many Families occupied.	Building.	Uninhabited.	OCCUPATIONS. Families chiefly employed in Agriculture.	Families chiefly employed in Trade, Manufactures, or Handicraft.	All other Families not comprised in the Two preceding Classes.	PERSONS. Males.	Females.	Total of Persons.
GARTRE (continued).	Brought forward	1,262	1,339	2	43	583	597	159	2,813	2,969	5,782
Horninghold — — — —	Parish — —	20	20	—	2	16	3	1	41	42	83
Houghton-on-the-Hill — —	Ditto — —	79	80	2	1	37	25	18	156	173	329
Husbands-Bosworth — —	Ditto — —	155	155	—	2	96	56	3	519	505	1,024
Illston-on-the-Hill k — —	Township —	28	29	—	2	24	1	4	54	64	118
Ingarsby f — — —	Hamlet —	—	—	—	—	—	—	—	13	7	20
Keythorpe P — — — —	Liberty — —	3	3	—	—	3	—	—	263	292	555
Kibworth-Beauchamp q — —	Parish — —	115	119	—	6	36	69	14	263	292	555
Kibworth-Harcourt q — —	Township —	91	96	—	1	17	76	3	185	200	385
Knossington — — —	Parish — —	31	34	—	—	12	18	4	76	74	150
Langton, East r — — —	Township —	65	69	—	3	31	27	11	127	138	265
Langton, West r — — —	Ditto — —	17	17	—	—	10	5	2	32	46	78
Laughton — — — —	Parish — —	34	37	—	1	26	10	1	75	77	152
Lubbenham — — — —	Ditto — —	112	112	1	6	61	51	—	223	254	477
Market-Harborough h — —	Ditto — —	335	343	1	7	8	209	126	788	916	1,704
Marefield s — — — —	Township —	5	5	—	—	4	—	1	10	17	27
Medburne o — — —	Parish — —	103	112	1	3	83	27	2	191	229	420
Mowsley t — — — —	Chapelry —	55	58	—	1	46	11	1	114	115	229
Newton-Harcourt u — —	Township —	45	45	—	1	33	12	—	101	113	214
Norton k — — — —	Parish — —	15	15	—	—	9	5	1	34	39	73
Noseley — — — —	Extra-Paroch.	1	1	—	—	1	—	—	1	1	2
Owston with Newbold — —	Parish — —	44	44	—	—	42	1	1	104	112	216
Pickwell with Leesthorpe v —	Ditto — —	27	27	—	1	23	—	4	52	71	123
Rolleston g — — — —	Chapelry —	9	12	—	—	5	1	6	20	24	44
Sadington — — — —	Parish — —	52	52	1	2	22	17	13	107	108	215
Scraptoft — — — —	Ditto — —	26	27	—	—	3	3	21	43	67	110
Shankton — — — —	Ditto — —	7	7	—	2	7	—	—	17	19	36
Slawston — — — —	Ditto — —	49	49	—	5	31	11	7	97	106	203
Smeeton-Westerby q — —	Township —	77	86	—	2	25	52	9	174	199	373
Stonton-Wyvile — —	Parish — —	20	23	1	1	17	4	2	42	51	93
Stockerston — — —	Ditto — —	10	10	1	1	9	1	—	25	24	49
Stoughton j — — —	Township —	30	31	—	1	17	7	7	56	73	129
Stretton, Magna m — —	Ditto — —	3	3	—	1	3	—	—	13	11	24
Stretton, Parva k — —	Ditto — —	23	25	—	2	18	5	2	54	42	96
Thedingworth — — —	Parish — —	46	48	—	—	11	29	8	99	97	196
Thorpe-Langton r — —	Township —	42	48	—	1	36	12	—	89	91	180
Thurnby j — — — —	Parish — —	29	31	—	—	19	10	2	60	60	120
Tur-Langton r — — —	Township —	80	80	—	—	41	30	9	147	170	317
Welham — — — —	Parish — —	13	13	—	4	11	2	—	31	44	75
Wistow u — — — —	Ditto — —	2	2	—	—	2	—	—	6	5	11
		3,160	3,307	10	102	1,478	1,387	442	7,052	7,645	14,697
GOSCOTE, EAST.											
Allexton — — — —	Parish — —	17	18	—	3	15	1	2	37	47	84
Ashfordby — — — —	Ditto — —	86	88	—	1	35	28	25	184	183	367
Ashby-Folvile w — —	Ditto — —	37	37	—	—	25	5	7	65	80	145
Barkby x — — — —	Ditto — —	102	113	—	6	50	59	4	232	222	454
Barkby-Thorpe x — —	Township —	12	12	—	—	11	1	—	31	31	62
Barrow-upon-Soar y —	Parish — —	262	262	—	1	92	132	38	681	622	1,303
Baresby w — — — —	Township —	58	59	—	1	36	21	2	111	128	239
Beby — — — —	Parish — —	23	25	—	—	24	1	—	50	71	121
Belgrave z — — —	Ditto — —	121	122	—	2	9	36	77	299	332	631
Brokesby — — — —	Ditto — —	3	3	—	—	2	1	—	12	11	23
Burton-on-the-Woulds a —	Township —	80	90	—	1	60	16	14	183	201	384
Coates a — — — —	Ditto — —	16	16	—	—	13	3	—	38	45	83
Cossington — — —	Parish — —	65	66	—	1	44	16	6	132	156	288
Croxton, South — — —	Ditto — —	53	54	1	1	29	22	3	130	123	253
Dalby, Magna — — —	Ditto — —	65	74	—	1	62	12	—	185	193	378
Dalby-on-the-Woulds —	Ditto — —	54	66	—	—	28	12	26	159	161	320
Frisby-on-the-Wreke —	Ditto — —	82	83	—	1	35	30	17	175	169	344
Gaddesby — — — —	Ditto — —	49	53	1	1	42	10	1	109	121	230
Grimston — — — —	Ditto — —	36	38	—	2	25	8	5	83	84	167
Halstead b — — — —	Township —	31	33	—	—	29	3	1	67	71	138
Hoby — — — —	Parish — —	63	63	—	3	45	14	4	148	155	303
Hoton a — — — —	Township —	56	65	—	2	41	19	5	175	161	336
Humberston — — —	Parish — —	86	88	1	4	59	29	—	187	206	393
Hungerton c — — —	Ditto — —	46	46	—	1	22	8	16	98	102	200
Keyham d — — — —	Township —	36	43	1	3	29	13	1	75	132	207
Laund — — — —	Extra-Paroch.	5	6	—	—	5	—	1	20	20	40
Lodington b — — —	Parish — —	34	38	—	1	36	2	—	57	80	137
	Carried forward	1,578	1,660	4	35	903	502	255	3,723	3,907	7,630

[For Notes f g h j k m o see the preceding page.]

P In Tugby parish (East Goscote Hundred).——— q Kibworth-Harcourt and Smeeton-Westerby are in Kibworth-Beauchamp parish. ——— r The townships of East-Langton, West-Langton, Thorpe-Langton, and Tur-Langton, form the parish of Church-Langton.———s In Tilton parish (East-Goscote Hundred).——— t In Knaptoft parish (Guthlaxton Hundred). ——— u Newton-Harcourt is in Wistow parish.——— v Pickwell is a detached portion of the Hundred, North-eastward. ——— w Baresby is in Ashby-Folvile parish.——— x Barkby-Thorpe and North-Thurmaston are in Barkby parish. ——— y Barrow-upon-Soar contains Quorndon and Woodhouse; also part of Mountsorrell (see West-Goscote Hundred).——— z South-Thurmaston is in Belgrave parish; as is Burstall (see West-Goscote Hundred).——— a Burton-on-the-Woulds, Coates, and Hoton, are in Prestwould parish.——— b Whatborough is partly in Lodington, partly in Tilton parish. Halstead is in Tilton parish; as is Marefield (see Gartre Hundred).——— c Bagrave, part of this parish is in Gartre Hundred.——— d In Rothley parish (West Goscote Hundred), though locally situate in the middle of Framland Hundred.

COUNTY OF LEICESTER. — HUNDREDS.	PARISH, TOWNSHIP, OR EXTRA-PAROCHIAL PLACE.	HOUSES.				OCCUPATIONS.			PERSONS.		
		Inhabited.	By how many Families occupied.	Building.	Uninhabited.	Families chiefly employed in Agriculture.	Families chiefly employed in Trade, Manufactures, or Handicraft.	All other Families not comprised in the Two preceding Classes.	Males.	Females.	Total of Persons.
GOSCOTE, EAST (continued).	Brought forward	1,578	1,660	4	35	903	502	255	3,723	3,907	7,630
Lowesby e — — — —	Parish — —	15	17	—	—	7	1	9	40	39	79
Newton, Cold e — — —	Township —	21	21	—	—	21	—	—	54	57	111
Norton, East — — — —	Parish — —	25	27	—	4	16	3	8	60	67	127
Prestwould a — — —	Ditto — —	11	11	—	—	8	1	2	24	28	52
Queniborough — — — —	Ditto — —	94	96	2	2	50	46	—	217	229	446
Rakedale — — — —	Ditto — —	19	19	—	—	15	1	3	49	46	95
Radcliffe-on-the-Wreak —	Ditto — —	22	22	1	—	16	6	—	56	61	117
Rearsby — — — — —	Ditto — —	92	93	1	2	47	43	3	203	223	426
Rotherby — — — —	Ditto — —	25	25	—	—	16	7	2	53	57	110
Saxulby f — — — —	Ditto — —	21	21	—	—	10	6	5	44	56	100
Segrave — — — —	Ditto — —	72	74	—	—	53	20	1	183	182	365
Shoby f — — — —	Hamlet —	3	3	—	—	3	—	—	11	12	23
Sileby — — — —	Parish — —	253	257	—	7	61	187	9	558	642	1,200
Skeffington — — — —	Ditto — —	31	33	—	—	18	6	9	66	70	136
Syston — — — —	Ditto — —	264	273	—	3	68	186	19	593	630	1,223
Thorp-Satchvile g — —	Hamlet —	29	32	—	1	10	6	16	64	67	131
Thurmaston, North x — —	Township —	34	34	—	—	21	13	—	82	86	168
Thurmaston, South z — —	Ditto — —	138	139	—	1	58	79	2	326	348	674
Thrussington — — — —	Parish — —	92	92	—	4	54	37	1	214	203	417
Tilton b — — — —	Ditto — —	32	34	—	2	26	6	2	65	81	146
Tugby h — — — —	Ditto — —	51	51	—	1	39	12	—	107	123	230
Twyford g — — — —	Ditto — —	59	72	—	1	25	17	30	138	141	279
Walton-on-the-Woulds— —	Ditto — —	47	48	—	1	35	8	5	111	111	222
Wartnaby d — — — —	Township —	17	18	—	1	16	1	1	46	34	80
Whatborough b — — —	Liberty —	3	3	—	—	3	—	—	7	14	21
Wimeswould — — — —	Township —	204	208	4	5	32	88	88	493	509	1,002
Wycomb and Chadwell d —	Ditto — —	24	26	—	1	24	2	—	41	54	95
		3,276	3,409	12	71	1,655	1,284	470	7,628	8,077	15,705
GOSCOTE, WEST.											
Anstey i — — — —	Township —	142	157	1	2	23	130	4	373	374	747
Ashby-de-la-Zouch j — —	Parish — —	638	645	48	9	226	339	80	1,525	1,616	3,141
Beaumanor — — — —	Extra-Paroch.	11	11	1	—	11	—	—	38	35	73
Beaumont Leys — — —	Ditto — —	2	2	—	—	2	—	—	11	10	21
Belton (including Gracedieu)	Parish — —	119	119	—	—	71	44	4	267	287	554
Blackfordby j — — — —	Hamlet —	54	55	—	1	47	8	—	135	127	262
Bradgate — — — —	Extra-Paroch.	1	1	—	—	—	—	1	4	4	8
Bredon k — — — —	Parish — —	125	128	—	1	99	27	2	269	300	569
Burstall l — — — —	Township —	57	62	—	3	24	35	3	137	165	302
Charley — — — —	Ditto — —	10	10	—	—	9	1	—	24	25	49
Cole-Orton — — — —	Parish — —	201	211	1	14	59	142	10	422	488	910
Cropston i — — — —	Township —	20	20	—	1	9	11	—	55	45	100
Diseworth — — — —	Parish — —	132	152	—	1	81	67	4	334	322	656
Donington-Castle — — —	Ditto — —	481	493	1	12	200	274	19	1,081	1,227	2,308
Garendon — — — —	Extra-Paroch.	3	3	—	2	1	1	1	10	13	23
Gilroe. — — — —	Ditto — —	1	1	—	—	1	—	—	1	3	4
Hathern — — — —	Parish — —	209	209	1	3	60	141	8	536	562	1,098
Hemington m — — —	Township —	78	89	—	2	57	32	—	197	187	384
Isley-Walton n — — —	Ditto — —	10	10	—	—	10	—	—	32	23	55
Kegworth n — — — —	Parish — —	307	327	—	6	83	228	16	751	799	1,550
Knight-Thorpe o — — —	Township —	16	16	—	1	6	9	1	44	42	86
Langley Priory — — —	Extra-Paroch.	1	1	—	—	—	—	1	5	5	10
Leicester Abbey — — —	Ditto — —	2	2	—	—	2	—	—	14	5	19
Lockington m — — —	Parish — —	40	41	—	—	29	7	5	104	95	199
Loughborough o — — —	Ditto — —	1,128	1,179	8	12	186	847	146	2,612	2,788	5,400
Mountsorel, North & South p	Township —	277	292	—	4	4	278	10	743	759	1,502
Newtown-Linford — — —	Parish — —	72	90	—	2	54	34	2	195	208	403
Osgathorpe — — — —	Ditto — —	71	73	—	1	26	40	7	158	155	313
Packington with Snibston q	Ditto — —	88	92	—	1	56	19	17	220	235	455
Quorndon p — — — —	Township —	265	266	1	7	88	151	27	645	636	1,281
Ravenston r — — — —	Parish — —										
Rothley p — — — —	Ditto — —	186	196	1	4	77	113	6	433	424	857
Seile, Nether and Over s —	Ditto — —	208	217	1	1	142	53	22	489	502	991
Sheepshead — — — —	Ditto — —	544	548	—	3	109	415	24	1,578	1,448	3,026
Shermans-Grounds — —	Extra-Paroch.	1	1	—	—	1	—	—	4	3	7
Staunton-Harold k — —	Township —	49	56	—	1	31	18	7	146	135	281
Swannington t — — —	Ditto — —	95	97	—	5	46	49	2	193	234	427
Swebston with Newton —	Parish — —	109	109	1	—	67	37	5	255	265	520
Swithland — — — —	Ditto — —	58	62	—	5	30	31	1	155	150	305
Thorp Acre with Dishley —	Ditto — —	56	57	—	—	37	19	1	139	148	287
	Carried forward	5,867	6,100	65	104	2,064	3,600	436	14,334	14,849	29,183

[For Notes x z a b d see the preceding page.]

e Cold-Newton is in Lowesby parish. ———— f Shoby is in Saxulby parish. ———— g Thorpe-Satchvile is in Twyford parish. ———— h Containing Keythorpe (see Gartre Hundred). ———— i Anstey (including Anstey-Pasture, extra-parochial) and Cropston, are in Thurcaston parish. ———— j Blackfordby is in Ashby-de-la-Zouch parish.———— k Staunton-Harold, Tonge, Wilston, Worthington, and Newbold, are in Bredon parish. ———— l In Belgrave parish (East-Goscote Hundred). ———— m Hemington is in Lockington parish. ———— n Isley Walton is in Kegworth parish. ———— o Knight-Thorpe and Woodthorpe are in Loughborough parish. ———— p Quorndon and Woodhouse are in Barrow-upon-Soar parish (East-Goscote Hundred) ; Keyham, Wartnaby, and Wycomb (East-Goscote Hundred), are in Rothley parish ; and Mountsorel is in both of those parishes. ———— q Part of Packington is in Derbyshire (in Repton and Gresley Hundred). ———— r Partly in the Hundred of Repton and Gresley, in the county of Derby, where the whole is entered. ———— s Including part of Oakthorpe and Donisthorpe (Repton and Gresley Hundred), Derbyshire.———— t Swannington and Thringston are in Whitwick parish.

COUNTY OF LEICESTER. HUNDREDS.	PARISH, TOWNSHIP, OR EXTRA-PAROCHIAL PLACE.	HOUSES.				OCCUPATIONS.			PERSONS.		
		Inhabited.	By how many Families occupied.	Building.	Uninhabited.	Families chiefly employed in Agriculture.	Families chiefly employed in Trade, Manufactures, or Handicraft.	All other Families not comprised in the Two preceding Classes.	Males.	Females.	Total of Persons.
GOSCOTE, WEST *(continued).*	Brought forward	5,867	6,100	65	104	2,064	3,600	436	14,334	14,849	29,183
Thringston t — — —	Township —	202	215	2	5	39	176	—	450	498	948
Thurcaston i — — — —	Parish —	47	53	—	—	24	23	6	127	132	259
Tonge k — — — — —	Hamlet —	37	37	—	1	28	9	—	83	90	173
Ulvescroft — — — —	Extra-Paroch.	13	14	1	1	13	1	—	44	44	88
Wanlip — — — — —	Parish — —	23	25	—	—	18	5	2	68	58	126
Whatton, Long — — —	Ditto — —	147	147	—	—	46	88	13	414	368	782
Whitwick t — — — —	Ditto — —	189	205	—	2	62	138	5	433	462	895
Willson k — — — —	Hamlet —	33	33	—	—	30	3	—	80	86	166
Woodhouse p — — —	Parish — —	141	153	—	1	32	117	4	471	422	893
Woodthorpe o — — —	Hamlet —	14	14	—	—	14	—	—	35	35	70
Worthington and Newbold k	Liberty — —	237	237	—	—	124	111	2	543	570	1,113
		6,950	7,233	68	114	2,494	4,271	468	17,082	17,614	34,696
GUTHLAXTON.											
Arnsby — — — — —	Parish — —	84	96	—	1	52	43	1	195	205	400
Ashby, Magna — — —	Ditto — —	50	50	—	—	30	20	—	126	134	260
Ashby, Parva — — — —	Ditto — —	32	32	—	1	27	5	—	73	77	150
Aylestone u — — — —	Ditto — —	99	106	—	1	35	62	9	233	267	500
Bitteswell — — — —	Ditto — —	88	94	—	4	61	30	3	178	174	352
Bittesby v — — — —	Township —	1	1	—	—	1	—	—	3	2	5
Blaby w — — — — —	Parish — —	155	158	5	3	37	111	10	398	431	829
Broughton-Astley — — —	Ditto — —	132	137	—	3	73	60	4	286	299	585
Bruntingthorpe — — —	Ditto — —	69	76	—	—	36	36	4	171	161	332
Catthorpe — — — —	Ditto — —	34	36	—	—	14	18	4	90	77	167
Castle-View x — — — —	Extra-Paroch.	30	34	—	1	2	32	—	76	91	167
Claybrooke, Great v — —	Hamlet —	74	80	—	5	30	41	9	273	169	442
Claybrooke, Little v — —	Township —	14	14	—	—	6	—	8	26	35	61
Cosby with Little Thorpe —	Parish — —	160	162	4	3	39	115	8	432	394	826
Cottesbach — — — —	Ditto — —	17	17	1	—	16	—	1	51	47	98
Countess-Thorpe w — —	Hamlet —	116	116	1	—	31	83	2	286	307	593
Dunton-Bassett — — —	Parish — —	90	92	—	1	45	44	3	219	213	432
Foston — — — — —	Ditto — —	5	5	—	—	5	—	—	16	12	28
Frolesworth — — — —	Ditto — —	57	58	2	1	50	6	2	116	149	265
Gillmorton — — — —	Ditto — —	131	137	—	3	46	85	6	323	315	638
Glen, Parva u — — —	Township —	27	27	—	2	5	22	—	60	66	126
Kilby — — — — —	Parish — —	68	70	1	2	31	37	2	170	161	331
Kilworth, North — — —	Ditto — —	73	79	—	4	16	27	36	151	176	327
Kilworth, South — — —	Ditto — —	85	87	—	—	56	22	9	226	205	431
Kimcote with Walton y — —	Ditto — —	153	157	4	1	66	70	21	331	390	721
Knaptoft z — — — —	Ditto — —	6	6	—	—	6	—	—	29	23	52
Knighton a — — — —	Hamlet —	75	82	—	—	17	65	—	174	203	377
Leir — — — — —	Parish — —	93	94	1	4	23	71	—	197	221	418
Lutterworth — — — —	Ditto — —	410	410	—	15	115	278	17	861	984	1,845
Misterton b — — — —	Ditto — —	8	8	—	—	6	1	1	27	29	56
Oadby — — — — —	Ditto — —	150	158	—	6	19	139	—	369	397	766
Peatling, Magna — — —	Ditto — —	37	37	—	1	25	12	—	87	99	186
Peatling, Parva — — —	Ditto — —	25	28	—	—	17	6	5	58	78	136
Shawell — — — — —	Ditto — —	40	48	—	2	32	10	6	99	97	196
Shearsby z — — — —	Hamlet —	62	65	1	3	20	45	—	130	130	260
Swinford — — — —	Parish — —	85	89	—	2	47	32	10	198	212	410
Ullesthorpe v — — —	Hamlet —	100	104	—	2	35	64	5	218	252	470
Walcote and Poultney b —	Ditto — —	85	85	—	—	55	26	4	187	186	373
Westrill and Stormouth —	Extra-Paroch.	2	2	—	—	1	—	1	12	19	31
Whetstone — — — —	Parish — —	148	155	—	7	42	92	21	355	377	732
Wigston, Magna — — —	Ditto — —	373	394	2	15	63	306	25	926	975	1,901
Wigston, Parva v — —	Township —	11	16	—	—	12	2	2	34	35	69
Willoughby Waterless — —	Parish — —	52	58	—	4	19	30	9	143	135	278
		3,606	3,760	22	97	1,364	2,148	248	8,613	9,009	17,622

[*For Notes* i k o p t *see the preceding page.*]

u Glen Parva is in Aylestone Parish; as is Lubbesthorpe (see Sparkenhoe Hundred.) ———— v Great or Nether Claybrooke, Little or Over Claybrooke, Bittesby, Ullesthorpe, and Wigston Parva, form the Parish of Claybrooke. ———— w Countess-Thorpe is in Blaby Parish. ———— x Adjoining the Borough of Leicester, which is entered at the end of page 6. ———— y Including Cotes-Devile, and also Knaptoft in Walton. ———— z Shearsby is in Knaptoft Parish; as is Mawsley (see Gartree Hundred). ———— a Knighton is in the Parish of St. Margaret (Leicester). ———— b Walcote and Poultney are in Misterton Parish.

COUNTY OF LEICESTER. ⟶ HUNDREDS.	PARISH, TOWNSHIP, OR EXTRA-PAROCHIAL PLACE.	HOUSES.				OCCUPATIONS.			PERSONS.		
		Inhabited.	By how many Families occupied.	Building.	Uninhabited.	Families chiefly employed in Agriculture.	Families chiefly employed in Trade, Manufactures, or Handicraft.	All other Families not comprized in the Two preceding Classes.	Males.	Females.	Total of Persons.
SPARKENHOE.											
Appleby c — — — — —	Parish — —	214	220	—	3	180	34	6	469	654	1,123
Aston-Flamvile d — — —	Ditto — —	12	13	—	1	13	—	—	41	30	71
Atterton e — — — —	Hamlet — —	13	14	—	—	12	—	2	41	42	83
Bagworth, wth Bagworth-Park f	Ditto — —	61	61	—	—	31	30	—	186	185	371
Bardon-Park — — —	Extra-Paroch.	12	12	—	—	9	—	3	29	23	52
Barlston g — — — —	Chapelry —	107	107	—	1	37	70	—	285	273	558
Barrons-Park h — — —	Hamlet — —	2	2	—	—	2	—	—	9	6	15
Barton-in-the--Beans g t v	Township —	33	33	—	—	19	12	2	81	88	169
Barwell i — — — —	Parish — —	186	196	—	2	71	111	14	464	464	928
Bassett-House — — —	Extra-Paroch.	2	2	—	—	2	—	—	9	7	16
Bilstone j — — — —	Township —	27	30	—	2	28	2	—	68	77	145
Botcheston and Newton k —	Ditto — —	16	18	—	—	16	2	—	50	49	99
Braunstone l — — —	Chapelry —	38	38	—	3	36	2	—	103	90	193
Braunstone-Frith l — —	Liberty —	1	1	—	—	1	—	—	5	4	9
Burbach and Sketchley d —	Chapelry —	219	229	—	2	98	131	—	709	639	1,348
Cadeby m — — — —	Parish — —	30	30	—	2	18	12	—	51	72	123
Carlton g — — — —	Chapelry —	43	43	1	1	31	12	—	116	103	219
Congeston — — — —	Parish — —	42	53	—	2	30	14	9	120	124	244
Croft — — — — —	Ditto — —	47	47	—	1	24	23	—	132	116	248
Dadlington n — — —	Chapelry —	27	31	—	3	18	13	—	66	81	147
Desford h — — — —	Parish — —	143	147	1	8	65	70	12	361	368	729
Drayton-Fenny — — —	Ditto — —	23	23	—	—	19	3	1	69	70	139
Earl-Shilton o — — —	Chapelry —	307	309	1	3	65	221	23	758	775	1,533
Elmesthorpe — — — —	Parish — —	4	6	—	—	6	—	—	23	15	38
Enderby — — — —	Ditto — —	164	168	—	4	48	94	26	407	397	804
Glenfield l — — —	Ditto — —	79	79	—	—	34	44	1	163	184	347
Glenfield-Frith l — — —	Liberty —	1	1	—	—	1	—	—	3	1	4
Gopsal — — — — —	Extra-Paroch.	1	1	—	—	—	—	1	5	2	7
Groby k — — — —	Hamlet — —	64	64	—	—	29	31	4	158	164	322
Hether — — — — —	Parish — —	67	68	—	1	45	23	—	157	177	334
Higham-on-the-Hill, with Lindley — — — — }	Ditto — —	81	91	1	3	78	10	3	223	246	469
Hinckley n — — — —	Ditto — —	1,097	1,244	3	26	148	1,010	86	2,872	3,186	6,058
Hugglescote and Donington P	Township —	114	114	—	2	85	29	—	312	302	614
Huncote q — — — —	Hamlet — —	61	61	—	—	29	30	2	136	161	297
Ibstock P — — — —	Parish — —	157	163	—	3	75	71	17	392	444	836
Kirkby-Frith l — — —	Liberty —	2	2	—	—	2	—	—	9	9	18
Kirkby-Malory o — — —	Parish — —	51	53	—	2	48	3	2	122	126	248
Kirby-Muxloe l — — —	Chapelry —	46	46	—	2	32	12	2	107	124	231
Leicester-Forest — — —	Extra-Paroch.	10	11	—	—	11	—	—	36	34	70
Lubbesthorpe r — — —	Chapelry —	11	11	—	—	11	—	—	41	36	77
Market-Bosworth g — —	Parish — —	168	173	—	4	60	103	10	430	435	865
Markfield — — — —	Ditto — —	190	197	—	2	28	74	95	468	439	907
Marston-Potters i — — —	Chapelry —	3	3	—	—	3	—	—	5	9	14
Merevale s — — — —	—	—	—	—	—	—	—	—	—	—	—
Mythe — — — — —	Extra-Paroch.	2	2	—	—	2	—	—	7	8	15
Nailstone t — — — —	Parish — —	69	73	—	1	60	12	1	139	154	293
Narborough q — — —	Ditto — —	118	122	3	1	34	84	4	338	297	635
Newbold-Verdon — — —	Ditto — —	94	96	—	3	40	53	3	183	227	410
New Parks u — — —	Liberty —	2	2	—	—	2	—	—	9	9	18
Normanton-le-Heath t — —	Parish — —	36	36	—	—	34	2	—	98	104	202
Norton j — — — —	Ditto — —	60	62	2	2	44	15	3	125	164	289
Odstone v — — — —	Hamlet — —	32	37	—	1	30	7	—	87	84	171
Orton-on-the-Hill — — —	Parish — —	58	65	—	3	42	16	7	131	148	279
Osbaston g m — — —	Township —	36	36	—	—	24	9	3	91	88	179
Peckleton with Tooley — —	Parish — —	64	70	—	—	39	30	1	144	187	331
Ratby k — — — —	Ditto — —	107	118	1	1	55	60	3	266	275	541
Ratcliffe-Culey w — — —	Hamlet — —	40	41	—	1	30	11	—	94	107	201
Sapcote — — — —	Parish — —	120	127	2	2	42	81	4	346	346	692
Shakerston v — — —	Ditto — —	56	56	—	1	34	22	—	127	128	255
Sharnford — — — —	Ditto — —	85	90	—	1	48	35	7	188	206	394
Shepey-Magna w — — —	Ditto — —	73	73	—	5	49	15	9	182	181	363
Shepey-Parva — — —	Ditto — —	18	18	—	—	14	4	—	48	44	92
Shenton g — — — —	Chapelry —	39	39	—	1	36	2	1	90	95	185
Sibbeston x — — — —	Parish — —	42	43	—	1	39	3	1	86	105	191
Snareston v — — — —	Ditto — —	68	68	—	2	47	15	6	157	152	309
Stanton-Stoney — — —	Ditto — —	95	97	—	2	44	40	13	222	224	446
Stanton-under-Bardon, and Horsepool f — — }	Township —	53	53	—	—	15	14	24	158	132	290
Stapleton i — — — —	Hamlet — —	41	41	—	3	25	11	5	118	102	220
Stoke-Golding n — — —	Chapelry —	102	105	1	2	40	56	9	258	267	525
Sutton-Cheney g — — —	Ditto — —	72	79	—	1	46	32	1	172	167	339
Temple-Hall y — — —	Extra-Paroch.	9	10	—	—	9	1	—	38	32	70
Thornton f — — — —	Parish — —	68	69	—	1	35	30	4	202	165	367
Thurlaston u — — —	Ditto — —	88	88	—	—	42	43	3	232	237	469
Twycross — — — —	Ditto — —	63	64	—	1	44	20	—	148	144	292
Upton x — — — —	Township —	29	29	—	1	27	2	—	70	71	141
Witherley e — — — —	Parish — —	76	79	—	3	40	28	11	165	169	334
Wykin n — — — — —	Hamlet — —	—	—	—	—	—	—	—	—	—	—
		5,891	6,203	16	122	2,710	3,049	444	15,010	15,650	30,660

c Appleby is partly in Derbyshire (Repton and Gresley Hundred); but the whole is entered here.'———— d Burbach and Sketchley are in Aston-Flamvile parish.———— e Atterton is in Witherley parish. ———— f Bagworth, and Stanton-under-Bardon, are in Thornton parish.———— g Barlston, Carlton, Shenton, and Sutton-Cheney, are in Market-Bosworth parish; also Coton and Naneby, and

₊ *For the Remainder of the Notes see the following page.*

COUNTY OF LEICESTER. ——— HUNDREDS, &c.	PARISH, TOWNSHIP, OR EXTRA-PAROCHIAL PLACE.	HOUSES.				OCCUPATIONS.			PERSONS.		
		Inha-bited.	By how many Fami-lies oc-cupied.	Building.	Uninhabited.	Families chiefly employed in Agriculture.	Families chiefly employed in Trade, Manufactures, or Handicraft.	All other Families not comprized in the Two preeding Classes.	Males.	Females.	Total of Persons.
BOROUGH OF LEICESTER:											
All Saints — — — —	Parish — —	664	791	3	9	39	697	55	1,549	1,813	3,362
Leonard, St. with Abbey and Woodgate — — —}	Ditto — —	93	94	—	1	17	77	—	212	211	423
Margaret, St. with Bishop's Fee z — — — —}	Ditto — —	2,064	2,138	56	26	293	1,672	173	4,835	5,323	10,158
Martin, St. — — — —	Ditto — —	598	635	1	23	24	549	62	1,446	1,808	3,254
Mary, St. — — — —	Ditto — —	816	823	10	11	25	768	30	1,951	2,128	4,079
Nicholas, St. — — — —	Ditto — —	337	355	3	4	30	300	25	721	868	1,589
Newark a — — — —	Liberty — —	37	37	—	—	—	27	10	87	194	281
		4,609	4,873	73	74	428	4,090	355	10,801	12,345	23,146

SUMMARY.

HUNDRED OF											
FRAMLAND — — — — — — —		2,527	2,695	11	50	1,571	798	326	6,223	6,713	12,936
GARTRE — — — — — — —		3,160	3,307	10	102	1,478	1,387	442	7,052	7,645	14,697
GOSCOTE, EAST — — — — — —		3,276	3,409	12	71	1,655	1,284	470	7,628	8,077	15,705
GOSCOTE, WEST — — — — — —		6,950	7,233	68	114	2,494	4,271	468	17,082	17,614	34,696
GUTHLAXTON — — — — — —		3,606	3,760	22	97	1,364	2,148	248	8,613	9,009	17,622
SPARKENHOE — — — — — —		5,891	6,203	16	122	2,710	3,049	444	15,010	15,650	30,660
BOROUGH OF											
LEICESTER — — — — — —		4,609	4,873	73	74	428	4,090	355	10,801	12,345	23,146
Local Militia b — — — — —		—	—	—	—	—	—	—	957	—	957
TOTALS — — — — — —		30,019	31,480	212	630	11,700	17,027	2,753	73,366	77,053	150,419

and part of Barton-in-the-Beans, and of Osbaston. ——— h Barrons-Park is in Desford parish. ——— i Potters-Marston and Stapleton are in Barwell parish.——— j Bilstone is in Norton parish. ——— k Botcheston and Newton, and Groby, are in the parish of Ratby. ——— l Braunstone, Glenfield-Frith, Kirkby-Frith, and Kirby-Muxloe, are in Glenfield parish. ——— m Osbaston is partly in Cadeby parish. ——— n Dadlington, and Stoke Golding, are in Hinckley parish; in the Return of which are included Hinckley-Bond and Wykin. ——— o Earl-Shilton is in Kirby-Malory parish. ——— p Hugglescote and Donington are in Ibstock parish.——— q Huncote is in Narborough parish. ——— r In Aylestone parish (Guthlaxton Hundred). ——— s Partly in the Hundred of Hemlingford (Atherstone Division), county of Warwick, where the whole is entered. ——— t Normanton-le-Heath is in Nailstone parish; as is part of Barton-in-the-Beans. ——— u New Parks is in Thurlaston parish, the Return of which includes Normanton-Turvile. ——— v Shakerston contains Odstone, part of Barton-in-the-Beans, and part of Snareston. ——— w Ratcliffe-Culey is in Shepey Magna parish; which includes Moor-Barns.——— x Upton is in Sibbeston parish.——— y Wellsborough extra-parochial is returned with Temple-Hall.

z Containing Knighton (see Guthlaxton Hundred. ——— a Castle-View is entered in Guthlaxton Hundred.

b The First Regiment of Leicester Local Militia was assembled for fourteen days' exercise on the 15th of May 1811, to the number of 957 (officers included). This Regiment was furnished by the Town of Leicester and its vicinity, extending into all the Hundreds of the County, except Framland Hundred.

Abstract of Answers and Returns to the Population Acts of 1800 and 1811.

PARISH REGISTERS.

HUNDRED OF FRAMLAND.

Years	BAPTISMS Males	Females	Total	BURIALS Males	Females	Total
1700	172	178	350	104	91	195
1710	141	138	279	95	113	208
1720	122	108	230	179	189	368
1730	143	152	235	132	143	275
1740	150	135	285	93	120	213
1750	171	150	321	122	110	232
1760	159	156	315	94	115	209
1770	166	170	336	118	107	225
1780	142	146	288	137	121	258
1781	144	149	293	114	140	254
1782	139	126	265	100	119	219
1783	131	155	286	131	113	244
1784	150	137	287	140	140	280
1785	155	135	290	128	126	254
1786	164	135	299	111	115	226
1787	158	150	308	104	101	205
1788	176	148	324	106	106	212
1789	144	173	317	93	114	207
1790	169	146	315	100	74	174
1791	172	157	329	110	114	224
1792	158	146	304	102	86	188
1793	167	165	332	118	108	226
1794	161	134	295	83	89	172
1795	156	162	318	120	127	247
1796	163	182	345	97	88	185
1797	163	163	326	100	109	209
1798	165	157	322	84	104	188
1799	182	183	365	109	100	209
1800	149	151	300	111	108	219

Years	MARRIAGES
1754	61
1755	96
1756	96
1757	80
1758	93
1759	80
1760	81
1761	82
1762	88
1763	99
1764	86
1765	66
1766	53
1767	73
1768	80
1769	92
1770	71
1771	70
1772	71
1773	79
1774	78
1775	64
1776	96
1777	69
1778	84
1779	72
1780	83
1781	75
1782	74
1783	70
1784	75
1785	107
1786	89
1787	75
1788	90
1789	65
1790	75
1791	73
1792	77
1793	84
1794	85
1795	82
1796	68
1797	74
1798	85
1799	82
1800	88

HUNDRED OF GARTRE.

Years	BAPTISMS Males	Females	Total	BURIALS Males	Females	Total
1700	200	192	392	132	131	263
1710	155	160	315	159	129	288
1720	198	178	376	176	174	350
1730	189	185	374	184	177	361
1740	206	152	358	158	158	316
1750	213	194	407	157	167	324
1760	218	228	446	190	185	375
1770	241	202	443	204	264	468
1780	246	237	483	237	256	493
1781	244	234	478	211	219	430
1782	236	216	452	178	187	365
1783	216	221	437	201	200	401
1784	212	189	401	200	218	418
1785	218	228	446	220	235	455
1786	256	196	452	211	210	421
1787	206	230	436	180	189	369
1788	260	235	495	164	295	459
1789	266	265	531	159	186	345
1790	257	237	494	188	214	402
1791	272	271	543	198	187	385
1792	299	288	587	181	221	402
1793	305	256	561	190	200	390
1794	264	252	516	211	197	408
1795	276	272	548	189	235	424
1796	255	234	489	183	199	382
1797	261	315	576	207	184	391
1798	296	296	592	228	197	425
1799	270	263	533	191	157	348
1800	290	251	541	190	205	395

Years	MARRIAGES
1754	106
1755	130
1756	135
1757	131
1758	131
1759	113
1760	148
1761	158
1762	143
1763	144
1764	155
1765	123
1766	132
1767	97
1768	120
1769	130
1770	146
1771	156
1772	146
1773	129
1774	136
1775	131
1776	138
1777	154
1778	161
1779	151
1780	150
1781	140
1782	118
1783	143
1784	127
1785	152
1786	161
1787	176
1788	123
1789	162
1790	159
1791	152
1792	157
1793	165
1794	125
1795	155
1796	157
1797	168
1798	173
1799	142
1800	153

Register of Baptisms and Burials of Nether Broughton, defective in 1700;—of Eaton, in 1700, 1710, and 1720;—of the Roman Catholic chapel of Eastwell, from 1700 to 1780, inclusive;—of Hose, in 1700;—of Kirby Bellars, in 1700;—and of Somerby, in 1710.

Register of Baptisms and Burials of Carlton Curlieu, defective from 1700 to 1740, inclusive;—of Evington, from 1700 to 1740;—of Gumley, in 1700;—and of Laughton, from 1700 to 1750.

Register of Marriages of Stoughton, defective in 1754, 1756, 1758, 1760, 1761, 1762, 1765, 1780, and 1781, and from 1784 to 1786, inclusive; from 1791 to 1793, inclusive; in 1795, 1798, and 1800.

Observation.—The Curate of Great Bowden observes, " that the increase of Burials in 1785 was occasioned by the small-pox."

FRAMLAND (1801–1810)

Years	Males	Females	Total	Males	Females	Total		Marriages
1801	154	166	320	101	121	222	–	68
1802	177	190	367	129	121	250	–	93
1803	205	182	387	106	119	225	–	97
1804	202	188	390	89	85	174	–	93
1805	181	180	361	102	105	207	–	105
1806	211	186	397	79	83	162	–	78
1807	203	169	372	102	109	211	–	93
1808	227	196	423	100	97	197	–	73
1809	202	184	386	118	123	241	–	95
1810	205	202	407	111	106	217	–	86

GARTRE (1801–1810)

Years	Males	Females	Total	Males	Females	Total		Marriages
1801	162	151	313	124	163	287	–	101
1802	194	196	390	155	187	342	–	130
1803	213	201	414	160	150	310	–	128
1804	200	215	415	115	111	226	–	113
1805	199	161	360	124	108	232	–	96
1806	212	193	405	120	125	245	–	86
1807	206	179	385	139	152	291	–	92
1808	189	196	385	121	135	256	–	97
1809	181	195	376	113	132	245	–	83
1810	189	190	379	146	165	311	–	106

The above ABSTRACT is collected from the Registers of Abkettleby v. Barkstone v. Bottesford r. Branston r. Nether Broughton r. Buckminster v. Burton Lazars c. Claxton v. Coston r. Croxton Keyrial v. Little Dalby v. Eastwell r. Eaton v. Edmondthorpe r. Garthorpe v. Goadby Marwood r. Harby r. Horeston r. Hose r. Kirby Bellars c. Knipton r. Melton Mowbray v. Muston r. Cold Overton r. Plungar v. Redmile r. Saltby v. Saxby r. Scalford v. Somerby v. Sproxton v. Stapleford v. Stathern r. Stonisby v. Thorpe Arnold (with Brentingby) v. Waltham on the Wolds r. Withcote r. Wyfordby r. and of Wymondham r.

*** The Orthography of the different Parishes, in several instances, differs from that in the History; but the Parliamentary Returns are here strictly followed.

The above ABSTRACT is collected from the Registers of Billesdon v. Blaston[1] r. Husband's Bosworth r. Great Bowden c. Bringhurst v. Burrow r. Burton Overy r. Carlton Curlieu r. Cranoe r. Great Easton c. Evington c. Fleckney c. Foston v. Galby r. Great Glen v. Glooston r. Goadby c. Gumley r. Hallaton r. Market Harborough c. Horninghold v. Houghton on the Hill r. Ilston on the Hill c. Kibworth Beauchamp r. Knissington r. East Langton r. Thorpe Langton c. Tur Langton c. West Langton c. Langton r. Lubenham v. Medbourn and Holt r. Mowsley c. Norton by Galby v. Ouston c. Pickwell r. Rolleston Chapelry c. Saddington r. Scraptoft v. Shangton r. Slawston v. Staunton Wyville r. Stockerston r. Stoughton c. Great Stretton c. Little Stretton c. Thedingworth v. Thurnby v. Welham v. and of Wistow (with Newton Harcourt) v.

[1] No church-yard at Blaston.

HUNDRED OF EAST GOSCOTE.

Years	BAPTISMS. Males	Females	Total	BURIALS. Males	Females	Total
1700	139	152	291	65	116	181
1710	102	77	179	50	76	126
1720	199	99	298	99	98	197
1730	145	123	268	110	102	212
1740	119	126	245	67	91	158
1750	152	123	275	58	81	139
1760	143	116	259	86	81	167
1770	149	130	279	72	97	169
1780	169	260	429	119	161	280
1781	180	173	353	167	172	339
1782	178	197	375	160	158	318
1783	197	200	397	146	178	324
1784	184	175	359	160	160	320
1785	228	212	440	182	152	334
1786	198	225	423	147	170	317
1787	213	195	408	117	151	268
1788	213	200	413	162	135	297
1789	201	215	416	138	151	289
1790	220	240	460	128	172	300
1791	225	191	416	122	135	257
1792	207	201	408	121	141	262
1793	172	231	403	137	157	294
1794	213	213	426	141	157	298
1795	190	216	406	152	142	294
1796	187	198	385	117	141	258
1797	228	203	431	135	127	262
1798	203	215	418	110	146	256
1799	187	195	382	122	141	263
1800	198	206	404	129	105	234

MARRIAGES (East Goscote)

Years	Marriages
1754	55
1755	56
1756	86
1757	110
1758	103
1759	105
1760	120
1761	89
1762	79
1763	109
1764	100
1765	90
1766	78
1767	75
1768	82
1769	95
1770	106
1771	108
1772	92
1773	87
1774	95
1775	94
1776	98
1777	80
1778	105
1779	113
1780	107
1781	106
1782	111
1783	105
1784	112
1785	114
1786	90
1787	102
1788	107
1789	119
1790	104
1791	103
1792	105
1793	108
1794	115
1795	85
1796	118
1797	119
1798	111
1799	109
1800	99

HUNDRED OF WEST GOSCOTE.

Years	BAPTISMS. Males	Females	Total	BURIALS. Males	Females	Total
1700	234	180	414	183	158	341
1710	192	173	365	122	114	236
1720	218	216	434	180	164	344
1730	224	204	428	223	175	398
1740	251	223	474	173	179	352
1750	311	290	601	196	199	395
1760	284	260	544	181	180	361
1770	334	349	683	222	240	462
1780	368	379	747	242	241	483
1781	376	318	694	229	242	471
1782	366	337	703	244	232	476
1783	372	366	738	256	309	565
1784	339	352	691	289	289	578
1785	388	370	758	285	286	571
1786	406	358	764	291	290	581
1787	407	384	791	238	222	460
1788	382	371	753	252	265	517
1789	424	375	799	241	250	491
1790	413	386	799	283	248	531
1791	380	374	754	240	247	487
1792	460	406	866	258	268	526
1793	220	365	585	348	312	660
1794	395	424	819	262	257	519
1795	386	388	774	266	285	551
1796	375	355	730	264	263	527
1797	392	356	748	267	264	531
1798	379	396	775	233	257	490
1799	370	307	677	284	273	557
1800	361	315	676	289	267	556

MARRIAGES (West Goscote)

Years	Marriages
1754	88
1755	141
1756	151
1757	159
1758	174
1759	140
1760	202
1761	189
1762	182
1763	193
1764	186
1765	174
1766	161
1767	173
1768	197
1769	216
1770	189
1771	194
1772	146
1773	178
1774	166
1775	168
1776	182
1777	182
1778	193
1779	165
1780	163
1781	195
1782	190
1783	185
1784	210
1785	197
1786	214
1787	197
1788	200
1789	220
1790	211
1791	178
1792	333
1793	232
1794	248
1795	213
1796	197
1797	218
1798	227
1799	197
1800	190

Register of Baptisms and Burials of Brookesby, defective from 1700 to 1760, inclusive;—Dalby on the Wolds, in 1700, 1710, and 1720;—of Hoton, from 1700 to 1770;—of Keam, in 1700, and 1710;—of East Norton, from 1700 to 1730;—of Rearsby, in 1700 and 1710;—and of Thurmaston, in 1700 and 1710.

Register of Marriages of Brookesby, defective from 1754 to 1766, inclusive;—of Hoton, from 1754 to 1761;—and of Skeffington, from 1754 to 1762.

Observation.—The Register of Ragdale, prior to 1784, is in possession of earl Ferrers; and his lordship desired the Rev. William Casson, curate of the parish, to say, that it was mislaid.

Register of Baptisms and Burials of Newtown Linford, defective in 1760, 1783, and 1784;—of Ravenstone, in 1700;—and of Rothley, in 1700.

Register of Baptisms of Lockington, defective in 1784 and 1785; of Mountsorrel, in 1700;—and of Newtown Linford, in 1770.

Register of Marriages of Rothley, defective from 1779 to 1791, inclusive.

EAST GOSCOTE (1801–1810)

Years	Males	Females	Total	Males	Females	Total	Years	Marriages
1801	227	203	430	151	166	317	–	94
1802	234	242	476	122	148	270	–	102
1803	243	249	492	161	154	315	–	109
1804	279	226	505	115	132	247	–	123
1805	241	259	500	123	130	253	–	111
1806	224	221	445	116	163	279	–	96
1807	249	226	475	166	174	340	–	100
1808	229	245	474	102	125	227	–	107
1809	236	245	481	127	130	257	–	112
1810	252	235	487	148	127	275	–	110

WEST GOSCOTE (1801–1810)

Years	Males	Females	Total	Males	Females	Total	Years	Marriages
1801	387	358	745	287	285	572	–	231
1802	423	406	829	381	371	752	–	281
1803	426	395	821	305	295	600	–	281
1804	424	485	909	276	284	560	–	285
1805	420	402	822	268	270	538	–	253
1806	425	409	834	258	285	543	–	248
1807	447	390	837	247	265	512	–	285
1808	452	400	852	259	296	555	–	270
1809	399	374	773	296	286	582	–	263
1810	427	427	854	291	275	566	–	286

The above ABSTRACT is collected from the Registers of Alexton r. Asfordby r. Ashby Folville v. Baresby c. Barkby v. Barkby Thorpe c. Barrow upon Soar v. Beeby r. Belgrave v. Brooksby r. Cossington r. South Croxton r. Dalby Challacomb v. Dalby on the Wolds c. Frisby on the Wreak v. Gadsby c. Grimston c. Hoby r. Hoton c. Humberston v. Hungerton v. Keyham c. Loddington r. Lowesby (with Cold Newton) v. East Norton c. Prestwold v. Queneborough v. Ragdale c. Ratcliffe v. Rearsby r. Rotherby r. Saxelby r. Seagrave r. Sileby v. Skeffington r. Syston v. Thrussington v. Thurmaston North End c. Thurmaston South End c. Tilton v. Tugby v. Twyford v. Walton on the Wolds r. Wartnaby c. Wymeswold v. and of Wicomd and Caldwell c.

The above ABSTRACT[1] is collected from the Registers of Ansty c. Ashby-de-la-Zouch v. Belton v. Birstall c. Blackfordby c. Breedon v. Cole Orton r, Diseworth v. Diskby (with Thorpe Acre c. Castle Donington v. Hathern r. Isley Walton c. Kegworth r. Lockington (with Hemington) v. Loughborough r. Mountsorrel c. Newtown Linford c. Osgathorpe r. Packington v. Quarndon c. Rothley v. Scale r. Sheepshead v. Swepston r. Swithland r. Thurcaston[2] r. Wanlip r. Long Whatton r. Whitwick[3] v. Woodhouse c. and of Worthington[4] c.

[1] Staunton Harold, in this Hundred, is a domestic chapel.
[2] The chapel formerly at Cropston is demolished.
[3] Including Swannington and Thringstone.
[4] No church-yard at Worthington.

HUNDRED OF GUTHLAXTON.

Years	BAPTISMS Males	Females	Total	BURIALS Males	Females	Total
1700	114	142	256	103	89	192
1710	116	121	237	109	121	230
1720	143	151	294	135	127	262
1730	136	119	255	112	119	231
1740	145	106	251	86	83	169
1750	174	146	320	134	159	293
1760	174	159	333	126	117	243
1770	192	174	366	119	129	248
1780	195	183	378	147	157	304
1781	198	185	383	136	155	291
1782	198	191	389	156	139	295
1783	184	191	375	175	149	324
1784	179	176	355	195	183	378
1785	171	164	335	190	226	416
1786	205	201	406	194	185	379
1787	198	184	382	132	155	287
1788	224	210	434	138	158	296
1789	198	221	419	128	181	309
1790	212	166	378	124	161	285
1791	205	205	410	114	135	249
1792	215	212	427	123	149	272
1793	241	215	456	202	188	390
1794	209	217	426	155	167	322
1795	203	179	382	152	131	283
1796	228	220	448	133	146	279
1797	238	230	468	131	154	285
1798	213	206	419	132	127	259
1799	208	225	433	126	143	269
1800	211	215	426	157	146	303

MARRIAGES (Guthlaxton):

Years	Marriages
1754	54
1755	91
1756	91
1757	91
1758	94
1759	94
1760	87
1761	84
1762	100
1763	106
1764	107
1765	101
1766	89
1767	76
1768	86
1769	96
1770	109
1771	109
1772	108
1773	94
1774	84
1775	115
1776	95
1777	105
1778	103
1779	118
1780	120
1781	107
1782	90
1783	93
1784	87
1785	119
1786	115
1787	127
1788	100
1789	102
1790	95
1791	121
1792	106
1793	109
1794	104
1795	112
1796	113
1797	122
1798	138
1799	139
1800	102

HUNDRED OF SPARKENHOE.

Years	BAPTISMS Males	Females	Total	BURIALS Males	Females	Total
1700	176	172	348	121	124	245
1710	170	150	320	142	121	263
1720	192	176	368	140	118	258
1730	162	159	321	224	183	407
1740	182	191	373	179	196	375
1750	262	225	487	147	186	333
1760	243	252	495	137	147	284
1770	242	230	472	213	193	406
1780	269	262	531	186	192	378
1781	272	244	516	200	177	377
1782	245	243	488	187	182	369
1783	283	242	525	189	184	373
1784	214	202	416	226	246	472
1785	280	284	564	200	219	419
1786	254	276	530	208	225	433
1787	243	286	529	183	172	355
1788	273	264	537	222	215	437
1789	293	256	549	197	220	417
1790	304	289	593	189	224	413
1791	263	262	525	205	185	390
1792	483	472	955	313	340	653
1793	494	511	1,005	363	380	743
1794	592	460	1,052	367	360	727
1795	474	442	916	341	354	695
1796	468	462	930	399	410	809
1797	553	493	1,046	344	351	695
1798	472	500	972	295	348	643
1799	488	460	948	307	295	602
1800	454	475	929	360	340	700

MARRIAGES (Sparkenhoe):

Years	Marriages
1754	101
1755	113
1756	119
1757	113
1758	120
1759	145
1760	160
1761	135
1762	157
1763	169
1764	147
1765	144
1766	123
1767	158
1768	154
1769	156
1770	175
1771	160
1772	166
1773	132
1774	168
1775	137
1776	165
1777	169
1778	149
1779	168
1780	139
1781	156
1782	145
1783	146
1784	150
1785	155
1786	161
1787	198
1788	186
1789	196
1790	176
1791	190
1792	205
1793	177
1794	192
1795	147
1796	196
1797	216
1798	225
1799	195
1800	178

Registers of Baptisms and Burials of Little Ashby, defective in 1700 and 1710;—of Broughton Astley, in 1710;—of Claybrook, in 1700;—of Gilmorton, in 1700, 1710, and 1720;—of Kimcote and Walton, in 1700 and 1710;—of Knighton, in 1730;—of Little Peatling, from 1700 to 1786, inclusive;—of Shawell, in 1750;—and of Swinfield, from 1700 to 1740.

Register of Marriages of Leir, defective from 1754 to 1765, inclusive; and from 1767 to 1771;—of Little Peatling, in 1754 and 1755;—and of Shawell, from 1759 to 1765.

Register of Baptisms and Burials of Aston Flamville, defective from 1760 to 1780, inclusive; of Cadeby, in 1730 and 1740;—of Carlton, in 1700 and 1710;—of Dadlington, from 1700 to 1730;—of Grooby cum Ratby, from 1700 to 1783;—of Higham and Lindley, in 1700;—of Hugglescote, in 1700, 1710, and 1720;—of Kirby Muxloe, in 1700;—of Ratcliffe, in 1740;—of Great Sheepy, in 1700; and of Shenton, in 1800.

Register of Baptisms of Kirby Muxloe, defective in 1784.

Register of Burials of Hugglescote, defective from 1730 to 1790, inclusive;—and of Kirby Muxloe, in 1720.

Register of Marriages of Aston Flamvile, defective from 1755 to 1767, inclusive;—of Burbage from 1754 to 1768;—of Charlton, from 1754 to 1758;—of Earl Shilton, in 1754; and of Peckleton, from 1754 to 1769.

Guthlaxton 1801–1810

Years	BAPTISMS Males	Females	Total	BURIALS Males	Females	Total	Years	Marriages
1801	193	181	374	170	164	334	–	103
1802	247	214	461	174	192	366	–	138
1803	277	245	522	167	168	335	–	143
1804	256	217	473	146	170	316	–	141
1805	260	240	500	133	121	254	–	127
1806	233	248	481	149	132	281	–	115
1807	228	252	480	139	139	278	–	126
1808	246	239	485	128	138	266	–	140
1809	249	246	495	137	134	271	–	129
1810	251	238	489	168	152	320	–	151

Sparkenhoe 1801–1810

Years	BAPTISMS Males	Females	Total	BURIALS Males	Females	Total	Years	Marriages
1801	288	314	602	279	275	554	–	182
1802	334	314	648	284	288	572	–	246
1803	344	354	698	229	242	471	–	334
1804	395	388	783	163	169	332	–	225
1805	367	354	721	257	232	489	–	204
1806	354	357	711	193	199	392	–	228
1807	379	386	765	202	244	446	–	224
1808	387	371	758	246	209	483	–	216
1809	398	391	789	246	209	455	–	229
1810	358	365	723	236	273	509	–	227

The above ABSTRACT is collected from the Registers of Aileston r. Arnsby v. Great Ashby v. Little Ashby r. Bitteswell v. Blabye r. Broughton Astley r. Bruntingthorpe r. Catthorpe r. Great Claybrook c. Little Claybrook v. Cosby v. Cotesbach r. Countess Thorpe c. Dunton Basset v. Foston r. Frowlesworth r. Gilmorton r. Little Glen c. Kilby c. North Kelworth r. South Kelworth r. Kimcote r. Knighton r. Leire r. Lutterworth r. Misterton r. Oadby v. Great Peatling v. Little Peatling r. Shawell r. Shearsby¹ c. Swinford v. Ullesthorpe c. Whetstone c. Great Wigston v. Little Wigston c. and of Willoughby Waterless r.

¹ The church of Knaptoft being demolished, Shearsby chapel is used instead of it.

The above ABSTRACT is collected from the Registers of Appleby r. Aston Flamville r. Barlston c. Barwell (with Stapleton and Marston) r. Braunston c. Burbach c. Cadeby r. Carlton c. Conyerston r. Croft r. Dadlington c. Desford r. Fenny Drayton r. Enderby v. Glenfield r. Heather r. Higham on the Hill r. Hinckley v. Hugglescote c. Ibstock r. Kirby Mallory r. Kirby Muxloe c. Lubbesthorpe c. Market Bosworth r. Markfield r. Nailstone r. Narborough r. Newbold Verdon r. Normanton on the Heath c. Norton by Twycross r. Orton on the Hill v. Peckleton r. Ratby v. Ratcliffe Culey c. Sapcote r. Shackerston v. Sharnford r. Great and Little Sheepy r. Shenton c. Earl Shilton r. Sibstone r. Snareston c. Stoke Golding c. Stoney Stanton r. Sutton Cheney c. Thornton (with Bagworth) v. Thurlaston r. Twycross c. and of Witherley r.

TOWN OF LEICESTER.

Years	Baptisms Males	Baptisms Females	Baptisms Total	Burials Males	Burials Females	Burials Total
1700	83	80	163	61	59	120
1710	65	59	124	42	44	86
1720	67	70	137	73	67	140
1730	103	78	181	88	96	184
1740	98	89	187	109	76	185
1750	98	111	209	109	138	247
1760	93	97	190	137	171	308
1770	164	128	292	147	124	271
1780	141	137	278	135	121	256
1781	157	149	306	214	171	385
1782	132	135	267	120	158	278
1783	135	141	276	134	142	276
1784	151	134	285	135	151	286
1785	142	152	294	128	139	267
1786	153	144	297	138	143	281
1787	154	149	303	126	115	241
1788	163	153	316	180	175	355
1789	185	143	328	145	124	269
1790	159	149	308	156	151	307
1791	165	179	344	161	137	298
1792	171	156	327	162	157	319
1793	188	162	350	127	147	274
1794	181	165	346	167	193	360
1795	141	147	288	162	177	339
1796	132	130	262	127	128	255
1797	140	149	289	141	136	277
1798	151	151	302	145	177	322
1799	186	153	339	139	145	284
1800	155	179	334	143	155	298

Marriages (Town of Leicester):

Years	Marriages	Years	Marriages
1754	76	1777	103
1755	83	1778	82
1756	78	1779	107
1757	67	1780	82
1758	76	1781	84
1759	77	1782	91
1760	83	1783	77
1761	83	1784	100
1762	70	1785	118
1753	92	1786	116
1764	74	1787	123
1765	81	1788	120
1766	81	1789	107
1767	75	1790	114
1768	94	1791	108
1769	111	1792	143
1770	96	1793	114
1771	77	1794	98
1772	83	1795	94
1773	69	1796	105
1774	88	1797	130
1775	95	1798	120
1776	105	1799	124
		1800	116

Register of Baptisms and Burials of St. Leonard, defective in 1720.

Observation.—The vicar of the parish of St. Mary observes, " that the increase of the Burials in 1781 was owing to the small-pox;" and also, " that an infirmary, and an hospital for aged and infirm persons, occasion the Burials of that parish to bear a larger proportion in the Register."

Years	Males	Females	Total	Males	Females	Total	Years	Marriages
1801	250	241	491	287	316	603	–	191
1802	256	293	549	251	285	536	–	225
1803	336	329	665	219	210	429	–	348
1804	331	329	660	152	147	299	–	237
1805	326	320	646	197	193	390	–	188
1806	307	312	619	230	221	451	–	179
1807	344	310	654	249	241	490	–	198
1808	309	278	587	180	189	369	–	231
1809	400	338	738	328	284	612	–	218
1810	352	367	719	266	272	538	–	240

The above ABSTRACT is collected from the Registers of All Saints v. St. Leonard v. St. Margaret v. St. Martin v. St. Mary v. St. Nicholas v.

SUMMARY.

Years	Baptisms Males	Baptisms Females	Baptisms Total	Burials Males	Burials Females	Burials Total
1700	1,118	1,097	2,215	769	768	1,537
1710	941	878	1,819	712	718	1,430
1720	1,059	998	2,057	982	937	1,919
1730	1,042	920	1,962	1,073	995	2,068
1740	1,151	1,022	2,173	865	903	1,768
1750	1,381	1,239	2,620	893	1,040	1,933
1760	1,314	1,268	2,582	951	996	1,947
1770	1,488	1,383	2,871	1,095	1,154	2,249
1780	1,530	1,504	3,034	1,203	1,249	2,452
1781	1,571	1,452	2,023	1,271	1,276	2,547
1782	1,494	1,445	2,939	1,145	1,175	2,320
1783	1,518	1,516	3,034	1,232	1,275	2,507
1784	1,429	1,365	2,794	1,345	1,387	2,732
1785	1,582	1,545	3,127	1,333	1,383	2,716
1786	1,636	1,535	3,171	1,300	1,338	2,638
1787	1,579	1,578	3,157	1,080	1,105	2,185
1788	1,691	1,581	3,272	1,224	1,349	2,573
1789	1,711	1,648	3,359	1,101	1,226	2,327
1790	1,734	1,613	3,347	1,168	1,244	2,412
1791	1,682	1,639	3,321	1,150	1,140	2,290
1792	1,993	1,881	3,874	1,260	1,357	2,617
1793	1,987	1,905	3,892	1,485	1,492	2,977
1794	2,015	1,865	3,880	1,386	1,420	2,806
1795	1,826	1,806	3,632	1,382	1,451	2,833
1796	1,808	1,781	3,589	1,320	1,375	2,695
1797	1,975	1,909	3,884	1,325	1,325	2,650
1798	1,879	1,921	3,800	1,227	1,356	2,583
1799	1,891	1,786	3,677	1,278	1,254	2,532
1800	1,818	1,792	3,610	1,379	1,326	2,705

Marriages (Summary):

Years	Marriages	Years	Marriages
1754	541	1777	862
1755	710	1778	877
1756	756	1779	894
1757	751	1780	844
1758	791	1781	863
1759	754	1782	849
1760	881	1783	819
1761	820	1784	861
1762	819	1785	962
1763	912	1786	946
1764	855	1787	998
1765	779	1788	926
1766	717	1789	971
1767	727	1790	934
1768	813	1791	925
1769	896	1792	1026
1770	892	1793	989
1771	874	1794	967
1772	812	1795	888
1773	768	1796	954
1774	815	1797	1047
1775	804	1798	1079
1776	879	1799	983
		1800	926

The above ABSTRACT is collected from the Registers of two hundred and forty-eight parish churches and chapels, situate in the county of Leicester.

It is supposed that thirty Returns due from this County were not received at the Privy Council Office.

Years	Males	Females	Total	Males	Females	Total	Years	Marriages
1801	1,661	1,614	3,275	1,399	1,490	2,889	–	970
1802	1,865	1,855	3,720	1,496	1,592	3,088	–	1,215
1803	2,044	1,955	3,999	1,347	1,338	2,685	–	1,441
1804	2,087	2,048	4,135	1,056	1,098	2,154	–	1,217
1805	1,994	1,916	3,910	1,204	1,159	2,363	–	1,084
1806	1,966	1,926	3,892	1,145	1,208	2,353	–	1,030
1807	2,056	1,912	3,968	1,244	1,324	2,568	–	1,118
1808	2,039	1,925	3,964	1,136	1,217	2,353	–	1,134
1809	2,065	1,973	4,038	1,365	1,298	2,663	–	1,129
1810	2,034	2,024	4,058	1,366	1,370	2,736	–	1,206
Total	19,811	19,148	38,959	12,758	13,094	25,852	–	11,544

The SUMMARY of the County of Leicester is collected from the Registers of 259 parish churches and chapels; and it is believed that no Return whatever remains due.—Several Returns mention Unentered Baptisms and Burials, to the following amount, viz. annual average number of Unentered Baptisms 232—Burials 66.

INDEX

TO THE

NAMES IN THE FIRST VOLUME.

AARON the Jew, 97; 358: *App.* 38. *n.*
Abantes (the), 253.
Abbot, George, [95].
Abbott, rev. G. S. ix. *pref.*
Abel, Anthony, 352.
Abell, Joseph, 441.
Abney, Danet, 351.
—— Daniel, mayor, 428; 433.
—— sir Edward, 458.
—— Edmund, 411.
—— George, 430; 452.
—— John, mayor, 313; 352; 439; 442; 583.
—— rev. John, 445.
—— Philip, mayor, 354; 435.
—— Robert, 462.
—— Samuel - Bracebridge, 462.
Aboveton, Martha, cxx.
Abraham, Henry, *App.* 78.
Abrincis, Hugo de, liii.; *see* Earls of CHESTER.
Aburbury, Richard, 241.
Acham, Anthony, [117]; [122]; [124]; [126]; 468; 552; 595.
Ackland, sir Thomas-Dyke, 528. *n.*
Actæon, i. 9, 10.
Acton, Thomas, [26].
Ada, countess, 90.
Adam de . . . . , vicar, 322.
Adam of Newmarket, 183, 184; 187; 198; 207.
Adams, John, 451.
Adamthwaite, Dr., ix. *pref.*
Adcock, Thomas, 443. 445; 512.
Addison, Mr. 10.
Adela, queen, 59. *n.*
Adelais, 80, 81; 83; 85; 86; 91; 94.
Adelina, 22; 23; 24; 25.
Adeline, lady, 21. *n.*
Adeliza, lady, liii; 20; 21.
Ad Fontem, Adam, cxx.
Ad Molendinum, Johannes, cxx.
Adrian, pope, 12; 52.
Ægidius Bonomensis, *App.* 106. *n.*
—— Romanus, *App.* 102. *n.*; 105. *n.*
Ælfhere, duke, 15.
Ælfric, duke, 15.
Ælian Spartianus, 356.
Aelis, 80.
Æneas, 2.
Æthelfleda, lady, 14, 15. 356.
Æthelred, king, xxxv; 12; 15; 16; 216.
Æthelred, duke, 14; 15; 356.
Æthelric, king, 12.
Agamemnon, 9.
Aganippe, 2.
Agnes of Evreux, 99.
Agrippa, 9. *n.*; 356.
Aigle-blanche, Peter, 127; 130, 131, 132; 134, 135. (*See* Hereford, Peter, bishop of.)
Ailesbury, Robert Bruce earl of, 292.
Ailway, Jane, 614. *n.*
Aires, Hannah, 326.
Airy, Richard, [112].
Alanus de Insulis, *App.* 102. *n.*
Alban (St.), 12; 72; 161.
Albaniacho, Nicholas de, cxxiv.
Albany, duke of, 2.
Albe, Thomas, cxxiii.
ALBEMARLE, Earls of, and Countess.
— William de Albini, 49, 50.
— William de Fortibus, 149; 151; 152; 153; 167; 187.
— William, 221.
— Edward, 240.
— Richard Beauchamp, 544.
— Maud, liii.
VOL. I.

Albeney, William de, 97.
Alberic, li.
Albert of Bavaria, 232, 233.
Albert, cardinal, 125.
Albigensians, 101, &c.
Albini, Nigel de, liii.
—— William de, liii.
Albiniaco, Isabella de, *App.* 38. *n.*
Albion the Great, 1.
Albreda, abbess, 23; 98: *App.* 54.
Albumazar, *App.* 105.
Alchfrid, king, *App.* 2.
Alcock, Daniel, 326. *n.*
Aldelega, Adam, 459.
Aldithel, James de, 158.
Aldred, or Aldredus, bishop, 13; 356.
Aldridge, William, [60].
Aldulfus, archbishop, 12.
Aldwin, bishop, 13; 356.
Alefounder, Dr. 347.
Alexander, Edward, 529.
—— III. king, 199.
—— III. pope, 38; 47, 48, 49, 50, 51, 52, 53; 55; 61; 81; 277: *App.* 9.
—— IV. pope, 127; 131, 132, 133, 134, 135, 136; 142; 144; 167; 169, 170. *n.*; 173; 221; 300: *App.* 68.
—— bishop, 17; 25; 26; 254; 357; 567: *App.* 3; 15. *n.*; 53.
—— the Great, 253.
—— Severus, 356.
—— Trallianus, *Ap.* 106. *n.*
Alfonse, king, 227.
Alfounder, rev. Mr. 598; 606.
—— Mary, 606.
Alfred, king, xxxiii; xxxiv; xxxvi.; 3; 14; 22. *n.*; 137. *n.*; 153. *n.*; 174. *n.*; 356; 569. *n.*: *App.* 2.
Alfric (Alfrid), king, *App.* 2.
Algar, earl, li.
—— 15.
Alger, a monk, *App.* 103. *n.*
Algernoune, 260. *n.*
Algitha, 17.
Algyva, 15.
Alianor, queen, 69; 70, 71; 75, 76; 80; 82; 87, 88; 91; 94, 95. *n.*
Alianora of Provence, queen, 106; 108; 119. & note.; 121; 124; 125; 127; 128; 141; 143; 146; 148; 162; 166; 169. *n.*; 172. *n.*; 175, 176, 177, 178, 179, 180; 184; 192, 193, 194; 196. *n.*; 203; 210; 221; 224. & *n.*; 361: *App.* 34; 41.
—— of Spain (queen), 123; 127; 129; 138. *n.*: *App.* 34.
Alisander, Christopher, 416.
Alisia, 80.
Alithwerl, John de, 366.
Alkabucius, *App.* 105. *n.*
Allamand, or Allemand, John-Peter, 450; 558; 565.
Allen, Bridget, [22].
—— sir John, 272.
—— John, 351.
—— Ralph, [69]; [75].
—— Thomas, 615.
—— William, [89].
—— Mrs. 513.
Allibon, Mrs. [92].
Allin, Thomas, [78].
Allington, Mr. 492.
Allmanbury, William, 331; *App.* 111.
Allnutt, Richard, 543.
Allsop, Nicholas, 452.
—— rev. Thomas, [64].
B

Almaine, king of; *see* Richard earl of CORNWALL.
Almaine, sir Henry de; *see* Henry.
Almaric, 212.
Almasor, *App.* 105. *n.*
Almeneschis, John de, *App.* 9.
Almeric, bishop - elect; *see* Aylmer.
Almey, Robert, 444.
Alnei, William.
Alneto, Henry de, *App.* 47.
Alnetto, William de, 27.
Alnewyk, William, 372.
Alphonso, 109.
—— king, 120, 121, 122, 123; 125; 127; 137; 139; 140; 175.
AlredusRievallensis, *App.* 103. *n.*
Alsay, John, mayor, 364, 365.
Alselin, Goisfrid, xlvi.
—— Geoffrey, lii.
Alsis, John, mayor, 556.
Alsopp, John, [70].
Alsop, Mr. 352, 620.
—— rev. Mr. 347.
—— William, mayor, 434, 435; 580.
Alston, sir Thomas, 614.
—— Elizabeth, 614.
—— Frances, 614.
Alta-villa, William de, *App.* 71.
Alured de Lincoln, 155.
Aluric, xl; li.
Alveres, Peter, *App.* 105. *n.*
Alveva, countess, li.
Alwigus, bishop, *App.* 2.
Alwina, 15.
Aly, John, *App.* 78.
Alyngton, Robert, *App.* 104. *n.*
Alysander, William, 494.
Amandevil, Alexander de, 155.
Amatues, 251.
Amauri, count, 99.
Amauri de Montfort; *see* Earls of LEICESTER.
Ambolard, frier, 201.
Ambrose, Dr. Davies, 501.
Ambrosius, 279.
Amicia, 24; 48; 99.
—— countess, 24; 48, 90; 99.
—— heiress of Osbern, 71.
Amison, John, *App.* 77.
—— Richard, *App.* 100.
—— William, *App.* 100.
Ammonius, Andreas, 266. *n.*
Amyson, John, *App.* 100.
—— William, *App.* 77.
Anderson, lord, 407.
—— rev. George, 502, 503.
—— sir John, 528. *n.*
—— rev. John, 529, 530; 608, 609.
—— rev. Robert, 503.
—— William, 491.
Andervill, John de, cxxii.
Andesaure, William de, cxxii.
Andon, Eustachia de, *App.* 47.
Andrew of Bourgogne, 105.
Andrew, James, 340; 342; 343; 345; 409; 411; mayor, 420; 425, 426; 454; 601.
—— James, junior, 506.
—— Moses, 577.
—— Richard, 331, 332; 338.
Andrewe, James, 597.
Andrewes, Frances, 610.
—— Francis-Henry, 610.
—— rev. Gerrard, [132]; 347; 467; 512; 609, 610.
—— Dr. Gerrard, 512.
—— rev. Mr. 7.
—— Isabella, 610.
Andrews, James, [127]; [131].
—— rev. James, 595.
Anesti, John de, 511.
Angel, Alice, 501.

Angel, rev. John, 427; 429; 501, 502; 505; 578; 581; 609.
—— John, 490; 502, 503; 506; 512.
Angerville, John de, cxi.
Angervyle, Roger, *App.* 72.
Angles, 355.
Anglicus, Gilbertus, 277.
Anglo-Normans, 41; 213.
—— Saxons, 6.
Angos, Robert earl of, 224.
Anjou, Charles count of, 175; 183; 190; 194, 195.
—— Geoffry count of, 45.
—— Henry Fitz-Henry count of, 27.
Anne of Cleves, queen, 465.
—— of Denmark, queen, 417; 453.
—— (Stuart), queen, 439, 440, 441, 442, 443, 444; 502, 503: *App.* 8.
Annesley, sir John de, 237.
Annis, James, mayor, 441, 442; 552; 566.
—— Martha, 566.
Annius, 1.
Anselm, archbishop, 22; 35, 36, 37; 357.
Anstis, John, 297.
Ansty, John, 264; *App.* 64.
—— William de, *App.* 98.
Anteswesill, Thomas, 384.
Anthony (St.), 251.
Antonine, cxlvii; 4; 355, 356.
Antoninus Philosophus, 356.
—— Pius, clvii.
Aomar, *App.* 105. *n.*
Apollo, 10; 253.
Appleby, John de, 561.
Appleby, sir Edmund de, 455.
Apsley, Peter, 595.
Apulians, 133, 134; 136; 146.
Aquila, Gilbert de, 97; 359.
Aquitaine, John of Gaunt duke of, 239; 241.
Araby, Ralph de, *App.* 71.
Arcadius, 4*.
Archer, Richard, 407, 411.
—— Robert, 490.
—— Mrs. 491.
Archigallo, king, 8.
Arden, Edward, 284. *n.*
Arden, Hugh de, 260; 284: *App.* 66; 79, 80, 81.
—— John de, 256; 284: *App.* 79.
—— Thomas de, 286; 337: *App.* 80; 82.
—— William de, 285; *App.* 79.
Ardern, Robert, 460.
Arderne, John, cxxx.
Ardington, Thomas, 460.
Arecourte, Richard de, cxxiii.
Argenten, Ægidius de, 152; 205, 206; 363.
Argyle, Archibald Campbel earl of, 436.
—— John duke of, 543.
Aristotle, xli. *n.*; *App.* 103. *n.*
Arlot, master, 145, 146; 149; 154.
Armachanus, Richardus, or Richard of Armagh, *App.* 102. *n.*; 103. *n.*
Armanak, the earl of, 228.
Armeston, Thomas, 430; 458.
Armston, Dorothy, 564.
—— James, 462.
—— John, [87]; [101];* 446; 564.
—— widow, 440.
—— William, 553.
Armstrong, Alice, 599; 601?
—— Elizabeth, 602.
—— Gilbert, 349. *n.*; 599; 601, 602.

Arnold,

Cattisbie,

Jane de Valois, princess, 232.
———— countess, 232.
—— of Heynault, 232.
Januensis, James, *App.* 103. *n.*
Janus Bifrons, 2; 5; 355.
Japhet, 1.
Jaques, Elizabeth, 492.
———— Joseph, 493.
———— Richard-Spooner, 462.
Jaquis, William, 487.
Jarratt, Thomas, [69]; [75].
Jaruman, bishop, 13.
Jee, Thomas, 564.
—— William, 411.
—— Mr., ix. *pref.*
Jeffcut, Thomas, 450; mayor, 451.
Jefferies, lord-chancellor, high-steward, *App.* 7.
Jeffrey of Monmouth, cli.
Jenkinson, Thomas, 395; 458.
Jennens, Charles, [100]; [108]; [109]; 517.
Jenner, rev. Mr. 522.
Jennings, Joseph, [104].
Jennison, Christopher, 560.
Jephson, Roger, [29].
Jerdislaus, emperor, 98. *n.*
Jerome (St.), 505.
Jerveis, William, 461.
Jervis, Richard, 442.
Jesson, rev. Thomas, 609.
Jevon, Edward, 438; 440; 454.
Jews, 7, 8; 76; 112; 129; 178. *n.*; 185; 187; 206; 253; 361, 362: *App.* 38.
Joan, princess, 238.
Joanes, rev. John, 326.
Joceline, bishop, lv. *n.*
Johannitius, *App.* 105. *n.*
John (Lackland), prince, 69, 70; 82; 85; 86; 89; 94, 95; 104. *n.* 281. *See*
John, king, lviii. *n.*; 32; 77. *n.*; 90. *n.*; 95, 96, 97; 99, 100; 102, 103, 104; 120; 123. *n.*; 144; 148; 150. *n.*; 157. *n.*; 173. *n.*; 184; 193. *n.*; 214, 215, 216, 217, 218; 260; *App.* 58, 59; 279; 281; 358, 359, 360; 363; 393; 447. *n.*; 622, 623: *App.* 34; 58, 59.
—— the Good, king, 229, 230.
—— I. king of Portugal, 242.
—— mareschal, 42; 46.
—— abbot, cxlii; *App.* 18.
—— bishop, 264; *App.* 64, 65.
—— of Eltham, 365.
—— of Gaunt, 89: *see* Dukes of LANCASTER, &c.
—— at Halle, c.
—— of Hexham, 27.
—— of Heynault, 232.
—— de Lancaster, 222; *App.* 34.
—— of Leicester, a frier, 297.
—— of Salisbury, 48; 53, 54; 58. *n.*; 63; 66; 68.
—— de Sancto Ægidio, 123.
—— of Oxford, 47; 51, 52; 54, 55; 63.
Johns, Thomas, *App.* 47.
Johnson, Abraham, 466.
———— Edmund, mayor, 429; 438; 442; 445; 447.
———— Edmund, 313; 452.
———— Edward, 427; 489.
———— Ezechiel, 466.
———— Frances, 604.
———— George-William, 466.
———— Isaac, 466.
———— John, [89]; 444; 514; 527, 528; 531; 533, 534; 604.
———— Joseph, 445; 449; mayor, 450, 451; 531.
———— Mathias, [101].
———— Matthew, [32].
———— Maurice, 242. *n.*; 328. *n.*; 465.
———— Rebecca, [76].
———— Richard, [77]; [101].
———— Robert, archdeacon, 465, 466.
———— Robert, 327; 411; 451; 470; 466.
———— Dr. Samuel, 609. *n.*
———— Samuel, 448; mayor, 450; 466.
———— Thomas, 313; 404; 444; 446; 458.
———— William, 554.
———— Zachary, [76].

Johnson, rev. Mr. 403.
———— Mr. *App.* 3.
Johnsone, Stephen, 608.
Joigny, 104.
Jolliffe, Henry, 275.
Jolly, William, 457.
Jones, rev. Cadwallader, 508.
———— Cornelius, 492.
———— Elizabeth, 544.
———— John, 585.
———— Rowland, 2.
Jonson, Ben, 540.
———— Geffrey, 477; 480; 495; 501; 503.
———— William, *App.* 77.
Jonsone, William, *App.* 98; 100.
Jonys, Robert, mayor, 395.
Jordan, archdeacon, 39.
———— Giles, 264. *See* Jurdan.
———— Hannah, 553.
———— Hugh, 352.
———— Richard, 444.
———— Samuel, 529; 531.
———— William, 529; 531.
Jordain, Mary, 319.
———— Thomas, 319; 444; 454.
Jordaine, Thomas, 616.
Joyce, Thomas, 563.
———— William, [60].
Judd, Deane, [89].
—— John, 528. *n.*
—— Matthew, 352.
Judith, countess, xlii; liii; 17; 19, 20.
Julian, Robert, cxx.
Juliers, William VI. duke of, 232.
Julius Cæsar, clvii.
Jurdan, Giles, *App.* 64. *See* Jordan.
Jurdane, Thomas, 274.
Justinian, 9.
Jutes, 355.
Juxon, Abigail, 609. *n.*
———— rev. Joseph, 609.

K.

Kalewyken, William de, abbot, 275.
Kamvile, Thomas de, cxiii.
Karvile, Thomas de, cxiii.
Kateby, William de, cxvii.
Katerington, Thomas, 237.
Katharine, queen, 272.
Katineto, Robert de, 26. *n.*
Kaye, Mrs. [41].
Kaynnes, William de, 155.
Keate, sir John, 502.
Kebell, Elizabeth, 616.
———— John, 616,
Kebill, Thomas, 384; 389.
———— Walter, 389.
Keble, Francis, 371.
Keck, Anthony-James, 458; 517; 522.
Keene, Daniel, 436; 438; 512.
Kegworth, Margaret, 309, 310.
———— Robert de, 455.
Keightley, Elizabeth, 610.
———— John, 610.
Kelham, Mr. l.; 443.
Kelnemundescod, Adam de, cxiv.
Kemp, Elizabeth, [104].
Ken, William, *App.* 93.
Kendal, John of Lancaster, earl of, 369.
Kendall, Thomas, 274.
Kene, Stephen, *App.* 77.
Kenilworth, Robert de, cxxii.
Kenmure, William viscount, *App.* 7.
Kennell, Thomas, 382.
Kenning, Elizabeth, 616.
Kensington, Henry Rich lord, 341. *n.*
KENT, Earls of.
———— Godwyn earl of, 173. *n.*; *App.* 6.
— Hubert de Burgh, 295; *App.* 6.
— Edmund, 224, 225, 226.
— Thomas, 243.
— Edward, 370.
— Henry lord Grey, 456.
— Arthur, 470.
— Lucy, countess, 370.
Kent, Gregory, [112].

Kent, Jeffery, mayor, 366.
———— Peter de, 457.
———— Peter, mayor, 364.
Kenthorpe, Richard de, cxx.
Kentwode, rev. Reginald, 561.
Kenulph, *or* Kenwulf, king, 12, 13; 356. *n.*
Kerby, John, 452.
———— Robert de, 559.
———— William de, abbot, 264; 275.
———— William de, 260.
———— William, [23].
Kerdeston, Fulk de, 152.
Kerkeby, William de, cxiv; cxxiv.
Kestin, Richard, [18].
Kestven, Richard, 376.
Ketering, William, 240.
Kevelioc, Hugh de; *see* Earls of CHESTER.
Keysteyn, Henry, *App.* 78.
Keyte, Margaret, 616.
—— sir William, 616.
Keythorp, William de, 455.
Kiddier, Susannah, [71].
Kidyan, John, [59].
Kilby, rev. John, 444; 563.
—— John, 438, 439; 512.
—— Joseph, 438.
—— Roger, 457.
—— William, [106].
Kilbye, Mary, 563.
Killigrew, Dr. 293. *n.*
Killingworth, Robert de, 252.
Kilmarnock, William earl of, *App.* 7.
Kilwarby, Robert, archbishop, 295. *n.*
King, George, 352.
—— John, 492.
—— Thomas, 615. *n.*
Kingston, Elizabeth duchess of, *App.* 7.
———— sir William, 271, 272, 273.
Kinnoul, Thomas Hay, earl of, 546.
Kinns, rev. William, 509.
Kipping, Alicia, 388.
———— Cecilia, 388.
———— Simon, 388.
———— William, 388.
Kippis, Dr. 598. *n.*
Kirby, John, [23].
Kirk, John, [51].
Kirkby, Anne, [4].
—— John de, cxx.
—— rev. Robert, [53].
Kirkland, John, 452.
Kirton, Richard, 320.
Kitchin, Thomas, 351.
Knaptoft, William de, 555.
Knight, John, [27]; 406.
———— John, mayor, 364; *App.* 40.
———— William, dean, 335, 336; 338.
Knightcote, Richard, mayor, 368.
———— Roger, mayor, 366.
Knighton, Henry de; *see* Knyghton.
———— John de, 330; 455.
———— Richard, 457.
———— Roger, 457.
Knivet, John, cxxv; cxxvii, cxxviii.
Knitle, Robert de, cxviii.
Kniton, Philip de, 459.
Kniveton, sir Gilbert, 539; 544.
Knollys, sir Francis, 537.
Knott, Elizabeth, [4].
———— Mary, [4].
Knowles, William, 578.
———— Mrs. [111].
Knyghtley, Edmond, cxliii.
Knyghton, *or* Knighton, Henry de, 24; 48; 90; 100; 104; 106; 244; 255. *n.*; 256; 262; 323; 366, 367: *App.* 108.
Knythtecote, John de, 457.
Kylby, William de, *App.* 93.
Kylwardby, Robert, abp. *App.* 104. *n.*
Kymeringham, Peter de, 227.
Kyng, Gregory, 274.
———— William, *App.* 99.
Kynston, Henry de, 552.
Kynyngham, John, 241.
Kyriel, John, 152.
Kyrke, Richard, 259.
Kyttes, William, 337.

L.

L'Abbé, Geoffrey, *App.* 79.
———— Richard, 260.
La Beauvisme, Robert de, 285; *App.* 80.
Labrookes, John de, cxxii.
Lacer, William, [54].
———— Mrs. [127]; 308; 435.
Lacie, John, 274.
Lackland, John, king, 110; 216: *and see* John, king.
Lacy, Edmund de, *App.* 33.
—— John de, 220.
—— John, [127].
—— N. 461.
Lacum, Richard, 371.
La Ferte, Margaret de, *App.* 33.
La Haye, John de, 174.
La Marche, count de, 109.
La Mare, Robert, 231.
———— Wigan de, 261.
La Mere, Peter de, 237.
Lamb, sir John, 578.
Lambe, John, 475.
———— William, 282. *n.*
Lambarde, Mr., xxxix; 8.
Lambarte, Robert, *App.* 78.
Lamberd, Miles, mayor, 388.
Lambert, Anne, 553; 604.
——— John, 553; 604.
——— Margaret, 617.
——— Milo, 389.
——— Thomas, mayor, 446.
Lambrige, Christopher, 296.
Lancaster, William de, 260; *App.* 66.
LANCASTER, Earls of, and Countesses.
— Thomas de Holland, cxxv; cxxvii.
— Edmund Crouchback, 211; 220, 221, 222; 261; 363, 364; *App.* 6; 19; 21, 22, 23; 34; 42, 43; 61. (*See also* Edmund, prince.)
— Thomas Plantagenet, 222, 223, 224, 225, 226; 229; 248; 261; 284; 295; 300; 321; 329; 357; 364, 365; 369; 625; *App.* 6; 23, &c., 32, 33, 34; 43; 59.
— Henry Plantagenet, 222; 224, 225, 226, 227, 228; 239; 329; 336; 339; 348; 364, 365, 366: *App.* 26, &c.; 34; 44; 109.
— Henry Grismond, 227, 228, 229; 329; 365: *App.* 26; 44, 45; 109. (*See* Dukes, below).
— Aveline, 221; *App.* 34.
— Blanch, 222; *App.* 34.
— Alice, 222; 225; Margaret, 364, (Q.?); *App.* 34.
— Maud, 226, 227; *App.* 33, 34.
Dukes *and* Duchesses.
— Henry Grismond, 229, 230, 231, 232, 233, 234, 235; 239; 244; 262; 286; 295, 296; 329; 330; 332; 339; 348, 349; 365, 366, 367; *App.* 6; 26; 34; 45; 109.
— John of Gaunt, cxxvi; 211. *n.*; 231, 232; 234, 235, 236, 237, 238, 239, 240, 241, 242, 243, 244, 245, 246, 247, 248, 249, 250; 263; 265; 305; 321; 330, 331; 332; 337; 339; 367, 368; 380: *App.* 6; 27, 28; 33, 34; 45, 46; 110.
— Henry of Bolingbroke, 242; 250; 368; *App.* 7.
— Henry of Monmouth, *App.* 7.
— Isabel, 231; 235; 330; *App.* 34.
— Blanch, 231, 232; 234, 235, 236, 237; 239, 240, 241, 242; 244: *App.* 34; 46.
— Constance of Castile, 236, 237, 238, 239, 240, 241, 242; 244; 331; 339; 368.
— Catharine Swinford, 239, 240, 241, 242, 243, 244, 245.
Land, William, [43].
Landa, Bouth, cxx.
——— Thomas de, 285; *App.* 80.
Lane, John, cxliii; [28]; *App.* 77.
———— William, [53]; [63]; [81].
Laneham, Robert, 535.
                    Lanfranc,

GENERAL INDEX

TO THE

FIRST VOLUME.

B

lars of the battle at Bosworth-field between Richard the Third and Henry earl
of Richmond, 298, 299 ; 380, 381. See
also the article *Skirmishes*.)
Baudesert, baron ; see sir William *Paget*.
Bauthumley, Jacob, appointed serjeant-at-
mace for the borough of Leicester, 430.
———— Jacob, keeper of the town-
library of Leicester, wrote, and dedicated to the corporation of the town, a
history of the persecution of the church,
509.
Bavaria, William duke of ; see *William of
Heynault*.
Bayford, John, chaplain to Robert Matseyn
master of St. Leonard's hospital at Lei-
cester, sentenced to a singular penance
for infringing the rights of the abbot of
Leicester touching the administration of
the sacrament, 322 ; *App.* 65.
Bayley, Thomas, twice elected mayor of
Leicester, 368, 369.
Baylol ; see *Baliol*.
Baymond, John, chosen recorder of Leices-
ter, 391 ; 452.
Beadle of Leicester, his annual salary, 443 ;
467.
Beal, Richard, chamberlain of Leicester,
447.—Chosen mayor, 448.
Beamount, John, his letter to Thomas lord
Cromwell, concerning the abbey of Grace-
dieu, cxliii.
Bear-baitings, bear-wards, &c. ; orders of the
corporation of Leicester respecting, 402.
Bearas, the practice of shaving them,
among the monks and friers ; whence
originating, 252. — Why practised by
the warriors of classical antiquity, 253.
Bearne, countess of ; her evil character,
114.
Beasley, Ebenezer, chosen mace-bearer of
Leicester, 446.
Beast-market (The) of Leicester transferred
from the Saturday-market to the Cow-
lane, 408.—Removed to the Horse-fair,
450. *n.*
Beatrice, daughter of king Henry the
Third, espoused to John de Dreux, count
of Bretagne, 167 ; (165. *n.*)
Beatrice de Bourgogne-Viennois, married to
Amauri earl of Leicester, 105.
Beauchamp, Milo de, expelled from his dignity of earl of Bedford, 24.
———— John, a partisan of Montfort
II. earl of Leicester ; slain at the battle
of Evesham, 208.
———— Thomas, earl of Warwick, appointed protector during the minority
of king Richard the Second, 237.
———— lady Joan, her bequests to the
several sanctuaries in which her body
should rest in its peregrination to the
place of interment, 267 ; *App.* 72.
———— lady Isabel, her monumental
stone in the Black-Friers church at Leicester, noticed by Leland, 296.
Beauclerc, Henry, son to William the Conqueror, was the fourth who held the
office of Steward of England, 20 ;
App. 6. (See *Henry the First*.)
Beauforts (the), descendants of John of
Gaunt duke of Lancaster, by Catharine
Swinford his concubine ; their legitima-
tion, under that appellation, 239. *n.* ;
240 ; 245. (See their names, and particulars respecting them, in the four subsequent articles.)
Beaufort, John de, marquis of Dorset, and
earl of Somerset, marries Margaret Holland, daughter of the earl of Kent,
239. *n.* ; 240 ; 243.—His death, 243.—
Interred in Canterbury-cathedral, *ib.*—
His tomb and arms described, *ib. n.*—His
creation to the earldom of Somerset,
245.
———— Henry de, cardinal ; bishop of
Lincoln, and of Winchester ; twice chancellor of England, 239. *n.* ; 243 ; 264.—
Interred at Winchester : description of
his tomb, 243. *n.*—By him the collegiate
church of St. Mary in the Newark at
Leicester was interiorly decorated, 339.
—Lord-chancellor ; his theme and descant, on opening a session of parliament
at Leicester at the commencement of
the reign of his nephew Henry the Fifth,
369 : — and again, under Henry the
Sixth, 371.—Some particulars of the dis-
sensions betwixt him and Humphrey
duke of Gloucester, *ib.* & 372.—Resigns
his office of chancellor, 372.
———— Thomas de, duke of Exeter, earl
of Dorset, and admiral of England ; his
marriage, and death, 239. *n.* ; 243.—

Buried at St. Edmundsbury, 243.—His
corpse recently discovered, *ib.*—Particulars of his will, *ib. n.*—Restored to his
titles and honours by his nephew king
Henry the Fifth, 369.
Beaufort, Joan, her marriages, issue, and
death, 242. — Interred in Lincoln-cathe-
dral, *ib.* — Her tomb described, *ib.*—Her
epitaph and arms, *ib.*
———— Edmund, duke of Somerset, excites the discontents of the commons,
373.
Beaumont, the town of, in Gascogne, captured by Henry de Lancaster, earl of
Derby, 228.
———— lord, of Beaumanor, entertained
king Richard the Second and his queen,
on their journey to York, 368.
———— lady Jane, her epitaph, in St.
Mary's church at Leicester, 316.
———— lord, his tenure, under Wigston's
Hospital, 487.
———— lady, her donation of books to
the Town-library of Leicester, 506.
———— Edward, his tenure in Norton,
under Wigston's Hospital, 487.
———— sir George, appointed by the
corporation of Leicester to present a con-
gratulatory address to queen Anne, 442,
443.
———— Henry, lord of Folkingham, 231 ;
App. 34.
———— sir Henry, of Gracedieu, made
free of the borough of Leicester, 418.—
Chosen burgess of parliament for the
same, *ib.* ; 432 ; 458.—His death, 419.
———— Henry de, sells a parcel of wood
to the abbot and convent of Leicester,
262 ; *App.* 62.
———— John viscount, one of the commissioners of Leicestershire for raising
archers for defence of the realm at the
period of Blore-heath battle, 373.
———— John, chosen recorder of Leicester, 394 ; 452.
———— John, sold away the land given
by the bishop of Carlisle towards founding a school at Leicester, 394 ; 511.
———— John ; see William *Gyes*.
———— Thomas, constituted a trustee
and governor of Wigston's Hospital,
489.
Beaumont-Leas, memoranda of payments
for grass-land there for keep of certain
post-horses to the use of the corporation
of Leicester, 394 ; 571.
Beauville, count, a French officer, with several other prisoners, lodged at Leicester, 448.
Bebee, Thomas, elected mayor of Leicester,
367.
———— Henry, elected mayor of Leicester, 368 ; 371.
Bebi, its value at the Conqueror's survey,
xxxviii.—Pertained to the abbey of Croyland, li.
Becherell-castle, in Brittany, pawned for a
sum of money to king Edward the Third
by his son John of Gaunt, 236.
Becket, archbishop, his history, 32. & *seq.*
(See *Thomas à Becket*.)
———— Mr. of the Newark, Leicester, alderman ; a benefactor to Trinity-hospital there, 348.—His donation, 351.
———— Joseph, of Houghton ; his donation
to the same hospital, 350.
———— George, elected mayor of Leicester,
435 ; again, 438.—His death, 438.—His
and his wife Hannah's epitaph, in St.
Mary's church in that town, 314.
Bed, Gilbert de, his petition to king Edward the First, 267. *n.*
Bede (Venerable), the historian ; a remark
of his relative to the district of Lindsey,
misapplied by Matthew of Westminster,
App. 1.—The period in which he wrote
his History, *ib.*—His account of the precise boundaries of Lindsey ; very accurate, 2.
Bedehouse-mead, by Leicester, belonging to
the dissolved college of the Newark ;
purchased, with the Grange, by the corporation of that town, 339.
Bedell, William, founded a chantry in the
collegiate church of St. Mary in the Newark at Leicester, 337.
Bedell's Chantry, account of, 337.
Bedford, siege and capture of, 218.—An
action brought against that town by the
corporation of Leicester, 440.
———— the earldom of, given by king
Stephen to Hugh Pauper, 24.
Bedfordshire ; the possessions of Leicester-
abbey in that county, 280.

Bedingfield, Thomas, chancellor of the
duchy of Lancaster, his death, 546. *n.*
———— sir Thomas, attorney-general of
the duchy of Lancaster, relinquishes that
office, 546. *n.*—His death, *ib.*
Bedstead, king Richard the Third's, preserved at Leicester, traditional account
respecting it, and an engraved delineation, 380, 381 ; *Plate* XXXII.
Beeby, John, chosen bailiff of Leicester,
457 ; 451.—Appointed clerk of the statutes for that town, 428 ; 452.—Deprived
of his ministerial office in the court of
record, 451.
Beech-mast, formerly of great esteem for
the feeding of hogs, xliii. & *n.*
Beeston, Richard, one of the commissioners
of Leicester for levying a subsidy granted
to king Henry the Eighth, 389.—Elected
mayor of that town, *ib.*
Begging-friers ; see *Mendicants*.
Bek, Anthony, bishop of Durham ; his donation of land to the abbey of St. Mary
de Pratis at Leicester, 261 ; *App.* 61, 62.
Beler, Roger, founded a chantry at Kirkby-
upon-Wreke, xcix.
———— Roger, his tenures in the town of
Leicester, 364 ; 368.
———— Mary, wife of the above, her tenure,
368.
Belfry of St. Martin's church in Leicester ;
within it formerly there was a library,
574.—In this *library* was a grave-stone
with an inscription (transcribed) for
George Pilkington, of Stanton, Derbyshire, 606. [¶ This latter reference is
introduced, in order to shew that the
present *consistory-court* is not the part of
the church intended, as stated p. 606,
when it is said that the stone was heretofore in the *library :* the consistory-
court, we read in p. 591, is now held in
"Our Lady's chapel, or choir, at the East
end" of the church.—In pag. 576, we
have a receipt "for a gravestone for
Mr. Stafford Watts, carried out of the
church into the library." In the same
page, there is mention of a payment,
eight years after this receipt, " for the
seats in the belfry, which hold forty several people."—it may be worth while to
remark farther, that the *Town-library* was
not completed till about eight years after
the belfry had thus been furnished with
seats : what then became the receptacle
for the town-books (for they had several)
in the interim ? That some of them were
chained and *nailed* in or about the
church, appears from several entries ; see
the article *Chains*. In fine, it is probable
that the belfry-part of the church retained the name of *the Library* for some
years, even till the erection of the building called the *Town-library*, and that the
appellation afterwards gradually died
away.]
Belgrave, the men of, their disputes with
the abbot of Leicester, 256.
Belgrave, Roger, elected mayor of Leicester, 367.
———— Francis, gives two swans to the
borough of Leicester by way of fine, 416.
—His donation to the Town-library,
506.
———— George, chosen burgess of parliament for the town of Leicester, 416 ;
458.
———— George, his grant of a messuage
in the parish of All-Saints, Leicester, to
Robert Newcom, 549.
———— John, sells to John Wigston a tenement in the town of Leicester, on the
site whereof was afterwards built Wigston's Hospital, 504.
Belgrave-gate, a considerable street in Leicester ; description of it, 532 ; 555. *n.*—
Ineffectual attempt to establish a pig-
market there, cl. *n.*—In this street stands
the famous Roman milliary, cliii ; 532 ; 555.
n.—A messuage there granted by Richard
Elkesley to the corporation of Leicester,
379.—Early grants of messuages there
situate, 556 :—and certain rents thence
issuing, appropriated to charitable purposes, 557.—Antient rents for pieces
of land there, 562.—Various tenements
there antiently pertained to Leicester-
abbey ; rents or acknowledgements for the
same, *App.* 78.
Belinus asserted by Jeffrey of Monmouth
to have made the road called the Foss,
1 ; clii.
Bellamy, William, chamberlain of Leicester, 450.—Elected mayor, 451.
Belleholme.

Bohun, Eleanor, sister of the preceding; married to Thomas of Woodstock, 247.

Bois, William, enfeoffs dame Milicent de Montalt in his rent at Leicester, 364.

—— or De Bosco, Ernald; see Bosco.

Boisard's "Antiquities of Rome" presents an ample description and delineations of the bathing-houses of the Romans, 356. n.

Boley, John, elected town-clerk of Leicester, 440; 454.—Has a gratuity from the corporation on account of his faithful discharge of his office, ibid. — Admitted a freeman of the town without paying any fine, ibid. — Has a farther gratuity allowed him during his last illness, and the expences of his funeral borne by the town, 444.

Bolingbroke, Lincolnshire, the manor and soke of, with the castle, committed by the king, after the decease of Henry duke of Lancaster, to the care of the bishop of Lincoln, 231.—The castle, park, knights-fees, and advowsons thereof, granted by the said bishop, with the king's licence, to John of Gaunt earl of Richmond, 235; App. 27.⁋

—————— Henry de, earl of Derby, and duke of Hereford; see Plantagenet.

Bologna, John bishop of, sent to England on a negotiation between the pope and king Henry the Third, 132. — Commissioned to invest prince Edmund in the possession of the kingdom of Sicily, ib.

Bologne, Matthew count of, his death, 74.

Bolle, William, chosen mayor of Leicester, 390;—again 391.—Elected burgess of parliament for that borough, ib.; 432; 458.

Bolsworth Land, a place at Sowrdrop, in Bedfordshire; whence the abbey of Leicester received a rent, 286.

Bolting-mills, several destroyed in various towns of Leicestershire in consequence of the dearness of corn, 448.

Bolyvant, Nicholas, chosen town-clerk of the borough of Leicester, 425; 454.—Interred at St. Martin's in that town, 454.

Bonaventure, cardinal, brief notice respecting him, App. 101. n. 8.

Bond (John), his portrait preserved in the town-hall at Leicester; description of it and of his arms, 354.

Bond, Josiah, vicar of St. Mary's at Leicester, 308; 311.—His epitaph, 314.—Was also vicar of St. Nicholas's in that town, 609.—His agreement with the parishioners of St. Nicholas, ib. n.

Bond-street, Leicester; a society of Huntingtonians holden in a room there, 547.

Bondman, of feudal times, his very abject condition, 213.

Bondmen and Bondwomen, xliii. xliv.—The life of the former, and the chastity of the latter, protected by law from the violence of their master, xliii.—Numbers of them in Leicestershire at the Norman survey, xlviii.

Bones of animals, supposed victims in the sacrifices of the Romans; large quantities of them dug up at Leicester, particularly near the churches of St. Nicholas and St. Martin, *5. n.; 5; 8; 355; 605, 606.—Hence the place by St. Nicholas's church, called The Holybones, acquired its appellation: see that word.

Boney, Nottinghamshire; the manor of, purchased by Mr. Richard Parkins, recorder of Leicester, 452.—Mr. Parkins interred in the church there; his epitaph, and description of his monument, 453. & n.

Boniface, uncle to queen Alianor of Provence, obtruded into the primacy of England without the concurrence of the monks of Canterbury, 125.—Authorized by the pope to absolve king Henry the Third from his vow of going into the Holy Land, 132.—Highly displeases the barons, and stripped by them of his property, 179.—Appears at the great council of Boulogne, and vents his complaints against the earl of Leicester, 180.—Issues sentence of excommunication against divers persons, 181.—Obliged to flee from England, to save his life, 203.—Co-operated with queen Alianor and his brother Peter of Savoy in levying an army for invading England and reducing the barons, ib.; (192, 193).—Recalled to England, under certain restrictions, with the joint consent of the king and the barons, 203.

Boniface VIII. pope, his constitution prohibiting the giving any thing to laymen, 261.

Bonner, Edmund, installed archdeacon of Leicester, 466.—Was afterwards bishop of London, ib.—His parental descent and character, ib.

Bonner's-lane, Leicester; in a house there (now a barn) the Presbyterians of the town used to assemble for divine worship, 315. n.

Bonnet, Elizabeth, her donation of books to the Town-library of Leicester, 506.

Bonquer, William, sent to Rome by king Henry the Third to communicate his sentiments to the pope on the election of a king of the Romans, 135.

Bonu, in Gascogne, captured by Henry de Lancaster, earl of Derby, 228.

Book of Directions to the Mayor of Leicester; being a schedule of the annual salaries of town-officers, and of sundry charitable donations, 467, 468, 469.

Books, several given by Henry earl of Huntingdon to the town of Leicester, which, on the founding of the Town-library, were there reposited, 353; 505.—Catalogue of the principal books in this library, with the names of the donors, 505. to 509.

—————— a valuable collection of, formerly preserved in Leicester-abbey, 276.—Charyté's register or catalogue of them, App. 101. to 108.

Boots, black, worn by the monks of Leicester; substituted for shoes by abbot Clowne, 262; 276; App. 69; 71.

Bord, or Borde, import of the word, xliv.

Bordarii, xxxvii; xliii.—Various explanations of the term, xliv.

Bordars, number of, in Leicestershire, at the Norman survey, xlviii.

Bordland rents, xliv.

Bordlands, xliv. n.

Boresworth, Leicestershire; its antient fee and tenure, cxix, cxx.

Borlase, Dr. his derivation of the term Britain, 2.—An erroneous assertion of his refuted, ib.

Borma, John, master of a charity-school at Leicester (the founder thereof unknown,) his annual salary, 513.

Bornington, Walter de, instituted to the vicarage of St. Margaret's in Leicester, 559; 561.

Borough; see Burgh, and also the article City.

Borough-English, explanation of the law so called, 362.—Reversed at Leicester by procurement of earl Simon de Montfort, ib.—Example of its being enforced, 465.

Boroughe, John, prebendary of the collegiate-church of St. Mary de Castro at Leicester; his epitaph (formerly) in that church, 314.

Borrough, Martha, and John her son; their epitaph, in St. Mary's church at Leicester, 320.

Bosco (de), Ernald, steward of Robert Bellomont le Bossu earl of Leicester; his donations to the abbey of St. Mary de Pratis, 259; 284, 285, 286; App. 54, 55, 56; 79, 80; 82.—Specification also of the donations of three of his descendants of the same name, 259; App. 56, 57.

Boseworthe, Thomas de, has a conveyance made to him of half a toft of land in the suburb of Leicester by John Unly and others, 556.

Bossu, crook-backed or deformed, (not so properly rendered crouch-back; see that word;) remarks on the term, 321. n.; 357.

—————— or rather Le Bossu; a distinguished appellation of Robert Bellomont II. earl of Leicester; see Le Bossu.

Boston, Lincolnshire; possessions of Leicester-abbey there, 282.

Bosworth, Leicestershire, li.—Its antient fee and tenure, cxvi.—In Bosworth-field king Richard the Third was slain, 298.—Some account of the battle there, 298, 299; 380, 381. (See the particulars of this battle at large, vol. IV. pp. 549—564.)

Botanical remarks, clxxvii. & clxxviii.

Botany, writers on the subject, and the titles of their works, clxxviii. n.

Boteler (Pincerna), Ralph, augments the prebends of the church of St. Mary de

Castro at Leicester; granting and appropriating to it three other churches in that town, 22; 303; App. 54, &c.

Boteler, Edmund, created earl of Ormond by king Edward the Third, 365.

—————— Edward, installed prebendary of St. Margaret's in Leicester; his death and interment, 561. — Was also rector of Wintringham in Lincolnshire, ib.

Botevilayn, Roger, an adherent to the baronial party; taken prisoner by king Henry III. at Northampton, 186, 187.

Botham, or Bottom, Hugh, his donations to the poor of St. Mary's at Leicester, 313: —to the town in general, 467:—to St. Margaret's, 557:—to St. Martin's, 595.

Bottesford, Leicestershire, xlii; lii.—Possessions of Wigston's Hospital at that place, 487; 492.

Bottlesham, John de, archdeacon of Leicester; some account of him, 464.

Bouch of court, 224.—[¶ As the text referred to gives no explanation of this phrase, the following illustration may not be unacceptable to the reader. Bouche of Court, or (as the vulgar call it) budge of court, is, to have meat and drink scot-free there: for so is the French, avoir bouche à la cour, to be in ordinary at court. Sometimes it is extended only to bread, beer, and wine: and this was antiently in use as well in the houses of noblemen as in the king's court.—This bouche of court was also an allowance of diet, or belly-provision, from the king, or superior lord, to their knights, esquires, and other retinue, that attended them in any military expedition: from the French bouche, a mouth; or, rather, from the Gall. boughs, Lat. bulga, Eng. budget, of British original: for, the Welsh use bolgan, and the Irish bolgy, by metaphor, for bellows.—Cowel's Interpreter.]

Boughes, Yorkshire; charter granted by king Edward the Third to his son John of Gaunt, for a weekly market and annual fair there, 235.

Boughton, Robert, vicar of St. Martin's in Leicester, 595.—Deputed by the corporation of Leicester to re-purchase certain land given by the bishop of Carlisle towards founding a free-school in that town, 394; 511.—Employed also by the corporation to purchase for the town the patent of the bailiwick thereof, 394; 451.—Various items of payment to him, 571, 572.

Boulogne, the great council of, 180.

Boulter, William, his tenure in Great Wigston, under Wigston's Hospital, 487; 492.

Boune, Thomas, last dean of the collegiate church of St. Mary in the Newark at Leicester, 336; 338.—Subscribes to the supremacy of king Henry the Eighth, and is afterwards cited to convocation, 336.—His salary from the revenues of St. Mary's, ib.—Presented to the rectory of Hanslope in Buckinghamshire; his death, ib. & 338.

Bourbon, sir James de, honourably receives Henry duke of Lancaster, and attends him to Paris, 229.

—————— Lewis de, count of Vendôme, taken prisoner at the battle of Agincourt by sir John Cornwall, 243. n.

Bourchier, John, with Elizabeth his wife, invested by king Edward the Fourth in the honour of Winton, 624.—Some genealogical notices respecting this Elizabeth, ib.

—————— John, last abbot of Leicester, subscribes to the supremacy of king Henry the Eighth, 274;—and surrenders up his office, 275.—His character, 274; (cxliii.)—Nominated to the see of Gloucester by queen Mary, but by her death lost the promotion, 274, 275:—as king Henry her father had designed to have given him an episcopal see at Shrewsbury, 274.—Exchequered as a fugitive, but obtains a general pardon, 275.—Conjecture relative to him, 325. n.

Bourk, Richard, earl of Clanrickard and St. Albans, re-married Frances widow of sir Philip Sidney, and of Robert Devereux earl of Essex, 541. n.

Bourn, Alexander, chosen mayor of Leicester, 363.

Bovata, explanation of that term, App. 54. n.

Bovate, or oxgang; an antient measure of land, xlviii.

Bow-

nec in aliquos usus mitti debent, nisi in usus ecclesiæ. Statut. Ægid. episc. Sarisbur. anno 1256. —— The CHRISOM-PENCE *(Chrismatis denarii)* were paid to the diocesan, or his suffragan, by the parochial clergy for the *chrism* consecrated by them about Easter, for the holy uses of the year ensuing. This customary payment being made in Lent near Easter, was therefore in some places called *Quadragesimals*, and, in others, *Paschals* and *Easter-pence.* The bishops' exaction of it was condemned by pope Pius III. for simony and vile extortion: and therefore the custom was released and quitclaimed by some of our English bishops.—See farther, in Cowel's Interpreter.]

Christ-church, Canterbury, the monks of, received from Lewis le Jeune, king of France, on that monarch's visiting the shrine of archbishop Becket, a present of a hundred tuns of French wine; the like to be received by them annually for ever, *App.* 37. *n.*

Christ-church Oxford; library given to that foundation by archbishop Wake, li. *n.*

Christendom, spiritual monarchy of, described, 50.—Deluged with the monstrous corruptions of the (misnamed) holy see, 122.—Overspread with barbarism on the fall of the Roman empire, 256.

Christiana, countess of Devonshire; see *Bruce.*

Christianity, the early professors of that religion were exposed to great persecutions, 251.—Propagated in the district of Lindsey by bishop Paulinus, *App.* 1, 2.

Christians, the primitive, used to frequent the Roman baths, 9. *n.*; 356.

———— oppressed by the sultan Saladine, 81.—Their conflicts with the Turks in Palæstine, 92, 93.

———— of *St. Thomas*, 569. *n.*

Chronicle of Sir John Froissart; to whom the first volume of that valuable work was dedicated, 232.

———— of Knighton, when and where compiled; commendation of it, 262.

Chronicles of England often deficient in truth; the reason, 68. *n.*; 165.

[¶ *Chronology* of the Town of Leicester.
Built by king Leir . . . Before Christ 844
Walls built . . . . Since Christ 914
———— destroyed 1173
Abbey founded 1143
Charter granted 1207
First mayor 1258
Trinity-hospital founded 1332
Parliaments holden in Leicester 1400,
                              1421, & 1425.
Battle of Bosworth-field 1485
Wigston's Hospital founded 1490
Cardinal Wolsey died at Leicester-
abbey 1530
Sir Thomas White left £.10,000.
to the freemen 1556
A great plague . . . . 1610 & 1611
Besieged by king Charles the First 1645
Corporation-charter taken away, 1682;
and restored 1687
The Exchange built 1748
Mitford's contested election 1753
Grey and Coote's and Darker and
Palmer's contest 1767
The Infirmary built 1771
New walk formed . . . . , 1785
Parkyns's and Smith's election 1790
County-gaol built 1791
Leicester Navigation-bill obtained 1791.]

Church, John, elected mayor of Leicester, 369;—again, 371.

Church-ales, 305.—Were frequently kept in St. Margaret's church at Leicester; various sums received and expended at, 560; 569.

Church-door, endowment at, instance of, 225. [¶ *Dower ad ostium ecclesiæ* was made by the husband immediately after the marriage; who expressly named such particular lands, whereof his wife should be endowed: and the certainty of the land was openly declared, the wife, after her husband's decease, might enter upon the land of which she was so endowed, without any other assignment.]

Churches are not generally noticed in the Domesday record; why, xl.

———— in Leicestershire, patronage and valuation of, recorded in the Matriculus of Bishop Welles, lv. to lxii.—Procurations and taxation of, in the time of Edward the Third, lxiii. to lxxvi.—Names of those which were formerly ap-

propriate, lxxviii.—Value of those in the archdeaconry of Leicester, with pensions, synodals, and incumbents, in the reign of Henry the Eighth, lxxix. to lxxxiv.—Survey of the churches in the county, by the Parliamentary visitors, xcvi. to xcviii.—Ornaments, &c. in several, at the time of the dissolution of the religious houses; and the prices for which they were sold, cxxxvii. to cxxxix.

Churches of the town of Leicester in particular; how registered in the Matriculus of bishop Welles, lv.—Extracts from Charyté's Rentale relative to some of them, *App.* 113, 114. — (There are now five churches in Leicester, viz. that of *All-Saints*'; St. *Margaret*'s; St. *Martin*'s; that of St. *Mary de Castro*; and St. *Nicholas*'s: see them respectively in their proper places.)

———— demolished, at Leicester, account of, 328.

———— were often, in old time, erected in places where the reliques or bones of martyrs had been buried, 6 :—and oftentimes upon the sites of heathen temples and Roman roads, 7; 8.

Church-gate, 532. *n.*

Church-lands, restoration of, xxxv. *n.*—Those possessed by donation, burthened with military service, xxxviii.

Church-lane (St. Margaret's) at Leicester; six tenements for the accommodation of a few poor people erected there in lieu of those that had stood on the Cock-muckhill, 323; 557, 558. (See *Cock-muck hill.*)

Churchman, Francis, chosen mayor of Leicester, 426.

Churchmaster; thus the churchwarden of St. Martin's in Leicester is styled in a certain memorandum, 575.

Church-men were formerly practitioners in medicine and law, as well as in divinity, 123.

Churchwardens' Accompts relating to the town of Leicester; viz. observations on, and extracts from, those of St. Mary de Castro, 309, 310, 311. — Extracts from those of St. Margaret's, 560, 561. — From St. Martin's, 569. to 585.

Churl, or *Charl*, a clown or ploughman; derivation of the word, xlvii. *n.*; 213.

Chykenlane (Chicklane), at Smithfield, London; the abbot and convent of Leicester had there a parcel of land; its dimensions and yearly value, 282; *App.* 74.

Chyrch-lane, 533.

Cincture, military, 187. (And see the articles *Belt* and *Knighthood.*)

Cincture with a sword, the ceremonial badge of a duke's investiture in his dignity, 229.

Cinque-ports, the barons of, how denominated, 178. *n.*—The *libres hommes*, or citizens of, styled barons, 213.

———— the custody of, committed by king Henry the Third to Richard de Gray, 151. *n.*—This office, assumed by Hugh Bigot the high-justiciar, 162.—The wardens renew their oath of fealty to king Henry, 182.—The custody of them given to sir Henry de Montfort, 190.—Their freemen elected some of their order to represent them in the (parliament) grand council of the realm, 191. *n.*—Such representatives styled Barons, *ib.*—The inhabitants excommunicated by Guy the cardinal-legate, 195 : — commit great outrages in the Channel, 196 :—refuse to accede to terms of amity with king Henry; burn the town of Portsmouth, 210.—Headed by young Simon de Montfort, the barons hold out against the king till they obtain an amnesty for their outrages, and a confirmation of their charters and rights, *ib.*

Cioches, Gunfrid de, an antient land-owner at Moseley, lii.

Circular letter of king Henry the Third, sent to the several counties of England, 170, 171.—One from the Abbey of Leicester to the neighbouring churches; craving their prayers for the souls of the benefactors to the abbey, 267; *App.* 65, 66.

Cirset, *Cyrksceat*, church-rent, xl.

Cistertians, or White Monks, refuse to submit to the infamous exactions of the papal harpy Rustand, 136. — An abbey founded for them at Gerendon, in Leicestershire, by Robert Bellomont le Bossu, earl of Leicester, 48; 254: *App.* 53.

2 G

Citation to parliament, a right of the sovereign by virtue of the service of barony due to him; often issued to persons on pretence of their owing such service, 197; 214, 215.—Of abbots and priors to serve in parliament, largely explained, 254, 255.

Cities, twenty-eight in Britain antiently: these converted into bishops' sees, 3; 5.* *n.*—Were oftentimes cantoned into four divisions in respect to the number of orders of mendicant friers, 295.

———— and *burghs*, their common properties, 112. *n.* 113. *n.* — Some of these enjoyed great liberties, by prescriptive right, prior to the Conquest: what these liberties consisted in, 198. *n.*

———— and *Corporations* of England surrender their charters to king Charles the Second, 436. — Obtain a restitution of them from king James the Second, 437.

City, that word used promiscuously with *burgh* formerly, xxxvii; 112. *n.*—Every city a bishop's see, xxxvii.—Cities not having arable lands, were exempt from paying the geld, xxxviii. — Few cities antiently in England, and those thinly inhabited, xlviii.—Leicester was antiently called a city, xxxvii; xlii; 2; 3; 12; 19; 113. *n.*; 355.

City-seal (of London), affixed to an ordinance of the grand council of the realm, in the reign of Henry the Third, by the lord-mayor, 191. *n.*

Cives, the barons of the Cinque-ports sometimes so called, 178. *n.*

———— *magnates*, 148. *n.*; 177. *n.*

Civil-war, between king Henry the Second and the princes his sons, history of, 69, & *seq.*—Betwixt king Henry the Third and the English barons; its origin, 124; 221; — and progressive consequences, 168. & *seq.*; 178. & *seq.* 217, 218.—Under Charles the First, incidentally mentioned, 289, 290; 293; 323; 428, 429.

Civitas, that word formerly rendered by *burgh* or *city* promiscuously, xxxvii; 112. *n.*—*Nobiles civitatis*, burgesses holding lands of an earl, 72. *n.*

Clanney, William, chosen mayor of Leicester, 365.

Clarcke, Jacob, elected mayor of Leicester, 398.

Clare, Gilbert earl of, his decease, 27.

———— Roger earl of, refuses to do homage to archbishop Becket, 37.

———— Richard de, earl of Gloucester, marries Maud daughter of John (Lacy?) earl of Lincoln, 107.—Befriends Montfort earl of Leicester at his trial, 118.—Sent to Edinburgh to effect a cohabitation betwixt the young king and queen of Scotland, 132. — Was earl also of *Herts*, 137.—Commissioned to treat with the princes-electors of Germany concerning the advancement of the earl of Cornwall to the imperial dignity, 137, 138.—Entrusted with the conduct of an army into South Wales; retires from his post precipitately, 143. — Grossly affronted by William of Valence, the king's brother, 145.—Nominated one of the Council of Twenty-four for settling the disputes betwixt the king and the barons, 150.—Receives letters mandatory from the king, 151. *n.*—Poisoned at the table of the queen's uncle; sustains much bodily detriment, yet survives the baneful potion, 153, 154; 160; 175.—Has a sharp dispute with the earl of Leicester, and breaks with him, 159; 160; 162.—Joined in a commission to treat for peace with the king of France, 160, 161; 362. —Quarrels with prince Edward, 166.— Appointed guardian to the young earl of Albemarle, 167.—Reconciled to the earl of Leicester, and joins in a confederacy with him and prince Edward against the king, 169.—Recedes from the council of the earl of Leicester, and joins the party of the king, 171.—His death, 175. His epitaph, *ib.*—[Called *Robert* by mistake, and earl of Hereford, 365.]

———— William de, brother of the earl of Gloucester, made warden of the castle of Winton by king Henry the Third, 151. *n.* —His death, *ib.* — Farther particulars respecting his death; poisoned by Walter de Scotiney, 153; 160; 161. — His character, 153. *n.*

———— Gilbert de, succeeds his father Richard as earl of Gloucester, 175.—(Instructed by his father to maintain the Oxford ordinances, *ib.*)—Adheres faithfully to the baronial

about 1298, by Ralph Hosier and William Sabernes; the establishment of which was confirmed by king Edward the Third : it stood at the south-east corner of Hart-street near Tower-hill. Other religious-houses and hospitals in England bear a similar appellation. The words *crouched* and *crutched*, it is true, may be said to carry a slight vocal resemblance on hasty pronunciation; but that men, soberly and deliberately, could have written it so, appears truly strange.]

Crowmere, sir William, alderman of London, appointed judge of the company of merchants of the Hans Towns, 372.

Crown (meaning the king's dominions), a comprehensive term equal in import to the antient phrase, *the lands subject to the king*, 200. *n.*

Crown, the, (so to say) the great proprietor, whence the king himself held his royal demesne, 213.

Crown-patrimony ; see Patrimony.

Crown of England, antiently denominated a diadem, 29; 165.

———— English, the legal succession to, oppugned by Richard Cœur-de-Lion, 95.

Crown of Thorns ; see Thorn.

Crown of the head, remarks on the practice of shaving it, 252, 253.

Croxton lordship, an antient demesne ; holden by William the First, l.

Croxton, the abbot and convent of, were benefactors to the Spital at Leicester, 323.—Possessed an annual rent from St. Clement's church in that town, 328. *n.*— Schedule of the possessions of this abbey in the town of Leicester, 388.

Croyland, abbey of, in Lincolnshire, the true value and extent of its lands not set down in Domesday-book, xlix.— Founded by Ethelbald, king of Mercia, li. ; 16.—Its antient possessions in Leicestershire, li ; 19. — Had the priory of Benedictine monks at Freston annexed to it by Wido de Credun, lii :—and the lordship of Bernak in Northamptonshire, granted to it by earl Waltheof, liii. *n.*— The abbot Wulgate obtains a charter for founding and endowing the monastery of Spalding as a cell to the abbey, 17.— The regulations of their infirmary, 278, 279.—A charter of king Kenulph to the abbey was attested by Unwon bishop of Leicester, 356. *n.;* — and a charter of king Bertulph, by Rethun another bishop of Leicester, *ib.*

Crudworth, Warwickshire ; the church of St. Nicholas there, with divers chapels, &c. granted to Leicester-abbey by Hugh de Arden, 285; *App.* 80.

Crusades, account of, 81, 82 ; 91. to 94 :— against the Albigensians, 101. to 104 :— against the people of Nocera, 132, &c.

Cryche, William, prior of Mountagu in Somersetshire ; his petition to parliament, 370.

Cuckoo-Gap-close, 487.

Culinary and other expences of Thomas earl of Lancaster, in the reign of Edward the Second, 223.

Culloden, battle of, 447. *n.*

Cumberland, that county omitted in the Domesday survey ; why, xxxvi.

Cumyn, or *Comyn*, John ; see *Comyn*.

Cuneator, his office, [xli.] *n.*

Cunston, lands holden there by Aylene Pauke by the service of repeating the Lord's Prayer five times daily, xli. *n.*

Cupa, a hariot, 262.

Curetes, their politic practice of shaving their hair, 253.

Curfew-bell, the ringing of it revived at Leicester, on account of a murder committed in the town, in the reign of the first Mary, 394 : (and see pag. 375.)

Curia, the king's court, of what officers it consisted, 31 ; 78 ; 113. *n.* ; 153. *n.*

Curlewache, or *Curlewake*, Simon ; see William *Teynlo*.

Curtana, or principal sword, carried before the king at his coronation; the honour of bearing it appertained to the duke of Lancaster, 236, 237; *App.* 28. [¶Cowel informs us that the *curteyne*, or *curtana*, was the name of king Edward the Confessor's sword, and that it was carried before the king of this land at his coronation. He adds, that the point of it being broken is designed as an emblem of mercy.]

Curteen ; see Courteen.

Curteys, Peter, bailiff of Leicester, 373. *n.* ; 377 ; 451.—Obtains from king Edward

the Fourth a certain messuage, &c. in the High-street in that town, 376 ; (373.) —Chosen burgess of parliament for the borough of Leicester, 378 ; 432 ; 458.— Elected mayor of that town, 379.

Curthose, Robert, 20, 21.—(See particulars respecting him under *Robert*, duke of Normandy.)

Curtis, Anthony, appointed bailiff of Leicester, 430 ; 452.

Curtmantle, Henry, 216 : and see *Henry the Second*. [Qu. Was this, as in the page referred to, an appellation of this king ; or rather of his rebellious son Henry ? In Moll's Geography, folio edition, pag. 61, the prince, not his father, is expressly so called.]

Custom, antient, among the men of Berkeholt, xxxix.

Cuteler, (sir) Robert, purchases from king Edward the Sixth the lands belonging to the guilds of Corpus-Christi and St. Margaret's in Leicester, 562.

Cuthwinus constituted bishop of Leicester, 12.

Cyparissus, his story, 10.

Cyprus-tree, fable of, 10.

Cyricscet, import of that term, lviii. *n.*

Cyvelioc, or *Kevelioc*, Hugh de, fifth earl of Chester ; see *Kevelioc*.

D.

Dabbs, William, elected mayor of Leicester, 451.

Dackombe, (sir) John, appointed chancellor of the duchy of Lancaster, 343. *n.* ; 546.

Dudelington, Leicestershire ; its antient fee and tenure, cxii.

Daffy, Thomas, elected vicar of St. Martin's in Leicester, 578, 579.

Dakyn, William ; see Richard *Darker*.

Dalbi, xliii ; lii ; liii.

Dalby, Geffrey de, his donation to Leicester-abbey, 283.

———— Edward, prior of Woolsthorpe at the time of the Dissolution; remarkable for his piety, cxliii. & *n.*

———— Henry, elected steward of the court of record of the borough of Leicester, 454.

———— Martha, her epitaph, in St. Margaret's church-yard at Leicester, 566.

Dalby's Hospital in Okeham, re-established by Robert Johnson, archdeacon of Leicester, 466.

Dalliwater, Dorothy, her tenure in Redmyle, under Wigston's Hospital, 487 ; 492, 493.

Dallow, Mark-Anthony, appointed to repair the organ of St. Martin's church in Leicester ; his payment for the same, 585.

Dalton, Maurice, obtains, jointly with Thomas *Fisher* and Robert *Cowles*, a lease, under Wigston's Hospital, of the manor-house in Foston, Lincolnshire, 490.

———— Thomas, elected mayor of Leicester, 373.

Damasau, the castle of, in France, captured by Henry earl of Derby, 228.

Damnes-close, 487.

Damory, Thomas, knighted by John of Gaunt duke of Lancaster, 236.

Dane-geld, a tax imposed by king Æthelred, xxxv ; 15. — Why so called, xxxv ; 216.—Levied, and augmented by William the Conqueror, xxxv.—Actual rate of the tax, as levied by several kings, *ib.* —How long it continued to be collected, *ib.*—The demesne lands of the king and queen subject to payment of the tax, xxxviii. — The English grievously oppressed by that tax, 41.—The first general tax in England, 216.—When and by whom first imposed, *ib.*—Upon what levied, and for what end, *ib.*—Applied to a purpose diametrically contrary to that for which it was ostensibly levied, *ib.*— Discontinued in part by William the Conqueror ; revived by his successors ; abolished by charter under Stephen ; revived once more by Henry the Second, *ib.*

Dane Hew, "a munk of Leicestre, foure times slain and once hanged ;" reference to a poem respecting him, 287.

Danes, the subsidiary tribute called *Dane-gelt*, raised for them by king Æthelred, xxxv ; 15 ; 216.—Brought in the reckoning of money by *ores*, xxxix.—Defeat Burrhed king of Mercia, 13. — Confer

the government of that kingdom on Ceonwulf, 14.—Defeat the English at Hookenorton, *ib.* — Are themselves defeated near Leighton, *ib.* — Defeated at Derby by the lady Æthelfleda, 15 :—and by king Edmund, *ib.* ;—who wrested several cities from them, 356. *n.*—Make peace with the English, 15.—Murdered in great numbers, *ib.*—Make several incursions into England under kings Sweyn and Canute, *ib.* & 16.

Danet, Gerard and Mary, their epitaph, in St. Mary's church at Leicester, 316; (309.)

———— John, sells to Mr. John Stanford (for the use of the town) the patent of the bailiwick of Leicester, 401 ; 451.

———— John, a tenant, under Wigston's Hospital, of certain lands in Brankingsthorpe, has, in lieu of them, other lands assigned to him in Leicester-forest, 488.

———— Leonard, his arms, in St. Mary's church at Leicester, 312. — His epitaph there, 316.

———— Philip, grants to St. Leonard's Hospital at Leicester certain messuages, &c. at Frisby, 321 ; 625. — His donation to St. John's Hospital, 357.

———— Thomas, obtains a patent for holding for life the office of king's bailiff in the liberties of Leicester, 287.—Sells his patent to the town, 393 ; 451.

Danet's Assartum, in the suburbs of Leicester ; the tithes thereof demised to the abbey of St. Mary *de Pratis*, by the superior of St. Ebrulph's, 265 ; *App.* 73.

Danett, an antient family of Bronkinsthorpe in Leicester, 316. *n.*

Daniel, P. (Father Daniel), his opinion respecting king Henry the Second's motive for having his eldest son crowned in his own life-time, 60. — His character of Simon de Montfort I. earl of Leicester, 101 ; 104.

Dannet, Lucy, her tenure in the town of Leicester, under Wigston's Hospital, 488 ; 493.

Dapiferate, that office explained, 107.

Darby, Edward, archdeacon of Stow, founded a fellowship in Brazennose-college, Oxford, 607.

———— Henry, elected mayor of Leicester, 371.

Darker, John, member of parliament for Leicester ; description of his portrait in the Town-hall there, 354.—His donation to the Infirmary at Leicester, 517.

———— Richard, his deed of grant of a messuage and garden in St. Peter's parish, Leicester, to William Dakyn, 328.

Dart, Mr. his imperfect engraving of the monument of the countess Aveline, 221. *n.*

Daughters, antient custom of the men of Berkeholt respecting their marriage, xxxix.

Davenport, ensign Samuel, his epitaph, in St. Martin's church, in Leicester, 604.

———— John, vicar of St. Nicholas at Leicester, appointed head-master of the free grammar-school there, 512 ; 609.— His death, *ibid.*

———— William, son of the preceding, an erudite printer ; obtained Mr. Bowyer's annuity, 609. *n.*—His death, *ib.*

David, king of Scotland, confers the honour of knighthood on the count of Anjou, 27.

———— earl of Huntingdon, brother of William king of Scotland, chosen general and prince by the partisans of Blanchmaines earl of Leicester, 74 ; — and governor of the town and castle of Leicester, 219. *n.* ; 358. — Commits great ravages throughout the kingdom, 74.— Submits to king Henry the Second, 75. —Takes the cross, 81.—Bears one of the three golden swords at the coronation of Richard the First, 89.—His marriage and issue, 219 ; (18.)

———— brother of Llewellin, prince of Wales, does not venture to encounter the forces of the earl of Derby, 196.

———— *Bruce*, king of Scots, creates Henry Grismond (duke of Lancaster) earl of Moray, i. 232.

Davie, Edward, and Anne, their epitaph, in St. Margaret's church, Leicester, 563.

———— John, his annual donation towards the repairing of St. Martin's church in Leicester, 574.

Davies, R. curate of St. Margaret's at Leicester, appointed under-master of the free grammar-school there, 512. — To his exertions the new building of St. Margaret's

2 K

bedehouse in the Newark at Leicester, 336.

Five wounds (the), and other symbols of popish superstition, in the church of St. Mary *de Castro* at Leicester, 305.

Flagellation of Henry the Second at the tomb of Becket, strictures on, 75.

Flagon, a pewter one given to St. Martin's church in Leicester, by Mr. Thomas Manly, 576. [And there was another pewter flagon belonging to the church; but the donor's name, or whether it was a parish-purchase, does not appear: however,]—Two silver flagons were afterwards presented to the church by Mrs. Alice Barnes : and the *two* pewter flagons were thereupon ordered to be melted down, and the value of the pewter applied to the *repairs* of the church, 585.

Flamens, or high-priests, twenty-eight of them with three arch-flamens antiently resident in Britain, 3. — A flamen once belonged to the temple of Janus formerly at Leicester, 5 ; 355.

Flanders, Philip count of, besieges and wins Albemarle, and captures the earl, 71.—Does homage to young king Henry for the earldom of Kent, 74.—Solemnly engages to enter England in strong force, and subject it to the power of the young king, *ib.* — Separated from him at sea by a storm, and his army dispersed, 75.—Joins forces with the young king and Lewis le Jeune in the siege of Rouen, *ib.*—To quiet his conscience, he undertakes a voyage to Jerusalem, 76.

Flanders, Joan, countess of ; see *Joan.*

Flavia Maximiana Fausta, stifled by order of her husband Constantine the Great, 9 ; 356.

Fleckney, its value at the Conqueror's survey, xxxviii.—Enumeration of the possessions of Leicester-abbey at that place, *App.* 92.

Fleeces, by way of tithes, in the reception of the abbot and convent of St. Mary *de Pratis* at Leicester ; specification of their numbers, 262 ; *App.* 69.

Flemings, a large party of them brought over to England by Robert Blanchmaines earl of Leicester; defeated near St. Edmundsbury, 72 ; 358.

Flesh, the eating of it, even during Lent, permitted in monastic infirmaries, 277 ; 278. — Forbidden to be eaten by the monks generally, by bishop Grossetête, 279.—Certain places in monasteries set apart for the eating of it, *ib.* — The Augustine Friers obtain permission to eat it, 300.—Fines for eating it during Lent enforced at Leicester under queen Elizabeth, and given by her almoner to the mayor, to be distributed in alms, 406.

Flesh-'sayer (The) of Leicester, his official oath, 377.

Fletcher, Robert, elected mayor of Leicester, 395.

Flexdames, a meadow in Clifton, Warwickshire, granted to Leicester-abbey by divers persons, 285 ; *App.* 80.

Flodden-field, battle of, 540. *n.*

Floor, subterraneous, discovered at Leicester, 11.

Flora, the advantage of making an early one, cxcviii. *n.*

Flori, John, has certain land in Stocton assigned to him, in consideration of his homage and service, by the abbot and convent of Leicester, *App.* 95.— Farther statement of his tenures under that abbey, 99, 100.

Flower, Jane, purchases Mr. Carter's mills, &c. at Leicester, 447.

Foix, Bernard count de, affords protection to the Albigensian heretics, 101.—Compelled by the elder Montfort, earl of Leicester, to surrender Prissan, and renounce the heretical party, 102.

Foliot, Gilbert, translated from the see of Hereford to that of London, 39 ; 260.—Abbot of Leicester; by Matthew of Westminster, erroneously, stated to have been abbot of Gloucester, 255 ; 275. *n.*—Made bishop of Hereford, and afterwards of London, 260. — Twice excommunicated by archbishop Thomas à Becket, *ib.*—His resolute answer to a miraculous voice, *ib.*—His death, *ib.*—Wrote an Apology for king Henry the Second against Becket, *ib.*—Account of his other literary productions, *ib.* 261.

Folville, William de, his donation to Leicester-abbey, *App.* 71.

Folyot, Richard, appointed one of the three referees on the part of the barons in their dispute with king Henry the Third touching the election of shire-reeves, 174.

Fontinello-Putrell, Drogo de, unhorsed in a skirmish with the Turks, 93.

Foot, the exact number of inches of which it antiently consisted, diversely stated, xlviii.

Foot-measure of ground antiently estimated *per pedes sancti Pauli*, 282 ; *App.* 74. (See *Pes.*)

Foreigners, their great ascendancy in England, xxxv ; 127. — Invested with English benefices and dignities by pope Innocent the Fourth, 122.—Bishop Grossetête's computation of their revenues, 123.—Many introduced into England in the suite of Alianora the infanta of Spain, 138. *n.*—Their growing numbers and insolence threaten the kingdom with entire subversion, 144, 145.— Sent out of the kingdom, 153.—Many introduced by prince Edward Longshanks, to the great prejudice of the native English, 177.—Assailed by the confederate barons, and driven from their lands and possessions in England, 178, 179.—Those in the suite of prince Edward sent out of the kingdom, and escorted to the seaside by the barons, 180.—Re-admitted into the country by an award of the king of France, 184. — A prodigious army of them collected in France by queen Alianor for the invasion of England ; headed by her into Flanders, and prepare for embarkation ; the queen's finances failing, they gladly avail themselves of that pretence, and disperse, 192, 193, 194.—Proviso of the barons against the introduction of foreigners into the kingdom by either the king or the prince, 200.

Forest of Leicester ; see *Leicester.*

———, Charter of ; see *Charter.*

Forests of Leicestershire, perambulation of them taken by order of king Henry the Third, 360.

Forest-close (The), let on lease by the corporation of Leicester to Thomas Hall, 446.

Forfeiture of free lands to the king as capital lord ; whence resulting, 205. *n.*

Forrest, Miles, one of the villains employed by Tyrrel to murder king Edward the Fifth, 379.

Forsait, the town of, in Gascogne, captured by Henry de Lancaster, earl of Derby, 228.

Fortescue, sir John, master of the wardrobe to queen Elizabeth, and chancellor of the exchequer ; was also chancellor of the duchy of Lancaster, 546. — His death, *ib.*

Fortieth of all moveables, a talliage or subsidy granted to king Henry the Third, 214.

Fortrey, William, gave two additional bells to St. Margaret's church at Leicester, 558.

Forty-eight, Company of, of Leicester-borough, account of, 359.—Their institution, style, &c. 409, 410. & *seq.*; 421. & *seq.*—Names of the persons first incorporated, 411.—Their official oath, 430. (And see the articles *Corporation, Leicester* town, *Mayor*, &c.)

Forum porcorum, 556. See *Swines-market.*

Foss-road, in Leicestershire, observations respecting, cxlvii.—How it may now be traced, cxlviii. — Its route, cl. — Dr. Pegge's remarks on that road, cli.—Asserted by Geoffry of Monmouth to have been originally made by Belinus, *ib.*—Mr. Throsby's excursion and observations along the Foss, clii, cliii.—Observations on it by the Rev. Mr. Reynolds, cliv. — Supposed to have been made by order of Hadrian, 5. — The part of it over the river Soare stopped up by the men of Belgrave, 256.—Its route briefly traced, 355.

Fossil, various interpretations of the term, cciii.

Fossils, the several species of, found in the Vale of Belvoir, cc.–ccviii.

Foster, John, chaplain of Corpus-Christi guild at Leicester ; his annual stipend, 592.

Foston, xlvii ; lii.

Foston, Lincolnshire ; lands there demised, under Wigston's Hospital, to William Vincent, 490.—The manor-house let to Maurice Dalton and others, *ib.*

Fougeres, Radulph de ; see *Fulgers.*

Foundations, subterraneous, discovered at Leicester, 11.

——— antient, several discovered within the precincts of St. Martin's church in Leicester, 606.

Fountain, situated at Holborn-cross, granted by William de Langley to Leicester-abbey, 282.

Four-yard-lands, the farm so called, in St. Mary's fields, Leicester, leased by the corporation to George Bent, 441, 442.

Fowkes, William, appointed master of Newark-hospital at Leicester by patent, 339.—Disposes of his patent of mastership to Henry earl of Huntingdon, *ib.*; 420 ; 427 ; 625.

Fowler, Richard, canon of St. Mary's in the Newark at Leicester, and treasurer of that church ; appointed governor of the bede-house there, 336.

——— Richard, was chancellor of the duchy of Lancaster, 546.

——— Thomas, elected mayor of Leicester, 397.

Fownes, Lucy, her epitaph, in St. Mary's church at Leicester ; and her donation to the poor of that parish, 318.

Fox, the historian, his account of the proceedings against Philip de Repingdon, canon of Leicester, for espousing the doctrines of Wickliffe, 263.

—— Edward, installed archdeacon of Leicester, and afterwards made bishop of Hereford, 464.—His death, *ib.*

—— George, founder of the sect of Quakers, commenced his career in the county of Leicester, 547.

—— John, his epitaph, in St. Margaret's church in Leicester, 565.

[¶ John *Fox*, esq. was elected mayor of Leicester for the year 1812 ; James Rawson and William Forrester, gents. being chamberlains.]

Fox, William, curate first, and afterwards vicar of St. Mary's at Leicester ; appointed tenant of the church-yard by consent of common-hall, 308 ; 311 ; 410, 441.—This gentleman used to officiate as chaplain to Trinity-hospital in the Newark, 347.

Fox preaching to the geese ; a whimsical device in one of the windows of St. Martin's church in Leicester, 591 ; *Plate* XLIII. [¶ The words issuing from the fox's mouth render this design a burlesque, or pun delineated to the eye, upon a passage of the New Testament, where Paul commends his love to the Philippians ; *Philip.* i. 8. — This instance of exemplifying doctrines, precepts, or simple assertions, by *ocular demonstration*, is not a solitary relic : but why the artists made here their choice, is hard to say. The passage in question *wears* no obscurity : and the Scriptures are too important to be trifled with. In many of our Bible-histories, an *ad vivum* delineation, surely less *witty* than the above, (indeed a display of ignorance) highly offends common sense ; namely, our Lord's injunction, *Matt.* vii. 5. The mote is represented projecting from a man's eye, not as a small point merely indicative of a disorder, but a *moat* surrounding its castle in complete fortification : while his companion balances from one of his eyes a ponderous *beam*, or tree, nearly as large as himself. Besides the stupidity of such a design as this, others too gross to be noticed here, often occur : indecency characterizes the artist's selection.—No book succeeds these sorts of histories as a counterpart more faithfully perhaps than Quarles's Emblems, (an enlargement of Hugo's *Pia Desideria ;)* humour enough certainly some of them have, and the graver of Marshall furnished a grateful *regalé* to the amateurs of art. *Exempli gratiâ ;* Isaiah lxvi. 11. is thus illustrated : a prodigious globe by way of back-ground exhibits the world ; the world is represented as a *mater mammifera :* two hopeful children are feeding (not so exactly) on her bounty ; one a bloated *fool*, with his cap, hobby, and other insignia, is clinging leach-like to one breast ; portraying well enough the insatiable *glutton.*

pressed by the French phrase *libres hommes*, 88. *n.*

Freeholders of Leicestershire, in the reign of Charles the First, xcii–xcv.

Freeman, of feudal times, how demominated, 213.

Freeman (a tradesman) of Leicester; his oath on being admitted to the franchises of that borough, 431.

Freeman, Andrew, elected mayor of Leicester, 434;—again, 436.

—— Andrew, two of that name, their epitaphs, in St. Martin's church, Leicester, 602, 603.

Freemen of England, all subjected to William the Conqueror by oath of ligeance, 87; 205.—The whole body of freemen, how composed, 95. *n.*;—how styled, 147. *n.*—Formed, collectively, the Baronage of England, 190. *n.*; 213.

—— of Leicester, law respecting them, 435.—Retrospect of their privileges, &c. 447. *n.* & 448. *n.*

Freer, John, chamberlain of Leicester, his death, 450.

Free-school; certain lands in St. Margaret's parish at Leicester given by bishop Penny towards the founding of one in that town, 394; 511. (See *Free Grammar-School.)*

Free-school-Lane, Leicester; a meeting-house there, of the followers of Mr. Learnhoult Garrett, 457; 532.

Freind, Dr. his strictures on the monkish-clergy for their interference in the profession and practice of physic, 277.

Freman, William, and others, obtain licence from the king to grant certain messuages, &c. to the dean and canons of St. Mary *de Castro* at Leicester, 304.

French language, much spoken in England, both at the court and bar, in the reign of Henry the Third, 122.

Frenchmen, many, introduced into England by king Henry the Third, 184.

Fresiby, William de, his tenures under Leicester-abbey, *App.* 98, 99.

Freston, in Lincolnshire, a priory of Benedictine monks founded there by Wido de Credun, lii.

Fretheby, Leicestershire; its antient fee and tenure, cxx.

Friar-lane, Leicester, 532.—The meeting-house of the General Baptists there situated, 547.

Friday, Ralph, his tenures in Stocton; his donation to Leicester-abbey, and agreement with the abbot, *App.* 94, 95, 96; 98, 99.

——, Thomas, his tenures under Leicester-abbey, *App.* 99.

Fridiswide (St.) in Oxford, the canons of, obtain from earl Robert Blanchmaines the donation of Edmetone lordship, 89.

Friendly societies, number of, in the town of Leicester, 568.

Frieries were seldom endowed, though oftentimes large and stately buildings, and the burial-places of great personages, 295.

—— at Leicester, historical account of; with Mr. Staveley's introductory remarks, 251, & *seqq.*; 295; 297; 300; 302.

Friers, the several denominations of those religious, 252.—In what respects they differed from those denominated *monks*, ib.—Were by their profession mendicants, having no settled property, 295.

Friers de Pœnitentiâ Jesû Christi, an antient order of mendicant friers; their various appellations, 302.—Their introduction into England, and settlement there, ib.—From their first residence without Aldgate they had from king Henry the Third licence of free removal; with a grant of a Jewish synagogue in Lothbury, ib.—Their habit, rules, character, and privileges, ib.—The order proscribed by the council of Lyons, ib.—Ten houses of the order in England; one of which was at Leicester, ib.—Total suppression of the order, ib.—On the ruins of two hostels of this fraternity in Cambridge, Peter-house College was founded, ib. *n.*

Friers-Minors, a class of men formerly much employed in adjusting amicable negotiations betwixt contending nations and parties, 189.

Friers Minors; Walsingham's jocose description of their squabbles for the heart of queen Eleanor, 252.

Friers-Preachers, or Black-Friers, an order

of mendicants instituted by St. Dominick, and from him named Dominicans, 295.—The Franciscans, or Grey Friers, also thus styled, ib. *n.*

Friers, Augustine; see *Augustines.*

Friers, Black; see *Black Friers*, and *Dominicans.*

Friers-Eremite of St. Augustine; see *Eremites.*

Friers, Grey; see *Franciscans.*

Friers-Mendicant; see *Mendicants.*

Friers-Minorites; see *Minorites.*

Friers-Minors; see *Franciscans.*

Frisby, l.

Friseley, Richard, a Franciscan doctor, executed in his religious-habit, 297; 369. (Called *Triseley*, probably by mistake, in the latter reference.)

Frith (The) at Leicester, particulars respecting, 406, 407, 408; 416.

Frogmere-bridge, 533.

Froissart, sir John, the historian; to whom he dedicated the first volume of his Chronicle, 232.—To what cause he attributed the death of John of Gaunt, duke of Lancaster, 240.—His character of Henry of Bolingbroke, earl of Derby, 247.—His statement concerning the accusation of that earl by the duke of Norfolk, erroneous, 248.—His account of the conference betwixt king Richard the Second and his cousin Henry of Bolingbroke, 250. *n.*

Frolesworth, li.

Frost, a great one in England, 373. *n.*—A severe one, during which, at Leicester, a masquerade was performed on the river, 450.

Froste, Edmund, held, as tenant under queen Elizabeth, the tenement at Leicester called Talbot's House, 590.

Frysley, John, burgess of Leicester; singular entry in the corporation-records of that town respecting him, 373.—Mayor of the town, 375 : *sed quære ?*

—— William, elected mayor of Leicester, 384.

Fulgers or *Fougeres*, Ralph de, taken prisoner at Dol by king Henry the Second, 72; 76.—Joins the party of prince Richard Cœur de Lion, 86.

Fulk, bishop of London, heroically withstands the papal usurpation of the rights and property of the church, 134.—Appointed chief manager of the earl of Cornwall's English estates, 139.

Fuller, bishop, his verses on bishop Remigius, li.

—— Dr. Thomas, his character of the monkish cellarars, 276.—Was very minute in his description of the apartments of a religious house, ib.—His quaint remarks on king Henry the Eighth's seizure of the abbey-lands, 336. *n.*

Funeral, in the Grey-Friars church at Leicester, order of, 299.—That of a mayor of Leicester, described, 430.

Funeral-procession of Sir Philip Sidney, grand beyond all precedent, was engraved in a roll of thirty-eight feet in length; a description thereof given in "Queen Elizabeth's Progresses," 540. *n.*

Funeral-solemnities; see also *Interment.*

Fungi, the several species of, found in the Vale of Belvoir, cc.

Funus; a dialogue by Erasmus, humorously exhibiting the petty feuds of the monks and friers, 252.

Furlong, derivation of the word, xlviii.

Furmenteyn, Robert, abbot of Leicester, his election, 275. & *n.*

Furnys, Ralph, mayor of Leicester, 373.

Fustium; see *Parliamentum.*

Fysher, Henry, obtains from the feoffees of John Bellers, a grant of a messuage and garden in Saint Margaret's, in the suburb of Leicester; which he afterwards sold to John Berege, 556.

G.

Gables, in the fronts of houses, subjected to an annual payment called Gavel-pence, 357; (22).

Gaddesby, l.

Gaddisby, Robert, mayor's clerk of Leicester, 388.—Elected mayor, 392.

Gage, sir John, was chancellor of the duchy of Lancaster, 546.

Gainsborough, (The old) at Leicester; its site, 354; 395; 397.—Rejoicings kept up there on account of victories in the Netherlands, 440, 441 :—and on the accession of king George the First, 444.

—The shop under this building let on lease by the corporation to Samuel Brown, 443:—and the shops under the balcony let to two other tenants, 444.—Pulled down, 513. *n.*

Galby, Leicestershire, xlvi; l.—Its antient fee and tenure, cxx.

Galby; homage done for that lordship to sir Robert Burdett, in St. Peter's church, at Leicester, by sir William Marmion, 327.

Gale, Mr. chaplain to Christiana countess of Devonshire, assists his lady in her correspondence, in cypher, with the royalists in the interest of king Charles the Second, 289, 290.—His annual salary, 290.

Gale, Mr. [Roger], his observations on the Roman roads, cl.—His account of the Old Work of Wroxeter, 5. *n.*

Galeas, duke of Milan, sends over from Lombardy certain armourers to equip Henry of Bolingbroke for his combat with the duke of Norfolk, 248.

Galfridus Anglicus (or *Galfridus de Vinesalvo)*, notice of his writings, *App.* 104. *n.*

Gallery of heroic women; a work so intitled, written by Le Moyne, 291.

Gallow Dale, conjecture respecting, *App.* 4.

Gallowtree-gate, Galtree-gate, Gartree-gate, and *Goll-tree-gate*, various appellations for a considerable street in the town of Leicester, 532.

Gamage, Barbara, married to Robert Sidney earl of Leicester; her issue, and death, 541; 544.

Gamble, John, chamberlain of Leicester, 448.—Elected mayor, 449.—His epitaph in St. Martin's church, in Leicester, 603.

Gamble, Richard, his epitaph, in the church-yard of St. Mary's at Leicester, 320.

Gamelston, Richard, elected mayor of Leicester, 368.

Games, unlawful, prohibited at Leicester, 375.

Gamfrey, Thomas, elected mayor of Leicester, 364.

Gamul, John, his tenures under Leicester-abbey, *App.* 97, 98.

Gamult, or *Ganult*, John, his tenure in Stockton, under Leicester-abbey, *App.* 95.

Goal-delivery, commission of, appertaining to the justices in eyre, 136. *n.*

Gaols at Leicester, account of, at large, 529, 530, 531. (See *County-gaol, Town-gaol*, and *Bridewell.)*

Garden of St. Francis; see *St. Francis's Garden.*

Gardens were rated to the hidage tax, or carucage, 215.

Gardiner, Stephen, installed archdeacon of Leicester, 464.—Made bishop of Winchester; deprived of his bishoprick, but afterwards restored to it, ib.—His character, writings, and death, ib.

Garet, Henry, has a lease granted to him of a piece of ground near St. Margaret's church, bequeathed by widow Chetle for charitable purposes, 585; (577.)

Garland, Mr. his donation to the poor of St. Martin's in Leicester, 595.

Garle, Mr. purchases the mansion-house and gardens of the Grey-Friers priory at Leicester, 299.

Garment, one of curious fabric bequeathed by John of Gaunt, duke of Lancaster, to the church of St. Mary in the Newark at Leicester, 241; 330.

Garments, costly, the extravagant use of, prohibited in England, 153.—The wearing of those coloured, (*i. e.* die'd), deemed a reproach by the earl of Leicester and his party, 196.—Injunction of the Oxford statutes respecting the exclusive use, in England, of the woollen garments wrought in that country; and against profuseness in dress, ib. *n.*

Garnesterre (en); what meant by that phrase, 267. *n.*

Garrett, rev. Jeremiah-Learnhoult; a meeting-house for his followers situate in Free-school-lane, Leicester, 547.

Garrison, the brave, of Kenilworth-castle; their gallant defence of the place against king Henry the Third and his son Edward Longshanks, 211; (210).

Garrodon-church; ornaments, &c. therein at the time of the dissolution of religious-houses; the prices they respectively sold for, cxxxviii. & cxxxix.

Garter, Knights of the; names and arms of those of Leicestershire, [xlv.]—Institution of that Order, 228.

Garthwaite,

OF THE HISTORY OF LEICESTERSHIRE. 43

caster, and also surnamed ***Plantagenet*** ; son of Henry third earl of Lancaster ; obtains from his father a grant of the castle and town of Kidwelly, with divers other castles, towns, and manors, 227. —Accompanies king Edward the Third in an expedition against the Scots, and for his valour is rewarded with certain lands at Berwick-upon-Tweed ; and afterwards appointed captain-general of the king's army in the North, with the title of a banneret, *ib.* — Obtains from the king an assignment of a sum of money for the wages of himself and his men at arms, *ib.* —Advanced to the title and dignity of earl of Derby, *ib.* ;—and about this time he held a solemn tournament at Leicester, 366.—His annual pensions, 227.—Sent with forces to dispossess the French garrison of the isle of Cagant ; felled to the ground on the first encounter, but rescued by sir Walter Manney, *ib.*—Attends the king in his Flandrian and French expeditions, and in the naval fight with the French before Sluys, *ib.*—Was one of the commissioners for ratifying a truce with the French at Maletrete, *ib.* — Invested with a special commission to treat for peace with the Scots, *ib.* — Wounds William de Douglas in a tournament, *ib.* — Employed in another expedition into France ; description of his retinue, and the stipendiary allowances for himself and his knights, *ib.* — Has a thousand marks assigned to him for guarding the marches of Scotland, *ib.*—Obtains a grant of divers privileges (afterwards revoked,) *ib.*—Marches into Scotland, to raise the siege of Louhmabancastle, *ib.*—Appointed ambassador to Alfonse king of Castile, *ib.*—Sent to Rome, to treat in the presence of the pope concerning king Edward's right to the crown of France, *ib.*—Grants an annual rent to sir Roger de Chetwynd, *ib.*—Employed as the king's lieutenant in the duchy of Aquitaine, *ib.*—Entertained with solemn procession at Bourdeaux, *ib.* —Wins several places in High Gascogne, aided by sir Walter Manney, *ib.* & 228.—Confers the honour of knighthood on forty persons, 228. —While he is carrying all before him in France, his father dies in England, so that he could not attend at his funeral, *ib.* — Appointed the king's lieutenant in Aquitaine, *ib.* — —Created knight of the Garter, being the second knight-companion of the order, *ib.* — His farther exploits in France, *ib.*—After his victories, he returns with great booty and triumph to Bourdeaux, *ib.*—On king Edward's laying siege to Calais, he is sent with a choice number of men to keep Newland Bridge, *ib.*—Earl now of Lancaster and Leicester as well as of Derby, and also steward of England, he, with some other noble persons, is appointed by the king, to hear and determine all disputes touching arms, *ib.* — Decides a cause of this nature in favour of sir John de Warbelton, *ib.*—Account of his retinue and expenditure, *ib.*—Obtains from the king a grant of the castle and town of Brigerac, and of the lands and goods of the prisoners whom he had taken at St. John d'Angelyn, *ib.* ; *App.* 44.—Has also the castle of Horestan in Derbyshire, and an annual rent out of the town of Derby, granted to him, 228 ; *App.* 26.—Attends the tournament at Eltham in Kent, wearing a curious hood which the king had presented to him, 229. — Assigns over to his sister the countess of Ulster, by deed, the castle and manor of Melbourne, *ib.* : *App.* 45.—Employed by the king on divers negotiations and commissions in France and Flanders, 229.—Obtains a charter for free-warren in his lordships in Norfolk, *ib.*—Advanced to the title and dignity of earl of Lincoln, having an annual fee granted him in lieu of the *third penny* of the county, *ib.* —Appointed the king's lieutenant and captain-general in Poitou, *ib.*—Marches with a large army into Gascogne, and commits great ravages, capturing forty-two towns and castles, *ib.*—Challenges the men of Tholouse out to fight, which they declining, he fires the suburbs of the city, *ib.*—His several titles, *ib.*—Advanced to the higher dignity of DUKE of Lancaster ; his investiture and privileges described, *ib.*—Appointed admiral of the king's whole fleet, *ib.*—Obtains licence to take a journey into Syruse, to fight against the infidels ; surprized and taken prisoner by Otho duke of Brunswick ; constrained to pay a large sum for his liberty, *ib.* ; 233.—Openly resents the duke's injurious conduct, and accepts a challenge from him, 229.—On his arrival at Paris, the king and nobility vie with each other in doing him honour, *ib.* — Refuses to be reconciled to the duke of Brunswick on dishonourable terms, and enters the lists against him, *ib.*—Takes the oath prescribed to the duellists of those days (as does the duke of Brunswick), and mounts his horse for the combat (as likewise does the duke of Brunswick), *ib.*—Stands cheerfully in his place, awaiting the signal for the combat ; while the duke his adversary, through terror, is unable to wield his arms, *ib.* — Consents at length to refer the matter of quarrel to the king of France ; by whose award, he submits to be reconciled to his ungallant challenger, *ib.*—Entertained by the king of France, and gratified with a sight of that king's rarities, and receives from among them as a token of courtesy, a thorn ! out of the crown of our Saviour, *ib.* ; — which afterwards he left as a precious † relick to the collegiate church of St. Mary at Leicester, *ib.* ; 329.—Returns triumphantly to England, where he is honourably received by king Edward, 229.—Called, on account of his many and heroic virtues, (as noticed above) " the good duke of Lancaster," *ib.* — Grants licence to the abbot and convent of Leicester-abbey to impark their wood, and gives them deer to store it with, *ib.* ; 262. — Mediates personally with the pope for the appropriation of the churches of Humberston and Hungarton to the said Abbey, *ibid.* —Obtains from the abbot and convent, in requital of this last favour, a quitclaim of their right to a cart-load of wood daily from Leicester-forest, and of certain other of their rights, 262.—Receives special command from the king to guard the sea-coasts of Lancashire, 229.—Attends the king into France, *ib.* Sent to Avignon to the pope, to treat in his presence for a prolongation of peace with the French : his reception, retinue, and munificence, 230. — Narrowly escapes surprisal and capture by the French on his return ; arrives in England with safety and honour, *ib.* — Obtains a grant of certain privileges and exemptions, *ib.* — Constituted lieutenant and captain-general for the king, and for John de Montfort duke of Bretaigne, *ib.*—Escorts the duke to Bretaigne, *ib.* —Compels the French to abandon the siege of the castles of Pont d'Audomer and Bretoil, and supplies their garrisons with victuals ; captures the city and castle of Vernoil, *ib.* — Prepares to encounter the king of France : his reply to the two heralds sent to him by that monarch, *ib.* — Display of his gallantry at the broken bridge of St. Fremund, *ib.*— Besieges Reynnes in Bretaigne, and forces the inhabitants to capitulate, *ib.* —Captures divers places, *ib.*—Built the stately palace called the Savoy, in the suburbs of London, *ib.*—Sent again into France with an army to await the arrival of king Edward ; makes an ineffectual assault upon the town of Bray, *ib.* — Joins his forces with those brought over by the king ; captures several places, and returns in safety to the king at Calais, *ib.*—Obtains a charter from the king for altering the time of holding one of the annual fairs at Leicester, *ib.* ; 366, 367 ; *App.* 26, 27.—Sent by the king to the gates of Paris to offer a decisive battle to the French, 231. — — Among his numerous works of piety, which are detailed at length, may be enumerated the following : He completed the bede-house (in the Newark) at Leicester, which the earl his father had begun ; adding largely to its possessions and privileges, *ib.* ; 239 ; 329 ; 330. *n.* ; 339 ; 348, 349 ; 365 ; (226 ;) *App.* 109.—Within the precincts also of the Newark he founded, and amply endowed, a church in honour of the Virgin Mary, which he engrafted upon the said hospital, and which, by licence from the king and pope, he converted into a collegiate church, 231 ; 239 ; 329 ; 332 ; 339 ; 365 ; *App.* 109, 110.—Relinquishing the place of sepulture of his ancestors, he (as his father before him had done) fixed upon this hospital as his burial-place, 329.—His donation to the recluses of St. Helen's at Pontefract, 231.—His ample grants to the monks of Whalley, *ib.*—Lord of the honour of Pontefract, *ib.*—Lord also of Brigerac and Beaufort, *ib* —Items of his last will, *ib.* — Dies at Leicester of the pestilence, *ib.* ; 367. — His character, 231. — Interred, agreeably to his will, in the collegiate church of St. Mary in the Newark *ib.* ; 330 ; 339 ; 367 : — His legacy to that church, 231. — His issue, *ib.* : — and their vast possessions of inheritance, *ib* ; 232.—Bore the title also of earl of Moray, to which dignity he had been advanced by David Bruce king of Scots, 232.—His several titles enumerated, 235.—Was highly beloved by the people, 244.—Gave to the abbot of Leicester the churches of Humberston and Hungarton in exchange for certain lands at Everley in Wiltshire, 286 ; *App.* 55. — His grant to the Dominican priory at Leicester, 295, 296.— Additional particulars respecting him : His grants to his father's hospital and to his own collegiate church in the Newark recapitulated at length, 329, 330 ; *App.* 109, 110.—Afflicted by the loss of his only son, he quitted his favourite residence at Kempsford, and bestowed the manor on his collegiate church, 330.— On retiring from Kempsford, his horse cast its shoe, which was afterwards picked up, and fixed to the church-door, *ib.*—His character, *ib. n.* ; *App.* 44.— Several royal grants to him, both as earl and duke of Lancaster, *App.* 44, 45.

* Though this Duke is more than once in the course of these memoirs called earl of *Nicol* ; it does not seem to be any additional title. That he was earl of *Lincoln*, is several times distinctly mentioned. Now, it should seem that *Nicol* is no other than *Lincoln* ; which city was familiar to the Normans by the appellation of *Nicol* : and one of the places where the Duke is so styled, is a charter in the old or Norman French.] — — [† We read of another *precious relick* which passed through the hands of this great Duke.—" The coronation of Henry the Fourth was extraordinarily solemn and magnificent ; and he was anointed with a peculiar oil which a religious-man had given to *Henry* the first duke of Lancaster, with a certain prophecy ; That all kings anointed with it should be champions of the church. This oil coming into the hands of king Richard, as he was looking among his jewels (then going into Ireland,) he was desirous to be anointed with it ; but Arundel the archbishop prevented him, by assuring him, that it was not lawful to be anointed more than once. On his return into Wales, the archbishop got it into his own possession, and reserved it to the coronation of king Henry, who was the first king of the realm that was anointed with it." See Echard's History of England.]

Groby, Leicestershire ; its antient fee and tenure, cxvi.—Gave title of Baron to the Quinceys earls of Winchester, 98 ; 220. Description of its peculiar, or ecclesiastical jurisdiction, 624.

Groby, barons of, deduction of their genealogy, 545.

Groby, the castle of, surrendered to king Henry the Second, 75. — Demolished, 77 ; 358.

Grocers-Hall, Lothbury ; adjoining thereto formerly stood the chapel of the friers *de Pœnitentiâ*, 302. *n.*

Grocery, amount of charges for, *temp.* Edw. II, in the household of Thomas earl of Lancaster, 223.

Grosseteste (Grossetête, or *Greathead*), Robert, bishop of Lincoln ; his death ; his character, learning, and promotion, 122. —Rebuked pope Innocent to his face ; suspended from his episcopal office, *ib.* ; and see p. 361. — Caused a computation to be made of the English revenues of foreign ecclesiastics, 123. — His manner of

Hardil, Ralph, mayor of London, and his citizens, summoned before king Henry the Third, and amerced, 128.

Harding, John, his metrical story of king Leir, 2.—An error of his refuted by Mr. Burton, 355.

——— (sir) Robert, chosen recorder of Leicester, 433; 435; 453.

Hardreshull, Robert de, a confederate with Montfort II. earl of Leicester; slain in the battle at Evesham; his property seized by king Henry the Third: specification of his tenure in Leicestershire, *App.* 35.

Hardwick, rev. Robert, succeeds to the mastership of Wigston's Hospital, 497.— His death, 498.

Hardy, Joseph, chosen head-usher of the free-school at Leicester, 439; 512.—His death, 444; 512.

Hareston, l.

Harington, sir Henry, his tenure of the Bishop's Fee, or manor of Leicester, 567.

Hariot; see *Heriot*.

Harlaxton, Lincolnshire; possessions of Wigston's Hospital at that place, 488; 490.

Harlexton, John, of Leicester; a lease granted by him to John Seyton, of a messuage in the Senvey-gate, 549.

Harold Harefoot, son of Canute, advanced to the throne by earl Leofric, 16.

Harold, Henry, admitted a freeman, and appointed serjeant-at-mace, of the borough of Leicester, 427.

Harper's Pynghylls, 588.

Harrington, sir James, (ancestor of sir John Harrington,) married Lucy daughter of sir William Sidney, 540. *n.*

Harris, David, elected mayor of Leicester, 621.

——— John, his epitaph, in St. Mary's church at Leicester, 314.

——— William, of Leicester, one of the Forty-eight, has a gratuity from that company, 441; 443.

——— Mr. his donation to the poor widows of Bent's hospital at Leicester, 326.

——— Mrs. her donations to St. Margaret's Charity-school at Leicester, 513.

Harrowby, Dudley lord, appointed chancellor of the duchy of Lancaster, 546.

Harryman, John, rector of Peckleton, Leicestershire; his epitaph in St. Martin's church at Leicester, 598.—His donation of books to the Town-library of Leicester, 509.

Hartopp, sir William, chosen burgess of parliament for the borough of Leicester, 432; 458.

Hartshorn, Robert, elected mayor of Leicester, 435.

——— Robert, tenant, under Wigston's Hospital, of a messuage, &c. in the Bishop's Fee near Leicester; his annual rent, 493, 494.

——— Thomas, chosen mayor of Leicester, 440.

——— Thomas, (father probably of the preceding), alderman of Leicester; his epitaph, in St. Mary's church in that town, 319.

Harvest, the labours of, suspended by ordinance of king Henry the Third; the king's singular plea for enforcing the necessity of the command, 193.—The burgesses of a town owed personal service (or a payment in lieu thereof) to their earl in gathering-in the harvest: the burgesses of Leicester exonerated from this service by earl Robert Fitz-Parnell, 358;—and confirmed in this exemption by earl Simon de Montfort, 361: (called, in the latter place of reference, a release from all demand for the *reap of his domain.*)

Harvey, Francis, recorder of Leicester; some account of him, 340. & *n.* — His nomination and appointment to the recordership, 424; 425; 453.

——— Stephen, jointly with George *Tatam*, obtains a lease of the lands of the hospitals of St. Leonard and St. John at Leicester, 322.

——— lady Mary, her grant to the collegiate church of St. Mary in the Newark at Leicester, towards founding a chantry there, 331; 333; 337. — Her donation to the poor of the bede-house in the Newark, 336; 349.

Harwar, Nicholas, succeeds to the mastership of Wigston's Hospital; his death, 496.

Harward, Robert, appointed by the corporation of Leicester to purchase for the use of the town, standard measures and weights of brass, 389.—Elected mayor of the town, *ib.*

Harwold nunnery, Bedfordshire; report of the state of, in a letter to Thomas lord Cromwell, cxlii.

Haryngdon, the advowson (and manor) of, granted by Henry Grismond duke of Lancaster to the collegiate church of St. Mary in the Newark at Leicester: charter of free-warren there obtained by the dean and canons, 330; *App.* 109.

Haselrigg, Thomas, constituted a trustee and governor of Wigston's Hospital, 489.

Haselrigg, Haslerigge, Hazlerigg, &c.; see *Hesilrige*.

Hasloe, John, his communication with Mr. Carte on the subject of Cardinal Wolsey's burial-place, 273.

Hastings, antient fiefs of, cxxiii.

Hastings, Henry de, a confederate with the earl of Leicester against king Henry the Third; submits to be shorn in token of his cause, 177.—Excommunicated by archbishop Boniface, 181.—Joins battle against the royalists at Lewes; discouraged at the onset, he seeks safety by flight, 189. — Wounded and taken prisoner in the battle at Evesham, 208.— His possessions seized by king Henry: statement of those in Leicestershire, *App.* 35.

——— sir William, is by king Edward the Fourth appointed steward of the honour, manor, and castle of Leicester, &c.; created baron Hastings and made knight of the Garter, 322; 380.—Obtains also from that king a grant of the revenues of St. Leonard's hospital at Leicester, *ib.* — His covenant with dean Chauntre for celebrating his anniversary and keeping an obit for himself and his wife in the collegiate church of St. Mary in the Newark, *ib.*; 333.—Beheaded by order of Richard duke of Gloucester, 379. —His tenure in the town of Leicester, 380. —His arms placed on a stone against the wall of the church of St. Mary *de Castro* at Leicester, 305.—Description of them, *ib. n.*

——— Edward, second lord; his marriage, death, and issue, 305. *n.*

——— sir Edward, purchases the site of Leicester-abbey, 287.—Inventory of certain articles of confectionery presented to him by the corporation of Leicester, 407.

——— sir George, chosen burgess of parliament for the borough of Leicester, 426; 458.

——— George, was the first [of this name] earl of Huntingdon, 305. *n.*; 312.

——— Francis, second Earl of Huntingdon, his letters to the mayor of Leicester, 393.

——— Henry, third earl of Huntingdon, held at his death a ninth part of the honour of Winton, cxxxvi.—Purchased, and built a fair house upon, the site of Leicester-abbey, 287.

——— George, fourth earl of Huntingdon, charged six persons of Leicester to provide him a soldier, 416.—His funeral, 418.

——— Henry, fifth earl of Huntingdon, succeeding to the earldom of Huntingdon; has an honorary present sent to him by the mayor of Leicester, 418.— Causes the mayor to be confined to his house, 420.—Purchases from William Fowkes the patent of mastership of Newark-hospital; and disposes of the same to the corporation of Leicester, 339; 420; 427; 625.— Sumptuously entertained by the mayor of Leicester on account of the defeat of the Spanish Armada, 405.—Various instances of his interference in the affairs of the town of Leicester, 406, 407, 408.—Lord-lieutenant of the county of Leicester; ceremoniously precedes king James the First into the town of Leicester, and lodges him in his house, 424; and again lodges and entertains the king, 425.—Description of his portrait, which is preserved in the Town-hall of Leicester, and whereon his several benefactions to the town (a transcript of them here given) are recorded, 353;

476. *n.*—Obtained authority from queen Elizabeth to frame a code of laws for the government of Wigston's Hospital at Leicester: recital of these laws at length, 476. & 477. to 484.—His benefactions to the hospital stated in detail, 485, 486. — Was a benefactor likewise to the town by an ample donation of books, which afterwards on the founding of the public library were there reposited, 505; (353.)—His donations to the free-grammar-school at Leicester, 511; 513. —To this nobleman belonged the mansion (part of which yet remains) at Leicester, called Lord's-Place, 532. — He also purchased from John and Ralph Eaton the tenement in that town called Reynold's dwelling-house, *ib. n.* — On this nobleman's coming to reside in the town of Leicester, he was received with great demonstrations of joy, ringing of bells, &c. 576, 577.

Hastings, Henry, lord Loughborough, through envy caused Leicester-abbey to be burnt during the civil-wars, 293.

——— sir Henry, his suit concerning the North mills and the Newark mills at Leicester, 419.

——— John, of Countesthorpe, apprenticed to Samuel Jacome, fellmonger, of Leicester, 442.

——— sir Leonard, his tenure at Leicester, 373.

——— Mabell, interred in St. Mary's church at Leicester; Mr. Burton's commendation of her, 316.

——— sir Richard, a gallant companion of Henry earl of Derby and sir Walter Manney in their exploits in Gascogne, 228.

Hastinges, sir Richard, his tenure in Leicester, 373.

Hasty, William, chosen mayor of Leicester, 373.

Hat! of St. Thomas of Lancaster, a relic deemed a grand remedy for the headache, 225. *n.*

Hatfield, Yorkshire; the site, according to Mr. Johnson, of the antient episcopal see of Sidnacester, *App.* 35.

Hatfield Broadoak, in Essex, charitable bequest of John Gobert to the poor of that town, [15.]

Hathern, Leicestershire; the advowson of the church of, granted by the abbot and convent of Leicester to the sacrist and canons of St. Mary *de Castro*, 304.— Possessions of Wigston's Hospital at that place, 487.

Hatton, sir Christopher, obtains from queen Elizabeth a grant of certain tenements, &c. at Leicester, parcel of the possessions of the (then) late abbey of St. Mary *de Pratis*, 287.

Hawes; see *Halso*.

Hawes, Dr. William (the philanthropist,) assisted in promoting the establishment of a Humane-society at Leicester, 529.

Hawise, daughter of Hugh Kevelioc earl of Chester, had the earldom of Lincoln granted to her by earl Blundeville her brother, 220.—At her suit the honour was conferred upon John de Lacy, *ib.*

Hawk, that bird antiently valued at an extravagant price, xxxviii, xxxix. — The sum paid at Leicester to the Conqueror instead of one, xxxviii. *n.*—A single hawk worth ten pounds, xxxix.—Hawks from Norway highly prized, *ib.*—A large manor and estate given for a single hawk, *ib.*

Hawkesbury, Charles lord, (the present earl of Liverpool,) appointed chancellor of the duchy of Lancaster, 546.

Hawkins, Edward, chamberlain of Leicester, 446.—Elected mayor, 447.

——— Thomas, obtains from king Edward the Sixth a grant of a horse-mill, with a tenement, &c. at Leicester, 393.

Hawl, Mr. with his servant, murdered in the Sanctuary at Westminster, 237.

Hawthorn-bush, a singular variety of, presented to Thomas Bett mayor of Leicester, 391.

Hay, the castle of, besieged and won by prince Edward Longshanks, 185.

——— Thomas, (viscount Dupplin, and earl of Kinnoul,) was chancellor of the duchy of Lancaster, 546.

Haymarket (The), in Leicester, 532.

Hayne, rev. Thomas, a benefactor to the town of Leicester, 467, 468:—and particularly to the Town-library, 505.—

His

to

in-law, was buried, 239 ; 339. & n. ;
368.—A chantry was founded in this
church by the lady Mary Harvey, 331 :—
and another by Thomas de Langley,
bishop of Durham, ib. ; App. 65.—King
Henry the Fourth was a benefactor to
this church, 331 ; (241) ; App. 110, 111:
—who granted to it all the lands belonging to St. John's hospital, 357.—
Henry the Fifth and Sixth likewise confirmed its privileges, 331. — Farther
statement of the possessions of this
church, ib. ; 625.—Memoirs of several
eminent personages who enjoyed preferments in this church, ib. & 332. to
336.—The privileges of this church recognized and amply confirmed by king
Edward the Fourth ; his ordinance to
that effect, 332, 333.—The dean and
canons obtain from lord William Hastings grants of the lands and revenues
of the hospitals of St. John and St. Leonard, both in the town of Leicester,
333 ; (322) :—their indulgence, as proprietors or guardians, to the brethren
of St. John's hospital, 325.—The dean
and canons regularly incorporated by letters-patent of king Edward the Fourth,
333 ; App. 111, 112.—Form of a presentation to one of the prebends of this
church, 334.—Order of king Richard
the Third in favour of the dean and
canons, ib.—Process of founding a chantry here by William Wigston and others,
ib. & n. & 335 ; 471 ; 474: & App. 112.
(See WIGSTON'S HOSPITAL.) — Robert
Boune, the last dean of this church, subscribes to the supremacy of king Henry the
Eighth, 336.—Annual payments of the
church at that period, ib.; (lxxxii).—
State of the college, as reported to the
lord Cromwell by Mr. Richard Layton,
336 ; (cxlii). — The college dissolved,
336 ; 365 ; (322).—Account of the several chantries founded in the church,
337. — Members of the college, and
their salaries, at the dissolution, ib.—
This church and the abbey of St. Mary
de Pratis mutually bound in payments
to each other, ib. ;—particularized, App.
69.—A considerable part of the possessions of this church given by king Edward the Sixth to John Beaumont and
William Gyes, 337.—Lists of the deans
and prebendaries of this church, 338.
—The church visited by Leland, while
in its full splendour ; his description of
it, 339 ; 504.—Mr. Wyrley's account of it,
339.—The site of the church, in Mr.
Carte's time, was occupied as a garden
by Mr. Carter ; some years previously
to which, the foundations of it had been
dug up, 349.—Rental of the lands and
possessions of this church, as demised
by queen Elizabeth to Edward Holt,
and afterwards granted by her to the
corporation of Leicester, 351, 352.—
In what year the statutes of the foundation of this college were dated, 366.—
Compromise of the dean and canons
with king Henry the Eighth touching
certain closes, 406.—Recapitulation of
statements relative to the disposal of the
possessions of the college after its dissolution ; and process of its incorporation,
625.—The foundation-charter of this
college, App. 109.—Royal grants to the
college and hospital: of Edward the
Third, 109, 110 ;—of Henry the Fourth,
110, 111 ;—Henry the Sixth, 111 ;—
Edward the Fourth, 111, 112. — To
this church the rectory of Cranesley, in
Northamptonshire, was appropriated,
114.

Newark-mill purchased, with the Grange,
by the corporation of Leicester, 339.
Newark-upon-Trent, Nottinghamshire ; a
castle erected there in the time of king
Stephen, cxlix.—Supposed to have been
the Roman *Ad Pontem*, clii.—Was, according to Dr. Stukeley, the antient
episcopal-see of Sidnacester, App. 3.
Newbery, Alice, her epitaph, in St. Margaret's church-yard at Leicester, 566.
New Bigging, or Holme, a hamlet in Newton parish, Warwickshire, 285. (See
Holme.)
Newbold, Thomas, his tenure in Hatherne,
under Wigston's Hospital, 487.
Newburg, Robert de, gallantly rescues the
earl of Leicester in a skirmish with the
Turks, 93.

Newburgh, Henry de, first earl of Warwick, 98.
———— lord ; see Sir Edward *Barret*.
Newby, William, mayor of Leicester, 371 ;
373.—Occurs as witness to a grant of
a messuage, &c. in St. Margaret's, by
the abbot of Leicester, to John German,
556.
Newcastle, privilege conferred on that town
by Henry III, that no Jew should reside
therein, 8.
Newcastle-under-Lyne, the town of, yielded
by prince Edward Longshanks, in exchange, to Simon de Montfort II. earl
of Leicester, and the castle and honour
conveyed in fee to the said earl, 201 ;
363.—The town afterwards granted by
the said (king) Edward the First to his
brother Edmund Crouchback, 222.
New-close, 488.
New College at Leicester, a chantry added
thereto by John of Gaunt duke of Lancaster, 231 ; 241 ; 337.—The patronage
of the said chantry conferred upon the
abbot and convent of Leicester, 265.
Newcom, Robert, elected mayor of Leicester, 393.—Held a messuage in the parish
of All-Saints, Leicester, by purchase from
George Belgrave, 549.
Newcome, Robert, held by lease under
queen Elizabeth, the tenement and croft
in Leicester, called The Isle of the
Fenn, 590.
Newcomb, Thomas, the bell-founder who
cast the six great bells of St. Margaret's
in Leicester, was interred in the church
of All-Saints in that town, 552.
———— Thomas, another bell-founder,
of Leicester, was buried also in All-
Saints church, 552. n.—Part of his tomb,
shorn of its brasses, yet remains, 553 :
shewn, *Plate* XXXVIII.
Newcome, Edward, of Leicester, excused
from serving the office of mayor, 408.—
Elected mayor, 415.
———— Edward, serjeant-at-mace for
the town of Leicester ; placed in the
New Hospital, 429.
Newdigate, Elizabeth (Palmer), her epitaph, in St. Martin's church, Leicester,
602.
Newell's-close, 487.
New Forest, in Hampshire, why made,
xxxix.—The wardenship thereof assigned
by Henry earl of Arundel to Robert
Dudley earl of Leicester, 535.
Newgate, prison of, mentioned so early as
the reign of Henry the Third, 128.
Newhay, Warwickshire ; property of Lei-
cester-abbey at that place, 285 ; App. 81.
New Hospital ; see WIGSTON'S HOSPITAL.
Newinton, Robert de, an adherent to the
baronial party ; taken prisoner at North-
ampton by king Henry the Third, 186,
187.
Newport, in Monmouthshire, captured by
Montfort II. earl of Leicester, 206.—
Dreadful skirmish on the river (Uske)
before that town betwixt the baronials
and royalists, ib.
New Street, Leicester, erected upon the
site of the Grey-Friars priory, 299.—
Description of it, 533.
Newton, lii, liii.
———— Warwickshire ; property of Leicester-abbey at that place, 285 ; App.
81, 82.
Newton, Bertram de, his donation to Leicester-abbey, 285 ; App. 81.
———— Gabriel, chamberlain of Leicester,
446. — Elected mayor, 447.—Account
of the charity-school founded by him at
Leicester, 513, 514. — His epitaph, in
All-Saints church-yard in that town,
554, 555. — Summary account of his
charitable donations, and of his death
and interment, ibid. n.n.—This gentleman
gave a brass chandelier to St. Martin's
church at Leicester, 593.—Was a strenuous advocate for the doctrines of the
Athanasian Creed, 611, 612.—Characteristic memoirs of him, 611. n.—Specification of his charitable bequests, 611
—613. (See various other donations by
him at the pages referred to in brackets,
in the INDEX OF NAMES.)
———— Elizabeth, and Mary, the two
wives of the above ; their monument
described, and epitaph, in St. Martin's
church, Leicester, 597 ; *Plate* XLIII.
———— George, son of Gabriel Newton by
his first wife Elizabeth ; his epitaph, 598.

Newton, Alicia, an only daughter of the
above Gabriel ; *nata et denata* in one
year, 597.
———— Humfrey de, his grant to Leicester
abbey, 285 ; App. 80.
———— John, vicar of St. Martin's in Leicester, 504 ; 596.—Preached a sermon
to a woman condemned to be burnt for
the murder of her husband, 436. n. :—
the sermon afterwards published, 596. n.
— Appointed confrater of Wigston's
Hospital ; resigns the office, 502.—His
donation to the town-library, 504.—
Sundry items of payment to him, for
keeping the parish-register of St. Martin's, &c. 582, 583.—Farther notice respecting him, 596. n. — His arms described, and epitaph, in St. Nicholas's
church, Gloucester, 606.
———— Judith, wife of the above ; her epitaph, 606.
———— John, parish-clerk of St. Martin's
in Leicester ; various items of payment
to him, 579, 580.—Resigns his office, 581.
———— John, and Elizabeth, their epitaph, in St. Margaret's church, Leicester, 564, 565.
———— John, and William, their epitaph,
565.
———— Joseph, alderman of Leicester ;
his epitaph, in St. Nicholas's church, in
that town, 610.
———— Robert, his epitaph, in St. Margaret's church-yard, Leicester, 567.
Newton's (Alderman Gabriel) Charity-school
at Leicester, account of, 514.—Rebuilt
and enlarged by the corporation of Leicester, 610.—Abstract of the Alderman's
trust-deed for establishing schools, 611,
612, 613.
New Work (The), at Leicester ; see *Newark*.
Nicholas, archdeacon of Ely, appointed
chancellor of England, 167. —Dispos-
sessed of his office, 170.—Entrusted with
the great-seal during king Henry's journey to France, 181 ; 362.
———— bishop of Evreux, accepts the
charge of the abbey of Lira, on the resignation of abbot Ralph, App. 9.
Nicholas IV. pope, his licence to the abbot of Leicester for wearing a hat,
App. 68.
Nicholas, a barber, in the suite of the earl
of Leicester ; what passed betwixt him
and the earl prior to the battle of Evesham, 207.
Nicholas o' the Isle of Leicester ; see John
Unly.
St. NICHOLAS's *Church*, at Leicester, description and account of it, 608 : with
two engraved views, *Plate* XLV.—How
registered in the Matriculus of bishop
Welles, lv :—and in Charyté's Rentale,
App. 114.—Supposed to have been built
out of the ruins of a Roman-temple, 7 ;
355 :—(and see *Jewry-wall*.)—Dispute
betwixt the parishioners and the abbot and convent of St. Mary de Pratis,
concerning the presentation of a vicar,
261 ; App. 62.—The church, when first
provided with a cemetery, 304. n. —
Rated at nothing, in an early taxation,
322.—Account of the *parish*, 608, 609.
nn.—Computation of the number of families in the parish, and remarks on the
parish-register, 534.—Table of money
raised and disbursed on parochial occasions, 608.—List of benefactions to the
poor of this parish, ib. — Chronological
series of the vicars, ib. & 609.—Description of the coats of arms found in this
church by Mr. Burton, 609.—Epistolary
correspondence relative to the vicarage,
ib. n. — Monumental inscriptions, 609,
610.—Account at large of several Roman antiquities discovered here, 617,
618, 619 ; *Plates* XLV, XLVI ; (&
pp. 6—12 ; *Plates* IV—IX.)
NICHOLS, Mr. John, the author of this
" History of Leicestershire," projected
the types for printing the Domesday-
record, xxxvii.—Published, jointly with
Mr. Gough and Dr. Ducarel, an account of the *Alien Priories*, 265. n.
Nidd, Mr. his donations to the borough of
Leicester, 468.
Nightingale, that bird a stranger to Devonshire and Cornwall, cxci. n. — Seldom
heard in the woods round Belvoir, cxcii.
Nick-names, very common in antient
times ; remarks on the subject, 24 ;
321. n.

Nicol,

Noryce, William, elected mayor of Leicester, 397;—again, 401.—Fined for being absent at the time of his election, *ib.*

Norys, John, elected mayor of Leicester, 384.

Noseley-college, Leicestershire, founded by Roger de Martival archdeacon of Leicester, and his father, 463.

Nottingham; complaint of the burgesses thereof, on being deprived of their fishery, xl.—The town captured by the earl of Derby, 74.—Sir Thomas White's donation to the town, 353. *n.*—The (city) freed from the power of the Danes by king Edmund, 356. *n.* — This town, jointly with Leicester, carries on the manufacture of stockings to a large extent, 620.

Nottingham, the csatle of, committed to the wardship of William Bardulph by king Henry the Third, 151. *n.*—Made over by the king, in hostage, to the barons, 201; 363.

Nottingham, William, nineteenth provincial of the Grey Friers in England, buried in the Franciscan priory at Leicester, 297.— Had been canon and chanter of York cathedral, *ib. n.*—Wrote an Exposition on the Four Gospels, and other pieces, *ibid.*

Nottinghamshire; the possessions of Leicester-abbey in that county, 284.

Novo Mercato (De), William, his grant to Leicester-abbey, 286; *App.* 82.

Novum Opus, The New Work, or *Newark*, at Leicester; see *Newark.*

Novum Testamentum Græcè; see *Codex Leicestrensis.*

Nowsley, statement of the possessions of Leicester-abbey at that place, *App.* 93.

Nuisances, of various kinds specified, prohibited at Leicester by order of the common-hall, 375, 376.

Numa Pompilius, affirmed by some writers to have built the first temple in Rome to the honour of Janus Bifrons, 5; 355.

Nun-Eaton, in Warwickshire, a monastery there, founded by Robert le Bossu, earl of Leicester, 48; 254.—Charters relative to the said foundation, *App.* 15, 16. —Statement of the property of Leicester-abbey in the lordship of Nun-Eaton, 285: and see *App.* 15; 82.

Nuns, an useless class of females, xlviii.— Fair specimens of their *sanctity ! !*, cxlii.

Nurse, John, his donation to Trinity-hospital at Leicester, 350.

Nurses of Leicester Infirmary, their rules, 520.

Nutmeg-grater, a curious old one, called Queen Elizabeth's pocket-piece, preserved in Trinity-hospital at Leicester; moral inscription upon it, with an engraved representation, 348; *Plate* XXVIII.

Nutt, William, his epitaph, in St. Margaret's church, Leicester, 562.

Nutt, Mary, her epitaph, in the same church, 562.

O.

Oak, that tree estimated at a high value formerly, xliii.

—— Royal; see *Royal Oak.*

Oak-moths; the oaks in Stathern and Barston woods spoiled by those insects, cxcii.

Oath, singular, of king Henry the Third and his barons, 153.

—— of ligeance, remarks respecting, 87. *n.* 88. *n.*

Oaths (in the reign of Henry the Third) :— Of the community of England, 150.— Of the Twenty-four, *ib.*—Of the high-justice, *ib.*—Of the chancellor, 151.— Of the wardens of castles, *ib. n.* (These relative to the provisions or statutes of Oxford.)

—— mutually taken by the duellists of chivalric times prior to the encounter, 229.

—— official, of the mayor, recorder, chamberlains, bailiffs, &c. of the borough of Leicester; the several forms of, 377, 378; 425, 426; 430, 431, 432.—Of the trustees of Wigston's Hospital at Leicester, 489.

[*N. B.* It was the intention of the Compiler of this Index to have formed here an article referring to the *oaths* used antiently in animated or even common conversation, as the allusions therein tend much to illustrate obsolete *manners* and *customs:*

but really they are many of them (especially in the mouths of our kings Henry the Second and Third), so fearfully profane and blasphemous, that even gigantic infidelity itself cannot here but veil, and an apostate Julian be thrown into the background, vanquished at his own weapons by these *Christian* kings. Instead, therefore, of indicating them to the reader, it is judged far more expedient to consign them to dispersion and merited oblivion.]

Obelisk, as a standard to measure distances from; propriety of erecting one in the centre of London, clvi.

Obits; see *Anniversaries.*—Specification of the annual obits in St. Martin's church at Leicester, 569, 570.

Occupations (The) of the borough of Leicester; their oath to their ordinals, 378. —Official oath of the stewards and wardens thereof, 431. (And see *Trades.)*

Octavian, pope, his struggle for the papacy with his rival pope Alexander, 52.

—— the papal legate, takes the field against Manfroi, prince of Tarento, 131. —His army totally routed, 133.

Ode, written by Joseph Cradock, esq., and performed in St. Martin's church in Leicester, on the third anniversary of the opening of the town-infirmary, 523 :— performed a second time, 524.

Odeby, Leicestershire; possessions of Wigston's Hospital at that place, 487; 492.

Odiham-castle, voluntarily surrendered to king Henry the Third by Montfort II. earl of Leicester; part of the possessions of that earl, and repaired by him, 148.

Odiston, William de, his donation, of a rent from a tenement in the town of Leicester, to the abbot and convent of Croxton, 388.

Odo, bishop of Baïeux, trial betwixt him and archbishop Lanfranc, li.—Sent, with the bishop of Coutance, to suppress a rebellion of the earls of Hereford and Norfolk, *ib.*—Joins in the rebellion against king William Rufus, *ib.* & liv.

Officers, the mayor's, of Leicester, their initiatory oath, 378.

—— of Leicester-abbey, their titles and duties, 267, 268; 276.

—— *of horse and foot*, in Leicestershire, in 1681, list of, 470.

Oger the Briton, his antient tenure in Kilby, xlvii.—Held the lordship of Sileby, liii. —Was a baron, and tenant of the king *in capite*, *ib.*

Oil, consecrated, *(crisma,)* antiently used at baptism : this the parochial clergy were necessitated to receive from the cathedral or mother church, 285. *n.* (See *Chrisma.)*

Ointments, used in great profusion by the Romans in their bathing-houses, 356.

Okeham, a royal soke, l.

—— Rutlandshire; the free grammar-school and hospital in that town erected or re-established by Robert Johnson, archdeacon of Leicester, 466:

—— Jeffery, elected mayor of Leicester, 368.

Okethorpe, a hamlet of Seile in Leicestershire; certain lands and tenements there given by Thomas Lathbury to Leicester-abbey, 281.

Oldcastle, sir John, baron Cobham, executed under a pretence of heresy, 371.— (Where correct the parenthetical clause by omitting the word *and:* for *were*, read *was.)*

Oldfield, George, appointed to cast six new bells for St. Martin's church in Leicester, 580.

Oldham, William, chamberlain of Leicester, 449.—Elected mayor, 450.

Old Jewry, in London; why so named, 7.

Old Work, of Wroxeter, account of, 5. *n.*

Oleron, the island of, granted by king Henry the Third to his son prince Edward, 129.—Sold by the prince to his uncle Guy de Lesignan, 142.—Re-annexed to the crown of England, 153.

Olesthorpe, Leicestershire; its antient fee and tenure, cxvi.

Oliver, Samuel, chamberlain of Leicester, 448.—Elected mayor, 449;—and again, 450.—Appointed one of the auditors of Leicester-Infirmary, 517.—His epitaph, in St. Margaret's church-yard in Leicester, 567.

—— Margaret, wife, and Thomas-Bass, son, of the preceding; their epitaph, 567.

—— Thomas, for his services, had an

allowance made him by the corporation of Leicester, 442.

Olveston, ornaments remaining in the church of, at the time of the dissolution of religious houses; the prices they respectively sold for, cxxxvii.— Parcels of possessions of the monastery there, cxl.

Olyffe, William, elected mayor of Leicester, 392.

Omai, the Otaheitean, was one of the distinguished personages present at the performance of sacred musick in commemoration of the opening of Leicester-Infirmary, 523.

Omnes ad regnum spectantes; a phrase denoting the whole tenancy of the king, 214.

Omnes de regno; who comprehended under that phrase, 147. *n.*—*Omnes de regno nostro;* who? investigated, 214.

Onely, John, of Hinckley, chosen bailiff of Leicester, 437; 452.—Appointed seneschal of the borough of Leicester, 453.

Onlaf, king of Norway, invades England. 15.—Enters into treaty with king Edmund, *ib.*—His death, *ib.*

Onlip, Henry de, his donation to Leicester-abbey, *App.* 71.

Optimates, a general appellation for the nobles of the realm, 145. *n.*

Ora, Oræ, a term of ambiguous import, meaning a piece of money or an ounce-weight; method of reckoning money thereby, introduced by the Danes, xxxix. —Restricted, in Domesday-book, to the latter signification, *ib.* — Greater and lesser ora, respective value of each, *ib.*— Divers opinions respecting the term, *ib.*; and see pp. [xli]; 19.

Oration, Latin, delivered by Mr. Wincoll, counsellor of Leicester, on the ceremonious reception of king James the First into the town, 424: and again, 425.

Oratory; the privilege of having one in his own house granted to sir Guy de Bernangull by the abbot of Leicester, 284; *App.* 79.

Ord family, their pedigree, 615.

Ordeal, trial by, abrogated by Waldemar king of Denmark, 22. *n.*

Order, curious one, of king Richard the Third, in favour of the dean and canons of Saint Mary's in the Newark, 334.

Ordericus Vitalis, his character of Edwin earl of Leicester, 17.—His verses on the accidental drowning of the earl of Chester and his countess, 18.—Reports, that William Rufus measured the hides of England with a rope, 215.

Orders made at common-hall by Richard Gyllott, mayor of Leicester, regarding the inhabitants and tradesmen of the town, 375, 376.—Other orders of the common-hall under successive mayors, 384: 389, 390; & *seqq.* interspersedly, to 452.

Orders, monastic-religious, the several denominations of, 252.

Orestes, his story, 9.

Organ, a new one, by Snetzler, set up in St. Martin's church at Leicester, and first used in commemorating the anniversary of the opening of the town-infirmary, 523; 593. — Description of the instrument, 523. *n.*—Its total cost, 524. —Various memoranda relative to the old organ of this church, (from the year 1546,) 570, 571, 572, 573; 583, 584, 585; 593. — One erected in St. Margaret's church, by subscription among the parishioners; its cost, 559.

Oriel-college, Oxford, one fellowship founded therein by William Smyth, bishop of Lincoln, 607.

Oriol, a dining-parlour for visitors, in a monastery, 276.

Oriolanum, an apartment in a monastery, 278. *n.*

Orlande, John, his tenures under Leicester-abbey, *App.* 96.

Orlando, or Alexander III. pope; see *Alexander.*

Ornaments in several churches in Leicestershire at the time of the dissolution of the religious-houses, and the prices they were sold for, cxxxvii.—cxxxix.

Orpwood, Robert, and Elizabeth (Heyrick) his wife; their epitaphs in St. Martin's church, Leicester, 601.

Orson, Robert, his tenure in Bottesford, under Wigston's Hospital, 487; 492.

Orthography

2 Y

[¶If the reader be pleased to look back to letter *B*, he will see, that, in the article *Bible*, some remarks were promised under the present head. In consequence, these said remarks are here subjoined: and it is hoped that the importance of the subject will serve as an apology, if they be somewhat amplified.— In this all-improving age of ours, it must be confessed, much genuine information and many important discoveries have been brought to light: but *novelty* and real *improvement* are by no means always associated. Innovations in the more refined branches of knowledge are ushered in with indefinable terms; (or, if not entirely so, not satisfactorily soluble,) and dry metaphysical disquisitions, and cramp far-fetched epithets, perplex where simplicity is required, and repel the humble *tyro*, who would fain sit at the feet of Philosophy, and imbibe her native lessons *vivâ voce*. Not only does knowledge suffer under the influence of innovation; manners and customs also take the degenerate course; and in proportion as refinement, unrestrained, exalts its head, pride and daring insolence usurp ample sway over the minds of men. But to come to the point in hand, (for it would require a volume to descant at full on the subject of innovation); what effects do we witness in the typographical art which novelty has superinduced? Many, certainly, of very different shades and complexions.— A Bible, then, a *ruled Bible*, as that is the subject on which this digression takes its course, has some advantages, and those not trivial, over the unadorned modern-printed as well Bibles as other books. — These advantages need not be treated separately under so many distinct heads, but may be summarily comprised, *uno verbo*, in this, that they were *legible*: whereas, generally speaking, our modern-*stamped* (we must not say *printed)* Bibles vex the eyes, and obliterate the pleasure of perusal by the pains requisite to ascertain the reading, which merely here and there shines out of obscurity. I will not take upon me to decide whether the limitation of a margin by *red* lines, from the diversity of colour, relieves the sight (of the aged); certain I am that it conveys to the mind a satisfactory idea of a *finish*, to wit, that adequate pains have been taken with the book, to make it fitting for the purchaser and peruser.—But it may be said, that a Bible might be well printed, and yet the additional labour of ruling be spared. True: but the ruling secures these essentials; 1. A good substantial paper is requisite; 2. It is indispensable, that the printed sheets should be well dried, before they can be prepared for the operation of ruling. To apply this to our times. It is a lamentable but too certain fact, that, now, when an article is grievously advanced in price, it proportionally degenerates in quality: paper, among other commodities, (though this perhaps less so than the *necessaries* of life,) feels the diminution of its substance and the exaggeration of its price. The most ordinary book heretofore, if clad in a homely garb of coarse paper, yet did not shrink from the touch of the improving or correcting pen; while the flimsy meretricious face of our present paper presents a more fair appearance, but shrinks under the test of the uplifted plume, and, blushing, buries its imprinted superficies in the oblivion of deletion:—a fate, by-the-by, which much of our modern trash amply

merits. The hasty call for novel information is so imperious, that, as with newspapers, each book is almost taken into hand wet with the dew (not of heaven, which unction they too seldom can claim, but) of the *prelum impressorium*. To satisfy himself of the truth of these observations, a person had only need to look at the several things published for the last twenty years under the appellation of *Holy Bibles*: vile paper, illegitimate, and inaccurate orthography, &c. constitute a book; with, perhaps, a showy (book-binding too has suffered its eclipse) outside. For more than double the above-specified number of years, few small Bibles, (those called *Pocket-Bibles* I mean, of which, after their introduction by Field, prodigious numbers issued from the press in the latter half of the seventeenth century,) few, I say, of these little books have been given to the publick, which it is practicable to peruse. One, however, called *Pasham's Bible*, printed about thirty years ago, may well deserve the appellation of a pretty book, and may stand in competition with that printed by Field or any of his imitators: it is said, that each sheet of this book was hung up separately, until it was thoroughly dried; and the good effects of this care seem manifest in the general beautiful appearance of the book. Whereas, now, the printed sheets are laid together in heaps while wet, and huddled upon the drying-poles in clusters, ere the impression be well settled:—the causes of this negligence I do not design to investigate, nor to trace the ill effects thence resulting, farther than they have been already adverted to, in a general view. — — The ornamental finish of ruling seems to have been discontinued about the year 1720, or shortly after, and never, in recent times, had its revival been attempted, unless a single effort made by Corall, a few years ago, may be dignified with the appellation of a resuscitatory attempt: this was a pocket-bible, to enhance the value of which, red lines were drawn around the margin; but, instead of the brilliant gloss of old times, the colour seemed absorbed as by a sponge or blotting-paper. — — But the omission of ruling books is not the whole of the *improvement* which innovation has introduced: our title-pages heretofore, and that in times not long past, were wont to exhibit a display of characters red and black; the former marking the leading words or summary of the subject handled. The variety was, surely, not unpleasing, and stamped upon a book (as above remarked in respect to the ruling) a something like a *finish*; but, more than that, it preserved, as it were, a faint vestige of the rich adornments of our antient illuminated titles. In one work, indeed, of recent publication, the "Illustrations of Shakspeare," the learned author has shewn so much deference to old usages, as to re-instate in his title-pages the obsolete assemblage of red and black characters. — And truly, though many frivolous objections might be raised against a general revival of this practice, such as the uselessness thereof, the additional trouble and expence, and many similar arguments just as futile: yet, after all, we may infer, that, however rich the jewel may be that is contained within the casket, or however sumptuous the interior of the edifice, a graceful exterior can by no means be regarded as any disparagement. *Verbum sapienti.*—Having thus, as I trust, briefly illustrated my position, (though many other arguments on the subject might be adduced,) I conclude by soliciting the reader's indulgence for this digression.]

S.

Lines

of the corporation of Leicester, 447. *n.* & 448.*n.*

Strangers, or aliens; see *Foreigners.*

Strangford, viscount; see Thomas *Smith.*

———— Philip viscount, married Isabella daughter of Robert Sidney earl of Leicester, 544.

Strata of stone found in the Vale of Belvoir, account of, cciii. & *seq.*

Stratford, Nicholas, installed prebendary of St. Margaret's in Leicester; advanced to the see of Chester, 561.

Streatfield, Mrs. 543.*n.* See Anne *Sidney.*

Streets of Leicester, various regulations, and orders of the common-council of the town, for paving, cleansing, and keeping them in repair, 416, 417; 424; 439; 441; 445; 446; 447.—The paving of them undertaken by the inhabitants at their own expence, 450.—Particular description of them, 532, 533.

Street-Way, the present name of the Watling-street road, cli.

Strette, William, his tenure under Leicester-abbey, *App.* 74.

Stretton, Leicestershire, l.—Its antient fee and tenure, cxx.

Stretton, Warwickshire; what the abbey of Leicester possessed there, 286.

Stretton, William, of Whetstone; his donation to Richard Braunston, mayor of Leicester, 368.

Stringer, Thomas, elected churchwarden of St. Martin's in Leicester, 576.

———— William, chosen mayor of Leicester, 373.

Stubbing, William, alderman of Leicester; his donation to Trinity-hospital in the Newark, 351.

Stubbs, Mr.; an action brought against him by the corporation of Leicester for infringing their franchises, 447.*n.*

Stukeley, Dr. his conjectures respecting the Rawdikes near Leicester, 4*: and see his representation of the same in the plate facing that page.—His plan of Roman Leicester *(Plate* III.) deemed inaccurate by Mr. Ludlam, 5* *n.*:—Mr. Maurice Johnson's written remark on that plan, 328. *n.*—His remark on the Jewry-wall at Leicester, 6.—His hypothesis respecting the church erected by bishop Paulinus at Lindsey, *App.* 2. *n.*—His arguments relative to the site of the antient episcopal see of Sidnacester: objections to them, 3.—Fixed the Roman station *In Medium* at Kirton in Lincolnshire, 5.

Stukley, John de; see Peter *Burnell.*

Suabia, house of; their contest with the holy see, 124. & *seq.*

Suard, Richard, (in consideration of his liege-homage,) had from earl Simon de Montfort I. a grant of a certain rent in the prefecture of Leicester, 359; *App.*38.

Sub-cantor, his office in a monastery explained, 276.

Subditi, the *homines* or vassals of feudal lords, 205. *n.*

Subfeudatarii, under-tenants, xlx.

Sub-prior, his office explained, 276.

Subsidy, a tax originally imposed by king Henry the Second, 102.—Variously denominated, 214, 215, 216.—Styled a tax upon rents and moveables, 216.—A large one exacted from the clergy by king Edward the First, 261.—One demanded from the clergy by king Edward the Third, 365.—A general one of wool granted to king Edward the Third, 365, 366.—One on wine, granted to Henry the Fifth, 369.—One granted to queen Elizabeth; proportion of the same sustained by the corporation of Leicester, 402.—The origin of subsidies, 216.—Superseded the carucage and hidage, *ib.*—Specification of those levied by king John, 217:—and by Henry the Third, 218.

Sub-tenants, number of, in Leicestershire, at the Domesday-survey, xlviii.

Subterraneous buildings discovered at Leicester, description of, 11; 356; 618; *Plate* XLVI.

Suburbs (The) of Leicester; the antient fee and tenure thereof, cxx.—A moiety thereof granted by king John to Sayer de Quincey earl of Winton, 100; 360.—Specification of some antient tenures in the eastern suburb, 556.

Succentor, or sub-chanter, in the antient church-service, 266.*n.*

Suffolk, the duke? of, banished by king Edward the Third; beheaded at sea, 366.

Sughton, Leicestershire; its antient fee and tenure, cxviii.

Sumery, Roger de; see *Somery.*

Sumeter, his office explained, 267. *n.*

Sumner, John, his tenure in Bottesford, under Wigston's Hospital, 487; 492.

Sumpter-horse, the value of one at the time of the Domesday-survey, xxxix.

Sunday-schools at Leicester, account of, 514.

Sunderland, Henry earl of, married Dorothy daughter of Robert Sidney earl of Leicester, 544.

Superstition of antient times, some pretty fair specimens of, 225. & *n.*—Strong traits thereof, in some particulars of the will of John of Gaunt, duke of Lancaster, 240.

Supremacy, oath of, strictly required from every official member of the corporation of Leicester, 433, 434.

Supreme head of the church of England and Ireland; queen Mary I. so styled, 395.

Surcotes of silk, having the badges or marks of ancestorial achievements depicted on them, retained and worn hereditarily, 227.*n.*

Surgeons of Leicester-Infirmary, their rules, 519.

Surgeres, the town of, in Poitou, captured by Henry de Lancaster, earl of Derby, 228.

Surnames, not common when the Domesday-survey was taken, xlvi.—The want of them, in antient times, supplied by nicknames, 24.—These often borrowed from personal deformities, 321. *n.*

Surrey; the tenure of Leicester-abbey in that county, 284.

Survey, antient, as set down in the Domesday-Book, taken by Norman commissioners, vii. *n.* & xxxiv.—Called *Domesday* by the English, xxxiii. (See DOMESDAY-BOOK.)—King Alfred's survey of England, xxxiii. & *n.* & xxxiv.—Manner in which the Conqueror's survey was executed, xxxiv:—and the motives for which it was undertaken, xxxv.—A general survey of England taken by Henry the Eighth, xlix; 389.—Copy of one of the warrants for this latter survey, l.—Another survey attempted in Cromwell's time, but given up, *ib.*—Survey of churches and incumbents in Leicestershire, xcvi. to xcviii.

———— ecclesiastical, taken of the county of Leicester under king Henry the Eighth, 274; 391; 464.—The commissioners' return of the revenues of Leicester-abbey, 274.—The persons employed by the king to make this survey, 464.

———— of weights and measures, made by king Henry the Third, 138.

Suthvil, John, sent by king Henry the Third on confidential business to the king of France, 161.

Sutton antiently pertained to the abbey of Croyland, li.—Part of the king's eleemosinary lands, *ib.*

Sutton, Christopher, his fine for disobedience to the mayor of Leicester, 407.—Chosen chamberlain of the town; fined for absence, 408.—Put out of the Company of Forty-eight, and disfranchised, *ib.*

———— Edmund, elected mayor of Leicester, 435.

———— Edward, chosen mace-bearer of Leicester, 444.—His death, 446.

———— William, his donation to the Newark and St. John's Hospitals at Leicester, 469.—His epitaph, in St. Nicholas's church, in Leicester, 610.

Sutton-field, near Market-Bosworth in Leicestershire; account of the famous engagement there betwixt Richard the Third and Henry earl of Richmond, 381.

Svesbi, li.

Swan, Thomas, his tenures under Leicester-abbey, *App.* 96, 97.

———— Walter, and William *Mosse*, and Isabel relict of Fulco de *Penbruge*, obtain letters-patent from king Henry the Fourth for founding the collegiate church of Tonge in Shropshire, 369.

Swann, John, his epitaph, in St. Mary's church at Leicester, 316.

Swannington, Leicestershire; possessions of Wigston's Hospital in that place, 487.

Swanns-mill, 441, 442, 443.

Swedenborgians, a society of, holden in Sanvey-gate, 547.

Swepston, William de; see John de *Stockton.*

Sweyn, king of Denmark, slain by his own officers, 15, 16.

Swift, river, its rise and course described, l; clxi.

Swillington (or Swyllington), Ralph, made free of the town of Leicester, and admitted to be one of the co-burgesses, 388; 452.—(Recorder of the town, 390; 452:) appointed one of the commissioners for levying a subsidy granted to king Henry the Eighth, 389.—His death, 390.

Swillington, Robert, possessed a rent called Palfrey-silver, xl.

———— sir Robert de, his tenure in the town of Leicester, 368.

Swine-market, or *Swine's-market*, and sometimes written *Swyne-market*; (a narrow street in Leicester so named; formerly called Parchment-lane, 390; 532; 590;) certain messuages there conveyed by Charles Villars to Richard Reynolds and others, 308.—The *swine-market* was antiently kept in the High-street; but the place of holding it was changed to Parchment-lane by order of the common-hall, 390; 532.—A horse-mill, &c. there situate granted by king Edward the Sixth to Thomas Hawkins, 393.—Description of this street, 532.—Two tenements *in foro porcorum* let by the mayor and commonalty to John Whitewell, 556.—A messuage in the Swines-market granted by Hugh Whalley to Nicholas Reynolds, *ib.*

Swinfen, Edmund, chamberlain of Leicester, 450.—Elected mayor, 451.—Gave order for holding a meeting for furthering the institution of a Humane-society in the town, 529.

Swinford, Leicestershire, li.—Its antient fee and tenure, cxii.

Swinford, Catharine, the concubine of John of Gaunt duke of Lancaster, has certain lordships assigned to her by the duke by way of dower, 236:—which are afterwards confirmed to her, 240.—Dismissed by the duke from his house (where she had been brought up in her youth, 239. *n.*; 244: and entrusted with the care of the duke's children by his wife Blanch, 242; 247,) in pursuance of a vow made by him in his afflictions, 238; 244.—Married by the duke, 239. & *n.*; 240; 242; 244.—Her paternal descent, 239. *n.*; 244; (236).—Her history prior to her marriage with the duke, 239. *n.*—Excites no small share of envy among the great ladies by her elevation, *ib.*—Her character, *ib.*—Her monumental memorial, inscribed on the monument of the duke her husband in St. Paul's cathedral, 240.—Her death, 242.—Interred in the cathedral church at Lincoln, *ib.*—Her epitaph there, *ib.*—Her arms, *ib.*—Description of her tomb, *ib.*—Her issue, *ib.* & 243.; naturalized by papal and parliamentary authority, 239. *n.*; 240; 245.

Swingler, Nicholas, appointed bell-man of Leicester, 441.

Swithin, the monks of, murdered by the Wintonians, 178. *n.*

Sword, the being girded with one, by the hands of the sovereign, was the manner of investing an earl in his earldom, 91; 108. *n.*—By a similar cincture also a duke was initiated in his dignity, 229; 235.

———— of knighthood; see *Knighthood.*—Pleas of the *sword*; see *Pleas.*

Swords, three of gold, borne before Richard the First at his coronation, 89.—To whom the office of carrying the sword at such ceremonies of right appertained, *ib.*; and see p. 237. & *App.* 28; and the article *Curtana.*

Swyke, Thomas, elected mayor of Leicester, 382; 384.

Swyllington, Ralph; see *Swillington.*

Swyne-market, Leicester, 308: see *Swine-market.*

Swynerfled, Peter, eighth provincial of the Grey Friers in England, buried in the Franciscan priory at Leicester, 297.

Syleby, sir John, master of St. John's hospital at Leicester; his agreement with Richard Wigston, 324.

Symmes (or Simms), William, a Nonconformist, intruded by the parliament into the confraternity of Wigston's Hospital, but soon deprived of the same, 488; 502.—His death and interment, 502.

Symons, Matthew, his donation to Trinity-hospital at Leicester, 350. (See *Simons.)*

Synagogue,

END OF THE INDEX TO THE FIRST VOLUME.

INDEX TO THE ARMS

IN THE

FOUR VOLUMES

OF THE

HISTORY OF LEICESTERSHIRE.

---

4 B

GENERAL INDEX

TO THE

PEDIGREES.

Fitzherbert

PERSONAL INDEX

TO THE

SECOND, THIRD, AND FOURTH VOLUMES.

*** It has been found necessary, in compiling this Index, to reduce the number of references as far as was consistent with clearness and precision. For this reason the names of *all the Landholders* are given under this restriction, that when Lands or Manors remained for a century or more in a family bearing the *same name, that name* is seldom mentioned more than *once* in the same page, in the Index, though there may be ten or more members of the family noticed as succeeding to the property.

In pointing out the period when the persons lived, the actual dates are used, when given by the Author; in other cases, the dates of Inquisitions are substituted.

In those cases where a great number of references occur under the same name, the Christian names of John, James, &c. are kept together; but when the same Christian names again occur, more is said of the parties in MEMOIRS of their families in successive pages of the work.

It should also be remembered that antient names are spelt in several ways; as Eyrick, Heyrick; Boghan, Buchan, and Bucquan, &c.; these are referred to as occasion requires.

AARON of York, 1245, ii. 420.
―――― the Jew, of Lincoln, iii. 172.
Abbat, Rich. 1346, iv. 321.
Abdy, Ant. 1629, iv. 252, 258.
Abbé, Rich. l', iii. 44.
Abel, John, 1328, iii. 703.
Abell, Rev. John, 1602, iv. 823, 4.
―――― John, 1626, iv. 588.
―――― Matt. 1724, iv. 1034.
Abergavenny, Hen. lord, 1268, iv. 807.
―――――――― John de Hastyngs baron of, 1277, iv. 446.
―――――――― John de, earl of, 1296, iv. 452, 474, 810.
―――――――― John, lord of, 1324, ii. 869, iv. 712.
―――――――― Lawrence Hastings lord of, 1340, iv. 452.
Abington, Will. epit. of, and wife, 1720, 1750, ii. 254
Abkettleby, Alan of, 1331, ii. 10.
Abney, Rev. John, 1717, iii. 455.—epit. of, 1744, ib.
―――― family; particulars of a pedigree of, iii. 528.
―――― Tho. Esq. character of, iii. 606. n.
―――― Edward, Esq. 1800, iii. 783*.
―――― James, Esq. 1682, iii. 845.
―――― Will. Esq. 1802, iii. 1032.
―――― fam. memoirs of, iii. 1032.
―――― Damaris, epit. of, 1677, iii. 1032.
―――― of Willesley and Neuton Burguland, ped. of fam. of, iii. 1032.
―――― Robert, 1603, iii. 1042.
―――― Robert, iv. 592, 640.
―――― Sam. Bracebridge, Esq. iv. 593, 648.
―――― Paul, iv. 617.
―――― John, iv. 621, 964*.
―――― Sir Tho. Bart. 1749, iv. 850*.
―――― Christopher Edward, 1631, iv. 851*.
Abbot, Rev. Edward, 1689, ii. 436.
―――― fam. extracts from Galby Reg. concerning, ii. 570.
―――― Rev. Edward, 1674, ii. 572.
―――― Anne, 1730, ii. 719.
―――― Rev. Thomas, 1684, ii. 793.—Particulars of the life of, from Shankton Register, ii. 794.
Abbot of St. Peter *super Divam*, ii. 613.
―――― fam. epitaphs of, 1692, 1776. iii. 879.
―――― Sam. 1694, iv. 104-5.
Abbott, Edmund, 1710, ii. 534.
―――― Rich. and Mary, epitaph of, 1748, 1771, iii. 783.
―――― Rev. Lemuel, 1756, iii. 1082.—1773, iv. 984.
―――― Will. 1630, iv. 375.
―――― Rev. Geo. Stackhouse, 1794, iv. 982, 984.
Abbots, John, epit. of, 1781, iii. 92.
Abbotts, John, 1781, iii. 89.
Abraham fam. extracts from Stockerston Reg. concerning, ii. 819.
―――― John, epitaph of, 1671, ii. 822.

Abraham, Elizabeth, epitaph of, 1671, ii. 822.
―――― John, 1387, iv. 455, 807.
Abby, John, 1784, iii. 482.
Achardus, Magister, 1160, ii. 307.
Achison, Magister Dr. 1534, iii. 900.
Ackworth, Geo. priest, 1560, iv. 452.
Aclee, Walkelin de, iii. 457.
Acton, Tho. 1713, iv. 169.
―――― Will. 1584, iii. 129.
Acum, Will. priest, 1358, ii. 20.
Adam, Abbot, 1203, ii. 157.
―――― Tho. 1775, ii 464.
―――― Prior of Laund, 1200, iii. 308.
―――― Prior of Bredon, 1377, iii. 694.
―――― priest, 1219, iv. 211.
Adams, Rev. John, 1730, ii. 501.—1736, 891, 892.——1754, 145.
―――― Rev. Rich. 1661, iii. 275.
―――― Rev. Simon, 1790, iv. 478.
―――― Tho. priest, 1557, iv. 78.
Adamson, Anne, epit. of, 1764, iv. 779.
―――― Rev. . . . . epit. of, 1767, iv. 1000.
Adamthwaite, Rev. John, answers to the bishop of Lincoln's queries relative to Shakerston, iv. 912-13.
―――――――― historical remarks of, relative to Shakerston, iv. 909.
Adcock, Rich. priest, 1578, ii. 404, 6.
―――― John Johnson, 1777, iii. 46.
―――― Will. 1762, iii. 58.
―――― Will. epit. of, 1644, iii. 383.
―――― Rob. 1609, iii. 452.
―――― Hugh, 1707, iv. 441.
Aden, Ralph, 1608, iii. 99, 167*.
Adderley, Rob. epit. of, 1778, iii. 92.
―――― Humphrey, 1572, ii.**262, iii. 522.
―――― Humphry, iv. 631, 638, 640.—1632, 640.
―――― Rev. Tho. 1719, iv. 574.
―――― fam. epitaphs of, 1598, 1639, iv. 650.
Addington, Rev. Stephen, ii. 497.—memoirs of, 504.
Addison, Joseph, Esq. anecdotes of, iii. 238. n.
―――― Joseph, memoirs of, iv. 913. n.
―――― Rev. Lancelot, memoirs of, iv. 913. n.
―――― Dorothy, epit. of, 1719, iv. 913.
Addyson, Rob. priest, ii. 20.
Adkins, Rich. 1764, iv. 165.
Adlokeston, Peter of, iii. 231.
Adnut, John, 1770, iv. 878.—1777, iii. 46.
Adnutt, Rev. Tho. 1800, iii. 933.—1809, iv. 584, 585.
―――― Rev. . . . . . 1810, iv. 971.
―――― Edward, 1779, iv. 993.
Ætoun, Mat. priest, 1599, ii. 496.
Agar, Frances, 1775, ii. 512.
Agard, George, epit. of, iv. 546.
Agarde, Charles, Esq. 1646, ii. 805.
Agas, Walter, priest, 1413, ii. 20.
Agaz, Walter, priest, 1226, ii. 297, 423.
Ailesbury, Tho. 1418, iv. 713.

Ailesford, Heneage earl of, 1731, iii. 403, 405.
―――― Heneage earl of, 1764, iii. 403.
Ailston, ..., great age of, ii. 288.
Ainsworth, Will. 1630, iii. 1105.
―――― Tho. epit. of and wife, 1737, 1764, iii. 1023.
Aislabie, Will. Esq. 1727, memoirs of, iv. 492.
―――― Will. Esq. 1762, iii. 58, 186.
―――― John, Esq. tradition concerning, iv. 492. n.
Akers, Rev. J. D. 1796, iii. 1082.
Akerville, Will. de, priest, 1220, iv. 206.
Akethorpe, Ralph de, priest, 1241, ii. 555.
Alan, Rob. 1279, ii. 574.
―――― priest, 1220, ii. 13.—1223, iv. 330.
―――― Mat. token of, iii. 894.
Allanson, Mrs. 1800, iii. 176.
Allatt, John, 1670, token of, iii. 612.
Albans, St., Will de, priest, 1220, iv. 187.
―――― St., Dukes of, 1732, 1764, 1787, 1802. iv. 376, 381.
Albany, ii. 9.
Albemarle, Hawisia countess of. 1200, ii. 166.
―――― Will. 2nd earl of, 1216, ii. 394.
―――― Christopher, duke of, 1670, ii. 114.—II. duke, 1676, 121.
―――― Edward, duke of, iv. 671.
―――― Will. de, iv. 168.
Albeny, Oliver de, 1204, iv. 157.
Albi, Roger, priest, 1209, ii. 330.
Albin, Roger de, ii. 146.
―――― Saint Margery de, ii. 151.
Albiniaco, Odinell de, 1230, ii. 17, 296.
―――― Ralph de, Acolytus, nature of his ecclesiastical connection with the rectory of Bottesford, 1223, ii. 96 and n.
Albini family, memoirs of, ii. 24.
―――― Will. de, 1155, ii. 24, 76, 218.
―――― Will. de, II. 1165, number of Knights' fees held by, ii. 24, 86, 130, 213.
―――― Will. de, III. obstinate defence of Rochester castle by, temp. K. John, and epit. 1236, ii. 25, 26, 86, 96, 213, 355.
―――― Will. lord, 1251, ii. 355.
―――― Will. de, IV. seal of, ii. 23.—1427, ii. 27, 104, 299.—Supposed tomb of, 23, 98.
―――― family, pedigree of, ii. 27.
―――― Nich. de, priest, 1222, ii. 96.
―――― Eliz. 1294, ii. 194, 556. iv. 373.
―――― Brito Will. de, ii. 76.
―――― Invenus de, ii. 76.
―――― Nigell de, 1118, memoirs of, ii. 222, 239, 272, 277, iv. 756. (See Mowbray).
―――― Tho. 1296, ii. 209.
―――― of Belvoir, benefactions of family of to various religious houses, App. No. III. ii. 40.
―――― and Ros, additional charters of the families of, App. No. XII. ii. 105.
Alcock, George, epitaph of and wife, 1724, 1739, ii. 385.

Alcock,

4 D

Camville,

Ringe

Rose,

Watson,

5 A

Bardon,

Shilton,

SUPPLEMENTARY INDEX

TO

THE ADDITIONS AND CORRECTIONS, DOMESDAY, &c.

** Small Capitals indicate Names of Parishes, &c. The *Italic* Characters are the antient Names, both of Places and Possessors of Land, as spelt in Domesday Survey (given in Vol. I. Part I.) and the Figures and Letters refer to the Pages of the original Record.—ap. refers to the Appendix, and po. refers to the Population Return of 1811 (both given in Vol. II. Part II.)

Blunt.

†╂† *Italics* refer to DOMESDAY in Vol I. Part I.—po. to Population Return in Vol. I. Part II.

Blunt, Rev. Edward, 1645, iii. 1135.
——— William, 1588, i. ap. 117.
BOCHESTON, *Brocardescote,* 232, a. 1.—adtions to, iii. 4.
Bon Compagnon, ii. 32.
Bonsar, T, 1814, i. ap. 145.
Bond, Thomas, 1506, iii. 1131.
Boothby, of Broadlow, pedigree, corrections in, iv. 418.
Bosvile, Rev. Thomas, 1815, i. ap. 149.
BOSWORTH, HUSBANDS, *Basurde,* 234. a. 1. 2. *Baresworde,* 234. a. 2. 236. a. 1.—additions to, i. ap. 131 ; ii. 673, 1127 ; iii. 467, 528, 1127 ; iv. 399, 1045.—celts found at, iii. 1127.—extracts from charters of Selby Abbey, relating to, ii. app. No. XXI. 141.—possessions of Welford or Sulby Abbey in Bosworth and its neighbourhood, 142.—possessions of Leicester Abbey in Bosworth, 143.—po. i. 2.
BOSWORTH, MARKET, *Boseworde,* 231.b.1, 233. a 1.—additions to, i. ap. 145 ; iii. 4 ; iv. 1041.—po. i. 5.
BOSWORTH FIELD, additions to account of and present state, i. ap. 145, 149.
BOTCHESTON, *Brocardescote,* 232, a. 1.—po. i. 5.
BOTHE-THORPE, iii. 906.
BOTHORPE, *Bortrod,* 233. b. 1.
BOTTESFORD, *Bothesford, Holesford,* 233. b. 2. 234. a. 1.—additons to, i. ap. 128, 130; ii. 419, app. No. XXII. 148 ; iii. 517 ; iv. 1045.—po. i. 1.
Boune, Rob. dean, 1. Edw. VI. i. ap. 120.
Bourne family epitaphs, ii. 424.
BOWDEN MAGNA, *Bugedone,* 230. b. 1. 236. a. 2.—additions to, ii. 891 ; iv. 261.—po. i. 1. 7.
BOWDEN PARVA, additions to, ii. 478 : iii. 528.
Bowes, Jane, i. ap. 117.
BRADFORD, co. York, i. ap. 120.
BRADGATE, additions to, iii. 3. 1141.—view of Bradgate Ruins, iii. ap. 66.—po. i. 3.
BRADLEY, po. i. 1.
Bradshaigh, Roger, i. ap. 135.
BRASCOTE, iii. 3.
BRAUNSTON, in Framland, *Brantestone,* 231. a. 1.—additions to, iv. 396.—po. i. 1.
BRAUNSTON, in Sparkenhoe, *Brantestone,* 232. a. 1. b. 1.—additions to, iii. 4. 518, iv. *630.—po. i. 5.
BRAUNSTON FRITH, po. i. 5.
BREDON, additions to, iii. 3, 4, *6, 1141 ; iv. 261, 409.—po. i. 3.
Bren, Thomas, 1645, iii. 1135.
BRENTINGBY, additions to, iii.525.—po. i.1.
BRESCOTE, *Brocardescote,* 232. a. 1.
Breton, Rev. Dr. Clement, 16. . . iii. 537.
Breton, Rev. Wm. iv. 1041.
Brereton, Rev. Wm. 1812, i. ap. 132.
BRET's HALL, additions to, i. ap. 154.
Brett, account of family of, i. ap. 154.
Brewin, Rev. John, 1808, i. ap. 142.
BRIDGE CASTERTON, ii. 890. *n.*
Bright, Rev. . . .. 1814, i. ap. 138.
——— Edw. 1750, i. ap. 125.
Brindsley, Rev. Jonn, 1665, memoirs of, i. ap. 140.
BRINGHURST, inclosure, iv. 399.—po. i. 1.
BRISTOWE, iv. 417.
Brito, Manno, 236.
——— *Ogerius,* 236.
Brocke, Richard, i. ap. 117.
BROKESBY, *Brochesbi,* 236. b. 1. 237. a. 1.—additions to, i. ap. 134; iii. 3.—po. i. 2.
Brokesby, Rev. Abel, 1735, iv. 1043.
——— Bartholomew, ep.1466, i.ap.135.
——— Bartholomew, epit. of, and wife, 1543, i. ap. 131.
——— Bartholomew, 1603, iv. 415.
——— Rob. 1588, i. ap. 117.
——— Rob. i. ap. 133.
——— Wm. epit. 1505, i. ap. 136.
——— Pedigree corrected, iii. 1043.
BROMKINSTHORPE, *Brunestanestorp, Brunechinestorp, Brunestanestorp,* 230. a. 1. 232. a. 1. 232. a. 2.—additions to, iii. 3.
BROUGHTON ASTLEY, *Broctone, Broctone,* 230. a. 1. 231. b. 1. 232. b. 1. 236. a. 2.—additions to, i. ap. 142 ; iii. 3.—po.i.4.
BROUGHTON, NETHER, *Broctone,* 230. a. 2.—additions to, ii. 419; iii. 556.—po. i.1.
Brooke, Basel, i. ap. 117.
Brown, Rev. . . . . 1566, i. ap. 126.
——— Edward, epit. and char. of, i. ap.151.
——— Francis, 1814, i. ap. 122.
——— Rev. Matthew, 1812, i. ap. 146.
——— Mary, epit. 1786, i. ap. 151.
——— Rev. Wm. acc. of, 1814, i. ap.131.
——— Rev. Wm. 1814, i. ap. 150.
——— Brown, Wm. 1808, i. ap. 146.—character of, 147.

Browne, Thomas, 1808, i. ap. 122.
——— Sir Wm. 1605, iv, 415.
——— John-Cave, 1799, ii. 888 ; iii. 551.
Bruce, the Traveller, a plagiarist, iv. 396.
Brudenell, Sir Robert, iii. 525.
——— Thomas, epit. 1670, iii. 544.
——— arms, ii. 545.
——— pedigree corrected, iii. 544.
BRUISYARD, Suffolk, iii. 544.
BRUNTINGTHORPE, *Brandinestor,* 237. a. 2. —additions to, iii. 3.—po. i. 4.
Buci, Robertus de, 234.
BRUSSELS, English nuns at, ii. 413.
Buckingham, marquis, entertains James I. at Burley, 1621, iii. 1133.— Sir John Beaumont's verses on the occasion, *ib.*— his expedition to the Isle of Rhé 1627, *ib.*
——— duke of, 1651, iii. 556.
Buckley, Dorothy, 1813, account and character of, i. app. 153, *n.*
——— Richard, i, ap. 141.
BUCKMINSTER, *Bucheminstre,* 231. a. 1.— additions to, iii. 518.—pop. i. 1.
Bucknall, Richard, 1679, ii. 891.
Buenvaslet, 285.
BURBACH, *Burbece,* 231. a. 2.—additions to, i. ap. 145 ; iii. 3.—po. i. 5.
Burbidge, Joseph, 1807, i. ap. 122.
——— Thomas, 1813, i. ap. 123, 129.
Burdett, Anne, 1774, iv. 1041.
——— John, 1737, iv. 1041.
——— Rev. Theophilus, 1705, ii. 894.
Burg, Sanctus Petrus de, 231. 2.
BURGNESS, or BURGSEIT, iii. 332, 333.
Burkitt, John, 1814, i. ap. 141.
BURLEY PARK, additions to, iii. 4, 1133 ; iv. 415, 1049.
Burleton, Wm. 1791, i. ap. 157.
Burlington, countess of, 1721, iv. 403.
Burnaby, Edwin-Andrew, iii. 557.
——— Rev. Robert, 1807, i. ap. 141.
——— Rev. Archdeacon, 1812, account of, i. ap. 123, 135.
——— Mrs. i. ap. 123.
Burrough, Rev. John, 1645, ii. 894.
BURROW, *Burc, Burg,* 233. b. 1. 236. b. 2. (bis.)—additions to, i. ap. 131; ii. 673.—po. i. 1.
BURROW HILL, ii. 892.—view of, iii. ap. 66.
Burrows, Hannah, 1664, iv. 409.
BURSTALL, *Burstelle,* 230. a. 1. 232. a. 2. b. 2.—additions to, iii. 3, 4, *6.—po. i. 3.
BURTON LAZARS, *Burtone,* 234. b. 2. 235. b. 1.—additions to, ii. ap. No. XII. 112; iii. 523, 525, 526, 555 ; iv. 396.—cures performed by the waters there, iii. 524.—po. i. 1.
BURTON OVERY, *Burtone,* 232. a. 2. 237. a. 1.—additions to, i. ap. 131 ; iii. 531; iv. 1045.—po. i. 1.
BURTON ON THE WOULDS, *Bortone, Burtone,* 230. a. 1. 235. b. 236. b. 237. a.—additions to, ii. ap. No. XIII. 112 ; iii. 3, 1136 ; iv. 405.—po. i. 2.
Burton, Rev. Robert, additions to account of, iii. 1137.
——— William, Historian of Leicestershire, Portrait of, Frontispiece to vol. I. part. I.
——— Pedigree corrected, iv. 1042.
BUSHBY, po. i. 1.
BUSHMEAD PRIORY (not Wishmed or Newsted priory) ii. 32 ; iv. 395.
Rusli, Rogerus de, 234. b.
Butler, Mary, 1723, 1730, iii. 909, 1143.
——— Dr. 1703, iii. 1140.
Button, Edward, 1775, iv. 212, 418.
——— Humphrey, 1658, iv. 418.
Buxham, Rev. John, ii. 169.
Buxton, Thomas, 1811, i. ap. 122.
Byerly, Col. Robert, 1714, iv. 403.

C.

CADEBY, *Catebi,* 232. b. 1.—additions to, i. ap. 146; ii. ap. No. XIII. 116; iii. 3.—po. i. 5.
CALAIS, THE, iii. 561.
CALDECOTE, iii. 536.
Caldecote Pedigree corrected, i. ap. 142 ; iv. 1039.
Caldecott, Eliz. 1804, i. ap. 130.
CALDWELL, *Caldeuuelle,* 230. b. 1.—additions to, iii. 3.—po. i. 3.
Calf-running, iv. 123.
Cambrai, Godefridus de, 235. b. 2.
Camerarius, Hunfridus, 236.
Campden, Edward Noel, 2d viscount, 1618, iv. 405.
Cardigan, James Brudenell earl of, 1811, i. ap. 133.

CARLETON CURLIEU, *Carletone, Carlintone,* 230. b. 1. 232. a. 2.—additions to, iii. 532.—po. i. 1.
CARLETON, near Bosworth, additions to, iii. 3.—po. i. 5.
Carrick, Henry, 1809, i. ap. 126.
Carrington, lord, and family, 1644, iii. 552.
Carter, baron, i. ap. 120.
——— Isaac, 1804, i. ap. 132.
——— John-Edward, 1813, i. ap. 132, 149.
CASTERTON, LITTLE, co. Rutland, ii. 884.
CASTLE DONINGTON. See DONINGTON.
Castle-guard, ii. 10.
CASTLE-VIEW, iv. 69.—po. i. 4.
CAT-THORPE, *Torp,* 236. a. 1.—additions to, i. ap. 142 ; iii. 3 ; iv. 1039.—po. i. 4.
Cattwell, Andrew, 1721, iv. 403.
Cave, Brian, 1588, i. ap. 117.
——— Capt. 1645, iii. 1135.
——— Sir Thomas, his remarks on the difficulties of an historian's labours, iv. 421.
——— of Worcestershire, pedigree corrected, iv. 420.
CAVENDISH BRIDGE, iii. 779, 1142.
CHADWELL, po. i. 3.
Chambers, Joseph-Thos. 1812, i. ap. 142.
——— pedigree corrected, i. ap. 133, 136.
Chamberlayne's Manor, iii. 390.
Chancy alias Giles, Clement, epitaph of and wife, 1578, i. ap. 131.
Chantler, Mary, epitaph, 1585, i. ap. 131.
Chapman, Rev. John, 1562, ii. 420.
——— John, 1810, i. ap. 153.
CHARLEY, *Cernelega,* 237. a. 1.—additions to, iii. 4.—po. i. 3.
Charnock, John, F.S.A. 1807, iv. 418.
——— John and Frances, 1808, 1809, i. ap. 144.
CHARNWOOD FOREST, additions to, iii. 554.—new chapel in, i. ap. 149.
Chauncey, Rev. Wm. iv. 1041.
Cheselden, lieut.-col. Edward, acc. of, i.131.
Cheslyn, R. 1812, i. ap. 123.
——— Thomas, 1814, i. ap. 140.
Chessee, Rev. John, 1579, ii. 417.
Chiborne, 230. a. 1.
Chifflet, John, iii. 522.
Choyce, Margaret, aged 106, 1704, i. ap. 152.
Christmas, Gerard, 1634, i. ap. 151.
Churchill, Rev. Wm. account of, 1804, i. ap. 151.
Ciacconio, Alfonso, 1599, iii. 521. *n.*
Cioches, Gunfridus de, 235. b. 2.
Clark, William, 1804, iv. 399.
Clarke, Jonah, 1805, i. ap. 145.
——— Samuel, 1812, i. ap. 122.
——— Rev. Thomas, iv. ap. 138.
——— Pedigree continued, iv. 602.
CLAXTON, LONG, *Clachestone,* 233. b. 2. 235. a. 1. 237. a. 1.—additions to, ii. 420, 884 ; iii. 518.—po. i. 1.
CLAYBROOK, GREAT, *Claibroc,* 237. a. 2.—additions to, i. ap. 142 ; iii. 3 ; iv. 417. po. i. 4.
CLAYBROOK, LITTLE, additions to, i. ap. 142.—po. i. 4.
Clayton, Rev. Obadiah, 1810, acc. of, i. ap. 122.
Cliborne, 234. a. 1; i. 625 ; iv. page xi.
Clifford, Mrs. 1814, i. ap. 140.
Clifton, John, 1664, ii. 883.
Coal-mines, fires long burning in, iii. 739.—at Swannington described, iii. 1125*.
Coke, William, i. ap. 117.
COLD NEWTON, additions to, iii. 3.
COLD OVERTON, *Ovretone,* 236. a. 1. 234. b. 1.—additions to, i. ap. 130 ; ii. 420, 884 ; iii. 518, 1142.—po. i. 1.
COLE ORTON, *Ovretone,* 234. b. 1.—po. i. 3.
Cole, ... 1813, i. ap. 123.
Coleman, Henry, acc. of, 1794, i. ap. 123.
——— Henry, 1813, i. ap. 131.
——— Rev. James Sherard, 1808, i. ap. 132.
——— Henry, 1813, i. ap. 131.
Collier, Rev. Joseph, 1807, i. ap. 140.
COLSTON BASSETT, co. Notts, iv. 403.
CONGESTON, *Cuningeston,* 232. a. 2. 234. b. 2.—additions to, iii. 3.—po. i. 5.
CONNINGTGN, the seat of the Cotton family at, iii. 1140.
Constable, William, dean of York, 1535. ii. 97; iv. 396.
Constantiensis, Episcopus, 281.
Cooke, Rev. . . . . 1810, i. ap. 133.
Cooper, John, 1637, iv. 1041.
——— Rev. John Mawbey, 1814, i. ap. 152.
Cope, Thomas, 1578, iii. 557.
Copeland, John, i. ap. 117.

COSBY,

SUPPLEMENTARY INDEX. 19

†‡‡ *Italicks* refer to DOMESDAY, in Vol. I. Part II.—po. to Population Return in Vol. I. Part II.

20   S U P P L E M E N T A R Y   I N D E X.

†++ *Italics* refer to D**omesday**, in Vol. I. Part I.—po. to Population **R**eturn in Vol. I. Part II.

22   SUPPLEMENTARY INDEX.

†‡† *Italics* refer to DOMESDAY in Vol. I. Part I.—po. to Population Return in Vol. I. Part II.

SUPPLEMENTARY INDEX. 23

†++ *Italics* refer to DOMESDAY in Vol. I. Part I.—po. to Population Return in Vol. I. Part II.

QUENEBOROW, *Cuniburg*, 235. b. 2.—account of sepulchral relicks found at, i. ap. 136.—additions to, iii. 3.—po. i. 3.
QUORNDON, additions to, i. ap. 134; iii. 3, 4, *6, 1130; ii. ap. No. XIII. 115.—po. i. 3.
QUORNDON Hall, view of, iii. 1131.

R.

RADCLIFFE-ON-THE-WREKE, *Radeclive*, 234. b. 1.—additions to, i. ap. 136; ii. ap. No. XIII. ii. 114; iii. 3.—po. i. 3.
Radulphus filius Huberti, 235.
Rainbuedecurt, Wido de, 235. a. 1.
RAKEDALE, *Ragendele*, 234. b. 1.—additions to, i. ap. 136, 142; iii. 3.—po. i. 3.
RATBY, *Rotebi*, 232. a. 1.—additions to, iii. 4.—po. i. 5.
RATCLIFFE CULEY, *Redeclive*, 234. b. 2.—additions to, iii. 4.—po. i. 5.
Raven, John, 1623, ii. 419.
RAVENSTON, or RAUNSTON, *Ravenstun, Ravenstorp*, 278. a. 1. 235. a. 2.—additions to, iii. 3, 4, 1125.—po. i. 3.
Rawdon, Hon. John-Theophilus, 1808, i. ap. 139.
Rawlins, Thomas, his will, iii. 553.
Rawson, James, 1812, i. ap. 122.
Ray, Samuel, 1631, ii. 419.
READING ABBEY, extracts from Register of, iv. 417.
REDMILE, *Redmelde*, 233. b. 2.—additions to, ii. 424; iv. 397.—po. i. 1.
Redmile, Robert de, 1242, ii. Ap. 14; iii. 525.
Reeve, Mrs. 1808, i. ap. 130.
Registers. See Parish Registers.
Reinbudcurth, vel Rainbuedcurt, Wido de, 235.
Reppingham, Thomas de, priest. 1343. ii. 896.
RERESBY, *Redresbi, Reresbi*, 234. b. 1. 236. a. 2. 237. a. 1.—additions to, i. ap. 136; ii. Ap No. XIII. 113; iii. 3.—po. i. 3.
RICHARD's (King), or DICK's WELL, inscription on by Dr. Parr, i. ap. 145.
RIDGE-LANE, account of, i. ap. 158.
Riley, ... 1814, i. ap. 136.
RINGLETHORPE GRANGE, *Ricolthorp*, 236. a. 2. b. 2.
Roberts, Rev. J. 1814, i. ap. 153.
———— William, 1588, i. ap. 117.
———— Miss, 1800, iii. 560.
ROBIN-O'-TIPTOE, i. ap. 158.
Robinson, Sir James and lady, epitaphs, 1731, 1727, ii. 893.
———— Sir John, and family, epitaphs, 1713, ii. 893.
———— Rev. Thomas, 1813, memoirs of, i. ap. 119.—character of him as a preacher, 119, 120.—character of, by Mr. Hall, i. ap. 158.
———— Thomas, i. ap. 147.
———— .... aged 107, i. ap. 149.
———— of Stretton, pedigree, additions to, ii. 893.
Rochester, John Wilmot, earl of, 1660, ii. 392, 403.
ROCKINGHAM CASTLE, ii. 895.
Rogers, Rev. Samuel, 1790, i. ap. 131; ii. 468; iii. 528.
———— Stephen, 1588, i. ap. 117.
ROLLESTON, *Rovestone*, 235. b. 1.—additions to, i. ap. 131.—po. i. 2.
Ross, Rev. John-Dawes, 1814, i. ap. 138.
———— Family arms, iv. 396.
———— Pedigree, corrected, iii. 517.
ROTHERBY, *Redebi*, 237. a. 1.—additions to, iii. 3.—po. i. 3.
ROTHLEY, *Rodolei*, 230. a. 2.—additions to, i. ap. 141; iii. 3, 4, 5*; iv. 261.—suit between Rothley and Mountsorell, 1638, iii. 1125.—po. i. 3.
ROTHLEY INN, iv. 415.
ROTHLEY TEMPLE, iii. 3.
Rowlatt, John-Inckley, 1804, iv. 399.
Rozzel, William, 1813, i. ap. 125.
Ruding, Rev. Rogers, 1812, i. ap. 146.
———— Sarah, 1813, char. of, i. ap. 146.
———— Pedigree corrected, i. ap. 145, 146.
Russell, John, 1419, ii. 884.
Ru*sted*, Tobias, (not Ru*ffed*), 1690, iii. 702, 1141.
Rutland, Edward, third earl of, 1587, curious account of his funeral, i. ap. 127.
———— Francis, sixth earl of, account of, ii. 418.
———— John, first duke of, funeral poem to his memory, 1711, ii. ap. No. VIII. 67.
———— John-Henry, fifth and present duke of, 1814, his marriage and issue, i.

ap. 127. — his entertainment of the Prince Regent, &c. at Belvoir Castle, 128, 129.
Rutland, Thomas first earl of, 1532, i. ap. 127; ii. 423.
———— Dukes of, account of pedigree of, i. ap. 130.
Ryder, Hon. and Rev. Henry, 1814, i. ap. 143; iii. 1142.

S.

Sacheverell, Sir Henry and family, i. ap. 138, and *note.*
———— Joshua, his pedigree, iii. 510. —corrected, 560.
———— Richard, 1810, i. ap. 136.
———— Family epits. iii. 1139, 1140.
SADINGTON, *Sadintone, Setintone*, 230. a. 1. b. 1.—additions to, ii. 673, 789,895; iii. 543.—po. i. 2.
ST. MARY IN ARDEN. See Mary in Arden.
St. Nicholas family, account of, and extracts from Monk's Kirby register, iv. 419.
SALTBY, *Saltebi*, 234. b. 2.—additions to, i. ap. 131; ii. 424, 888; iii. 525; iv. 1045.—deeds relating to, ii. ap. No. XIX. 138.—po. i. 1.
Sandby, Rev. Chas. 1807, i. ap. 140.
Sanderson, Robt. bp. of Lincoln, ii. 887; iv. 397.
SANDON HOSPITAL, or PRIORY, in Esher, Surrey, iv. 418.
Sansome, Thomas, 1814, i. ap. 146.
SAPCOTE, *Scopecote*, 231. b. 1. 232. a. 1. b. 1. 233. a. 2.—additions to, i. ap. 152; iii. 3.—po. i. 5.
Saultby, William de, priest, ii. 884.
Savile, William, 1610, iv. 1039.
SAXBY, *Saxebi*, 236. b. 2.—additions to, ii. 888.—po. i. 1.
SAXULBY, *Saxelbi*, 230. b.—additions to, iii. 3.; iv. 261.—po. i. 3.
SCALFORD, *Scaldeford*, 234. b. 1. 236. b. 1.—additions to, i. ap. 142; iv. 397.
Scarborough. See Orton.
SCRAPTOFT, *Scrapentot*, 231. a. 2.—additions to, i. ap. 132.—po. i. 2.
Scrope, lord, iii. 524.
Seal used by Henry VII. and VIII. [not Henry III. as in iii. 432], iv. 406.
SEGRAVE, *Segrave, Setgrave, Satgrave*, 230. b. 1. 234. b. 1. 233. a. 2. 237. a. 1.—additions to, i. ap. 137; iii. 3, 557, 558, 1136, 1137.—extracts from the Chartulary of the Honour of, ii. ap. No. XIII. 108—120.—relating to the Town of Segrave, ii. ap. 111.—po. i. 3.
Segrave, Gilbert de, iv. 418.
———— Sir John de, 1311, ii. 420.
———— Stephen de, iv. 417.
———— Family, iv. 1040.
SEILE, NETHER, *Sela*, 233. b. 1. 236. a. 1. —additions to, iii. 3, 4.—po. i. 3.
SEILE, OVER, additions to, iii. 3, 4. — po. i. 3.
SELBY ABBEY, account of, ii. 897. *n.*
SERLETHORP, iii. 3.
Servientes Regis, 236. b. 2.
SEWESBY, ii. ap. No. XIII. 114.
SEWSTERN, *Sewesten*, 235. b. 1.—additions to, ii. 419, 420; iii. 510; iv. 396.—po. i. 1.
Seyntcler, Thomas, 3 Hen. VI. iv. 417.
SHAKERSTON, *Sacrestone*, 234. b. 2.—additions to, iii. 3.—po. i. 5.
SHANKTON, *Sanctone, Santone*, 230. b. 1. 232. b. 2. 234. a. 2.—po. i. 2.
SHARNFORD, *Sceneford, Scerneford, Sterneforde*, 231. a. 2. 231. a. 1. 232. a. 1. 236. a. 2. b. 2.—additions to, iii. 3.—po. i. 5.
Sharp, John, epitaph, 1578, i. ap. 135.
Sharpe, William, 1645, ii. 891.
SHAWELL, *Sawelle*, 237. a. 2.—additions to, i. ap. 144; iii. 3, *6.—po. i. 4.
SHEARSBY, *Svesbi, Svevesby, Sevesby*, 231. a. 2. b. 1. 232. b. 1.—additions to, iii. 3.—po. i. 4, 9.
Sheeles, William, iii. 938; iv. 415.
SHENTON, *Scentone*, 231. b. 1. 233. a. 2. 234. a. 1.—additions to, iii. 3.—po. i. 5.
SHEPEY MAGNA, *Scepa, Scepehe*, 232. b. 2. 233. a. 2.—additions to, iii. 3.—po. i. 5.
SHEPEY PARVA, additions to, iii. 3.—po. i. 5.
SHEPESHED, *Scepehefde, Scepeshefde*, 230. a. 1. b. 233. a. 2.—additions to, iii. 3, 4, *6, 1125.—po. i. 3.
Sherard, Francis, 1588, i. ap. 117.
Sheriffs of Leicestershire, continued, i. ap. 123, 158.

SHERMAN's LODGE, described, i. ap. 152.—po. i. 3.
Sherrier, Rev. Edward, 1731, i. ap. 144.
Shevington, Giles, abbot, iii. 532.
SHILTON, EARL's, *Sceltone*, 230. a. 1. 232. a. 1.—additions to, iii. 3.—po. i. 5.
Shipman, John, 1811, i. ap. 146.
Shirley, sir Anthony, 1594, iv. 410.
———— Ferrers, Latin lines on, by bp. Atterbury, iv. 410.
———— sir Thomas, 1607, iv. 410. 417.
———— Rev. Walter, 1769, his family, iv. 410.
SHORTLEY, co. Warwick, ii. 884.
SHOULBY, *Seoldesberie*, 231. b. 2.—additions to, i. ap. 136.—po. i. 3.
Shuttlewood, John, 1802, iii. 1136.
SIBBESDON, *Sibetestone*, 231. b. 1.—additions to, iii. 3.—po. i. 5.
SILEBY, *Seglebi, Siglebi, Siglesbie*, 230. a. 1. b. 1. 233. a. 1. 237. a. 1.—additions to, i. ap. 137, 140; ii. ap. No. XIII. 116; iii. 3, 559, 1138.—po. i. 3.
Simpson, Mrs. .... 1811, i. ap. 122.
Sims, Rev. William, 1651, i. ap. 121.
SISONBY GRANGE, ii. ap. No. XVII. 136.
Sixtus Quintus, Pope, 1584, Mr. Burton's eulogium on, iii. 521.
SKEFFINGTON, *Sciftitone*, 230. b. 1.—additions to, i. ap. 138; iii. 3, 559, 1138.—po. i. 3.
Skeffington, Catharine-Josepha, lady, 1811, i. ap. 138.
———— Sir William-Charles Farrell, 1815, account of, i. ap. 138; iv. 406.—and of his family, i. ap. 138.
Skeles, Rev. Mr. 1800, iv. 396.
SKELTHORPE, or SHELTHORPE, additions to, iii. 911.
SKETCHLEY, additions to, i. ap. 147; iii. 3.—po. i. 5.
SLAWSTON, *Slachestone, Slagestone*, 234. a. 2.—additions to, i. ap. 132.—po. i. 2.
SMEETON-WESTERBY, *Smitone, Smitetone, Esmeditone*, 230. b. 1. 232. a. 2. 234. b. 2. Q. *Witenesta*, 235. a. 1.—additions to, iv. 1045.—po. i. 2.
Smith, Dorothy, iii. 521.
———— Henry, alderman, ii. 882.
———— Rev. John, 1660, acc. of, iv. 416.
———— Rev. John, 1706, iii. 1136.
———— John, 1812, i. ap. 140.
———— Lord Chief Baron John, character of, iv. 418.
———— Joseph, 1808, i. ap. 152.—epit. iv. 1044.
———— William, 1667, ii. 884.
———— William, 1711, his charities, ii. 150; iv. 396.
———— William, 1804, iv. 399.
———— alias Heriz family, Mr. Burton's account of, iii. 526.
———— alias Moor, Thomas, 1643, will of, iii. 537.
Smithe, Erasmus, 1588, i. ap. 117.
———— Francis, 1588, i. ap. 117.
SMOCKINGTON, *Snochantone*, 233. a. 2.
Smythe, Benjamin, 1679, iv. 396.
———— Hannah, her will, 1679, iv. 396.
SNARESTON, *Snarchetone*, 234. b. 1.—additions to, iii. 3; iv. 1049.—po. i. 5.
SNIBSTON, additions to, iii. 3, 4, 1125.—po. i. 3.
SOMERBY, *Sumerdeberie, Sumerdebie, Sumerlidebie*, 230. b. 1. 233. b. 1. 235. a. 1. b. 2.—additions to, i. ap. 131; ii. 424; iii. 525.—po. i. 1.
Somner, John, 1675, ii. 883.
Sondes, Thomas lord, 1804, iv. 399.
Soules, Francis, his death, 1792, i. ap. 121.
SOUTH MARKFIELD. See Markfield, in Local Index, p. 10, 21.
SOUTH CROXTON. See Croxton, in Local Index, pp. 5, 19.
Spalding, Robert de, monk, 1310, ii. 420.
Sparke, Rev. Bowyer-Edward, D.D. bp. of Ely, account of, i. ap. 131.
SPARKENHOE HUNDRED, additions to, i. ap. 144—158.— population of parishes in, i. part ii.—abstract of Parish Registers of Parishes in, 1700—1810, 9.
Spanish Armada, 1588, gentry of Leicestershire, who contributed to the defence of their country at that time, i. ap. 117.
Spencer, Thomas, and family, epit. 1810, iv. 1044.
Stamford and Warrington, George-Harry earl of, i. ap. 149.—character of, 144.—his portrait, Frontispiece to vol. IV. part II.
———— Thomas earl of, his children, iii. 1141.
SPROXTON, *Sprotone*, 235. b. 2. 236. b. 2. additions to, ii. 888; iii. 525.—po. i. 1.
STANFORD, *Stanford*, 235. a. 2. 236. b. 1.—account of corrected, iv. 420.

Stanford,

24   SUPPLEMENTARY INDEX.

†‡† *Italics* refer to DOMESDAY in Vol. I. Part I.—po. to Population Return in Vol. I. Part II.

SUPPLEMENTARY INDEX.
25

†‡† *Italics* refer to Domesday in Vol. I. Part I.—po to Population Return in Vol. I. Part II.

ARRANGEMENT OF THE INDEXES.

NICHOLS'S HISTORY of LEICESTERSHIRE.

DIRECTIONS TO THE BINDER.

FEBRUARY 14, 1815.

The Work consists of Four very large Volumes, divided into Eight Parts ; viz.

(Lettering.)

Vol. I. Part I.—INTRODUCTION—TOWN of LEICESTER.

For a List of the Plates and Signatures in this Part, see at the back of the Preface, p. xii.

Place the Portrait of Mr. Burton (given with Sparkenhoe Hundred) facing the Title to this Part;—and signatures [d d d] to [h h h], Natural History of the Vale of Belvoir, with Three Plates, (given with Sparkenhoe Hundred), in their proper situation.

(Lettering.)

Vol. I. Part II.—TOWN of LEICESTER — GENERAL INDEXES.

For the Contents and List of Plates to this Part, see p. viii.

Place the Portrait of Mr. Nichols (given with Sparkenhoe Hundred), as a Frontispiece to this Part.

*** Pages 251 to 354 of this Part, were published at the end of Gartre Hundred; pages 355 to 548, at the end of Guthlaxton Hundred; pages 549 to 626, at the end of Sparkenhoe Hundred; Appendix, pages 53 to 116, at the end of Gartre Hundred; and pages 117 to 158, and 1 to 10 (Population), were published with the General Indexes.

Signatures: Title and Preface i to viii; [T t t] to [4 I]; [4 K] (misprinted 6 K) half sheet; [4 L] to [4 Y] half sheet; [4 Z] to [6 C]; [6 D 1, 2, 3]; [6 E] to [7 B] half sheet; [7 C] to [7 Y] half sheet.—Appendix P to S s.—Population, A 1 to 5.—Indexes, B to H.—2 B to 3 G.—4 A to 4 Y.—5 A to 5 G.

(Lettering.)

VOL. II. Part I. — FRAMLAND HUNDRED.

For the List of Plates in this Part, see p. xiii. at beginning of Vol. I. Part I.; and for a List of the Signatures, see p. xii. of Vol. I. Part I.

Place the large folding Map of the County (given with the General Indexes) as a Frontispiece to this Part.

The Leaf of Index, pp. 425, 426, had better be placed after the Appendix, p. 140, at the end of the Part.

(Lettering.)

Vol. II. Part II. — GARTRE HUNDRED.

For the List of Plates in this Part, see Vol. II. Appendix, p. 150.

Signatures : Title and Dedication ; 5 S to 5 X 1, 2, 3; 5 Y to 6 D 1, 2, 3, 4; 6 E to 7 Y 1, 2, 3, 4; 7 Z to 10 T; App. N n to P p.

(Lettering.)

Vol. III. Part I. — EAST GOSCOTE HUNDRED.

For the Lists of Plates and Signatures in this Part, see the Appendix, p. 16.

Place the additional Pedigree of Ashby of Quenby (given with the General Indexes) facing p. 300.

(Lettering.)

Vol. III. Part II. — WEST GOSCOTE HUNDRED.

For the List of Plates in this Part, see page 1126; and for the List of Signatures, see Appendix, p. 72.

Place the Portrait of Francis Earl of Moira as a Frontispiece to this Part; and the Sheet of Babington Pedigrees, between pages 954 and 955. They are both given with the General Indexes.

(Lettering.)

Vol. IV. Part I. — GUTHLAXTON HUNDRED.

For the List of Plates in this Part, see p. 424.

Signatures : Title and Dedication; B to 4 E; Pedigree of Fielding; 4 F to 5 P.

Place the Portrait of the Rev. Dr. Farmer (given with the General Indexes) as a Frontispiece to this Part. A Memoir of him is given in p. 943 of this Volume.

(Lettering.)

Vol. IV. Part II.—SPARKENHOE HUNDRED.

For the List of Plates in this Part, see p. 1054; and for the List of Signatures, see p. 1053.

Place the Portrait of the Earl of Stamford and Warrington (given with the General Indexes), as a Frontispiece to this Part.

Place the additional Pedigree of Jervoise Clarke Jervoise (given in the General Indexes) facing p. 602.

END of VOL. I.

Printed by NICHOLS, SON, and BENTLEY,
Red Lion Passage, Fleet Street, London.